THE FIELD DAY ANTHOLOGY
OF IRISH WRITING

THE FIELD DAY ANTHOLOGY OF IRISH WRITING

VOLUME IV

IRISH WOMEN'S WRITING AND TRADITIONS

Edited by

Angela Bourke, Siobhán Kilfeather, Maria Luddy, Margaret Mac Curtain, Gerardine Meaney,
Máirín Ní Dhonnchadha, Mary O'Dowd, and Clair Wills

New York University Press
Washington Square, New York

Published in the U.S.A. and Canada 2002 by
New York University Press
Washington Square
New York, NY 10003

www.nyupress.org

Published in Ireland, UK and Europe by Cork University Press, Ireland.

THE FIELD DAY ANTHOLOGY OF IRISH WRITING VOLUME IV AND V
ISBN 0–8147–9906–X   Vol. IV
ISBN 0–8147–9907–8   Vol. V
ISBN 0–8147–9908–6   Set

A Catalogue-in-Publication record is available from the Library of Congress

Typeset by Mick Lynam and Noel Murphy at Phototype-Set Ltd, Dublin, Ireland
Printed by MPG Books Ltd, Cornwall, England

Contents

Sexuality, 1685–2001

SIOBHÁN KILFEATHER, *Editor*

SEXUAL DISCOURSE IN ENGLISH BEFORE THE ACT OF UNION: PRESCRIPTION AND DISSENT, 1685–1801

SIOBHÁN KILFEATHER, *Editor*

CONTENTS xvii

Oral Traditions

ANGELA BOURKE, *Editor*

LIFE STORIES

ANGELA BOURKE and PATRICIA LYSAGHT,
Editors

INTERNATIONAL FOLKTALES

ÉILÍS NÍ DHUIBHNE, *Editor*

THE SONG TRADITION

Ríonach Uí Ógáin and Tom Munnelly,
Editors

LIST OF CONTRIBUTING EDITORS
VOLUME IV and VOLUME V

Ursula Barry teaches at the Women's Education Research and Resource Centre (WERRC) at University College Dublin. She is a feminist and social economist with wide-ranging experience as a researcher and policy analyst in the area of equality (in particular, gender equality in Ireland) She has published widely on the economic and social situation of women in Ireland and among many other activities represents women's interests on various national bodies.

Angela Bourke, born in Dublin, 1952, graduated in Celtic Studies but works now in interdisciplinary Irish Studies, specialising in oral traditions in Irish. Her 1999 book, *The Burning of Bridget Cleary: A True Story* has won several awards. A Senior Lecturer in Irish at University College Dublin, her scholarship and fiction are published in Irish and English.

Ruth Carr (formerly Hooley) lectures for the Belfast Institute of Further & Higher Education. She has edited various anthologies and group publications including *The Female line* (NIWRM, 1985), *Write to the core* (Greenway Women's Press, 1992) and *I know a woman* (The Spellweavers, 1997). She has been production editor and, more recently, associate editor of *HU* poetry magazine since 1986. Her first collection of poetry, *There is a house,* was published by Summer Palace Press in 1999.

Caitriona Clear lectures in history at National University of Ireland, Galway. Women of the House: women's household work in Ireland 1922-1961 (Irish Academic Press 2000) is her most recent book. She is currently interested in oral history and in the Irish writer Maura Laverty.

Mary Condren is currently director of the Institute for Feminism and Religion in Ireland and a Research Associate in the Centre for Gender and Women's Studies at Trinity College Dublin, and also works as a communications consultant. Her current research and writing focuses on the complementary roles women and men in war. Her critically acclaimed book *The Serpent and the Goddess: Women, Religion, and Power in Celtic Ireland* published by Harper & Row in 1989 has just been published for the first time in Ireland by New Island Books, 2002.

Alpha Connelly has worked as a lecturer in University College Dublin and as a legal advisor in the Department of Foreign Affairs in Dublin. She is editor of *Gender and the Law in Ireland* (1993). Dr Connolly was appointed Chief Executive Officer with the Human Rights Commission in Dublin in 2002.

Anne Crilly is a film maker whose career began in her native Derry, where she was a founder of the Derry Film and Video Workshop. She won awards for her pioneering documentary, *Mother Ireland* (1989). She taught for several years at Dublin City University and currently teaches Media Studies at the University of Ulster. Her latest film is *Limbo* (2001).

Mary Cullen taught for a number of years in the Modern History Department at NUI Maynooth. She is currently a research associate at the Centre for Gender and Women's Studies, Trinity College, Dublin.

Mary E. Daly is Chair of the Interim Board of the Humanities Institute of Ireland, based at UCD, secretary of the Royal Irish Academy, and a member of the History Department at UCD. She is the author of numerous journal articles and has contributed to *Women and Irish History* (Dublin, Wolfhound, 1997) and *Gender and Sexuality in Modern Ireland* (Amherst, MA 1998)

Emma Donoghue is a novelist, biographer, playwright and literary historian. She has published numerous books, including her latest novel, *Slammerkin* (2000), and has edited anthologies of lesbian writing. She now lives in London, Ontario.

Frances Gardiner has lectured in Politics at UCD and TCD, and currently provides a political-legal briefing service for politicians, diplomats, business and voluntary sectors. Author of numerous articles on women and politics, contributing editor of *Sex Equality Policy in Western Europe* (Routledge) and co-author of *Achieving the Advancement of Women in the Post-Beijing Era,* she was the Irish representative on the EU Commission '*Women in Decision-Making*' Network 1996-2000.

Hazel Gordon was born in Belfast in 1946. She worked in the Belfast community sector before taking up a teaching post in further education. In 2000 she completed a career break to carry out research in learning disability and human rights. She is currently working as a freelance consultant researcher.

Máire Herbert is a Professor of Early and Medieval Irish at University College, Cork. She has written extensively on medieval Irish literature and history and Hiberno-Latin texts. Her publications include *Iona, Kells and Derry: The History and Hagiography of the Monastic Familia of Columba* (Dublin: Four Courts Press, 1996), and (with Pádraig Ó Riain) *Betha Adamnáin: The Irish Life of Adamnán* (London: Irish Texts Society 1988).

Janice Holmes studied history in universities of Guelph and Queen's, Kingston, Canada, now lectures in University of Ulster at Coleraine, Northern Ireland. She co-edited (with Diane Urquhart) *Coming into the Light The Work, Politics and Religion of Women in Ulster 1840–1940* (Belfast: Institute Irish Studies, QUB, 1994) and is currently researching popular protestantism and religious revivalism.

Marjorie Howes was born in Ann Arbor, Michigan. Her BA is from the University of Michigan (1984) and her PhD from Princeton (1990). She is the author of *Yeats's Nations: Gender, Class, and Irishness* (Cambridge: Cambridge UP, 1996) and co-editor (with Derek Attridge) of *Semicolonial Joyce* (Cambridge: Cambridge UP, 2000). She is Associate Professor of English and Irish Studies, Boston College.

Margaret Kelleher lectures in the English Department, National University of Ireland, Maynooth. She is the author of *The Feminization of Famine* (Cork U.P. and Duke U.P., 1997) and co-editor (with James H. Murphy) of *Gender Perspectives in Nineteenth-Century Ireland* (Irish Academic Press, 1997). She is co-editor (with Philip O'Leary) of the forthcoming *Cambridge History of Irish Literature.*

Siobhán Kilfeather grew up in Belfast. Her PhD thesis for Princeton (1989) was on eighteenth-century Irish women's writing. She teaches English at the University of Sussex.

Phil Kilroy is a member of the Society of the Sacred Heart and author of *Protestant Dissent and Controversy in Ireland 1660-1714* (Cork U.P. 1994) and of numerous articles on religious dissent in 17th century Ireland. Her most recent publication is a scholarly biography of *Madeleine Sophie Barat. A Life* (Cork U.P. 2000), which has also appeared in French and Spanish. She is currently preparing a book on the Counter-Enlightenment and Counter-Revolution in the early years of the Society of the Sacred Heart.

Jo Murphy Lawless is a sociologist and author of *Reading Birth and Death: A History of Obstetric Thinking* (Cork U.P., 1998). Her most recent book is *Fighting Back: Women and the Impact of Drug Abuse on Families and Communities* (The Liffey Press, 2002).

June Levine is a well-known writer and activist who currently works in television production. She is the co-author of *Lyn: A Story of Prostitution.* Her full biography can be found on p. 1139.

Rena Lohan has worked as an archivist in The National Archives of Ireland, Dublin, and as College Archivist in University College, Dublin. She is currently Freedom of Information Officer in UCD.

Patricia Lysaght is a professor in the Department of Irish Folklore, University College Dublin. Well known internationally as a scholar and lecturer, the second edition of her book *The Banshee: The Irish Supernatural Death-Messenger* was published in 1996. She is a member of the Royal Gustavus Adolphus Academy for Swedish Folk Culture, Uppsala.

Margaret Mac Curtain was born in 1929 and joined the Dominican Cabra Congregation in 1950. She played a pivotal role in the emergence of the study of women in Irish History during her academic career in UCD, from which she retired in 1995 as lecturer in Irish History. In 1997 she was appointed Chair of the National Archives Advisory Council. Her publications include *Women in Early Modern Ireland* (co-edited with Mary O Dowd, Dublin: Wolfhound Press 1979). She is the recipient of Honorary doctorates from several American universities.

Sarah MacDonald was born in Dublin in 1968. Her M.A. was in Etruscan Archaeology from University College Dublin, (awarded 1994). She has worked in publishing and broadcasting and currently works as an Interactive Journalist with R.T.E. and freelances for a number of religious publications.

Elizabeth Malcolm studied at Trinity College, Dublin, and worked at Queen's University, Belfast, and the University of Liverpool, before being appointed Professor of Irish Studies at the University of Melbourne in 2000. She has published books and articles on Irish mental illness, women's health, migration, crime and policing and drink and temperance.

Dympna McLoughlin teaches in the Department of Modern History at NUI Maynooth. Her research interests include women and workhouses in nineteenth-century Ireland, infanticide and the history of children in Irish society.

Anna McMullan is Director of the M.Phil. in Irish Theatre and Film at the School of Drama, Trinity College, Dublin and author of *Theatre on Trial: Samuel Beckett's Later Drama* (London: Routledge, 1993). She is also the author of numerous articles on Beckett's drama and contemporary Irish theatre including contributions to *Druids, Beauty Queens and Dudes: The Changing Face of Irish Theatre*, (Dublin: New Island Books, 2001); and *Theatre Stuff: Critical Essays on Contemporary Irish Theatre*, ed. Eamonn Jordan (Dublin: Carysfort Press in 2000).

Monica McWilliams is a founder member of the Northern Ireland Women's Coalition and has represented the party in the Northern Ireland Assembly since 1998. She is also Professor of Women's Studies and Social Policy at the University of Ulster and has researched and published extensively on women in Northern Ireland since 1968.

Geradine Meaney lectures in Film Studies, Women's Studies and English at University College Dublin. She is the author of *(Un)like Subjects: Women, Theory, Fiction* (Routledge, 1993) and of numerous articles on gender in Irish culture. She is also author of a forthcoming volume on Pat Murphy's film, *Nora*, in the Ireland into Film series (Cork University Press).

Tom Munnelly was born in Dublin in 1944. As a collector of folksongs since early 60 he began collecting professionally for the Department of Education 1971. From 1974 he was employed as archivist/collector by the Department of Irish Folklore, UCD. Based in Miltown Mallbay, Co. Clare since 1978 he has worked all around Ireland, and has written and published widely on English-language folksong in Ireland.

Máire Ní Annracháin is Senior Lecturer in the Department of Modern Irish, National University of Ireland, Maynooth. She is author of a study of the Scottish Gaelic poet Somhairle MacGill-Eain, *Aisling agus Tóir: An Slánú i bhFilíocht Shomhairle MhicGhill-Eain* and co-editor of *Téacs agus Comhthéacs: Gnéithe de Chritic na Gaeilge*. Her academic interests include the reading of Irish-language literature in the light of contemporary literary theory, and modern Scottish Gaelic literature.

Nuala Ní Dhomhnaill is a critically acclaimed poet writing in Irish. Her work is published by Gallery Press and by Wake Forest in the U.S. Her most recent collection is *The Waterhorse* (1999) with translations by Medbh McGuckian and Eiléan Ní Chuilleanáin. For additional information see p. 640.

Máirín Ní Dhonnchadha is Professor of Old and Middle Irish and Celtic Philology at the National University of Ireland, Galway. Her publications include *Nua-Léamha: Gnéithe de Chultúr, Stair agus Polaitíocht na hÉireann 1570–1900* (Baile Átha Cliath: An Clóchomhar, 1996], and (co-edited with Theo Dorgan) *Revising the Rising* (Derry: Field Day, 1991).

Éilís Ní Dhuibhne was born in Dublin, in 1954 and is a graduate of University College Dublin, where she studied Old and Modern English, and Irish Folklore. She was awarded a Ph.D. in 1982 and is the author of many articles on folklore topics and also a well known writer of fiction and drama. She works as an Assistant Keeper in the National Library of Ireland.

Bairbre Ní Fhloinn works as an archivist/collector in the Department of Irish Folklore in University College Dublin. She has worked in co-operation with Pavee Point, the Dublin Travellers' Centre, on a number of projects concerning the oral traditions of Travellers. She has published several articles and has recorded material from singers and storytellers in many parts of Ireland.

Bríona Nic Dhiarmada was educated at Trinity College, Dublin and at UCD where she completed her Ph.D. on the poetry of Nuala Ní Dhomhnaill. She is co-editor of *Téacs agus Comhthéacs* (Cork: Cork University Press, 1988). Formerly a lecturer in the Department of Irish in UCD, she now works in television as a writer and producer/director.

Aoibheann Nic Dhonnchadha is an Assistant Professor at the School of Celtic Studies, Dublin Institute for Advanced Studies. She has carried out extensive research on Irish medical texts. Her most recent publication is 'Medical writing in Irish', in *2000 years of Irish medicine* (ed. J.B. Lyons) (Dublin: Eireann Healthcare Publications, 1999)

Máirín Nic Eoin is a lecturer in the Department of Irish at St Patrick's College, Drumcondra, Dublin. She has published extensively on modern and contemporary literature in Irish. Her most recent book is *B'Ait Leo Bean: Gnéithe den Idé-Eolaíocht Inscne i dTraidisiún Liteartha na Gaeilge* (Baile Átha Cliath: An Clóchomhar, 1998). It won the Irish Times Prize for Literature in the Irish Language.

Margaret O'Callaghan is an historian in the School of Politics at QUB. She is the author of *British High Politics and a Nationalist Ireland; Criminality, Land and the Law under Forster and Balfour* (Cork U.P. 1994) and a wide range of articles on nationalism and Unionism in 19th and 20th century Ireland. She has taught Modern British History at Cambridge University and has been Visiting Associate Professor of Government and International Relations and a Fellow of the Keough Institute at the University of Notre Dame, Indiana.

Anne O'Connor has spent most of her working life as a secondary school teacher in Alexandra College, Dublin, where she taught History. She began research into girl's secondary education in Ireland as part of her M.A. thesis and subsequently contributed to various publications on women's history including *Women Power and Consciousness* (Dublin, Attic Press 1995) and the forthcoming Encyclopaedia of Ireland (Dublin, Gill and Macmillan, 2003)

Donnchadh Ó Corráin is Professor of Medieval History at University College, Cork; founder and editor of *Peritia: Journal of the Medieval Academy of Ireland* (1981–, 13 volumes); and founder and director of CELT: Corpus of Electronic Texts (*http:www.ucc.ie/celt/*). He has authored and edited numerous works on various aspects of medieval Irish and medieval European history.

Mary O'Dowd is a senior lecturer in History at Queen's University Belfast. She is author of *Power, Politics and Land: Sligo 1568-1688* (1991) and editor of a number of collections of essays on Irish women's history. She was appointed President of the International Federation for Research in Women's History in 2000. She is currently completing a book on women in early modern Ireland.

Riana O'Dwyer is a lecturer in English at the National University of Ireland, Galway. Current research interests are nineteenth century Irish fiction and contemporary Irish drama. Her doctoral thesis was on Joyce's use of Irish history in *Finnegans Wake*. She has also written on recent Irish and Canadian literature.

Ríonach uí Ógáin is a lecturer/archivist in the Department of Irish Folklore, University College Dublin. Her 1995 book, *Immortal Dan: Daniel*

O'Connell in Irish Folk Tradition, was based on her doctoral thesis. She has lectured and published widely on Irish traditional music and song and on other aspects of Irish folklore.

Susan M. Parkes, FTCD is an Emeritus Fellow and a former Senior Lecturer in Education, Trinity College, Dublin. Her research interests are in the history of education and women's history. Recent publications include contributions to *Women in Higher Education, past, present and future* (eds M.R. Mason and D. Simmonds (Aberdeen University Press, 1996); *The Blackwell Companion to Irish Culture*, ed. W.J McCormack (Blackwell, 1999). She is currently working as editor of a history of women in Trinity College to mark the centenary of the admission of women in 1904.

Antoinette Quinn was a founder member of the Centre for Gender and Women's Studies at Trinity College Dublin and was until recently a Senior Lecturer in the English Department there. She has published numerous articles on women's writing. She is the author of *Patrick Kavanagh: A Biography* (Gill And Macmillan, 2001*).

Rosemary Raughter has published a number of articles on 18th-century female philanthropy and on women and religion, and is currently researching a biography of Lady Arbella Denny. She is a member of the committee of the Women's History Association of Ireland and of the Women's History Project.

Márie Rogers was born in Belfast in 1944. She took received a BSc Hons from University College Dublin in 1969 and an MA in Education from the New University of Ulster in 1983. She was a Dominican Sister for 20 years and taught in schools before lecturing in Mathematics Education at the University of Ulster at Coleraine until 1987. She retrained and is now practising as an AOC Registered Aromatherapist.

Eilish Rooney is currently chairperson of several community and education action groups and co-editor of Community Development, Democracy and Citizenship (1996).

Ruth Taillon is author of *When History Was Made: The Women Of 1916*, and editor of the Woodfield Press *'Activist To Activist' Biographical series on Irish women*. Ruth works as a researcher and is also author of a number of reports on contemporary Irish women's organisations.

Diane Urquhart is a lecturer in modern Irish history at the Institute of Irish Studies of the University of Liverpool. She is a graduate of Queen's University Belfast and a former postgraduate fellow of the Institute of Irish Studies at Queen's. She has also worked as a researcher for the Women's History Project. She is the author of *Women in Ulster Politics, 1890–1940: a History Not Yet Told* (Dublin, 2000).

Éibhear Walshe lectures in the Department of Modern English at University College, Cork and had edited *Ordinary People Dancing: Essays on Kate O'Brien* (Cork U.P. 1993), *Sex, Nation and Dissent* (Cork U.P. 1997) and *Elizabeth Bowen Remembered* (1999). He has completed a study of the Irish novelist, Kate O'Brien and is working on a book on Oscar Wilde and Ireland.

Caroline Williams was a founding member and producer with Glasshouse Productions. She devised their stage presentations 'There are no Irish women Playwrights' 1 and 2. She has worked as a literary researcher for RTE, BBC and Tyrone Productions.

Clair Wills is reader in Modern Poetry at Queen Mary, University of London. She has published widely on twentieth century Irish literature and on contemporary poetry, including *Improprieties: Politics and Sexuality in Northern Irish Poetry* (Oxford, 1993), and Reading Paul Muldoon (Bloodaxe Books, 1998). She is currently completing a study of Irish writing and the Second World War.

Preface

VOLUME IV and VOLUME V

These two volumes of women's writing and traditions invite readers to approach the written word in new ways. Irish literature, history and culture are human constructs, not natural phenomena; their presentation in print has usually been conditioned by ways of thinking and writing developed through generations of scholarship, and the underlying assumption of much of that scholarship has been that both reader and writer are male. Words written and spoken by and about women, from a variety of sources, over many centuries, are presented here with detailed notes on their contexts. They offer a multifaceted view of women who belong to different times and different social classes, whose economic circumstances and access to education have varied, as have their ways of using the languages of Ireland, their politics, their life choices and their sexualities. The work of editing their words has brought together a range of disciplines, scholarship and material, and produced a new kind of anthology. These volumes set out to challenge existing canons of Irish writing. They question received versions of history, and reinterpret cultural myths, while their shape reflects the collaborative and interdisciplinary nature of our editorial structure. *The Field Day Anthology of Irish Writing*, volumes IV and V, is the first attempt to bring together a substantial body of written documents produced by and about women since writing began in Ireland.

There are many ways of making anthologies, but in most methods one can trace the interests and judgements of the anthologist — that is, indeed, part of the pleasure for the reader. One of this project's distinctive features, however, is that its team of editors, drawn from several different disciplines, has in turn benefited from the contributions and expertise of a large number of contributing editors. The first three volumes of the *Field Day Anthology*, published in 1991, were exemplary in this regard, demonstrating the benefits of recruiting expert and enthusiastic editors to present areas of Irish history or ideas which may be little known outside a small academic community. The initial proposal for the present work emerged after the publication of that three-volume anthology, which coincided with a perceived flowering of women's writing, political activism and feminist scholarship in Ireland, and led to an intense debate about the position accorded to women in the formation of literary canons. In the ten years the work has been in progress, it has become both encyclopaedic and kaleidoscopic, combining many hundreds of texts with dozens of ways of reading them.

The first three volumes of the *Field Day Anthology* were not originally conceived with a sequel in view, but their publication alerted readers to the lack of adequate representation of women in editorial practice. A number of editors had been involved in volumes I-III and they answered the critics in a variety of ways. The response of the General Editor, Seamus Deane, was to invite some women scholars who had found fault with the anthology to meet him to discuss the possibility of producing a supplementary volume under the auspices of the Field Day Company. After a series of preliminary meetings, a panel of eight editors with a shared commitment to feminist work undertook the making of a new anthology. Coming from a variety of disciplinary backgrounds, most of us had not worked together before, and some of us met for the first time as the project began. We soon decided that the new work should have a broadly thematic organization and that each of us should take responsibility for one section.

What had originally been intended as a single volume of women's writings, supplementing and interrogating the 1991 *Field Day Anthology*, and operating within similar parameters, quickly developed into a much larger, multidisciplinary project involving contributions from people with many kinds of qualification. Although all of us had worked extensively on aspects of Irish women's history or cultural production, we were surprised by the volume of interesting, important and exciting material that emerged even on our first investigations. Every meeting produced compelling reasons to increase the number of texts included as we learned about forgotten debates and read long-neglected writers. Many more texts could have been included, had space allowed, but editors must make choices and we are heartened by the growth in women's publishing in Ireland since the project began.

We have sometimes been asked why we elected to produce an anthology about women under the auspices of the Field Day Company. A simple answer is that Field Day provided the opportunity: it would have been all but impossible for us to fund such a large and complex project privately or to persuade another publisher to invest in it in its early stages. Through the fourteen centuries we survey, women have struggled to produce their work in a material world. The story of women's exclusion from power and from modes of representation is first of all a story about property: about labour, money, markets, exchange, self-determination, and living in the female body. Women's cultural production has always depended on negotiations about time and money, and the making of this anthology has required a significant investment of both. While our university positions afforded us some of the time needed, Field Day offered the funding and experience that made possible the project of assembling, editing and annotating texts. Aside from this very practical reason for partnership with the Field Day Company, we share with the editors of the original three volumes a belief in the importance for Irish and other readers of recovering and representing literary and historical texts and making them accessible to a wider public, so as to ground fresh attitudes to the future in new understandings of the past. In the last three years Cork University Press has taken on the burden of putting the book into production, and we are grateful for the imagination and generosity it has shown in allowing us to expand from one to two volumes. Two people with vision, Seamus Deane of Field Day and Sara Wilbourne of Cork University Press, deserve our particular thanks: they persuaded their organizations to risk putting their energies behind our project, not for profit, but because they believed it was valuable and worthwhile.

What is an anthology of Irish writing? In his General Introduction to volumes I-III, Seamus Deane suggests that he is using the term 'writing' to avoid 'the narrow sense of the word "literature",' (p. xix), but most of volumes I-III can be classified as 'literature' in the broad sense, particularly as literary studies have redefined themselves as cultural studies in the last thirty years. Most of the contributing editors to volumes I-III were members of university literature departments. Volumes IV-V further broaden the category of 'writing', not simply because our editorial board includes several historians and an expert on oral traditions, but also because the contributing editors include political activists, journalists, theologians, poets and novelists, as well as scholars from a number of disciplines. The sense in which we have understood 'writing' has been redefined as 'the ways people use words'. At times we glance at the ways in which words entwine with music and visual imagery to produce meaning in Irish life — the presence of music is particularly felt in 'Oral Traditions' — but the resources were not available to combine all fields of narrative possibility, so we have worked with words. Literature is central to Irish cultural expression and is therefore central to this anthology. As well as selecting excerpts from the most interesting and accomplished Irish writings, however, we have chosen material which will provide a set of contexts for understanding how women have lived in Ireland.

Some of the writers included here might be claimed by anthologies of other national literatures. People live their lives in more than one place and in more than one imagined relation. We have developed a loose and, we hope, generous sense of what it means to be Irish, looking at words produced in Ireland, and words used by Irish people in other places. It is almost always clear why a text is considered as Irish, but in borderline cases editors have made sometimes intuitive judgements about a text's relationship to a sense of Ireland: nothing was excluded as being insufficiently Irish.

Early in the work we debated whether or not to include texts from Scotland written in classical Modern Irish, the standard language used by the school-trained Gaelic poets both there and in Ireland. Although the very existence of such a standard points to a shared cultural world, we decided that we were not entitled to appropriate Scottish texts for an anthology of Irish writing.

One major exclusion from this anthology deserves explanation: we have not attempted to do justice to diasporic writings. Diaspora involves an experience not only of dislocation but of relocation, and when we began to plan this anthology we could not imagine the resources we might need to make a responsible, rather than a token, exploration of Irish diasporas. It might be argued that as we have made ample provision for Irish writers living and working in other European countries, we ought to have done the same for Argentina, Australia, Canada, Southern Africa or the United States. We can only respond that we did not have the resources to do so.

Most of the groundwork for these volumes was laid prior to the 1990s. It was possible for critics to challenge the 1991 *Field Day Anthology* precisely because so many readers were by then aware of women's work in literature, politics and culture. In the 1970s and 1980s, by contrast, the project of defining and redefining Ireland did not accommodate the re-evaluation and recovery of women's words and history. Had gender been considered then as an element in the making of national and political identity, literary canons and historical priorities might not have been framed as they were. As the debates surrounding the publication of volumes I-III made clear, even writers and critics well disposed to and welcoming of feminist scholarship at that time failed to take adequate account of women's literary, social and political history. We have produced these two volumes to demonstrate that women's lives and imaginations in Ireland have been infinitely more rich and diverse than stereotypes suggest, while investigating the origins of many of those same stereotypes. We have not attempted to erase or minimize political or cultural differences between Irish women, now or in the past. As editors, we bring a variety of approaches to the material we present, but while we have not always been of one mind about the selection or interpretation of texts, we have worked in close collaboration throughout, increasing our own understanding through discussion and cross-referencing.

There are contentious areas in Irish life where we would have liked to have able to balance opinions, but were thwarted by a lack of written material. We had decided at the outset that this type of large historical anthology should select from material previously written and recorded. Although the subsections are preceded by short interpretative essays, therefore, we have resisted the temptation to commission new contributions to debate. This means that sections on recent writing from Northern Ireland, for example, contain a greater body of texts from a broadly nationalist than from a unionist perspective. Similarly, from the 1960s onwards, ways of thinking about sexuality have been debated intensely in Ireland as elsewhere; however, almost no writings have emerged on the merits of radical separatism, or on the pornography debate, to name but two areas.

Our sources include manuscripts and original sound recordings; we draw on work that has previously been read or performed only to a coterie audience, as for example at a lesbian poetry reading; we include interviews with prisoners distributed in a community newsletter. The decision to follow the example of traditional anthologies in choosing from what we could find, rather than attempt to represent every possible constituency, comes at a price: certain groups of women, such as recent immigrants, including refugees and asylum-seekers, do not get the attention they merit in these pages.

The two volumes are organized into eight large sections. These are 'Medieval to Modern, 600–1900'; 'Religion, Science, Theology and Ethics, 1500–2000'; 'Sexuality 1600–2001'; 'Oral Traditions; Women in Irish Society, 1200–2000'; 'Politics, 1500–2000'; 'Women's Writing, 1700–1960'; and 'Contemporary Writing, 1960–2001'. Each section has been designed by its editor as part of a wider process of recovery of documentary resources and the development of new approaches to them. Each of the eight major sections is divided into sub-sections and accommodates the work of a number of contributing editors, while cross-referencing within and between the various sub-sections and sections means that the work may be read in a number of directions. There is nothing natural or inevitable about the divisions we have imposed. We looked at volumes I-III and decided to dismiss opportunities to organize the material in terms of literary genres, major authors, or historical events.

We could not so easily dismiss the principle of chronological presentation; where appropriate, therefore, each section traces recognizable chronologies within its borders.

Ireland has a long and rich tradition of collective cultural production and a very different relationship with print culture to that found in Britain or North America, for example. The nineteenth- and twentieth-century version of a bourgeois female tradition of women's writing is not appropriate here. From earliest times until the twentieth century, most poetry in Irish was addressed to individuals — patrons, patrons' spouses, fellow-poets and individuals in the writer's community — while in the period 1500–1900, writing in Gaelic Ireland derived from communal exchange and activity to a degree not found, say, in Wales or Scotland. 'Medieval to Modern, 600–1900', edited by Máirín Ní Dhonnchadha, discusses these and other aspects of the literary forms used in Gaelic Ireland down to modern times, while 'Oral Traditions', edited by Angela Bourke, demonstrates some of the diverse and complex ways in which authorship needs to be understood in an Irish context.

Irish women in the modern era have been influenced by and have adapted models of action and interpretation from other places. The section on 'Women and Writing, 1700–1960', edited by Gerardine Meaney, concentrates on poetry, fiction, drama and criticism by Irish women, exploring that which is recognisable from the rise of women's writing elsewhere and what is particular to Irish culture during this period. Like this section, 'Contemporary Writing, 1960–2001', edited by Clair Wills, includes only writing by women. Elsewhere, we have found that the best explanatory model for each theme has been to show how women and men have created meaning around experience, gender and sexuality, but throughout this anthology, women's own accounts of their lives and ideas have priority. In the earlier historical periods especially, many texts are anonymous. Parliamentary reports, Commissions of Enquiry, newspaper reports, medical reports and legal documents, almost all of which were authored by men until about 1900, are often anonymous too, but their anonymity differs from that of an unsigned novel or poem.

Women were, and are, to be found in almost all the institutions which make up society: family, politics, church, work; our lives are structured not only by events, but by ways of thinking, speaking and writing. 'Women and Society, 1200–2000', edited by Maria Luddy, deals chronologically and thematically with major issues relating to women in the economy, in education and experiencing emigration. 'Politics, 1500–2000', edited by Mary O'Dowd, traces the emergence of women's political voices from early Tudor Ireland through to the twentieth century.

Since the seventeenth century the various governments of Ireland have taken a strong interest in regulating sexuality, promoting some kinds of reproduction, family life and social intercourse, and discouraging others, and this state surveillance has prompted a response from writers, intellectuals and political activists demanding a more open public debate about sex in Ireland: what it has been and what it might become. For the purposes of this anthology we considered the variety of times and places where sexuality is part of other discourses: subject to examination by courts, doctors, journalists and religious leaders; discussed in the intimacy of personal letters and diaries; imagined in novels, poems, plays and ballads. 'Sexuality', edited by Siobhán Kilfeather, offers little-known texts and unexpected readings of familiar ones. 'Religion, Science, Theology and Ethics, 1500–2000', edited by Margaret Mac Curtain, explores women's religious and spiritual experiences in the aftermath of the sixteenth-century religious Reformation, and their growing competence in expressing scientific and theological thinking.

In each of the eight sections, editors explain how they have selected the material appropriate to the particular theme. No anthology could claim fully to represent all the people who have lived in Ireland. Testimonies from a small number of women philanthropists, travellers and members of the landowning and middle classes describe the Famine of the mid-nineteenth century, for instance, but almost no documents survive from those who starved, though some echoes of their voices may perhaps be heard in the songs and stories of 'Oral Traditions'.

Over the ten years this anthology has been in preparation, the eight sections we originally designed have set challenges and provoked debate among us. Feminist studies have developed considerably since 1992, stimulating new questions and opening new fields of study. We have attempted to respond to this flowering of inquiry through an elaborate system of cross references which will facilitate the exploration of themes such as women's work in translation or in children's literature, and allow the texts and accompanying material to be read in a number of configurations. The indigenous tradition of *dindsheanchas*, lore of places, which long precedes the eco-feminist concern with women's relation to the natural world, is just one starting point: the materials presented here offer a many-voiced narrative of place and environment for women in Ireland.

While editorial practice and the criteria for selection differ according to materials and disciplines, and while the system of footnoting and referencing is discrete to each section, certain broad editorial principles have informed all of the sections. Authors well represented in volumes I–III are not usually represented again here, and exceptions are intended to propose either a re-evaluation of authors whose reputation previously rested on an unrepresentative or restricted sample of their work, or a repositioning of well-known texts. Each section editor was the final arbiter of the contents of her section, but we frequently discussed overall patterns and took group decisions to move, increase, or decrease particular selections in order to strengthen thematic concerns. Excerpts are included here, often for the first time in print, from texts which are centuries old, little read and long unavailable, together with the more familiar issues, debates and literary movements of recent centuries. Our ambition throughout has been to present a broad range of texts in a format accessible to the general reader.

Until recently, women's writings and women writers were neglected in most works of reference; the contributing editors have pursued scraps of information, traced scholars and enthusiasts, even tracked down relatives and descendants of little-known authors. It was often as difficult to discover information about contemporary writers as about those long dead. We have made every effort to provide full biographical and bibliographical notes on the people whose literary, historical or political writing is included, or from whom folklore has been collected. There are cases where anonymity or obscurity have made this impossible, however, and we hope that readers who spot errors will share their knowledge with us. We have attempted to trace all living writers and performers represented, and all holders of copyright, but for some material we have only a name, and for many texts, not even that. We welcome further information, and will correct errors in later editions of this work. The material presented here stretches to cover many areas previously neglected, but we are perhaps proudest of the fact that it shows where the gaps are: we look forward therefore to new research on Ireland which will be developed and produced by new generations of feminist scholarship.

A major concern throughout our work has been to illustrate women's lives as expressed through both of the languages spoken and written in Ireland. We provide English translations of texts in Irish, many of them new and some specially commissioned. Early modern texts in English have been standardized where necessary. Writers, singers and storytellers are included under the names by which they are best known, but all known variants of birth names, marriage names and pseudonyms are included in the Index. Proper names have been standardized in some sections, especially in early material, but all versions used appear in the Index.

Poet Eiléan Ní Chuilleanáin has commented of one poetic protagonist lost in history that 'Her name lay under the surface'.[1] The surface has changed, and new names are emerging from beneath it. In ranging so broadly across forms of writing, historical records and oral traditions, where the words of poets jostle with those of paupers and politicians, these volumes seek to do more than propose a new or extended canon of Irish writing, or a subaltern history for academics. Irish women are entitled to know about their history, culture and traditions. We offer this anthology to all our readers as a sampler of texts which are historically interesting, aesthetically accomplished and politically indispensable.

May 2002

---

1. Eiléan Ní Chuilleanáin 'J'ai Mal a nos Dents', *The Magdalene Sermon* (Loughcrew: Gallery, 1989).

Réamhrá

Tugann an dá imleabhar seo de scríbhinní agus de thraidisiúin na mban cuireadh don léitheoir dul i ngleic leis an bhfocal scríofa ar bhealaí nua. Is déantúis, seachas feiniméin nádúrtha, iad litríocht, stair agus cultúr na hÉireann; tá a gcur i láthair i bprionda múnlaithe cuid mhaith ag modhanna machnaimh agus scríbhneoireachta atá tagtha chun cinn trí na glúnta scoláireachta, agus is buntuiscint don scoláireacht sin gur fireannaigh an léitheoir agus an scríbhneoir araon. Focail atá scríofa agus ráite ag mná leis na céadta bliain anuas atá cnuasaithe anseo as foinsí éagsúla, chomh maith le focail a scríobhadh agus a dúradh faoi mhná, agus nótaí faoina gcomhthéacs. Tugtar léargas fairsing ar mhná ó aoiseanna éagsúla agus aicmí éagsúla, ar mhná nach ionann stádas eacnamaíochta dóibh, ná stádas oideachais, ná teanga, ná polaitíocht, ná rogha faoin saol, ná cineál collaíochta. Thug eagarthóireacht a gcuid focal réimse disciplíní, scoláireachta agus ábhair le chéile, agus tháinig cnuasach de chineál nua chun cinn. Tugann na himleabhair seo dúshlán na gcanónacha scríbhneoireachta atá coitianta in Éirinn. Ceistíonn siad leaganacha den stair a nglactar go forleathan leo agus baineann siad ciall nua as miotais chultúrtha; léiríonn a leagan amach an struchtúr comhpháirteach, idirdhisciplíneach a bhí ar an gcomhar eagarthóireachta. Is é *The Field Day Anthology of Irish Writing*, Iml. IV agus V, an chéad iarracht ar lear mór de na cáipéisí a bhaineann le mná a thabhairt le chéile ó thosaigh an léamh agus an scríobh in Éirinn.

Is iomaí bealach le cnuasach a chur le chéile, ach is iondúil gur féidir réimse spéise agus breithiúnas an eagarthóra aonair a aithint — sin, ar ndóigh, cuid de phléisiúr an léitheora. Saintréith de chuid an chnuasaigh seo, áfach, ní amháin gur as réimsí éagsúla léinn a tháinig an fhoireann eagarthóirí, ach go raibh meitheal saineolaithe mar eagarthóirí cúnta ag tacú le gach duine againn. Ba réalt eolais dúinn an chéad trí imleabhar den chnuasach sa mhéid sin: léirigh siad sin a mhéid agus is fiú eagarthóirí saineolacha a cheapadh a bhfuil a gcroí istigh san obair, chun gnéithe den stair nó den mhachnamh a léiriú nach bhfuil eolas go forleathan orthu taobh amuigh de phobal beag acadúil. Is i ndiaidh do thrí imleabhar an chnuasaigh sin teacht amach a tháinig an togra seo chun cinn don chéad uair. Bhí bláthú as cuimse ar scríbhneoireacht agus ar ghníomhaíocht pholaitiúil na mban in Éirinn san am sin, chomh maith le borradh ar an léann feimineach, agus thosaigh diandhíospóireacht faoin áit a bhíonn ag mná i bhforbairt chanónacha litríochta. Ó thosaigh an obair seo breis is deich mbliana ó shin, tá fás agus forleathnú tagtha uirthi, go dtí go bhfeidhmníonn sí anois, b'fhéidir, mar a dhéanfadh ciclipéid nó cailéadascóp le léargas a thabhairt ar na céadta téacs agus ar na scórtha bealach len iad a léamh.

Nuair a cuireadh an chéad trí imleabhar den *Field Day Anthology* in eagar, ní raibh sé i gceist go mbeadh aon imleabhar breise ann, ach a luaithe is a foilsíodh iad thuig léitheoirí chomh gann is a bhí léiriú ar na mná iontu. Bhí scata eagarthóirí i gceist le hImleabhair I-III, agus d'fhreagair siad na léirmheastóirí ar bhealaí éagsúla. Ba é a rinne Séamus Deane, an tEagarthóir Ginearálta, cuireadh a thabhairt do chuid de na scoláirí ban a raibh an cnuasach cáinte acu bualadh leis, féachaint arbh fhéidir imleabhar breise a chur le chéile faoi choimirce Chomhlucht Field Day. Tar éis sraith de chruinnithe tionscnaimh, thug foireann ochtar eagarthóirí, a raibh luí acu ar fad leis an léann feimineach, faoi chnuasach nua. Ó tharla nárbh ionann cúlra acadúil dúinn, ní raibh aon taithí ag an gcuid is mó againn ar a bheith ag obair as lámh a chéile, agus bhí cuid againn ag cur aithne ar a chéile den chéad uair agus an obair ag tosú. Shocraíomar go luath go mba cheart an saothar nua a leagan amach ar bhonn téamúil, tríd is tríd, agus go nglacfadh gach duine den ochtar cúram roinne amháin de.

An togra a leagadh amach an chéad lá mar imleabhar amháin de scríbhinní ban, a cheisteodh agus a chuirfeadh le cnuasach 1991, agus a d'oibreodh de réir na bparaméadar céanna leis, rinne tionscnamh idirdhisciplíneach i bhfad níos mó de, agus ionchur ó dhaoine ann a raibh cáilíochtaí uilechineálacha acu. Tar éis go raibh go leor taithí ag gach duine againn ar bheith ag obair ar ghnéithe de stair agus de chultúr na mban in Éirinn, chuir líon an ábhair spéisiúil, thábhachtaigh, spreagúil a tháinig chun solais go luath iontas orainn. Bhí brú orainn ag gach cruinniú cur le líon ár dtéacsanna, de réir mar a fuaireamar amach faoi dhíospóireachtaí práinneacha a bhí ina dtost leis na blianta, agus de réir mar a léamar scríbhneoirí a bhí i bhfad ligthe i ndearmad. D'fhéadfaí go leor téacsanna eile a chur i gcló anseo, dá mbeadh an spás againn, ach is é dualgas eagarthóirí rogha a dhéanamh, agus tugann fás na foilsitheoireachta i measc na mban in Éirinn ó thosaigh an obair seo an-uchtach dúinn.

Fiafraíodh dínn ó am go chéile, cén fáth gur le Comhlucht Field Day a roghnaíomar cnuasach scríbhinní faoi mhná a chur le chéile. Freagra simplí, gurb é Field Day a thug an deis dúinn: ar éigin ar fad a d'éireodh linn tionscnamh chomh mór casta a mhaoiniú ar bhonn príobháideach, ná tabhairt ar fhoilsitheoir eile ineistiú ann i dtús na hoibre. Ó thús na tréimhse 1,400 bliain a dtugaimid tuairisc uirthi, tá na mná ag streachailt leis an saol ábharach agus iad ag iarraidh saothar a chur i gcrích. An scéal atá le hinsint faoin gcaoi a gcoinnítear na mná amach ó réimsí cumhachta, is scéal é go bunúsach faoi chúrsaí úinéarachta: faoin saothar, faoin airgead, faoi mhalartú earraí, faoin bhféinteorannú agus faoi mhaireachtáil i gcorp baineann. Bhí táirge cultúrtha na mban ag brath riamh ar mhargáil faoi am agus faoi airgead, agus bhí cuid mhaith den dá rud ag teastáil leis an gcnuasach seo a dhéanamh. Cé gur cheadaigh ár gcuid post ollscoile cuid den acmhainn ama a bhí ag teastáil, chuir Field Day an maoiniú agus an saineolas ar fáil a lig dúinn téacsanna a chnuasach agus a chur in eagar agus nótaí a chur leo. Anuas ar an gcúis phraicticiúil seo le dul i bpáirtíocht le Comhlucht Field Day, táimid ar aon intinn le heagarthóirí na chéad dtrí imleabhar faoi a thábhachtaí is atá sé do léitheoirí in Éirinn agus in áiteanna eile téacsanna litríochta agus staire a athghabháil agus a athléiriú, agus a chur ar fáil go forleathan, chun gur féidir le dearctha úra ar an todhchaí fás as tuiscintí nua ar an am atá caite. Le trí bliana anuas is ar Chló Ollscoil Chorcaí atá ualach na hoibre tite, ó thaobh an leabhar féin a thabhairt amach, agus is mór linn an tsamhlaíocht agus an fhlaithiúlacht atá léirithe acu agus dhá imleabhar a dhéanamh in áit aon cheann amháin. Tá ár mórbhuíochas tuilte go háirithe ag beirt a bhí tuisceanach thar an gcoitiantacht, Seamus Deane, ó Field Day agus Sara Wilbourne ó Chló Ollscoil Chorcaí: thugadar ar a gcuid eagraíochtaí dul sa seans agus tacaíocht a thabhairt don tionscnamh, ní ar mhaithe le brabús, ach toisc gur chreideadar go mba luachmhar é agus go mb'fhiú tabhairt faoi.

Cad atá i gceist le cnuasach de scríbhinní na hÉireann? Ina réamhrá le hImleabhar I (lch xix), luann Seamus Deane go bhfuil an focal *writing* (scríbhinní) á úsáid aige mar bhealach leis an gciall is teoranta den fhocal *literature* (litríocht) a sheachaint, ach is féidir 'litríocht' sa chiall is leithne a thabhairt ar an gcuid is mó dá bhfuil in Imleabhair I-III, go háirithe agus léann na litríochta á thuiscint go forleathan mar léann cultúrtha le tríocha bliain anuas. Ba bhaill de ranna litríochta in ollscoileanna formhór eagarthóirí Imleabhar I-III. Leathnaítear an tuiscint ar 'scríbhinní' arís in Imleabhair 4-5, ní amháin toisc roinnt staraithe agus saineolaí amháin ar an litríocht bhéil a bheith ar an bhfoireann eagarthóireachta, ach toisc go bhfuil gníomhaithe polaitíochta, iriseoirí, diagairí, filí agus úrscéalaithe, chomh maith le scoláirí as réimsí éagsúla, i measc na n-eagarthóirí cúnta. Is í an chiall a bhainimid as 'scríbhinní', 'na bealaí a n-úsáidtear focail'. Ó am go chéile tugaimid sracfhéachaint ar an gcaoi a mbíonn an ceol agus an t-íomháineachas á bhfí leis na focail agus brí á forbairt i saol na hÉireann — sa roinn faoi thraidisiúin bhéil, 'Oral Traditions', go háirithe a thagann an ceol i gceist — ach ní raibh na hacmhainní againn dul i ngleic leis na bealaí ar fad ar féidir scéal a insint; agus is le focail a phléimid anseo. Tá áit lárnach ag an litríocht i saol cultúrtha na hÉireann, agus áit lárnach aici anseo dá réir sin. Ní amháin go bhfuil sleachta roghnaithe againn as an gcuid is slachtmhaire agus is spéisiúla de scríbhneoireacht na hÉireann, áfach, ach tá ábhar tofa againn a léireoidh sraith comhthéacsanna do thuiscint chuimsitheach ar an saol atá caite ag mná in Éirinn.

D'fhéadfaí cuid de na scríbhneoirí a bhfuil saothar leo anseo a áireamh i measc lucht litríochta thíortha eile. Ní san áit chéanna a chaitheann daoine a saol ar fad, ná ní leor leo i gcónaí aon dúchas amháin. Tá tuiscint fhairsing againn anseo ar an méid atá i gceist le bheith Éireannach, agus súil againn gur tuiscint fháilteach í, agus muid ag féachaint ar na focail a úsáideadh in Éirinn agus a d'úsáid Éireannaigh in áiteanna eile. Is léir go hiondúil cén fáth gur tuigeadh téacs a bheith Éireannach, ach bhí ar na heagarthóirí ó am go chéile breith a thabhairt as a stuaim féin ar an mbaint a bhí ag téacs le hÉirinn: níor caitheadh ceann ar bith amach toisc gan a bheith sách Éireannach. I dtús na hoibre phléamar téacsanna Albanacha atá scríofa sa Ghaeilge Chlasaiceach, an teanga chaighdeánach a bhí ag filí na scol in Éirinn agus in Albain. Cé gur fianaise í an caighdeán céanna gurb aon saol cultúrtha a bhí sa dá áit, bheartaíomar nár chóir téacsanna a fhuadach as Albain do chnuasach Éireannach.

Is ceart míniú a thabhairt maidir le bearna mhór amháin sa saothar seo: bhí orainn faillí a dhéanamh i scríbhinní *diaspora* na hÉireann. Bíonn idir stoitheadh agus athphlandáil i gceist leis an imirce, agus nuair a thosaíomar ar an obair seo ní fhéadfaimis na hacmhainní a shamhlú a ligfeadh dúinn eolas cuimsitheach, seachas smeareolas, a sholáthar faoi imircigh na hÉireann. Léirímid scríbhneoirí Éireannacha san Eoraip go fial, agus d'fhéadfaí a áiteamh go mba cheart an freastal céanna a dhéanamh ar an Airgintín, ar an Astráil, ar Cheanada, ar an Afraic Theas nó ar na Stáit Aontaithe. Níl de leithscéal againn ach nach raibh na hacmahinní againn len é sin a dhéanamh.

Roimh na 1990í a baineadh an scraith don obair seo. Bhí caoi ag léirmheastóirí locht a fháil ar an *Field Day Anthology* 1991 ar an ábhar go raibh an oiread sin léitheoirí ar an eolas faoin am sin faoi shaothar na mban sa litríocht, sa pholaitíocht agus sa chultúr. Sna 1970í agus sna 1980í, ar an taobh eile, níor tugadh athshealbhú ná athbhreithniú ar fhriotal ná ar stair na mban san áireamh agus tuiscintí ar Éirinn á bplé agus á bhforbairt. Dá mbeadh cúrsaí inscne i gceist ansin mar ghné den fhéiniúlacht náisiúnta agus pholaitiúil, seans nach leagfaí amach canónacha litríochta ná insintí ar an stair mar a leagadh. Mar a léirigh an díospóireacht i ndiaidh do Imleabhair I–III teacht amach, bhí faillí á ndéanamh i stair litearta, shóisialta agus chultúrtha na mban fiú amháin ag na criticeoirí sin a bhí báúil leis an bhfeimineachas agus le léann na mban. Tá an dá imleabhar seo curtha le chéile againn lena léiriú gur fairsinge agus gur éagsúla saol agus samhlaíocht na mban in Éirinn ná mar a thugann steiritípeanna le tuiscint, agus mar iniúchadh ar bhunús go leor de na steiritípeanna céanna. Níl aon iarracht déanta againn na difríochtaí cultúrtha agus polaitíochta idir mná na hÉireann, inniu ná san am atá caite, a cheilt ná a chur ar ceal. Mar eagarthóirí, tugaimid faoi na téacsanna a chuirimid i láthair ar bhealaí éagsúla, ach cé nach rabhamar i gcónaí ar aon intinn faoi na téacsanna ba cheart a roghnú, ná faoin gciall a bhí le baint astu, táimid ag obair as lámh a chéile ón tús, agus ag cur lenár gcuid eolais féin trí phlé agus trí chrosthagairtí.

Tá réimsí achrannacha i saol na hÉireann inar mhaith linn cothrom Féinne a thabhairt do thuairimí ón dá thaobh, ach nár éirigh linn, de cheal ábhair. Bhíomar tar éis aontú ón tús gur ar ábhar a bhí scríofa nó taifeadta cheana ba cheart a leithéid seo de chnuasach mór stairiúil a bheith bunaithe. Cé go bhfuil réamhaistí gearra anseo ag ciallú na rannóg éagsúla, mar sin, níor ghéilleamar don chathú a bhí orainn ráitis nua díospóireachta a choimisiúnú. Fágann sé seo gur mó a léirítear meon náisiúnaíoch ná meon aontachtach sna rannóga faoin scríbhneoireacht is déanaí as Tuaisceart Éireann, mar shampla. Ar an gcaoi chéanna, cé go bhfuil an-chuid díospóireachta déanta in Éirinn faoi chúrsaí collaíochta ó na 1960í ar aghaidh, díreach mar a tharla in áiteanna eile, is ar éigin atá aon scríbhinní tagtha chun cinn faoin leithleachas radacach, nó faoin bpornagrafaíocht, gan ach dhá shampla a lua.

Tá idir lámhscríbhinní agus fuaimthaifid phríomha i measc ár bhfoinsí, agus tarraingímid as obair nár cuireadh ar fáil roimhe seo ach do phobal teoranta, mar a bhíonn i gceist, mar shampla, ag léamh leisbiach filíochta, nó i gcás agallamh le príosúnaithe a fhoilsítear i nuachtlitir áitiúil. Míbhuntáiste amháin a bhaineann leis an gcur chuige traidisiúnta a leanamar — ábhar a tharraingt as a raibh ar fáil, seachas dul as an mbealach le freastal ar gach tráth dá bhfuil — go ndéantar faillí i ngrúpaí áirithe ban, mar na himircigh atá tagtha le déanaí, teifigh agus iarratasóirí tearmainn ina measc.

Ocht roinn atá sa saothar seo: Lorg na Meánaoiseanna *600–1900* ('Medieval to Modern'); *An Creideamh, an Eolaíocht, an Diagacht agus an Eitic, 1500–2000* ('Religion, Science, Theology and Ethics'); *An Chollaíocht* ('Sexuality'); *Traidisiúin Bhéil* ('Oral Traditions'); *Na Mná i Sochaí na hÉireann,*

1200–2000 ('Women in Irish Society'); *An Pholaitíocht, 1500–2000* ('Politics'); *Scríbhinní na mBan, 1700–1960* ('Women's Writing'), agus *Scríbhinní Comhaimseartha, 1960–2001* ('Contemporary Writing'). Tá gach roinn leagtha amach ag a heagarthóir mar chuid de phróiseas níos leithne, cáipéisí de chineálacha éagsúla a athshealbhú agus bealaí nua a fhorbairt le dul i ngleic leo. Tá gach roinn briste ina rannóga a chuimsíonn obair na n-eagarthóirí cúnta, agus is féidir an saothar a léamh i dtreonna éagsúla de bharr na gcrostagairtí ó roinn go roinn agus ó rannóg go rannóg. Ní áitímid gur rangú cinniúnach ná nádúrtha é seo atá buailte anuas ar an ábhar againn. Bhreathnaíomar ar Imleabhair I–III agus shocraíomar gan an t-ábhar nua a roinnt de réir *genres* liteartha, ná mórúdar, ná imeachtaí staire. Níorbh fhéidir cúl a thabhairt chomh saoráideach céanna le prionsabal na cróineolaíochta, áfach, agus leanann gach roinn fráma ama de réir mar is cuí.

Is fada siar a théann an nós in Éirinn gur i bpáirt a chruthaítear cuid den táirge cultúrtha is saibhre, agus ní hionann an áit atá ag cultúr an phrionda in Éirinn agus sa Bhreatain, nó i Meiriceá, mar shampla. Tuiscint an 19ú agus an 20ú haois ar an scríbhneoireacht mar thraidisiún buirgéiseach ban, ní oireann sí don chás seo, mar sin. Ó thús ama go dtí an 20ú haois, bhí an chuid is mó den fhilíocht in Éirinn sa tuiseal gairmeach: dírithe ar phátrúin nó ar a gcéilí cnis, ar fhilí eile, nó ar dhaoine aonaracha i bpobal an fhile. Sa tréimhse 1500–1900, bhí scríobh na Gaeilge in Éirinn fréamhaithe i bhfad níos daingne sa chumarsáid idir daoine ná mar a bhí a leithéid in Albain, mar shampla, ná i mBreatnais sa Bhreatain Bheag. Pléitear na pointí seo, agus gnéithe eile den litríocht in Éire Ghaelach anuas go dtí an nua-aimsir, in Lorg na Meánaoiseanna, *600–1900*, atá curtha in eagar ag Máirín Ní Dhonnchadha. Léiríonn *Traidisiún Béil*, atá curtha in eagar ag Angela Bourke, cuid de na bealaí éagsúla ilchasta is gá a úsáid le dul i ngleic leis an méid a thuigtear le húdar i gcomhthéacs na hÉireann.

Is minic mná na linne seo in Éirinn faoi anáil ag modhanna gníomhaíochta agus tuisceana ó áiteanna eile, agus na modhanna sin á gcur in oiriúint acu dá riachtanaisí féin. Filíocht, ficsean, dráma agus critic le mná Éireannacha is ábhar do *Scríbhinní na mBan, 1700–1960*, atá curtha in eagar ag Gerardine Meaney, agus déantar iniúchadh ann ar an dúchas agus an iasacht faoi mar a fheictear iad i scríbhneoireacht na mban. Is le mná amháin freisin na scríbhinní sa roinn *Scríbhinní Comhaimseartha, 1960–2001*, atá curtha in eagar ag Clair Wills. I ranna eile, thuigeamar gurb é an leagan amach ab fhearr a léireodh gach téama, mná agus fir a thaispeáint ag cruthú céille thart ar a dtaithí féin, ar an inscne agus ar an gcollaíocht, ach is do thuairisc na mban féin ar a saol agus ar a n-intinn a thugtar tús áite tríd síos. Téacsanna gan ainm cuid mhaith dá bhfuil againn ó na luath-thréimhsí staire go háirithe. Bíonn tuarascála parlaiminte, Coimisiúin Fhiosraithe, tuairiscí nuachtán, tuairiscí leighis agus cáipéisí dlí gan ainm go minic freisin; fir a scríobh a bhformhór, ach ní hionann cás dóibh agus do dhán nó úrscéal gan ainm.

Bhí agus tá mná le fáil i mbeagnach gach ceann de na hinstitiúidí as a ndéantar an tsochaí: an chlann, an pholaitíocht, an eaglais, an obair; ní ó na rudaí a tharlaíonn amháin a thagann crut ar an saol dúinn, ach ó na rudaí a thuigtear, a deirtear agus a scríobhtar. Pléann *Na Mná i Sochaí na hÉireann, 1200–2000*, atá curtha in eagar ag Maria Luddy, ar bhonn téamúil agus cróineolaíoch le mórcheisteanna eacnamaíochta, oideachais agus imirce i dtaca le saol na mban. Is é atá in *An Pholaitíocht, 1500–2000*, atá curtha in eagar ag Mary O'Dowd, léiriú ar ghuthanna na mban sa pholaitíocht ó thús ré na dTúdarach go dtí deireadh an fhichiú haois in Éirinn.

Ón seachtú haois déag i leith, tá mórspéis léirithe ag rialtais éagsúla Éireann i rialú na collaíochta: ag tacú le cineálacha áirithe giniúna, saol teaghlaigh agus caidrimh, agus ag cur in aghaidh chineálacha eile. Seasann scríbhneoirí, intleachtóirí agus gníomhaithe polaitiúla mar fhreasúra le faire seo an stáit, agus díospóireacht níos poiblí agus níos oscailte á héileamh acu faoin ngnéas in Éirinn: céard atá i gceist leis, nó céard a d'fhéadfadh a bheith. Agus an cnuasach seo á chur le chéile, thugamar san áireamh an réimse ama agus áite ina bhfuil caint ar an gcollaíocht mar chuid de dhioscúrsaí eile: í á scrúdú ag cúirteanna dlí, ag lucht leighis, ag iriseoirí agus ag ceannairí creidimh; á plé i bpríobháid litreacha agus dialann; á samhlú in úrscéalata, i ndánta, i ndrámaí agus i mbailéid. Tá idir théacsanna anaithnid agus léargas nua ar théacsanna seanaitheanta sa roinn *An Chollaíocht*, atá curtha in eagar ag Siobhán Kilfeather. Is é atá in *An Creideamh, an Eolaíocht, an Diagacht agus an Eitic, 1500–2000*, atá curtha in eagar ag Margaret MacCurtain, taiscéaladh ar spioradáltacht agus ar chreideamh na mban i ndiaidh Reifirméisin Chreidimh an séú haois déag, agus mná ag teacht i dtír de réir a chéile ar an machnamh eolaíochta agus diagachta a chur in iúl.

I ngach ceann den ocht roinn, míníonn na heagarthóirí an bunús a bhí le roghnú ábhair don téama atá faoi chaibidil. Ní fhéadfadh cnuasach ar bith freastal go hiomlán ar na daoine ar fad a bhfuil saol caite acu in Éirinn. I gcás Ghorta an naoú haois déag, mar shampla, tá fianaise scríofa againn ó dhornán daoncharad agus taistealaithe ban, agus ó roinnt ban a bhain le haicme na n-úinéirí talaimh nó leis an meánaicme, ach is ar éigin a mhaireann cáipéisí ón dream a cailleadh leis an ocras, cé go mb'fhéidir go bhfuil macalla dá nglór le fáil sna scéalta agus sna hamhráin in *Traidisiún Bhéil*.

Sna deich mbliana ó thosaíomar ar an obair, is iomaí dúshlán agus díospóireacht a spreag leagan amach na n-ocht roinn seo eadrainn. Tá fás agus forbairt tagtha ar an léann feimineach ó 1992 i leith: ceisteanna nua tagtha chun cinn agus réimsí nua staidéir á n-oscailt. Tá iarracht déanta againn freastal ar an mbláthú seo i gcuartú an eolais trí chóras crostagairtí a fhorbairt a threoróidh léitheoireacht ar théamaí cosúil le cuid na mban den aistriúchán nó den litríocht do pháistí, agus a ligfidh do léitheoirí na téacsanna agus an t-ábhar a théann leo a cheadú ar go leor bealaí éagsúla. Pointe tosaigh amháin, b'fhéidir, traidisiún dúchasach an dinnseanchais, arbh ann dó i bhfad roimh an mbuairt éiceafeimineach faoi chaidreamh na mban leis an dúlra: insíonn ábhar an chnuasaigh seo scéal ilghlórach faoi chúrsaí áite agus faoi chúrsaí timpeallachta do mhná in Éirinn.

Cé nach ionann go baileach an cur chuige eagarthóireachta ná na slata tomhais a chuirtear i bhfeidhm anseo ó chineál amháin ábhair go dtí cineál eile, ná ó dhisciplín go disciplín, agus cé go bhfuil na ranna neamhspleách ar a chéile ó thaobh fonótaí agus tagairtí, baineann mórphrionsabail áirithe eagarthóireachta leis an saothar tríd síos. Ní nós linn údair a léiriú anseo atá léirithe go maith in Imleabhair I-III, ach amháin sa chás go molaimid athbhreithniú orthu siúd a bhfuil a gcáil bunaithe ar shampla teoranta nó neamhthipiciúil dá saothar, nó gur dóigh linn gur gá téacsanna seanaitheanta a lonnú as an nua. Is í eagarthóir gach roinne atá freagrach ar deireadh as a bhfuil ina roinn féin, ach is minic a phléamar leagan amach na n-imleabhar trí chéile, agus a chinneamar mar fhoireann ar ábhar a aistriú ó roinn go roinn, a mhéadú nó a laghdú, chun freastal ar théamaí éagsúla. Tá sleachta anseo, cuid mhaith acu i gcló den chéad uair, as seantéacsanna a léitear go fíor-annamh agus nach bhfuil fáil orthu le fada, chomh maith le téacsanna faoi chonspóidí agus díospóireachtaí agus gluaiseachtaí liteartha ár linne féin. Ba é a chuireamar romhainn ón tús, réimse fairsing téacsanna a chur ar fáil i bhfoirm sholéite.

Go dtí le déanaí, is beag an t-eolas a bhí le fáil faoi scríbhneoirí ná faoi scríbhinní ban i saothair thagartha; tá dúthracht caite ag na heagarthóirí cúnta ar fad chun teacht ar bhlúirí eolais, ar scoláirí agus ar shaineolaithe, agus fiú amháin ar mhuintir na scríbhneoirí ba lú aithne orthu. Ba dheacra, uaireanta, eolas a aimsiú faoi scríbhneoirí comhaimseartha ná futhu siúd atá caillte le fada. Tá gach iarracht déanta againn nótaí cuimsitheacha beathaisnéise agus leabhareolais a sholáthar faoi scríbhneoirí agus aithriseoirí a bhfuil ábhar leo anseo. I gcásanna áirithe, tá teipthe orainn de cheal eolais, nó toisc téacsanna a bheith gan ainm, agus tá súil againn, má thugtar lúb ar lár faoi deara, go gcuirfear eolas ar fáil dúinn. Tá iarracht déanta againn teacht suas leis na scríbhneoirí agus na haithriseoirí a mhaireann, agus le sealbhóirí cóipchirt, ach i gcásanna áirithe níl againn ach ainm, agus i gcásanna eile, níl an méid sin féin againn. Cuirfimid fáilte roimh eolas breise, mar sin, agus ceartófar earráidí in eagráin eile den saothar seo. Clúdaíonn an t-ábhar seo go leor réimsí nár saothraíodh mórán go dtí seo, ach is é is mó a thugann sásamh dúinn, a shoiléire is a fheictear na háiteanna a bhfuil an brat tanaí, agus táimid ag súil go mór leis na glúnta nua scoláireachta a dhéanfaidh iniúchadh ar scéal na mban in Éirinn.

Cúram faoi leith a ghlacamar orainn féin tríd síos, saol na mban a léiriú sa dá theanga, agus chuireamar aistriúcháin Bhéarla ar fáil — cinn úrnua, cuid acu — ar théacsanna Gaeilge; rinneadh caighdeánú ar luath-théacsanna Béarla nuair ba ghá. Tugtar ainmneacha scríbhneoirí, amhránaithe agus scéalaithe de réir mar is fearr aithne orthu, ach gheofar gach ainm a bhíonn in úsáid san Innéacs, idir ainmneacha breithe agus pósta, agus ainmneacha cleite. Tá caighdeánú déanta ar ainmneacha dílse i gcuid de na ranna, ach gheofar gach leagan san Innéacs.

Ag trácht di ar fhile anaithnid mná ón stair, deir Eiléan Ní Chuilleanáin, file, gur 'faoin dromchla' a mhair a hainm.[1] Tá an dromchla féin athraithe, agus tá ainmneacha nua ag borradh aníos tríd. Is siúlach an saothar é seo, a thugann cuairt ar an-chuid foirmeacha scríbhneoireachta, ar cháipéisí staire agus ar thraidisiúin bhéil, áit a mbíonn friotal na bhfilí ag bualadh le caint na mbocht agus le reitric na bpolaiteoirí, agus ní leor linn cur le canóin scríbhinní na hÉireann, nó ceann nua a mholadh, nó stair 'íseal le huasal' a chur ar fáil do lucht ollscoile. Tá sé de cheart ag mná na hÉireann eolas a chur ar an stair agus ar an gcultúr a bhaineann leo féin. Tairgímid an saothar seo dár léitheoirí ar fad mar chnuasach téacsanna atá spéisiúil ó thaobh na staire, snasta ó thaobh ealaíne, agus riachtanach ó thaobh na polaitíochta.

Bealtaine 2002.

---

1. 'Her name lay under the surface', Eiléan Ní Chuilleanáin, 'J'ai Mal a nos Dents', *The Magdalene Sermon* (Loughcrew: Gallery Press, 1989)

Acknowledgments

The Editors and the Publishers wish to thank the following for their help in the production of the Anthology:

Marianne McDonald and the Lannan Foundation for their generous support of the Field Day Anthology enterprise and Seamus Deane of Field Day Publications Ltd for creating the space for development of Volume IV of the *Field Day Anthology of Irish Writing*. Seamus Deane brought us together, raised funds for the project, gave expert advice on many aspects of editorial practice, facilitated at numerous meetings, read through some material as we developed the shape of the anthology, and was unstinting with his help and encouragement. Sara Wilbourne of Cork University Press has been a remarkable publisher and a friend to this project, taking extraordinary amounts of work on herself in order to bring everything to completion.

The editors of each section, and the subsection editors received invaluable help from a broad community of scholars and friends. In many cases the following people provided texts for inclusion, sought out dates and bibliographical information, wrote headnotes, provided leads to help locate hitherto undiscovered details about the authors in the Anthology, or offered less direct but no less valuable forms of support. We would like to say thank you to:

Jean Agnew, Bo Almqvist, John Archer, Wanda Balzano, David Berman, Angela Bolster, RM, Maryrose Bourke, Margaret Brindley, Terence Brown, Ivor Browne, M.T. Bruck, Tony Buckley, James Buxton, David Cannon, John Carey, Andrew Carpenter, Pam Charlton, Mary Clark, Joe Cleary, Kathleen Clune, Claire Connolly, Anne Connon, Evelyn Conlon, Roisín Conroy, Marie-Louise Coolahan, Karen Corrigan, Goretti Corway, Michael Cronin, Virginia Crossman, Patrick Crotty, Fintan Cullen, Rosemary Cullen-Owens, Monica Cullinan, Brendan Dalton, Peter Dews, James Donnelly, Margaret Anne Doody, Dolores Dooley, Jo Dorran O.P., Aileen Douglas, Gerry Dowling, Gráinne Dowling, Damien Doyle, Mary Dunne, Fraser Easton, Marcella Edwards, Richard English, Jennifer Fitzgerald, Claudia FitzHerbert, Elizabeth FitzPatrick, Christopher Fitzsimon, Marie Therese Flanagan, Maggie Fleming, Anne Fogarty, Tadgh Foley, Rachel Furmston, Catherine Gandy, Nessa Gardiner, Tom Garvin, Dolores Gibbons, Luke Gibbons, William Gillies, Chris GoGwilt, Fiana Griffin, Isobel Grundy, Jane Hall, Judith Hawley, Michael Hayes, David Hayton, Brian Henry, Patrick Hilary, Philip Horne, Peter Jameson, Norma Jessop, Liane Jones, Robert Jones, Helen Kahn, Fergus Kelly, James Kelly, Patricia Kelly, Patricia Kennedy, John Kilfeather, Rachel Kilfeather, Sylke Lehane, Jayne Lewis, Brian Leyden, Rolf Loeber, Geraldine Luddy, Máire MacAongusa, Caoimhín Mac Giolla Leith, Mícheál Mac Craith, Pádraig Mac Gréine, Alen MacWeeney, Eoin Magennis, Magda Majkowska, Richard Maxwell, John McCafferty, Nell McCafferty, Charles McCarthy, Peggy McCarthy,

W.J. McCormack, Lucy McDiarmid, James McGeachie, Medbh McGuckian, Neil McKenna, Helen Miles, Lia Mills, Theresa Moriarty, Deirdre Morrissey, Dorothea von Mücke, Paul Muldoon, James H. Murphy, James Murphy, Maureen Murphy, Christopher Murray, Éilis Ní Dhuibhne, Siobhán Ní Laoire, Máirín Nic Eoin, Michelle Nic Leoid, Eoghan Ó hAnluain, Brendán Ó Caoláin, Séamas Ó Catháin, Anne O'Connor, Gearóid Ó Crualaoich, Dáibhí Ó Cróinín, Pádraigín O'Donoghue, Anne O'Dowd, Pius O'Farrell PBVM, Cathal O'Hainle, Tom O'Loughlin, Diarmaid Ó Muirithe, Nollaig Ó Muraíle, Máirtín Ó Murchú, Kevin O'Neill, Dáithí Ó hÓgáin, Ruairí Ó hUiginn, Tina O'Toole, Kathy Overfield, Vincent Quinn, Marie Redmond, Nini Rodgers, Nell Regan, Avril Reynolds FMSA, Ian Campbell Ross, Jonathan Sachs, Mary Salmon, Catherine Santoro, Caitríona Scanlan, Hugh Shields, Mary Shine, Elaine Showalter, Sinéad Ní Shúinéar, Philippe Similon, Katharine Simms, Alan Sinfield, Ailbhe Smyth, Magda Stouthamer-Loeber, Betsy Thompson, Colm Tobin, Katie Trumpener, Diane Urqhardt, Norman Vance, Karen Van Dyck, Brian Walker, Margaret Ward, Bernadette Whelan, Kevin Whelan, Norman White, Sean White, Jonathan Williams, Bernard Wills, Philomena Wills, Rachel Wilshaw, Susan Winnett.

The editors and subsection Editors owe a special debt of thanks to those who created new editions or translations of texts for Volumes IV and V. Their names are to be found in the headnotes to the texts in question and in the index.

The Editors would like to thank: Cormac Deane, Emer Deane and Colette Nelis for their secretarial and administrative support and extend a special thank you to Moynagh Sullivan for editorial assistance. Numerous institutions helped with library, archival and administrative support. We would also like to thank:

The staff of the National Library of Ireland; the Munby Rare Books Room, Cambridge University Library; Marsh's Library, Dublin; University College Dublin Library; the Royal Irish Academy; the Archives of the Medical Missionaries of Mary Drogheda; the Central Library, Belfast; the Gilbert Library, Dublin; the Linenhall Library, Belfast (especially John Killen and John Gray); Mary Doran and staff at the British Library; the Public Record Office of Northern Ireland; the Queen's Library with special thanks to the staff in the Special Collection Library; the Manuscript Room of Trinity College, Dublin; The Department of Irish Folklore, UCD; Pavee Point; The School of Celtic Studies of the Dublin Institute for Advanced Studies. The staff of Beinecke Library, Yale University; Belfast Public Library; Birmingham Public Library; University of Chicago Library; Columbia University Library; London Library; Newberry Library, Chicago; New York Public Library; Princeton University Library; and Sussex University Library.

The publishers and editors wish to acknowledge the immense contribution made towards the project by Hilary Bell who undertook the daunting task of copyediting the final text. Her skill, accuracy and patience made an incalcuable contribution to these volumes. We would like to say a special thank you to Deborah Marshall, who along with Madeleine D'Arcy expertly read and checked thousands of proof pages throughout production. Thanks to Eileen O'Carroll who took on the burden of collating and proof-reading in the early stages of production, and also to Fintan Lane who proofed last minute additions at short notice. Thanks to Síne Quinn who ably and persistently tracked down missing data on writers. Two of Ireland's finest indexers took on the considerable task of indexing 3,300 pages in twenty days: Gloria Greenwood and Yann Kelly, thank you. We would also like to say a special thank you to Mick Lynam and Noel Murphy of Phototype-Set (who produced the first three volumes of the Anthology in the late 1980's without the benefits of desk-top typesetting technology). Thank you for your skill and professionalism throughout the long duration of the typesetting process.

COPYRIGHT ACKNOWLEDGMENTS

The Publishers are grateful to the following for giving permission to use copyright material in Volume IV and V of *The Field Day Anthology of Irish Writing*. The following list constitutes acknowledgment of permissions granted for both volumes. While we have made very effort to trace copyright in all cases where rights are held, we have not been able to contact the rights holder in all cases. We would be grateful if rights holders could inform us so that we can correct any errors in future editions.

Archer, Nuala, *The Hour of Panama* (Salmon Press, 1992)

Archer, Nuala, "Hunting the Sloth" and "Whale on the line" from *Whale on the Line,* 1981, by kind permission of the author and The Gallery Press, Loughcrew, Oldcastle, County Meath, Ireland

Aron, Geraldine, *A Galway Girl* (Samuel French Inc, New York, 1979)

Bardwell, Leland "Dvostoevsky's Grave" (Dedalus 1991)

Beckett, Mary, *A Belfast Woman* (Poolbeg Press, 1973)

Behan, Brendan, extract from *After The Wake* published by The O'Brien Press Ltd, Dublin, © Copyright Brendan Behan

Boland, Eavan, from *The Journey and Other Poems* (Carcanet Press Ltd, Manchester, 1987)

Bourke, Angela, by kind permission of The Jonathan Williams Literary Agency

Bowen, Elizabeth, extracts from *Disloyalties* and *Why Do I Write*, © Elizabeth Bowen, reproduced by permission of Curtis Brown Ltd

Boylan, Clare, *Concerning Virgins* (Hamish Hamilton, 1989, Copyright © Clare Boylan, 1989. Reproduced by permission of the author c/o Rogers, Coleridge & White Ltd, 20 Powis Mews, London, W11 1JN

Breen, Suzanne, "Mandarin Mayhew" *Fortnight,* March, 1999

Brennan, Maeve, *The Springs of Affection* reprinted by permission of Harper Collins Publishers Ltd © Maeve Brennan 1997

Browne, Ivor, Paddy Torpey Killoughry "The Holy Church of Rome" reprinted by kind permission of Professor Ivor Browne

Buckley, John, "Cinderella dressed in yella." *The Irish Times* 24 September, 1982

Buckley, Suzanne, and Pamela Lonegran "Women and the Troubles" from *Terrorism in Ireland* (Routledge, London, 1984, reprinted by permission of Taylor & Francis Ltd)

Burc, Patrick A., *Bean Phaidin* (1986) reprinted by permission of the Head of the Department of Irish Folklore, University College Dublin.

Burc, Eamon A., Eamon a Burc, *Scealta* (An Clochomhar, 1983)

Burke Brogan, Patricia., "Eclipsed" (Salmon Press, 1992)

Callaghan, Louise C., "The Puzzle Heart" (Salmon Press, 1999)

Campbell, Siobhan, *The Permanant Wave* (Blackstaff Press, 1996)

Cannon, Moya, "Holy well"; "Oar"; "Taom"; "Nest"; and "Hills" from *Oar,* 2000, by kind permission of the author and The Gallery Press, Loughcrew, Oldcastle, County Meath, Ireland

Carr, Ellie, "Account of May Dew" *Traveller Ways, Traveller Words* (Pavee Point Travellers' Centre, 1992)

Carr, Marina, from *The Mai* 1995, by kind permission of the author and The Gallery Press, Loughcrew, Oldcastle, County Meath, Ireland

Chonaire, Brid Ni, An Sagairin (1986) reprinted by permission of the Head of the Department of Irish Folklore, University College Dublin

Chuilleanain, Eilean Ni, "J'ai mal a nos dents"; "The Informant"; "Street"; "The Liturgy"; "Pygmalion's Image"; and "St Mary Magdalene" all from *The Magdalene Sermon and Earlier Poems* (Wake Forest University Press, Winston-Salem, N.C.), and by kind permission of the author and The Gallery Press, Lougtherew, Oldcastle, County Meath, Ireland

Clarke, Kathleen, extract from *Revolutionary Woman - My Fight for Ireland's Freedom* published by The O'Brien Press Ltd, Dublin, © Copyright Kathleen Clarke

Cleary, Catherine, "Women at War" *Sunday Tribune* 4 July 1999

Cleary, Nora, 'The Bold Trooper' (1975) reprinted by permission of the Head of the Department of Irish Folklore, University College Dublin

Colum, Mary, *Life and the Dream* (Macmillan, London, 1928)

Condren, Mary, *The Serpent and the Goddess* (new edition New Island Press, Dublin, 2002)

Connolly, Susan, "How high the moon" (Dedalus 1991)

Conway, Joan, "Too late for me" reprinted by permission of *The Irish Times* 1971

Coughlan, Patricia, "Bog Queens: the representation of women in the poetry of John Monague and Seamus Heaney" from *Gender in Irish Writing* (ed. Toni O'Brien Johnson and David Cairns) (Open University Press, 1991)

Coulter, Carol, "Hello Divorce, goodbye Daddy" from *Gender and Sexuality in Modern Ireland* (eds. Anthony Bradley and Maryann Valiulia) (University of Massachusetts Press, Amherst, 1997): "Feminism and Nationalism in Ireland" from *Rethinking Northern Ireland Culture, Ideology and Colonialism* (ed. David Miller) © Addison Wesley Longman Limited 1998, reprinted by permission of Pearson Education Limited

Court, Artelia, "A fortune" from *Puck of the Droms: The Lives and Literature of the Irish Tinkers* (The University of California Press, Berkeley, 1985)

Court, Artelia, "The man who caught the mermaid" from *Puck of the Droms: The Lives and Literature of the Irish Tinkers* (The University of California Press, Berkeley, 1985)

Cowman, Roz, "The Goose Herd" (Salmon Press, 1989)

Coyle, Kathleen, *Liv* (Jonathan Cape, London, 1928, used by permission of The Random House Group Limited)

Crone, Joni, *Lesbian and the Gay Visions of Ireland* (Cassell, 1995)

Cronin, Elizabeth (Bess), "Cuc-A-Nandy" BBC Sound Archive 1947

Cummins, Mary, reprinted by permission of The *Irish Times* 1995

D'Arcy, Margaretta, "The Little Gray Home in the West" from *Arden & D'Arcy Plays 1* (Methuen Publishing, London, 1972)

Deevy, Teresa, *The King of Spain's daughter* (Macmillan, London, 1939)

Devlin, Anne, *The Way Paver* (Faber & Faber Ltd, London 1986): *Ourselves Alone* (Faber & Faber Ltd, London, 1985)

Devlin, Polly, *All Of Us There* (Weidenfeld and Nicolson, London, 1983)

Dhiubhne, Éilís Ni, *The Women's Fort is On Fire* (Poolbeg Press, 1994)

Dhomhnaill, Nuala Ni, Ceol Irish Traditional Music Archive, 1982: "Ceist na Teangan" (trans. Paul Muldoon "The Language Issue"): "Fear Suaithinseach" (trans. Seamus Heaney "Miraculous Grass") by kind permission of the author and The Gallery Press, Loughcrew, Oldcastle, County Meath, Ireland, from *Pharaoh's Daughter* 1990

Doherty, Kate 'Dineery', "The Dark eyed Sailor" (1984) reprinted by permission of the Head of the Department of Irish Folklore, University College Dublin

Doherty, Eileen., *Bloody Sunday in Derry: What Really Happened* (Brandon Press, Dingle, 1992)

Dolan, Mary, "Jimmy Whelan" (1971) reprinted by permission of the Head of the Department of Irish Folklore, University College Dublin

Donegan, Bill, "The Nobleman's Wedding" (1975) reprinted by permission of the Head of the Department of Irish Folklore, University College Dublin

Donoghue, Emma, "The tale of the shoe" from *Kissing the Witch* (Hamish Hamilton, 1997)

Donovan, Katie, *Watermelon Man* (Bloodaxe Books, 1993)

Dorcey, Mary, "Beginning"; "Friendship"; and "Come quietly or the neighbours will hear" from *Moving into the Space Cleared by Our Mothers* (Salmon Press, 1991): "A Country Dance" from *A Noise in the Woodshed* (Onlywomen Press, London, 1989)

Dougan, Sally, *Only The Rivers Run Free* (Pluto Press, London, 1984)

Duffy, Catherine, "The erratic behaviour of tides" (Dedalus 1998)

Earlham College, "Charles F Coffin: Notes on Prisons, Reformatories, Gaols, Etc. Through

Ireland and Great Britain (1871)"; from Lilly Library, Earlham College, Richmond, Virginia,

Enright, Anne, *The Portable Virgin* (Secker & Warburg, 1991, copyright © Anne Enright 1991. Reproduced by permission of the author c/o Rogers, Coleridge & White Ltd. 20 Powis Mews, London, W11 1JN

Eoin, Mairin, nic., *B'Ait Leo Bean* (An Clochomhar 1971)

Evans, Martina, "Limbo", "One Evening in July", "Christmas Days" and "The Smell" from *All Alcoholics are Charmers* by Martina Evans (Anvil Press Poetry 1998)

Ferguson, Rosaleen, *Force 10* 10 (1991)

Fhionnlaoich, Maire Mhic, *The Giant Killer and His Dog* (Bluebeard) (1938) reprinted by permission of the Head of the Department of Irish Folklore, University College Dublin

Friends' Historical Archives "Letter to Ann Shannon (1786)", from Friends' Historical Library, Dublin

Gaffney, Maureen, extract from *The Way We Live Now,* reproduced by kind permission of the Jonathan Williams Literary Agency

Ghallchobhair, Brid Ui, "Abhainn Mhor" (1956) reprinted by permission of the Head of the Department of Irish Folklore, University College Dublin

Ghallchobhair, Sile ni, "An Seanduine Doite" BBC Sound Archive 1953

Ghrianna, Sorcha Mhic, "Ri Na Fasaighe Duibhe" (1956) reprinted by permission of the Head of the Department of Irish Folklore, University College Dublin

Ghuairim, Sorcha, Ni, "An Sceil;pin Droighneach" (1940) ; and "Maile Ni Maoileoin" (1957) reprinted by permission of the Head of the Department of Irish Folklore, University College Dublin

Gillespie, Elgy, reprinted by permission of *The Irish Times* 1971

Groarke, Vona, "The Idea of the Atlantic"; "Patronage"; and "The Family Photograph" from *Shale* 1994, by kind permission of the author and The Gallery Press, Loughcrew, Oldcastle, County Meath, Ireland

Hardie, Kerry, "The young woman stands on the edge of her life"; "May"; "The husband's tale"; "Ship of Death"; and "Interlude" from *A Furious Place* 1996, all by kind permission of the author and The Gallery Press, Loughcrew,

Oldcastle, County Meath, Ireland

Hartigan, Anne le Marquand, "Immortal Sins" (Salmon Press, 1993)

Haverty, Anne., *The Beauty of the Moon* (Chatto & Windus Ltd., 1999: *One Day As A Tiger* (Chatto & Windus Ltd, 1978. Used by permission of The Random House Group Limited)

Hayes, Joanne, *My Story* (Brandon Press, Dingle, 1985)

Hinds, Bronagh, "Women working for peace in N.I." from *Contesting Politics* (eds. Yvonne Galligan and Ellis Ward) (Westview Press, 1997, copyright © 1997 by Westview Press, reprinted by permission of Westview Press, a member of Perseus Books, L.L.C.)

Hogan, Linda, *Occupying a Precarious Position: Women in Culture and Church in Ireland* (Columba Press, Blacknock, Co Dublin, 2000)

Holland, Mary, "Girl on a Nation's Conscience" *The Observer* 1992: extract reprinted by permission of *The Irish Times* 1999: "Mary the Mother and Her Impact on Irish Politics"; reprinted by permission of *The Irish Times* 1979: "Why the Flynn case is so important" reprinted by permission of *The Irish Times* 1985

Hooley, Ruth, "Sleeping with Monsters: Conversations with Scottish and Irish Women Poets" (Wolfhound Press, 1990)

Hoult, Norah, *Holy Ireland* (William Heinemann, 1935. Used by permission of The Random House Group Limited)

Jones, Marie, *Women on the Verge of HRT* (Nick Hern Books, 1995)

Joyce, Nan, *Traveller: An Autobiography* (Gill & Macmillan, 1985, © Nan Joyce and Anna Farmer, Dublin)

Joyce, Nellie, "The enchanted hare" *Traveller Ways, Traveller Words* (Pavee Point Travellers' Centre, 1992)

Kelly, Meave, *Necessary Treasons* (Blackstaff Press, 1985, copyright Michael Joseph, London)

Kennedy, Stanislaus, *Spiritual Journeys* (Veritas, 1997)

Kuti, Elizabeth., *Treehouses* (Methuen Publishing Limited, London, 2000)

Laverty, Maura, *Alone We Embark* (Longman, 1943)

Lennon, Tom, extract from *Crazy Love* published by The O'Brien Press Ltd, Dublin, © Copyright Tom Lennon

Lentin, Ronit, extract from 'Emerging Irish Identities' (1999) and 'Where did the journey begin?' (1987) reproduced with the kind permission of the author

Limerick Poor Law Union, "Minute Book" (1852, 1854, 1865) from Limerick Regional Archives, Limerick

Lingard, Joan, "Across the barricades" from *The Twelfth Day of July* (Hamish Hamilton, 1972)

Luain, Anna Nic an. "Na Cruacha: Scealta Agus Seanchasd" (1985) reprinted by permission of the Head of the Department of Irish Folklore, University College Dublin

Luddy, Maria, *Women Surviving: Studies in Irishwomen's History in the 19th and 20th Centuries* (Poolbeg Press, 1989)

Lynch, Nonie, *My Good-looking Man* (1992) reprinted by permission of the Head of the Department of Irish Folklore, University College Dublin

Lynch, Siobhan, "The farmer wants a wife" *Bealoideas* 1979

MacCarthy, Catherine Phil, "The Moment it Stopped"; "Charms"; "Lucy's Song"; "Spring Cleaning", from *The Blue Globe* (Salmon Press, 1998)

MacNeill, Maire, "The festival of Lughnasa" *Bealoideas* 1962

MacNeill, Maire, "Poll na seantuinne and poll tigh" *Bealoideas* 1971-3

Madden, Deirdre, *The Birds of the Innocent Wood* (Faber & Faber Ltd, London, 1988)

Maher, Mary, from *The Irish Times* 1971; and "Deserted Wives" reprinted by permission of *The Irish Times* 1970

Mahon, Brid, "Land of Milk and Honey: The Story of traditional Irish food and drink" from *Irish Folk Ways* (Routledge and Kegan Paul, London, 1957) reproduced by kind permissin of The Jonathan Williams Literary Agency

Makem, Sarah, "The Factory Girl" from *Who's that at My Bed Window* (Topic TSCD660, reprinted by permission of Topic Recods Ltd, London, 1968) and "Barbara Allen" from It Fell on a Day, A Bonny Summer Day (Topic TSCD667, reprinted by permission of Topic Records Ltd, London, 1980)

Malone, Mary, *Reading Women into History* (Columba Press, Blacknock, Co Dublin, 2000)

Manning, Olivia, *The Danger Tree* (Weidenfeld and Nicolson, London,1977): *A Romantic Hero* (William Heinemann, 1967. Used by permission of The Random House Group Limited)

McBreen, Joan, "A Walled Garden in Moylough" (Salmon Press, 1995)

McClenaghan, Brendi, "Invisible Comrades" (An Glor Gafa 1991)

McCrory, Moy, *Bleeding Sinners* (Methuen, London, 1988m copyright Sheil Land Associates Ltd)

McDiarmid, Lucy, *Gender and Sexuality in Modern Ireland* (University of Massachusetts Press, Amherst, 1997)

McDonagh, Margaret, *Moving Stories: Traveller Women Write* (Southwark Traveller Women's Group)

McDowell, Florence., *Other Days Around Me* (Blackstaff Press, 1966, copyright Campbell Thomson and McLaughlin, London for the author's estate)

McGuckian, Medbh, "A dream in three colours"; and "The dream language of Fergus", from *On Ballycastle Beach* 1995: "The man with two women"; "The book room"; and "Marconi's Cottage" from *Marconi's Cottage* 1991: "Captain Lavender" from *Captain Lavender* 1994: "The feminine Christs" from *Shelmalier* 1998: "The Moses room" from *Drawing Ballerinas* 2001 all by kind permission of the author and The Gallery Press, Loughcrew, Oldcastle, County Meath, Ireland

McKay, Susan, extract fro 'Interview with Róisín McAliskey' (1997) and 'Rest in Peace' (1997) reproduced by kind permission of the author

Medbh, Maighread, "Tenant" (Salmon Press, 1999); *The Making of a Pagan* (Blackstaff Press, 1990)

Meehan, Paula, "The statue of the Virgin at Granard speaks"; "The man who was marked by winter"; "The leaving"; and "The pattern", from *The Man Who Was Marked by Winter* 1991: "Would you jump into my grave as quick?" from *Pillow Talk* 1994. All poems appear by kind permission of the author and The Gallery Press, Loughcrew, Oldcastle, County Meath, Ireland

Mhuimhneachain, Cait Ni, "Ari Jug Mor Is E

Lan" (1941) reprinted by permission of the Head of the Department of Irish Folklore, University College Dublin

Miller, Aine, "Goldfish in a baby bath" (Salmon Press, 1994)

Mills, Lia, *Another Alice* (Poolbeg Press, 1996)

Minute Book of Dr Stevens' Hospital(1717-1906) and Westmoreland Lock Hospital, Patients' Register (1857-1868) from Royal College of Physicians of Ireland Library, Dublin

Morrissy, Mary, *Mother of Pearl* (Jonathan Cape, London, 1996, used by permission of The Random House Group Limited Copyright © Mary Morrissy 1996, Greene & Heaton Limited

Morrissey, Sinead, *There Was a Fire in Vancouver* (Carcanet Press Ltd, Manchester, 1996

Mother Catherine's Diary (1812-1825) and "Annals (1854-82) from Sisters of Charity Archives, Sandymount, Dublin

Moxley, Gina, *Danti-Dan* (Faber & Faber Ltd, London, 1995)

Murdoch, Iris, *Metaphysics as a Guide to Morals* (Chatto & Windus Ltd., 1992). Used by permission of The Random House Group Limited and Ed Victor Ltd.): *The Sea, The Sea* (Chatto & Windus Ltd., 1992. Used by permission of The Random House Group Limited and Ed Victor Ltd.)

Murphy., Brenda, "The Curse" from *The Female Line* (The Northern Ireland Women's Rights Movement, Belfast)

Murphy, Dervla., *Wheels Within Wheels* (John Murray (Publishers) Ltd, 1979)

Murphy, Pat, "Interview with Pat Murphy" *Screen* (1981)

National Library of Ireland, Ms 13.022; Ms 5985; Ms 4810; Ms 989 *Commission on Civil Service 1932-35*, property of the National Library of Ireland. Reproduced with the permission of the Council of Trustees of the National Library of Ireland

Newman, Joan, extracts from *Coming of Age* (Blackstaff Press, 1995); *Thin Ice* (Blackstaff Press, 1998)

O'Brien, Breda., reprinted by permission of *The Irish Times* 2000

O'Brien, Edna, extract from *The Love Object* (Jonathan Cape, 1968, copyright David Godwin Associates on behalf of the author's estate

O'Brien, Kate, *Mary Lavelle* (Heinemann, London, 1936); *My Heart and I* (Heinemann, London, 1955)

O'Cadhla, Labhras, "A Mhamai, Nach Tu An Cladhaire" (1954) reprinted by permission of the Head of the Department of Irish Folklore, University College Dublin

O'Connor, Clairr, "When you need them" (Salmon Press, 1989)

O'Cualain, Coilin, "Mainistir na Buille" (1986) reprinted by permission of the Head of the Department of Irish Folklore, University College Dublin

O'Donnell, Mary, "Reading the Sunflowers in September" and "Spiderwoman's Third Avenue Rhapsody" (Salmon Press, 1990 and 1993)

O'Faolain, Nuala, "Putting reality before idealism on the abortion issue" reprinted by permission of *The Irish Times* 1992

O'Hagan, Sheila, "The Troubled House" (Salmon Press, 1995)

O'Halloran, Maura 'Soshin' *Pure Heart, Enlightened Mind: The Zen Journal and Letters of an Irish Woman in Japan* (Tuttle Publishing, Boston, 1994)

O'Hanlon, Eilis, extract from *Sunday Independent* 21 September 1997

O'Leary, Olivia, *Sunday Tribune* 3 December 1995

O'Malley, Mary, "Where the Rocks Float" (Salmon Press, 1993)

O'Neill, Onora, "Women's rights whost obligations? from *Women's Voices, Women's Right* (ed. Alison Jeffries) (Westview Press, 1998, copyright © 1998 by Westview Press, reprinted by permission of Westview Press, a member of Perseus Books, L.L.C.)

O'Reilly, Emily, 'Anne Lovett: a teenage pregnancy could not have gone Unnoticed' (1984) and extract from *Magill* (1999) reproduced by kind permission of the author

Parker, Tony, *May the Lord in His Mercy be Kind to Belfast* (Jonathan Cape, London, 1993. Copyright © 1993. Reproduced by permission of the author c/o Rogers, Coleridge & White Ltd, 20 Powis Mews, London, W11 1JN

Paterson, Evangeline, "Lucifer with angels" (Dedalus 1994)

Power, Brenda, "Interview with Rosemary Scallon", *Sunday Tribune* 12 December 1999;

"Abortion brings out the ostrich in us" *Sunday Tribune* 17 December 2000

Power, Nora 'Oney', "The Fiery Dragon" (c. 1930); "Strange Adventure of the Storyteller with The Enchanted Man" (1930) reprinted by permission of the Head of the Department of Irish Folklore, University College Dublin

Prendiville, Monica, "Irish Countrywomen's Association Press Release 1993" and "Address to National Council of Irish Countrywomen's Association 1994" reprinted by permission of Irish Countrywomen's Association and the author

Presentation Convent Archives "Teresa Mulally: an address to the Charitable of St Michan's Parish (1766)" and "Letter to Archbishop Troy (c. 1802)" Presentation Convent Archives, George's Hill, Dublin

Price, Katherine Arnold, "Curithir and Liadan" (*Dubliner* 1963)

Primavesi, Anna, 'Theology and Earth System Science" from *Challenging Women's Orthodoxies in the Context of Faith* (ed. Susan F Parsons) (Ashgate Publishing, Aldershot, 2000)

Quinn, Vincent, "On the borders of allegiance: identity politics in Ulster" from *De-centring Sexualities* (eds. Richard Phillips, David Shuttleton and Diane Watt) (Routledge, London, 2000)

Reid, Christina, "Tea in a China Cup" from *Reid Plays 1* (Methuen Publishing Ltd., 1983)

Ridgway, Keith, *The Long Falling* (Faber & Faber Ltd, 1998)

Rooney, Eilish, "Learning to remember and remembering to forget" from *Devolving Identities: Feminist Readings i Home and Belonging* (ed. Lynne Pearce) (Ashgate Publishing, Aldershot, 2000)

Rooney, Phyllis, "The Maleness of Reason" *American Philosophical Quarterly* 31(1) 1994

Ruane, Medh, extract reprinted by permission of *The Irish Times* 1999

Ruiseal, Maire, "Scal an ghabhairn Bhain", (1936) reprinted by permission of the Head of the Department of Irish Folklore, University College Dublin.

Saint Patrick's Hospital "Letter to the Governors and Guardians of St Patrick's Hospital, Dublin" Archives of St Patrick's Hospital, Dublin

Sayers, Peig, *Peig: A Sceal Fein* (Talbot Press, 1936)

Sayers, Peig, "An Chaibidil Dheireannach" from *An Old Woman's Reflections* (trans. Seamus Ennis) (Oxford University Press, London, 1962)

Seale, Mary, "The Old Oak Tree" reprinted by permission of the Head of the Department of Irish Folklore, University College Dublin

Shighil, Anna Ui, "Ni Mhaol Dhonn Ni Mhaol Fhionn, Agus Ni Mhaol Charach" (1939) reprinted by permission of the Head of the Department of Irish Folklore, University College Dublin

Shannon, Elizabeth, *I am of Ireland: Women of the North Speak Out* (The University of Massachusetts Press, Amherst, 1997)

Shepperson, Janet, "The Aphrodite Stone" (Salmon Press, 1995)

Sheridan, Kathy, extract reprinted by permission of *The Irish Times* 1997

Siggins, Lorna, *Mary Robinson: The Woman Who took Power to the Park* (1997) reproduced th kind permission of The Jonathan Williams Literary Agency

Stewart, Thomas H., "The flower of Gortade" from *Sam Henry's Songs of the People* (University of Georgia Press, 1990 copyright kindly granted from the author's estate, Mrs Olive Craig and family

Stopes, Marie, "Dear Dr Stopes: Sex in the 1920s" (1928) from *Married Love* (ed. Ruth Hall) (Andre Deutsch, 1978)

Sullivan, Breda, "After the Ball" (Salmon Press, 1998)

Sweetman, Rosita, *On Our Backs* (Macmillan Publishers, London, 1979)

Taylor, Alice, *To School Through the Fields* (St Martin's Press, New York, 1988)

Thurston, Anne, "In birth" from *Because of Her Testimony* (The Crossroad Publishing Co., New York, 1995)

Tunney, Brigid, "As I Roved Out" BBC Sound Archive, 1953

Tynana, Maol Muire, extract from *Sunday Business Post* 6 Feb. 20000

Ursuline Convent Archives " Licence to a Papist Schoolmistress at Thurles, Co. Tipperary (1799)" Archives of the Ursuline Convent, Thurles

Walsh, Liz, "Women at War driven by Politics not Passion" by kind permission The Jonathan Williams Literary Agency

Ward, Chrissie, "Womens' work" and "Musha Mary daughter" *Pavee Pictures* (Pavee Point Travellers' Centre, 1991)

Wilford, Rick and Yvonne Galligan, "Gender and Party Politics in N.I." from *Contesting Politics* (eds. Yvonne Galligan and Ellis Ward) (Westview Press, 1997, copyright © 1997 by Westview Press, reprinted by permission of Westview Press, a member of Perseus Books, L.L.C.)

Wyley, Enda, "Eating baby Jesus" (Dedalus 1994)

Zell, Ann, "Weathering" (Salmon Press, 1998)

MÁIRÍN NÍ DHONNCHADHA, *Editor*

Medieval to Modern, 600–1900

Writing in Irish covers a longer time-span than writing in any of the other languages used in Ireland since alphabetic characters were first incised in the fourth or fifth century. Despite its quantity and diversity, this writing is very poorly served by print and secondary sources. There is no single anthology of Gaelic literature, and very few anthologies dealing with particular genres, themes or chronological periods. There is only one English-language literary history in print dealing with the full span of Gaelic tradition: J.E. Caerwyn Williams and Patrick K. Ford, *The Irish Literary Tradition* (Cardiff: University of Wales Press and Belmont, Mass.: Ford & Bailie, 1992). A heroic-romantic vision of women in Gaelic Ireland, derived from scholarly editions and literary translations of a limited selection of early Irish sagas and poetry, has endured in popular imagination since the early twentieth century. One flattering implication of this vision is that native Gaelic society was remarkably well disposed towards women. It is still widely believed that Ireland was less patriarchal at the dawn of the historic era than it would become under the influence of Christianity, that there was a 'Celtic' stage when Irishwomen enjoyed freedoms, privileges and respect which were without parallel in other cultures, and that elements of this regime survived the experience of christianization and colonization.

The aim in 'Medieval to Modern, 600–1900' is not to engage with the heroic-romantic vision of women but to approach a larger and more heterogeneous body of texts than the one on which that vision was based with the kinds of questions that critics and literary historians — and readers — alert to feminist perspectives tend to ask. Are texts by female authors known to have survived? What kind of texts are they? How is Gaelic tradition to be reconceptualized in the

light of such work? What can be learned from texts and literary forms about female subjectivity as a collectively and culturally constructed identity? Which belief systems underlie literary representations of women? Do these belief systems support particular power formations? What insights can be gained from bringing an awareness of gender as a product of cultural and linguistic practice to bear on the literature?

A reader would be right to suspect the prescriptive nature of this list of questions: like much prefatory material compiled after the work is done, it suggests a more focused beginning than was in fact the case. Questions of this kind were undoubtedly asked, but the process of refining them in response to the materials was continuous. Other questions were asked but eliminated when they proved less productive, while others again which are not included in the list were prompted by the particularity of the Irish texts.

While the section focuses mainly on medieval traditions it also addresses some of their consequences, and this accounts for its long temporal range. In many respects the key period was that between 650 and 850. The reservoir of myths, legends and dramatis personae established during this time was drawn on by story-tellers and poets for over a millennium. Irish law, in Latin and Irish, was codified, and the first great collections of annals and genealogies were compiled. The earliest documents, such as the writings of fifth-century Saint Patrick, were in Latin. A standard form of Irish (Classical Old Irish) was evolved from the Irish of the sixth and seventh centuries, and remained in use for over three hundred years, allowing the earliest literary achievements in that language to be consolidated and built upon. From the beginning, linguistic diversity was an essential feature of Irish literary

1

culture. Recognizing this helps one to see the extent to which the foundations for later traditions were in place by 850. In the early medieval period, there was continuous interchange between Latin and Irish. The earliest recorded lives of Ireland's three patron saints — Patrick, Brigit and Colum Cille — were written in Latin towards the end of the seventh century. There are lives of Patrick and Brigit in Irish from the ninth century, and one for Colum Cille from the twelfth. The lives of the native female saints excerpted in the following pages — Brigit, Íte, Darerca and Samthann — are mainly but not exclusively in Latin, while the material interwoven between the lives is mainly in Irish. Samthann, who died in 739, is the latest of the numerous Irish saints of the early medieval period. The next Irish saint belonged to a different era: Laurence O'Toole, who died in 1180, was canonized in 1225. There is an even larger gap between him and the succeeding Irish saint: Oliver Plunkett, who died in 1681 and was canonized in 1976. The company of Irish saints was almost complete by the mid-eighth century. The chronology is worth noting, since devotion to saints occasioned a significant portion of all recorded literature, both written and oral.

By the late eighth century, Armagh (Ard Macha) had arrogated the primacy of the Irish church to itself, through promoting Saint Patrick as Ireland's greatest saint while simultaneously associating his cult with its church above all others. One might think of the outstanding warrior Cú Chulainn as a secular counterpart to Ireland's chief apostle, and it has been suggested that he was developed as such by writers also associated with Armagh. The cycle of heroic tales concerning Cú Chulainn and his Ulster brothers in arms locates their royal capital at Emain Macha, a great ceremonial site located two miles west of the city. Secular and saintly heroes have much in common. They share the function of exemplarity. Their biographies tend to be structured in a similar manner, and they frequently employ the same tropes and motifs. The range of exemplars and images influencing medieval men and women derived alike from secular writing and hagiography.

Heroines are not the female equivalent of the heroes of saga: they do not have superhuman strength or a record of extraordinary physical achievements, and their proper element is romance rather than saga. They share with the saints something of the function of exemplarity,

however: the women addressed in bardic poetry, for example, are regularly compared to such heroines. Clearly, the Irish spectrum of female representations includes not just the saints mentioned above (along with many less distinguished ones) but also iconic secular figures such as Medb, Deirdre, Emer, Aífe, Gráinne and Ailbe. These secular heroines comprised the core cast of female characters in Gaelic traditional tales. Much of the lore concerning them which was familiar to Gaelic-speaking communities until very recently can be traced back to the eighth and ninth centuries, revealing once again the durability of the early medieval traditions.

Medieval Irish writers also used the lives of historical men and women — or, more precisely, historical kings and queens. The last historical king to have his deeds cast in heroic saga form was Fergal mac Máile Dúin, king of Tara, who died in 722. From the eighth century onwards, narratives based on real characters tended to take the form of political propaganda or historical fiction. Some important narratives of this kind appear in the following pages. The most notable are those involving Queen Gormlaith (died 1030), one-time wife of great Brían Bóruma (Brian Boru), and Queen Derbforgaill (Devorgilla; died 1193), whose abduction by Diarmait Mac Murchada, King of Leinster, has been depicted in myriad sources down to the twentieth century as the cause of the Norman Invasion of Ireland.

The five texts concerning Gormlaith and Derbforgaill which are excerpted below include the thirteenth-century Norse *Njáls saga* and the Norman French poem commonly titled *The Song of Dermot and the Earl*. These two works exemplify a linguistic diversity that goes well beyond Latin and Irish. The author of *The Song of Dermot and the Earl* based his text on materials he took from the man who acted as Diarmait (Dermot) mac Murchada's interpreter; these may have been in Norman French, in Latin or, perhaps most likely of all, in Irish. The bold but plausible suggestion has been made that the twelfth-century Norse text underlying *Njáls saga* was written not in Iceland but in Ireland. The characterization of Gormlaith and Derbforgaill differs from one text to the next within each of the two selections concerning them, and the prejudices of the individual authors soon become apparent when one reads the texts in sequence.

Hagiography, romance, political propaganda, historical fiction and legal tracts accommodate only some of the female figures who are represented — and re-presented — in the following pages. There is a rich additional literature drawing on a mythology in which key supernatural forces or transcendent powers were imaged as female bodies — the earth mother, the death messenger and the sovereignty goddess, to take perhaps the most prominent examples. Over time, the meanings invested in these images, like the stories attached to them, changed in accordance with cultural and political needs. The large literature embodying this process was mainly an Irish-language one until the eighteenth century, but fundamental images and metaphors were carried over into English at that point. Consequently, this field of representation shows remarkable continuity. It was with a view to demonstrating this continuity that the range of 'Medieval to Modern' was extended to 1900. (Later uses of mythological material can be traced elsewhere in this anthology).

The medicalized female body provides the subject for another kind of writing. A portion of this is found in the law texts of the early medieval period, where the emphasis is on the tariffs of fines for injuries and other forms of maltreatment which result in ill-health. The texts in question give some insight into indigenous thinking on medicine. A new literature on the subject reached Ireland in the fourteenth century. It was a mix of classical Greek and Roman medicine and Arabian folk influences, and it developed in close association with Aristotelian philosophy. Reading, rather than practical experience of diagnosis, was regarded as the source of prestige medical knowledge at this time, and the books of the physicians had direct and indirect influence on the minds and bodies of women and men. Women's interest in the new medical literature repays investigation as a form of scholarly patronage. One might compare the scribes of medical manuscripts who worked to supply commissions from women with other classes of professionals who produced texts for them — poets, lawyers and clerical writers, for example.

Clearly, there was no shortage of material on which to test the questions outlined at the beginning of this introduction. The challenge was to organize the material into categories that medieval people would have found meaningful while simultaneously offering the modern reader a critical perspective on those categories. This eventuated in the following eight selections of texts, each of which is preceded by a substantial introduction which aims to supply a contextualizing, interrogative framework — and obviates the need to attempt the same here. The selections are generically, discursively or chronologically distinct from each other. 'Early Medieval Law, c. 700–1200', edited by Donnchadh Ó Corráin, addresses Ireland's uniquely rich corpus of early medieval law-texts concerning women. In addition to canon law in Latin and law-tracts in Old Irish, the editor presents various literary narratives in which legal rules are embedded, and key texts by the eleventh-century reformers of canon law on marriage. Three ideas structure the second selection, titled 'Mary, Eve and the Church, c. 700–1800'. The first is the idea that the model of Christian life specifically appropriate to the female sex is not 'imitation of Christ' but 'imitation of Mary' (*imitatio Mariae*). The second and related idea is that virginity is superexcellent. The third idea is that a threefold order of virgins, penitent spouses (holy widows) and married people encompasses all of Christian society, and elements which do not fit into one or other of these categories are disorderly. Hegemonic views on the roles of women in society are represented forcefully and at length in many texts in these first two selections, but the reader may be surprised to find other texts in which these views are countered.

The selection titled 'Gormlaith and her Sisters, c. 750–1800' presents a range of material in which the Christian world view is not predominant. Many of the texts here are richly revealing of the ways in which proactive female sexuality was constructed. The selection is divided in two: 'A Place in the World' mainly concerns female association with the public sphere while 'Natural and Unnatural Women' focuses primarily on private relations.

The selection titled 'Society and Myth, c. 700–1300' is edited by Máire Herbert. It focuses on a broad range of mythic images of supernatural females and their cultural meanings, carefully distinguishing throughout between primary and secondary forms of myth. It is succeeded by 'Sovereignty and Politics, c. 1300–1900', edited by Máirín Nic Eoin. Sovereignty, which is one topic among many in the previous selection, becomes centrally important here. The landscape of *dinnsheanchas* ('lore of important places'), the *mise en scène* for the colonization of Ireland by the Gaels, is usually empty of other human beings: any resistance they encounter comes from the land herself (personified as a woman), from fellow Gaels, or from earlier and supernatural inhabitants. The landscape of 'Sovereignty and Politics' is more densely populated by humans, as the wooers of Éire contend with the wooers of Irena. In this selection, texts illustrating a Gaelic and later a nationalist perspective run the gamut of emotions between jubilation and despair over the rights to colonize the body of Ireland.

For all the diversity of the material gathered here, disappointingly little of it was actually written by women. There are important references to historical female poets, there are texts attributed to such poets which were actually composed after their time (though some of them may be based on their original work), but there is not one complete text which can be attributed with absolute certainty to a historical woman until the early seventeenth century. There is the unique case of the Old Irish poem attributed to Digde, however: it is argued below that the introductory material to this poem offers strong presumptive evidence that it was actually composed by a woman of this name (pp. 111–15).

Authorship aside, women had a large stake in literature as readers and auditors, recipients and patrons. One way of conveying this interest was to present a sequence of poems addressed to historical women. The apostrophic mode was dominant in Gaelic poetry throughout the medieval and most of the modern period, and it proved possible to compile a sequence of poems addressed to named women from the mid-tenth century onwards. The sequence is divided between two selections, titled 'Courts and Coteries I, c. 900–1600', and 'Courts and Coteries II, c. 1500–1800' (poems addressed to women, in Latin as well as Irish, are also found in 'Mary, Eve and the Church'). In some cases the address is oblique or implicit rather than direct: the poet may speak as though to a third party, for example. Other kinds of texts which bear on women's participation in literary culture are also represented. The view on Gaelic literary history afforded by these two selections challenges the frequently made claim that written literature before the eighteenth century was of little interest or relevance to women. In addition, the selections provide a context for the sequence of poems by named women which can be traced from the seventeenth century onwards, and which constitutes a large part of 'Courts and Coteries II'. Some of the anonymous courtly love poems included there may also have been composed by women and could conceivably date from before the seventeenth century.

'Irish Medical Writing, 1400–1600', edited by Aoibheann Nic Dhonnchadha, appears, with chronological appropriateness, between 'Courts and Coteries I' and 'Courts and Coteries II'. Its placing also points up the link between women's patronage of medical writing and poetry. Furthermore, the texts themselves suggest connections between medical and other kinds of written discourse. The selection exemplifies a complex translation process: the Irish 'originals' which are translated into English here were previously translated from Latin 'originals', and some of these are underlain in turn by 'originals' in Greek and Arabic.

The division of the poetry into two selections, and the overlap created between them, had another aim: to challenge the still pervasive view that the year 1600 marked a watershed in Gaelic literary culture. This date of course is shorthand for the events of the Nine Years War (1593–1603) and their aftermath. A belief that these events did not have as devastating an impact on cultural production as they are conventionally said to have had, particularly in nationalist historiography, underpins 'Courts and Coteries II'. Most anthologies of Irish poetry in English suggest, through their choice of poems, that an aristocratic Gaelic civilization was suddenly overthrown in the early seventeenth century, leaving a void which the rest of the Gaelic population never adequately filled. One must beware of the false obviousness of history, however, of the danger of reading the outcome back into the past. It is arguable indeed that the first half of the seventeenth century held out greater promise for the future of Gaelic literature than any preceding period. It is certainly true that Gaelic literary culture remained vibrant in many parts of the country throughout the eighteenth century. In 'Courts and Coteries II', an attempt is made to encounter the seventeenth and eighteenth centuries on their own terms rather than in terms of retrospective nostalgia.

This is not to deny the troubled history of relations between the Irish and the English — the people, the cultures and the languages. It is to say rather that their story should not be told at the expense of detail. It is to encourage examination of different stretches of the past, to look for designs other than the ones that traditional perspectives have naturalized. It has been argued that the historical particularities of the Irish colonial situation are in danger of being over-looked when it is viewed exclusively in a global colonialist frame. It has also been suggested that in much of the debate about the Anglo-Irish colonial relationship, the propinquity of England and Ireland and the heritage shared by the two countries on that account have not had due attention. Certainly, the trend in most accounts of Gaelic literary history has been to stress the deleterious aspects of the encounter with England. It is as if an alternative outcome to the current balance of power between the Irish and English languages was never possible, despite Ireland's and England's common experience of such major forces as christianization and European cultural influences.

Language is a crucial component of the discourse of civility and barbarism as it relates to the early modern Anglo-Irish colonial situation. Formulation of the idea of the barbaric otherness of the Irish is usually credited to Giraldus Cambrensis in the twelfth century. It is easy to show that attitudes were quite different in the early medieval period. It may be recalled, for example, that Irish was spoken and used as a prestige language in Britain in the sixth and seventh centuries, as inscriptions in the Irish *ogam* alphabet on standing stones in Wales, the west of England and the Isle of Man testify; the expansion of the Irish from Dál Ríata in Antrim to Scottish Dál Ríata was not the only one that produced the sea-divided Gael. Bede, in his *Ecclesiastical History of the English People*, counted Irish as one of the five estimable languages of Britain since it had been used to expound the Gospel. One can hardly read his account of abbess, Hild, who encouraged the bashful Cædmon to compose poetry, 'in English, which was his own tongue', without seeing at her shoulder the figure of her mentor, the Irish-speaking Aedán.

Certainly, the evidence for the systematic oppression of the Irish language in later centuries cannot be gainsaid. This oppression undoubtedly arrested what would have been the natural development of Gaelic literature. Nevertheless, Gaelic literary culture was more vigorous, dynamic and flexible — and more attractive to English-speakers — in medieval, early modern

and later times than has been generally realised, either by its detractors (such as James Joyce, who characterized the Irish as 'a nation which never advanced so far as a miracle-play), or its vindicators who would relate its history as a story of continuous oppression and decline.

Feminist perspectives provide new ways of reading familiar texts and a context for the reconsideration of neglected ones. They highlight the fact that tradition is a continuous work of invention, amenable to incorporating new insights and discoveries. Irish literary culture in all its languages is characterized by plurality and hybridity, though the persistence of these qualities in the Gaelic tradition has been insufficiently noticed. The recuperation of 'other traditions' is essential to feminism. Many of the texts in 'Medieval to Modern' are published for the first time. Almost half of the material had not been translated into English previously and much of the rest was newly translated. New literary translations were commissioned for quite a few texts, in an effort to give the aesthetic status of the originals its due. With few exceptions, the originals of verse-texts are provided, but con-siderations of space ruled against this in the case of prose. (All unattributed translations are by the present writer.) Where existing translations were concerned, twentieth-century translations were generally preferred. The work of Frank O'Connor and Thomas Kinsella, two poets whose commitment to translating Gaelic literature has been outstanding, is well represented. Many of the new translations are by well known writers. To them and to their less-well known colleagues, the editor owes a particular debt of gratitude.

Finally, a word about editorial conventions. The selections include Irish-language texts in Old and Middle Irish (600–1200), Classical (Early) Modern Irish (1200–1600), and Post-Classical Modern Irish, down to the turn of the twentieth century. In translations of Irish-language material, one norm is applied to names deriving from Old and Middle Irish originals, another to names deriving from texts of a later date. The same practice has been adopted in the case of names, words and phrases in Irish which are cited in the introductory essays and headnotes. This accounts for such diverse spellings as Finn mac Cumaill and Fionn mac Cumhaill, *áes dána* and *aos dána*, *síd* and *síodh*.

DONNCHADH Ó CORRÁIN, *Editor*

Early Medieval Law,
c. 700–1200

The early medieval Irish law tracts, in Latin and Irish, date from the seventh, eighth and early ninth centuries, and they contain a great deal of information on the lives of women and their status at law in the early Middle Ages, when a remarkable Christian culture flourished in Ireland.

The principal Latin law book is the *Hibernensis*, one of the three great collections of church law produced in the western church before AD 800. It deals with all aspects of canon law and, apart from many references to women in passing, it devotes two books to them: 'Concerning Questions of Women' and 'On Marriage'. The work was put together by learned Irish clerics in the early eighth century and based on much more extensive and earlier texts. Its arrangement was brilliant and innovative: this first systematic canon-law collection was brought all over Europe by Irish missionaries, and was very influential for centuries. It based its rules on very many sources: canons of council, papal decretals and Church Fathers — Origen, Saint Jerome, Saint Augustine, Gregory the Great and Isidore of Seville are cited throughout — but also the Bible, the Old Testament as well as the New. The Irish savants saw the Bible and the Fathers as a source of positive law, and some of their legal thinking is still present in the canon law of the Catholic church.

The *Hibernensis* is important evidence for the legal framework of early medieval Ireland: it combined elements of Roman law and Christian teaching with law ultimately inherited from the pagan past. Its position on women reflects the basic attitudes of a patriarchal society, but also the rigorist stance of the dominant theologians of

the Latin church, in particular Saint Jerome (d. 420) and Saint Augustine (d. 430) and the puritan tradition that followed them. Classical attitudes to women, Stoic concepts of sexuality, and Christian views of the culpable role of woman in the drama of the Fall and Redemption combined to produce a negative image of women and of sexual love: men were privileged over women, celibacy preferred to marriage, continence to sexual love, and sex itself, powerfully associated with passion, baseness and sordidity, was redeemed only by procreation within Christian marriage. The Fathers were obsessed with the control of women: they insisted they should be virgins until marriage (and tried to apply the same rule to men); that men have no concubines, before or during marriage; that a man may put away his wife for adultery but neither may remarry while the other lives; that widowers and widows should remarry (and then be faithful) lest they satisfy their lust in many sexual relationships; that elderly widows in the care of the church be closely supervised by the clergy, and not given to gossip or drinking; and they condemned contraception and abortion, which they equated with murder, in strikingly violent language.

Some rules reveal the problems of the churchmen and inconsistencies in their attitudes. Nearly always, they give the hard line, their ideal of restraint in a sinful world. Licit sex can take place on less than a hundred days of the year, it must be procreative, and it can only occur within Christian marriage, as defined by Pope Leo the Great (d. 461). Anything else is sinful. Again and again, they condemn concubinage — and this shows that many lived in sexual relationships that were not marriages in the eyes of the church, and this was perhaps the norm, in Ireland as elsewhere. They cite Scripture to justify throwing out concubines and their children, precisely because this is what Irish kings and nobles refused to do. Yet on some points they are equivocal. Sterility is no good reason for divorce, but men in a childless marriage could do as Abraham and Jacob and have children blamelessly by their slave girls. A woman should follow her husband if he takes a religious vow, but when men or women enter the religious life, their spouses may remarry, provided they marry young persons, presumably virgins. They demand that the adulterous wife should be ejected (in the words of the prophet Isaiah), but practical considerations can intervene: the natural father may obtain the child he has had by another's adulterous wife by paying the necessary compensation and the price of its fosterage, but for simple adultery the cuckold gets nothing. And the sanctions for breaking the rules are excommunication and penance, not the savage punishments of the Old Testament.

Traditional Irish society, like all ancient and medieval European societies, was patriarchal. Formally, legal, political and social life was ruled by men and most women lived out their lives in a state of dependence. This inherited social structure was reinforced by Christianity, which had achieved a dominant cultural position in Ireland in the fifth and sixth centuries. Patriarchal ideology was given a divine sanction in Scripture and elaborated by the Church Fathers who added their peculiar misogyny.

Patriarchal societies are concerned with the transmission of property, status and social roles through descent in the male line. Therefore they insist that women should be virgins until marriage and faithful in marriage. However, men make rules they cannot keep, and there is always a double standard. Men have non-marital or extra-marital sex, but if all women are to be virgins or faithful wives, who are their partners? The solution is to divide women into two classes, the good who are not available and the bad who are. Some women (the dishonest) are exploited sexually as concubines, whores, compliant servants, slave girls and the like, whilst others (the honest) are exploited as the chaste mothers of patriarchy's heirs and given social position,

esteem and sometimes wealth in return for sexual restraint, and many women internalize these values, at least overtly. In general, these are the values of early medieval Irish society, and its clerical lawyers, who shaped its laws (in Latin and in the vernacular), had to look no further than the patriarchs of the Old Testament to validate them, at least in outline. Where the Irish did tend to differ from contemporary patriarchal societies was in blurring these distinctions to a degree — for example, they had a somewhat relaxed attitude to legitimacy and inheritance, they were more tolerant of divorce, remarriage, and polygyny than outside observers thought proper, and they were less likely to punish severely women who broke the rules.

Some basic concepts of Irish law need to be explained before one can understand its legal rules. Medieval Irish society was class-ridden: one's status, usually based on wealth and birth, determines one's legal capacity, and this is expressed in honour-price (*enech, eneclann*, originally 'face', later 'honour, status'). Honour-price expresses one's social value, one's status or rank in society. It varied from person to person; for example, a substantial farmer (*bóaire*) had an honour-price of two and a half milking cows, a provincial king forty-two milking cows. Values were calculated on the basis of the *sét* 'valuable', normally equal to a heifer or half a milking cow. A higher unit, *cumal* 'slave girl', is the equal of three milking cows. Compensations for injury, damage and insult were calculated as a fraction or a multiple of honour-price. One could not go bond for more than one's honour-price nor make a contract for a greater amount. In law suits, the worth of one's oath and one's evidence was limited to one's honour-price. For most women, their honour-price (and thus their status at law) was half that of their husband, for some it was lower — the honour-price of concubines, paramours and other socially and sexually exploited dependent women is a quarter or less of their male partner's. A man's lawfully contracted spouse has the same status as a son or a daughter. This represents a severe social disability: the extent of one's contracts, the amount of compensation paid for offences, outrages and injuries against one (including compensation for unlawful killing), and one's general entitlements at law were seriously reduced. This meant that in the very structure of society there was a built-in discrimination against women that operated at all levels — a woman's word carried less weight, her life was less valuable, and her entitlements were usually half those of her male equivalent. But this is not the case for all wives.

In Irish law, criminal offences are paid off or compounded for. According to some tracts, the fixed penalty for homicide (*éraic*) is twenty-one milking cows for any freeman regardless of rank. Other tracts base compensation for homicide on the honour-price of the victim or, in the case of a dependant, the victim's guardian. *Éraic* is paid to the victim's extended family but, in addition to the *éraic*, the honour-price of the victim must be paid and it is distributed in fixed proportions among the paternal and maternal relatives. Another term, *díre* 'off-payment', has the meaning 'honour-price', and the more general meaning of 'penalty, fine, payment in atonement'.

The term commonly used for husband and wife in formal marriage is *cétmuinter*. This is a compound of *cét* 'with, together' and *muinter* 'community', seen as a singular, and meaning 'spouse'. This word is a Christian term meant to convey 'husband' and 'wife' in the Christian understanding of these terms — the exclusive partners in monogamic marriage. Ironically, the first part was later re-analysed as *cét* 'first' and came to be understood to mean first or principal spouse as distinct from the secondary partners of various kinds that were common in early medieval Irish society. Churchmen called a secondary wife *adaltrach*, literally 'adulteress', but there were other earlier and less condemnatory terms for differing grades of concubines that are dealt with in some detail in the laws. What is extraordinary about this is not that there should be many kinds of women in different kinds of sexual relationships — these are to be found in many societies — but the level of social analysis by lawyers who were mostly clerics.

As in other northern European countries and as in the patriarchal societies of the ancient Near East (including the Hebrews), the earliest form of marriage appears to have been bridewealth marriage. Bridewealth is the formal agreed payment made by the husband-to-be to the father or guardian of the bride-to-be, and this starts off the exchanges and legal formalities that bring about a marriage. Custom differed in time and place: none, part or all of this payment may ultimately be passed on to the bride. The oldest term for bridewealth is *tinnscra*, common in the sagas but very rare in the Laws. The usual word in the Laws is *coibche*, in the first instance, 'contract', then, 'marriage contract', and lastly, the principal payment made in early marriage contracts, namely, the bridewealth. The meaning of *coibche* changed over time. As bridewealth marriage lost status — and this had happened by 700 — *coibche* came to mean, on some occasions, a payment made directly by a man to a woman to induce her to become his concubine. Later still, it seems to mean a payment made by the man, which forms part of the marriage goods held in common, and which falls to the innocent party on divorce. Marriage with dowry, between partners of equal social standing, and celebrated in public nuptials is what the church advocated from early times, in the Latin and Irish Laws, and this is the principal form of marriage in all the law tracts.

One of the most remarkable law texts is *Cáin Adomnán*, the Law of Adomnán, also called the Law of the Innocents, which was publicly enacted at Birr, a great church on the borders of Munster and Uí Néill in 697, in the presence of a great assembly of lay and clerical leaders, at the behest of Adomnán (d. 704), 9th Abbot of Iona, the most influential cleric in Ireland and Britain. Essentially, it is the work of Adomnán and it was intended to be effective in Britain as well as Ireland. It was drafted by professional clerical lawyers who had a thorough knowledge of the vernacular law. It extends special protection to 'innocents': women, clerics and young boys, thus limiting acts of war. In its concern for the dignity of women, sympathy for their lives and sufferings, and in its punishment of sexual harassment, whether physical or verbal, it is the first of its kind in western Europe. In background and intent, and especially in its emphasis on Christian monogamic marriage, it belongs with the *Hibernensis*.

The principal Old Irish law tract on marriage, *Cáin Lánamna*, the Law of Couples, was written about 700 and belongs to the law collection called *Senchas Már*. It is the work of Christian lawyers. So much is clear from references to the church setting, the mention of the celebration of religious festivals, the statement that their parish churches continued to have rights over both partners, the references to the *debitum conjugale* (marital debt), the special mention of penalties for the rape of a nun, and the use of the term *adaltrach* for a secondary wife, that is, a wife whose status is not valid in the law of the church. It contains a great deal of valuable information on marriage but it and other Old Irish legal sources are difficult to interpret because the style is condensed and the terminology differs greatly from that in the Latin law tracts. Three primary types of marriage are described: *lánamnas comthinchuir*, 'marriage of common contribution', *lánamnas for ferthinchur*, 'marriage on man-contribution', and *lánamnas for bantinchur*, 'marriage on woman-contribution'. The last is a special case, namely the marriage of an heiress to a man of little or no property. All three are considered to be contractual relationships between the spouses in regard to marital rights and to rights over property used in common. The lawyers see the rights of spouses over marital property as being analogous to those of others who have the use of property in common and who, on occasion at least, share a common table — a foster-father and his foster-son, a teacher and his pupil, a church and its tenantry, a lord and his base clients. Each partner retains ownership of the property brought into the relationship, that property is used in common, but its use is subject to fair dealing and to fair division should the partnership end.

A woman's right to own personal private property and her right to the property she contributes to the common marital fund is not extinguished by marriage. In fact, it is legally protected. What each of the partners may have given the other, consumed, or spent in good faith, cannot give rise to a legal action for recovery. What has been taken without permission must be replaced if a complaint is made about it. Legal penalties arise only when a justified complaint (and the legal procedures that must follow it) is ignored or when property is removed by theft or violence.

Lánamnas comthinchuir, the most common type of marriage between persons of property, is a canon-law marriage that owes most to late Roman law as interpreted by Leo the Great. Irish canon lawyers (such as those who compiled the *Hibernensis*) applied these rules to Irish conditions. The matching contribution of husband and wife may have an earlier history, but it is interpreted in the light of late Roman custom: the husband made his wife-to-be a payment from his own resources (*donatio propter nuptias*) and she brought into marriage an amount equal to that payment, called dowry (*dos*). In Leo's terms (quoted in the *Hibernensis*) the couple must be free-born and equal, the woman must have a dowry, and the marriage must be celebrated publicly. In Roman society, by custom though not by law, the dowry distinguished legal marriage from concubinage. Dowry was made mandatory for a short period (458–63) and this requirement passed into the law of the church, and into Irish canon law. These conditions govern *lánamnas comthinchuir* (and *lánamnas for ferthinchur* when that form of marriage is a canonical marriage). The act that establishes a formal marriage is *airnaidm* 'binding', a contract with witnesses and guarantors, made between the couple and between their respective families. This contract meets the requirements of Leo the Great.

Lánamnas for ferthinchur reflects the more traditional bridewealth marriage, but it has already come under the influence of the church in that this marriage can be canonical, but it is more usually a relationship of concubinage or at least one of an uncanonical nature. *Lánamnas for bantinchur* occurs when an heiress without male siblings inherits her father's estate and marries a non-inheriting male. This may or may not be a canonical marriage. An heiress held only a life interest in her father's estate: on her death, it had to revert to the male heirs of her father. Only by marrying one of these, usually a first or second cousin, could she pass on part of her estates to her children. Technically, marriage to such close relatives was forbidden by canon law, but Irish lawyers were able to work their way around this. In all these kinds of marriage, the wife in canonical marriage is privileged and her rights in regard to contract, property and other important matters are more extensive.

But the vision of the compilers extends far beyond the moral prescriptions of the medieval church. *Cáin Lánamna* is not intended as a complete treatise on marriage — it is complementary to the Latin canon-law tracts. Its themes are quite limited, but its focus is sharp and its social analysis acute. It deals principally with the rights of marriage partners, the holding and management of marital property in canonical marriage and in other types of procreative sexual unions, and its equitable distribution when these relationships terminate, by mutual consent or otherwise. It offers a useful classification of marital unions (which it sees in the context of other social units that share a common economy and a common table), based largely on property relationships but also on the legal standing and intention of the partners. It is pragmatic — it deals with everyday reality, hardly at all with abstract moral prescriptions, and for that reason it is an invaluable social commentary.

Remarkably, various kinds of sexual unions — permanent, semi-permanent and transitory — are given legal status in that the partners are recognized as having rights at law in regard to each other, and against others. The lawyers attempt to classify these relationships in different ways. One text divides women's relationships into five classes, three legitimate and two not. The legitimate group are a *cétmuinter* with sons, a *cétmuinter* without sons and a 'woman who is recognized and betrothed by her family', that is, a duly contracted secondary wife, evidently fully recognized as wife in secular society but not by the church. The rights and duties of all three in regard to their natal family, their husband and their children (if any) are set out clearly in the law. The more formal the marriage, the more closely bound are they to their husband's family. The non-legitimate are: 'the woman who is recognized but who is not betrothed nor ordered into the relationship by her kindred', that is, a woman who has no marriage contract; and 'the woman who is abducted in defiance of her father or family'. In this last case, her natal family takes all her assets, and her partner bears all her liabilities. Amongst the lowest sexual unions, occupying a social position just above rape, is the marriage of wandering mercenaries. We may have here an echo of Roman law — an early imperial law, apparently abrogated by Septimus Severus, forbade soldiers to marry and soldiering made a previous marriage invalid.

Divorce, the dissolution of the bond of a valid marriage, posed a difficult problem for the Fathers of the Church because of the ambiguity of Scripture. Saint Augustine, the greatest Christian theoretician of marriage, returned to the question again and again. He wrote: 'The matter is quite obscure in the divine Scriptures [Matthew 5:31–2, 19:3–11]: he to whom without doubt it is permitted to repudiate his adulterous spouse, is he to be considered an adulterer if he remarries? The difficulty is so great that as far as I am concerned here one commits a venial sin.' Augustine's second book on the subject was published a mere eleven years before the first date in Irish church history — 431, when the missionary Palladius was sent to Ireland. Legal concepts of marriage were brought into Ireland by missionaries from Britain and Gaul, areas of late Vulgar Roman law, who knew little of Augustine's thought, and they very likely brought with them the prudent tolerance in regard to divorce and re-marriage evident in the synods of the fifth century.

How much Irish divorce law reflects inherited native custom is a moot point. Late Roman law and the sixth-century legislation of the Emperor Justinian (d. 565) regarded marriage as being dissoluble by mutual consent or unilaterally. In the latter case, sickness, insanity, sterility, impotence and adultery of the wife were all adequate grounds. Captivity and enslavement allowed the free partner to re-marry. In Irish law *inscuchad* ('removal') ended cohabitation and broke the bond, as it did in Roman law. The letter of divorce (*libellus repudii*) became the most common divorce procedure under the emperors Theodosius II and Valerian III in the first half of the fifth century. Irish canon lawyers mention the Mosaic law in this respect (Deuteronomy 24:1–4) and they may be doing so to condemn a practice they were familiar with from late Roman law. In the East, the legislation of the Emperor Justinian codified grounds for divorce, and provisions like his appear in Irish law: divorce on grounds of impotence of the husband, and on grounds of abortion, immoral acts, or adultery on the part of the wife. The Greek Archbishop of Canterbury, Theodore of Tarsus (d. 690), apparently brought some of these ideas to the West and the Irish were his apt pupils. His Penitential allows divorce and subsequent re-marriage along the lines of the civil legislation of the East. The Irish scholars were well informed on patristics and they knew thoroughly the writings of Leo the Great, Augustine, Jerome, Caesarius of Arles, and others. Their texts provide the rigorist theory, but the practice was a good deal more latitudinarian. From the point of view of the church, there could be three types of unions: illicit unions, unions in which there were grounds for canon-law annulment, and canonical marriages. Whatever the outward appearances, the tricky question of divorce in the canonical sense arose only in the case of the last, and here the rules remained unclear and authorities divided throughout the early Middle Ages.

Far stricter rules of marriage applied to the learned and clerical castes — clerics, poets, judges and other members of the professional class — and to the tenants of church lands who had the church for a lord. Drawing on the Old Testament, the lawyers applied the rules governing the Levites to the learned classes. They were allowed one spouse only, and they could not re-marry if that spouse died. Members of the learned classes should marry only virgins and should strictly avoid women with previous sexual experience — the widow, the divorcée and the whore. In regard to the poet, for example, *Uraicecht na Ríar*, a tract on the poetic grades in early Ireland, states:

> How is a grade conferred on a poet? Answer. He shows his compositions to an *ollam* (and he has the seven grades of knowledge) and the king receives him in his full grade in which the *ollam* declares him to be on the basis of his compositions, his guiltlessness and his purity — purity of learning and purity of mouth and purity of hand and marital union, and the purity of being innocent of theft and plunder and illegality, and purity of body, that he have only one wife, for one perishes through illicit cohabitation aside from one chaste woman on lawful nights.

Continence was obligatory for married couples during Advent, Lent and the forty days after Pentecost, on Wednesdays, Fridays, Saturdays and Sundays, and on the major religious feasts. It was also obligatory during pregnancy, that is, from the time the child first moves in the womb until birth; and after birth, a lengthy purification period, based on but not exactly identical with the prescriptions of the Old Testament (Leviticus 12:14), is to be observed — thirty-six days in the case of a male child, forty-six in the case of a female. Some of these restrictions occur in the Fathers but they were greatly expanded by Irish confessors and canon lawyers. They tried to extend some of these strict rules to the laity in general — 'lords, poets, commoners are impaired by illicit cohabitation', declares one legal text — but evidently without much success.

The rules applied to the laity were much laxer. Divorce and re-marriage were allowed and, as elsewhere, the rules were stretched to accommodate the dynastic needs of kings and aristocrats and, lower down on the scale, the strategies of heirship and property management of gentry and farmers. Even the *Hibernensis* allows a man without an heir to have children by his slave girl, like Abraham in the Old Testament. The *Hibernensis* and related texts give us the rigorist ideal, but practice was more easygoing, as it was everywhere at least unofficially.

Some rules of law are embedded in literary narratives and these form a minor though interesting genre in early medieval literature which shows how close the makers of literature and law were. Four of these narratives are provided here. The first concerns the alleged infidelity of Sadb, daughter of Conn Cétchathach, her legal suit against her former husband and the judgment which forced her to surrender her children to him. The second deals with the decision of Gráinne, daughter of Cormac, to leave the aged warrior Finn, and describes the moral and material support her father gives her to leave her unhappy marriage. The story of Corc's exile and his relations with the daughter of the King of Alba illustrates the legal process of affiliation, that is, attaching a child to its father and thus establishing its legitimacy. The last describes the famous pillow-talk between Medb and Ailill, a legalistic argument which ultimately led to the Cattle Raid of Cúailnge. In the sagas there are complex images of women and their social and sexual roles. This literature represents a world of high dramatic heroism, sometimes in the grand mode, sometimes in the burlesque. One may infer that it echoes, in a heightened literary mode, some of the social values of the aristocracy and the underlying legal framework of society.

In continental Europe, marriage became more and more a matter for the church, which showed a marked tendency towards innovation — in regard to kindred, marriage taboos, concubinage, divorce, adoption and inheritance. Between the ninth and eleventh centuries, the church established its exclusive competence in regard to marriage law — the conditions of the contract, the circumstances of invalidity and nullity, the forbidden degrees of kindred (an ever-widening circle), the rules defining bastardry and the exclusion of bastards from inheritance — and brought about a legal revolution that was refined and systematized by the new canon lawyers. Ireland remained set in the older ways, to the righteous horror of twelfth-century reformers and Elizabethan administrators.

ANONYMOUS

from:
THE HIBERNENSIS
(Irish Canons) (*c.* 716–25)

[By the end of the fourth century there was a standard negative attitude to sex and women in the Western church, based on classical views, the Old Testament and especially the story of Eve's role in the Fall, and the exalting of sexual continence in the New Testament. Just as in the Western church as a whole, this is the stance of the *Hibernensis*, the early eighth-century compendium of Irish canon law, compiled from the Bible, the Fathers, church councils, and occasionally some Irish synods. Its chief compilers were Ruben (d. 725) of Dairinis (now Molana), a church on the Blackwater above Youghal in County Cork, who is called 'scribe of Munster' in the annals, meaning principal canon lawyer of the province; and Cú Chuimne the Wise (d. 747) of Iona in Scotland, the author of the earliest hymn in honour of the Blessed Virgin in the Western church.[1] There are two editions, an earlier one by Ruben and a corrected and expanded version that may be the work of Cú Chuimne and the school of Iona. The *Hibernensis* normally expresses the puritanical clerical ideal. However, for most people, including many clerics, the social reality was quite otherwise. The text is here translated by Thomas O'Loughlin from Herrmann Wasserschleben, *Die irische Kanonensammlung*, 2nd ed. (Leipzig: Tauchnitz, 1885), pp. 185–95. The heading of each section, given below in italic, is part of the text: it gives the subject or the legal principle in question. Scriptural references have been supplied in the translations. On other references see Thomas O'Loughlin, 'Marriage and Sexuality in the *Hibernensis*', *Peritia*, vol. 11 (1997), pp. 188–206.]

---

1. 'Hymn to Mary' by Cú Chuimne of Iona, in 'Mary, Eve and the Church', pp. 59–60.

BOOK 46: ON MARRIAGE

1. *In praise of marriage*
Jerome: If there were no marriage, there would be no virginity; the earth is populated by marriage, heaven by virginity.

2. *Qualities a wife should have in marriage*
Augustine: According to the Law what ought a wife to be? She is a chaste virgin, betrothed in virginity, given dowry in accordance with law, and handed over by her parents, and accepted by the groom and his female attendants. According to the Law and the Gospel, she is received honestly, in public nuptials, into lawful matrimony, and for all the days of her life she is not to be separated from her husband, 'except for the reason of fornication' [Matthew 19:9], apart from separation by mutual consent and to serve God. If she commits fornication, she is to be abandoned, but her husband may not take another wife as long as she lives for those who commit adultery shall not possess the kingdom of God.

3. *On the three kinds of lawful union*
Jerome: We read of three types of lawful marriage in scripture. First, the union of a chaste virgin, betrothed from virginity and given with a lawful dowry to her husband. Second, when someone seizes a virgin in the city and copulates with her by force; if her father consents, he shall give her bride-price in the form of fifty silver shekels paid to her father, or however much the father shall judge, and the man shall pay her the price of her chastity [cf. Deuteronomy 22:29]. If, however,

she had a husband before she was seized, the price that shall be given by him is whatever is willed by the father and the daughter. Third, when a daughter is seized as in the previous case, but her father does not consent, she will not, in this case, be joined to her corrupter but to whomsoever the father will choose for her and he will pay her bride-price, and the matter will be lawful [cf. Exodus 22:16–17]. Of these two kinds of marriage, the first is preferable.

4. *On the fourth kind of union*
Jerome: A fourth kind of marriage is added. When a man's wife dies it is lawful for him to marry another, but she must not be a widow, nor a divorced woman, nor someone who is betrothed, but a virgin. The like applies in the case of a woman. Thus Paul says: She who is under the power of the man is bound by law to her husband as long as he lives . . . Thus, she will be called an adulteress if she lives with another man while her husband is alive. But if her husband dies she is free from that law, and she is not an adulteress if she lives with another man [Romans 7:2–3].

5. *On the fifth kind of union*
Jerome: A fifth kind is added. If a man or a woman, with consent, enters the religious life, it is lawful for the other to accept a spouse, but it is to be a young woman or a young man.

6. *On avoiding adultery, even in lawful unions*
1. Jerome: In a lawful union adultery is avoided; what is sought is not what lust may demand but what is proper to nature and for the procreation of children.
2. Again: It is not lawful for a man to have another wife apart from his own; if he does have another woman, what was lawful will no longer be lawful.
3. Paul says: Every [other] sin which a man commits is outside the body; but the man who fornicates sins in his own body [1 Corinthians 6:18], that is, his wife will be stained and she will no longer be lawful for him, but adulterous.

7. *On the pollution in a union without blame*
It is asked whether there is any occasion when it is licit for a woman to have intercourse with another while her husband is alive. There are three such cases. First, if she is coerced into intercourse with another, this does not break the marriage bond. Second, if it occurs because of a given advantage, as what Sarah did lest Abraham be killed by the wicked king [Genesis 12:11–20]. Augustine says: Or, as happened recently, when a rich man demanded a gold coin from a man who had none to pay. Now a certain wealthy young man said to his wife that if she would have intercourse with him, he would give her the coin. Now she, knowing that she had not power over her own body [1 Corinthians 7:4], spoke to her husband about this. The husband gave thanks and permitted her to do this, considering that where there was no desire there was no adultery. Third, if she be sterile, as one reads in Genesis of Abraham and Jacob, that they took their slave girls in marriage [Genesis 16:1-7; 29:21–35].

8. *On the woman who is repudiated*
Moses says: If your wife displeases you, write her a bill of divorce [Deuteronomy 24:1]. Note that he does not prescribe that she be thrown out absolutely, but that a bill of divorce be given to her. Hence the Lord in the Gospels says: A man is not to put aside his wife except for fornication [Matthew 19:9].

9. *On the matters that a bill of divorce recounts*
Augustine: These are the matters that a bill of divorce recounts: that is, whether she is drunken, irascible, wanton, quarrelsome, gluttonous, slanderous, or one who is found not to be a virgin; but if these charges be false, that husband shall give his wife one hundred pounds of silver.

10. *That a wife may not be repudiated under the New Law even for good reasons*
Isidore: What then if she is sterile, deformed, somewhat advanced in years, stinking, drunken, irascible, if she has bad habits, is wanton, gluttonous, quarrelsome and slanderous: is she to be kept or put aside? Whether you like it or not, whatever sort she is, once accepted, she must be kept.

11. *On the periods when spouses ought to remain continent*
1. The Irish Synod: During the three Lents in the year and on Sundays, Wednesdays and Fridays couples ought to keep themselves continent.

2. And again: On all solemn feast-days and in the period when the wife is pregnant (that is, from the day that the child first moves in the womb until the day of its birth).

3. And again: For 36 days after a birth, if a male child; for 46 days, if a female.

4. Again: sexual intercourse is not permitted to those in a religious habit.

12. *Of men and women who are not to be received in matrimony*

Augustine: Wives do not have husbands whose previous wives are still alive — such marriages are adulterous; nor are we allowed to marry that woman who left her husband because of repudiation as long as her husband is alive.

13. *Second marriages are not prohibited*

1. Augustine: Because of incontinence the apostle orders second marriages saying: 'it is better for a man to marry' [1 Corinthians 7:9] than that he should satisfy his lust fornicating with many women; more often, indeed, the freedom to marry is exercised not for religious but sinful motives.

2. Hermas:[2] I asked [the angel] saying: 'Sir, a husband or wife, if one of them dies, and the one marries again after the death of the other, does the one who so does sin or not?' And he replied: 'In my opinion he does not sin; but if he were continent and remained so, he would acquire great glory before God, but if he marries he does not sin.'

14. *That a wife is not to be taken while a previous wife is still alive, even if she is an adulteress*

The Synod of Arles: It is decreed that if young men catch their wives in adultery, while those wives, even if they are adulteresses, still live they may not take others; this is to be done lest when they do penance this should exclude them from the place of penance and lest they stain themselves with many sexual relationships.

15. *That the adultery of the wife is not to be concealed; that one must accept her penitence, and one may not marry another wife*

2. In the manuscripts, this and no. 15 are wrongly ascribed to Jeremiah (*Hieremias*). In fact, they derive from a second-century Greek Christian work known as *The Shepherd*, an account of a vision that one Hermas had in which he discussed many issues with an angel.

Hermas said to the angel shepherd: 'Sir, may I ask you some more questions?' 'Speak,' he replied. 'Sir, if a man had a faithful wife in his house, and later found her committing adultery, does her husband sin if he continues to live with her?' He said to me: 'As long as he is unaware of her sins, he does not sin; but if he knows of her sin and she does not do penance but perseveres in her wickedness, then the man by continuing to live with her fails in his duty and shares in her guilt.' 'What,' I asked, 'is the husband to do if she continues in her vice?' 'Let him dismiss her,' he said, 'and remain continent himself; if, after dismissing her he takes another wife, then he, too, commits adultery.' 'If however, sir,' I said, 'after being sent away, she does penance and wishes to return to her true husband and she is not taken back?' And he replied to me: 'If she is not taken back, her husband sins, and he brings a great sin upon himself. Everyone who does penance for his sins receives forgiveness. However, pardon occurs but once for the Servants of God. The husband, after repudiating his wife, must not marry another, lest he take away from his wife the opportunity of doing penance. This ruling applies equally to the husband and to the wife.'

16. *On the chastity of spouses before marriage*

Augustine: Just as he who chooses to take a wife wants to find her a virgin, likewise he must keep his virginity before marriage, for it is so great an evil to violate it before marriage that when he marries he does not deserve to receive the blessings with his wife and here is fulfilled 'he would not be willing to be blessed and it shall be far from him' [Psalms 108:17]. Since man (*vir*) gets his name from strength (*virtus*) and woman (*mulier*) from weakness (*mollitas*), why should anyone want his wife to be victorious over that most cruel beast of lust when he himself falls victim to the first blow of passion? Now whatever is against Catholic faith and is unlawful for women is equally unlawful for men.

17. *That concubines are not to be kept prior to marriage*

Augustine: How is this that many men have recourse to concubines before they marry and they are not ashamed; then after years they dismiss them and take lawful wives? In the presence of God and his angels I testify about these men and denounce them, for these unions have always been prohibited by God and have never pleased him. To have concubines, especially in these Christian times, never has been lawful, never is lawful, and never will be lawful.

18. *That concubines are not to be kept alongside legitimate wives*
1. Jerome: No one seeks a number of women except to practise a superfluity of lust.
2. The same author also says: Whoever desires a number of women mixes the lawful with the unlawful; thus says the apostle: 'he who joins himself to a prostitute becomes one body with her' [1 Corinthians 6:16].

19. *That a free-born woman and a free-born man ought to marry and the concubine should be abandoned*
1. The Synod of Narbonne: To eject the slave girl from the bed and marry a wife of known free-born birth: this is not a second union but a growth in honesty.
2. The same synod: Girls who marry men who have concubines, if wedded in accordance with the will of their fathers to men who keep concubines, are without fault if the women kept by such men were not married to them: for a wife is one thing, a concubine quite another.
3. The same synod: Regarding the priest or deacon who gives his virgin daughter in marriage to a man who is already joined to a woman who has even already given him sons. Not every woman joined to a man is his wife, for not every son is the heir of his father. Marriage contracts are legitimate between free-born people who, at the same time, are equals, for the Lord established this before the beginning of Roman law. Thus a wife is one thing, a concubine quite another, just as a free woman is one thing, and a slave girl another. And a little later: Therefore, if a cleric of any cure gives his daughter in marriage to a man who has a concubine, she is not to be accepted as if he had given her properly in marriage unless that woman is free-born, given a legitimate dowry, and seen to be properly validated in a public marriage ceremony. The Roman rule, which prohibits marriage if it is previously corrupted, does not permit this arrangement, constituted from the beginning.

20. *That a woman ought to follow her husband if he takes refuge in a Christian vow*
Origen: Let women learn from the example of the wives of the patriarchs who followed their husbands. It is not for nothing that it is written that Sarah stood behind Abraham [Genesis 18:10]. This was done to show that if a man goes before the Lord, his wife ought to follow him. Thus I say that a woman ought to follow her husband, if standing with him she wants to see God.

21. *That coercion cannot taint virginity in the New Testament*
Jerome in his commentary on Matthew says: What is sought in the Gospel is the presence of will: so if someone has an evil intention, even if an evil deed does not result, then the prize of grace is withheld. The Old Law on the other hand does not judge at the level of intention but according to the things that actually happen. An example of this is the case of a virgin who as a result of persecution is made into a prostitute. According to the Gospel she is still a virgin since she did not will it; while according to the Old Law which judges by effects she is now corrupt and to be repudiated.

22. *On rendering the debt between man and woman*
1. Paul: The husband should render the debt to his wife, and likewise the wife to her husband [1 Corinthians 7:3].
2. And again: Do not defraud one another except perhaps by consent for a time, that you may free yourselves for prayer; but then come together again, lest Satan tempt you through lack of self-control [1 Corinthians 7:5].

23. *That neither a woman nor a man has control over her/his own body*
Paul: For the wife does not have power over her own body, but the husband does; likewise the husband does not have power over his own body, but the wife does [1 Corinthians 7:4].

24. *That wives are to obey their husbands*
Paul: Wives, be subject to your husbands, as to the Lord [Colossians 3:18].

25. *On the names of the sexes*
Augustine: The name 'man' (*vir*) comes from 'strength' (*virtus*), that is, for making war, working, defending, ruling and public speaking; the name 'woman' (*mulier*), on the other hand, is derived from 'softness' (*mollitia*), that is, from fragility, weakness, lowliness and subjection.

26. *That a wife should be ejected on account of adultery*
Isaiah says: Our bed is so narrow that one must fall out, and a short covering cannot cover both [Isaiah 28:20].

27. *Concerning the adulterer who abandons his wife, except on account of fornication; and the fool who retains an adulterous wife*
1. The Lord in the Gospel says: And I say to you: whoever puts away his wife, except for the reason of fornication, and marries another, commits adultery [Matthew 19:9].
2. Jerome says: When a woman divides one flesh in two and by fornication becomes separated from her husband, she ought not be kept lest the husband fall under the same curse because Scripture says: he who keeps an adulteress is a fool and impious [Proverbs 18:22].[3]

28. *Of the prostitute who does not have her own husband*
1. Christ in John's Gospel says: 'Call your husband.' The woman replied: 'I have no husband'; Jesus said: 'You have spoken well for you have had five husbands and the one you now have is not your husband' [John 4:16–18].
2. Jerome: Where there is a number of husbands, there the man who is husband of his proper wife ceases to be such.

29. *That a wife is not to be dismissed at baptism*
The Roman Synod says: He who had his first virgin wife before baptism may not, as long as she is alive, have a second wife; for while crimes are dissolved in baptism, a legitimate marriage is not.

30. *That the sons of adulteresses not born in legitimate marriage are to be expelled*

---

3. This verse is found only as a variant in critical editions of the Vulgate.

1. Ezekiel: I have cast out your fornicating mother and the sons of fornication [cf. Hosea 1:2; 2:2].
2. Augustine: The adulteress is to be dismissed with the fruit of adultery, lest the blessed offspring be contaminated. Note that Abraham separated himself from Lot and his seed foreseeing that the seed of Lot would be cursed [cf. Genesis 13:8–13]; and he threw out Hagar with her son lest she be with the blessed seed [cf. Genesis 21:8–18].
3. The Irish Synod: If someone corrupts the legitimate spouse of another and oversows his seed so that the woman becomes pregnant, that child will be the son of the body from which it was generated, and moreover he [the natural father] shall pay the price of that son and of its fosterage, as much as the judges decide; if, however, he oversows his seed in adultery, the corrupter pays nothing nor must the adulterer give the cuckold anything except, when the fathering of a child has been admitted, the fee for its fosterage.

31 *Adulterers are to be excommunicated*
The Irish Synod says: Every adulterer, until he has done penance, is to be excluded from concelebration, communion at the table, cohabitation, blessing, conversation, and companionship.

32. *On taking back an adulterous woman after penance and the amount of her penance*
1. Synod: We decree that if a woman has sexual relations with another man in adultery she is to be excommunicated until she does penance; and after penance she is to be reconciled to her own husband.
2. Patrick: If someone's wife commits fornication with another man, let him not take another wife while the first wife is alive; but if she changes her life and does penance let him take her back and let her serve him while she lives as slave girl. Let her do a full year's penance on a measured amount of bread and water, nor shall they remain in the one bed.
3. In another synod it says: Let her do penance for seven years: three of these in the strict form and four in the slack form; and let it be understood that this also applies to a man if he commits adultery.

33. *On the chastity of the penitent spouse*
Augustine: Her penitence is to be accepted, but both are to live in a chaste state as long as she lives.

34. *That the husband of an intact wife is not to go to war*
The Law says: That man to whom a wife is betrothed, and who has not yet consummated the marriage with her, let him go and return to his house lest perhaps he die in battle and another man take her [Deuteronomy 20:7].

35. *That a man is not to go into the marriage bed of his dead brother*
1. The Synod of Arles says: No surviving brother is to go into the marriage bed of his dead brother; if he does this, let him be excommunicated.
2. The Romans say: A surviving brother must not go into the marriage bed of a dead brother, as the Lord says: 'The two shall be one flesh' [Matthew 19:5]. Therefore, your brother's wife is your sister.
3. Again others say: A woman who has been joined to two brothers is to be excommunicated, unless she does penance.
4. Jerome: A woman shall not go into the marriage bed of two brothers; if she does so, she commits adultery.

36. *Concerning girls betrothed in marriage who have been seduced by others*
Synod: It is decreed that girls who, after being betrothed in marriage are seduced by others, are to be sought out and returned to those to whom they were already betrothed.

37. *About wives suspected of adultery*
The Law says: If any man's wife goes astray and, despising her husband, sleeps with another man, and her husband cannot discover it because the adultery of the woman is hidden, and it cannot be proved by witnesses since she was not caught in the adultery; if the spirit of jealousy stir up the man against his wife, who is either polluted or is charged with false suspicion, then he shall bring her to the priest, and make an offering for her, a tenth of a measure of barley meal; he shall not pour oil upon it nor place incense on it, for it is a sacrifice of jealousy, and an offering investigating adultery. So let the priest offer it, and set it before the Lord and take holy water in an earthen vessel, and take a little of the earth that is on the floor of the tabernacle and put a tenth part of it into the water. And the woman shall stand before the Lord, he shall uncover her head, and place upon her hands the sacrifice of remembrance, and the offering of jealousy. The priest himself shall hold the waters of bitterness on which he has heaped curses with execration and the priest shall adjure her, saying: 'If no other man has slept with you, and if you are not unclean on account of deserting the marriage bed, these most bitter waters upon which I have heaped up curses will not harm you. But if you have wandered from your husband and are defiled and you have lain with another man, then these curses will strike you. May the Lord put on you a curse as an example to all his people; and may he make your thigh to rot and may your womb swell and burst open. Let the cursed waters enter your belly, make your womb swell, and your thigh rot.' And the woman shall reply: 'Amen, Amen.' And the priest shall write these curses in a little book, and shall wash them out with the most bitter waters and he shall give her the waters to drink. When she has drunk them, the priest shall take from her hands the sacrifice of jealousy and shall hold it high in the presence of the Lord and place it upon the altar. But first he is to take a handful of the sacrifice offered and burn it upon the altar, and thus give the drink of the bitterest waters to the woman. When she has drunk it, if she is defiled and, having despised her husband, is guilty of adultery, the waters of cursing shall go through her and her belly will swell and her thigh rot, and the woman will become a curse as an example to all the people. But if the woman is not defiled, she will be unharmed, and she shall bear children. This is the law of jealousy.[4]

38. *That it is not possible for a wife to accuse her husband of an uncertain adultery*
The Roman Synod: A woman may not accuse her husband of adultery, and the hidden sins are not punished. However, the husband has the ability to report his adulterous wife to the priest.

---

4. Numbers 5:12–29; this passage is corrupt in the Vulgate, and it is further altered in the *Hibernensis*.

from:
CÁIN ADOMNÁN
(The Law of Adomnán) (697)

[*Cáin Adomnán*, the Law of Adomnán, otherwise known as *Lex Innocentium*, the Law of the Innocents, is the earliest known European law enacted to safeguard women and to improve their lot in society. It was proclaimed at Birr, County Offaly, in 697. Adomnán, Abbot of Iona and head of the Columban federation of churches in Scotland and Ireland, and ninety-one other leading male figures from the church and the laity pledged themselves and society at large to give special protection henceforth to three categories of people: women, clerics and children. The Law bracketed these categories together on the basis that all three were exempt from military service, and specified penalties for a range of offences against them. However, by far the most severe and the most detailed related to offences against women, so much so that it is fair to say that the Law is primarily concerned with women's welfare.

Medieval concepts of the just war lie behind this association of women, clerics and children. While Christians in general were expected to support just wars, certain groups were regarded as 'innocent' — not arms-bearing. There are many precedents for the exclusion of clerics from military service because it would interfere with their pastoral responsibilities. The exemption of male children was only temporary, until they reached adulthood, unless they then took clerical vows. The Law's exemption of women from military service is more complex. Almost all accounts of Irish female warriors belong to the realm of legend. Yet when a district was hard-pressed by sudden attacks, it is likely that women as well as men were called on to take defensive action and, in some circumstances, the line between defensive and offensive action must have been thin. Nevertheless, the Law is far more concerned with women as victims rather than as agents of violence.

Women's potential role as mothers is an outstanding preoccupation. Indeed, the Law implies an opposition between men as takers of life (when there is just cause) and women as givers of life. In a preamble added to the Law in the Middle Irish period, the perceived incompatibility of the two roles is presented as the rationale for excluding women from warring. We are told that an image vividly illustrating this incompatibility, which Adomnán and his mother supposedly saw on a battlefield, drove him eventually to enact his Law: 'Though they beheld the massacre, they saw nothing which they thought more pitiful than a woman's head on one bank and her body on the opposite bank with a child asleep at her breast, a stream of milk on one cheek and a stream of blood on the other.' In the law-text proper, women's role as givers of life is valorized through assimilation to the role of Mary, mother of Christ. As all women are sisters of Mary, so all of them share in her

motherhood of Christ (§6). This idea is frequently broached in relation to the virgin saints (cf. subsection 'Mary, Eve and the Church', *passim*). The exaltation of women as givers of life probably explains why the Law exempts women who are themselves guilty of murder from capital punishment (§18).

Men are exempt from liability for women's deaths in one noteworthy case, that is, if a woman should die as a result of 'an act of God or proper lawful union' (§15; cf. §6), in other words, in childbirth within lawful Christian marriage. In fact, there is a clear subtext in the Law whereby all laywomen (and laymen) are called upon to accommodate themselves to Christian marriage and to abandon unorthodox unions. This echoes the views expressed more fully in Adomnán's Life of Columba (*Vita Columbae*) (pp. 102–3), and in *Hibernensis* (pp. 12–17), which cites him as a source.

The Law was not just an influential formulation: it was to be implemented systematically and efficiently. An unusual but not entirely unprecedented jurisdiction was claimed for it: the two islands of Ireland and Britain. In the case of Britain, presumably only those areas in which the Columban church had influence were targeted. The first-listed of the forty ecclesiastical guarantors of the Law was Flann Febla, the Bishop of Armagh, the most powerful church figure in the country after Adomnán. The first-listed of the fifty-one secular guarantors was Loingsech, who became King of Tara in 696. One representative or more figures in the list for every major kingship, over-kingship and monastic centre in the country. The list also includes Coeddi, Bishop of Iona, Curetán, Bishop of Rosemarkie in Scotland, and Uuictberct, an English cleric living in the English colony at Clonmelsh near Carlow in Ireland. The procedures to be adopted to bring offenders to justice would have been readily understood, as most of them were founded on established practice in Irish customary law. One exception is the order of psalms which the text claims to have been established by Adomnán for chanting in a ritual of malediction, to excommunicate malefactors (§5).

The text was first edited and translated by Kuno Meyer as *Cain Adamnain: An Old Irish Treatise on the Law of Adamnan* (Oxford: Clarendon Press, 1905). This translation is based on a new edition by the present writer (the paragraph numbers correspond to §§28–52 in Meyer), M. Ní Dh.]

§1. This is the enactment of the Law of Adomnán of Iona. At Birr this enactment has been enjoined upon the men of Ireland and Britain as a perpetual law until Doom, by order of their nobles, clerical and lay, together with their lords and *ollams*[1] and bishops and sages and confessors, including: Fland Febla sage-bishop of Armagh . . .[2]

---

1. This probably refers to kings of the highest grade.
2. The names of the remaining ninety guarantors are omitted here.

§2. All have sworn, therefore, both lay persons and clerics, to fulfil the entirety of the Law of Adomnán until Doom. They have offered the whole *éraic*-fine of their female deaths to Adomnán, and to every heir who will be in his seat until Doom, and Adomnán does not steal fines from lord or church or kindred to whom [their payment] is due.

§3. Now, all the holy churches of Ireland together with Adomnán have besought the unity of the divinity of Father and Son and Holy Spirit and the heavenly host and the saints of the earth, that whoever fulfils this Law, with respect to exacting and enforcing and effecting and *éraic*-fine, may be long-lived and prosperous, and held in honour by God and humankind, and may be glorified in heaven and on earth.

§4. Now, all the holy churches of Ireland together with Adomnán have besought God with the orders of heaven and the saints of the earth, that whoever shall violate the Law of Adomnán, including lay persons and clerics, who shall not exact it nor effect it to the best of his ability and power, and who shall not enforce it on every one, both lordship and church — that his life may be short, with suffering and dishonour, leaving neither heavenly nor earthly inheritance to those [descended] from them.

§5. Adomnán moreover has established an order of malediction for them, to wit, a psalm for each day until the end of twenty days and an apostle or a noble saint besides to be invoked each day, that is:

Quare and Peter;
Domine, quid multiplicati and John;
Verba mea and Philip;
Domine Deus meus and Bartholomew;
Dixit insipiens and Thomas;
Deus, Deus meus, respice and Matthew;
Iudica me, Domine and Jacob;
Dixit iniustus and Simon;
Domine, ne in furore and Thaddeus;
Dixi: Custodiam and Madian;
Deus deorum and Mark;
Quid gloriaris and Luke;
Dixit insipiens and Stephen;
Exurgat Deus and Ambrose;

Saluum me and Gregory of Rome;
Deus, uenerunt gentes and Martin;
Deus, quis similis erit and Old Paul;
Deus, laudem meam and George;
Audite, cæli, quae loquor;
Non nobis, Domine, non nobis; sed nomini tuo et cetera.

§6. Here begins the angel's directive to Adomnán.

After fourteen years[3] Adomnán obtained this Law from God and this is the cause. On Pentecost eve a holy angel of the Lord came to him, and again at Pentecost after a year, and took a staff and struck his side and said to him: 'Go forth into Ireland and make a law that women be not killed in any manner by man, whether through slaughter or any other death, either by poison or in water or in fire or by any beast or in a pit or by dogs, except [they die in childbirth] in lawful bed. You shall establish a law in Ireland and Britain for the sake of the mother of each one, because a mother has borne each one, and for the sake of Mary, the mother of Jesus Christ through whom the whole [human race] is.' Mary along with Adomnán besought her Son about this Law.

And whoever kills a woman shall be condemned to a twofold punishment, that is, before death, his right hand and his left foot shall be cut off and after that he shall die and his kin shall pay seven full *cumal*s and [the commutation for] seven years of penance. If a payment has been imposed instead of life and amputation, [the commutation for] fourteen years of penance and fourteen *cumal*s shall be paid. However, if a multitude has done it, every fifth man up to three hundred shall be condemned to that retribution. If few, they shall be divided into three parts. The first part of them shall be put to death by lot, hand and foot having been cut off. The second shall pay fourteen full *cumal*s. The third shall be cast out into alienage beyond the sea, under the rule of hard regimen. For great is the sin when anyone kills one who is mother, and sister to Christ's mother, and mother of Christ, who labours in carrying the distaff and in clothing everyone. But from this day forward, he that shall put a woman to death, and not do penance in

---

3. i.e. in the abbacy of Iona which Adomnán held from 679.

accordance with this Law, shall not only perish in eternity and be cursed by God and Adomnán, but all that have heard and do not curse him, and do not censure him according to the judgement of this Law, shall be cursed.

This is the angel's directive to Adomnán.

§7. This is the enactment of the Law of Adomnán in Ireland and in Britain: the immunity[4] of the church of God together with her community and her insignia and her sanctuaries and all the property, animate and inanimate, and her law-abiding laymen with their legitimate spouses who abide by the will of Adomnán and a proper, wise and holy confessor. The enactment of this Law of Adomnán enjoins a perpetual law on behalf of clerics, and laywomen, and innocent children until they are capable of killing a person,[5] and of taking their place in the *túath*, and until their drove[6] be known.

§8. Whoever wounds and kills a clerical student or an innocent child in transgression of the Law of Adomnán, eight *cumal*s and eight years of penance for it for every hand involved, up to three hundred; one *cumal* and one year of penance for it for each one from three hundred to a thousand; and it is the same fine for the one who commits it and the one who sees it and does not prevent it to the best of his ability. If there be inadvertence or ignorance, half-fine for it, and there shall be an oath-equivalent[7] that it is inadvertence and ignorance.

§9. The enactment of this Law enjoins full *díre* to every church which is in proper discipline; half-*díre* to it for [crimes in] its confines beyond the green; full *díre* to it for [crimes against] every grade, with respect to wounding and theft and burning; half-*díre* for its exempt[8] sanctuaries; half-*díre* for merely threatening a cleric, without wounding or theft. Every church deserves full *díre* for the violation of its insignia, no matter where it is done.

§10. These are the judges of the Law of Adomnán in every church and in every territory, to wit, the clerics whom the *familia*[9] of Adomnán chooses and to whom they entrust the enactment of his Law.

§11. These are the pledges of this Law: a one-third pledge in bronze or silver according to the estimation of each territory from the entitlement of every case. The pledge [to be given] before [the end of] the three-day period, judgement before [the end of] the five-day period, payment before [the end of] the ten-day period in all other cases. The pledge immediately, judgement before [the end of] the three-day period, payment before [the end of] the five-day period in this case.

§12. The enactment of this Law enjoins that a hostage-surety is to be appointed with respect to every suit, both for the grades of the laity and the grades of the church, for fines small and large according to Adomnán's stipulation. [There shall be] proclaiming of enactment and the Law of Adomnán and his *familia* does not become extinct.

§13. The enactment of this Law enjoins that if innocent children or clerics are killed, it is to their burial-tombs that their fines[10] come, and their fines under customary law to their lords and to their kindreds.

§14. The enactment of the Law enjoins that payment in full fines is to be made for every laywoman that has been killed, whether a human had a part in it, or animals or dogs or fire or a ditch or a building. For in *cáin*-law every construction is to be paid for, including ditch and pit and bridge and hearth and step and pool and kiln and every hardship besides, if a laywoman should die on account of it. But one-third is remitted for fore-maintenance if it be a person of unsound mind that die on account of it.[11] Of the other two-thirds, one-third belongs to whomsoever is entitled to it.[12]

---

4. i.e. immunity from legal claim while in good standing.
5. i.e. in battle, an ability/characteristic of adult laymen.
6. i.e. a migration to establish a new home, for seasonal transhumance or permanently.
7. i.e. the process whereby 'oath-helpers' swear on behalf of someone whose oath is inadmissible, through criminality or other incapacity.
8. i.e. from secular imposition.

9. *familia* (of Adomnán): the community of churches (having allegiance to Adomnán and his successor).
10. i.e. under *cáin*-law.
11. i.e. one-third of the fines due for her death is given to those who have cared hitherto for the woman of unsound mind.
12. This refers to the third due to the person who levies the fines.

§15.Whatever violent death a laywoman may die, excepting [that which results from] an act of God or proper lawful union, it is paid for in full fines to Adomnán, including slaying and drowning and burning and poison and crushing and submerging and wounding by domesticated animals, and pigs and cattle. If it be the first crime on the part of the cattle or the pigs or the dogs, they are to be killed at once and half the fine for human hand for it. If not the first crime, payment is made in full fines.

§16. There shall be no counter-claiming or balancing of liabilities but everyone shall pay for the crimes committed by him. The *familia* of Adomnán is entitled to a superlevy for each trespass which is committed in respect to the Law of Adomnán apart from [that against] laywomen, be it [against] innocent children or clerics, or [it is owing] from him to whom they commit it,[13] that is, a *cumal* in superlevy to the *familia* of Adomnán where seven *cumal*s are paid and one half-*cumal* from half of seven *cumal*s. Six *sét*s on thirty *sét*s and three *sét*s on fifteen *sét*s.

§17. One eighth of everything small and large [is to be paid] to the *familia* of Adomnán for the murder of clerics and innocent children. If it be a non-mortal wound that anyone inflict on a laywoman or a cleric or an innocent child, half seven *cumal*s from him, fifteen *sét*s from [related] kindred and unrelated[14] kindred for their accompliceship. Three *sét*s for every white blow, five *sét*s for every spilling of blood, seven *sét*s for every wound requiring a staunch, a *cumal* for every injury requiring attendance and the leech's fee besides. It amounts to half of the fines for murdering someone if it be more serious than that. If it be a blow with the palm or the fist, an ounce of silver for it. If it be a livid or red mark or a swelling, six scruples and one ounce [of silver] for it. Women's hair-fights, five wethers for it. If it be woman-combat with degradation, three wethers for it.

§18. Men and women are equally liable, therefore, for all fines, small and large, from this up to woman-combat, except [it result in]

outright death. For this is the death that a laywoman deserves for her killing of a man or a woman, or for ministering poison from which one dies, or for arson, or for digging beneath a church, to wit, to be put in a boat of one paddle at a sea-marking out at sea, to [see if she will] go ashore with the winds. Judgement on her in that regard [rests] with God.

§19. Should it be charms from which one dies that anyone give to another, fines for body-concealment for it. Dire mutilations and dismemberments which are discovered in [one of] the four [nearest] uplands, if [that one of] the four [nearest] uplands cannot charge it to anyone in particular, they deny by oath that they know it of anyone and they make payment for it themselves. If they lay a charge of suspicion on a person, having evidence, it is he who will be liable. If the suspicion lie between two or a greater number, their names are written on leaves. Each leaf is fixed around a lot and the lots are put into a chalice on the altar. The one on whom the lot falls, it is he who is liable.

§20. If the criminals who violate the Law are not apprehendable, the kindred pays their full fines in accordance with the extent of their crimes, and their[15] forfeiture [of legal rights] is proclaimed, and thereafter let them be expelled[16] until the end of the Law. Half of seven *cumal*s [is due] for their accompliceship[17] after that from every [related] kindred and unrelated kindred. If there be maintenance or protection or connivance, [the penalty] for it is death, but that [same amount] which applies to fines applies to accompliceship.

§21.The enactment of the Law enjoins: they shall feed the steward of the Law of Adomnán, for whatever period [is required], with the noble refection of his company, that is, the surety as one of [a party of] five and refection [also] for every one who shall levy the fines of the Law [shall be provided] according to the rank of each, be he lord or cleric or layman. One *cumal* for refusing food to any one of them while fines are being levied; and [when proven guilty] it is the

13. i.e. the levying of the Law.
14. i.e. to the victim.

15. i.e. the criminals' forfeiture.
16. i.e. from the territory.
17. Here, in the sense of having failed to bring the criminals to justice.

offenders who must feed them, and they are liable for a joint bond of fines. If they do not feed them, two *cumal*s to them[18] from offenders.

§22. This, then, is the immunity of every hostage-surety who takes up the joint levying of this Law: they bear no liability for the kindred's crime, so long as they uphold [their] suretyship[19] and remain in position and do not default, apart from their own crime, or that of the family, or their offspring or their hirelings.

§23. If it be forcible rape of a girl, twice[?][20] seven *cumal*s for it. If it be a hand against her or on her belt, ten ounces for it. If it be knocking a laywoman down with intention to injure, one *cumal* and seven ounces for it. If it be a hand under her clothing to dishonour her, one *cumal* and three ounces for it. If there be a defect in head or eye or face or ear or nose or tooth or tongue or foot or hand, there are seven *cumal*s for it. If it be a defect in another part of the body, half of seven *cumal*s for it.

§24. If it be insulting a good woman by [accusing her of] lust or by denying her child, there are seven *cumal*s for it [for every woman] down to [the wife of] an *aire désa*.[21] Half of seven *cumal*s if it be the wife of an *aire désa*. From that down to a castaway[?], there are seven ounces for it.

§25. If it be making use of laywomen in a massacre or a muster or a raid, seven *cumal*s for every hand [involved] as far as seven, and [it is reckoned as] the crime of one man from that onwards. If a laywoman has been made pregnant through fornication, without contract, without property, without brideprice, without betrothal, full fines for it. Whatever reckoning is made for the [finished] hand-produce, however great or small, the same is made for the madder and the woad and the onion plant; if it be the red dye of a cloak, the value of a cloak [is paid] for it.[22]

---

18. i.e. the leviers.
19. i.e. if the offenders abscond.
20. The text reads 'half of seven *cumal*s' but this seems incorrect.
21. *aire désa*, 'lord of vassalry, ordinary lord'.
22. This echoes statements found elsewhere on the division of property when a couple separate; whether introduced here in error or as an aside is not clear.

§26. Three hostage-sureties for every principal church for the Law of Adomnán, to wit, the prior and the cook and the guest-master, and a hostage-surety for every kindred throughout Ireland, and two hostage-sureties for noble lords, and a hostage as warrant for levying it, if there be the evidence[23] of laywomen.

---

23. Evidence, presumably, that the Law has been breached.

CÁIN LÁNAMNA
(The Law of Couples) (*c.* 700)

[*Cáin Lánamna*, 'The Law of Couples', is the most extensive Old Irish tract on marriage. It was written about 700, and copied and glossed for centuries to come. The author of the twelfth-century tale that serves as an introduction to *Táin Bó Cúailnge* was thoroughly familiar with its text and glosses, and constructed his plot about its provisions (see p. 38). On internal evidence, *Cáin Lánamna* was written by clerics. It even has a principle borrowed from a rule of Roman law that occurs in the *Codex Theodosianus* and in the Visigothic *Lex Romana* and these may have reached the Irish in the seventh century. The type of marriage it privileges is *lánamnas comthinchuir*, a form that meets the requirements of canon law, but it also treats of others that were far from canonical. It does not touch on *airnaidm*, 'binding', the formal act that creates a formal marriage contract, nor does it give details about the guarantors who enforce the contract. It is pragmatic, not preachy. It categorizes sexual relationships on a descending scale, beginning with canonical marriage and ending with abduction and rape. It deals with the partners' rights, especially in regard to property, fair use by a partner of the other's property and its fair division at divorce, by mutual consent or otherwise. It is not a complete treatise on marriage — it does not deal at all with issues of sexual morality but concentrates, in a very practical way, on the realities of everyday life.

Perhaps one should argue that a large body of the Irish lawyer-clerics — unlike the compilers of the *Hibernensis* — showed themselves sensible and relatively humane in not adopting the bleak and guilt-ridden Augustinian teaching on marriage. They took rather a practical view of a complex human institution and spent their efforts on making rules to ensure equity and mutual respect.

This text was first translated into English in 1869. It was edited and translated into German by Rudolf Thurneysen in D.A. Binchy (ed.), *Studies in Early Irish Law* (Dublin: Royal Irish Academy, 1936), pp. 1–80. This new and rather literal translation owes much to

Thurneysen's. The paragraph numbering is that of his edition. Omitted extraneous material is indicated by ellipses. Explanatory material is added from time to time in square brackets. Sub-headings are added to make the text easier to follow and are not part of the original.]

I. *Couples in Irish law*

§1. Exempt from legal suit for each is what each may have used or have consumed as against the other, except what . . . lien, obligation or loan may have imposed, or what one of them may have misappropriated from the other. Exempt from legal suit is everything useful to the partnership, everything done in good faith; liable [to legal claim] is everything done in bad faith in the law of the couple.

§2. Question. How many couplings are there in Irish law? Answer. Eight: a lord and his base clients, a church and its tenantry, a father and his daughter, a girl and her brother, a son and his mother, a foster-son and his foster-mother, a teacher and his pupil, a man and his wife.

§3. Equally exempt from legal suit for each is whatever one of them may have given the other, whatever one of them may have used as against the other, without violent crime, without stealth. Everything taken without permission, that is complained about, is repaid by simple replacement of the object until the matter goes as far as the legal remedy of fasting,[1] except in the case of the church. Repayment, by simple replacement, of what is taken without permission and complained about is all that is required until there is evasion of the legal obligations that arise from fasting, or legal default. Anything taken by stealth, by violent crime, anything taken without permission, that is complained about and ignored, is levied with its penalty fine.

§4. Question. How many couples of cohabitation and procreation are there in Irish law? Answer. Ten: union of common contribution; union of a woman on a man's contribution; union of a man on a woman's contribution with service; union of a woman who accepts a man's solicitation; union of a man who visits the woman, without work, without solicitation, without provision, without

material contribution; union by abduction; union of wandering mercenaries; union by criminal seduction; union by rape; union of mockery.

II. *Union of common contribution*

§5. Union of common contribution: if it is a union with land and stock and household equipment, and if their marital relationship is one of equal status and equal propriety — and such a woman is called a woman of joint dominion — no contract of either is valid without the consent of the other, except for contracts that benefit their establishment. These are: an agreement for common ploughing with proper kinsmen when they do not themselves have a full ploughing team; [paying for] the leasing of land; getting together food for a coshering;[2] getting food for feast-days; paying stud fees; fitting out the household; making an agreement for joint husbandry; the purchase of any essentials that they lack. Every contract shall be without neglect, an advantageous contract, conscientious, in accordance with right and propriety, with acknowledgement on both sides that the ownership of what is acquired belongs to the person whose property was alienated to acquire it.

§6. Anything, the lack of which brings loss on the household, cannot be sold without common counsel, consultation, and mutual concession. For the impairment of the joint economy in a union of common contribution is not proper without mutual concession.

§7. Putting children in a well-befriended and good fosterage is a contract in accord with all propriety that brings well-being into the community of their common household.

§8. Every contract shall be without cheating. Either of them may dissolve the bad contracts of the other. The one does not dissolve the good contracts of the other in the case of those matters that have been listed, if the joint husbandry is without mutual friction, without mutual inculpation, in good partnership, in good faith.

§9. If they divorce, each divorce shall be without mutual defrauding. If they divorce by mutual consent, let them divide their property in accordance with legal propriety.

---

1. Ritual fast (a kind of hunger strike) is a means of bringing the defendant to submit the case to arbitration.

§10. A third of all proceeds belongs to the [owner of the] land, except for handiwork;³ a third of the cattle dropped during the union belongs to the [owner of] the stock from which they are sprung; a third to [whoever did] the labour. Division is made in proportion to the entitlement of each in regard to land, stock and labour. If the conduct of each is equally good or equally bad, this is the way they divide their thirds.

§11. The third assigned to labour of the proceeds of the cattle is further divided into thirds: a third to the master of the house, a third to the mistress of the house, a third to the workers, that is, the herders.⁴ . . .

§12. Likewise dairy produce: it is divided in three between land [$^{12}/_{36}$], stock [$^{12}/_{36}$] and labour [$^{12}/_{36}$]. The labour third: half goes to the woman who does the work [$^{6}/_{36}$]; a twelfth goes to dairy vessels [$^{3}/_{36}$];⁵ two-thirds of the remaining half go to the master of the house [$^{2}/_{36}$], a third to the dairy workers [$^{1}/_{36}$].⁶

§13. If one of them is ill-behaved, the labour portion of the ill-behaved falls to the well-behaved, but the portions due to land and stock are not diminished.

§14. The labour third of the fodder corn and salt meat:⁷ let it be divided in three i.e. a third [$^{1}/_{9}$] to the wife who is responsible for ploughing and reaping⁸ and for looking after the pig-sties, for feeding and for fattening the pigs, unless they are fattened on milk. In that case, the wife gets two-thirds [$^{2}/_{9}$]. For only spring-work in regard to ploughing and looking after the sties, the wife is entitled to two-thirds of a third [$^{2}/_{27}$].

§15. The wife takes a half of clothing and of woven fabric, a third of fibre combed and ready

for spinning; a sixth of fleeces and sheaves of flax; a third of woad in steeping vats, half if it is caked.

§16. Anything that either of them may consume from [what belongs to] the other is exempt from liability if it is by mutual consent. Whence is said: Without penalty is anything mutually discussed, mutually conceded.

§17. Every defrauding is paid off by replacement in kind unless the person entitled waives claim, or else compensation is paid on the day of parting.

§18. Anything taken by stealth, or despite mild or forceful protest, or by violent seizure, is repaid with its interest and with double its replacement if dry goods; if it is livestock, it is repaid with milk and young,⁹ with double replacement, and with interest.

§19. Exempt from liability is every loan, every lease, every sale, every purchase, without mutual defrauding by either, made with the private property of each up to the amount of the honour-price of each, in accordance with the contracting rights of each.

§20. Hospitality and refection is a duty of each of them according to rank . . . Each of them gives hospitality to his/her own lord, to his/her own church and friends and relations.

III. *Union on a man's contribution*
§21. Union of a woman on a man's contribution: the man's contract is a valid contract without the wife's consent, except for the sale of clothing and food; and the sale of cattle and sheep, if she is a duly contracted wife who is not a *cétmuinter*.¹⁰

§22. If she is a woman who is a proper *cétmuinter*, equally good and equally well-bred — for everyone of equal goodness is of equal birth — she impugns all his contracts if they are foolish — for immunity from suit does not attach to defrauding and to what is forcefully protested against — and her sureties annul them.¹¹

2. Old Irish *coí*, the obligatory hospitality of a client to the lord and his retinue.
3. The wife gets half the handiwork (§27). This is to be understood as textiles, and perhaps other hand-crafted objects.
4. i.e. to the person who hired and paid for the herders.
5. i.e. to the person who provided the dairy vessels, expensive and high-quality wooden containers.
6. i.e. to the person who hired and paid the dairy workers.
7. The other thirds go to the person who provided the stock and the land.
8. i.e. who pays for the ploughing and reaping to provide barley as pig-feed.

9. i.e. the livestock and what they produced during the time they were wrongfully detained.
10. i.e. given by her family in a marriage based on a marriage contract (*airnaidm*), but not a *cétmuinter*.
11. The sureties in question here are the original guarantors and witnesses of her marriage contract.

§23. If he gives bridewealth to [acquire] another woman, even from his own private property, that bridewealth is forfeit to his *cétmuinter* if she carries out her marital obligations. Every secondary wife[12] who comes 'over the head' of a *cétmuinter* is liable to penalty: she pays the honour-price of the *cétmuinter*.

§24. The wife gives hospitality to half as many people as her husband, in accordance with the social status of her husband . . .

§25. . . . Everybody is fed and hospitality is not refused up to the legal number of his/her retinue. Refusal of hospitality in the case of a guest accompanied by a excessive retinue does not damage one's honour for, though one refuse, this is not [deemed] refusal of hospitality if the retinue is excessive.

§26. If they divorce and the divorce is by mutual consent and their behaviour is equally good at the time of parting, what the one may have freely consumed as against the other is without penalty at the time of parting if it is done without bad faith and with consent, so that they may not defraud each other. Every replacement in kind shall be as that consumed, with milk and young and dung and with interest. Everything taken by stealth, by force, by secret removal, without consent, without recompense, without asking pardon, is levied with its penalty fine.

§27. The wife receives half the handiwork, as we said in the first type of union we discussed; a sixth of the dairy produce with the same proportions as previously between land and cows and vessels and servants. She receives a ninth of the cattle dropped during the union, a ninth of the corn, and a ninth of the salt meat, if she is a great worker.

§28. She receives a sack of corn for every month that remains until the year end i.e. until the first of May next, following the time they part.[13]

IV. *Union of an heiress*
§29. Union of a man on a woman's contribution: in that case, the husband goes in the track of the wife and the wife in the track of the husband. If he is a man of service he receives a ninth of the corn; and of the salt meat, if he is a 'head of counsel' who controls the people of the household with advice of equal standing. The sixth of milk produce is divided in two: one half ($1/_{12}$) goes to the vessels; of the other half, the husband receives two-thirds ($1/_{18}$). He receives a ninth of the handicraft when they divorce. If they divorce by mutual consent, they part in this way.

§30. If either of them is badly behaved, the labour third of the badly-behaved partner is forfeit to the well-behaved one. In the case of a *cétmuinter*, [the profit from] everything is forfeit to the party that carries out his/her marital duties, apart from what the other is entitled to of land and breeding stock [originally contributed to the marital fund].[14] But they part as they came together: what survives of what each brought in to the other, that is what each brings away on parting, or its replacement out of [that person's] profits if it no longer survives.

§31. But he is a husband who is paid honour-price in accordance with his wife's status if she holds all the property, unless he has higher property qualifications [in his own right] than his wife or is more godly, more high-born or more estimable than she.

V. *Other unions*
§32. Union of a man who visits the woman, without provision, without work: a fifth of the handiwork is the portion of the man (i.e. of the partner) when they part if the handiwork is hers to dispose of — for a fifth is the proportion of the compensation due to him for her being dishonoured;[15] if an offence is committed against her, that is the compensation he is paid for it.

§33. Union on accepting the inducement of the man: in that case the man receives a quarter of her handiwork. If it is a union with stock on land, let them divide by the proportions of land, labour and breeding stock, in accordance with what each owns.

---

12. Here the text uses the pejorative term *adaltrach*, 'adulteress'.
13. May Day is the time for entering into new contracts, including marriage contracts.
14. Both husband and wife have the status of *cétmuinter*.
15. i.e. in the case of off-payments for offences against her, her partner takes one-fifth of the amount because offences against her are considered to be offences against him also.

§34. Union by abduction and union in secret: they have no stock or dry goods to divide on parting, only offspring. If a woman abducted from her family grants property to her partner who has abducted her, that grant is invalid from the point of view of her family and it is thus repaid: it is paid off with half penalty-fine if what was given belonged [wholly] to the woman; if a third party owns a share in it, it is paid off with full penalty-fine. The same holds good for union by criminal seduction in secret.

§35. Union by rape or by stealth: they [the partners] possess nothing but offspring. Full *éraic* is paid for a virgin, for a young nun who does not reject her veil,[16] and for a *cétmuinter*; half *éraic* for secondary wives[17] — all this is without the co-operation of the woman — together with the full honour-price of the man of highest rank who has authority over her of those to whom she specially belongs.

§36. Union of mockery: union of a lunatic or madman with a deranged woman or madwoman. Neither of them is bound to take or to make payments. The person who brings them together for fun and the responsible person in whose presence this takes place, theirs is the offspring, if offspring there be; its rearing, compensation for its offences, and its suretyship falls on both of them. The *éraic* and the legacy of such persons is divided between the king, the church and the family.

16. i.e. a novice nun who is a virgin.
17. *adaltracha*, literally 'adulteresses'.

these attitudes represent the oldest state of affairs, and texts that allow women independent capacity at law are later, but there is no real evidence for this distinction and it is better to treat this text as an extreme statement of general principles, to which there are exceptions, as in *Cáin Lánamna*.

Here there is another classification of married women: (i) *cétmuinter* with or without sons; (ii) a wife who is contracted in marriage and recognized by her family (but not a *cétmuinter*); (iii) a wife without a marriage contract but whose family accepts her *de facto* relationship; and (iv) a wife living in a union based on abduction, despite the prohibition of her family. The third relationship is poorly regarded: the term for her children, *bronnfine*, literally 'belly-children', is disparaging. The fourth is seen as illegal, and this is expressed in very practical terms: the wife's assets are her natal family's, her liabilities are her partner's. In the suing out of her rights a *cétmuinter*'s husband acts for her unless he is badly behaved within marriage, and for that she can divorce him. Other women, less closely bound to their husbands, are free to select others to do so.

A woman may leave the product of her labour to the church, provided it is wholly her own and provided she has left no undischarged liabilities in the community. This leads the lawyer to a more general observation on the grant of property to the church: 'it is no commandment of God to neglect one's family' by granting its property to the church (§9). Far from being evidence of conservatively pagan attitudes, such views are expressed in fifth-century imperial legislation and in the writings of Fathers such as Augustine and Jerome. The present strictures may be directed against clerics who tried to have undue influence on women.

This text is edited and translated into German by Rudolf Thurneysen, *Irisches Recht* (Berlin: Akademie der Wissenschaften, 1931), pp. 27–37, §§27–38. It is also edited (without translation) by D.A. Binchy in *Corpus Iuris Hibernici* (Dublin: Dublin Institute for Advanced Studies, 1978), pp. 440–4. This is a new translation from the latter edition, but it owes much to Thurneysen's work.]

DÍRE
(Marriage and Families) (*c.* 700)

[This text is probably contemporary with *Cáin Lánamna*. It gives graphic expression to the general legal incapacity of women in regard to contracts. The same views occur elsewhere: 'Thou shalt not buy from one who is senseless in Irish law: a woman, a captive, a slave . . . There are three who are not capable of individual contract: the son of a living father, a legally married woman, a lord's base client.' This is an almost unqualified general statement of women's inability to contract. Some have argued that

§1. How many class-divisions have been established in Irish law in regard to the *díre* of women? How are their offences off-paid? Who receives their *éraics* and legacies?

§2. Payment for the offence of a *cétmuinter* falls on her sons, a third on her [natal] family. The same proportions hold good for her *éraic* and her legacy.

§3. If she is a *cétmuinter* who did not have sons, payment for her offence is divided in two between her [natal] family and her spouse. The same proportions hold good for her *éraic* and her legacy.

§4. And a wife who is recognized and contracted in marriage by her family: payment for her offence is divided between her sons and her [natal] family. The same proportions hold good for her *éraic* and her legacy.

§5. And a wife who is recognized but who is not contracted in marriage and who is not commanded to form the relationship [by her family], two-thirds of the payment for her offence falls on her [natal] family, a third on her natural children. The same proportions hold good for her *éraic* and her legacy.

§6. And the woman who is in a union of abduction despite the prohibition of her father or her family: her *éraic* and her legacy belong to her [natal] family, liability for payment for her offence and for her children fall on the man who abducts her.

§7. The mother's family has no right in sons — except for the son of a foreigner and the son of a man without property[1] — apart from the *cumal aireir*[2] which does not diminish the *éraic*. This is assigned to off-pay vengeance and to discharge the cost of fosterage paid by the mother's family.

§8. Every woman who has not left liabilities for her offence, children, or other burden on the community is entitled to grant the product of her own hands to the church, but not a product in which others had a part.

§9. Nobody grants away anything without the consent of his/her family, for it is no commandment of God to neglect one's family from which one has one's birth, which supports the liability for one's offences, which fosters one until adulthood, and not to leave to it what is its due.

§10. The levying share of the suing out of everyone's rights belongs to one's kindred, except when legal proceedings for malfeasance are in

1. Such sons really belong to their mother's family.
2. An additional payment (equal to three milking cows) that is the equivalent of a seventh of the *éraic* made to the mother's family.

progress against the head of the kindred. In that circumstance, the head of the kindred is deprived of the levying share [a third] because of malfeasance.

§11. Every woman is competent to decide whether the suing out of her rights should belong to her son,[3] her [natal] family, or the man she is sleeping with, except for a *cétmuinter*; for the suing out of her rights belongs to every proper *cétmuinter* [husband] unless his misdeeds in marriage pollute him. When they do, she is entitled to part from him.

§12. The worst of transactions are women's contracts. For a woman is not capable of selling anything without the consent of one of those who has authority over her: her father looks after her when she is a girl; her *cétmuinter* [husband] looks after her when she is a *cétmuinter*; her sons look after her when she is a widow with children; her [natal] family looks after her when she is a woman of the family;[4] the church looks after her when she is a woman of the church. She is not capable of selling or buying or contract or transaction without the consent of one of those who has authority over her, apart from a proper gift to one of those authorities with agreement and without neglect.

3. 'Guarantor' of the conditions of her marriage contract is also a possible translation.
4. i.e. a widow without living father, spouse or children, who has returned to her natal family.

HONOUR-PRICE — SOME EXCEPTIONS (*c.* 700)

[For most women, their honour-price (and thus their status at law) was half that of their husband, for some it was lower (see pp. 7–8). But this is not the case for all wives, as the text below indicates. However, even here the man who marries an outland woman (and is wholly dependent on her for his rights in his adoptive community) is an object of disdain, as is the hero Fergus, illicit lover of Queen Medb in the sagas. This text is edited and translated by Rudolf Thurneysen in *Irisches Recht*, p. 64, §4, and D.A. Binchy in *Studies in Early Irish Law*, p. 215. This is a new translation.]

In the case of all kinds of men in Irish law, except for three alone, their wives have half their honour-price: a man without land without property who is married to an heiress — he is paid honour-price according to the honour-price of his wife; a man who follows his wife's arse over a border — he is paid honour-price according to the honour-price of his wife; and a foreigner from overseas — he is paid honour-price according to the honour-price of his wife; she pays for his offences if she is contracted in marriage or recognized by her [natal] family. These three women are capable of impugning the contracts of their husbands, so that these latter are not competent to sell or buy without their wives, but they can do only what their wives authorize.

DIVORCE
(*c.* 700)

[Divorce was a perennial problem for the medieval church. The Old Irish laws cite Christ's words: 'What therefore God hath joined together, let no man put asunder' (Matthew 19:6) and while there are some ringing assertions of the lifelong and indissoluble nature of marriage in the Laws, divorce and re-marriage are tolerated in the case of serious faults and failings. They reflect the ambivalence of the Old and New Testaments, and the difficulty in deriving Scripture-based rules for Augustinian theology. Besides, they are influenced by Roman civil law and no doubt by indigenous Irish custom inherited from a pagan past.

The first text is from Binchy, *Corpus Iuris Hibernici*, pp. 1823–4, 1883–4. The second is to be found, ibid., pp. 47 and 1848. The third is to be found, ibid., p. 2198; it is edited and translated into German by Rudolf Thurneysen in *Zeitschrift für celtische Philologie*, vol. 15 (1925), p. 356, §44. The fourth is from *Bretha Nemed* in *Corpus Iuris Hibernici*, pp. 2230–1.]

§1. There are seven men in the community whom the rule of marriage excludes and their wives turn from them out of marriage, and what they [the wives] have received is forfeit to them [the wives]: an infertile husband, an impotent husband, a husband in holy orders, a husband who is a churchman, a husband without assets, an obese husband, a husband who talks about the marriage bed. For an infertile husband has

no offspring, an impotent husband cannot have a wife, it is not right that a son should be on the roadside, it is impossible to have equal right with the church, an obese husband is not capable of the sexual act, a man who talks about the marriage bed should not be under the sheets.

§2. There are seven women in Irish law who, though their marriage contract is bound by enforcing surety and paying surety, are entitled to leave their marriage any time they like and what is given them in their bridewealth is theirs: a woman whose husband spreads slander about her, a woman whose husband inflicts humiliation upon her so that she becomes an object of derision, a woman on whom is inflicted the mark of beating, a woman who is repudiated and abandoned for another woman, a woman whose bed is spurned and whose husband prefers to sleep with boys unless he have cause,[1] a wife to whom her husband gives charms while wooing her and excites her to fornicate, a woman who does not receive her needs in the marriage partnership, for every woman who is married in Irish law is entitled to her needs . . .

§3. These are the seven offences that give a man full right to divorce his wife: the betrayal of her husband, persisting in a forbidden relationship, abortion of that which she bears, bringing disgrace upon his honour, infanticide, barrenness because of disease, spoiling everything [in her domestic work].

§4. These are the three that do not sever their partnership until death: a client from his lord after taking chattels [a fief] from his hand, a monastic tenant from his superior, and a legal *cétmuinter* from his/her partner after a marriage contract witnessed by two firm sureties, for they are indissoluble after sexual intercourse and sleeping together. Until the hand part from the side, the head from the body, and the tongue from speech and as they do not part until death, so a monastic tenant does not part from his superior until death, a client does not part from his lord or a legal *cétmuinter* from his/her partner until they are both in the grave.

---

1. This clause is ambivalent in original: *gilla* means 'youth' or 'servant'.

RAPE (*c.* 700)

[The Irish lawyers treat rape and *sleith* as heinous crimes. *Sleith* means non-consensual sexual intercourse with a woman who is sleeping, in a drunken stupor, or comatose for whatever reason. Some of the rules about rape (and *sleith* is merely a variety of rape) do not derive from any traditional Irish law but from Hebrew law as set out in Deuteronomy 22:23–7, and repeated in the *Hibernensis*. Here Irish law takes over the principle of Hebrew law, but not its harsh penalties. The woman who does not cry out at her rape when there are people in the vicinity loses her honour and her entitlement to any compensation. There are other women who are not entitled to any compensation for rape: the common prostitute (until she reforms), the woman who conceals her rape, an adulterous wife, a woman who makes illicit trysts, a woman who uses sex for legal favours, a woman who offers herself frivolously.

The usual punishments for rape are serious, but the lawyers base punishments and compensations on the social status of the woman raped: 'Full *éraic* is paid for a virgin, for a young nun who does not reject her veil and for a *cétmuinter*; half *éraic* for secondary wives — all this is without the co-operation of the woman — together with the full honour-price of the man of highest rank who has authority over her of those to whom she specially belongs.' *Éraic*, the fixed penalty for homicide, is payable for rape. The first penalty, then, for the rape of a virgin, a young nun, or a *cétmuinter* is twenty-one milch cows. The second penalty is the honour-price of the man of highest rank who is in authority over the woman — her father, grandfather, husband, guardian or, in the case of a nun, her religious superior. A secondary wife receives half-*éraic* (still a substantial sum), and the same provision about the honour-price of the woman's superior applies, but her diminished compensation points to the church's disapproval of concubinage. Non-resistance to the rapist or contributory negligence in the case of *sleith* lost a woman her right to compensation, and her honour. Passages four and five are taken from *Gúbretha Caratniad*, 'The False Judgements of Caratnia', a text that deals with conflicts between legal principles and equity — hence the unusual format.

For the Irish text of the first passage, see *Corpus Iuris Hibernici*, pp. 15, 538. For the second, ibid., p. 42 (cf. p. 1845). For the third, ibid., p. 827. For the fourth and fifth, see Rudolf Thurneysen, *Zeitschrift für celtische Philologie*, vol. 14 (1925), pp. 350–1.]

§1. There are seven women in Irish law who are not entitled to penalty-fine or honour-price from anybody: a woman who thieves, a woman who lampoons every class of person, a woman who betrays, a tale-bearer until her slanders are off-paid by her family, a whore in the bushes, a woman who slays, a woman who refuses hospitality to every class of person.

§2. There are seven[1] women in Irish law who are liable in their encounters and who are not entitled to penalty-fine or honour-price for their *sleith*: they are not entitled to fines or *éraic* for rape whosoever may have done so: a whore who offers her body to all, until she becomes chaste, a woman who stays silent about her *sleith*, a woman who conceals her rape, a woman who is raped in a town and who does not cry out until the rapist has got away, a woman who agrees to have illicit intercourse in despite of her husband, a woman who trysts with a man in the bushes or in bed, a woman who invokes a hostage-surety, clerical or lay, by offering her body, a woman who offers herself for something trivial. These are seven women who are capable of giving their bodies in sexual intercourse, provided they do not fail in their duties. Their children do not belong to the family and they are not entitled to the profits arising from cohabitation.

§3. This is when sexual intercourse by stealth perpetrated on a woman is not actionable and is without *éraic* i.e. if the woman fell asleep at a fair or in an ale-house without a witness to testify, there is no *éraic* for sexual intercourse by stealth.

§4. I granted *éraic* to a woman who did not cry out at her rape. It was technically incorrect but it was equitable, because she was raped in a desert place.

§5. I discharged an action for sexual intercourse by stealth perpetrated upon a single woman in a mead-house. It was technically incorrect, but it was equitable, because it was wrong for a woman to be amongst a houseful without her partner to watch over her.

1. This 'heptad' in fact lists eight kinds of women.

CHILDREN AND CHILD-REARING (*c.* 700)

[Normally, man and wife shared in the responsibility and expense of rearing their offspring. Children of nobles were usually fostered and the setting up of a suitable fosterage contract was an important aspect of parental duties. This practice was so widespread that the familiar forms, *muimme* 'mummy' and *aite* 'daddy', are used for foster-mother and foster-father, not for natural parents. There are reasons for this arrangement. Royals were fostered by the great families of the kingdom, children of leading nobles were brought up in court. This provided the young royal with enduring friendships and alliances in future social and political life and the children of great nobles with lifelong patrons at court. It also helped to reduce a sibling rivalry that was very keen in a polygynous aristocratic society. It created cross-links between the great lineages. That was all the more necessary because inter-dynastic marriage was perhaps a more fragile social cement in Ireland than elsewhere. Similar considerations — the search for patrons, social connections, alliances and support — applied lower down in society.

The fosterage fee varied according to the rank of the child's father. Girls were more expensive (generally one-third more) to foster than boys because their needs were seen as more complex. The daughter of a farmer was taught how to run a house — the use of the quern, the kneading-trough and the sieve, and how to herd lambs and kids. An upper-class girl was taught sewing, cutting out, and embroidery (and this was a highly valued skill). Fosterage ended at the age of consent: usually fourteen for a girl, seventeen for a boy. A child in fosterage could make no legal contract and its foster-parents were responsible for any fines incurred by it. Intimate relationships and warm affections existed between fosterer and fostered long after the contract was over: the 'avenging of a foster-son of the kin' is one of the four legitimate killings in Irish law.

Some women did not share the duty of contributing to the fosterage of their children because of illness or the social circumstances of the child's birth. Some fathers did not share in this duty: certain high status persons exempt because of their exalted positions, those disqualified by madness or by their precarious legal position. Some of these provisions are purely practical, others betray firmly held social values, and the rules about the slave girl's child may reflect late Roman law inherited through early canon law. Children whose fathers played no part in arranging their fosterage were severely disadvantaged in society. These texts were edited and translated by Kathleen Mulchrone in *Studies in Early Irish Law*, pp. 191–5, and the present translation is based on her work.]

§1. There are seven women in Irish law who do not engage in joint fosterage with men, for it is the men who foster what they [the women] bear and the women are not liable for half the fosterage fee: a child begotten on a slave girl by illegal sexual intercourse without the assent of her lord, the child of a madwoman, the child begotten by rape, a child begotten on a girl in despite of her father's prohibition; the child returned to his father's family when its mother dies in childbirth, the child begotten on a *cétmuinter* in despite of her husband's prohibition, the child of a woman who is ill. Just cause allows it in this case.

§2. How many kinds of children are there in Irish law whose mothers do not share in the responsibility for their fosterage? Answer, twelve:[1] the child of a slave girl, the child of rape, the child of violation by stealth, the child of a woman repudiated by her family, the child of a deaf woman, the child of a blind woman, the child of a consumptive, the child of a woman-satirist, the child of a foreigner, the child of a madwoman, the child of a woman-hireling.

§3. There are seven[2] women in Irish law whose men do not share responsibility for the fosterage of their children and the women raise what they bear: the child that a free woman bears to a slave through illegal sexual intercourse without the consent of his lord, the child of a man whom his family has repudiated, the child that a woman bears to the son of a living father in despite of his father's prohibition, the child of a whore, the child of a foreigner, the child of a satirist who does not allow right or entitlement to anybody, the child of [a woman who is] an outcast from her family, the child of a man who sins in holy orders, who does not laicize but who does penance.

§4. How many kinds of children are there whose fathers do not share in the responsibility for their fosterage? Answer, nine: the child of a madman, the child of a foreigner, the child of an imbecile, the child of a man repudiated by his father because of his habitual viciousness, the child of a wise man [i.e. the son of a judge], the child of a satirist, the child of an alien, the child of one who carries his book in front of him [i.e. a cleric in holy orders], the child of rape.[3]

1. The text lists only eleven.
2. This heptad in fact lists eight.
3. This last is probably an error, unless the man is perceived here as the victim of rape.

from:
BRETHA CRÓLIGE
(Judgements on Sick-Maintenance)
(first half of 8th century)

[There were no hospitals (public or private) in early Ireland and the sick were usually tended by physicians in private houses. Illegal personal injuries — deliberate wounding with weapons or injury as a result of negligence — were dealt with through an early social institution, sick-maintenance, which worked as follows. First, the victim was removed to his/her own home where s/he was tended by a physician and by his/her family. If s/he died within nine days, full fine for killing became payable. If the patient survived for nine days, s/he was forensically examined by the physician and if further nursing was required s/he was conveyed to the house of a third party (to a 'high sanctuary', obviously a church foundation, in the case of a cleric), where s/he was nursed back to health at the expense of the culprit and under very strict legal and physical conditions. The culprit had to pay for all medical attention, for suitable accommodation (there must be no loud and foolish talk, rows, screaming children, barking dogs, squealing pigs), and for the minutely prescribed food for the patient and the patient's specified number of visitors. The visitors allowed and the quality of food varied with the social class of the victim. In addition, the culprit usually had to supply a person to do the work normally done by the victim.

There were disagreements among the lawyers about those who should be excluded from sick-maintenance. One text declares: 'Neither lawful principal spouse nor virgin maid below the age of consent, nor king, nor royal poet, nor abbot, nor bishop, nor nobleman, nor "exile of God", nor senior, nor antiquary . . . go on sick maintenance — the wife lest she be debauched, the virgin lest she be seduced.' The text insists that all women be accompanied and this provision has more to do with distrust than with care.

The lawyers saw the sick-maintenance of women as problematic and they had detailed rules about it. These reflect male concerns about control over women and over their fertility. The provision for dependants is estimated as a fraction of the entitlement of those on whom they depend. This rule is applied to women, with socially reprehensible consequences: a *cétmuinter* is entitled to half what her husband gets, a secondary wife a third, and any other kind of concubine a fourth. Women who do not consider themselves to have a marriage partner are estimated in terms of their own dignity and possessions. Some men — those accused of excessive lust and the constant sinner (understood by the glossators as a man given to masturbation) — are accompanied by their women, but no corresponding provision is made for women's sexual needs.

Some women are excluded from sick-maintenance, and these are of two kinds. One category is women of high social status — 'a woman who turns back the streams of war, a woman who is a ruler holding hostages, a woman abundant in miracles, a woman satirist, a woman wright, a woman revered by the community, the woman doctor of the community'. The first of these is understood variously: some commentators think of a military leader (such as Medb, who commanded the troops of Ireland in *Táin Bó Cúailnge*); others suggest heads of great female houses, such as the Abbess of Kildare, always an aristocrat as well as the controller of vast resources in lands and income. Holding hostages is holding political power, and such a woman would have political authority. There were, of course, women poets, though a satirist is not at all the most respectable. The others are women honoured by the community because of their professional or personal qualities. The second category of excluded women are those seen as difficult — promiscuous women, whores, viragos, lunatics, thieves, and those powerful, feared women whose practices fall outside the bounds of social approval.

Compensation for the disruption of a married couple's sexual life is another cost to be borne by the culprit.

What follows is a selection of excerpts from *Bretha Crólige*, the principal tract on sick-maintenance. They correspond to D.A. Binchy, 'Bretha Crólige', *Ériu*, vol. 12 (1938), pp. 1–77, §§29–40, 44, 56–7.]

§1. There are three persons in the community whose women-folk accompany them on sick-maintenance: a man who is accused of excessive lust, a man constant in sinning, the mother of every child at the breast.

§2. Most difficult in the Irish law of sick-maintenance is the nursing of women. How are they brought away on sick-maintenance? And how are they maintained? And how many of them are debarred? Half the food of every man on sick-maintenance is due to his wife.

§3. There is moreover in Irish law a woman who is entitled to have three judges to estimate her maintenance: a judge who is knowledgeable about food, a judge of the language of the law, and a judge of common custom. She who is entitled to have these three to estimate her sick-maintenance is a woman of handicraft.[1]

§4. There are twelve women in the community whom the rule of sick-maintenance in Irish law

---

1. A skilled worker such as an embroideress or maker of textiles.

excludes: a woman who turns back the streams of war, a woman who is a ruler holding hostages, a woman abundant in miracles, a woman satirist, a woman wright, a woman revered by the community, the woman doctor of the community, a sharp-tongued virago, a vagrant woman, a werewolf in wolf-shape, an idiot, a lunatic. These women are compensated by a fee paid to their families: they are not brought on sick-maintenance.

§5. The payment for them is in proportion to that due to men whom the rule of sick-maintenance excludes. If these women consider themselves to be persons without a marriage partner, they are paid compensation in accordance with their own dignities and property, in accordance with the judgement of the judge of the community.

§6. There are three of these women whose sick-maintenance fee is paid according to the dignity of their marriage:[2] a sharp-tongued virago, a werewolf, and a vagrant woman. The reason why they are not brought on sick-maintenance is that one dare not take responsibility for a crime of their audacity.

§7. Every other woman debarred from being brought on sick-maintenance is paid honour-price according to her worth and property, in the same way as a man is entitled to sick-maintenance in Irish law.

§8. Every woman who goes on sick-maintenance is entitled to have half the retinue proper to her husband with her on sick-maintenance.

§9. There are moreover two women in the community who are entitled to be brought on sick-maintenance though no wrong has been done them: a witness accompanying the woman to whom injury has been done to guard her, and a witness accompanying the woman who goes to do the work of the woman against whom injury has been done, for it is a great foolishness and every compensation perishes if such women are let go without guarding, so that it is necessary that a witness go with every woman who is brought away on sick-maintenance in Irish law.

§10. Most difficult in the judgement of sick-maintenance is the barring of sexual intercourse if it occurs in the fertile period. For it is one of the oaths that are sworn by women in Irish law that their fertile periods have come.

§11. Three *sét*s are due for the barring of sexual intercourse of a king of over-kings and a petty king. Two *sét*s for barring of the sexual intercourse of an *aire ard*.[3] It is the same amount from the latter down to the *aire itir dá airig*[4] inclusive. One *sét* for the barring of sexual intercourse of everyone from an *aire itir dá airig* to a *fer midboth*.[5]

§12. Moreover, there is the same penalty for barring of sexual intercourse for women because of injury to their husbands — except that here women dignitaries prove it by giving evidence — and this penalty does not diminish the obligations of sick-maintenance in Irish law wherever these debts may accrue . . .

§13. There are three women in the community who have no right to sick-maintenance or fines, although injury has been done them: a woman who does not care who she sleeps with, a woman who steals from everybody, and a sorceress who traffics in charms . . .

§14. Every woman who is living in a proper marital union is entitled to half the food of her husband in sick-maintenance. Every secondary wife is entitled to a third of the food of her husband in sick-maintenance. Every other woman is entitled to a fourth of the food of her husband. For in Irish law nobody has been left without a right to compensation-fine but the person who deserves evil because of his/her conduct.

---

2. i.e. on the basis of the status of their marriage partners, unlike the other women debarred from sick-maintenance (§7).

3. i.e. 'high *aire*' (lord).

4. An *aire* of intermediate rank between lord and commoner (literally, 'an *aire* between two *aire*s').

5. A *sét*, 'chattel', has the value of a heifer. Payment is listed in a descending scale from a king of over-kings (provincial king) down through the nobility to a *fer midboth*, a low level commoner who had not yet inherited his farm. The barring of sexual intercourse is due to injury to these men's wives.

§15. Everybody is paid compensation for his/her marital union [for offences against his/her spouse] according to the customary law of the island of Ireland, whether it be many or one. For there is a dispute in Irish law as to which is more proper, whether many sexual unions or a single one; since the chosen people of God lived in polygamy, it is no easier to condemn it than to praise it.

PICA
(mid-9th century; Early Modern Irish)

[Pica, known since ancient times, is an extreme craving for normal food or for non-food substances. It is not limited to race, sex or class, but it is commonest in pregnant women. It seems to be related to increased nutritional needs in pregnancy. However, famine and undernourishment were chronic (often acute) in Ireland, as elsewhere, in the Middle Ages and, in any case, the medieval Irish diet led to grave imbalances in nutrition. The winter diet of corned meat, heavily salted butter and grain (taken mostly as porridge) was deficient in necessary vitamins and minerals. As a result, pica in pregnancy, especially in winter, was likely to be common and socially significant. The first extract comes from *The Tripartite Life of St Patrick* (mid-ninth century) and the clinically acute observation and soundly based therapy suggest a clerical medical practitioner. Two other points may be noted. First, nocturnal searching, anxiety, and dreaming about the craved food are well known clinically. Second, chives are the earliest of the onion family to provide edible leaves in spring and contain important nutrients — iron, pungent volatile oils, pectin and a small quantity of sulphur.

Pica is also treated of in a later medieval legal tract that may date to some time between the twelfth and the fifteenth century, but there are enough traces of older language to indicate that the lawyers were considering the problem in the Old Irish period. Pica is given a legal standing as a condition of pregnancy. The rules of private property are relaxed, to a degree, in favour of the sufferer and, given the scarcities of the Middle Ages, this is significant. A sufferer from pica may consume the equivalent of three meals of anyone's food without incurring any liability. If, in a case of genuine craving, she exceeds that amount, replacement of the excess consumed is all that is required of her. Penalties begin with evident abuse.

The lawyer then discusses three different cases in regard to husband and wife: on the part of the husband,

(i) his criminal refusal to give the food craved (in order to bring about abortion), (ii) his neglect, and (iii) his simple refusal of the food craved without other motive; on the part of the wife, (i) her criminal failure to ask for the food craved (in order to bring about abortion), (ii) her neglect, and (iii) her simple failure to ask due to shame. First, the ideology is very strongly patriarchal: the loss of the child (and in the text that follows, the loss of the child is assumed) is seen as serious damage to the patrilineage to which the child legally belongs, and the patri-family in consequence takes the most of the compensation. The *éraic* is seven *cumal*s, the usual compensation for homicide. The matri-kin is entitled to an additional seventh of the compensation for the perceived damage to it, and this is the ancient proportion. Second, the offence, in whatever degree, is seen as a marital offence of one partner against the other, and the guilty or negligent partner must compensate the other. Were these rules enforced or enforceable? It is difficult to know, but at the very least one can take them as a piece of advanced legal thinking, an attempt to grapple with a delicate and socially significant problem, and write legal rules to deal with it.

The first text is from Whitley Stokes, *The Tripartite Life of St Patrick*, 2 vols (London: Stationery Office, 1887), vol. 1, pp. 200–1. The second is translated from D.A. Binchy, *Corpus Iuris Hibernici*, pp. 940–1, 1256–7.]

I.

It was then that sickness seized Ailill's pregnant wife and she was near to death. Patrick asked what was wrong with her. The woman replied: 'There is a herb that I saw in the air and I have not seen its like on the ground, and I will die or the child in my womb will die or we will both die unless I eat that herb.' Patrick said to her: 'What kind of herb is it?' 'Like rushes,' said the woman. Patrick blessed the rushes and they became chives. The woman ate them, then she was cured immediately; and presently she gave birth to a son, and she blessed Patrick. And it is said that Patrick said, 'All women who eat this herb will be cured.'

II.

§1. Exempt from legal liability for the woman suffering from cravings is that which overcomes her cravings: three full meals of his [her husband's] own food or three portions of somebody else's food, provided she does not eat in excess of that, and if she does eat in excess of that, it is held to be a culpable act in respect of compensation [i.e. simple replacement is required of her]. She did not get satisfaction of her cravings where replacement is the case. Or it may be the penalty for theft: she had got satisfaction of her cravings in the case in which penalty for theft is payable by her in respect of the excess. On the other hand, however much of his own food she consumes, no charges arise, except for the festival food of Easter or Christmas[1] and a fine for damages is payable in that case.

§2. Why is she not obliged to pay the penalty for the total amount as is the case with the *aire échta*[2] when he has consumed an excess beyond his legal entitlement? The reason for this is: he sooner did what was unlawful than what was lawful i.e. he sooner consumed the food than avenged injuries to his kindred. Here, however, the woman sooner did what was lawful than what was unlawful i.e. she sooner expressed [?] the craving than consumed the food and that is why she is obliged to pay the penalty for theft only in respect of the excess.

§3. If she asked for the food and it was not given to her, and in our opinion it is the man who refused to give the food in this case, and the reason why it was not given to her was to abort her, *éraic* and honour-price is due [from the father] in respect of the child i.e. to the family of the father, and a *cumal* to the woman's family; and *coibche*[3] and honour-price are due to the woman; and that is when only the killing of the child is intended; if it was to kill them both, the woman and the child, *éraic* is payable in respect of that one and *aithgin*[4] in respect of the other.

§4. If it [failure to provide the food, and its consequences] occurred because of heedlessness, and

the heedlessness in question was his idle amusement, half *éraic* is payable for the child, and half a *cumal* to the mother's family, and *coibche* is payable to the woman if she is alive; and it was not in respect of the child directly that the heedlessness took place; and if it were it would be heedlessness of foul play and full fine is payable for that.

§5. If it was through hardness or niggardliness the food was refused, that is regarded as a culpable act in respect of compensation for it — a *cumal* is payable to the father's family for it, a seventh of a *cumal* to the mother's family, and *coibche* to the wife. That is so in the case of a married person; it is the same in the case of a person who is not married, but *coibche* is not paid by a person who is not married.

§6. If she did not ask for the food and the reason why she did not ask was to abort herself, i.e. in order to kill the child, she is liable to *éraic* and honour-price in respect of the child and she is to pay it to the father's family, and she is to pay a *cumal* to the mother's family, and *coibche* and honour-price to her own husband.

§7. If it [failure to ask for food, and its consequences] occurred because of heedlessness, and the heedlessness in question was her idle amusement, and it was not heedlessness in respect of the child, half *éraic* is payable by her in respect of the child to the father's family, half a *cumal* to the mother's family, and *coibche* to her own husband, and this was not heedlessness in respect of the child directly; and if it were it would be heedlessness of foul play and full fine [is payable for that].

§8. If she did not ask for the food because of shyness or shame,[5] that is regarded as a culpable act in respect of compensation for it — a *cumal* is payable to the father's family and one-seventh of a *cumal* to the mother's family and *coibche* to her own husband . . .

---

1. Special stores of food were set aside for these two major feasts.
2. A member of the kindred with the special duty of avenging the killing of any of its members. His activities were governed by complex rules.
3. Literally, 'bridewealth', but in later law tracts apparently a unit of account in which marital compensation is paid. That is to say, marital compensations were paid in fractions or multiples of a notional 'bridewealth'.
4. This is a very unusual use of a technical term meaning simple replacement.

5. Modern clinicians lay great stress on the reluctance of patients to admit the practice of pica.

IMMATHCHOR nAILELLA OCUS AIRT
(Ailill's and Art's Mutual Restitution) (*c.* 700)

[This difficult text, which dates from about 700, is a literary example of a legal suit before a judge, embedded in a narrative about the legendary ancestors of the leading families of Ireland. This is a genre inherited from antiquity. Eogan Már and his sister Inderb are children of Ailill Ólom, ancestor of the Kings of Munster, and Sadb, daughter of Conn Cétchathach, ancestor of the Kings of Tara. Ailill expelled his wife because of alleged infidelity and she reared the children on her own. Sadb's claim to *comaltar*, namely, that husband and wife should share in the rearing of children, is sued out by her brother Art on her behalf. He states that she is of noble status and that a woman is entitled to *comaltar* even when she has been expelled from the common household. Ailill counters by saying that Sadb is a *cétmuinter* and that the children of such a woman belong to her husband. Ailill refers to his means of enforcing his rights by sureties, and claims personal and sexual integrity. The children are assigned to Ailill, who is allowed to enforce their surrender to him. The last (and very difficult) section deals with affiliation of children whose paternity is in doubt and the inadmissibility of the unreliable oaths of women in this regard. The present translation is from Johan Corthals, 'Affiliation of Children: *Immathchor nAilella ocus Airt*', *Peritia*, vol. 9 (1995), pp. 92–124, with some verbal changes and reinterpretations.]

§1. Ailill Ólom repudiated his wife, i.e. Sadb, daughter of Conn Cétchathach, after she had borne him twins,[1] i.e. Eogan Már and Inderb, and Sadb fostered them in Comalt Uaithne, and this is why that mountain was called Comalt: because she had fostered her son and her daughter together (*con-alt*) there. Her brother Art came to affiliate his children to Ailill,[2] and they appealed to the judgement of Ollam, the judge of Ireland, on the matter of joint responsibility for their fosterage.

'Plead your case,' said Ollam.
'Which of us two will plead first?'
'Easy to say,' said Ollam: 'The plaintiff.'
'Then let Art plead first,' said Ailill.

1. The belief that the conception of twins resulted from infidelity of the wife was widespread.
2. i.e. to assign the children legally to Ailill as his lawful offspring.

§2. 'I plead thus,' said Art:

'Very noble is the law concerning Sadb, which extolled her beyond a base woman. If strife should have expelled her, joint fosterage is swiftly due to every wife that is expelled from her central quarters of common supply, common living, common conversation in the ale-house.'

§3. 'And you, what do you plead, Ailill?' said Ollam.
'I plead thus,' said Ailill:

'Forfeited are the children of a woman bound by marriage, by which offspring of common supply, common sleeping, common union is bound. To me belongs my fair *cétmuinter* without any abrogation, to me belongs that which she rears, to me belongs what is fostered in that place.'

§4. Art answered:

'It is true that they are forfeited, the children of a woman bound by marriage, by which the offspring of common sleeping, common union, common provision are bound. Not, however, those of a marriage of violation, of disgrace, of hurt, of landlessness, of neglect. For such a marriage is like contracting hurt.'

§5. Ollam the judge answered:

'I pronounce on men, by whom noble women are passed over, by whom noble thighs are outraged, in order that they be not endowed by them with dishonour, a ready judgement, that will last forever.'

§6. Ailill answered:

'To me belongs my son, to me belongs my daughter. Let evidence be given by witnesses of the enforcing sureties. Hostages, that I should have selected to warrant my right of ownership, should be taken. Hostages should be taken pledging from the people's supply. My children should be given to me by the end of the month with their joint right of belonging to a hero, in order that, being without progeny of sin, I may not be punished by their being taken away by their mother, my fair *cétmuinter,* who makes wily contracts and gives bad advice.'

§7. Ollam said:

'Ailill's brilliant speech, it overcomes the guilt and wins his children, so that they should be surrendered by the people's good enforcing sureties, by which selection [of hostages?] should be made. Let me plead the great number of oaths of the untrustworthy woman that suffocate the trust of marriage after the . . .[3] of honour.

'A great number of bold oaths by unsteady women do not assign [to the father's family] the offspring of the womb. An unlawful conception without inalienable right is not entitled to be placed in the [father's] kindred. It is fixed by payment of *cumal*s so that the ordeal of the cauldron, of the duelling block, of lot, of the *cain*[?] of the adze, of the threefold stone . . .[4] is escaped from.'[5]

3. The sense of the original is unclear to me at this point.
4. Ditto.
5. These are ordeals (some obscure) that a woman underwent to establish the paternity of her child, and its consequent rights as an heir.

THE SEPARATION OF FINN AND GRÁINNE
(Middle Irish)

[This is another example of a legal case embedded in a narrative. Gráinne, daughter of Cormac mac Airt, was unhappily and unwillingly married to the aged warrior Finn. This is the theme of a number of tales and poems, the best known of which is *Tóraíocht Dhiarmada agus Ghráinne,* 'The Pursuit of Diarmaid and Gráinne'; see Volume I, pp. 313–17, and below, pp. 225–6. Here, Gráinne is unwilling to marry Finn and she demands of him a bridewealth that is impossible: a couple of every wild creature in Ireland. However, Caílte, the fleet-footed follower of Finn, collects the animals and Gráinne is married to Finn, and becomes increasingly unhappy. At

the Feast of Tara Cormac observes his daughter's deep distress. Her brother Coirpre says that it would be no dishonour for Cormac to return the bridewealth and thus end Gráinne's marriage. Cormac declares his responsibilities in her respect, undertakes to meet them, and have her returned to her natal family. Finn overhears this and speaks. Some general moralistic statements about marriage are attributed to him and he agrees that marriage partners with insuperable difficulties should part without defrauding. See Johan Corthals, 'Die Trennung von Finn und Gráinne', *Zeitschrift für celtische Philologie,* vol. 49–50 (1997), pp. 71–91 (with translation into German). The present translation is based on Corthals's with some minor changes and reinterpretations.]

Finn úa Baíscne went to court Gráinne, daughter of Cormac son of Conn. But she said she would not sleep with him unless he gave the bridewealth she would ask of him. She intended to demand something burdensome of him so that she might not be united with him. However, Finn answered that he would give her whatever she wished, whether near or far. The girl said that she would not accept any bridewealth from him other than a couple of every wild animal that lived in Ireland, to be conveyed in one drove to the meadow of Tara, and she vowed that unless she was given that drove they would not be united. 'I will see to it,' Finn said. 'No! I will see to it,' swift-footed Caílte said, the son of Oisgen or Coisgen of the Cerdrige of Múscraige Dotrut. He was the son of Cumall's daughter.

Then Caílte went and collected a couple of every wild animal and conducted that odd herd to the meadow of Tara. He went to where Cormac was and he told him that his daughter's bridewealth was in the meadow of Tara. 'Which was the most difficult for you to bring?' said Cormac. 'Easy to say. The white-tailed fox dodged me,' Caílte said.

Gráinne was then given in marriage to Finn, and that was no portent of peace, for they were unhappy until they separated. The girl hated Finn, and so great was her hatred that it made her sick. Cormac held the Feast of Tara and the men of Ireland set out for it from every direction. And they were consuming the Feast of Tara: the men of Ireland about Cormac in his royal house; and Finn, for his part, with his warrior bands like everyone else. As Gráinne went past Cormac, he noticed a gloomy look about her.

'Is there something the matter with you, woman?' said Cormac. Then she said in a very low voice past the head of his bed: 'So there should be, dear Cormac. I have a lump of gore under my heart the same size as the grease and fat of my husband, and hatred of him, so that the sinews of my body are taut.'

'Alas Gráinne is downcast. She has abstained too long from the common bed, from common lying, and from the sound of familiar things. Every living being is driven to union and love, every one who hates is dead.' Coirpre said, 'There is no shame on you if, with the help of a surety, you return Gráinne's bridewealth.'

Cormac declaimed: 'I am liable for Gráinne's debt. Of my body and my kin is the choicest of my children. Let it be collected together, let it be handed over. I am liable for one and a half times the bridewealth together with full fines. Let her be released today to her father's family.'

Finn heard this and he knew the girl hated him and then he said:

'It is time for us to part from the shame of great lust; I will bring you before the judge; nothing raw come out of the cauldron; gore should not be drunk; nothing foul should be sued by ordeal; great the hatred of the absconder[1] who dissolves legal matrimony between people who are wed. Physical beauty, love affairs with free women and the breaching[2] of chastity should be avoided . . .[3] Let there not be sexual intercourse in violation of the body, let a woman's hatred not be striven against. When the truth of any strife has been established by lot, then let the partners divorce without defrauding.'

1. *Malartach*, 'destroyer', is a synonym of *cumscaigthech*, 'somebody who abandons his/her marriage' (justly or otherwise).
2. Reading *fuidbech* for *fidbad*.
3. The sense of the original is unclear at this point.

from:
THE EXILE OF CONALL CORC (*c.* 1000)

[Corc of Cashel was sent to his death overseas to Feradach Find Fechtnach, King of Alba, with a secret message written on his shield in ogam: if he arrived by day he was

to be killed by evening, if by night, he was to be killed by morning. Gruibne, the scholar-poet of Feradach, whom Corc had previously liberated from captivity, found him in the wilderness dying of exposure, revived him, and read the inscription. He altered the inscription in Corc's favour and presented him to Feradach, whose daughter he slept with and made pregnant. The text deals with two things: punishment for fornication, and filiation. There are occasional literary references to burning women at the stake for fornication, or adultery, but there is no good evidence that this represents ancient custom. It seems rather to be a literary motif. It is true that the *Canones Wallici* state: 'If any man commits fornication with another's wife or sister or daughter, he shall be put to death; and he who slays him, let him not fear that he will have any lawsuit.' This is probably a British text and, in any case, it is merely an uncongenial and unusual extension to the Middle Ages of Old Testament provisions (Leviticus 20:10). Delaying a decision about filiation in cases of dubious paternity is a common practice in Irish law: the lawyers advocate a stay until family characteristics appear.

In its present form the tale belongs to *c.* 1000, but it is a re-telling of earlier material. The text is published in R.I. Best and M.A. O'Brien (eds), *The Book of Leinster*, 6 vols (Dublin: Dublin Institute for Advanced Studies, 1954–83 [1965]), vol. 4, p. 1250; and it is edited and translated by Vernam Hull, 'The Exile of Conall Corc', *Proceedings of the Modern Language Association*, vol. 56 (1941), pp. 937–50. This translation is based on Hull's but with numerous changes.]

'Who equipped you with that ogam writing that is on your shield? It indicated no good fortune.'

'What is there?' said Corc. 'This is what is there: if you go to Feradach by day, that your head be off before evening; if you go by night, that your head be off before morning. This is not the way it is going to be.'

He [Gruibne] brings him to his own house, with a litter under him, and eight men bearing the litter. A month later, he went to speak to Feradach, and he left Corc outside. He told him the whole story, how he had gone in search of his pigs and he said he intended to kill the man [he found]. When he saw the ogam writing on the shield he was reluctant to kill him, for this is what it said: 'The son of the King of Munster has come to you. If he comes by day, give him your daughter before evening; if he comes by night, she is to sleep with him before morning.'

'This is bad news,' said Feradach. 'A pity that you have brought him here alive.' He binds his own weight of silver on Feradach and he brings him [Corc] in. Feradach made him very welcome. The girl was not given to him, however, for Feradach said he would not give his daughter to a mercenary soldier from abroad.[1] This did not do him much good: the couple had sexual intercourse and the woman became pregnant by him, and she was brought to bed and bore him a son. She did not admit that it was Corc's. They intended to burn her [and] the men of Alba came for the burning. It was formerly a custom that any maiden who had illicit sex before betrothal in marriage was burnt. Hence these hills are [named] Mag Breo,[2] that is, Mag Breg. Then the men of Scotland sought a delay for the girl to the end of a year until the boy displayed family form, or family voice, or family habit.

At the end of year they come to burn her. 'Will I give your son to you?' said she [to Corc]. 'You shall give him, then,' said he, 'in the presence of Feradach.' When she was about to be burned, she brought him before both of them. 'O woman,' said Feradach, 'does the boy belong to Corc?' 'He does,' said the woman. 'I will not take him from you,' said Corc, 'because he is a bastard until his grandfather gives him.' 'I do indeed give him to you,' said Feradach. 'The son is yours.' 'Now he will be accepted,' said Corc. 'Go away, woman,' said Feradach, 'and may you have no luck.' 'She will not go,' said Corc, 'because she is not guilty.'

'She is guilty,' said Feradach. 'But she is not guilty,' said Corc, 'to every son his mother. Her liability falls on her son, that is, on her womb.' 'He shall not be expelled, indeed,' said Corc, 'since that youth has not attained manhood. For the son will pay for her liability.' 'You have saved them both,' said Feradach. 'Good,' said Corc. 'Well, Corc, sleep with your wife. It is you we would have chosen for her, if we had a choice.' 'I will pay her price to the men of Alba,' [said Corc].

That is done, and he stayed in the east until she bore him three sons. 'Well, Corc,' said Feradach, 'take your sons and your wife with you to your country for it is sad they should be outside their own land. Take what silver three men can bear with you. Let thirty warriors go with you.' That is done.

---

1. The original is illegible in the manuscript at this point — my translation is a likely guess.
2. Mag Breo means, literally, 'Plain of Burning'.

from:
TÁIN BÓ CÚALNGE (THE CATTLE RAID OF CÚALNGE)
(*c.* 1125)

[The famous pillow-talk between Medb and Ailill serves as an artistic introduction to, and motivation for, Medb's quest for the famous bull Donn Cúailnge, and thus the action of *Táin Bó Cúailnge*. Thurneysen attributed it to the writer who composed the version of *Táin Bó Cúailnge* in the Book of Leinster and he dates it to the first third or quarter of the twelfth century. Only Thurneysen seems to savour the writer's creative gifts and humour, and nobody has thought much of his knowledge of the law concerning women. In fact, he uses contemporary legal language flawlessly, the high comic effect of the episode turns on his precision, and the legal terminology is used to deepen and sharpen what may be one of the main points of the episode, that upset of the patriarchal order of society leads to conflict, even calamity. However seriously or not one takes the paradigm, it provides the tension-giving framework within which the comic dramatic episode is very skilfully developed.

The heart of the matter is a lively husband–wife wrangle that refers back constantly to Irish marriage law. Ailill had married Medb, heiress to the kingdom of Connacht, and is really king in right of wife. When he makes the foolhardy and smug remark that his wife is well-off because she is married to him he starts an argument in which he is humiliated. Medb was a *banchomarba*: when she married a lackland (such as Ailill), her marriage is *lánamnas for bantinchur* and here 'the husband goes in the track of the wife and the wife in the track of the husband' (*Cáin lánamna* §29, see p. 25). Such a man has no independent honour-price in some circumstances: 'But he is a husband who is paid honour-price in accordance with his wife's status if she holds all the property, unless he has higher property qualifications [in his own right] than his wife or is more godly, more high-born or more estimable than she' (ibid. §31). Medb, as the daughter of the King of Tara, is of higher status than Ailill, she is heiress to Connacht (she was given it by her father) and Ailill is therefore 'a man who follows his wife's arse over a border', therefore without independent honour-price, as she tauntingly reminds him. Role reversal is pressed further: she claims to have given him bridewealth (a male prerogative), almost implying that he is a kept man. Hence the keen competition between them over moveable wealth, and Medb's intense irritation when she finds that she has no bull to equal Findbennach. Ailill makes his point, but here again there is an irony: the bull, unlike his royal owner, is too male to be kept by a woman. There are ironies, too, in regard to Medb's promiscuity and ruthlessness. What she offers Dáire for his bull echoes what she offered Ailill in marriage: sex and a chariot worth thrice seven bond maids. But she offers too much, and this is marked by Dáire's prodigious laughter as he lies abed. Yet she fails of her purpose, and stubbornly brings disaster on all.

Though this tale is placed conventionally in the pagan past it is full of contemporary resonances. It owes much to Christian misogyny and to patristic ideas about female lust and the waywardness of female character. At one level, the text warns of dire consequences when women are independent and usurp the male role in society: they should be chaste and obedient, and not take part in political and military matters. The twelfth-century preoccupation with marriage law and reform finds an echo here. But there are other levels: women in the state of nature and before the saving effect of Christian grace have their points — Medb's character is drawn with a flourish that does not wholly lack sympathy. And the imagined court of Connacht is pointedly the very opposite of what it was in the writer's time, when the great warrior-king and philanderer, the much-married Tairdelbach Úa Conchobair, was winning the kingship of Ireland for himself — and this is yet another irony that contemporaries may have savoured. Cecile O'Rahilly, *Táin Bó Cúalnge from the Book of Leinster* (Dublin: Dublin Institute for Advanced Studies, 1967), pp. 1–3 (text), pp. 137–40 (translation). This is a new translation.]

THE PILLOW-TALK

One time it happened Ailill and Medb that when their royal bed had been made for them in Ráth Crúachan of Connacht, they spoke together as they lay on their pillow.

'It is a true saying, woman,' said Ailill, 'she is a well-off woman who is the wife of a man of substance.'

'Indeed,' said the lady. 'Why do you think so?'

'I think so,' said Ailill, 'because you are better off today than when I married you.'

'I was well-off before you,' said Medb.

'It was wealth that we had not heard of and did not know about,' said Ailill, 'but you were an heiress and enemies from the lands about you were carrying off spoils and booty from you.'

'Not so was I,' said Medb, 'but my father held the high-kingship of Ireland — Eochu Feidlech mac Find meic Findomain meic Fineóin meic Findguill meic Rotha meic Rigeóin meic Bláthachta meic Béothechta meic Énna Aignig meic Óengusa Turbig. He had six fine daughters: Derbriu, Ethne and Éle, Clothru, Mugain and Medb. I was the noblest and worthiest of them. I was the most generous of them in bounty and gift-giving. I was the best of them in battle and fight and combat. I had fifteen hundred royal mercenaries of the sons of strangers exiled from the outland and as many of the sons of native freemen from within. And there were ten men for each mercenary of these, and nine men for every mercenary, and eight men for every mercenary, and seven for every mercenary, and six for every mercenary, and five for every mercenary, and four for every mercenary, and three for every mercenary, and two for every mercenary, and one mercenary for every mercenary. I had these for my standing household troops,' said Medb, 'and for that reason my father gave me one of the provinces of Ireland, namely, the province of Crúachu. Whence I am called Medb of Crúachu.

'Messengers came from Find mac Rosa Rúaid, King of Leinster, asking for my hand in marriage, and from Cairbre Nia Fer, King of Tara, and they came from Conchobar mac Fachtna, King of Ulster, and they came from Eochu Bec. But I did not consent, for I demanded a strange bridewealth that no woman before me had asked of any of the men of Ireland, namely, a husband without meanness, without jealousy, without fear. If my husband were mean, it would not be fitting for us to be together, for I am generous in largess and in gift-giving and it would be a reproach for my husband that I should be more generous than he, but it would be no reproach if we were equally generous provided both of us were generous. If my husband were timorous, neither would it be fitting for us to be together, for single-handed, I am victorious in battles and contests and combats, and it would be a reproach to my husband that his wife should be more courageous than he, but it is no reproach if they are equally courageous provided they are both courageous. If my man were jealous, that would not be fitting either, for I was never without one lover in the shadow of another.

'Now such a husband have I got in you, Ailill mac Rosa Rúaid of Leinster. You are not niggardly, you are not jealous, you are not sluggish. I gave you a marriage of contract and bridewealth as best befits a woman, namely, the raiment of twelve men, a chariot worth thrice seven bond maids, the breadth of your face in red gold, the weight of your left arm in white bronze. Whoever brings shame and annoyance and confusion on you, you have no claim for compensation or for honour-price for it except what claim I have,' said Medb, 'for you are a man dependent on a woman's marriage-portion.'

'Not so was I,' said Ailill, 'but I had two brothers, one of them reigning in Tara, the other in Leinster, namely, Find over Leinster and Cairbre over Tara. I left the kingship to them because they were older, but they were no better in bounty and in gift-giving than I. And I heard of no province in Ireland being a woman's inheritance except this province alone, so I came and assumed the kingship here in virtue of my mother's rights, for Máta Muirisc the daughter of Mága was my mother. And what better queen could I have than you, for you are the daughter of the high-king of Ireland.'

'Nevertheless,' said Medb, 'my property is greater than yours.'

'I am surprised at that,' said Ailill, 'for there is no one who has greater possessions and riches and wealth than I, and I know that there is not.'

There were brought to them what was least valuable among their possessions that they might know which of them had more goods and riches and wealth. There were brought to them their wooden cups and their vats and their iron vessels, their cans, their washing-basins and their tubs. There were brought to them their rings and their bracelets and their thumb-rings, their treasures of gold and their garments, as well purple as blue and black and green, yellow and variegated and grey, dun and chequered and striped.

Their great flocks of sheep were brought from fields and pastures and open plains. They were counted and reckoned and it was recognized that they were equal, of the same size and the same number. There was a splendid breeding ram among Medb's sheep and he was worth a bond maid, but there was an equally good ram among Ailill's sheep.

From grazing lands and paddocks were brought their stallions and steeds and studs. In Medb's stud there was a splendid stallion at stud and he was worth a bond maid. Ailill had a stallion at stud to match him.

Then their great herds of swine were brought from woods and sloping glens and remote places. They were counted and reckoned and recognized. Medb had a splendid breeding boar, and Ailill had another.

Then their herds of cows, their cattle and their droves were brought to them from the woods and waste places of the province. They were counted and reckoned and recognized, and they were of equal size and equal number. But there was a splendid breeding bull among Ailill's cows. He was a calf of one of Medb's cows, and his name was Findbennach. But he considered it unworthy of himself to be counted as women's property, and he went and took his place as bull to the king's cows. For Medb it was as if she had not a pennyworth of possessions since she had not a bull as great as that for her cows.

Then Mac Roth the herald was summoned to Medb and she asked him to find out where in any of the provinces of Ireland there might be a bull such as he. 'I know indeed,' said Mac Roth, 'where there is a bull even better and more excellent again, in the province of Ulster in the cantred of Cúailnge in the house of Dáire mac Fiachna. Donn Cúailnge is his name.'

'Go there, Mac Roth, and ask of Dáire for me a year's loan of Donn Cúailnge. And he will get the fee for the loan of the bull at the end of the year — fifty heifers, and the return of Donn Cúailnge himself. And take another offer of partnership with you, Mac Roth: if the people of that land and country object to giving that precious possession, Donn Cúailnge, let Dáire himself come with his bull. He shall have the extent of his own lands in the level plain of Mag nAí and a chariot worth thrice seven bond maids, and he shall sleep with me.'

Then the messengers went to the house of Dáire mac Fiachna. The number of Mac Roth's embassy was nine messengers. Then Mac Roth was welcomed in the house of Dáire. That was only right because Mac Roth was the chief herald of all. Dáire asked Mac Roth what was the cause of his journey and why he had come. The herald told him what he had come about and related the contention between Medb and Ailill.

'And it is to ask for a loan of the Donn Cúailnge to match Findbennach that I have come,' said he, 'and you shall get the fee for his loan — fifty heifers and the return of the Donn Cúailnge himself. And there is something else besides: come yourself with your bull and you shall get an area equal to your own lands in the level plain of Mag nAí and a chariot worth thrice seven bond maids and you will sleep with Medb to boot.'

Dáire was delighted with that and he shook himself so violently with pleasure that the seams of the featherbed beneath him burst apart; and he said: 'By God, even if the Ulstermen object, this precious possession, Donn Cúailnge, will now be taken to Ailill and Medb in the land of Connacht.' Mac Roth was pleased to hear what Mac Fiachna said.

Then they were attended upon, and fresh rushes were spread underfoot for them. They were given fine food and served a drinking feast until they were drunk and boisterous. And this conversation took place between two of the messengers.

'It is true,' said one, 'he is a generous man, the man of this house.'

'Indeed he is,' said the other.

'Is there any Ulsterman more generous than he?' said the first messenger.

'Indeed there is,' said the second messenger.

'Conchobar his lord is more generous, and if all the Ulstermen rallied round him it would be no shame to them.'

'It is great generosity to give the Donn Cúailnge to us, to nine messengers, and it would take the four great provinces of Ireland to bring that out of Ulster.'

A third messenger joined their conversation.

'What are you saying?' said he.

'That messenger there says that the man of this house is a generous man. Indeed, says the other. Is there a better Ulsterman than he? says the first messenger then. There is indeed, says the second messenger. His lord Conchobar is more generous, and if all the Ulstermen rallied round him it would be no shame to them. And it is a great generosity to give us, nine messengers, what it would take the four great provinces of Ireland to bring out of Ulster. I'd like to see a gush of gore and blood in the mouth that that kind of talk comes from, for if he wasn't given willingly he would be given under force.'

Just then Dáire mac Fiachna's butler came into the house with a man bearing drink and a man bearing food, and he heard what they had said, and he flew into a rage. He put down the drink and the food for them, and he did not tell them to partake or not. He went then to the house where Dáire mac Fiachna was and he said:

'Was it you who gave that prize possession, Donn Cúailnge, to the messengers?'

'Indeed it was I,' said Dáire.

'May there be no kingship where he was given, for what they say is true, if you do not give him willingly you will be forced to give him because of the armies of Ailill and Medb and the guidance of Fergus mac Róig.'

'I swear by the gods I adore that unless they take him like that by force, they will not take him by fair means.'

They sleep thus until morning. Early next morning the messengers arose and went to the house where Dáire was.

'Guide us, sir, to where Donn Cúailnge is.'

'Certainly not,' said Dáire, 'and if treachery to messengers, travellers and those who pass this way were my practice not one of you would leave here alive.'

'What is this about?' said Mac Roth.

'There is good reason for it,' said Dáire. 'You said that if I did not give him willingly I would give him under force because of the armies of Ailill and Medb and the guidance of Fergus.'

'Not so,' said Mac Roth, 'whatever messengers were saying after indulging in your food and drink is not a matter for heed or notice or for reproach to Ailill and Medb.'

'Nevertheless, I will not give my bull on this occasion, if I can help.'

The messengers returned under these conditions and they came to Rath Crúachan of Connacht. Medb asked news of them. Mac Roth told her they had not brought Dáire's bull.

'Why?' said Medb.

Mac Roth explained why.

'There is no need for soft talk, Mac Roth,' said Medb, 'for we knew that he would not be given willingly if he were not given under threat of force, and so he shall.'

ELEVENTH-CENTURY REFORMERS — FOREIGN AND IRISH

[In the eleventh century the church developed an increasingly coherent and strict canon law of marriage and it sought to impose a rigorous sexual ethic. Divorce, in the proper sense of the word, was of course strictly forbidden, and the rules about decrees of nullity became more exacting. Marriage to close kindred came under increasing attack. In 1059 marriage with the seventh degree was forbidden and made punishable by excommunication. Shortly after, the church moved from the Roman to the Germanic method of reckoning relationships — one's sixth cousin was now counted as belonging to the seventh degree — and many more possible marriage partners were ruled out. These prohibitions applied to relations by marriage as well as by blood. In a land-based society where there was little mobility these rules were difficult to enforce. In a society where dynastic marriage strategies were seen as vital and where relatives married in order to preserve and consolidate family property (as in Ireland) they were burdensome and impractical, and led to social conflict.

In this new climate of opinion, usages long tolerated by the Irish church appeared corrupt and outlandish. A very active reform party targeted these practices, especially divorce and marriage to close kin, condemned them vigorously, and brought them to the attention of popes and other authorities — perhaps too successfully for these reports of Irish vice were used by popes Adrian IV (1154–9) and Alexander III (1159–81) in a different context. Adrian IV, with some prompting from the king's chancery, can describe Henry II's projected invasion of Ireland as directed to 'extending the bounds of the church, declaring the truth of the faith to untaught and primitive peoples, and rooting out the weeds of vice from the fields of the Lord'. Alexander III speaks of enormities of vice, made known to him by the letters of the prelates — unlawful sexual relations among them — and he commands the bishops to help Henry II exterminate those abominable practices.

Irish royal lineages and aristocratic families were much married and much divorced, and their lives were far from the ideals of the church. One could cite the extreme instance of Magnus Mac Duinn Shlébe, King of Ulaid, who was killed in 1170: 'and that Magnus was slain shortly after by Donn Slébe, his own brother, . . . in Downpatrick, after he had done many wicked deeds: he left his own wife, he seized the wife of his foster-father, Cú Maige Ó Floinn, and she had previously been married to his brother, Áed; he raped the wife of his other brother, Eochaid; and he outraged bell and crozier, cleric and church'. But the life style of many fitted in better with that of their European feudal contemporaries than one might gather from the repetitious and overdone complaints of the reformers. When the bishops met in council at Cashel in 1172, at the instance of Henry II, their first decree was 'that all the faithful throughout Ireland should repudiate cohabitation between those related by kinship or marriage, and should enter into and abide by lawful marriage contracts' — the common and much-ignored ruling of many eleventh- and twelfth-century councils throughout western Europe.

The first extract below is from Helen Clover and Margaret Gibson, *The Letters of Lanfranc, Archbishop of*

Canterbury (Oxford: Clarendon Press, 1979), pp. 65–7; the second, ibid., p. 69; the third, ibid., pp. 71–3; the fourth, from Aubrey Gwynn, *The Irish Church in the Eleventh and Twelfth Centuries* (Dublin: Four Courts Press, 1992), p. 108; and the fifth from Standish O'Grady, *Caithréim Thoirdhealbhaigh*, 2 vols (London: Irish Texts Society, 1929), vol. 2, p. 185.]

I. Pope Gregory VII to Lanfranc, Archbishop of Canterbury (1073)

Though you, brother, need no guide, still we are moved by our own pastoral concern to remind you to endeavour to extirpate serious moral offences wherever they occur, specifically and pre-eminently that you strive by every means open to you to ban the wicked practice which we have heard rumoured about the Irish: namely that many of them not only desert their lawful wives but even sell them. In these matters we wish you to be sustained with apostolic authority, so that you may punish this crime with stern chastisement not only among the Irish but also among others, too, if you know of any such men in the island of the English, and be prompt to cut out the roots of such a great evil completely with the skilful hoe of discipline.

II. Lanfranc to Gofraid, King of Dublin (1073–4)

There are said to be men in your kingdom who take wives from either their own kindred or that of their deceased wives; others who by their own will and authority abandon the wives who are legally married to them; some who give their own wives to others and by an abominable exchange receive the wives of other men instead. For the sake of God and your own soul command that these offences and any others like them be corrected throughout the land which you rule, and with God's help so treat your subjects that those who love good may cherish it the more and those who lust after evil may never venture to do wrong.

III. Lanfranc to Tairdelbach Úa Briain, King of Munster (*c.* 1074)

But among many things which are commendable certain reports have reached us which are quite the opposite: namely that in your kingdom a man abandons at his own discretion and without any grounds in canon law the wife who is lawfully married to him, not hesitating to form a criminal alliance — by the law of marriage or rather by the law of fornication — with any other woman he pleases, either a relative of his own or of his deserted wife or a woman whom someone else has abandoned in an equally disgraceful way. Bishops are consecrated by a single bishop; many are ordained to villages or small towns; infants are baptised without the use of chrism; holy orders are conferred by bishops for money. No one who has the least familiarity with Christian learning is unaware that all these abuses and others like them are contrary to the Gospels and to apostolic teaching, that they are prohibited by canon law and are contrary to what has been established by all the orthodox Fathers who have gone before us. The more appalling they are in the sight of God and his saints, the more uncompromisingly should such practices be forbidden at once by your edicts and punished, if they are not set right, by the harshest measures possible.

IV. Anselm Archbishop of Canterbury to Muirchertach Úa Briain, King of Ireland (*c.* 1097)

One thing seems to be common among people you have undertaken to rule, which is urgently in need of correction as being altogether contrary to Christian religion. It has been said to us that men exchange their wives for the wives of others as freely and publicly as a man might exchange his horse for a horse or any other property; and that they abandon their wives at will and without any cause. How evil this is any man who knows the law of Christ will understand. If Your Excellency is unable himself to read the passages of Holy Writ which condemn this wicked traffic, give an order to the bishops and religious clerks in your kingdom to expound them to you: so that, having known their teaching, you may know with what zeal you must be vigilant to correct this abuse.

V. Decrees of the Synod of Cashel (1101)

A council and great assembly of the men of Ireland, laymen, clerics and the learned, at Cashel, to make law and rule for the whole of Ireland, thus: that ex-cleric and ex-layman should not make traffic of God's church; that neither rent nor tribute should be paid by the church to king or lord in Ireland forever; that lay people should not be superiors of churches; that no church should have two superiors except where two provinces march; that no superior of a church should have a wife; that those who kill by treachery and kin-slayers should not have sanctuary; that the share of a cleric or a poet should not be given to a lay person; that in Ireland none should have to wife either his father's wife or his grandfather's,[1] her sister or her daughter, or his brother's wife, or any woman at all so near related.

---

1. i.e. his stepmother and stepgrandmother.

Biographies/Bibliographies

Ruben

LIFE. Canon lawyer, scribe and ecclesiastical scholar of Dairinis (Molana), on the Blackwater, below Lismore. Joint-compiler (with Cú Chuimne, below) of the *Collectio Canonum Hibernensis* (perhaps the B-recension). He died in 725.

CHIEF WRITINGS. *Collectio Canonum Hibernensis* (Hermann Wasserschleben, ed., *Die irische Kanonensammlung* [Leipzig: Tauchnitz, 1885; rpr. Aalen 1966]).

BIOGRAPHY AND CRITICISM. Bart Jaski, 'Cú Chuimne, Ruben and the Compilation of the *Collectio Canonum Hibernensis*', *Peritia*, vol. 14 (2000), pp. 51–69; Thomas O'Loughlin, 'Marriage and Sexuality in the *Hibernensis*', *Peritia*, vol. 11 (1997), pp. 188–206.

Cú Chuimne of Iona

LIFE. Canon lawyer, poet, and ecclesiastical scholar of Iona. Joint-compiler (with Ruben, above) of the *Collectio Canonum Hibernensis* (perhaps the A-recension). Author of the oldest extant Latin hymn in honour of the Virgin. He died in 747.

CHIEF WRITINGS. *Collectio Canonum Hibernensis* (Hermann Wasserschleben, ed., *Die irische Kanonensammlung* [Leipzig: Tauchnitz, 1885; rpr. Aalen 1966]); hymn 'Cantemus in Omni Die' (hymn to the Virgin).

BIOGRAPHY AND CRITICISM. Rudolf Thurneysen, 'Zur irischen Kanonensammlung', *Zeitschrift für Celtische Philologie*, vol. 6 (1908), pp. 1–5; David Howlett, 'Five Experiments in Textual Reconstruction and Analysis', *Peritia*, vol. 9 (1995), pp. 1–50: T.O. Clancy and G. Márkus, *Iona: The Earliest Poetry of a Celtic Monastery* (Edinburgh: Edinburgh University Press, 1995), pp. 181–92; Bart Jaski, 'Cú Chuimne, Ruben and the Compilation of the *Collectio Canonum Hibernensis*', *Peritia*, vol. 14 (2000), pp. 51–69.

Adomnán

For biography and bibliography, see Volume I, p. 138.

Gregory VII

LIFE. Born in Tuscany *c.* 1015; educated in Rome and took monastic vows; became an austere reformer and papal administrator; pope from 1073 to his death in 1085, and an extreme proponent of church reform who precipitated major conflict with the German emperor.

CHIEF WRITINGS. His letters (E. Caspar (ed.), *Das Register Gregors VII*, Monumenta Germaniae Historica. Epistolae Selectae 2 [1920–3]).

BIOGRAPHY AND CRITICISM. A. Fliche, *La réforme grégorienne* (Paris: E. Champion, 1924–37); C. Morris, *The Papal Monarchy: The Western Church from 1050–1250* (Oxford: Clarendon Press, 1989); Aubrey Gwynn, 'Gregory VII and the Irish Church', *Studi Gregoriani*, vol. 3 (1948), pp. 105–28 (rpr. in A. Gwynn, *The Irish Church in the Eleventh and Twelfth Centuries*, ed. Gerard O'Brien [Dublin: Four Courts Press, 1992], pp. 84–98).

Lanfranc

LIFE. Born at Pavia *c.* 1010, monk at Bec and Abbot of Caen in Normandy, Archbishop of Canterbury (1070–89). A learned canon lawyer, brilliant administrator, and reformer (he strongly opposed simony and clerical marriage); he claimed primatial jurisdiction over Ireland and corresponded with Irish kings and bishops, urging reform of church administration and marriage. Died 28 May 1089 at Canterbury.

CHIEF WRITINGS. *Concerning the Body and Blood of the Lord* (an influential tract on the Eucharist) and his letters.

BIOGRAPHY AND CRITICISM. Margaret Gibson, *Lanfranc of Bec* (Oxford: Clarendon Press, 1978); Frank Barlow, *The English Church, 1000–1066* (London: Longman, 1963); Helen Clover and Margaret Gibson (ed. and tr.), *The Letters of Lanfranc, Archbishop of Canterbury* (Oxford: Clarendon Press, 1979); Aubrey Gwynn, 'Lanfranc and the Irish Church', *Irish Ecclesiastical Record*, vol. 57 (1941), pp. 481–500, vol. 58 (1941), pp. 1–15.

Saint Anselm

LIFE. Born at Aosta in Piedmont, *c.* 1033, he studied at Bec under Lanfranc (see above), whom he succeeded as Prior and Abbot of Bec. One of the leading medieval thinkers and a distinguished theologian and philosopher, he succeeded Lanfranc as Archbishop of Canterbury, which he ruled from 1093 to his death in 1109. He continued Lanfranc's policies towards the Irish church, but more moderately.

CHIEF WRITINGS. These are principally theological and philosophical works, the most important of which are *Monologion* and *Proslogion* (1078–9); *De Incarnatione Verbi* (1095); *Cur Deus Homo* (1098). His works are edited by Dom F.S. Schmitt, Edinburgh: T. Nelson, 6 vols, 1946–61.

BIOGRAPHY AND CRITICISM. R.W. Southern, *Saint Anselm and His Biographer* (Cambridge: Cambridge University Press, 1963); *Saint Anselm: A Portrait in a Landscape* (Cambridge: Cambridge University Press, 1990).

Mary, Eve and the Church, c. 600–1800

Virginity is the dominant theme in the following selection of texts. Much of the Irish literature on virginity is informed by concepts developed by early Christians. These concepts are grounded in Old Testament references to the daughter of Zion as a personification of the people of Israel, a virgin beloved by God but subjected by him to travail before her deliverance. They ramify through the medieval literature of the Church, pervading Christian thought, of the learned and the unlettered alike. They are vital to understanding notions such as the Church as Bride of Christ, the fecund virginity of Mary, Mother of God, and the spiritual motherhood of vowed virgins, while the development of the female saint's Life is also predicated on them. They prove remarkably durable, and are easily traced down to the contemporary period. Categories such as the Child of Mary, the Magdalen in her Laundry, and the Good Christian Wife are current or recent aspects of their legacy.

In Ireland in the early Christian period, the identity of Mary as Virgin Mother of God and of the whole human race was given a local projection in Saint Brigit, who thus became another Virgin Mother of God and 'Mary of the Gael'. Brigit's identity as spiritual mother of the Irish may have helped the emergence of Saint Patrick as spiritual father. In a letter written around 633 by one Cummian, an Irishman, Patrick is described as *papa noster*. As *papa* at this stage did not have the specialized sense of 'pope, primate', the phrase probably meant 'our [spiritual] father'. There was a time when Brigit and Patrick were imaged as the sky's two pillars (pp. 62–3). This monument to male-female

equilibrium was severely damaged in the battle for primacy of the Irish church. Kildare, Brigit's foundation, claimed primacy for its 'episcopal and female virginal see' (*cathedra episcopalis et puellaris*) but Patrick's foundation at Armagh won the day, and the feast celebrated worldwide is not that of Brigit but of Patrick, Ireland's apostle from Britain.

The application of the idea of the virgin mother to Brigit is recognizably Irish, but the idea produced other effects also. For example, the belief that it was the special prerogative of *all* women to share in Mary's motherhood of Christ was used, at the end of the seventh century, as validation for the Law of Adomnán, the earliest known European law to be enacted on behalf of women (see above, pp. 18–22). In the following selection, the earliest texts predate the Law of Adomnán, while the latest was written in 1820. Though the materials are highly diverse, the key concepts of virginity as they were established in Ireland in the Early Middle Ages recur time and again. One major distinction accounts for the allocation of texts under either of two subheadings. The texts on pp. 57–95 concern 'Mary and the Virgin Saints', those whose perfect imitation of her entitles them to be ranked beside her. The texts appearing under the rubric of 'Eve and her Sisters' on pp. 95–163 deal with more ordinary women and their moral frailties and strengths: their imitation of Mary is imperfect. Although the latest text in 'Mary and the Virgin Saints' dates from the thirteenth century, like many of the others it was copied down to modern times. Broadly speaking, one may assume that the ideas in these texts were current alongside the ideas in the texts in the 'Eve and her Sisters' material, although much of the latter was composed later in time.

Only one text comes with an attribution to a female author; coincidentally, it is regarded by many as one of the finest medieval Irish poems still extant (see pp. 111–15). One can take it for granted that most of the other texts below, whether attributed or anonymous, were authored by men. While they communicate male representations of women, they are also rich in detail on the structures — material, social and mental — in which women and, to a lesser degree, men, lived their lives in the church. This latter distinction is often important. In theory, for example, the frequently-mentioned threefold order of Christians in the categories of virgins, penitent spouses, and married people applied equally to men and women. Chastity of a different kind was expected from each category, in a descending scale of merit. Those who aspired to the status of virgins vowed themselves to perpetual celibacy. Penitent spouses were those who had taken a vow of celibacy after a period as sexually active adults; many of them were either widowed or had separated from their spouses by mutual consent. They are often described as 'holy widows'. A form of chastity or continence was also expected of married people: they were to be monogamous, and celibate in periods strictly ordained by the church (see above, pp. 13–14). Comparison with the seeds in the Gospel which brought forth one hundredfold, sixtyfold and thirtyfold, as in Matthew 13:23, Mark 4:8, and Mark 4:20, was a commonplace in Christian writings. Yet most references to the threefold order in the following texts, as in medieval Irish writing in general, concern women, because issues relating to virginity, chastity and continence fixed largely on female sexuality, on controlling it and on deflecting its perceived threat to men. In other words, when looking at texts which describe structures such as the threefold order, one may find an ideology, aspects of which are inherent in the text and possibly legitimated by it.

This selection aligns Mary, Eve, female saints and less than saintly females. The underlying justification for this is biblical typology, an idea which must be referred to the Christian concept of time. The Incarnation, which united the divine and the human in the person of Christ, showed that an historical event could have transhistorical meaning. This event occurred in time, but its consequence was transhistorical, transtemporal: it ensured humanity's redemption, once and for all. It pointed to a reality beyond finite time, a world without end; in the process, it redeemed time itself. The bible's history of the Jewish and Judaeo-Christian communities was therefore taken to exemplify relations between God and humanity throughout *all* time. The providential nature of history was to be inferred from transhistorical and transtemporal images and correspondences. Biblical typology posits continuity between the Old and the New Testaments. The New is prefigured in the Old, and the events described in both are seen as part of a single development, albeit in two stages.

Typological continuity is illustrated, for example, in the teaching that Christ is the New Adam: death came into the world on account of Adam's sin, but life is restored to mankind through Christ's sacrifice. Similarly, it is illustrated in the early Christians' description of themselves as a type of Israel, the new Chosen People. Prophecy is an essential feature of biblical typology. In broad terms, Old Testament prophecy in its entirety was viewed by New Testament writers as a prediction of Christ. More specifically, the prophets of the Old Testament were identified as continuous with those of the New, including the supreme prophet, Christ. All of them were further linked with the prophets of the early church, whose role was to reveal the divine mysteries and to proclaim salvation.

Exegesis of Mary's significance in the continuity between the Old and the New Testaments is part of the earliest traditions of Christianity, as Marina Warner has shown in her classic account of her myth and cult.[1] Mary is the second Eve, prefigured in Eve, the virgin whose sin had condemned humanity to death. The idea of the virgin who gives birth to the redeemer of the human race was enormously appealing. In Mary, the guile of the serpent is overcome by the simplicity of the dove. Ephrem of Syria (d. 373) spoke eloquently of Creation clothed once more 'in a robe of flowers/and a tunic of blossoms' at

1. Marina Warner, *Alone of All Her Sex: The Myth and the Cult of the Virgin Mary* (London: Pan Books, 1985).

the moment of the Annunciation. Eve 'had covered Adam in a shameful coat of skins, but Mary had woven a new garment of salvation . . . The wine Eve pressed for mankind poisoned them; the vine that grew in Mary nourishes and saves the world.' In Warner's words: 'To this day it is a specially graceful analogue, architectural in its harmoniousness, a great vault thrown over the history of western attitudes to women, the whole mighty span resting on Eve the temptress on one side, and Mary the paragon on the other'.[2]

The concept of typology was extended not only to Mary but to humanity at large. By aligning their lives with that of Christ, Christians think to involve themselves in the transtemporal drama of salvation. Hagiography is based on a related idea, the idea of *imitatio Christi*, 'imitation of Christ'. For Christians, the saints are proof that human beings can be transformed into likenesses of Christ. Yet while *imitatio Christi* is available to all, a more circuitous route to Christ-likeness is held out to women: *imitatio Mariae*. The *vita*, 'life', of a female saint is a literary expression of *imitatio Mariae*. And since Mary is the fulfilment of the Old Testament heroines as well as the prototype for all female saints, a woman who seeks to imitate her will find a moral life mirrored back from many points in biblical history.

The cult of Mary was on a rising tide when Christianity was first introduced to Ireland. The idea of her perfect virginity had been established since about 200. Following intense controversy, she was jubilantly proclaimed *Theotokos*, 'Mother of God', at the Council of Ephesus in 431. Ironically, this year is often described as the first secure date in Irish history: it was the year, according to the Chronicle of Prosper of Aquitaine, in which Christianity was officially introduced into Ireland: 'To the Irish believing in Christ, Palladius, having been ordained by Pope Celestine, is sent as first bishop'. After Ephesus, physical corruption appeared increasingly incompatible with Mary's dignity as *Theotokos* and accounts of her 'dormition' and bodily assumption into heaven began to appear. If the apocryphon from which the Irish material on the death and assumption of Mary (*Transitus Mariae*) derives did indeed reach Ireland in the

seventh century, as has been argued, then this Syriac apocryphon has its earliest witness in the West in Europe's most westerly island. The feast of Mary's translation to heaven has been celebrated on 15 August by East and West since the seventh century.

The first text below, 'The Monastery of Bangor', also dates from the seventh century. This poem describes the character which by then defined Mary but assigns its features not to her but to a monastery and its rule. The poem is founded on awareness of Mary's figural significance as a type of the church and its typological continuity with many Old Testament passages concerning the daughter of Zion. As the daughter of Zion is a figure of Israel, Mary is a figure of the church which, in this instance, is represented by Bangor monastery. The promise of deliverance to the daughter of Zion on the coming of the Lord prefigured Gabriel's words to Mary at the Annunciation. The community at Bangor, probably an all-male one, living a life of renunciation in preparation for the coming kingdom, is also a 'Virgin most fruitful/And yet an inviolable Mother,/Joyous and trembling/Prepared for the word of God.' The monks, imitating Mary, have themselves become mothers of Christ. Clearly, spiritual fecundity was not restricted to women.

Feminine figuration of this kind has powerful resonances in Irish literature. For example, some medieval tales which describe a man being overcome by desire for a beautiful woman and departing with her to an apparently pagan otherworld may be read allegorically as messianic prophecy: the otherworldly beauty, like the daughter of Zion and Mary, is then a figure of the Chosen People and the church. The man's desire to join her brings him to the Promised Land or sometimes, more specifically, to the monastic life.[3] Instead of the Israelites' journey through the wilderness, such tales often describe a journey on the ocean — the Irish desert — by way of island-stations which recall the monastic settlements which criss-crossed the waterways between Ireland, Britain, and Iceland, and places further afield. The mariners in these tales are male and their boat is often a microcosm of the monastery

---

2. Ibid., p. 60.

3. See, for example, *Echtrae Chonnlai*, 'The Adventure of Connlae', at pp. 268–9 below.

(as in the Voyage of Brendan, for example), but on occasion they visit islands inhabited by women. In fact, *Tír inna mBan*, 'The Land of Women', is found as a synonym for *Tír Tairngire*, 'The Promised Land'. Typically, however, the beautiful women of the medieval voyage-tales augur mystical rather than sexual union.

In Modern Irish, elements of apocalyptic and messianic vision (*aisling*) and prophecy which may be traced to the nexus of ideas associated with the daughter of Zion appear in the genre of political poetry known as the *aisling*. In some *aisling*-poems, the poet has as interlocutor a *spéirbhean* ('heavenly woman, beautiful woman') who is clearly virginal, while in others (the majority), the virgin has been crossed with, or replaced by, the figure of the sovereignty goddess whose role as sovereign's mate demands non-virginity.[4] In others again, the vision or prophecy is conveyed without any female actually presenting herself. Nevertheless, the same biblical *figura* lies behind these diverse effects and can account for them all.

In the early Christian period, a highly complex ideology of virginity flourished as it intertwined with ideas of asceticism which in turn had been grafted on a new concept of martyrdom. The roots of the ideology are found in Jesus's forswearing of family: 'My mother and my brothers are those who hear the word of God and do it' (Luke 8:21). By the fourth century, the practice of celibacy was being adopted by an astonishing number of people. It has been noted that this new fervour for celibacy coincided with the end of the persecutions of Christians and increasingly it is accepted that this was the context in which lifelong virginity, a key feature of monasticism, recommended itself as a new kind of martyrdom. The unattainable ideal of blood-martyrdom was replaced by asceticism, and consecrated virgins became martyr-surrogates. The assimilation was evidenced in the use of *passio*, 'martyrdom', in the sense *vita*. For women especially, the lifelong, self-imposed martyrdom of virginity became the main route to sainthood. Significantly, the lives of the four great female martyrs of the Latin Church, Agatha, Lucy, Agnes and Cecilia, give equal weight to their virginity and their martyrdom. The Virgin

4. See 'Sovereignty and Politics, *c.* 1300–1900', pp. 273–92.

Mary, of course, was the ultimate standard for all who aspired to the sanctity of the martyrs.

Saint Patrick, like many of his contemporaries, described women in particular as eager to opt for virginity. He too took his terms from the lexicon of martyrdom: 'Not that their fathers agree with them; no — they often suffer persecution and undeserved reproaches from their parents; and yet their number is ever increasing. How many have been reborn there so as to be of our kind, I do not know — not to mention widows and those who practice continence' (Volume I, p. 68). Saint Columbanus called the ascetic life 'this bliss of martyrdom' (Volume I, p. 89). When the daughters of King Loígaire, after baptism, asked to see the face of their 'bridegroom', the virgin Christ, they immediately died (Volume I, pp. 74–5). There is a similar outcome to the tale of Holy Monesan (see pp. 98–9). The Calendar of Óengus, compiled *c.* 800, describes Saint Brigit and Ireland's nuns as a 'shower of martyrs'. One might think of 'The Children of Lir' as having endured the longest martyrdom of all time, and their arrested development as a kind of enforced virginity (pp. 150–6).

As in Revelation 7:14, the white of virginity and the red of blood martyrdom went together: the redeemed 'have come out of the great ordeal; they have washed their robes and made them white in the blood of the Lamb'. This and Revelation 14:4 were favourite citations in texts about virgins (for example, p. 100) and virgin saints (for example, p. 73). The Irish were noted for their interest in penitential concepts and practices. They have also been credited with augmenting the dyad of red and white martyrdom (*dergmartrae*, *bánmartrae*) with a third kind: grey martyrdom (*glasmartrae*, sometimes translated 'blue martyrdom'), a kind associated with the mortificatory regime of penitents. The twofold classification is commoner, however, and is the only one represented below (see, for example, pp. 105–6, §§ 60, 61).

Constructs of virginity, and something of the ways in which they were experienced by women, have been recovered from an extensive literature, encompassing the Apocryphal Acts of the Apostles, treatises and homilies on virginity and renunciation, letters to virgins and holy women from such important church fathers as Jerome

(c. 341–420), Paulinus of Nola (d. 431), John Chrysostom (347–407), and Basil (c. 327–79), and the lives of remarkable and influential intellectuals and ascetics such as Macrina (c. 330–80), elder sister of Basil who converted him to asceticism, Olympias (c. 367–408), spiritual daughter and supporter of John Chrysostom, and Melania the Younger (c. 383–448). All the salient ideas in that literature, recently reviewed thoroughly and sensitively by Elizabeth Castelli,[5] are echoed in the texts which follow below: the ascetic as athlete (like the martyrs in their fatal arena); virginity as a struggle against the tyranny of feminine nature; virginity as deliverance from the tribulations of marriage; the equation of *pathos*, 'passion', and femininity, which accounts for the belief in women's greater disposition to sinfulness; the ideal of total liberation from the passions (*apatheia*), and denial of the flesh in favour of an insensate existence adumbrating bodily death; the substitution of celestial marriage (often presented in erotic language) and spiritual fecundity for their human precursors.

As we have seen, 'The Monastery of Bangor' praises the spiritual fecundity of Bangor's monks. Nonetheless, spiritual fecundity in Irish tradition is primarily associated with women, particularly the virgin saints, because they most closely resemble Mary. The idea is found in the very earliest reference to Mary in Irish literature. This occurs in early seventh-century genealogical material concerning Leinster, in a poem prophesying Leinster's greatest saint, Brigit. It says of her: 'A fair birth, fair dignity will come . . . who shall be called, from her great virtues, truly pious Brigit; she will be another Mary, mother of the great Lord'. In what may be the oldest extant Irish-language hymn, Brigit is titled 'the mother of Jesus' (pp. 62–3). *Vita Prima* calls her 'holy Mary' and 'a type of Mary' (p. 66, §15.2, 3). The obituary notice for Saint Íte in the Annals of Innisfallen reads: 'Repose of Íte of Cluain, i.e. the fostermother of Jesus Christ and of Brénainn [Saint Brendan]'. Her foster-motherhood of Jesus is literalized in a famous

Old Irish poem (pp. 80–1). Down to the present day, the Munster saint, Íte, is to Brigit as Brigit is to Mary: Brigit is *Muire na nGael*, Íte is *Muire na Mumhan*, 'Mary of Munster'. It is noticeable that, whereas medieval Irish writers name their female virgins and saints by reference to Mary, late patristic writers frequently describe theirs as 'second Theclas' or 'new Theclas' (Thecla, legendary disciple of Saint Paul, was miraculously saved from martyrdom by burning, after which she lived a long life of exemplary renunciation). Irish writers, although they certainly imbibed the spirit of late patristic writings on virginity and renunciation, were possibly not familiar with all the literature, particularly the biographies. Ireland had little experience of blood martyrdom. For the Irish, the white martyrdom of virginity was what really counted, its paragon was Mary, and the local paragon was Brigit.

The remarkable thing is that much of what was written about Brigit over the last century, by scholars and others, evinces little or no awareness of the fact that her life was constructed and interpreted in the preceding centuries as *imitatio Mariae*, thus reflecting the belief that the *real* Brigit was a saint who actually fitted this mould. Instead, the cult of Brigit at Kildare has been represented by most writers in the twentieth century as either the cult of a pagan deity who took on a little of the identity of a (historical or non-historical) saint, or the cult of a saint (historical or non-historical) who took on a lot of the characteristics of a pagan divinity. As we have seen, Brigit's cult is in ways the prototype for that of other female saints. Anyone who was unaware of her fundamental relation to Mary was also unlikely to give due weight to the relation between other female saints and Mary.

Various factors helped bring a goddess named Brigit to the fore at the expense of Saint Brigit. The historicity of Ireland's other two patron-saints has never been doubted, and Brigit's claims to historicity (although this is rarely stated) have suffered by comparison with them. By a great fluke, two of the writings of Saint Patrick (?died c. 492) survived (see Volume I, pp. 67–71). The Life of Saint Colum Cille (*Vita Columbae*), written by his kinsman and successor in the abbacy of Iona, Adomnán (c. 624–704), for all that it is hagiography, clearly has a historical

5. Elizabeth Castelli, 'Virginity and its Meaning for Women's Sexuality in Early Christianity', *Journal of Feminist Studies in Religion*, vol. 2 (1986), pp. 61–88.

person at its centre. There are no writings by Brigit and, compared to Patrick and Colum Cille, little is known of the details of her life. Also, popular and folkloric elements are strong in her *vitae*. Rather than being accounted to the vacuum in the information about the saint, or the vigour of her cult, these are often presented as further arguments for the pagan goddess. The fact that Cogitosus, author of her earliest extant *vita*, described Brigit's body as lying in honour in an elaborate tomb in Kildare's great church did nothing to diminish enthusiasm for her.

The historical Brigit is located between Patrick and Colum Cille: her obit is recorded variously for 524, 526 and 528. Her cult seems to have flourished before that of Patrick. Patrick is not even mentioned in Cogitosus's Life of Brigit, written in the second half of the seventh century. Cogitosus's Life is the earliest extant *vita* of any Irish saint, male or female. It, and what is generally accepted to be a later Life (although confusingly titled *Vita Prima*), were extremely popular: there are around 25 copies of *Vita Prima* and over sixty of Cogitosus's Life. The fact that all of these are preserved on the continent points up the popularity of Brigit's cult in the world beyond Ireland. In fact, her lives seem to have been the most frequently copied of *all* early medieval female saints' lives. Interestingly, the earliest record of Brigit's feast is in a martyrology compiled for the Englishman, Willibrord, which is known to have been at Echternach (in modern Luxembourg) by about 700. It is also noted in later continental martyrologies, including the *Martyrologium Romanum* itself. As Pádraig Ó Riain has pointed out, no other Irish saint compares with Brigit in having such early continental martyrological witness, not even Patrick. Ó Riain's was the first voice of dissent from the orthodox view that the Kildare saint acquired her elevated status through assimilation to a goddess.[6]

True, Brigit was the name of a goddess, or goddesses. The *locus classicus* for the mythological Brigit is a passage in *Sanas Cormaic*, the glossary attributed to Cormac mac Cuilennáin (d. 908), which may be translated as follows:

Brigit, i.e. the woman poet, daughter of the Dagda. This is Brigit the woman poet (*banéces*) or woman of poetry (*bé n-éicse*), i.e. Brigit, a goddess whom the poets used to worship, for their [or 'her'] attendance was very great and very wonderful. It is for that reason they call her the goddess of poets by this title. Her sisters were Brigit woman of healing [and] Brigit woman of smith-work, i.e. goddesses, i.e. those who are the three daughters of the Dagda, from whose names a goddess used to be called Brigit among all the Irish. Brigit, then, i.e. 'she blazes' or 'a fiery arrow'.

There is no apparent link between the goddess(es) of this passage and Saint Brigit or Kildare. Indeed, the fact that there is a separate entry in *Sanas Cormaic* for '*sanct Brigit*' strongly suggests that Cormac mac Cuilennáin distinguished them. This important early counter to arguments for identifying them with each other has been pointed out in a ground-breaking study by Catherine McKenna of the way in which Brigit's cult developed in recent centuries in response to religious, political and cultural forces.[7] As McKenna noted, the first writer to identify the Kildare abbess with the goddess was d'Arbois de Jubainville. That was in 1880. For d'Arbois de Jubainville, she was heir to some features originally associated with the goddess, not her embodiment, but later writers often took a less cautious view. Brigit of Kildare very quickly developed a dual aspect. It now seemed that she was both Christian saint and pagan Celtic goddess. She was a virgin and a fertility symbol, not spiritualised fertility but the kind suggested by the co-incidence of her feast on 1 February with the beginning of Spring and the pagan festival of *Imbolc*. The fire her nuns tended in Kildare was also a vestal fire, with the latter aspect supported by the dubious authority of Giraldus (see pp. 75–6). Her femininity was simultaneously Christian and of an essential, primordial kind.

McKenna has described how all this came into play in 1900 when *Inghinidhe na hÉireann*,

6. Pádraig Ó Riain, 'Pagan Example and Christian Practice: A Reconsideration', in Doris Edel (ed.), *Cultural Identity and Cultural Integration: Ireland and Europe in the Early Middle Ages* (Dublin: Four Courts Press, 1995), pp. 144–56 at 154-5.

7. Catherine McKenna, 'Apotheosis and Evanescence: The Fortunes of Saint Brigit in the Nineteenth and Twentieth Centuries', in Joseph Falaky Nagy (ed.), *The Individual in Celtic Literatures. CSANA Yearbook 1* (Dublin: Four Courts Press, 2001), pp. 74–108.

Ireland's first nationalist women's organization was founded (see also Volume V, pp. 69–74), and Brigit was chosen as patron of its Central Branch. As Maud Gonne, president of the organization, made clear, this was Brigit 'in her dual character of Goddess and Saint', but Gonne herself was more interested in the goddess-aspect. In a paper she read at the organization's first *céilí* in October 1900, Gonne characterized Brigit as 'the apotheosis in Irish mythology of the feminine, the aesthetic, and the rural . . . an apt symbol of the Irish people as she would have them', tacitly construing the goddess as 'a counterpoint to the imperial values represented by that other seemingly eternal feminine, Queen Victoria'.[8]

Gonne needed a unifying symbol, a feminist icon that would appeal to all Irishwomen. During the nineteenth century, and especially after Catholic Emancipation, the medieval Irish saints were increasingly being appropriated for the Catholic church. At the same time, the Catholic hierarchy was distancing itself from practices it regarded as superstitious or licentious. A new Brigit emerged in popular Catholic hagiography: her thaumaturgical wings clipped, her scandalous actions and origins tidied away. Gonne's Celtic goddess-saint, on the other hand, was capable of overriding the denominational divide without losing her appeal for Catholics. She impressed proponents of submissive and independent-minded behaviour in women. For some, she was saintly submissive, for others she was a rebel against parents, clergy and class. Embedded in folk tradition, she suited the cultural nationalist agenda, and yet she was exotic and strange. As the interest in her mythological face increased, however, she began to slip the loop of the historical abbess of Kildare, a process that has continued to this day.

One of the aims of the following selection is to re-present Brigit as she was before the 'discovery' of Kildare goddess, and to re-establish her relationship to other Irish female saints, particularly Íte, Darerca and Samthann, the three others for whom there is a significant medieval dossier, and whose *vitae* are excerpted below. Fortunately, there is another context in which to view these saints, the larger one of the

western archipelago of Britain and Ireland. In the cross-light of the culture of these two islands, it is easier to see these saints as they were originally drawn. There were close and frequent contacts between the churches of Britain and Ireland until the ninth century — and they did not end then — but the time of greatest mutual influence was the seventh and eight centuries. The *vitae* of Brigit, Íte, Darerca and Samthann were composed in, or are based on materials dating from, the seventh and eighth centuries also.

The English historian Bede (673–735), in his *Ecclesiastical History of the English People*, gave great praise to the Irish for having preached the gospel to the English. The Irish were gospel-prodigal: when the English came to Ireland in their droves, 'The Irish welcomed them all gladly, gave them their daily food, and also provided them with books to read and with instruction, without asking for any payment.' Bede counted Irish as one of the five languages of Britain, all estimable since they were used to seek and expound 'the knowledge of sublime truth and true sublimity'. The names of many Englishmen who spent lengthy periods in Ireland are known.

The traffic went both ways. Saint Fursa joined his Irish brothers, Fáelán and Ultán, in East Anglia some time after 630. Dímma and Cellach, the first two bishops of the Middle Angles and Mercians, were also Irish. An Irish mission to Northumbria began when Oswald (d. 642), who had been baptised on Iona, became king and sent to Iona for a bishop. The Irishman Aedán (Aidan) (d. 651) arrived from Iona in 634 and was given the island of Lindisfarne for his episcopal see. Oswald, who had a acquired an excellent command of Irish, acted as interpreter when Aedán preached to the court. The Lindisfarne-Iona connection opened an arena of cultural exchange between Ireland and Northern Britain which resulted in *insular* art, *insular* script, and other proofs of cultural fusion. Aedán was succeeded at Lindisfarne by the Irish bishops Fínán (d. 661), and Colmán (d. 676).

Roll-calls of Anglo-Saxon and Irish names convey not just ethnicity but sex, and most of the names we know were men's. From an Irish perspective, it takes effort to imagine the degree to which women, also, must have been caught up in the radical movement of conversion. Undoubtedly, Irishwomen travelled abroad far

8. McKenna, 'Apotheosis and Evanescence', p. 82.

less often than Irishmen — this is the only assumption one can draw from the paucity of references to Irishwomen crossing the Irish Sea, never mind the English Channel. Yet they must have had significant influence in the conversion period, and this was not necessarily confined to Ireland. The extent and nature of that influence have yet to be explored fully. Here again, it may prove useful to view Ireland in the context of the western archipelago. The importance of queens and other royal women in converting kings, and in supporting and managing monasteries, has long been recognized for Britain, and the continent. Ironically, although some *vitae* and other documents composed by women of the early English church survive, no independent lives of early English female saints have been transmitted. Nonetheless, so much information about these saints has been preserved, in Bede's *History*, in the lives of male saints, and in a variety of other documents, that one can almost feel one knows what some of them were like as individuals. As we shall see, their Irish contemporaries were interested in them and shared common ground with them, sometimes literally.

Take the case of Saint Æthelthryth (d. 679), celibate throughout two marriages, whose second husband was King Ecgfrith of Northumbria (d. 685). She withdrew from this marriage to the double monastery of Coldingham and not long afterwards, in 673, she founded a double monastery (one which housed both female and male monastics, normally ruled by an abbess) at Ely. We know from Bede of two Irishmen who lived for a time at Coldingham, a monk and a priest. One should not rule out the possibility that some Irishwomen journeyed to monasteries such as Coldingham. By the end of the seventh century, there were double houses also at Barking, Bardney, Hartlepool, Munch Wenlock, Repton, Thanet, Wimbourne and Whitby. Sixteen years after she died, Æthehthryth's body was found uncorrupt, a sign of her virginity which was reported in the Irish annals. Bede wrote a hymn in honour of this 'queen and bride of Christ'. Beginning with Mary, 'God's wicket-gate', it sings the praise of virgin-martyrs, naming Agatha, Eulalia, Thecla, Euphemia, Agnes, and Cecily before speaking of Æthelthryth in terms an Irish audience would have found

wholly familiar: 'Royal Mother of Heaven's King your leader now;/You too, maybe, a mother of Heaven's King'.

King Ecgfrith's sister, Ælflaed, and half-brother, Aldfrith (d. 705), also interested the Irish. Ælflaed's death in 714 is noted in the Annals of Ulster. She was abbess of the double monastery of Whitby; she and her mother, Eanflaed (d. *c*. 704), had ruled it jointly before her mother's death. It was here that the decisive Synod of Whitby was held in 664. It was hosted by the abbess of the time, Hild (614–80). 'All who knew Hild', says Bede, 'used to call her mother because of her outstanding devotion and grace'. It was she who nurtured the creative talent of Cædmon, the tongue-tied monk whom an angel enjoined to 'sing about the beginning of created things', which he did — 'in English, which was his own tongue'. Hild's ears may have been attuned to another vernacular also, Irish. When, at the age of thirty-three, she decided on a monastic life, her plan was 'to cross over to Gaul, leaving her home and all that she had, to live as a stranger for the Lord's sake in the monastery of Chelles'. The Irish bishop from Iona, Aedán, persuaded her to remain at home. She became abbess, firstly of Hartlepool, in 649 or thereabouts, and she established a rule for this monastery which was 'in all respects' like that she had been taught by Aedán and 'other devout men', who may also have been Irish. Bede says that Hartlepool had been founded 'not long before by Heiu, a devoted handmaid of Christ, who is said to have been the first woman in the Northumbrian kingdom to take the vows and habit of a nun, having been ordained by Bishop Aidan'.

Bede's remark is highly significant. It claims that monasticism for women was first introduced into Northumbria by an Irishman, long after it had become established in Ireland. It describes female monasticism as making its first appearance in Britain in a double monastery, an institution which Cogitosus described as existing at Kildare since Brigit's time (see Volume I, pp. 76–7; cf. the double monastery in the Life of Darerca, p. 83). A tradition of the prior existence in Ireland of some kind of institutional structures for women may underlie the tale of Holy Monesan, the princess who journeyed there from Britain (p. 99). Structures were bound to follow the abstract order of virgins, widows, and continent wives, and Patrick's own words, cited above, show that this order was already known in Ireland in his day. An early medieval Irish and Latin text detailing 'Saint Brigit's Subjects' (*Brigitae Sanctae Subiectae*) — presumably meaning those who owed allegiance to the church at Kildare — lists women and men in a variety of structures: some individuals apparently living alone, like hermits, others in single-sex groups, others again in small or large groups, consisting of both males and females.

In short, one has to contend with the possibility that Ireland had significant influence on the development of female monasticism, and the double monastery, in Britain. It must be acknowledged, of course, that the double monasteries of Merovingian Francia also provided inspiration and models. In fact, according to Bede, it was to monasteries such as Faremoutiers, Chelles and Andelys outside Paris that the young female royals and nobles of the Anglo-Saxons were often sent for education, for lack of comparable foundations at home. Yet what was probably the first Frankish double monastery, at Faremoutiers, was not founded until 617 or thereabouts. More importantly, it was under the influence of the Irishman, Saint Columbanus (*c.* 543–615), that a new attitude towards women developed within the Frankish church, which now welcomed them as collaborators and spiritual equals to the point where double monasteries were promoted.

One last pivotal figure in Irish-English relations may be mentioned briefly, since his mediation may have been crucial in transmitting ideas about Mary and virginity. This is Aldfrith, son of Oswiu and half-brother of Ecgfrith and Ælflaed. Aldfrith's mother was Irish, of the Northern Uí Néill dynasty of Cenél nEógain. He also had an Irish name, Flann Fína, under which various texts in Irish are attributed to him. Contemporary sources say that he spent many years among the Irish and consequently became 'most learned in the Scriptures', and it appears he was on Iona shortly before succeeding Ecgfrith as King of Northumbria in 686. The evidence suggests that he came to power with the backing of his maternal kin, the Uí Néill, who were also, ultimately, the kin of Adomnán, whose extraordinary Law on behalf of women was proclaimed in 697. In fact, Adomnán counted Aldfrith as a friend. He paid a number of visits to his court, and presented the king on one occasion with a copy of his book on Christianity's Holy Places, *De Locis Sanctis*, which contains, among other things, an interesting section on Mary (see Volume I, pp. 101–2).

Aldfrith may be pivoted in another direction. He was sponsored at confirmation by Aldhelm (d. 708 or 710), abbot of Malmesbury, 'the first English man of letters', author of a considerable body of Latin writing in prose and verse, which evidences a familiarity with works of Irish provenance and with the education available in Irish schools. Michael Lapidge, who translated his long, convoluted prose-work on virginity, *De Virginitate*, judged it to be Aldhelm's most influential work.[9] He suggested it may date from some time after 675 or 680. Since a treatise on metre which Aldhelm wrote some years later (*c.* 685–95) is addressed to Aldfrith, the Northumbrian king was probably also familiar with *De Virginitate*. This work is wholly continuous with patristic writings on virginity as summarised above. It ranges down through biblical history, covering Old Testament virgin-prophets, New Testament apostles, male martyrs, Mary, female martyrs and the virgins of the church who are heirs to them all. It proves that the ideas on virginity which often appear sketchily in contemporary Irish texts also received extended, complex treatment, and one may suspect that they circulated among the Irish, as much as the English, in this form. Adomnán surely knew this text. His Law is instinct with its thinking and, in this context, the Law's claim to force in Ireland and Britain takes on a new significance.

Aldhelm dedicated *De Virginitate* to abbess Hildelith and other women in the monastery at Barking, Essex. His attitude to them is deferential, that of brother to sisters rather than of master to pupils. He asks them to let him know if his style is 'pleasing to [their] intelligence'. He describes them 'roaming widely through the flowering fields of scripture', exploring the work of historians, chroniclers, grammarians and experts on metrics. He thanks them for their

9. Michael Lapidge, *Aldhelm: The Prose Works* (Cambridge [England]: D.S. Brewer, 1979).

letters, admires their eloquence, and hopes they will send him more. The extraordinarily convoluted style of *De Virginitate* found many imitators. They included Eadburg, abbess of Thanet, with whom Boniface corresponded. She was a highly skilled scribe, whom Boniface addressed in one letter as his 'dearest sister who has brought light and consolation to an exile in Germany by sending him gifts of spiritual books'. He asks that 'she will continue the good work ... by copying out for me in gold the epistles of my lord St Peter'.[10]

One cannot deny that there may have been major differences in levels of female literacy in Britain and Ireland at this time but the issue has yet to explored seriously. These references to the nuns at Barking and Thanet remind one that the following texts from Ireland, some of which emanated from women's monasteries and double monasteries, may also reflect something of the reality of the lives lived in them. The work of scholars of the early Irish church generally conveys extremely low expectations of medieval Irish women (as opposed to men) in respect to literary skills and even basic literacy. This has not helped promote an interest in these texts as sources for the history of medieval Irishwomen.

There are many affinities between the lives of women within the church in both islands. Much of the data on women in the Irish church has yet to be gathered and co-ordinated, however, from sources not easily represented in an anthology such as this. These include notices in annals, which tend to be extremely terse in the early medieval period, genealogies, lists of abbesses, lists of affiliates such as 'Saint Brigit's Subjects', and a wide range of sources containing other data such as place-names. Very little work has been done on individual foundations since the publication of Aubrey Gwynn's and R.N. Hadcock's magisterial work, *Medieval Religious Houses. Ireland* (Bristol: Longman, 1970). Nonetheless, some general comparisons can be made at this stage. Early Irish female saints tend to be of royal or noble blood even more often than their counterparts in Britain. In fact, Brigit is most unusual in being a slave by birth. This begs the question of how the monasteries were endowed and whether offices

within them remained the preserve of certain families. The two issues are related, since hereditary office tends both to encourage endowments from relations of those in office and to concentrate the assets. Women's houses and double houses seem to have behaved in much the same way as men's ones. For example, the Fothairt, a group situated mainly in Leinster who were in long decline, claimed Brigit as one of their own. Despite their political unimportance, they supplied many of the identified abbesses of Kildare in the eighth, ninth, tenth and eleventh centuries, and some of those whose descent is unknown were probably also of the Fothairt. The case of a ninth-century Kildare abbess, Muirenn (d. 831), daughter of Cellach mac Dúnchada, king of Leinster (760–66), and sister of a later king of Leinster, Fínnechtae Cetharderc (795–808), illustrates the link between secular and ecclesiastical power. Three other brothers of hers succeeded each other as abbots of Kildare in the early ninth century. An early list of the abbesses of Kileevy monastery, Saint Darerca's foundation, exemplifies hereditary office also: the eighth abbess was the grandniece of the fifth, and the ninth and tenth were sisters, and nieces of the eighth.

This list was probably compiled at Kileevy. If so, it is only one of a number of early texts to emerge from this women's monastery, all augmenting the case for some degree of literacy among female monastics. A number of the following texts speak of men who received their elementary education from women. The less typical case of Digde, to whom the famous poem beginning 'Aithbe Damsa Bés Mara', is attributed, and the three 'wonderful nuns' with whom she is associated, at least two of whom were also poets, is also found below (pp. 111–15). Samthann apparently advocated the spiritual benefits of study (pp. 87–8). The tradition that Mary was a contemplative since early childhood helped make a studious disposition in women acceptable. In fact, accounts of Mary's years in the Temple by early apocryphal writers and church fathers gradually evolved into an ideal of Christian life for secular as well as monastic women. Mary was modest in mind and body, spare in diet, never loud, devoted to reading, prayerful, quick to learn but hesitant to advise, reverent to her elders, beautiful. These same qualities, in various arrangements, appear in the

10. See Christine Fell, *Women in Anglo-Saxon England* (Oxford: Blackwell, 1986), pp. 109–28.

seventh-century moral theological tract known as *De Duodecim Abusivis Saeculi* in the account of 'The Woman Without Modesty' (pp. 96–7), and in Sedulius Scottus's tract, 'On Christian Rulers', in describing the ideal consort (pp. 107–9). Some of them become standard in bardic poems addressed to noblewomen, and in their annalistic obituaries (pp. 332–40). One might even argue that they are found, vestigially, in modern advertising.

The female saint, being in the image of Mary, was mother of her people and in this role she is often described as their protector in battle — after her death. The living aspirant to sainthood, as we read below, had an important role as broker of peace. This tallies with references in the law-tracts. One tract which speaks of 'a woman who turns back the streams of war' glosses this phrase as 'the abbess of Kildare' (p. 31). In the early ninth century the Law of Dar Í was enacted in turn over Munster, Uí Néill and Connacht. This holy woman was from Connacht and her Law was directed against killing cattle, an activity one might think from the literature was endemic in her province.

Conspicuously wealthy monasteries were obvious targets for brigands and people in dire straits. Association with ruling dynasties left monasteries open to attack from their enemies. It was not uncommon for feuding clerics to introduce violence into their confines. The annals show that women's houses were not immune to any of these, and they undoubtedly account for the disappearance of some nunneries and the coalescence of others with male foundations. Women's houses were also particularly vulnerable to the depredations wrought by the Vikings. However, the following texts mainly portray life in less violent times and turn on such quotidian occupations as prayer, preaching and providing hospitality. Charity to the poor is represented as the particular prerogative of women, both secular and monastic, but so is hospitality to honoured guests: it was owed alike to *dám ocus deórad*, 'retinue (of a dignitary) and stranger'. As ever, women are closely identified with food-production, especially dairying and sheep-rearing. 'Brigit's kitchen' figures in prayer down through the ages, and was represented on kitchen wall-plaques until recently.

A favourite theme is the residency of former wives, or former seculars, in the monastery. It is found in some of the most highly regarded texts, including the poem by Digde, the tale of the Union of Líadan and Cuirither, and the poems attributed to Queen Gormlaith (pp. 111–15, 115–18, 133–8). Many aristocratic women retired to monasteries they had founded or endowed in earlier life, and this is borne out in their obituary notices (see pp. 332–40). The practice, established in the early medieval period, continued after the introduction of the new foreign orders. The Cistercian Order, for example, was established at Mellifont in County Louth in 1142. When the church there was dedicated in 1157, Derbforgaill, daughter of Úa Rúairc, was among those who made a lavish bequest. Later, having achieved great notoriety, she retired to Mellifont and it was there she died in 1193 (pp. 192–7, 334).

Undoubtedly the most vivid theme in 'Eve and her Sisters' is women's innate sinfulness and its corollary, clerical distrust. It is a theme which gathers force as time progresses. The more women come to be regarded as a threat to male, and especially clerical, virtue, the more virginity as a form of heroism becomes associated with men. Many texts portray celibacy as a clerical, and therefore male, prerogative, and repudiation of women as a virtue although, occasionally, the older tradition reappears (pp. 127–8). Clerical antipathy to women is probably the main explanation for the gradual demise of the double monasteries, although they lasted longer in Ireland than elsewhere, and consequently became the target of church reformers of the twelfth and later centuries. When these were not an issue, assiduous reformers were able to turn their attentions to clerical 'concubines' as, for example, in the fifteenth-century *Riaghail na Sagart*, 'The Priests' Rule' (pp. 148–50). This text was copied, or perhaps adapted, by Uilliam Mac an Leagha who was a prolific scribe, a translator of texts from English, and probably an author in his own right. The antipathy to priests' consorts in *Riaghail na Sagart* is muted by comparison with that expressed in *Betha Mhaighnenn* 'The Life of Saint Maighnenn', the text of which is also in Mac an Leagha's hand. It accounts these words to Maighnenn:

> If any young woman should be desirous of a man in holy orders, I deem that the same as if she had not kept herself from any man in

the three divisions of the world. . . . Woe is he who gets her as a prize after the priest, for to know her and to be intimate with her is [thrusting one's] head into the mire, and [having] relations with a serpent, it is a renunciation of baptism and faith and piety, it is a pact with Lucifer and Dathan, and with Abiron and Pluto, and with Beelzebub, and with Malemantus and with the swart sow, and with the captains of Hell's host.

Over time, the fashion in saints changed, as did the literary forms associated with them. Early hagiography shares its aesthetic with the icon: a saint's *vita* was a verbal representation of the *imago*, the static, emblematic image of virtue which the saint embodied, whole and entire, since birth. After the coming of the Normans, the cults of the older saints continued side by side with those of newly introduced ones, whose lives are often closer to the genre of romance than to the early medieval *vita*. Among the most popular were the legendary saints, Margaret of Antioch, Catherine of Alexandria, and Mary of Egypt, and the composite saint, Mary Magdalen. A 'book of piety' which Máire, daughter of Eoghan Ó Máille, wife of Mac Suibhne of Fanad, had made for herself in 1513–4 contains translations into Irish of the Lives of Saints Margaret and Catherine, and contemporary Christian doctrine, as well as traditional material such as the Life of Colum Cille. An obituary notice for Máire which was later written into the manuscript gives an exceptionally detailed account of a woman's devotional practice (see pp. 337–8). Mary Magdalen, the penitent *par excellence*, became the model for penitent women. Both she and Mary of Egypt, a former nymphomaniac, presented particularly good examples of peripety — a complete change, from sinfulness to virtue — and progress, from the depths of depravity to the heights of holiness (pp. 143–8).[11] There are rare examples in Irish of this kind of narrative from pre-Norman times, such as 'The Fate of the Sinful Greek Girl' (pp. 119–21). The idea of progress in holiness is also central to the later and

deservedly famous tale of 'The Children of Lir'. Tales such as these were enormously appealing. Assessments of how they influenced Irishwomen's attitudes and religiosity must take into account change in translation practices and linguistic competences. In the late medieval period, women had varying degrees of access to devotional literature which originated in Irish and to Irish translations and adaptations of Latin and English texts; a tiny minority of privileged noblewomen were also competent to read texts in Latin. From the sixteenth century onwards, many texts written in English were being read in the same language, as Ireland's ruling classes became increasingly bilingual. Figural sculpture, and wall-paintings (of which there are some poorly preserved examples in churches and tower-houses), give further insights into Irishwomen's religious devotion and have the benefit of evidencing what was common to the literate and the unlettered alike.

Devotion to Mary, which was a constant, acquired a virulent political and sectarian dimension at the time of the Reformation and Counter-Reformation. The fires of Catholic antipathy to apostates were stoked by influential preachers such as the Franciscan friar, Eoghan Ó Dubhthaigh. The poem of his excerpted below, a kind of verse-sermon, dates from the beginning of a tradition of savagely critical verse in Irish about named clerics and the women for whom they abandoned the celibate priesthood of the Roman Catholic church (pp. 156–9). This tradition runs in parallel with another, which represents Ireland under Protestant influence or domination as a victimised virgin, an adulteress, or a whore (see pp. 277–81). Ó Dubhthaigh's poem is one of three sermon-type texts which conclude the selection. Domhnall Ó Colmáin's text, *Párliament na mBan* (*The Parliament of Women*), dates from the beginning of the period of the Penal Laws or, as they were commonly known at the time, the Popery Laws. In this text, it is the women who assume the mantle of the preacher, as if to illustrate what historians have shown: when structures of authority are fluid or weak, women are allowed a more central role in church affairs (see pp. 459–64).

The final text is an early nineteenth-century sermon by a Catholic priest which names its subject — *Cáit na gCupán* 'Kate of the Cups' —

11. See Erich Poppe and Bianca Ross (eds.), *The Legend of Mary of Egypt in Medieval Insular Hagiography* (Dublin: Four Courts Press, 1996), especially Jane Stevenson, 'The Holy Sinner: The Life of Mary of Egypt', ibid., pp. 19–50.

while clearly conveying that no response is expected from her to the attack it makes on her. Irish-language tradition provides abundant evidence of the perpetuation of unofficial forms of Catholicism. The class most resistant to the emergence of orthodox Catholicism (a movement termed 'the devotional revolution' by historians who see the Great Famine of 1845–9 as the crucial watershed, and 'the Tridentine evolution' by historians taking a longer chronological perspective) was that of the labourers and cottiers. From the late eighteenth century onwards, the majority of Irish speakers belonged to this class. Many women who were staunch supporters of the clergy and the official church showed their support in what had come to be regarded as unofficial forms: a large number of the *caointe* recorded from oral tradition in the twentieth century were composed by women for the priests of their parishes; women transposed church teaching into poems such as '*An Peacach*' ('The Sinner') by Máire Ní Dhonnagáin (*fl.* 1760) (pp. 438–40); others upheld Catholic morale with poems that might be classed as sectarian (pp. 444–5).

Over time, as the borders of Gaelic Ireland contracted, the interest in knowing and recording its traditions began to increase. The variety of ways in which women developed a personal religious voice, in Irish and English alike, can be traced in other selections in this anthology. See especially the selections in 'Religion, Science, Theology and Ethics, 1500–2000' (pp. 459–754) and 'Oral Traditions' (pp. 1191–1548).

A. Mary and the Virgin Saints, *c.* 600–1200

ANONYMOUS

VERSICULI FAMILIAE BENCHUIR
(On the Monastery of Bangor)
(7th century)

[In this hymn the monastic rule of Bangor, and the monastery itself, are figured in imagery used also of Mary: Bangor is the Virgin Bride of Christ, Mother of Christ's flock, and type of the Church. Bangor, on Belfast Lough, was founded by Saint Comgall (d. 602).

The hymn, composed sometime in the seventh century, is preserved in Antiphonary of Bangor. This is the oldest Irish manuscript to which precise dates can, with probability, be assigned: it was written apparently between 680 and 691.

Text: F.E. Warren, *The Antiphonary of Bangor*, 2 vols (London: Harrison, 1893), vol. 2, p. 28. Translation: Peter O'Dwyer, *Mary: A History of Devotion in Ireland* (Dublin: Four Courts Press, 1988), pp. 35–6.]

1
Benchuir bona regula
Recta, atque divina,

Stricta, sancta, sedula,
Summa, iusta ac mira.

2
Munter Benchuir beata
Fide fundata certa,
Spe salutis ornata,
Caritate perfecta.

3
Navis nunquam turbata
Quamvis fluctibus tonsa
Nuptiis quoque parata
Regi domino sponsa.

4
Domus deliciis plena,
Super petram constructa,
Necnon vinea vera
Ex Aegypto transducta.

5
Certa civitas firma,
Fortis atque unita,

Gloriosa ac digna,
Supra montem posita.

6
Arca Cherubin tecta
Omni parte aurata,
Sacrosanctis reperta,
Viris quatuor portata.

7
Christo regina apta,
Solis luce amicta,
Simplex simulque docta,
Undecumque invicta.

8
Vera regalis aula
Variis gemmis ornata,
Gregisque Christi caula
Patre summo servata.

9
Virgo valde fecunda
Haec, et mater intacta,
Laeta ac tremebunda,
Verbo Dei subacta.

10
Cui beata vita
Cum perfectis futura
Deo Patre parata
Sine fine mansura.

TRANSLATION

The Rule of Bangor is good,
Right and divine,
Strict, holy, zealous,
Very lofty, just and wonderful.

The community of Bangor is happy —
Founded on sure faith,

Embellished with the hope of salvation,
Perfected by charity.

Ship that was never tossed
Though buffeted by the waves;
Also bride prepared
For nuptials with the King and Lord.

House full of delights —
Built on rock
Likewise the true vine
Transferred from Egypt.

Surely a firm city,
Strong and united,
Glorious and worthy,
Situated on a mountain.

Ark covered by the Cherubim
Gilded on all sides
Containing most holy things
Carried by four men.

Meet queen for Christ
Clothed in the light of the sun
Simple, yet learned,
Unconquered on all sides.

True royal palace
Adorned with different jewels,
And fold of the flock of Christ
Preserved by God the Father.

Virgin most fruitful
And yet an inviolable Mother,
Joyous and trembling
Prepared for the word of God.

To which (whom) will be happy life
With the perfect,
Prepared by God the Father —
It will last forever.

CÚ CHUIMNE OF IONA

(?–747)

CANTEMUS IN OMNI DIE
(Hymn to Mary)
(first half of 8th century)

[This is the earliest hymn in honour of Mary in the Western church and an outstanding example of Hiberno-Latin versification. Its author was Cú Chuimne, Sage (*Sapiens*) of Iona, one of the chief compilers of the *Hibernensis* (see pp. 12–17 and 99–102). It focuses more on Mary's motherhood and its part in human redemption than on her virginal conception of Christ and her own unique holiness. The Mary–Eve contrast is signified by the tree, both Cross and Tree of Knowledge. Verbal echoes recall Luke 1:26–55, and the tone suggests something of the elation in the Magnificat; the hymn, however, is jubiliantly choral and antiphonal. Edition and translation are by David Howlett; see his 'Five Experiments in Textual Reconstruction and Analysis', *Peritia*, vol. 9 (1995), pp. 1–50 at 19–30.]

Cantemus in omni die concinnantes uarie
conclamantes Deo dignum ymnum Sancte Marie.
Bis per chorum hinc et inde conlaudemus
    Mariam
ut uox pulset omnem aurem per laudem
    uicariam.
Maria de tribu Iuda Summi mater Domini
oportunam dedit curam egrotanti homini.
Gabriel aduexit Verbum sinu prius Paterno
quod conceptum et susceptum in utero materno.
Hec est summa, hec est sancta uirgo uenerabilis,
que ex fide non recessit sed exstetit stabilis.
Huïc matri nec inuenta ante nec post similis
nec de prole fuit plane humane originis.
Per mulierem et lignum mundus prius periit;
per mulieris uirtutem ad salutem rediit.
Maria mater miranda Patrem suum edidit
per quem aqua late lotus totus mundus credidit.
Hec concepit margaritam — non sunt uana
    somnia —
pro qua sani Christiani uendunt sua omnia.
Tunicam per totum textam Christi mater fecerat
que peracta Christi morte sorte statim steterat.
Induamus arma lucis loricam et galiam
ut simus Deo perfecti suscepti per Mariam.
Amen, Amen, adiuramus merita puerpere

ut non possit flamma pire nos dire decerpere.
Christi nomen inuocamus angelis sub testibus
ut fruamur et scribamur litteris celestibus.
    Sance Marie meritum
    imploramus dignissimum
    ut mereamur solium
    habitare altissimum.
        Amen.

TRANSLATION

Let us sing on every day, putting together
    variously,
shouting together to God a hymn worthy of
    Saint Mary.
Twice in a chorus on this side and that let us
    together praise Mary,
so that the sound may strike every ear in
    successive praise.
Mary from the tribe of Judah, mother of the
    Highest Lord,
gave an advantageous cure to ailing man.
Gabriel conveyed first from the Father's bosom
    the Word,
Which [was] conceived and received in the
    mother's womb.
This is the highest, this the holy venerable virgin,
who has not drawn back from the faith, but
    stood out stable.
To this mother a like has been found neither
    before nor since
nor after her offspring of fully human birth.
By a woman and a tree the world first perished;
by the virtue of a woman it came back to
    salvation.
Mary the wondrous mother brought forth her
    own Father,
through Whom the whole world far and wide
    washed by water [in baptism] has believed.
This woman conceived a pearl — these are not
    empty dreams —
for which sane Christians sell all their own
    possessions.
The mother of Christ has made a garment
    woven throughout,

which, when Christ's death was brought about,
  had remained constant in its order.
Let us put on the arms of light, breastplate, and
  helmet,
that we may be perfect for God, received
  through Mary.
Amen. Amen. We affirm on oath the merits of
  the child-bearer,
so that the flame of the dreadful pyre cannot
  snatch us away.

We invoke the name of Christ with angels as
  witnesses,
so that we may enjoy and be written in celestial
  letters.
We beseech the most worthy
  merit of Saint Mary
that we may be worthy
  to inhabit the loftiest throne.
    Amen.

BLATHMAC SON OF CÚ BRETTAN

(fl. 750)

from:
TAIR CUCUM, A MAIRE BOÍD
(Come to Me, Loving Mary)
(c. 750)

[Lamenting the dead has long been regarded as 'women's work' and the church has censured extravagant displays of grief since earliest times. Irish canons and penitential documents specifying penalties for keening (from Irish *caíned*, later *caoineadh*) the dead are extant from the seventh century onwards. The higher the status of the deceased, the less the penalty and, not surprisingly, the church approved of mourning for the crucified Christ. However, church Fathers were at pains to convey the seemly nature of Mary's grief for her Son, differentiating it from the violent mourning of those of lesser faith. By contrast, the poet here asks to mourn unrestrainedly along with Mary, simultaneously identifying himself and her with the affective piety of women. He writes in a simple style that might have appealed to a popular audience.

In the long verse sequence from which the following extracts are taken, Blathmac recounts Christ's life and death in terms of Irish social institutions. Had the Jews remembered God the Father's deliverance of their ancestors, they could not have crucified the Son. But worse, they had ignored the special relationship between a son and his maternal kin. Encapsulated in the phrase 'the sister's son', this relationship was highly valued in medieval Irish society. The specific bond (the 'avunculate') was between a maternal uncle and his sister's son. As Mary was sister to the whole Jewish race, the Jews had committed *fingal*, 'kin-slaying', against their own sister's son, who was also the ultimate Sister's Son. Finally, 'the

Jews did not suffer that Christ should be mourned by his own people' (quatrain 128). The present quatrains (qq. 1–2; 100–7; 144–9) are from: James Carney (ed. and trans.), *The Poems of Blathmac son of Cú Brettan*, Irish Texts Society, vol. 47 (Dublin: Educational Company of Ireland for Irish Text Society, 1964). For further extracts, see Volume I, pp. 40–1.]

Tair cucum, a Maire boíd,
do choíniuth frit do rochoím;
dirsan dul fri croich dot mac
ba mind már, ba masgérat.

Co tochmurr frit mo di láim
ar do macind irgabáil;
Ísu con-atoí do brú,
nícon fochmai th'ógai-siu . . .

A scél ad-chuäd co glé
is do chairiugud Iudae
dég ro-crochsat — cáin fethal! —
corp Críst, maic a ndeirbsethar.

Ro-rairngred don-icfed de
ind flesc do chlaind Iëse;
ro-sloinded uadib is glé
in leü di thrib Iudae.

I nIerosalem nuall na mac,
is d'ó Dauíd da-bertat;
fersait díchru — ba cain chlú! —
fáilti uili fri hÍsu.

Ainbli gnúisi, condai fir
ro-fersat in fingail-sin;
céin ba diïb a máthair
ba diäll for firbráthair.

Cenmothá, mac Dé athar,
Críst ar ruiri rígrathach,
ronda-hír meinic iar sin
áilib ilib adamraib.

Ísu, ósar na huagae
do-roächt gním nglanbuadae:
de íc cenéli doíne
don-etarraith mórchloíne.

Cach feb tecomnacht in rí
do Iudib ara célsini,
batar moíni do mogaib;
ro-coillset a cobfolaid . . .

Dot-gaur co foclaib fíraib,
a Maire, a maisrígain,
con roirem cobrai ma tú
do airchisecht do chridi-siu.

Conro-choíner Críst as glé
frit-su tucht bas n-incride,
a lië lógmar laindrech,
a máthair in mórchoimdeth.

Ce chon-messinn co cach rian
doíni betho fo moenmiad
do-regtis lim ocus lat
conro-choíntis do rígmac.

Do lámchomairt cen moraich
mnáib macaib ferolaib
conro-choíntis for cach dind
ríg do-rósat cach n-oenrind.

Nacha cumgaim; ciche féin
do mac frit-su co daigléir
acht do-dichis-siu nach ré
do chélidiu cucum-sae.

Do airchisecht chridi cen on
con roirem ar ndiäbor,
a chond na creitme glaine,
tair cucum, a boídMaire. Tair.

TRANSLATION

Come to me, loving Mary, that I may keen with you your very dear one. Alas that your son should go to the cross, he who was a great diadem, a beautiful hero.

That with you I may beat my two hands for the captivity of your beautiful son: your womb has conceived Jesus — it has not marred your virginity . . .

The story I have told clearly is for the purpose of censuring the Jews; for they have crucified (beautiful form!) the body of Christ, their sister's son.

It had been prophesied that there would come of them the rod of the plant of Jesse; it is clear that he has been named from the lion of the tribe of Judah.

The acclamation of the youths in Jerusalem — it was to the descendant of David that they gave it; they all (fair the fame!) welcomed Jesus zealously.

Of shameless countenance and wolf-like were the men who perpetrated that kin-slaying; since his mother was of them it was treachery towards a true kinsman.

Besides that the son of God the Father, Christ, our royal gracious king, had granted to them often after that many wonderful requests.

Jesus, darling son of the virgin, achieved a deed of pure victory; from him the salvation of the human race which great perversity encompassed.

Every advantage that the King had bestowed upon the Jews in return for their clientship was 'wealth to slaves'; they violated their counter-obligations . . .

I call you with true words, Mary, beautiful queen, that we may hold converse together to pity your heart's darling.

So that I may keen the bright Christ with you in the most heartfelt way, shining precious jewel, mother of the great Lord.

Had I, being rich and honoured, power over the people of the world as far as every sea, they would come with you and me to keen your royal son.

So that with beating of hands without . . .(?) with women, children and men, they might keen on every hill-top the King who created every single star.

Indeed, I have not power over them; I myself will lament your son with you with all good diligence if only, at some time, you come on a visit to me.

Come to me, loving Mary, head of pure faith, that we may hold converse with the compassion of unblemished heart. Come.

?ULTÁN OF ARDBRACCAN

(?–657 or 663)

BRIGIT BÉ BITHMAITH
(Hymn to Saint Brigit)
(?*c.* 650)

[Brigit, 'the mother of Jesus', is the sole focus of this extravagant eulogy, apart from a brief reference to Patrick as her coequal — or perhaps her male counterpart — in the Kingdom on earth. The hymn may be the oldest of the extant hymns in the Irish language. It is found in the eleventh-century *Liber Hymnorum*, where its preface attributes it to various sixth- and seventh-century ecclesiastics. As author, the most plausible of these is Ultán, Bishop of Ardbraccan, near Navan in County Meath, an early biographer of Brigit and Patrick.

Text (with translation): Whitley Stokes and John Strachan (eds and trans.), *Thesaurus Paleohibernicus*, 2 vols. (Cambridge: Cambridge University Press, 1901, 1903; rpr. Dublin: Dublin Institute for Advanced Studies, 1975), vol. 2, pp. 325–6. This is a new translation.]

1
Brigit bé bithmaith
breó órde óiblech,
donfé don bithflaith
in grén tind tóidlech.

2
Ronsóira Brigit
sech drungu demne:
roróina reunn
cathu cach thedme.

3
Dirodba indiunn
ar colno císu,

in chróib co mbláthib,
in máthir Ísu.

4
Ind fíróg inmain
co norddon adbil,
bé sóir cech inbaid
lam nóib di Laignib.

5
Lethcholbe flatho
la Pátricc prímde,
in tlacht ós lígib,
ind rígin rígde.

6
Robet ér sinit
ar cuirp hi cilicc;
dia rath ronbróina
ronsóira Brigit.

TRANSLATION

Brigit, eternally good lady,
golden sparkling flame,
may she lead us to the eternal kingdom,
the dazzling shining sun!

May Brigit deliver us
past throngs of devils:
may she rout before us
the temptations of each attack.

May she destroy within us
the taxes of our flesh,
the branch with blossoms,
the mother of Jesus.

The dear, true virgin
of immense honour,
I shall always be safe
with my saint from Leinster.

She and prime Patrick
are the kingdom's two columns;
she the beautiful calyx,
the regal queen.

After reaching old age
may our bodies be in sackcloth;
may she rain her grace on us,
save us, Brigit!

ANONYMOUS

from:
VITA PRIMA SANCTAE BRIGITAE
(Latin Life of Saint Brigit)
(c. 750)

[The date of Saint Brigit's death is variously recorded as 524, 526 and 528. The Life excerpted here is known as *Vita Prima* because it is the first of five lives printed in the Bollandists' *Acta Sanctorum*. However, it is generally accepted that it dates from about the middle of the eighth century and is thus almost a century later than the Latin Life of Brigit written by Cogitosus in the second half of the seventh century.

The excerpt from Cogitosus's Life in Volume I, pp. 76–7, evidences in miniature the striking contrast between his concerns and those of the anonymous author of *Vita Prima*. Cogitosus's Life was designed as much to articulate Kildare's claims to primatial status and supremacy over all the churches of Ireland as it was to gild Brigit's reputation as a saint. The 'reverences', 'brethren' and 'readers' to whom Cogitosus addressed his literary Latin were undoubtedly equipped to sustain, or oppose, those claims. *Vita Prima* is a miscellaneous compilation of Brigidine traditions from many sources, including the earlier writings of Cogitosus, Ultán of Ardbraccan (see preceding poem), and others. Its Latin is plain, its narrative lines simple. It was probably composed in Southern Uí Néill and shows no particular interest in Kildare. Rather, it draws on anecdotes from places throughout Ireland, and frames much of the narrative by reference to Brigit's various itineraries. The founder of the monastery for which claims to primatial exclusivity had been advanced in the seventh century is here an itinerant saint for all the people.

There are other striking differences. Cogitosus highlights the fact that Kildare was a double house without conceding anything of the powers associated with the male clergy to the saint or her female community. The roles of abbess and bishop are carefully delimited. Thus, when Brigit 'reflected that she could not be without a high priest to consecrate churches and confer ecclesiastical orders in them, she sent for Conleth, a famous man and a hermit endowed with every good disposition . . . in order that he might govern the Church with her in the office of bishop and that her churches might lack nothing as regards priestly orders' (Preface, §5). *Vita Prima* brings Brigit into association with various bishops, including Patrick. It portrays Brigit and Patrick as not merely supportive of each other, but as equally deferential (for example, §§38–9, 42 below).

More tellingly, *Vita Prima*, unlike Cogitosus's Life, is replete with incidents involving nuns and the secular women with whom they had contact (for example, §§20–8 below). Relatively, a greater proportion of its miracles relates to Brigit's dealings with the poor and the sick. Its author portrays Brigit as willing to use her power equally on behalf of the mother of the mongoloid child, the nun with the unwelcome pregnancy, and wife who could not conceive (§§100, 103, 109). Finally, while Cogitosus briefly alludes to Brigit's birth 'of Christian and noble parents' named Dubthach and Broicsech (§1), *Vita Prima* highlights Broicsech's slave status and the fact that Dubthach had a wife (§§1–18 below). Slavery and sexual exploitation impinged more on women than on men. In short, the possibility that *Vita Prima* was composed by a female author, or on behalf of a female audience, begs consideration. At very least it can be said that its author had more interest in the lives of women and less in the mandarins of the church than did Cogitosus.

The following excerpts are from the translation of the full text by Seán Connolly, '*Vita Prima Sanctae Brigitae*. Background and Historical Value', *Journal of the Royal Society of Antiquaries of Ireland*, vol. 19 (1989), pp. 5–49, at pp. 14–19, 22–4, and 44–6.]

§1

1. There was a nobleman of Leinster stock named Dubthach. He bought a bondmaid named Broicsech and she was of comely appearance, good-living and a good slave.
2. Her master Dubthach desired her and slept with her and she became pregnant by him.
3. When Dubthach's wife came to know of this she was sorely aggrieved and said to her husband, 'Cast out this bondmaid[1] and sell her lest her offspring surpass my offspring.'
4. But her husband refused to sell the maid since he loved her dearly, for she was a person of quite irreproachable conduct.

§2

1. Now one day both of them, man and maid, sat in a chariot and drove past the house of a certain druid. Hearing the sound of the chariot the druid said to his servants, 'See who is sitting in the chariot for the chariot sounds as if it is carrying a king.' Then the servant said, 'We can see no one but Dubthach in the chariot.' The druid said, 'Summon him to me.'
2. And when he had been summoned the druid said to him, 'This woman who is sitting behind you in the chariot, is she with child?' Dubthach replied, 'Yes.' The druid said, 'Woman, by what man have you conceived?' She replied, 'By my master, Dubthach.'
3. The druid said to him, 'Take good care of this woman, for the child she has conceived will be extraordinary.' Dubthach replied, 'My wife is trying to force me to sell this bondmaid because she is afraid of her progeny.' The druid said, 'Your wife's progeny will serve your bondmaid's progeny until the end of the world.'
4. To the bondmaid, however, the druid said, 'Keep your spirit up; no one can harm you; the grace of your little infant will set you free. You will give birth to an illustrious daughter who will shine in the world like the sun in the vault of heaven.' Dubthach said, 'I am grateful to God because until now I have not had a daughter but only sons.'
5. Dubthach and his bondmaid returned to his house but Dubthach loved his bondmaid all the more after the druid's words.

6. Then in a rage his wife together with her brothers urgently pressed Dubthach to sell the maid in a distant region.

§3. In those days two holy bishops from Britain came at God's prompting and entered Dubthach's house. One was called Mel, the other Melchu. And Mel said to Dubthach's wife, 'Why are you so sad? The offspring of your bondmaid will excel you and your progeny. Nevertheless love the bondmaid as you do your sons because her offspring will greatly benefit your children.'

§4

1. So as the wife persisted in her rage, there came a certain poet of the Uí Néill at God's inspiration and bought the bondmaid off Dubthach. The latter, however, did not sell the offspring which she had in her womb.
2. So the poet went with the bondmaid to his own region and that night when he entered his house there came a certain guest, a holy man who prayed to God all through the night, and during the night he often saw a ball of fire in the place where the bondmaid slept and he reported this to the poet in the morning.

§5. At that time a certain druid came from the north to this poet's house and he sold this bondmaid and gave her to the druid.

§6

1. One day the druid invited his king and queen to supper but the queen was near childbirth.
2. Then the king's friends and servants began to ask a certain prophet at what hour the queen was due to give birth to the baby. The druid said, 'Were it born tomorrow at daybreak, it would have no equal on earth.' But the queen gave birth to a son ahead of time.
3. When morning came and the sun had risen, the druid's bondmaid came to the house carrying a vessel full of milk which had just been milked, and when she had put one foot across the threshold of the house and the other foot outside, she fell astride the threshold and gave birth to a daughter.
4. That is how the prophet said this bondmaid would give birth, neither in the house nor

1. Genesis 21:10; cf. Galatians 4:30.

outside the house, and the infant's body was washed with the warm milk which she was carrying.

§7
1. After this the druid went with the bondmaid to the region of the Connachta and lived there because the druid's mother was of the Connachta but his father from Muma.[2]
2. One day the bondmaid went off to milk cows a long distance away and left her daughter asleep in the house on her own. Then the house appeared to be on fire and everyone ran to put out the fire but when they got near the house there was no sign of the fire and they saw the girl in the house rejoicing with a lovely expression and rosy cheeks and they all said, 'This girl is full of the Holy Spirit.'

§8. One day when the others also were with them, the druid and bondmaid were sitting in a certain place and suddenly saw a piece of cloth, which was touching the girl's head, glow with fiery flame but when they quickly reached out their hands they could not see the fire.

§9. The same druid also as he was asleep one day saw two clerics clothed in white garments pouring oil on the girl's head. They were performing the rite of baptism in the customary way. One of them said, 'Call this virgin Brigit.'

§10. One night this druid stayed up, as his practice was, to study the stars in the sky, and all through the night he saw a glowing column of fire rising from the little house in which the bondmaid with her daughter was sleeping and he called a certain man and he likewise saw it.

§11
1. One day the infant's voice was heard. She was praying to God and stretching out her hands to heaven.
2. A man greeted her and she replied, 'This will be mine; this will be mine.' The druid on hearing this said, 'The answer which the infant has given is a true prophecy, because this place will be hers for ever.'

3. Which later proved true, for today saint Brigit has a large *paruchia*[3] in those regions.
4. When the inhabitants of that area heard this they flocked to the druid and said to him, 'You stay with us but let the girl who is prophesying that our territories will be hers depart from us.' The druid replied, 'The bondmaid and her daughter I'm not going to leave. Rather what I am going to do is turn my back on your country.'
5. Then the druid with all his people went to his native place which is in the territory of the Muma where he had inheritance of his father.
6. The holy maiden felt a loathing for the druid's food and used to vomit daily. Observing this the druid carefully investigated the cause of the nausea, and, when he discovered it, said, 'I am unclean, but this girl is filled with the Holy Spirit.[4] She can't endure my food.'
7. Thereupon he chose a white cow and set it aside for the girl, and a certain Christian woman, a very God-fearing virgin, used to milk the cow and the girl used to drink the cow's milk and not vomit it up as her stomach had been healed. Moreover this Christian woman fostered the girl.
8. When the holy maiden grew up she served in the house and any food her hand touched or her eye saw would multiply.

§12
1. Later on the thought entered her heart of returning to her father. When the druid found this out, he sent messengers to him to tell him to take his daughter back as a free person.
2. Whereupon he was overjoyed and came to the druid's house and took his daughter away and her Christian foster-mother accompanied her.

§13
1. As her foster-mother was ill she sent Brigit and another girl with her to the house of a certain man to ask for a drink of beer for the sick woman, but receiving nothing from him they returned to their own home.

2. i.e. Munster.

3. A federation of churches.
4. cf. Acts 6:5.

2. Then saint Brigit went to a well and filled her vessel with water and it became excellent beer, and after her foster-mother tasted it she got up cured.

§14
1. Not long afterwards a certain respected guest came to her father's house. Her father arranged for meat to be cooked for him and gave his daughter five portions to cook. Now he went out but the guest was asleep inside.
2. Then a hungry dog came into the house and Brigit gave it one portion; the dog came a second time and she gave it another portion. The guest saw this but said nothing. She for her part thought he was asleep.
3. Later the father came into the house and found the five portions intact and the guest told him what he had seen and they said to one another, 'We are unworthy to eat this food. It is better that it be given to the poor instead.'

§15
1. A certain God-fearing widow who lived in the next village asked her father if saint Brigit could go with her to the synod which was assembled in Mag Life. The father gave permission and off they went.
2. Then a holy man at the synod saw a vision in his sleep and when he got up said, 'I have seen Mary and a certain man standing beside her who said to me, "This is holy Mary who has been dwelling among you."'
3. No sooner had the holy man related this at the synod than the widow accompanied by saint Brigit arrived on the scene. Whereat the holy man said, 'This is the Mary whom I saw, for I clearly recognise her features.' Thereupon they all glorified her as a type of Mary.

§16
1. Brigit subsequently went off to visit her mother whom she had left with the aforesaid druid.
2. However her mother was a long way from the druid's house at the time and had twelve cows for making butter. After coming to her mother saint Brigit would distribute butter to the poor and the guests every day and divide the butter into twelve parts as if for the twelve

apostles and one part would be larger as if for Christ.
3. For she used to say, 'Every guest is Christ.'

§17
1. One day the druid and his wife came with a large vessel to have it filled with butter. When Brigit saw the large vessel her face blushed with embarrassment. All the butter she had was the amount required for one day and for the half of another.
2. When they entered the house the maiden served them cheerfully, washed their feet, set food before them and regaled them generously.
3. Later she went into her pantry and prayed to the Lord and from it brought out the little butter she had.
4. When the druid's wife saw this she scorned it and said with a sneer, 'The amount you have brought out is paltry.' The maiden said in reply, 'Fill the vessel and you will have butter.' Then by God's power the big vessel was filled with this meagre amount of butter.
5. When the druid saw this marvel he said to saint Brigit, 'Let this vessel filled with mysterious butter be yours and let the twelve cows which you have milked be yours.'
6. Brigit said, 'You can have your cows. Let me have my mother back as a free woman.' The druid said, 'Here, I offer you the butter and the cows and your mother as a free woman.'
7. Then the druid believed in the Lord and was baptized. But saint Brigit gave to the poor all that had been offered her by the druid and returned with her mother to her father.

§18
1. After this Dubthach began to contemplate selling his daughter because she was committing many thefts, for everything she saw she secretly gave to the poor.
2. Now one day he took her with him in the chariot to visit the king. And when they reached the king's palace, Dubthach left the chariot in her charge and went to the king.
3. And a poor man came to saint Brigit and she gave him her father's royal sword which the king had given him.
4. Then Dubthach said to the king, 'Buy my daughter to be your slave.' The king replied,

'Why are you selling her?' Dubthach said, 'Whatever she lays her hand on she steals.' And the king said, 'Let her come to us.'

5. Dubthach went out to her and said, 'Where is my sword?' She replied, 'I gave it to Christ.'

6. Her father became furious and felt like killing the maiden. But the king said to her, 'Why did you give my sword and your father's to the poor?' She replied, 'If God were to ask me for yourself and him, I would give you and all you have to him if I could.'

7. Then the king said, 'This daughter of yours, Dubthach, it seems to me, is a great responsibility for me to buy and a greater one for you to sell.' Then the king gave the maiden another sword to give to her father. And Dubthach returned home with his daughter rejoicing.

§19

1. Shortly afterwards a certain man of honourable birth came to Dubthach to seek his daughter in marriage, which pleased her father and brothers. Brigit however turned him down.

2. And when they began to put great pressure on her to marry the man, saint Brigit asked God to afflict her body with some deformity in order that men might stop paying suit to her.

3. Thereupon one of her eyes burst and liquefied in her head. For she preferred to lose her bodily eye than the eye of her soul and loved beauty of soul more than that of the body.

4. When her father saw this he allowed her to take the veil and her eye was restored and she was healed on taking the veil as is related below.

§20

1. Then saint Brigit taking three nuns with her went to the territory of the Uí Néill to the two holy bishops, Mel and Melchu, who were disciples of St Patrick and lived in the towns of Mide.[5] And they had a certain disciple called Mac Caille who said to Mel, 'Look, there are holy virgins outside who wish to receive the veil of virginity from your hands.'

5. Anglicized 'Meath'.

2. Then he ushered them into the bishop's presence, and while bishop Mel was gazing intently at them, a column of fire suddenly appeared rising from Brigit's head up to the very top of the church in which she dwelt.

3. Then the holy bishop placed the veil on saint Brigit's head and when the prayers had been read Brigit bowed her head and seized the wooden foot of the altar in her hand and since that moment the altar foot has permanently remained fresh without any decay or blemish. And saint Brigit's eye was healed forthwith when she received the veil.

4. Then eight other virgins also received the veil together with saint Brigit and the virgins with their parents said, 'Don't leave us. Instead stay with us and make your home in these parts.'

5. Thereafter saint Brigit stayed with them.

§21

1. One day there came to Brigit and her nuns three devout men who were pilgrims and she regaled them with bread and cooked bacon. The men ate the bread but hid the three portions of bacon as they did not want to eat it.

2. The following day Brigit greeted them and said, 'See how much bread you have left over!' When they looked they saw that the three portions of bacon were three loaves of bread.

§22

1. Another day two of these men went out to the work they had to do for a living. The third, the youngest, stayed behind and when Brigit saw him she said to him, 'Why didn't you go out to work with your brothers?' He answered, 'Because I am missing one of my hands and can't work.'

2. When she realised that his hand was missing Brigit healed him and at once he went out after his companions to work.

§23

1. As Easter Day was approaching, saint Brigit wanted to give a banquet for all the churches which were near her in the surrounding towns of Mide.

2. However, she had not the wherewithal for a banquet except for a single vat of beer, for

there was a shortage of provisions in those parts at the time.

3. Now she put the beer from the vat into two basins, for she had no other vessels.

4. And the beer was divided up and taken by Brigit to the eighteen surrounding churches and there was enough for them all for Holy Thursday and Easter Sunday and the week up to the end of Easter.

5. The same Easter a leper came to saint Brigit and as he was covered with leprosy he asked Brigit for a cow.

6. Not having a cow she said to him, 'Would you like us to pray to God for you to be cured of your leprosy?' He replied, 'That to me would be the best gift of all.'

7. Then the holy virgin blessed water and sprinkled it on the leper's body and he was cured.

8. He gave thanks to God and stayed with Brigit till his death . . .

§38

1. Then the holy bishops Mel and Melchu said to saint Brigit, 'Would you like to come with us to Mag Breg[6] to visit the holy bishop Patrick?' Brigit replied, 'I'd like to speak to him so that he may bless me.'

2. Then the bishops and saint Brigit went on their way but a certain cleric with a large entourage, cows, carts and a great deal of baggage, asked if he might go with them to Mag Breg.

3. But the bishops demurred in case the amount of cattle and baggage he had should slow them down on their journey. And Brigit said to them, 'You go on ahead of us, I'll stay behind and comfort these folk.' So she stayed behind and said to the domestics, 'Why not put the baggage in the carts?' They said, 'Because our crippled brother and blind sister are lying sick in the carts.'

4. So night fell and they had something to eat and drink. But Brigit alone fasted and stayed awake, and in the morning she poured the morning dew on the cripple's feet and immediately he rose to his feet cured and the blind woman got back her sight.

5. Then they put their baggage in the carts and continued their journey giving thanks to God. As they were walking along the road they saw a certain countryman who was milking cows on his own with exceptional hardship, and Brigit said, 'Ask him why he is toiling away on his own without a helper.' He said, 'Because my whole household is ill; there are twelve people down with illness in the one house.'

6. Thereupon Brigit told the nuns to milk the cows with him. Then the countryman asked them to have dinner in return for their pains, and they accepted and ate by the bank of a certain river, all except Brigit who remained fasting.

7. Then saint Brigit blessed water and sprinkled the countryman's house and cured all the sick who were in it.

§39

1. From there they went directly to a place called Tailtiu. There a holy bishop was in session with an assembly of many bishops and in the council there was a big discussion.

2. A certain virgin who had fallen into sin was alleging that the baby she had borne was by a certain bishop from among the disciples of St Patrick named Brón. He, however, was repudiating the allegation.

3. Then all who were at the council, having heard of the wonderful works of saint Brigit, said, 'This matter can be settled by her.'

4. Accordingly the woman with her baby in her arms was brought to Brigit outside the council. Brigit said to her, 'By whom did you conceive this baby?' 'By Bishop Brón,' she replied. Brigit said, 'That's not what I think.'

5. Then Brigit bowing low to St Patrick, said, 'Father, it is for you to settle this matter.' Patrick said in reply, 'My most beloved daughter, holy Brigit, do us the honour of revealing the truth.'

6. And so saint Brigit made the sign of the cross of Christ on the woman's mouth and at once her whole head and tongue swelled up, but even at that she did not repent.

7. Then Brigit blessed the baby's tongue and said to him, 'Who is your father?' He replied as he walked along, 'My father is not Bishop Brón but a certain fellow who is sitting

6. The Plain of Brega, through which the Boyne flows.

furthest away at the very end of the council-hall, a most despicable type, base and depraved.'

8. Thereupon they all gave thanks to God, and Brigit was extolled, and the woman repented . . .

§42

1. At this time saint Brigit was a guest at the monastery of St Laisre. Now one day towards evening St Patrick came with a large crowd to put up at that monastery.

2. Thereupon the local community was worried and said to Brigit, 'What are we going to do? We don't have food for such a large crowd.' But Brigit said to them, 'How much do you have?' They said to her, 'All we have is twelve loaves and a little milk and one sheep which we have cooked for you and your folk.' But Brigit said, 'These will be enough for the whole lot of us, for the sacred scriptures will be read to us, thanks to which we will forget about bodily food.'

3. Whereupon the two groups of people, namely, Patrick's and Brigit's, ate together and had their fill and the amount of scraps they had left over was greater than the supplies which St Laisre offered them in the first place, and later St Laisre offered herself and her place to saint Brigit in perpetuity . . .

§100

1. Another day a woman came to saint Brigit and said, 'What am I to do about my child? You see, his father wants to kill him because he is almost a stillborn child for he is blind from birth and mongoloid.'

2. Thereupon Brigit took pity on the woman. She told her to wash the child's face in the water nearby and at once the boy who was called a cretin became normal and they say that until his death he had no eye-disease but always had healthy eyes.

§101

1. Likewise another day a prankish boy came to saint Brigit knowing her to be compassionate towards the poor. For a joke and at the mischievous suggestions of others, he went to her in the guise of a poor person and asked her for a sheep from her flock, and she gave him the sheep. He came back seven times and asked her in the Lord's name for seven sheep, cunningly coming in the guise of a poor person, and got from her what he wanted.

2. But when evening came and the flock was counted, the tally was found to be correct. Moreover when the seven sheep were added to the flock on the night the prank was played no extra ones were found in the morning.

§102. By an extraordinary turn of events lepers came to Brigit asking for beer. Not having any and seeing some water which had been brought in for the bath, she blessed it by the power of faith and turned it into the finest beer and drew it in abundance for the thirsty people.

§103. Another day saint Brigit by the very powerful strength of her faith blessed a woman who had fallen after a vow of integrity and whose womb was pregnant and swelling and the conception in the woman's womb decreased and she restored her to health and repentance without childbirth or its pangs. The woman was healed and gave thanks to God . . .

§109

1. Another night in the guest-lodge at Brigit's place there was a layman, a dear friend of hers, with his wife. He asked Brigit to make the sign of the cross over his wife's womb that she might have a son. Brigit did so and that very night he slept with his wife. As a result Étchén, a remarkably holy man, was born.

2. That night a maidservant stole a silver lunula[7] belonging to the layman's wife and the following day, as she was pursued by a lot of people, she threw the lunula into a very big river and immediately an abnormally large fish swallowed it.

3. Just then fishermen caught the fish in their nets and at once brought the fish as an offering to saint Brigit. But when the fish was cut open Brigit gave her lunula back to the layman's wife. Thereupon he and his pregnant wife gave thanks to God and Brigit and went on their way . . .

7. A crescent-shaped neck ornament.

from:
BETHU BRIGTE
(The Old Irish Life of Brigit)
(9th century)

[This Life, written largely in Irish and dated to the ninth century, is the earliest source for the tradition that when Saint Brigit sought to become a veiled nun, she was instead ordained bishop. Earlier awareness of it is indicated in the preceding text, which relates that she and her companions sought out clerics of episcopal rank when they wished to be veiled (§20). A later Irish life of the saint, which may date from the late twelfth century, substitutes for Bishop Mel's prophecy that Brigit alone will have this status the claim that all her successors 'from that time to this' also enjoyed it. The synod of Kells-Mellifont in 1152 deprived the Abbess of Kildare of her privilege of precedence over bishops.

The following paragraphs (here with minor changes in presentation) are from: Donncha Ó hAodha (ed. and trans.), *Bethu Brigte* (Dublin: Dublin Institute for Advanced Studies, 1978), p. 24.]

§16. Dubthach said to her: 'Take the veil then, my daughter, for this is what you desire. Distribute this holding to God and man.' 'Thanks be to God,' said Brigit.

§17. On a certain day she goes with seven virgins to take the veil to a foundation on the side of Cróchán of Brí Éile, where she thought that Mel the bishop dwelt. There she greets two virgins, Tol and Etol, who dwelt there. They said: 'The bishop is not here, but in the churches of Mag Taulach.' While saying this they behold a youth called Mac Caille, a pupil of Mel the bishop. They asked him to lead them to the bishop. He said: 'The way is trackless, with marshes, deserts, bogs and pools.' The saint said: 'Extricate us [from our difficulty].' As they proceeded on their way, he could see afterwards a straight bridge there.

§18. The hour of consecration having arrived, the veil was raised by angels from the hand of Mac Caille, the minister, and is placed on the head of saint Brigit. Bent down moreover during the prayers she held the ash beam which supported the altar. It was afterwards changed into acacia, which is neither consumed by fire nor does it grow old through centuries. Three times the church was burned down, but the beam remained intact under the ashes.

§19. The bishop being intoxicated with the grace of God there did not recognise what he was reciting from his book, for he consecrated Brigit with the orders of a bishop. 'This virgin alone in Ireland,' said Mel, 'will hold the episcopal ordination.' While she was being consecrated a fiery column ascended from her head.

?ORTHANACH ÚA COÍLLÁMA

(?–*c.* 839)

from:
SLÁN SEISS, A BRIGIT
CO ᴍBÚAID
(Hail Brigit) (9th century)

[The poem from which these triumphalistic quatrains derive may have been written by Orthanach úa Coílláma, Bishop of Kildare. Brigit's permanent sway over Leinster is contrasted with the fleeting powers of the secular rulers of the province. Those named below range from the first conqueror, Labraid Loingsech, to late seventh-century Uí Dúnlainge Kings of Leinster. The reference to 'virgin Ireland' in quatrain 2 is noteworthy.

Apart from minor changes in presentation, the text is as in Kuno Meyer, *Hail Brigit: An Old-Irish Poem on the Hill of Allen* (Halle a S.: Max Niemeyer; Dublin: Hodges, Figgis, 1912), and this new translation is indebted to his.]

1

Slán seiss, a Brigit co mbúaid,
for grúaid Lifi lir co tráig,
is tú banfhlaith buidnib slúaig
fil for clannaib Catháir Máir.

2

Ba móu epert in cach ré
airle Dé fri hÉrind n-úaig,
indiu cid latt Liphe líg,
ropo thír cáich ala n-úair . . .

4

Ba rí Lóegaire co ler,
Ailill Áne, adbol cor,
marid Currech cona lí,
ní mair nach rí rodboí for.

5

Ní mair Labraid Longsech lán
íar tundsem a tríchait chóim,
i nDind Ríg, ba hadba gnáth,
ó thuc bráth do Chobthach Chóil.

6

Gabais hÉrind húae Luirc,
Óengus Róirend, réim co sairc,[1]
rolá flathi dar a feirt,
Maistiu munbrecc Moga Airt.

7

Ailend aurdairc, álaind fius,
fail mór flathi fo a crius,
ba mó foscnad tan atchess
Crimthan Coscrach ina crius . . .

24

Ba slicht flatha Fáelán find,
Fíannamail fri forbud fland,
Bran mac Conaill co llín glond,
ba sí in tond dar cach n-ald.

25

A Brigit 'sa tír atchíu,
is cách a úair immudrá,
rogab do chlú for a chlú
ind ríg, is tú fordatá.

26

Táthut bithfhlaith lasin Rí
cen a tír i fail do rúaim,
a úe Bresail maic Déin,
slán seiss, a Brigit go mbúaid!

TRANSLATION

1

Sit safely enthroned, victorious Brigit,
On Liffey plain far as the sea's shore:
You are the sovereign with legion bands
Who rules the children of Catháir the Great.

2

Beyond telling at all times
Was God's counsel for virgin Ireland.
Although bright Liffey is yours today
It has been the land of others in their turn . . .

4

Lóegaire was king as far as the sea,
Ailill Áne — terrible reversal!
The Curragh[1] with its loveliness lives on,
No king remains that ruled it.

5

Great Labraid Loingsech lives no more,
Having trod his fair thirty years,
Since he dealt doom to Cobthach Cóel
In Dinn Ríg[2] — a constant abode.

6

Lorc's grandson, Óengus of Roíriu,[3]
Seized the rule of Ireland, a difficult course!
Maistiu[4] of the freckled neck, son of Mug Airt,
Toppled princes on their graves.

7

Illustrious Aileann[5] — dear the lore —
Many princes are beneath its face.
Difficult to fathom when once was seen
Victorious Crimthann above its surface . . .

1. In County Kildare.
2. A large hill-fort near Leighlinbridge, County Carlow.
3. North of Ballaghmoon, in County Kildare.
4. A personal name extrapolated from the homonymic place-name
   Maistiu, the seat of the Uí Dúnlainge kingship, County Kildare.
5. Modern Knockaulin, Leinster's pre-eminent hill-fort, south of
   Kildare town.

1. In translating, MS *co sairc* is interpreted as *co n-airc*.

24
Fair Fáelán was a track of lordship,
Fiannamail for bloody smiting,
Bran son of Conall with many deeds —
He was the wave over every cliff.

25
O Brigit whose land I see,
Where each in turn has lived,

Your fame has surpassed the king's fame —
You transcend them all.

26
You share sovereignty with the king
Except for the land where your sanctuary is.
Grand-child of Bresal son of Dian,
Sit safely enthroned, victorious Brigit!

ANONYMOUS

BRIGIT BÚADACH
(Glorious Brigit)
(Old Irish)

[Saint Brigit is celebrated here as Christ's kinswoman, and 'mother of the Gaels'. These verses are cited in a metrical tract in exemplification of a metre associated with the *fochloc*, one of the lowest grades of poets. Text: Kuno Meyer, *Miscellanea Hibernica* (Urbana: University of Illinois, 1917), p. 45. This is a new translation.]

Brigit búadach,
búaid na fine,
siur Ríg nime,
nár in duine,
    eslind luige,
        lethan bréo.

Rosíacht nóibnem
mumme Góidel,
ríar na n-óiged,
óibel ecnai,
ingen Dubthaig,
duine úallach,
Brigit búadach,
    bethad béo.

TRANSLATION

Glorious Brigit,
glory of the kindred,
King of Heaven's sister,

righteous person,
perjury's peril,
    flagrant fire.

She has reached holy heaven —
mother of the Gaels,
hospitaller of guests,
seed of wisdom,
Dubthach's daughter,
proud mortal,
glorious Brigit,
    living one of life.

SAINT BRIGIT'S RULE
(Middle Irish)

[According to her so-called *Vita Prima*, written in the eighth century (see pp. 63–9), Saint Brigit awoke one time from a prayer-trance and declared that she had heard the liturgy then in use in far-off Rome: '"I heard the masses in Rome at the tombs of Sts. Peter and Paul and it is my earnest wish that the order of this mass and of the universal rule be brought to me." Then saint Brigit sent experts to Rome and from there they brought the masses and the rule. Again after some time she said to the men, "I discern that certain things have been changed in the mass in Rome since you returned from there. Go back again." And they went and brought it back as they had found it.' (cf. Seán Connolly, 'Vita Prima Sanctae Brigitae', pp. 5–49 at p. 41).
    The following Middle Irish version of the same incident overturns the saint's identification with scholastic, textual and papal authority. This version occurs as a note on the

name *Plea*, a place supposedly visited by some of Brigit's community when seeking the 'Rule of Peter and Paul'. Brigit is expressly debarred from travelling to Rome, but acquires the Rule — and more — from a blind illiterate boy who never sets foot on dry land beyond Ireland. Translation: Whitley Stokes and John Strachan (eds and trans.), *Thesaurus Paleohibernicus*, vol. 2, pp. 328–9. See ibid. for original.]

Plea, a monastery which Brigit has on the Sea of Wight, or it is its Rule that the community of Brigit have: Brigit sent seven men to Rome to learn the Rule of Peter and Paul, since God did not allow that she should go herself. When they returned to her, they did not recall a single word of the Rule. 'The Son of the Virgin knows,' said Brigit, 'that for all your effort your gain is small.' She sent another seven men, and the same thing happened to them, and then she sent a further seven accompanied by her blind lad, for whatever he heard he memorised at once. When they reached the Sea of Wight, a storm came on and they let down their anchor. It stuck on the apex of the oratory and they drew lots to see who should go down. It fell to the blind lad and he descended and freed the anchor, and then remained there for a year, learning the Rule, until the rest of the company returned from the East. Again, a great storm blew up in the same place, and they let down the anchor once more and their blind lad ascended from below, bringing with him that church's Mass-Rule. He also brought up a bell, and that today is the 'Bell of Blind Lad' in Brigit's community, and the Rule that they have is the Rule that he brought with him from Plea.

from:
A HOMILY ON THE LIFE OF SAINT BRIGIT
(Middle Irish)

[Many of the key images found in the preceding texts are reprised in this short extract from a Middle Irish homily on the text of Revelation 14:4. The homily frames the life of Brigit. The excerpt is translated from: Whitley Stokes, *Three Middle Irish Homilies* (Calcutta: privately printed, 1877), p. 84.]

Now there has never been anyone more bashful or more modest than that holy virgin. She never washed her hands or her feet or her head in the company of men. She never looked into a man's face. She never spoke without blushing. She was abstinent, innocent, liberal, patient, rejoicing in God's commandments, steadfast, humble, forgiving, charitable. She was a Consecrated Casket for the keeping of Christ's Body. She was a Temple of God. Her heart and her mind were a Throne of Rest for the Holy Spirit. She was meek before God. She was sad with the wretched. She was splendid in miracles. For that reason her type among created things is the Dove among birds, the Vine among trees, the Sun above stars.

This holy virgin's father is the Heavenly Father. Jesus Christ is her son. The Holy Spirit is her fosterer. And that is why this holy virgin does these great innumerable miracles.

It is she that helps everyone who is in difficulty and in peril. It is she that abates the attacks. It is she that quells the roaring and the anger of the great sea. This is the prophetess of Christ. She is the Queen of the South.[1] She is the Mary of the Gael.

1. Matthew 12:42; Luke 11:31.

ROPAD MAITH LEMM
(Saint Brigit's Alefeast)
(Middle Irish)

[Generosity was the mark of nobility, and one who freely dispensed ale, to clients or overlords, was deemed to be *flaithiúlach,* which means both 'generous' and 'lordly' (from Irish *flaith* 'lord'). Brigit's hospitality typically was to the poor and needy. Appropriately enough, her ale-feast in this Middle Irish poem is a holy fast, an excess of asceticism.

The Irish text is a normalized version of that published by David Greene, and incorporates his suggested emendations: 'St Brigid's Alefeast', *Celtica*, vol. 2 (1952), pp. 150–3. This is a new translation.]

Ropad maith lemm
  coirmlinn mór do Ríg na ríg,
muintir Nime
  aca ól tre bithu sír.

Ropad maith lemm
  turtha creitme, crábaid glain,
ropad maith lemm
  sústa etla oc mo threib.

Ropad maith lemm
  fir Nime im' thegdais féin,
ropad maith lemm
  dabcha ainmnet do a réir.

Ropad maith lemm
  lestra déirce do dáil,
ropad maith lemm
  escra trócaire don dáim.

Ropad maith lemm
  soichell do bith ina luss,
ropad maith lemm
  Ísu beós do beith i fuss.

Ropad maith lemm
  na teóra Maire, míad clú!
ropad maith lemm
  muintir Nime de cech dú.

Ropad maith lemm
  corbam císaige don fhlaith.
Mad chés imned
  forsa tibred, bendacht maith.

I'd like a great ale-feast for the King of kings
and the folk of heaven drinking it for all
  eternity.

I'd like malts of faith, of pure piety,
I'd like threshels of penitence for my hall.

I'd like the men of Heaven in my own house,
I'd like casks of forbearance to serve them.

I'd like to pour out cups of charity,
I'd like jorums of mercy for the company.

I'd like largess for their sake,
I'd like Jesus to be here for ever more.

I'd like to have the three Marys[1] — proud boast!
I'd like heaven's folk from every quarter.

I'd like to be a vassal of the Lord's.
Happily has he endured suffering to whom He'd
  grant it — a blessed fief!

---

1. Tradition accords three daughters named Mary to Anna, the
   Virgin's mother; cf. the poem 'Éistidh Riomsa a Mhuire
   Mhór/Mighty Mary, Hear Me', p. 91, p. 93, §§3–9.

GIRALDUS CAMBRENSIS (GERALD OF WALES)

(c. 1146–1223)

from:
TOPOGRAPHIA HIBERNIAE
(The History and Topography of Ireland) (c. 1187)

[On his second visit to Ireland, between April 1185 and Easter 1186, Gerald visited Meath and Kildare. Part II (chapters 33–83) of his *History and Topography* deals firstly with wonders of the natural world, and then with miracles of the saints. Many of the miracles concern punishments inflicted by the Irish saints on Anglo-Norman soldiers and army leaders who had committed outrages against the church. His dim view of Irish Christianity and his identification with the invaders are combined in the heading to his concluding remarks: 'That the saints of this country seem to be of a vindictive cast of mind' (chapter 83).

Almost a third of the section on miracles is given over to Saint Brigit, the only female saint included; about half of this material appears below. Gerald's admiration for her is remarkable. Yet, when speaking of her, his concern for the separation of the sexes in the church takes precedence over other politics. His representation of Kildare's falcon as an example to clerics who should avoid polluting the church through contact with women is particularly striking. In short, Brigit and Kildare seem to have interested Gerald, an avid supporter of church reform, as rhetorical ammunition in the battle for clerical celibacy. The literature abounds with tales of precincts from which women were excluded by male saints or clerics. Gerald pays Brigit a large compliment by fitting his account of the space around her fire into this mould while simultaneously managing to depict the Irish as benighted by association with yet another tall tale.

These excerpts derive from: *Gerald of Wales: The History and Topography of Ireland*, trans. John J. O'Meara (Harmondsworth, Middlesex: Penguin Books, 1982), pp. 81–8.]

CHAPTER 67

Various miracles in Kildare; and first about the fire that never goes out and whose ashes do not increase

In Kildare, in Leinster, which the glorious Brigid has made famous, there are many miracles worthy of being remembered. And the first of them that occurs to one is the fire of Brigid which, they say, is inextinguishable. It is not that it is strictly speaking inextinguishable, but that the nuns and holy women have so carefully and diligently kept and fed it with enough material, that through all the years from the time of the virgin saint until now it has never been extinguished. And although such an amount of wood over such a long time has been burned there, nevertheless the ashes have never increased.

CHAPTER 68

How Brigid keeps the fire on her own night

Although in the time of Brigid there were twenty servants of the Lord there, Brigid herself being the twentieth, only nineteen have ever been here after her death until now, and the number has never increased. They all, however, take their turns, one each night, in guarding the fire. When the twentieth night comes, the nineteenth nun puts the logs beside the fire and says:

'Brigid, guard your fire. This is your night.'

And in this way the fire is left there, and in the morning the wood, as usual, has been burnt and the fire is still alight.

CHAPTER 69

The hedge around the fire that no male may cross

This fire is surrounded by a hedge which is circular and made of withies, and which no male may cross. And if by chance one does dare to enter — and some rash people have at times tried it — he does not escape the divine vengeance. Only women are allowed to blow the fire, and then not with the breath of their mouths, but only with bellows or winnowing forks. Moreover, because of a curse of the saint, goats never have young here.

There are very fine plains hereabouts which are called 'Brigid's pastures', but no one dared to put a plough into them. It is regarded as miraculous that these pastures, even though all the animals of the whole province have eaten the grass down to the ground, nevertheless when morning comes have just as much grass as ever. One might say that of these pastures was it written:

> And all the day-long browsing of thy herds
> Shall the cool dews of one brief night
> repair.[1]

CHAPTER 70

The falcon in Kildare that was tamed and domesticated

From the time of Brigid a noble falcon was accustomed to frequent the place, and to perch on the top of the tower of a church. Accordingly it was called by the people 'Brigid's bird', and it was held in a certain respect by all.

This bird used to do the bidding of the townspeople or the soldiers of the castle, just as if it were tamed and trained in chasing, and because of its own speed, forcing duck and other birds of the land and rivers of the plain of Kildare from the air down to the ground to the great delight of the onlookers. For what place was left to the poor little birds, when men held the land and the waters, and a hostile and terrible tyrant of a bird endangered the air?

A remarkable thing about this bird was that it did not allow any mate into the precincts of the church where it used to live. When the season of mating came, it went far away from its accustomed haunts and, finding a mate in the usual manner in

1. Virgil, *Georgics*, Book II, lines 201–2.

the mountains near Glendalough, indulged its natural instincts there. When that was finished it returned alone to the church.

In this it showed a good example of honour to churchmen, especially when they are entrusted with divine office within the precincts of the church . . .

CHAPTER 77

How an archer who crossed the hedge of Brigid went mad and how another lost his leg

At Kildare an archer of the household of earl Richard crossed over the hedge and blew upon Brigid's fire. He jumped back immediately, and went mad. Whomsoever he met, he blew upon his face and said:

'See! That is how I blew on Brigid's fire.'

And so he ran through all the houses of the whole settlement, and wherever he saw a fire he blew upon it using the same words. Eventually he was caught and bound by his companions, but asked to be brought to the nearest water. As soon as he was brought there, his mouth was so parched that he drank so much that, while still in their hands, he burst in the middle and died.

Another who, upon crossing over to the fire, had put one shin over the hedge, was hauled back and restrained by his companions. Nevertheless the foot that had crossed perished immediately with its shank. Ever afterwards, while he lived, he was lame and feeble as a consequence.

ANONYMOUS

from:
THE LATIN LIFE OF
SAINT ÍTE
(13th century MS)

[Saint Íte's death is recorded in the Annals of Ulster for both 570 and 577. Her feast-day is 15 January. The Latin Life excerpted here derives from the fifteenth-century collection of Irish hagiography known as the Codex Kilkenniensis. However, it is based on very early materials, as the miracle about Brigit's contemporary, a man named Fergus 'whose son still lives', indicates, and it contains few anachronisms.

The beginning of the Life describes Íte's noble parentage and prodigious childhood piety. Originally of the Déisi, an angel reveals to her that she will found a church in Uí Chonaill territory. This was Clúain Credail (Holy Meadow), later known as Cill Íte, anglicized Kileedy, five miles south of Newcastle, County Limerick. It appears to have been an all-female community at the time the Life was written: the text states that as her death approached, Íte 'gathered her virgins about her'. Clearly its date of composition was somewhat later than 570–7, given the reference in it to Íte's tomb and the 'miracles (which still continue there)'.

Female sanctity and spiritual mentoring are represented as normal. Male saints and bishops are happy to avail of Íte's counsel. Clúain Credail is shown to be part of a network of powerful monasteries, while having a special relationship with Clonmacnoise. Since the Life clearly was not written at Clúain Credail itself, Clonmacnoise might be considered as its source.

As Brigit is 'a second Mary' and 'mother of the Gaels', so Íte in this Life is described as 'a second Brigit' and 'mother of the Uí Chonaill'. Particularly noteworthy is her role as protector of the Uí Chonaill in battle, a role referred to also in the annals. In later tradition, Íte comes to be known as Muire na Mumhan, 'Mary of Munster'.

For the Latin original see: Carolus Plummer, *Vitae Sanctorum Hiberniae*, 2 vols (Oxford: Clarendon Press, 1910), pp. 116–30. The following excerpts are derived from a first translation of the entire Life by the late Liam de Paor.]

One day the most blessed virgin Íte went to her mother and, instructed by the Holy Spirit, preached the Divine commands to her. And she asked her mother to speak to her father on her behalf to ask that she, with her father's permission, might be consecrated to Christ. But her father would on no account give such permission, because a powerful young nobleman had asked him for her. This greatly displeased her mother. And he also refused with oaths when others pleaded. At that, Saint Íte, filled with the spirit of prophecy, said to all: 'Leave my father be for the moment. Now he forbids my consecration to Christ. Shortly he will urge and command it.

For he will be forced by my Lord Jesus Christ to send me where I wish to go, to the service of God.' And so it came to pass . . .

Hearing of her great sanctity, the people of Uí Chonaill came with their chief and wished to give all the land round her church to Íte and to God in perpetuity. However, the servant of the Lord had no interest in worldly things and refused to accept any land except four *jugera*[1] for use as a garden. This greatly displeased the chief and his followers, who said: 'Since you don't want to accept this now, it will be given to you after you have gone to heaven.' And so it came to pass. At that time the whole people of Uí Chonaill accepted Saint Íte then and forever as their mother, as the angel had foretold. And the beatific Íte blessed the people and their land with many benedictions, which are fulfilled always. When they had brought great gifts and alms and donations to that church for the use of the holy virgins within it, in perpetual honour of Saint Íte, they returned to their homes greatly rejoicing.

The most blessed virgin Íte assiduously practised fasting, for two, three, or often four days at a time. One day, when she was exhausted from hunger, an angel of the Lord came to her and said: 'You afflict your body without measure: don't do so.' Since she was reluctant to ease the burden of fasting, the angel said: 'God has given you this great grace; that from today until your death you will be fed on heavenly food. And whenever an angel comes offering you a meal, you will be unable not to eat it.' Prostrating herself, blessed Íte gave thanks to God; and she gave of that food to others, whom she considered worthy, to eat. So — there is no doubt about this — until her death she lived on heavenly rations, supplied by angels.

One day a holy virgin in religion came to her and they talked of divine things. And, as they conversed, this virgin said: 'Show us in God's name why you are singled out by God more than the other virgins we know of in this world. It is to you that heavenly bread is given by God; it is your prayers that cure all infirmities; it is you who tell of the past and the future; it is you who rout demons everywhere; it is to you that God's angels speak daily; it is you who continue always without difficulty meditating and praying on the Holy

Trinity.' At which Saint Íte replied: 'You answered your own question when you said: "You continue always without difficulty praying and meditating on the Holy Trinity." God will always be with the person who does that; and since I have done so from infancy, all the other things you have spoken of apply to me.' And that holy virgin, hearing this about prayer and meditation on God from the blessed Íte, returned joyfully to her convent . . .

There came a certain layman, very rich and plausible, to the blessed Íte with a great alms of silver which he laid at the feet of the most holy virgin. She touched the silver in reaching out her hand, and pushed it contemptuously from her feet, not wishing to see it with mind or eye. After she, the handmaid of God, had touched it with her hands, she said to her servants: 'Give me water, so that I may wash the hand that touched the destructive silver.' She hated to touch gold or silver — and all worldly wealth — as if it were dirt. Afterwards, the man who had given the gift questioned the blessed Íte, asking: 'To whom should the offering be given; to the rich and powerful or to the poor and to wayfarers?' God's servant answered: 'What do you ask? To the rich and powerful, for earthly honour? Or to the poor and wayfarers for a return in heaven?' 'If I can't give it to either, what should I do?' asked the man. She answered: 'It is in human power to give one's property for worldly honour or to God for eternal life.' He received her blessing and withdrew, edified by these sayings . . .

A certain holy virgin, wishing to find out how the most holy Íte lived, once went at a certain time to a very secret place where Saint Íte was accustomed to spend some time alone with God, to observe her. Arriving here, she saw three most brilliant suns, just like the sun of this world, lighting up the whole area around. Her terror was such that she could not approach, but turned and fled. The mystery of this portent must remain hidden from us, unless they were the gifts of the Holy Trinity, who made all from nothing and whom the most blessed Íte served assiduously in soul and body.

There was a certain virgin in Mag Life,[2] Rícenn[3] by name, who had a holy fosterling

---

1. i.e. four 'yokes', the ploughland of four oxen, roughly a hectare.

2. Liffey Plain, through which the river Liffey flows.
3. For another story of Rícenn, see pp. 129–30.

named Colmán. This Colmán proceeded to Iona, to Saint Columba, and there was raised to the rank of bishop, and then returned to his homeland. When he came back to his foster-mother, that blessed virgin said to him: 'My son, a grave sickness afflicts a dear daughter of mine. Come with me therefore to Saint Íte, that she may bless you and help your colleague.' He gladly agreed. The chariot horses were yoked and the bishop and his nurturer with their companions took the road. But the devil laid a great ambush for them on the way. The blessed prophetess Íte said to her community: 'Prepare a bath and a meal, because today holy guests are coming to us from the far land of Leinster.' They arrived that day, and Saint Íte said at once: 'Let the bishop come to me and place his hand in blessing on my head.' They marvelled at this, that God's saint knew he was a bishop, which had been told to no one. When they had blessed each other — as it pleased the bishop — Saint Íte, who had not been told about the sick virgin, said: 'Your daughter, whom you have reared: choose whether she should be sound in body and die in sin, or be in pain here but enjoy eternal life; as the apostle said: "My strength is made perfect in weakness."' And they chose, with the girl, that she should suffer now but live forever. And so it came to pass. Turning to Saint Rícenn, Saint Íte said: 'Handmaid of God, your journey would not have gone well had not the bishop been with you, because the demons greatly ensnare our sex.' And when they had spent some days with Saint Íte in true love, they decided to return. Then Saint Rícenn said to the blessed Íte: 'There is a virgin dear to me in the southern part of Ireland. Tell me, my lady, should I go to her now?' Saint Íte said: 'No. Go on with your people on the direct way to your convent, and that virgin will meet you on the border land of Munster and Leinster, since she wishes to join you.' And so it happened. They went their way with her blessing, and at that place the virgin in question met them. And, rejoicing among themselves, they blessed Íte the prophetess . . .

Another time, there was a troublesome business in a house of nuns called Daire Chuiscrig,[4] because of a theft which occurred there. Each of the nuns was questioned about it. Since they all denied it, the abbess of that place said to her daughters: 'Let us go to the blessed Íte, and I believe that this mystery will be cleared up by her.' She was troubled because all opinion had fixed on one innocent virgin of Christ as the culprit. She set out to visit the blessed Íte, and Íte prophetically said to her community: 'Make ready food and a bath, because handmaids of Christ are coming to us today.' When they had arrived, they came in to Saint Íte and kissed her. However, she who was the suspect didn't dare to approach God's handmaid, although she was innocent and had a clear conscience. Then the blessed Íte said to her: 'Come, most innocent virgin of Christ, give me a kiss; it is certain that you are not guilty of the crime for which you are blamed.' As a result of this, the virgins in Christ asked Saint Íte to tell who it was who had stolen that property. She answered: 'She who has been placed among you in penance for another fault; she has done this theft and she has hidden what she stole between the wood screen and the meadow.' And she added: 'It will be found intact, but she who committed the theft will not stay in your convent. For, as the prophet says, "she has a whore's forehead."' And so it all happened. The stolen property was found, and the wretched one abandoned her habit and lived in fornication, ravished by woodsmen.

Another time a certain man called Fergus, whose son still lives, was brought to Saint Íte suffering from the most grievous afflictions of eyes and body. It was hard to tell if he was alive or dead. But he, who had been sick to death, his eyes blind, given up by those around him, was returned sound in body and with the keenest sight, and until his death lived in good bodily health through the prayer and blessing of the most saintly Íte . . .

Another time the abbots Saint Lugthigern[5] and Saint Laisrén[6] said to one another: 'Let us go to visit the servant of God Saint Íte.' At which a foolish youth said to them: 'Why are you, great and wise men, going to that old hag?' They rebuked him, saying: 'You speak badly, brother; but the prophetess of God will know now what

---

4. A monastery in Munster.

5. A saint associated with Thomond (north Munster) whose feast is on 28 April.
6. Possibly the sixth-century saint known also as Mo-Laisse, and associated with Devinish, an island in lower Lough Erne, near Enniskillen, County Fermanagh.

you have said.' The saints then set off to Saint Íte, bringing the youth with them. When they arrived at the gate of the monastery, the virgins knew Lugthigern, because he had often visited the most blessed Íte, and they went in and announced the arrival to Christ's spouse, Saint Íte, saying: 'This is a good day for us, because Saint Lugthigern visits you.' The holy mother replied: 'He is not less in the sight of God who comes with him, and whom you didn't greet because you don't know him, Laisrén son of Colmán.' Saint Íte had never seen him but through the Spirit she knew him by name and merit. And when they came in to the blessed Íte for her blessing, she said to the youth: 'Why have you come to the old hag, when you asked what brings the saints to me?' Then the saints pleaded on his behalf and he did penance. Having stayed three days they returned home with Saint Íte's permission and blessing . . .

After these events war was waged on Uí Chonaill by many enemies. In the presence of their mother, the blessed Íte, this people, through her, prayed for God's help against the great multitude of their enemies. Then the blessed Íte, in her compassion for them, prayed, saying: 'Holy Trinity and inseparable Unity, Father, Son and Holy Spirit, help these few unfortunate people of mine, who kindly received me into their territory in your name and accepted me as their mother; for no human aid can avail against this great host from West Munster.' The Uí Chonaill, trusting in the prayer of the most blessed Íte, went out boldly against the host of enemies and fought furiously. And, boldly exchanging mutual wounds, they routed the enemy, obviously by God's help through the most holy Íte's prayers; the Uí Chonaill did great slaughter among them. And, returning after their great victory, they gave thanks to God and to the most blessed Íte their mother for the victory she had brought them. The few were Christ's victors over the many because Saint Íte prayed for them . . .

One day Saint Íte said to her daughters: 'At this hour a soul in our community is being stained. Go and enquire closely as to which of us is being carried off from our flock by the insidious wolf.' Then the community of the most blessed virgin investigated to see what wicked-ness had been committed, but they were unable to discover who among them had sinned.

Gathered before the blessed Íte, the whole community one by one declared: 'It was not I who committed that sin.' Saint Íte, filled with the spirit of prophecy, said to one who denied like the rest that she was guilty: 'You committed fornication today.' And she wouldn't repent or confess, but left, with the shame of her sin. She wandered through many places and, being made a slave-woman in Connacht, she bore a daughter. After a long time had passed Saint Íte said to her community: 'Our sister, who was once free but is now enslaved in the household of a druid in Connacht, is now repentant, and if she were free she would faithfully make amends.' After this Saint Íte sent messengers to the blessed Brendan the abbot, who lived in the province of Connacht, asking that he might demand the freeing of that woman. And Brendan, humbly obedient to the instructions of the spouse of Christ, went to the King of Connacht on her behalf and secured the freeing of the woman and her daughter. He sent her and her daughter to the blessed Íte, who received them joyfully. And that woman, penitent, remained in the monastery of the most pious mother Íte in holiness with her daughter until her death.

One day the venerable and aged virgin Íte gathered her virgins about her and told them her death was near, saying gently to them: 'The Abbot of Clonmacnoise, Mac Nisse, has sent messengers to me to collect water blessed by me and bring it back to Abbot Óengus, who is very ill, hoping to cure his illness if he should drink water I have blessed. I will bless the water right away; the messengers are sad, and you are to tell them that I blessed this water. If I should die before they arrive here, and before they return home, Saint Óengus will go to heaven.' And that is what happened, just as the most blessed and prophetic Íte had foretold.

After this, the most holy mother Íte was seized by illness and began blessing and counselling her city and the people of Uí Chonaill who had accepted her as their mother. She was visited by numerous saints of both sexes, and the most glorious virgin, enjoying the sight of the Holy Trinity, passed away on January 15 among choirs of saints and her soul, replete with numberless virtues and wonders, was met by rejoicing angels. The multitudes gathered in from all around, miracles (which still continue there) were worked, and after the solemnity of masses, her most blessed body was brought to the tomb in her monastery which she, Saint Íte, a second Saint Brigit, had made exemplary by her merits and she entered the kingdom of Our Lord Jesus Christ, who lives and reigns with God the Father and the Holy Spirit, God for ever and ever. Amen.

ÍSUCÁN
(Saint Íte and the Child Jesus)
(Old Irish)

[The teaching that all women shared figuratively in Mary's motherhood of Christ was sometimes literalized, no doubt helped by the fact that babies and young children were fostered in women's monastic houses. Most copies of the following late Old Irish poem, supposedly spoken by Saint Íte (modern 'Íde'), are accompanied by the intriguing anecdote which precedes it here. In this, she is named by the familiar form 'M'Íde', literally 'My Íde'. The anecdote describes how Íte earned the privilege of becoming nurse to Christ by first being host to a grotesque familiar. It is tempting to interpret her illness as a medieval rationalization of the ravages of untreated breast cancer.

The anecdote is translated from the Book of Lecan, f. 166v. For a comprehensive discussion (with edition and translation) of the poem, see E.G. Quin, 'The Early Irish Poem *Ísucán*', *Cambridge Medieval Celtic Studies*, no. 1 (summer 1981), pp. 39–52. This new translation is much indebted to his work.]

M'Íde daughter of Cenn Fáelad, son of Cormac son of Conchobar son of Conall son of Óengus son of Art Corp son of Cairpre Rígrón son of Fiachu Suidge. One day, M'Íde was out on her rampart and God endowed her with miraculous power, or else much illness from the wretched people of the world beset her and she herself took ill, i.e. a beetle was sucking her and it was as big as a lapdog and it gnawed away her whole side. And yet no one knew that was happening to her except God. Once she went out and the beetle came out of its den after her. The nuns saw it and they killed it. Then, because the beetle did not come, she came and asked: 'Where has my little fosterling gone and who has interfered with it?' 'Do not deprive us of heaven,' said the nuns, 'it is

we who killed it for we did not know that it was not harmful.' 'However that may be,' said she, 'on account of that deed no nun [of you] will ever be my successor, and I will take nothing from my Lord,' said she, 'unless He give me His son in the form of a child to foster.' And the angel who used come and go from her to God visited her. 'It is high time for me,' she said to him on each occasion he came to address her. And he said to her: 'You will be given everything you ask.' And Christ came to her in the form of a child. And then she said:

Ísucán
  alar limm im dísertán
cía beith clérech co llín sét
  is bréc uile acht Ísucán.

Altram alar limm im thaig
  ní altram nach doér-rathaig
Ísu co Feraib Nime
  frim chride cach n-oénadaig.

Ísucán oc mo bithmaith
  ernaid ocus ní maithmech
in rí con-icc na uili
  cen a guidi bid aithrech.

Ísu úasal ainglide
  nícon clérech dergnaide
alar lemm im dísertán
  Ísu mac na Ebraide.

Maic na ruirech maic na ríg
  im thír cía do-ísatán
ní úaidib saílim sochor
  is tochu limm Ísucán.

Canaid cóir a ingena
  d'fhiur dliges for císucán
attá na purt túasacán
  cía beith im ucht Ísucán.

TRANSLATION

Jesukin
is whom I have as fosterling,
great wealth a cleric-child might bring
but all is false save Jesukin.

The fosterage I undertake
is not of any bondsman's child:
Jesu and the Folk of Heaven
are next my heart all through the night.

Jesu, for my eternal good,
bestows but looks for due return;
all will rue who do not pray
the Omnipotent King.

It is no ordinary child
I foster in my little cell
but Jesu, noble, angel-like,
son of the Judaean girl.

Sons of sovereigns and kings
may come to me for coshering,
but I set little store by them —
I've hopes of more from Jesukin.

For Him to whom your render is due,
maidens, sing in unison!
Jesu is at home on high,
yet here He lies — in my bosom.

from:
THE IRISH LIFE OF
SAINT BRENDAN
(17th century MS)

[Saint Brendan of Clonfert died, according to the annals, in either 577 or 583. He was reputed to have made the voyage described (and disseminated throughout medieval Europe) in the Latin text *Navigatio Brendani*. The Life from which the following extracts are taken says that, before setting out on the ocean, he took advice from his foster-mother, Saint Íte. She had fostered him until he was old enough to learn to read, and he returned to her when the time came to found a monastery of his own. The implication is that he expected the abbess to devise a monastic rule for him. Not only does she disappoint him in this, she warns him against taking his rule from any woman whatsoever. The solution to Brendan's dilemma — since it is does not occur to him to derive a rule from a male monastery — is provided by the angel.

The Early Modern Irish Life, which conflates older materials and traditions, was edited and translated by Charles Plummer, *Bethada Náem nÉrenn. Lives of the Irish*

Saints, 2 vols (Oxford: Oxford University Press, 1922, 1992), vol. 1, pp. 44–95; vol. 2, pp. 44–92. The following extracts (with minor changes in presentation) are from vol. 2, pp. 45–8.]

§9. [After Brendan's birth] his family took him with them, and he was with them for a year being nurtured. At the end of the year Bishop Erc took him to his foster-mother, Íte, and he was with her [five] years. And the nun loved him exceedingly, because she saw the attendance of angels above him, and the grace of the Holy Spirit evidently abiding on him. And Brendan was always smiling at the nun whenever he saw her.

§10. So one day Íte asked him: 'What is it that pleases thee, O holy child?' said she. He answered: 'Thou,' said he, 'I see thee talking to me continuously, and numberless other virgins like thee, nurturing me in turn.' But these were really angels in the form of virgins.

§11. After this, at the end of his five years, Brendan studied with Bishop Erc; and to Íte the time seemed long without him. Then he learnt his psalms . . .

§18. Now after learning the canon of the Old and New Testaments, Brendan wished to write out and learn the rule of the saints of Erin. Bishop Erc gave him leave to go and learn this rule, for he knew that it was of God that this counsel had come to him. And he said to him: 'Come back to me, and bring the rules with thee, that thou mayest receive orders at my hands.'

§19. When he went to consult his foster-mother, Íte, she said the same thing to him, viz., that he should learn the rule of the saints of Ireland. And she said to him: 'Do not learn of women or of virgins, lest thou be reproached in regard to them' . . .

§23. . . . Brendan proceeded to Magh nAí.[1] An angel met him on the road, and said to him: 'Write down,' said he, 'from my mouth the words of devotion.' Brendan wrote from the mouth of the angel all the rules of holy Church, and all these rules are still extant.

---

1.   The plain around Croghan (Crúachain), County Roscommon.

from:
THE LATIN LIFE OF SAINT DARERCA ALIAS MO-NINNE
(14th century MS)

[The death of Saint Darerca is recorded under the year 517. Her feast day is 6 July. She founded the monastery of Cell Sléibe Cuilinn (Church of Slieve Gullion), anglicized Killeevy, in modern County Armagh.

The Latin Life excerpted here describes her as a woman who was willingly counselled by holy men and who deferred at all times to episcopal authority. It relates her career as a progress: first of all, she lived a regulated life in her parents' house; later, together with eight virgins and a widow, she joined a double-house ruled by an abbot; later still, she served in a community of 150 nuns in her home territory; finally, she withdrew to a more remote place at the foot of Slieve Gullion and founded her own monastery. Darerca is ascribed a strong character — strongly conformist but highly intelligent and an advocate of learning, keen to withdraw from the world but an able administrator, submissive to the clerical grades but 'within her woman's body a manlike spirit'.

The Life is found in the fourteenth-century Codex Salmanticensis. It is an abridgement of an earlier document which, in turn, reproduces a document which may well date back to the early seventh century. The final sections describing events that happened after Darerca's death seem to consist of a series of notes added to the text of the Life in the monastery at Killeevy. The record of the first three abbesses to succeed her there was probably completed during the rule of the fourth who, according to a later list, died in 624. Thus the original Life was probably written before that date.

The original text was published by W.W. Heist (ed.), *Vitae Sanctorum Hiberniae ex codice olim Salmanticensi nunc Bruxellensi* (Brussels: Société des Bollandistes, 1965), pp. 83–95. A translation of all but §§20 and 21 of this was provided by Liam de Paor in his *St Patrick's World* (Dublin: Four Courts Press, 1993), pp. 281–94. The following extracts are found ibid. Footnotes 2–15 are by de Paor.]

[Her childhood and her baptism by St Patrick]

The venerable virgin named Darerca, also known as Moninna,[1] descended from the Conaille.[2] Her father was an excellent man named Mocteus. She was born in Mag Coba,[3] and fostered, as was befitting, in the care of conscientious parents. By the inspiration of God's grace, she determined at a tender age to preserve the unfading flower of virginity, from infancy for as long as she might live. Some years after her birth it came to pass that St Patrick arrived in the province in which she had been born. There, when a number of people had been brought to him through the good offices of devout men, to be washed at the baptismal font and confirmed in faith by the imposition of hands, one of the gathering crowd was St Darerca, who came and made herself known to the bishop. The saintly pontiff was filled with the Holy Spirit: he observed her closely and understood her fervent desire to serve God. Having distributed blessings, along with suitable counsel, he received her — who was already confirmed by her own virginal state — at the pool of Bríu,[4] whose name, translated into Latin, means 'generosity' or 'abundance'. This signifies that she was to be a fountain of living waters of the spirit from which many measures of life would be drawn.

[St Patrick forms a community of pious women]

The same pontiff, then, having commenced her instruction in the way of salvation, approved her virginal style of living as a worthy one, and directed her to come together with other virgins to whom she should teach the fear of God, so that — supported by their help and encouraged by their comfort — she could better bring to a conclusion the good work that she had undertaken. Then he entrusted the responsibility of protecting them and teaching them the psalms to a devout priest who lived near her parents. She spent a little time under this master, understanding what she was told without any difficulty because of the natural subtlety of her intelligence, and tenaciously retaining what she was taught because of the capacity of her memory; and within a short space of time she had learnt a great deal. There were with her at first, as they tell, eight virgins, as well as one widow who had a small boy named Luger. Darerca adopted the child as her foster son and when she had thoroughly accustomed him to the ways of the church, she raised him to the high dignity of a bishop. He

---

1. A Latinization of the Irish name Mo-Ninne.
2. In north County Louth.
3. The plain of Coba, in northwestern County Down.
4. Not known: somewhere in Mag Coba.

crowned his good works as a leader of the whole of his people — the Conaille — by building the church of Rúscach[5] in honour of God.

[She goes to stay with St Ibar]

So this virgin lived for some time with her parents; but since she could find no convents of nuns in her own country — although it had been converted to the Faith — she decided to leave her parents and relations and go away. In fact she did not wish to have her devout intentions vitiated through empty discussions and inept conversations with lay people or through frequent encounters with her parents. Therefore the virgin of Christ, placing her trust in the Lord, set out, along with the eight other virgins and the widow — together with some others — to make her way to the reverend pontiff Ibar, who was settled in the western islands of Ireland; for that is what she had longed to do. When St Darerca with her company reached the man of God, she spent a long time under his rule with many other virgins.

[She visits St Brigid]

Afterwards this bishop moved from those islands, crossed the south of Ireland and arrived at the island they call 'Little Ireland'[6] (where finally he died). Christ's sheep followed their shepherd. When they arrived in the country of the Lagin, the people told them of the fame of the holy virgin Brigid. Learning this, St Darerca, with her virgins, obtained their master's permission and turned aside to visit St Brigid. And it is said that she spent some time with her, accepting no honour but always acting with humility. She lowered herself to such an extent that God raised her correspondingly so much above all others — through the merit of her wonderful works — so that she is even reckoned second only to Brigid for holiness, for worthy practices and for her gift of virtue.

[She receives gifts and gives them to the poor]

Then, in her obedience to the regulations of the nuns, she was made keeper of the guesthouse, on the instructions of the abbess. And she performed the duties of this office diligently, and was agreeable in all matters. The All-Highest indeed conferred on her the grace to bring health to the sick and to expel demons from those who were possessed. Such reputation for signs and wonders did she have among the ordinary people, that she was revered by all, so much so that every day, because of her sanctity, many came to her with food and offerings; but, placing her trust in God, she kept none of this to herself, but gave it all, for Christ, to the poor who approached her . . .

[She returns to St Ibar]

After this, she went on to the bishop, Ibar, and lived under his direction in Ard Conais.[7] There were many virgins and widows in the community there, as well as queens and noble matrons who gathered round her, to whom she was mistress, showing them by word and deed how to live well in all goodness . . .

[She turns water into wine]

Afterwards the virgin of Christ left for the northern part of Ireland to visit her relations, like the lost sheep of the house of Israel. At the end of her journey she came at last to the plain of Muirtheimhne,[8] where the dwelling place of her people formerly was. This people, endowed in ancient times more than the neighbouring tribes with skill in the magical arts, had nevertheless become Christian, by God's grace operating through St Patrick. Then — it is told with complete certainty — when the virgin of Christ lived here, she never looked at a man. If she had to leave her cell for some compelling necessity, such as, for example, to visit the sick, or to free a captive from prison, either by persuasion or by paying a ransom, she made her journey by night; and it was her custom to keep her face veiled in case she might encounter someone on the way . . .

[She spends a time at Faughart and moves to Killeevy]

It is said that when the holy virgin returned (as we have already told) to her native province, she

---

5. Rooskey, Cooley, County Louth.
6. Beg Ériu, now Beggary, at the mouth of Wexford harbour.
7. Not known: presumably near Wexford.
8. In County Louth.

first lived on the mountain of Facharta.[9] In that place she faithfully served God with her sisters, to the number of one hundred and fifty. One night she heard the sounds of a wedding feast and feared the large number of voices she seemed to hear. In the end she crossed over to a certain place situated on the slope of the mountain of Culind,[10] so that there she could listen to the sweet discourse of her Spouse without any earthly impediment. And there she laid the foundations of her church for the handmaids of Christ.[11]

It is said that, like a daughter of John the Baptist, or the prophet Elijah, she waged war most strenuously in this desert place, clad in sackcloth like a stern hermit, while bound indissolubly to her sisters by their most steady love and support. It is not to be doubted, indeed, that, like a taper placed on a candlestick, shining with the light of her miracles, she drove away by the effect of her devoted prayers the foul clouds of northern darkness. It is not possible, however, to reckon up or to know in full how many the prayers and vigils, how great and how frequent the manual works she imposed on herself, or how fierce the battles in which she sweated to overcome demons, or how brilliantly she shone through her miracles. For she did her best, as far as she could, to conceal the good deeds she did from public notice, except for those which dire necessity compelled her to reveal. She followed in the footsteps of the earlier hermits to such an extent that she dug the earth and sowed it with her own hands: she contained within her woman's body a manlike spirit. The hoe she used for digging was kept for many years after her death in her monastery in her honour. They also kept for a long time, with great reverence, her badger-skin garment — more precious than gowns of silk — and the wooden comb with which, once a year (on the Feast of the Lord), it was her custom to comb her hair . . .

[She sends the nun Brignat to Whithorn for a while]

It is said that a certain virgin named Brignat, among other handmaids of God, lived with the holy virgin. Darerca, contemplating the signs of this woman's future sanctity, was inspired to send her to the island of Britain to follow the rules of the community of the monastery of Rosnatense.[12] Brignat, since she was subject to holy obedience, set out without delay and arrived at the designated place without any pause on the way. She was careful to comply with the direction of her holy mother, and she stayed in that monastery, in a certain little lodging in which she read the Psalms and other necessary books. To fulfil holy obedience, with God's help she made the return voyage safely just as she had made the outward passage, and came back to her abbey.

[She revives a novice who died suddenly]

After this, St Darerca, by her devoted prayers, was found worthy to bring to life a certain girl, a novice, who had been suddenly struck dead. And the girl lived for many years after that.

[A nun who accepted shoes from a man causes the visits of angels to cease in Killeevy]

Furthermore, as is proven to be true by the witness of those who knew her, angels often visited her and held familiar conversations with her. This is shown with certainty by the following miracle. For one night, when the sisters were coming in to celebrate Matins but had not yet begun the sacred office, she clapped her hands and called for silence, saying 'O blessed Lord, we must not pass over in silence what has happened to us tonight! For our prayers up to now could barely rise above the ridge of the church roof before angels would come as guests to visit us; now, however, tonight I don't see them. I have no doubt that this has happened to us because of sins we have committed. Let us examine our consciences as best we can.' Hearing this, the terror-stricken nuns, trusting more in their mistress than in themselves, threw themselves to the ground. One of the widows, who had only lately come from worldly society, stood up and said: 'Oh, mistress, I admit that my sin is the cause of this business. I confess that I accepted a pair of shoes from a man with whom I was unlawfully joined. I forgot that I had not your

9. Faughart, County Louth.
10. Slieve Gullion, in County Armagh.
11. Cell Sléibe Cuilinn; Killeevy, County Armagh.

12. Whithorn, in Galloway.

permission, and I have them on my feet because of the cold.' The holy prophetess said to her: 'It would be better that these shoes should be dropped into the depths of the sea rather than that we should suffer the absence of the angels because of them.' And one of the sisters — the same Brignat whom we mentioned a short while ago — supported by some of the others, said to St Darerca: 'Go and hide those shoes in some abyss, where no one could find them.' While they went to follow this advice, the other nuns completed the vigil. At the end, the blessed virgin said: 'We should give thanks to God from devout hearts, because now our prayers, with nothing to impede them, can reach heaven, and because our dear guests are no longer unwilling to be present — since that which met divine displeasure has been disposed of.' From this it is plain that she understood the principle of keeping morally pure, how she perceived clearly that her prayers were being impeded by minor sins, and how she was as quick to see to the correction of small matters as she was to prevent the growth of major faults . . .

[She speaks to her people on her death-bed]

After these happenings, as the day approached on which St Darerca was to pay the ultimate debt of nature, the worsening of her illness, which had long been hidden, was made known and caused enormous grief in the surrounding populace. As a result the king Eugenius son of Conaille, who at this time ruled over three territories — Muirtheimne,[13] Cuailgne[14] and Cobha[15] — along with the magnates of other peoples, and with great crowds, came as far as the immediate vicinity of the monastery, all having the same wish to visit her. And they all appealed to the bishop Herbeus, whom we have already mentioned, to go to the virgin Darerca, and faithfully to convey to her the message of the whole people, saying as follows: 'Lady, we appeal to you on the grounds of our common blood' (many of her own people were there, the king Eugenius himself being of the Conaille on his mother's side) 'through which we have an affinity

both in the flesh and in the spirit, to go so far as to grant us the space of one year in which you will live still with us on this earth. And that you will not orphan us by dying this year. For we are quite certain that whatever you ask of God you will straightaway obtain. In fact, anyone among us who is a man of substance will give a handmaid free to the Lord in exchange for your life. And every man at arms will gladly give a cow of full age.'

To them she replied, through the bishop: 'May you be blessed by the Lord Who made heaven and earth, you who lowered yourselves to come and visit me in my infirmity. If you had asked this yesterday or the day before yesterday, perhaps God's mercy would have granted your request, but today I am unable to accede to you. Venerable guests who are listening to our dialogue, Peter and Paul, have been sent to guide my soul worthily to God, and they are now here present with me. I see them holding between them a kind of linen cloth, made with marvellous art and interwoven with gold. I must go with them to my Lord Who sent them for me. But Almighty God, to whom a ready good will is as good as the deed, will return you suitable compensation. God further will grant to you what you asked for me — that my life be redeemed — but will give a life instead to one of you. Bless you in the name of the Lord Who created heaven and earth and all things: bless you, I say, and your wives and children and your possessions. I leave you my badgerskin garment and my rake and some other tools. Have no doubt that if you carry these with you against enemies who come to plunder your territories, God will grant you, through them to be victorious. But do not presume to cross your borders in order to ravage other territories (unless perhaps you are compelled by superior power) or the just punishment of God will descend upon you. Do not be sad at my departure. For I believe that Christ, with Whom I now go to stay, will give you whatever I ask of Him in heaven no less than when I prayed to Him on earth.'

[Her death]

Having passed on these and similar words through the bishop Herbeus, she said farewell

13. North County Louth.
14. The Cooley peninsula in north-east County Louth.
15. North-west County Down.

one by one, calling each person by name. But the populace, hearing this, cast away their weapons, lamenting and keening, and raised an enormous wail to the sky. Finally, comforted by the address of the bishop, they returned to their own homes. Having arranged everything for the future of her monastery, and having foretold, by the spirit of prophecy, the sequence of many things that would happen in time to come, then, on the day on which these things were concluded, that is the 6th of July, the octave of the feast of the blessed apostles Peter and Paul — her good fight fought and her course happily completed — she migrated to Christ, with Whom she reigns for ever and ever. Amen . . .

[St Darerca in heaven moves a tree for Abbess Derlasra]

After the death of St Darerca, Bia was abbess, as Darerca herself had directed; then Indiu; then Derlasra, who was forty years at the head of the monastery. In her time a famous miracle occurred. She had almost finished a work which she had begun — the building of a church, in the style of the Irish nation, of planed planks, with careful workmanship, in the monastery of St Darerca. However, a timber was missing up to now: the piece called *spina* in Latin ['spine', that is, 'druimm' — 'ridge-pole'], the member which was placed on the apex of a building to join together the two planes of the pitched rood. The craftsmen had to go into the woods to find a suitable piece to solve this problem. They found it at last, but in a remote and difficult place. There was no way in which they could remove the felled tree because of the impracticability of the place. The abbess knew of this and was losing hope of getting the timber to the monastery; so she applied to St Darerca as advocate, and said: 'St Darerca, then, for whom this house is being built on earth, is now living in heaven. She can help us if she will.'

The very next day the ridge-pole already mentioned was discovered, located on a level spot beside the monastery, where harm could come neither to beasts of burden nor to humans. Afterwards, the carpenters were curious to see if there were any traces along the way of the passage of this pole: they found some broken branches near the top of the tree-trunk. From

this it is to be understood that divine power, through the service of angels, had done what was beyond human power. That tree, found on the highest crags, could not have been brought over the terrain from so steep and high a place by human art, but was borne down through the air without difficulty by the art of angels.

from:
THE LATIN LIFE OF SAMTHANN
(14th century MS)

[Saint Samthann, who died in 739, is the latest in time of the Irish female saints. Her feast day is 19 December. She was abbess of the monastery of Clonbroney (Clúain Brónaig), near Granard, County Longford, which, according to her Life, was founded by Saint Fainche. An early list of the communities subject to Saint Brigit includes Clonbroney and names Fainder as its head; this may be an error for Fainche, or vice versa.

Overcoming parental objections to a vow of virginity or evading the plans of those who stood to profit from her marriage is standard in the female saint's life, but none of the other Irish lives begins the narrative at this point or presents the issue as artfully. Adaptation of an anecdote deriving from the Life of Saint Martin of Tours for use in reference to Samthann (§3) is further evidence of the Life's literariness. Yet Samthann's Life contains many historical data and there is no evidence that those named as her contemporaries were otherwise. The miracle involving Níall (d. 778) son of Fergal, king of Tara, may be understood to have happened after Samthann's death. The fact that Níall is spoken of in the past tense indicates that the Life was written sometime after his death. Samthann's advocacy of learning as a basis for spirituality is noteworthy. Elsewhere, she is portrayed as having been an inspiration to the leaders of the *Céli Dé* movement (p. 106).

The following excerpts were translated by Colm Luibhéid from the Latin original in: Carolus Plummer, *Vitae Sanctorum Hiberniae*, vol. 2, pp. 253–4; 258; 260–1.]

§1. The holy and admirable virgin Samthann came of Ulster stock. Her father was Díamrán and her mother was called Columb. Crídán, king of Cairpre[1] was her fosterer and when she was growing up he betrothed her to a noble. Before

---

1. A kingdom in Tethbae (in Southern Uí Néill); Clúain Brónaig is situated in it.

the marriage rites were celebrated this man, in the middle of night, gazed with open eyes on what seemed a ray of sunlight which came through the roof of the house and on to the bed in which Samthann and the two daughters of the king were lying. Astounded by the vision of unexpected light at such an hour, he quickly got up and approached the bed of his betrothed. He found that her face was suffused with that ray of light. It was the greatest joy to him that he should acquire such a wife, someone on whom such heavenly light was poured out. On the following night, after the marriage celebrations, the two of them entered the bedchamber in accordance with custom. Her husband said to her: 'Take your clothes off, so that we may come together as one'. But she answered: 'Please grant me a respite until all those in the house are asleep.' The husband agreed and after a little while he fell asleep. She then began to pray intensely, beating at the doors of divine mercy, asking that God keep her virginity unharmed. And God heard her prayers and the Lord accepted her plea. Around midnight their fortification was seen by those outside to be on fire and an immense flame ascended from the mouth of the holy virgin to the roof of the house. A great clamour arose outside in the fortification. Everyone in the house was awakened from sleep and all rushed to put out the fire.

§2. Meanwhile the holy virgin Samthann fled, and she went into hiding among nearby ferns. The fire disappeared straightaway without having harmed the fortification. In the morning her fosterer, the king of Cairpre, got up and went to look for the virgin. When he had found her she said to the king: 'Was your fortification burnt during the past night?' 'No.' 'I thank God it was not destroyed by fire,' she said. Then she addressed the king: 'Why have you wished to hand over this poor servant of Almighty God in betrothal to someone and without her consent?' Then the king said: 'I will not hand you over to another man. Let the decision be in your hands.' And she said: 'This is my decision, that you offer me as a bride not to a man but to God.' Then, bending the knee, the king declared: 'We join you to the God whom you have chosen and we offer you to Him as a bride.' Freed now to be a dedicated virgin, she entered the monastery of

Cocnat, which is called Ernaide.[2] Spending some time there she fulfilled the duties of stewardship eagerly and faithfully.

§3. One day the holy virgin Samthann got up at very early dawn. She heard the voice of a leper coming from the other side of the pond and crying to be brought across the water. Obeying his wishes, the faithful virgin, guiding a small raft with her staff, carried him over. He lamented his poverty and his nakedness, and she gave him a cow and calf together with the greater part of her own cloak. She was like another Martin.[3] When she asked him where he had come from, he answered that it was from the monastery of Saint Ultán.[4] Having said this he vanished. Then something amazing happened. The cow and calf which the leper had received were found in the byre where they had been previously. And in the dress of holy Samthann there was not a trace of it having been torn . . .

§17. Níall son of Fergal,[5] king of Ireland, sought the staff of the holy virgin Samthann so that he might adorn it with gold and silver. But because the wood in it was bent and old, the work of ornamentation seemed to the craftsmen to be inappropriate. On the following night the staff was placed on the wall above the bed of the king. But because of the devotion of the faithful king and because of the merits of his servant Samthann, Christ made straight the wood which had been previously crooked, and no trace appeared of its having been bent. The delight of the king was great because faithfulness to God had done what human ability could not do. And that was why the king and all his people held the staff in the greatest honour . . .

§24. A teacher named Tairchellach[6] came once to the virgin and said to her: 'I am planning to leave

---

2. A monastery near Lifford, County Donegal, anglicized 'Urney'. Cocnat is probably identical with the Cocnat named in the 'Litany of the Virgins', p. 88.
3. i.e. Saint Martin of Tours.
4. Almost certainly Ultán, brother of the Irishman Saint Fursa (d. c. 649), who was buried at Péronne in north-east France, where Ultán became abbot.
5. Niall Frassach (d. 778), son of Fergal, Cenél nEógain King of Tara. For a tale about him, see 'Niall Frassach's Act of Truth', p. 220.
6. Perhaps Tairchelltach *Sapiens* 'Sage' who died in 760 (Annals of Ulster).

aside my study and to give up teaching.' She said to him: 'If you neglect the study of things spiritual what can concentrate your mind so as to keep it from wandering?' Again the teacher spoke: 'I want to travel on a pilgrimage.' She replied: 'If God cannot be found on this side of the sea then let us all go travelling. But God is near to all those who call on Him, and so there is no need for us to travel. For one can reach the kingdom of heaven from every land.'

§25. These few things must be said, for who could list all the riches God gave her? She was filled with the grace of good works and adorned with the beauty of every virtue. All of her life was enriched by good example. She was a faithful guide to those under her authority and a servant of most humble demeanour. She was poor in spirit and in worldly goods. She refused to own land, and at any one time she never had more than six cows. She looked after everyone — and her servants especially — with eager charity. As one example among many of this, alms offered to her were divided among her sisters and her own share was added in; however many sisters were living together her portion was reckoned in with theirs. She was cheerful in giving help, modest in receiving, faithful in peace-making, efficient in assistance. Why list everything? No task of piety passed her by. And so it was that holy and just as she was in the presence of Christ, her betrothed, she completed her journey through this present life and received from him the crown which from eternity he had prepared for those who love Him.

§26. On the night when she yielded her spirit to heaven the holy abbot Laisrén whom we have mentioned above[7] . . . saw two moons, one of which came down to him . . . Recognising her to be beautiful as a star he said: 'Blessed are you, Samthann, faithful servant of God, for you are about to enter into the joy of the Lord, your betrothed.' At that she vanished, ascended into heaven, where she enjoys eternal life forever.

7. i.e. in §10 of the Life which refers to the 'abbot of Daiminis' without naming him. Daiminis monastery was founded by Saint Laisrén alias Molaisse, who died in 564 or 571. It seems likely that a later abbot of the same name is intended here. A Molaisse of Daiminis appears in 'Notes on the Customs of Tallaght', as does Samthann see pp. 105–6. A Molaisse of Daiminis who is contemporary with Diarmaid (d. 664), son of Áed Sláne, is found in 'The Wooing of Becfhola'; see pp. 210–13.

LITANY OF THE VIRGINS
(Old Irish)

[This litany, or *lorica*, is found in the twelfth-century Book of Leinster. All these saints probably had well-established cults but, apart from Brigit, Íte (if 'Midnat' is a pet form of her name), Darerca (here called Mo-Ninne) and Samthann, whose lives are excerpted above, they cannot now be identified with certainty. Cocnat is probably the person of that name in §2 of the Life of Samthann (p. 87), and Lasair is probably the patron of Kilronan (Cell Rónáin), County Roscommon (whose Irish-language Life is published in *Ériu*, vol. 5 [1911], pp. 73–108).

The text was edited and translated by Charles Plummer, who also suggested various possible identifications: see his *Irish Litanies* (London [*s.n.*], 1925), pp. 92–3, 121–3. Apart from the normalization of name-forms, the following translation is as ibid.]

I place myself under the protection
Of Mary the pure Virgin,
Of Brigit, bright and glowing,
Of Cúach of great purity,
Of Mo-Ninne and Mídnat,
Of Scíre, Sinche, and Samthann,
Of Caite, Cúach, and Coímell,
Of Craine, Cop and Cocnat,
Of Ness the glorious of Ernaide,[1]
Of Derfáilind and Becnat,
Of Cíar and Cróine and Coílfhind,
Of Lasair, Lóch and Luaithrinn,
Of Ronn, Rónnat and Rígnach,
Of Sárnat, Segnat and Soidelb,
And of the virgins all together
    North, South, East, West.

I place myself under the protection
Of the excellent Trinity,
Of the prophets, of the true apostles,
Of the monks, of the martyrs,
Of the widows and the confessors,
Of the virgins, of the faithful,
Of the saints and the holy angels;
To protect me against every ill,
Against demons and evil men,
Against thunder (?) and bad weather,
Against sickness and false lips,

1. For another reference to this monastery, see p. 87, n. 2.

Against cold and hunger,
Against distress and dishonour,
Against contempt and despair,
Against misfortune and wandering,
Against the plague of the tempestuous doom,
Against the evil of hell with its many monsters.
And its multitude of torments.

from:
THE INFANCY GOSPEL
(Late Middle Irish)

[The most important collection of stories about Mary's birth, upbringing and adulthood was the work known as the Gospel (or Protoevangelium) of Saint James, originally written in Hebrew. A Latin form of this apocryphal text was known in Ireland from the twelfth century, and perhaps from the ninth. A Late Middle Irish version of it is found in the fifteenth-century manuscript *Liber Flavus Fergusiorum*, and the following extract (in translation) derives from this source.

The extract gives an arresting account of the actual birth of Christ — the reality of Mary's maternity — in the words of the midwife who attended her. The preceding paragraphs tell that Joseph and Mary, together with Joseph's three sons — Simeon, Ameon and James of the Knees — travelled from Nazareth in Galilee to Bethlehem in Judah to pay Caesar's tribute. When they reached the outskirts of Bethlehem, Joseph brought his entourage to a cave lodging, so that Mary could rest before giving birth.

The translation is from: Máire Herbert and Martin McNamara, *Irish Biblical Apocrypha. Selected Texts in Translation* (Edinburgh: T. and T. Clark, 1989), pp. 29–32.]

§9. Joseph told her to go to her bed and rest. 'O Simeon,' said he, 'anoint the virgin's feet with oil.' Simeon did so, and after Joseph had gone out Simeon followed him, and said: 'The virgin is rapidly being overcome by debility, and I think that she will give birth without delay.' 'I will not leave her,' said Joseph. 'Since you are more agile than I am, let you go around the city in search of a midwife for her, for a competent midwife greatly assists a woman in childbirth.' 'How am I to do that since I know neither the city nor its people? Yet I will go, for I am sure that God will provide a midwife for her, and everything else that she needs, for He has a special concern for her.'

§10. As they ceased their conversation, they saw a gentle, steady-eyed girl approach swiftly, carrying a chair. 'Who are you, girl?' asked Joseph, 'and what is the chair which you have?' 'It is a chair for women in childbirth,' said she. 'My mistress sent me to bring it to you, and she will follow me herself without delay, for a beautiful handsome youth came to guide us speedily to the virgin who is with you, to assist her in giving birth to the noble king.' This amazed them. Joseph looked at the nearby mountain, and he saw a tall venerable woman at the summit, vigorously traversing the hill with swift steps until she speedily reached the place in which was the noble senior of Israel, Joseph.

§11. As Joseph saw her approach him he went forward to speak to her, and they greeted each other. The woman said to Joseph: 'Where are you going?' 'I am going to seek a Hebrew woman who will attend to the virgin who is about to give birth to the true God and true man, the beneficent king who is the creator of the four elements,' said Joseph. 'Here I am,' said the woman, 'for I am the best midwife of the Jewish people. Tell me, good man, are you an Israelite yourself?' 'I am, indeed,' said Joseph. 'Who is this young woman brought to a cave lodging?' she asked. 'She is married to me,' said Joseph. 'She is not your wife at all,' said she. 'She is called the Virgin Mary, she was reared in the temple of the Lord, and it fell to you by lot to look after and protect her.' 'That is true,' said Joseph, 'and since the Lord has revealed these things to you, I shall not conceal them. Let us go in to see Mary,' said Joseph.

§12. When they went to the door of the house they saw a shining bright cloud above the cave, and such was the illumination, both inside the cave and over the outside, that human eyes could not gaze on it. 'Enter,' said Joseph. 'I will,' said she, 'and may the hand of God be with me. And do not show me any disrespect,' she said. 'For there is no midwife who is my equal throughout the land of the Jews.' 'We should rather give thanks to God that through his grace you were found thus,' said Joseph. 'He who does not esteem God's providence and does not show gratitude, commits a sin against the Lord.' Then Simeon said to Joseph: 'You have been blessed, beloved father, and the saints of heaven and the everlasting joy of all joys are with you, and your helper, from the God of gods, the Lord of lords, who is without pride . . .'

§13. The woman went in, and shortly afterwards Joseph followed her. When they came out again Simeon was waiting at the entrance of the cave, and he asked the midwife for news. 'Woman,' said Simeon, 'how is the virgin, and is there hope that she will live?' 'I have news, indeed,' she said '. . . I bless my God and Lord who revealed these things to me, his servant, unworthy though I am to witness them. And how am I to relate them,' said she, 'since they are new and extraordinary things, like nothing experienced ever before?' 'I beseech you for the love of God to disclose them to me,' said Simeon. 'They will not be concealed from you,' said she, 'for in time, they will be commonly known throughout the whole world, but they have been secret up to now. Heed these words and affix them in your heart, son,' she said.

§14. 'When I came to the place where the virgin was, I saw her praying and blessing the Lord. I asked her if she were in distress of body or mind. She did not answer, but remained immobile as a rock, with her eyes directed towards heaven, praying unceasingly. Then all of creation stood still, the wind ceased its storms, the ocean its roar. The sea was quiet, the wave soundless, the land untraversed, swift-flowing rivers became like pools, streams reposed as if in sleep, fish remained still. There was not a quiver in the woods, leaves were motionless, animals stood at rest, birds did not fly, people could not speak or work during the sacred time while the virgin was giving birth to the everlasting Lord. Assuredly the four elements recognized their creator . . . The inhabitants of hell were held fast, motionless and miserable, without the ability to do evil or harm against creature or devout person fashioned by God on that night of the divine birth . . .'

§15. 'The virgin was looking upwards, praying constantly . . . And we saw a bright light from her shine throughout the cave, so that she was like a single glorious radiance . . . Many angelic voices were heard above the cave praising the great Lord, and giving strength to the virgin inside. And the brightness outshone the light of the sun and all the stars. Moreover, a fragrance reached us which would delight everyone everlastingly, with the perfume of all the fruit, wax, saffron, and beautiful ointments in the world, all the herbs and plants and beautiful fruits that ever existed in holy Paradise. More wonderful than all of these, indeed, was the pleasure derived from that fragrance. And heavenly angels were unceasingly in attendance, since there is no human born who could not worthily partake of that mystery, except for the Virgin Mary herself.'

§16. 'Deep silence overcame me, and I was seized by fear and terror at the sight of these miraculous events, for the infant was like a sphere of light, such that human eyes could not look on. He was briefly in this form before assuming the shape and appearance of a child, and my mind grew animated as I looked on him, and I bent down and raised him up. He weighed nothing, unlike an ordinary child, and as I examined him attentively, I could find neither blemish nor mark nor trace of blood on him. It was as if he were washed in the gentle beautiful dew of the noble Heavenly Father. No known body was so radiant, no infant so weightless to carry, no human being was ever seen whose beauty was more resplendent. I marvelled that his nature was not like that of any other child, for he did not cry or wail, except for a little as he was being put in the manger. He was without the weakness of infancy, and as I looked in his face, he smiled at me, and no worldly delight was ever as pleasing. The flash of light from his eyes overshadowed the sunlight which reached throughout the cave at dawn from the east.'

§17. When Simeon heard these words he said: 'You are blessed and ever-fortunate, O devout and astute woman, and though I am the lowliest, it is propitious for me to have heard of these wonders, though I did not see them. And I believe all that you relate,' said Simeon.

MUIREADHACH ALBANACH Ó DÁLAIGH

(*fl.* early 13th century)

ÉISTIDH RIOMSA A MHUIRE MHÓR
(Mighty Mary, Hear Me)
(*c.* 1200)

[Many of the best Irish religious poems of the early and late
Middle Ages are addressed to Mary. The narrative in the
opening quatrains of this fine one segues into an imagistic
dreaminess one might associate with long contemplation of
an icon. Mary's youthful beauty is emphasized — a feature
dating back to texts of the early Christian period — and
there is much play on her complex relations, and hence the
poet's, to the deity: she is the Creator's spouse, mother and
child. Muireadhach Albanach's elegy for his wife is printed
in Volume I, pp. 43–4.

Text: Osborn Bergin (ed. and trans.), *Irish Bardic
Poetry*, compiled and edited by David Greene and Fergus
Kelly (Dublin: Dublin Institute for Advanced Studies,
1970), pp. 94–100. Translation: Thomas Kinsella (ed.),
The New Oxford Book of Irish Verse (Oxford: Oxford
University Press, 1986), pp. 87–91.]

Éistidh riomsa, a Mhuire mhór,
  do ghuidhe is liomsa badh lúdh:
do dhruim réd bhráthair ná bíodh,
  a Mháthair Ríogh duinn na ndúl.

Sgél do mháthar meabhair liom,
  'na dheaghaidh atáthar treall.
inghean mhilis mhalach ndonn,
  trilis trom chladhach fá ceann.

Anna sein, seanmháthair Dé,
  óa gealbhráthair do ghein rí,
níor ghiall a meadhair do mhnaoi,
  gur fhaoi lé triar d'fhearaibh í.

Rug inghean gach dheighfhir dhíobh,
  geibhidh aca an fhinngheal úr,
teóra inghean a clann chaomh,
  slimgheal a dtaobh, cam a gcúl.

Gorma a súile, suairc a ngné,
  a gcuairt nochar chuairt gan ghnaoi,
na sluaigh uile atá ar a dtí,
  trí mná agus Muire ar gach mnaoi.

Tugsad trí fir thoighe a dtriúr
  na trí Mhoire ó nimh na naomh,
gur thráchtmhall torrach an triar
  na gciabh ndrongach snátrom saor.

Rugsad trí maca na mná,
  aca roba lia 'sa lia:
(cá seisear mín doba mhó?)
  eisean roba só dhíbh Dia.

Máthair Iacóibh inghean díbh,
  sgiathdóigh ar gach n-imneadh fhuair,
bean díobh Muire máthair Eóin,
  geóil nár ghnáthaigh duine i nduain.

Tusa Muire Máthair Dé,
  duine níor ghnáthaigh do ghnaoi,
ríghbhile arna roinn ar thrí,
  Rí fírnimhe id bhroinn do bhaoi.

Mise ar bhar n-aithnibh ar-aon,
  id dhaighthigh agus id dhún,
a anam, a Mhuire mhór,
  a ór buidhe, a abhall úr.

A bhiadh, a édach ar h'iocht,
  a chiabh ghégach mar an ngort.
A Mháthair, a Shiúr, a Shearc,
  stiúr go ceart an bráthair bocht.

Bráthair dhamhsa do Mhac mór,
  a shlat mhallsa, a Mháthair shaor,
deaghbhráthair cóir ar bhar gcúl,
  seanmháthair úr róibh a-raon.

Go ndearna m'ionghaire ar h'Fhear,
  a fhionn Mhuire, a earla tiogh,
iomdha im chridhe crithir dhubh,
  mithigh dul dá nighe aniogh.

A Mháthair Dé, dénam síodh,
  ósa ghlédhonn gné do chiabh,
ciúnaigh h'fhearg, a Mhoire mhór,
  a ór dearg i gcoire chriadh.

Do nimh thánaig, a thaobh geal,
  a láraig, saor mar an sriobh.

Cá beag liom do dhúthchas damh,
  a chúlchas ghlan fhionn, ót Fhior?

A Thríonóid, a Mhuire mhín,
  tuile gach glóir acht bhar nglóir;
a Cheathrair, caistidh rém dhuain,
  ní geabhthair uaibh aisgidh óir.

A ÓghMhuire, a abhra dubh,
  a mhórmhuine, a ghardha geal,
tug, a cheann báidhe na mban,
  damh tar ceann mo náire neamh.

Do chloinn Dáibhíodh thú, a mhall mhór,
  gan chrann mar thú rébhar dtúr,
do chloinn Abhrán h'urla claon,
  gabhlán craobh gcumhra ar do chúl.

H'Fhear is do Mhac ar do mhuin,
  geal a ghlac is geal a righ,
t'Fhearathair réd thaobh as-toigh,
  ag soin taom d'ealathain t'Fhir.

Dalta iongnadh dot ucht bhán,
  agus dot fhult fhionnghlan úr,
do Mhac agus t'Fhear ar-aon,
  a shlat shaor gheal ar do ghlún.

Do bhábhair dias aobhdha ann
  dábhar gcaomhna ó ghlionn do ghlionn,
Mac malachdhubh dóidgheal donn,
  óigbhean trom anathlamh fhionn.

Do-ní sé casadh do chiabh,
  do dhuadh é ar t'asal dá dhíon,
do bhas, a ógMhuire úr,
  do chas cúl ródbhuidhe an Ríogh.

Tú do shíor doba shámh leis,
  is do chíogh bán ar a bhois,
an uair do nightheá an gcraoibh gcais,
  do ligtheá an mbais gcaoimh 's an gcois.

Fraoch buidhe ar h'úrbharr mar ór,
  a Mhuire shúlmhall, a Shiúr,
cíoch geilmhín trom as do thaobh,
  Leinbhín saor donn agá diúl.

Mairg do oiligh h'earla glan,
  doiligh, ór ní dhearna cion;
munab ionnraic do bhrú, a Bhean,
  ní headh cnú ar fionnshlait i bhfiodh.

Easbach clann ladrann do luadh,
  a lagbharr fleasgach cam claon,
amharas dob olc an chiall
  ort, a chiabh chladhsholas chaomh.

Do bhrú aníos ba lomlán leat,
  mar bhíos a bhronnlár 'san bhrioc,
an Coimdhe 's gan loighe lat,
  Mac Moire do-roighne riot.

Acht tú féin, a Mhuire mhór,
  nochar léir do dhuine dhaor,
suaimhnighe ar fhear, a fholt fiar,
  nach biadh is bean olc ar-aon.

Cosmhail h'aonMhac réd chúl gcam,
  a shaorshlat an dá shúl chorr,
do ghlaca ag an Ghiolla shiong,
  is t'ionga fhionn data dhonn.

Coinnleach gormshúileach do ghruadh,
  abhra donnghlúineach 'gá dhíon,
geilghégach leabhair do lámh,
  dán neimbrégach dleaghair dhíom.

Glann fallán buidhe do bharr,
  mar mhuine camán fád cheann,
glan do bhas chaoilmhérdha chorr,
  a chas donn shaoirdhénmha sheang.

Ní dheachaidh d'ég h'aithghin mhná,
  do shaighthin — ní brég — ní bhia,
níor bhlas beathaidh bean mar thú,
  a bhrú gheal i ndeachaidh Dia.

Tugaidh dhún leabaidh is lionn,
  a chúl ris nach teagaimh tonn,
an bhréigfhleadh ar nach bí ceann,
  nárab leam í a dhéidgheal donn.

Guidheadh go hán h'abhra dubh,
  ar ghrádh bhar n-anma, a ghrádh glan,
a Mhuire, ní hédmhar h'Fhear
  fád ghuidhe, a gheal dédghlan, damh.

A fholt buidhe cladhach cam.
  A Mhuire na malach seang,
ná leig do bhreith oile ionn,
  feith lionn do chroidhe fár gceann.

Dénam feis, a mheardha mhór,
  dod deis dealbhdha, taobh ré taobh,

gabh m'fhorthain deaghrann is duan
    uam, a ghealmhall shochraidh shaor.

Ní rabh bean acht tusa im thigh,
    gomadh tusa bhus fhear air,
na mná fallsa ad-chiú 's na cruidh,
    a bhfuil damhsa riú ná raibh.

Gan spéis i gconaibh ná i gcrodh,
    ná i sgoraibh, a ghéis ghlan,
easbhaidh chorn cáich is a gcon,
    orm is a sgor mbláith 's a mban.

Tógaibh an malaigh nduibh dhúin,
    is an aghaidh mar fhuil laoigh,
tógaibh, go ros faicinn féin,
    an gcéibh ródaigh slaitfhinn saoir.

Tógaibh dhún an bonn 's an mbois,
    agus an cúl donn go ndeis,
'gus an súil n-ógcruinn ngéir nglais,
    réd chéibh dtais go bhfóbrainn feis.

TRANSLATION

Mighty Mary, hear me.
    To you I would wish to pray.
Turn not your back on your brother,
    mother of the high elemental King.

I recall your mother's story.
    For long it has been told:
a gentle girl with dark brows
    and tresses heavy about her head.

Anna she was, grandmother of God,
    whose bright brother begot a king.
She yielded in cheer to no woman
    and to three men she was wed.

To each good man she bore a daughter.
    Fair, bright, noble, she conceived
three daughters, her children dear,
    with slim bright sides and waving hair.

Blue their eyes, their manners pleasing,
    never a scandal touching them,
three ladies sought by the whole world
    and Mary the name of each.

Three husbands they took, the three of them,
    three Maries from saintly Heaven.
Pregnant, slow-paced, the three became,
    with thick and rich tress-heavy hair.

The women bore three sons
    who grew from strength to strength.
Where find a mightier, modest six?
    And the youngest of these was God.

One girl the mother of James,
    shielded from every care.
One Mary the mother of John
    (no usual theme in verse).

And you, Mary, the mother of God,
    no usual beauty yours,
triple-branched royal stem:
    in your womb true Heaven's King.

Summon me, both of you,
    to your fine house and your fort,
mighty Mary, my soul,
    yellow gold, rich apple tree!

Food and clothes, by your clemency,
    O branched locks like a garden;
Mother, Sister, Beloved,
    guide this wretched brother well.

Your great son is my brother,
    noble mother, stately branch.
Guard this good brother, it is right;
    one fair grandmother had we both.

Till I put myself in your Husband's hands,
    fair Mary, O tresses thick,
black coals a-plenty were in my heart.
    It is right I should cleanse them now.

Let us make peace, mother of God
    — bright brown in hue your hair.
Mighty Mary, calm your wrath,
    red gold in vessel of clay.

From Heaven He came, that fair body,
    that waist like the noble stream.
No little kinship I have with Him,
    O fair, pure, curling locks.

O Trinity, O Mary mild,
all glory ebbs but yours.
Four Persons, hear my poem.
I will take no gold in payment:

Virgin Mary, dark of brow,
mighty vine, O garden bright,
grant, of women most beloved,
Heaven for my humility!

Sedate and great, of David's line,
there is no tree but you.
From Abraham your waving locks,
sweet branching tresses about your head.

Husband and Son within your womb
— bright His fist and bright His wrist!
Your Husbandfather in your side:
so your Husband's art is shown.

A wondrous child at your white breast,
your fresh and fair pure hair;
a Son and Husband both in one
on your knee, bright noble branch.

A pleasant pair indeed you were
as you fled from vale to vale;
a black-browed, white-gripped noble Son,
a gravid, fair unhurried girl.

And while you curled His locks
and minded Him on the ass
your palm, pure Virgin Mary,
curled yellow paths in a King's hair!

Always you were His peace,
your white breast in His palm.
When you washed that graceful Branch
you kissed His dear palm and foot.

A yellow-gold heath your noble head,
my sister Mary of the slow eyes.
A smooth, bright, heavy breast on your side
and a high-born Baby suckling it.

Accursed who rebukes your pure locks
— no easy thing, for you never sinned.
If your womb, lady, is not pure
there's no nut on a lovely branch in the wood.

Robbers' children we will not mention,
soft-tipped, ringleted, curling hair:
who with any wit could doubt you,
beloved locks, all ridged with light?

Your womb below filled full
like the mid-belly of a trout:
the Lord, though He never lay with you,
made with you the Son of Mary.

Mighty Mary, but for you
wretched man would never know
his greater peace — O curling hair —
is never to go with wicked women.

Your only Son has your waving hair,
noble sapling with rounded eyes.
He has your hands, that slender Boy,
and your fair nails shaded brown.

Blue-eyed, gleaming, is your face,
with dark-ridged eyebrow over it;
fair-branching, slender, is your hand:
I owe a poem that does not lie.

Pure, wholesome, yellow hair,
a vine of curls about your head;
round, thin-fingered, pure palm,
O firm, slim, well-shaped foot.

No like-born woman ever was;
your like (no lie) will never be.
Woman like you ne'er tasted life,
bright womb where God has gone.

Give me beer and bed,
O head untouched by soil.
The false feast that has no end
be it not mine, O strong white teeth.

May your dark brow nobly plead,
pure love, for the love of your soul.
(If I pray to your white bright teeth,
Mary, that Man will not be jealous.)

O curled, ridged, yellow hair,
Mary of slender brows,
give me no other judge
but the welcome of your heart.

Let us feast to your shapely figure
  — swift, mighty — side by side.
Accept my best poems and songs,
  bright-languid, noble, decorous one.

No woman but you in my home;
  its mistress may you be.
False women and all the wealth I see,
  none of mine will pay them heed.

May I never care for wealth
  or horses or hounds, pure swan,

or others' hounds or drinking horns
  or women, or choice pastures.

Turn your dark brow towards me,
  your face calves' blood in colour.
Turn it so I may see
  your noble fair locks' branching paths.

Turn towards me your sole and palm
  and your brown hair in beauty,
your keen green young round eye
  — may I fall in feast on your moist locks!

B. Eve and Her Sisters, *c.* 550–1800

SAINT FINNIAN

(?–549 or 579)

from:
THE PENITENTIAL OF FINNIAN
(mid-6th century)

[The Penitentials were mainly concerned with regulating the lives of clerics and monks. What few references they contain to women usually concern the threat they posed to churchmen by living near, and more especially in, their community. The following extracts derive from the earliest extant Irish penitential. The author identifies himself in a postscript as 'Vinnianus', who 'adapted his work for the sons of his bowels, out of affection and in the interest of religion'. It is generally agreed that this must be either Saint Finnian of Clonard (d. 549) or, more likely, Saint Finnian of Moville (d. 579). The unqualified term 'woman' in §§20 and 21 refers to a vowed virgin nun. In §27 'mate' (Latin *clentella, clientella*) describes a woman who was formerly married but who has renounced this state, together with her husband, for spiritual marriage.
  Text: Ludwig Bieler (ed.), *The Irish Penitentials* (Dublin: Dublin Institute for Advanced Studies, 1975), pp. 79, 81, 83, 89.]

§20. If a woman by her magic destroys the child she has conceived of somebody, she shall do penance for half a year with an allowance of bread and water, and abstain for two years from wine and meat and fast for the six forty-day periods with bread and water.

§21. But if, as we have said, she bears a child and her sin is manifest [she shall do penance] for six years [with bread and water], as is the judgment in the case of a cleric, and in the seventh year she shall be joined to the altar, and then we say her crown can be restored and she may don a white robe and be pronounced a virgin. So a cleric who has fallen ought likewise to receive the clerical office in the seventh year after the labour of penance, as saith Scripture: *Seven times a just man falleth and ariseth*, that is, after seven years of penance he who fell can be called 'just' and in the eighth year evil shall not lay hold on him, but for the remainder (of his life) let him preserve himself carefully lest he fall, since, as Solomon saith, *as a dog returning to his vomit becomes odious, so is he who through his own negligence reverts to his sin . . .*

§27. If anyone is a cleric of the rank of a deacon or of any rank, and if he formerly was a layman, and if he lives with his sons and daughters and with his mate, and if he returns to carnal desire and begets a son with his own mate, as he might say, let him know that he has fallen to the depths of ruin and ought to rise; his sin is not less than it would be if he had been a cleric from his youth and sinned with a strange girl, since they have sinned after their vow and after they were consecrated to God, and then they have made their vow void. They shall do penance for three years on an allowance of bread and water and shall abstain for three years more from wine and meat, and they shall not do penance together, but separately, and then in the seventh year they shall be joined to the altar and receive their rank . . .

§37. If any layman has defiled a vowed virgin, and she has lost her crown and he has begotten a child by her, let such a layman do penance for three years; in the first year he shall go on an allowance of bread and water and unarmed and shall not have intercourse with his own wife, and for two years he shall abstain from wine and meat and shall not have intercourse with his wife.

§38. If, however, he does not beget a child of her, but nevertheless has defiled the virgin, he shall do penance for an entire year and a half, an entire year on an allowance of bread and water, and for half a year he shall abstain from wine and meat, and he shall not have intercourse with his wife until his penance is completed.

ANONYMOUS

from:
DE DUODECIM ABUSIVIS SAECULI
(Of the Twelve Abuses of the World)
(early 7th century)

[*De Duodecim Abusivis Saeculi* is a moral theological tract on the chief sources of evil in the world. Its author is unknown, though many of the manuscripts ascribe it to Cyprian or Augustine. Internal evidence indicates that it was composed in Ireland in the early seventh century. The author was a man of considerable learning and his succinct and skilful portraits of the various types of moral evil (for example, 'the preacher of good works', 'the unjust king') made his text a best-seller throughout the Middle Ages, and it was translated into many languages. The fifth abuse, 'the woman without modesty', praises this virtue as the source of all good behaviour in women, whether married, single or widowed. From his very full enumeration of its characteristics, it is clear that modesty, or purity, was not simply sexual abstinence, but something that touched on all aspects of a woman's mental, moral and spiritual being. It was manifested both through the exterior physical sense and their five interior, or spiritual, counterparts. The end result was not only edifying to others, but pleasing to God and a promise of future salvation.

There is an undoubted nobility of thought in the author's description of ideal womanhood, which contrasts sharply with the misogynist sentiments of famous Church Fathers like Jerome and Augustine. Although it is clearly the product of an ascetic, monastic environment, it reveals an attitude to woman which, in the medieval context, is remarkably free of male prejudice.

Translation: Aidan Breen, 'De XII Abusivis: A Critical Edition with Translation and Introduction' (unpublished Ph.D. thesis, 1988), pp. 363–73. Headnote also by Aidan Breen.]

Of the woman without modesty
The fifth abuse is a woman without modesty. Just as prudence procures and keeps all good manners in men, so modesty nourishes, cherishes and sustains all good and honest actions in women. For modesty [guards chastity,] restrains avarice, avoids litigation and strife, assuages anger, keeps sexual desire in check, moderates passionate desires of the mind, chastens wanton behaviour, guards against drunkenness, makes few words, resists the greedy appetites of the gut and utterly condemns theft. What more? It bridles every vice, and nourishes every virtue, and whatsoever is praiseworthy in the sight of God and before virtuous men. For a life that is unchaste can expect neither praise from men in this world nor a reward from God in the next. But a chaste life is well spoken of by men, and rejoices in the hope of the bliss to come. It wins the admiration of all who perceive it and leaves a good example to those who come after; it delights always in good manners and agrees with them; it directs and stabilises the mind through continual reading of

and meditation upon Scripture; it keeps the example of good men who have gone before and is always acquainted with and keeps the company of those who are good and perfect.

Modesty is therefore practised in two ways, that is, in the outward behaviour and appearance of the body and in the inward affection and disposition of the mind. In the outward manner it gives, as the Apostle says, good example to men, and through the interior manner we provide good works before God. Physical modesty therefore is not to covet the goods of others, to avoid all impurity, not to wish to eat before the proper time, not to be a giggler or to provoke laughter, not to utter false or vain words, to be of such behaviour and determination of mind as is in every way orderly and befitting one who is as it were clothed in garments of hair [i.e. in ascetic garb], not to keep the company of unworthy persons, to look upon no one with a haughty regard, not to permit the eyes to wander, not to walk with a showy or seductive gait, to appear [to be] inferior to no one in beginning good works, to be an occasion of reproach or shame to no one, to blaspheme nobody, not to make fun of the old, not to engage in dispute with one's betters, not to discourse upon things of which you know nothing nor even make display of that which you do know. These qualities render one beloved of one's fellow man and make one acceptable to God.

But modesty of the soul rather is to do all things more for the sight of God than to be seen by men, to curb the inclination to evil or filthy thoughts, to esteem everyone to be better [than oneself]. To envy no one, to presume nothing of oneself, always to place one's trust in everything in God, to be always mindful of God's presence, not to infect one's judgement with heretical perversity, to agree in everything with them who are of the Catholic faith, to cleave only to God, to offer up to the Lord Christ the chastity of the inward mind, never to cease from doing good works during this life, with a strong heart to despise present tribulations of the spirit, to love nothing of this world before one's fellow man, to lay up all the treasure of one's love in heaven and finally to hope for a heavenly reward from God for all good works.

Modesty is the adornment of noble persons, the raising up of the lowly, the ennobling of the classless, the beauty of the enfeebled and handicapped, the prosperity of the able-bodied, the consolation of the bereaved, the enhancement of every [kind of] beauty, the adornment of religion, the defence against [false] charges, the multiplication of merits and, in final, it is the darling of God, the creator of all.

JONAS OF BOBBIO

(d. 659)

from:
THE LIFE OF COLUMBANUS
(c. 642)

[Jonas was an Italian monk who joined the monastery of Bobbio in 618, three years after the death of its founder, Columbanus. He remained associated with it until his death. His Life of Columbanus, his best-known work, was completed about 642 and was largely compiled from the recollections of older monks of Bobbio concerning Columbanus. It is therefore an excellent historical source for the life of one of Ireland's greatest *peregrini*, though there is much that it does not tell us, especially about Columbanus's early career in Ireland and his first missionary years in Gaul. The following excerpt describes the handsome saint's temptations from young women, his resort to a woman hermit for advice and, acting upon that advice, his final abandonment of home and family, against his mother's entreaties, for 'a place of greater exile'.

For the Latin original see: Bernhard Krusch (ed.), *Ionae Vitae Sanctorum Columbani, Vedastis, Iohannis*, Scriptores Rerum Germanicarum in usum scholarum ex Monumentis Germaniae Historicis separatim editi (Hannoverae: Impensis Bibliopolii Hahniana, 1902), pp. 432–49. Translation and headnote by Aidan Breen.]

Having passed his childhood, and growing into adolescence, he began to devote himself enthusiastically to the study of grammar and the sciences, which he pursued with fruitful zeal all through his boyhood and youth until he became a man. But as the handsomeness of his form, especially his white complexion and noble manliness, made him loved by all, the old enemy began finally to aim his deadly weapons at him in order to ensnare in his bonds this youth, whom he saw grow so much in grace. And he aroused against him the lusts of lascivious maidens, especially of those whose figure and superficial beauty are wont to enkindle with terrible desire the souls of wretched men.

But when that excellent soldier saw that he was pressed on all sides by so many legions, and had perceived the glistening dagger and shrewdness of the enemy fighting against him, and that by an act of human frailty he might quickly be destroyed by a fall into the precipice ... holding in his left hand the shield of the gospel, and bearing in his right the two-edged sword, he prepared to advance and attack the threatening hosts of the enemy. He feared that, ensnared by the lusts of the world, he should in vain have spent so much labour in the study of grammar, rhetoric, geometry and the holy Scriptures. And [in these perils] he was strengthened by a particular aid.

While he was still meditating upon his purpose, he came to the dwelling of a holy nun, devoted to God. He at first addressed her humbly; afterwards he approached and began to castigate her, as far as he could, with youthful exhortation. As she saw the increasing strength of the youth she said: 'I have gone forth to the strife, so far as it was in my power. Lo, fifteen years have passed since I have been far from home and have sought out the place of pilgrimage. And never since then, with the aid of Christ, having put my hand to the plough, have I looked back. And if the weakness of my sex had not prevented me, I would have crossed the sea and sought a better place of exile. But you, glowing with the fire of youth, stay [quietly] on your native soil. Out of weakness, even against your will, you lend your ear to the voice of the flesh; and do you think that you can associate with the female sex freely [without sin]? Do you not recall that by the wiles of Eve Adam fell, that Samson was deceived by Delilah, that David was corrupted from former righteousness by the beauty of Bathsheba, and that the most wise Solomon was ensnared by the love of women? Away, o youth! away! Flee that corruption through which many, as you know, have fallen. Forsake the path which leads to the gates of hell.'

The youth, stirred by these words which were such as to terrify a young man, thanked her for warning him thus, took leave of his companions and set out. His mother in anguish begged him not to leave her. But he said: 'Have you not heard, "he that loves father and mother more than me is not worthy of me"?' He begged his mother, who placed herself in his way and held the door-post, to let him go. Weeping, and stretched upon the floor, she said she would not permit it. Then he stepped over his mother across the threshold, and begged his mother to be joyful: she would never see him again in this life, but wherever the way of salvation led him, there he would go.

MUIRCHÚ MOCCU MACTHÉNI

(*fl.* late 7th century)

from:
VITA SANCTI PATRICII
(The Life of Patrick)
(late 7th century)

[Monesan followed in the steps of Abraham and arrived at a knowledge of good through innate grace. Thereafter her life adumbrated that of Mary, itself a fulfilment of the Old Testament, and the virgin saints. Monesan preserved her virginity from youth, rendered her body insensate, and swiftly underwent the ultimate social alienation of death. A strikingly similar tale is told by Muirchú's contemporary, Tírechán, of the daughters of King Lóegaire: see Volume I, pp. 74–5.

Translation: Ludwig Bieler (ed.), *The Patrician Texts in the Book of Armagh* (Dublin: Dublin Institute for Advanced Studies, 1979), pp. 99, 101.]

HOLY MONESAN

At a time, then, when all Britain was still frozen in the cold of unbelief, the illustrious daughter of some king — her name was Monesan — was full of the Holy Spirit. Assisted by Him, although many desired to marry her, she accepted no proposal. Not even when floods of water were frequently poured over her could she be forced to do what she did not want and what was less valuable. When, in between beatings and soakings with water, she was insistently urged [to do so] she kept asking her mother and her nurse whether they knew the maker of the wheel by which the world is illumined, and when she received the answer that the maker of the sun was he whose throne was in heaven, she, frequently urged to enter into the bond of marriage, said, enlightened by the luminous counsel of the Holy Spirit: 'I shall never do that.' For through nature she searched the maker of all that is created, following in this the example of Abraham the patriarch. Her parents, deliberating in their great sorrow, on hearing that Patrick, a just man, was visited by eternal God every seventh day, went with their daughter to Ireland and after such a great effort met Patrick. He asked them why they had come. Then the travellers told him in excited tones: 'The ardent desire of our daughter to see God has forced us to come to you.' He then, full of the Holy Spirit, raised his voice and said to her: 'Do you believe in God?' And she said: 'I do believe.' Then he bathed her in the bath of the Holy Spirit and the water. Immediately afterwards she fell to the ground and gave up her spirit into the hands of the angels. She was buried on the spot where she died. Then Patrick prophesied that after twenty years her body would be conveyed to a near-by chapel with great ceremony. This was done afterwards, and the relics of the maiden from across the sea are there an object of worship to the present day.

ANONYMOUS

from:
THE HIBERNENSIS
(Irish Canons)
(*c.* 716–25)

[Two of the sixty-seven books which comprise the *Hibernensis* concern women, Books 45 and 46. The title of Book 45, 'Concerning Questions of Women', may be taken to cover both it and Book 46, 'On Marriage', for which see pp. 12–17. The scheme of the three orders of virgins, penitent spouses and the legitimately married is neatly reproduced here, with virgins and penitent spouses (under the aliases of 'widows' and 'penitents') assigned to Book 45, and married women to Book 46. The opening statement below, 'That virginity is to be praised in either sex', is special pleading because in reality the Book treats of female virginity only.

In common with the Penitentials, Book 45 evidences a particular interest in the sexual sins of women who have taken vows of virginity or sexual abstinence. Abortion is treated in detail and the text provides a rare reference to contraception. It may be noted that penalties for abortion are far more severe than those specified in earlier texts, such as the sixth-century Penitential of Finnian (see p. 95). Abstract virginity is assigned personal traits similar to those ascribed to the Virgin Mary and the virgin saints, and a temperament appropriate to the widow is also defined. There is a dismal logic to the way the text proceeds from discussion of veiling through the topics of segregation, enclosure, rejection of women's right to teach men, their obligation to silence in church and, finally, the total denial to them of male and priestly office.

The text is here translated by Thomas O'Loughlin from Herrmann Wasserschleben, *Die irische Kanonensammlung*, pp. 180–4. The heading of each section, given below in italic, is part of the text: it gives the subject or the legal principle in question. Scriptural references have been supplied in the translations.]

BOOK 45: CONCERNING QUESTIONS OF WOMEN

1. *That virginity is to be praised in either sex*
Jerome: Virginity is the beauty of the church, the flower of modesty, the path to life, the guardian of sobriety, the patroness of innocence, the darling of justice. She eradicates vices and is the

conqueror of lust. Virginity is strong in abstinence, constant in humility, sincere in charity,
gives substance to prayer, is careful in vigils,
eager in fasts, victorious in life, is the companion
of the angels [Matthew 22:30]. Virginity follows
the Lamb wherever He goes [Revelation 14:4]
and remains always in the gaze of the Creator.
Virginity is sublime above all else, and the Lord
does not dare to demand it. For He says: Not
everyone can receive this word, but to whom it is
given [Matthew 19:11] by my Father.

2. *Warning against the danger of pride arising from
   continence*
1. The Synod of Gangra said: If anyone from
   among those preserving virginity for the
   Lord's sake is extolled at the expense of
   married people, let him be anathema.
2. Again: Each person who guards his virginity
   is to do this for the Lord's sake and not in
   order to deplore marriage; for anyone who
   thinks that the faithful husband and the
   religious woman are to be detested or that
   they are blameworthy is to be anathema.

3. *On the habits of those who pretend to be virgins*
Jerome: I am ashamed to speak of what is a
lamentable crime, but it is the case. Some women
walk with heads held high and with a mincing
gait; some drink [potions] to make themselves
sterile, and do murder to the yet unborn human
child. Still others when they become aware that
they have conceived plan poison for the crime of
abortion, and often for themselves also. When
they are dead they are led down to Hell guilty of
three crimes: the murder of themselves and of
Christ, adultery, and the murder of the unborn
child.[1]

4. *On women who have abortions*
1. Jerome in his letters says: Any woman who
   commits this detestable act is guilty on two
   counts: that of the murder of her own soul,
   and the murder of her son. Hence we
   prescribe for her that she should do 14 years'
   penance.
2. Augustine in his Homilies says: A woman
   who either destroys her pregnancy or who
   kills her son has committed murder; any man

or woman who was in agreement with her has
sinned and must do 7 years' strict penance.
3. Again: Let no woman accept a potion lest her
   children (whether conceived or already born)
   be killed. Let any woman who does this know
   that (along with murderers) she will have to
   give an account before the court of Christ
   [2 Corinthians 5:10].
4. Again: Women ought to take no diabolical
   potions which might make it impossible to
   conceive; let any woman who does this know
   that she is guilty of the same number of
   murders as the number of children she would
   have conceived and given birth to.

5. *On the penance for those who have abortions*
The Synod of Ancyra: Regarding women who
commit fornication and then kill their offspring
when they are born or those who expel what they
have conceived in the womb, an ancient decision
says that they must be removed from the church
until the end of their lives; however, we now give
a more humane judgement: they shall be given
14 years of graded penance.

6. *On the origins [of the state] of widowhood*
The first widow was Dinah the daughter of Jacob
[Genesis 34:26]; the second was Naomi [Ruth
1:3]; the third was she to whom Elijah was sent
in Zarephath belonging to Sidon [1 Kings 17:9;
Luke 4:26]; the fourth was the Shunammite who
used to welcome Elisha and served him food
[2 Kings 4:12]; the fifth was Esther [cf. Esther];
the sixth was Judith who triumphed over
Holofernes the Assyrian king [cf. Judith]. Now
Anna, who recognised the Lord as an infant, was
the first widow in the New Testament [Luke
2:36].

7. *Regarding true widows*
1. Paul says: 'Let a widow be enrolled if she is
   not less than sixty years of age, having been
   the wife of one husband' [1 Timothy 5:9]; but
   note that if she had several husbands she
   cannot be a widow; widows are chosen from
   the sixty-year-olds.
2. Jerome: These rules apply to widows who are
   fed on the alms of the church, and that is why
   the age is prescribed, so that only those who
   cannot work receive the food of the poor.
   Likewise, keep in mind that a woman who

1. Cf. Jerome, Epistle 22 (To Eustochius), §§13, 14.

had husbands, even if she be old, decrepit and needy, does not deserve to receive the church's alms; for if she is deprived of the bread of charity, how much more should she be deprived of that bread which descends from heaven, [cf. John 6:33] since whoever eats that unworthily is guilty of violating the body and blood of Christ [1 Corinthians 11:27].

3. A woman is chosen as a [holy] widow subject to these conditions: if she is proven in good works; has instructed her children thoroughly; received with hospitality; washed the feet of the saints etc.

4. They ought to be holy in dress, in movement, and in gait, not slanderers, not chatterers, nor with a taste for much wine.

5. A synod decrees: Widows, who are sustained on the alms of the church, ought to be so assiduous in the work of God [that they prove a help to] the church with their prayers and merits.

8. *That the church ought to support virgins who are weak*
The Synod of Carthage: Young widows who are sick in body are to be taken care of and supported by the church whose widows they are.

9. *Regarding young widows*
1. Paul: Let young women choose to marry whom they will, but only in the Lord, or, let them dedicate themselves and be far from men.

2. Jerome: Let clerics be careful lest they become neighbours of the houses of widows; and let the widows be careful that they are kept from the view of clerics; view defiles view.

10. *On the name 'palliata' or 'veiled woman'*
The word *pallium* 'veil' comes from *palliditas* 'paleness', hence comes the word *palliata* 'veiled woman'; or, it comes from the goddess Pallas, that is Minerva, whose temple[2] was *palladium* 'draped' and whose priestesses were virgins who were *palliatae*, that is 'veiled women'. With a change in meaning the word may be kept and one who under the New Law is veiled may be called *palliata*.

11. *The age at which virgins should be veiled*
Synod: Nuns, however proven their life and morals may be, are not to be veiled before their twelfth or fifteenth year.

12. *On the two kinds of veiled women*
1. Augustine, in his book *De virgine sincletica*,[3] says: There are two kinds of veiled women: firstly virgins who imitate Mary in body and nature; secondly penitents who imitate Anna and who ought to remain under the hand of the pastor until death [Luke 2:37]. Wherever these are, there the church is. The first kind can be likened and compared to bishops, the second grade to presbyters, that is, to elders.

2. Jerome: As there are two kinds of men — saints and penitents, so there are two kinds of women — virgins and penitents.

13. *On the honour due to veiled religious women*
The Roman Synod says: Veiled women (*palliatae*) have great honour for they have conquered their sex, that is, their fragility, and have renounced the doings of the world.

14. *How the two kinds[4] of veiled women ought to live*
The Romans say: It is proper that women, since they accept the fragility of their sex, should always live strictly, subject to a pastoral regimen. Virgins adorned with the dress of virginity should be segregated from the view of all men; and they should live in this way until death. Penitents, also, are to be under obedience, and the more they have experienced their fragility, the more careful they ought to be.

15. *Regarding women who are bad penitents*
Jerome: There are other women who are unwilling to live the life of penitence; they are wicked, talkative, wandering, full of tales, harsh, and they never provide anything useful to others.

16. *On the lifestyle of young women*
The Synod of Arles: Young women, you should live thus: knowing nothing beyond home and parents; and, if you should be separated from your parents, you should live an enclosed life, until death, under the authority of a priest.

2. The Palladium, which was 'draped' in olive branches.

3. Unidentified work.
4. That is, virgins and penitents.

17. *That nuns cannot be tainted by the use of oppressive force*
1. Jerome: It is not force, but the will, which stains the body of a woman.
2. The same man says again: If the purity of a nun's body is lost by being violated, the purity of her soul remains intact, even if her body is oppressed; on the other hand, if the purity of the soul is lost, the holiness of her body is violated, even though her body remains intact.[5]

18. *That women are not to teach men*
1. Paul to Timothy: I do not permit women to teach [1 Timothy 2:12].

2. Jerome: Others, I am ashamed to say, go and teach to men what they have learned from women!

19. *That women are to be silent in church*
Paul to the Corinthians: Your women should keep silent in the church. For they are not permitted to speak, but should be submissive, as the law says. But if there is anything they desire to know, let them ask their husbands at home. For it is shameful for a woman to speak in the church [1 Corinthians 14:34–5].

20. *That women of any kind are not to receive any male or priestly office*
Isidore: It is not permitted for women to speak or teach in church [1 Corinthians 14:34]; nor to have any part in, or carry out, any of the duties of a man or to assume for themselves the lot of the priestly office.

5. Cf. Book 46, 21 of the *Hibernensis* (p. 15).

ADOMNÁN OF IONA

(*c.* 628–704)

from:
VITA COLUMBAE
(The Life of Columba)
(*c.* 700)

Translation from: A.O and M.O Anderson (eds, revised by M.O. Anderson), *Adomnan's Life of Columba* (Oxford: Clarendon Press, 1991), pp. 165, 167.]

[Adomnán's *Vita Columbae*, ostensibly a biography of Columba, founder of Iona, was also a vehicle for his own views. In it, we find his ideas on Christian marriage presented with the endorsement of his saintly predecessor. It has been suggested that Adomnán's Law has a clear subtext whereby the laity and, in particular, laywomen are called upon to accommodate themselves to Christian marriage (see pp. 18–22). Something of this agenda is also reflected in the following statement associated with Adomnán: 'Of a wife who is a harlot, thus the same man explained, that she will be harlot who has cast off the yoke of her own husband, and is joined to a second husband or a third' (cf. Ludwig Bieler (ed.), *The Irish Penitentials*, pp. 178–9). The longest narrative concerning a woman in the *Vita* tells how Columba miraculously restored a wife's affection for a husband she had previously found repulsive.

CONCERNING A CERTAIN LUGNE, A PILOT SURNAMED TUDICLA, WHO LIVED IN THE ISLAND OF RECHRU, AND WHOM HIS WIFE HELD IN AVERSION BECAUSE HE WAS VERY UGLY

At another time, when the holy man was a guest in the island of Rechru [Rathlin], a certain layman came to him and complained regarding his wife, who, as he said, had an aversion to him, and would not allow him to enter into marital relations. Hearing this, the saint bade the wife approach, and began to chide her as well as he could on that account, saying: 'Why, woman, do you attempt to put from you your own flesh? The

Lord says: "Two shall be in one flesh".[1] Therefore the flesh of your husband is your flesh.' She replied: 'I am ready to perform all things whatsoever that you may enjoin on me, however burdensome: save one thing, that you do not constrain me to sleep in one bed with Lugne. I do not refuse to carry on the whole management of the house; or, if you command it, even to cross the seas, and remain in some monastery of nuns.' Then the saint said: 'What you suggest cannot rightly be done. Since your husband is still alive, you are bound by the law of the husband; for it is forbidden that that should be separated, which God has lawfully joined.' After saying this, he continued: 'On this day let us three, myself, and the husband with his wife, pray to the Lord, fasting.' Then she said: 'I know it will not be impossible that things appearing difficult or even impossible may be granted by God to you, when you ask for them.'

In short, the wife agreed to fast on the same day, and the husband also, with the saint. And on the night following, in sleep, the saint prayed for them. On the next day the saint thus addressed the wife, in the presence of her husband: 'Woman, are you today, as you said yesterday, ready to depart to a monastery of nuns?' She said: 'I know now that your prayer concerning me has been heard by God. For him whom I loathed yesterday I love today. In this past night, (how, I do not know) my heart has been changed in me from hate to love.'

Let us pass on. From that day until the day of her death, that wife's affections were indissolubly set in love of her husband; so that the dues of the marriage-bed, which she had formerly refused to grant, she never again denied.

1. Matthew 19:5; Mark 10:8.

ANONYMOUS

HUSBAND AND WIFE DEBATE
(late 7th century)

[A late seventh-century date has been proposed for this Insular Latin lyric. Although its country of origin is not known, there is clear evidence of contemporary Irish interest in its theme — the plight of a couple when one seeks a separation 'to serve God', while the other wishes to remain married — in the *Hibernensis*. It is stated there that a wife is to remain with her husband all the days of her life unless they separate 'by mutual consent and to serve God' (see p. 12).

Text and translation: Peter Dronke, '"*Ad Deum Meum Convertere Volo*" and Early Irish Evidence for Lyrical Dialogues', *Cambridge Medieval Celtic Studies*, no. 12 (winter 1986), pp. 23–32.]

'Ad deum meum convertere volo:
uxorem meam ego nolo.
Domine, hoc tibi rogo:

tibi soli servire volo,
    Recede a me, uxor!'

'Bene nos iunxærat deus,
congaudet animus meus;
placuisset hoc in deum:
maritus in latus meum,
    dulcis iugalis meus!'

'Calamitas, de me recede —
ista verba nolo audire!
Si tibi dilectat nubere,
alium perquire!
    Recede a me, uxor!'

'Die ac nocte doleo et fleo
propter carum virum meum.
Si tibi me fraudat deus,
non iaces in latus,
    dulcis iugalis meus!'

TRANSLATION

'I want to turn to my God:
I do not want my wife.
Oh Lord, I ask this of you —
I long to serve you alone.
    Wife, depart from me!'

'God has joined us fairly,
my mind takes joy in that;
it would have been pleasing to God —
my husband at my side,
    my gentle husband!'

'Depart from me, you calamity —
I'll not hear these words of yours!
If marrying gives you delight,
seek out another husband!
    Wife, depart from me!'

'Day and night I grieve and weep
because of my dear husband.
If God tricks me out of you,
you won't lie at my side,
    my gentle husband!'

THE POWER OF WOMEN
(Old Irish)

[Woman is the Devil Incarnate, as these men enjoy telling each other. The tale is a version of the apocryphal work 1 Esdras 3:1–4:32. From: Máire Herbert and Martin McNamara, *Irish Biblical Apocrypha: Selected Texts in Translation*, pp. 23–4.]

1. There was a famous king of the Greeks called Solomon. A great feast was prepared for him by a king from one of his tribes. They all grew very drunk. There were untrustworthy persons close to the king. 'Let me be guarded by you tonight,' he told three friends from his [own] household. 'That will be done,' they replied. In this manner they were engaged in their watch, with a barrel of wine beside them, and a servant holding a candle in their direction. They were all attending to each other. 'Indeed, it is well for us,' said one of the three men. 'Let us give thanks to our lord. Except in one regard, our bodily senses are in a favourable

state. The feet rejoice in being stretched out without motion. The hands rejoice in dispensing [food] to the body. The eyes rejoice in viewing the preparation. Noses revel in the aroma, lips, in the taste. One area, however, is not being pleased, and that is our hearing, for none of us hears agreeable sayings being passed from one to another.'

2. The question is put: 'What will we discuss?' 'Not difficult the resolution. We will seek to ascertain what power on earth is strongest.' 'I know,' said the Roman warrior. 'It is wine. For it is wine which intoxicated the host, leaving them without reason or sense, so that they were dementedly drunk, cast into sleep, and at the mercy of their enemies.'

3. 'That is a good case,' said the Greek, 'but it seems to me that the stronger power is that of the ruler by whom the wine was given. The ruler is stronger than ordinary men, and man more estimable than the rest of creation. It is his power which causes us to be sober and sleepless, even though we are drinking wine.'

4. 'Well,' said the Jewish warrior, whose name was Nemiasserus, 'those were good propositions. Yet it appears to me that the power of women is the greatest. It would be no wonder if this is what you remember on the morrow.' They remained there until the morning.

5. 'So now, what judgements were passed among you last night?' asked the king. 'This one, indeed. We were considering what was the greatest power on earth.' 'I said that it was the power of wine,' said the Roman. 'I said that it was the power of a king,' said the Greek. 'I said that it was the power of woman,' said the Jew.

6. The queen was at the king's side. The king himself was wearing his golden crown. 'Wine is the stronger,' said one man. 'The power of the king is stronger,' said another. 'Is it the case that I am without power?' asked the queen, striking the king's headgear with the palm of her hand, so that [the crown] fell on the floor of the house. 'She should be put to death,' said everyone. The king looked over at her. Then the queen smiled. The king immediately smiled too. 'No harm will be done to the woman,' said the king. 'There it is,

then,' said Nemiasserus, 'that is a mighty power.' 'It is true,' said the king, 'the power of woman is more powerful than all others. For on her brow is her accompanying Satan, so that one cannot reproach her for anything she does.'

from:
NOTES ON THE CUSTOMS OF TALLAGHT
(*c.* 840)

[The Céli Dé (literally, 'Clients of God') were religious who spearheaded a movement for reform in the Irish church from the mid-eighth century to the late ninth. Máel Ruain (d. 792), Abbot of Tallaght, now a suburb of Dublin, was the movement's leader. Other key figures included the bishops Caenchomrac (d. 791) and Dublitir (d. 796) of Finglas, also a suburb of Dublin; Fer Dá Chrích (d. 747), Abbot of Dairinis (probably the island of that name near Youghal, County Waterford); and Máel Díthruib (d. 840), an anchorite of Terryglass (Tír Dá Glas), County Tipperary. All these are referred to below. Molaisse of Daiminis who is also named below may have been a contemporary of this group (see p. 88, note 7). The following excerpts derive from a commonplace book written by a disciple of Máel Díthruib's, who was keenly interested in the teachings of Máel Ruain. Máel Díthruib is the 'he' referred to once in §32, and repeatedly in §62.

Although the Céli Dé were opposed to materialism and secularization, they did not favour extremes of austerity. They advocated moderation, and humane remedies for human frailties. On the evidence of the extracts below, they may also have sought to counter the misogynistic tendencies which were being continuously reinforced within the church. While women are said to have stronger sexual desire than men, this is accounted to physiology rather than to an inherently more sinful nature. Although Máel Ruain is said to have 'blushed down to his breast' when Samthann tested the sincerity of his response to women with doubletalk, nevertheless he resolutely accepted her as a sister in Christ. It is Samthann who advocates the hard-line approach and who seems to be most distrustful of women's nature.

These excerpts (with minor changes in presentation and standardization of names) are from: E.J. Gwynn and W.J. Purton, 'The Monastery of Tallaght', *Proceedings of the Royal Irish Academy*, vol. 29, series C (March 1911), pp. 115–80.]

§7. There was a certain bishop of the Déisi at Finglas named Caenchomrac: he was Dublitir's confessor. One day the two came in front of the brethren out of the garden over the stile into the field. There was a certain poor old woman waiting for Dublitir in the field to pray him to let her sleep in the nuns' hostel. Presently the old woman wearied him with her loud praying to God. 'Be off with you then!' said he; 'misfortune take your face!' Instantly thereupon Caenchomrac bowed himself to the ground. 'What is this?' said Dublitir. 'Alas! it is a dreadful deed that thou hast committed,' said Caenchomrac, 'to revile the poor old woman.' Then he bowed himself *statim*.[1] 'Thine award therefor?' said Dublitir. 'This is my award,' said Caenchomrac, 'that she go into the women's hostel, and be given a milch cow and a cloak. Moreover, we will settle here and now the penance that is meet for thee'. 'It shall be done,' said Dublitir . . .

§32. There was a certain nun from Caill Uaitne[2] endowed with the grace of God. She would not rise without singing a *pater*. She would not sit down without chanting a *pater*. When she rose to recite the divisions [of the psalms] she used to recite a *pater* immediately after rising, and then she would begin the division. Then when that division was finished she would sit down and she would recite a *pater* immediately after sitting down, and then she would begin to recite the [next] division sitting down. It is by her example that he appoints [?] the *pater* at the end of each division. It is his constant usage to sing a *pater* whenever he rises, and a *pater* whenever he sits down . . .

§59. Persons whose desires are excited, it may be through hearing confessions, or merely with meditating, or through youth, need strict abstinence to subdue them, because it is excess of blood in their body that is the cause. Afterwards, when the blood fails, then lust and desire fail.

§60. Molaisse of Daiminis had a sister named Copar. Now desire lay heavy upon the girl, for it is a third part as strong again in women as in men. Then he regulates her portion and her pittance for a year: that is, a measured pittance.

---

1. i.e. immediately.
2. Unidentified.

On that day year[3] she came to him, and confessed that her desire still persisted. Now he was busy sewing before her. Then he thrust the needle thrice into her palm, and three streams of blood flowed from her hand. Then said he, 'No wonder,' said he, 'if it is hard for the body, wherein are these strong currents, to contain itself.' Then he diminished her meals a second time. She was on that ration for a year, and her desire still persisted. So after that time he thrusts the needle into her hand thrice, and three streams of blood flowed from it. So he reduced her meals again for a year, and at the end of that time he thrust the needle [again into her hand]. This time, however, not a drop of blood came out of her. Then he said to her: 'In future,' said he, 'keep on this pittance until thy death.'

§61. There was a certain itinerant pedlar in Munster in the time of Samthann, who used to carry greetings from her to the 'sons of life'[4] in that country. Once she called him to her and bound him not to add to nor take away a single word that she said, nor a word that anyone should say to whom he was sent. Then she said to him: 'Say to Máel Ruain for me,' said she (or to Fer Dá Chrích, and this latter is more likely, since Máel Ruain was more venerable than Samthann), 'that he is my favourite[5] among the clerics of the Desert,[6] and another thing thou shalt say to him: ask, does he receive womankind to his confession, and will he accept my soul-friendship?' The pedlar took this message. But when he told him he was Samthann's favourite, he rose at once and raised both hands as in a cross-vigil and gave thanks to God. When the pedlar next asked him whether women took counsel of him, and whether he would accept Samthann's soul-friendship, he blushed down to his breast, and made three genuflections, and fell silent for a long time. Then he said: 'Tell her,' said he, 'that I will seek counsel from her.' Then the pedlar told all these sayings to Samthann, and she said: 'I trow,' said she, 'something will come of that youth.' Then she draws her brooch out of her mantle and drives it into her cheek till it stuck in the bone, and then there came out two filaments of milk: yet not a single drop of blood came out. At that sight the pedlar began to weep and wail. Then she took the wound between two fingers and began to squeeze it for a long time, and not a drop was wrung from it. Then at the last by reason of the long squeezing out came a little tiny drop. It was a little drop of water, and there was a little yellow on the surface enough to change its colour. Then she put this little driblet on her nail, and she said: 'So long,' said she, 'as there is this much juice in his body, let him bestow no friendship nor confidence upon womankind.'

§62. Devout young nuns he thinks it [right] to go and converse with and to confirm their faith, but without looking at their faces, and taking an elder nun in thy company: and it is right to converse with them standing on the slab by the cross in front of the hostel,[7] or in the retreat[8] where they live. And the elder who goes with thee, and the senior nun who lives in company with the young nuns, should be present and not far from you, where they are. When ill desire or ill thoughts overtake thee, through seeing women or in converse with them, if . . .[9] that is not to be indulged by thee even as an idle thought [?], then he considers that such desire is no great matter: it is meritorious, however, if a man gets clear of it. When the thoughts are constantly straying towards ill meditations, they must be checked and recalled as far as possible; and he should resort to reading or to examining himself against it, and keep his mind fixed on prayer. He does not consider it easy to fix any penance for such straying of the thoughts; for . . .[10] not much about it here at all.

---

3. i.e. on the same day one year later.
4. Irish *maic bethad*.
5. Irish *sainserc*, from *serc* which usually connotes 'physical love'.
6. i.e. the south of Ireland: Samthann is speaking from the north, at Clonbroney.
7. Irish *les*.
8. Irish *disert*.
9. There is a difficulty in the original at this point.
10. There is something lost here.

SEDULIUS SCOTTUS

(fl. 860)

FOR BERTA, ABBESS OF AVENAY

(c. 860)

[The monk Sedulius Scottus, one of the foremost scholars of the Carolingian Renaissance, arrived in Liège in the mid-ninth century when Irish influence in European scholastic circles was reaching its zenith. He wrote works on grammar, theology, philosophy and politics. He was also a prolific poet and an adept at winning influential patrons. The question of how much of his scholarship was acquired by him before he left Ireland is the subject of ongoing debate. In that context, it is worth noting that the extract cited here reflects ideas that had long been current in Ireland, and which are threaded through the selection on 'Mary and the Virgin Saints'.

Many of his poems are addressed to the rulers of the Carolingian dominions, including the three sons of Louis the Pious, namely, Lothar I (d. 855), who ruled as emperor from 840, Louis the German (d. 876), and Charles the Bald (d. 877). He also addressed poems to Irmingard, queen of Lothar I, and to their children. The following poem is one of a number addressed to their daughter Berta. After her husband's death, she became Abbess of Avenay, in the diocese of Rheims. Thus she moved from marriage (the thirtyfold) through widowhood (the sixtyfold) to the new virginity of the spouse of Christ (the hundredfold). Very diplomatically, the poem inflects the sequence so that Berta's feelings for her earthly husband may also be honoured. 'Bobila' was probably Berta's daughter.

Translation: Edward Gerard Doyle, *Sedulius Scottus: On Christian Rulers and The Poems*, Medieval and Renaissance Texts and Studies, vol. 17 (Binghampton, New York: State University of New York, 1983), p. 170.]

Let us duly give thanks and praise to God,
who always honours his people on earth!
For, as he illumined the heavens with starlight
and decked the land with verdant flowers,
so our bounteous Creator adorns his church
with virgins, widows, and pious wives.
Thus, the saints' threefold fruit prospers,
a glorious harvest which paradise reaps.
Marriage glitters first in sacred rank,
then come widowhood and fair virginity.

Blessed woman, yours is the highest honour,
whence you observed marriage's chaste laws.
You bore a flourishing son and noble light,
but that youthful heir of the Franks has perished.
Alas that cruel death struck your royal scion —
yet paradise now rejoices in his presence!
Hateful death seized your earthly husband,
but in his stead comes a heavenly spouse.
Your groom is richer than all the earth's kings,
and fairer even than violets and roses.
The sun and golden moon marvel at his beauty,
and the angelic chorus praises him on high.
His yoke is light and compassion sweet —
Bobila, too, exults in such a spouse!
He showers you with gems of virtue,
and prepares for you eternal treasures.
Whatever you cheerfully give to the poor,
will be forever inscribed in the Book of Life.
In heaven sumptuous riches await you,
which will never pass away, but eternally endure.

from:
DE RECTORIBUS CHRISTIANIS
(On Christian Rulers) *(c. 855)*

[The genre of *Speculum Principum*, 'Mirror for Princes', to which this tract belongs, served as a vehicle for much of the political writing of the Middle Ages. Sedulius wrote his treatise sometime between 855 and 859 for Lothar II (see preceding note). In it, the king is represented as Christ's vicar on earth, deriving his power directly from God, and ruling a society that should be a model of *civitas Dei*, the 'city of God'.

Despite its title, the following section treats mainly of wives. In describing his ideal, Sedulius renewed key terms from the cult of the Virgin which had come to be recommended to Christian women in general; cf. the 'modest woman' of the anonymous, early seventh-century Irish tract, *De Duodecim Abusivis Saeculi* (see pp. 96–7). Theodosius (the Great), who ruled as Emperor of the East during the years 379–92 and as Emperor of East and West from 392 until his death in 395, was regarded by Christians as ruling by the grace of God. As Theodosius and his wife, Placilla, are typologically equivalent to Christ and his church, Placilla and therefore all noble wives are to be seen as types of the Virgin. It is sobering to compare the attitude to women displayed in the vernacular *Speculum Principum* known as *Tecosca Cormaic* (see pp. 199–200) with Sedulius's text.

Translation: Edward Gerard Doyle, *Sedulius Scottus: On Christian Rulers and The Poems*, pp. 59–61.]

'THE DUTY OF PIOUS GUIDANCE WHICH A RULER OUGHT TO FULFIL WITH REGARD TO HIS WIFE, HIS CHILDREN, AND HIS HOUSEHOLD.'

A pious and wise king performs the office of ruling in three ways: as we have shown above, he should first rule himself with reasonable and meritorious discipline; second, his wife, his children, and his household; and third, the people entrusted to him. Hence, a just prince must not only rule himself, while he rejects evils and chooses and firmly upholds what is good, but he must also direct others more closely related to him, namely, his wife, his children, and his household with prudent care and familial affection. And by accomplishing this, a prince attains a double palm of glory in that when he himself is just and holy, he makes others related to him just and holy too, in accordance with the psalmist who said: 'You will be pure with the pure and blameless with the man who is blameless' [Psalms 18:26]. For it does not suffice to possess personal honour, unless it is embellished with the propriety of a chaste and modest wife, and with the propriety of children, friends, and servants, as David said: 'He who walks in immaculate ways served me' [Psalms 101:6]. Just as a lily of the field is enhanced in beauty by the manifold beauty of other plants and of violets and just as the moon shines more pleasingly in the glow of the surrounding stars, so, truly, a just king is greatly adorned by the fellowship of other good men.

A ruler, therefore, should perspicaciously endeavor to have a wife who is not only noble, beautiful and wealthy, but also chaste, prudent, and compliant in holy virtues. For, so much as a wife is closer (to a man) in law, to that extent she becomes either noxious with the poison of wickedness or pleasing with the sweetness of morals. To be sure, a foolish wife is the ruin of a household, the exhaustion of wealth, the fullness of crimes, and the abode of all evils and vices, who ornaments her exterior mien with diverse observances, but who knows not how to adorn the interior beauty of her soul. Whomever she loves today, she hates tomorrow, just as a certain man once said: 'A wife unfaithful to her husband is the shipwreck of all things.' However, a chaste and prudent wife, diligently attending to useful matters with a humble demeanor and cheerful speech, peacefully manages her children and family; and, on behalf of her husband's welfare, if necessary, she sets her life against death and defends his wealth with an honorable reputation. Whoever was her friend yesterday is her friend today. In effect, she becomes the increase of wealth, the support of the household, the delight of her husband, the glory of the family, and the union of all virtues. Indeed, it is proper for such a one not only to be bound and subservient to her husband with a chaste bond, but also to reflect always an image of holiness and pious behavior, and to be an inventress of prudent counsels. Just as by the persuasion of an evil wife pernicious dangers are begotten, so by the counsel of a prudent wife many benefits are produced that are pleasing to the Almighty, whence the apostle said: 'The unbelieving husband will be saved by a believing wife' [1 Corinthians 7:14].

Not only unbelieving but also pious and orthodox princes often ponder and give heed to the marvellous prudence in their wives, not reflecting on their fragile sex, but, rather, plucking the fruit of their good counsels. Hence, it is said about Placilla, the venerable wife of the glorious emperor Theodosius, that through her the prince, though he himself was upright, just and wise, enjoyed another useful opportunity by which he might triumph from good works. His wife, having instructed herself completely beforehand, often admonished the prince concerning divine laws. She was not puffed up by the dignities of royal power but was inflamed by divine love. In fact, the abundance of blessings she received increased her love for her benefactor; and indeed, she came unexpectedly to high station. She took the greatest care of the crippled and lame, but not by using slaves or other servants; rather, she acted through herself, coming to their dwellings and offering to each what he needed. In this way visiting the hospitals of the churches, she ministered to the sick with her own hands, cleaning their pots, tasting broth, offering spoonfuls, breaking bread, serving food, washing cups, and doing all the other things which are customarily performed by slaves and servants. To those who tried to restrain her from such things she would say: 'It is the office of our emperor to distribute gold; but I offer this service on behalf of that Emperor who has conferred upon me so many blessings.' Moreover, to her husband she would often say: 'You should always remember, my husband, what you once were and what you are now. If you always remember these things, you will never be ungrateful to your benefactor, but will lawfully rule the empire you have received and will appease the author of all these things.' And, with such words, she presented to her husband some useful profit and abundant virtue.

A pious and wise king rules himself, his family,
     and his subjects with threefold direction.
A wife virtuous in morals stands forth as the
     glory of the king like a fruitful vine.
Nobility in threefold virtue should beautify her
     with the roses of a chaste heart;
for if milk-white necks glisten with lovely
     elegance, chastity should glisten even more.
As Christ united the Church to him with a
     chaste love, so a wife should cleave to her
     husband;
in her heart gentle simplicity like the beauty of a
     dove should always abound.
Piety, prudence, and sacred authority should
     adorn her, just as gracious Esther shone.
A king and queen should cherish the bonds of
     peace; in both there should be agreement
     and concord.
Hateful discord must not separate the pair
     whom the divine law of peace has joined
     together.
Discipline should rule their glorious offshoots
     so that seemly branches may flourish.
A withered young branch never thrives on a
     vigorous tree. A good cultivator provides
     for this:
if a ruler and his queen are to rule the people
     justly, let them first rule their own family.
Let them decorate the heavens with
     descendants created as if from the noble
     stock of Abraham.

DANIÉL ÚA LÍATHAITI

(d. 863)

A BEN, BENNACHT FORT —
NÁ RÁID!
(Sell Not Heaven for Sin)
(c. 850)

[The Annals of Innisfallen describe Daniél úa Líathaiti as Abbot of Lismore and Cork. Text and translation: Gerard Murphy (ed. and trans.), *Early Irish Lyrics: Eighth to Twelfth Century* (Oxford: Clarendon Press, 1956), pp. 6–9.]

At-rubairt Daniél ua Líathaiti, airchinnech Lis Móir, oca guide don mnaí. Esseom ropo anmchara disi. Baí-si immurgu ocá thothlugud-som. Is and as-bert-som:

1
A ben, bennacht fort — ná ráid!
     Imráidem dáil mbrátha búain.
A-tá irchra for cach ndúil:
     ad-águr dul i n-úir n-úair.

2
Im-ráidi baís cen bríg mbaí:
     is súaichnid ní gaís fris-ngní.
A n-asbir-siu bid rád fás:
     bid nessa ar mbás 'siú 'ma-rrí.

3
A n-airchenn fil ar ar cinn
     bad mebor linn (éirim ngann):
sunn cía na-cráidem in Ríg,
     bami aithrig is tír thall.

4

Ríched ní renaim ar chol;
    dam ad-fíther cía do-gnem.
Ní nád faigbe síu íar sin
    ní thaibre ar bin, a ben.

5

Léic úait a n-í condat-shil;
    do chuit i nnim náchas-ren;
for fóesam nDé eirg dot treib
    bendacht úaim-se beir, a ben.

6

Messu tussu, tussu mé,
    águr, áigthe Fíadait fó;
guid-siu, gigsea Coimdid cáid:
    a ben, ná ráid ní bas mó.

7

Ná bí for seilg neich nád maith
    dáig fot-cheird ind Fhlaith for cel;
áigthe, águr Críst cen chin
    ná ro-lámur tríst, a ben.

'Bid fír ón,' or sisi. Ro shlécht-si for a bith-denma-som in eret ro boí i mbethaid.

TRANSLATION

Daniel grandson of Líathaite, abbot of Lismore, spoke these verses when a woman was entreating him. He was her confessor, but she was soliciting him. Then he said:

1

O woman, a blessing on thee — say it not! Let us think on the court of eternal judgement. Decay is the fate of every creature: I fear going into cold clay.

2

Thy mind is set on profitless folly: clearly it is not wisdom thou pursuest. What thou sayest will be empty speech: our death will be nearer before it comes to pass.

3

Let us remember the fated end that awaits us (short journey!): if we afflict the King here, we shall rue it in the land beyond.

4

I sell not Heaven for sin: if I do so retribution will be made me. O woman, give not for wrongdoing that which thou shalt never recover here.

5

Abandon that which will injure thee; sell not thy share in Heaven; under God's protection go to thy home; take from me a blessing, O woman.

6

I and thou, thou and I, let me dread, dread thou the good Lord; pray thou, I shall pray the holy King; O woman, say no more.

7

Pursue not that which is not good, for the Lord will bring thee to nought; dread, and let me dread, sinless Christ, whose malediction I have not risked, O woman.

'Thus shall it be,' said she. She bowed before his perpetual purity as long as she lived.

DIGDE

(fl. 900)

AITHBE DAMSA BÉS MARA
(Digde's Lament)
(c. 900)

[Many poets and scholars have made translations of this intriguing Old Irish poem. Until recently, its attribution to a woman was almost invariably ignored or disbelieved, and its speaker, thought to be the Caillech Béirre, was identified as a goddess of the land and of sovereignty. In fact, Gaelic tradition, medieval and modern, learned and popular, represents the Caillech Béirre as a revenant who enjoyed extraordinary longevity and survived serial epochs and historical ruptures; other such revenants are Tuán mac Stairn and Mongán mac Fiachna. In the poem, she has become at last an ordinary mortal who cannot postpone death, and is living out her span in a monastery of women: she is now the 'Caillech Béirre that was' ('Is mé Caillech Béirre boí', quatrain 2a), the *former* Caillech Béirre. Her bleak vision of the transience of all worldly pleasure is tempered by belief in the Christian heaven. The poem turns on consideration of different modalities of time: the linear, finite time of humankind, the cyclical time of Nature, and the eternity promised to Christians.

The poem is pervaded by the range of meanings associated with the word *caillech* (from Latin *pallium*, 'veil'): 'spouse', 'nun', 'widow', 'penitent spouse' (a nun who was formerly married), and 'ancient crone'. Béirre (anglicized Beare) is a peninsula in west County Cork. Some copies of the poem have prose introductions. In these, the identities of the author, the speaker (a 'penitent spouse'), and the speaker's former self (the Caillech Béirre), are partially conflated but can still be separated out. The following details are given about the author: her name was Digde (with variants 'Dige' and 'Duineach'). She was of the Corco Duibne, a people associated with the modern Dingle peninsula in County Kerry. She was comparable to three 'wondrous *caillech*s' of the Corco Duibne: Brigit daughter of Iustán, Líadan wife of Cuirither, and Úallach daughter of Muimnechán.

Brigit daughter of Iustán is otherwise unknown. Líadan is elsewhere said to have been a poet and is portrayed as a 'penitent spouse' or, as in the text which follows this poem, as a spouse in a spiritual marriage. Úallach daughter of Muimnechán is described as *banfhile Herend* 'Ireland's woman-poet' in her death-notice in the Annals of Innisfallen under the year 934. These details argue strongly that the poem was indeed composed by a female poet named Digde, of the Corco Duibne, who, at some stage in her life, became a nun.

The poem is found already in Volume I, 'Caillech Bérri/The Old Woman of Beare', pp. 32–4, in Gerard Murphy's edition, with a translation by David Greene and Frank O'Connor. In essence, the present edition is that of Donncha Ó hAodha, but variant readings have been adopted for lines 2a, 4b, 6b, 14d, 24a and 30c. See his 'The Lament of the Old Woman of Beare', in *Sages, Saints and Storytellers: Celtic Studies in Honour of Professor James Carney*, eds Donnchadh Ó Corráin, Liam Breatnach and Kim McCone (Maynooth: An Sagart, 1989), pp. 308–31. This is a new translation by Seamus Deane.]

1
Aithbe damsa bés mara;
sentu fom-dera croan;
toirsi oca ce do-gnéo,
sona do-táet a loan.

2
Is mé Caillech Bérre boí,
do-meilinn léne mbithnuí;
indíu táthum dom shémi
ná melainn cid athléni.

3
It moíni
charthar lib, nidat doíni;
ind inbaid i mmarsamar
batar doíni carsamar.

4
Batar inmaini doíni
ata maige 'ma-ríadam;
ba maith no meilmis leo,
ba bec no moítis íaram.

5
Indíu trá caín-timargat,
ocus ní mór nond-oídet;
cíasu bec do-n-idnaiget,
is mór a mét no-moídet.

6
Carpait lúaith
ocus eich no beirtis búaid,
ro boí, denus, tuile díb:
bennacht ar Ríg roda-úaid.

7
Tocair mo chorp co n-aichri
dochum adba díar aichni;
tan bas mithig la Mac nDé
do-té do breith a aithni.

8
Ot é cnámacha cáela
ó do-éctar mo láma —
ba hinmainiu, tan, gnítis
bítis im ríga ána.

9
Ó do-éctar mo láma
ot é cnámacha cáela,
nidat fiu turcbáil, taccu,
súas tarna maccu cáema.

10
It fáilti na hingena
ó thic dóib co Beltaine;
is deithbiriu damsa brón:
sech am tróg, am sentaine.

11
Ni feraim cobra milis:
ni marbtar muilt im banais;
is bec, is líath mo thrilis,
ní liach drochcaille tarais.

12
Ní holc lim
ce beth caille finn form chinn;
boí mór meither cech datha
form chinn ic ól daglatha.

13
Nim-geib format fri nach sen
inge nammá fri Femen;
meisse, ro melt forbuid sin,
buide beus barr Femin.

14
Lia na Ríg i Femun,
Cathair Rónáin i mBregun:
cían ó ro-síachtsat sína,
a llecne, nít senchrína.

15
Is labar tonn mara máir,
ros-gab in gaim comgabáil;

16
fer muid, mac moga, indíu
ni frescim do chéilidiu.

16
Is éol dam a ndo-gniat,
rait ocus do-raat;
curchasa Átha Alma,
is fúar in adba i faat.

17
Is mó láu
nát muir n-oíted ima-ráu;
testa mór mblíadnae dom chruth,
dáig fo-rromled mo chétluth.

18
Is mó dé
damsa indiú, cé bé-de;
gaibthium étach, cid fri gréin,
do-fil áes dam, at-gén féin.

19
Sam oíted i rrabamar
do-melt cona fhogamur;
gaim aís báides cech duine,
domm-ánic a fhochmuine.

20
Ro milt m'oítid ar thuus,
is buide lem ro-ngleus;
cid bec mo léim dar duae,
níba nuae in brat beus.

21
Is álainn in brat úaine
ro scar mo Rí tar Drummain;
is sáer in Fer rod-lúaidi,
do-rat loí fair íar lummain.

22
A minecán morúar dam
— cech dercoin is erchraide —
íar feis fri condlib sorchaib
bith i ndorchaib derrthaige.

23
Rom-boí denus la ríga
ic ól meda is fína;
indíu ibim medcuisce
itir sentanaib crína.

24
Robat mo chuirm coidin midc,
ropo toil Dé cecham-theirp;
ocot guide-si, a Dé bí,
do-rata cró clí fri feirg.

25
At-chiú form brat brodrad n-aís;
ro gab mo chíall mo thogaís;
líath a finn ásas trim thuinn,
is samlaid crotball senchroinn.

26
Rucad úaim-se mo shúil des
dá reic ar thír mbithdíles;
ocus rucad int shúil chlé
do fhormach a fhoirdílse.

27
Trí thuile
tascnat dún Arda Ruide:
tuile n-ooc, tuile n-ech,
tuile mílchon mac Luigdech.

28
Tonn tuili
ocus ind í aithbi áin:
a tabair tonn tuili dait
beirid tonn aithbi as do láim.

29
Tonn tuili
ocus ind aile aithbi:
dom-áncatarsa uili
conda éolach a n-aichni.

30
Tonn tuili,
nícos-toir socht mo chuili;
cid mór mo dám fo deimi,
fo-cres lám forru uili.

31
Ma rro-fessed Mac Muire
co mbeth fo chlí mo chuile:
cinco ndernus gart chena,
ní érbart 'nac' fri duine.

32
Tróg n-uile,
daírib dúilib, do duine,
ná déccas a n-aithbesi
feb ro-déccas a tuile.

33
Mo thuile,
is maith con-roíter m'aithne:
ro-sháer Ísu Mac Muire
conám toirsech co aithbe.

34
Céin-mair ailén mara máir,
dos-n-ic tuile íarna tráig;
is mé, ni frescu dom-í
tuile tar éisi aithbi.

35
Is súaill mennatán indíu
ara tabrainnse aithgne;
a n-í ro boí for tuile
atá uile for aithbe.

TRANSLATION

As the sea ebbs
so my youth recedes;
no matter how I grieve
my body concedes.
It is no more than food
to the sea. Now, this hood
of age that time leaves
on my sunken frame,
covers but a wraith.
Caillech Béirre was my name,
I here assert a mortal's faith
in what I was. But I'm so thin
now even a cast-off shift
would survive my frame.

You living nowadays love
wealth, and crave more.
But we who lived before
you put people above
riches, and lived well
on the time-plains we cross.
Then people gave
without fuss, did not sell
themselves nor were lost
in claims of what they gave,
while hugging their gold.
Now all's bought and sold
and people boast
how much their giving cost.

There was another time
when chariots and steeds,
prized and swift, in a line
without end, bespoke
the glory of the king
who could boast
that he could bring
such untold blessings,
and win great praise.
But now my body pleads,
at the bitter end of its days
to go where it will be known,
to the time where time has flown.
When the Son of God will deem it right,

let him take into his eternal light
what he gave me, the grace of life.
These scrawny bones that jut
from arms that would once embrace
desirous and desiring kings
are no longer thought
wondrous limbs, worthy to enfold
the dear sons of men, of Adam's race.
When the young maidens come
to the May-Day feast, they walk in joy.
But old and wretched have I become,
a walking misery, the feast's kill-joy.
I have no sweet talk, no sheep are slain
for the wedding I've come to make.

My veil is unembroidered, plain,
to hide thin hair, not overawe
by its beauty. Now my head is covered.
But I don't mind. Once it was swathed
in every colour cloth could draw
from dyes and tinctures and men raved
in feasting sessions at my style.
Now only Feimen[1] wakes my bile,
for Feimen ages and stays golden-fringed
while I shrivel, and even Feimen's kings'
Inauguration Stone, Rónán's Fort[2]
in Bregon,[3] all show the stress and hurt
of time and storm. My short story
of bright pleasure is also curt,

a dark oratory hears its dying fall.
I whose pleasure was with kings

now wait no more for a call
from royalty, nor from the lowly.
On the quick-rising waves
winter has begun to fall
and they break, break slowly.
All those people and their deeds
fade across Alma's Ford.[4]
Like ghosts among the reeds,
they depart without a word.
They row away into the cold,
into the fastness of sleep.
It is so long ago, so old

a time now, when I rode
on the tide of youth,
knew its intimacies, its sex
as intensities and truth.
Now, even the sunlight can vex
me, when I still feel cold
in its warmth, and need my cloak.
I lived the summer of youth,
I felt autumn's first taint,
and now the wintry truth
that steals at first as a faint
chill on me, and on everyone,
has come. I enjoyed my youth,
and am glad it was so.

It was a small release
then, to jump the traces
as I did. Youth briefly blazes,
and play or no play,
the cloak, with time's increase,
would wear out anyway.
It is not at all like the green
my King has woven on Drummain.[5]
The craftsman who wove that cover
knew what he was about, a fuller
who turned the hills' serge
into fine-spun wool. Ah, the dirge
of my sorrow! Both the folk and the fool
know every acorn that grows decays.

I, who once drank mead and wine,
am now in such sharp decline
that whey water is all I taste
among women gone to waste.
Yet may my goblets be whey-cups,
may what vexes me be fresh

---

1. Feimen, a plain south of Cashel, is sometimes used in reference to all Munster and, more rarely, Ireland.
2. A royal residence, probably that of Rónán Mór of Múscraige Bregoin who lived in the early eighth century.
3. A place in Feimen.

4. Unidentified.
5. Unidentified.

occasion to accept God's will;
and between these humble sups
may Christ's blood intervene
to calm God's anger and redeem
with the fading of my flesh
my spirit in its fierce unrest.
My reason weakens, my cloak is stained,
I wince like a tree in wind and rain.

Grey and raddled, my right eye blind,
the better to have sight of heaven;
the left eye unsighted next, resigned
from the world, I am assured, more even
than before, of my eternal place.
The fort of Ard Ruide[6] was mobbed
by warriors, steeds and there sobbed
among them the excited hounds,
almost numberless, of Lugaid's race.[7]
Three flood and three ebb tides!
What the one brings to you the other
bears away. I have seen both sides,
flood and ebb, nothing will smother
their advance, retreat. Nothing abides.

My silent kitchen! Gone forever
my friends of old! Yet I aver,
had I known as now I know
the Son of Mary dwelt within,

6. Probably in Munster.
7. Perhaps Lugaid, who was son of the Munster King Óengus mac
   Nad Froích (d. 490/2).

under the roof-tree of my house,
my charity that once was thin
would have known no bounds.
I would never have refused
anyone, not the least of humankind.
It's sad we were so wholly blind
to the ebb's arrival, the grounds
of hope withdrawing for good,
because it was only flood
we saw, and not the counter-flow.

The flood-tide of my life
has preserved for me
the rich deposit Jesus Christ
bestowed so freely
until now the ebb has come.
How fortunate the isle
that enjoys once more
high water, running tide,
after the dried shore
of the ebbing main.
I do not expect or abide
such a returning flow;
once the ebbing-time
has come, there is no more.

Today, there isn't a home
standing that I would know.
All the life that crested
on the full tide-foam
is abandoned, bested
by the counter-flow.

ANONYMOUS

COMRAC LÍADAINE OCUS CHUIRITHIR
(The Union of Líadan and Cuirither)
(10th century)

[The tale of Líadan and Cuirither, the lovers separated by their love of God, is one of the most appealing in medieval Irish. The text as it survives is possibly no more than a synopsis. The literary quality of the final poem, in particular, prompts thoughts of a fuller sequence of monologues — a kind of play for voices, needing little action to support the unfolding drama.

It is clear from references elsewhere that the story was well known to readers and auditors of medieval Irish literature, who would have readily understood the following text despite its laconic character. Both Líadan and Cuirither are said to have been notable poets, dedicated to their craft (§1). (A single quatrain attributed to Líadan survives; nothing is known of Cuirither's work.) They postpone the consummation of their love until after the completion of their rounds to their patrons. Then Cuirither mac Doburchon (Cuirither 'Son of Otter'), comes to Líadan's house to claim her for his bride (§2).

The secular nature of his quest is indicated by his dress and his spearshafts: only the laity bore arms. Courteously, he has his arrival announced. The messenger, appropriately, is Mac Da Cherdae, 'Son of Two Arts', a poet and holy fool, giddy with love. His allusive speech with its invitation to a love-union is understood by Líadan alone, who is alert to the pun on her name, 'the grey one', from Irish *liath* 'grey'. Sadly, he has also already intuited that her love has changed: she is now more drawn to God than to Cuirither.

For Cuirither, and to a lesser extent Líadan, their dilemma is beyond remedy, and their efforts to neutralize it by entering on a spiritual union in a double monastery are fraught from the beginning and end in frustrated loneliness and separation. By testing their virtue in an absurd ordeal, the rigorist Saint Cummaíne (in life the author of a penitential rule) makes a mockery of love, both divine and human.

The church of Cill Chonchinn, alias Cill Achaid Chonchinn, anglicized Killaha, is in the barony of Magunihy, County Kerry. The indications are that Líadan and Cuirither lived in the seventh century. The text, in its entirety, dates perhaps from the tenth century and there seem to be no grounds for dating any of the verse to earlier than the ninth.

The final poem, in the original and with a translation by David Greene and Frank O'Connor, is in Volume I, pp. 48–9. (See also 'Curithir and Liadain' by Katherine Arnold Price in Volume V, pp. 1026–8.) This new translation of the entire text is by Seamus Deane. It is based on a forthcoming new edition.]

§1. Líadan, a woman of the Corco Duibne,[1] was a woman poet. She went on a poet's circuit into the territory of Connacht. Now Cuirither mac Doburchon, himself a poet, was a Connacht man. He prepared an ale-feast for Líadan. 'Why should we not come together, Líadan?' Cuirither asked. 'A child of ours would be remarkable.' 'No, we won't do that,' she says, 'in case my circuit is thereby ruined. But if you come to seek me at my house, I shall come with you.'

§2. And so it happened. He went south with a single servant, his clothing in a bag on the servant's back. He himself was poorly dressed. His spearheads were also in the servant's bag. So he travelled until he came to the well beside the *lios*. Then he put on his formal, purple clothing and the spearheads were fixed to their shafts.

---

1. The people who occupied what is now Dingle peninsula, County Kerry.

As he stood brandishing the spears, he saw Mac Da Cherdae coming towards him. This man was a fool, the son of Máel-Ochtraig, of the Déisi of Munster. Dryshod, he regularly travelled over land and sea alike. He was the chief poet and the fool of all Ireland. Up he comes to Cuirither. 'Well met!' said Mac Da Cherdae. 'Well met indeed!' answered Cuirither. 'Are you the man of the *lios*?' asked Mac Da Cherdae. 'I am not,' replied Cuirither. 'Where are you from?' 'That's easy to tell. I am the poor fool, that is to say Mac Da Cherdae of the Déisi.' 'I've heard of you,' says Cuirither, 'Are you going into the *lios*?' 'I am,' he answered. 'Do me a favour,' says Cuirither. 'Tell that tall woman yonder to come to this well. Find a way of your own to tell her.' 'What is her name?' 'Líadan.' 'And what is your name?' 'Cuirither mac Doburchon.' 'Right,' he said.

So he goes into the house. She was in her chamber with three women. He sat down; no one paid any attention to him. Then he said:

'If in this great pillared *lios*
There is anyone who is
Arranging a tryst, to be met,
The command is, when the sun sets,
That would be a time to arrive
At the well, a time to contrive
To be met in front of the house,
When birds fly like sparks
Around it, sweet darting larks.
Darkness has assailed my eyes,
I am insensible to every sign.
There's no woman I recognize
Here, but I address Líadan blind.
In the great choir there is none
Physically like you, the grey one,
Nor is there a veiled nun
To match your dedication.
Cuirither, son of the otter,
Who stays at night under water,
Waits for you, his spear-shafts
Pointed, his warrior die cast.'

§3. After that she went with him and the couple became spiritual partners under the aegis of Cummaíne Fota. 'Good,' said Cummaíne. 'Many come to me, raw, untested by spiritual discipline. May the strength of soul-friendship be granted to you. What shall you choose — to look on one another or to talk together?' 'For us, talking together,' said Cuirither, 'what will come of that will be better. We looked on one another before now.'

After that, whenever he made the rounds of the gravestones of the saints, she would be closed up in her cell. Similarly, when she made the rounds, he would be closed up in his cell. It is then that she said:

'I loved Cuirither, who once wrote verse,
Less for me a blessing than a curse.
He was so dear to me, the lord of the spear,
It will be sad to be forever so near,
Celibate, though not to him averse.

'Each day I often go to the oratory
To where he has been, on the flagstone
In the south corner. It is the territory
I hold after the victory I have won
In prayer from my body's mourn.

'He shall have neither cow nor heifer
Nor bull-calf. There shall be none
To sleep by him, never any one
For this cleric who is alone;
No wife, no daughter, no son.'

[Cuirither said:]

'Dear is the voice that I hear,
To take pleasure in it, I fear.
I do not dare rejoice
But say only, "Dear is this voice!"'

The woman said:

'The voice that reaches me
Through the wooden wall,
Rebukes the desire in me.
And its appeal is deep
It begins to appall
That it will not let me sleep.'

§4.

'Sir, it's an evil accusation
That Cuirither and I sinned.
That he came from Loch Seng's[2]
Bank and I from Cill Chonchinn
For carnal delectation.'

2. Unidentified.

'You two are to sleep together tonight,' said Cummaíne, 'and let a young scholar sleep between you in case you do anything foolish.' It was then that Cuirither said:

'If you say it is for one night
That I shall sleep with Líadan,
Imagine how any layman
Would prize such a plight,
As it is for me. It would so arouse
Him I bet he would not drowse.'

It is then Líadan said:

'If it be for one night sir
That I sleep with Cuirither
It would be to me no fear
Were it to be for a year.
I would not run out
Of things to talk about.'

They slept together that night. On the following day, the little boy is brought in to be questioned by Cummaíne. 'I advise you to conceal nothing. I shall kill you if you do.' It is all the same to the young boy. He will tell the truth though he should die for doing so. 'I shall kill you unless you affirm and acknowledge the truth.'

§5. Cuirither was brought then to another church. It was there that he said:

'Of late, since I parted
From Líadan, every day
Is as long as a month.
Every month as a year.'

[Líadan said:]

'If Cuirither has today
Gone to teach the scholars,
Who will get what he'll say?
They don't know him. It bothers
Me they'll think his wits astray.'

Cummaíne said:

'I do not like what you say,
Líadan, wife of Cuirither.
He was here, he was not astray
In his wits, that I can aver,
Any more than on the day
He first came as a visitor.'

[Líadan said:]

'That Friday, we lay on no carnal bed.
We made no love on the fleece
Of my bright coverlet. Whatever is said
I did not go into such sleep
In the arms of Cuirither.'

§6. Cuirither travelled then until he came to Cill Leitrech[3] in the land of the Déisi on his pilgrimage into solitude. She went in search of him and she said:

'Without joy is the deed
That I have done. To augment
My love was my creed.
It has finished in torment.

'It would have been madness
Not to sleep with him. The pain
Had to be overcome, the gladness
That I pleased the King of Heaven.

'I deprived him of no prize,
For my desired tryst
With him was in Paradise,
Beyond pain's twist.

'The phantom of the flesh
Turned Cuirither against me.
But I had a tenderness
For him greater than he for me.

'I am Líadan, I have loved
Cuirither. This is the case.
Nothing is truer below or above
Than the story I relate.

'It was for a short time
I had Cuirither with me,
And for that while
Sweet was our intimacy.

'With Cuirither I heard
The song of the trees
And the sound of the seas
Falling blood-red.

'It was my belief
That nothing I chose
Would cause Cuirither grief,
Would make us like foes.

'It shall not be hidden!
He was my heart's love,
Although I am bidden
To love all from above.

'A blast of flame
Has scorched my heart.
It will not beat again
Now we're apart.'

This then was the reason for his torment — the speed with which she took the veil. When he was in the west and heard of her coming, he set off in a curragh on the sea and went on his pilgrimage. So she never saw him again. 'He has truly gone this time,' she said. She lay on that flagstone on which he used to pray until she died and her soul went to heaven. And it was that flagstone that was laid on the grave over her face. And that is the story of the Union of Líadan and Cuirither.

SAINT MOLAISSE AND HIS SISTER
(10th century)

[The lovers in the previous text, the Union of Líadan and Cuirither, are not said to have had a child. This text dramatizes the ecclesiastical ostracization of a couple who did. The casual attitude to the unequal punishments suffered by the two individuals is remarkable. The didactic purpose of the text — to demonstrate the efficacy of Psalm 118 in procuring the release of souls from hell — only serves to reinforce the impression that the woman herself is mainly to blame for the sin of her pregnancy.

This story has been dated to the early tenth century. The death of Molaisse moccu Dímma (alternatively, 'moccu Imdae') of Leighlin is recorded in the annals for the year 639. The Annals of Ulster describe him as abbot of that church. Leighlin, in present-day County Carlow, was one of the principal churches of the Leinster people. This translation is based on the edition (with German translation) by Julius Pokorny, 'Eine altirische Legende aus dem Buch von Leinster', in *Miscellany Presented to Kuno Meyer*, eds Osborn Bergin and Carl Marstrander (Halle a S: Max Niemeyer, 1912), pp. 207–15.]

3. Possibly the same as Dún Leitrech, on the River Suir, in south County Tipperary.

The sister of Saint Molaisse of Leighlin was studying with him. Moreover, it was she who looked after the cleric. Now there was a clerical student in the saint's community. He and the young nun had intercourse and so she became pregnant.

'There will be trouble on account of this,' said the woman, 'if the cleric should find out. He will heap odium on us so that we shall have neither heaven nor earth. But it is enough that *I* am ruined,' she said; 'go you and avoid him.' 'Then may you not speak of me, girl,' said the student. 'I shall not,' she said, 'unless it comes out through my side. Say my requiem well.' 'If I live,' he said, 'you shall not be in hell.' 'Go in God's care, then,' said she. He travelled after that until he came to Armagh.

After a time, someone in the place said to Molaisse: 'Cleric, the young nun is in labour.' 'May that be labour of swift death,' says the cleric Molaisse, and he deprives her of heaven and earth. That came to pass. She did not receive communion. She died and went to hell. The cleric did not allow her burial in the cemetery, and so she was buried in the bog below the church.

A clerical student of the Leinstermen came to him in Armagh. 'How are things with Molaisse?' he said. 'Fine,' said the student. 'And the young nun?' 'It is like this,' he said, 'she died and went to hell. No one knows who has caused this.' 'Fair enough,' he said. Thereupon he began to say her requiem, that is to say, he recited the *Beati*[1] seven times daily, with one hundred genuflexions and the three fifties.[2] Then he journeyed southwards. He greeted Molaisse, and the cleric questioned him about everything. 'What I request,' said the student, 'is a secluded hut outside the church in which I might entreat God.' 'All right,' said the cleric.

The student built a hut close to the grave, and he spent a year there. On one occasion he saw the young nun approach him. 'A blessing on your soul!' she said. 'You are good to me: I am almost redeemed.' 'What most of all has redeemed you?' asked the student. 'The *Beati*,' she replied, and then she said:

'When one sings it long and fervently,
the *Beati* is a prayer most dear;

1. Psalm 118 (119 in some version of the Bible), the opening words of which are '*Beati immaculati*'.
2. i.e. the full complement of 150 psalms.

I would not be damned for long,
were it sung zealously for me.

'The *Beati* is a prayer most dear —
happy the soul for which it is sung —
accounted two score cows in worth
by Him who watches over us, our King.'

'Truly,' she said, 'it is the *Beati* that succours me.'

Then at one time the pious Fursa[3] visited the church and he saw a ministration of angels coming to the grave in the bog. 'Well then, Molaisse,' said Fursa, 'who is the saint who lies in the bog?' 'It is a demon,' said Molaisse, 'a diabolical nun.' 'Look at this, Molaisse!' said Fursa. And Molaisse saw a ministration of angels rising heavenwards from the grave. After that, the body was taken from the bog and buried in the cemetery. And Fursa took the clerical student under his care and he became a saint and went to heaven.

And so it follows that the *Beati* is better than all prayers.

3. Saint Fursa who died at Péronne *c.* 649 is probably intended.

THE FATE OF THE SINFUL GREEK GIRL
(Early Middle Irish)

[The burden of this text is that even the greatest sinners can repent and become saints: the sinful Greek girl, in her youth, had compounded her sin of lust with a double murder. The dense plot, complicated shifts and Greek setting all suggest that the Irish text originated as a translation, probably from Latin.

The following translation into English is made from the Irish text in: R.I. Best and M.A. O'Brien (eds), *The Book of Leinster*, vol. 5 (1967), pp. 1224–6.]

Once upon a time there was a distinguished Greek king in an encampment. The kings in the east always had an encampment. When stationary, the queens were wont to spend their time drinking and feasting. A message arrived for the king. 'Honour and dignity to you, O king! A daughter was born to you last night.' 'May it be a good portent,' said the king; 'a blessing on the womb that bore her.' 'Honour to you, O king,' said a young lord who was there. 'A son was born to me last night.' 'Give the girl to her then,' said the king. It was always their custom when a boy was born on the same night as a girl that one was betrothed to the other. If either one died forthwith, the one who survived was to remain chaste for ever more and never to sleep with any one else.

The king's daughter was betrothed then to the lord's son. And the daughter was brought up impeccably in learning and wisdom and art, so much so that her father used to direct his questions to her and seek her counsel. And she lived in a house apart, and no one dared to enter it except for the person who waited on her. It was she who used to distribute the last drink every night. In order that there would be sociability and blessing, no matter what should befall them from one day to the next, she used to come in her broad shoes and take the pitcher and fill the goblets. She used to go back out again after that.

A handsome youth who was part of the household fell in love with her. She invited him one time into her house with the girls. He did not come out of the house until he and the girl were lovers. One time when he had lain with the girl in the house, the king came to the door. 'Open up!' said the king. The girl got up and placed the quilt over the youth. The king came and sat on the quilt. She sat herself down beside him and they conversed into the afternoon. The king went out. The man under the quilt was dead. The girls were dismayed at that. Then a brawny herdsman came to the door of the girls' house. They call him in. They give him food. 'Take away that load from us. You'll get a reward for it.' Then he is trussed up. 'Throw it over the cliff. It will be all the better if I go with you.' She goes with him. 'Throw it over the cliff.' When the herdsman was at the cliff, she pressed her two hands against them both and pushed them into the abyss. 'Your secret will be all the better for it!' said she.

'Well now,' said the lord, 'it's time the girl was given to this boy.' 'Let her be given to him then,' said the king. 'Here's a young, beautiful girl, of good family and well-educated.' So he comes to lie with her. 'What will I do?' said she. 'He'll discover my misdeed and I'll be burnt on the spot. Help me!' said she to her companion, 'that is to say, lie with the man as if you're me. If he couples with you again, I'll take your place.' 'I too

have been betrothed to a man,' said she,[1] 'and I'll give some advice to you about that.'

He is brought into a house to them — that is, a dark house so that none of them was seen by the others until the following day. He was allowed into their presence. 'You're welcome,' said she;[2] 'come to your young queen that there may be good fortune and prosperity for you and your sons and daughters.' The other woman[3] sleeps alone until the pair have lain together. 'Let me into that place now,' said she, when the youth had fallen asleep. 'No,' said her companion, 'not until everyone sees the man who lay with me.' 'All right,' said she. They fall asleep. She goes out. She looks for a candle and she sets it under the roof so that the house would take fire. The youth got up to save the house. 'Bring water from the vat,' said she to her companion. The girl went to the vat. She followed her. When the companion was stooping to get the water, she seized her two feet and thrust her head under the water so that she killed her. She did not let her come to the surface. Before she had finished, the youth came to the rescue. 'Where's my companion?' said she. 'O woe if she's drowned!' They saw that she was dead. She knelt down to keen over her. 'Little you care!' said the youth. After that, she slept with him. She went away with him to his country.

Subsequently, her father died. Another high-king came to power in the land. Her partner also died. The king who ruled there was very distinguished. She too was very distinguished. And she was summoned to the king so that gifts might be bestowed on her. She came to the king. He gives her a great welcome. She takes her meals with him. 'Have you a soul-friend?' she said. 'I have,' said the king, 'a wonderful man.' 'He'll be soul-friend to me also,' said she. Then she goes to undertake soul-friendship. Everyone is sent out. She confesses everything without concealment. When the cleric heard that she had succumbed to lust, and saw how beautiful she was, he began to solicit her. 'No!' said she. 'Whatever has been done already, doubtless I haven't atoned for it. I won't add to it.' The cleric did not continue with the confession. She bade farewell to the king.

The king went to speak with the soul-friend. He reports the woman's confession to the king.

1. i.e. the companion of the king's daughter.
2. i.e. the companion of the king's daughter.
3. i.e. the king's daughter.

'That's not good.' She was summoned to the king once more. 'Well, woman,' said he, 'did you make your confession?' 'I did,' said she. 'Did the cleric solicit you?' 'It won't be me that tells.' 'Not good. Depart, cleric,' said he, 'to a place where I may not hear of you.' He took the woman away and, at the meeting of three roads, he built an oak house for her that had small windows only and no exit. She was left there. Pious people used to bring morsels there to her. Seven years she spent in that way so that she became an emaciated poor wretch.

It was reported to the king that she was still alive. She was released. And she was taken into his care and cared for until she became the greatest beauty ever. 'You're fit for a king,' said the king himself; 'and may you go to him[4] and I'll take soul-friendship from you.' 'I've been given to a King,' said she, 'that is, to the Lord. No king to whom one will go in this life will prove better. I won't forsake Him as long as I live. You must build me a hermitage and a church.'

That much was done. The hermitage was filled with cows and oxen and horses and gold and silver. 'Come now to what has been built for you,' said the king. 'May a cleric precede me into it, that is, a soul-friend,' said she. 'Who?' said the king. 'My own soul-friend,' said she, 'whom I rebuked. Now, however, he is a saint, on account of the repentance he has made.' He was brought to her. And they were in their hermitage until they went to heaven, and great miracles used to be performed on their account. And the place founded for them is the Greeks' greatest city of refuge. That, then, was the fate of the sinful Greek girl.

4. i.e. to the king who is speaking.

from:
SALTAIR NA RANN
(The Psalter of Verses)
(*c.* 987)

[*Saltair na Rann* is a sacred history of the world, as found in the Bible and some apocryphal texts. The body of the work consists of 150 cantos (7,788 lines), hence the title *Saltair* 'Psalter'. The entire work is written in quatrains in syllabic *deibhidhe*-metre. The Adam and Eve story (Cantos IV–XII) contains a large amount of dialogue, thus affording Eve a greater say than she has anywhere else in medieval Irish literature.

The brief extracts provided here derive from Canto XI. They concern, in turn, the expulsion of Adam and Eve from Paradise after the Fall, their penance, and the second temptation of Eve. The main source underlying Canto XI is *Vita Adae et Evae*, but with variations which may derive from other Latin versions which are no longer extant. Some of these variations are attested in other vernacular versions. The following quatrains have been selected to reflect two aspects of the Irish version which seem attributable to the Irish poet. The first is Eve's forceful self-accusation (also found in the poem 'Mé Éba', p. 125). The second is the Devil's reliance on Eve's acting before she has time to reflect, as he encourages her to abandon her penance in the River Tigris prematurely. When she hesitates, he complains, 'O Eve, what is the matter with you? You are thinking greatly.'

Text and translation (here minus textual notes and with minor changes in presentation): David Greene and Fergus Kelly (eds and trans.), *The Irish Adam and Eve Story from Saltair na Rann*, 2 vols (Dublin: Dublin Institute for Advanced Studies, 1976), vol. 1, pp. 54–73. For detailed commentary on the sources and analogues of Cantos IV–XII, see ibid., vol. 2: *Commentary* by Brian Murdoch.]

from: Canto XI

Baí Ádam sechtmain i fos
iarna thathchor a Pardos,
    fri toirsi, cen tein, cen tech,
    cen dig, cen biäd, cen héted.

Húair ro mbátar i mbochtai
do-chúatar i n-húachtgortai;
    mór do imaithbeur in cach than
    baí eter Eua is Ádam.

'A Eua chóir crotha cain
ar tróig trá dot impartain;
    fua-rír, ron-lád a Pardos
    triat mígním, triat immarbos . . .

Ro ráid Eua, ar baí hi cacht,
hi trúage iar tarimthecht:
    'A Ádaim amrai ós cach maig
    cid nacha[m] marbai im chintaib?

Is mé do-chóid darsin smacht,
is mé do-róni in tarmthecht,
    cóir duit mo marbad di shain,
    a mo thigerna, a Ádaim.

Acht co torchror-sa, delm cert,
im chinaid, im tharimthecht,
　　móte do-géntar co glé
　　orot o Día trócaire.

'Is lór ro chráidsem ind ríg',
ar sé, ar Ádam, cen dimbríg,
　　'a ben, ní dén fingail fort
　　cia beó i ngortai, ciam toebnocht.

Ní himmér mo láim, lúad n-éim,
for m'fhuil nach for m'fheóil fo-déin;
　　cid mór do locht, línaib gal,
　　is dom chorp for-coemnacar . . .

A Eua, dénam go glé
pennait buan is atheirge,
　　cor glanmais fiad Ríg na recht
　　ní diar cintaib, diar tarmtecht.'

'Déna mo thinchosc di shain,
a mo thigernai, a Ádaim,
　　húair nach fetar fiad cach rainn
　　cinnas do-gníther pennaind.

Déna mo thinchosc co léir
iar th'intliucht, iar do glanchéil.
　　ná dern féin forcraid nach thur,
　　ná raib form essbaid d'oenmud.'

'Adram in Coimdid 'mo-le
hi toë, cen chomlabrae,
　　eirgg-siu i sruth Tigir trén
　　is rag-sa i sruth n-Iordanén.

Trí lá tríchat, tórainn ndil,
do bith duit-siu i sruth Tigir;
　　messe i n-Iordanén fo smacht
　　secht lá caíne cethrachat.

Beir let licc clochi cobsaid
fot shuidi, fot choemchossaib,
　　co ruc-sa limm licc n-aili
　　fo chumma, fo chosmaile.

Córaig in cloich isin tsruth,
déna fuirri fothrucud,
　　— ba tuicse amal bíæ co mblait —
　　co ríæ ina usce do brágait.

Th'fholt scaílti cech cruth cen meth
iarsin sruth for cach n-oenleth;

bí hi tost fri sním snéid sain,
do rosc féig frisna nemdaib.

Suidig do da láim cech thráth
fri ruirig nime noe ngrád;
　　guid iar fírdul, cia bé hi toss,
　　im dílgud dot immarbos . . .

Ro gáid Ádam, hitgi thrén,
iarum for sruth n-Iordanén,
　　co troisced lais for Dia ndil
　　cona huilib hilmílaib.

Tarrasair in sruth 'na thoss
dia rémim, dia anfhoros,
　　in rígshruth dia rith ro an
　　co tarddad dílgud d'Ádam.

Iarsin targlammair in sruth
cech míl beó baí 'na crisluch,
　　lín a cuiri cruth ros gab
　　co mbáthar huili im Ádam.

Ro gádatar dib-línaib
Ádam is sruth, hilmílaib;
　　trúag ro fhersat a nnúal n-án
　　fri slúag n-úag na noí noebgrád.

Cor guiditis leo cen chlith
na huili grád a Coimdid,
　　co tardad Dia dílgud nglan
　　cen nach ndíbdud do Ádam.

Gádatar Día cotas-geib,
na noí ngrád cona n-airbreib,
　　im dílgud d'Ádaum hi fus
　　dia gábud, dia immarbus.

Do-rigni Dia ar a grádaib
slándílgud cinad Ádaim,
　　co n-aittreib thalman cech than,
　　co nnim nallglan noebúasal.

Ocus ro dílig iar sin
dia chlannaib, dia chinedaib;
　　acht int hé na tibri cert,
　　téis dar réir nDé i n-anrecht.

Mar ro-chúala Demun dub
dilgud do thabairt d'Ádaum:
　　'Rag-sa iar febai co glé
　　dochumm nEuae do-ríse,

Conos tuc ast shruth tri thlás,
conas rucur rith forbás,
  coro bádur ní dia mud
  'ma crábud do chumscugud.'

Do-luid Lucifer lúath laind,
in faíl feochair fírthúachaill,
  mar hela, i rricht angil gil,
  co Eua do shruth Tigir.

Ro ráid ría in t-angel ros mert
— dar lía, ba dia airchisecht —:
  'A Eua fhíal c[h]rotha gil
  is cían a-taí i sruth Tigir.

A ben, ciarbo glé do chruth,
ro choemcláis gné 'sin garbshruth;
  cen nach mbríg mbladbrais ro feis
  rot marbais, rot mudaigeis.

A ben, tair ar do Día ass,
ná bí ní sía ist shruth amnas,
  do rí rúad rom fhaíd for fecht,
  úad tánac dott' airchissecht.'

Iar sin tic Eua asint shruth,
baí for tír 'ca tírmugud,
  dos-fánic nél iar sét shain
  co tarmairt héc cen anmain.

Ní haithgén Eua co glé
Lucifer línib hilgné,
  don banscáil fhebdai bá hairc,
  bæ a menmai i cumtabairt.

'A Eua, cid arnot geib?
Is mór do-gní d'imráteib;
  cucut gléthánac do nim
  la forngairi Dé derbdil.

Tíagum ass dochum n-Ádaim,
a ben, ná bí ic hildálaib;
  gádamar huili Dia ndil
  im dílgud in for cintaib.'

Iar sain do-chúatar co trén
co-rice sruth n-Iordanén
  co Ádam, húas treba tor,
  Eua án is Lucifor.

Mar ro deircc Ádam ast shruth
for Eua, for Lucifur,

ron gab crith, ba lán do gail,
ro llín gráin gnúisi Díabuil.

'Mon-úar, a Eua fhechtai,
rot mera do thuicthechtai;
  fer thánic lat for fecht foss,
  is hé rot mert hi Pardos.

A Eua trúag, cen tucht ndil,
cid dot-fhuc o shruth Tigir,
  cen forngaire Ríg rechta,
  cen angel nglan coemthechta?'

Mar at-chúala Eua in sain,
reba adchosain Ádaim,
  dos-fuit for lár, luid i ssás,
  is becc ná dechaid díanbás . . .

TRANSLATION

Adam was a week on earth after his expulsion from Paradise, sorrowing without fire or shelter, without food or drink or clothing.

After that they were in poverty, they fell into cold and hunger; there was much reproach at all times between Adam and Eve.

'O generous Eve of fair shape, we are wretched as a result of your disgrace [?]; alas, we have been put out of Paradise through your misdeed, your transgression . . .'

Eve said, since she was in trouble, in misery after transgression: 'O Adam, famous over every plain, why do you not kill me for my sins?

'It is I who broke the law, it is I who made the transgression, it is right for you to kill me for that, O my lord Adam.

'If I fall, righteous fame, for my crime and my transgression, it is more likely that God will clearly show mercy to you.'

'Sufficiently have we grieved the king,' said he, said Adam with good sense, 'O woman, I will not kill my own kin, though I be in hunger, though I be naked.

'I will not ply my hand, swift movement, on my own flesh or blood; though your fault be great, with hosts of battles, it is from my body you have come . . .

'O Eve, let us make lasting penance and repentance, so that we might, before the King of laws, cleanse away something of our sins, of our transgression.'

'Instruct us about that, my lord Adam, since I do not know, before every quarter, how penance is done.

'Instruct me diligently according to your understanding, your pure sense, so that I may not exceed by any amount [?], so that I may not be lacking in any way.'

'Let us worship the Lord together, in silence without speaking together; go you into the strong river Tigris, and I will go into the river Jordan.

'Thirty-three days, a dear measure, for you to be in the river Tigris; I in the river Jordan under correction forty-seven fair days.

'Take with you a solid flagstone, under your seat, under your fair feet, while I take another of the same kind, similar.

'Arrange the stone in the river and immerse yourself upon it — let it be chosen so that you will be with strength — until the water reaches your neck.

'Your hair spread faultlessly along the stream on every side, be silent with especial swift torment, your keen eye towards the heavens.

'Lift your hands every hour to the heavenly lord of the nine orders; pray in a true manner, though you be motionless, for forgiveness of your sin . . .'

Adam then prayed, a strong request, the river Jordan, that it, with all its many animals, should fast with him against dear God.

The stream stopped motionless from its movement and its activity; the royal stream abstained from running that [God] might forgive Adam.

Then the stream collected every living creature that was in its womb, all of them as it possessed them, so that they were all around Adam.

They both prayed, Adam and the stream with many creatures; pitifully they poured out their noble lamentation to the pure host of the nine holy orders.

That all the orders should pray to them to their Lord without concealment that God should give pure forgiveness to Adam, and not destroy [him].

The nine orders with their hosts prayed God who maintains them to forgive Adam in this world for his danger, for his sin.

For the sake of his orders God fully forgave the sin of Adam, with the habitation of the earth at all times, with high pure holy noble heaven.

And he forgave after that his children and descendants; but he who does not do right, let him go into injustice against God's command.

When the black Devil heard that Adam had been forgiven: 'I will go in good shape and brilliantly to Eve again,

'So that I may take her out of the river through weakness, so that I may bring her on a vain journey, so that I may destroy something of her work and disturb her devotion.'

Swift joyful Lucifer, the fierce truly cunning wolf, came like a swan, in the shape of a bright angel, to Eve, to the river Tigris.

The angel who had betrayed her said to her — in pity for her, as she thought: 'O modest Eve of bright form, you have been for a long time in the river Tigris.

'O woman, though your shape was bright, you have changed form in the rough river; without any strength of great fame in sleeping, you have killed yourself, you have ruined yourself.

'O woman, come out of it for the sake of your God, do not be any longer in the cruel river; your strong king has sent me on a journey, it is from him I have come to show pity to you.'

Eve did not recognise clearly Lucifer with all his disguises; it was a difficulty for the excellent woman, her mind was in doubt.

'O Eve, what is the matter with you? You are thinking greatly; I came clearly to you from Heaven at the order of very dear God.

'Let us go off to Adam, O woman, do not be wavering; we have all prayed to dear God for the forgiveness of your sins.'

After that they went strongly to the river Jordan, to Adam, chief above dwellings, noble Eve and Lucifer.

When Adam looked out of the river at Eve and Lucifer, he began to tremble, he was full of fury, horror of the Devil's face filled him.

'Alas, O journeying [?] Eve, your reason has led you astray [?]; the man who came firmly with you on a journey, it is he who betrayed you in Paradise.

'O miserable Eve, without dear beauty, what brought you out of the river Tigris without the command of the King of justice, without a pure guardian angel?'

When Eve heard that, Adam's outbursts of reproach, she fell to the ground, she was trapped, she nearly died speedily . . .

MÉ ÉBA
(I am the wife of Adam, Eve)
(11th century)

[Text: Gerard Murphy (ed. and trans.), *Early Irish Lyrics: Eighth to Twelfth Century*, pp. 50, 52. Translation: Frank O'Connor, *The Little Monasteries* (Dublin: Dolmen Press, 1976), p. 42.]

Mé Éba, ben Ádaim uill;
  mé ro sháraig Ísu thall;
mé ro thall nem ar mo chloinn:
  cóir is mé do-chóid sa crann.

Ropa lem rígtheg dom réir;
  olc in míthoga rom-thár;
olc in cosc cinad rom-chrín:
  for-ír! ní hidan mo lám.

Mé tuc in n-uball an-úas;
  do-chúaid tar cumang mo chraís;
in céin marat-sam re lá
  de ní scarat mná re baís.

Ní bíad eigred in cach dú;
  ní bíad geimred gáethmar glé;
ní bíad iffern; ní bíad brón;
  ní bíad oman, minbad mé.

TRANSLATION

I am the wife of Adam, Eve;
  For my transgression Jesus died;
I stole Heaven from those I leave;
  'Tis me they should have crucified.

Dreadful was the choice I made,
  I who was once a mighty queen;
Dreadful, too, the price I paid —
  Woe, my hand is still unclean!

I plucked the apple from the spray
  Because of greed I could not rule;
Even until their final day
  Women still will play the fool.

Ice would not be anywhere
  Wild white winter would not be;
There would be no hell, no fear
  And no sorrow but for me.

SAINT SCOTHÍN AND THE GIRLS
(Middle Irish)

[The feast of Saint Scothín of Tiscoffin (Tech Scothín), County Kilkenny, falls on 2 January. It is not known when he lived. This Middle Irish anecdote, describing his heroic virginity, is found in the notes to the calendar *Félire Óenguso*, under his feast. The belief that virgins could carry fire and walk over live coals without being burnt was widespread; cf. Proverbs 6:27–8.

This translation is based on Whitley Stokes, *Felire Oengusso Céli Dé: The Martyrology of Oengus the Culdee* (London: Henry Bradshaw Society, vol. 29, 1905), pp. 40–1.]

Now two girls with pointed breasts used to lie with him each night that his battle with the Devil would be all the greater. And it was proposed to make accusation of him on that score. So Brénainn came to test him, and Scothín said, 'Let the cleric lie in my bed tonight,' said he. So afterwards when Brénainn reached the resting-hour the girls came into the house where he was, with their lapfuls of glowing embers in their chasubles, and the fire did not burn them. 'What's this?' said Brénainn. 'This is what we do every night,' said the girls. They lie down beside Brénainn and no way could he sleep with the longing. 'Cleric, that's not perfect,' said the girls, 'he who's here every night feels nothing at all. Why don't you get into the tub [of cold water], cleric, if that would make it easier for you? The cleric often visits it' — that is, Scothín. 'Well,' said Brénainn, 'it's wrong for us [to seek] this proof, this man is better than I am.' They make their union and their covenant after that, and they part felicitously.

THE CONCEPTION OF SAINT FÍNÁN CAM
(Middle Irish)

[The secular hero is often a product of a violent or incestuous union. For the conception or birth of an ecclesiastical hero to be remarkable, it usually needed only to defy the church requirement that parents be married: all sex outside marriage was taboo. Yet some tales of male saints' births and conceptions which at first seem ripe with illicit sex turn out otherwise: it transpires that the saint's origins are pure after all. The following Middle Irish anecdote concerns the early seventh-century saint, Fínán Cam, patron of the Corco Duibne in Kerry and founder of the monastery of Kinnity, County Offaly, and his mother, Becnait. It appears in the notes to the calendar entry for his feast on 7 April. The salmon is a version of the fish as Christian symbol. For another tale of a woman conceiving of a salmon, see pp. 182–4.

Text (with minor changes in presentation): Whitley Stokes, *On the Calendar of Oengus* (Dublin: Royal Irish Academy, 1880), p. lxxiii. The translation of the first quatrain is taken from John Montague ('Sunset', *Collected Poems* (Oldcastle, County Meath: Gallery Press, 1995), p. 102).]

Fínán Cam Chindetig —
    Éigne dergoir tarlustar
    laistiar iar fuined gréni
    ra broind Becnaite báine
    comba hesium a céli.
.i. dia roibe oca fothrucad i lLoch Léin, ut dicitur:
    Nis fil athair talmanta lat
    in Spirut Nóem rot saer, rot alt.
Inde alius dixit:
    Becnait ingen ídgna adbail
    in lia lógmar nárbo gand,
    fo chosmailius Mec na hÓige
    genair uaithe Fínán Cam.

    I mbrú Becnaite ro bui re ré
    orat coimpred tria bréthir Dé
    nis fil athair talmanta lat
    in Spirut Náem rot saer rot nalt.

TRANSLATION

Fínán Cam of Kinnity —
    In Loch Lene
    a queen went swimming;
    a redgold salmon
    flowed into her
    at full of evening.
i.e. when she was at her bathing in Loch Lene, as is said:
    Earthly father you have not,
    The Holy Spirit has freed, has raised you.
Concerning which another said:
    Becnait, daughter of great Idgna,
    Precious stone, not niggardly,
    In the manner of the Virgin's Son
    Was Fínán Cam born of her.

    In Becnait's womb you were for a time
    for you were conceived through the word of
        God
    Earthly father you have not,
    The Holy Spirit has freed, has raised you.

THE CONCEPTION OF SAINT BÓETHÍNE
(Middle Irish)

[Translated from: Whitley Stokes, *On the Calendar of Oengus*, p. lxxxix.]

Bóethíne son of Findach, of Inis Bóethíne in west Leinster. And Créd daughter of Rónán, King of Leinster, was mother of Bóethíne son of Findach. And this is how Bóethíne was conceived: one day a robber, Finnach, happened to be atop a thorntree over the well, about to commit a robbery on the church. And Créd came to the well to wash her hands. When Finnach saw the virgin, he lusted after her and the desire of his body flowed from him onto the watercress that lay beneath him. The girl ate the plant on which the semen was, and thence was Bóethíne born.

A CHRÍNÓC, CUBAID DO CHEÓL
(To an Old Psalm-Book)
(11th century)

[For many years it was believed this poem addressed one of the religious women who lived in spiritual marriage with clerics or ascetics. James Carney's reading of it as an address to a psalter, the primer of the medieval schoolchild, gave a better solution to its enigma: the poem is an allegorization of spiritual marriage. Crínóc is an attested female personal name. It might be translated literally as 'Little Old One' and compared to the name 'Sophia' in its connotations of wisdom: the speaker's psalter is full of wisdom, music and piety.

Tomás Ó Broin suggested the poem is a clerical, Christianized version of Horace's light-hearted epilogue to his Epistles, Book I ('The Genesis of "An Chrínóc"', *Éigse*, vol. 9, Part I [spring 1958], pp. 1–3). Although there is no evidence to support Carney's attribution of the Irish poem to Máel Ísu Úa Brolcháin (d. 1086), it would not be surprising if he had written it as his obituary describes him as 'master of wisdom and of piety and in *filidecht* in both languages', i.e. Irish and Latin.

Text and translation: James Carney, *Medieval Irish Lyrics with the Irish Bardic Poet* (Mountrath, Portlaoise: Dolmen Press, 1985), pp. 74–9.]

A Chrínóc, cubaid do cheól,
    cenco bat fíróc at fíal;
ro-mósam túaid i tír Néill
    tan do-rónsam feis réid ríam.

Rop hí m'áes tan ro-foís lem,
    a bé níata in gáesa grinn,
daltán clíabglan cáem nád camm,
    maccán mall secht mbliadan mbinn.

Bámar for bith Banba bailc
    cen éilniud anma ná cuirp,
mo lí lasrach lán dot sheirc
    amail geilt cen aslach uilc.

Erlam do chomairle chóir,
    dóig nos-togamne in cech tír
is ferr rográd dot gaeis géir,
    ar comrád réid frisin Ríg.

Ro-foís la cethrar íar sin
    im díaid cen nach methlad mer,
ro-fetar, is beóda in blad,
    at glan cen phecad fri fer.

Fo deóid dom rúachtais do-rís
    íar cúartaib scís, gleó co ngaeis;
do-dechaid temel tart gnúis,
    cen drúis is dered dot aeis.

At inmain lem-sa cen locht,
    rot-bía mo chen-sa cen cacht;
ni léicfe ar mbádud i péin,
    fo-gabam crábud léir lat.

Lán dot labrad in bith búan,
    adbal do rith tar cach rían;
día seichmis cech día do dán
    ro-seismis slán co Día ndían.

Do-beire do thimna in toí
    do chách co himda ar bith ché,
síthlai dúin uile in cech ló
    ní gó guide díchra Dé.

Do-rata Día dellraid dúin
    a ré frit ar menmain mín
rop rolainn frinn gnúis Ríg réil
    íar n-ar léimm ór colainn chrín.

TRANSLATION

Crínóc, lady of measured melody,
    not young, but with modest maiden mind,
together once in Niall's northern land
    we slept, we two, as man and womankind.

You came and slept with me for that first time,
    (skilled wise amazon annihilating fears)
and I a fresh-faced boy, not bent as now,
    a gentle lad of seven melodious years.

There we were then on that firm Irish earth
    desirous, but in pure and mystic sense;
burning with love my flesh, still free from fault
    as fool of God in smitten innocence.

Your counsel is ever there to hand,
    we chose it, following you in everything;
love of your word is the best of loves,
    our gentle conversation with the King.

Guiltless you are of any sin with man,
    fair is your name, and bright, and without
        stain,
although I know that when you went from me
    each in his turn, four lay where I had lain.

And now you come, your final pilgrimage,
    wearied with toil and travel, grimed with
        dust,
wise still but body not immaculate:
    time it is that ravished you, not lust.

Again I offer you a faultless love,
    a love unfettered for which surely we
will not be punished in the depths of hell
    but together ever walk in piety.

Seeking the presence of elusive God
    wandering we stray, but the way is found,
following the mighty melodies that with you
    throughout the pathways of the world
        resound.

Not ever silent, you bring the word of God
    to all who in the present world abide,
and then through you, through finest mesh,
    Man's earnest prayer to God is purified.

May the King give us beauty back again
    who ever did his will with quiet mind,
may he look on us with eagerness and love,
    our old and perished bodies left behind.

THE THREE ORDERS OF THE CHURCH
(14th century MS)

[The text excerpted here deals not with virgins, widows and married folk but with a different triad of orders. While it has chronological inconsistences and some dubious details, it is a valuable witness to the belief that the Irish church treated men and women with equal respect only in its earliest stages and that thereafter, the consolidation of patriarchy ensured women were pushed ever further from the centre.

It is found in the fourteenth-century Codex Salmanticensis. This collection, consisting almost exclusively of saints' lives, is believed to have been compiled in Ireland, in a community of English or Anglo-Norman religious. The motive seems to have been to make a national collection, although the materials seem otherwise to have been amassed indiscriminately. The text provides no evidence by which a date, other than that of the manuscript, might be assigned to it. The following excerpts derive from: Liam de Paor, *St Patrick's World*, pp. 225–6.]

[The first order]

The first order of saints was in the time of Patrick. They were all bishops, eminent and holy and filled with the Holy Spirit, numbering three hundred and fifty. They were founders of churches, who worshipped one head, Christ, followed one leader, Patrick, had one tonsure and one liturgy of the Mass, and celebrated one Easter (that is, after the spring equinox). What was excluded from the communion of one church, all excluded. They did not reject the government and the company of women because, since their foundation was the rock, Christ, they did not fear the wind of temptation. This order lasted through four reigns: that is, from the time of Loeguire[1] son of Niall, who reigned thirty-seven years, and Ailill[2] surnamed Molt, who

1. d. *c.* 463.
2. d. *c.* 482.

reigned thirty years, and Lugaid,[3] who reigned seven years. And this order of saints lasted until the end of the time of Tuathal Maelgarb.[4] They all continued to be holy bishops, and for the greater part they were of Frankish and Roman and British and Irish origin.

[The second order]

The second order of saints was as follows. In this second order there were in fact few bishops but many priests, to the number of three hundred. They worshipped one God as their head. They had diverse liturgies and diverse rules of life, but they celebrated one Easter (that is, on the fourteenth of the moon), and they practised one tonsure, from ear to ear. They shunned the company and the services of women and excluded them from their monasteries. This order lasted as far as four reigns, that is, from the end of the reign of Tuathal Maelgarb through the thirty years in which Diarmait[5] son of Cerrbél reigned, through the time of the two descendants of Muiredach,[6] who reigned for seven years, and through the time of Áed[7] son of Ainmere, who reigned thirty years. These accepted their ritual of the Mass from holy men of Britain: Saint David and Saint Gildas and Saint Doc. And their names are: Finnian, Énda, Colmán, Comgal, Áed, Ciarán, Columba, Brendan, Brichin, Cainnech, Cóemgen, Laisrén, Lugid, Barra, and many others who were of the second rank of saints.

[The third order]

The third order of saints was as follows. They were holy priests, few of them bishops, to the number of one hundred, and they settled in uninhabited places. They lived on herbs and water and on the alms of the faithful; they despised all earthly goods and they utterly avoided every murmur and distraction . . .

3. d. c. 507.
4. d. c. 544.
5. d. c. 565.
6. i.e. Báetán (d. c. 586) son of Muirchertach, and Eochu (d. c. 572) grandson of Muirchertach.
7. d. c. 598.

[The hierarchy of the orders]

Note that the first order was the holiest, the second holier than the third, the third holy. The first blazed like the sun in the heat of love; the second shone with a paler light like the moon; the third glowed like gold. The blessed Patrick, taught by heavenly inspiration, discerned these three orders when — in his prophetic vision — he saw the whole of Ireland filled with the flames of fire; then, afterwards, the mountains as if they were burning; then lighted lamps in the valleys. This is taken from the old Life of Patrick . . .

RÍCENN AND CAIRECH DERCÁIN
(Middle Irish)

[The different states of virginity, marriage and holy widowhood are encapsulated in the tale of these two pious women who, between them, rendered the 'threefold territory' to God. Translated from the Middle Irish original published by Kuno Meyer in *Archiv für celtische Lexicographie*, vol. 3 (1907), pp. 308–9.]

Crimthann son of Lugaid, from whom the Crimthainn in Uí Maine[1] are descended, was the first man of the Connacht people who murdered a woman after the coming of the faith. A daughter was born to Crimthann. She was brought to Mac Raith son of Naingen for baptism and he baptized her. 'Cleric,' said Crimthann, 'I give this girl to you and to the Lord in atonement for the woman I murdered in transgression against God.' The cleric took the girl with him then. He rears her for seven years and brings her to Cairech Dercáin and he heartily commends the girl to her to be schooled by her. The girl grew apace in purity, artistry, learning, shapeliness, form, manner and speech. Cairech Dercáin was more beautiful than all of womankind at that time, except for the girl. Cairech Dercáin used be among the people every day, while the girl, attending to her studies and handiwork, used not be seen.

1. An over-kingdom in east Connacht.

The King of Thomond, namely Tipraite son of Foramán, is told that there is a young nun, namely Cairech Dercáin, in Cluain Bairenn[2] who would make a fitting consort for a king. He sends one of his officials to take stock of Cairech's looks. He arrived at the place where the nun lived. She was in the church, singing her psalms, and the church was locked. The man observed her through the keyhole. The virgin noticed that. 'May injury soon afflict you, brother, that will take the eye out of your head!' said she. Afterwards, a pet crane which was in the monastery came and swiftly took the eye out of his head. Then youth went to his lord and he told him that there was no woman in the world more beautiful than the woman he had seen.

The king sent a fleet along the Shannon to Cluain Bairenn to fetch the girl. It was revealed to the nun that they were coming for her. Cairech closed up the church on herself and the squadron arrived at the door. 'Come out,' said they. 'Give me a respite of three days and three nights,' said she, 'and I'll go then.' She is granted that. After three days she said to Rícenn: 'Take my blessing and go to that man in place of me for I've dedicated my virginity to the Lord. But you're a girl and you haven't dedicated your virginity as yet. For God's sake, then, go out in my place. I warrant you by the Lord that your reward in heaven and on earth will be no less on account of it.' The girl binds her to that.

Then she went out to them and she said: 'I'll sleep with him only in my own country and land and I won't go with him like a wanton woman'. For that reason she was taken as far as the Shannon. She gets onto a rock there. The ship is sent after her. She raises the rock aloft above the ship. Thus nothing could be done. They sent messengers then to their lord and they told him about that. 'Let her come with me to Maenmag.'[3] This news reached her. 'I can't go without a horse,' said she. 'We have no horses,' said they. 'I command that this rock on which I am should convey me along the route you mention,' said she. The rock proceeded before them until it reached Maenmag and there it stopped. And that today is 'Rícenn's Stone' and it is around it that the northern church was founded. Tipraite came

southwards to the plain where the southern church stands today. She said that she would not unite with him in the northern church, and it is for that reason that the southern church was built. Subsequently, she was taken southwards and she bore a son to Tipraite, namely Dúngal, from whom Cenél Dúngaile[4] are descended, and the southern church is built, namely, Clúain Cenéoil Dúngaile.[5]

After a time, Rícenn became a pious widow, and it was that which gave the threefold territory (*trichait in tredual*) to Ciarán[6] and to God and to Cairech.

4. A sept in east County Clare, near Killaloe.
5. Unidentified.
6. Founder of the monastery of Clonmacnoise on the Shannon, not far from Killaloe.

CIODH MÁ nDEILIGHE MO MHAC GRÁDHACH RIOM?
(Massacre of the Innocents)
(Late Middle Irish)

[This eleventh- or twelfth-century lament dramatically enacts the keening of four mothers over their children, massacred at Bethlehem. Found within a series of homilies on the story of Christ's childhood in the *Leabhar Breac*, its rhythmic chant would have strongly affected the preacher's audience. Text and translation are from: David Greene and Frank O'Connor, *A Golden Treasury of Irish Verse* (Macmillan, 1967; Dingle: Brandon, 1990), pp. 190–4.]

Ciodh má ndeilighe mo mhac grádhach riom?
Toradh mo bhronn,
mé ro thuisimh,
mo chích ro ibh
mo bhrú ros iomarchar,
m'inne ro shúigh,
mo chridhe ro shás,
mo bheatha rob é,
mo bhás a bhreith uaim;
mo neart ro thráigh,
m'innscne ro shocht,
mo shúile ro dhall.

2. Today Cloonburren in County Roscommon.
3. Anglicized as Moyno, near Killaloe, County Clare.

Mo mhac bheire uaim,
ní hé do-ní an t-olc,
marbh didhiu mé féin,
ná marbh mo mhac!
Mo chíocha gan loim,
mo shúile go fliuch,
mo lámha ar crith,
mo chorpán gan níth,
mo chéile gan mhac,
mé féine gan neart,
mo bheatha is fiú bás!
Uch, m'aonmhac, a Dhé!
M'fhaoidhe gan luach,
mo ghalar gan ghein,
gan díoghail go bráth;
mo chíocha 'na dtost,
mo chridhe ro chrom.

Aon shiorthaoi dá mharbhadh,
sochaidhe mharbhthaoi,
naoidhin bhuailtí,
na haithreacha ghontaoi,
na máithreacha mharbhthaoi,
ifreann ro líon sibh
neamh ro dhún sibh,
fola firén ro dhoirtseabhar gan chionaidh.

Tair chugam, a Chríost,
beir m'anmain go luath
maraon is mo mhac!
Uch, a Mhuire mhór,
Máthair Mheic Dé,
ciodh do-dhéan gan mhac?

Tríd Mhacsa ro marbhadh
mo chonn is mo chiall;
do-rinne bean bhaoth díom
i ndiaidh mo mheic;
mo chridhe is caob cró
a haithle an áir thruaigh
ó 'ndiu go dtí bráth.

TRANSLATION

[A woman:] Why do you part me from my darling son? The fruit of my womb, it was I who bore him, he drank from my breast, my womb carried him, he sucked my bowels, he was my life, it is my death to take him from me. It has sapped my strength, it has stilled my speech, it has blinded my eyes.

[Another:] You take my son from me, it is not he who does the wrong; kill me then, do not kill my son! My breasts without milk, my eyes wet, my hands shaking, my body without mettle, my husband without a son, myself without strength, my life is but death! O God, my only son, my journey [?] without reward, my labour without birth, unrevenged until Doomsday. My breasts are stilled, my heart is bowed down.

[Another:] You seek one to kill, you kill many; you strike down the babies, you wound the fathers, you kill the mothers. You have filled hell, you have shut heaven, you have spilt the blood of the righteous without a cause.

[Another:] Come to me, Christ! Take my life quickly along with my son. O great Mary, Mother of God's Son, what shall I do without a son? On account of your Son my sense and mind have been killed; I have been made a mad woman after my son. My heart is a clot of blood after the tragic slaughter from today until the judgement comes.

THE ABBOT OF DRIMNAGH WHO WAS CHANGED INTO A WOMAN
(Middle Irish)

[This humorous Middle Irish tale is somewhat akin to the legend of Tiresias. He was changed into a woman on account of killing the female of a pair of mating snakes and did not recover his own sex until he had killed the male. In the Irish fantasy, the married abbot who undergoes a sex-change appears to have done no wrong. The intention may be to mock clerical anxieties about womanishness and transvestism.

The original text was edited by Kuno Meyer, *Anecdota from Irish Manuscripts*, vol. 1 (1907), pp. 76–9. The following translation, by John Montague, is in *Mounts of Venus: The Picador Book of Erotic Prose* (London: Pan Books, 1980), pp. 57–8.]

A certain young man who was Abbot of Drimnagh set about preparing a generous feast to celebrate Easter. When it was ready he left the banqueting hall and climbed a high, beautiful hill which overlooked the town. And the young man wore a fine linen hood, a close-fitting shirt of royal satin next his bright skin, an elegant mantle with a dark brown cloak lined with scarlet, billowing around him, and a gold-hilted ceremonial sword under his hand. When he reached the top of the hill, he placed his head in the crook of his elbow, and fell fast asleep.

When he woke and reached to grasp his sword, he found a woman's weapon, a distaff, in its place. And when he reached downwards he found a woman's skirt about his waist and his shirt lengthened to a great gown sweeping the ground. And when he reached upwards he found a woman's hair, long and golden ringlets which fell around a smooth face, with no bristles upon it, neither whiskers nor beard. But when he placed his hands between his thighs he found the thatched sign of womanhood there.

Despite all this evidence, the young man could not believe in these strange changes, and thought a spell had been cast upon him. After a while a large woman came by, hideous and yellow-complexioned, with long grey hair and sunken eyes, a right hag. 'And what,' said she, addressing the young man, 'is a likely young lassie like yourself, with your nice yellow hair, doing up here alone on the hill at twilight, with night coming on?' He was utterly downcast and tearful at such a greeting. 'I don't know,' he wondered sadly, 'where I can go now. If I go home to the community they won't recognize me, and if I wander on, there's no knowing what might happen to a single girl on her own. However, it is all in God's hands, for it was he who deformed my shape and put me in this fix, so I'll push on and see what judgement falls on me.

'If it is his work — though I solemnly swear before him that I hanged or betrayed no one, that I never violated bell, relic or crozier, that I never persecuted any cleric, that I never wished evil on anyone, and that no guest ever left my house unsatisfied.'

So he rose up and from the slopes of that beautiful hill he uttered a plaintive lament, a last cry of grief and sadness. 'It is a great pity,' he sobbed, 'that the smooth mound of this hill does not swallow me now, for I don't know what I'll do or where I'll go.'

Then *she* set out westward across the slope of the hill towards the green of Crumlin, the church to the west of Drimnagh. And who should she meet on the green but a tall soldierly young man who fell completely in love with her on the spot. His desire was so irresistible that he would not leave until they made love. And as they lay there the young man asked the girl where she came from and what her name was. She replied that he would never learn that from her, however long or short their time together. 'But,' said the handsome young man, 'I must tell you who I am. Do you see this church called Crumlin? Well, I am its abbot and I have been in need of a wife for two years. Now you can be mine, for we are of an age.'

And when they went together into the house of the abbot the whole community gave them a loving and kindly welcome. And for seven years she lived with him as wife and spouse, during which time she bore him seven children.

When the seven years were up there came a message from the community and congregation of Drimnagh inviting the abbot for that Easter. His wife travelled with him, and when they came to the hill where her appearance had changed she lay down to rest while the abbot and his company went ahead to the monastery. When the girl awoke from her sleep she found she had reverted to her first shape. On her knees she found the gold-hilted and embellished sword and cried out again:

'O great God, terrible is the position in which you keep placing me.'

And after much tearful lamentation he found his way back to his first home. There his wife said to him: 'You shouldn't have stayed so long.' His seat was still waiting in the banqueting hall and he recounted the whole remarkable story to his double audience. But he was not believed at home because his wife said he had not been missing for more than an hour.

But eventually, after many remarkable proofs had been given, his story was accepted and judgement given between himself and the Abbot of Crumlin. It was decided that the family should be divided into two, but since this left a son over and above, he was given to the abbot for fosterage. Thus the abbots of Drimnagh and Crumlin parted from each other.

ÉIRIGH A INGHEAN AN RÍOGH
(To Gormlaith, Daughter of Flann Sinna)
(Late Middle Irish)

[Texts concerning Gormlaith (d. 947), daughter of the Uí Néill high-king Flann Sinna (d. 916), although mainly not of a 'historical' kind, constitute the largest dossier there is for an Irish woman from before the twelfth century. At least eighteen poems are extant, spoken, as it were, in her voice, and attributed to her, but linguistic criteria show that all of them postdate her by at least two centuries (two of them are printed below, after the present poem). Nevertheless the tradition that she was a poet is solid, and her own work may well underlie some of these later poems. In addition, a few stray quatrains in earlier Irish attributed to her may derive from poems actually composed by her.

Gormlaith is credited with marriages to three men, all of whom she outlived by many years. In most texts, the sequence of her husbands is: Cormac mac Cuilennáin (d. 908) of Munster, Cerball mac Muirecáin (d. 909) of Leinster, and Níall Glúndub (d. 919) of Uí Néill. The fact that the broad outline of her life was of more interest than the detail by the time the Annals of Clonmacnoise were written accounts for the different order there (see pp. 138–9). Her marriage to Níall Glúndub is the only one concerning which there is no doubt. It is probable, but not proven, that she had been married previously to Cerball mac Muirecáin.

The tradition, evidenced in the following poem, that she first contracted marriage with Cormac mac Cuilennáin, king-bishop of Cashel, is pure fabrication. The point was to cast Gormlaith as a force antithetical to celibacy as a clerical and therefore male ideal and prerogative. This was possible because Gormlaith had become an exemplar of the erstwhile happy wife by the time the poem was written. The language of the poem is Late Middle Irish. The author's aim may have been to endorse the twelfth-century church reformers' advocacy of celibacy for all clerics. Cormac and the other males named in the poem personify saintliness, yet their only semblance of personality is the single, shared act of repudiating women. Quatrain 4 refers to the disciple John. Although he had forsworn all women, Christ, on the Cross, entrusted his mother to his care. He is thus the celibate *par excellence*.

The text is edited from two manuscripts in the Bibliothèque Royale, Brussels: MS 20, 978–9, f. 54v and MS 5100–4, p. 44. The poem is translated by Seamus Deane.]

1
Éirigh a inghean an ríogh,
ná bíodh t'aigneadh i n-imshníomh;
atá bean eile id' aghaidh,
a bhéalchorcra bhanamhail.

2
Is í bean atá 'gom chrádh,
eaglas Dé dá ndéantar dán —
agus smuaintighthe eile
ima ndéanta aithrighe.

3
Rug leath feise, a inghean fhial,
mo bhean-sa san ail-se thiar;
béaraidh uait in leath eile
m'fhíormhuintear is m'fhíorghuidhe.

4
Do smuaineas an mnaoi tug Eoin,
do cheadaigh Dia dá dheighdheoin,
dár ling óighe mo bhruinne
ar fhaicsin na haislinge.

5
Do smuaineas Bairre buadhach,
'ga bhfuil an t-aigneadh uallach,
dár ob in ríoghain reabhaigh,
inghin Dúnghail d'Uíbh Eannaigh.

6
Do smuaineas Ciarán Cluana
— mór dá chrábhadh ad-chuala —
dár ob Aillinn inghin mBrain,
is fa cíoghaibh ro chodail.

7
Do smuaineas in crábhadh cóir
Scoithín Sléibhe Mairghe Móir,
luigheadh — grádh Dé fo-deara —
sé idir ainnribh uichtgheala.

8
Do smuaineas Colum Cille,
ar ghrádh Ríogh na fírinne
dár ob sé, gér mhór a gcáil,
ingheana áille Aodháin.

9
Do smuaineas-sa Mo-Laise
— dó-somh ba mhór a mhaise —

dár chin Éadaoin a hóighe,
tré choibleadh na Canóine.

10
Do smuaineas Pádraig na bpeann,
ardapsdal uasal Éireann,
dár ob an luchair leannghlain,
inghin Míolchon móirmeanmnaig.

11
Do-radas-sa inghin bhFloinn
mhic Mhaoil Sheachlainn mhic Dhomnaill,
tugas trí chéad mbó mbeannach
'na connradh, 'na céadcheannach.

12
Tugas fichid n-uinge n-óir
agus fichid gcorn gcomhóil,
nochan fheadar a dheimhin,
in neoch rug uaim d'innilibh.

13
Dar an anmain atá im' chorp,
nocha dearnas-sa ria d'olc,
acht madh éanphóg re n-éirghe
do dhéanamh na hiairmhéirghe.

14
Do ghabhas trí caoigde salm,
i dtiobraid Locha na dTarbh,
tiocfadh riom, munbadh m'óighe,
adhailge na haonphóige.

15
Do-ghéan-sa do dháil go bog,
uair ní tusa riamh ro ob;
is ris do-ghéantar do dháil,
re Cearbhall mac Muireagáin.

16
Nochar chubhaidh d'inghin Fhloinn,
m'ionar ro innigh fá choim;
an corp 'ma bhfuil an t-ionar,
go nglana Dia a chuid cionadh.

17
Mithidh duit-se feis re fear,
a inghean luchair láingheal;
tugas m'óighe do Dhia dhil,
gabh umat agus éirigh.
                    Éirigh.

TRANSLATION

Arise, daughter of the king.
No need to be puzzled any more.
You *do* have a woman rivalling you,
For all your red mouth's allure.

It is the Church of God that torments
Me, it's for her poems should be made.
To her I should make repentance
For letting worldly thoughts invade.

She has taken up house with me, daughter,
Our bed is the flagstone over there;
She is my family and I have besought her
So, that she shall have all my care.

I thought of John, to Mary wed,
With Christ's blessing. My heart
Leapt at what they embodied,
That pure vision, a couple apart.

On Bairre's triumph, one of many,
When he refused the queenly
Daughter of Dúnghal of Iveanny,
I pondered. It was noble, seemly.

And on Ciarán of Clonmacnoise
Who refused Aillenn, daughter of Bran
Though he lay with her. That choice
Was right for so pious a man.

And on Scoithín of great Slieve Margy —
Known for his holy rigour,
Who, to test his love of God, lay
Between young girls and was pure.

Of Colum Cille too, I thought,
Refusing the daughters of Aodhán,
Famed for beauty and much sought
After, for the King of Truth's hand.

Molaisse was honoured too
By Éadaoin's dedication
Of her virgin life to Him who
Wrote the book of Creation.

Patrick of the pens, the scribe
And apostle of Ireland's isle,
Would not have as bride
Míolchú's daughter, radiant and wild.

The daughter of Flann I married,
Son of Maoil Sheachlainn, son of Domhnall.
Three hundred horned cattle I carried
To her as bridewealth. The total

I gave away, I don't know.
Twenty ounces of gold, any amount
Of drinking horns, a steady flow
Of gifts. I didn't count.

I swear by my body's soul
I wronged her in no way.
A single kiss was the whole
Of it, before I rose to pray.

I stood in Loch na dTarbh's cold.
I recited psalm upon psalm,
For that kiss I learned to scold
Myself until desire was banned.

I will pledge your troth for you
Because you never reneged
On marriage. To Cearbhall mac Muireagáin
As spouse you'll be engaged.

If I allege anything, it's that you
Made my wedding-tunic in secret.
May God clean it of sin, renew
The body that wore it, so decree it.

The time to lie with a man
Has come for you, O radiant eyes!
I am given to God; so now you can
Dress and prepare, and arise.
                                    Arise.

RO CHARAS TRÍOCHA FO THRÍ
(Gormlaith Speaks)
(Early Modern Irish)

[Gormlaith was a widow for almost thirty years (see preceding headnote). Tradition has it that, like many other royal widows, she took up residence in a monastery, where her status was that of the 'penitent spouse' (alias 'holy widow'). The texts mostly indicate that the monastery in question was Kells in the Southern Uí Néill territory of Clann Cholmáin, an appropriate choice for Gormlaith, whose father, Flann Sinna, was king of Clann Cholmáin and high-king of Uí Néill. There are some eighteen poems supposedly composed by Gormlaith during her years as a widow. Níall Glúndub is portrayed in them as her clear favourite of her three husbands. Typically, the poems emphasize the denigration suffered by a widow after the death of her lordly husband, the loneliness and jealousy of old age, the endless slights from a younger generation who did not know the widow in her heyday. In some poems, Gormlaith mourns the loss of male company, hearing nothing now but *baothghlór ban*, 'women's foolish talk'. In others, she complains of the harsh regime of the monastery, contrasting it with the luxury she had known in her youth — thus echoing the words of the penitent, Digde (see above, pp. 111–15). The poems as transmitted are in very Late Middle Irish or Early Modern Irish. They remained popular, copies of them being made down to the nineteenth century.

The following poem was previously edited and translated by Osborn Bergin: see his *Irish Bardic Poetry*, pp. 212–4. This is a new edition, based on Royal Irish Academy, MS 23 F 16 (used by Bergin) and Trinity College Dublin, MS G 200, pp. 156–9, together with a new translation. It is implied that the woman named Mór, now the wife of the Abbot of Kells, was known to Gormlaith since her young days; the abbot is said to have hailed from Tullylease.]

1
Ro charas tríocha fo thrí,
    ro charas a naoi fo naoi;
gé no charfainn fiche fear,
    nocho n-eadh do mheallfadh mnaoi.

2
Do thréigeas íad sin ar Niall,
    dob é mo mhían bheith dá réir,
ciodh nach dtréigfinn-se gach fear —
    mór mban do mhear mac uí Néill.

3
Gér líonmhar laoich Leithe Cuinn,
    ní bhfuil drong ar nár ghabh greim;
ba fearr damh a bhfúaras d'olc
    go mba ag fear bocht do bheinn.

4
A bhruit dhatha, a fhailghe óir,
    a eich mhaithe bhaoi 'gan mbúaidh —
mór do thráigh a thuile shéad,
    do-chuaidh uile d'éag ar n-úair.

5
Gan agam ó nimh go lár
  ach léine bhán is brat cíar;
i gCeannanas na gcéad ríogh
  beag an bhrígh mo bheith gan bhíadh.

6
Domhnach do bhámar san chill,
  mé 's mo chodhnach 'gan gcloich thuill,
i gCeanannas 'gan gcrois mhóir
  ag fógra lóin Leithe Cuinn.

7
A-dubhairt riomsa mo rí,
  rom-bhuail go mín dá bhais chlé:
'Eirg don teampall i mbí cách
  ina ngnáth adhradh Mic Dé'.

8
Tiagham ann sin, is ní bréag,
  dá fhichid déag inghean óg;
gluaisidh Mór romham 'na réim
  thairgeas damhsa beinn mo bhróg.

9
Do mhnaoi abadh Coluim chaoimh
  tugas cíor go bhfalaigh n-óir
is dá fhichid bó do bhúaibh
  ar shlios thúaidh an teampaill mhóir.

10
Tugas dí gallchochall gorm
  agus corn séadach na salm,
agus tríocha uinge óir,
  mairid ag Móir Mhuighe Sanbh.

11
Tug sise damhsa anocht —
  nocha maith cumann nach ceart —
dá dheachmhadh do choirce chruaidh
dá ugh chirce iar mbuain dá beart.

12
Dar an Rígh do shoillsigh grían,
  dá maireadh Niall an Ghlúin Duibh,
a bhean abadh Tolcha Léis
  ní bhíadh mo spéis id' dhá uigh.

13
Fuaras ceanbharr, fuaras cíor,
  fuaras anairt mhín ó Mhóir;

tugas di-se an Teach Ruadh
  agus cuach go n-ubhlaibh óir.

14
Mairg do-ní díomas as ór,
  's is mairg do Mhóir bhíos go neóid;
do bhádhas ag díol na gcliar,
  nó go rug an Triath mo sheoid.

15
Fear do-bheireadh eich ar dhuan,
  go dtabhra Dia a luach sin dó!
dá n-abrainn-se maith re Niall,
  a-déaradh an chliar maith badh ró.

TRANSLATION

'*I* have loved three times thirty,'
'*I* have loved nine times nine' —
though I should love twenty men
that's not how a woman is won.

All of them I left for Níall,
my one desire to do his will,
why should I not forsake all men? —
Níall's Níall[1] turned many women's heads.

Though Leath Chuinn's warriors were legion
no band was beyond his grip;
better for me, after all I suffered,
had I been a poor man's wife.

His coloured cloaks, his rings of gold,
his fine horses that won the prize —
his flood of wealth has greatly ebbed,
all in turn come to an end.

I own nothing between heaven and earth
but a white shift and a dark cloak;
in Kells of the hundred kings
who cares that I have no food?

One Sunday we were in the church,
I and my lord at the hollowed stone,[2]
in Kells, by the Great Cross,
proclaiming the feast of Leath Chuinn.

---

1. Interpreting '*mac uí Néill*' as 'son of the descendant of Níall (Noígíallach)'.
2. Perhaps a stone at which covenants were sworn.

My king did say to me,
he struck me gently with his left hand,
'Go to the church where the people are,
where folk worship the Son of God.'

Then we process, this is no lie,
twelve score young girls;
Mór sweeping along before me
made me put my best foot forward!

To the wife of Colum's abbot[3]
I gave a comb with a gold ring,
that and two score cattle
on the north side of the great church.

I gave her a blue Norse hood
and the costly horn of the psalms
and thirty ounces of gold —
Mór of Magh Sanbh[4] has them yet.

She gave to me this night —
mismatched kindness is not good —
two tenths of hard oats,
two hen's eggs from her clutch!

By the King who gave light to the sun
if Níall Glúndubh were alive
I'd spare no thought for your two eggs,
Tullylease[5] abbot's wife!

I got a coif, I got a comb,
I got smooth linen from Mór;
to her I gave the Red House[6]
and a goblet with orbs of gold.

Woe to all who take pride in gold
and woe to Mór in her stinginess:
I had the poets in my pay
until the Lord took my wealth.

A man who used give steeds for a poem —
may God give him due reward!
were I to speak in praise of Níall
the poets would have much to add.

3. Saint Colum (Cille) was patron of Kells.
4. Apparently in Meath, perhaps near Kells.
5. In County Cork.
6. Perhaps the name of a reliquary.

BEIR A MHANAIGH LEAT AN CHOIS
(Monk, Step Further Off)
(Early Modern Irish)

[For context, see preceding headnote. Text: Osborn Bergin, *Irish Bardic Poetry*, pp. 209–10. Translation: Thomas Kinsella (ed.), *The New Oxford Book of Irish Verse* (Oxford: Oxford University Press, 1986), pp. 129–30.]

1
Beir a mhanaigh leat an chois
  tóccaibh anos do tháobh Néill:
as rothrom chuireas tú an chré,
  ar an té re luighinn féain.

2
Fada a mhanaigh atáoi thíar,
  acc cúr na críadh ar Níall nár;
fada liom é a ccomhraidh dhuinn,
  'snach roichid a bhuinn an clár.

3
Mac Aodha Finnléith an óil,
  ní dom dhéaon atá fa chrois;
sín ar a leabaidh an leac,
  beir a mhanaigh leat an chois.

4
Fa Chloinn Uisnigh dob fhearr clú
  do bhí Deirdre mar tú anois,
a croidhe ina clíaph gur att —
  beir a manaigh leat an ccois.

5
As mé Gormlaith chumas rainn,
  deaghinghean Fhloinn ó Dhúin Rois;
trúagh nach orom atá an leac —
  beir a mhanaigh leat an ccois.

TRANSLATION

'Monk, step further off.
Move away from Níall's side.
You settle the clay too heavy
on him with whom I have lain.

'You linger here so long
settling the clay on noble Niall:
he seems a long while in the coffin
where his soles don't reach the boards.

'Aed Finnliath's son, of the drinking feasts,
under a cross — it is not my will.
Stretch the slab upon his bed.
Monk, step further off.

'Over Uisnech's famous family
Deirdre stood as I do now,
till her heart swelled in her side.
Monk, step further off.

'I am Gormlaith, maker of verses,
Flann's noble daughter from Dún Rois.
My grief that slab is not above me!
Monk, step further off.'

from:
THE ANNALS OF CLONMACNOISE
(17th century)

[The two preceding poems portray Gormlaith as a woman who lost everything when her husband, Níall Glúndub died. Tradition represents her as having been married three times in all (see headnote to 'To Gormlaith, Daughter of Flann Sinna', p. 133). Many royal women in medieval Ireland were serially married, *de jure* or *de facto*. When such unions were motivated by political advantage, women were more liable to be exposed to the use of intimidation and force by their own kin, as well as by those who sought them as consorts or wives.

Whatever the reality of Gormlaith's life and her own experiences, various texts, most notably the following one, represent her as having been brutally treated when married to Cerball mac Muirecáin. It may be that this tradition originated as a foil to the tradition, or reality, of a remarkably happy marriage to Níall Glúndub. If based on truth, the text excerpted here is not the best possible witness. For example, its claim that Níall predeceased Cerball mac Muirecáin is incorrect. On the other hand, the tradition that Muirchertach son of Níall Glúndub had chess pieces made out of Cerball's bones is attested in other texts, from the thirteenth century and later.

The original Irish-language Annals of Clonmacnoise are no longer extant. The following extracts derive from a copy of the seventeenth-century translation into English made by Conall Mageoghagan of Lismoyne, County Westmeath (part of the over-kingdom which Gormlaith's father had ruled) in 1627. The portion between double asterisks was expunged from Denis Murphy's published edition but is restored here from Trinity College Dublin, MS F.3.19. For the surrounding material see: Denis Murphy (ed.), *The Annals of Clonmacnoise, Being Annals of Ireland from the Earliest Period to A.D. 1408* (Dublin: Royal Society of Antiquaries of Ireland, 1896), pp. 145, 153–5. Forms of personal names have been normalized.]

Sub anno 905:
. . . Níall Glúndub was king three years and was married to the lady Gormlaith, daughter to king Flann, who was a very faire, vertuous, and learned damozell, was first married to Cormac mac Cuillennáin king of Mounster, secondly to king Níall, by whome she had issue a sonn called prince Domhnall who was drowned, upon whose death she made many pittifull and learned dittyes in Irish, and lastly shee was married to Cerball mac Muirecáin king of Leinster, after all which royall marriages she begged from doore to doore, forsaken of all her friends and allies, and glad to be relieved by her inferiours . . .

Sub anno 936:
. . . Gormlaith (of whome mentione is made before) Queen of Ireland and wife to Níall Glúndub after that king Níall was slain in the battle of Dublin by Danes and Leinster men, the king of Leinster **caused privily kinge Níall's stones irreverently to bee cutt off, and their cover to bee fleyed and conveyghed to his house of Naase,[1] there to be kept as a monument to keepe tablemen in. After the death of kinge Níall, Queene Gormlaith married the k. of Leinster, whose name was Cerball mac Muirecáin, and vpon a time as the kinge of Leinster and Queene Gormlaith were playeinge of tables in Naase aforesaid with condition y^t whomsoever would loose the game should beare this bagge of tablemen in his mouth vntill hee had wonne one game, wch fell that Queene Gormlaith lost the game, wherevpon shee was driven to putt the bagge to her mouth, little knowing what itt was or meant, save onely that it was a bagge. The k. seeing her in hand with the bagg, said bawdly, that now shee carried in her mouth, that shee

---

1. In County Kildare.

received below diverse times before, and revealed vnto her how this bagg was k. Níall's cover of his stones that he kept as a monument in despight of all Vlstermen**, whereupon she begott somewhat interiorly grieved concealed her griefe for a time, and sent privately to Muirchertach mac Néill, who came with a company of Lusty and choice Ulstermen, who clad themselves with cowhides, and lay in the king of Lynsters parcke at Naas neare his pallace in their hides like cowes, to the end that the king upon sight of them, would take them for cowes, the king after he had gotten out of his bedd looked out of the windowe of his pallace, and seeing soe many cowes lye couchant in his park, as Muirchertach brought men out Ulster or the North to be Revenged, and thinking they had layne there all night, hee fell in a rage, and went himself among the cowes, and was miserably killed. Muirchertach and his Ulstermen carried his bones with them to the north, and there artificially caused them to be made a payer of tables of the said kings bones, which for a very longe time after was kept as a monument in the king of Ulsters house, and of these cowhides Muirchertach was ever after during his life named Muirchertach of the Leathercoates.[2]

Sub anno 943:
Gormlaith daughter of king Flann mac Maílechlainn and Queen of Ireland died of a long and grievous wound which happened in this manner. Shee dreamed that she sawe king Níall Glúndub, whereupon she gott up and sate in her bedd to behould him, whom hee for anger would forsake and leave the chamber, and as hee was departing in that angry motion (as shee thought) shee gave a snatch after him, thinking to have taken him by the mantle, to keep him with her, and fell upon one of the beddstickes of the bedd that it pearsed her breast, eaven to her very hart, which received no cure untill she Died thereof.

2. In Irish '*Muirchertach na gCochall gCroicenn*'.

INSTRUCTIO PIE VIVENDI ET SUPERNA MEDITANDI
(Holy Life and Heavenly Thought)
(15th century)

[These extracts afford a glimpse of the conventual ideal, and mystical experience, here figured as swooning drunkenness, in the pre-Reformation period. They derive from a treatise composed by a spiritual adviser for a nun. The original text, dating from the fourteenth century, was written in Latin and came from the House of Saint Victor in Paris which belonged to the Augustinian Canons. It was the location of a school of religious teaching which was highly mystical in tone and opposed to scholasticism. The Augustinian Canons, also known as the Black Canons, were extremely popular in Ireland. Some of their earliest foundations were in County Tipperary. Hore Abbey, also known as Saint Mary's Abbey of the Rock of Cashel, was founded in 1272 with a colony of Cistercians. It maintained links with France until the fourteenth century at least, through which the Latin text possibly reached Ireland, if it had not already done so through the Augustinian Canons. It was translated into Irish, more or less faithfully, in the late fifteenth century by Uilliam Mac an Leagha. (For his adaptation of the Life of Mary of Egypt see pp. 143–8). A note in the manuscript in a nineteenth-century hand, which claims that it was found in the walls of Hore Abbey 'some 40 Years ago', may have some foundation in fact.
From: John McKechnie, *Instructio Pie Vivendi et Superna Meditandi*, Irish Texts Society, vol. 29 (nos 1 and 2) (Dublin: Educational Company of Ireland for Irish Texts Society, 1933 [1927] and 1946 [1927]), pp. xv, 24–7, 86–7, 98–100.]

Quoniam in felici captione Domini sum reclusus, i.e. since I am in my Lord's blissful bondage and that we cannot speak together, I have prepared for you a salvation full of solace, which is more profitable than that we should be together. As any opportunity of our being together would be rare and shorter than we would wish, I have, therefore, written this brief, profitable Instruction for you, in order that you may live compassionately and meditate upon heavenly things. By means of this Instruction, I will speak briefly to you, whenever you please and desire it. If you examine this Instruction prudently you will find in it how to live peacefully, humbly, dutifully and discreetly, how to fashion your character beautifully, wisely guard your senses both extrinsic and intrinsic, keep the Catholic faith firmly, be prudent in every situation in which you shall be placed, rightly invoke the saints and the heavenly spirits, meditate upon the divine substance and subsistence with joy and constant thanksgiving for your gifts, and eagerly desire the heavenly bliss. Satisfied, then, by this spiritual colloquy, do not ask for my presence with you again, because I can speak no better or more effectively than this in order to refresh you in the love and bondage of your own sweet beloved Spouse for ever; and so I now steadfastly beseech you to answer me with deeds in these matters — you have often said that you desired to converse with me — since I am giving you what you desire.

DE LUXURIA, i.e. OF LUST

Lust arises from excessive revelling in food and drink, and for many reasons it is right to avoid it. The first reason: because it defiles the body; as the apostle says, every sin is outwith the body, but one sins within it by lust. The second reason: this sin is foul in the presence of God and of the angels, and so Genesis says that God inflicted punishment for this sin upon the lustful by means of an avenging stream of evil-smelling fire. The third reason: indulgence in it satisfies no one, while its commission tortures the mind. The fourth reason: when a man commits this sin he then hates the woman whom he loved most in all the world, as is proved in the case of Tamar.[1] The fifth reason: this sin makes a dwelling-place for the Devil of the well-beloved spouse of Christ. The sixth reason: the soul, which was at first satisfied by sweet steadfast thoughts of the heavenly joy, is grievously polluted in this sin by unclean thoughts and by the commission of the transgression. The seventh reason: no good thing done without chastity profits. The eighth reason: it despoils one of virgin modesty which can never be restored; with regard to this Jerome says, 'Cum omnia possit Deus, virginem non potest suscitare post ruinam,' i.e. although God is omnipotent yet He cannot restore to virginity the woman who has been once defiled: He can, however, free her from punishment although He does not desire to give her the crown of virginity. The ninth reason for

1. See p. 170.

which it is right to cherish virginity is because it partakes of angelic qualities. Jerome says, 'Profecto in carne praeter carnem vivere non terrena vita est sed celestis,' i.e. to live in the flesh and yet be independent of the flesh is the same as to live in the heavenly life after spurning the earthly. I assert, then, that is a greater merit to attain the angelic life by virtue of good morals than to have it naturally; it is bliss to be an angel, but to be a virgin is a virtue. Understand that it is on account of his virtues that a man obtains the bliss which the angel has naturally, and that both come by these through the gift of God. If you will carefully consider these matters, you will thereafter have no love for unchastity.

DE TACTU, i.e. OF THE SENSE OF TOUCH

First of all keep your hands from every forbidden thing. Neither give nor take anything without your superior's permission — indeed, do nothing without his permission. Do not touch a woman whether she is a relative, aged, or a religious. Do not put your arm round her neck or waist, and do not clasp her hand or gaze into her face. Never do to another what you would not wish done to yourself. You say in answer to this, 'I do not want that advice to be given to me, for my conscience is strong.' My answer to you is that, although such conduct does not harm you, it may harm your companion or neighbour, and even although it should harm no one, yet it is unseemly. In this regard the apostle says, 'Avoid every appearance of evil,' i.e. avoid not only the act condemned, but also every appearance of it. The reason for this is that every time you cause scandal to another, you condemn yourself in particular. I enjoin upon you, therefore, never to be alone with a man, whether he is a relative or a religious. Do not make many signs for to do so reveals that women are inane. When making use of these signs, do not speak or utter cant sayings whence there might be discerned in you the boldness of inanity and impiety. While you are speaking, do not stretch forth your finger, and practise no tricks with your hands. Do not catch hold of a woman's thighs, indeed, do not catch hold of her anywhere, for these acts show that the religious woman is bold and shameless. Never stretch out your hand to anyone. Do not let your hand be seen uncovered, except through necessity, for the religious woman ought to be firm and modest in body and mind.

DE HABITU CORPORIS, i.e. OF THE DEPORTMENT OF THE BODY

It is right to watch the deportment of the body carefully, so that nothing might be apparent in it which would cause shame to another. I enjoin upon you, then, that your manner of walking should not be fatuous, self-complacent, futile or dissolute, but calm, grave, steadfast, slow, temperate and modest. Do not let your body be unsteady or unclean, but seemly, correct, well-ruled. Do not let your shoulders be erect or firm, but moderately low and bent, and do not let your neck be held up proudly, but keep it bent downwards. Do not let your head be ever turning, but steady, submissive and modest. Do not let your countenance be restless, foolish and shameless, but resolute, sober, agreeable and harmless. Do not let your clothing be conspicuous or excessive, but sufficient and reasonable. Do not let the material of your clothing be expensive or mean, but ordinary and moderate. Do not let your clothing be soiled or too beautiful or conspicuous, for of such clothing, the one reveals want of taste or else too much vain glory, the other, meanness and baseness. Excessive cleanliness or ugly sordidness is unsuitable for a nun. Do not let your clothing be too long, for a train on the clothing of a nun is unseemly, but still, do not let it be too short, but moderately measured. Do not let your boots be too narrow or too ornamental, but broad and neatly arranged. Have no binding or variegated painting upon your girdle, stockings, or the borders of your sleeves, but make choice of what is ordinary among all these things and have no variety of a conspicuous nature. Make no excessive mirth with the mirthful, nor excessive mourning with the mournful. Do not be overcome by mischance, or exalt yourself on account of quietness if you should get it. I tell you, at every time and in every way be inwardly instructed by the signs of virtue, ready for perfection. Cast no reproach or scandal upon the undisciplined, but guide them by your own example to better things. If you thus carefully guard the outward senses, the inner sense ought to be perfectly guarded, and through this watchfulness the heart is thoroughly guarded . . .

DE EUNDO IN VIA, i.e. OF TRAVELLING

Go rarely, sadly and unwillingly out of your monastery, and if it is necessary for you to leave it for a time, return as soon as you can. You ought always to know that the time you have spent outside of your monastery has gone, and you should feel great sorrow for whatever time you have let slip past unprofitably. While you are outside do not spend much, and do not permit anyone to spend much on your behalf. Never be alone with any man at all; do not sit or speak with one so as not to give others an opportunity of doing harm to themselves, and never part with the companionship of another woman lest each of you should incur scandal. Give an example in words, manners and deeds to all. Make no alliance with worldly folks, and attach no importance to any particular person's advice in the matter of piety or impiety, for to do so is to subvert and to destroy your faith and rule. Do not ask for the interpretation of a dream or for a spell. Do not expose your affairs to fickleness and instability, but devote your life to good deeds and to many virtues and let it shine therein, for the pious marks all vain forbidden things as signs of irresolution and of heterodoxy, and indeed, such are neither virtues nor truths of the faith. One is drawn away from asking the help of the pious when alone for fear of back-biting. By making sure of these things he[2] has mentioned, the sweet first-fruits of eternal glory are obtained. The pious ought not to read to, or to pray on behalf of, others, for fear of back-biting about the reward, or about neglect of the proper time, and for that very reason we counsel you to avoid carefully a peril that might result in danger to yourself or to others, and to be quiet, pious and retired in your own house . . .

DE EBRIETATE SPIRITUALI, i.e. OF SPIRITUAL INTOXICATION

This is the true felicity of the soul, and the blessed soul which possesses the spiritual felicity

---

2. i.e. the author of the Latin original.

wholly is the one which has endeavoured to turn frequently the mouth of the heart to drink from the precious vessel, i.e. the body of the Lord, which was pierced and often tormented so that the beloved disciple might drink all that he required from it and be filled with the temperate nourishment and spiritual intoxication which contains the bliss of the soul fully. By means of this holy wine mingled with the water of perfect righteousness the beloved blessed soul can now satisfy its desire for eternal salvation if, bending down humbly to these holy feet, it bows to them, praying eagerly and in spirit, and drinks from the wound in the left foot the fear of judgment, the dread of Hell and the pure wine of contrition and penance, and from the wounds in the right foot, the wine of joy and eternal satisfaction wherein mercy and the hope of goodness are assured. The blessed soul now rises peacefully, bowing honourably to these precious holy hands, and drinks from the cleansing wounds in the left hand and drives out sins by means of the wine of desire and joy. Gather together and guard the grace from the wound in the right hand by drinking the wine of strength and salvation from the cup filled with the pure mixed wine, which has been bestowed upon you by the hands of the Lord. Thus the blessed soul can become intoxicated with bliss. Should the soul wholly immerse itself by hastening fervently to the glorious wound in Christ's side and drinking from it security of heart and mildness of spirit, i.e. the wine of devotion and pure meditation, it can be thoroughly filled with this gracious intoxication by partaking of this precious claret and various chosen kinds of these ineffable heavenly types divinely repeated and mingled with the blessed joy. Whoever you are, O honourable and blessed soul, which yearns for the materials for this spiritual intoxication, while constantly drinking from these precious wounds sweetly, abundantly and incessantly, you must imitate bodily intoxication in every way. As the drunkard weeps, be you afflicted by tears of devotion, but as the drunkard rejoices, be you joyful through your gratitude to the Lord. As the drunkard sings, rejoice in the melody of your heart particularly. As the drunkard laughs, fill yourself with the heavenly joy. As the drunkard

thinks that he is fortunate and elegant in his habits and is optimistic in his all-golden prosperity[3] . . . and as the drunkard frequently falls in the mud, mourn and sigh because your dwelling is in this mud as long as you dwell in a human body, and meditate upon the speed and difficulty involved in reaching heavenly things. As the drunkard is held up in case he should fall, you to your joy, are being invited into the kingdom of God. The drunkard is guided in case he should go astray, cleave, then, to the Holy Ghost whom you know. As the drunkard keeps nothing for himself, cast yourself wholly upon God and spurn everything else. As the drunkard speaks extravagantly, be you filled incessantly with the heavenly glory. As the drunkard is not quite at himself, let nothing be at your own disposal, but be you completely cast upon God. As the drunkard is quarrelsome or obstinate, be you obstinate and contentious in gaining a battle-contest over yourself, and cast yourself wholly upon God in true glory. As the drunkard fears nothing, see that you have no fear of want or failure should such be your lot while you are travelling towards God. As the drunkard cannot speak a single word, be you unskilled in the tongues of the world, but filled abundantly with the heavenly language. As the drunkard thinks himself powerful, rejoice greatly at seeing the bliss and glory of your own Father, and because you are exalted high above all earthly things. As the drunkard thinks that he is noble, boast with regard to the queenship of Heaven. As the drunkard leaps and shouts, leap and advance from virtue to virtue, and sing and make melody in your mind while meditating upon the delightfulness of your own sweet harmonious Creator. As the drunkard willingly falls asleep, you will be comforted, when your bodily senses sleep, by the heavenly rest that arises between God's will and your own while you are embracing and touching your own blessed Spouse. You can be instructed more fully and more learnedly by this spiritual draught he[4] mentions, than by letter or by writing of earthly words.

3. In the original, some words have been lost at this point.
4. i.e. the author of Latin original.

from:
BEATHA MHUIRE
ÉIGIPTEACHDHA
(Life of Mary of Egypt)
(15th century)

[The legend of Mary of Egypt, the nymphomaniac who became a saint, was invented in Palestine in the sixth century, and reached the West in the eighth, when it was translated from Greek into Latin by a scholar-monk of Monte Cassino, Paul the Deacon (d. *c.* 799). Thereafter it became widely known in the West, in Latin and the vernaculars. It is an arresting illustration of the gendered nature of penitence. There are three different recensions in Irish, the longest of which is excerpted here.

The sixth-century legend derived from the same context as that which produced early Byzantine lives of 'harlots of the desert', such as the actress Pelagia and the courtesan Thaïs. Mary's Egyptian origins also gave the legend an Old Testament resonance: as one who in her youth had 'played the whore in Egypt' (Ezekiel 23:2), she was a type of the Chosen People who turned away from God. The sixth-century version opens with an account of the holy man Zosimus and his encounter with Mary. Zosimus both narrates and participates in Mary's peripety — her complete about-turn from a life of sin to intensely felt penitence. He is both shocked and edified by Mary's journey from the depths of depravity to the heights of holiness, and consequently loses his own undue self-satisfaction. Zosimus also figures the idea of ecclesiastical community as opposed to eremitical life: he is needed to administer the Eucharist to Mary at the end of her days as a solitary desert penitent. Thus Mary and Zosimus are seen to be two different but complementary types.

Only one of the three Irish recensions opens with an account of Zosimus. This follows the version found in the thirteenth-century Latin collection known as the *Legenda Aurea* (Golden Legend). The other two focus immediately on Mary, and Zosimus appears at a late stage and in a supporting role; these are more concerned with Mary as an individual than with the counterbalanced roles of Mary and Zosimus. The prologue to the longer of the two (below, §1) associates her with Mary Magdalen, who was not only the model for penitent prostitutes but the penitent *par excellence*. This saint's reputation in the Roman church as a reformed prostitute derived from the conflation of three distinct women: Mary of Bethany, sister of Lazarus, the unnamed female sinner of Luke 7:37, and Mary of Magdala from whom Christ had cast out seven demons (Mark 16:9). The propensity to shed copious tears which the evangelists ascribed to Mary of Bethany carried over to the composite Magdalen, and was as important (at least) as the sexual nature of her sin in her construction as model penitent.

The subject of penance was central to the preaching of the mendicant orders, particularly the Dominicans. In five sermons he wrote for the Magdalen's feast-day, Jacobus de Voragine, Dominican Archbishop of Genoa and author of the *Legenda Aurea*, 'distinguished the Magdalen's tears according to their nature: those of compunction in keeping with the memory of her sins; those of compassion for her dead brother Lazarus; those of contrition at the Crucifixion; those of love, wept while standing outside the sepulchre'. As K.L. Jansen has shown, his schema illuminates 'the late medieval notion of penance in all its manifold configurations' ('Mary Magdalen and the Mendicants: The Preaching of Penance in the Late Middle Ages', *Journal of Medieval History*, vol. 21 [1995], pp. 1–25, at p. 6).

Mary of Egypt also sheds many tears which, in her case, are proof of a change of heart. From that point forward she is dry-eyed but her life exemplifies due progress through the stages of contrition, confession, penance and absolution. Only then can she receive the Eucharist, which is the guarantee of her salvation. The monk who brings it to her (named Damsosmais rather than Zosimus) encounters her when he himself is a penitent, having retreated to the desert on Ash Wednesday after hearing a sermon on the Last Judgment. Clearly then, despite her many riveting adventures, Mary of Egypt's Life is less a romance than a discourse on sin and repentance.

The topic of virginity is also important. Mary of Egypt contrasts herself with the Virgin Mary: she, 'a sink of corruption, impure and abominable', is not worthy to receive Christ, whereas his Mother is the 'virgin undefiled before and after' (§6). Yet it is to the Virgin that she dares to pray, asking her to intercede with Christ on her behalf. Consequently, the former harlot eventually receives the Sacred Body, after which she is recuperated as a virgin (§§14–16).

The Irish Life excerpted here (in translation) is found in a manuscript written by the fifteenth-century Uilliam Mac an Leagha (British Library, MS Additional 30,512). There is compelling evidence that Mac an Leagha did not merely copy the text but actually translated or adapted it, from an unidentified English source. One feature which seems unique to his text is his description of Mary in the desert as grown bestial, like the legendary deranged Mis in the wilderness (see pp. 238–41). Mac an Leagha's text was edited and translated by A. Martin Freeman, 'Betha Mhuire Eigiptacdha', *Études Celtiques*, vol. 1 (1936), pp. 78–113. The following excerpts from Freeman's translation, with minor changes in presentation, admirably convey the style of Mac an Leagha's text.]

§1. *Incipit uita Mariae Aegyptianae*, that is, Here beginneth the life of Mary of Egypt. When the Lark ceases her singing at eventide her heart mourns for the day in sadness and sorrow; for she hath no love or liking for the night but is lonely for the day all the while. Even so the man who has no pleasure [?] in praising another but regards not his good deeds and disdains his virtues; that man is lonely for the great glory compact of glories, the noble house of Heaven, where is life without death, love without darkness, cheer without gloom and all other glories besides. For tongue cannot tell, nor eye attain, nor ear receive, nor heart meditate the glory of that house; and he who is not in deadly sin will have his share of that glory. No man can sleep or rest, sit or stand, fast or feast, without sin; but, O mortal, if thou sin, be not downcast and despairing of God's mercy, but make confession quickly afterwards and God will forgive thee thy vices. For consider how Peter sinned, and Paul and Longinus and Mary Magdalene and Mary of Egypt and many others likewise; yet these were all saved after repentence, since God longeth more for the sinner to pray that his sins may be forgiven than doth the sinner to obtain forgiveness.

§2. There was a King in Egypt, rich, happy and agreeable, prudent, wise and very chaste, who was married to a worthy wellborn lady, and there was born to them an illustrious daughter, Mary by name. The child was nursed and nurtured in great splendour, [being clothed] in beautiful silken dresses and lovely cloaks of golden thread. She waxed and grew very quickly and became fairer of form than any other woman in the world at that time. She had long, light-yellow hair of the hue of refined gold or of the sun at evening; eyes very regal, very beautiful; brows black and slender above them; a comely, winning face; lovely alluring lips coloured like the red rose; two little hills, a pure-white pair, on her bosom; fair fine fingers on her white hands, with long narrow nails at their tips; tall slender sides; and all her body was beautifully white like ermine or lily. No man looked upon this maiden of many charms without loving her passionately, and she looked upon no man without desiring intercourse with him; for she would abide with no man but passed from one mate to another. Now her mother began to correct her unceasingly with soft speech, but her daughter only called her an ignorant, witless woman, disregarding and despising the discourse of the gentle queen. Her father then admonished her sharply, saying. 'Thou headstrong girl, desist

from this scandalous, impure practice, for thou mayest readily have whomsoever thou wilt in honourable wedlock. It is a sorrow and a misfortune for me that thou art my child, and in an unblessed hour wast thou begotten.' And many more sorrowful and scornful words did he speak to his daughter, but she heeded not his mighty displeasure. As for the adulteress after this, since she accepted not counsel or correction from her parents or kindred, they conceived hatred and abhorrence of the wanton and could not suffer the sight of her thenceforth.

§3. She then began to indulge her passions in sinful lust and could not satisfy her will in all Egypt till she went to Alexandria. In that wealthy, well-favoured city she took a house, and the perverse harlots of the town gathered round her and made her the leader of their corruption and ill dealing, because of her boldness and her beauty. And Mary in her headlong perversity kept not herself from the married men of that city, nor its religious nor its priests, nor from any two that were brothers, or father and son, or from any class of incest, even at the most holy seasons. Moreover the city merchants used to bring cool sweet wines and dainty drinks and sell them in the house with the adulteress and hold a market and merrymaking around her, while all in turn entered in unto her; and every man who saw her desired to go with her because of the lively light of love in her face. And she was so full of craving for men that she would hale them by the head out of the streets, to have satisfaction of them. Afterwards there was made for her a costly cloak of the purest golden thread, and on it were set four fair gems of great price; then jewelled sandals of Cordovan were made for her, supple and set with gleaming, glancing gems; and every man who saw her in this splendour would rather have his will of her than be possessed of vast riches. Now there came terrible poverty and evil plight upon the land, and assuredly upon the city, through the multitudes that came to seek out and see this witless, wicked adulteress; and the wise men said that God himself had allowed the want and hunger, poverty and penury to visit the land and city as a punishment for this impiety and pollution. Seven years did this vicious woman dwell in Alexandria, freely following every lust and uncleanness and transgression.

§4. One day early in the month of May this head-strong, evil-living woman was on the battlements at the top of the town, and looking upon the sea she saw a ship, wide-hulled and well-timbered, making port and standing in towards the strand, and in it a jolly, jovial crew, a courageous company of mighty men, fine, well-favoured folk, and thought in her erring mind that she would fain be among those virile fellows so that they might work her will. She walked boldly and swiftly through the noisy city and on her way she met an ancient senior and asked him from what parts or from what people came that full vessel which lay snugly sheltered in the city's harbour. 'From Jerusalem city,' answered the old man, fair and friendly. 'Would ye take me with you in that ship to Jerusalem city?' said the woman. Said the old man: 'We will, if we receive the price of our labour.' The lady said she had nothing but her body to bestow upon them, but that she would give herself unsparingly. At this the old man smiled and went his way. But the erring woman went quickly onto the ship and saluted the sailors and said: 'Take me with you for God's honour to the city of Christ's Passion and penance!' The crew asked her what she would give them for carrying her to Jerusalem city. The adulteress said that she had no worldly wealth save her clothes, but that she would not be niggardly of yielding her body and smooth skin to them. But the sailors were abashed at the wanton words of the wicked woman and bade her enter quickly into the ship, for they would carry her to Jerusalem city. So she went in and they sailed swiftly away over the wave-walled, dense, dark, sudden-stormy sea, and she was taking the sailors by turns below the ship's hatches to seduce them. But now the wild winds, dangerous and dreadful, fell with violence upon the vessel, so that the mast was splintered, the sails blown down, the ropes strained and snapped, the hull holed and battered, and the great and courageous crew were filled with fear and daunted by the danger. But not so was Mary: she was untouched by terror and free from fear, for a devil was impudently prompting her to ill and she was haling the mariners by the head under the hatches to work her will.

§5. Afterwards they made port in Jerusalem and landed among that pleasing, prosperous people. The sinful woman went with them, but none of them desired to have dealing or dalliance with her in that country. The adulteress, uneasy in mind, sat herself on a stone, but since no one accosted her she entered into the city and joined herself to the public women. Thus she lived from the beginning of May till Ascension Day, saying nay to no man whom she might have. But on that very day, the Thursday of the Ascension, she saw the congregation of the city going to the temple of Solomon to hear a service and to walk in procession, and she followed them: not from any desire of piety or cause of conscience, but that she might bring some of them back to her room and have her will of them. But when she saw all the people climbing the steep steps of the smooth-polished marble stairway [and] wished to go there herself likewise, she was met by a company, fair of form and with drawn swords in their hands, threatening her, and she was afraid and went back the way she had come. Four times did Mary seek to mount the stairway, that she might look upon the sports and pretty pastimes of the temple, but always that same company threatened her; and they did not except or disdain any other who offered to enter, but her alone.

§6. Then Mary went to a desolate dark spot and reflected in her mind that they were holy angels of heaven that had hindered her from entering the upper chambers of the temple by reason of her manifold vices and misdeeds. Then began she to tear her hair and to make loud lamentation in her sorrow and affliction. Afterwards she saw a beautiful altar nearby and an image of Mary on it. And the sinner approached and made a cross-vigil before it and said: 'O Mary, mother of grace and mercy, behold me suing for Thy protection and the succour of Thy Son. Let Thy heart be moved towards me, pray Thy Son for my sake and pity me. For Thy Son, the only Son of God, vouchsafed to enter Thy body by reason of Thy humility and lowliness and piety and meekness and chastity and purity. Not thus am I, for my manifold misdeeds. I am not worthy that He should enter my bosom, for I am a sink of corruption, impure and abominable, filled full with all revolting vices and iniquitous deadly sins.' Furthermore the sinful woman said: 'Gracious Mary, to Thee came the archangel Gabriel in the shape of a fair gentle dove and greeted Thee, and by his power infused pregnancy of the Holy Spirit through Thy right ear, leaving with Thee the blessing of the heavenly Father. And God's Son was nine months in Thy womb, and at the end of that time Thou didst bear Him in the lowly stall of the ox and the ass and wast a virgin undefiled both before and after. Afterwards Gabriel came to Thee and bade Thee flee with Thy son into Egypt, for fear of Herod; for he had commanded the children to be slain, hoping to slay Thy Son among them. Thou wast for a while in Egypt till Gabriel directed Thee to go back again to Thy hereditary home, and Thou, with Thy Son and Joseph and your feeble folk, didst return. Thirty and three years was Thy Son in this world suffering humiliation, without shoes to His feet, and afterwards He willingly suffered death on the cruel cross to redeem the race of mankind. He went to Hell and harrowed it; on the third day after the Passion He rose from the dead and was with the apostles until the day with today's name; afterwards He ascended into the kingdom of God before the eyes of the multitudes and sat at the right hand of the heavenly Father; after that He sent the Holy Spirit on Whitsunday among the apostles to teach and comfort them. And Thy Son, O Mary, left behind Him in this world a new law and righteous ordinance and ten most noble commandments. And I believe that this Son will come to judge both quick and dead in doom; and in that day do I fear to meet my God and my Lord. Furthermore it is presumptuous in me to expect salvation because of the multitude of my misdeeds, save for this one thing, that the mercy of my God is greater than the sin of all the seed of Adam.' And again she said: 'O merciful Mary, since before Thy image I am imploring Thee, pray Thy Son earnestly and fervently for my sake!' Said an angel on high: 'Egyptian Mary, God hath forgiven thee thy vices for thy repentance. Yet must thou suffer sorrow and oppression and penance. Arise now and hear Mass.'

§7. Then Mary went to hear Mass, and after witnessing the Consecration she bought bread for three halfpence and went out from Jerusalem city, and one met her who put a small staff into her hand and bade her keep it. Thereafter she journeyed through the wild wilderness and neither stopped nor stayed until she came to the bank and brink of the wonderful river Jordan. Then she saw a pleasant chapel, a strongly built, holy house of prayer, placed there long ages before for John Baptist of the melodius mouth, and she tried to enter it but could not. She went again to the stream and washed her body with its water. After this she left her staff behind and going under a tree bewept her vices in sadness and sorrow. Her clothes were cold and wet about her, for it was rainy weather, and the desert, deep and impassable, [surrounded her.] Then she drew out the scanty store of bread and ate one loaf, and slept awhile under the tree with her ear to a stone. In the morning she heard a bell ringing from the chapel of John Baptist, and entering the oratory she listened to the service, earnestly, devoutly, with tormented heart. Afterwards she begged the priest to hear her confession devoutly for the love of God. Then did Mary confess her faults in full to the priest, from the time of her childhood until that hour, and asked him for God's sake to give her absolution and remission of sins. This she received from the priest charitably and without scorning, for he forgave her all her transgressions . . .

§9. Now as for Mary of Egypt, she was forty-seven years without any provision of food save three-halfpennyworth of bread. And for seventeen of those years she had no food or drink but grass and roots and small grapes and water. And she ranged the desert on her feet and hands; her smooth body put forth a long hideous hairy coat, so that her own fur was her covering in place of clothes. The polished rosy nails fell from her toes and fingers and she grew long, sloping, sharp, savage nails after the likeness of the hideous hooves of a goat. And she did not trust any one of all mankind but was like any other wild beast and abode constantly in the desert.

§10. Now there was a monastery in the Egyptian desert at that time. Its abbot was named John, and he had with him a pious community. They lived always on poor barley bread and earthy, stagnant water, for they would not indulge their flesh with spring-water to drink. Each monk wore a harsh hair-shirt next his skin; on Fridays they took no food but berries and water and washed each other's feet and kissed each other; and no words were spoken among them save prayers.

§11. Now Lent came upon them and they confessed their lives to the abbot on Ash Wednesday and took the communion and sacrifice of the Church. Then the abbot preached to them a sermon about the day of Judgment, saying that sun and moon would be of the colour of smith's coal on that day for dread of the Son of God; that the angels would be terrified at the wrath of the Lord; that fluttering, flashing flames and lightning, portentous and mighty, would issue from Hell; that dread hideous devils of hell would be brilliantly blazing on the Lord's left hand; that sinners would send forth horrific howlings as they were haled to Hell; and many hard sayings did he add about the day of doom. When the monks heard these things they screamed and burst into tears, and they begged the abbot's leave to depart into the desert, that they might mortify the flesh until Palm Sunday. The abbot gave them this permission and said that no two of them must be together during that time. Then the monks, having heard his words, hastened out into the wilderness, all going different ways, North, South, East and West, and each of them went apart into a small cave in the mountain side and prayed until Palm Sunday; and all that time only one monk remained with the abbot. But on Palm Sunday they came out of the desert and met together, yet no monk spoke to another till Maundy Thursday. On that day the abbot washed all their feet and gave them Communion and Sacrifice, and they performed the Easter celebrations with proper piety.

§12. They then passed the following summer and autumn and winter until Ash Wednesday, with no speech or song but prayer alone. The abbot gave them Communion and Sacrifice, heard their confessions and gave them absolution afterwards and preached before them; and each monk separately, having asked the abbot's leave, went out into the desert of Egypt. And the monk whose name was Damsosmais went far apart from the rest and was for thirty days walking in the mountains and the desolate solitudes. Higher and higher, rougher and rougher, colder and colder every day he [found] the gloomy overgrown highland and the desert depths.

§13. One day as this monk was walking he saw nearby a misshapen creature in the likeness of a terrifying animal, a horrid hateful beast, eating the grass. The animal fled from him on its four foul, dusky feet, and though he pursued it with the utmost speed of his running he could not come up with it because of the denseness of the desert growth. Then he adjured the marvellous uncouth monster by the Passion of Christ to wait for him. On hearing this the beast halted, obedient and biddable, and dropped on her . . . knees before him, saying: 'I give thanks to the only God of Heaven that I have heard the name of my Lord pronounced in my presence! For I have not heard my Lord's name for seven and forty years, save that I often speak it in my mind.' Said the monk: 'Give account, for God's sake, and tell me what thou art!' 'I will,' said the animal, 'and do thou put somewhat of thy clothing about me while I tell my tale, for I am wearing nothing to hide my nakedness.' The monk threw her his frock and she quickly wrapped it about her and stood upright and told him that she was Mary of Egypt; and she told the monk her whole story, from first to last . . .

§15. After this Damsosmais returned to the monastery and attended the Easter celebrations therein, and so remained until the following Lent, increasing in prayer every day. Ash Wednesday came round and the devout community made Communion and Sacrifice and confession of sin, listened to a sermon from the abbot and afterwards scattered into the desert. Damsosmais ranged the wilderness, looking for the holy woman, walking every day and night. And one midnight he beheld a bright light afar off, and it seemed to him seven times stronger than the shining, scorching, splendid sun, and he thought it was a smooth white marble stone. He walked towards it until the full light of day came upon him, when he found a shining, snowy substance and a deal of fragrant spices sprinkled all about it and flocks of most melodious birds of paradise chanting around it. And it seemed to him that the sick and wounded of the whole world would fall asleep on hearing the ever-living, ever-lovely lays which he now heard from those birds on every hand. Yet he did not understand what was the light or what caused them so to sing round about it. And because he had not found the holy woman he returned to the monastery and told the story of this virgin to the abbot and his community. The monks asked him what was the holy woman's name, but Damsosmais said he had not asked it of her. Then the abbot and all the monks fell upon their knees and besought God very fervently that they might know the virgin's name, and they beheld it written upon a flagstone before their faces and returned thanks to God.

§16. Damsosmais then, saying that he thought the very bright thing he had seen in the desert was the body of the virgin, went again to look at it and found the body of the holy woman in that same place, with birds of paradise surrounding it and singing. Now he had no tool, of iron or of wood, wherewith to commit that body to the earth, and at that season the ground was hard and firm and ill to dig. But just then he saw coming towards him a sharp-toothed lion and was filled with great fear of the unbiddable beast; for now he would grimly grind his teeth, and anon he was mild and showed friendship when the fur lay flat on his tick-rooted [*sic*], tight-pointed tail. The monk, however, determined to await the coming of the lion, and the lion approached and fell upon his knees before the monk and gave the kiss of peace upon his feet. He then dug a pit, deep and ill to dig, with his forceful fore-feet and cast out the clay with his hefty hind-feet. Afterwards he took the feet of the holy woman between his fore-feet, while the monk took her head in his hands, and together they laid her in the grave, and the lion quickly covered her up with earth. Then the lion gave a kiss of peace on the monk's feet and the monk blessed the lion and the lion went his way into the forest fastnesses. After this the monk returned to his monastery and related the tidings of the holy woman to the abbot and his community and they all said a Mass for the soul of the faithful pious one. Moreover they prayed to God fervently and trustfully that their own lives might reach a like good end. For ever and ever, amen. The end. I, William, who wrote this, pray for mercy.

from:
RIAGHAIL NA SAGART
(The Priests' Rule)
(15th century)

[Various decrees were issued by the Irish church in the fifteenth century, as in earlier ones, ordering priests to put away their 'wives'. Under canon law all women who had a sexual liaison with clerics were concubines, even though the annals show that women in long-standing relationships might be held in the highest regard (for example, under the years 1419 and 1427 at p. 336). Clearly the drive for a celibate clergy was unevenly applied in different sectors of the Irish church, and no doubt the experience of 'correction' was also differently felt by clerics on the one hand, and by their consorts and families on the other. The rhetoric of an inherently sinful female nature would have helped shift the blame from errant males to their 'temptresses'. Furthermore, to deprive a cleric and his consort of *her* property (for redistribution among the poor or the faithful) did less to undermine church stability than to strip him of his privileges and benefice.

Victimization of non-celibate clerics and their consorts worsened when the laity, through zeal or greed, became involved in pursuing miscreants. Evidently such intervention was on the increase in fifteenth-century Ireland. One instance of it is 'The Priests' Rule', an inflammatory appeal to the Irish laity, especially the chiefs, to take action against bad priests, particularly those who cohabited with women. Internal references show that its author was a layman. The earliest extant version is found in *Liber Flavus Fergusiorum*, a manuscript dated *c.* 1437–40. It was addressed to Maghnus Mac Mathghamhna (d. 1443), heir-apparent (*adhbhar riogh*) of Oriel in the Northern Half. He was a sometime ally of the Great O'Neill, Eoghan Ó Néill. This lord's sons had to be censured for profiteering from penalizing clerics' consorts. A grant made to his heir, Henry, to arrest priests' concubines and to confiscate their goods throughout Ulster was revoked by the church in 1455 because Henry was 'moved not by zeal or the intention of bringing about a salutary correction, but by his notorious covetousness, avarice or greed, whereby at the devil's prompting he had long plotted to acquire for himself not only [the concubines'] goods, but the goods of others also' (see Katherine Simms, 'The Concordat between Primate John Mey and Henry O'Neill [1455]', *Archivium Hibernicum*, vol. 34 [1977], pp. 71–82 at p. 75).

A somewhat different version of 'The Priests' Rule' is found in a manuscript written by the fifteenth-century scribe and author Uilliam Mac an Leagha: British Library, MS Egerton 81, ff. 16–20. It may represent an adaptation to suit an audience in the Southern Half. The following extract is translated from a nineteenth-century copy of that version, in Maynooth, Saint Patrick's College Library, MS 2 G 11, pp. 97–130. Other extracts were published anonymously (in Irish only) in *Irisleabhar Muighe Nuadhad*, 1919, pp. 73–9.]

As regards the priests' women, the offspring of those who are your subjects as lords, it is right that you should take them from them by force, so long as you do this for the love of God and for the good of the church. And should they have a personal dowry, provided they abide henceforth by the counsel of the church and are good-living, let them retain possession of what is theirs. If they do not do so, however, let you divide the dowry among God's poor and His labourers.

As regards the persons of the clerics and the priests, and the private property of the church, they are to remain subject to the rule of the superior[1] himself. And should the superiors be just the same, the wisest course is to complain them to the Pope and to seek remedy from God and from the Pope for those cases.

And we say to the people to shun their masses and their sacrament, because if you do not do so, it is a mortal sin on your part and it merits Hell.

And we say to go to the parish church, every Sunday and Holy Day, to show obeisance and honour to God and to the church and, should the priests offer to say mass, to flee from them instantly, for that Christ could charge you with aiding in his crucifixion. For it is certain that whosoever hears their masses sins as gravely as the Jews who were present at the place of Christ's crucifixion and did not prevent his crucifixion. For those that act and those that give assent bear the same sin. For not to tempt bad-living people to error is to help them, and when the truth is not proclaimed it is suppressed. Therefore, as their sin is of equal gravity, so should their pain be.

And further, as regards the priests who keep the mothers of their offspring in their houses, even though they might be old, or in a black coif, and especially those who spend their youth and health in that sin, we say that their sacraments should be shunned, for two reasons. The first reason: that Canon Law forbids that any woman whatsoever should reside in the houses of priests. And should the priests say that what is to be understood here is such time when the women and priests are young and when there might be a suspicion of the evil business, our answer is that how this is to be understood is: when the priests live celibately from the time of their youth to their old age. And how can they keep the women with whom they have spent their lives in their houses without sinning?

And it is on account of this that Augustine says: 'if you have laid the sins aside when you are incapable of committing them, it is the sins that have abandoned you, not you that have abandoned them'. Therefore, the priests who have not yet abandoned their sins and who maintain the old women nourish the devils both in their youth and in their old age.

And should they say that they repent it, we do not believe that, and we do not countenance it, while the women are in residence. For the Scripture says that what sin requires is the pouring of water, for when the water is poured, it leaves no colour or taste or scent. For the same reason it is right to separate from sin: [to be] without its colour, that is, not to see its cause; and without its scent, that is, not to have desire of it in his heart; and without its taste, that is, not to recall it in his mind.

How, then, can the priests, who have before them these same women who had their affections and with whom they would associate, acquit themselves before God and before people?

Further, the second matter. We say that her wearing of the coif or the cap does not save the woman from the priest for, were she a true nun, she would be found in a monastery or among pious black nuns. Where she should be is in an enclosure, living a life of hardship and chastity in obedience to an abbess or a prioress, as the text of Canon Law says.

Therefore, as the nuns who remain in sin are without rule, without obedience, without master, our understanding is that their authority is the Devil. And still less again does the deceitful cap avail the 'wife', for that is nothing more than evil enveloped. And the doctors say that the sin of this evil is greater than that of the evil which is not enveloped, and apparent propriety is in fact a double impropriety. Therefore, since the coifs and the caps are adopted merely as envelopes and covers, the sin is greater for their presence than for their absence.

Therefore, the upshot of what I say is this: no matter what the colour or aspect of the priests'

---

1. i.e. 'church superior'.

women in their houses, their masses cannot be heard and the sacraments of the church cannot be received from them, and whosoever would hear mass or receive the sacraments commits a mortal sin. And so I say to you to honour the good priests as if they were kings or consecrated bishops and further, should they be evil and yet give good instruction, to accept that good instruction, and to let them keep their own evil.

The third thing we say to you: as regards the priests who are found guilty of the sin of women on any of the three counts which render · it manifest, that is, through its being made public, or through its being confessed, or through his being subdued in his sin canonically, shun their masses if you desire not to be in pledge to their sin.

The fourth thing: when the sin is manifest as we have said and when . . .[2]

The fifth thing: when the woman is in residence, even though she be old, or in a black coif, or a false cap, to shun her then as she[3] would be shunned if she were in childbirth.

And we say to you to observe those teachings, and to cherish the eternal kingdom, through the Holy Spirit. AMEN.

2. The MS is defective here.
3. Reading *i* for MS *é*.

THE BURIAL OF THE PRIEST'S CONCUBINE
(15th century)

[The preceding extract evidences the defamation, even demonization, of clerics' consorts by the literate, upper echelons in the fifteenth century. Contemporaneous versions of the following learned popular tale show that such attitudes also filtered down to the populace.

Translation: Kenneth Hurlstone Jackson, *A Celtic Miscellany* (Harmondsworth, Middlesex: Penguin Books, 1971), pp. 165–6.]

This is a tale about a priest's concubine when she died. Many people came to her to carry her away to bury her, and they could not lift her because she was so heavy. And they all wondered greatly at this, and everyone said, 'O One God, Almighty Father, how shall she be taken to be buried?' And

they consulted a cunning professor, and the professor said to them as follows: 'Bring two priests' concubines to us to carry her away to the church.' And they were brought, and they carried her away very lightly to the church; and the people wondered greatly at this, and the professor said to them, 'There is no cause for you to wonder at their actions, O people; that is, that two devils should carry off one devil with them.' *Finit.*

from:
OIDHEADH CHLAINNE LIR
(The Children of Lir)
(15th century)

[Until recently, this renowned tale was regarded by most as primarily mythological but work by Caoimhín Breatnach has shown that it is thoroughly imbued with the notions of suffering and salvation disseminated by the church, particularly the preaching orders, in the fifteenth and sixteenth centuries ('The Religious Significance of *Oidheadh Chloinne Lir*', *Ériu*, vol. 50 [1999], pp. 1–40). The tale seems to date from the fifteenth century.

The story unfolds in remote pre-Christian times, when the supernatural Tuatha Dé Danann (Tribes of the God Danu) still walk the earth, sharing Ireland with the human descendants of Míl, ancestor of the Irish. Bodhbh Dearg rules over the Tuatha Dé Danann. There is tension between him and Lir, also of the Tuatha Dé Danann and a former contender for the sovereignty. To lessen it, Bodhbh Dearg offers Lir his choice of his three foster-daughters, Aobh, Aoife and Ailbhe, in marriage. Lir chooses Aobh and their union is happy, and blessed with children — two sets of twins — but Aobh dies in childbirth. The tale concerns the terrible fate suffered thereafter by the four children of Lir and Aobh, and their ultimate deliverance.

Their new stepmother, Aoife — their own mother's sister – is thoroughly evil and almost without remorse, whereas the children are wholly loveable. In no way do they earn the injustice she visits on them. The moral is that the innocent often suffer most in this world yet no tyrant can touch their immortal soul, and any pain they endure in this world is as nothing compared to the hell from which their fortitude delivers them.

The children move freely between their father's fairy residence, Síodh Fionnachaidh, alias Síodh Lir, in the Fews mountains (County Armagh), and Bodhbh's *síodh*, on the brink of Lough Derg (near Killaloe, County Clare). It is when travelling south to Bodhbh's *síodh* that Aoife transforms them into swans. Their colour and their bird-form point up their innocence: in the Voyage-Tales, for example, beautiful birds often represent innocent souls awaiting sight of the face of God. She passes a cruelly long sentence on them: they are to spend 900 years out of their human shape, 300 of them on Loch Dairbhreach (Lake Derryvarragh, County Westmeath), 300 on Sruth na Maoile (the sea between Ireland and Scotland's Mull (Maoil) of Kintyre), and the remainder at Iorrus Domhnann (Erris Bay, County Mayo). Even their Tuatha Dé Danann kin, who consume the 'Feast of Age' to extend their preternatural span, are dead before this sentence is complete.

Their mortification, like that of the desert ascetics or the martyrs, intensifies continuously. The cold they experience is scarifying, as in the Pit of Cocytus in Dante's Inferno. When it seems they can endure no more, Fionnghuala urges her three brothers to believe and trust in God (§54). Like Monesan in pagan Britain, they, in pagan Ireland, arrive at belief through innate grace, not evangelization (see pp. 98–9). Like her, they die immediately after baptism. All suffering ended, they are released from their aged bodies into eternal bliss.

There is as yet no good translation of this tale. It was first edited and translated by Eugene O'Curry, 'The Fate of the Children of Lir', *Atlantis*, vol. 4 (1863), pp. 113–57. Richard O'Duffy produced a modified edition and translation based on O'Curry's work: *Oidhe Chloinne Lir: The Fate of the Children of Lir* (Dublin: M.H. Gill, 1894). The following extracts are found ibid., pp. 43–9, 54–65, 67–78. Almost all the verse-passages in them are omitted below. Minor changes and corrections have also been made and the forms of names have been normalized.]

§10. ... [Lir's] wife became pregnant, and she brought forth two children at a birth, a daughter and a son; Fionnghuala and Aodh were their names. And she became pregnant again, and brought forth two sons; Fiachra and Conn were their names; and she herself died at their birth. And that preyed greatly upon Lir; and were it not for the greatness [of love] with which his mind rested upon his four children, he would almost have died of grief.

§11. That news [soon] reached the Síodh of Bodhbh Dearg; and the people of the Síodh raised three shouts loudly lamenting their nurseling. And Bodhbh Dearg said: 'We grieve for that girl, on account of the good man to whom we gave her, because we are grateful for his friendship and his constancy; however, our friendship for each other shall not be rent asunder, for I shall give him her other sister as a wife, namely, Aoife.'

§12. When Lir heard that, he repaired immediately to espouse her; and they were united together; and he took her with him to his house. And Aoife felt honour and affection for the Children of Lir and of her own sister; and [indeed] every one who should see these four children could not help giving them the love of his soul.

§13. And Bodhbh Dearg used often to come to Síodh Lir, for love of these children; and he used to take them with him to his own house for a long while, and then to let them return to their own home again. And the Túatha Dé Danann were at that time consuming the Feast of Age in each Síodh in turn ; and when they went to Síodh Lir, these four were their joy and their delight, for the beauty and symmetry of their form; and where they constantly slept was in beds in front of their father; and he used to rise at early dawn of every morning, and lie down among his children.

§14. But the consequence of all this was, that a dart of jealousy passed into Aoife on account of this, and she regarded the children of her sister with hatred and through enmity. Then she assumed a feigned illness, under the influence of which she continued the greater part of a year. And it is after that she perpetrated an act of hateful treachery, as well as of unfaithful jealousy, against the Children of Lir.

§15. And one day her chariot was yoked for her, and she took with her the four Children of Lir in the chariot; and she went forward in that way towards the house of Bodhbh Dearg and Fionnghuala was not willing to go with her on the journey; for she knew by her that she had some intention of ruining, or of killing them; for she dreamed of a treachery and fratricide in the mind of Aoife. But, however, she was not able to avoid the misfortune and fate that were in destiny for her.

§16. And so Aoife set out from Síodh Fionnachaidh; and (on the way) Aoife said to her people: 'Kill,' said she, 'the four Children of Lir, for whom my love has been abandoned by their father, and I shall give you your own reward of every kind in the world.' 'Not so, indeed,' said they; 'they shall not be killed by us; and it is an evil deed you have thought of, and evil will it be to you to have mentioned it.'

§17. And when they did not consent to do this, she herself drew forth a sword to kill and destroy the Children of Lir; but her womanhood, and her natural cowardice, and the weakness of her mind prevented her. And so they went westward to the shore of Loch Dairbhreach; and their horses were halted there. And she [Aoife] desired the Children of Lir to bathe, and go out to swim upon the lake; and they did as Aoife told them. And as soon as Aoife found them upon the lake, she struck them with a metamorphosing druidical wand, and so put them into forms of four beautiful perfectly white swans . . .

§20. And then repentance seized upon Aoife, and she said: 'Since I am not able to afford you any other relief henceforth, ye shall retain your own speech; and ye shall sing plaintive music, at which the men of the Earth would sleep, and there shall be no music in the world its equal . . .'

[Loch Dairbhreach]

§33. As for Bodhbh Dearg and the Túatha Dé Danann they came to the shore of Loch Dairbhreach, and they took up an encampment there, listening to the music of the swans. And as for the Milesian Clanns, too, no less did they come from every point of Erinn that they might take up an encampment at Loch Dairbhreach in like manner; for historians do not count any music or delight that ever was heard in Erinn in comparison to the music of these swans; and they used to be telling stories and conversing with the men of Erinn each day, and discoursing with their tutors and their fellow-pupils, and with all their friends in like manner; and they used to chant very sweet, fairy music every night; and every one who used to hear that music slept soundly and easily, no matter what disease or long illness might be upon him; for happy and delighted after the music the birds chanted was every one who heard it.

§34. Well, then, these two encampments of the sons of Míl[1] and the Túatha Dé Danann continued to be around Loch Dairbhreach for the space of three hundred years. And it is then Fionnghuala said to her brothers: 'Do ye know, O youths!' said she, 'that ye have come to the end of your term here, all but this night only?' And distress and very great sorrow seized upon the sons of Lir when they heard that news; for they thought it the same as being human beings, to be upon Loch Dairbhreach discoursing with their friends and their companions, in comparison with going upon the angry, quarrelsome sea of the Maoil in the North.

§35. And they came early on the next day to speak to their foster-father and their father; and they bade them adieu; and Fionnghuala made this lay:—

> Adieu to thee, O Bodhbh Dearg!
> Thou man to whom all science has done
>   homage,
> Adieu to thee, together with our father,
> Lir of the famous Síodh Fionnachaidh . . .

[Sruth na Maoile]

§36. After that lay, they took to flight; flying highly, lightly, aerially, until they reached Sruth na Maoile between Erinn and Albain; and the men of Erinn were grieved at this, and it was proclaimed by them throughout Erinn, that no swan should be killed, however great the power which they might have to do it from that out.

§37. It was a bad residence for the Children of Lir, to live upon Sruth na Maoile. When they saw the shore of the extensive coast around them, they became filled with cold, and grief, and regret; and they thought nothing of any evil which they had before suffered, compared with that which they suffered upon that current.

§38. And they remained there upon Sruth na Maoile, until one night a thick tempest came upon them, and Fionnghuala said: 'My beloved brothers,' said she, 'bad is the preparation we make, for it is certain that the tempest of this night will separate us from one another; therefore let us appoint a particular place of meeting to which we shall repair, if God shall cause us to separate from each other.' 'Let us settle, O sister,' said they, 'an appointed place of meeting at Carraig na Rón,[2] for we are all equally acquainted with it.'

---

1. Ancestor of the Irish or Milesian people.

2. Literally, 'The Rock of the Seals'.

§39. However, when the midnight came to them, the wind descended with it, and the waves increased their violence and their thunder; and the lightnings flashed; and a rough sweeping tempest passed all over the sea, so that the Children of Lir were scattered from each other over the great sea; and they were set astray from the extensive shore, so that not one of them knew what way or what path the rest went. There came, however, a placid-calm upon the sea after that great tempest; and Fionnghuala was alone upon the current; and she observed that her brothers were absent . . . and she lamented them greatly . . .

§40. As for Fionnghuala she was that night upon the rock, until the rising of the day upon the morrow, watching the sea in all directions around her, until she saw Conn coming towards her, with heavy head, and drenched feathers; and the heart of the daughter greatly welcomed him; and Fiachra came also, cold, wet, and quite faint; and neither word nor speech of his was understood, such was the excess of cold and hardship which he had suffered; and she put him under her wings, and said: 'If Aodh would but come to us now, how happy should we be!'

§41. It was not long after that, when they saw Aodh coming towards them, with dry head and beautiful feathers; and Fionnghuala welcomed him greatly; and she put him under the feathers of her breast and chest; and Fiachra under her right wing; and Conn under her left wing; and she disposed her feathers over them in that way. 'O youths,' said Fionnghuala, 'though evil ye may think this last night, many of its like shall ye find from this time forwards.'

§42. The Children of Lir after that continued a long time there, suffering cold and wretchedness upon the current of the Maoil; until at last a night came upon them so cold that never before did they experience anything like the frost, and the cold, the snow and the wind of that night . . .

§43. Thus were the Children of Lir for a long time suffering a life of extreme cold to the end of a year, upon the current of the Maoil, until at last a night came upon them, upon the pinnacle of Carraig na Rón; and the time was in the Calends of January; and the waters congealed, and each of them became chilled in his place; and as they lay upon the rock, their feet, and their feathers, and their wings adhered to the rock, so that they were not able to move them from where they were; and they made such vehement efforts with their bodies to move away, that they left there the skin of their feet, and the feathers of their breasts, and the tips of their wings attached to the rock.

§44. 'Alas! O Children of Lir,' said Fionnghuala, 'evil indeed is our condition now, for we cannot support the salt-water, and yet it is prohibited to us to be absent from it; and if the salt-water enters into our sores, we shall die . . .'

§45. However, they came again upon the current of the Maoil; and though the sea-water was extremely distressing, and sharp, and bitter to them, they were not able to avoid it, or to shelter themselves effectually from it. And so they were in that misery by the shore until their feathers grew anew, and their wings, and until their sores were perfectly healed; and then they used to go every day to the shore of Erinn and of Albain; and they used to go to the current of the Maoil each night, for it was their original . . . place of abode.

§46. They came one day to the mouth of the Banna in the north; and they saw a splendid one-coloured cavalcade, with trained pure-white steeds under them, constantly walking upon the road directly from the south-west. 'Do ye know yonder cavalcade, O Children of Lir?' said Fionnghuala. 'We do not know them,' said they; 'but it is most probable that they are some party of the sons of Míl, or of the Túatha Dé Danann that are there.'

§47. They moved then to the border of the shore, that they might be able to recognize them; and when the cavalcade on their side saw them, they moved towards them also to meet them, until they reached the place of mutual converse to each other.

§48. The chief men of those who were in that cavalcade were: Aodh Aithfhiosach, and Ferghus Fithchiollach, that is, the two sons of Bodhbh Dearg, and a third division of the Fairy cavalcade along with them; and that cavalcade had been seeking the swans for a long time before that; and when they reached each other, lovingly and friendly did they bid each other a truly affable welcome; and the Children of Lir inquired how the Túatha Dé Danann were, and particularly Lir, and Bodhbh Dearg, and their people besides.

§49. 'They are well; in one place,' said they, 'in the house of your father, in Síodh Fionnachaidh, and the Túatha Dé Danann along with them there, consuming the Feast of Age, merrily and happily, without fatigue and without uneasiness, except for being without you, and not having known where ye had gone to from them, from the day upon which ye left Loch Dairbhreach.' 'That is not the record of our lives,' said Fionnghuala, 'for much indeed of evil and suffering and misery have we endured on the tide of the current of the Maoil to this day . . .'

§51. As to the Children of Lir, they went towards their original home in the north upon the current of the Maoil; and they were there until the time they had to spend there expired; and then Fionnghuala said: 'It is time for us to leave this place, for our time here has come,' and she sang this lay:

Our time has come here, indeed,
It is time to depart,
From this shore which we have frequented
Three hundred years of lasting light . . .

[Iorrus Domhnann]

§52. The Children of Lir then, accordingly, left the current of the Maoil in that manner, and they passed on to the point of Iorrus Domhnann; and there they were for a long period of time, suffering cold and a life of chilling, until at last it happened to them that they met a young man, of a good family, one of the occupants of the lands whose name was Aibhric. And his attention was often attracted to the birds, and their singing was sweet to him, so that he loved them greatly, and they loved him; and this is the young man who arranged in order and narrated all their adventures.

§53. But at last it happened that the Children of Lir, one night that they were there, at Iorrus,

experienced a night such as they never experienced any night before or after it, for the intensity of its frost and its snow; for a flag of ice grew upon the whole of the current between Iorrus and Acaill,[3] and their feet adhered to the ice flag, so that they were not able to stir, and the brothers fell to moaning greatly, and to lamenting greatly, and to grieving intensely; and Fionnghuala was checking them, and she could not, and she recited the lay:

Pitiful the lament of the swans this night . . .

§54. 'My brethren,' said Fionnghuala, 'believe ye the truly splendid God of truth, who made Heaven with its clouds, and Earth with its fruits, and the sea with its wonders; and ye shall receive help and full relief from the Lord.' 'We do believe,' said they. 'And I believe with you,' said Fionnghuala, 'in the true God, perfect, truly, intelligent.' And they believed at the proper hour; and they received help and protection from the Lord after that; and neither tempest nor bad weather affected them from that time out.

§55. And they were in the point of Iorrus Domhnann until the time they had to spend there expired. And then Fionnghuala said: 'It is time for us to go to Síodh Fionnachaidh, where Lir is with his household, and all our people.' 'We like that,' said they.

§56. And they set out forward, lightly and airily, until they reached Síodh Fionnachaidh; and they found the place deserted and empty before them, with nothing but unroofed green raths, and forests of nettles there; without a house, without a fire, without a residence. And the four came close together, and they raised three shouts of lamentations aloud; and Fionnghuala spoke the poem:—

A wonder to me is this place —
How it is without house, without dwellings?
As I see this place —
Uchone, it is bitterness to my heart . . .

§57. However, the Children of Lir were that night in the place of their father and their grandfather,

3. Achill Island.

where they had been nursed; and they chanted very sweet, fairy music; and they arose at early morning next day, and they set out forward to Inis Gluaire[4] of Bréanainn; and the birds of the country in general congregated near them upon the Lake of the Birds in Inis Gluaire of Bréanainn. And they used to go forth to feed each day to the remote points of the country, namely, to Inis Géadh,[5] and to Acaill, and to Teach nDuinn,[6] and to the other western islands in like manner; and they used to go to Inis Gluaire of Bréanainn each night.

§58. And they were in that state for a long period of time, till the time of the faith of Christ, and until holy Patrick came into Erinn; and until holy Mochaomhóg[7] came to Inis Gluaire of Bréanainn. And the first night he came to the island, the Children of Lir heard the voice of his bell, ringing at matins, near them; so that they started, and leaped about in terror at hearing it; and her brothers left Fionnghuala alone.

§59. 'What is that, O beloved brothers?' she says. 'We know not,' say they, 'what faint fearful voice it is we have heard.' 'That is the voice of the Bell of Mochaomhóg,' Fionnghuala says; 'and it is that bell that shall liberate you from suffering and from pain, and shall relieve you according to the will of God.' . . .

§60. The Children of Lir, therefore, were listening to that music which the cleric performed, until he had finished his matins. 'Let us chant our music now,' said Fionnghuala, 'to the High King of Heaven and Earth.' And they immediately chanted a plaintive, slow-sweet, fairy music, praising the Lord, and adoring the High King.

§61. And Mochaomhóg was listening to them, and he prayed God fervently to reveal to him who chanted that music; and it was revealed unto him that it was the Children of Lir who

performed it. And upon the coming of the morning of the next day, Mochaomhóg went forward to the Lake of the Birds; and he saw the birds from him[8] upon the lake; and he went to the brink of the shore where he saw them, and he inquired of them: 'Are ye the Children of Lir?' he says. 'We are, indeed,' they say. 'I return thanks to God for it,' Mochaomhóg says, 'for it is for your sakes that I have come to this island beyond every other island in Erinn; and come ye to land now, and put your trust in me, for it is here it is in destiny for you to perform good works, and separate from your sins.'

§62. They came to land after that, and they put trust in the cleric; and he took them with him to his own abode, and they were keeping the canonical hours there, and hearing mass along with the cleric. And Mochaomhóg took a good artificer to him, and he ordered him to make chains of bright white silver for them; and he put a chain between Aodh and Fionnghuala, and a chain between Conn and Fiachra; and the four of them were rejoicing the mind and increasing the spirits of the cleric; and no danger nor distress in which the birds had been hitherto caused them any fatigue or distress now.

§63. He who was King of Connacht at that time was Lairgnéan, the son of Colmán, son of Cobhthach, and Deoch, the daughter of Fínghin, son of Aodh Alláin, that is, the daughter of the King of Munster, was his wife.

§64. And the woman heard the account of the birds, and she became filled with affection and fast love for them; and she entreated of Lairgnéan to procure the birds for her. And Lairgnéan said that he would not ask them of Mochaomhóg. And Deoch pledged her word that she would not be one night longer with Lairgnéan if she did not obtain the birds; and she set out from her residence. And Lairgnéan sent messengers quickly to pursue her, and she was not overtaken till she reached Cill Dalua.[9] And she went back to the residence then; and Lairgnéan sent messengers to ask the birds from Mochaomhóg; and he did not get them.

---

4. Inisglory, or Glory Island, in the Bay of Erris. Saint Brendan (Bréanainn) is said to have visited it before setting out on his westward voyage.
5. In English 'Goose Island', probably in Erris Bay.
6. 'House of Donn', Donn being god of the underworld; usually identified with Dursey Island at the tip of the Beare peninsula, County Cork.
7. Not identified. Evidently later than Saint Brendan, who died in 577 or 583.

8. i.e. at a distance before him.
9. Killaloe, County Clare.

§65. Great anger seized upon Lairgnéan on that account, and he came himself to the place where Mochaomhóg was, and he asked him if it was true that he had refused him the birds. 'It is true, indeed,' said Mochaomhóg. Then Lairgnéan arose, and grasped at the birds, and snatched them to him off the altar, namely, two birds in each hand; and he went forth towards the place in which Deoch was; and Mochaomhóg followed him; but as soon as he had laid hands on the birds their feathery coats fell off them, and of the sons were made three withered, bony old men, and of the daughter a lean, withered old woman, without blood or flesh.

§66. And Lairgnéan started at this, and he went out of the place.

§67. It was then that Fionnghuala said: 'Come to baptize us, O cleric, for our death is near; and it is certain that you do not think worse of parting with us than we do at parting with you; therefore make our grave afterwards, and place Conn at my right side, and Fiachra on my left side, and Aodh before my face' . . . [T]he Children of Lir were baptized; and they died, and were buried; and Fiachra and Conn were placed at either side of Fionnghuala, and Aodh before her face, as Fionnghuala ordered; and their tombstone was raised over their tomb, and their *ogham*-names were written; and their lamentation rites were performed; and heaven was obtained for their souls. And Mochaomhóg was sorrowful and distressed after them.

And that is the fate of the Children of Lir, so far.

EOGHAN Ó DUBHTHAIGH

(d. 1590)

from:
AN CHLIAR GHLIOGAIR
(A Satire)
(*c.* 1578)

[Donatus Mooney, historian of the Franciscan order and a younger contemporary of the Franciscan friar Eoghan Ó Dubhthaigh, described him as 'a most renowned preacher, and not less distinguished for his austere and saintly life. His fame extended to the most remote parts of the kingdom . . .' Of his preaching he said: 'While delivering his discourse he never looked in the faces of his audience, nor even opened his eyes. He rebuked the evildoer with great severity, and his words were seldom without effect. Yet in his sermons he was mild and gentle, rarely giving offence to individuals . . . At the conclusion of each sermon, even of the longest, he was in the habit of reciting elegant verses in the Irish language, which contained the pith of what he had said. These verses were so fruitful of good that they appear to have been inspired less by the spirit of poetry than by the unction of the Holy Ghost' (cf. Brendan Jennings (ed.), 'Donatus Moneyus: De Provincia Hiberniae S. Francisci', *Analecta Hibernica*, vol. 6 [1934], pp. 49–50; translated anonymously in *Franciscan Tertiary*, vol. 5 [1894], pp. 196–7).

The spirit behind the poem excerpted here was not so benign. It interweaves a eulogy of the Virgin Mary (part of which is still sung as a hymn), a vituperative and coarse attack on three notorious apostate clerics, and a defence of the Virgin Birth. The three clerics were William Casey (Uilliam Ó Cathasaigh), who served two periods as Protestant Bishop of Limerick; Matthew (Master) Sheyne (Mathghamhain [Maighisdir] Seidhin), Protestant Bishop of Cork; and Maol Muire Mac Craith (Myler Magrath), Protestant Bishop of Cashel. Ó Dubhthaigh apparently wrote it in response to a sermon preached by Sheyne in Cork in October 1578, in which he repudiated the Virgin Birth. Nothing is known of Sheyne's wife. Casey's wife was later granted absolution by the papal legate. According to the contemporary Catholic historian Philip O'Sullivan Beare, Ó Dubhthaigh used to call in person on Mac Craith's wife, Áine Ní Mheadhra (Annie O'Meara), urging her to re-convert to Catholicism.

The composite edition consists of over 100 quatrains in loose syllabic form. The scurrilous opening address to Master Sheyne is followed by the present excerpt. Many of the insults here turn on the name 'Maol Muire'. The word *maol* means 'tonsure'; 'Maol Muire' means 'tonsured one/devotee of Mary (Muire)'. The Protestant Maol Muire Mac Craith is 'Maol *gan*, "without", Muire'. The word *maol* is also used in the sense 'bald; baldness'. The extension of *portús*, 'breviary, pocket prayer-book', to mean 'female genitals' is frequently attested in the eighteenth century. The examples below may be the earliest and, given the great popularity of Ó Dubhthaigh's poem, the original examples of same.

Text (here with minor changes) and translation: Cuthbert Mhág Craith (ed. and trans.), *Dán na mBráthar Mionúr*, 2 vols (Dublin: Dublin Institute for Advanced Studies, 1967; 1980), vol. 1, pp. 133–8; vol. 2, pp. 60–2.]

'Uilliam, is 'Mhathghamhain nach caoin,
   'Mhaol gan Mhuire is Maol nach glan,
is fearr máthair Ríogh na ndúl
   ná sibh féin is bhar dtriúr ban.

Rug Muire mac do Dhia,
   Íosa Críost, triath na rann,
's mairidh tar a éis 'na hóigh —
   an bhean is dóigh dá gach dall.

Rug do mháthair ('s ní 'na hóigh)
   mac nach cóir (is ní do Dhia);
thusa, a Mhaighistir, an mac úd:
   sé Belsebúb ort is triath.

An chliar-sa anois tig anall,
   cliar dhall ar a ndeachaidh ceo,
ní mó leo Muire ná *dog*;
   dar *by God*, ní rachaidh leo.

'S ar mháthair Airdríogh na ndúl,
   ríoghan úr dárab oighre Dia —
ní fhuighe acht dorn ar a dúid,
   istigh i gcúirt Átha Cliath.

Bhur dtriur máthar, bhur dtriur ban,
   bhur dtriur easbog nach glan gníomh,
bhur dtriur cloinne nach clann chóir —
   ní connchlann don óigh na trír.

Ní hí sin, dar linne, an chóir,
   's í ina máthair 's 'na hóigh glain,
's mná na n-easbog fá chion ann —
   do cuireadh sin mar bharr air.

Buime is máthair Mheic Dé Bhí —
   bean mar í ní fhacaidh súil:
bean lér hosgladh flaithios Dé,
   gnáth-mholfas mé ós gach dúil.

A chliar ghliogair ara bhfuil ceo,
   beithí i n-ifrionn go beo marbh,
is cliar Mhuire fá sgoith chnuas,
   i bhflaithios Dé, thuas go hard.

A Mhaoil gan Mhuire, ataoi leamh,
   dul ar neamh ní hé do thriall;
Maol gan Aifrionn, Maol gan ord,
   Maol go hIfrionn is borb pian.

A Mhaoil gan chreidiomh, a Mhaoil gan Dia,
   a Mhaoil gan Íosa is sia neart,
rachair síos go lasair ghéir
   's do bhean féin ar leath-láimh leat.

Lán do ghorta, lán do thart,
   i mbrugh ifrinn — ní smacht gann! —
gan sholas, gan fhíon, gan cheol;
   ní fhuighthí feoil Aoine ann.

Tigh *Lucifer*, carcair bhréan
   — is nimh-ghéar do réir an tsailm —
lá Cásga, biadh iná deoch
   ní fhuighe neoch dá mhéid gairm.

Ní fhuighe aird-easbog ná a bhean
   ná suib-easbog nach glan gníomh,
bhrisios trosgadh, loisgios dealbh,
   acht teine shuthain shearbh shíor.

Ré creidiomh ó chuiris druim,
   ní fhuil mo shuim i bhfear mar sibh;
Maol gan Mhuire is Muire gan Mhaol —
   t'ainm baisde sgaoil mar sin.

Maith an aithrighe, maith an déirc,
   maith an urnaidhe shíor gan cheo:
an drong adeir nach maith an trosgadh
   tiucfaidh lá bhus losgadh leo.

Mar do thriall Neamhruadh mhac Cúis
   dol do bharr a dhúin go Dia,
Maol gan Mhuire ag tochailt díog
   d'íochtar Ifrinn síos go ria!

A Mhuire mhór, a bhláth nach críon,
   leabaidh Ríogh na Ríogh do bhrú;
a ghrádh croidhe, a chnú ghaoil,
   bheith gan Mhaoil go maire tú.

Maol mór reamhar gránna dubh —
   ní maith ar mhnaoi go gcruth chaomh:
do réir fhiadhnaise na bhfear,
   ní maith bean ar a mbí Maol.

A Mhaoil gan Mhuire, ná bí borb;
   ná labhair ré Muire go garg;

feoil Chorghois is bean ar bord
  olc an t-ord ag easbog ard.

Ringce, imirt, agus ól,
  is bean óg dá fásgadh ribh,
bruidhean, meisge, fíon Spáinneach —
  ní *instrument* crábhaidh sin.

Do léigis amudha portús Dé
  is portús Mhuire — clé an ceart;
och, mo náire! a chroidhe fhallsa,
  portús Áine is annsa leat.

Ar phortús Áine 's an diabhuil
  — olc an riaghail fhir chrábhaidh —
do léigis, a Mhaoil gan Mhuire,
  portús Mhuire ré fánaidh.

Leamsa ní hionmhuin bhur dtréan;
  bhur gcreidiomh ní creidiomh cóir;
a dhream do chuir an chanóin ar gcúl,
  beithí i ndún Mhamóin mhóir.

Do mhill bhur mbantracht an pobal;
  lé conntracht fríoth bhur dtiodail;
do-chuaidh sin ó chéill chogair,
  a chliar shodair 's tréan gliogar.

A Mhaighisdir Seidhin, coisg do Mhuire;
  ataoi ar buile gé ataoi liath;
ná habair seanmóir lochtach;
  ní fiu Corcach dul ó Dhia . . .

TRANSLATION

O William and rough Matthew and dirty Maryless Maol, the mother of the King of the elements is above you and your three wives.

Mary bore a son to God, Jesus Christ, the lord of the constellations, and remains a virgin still — the woman who is the hope of the blind.

Your mother (and not as a virgin) bore a son (and not to God): you, Master, are that son, and Beelzebub is your lord.

These clergymen who have come from the other side — blind clergy, enveloped in fog, respect a dog more than Mary. And, by heaven, they shall not get away with it.

The mother of the High-king of the elements, young queen who had God for heir, would receive only a slap on the face in Dublin Castle.

Your three mothers, your three wives, your three bishops of unclean life, your three illegitimate families — the trios are no equal to the Virgin.

We do not consider that fair, seeing that she is both a mother and a pure virgin. And the wives of the bishops are respected there.[1] That crowns all.

Nurse and mother of the Son of the Living God — the eye of man never beheld her like. The woman, through whom heaven was opened, shall always be praised by me above every creature.

You empty, befogged churchmen, dead, you shall live in hell; whilst Mary's clergy shall flourish fruitfully, high up in God's heaven.

Maol-without-Mary, you are a fool. You journey not towards heaven. A Maol-without-Mass, a Maol-without-Canonical-Hours is a Maol destined for hell with its savage pain.

Maol without faith, Maol without God, Maol without most influential Jesus, you shall descend to piercing flame, holding your wife by the hand.

In hell's palace, you shall be full of hunger, full of thirst — no mean torture; without light, without wine, without music; you shall have no Friday's meat there.

In Lucifer's house, putrid prison — it is bitter like poison, according to the scripture — [even] at Easter no one shall enjoy food or drink, no matter now great his dignity.

An archbishop and his wife, and a suffragan of unclean life, who breaks the fast and burns statues, shall have only bitter fire for ever and ever.

Since you have renounced the faith, I respect you not. A Maolless Mary means a Maryless Maol — interpret your name thus.

Penance is good; charity is good; orthodox,

1. i.e. in Dublin Castle.

constant prayer is good. Those who say that fasting is not good, the time will come when burning shall be their lot.

Whereas Nemrod son of Cus endeavoured to go up to God, from the top of his tower, Maol without Mary is digging a pit, so that he may reach the bottom of hell.

O great Mary, O fresh flower, your womb was a resting place for the King of kings. O love of my heart, O dearest, I congratulate you on being rid of Maol.

A big, fat, ugly Maol is loathsome on a fair woman: men say that it is bad for a woman to suffer from baldness.

Maol without Mary, be not coarse; speak not ribaldly about Mary. Meat in Lent and cohabitation with a woman are an unbecoming observance for an archbishop.

Dancing, play, drink, and your embracing a young woman; riot, drunkenness, and Spanish wine — that is no aid to piety.

You have abandoned God's breviary and Mary's — a wrong rite! Shame, alas! treacherous heart, that you prefer the breviary of Annie.

For the breviary of Annie and the devil, Maol without Mary, you have cast down the breviary of Mary — a bad rule of life for a man of religion.

I hate your elation. Your religion is false. Men, who have brought scripture to naught, you shall be in great Mammon's abode.

Your woman-folk have ruined the people. Your titles have been obtained by sorcery (?) — so it has been whispered abroad, obsequious clergy of colossal prententiousness.

Master Sheyne, leave Mary alone. Though an old man, you have no sense. Do not be delivering erroneous sermons. Cork is no recompense for abandoning God . . .

DOMHNALL Ó COLMÁIN

(fl. 1670–1704)

from:
PÁRLIAMENT NA mBAN
(The Parliament of Women)
(c. 1703)

[The theme of this work is the convening of a parliament of noblewomen at Glanmire, County Cork, to consider the role of women in general in society. The main text consists of 32 (in some versions, 33) speeches delivered by the ladies. The first nine comprise a substantially faithful translation into Irish, from Latin, of 'The Council of Women', one of the Colloquia of Desiderius Erasmus (?1466–1536). Ó Colmáin, Catholic parish priest in the Glanmire neighbourhood, created the remaining speeches out of the range of materials a Catholic preacher would have had to hand; in fact, most of these speeches appear elsewhere in sermon form.

Ó Colmáin apparently made three versions of his work. The original version is not extant. He addressed the second version, made in 1697, to his eight-year-old pupil James Cotter, son of Sir James Cotter (d. 1705), Munster's leading Jacobite and a notable defender of the Catholic clergy. Internal references indicate that his third version, the one excerpted here, was made with a female readership in mind.

Erasmus himself had been a tutor to the sons of nobles and his Instructio Principis Christiani (1516) concerns the education of a Christian prince. On one level his 'Council of Women' was a gentleman's joke: the idea of an all-female parliament was absurd. On a more subtle level, it called attention to the perennial question of inequality, between the sexes and within the female sex, as the parliamentarians themselves avidly exclude the lower orders. Erasmus's text, however entertaining, was thus an important commentary on political privilege.

Ó Colmáin's adaptation reflects another aspect of Erasmus's thinking: his belief in the cultivation of personal piety. Erasmus wished that every woman might read the Gospel; Ó Colmáin presented devotional reading in a manner calculated to appeal to women. Yet Ó Colmáin's work was significantly more conservative and more reductive of women than that of Erasmus. For one thing, his women have nothing of the astringent humour which Erasmus credits to his. Often they are imaged in uncouth terms. For example, Ó Colmáin describes women with a fondness for dancing as pigs, and the piper as a devilish pigherd who takes up his 'screech-bag' (*bolgán béice*) to call them together. He gives names to some of the speakers in the version he addressed to his young (male) pupil which undermine the message they are conveying, for example Fionnghuala Ní Stanganéifeacht, 'Useless Fionnghuala'; Caitríona Ní Chosarasair, 'Caitríona Trampled-Underfoot'; Gobnuit An Fhuadair, 'Hasty Gobnuit'; Treasa Thromchúiseach, 'Self-important Treasa'. The thirty-second and original concluding speech is a version of the apocryphon on the relative power of wine, kings, women and truth. This version casts the power of women as a tyrannizing but ultimately inferior force (for an earlier version which demonizes women but accords them superior force see pp. 104–5).

Ó Colmáin's third version replaces the derogatory nicknames with surnames, mainly of recognizable Munster aristocratic families: for example, the Gibbonses (Fitzgibbonses), were associated with Mitchelstown in the early 1700s. This alteration, and the incorporation of references to the 1697 Act of Banishment (of religious orders), and the new section on Máire Lawless, a vowed virgin living in the community, suggest that the third version may have been prepared as a devotional text for Catholic ladies, including would-be nuns, as the regime of the Penal Laws against Catholics took hold.

The text was edited in full by Brian Ó Cuív, *Párliament na mBan* (Dublin: Dublin Institute for Advanced Studies, 1952). The following extracts are translated from ibid., pp. 83–5, 118–20.]

The Oration of good Grace Gibbons, i.e. Lady Mitchelstown

It was then that good Grace Gibbons rose to her feet before the Parliament and said that it behoved them to order the Parliament correctly in accordance with the law, so that what often happens kings and other parliaments who fall out with each other long before they sit should not happen them. After that the ladies laid down fixed rules in the Parliament, i.e. to give precedence to the ladies who were of highest honour with respect to blood and learning, that is to say, to the ladies of the line of Éibhear Fionn[1] who were

present, and next to the ladies of the Old English — the Geraldines, the Barrys, the Roches, and so on and so forth and, in addition, to the ladies of ignoble birth who had achieved high rank on account of their husbands, so that each and everyone of the aforesaid women would be assured of her place in the Parliament.

'And now,' said she, 'it is right that we order and rank the commoner sort, giving precedence to those of them who bear most children, and should their offspring be equal in number, let the older women be first. And let widows sit with them if they have children. Similarly, let third place be given to women who are married and have no children, and the last place to the infertile women, i.e. the women who are not reproductive.'

'And what shall we do about the commoner-women who ascend on account of their perverted polluted bodies?' asked one of the ladies. Grace Gibbons said that they would allow no such woman into their conference, lest they infect the others who were respectable ladies.

'And lest our Parliament be held in contempt, let us order everything correctly in accordance with the law and let us elect a lady-clerk who will note down every statute that we will agree in this Parliament.'

Then they ordained that no woman should speak a word [until requested to do so; and that any woman who should speak][2] without permission was to be ejected from the Parliament and fined. And that everyone who broadcast any matter discussed in Parliament should be bound to silence for three months, and fined five pounds.

At that point they said that it behoved them to discuss such matters as might bear on their dignity, and that their dignity depended in large part on ensuring that they had a style of dress and the wearing of it.

'There is no doubt,' said one of them, 'that parliament attire is what we ought to wear here. As for the other costumes which we should wear, we have greatly neglected that practice, so that they have become the badge for the quern-maid as much as the high-born lady, the respectable woman as much as the harlot. Likewise, provided they have the wealth or the wherewithal, the daughter of an inferior person or a yokel has the

---

1. Ancestor of the people of Leath Mogha, the Southern Half of Ireland.

2. Words within parentheses have been supplied from another version where the main MS is defective.

same mode of dress as the daughter of a lord or noble. We see the shovel-maid putting silk or holland on her domestic's black. They wear gold on their wrists and amber or jet bracelets at their throats, and enormous headdresses atop their mops when they should be content with rough tow. So that two ill-effects [derive from the wearing of genteel dress by the lower orders. Firstly,] their wealth and substance [is diminished] in the buying of the best material. And secondly, to have something in common with the rough serving-women disparages the ladies. Not alone that, some of the base-born women insist on wearing every token of honour that they can get hold of, so much so that if we tolerate these things, we will have no token of honour over and above their sort . . .'

Here follows the Oration of Good Máire, daughter of Walter Lawless, Lady Poulacurry

This noblewoman was raised from infancy until the end of her sixteenth year in the city of Cork in the care of the most pious of noblewomen. Then she bound herself by an oath of chastity to remain a black-veiled nun for as long as she lived. And because that angelic flock which are called black-veiled or cloistered nuns had not existed for a long time, and were not tolerated — and still are not — since Henry VIII perverted his religious vow, the aforesaid noblewoman resolved that the most suitable place for her to be, since none of the remaining orders in the country had an appointed cloister, was with the religious folk that were in Cork at that time. And there she passed her days until, alas, it was decreed by Act of Parliament to destroy that religious body and blessed band and expel it from this isle of Ireland. And after that, she served that goodly prelate, the man who excelled all his contemporaries in knowledge and wisdom, and in high scholarship, piety and godly intercourse, namely, the angelic and noble Eoin Mac Sleighne, the soft-spoken, gentle bishop of Cork in Munster, of Colman's Cloyne and of Rosscarbery, who was imprisoned in the city of Cork in Munster on account of the aforesaid act. For clearly that act was aimed at the expulsion of every prelate, bishop and vicar, as it had been aimed previously at the expulsion of the Friars Minor.

The well-mannered virgin spent her days honourably in the company of that prelate until God deigned to send him from her to Portugal in this year of Our Lord 1702. And since we have few remaining religious apart from a small number of priests, she associated herself with Father Donnchadh Mac Carthaigh who now has the care of souls in Cork. However that may be, after the expulsion of the brothers from this very noble lady, and before the aforementioned bishop had been imprisoned in Cork on account of his faith, she went on her pilgrimage to Ballvourney and spent a period of her life there in the lonely solitude of a secret place, and from there she went to Cullen to pay obesiance to the female saint to whom the place is consecrated, i.e. Laitiarann. And Dundareirke[3] lies on the road between Ballyvourney and Cullen, clear to all who reconnoitre it. And she chanced to arrive in the assembly among the people on that day. And all agreed, on account of her association with the flower of clerics, i.e. the same Eoin we have mentioned, to accept her as a member of the Parliament. And this is what she said, in ever loving and mannerly words: 'O prudent sisters and friends and dear religious associates who are gathered here, there is a sin which you have not yet mentioned and which is not named for certain as one of the seven deadly sins. Nevertheless, it is clearly a serious sin, i.e. mockery. "Let God abhor those who mock".

'And we all should avoid this sin because mockery is not a praiseworthy trait in anyone and, also, because mockery occasionally leads one into as much temptation as any other trespass. And again, this sin should also be abandoned on account of the obeisance we are bound to show God whose creatures are made in His likeness and image.

'You are aware that Shem was cursed because he made a mockery of his own father. One also reads in Scripture that two bears killed the crowd that were mocking the prophet Elizeus.

'These are the four types who are wont to mock: the flatterer, the hypocrite, the devil and the mocker. For the flatterer deceives with honeyed words, the hypocrite with deeds, the devil with calumny, and the mocker with jeering and ridiculing.'

---

3. In Kilnamartry parish, south of Ballyvourney.

PATRICK WALL

(*fl.* 1814–34)

A SERMON (1820)

[His autography copy indicates that Father Wall preached this sermon, in Irish, at Clonea, near Dungarvan, County Waterford, in 1820. It is quite unlike what was being promoted as an orthodox Catholic sermon in the early nineteenth century, for which printed sermon-books provided models. Its content indicates that Wall's intended congregation consisted mainly of the labourer, cottier and poor farmer class, most of whom would have been illiterate, and monoglot Irish-speakers. His sermon does not deal with a specific abuse such as drunkenness, swearing or brawling, staples of rural preaching in his day, much less does it expound on a biblical text or doctrinal statement. It is a personalized attack on a clearly identified woman, and her supporters, but it is the woman herself who is held up as the most notorious sinner and malefactor. The name Cáit na gCupán, 'Kate of the Cups', suggests she was involved in fortune-telling, one activity for which she is not specifically criticized.

Most of Wall's sermons are written in a peculiar phonetic spelling. This one was transliterated into normalized spelling and translated into English by Diarmuid Ó hAirt, from Dublin, Royal Irish Academy Library, MS No. 1005 (23 H 17), pp. 85–7.]

It is very sad and painful news at this time, when most people in the world are trying to gain best advantage from this Blessed Indulgence, when most are doing penance and giving strength to their souls with the food of virtue and the favour of good deeds, that certain unfortunates exist, who, though this same Indulgence will never be got again in their lifetime or in their country, although they will be dead and likely damned, when the Doors of Heaven are again opened and God's grace and Heaven's blessing showered again in floods as at present — despite all this they are increasing in their guilt and wrong doing. Far from turning towards the Lord and Penance, placing themselves under His care, seeking His grace to gain the advantage now offered, they are becoming hard and confirmed in their sins, giving freer rein to their more base desires, offering insult to God, disrespect and contempt for His commandments and giving public and private scandal and bad example to fellow Christians.

But beyond all others, none are more damnable, none have so forsaken good fortune, God's Kingdom, their own best interests, their own welfare and goodwill than those of certain cabins in the Buaile yonder. I feel that the Devil has them deeply in his clutches so that neither God's grace or man can awaken them. So blindly are they immersed in mortal sin that they never seek God or Mary or the salvation of their souls. That village and that street are the Hell of this parish and gives more scandal and bad example than all others in my care. The wounds which they have inflicted on the Faith of Christ are more than may be cured by the penance of the saints who are not martyrs. It is in their power to draw the wrath of Heaven upon themselves and their descendants.

Here you will find all the very worst scamps and vagabonds, the sheep-stealer, the clothes-stealer, the potato-stealer, and every wandering whore, here she will lodge. And not alone that, if some scoundrel arrived from the remotest corner of Ulster he would be made feel welcome in the Buaile because it is here that the Devil lies down and awakens. It is his natural habitat — the abode of his most loyal servants.

Is there anyone among you who has not heard of Cáit na gCupán? That abomination, that devil's disciple, it is she who has robbed and plundered the neighbourhood, having first destroyed people in soul and body wherever she goes or settles. Particularly the people of the Buaile — because of her their reputation has been broadcast far and near. Only recently she perjured herself attempting to have one of them hanged. And indeed he would have been hanged or maybe transported were it not for his good connections. I read her affidavit myself and must confirm that almost every line contained some lying testimony against him. This woman is a floodgate for all kinds of evil. An act of perjury twenty times over would mean no more to her than stealing a barrel of potatoes. I wouldn't wonder if the grass were to wither and burn wherever she lays her foot! Wicked though people may be, could you really imagine that any miserable wretch could seek to defend such a creature? A man came who was in the habit of giving this person accommodation — he appeared in front of the judge to sell his soul to the Devil, to perjure himself on her behalf, to support and strengthen the lies of this whore. Oh, if you saw his change of colour and facial expression when I unexpectedly arrived on the scene! This is the effect that this blackguard, this prostitute had on one of the villagers. Not that I offer them much sympathy as they should have united long ago and lashed this miscreant out of their village along with those who provide her with lodgings.

Now who should take the blame for this virago, this whore, this cut-throat, going foot-loose among the people of the Buaile? Herself, is she to blame? Not at all. But the two households who provide her with accommodation and encouragement. Blame these. These are as evil and as thieving as herself.

I have information that one of these has lived throughout the winter on the proceeds of her vice and larceny. He has not been seen near a potato patch but may be likened to the man who didn't steal the fat pig but sent his lackey to do so. If he doesn't steal himself he encourages her in order to have half-share of everything she robs. It would be long before he would maintain her likes if he were not obtaining some benefit as a result.

I have before this warned the people of these cabins not to provide lodgings or encouragement to that wicked devil who has brought so much misfortune and suffering into the parish, and I warn them again — before I bind them under the Combined General Curse of God and the Congregation. I ask God today that anyone who receives this creature under his roof may have no good fortune or happiness but rather that God and the Company of Heaven bring down their curse upon him! May wrath and destruction descend on that person and on his descendants after him!

Biographies/Bibliographies

Cú Chuimne of Iona

For biography and bibliography, see p. 43.

Blathmac son of Cú Brettan

LIFE. Blathmac son of Cú Brettan flourished in the mid- or late eighth century: the Annals of Ulster record his father's death for the year 740 and that of his brother, Donn Bó, for 759. They were of the Fir Roiss, who were located in an area in modern counties Monaghan and Louth. It is evident from the two long poems of his that survive (each of which may originally have had 150 quatrains) that he was an educated monk, well read in scriptural and apocryphal material. His poems envisage salvation in terms of a relationship of *célsine*, 'clientship' between God and man, and Blathmac has been identified with the Céli Dé church reform movement of the second half of the eighth century.

CHIEF WRITINGS. James Carney (ed. and trans.), *The Poems of Blathmac son of Cú Brettan*, Irish Texts Society, vol. 47 (Dublin: Educational Company of Ireland for the Irish Texts Society, 1964).

BIOGRAPHY AND CRITICISM. James Good, 'The Mariology of the Blathmac Poems', *Irish Ecclesiastical Record*, vol. 104 (1965), pp. 1–7; Brian Lambkin, 'The Structure of the Blathmac Poems', *Studia Celtica*, vols 20–21 (1985–6), pp. 67–77; Brian Lambkin, 'Blathmac and the Céli Dé: A Reappraisal', *Celtica*, vol. 23 (1999), pp. 132–54.

Ultán of Ardbraccan

LIFE. As his name indicates, Ultán moccu Conchobair was of Dál Conchobair in Déisi Breg, modern County Meath. He became Bishop of Ardbraccan (Ard mBreccáin), near Navan, County Meath. He was revered as a saint; the Martyrology of Tallagh records his feast as 4 September. The annals record his death for 657 and, from another source, for 663. An eighth- or early ninth-century Latin elegiac poem provides indisputable evidence that Ultán composed a significant work on the miracles of Saint Brigit. Brigit's mother, Broicsech, was said to have been a daughter of Dallbrónach of Dál Conchobair. Bishop Tírechán, author of a memoir on Saint Patrick preserved in the Book of Armagh, studied under Ultán and drew on a book belonging to him in compiling his memoir. The early tenth-century Tripartite Life of Patrick also mentions Ultán in a list of those who narrated Patrick's miracles. Broccán Clóen (d. 17 September 650), to whom another hymn on Brigit is conventionally ascribed, is also said to have been his pupil.

CHIEF WRITINGS. The poem at pp. 62–3 is all that remains of the work that may plausibly be ascribed to Ultán.

BIOGRAPHY AND CRITICISM. J.F. Kenney, *The Sources for the Early History of Ireland: Ecclesiastical* (New York: Columbia University Press, 1929); Kim McCone, 'Brigit in the Seventh Century: A Saint with Three Lives?', *Peritia*, vol. 1 (1982), pp. 107–45.

Orthanach úa Coílláma

LIFE. In one of three poems ascribed to him, Orthanach is described as '.h. Caellama Cuirrich', i.e. grandson of Cáellám of the Curragh (of Kildare). He is titled Bishop of Kildare in his obituary notice in the Annals of the Four Masters, under the year 839.

CHIEF WRITINGS. (In addition to the poem at pp. 70–2) 'A Chóicid choín Chairpri Crúaid', ed. Máirín O'Daly, *Éigse*, vol. 10, Part 3 (1962–3), pp. 178–97; 'Masu de chlaind Echdach ard', ed. Kuno Meyer, *Zeitschrift für celtische Philologie*, vol. 11 (1917), pp. 107–13.

BIOGRAPHY AND CRITICISM. O'Daly and Meyer, art. cit.

Giraldus Cambrensis (Gerald of Wales)

For biography and bibliography, see Volume I, pp. 270–1.

Muireadhach Albanach Ó Dálaigh

LIFE. Muireadhach Albanach, one of the most famous of the Ó Dálaigh line of hereditary professional poets, was probably born in Meath (Irish, Midhe): this would account for one of his sobriquets: Muireadhach Midhe. His dates are not known but his older brother, Donnchadh Mór, an outstanding religious poet, died in 1244. In 1213 Muireadhach was resident at Lios an Doill (Lisadell), County Sligo, where he may have been *ollamh* to Ó Conchobhair Cairbre (Carbury). Having murdered a steward of Domhnall Ó Domhnaill, King of Tír Conaill, who was then raiding Cairbre, he fled, firstly to Riocard Búrc in Clanrickard in Galway, then to Donnchadh Ó Briain in Thomond, and lastly to Dublin. When Ó Domhnaill pursued him to Dublin, he escaped to Scotland and lived there for a long time, hence the sobriquet 'Albanach', 'of Scotland'. The MacVuirichs, perhaps Scotland's leading line of Gaelic poets, descended from him. Some of his poems, including 'Éistidh riomsa, a Mhuire Mhór', are known only from the Scottish Book of the Dean of Lismore. From Scotland he visited the Continent and possibly the Holy Land. Three of his extant poems were addressed to Ó Domhnaill in the hope of regaining his favour. They eventually made their peace. A moving elegy for Maoil Mheadha, his wife of twenty years with whom he had eleven children, is extant (see Volume I, pp. 43–4). Tradition has it that he ended his days in a monastery in Connacht.

CHIEF WRITINGS. Osborn Bergin (ed. and trans.), *Irish Bardic Poetry*, compiled and edited by David Greene and Fergus Kelly (Dublin: Dublin Institute for Advanced Studies, 1970), pp. 88–107; Brian Ó Cuív, 'A Poem Attributed to Muireadhach Albanach Ó Dálaigh', in *Celtic Studies: Essays in Memory of Angus Matheson, 1912–1962*, eds James Carney and David Greene (London: Routledge and Kegan Paul, 1968), pp. 92–8; Brian Ó Cuív, 'A Pilgrim's Poem', *Éigse*, vol. 13 (1969–70), pp. 105–9; Gerard Murphy, 'Two Irish Poems Written from the Mediterranean', *Éigse*, vol. 7, Part 2 (1953–5), pp. 71–9; Lambert McKenna (ed.), *Aithdioghluim Dána*, 2 vols (Irish Texts Society, vols 37 and 40) (London: Irish Texts Society, 1939 and 1940), vol. 1, pp. 172–4, vol. 2, pp. 102–3; vol. 1, pp. 174–6, vol. 2, p. 103; vol. 1, pp. 266–70, vol. 2, pp. 162–4); Láimhbheartach Mac Cionnaith (Lambert McKenna) (ed.), *Dioghluim Dána* (Baile Átha Cliath: Oifig an tSoláthair, 1939), pp. 124–9; A.J. Goedheer, *Irish and Norse Traditions about the Battle of Clontarf* (Haarlem: H.D. Tjeenk Willink, 1938), pp. 45–50; Standish Hayes O'Grady, *Catalogue of the Irish Manuscripts in the British Museum* (London: British Museum, 1926), pp. 331–2, pp. 336–8; E.C. Quiggin, 'Prolegomena to the Study of the Later Irish Bards, 1200–1500', *Proceedings of the British Academy*, vol. 5 (1911–12), pp. 131–3.

BIOGRAPHY AND CRITICISM. William Gillies, 'A Religious Poem Ascribed to Muireadhach Albanach Ó Dálaigh', *Studia Celtica*, vols 14–15 (1979–80), pp. 81–6; Brian Ó Cuív, 'Eachtra Mhuireadhaigh Uí Dhálaigh', *Studia Hibernica*, vol. 1 (1961), pp. 56–69; Robin Flower, *The Irish Tradition* (Oxford: Oxford University Press, 1947), pp. 85–8; Lambert McKenna (ed.), *Aithdioghluim Dána*, vol. 1, pp. xxxii–xxxiii.

Finnian of Clonard or Moville

LIFE. Finnian, the founder of Clonard (Clúain Iraird) in County Meath, is named Finnio maccu Thelduib in his obituary in the Annals of Ulster. He died in 549 of the Great Plague. Clonard was one of the most important of the ancient Irish churches. The surrounding territory had belonged to Leinster but had been claimed by the Uí Néill since 515. Finnian had early associations with Leinster, where he is reputed to have founded various churches. Clonard eclipsed them in importance and came to be regarded as the head of his *paruchia*, and Finnian himself was seen primarily as an Uí Néill rather than a Leinster saint. His cult spread widely. According to later tradition, Finnian was 'master of the saints of Ireland', and those who had been educated by him at Clonard were said to include Columb Cille of Iona, and Ciarán of Clonmacnoise.

Some scholars believe that the cult of Saint Finnian of Clonard is ultimately no more than a localization of a single original cult which also manifested as that of Saint Finnian of Moville. Others believe that two distinct historical Finnians had separate cults, the details of which have become somewhat entangled. Moville (Mag mBili) was one of the major episcopal churches of Ulster. It is now a suburb of Newtownards in County Down. The founder of its earliest church was a bishop who died in 579. The sources give his name in different forms, including Finnio, Findbarr and Vinnianus. There is no agreement as to his origins. Some argue that he was British, others say he was Irish. Recently the compelling suggestion has been made that he was one of the transmarine Irish who came to Ireland from Britain. The genealogies associate him with the Dál Fíatach of Ulster. As he had a reputation as a scriptural scholar, there are reasonable grounds for identifying him with the Findbarr (alias Finnio, Vinniauus) who, according to Adomnán's Life of Colum Cille, was one of the teachers of the latter saint. For the same reason, and given his name and associations with Britain, there are grounds for supposing that he was the Vinnian who composed a Penitential which derives from the British tradition of penitentials.

CHIEF WRITINGS. There is no early work extant which may plausibly be attributed to either Finnian apart from the Penitential excerpted above, pp. 95–6.

BIOGRAPHY AND CRITICISM. Thomas Charles Edwards, *Early Christian Ireland* (Cambridge: Cambridge University Press, 2000), pp. 290–3; Pádraig Ó Riain, 'Finnio and Winniau: A Return to the Subject', in *Ildánach, Ildírech: A Festschrift for Proinsias Mac Cana*, eds John Carey, J.T. Koch and P.-Y. Lambert (Andover, Mass., and Aberystwyth: Celtic Studies Publications, 1999), pp. 187–202; L. Fleuriot, 'Le "saint" breton *Winniau* et le pénitentiel dit "de Finnian"', *Études Celtiques*, vol. 15 (1976–8), pp. 607–14; D.N. Dumville, 'Gildas and Uinniau', in *Gildas: New Approaches*, eds Michael Lapidge and D.N. Dumville (Woodbridge: Boydell Press, 1984), pp. 207–14; Kathleen Hughes, 'The Historical Value of the Lives of Saint Finnian of Clonard', *English Historical Record*, vol. 69 (1954), pp. 353–72, and 'The Cult of Saint Finnian of Clonard from the Eighth to the Eleventh Century', *Irish Historical Studies*, vol. 9 (1954–5), pp. 13–27.

Jonas of Bobbio

LIFE. Jonas entered the monastery of Bobbio, in the Appenines north-east of Genoa, shortly after its founder, Saint Columbanus, had died there in November 615. He remained at Bobbio for about ten years. He made the acquaintance of men who had been intimates of the saint, including three who had acted as personal assistant to him and one named Gall who was of the band which originally travelled from Bangor to the Continent with Columbanus. From these and others he gathered a wealth of personal information on the saint. Later, perhaps in the early 630s, Jonas's base seems to have shifted to north Francia. Around 639 Bertulf, Abbot of Bobbio, commissioned him to write the Life. The work he produced was in two books. Book I contains the saint's life, and concludes with a poem and a hymn in his honour. The materials in Book II are heterogeneous. They include 6 chapters on Athala, Columbanus's successor as Abbot of Bobbio; 4 chapters on Eusasius, the saint's successor at Luxeuil; 12 chapters on the double monastery of Evoriacas (Faremoutiers), presided over by Burgundofara; and a concluding section on Bobbio during the abbacies of Athala and Bertulf. Jonas seems to have ended his days as Abbot of Marchiennes, a predominantly female community near Saint-Amand. He died in 659.

CHIEF WRITINGS. Bernhard Krusch (ed.), *Ionae Vitae Sanctorum Columbani, Vedastis, Iohannis*, Scriptores Rerum Germanicarum in usum scholarum ex MGH separatim editi (Hanover and Leipzig, 1902), pp. 432–49.

BIOGRAPHY AND CRITICISM. Clare Stancliffe, 'Jonas's *Life of Columbanus and His Disciples*', in *Saints and Scholars*, eds John Carey, Máire Herbert and Pádraig Ó Riain (Dublin: Four Courts Press, 2001), pp. 189–200; Walter Berschin, *Biographie und Epochenstil im lateinischen Mittelalter*, 2 vols (Stuttgart: A. Hiersemann, 1988), vol. 2, pp. 26–41; Christian Rohr, 'Hagiographie als historische Quelle: Ereignisgeschichte und Wunderberichte in der Vita Columbani des Ionas von Bobbio', *Mitteilungen des Instituts für Österreichische Geschichtsforschung*, vol. 103 (1995), pp. 229–64.

Muirchú moccu Macthéni

For biography and bibliography, see Volume I, p. 137.

Adomnán of Iona

For biography and bibliography, see Volume I, p. 138.

Sedulius Scottus

For biography and bibliography, see Volume I, pp. 139–40.

Daniél úa Líathaiti

LIFE. The Annals of Innisfallen record the 'Repose of Daniél, abbot of Les Mór [Lismore, County Waterford] and Corcach [Cork]' in 863. The Annals of the Four Masters call him 'Úa Liaithide', and say he was mortally wounded. Nothing further is known of him, apart from what is stated in the preface to the poem above, at pp. 109–10.

Digde

LIFE. For all that is known of this putative author, see the headnote to 'Aithbe damsa bés mara' (Digde's Lament), p. 111.

Eoghan Ó Dubhthaigh

LIFE. The Franciscan Ó Dubhthaigh was possibly the most influential Irish Counter-Reformation preacher. He had acquired a name as a poet also by 1577, when Richard Stanyhurst described him as 'a preacher and maker in Irish'. He belonged to Cavan Friary, and was probably born in the vicinity of Cavan. From 1580 to 1583 he was Provincial of the Friars Minor in Ireland. He died in 1590. Stories of his efforts to re-convert apostates were still current in the late nineteenth century. At least two poems other than that at pp. 156–9 are attributed to him: an address to the Virgin Mary, and an exhortation to Ireland to stand firm against 'Captain Luther and Captain Calvin'.

CHIEF WRITINGS. Cuthbert Mhág Craith (ed.), *Dán na mBráthar Mionúr*, 2 vols (Dublin: Dublin Institute for Advanced Studies, 1967; 1980), vol. 1, pp. 127–53, vol. 2, pp. 58–67; Dublin, Royal Irish Academy Library, MS 23 N 13, p. 162.

BIOGRAPHY AND CRITICISM. Cuthbert Mhág Craith (ed.), *Dán na mBráthar Mionúr*, 2 vols, vol. 2, pp. 160–87; Anon., *The Franciscan Tertiary*, vol. 5 (1894), pp. 161, 163, 196–7.

Domhnall Ó Colmáin

LIFE. Unless more than one priest of the name is in question, ecclesiastical sources indicate that Father Domhnall Ó Colmáin was parish priest of Glounthane, near Cork city, c. 1670, of St Finbarr's parish in Cork city in 1700, and of Knockraha, north of Cork city, in 1704. A colophon in one manuscript of *Párliament na mBan* describes him as a Doctor of Canon Law. He was well read in classical, patristic and scriptural sources. Conchúr Mac Cairteáin, who translated from Latin a catechism which he titled *Agallamh na bhFioraon*, named Ó Colmáin as one of the 'great experts in Irish' who assisted him. Ó Colmáin also knew French. He was on intimate terms with Cork's leading Gaelic poets and their patrons, including Dr Eoin Baiste Mac Sleighne, Bishop of Cork and Cloyne, and Sir James Cotter, whom Ó Colmáin described as 'protector of the clergy'. He was tutor to Sir James's son. He concludes many of the speeches in *Párliament na mBan* with pithy quatrains, apparently of his own composition.

CHIEF WRITINGS. Brian Ó Cuív (ed.), *Párliament na mBan* (Dublin: Dublin Institute for Advanced Studies, 1952).

BIOGRAPHY AND CRITICISM. Breandán Ó Conchúir, *Scríobhaithe Chorcai 1700–1850* (Baile Átha Cliath: An Clóchomhar, 1982), pp. 18, 212–16, 236; Breandán Ó Buachalla, 'The Making of a Cork Jacobite', in *Cork History and Society*, eds. Patrick Flanagan and C.G. Buttimer (Dublin: Geography Publications, 1993), pp. 469–98.

Patrick Wall

LIFE. Father Patrick Wall was an occasional scribe, translator and author of sermons: all his literary activities seem to have been related to his work as a Catholic priest. From 1814 to 1821 he officiated at Carrickbeg and Windgap, from 1822 to 1829 he was parish priest of Clonea and Rathgormick (Mothill), and from 1830 to 1833 he was parish priest of Stradbally, all in County Waterford. He co-operated with Philip Barron (c. 1801–44), whom Eoin Mac Néill described as 'The First Gaelic Leaguer', in founding an Irish College at Seafield, Bunmahon, County Waterford, c. 1834.

CHIEF WRITINGS. (Sermons) Dublin, Royal Irish Academy Library, MS 1005.

BIOGRAPHY AND CRITICISM. See T.F. O'Rahilly et al., *Catalogue of Irish Manuscripts in the Royal Irish Academy* (1926–70), pp. 381–2, 2864–5.

MÁIRÍN NÍ DHONNCHADHA, *Editor*

Gormlaith and her Sisters, c. 750–1800

The texts in the following selection know almost nothing of the discourse of virginity which dominated the previous selection, and its one shy virgin, the speaker in *Cúirt an Mheon-Oíche* identified in a broad hint as Brian Merriman, is on the defensive. That women and men have need of sex is a given here, and the tales and poems show the diverse ways in which proactive sexuality was constructed and gendered. Many of them concern the threat posed to society by misdirected sexual drives. Generally, the literature shows little concern with representing sexual contentment. Gormlaith, which means 'Illustrious (literally "Blue") Sovereignty', was a popular choice of name for girls among Gaelic aristocrats. There does not appear to have been any saint of the name, and its use in the title is meant to suggest that not all thinking about women was pervaded by images of Mary, Eve and those associated with them. The full title, 'Gormlaith and her Sisters', also implies a particular perspective, a habit of viewing women as a group.

There is a convention that medieval Irish storytellers categorized their narratives thematically as destructions, cattle-raids, wooings, battles, terrors, voyages, death-tales, sieges, adventures, elopements, plunderings, feasts, and so forth. Two medieval tale-lists remain, and the titles in them often identify the main protagonists as well as the theme. From these lists and from what remains of the literature, it is clear that women figured prominently in wooing-tales (*tochmarca*) and love-tales (*serca*). Examples of both appear below. Female roles are also important, however, in three examples of a category one might not immediately associate with women — the death-tale (*aided*). It is dangerous to presume that many tales in other categories of which only the titles now remain

were written or narrated exclusively or primarily for a male audience. Two texts below concern the birth (*geinemain*) of famous men. There may have been a tradition of birth-tales, although *geinemain* does not appear as a thematic title in the medieval lists. It is easy to imagine that such tales, like genethliacons (see, for example, pp. 432–3), would have held a particular appeal for women.

In the narratives dating from the medieval period, little or nothing of the individual's inner life is described. Psychology is externalized to a large degree into plot and speech. The protagonists are usually famous and emblematic; the name Deirdre, for example, would have conjured both the history of the individual of that name whose elopement with Noísiu brought tragedy to Ulster, and the character associated with her: beautiful, wilful, fatalistic. When the emotions of a figure such as Deirdre, typically expressed in poetic language, were thought to epitomize those experienced by real people in circumstances regarded as somehow similar, this figure might function as a poetic mask. Maria Tymoczko has suggested that the absence of direct personal expression by Celtic-speaking poets in the medieval period is due to their preference for projecting emotions through such masks. She attributed the Celtic predilection for female masks in particular to the opportunity they afforded male poets to express emotions or views normally repressed or socially censured in males. 'Where the heroic ethic hung on and was slow to die, feelings of love, grief, dismay over societal disintegration and defeat, fear of aging, and self-pity were charged; by putting on a mask and projecting these feelings outwards, particularly onto females, the poet could free himself — and his audience — to consider and express aspects of life that were, if not forbidden, then at least difficult'.[1]

This attractive suggestion does not rule out the use of female masks by female authors of course. Unfortunately, the great majority of texts in medieval Irish are anonymous, the poem attributed to Digde (who is not obviously of a different time to that when it was composed) being all too rare a case (see pp. 111–15). As it happens, none of the following texts, including those employing male and female masks (notably the legendary Cú Chulainn, Gráinne and Suibne), has an attribution to a female author, and most of them, though anonymous, were probably composed by male authors. Two texts deserving special mention are those concerning Derbforgaill, daughter of Murchad Úa Máil Shechnaill, the woman charged by tradition with being the ultimate agent of the Norman Invasion of Ireland. The authors of these texts were coeval with Derbforgaill, yet their accounts of her part in the Invasion are quite contradictory. She was certainly still alive when the more critical account, by Giraldus Cambrensis, was written, a fact which shows that a woman could be enlisted in the annals of immorality in her own lifetime.

The selection's two halves are not entirely discrete. 'A Place in the World' mainly concerns female association with the public sphere while 'Natural and Unnatural Women' focuses primarily on private relations. Quite a few texts, however, describe a troubled relationship to both public and private spheres. Women were deeply implicated in the idea of the private sphere. Almost invariably, a negative representation is given to a quest by a woman for an association with — or freedom of action in — the public sphere equal to men's. The higher the stakes, the more vehement the criticism becomes, as we find in the texts concerning Gormlaith, wife of three outstanding kings including the great Brían Bórama, and Bébinn, whose attempted association with King Cellachán of Munster came to nothing (pp. 188–92). These texts or their underlying materials all date from the twelfth century. Taken together with the twelfth-century accounts of Queen Medb's calamitous leadership of the Cattle-Raid of Cúailnge (pp. 38–41, and especially pp. 174–7), they suggest that women's power in the public sphere had increased significantly and moreover, that there was a hardening resistance to it from some quarters. Non-condemnatory historical evidence of royal wives and daughters exercising influence on politics in the eleventh and twelfth centuries is plentiful, although there is no example of a woman inheriting political office or governing as an independent ruler. As Marie Therese Flanagan has noted, Diarmait Mac Murchadha's offer to Strongbow of his daughter, Aífe, in marriage together with the kingship of Leinster, when he recruited Strongbow to help him recover it, may be placed in a context where direct male descent within a hereditary royal dynasty was not invariable. She points out that the political significance royal women had acquired by the twelfth century was significantly greater than that described in the Early Irish law-tracts.[2] On the position later than the twelfth century, see Vol. V, pp. 1–5, and pp. 464–529.

In recent years researchers have begun to focus on the realities of queenly consortship and regency in the Early Middle Ages: a detailed picture for the pre-twelfth century period can be expected from their work. The related subject of the symbolism of sovereignty is taken up below, in two separate selections of texts (pp. 250–72, 273–92). The figure of the sovereignty goddess looms large in medieval Irish literature. In popular imagination, she and the figure of the historical queen sometimes blend into one, bolstering ahistorical ideas of matriarchy, superhuman battle-queens and extraordinarily powerful regents. On the symbolic level, the sovereignty goddess is indeed powerful. It is recognized, however, that sovereignty is a site of gender transgression — for example, female figures can temporarily assume an unwonted power. What the pliancy of sovereignty point to is the need to represent inclusivity. While the sovereign must exceed — be greater than — all the subjects, thus asserting exclusivity, he (only the masculine pronoun applies in the Irish

1. Maria Tymoczko, 'A Poetry of Masks: The Poet's Persona in Early Celtic Poetry', in *A Celtic Florilegium. Studies in Memory of Brendan O Hehir*, eds K.A. Klar, E.E. Sweetser and Claire Thomas (Lawrence and Andover: Celtic Studies Publications, 1996), pp. 187–209.

2. Marie Therese Flanagan, *Irish Society, Anglo-Norman Settlers, Angevin Kingship. Interactions in Ireland in the Late 12th Century* (Oxford: Clarendon Press, 1998), pp. 80–105.

situation) must also embody them all. Rituals such as the sacral marriage of the king to the sovereignty goddess symbolize sovereignty's inclusivity of male and female, but do not necessarily confirm the power of queens in real life. Only historical research will deliver a definitive picture of the power of queens.

Women's reproductive capacity is represented in vernacular medieval Irish literature as the crucial distinction between men and women, the most obvious marker of sex difference. The desire to have children is portrayed as innate in women, their libido is supposedly driven in large part by it, and they are credited with a natural facility for rearing children. Women gave life. This characteristic was not seen as marking them off from those of their own sex who did not have children but from men: men were natural warriors whose prerogative it was to *take* life. No doubt the particular association of spiritual fecundity with women helped reinforce the idea of women as life-givers (see pp. 47–9). The differentiation between life-givers and life-takers which reinforced ideas of the heroic warrior was also productive of an anti-heroic and counter-heroic discourse.

The idea of the warring male as protector of the progenitive female is given clear expression in a very early text which had the endorsement of the highest ecclesiastical and secular powers: the Law of Adomnán, first enacted in 697 (pp. 18–22). Much of the Ulster Cycle gives a positive value to the warrior ethic without any reference to the dualism of protector and protected, life-taker and life-giver. Whenever the idea does occur, however, it acts to call into question the whole enterprise of warfare and the heroic code that upholds it. Adomnán's Law propounded the idea of a fundamental division in secular society: on one side, women and children, marked by their physical vulnerability, on the other, men, whose strength obliges them to protect the weaker group. The idea is turned on its head in the tradition of the debility with which the Ulster goddess, Macha, cursed the warriors of the province (pp. 173–4). An Ulsterman had failed her when she had most need of protection — at the point of giving birth — and so she damned all Ulstermen with a debility comparable to the weakness of childbed (*cess noínden* 'nine-fold period of weakness', re-interpreted as *cess noíden* 'weakness of child[-bearing]') whenever they had most need

of physical prowess. Consequently, the Ulstermen are doomed from the outset of the Cattle-Raid of Cúailnge. Another story explains the debility differently: Cú Chulainn lived for a year with beautiful Feidelm Foltcháin of the *síd*. She appeared naked before the Ulstermen and they became afflicted with this debility, presumably on this occasion as a result of Cú Chulainn's failure to protect her from their astonished stare.

Macha's curse is often cited as a measure of the effete warrior. In *Fled Bricrenn*, for example, Emer jibes that 'all the strong ones of Ulster are as a woman in labour, except for my husband, Cú Chulainn'. The effect of her words is ironic, though, as *Fled Bricrenn* is a parody of the heroic tale (see Volume I, pp. 22–4). Usually, the appearance of female characters in Ulster tales signals not the endorsement of heroic values but the opposite. The tale of the Death of Aífe's One Son, for example, is an eloquent rebuke to the idea of heroic sacrifice and declaration for a protective maternalism (pp. 177–9). The story of Cú Chulainn's Boyhood Deeds tells that that most potent symbol, the naked female breast, is enough to dissipate the furor of the young warrior (Volume I, pp. 11–2). There are texts depicting bellicose women but they usually contain a suggestion that these women have been traumatized or denatured in some significant way (pp. 179-81). The outstanding example, of course, is Queen Medb. The message that her dismal failure as a military leader is due to her sex is driven home by constant references to bodily functions, sexual acts and animal parallels (pp. 174–7). Medb may have been a failure as a mother — she was not adverse to baiting men with her daughter, Findabair, for example — but she was a mother nonetheless. It is maternity in particular which debars women from warring whereas virginity, at least in ecclesiastical discourse, may be associated with valour and athleticism: virgins, by renouncing maternity, overcome the weakness of their sex (see pp. 48–9).

Although women were life-givers in their own sphere, the literature suggests an anxiety that they would drain men of strength if encountered in the ambit of battle. Warriors are seen to go more willingly to tryst with death than to tryst with women (see, for example, Volume I, pp. 37–40). Although the challenge of over-mastering a woman pales by comparison with the challenge of the battlefield, the lesser challenge also presages the greater one and is therefore taboo at that crucial time before going into the fray: the superstition is that the beautiful woman will transform herself into the death-goddess (see pp. 252, 263–6). The warrior may still boast of victory in the woman-tryst, however. For example, after his death on the battlefield Cú Chulainn, appears, in soul, to the fifty women whom he had violated on the previous day.

Individualized sexuality hardly features at all in literary texts although it was discussed in other kinds of writing, notably the penitentials. Rather, sexuality appears as a social matter, a determinant of social integration or exclusion. To bear children and especially sons to a reputable father who was willing to acknowledge them as his own was the measure of a woman's social success and numerous texts concern the difficulties that lay in the way of achieving it. Infertility is central to the comical tale of the Birth of Áed Sláine, for example, whose mother resorted to the saints to cure her (pp. 182–4). In hagiographical texts, this is perhaps the commonest miracle performed by saints on women's behalf. A long poem on the Birth of Áedán mac Gabráin vividly conveys that daughters were less desirable than sons, at least in an aristocratic context (pp. 184–8).

That great importance was attached to the identity of the mothers of outstanding figures such as saints, kings and queens is proven by the existence of compilations such as that on 'The Mothers of Irish Saints', and the *Banshenchas* ('Lore of Women'). The latter exists in two versions, a metrical one composed in 1147 by Gilla Moduta Ó Caiside of Ardbrackan in Mide (now County Meath), and an anonymous prose one, also dating from the twelfth century. Since Ó Caiside ends his version with a tribute to Tigernán Úa Rúairc, his wife, Derbforgaill, daughter of the king of Mide, whom we have encountered already, and Derbforgaill's parents, it is quite possible that he composed this unique metrical work for Derbforgaill herself.[3] The *Banshenchas* texts detail royal women's marriages and offspring, and they are a revelation in regard to the number of alliances contracted by such women as they record far more of them than do the annals. The *Banshenchas* texts describe many women as marrying two or three times and having children by each marriage. In one instance, a woman had married six times and had children by all husbands. Daughters as well as sons are named, the daughters mainly on account of later becoming the consorts of kings and, consequently, the mothers of kings in the next generation. Accounts of the dreams women supposedly had of the future greatness of their children, are another indication of the respect which accrued to the mothers of famous men and women. Samples of these appear below (pp. 181–2, p. 190).

It is suggested that the enigmatic poem, 'Gas Lossa', concerns the distress of an abandoned mother who plans to kill herself. Suicide is the theme of quite a few medieval Irish texts and almost invariably, the person in question is a woman. The most famous suicide is probably Deirdre, who killed herself after the death of her lover, Noísiu, rather than submit to the hated Conchobar and Eogan mac Durthacht — Conchobar who gloated that 'it is a sheep's eye between two rams that you make between me and Eogan' (cf. Volume 1, p. 17). In the literature, female suicide is characterized by association with the threat or actuality of sexual violation. This suggests an understanding that female identity was so closely bound up with sexual integrity that such violation led naturally to personal disintegration and complete loss of self in suicide. Thinking along these lines also seems implicit in the exculpation by some of the Fathers of the Church of suicide committed in the face of rape. Although difficult to pursue, the contribution of the authoritative voice of the Church to the literary troping of suicide would probably repay investigation.

Various voices can be heard in the texts on the subject of erotic love, suggesting a range of influences emanating from different sources. The idea of love as a medically defined condition, a sickness amenable to diagnosis and treatment though also potentially fatal, is well represented. Three classic medieval Irish texts on love-sickness are presented in Volume I. They are *Aislinge Óenguso*, 'The Vision of Óengus', *Serglige Con Culainn*, 'The Wasting Sickness of Cú

---

3. Muireann Ní Bhrolcháin, 'The *Banshenchas* Revisited', in *Chattel, Servant or Citizen. Women's Status in Church, State and Society*, eds. Mary O'Dowd and Sabine Wichert (Belfast: Institute of Irish Studies, Queen's University of Belfast, 1995) pp. 70–81.

Chulainn', and *Tochmarc Étaíne*, 'The Wooing of Étaín' (ibid., pp. 18–9, 26–9). These texts date from the eighth and ninth centuries, a period roughly midway between the disintegration of the Roman Empire, when the ancient medical tradition of lovesickness developed by writers such as Galen (129–*c.* 216) largely disappeared from European culture, and the upsurge of interest in the disease in the eleventh and twelfth centuries. Ancient medicine was not the only source for ideas of lovesickness, however: they were found also in classical literature, in the Bible and biblical commentaries, and in the work of influential medieval encyclopaedists such as Isidore (*c.* 560–636) of Seville. As Mary Wack has noted, the two key biblical texts were the story of Amnon and Tamar in 2 Samuel 13, and the refrain in the Song of Solomon 2:5 and 5:8, 'for I am sick with love'.[4]

Amnon fell ill from love of his sister, Tamar. When she came to minister to him, he laid hold of her, to force her to lie with him. She pleaded with him not to commit folly but he would not listen. Afterwards, Amnon despised her, 'so that the hatred wherewith he hated her was greater than the love wherewith he had loved her'. 'The Wooing of Étaín' may be a sanitized version of this story. It is interesting that the physician treating the Irish patient, Ailill Ánguba, gives the following diagnosis: 'One of the two pains thou hast that no physician can heal, the pain of love and the pain of jealousy' (Volume I, p. 28). The idea that love and hatred, like two sides of the one coin, are simultaneously opposite and related, which is well brought out in the fact that English 'zeal' and 'jealousy' are at root the same word, is even more evident in the use of Irish *cais* for both 'love' and 'hatred'. This dualism is not found in the main Irish words for love, *serc* (later *searc*), and *grád* (later *grádh* and *grá*), a borrowing of Latin *gradus*, 'rank, honour'.

In medieval Irish literature, as in medieval literature in general, lovesickness has mainly to do with men. It is they who are enraptured, immobilised in love-languor, becoming emaciated and silent, even aphasic. Women also fall in love, but not with the same catastrophic

consequences for their health and they not only retain the power of speech but become eloquent on the subject of love, as we see below in accounts of Ailbe, Gráinne and Deirdre (pp. 206–10, 225–6, 234–6). Various factors contributed to making eloquence a desirable quality in women, such as the common idea that verbal skills in women complemented physical strength in men, or the association of wise speech with the Virgin Mary. In this case, eloquence suggests an *absence*, a lack of susceptibility to one of the classic symptoms of lovesickness.

There is one notable instance of a woman suffering from lovesickness, however, in the Middle Irish tale of 'The Separation of Finn and Gráinne' (pp. 36–7). Here, Gráinne's malady derives not from love but from its potential sequel, hatred. It is properly diagnosed by her father and she is cured by the remedy of divorce from the hated partner, Finn. This text is exceptional, if one allows that 'The Story of Mis and Dubh Rois', although it may involve a misdirected sexual drive, is not a classic case of lovesickness. In the Irish medical tradition of the later Middle Ages, lovesickness was still presented as a disease primarily affecting males (pp. 352–3). Later again, in courtly *dánta grádha* ('poems of love'), there is little sign of any change in this regard (pp. 360–1). As Mary Wack has noted, the concepts underlying both lovesickness and courtliness in vernacular literature suggested ways of 'constraining and yet indulging in potentially disruptive erotic impulses'.[5] Consequently it is perhaps unsurprising that both discourses present the male as the primary sufferer.

Female readers and auditors of this literature may have indulged an impulse to identify with the love-visitant, with her beauty, her power over men, and her affiliation with the *síd* (later *sí*) 'Otherworld'. Like the *leannán sí* ('fairy lover') of song and poem, the love-visitants to Óengus, Cú Chulainn and Ailill Ánguba are all bewitchingly beautiful, as are those who tryst with the kings, Díarmait and Muirchertach, in 'The Wooing of Becfhola' and 'The Death of Muirchertach mac Erca' (pp. 210–13, 213–8). Later, in texts such as the *dánta grádha* and the *aislingí*, these visitants often appear alongside more strictly localized

4. Mary Frances Wack, *Lovesickness in the Middle Ages. The Viaticum and Its Commentaries* (Philadelphia: University of Pennsylvania Press, 1990), p. 19.

5. Ibid., p. 30.

goddesses such as Aoibheall of Thomond and Clíona of Fermoy, as well as figures from classical literature such as Venus, Diana and Helen of Troy.

One version of 'The Wasting Sickness of Cú Chulainn' links the power of his visitant to a pagan, diabolical source. It concludes:

> That is the ruinous vision [shown] to Cú Chulainn by the people of the *síd*. For the demonic power was great before the Faith, and it was so great that demons used to fight in bodily form against men, and used to show them delights and mysteries, as if they were real. And so they were believed in.

The author of the seventh-century Hiberno-Latin text, *De Ordine Creaturarum*, speaks as though demonic power were still believed in:

> But those lying and impure spirits, fleeting and insubstantial, are capable of sensation and, clothed in bodies of air, never grow old and swell with pride as they wage war with men. Liars, and skilled in deceit, they move the sense of men, filling mortals with fear, troubling their lives with disturbances in their dreams and with movements and twistings of their limbs, concocting apparitions and oracles, and governing the casting of lots. They fill human hearts with yearning for unlawful love and desire; telling lies which seem like truth, they put on the appearance and the radiance of good angels.[6]

There was plenty potential for confusing aerial demons or fallen angels with folk of the *síd* and female witches, despite Church denials of the efficacy of sorcery and severe penalties for making accusations against so-called witches. The so-called 'First Synod of St. Patrick' declares:

> A Christian who believes that there is such a thing in the world as a vampire [*lamia*], that is to say, a witch [*striga*], is to be anathematized — anyone who puts a living soul under such a reputation; and he must

not be received again into the Church before he has undone by his own word the crime that he has committed, and so does penance with all diligence.

But such belief dies hard, as the renowned case of the burning of the Bridget Cleary in Ballyvadlea, County Tipperary, in 1895 shows.[7]

Clerics play little part in the pre-eleventh century narratives, either to oppose women or to reconcile them to their life. The Church figures largely, however, in the outstanding literary work of the twelfth century, that great collection of tales structured by a sequence of encounters between Saint Patrick and the last remaining *fianna* 'fenians' (members of the legendary warrior-band [*fian(n)*] of Finn mac Cumaill) which is known as *Acallam na Senórach* (The Colloquy of the Ancients). There is nothing to match the refined courtliness of the *Acallam* in earlier Irish tradition, nor anything corresponding to its sensitive treatment of the feelings associated with love. In this work the Church, mainly in the person of Saint Patrick, gives ear to the confessions of many lovers, sometimes at one remove through the voice of a story-teller. Saint Patrick is usually touched by what he hears but his responses, nonetheless, are governed by the teachings of the Church on love within marriage in the permitted degrees, and all other affections are disallowed, gently but firmly. The three tales from the *Acallam*, here presented and translated by Ann Dooley, are among its most poignant (pp. 228–33).

Overall, in the following texts, very few women are seen to have their way although many speak their mind and state their wants. In one unusual case, all that is asked is an explanation, to account for a pregnancy in a woman whose sexual partner is also female. This is one of the few texts concerning female homoeroticism to come to light (p. 220). Men also speak in the following texts, sometimes as representatives of the male group. A poem such as '*Moladh na Pite*' ('Quim Praise') can work like the misogynistic diatribe attributed to Cormac mac Airt to assert the cohesion of the group (pp. 241–2, 199–200). Male poets also spoke in their own name, to

---

6. Cited from John Carey, 'The Uses of Tradition in *Serglige Con Culainn*', in *Ulidia. Proceedings of the First International Conference of the Ulster Cycle of Tales*, eds J.P. Mallory and G. Stockman (Belfast: December Publications, 1994), pp. 77–84.

7. Angela Bourke, *The Burning of Bridget Cleary. A True Story* (London: Pimlico, 1999).

praise and dispraise women. The poem by Dáibhidh Ó Bruadair given below (pp. 237–8) is an attack on a woman. As she is unnamed, one must allow that this may be a set piece but it may be noted that he also wrote at least one poem in defence of a woman whom he named.

'*Moladh na Pite*' was composed by the Clare poet, Aindrias Mac Cruitín. Writing in Irish was particularly vibrant in his county in the eighteenth century and even into the nineteenth. A significant amount it has been preserved, partly due to the efforts of a great Clare scholar of Irish, Eugene O'Curry (1794–1862). The *cúirt éigse* 'court of poetry' was a mainstay of Irish-language writing in the eighteenth century. County Clare had its own, firstly at Ennis and later, apparently, at Quin. Some of the poets associated with the Clare *cúirt éigse* are notable for their contribution to the tradition of bawdry and Aindrias Mac Cruitín's poem might be seen as an earlier poem in the same tradition. A feature of Clare bawdry is that some of the poems concern named (and identifiable) women, and a few of them are written as though by the women themselves. The *cúirt éigse* was a near equivalent to a male club, and its atmosphere may have been conducive to the writing of ribald and even misogynistic verse.

The *cúirt éigse* is generally seen as important for having promoted literary activity in Irish while providing a focus for sociable gatherings. It has yet to be acknowledged that it also acted to boost Catholic morale in Munster throughout most of the eighteenth century, especially in Counties Cork, Limerick, and Clare. Catholics were excluded from the legal profession for much of the eighteenth century by the Penal Laws. Catholic priests were prominent among the writers and 'functionaries' associated with this simulacrum of the real law-court. Clerics who apostatized, particularly those who did so to marry, were sometimes publicly ridiculed or condemned by the *cúirt éigse*. Condemnatory poems and mock warrants were also issued against secular Catholics who apostatized to gain entry to a profession or to advance themselves in the world.

Brian Merriman's '*Cúirt*', presented here by Patrick Crotty, is of a different kind. For a start, all its functionaries are female, from the terrifying bailiff who has a warrant for the poet's arrest to Aoibheall, gracious *sibhean* of Craigliath, who sits on the bench. Most commentators on the *Cúirt*, including those who regard it as radically engaged with the 'new world' of the eighteenth century, see it as embedded in the medieval Court of Love tradition. One might argue that Merriman's *Cúirt* owes as much, if not more, to the contemporary *cúirt éigse*, and that it works in fact by quarrelling with the male-bonded structure and Catholic identity-politics of the latter. Despite Frank O'Connor's provocative description of Merriman as an 'intellectual Protestant', there is an unspoken — and unsubstantiated — assumption among commentators that he was a Catholic. Irrespective of his religion, it is remarkable that all the speakers in his *Cúirt* — plaintiff, defendant, judge and jury — argue against aspects of orthodox Catholic teaching on love, marriage, bastardy and clerical celibacy. For instance, even the old man who complains that his wife was pregnant by someone else before they married vehemently opposes the stigmatization of bastards. Some critics have seen the common ground between the speakers as a weakness in the poem, as though it had been better if only one group — the female sex — had spoken in favour of free love. It may be that a desire to have a cast unanimous in opposing Tridentine teaching weakened Merriman's plot. Liam P. Ó Murchú has recently discovered that Merriman made extensive borrowings of words and phrases from a series of religious poems in Counter-Reformation mode by an earlier Clare poet, Murchadh Riabhach Mac Namara (*fl.* 1687–8).[8] Consequently, we know that Merriman was aware of the irony of putting them to use in speeches opposed to Counter-Reformation thinking.

The 'Vision of Liberation' which Gearóid Ó Crualaoich finds in the *Cúirt* has much to recommend it.[9] Yet at the end of the poem, female 'liberation' is associated with anarchy and poses a threat to the narrator and, by extension, to the male sex. Ultimately, it is as if no court can deliver the liberation that is desired, by women or by men.

8. 'Cúlra agus Múnla Liteartha do *Chúirt* Mherriman', in *Saoi na hÉigse: Aistí in Ómós do Sheán Ó Tuama*, eds Pádraigín Riggs, Breandán Ó Conchúir and Seán Ó Coileáin (Baile Átha Cliath: An Clóchomhar, 2000), pp. 169–96.
9. 'The Vision of Liberation in *Cúirt an Mheán Oíche*', in *Folia Gadelica: Essays Presented to . . . R.A. Breatnach* (Cork: Cork University Press, 1983), pp. 95–104.

A. A Place in the World

ANONYMOUS

NOÍNDEN ULAD
(The Debility of the Ulidians)
(9th century)

[This tale purports to explain why the warriors of Ulster, with the exception of Cú Chulainn, succumbed to an affliction as debilitating as the pains of childbirth when they had most need of their strength (an implicit reference to the Cattle Raid led by Medb). It has been suggested that the debility of the Ulstermen is a literary reflex of the social practice of couvade. An alternative interpretation equates the debility with seasonal death within a vegetation cult: the goddess who overcomes seasonal death — winter — by giving birth to the spring is propitiated by men who mime her travail. Elsewhere in this volume we find that warring and giving birth are contraposed as spheres of activity: those who give life should not be involved in taking it (cf. p. 18). This view suggests a third way of reading the present tale. Just as Macha, the exemplary wife — silent, industrious and supportive — should remain at home, away from the royal assembly — which is tumultuous, ceremonial and competitive — so should the domestic and public spheres be preserved distinct from one another. Macha's acute need of separation figures the needs of hearth and home. By failing her, Crunnchu brings future catastrophe to all of Ulster: Macha names not just the real woman but a goddess of the province, and the twin children she bears are 'The Twins of Macha', in Old Irish *Emain Macha*, from whom the capital is named. The gendering of the private and public spheres normalizes movement from one to the other by males. The text was edited and translated by Vernam Hull (who dated it to the ninth century): '*Noínden Ulad*: The Debility of the Ulidians', *Celtica*, vol. 8 (1968), pp. 1–42, at 36–8. This translation is his.]

Why was the affliction brought upon the Ulidians? It is not hard to relate.

There was a wealthy peasant of the Ulidians who lived on the heights of mountain-ranges and of wildernesses. The name of that one was Crunnchu mac Agnomain. As an inhabitant of the wilderness, great wealth had accrued to him. Moreover, he had many sons around him. The woman who had cohabited with him, namely the mother of his children, died. For a long time he was without a wife. One day while he was alone on his couch in his house, he saw coming towards him into the main building a shapely woman excellent in appearance, apparel, and aspect. The woman sat down on a seat at the fireplace and kindled a fire. Until the end of the day, they remained there without mutual converse on their part. Then she fetched a kneading trough for herself and a sieve and set about preparing food in the house. When the end of the day had arrived, she brought pails with her and milked the cows without asking leave.

After she had come into the house, she turned righthandwise[1] and went into his kitchen. She ministered to his household and sat down on a seat beside Crunnchu. Then every one went onto his couch. She remained after every one else, slacked down (?) the fire, turned righthandwise, went to him under his covering, and laid a hand on his privy parts. They remained in union until she became pregnant through him. Now from union with her, his wealth was all the greater. His flourishing aspect and his trappings were pleasing to her.

Now the Ulidians used to hold great and frequent encampments and assemblies. All the people of Ulidia, both men and women of those who could go to it, used to go to the assembly. 'I shall go,' Crunnchu said to his wife, 'like every one else to the assembly.' 'You shall not go,' the woman said, 'lest danger dog you from mentioning us, for our union will be at an end if you mention me in the assembly.' 'I shall not speak there at all,' Crunnchu said.

The Ulidians came to the assembly. Like every one else, Crunnchu came as well. The assembly was splendid, including people and horses and costumes. At the assembly were held horse-races, combats, casting and shooting matches, chariot-races, and processions. In the mid-afternoon the king's chariot was brought to the course, and his horses gained the victory of the assembly. Thereafter the eulogists came to eulogize the

---

1. i.e. to bring luck.

king, the queen, the seers, the druids, the retinue, the host, and all the assembly. 'Never has come to the assembly,' the eulogists said, 'two horses like these two steeds of the king, for there is not a swifter pair in Ireland.' 'My wife is swifter,' Crunnchu said, 'than those two steeds.' 'Seize the man,' the king said, 'in order that the woman come to answer for the boast.'

He was seized, and messengers were sent by the king to the woman. She bade the messengers welcome and asked what had impelled them to come. 'We have come in order that you go to release your husband who has been seized by the king, for he has said that you were swifter than the two steeds of the king.' 'This indeed was bad,' she said, 'for that remark was not seemly.' 'In sooth, that for me is a ground for exemption,' she added, 'in that I am pregnant with the pangs of childbirth.' 'Even so,' the messengers said, 'he will be slain unless you come.' 'Needs then must be,' she said.

Thereupon she went with them to the assembly. Every one then came to gaze upon her. 'It is not meet,' she said, 'to gaze upon my shape.' 'Wherefore have I been brought hither?' she asked. 'To race with the two steeds of the king,' every one said. 'That is a ground for exemption,' she said, 'for I am in the pangs of childbirth.' 'Then ply swords upon the peasant,' the king said. 'Wait for me but a little while,' she said, 'until I have been delivered.' 'No,' the king said. 'It is indeed a cause of shame to you not to grant me a small favour (?). Since you do not grant it, I shall bring an even greater shame for that upon you. Now let loose,' she said, 'the horses alongside me.'

That was done, and at the end of the course she was across in front of them. Thereupon a scream arose from her on account of the pain of the travail. Forthwith God cleared it away for her, and she bore a boy and a girl at one birth. As soon as all the people heard the scream of the woman, it laid them low so that the strength of all of them was the same as that of the woman who was in travail. 'The shame that you have inflicted upon me,' she said, 'shall be indeed a disgrace to you from now on. When things shall be most difficult for you, all those of you who guard this province shall have only the strength of a woman in childbirth; and as long as a woman is in childbirth, so long shall you likewise be, namely to the end of five days and four nights, and, moreover, it shall be

on you unto the ninth generation, that is to say, for the lifespan of nine persons.'

That indeed fell true. It has dogged them from the time of Crunnchu to the time of Fergus mac Domnaill. This affliction, however, did not used to be upon women and boys and upon Cú Chulainn, for he was not one of the Ulidians, nor upon every one who used to be outside of the territory.

For that reason, then, it is that the affliction has been upon the Ulidians.

from:
TÁIN BÓ CÚAILNGE
(The Cattle Raid of Cúailnge. Recension I) (9th century; 12th century)

[An argument about property between Queen Medb and her royal consort, Ailill, provides the motivation for the Cattle Raid of Cúailnge in the second recension of the epic, the so-called 'pillow-talk', which dates from the early twelfth century (see pp. 38–41). The opening section of the first recension, the first of three excerpted here, is believed to date back to the ninth century. In it, we are told that Ailill and Medb have mustered armies from the four provinces but their quest is not stated explicitly. Instead, the opening focuses on the fact that the expedition is doomed from the outset because it is lead by Medb. Patricia Kelly has shown that the theme of her usurpation of male authority and its dire consequences for society is woven through this otherwise episodic recension and is recapitulated forcefully in its concluding section, also excerpted here ('The Táin as Literature', in *Aspects of the Táin*, ed. J.P. Mallory [Belfast: December Publications, 1992], pp. 69–102). Medb ignores the altogether ominous prophecy of the woman-poet Feidelm (this instance of female divination is noteworthy). She also disregards Fergus's estimate of the strength of Cú Chulainn, although he was well qualified to make it, being an exile from Cú Chulainn's province, Ulster. Medb depended on retaining Fergus's military support throughout the Cattle Raid by doling out her sexual favours to him, and Ailill colluded in this. Fergus's gigantic stature and enormous appetites are thematized elsewhere. According to one text, there were 'seven feet between his ears and his lips, and seven half-feet between his eyes, and the same in the length of his nose, and of his lips . . . and of his penis, and his scrotum was a bushel in weight'. According to another, it used to take seven women to satisfy him 'until he came to Crúachain and had the run of Medb'. The loss of his sword signifies that Medb has unmanned him. In some respects he is Medb's male alter ego but, unlike her, he is ultimately restored to grace.

In the final scene, when Conall Cernach taunts him with 'following a wanton woman', Fergus's primary allegiance to the male group and to Ulster is reasserted and he averts his battle fury from them, spending it instead on the hills of Meath. Echoing Conall Cernach, he says that the people's downfall was to 'follow [the arse of] a woman who has misled them'. The bracketed words correspond to what is found in the original and convey an important legal resonance (see p. 27 and pp. 38–41). The text was edited and translated by Cecile O'Rahilly, *Táin Bó Cúailnge. Recension I* (Dublin: Dublin Institute for Advanced Studies, 1976). The three excerpts are from ibid., pp. 125–7 and 129; pp. 154–5; pp. 235–7.]

A great army was mustered by the Connachtmen, that is, by Ailill and Medb, and word went from them to the three other provinces. And Ailill sent messengers to the seven sons of Mágu: Ailill, Anlúan, Moccorb, Cet, Én, Bascall and Dóche, each with his fighting force of three thousand, and also to Cormac Conn Longas the son of Conchobor, who was billeted with his three hundred men in Connacht. They all came on then until they reached Crúachain Aí[1] . . .

So then the four provinces of Ireland were gathered together in Crúachain Aí. Their prophets and druids did not permit them to go thence, but kept them for a fortnight awaiting an auspicious omen.

Then, on the day that they set forth, Medb said to her charioteer:

'All those who part here today from comrade and friend will curse me for it is I who have mustered this hosting.'

'Wait then,' said the charioteer, 'until the chariot has turned right-handwise to strengthen the good omen so that we may come back again.'

When the charioteer turned back the chariot and they were about to descend, they saw in front of them a grown maiden. She had yellow hair. She wore a vari-coloured cloak with a golden pin in it and a hooded tunic with red embroidery. She had shoes with golden fastenings. Her face was oval, narrow below, broad above. Her eyebrows were dark and black. Her beautiful black eyelashes cast a shadow on to the middle of her cheeks. Her lips seemed to be made of *partaing*.[2] Her teeth were like a shower of pearls between her lips. She had three plaits of hair: two plaits wound around her head, the third hanging down her back, touching her calves behind. In her hand she carried a weaver's beam of white bronze, with golden inlay.

There were three pupils in each of her two eyes. The maiden was armed and her chariot was drawn by two black horses.

'What is your name?' asked Medb of the maiden.

'I am Feidelm, the poetess of Connacht,' said the maiden.

'Whence do you come?' asked Medb.

'From Albion after learning the art of divination,' answered the maiden.

'Have you the power of prophecy called *imbas forosna*?'[3]

'I have indeed,' said the maiden.

'Look for me then and tell me how it will fare with my hosting.'

Then the maiden looked and Medb said:

'O Feidelm Prophetess, how do you see the fate of the army?'

Feidelm answered and said: 'I see it bloody, I see it red.'

'That is not so,' said Medb, 'for Conchobor lies in his debility in Emain[4] together with the Ulstermen and all the mightiest of their warriors, and my messengers have come and brought me tidings of them. O Feidelm Prophetess, how do you see our host?' asked Medb again.

'I see it blood-stained, I see it red,' said the maiden.

'That is not so,' said Medb, 'for Celtchar mac Uthidir is in Dún Lethglaise[5] together with a third of the men of Ulster, and Fergus mac Roeich meic Echdach is here in exile with us with three thousand men. O Feidelm Prophetess, how do you see our host?'

'I see it blood-stained, I see it red,' answered the maiden.

'That matters not indeed,' said Medb, 'for in every muster and in every army assembled in a great encampment there are quarrels and strife

---

1. Anglicized as Croghan and Rathcroghan, in present-day County Roscommon.

2. Meaning doubtful; apparently 'some bright crimson or scarlet substance'.

3. Literally, 'knowledge which illuminates'.

4. Ulster's royal capital, now known as Navan Fort, beside Armagh.

5. Now Downpatrick, County Down.

and bloody woundings. So look once more for us, and tell us the truth. O Feidelm Prophetess, how do you see our host?'

'I see it blood-stained, I see it red,' said Feidelm . . .

On the Monday after the autumn festival of Samain they set out . . .

. . . . . .

When they had all arrived with their booty and assembled at Findabair Cúailnge, Medb said:

'Let the army be divided here. All the cattle cannot be taken by one route. Let Ailill go with half of them by Slige Midlúachra. Fergus and I will go by Bernas Bó nUlad.'

'The half of the drove that has fallen to our share is not lucky for us,' said Fergus. 'The cattle cannot be taken across the mountain unless they are divided.'

So it was done. Whence comes the name Bernas Bó nUlad.

Then Ailill came to Cuillius, his charioteer:

'Spy for me today on Medb and Fergus. I do not know what has brought them together. I shall be glad if you can bring me a proof.'

Cuillius arrived when they were in Cluichri. The lovers remained behind while the warriors went on ahead. Cuillius came to where they were, but they did not hear the spy. Fergus's sword happened to be beside him and Cuillius drew it out of its scabbard, leaving the scabbard empty. Then he came back to Ailill.

'Well?' said Ailill.

'Well indeed,' said Cuillius. 'Here is the proof for you.'

'That is well,' said Ailill.

They exchanged smiles.

'As you thought,' said Cuillius, 'I found them both lying together.'

'She is right (to behave thus),' said Ailill. 'She did it to help in the cattle-driving. Make sure that the sword remains in good condition. Put it under your seat in the chariot, wrapped in a linen cloth.'

Then Fergus rose up to look for his sword.

'Alas!' he cried.

'What ails you?' asked Medb.

'I have wronged Ailill,' said he. 'Wait here until I come out of the wood, and do not wonder if it is a long time until I return.'

Now in fact Medb did not know of the loss of

the sword. Fergus went off, taking his charioteer's sword in his hand. In the wood he cut a wooden sword. Hence the Ulstermen have the place-name Fid Mórdrúalle.

'Let us go on after the others,' said Fergus.

All their hosts met in the plain. They pitched their tents. Fergus was summoned to Ailill to play chess. When he came into the tent Ailill began to laugh at him.

Fergus said:

'Well for the man who is being laughed at if he be not deluded by the foolish violence of his fateful deed. By the point of my sword, halidom of Macha, swiftly shall we wreak vengeance on swords following on a cry (for help) from the Gaileóin had not a woman's triumph misdirected (me); following on a tryst bloody and grave-strewn and with blunt-edged spears between a great host with [their] commanders, there shall be fought a battle [extending] to the mountain of Nessa's grandson (Cú Chulainn) by a stout host, and the battle shall scatter the headless trunks of men.' . . .

. . . . .

'Too great is that force which you exert against (your own) people and race, following a wanton woman as you do,' said Conall Cernach.

'What shall I do, O warrior?' asked Fergus.

'Strike the hills beyond them and the trees about them,' said Conall Cernach.

Then Fergus smote the hills and with three blows struck off the (tops of the) three hills in Meath (now called) Máela Midi, the flat-topped hills of Meath. Cú Chulainn heard the blows which Fergus had struck on the hills, or (those he had struck) on the shield of Conchobar.

'Who strikes those great strong blows in the distance?' asked Cú Chulainn. 'Blood seals up the heart. Anger destroys the world. Quickly it loosens the dressings of my wounds.' . . .

'Turn hither, master Fergus!' cried Cú Chulainn, but (though he said this) three times Fergus did not answer.

'I swear by the god by whom Ulstermen swear,' said Cú Chulainn, 'that I shall drub you as flax-heads (?) are beaten in a pool. I shall go over you as a tail[6] goes over a cat. I shall smite you as a fond woman smites her son.'

6. Better 'club' or some such word.

'Who among the men of Ireland speaks to me thus?' said Fergus.

'Cú Chulainn mac Súaltaim, the son of Conchobar's sister,' said Cú Chulainn, 'and hold back from me now.'

'I have promised to do that,' said Fergus.

'Begone then,' said Cú Chulainn.

'I agree,' said Fergus, 'for you refused to encounter me when you were pierced with wounds.'

So at that juncture Fergus and his division of three thousand went away. The men of Leinster and the men of Munster went away too, and nine divisions, those of Medb and Ailill and of their seven sons, were left in the battle. It was midday when Cú Chulainn came to the battle. When the sun was sinking behind the trees in the wood, he overcame the last of the bands, and of the chariot there remained only a handful of the ribs of the framework and a handful of the shafts round the wheel.

Then Cú Chulainn overtook Medb going from the battle-field.

'Spare me!' cried Medb.

'If I were to kill you, it would be only right for me,' said Cú Chulainn. But he spared her life then because he used not to kill women. He convoyed them west to Áth Lúain and across the ford too. He struck three blows of his sword upon the flagstone in Áth Lúain. They (i.e. the hills) are called Máelana Átha Lúain.

Now when they were finally routed Medb said to Fergus:

'Men and lesser men (?) meet here today, Fergus.'

'That is what usually happens,' said Fergus, 'to a herd of horses led by a mare. Their substance is taken and carried off and guarded as they follow a woman who has misled them.'

AIDED ÓENFHIR AÍFE
(The Death of Aífe's One Son)
(9th or 10th century)

[Heroic literature tends to portray bloodletting as regenerative of virility but contact with women as destructive of it. The *furor* of the child Cú Chulainn was dissipated when he encountered bare-breasted women (see Volume I,

pp. 11–12). Here, the adult Cú Chulainn pushes his wife Emer aside as bloodlust drives him onward to murder his own son, Connla. This child was born of his union with Aífe, one of two women from whom he received his training in arms in Scotland before returning to Ireland to marry Emer. As Joanne Findon has argued, while Emer's words do not stay Cú Chulainn's hand, her maternal empathy is a rebuke to his heroic sacrifice and to the heroic code in general. The implied lowing of the separated cows and calves is its echo ('A Woman's Words: Emer versus Cú Chulainn in Aided Oenfir Aífe', in *Ulidia. Proceedings of the First International Conference on the Ulster Cycle of Tales*, eds J.P. Mallory and G. Stockman (Belfast: December Publications, 1994), pp. 134–49). Emer does not figure in the play which Yeats based on this tale, *On Baile's Strand*. The original tale is dated to the later ninth or tenth century; see A.G. Van Hamel (ed.), *Compert Con Culainn and Other Stories* (Dublin: Dublin Institute for Advanced Studies, 1933), pp. 9–15. This translation is from: Thomas Kinsella, *The Táin. Translated from the Irish Epic Táin Bó Cuailnge* (Mountrath, Portlaoise: Dolmen Press, 1969; Oxford: Oxford University Press, 1970), pp. 39–45.]

What caused Cúchulainn to kill his son? It is soon told.

Seven years to the day after Cúchulainn left Aífe, the boy came looking for his father. The men of Ulster were gathered at Tracht Esi, the Strand where the Mark is, when he came. They saw the boy coming toward them over the ocean in a little boat of bronze with gilt oars in his hands.

There was a pile of stones beside him in the boat. He put a stone in his sling and sent it humming at the sea birds, and stunned them without killing them. Then he let them escape into the air again. Then he did a feat with his jaws, between his hands, faster than the eye could follow, tuning his voice to bring them down a second time. Then he roused them again.

'Well,' Conchobor said, 'I pity the country that boy is heading for. I don't know what island he comes from, but their grown men can grind us into dust if one of their young boys can do that. Someone go out to meet him. Don't let him ashore.'

'Who ought to meet him?'

'Who but Condere mac Echach?' Conchobor said.

'And why Condere?' they all asked.

'Clearly,' Conchobor said, 'where there is a need for good sense and eloquence, Condere is the right person.'

'I'll go and meet him,' Condere said.

Condere went up to the boy just as he reached the strand.

'You have come far enough, young man,' Condere said, 'until we find out where you come from and who your people are.'

'I'll give my name to no man,' the boy said, 'and I'll make way for no man.'

'You can't land,' Condere said, 'unless you give your name.'

'I am going where I am going,' the boy said.

The boy moved to pass him, but Condere said:

'Heed me my son.
Mighty are your acts
   manly your blood
you have the pride
   of an Ulster warrior
Conchobor would protect you
   but you bare your jaws
and dare us with your little spears
   and annoy our warriors
you have come to Conchobor
   let him grant you protection.
Listen, pay heed.
Come to Conchobor
   Nes's swift son
to Sencha mac Ailella
   full of victories
to Fintan's son Cethern
   of the crimson blade
the fire that burns battalions
   to the poet Amargin
to Cúscraid of the huge hosts
   come into the care
of Conall Cernach
   above story or song
or the shouts of heroes
   gathered together
Blai Briuga would dislike it
   if you pushed past him
or any warrior
   however fine
the insult would hurt him
   come let it be said
that Condere himself
   arose and approached
the warlike boy
   and held him back.

'I have sworn to oppose you, a beardless, unfledged boy,' Condere said, 'if you won't heed the men of Ulster.'

'You have come and spoken well,' the boy said, 'so I will answer you:

'I tuned my voice:
from little jaws
   a straight shot sped
with my little spears
   flung from afar
I gathered together
   a lovely bird flock
no need of my hero's
   salmon leap
by such brave acts
   I have sworn no man
will stand in my way
   go back to Ulster
and say I'll fight them
   singly or together.

'Turn aside,' the boy said, 'for even though you had the strength of a hundred men you couldn't hold me back.'

'Very well,' Condere said, 'someone else can try.'

Condere went back to the men of Ulster and told them.

'No one makes little of Ulster's honour while I live,' Conall Cernach said. 'I won't permit it.'

He went out to meet the boy.

'Those were pretty games, boy,' Conall said.

'They'll work just as nicely on you,' the boy said.

He set a stone in his sling and sent it in a stunning-shot into the sky. The roar of its thunder as it rose reached Conall and knocked him headlong. Before he could rise the boy had the shield-strap tied around Conall's arms.

'Send out someone else!' Conall said, but the whole army was put to shame.

Then Cúchulainn advanced on the boy, performing his feats as he came. Forgall's daughter Emer had her arm round his neck. She said:

'Don't go down!
It is your own son there
   don't murder your son
the wild and well born
   son let him be
is it good or wise
   for you to fall

on your marvellous son
   of the mighty acts
remember Scáthach's
   strict warning and turn
from this flesh agony
   this twig from your tree
if Connla has dared us
   he has justified it.

Turn back, hear me!
My restraint is reason
   Cúchulainn hear it
we know his name
   if he is really Connla
the boy is Aife's
   one son.'

Then Cúchulainn said:

'Be quiet, wife.
   It isn't a woman
that I need now
   to hold me back
in the face of these feats
   and shining triumph
I want no woman's
   help with my work
victorious deeds
   are what we need
to fill the eyes
   of a great king
the blood of Connla's
   body will flush
my skin with power
   little spear so fine
to be finely sucked
   by my own spears!

'No matter who he is, wife,' Cúchulainn said, 'I must kill him for the honour of Ulster.'

So he went down to meet him.

'Those were pretty games, boy,' he said.

'Prettier than the games I'm finding here,' the young boy said. 'Two of you have come down here and still I haven't named myself.'

'Maybe you were meant to meet me,' Cúchulainn said. 'Name yourself, or you die.'

'So be it!' the boy said.

The boy set upon him and they struck at one another. The boy cut him bald-headed with his sword, in the stroke of precision.

'The joking has come to a head!' Cúchulainn said. 'Now we'll wrestle.'

'I can't reach up to your belt,' the boy said.

He climbed up onto two standing stones. Without moving a foot he trust [*sic*] Cúchulainn three times between the two stones. His feet sank in the stone up to the ankle. The marks of his feet are there still, which is why the people of Ulster call it Tráig, or Tracht, Esi, the Strand of the Mark.

They went down into the sea to drown each other, and the boy submerged him twice. Then Cúchulainn turned and played the boy foul in the water with the *gae bolga*,[1] that Scáthach had taught to no one but him. He sent it speeding over the water at him and brought his bowels down around his feet.

'There is something Scáthach didn't teach me,' the boy said. 'You have wounded me woefully.'

'I have,' Cúchulainn said.

He took the boy in his arms and carried him away from the place and brought him and laid him down before the people of Ulster.

'My son, men of Ulster,' he said. 'Here you are.'

'Alas, alas!' said all Ulster.

'It is the truth,' the boy said. 'If only I had five years among you I would slaughter the warriors of the world for you. You would rule as far as Rome. But since it is like this, point me out the famous men around me. I would like to salute them.'

He put his arms round the neck of each man in turn, and saluted his father, and then died. Then a loud lament was uttered for him. His grave was made and the grave-stone set. For the space of three days and nights no calf in Ulster was let go to its cow on account of his death.

---

1. *gae bolga*, 'spear of *bolga*' (or Bulga), a deadly spear acquired by Cú Chulainn from the female warrior Scáthach, or her double, Aife.

CREIDNE THE SHE-WARRIOR
(Early Middle Irish)

[This Early Middle Irish anecdote, preserved in genealogical material, provides a rare account of a female warrior, depicted here as the product of extreme circumstances. From: Kuno Meyer, *Fianaigecht: Irish Poems and Tales Relating to Finn and His Fiana, with an English Translation* (Dublin: Dublin Institute for Advanced Studies, 1910), p. xii.]

The Conaille Murthemne[1] are of the race of Conall Cernach. The Dál Runtair and Glasraige in Coolney and the Dál nImda are of the race of Conall Costamail. Glas and Runtar and Imda were the three sons of Conall Costamail (or Cosdub, 'Blackfoot'). His own daughter had borne them to him, viz., Creidne the she-*fénid*[2] was their mother. He was ashamed that his daughter should have borne the sons to him. Thereupon the sons were taken from him into the outer parts of his land and his kindred, for it was necessary for Conall that he should part with these sons on account of his queen, Aife. For great was the strife between Aife and Creidne. Then Creidne went on the warpath to despoil her father and her step-mother on account of her sons being outside their proper kindred. She had three bands of nine men with her on the warpath. She used to wear the hair of her back plaited. She would fight equally on sea and on land. Hence she was called Creidne that was a *fénid*. She had been seven years in exile, both in Ireland and Alba, when she made peace with her father. This Conall said to his daughter, through prophecy and augury: 'There will be destruction on the men of Ulster,' said Conall, 'and they will be driven from their land. And thy sons, O Creidne, shall possess to the day of Doom the lands into which they have gone, and they will not be moved (thence), and they shall have wealth and plenty of success in war.'

1. These, and the other groups in the text, were located in Louth.
2. *fénid*, 'member of a *fian*-band, a warrior'.

from:
FRAGMENTARY ANNALS
OF IRELAND
(11th century)

[This anecdote, from a set of annals of which the original dates back to the eleventh century, contains ideas that would have been familiar to an educated élite. It suggests that the male generative contribution is the significant one in the production of a warrior. Such a view adumbrates an Aristotelian single-seed system of active male form and passive female matter. Yet innate character requires nurturing before it can be realized and the female contribution is portrayed as paramount here. From: Joan Newlon Rader (ed. and trans.), *Fragmentary Annals of Ireland* (Dublin: Dublin Institute for Advanced Studies, 1978), p. 11.]

One day, as Fiachna, the father of that Suibne, was going to inspect his plowing — for he himself was not a king at all — he brought to his mind how each person succeeded another in the kingship of Ireland. Pride and great arrogance came over him, and greed to seize the sovereignty of Ireland, and he came home and told this to his wife, and this is what his wife said to him: 'Since you have not attempted that before now,' she said, 'I do not see that it is suitable for a man of your age and antiquity to be fighting at this time for a kingdom. For it is not . . .'[1]

'Be quiet,' said he, 'don't get in my way; but have food and drink brought in,' said he, 'and let the noblemen be invited out to visit us, and let them be given their fill.' And he summoned his wife to him then, and he lay with her, and every plan that had been in his mind before he put away from him through the act of procreation, and after that it was his wife who possessed the intentions that he had had, and it was then that this Suibne Menn was conceived in the womb of his mother.

When he rose from the woman, she asked, 'Shall everyone be invited in?'

'No,' said Fiachna, 'we will not make ourselves ridiculous — that is, by fighting for the kingship henceforward.' Now from that it is to be understood that it is from the pre-existing great ambitions of parents that children with great ambitions are born.

Now, one day when this Suibne, as a young man, was in his house with his wife, he said to his wife, 'I am amazed,' he said, 'that so few of the Cenél Eógain have taken the lordship over all, up to this time.'

His wife replied, with a kind of sarcasm, 'What's wrong with you, that you don't use force, and go before them to fight with everyone, and win frequent victories?'

1. Space for a few letters here in the MS.

'That's the way it will be,' he said. Consequently he came out armed the following morning, and he met a warrior of the people of the [country], who was armed, and he gave battle to him until the warrior submitted to him at spear-point; and a huge host submitted to him in that manner, and he took the kingship of Ireland.

EITHNE'S DREAM
(c. 700)

[Dreams loom large in medieval literature, particularly in Celtic and Norse literatures which provide extensive evidence of the deliberate cultivation of subjective dreams and of objective, projected visions (the distinction between them is often unclear). Dreams functioned to disclose the future, to bestow insight which helped in problem-solving, and to procure poetic inspiration. Techniques to induce them are usually portrayed as a male prerogative, but there are exceptions (for example, pp. 174–6). For the most part, women's dreams and visions are involuntary and are restricted to prophesying the future of their husbands and sons, and women are depicted dreaming of other women only very rarely (cf. p. 190 (iii)). Adomnán, in his biography of Saint Columba written c. 700, relates that the following 'angelic vision' was beheld by the saint's mother, Eithne. The excerpt is from: A.O. and M.O. Anderson (ed. and trans.; revised by M.O. Anderson), Adomnan's Life of Columba, pp. 183, 185.]

An angel of the Lord appeared to the mother of the venerable man in a dream, one night between his conception and his birth; and standing there, gave her, as it seemed, a robe of marvellous beauty, in which there appeared embroidered splendid colours, as it were of all kinds of flowers. And after some little space, asking it back, he took it from her hands. And raising it, and spreading it out, he let it go in the empty air. Grieved by losing it, she spoke thus to that man of reverend aspect: 'Why do you so quickly take from me this joyous mantle?' Then he said: 'For the reason that this cloak is of very glorious honour, you will not be able to keep it longer with you.'

After these words, the woman saw that robe gradually recede from her in flight, grow greater, and surpass the breadth of the plains, and excel in its greater measure the mountains and woods. And she heard a voice that followed, speaking thus: 'Woman, do not grieve, for you will bear to the man to whom you are joined by [the bond of] marriage a son, of such grace that he, as though one of the prophets of God, shall be counted in their number; and he has been predestined by God to be a leader of innumerable souls to the heavenly country.' While she heard this voice, the woman awoke.

ÓEBFHINN'S DREAM
(Old Irish)

[This dream is recounted in Old Irish genealogical material. Óebfhinn is wife to Conall Corc, legendary founder of Cashel, seat of Munster's high-kingship, and mother of the Eóganachta, the province's leading dynasties. The relative importance of these dynasties to each other is signified by the different liquids in which she bathes her sons in her dream. Cairpre Cruithnechán, 'The Little Pict', their half-brother by another mother, is the outsider who poses a threat to her authority as royal matron. This new translation is based on: M.A. O'Brien (ed.), Corpus Genealogiarum Hiberniae (Dublin: Dublin Institute for Advanced Studies, 1976), pp. 195–6.]

Now the four sons of Óebfhinn daughter of Óengus Bolg, king of Corcu Loígde: (i) Nad-Fraích from whom are descended Mac-Láre and the Eóganacht of Cashel and the Eóganacht Áine and the Eóganacht Glendamnach and the Eóganacht Durlais Airthir Chliach; (ii) Macc-cass from whom are descended the Uí Echach; (iii) Macc-Bróc from whom are descended the Uí Threna; (iv) Macc-Iair from whom are descended the Uí Meicc Iair. [A fifth son is] Cairpre Cruithnechán 'The Little Pict' from whom are descended the Eóganacht Maige Gerrgind in Scotland.

This is the same Óebfhinn who saw the aisling on the first night that she slept with the king of Cashel, that is, she saw that she gave birth to four wolf-cubs. And she bathed the first cub in wine, namely Nad-Fraích. She bathed the second in ale, namely Macc-cass. She bathed the third in new milk, namely Macc-Bróc. She bathed the fourth in water, namely Macc-Iair. The fifth cub came to her in her bed from without and she bathed him in blood. This same was Cairpre Cruithnechán 'The Little Pict' and he turned on her and gnawed her breasts from her body.

SÉATHRÚN CÉITINN (GEOFFREY KEATING)

(*c.* 1580–*c.* 1644)

ÉACHTACH'S DREAM
(17th century)

[Various texts relate that Cormac mac Airt was conceived as a result of a fortuitous encounter between his parents on the night before his father's death in the Battle of Mucrama. In *Forus Feasa ar Éirinn* (The History of Ireland) the Counter-Reformation historian Séathrún Céitinn (*c.* 1580–*c.* 1650) portrays Cormac as the off-spring of a legitimate union, substituting a prophetic dream for the prodigious extramarital conception. As his account may well have drawn on an earlier source, it is included here. The excerpt is newly translated from the text in: P.S. Dineen (ed. and trans.), *Foras Feasa ar Éirinn. The History of Ireland*, 4 vols (London: Irish Texts Society, 1901, 1908, 1914), vol. 2 (1908), pp. 298, 300.]

Wonderful is the *aisling* that this Éachtach — Cormac's mother — had. Once upon a time while asleep beside Art it seemed to her that her head was cut from her body and that a great tree grew out of her neck and spread its branches across the whole of Ireland. And the sea rose above that tree and laid it low. And after that, another tree grew out of the root of the first tree, and a fairy wind came from the west which knocked it down. And on seeing that *aisling* the woman started and woke from her sleep, and recounted the substance of the *aisling* to Art.

'That is true,' said Art. 'Every woman's head is her husband and I will be taken from you in the battle of Magh Mhucramha.[1] And the tree that will grow out of you is the son you will bear to me who will be king of Ireland. And the sea that will drown him is a fishbone that he will swallow which will choke him there and then. And the tree that will grow out of the root of the first tree is the son that will be born to him who will be king of Ireland. And the fairy wind from the west that will overthrow him is a battle that will be fought between him and the *fian*-band[2], and he will fall at the hands of the *fian*-band in that battle. But if so, the *fian*-band will not have luck from that time forward.'

And that *aisling* came to pass for Cormac and for his son, for it was when he was swallowing a fishbone that the demons choked him, and it was at the hands of the *fian*-band that Cairbre Lifeachair died in the Battle of Gabhair.[3]

1. Near Athenry, County Galway.
2. The *fian*, 'warrior band', of Fonn mac Cumhaill is intended.
3. An area in Leinster around the River Liffey.

ANONYMOUS

THE BIRTH OF ÁED SLÁINE
(11th century)

[This comic eleventh-century tale describes the tribulations of rival consorts, driven to extremes to retain their place in the royal household and to produce male heirs. It is accompanied in the manuscript by a poem on the same subject attributed to Flann Mainistrech (d. 1056), an historian of the Ciannachta in Síl nÁeda Sláine who became head of the monastic school at Monasterboice in County Louth; it is possible that he was the author of both prose and verse. If so, perhaps he was making fun of unnamed female contemporaries from Síl nÁeda Sláine — the dynasty claiming descent from Áed Sláine — by recounting an absurd tale about their predecessors.

The account of Mugain's odd brood of lamb, salmon and, finally, Áed Sláine, is narrated pietistically in the Life of Saint Áed mac Bric which predates our tale. In an Early Modern poem beginning *Fuigheall beannacht brú Mhuire*, 'Mary's womb is replete with blessings', the Virgin is said to have given birth to Christ who is the Child, the Lamb, and 'the Salmon of the well of mercy' — here, the fish as Christian symbol is given a little native colouring. A Middle Irish anecdote above, at p. 126, equates the Holy Spirit with a salmon. The equation of Áed Sláine with Christ and Mugain with the Virgin, if implicit in our tale, is a bold stroke. The association of Mugain's prodigious progeny with the account of Mairenn the Bald ensures the mode is pietistic rather than droll. This new translation is from the Irish original published in: R.I. Best and Osborn Bergin (eds), *Lebor na hUidre. Book of the Dun Cow* (Dublin: Dublin Institute of Advanced Studies, 1929), pp. 133–5.]

Tara of the Kings was the estate reserved for all kings who used to rule Ireland, and it was common practice for them to have the *cáin*-fines and penalties and rents of the men of Ireland brought to them there. It was common practice moreover for the men of Ireland to come from every quarter to Tara to partake of the Feast of Tara at *Samain*.[1] For the two renowned gatherings which the men of Ireland had were the Feast of Tara every *Samain*, for that was the pagans' Easter, and the Fair of Tailtiu[2] every *Lugnasad*.[3] During the course of the year, no one dared infringe any penalty or law that was ordained by the men of Ireland on either of those dates.

On one occasion, the Gaels held an extraordinary great fair at Tailtiu. The King of Ireland at that time was Diarmait son of Fergus Cerrbéoil.[4] The men of Ireland were arrayed on the mounds of the Fair, with everyone ranged according to honours and arts and entitlement as was customary at that time. Moreover there was a separate mound for the king's women, ranged around his two consorts. The queens who were with Diarmait at that time were Mairenn the Bald, and Mugain daughter of Conchrad son of Duach Donn[5] of the Munster men. Mugain was very envious of Mairenn, and she said to the woman-satirist that she would give her whatever she requested if only she would remove the queen's golden crown from her head for, as it happens, Mairenn had no hair and a queen's crown is what used to cover her defect.

Then the woman-satirist came to where Mairenn was and was demanding something from her. The queen said that she did not have it. 'I'll[6] have this,' said she, as she pulled the golden headdress from her head. 'God and Ciarán help me in this!' said Mairenn, covering her head with her two hands. Scarcely had anyone in the crowd glanced at her when down to her two shoulders fell the smooth wavy golden hair that grew on her through Ciarán's power. The crowd were amazed at the miracle, and pleased that the queen had not been put to shame. 'I call on God that you may be disgraced for this before the men of Ireland!' said Mairenn, and that came to pass.

Later, Mugain was with Diarmait, and she was barren. Mugain was unhappy because of that, for the king thought of abandoning her altogether. She was also unhappy at the fact that the other women that the king had were bearing children, namely, Eithne, daughter of Brénainn the Blind, of the Conmaicne of Cúl Tolad[7] specifically; she was the mother of Colmán Mór.[8] And Brea, daughter of Colmán son of Nemán from Dún Súaine,[9] the mother of Colmán Bec.[10] Mugain was dejected because of that — that is, because of having no son or daughter and because the king was threatening to abandon her.

It came about that Finnian of Mag Bile[11] and Bishop Áed son of Brec[12] were in Brega. The queen sought them out and she was imploring the clerics to help her. Finnian and Bishop Áed blessed water and gave it to her to drink, and she became pregnant from that. What she produced from that pregnancy was — a lamb! 'I'm ruined,' said Mugain, 'to have given birth to a quadruped — for I won't be acceptable to anyone after this.' 'That won't be so,' said Finnian, 'for that thing will be a consecration of your womb, a likeness namely of the blameless Lamb that was offered up for the human race.' The cleric blessed water on her behalf once more and she became pregnant from that, and what she bore then was a silvered salmon. 'This has me ruined,' said she. 'Whatever you do, clerics, I'm the worse for it, seeing as these two births will be notorious among the men of Ireland and I've had no good at all out of this.' 'That won't be so,' said the cleric, 'because I'll take the silvered salmon and my insignia will be made out of it, and you will

---

1. 1 November, the great Celtic and Christian feast of the dead.
2. Modern Teltown, County Meath.
3. 1 August, a feast named for the god Lug.
4. Alias Diarmait mac Cerbaill (d. 565).
5. Ancestor of Uí Duach of Ossory, in modern County Kilkenny.
6. Reading *Bíaid ocum* for *Bíaid ocut*.

7. Corresponds roughly to the modern barony of Kilmaine, County Mayo.
8. Ancestor of the Clann Cholmáin kings of Brega, d. 555–8.
9. Possibly in Cúl Tolad.
10. Ancestor of the Caílle Follamain kings of Brega, d. 587.
11. A late sixth-century Uí Néill saint; Mag Bile is modern Moville, County Down.
12. An Uí Néill saint; d. 589 or 595.

bear a son as a result. And he will surpass his brothers and more kings descended from him will rule Ireland than from the other sons.' 'I'm happy with that,' said Mugain, 'provided that what you say can be put into effect for me.' 'Let it be done!' said the cleric.

After that, Finnian performed the blessing of the queen and of the seed that would be born of her. And he placed water into his cup and he gave it to the queen and she drank, and washed out of it. The queen became pregnant through this, and she bore a son and that was Áed Sláine. Good indeed was the child that was born there, namely, Áed Sláine, and good are his offspring, that is, the men of Brega, as regards generosity, glory, honour, toughness, *cáin*-laws, supremacy, rectitude, heroism, brilliancy, church-orders, hospitallership, compassionateness, customs, practice, pride, fame, boastfulness, warmth, handsomeness, sense, understanding, dignity, goodness and cheer. For the seed of Áed Sláine ruling the Plain of Brega were 'the rod of gold atop the board of *findruine*'.[13] For every good thing, even the most grandly organized great household, it is to that of Áed Sláine that it is compared.

13. An amalgam, possibly of gold or silver, with bronze.

from:
THE BIRTH OF ÁEDÁN
MAC GABRÁIN
(*c.* 1100)

[These quatrains are from a syllabic poem in almost perfect *deibhidhe* metre, written *c.* 1100. Its graceful expression and form support the image of the two main protagonists gracefully acceding to the patrilineal order. They are the wives of the kings of Scotland and Leinster, and they each give birth to twins. Modern readers will be alert to the downgrading of female offspring but the positive representation of relations between the sons who, in this case, are uterine brothers may have been of greater moment for the medieval audience. Since they had different fathers, uterine brothers were not usually in competition for the same succession. The relationship is frequently invoked to thematize solidarity between men of different agnatic lines.

The legend that the historical Áedán son of Gabrán, King of Scotland (d. 606), and Brandub son of Eochu,

King of Leinster (d. 605), were twins is found in other sources also. The basis for it is unknown. In the course of the struggle for the kingship of Leinster, Eochu may have been forced to take refuge in Scotland and may have allied himself there with Gabrán. If so, perhaps both men's sons were born in Scotland around the same time and were fostered together. The poem was edited and translated by M.A. O'Brien: 'A Middle-Irish Poem on the Birth of Áedán mac Gabráin and Brandub mac Echach', *Ériu*, vol. 16 (1952), pp. 157–70. Apart from minor changes in presentation, this excerpt is as found there, at pp. 162–70 (quatrains 17–53).]

Maith in ben ben Echach féil;
Eochu nír duine dochéil[l],
ro-s-fuc co tech nGabráin géir
ara ragrád hi rochéin.

Ropo cheist la Gabrán ngel
la ríg nAlban na n-órmed;
acco nír cheiled in chned
ná beired macco a mórben.

Rí Alban álaind a graig
ro char ríg Liphi línmair,
cumthanas nár thana thair
do-rala eter na rígnaib.

Dona romnáib do-rala
a toirrched cen tirbada;
na mná cen tóebhuail tana
ros-lá i n-óenhuair n-inbada.

Do-chuaid-sium ar sluaged sel
Gabrán ria ngasraid Goídel —
ar chrechaib nír cheis in fer —
ruc leis Echaid na n-oíged.

Dar héis na fer ic Foirthe —
cia caingen bad cháems[h]oirthe? —
na mná cen chosaít chaidche
a n-osaít i n-óenaidche.

Dá mac robo mó fo nim
ruc ben Echach in Inbir;
ruc — gním cen fharddal a fhir —
ben ríg Alban dá hingin.

Cethrur dóib — derb ind áirim —
dias brónach, dias bithfháilid,
dias tuí na cích nár cháinid
dí mnuí fríth co[a] fritháilim.

Fáilid ben Echach Enaig
ria maccaib cen minmebail;
brónach ben Gabráin gregaig
hic amrán dia hingenaib.

[. . .]
ro mnaí Echach co n-attain
'beir ingin latt ocus laig
is tuc dam mac dot maccaib.'

'Maith na beimmis ar ndís de,
a ben Echach na huaille,
mac is ingen cechtar de
dia nertad imned huainne.'

'Mad ferr de dait ocus dam
guth Feideilmthe ro fírad,
cobair fo-géba co glan
béra rogain, a rígan.'

Do-rat comartha, ní chél,
inna mac find dar fin[n]én;
tuc gráinne d'ór na nGall ngér
cen brón fo barr a s[h]linnén.

Ro-lá huaide a mac co mer
do mnaí Gabráin na ngemel;
ro gab ingin mbuain a ben
co ngruaid tibrig cen temel.

Do-ruacht rí Alban na n-ech
iar snaidm ríge ocus rochrech
co cnis béoda, déoda an drech,
d'fhis na séola co soichlech.

'Gairmther mo druíd co ndaithe,'
ar Gabrán na gargmaiche,
'cacrad na macco maithi
aprad inbat arddfhlaithe.'

'hEirged in fer gráid cen geis,'
ar in druí óg cen aitheis;
'cen ocla nos-légad leis
dénad co brotla in mbaitheis.'

'Baistiter na meic immuich,
a rí Monaid in marggaid;
gébait ríge nglébind nglain
for hÉrind is for Albain.'

'Emain na meic hút, a f[h]ir,'
ar in druí ó Dún hInbeir;

'a mná, nábad mebul lib,
is hemun in dá hingein.

Nír báeth in druí, dar mo dán,
d'fhir dia n-adair ní radráb;
nír sluind in cairddes cen chrád
acht don gargdes do Gabrán.

'Rí bas ferr, a Gabráin glain,
ní ragaib Albain áthaich;
allud ar hú Da-thí thair
bid rí Brandub a bráthair.'

Ro gab Eochu triall dia thich
a llurg ríg Alban airig;
airm cen chammud 'na deis dil,
ruc leis Brandub dia bailib.

For-fhácaib Áedán inn óir
i nAlbain na corn comóil;
i nAlbain dár cáemán c[h]óir
nochorb Áedán cen honóir.

Ní fitir Áed amnas án
ro gab Albain na n-argán —
ro chind sain ar cach sluag slán —
nach huad ro chin á Gabrán.

Ro-ngairm ben Gabráin co glan
ro innis d'Áed co hidan
tráth buí hic héc — is éol dam —
náro fét acht cóe a cinad.

'Gabrán ro gab giallo Gall
ainm th'aite, a Áedáin Arann,
a s[h]eisse na tuinne thall,
meisse do muimmi, a m'anam.'

'Do máthair a Cruachain cháem
do chlaind Da-thí cen tatháer
athair Branduib roba baíd
t'athair do chlannaib Catháer.'

In comrád-sin cen chur de
cuman ra hÁedán nÍle;
tánic for eoch luath ille
d'acallaim tuath a thíre.

Tánic hi Laignib cen lag
d'acallaim meic a máthar,
in drech ro mannair cach mag,
co tech mBranduib a bráthar.

Ro báe a máthair féin hi fus
ar cind in meicc ro molus,
maith do chaicill chliar is chros,
ro-s-aicill tiar don tirus.

Co tech Feideilme finne
tánic dar druim ndílinne;
don chais co mbriathraibh binne
ro iarfaig frais firinne.

'Eochu th'athair, ard a graig,
ocus Brandub do bráthair;
dar in leicc is treisse thair
is meisse, a meic, do máthair.'

'Ro bá co cenn noí mís mór,
a rí Forthe na fledól,
ar óen is Brandub cen brón
cen for mandur im medón.'

Fuair ann Feidelm na fodla
in gráinne d'ór olorda
tuc i nÁed a hÁth Gabla
cáem la cách in comarda.

'Méraid co lá brátha bil
for nós, a Áedáin fhailgich,
ní dam is rádbraisse rib
bid lánmaisse do Laignib.'

Cid maith do mnáib is d'fheraib
sluaig Gálián ór geinsebair;
róit for n-ech seng co Slemain
ferr fo chóic d'Uíb Ceindselaig.'

Áedán is Brandub co mblad
ó Laignib noco látar;
for Albain na ngarda nglan
is for Banba ro bátar.

TRANSLATION

Generous Eochu's wife was a goodly woman and Eochu being wise took her far away with him to the vigorous Gabrán on account of his great love for her.

Bright Gabrán king of Alba of the gold lances had one source of grief which they never concealed, namely, that his wonderful wife never gave birth to boys.

The king of Alba whose steeds were fine grew to love the king of Liphe[1] of the hosts; between the two queens there grew up a deep friendship over in Alba.

Both noble women had become pregnant without hindrance and both without even a slight cry of pain were brought to bed at the same time.

Gabrán at the head of his band of Goídil[2] went on an expedition — he never complained of having to make raids — and took with him hospitable Eochu.

The women left behind by their husbands at Forth[3] and still without any complaining were both brought to bed on the same night, what could be more propitious?

The wife of Eochu of the Inver[4] gave birth to two fine boys; the wife of the king of Alba bore two daughters — no errant deed — O man.

Four there were — certain the count — two sad and two joyful; two others silent with blameless breasts, the two women who had been procured to attend them.

Joyful was the wife of Eochu of Enach[5] at the sight of her sons without the slightest deceit; sorrowful was the wife of Gabrán of the steeds while singing to her daughters.

...[6] to the wife of Eochu, 'Take one of my daughters and lie down, and give me one of your sons.

'We should both be all the better in consequence, O wife of proud Eochu, each of us with a son and daughter to drive away our worries.'

1. The plain in Leinster through which the River Liffey flows.
2. i.e. the Gaels.
3. North of Edinburgh, in Scotland.
4. Probably Inber Domnann, near Arklow, County Wicklow.
5. Presumably in Leinster.
6. Words lost from MS; perhaps 'The wife of Gabrán said'.

'If it be better for you and me, Feidlimid's[7] prophecy has been fulfilled, you shall be comforted and shall take your choice, O queen.'

She put a mark in her son fairer than '*finnén*'[8] — I shall not conceal it — namely, a grain of gold of the furious foreigners under the top of his shoulder blade.

Quickly she handed over her son to the wife of Gabrán who held many hostages and took in exchange a vigorous girl with bright smiling cheek.

Having united kingdoms and made great raids, the kings of Alba of the steeds returned safely with lively cheeks — to inquire concerning the birth.

'Let my druid be quickly called,' said Gabrán of the rude fields, 'let him consider the goodly youths, and let him say whether they will be supreme rulers.'

'Let the priest proceed with lucky omen,' said the blameless learned druid, 'let him read the service calmly and let him perform the baptism speedily.

'Let the youths be baptized outside, O king of Monad[9] of the market, they will be famous kings of Ireland and Alba.

'Those boys, O king, are twins,' said the druid from Dún Inbir,[10] 'and, you women, let it not cause you shame, these two girls are also twins.'

Not foolish was the druid, by my art, though I shall not worship the god he does; he only revealed the relationship (of the children) to fierce beautiful Gabrán.

'A better king, O pure Gabrán, has never ruled Alba of the fords, the descendant of Dathí[11] will be famous in Alba and Brandub his brother will also be king.'

Eochu set out for his home in the track of the noble king of Alba; bearing in his right hand his weapons that had never been bent he brought Brandub to his own land.

He left Áedán of the gold in Alba the land of the feast goblets; our dear young friend Áedán was not without honour there.

Áedán, noble and fierce, who seized Alba of the organs and excelled every vigorous host did not know that he was not the son of Gabrán.

With honest intent Gabrán's wife when dying — I know it well — and was only able to bemoan her sin, called him to her and truthfully revealed the whole thing to Áedán.

'O Áedán of Arann,[12] O comrade of the eastern wave, Gabrán who has taken the hostages of the foreigners is only your fosterfather, and I, my dear one, am only your fostermother.

'Your real mother is from fair Cruachain[13] of the race of blameless Dathí, your real father is of the children of Cathaír[14] and is also the father of loving Brandub.'

Áedán of Íle[15] keeps this conversation well in mind; he comes over from Scotland on a swift steed to have converse with the peoples of his land.

To Leinster he who spoiled every plain came without delay (?) to have speech with his mother's son, to the house of Brandub his brother.

His real mother good at cherishing clergy and crosses was here to meet the son I have praised; he addressed her here in Ireland after his journey.

To the house of fair-haired Fedelm he comes over the sea's ridge; of the curly-haired woman

---

7. Fedelm's father was called Feidlimid.
8. Literally, 'little white one'; used of shields (perhaps from practice of whitening them).
9. The Mounth, extending from Ben Nevis to the head of the River Dee, in Scotland.
10. Unidentified.
11. A legendary King of Connacht from whom the twins' mother was descended.
12. In the Firth of Clyde.
13. Royal capital of Connacht, where Dathí is supposedly buried.
14. A legendary King of Leinster.
15. Islay off west coast of Scotland.

with musical words he demands the whole[16] truth.

'Eochu whose steeds are noble is your father, and Brandub is your brother; by the most potent flagstone[17] in Scotland I swear I am, O son, your mother.

'For nine long months, you and fortunate Brandub, O king of Forth of the carousals, were together in my womb without any harm having been done to you.'

Generous Fedelm found the bright grain of gold which she had put in Áed from Áth Gabla.[18] Everyone deemed it a fair sign.

'Your fame, O Áedán of the rings, will abide to the good day of Doom; what I say to you is no vain boasting, it will be a full ornament for the Laigin.[19]

'Though good for men and women are the hosts of the Gáiléoin[20] from whom you are descended, better five times for the Uí Cheindselaig[21] are the tracks of your slender steeds extending as far as Slemain.'[22]

Áedán and far-famed Brandub are being kept[23] amongst the Laigin; they ruled, the one over Alba of the pleasant enclosure, the other over Leinster.

16. M.A. O'Brien's note: Lit. 'a shower of'.
17. Perhaps a reference to the coronation stone of the kings of Scotland.
18. Unidentified.
19. The people of Leinster.
20. A term for the people of Leinster.
21. A Leinster dynasty.
22. Probably Slane (Slemain Mide), County Westmeath, close to the Connacht border.
23. i.e. 'their memory is preserved'.

GORMLAITH, WIFE OF BRÍAN BÓRUMA
(12th, 13th century)

[Gormlaith daughter of Murchad mac Finn, a Leinster King of the Uí Fháeláin line (around Naas, County Kildare), was the consort of three outstanding kings. The

third of these, Brían Bóruma, became legendary as the deliverer of the Irish from foreign oppression, while Gormlaith's story illustrated the threat posed by women, ever liable to have relations with the country's enemies.

Gormlaith found a place in literature when — and probably because — her descendants had become historically unimportant. Her first husband was the Viking Amlaíb Cúarán (alias Óláfr Sigtryggson, d. 981), ruler of Dublin and one-time ruler of York, by whom Gormlaith had Sitriuc Silkenbeard, probably in the 970s. The second was Máel Sechnaill mac Domnaill (d. 1022), Ireland's pre-eminent ruler as King of Tara, from 980 until 1002, when he was forced to submit to Brían Bóruma. This led to the acceptance of Brían as King of Ireland. Brían's meteoric rise, his long and very successful career and the historiography produced by his descendants, earned him his reputation as one of Ireland's greatest kings. It is likely that Gormlaith was wife to Máel Sechnaill in the early 980s, and became Brían's wife some few years later. Apparently this third marriage had ended by the early 990s. Gormlaith also had sons by Máel Sechnaill and Brían, named, respectively, Conchobar and Donnchad. She outlived her three husbands, dying in 1030. Her highest accolade in the contemporary annals is the title 'Queen of Munster', hers by right of having been Brían's consort while he was king of that province. Yet the first two texts excerpted here represent her as wholly inimical to him. How should these accounts be regarded? There is no evidence to counter the suspicion that they are entirely fictive.

Gormlaith is nowhere given credit for the fact that her son Donnchad (by Brían) supported Brían in the campaign which ended at Clontarf. Her son Conchobar (by Máel Sechnaill) is not recorded as having been immediately involved. Her notoriety derives from inciting her brother, Murchad, and her son, Sitriuc Silkenbeard (then aged around forty), to fight against Brían at Clontarf. The first of the three excerpts below derives from *Cogadh Gaedhel re Gallaibh* (The Wars of the Gaedhil with the Gaill), written in the first decade of the twelfth century or thereabouts. This work, more historical saga than history, is concerned to show how Brían and his kinsmen saved Ireland from Viking oppression. The Battle of Clontarf is presented as the culmination of a national struggle against the Viking enemy — the Foreigners. This is a false view of history: Clontarf was part of an internal struggle for sovereignty. Leinster was in revolt against the dominance of Brían, and the Dublin Vikings were necessary allies if the province was to re-assert its independence.

The text was written during the reign of Muirchertach Úa Bríain (d. 1119), great-grandson of Brían and aspirant King of Ireland. He was not a descendant of Gormlaith's; in fact, her descendants played no part in dynastic power-struggles beyond the first generation, and her line was by now an excluded segment. Donnchadh Ó Corráin has made the plausible suggestion that the text was inspired by the westward enterprise of Magnus Barelegs, King of Norway, in 1098. He exerted his authority over the Orkneys, the Hebrides, Man and other places in the Irish Sea littoral, and may have alarmed Muirchertach's party into producing a text which asserted its power, particularly over Dublin, and suppressed any tendencies there might have been in the Viking element there to accept Magnus Barelegs as suzerain. With the benefit of hindsight, the Leinsterfolk are taught the folly of abandoning Úa Bríain rule for the 'Foreigner'. Gormlaith, the Leinster princess who took the enemy's part and whose descendants are no longer of any importance to the Uí Bríain, aptly illustrates the lesson. The incident described in the excerpt supposedly occurred in 1013. The implication that Gormlaith was at Brían's home-base at Kincora, County Clare, so long after her marriage gives the account an added air of untruth. (Donnchadh Ó Corráin, 'Viking Ireland — Afterthoughts', in *Ireland and Scandinavia in the Early Viking Age*, eds. H.B. Clarke, M. Ní Mhaonaigh and Raghnall Ó Floinn (Dublin: Four Courts Press, 1998), pp. 421–52).

The second excerpt is from the Old Norse *Njáls saga*, written between *c.* 1250 and *c.* 1280. Underlying this is an earlier text, usually titled *Bryáns saga*. This seems to have been written not in Iceland but in Ireland, possibly in Dublin, by someone who had an accurate knowledge of contemporary politics. Donnchadh Ó Corráin argued that *Bryáns saga* was composed in almost immediate response to *Cogadh Gaedhel re Gallaibh*, as a declaration of loyalty by the Dubliners to the Uí Bríain (*art. cit.*). *Bryáns saga* lays the blame for Clontarf and Brían's death almost exclusively on the 'Foreigners' from the Orkneys, the Hebrides and Man — and on Gormlaith (Kormlod), whose guilt in recruiting them serves to exculpate the Dubliners. The author distances her from the Uí Bríain by claiming — wrongly — that she was not the mother of any of Brían's sons. She is a monotype of evil, 'utterly wicked'; therefore, although she is a Leinster princess, she alone of the province bears responsibility for her actions.

In striking contrast, the final item, which derives from genealogical material in the twelfth-century Book of Leinster, suggests that Gormlaith was highly regarded in her home province, not least because of her marriage to Brían. At the time of their making, her three alliances would have served a political purpose for Leinster. Perhaps the 'three leaps' originally signified the quickening of her sons in the womb, and not shifts to ever more powerful partners. In support of this, we may note that the same figure is applied to a much earlier Leinster royal named Cúach, whose 'three leaps' were the three sons she bore to the one man, named Dúnlang, eponym of the Uí Dúnlainge dynasty.

This item may date from the same period as the previous two. The later occlusion of Gormlaith's line seems to be inscribed in the text: the most likely explanation for the author's 'conferral' of the kingship of

Ireland on Gormlaith is that he knew that none of her sons had attained to it. Of course, Gormlaith was Brían's consort only while he was King of Munster. He and Gormlaith had separated long before he became King of Ireland, and so the author is dwelling on what might have been, rather than on what eventuated. The account of a mother dreaming of her daughter's future greatness and the reference to the legal judgement made on foot of an *aisling* are remarkable, and perhaps unique in Irish sources.

The first excerpt is translated from: Anne O'Sullivan (ed.), *The Book of Leinster*, 6 vols (Dublin: Dublin Institute for Advanced Studies, 1954–83 [1983]), vol. 6, pp. 1462–3 (lines 44,258–44,276). The second is taken from: Magnus Magnusson and Hermann Pálsson, *Njal's Saga* (Harmondsworth, Middlesex: Penguin Books), pp. 342, 344. The third is translated from: J.H. Todd (ed. and trans), *Cogadh Gaedhel re Gallaibh. The Wars of the Gaedhil with the Gaill* (London: Longmans, Green, Reader, and Dyer, 1867), p. 143.]

(i)

Afterwards Máelmórda[1] son of Murchad, King of Leinster, set out to convey three masts of pine from the wood of Fid Gaible[2] to Brían at Kincora,[3] that is, a mast from the Uí Fhailge[4] and a mast from the Uí Fháeláin and a mast from the Uí Muiredaig.[5] And a dispute arose among them while they were ascending a boggy mountain, and the king himself — Máelmórda — put his shoulder to the Uí Fháeláin mast, and a silk tunic with a gold fringe and silver buttons which Brían had given to him sometime before, that is what he was wearing, and one of the buttons broke from the exertion. Now when they had reached Kincora, the king took off his tunic and it was brought to his sister to have a silver button put in it, that is, to Gormlaith daughter of Murchad, Brían's wife, and she was the mother of Donnchad son of Brían. The queen seized the tunic and cast it into the fire, and she began to reproach her brother and to incite him, for she hated to yield service and bondage to anyone or to suffer oppression, or that he should yield what his father and grandfather had not yielded. And she said that Brían's son would demand the same from his son.

1. Gormlaith's brother.
2. Between Rathangan and Edenderry, County Offaly.
3. Beside Killaloe, County Clare.
4. Leinster sept in area now in counties Laois and Offaly.
5. Leinster sept in area now partly in County Wicklow.

(ii)

[Kormlod] was endowed with great beauty and all those attributes which were outside her own control, but it is said that in all the characteristics for which she herself was responsible, she was utterly wicked. She had been married to a king called Brian, but now they were divorced. He was the noblest of all kings, and lived in Kincora in Ireland . . . Kormlod was not the mother of King Brian's sons. She was so filled with hate against him after their divorce that she wished him dead. King Brian would always forgive men he had sentenced to outlawry, even when they committed the same offence thrice; but if they transgressed yet again, he let the law take its course. From this it can be judged what kind of a king he was.

Kormlod kept urging her son Sigtrygg to kill King Brian. For that purpose she sent him to Earl Sigurd to ask for support. King Sigtrygg arrived in Orkney before Christmas . . . King Sigtrygg then raised the matter of his mission to Earl Sigurd, and asked him to go to war with him against King Brian. The earl was stubborn for a long time. Finally he agreed, but only on condition that he should marry Sigtrygg's mother, Kormlod, and become King of Ireland if they defeated Brian. All his men urged him against the expedition, but without success. When they parted, Earl Sigurd had promised to take part in the expedition, and King Sigtrygg had promised him his mother and the kingdom. It was agreed that Earl Sigurd should come with all his army to Dublin on Palm Sunday. Sigtrygg sailed south to Ireland and told his mother that the earl had joined forces with them, and told her what he himself had committed them to. She was pleased at this, but said that they would have to amass an even larger force. Sigtrygg asked where they could expect to get that.

Kormlod replied, 'There are two Vikings lying off the Isle of Man with thirty ships, and they are so formidable that no one can withstand them. They are called Ospak and Brodir. Go and meet them, and spare nothing to induce them to join you, whatever conditions they demand.'

King Sigtrygg went in search of the Vikings and found them off Man. He stated the purpose of his visit at once, but Brodir refused to have anything to do with the scheme until Sigtrygg promised him the kingdom and his mother. This was to be kept quite secret, to prevent Earl Sigurd from hearing of it. Brodir was to come to Dublin before Palm Sunday. Sigtrygg went back home and told his mother.

(iii)

The four sons of Murchad mac Finn: Fáelán Senior and Máel Mórda and Muiredach . . . And Máel Carmain (son of the female slave). And Gormlaith wife of Brian. She is the one who leapt the three leaps of which was said:

> Three leaps did Gormlaith make —
> we'll not see the like again —
> a leap in Dublin, a leap in Tara,
> a leap in Cashel, topmost plain!

Amlaíb Cúarán was her husband and, after a time, Máel Sechnaill son of Domnall, and Brían.

It is the mother of Gormlaith daughter of Murchad who saw in an *aisling* that she would sleep with the King of Leinster and that she would bear him a son and that he would take the kingship of Leinster. And that she would bear a daughter to the same king and that she would take the kingship of Ireland. Those two are Máelmórda and Gormlaith. And it is on that account that the over-king of Leinster, namely Murchad, took her by lawful arrangement from the kings of the other provinces who were soliciting her. As regards the mother, she was the daughter of the King of Connacht. These, then, are the judges who gave that judgment: Éicnechán and Bladmasán and Brígán and Mac-Cinad.

from:
CAITHRÉIM CHEALLACHÁIN CHAISIL
(The Victorious Career of Cellachán of Cashel)
(*c.* 1127)

[The perennial allure of women which can undo the most stalwart rulers is intensified in the case of foreign women — the extravagantly Other — such as the attractive Viking women below. King Cellachán (d. 954) belonged to the

Eóganachta, who had long dominated the kingship of Cashel. His lineal descendants were the Meic Carthaig (MacCarthys), and the text was probably written during the reign of Cormac Mac Carthaig, King of Munster between 1127 and 1134. The text, by glorifying Cellachán, gave the Meic Carthaig a history that justified their rise to power. Cormac's rule was apparently accepted by the Uí Bríain of Dál Cais as well as the Eóganachta, and this is reflected in the fact that Cellachán is portrayed below as sharing the booty of foreign women with Cormac's ancestor, Donnchúan son of Cennétig.

The text begins by describing Cellachán's circuit of Munster, during which he has many victorious encounters with the Vikings (the Lochlannachs). His greatness proven, he becomes King of Munster, but then falls victim to a Viking plot: he is lured to Dublin by the promise of Bébinn, daughter of Turgesius (Turgeis), a legendary super-Viking. Before entering Dublin, he is warned of impending danger by Mór, 'daughter of the king of the Islands of the Foreigners', the wife of Sitriuc son of Turgesius. Later, however, the Vikings succeed in capturing Cellachán but he is rescued next by an alliance of the Eóganachta and the Dál Cais who ultimately defeat the Vikings. Cellachán and his allies march on Dublin, where he and Donnchúan reward themselves with their choice of Viking women. Apart from minor changes in presentation and the introduction of length-marks, the excerpts are as in Alexander Bugge (ed. and trans.), *Caithreim Cellachain Caisil: The Victorious Career of Cellachan of Cashel* (Christiana: J.Chr. Gendersens Bogtrykkeri, 1905), pp. 74–5, 113–4. The spelling has been normalized also in the title preceding this headnote.]

When Cellachán had made order in the districts and destroyed his enemies, the direction the Lochlannachs took was to Áth Cliath,[1] and they hold counsel there ... And that is what they decided, namely, to send messengers to Cellachán, and to promise him Bébinn, the daughter of Turgeis, and to tell him to go to Áth Cliath to marry her, and [to inform him] that they leave him the territory of Munster without contest.

The reason why they did this was the hope of capturing Cellachán and of killing those who accompanied him. They made known the plan that was formed in the bosom of the Lochlannachs to the king of Erin, viz. to Donnchad, son of Flann, king of Tara. For Cellachán had not consented to pay tax or tribute to him. The king of Erin agreed with this plan, and they sent messengers to Cellachán ...

That night there happened to be a discourse between Sitric, the son of Turgeis, and his wife. And his wife asked him why he gave his sister to Cellachán, as it was he who had destroyed the Lochlannachs. He answered that it was not out of kindness to him, but in order to capture himself and to slay his people. The woman arose early the next morning, and put a bond-maid's dress round her. For this discourse which she had heard was grievous to her as she herself greatly loved Cellachán. She left the town, and came upon the road where she supposed that the Munstermen would come. And as she stayed there she beheld Cellachán approaching, and the woman told the news to him. Cellachán asked her who she herself was. 'Mór, daughter of Áed, son of Echu, am I,' said the woman, 'daughter of the king of the Islands of the Foreigners (i.e. the Hebrides), and my husband is Sitric, son of Turgeis, of the Fair Lochlannachs. And I fell in love with you the day I saw you at Port Láirge.' ...[2]

Then[3] the men of Munster set out on their way and journey and expedition orderly, bravely, and prudently. They plundered each territory, and burned each fortress and town that they met on their straight way from Dundalk to Áth Cliath. There came a message before them to the royal town, and it was told to the women of the Norsemen that their husbands were slain, and that Cellachán was taken from them by force.

Then the wife of Tora, son of Turgeis, namely Mór, the daughter of Donnchad, said: 'I know,' said she, 'a plot that will result in the death of Cellachán and in the destruction of the Munstermen: let us even go to the summerhouse where Mór, the daughter of Áed, son of Echu, is, the woman who loves Cellachán, and tell her that Cellachán has perished, and that the Munstermen are slain, and she will die from grief for Cellachán, and he himself will die from grief for her, and the Munstermen will be routed, when he has died.' 'Let this be done,' said the women, and they told the young woman those tidings. 'It is not true for you, O women,' said Mór, 'and it would be better for you if that story were true. And it is certain that Cellachán would die, if I should die. But I get news of him every

---

1. i.e. Dublin.

2. i.e. Waterford.
3. i.e. after the Munstermen have rescued Cellachán and routed the Vikings.

night in my bed, and yet I am not his wife,' said the woman.

Then the van of the Munster army reached the town, and they collected the cows and cattle-droves of the town, and its gold, and silver, and many riches, and brought the women and young men of the town together. Mór, daughter of Áed, son of Echu, and Bébinn, the daughter of Turgeis, were brought to Cellachán, who said to Donnchúan, son of Cennétig, that he should take Bébinn to his wife. And so it was done by them, and each man of them likewise had his choice of women afterwards. They spent a week in arranging this. And as they went away they burned the town.

from:
THE SONG OF DERMOT AND THE EARL
(*c.* 1200–25)

[This, and the next excerpt, concern the abduction of Derbforgaill (Devorgilla), daughter of Murchad Úa Máil Shechnaill, King of Mide (Meath). 'Almost all the world's most notable catastrophes have been caused by women' was the response of Giraldus Cambrensis, one of her contemporaries. She has had negative press ever since.

Her abductor, Diarmait Mac Murchada (Dermot Mac Murrough), King of Leinster, was expelled from Ireland in 1166. On 1 August of that year, he set sail for Bristol with his wife, his daughter and a small band of supporters. Within a year, he had regained power, and Ireland was facing invasion from Britain by a group of people whose roots were in England, Wales, Northern France and the Low Countries, but who are commonly termed English in contemporary sources. The term most frequently used in modern times to describe their arrival in Ireland is the 'Norman Invasion'.

The political upheavals which occurred in the year preceding Diarmait's expulsion were the death of his most important ally, Muirchertach Mac Lochlainn of Cenél nEógain, the most powerful king in Ireland, the accession of the then inimical Ruaidrí Úa Conchobair, King of Connacht, in his place, and the harrying of Diarmait by his greatest enemy, Tigernán Úa Ruairc, King of Bréifne, who had joined forces with the Dublin Vikings and Diarmait's own rebellious vassals in Leinster. Defenceless, Diarmait sought out Henry II, swore fealty to him and agreed to hold his Leinster kingdom as a fief of the crown of England, once Henry's vassals had helped him regain it.

Diarmait must have given long consideration to this course of action, which, unsurprisingly, had far-reaching consequences for Ireland. The sources imply that he was not driven to it by the events of the preceding year alone. Twelfth- and thirteenth-century sources in Latin, French and Irish, in a most striking illustration of the importance of women to politics and political discourse, associate Diarmait's expulsion and the beginning of the invasion not with the recent political upheavals but with Diarmait's abduction, in 1152, of Derbforgaill, wife of Tigernán Úa Ruairc, Diarmait's arch-enemy. This is not to say that women such as Derbforgaill controlled the way in which politics were shaped by them; they were often mere puppets of others, particularly their own kinsmen, in their quest for power. The two most important sources for the history of the invasion charge Derbforgaill with varying degrees of responsibility for her abduction by Diarmait, initiating a tradition which blames her for the 'catastrophe' which befell Ireland. Extraordinarily, Derbforgaill was coeval with the writers of both sources, yet they are quite contradictory about her role and motives. The first source is the *chanson de geste* known as *The Song of Dermot and the Earl*, which dates from *c.* 1200–25 but is based on material supplied to the author by Morice Regan, Diarmait's friend and interpreter. Giraldus's history of the invasion, *Expugnatio Hibernica*, was written in 1189.

Both sources justify the invasion. The *Song*, by an anonymous Irish author, glorifies Diarmait and his allies for their part in it. It tells that Derbforgaill loved Diarmait and willingly made herself available to him — the romantic turn fits with the *chanson*-form. Far from censuring him for his unfeeling abuse of her, it implies that politics might be thought to justify a king's exploitation of high status women. Giraldus describes the invasion from the English point of view: that the Irish needed the conqueror's steadying rule was demonstrated by abductor and abductee. As Diarmait's 'burning with love' is consistent with his furious nature and as Derbforgaill is 'fickle' in her feelings for her husband (cf. below), so all the Irish are 'consistent only in their fickleness' (cf. p. 135 of the edition exerpted below).

The Irish annals show the abduction in a quite different light. An ongoing cause of hostility between Tigernán Úa Ruairc and Diarmait was their contention over the kingdom of Meath, sandwiched between Bréifne and Leinster. As Derbforgaill was Úa Ruairc's wife as well as the daughter of the King of Meath, to abduct her was to insult Úa Ruairc and simultaneously to stake a claim to her father's kingdom. Diarmait had the support of his over-king, Ruaidri Úa Conchobair, King of Connacht, in his struggle with Úa Ruairc over Meath. The Annals of Tigernach, the only contemporaneous account, offer what is very likely the most trustworthy version: in 1152 there was 'a hosting by Toirdelbach Húa Conchobair and by Diarmaid Mac Murchada against Tigernán Húa Ruairc ... And Diarmait Mac Murchada, king of Leinster, carried off from Mide *by force* the wife of Úa Ruairc, namely Derbforgaill daughter of Murchad, and her wealth'. In the following year, 'the daughter of Murchad Úa Máelechlainn returned again to Úa Ruairc *having escaped from the Leinster folk*' (my emphasis). The Annals of Clonmacnoise (a seventeenth-century English translation of an Irish text) relate that 'Dermott mcMurrough king of Leinster tooke the lady Dervorgill, daughter of . . . Morrogh o'Melaghlin, and wife of Tyernan o'Rourke, with her cattle with him, and kept her for a long space to satisfie his insatiable, carnall and adulterous lust, shee was procured and enduced thereunto by her unadvised brother Melaghlin for some abuses of her husband Tyernan don before'.

The words 'enduced thereunto' offer doubtful support for the argument that Derbforgaill was willingly abducted: they may derive from the translator and not the original annals, and the meaning of 'enduced' is ambiguous. Nevertheless, modern commentators have used them to shore up the case against Derbforgaill. Diarmait has been described as a great modernizer, progressive in church affairs, outward-looking and abreast of European trends, and at least one historian has implied that Derbforgaill would have found him more attractive than her husband, whose world was the small, inland kingdom of Bréifne. F.X. Martin interpreted the 'abuses of her husband Tyernan don before' to mean that 'she was apparently a battered wife' (*No Hero in the House: Diarmait Mac Murchada and the Coming of the Normans to Ireland. O'Donnell Lecture Delivered at University College Dublin, December, 1975* [Dublin: National University of Ireland, n.d.], p. 17). It is surely more credible that the abuses were inflicted by Tigernán Úa Ruairc on Derbforgaill's brother and perhaps on other kinsmen in Mide, possibly in the struggle for control over their kingdom, and were what led to her being 'procured' for abduction.

At any rate Úa Ruairc was seriously aggrieved: fourteen years later, when he and his allies invaded Diarmait's home territory, laid it waste and drove Diarmait into exile, they did so, according to the Annals of Tigernach, 'in order to take vengeance on him for Úa Ruairc's wife'. When Diarmait returned to Ireland in 1167, he was initially forced to submit to Ruaidrí Úa Conchobair and his allies; he then 'gave one hundred ounces of gold as a peace-offering to Úa Ruairc in atonement for his wife' (*s.a.* 1167). The level of compensation weakens further the case that Derbforgaill was party to her abduction.

The Song of Dermot and the Earl and the *Expugnatio* ignore completely the gap of fourteen years between the abduction in 1152 and Diarmait's expulsion in 1166. Thus, all three twelfth-century sources concur that Úa Ruairc harboured such a grudge that it caused Diarmait's expulsion fourteen years later, leading in turn to the invasion. In the meantime — within a year, in fact, of her abduction — Derbforgaill had been returned to her husband. There is no suggestion in the annals of resentment on his part towards her.

Apparently she continued to live with Úa Ruairc until his death in 1171, some time after which she retired to the Cistercian monastery at Mellifont where she died in 1193.

Derbforgaill's blameworthiness became fixed in history and literature. In his widely disseminated history of Ireland, *Forus Feasa ar Éirinn*, the Counter-Reformation scholar-priest Séathrún Céitinn stressed the reformist force of the invasion. It was in his interests to present Derbforgaill in that work more as a pro-active adulterer than as Mac Murchada's prey, since he invited the invaders in. Interestingly, his theological work on death, *Trí Bior-Ghaoithe an Bháis*, which is concerned more with contemporary morality than with history, holds Diarmait fully accountable for 'his abduction of the wife of Tighearnán Ó Ruairc which caused every hurt that he did to himself and to Ireland': cf. pp. 278–9. The idea of Derbforgaill's willingness was perpetrated by nineteenth-century writers, including John Quincy Adams, sixth President of the United States of America (1825–9) who, in 1832, published a long romantic narrative poem on Derbforgaill's 'elopement' as 'a moral tale . . . of a country sold to a foreign invader by the joint agency of violated marriage vows, unprincipled ambition, and religious imposture' (*Dermot Mac Morrogh; or, The Conquest of Ireland. An Historical Tale of the Twelfth Century in Four Cantos* [Boston: Carter and Hendee, 1832]). Lady Gregory's one act play, *Dervorgilla* (1907), set twenty years after the abduction, has the queen living out her years at Mellifont, full of remorse for the catastrophic violence that ensued from her lust. In Yeats's play *The Dreaming of the Bones* (1919), set at Corcomroe Abbey in County Clare in 1916, a young Republican who has fought in the Easter Rising refuses the adulterous couple the absolution and forgiveness that would bring them peace.

The following excerpt is from Goddard Henry Orpen (ed. and trans.), *The Song of Dermot and the Earl: An Old French Poem* (Oxford: Clarendon Press, 1892), pp. 2–11.]

Del rei dermod *vus* voil cont*er.*

En yrland, a icel ior,
Ni out reis de tel valur:
Asez esteit manans *e* richez,
Amale francs, hailes chiches.
Icil par vn poste
Aveit pr*is e* conqu*e*ste
Oneil *e* mithe p*ar* sa guerre,
Ostages menad en laynest*e*re:
O sei amenad okaruel,
Le fiz le rei de yriel.

Mes en leschoin iout vn reis,
Ororic out nu*n* en yrreis,
En tirbrun mist la hiduse,

Tere lede *e* boschaguse;
Mes ororic, li riche reis,
Femme aueit bele a celefeis,
La fille al rei malathlin,
A ki mithe esteit enclin;
Melathlin de mithe iert sire.
Ki la uerite *vus* ueut dire,
Icel esteit de truin
Del bon veil malathlin;
Estreit cil ert de linage
Malathlin al fier corage,
Fiz coleman, le riche reis,
Ke tant se*n*gnes *e* curteis.
De malathlin uoil lesser,
Del rei dermod voil cont*er*.

De leynest*er* reis dermod,
Ki cel dame tant amout,
De amer li fist bel semblant,
Mes nel ama tant ne q*u*ant,
Ne mes q*u*il uout a sun poer
La gra*n*t hunte, sil pout, ueng*er*
Que cil de lethcoin firent ia dis
A ces de lethunthe en son pais.
Li reis dermod souent manda
A la dame, q*u*il tant ama —
P*ar* bref *e* par messagers,
Souent fist li rei mander
Ke ele en fin p*ur* ueir esteit
La reigne del siecle q*u*il pl*us* ameit;
Si la requ*i*st m*u*lt souent
De fin amur cou*er*tement.
E la dame li ad mande
P*ar* vn messager priue
Que tut freit sa uolunte,
Al rei ke tant est p*re*ise
E si remande de richef
E par buche *e* par bref
Que pur lui uenit en tiel man*er*e
Od tut lost de leynest*er*e,
E par force *e* par guerre
Od lui la ramist tote la t*er*re;
Sauer al rei dermod freit
En q*u*el lui la prendreit
U ele serreit pr*i*uement,
Que prendre la pust q*u*itement:
En q*u*el lui en fin serreit
V q*u*ite prendre la pu*er*reit.

Li reis manda hastiueme*n*t
Par leynest*er*e tute sa gent

Que alui uiengent san de mure
De osseri *e* de leynest*er*e;
Si lur feisteit a tuz sauer
Vers lethcoin q*u*il uout aler
La hunte, sil pust, ueng*er*
Que cil firent iadis p*re*mer:
La hunte q*ue* cil firent iadis
En lethunthe, en son païs.

Icil uindrent deliuerement
P*ar* le rei com*m*andement.
Quant tuz furent assemblez,
Vers lethcoin su*n*t dreit tur*n*ez;
Nuit e ior errent auant
Riche e poure, petit e g*r*ant.
Que *vus* irrai pl*us* contant?
En tirbrun uint li reis uailla*n*t;
E la dame mande aueit
Al rei dermot v ele esteit,
Que il nemist od sa gent,
Si la prest deliuerement.
Li reis dermot meintenant
En la place uint errant
V la dame aueit mande
Quele serreit ap*re*ste.
En cele manere de*r*mot li reis
La dame p*r*ist acele feis.

Ororic forment se pleniout
P*ur* sa femme q*ue* p*er*du out:
Mes mut rendi bataille fere
A la gent de laynist*er*e.
Mes, seingn*ur*s, li re de*r*mot
La dame lores od sei menout,
De errer vnq*ue*s ne finat
De ci ke mi kencelath.
E la dame m*u*lt longement
Iloc estoit asoiorn mise,
Solu*m* la gent, en tel guise.

Ororic, m*u*lt dolusant,
Vers co*n*noth tendi tut bata*n*t;
Al rei de co*n*noth tut p*ar*cunte,
Forme*n*t se pleint de la hunte
Cu*m* li reis de leynist*er*e
Sur lui uint en tele manere,
Sa fe*m*me aforce sur lui p*r*ise,
A fernes lad asoiorn mise.
Al rei de co*n*noth de hu*n*tage
Forme*n*t se pleint del damage;
M*u*lt li requ*i*st ententiuement

De la meyne e de sa gent
Que lui feseit aprester
Ki sa hunte pout uenger.

TRANSLATION

About King Dermot I will tell you.

In Ireland, at this day,
There was no more worthy king:
Very rich and powerful he was;
He loved the generous, he hated the mean.
He by his power
Had taken and conquered
O'Neil[1] and Meath in his war;
Hostages he brought into Leinster:
He brought with him O'Carroll,[2]
The son of the king of Uriel.

Now in Leath-Cuinn[3] there was a king,
O'Rourke he was called in Irish,
In Tirbrun,[4] the barren, he dwelt,
A waste and woody land.
But O'Rourke, the rich king,
Had a beautiful wife at this time,
The daughter of King Melaghlin[5]
To whom Meath was subject.
Melaghlin was lord of Meath;
Whoever would tell you the truth,
She was of the stock
Of the good old Melaghlin;
He was sprung from the lineage
Of Melaghlin of the bold heart,
The son of Coleman,[6] the rich king,
Who was so well bred and courteous.
About Melaghlin I will leave off,
About King Dermot I will tell.

Dermot, king of Leinster,
Whom this lady loved so much,
Made pretence to her of loving,
While he did not love her at all,

But only wished to the utmost of his power
To avenge, if he could, the great shame
Which the men of Leath-Cuinn wrought of old
On the men of Leath-Mogha[7] in his territory.
King Dermot often sent word
To the lady whom he so loved —
By letter and by messenger,
Often did the king send word
That she was altogether, in truth,
The thing in the world he most loved:
Thus he besought her very often
For her true love covertly.
And the lady sent him word
By a secret messenger
That she would do all his will:
To the king who is so renowned
She returns answer again,
Both by word of mouth and by letter,
That he should come for her in such manner
With all the host of Leinster
And by force and by war
Should carry her away with him from the land;
That she would let King Dermot know
In what place he should take her
Where she would be in concealment,
That he might freely carry her off:
In what place, in short, she would be
Where he might freely carry her off.

The king summoned speedily
All his men throughout Leinster,
To come to him without delay
From Ossory[8] and from Leinster;
And he let them all know
That he wished to go against Leath-Cuinn,
To avenge, if he could, the shame
Which these men wrought of yore:
The shame which they had wrought of yore
In Leath-Mogha, in his territory.

Promptly they came
At the king's command.
When all were assembled,
Against Leath-Cuinn they turned straightaway;
Night and day they marched forward
Rich and poor, small and great.
Why should I go on telling you more?

1. Probably refers to the over-king of the Southern Uí Néill.
2. Úa Cerbaill was King of Airgialla (Uriel), a territory comprising the present counties Louth, Armagh and Monaghan.
3. English 'Conn's Half', i.e. the Northern Half of Ireland.
4. Irish Tír Briúin, the seat of Úa Ruairc, comprises the present counties Leitrim and Cavan.
5. More properly Murchad son of Máelechlainn, King of Mide (Meath), Derbforgaill's father.
6. A remote ancestor of Máelechlainn.
7. English 'Mog's Half', i.e. the Southern Half of Ireland.
8. Irish Osraige, co-extensive with modern diocese of Ossory, in counties Tipperary and Offaly.

Into Tirbrun came the valiant king.
Now the lady had sent word
To King Dermot where she was,
That he should come with his men
And promptly carry her off.
King Dermot immediately
Came marching to the place
Where the lady had sent word
That she would be ready.
In this way Dermot the king
Carried off the lady at this time.

O'Rourke bitterly complained
For his wife whom he had lost;
While he offered very fierce battle
To the men of Leinster.
But, my lords, King Dermot
Then brought the lady away with him,
Nor ever ceased marching
From thence to the midst of Hy-Kinsellagh.[9]

And the lady for a good long time
Was there, as people say:
At Ferns[10] she was placed for her abode,
As people say, in this manner.

O'Rourke, much grieving,
To Connaught went in all haste.
To the king of Connaught he relates all;
Bitterly he complains of the shame,
How the king of Leinster
Came upon him in such manner,
Took his wife by force from him,
And placed her at Ferns for her abode.
To the king of Connaught of the outrage
Bitterly he complains, and of the injury:
Very earnestly he besought him
To make ready for him
Some of his household and of his men
So that he could avenge his shame.

9. Irish Uí Cheinnselaig, co-extensive with modern diocese of Ferns, in south Leinster — Diarmait's home territory.

10. County Wexford.

GIRALDUS CAMBRENSIS (GERALD OF WALES)

(c. 1146–1223)

from:
EXPUGNATIO HIBERNICA
(The Conquest of Ireland)
(1189)

[From A.B. Scott and F.X. Martin (ed. and trans.), *Expugnatio Hibernica: The Conquest of Ireland by Giraldus Cambrensis* (Dublin: Royal Irish Academy, 1978), pp. 25–7, 29. For details, see preceding headnote.]

Diarmait Mac Murchada, prince of Leinster and ruler of that fifth part of Ireland, held in our time the eastern seaboard of the island adjacent to Great Britain, with only the sea separating the two. From his earliest youth and his first taking on the kingship he oppressed his nobles, and raged against the chief men of his kingdom with a tyranny grievous and impossible to bear. There was another unfortunate factor. On an occasion when Ua Ruairc king of Meath had gone off on an expedition to far distant parts, his wife, Ua Máelechlainn's daughter, whom he had left on an island in Meath, was abducted by the aforesaid Diarmait, who had long been burning with love for her and took advantage of her husband's absence. No doubt she was abducted because she wanted to be and, since 'woman is always a fickle and inconstant creature',[1] she herself arranged that she should become the kidnapper's prize.

Almost all the world's most notable catastrophes have been caused by women, witness Mark Antony and Troy. King Ua Ruairc was stirred to extreme anger on two counts, of which however the disgrace, rather than the loss of his

1. The saying in Latin is 'Varium et mutabile semper femina'.

wife, grieved him more deeply, and he vented all the venom of his fury with a view to revenge. And so he called together and mustered his own forces and those of neighbouring peoples, and roused to the same purpose Ruaidrí, prince of Connacht and at that time supreme ruler of all Ireland. The men of Leinster, seeing that their prince was now in a difficult position and surrounded on all sides by his enemies' forces, sought to pay him back, and recalled to mind injustices which they had long concealed and stored deep in their hearts. They made common cause with his enemies, and the men of rank among his people deserted Mac Murchada along with his good fortune. He saw that his forces were melting away on all sides and that he was now in desperate straits, for Fate had completely turned her back on him, and Fortune had withdrawn her favour. So after many fierce clashes with the enemy in which the odds were stacked against him, he finally trusted his life to the sea in flight, and so to speak had recourse to this last hope of saving himself . . .

Diarmait returned by way of Great Britain and, although very much honoured and weighed down by gifts, the evidence of the king's[2] generosity, he was much more elated by expectations aroused than by any concrete result. He travelled to the noble town of Bristol and spent some time there, supported in fitting style at the public expense, in expectation of the chance visit of ships which, coming from Ireland, had often in the past berthed in that port. For he was eager to learn from these the state of affairs in his country and among his own people. And when he had often caused the king's letter to be read in the hearing of many there, and had made many promises of money and lands to many people, all to no purpose, at last earl Richard lord of Strigoil, son of earl Gilbert, came to speak with him. On that occasion they got so far in their conversation as to give firm undertakings, the earl that he would help in restoring Diarmait the following spring, and Diarmait that he would give his eldest daughter[3] to the earl in marriage, together with succession to his kingdom.

2. i.e. Henry II.
3. i.e. Aife (modern 'Aoife', traditionally anglicized 'Eva'), Diarmait's daughter by his wife, Mór.

B. Natural and Unnatural Women

ANONYMOUS

AD-MUINIUR SECHT nINGENA TRETHAN
(I Invoke the Seven Daughters of the Sea)
(8th century)

[The dual aspects of female supernatural power — to protect and destroy — are well illustrated here. It is difficult to say for certain whether the Christian elements in this lorica are intrinsic or accretions. The word *trethan* in the first line means 'sea' but also 'fury'. Although there is no supporting evidence, it is tempting to see a reference here to a heptad of Furies. Prefacing the lorica is the comment: 'May Fer Fio's cry protect me on the way, as I make my circuit of the Plain of Life' (passsage through this world is often figured as a journey across a plain). The annals record the death of Fer Fio mac Fabri, Sage (*Sapiens*), and Abbot of Conry, County Meath, under the year 762. As the name Fer Fio is unusual, there is a reasonable chance that he was the author of the lorica as we have it.

Text and translation: P.L. Henry (ed. and trans.), *Dánta Ban: Poems of Irish Women, Early and Modern* (Cork: Mercier Press, 1991), pp. 38–41.]

Ad-muiniur secht n-ingena trethan
dolbtae snáithi macc n-áesmar.
Trí bás úaimm ro-ucaiter,
trí áes dom do-rataiter,
secht tonna tocaid dom do-ro-dáilter!
Ním chollet messe fom chúairt
i llúrig Lasréin cen léiniud!
Ní nassar mo chlú ar chel!
dom-í-áes;
ním thí bás comba sen!

Ad-muiniur m'Argetnia
nád bá nád bebe;
amser dom do-r-indnastar
findruini febe!
Ro orthar mo richt,
ro saerthar mo recht,
ro mórthar mo nert,
níp ellam mo lecht,
ním thí bás for fecht,
ro fírthar mo thecht!
Ním ragba nathair díchonn,
ná dorb dúrglass,
ná doel díchuinn!
Ním millither téol,
ná cuire ban,
ná cuire buiden!
Dom-í urchar n-aimsire
ó Ríg inna n-uile!

Ad-muiniur Senach sechtaimserach
con-altatar mná síde
for bruinnib búais.
Ní báitter mo shechtchaindel!
Am dún díthogail,
am ail anscuichthe,
am lia lógmar,
am sén sechtmaínech.
Roba chétach
cétbliadnach,
cach cét diib ar úair.

Cota-gaur cucum mo lessa;
ro bé rath in Spiurto Noíb formsa.
Domini est salus.
Christis est salus.
Super populum tuum, Domine, benedictio tua.

TRANSLATION

I invoke the seven daughters of the Sea
Who fashion the threads of the sons of long life.
May three deaths be removed from me,
Three lifetimes granted to me,
Seven waves of good fortune conferred on me!
May phantoms not harm me on my journey
In S. Laserian's corslet without hindrance!
May my name not be pledged in vain!
May old age not come to me!
May death not come to me until I am old!

I invoke my Silver Champion
Who dies not, who will not die;
May a time be granted to me
Of the excellence of white bronze!
May my form be arranged,
May my right be exalted,
May my strength be increased,
May my tomb not be readied,
May I not die on my journey,
May my return be confirmed!
May the headless serpent not seize me,
Nor the hard grey worm,
Nor the senseless chafer!
May no thief harm me,
Nor band of women,
Nor warrior band!
May increase of time not come to me
From the King of the Universe!

I invoke seven-cycled Senach[1]
Whom fairywomen suckled
On the paps of mystic lore.
May my seven candles not be quenched!
I am an invincible fortress,
I am an immoveable rock,
I am a precious stone,
I am the symbol of seven treasures.
May my wealth be in hundreds,
My years in hundreds,
Each hundred after the other!

My benefits I call to me:
The grace of the Holy Spirit be upon me!
Wholeness is the Lord's.
Wholeness is Christ's.
Bless, O Lord, Your people!

---

1. Unidentified.

from:
TECOSCA CORMAIC
(The Instructions of
King Cormac)
(*c.* 800)

[This torrent of invective derives from one of the so-called Irish 'wisdom texts', a genre characterized by a question-and-answer format in which an older man instructs a younger one, on the conduct and attitudes proper to his office. The younger man is often a prospective king, in which case the text may also be classified as a *Speculum Principum*, 'Mirror for Princes'. Cormac (mac Airt) is the ideal king and the Solomon of the Irish; Carbre is his son. While the following excerpt recalls passages in Proverbs, Ecclesiastes and Ecclesiasticus, content and expression are sufficiently distinctive to belie scriptural origin. The female sex *en masse* is targeted in an unstructured list of allegations leading to a disturbing conclusion that resists definition as a mere rhetorical posture. The lack of structure is a common feature of medieval anti-feminist texts, and the charges against women that are found here — pernicious surliness, greed and deceitfulness — predominate in that literature. The translation is from: Kuno Meyer (ed. and trans.), *The Instructions of King Cormac mac Airt*, Todd Lecture Series XV (Dublin: Hodges, Figgis, 1909), pp. 29–35.]

'O grandson of Conn, O Cormac,' said Carbre, 'how do you distinguish women?'

'Not hard to tell,' said Cormac. 'I distinguish them, but I make no difference among them.

They are crabbed as constant companions,
haughty when visited,
lewd when neglected,
silly counsellors,
greedy of increase,
they have tell-tale faces,
they are quarrelsome in company,
desirous of letting go,
greedy of gifts,
putting up with exaggeration,
hard and grasping,
steadfast in hate,
forgetful of love,
thirsting (?) for lust,
anxious for alliance,
accustomed to slander,
dishonest in an assembly,
stubborn in a quarrel,
not to be trusted with a secret,
ever intent on pilfering,
boisterous in their jealousy,
every ready for an excuse,
on the pursuit of folly,
quick to engage,
ready to pledge,
neglectful of earning,
ready to injure,
never ready to heal,
they check what they do not attain,
they betray what they do not save,
haughty when wooed,
slanderers of worth,
slow to make use of things,
scamping their work,
stiff when paying a visit,
disdainful of good men,
gloomy and stubborn,
forgetful of restraint,
mindful of strife,
feeble in a contest,
viragos in strife,
prodigal at a feast,
sorrowful in an ale-house,
sturdy in wrangling,
indolent of exertion,
tearful during music,
lustful in bed,
arrogant and disingenuous,
abettors of strife,
niggardly with food,
incredulous of speech,
rejecting wisdom,
vigorous of speech,
quick to revile,
tenacious in cohabitation,
setting themselves against comfort,
alive to discomfort,
indolent in gathering,
ever in the company of folly,
quick to promise,
harbouring evil thoughts,
eager to go into society,
sulky on a journey,
troublesome bedfellows,
deaf to instruction,
blind to good advice,
fatuous in society,
craving for delicacies,
small givers,
chary in their presents,

languid when being solicited,
exceeding all bounds when keeping others
    waiting,
shameless on visits,
tedious talkers,
persevering in lust,
close practitioners,
skilled in pleasure-seeking,
unskilled in obedience,
prattling . . .
dumb on useful matters,
eloquent on trifles,
painstaking about an elegant head-dress,
they utter what they do not perform,
they attempt what they do not finish,
they watch what they do not get,
they turn aside what they do not secure,
they vow what they do not make true,
they promise what they do not fulfil,
they separate what they do not redeem (?),
they destroy what they do not save,
they scatter what they do not gather,
they affirm what they cannot do,
they strive after what they do not effect,
they break up what they cannot collect,
they give away what they do not levy,
they lavish what they cannot husband . . .
happy he who does not yield to them,
they should be dreaded like fire,
they should be feared like wild beasts,
women are capricious beasts . . .
woe to him who humours them,
better to whip them than to humour them,
better to scourge them than to gladden them,
better to beat them than to coddle them,
better to smite them than to please them,
better to beware of them than to trust them,
better to trample upon them than to fondle
    them,
better to crush them than to cherish them —
he will have neither honour nor life nor fame
    who listens to bad women,' said Cormac
    to Carbre.
'They are waves that drown you,
they are fire that burns you,
they are two-edged weapons that cut you,
they are moths for sticking to one,
they are serpents for cunning,
they are darkness in light,
they are bad among the good,
they are worse among the bad.'

FINGAL RÓNÁIN
(The Kin-Slaying of Rónán)
(early 10th century)

[This fine tale is often described as a version of the Phaedra and Hippolytus tragedy but its naturalism marks it off from classical treatments of the theme. Phaedra's Irish congener lusts after her stepson not because the gods have so decreed but because his aged father, Rónán, the King of Leinster, is incapable of satisfying her. There is no fool like an old fool and none as quick to exploit him as Woman. The Irish Phaedra has no name of her own but is styled 'Echaid's daughter', 'whore', 'evil woman' and 'wanton woman'. Granted that wantonness is innate in her sex, her real crime is covetousness of the role of royal consort when she knows that marriage must bring shame to this king. Her family had betrothed her to his desirable son, Máel Fothartaig, and would still condone her eloping with him. She stays put, posing a threat to Rónán's honour, and to that of Máel Fothartaig.

Máel Fothartaig's dread of encountering her in person may seem puzzling in view of the incest taboo. Furthermore, he is no chaste devotee of Artemis, nervous of succumbing to his first opportunity for conquest. Why, then, does he refuse to meet her? As Thomas Charles-Edwards has argued, values in medieval society were upheld in large part by rituals of shaming, effected by the delivery of solemn statements in public, often before an audience or witnesses (see T.M. Charles-Edwards, 'Honour and Status in Some Irish and Welsh Prose Tales', *Ériu*, vol. 29 (1978), pp. 123–41). Máel Fothartaig dare not hear such a statement. Gaelic literature offers many examples of warriors who succumb to a woman's formal advances rather than invite disgrace (cf. Volume I, pp. 14–15). For Máel Fothartaig, however, the truly awful consequence of hearing out his stepmother's declaration may not be the threat posed to his own honour, but rather the exposé of the king's sham marriage, the publicization of his failure to satisfy his wife, a shame intolerable to so loyal a prince. Rónán's tragedy is that he answers his son's loyalty with *fingal*, 'kin-slaying'. This kind of murder was regarded as particularly heinous because the business of seeking retaliation was complicated by the fact that the agent's kin and the victim's kin were one and the same.

The story was first edited and translated by Kuno Meyer, and has been the subject of much commentary since then. Séamus Ó Néill based a modern drama on it: *Iníon Rí Dhún Sobhairche. Tragóid Trí Ghníomh* (Baile Átha Cliath: Sáirséal agus Dill, 1960). This new translation is based on the edition by David Greene (ed.), *Fingal Rónáin and Other Stories* (Dublin: Dublin Institute for Advanced Studies, 1975), pp. 3–11.]

A wonderful king reigned in Leinster, namely, Rónán son of Áed, and his consort was Eithne daughter of Cummascach son of Eógan of the Déisi of Munster. And she bore him a son, namely, Máel Fothartaig son of Rónán, the best youth that ever came of the Leinster folk. On his account they used to set out for meetings and camps and games and assemblies and fights and shooting matches. Máel Fothartaig was the desire of all their daughters and the darling of all their young women.

His mother died. Rónán was without a wife for a long time. 'Why don't you take a wife?' said his son. 'It would be better for you to have a wife.' 'I'm told,' said Rónán, 'that Echaid (that is, the King of Dunseverick in the North) has a lovely daughter.' 'But you're no husband for a young girl,' said the lad. 'Why won't you marry a settled woman?'

It was impossible to oppose him, and he went and slept with her in the North and brought her hither with him. Máel Fothartaig, however, went off on a circuit in south Leinster. She arrives from the North. 'Where's your son, Rónán?' said she, 'I'm told you have a fine son.' 'I have indeed,' said Rónán, 'the best there is in Leinster.' 'Then let him be summoned to me, so that he can receive me and receive my people and my treasures and my wealth.' 'He shall come indeed,' said Rónán. Later, he arrives and he gives her a great welcome. 'You shall have honour,' said the lad. 'Whatever we'll obtain of wealth and treasures will be yours in honour of Rónán.' 'It pleases me,' said she 'that you should act in my interest.'

She had a lovely young woman as her companion. She sent her to him forthwith to solicit him (that is, Máel Fothartaig). The young woman didn't dare to say it, lest Máel Fothartaig should kill her, and *she* threatened to cut her head off should she *not* say it. One time Máel Fothartaig was playing *fidchell*[1] with his two foster-brothers, Dond and Congal, the two sons of his foster-father; they used be with him constantly. The young woman went over to them and was playing *fidchell* with them. She used to try to say it, fail, and blush. The men noticed that. Máel Fothartaig went away from them.

'What do you wish to say?' said Congal to the woman. 'It's not me that wishes it,' said she, 'but Echaid's daughter, who'd like to have Máel Fothartaig as her lover.' 'Don't say it, woman!' said Congal. 'You'll be dead if Máel Fothartaig hears you. But I'll act in your own interest with him, if you wish.' The young woman tells that to her. 'I like it,' said she, 'for you'll dare to make the declaration once you've had an encounter with him; and act in my interest with him afterwards.'

That comes to pass. The young woman sleeps with him — that is, with Máel Fothartaig. 'Well, well!' said she,[2] 'you don't act on my behalf on this occasion! You prefer to have that man all to yourself. I'll have you killed then.' One day the woman turned to Máel Fothartaig, crying. 'What's upsetting you, woman?' said he. 'That Echaid's daughter is threatening to kill me,' said she, 'because I don't act in her interest with you, so that she may lie with you.' 'Likely true,' said he. 'It was no mistake on your part,' said he, 'that you took protection. If I were thrust three times into a burning pyre so that I became dust and ashes, I still wouldn't have an encounter with Rónán's wife, even if that should protect me from all that. I'll leave,' said he, 'in order to avoid her.'

After that, he went in a party of fifty warriors until he reached Scotland. He got a great welcome from the King of Scotland. He had hounds for hares, hounds for pigs, hounds for deer. But Doílín and Daithlend, Máel Fothartaig's two hounds, used to kill every quarry in turn before the eyes of all. In every battle and fight that was won by the King of Scotland, it was Máel Fothartaig who carried the day.

'What's this, Rónán?' said the Leinster men. 'Was it you that sent Máel Fothartaig out of the country? We'll kill you should he not come back again.' That was told to Máel Fothartaig and he returned from the east once more. As it turned out, the place he came to, from the east, was Dunseverick. He was given a great welcome. 'It's bad for you, Máel Fothartaig, that you didn't sleep with our daughter. It was to you we gave her, and not to that old boor.' 'A bad thing indeed,' said Máel Fothartaig.

1. A type of board-game, usually — though inaccurately — translated 'chess'.

2. i.e. Echaid's daughter.

Máel Fothartaig reaches Leinster and they give him a great welcome. The same young woman sleeps with him. 'Give up that man to me,' said Echaid's daughter to her companion, 'or you die!'³ She told Máel Fothartaig. 'What will I do about this, Congal?' said Máel Fothartaig. 'Give me the reward for it,' said Congal, 'and I'll keep her away from you so that she won't as much as mention you.' 'You'll have my horse with its bridle and my cloak.' 'I'll accept nothing other than the two hounds,' said Congal, 'that they may be mine alone.' 'You'll have them,' said Máel Fothartaig.

'Go then tomorrow,' said Congal, 'as far as the Cows of Aífe as if to hunt.' (The 'Cows of Aífe', that is, rocks on the mountain-side: they look like white cows from a distance. On the 'side' (*aífe*) of the mountain is where they are.) 'Go then, as though you could be there giving chase. And the woman will arrange for her companion to meet us, and I'll rid you of her.'⁴

And so it happened. Her companion said it to her. She felt it long till morning-time. On the morrow, they went to their tryst. They saw Congal before them. 'What brings you here, you whore?' said he. 'It does you no good to travel about alone — that is, unless you're going to meet a man. Go back home,' said he, 'and take a curse with you.' Congal conveyed her to her house.

They saw her approach them again. 'So!' said Congal. 'What you want is to bring shame on the King of Leinster, evil woman! If I see you again,' said he, 'I'll take your head off and set it on a stake in front of Rónán. Evil woman! shaming him in ditches and bushes, out all alone to meet with a lad!' He attacked her with a horse-whip and drove her back inside her house. 'I'll bring a gush of blood to your lips!' said she.

Rónán returned to his house. Máel Fothartaig's folk arrived in before him. He stayed out on his own, hunting. 'Where's Máel Fothartaig tonight, Congal?' said Rónán. 'He's still out,' said Congal. 'O pity! my son out alone, for all that he is good to so many.' 'You've made us deaf,' said she, 'with talk of your son.' 'It's only right to talk of him,' said Rónán, 'for there isn't a son in Ireland better at carrying out his father's wishes. For he is

equally jealous of my name with man and woman alike, at Áth Cliath and at Clár Daire Móir⁵ and at Drochet Carpri,⁶ just as if his own were pledged on my behalf. So you and I may rest easy, wife,' said Rónán. 'He doesn't get the ease he wants from me,' said she, 'which is to have an encounter with me in spite of you. I won't hold out against him much longer: Congal brought me to him three times since morning, so that I've only barely escaped from his clutches.' 'A curse on your mouth, evil woman!' said Rónán. 'You speak false!' 'Well, you'll see proof of it now,' said she. 'I'll recite a half-quatrain to see if it will fit with what he'll recite.' (He used to do that every night to amuse her: he'd recite one half-quatrain, she'd recite the other.)

So then he came in and was drying his shins at the fire, and Congal was with him. Máel Fothartaig's jester, that is, Mac Glass, was trick-acting on the floor of the house. Then, because the day was cold, he said:

'It is cold against the whirlwind
for one who herds the Cows of Aífe.'

'Hear this, Rónán,' said she. 'Say that again,' said she.

'It is cold against the whirlwind
for one who herds the Cows of Aífe.'
'It is herding in vain,' said she,
'without cows, without anyone you love.'

(i.e. 'although I did not come, nor did you take the cows away with you').⁷

'It's true then,' said Rónán.

There was a warrior by Rónán's side, namely, Áedán son of Fiachna Lára. 'Áedán,' said he, 'stick a spear in Máel Fothartaig and give something to Congal also!' When Máel Fothartaig's back was turned to them at the fire, Áedán thrust the spear into him and drew its points out through him so that he was in a sitting position. As Congal rose,

---

3. Literally, 'or death on your lips'.
4. Presumably Echaid's daughter, who will come to the tryst unannounced.

5. In the barony of Clonlisk, County Offaly.
6. Drehid, County Kildare.
7. 'Cows' echoes the place-name, 'Aífe's Cows', refers to actual cows (the presence of which would have provided Máel Fothartaig with an alibi), and refers to Echaid's daughter since women are often figured as cows in the literature. The implication is that Máel Fothartaig had been disappointed of his expectation of finding Echaid's daughter on the hill, and so had failed to carry her, or any others, off.

Áedán stuck the spear in him and it went through his heart. The jester leapt up. Áedán sent the spear flying after him and disembowelled him. 'You've inflicted enough on the men, Áedán,' said Máel Fothartaig.

'How well for you,' said Rónán, 'that you found no other woman to solicit but my wife.' 'That was a sorry lie that was told to you, Rónán,' said the lad, 'to kill your own son when there was no guilt By your honour, and by the tryst to which I go — the tryst with death — I am no more guilty of suggesting an encounter with her than that I should have an encounter with my mother. But she has been entreating me since she reached these parts, and Congal has brought her back three times today so that she might not meet me. Congal didn't deserve to be killed.'

The raven was drawing the jester's bowels away to a causeway. The jester was grimacing. The folk were laughing. Máel Fothartaig was shamed. Then he said:

'O Mac Glass,
gather in your bowels,
why do you know no shame?
the folk are laughing at you.'

The three died afterwards. They were taken to a house apart. Rónán went and stood at his son's head for three days and three nights.

Then Dond, Máel Fothartaig's foster-brother and Congal's kinsman, went in a party of twenty horsemen to Dunseverick, and they duped Echaid into coming to the border, as it were to meet Máel Fothartaig who had eloped with his daughter, and they carried off his head and the head of his son and his wife.

Then, standing at his son's head, Rónán said:

'It is cold against the whirlwind
for one who herds the Cows of Aífe;
it is herding in vain,
with no cows, with none you might love.

'Cold the wind
in front of the warriors' house;
dear were the warriors
that used shield us from the wind.

'Sleep, daughter of Echaid,
the wind's sting is great;

I grieve that Máel Fothartaig should die
for the crime of a wanton woman.

'Sleep, daughter of Echaid,
while you sleep it gives me no peace
to see Máel Fothartaig
in his shirt full of gore.'

Echaid's daughter:

'Alas! O corpse in the corner
that many an eye once marked,
whatever much we did of wrong,
that was your torment after your rejection.'

Rónán:

'Sleep, daughter of Echaid,
the people are not mad!
though you shed tears on your cloak
it is not my son you keen.'

Then Dond arrived and he threw before her her father's head, and her mother's head, and the head of her brother. After that, she got up and she threw herself on her knife so that it came out through her back. Then Rónán said:

'Echaid has got one shirt only,
having been in a soft, warm cloak;
the sadness that is over Dún Áis
is also over Dunseverick.

'Give ye food, give ye drink
to the hounds of Máel Fothartaig,
and let someone else give
food to the hounds of Congal.

'I grieve for the flogging of Daithlenn
with stinging whips along her sides;
she does not bear our reproach,
it was not she who sold our dear ones.

'Doílín,
to me you have given service;
her head on each person's lap in turn
seeking one she will not find.

'The men, the youths, the horses
that used to be around Máel Fothartaig,
they envied no one's cheer
in the lifetime of their lord.

'The men, the youths, the horses
that used to be around Máel Fothartaig,
they ranged freely on the plain,
they enjoyed horse-racing.

'The men, the youths, the horses
that used to be around Máel Fothartaig,
many is the time they were
clamorous after great victories.

'The folk of Máel Fothartaig,
granted they were not dishonoured, yet
they did not stand by the man
who used to provide for all their needs.

'My own son Máel Fothartaig
for whom the wide wood was home,
neither kings nor princes
used to trespass against him lightly.

'My own son Máel Fothartaig
who traversed sea-boarded Scotland,
he was a hero among heroes,
he held sway over them all.

'My own son Máel Fothartaig,
he was the champion of the pack,
a bright, tall, radiant yew,
he has found a cold abode. Cold.'

Afterwards, the Leinster folk were around
Rónán at the keening. Rónán is pushed backwards.
Áedán is attacked and seized by the two sons of
Máel Fothartaig, that is, Áed and Máel Tuile. Áed
stabbed him until he made a wasp's honeycomb
out of him. 'Let me get up, lads,' said Rónán,
'unless you want to kill me.' 'Is the man dead?' he
asked. 'Dead indeed,' said the warriors. 'Was it
Máel Tuile who struck him?' 'No,' said the
warriors. 'May he not kill anyone until doom!' said
he. 'But the palm of valour and arms to the youth
who struck him.' It is then that Rónán said:

'It is a grave thing
for the son of a churl to kill the son of a king;
that was clear on the day of his tryst[8]
to Áedán son of Fíachna Lára.'

8. i.e. with death.

Then the battle was moved to where he was in
front of the house. At that he said:

'This battle on the plain,
woe! without Máel Fothartaig;
awaiting the new fight
the old warrior does not endure.'

With that, a gush of blood burst from his lips
and at once he died. That is the Kin-slaying of
Rónán.

THE DEATHS OF LUGAID AND DERBFORGAILL
(early 10th century)

[A number of themes and literary devices are combined to
great effect in this complex and poignant tale. Scholars
have commented on the pattern of mythological thinking
behind the presentation of Derbforgaill's sexuality, and
have discerned in it aspects of the saga-image of a
powerful cosmic goddess not unlike her Norse sisters.
However, the question of power and women in a saga
world is much more problematically set here. The motif of
the woman empowered by the Otherworld is countered by
a stress on the emotional pathos of the love story and the
vulnerability of the heroine. Wounded, ravished and
slighted by Cú Chulainn, she accepts a lesser role as
exemplary wife to Lugaid and much of the 'mythic'
efficacy of the story resides in the reader's understanding
of the Mélusine-type pattern underlying the subsequent
unfolding of the tale. But it is the power of transgressive
behaviour, of women pissing like men, of women's
collective rage, jealousy and violence, that truly shocks.
What is observed elsewhere by Boniface as collective legal
punishment among German tribes — the mutilation by
her peers of a deviant woman — becomes itself the final
horror to which the hero must respond with a Samson-like
Old Testament destruction of these same women. What we
are finally left with, however, is the quiet strength of
Derbforgaill's lament. Her poem places her firmly before
us as one of the most appealing figures in the whole
repertoire of Irish literary women. The text was edited and
translated by Carl Marstrander, 'The Deaths of Lugaid
and Derbforgaill', *Ériu*, vol. 5 (1911), pp. 201–18. This
new translation and headnote are by Ann Dooley.]

Derbforgaill fell in love with Cú Chulainn
because of the extraordinary stories told about

him. She and her maidservant set out from the east, in the form of two swans linked by a chain of gold, and they alighted on Loch Cuan. As Cú Chulainn and his foster-son, Lugaid son of the three Findemna, were by the lake one day they saw the birds. 'Take a shot at the birds,' said Lugaid. Cú Chulainn threw a stone in such a way that it went between her ribs and lodged in her womb. Straightaway the birds were turned into human shape on the edge of the water. 'You have done me wrong,' said the girl, 'and it was to you I was coming.' 'You are right,' said Cú Chulainn. Then he sucked the stone from the girl's side until it was in his mouth with the clot of blood that had formed around it. 'It was in search of you that I came,' the girl reminded him. 'That is impossible,' replied Cú Chulainn. 'The one whose side I have sucked I cannot ever sleep with.' 'Then I am yours to give to whomever it pleases you.' 'I would like you,' he said, 'to go to the noblest young man in Ireland, that is to Lugaid of the Red Stripes.' 'I will agree to that,' she said, 'provided I am always able to see you.' So she went to Lugaid and bore children to him.

Then a day came towards the end of winter, a day of heavy snow. The men made big mounds of the snow. After the men the women got up on the mounds. This was the game they played: 'Let's piss on the mound to see which one's piss can go farthest into it. The woman who can get it to go all the way, she is the sexiest of us!' However, none of them quite succeeded in doing it. Then they called Derbforgaill. She did not want to play the game because she was not a lewd woman. Nevertheless she got up on the pillar and her piss went all the way to the ground.

'If the men get to know about this there is only one woman they will lust after. Let's gouge out her eyes, cut off her nose, her two ears, her hair and her buttocks. She won't be sexually attractive then!'

She was tortured in this way and then brought back to her house. Meanwhile the men were chatting togther on a little hill above Emain Macha. 'I'm surprised, Lugaid,' remarked Cú Chulainn, 'to see snow still on Derbforgaill's house.' 'If that is so, then she is at the point of death,' said Lugaid. They rushed with one accord to the house. But when she heard them she went and locked the door on herself. 'Open up!' cried Cú Chulainn. 'Lovely the bloom in which we parted,' she cried out. 'Never will you see me again.' And then bidding him farewell she sang this brief song:

'Cú Chulainn's farewell has reached me
from the places that were familiar to me;
and swift Lugaid's also,
whose love bond cannot hold me.

'I must go away now;
dark the journey destined for me;
I would still have to part from them,
even if certain death had not come to me.

'With Cú Chulainn and with Lugaid
who had neither fear nor terror,
were it not for rebuke and punishment
our union were no cause for regret.

'A broken union with Red-stripe
is a thorn in the heart, a wounding of the
    body;
to be separated from Cú Chulainn
is bitter unless revenge attends it.

'Unless Lugaid's shaming be avenged
to whom every setback was small till now,
too soon has come my tragedy
for the son of the three Findemna.

'That I do not see Cú Chulainn
and that I must part from Lugaid,
I am tearful and sad from it;
cut off from my people, alas for the living!

'My *fian* friend Cú Chulainn did not betray
    me
Cú Chulainn boastful to a friend;
Lugaid the son of Clothar of Cruachu
was a noble and pleasing husband.

'His form gave Cú Chulainn first place
in heroic ardour, in athletic feats;
to Lugaid went pre-eminence in arms,
and to me beauty beyond all women.

'Every fulfilment eventually becomes a
    burden,
though you ardently desired it;
all wealth is a total liability,
every strength is pitiful or is doomed.

'This transitory world is a deceitful
   encounter,
it is not a neutral token;
beyond all else, the tryst with death destroys
a beautiful face however lovely.

'Unhappy he of the steadfast heart
who trusts one of another land;
because appearances can change so often
of a face in the time of misfortune.'

'When we rode around in Emain,
or in Tara, that was no weak display;
Cú Chulainn there in high spirits
and Lugaid son of Clothru.

'Cú Chulainn speaking to me —
he of the great heroic deeds;
that was what satisfied my heart,
as well as sleeping with Lugaid.

'We have taken leave of the sporting
that used to fill our days;
it may be that we shall never meet again,
I have been fated to die.'

This is what people said, that when they made
their way inside, her spirit was no longer in her
body. And then, they said, Lugaid died on seeing
her. Cú Chulainn stormed out of the house to
the building where the women were and he
overturned it on them so that neither man nor
woman came alive out of that house — that is of
the one hundred and fifty ladies — but he killed
them all. Then Cú Chulainn sang:

'Derbforgaill, fair and lovely girl
who came to me from across the sea waves;
she honoured me with friendship,
the daughter of a king from great Norway.

'Being here between two graves
the hurt makes my heart bleed;
the face of Derbforgaill under a broad stone
and Lugaid Red-stripe, alas for him.

'Great was Lugaid's glory once,
he was skilled above his spear-shafts;
fifty grave woundings attributed to him alone,
an inspiration in every situation.

'Derbforgaill, famous for wealth;
for modesty and for generosity;
never did a haughty look
cloud her face at her husband's shoulder.

'One hundred and fifty women in Emain
it was I who slaughtered them;
though an over-king were to estimate it,
they are worthless compared to Derbforgaill.'

Der Forgaill, that is, 'the daughter of Forgall',
King of Norway. Cú Chulainn had their burial
mounds and their graves made, and it was he
who lamented them and raised their commemorative stones. This is 'The Deaths of
Lugaid and Derbforgaill'.

from:
TOCHMARC AILBE
(The Wooing of Ailbe)
(10th century)

[The category of *tochmarc*, or 'wooing tale', is well
represented in the earliest Irish tale-lists. Typically, wooing
tales describe the courting of a quick-witted and strong-
minded young woman by a suitor who has to appease a
jealous or unwilling father, husband or other relative and
accomplish a series of tasks, normally set for him by the
woman herself. The Wooing of Ailbe is remarkable for the
attention it pays to the woman's response to her suitor,
and to father–daughter relations.

The male protagonists are the two senior males in
Ossianic literature, Cormac mac Airt, King of Tara, and
Finn mac Cumaill, leader of his *fian*-band. They fall out
when Cormac's eldest daughter, the reckless and beautiful
Gráinne who had eloped with Finn, begins to hate her
husband. Peace is restored between the two men when she
and Finn are formally divorced (see. pp. 36–7). In the hope
of strengthening it, Cormac encourages his remaining
daughters to consider Finn as a consort. Meanwhile, his
youngest daughter, Ailbe Grúadbricc, 'Freckle-faced' (the
epithet suggesting plainness), is anxious to marry. The
druid tells her that her fated husband will arrive at the
court on the morrow, to attend the great Feast of Tara, and
he gives her a potion which enables her to see him in a
dream. Both Ailbe and her father, then, in a departure from
the typical pattern, are positively disposed towards Finn as
a suitor before he visits Tara. Where they disagree is on his
marrying Ailbe, whom Cormac considers far too young for
the 'greybeard', Finn.

Our excerpt begins with an account of the arrangements for the great feast in which the complementarity of the sexes is highlighted. Cormac, a model of the attentive father, quickly intuits Ailbe's intentions towards Finn. Far from opposing her outright, he engages with her arguments reasonably, eventually conceding that his headstrong daughter has made the right decision and must leave 'the bull that loved her' for 'the great ox'. Here, as in many other texts, the proof of a woman's intelligence is in her conversation. Ailbe excels again in her exchange with Finn, with which our excerpt concludes. That her excellence is of an intellectual kind is just as well, given Finn's age: what he offers her, in a delightful idyll (cf. the edition by R. Thurneysen, cited below, pp. 276–8), is a safely exuberant life in the green woods, not the dangerous excitement he knew as a young warrior. In fact, Finn's character in this tale is distinctly meek in comparison to Ailbe's. When he says that her willingness to exile herself from court for his sake is acceptable to him only as long as this does not infringe 'Cormac's law', she responds defiantly: 'We'll do Cormac's will here at home provided we have done our own first of all.' Finn concludes that he dare not refuse the daughter of the King of Ireland her own choice of husband. And so 'the girl went to Finn with Cormac's goodwill after that and Finn paid seven *cumal*s for her brideprice'. Nor did Finn live to regret it. They lived happily together, Ailbe bore him three sons, and three wonders were wrought in him on account of Ailbe: 'He slept on Sadb's stream' (perhaps a reference to poetic inspiration). 'A white-purple blister that had the brilliance of a carbuncle was formed below his breasts. His hair turned blond, blond as burnished gold-dust on gems, and a cup-shaped filament was laid down at the back of his head, round as an apple of white gold, and it was never loosened in his lifetime.'

This new translation is based on the edition, with German translation, by Rudolf Thurneysen ('Tochmarc Ailbe "Das Werben um Ailbe"', *Zeitschrift für celtische Philologie*, vol. 13 (1920–1), pp. 251–82). It incorporates most of his suggested emendations, including ones in later publications, and a number of additional ones by the present editor. It also draws on an unpublished translation of the full text kindly made available by John Carey.]

One time the Feast of Tara was prepared by Cormac for the hosts of the whole of Ireland. In like manner there used to come to that Feast kings and royal candidates, hospitallers and chief poets and *fian*-members and marauders and brigands and trappers, and the *áes dána* of all Ireland, and her noble families, small and great. For seven years they used to prepare to consume the great Feast of Tara, when the men of all Ireland used to come to the carousal. And kings and high princes used to make preparations for it for a year and they used to be consuming it for seven nights.

There used not to go to the carousal any king without a queen, nor any champion without a female champion, nor any *fian*-member without an arms-bearer [?], nor any jester without a female jester nor any hospitaller without a companion, nor any youth without a sweetheart nor any maiden without a lover nor any person without an art.

The kings and the chief poets used to be arrayed around the King of Tara, Cormac mac Airt, that is, the kings and the chief poets to one side, the *fian*-members and the marauders together, the youths and the maidens and the foolish boisterous folk around the doors. And to every one of them was given his proper portion, that is, small tree-fruit and oxen and boars and bacon-flitches for kings, chief poets, and for the noble, aristocratic venerables of the men of Ireland also; stewards and female stewards doing the carving and serving for them. Then, red meat from spits of iron, pure malt-brew and both new ale and old for *fian*-bands and marauders; jesters and cup-bearers doing the dividing and serving for them. There was veal there, too, and lamb and piglet, and the seventh distribution — not counting the mead — for youths and maidens, for their youthful chatter used to entertain them. And their morsels used be set before them; male and female servants dividing and serving for them.

The men of Ireland came from every quarter to the Feast of Tara. And Finn came too, along with the *fian*-bands, to the green of Tara's enclosure. And they made the *fian*-drone against the shafts of their spears, and of all the music of Ireland no music or drone was sweeter than this. It was there too that the girl chanced to be, in a private chamber, working knotted thread of gold on Cormac's — her father's — helmet. Now, when the disputes of the men of Ireland weighed on him, it was ever Cormac's wont to go out to see the girl, on account of his great love for her and the excellence of her handiwork for him. For at that time no other girl could equal her in working gold and silver, or in intelligence and beauty and ancestry, and wisdom and speech and poetry. However, her mind was so perturbed on hearing the *fian*-band that the handiwork she was doing went crooked and awry. Cormac noticed the slip she was making. He set to instructing her, concerning which the poet said:

[Cormac]
'What excites you, girl, what engagement of the mind? Let your thinking not be swayed by the sound of the *fian*-bands on Tara's ground.'
[Ailbe]
'A greybeard's drone I have heard, a shout of triumph, with incitements in verse. After victory in keen-run races he routed your assembly.'
[Cormac]
'If all you young women hearken: greybeards are not to be listened to! They may make a fine sound but they do not discharge their obligations.'
[Ailbe]
'A greybeard with a bald head is the one with keen wits. Every assembly to which he belongs is more experienced than the warrior of the hostage-band.'[1]
[Cormac]
'In a place where raiding occurs, your liking is for lively horses; whenever you turn to the old horse, it does not gladden the mind.'[2]
[Ailbe]
'A good horse, not wild, is better for the course — on such the warrior escapes. The colt — a puny thing — runs, he stumbles and breaks his bones.'
[Cormac]
'I heard a wondrous thing today, in the early morning after daybreak: a heifer disregarding the bull[3] that loved her — headlong you bring yourself to the great ox.'
[Ailbe]
'By the ox that knows the cart is the barn swiftly filled. Although a bull is high-spirited at the head of a herd, no litter of piglets is reared.'
[Cormac]
'. . .[4] To spread a bed for the greybeard rather than the lad will bring you to bad woman-state.'
[Ailbe]
'I know, though I visited no wood, that the acorns of the knotty tree are better. The tender sapling has no right to love; it will bear but little fruit.'

[Cormac]
'I have heard of an arrangement that is not wise: a girl going to an old warrior. Ill is what I fear will come of it — a time in the drought of hate.'
[Ailbe]
'This is why I love an old man: because the blow he strikes is not too light. A tremoring in his side is rare, whatever about his body-beauty.
'Better Tara's aged rampart — undoubtedly its merit is enduring — than yesterday's new rampart that was razed by Arrtaile's son.'
[Cormac]
'Is it right to put the fresh branch in the shade of the great oak — since plants decay there, without heat, under great-acorned oaks?
'Let your deeds not be injurious — like a bird round which a trap closes. You can not unmake your bed even though you regret it.'
[Ailbe]
'Why do you lure the bird of flawless plumage into traps? I would not place my foot into a trap where I would expect to meet my death.'
[Cormac]
'I am not unhappy with the arrangement on your account — [but] it is hard for a grey-faced warrior.[5] It will make you mature; it will bring all good things to a girl.'
[Ailbe]
'I am certain, whatever I should do — even to refuse the grey-haired warrior — my father could not accuse me, after my departure to the pure *fian*-band.'
[Cormac]
'Although I say to you, "don't love the old man", that is what a good woman will do. I could not fail to provide dues of valour for a good man.'[6]
[Ailbe]
'Why should we two not dispute when it can cause no strife? If a woman's deeds can be good, then good is what I have heard.'

After that, a party went from Cormac to enquire of Finn what art he had that he might bring to Tara. 'In truth,' said Finn, 'I am good at old sayings and at pronouncing witticisms.' 'We regard that as the art of goslings and girls', said Cormac. 'Let me be called a gosling then,' said Finn, 'that doesn't stop me: I'll create a

1. Royal hostages were usually young.
2. The second sentence is conjectural.
3. i.e. Cormac.
4. Sentence omitted; I cannot make sense of it.

5. i.e. Cormac.
6. i.e. for Finn. Next verse omitted; I cannot make sense of it.

disputation that will be art enough to woo women and girls.' 'Into this stronghold there comes no king without a queen, nor any *fian*-warrior without a female warrior, nor any hospitaller without a consort, nor any jester without a female jester, nor any youth without a sweetheart, nor any girl without a lover, nor any person without an art.' 'In truth,' said Finn, 'I've brought about thrice fifty matches so far for the daughters of Ireland's and Britain's lords, and all of them used to give themselves to the *fian*-bands of Ireland, so that there's not a half-coupled yoke nor a half-empty bed in existence save only that I myself am alone. If you have among you any noblewoman who is not a feigned noblewoman, let her be given to me by you.' 'Make the enquiry yourself,' said Cormac 'in the noblewomen's circuit, to see if any of them answer you and play the game of witticisms with you.' After that, Finn himself went into the stronghold, and came to the courtyard where Cormac's daughters were, in a covered bower, weaving fringes and knotted thread of gold and silver on cloth of every hue. And it was there that Finn said this string of eloquence.

'Girls,' said Finn, 'would any of you know the following? What water is wider than every sea?' 'Dew is wider,' said Freckle-faced Ailbe daughter of Cormac. It is she who answered, for there was none in the house more clever than she — among the women — and therefore, it was to her the witticism was put.

'What is sweeter than mead?' said Finn. 'Confidential talk,' said the girl.

'What is redder than blood?' said Finn. 'The blushing of noble offspring,' said the girl, 'when they are praised or satirized.'

'What is blacker than the raven?' said Finn. 'Death is blacker,' said the girl.

'What is brighter than snow?' said Finn. 'Truth,' said the girl.

'What is swifter than the wind?' said Finn. 'Intellect,' said the girl.

'What is hotter than fire?' said Finn. 'The face of a hospitaller to whom the arrival of guests at his house is announced, should he have nothing to give them,' said the girl.

'What is oilier than the flesh of a boar raised on acorns?' said Finn. 'The hatred of a man if one cease to love him,' said the girl.

'What is heavier than layers?' said Finn. 'The cold,' said the girl.

'What is sharper than a sword?' said Finn. 'Sense,' said the girl.

'What is more brittle than a nut?' said Finn. 'The mind of a jealous woman,' said the girl.

'What is lighter than a particle?' said Finn. 'The sense of a woman undecided between two,' said the girl.

'What is rougher than the strand?' said Finn. 'A rock,' said the girl.

'What porridge is boiled for every company?' said Finn. 'The smith's tongs,' said the girl.

'What living child is born from a dead woman?' said Finn. 'A spark on the edge of a flintstone,' said the girl.

'What is lovelier than foxglove?' said Finn. 'Treachery's cheek,' said the girl, 'the cheek of deceit: when its wish is to betray you, then its aspect towards you is fairest.'

'How many trees are there in Asal?'[7] said Finn. 'Two,' said the girl, 'green and withered.'.

'How many horses come to Tailtiu?'[8] said Finn. 'Two,' said the girl, 'female and male.'

'What is the best of treasures?' said Finn. 'A knife,' said the girl, 'for it is compared to sense.'

'What is best in a warrior?' said Finn. 'A lofty deed and a lowly pride,' said the girl.

'What is best in a woman?' said Finn. 'Gentleness, steadiness, modesty, silence, eloquence,' said the girl.

'What is the best food?' said Finn. 'Milk,' said the girl, 'for it is good new, it is good old, it is good thickened, it is good thin, it nourishes the baby, it sustains the old man.'

'What is the worst food?' said Finn. 'A scrawny rib, rancid fat,' said the girl; 'where you find it, throw it away.'

'What is it that neither lock nor chain holds fast?' said Finn. 'The eye of a pretty girl following her beloved,' said the girl.

'What is best in speech?' said Finn. 'Wisdom. Brevity,' said the girl.

'What is best for an eye?' said Finn. 'Cold, satiety, darkness,' said the girl.

'What is worst for an eye?' said Finn. 'Heat, irritation, hunger,' said the girl.

7. A large area, roughly between Tara and Mullingar.
8. Modern Teltown, County Meath.

'What is more bitter than poison?' said Finn. 'An enemy's insult,' said the girl.

'What is more restless than a squirrel?' said Finn. 'The mind or the advice of a foolish man,' said the girl.

'What is softer than down?' said Finn. 'A palm against a cheek,' said the girl.

'Perhaps the folk of Tara think our banter here has gone on long enough, girl,' said Finn. 'Well indeed, if that's so, it was you began the conversation and it's your prerogative to pronounce the *coup de grâce*.' 'If you'd like to go with me to my bed and sleep with me, girl, the life you'll enjoy with me afterwards will be described for you forthwith, and you'll not be refused it. And should you not like what is offered to you, stay with your people, lest you regret it later.'

TOCHMARC BECFHOLA
(The Wooing of Becfhola)
(Early Middle Irish)

[A beautiful and sexually available Otherworld woman embodies immorality in this Early Middle Irish tale. The threat she poses to society is activated when the king woos her before he has determined her origins. His foster-son narrowly escapes her clutches by bowing to Christian teaching. As the clues to Becfhola's true nature accumulate, her own desires are assuaged in an encounter with a man in an Otherworld setting. The tale's conclusion — its *doppelgängers* and weird symmetries notwithstanding — implies that the danger admitted into the worldly sphere along with Becfhola has been resisted. By eliding this ending, Austin Clarke's treatment of the tale in his narrative poem, 'The Wooing of Becfola' (1974), refuses the moralizing of the original and, instead, celebrates Becfhola's ability to evade society's pleasure-denying strictures.

Diarmaid died in 664. Saint Mo Laise (also Molaisse), founder of the monastery of Daiminis (Devenish), died in 563 or 571. It follows that a later Mo Laise, also associated with Daiminis, may be in question here. It may be noted that a Molaisse of Daiminis is mentioned as a contemporary of Saint Samthann (d. 739) in her Life (see p. 88). On the other hand, there is no evidence to indicate that Cluain Dá Chailech (perhaps 'Glade of Two Goblets'), the characters Flann and his grandfather Fedach mac in Daill, and the latter's island, are not all fictitious. The text was edited and translated by Máire

Bhreathnach, 'A New Edition of Tochmarc Becfhola', *Ériu*, vol. 35 (1984), pp. 59–92. The present translation is hers.]

§1. Díarmait, son of Áed Sláne, held the kingship of Temair.[1] Crimthann, son of Áed, was in fosterage with him and taken in hostageship by him from the Laigin.[2] He and his foster-son, Crimthann, journeyed one day to Áth Truim[3] in the territory of Cenél Lóegaire,[4] accompanied by a single attendant. They beheld a woman coming from the west across the ford in a chariot. She wore rounded sandals of white bronze, inset with two jewels of precious stone; a tunic covered with red-gold embroidery about her; a crimson mantle on her; a brooch in fully-wrought gold with shimmering gems of many hues fastening the mantle over her breast; necklets of refined gold around her neck; a golden circlet upon her head; two dark-grey horses drew her chariot, (harnessed) with a pair of golden bridles, yokes with animal designs worked in silver upon them.

§2. 'Whence have you come, woman?' asked Díarmait.

'It is not from any distance,' she said.

'Why do you come?' asked Díarmait.

'To seek seed-wheat,' said she. 'I have good arable land but lack seed which is suitable for it.'

'If it be the seed of this territory that you desire,' said Díarmait, 'your destiny does not lie beyond me.'

'Indeed, I shall not refuse,' replied she, 'provided that I get the price.'

'You shall have this little brooch,' answered Díarmait.

'It will indeed be accepted,' said she.

§3. And he brings her with him to Temair.

'Who is the woman, Díarmait?' asked everyone.

'Indeed she has not told me who she is,' replied Díarmait.

'What have you given as her bride-price?' asked everyone.

'My little brooch,' said Díarmait.

'That is little value,'[5] they all said.

---

1. Modern Tara, County Meath.
2. The Leinster folk.
3. Modern Trim, County Meath.
4. In the vicinity of Trim.
5. Or perhaps 'That is a small offence'.

'That will be her name then,' said the druid, 'Becfhola.'[6]

§4. She, however, had her heart set on his foster-son, on Crimthann, son of Áed. She solicited him and yearned for him for a long time. At last the lad was prevailed upon to tryst with her at Cluain Dá Chaileach, at sunrise on Sunday, in order to elope with her. This he mentioned to his people. Thereupon his people forbade him, (saying) that he should not elope with her, the wife of the high-king of Ireland.

§5. However, she arose early on the morning of the Sunday from Díarmait's side.
'What is this, woman?' asked Díarmait.
'It is nothing good,' she replied, 'there are possessions of mine at Cluain Dá Chaileach. The servants left them there and fled.'
'What possessions?' asked Díarmait.
'Seven embroidered tunics, seven gold brooches, three circlets of gold. It is a pity to have them go astray.'
'Don't go on Sunday,' said Díarmait, 'a journey on Sunday is not auspicious.'
'Let someone go forth with me,' she said.
'He will certainly not come from me,' answered Díarmait.

§6. She and her handmaid set out from Temair southwards, until they reached Dubthor Lagen.[7] There they went astray until nightfall, when wolves came upon them and killed the handmaid. She herself took refuge in a tree. While she was in the tree she saw a fire in the middle of the forest. She went towards the fire and saw a warrior cooking a pig by the fire. He was clad in a silken tunic with a bright border, embroidered with circular designs of gold and silver. A helmet of gold, silver and crystal was on his head, clusters and loops of gold around every lock of his hair, which hung down to his shoulder-blades. Two golden balls were at the parting of his braids, each one of them the size of a man's fist. His golden-hilted sword on his belt. His two five-barbed spears lay on his shield of belly-leather which was embossed in white bronze. A cloak of many hues lay beside him. His two arms were laden to the elbows with gold and silver bracelets.

§7. She went and sat beside him at the fire. He looked and was unconcerned until he had finished cooking the pig. He made a meal off [sic] the pig, then washed his hands and left the fire. She followed him as far as the lake. There was a boat of bronze in the middle of the lake. A woven bronze chain from the boat was attached to the shore and another to the island in the middle of the lake. The warrior hauled in the boat. She got into the boat before him. The boat was left in a boathouse of clay in front of the island.

§8. She went before him into the house. This was a fine house with both cubicles and beds. He sat down. Then she sat down beside him. He reached out his hand as he sat and brought forth a dish of food for them. They both ate and drank and neither of them was drunk. There was no one in the house. They did not speak to each other. He went to bed. She slipped in beneath his cloak, between him and the wall. However, he did not turn towards her throughout the night, until they heard the call in the early morning from the jetty of the island, i.e. 'Come out, Flann, here come the men.' He arose immediately, donned his armour and strode out. She saw three others at the jetty, who resembled him in form, age and comeliness. She also saw four others at the jetty of the island, their shields held on guard. Then he and the three others went forth (to meet them). They smote one another until each was red with the blood of the other, then each one went his way, injured.

§9. He went out to his island again.
'May you have the victory of your valour,' said she, 'that was an heroic combat.'
'It would indeed be good if it were against enemies,' said he.
'Who are the warriors?' she asked.
'The sons of my father's brother,' he answered, 'the others are my own three brothers.'
'What have you been fighting about?' asked the woman.
'For this island,' he said.
'What is the name of the island?' she asked.
'The island of Fedach mac in Daill,'[8] he said.

---

6. Either 'Little Value' (from *fola(d)*) or 'Small Offence' (from *fola*); cf. footnote 5.
7. South of Tara.

8. The name means 'Wood son of Blind Man'.

'And what is your name?' she asked.

'Flann,[9] grandson of Fedach,' he replied. 'It is the grandsons of Fedach who are in contention. The island is indeed bountiful. It provides a meal sufficient for a hundred men, with both food and ale, every evening without human attendance. Should there be only two people on it, they receive only what can suffice them.'

'Why don't I remain with you?' she asked.

'It is indeed a bad union for you,' he answered, 'to stay with me and to forsake the king of Ireland and to follow me in soldiering and in exile.'

'Why don't we become lovers?' she asked.

'Not this time,' he replied. 'However, if the island becomes mine and if we are alive, I shall go to fetch you and you are the woman who will be with me always. But go now!'

'It distresses me to leave my handmaid,' she said.

'She is alive at the foot of the same tree,' he said, 'because the warriors of the island protected her, and you will be escorted (home).'
This was so.

§10. She arrived home to find Díarmait getting up on the same Sunday.

'That is a wonder, wife,' said Díarmait, 'that you have not made a Sunday journey in defiance of our prohibition.'

'I dare not defy your command,' said she, as if she had not gone at all.

From that time onwards the habitual saying of Becfhola was:

'I spent a night in the forest,
In the house of the island of Mac in Daill,
Although it was with a man, it was no sin,
It was too soon when we parted.

'Inis Fedaig mac in Daill
In Dubthor, in Leinster,
Although it lies close to the road
Bearded warriors do not find it.'

Everyone wondered at that poem.

§11. Now, on that same day one year later, Díarmait was lying in bed with his wife Becfhola, when they saw a man go past the door of the house, and he was severely wounded. It was Flann. Then Becfhola said:

'I am suspicious about feats of men
At the battle in Daiminis,[10]
Was it the four (warriors) who defeated
Four in Daiminis?'

Then Flann replied:

'O woman, do not direct reproachful anger
At the warriors concerning their result
It was not the valorous feats of men that he overcame
But men with charmed spears.'

'I am unable,' said she,
'To hold out against the fighting of a man
When it was Flann that was wounded
In the conflict of the equally-matched eight.'

With that he (Díarmait) let her go from them out of the house after him, so that she was not overtaken.

'Let her go,' said Díarmait, 'the evil one, for one knows not whither she goes nor whence she came.'

§12. While they were saying this, they saw four clerics come into the house.

'What then,' cried Díarmait, 'the clergy travelling on Sunday!'

He drew his cloak over his head so that he might not see them at all.

'It is the order of our superiors that has brought us,' said the clerics, 'not wilfulness. Mo Laise of Daiminis has sent us to speak with you. A respected member of the community of Daiminis was rousing his cows this morning and he saw four armed warriors with their shields on guard advancing along the island. Then he saw the other four waiting for them. They smote each other so that the noise of the shields in battle echoed over the whole island, until they were all slain on both sides save one man, severely wounded, who alone survived. The other seven were buried by Molaisse. However, they left behind as much gold and silver as two of us could

---

9. The name means 'Blood-red'.

10. Modern Devinish, an island in Lough Erne, County Fermanagh.

carry, of all that was beneath their cloaks and about their swords and on their arms and on their tunics. (We come) that you may know of your share in that gold and silver.'

'Nay,' said Díarmait, 'I will not share in what God has given to him. Let his sacred emblems be made with it.'

This was done. It is from this silver and gold that the sacred reliquaries of Mo Laise were made, that is, his shrine and his travelling service and his crozier. But Becfhola went off with Flann, grandson of Fedach, and has not returned since then. That is the wooing of Becfhola.

from:
AIDED MUIRCHERTAICH MEIC ERCA
(The Death of Muirchertach mac Erca)
(Late Middle Irish)

[The beautiful Sín is the best delineated witch in medieval Irish tradition. This dramatic tale, in Late Middle Irish, relates how her powers caused the death of the Northern Uí Néill king, Muirchertach mac Erca. Although the Annals of Ulster record his death under the year 536, there is some doubt about his historicity.

The early church accepted the existence of demons and their ability to induce delusions, especially in pagan times or in people whose faith was weak. In Ireland, demons, who belonged to the aerial regions, were assimilated to the *áes síde* (Modern *aos sí*), 'folk of the *síd* (Otherworld); fairies'. The tale *Serglige Con Culainn*, 'The Wasting Sickness of Cú Chulainn', recounts how the great pagan warrior was almost destroyed by his encounter with the fairy lover Fand (see Volume I, pp. 26–8). One version concludes: 'That is the ruinous vision shown to Cú Chulainn by the *áes síde*. For the demonic power was great before the faith, and it was so great that the demons used to fight in bodily form with men, and show them delights and wonders as if they were real.' Assertions by the church that humans could not access demonic powers were undermined by popular beliefs that certain people, in particular witches and 'wise women' (*mná feasa*), communicated with the folk of the *síd*, or, as the phrase has it, spent time 'away with the fairies'.

Sín, who describes herself as 'the daughter of a man and a woman / of the race of Eve and Adam', is undoubtedly a witch rather than a demon or one of the *áes síde*. She does

not reveal the cause of her antipathy to Muirchertach until after his death, when she confesses to the clerics against whom she has pitted her powers all along that Muirchertach had murdered her father, mother and sister and destroyed their homeland. An ever more frightening phantasmagoria leads him on to his own death. His multiple offences — murder, witchcraft and the repudiation of his wife in favour of Sín — are requited by the manner it takes: he dies a triple death of simultaneous wounding, burning and drowning. His wife dies of grief for him, as does Sín, but not before she has repented. The imperturbable sang-froid maintained by the clerics through all of this distinguishes them as the ultimate winners in this contest of supernatural powers.

Whitley Stokes edited and translated the text, omitting most of the interspersed verse passages: 'The Death of Muirchertach mac Erca', *Revue Celtique*, vol. 23 (1902), pp. 395–437; vol. 24 (1903), p. 349. For the full text, without translation, see Lil Nic Dhonnchadha, *Aided Muirchertaig Meic Erca* (Dublin: Dublin Institute for Advanced Studies, 1980). The present text is excerpted from Stokes; name-forms have been normalized, and there are minor changes in presentation. A crucial emendation has been adopted from Tomás Ó Concheanainn, 'The Act of Wounding in the Death of Muirchertach mac Erca', *Éigse*, vol. 15, Part 2 (winter 1973), pp. 141–5.]

When Muirchertach son of Muiredach, son of Eógan, King of Ireland, was in the House of Clettech, over the brink of Boyne of the Brug[1] — and he had a spouse, Dúaibsech daughter of Duach Brazentongue, King of Connacht — that king came forth one day to hunt on the border of the Brug, and his hunting companions left him alone on his hunting mound.

He had not been there long when he saw a solitary damsel beautifully formed, fair-headed, bright-skinned, with a green mantle about her, sitting near him on the turfen mound; and it seemed to him that of womankind he had never beheld her equal in beauty and refinement. So that all his body and his nature filled with love for her, for gazing at her it seemed to him that he would give the whole of Ireland for one night's loan of her, so utterly did he love her at first sight. And he welcomed her as if she were known to him, and he asked tidings of her.

'I will tell thee,' she said. 'I am the darling of Muirchertach mac Erca, King of Erin, and to seek him I came here.' That seemed good to Muirchertach, and he said to her, 'Dost thou know

1. i.e. Brug na Bóinne, the prehistoric necropolis of Newgrange.

me, O damsel?' 'I do,' she answers; 'for skilled am I in places more secret than this, and known to me art thou and the other men of Erin.' 'Wilt thou come with me, O damsel?' said Muirchertach. 'I would go,' she answered, 'provided my guerdon be good.' 'I will give thee power over me, O damsel,' said Muirchertach. 'Thy word for this!' rejoined the damsel. And he gave it at once . . .

'I will give thee a hundred of every herd, and a hundred drinking-horns, and a hundred cups, and a hundred rings of gold, and a feast every other night in the House of Clettech.' 'Nay,' said the damsel. 'Not so shall it be. But my name must never be uttered by thee, and Dúaibsech, the mother of thy children, must not be in my sight, and clerics must never enter the house that I am in.' 'All this shalt thou have,' said the king, 'for I pledged thee my word; but it would be easier for me to give thee half of Ireland. And tell me truly,' said the king, 'what name is on thee, so that we may avoid it by not uttering it.' And she said, '[*Osnad, Esnad, Sín, Gáeth Garb, Gamadaig, Ochsat, Íachtad, Táethen*] Sigh, Sough, Storm, Rough Wind, Winter-Night, Cry, Wail, Groan.'

Each of these things was promised to her, and thus he pledged himself. Then they went together to the House of Clettech. Good was the arrangement of that house, and good were its family and its household, and all the nobles of the Children of Níall cheerfully and spiritedly, gaily and gladly consuming the tribute and wealth of every province in the trophied House of Clettech above the brink of the salmonful, ever-beautiful Boyne, and over the border of the green-topped Brug.

Now when Sín saw the house with its family she said: 'Good is the house we have come to!' quoth she. 'It is good,' says the king; 'and never has there been built for Tara or for Naas or for Cráeb Ruad[2] or for Emain Macha or for Ailech Néit[3] or for Clettech a house the like of it.' . . .

'What shall be done here now?' demands the damsel. 'That which thou desirest,' replied Muirchertach. 'If so,' said Sín, 'let Dúaibsech and her children go forth from the house, and let a man of every craft and art in Ireland come with

his wife into the drinking-hall.' Thus it was done, and each began praising his own craft and art, and a stave was made by every craftsman and artist who was therein . . .

When the drinking ended Sín said to Muirchertach, 'It is now time to leave the House to me, as hath been promised.' Then she put the Clans of Níall, and Dúaibsech with her children, forth out of Clettech; and this is their number of them, both men and women, two equally great and gallant battalions. Dúaibsech went with her children from Clettech to Tuilén,[4] to seek her soul-friend, the holy bishop Cairnech.[5] When she got to Cairnech she uttered these words:

'O cleric, bless my body,
I am afraid of death tonight . . .

'Go thou thyself, O cleric, there
To the children of Eogan and Conall . . .'[6]

Thereafter Cairnech came to the Children of Eogan and Conall, and they went back together to Clettech, but Sín would not let them near the fortress. At this act the Clan of Níall were distressed and mournful. Then Cairnech is greatly angered, and he cursed the steading, and made a grave for the king, and said, 'He whose grave this is hath finished; and truly it is an end to his realm and his princedom!' . . .

The king sits on his throne, and Sín sits on his right, and never on earth had there come a woman better than she in shape and appearance. When the king looked on her, he was seeking knowledge and asking questions of her, for it seemed to him that she was a goddess of great power; and he asked her what was the power that she had. So then he spake and she answered:

Muirchertach:

'Tell me, thou ready damsel,
believest thou in the God of the clerics?
or from whom hast thou sprung in this
     world?
tell us thy origin.'

---

2. 'The Red Branch', the warriors under command of King Conchobar in Ulster.
3. Also Ailech (Grianán Ailigh), on Inishowen peninsula.

4. Dulane, north of Kells, County Meath.
5. Founder of monastery of Dulane.
6. Sons of Níall Noígiallach.

Sín:

> 'I believe in the same true God
> helper of my body against death's attack;
> ye cannot work in this world a miracle
> of which I could not work its like.
> I am the daughter of a man and a woman
> of the race of Eve and Adam;
> I am fit for thee here,
> let no regret seize thee.
> I could create a sun and a moon,
> and radiant stars:
> I could create men fiercely
> fighting in conflict.
> I could make wine — no falsehood —
> of the Boyne, as I can obtain it,
> and sheep of stones,
> and swine of ferns.
> I could make silver and gold
> in the presence of the great hosts:
> I could make famous men
> now for thee.'

'Work for us,' said the king, 'some of these great miracles.' Then Sín went forth and arrayed two battalions equally great, equally strong, equally gallant; and it seemed to them that never came on earth two battalions that were bolder and more heroic than they, slaughtering and maiming and swiftly killing each other in the presence of every one. 'Seest thou yon?' says the damsel; 'and meseems that my power is in no wise a fraud.' 'I see,' said Muirchertach . . .

Then the king with his household comes into the fortress. When they had been a while seeing the fighting, some of the water of the Boyne was brought to them, and the king told the damsel to make wine thereout. The damsel then filled three casks with water, and casts a spell into them; and it seemed to the king and his household that never came on earth wine of better taste or strength. So of the fern she made fictitious swine of enchantment, and then she gave the wine and the swine to the host, and they partook of them until, as they supposed, they were sated. Howbeit, she promised that she would give them forever and forever the same amount . . .

Then the king said to her, 'Shew us something of thine art, O damsel!' 'I will do so indeed,' quoth she. They fared forth, that is,

Muirchertach and all the hosts in his presence. Then Sín made of the stones blue men, and others with heads of goats; so that there were four great battalions under arms before him on the green of the Brug. Muirchertach then seizes his arms and his battledress and went among them like a swift, angry, mad bull, and forthwith takes to slaughtering them and maiming them, and every man of them that he killed used to rise up after him at once. And thus he was killing them through the fair day till night . . .

So when the king was weary fighting and smiting the hosts, he comes sadly into the fort, and Sín gave him magical wine and magical swine. He and his household partake of them, and at the end he sleeps heavily till morning, and when rising there on the morrow he had neither strength nor vigour . . . They heard the heavy shout of the hosts and the multitudes, calling Muirchertach forth and challenging him to battle. Then in his presence in the Brug were two battalions equally great, to wit, blue men in one of the two and headless men in the other. Muirchertach was enraged at the challenge of the hosts, and he rose up suddenly, and fell strengthlessly on the floor . . .

Then he went into the Brug and charged through the hosts, and took to slaughtering and maiming them lengthily for the day. There came Sín to them and gave Muirchertach kingship over them, and he rests from battling. Thereafter the king fares forth to Clettech, and Sín formed two great battalions between him and the fortress. When he saw them he charged through them and began to do battle against them.

Now when he was delivering that battle, then Cairnech sent Masán and Casán and Crídán to seek him, so that he might have God's assistance, for the high saint knew of the oppression which he suffered at that time. Thereafter the clerics meet him in the Brug, while he is hacking the stones and the sods and the stalks besides, so then one of the clerics said:

Cleric:

> 'Wherefore dost thou fell the stones,
> O Muirchertach, without ground?
> we are sad that thou art strengthless
> according to the will of an idolater working
>   magic.'

Muirchertach:

> 'The cleric who attacked (?) me,
> I came into conflict with him:
> I know not furthermore
> that the stones are not alive.'

Cleric:

> 'Put Christ's mysterious Cross
> now over thine eyes:
> abate for a time thy furies:
> wherefore dost thou fell the stones?'

Then the royal soldier's wrath ceases, and his sense came to him, and he put the sign of the Cross over his face, and then he saw nothing there save the stones and sods of the earth. Thereafter he asked tidings of the clerics, and said: 'Why come ye?' 'We came,' they answered, 'to meet thy corpse, for death is near thee.' . . .

The clerics marked out a church there in the Brug, and told him to dig its trench in honour of the great Lord of the Elements. 'It shall be done,' said he. Then he began digging the trench, so that it was then for the first time that the green of the Brug was injured. And he was telling the clerics his own tidings, and making God a fervent repentance . . .

Now after this confession the clerics blessed water for him, and he partook of the Body of Christ, and made to God a fervent repentance. And he told them to relate to Cairnech how he had made his confession and repentance . . . The clerics remain for that night in the church of the Brug, and the king goes to Clettech, and sat there on his lady's right hand. Sín asked him what had interrupted his combat on that day. 'The clerics came to me,' he answered, 'and they put the sign of the Cross of Christ over my face, and then I saw nothing save fern and stones and puff-balls and sprigs of *sanas* (?). And since there was no one there to fight me, I came away.' Then Sín said:

> 'Never believe the clerics,
> for they chant nothing save unreason:
> follow not their unmelodious stave,
> for they do not reverence righteousness.

> 'Cleave not to the clerics of churches,
> if thou desire life without treachery:

> better am I as a friend here:
> let not repentance come to thee.'

Muirchertach:

> 'I will be always along with thee,
> O fair damsel without evil plight;
> likelier to me is thy countenance
> than the churches of the clerics.'

Then Sín beguiled his mind and came between him and the teachings of the clerics, and on that night she made a magical wine for the king and his troops. The seventh night she was at her magic, on the eve of Wednesday after All-saints-day[7] precisely. When the hosts were intoxicated there comes the sigh of a great wind. 'This is the sigh (*osnad*) of a winter-night (*gemadaig*),' said the king. And Sín said:

> ''Tis I am the Rough Wind [*Gáeth Garb*],
> a daughter of fair nobles:
> Winter-Night [*Gamadaig*] is my name, for
> every place together.
> Sigh [*Osnad*] and Wind [*Gáeth*]: Winter-
> Night [*Gamadaig*] thus.'

After that she caused a great snow-storm there; and never had come a noise of battle that was greater than the shower of thick snow that poured there at that time, and from the northwest precisely it came . . . When the feasting ended, then the hosts lay down, and in no one of them was the strength of a woman in childbed. Then the king lies down on his couch, and a heavy sleep falls upon him. So he makes a great screaming out of his slumber and awoke from his sleep. 'What is that?' says the damsel. 'A great host of demons has appeared to me,' he answers . . . The king rises up, for the vision which he beheld did not let him sleep, and he came forth out of the house, and in the church of the Brug he sees a little fire by the clerics. To them then he came and said: 'There is neither strength nor vigour in me tonight.' And he related his vision and his dream. 'And 'tis hard for me,' quoth he, 'to shew prowess tonight even though hosts of outlanders should attack me, because of the weakness in which we are and the badness of the

---

7. The feast of *Samain*.

night.' So then the clerics began instructing him. He came in at once and there he said:

> 'Full evil is this storm [*sín*] tonight
> to the clerics in their camp;
> they dare not ever sleep
> from the roughness of the night's storms
> [*sín*] . . .'

Then he went into his bed and asked the damsel for a drink, and she cast a sleep-charm upon that deceptive wine, so that he drank a draught of it, and it made him drunk and feeble, without sap or strength. Then he slept heavily and he sees a vision there, to wit, that he went in a ship to sea, and his ship foundered, and a taloned griffin came to him and carried him into her nest, and then he and the nest were burnt, and the griffin fell with him.

The king awoke and ordered his vision to be taken to his foster-brother Dub Dá Rinn, the son of the druid Saignén, and Dub Dá Rinn gave the rede thereof (thus): 'This is the ship wherein thou has been,' quoth he, 'to wit, the ship of thy princedom on the sea of life, and thou a-steering the princedom; and this is the ship that foundered, thou to be offered and thy life to come to an end. This is the taloned griffin that has carried thee into her nest, the woman that is in thy company, to make thee intoxicated, and to bring thee with her into her bed, and to detain thee in the house of Clettech so that it will be burnt upon thee. Now the griffin that fell with thee is the woman who will die by reason of thee. This then is the rede of that vision.'

The king then sleeps heavily after Sín had cast the sleep-charm upon him. Now while he was in that sleep Sín rose up and arranged the spears and the javelins of the hosts in readiness in the doors, and then turned all their points toward the house. She forms (by magic) many crowds and multitudes around the fortress. She herself goes in and scatters fire in every direction throughout the house and the side-walls, and then she enters the bed.

'Twas then the king awoke from his sleep. 'What is that?' asked the damsel. 'A host of demons has appeared to me, burning the house upon me, and slaughtering my people at the door.' 'Thou has no hurt from that,' says the damsel, 'save that it has appeared.'

Now when they were thus in converse they heard the crash of the burning house, and the shout of the host of demons and wizardry around it. 'Who is around the house?' asked the king. Says Sín: 'Túathal Máelgarb,[8] son of Cormac Cáech son of Cairpre son of Níall, with his armies. He is there taking vengeance on thee for the battle of Granard.' And the king knew not that this was untrue, and that no corporeal host was surrounding the house.

Then he rises swiftly and comes to seek his arms, and found no one to answer him. The damsel goes forth from the house, and he follows her at once, and a spear hits him in his chest and goes right through him.[9] From the door he returns to his bed. The hosts thereupon went forth, and no one of them escaped without wounding or burning.

Then the king came again towards the door, and between him and it were the embers and the hails of fire. When the fire had filled the doorway and all the house around, and he found no shelter for himself, he got into a cask of wine, and therein he is drowned, as he went under it every second hour[10] for dread of the fire. Then the fire falls on his head, and five feet . . . of him is burnt; but the wine kept the rest of his body without burning.

The day after, when the morning came, the clerics Masán and Casán and Crídán go before the king, and carry him to the Boyne and wash his corpse therein. So Cairnech with his monks thereupon visits him, and the saint himself made great grief in bewailing him, and bore witness of him, and said: 'A great loss to Ireland today is Mac Erca, one of the four best men that have gained possession of Erin without trickery and without force, namely Muirchertach mac Erca, and Níall Noígíallach, Conn Cétchathach, and Úgaine Mór.'[11]

The body is afterwards lifted up by Cairnech, to be carried to Tuilén and there interred. Then Dúaibsech, the wife of Muirchertach, met the clerics while the corpse was among them, and she made a great, mournful lamentation, and struck

---

8. Great-grandson of Níall Noigiallach and kinsman of Muirchertach, d. 544.
9. The words 'and a spear . . . through him' derive from an emendation by T. Ó Concheanainn (*Éigse*, vol. 15, Part 2, pp. 141–4).
10. Read 'moment'.
11. The last three mentioned are prehistoric kings.

her palms together, and leant her back against the ancient tree in Óenach Réil;[12] and a burst of gore broke from her heart in her chest, and straightaway she died of grief for her husband. Then the clerics put the queen's corpse along with the corpse of the king. And then said Cairnech:

'Dúaibsech, Mac Erca's noble wife,
let her grave be dug by you here . . .'

Thereafter the queen is buried and her grave is dug. Then the king is buried near the temple on the north side, and Cairnech was declaring the king's character, and uttered this lay:

'The grave of the King of Ailech will abide forever,
in Tuilén, every one will hear of it . . .'

When the clerics had finished the burial they saw coming toward them a lonely woman, beautiful and shining, robed in a green mantle with its fringe of golden thread. A smock of priceless silk was about her. She reached the place wherein the clerics were, and saluted them, and so the clerics saluted her. And they perceived upon her an appearance of sadness and sorrow, and they recognized that she it was that had ruined the king . . . Then the clerics were asking her who she herself was, or who was her father or her mother, and what cause she had from the king when she ruined him as aforesaid. 'Sín,' she replied, 'is my name, and Sige son of Dían son of Trén is my father. Muirchertach mac Erca killed my father, my mother and my sister in the battle of Cerb on Boyne, and also destroyed in that battle all the Old Tribes of Tara and my fatherland.' . . .

Then she confessed to Cairnech, and to God she made fervent repentance, as had been taught her, and she went in obedience to Cairnech, and straightaway died there of grief for the king. So Cairnech said that a grave should be made for her, and that she should be put under the sward of the earth. It was done as the cleric ordered . . .

Touching Cairnech, now, he shewed great care for Muirchertach's soul, but he did not bring it out of hell. Howbeit he composed a prayer which from its beginning is called *Parce mihi Domine*,[13]

etc., and he repeated it continually for sake of the soul of the king, so that (at last) the soul was given to him out of hell. Whereupon the angel came to Cairnech and told him that whoever should sing that prayer continually would without doubt be a dweller in heaven. So then said the angel:

'Whoever should sing strongly
the prayer of Cairnech of the mysteries
'twould be enough to succour
Judas, who was the worst ever born, etc.'

So far the Death of Muirchertach, as Cairnech related it, and Tigernach, and Ciarán, and Mochta,[14] and Túathal Máelgarb; and it was written and revised by those holy clerics, commemorating it for every one from that time to this.

14. Tigernach, Ciarán and Mochta are sixth-century saints associated, respectively, with Clones, County Monaghan, Clonmacnoise, County Offaly, and Louth, County Louth.

BAILE THE SWEET-SPOKEN, SON OF BÚAN
(Middle Irish)

[The phantasm of ideal love and the longing for constancy it provokes are suggested in the name of Baile son of Búan, 'Illusion son of Immutability'. This story is found in many cultures, ancient and modern: lovers part, but one tree will take another in her arms and hold. This Irish version is not later than the eleventh century. The transmutation of the lovers into writing tablets on which the fictions of love are preserved may be an Irish flourish. The story was published and translated by Eugene O'Curry, *Lectures on the Manuscript Materials of Ancient Irish History* (Dublin, 1861; rpr. Dublin: Four Courts Press, 1995), pp. 472–5. Apart from minor changes in presentation and the normalization of name-forms, the present translation corresponds to his.]

The three grandsons of Capa, son of Cinga, son of Ros, son of Rudraige, were Monach, and Búan[1] and Fer-Corb, a quibus[2] Dál mBúain and Dál Cuirb, and the Monachs of Arad.[3]

1. MS 'Baile' is corrected to 'Buan'.
2. i.e. 'from whom are'.
3. All these territories are in County Down.

12. Unidentified.
13. 'Spare me O Lord'.

Búan's only son was Baile; he was the specially beloved of Aillinn, the daughter of Lugaid son of Fergus Fairge[4] (or the daughter of Éogan, the son of Dathí).[5] And he was the specially beloved of every one who saw or heard him, both men and women, on account of his novel stories. And they made an appointment to meet at Ros na Ríg,[6] at Lann Máelduib, on the brink of the Boyne in Brega.

The man[7] came from the north to meet her, from Emain Macha, over Slíab Fúaid,[8] over Muirtheimne[9] to Tráig Baile.[10] Here they unyoked their chariots, sent their horses out to graze, and turned themselves to pleasure and happiness.

While there, they saw a horrible spectral personage coming towards them from the south. Vehement was his step and his rapid progress. The manner in which he sped over the earth might be compared to the darting of a hawk down a cliff; or to wind from off the green sea. His left was towards the land.

'Let him be met,' said Baile, 'to ask him where he goes, and where he comes from, and what is the cause of his haste.' 'To Túag Inbir[11] I go back, to the north, now, from Slíab Suide Laigen,[12] and I have no news but of the daughter of Lugaid son of Fergus, who had fallen in love with Baile son of Búan, and was coming to meet him, until the youths of Leinster overtook her, and she was killed by the forcible detention, as it was promised by druids and good prophets for them, and that they would not part for ever after. This is my news.' And he darted away from them like a blast of wind over the green sea, and they were not able to detain him.

When Baile heard this, he fell dead without life, and his tomb was raised, and his *ráth*,[13] and his tombstone was set up, and his fair of lamentation was held by the Ultonians. And a yew tree grew up through his grave, and the form and shape of Baile's head was visible on top of it, hence Tráig Baile.

Afterwards the same man went to the south to where the maiden Aillinn was, and went into the *grianán*.[14] 'Whence comes the man that we do not know?' said the maiden. 'From the northern half of Erinn, from Túag Inbir, and past this place to Slíab Suide Laigen.' 'Have you news?' said the maiden. 'I have no news worth relating now, but that I have seen the Ultonians holding a fair of lamentation, and raising a *ráth*, and erecting a stone, and writing his name, to Baile son of Búan, the *rígdamna*[15] of Ulster, by the side of Tráig Baile, [who died] whilst he was coming to meet a favourite and beloved woman to whom he had given love; for it is not destined for them that they should reach each other alive, or that one of them should see the other alive.' He darted off after telling the evil news. Aillinn fell dead without life, and her tomb was raised, etc. And an apple-tree grew through her grave, and became a great tree at the end of seven years, and the shape of Aillinn's head upon its top.

At the end of seven years, poets and prophets and visioners cut down the yew which was over the grave of Baile, and they made a poet's tablet of it, and they wrote the visions and the espousals and the loves and the courtships of Ulster in it. [The apple-tree which grew over Aillinn was also cut down and] in the same way the courtships of Leinster were written in it.

When *Samain* had arrived, afterwards, and its festival was made by Art the son of Conn, the poets and the professors of every art came to that feast, as it was their custom, and they brought their tablets with them. And these tablets also came there, and Art saw them, and when he saw them he asked for them. And the two tablets were brought, and he held them in his hands face to face. Suddenly the one tablet of them sprang upon the other, and they became united the same as woodbine around a twig, and it was not possible to separate them. And they were preserved like every other jewel in the treasury at Tara, until it was burned by Dúnlang the son of Énna,[16] namely, at the time that he burned the princesses at Tara.

---

4. Descended from Núadu Necht, legendary ancestor of most Irish dynasties.
5. An alternative descent; the identity of Éogan and Dathí is uncertain.
6. Rosnaree, a ford on the Boyne, near Slane, County Meath.
7. i.e. Baile.
8. Fews mountains, County Armagh.
9. Muirtheimne Plain, extending from Drogheda to Dundalk, County Louth.
10. In English, 'Baile's Strand', at Dundalk.
11. Estuary of the Bann, County Derry.
12. Mount Leinster, in the barony of Ferns, County Wexford.
13. English 'rath, enclosure'.

14. English 'sunny chamber'.
15. English 'royal heir'.
16. An early Leinster king, reputed to have burned thirty princesses with their retinues, on account of which the Bóruma tribute was re-imposed.

NÍALL FRASSACH'S ACT
OF TRUTH
(Middle Irish)

[A king divines the mysteries of surrogate motherhood and remote paternity in an 'Act of Truth' that proves his rule has direct sanction from the supernatural realm. For good measure, his Act of Truth releases a priest from demonic bondage in the upper regions, who falls down to earth before the assembly. In this Middle Irish tale, women's sexual gratification of each other, if unusual, is unproblematic, all the more so when contrasted with the priest's homage to his demon woodworker. A later version of the tale in the sixteenth-century *Leabhar Eoghanach* is more vaunty. There, King Níall Frassach asks the woman: 'What business had she with you?' She answers: 'That her husband lay with her and didn't satisfy her need — so she lay with me to finish her pleasure.' The present translation is from: David Greene (ed. and trans.), 'The "Act of Truth" in a Middle Irish Story', *Saga och Sed* (1979), pp. 30–7.]

There was a fine, firm, righteous, generous princely king ruling over Ireland, Niall Frassach, son of Fergal. Ireland was prosperous during his reign. There was fruit and fatness, corn and milk in his time, and he had everyone settled on his own land. He called a great assembly in Tailtiu[1] once, and had the cream of the men of Ireland around him. Great kings and wide-eyed queens and the chiefs and nobles of the territories were ranged on the stately seats of the assembly. There were boys and jesters and the heroes of the Irish in strong eager bands racing their horses in the assembly.

While they were there, a woman came to the king carrying a boy-child, and put him into the king's arms. 'For your kingship and your sovereignty,' said she, 'find out for me through your ruler's truth who the carnal father of this boy is, for I do not know myself. For I swear by your ruler's truth, and by the King who governs every created thing that I have not known guilt with a man for many years now.'

The king was silent then. 'Have you had playful mating with another woman?' said he, 'and do not conceal it if you have.' 'I will not

conceal it,' said she; 'I have.' 'It is true,' said the king. 'That woman had mated with a man just before, and the semen which he left with her, she put it into your womb in the tumbling, so that it was begotten in your womb. That man is the father of your child, and let it be found out who he is.'

While they were there they heard a noise coming towards them out of the sky, and they saw a strange malignant spectre falling to the floor of the assembly, putting men and horses to flight; nobody stayed in the assembly but the king and a few people around him. 'What are you?' said the king. 'A human being,' said he. 'What put you in that plight?' said the king. 'I will tell you,' said he. 'I am in fact the priest of Inis Bó Finne,[1] and I had built a house, and there was no craftsman in the world that I thought good enough to make the woodwork. And a demon came to me in the shape of a man, and he made the woodwork in the house, and he would take no payment except that I should bow down to him. And I bowed down to him then, and I was seized by swelling pride and a wave of vainglory and I was caught up into flight and the demons took me away with them, and they have been ruling me for seven years now. But when you gave that fine righteous judgment this morning on the woman who came to plead with you, we happened to be above you at that time. The vapour, then, which arose from you when you became red flew up and scattered the demons in all directions, and they were unable to hold me in the air, so that I fell down through the truth of your rulership — the true judgment you gave on the child.'

The priest was saved and the father of the child was ascertained through the king's judgment in that way. It was at the birth of that king that the three showers fell: a shower of white silver (it is from that that the shrines and emblems of the saints of Ireland were made) and a shower of blood in Glenn Lagen,[2] and a shower of wheat. Hence Níall[3] *Frassach* 'of the Showers'.

---

1. Inishbofin, an island off County Mayo.
2. Unidentified.
3. The Irish actually has 'Fland' here (a slip).

GAS LOSSA
(A Sprig of Herb)
(*c.* 1000)

[James Carney edited the following allusive poem and provided a literal translation, but confessed to finding its meaning obscure ('*Gas Lossa*', *Éigse*, vol. 13 [spring 1970], pp. 99–103). He dated it to *c.* 1000. One possibility is to read it as a declaration of intent by a deserted woman, jealous of her former lover's affections, who threatens to kill their love-child and then herself. The 'herbal sprig' may have a double meaning: both the poisonous plant which will bring about their deaths (*los* is Irish for plants of the water-dropwort type, of which hemlock is one), and the child the father does not acknowledge, whose birth has brought her to this crisis. In support of the latter interpretation, we may note that in the eighth-century legal text *Bretha Nemed Tóisech*, the following allusive passage uses another term for a plant of the water-dropwort type to refer to the 'son of a wanton woman' who is an embarrassment to the kin because he is not recognized by his father: 'A stake of wood in a fence of silver, water-dropwort in brooklime, is the son of a wanton woman who is joined to the bosom of the family other than by propriety [and] fittingness.' Translated from: D.A. Binchy (ed.), *Corpus Iuris Hibernici*, vol. 6, p. 2230, lines 3–4. This new translation of the poem is by Seamus Deane.]

Gas lossa
cona duilli barruaini
tucc duine dam ind-ossa.

Na cella
cid occu ro throiscemmar
ní fuarammar co[1] gremma.

Muir uaine
port na hinse i n-athaigenn,
commór ticc is téit uaide.

Muir aithbech
mo-génar dian comdúthaig
ma-raen is talam tairthech.

Ro-fetar
is imda tonn trethanglas
imm dúnad meic ríg Bretan.

Rom-úraig
fairrge uaine ailénach
etrumm is fer in dúnaid.

Rom-bánaig
ben buide is sí drochlámach
d'fhaicsin occai 'na grádaib.

Rom-lochraig
étach uaine ildathach
d'fhaicsin imm duine ndochraid.

Mo lennán
iar tuidecht ónd fhírthiprait
iar n-innlut a dá gel-lám.

Is brígmar
folt 'na ualach lethorlach
cen anad icá chírad.

Druim nUball,
is doilge cech ndédenach,
is usa écc[2] ná a fhulang.

---

1. Restoring MS *co* here, against Carney's *cen*.

2. MS: 'as usa aeg'. It seems preferable to interpret this as 'is usa éc' than as 'is usa a écc' with Carney.

TRANSLATION

Not long ago
Someone gave
Me a sprig of herb
With green
Fangs at its tip.

I have done
Church fastings
That are less lethal
Than that sprig
In their effects.

In the green sea
The island
Lies and the tide goes
In and out
Alike from its shore.

Happy that one
Equally
At home on
The sea and the land.
In this, unlike me.

1 know there is many
A green wave
Furled round the fort
Of the king
Of Britain's son.

It has cut me deep
That the isled
Sea lies between
Me and him
Who lives in the fort.

It has made me blanch
To observe
A sly, sallow one,
That woman,
So close with him.

It has killed
Me to see
Green-shaded clothing
Draped on
Her ugly person.

Loved bye-child!
I come from
The well, after washing
His two bright
Hands. My own love!

His head a mass
Of tresses,
Thick, unruly, always
Tended by
The stroke of my comb.

Ah, Drumnoole!
This last thing
Is worst of all. My death
At least is
Easier than this.

from:
CERT A MNÁ RÉ PARTHOLÁN
(The First Lawcase)
(Late Middle Irish)

[Anxieties about virility and accusations of female frailty are brought together and presented as foundational in the schema of Irish mytho-history which received its distinctive form in the late eleventh-century *Lebar Gabála Érenn*, 'The Book of the Taking of Ireland'. Ireland's first invasion was led by the woman Cesair. She and fifty other women (some accounts say forty-nine) embark on an expedition to avoid the Deluge. They are joined by Bith, Ladra and Findtan, three men who were refused a place on Noah's ark. Sailing by way of Egypt and Spain, they reach Ireland where the men divide the tally of women among them. Bith dies of 'woman demand', soon followed by Ladra, and Findtan flees from the lascivious women and is transformed into a salmon. All the women are drowned and Ireland lies waste for hundreds of years until the second invasion, which is led by Partholán. One day when his back is turned, his wife Delgnat commits Ireland's first adultery. When accused, she cites precedents in her defence and wins her case. Yet behind these lurks the precedent of Eve, who did not go unpunished for her sin. A prose version in the Book of Lecan (f. 275a) has Partholán declare: 'Ever since Eve committed the transgression of the apple for which the human race was condemned and expelled from Paradise, no restitution has been made for your crime. Great are your crimes of intention. Your guilt deserves penalties.' Such considerations are eschewed in the present playful version.

For the full Irish text, see: R.A.S. Macalister (ed. and trans.), *Lebor Gabála Érenn. The Book of the Taking of Ireland, Part III*, Irish Texts Society, vol. 39 (Dublin: Irish Texts Society, 1940), pp. 60–72. This translation is by John Montague (ed.), *The Faber Book of Irish Verse* (London: Faber and Faber, 1974) 42–4.]

Parthalón luid laithi amach.
do cuairt a thíri torbach:
a ben sa ghilla immale,
fácaid da éis san indsi.

Amail robatar na tig,
in días, ingnad anaichnig,
saichis for in ngilla nglé,
ocus ni rosaig fuirre.

Húaire na rosfreccair co féig
in gilla, decair doméin,
nosnochtand tria tristib trá,
ro po obair díscir deg-mná!

Atraig in gilla cen acht,
Abrisc in raid in dáenacht! —
ocus doluid, rád cen ail,
co Delgnait na coim-lepaigg. [. . .]

Bái ic Parthalón, ba fer fis,
lestar do lind somilis:
as na fétad nech ní d'ól
acht tré chuislind do derg-ór.

Nosgeib íta íar sin ngním,
Toba ocus Delgnait íar fír;
cor ibidar adangeim
a dá ndig is a cuislind. [. . .]

Do roich Parthalón imuig,
íar cur do cúaird in ássaig,
Dobert dó, ba sestan seng,
a lestar is a cuislenn. [. . .]

Ro fhaillsig demun dub duairc
in gním n-olc n-étigh n-an-suairc;
'Blas beóil Toba sund' ar sé,
'Ocus blas beóil Delgnaite'. [. . .]

Ro frecair Delgnait dia fir:
'Noco n-acaind atá in cin,
cid serb lat a rád damsa,
co derb, ach is acat-so. [. . .]

Mil la mnái, lemnacht la cat,
biad la fial, carna la mac,
sáer istig ocus fáebar,
áen re n-áen, is ro-báegal.

Blaisfid in ben in mil m[b]alc,
íbaid in cat in lemnacht,
dobéra in fial in biad bán,
toméla an carna in macám.

Imeoraid fáebar in sáer
conricfa in táen ris an áen;
conid airi sin is chóir
a n-imcoiméd a cétóir.

Is í sin cét drúis ro clos
do rignid ar tús i fos:
ben Parthalóin, fír a raid,
do techt do gillai n-iarraith. [. . .]

Acas is í sin, can meng,
cét breth rucad an Érinn:

conad dé atá, re racht rán,
Cert a mná ré Partholán.

TRANSLATION

Partholan went out one day
To tour his wide spread lands;
Leaving his wife and servant,
Both bound by his commands.

Long they waited in his house,
Until the lady, feeling desperate —
A state before unheard of —
Propositioned the pure servant.

Rightly he ignored her,
Stubborn against temptation,
Until she removed her clothes:
Strange work for a decent woman!

Then, so frail is humanity,
Long limbed Topa rose,
And joined the lovely Delgnat,
Lonely upon her couch.

Wise Partholan possessed
A vat of ale, cool and sweet,
From which none might drink
Save through a golden spigot.

Thirsty after their actions,
Topa and Delgnat, truth to tell,
Leapt from bed so urgently
Their mouths met on the barrel.

When Partholan returned
From wandering his wide fields
A surly black demon revealed
The stains on the golden tube.

'Look, the track of the mouth
Of Topa, as low down as this,
And beside it the smear left
By married Delgnat's kiss!'

Whereupon his wife replied:
'Surely the right to complain
Is mine, innocently left
To confront another man.

'Honey with a woman, milk with a cat,
A sharp tool with a craftsman,
Goods with a child or spendthrift:
Never couple things like that.

'The woman will eat the honey,
The cat lap the new milk,
While the child destroys the things
Not bestowed by the spendthrift.

'The craftsman will use the tool,
Because one and one make two:
So never leave your belongings
Long unguarded, without you.'

That is the first adultery
To be heard of in Ireland.
Likewise the first lawcase:
The right of his wife against Partholan.

CINEAD, CÁ CIN RO BUÍ DÚINN?
(A Protest)
(Late Middle Irish)

[This protest of innocence vaunts the pleasure of guilt. It was dated to the Late Middle Irish period by Brian Ó Cuív, who edited and translated it in 'Three Middle Irish Poems', *Éigse*, vol.16 (1975–6), pp. 11–13. This new translation is by Seamus Deane.]

Cinaed, cá cin ro buí dúinn
        cár n-innarba a crích Néill,
óir ní dingnainn re mnaí mín
        acht a ndingnainn rem mnaí féin?

Fer liath ro lí orm a mnaí,
        ní ro tarbaige Dia dó
óir ní ragainn-si fó brat
        co n-ebad cat lemlacht bó,

co linged os airbe n-aird
        co n-éirged eo a buinne bedg,
co ndernadh ben dolbad duilb,
        co n-ebtha cuirm a corn cerb.

Cid isi ro léiced dam
        ní dingnainn ar apa a fir
co lenad torc trom a threoit
        co n-ebad leoit deoch do mil.

Fóill apa 'mar lied orm
        Gormfhlaith fhial ó Áth dá Rinn,
ar aoi gluasachta a dá les,
        meise 's mo lám des fó cinn.

Ar ar faicsin ima raen
        ar in raen fonnglas fér
fóill adbar d'innisin sceóil
        faicsin a beóil ar mo bél.

Nochar chert do Chinaed chain
        ar corn comóil, ce mad mid,
ingen ríg na n-étach ndrol
        d'écnach rim cen col cen cin.

TRANSLATION

Why was I banished Cinaed, why?
Why sent out from Niall's country?

I would not, I tell you, do anything
With any decent woman, nothing,

That I would not do with my wife.
It was an old man who accused me

Of being intimate with his wife. Damn
Him! I'd no sooner go with her than

Would a cat drink new milk,
Than a deer jump a high fence,

Than a salmon leap from a stream,
Than a woman perform sorcery,

Than ale be drunk from a silver cup.
Even were she to allow me, I would

Not sleep with her, not even to spite
Her husband, not until a boar would

Follow its herd, a woman drink honey.
It was for a trivial reason

I was accused of violating Gormflaith.
Because of the way she was moving

Her slow thighs, because my hand
Was under her head, because we were

Seen together on the grassy pathway.
It was a trivial reason, I tell you.

Her lips on mine, they said!
It was not right for Cinaed,

Just because we had a drink together,
Even if it was mead, to accuse me,

I who am wholly innocent, without sin,
Of having been intimate with her,

The King's daughter, her of the fancy
Fringed garments. Not right, I tell you.

CODAIL BEAGÁN, BEAGÁN BEAG
(Lullaby of Adventurous Love)
(12th century)

[In the earliest tradition about Gráinne, her love for the young warrior Díarmait úa Duibne is fearless and unconditional. A secondary tradition in which the image of free love associated with Gráinne is contested is found in various texts from the tenth century onwards. 'The Wooing of Ailbe' reasserts the values of domestic stability (cf. pp. 206–10), while 'The Separation of Finn and Gráinne' concerns the restoration of order after marital breakdown (cf. pp. 36–7). Dealing a further blow to the tradition of free love, Díarmait, in the Early Modern Irish tale 'The Pursuit of Diarmaid and Gráinne', claims that it was sorcery which caused him to abscond with Gráinne (cf. Volume I, pp. 314, 316). In the following poem, which dates from the twelfth century or thereabouts and may be the remnant of a tale from that period, neither lover is manipulated by the other. The lines between abduction and elopement, between sleep and wakefulness, blur to suggest that the relationship between the lovers is complementary. The poem was adapted and re-mythologized by Yeats as 'Lullaby'. Text and translation are from David Greene and Frank O'Connor (ed. and trans.), *A Golden Treasury of Irish Poetry*, pp. 184–8.]

Codail beagán beagán beag,
uair ní heagail duit a bheag,
  a giolla dá dtardas seirc,
  a mhic Uí Dhuibhne, a Dhiarmaid.

Codailse sonn go sáimh sáimh,
a Uí Dhuibhne, a Dhiarmaid áin:
  do-ghéan-sa t'fhoraire de,
  a Mheic Uí dhealbhdha Dhuibhne.

Codail beagán, beannacht fort,
ós uisce Tobráin Tréanghort,
  a uanáin uachtair locha
  do bhrú Thíre Tréanshrotha.

Rob ionann is codladh teas
deighFhiodhaigh na n-airdéigeas,
  dá dtug inghin Morainn bhuain
  tar ceann Conaill ón Chraobhruaidh.

Rob ionann is codladh tuaidh
Fionnchaidh Fhionnchaoimh Easa Ruaidh,
  dá dtug Sláinghe, séaghdha rainn,
  tar ceann Fáilbhe Chotatchinn.

Rob ionann is codladh tiar
Áine inghine Gáilían,
  feacht do-luidh céim fo thrilis
  la Dubhthach ó Dhairinis.

Rob ionann is codladh tair
Deadhadh dána dhíomasaigh,
  dá dtug Coinchinn inghin Binn
  tar ceann Deichill déin duibhrinn.

A chró gaile iarthair Ghréag,
anfad-sa dot fhorchoimhéad;
  maidhfidh mo chroidhe-se acht súaill
  monat fhaicear re hénuair.

Ar scaradh ar ndís 'ma-le
scaradh leanabh aonbhaile,
  is scaradh cuirp re hanmain,
  a laoich Locha fionnCharmain.

Léigfidhear caoinche ar do lorg,
rith Caoilte ní budh hanord;
  nachat tair bás ná broghadh,
  nachat léige i sírchodladh.

Ní chodail in damh-sa sair,
ní scuireann do bhúirfeadhaigh;
  cia bheith um dhoiribh na lon
  ní fuil 'na mheanmain codladh.

Ní chodail an eilit mhaol
ag búirfeadhaigh fá breaclaogh;
   do-ní rith tar barraibh tor;
   ní dhéan 'na hadhbhaidh codal.

Ní chodail an chaoinche bhras
ós barraibh na gcrann gcaomhchas;
   is glórach a-táthar ann;
   gi bé an smólach ní chodlann.

Ní chodail an lacha lán;
maith a láthar re deaghshnámh;
   ní dhéan súan ná sáimhe ann,
   ina hadhbhaidh ní chodlann.

A-nocht ní chodail an ghearg
ós fhraochaibh anfaidh iomard;
   binn foghar a gotha glain
   eidhir shrotha ní chodail.

TRANSLATION

Sleep a little, a little little, for you have little to fear, lad I gave love to, Díarmait son of Ó Duibne.

Sleep here, quietly, quietly, grandson of Duibne, noble Díarmait. I shall be your watchman, shapely son of Ó Duibne.

Sleep a little, bless you, over the water of Toprán Tréngort. O foam on the lake's surface from the edge of Tír Trénshrotha.

May it be like the southern sleep of great Fidach of the high poets who carried off the daughter of enduring Morann against Conall of the Red Branch.

Let it be like the northern sleep of fair Finnchad of Assaroe when he carried off Sláine, happy choice, from Fáilbe Hardhead.

May it be like the western sleep of Aine, daughter of Gailian, when she eloped into the woods with Dubthach from Dernish.

May it be like the eastern sleep of proud arrogant Dedad when he carried off Coíchenn, daughter of Binn, against stern Deichill Duibrinn.

Fold of valour west of Greece, I shall remain and keep guard; my heart will all but break if at any time I do not see you.

The parting of us two is like the parting of children of one home; it is like the parting of body and soul, hero of fair Loch Carman.

A spell will be laid on your path; Caoilte's race[1] will not be in vain, so that neither death nor grief may come to you, nor lay you in eternal sleep.

This stag eastward does not sleep; he does not cease from bellowing; even though he is in the blackbirds' grove he does not have it in his mind to sleep.

The hornless hind does not sleep, crying for her speckled fawn; she races over the tops of the bushes and does not sleep in her lair.

The flighty linnet does not sleep in the tops of the lovely tangled trees; everything there gives voice, and even the thrush does not sleep.

The heavy duck does not sleep, but plans to swim boldly; she does not rest or linger; in her nest she does not sleep.

The curlew does not sleep tonight over the raging of the wild storm; the sound of his clear voice is sweet; he does not sleep among the streams.

1. Cf. pp. 36–7.

from:
BUILE SHUIBHNE
(Sweeney Astray)
(12th century)

[Suibne *gelt*, Sweeney the madman, figures in Irish literature from the ninth century onwards but the key text for his legend, *Buile Shuibhne*, dates from the very end of the Middle Irish period. It tells how a saint's curse causes Sweeney's descent — or rather flight — into madness in the Battle of Mag Rath (Moira, County Down) in 637, and it describes the life he led subsequently, in which his nakedness, extraordinary agility, and inspired ravings about the natural world combine to mark him out as a classic Wild Man figure. Middle Irish commentary on the law-tract *Bretha Étgid* states that there were three great virtues associated with the Battle of Mag Rath, the chief of which was Sweeney's madness, but adds that the virtue consisted not in 'the fact of his going mad but rather in all the stories and poems he left after him in Ireland' (cf. D.A. Binchy [ed.], *Corpus Iuris Hibernici*, vol. 1, p. 250).

The Sweeney legend is one of the great formulations of the plight of the artist who earns his gift at the cost of alienation and dispossession. Robert Graves deemed it 'the most ruthless and bitter description in all European literature of an obsessed poet's predicament' (*The White Goddess: A Historical Grammar of Poetic Myth* [revised and enlarged edition, London: Faber and Faber, 1961], p. 455). Sweeney forfeits church, kingship, and marriage. Twice in the course of his wild life, however, he returns to his wife, Eorann. The following excerpt, from the translation of *Buile Shuibhne* by Seamus Heaney, *Sweeney Astray* (Derry: Field Day, 1983, and London: Faber and Faber, 1984), pp. 25–8), describes the first occasion.]

When Sweeney deserted his kingship, his wife had gone to live with Guaire. There had been two kinsmen with equal rights to the kingship Sweeney had abandoned, two grandsons of Scannlan's called Guaire and Eochaidh. At that time, Eorann was with Guaire and they had gone hunting through the Fews towards Edenterriff in Cavan. His camp was near Glen Bolcain, on a plain in the Armagh district.

Sweeney landed on the lintel of Eorann's hut and spoke to her:

— Do you remember, lady, the great love we shared when we were together? Life is still a pleasure to you but not to me.

And this exchange ensued between them:

Sweeney: Restless as wingbeats
of memory, I hover
above you, and your bed
still warm from your lover.

Remember when you played
the promise-game with me?
Sun and moon would have died
if ever you lost your Sweeney!

But you have broken trust,
unmade it like a bed —
not mine in the dawn frost
but yours, that he invaded.

Eorann: Welcome here, my crazy dote,
my first and last and favourite!
I am easy now, and yet I wasted
at the cruel news of your being bested.

Sweeney: There's more welcome for the prince
who preens for you and struts
to those amorous banquets
where Sweeney feasted once.

Eorann: All the same, I would prefer
a hollow tree and Sweeney bare —
that sweetest game we used to play —
to banqueting with him to-day.

I tell you, Sweeney, if I were given
the pick of all in earth and Ireland
I'd rather go with you, live sinless
and sup on water and watercress.

Sweeney: But cold and hard as stone
lies Sweeney's path
through the beds of Lisardowlin.
There I go to earth

in panic, starved and bare,
a rickle of skin and bones.
I am yours no longer.
And you are another man's.

Eorann: My poor tormented lunatic!
When I see you like this it makes me sick,
your cheek gone pale, your skin all scars,
ripped and scored by thorns and briars.

Sweeney: And yet I hold no grudge,
my gentle one.
Christ ordained my bondage
and exhaustion.

Eorann: I wish we could fly away together,
be rolling stones, birds of a feather:
I'd swoop to pleasure you in flight
and huddle close on the roost at night.

Sweeney: I have gone north and south.
One night I was in the Mournes.
I have wandered as far as the Bann mouth
and Kilsooney.

They had no sooner finished than the army swept into the camp from every side, and as usual, he was away in a panic, never stopping until twilight, when he arrived at Ros Bearaigh — that church where he had first halted after the battle of Moira — and again he went into the yew tree of the church.

from:
ACALLAM NA SENÓRACH
(The Colloquy of the Ancients)
(c. 1200)

[One might describe the *Acallam*, the great collection of Fenian stories in prose and verse from the end of the twelfth century, as a high chivalric text with the same underlying cultural assumptions as can be posited for romances of chivalry elsewhere in twelfth-century Europe. A new European preoccupation with the interpersonal and discursive proprieties attendant on the social position of women has left its mark on the traditional materials and newly invented stories of which it is composed. As befits a chivalric romance sensibility, there is considerable interest in stories of refined love for their own sake, and so one finds the love interest painted in with considerable aesthetic delicacy and care. The famous story of the tragic lovers Créide and Cáel, told near the beginning of the collection, is a case in point and the fact that this segment has been frequently anthologized and translated attests to its power as a story of doomed love. Here as elsewhere in the *Acallam*, however, the simple agenda of a pathetic 'romance' theme is rendered complex by its association with other problematic issues of construing the feminine: tales such as these privilege a male-dominated discursive agenda at the same time as they implicitly acknowledge the necessity of mapping the feminine. Thus Créide is both a desirable and a dangerously problematic figure. Acting as her own marriage broker and economically self-sufficient, she is enormously attractive: to the young man as the alluring 'other' and — on the scene of his developing socialization and absorption into the male-bonded world of the Fíanna — to his military companions, Créide is an opportune supplier of the needed back-up of provisions and medical help in time of war. Her challenge to suitors also has aspects of the traditional story-type of the death-dealing seductress as exemplified in European romance codes, for example, in the *Joi de la Cour* episode in Chretien de Troyes's *Erec et Enide*. To neutralize the danger of the feminine, and to win this prize of the independent woman, Cáel plots to approach her through a female path of discourse, through the poem of praise supplied by a woman mentor. Yet one

may still trace an ongoing and fatal thread of danger in this resort to feminine help; the first line of the poem encodes a traditional taboo, journeys on a Friday. Cáel's enterprise is compromised and doomed by feminine discourse and the pathos of the tragic romance closure, where the woman too dies of grief, cannot fully elide the perception of danger in a young man's trust that female authored words can be borrowed and spoken and be effective in the dangerously pleasurable world of courtship.

The completed love affair between Manannán and Aillén's sister is another example of a 'romantic' love tale but it displays the author's undercurrent of unease at the conspicuous lightheartedness with which these denizens of Otherworlds — as stand-ins for contemporary Irish aristocrats — manage their complex love affairs. Patrick's comment on this tale is also light but brings some of the church's ambivalence on the matter of secular narrative and secular marriage customs together into a single ironic judgement. Tales of romance are indeed, as Patrick says, complicated affairs requiring complicated responses.

The controlling role that the reformed church of the twelfth century wished to wield through the production of chivalric texts such as the *Acallam* is most obvious in the numerous tales that enjoin monogamy on their protagonists. This may receive a straightforward chivalric frame, as in the story of the two wives of the chiefs of Fermoy who were abandoned by their husbands and then transformed by Caílte's agency into paragons of irresistible allure. It may also mediate the role of the feminine in narrative through the much more ambitious structuring of stories around the amalgam of ecclesiastical control and politic ambitions of the great regional dynasties. Of these, the series of stories dealing with various members of the family of the King of Connacht — an obvious reference to the importance of the Síl Muireadaig kings in the twelfth and early thirteenth centuries — is the most significant. Indeed the interlacing of this cycle of tales is the most ambitious structuring achievement of the *Acallam*. The tale begins with the healing of the king's son, Áed, by Patrick at the intercession of his mother; it continues through a related sequence of stories which culminates in the blessing of the Síl Muireadaig inauguration site at Carn Fraích, a moment in the text when, gratuitously, the occasion of Finn's belief in the one true God is recalled. Towards the end of the collection, the story of the same Áed's love for the Túatha Dé Danann girl, Aillén, is introduced in a fashion that breaks the usual sequencing of tales by reference to *dindshenchas* (place-name lore). As the king's wife is still alive, he declares himself obedient to Patrick's dictate that he remain monogamous on account of the old debt he owes the saint for his healing. The pathos of the story resides in the fact that, although movingly enunciated by both Áed and Aillén, this mutual love is real but irregular, a fact symbolized in the liminal valency of the woman — she is both real and from the Otherworld. But there is a happy outcome which also forms a virtual ending for the text of the *Acallam* as we have it. Patrick solemnly blesses the two lovers, when they are eventually free to marry and, furthermore, proclaims a future blessing on the dynastic line. Ironically, it is a matter of historical record that the Connacht king who is traditionally reputed to have lost Ireland to the Anglo-Normans, Ruaidrí, is blamed by the monastic chroniclers as having lost the blessing because he ignored the new climate of sexual conformity introduced by the reformers and strongly endorsed by the *Acallam*.

For a recent translation of the entire *Acallam*, see: Ann Dooley and Harry Roe, *Tales of the Elders of Ireland (Acallam na Senórach)* (Oxford: Oxford University Press, 1999). The following excerpts have been newly translated here by the present writer, Ann Dooley. For a note on the treatment of place-names and personal names, see Dooley and Roe, p. xxxiii.]

(i) THE STORY OF CÁEL AND CRÉIDE

On our way to fight the battle of Ventry we saw a young warrior coming towards us, Cáel, the Brave and Battle-hardy descendant of Nemnann. 'Where are you coming from, Cáel?' asked Finn. 'From the dew-dappled northern Brug,' he replied. 'What were you looking for?' 'To speak with my old nurse, Muirenn, daughter of Derc.' 'Why so?' 'Because of a fairy lover, a special courtship, and because of a vision vouchsafed to me.' 'I can tell you who it is,' said Finn, 'Créide daughter of Cairbre the fair-cheeked, daughter of the King of the Ciarraige Luachra. But you should know, Cáel,' said Finn, 'that she is the most dangerously attractive woman in Ireland, because many is the great treasure hoard that she has inveigled into her stronghold and her fine house.' 'Do you know the task she sets everyone?' asked Cáel. 'I do,' said Finn. 'Whoever comes to recite a poem or song to her must describe her cups and horns and goblets, her vessels and dishes, and her great house.' 'That is all prepared for,' replied Cáel, 'for I got it from Muirenn, my own nurse.'

So we turned aside from the battle for this matter in hand and we crossed mountainsides, crags and hills till we reached Loch Cuire in the west of Ireland. We went up to the door of the fairy mound and sang as Fíanna do, striking the shafts of our tall golden spears. Then fine, young golden-haired girls appeared, clustering on the balconies of the pavilions. Créide herself came to talk to us with one hundred and fifty maidens and our high chieftain said to her, 'We have come to make our choice of you and to woo you.' The

girl asked who exactly wished to woo her. 'Cáel, the keen battler, of the people of Nemnann, son of a King of Leinster,' she was told. 'We have heard tell of him though we never saw him,' said the girl. 'Now, does he have my poem?' 'I have so,' said Cáel. He stood up and recited his poem:

I travel a Friday's journey,
Privileged, I am here a suppliant.
To Créide's house in its fastness,
In the curve of the north-east mountain.

It is my destiny to go there,
To Créide of the Paps of Anu.
A time of testing there,
Four days of a week.

Splendid this house of hers,
With fine women, lads and men;
With clowns and musicians
With butler and dispenser.

With attentive stable boys
With carvers for the serving.
All of these in attendance,
On Créide the golden-haired.

A fine life for me with her,
Under quilts and bolsters.
If what Créide hears moves her,
Fine too would be my journey.

The great vat for fruit juices,
Brings crowds flocking on the lawns;
Glass vessels for liquor,
Cups and wine-pitchers.

In the lime-white mansion,
Are quilts and rush beds;
Silks and blue cloaks,
Red gold for the drinking horns.

Her bower by Loch Cuire
Of silver and yellow gold;
Her peaked thatched roof
Of brown and purple feathers.

Créide's chair is to the left,
And — O bliss after bliss! —
the covering of Alpine gold
At the foot of her soft bed.

The bed, brightly arrayed,
Stands beyond the chair;
The work of Turbe the smith,
Of yellow gold and jewels.

I see another bed to the right
Of flawless gold and silver,
With curtains in bright colours
And slender bronze rods.

As for her household folk,
They are the most fortunate;
Their cloaks are not frayed or faded,
But full-textured and bright as new.

A wounded man in his gore
Would sleep soundly on,
Lulled by fairy birdsong
In that sun-filled pavilion.

If I should please my lady,
For whom the cuckoo sings;
She would never lack a poem,
If she would just pay me now.

If Cairbre's daughter so desires it
She should not leave me hanging on,
But declare it now and openly:
'Welcome, welcome to my house!'

Créide's house is one hundred paces
From one end to the other;
And twenty feet in width
From door to door.

Her thatching and her roof
Of yellow and green feathers;
Of crystal and carbuncle
The platform by the well.

Four pillars round the bed
Of gold and silver fine work;
A crystal gem at each bedpost's top,
What joyful work is here!

In a vat of red-enamel work
The fermenting juices flow;
An apple-tree bends over the vat,
Bending under its crop.

When Créide's cup is filled
With drink from this vessel,

Four apples fall down
Straight into the cup.

The servers I just spoke of
Begin dispensing drink;
And they then pour out
Four drinks, each with an apple.
The woman who owns all this
Between ebb and flood,
Créide from the three hills
Makes all women mad with envy.

This poem then is no clever snare,
Nor flattery done to a formula;
Simply, my song to lovely Créide —
May my journey give her joy.

Then the couple slept the night in the beautifully dressed bed and they spent seven days drinking, feasting and taking their pleasure. Indeed none of us had any lack of food or drink or attention. The only anxiety Finn had was the presence of the foreigners at Ventry. Créide gave each one a fine serviceable cloak and so we assembled to bid each other farewell. Then Finn said, 'The girl must come with us so that we may know who is going to come out well or ill from this venture.' Créide brought great herds of cattle with her and attended those who were sick or wounded. The battle of Ventry went on for seventeen days. And the girl supplied us with food and fresh buttermilk and looked after the sick and invalided of the Fíanna. Indeed, just as she surpassed all the women of the Fíanna in service, so her husband Cáel surpassed all the three battalions of the Fíanna in bravery. A great tragedy occurred on the last day of battle: Cáel was drowned as he pursued his adversary out into the water; and fighting there, Cáel drowned and the wave that drowned him washed him ashore. And all the creatures who were born at the same time as he died of sorrow for him. The girl and the Fenian leaders went out to where he was and they brought him up on to the strand to the south of Ventry. That spot was called Cáel's Cove and Cáel's Grave ever after. Créide came and stretched herself out beside him and began to lament in great sorrow. 'Why should I not die in this spot of grief for my husband when the wild flying creatures are dying in grief for him?' And she uttered this lament:

The whole harbour laments,
Over the torrents of Two-boat Rinn;
The hero from Two-dog Lake has drowned,
This torments the ebbing tide.

The crane's call
Over the marsh of Two-force Ridge;
No more can she save her brood
The pale-red fox hunts down her chicks.

Lonely the note
The thrush sings on Druim Chaín;
And lonely the cry the blackbird gives
At Leittir Láeig.

Sad the stag,
Belling from Two-hut Ridge,
The death of Druim Sílenn's doe,
Bitter the stag's laments.

A torment for me,
He whom I lay with lies dead;
The son of the Doire Dá Doss woman,
Lying on his deathbed.

A torment to me is Cáel
Lying dead beside me;
The wave caressing his fair side,
That is my torment, his loveliness.

Desolate the cry,
Of ebb-tide on shore;
Since it drowned the noble hero
It washed over Cáel, that is my torment.

Poignant the sound
Of wave on northern shore;
Surging around the fair rock;
Lamenting Cáel who went from us.

Lonely the sound,
Of the wave on the southern shore;
For me, my joy is over,
My face is torn with keening.

Compelling the spell,
Of the heavy wave of Tulach Léis;
I am utterly bereft
The tragic news has broken me.

Créide then lay down beside Cáel and died of sorrow; they were buried together in one grave and a stone erected on their grave.

This is the story of The Grave of Cáel and Créide.

(ii) THE STORY OF MANANNÁN'S WIVES

[Caílte is asked to explain to a group that includes Patrick the meaning of the placename, Carn Manannáin, the Mound of Manannán, or, in another version, the Mound of Manannán's Seduction.]

'There was a warrior of the Túatha Dé Danann,' said Caílte, 'Aillén son of Eógabal by name, who fell in love with the wife of Manannán, son of Ler, and Manannán fell in love with his sister, that is, Áine, daughter of Eógabal, and she was dearer to Manannán than all the world. Áine, then, began to quiz her brother: "What has caused your great kingly appearance to lose its lustre?" "By my word, girl," said Aillén, "there is no one in the world in whom I could confide this but you alone." So he told her. "I have fallen in love," he said, "with Uchtdelb, the daughter of Óengus Find, the wife of Manannán." "Well, the remedy for that happens to lie in my hands," replied Áine, "since Manannán has declared his love for me; so, in order to help you, I would sleep with him if he were to give his wife to you." And so Aillén and Áine came,' said Caílte, 'to this hill and Manannán also came here with his wife. Áine sat down at Manannán's right and gave him three passionate deep kisses, and they told each other how things were for each of them. No sooner had Manannán's wife seen Aillén than she fell instantly in love with him and they too proceeded to get acquainted with each other.'

Then Patrick declared, 'This bit of storytelling is a most complicated affair!' — that is, Aillén's sister in love with Manannán and Manannán's wife in love with Aillén. From this derives the old saying, 'Storytelling is a very intricate business.'

'So Manannán gave his wife to Aillén and took for himself Áine, the sister of Aillén.'

And Caílte told them how Áine, daughter of Eógabal, used to entice Manannán and how, to that end, she composed the following poem:

O son of Ler come away with me
To the oakwood of Dairbre in the heights;

The woodcock will call, a blackbird's song
   will carry,
If you but reach the Causeway of the Two
   Curs.

Much music will be played for you,
Music both familiar and strange;
The cuckoo's song will spring from the
   dark wood
At the lead stag's belling.

The lure of faint forest piping,
The woodpecker's drumming on a tree
   trunk,
Stags calling into the bracing wind,
Heather grouse in the cold night.

Listening to such soothing music
With its many-noted performance;
And with lovely girls in our house —
All this will be yours, son of Ler.

And Aillén took the wife of Manannán to the
fairy mound of Eógabal and Manannán brought
Áine, Eógabal's daughter, away with him to the
Land of Promise.

(iii) THE STORY OF ÁED AND AILLÉN

[This is one of a series of stories concerning the family of
the kings of Connacht and may be symbolic of close co-
operation between the reforming church of the twelfth
century and the Síl Muireadaig dynasty.]

At that time the King of Connacht, Áed son of
Muiredach, son of Fínnachta, was at Dún Leóda
Loingsig partaking of a great feast. One evening he
went out at sunset into the grassy forecourt of the
house with the nobles of his household about him.
And while he was there he saw a lovely yellow-
haired girl coming towards him unobtrusively.
None of the group could see her but the king
alone and he marvelled at the manner of her
approach. 'Where have you come from, girl?'
asked the King of Connacht. 'From the light-
dappled mansion to the east,' she replied. 'Why
have you come?' asked the king. 'I am in love with
you,' she replied. 'Whose daughter are you?' asked
the king, 'and what is your name?' 'I am Aillén, the
many-shaped one,' replied the girl, 'and I am the

daughter of Bodb the red, the Dagda's son.' The
king replied, 'You should be aware, my dear Aillén,
that once I fell ill with a terrible sickness, and
though my parents succumbed to it as if to a
draught of death, it was holy Patrick who restored
me to life. He enjoined on me the obligation to
have only one wife, Aífe the many-shaped,
daughter of Eógan Lethderg, King of Leinster. Yet
I declare,' the king added, 'were it not for the
power the cleric has over me and my fear of the
King of Heaven and Earth, there is no woman on
earth whom I have ever seen that I would rather
have than you. And now, dear girl, would you like
to make yourself visible to the nobles of the
province?' 'I would like to do that,' replied the girl,
'for I am not a bewitching woman of the
Otherworld [*síd*], but I am in my own real body,
even if I am one of the Túatha Dé Danann.' So the
girl showed herself to the crowd and they had
never seen before or since a woman lovelier than
she. 'Well, King of Connacht, what have you
decided about me?' asked the girl. 'I will abide by
the judgement that the holy Patrick will give and I
will convey that to you,' he replied.

Then the king asked seven of his retainers to
go and seek out Patrick from the Stronghold of
the Crooked Rampart to the south, to the
summit of Sliabh Mis. And they went in search of
him and found him accordingly. At that time
Patrick had taken his leave of the two provinces
of Munster and had left a blessing on them. He
joined the messengers and they went together to
Benn an Bailb — now called Benn Gulban — in
Máenmag, Áed, King of Connacht having
arrived there from Dún Leóda Loingsig to meet
him. And the King of Connacht put his head on
Patrick's breast and did homage to him and gave
the authority of the whole province to him, both
great and small.

Then the king began to tell the story of the girl
to Patrick. 'Are you the girl who has fallen in love
with the King of Connacht?' asked Patrick. 'I am,'
said the girl. 'Well my dear girl,' said Patrick, 'you
are indeed beautiful in form and appearance.
What is it that preserves your kind in the peak of
shape and condition?' 'Everyone of us who drank
at Goibniu's feast,' replied the girl, 'never
experiences sickness or disease. And now, holy
cleric,' said the girl, 'what is to be your judgement
on the case of the King of Connacht and myself?'
'My judgement is a fair one,' replied Patrick; 'he

vowed to God and to me that he would be faithful to one wife and we are not going to gainsay that vow.' 'But what about me?' asked the girl, 'what am I to do?' 'You must go to your own country and to your Otherworld dwelling,' replied Patrick; 'and if the King of Leinster's daughter were not already his wife, you would be his only wife from now on, you who have brought him your great love and devotion. But if, by day or by night, you make an attempt to harm him or his wife, I will mutilate you so that not even your own mother or father, nurse or foster-father could bear to look at you.'

Then Patrick chanted:

O Aillén of the purple veil,
O daughter of Bodb,
I see no good result for you,
Go back to your feasting.

Not by the direction of a fairy host
Will you come to Benn Bailb,
Not by tracking like a hunting dog
Will you get your reward.

May she accept our protection gracefully
The girl from far away;
With the Gospels of mighty Christ
Protecting us from harm.

I will bless this province
Through my wisdom and power;
So that outsiders cannot harm it
Without destroying themselves.

Do not try to bribe us,
O sweet lovely girl;
Arise and take my blessing
And go now in peace.

'And is that your final judgement on the matter?' asked the girl, 'that you will not give me to the king as long as he has that wife?' 'It is indeed,' replied Patrick. 'Is this how it is then, on your word of honour, holy cleric, that if the king's wife dies before me, then I would then be given to him?' 'As my own truth is a witness to me,' replied Patrick, 'if she were to die first, then you would be given to him.'

And then the girl wept copious and bitter tears of real sorrow. 'Do you really love me so much, girl?' the king asked her. 'I really do,' she replied, 'there is not one of the whole human race dearer to me than you. But I am unable to prevail against the arrangements and the sanctions of the Adzehead[1] and of God.' With that, the girl betook herself off to her fairy dwelling until such time as the story has occasion to return to her again . . .

They had not been there long before they saw Aillén of the purple veils, daughter of Bodb the red, son of the Dagda coming towards them with one hundred and fifty women of the Túatha Dé Danann in her retinue and they all seated themselves on the sodded bank in the presence of Patrick and the King of Connacht. The girl told them why she had come. 'What have you to say to her, King of Connacht?' asked Patrick. 'What have I to say? I will do whatever you approve of,' replied the king. 'What I approve is that she be yours,' replied Patrick, 'for I promised her that I would give her to you provided that she do homage to the Gospel of the King of Heaven and Earth.' 'Are you agreeable to that?' the king asked the girl. 'I am,' she replied. Then the girl rose up with all her women and they did homage to Patrick, and Patrick joined the two of them in holy matrimony. And learned authors reckon that that was the first couple that Adzehead married in Ireland.

'What payment is due for the marriage?' asked Benén the great, son of Áed. 'I will give,' said the king, 'the best townsland in every locality from the stone of Lemanegh (called Limerick) to the Stone of Assaroe.' 'What will be your gift to the people of the province in return, Patrick?' asked Benén. 'I will give the following,' said Patrick; 'three kings of theirs will take the kingship of all Ireland and the revenue of Ireland will eventually be theirs forever.' Brocán recorded these bequests to the province of Connacht and also recorded what was given to Patrick. And the happy couple celebrated their wedding night sleeping in the nuptial bed prepared for them.

---

1. A nickname for Saint Patrick, or any priest, suggested by the clerical tonsure.

DEIRDRE'S DEPARTURE WITH NAOISE AND THE DEATH OF THE SONS OF UISNEACH
(Early Modern Irish)

[The following excerpt is from the longest and one of the latest literary redactions of the tale of Deirdre. Most of the earliest version, from the eighth or ninth century, is found in Volume I, pp. 13–17. It described an austere, extreme world, in which human actions were judged pitilessly by the warrior code. The fates decreed before her birth that tragedy would follow Deirdre, and her love for Naoise was reflexive, yet she was blamed and blamed herself for the slaughter that ensued, and took her own life. She knew ecstasy and grief but no modulation of feeling in between.

The cast of the present redaction are not proud, tragic figures, estranged from the world and each other. Deirdre's sensibility is particularly well developed, and especially so in the exchanges with her loyal nurse, Leabharcham, which occur in the opening section, which shows more signs of innovation than any other part of the text. The saga's fixated adult has become the impressionable, vulnerable protagonist of a romance. The unique manuscript witness contains Old, Middle and Early Modern Irish forms, with an admixture of East Ulster dialect forms. The text probably dates from the Early Modern Irish period, acquiring the later dialect forms in the copying process. The opening section was transcribed and translated by Douglas Hyde, 'Déirdre', *Zeitschrift für celtische Philologie*, vol. 2 (1899), pp. 138–55. A long excerpt from his translation is reproduced here, with name-forms normalized and minor changes in presentation. For the full text (in Irish only), see Breandán Ó Buachalla, 'Imthiacht Dheirdre la Naoise agus Oidhe Chloinne Uisneach', *Zeitschrift für celtische Philologie*, vol. 29 (1962–4), pp. 114–54.]

As for the girl, Conchobhar took her under his own protection, and placed her in a moat apart, to be brought up by his nurse, whose name was Leabharcham, in a fortress of the Red Branch,[1] and Conchobhar and Cathbhadh the Druid gave her the name of Deirdre. Afterwards Deirdre was being generously nurtured under Leabharcham, and under [other] ladies, perfecting her in every science that was fitting for the daughter of a high prince, until she grew up a blossom-bearing sapling, and until her beauty was beyond every

degree surpassing. Moreover she was nurtured with excessive luxury of food and drink that her stature and ripeness might be the greater for it, and that she might be the sooner marriageable. This is how Deirdre's abode was [situated, namely] in a fortress of the Branch, according to the king's command, every aperture for light closed in the fort of the *dún*, and the windows of the back ordered to be open. A beautiful orchard full of fruit [lay] at the back of the fort, in which Deirdre might be walking for a while under the eye of her tutor, at the beginning and the end of the day; under a shade of the fresh boughs and branches, and by the side of a running meandering stream that was winding softly through the middle of the walled garden. A high, tremendous, spacious wall, not easy to surmount, [was] surrounding that spacious habitation, and four savage man-hounds [sent] from Conchobhar [were] on constant guard there, and his life were in peril for the man who should venture to approach it.

For it was not permitted to any male to come next nor near to Deirdre, nor even to look at her; but [only] to her tutor whose name was Cailcín and to king Conchobhar himself. Prosperous was Conchobhar's sway, and valiant was the fame . . . of the Red Branch defending the province of Ulster against foreigners and against every other province in Erin in his time; and there were no three in the household of Eamhain nor throughout all Banba[2] more valiant than the sons of Uisneach, nor heroes of higher fame than they, Naoise, Ainle, and Ardán.

As for Deirdre, when she was fourteen years of age she was found marriageable, and Conchobhar designed to take her to his own Royal couch. About this time a sadness and a heavy flood of melancholy lay upon the young queen, without gentle sleep, without sufficient food, without sprightliness — as had been her wont.

Until it chanced of a day, while the snow was lying on [the ground] in the winter, that Cailcín, Deirdre's tutor, went to kill a calf to get ready food for her, and after shedding the blood of the calf out upon the snow, a raven stoops upon it to drink it, and as Deirdre perceives that, — and she watching through a window of the fortress, — she heaved a heavy sigh so that Cailcín heard her.

---

1. The order of Ulster warriors led by King Conchobhar.

2. A name for Ireland.

'Wherefore thy melancholy, girl?' said he. 'Alas that I have not yonder thing as I see it,' said she. 'Thou shalt have that if it be possible,' said he, drawing his hand dexterously, so that he gave an unerring cast of his knife at the raven, so that he cut one foot off it, and after that he takes the bird and throws it over near Deirdre. The girl started at once, and fell into a faint, until Leabharcham came up to help her. 'Why art thou as I see thee, dear daughter?' said she, 'for thy countenance is pitiable ever since yesterday.' 'A desire I chanced to have,' said Deirdre. 'What is that desire?' said Leabharcham. 'Three colours that I saw,' said Deirdre, 'namely the blackness of the raven, the redness of the blood, and the whiteness of the snow.' 'It is easy to get that for thee now,' said Leabharcham; she arose [and went] out without delay; and she gathered the full of a vessel of snow, and half the full of a cup of the calf's blood, and she pulls three feathers out of the wing of the raven, and she laid them down on the table before the girl. Deirdre began as though she were eating the snow, and lazily tasting the blood with the top of the raven's feather, with her nurse closely scrutinizing her, until Deirdre asked Leabharcham to leave her alone by herself for a while. Leabharcham departs, and again returns, and this is how she found Deirdre — shaping a ball of snow in the likeness of a man's head, and mottling it with the top of the raven's feather out of the blood of the calf, and putting the small black plumage as hair upon it, and she never perceived her nurse scanning her until she had finished. 'Whose likeness is that?' said Leabharcham. Deirdre starts, and she said, 'It is a work easily destroyed.' 'That work is a great wonder to me, girl,' said Leabharcham, 'because it was not thy wont to draw pictures of a man, [and] it was not permitted to the women of Eamhain to teach thee any similitude but that of Conchobhar only.' 'I saw a face in my dream,' said Deirdre, 'that was of brighter countenance than the king's face or Cailcín's, and it was in it that I saw the three colours that pained me, namely the whiteness of the snow on his skin, the blackness of the raven on his hair, and the redness of the blood upon his countenance, and O woe! my life will not last unless I get my desire.' 'Alas for thy desire, my darling (?),' said Leabharcham. 'My desire, gentle nurse,' said Deirdre. 'Alas! 'tis a pity thy desire, it is difficult to get it,' said Leabharcham, 'for fast

and close is the fortress of the Branch, and high and difficult is the enclosure round about, and [there is] the sharp watch of the fierce man-hounds in it.' 'The hounds are no danger to us,' said Deirdre. 'Where did you behold that face?' said Leabharcham. 'In a dream yesterday,' said Deirdre, and she weeping, after hiding her face in her nurse's bosom, and shedding tears plentifully. 'Rise up from me, dear pupil,' said Leabharcham, 'and restrain thy tears henceforth, till thou eatest food and takest a drink, and after Cailcín's eating his meal we shall talk together about the dream.' Her nurse lifts up Deirdre's head, 'Take courage, daughter,' said she, 'and be patient for I am certain that thou shalt get thy desire, for according to human age and life, Conchobhar's time beside thee is not [to be] long or lasting.'

After Leabharcham's departing from her, she [Leabharcham] perceived a green mantle hung in the front of a closed-up window on the head of a brass club and the point of a spear thrust through the wall of the mansion. Leabharcham puts her hand to it, so that it readily came away with her, and stones and moss fell down after it, so that the light of day, and the grassy lawn, and the plain of the champions in front of the face of the mansion, and the heroes at their feats of activity outside, were visible. 'I understand now, my pupil,' said Leabharcham, 'that it was here you saw that dream!' but Deirdre did not answer her. Her nurse left food and ale on the table before Deirdre, and departed from her without speaking, for the boring-through of the window did not please Leabharcham, for fear of Conchobhar or Cailcín coming to the knowledge of it. As for Deirdre, she ate not her food, but she quenched her thirst out of a beaker of ale, and she takes with her the flesh of the calf, after covering it under a corner of her mantle, and she went to her tutor, and asks leave of him to go out for a while [to walk] at the back of the mansion. 'The day is cold, and there is snow darkening in [the air], daughter,' said Cailcín, 'but you can walk for a while under the shelter of the walls of the mansion, but mind the . . . house of the hounds.' Deirdre went out, and no stop was made by her until she passed down through the middle of the snow to where the den of the man-hounds was, and as soon as the hounds recognized her and the smell of the meat, they did not touch her, and they made no barking till she divided her food amongst them, and she returns into the house afterwards. Thereupon came Leabharcham, and found Deirdre lying on one side of her couch, and she sighing heavily and shedding tears. Her nurse stood silent for a while, observing her, till her heart was softened to compassion, and till her anger departed from her. She stretches out her hand and 'twas what she said: 'Rise up, modest daughter, that we may be talking about the dream, and tell me did you ever see that black hero of the dream before yesterday?' said Leabharcham. 'White hero, gentle nurse, hero of the pleasant crimson cheeks,' said Deirdre. 'Tell me without falsehood,' said Leabharcham, 'did you ever see that warrior before yesterday, or before you bored through the window-work with the head of a spear and with a brass club, and till you looked out through it on the warriors of the Branch when they were at their feats of activity, on the Champions' plain, and till you saw all the dream you spoke of.' Deirdre hides her face in her nurse's bosom, weeping, till she said: 'O gentle mother and nurturer of my heart, do not tell that to my tutor, and I shall not conceal from thee that I saw him on the lawn of Eamhain playing games with the boys and learning feats of valour, and och! he had the beautiful countenance that time, and very lovely was it yesterday.' 'Daughter,' said Leabharcham, 'you did not see the boys on the green of Eamhain from the time you were seven years of age, and that is seven years ago.' 'Seven bitter years,' said Deirdre, 'since I beheld the delights of the Green, and the playing of the boys, and surely moreover Naoise surpassed all the youths of Eamhain.' 'Naoise the son of Uisneach?' said Leabharcham. 'Naoise is his name, as he told me,' said Deirdre, 'when he made a throw of a ball, by a miscast, backwards, transversely over the heads of the bands of maidens that were standing on the Green, and I rose from amongst them all, till I lifted the ball, and I delivered it to him, and he pressed my hand joyously.' 'He pressed your hand, girl!' said Leabharcham. 'He pressed it lovingly, and said that he would see me again, but it was difficult for him, and I did not see him since, until yesterday; and O gentle nurse, if you wish me to be alive take a message to him from me, and tell him to come to visit me and talk with me secretly tonight, without the knowledge of Cailcín or any other person.' 'O girl,' said Leabharcham, 'it is a very dangerous mission to gain the quenching of thy desire [being in peril] from the anger of the king, under the sharp watch of Cailcín, considering the fierceness of the savage man-hounds, and considering the difficulty of [scaling] the enclosure round about.' 'The hounds are no danger to us,' said Deirdre. 'Then too,' said Leabharcham, 'great is Conchobhar's love for the Children of Uisneach, and there is in the Red Branch no hero more dear to him than Naoise.' 'If he is the son of Uisneach,' said Deirdre, 'I heard the report of him from the women of Eamhain, and that great are his own territories on the west of Alba,[3] outside of Conchobhar's sway; and gentle nurse go to find Naoise, and you can tell him how I am, and how much greater my love for him is than for Conchobhar.' 'Tell him that yourself, if you can,' said Leabharcham, and she went out thereupon to seek Naoise, till he was found, and till he came with her to Deirdre's dwelling, in the beginning of the night without Cailcín's knowledge. When Naoise beheld the splendour of the girl's countenance, he is filled with a flood of love, and Deirdre beseeches him to take her and escape to Alba. But Naoise thought that too difficult an [enterprise] for fear of Conchobhar, but in the course (?) of the night Deirdre gained the victory over him, so that he consented to her [wish], and they determined to depart on the night of the morrow.

Deirdre escaped in the middle of the night without the knowledge of her tutor or her nurse, for Naoise came at that time and his two brothers along with him, so that he bored a gap at the back of the hounds' den, for the dogs were dead already, through poison from Deirdre.

They lifted the girl across the walls, through every rough impediment, so that her mantle and the extremity of her dress were all torn to pieces, and he set her upon a steed's back, and no stop was made by them till [they reached] Sliabh Fuaid[4] and Fionncharn[5] of the watch, till they came to the harbour and went aboard a ship and were driven by a south wind across the ocean-waters, and over the back-ridges of the deep sea, to Loch nEathaigh[6] in the west of Alba, and thrice fifty valiant champions sailed along with them, namely fifty with each of three brothers, Naoise, Ainle and Ardán.

3. Scotland.
4. The Fews, a mountain range in County Armagh.
5. Name of a peak in the Fews.
6. Unidentified.

DRUMAÍ MHIC CARTHAIGH
(McCarthy's Drums)
(early 17th century)

[This text must stand for the numerous poems and songs, dating from the sixteenth century onwards, which deride or criticize the sexual activities of named or otherwise identified individuals. It (or an earlier form of it) probably comes from the beginning of the seventeenth century: a poem from the early 1600s quotes from and refers to it (cf. National Library of Ireland, MS G 200, p. 325). The poem in question, of south-east Ulster origin, satirizes as effete a soldier named Eoghan Mac Criostail. Its military associations suggest that 'McCarthy's drums' in this poem refer, in the literal sense, to army drums.

McCarthy, it seems, was an officer and a gentleman. A short note prefaces this squib in the manuscripts: 'A surly, brittle old man married a lovely, cheery young woman and the story goes that she didn't observe her marriage bond and the local grandee used be getting up on her — he was a McCarthy. And a well-educated young fellow from the locality got wind of the transgression. He came up to the old man's house one Sunday morning as he and his wife were in the back room dressing themselves for Mass, and this is what the young fellow said to them, as he stood there in the kitchen . . .' The text below presents, in normalized spelling, that published by Brian Ó Cuív: 'An Ornamental Device in Irish Verse', *Éigse*, vol. 23 (1989), pp. 45–56, at pp. 48–9. The translation is by Patrick Crotty.]

Mo smidín do smigín bheag bhearrtha liath —
gan tábhacht,
's do stocaí a bhfuil clocaí iontu gearrtha ar fiar
— le snáithe,

do chloigín nár chuir comaoin ar mhnáibh
ariamh — le sásamh,
is do chuid díobh mar phillín ag Mac Cárthaigh
thiar — mo náire!

Mo smidín tu, a mhuirnín is áille ciabh — 's is
deise gáire,
's do phisín a chuir comaoin ar a lán ariamh —
ar do thár in airde,
do phoillín a mbíobh cloigíní uirthi a' fáisgeadh
thiar — insna garrdhtha,
's go mba chosamhail iad le drummaí Mhic
Cárthaigh a' tiacht — ón Maolairdne.

TRANSLATION

Fellow with the grey, cropped, unimposing chin
Whose stockings have clocks on them, threaded
with fuss,
Whose knob never coaxed pleasure's sobs from
a woman —
McCarthy is the pillow in your wife's pillow-
case.

Woman with the bright face and abundant hair
Whose pusseen has coaxed many, thrust
pouting on high,
Your dingleberries jig on the grass blades
To McCarthy's drumming, whose coming
shakes the sky.

DÁIBHIDH Ó BRUADAIR
(*c.* 1625–98)

SEIRBHÍSEACH SEIRGTHE
ÍOGAIR SRÓNACH SEASC
(A shrewish, barren, bony, nosey
servant) (17th century)

[Many of Ó Bruadair's generation of poets still felt they had every right to crush the minions who dared to cross them. Poems destroyed many reputations, but few were

quite as stinging as this one. If not a set piece, then it must have been regarded as truly offensive. Text and translation from: Seán Ó Tuama and Thomas Kinsella (ed. and trans.), *An Duanaire 1600–1900: Poems of the Dispossessed* (Mountrath, Portlaoise: Dolmen, 1981), pp. 116–17.]

Seirbhíseach seirgthe íogair srónach seasc
d'eitigh sinn is eibear íota im scornain feacht,
beireadh síobhra d'eitill í gan lón tar lear,
an deilbhín gan deirglí nár fhóir mo thart.

Dá reicinn í 's a feileghníomh do-gheobhadh
    ceacht,
is beirt an tí go leigfidís im scórsa casc;
ó cheisnimh sí go bhfeirg linn is beoir 'na gar
don steiling í nár leige Rí na glóire i bhfad.

Meirgíneach bheirbhthe í gan cheol 'na cab
do theilg sinn le greidimín sa bpóirse amach;
cé cheilim ríomh a peidigraoi mar fhógras
    reacht,
ba bheag an díth dá mbeireadh sí do ghósta cat.

Reilgín an eilitín nach d'ord na mban
is seisce gnaoi dá bhfeicimíd sa ród ré maith;
a beith 'na daoi ós deimhin dí go deo na dtreabh
san leitin síos go leige sí mar neoid a cac.

TRANSLATION

A shrewish, barren, bony, nosey servant
refused me when my throat was parched in
    crisis.
May a phantom fly her starving over the sea,
the bloodless midget that wouldn't attend my
    thirst.

If I cursed her crime and herself, she'd learn a
    lesson.
The couple she serves would give me a cask on
    credit
but she growled at me in anger, and the beer
    nearby.
May the King of Glory not leave her long at her
    barrels.

A rusty little boiling with a musicless mouth,
she hurled me out with insult through the
    porch.
The Law requires I gloss over her pedigree
— but little harm if she bore a cat to a ghost.

She's a club-footed slut and not a woman at all,
with the barrenest face you would meet on the
    open road,
and certain to be a fool to the end of the world.
May she drop her dung down stupidly into the
    porridge!

ANONYMOUS

THE STORY OF MIS
AND DUBH ROIS
(18th century)

[This is a lively treatment of the idea of sexual healing (cp. pp. 1388–90). Mis was originally the goddess associated with Slieve Mis, the mountain range south of Tralee, County Kerry (at least one similarly named mountain elsewhere in Ireland had its own local goddess). In modern tradition she figures as a *bean sí*, in the sense of both 'fairy woman' and 'supernatural death-messenger', in the company of other *mná sí* with Munster associations such as Aoibheall of Craig Léith in County Clare. On one level, the present tale naturalizes Mis. However, her father's violent death causes the protagonist of the tale to become deranged and to take the role of *bean chaointe*, 'keening woman', to unnatural extremes. The *bean sí* as harbinger of death, in any case, imitates the keening woman's doleful cry, dishevelled appearance and wild movement, so the grieving protagonist cannot but adumbrate the original character of Mis.

Dubh Rois, her saviour, is presented as a contemporary of Feidhlimidh mac Criomhthainn, King of Munster (d. 847), but he also has a mythic counterpart, a prodigious leaper associated with landscape features in County Cork. His landscape leaping may have suggested the idea of a more ludic leaping with Mis.

The present version of the tale, in the hand of the Cork poet Piaras Mac Gearailt (1702–95), is probably a copy of an eighteenth-century exemplar. In this and in the only other known version of the tale, it serves as an introduction to a formal elegy in syllabic metre (of which only the first line is cited below). This elegy, by a male poet for a friend and patron whose name was Dubh Rois, exists separately in multiple manuscript copies. It appears to have been brought into association with the tale on account of the coincidence of the name Dubh Rois. In Mis's mouth, the poet's masculinst praise of Dubh Rois sounds an incongruous note.

Mis offers a striking contrast to Sweeney the madman (see pp. 226–8). Her psychosis is cured by the ministrations of Dubh Rois, and her domestic contentedness leads ultimately to a gift for poetry. Yet its humour and grotesquerie preclude the tale from becoming a paean to marriage.

In the poem which Austin Clarke based on this tale, 'The Healing of Mis' (1970), Mis must dispel a carnal dream of her father before she can be at peace. Another father figure engrossed Piaras Mac Gearailt as he inscribed his version: he wrote it into a manuscript anthology he compiled in 1769 to entertain the father of a young woman he claimed to love. His dedication of it to her reads, in part: 'I trust that the affable Mr Butler will not be insulted by this poor little gathering or collection that I have compiled, for it is out of good will and respect for you and for that gracious fair man that I undertook, in my sixtieth year, to write so much in a single week, besides which I am not yet free of pain, i.e. the gravel, and various other ailments which have been wearing me down for a long time and which account for this small share of writing being so illegible and defective. Still, my sore cry, my sorrow, my woe is that I'm not thirty years of age, and that I don't have a solid, assured estate worth ten thousand guineas a year, in the hope that I might have the favour, the honour, the fortune, the worldly delight and the solace of your accepting from me that which you stole from me, namely, my heart ... Your prisoner and servant, devoted, despondent, depleted and discontent for evermore until I see your radiant, precious face that is not of creaturekind.' (Translated from St Patrick's College, Maynooth, Murphy MS 58, p. 69.)

The tale was edited by Brian Ó Cuív, 'The Romance of Mis and Dubh Ruis', *Celtica* vol. 2, no. 2 (1954), pp. 325–33. He appended only the first line of the elegy to his text. This first translation of the tale is based on his work.]

Mis the daughter of Dáire Dóidgheal sang this when lamenting her husband and companion, that is, Dubh Rois, the melodious harpist of Feidhlimidh mac Criomhthainn, King of Munster. For the kerne of Clanmaurice killed this Dubh Rois when he went to exact the great cess from them which King Feidhlimidh had granted him for taming Mis, the daughter of Dáire, and for bringing her to her senses. She was a madwoman for seven score years (or three hundred years according to others) on Slieve Mis in the barony of Clanmaurice beside Tralee in County Kerry since the day her father, Dáire Dóidgheal, who came to make conquest of Ireland in the Battle of Ventry, was killed. He brought her with him as she was his only daughter, and after the battle she came with a multitude searching through the slaughter for her father's body, and having found the severely wounded body, she began to suck and drink the

blood from the wounds so that eventually in a fever of lunacy she rose aloft and flew to Slieve Mis, and remained there for the aforesaid time, and there grew on her whiskers and hair of such length that they used to scour the ground behind her. Moreover, the nails of her feet and hands curved inwards so much that no man or beast encountered her that was not torn apart on the spot.

Furthermore, her lunatic frenzy caused her to move at such speed that she ran like the wind and so she used to outstrip whatever she wished. And she did not hesitate to eat each and every animal and person that she killed, and to drink as much as she wanted of their flesh and blood, so much so that the region called the barony of Clanmaurice became a wilderness with scant population and stock for fear of her, because King Feidhlimidh issued a general edict that she was not to be killed on any account. However, he offered large rewards as well as the barony's great cess to whoever would succeed in capturing her or taking her alive.

Over time, many people approached her and most of them died at her hands on the expedition. Eventually, however, the harpist Dubh Rois said to Feidhlimidh, the king, that he himself would go to meet her with his harp, and the king laughed at him. And Dubh Rois asked him for a fistful of gold and a fistful of silver — that these were needed for the expedition, and that he would approach her. The king gave him the gold and the silver and he made no delay until he reached Slieve Mis. And when he had climbed the mountain, he sat down in the place where he expected to catch her, he spread his mantle or cloak under himself, and he scattered the gold and silver on the edges of the mantle. He lay on his back. He drew the harp to his body. He opened his trousers or, if you will, his breeks and he exposed himself, for he thought to himself that if only he could manage to lie with her and make love to her, this would prove a good measure or manoeuvre for bringing her to her senses or her natural reason. He was not like that for long before she appeared, having heard the music, and she stood there fiercely, listening to him and looking at him. 'Aren't you a human?' she asked. 'That's right,' he said. 'What's this?' she said, as she put her hand on the harp. 'A harp,' said he. 'Oh ho!' said she, 'I remember the harp. My father had one like it. Play it for me.' 'I will,' he said, 'but don't hurt or harm me.' 'I won't,' said she. She looked then at the gold and silver and said: 'What are these?' 'Gold and silver,' he said. 'I remember,' said she. 'My father used to have gold. Ochone ochone!'

When she gave a side-glance, she caught sight of his fine nakedness and the sporting pieces. 'What are these?' she asked, of his pouch or nest-eggs,[1] and he told her. 'What's this?' she asked, of the other thing that she saw. 'That,' said he, 'is a tricking staff.'[2] 'I don't remember that,' said she. 'My father didn't have the like.' 'A tricking staff,' she said again; 'what's the trick?' 'Sit beside me,' said he, 'and I'll do that staff's trick for you.' 'I will,' said she, 'and stay with me.' 'I will,' he said, and he lay with her and made love to her, and she said: 'Ah! ha! bah, bah — aaah! That's a fine trick, do it again!' 'Yes,' he said, 'but first of all I'll play the harp for you.' 'Don't mind the harp,' said she, 'but do the trick.' 'I'd like to eat some food or vitals,' said he, 'for I'm hungry.' 'I'll get a deer for you,' said she. 'Do that,' said he, 'and I've got bread myself.' 'Where is it?' she asked. 'Here it is,' said he. 'Ha ha! I remember the bread; my father used to have it,' said she. 'Don't leave me,' she said. 'No, I won't,' said he.

She hadn't been away from him for long when she returned with a stunned deer under her oxter (I told you that she used to run like the wind on account of her lunatic frenzy), and she was of a mind to tear the deer asunder and eat it as it was until Dubh Rois said to her: 'Hold on,' said he, 'until I slaughter the deer and cook the meat.' With that, he cut the deer's throat and he skinned it. Then he made a huge fire of the dry wood of the forest, and he collected a pile of granite rocks and put them in the fire. He made a pit in the ground of equal length and depth and he filled it with water. He cut up his meat and he wrapped it in a sheaf of sedge-grass tied with a *súgán* and he put it in the water. Then he proceeded to feed those glowing, well-fired stones into the water so that he kept it on the boil continuously until their meat was done. He took it out of the pit and he put the fat of the deer into the boiling water then so that it liquefied in the water. He arranged his bread and his meat before him on the deer-skin

and he told her to come and eat her meal. She had been eyeing and observing him quietly and thoughtfully all the while. 'I recall,' said she, 'that it was cooked meat my father used to have, and now I know that it's best like that and not the way I've been having it.' Then, Dubh Rois broke the bread and cut the meat for her and he induced her to eat her fill, peacefully and pleasurably, whereupon she said to him that she would do everything he asked of her provided that he stayed with her. And he gave her his word on that. Then he brought her fresh water in his mantle or in his cap and she drank her fill of it.

After that he brought her to the pit which had the tepid broth and the deer's fat liquefied in it, and he stood her in it. He took the tallow of the deer and he massaged and kneaded all the joints and bones of her body, and he set about scouring them and scraping them and smoothing them with the deer's fat and the broth until he had cleansed her greatly and drawn streams of sweat from her. He gathered leaves and moss and green rushes, and he prepared a bed for her. He spread the deer-skin beneath her and his cloak above her. He himself lay beside her and made love to her, and so they slept until morning. But in the morning he could not wake her, so he rose and covered her over and he made a bothy or a screen of tree-tops and branches around her. She did not wake until evening, and when she did not find him beside her she began to keen him, while he listened to her unbeknownst and among other things, heard her say this of himself:

> It's not the gold I'm keening, nor the sweet
>   harp, nor the nest-eggs,
> but the tricking staff of Dubh Rois son of
>   Raghnall.

He remained with her in this way on the mountain for two months and by the end of that time, the whiskers had fallen off her completely, because of his scouring and cleansing her as we have said, and furthermore, her sense and her memory, her mind and her natural reason returned, and Dubh Rois put suitable garments on her before he brought her home. And it is written also that she had the shape and the form and also the same age as she had on the day when she took to lunacy on the mountain. And Dubh Rois married her and she gave him four children,

---

1. The Irish (*eoin eadhbhair*) is obscure, possibly deliberately. Either of two literal meanings may underlie it: 'bird materials' or 'little eggs of substance', i.e. 'testicles'.
2. The Irish term is *crann clis*.

and she was among the most beautiful and gracious women of Munster in her time. Be that as it may, when at last Dubh Rois went one time to demand the aforesaid great cess, the kerne of Clanmaurice seized him by the throat and so he died as we have said and she made these lays after the manner of a keen over his body:

'Dubh Rois whose countenance was royal . . .'

AINDRIAS MAC CRUITÍN

(?1650–?1738)

MOLADH NA PITE
(Quim Praise) (? c. 1700)

[Mac Cruitín's lines are reminiscent of Rochester's: 'It is the workhouse of the world's great trade: / On this soft anvil all mankind was made' (John Adlard (ed.), *The Debt to Pleasure: John Wilmot, Earl of Rochester, in the Eyes of His Contemporaries and His Own Poetry and Prose* [Cheadle: Carcanet Press, 1974], p. 49). The Irish text was published by Pádraig Ó Fiannachta in his *Léas Eile ar an Litríocht* (Maigh Nuad: An Sagart, 1982), pp. 240–1. The translation is by Patrick Crotty.]

1
Tá clúid sheascair shuite, gan bhrú ar bith ná
   briseadh,
'Na dtionscnaid an cine daonna de ghnáth
Dá cumhdach go cliste, dá sciúradh le huisce,
I bhfothnochta bruinne is caomhanta cáil.

2
Ar amhlus na muice ar dtúis bhí ag Tuireann,
Púiribh na cruinne leigheasfadh gach tráth;
Amhras doráigh mise, pé spíonfadh a ciste,
Go dúnadh gach druinge nach baol dó an bás.

3
Is cumtha 's is cliste a cúl is a himeall,
A hurla, a grinneall, 's a béal leabharbhláth.
Is súgach 's is frithir d'iomcharann sise
A brú is a briseadh, a réabadh 's a sá.

4
Níl údar dá ghlice do scrúdfadh a himeall,
A fiúntas, a hinneach, a féile is a cáil,
I gcúngracht, i gclisteacht, i gcumharthacht, i
   misneach,
Siúd agus tuilleadh dá béasa nárbh fhearr.

5
Tá crógacht is clisteacht, mórgacht is misneach,
Móriomad oinigh is séimhe gan tlás
Insa tseoid úd 'na ngeintear mórshliocht na
   cruinne
Is a comhachta nach dtuigeann éigse agus baird.

6
Cidh mómhrach na ríthe 'na cóngar tan tigid
Le spóirt di go ndinid sléachtain ar lár;
Ba glórmhar an duine ghéabhas eolas dá ciste,
Is go bhfóirfeadh ón uile ghéarghoin go brách.

7
Is ceolmhar le binneas, is somplach le muirinn
Is cróga na nithe, le béasa gan cháim,
Seoltar le foithin le heolas gan tuirinn
As an tseoid úd 'nar geineadh na Caesars dob
   fhearr.

8
Is dóigh liom gur duine neamheolach 'na
   thuigsin
Nach mórga do chuirfeadh 'na caomhnadh gan
   tlás,
'Na cóngar go cluthair gan teorainn gan deifir,
An béal sin le cumas nach géilleann san ár.

TRANSLATION

I sing the cosy covert where you'll neither
   bruise nor break,
There the sons of men are happy to foregather;
Cleverly they shield it before they pour their
   blessing
In that body-cleft of everlasting fame.

Like Tuireann's famous pig, in the story long ago,
It can cure every sorrow in the world;
There's reason to believe, whoever learns to
tune it
Will have long bliss amid the angelic choirs.

Supple and most shapely are its depths and sides,
Its tuft, its floor, its mouth all silken-soft.
And gladly will it take you and smilingly endure
As you try to bruise and break it for your
pleasure.

Where is the tribunal that could regard its shape,
Its worth, its warmth, its welcome and its fame,
Its tightness, its swiftness, its ardour and its
fragrance,
And not find it peerless in all these?

Ardent and alert, noble and courageous,
Forever taut and tender is that treasure,
That seam where every person living was
conceived,
Whose power no poet nor gleeman understands.

The king who would approach it, mighty
though he be,
Must prostrate himself in order to get near;
Any man who'd mine its ores must be glorious
And it would help him with his digging
evermore.

Musical with sweetness, exemplary as offspring
Are those brave ones with the seamless
manners
Who are conveyed so expertly, so smoothly
without bruising
From that treasure where even Caesars were
engendered.

It's clear only a clodhopper, of darkened
understanding,
Would fail to cherish it hugely and with
firmness,
Cosying up to it, without hurry, without
hindrance —
That lovely mouth that never flees from
combat.

BRIAN MERRIMAN

(*c.* 1749–1805)

from:
CÚIRT AN MHEON-OÍCHE
(The Midnight Court)
(1780)

[The considerable secondary literature excited by *Cúirt an Mheón-Oíche* is notably lacking in consensus. The fact that we know little of Brian Merriman's life has compounded the difficulty of contextualizing the poem. The *Cúirt* has been seen variously as standing apart from the rest of Gaelic literature, as extending the motifs of the medieval Court of Love and Parliament of Women traditions into the eighteenth century, as ironizing the Jacobite pieties of the *aisling* tradition, as endorsing the values of the Enlightenment and as re-animating the trope of the Sovereignty goddess. (Indispensable accounts of the poem's contexts and reception are provided by Gearóid Ó Crualaoich, 'The Vision of Liberation in *Cúirt an Mheán*

Oíche (*Folia Gadelica*, eds Pádraig de Brún, Seán Ó Coileáin and Pádraig Ó Riain (Cork: Cork University Press, 1983), pp. 95–104), and Alan Titley, 'An Breithiúnas ar *Cúirt an Mheán-Oíche*' (*Studia Hibernica*, vol. 25 (1990), pp. 105–33).)

Key formal considerations relate the *Cúirt* to the anglophone verse of its own time. The poem's status as a satire committed to rhyming couplets links it to the dominant poetic genre of the English eighteenth century. Its parody of the *aisling* is directly continuous with the Mock mode of Augustan literature. The turning of the convention of visitation by a visionary *spéirbhean* against itself in the account of the speaker's entrapment by a titanic female horror may be said to lend the opening section (lines 1–166) — if not the entire poem — the status of a mock *aisling* to set beside Pope's mock epic, *The Rape of the Lock* (1712; 1714) and Burns's mock moral tale, *Tam o' Shanter* (1790). Merriman's poem can be seen to advocate an amoral emancipatory philosophy similar to Burns's, which is presumably one of the reasons why Frank O'Connor argued in the face of evidence dating the poem to 1780 that Merriman 'must derive from Burns'. (Frank O'Connor, *Kings, Lords, & Commons: An Anthology from the Irish* [2nd ed. Dublin: Gill and Macmillan, 1970], p.xiv.) It might have been more convincing to claim that Merriman and Burns have a common root in Alexander Pope, and that both the *Cúirt* and *Tam o' Shanter* represent a marriage between one of the vernacular literary traditions of these islands and the increasingly unignorable English one centred on London — though the Gaelic tradition is clearly the more powerful partner in the canonical nuptials of the *Cúirt*, whereas the Scots and English traditions achieve a more or less exact balance in Burns's poem.

Commentators familiar with the *Cúirt* only in translation, however, can overstate its Augustanism. Though written in tetrameter couplets, it is driven forward by its assonantal, and frequently alliterative, stresses rather than its end-rhymes, and the poem consequently sets up a more turbulent acoustic than most of the attempts to render it in English suggest. The furious and at times almost grotesque energy of the *Cúirt* — a matter of verbal extravagance as well as of 'vision' — takes it well beyond the ambit of eighteenth-century notions of literary decorum. The sexual frankness of the poem is of a different order from that of the self-consciously transgressive 'unofficial' literature of post-Restoration Britain, being entirely free of the libertine *machismo* of Rochester's verse or of Burns's *Merry Muses of Caledonia*. Merriman's celebrated bawdiness has sometimes been seen as providing an instance of the libertarian daring of the Revolutionary period, but it has at least as much in common with the medieval earthiness preserved in the poetry of County Clare.

Critics have been as divided about the meaning of the poem as about its relationship to tradition. Some have concentrated on its apparent concern with agrarian decay, interpreting its overt thematic treatment of sexual disharmony in terms of the fertility of the land, and seeing Aoibheall of Craig Liath, who presides over the Midnight Court, as a version of the Sovereignty goddess responsible for the welfare alike of land and people. The fact that the population explosion which would culminate in the Great Famine was already palpably in progress in the 1770s has made the poem's complaint against depopulation difficult to historicize, and indeed the central charge laid against men in the Court session itself — that they marry too late — is at odds with a wealth of evidence pointing to what were by European standards the unusually early marriages of the Irish rural poor. Others have construed the poem's concern with marriage and paternity in the light of Merriman's reputed bastardy. The text's implicit mockery of Jacobite rhetoric and its eschewal of more than glancing reference to specifically national resentments have been taken to indicate either callousness or despair on the author's part in relation to the Matter of Ireland.

Though the *Cúirt* is openly concerned with gender politics, this aspect of the poem has only come to be commented upon centrally since the rise of feminist criticism. The testimony of the young woman who delivers two of the three long monologues which constitute the main body of the *Cúirt* can be construed alternatively as a recognition by a male poet of the validity of female desire or as an elaboration of male sexual fantasy. Máirín de Búrca took the latter view in a lecture at the Merriman Summer School in 1980, when she condemned the entire poem as 'sexist rubbish' (see Volume V, pp. 1588–91). It should be noted, however, that the woman is presented much more sympathetically than her detractor, the foul-mouthed old man who speaks the intervening monologue: he fetishizes sexuality in terms of economic exchange, whereas she sees it as its own justification. Merriman's comic gusto and in particular his gleeful debunking of the ethereality of the *aisling* should make us slow to detect a fear of women behind the description of the gigantic female bailiff in the opening section. The concluding section, however, when the bailiff and the young woman move to carry out on the poet himself Aoibheall's judgement on men who have remained unmarried after twenty-one, is suggestive of extreme anxiety in the face of female licentiousness. (The speaker is now identified not only as Brian but, by way of a punning clue, as Brian Merriman.)

Noting that the speaker is condemned not just for his virginity but for his poetic disposition — 'Seinm ar cheolta, spórt is aoibhneas', 'Playing his tunes, on sprees and batters' — Seamus Heaney has highlighted a possible connection between the end of the poem and the myth of Orpheus, torn apart by the Thracian women he had spurned in favour of his art. More slyly, perhaps, he has recruited Merriman as a defence witness in the gender trials of contemporary poetry criticism: 'Merriman deserves a specially lenient hearing in the women's court, if only for having envisaged his own prosecution ahead of time and for having provided the outline of a case against himself. He was surely something of a progressive when it came to the representation of women. He gave them bodies and brains and let them speak as if they lived by them' ('Orpheus in Ireland', in Seamus Heaney, *The Redress of Poetry: Oxford Lectures* [London: Faber and Faber, 1995], pp. 60, 55]).

The extracts which follow include the mock *aisling* opening of the poem, part of the second testimony of the ignored young woman, and most of the closing section. The three Irish excerpts are from Liam P. Ó Murchú (ed.), *Cúirt an Mheon-Oíche* (Baile Átha Cliath: An Clóchomhar, 1982), pp. 19–20, lines 1–60; pp. 37–8, lines 679–718; pp. 42–6, lines 855–1014. The corresponding translations are from: (i) Seamus Heaney, *The Midnight Verdict* (Loughcrew: Gallery Press, 1993), pp. 23–5 (p. 23, line 1, to p. 25, line 6); (ii) Thomas Kinsella (ed.), *The New Oxford Book of Irish Verse*, pp. 238–9 (p. 238, line 30, to p. 239, line 29); and (iii) Seamus Heaney, *The Midnight Verdict*, pp. 30–3 (p. 30, line 1, to p. 33, line 29). For further excerpts, with translation by Dennis Woulfe, see Volume I, pp. 297–303. Selection of and headnote to the following excerpts: Patrick Crotty.]

BA GNÁTH me ag siúl le ciumhais na habhann
Ar bháinseach úr 's an drúcht go trom,
In aice na gcoillte i gcoim an tsléibhe
Gan mhairg gan mhoill ar shoilse an lae.
Do ghealadh mo chroí an uair chínn Loch
   Gréine,
An talamh 's an tír is íor na spéire,
Taitneamhacht aoibhinn suíomh na sléibhte
Ag bagairt a gcinn thar dhroim a chéile.
Do ghealfadh an croí bheadh críon le cianta
Caite gan bhrí nó líonta 'o phianta,
An séithleach searbh gan sealbh gan saibhreas
D'fhéachfadh tamall thar bharra na gcoillte
Ar lachain 'na scuainte ar chuan gan ceo
Is an eala ar a bhfuaid 's í ag gluaiseacht leo,
Na héisc le meidhir ag eirghe in airde,
Péirse im radhairc go taibhseach tarrbhreac,
Dath an locha agus gorm na dtonn
Ag teacht go tolgach torannach trom
Bhíodh éanla i gcrainn go meidhreach mómhar
Is léimreach eilte i gcoillte im chóngar,
Géimreach adharc is radharc ar shlóite,
Tréanrith gadhar is *Reynard* rompu.

AR MAIDIN inné bhí an spéir gan ceo,
Bhí *Cancer* ón ngréin 'na caorthaibh teo
Is í gofa chum saothair tar éis na hoíche
Is obair an lae sin réimpi sínte.
Bhí duilleabhar craobh ar ghéaga im thimpeall,
Fiorthann is féar 'na shlaodach taoibh liom
Glasra fáis is bláth is luibheanna
Scaipfeadh le fán dá chráiteacht smaointe.
Bhí me cortha is an codladh dom thraochadh
Is shín me thoram ar cothrom sa bhféar glas
In aice na gcrann i dteannta trinse,
Taca lem cheann 's mo hanlaibh sínte.
Ar cheangal mo shúl go dlúth le chéile,
Greamaithe dúnta i ndúghlas néalta
Is m'aghaidh agam foilithe ó chuile go sásta
I dtaibhreamh d'fhuiling me an cuilithe cráite
Chorraigh do lom do pholl go hae me
Im chodladh go trom gan mheabhair gan éirim.

BA GAIRID mo shuan nuair chualas, shíl me
An talamh máguaird ar luascadh im thimpeall
Anfa aduaidh is fuadach fíochmhar
Is calaithe an chuain ag tuargaint tinte.
Siolla dhom shúil dár shamhlaíos uaim
Do chonairc me chúm le ciumhais an chuain
An mhásach bholgach tholgach thaibhseach
Chnámhach cholgach dhoirrgeach ghaibhdeach.

A haeirde cheart má mheas me díreach,
Sé nó seacht do shlata is fuilleach,
Péirse beacht dá brat ag sraoilleadh
Léi sa tslab le drab is ríobal.
Ba mhuar ba mhiar ba fiain le féachaint
Suas 'na héadan créachtach créimeach,
B'anfa ceantair, scanradh saolta,
A draid is a drandal mantach méirsceach.
A Rí gach má! ba láidir líofa
A bíoma láimhe is lánstaf inti
Is comhartha práis 'na barr ar spíce
Is comhachta báille in airde air scríofa.

TRANSLATION (i)

I used to wade through heavy dews
On the riverbank, in the grassy meadows,
Beside the woods, in a glen apart
As the morning light lit sky and heart
And sky and heart kept growing lighter
At the sight of Graney's clear lough water.
The lift of the mountains there! Their brows
Shining and stern in serried rows!
My withered heart would start to quicken,
Everything small in me, hardbitten,
Everything hurt and needy and shrewd
Lifted its eyes to the top of the wood
Past flocks of ducks on a glassy bay
And a swan there too in all her glory:
Jumping fish in the heady light
And the perch's belly flashing light.
The sheen of the lough, the grumble and roar
Of the blue-black waves as they rolled ashore.
There'd be chirruping birds from tree to tree
And leaping deer in the woods nearby,
Sounding of horns, the dashing crowd
As the hounds gave tongue and Reynard fled.

Yesterday morning the sky was clear,
The sun flamed up in the house of Cancer
With the night behind it, fit to take on
The work of the day that had to be done.
Leafy branches were all around me,
Shooting grasses and growths abounded;
There were green plants climbing and worts
   and weeds
That would gladden your mind and clear your
   head.
I was tired out, dead sleepy and slack,
So I lay at my length on the flat of my back

With my head well propped, my limbs at ease
In a nest in a ditch beside the trees.
The minute I closed my eyes, I drowsed.
My lids were locked, I couldn't be roused.
I was hidden from flies, felt safe and sound
When a nightmare swarmed and gathered
    around,
Battered me, flattened me, dragged me down
Through weltering sleep and left me stunned.
But my rest was short for next there comes
A sound from the ground like the roll of drums,
A wind from the north, a furious rout
And the lough in a sulphurous thunderlight.
And then comes looming into view
And steering towards me along the bay
This hefty menacing dangerwoman,
Bony and huge, a terrible hallion.
Her height, I'd say, to the nearest measure,
Was six or seven yards or more,
With a swatch of her shawl all japs and glar
Streeling behind in the muck and mire.
It was awe-inspiring just to see her,
So hatchet-faced and scarred and sour —
With her ganting gums and her mouth in a twist
She'd have put the wind up man or beast.
And Lord of Fates! Her hand was a vise
Clamped on a towering staff or mace
With a spike on top and a flange of brass
That indicated her bailiff's powers.

★   ★   ★   ★   ★

Ba dubhach an fuadar suairceas oíche,
Smúit is ualach, duais is líonadh,
Lúithní lua agus guaille caola
Is glúine crua comh fuar le oighre,
Cosa feoite dóite ón ngríosaigh
Is colann bhreoite dhreoite chríonna.
An bhfuil stuaire beo ná feofadh liath
Ag cuail dá shórt bheith pósta riamh
Nár chuartaigh fós fá dhó le bliain
Cé buachaill óg í, feoil nó iasc,
'S an feoiteach fuar seo suas léi sínte
Dreoite duairc, gan bhua gan bhíogadh?
Och, cár mhuar dhi bualadh bríomhar
Ar nós an diabhail de uair gach oíche.
Ní dóch go dtuigir gurb ise ba chiontach
Ná fós go gclisfeadh ar laige le tamhandacht,
An maighre mascalach carthanach ciúintais,
Is deimhin go bhfeaca sí a mhalairt do
    mhúnadh.

Ní labharfadh focal dá mb'obair an oíche
Is thabharfadh cothrom do stollaire bríomhar,
Go brách ar siúl níos dhiúltaigh riamh é
Ar chnáimh a cúil 's a súilibh iata.
Ní thabharfadh preab le stailc mhíchuíosach,
Fobha mar chat nó sraic nó scríob air,
Acht í go léir 'na slaod comh sínte
Taobh ar thaobh 's a géag 'na thimpeall,
Ó scéal go scéal ag bréagadh a smaointe
Béal ar bhéal 's ag méaracht síos air.
Is minic do chuir sí a cos dtaobh anonn de
Is chuimil a *brush* ó chrios go glún de,
Sciobadh an phluid 's an chuilt dá ghúnga
Ag spriongar 's ag sult le moirt gan subhachas
Níor chabhair di cigilt ná cuimilt ná fáscadh,
Fobha dá hingin, dá huilinn ná a sála,
Is nár dom aithris mar chaitheadh sí an oíche
Ag fáscadh an chnaiste 's ag searradh 's ag
    síneadh,
Ag feacadh na ngéag 's an t-éadach fúithi,
A ballaibh go léir 's a déid ar lúthchrith,
Go loinnir an lae gan néall do dhubhadh uirthi
Ag imirt ó thaobh go taobh 's ag únfairt.

TRANSLATION (ii)

It was gloomy doings, the nightly joy
— oppression and burden, trouble and fright:
legs of lead and skinny shoulders,
iron knees as cold as ice,
shrunken feet by embers scorched,
an old man's ailing, wasting body.
What handsome woman would not go grey
at the thought of being wed to a bundle of bones
that wouldn't enquire, not twice in the year,
was she half-grown boy or meat or fish?
— this dry cold thing stretched out across her
surly and spent, without power or bounce.
O what to her was a lively hammering
hard as the Devil, and twice a night!
It won't, I hope, be thought she was guilty
or might fall down weak, worn out by the like,
this vigorous, handsome, kind, sweet girl.
She certainly met with the opposite rearing:
she'd never complain at a night of work
but give a brave slasher as good as she got.
She'd never refuse, any time or place,
on bone of her back with her eyes shut tight,
with never a balk or immoderate sulk
nor attack like a cat, nor scrape nor scratch,

but stretched her all like a sheaf beside him
flank on flank, with her legs around him
coaxing his thoughts by easy stages,
fingering down on him, mouth on mouth,
putting her leg across him often,
rubbing her brush from waist to knee,
or snatching the blanket or quilt from his loins
to fiddle and play with the juiceless lump.
But useless to tickle or squeeze or rub
or attack with her elbows, nails or heels.
I'm ashamed to relate how she passed the night
squeezing the sluggard, shuddering, sprawling,
tossing her limbs and the bedding beneath her,
her teeth and her members all a-shiver,
not sleeping a wink till the dawn of day,
performing and tossing from side to side.
Lightly this leper may talk of women
with no force in his spine and no power in his
    bones . . .!

★ ★ ★ ★ ★

D'EIRGHE an mhánla ar bharr an bhinse,
Shoilsigh an lá is an áit ina timpeall,
B'álainn óg a cló is a caoindreach,
B'ard a glór, ba bheo is ba bhíogthach,
D'fháisc a doirne is d'ordaigh deimhneach
Báille ar bord ag fógairt *Silence*,
Dúirt a béal bhí ag séideadh soilse,
An chúirt go léir go faon ag eisteacht:

'GHEIBHIMSE díreach brí chum buaite
Is feidhm id chaintse, a bhrídeach bhuartha,
Chím 's is dóch gur dóite an radharc liom
Síolrach Órla, Mhóire is Mheidhbhe,
An seifteoir caol 's an créatúir cladhartha
An ceisteoir claon 's an déirceoir daigheartha,
Sú na táire is tál na coimse
Ag súil le sárfhuil sámh na saoithe.
Achtaimíd mar dhlí do bhéithe
An seacht fó thrí gan cuibhreach céile
Tharraingt ar cheann go teann gan trua
Is a cheangal don chrann seo i dteannta an
    tuama.
Bainigí lom de a chabhail 's a chóta
Is feannaigí a dhrom 's a chom le corda.
'On chuid acu tharla báite i mblianta
Is cheileann go táir an tairne tiarpa,
Chuireas amú gan subhachas d'éinne
Buile na hútha is lúth a ngéaga,
Mheilleas a gcáil is fáil ar mhnaoi acu

Ag feitheamh gan fáth ar bharr na craoibhe,
Fágaim fúibhse tionscailt páise,
A mhná na dúla, dubhadh le dálgas,
Ceapaigí fíornimh tinte is tairnibh,
Caithigí smaointe is intleacht mná leis,
Cuiridh bhur gcomhairle i gcomhar le chéile
Is tugaimse comhachta an fórsa dhéanamh,
Bheirim gan spás díbh páis na gciantach
Is beag liom bás gan barrghoin pian dóibh.

NÍ CHUIRIMSE i bhfáth 'o bharr mo chainte
An foirfeach fálta cáslag cloíte,
An gabhal gan gotha ná an gola gan geall suilt,
Toll gan toradh ná an tormach falsa,
Acht léigthear an óige i gcóir chum síolraigh
Is déanadh an sórt seo clóca is díon dóibh.
Is minic do chímse righinsigh bhaotha
Ag tuitim le tíos is bímse baoch dhíobh,
Gofa le mná do lá agus d'oíche
Ag cosnamh a gcáil 's ar scáth a ngníomhartha,
Ag seasamh 'na bhfeighil 's a bhfeidhm go fálta,
A n-ainm ar chloinn is bheinnse sásta.

CHUALA siolla is do cuireadh i bhásta é,
Is fuath liom baineannach iomadach ráiteach,
Labhair go réidh is glaoigh go híseal,
Bas ar do bhéal is baol bheith cainteach.
Seachain go fóill na comhachtaigh íogmhar
Is caithfid siad pósadh fós pé chífeas,
Tiocfaidh an lá le lánchead comhairle
Is cuirfidh an Pápa lámh na gcomhacht air,
Suífidh an chuideachta ar thubaist na dtíortha
Is scaoilfear chugaibh fá urchall cuibhrigh
Fiantas fola agus fothrom na feola
Is mian bhur dtoile, na tollairí teo so.
Aon duine eile dár hoileadh ó mhnaoi ar bith,
Léigh a ndeirim is feicim do bhíogadh,
Ar shlí mo chumais ná fuiling i gcaoi ar bith
Sraoill gan urraim ná Murainn i mbríste,
Acht leanaig sa tóir na feoitigh liatha
Is glanaigí Fódla ón sórt so fiale.

CAITHFEADSA gluaiseacht uaibh chum siúil,
Is fada mo chuairdse ar fuaid na Mumhan,
An turas tá romham ní fhónann moill do
Is iomad dom ghnó anso fós gan eisteacht.
Casfaidh me arís 's is fíor nách fáilteach,
D'fhearaibh nách binn mo thíocht don áit seo.
An chuid acu atá go táir 'na smaointe,
Foireann nách foláir leo a gcáil bheith sínte,
Mhaíos le fothrom a gcothrom ar bhéithe,

Chífe an pobal a gcogar 's a sméideadh.
Is taitneamhach leo is is dóil gur laochas
Scannal na hóige pósta is aonta,
Mian a dtoile ní sporann a gcionta,
Bréantas fola ná borradh na drúise,
Taitneamh don ghníomh ná fíoch na féithe
Acht magadh na mílte ag maíomh na n-éachta.
Ní saint dá só bheir leo na céadta
Acht caint is gleo agus mórtas laochais,
Mustar is ábhacht is ráig gan riail
Is a gcumas go tláith gan tál gan triall,
Go tuisealach tarrlag támh 'na n-iall
Is cuthach le gá ar a mná ina ndiaidh.
Glacfad go réidh an méid seo láithreach,
Caithfidh me géilleadh 'o mhéid mo phráinneach,
Cuirfidh me an bhuíon so i gcuing 's in úim
Nuair thiocfaidh me arís sa mí seo chúinn'.

DO BHREATHAIN me cruinn an ríbhean réaltach,
Lagaigh mo chroí le linn bheith réidh dhi,
D'airigh me dásacht ghránmhar éigin
Is pairithis bháis im chnámha is im chéadfa,
Chonairc me an tír 's an tíos ar luascadh
Is fuinneamh a cainte ag rince im chluasa.
Tagann an bíoma bíogthach báille
Is leathain mo líthe ar shíneadh a láimhe,
Tharraing ar chluais go stuacach storrtha
Stracaithe suas léi ar uachtar boird me.
Preabann an báb so chráigh an t-aonta,
Greadann a lámha is is ard do léim sí,
Is aibigh adúirt, 'a chrústa chríonna,
Is fada me ag súil led chúlsa chíoradh.
Is minic do slaíodh thu, a chroí gan daonnacht,
Is mithid duit stríocadh 'o dhlí na mbéithe.
Cosaint cá bhfaighidh tú in aghaidh na cúise?
Focal níor thuill tá a leadhb gan lúthchlis.
Ca bhfuil do shaothar saor le suíochant?
Ca bhfuil na béithe baoch dod ghníomhartha?
Breathainse a bhaill seo, a mhaighdean
    mhaorga,
Ainimh ní bhfaighimse mhill ar bhéithe é,
Breathain go cruinn a ghnaoi is a ghéaga
Ó bhaitheas a chinn go boinn a chaolchos.
Bíodh gurb ainmheach an-mhíchumtha é
Chímse ceangailte a bharra gan diúltadh,
Gile ní ghráfainn, b'fhearr liom buí é,
Is cuma na gcnámh ní cháinfinn choíche.
Duine a mbeadh dronn 'na dhrom is fána —
Is minic sin togha fir cromshlinneánach,
Is minic sin gambach lansa gníomhach
Is ioscada cam ag strampa bríomhar.

Is fáthaibh foilitheach uireaspach éigin
D'fhág an doirfeach foirfe in aonta
Is méid a cheana idir mhaithibh na tíre,
A réim le sealad i gcaradas daoine
Ag seinm ar cheolta, spórt is aoibhneas,
Imirt is ól ar bhord na saoithe
I gcomhar na foirinne fuineadh as féile —
An snamhaire! b'fhurus dom urraimse ghéilleadh.
Is taibhseach taitneamhach tairbheach
    tréitheach
Meidhreach meanmnach a ainm 's is aerach.
Ainmhí 'od shórt níor ordaigh an Tiarna
Geanmnaí fós i gcóngar liaithe,
Creathaim go bonn le fonn do dhaortha
Is gairid an chabhair do labhartha baotha,
Is coir mós díreach, suíte an t-éadan,
Deich fó thrí gan cuibhreach céile.

EISTIG liomsa, a chlú na foighne,
Faighimse cúnamh i gcúis na maidhme,
An crá is an dúla mhúch gan bhrí me,
A mhná na muirne, is rún liom íoc air.
Cúnamh adeirim libh, beirig air, tóg é,
'Úna, goirim thu is faigh dhom an corda,
Ca bhfuil tú, 'Áine, ná bí ar iarraidh,
Ceangailse, a Mháire, a lámha ar dtaobh thiar
    dhe,
A Mhurainn, a Mheidhbh, a Shaidhbh 's a Shíle,
Cuirigí i bhfeidhm le daighearthaibh díocais
Barr gach scóla d'ordaigh an tsíbhean,
Báidh sa bhfeoil gach corda snaimdhmeach,
Tomhais go fial na pianta is crua
Le tóin 's le tiarpa Bhriain gan trua ar bith,
Tóg na lámha is ardaigh an sciúirse,
Is sómpla sámh é, a mhná na muirne,
Gearraigí doimhin, níor thuill sé fábhar,
Bainigí an leadhb ó rinn go sáil de,
Cloistear a chlinn i gcríochaibh Éibhir
Is critheadh a gcroí insna críontaigh aonta.

TRANSLATION (iii)

Bathed in an aura of morning light,
Her Grace on the bench got up to her feet;
Beautiful, youthful, full of poise,
She cleared her throat and raised her voice,
Then clenched her fists with definite menace
And ordered the bailiff to call for silence.
The court complied; they sat entranced
As her lovely fluent lips pronounced:

'To my mind, girl, you've stated your case
With point and force. You deserve redress.
So I here enact a law for women:
Unmated men turned twenty-one
To be sought, pursued, and hunted down,
Tied to this tree beside the headstone,
Their vests stripped off, their jackets ripped,
Their backs and asses scourged and whipped.
But the long-in-the-tooth and the dry-in-
      marrow,
The ones whose harrow-pins won't harrow,
Who pen the pent and lock away
The ram that's rampant in their body,
Keeping in hand what should go the rounds
And fencing off the pleasure grounds —
Their nemesis I leave to you
Whose hearths they'd neither fan nor blow.
Dear natural sexual women, think!
Consult your gender, mind and instinct.
Take cognizance. Co-operate.
For I here invest you with the right
(To be exercised to the breaking point)
And powers of violent punishment.

'Yet who gives a damn in the end of all
For them and their dribbling stroup and fall?
With forks collapsed and the feeling gone,
Their hardest part is a pubic bone.
So let them connive, sing dumb and smile
If ever a young man rings their bell
For it seems to me that the best solution
For men past making a contribution
Is not to resent their conjugal plight
But stand by their wives when they put it about,
Facilitate their womanly drives
And lend their name when the baby arrives.
And that, for the moment, will have to do.
I'm on the circuit, and overdue
In another part of Munster. So:
My verdict's short because I go.
But I'll be back, and God help then
Recalcitrant, male-bonded men.'

She stopped, but still her starry gaze
Transfixed me in a kind of daze
I couldn't shake off. My head went light,
I suffered cramps and a fainting fit.
The whole earth seemed to tilt and swing,
My two ears sang from the tongue-lashing
And then the awful targe who'd brought me,
The plank-armed bailiff, reached and caught me

Up by the ears and scruff of the neck
And dragged me struggling into the dock.
Where next comes skipping, clapping hands,
The lass who had aired her love-demands
And says to my face, 'You hardened chaw,
I've waited long, now I'll curry you raw!
You've had your warnings, you cold-rifed blirt.
But now you're caught in a woman's court
And nobody's here to plead your case.
Where is the credit you've earned with us?
Is there anyone here your action's eased?
One that your input's roused or pleased?
Observe him closely, Madam Judge.
From head to toe, he's your average
Passable male — no paragon
But nothing a woman wouldn't take on.
Unshapely, yes, and off the plumb,
But with all his kit of tools about him.
A shade whey-faced and pale and wan,
But what about it? There's bone and brawn.
For it's him and his likes with their humps and
      stoops
Can shoulder doors and flutter the coops;
As long as a man is randy and game,
Who gives a damn if he's bandy or lame?
So why is he single? Some secret wound
Or problem back in the family background?
And him the quality's darling boy,
All smiles and friends with everybody,
Playing his tunes, on sprees and batters
With his intellectual and social betters.
Wining and dining, day in, day out —
The creep, I can see why they think he's great!
A star bucklepper, the very man
You'd be apt to nickname 'merry man',
But the kind of man I would sweep away,
The virgin merry, going grey.
It bothers me deeply. I've come to hate
His plausible, capable, charming note
And his beaming, bland, unfurrowed forehead:
Thirty years old, and never bedded.

'So hear me now, long-suffering judge!
My own long hurt and ingrown grudge
Have me desolated. I hereby claim
A woman's right to punish him.
And you, dear women, you must assist.
So rope him Una, and all the rest —
Anna, Maura — take hold and bind him.
Double twist his arms behind him.
Remember all the sentence called for

And execute it to the letter.
Maeve and Sive and Sheila! Maureen!
Knot the rope till it tears the skin.
Let Mr Brian take what we give,
Let him have it. Flay him alive
And don't draw back when you're drawing blood.
Test all of your whips against his manhood.
Cut deep. No mercy. Make him squeal.
Leave him in strips from head to heel
Until every single mother's son
In the land of Ireland learns the lesson.'

Biographies/Bibliographies

Séathrún Céitinn (Geoffrey Keating)

For biography and bibliography, see Volume I, pp. 272.

CRITICISM. (relating to *Trí Bior-Ghaoithe an Bháis*) Tadhg Ó Dúshláine, 'Seathrún Céitinn agus an stil Bharócach a thug sé go hÉirinn', in *Dúchas* (Baile Átha Cliath: Coiscéim, 1983–5), pp. 43–55; Breandán Ó Buachalla, 'Na Stíobhartaigh agus an tAos Léinn: Cing Séamas', *Proceedings of the Royal Irish Academy*, vol. 83, series C (1983), pp. 81–134; Bernadette Cunningham, *The World of Geoffrey Keating: History, Myth and Religion in Seventeenth-Century Ireland* (Dublin: Four Courts Press, 2000).

Giraldus Cambrensis (Gerald of Wales)

For biography and bibliography, see Volume I, pp. 270–1.

Dáibhidh Ó Bruadair

For biography, see Volume I, p. 325.

CHIEF WRITINGS. Standard edition: *Duanaire Dháibhidh Uí Bhruadair*, ed. and trans. J.C. McErlean, 3 vols (London: Irish Texts Society, 1910, 1913, 1917). Poems in translation, with Introduction: Michael Hartnett, *Ó Bruadair* (Loughcrew: Gallery Books 1985).

BIOGRAPHY AND CRITICISM. Gerard Murphy, 'David Ó Bruadair', *Irish Ecclesiastical Record*, 5th series, vol. 78 (1952), pp. 340–57; Pádraig Ó Fiannachta, 'Dáiví Ó Bruadair', in *Idem.*, *Léas ar ár Litríocht* (Má Nuad: An Sagart, 1974), pp. 155–66; Art Ó Beoláin, 'Dáibhí Ó Bruadair', in *Merriman agus Filí Eile* (Baile Átha Cliath: An Clóchomhar, 1985), pp. 65–76; J.E. Caerwyn Williams and Patrick Ford, *The Irish Literary Tradition* (Cardiff: University of Wales Press, 1992), pp. 213–6.

Aindrias Mac Cruitín

LIFE. Aindrias Mac Cruitín, poet, scribe and teacher, came of a hereditary learned family which is known to have professed *seanchas* ('traditional history') for the lords of Thomond in the fourteenth and fifteenth centuries. In Aindrias's time, the family was associated particularly with poetry. Writing in 1847, Séamas Mac Cruitín, a later descendant, stated that Aindrias was born at Moyglass in the parish of Kilmurry-Ibricane, in west County Clare. His family appears to have been in comfortable circumstances, yet not so wealthy that Aindrias did not have to earn his living; at one or more stages of his life, he was employed as a teacher. While it is not known where he received his education, it is clear that it encompassed the traditional modes of Gaelic poetry. He wrote syllabic poems in *dán díreach* but also poems in the newly favoured accentual song-metres (*amhrán*). He is reputed to have tutored his better-known kinsman, the poet Aodh Buí Mac Cruitín (see pp. 429–30), to whom he was distantly related. Aindrias was a prolific scribe, and a number of manuscripts in his hand are still extant. One of the most important is a *duanaire* of poems composed for the Ó Lochlainn family of the Burren in County Clare (Royal Irish Academy Library, MS E.iv.3). He also worked as a genealogist, and inscribed pedigrees for many of the noble families of Munster, including the O'Briens of Thomond. Edward O'Brien of Ennistymon and Somhairle Mac Domhnaill of Kilkee seem to have been his major patrons. Aodh Buí composed a syllabic elegy on his death, beginning 'Ní buan brón go bás ollaimh'. It is preserved in the Library of Trinity College, Dublin, in MS H.6.11, p. 23. At least six manuscripts in his hand are still extant, and forty-three or more poems with attributions to him are recorded.

CHIEF WRITINGS. 'Fada mo thnúth re triall / re duanóg', in *A Collection of Poems . . . by the Clare Bards*, ed. and trans. Brian O'Looney (Dublin: O'Daly, 1863), pp. 5–25; T.F. O'Rahilly (ed.), 'Deasgán Tuanach: Selections from Modern Clare Poets', *Irish Monthly*, vol. 52–3 (1924–5).

BIOGRAPHY AND CRITICISM. Máire Ní Mhurchú agus Diarmuid Breathnach, *1560–1781: Beathaisnéis* (Baile Átha Cliath: An Clóchomhar, 2001), pp. 70–1; Vincent Morley, *An Crann os Coill: Aodh Buí Mac Cruitín c.1680-1755* (Baile Átha Cliath: Coiscéim, 1995), *passim.*; Pádraig Ó Fiannachta, *Léas Eile ar ár Litríocht* (Maigh Nuad: An Sagart, 1982), pp. 229–46; Eilís Ní Dheá, 'Lucht Scríofa Lámhscríbhinní i gContae an Chláir san 18ú Aois', *Dál gCais*, vol. 10 (1991), pp. 51–7; Breandán Ó Buachalla, *Aisling Ghéar: Na Stíobhartaigh agus an tAos Léinn 1603–1788* (Baile Átha Cliath: An Clóchomhar, 1996), *passim.*

Brian Merriman

For biography, see Volume I, p. 325.

BIOGRAPHY AND CRITICISM. Liam P. Ó Murchú, 'Cúlra agus Múnla Liteartha do *Chúirt* Merriman', in *Saoi na hÉigse. Aistí in ómós do Sheán Ó Tuama*, eds Pádraigín Riggs, Breandán Ó Conchúir and Seán Ó Coileáin (Baile Átha Cliath: An Clóchomhar, 2000), pp. 169–95.

MÁIRE HERBERT, *Editor*

Society and Myth, c. 700–1300

We do not have direct access to Irish mythology in its primary form. Our earliest evidence survives in tales redacted in writing in the Early Christian period. In these written works, mythic concern with the religious significance of foundational events has been transmuted to a historical concern with the re-telling of the past. Yet some of the underlying myths are still discernible, embedded in the stories, and particularly in their images and metaphors. We receive glimpses, rather than a complete view, of the manner in which manifestations of the supernatural were delineated in pre-Christian Ireland.

The use of imagery is fundamental to the expression of myth, and gender plays an important role in this process. We must keep in mind, however, that gender representations in myth function at the level of the metaphoric, not the literal. Moreover, the symbolism of myth is always multivalent. Thus, while divinities may be represented as male and female, their functions are not limited by social constructions of gender roles. Comparative mythology enables us to elucidate aspects of the Irish evidence through analogy with recognized patterns. Yet Irish female divinities are not simply reflections of Indo-European goddesses, nor transhistorical images of feminine power. We must be alert to the particular manner in which female representations are articulated in their specific Irish setting.

We must be aware, also, that mythic images are open, not fixed. As perceptions regarding the sources of power in the universe could shift, so too could perceptions regarding the divinities who embodied these powers. Thus, changes in society are likely to have led to changes in the interpretation and cultural meanings ascribed to its

myths. The Irish texts bear the impress of multiple layers of meaning. Narratives orally recounted as expressions of the sacred now survive in written texts which occlude their mythic meanings. Christianity may be the most evident influence on their present formulation, but we cannot assume that it has been the sole agent of change in the representation of gendered divine powers.

This section does not presume to give a full catalogue of Irish supernatural females, nor to discuss every surviving item of evidence. Instead, it focuses on the aspects of female representation which are best attested in the literature, recognizing that there is no necessary correlation between the date at which the material was first shaped into story, and the date of the surviving textual witnesses. As with myth itself, the narratives which preserve our materials are concerned with matters of fundamental import. They deal with the physical world and its society, the formation of the landscape, the sources of royal power, the fortunes of those involved in warfare, and the relations between mortals and immortals. Moreover, either implicitly or explicitly, they witness to the complex process of negotiation between native and Christian ideologies in the early historical period in Ireland.

THE VISIBLE WORLD (pp. 253–8)

The association of female divinities with the land and its physical features seems to have been an important feature of primal religious thought. Unfortunately, no Early Irish myth of creation survives, but tantalizing glimpses in Early Irish literature point to identification between the body of a goddess and the contours of the land. The ninth-century Christian glossator Cormac mac Cuilennáin, mentions Ana, *mater deorum Hibernensium,* 'mother of the gods of Ireland', from whom the hills called 'the two breasts of Ana' are named. The word *ériu,* which seems to mean 'land', is also the name of a goddess who requested that the whole island be called after her. In the first extract below, the naming of the land of Ireland by Ériu and by her female companions Banba and Fótla may be seen as a later reformulation of the mythic idea of a feminized land.

The *Dindshenchas,* 'The Lore of Places', is more concerned with recounting how features of the landscape came to be named than with describing their genesis. Yet it preserves the origin legends of Ireland's great rivers, the Boyne (Bóand) and the Shannon (Sinann). In the extracts concerning them, we see that the rivers are brought forth by female action, and they subsume, and fuse identity with, female bodies. However, both Bóann and Sinann receive their river embodiments as punishment. Both challenged prohibitions placed on them. Does this mean that their fate was decreed by their having sought capabilities beyond their sphere? Do we have here a prehistoric shift in the power relations between male and female divinities?

Similar transmutations are certainly discernible elsewhere. The *Dindshenchas,* while revealing something of the feminine aspect of the natural world, also associates the female with the transformation of natural landscape into social space. The creation of the great assembly sites of Tailtiu and Carman is attributed to females. These are depicted as figures who lose their former powerful position and die in captivity. They are commemorated at the sites which enclose their bodies and bear their names. Great fairs are held annually at these sites. Yet the fairs, while named for the goddesses, are said to have been held at Lugnasad, the feast of the god Lug. The ambivalence in the status accorded to Tailtiu and Carman here would seem to indicate that the texts are seeking to accommodate different levels of mythic significance. There is acknowledgment that assembly places have a tradition of association with female divinity but it is evident that their ritual celebration of the female was superseded by that of the male.

SOVEREIGNTY (pp. 259–62)

Through association with social as well as natural space, the sphere of female divinity extended from the physical universe to the ordering of human existence in this universe. Thus, a divine female was influential in society's central institution of kingship. In Irish mythic thought, the goddess of the land was depicted as choosing the mortal who would be king. Immortal and mortal were united in a relationship symbolized as a marriage. By his espousal to the goddess of the land, the male chosen as sovereign participated in divine power. The fruitfulness of his kingdom, as well as peace and harmony among its people, was ensured by his observance of the obligations which intimate association with the divinity had laid on him. According to mythic thought, it was the goddess of the land who validated its sovereignty and bestowed the fruits of his rule on the sovereign.

In our first text, Medb's depiction as sought-after royal female is a demythologized version of her primary role as female sovereignty with whom all successful kings must be harmoniously united. The ritual counterpart of the myth, the sacred marriage ceremony itself, appears to be described in the account by Giraldus Cambrensis. There, the ruler is mated with the goddess's animal surrogate. Certainly we may doubt the validity of the account as representative of contemporary inauguration rites in twelfth-century Ireland. Nevertheless, we should bear in mind that kingship was the prime societal institution in Ireland which survived from pre-Christian into Christian times, and that this continuity seems to be matched by continuity in the use of the symbols and metaphors through which the concept of rule was expressed. Thus an early fourteenth-century annalist still refers to royal inauguration in terms of the king's marriage to his land.

However, the social function of kingship in Ireland changed over the centuries, and so too we find that its metaphoric representations reflect change. The attainment of sovereignty came to be viewed as the result of personal achievement rather than of divine assignation, and, in gendered representations in literature, the female, formerly dominant in her role as locus of power, loses this dominance to the male.

This is indicated below in the representation of the designation of future kings in *Baile in Scáil,*

'The Vision of the Spectre'. Here, the female bestower of sovereignty is accompanied by the god Lug, and must await his prompt in order to offer the drink of espousal to royal candidates. In the following instance, the story of Niall and the 'Loathly Lady', ostensibly we again have the mating between female sovereignty and male royal aspirant. Now, however, the female is dependent on the action of the male in order to be restored to her rightful form and beauty. As the government of society came to be realized in terms of real power rather than of symbolic authority, so too in the mythic marriage the divine female, no longer autocratic, instead becomes the more passive partner.

WARFARE AND DEATH (pp. 262–6)

Feminized power, as well as being associated with kingship, is also associated with society's other important institution, that of warriorhood. The supernatural female involved in tales about battles is most frequently named as the Mórrígan ('great queen'). Her alternate identity is as Badb ('scald-crow'), whose appearance as a black bird of prey causes terror on the battlefield. In *Lebar Gabála*, 'The Book of Invasions', a trio of goddesses, Badb, Macha and the Mórrígan, are depicted as belonging to the Otherworld people, the Túatha Dé Danann. This schematization seems to be late, however, and our earliest texts usually depict a solitary supernatural female, with multiple names and guises, intervening on occasions of battle, or of impending violent death.

It is in the action of heroic tales that we most frequently find this divine female. In the extract from *Táin Bó Regamna*, 'The Cattle Raid of Regamain', the Mórrígan's role seems designed to check unwarranted arrogance on the part of Cú Chulainn, the warrior *par excellence*. The heroic life is destined to end in early death and, as we see below, the depiction of the bird perched beside the dead Cú Chulainn recalls the previous appearance of the goddess in *Táin Bó Regamna*, as she promises the warrior to be 'guardian of his death'.

Indeed, it is a prime function of the female divinity to be both prophet and visible presage of battle-outcome and death. At the close of the tale of the Battle of Mag Tuired, the Mórrígan

prophesies future disaster, while in *Táin Bó Cúailnge*, the mere sight and sound of Badb, the carrion crow, causes fatal terror among the hosts. In extracts below, the death of besieged kings is foreshadowed by female prophecy which is both verbal and visual. The supernatural female assumes a striking pose as she foretells the doom of Conaire and of Cormac, while, in her guise as washerwoman at the ford, she presents a gruesome tableau of death in battle to accompany her foreboding words.

As the outcome of battle came to be regarded more as a matter of human competence than of divine involvement, it is to be expected that the mythic component of battle-narratives might diminish. Yet fear of death in battle remained inescapable, though societal attitudes might change. Moreover, this fear retained its terrifying female aspect. As the final extract indicates, the cry of the avian Badb and the appearance of the washerwoman at her bloody task long retained their narrative potency as harbingers of approaching disaster.

THE OTHERWORLD (pp. 267–72)

The overall evidence of Early Irish literature points to belief in a paradisiacal Otherworld which existed in close relation to the mortal world, with a social structure replicated in human society. An invitation to an Otherworld realm to display prowess and to receive enhanced powers seems to have been part of the heroic life-cycle of great kings and warriors. We have here the positive aspect of human contact with divine power, accessed in this instance by entering the realms of the supernatural world. In the original myth, the return of the hero and his reintegration into human society would seem to have been the norm. However, there was risk involved in supernatural contact. This came to be epitomized in terms of the mortal being attracted to remain in the Otherworld.

In our examples below, Láegaire mac Crimthainn, who had responded to an Otherworld request for military help, chooses to remain there, explaining how much his Otherworld existence represents an enhancement of earthly life. For Láegaire and his company, as for all male heroes, beautiful, freely available women were an important aspect of the allure of the Otherworld. It would seem, however, that the seduction of men from their earthly lives to an Otherworld existence began to develop an entirely female aspect.

In the narrative of Connlae a supernatural female is seen to invite a male simply because she has fallen in love with him. She lures him by her magic as well as by her beauty to an Otherworld now identified as a Land of Women, a realm which is enticing but entrapping. In the tale of Connlae we see representatives of human society struggle in vain against the Otherworld power embodied by the woman. Desire overcomes Connlae's love for his people, and the overwhelming sense is that of earthly loss. In the renowned Old Irish tale 'The Voyage of Bran' (*Immram Brain*) (see Volume I, pp. 45–7), the voyager's journey back to Ireland also involves this sense of loss, the impossibility of return and reintegration into mortal life. Thus, contact with a feminized Otherworld now comes to acquire a negative value in the eyes of human society.

Indeed, in the passage from 'The Voyage of Máel Dúin's Boat', what is retained of the traditional theme of Otherworld encounter is a dramatic portrayal of a female-dominated realm whence ensnared males could make their escape only by drastic measures. Woman now represents what is seductively, but destructively, 'other', a supernatural world which no longer validated the social order of this world.

Access to the supernatural world is often associated with sea-journeying. The sea is regarded as a liminal realm between two worlds, and is itself a scene of contact with Otherworld beings. Here, also, the potential perils of such contact come to be realized in female form. Beautiful women may entrap the male voyager, with devastating results. As we see below, life-enhancing Otherworld encounters are now depicted as death-dealing. From the male perspective of the storytellers, men like Rúad and Rot are portrayed as victims of the malevolence of female immortals.

Yet not all sea-dwelling females are represented as malevolent. It is related of Lí Ban that, after a submarine existence of three hundred years following the great innundation which formed Lough Neagh, she encounters Christian clerics, who compete for association with her. Not only does this representative of the pagan supernatural make the transition into Christendom through her baptism, she is ultimately elevated to sanctity, being identified with Muirgein, whose feast is recorded on 27 January in the early ninth-century Martyrology of Óengus.

A. The Visible World

ANONYMOUS

from:
LEBAR GABÁLA
(The Book of Invasions)
(Middle Irish)

[The text known as Lebar Gabála represents itself as the summation of knowledge about Ireland's past, from the beginning of time until the settlement of the Gaédil (i.e. the Gaels). What survives, however, is a work of medieval scholarship which ultimately provides more insight into Christian revisionism of myth than it does into myth itself. The following extract presents a historicized account of the encounter between the invading sons of Míl (the Milesians, claimed as the ancestors of the Gaédil) and the trio of tutelary goddesses of the land. The text which I have translated is from the twelfth-century Book of Leinster, in the diplomatic edition by R.I. Best, Osborn Bergin and M.A. O'Brien, *The Book of Leinster*, vol. 1 (1954), p. 50, lines 1589–1604.]

The sons of Míl conversed with Banba on Sliab Mis. She said to them: 'If the purpose of your coming be to seize Ireland, may it not be well-favoured.' 'Certainly that is the purpose,' said Amairgen Glúngel, the poet. 'Let me have a favour from you, then,' she said. 'What favour?' they asked. 'That my name be on this island,' she said. 'It will be a name for the island,' said Amairgen. They spoke to Fótla in Eblinn. She said the same thing to them, and asked that her name be on the island. Amairgen said that Fótla would be a name for this island. They had a conversation with Ériu in Uisnech. She said to them: 'Warriors, you are welcome. Long since, seers have known of your coming. This island will be yours forever, and as far as the eastern part of the world there will be no island better. No race will be more excellent than yours.' 'That is auspicious,' said Amairgen. 'The prophecy is good.' 'It is not to her that we are to be grateful, but to our own gods, and our own powers,' said Eber Donn, the senior of the sons of Míl. 'It does not matter, as far as you are concerned,' said Ériu. 'Neither you nor your family will have any of the benefit of this island. Grant me the favour, sons of Míl and offspring of Bregon, that my name be on the island,' said she. 'It will be the principal name for it,' said Amairgen.

from:
THE DINDSHENCHAS
OF BÓAND
(The River Boyne)
(Middle Irish)

[The *Dindshenchas* collection of place-name legends in prose and verse survives in various recensions, the earliest of which was probably compiled about the beginning of the eleventh century. The account here of the naming of the Boyne, and the following passage on the river Shannon, are both preserved in verse of the Middle Irish period. The edition is that of Edward Gwynn, *The Metrical Dindshenchas*, Part III (Dublin,: Royal Irish Academy, 1913), pp. 26–30. The present translation is my emended version of his, ibid., pp. 27–31.]

Síd Nechtain sund forsin tshléib,
lecht mic Labrada lán-géir,
assa silenn in sruth slán
dianid ainm Bóand bith-lán.

Cóic anmand déc, demne drend,
forsin tshruth-sin adrímem,
otá Síd Nechtain asmaig
co roshaig pardus Adaim.

. . . . . .

Bóand a h-ainm coitchend cain
otá in síd co fairge fraig:
mebur lim aní diatá
usce mná mic Labrada.

Nechtain mac Labrada laind,
diarbo ben Bóand, bágaimm,
topur diamair bói 'na dún,
assa maided cech mí-rún.

Ní fhail nodécced dia lár
nach maided a dá rosc rán:
dia ngluased do chlí nó deis,
ní thargad úad cen athis.

Aire níslaimed nech de
acht Nechtain 's a deogbaire:
it é a n-anmand, fri gním nglan,
Flesc is Lam ocus Luäm.

Fecht and dolluid Bóand bán —
dosfuargaib a dímus n-án —
cosin topur cen tarta
d'airigud a chumachta.

Immar rothimchill fo thrí
in topur co n-étuachli,
maidit teora tonna de
dia tánic aided Bóinne.

Rosiacht cach tond díb ria chuit,
romillset in mnaí mbláth-buic:
tond ria cois, tond ria súil sláin,
tres tond brisid a leth-láim.

Rethis co fairgi, ferr de,
d'imgabáil a hathise,
ar nách acced nech a cned:
furri féin a himathber.

Cach conair dolluid in ben
moslúi in t-usce úar imgel:
ón tshíd co fairgi nách fand,
conid di gairthir Bóand.

TRANSLATION

Síd Nechtain here on the hill,
is the grave of the fierce son of Labraid,
from which flows the perfect river
whose name is ever-full Bóand.

There are fifteen names, indisputably,
on this stream, as we enumerate,
from Síd Nechtain as it breaks forth
until it reaches the paradise of Adam.

. . . . . .

Bóand is its general pleasant name
from the Síd to the sea-wall;
I remember the reason for naming
the water of the wife of Labraid's son.

Nechtan son of bold Labraid
whose wife was Bóand, I declare;
had a secret well in his enclosure,
from which gushed forth every occult evil.

There was none that would look to its bottom
but his two splendid eyes would burst:
whether he moved to left or right,
he would not depart from it without blemish.

Therefore none dared approach it
save Nechtan and his cup-bearers:
these are their names, for assiduity,
Flesc and Lam and Luam.

On one occasion fair Bóand came
(her noble pride uplifted her),
to the never-failing well
to make trial of its power.

As thrice she walked round
about the well rashly,
three waves burst from it,
from which came the death of Bóand.

Each wave of them struck a bodily part,
they disfigured the soft-blooming woman;
a wave against her foot, a wave against her
    perfect eye,
the third wave shatters one hand.

She rushed to the sea (it was better for her)
to escape her blemish,

so that none might see her mutilation;
on herself fell her reproach.

Every way the woman went
the cold white water followed
from the Síd to the forceful sea,
and thereby it is called Bóand.

from:
THE DINDSHENCHAS OF SINANN
(The River Shannon)
(Middle Irish)

[The edition is by Edward Gwynn, *The Metrical Dindshenchas*, III, pp. 286–90. The translation is my emended version of his, ibid., pp. 287–91.]

Sáer-ainm Sinna saigid dún,
dáig rolaimid a lom-thúr:
nirb imfhann a gním 's a gleó
dia mbói Sinann co slán-béo.

Rop ingen rogasta ríam
Sinann sholasta shír-fhíal,
co fúair cach ndodáil nduthain
ingen Lodáin láech-Luchair.

Hi tír tarngire co túi,
ná geib anbthine imchrúi,
fúair in suthain blaid rosmill
ingen Luchair glain lúaidimm.

Tipra nad meirb fon muir mass
for seilb Chondlai, ba comdass,
feib adrímem ria rélad,
luid Sinann dia sír-fhégad.

Topur co mbara búaine
ar ur aba indúaire,
feib arsluinnet a clotha,
asmbruinnet secht prím-shrotha.

Immas na Segsa so dait
co febsa fond fhír-thiprait:
ós topur na tond tréorach
fail coll n-écsi n-ilcheólach.

Síltair sopur na Segsa
for topur na trén-chennsa,
ó thuitit cnói Crínmoind cain
fora ríg-broind réil roglain.

In óen-fhecht n-a tuile thrumm
turcbat uile don chóem-chrund,
duille ocus bláth ocus mess,
do chách uile ní hamdess.

Is amlaid-sin, cen góe nglé,
tuitit n-a róe dorise
for topur sográid Segsa
fo chomdáil, fo chomfhebsa.

Tecait co húais, ra gním nglé,
secht srotha, búais cen búaidre,
dorís isin topur the
dianid cocur ceól-éicse.

Adrímem in uide n-úag
dia luid Sinann co sóer-lúad
co lind mná Féile fuinid
cona gléire glan-fhuirid.

Ní thesta máin bad maith linn
for in sáir-sin na sáel-fhind,
acht immas sóis co srethaib,
ba gním nóis dia núa-bethaid.

Rotheich in topur, toirm nglé,
tria chocur na ceól-éicse,
re Sinainn, rothadaill túaid,
cor-riacht ina n-abainn n-indúair.

Rolen sruthair na Segsa
ben Luchair na lán-chennsa
cor-riacht huru na haba
co fúair mudu is mór-mada.

Andsin robáided in breiss,
is rothráiged fo throm-greiss:
cid marb in ben co mbruth baidb
rolen dia sruth a sáer-ainm.

Desin fri déine ndile
lind mná Féile fír-gile:
fail cech óen-airm, cúairt n-assa,
sáer-ainm súairc na Sinna-sa.

TRANSLATION

The noble name of Sinann, search it out for us,
since you venture to lay bare its origin:
not paltry was the action and the struggle
whereby the name of Sinann became immortal.

Sinann, radiant, ever-generous,
was once a maiden of great accomplishment,
till all earthly misfortune came upon her,
the daughter of Lodán from heroic Luchar.

In the still Land of Promise
that no storm of bloodshed mars,
she gained the eternal fame that was her undoing,
the girl from bright Luchar, whom I celebrate.

There is an active spring under the pleasant sea
in the domain of Condla,[1] as was fitting,
thus we recount, to set it out clearly,
Sinann went to look intently at it.

A well of lasting vehemence
is by the edge of a chilly river,
as its tidings relate,
seven great streams gush forth from it.

Here you find the magic lore of Segais[2]
with excellence, under the true spring:
above the well of mighty waters
stands the hazel of the many-melodied poets.

The spray of the Segais is sprinkled
on the well of great stillness,
as the nuts of fair Crínmond fall
on its royal bosom, bright and pure.

Together in lavish abundance
they all spring forth from the fair tree
leaf and flower and fruit,
delightful to everyone.

In this manner, without evident falsehood,
they fall again in their season,
upon the honoured well of Segais,
in unison, with like excellence.

1. The reference may be to the tale *Echtrae Chonnlai* (see pp. 268–9) below).
2. Over Segais, the source of the river, grew a tree of magical lore which shed its nuts into the stream.

Nobly, with clear action,
the seven streams, in unhindered gush,
come back into the well,
from whence arises secret lore, melodiously
    versed.

Let us recount the entire journey,
as Sinann nobly travelled
to Lind Mná Féile[3] in the west,
in her most excellent array.

The excellent woman lacked no possession
which we might desire . . .
save for occult knowledge in its sequences,
it was the noteworthy event of her young life.

Because of the secrecy of melodic poetics
the well retreated — loud the sound —
before Sinann, who approached it in the north,
until it reached the chilly river.

The calm woman of Luchar
pursued the waters of Segais
until she came to the river-brink
and met with destruction and extinction.

There the beauty was drowned
and laid low in a fierce onset,
yet though the woman of ill-fated ardour is
    dead,
her noble name has adhered to her river.

Thus, with zealous affection,
the resplendent Lind Mná Féile is named:
while in every place traversible
the noble pleasant name of Sinann is known.

3. Literally, 'The Pool of the Noblewoman'. The exact location by the
   Shannon is unknown.

from:
THE DINDSHENCHAS
OF TAILTIU
(Teltown) (1007)

[In the early historical period, the Fair of Tailtiu (Teltown,
County Meath) was an assembly to be convened annually
by the King of Tara. Its celebration was often intermitted,
however, in times of political crisis. The following extract,
setting out the fair's mythic origin, is part of a long poem
composed in the year 1007 on the occasion of the revival
of the fair after a lapse of about eighty years. The text and
abridged translation, with some alterations and
emendations, are those of Edward Gwynn, *The Metrical
Dindshenchas*, IV, pp. 146–51.]

A chóemu críche Cuind chain
éitsid bic ar bennachtain;
co n-écius duíb senchas sen
suidigthe óenaig Thalten.

Trí chét blíadan, fodagaib,
teora blíadna do blíadnaib
co gein Críst, coistid rissein,
ón chét-óenuch i Taltein.

Taltiu ingen Magmóir maill,
ben Echach gairb maic Dúach daill,
tánic sund ria slúag Fer mBolg
co Caill Cúan iar cath chomard . . .

Mór in mod dorigned sin
al-los túagi la Taltin
athnúd achaid don chaill chóir
la Taltin ingin Magmóir.

Ó thopacht aicce in chaill chain
cona frémaib as talmain,
ria cind blíadna ba Bregmag,
ba mag scothach scoth-shemrach.

Scaílis a cride 'na curp
iarna rige fo ríg-bruttd
fír nach follán gnúis fri gúal,
ní ar feda ná fid-uál.

Fota a cuma, fota a cur
i tám Thalten iar trom-thur;
dollotar fir, diamboí i cacht,
inse hÉrend fria hedacht.

Roráid-si riu 'na galur,
ciarb énairt nírb amlabur,
ara nderntais, díchra in mod,
cluiche caíntech dia caíniod.

Im kalaind Auguist atbath,
dia lúain, Loga Lugnasad;
imman lecht ón lúan ille
prím-óenach hÉrend áine . . .

TRANSLATION

O nobles of the land of Conn, hearken a while for a blessing, till I tell you the legend of the elders about the establishment of Tailtiu's Fair.

Listen to this. There are three hundred and three years from the first Fair at Tailtiu to the birth of Christ.

Tailtiu, daughter of gentle Magmór, wife of Eochu Garb son of Dúi Dall, came hither to the Wood of Cuan in the forefront of the host of the Fir Bolg after noble battle . . .

Great was the work done by Tailtiu with an axe. The reclaiming of meadowland from the even wood was accomplished by Tailtiu, daughter of Magmór.

When the fair wood was cut down by her, and its roots taken from the ground, before the year's end it was known as Bregmag, a plain blossoming with clover.

Her heart beneath her royal mantle burst in her body from the strain. It was, indeed, destructive of well-being . . .

Long was her sorrow, long her weariness, long Tailtiu's infirmity after a burdensome endeavour. The men of the island of Ireland, to whom she was in bondage, came for her final behest.

In her illness she told them — though weak, she was not speechless — that, with earnest effort, they should hold funeral games to lament her.

On the first of August she died, on a Monday, on the festival of Lug. Round her grave from that Monday forth is held the chief fair of glorious Ireland . . .

from:
THE DINDSHENCHAS OF CARMAN
(11th century)

[The Fair of Carman was the traditional assembly of Leinster kings. As was the case with the Fair of Tailtiu, its surviving origin legend seems to have been redacted at the time of an eleventh-century revival of the fair. The present translation is an emended version of that of Whitley Stokes, from his edition in 'The Prose Tales in the Rennes *Dindshenchas*', *Revue Celtique*, vol. 15 (1894), pp. 311–13.]

There were three men who came from Athens, and one woman with them. The men were the sons of Díbad son of Doirche, son of Ainces, and their names were Dian and Dub and Dothur. The name of their mother was Carman.

By spells and charms and incantations the mother ruined every place. By plundering and dishonesty the men destroyed. So they went to Ireland to bring harm on the Túatha Dé Danann by blighting the corn of the island upon them. The Túatha Dé Danann thought this evil. So Aí son of Ollam from their poets, and Cridenbél from the satirists, and Lugh Laebach from the druids, and Bé Chuílle from their witches went to chant spells over them. They did not cease until they had driven the three men overseas, leaving behind, as a pledge against their returning to Ireland, their mother, Carman, as well as the seven things which they served, to ensure that they would not come back for as long as sea surrounded Ireland.

Their mother died of grief here in her hostageship, and she asked the Túatha Dé Danann to hold a fair at her burial place, and that her name would be forever on the fair, and on that place. From thence is named Carman, and the Fair of Carman . . .

The Leinster men entered the fair on the kalends (first) of August and left it on the sixth of the ides (eighth) of August. Every third year they held it, two years being given to preparing it . . . For holding the fair, they were promised corn and milk, and freedom from control of any province in Ireland, that they should have men who were warriors and women who were fertile, good cheer in every household, every fruit to be spectacular, and full nets from rivers. If they did not hold it, however, they would endure decay and early greyness and young kings.

B. Sovereignty

ANONYMOUS

from:
FERCHUITRED MEDBA
(Medb's Husband-Allowance)
(Late Middle Irish)

[The text is titled *Cath Bóinde*, 'The Battle of the Boyne', in one manuscript and, more expressively, *Ferchuitred Medba*, 'Medb's Husband-Allowance', in the other. The following translation is an abridgement, with some minor emendations, of that of Joseph O'Neill in *Ériu*, vol. 2 (1905), pp. 174–84. O'Neill dated the surviving text to the Late Middle Irish period.]

Medb of Cruachain was a daughter of Eochaid Feidlech . . . Conchobar was Medb's first husband, and Medb forsook Conchobar through pride of mind . . . and the first cause of the stirring up of the Cattle Raid of Cúailnge was the desertion of Conchobar by Medb against his will.

Tindi, son of Conra Cas of the Fir Domnand,[1] was King of Connacht at that time, and Eochaid Dála and Fidech mac Féicc, of the Gamanraidi, were laying claim to the kingship. Fidech mac Féicc goes to Tara to assemble the kings for himself, and he asked Medb of Eochaid Feidlech. Tindi, Conra's son, got word of this story and lay in ambush for Fidech. They met over the Shannon streams, and the children of Conra, and Monodar, Conra's son, slew Fidech . . . Eochaid Feidlech executed a prince's injustice on Tindi, and drove him into the deserts of Connacht . . . It fell out, however, that Tindi was a visitor with Medb for a long time after that, so that it was in Cruachain with Medb the fairs of Ireland were wont to be held . . .

The festival of Tara was held by Eochaid Feidlech, with the provinces of Ireland about him, except Medb and Tindi. The men of Ireland bade Eochaid bring Medb to the gathering. Eochaid sent Searbluath, his female messenger,

to Cruachain for Medb. Medb went on the morrow to Tara, and the fair-races were run by them for a fortnight and a month. Thereafter the men of Ireland dispersed. Conchobar stayed after the others in the fair, watching Medb, and, as Medb happened to go to the Boyne to bathe, Conchobar met her there, overcame her, and violated her. When the tale was told in Tara, the kings of Ireland rose forth from Tara, and Tindi mac Conrach and Eochaid Dála with them . . . Tindi, son of Conra, challenged Conchobar to fight . . . Tindi fell in the conflict . . .

Eochaid Dála took up the yoke of battle across Meath, over the green-streamed Shannon, and brought Medb and Connacht safe with him through dint of fighting, so that he was not dared from the Boyne to the Shannon. The Fir Domnand and the Dál nDruithni and the Fir Chraíbi, from whom sprang Eochaid Dála, came to Cruachain after the slaying of Tindi . . . The counsel they decided on was to appoint Eochaid Dála to the kingship of Connacht with the consent of Medb. Medb consents to that on condition that he should marry her, and that he should have neither jealousy, fear, nor niggardliness, for it was a *geis* (prohibition) to her to marry a man who should have these three qualities. Eochaid Dála was made king thereby, and was a while in Cruachain as Medb's husband.

At that time Ailill son of Máta, son of Sraibgend of the Erna, came to Cruachain, and Ailill was then a young child . . . Thereafter, Ailill was reared in Cruachain until he was a great spirited warrior in battles and conflicts, and a battle-sustaining tower against Conchobar, defending the province of Medb, so that he was the chief of Medb's household afterwards, and Medb loved him for his virtues, and he was united to her, and became her lover in place of Eochaid Dála.

Eochaid Dála grew jealous because of this, and all the Fir Domnand shared in his jealousy through affection, so that they thought to banish Ailill, and all the Erna who were with him, out of Connacht, but Medb did not permit the doing of that deed, for she loved Ailill better than

---

1. All of the peoples mentioned in the text are Connacht population groups.

Eochaid. When Eochaid saw Medb's partiality, he challenged Ailill to fight for the kingdom and his wife. They fought a fierce fight, and Eochaid Dála fell in that conflict by Ailill mac Máta through the wiles of Medb. Ailill assumed the kingship of Connacht thereafter, with the consent of Medb, and it was he who was King of Connacht at the time of the royal inauguration of Conaire the Great and the beginning of the cattle raid against the Ulster men.

from:
BAILE IN SCÁIL
(The Vision of the Spectre)
(Middle Irish)

[This text belongs to a genre in which prophetic revelation is derived from a visionary experience. Here, it is the legendary King of Tara, Conn of the Hundred Battles, who is depicted as being granted foreknowledge of his kingship, and that of his successors. My translation is based on texts edited by Kuno Meyer, *Zeitschrift für celtische Philologie*, vol. 3 (1901), pp. 457–66, and Rudolf Thurneysen, ibid., vol. 20 (1935), pp. 213–27, and Eugene O'Curry's translation, *Lectures on the Manuscript Materials of Ancient Irish History* (Dublin: W.A. Hinch, 1861), pp. 618–22.]

One day, in the absence of the kings, when Conn was in Tara, in the early morning, before sunrise, he went up on the rampart of Tara with his three druids, Maol, Bloc, and Bluicne, and his three poets, Ethain, Corb, and Cesarn. The reason that he went up every day with that number was to keep a look-out, lest any Otherworld dwellers came to Ireland without his knowledge . . .

Then, as they were there, they noticed a great mist round about them, and such was the darkness that descended that they did not know where they were going. They heard the sound of a horseman approaching them. 'Woe betide us, if we are being brought to a strange land,' said Conn. Then the horseman made three casts at them, and the last cast was swifter than the first.

'He is assaulting a king, whoever aims at Conn in Tara,' said the druid. The horseman then stopped his casts, and came to them. He welcomed Conn, and escorted him to his dwelling.

They travelled until they reached a beautiful plain, and saw the royal fortress, with a golden tree at its entrance. They saw a wonderful house there, with a ridge-pole of white bronze. It was thirty feet long. Then they entered the house, and saw a young woman inside, with a golden diadem on her head. There was a silver vat with hoops of gold around it, full of red ale. There was a golden serving-vessel beside it, and an upended golden cup. They saw the Spectre himself, in his royal seat, before them in the house. Never had there been in Tara a man of his size, handsomeness, beautiful form, and wondrous appearance.

He addressed them, and said: 'I am not a phantom, nor an Otherworldly apparition. I have been revealed to you as one who has come back from the dead, and I am of the race of Adam. My name is Lug, son of Ethliu, son of Tigernmas.[1] For this reason I have come, to tell you the duration of your own rule, and that of every future ruler in Tara.'

The girl who was before them in the house was the eternal Sovereignty of Ireland. It was she who gave this repast to Conn, an ox-rib and the rib of a boar. The ox-rib was twenty-four feet long, and there were eight feet between its flank and the ground.

When the girl went to distribute the drink, she asked: 'To whom is this cup to be given?' The Spectre answered her. He named every ruler in turn from Conn's time until Doomsday. It was difficult for Cesarn the poet to chant the incantation immediately until it was rendered in *ogham*[2] on four staves of yew, each of which was twenty-four feet long, and eight ridges on each. Then the company was cast in the shadow of the Spectre, so that they saw no more neither fortress nor house. However, Conn was left with the vat, the golden ladle and cup, and the *ogham* staves.

---

1. Despite the claimed descent from Adam, the pedigree indicates the identity of the deity Lug.
2. The Irish *ogham* alphabet is attested particularly on standing stones.

from:
ECHTRA MAC NECHACH MUIGMEDÓIN
(The Adventure of the Sons of Eochaid Muigmedón) (Middle Irish)

[The following is an extract from a tale recounting the manner in which the claim to kingship of Niall of the Nine Hostages was vindicated over that of his brothers. The translation is an emended version of that in Whitley Stokes's edition, *Revue Celtique*, vol. 24 (1903), pp. 190–203.]

The sons went to hunt. Then they wandered greatly astray, as every direction became impenetrable. When they stopped straying, they lit a fire, cooked some of their prey, and ate till they were satisfied. Then they were in great thirst and drought after the cooked food. 'Let one of us go and seek water,' they said. 'I will go,' said Fergus. The lad went to get water, and came upon a well. He saw an old woman guarding the well.

Thus was the hag: every joint and limb of her from the top of her head to the ground was as black as coal. Like the tail of a wild horse was the grey bristly mane that came through the upper part of her head. A green laden branch of oak could be severed by the sickle of greenish teeth that filled her head as far as her ears. Dark, smoky eyes she had, and a nose crooked and cavernous. Her middle was fibrous, spotted with pustules, and diseased. Her shins were distorted and crooked, gnarled, and broad like shovels. She was big-kneed and taloned. Loathsome, indeed, was the hag's appearance.

'Well,' said the lad. 'Well, indeed,' said she. 'Are you guarding the well?' asked the lad. 'I am,' said she. 'Will you permit me to take away some of the water with me?' asked the lad. 'I will,' said she, 'provided that I get one kiss on the cheek from you.' 'No,' said he. 'You will take no water from me,' she said. 'On my word,' said he, 'I would sooner die of thirst than kiss you.'

The lad came to where his brothers were, and told them than he had not found water. Then Ailill went to get water, chanced on the same well, refused to kiss the hag, and returned without water. Brian, the eldest of the sons, went to seek water, found the same well, refused to kiss the old woman, and returned waterless. Fiachra went, found the well and hag, and asked her for water. 'Give me a kiss, and I will give it,' said she. 'I would offer a very small amount of kissing for it.' 'You shall visit Tara,' said she. That proved true, for two of his race took the kingship of Ireland . . . But Fiachra returned without water.

Niall went then to seek water, and reached the same well. 'Give me water, woman,' said he. 'Give me a kiss, and I will give it,' she answered. 'As well as giving you a kiss I will lie with you,' said he. Then he bent down over her and kissed her. Afterwards, however, when he looked at her, there was not in the world a girl fairer than her in appearance or form. Like the snowy residue in ditches was every bodily joint from head to sole. She had rounded queenly arms, graceful long fingers, straight, beautiful legs, and two rounded slippers of white bronze between her little soft-white feet and the ground. A costly purple mantle was around her, adorned with a bright silver brooch. She had shining pearly teeth, large queenly eyes, and lips red as rowan berries.

'You have many forms, woman,' said the young man. 'True,' said she. 'Who are you?' asked the lad. 'I am Sovereignty,' said she.

GIRALDUS CAMBRENSIS (GERALD OF WALES)

(*c.* 1146–1223)

from:
TOPOGRAPHIA HIBERNIAE
(The History and Topography
of Ireland) (*c.* 1187)

[The cleric Giraldus Cambrensis was a member of one of
the leading families involved in the Norman incursions
into Ireland. His *Topographia*, an account of the country
and its people, dates from *c.* 1187. The translation is by
John J. O'Meara from *Gerald of Wales: The History and
Topography of Ireland*, pp. 109–10.]

There are some things which, if the exigencies of
my account did not demand it, shame would dis-
countenance their being described. But the
austere discipline of history spares neither truth
nor modesty.

There is in the northern and farther part of
Ulster, namely Kenelcunill[1] a certain people

1. Irish Cenél Conaill, corresponding to modern County Donegal.

which is accustomed to appoint its king with a
rite altogether outlandish and abominable. When
the whole people of that land is gathered together
in one place, a white mare is brought forward
into the middle of the assembly. He who is to be
inaugurated, not as chief, but as beast, not as
king, but as an outlaw, has bestial intercourse
with her before all, professing himself to be a
beast also.

The mare is then killed immediately, cut up in
pieces, and boiled in water. A bath is prepared for
the man afterwards in the same water. He sits in
the bath surrounded by all his people, and all, he
and they, eat of the meat of the mare which is
brought to them. He quaffs and drinks of the
broth in which he is bathed, not in any cup, or
using his hand, but just dipping his mouth into it
round about him. When this unrighteous rite has
been carried out, his kingship and domination
have been conferred.

ANONYMOUS

from:
ANNÁLA CONNACHT
(The Annals of Connacht) (1310)

[This chronicle provides a year by year account of events in
Ireland, and particularly in Connacht, from the early
decades of the thirteenth century to the early sixteenth
century. The following extract forms part of the entry for
the year 1310. The translation is that of A. Martin Freeman
(ed.), *Annála Connacht, The Annals of Connacht,* A.D.
1224–1554 (Dublin: Royal Irish Academy, 1944), p. 223.]

Maelruanaid Mac Diarmata, seeing the
exclusion of his foster-son from his patrimony
and the heavy exactions on each *tuath* about him,
and much resenting the action of the Galls[1] in

1. The foreigners, i.e. the Anglo-Normans.

restricting and diminishing his power — for the
Galls felt sure that if this one man were weak the
whole province of Connacht would be in their
own hands — determined, like the warrior he
was, to take his foster-son boldly and make him
king by force. So he carried him to Carnfree and
installed him on the mound according to the
practice of the saints, and of Da Conna of Assylin
in particular; and he, Fedlimid mac Aeda meic
Eogain, was proclaimed in a style as royal, as
lordly and as public as any of his race from the
time of Brian son of Eochu Muigmedoin till that
day. And when Fedlimid mac Aeda meic Eogain
had married the Province of Connacht his foster-
brother waited upon him during the night in the
manner remembered by the old men and
recorded in the old books; and this was the most
splendid kingship-marriage ever celebrated in
Connacht down to that day.

C. Warfare and Death

ANONYMOUS

from:
TÁIN BÓ REGAMNA
(The Cattle Raid of Regamain)
(Early Middle Irish)

[Despite the title, the main focus of the tale is on an encounter between the Mórrígan and Cú Chulainn. My translation is indebted to that of Eleanor Hull, *The Cuchullin Saga* (London, 1898), pp. 101–7, and to the edition with German translation by Johan Corthals, *Táin Bó Regamna* (Wien: Österreichische Akademie der Wissenschafter, 1987).]

When Cú Chulainn was in Dún Imrid[1] he heard a shout. It so roused him from his sleep that he fell out of the bed in a heap onto the apartment floor. Then he rushed outside, his wife following with his clothing and weapons. He saw before him Lóeg, in his harnessed chariot, at Ferta Loíg[2] in the north. 'What brought you here?' Cú Chulainn asked Lóeg. 'A cry which I heard in the plain,' said Lóeg. 'In what direction?' asked Cú Chulainn. 'From the north-west,' said Lóeg. 'Let us pursue it,' said Cú Chulainn.

They set out then to Áth da Fherta.[3] As they got there, they heard the rumbling of a chariot beside Grellach Culgairi.[4] They went towards it, and saw the chariot before them. It was drawn by a single red horse, which was one-legged. The chariot-pole passed through the horse so that the wooden block entered from the front through his forehead. There was a red woman in the chariot, wearing a red cloak. She had red eyebrows. Her cloak trailed back between the two shafts of the chariot, so that it swept along the ground behind her. There was a big man alongside the chariot. He wore a good tunic, and he was driving a cow with a pronged pole of white hazel.

1. Cú Chulainn's fort in Muirtheimne Plain, in north County Louth.
2. Literally, 'Lóeg's Mound'; clearly north of Dún Imrid.
3. Unidentified.
4. Literally, 'Marsh of the Chariot-Rumble'; probably one and the same as Grellach Dolluid, an unidentified place in or near Muirtheimne Plain, mentioned later in the text.

'The cow is not pleased to be driven by you,' said Cú Chulainn. 'It is not your right to expound about this cow,' said the woman. 'She is not the cow of any friend or companion of yours.' 'But all the cows of Ulster belong to me,' said Cú Chulainn. 'You make inordinate pronouncements, Cú,' she said. 'Why is it the woman who speaks to me?' asked Cú Chulainn. 'Why is it not the man?' 'Is it the man whom you address?' asked the woman. 'Certainly it is,' said Cú Chulainn, 'yet it is you who speaks for him.' 'Cold Wind and Rushes . . . is that man's name,' said she. 'Truly, that is a surprisingly long name,' said Cú Chulainn.

'Now, this time,' he said, 'let it really be you who answers me, since the man does not. What is your own name?' 'Easy,' said the man. 'That woman whom you address is named Sharpness in Few Words — Insignificant Body — Spiky Hair — Short and Horrible.' 'You are making a fool of me with this behaviour,' said Cú Chulainn.

Thereupon, he leapt into the chariot and placed his two feet on her two knees, and his javelin on the crown of her head. 'Do not play games with me,' said Cú Chulainn. 'Get away from me now,' said she. 'I am a female satirist, and I have brought this cow from Dáire mac Fiachna[5] from Cúailnge as recompense for a poem.' 'Let me hear your poem, then,' said Cú Chulainn. 'Just move away from me,' said the woman. 'It does you no good to brandish that thing over my head,' said she. Then Cú Chulainn moved till he was between the two shafts of the chariot. She chanted the verse . . .

Afterwards Cú Chulainn jumped into his own chariot, whereupon nothing of them remained, neither woman nor chariot, nor horse, neither man nor cow. Then he saw that she was a black bird on the branch beside him. 'If I had known that it was you, we would not have parted thus,' said Cú Chulainn. 'Whatever you might do, evil will come of it,' said she. 'You cannot harm me,'

5. Owner of the bull known as the Donn Cúailnge, desire for which sparked the famous Cattle Raid of Cúailnge; see pp. 38–41.

said Cú Chulainn. 'I certainly can,' said the woman. 'I am, and will be, guardian of your death. I have brought this cow from the *Síd*[6] of Cruachain,[7] said she, 'so that, while in my possession, the Donn Cúailnge, the bull of Dáire mac Fiachna, might impregnate her, and your life-time will last until the calf she is carrying has become a yearling, and it is that animal which will cause the Cattle Raid of Cúailnge.'

'I will be all the more famous because of
    that Cattle Raid,' said Cú Chulainn.
'I will wound their champions,
I will rout their battalions,
I will be the survivor of the Raid.'

'How will you accomplish that?' asked the woman, 'for when you are in combat with a man equally strong and shapely, equally enterprising, swift and agile, of equal kindred, valour and size, then I will be an eel, and I will coil around your legs in the ford, so that you are greatly outmatched.' 'I swear by the god by whom the Ulster men swear,' said Cú Chulainn, 'I will trample you against the grey stones of the ford, and you will never get any relief from me unless you entreat my pardon.'

'I will be a grey she-wolf for you,' said she, 'and I will tear from your right arm to your left.' 'I swear by the god by whom the Ulster men swear,' said Cú Chulainn, 'I will strike with my javelin to shatter the eye in your head, and you will never be healed by me unless you beg my forgiveness.' 'I will be a white red-eared heifer,' said she, 'and I will enter the pool beside the ford whenever you are in conflict with a man of equal feats. I will be followed by a hundred white red-eared cows, and the whole herd will burst into the ford after me. On that day, you will get no fair play, and you will be beheaded in that ford.' 'I swear by the god by whom the Ulster men swear, I will cast a shot from my sling at you, to break the leg beneath you, and you will never get relief from me unless you entreat my pardon, and I will not be wounded at all on that day,' said Cú Chulainn.

They parted thereafter. Cú Chulainn went back again to Dún Imrid, and the Mórrígan and her cow went into the *Síd* of Cruachain in Connacht.

6. Otherworld dwelling.
7. Now Rathcroghan in County Roscommon.

from :
AIDED CON CULAINN
(The Death of Cú Chulainn)
(Early Modern Irish)

[The story of the death of Cú Chulainn has come down in two versions, a fragmentary early account and an Early Modern Irish text, generally titled *Brislech Mór Maige Muirtheimne* (The Great Defeat of Muirtheimne Plain). My translation of a passage from the latter version is based on the edition by A.G. Van Hamel, *Compert Con Culainn and Other Stories*, pp. 72–133, at p. 113.]

'Go,' said Medb, 'and find out for me whether Cú Chulainn is alive or dead.' 'I will go,' said Badb, 'despite the evil I may encounter as a result.' The form in which she went was that of a bird hovering in the air overhead. 'If he is alive, I risk being struck down with the first shot out of his sling, for no bird or creature ever came between him and the air above that he did not kill. If he is dead, I will descend near him, and you will hear my cry.'

She came, then, in the guise of a scald-crow, from the high vault of the firmament, to hover over his head, and she made her approach gradually until she was close to him. Then she uttered three loud screeches above his head, and she alighted on the bush in front of him. And thus that bush in the Plain of Muirtheimne is called 'The Scald-Crow's Bush'.

When the men of Ireland saw what happened, they said: 'It is indeed true. Cú Chulainn is dead.'

from:
TOGAIL BRUIDNE DA DERGA
(The Destruction of Da Derga's Hostel)
(11th century)

[This tale tells of the slaying of Conaire, King of Tara, in a raid on the house of the legendary hospitaller Da Derga. The king's own foster-brothers, to whom he had shown undue leniency, are implicated in the raid. Omens of impending disaster had begun to gather after the king's fateful decision regarding his foster-brothers, and again the sense of foreboding is reinforced by the supernatural female who appears as the king enters his doomed lodging. The text seems to be an eleventh-century compilation, based on material of the ninth century. It was edited and translated by Whitley Stokes, 'The Destruction of Da Derga's Hostel', *Revue Celtique*, vol. 22 (1902), pp. 8–61, and the present translation is based on his work (see pp. 57 and 59).]

They saw a lone woman coming to the door of the Hostel after sunset, and seeking to be let in. As long as a weaver's beam was each of her two shins, and they were as dark as the back of a stag-beetle. She wore a dingy fleecy cloak. Her pubic hair reached as far as her knee. Her mouth was to one side of her head.

She came and put one of her shoulders against the doorpost of the house, casting the evil eye on the king and the youths who surrounded him in the Hostel. The king himself addressed her from within. 'Well, woman,' said Conaire, 'if you are a seer, what do you see in store for us?' 'For you I see that neither body nor flesh of yours will escape from the place to which you have come, save what birds will carry off in their claws,' said she. 'We had not anticipated a bad prediction, woman; you do not augur for us usually,' said the king. 'You will never again be our oracle.'

'What is your name, woman?' he asked. 'Cailb,' she said. 'That is not much of a name,' said Conaire. 'Look out! I have many names besides,' said the woman. 'What are they?' asked Conaire. 'That is easy,' said she, 'Samon, Sinand, Seisclend, Sodb, Caill, Coll, Díchóem, Díchiúil, Díthím, Díchuimne, Dichruidne, Dairne, Dárine, Déruaine, Égem, Agam, Ethamne, Gním, Cluiche, Cethardam, Níth, Némain, Nóennen, Badb, Blosc, Bloár, Huae, óe Aife la Sruth, Mache, Médé, Mod.'[1]

Standing on one foot, with one hand raised, and in a single breath, she chanted all this to them from the doorway of the house.

from:
TOGAIL BRUIDNE DA CHOCA
(The Destruction of Da Choca's Hostel)
(Middle Irish)

[This Middle Irish tale recounts the death in the besieged hostel of Da Choca of Cormac Conn Loinges, son of the Ulster King Conchobar mac Nessa. The site of the hostel is now known as Breenmore, about six miles north-east of Athlone in County Westmeath, and Cormac was on his way from exile in Connacht to take up the kingship of Ulster. On his journey he unwillingly breaks *gesa* (prohibitions) placed on him, and the appearance of the supernatural female reinforces the sense of fatalism that attaches to his expedition. My translation is indebted to the edition of Whitley Stokes, 'Da Choca's Hostel', *Revue Celtique*, vol. 21 (1900), p. 157, and also draws on readings from Trinity College Dublin Library, Manuscript H.3.18, for the verse.]

They came to Druim Airthir,[1] which is called In Garman,[2] beside Athlone. Then they unyoked their horses. When they got there, they saw a red woman at the edge of the ford, washing her chariot, its covering, and armour. When she lowered her hand, the current ran red with gore and blood. When she raised her hand over the riverbank, there was not a drop in the river that was not lifted up, so that one could cross dryshod over the river-water.

'Fearsome is the action of the woman,' said Cormac. 'Let one of you go to ask her what she is doing.' Then she chanted to them, standing on one foot, with one eye closed, and she said to the illustrious champion of the Ulster men:

'I wash the war-gear of a king who will die
against a remnant of the men of Connacht.
Lamentation will be raised for champions
through the malevolence of Medb and
    Ailill.
From intelligence gained from Fergus,
ravenous black ravens will drink in a lake
    of blood,

---

1. Most of this incantation comprises personal names and names for natural features.

1. On the River Shannon, near Athlone.
2. Literally, 'The Beam' or 'The Pole'.

because of the virulence of the men of dark
   spears
the spearmen of Da Choca's house will
   perish,
and as soon as they die, devils will be
   mocking
on this dreadful night tonight,
where there will be pools of blood,
blood over fair bodies there,
all horror being washed.'

from:
CAITHRÉIM
THOIRDHEALBHAIGH
(The Triumphs of Turlough)
(mid-14th century)

[This mid-fourteenth-century text has been ascribed to the
poet Seán (son of Ruaidhrí, d. 1343) Mac Craith. It
describes the internecine strife between two branches of the
O'Briens, the Munster dynasty which claimed descent from
Brian Bóruma, Clann Taidg and Clann Briain Ruaid ('clan-
Brian-Rua' below). The hero of the text, Turlough, is of
Clann Taidg, and the narrative of his military triumphs is
calculated to prove his branch's natural qualification to rule.
However, the text is replete with portents of doom and
defeat for Clann Briain Ruaid, most obviously in the
prelude to the climactic Battle of Corcomroe in 1317. As
they marched to Corcomroe, in the Burren in north County
Clare, their encounter with the war-goddess at nearby
Lough Rask is represented as sealing their fate. The text was
edited and translated by Standish Hayes O'Grady,
Caithréim Thoirdhealbhaigh. Irish Texts Society, Volumes 26
and 27 (London: Irish Texts Society, 1929). The extract
below is from vol. 27, pp. 93–4.]

Quietly the broad-sworded warriors [of clan-
Brian-Rua], many in number, in closest order,
came hard by Loch Rask; all together they looked
on the shining mere, and there they saw the
monstrous and distorted form of a lone ancient
hideous hag that stooped over the bright loch's
shore. The loathly creature's semblance was this:
she was thatched with elf-locks foxy-grey and
rough as heather, long as sea-wrack, inextricably
tangled; had a bossy, wrinkled, foully-ulcerated
forehead; every hair of her eyebrows was like a
strong fish-hook, and, from under them, bleary,
dripping eyes peered with malignant fire between

lids all rawly crimson-edged. She had a huge
blueish nose, flattened and wide, copiously and
snortingly catarrhous; lips livid, white-rimmed,
pustulous, that outwards turned up to her snout,
and downward to a stubby beard . . .

The crone had a cairn of heads, a pile of arms
and legs, a load of spoils, all of which she rinsed
and diligently washed, so that by her labour the
water in its whole extension was covered with
hair and gory brains. The army, hushed, intently
and long gazes at her; but dauntlessly the chief
accosts the beldam: 'What name affectest thou,
or of what people are thine immediate friends, or
to whom are kin these so maltreated dead on this
moist shore?' And she nothing loath replies: 'The
Dismal of Burren I am named always; 'tis of the
Túatha dé Danann I declare myself and, royal
chief,' (the withered crone went on), 'this
carnage here stand for your [army's] heads with,
in their very midst, thine own head: the which
though now thou carriest it, yet no longer is it
thine. Proudly as thou goest to the battle's field,
the time is not far from you when, all to a very
few, ye must be slain.' By the perverse wretch's
bitter forecast the host was startled, and with
javelins straightway would have cast at her; but
on the rushing wind she rose above them and,
being well aloft, delivered herself thus defiantly:

Ill betide all that march here! a baneful trip
'twill be, an effort big with wrath! the combat
will be rude; till Doom 'twill ring how such an
host rushed into fight; there will abound both
pointless spears and swords [shivered] to the
bone[-hilt], sighs, moans and grief for clan-
Cas[1] slain, a woeful tale; the red chief's clan,[2]
'tis they must fail, must sink at last; their
prince shall fall; thou, comely Donough,[3]
thou com'st not back; smooth Brian of
Berra[4] shall supine be left; Murtough More[5]
though fierce is stricken, his body pruned. I
tell you all, your march bodes ill, your
eastward course will breed much woe!

1. The ultimate ancestor of the O'Briens was (Cormac) Cas. Here,
   'clan-Cas' refers to Clann Briain Ruaid.
2. i.e. the descendants of Brian Ruad, whose epithet means 'red, red-
   haired'.
3. i.e. Donnchad son of Domnall and grandson of Brian Ruad.
4. i.e. Brian son of Conchobar Ó Briain. Berra, which corresponds to
   the Beare peninsula in west Cork, is here a metonym for Munster.
5. i.e. Muirchertach son of Donnchad son of Domnall, and thus a
   great-grandson of Brian Ruad.

D. The Otherworld

ANONYMOUS

from:
ECHTRA LÁEGAIRE MAIC CRIMTHAINN CO MAG MELL
(The Adventure of Láegaire mac Crimthainn to the Plain of Delights)
(late 9th century)

[This text, dated to the late ninth century, begins with the arrival in Connacht of Fiachna, an Otherworld warrior, to ask for troops to assist him in the recovery of his abducted wife, Osnad. Láegaire, son of the Connacht King Crimthann Cass, was first to volunteer, and with fifty other warriors, he followed the Otherworld visitant down under a lake. There they fought successfully, and captured the fort where Osnad was held. The extract below begins as Láegaire returns Osnad to Fiachna. The translation (with minor alterations) is from that by Kenneth Jackson, 'The Adventure of Laeghaire mac Crimthainn', *Speculum*, vol. 17 (1942), pp. 377–89, at pp. 385 and 387.]

Láegaire went after that and put [Osnad's] hand in the hand of Fiachna; and there sleeps with Láegaire that night Dér Gréine daughter of Fiachna, and fifty women were given to his fifty warriors. They stay with them till the end of a year. 'Let us go to find out news of our country,' said Láegaire. 'If you would come back again,' said Fiachna, 'take horses with you, and do not dismount from them.' This is done. They went till they reached the place of assembly. The men of Connacht had been there a whole year bewailing him, so that they found them assembled together before them. The men of Connacht leaped up to welcome them. 'Do not approach,' said Láegaire; 'we have come to say farewell to you.' 'Do not leave me,' said Crimthann; 'you shall have the

kingship of the Three Connachts, their gold and their silver, their horses and their bridles, and their fair women at your pleasure; and do not leave us.' It is then Láegaire said:

'Wonderful it is, Crimthann Cass!
We love travelling on every shower,
leading an army of a hundred thousand,
going from kingdom to kingdom.

'Fine plaintive fairy music,
going from kingdom to kingdom,
drinking mead from bright vessels,
talking with the one you love.

'We mingle a set of men of yellow gold
on chessboards of white bronze;
we have drinking of clear mead
along with a proud armed warrior.

'My own wife
is the daughter of Fiachna, Dér Gréine;
then, that I may tell you,
a wife for every man of my fifty.

'We took from the fort of Mag Mell
thirty cauldrons, thirty drinking-horns;
we took Osnad with all that survived,
daughter of Eochu Amlabar.

'Wonderful it is, Crimthann Cass!
I was master of a blue sword;
one night of the fairy nights
I will not exchange for your kingdom.'

After that he turned from them into the fairy mound again; and he shares the kingship of the fairy mound with Fiachna son of Réda, that is, in the fort of Mag Mell, and Fiachna's daughter along with him; and he has not come out yet.

from:
ECHTRAE CHONNLAI
(The Adventure of Connlae)
(8th century)

[This text is framed as an answer to the question 'Why is Art Óenfer (Art, the Lone) so called?' It explains how Art's brother, Connlae, came to leave the kingdom. The tale may be as old as the eighth century. The translation is that of James Carney, in 'The Deeper Level of Early Irish Literature', *Capuchin Annual* (1969), pp. 160–71.]

One day Connlae the Red-haired, son of Conn Cétchathach, was beside his father on the top of the Hill of Uisnech. Suddenly he saw a woman in strange dress coming toward him. 'Where have you come from, woman?' he asked. 'I come,' said the woman, 'from the Lands of the Living, where there is neither sin, nor death, nor transgression. We eat everlasting feasts without their needing to be served. We have gentle contest without strife. We are in great peace, and from this we are called *aés síde*.'[1]

'Who are you talking to?' asked Conn of his son, for no one saw the woman except Connlae alone. The woman answered: 'He speaks to a beautiful young woman of noble race who looks forward to neither death nor old age. I have loved Connlae the Red-haired. I call him to the Plain of Delights where the eternal Boadag is king, having had no weeping nor woe in his land since he took sovereignty.'

'Come with me, Connlae the Red-haired, of freckled neck, shining like a candle-flame. The golden diadem of hair over your gleaming face will be a sign of your royal aspect. If you come with me, your form will not lose its youth and beauty until the Day of Doom.'

Conn said to his druid, whose name was Corán, for all had heard what the woman said, although they did not see her: 'I beseech you, Corán, great in song, great in art. Trouble has come upon me that is greater than my counsel, greater than my strength, a trial such as has not happened to me since I took sovereignty. An invisible form is forcing me, seeking to steal my fair son by evil acts, taking him from the king's side by women's spells.'

The druid then chanted a spell against the voice of the woman so that no one heard her voice, nor did Connlae hear her from that time. When the woman was departing, forced by the great spell of the druid, she threw an apple to Connlae. Connlae spent a month without a bite, neither drink nor food. No other food seemed worth eating but his apple. However much he ate of it, it grew no less, but remained still whole and perfect.

Connlae began to feel longing for the woman he had seen. On the day when a month had passed, Connlae was beside his father in Mag ar Chommin[2] when he saw coming towards him the same woman, who said to him: 'Connlae sits on a high seat amongst the doomed, waiting for horror-inspiring death. The eternal living ones invite you. You are a champion for the people of Tethra,[3] who watch you every day amongst your dear familiars in the assemblies of your fatherland.'

When Conn heard the woman's voice, he said to his people: 'Call the druid to me. I see her speech has been given back to her to-day.' Then the woman said: 'Conn of the Hundred Battles, do not give honour to druidry — it accomplishes few judgments upon the Great Strand. In a short time there will come a just man with many wonderful households. His law will destroy the spells of druids despite the evil magic-working Devil.'

Now Conn wondered that Connlae would answer no one, wanting only that the woman should come. 'Has what the woman says touched your heart, Connlae?' asked Conn. Connlae answered: 'It is not easy for me. I love my people beyond all. But I have been seized by a loneliness for the woman.' The woman then answered, saying this: 'You are struggling to get away from them against the wave of your love of home, so that in my crystal boat we might come to the Otherworld dwelling of Boadag, if we should reach it.

'There is another land which it would be better to seek. I see the sun is setting — though

---

1. The word *sid* means both 'peace' and 'Otherworld dwelling; fairy mound', so *aés síde* means both 'people of peace' and 'people of the Otherworld'.

2. Unidentified.
3. The Otherworld.

it is far we will reach it before nightfall. It is the land that rejoices the mind of all who walk about it. There is no race there but women and maidens.'

When the woman had finished her speech, Connlae leapt away from them into the crystal boat. They saw him gradually disappear, as far as the eye could reach. They then rowed away from them, and were never seen from that time forward, and nobody knew where they went.

from:
IMMRAM CURAIG MÁELE DÚIN
(The Voyage of Máel Dúin's Boat)
(9th or 10th century)

[*Immram*-narratives describe the variety of marvels encountered by sea-voyagers, who are usually either pilgrims or penitents. The Latin *Navigatio Brendani* (The Voyage of Brendan) is probably the best-known example of this type of composition. The text excerpted here belongs to the ninth or tenth century. It describes the journey of Máel Dúin and his company to many strange islands, and the extract below takes up the story after their arrival on an island of women. The present translation is an abbreviated and emended version of that by H.P.A. Oskamp, *The Voyage of Máel Dúin* (Groningen: Wolters-Noordhoff Publishing, 1970), pp. 154–7.]

They entered the fort then. They all bathed. The queen sat on one side of the house, with her seventeen girls around her. Máel Dúin sat opposite the queen, on the other side, surrounded by his seventeen men. A dish of fine food was brought to Máel Dúin, with a crystal vessel of good liquor, and there was also a dish and goblet for every three of his people. When they had eaten, the queen asked: 'How shall the guests sleep?' 'As you say,' said Máel Dúin . . . 'Let each of you take the woman opposite him, and go into the chamber behind her,' said she. For there were seventeen ornamented cubicles in the house,

with beds well made up. Then the seventeen men slept with the seventeen nubile girls, and Máel Dúin slept with the queen. They slumbered until the following morning. They got up in the afternoon.

'Stay here,' said the queen, 'and you will not grow old beyond the age which you have attained. You will have lasting life forever, and your experience last night will be yours every night, without any effort. Wander no longer from island to island on the ocean!' . . .

Then they remained in that island for the three months of winter, and it seemed to them that they had been there for three years. 'Long is our stay here,' said one of his company to Máel Dúin. 'Why do we not set out for our own country?' 'It is not right to say that,' said Máel Dúin, 'for we will not find anything in our own country that is better than what we have here.' His people began murmuring greatly against Máel Dúin, and they said: 'Great is Máel Dúin's love for his woman. Let him stay with her, then, if he so wishes. We will go home.' 'I will not remain after you,' said Máel Dúin.

One day, then, as the queen went to give judgment as she did every day, they went back to their boat. Thereupon, she arrived on her horse, and she threw a ball of thread after them. Máel Dúin caught it, and it adhered to his hand. She held the end-thread, and with it she drew the boat to her, back into port.

They stayed there with her after that for thrice three months. Then they reached a decision. 'We are convinced that Máel Dúin greatly loves his woman,' said his company. 'For that reason, he anticipates the ball of thread, so that it clings to his hand and brings us back to the fort.' 'Let someone else look out for the ball of thread,' said Máel Dúin, 'and if it sticks to his hand, let his hand be cut off.'

Then they boarded their boat. She threw the ball of thread after them. Another man of the crew caught it, and it clung to his hand. Diurán cut off his hand, and it fell, along with the thread. When she saw that, immediately she began to wail and shriek, so that all the land was one cry and screech and scream. And thus they made their escape from her out of the island.

from:
THE STORY OF INBER
NAILBINE
(*c.* 9th century)

[The following extract is one of a series of place-name explanations extraneous to the main plot of the wooing tale *Tochmarc Emire* (The Wooing of Emer). Its explanation of the place-name Inber nAilbine as equivalent to Inber nOllbine, 'Estuary of the Great Crime' also occurs in the *Dindshenchas*. The text may be of ninth century date. My translation is indebted to that of Kenneth Jackson, *A Celtic Miscellany* (Harmondsworth, Middlesex: Penguin Books, 1971), pp. 150–1, and to the edition of the original by A.G. Van Hamel, *Compert Con Culainn and Other Stories*, pp. 39–41.]

There was a famous king here in Ireland, Rúad son of Rígdonn of Munster. He had a meeting arranged with the Foreigners. He went to his meeting with them round Britain from the south, with three ships. There were thirty men in each ship. In the midst of the ocean, his fleet became stuck fast from below, and no amount of wealth or treasure thrown into the sea succeeded in setting it free. They cast lots to see which of them would descend under the sea to find out what was detaining them. The lot fell on the king himself. So the king, Rúad son of Rígdonn, leaped into the sea, and was immediately covered by it.

He arrived in a large plain, and found nine beautiful females there. They admitted to him that it was they who had held up the ships, in order that he might come to them. They offered him nine ships of gold in return for sleeping with them for nine nights, a night with each of them. He did so. Meanwhile, his crew were unable to leave, because of the powers of the women. One of the women said that it was her time of conception, and that she would bear a son, and that he should revisit them on his return from the east, in order to fetch the boy.

Thereafter he rejoined his company, and they journeyed on. They remained with their friends for seven years, and came back by another route. They did not revisit the same spot, and they eventually reached Inber nAilbine. It was there that the women came upon them. As they were berthing their fleet, the men heard the wailing in the women's bronze boat. The women came

ashore, and they threw the boy from them into the distance. The harbour was full of stones and rocks. The boy hit against one of the stones, and perished as a result. The women retreated, all calling out '*Ollbine, Ollbine*', that is, '*bine oll*', 'great crime'. And from that the place is named.

from:
THE DINDSHENCHAS OF
PORT LÁIRGE
(*c.* 10th century)

[This anecdote is founded on the literal meaning of the place name Port Láirge (now Waterford), 'The Port of the Thigh-bone'. It is preserved in verse of about the tenth century. The edition is that of Edward Gwynn, *The Metrical Dindshenchas*, III pp. 190–2. The present translation is indebted to his, ibid., pp. 191–3.]

Fil sund áirge do churp ríg;
dafuc sáile dar srib-gním
fri sóer-sheirc sith-baill suilig
óen-meicc Cithaing cét-guinig.

A hInis Áine na n-arg
ruc Rot a báire bith-garg,
in taur testa cach thíre:
ba caur cnesta cocríche.

Etir tír ocus tuind tig
cechaing mac in duind déinmig:
a chlé fri muir nIcht n-etal,
a dess fri bruig mbúan-Bretan.

Cocúala in fagur andsin,
ropo magur co mór-nim,
muirn na mur-duchand mara
ós na tonnaib tóeb-glana.

Cáine suire fri cach seilb;
ba cáime cech duine-deilb
a cuirp ós tonnaib tuile,
cona mongaib ór-buide.

Tuilfitis slóig in betha
ria nglóir is ria nglan-gretha:
nístibred im báig mbíthe
dáil fria cness fria cóem-chíche.

Ina mbíd fo uisce díb
ropo chuiscle cen cháin-bríg:
métithir tulaig tend-glain
do muraig do mór-fhemnaig.

Tuc mac Cithaing sain-sheirc sáir;
ní fríth serc dó 'na chommáin:
fuair Rot, cen grés ria nguide,
olc ba bés don ban-chuire.

Romúchad, romarbad Rot,
is rodamnad a dond-chorp;
cen bad buidech, mar báigid,
dia bith marb 'na min-áigib.

Doriacht anair dar sál seng
corogab íath-port nÉrenn
lárac ós bund, mar báige,
co fil sund a sóer-áige.

Desin is ráitte cach íath
Port Láirgge nal-lethan-scíath:
dáine is dían ar gurt mad glecc
dóig is lucht fial co failet.

TRANSLATION

Here is a limb from a king's body
which the sea bore in flowing currents
towards the tall, pleasant, noble sweetheart
of the wound-dealing only son of Cithang.

From Inis Áine of the champions
Rot set out on his mettlesome course,
the hero reputed in every land,
he was a worthy warrior of the border-land.

By land and fair sea alike,
the son of the noble ruler travelled:
his left-hand side toward the clear Channel,
his right toward the steadfast land of the Britons.

Then he heard the sound,
it was a baneful blandishment,
the chorus of the mermaids of the sea
over the bright-sided waves.

As lovely as all precious things,
fairer than any human shape
their bodies above the waves of the tide,
with their tresses of golden yellow.

The hosts of the world would be lulled asleep
by their voices and clear sounds;
he would not give up under violent threat
union with their bodies, with their fair bosoms.

What there was of them under water —
it was a secret with unwelcome power —
was as big as a substantial hill
of shell-fish and large sea-weed.

The son of Cithang loved nobly and truly,
no love was received in return:
without opportunity to entreat them, Rot
   succumbed
to the evil which was customary to the females.

Rot was suffocated and killed,
and his princely body was conquered,
nor was there satisfaction, according to report,
till he was dead and dismembered.

From the east, across the narrow sea,
until it reached the shore of Ireland,
there came a thigh-bone turned upward,
and here lies his noble limb.

Therefore, in every land,
Port Láirge of the broad shields is to be named:
those who are swift on the field in conflict
are likely to be honourable people.

from:
AIDED ECHACH MAIC MAIREDA
(The Death of Eochu mac Maireda)
(Middle Irish)

[This narrative forms part of the legend of the formation
of Lough Neagh (Loch nEchach, literally, the lake of
Eochu). Failure to fulfil an Otherworld injunction led to
the irruption of a spring well. Despite Eochu's
precautions, this well eventually overflowed to form the
lake which bore his name. The narrative focus then shifts
to Eochu's daughter, Lí Ban, who survived the innundation which overwhelmed her family. The text below is

indebted to the edition and translation by Standish Hayes O'Grady, *Silva Gadelica*, 2 vols (London: Williams and Norgate, 1892), vol. 1, pp. 233–7; vol. 2, pp. 265–9.]

For a full year Lí Ban remained in her bower beneath the lake, with her pet dog along with her, and she was being protected by God from the waters of Lough Neagh. One day she said: 'Lord, it would be pleasant to be in the form of the salmon, to be swimming along with them.' Thereafter, she was changed into salmon shape, and her lap-dog was changed into an otter who followed her under the waters and seas everywhere she went. Thus was her existence from the time of Eochu mac Maireda to that of Comgall of Bangor.[1]

Comgall had sent Beoán mac Innle[2] from Tech Dabeóc[3] to Rome, to speak with Gregory[4] about observance and rules. As Beoán's crew were traversing the sea, they heard angelic chanting under the boat. 'Where does that chant come from?' asked Beoán. 'It is I,' said Lí Ban. 'Who are you?' said Beoán. 'I am Lí Ban, daughter of Eochu mac Maireda,' said she. 'What has caused you to be like this?' asked he. 'I have been under the sea for three hundred years,' she said, 'and for this reason I have come, to tell you that I will go to meet you, westward to Inber Ollorba.[5] Let you receive me, in the company of the saints of Dál nAraide,[6] a year from this day. Tell this to Comgall, and to the other saints.' 'I will not,' said Beoán, 'unless I am rewarded.' 'What reward do you seek?' asked she. 'That I have you buried in my own monastery.' 'You shall have that,' she said. Beoán came from the east thereafter, and told the story of the sea-wanderer to Comgall and the other clerics.

The year ended, and the nets were prepared. She was caught in the net of Fergus from Mílecc.[7] Then she was brought to land, and her appearance and form were marvelled at. Crowds came to look as she was in the boat, with water round about her . . .

Then there was a dispute about her. Comgall said that she was his, because it was in his territory that she had been caught. Fergus, however, said that she was his, because it was in his net that she had been captured. Beoán, meanwhile, claimed that she was his, because she had herself promised him. All of those saints then fasted, so that God might judge between them in their quarrel.

An angel said to a certain person there: 'Two stags will come tomorrow from Carn Airenn.[8] Yoke them to the chariot, and, whatever direction they take her, let them be.' The stags came next day, as the angel prophesied, and they took her to Tech Dabeóc. The clerics then offered her a choice, to be baptized, and to go to heaven immediately, or to wait for as long again, and to go to heaven after a lengthy lifetime. The choice she made was to die there and then. Comgall baptized her, and gave her the name Muirgein, that is, 'sea-birth', or perhaps Muirgeilt, 'sea-wanderer'. Fuinche was another name for her.

Many wonders and miracles are performed in that place through her agency, and, like every holy virgin, she is accorded honour and reverence, just as God in heaven bestowed on her.

7. Perhaps Meeleg land (and well), beside Camlin river near Crumlin, County Down.
8. Probably the hill called Carnearny, in the parish of Connor, *c.* 5 miles north of Antrim and Lough Neagh.

1. The saint who reputedly founded the monastery of Bangor in County Down, probably in the sixth century.
2. Unidentified.
3. Perhaps the church associated with Saint Beoán, at Lough Brickland, County Down.
4. Pope Gregory the Great, d. 604.
5. At Larne, County Antrim.
6. A kingdom of Ulster, corresponding to the present south and south-east Antrim, and much of County Down.

Biographies/Bibliographies

Giraldus Cambrensis (Gerald of Wales)

For biography and bibliography, see Volume I, pp. 270–1.

MÁIRÍN NIC EOIN, *Editor*

Sovereignty and Politics, c. 1300–1900

The female image of sovereignty was employed allegorically in Irish political writing from the medieval period onwards. The vast body of bardic eulogy, the central poetic genre of the classical period (*c.* 1200–1600), for example, draws repeatedly on the pre-colonial sovereignty goddess tradition in works in which the particular lord being addressed — whether of native Irish, Norman or Old English stock — is depicted as a worthy spouse, who will look after Éire's welfare and overthrow her enemies. It has been argued that the monologic use of the sovereignty theme during this period reflects a sense of cultural identity largely unaffected by Ireland's colonial status. While the image of sovereignty could function as an impelling symbol of cultural unity, the political focus of the praise poetry was local and dynastic. Indeed, many of the professional poets' addressees were relatively minor provincial figures with few political aspirations beyond the defence of their dynastic lands from local rivals. The Donegal Lord Conn Ó Domhnaill (d. 1583), the subject of a lavish eulogy by Tadhg Dall Ó hUiginn (d. 1591) (see Volume I, pp. 51–4), for example, was a rather undistinguished minor chieftain who was certainly never a likely candidate for the mission outlined for him in the poem: 'to free the country of Banbha from its fetters'. Though an elaborate allegorical narrative is central to the structure of that particular poem, the more common practice in classical praise poetry is for the notion of a marriage union to emerge as one element in a whole series of stock phrases and images. This is the case in the poem by Gofraidh Fionn Ó Dálaigh (d. 1387), an excerpt from which is included below, where the emphasis is placed typically on the question of the subject's kingly potential.

It is only during the period of late Tudor expansionism and in the context of Counter-Reformation thinking that one finds a burgeoning sense of Irish national identity, as new ethnically inclusive concepts of Irishness — centred predominantly on the question of religious affiliation — begin to take shape. The post-bardic poetry of the seventeenth century, much of which was produced by clerics of Gaelicized Old English background, presents contemporary political events through the moralistic lens of post-Tridentine teaching. Ireland's woes during the Cromwellian period, for example, are accounted for in terms of divine providence and of moral degeneracy. In this period Éire, or 'the wife of Conn' in Brian Mac Giolla Phádraig's poem below, for long the passive partner in the symbolic union of sovereign and territory, comes to be presented as morally reprehensible — as a shameless whore or an adulteress, or as a bad mother who rejects her own offspring and suckles the foreign horde. A preoccupation with legitimacy becomes part of a wider concern about sinfulness and sexuality. Séathrún Céitinn's tract on death *Trí Bior-Ghaoithe an Bháis* includes a section devoted explicitly to sexual infidelity and to its political consequences, drawing for his examples on the experiences of prominent contemporaries and on the moral lessons to be gleaned from an examination of twelfth-century sexual liaisons and military and political alliances. While fundamentally a moral treatise by a post-Tridentine priest, this text supplements Céitinn's treatment of the same material in his history *Foras Feasa ar*

Éirinn and is a key source for an understanding of seventeenth-century and subsequent native interpretations of colonial relations.

The female image of sovereignty is altered once again in the allegorical *aisling* poetry of the eighteenth century, where Éire now becomes the grieving widow or forlorn wife awaiting the return of her rightful partner. The fact that the partner involved is now a Stuart prince has its origins in the acceptance by the Irish intelligentsia of James I as rightful King of Ireland on his accession to the crown of the three kingdoms in 1603. Irish espousal of the Jacobite cause survived the vicissitudes of the seventeenth century, and was strengthened in particular by the accession of the Catholic James II to the crown in 1685. It involved an acceptance of primogeniture in place of native succession practices (where various members of an extended kin-group were entitled to stake a claim to succession of a lordship), and was the basis of a literary tradition particularly strong in Munster in the period after 1690. An exiled Stuart claimant — and not an Irish lord — was now presented as the legitimate spouse who would deliver Éire from her present affliction. Aogán Ó Rathaille's 'Gile na Gile', 'The Glamouring', and Seán Clárach Mac Domhnaill's 'Bímse buan ar buairt gach ló', 'My heart is sore with sorrow deep', are early and mid-eighteenth-century examples of the genre and emphasis is placed in both on the ill-treatment and abuse meted out to Éire in the absence of her true protector.

An interesting development of the image occurs in eighteenth-century folk poetry where the sovereignty figure is addressed by names in the vernacular such as Caitilín Ní Uallacháin or Síle Ní Ghadhra (as in the examples presented here), Cáit Ní Dhuibhir or Móirín Ní Chuileannáin. She is also referred to in eighteenth-century Gaelic Jacobite song as Gráinne Mhaol, 'Bare-headed Gráinne', the name most commonly applied in popular tradition to the infamous sixteenth-century Mayo woman Gráinne Ní Mháille (Grace O'Malley, *c.* 1530–*c.* 1603). Scholars and commentators have propounded a number of explanatory theories for the emergence and apparent success of such popular names as political signifiers. The first of these claims that the use of vernacular names in political song

texts occurred when well-known song tunes, in the titles of which these names appeared, were employed in an eighteenth-century political context. Though there is no doubt but that song tunes bearing the names existed and that some, such as the airs 'Gráinne Mhaol' and 'Móirín Ní Chuileannáin' were associated with the Jacobite cause, nevertheless the association of certain tunes with Jacobitism does not explain sufficiently how vernacular names in themselves came to be given such a central political significance. A related theory states that eighteenth-century poets reworked what were originally love songs addressed by male poets/narrators to female loved ones, though the lack of evidence for the existence of such songs makes this theory rather implausible. As an explanation it is also inadequate in accounting for the use of the historically significant name Gráinne Mhaol. A third theory, which was particularly attractive to nineteenth-century commentators, postulates that the use of female names in eighteenth-century political songs was a form of disguise, used to shroud the songs' treasonable political message and comparable to the other forms of disguise employed both in Jacobite verse and in Jacobite popular culture. This theory has been quite rightly rejected by twentieth-century scholars, who point to the poets' unrestrained expression of politically motivated sentiments and to unambiguous references in many of the songs to members of the Stuart family. While one must accept that, in a very general sense, female personification was part and parcel of a form of political discourse which was forced by circumstance into a covert mode, the clear effectiveness of such personification must be explained, however, by addressing the significance of the female as a site of representation in the Irish literary tradition and the new uses to which female imagery is put in the eighteenth century.

In using vernacular names, eighteenth-century poets were above all harnessing the emotive force of the traditional female sovereignty figure and reclaiming the positive potential of the image after the denigration of seventeenth-century depictions. The allegorical image becomes less a metaphorical representation of Ireland, and more a metonym for the oppressed Catholic population familiar to the poets. Her function as an aid to popular mobilization and as a signifier of economic and religious injustice is clear in the allegorical use of female names by the Whiteboys in the 1760s, as evidenced in the excerpt from *A Short Narrative* relating to violent Whiteboy activities of the period 1761–2. Ironically, however, while allegory may be associated both in literature and in popular culture with the politics of resistance, the force and extent of that resistance may also have been limited by those same allegorical forms employed to give it voice, especially when they served to avoid or obscure the central question of agency. It is in this context that the relevance of the love-song tradition to the analysis of political song becomes apparent, as most of the love-songs in the Irish language are not songs of consummated love, but rather expressions of unfulfilled or frustrated desire, of loss and regret. Similarly, in the political song tradition, the woman as signifier becomes a site of representation on which are projected political yearnings and hopes as well as deep feelings of historical loss and grievance. The prophetic message, though reiterated again and again, always remains in the sphere of possibility, as little indication is given as to how the projected reversion of power relations will be achieved, or who exactly will be instrumental in bringing it about. From the political perspective of Máire Bhuidhe Ní Laoghaire composing her *aisling* 'Ar Leacain na Gréine', 'On the Sunny Slopes', in 1797, for example, it is irrelevant that 'An Laoiseach' (Louis XVI, 1754–93), whose support for the Catholic Irish is taken for granted, is in fact dead and that the French fleet dispersed off the Bantry coast had been sent to offer military support to a revolutionary movement in which republican principles would replace the familiar ideology of kingship on which the *aisling* as a literary form depended. Of course, unlike this particular song, many eighteenth-century political songs in Irish are impossible to date accurately, again illustrating that while political song could and did serve as a powerful channel of discontent and disaffection, its power lay more in its emotive thrust than in its overt historical or ideological content.

The female figure of Gaelic *aisling* poetry made its way into eighteenth-century Irish Jacobite song in English (see Volume I, pp. 474, 476), outlived the collapse of Stuart hopes in 1745 and was adopted and adapted to give voice to almost every subsequent national movement of significance. The 'Seanbhean Bhocht' (the 'Poor Old Woman', anglicized as the 'Shan Van Vocht') first appears in Irish political balladry in 1797 (see Volume II, pp. 109–10). Gráinne Mhaol (anglicized as Granuaile, Granu waile, Grana Uaile, Grania, etc.) is one of the most popular borrowings from the Gaelic tradition in nineteenth-century patriotic balladry and appears again in Irish in Patrick Pearse's adaptation for the Irish Volunteers of a Jacobite marching song. The female image becomes a potent element in nationalistic rhetoric through the publications of the Young Ireland movement, while in the visual arts a woman appears alongside the round tower, harp and other symbols of Irish identity. Through the translations of Jacobite poetry by James Clarence Mangan, John D'Alton and others, Caitlín Ní Uallacháin and her contemporaries enter the literature of the Anglo-Irish cultural revival. The all-pervasiveness of the image lends strength to the Celticist notion of an 'essentially feminine race', while amongst nationalists only hard-headed pragmatists such as Eoin Mac Néill recognize the danger implicit in a dream image whose force is emotional rather than rational. Mac Néill felt it necessary to include the following warning in a memorandum sent to Pearse and other members of the executive of the Irish Volunteers in February 1916:

> We have to remember that what we call our country is not a poetical abstraction, as some of us, perhaps all of us, in the exercise of our highly developed capacity for figurative thought, are sometimes apt to imagine — with the help of our patriotic literature. There is no such person as Caitlín Ní Uallacháin or Róisín Dubh or the *Seanbhean Bhocht*, who is calling upon us to serve her. What we call our country is the Irish nation, which is a concrete and visible reality.

Pearse himself, in the poem included below, gives subtle expression to the emotional pain involved in rejecting the aesthetic allure of the *aisling* tradition, in favour of the concrete reality of military rebellion.

It is only in relatively recent years that the use of female imagery in Irish political discourse has become a subject for critical analysis, and it is interesting that much of that analysis to date has taken place in and around the work of visual artists, poets and film-makers, both male and female. A major source of concern has been the manner in which the female body has been used as a site of representation and the effect this has had on women's ability to articulate their own cultural and political messages.

GOFRAIDH FIONN Ó DÁLAIGH

(?–1387)

from:
FUIRIGH GO FÓILL, A ÉIRE
(Wait a Little While, Dear Éire)
(14th century)

[The following lines form the opening stanzas of a praise poem addressed to Tadhg 'Mainistreach' (Mac Domhnaill) Mac Carthaigh (d. 1413), one of the McCarthys of Desmond. Tadhg was a youth at the time of composition and is referred to as such throughout the poem. In these stanzas the poet advises Éire (who is variously addressed through the use of metonyms — the fort of Tara, the plain of Uisneach, the mound of legendary high-kings Cormac mac Airt and his son Cairbre — or as wife of legendary kings Niall Naoighiallach, Tuathal Teachtmar, Art Éinfhir) to be patient, as a man worthy to be her husband will soon reach maturity. Later in the poem allusion is made to a prophecy relating to the McCarthy clan and the poem ends by inciting Tadhg to demonstrate his kingly potential by taking up arms against his rivals. The text is from: Láimhbheartach Mac Cionnaith (ed.) *Dioghluim Dána* (Baile Átha Cliath: Oifig an tSoláthair, 1938), p. 321. The translation is by M. Nic E.]

Fuirigh go fóill, a Éire,
gearr go bhfuighe fírchéile;
do chéile ní fear foirbhthe,
a Éire, a threabh théagairthe.

A fhionnráith Teamhra Dá Thí,
aithnim an fear dá bhfuiltí;
triath d'óigleanabh do b'áil libh,
a chláir fhóidleabhair Uisnigh.

Fada nach fuarais, a bhean,
aoinfhear d'aicme na naoidhean;
fad do chairde is dubhach dhuit,
a Thulach Chairbre is Chormuic.

A-tá fear i n-aois leinibh
— gearr go bhfuighe fóiridhin —
i ráith na ngéigbheangán ngeal
a chéidleannán mac Míleadh.

Tánaig an té taoi d'iarraidh,
a fhinnbhean Néill Naoighiallaigh,
dar dhual Bóinn bhraontana bhinn;
aontamha go fóill fuiling.

Eidhre ó gCarthaigh, ceann Gaoidheal,
gearr bhias i mbeirt ógnaoidhean;
feith, a Bhanbha, a bhean Tuathail,
go bhfaghbha th'fhear ionnuachair.

D'éis dealuighthe go réidh ruibh
d'fhuil Chuinn is d'fhíorfhuil Eoghain,
a bhean naoidhe an Chláir choimhthe
an áil naoidhe neamhfhoirbhthe?

Meinic riamh seanbhean mar sin,
a leannáin Airt Éinfhir,
do ghnáth ag iarraidh fhear n-óg,
a threabh dhiamhair na ndeargród . . .

TRANSLATION 1

Wait a little while, dear Éire,
soon you'll find a worthy spouse;
your husband is not yet mature,
O Éire of the stalwart tribes.

O bright fort of Dá Thí's Tara
I can see the man for you;
a youthful lord is your desire,
O plain of Uisneach, of surface smooth.

It's a long time, dearest woman,
since you had a man to match this child;
your long wait has brought you sorrow,
O mound of Cormac and of Cairbre.

There lives a man of tender years
— soon help will come your way —
in the fort of the bright branches
O first lover of the sons of Míl.

He has come whom you're awaiting,
O lovely wife of Niall Naoighiallach,
one deserving of the Boyne's sweet waters;
so remain unmarried yet awhile.

The heir of Carthach's seed, leader of the Gael,
will not be a young child for long;

wait, O Banba, wife of Tuathal,
'til a worthy spouse for you is found.

As the seed of Conn and of pure-blooded
 Eoghan[1]
have departed from you one by one,
O tender woman of the fertile Plain,
could you desire a raw young man?

An old woman is often like that,
O lover of Art Éinfhir,
forever seeking young men
O dark tribe of the red roadways . . .

---

1. Conn Céadchathach ('of the Hundred Battles'), eponymous
ancestor of the Connachta, and Eoghan Mór, eponymous ancestor
of the dominant dynasty in medieval Munster, the Eoghanachta.

BRIAN MAC GIOLLA PHÁDRAIG

(c. 1580–c. 1652)

ÁBHAR DEARGTHA LEACAN DO MHNAOI CHUINN É
(The Wife of Conn Should Blush Red with Disgrace) (c. 1652)

[Though the exact date of this poem is unknown, it was more than likely written after the commencement of the Cromwellian settlement in 1652. The 'wife of Conn' is depicted in the poem as a mother and a harlot who has rejected her own family in favour of newcomers of dubious pedigree. The text is from: Pádraig de Brún, Breandán Ó Buachalla, Tomás Ó Concheanainn (eds), *Nua-Dhuanaire*, vol. 1 (Dublin: Dublin Institute for Advanced Studies, 1971), p. 12. The translation is by M. Nic E.]

Ábhar deargtha leacan do mhnaoi Chuinn é
táir is tarcaisne a thabhairt dá saorchlainn féin,
grá a hanama is altram a cíoch cruinn caomh
do thál ar bhastard nach feadair cé díobh puinn é.

A Éire, a chailleach is malartach bréagach foinn,
a mheirdreach bhradach le sealad nár éim' ach
 sinn,
do léigis farat na Galla-sa i réim id eing
do léirscrios seachad mar bhastard gach aon
 ded chlainn.

A rúin mo chroí, a Rí na ndúl 's a pháirt,
an dúch nó an díth leat Gaoil dá mbrú ag cách,
a ndúiche, a roinn, a maoin dá n-útamáil
ag rút mac tíre tríothu ag rúcam rác?

Gan bú ná brí i mic Gaoil ach súil gach lá
le cúrsa gaoithe shaoilid chúcu d'fháil;
ailiú lem chroí! 'mbiam choíche ag umhlacht
 dáibh
nó an dtiubhra an bríste díol don triús go
 brách?

TRANSLATION

The wife of Conn should blush red with disgrace
to have shown such contempt for her own noble
    race;
her love and the milk of her round soft breasts
    she chose
to bestow on a bastard whose ancestry nobody
    knows.

O Éire, you lying old hag who keeps changing
    her tune,
you whore who of late turns no one away but
    her own,
it was you let the English wield power in your
    land,
while destroying like bastards all your own clan.

O sweetheart! and O King of Creation most
    blessed!
does it pain you that Gaels are on all sides
    oppressed?
that their lands and their food and their wealth
    are now plundered
by an armed band of wolves who are wreaking
    destruction?

The sons of the Gael are left without force,
expecting each day that the wind will change
    course,
alas! will we always so meekly surrender —
or will the breeks forever pay rent to the trews?[1]

1. The contemporary fashion in legware among Irish and English males respectively.

SÉATHRÚN CÉITINN (GEOFFREY KEATING)

(*c.* 1580–*c.* 1644)

from:
TRÍ BIOR-GHAOITHE AN BHÁIS
(The Three Shafts of Death)
(1631)

[This Counter-Reformation text on sinfulness and death, which Céitinn completed in 1631, links political misfortune with adultery. The references to Ruaidhrí Ó Conchobhair (Rory O'Connor), King of Connacht 1156–1186 (d. 1198) and Diarmaid Mac Murchadha (Dermot Mac Murrough, d. 1171), King of Leinster hark back to the events surrounding the earliest Norman encroachment on Ireland, and firmly place a narrative of sexual infidelity at the very beginning of Irish colonial history. The excerpt is translated from: Osborn Bergin (ed.), *Trí Bior-Ghaoithe an Bháis* (Dublin: Royal Irish Academy, 1931), pp. 170–2. The translation is by M. Ní Dh.]

Understand, O mortal, that one is usually affected by some one or other of four evil consequences which flow from adultery. The first evil consequence is extreme poverty which deprives one of his temporal wealth and plunges him into useless debts. And many a boasting, blustering braggart was oppressed and brought low in our own day in Ireland by this scourge, when God suffered them to over-encumber themselves as a result of corrupting married women. The second evil consequence is a disfiguring loss of limb. For God often suffers the adulterer to lose an eye or a leg or an arm in requital for the sin and as an admonition to others to guard against the same crime. The third misfortune is sudden death without repentance, that is, to be burned in a fire, or drowned in water, or wounded by a weapon, or to be carried off by some such sudden death. The fourth evil consequence is to have no son to inherit from him. And were it not for fear of the enmity it would cause, I might list many another clear and positive sign which has been seen in our own time in Ireland, of which I make no mention on this occasion.

However, as a warning to the reader I will name here, though I am loath to do so, some few of those who were afflicted (alas) by this misfortune and left without a son to inherit from them, viz., Gearóid, Earl of Kildare; Tomás Builtéar, Earl of Ormond and Ossory; Domhnall Mac Carthaigh, Earl of Valentia; Muiris Mac

Gearailt, Lord of the Déise; and Roland Eustace, Lord of Eustace country; Éamonn Mac Giobúin who was known as the White Earl; and Calbhach Ó Cearbhaill, who was known as Lord of Ely. And were it not for the fact that those I have mentioned were so blatantly guilty of this crime that their acts in that respect are on everyone's lips, I would have left them without remark, like all the others. And it was regarding this that some poet composed the following quatrain:

> Each wicked king who fornicates
> (a sin that takes his eye off governance) —
> it is that deed above all
> which destroys his prosperity and posterity.

Thus it is my understanding that it was in vengeance for the adultery of Ruaidhrí son of Toirdhealbhach Ó Conchobhair, King of Connacht, and the adultery of Diarmaid Mac Murchadha, King of Leinster, that God allowed the chieftainship of Ireland to be taken from the Gaels and that they be conquered by the Foreigners. For one reads that Ruaidhrí Ó Conchobhair was not satisfied with having six lovers, but had to have his way also with every other woman in his country of whom he might be enamoured, whether married or unmarried. And clearly, in the case of Diarmaid Mac Murchadha it was his abduction of the wife of Tighearnán Ó Ruairc which caused every hurt that he did to himself and to Ireland.[1] Why say more? — many extensive kingdoms and right noble, gracious royal families were overthrown overnight on account of this sin, as is manifest from the histories and annals of the great rulers of yore.

1. See pp. 192–6.

AOGÁN Ó RATHAILLE

(c. 1670–c. 1728)

GILE NA GILE
(The Glamouring)
(c. 1715)

[This early eighteenth-century political *aisling*, composed more than likely around the time of the 1715 Jacobite rebellion, is one of the most stylistically brilliant examples of the genre. The allegorical maiden is presented as a beautiful though pitiful figure who, as she awaits the return of her true mate, is subjected to sexual abuse by louts and boors. The political context of the poem is provided by the popular Jacobite reference to George I as 'adharcach' (a cuckold), or 'a hornmaster' in Seamus Heaney's translation, and the note of veiled optimism in the final line. The text is from: Seán Ó Tuama and Thomas Kinsella (ed. and trans.), *An Duanaire 1600–1900: Poems of the Dispossessed*, pp. 150, 152. The translation, by Seamus Heaney, is from: Louis de Paor (ed.), *Leabhar Sheáin Uí Thuama* (Baile Átha Cliath: Coiscéim, 1997), pp. 104–5.]

Gile na gile do chonnarc ar slí in uaigneas,
criostal an chriostail a gormroisc rinn-uaine,
binneas an bhinnis a friotal nár chríonghruama,
deirge is finne do fionnadh 'na gríosghruannaibh.

Caise na caise i ngach ribe dá buí-chuachaibh,
bhaineas an cruinneac den rinneac le rinnscuabadh,
iorra ba ghlaine ná gloine ar a broinn bhuacaigh,
do gineadh ar ghineamhain di-se san tír uachtraigh.

Fios fiosach dom d'inis, is ise go fíor-uaigneach,
fios filleadh don duine don ionad ba rí-dhualgas,
fios milleadh na droinge chuir eisean ar rinnruagairt,
's fios eile ná cuirfead im laoithibh le fíor-uamhan.

Leimhe na leimhe dom druidim 'na cruinn-tuairim,
im chime ag an gcime do snaidhmeadh go fíorchrua me;
ar ghoirm Mhic Mhuire dom fhortacht, do bhíog uaimse,
is d'imigh an bhruinneal 'na luisne go bruín Luachra.

Rithim le rith mire im rithibh go croí-luaimneach,
trí imeallaibh corraigh, trí mhongaibh, trí
    shlímruaitigh;
don tinne-bhrugh tigim — ní thuigim cén tslí
    fuaras —
go hionad na n-ionad do cumadh le draíocht
    dhruaga.

Brisid fá scige go scigeamhail buíon ghruagach,
is foireann de bhruinnealaibh sioscaithe dlaoi-
    chuachach;
i ngeimhealaibh geimheal me cuirid gan puinn
    suaimhnis,
's mo bhruinneal ar broinnibh ag broinnire
    broinnstuacach.

D'iniseas di-se, san bhfriotal dob fhíor uaimse,
nár chuibhe di snaidhmeadh le slibire
    slímbhuartha
's an duine ba ghile ar shliocht chine Scoit trí
    huaire
ag feitheamh ar ise bheith aige mar chaoin-
    nuachar.

Ar chloistin mo ghutha di goileann go fíor-
    uaibhreach
is sileadh ag an bhfliche go life as a
    gríosghruannaibh;
cuireann liom giolla dom choimirc ón mbruín
    uaithi —
's í gile na gile do chonnarc ar slí in uaignes.

An Ceangal

Mo threighid, mo thubaist, mo thurainn, mo
    bhrón, mo dhíth!
an soilseach muirneach miochairgheal beoltais
    caoin
ag adharcach foireanndubh mioscaiseach
    cóirneach buí,
's gan leigheas 'na goire go bhfillid na leoin tar
    toinn.

TRANSLATION

Brightening brightness, lonely, astray, she appears.
Crystalline crystal and sparkle of blue in green
    eyes,
Sweetness of sweetness in her unembittered
    young voice

And a high colour dawning behind the pearl of
    her face.

Ringlets and ringlets, a curl in every tress
Of her fair hair trailing and brushing the dew
    on the grass;
And a gem from her birthplace far in the high
    universe
Outglittering glass and gracing the groove of her
    breasts.

News that was secret she whispered to soothe
    her aloneness,
News of one due to return and reclaim his true
    place,
News of the ruin of those who had cast him in
    darkness,
News too awesome for me to utter in verse.

My head got lighter and lighter but still I
    approached her,
Enthralled by the thraldom, helplessly held and
    bewildered,
Choking and calling Christ's name: then she
    fled in a shimmer
To Luachra Fort where only the glamoured can
    enter.

I hurtled and hurled myself madly following
    after
Over keshes and marshes and mosses and
    treacherous moors
And arrived at that stronghold unsure about
    how I had got there,
That earthwork of earth the orders of magic
    once reared.

A gang of thick louts were shouting loud insults
    and jeering
And a curly-haired coven in fits of sniggers and
    sneers:
Next thing I was taken and cruelly shackled in
    fetters
As the breasts of the maiden were groped by a
    thick-witted boor.

I tried then as hard as I could to make her hear
    truth.
How wrong she was to be linked to that
    lazarous swine

When the pride of the pure Scottish stock, a
   prince of her blood,[1]
Was ardent and eager to wed her and make her
   his bride.

When she heard me, she started to weep, but
   pride was the cause
Of those tears that came wetting her cheeks and
   shone in her eyes;
Then she sent me a guard to guide me out of
   the fortress,

1. The Old Pretender, James Francis Edward Stuart (1688–1766).

Who'd appeared to me, lonely, astray, a
   brightening brightness.

. . . . . .

Calamity, shock, collapse, heartbreak and grief
To think of her sweetness, her beauty, her
   mildness, her life
Defiled at the hands of a hornmaster sprung
   from riff-raff,
And no hope of redress till the lions ride back
   on the wave.

ANONYMOUS

CAITILÍN NÍ UALLACHÁIN
(Kathaleen Ny-Houlahan)
(c. 1719)

[This song, though often attributed to the Tipperary poet
Liam Dall Ó hIfearnáin (c. 1720–c. 1803), was composed
in reality around the time of his birth. Together with a
companion piece which contains a more explicit reference
to the Jacobite plots of 1719, the song is an early example
of the attachment of allegorical significance to vernacular
names in Irish political poetry. James Clarence Mangan's
English translations of these songs were the source for
W.B. Yeats's re-workings in his poem 'Red Hanrahan's
Song about Ireland' and in his celebrated play Cathleen ni
Houlihan. The text is from: Risteárd Ó Foghludha (ed.),
Ar Bhruach na Coille Muaire (Baile Átha Cliath: Oifig an
tSoláthair, 1939), p. 42. The translation, by Mangan, is
from: D.J. O'Donoguhe (ed.), Poems of James Clarence
Mangan (Dublin: M.H. Gill, 1903), pp. 16–17. There is no
equivalent in the Irish for the fourth verse in Mangan's
poem.]

Is fada mílte á chartadh síos is suas ar fán,
Is clanna saoithe ar easbhaidh grinn gan chluain
   gan stát;
Gan chanadh díodhacht gan fleadh gan fíon gan
   chnuas gan cheárd,
Ag braith arís ar Chaitilín Ní Uallacháin.

Ná measaigí gur chaile chríon ná guaireachán,
Ná caillichín an ainnir mhín-tais bhuacach mná;
Is fada arís budh banaltra í is budh muar a hál
Dá mbeadh mac an ríogh ag Caitilín Ní
   Uallacháin.

Budh deas a gnaoi dá mairimís le ruagairt
   námhad,
A brata síoda ag tarraingt gaoithe is buadh
   chum báb;
Plaid go groidhe ó bhaitheas cinn anuas ag
   trácht
Ag mac an ríogh ar Chaitilín Ní Uallacháin.

Screadaimíd le hathchuinghí chum Uain na
   nGrás,
Do cheap na tíortha, talamh trím, is cruachaibh
   árd;
Do scaip 'na dtimcheall fairrgí geal-chuanta is
   trágha
Ag cur malairt críche ar Chaitilín Ní Uallacháin.

An Té tharraing Ísrael tarsna Taoide Ruaidhe ón
   námhaid
Is do bheathuigh daoine dathad geimhreadh
   anuas le arán;
Do neartuigh Maois ameasc a naímhde, fuascail
   tráth
Is tabhair díon do Chaitilín Ní Uallacháin.

TRANSLATION

Long they pine in weary woe, the nobles of our
land,
Long they wander to and fro, proscribed, alas!
and banned;
Feastless, houseless, altarless, they bear the
exile's brand,
But their hope is in the coming-to of
Kathaleen Ny-Houlahan!

Think her not a ghastly hag, too hideous to be
seen,
Call her not unseemly names, our matchless
Kathaleen;
Young she is, and fair she is, and would be
crowned a queen,
Were the king's son[1] at home here with
Kathaleen Ny-Houlahan!

Sweet and mild would look her face, O, none so
sweet and mild,
Could she crush the foes by whom her beauty is
reviled;
Woollen plaids would grace herself and robes of
silk her child,
If the king's son were living here with
Kathaleen Ny-Houlahan!

Sore disgrace it is to see the Arbitress of thrones,
Vassal to a *Saxoneen* of cold and sapless bones!
Bitter anguish wrings our souls — with heavy
sighs and groans
We wait the Young Deliverer of Kathaleen
Ny-Houlahan!

Let us pray to Him who holds life's issues in
His hands —
Him who formed the mighty globe, with all its
thousand lands;
Girding them with sea and mountains, rivers
deep, and strands,
To cast a look of pity upon Kathaleen
Ny-Houlahan!

He, who over sands and waves led Israel
along —
He, who fed, with heavenly bread, that chosen
tribe and throng;

1. The Old Pretender.

He who stood by Moses, when his foes were
fierce and strong — May
He show forth His might in saving Kathaleen
Ny-Houlahan!

SÍLE NÍ GHADHRA
(Sheela na Guire)
(*c.* 1740)

[The 'Síle Ní Ghadhra' of this anonymous song is one of the
most popular synonyms for Ireland to appear in eighteenth-
and nineteenth-century Gaelic verse. The name is
associated more commonly with the Young Pretender than
with his father and this particular song was more than likely
composed in the period before 1745 when hopes of a
Jacobite reinstatement still ran high. References to the
O'Briens of Ara (in the Castlelyons area of County Cork)
and to 'the Major' (a member of the Tipperary branch of the
O'Briens) link the author to one of the most important
eighteenth-century Catholic families, while also possibly
associating the song's message with those of the O'Briens
who served in the Jacobite Regiment of Clare in France.
The song departs substantially from the classic *aisling* form,
and the tone throughout is optimistic, as the language of
marriage and celebration merges with that of military
triumph. As in many songs by anonymous eighteenth-
century authors, political subjection is expressed in terms of
abduction and rape, while anti-Hanoverian sentiment is
boldly presented in the language of sexual disparagement,
masked somewhat in James D'Alton's subdued translation,
which appeared alongside the earliest published version of
the original in James Hardiman's *Irish Minstrelsy*. The Irish
edition here is from: Diarmaid Ó Doibhlin (ed.), *Duanaire
Gaedhilge Róis Ní Ógáin* (Baile Átha Cliath: An
Clóchomhar, 1995), pp. 86–8. D'Alton's translation is
from: James Hardiman (ed.), *Irish Minstrelsy*, 2 vols
(London: Joseph Robins, 1831), vol. 2, pp. 55–63.]

Is é deir Dónall Ó Mórdha, is é ar ard Leasa
Gréine
Gur fada tá an ógbhean gan pósadh le Séarlas,
Ó milleadh, ó leonadh, ó seoladh thar tréanmhuir
Na fearachoin chróga de chóirshliocht Mhilésius.
Lasfaimid tóirsí a dhóighfeas an saol,
Is bainfimid toirneach as crónphoic le faobhar,
Glanfam clár Fódla ó na cóbaigh go léir!
Beidh slóite ar na bóithre go mómharach
meidhreach
Ag triall chun do phósta-sa, a Shíle Ní Ghadhra.

Sin teachtaire tráthúil gan spás chun an *Mhajor*
Go scríobhfadh go fáidhghlic chun arda na
    hÉireann,
Gach file, gach fáidh glic, gach sárfhear dá
    thréine,
Bheith bailithe an lá úd ar ard Leasa Gréine;
Punch is fíon caordhearg dá thaoscadh mar
    shaighead,
Drumaí dá bpléascadh, dá ngréasú chun *siege*,
Séarlas ceann feadhna bhfear Éireann gan
    mhoill
Mac Uí Bhriain Ara go calma meidhreach
Ag triall chun do phósta-sa, a Shíle Ní Ghadhra.

Ar luadhan a ghrá geal go hálainn le Síle
Cualadh a gáire ar ard na dtrí ríochta;
Cualadh sa Spáinn í le háthas dá insint,
Cualadh san Iodáil í, 'gus ar ardbhailte
    Laoisigh;
Cualadh in Éirinn le féile á mhaíomh,
Go gcuirfí na Gaeil bhocht' 'na réimcheart arís,
Nach mbeadh sí 'na strae bhocht idir mhéirligh
    mar bhí,
Go dtraochfadh sí Galla, an aicme gan bhéasa,
Is go bpósfadh sí a cara le dlí cheart na cléire.

Cibé chífeadh an sárfhear breá álainn, an *Major*,
Ar ghillín ag ceáfráil go stáidmhear chun
    scléipe,
Lena chlaíomh leathan láidir 'na lámh dheas is
    faobhar air,
Ag fuascailt na mná úd is dá gráchan le Séarlas.
Cá bhfuil tú a Shéarlais? Ná déansa aon mhoill!
Díbir thar tréanmhuir go héasca na Gaill.
Bain fuaim as gach bréanphoc, is séid suas an
    adharc;
Suas leis na ceolta go mómharach meidhreach
Ag triall chun do phósta-sa, a Shíle Ní
    Ghadhra!

Tá fásach 'na slaoda ar shléibhte is ar
    mhaoilinn,
Agus binnghuth na n-éanlaith ar ghéaga san
    oíche;
Le dianteas na gréine bhí an chraobh ghlas sa
    gheimhreadh ann,
Is nach breá deas atá Phoébus ag séid' a chuid
    soilse!
Preabaig' in éineacht, an méidse Shíol mBriain!

Leanaig' a chéile agus féachaig' bhur dtriath!
Machnaig' ar ghéarghoin, bhur gcéasadh le cian!
A shíl na bhfear calma leanaig' bhur léidfhear
Ag feoilchoscairt bodach as Fódla-chlár Éibhir!

A Shíle na gcumann ná fulaing mé i bpéin,
Fóir ar mo ghlasa 's ar mo dhanaid má fhéadair;
Ná foighnigh mé a'm' stracadh idir ghasraí
    diabhal,
Mo shúil leis i gcónaí is gan gnó dhom á
    iarraidh.
Tá mo dhóichse le Peadar go scarfar an bháb
Leis an léicese, a dhealbh nach ait leis na mná;
Má luadh leis mar chéile í níor réitigh sé a cás,
An Gallphoc mallaithe! stracfaimid a adharca,
Is cuirfeam bodaigh chun sodair as Síle Ní
    Ghadhra.

Is mór an chúis éad' dom gach lae nuair a
    smaoinim
Ar ghruagach neamhbhéasach neamhaerach
    neamhaoibhinn,
Gan shuáilce, gan tréithe gan fhéile gan
    chaoineas,
Ach ag fuadach mo chéile 'gus dá héigean ar
    choillte.
Is mé an draoi is óige is is sine sa tír,
Is mé phógfas an ógbhean agus tiocfaidh sí linn,
Is í thógfas an smúitse is an tuirse dem chroí,
A óigh mhilis chiúin tais mar a luaitear ag
    Laoiseach,
Agus pósfad mo chailín le Cathaoir gan aimhreas.

Is é Cathaoir dob fhearr liom ag trácht liom sa
    ní úd,
Agus rí geal na Spáinne is a gharda bheith im
    thimpeall,
Is é 'bhuafas gan dualgas le huaisle na tíre,
Agus sinne — lá dubhach é ag búra d'ár
    gcoimheascar!
Troidig'-se an meirleach nach féidir a chloí
Go dtiocfaidh an Francach is a bhantracht thar
    toinn,
Is é 'fhágfas gan amhras iad go fannlag gan
    bhrí.
Nuair a thiocfaidh an dream úd go teann lena
    chéile
Beidh Aifreann cantaireacht' i dteampaill na
    hÉireann.

TRANSLATION

On the height of Lisgreny[1] cried Daniel O'More,[2]
'Oh, Erin! dear maiden, how long shall it be,
Ere thy bridesman in triumph will come to thy
    shore? —
But ruin has fallen on thy warriors — and thee!
Yet the torch, that must kindle a world in thy
    cause,
May haply the zeal of our cannons inspire,
Against those who would trample thy freedom
    and laws,
And flout at the wedding of *Sheela na Guire*.

'These vallies shall ring with the triumph of hosts!
The signals shall flash — and the thousands obey!
Bards, heroes, they hear me — they flow from
    their coasts —
Proud hill of Lisgreny! thou'lt triumph that day.
Echo will forward the beat of our drum,
What chiefs in the hearts of our mountains
    'twill fire!
O'Brien of Ara, exulting will come,
And Charles the bridesman bless — *Sheela na
Guire*.

'When to Erin was whispered the name of her
    spouse,
The laugh of her heart over Europe was heard;
In Spain 'twas received with a kindred carouse,
And in France and in Italy gladly declared.[3]
The homes, that our fathers — our childhood
    endeared,
That our memories cling to with pining desire,
Shall be ours — ours again — and the brave
    will be heard,
The long exiled brave — cheering *Sheela na
Guire*.

'And will not our heart's pulse triumphantly
    dance,
When the Major, the gallant, the graceful, the
    brave,
With his chivalrous comrades shall fearless
    advance
A tyrant to crush — and a country to save! —
Where art thou our Charles! ah, linger no more,
One flash of thy sword — and our foes shall
    retire;

A clang of thy trumpet once heard on our
    shore, —
And we'll start to thy wedding with *Sheela na
Guire*.

'The spring flowers are budding — the
    blossoms look gay
But the winter of tyranny never departs;
The birds warble sweet from each feathery spray,
But 'tis night — starless night, o'er our hopes
    and our hearts.
All nature's awake! — and will not the fame
Of heroes, your fathers — O'Brien your sire,
Arouse you to glory — to vengeance — or shame?
Shall the base churls still mock your own *Sheela
na Guire*?

'Her vallies but echo the voice of her woe,
In the fears of her people I hear her upbraid,
How long shall I bleed to a merciless foe?
How long shall my heart's secret wish be delayed?
But Saint Peter will sanction the welcome
    divorce,
From him who would ne'er be our maiden's
    desire;
A monster whose bonds are the fetters of force,
Ne'er by heaven designed for our *Sheela na Guire*.

'My heart, how it pines when I think of the
    wretch,
Without honour or principle, virtue, or truth;
Whose guilt could design, and whose power
    could reach
To assail our beloved in the hills of her youth.
I'm the oldest — the last of her sages confest,
And she, dearest maid, can alone still inspire
A joy and content o'er the gloom of my breast,
When Charles shall espouse her, my *Sheela na
Guire!*

'Speak only to me of the days when ere long,
Proud Spain and his guards in transplendent
    array,
Shall environ our cause — when our chiefs shall
    be strong,
And no tribute or fealty to tyranny pay.
When France and his hosts shall horse the
    broad main,
And the Despot shall crumble — while nations
    in choir
Awake the glad heavens with liberty's strain,
And light up the churches of *Sheela na Guire*.'

1. D'Alton's note: A well-known hill in the South of Ireland.
2. Unidentified.
3. References to the major Catholic powers from whom the Stuart
   claimant could expect support.

SEÁN CLÁRACH MAC DOMHNAILL

(1691–1754)

BÍMSE BUAN AR BUAIRT GACH LÓ
(My Heart is Sore with Sorrow Deep)
(c. 1746)

[The following poem laments the final defeat of the Stuart cause in Scotland in 1746, and the subsequent exile of the young Prince Charles Edward Stuart (1720–88). It is voiced by the sovereignty figure herself, who compares her Stuart hero to the Gaelic heroes of old. The text is from: Risteárd Ó Foghludha (ed.) *Seán Clárach* (Baile Átha Cliath: Oifig an tSoláthair, 1934), pp. 45–7. The translation, by Colm Breathnach, is from: Sean McMahon, Jo O'Donoghue (eds), *Taisce Duan* (Dublin: Poolbeg Press, 1992), pp. 55–9.]

Bímse buan ar buairt gach ló
Ag caoidh go cruaidh 's ag tuar na ndeór
Mar scaoileadh uainn an buachaill beó
Is ná ríomhtar tuairisc uaidh, mo bhrón.
    Isé mo laoch mo ghille mear,
    Isé mo Chaesar gille mear,
    Ní fhuaireas féin éantsuan ar séan
    Ó chuaidh i gcéin mo ghille mear.

Ní haoibhinn cuach ba suairc ar neóin,
Táid fíorchoin uaisle ar uathadh spóirt,
Táid saoithe suadha i mbuairt 's i mbrón
Ó scaoileadh uainn an buachaill beó.
    Isé mo laoch mo ghille mear, &c.

Níor éirigh Phoebus féin ar cóir,
Ar chaomhchneas ré tá daolbhrat bróin,
Tá saobhadh ar spéir is spéirling mhór
Chum sléibhte i gcéin mar d'éala' an leóghan
    Isé mo laoch mó ghille mear, &c.

Níl séis go suairc ar chruadhchruit cheóil,
Tá an éigse i ngruaim gan uaim 'n-a mbeól,
Táid béithe buan ar buairt gach ló
Ó théarnaidh uainn an buachaill beó.
    Isé mo laoch mo ghille mear, &c.

Marcach uasal uaibhreach óg,
Gas gan ghruaim is suairce snódh,
Glaic is luaimneach luath i ngleó
Ag teascadh an tsluaigh 's ag tuargain treón.
    Isé mo laoch mo ghille mear, &c.

Is glas a shúil mhear mhúirneach mhódhmhail
Mar leagadh an drúchta ar chiumhais an róis;
Tá Mars is Cúipid dlúth i gcomhar
I bpearsain úir 's i ngnúis mo stóir.
    Isé mo laoch mo ghille mear, &c.

Is cas a chúl 's is cúrsach cóir,
Is dlathach dlúth is is búclach borr,
Is feacach fionn ar lonnradh an óir
Ó bhaitheas úr go com mo stór.
    Isé mo laoch mo ghille mear, &c.

Is cosmhail é le hAonghus óg,
Le Lughaidh mac Chéin na mbéimeann mór,
Le Cúraoi árdmhac Dáire an óir —
Taoiseach éirligh tréan ar tóir.
    Isé mo laoch mo ghille mear, &c.

Le Conall Cearnach bhearnadh póirt,
Le Fearghus fiúntach fionn Mac Róigh,
Le Conchubhar cáidhmhac Neás' na nós —
Taoiseach aoibhinn Chraoibhe an cheóil.
    Isé mo laoch mo ghille mear, &c.

Ní mhaoidhfead féin cé hé mo stór,
Tá innsint scéil 'n-a dhéidh go leór;
Acht guidhim chum Aenmhic Dé na gcomhacht
Go dtíghe mo laoch gan bhaogal beó.
    Isé mo laoch mo ghille mear, &c.

Acht seinntear stáir ar chláirsigh cheóil
Is líontar táinte cárt ar bórd
Le hintinn árd gan cháim gan cheó
Chum saoghal is sláinte dfhagháil dom leóghan
    Isé mo laoch mo ghille mear!
    Isé mo Chaesar gille mear!
    Mo chruadhtan féin a luadh tré léan
    Mar chuaidh i gcéin mo ghille mear!

TRANSLATION

My heart is sore with sorrow deep,
Lamenting hard, so long I weep,
Because he's gone who is so sweet
And news of him we do not hear.

Chorus
He is my hero, fair and fleet;
He is my Caesar, fair and fleet;
I get no rest, I cannot sleep
Since he crossed the ocean, fair and fleet.

The cuckoo speaks at noon no more.
The noble hounds, they know no sport,
And learned men are left in woe
Since the fair one left these shores.

Phoebus hasn't risen right,
His fair face a black pall hides,
Storming winds have rent the sky
Since he fled to the far hills high.

The tuneful harps no longer play,
The poets don't make their rhyming staves;
Fair maids sorrow throughout the day
Since our bright one went away.

A young noble proud horseman he,
Scion without sadness, of countenance sweet.
His arm is quick in the battle's heat,
Hacking in the crush and battering the fierce.

His loving quick mild eye is green
Like the dew on the edge of a rose's leaf;

Mars and Cupid both are seen
In the face and person of my loved-one sweet.

His winding hair is flowing and free,
His heavy locks are curled and neat,
Are fair and wavy with a golden sheen
From the top of the head to the waist of my
    sweet.

He is like Aonghus Óg,
Like Lughaidh, son of Cian of the terrible blows,
Like Cú Raoi, son of Dáire of the gold,
Leader of the Éarainn, in the chase well known.

Like Conall victorious, sacker of forts,
Like fair and worthy Fearghus, son of Rogh,
Like Conchubhar, noble son of Nás renowned,
The pleasant leader of the musical host.

Who my treasure is, I will not say —
There are many others to tell his name —
To God's only Son, most high, I pray
My love protect and keep him safe.

So let the harpers strike up and play
And fill the glasses to brimming with ale;
With spirits raised and undismayed,
Here's health and long life to my lion brave.

Chorus
He is my hero, fair and fleet;
He is my Caesar, fair and fleet;
In desolation now I grieve
'Cause he crossed the ocean, fair and fleet.

ANONYMOUS

from:
A SHORT NARRATIVE OF SOME DISTURBANCES WHICH HAPPENED IN THE COUNTIES OF LIMERICK, CORK, TIPPERARY AND WATERFORD, FROM THE MONTH OF NOVEMBER 1761 TO THE MONTH OF APRIL 1762 (1762)

[This excerpt illustrates the use of the popular sovereignty figure Queen Sive Oultagh by the agrarian secret society the Whiteboys in the early 1760s. Sive (in Irish, Sadhbh) was the daughter of Conn Céadchathach, ancestor of the kings of Tara, and wife of Ailill Ólom, ancestor of the Munster kings (see pp. 35–6). She came to be associated with the borderlands of Munster and the Northern Half, and she emerges as an important figure in the literature of Whiteboy disturbances of the southern Midlands. Female personification is here employed as an aid to popular mobilization and Queen Sive's law is associated with the administration of 'rough justice' in an environment of class and sectarian conflict. The text is from: James Kelly, 'The Whiteboys in 1762: A Contemporary Account', *Journal of the Cork Historical and Archaeological Society*, vol. 94, no. 253 (January–December 1989), pp. 21–3.]

About the month of November 1761, began to assemble a Set of people, in the County of Limerick and Kingdom of Ireland who under the favor of the night, formed themselves into bodies all disguised by wearing white Shirts, Sheets, or white Waistcoats, over their common cloathes, something White over their hats which on occasion would likewise cover their faces, and white Cockades. From thence Sometime before Christmas, they extended into the County of Tipperary, Thence to the County of Cork, and about the 2d or 3d Week in January 1762, began to give proofs of their having entered into the Same Scheme in the Western part of the County of Waterford, to the transactions in which County the following narrative will be confined.

Their pretence for meeting was to redress the grievances imposed upon the poor (as they termed it) by the Commons being inclosed. At first they Executed their designs by levelling fences in the most private manner, in the dead time of the night, and at the places most remote from Towns, but finding their numbers increase, their oath of secrecy inviolably observed, and their persons thereby Secured from discovery, they quickly began to enlarge their designs, by declaring that no one Should presume to take any lands that were out of lease, until they had laid Waste for three years.

That no one Should give, or Set out, or take any Tithes under the penalty of death or destruction, that they would punish in the Severest Manner, any person who should presume to Speak in the least disrespectfully of their Queen Sive Oultagh, her children, or their Midnight operations, or any proprietor of the Lands thrown open, that Should attempt to impound any cattle found there, or should repair any of the levelled fences.

They established councils at Stated places, where a president, Secretary and Members, considered of Everything relative to her Majesty Queen Sive's interests, received petitions, gave answers to them, issued out menacing letters to creditors not to demand their just debts, to some Landlords to remit their Rents, to others to restore cattle &c, many years since distrained and Sold for rent, to some people to give up their Farms. Others to desist from taking any, though destitute of a place at the approaching Lady day to carry their families to. The Council summoneth persons, Swore them to secrecy, and allegiance to the Sovereign Queen Sive Oultagh, issued orders in her Royal Highness's name, for all operations where fences should be levelled, where Orchards Should be torn up, rooted out and destroyed, where timber trees Should be cut down, what houses Should be burned, or thrown down, what corn mills and public Pounds Should be demolished, What persons Should be taken out of their beds at midnight, and carried to a distance from home naked, upon thorns and Briars, upon a kind of hand-barrow and there buried alive in Graves dug on purpose, and erected gallows in many places to hang people on; and this in the severest cold on the winter nights.

From these Councils issued Menacing letters on all occasions among others to all inhabitants of every rank to send their horses, ready saddled and bridled, on mentioned nights to appointed places to carry her Majesty and her Children through such parts of her dominions as she should deem necessary to be visited by her highness. Thus from their first operation of levelling a ditch in the Western part of Waterford County, which happened early in January to the latter end of February, they proceeded very successfully, levelling ditches in all the western parts, every Monday, Wednesday, & Friday nights, without interruption of discovery, Those being the nights fixed on in each Week by their leaders to assemble. For now the party was grown So Strong, and so concerted by Oaths of Secrecy and Allegiance, that no magistrate could possibly get any intelligence, or if he did he could get no assistance. People of all ranks were so threatened and terrified. The very secrets of every protestant family were Constantly discovered by some of their Servants, all or most in every house being sworn to Secrecy and allegiance to Queen Sive, and that they would discover Everything that Should come to their knowledge, in the least relative to her Highness or adherents.

They now began to be so audacious as to march at nights with music playing disaffected and treasonable tunes, give regular orders of command, draw up in form and fire Shots, particularly in the night of Monday the 1st of March. A large body of those rioters, forced in the door of the protestant parish clerk of the Church of Affane, took him out of bed, and in his Shirt placed him upon thorns, on a kind of hand-barrow, which breaking disappointed this project so far. However they forced him naked along

with them to the town of Cappoquin about two English miles, having in the road greatly added to the Terror he was already in by digging a grave, and threatening to bury him alive; When at Cappoquin they dismissed him almost dead with cold and fear. They then entered the Town in Triumph with pipers and Fidlers playing disaffected tunes, drew up in an open part of the Town, Fired Several Shots, paraded up and down the Streets, Went to the Barracks gates in the most insulting manner, Shouting, and huzzaing, where a troop of Dragoons were there quartered (who gave them no molestation, having at that time no orders from the Government) and then dispersed in the most triumphant manner.

This success encouraged them to that degree, as to throw off almost all restraint, to meet in very numerous bodies early in the evenings, to make public reports of their intended rendezvous, to commit ravages in many different places in the same night, To Speak very Slightly of his Majesty's Troops, To threaten any who should make complaint, and the Magistrates that would dare to receive any or encourage any discoveries, with the cruellest tortures and punishments imaginable; They now began to Shew the utmost insolence towards the protestants in the Towns of Cappoquin, Lismore and Tallow, and in the Country adjoining, and having almost wore out their own horses, and themselves in these long continued midnight Violences, they now issued out menacing letters, to the protestant gentlemen and others, demanding their horses to be sent to appointed places, ready saddled and bridled for the use of Queen Sive and her Majesty's children and wearied Troops, as they termed them, going to visit her royal Highness's dominions.

MÁIRE BHUIDHE NÍ LAOGHAIRE

(1774–*c.* 1849)

AR LEACAIN NA GRÉINE
(On the Sunny Slopes) (*c.* 1796)

[This *aisling* was composed by Cork poet Máire Bhuidhe Ní Laoghaire in the aftermath of the French attempt to

provide military aid to the United Irishmen in December 1796. The French fleet, under General Hoche, set out for Ireland on 14 December but was scattered due to violent weather off the Bantry coast. Those vessels which did land were forced to return to France on 28 December. The reference to Louis XVI in the penultimate stanza exposes the limitations of the traditional *aisling* form as a vehicle for republican ideals. The song carries a message of hope, however, and is particularly interesting in its depiction of a social vision which includes the popular ideals of land 'without rent, without tax or dispute'. The text is from: Donncha Ó Donnchú (ed.), *Filíocht Mháire Bhuidhe Ní Laoghaire* (Baile Átha Cliath: Oifig an tSoláthair, 1933), pp. 37–9. The translation is from: Brian Brennan, *Máire Bhuí Ní Laoire: A Poet of Her People* (Cork: Collins Press, 2000), pp. 55, 57.

Ar leacain na gréine indé
  is mé ag múscailt mo bhó
'Seadh dhearcas-sa lem thaobh
  an spéirbhean mhodhmhail mhúinte dheas óg
Do bhí lasadh na gcaor 'na gné
  agus a gnúis mar an rós,
Agus a cúl carnfholt péarlach léi
  go dúnaibh a bróg.

Níor dhanaid liom féin teacht fé n-a déin
  le n-a fáilte is le n-a póig
Ach ar eagla nárbh aon bhean tsaoghalta
  a thárlaidh im threo,
Níorbh aithnid liom féin dá mhéid é
  a trácht insa chóig
Ach a pearsa agus a méinn
  a scéimh, a cáil, is a clódh.

Is 'na haice siúd do shuidheas
  is do luigheas ar phlámaireacht léi
Is is gairid arís gur shaoileas
  bheith páirteach seal léi.
'Má taoi tuirseach ón tslighe dein moill
  is go lá tar liom féin
Is gheobhair leabaidh nách tuighe ar feadh mí
  má's áil leat gabháil léi.'

'Tá magadh ort, a mhaoin,' adubhairt sí,
  'is ní hádhbhar duit mé,
Agus ná feadar cá luigheann
  do thigheas ná t'áitreabh féin;
Mar caithfead dul síos go híochtar
  Clár Luirc lem scéal
Go bhfeaca-sa an Fleet i bhFaoide
  'na lánchumas tréan.

'A mhascalaigh mhín thar an bhFleet
  ná trácht liom go héag,
Mar is le hanacra do chím-se na mílte
  i ngátar 'na déidh;

Tháinig scaipeadh ortha ón ngaoith fóríor!
  chuir a lán aca ar strae
Agus i nglasaibh 'seadh do shuidhid
  mar an ríghbhean seo thárlaidh i gcéin.

'Gach duine aca chífir mínigh dóibh
  brigh mo scéil,
Go bhfuilid ag tíocht go buidheanmhar
  fí ghrán is fí philéar –
Gearrthacaigh ghroidhe an Laoiseach,
  san Spáinneach dá réir,
Go Banba ag tíocht gan mhoill
  le grásta Mhic Dé.'

'Go deimhin má's fíor do laoithe,
  a stáidbhruinneal shéimh,
Beidh talamh gan chíos gan íoc
  gan cháin is gan phléidhe
Beidh cruithneacht is im is saill
  ar an gclár againn féin,
Agus gasra an ghrinn ag díogadh
  na gcárt agus dá nglaodhach.'

TRANSLATION

On a sunny hillside yesterday, as I was walking
  my cows,
A fair lady I saw, modest, well-mannered,
  comely and young.
The blush of berries was on her face, and her
  countenance like the rose,
And her abundant tresses flowed down to the
  clasps of her shoes.

I would gladly have come over to her to
  welcome her with a kiss,
But I feared she might be some ethereal woman
  who had happened my way.
I did not recognise her despite all that was said
  in the Province about her —
Her person, her visage, her beauty, her fame
  and her form.

I sat down beside her and started to flatter her.
And, again, soon after, I thought of sharing
  friendship with her:
'If you're tired from travelling, stop off and
  come with me for the day.
And you'll get a bed — not a straw one — for a
  month, if you wish it that way.'

'You are jesting, my dear,' said she. 'And you
    have no cause to do so with me,
Seeing that I do not know where lies your home
    or your habitation.
For I must go to the North of Lorc's Plain[1] with
    the news
That I have seen the Fleet in Whiddy[2] equipped
    in full power.'

'O gentle, strong one of the Fleet, do not speak
    to me till I die.
For it pains me to see the thousands that are
    distressed in its wake.
They were scattered, alas, by the wind which
    sent many of them astray.

1. Lorc's Plain is a poetic name for Ireland; Lorc was an ancestor of
    the Leinster people.
2. Whiddy Island is in Bantry Bay, County Cork.

And in shackles they sit, as happened to the
    regal lady far away.'

'Each one that you see, explain to them the gist
    of the news
That in full strength they are coming, well-
    supplied with bullets and shot —
Stout-hearted supporters, hastening, Louis, and
    the Spaniard complying —
To Banba they are coming, without delay, by
    the grace of God's son.'

'Indeed, if your descriptions are true, my stately,
    gentle maiden,
We shall have land without rent, without tax or
    dispute.
We shall have wheat and butter and salted meat
    on the table for ourselves.
And merrymakers will be draining the quarts,
    and calling for more.'

ANONYMOUS

POOR OLD GRANUAILE
(1870s)

[In this *aisling*-type ballad, Gráinne Mhaol (Granuaile)
appears as a nationalist icon dressed in green and bearing
a harp. While presented as a beautiful young woman, the
'Shan Van Vocht' theme is evoked in the references to 'poor
old Granuaile', who in this instance plays patriotic tunes
and predicts the achievement of Home Rule. The text is
from: Georges-Denis Zimmerman (ed.), *Songs of Irish
Rebellion* (Dublin: Allen Figgis, 1967), p. 182.]

My dream to some comes true, and comes with
    grief no more,
As it did to me, my country, that dear old Erin's
    shore.
I dreamt I was upon a hill beside a lovely vale,
And it's there I spied a comely maid and her
    name was Granuaile.

Her lovely hair hung down her neck as she was
    dressed in green,
I thought she was the fairest soul that e'er my
    eyes had seen;

As I drew near I then could hear by the pleasant
    morning gale,
As she went along she sang her song, saying I'm
    poor old Granuaile.

In O'Connell's time, in '29,[1] we had no braver
    men,
They struggled hard both day and night to gain
    our rights again;
Still, by coercion we were bound and our sons
    were sent to jail,
You need not fret, we'll Home Rule get, says
    poor old Granuaile.

I thought she had a splendid harp, by her side
    she let it fall,
She played the tunes called 'Brian Boru',
    'Garryowen', and 'Tara's Hall'.
Then 'God Save Ireland' was the next, and 'Our
    Martyrs who died in Jail',
You need not fret, we'll have Home Rule yet,
    says poor old Granuaile.

1. i.e. 1829, the year of Catholic emancipation.

When I awakened from my slumber and excited by my sight,
I thought it was the clear daylight, and I found it was night,

I looked all around and could not see but the walls of a lonely jail,
And that was the last I've seen of poor old Granuaile.

PATRICK PEARSE

(1879–1916)

FORNOCHT DO CHONAC THÚ
(Renunciation)
(1912)

[This poem is one of Pearse's best-known works, and was first published in 1912. Though obviously indebted to the *aisling* tradition, and in particular to Aogán Ó Rathaille's 'Gile na Gile' (see pp. 279–81), the poem subverts that tradition by proclaiming the revolutionary's compulsion to renounce that very vision of freedom, in all its beauty, which has been his inspiration. The Irish text is from: Ciarán Ó Coigligh (ed.), *Filíocht Ghaeilge Phádraig Mhic Phiarais* (Baile Átha Cliath: An Clóchomhar, 1981), p. 35; the translation, by Pearse himself, is from: Desmond Ryan (ed.), *The 1916 Poets* (Dublin: Allen Figgis, 1963), p. 18.]

Fornocht do chonac thú,
A áille na háille,
Is do dhallas mo shúil
Ar eagla go stánfainn.

Do chualas do cheol,
A bhinne na binne,
Is do dhúnas mo chluas
Ar eagla go gclisfinn.

Do bhlaiseas do bhéal,
A mhilse na milse,
Is do chruas mo chroí
Ar eagla mo mhillte.

Do dhallas mo shúil
Is mo chluas do dhúnas,
Do chruas mo chroí
Is mo mhian do mhúchas;

Do thugas mo chúl
Ar an aisling do chumas,

'S ar an ród seo romham
M'aghaidh do thugas.

Do thugas mo ghnúis
Ar an ród seo romham,
Ar an ngníomh do-chím,
'S ar an mbás do-gheobhad.

TRANSLATION

Naked I saw thee,
O beauty of beauty,
And I blinded my eyes
For fear I should fail.

I heard thy music,
O melody of melody,
And I closed my ears
For fear I should falter.

I tasted thy mouth,
O sweetness of sweetness,
And I hardened my heart
For fear of my slaying.

I blinded my eyes,
And I closed my ears,
I hardened my heart
And I smothered my desire.

I turned my back
On the vision I had shaped,
And to this road before me
I turned my face.

I have turned my face
To this road before me,
To the deed that I see
And the death I shall die.

Biographies/Bibliographies

Gofraidh Fionn Ó Dálaigh

LIFE. Gofraidh Fionn Ó Dálaigh, of Duhallow, County Cork, was one of the most important professional poets of fourteenth-century Ireland. His principal patrons were the McCarthys of Desmond, the O'Briens of Thomond and the Earls of Desmond. He is referred to by poets of later ages as a model composer, and the grammarians cite his opinions on syntax. He died in 1387.

Gofraidh Fionn's best-known poem is probably 'Filidh Éirionn go Haointeach' in praise of a Connacht chieftain Uilliam Ó Ceallaigh. His ironic lines depicting the professional poet's role in the colonial period are frequently cited: 'I ndán na nGall gealltar linn / Gaoidhil d'ionnarba a hÉirinn;/ Goill do shraoineadh tar sál soir / i ndán na nGaoidheal gealltair', 'In poetry for the Foreigners we promise to expel the Gaels from Ireland; in poetry for the Gaels, it is promised to drive the Foreigners over the sea eastwards' (for text see *Dioghluim Dána*, pp. 201–6, at 206). Also well known is his moving lament for his son (for text see: *Dioghluim Dána*, pp. 196–9).

CHIEF WRITINGS. Eleanor Knott 'Filidh Éirionn go Haointeach', *Ériu*, vol. 5 (1911), pp. 50–69; Osborn Bergin (ed.), *Irish Bardic Poetry* (Dublin: Dublin Institute for Advanced Studies, 1970), pp. 66–81; Láimhbheartach Mac Cionnaith (ed.), *Dioghluim Dána* (Baile Átha Cliath: Oifig an tSoláthair, 1938), pp. 109–13 (see also pp. 321–4), 192–206, 228–35, 274–83, 296–301, 321–5, 330–4, 338–44, 355–9, 400–2; Lambert McKenna (ed.), *Aithdioghluim Dána* (Dublin: Irish Texts Society, 1939), pp. 262–6.

BIOGRAPHY AND CRITICISM. No full biography exists. See Aodh de Blácam, *Gaelic Literature Surveyed* (Dublin: Talbot Press, 1973), pp. 118–19; J.E. Caerwyn Williams and Máirín Ní Mhuiríosa, *Traidisiún Liteartha na nGael* (Baile Átha Cliath: An Clóchomhar, 1979), pp. 160, 165, 174, 189, 190.

Brian Mac Giolla Phádraig

LIFE. Born *c*. 1580, grandson of Brian Mac Giolla Phádraig (d. 1575), first Baron of Ossory. He was ordained in 1610 and left the country for a period in 1615. He was appointed Vicar General and Vicar Apostolic of the Diocese of Ossory *c*. 1651, but was murdered soon afterwards by Cromwellian supporters. Eight of his poems survive, a long religious poem 'Psaltair na Rann' and seven short poems, mainly on political themes.

CHIEF WRITINGS. Cuthbert Mhág Craith, 'Brian Mac Giolla Phádraig', *Celtica*, vol. 4 (1958), pp. 103–205; Thomas F. O'Rahilly (ed.), *Measgra Dánta*, vol. 2 (Cork: Cló Ollscoile Chorcaí, 1977), pp. 136–9; Pádraig de Brún, Breandán Ó Buachalla, Tomás Ó Concheanainn (eds), *Nua-Dhuanaire*, vol. 1 (Dublin: Dublin Institute for Advanced Studies, 1971), pp. 10–11; R. Mac Cionnaith, 'Sagart maith cct.: amhráin Bhriain Mhic Giolla Phádraig', *Irisleabhar Muighe Nuadhat* (1955), pp. 75–9.

BIOGRAPHY AND CRITICISM. No full biography exists. See preceding references for biographical information.

Séathrún Céitinn (Geoffrey Keating)

For biography and bibliography, see Volume I, p. 272, and Volume IV, p. 249.

Aogán Ó Rathaille

For biography, see Volume I, p. 325.

CHIEF WRITINGS. Patrick S. Dinneen and Tadhg Ó Donoghue (eds), *Dánta Aodhagáin Uí Rathaille*, Irish Texts Society Volume 3 (London: Irish Texts Society, 1911).

BIOGRAPHY AND CRITICISM. Dineen and O'Donoghue, *op. cit.*; Seán Ó Tuama, *Filí faoi Sceimhle* (Baile Átha Cliath: An Gúm, 1978); Seán Ó Tuama, 'The World of Aogán Ó Rathaille', in *Idem.*, *Repossessions: Selected Essays on Irish Literary Heritage* (Cork: Cork University Press, 1995), pp. 101–18; Breandán Ó Buachalla, 'Ó Rathaille, na Cárthaigh agus na Brúnaigh', *Studia Hibernica*, vol. 31 (2000–1), pp. 119–38.

Seán Clárach Mac Domhnaill

LIFE. Born in 1691 near Charleville, County Cork, Mac Domhnaill was a poet, scribe and teacher who could read Latin and Greek and who had a detailed knowledge of contemporary national and international affairs. He was one of the most prominent members of the well-known poetic fraternity associated with the eighteenth-century Munster courts of poetry, and was an ardent supporter of the Jacobite cause. Best known for his Jacobite poetry and for his satire on the infamous Tipperary landlord Colonel James Dawson (d. 1737). He died in 1754.

CHIEF WRITINGS. Risteárd Ó Foghludha (ed.), *Seán Clárach* (Baile Átha Cliath: Oifig an tSoláthair, 1934); John Daly (ed.), *Reliques of Irish Jacobite Poetry* (Dublin: Samuel J. Machen, 1844), pp. 4–39; James Hardiman (ed.), *Irish Minstrelsy*, vol. 2 (London: Joseph Robins, 1831), pp. 64–76, 140–7.

BIOGRAPHY AND CRITICISM. See the three aforementioned works, *passim*.

Máire Bhuidhe Ní Laoghaire

LIFE. Born in Tureenanane in County Cork in 1774, Máire Bhuidhe Ní Laoghaire spent most of her life in Inchimore beside Keimaneigh, where she and her husband Seán de Búrca worked a 150-acre farm and raised nine children. Though they were reasonably well-off for most of their lives, they lost much of their wealth in later years, and suffered greatly during the Great Famine. Máire Bhuí died *c*. 1849.

Máire Bhuidhe Ní Laoghaire is best known for her political poetry. She adapted the *aisling* form to treat of contemporary affairs and her most famous work 'Cath Chéim an Fhia' (The Battle of Keimaneigh) describes the events of 1822 when a fight broke out between members of the Muskerry Yeomanry and a group of local Whiteboys. Máire Bhuí was illiterate but her poetry survived in the oral tradition until it was collected in the late nineteenth century.

CHIEF WRITINGS. Donncha Ó Donnchú (ed.), *Filíocht Mháire Bhuidhe Ní Laoghaire* (Baile Átha Cliath: Oifig an tSoláthair, 1933); Brian Brennan (ed.), *Máire Bhuí Ní Laoire: A Poet of Her People* (Cork: Collins Press, 2000).

BIOGRAPHY AND CRITICISM. Ó Donnchú, *Filíocht Mháire Bhuidhe Ní Laoghaire*, pp. 5–36; Brennan, *Máire Bhuí Ní Laoire: A Poet of Her People*, pp. v–viii, 1–53.

Patrick Pearse

For biography and bibliography, see Volume III, p. 932.

MÁIRÍN NÍ DHONNCHADHA, *Editor*

Courts and Coteries I,
900–1600

Female poets associated primarily with a monastic context have been encountered in the earlier selections — Digde and Líadan of the Corco Duibne, for example, or the widowed Queen Gormlaith, all of whom who are reputed to have spent much of their lives in nunneries or monasteries in retirement from the world (pp. 111–18, 133–9). The present selection and the two which follow it form a kind of triptych on the theme of women's interaction with secular poets and scholars in Gaelic Ireland, and their occasional appearances among their ranks. The three selections together draw on nine hundred years of Gaelic writing. Throughout this time, women were usually the subjects rather than the authors of texts. A broad survey of tradition raises questions as to why almost all of the small minority of women who were literate have left no written legacy. One might put this more positively and say that one is reminded that literary tradition belonged to women not just in right of authorship: they were also readers and auditors, recipients and patrons of all kinds of writing. They were arbiters of taste in praise-poems, love-poems, religious manuals and fictional tales, and they had influence on medical texts, obituary notices and other written forms. The following three selections of texts concerning women, addressed to women, or authored by women attempt to map a path through Gaelic tradition which will give something of its due honour to their contribution.

The selection of texts titled 'Irish Medical Writing 1400–1600' comes between 'Courts and Coteries I, 900–1600' and 'Courts and Coteries II, 1500–1800'. Irish physicians travelled to the emerging European centres of medicine at

places like Salerno and Montpellier from at least as early as the opening decades of the fourteenth century. The tradition of Irish translations and adaptations of the 'new' medicine (which was in fact the rediscovered classical Greek and Roman medicine, modified by an accretion of Arabic medicine and other influences) also dates back to the fourteenth century. The current view of scholarship is that contemporary Irishwomen had little or no access either to the native schools or the British and continental schools of medicine, although they were skilled at midwifery and some aspects of healing and herbal medicine: the *bean chabhartha* 'midwife' and *bean feasa* 'wise woman' were indispensable and honoured members of the community.

Exclusion from professional medicine does not mean that the profession's texts were not of interest to women. For one thing, the physician's authority for diagnosing and treating women's complaints derived partly from his supposed acquaintance with these texts, whatever the limits of their utility. The intimate encounter between doctor and patient might be a point of transfer for even the most arcane information. Less arcane information was not necessarily less interesting: it is easy to imagine that many female patients would have been willingly regaled with the views of Magninus of Milan on the best conditions for conception, the benefits of breastfeeding, and the character and physique of the ideal wet-nurse (pp. 350–2). The resonances of medical discourse in other kinds of writing contributed to its accessibility. To cite the most obvious example, the symptoms of *amor hereos* 'obsessive love', as described by Bernard of Gordon (pp. 353–3), are continuous both with those described in Old Irish tales about lovesickness (Volume 1, pp. 18–9, pp. 26–9, and cf. pp. 169–70 and those in courtly love-lyrics (*dánta grádha*) of the sixteenth century and later. A broad sample of these love-lyrics is found in 'Courts and Coteries II'.

An extensive sample from the Irish annals appears on pp. 332–40. Of monastic origin, many annalistic compilations are continued down into the early modern period when Gaelic learning was dominated by seculars. More necrologies than chronicles, they stand in close relationship to praise-poetry. Elegy was a fundamental aspect of the panegyric code, as was the idea that a person's fame had to be voiced and heard. The annalists commemorate the dead silently but use ideas and terms that would have been familiar from bardic praise-poems. The adulatory tone they take towards Gaelic Irishwomen counterbalances the attitudes expressed in early modern tracts written by Old English and New English writers. These range from the ambivalent — as in Richard Stanihurst's 'Description of Ireland', first published in 1577 — to the flagrantly misogynistic — as in Barnaby Rich's *A New Descriptione of Ireland* (1610). The annals are also rich in kinds of information not found in these tracts, whose authors were ideologically predisposed to a narrow focus of enquiry. One point on which annals and tracts agree is that the wives of nobles in early modern Gaelic Ireland had considerable political and social influence (cf. pp. 6–12).

The end-date of 1600 for 'Courts and Coteries I' derives from the fact that the last compilation of Irish annals dates from the seventeenth century, but 'Courts and Coteries II' returns to 1500 for its starting point. The popular view that the Nine Years War (1593–1603) and its aftermath effected one of the most significant transitions in Gaelic literary history is dangerously simplistic. The so-called Flight of the Earls (all two of them) and their followers in 1607 did not entail the withdrawal of the top layer of aristocratic patrons from Ireland, nor lead to the sudden collapse of the bardic order and the rapid ascendancy of poetry in stress metres, liberated from the officious formality which is often seen as characteristic of the poets of the Early Modern Irish period (this linguistic period is usually dated from 1200 to 1600). For one thing, Gaelic

poets as a group had been severely oppressed under the Tudors from the outset of their conquest of Ireland, a conquest that was avowedly cultural as well as territorial; in fact, Elizabeth I showed a more positive attitude to Gaelic language than her predecessors. The main implication of choosing 1500 as a starting point for 'Courts and Coteries II' is that significant changes in literary culture were well in train before the mid-sixteenth century.

It is often said that poetry in Early Modern Irish represents a remarkably sterile phase in Gaelic tradition. True, the Church Reformists of the eleventh and twelfth centuries helped drive a wedge between Latin and native learning, and the Anglo-Normans plundered and demolished many of the great monastic centres. When Gaelic literature needed a new home, it found it in secular schools with a much narrower remit than the monastic ones. The poetic tradition of these schools was unquestionably conservative, but one may get a better sense of tradition as perceived by the poets themselves by not corralling the poetry in a time-frame which separates it from earlier tradition. The date 1200 is as spurious a starting point as 1600. This selection begins in the tenth century, with the earliest known poem in Gaelic tradition composed for an identified historical woman. It is a poem of consolation which a Connacht poet, Irard mac Coisse, addressed to Der Fáil on the death of her son, Áed, in 956 or thereabouts (pp. 305–7).

The idea of the 'ancestral stair' is fundamental to eulogy. These lines from a poem for a Leinster king named Áed, probably dating from the ninth century, put it well:

Oc cormaim gaibtir dúana,
drengaitir dreppa dáena,
arbeitet bairtni bindi
tri laithlinni ainm nÁeda.

At the ale-feast poems are chanted,
human stairs are climbed,
tuneful bardisms modulate
through ale-pools Áed's name.[1]

The patrons' genealogical ladders were propped against another frame, that of literary

---

1. Translations are by the present writer, unless otherwise stated.

tradition. The later poets echo, paraphrase and quote earlier ones extensively, making a dense interweave of medieval and early modern allusions. Even in its attenuated form, the tradition still preserves traces of this intricacy. For example, nearly five hundred years after the death of the son of Der Fáil, Queen of Tara, a Connacht poet attempting to console another royal mother who had lost a son invoked the poem written for Der Fáil, calling tradition and the generations of grieving mothers to his aid (pp. 326–9).

Even when the links with earlier literature are not explicit as in this case, one can sense a poem's rootedness in tradition. Another consolatory poem, possibly by Cathal MacMhuirich (*fl.* 1625), for Séonóid, daughter of Kenneth, 1st Lord MacKenzie of Kintail in Scotland, on the death of her daughter, Caitir Fhíona (*A Sheónóid méadaigh meanma*), sets up an echo from a different country and from the latter end of the period usually described as bardic. The work of the professional bards resounds also in poems written much later than this and some of these later poems are very revealing of the place of women in the tradition, in terms alike of what the poetry meant to women and of what kinds of work were written for them.

For example, 'Courts and Coteries II' includes a genethliacon which Seán de hÓra wrote to celebrate the birth of Séarlas, son of Isibéal Ní Bhriain and her husband, Somhairle Mac Domhnaill, in 1736 (pp. 432–3). The birth of a child was an obvious occasion to quicken a poet's impulse to honour the lord's wife, especially if she herself was an important patron. A poem by Seán Ó Gadhra (*fl.* 1722) has an interesting list of the kinds of poems a professional was expected to produce: the genethliacon, the praise-poem, the settlement-poem, the love-poem, the historical poem, and the elegy (*duain leanbaidheacht, duain mholta, duain reidhte,/duain chumainn, duain tseanchais gan chlaenadh / . . . is marbhna tar aimsir an éaga*).[2] Yet the earliest known example of a genethliacon dates back no further than the seventeenth century: it was composed by Eoghan Ruadh Mac an Bhaird on the birth of a son to Brighid, daughter of Éinrí

Mac Gearailt, and Rudhraighe Ó Domhnaill, in Autumn 1606. As Brighid is the reputed author of a poem that still survives and as Rudhraighe is said to have been a good critic of poetry (pp. 384–9), this couple may have been the ideal recipients of a genethliacon.

Examples of all the categories listed by Ó Gadhra are found among the poems composed for women during the bardic period as traditionally dated, with the possible exceptions of the *duain tseanchais* and the *duain chumainn*. When all the extant bardic poems are published, these too may be represented. One can only speculate as to what Ó Gadhra meant by *duain chumainn*, a term which may be translated loosely as 'love-poem'. It may have encompassed poems such as the amorously complimentary address below to Fionnghuala, daughter of Maghnus Ó Conchobhair (pp. 311–16). If it referred to an epithalamium on the patron's marriage, then again one has to go outside the period of 1200–1600 to find examples. The epithilamion for Vailintín Brún and Onóra Butler by Aogán Ó Rathaille is included in 'Courts and Coteries II' as a possible late version of the traditional type (pp. 430–2).

Poems for women constitute a very small part of the surviving body of bardic poems: it has been estimated that there are some two thousand poems from the period 1200–1600, of which just over half are formal addresses to earthly patrons. What the actual balance was between the numbers of compositions for men and for women is not at all clear, but their function as rulers probably ensured that men always received the larger share. For the same reason, poems for men are likely to be disproportionately represented among the survivals. The *duanaire* (an anthology of poems), comprising a manuscript or part thereof, is a common location for them. There were various kinds of *duanaire*. The function of one important kind was to honour the different generations of a single ruling family, and the focus in such a case would obviously have been on those who ruled — the men. Nevertheless, even this kind of *duanaire* is likely to contain a sprinkling of poems about the lords' wives, daughters and other female relations, poems which confound traditional impressions of bardic eulogy. To read these is to find a world that is not dominated by the masculinist concerns of warfare and kingship. One of the poems below is

---

2. See Pádraig A. Breatnach, 'Dhá Dhuain Leanbaíochta', *Éigse*, vol. 22 (1987), pp. 111–23 at p. 111.

from the fourteenth-century Mág Shamhradháin family *duanaire*. It is a eulogy for Sadhbh, wife of Niall Mág Shamhradháin, and Niall himself (pp. 316–21). Two other poems in the same *duanaire* which concern Sadhbh alone seem to have been written while she was married to an earlier husband, an Ó Ruairc. Their inclusion in the Mág Shamhradháin *duanaire* suggests she significantly influenced its compilation. As it happens, the eulogy for herself and Niall turns on the complementary nature of their roles in lordship.

The centre of civility in medieval and early modern Ireland was the royal or aristocratic house. In Irish, this went by many terms. The terms *caisléan* 'castle' and *cúirt* 'court' are not those commonly used but the enclosed space did function as a court in the sense of a place identified with civility and culture as opposed to wildness and nature. Since Ireland had a network of such 'courts', cultural definition was more low-key than would be the case with a single centralized court.[3] The house was associated with order, feasts, alms-giving, poetry, music, reading, religious observance, luxury, beautiful objects. In Gaeldom, however, culture was simultaneously identified with a world outdoors, or rather with focal cultural sites on the landscape, chief of which was the *tulach tionóil* 'hill of gathering, assembly site'. Hallowed by long use as the site of royal inauguration-rites at which the lord's poet or a leading ecclesiastic or an overlord presided, the *tulach tionóil* also witnessed legal courts at which the lord's *breitheamh* 'brehon, judge' made pronouncements. Some of these hillside assemblies were attended by both men and women, but the inauguration rites in particular seem to have entailed a gathering that was predominantly, and sometimes exclusively, male. Considered as a Christian site, the *tulach tionóil* called to mind Psalms 2:6: 'Yet have I set my king upon my holy hill of Zion'. As a result of all its associations with men, it was possible to view the assembly site as a male space and the lord's body could itself be figured as an assembly site. Addressing his patron, Aodh Mág Uidhir, Eochaidh Ó hEodhasa (?1560–1612) said: 'Of you alone have

the poets of Ireland made a gathering-mound' (*ráth aonaigh*). A poem in Early Modern Irish on Alexander the Great describes him as 'Zion towering over every mountain' (*Sliabh Sion-óin ós gach sliabh slán*).

On the other hand, poems occasionally personify the castle or house as a woman, and it is characterized as the domain in which it was appropriate for women to excel. Of course, most women in bardic poems are wives, and marriage also brings their husbands into association with the house. The chief's poet passed freely between the two domains. The fact that the public recital of his poems occurred in the house was obviously an additional impetus to bestow lavish praise on this space. Yet within it, his bond with a male homosocial world might also be reasserted.

The gendering of the bond between the poet and his male patron calls for comment here as it has a potential bearing on his relationship with his female patron and the ways in which the latter is represented. Although this gender issue has been discussed frequently, its interpretation remains controversial. The typical bardic poem is one which apostrophizes the lord, or one which slips between apostrophizing him and speaking of him in the third person, to an implicitly intimate audience. Speaking man to man, the poets laid considerable stress on the physical: on the lord's beauty, on his attractiveness to men and women alike, and on the poet's desire to be near him. An unselfconscious association of male beauty, especially in friends, with a desire for closeness is found in Irish literature from an early date. For example, in the earliest recorded letter in Irish, addressed by Finn Úa Gormáin (d. 1160), bishop of Kildare, to Áed mac Crimthainn, abbot of Terryglas, has this quatrain:

Cu cinte duit a Aed amnais
A fhir cosinn aeb ollmais,
Cian gar dom beith it hingnais
Mían dam do bith im comgnais.

O keen Áed, know for sure,
Man of great beauty,
However long I am without you,
My wish is to have you with me.

The beauty of the ruler, the king in the earlier period and the lord in later times, has an added

---

3. See Joep Leerssen, 'Wildness, Wilderness, and Ireland: Medieval and Early-Modern Patterns in the Demarcation of Civility', *Journal of the History of Ideas*, vol. 56 (1995), pp. 25–39.

dimension. Beauty is to be expected in the ruler who is bridegroom to the sovereignty goddess; the rites of sacral marriage are a form of legitimation based on heterosexual symbolism. Another kind of legitimation is associated with the idea of the ruler's bodily integrity: in his integrity he embodies *all*, a totality which may be seen to incorporate male and female, for example. But the fetishization of the king's or lord's beauty in bardic poetry need not be referred to a heterosexual frame of reference, as many have suggested. It can be seen as a form of male homosocial bonding which in asserting men's right to rule acts to reinforce the patriarchal order. 'Lord, you are beautiful!' can mean 'Lord, *we* are beautiful, and fit to rule'. At any rate, the fetishization of male beauty is commonplace in bardic poetry. This is how Muireadhach Albanach Ó Dálaigh, writing sometime between 1213 and 1224, speaks of Cathal Croibhdhearg Ó Conchobhair, King of Connacht:

Ionar corcra mar chaoir nduinn
matal sgarlóid, sgiamh ndíoghainn,
is léini chaol mar chailc ngil
fá dhá thaobh uí Airt Aoinfhir.

Diobhruigis sgoth a sgingi
uaidh ag imirt fhithchille:
cúl réidhshleamhain tais do theilg
dá bhais mhéirleabhair mhíndeirg.

Súil chochlach uaine aga,
dá bhais mhíne mhérfhada,
is bonn tana saor sleamhain,
mala chaol donn druimleabhair. . . .

A crimson tunic like the red berry,
a scarlet mantle, massy beauty,
and a fine shirt like bright chalk
about the descendant of Art Aoinfhear.

He casts his fine apparel off
while playing chess,
his silky hair he sleeks back
with his smooth-fingered soft-ruddy hand.

A deep-set blue eye he has,
Two smooth long-fingered hands,
A foot slender, noble, smooth,
A brow delicate, dark, long-ridged. . . .

Clearly, the poets came under pressure to see beauty in the most unpromising subjects as their willingness to oblige is occasionally satirized. A fourteenth- or fifteenth-century poet accuses:

Cuirthí urla cruthach caomh
ar éadan mhaol, mór an oil,
cumthaoi d'fhior chriothshúileach cham
go mbí a rosg mall mar an ngloin.

Shapely, lovely hair dreamt up
For a bald pate — it's a disgrace!
A bug-eyed squinter reinvented
So his eye is slow and crystal!

Fetishized beauty is only one aspect of the ruler's aura, which derives mainly from his power over his subjects and draws them to him. In Gaelic culture, the special favour or love bestowed on the poet by the ruler is implicit in terms such as *fear grádha* 'favourite'. It is made explicit in various ways, most obviously by lavish gifts, but also by privileges which are simultaneously tokens: the ceremonial drink from the lord's cup, the public kiss, the right to sleep with the lord. In an anonymous poem addressed to Tomás Mág Shamhradháin (d. 1298), the poet, seeking reconciliation with this lord, says:

Mo bhéal red bhéal tana teann
mar a-déar, a mhala mhall;
teanntar an corp rabhán riom,
a fholt fionn na gcabhán gcam.

Let my mouth be on your delicate firm one
As I say, O stately brow,
Let your white body be pressed to mine,
O fair head of curling ringlets.

An elegy of uncertain authorship for the same lord has these lines:

Anaoibhinn damh fo-dheachta
i n-éagmhais m'fhir aoinleaptha;
gairid liom lámh re hó Cuinn
's a lámh fam chionn n'a cearchuill

Henceforth my life is misery
Without my one bed-fellow;
Too short my time with Conn's scion,
His arm a pillow for my head.

The orthodox interpretation of lines such as these is that they contain an ancient conceit figuring the poet as the lord's wife and the relationship between poet and lord as marriage. The idea of the lord and poet as bed-fellows is certainly pervasive, but if it were a heterosexual conceit, one might expect it to impinge on the representation of the actual marriage of lord and wife, which it does not in fact appear to do. Admittedly, there are numerous clear instances from the sixteenth century of Gaelic poets referring heterosexual conceits of marital and other liaisons to the relationship between themselves and their male patrons (see pp. 365–6). But in this writer's opinion, they represent a departure from tradition, partly under the influence of literature in Latin and English, and this departure coincides with a new ambivalence and self-consciousness in Gaelic culture in regard to homoeroticism. There seems to be no argument against reading all earlier representations of the bond between lord and poet as a male homosocial one, and therefore instinct with the homoerotic possibilities in the spectrum of male affection. Significantly, homoeroticism is not confined to relations between the lord and his professional poet: it is prominent also in the representation of friendship between males who are not bound to each other by formal contract. It is strongly associated with literary types, especially friends who are poets. For example, there are clear hints of homoeroticism in the poems which the amateur poet, Gearóid (Iarla) Mac Gearailt (d. 1398), 3rd Earl of Kildare, wrote for his friend, Diarmaid Mac Carthaigh (for two poems by Mac Gearailt on female subjects see pp. 321–6). And this is how Tadhg Óg Ó hUiginn (d. 1448), in a moving elegy for his elder brother and teacher, begins his description of the break-up of his brother's school:

Anocht sgaoilid na sgola,
leabtha uadha a n-aontomha:
do-ghéna lucht gach leabtha
déra re hucht n-imtheachta.

Tonight the schools break up,
leaving the beds unwed;
all who were bed-fellows
will shed tears at parting.

Behind the metaphor lies the reality of bed-sharing, not only in bardic schools but in the lord's house, as non-native as well as native writers attest. For example, Luke Gearnon, a Limerick resident writing in 1620 of his experience of Irish castles noted: 'Supper being ended, it is at your liberty to sitt up, or to depart to your lodging, you shall have company in both kind. When you come to your chamber, do not expect canopy and curtaynes. It is very well if your bedd content you, and if the company be great, you may happen to be bodkin in the middle'. Depending on the context, a term such as *fear éinleaptha* may have a more precise meaning than 'bedfellow'. In a poem written around 1588, Black Thomas Butler, 10th Earl of Ormond, is described as former *fear éinleaptha* to Edward VI (1537–53). In this instance, it may denote an official status as 'gentleman of the bedchamber'.

It may now be clear that male homosocial bonds and homoeroticism are fundamental to formal bardic poetry in a way that heteroeroticism is not, although the latter can also be invoked to embellish the lord's image and to uphold patriarchal power. Heteroeroticism features centrally only in courtly love-poems (see 'Courts and Coteries II'), and long bardic addresses to young unmarried women. A poem such as that for Fionnghuala, the unmarried daughter of Maghnus Ó Conchobhair, is a kind of next of kin to the courtly lyric (pp. 311–16). In formal addresses to the lord's wife, or to both lord and wife together, suggestions of sexual attraction are remarkably muted: marriage comes across as a decorous and dutiful affair, the spouses beautiful but not exciting passion, the wives quite like their chaste counterparts in the annalistic obituaries (see pp. 332–40). It is all the more striking, then, that quite a few formal bardic poems refer to the lord's attractiveness to women to whom he is not married. If he is single, such poems are likely to refer to nubile noblewomen who would willingly marry him; if he is married, references to high-born women who wish to become his 'secret lovers' (*mná taídhe*), or to 'harlots' whose venality does not diminish their admiration for him, are more common. Without compromising him, it is intimated that the lord's sexual magnetism and energy are extraordinary. Thus, Caitilín Dubh speaks of the many harlots (*iomdha meirdreach*) who keen the death of Diarmaid Ó Briain, while noting that he was not known to love any other man's partner excessively (*nár char bean tar cheart a caoimhthigh*) (pp. 403–5). It seems that acting as pander to their husbands was condoned by at least some of the ladies. For example, a poet writing around 1600 praises Lady Gráinne, wife of Éamonn Butler of Mountgarret, for keeping her menfolk supplied with naked 'merry-arsed' women (*díol méirdreach/bhíos go taobhnocht tónluaimneach*, pp. 382–4). If many poets approved of the lords' amours, seeing them as the prerogative of the nobility — which they may have enjoyed themselves — Counter-Reformation writers and English writers intent on justifying their various reform programmes were indignant. In his *View of the Present State of Ireland*, Edmund Spenser held the professional poet responsible for lordly immorality because his poems celebrated the fact that the lord 'loved not to lye longe woinge of wentches to yeild to him, but where he came he tooke by force the spoyle of other mens love, and left but lamentacion to theire lovers'. On the other hand, Sir John Harington, a distinguished courtier and godson of Elizabeth I whose attitude to the Irish character was far more positive, faulted them for being 'much given to whoredome' but acknowledged that one could find in Ireland excellent examples of 'love and chastyte in matrons'. In the following remarks by Luke Gearnon, it is not clear in what sense he is using 'wench' (probably 'young girl') but there is no doubt about his claims regarding the continence of Irish wives: 'The yong wenches salute you, conferre wth you, drinke wth you w^thout controll. They are not so reserved as the English, yett very honest. Cuckoldry is a thing almost unknowne among the Irish'.

The combined references of insiders and outsiders suggest that the ladies in Gaelic Ireland chose or were expected to remain chaste while the lords might have liaisons with women of lower rank.   Such an arrangement is also coherent with the lords' noted willingness to acknowledge their illegitimate offspring and zeal on the mothers' part for fathering them on the aristocracy (cp. p. 331)

There was more to poetry than eroticism, of whatever kind. Many male patrons were genuinely appreciative of their poets' work and its craft. Eochaidh Ó hEodhasa's high regard for the criticial judgment of his friend, Rudhraighe Ó Domhnaill, is a case in point (p. 384). Some patrons were poets themselves, at a time when to be an amateur meant not to be bound by the straitjacket of *dán díreach*, the stinting metres of the school-trained poets. (Irish *dán* 'poem' is cognate with Latin *donum* 'gift', while *díreach* is an adjective based on *díre* 'honour-price'. Thus the phrase originally meant 'art deserving of honour-price'. By the early modern period, however, the adjective had been assimilated to he homonymic adjective, *díreach* 'straight', and the phrase was generally understood to refer to the poems' 'straight' classical forms). Very little survives of the work of such amateurs as Éamonn Butler, who reputedly made *óglách as* 'amateur poetry' *d'éigsibh Éireann* 'for the poets of Ireland' (pp. 382, 383). The survival of a *duanaire* containing thirty of the poems of Gearóid (Iarla) Mac Gearailt tantalizes with the possibility that non-professional poetry was much less poorly regarded than modern commentators suggest. No *duanaire* of a female poet's work exists, nor is there any record of one, but there are abundant references to women's receptivity to poetry, in a wide variety of forms, not just *dán díreach* and *óglách as* but also *laoi* 'lay', *roscadh* 'speech-poem', and *rann* 'quatrain'. Perhaps women were more open than men to popular forms, or at least more familiar with them, since the house was the most likely site for their performance. Yet the poetic exchange between Brighid, wife of Rudhraighe Ó Domhnaill, and the outstanding poet, Eochaidh Ó hEodhasa, is a salutary warning against typing women as uninterested in high cultural forms.

The sender of the first recorded letter in Irish, which has been referred to above, asked that the *duanaire* of 'mac Lonáin' be forwarded to him. This 'mac Lonáin' is thought to be Flann mac Lonáin (d. 896), a Connacht poet whom the annalists described as the 'Virgil of the Gaels' and 'royal poet of Ireland'. All that remains of his work is a handful of stray quatrains. But Flann mac Lonáin is of interest on account of his mother as well as himself. She is named in various texts as Laitheog Laídech 'Laitheog of the Lays'. A poem supposedly spoken by her (though written long after her time) states that Flann's claim on poetry derived from her. Poetry was a hereditary business and the poets took their maternal connections seriously. A list of writings by another Connacht poet, Irard mac Coisse (d. 990) includes a reference to *Lánlabrad Laídich[e]* 'Láidech's Grandiloquence' immediately after one to *Molta maic Lonáin* 'mac Lonáin's Eulogies'.

One may never know for sure whether Laitheog Laídech hides behind this reference, whether she was a poet of note and, if so, whether she was literate. What can be said is that the secular women most likely to acquire literacy skills in Gaelic Ireland throughout the Middle Ages were those who belonged to, or married into, hereditary learned families. Annalistic obituaries show that daughters of poets and scholars tended to marry their own kind. Did these women go to school, or did they merely meet the scholars coming home? A significant gap in our information concerns the ground-plans of the schools: work on the excavation of the sites of medieval schools is only beginning. One can often tell the townland in which a poet or scribe worked and taught, but not whether his living quarters were part of the school complex, and if so, whether they were off limits to his female relations. Colophons in manuscripts written in the schools generally fall short of giving specific information. This intriguing one is from a legal manuscript written at the O'Davoren law-school at Cathair Mhic Neachtain in the Burren, County Clare: 'My curse, and God's into the bargain, I bestow on the women who have muddled up together all that I possessed in the way of ink, of colours, and of books. God's curse on him too that shall read this and fail to curse them. My God, this is a wretched piece of business!' An account of a prototypical bardic school in a dissertation written in English in 1722 intimates that all the students were male but is unhelpfully vague on the question of the teachers and their families (see Volume I, pp. 972–3).

The wives of one type of poet had the opportunity to play a very influential role in cultural affairs. These were the wives of poets who maintained a *teach oígheadh* (earlier *tech n-oíged*) 'guest-house' in which certain dignitaries and others of lesser rank down to that of the beggar were entitled to receive hospitality. In addition to providing continuous hospitality to visitors, the proprietors of guest-houses — like nobles in general — hosted occasional feasts for invited guests.[4] Some feasts were celebrations exclusively for poets, musicians and scholars. The feast hosted by Mairgréag, daughter of Tadhg Ó Cearbhaill (Margaret O'Carroll), wife of Ó Conchobhair Failghe, at which the names of two thousand and seven hundred guests associated 'with the arts of *dán* or poetry, music and antiquity' were recorded, not counting the 'gamesters and poor men' who also attended, is a spectacular example (Vol. v, pp. 622–3; cp. p. 336). Although the feasts held at poets' guest-houses for the various classes of entertainers were presumably on a smaller scale, they may have counted for more as the true courts for adjudging poetry, in which expert opinion ruled. The use of the term *gairm scoile* 'school invitation' for the summons to these feasts suggests a close link between the guest-houses and the schools of poetry. That the poet's wife might assume a central role in both is suggested by annalistic obituaries such as the one under the year 1427 for Siobhán, wife of Muiris Mac Uidhir, 'one who maintained a guest-house . . . for six and fifty years reputably, humanely [and] charitably', or that under 1524 for Mór, daughter of Ó Briain, 'a woman who kept a general house of hospitality' (p. 336, 338).

A common term for the lady who was hospitable to poets and scholars was *buime na cléire* 'nurse of the clerisy'. Who is to say that none of these women became respected arbiters of poetry? The term *ollamh*, literally 'greatest', was used of poets, historians and other professionally trained men who were regarded as leaders in their field, and often designated the man who had been appointed 'chief poet', 'chief historian', etc., in a particular lordship. Exceptionally, the term *banollamh* 'woman-*ollamh*' is used of Sadhbh, wife of Maoilín Ó Maolchonaire, in her obituary under the year 1447: '*banollamh* of Síol Muireadhaigh and a nurse of all guests and strangers, and of all the learned men in Ireland' (p. 337). What exactly *banollamh* means here is not clear. Her husband, Maoilín Ó Maolchonaire, who predeceased her in 1441, had been *ollamh* of history in Síol Muireadhaigh. At very least, the use of *banollamh* suggests an attempt to honour Sadhbh as the

4. See Katharine Simms, 'Guesting and Feasting in Gaelic Ireland', *Journal of the Royal Society of Antiquaries of Ireland*, vol. 108 (1978), pp. 67–100.

suitably intellectual partner of her historian husband, but a more proactive involvement in scholarship cannot be dismissed since there are examples of *ban-* in compound with *ab* 'abbot' and *airchennach* 'church-superior' in the sense 'abbess' and 'female church-superior'. Perhaps Sadhbh was an outstanding scholar or poet. It is worth recalling the role of Créide in the literary masterpiece, *Acallam na Senórach*: Créide presides over a very fine hostel to which poets are invited, she presumes to judge the poetry of others, and she herself is a fine poet (pp. 229–31).

This Introduction cannot be concluded without some mention of the itinerant classes of poets and entertainers and in fact, the very first text in the following selection concerns a travelling poet, the daughter of úa Dulsaine. Even settled poets who held lands by virtue of their appointment to a particular lord made occasional progresses through the territory, accompanied by a motley retinue (*dám*, later *dámh*) of lesser poets and other kinds of entertainers. When attending great feasts, they often met up with large numbers of itinerant beggars who constituted much of the 'stranger' (*deórad*) element among the party with whom the hosts felt obliged to share their hospitality. Commentators were prone to seeing both kinds of travellers as an undifferentiated group.

There are few sympathetic descriptions of these mixed groups. A stock theme in native Irish writing from earliest times is the material depredations of the visiting poets and their associates. Puritanical churchmen had always abhorred their disorderly, carnivalesque aspect. Officials of the English Crown regarded travelling poets as even greater fomenters of treason than those who stayed at home, and saw all who associated with them as potential spies; these impressions grew ever sharper during the Tudor period.

A fairly vivid picture of the women who were associated with the poets' retinues emerges from a collation of the native and non-native sources. Some of the women were poets, associated particularly with the composition of popular forms such as *amhráin* 'songs' (singular *amhrán*). The earliest extant examples of poems in *amhrán* metres (natural-stress metres) date from the end of the sixteenth century, but the fourteenth-century author of the following quatrains was already complaining of the inroads which these popular forms were making on the traditional entitlements of the makers of *dán díreach*:

> *Is é an t-abhrán ro fhalaigh*
> *a n-éadáil a n-ealadhain;*
> *do sgar an daghdhán re a dhath*
> *abhrán ban agus bhachlach.*
>
> *Le ríoghaibh caigillte an chruidh*
> *nach tabhair treas ar mianaibh*
> *binne an chliar abhrán fholtach*
> *'s an camdhán fiar fíorlochtach.*
>
> *'Siad a nduasa a ndúthaig dáibh*
> *biadh óna mbairdne d'aghbháil;*
> *mór an ceannach ar a gcuid,*
> *ór ná heallach ní iarraid.*

It is *amhrán* that has eclipsed
Their art and entitlement;
The *amhrán* of women and strollers
Has robbed real poetry of its worth.

Princes who are frugal,
Ignoring poets' desires,
Prefer the long-haired band of *amhrán*ers
And crooked faulty *dán*.

For their bardism — just desert —
Their only prize is their rations;
Their wares are in great demand:
They don't seek gold or cattle.

The women associated with *amhráin* and bardism (*bairdne*) are presumably those elsewhere designated *bairdseach* 'female bard' and *bean tsiubhail* 'walking woman'. Historically speaking, the terms 'bard' and 'bardic poetry' are misnomers for professional poets and their high art, although they now have the sanction of long use. In Medieval and Early Modern Irish, *bard* designated a poet with rudimentary training, who may even have been unlettered, and *bairdseach* was the equivalent term for a female. Yet as the preceding quatrains and many other references show, the purveyors of popular art found enthusiastic audiences. The plausible suggestion has been made that Agnes Carkill, 'barde wife', who performed for King James IV of Scotland in 1512 may have been of the Antrim family of Mac Fheargail and may have entertained the king in

Gaelic.[5] The Englishman Thomas Smyth, writing in the sixteenth century, refers to Ireland's 'Mannigscoule' (from Irish *mná siubhail*, plural of *bean tsiubhail*), whose 'order is for to singe' (p. 331). A presentment made by a Cork jury in 1584 which lists seventy-two persons who were living as 'poets, chroniclers, and rhymers' includes 'Mary-ny-Donoghue, a she-barde; and Mary-ny-Clancy, rymer'.

Male entertainers typically associated with a poet's retinue included dice-throwers, jugglers, mimes, actors, drummers, jokers, jesters and harpers. This terminological variety is not found in reference to women, who are mentioned less frequently in this context in any case. The terms most commonly used of female entertainers are *óinseach* 'lamb-like one', *óinmhid* 'lamb-witted one', and *amaid* 'witless one'.

As well as composing their own verse and songs, the lower-grade poets disseminated the more arcane compositions of poets of higher rank. Many of them had phenomenal memories and scribes with ambitions to compile verse collections of one kind or another often had recourse to them. For example, the basis for the sixteenth-century Scottish manuscript-anthology known as the Book of the Dean of Lismore was laid when Fionnlagh Mac an Aba, chief of the Macnabs, gathered material from packmen, and he urged that strolling bards (*lorgánaigh*) be approached for further material.

Accounts of a notable eighteenth-century carrier of poems from one poet to another may be mentioned here. The person in question was named Anna Príor, and she apparently travelled widely in Munster, carrying poems which she had memorized back and forth between some of the leading Gaelic poets, including Seán Ó Murchadha na Ráithíneach (1700–62), Uilliam Inglis (*c.* 1709–78), Séamas Mac Coitir (*fl.c.* 1740) and Nioclás Ó Domhnaill (*c.* 1700–59). She is known only from the poems which were written about her. Some of them describe her as a cross-dresser, while others seem to suggest that she was a hermaphrodite. Gaelic poets of this time were in the habit of sending each other verse salutations which played on the homonymy of

beannacht 'blessing' and *bean nocht* 'naked woman'. One begins to wonder whether Anna Príor really did exist, or was merely a persistent literary fantasy.

The more popular aspect of Gaelic poetic tradition — what may be described in historically accurate terms as 'bardic' — has been extraordinarily long-lived in Scotland and Ireland. The following details are extracted from a letter written to the Englishman John Aubrey (1626–97), author of *Brief Lives*:

A Bard in common Irish signifies a little poet or a rhymer, they used to travel thorow countries and coming into ane house, salute with a rhym called in Irish *Beanacha a baird*, i.e. the Bard's salutation qch is onlie a short verse or rhym touching the praise of the master and mistris of the house. The inferior sort of them are counted amongst the beggers . . .

This inferior sort, otherwise called beggers makes few or no verses or rhyms of their own, but onlie makes use of such as hath been composed by others . . .

He thats extraordinaries sharp of these bards is named *phili* [Irish *file*], i.e. ane excellent poet, these frequent onlie the company of persons of qualitie & each of them hes some particular person whom he owns his master . . . These bards in former times used to travel in companies, sometimes 40, 50, 60 persons between men, wives & childrene . . . The whol caball was called *Chlearheanachi* . . .

The form *Chlearheanachi* is a corruption of *Cliar Sheanchái*, 'Seanchán's Clerisy', the Seanchán in question being one and the same as Senchán Torpéist who appears in the first text in the following selection.

It is to be expected that elements of bardic culture will cross linguistic and territorial boundaries. Presumably the *lorgánaigh* whom Fionnlagh Mac an Aba recommended as informants are cousins to the 'summer walkers' of the modern Scottish north-east. The bards and beggars described by Aubrey were undoubtedly related to the itinerant bards and beggars of seventeenth-century Ireland. Well into the twentieth century, many Irish travellers, both

---

5. Thomas Owen Clancy, 'Women Poets in Early Medieval Ireland: Stating the Case', in *The Fragility of Her Sex*, eds C.E. Meek and M.K. Simms (Dublin: Four Courts Press, 1996), pp. 43–72 at p. 55.

Irish-speaking and English-speaking, used rhymed salutations and were held in high regard as singers, song-makers and musicians. It seems likely to this writer that future research will reveal closer links than are currently recognized between some of the traveller-families of contemporary Ireland and an order of poets that can be traced back to the beginnings of Gaelic history. For 'Storytelling Traditions of the Irish Travellers' see below, pp. 1263–70.

A problematic dimension of the life of some of the *mná siubhail* is highlighted by the representation of Irish mores by one of the protagonists of the Tudor conquest. According to Edmund Spenser, singing was not the chief role of the *bean tsiubhail*, as Thomas Smyth held. His description of the *bean tsiubhail* in *A View of the Present State of Ireland* (1596) is now notorious:

> . . . in summer you shall find her arrayed in her smock and mantle, to be more ready for her light services; in winter and in her travails, it is her cloak and safeguard, and also a cover for her lewd exercise. And when she hath filled herself under it, she can hide both her burden and her blame; yea, and when her bastard is born, it serves instead of swaddling clouts.

There is a category in Smyth's text corresponding to the *bean tsiubhail*: the 'goyng women' who 'are comen to all men; and if any of them happen to be with childe, she will say that it is the greatest Lorde adjoining, whereof the Lordes ar glad, and doth appoincte them to be nurysed' (p. 331). Other English writers of the period might be cited who associated what they saw as the lewdness of the Irish with the 'idle' itinerant element. If they refer to the matter at all, Irish-language poems of the period which were written for aristocratic patrons are insouciant about the sexual exploitation of women associated with itinerant poets and entertainers. A telling instance of a lord's wife who was praised as a procuress of other women's sexual services by a male poet has been referred to already, as has the fact that the female poet, Caitilín Dubh, refers unjudgmentally in her *caoineadh* for Diarmaid Ó Briain to harlots whom she mentions along with types such as the *óinseach*, the poet (*file*), the *bard*, the fool (*amadán*) and the *ollamh*. All persuasions of the Church took a more critical view, of course, and continued to do so as long as they perceived a link between itinerant entertainers and sexual services. No doubt there was often a gap between perception and reality. It is disturbing to note that an Irish-language sermon preached in 1820 against one *Cáit na gCupán* 'Kate of the Cups' shows that a travelling fortune-teller (taking 'Cups' to refer to this trade), living by her wits among the poor, could still attract the full battery of charges which English commentators in the seventeenth century were wont to visit on the female element of the poets' *dámh* (pp. 162–3).

CORMAC MAC CUILENNÁIN

(d. 908)

from:
SANAS CORMAIC
(Cormac's Glossary)
(*c.* 900)

[With remarkable nonchalance, a female poet is shown to belong in the ranks of the *áes dána*. In this densely allusive text, she encounters a distinguished male poet, Senchán Torpéist, and puts him on his mettle.

The daughter of úa Dulsaine, a *leiccerd* (probably a compound of *liaig*, 'leech, physician', and *cerd*, 'artist') who comes of a family of poets, goes abroad on an extensive tour with her retinue. An unspecified disaster befalls them which only she survives. Physically ravaged by it, and her only hope of being identified rests on encountering a poet who will recognize her intellectual prowess. This much might have been expected of Senchán. Tradition tells that he succeeded Dallán Forgaill (reputed author of the extraordinary elegy for Colum Cille (d. 597), *Amra Coluim Chille*) as head of Ireland's *áes dána*. He is credited with recovering the epic tale *Táin Bó Cúailnge* after it had been lost to living memory. Yet when chance brings him face to face with the daughter of úa Dulsaine, Senchán is found wanting: he is unable to contribute to the antiphonal exchange by which she hopes to prove her identity. The creative force comes to the rescue, personified as a rebarbative male figure. When the woman poet speaks of gathering seaweed, he interprets this correctly as a reference to salt production from the burnt ash of seaweed. When she speaks of her burning ears — caused by her degradation — he palliates her shame by giving her back her identity: he recognizes that she is the 'child of úa Dulsaine', a credited poet. He arrives at this conclusion by associating her oblique reference to shame with her name: the word *dulsaine* means 'mockery'. It also means 'satire', an activity frequently associated with female poets. Her true identity is revealed and the act of revelation makes poetry itself — figured here as the Spirit of Poetry — beautiful.

The text derives from *Sanas Cormaic*, a glossary with illustrative citations. A few of the citations, including the following one which appears under the Irish headword *prull*, constitute anecdotes. The present translation is based on the edition (with a German translation) by Rudolf Thurneysen, 'Zu Cormacs Glossar', *Festschrift für Ernst Windisch* (Leipzig, 1914), pp. 8–37, at pp. 11–23.]

THE SPIRIT OF POETRY

Prull, i.e. 'increase' and 'augmentation', as the woman-*leiccerd*, daughter of úa Dulsaine, said to Senchán Torpéist in the Isle of Man:
'My two ears burn me greatly (*prull*).'
Thereupon, the 'novice-poet' from Senchán's retinue responded, i.e.
'the *cerd*, child of úa Dulsaine,
from Lia Toll Taursaige'.[1]
This is why that happened to Senchán. He chanced to go to the Isle of Man, on a pleasure-trip with the purpose of making a circuit[2] there. [His retinue] numbered fifty poets, excluding apprentices. Hardly any poet before that had worn the like of Senchán's clothing, not to mention his sage's mantle etc. What was finest of the clothing of the nobles of the Gaels, this is what the poets put on.

When they put out to sea and set the stern towards land, a lad of unnatural appearance called after them from the shore. 'Let me go with you,' he said. They all look at the lad. They did not wish to let him join them for they thought

that he was not a bird fit for their flock because his appearance was hideous. To begin with, when one put a finger to his forehead, a spurt of putrid matter used to pour down the back of his neck. He had suppuration [?] from the crown of his head to the gristle of his shoulders. Anyone who saw it would think that it was the clots of his brain that had broken through his skull. Each of his two eyes was as round as a blackbird's egg, as black as death, as quick as a cat.[3] The points of his teeth were as yellow as gold, their roots were as green as the stock of a holly tree. Two bare, spindly shanks with two spiky, speckle-dark heels under him. If the rag he wore were stripped off him, it would have had little difficulty in setting out on its own, unless a stone were placed on it, on account of its teeming vermin.

He shouted loudly at Senchán and he said to him: 'I'll be of greater use to you,' he said, 'than the arrogant foolish crew that's around you.' 'Can you come along the rudder into the currach?' 'I'll try,' he said. Then he stepped along the rudder into the currach, as fast as a mouse along a loom-beam, and he was aboard. The currach with its load all but went under, because the poets pressed forward before him from one end of the vessel to the other, and they said as though from one mouth: 'A monster has reached you, Senchán! He'll be your sole company, if only we can make our escape ashore.' It is on account of that that he was called Senchán *Torpéist*, that is, 'Senchán whom the monster reached'.[4]

They reached the Isle of Man after that. They brought their vessel ashore. When they were going along the strand, they saw the tall grey-haired old woman on the rock gathering seaweed together with sea-produce. Excellent and noble were her feet and hands, except that she did not have fine clothing and the emaciation of famine was on her. And that was pitiful, for this was the woman-*leiccerd*, daughter of úa Dulsaine, from Múscraige of Lia Toll in the territory of Uí Fhidgenti.[5] She had gone on a circuit of Ireland and Britain and Man, and all her retinue were dead. Her brother, the son of úa Dulsaine — an eminent *cerd* also — was searching for her throughout the territories of Ireland and he did not find her etc.

---

1. In County Limerick, in the area around Croom.
2. A visitation made by poets to patrons.

3. Irish *fiamuin*, a swift-footed animal of uncertain identity.
4. Irish *do-rorpai péist*, a fanciful etymology of the element *Torpéist*.
5. In County Limerick.

When the old woman saw the poets, she asked them who they were. One of them said: 'Whoever asks this is from another country — this is Senchán, the poet of all Ireland!'

'Will you be so gracious, Senchán, as to stay and hear what I have to say?'

'I will indeed,' said Senchán.

> 'I was not accustomed to knotty tribulation,
>   although I gather blistered seaweed.

What's the other half-quatrain?'

Then Senchán grows silent, as do all the poets. With that, the aforementioned lad bounds out in front of Senchán and he said: 'Silence, old woman! Don't address Senchán. It's not appropriate for you. Address yourself to me, since no one else from the retinue will speak to you.'

'If that's so,' said the woman-*leiccerd*, 'what's the other half-quatrain?'

'Not difficult,' said he:

> 'From the top of a rock in the Sea of Man,
>   much salt has been made here.'

'True,' said she, 'and now for this half-quatrain:

> 'My two ears burn me greatly.[6]

What's the other half-quatrain, Senchán?'

'What! you still seek to address Senchán! He won't speak to you.'

'Well, then, what do you think it is?' said she.

'Not difficult,' he said.

> 'The *cerd*, child of úa Dulsaine,
>   from Lía Toll Taursaige.'

'That is true!' said Senchán. 'Are you the daughter of úa Dulsaine, the woman-*leiccerd* who is being sought throughout Ireland?'

'I am indeed,' said she. Then she was bathed by Senchán and she was dressed in wondrous clothing and she came with Senchán to Ireland.

When Senchán reached Ireland, they saw the aforementioned lad: he was now a youth with golden yellow hair, wavy as the scrollings [?] on harps. He was clad in royal apparel, and he had the finest appearance ever seen on any man. He comes right-hand wise[7] around Senchán and his retinue, and he has never appeared since that time. And thus it is certain that he was the Spirit of Poetry.

---

6. Only one line is given in the Irish.

7. This direction indicates a favourable outcome.

IRARD MAC COISSE

(d. 990)

APAIR DAMSA RE DER FÁIL
(On My Behalf Tell Der Fáil)
(*c.* 956)

[This, the earliest known Irish poem for an identified woman, is a condolence for Der Fáil (d. 1010), Queen of Tara, whose son Áed has died. The Connacht poet Irard mac Coisse is styled 'Ireland's chief poet' in his death-notices. Der Fáil was the daughter of Tadg mac Cathail (d. 956), King of Connacht. As a young woman, probably in her mid-teens, she married Domnall úa Néill, who was to become King of Tara in 956, and they remained together until his death in 980. It is almost certain that Áed was her first-born son, and that his death occurred *c.* 956, when he was hardly more than eleven or twelve years of age. What caused his death is now unknown. Almost five hundred years later another Connacht poet, also addressing a grieving mother, paraphrased Irard's address to Der Fáil at length (for the later poem, see pp. 326–9).

Irard seems to have depended on secular nobles for patronage. After Domnall's death, he turned to his successor in the Tara kingship, Máelsechnaill mac Domnaill (d. 1022) — and his consort. In fact, the resemblance between a poem addressed to the wife of Máelsechnaill, named Mór daughter of Donnchad, and the present one is so close, in language, style and references, that a reasonable argument may be made for its having been composed by Irard, although it is without ascription. (For text and translation see: Gerard Murphy, *Early Irish Lyrics: Eighth to Twelfth Century* (Oxford: Clarendon Press, 1956), pp. 88–91.) However, there is one major difference: Mór's cause of lamentation is the death of a goose. Since Der Fáil was alive when this poem was composed, it may be that she and Mór moved in different circles as, otherwise, Irard might have had to contend with charges of insincerity. Alternatively, perhaps the address to Mór on the death of her goose was written by another poet to mock Irard's endeavours.

The text is edited from Brussels, Bibliothèque Royale, MS 5100, p. 6, and Dublin, National Library MS G 131, pp. 225–6. The translation is by Moya Cannon.]

1

Apair damsa re Der Fáil,
  tacair re hingin Taidc thúaid,
ná dénad díthre dí féin,
  ní lé féin in fríthe fúair

2

Ná ferad debaid re Día,
  re Ríg belaig bethad cé;
adrad dont shlicht fora-tú,
  ná labrad don nech nár lé.

3

Léiced in rígan a recht,
  tréiced bith mbrecht is a bruc;
gé chaíne cach ben a mac,
  int í do-rat, is É ruc.

4

Cár doilge do ingin Taidc
  éc Áeda aird, aidble uird,
iná d'Échtaig a bás bróin
  Cormaic huí Chuinn ón mBóinn mbuirb.

5

Ocus ní luga ro leth
  cuma dar Saidb, soilse dath,
lá íar tuitim Eógain uill
  ocus Airt maic Cuinn i cath.

6

Nochar íslig BéFinn bláith
  faíd a guil gnáith risin ngéic,
dar marb Cú Chulainn grinn gaéth
  a mac Fraéch for Linn finn Féic.

7

Nocha luga ro chaí in ben
  Caíntigern dá treib dá tail
bás Mongáin i nGartúir gloin
  don oil ro theilc Artúir air.

8

Nocharb ferr la rígna ráin
  bás Laégaire maic náir Néill,
in bail i tá lecht in laích
  ro selt ó gaíth is ó gréin.

9

Nírb ferr la Feidlim in beirt,
  esbaid Eirc, inmain lé a mac,
dar thuit mac Coirpre Nia Fer
  la Conall ar Muig Breg balc.

10

Ó't-chúala Écuba in ngním,
  de nocha derna sním súaill,
den raichéim ruc Echtair án,
  dar gab fa gáib Aichéil úair.

11

Cid mór de máithrib mac ríg
  ro ráthaig in ngním co nglíaid,
fata a-táthar ar a ráin,
  dáil a máthar ina ndíaid.

12

Nach cúala DerFáil, dar Día,
  nach mó la Críst cáid co ceól,
gémad grúc leis cach rí rán
  ná ro lád a drúcht don fheór?

13

Ní mó leis bláth droigin duib,
  ocus cách do chur 'na chin,
etir thuile is tráig is tor
  iná duille do chor d'fhid.

14

Léiced a dagmac do Día,
  bad é fíach dá n-adrad í;
mét gráda a maic lennaig lé,
  bad é mét a chennaig dí.

15

Tabrad cros Chríst dar a hucht,
  adrad don Ríg darab cet,
sechnad sech iffern ngarb ngrot
  co port na n-apstal 's na n-ap.

TRANSLATION

On my behalf tell Der Fáil,
go north and beg Tadg's daughter
not to let sorrow destroy her —
her treasure was just on loan.

Let her not contend with God,
with the King of this world's road,
let her follow the path I go
and not speak of what she did not own.

Let the queen leave her keening now,
not heed the shifting world of cares,
though every woman may mourn her son
it's He who gave who took away.

For Tadg's daughter was it harder,
noble Áed's end, fate's awful order,
than for Échtach the death in sorrow
of Cormac úa Cuinn from the rough Boyne.

And it was no less a sorrow
which struck Sadb of the shining colours,
that day after they fell in battle
great Eógan and Art mac Cuinn.

Gentle BéFinn did not stanch
her tears, lamenting over the branch
with which keen Cú Chulainn slew
her son Fraéch on bright Linn Féic.

No smaller grief caused Caíntigern
to cry her heart out for her son
when Mongán died in fresh Gartúir,
levelled by the stone that Artúir threw.

No easier for a noble queen
was the death of mild Laégaire mac Néill,
the place the hero's gravestone marks
where he was felled by wind and sun.

No better was Feidelm pleased
when she lost Erc, the son she loved,
when on the ground of proud Mag Breg
Conall killed the son of Coirpre Nia Fer.

When Hecuba was brought word,
anguished, she cried her fill of tears,
that dreadful death great Hector met
when Achilles caught him off his guard.

Though many a prince's mother
has witnessed such deed with wailing,
in floods of tears they still suffer
who live to keen a son's killing.

In God's name, has Der Fáil never heard
it weighs no more with tuneful Christ
— though every king deserve His wrath —
than that the grass should shed its dew.

The blackthorn flower is no more to Him,
nor anything could be put with it,
flood nor ebb nor the human crowd,
than the dropping of a leaf in the wood.

Let her yield her dear son to God,
let that be the penance she must bear
and let the measure of her love
be the measure of the ransoming.

Let her raise Christ's cross above her breast,
follow the King who allowed such deeds,
avoid harsh hell with all its pain
and gain harbour with abbots and with saints.

SCANDLÁN MÓR

ADVICE TO LOVERS
(Middle Irish)

[Pre-Norman tradition had something of the badinage found later in the *dánta grádha*, as this Middle Irish poem shows. 'Scandlán Mór' on whom the poem is fathered is unidentified; if indeed the author, he was not overly concerned with metrical regularity. Kuno Meyer published the text in *Zeitschrift für celtische Philologie*, vol. 3 (1899), p. 37. The translation is from: Frank O'Connor, *The Little Monasteries* (Dublin: Dolmen Press, 1963, 1976), p. 17.]

Is É Mo Shámud re Mnái

Is é mo shámud re mnái
    amal bís cámull hi ceó,
cen co hana lim is cet,
    cet lim cid marb, cet cid beó.

Cett lim cía rabur 'na gnáis,
    cet lim cía hanur dia héis,
is ed rofácbad do mnái,
    is cet cía thái, cet cía théis.

Advice to Lovers

The way to get on with a girl
　Is to drift like a man in a mist,
Happy enough to be caught,
　Happy to be dismissed.

Glad to be out of her way,
　Glad to rejoin her in bed,
Equally grieved or gay
　To learn that she's living or dead.

GIOLLA BRIGHDE MAC CON MIDHE

(d. before 1281)

TEASTÁ EOCHAIR GHLAIS GHAOIDHEAL

(All Ireland is in Mourning)
(early 13th century)

['The only real hell is being childless' (*Ní fhuil ann mar ifearn bunaidh / ach bheith gan chloinn*), wrote Giolla Brighde Mac Con Midhe in an appeal to the Trinity to grant him and his wife another son, after all their children had died. This appeal, and the following elegy, are almost all we have of pre-modern Gaelic poems concerning children. Gormlaith, daughter of Domhnall Mór Ó Domhnaill, King of Tír Conaill (modern County Donegal), died of an illness at the age of five. She had been fostered out to another Domhnall 'in the east', possibly Domhnall (d. 1234), son of Aodh Úa Néill and King of Tír Eoghain (Tyrone). If not this man, Gormlaith's foster-father was almost certainly a kinsman of his. When Giolla Brighde says that Gormlaith's fosterage closed the doors of war, we may assume that he is referring to these often antagonistic neighbouring kingdoms.

The poem offers no consolation. It tells rather of inconsolable grief and irretrievable loss. Gormlaith embodied not only the fond parental hopes of two households, but also the desire for peace between Tír Conaill and Tír Eoghain. Many professional poets tended to blow with the prevailing political winds, but Giolla Brighde was constant in pressing for this peace in his work. His mother belonged to Ceinéal Conaill, while the Mac Con Midhe stock was of Ceinéal Eoghain. The poem radiates the hurt of the child's death across this broad community.

The poems of Giolla Brighde have been edited and translated by N.J.A. Williams, *The Poems of Giolla Brighde Mac Con Midhe*, vol. 51 (Dublin: Irish Texts Society, 1980). The present text is as ibid., pp. 22–8, apart from a small number of readings derived from an earlier edition. This new translation is by Seamus Deane.]

1
Teastá eochair ghlais Ghaoidheal;
fa Éirinn do héagcaoineadh;
budh anbhfann dóibh greim an ghlais
is a sheim óir 'na fhéagmhais.

2
Teastá eochair a iata;
síoth Éireann budh ainriata;
ó dhul as nochan fhuair síth;
a glas do-chuaidh don choigcrích.

3
Eochair shíothchána Shíl Chuinn
altrom inghine Í Dhomhnuill;
breith Ghormladha tar sliabh soir
do iadh comhladha an chogoidh.

4
Dob athair di an Domhnall thiar —
tug a n-aigneadh ar éinrian;
dob oide di an Domhnall thoir —
dob í conghlann a gceangoil.

5
Dá mbeidís ar tí tachair
a hoide 's a hardathair,
aghadh na naoidhean do-níodh
sgaoileadh fhaladh na n-airdríogh.

6
Fríoth lé buar is brat naoidhe,
fríoth sochar is somhaoine;
a cumha i gceann a solaidh
earr umha ar na hasgadhaibh.

7
Má táid fa a cumhaidh i gceas
gach fréamh re bhfuil a cairdeas,
tearc adhbhar ríoghna nó ríogh
gan íorna adhbhal d'imshníomh.

8
Biaidh a cuidigh dá cumhaidh
ar chlannmhaicne Chonchubhair;
ar aicme Briain biaidh cumha
's biaidh ar mhaicne Murchudha.

9
Conall, Eoghan dár fhoghain,
Clann Bhriain is Clann Chonchobhair,
bláth do Ghormlaith gach Gaoidheal;
comhdhaith cách dá comhchaoineadh.

10
Éagcóir iomarchar muirne
fa mhacámh an mhórChoimdhe;
teagaimh nach é ar a mbiadh bail
an té budh mian do mharthain.

11
Saoghal dí — ní dál fhoirbhthe —
do iarraidh gach éanoidhche;
an dligheadh uile ní fhuil
duine do shireadh shaoghuil.

12
Gairid beag do bhí i gcolainn
macámh Clainne caomhChonaill;
do sheal — céillidhe an cridhe —
feadh éindighe is aidhbhsighe.

13
Ag éag dot aghaidh niamhdha
nír shlán acht cúig ceirbhliadhna;
a ríoghan óg Muaidhe, is moch
fód na huaighe dot fholoch.

14
Baladh na n-ubhall n-abuidh
ar an uichtghil n-abhradhuibh;
fríoth fios balaidh an bhrogha
ar slios galair Gormladha.

15
Treas dá buime ag déanamh déar,
treas ag innisin uirsgéal;

gá meabhair budh duilghe dhi
cuimhne a meadhair 'gá muime?

16
Dealuchadh re a dreich mballaigh
díoghlaidh ar a dearnannaibh;
Gormlaidh do bhreith ó a buime
bodhraidh dreich a dearnuinne.

17
Ní thabhair adhbhann dá haoidh,
ní cheis re comhrádh macaoimh;
ní bhí a-muigh uirre omhan
a buime ód-chluin criothnoghadh.

18
Do báitheadh isan mBanbha
éanmhacámh a hionnamhla;
fa béin úraigh slat mar sain,
mac Néill Ghlúnduibh re Gormlaidh.

19
Nír bhuail macámh mná eile,
nír thuill osnadh inghine;
a doimheanma ar chách do-chím,
fáth a hoileamhna ón airdrígh.

20
As a croidhe nochar chuir
osnadh inghine Cathuil;
ní gan a dhula ó dhuine
ní bhí acht cumha cholluidhe.

21
Inghean inghine Cathail
is easbhach dá hardathair,
folt maothchaomh géagnúidhe glan
baothlaogh céadúidhe Cruachan.

22
Ubhall abhla Cruachan Cuinn
fa úir dheirg Dhoire Choluim,
aoighe caomh i gcriaidh Doire,
caor chraoibhe Briain Bhóroimhe.

23
Re a fás gion go bhfuil ar súil
do ba gráinne donn deargthúir;
tig síol is táire is ní thig
gráinne ríogh isan roilig.

24

Banua Cathail a Cruachain,
ua do Mhóir a Miodhluachair,
ua Móire Mumhan ní mhair;
pudhar budh fhóille is easbhaidh.

25

Banua Cathail an chruibh dhuinn,
inghean Domhnaill Í Dhomhnuill,
easbhaidh leam an tí theastá
is í i gceann a céidteasta.

TRANSLATION

All Ireland is in mourning,
For the key that would lock
Peace within it has gone.
Without that golden rivet,
It will not hold. A return
To strife has come with the shock
Of this death and Ireland has seen
The prospect of peace migrate
Across the border to the beyond.

Conn's seed[1] wholly depended
On bringing Gormlaith east
Across the mountain, fostering
A family bond, having blended
Father and foster-father,
The Domhnalls of the west and east,
In her and through her ended
War and anger. All that prattle
Between high-kings would come

To nothing. But now, alas,
After opening the avenues
To peace, all the cattle
And bright clothing, revenues
And assets that attended
Her coming, all have turned
To loss, hope is spurned
By grief and all is brass.
If the tremor of sorrow

Has shaken every leaf
And branch of her family tree,
There's no future king or queen
Left unafflicted. Their grief

Will ramify through the seed
Of Conchubhar, of Brian's breed,
Murcadh's sons, the race of Eoghan
And of Conall.[2] All will keen
And clamour to keen her,

The Gaels, touched by her fate
And name. The 'noble sovereignty'[3]
That 'Gormlaith' signifies,
The ideal that she graced,
Now interfuses grief with fame
In the grave in which she lies.
It is wrong, is out of place
To lament with prolonged cries
For the Lord's child. Still, it's rare

That people plead the great Lord spare
The sturdy child. Wrong it may be,
Yet every night the people prayed
For her survival though the law
Nowhere allows that one should plea
For a death to be stayed.
Though the bodily life we saw
In Conall's daughter[4] was brief,
The intensity of its blaze

Was the fiercest we have known,
The deepest occasion of grief.
O, little queen of the Moy,[5]
For five full years you had grown
Before your dying days
Dimmed the lustrous joy
Of your shining face,
Laid in its resting-place.
Essence of apple-scent

Drowsed on her white breast,
The fragrance of paradise
Rose from her corpse when we bent
Over Gormlaith's dark-browed eyes.
Her foster-mother spent
Long nights in weeping for her,
Long days in stories of her.
No memory made her agonise
More that Gormlaith's gaiety.

---

1. The people of Ireland's Northern Half.

2. The names denote Gormlaith's various ancestral affiliations.
3. From *gorm*, 'noble', and *flaith*, 'sovereignty'.
4. Gormlaith, being of Tír Conaill, is 'Conall's daughter'.
5. The Moy flows into Kilalla Bay, County Mayo, in Connacht. Gráinne's claim to Connacht blood was through her mother, Lasairfhíona (d. 1240), daughter of Cathal Croibhdhearg Úa Conchobhair.

She batters the palms of her hands
To stun the remembered sense
Of Gormlaith's freckled face
Between them. So dumb, so dense
Her grief that nothing leaves a trace
Of response in her. Not melody,
A chattering child, a fearful noise
Outdoors. Nothing. Not a voice
Since the quenching in Banbha's

Land of this child, her like and life,
The cutting, as by a knife,
Of a fresh growth, as long ago
The son of Niall Glúndubh's wife,
Also Gormlaith,[6] was brought low.
This child never struck another,
Her budding pains lost to her mother.
In every voice I hear the ring
Of despair for the high-king's

Child, for her mother, daughter
Of Cathal, heart-sick with the sting
Of a sorrow that has caught her
Too deep for cure, a grief
That will not pass like any other,
For the bright head, waved hair
Of the pet child, Cruachain's[7]

Prime care, now lost to her father.
From Conn of Cruachain's tree,

From Brian Bóroimhe's branch,
Has fallen an apple, has shaken
A berry, into the red earth
Of Columb's Derry,[8] there to rest,
An honour'd guest, life-forsaken.
We can no longer think to see
This noble grain's growth
In the vermilion earth.
Now a humbler seed sprouts

While the regal line dies out
In the graveyard. She does not live.
We could not grieve more, nor less.
Less would be hard to forgive,
More is inadequate. Yes,
Grand-daughter of Cathal
Of Cruachain, grand-child of Mór[9]
Of Luachair and Munster,
Of Cathal of the red hand;

Daughter of Domhnall Ó Domhnaill,
You are gone, your first praise hand-
in-hand with your last, and I mourn
You, as does Ireland, as do all.

---

6. On Gormlaith, wife of Niall Glúndubh, see pp. 133–9.
7. In County Roscommon.

8. Saint Colum Cille is the reputed founder of the monastery of Derry.
9. Mór Mumhan 'Mór of Munster' (d. 1218) was Gormlaith's maternal grandmother.

TADHG MÓR Ó hUIGINN

(d. 1315)

SLÁN FÁT FHOLCADH
(For Fionnghuala, Daughter of Maghnus Ó Conchobhair)
(c. 1300)

[The undulating metre of this poem — the uncommon *ollbhairdne* — seems particularly suited to praise of a woman's hair and to the downward caress which follows it in the poem's *duinedhíolaim*, 'body-compendium'. After delivering his praises, the poet confidently states what he expects to glean in return.

The Ó hUiginn family of Connacht was one of the most eminent bardic families of the pre-modern period. The addressee's father, Maghnus Ó Conchobhair, was Lord of Connacht, and Tadhg Mór, who had tutored him when he was young, was his poet. Fionnghuala (d. 1310) married Brian Mág Shamhradháin (d. 1298), Lord of Tullyhaw (Teallach nEachach) in present-day County Cavan. As he is not referred to in the poem, she was probably not yet married to him when it was composed. Tadhg Mór wrote an elegy on her husband's death, and was almost certainly the author of other poems to members of his family. It is likely that Tadhg's former bond with Fionnghuala led to his gaining Mág Shamhradháin patronage after her marriage.

The present poem is the first in a series of three which celebrate blonde-haired beauties associated with, or born into, the Mág Shamhradháin family. The second was written for Brian's daughter, Gormlaith (d. 1305). The record does not show whether Fionnghuala, or Brian's second wife, was her mother. His second wife was Maoil Mheádha (d. 1323), daughter of Mac Tighearnáin. Maoil Mheádha's and Brian's son Tomás acceded to the lordship of Tullyhaw, as did his son Niall. It was for Niall's wife, Sadhbh, that the third poem in praise of blond beauty was written. The next poem in this anthology is also addressed to the same Sadhbh.

The text was edited twice by Lambert McKenna (Láimhbheartach Mac Cionnaith): in the *Irish Monthly*, vol. 48 (1920), pp. 163–7 (with translation), and in his *Dioghluim Dána* (Baile Átha Cliath: Oifig an tSoláthair, 1939), pp. 394–8. This new prose version is largely based on McKenna's translation. Unfortunately, the lyricism of the original, which may have counted for much with 'musical' Fionnghuala, is lost in the English.]

1
Slán fat fholcadh
a Fhionnghuala réidh roicheolchar;
t'fholt idir é
ní fhidir mé nach moitheochthar.

2
Slán fat fholcadh
's fa fhighe th'fhuilt fhiarchlaidhigh
sé is th'óige ort
[is] móide ar an fholt mh'fhiafraighidh.

3
Slán fá dhíorghadh
do dhísleachta shlim shlaitleabhair,
a mhall mhilis,
a bharr 'n-a thrilis taitneamhail.

4
Slán fa chíoradh
do chúil as caomh re a shíorfhaicsin;
gurab soraidh
gurab [cobhuidh] don chíoraidh-sin.

5
Ar gcíoradh th'fhuilt
usuide dhamh a dheaghmholadh
gach clann chleachtach
id bharr leabthach ag leabhroghadh.

6
Gach uair fhoilce
th'earla bhíos ag breith ailtbhisigh
mar ghréin ngairthe
do néimh a haithle an fhailcei-sin.

7
Cros Críosd thorad
tearc th'aithghin ar bioth barrbhuidhe;
ná rabh trésan bhfolt bhfionnbhuidhe
ort amhghoire.

8
Aigmhéil dá bharr
béim súl ar chách re a chladhfhaicsin;
tú as caoimhe i gcurp
naoidhe fan fhult an aghaidh-sin.

9
An aghaidh óg
fan fholt bhíos 'n-a bharr dhronglánach
bíd is beid dí go deaghshnuadhach
's sí soghrádhach.

10
Soghrádhach thú
ós do thír lisleabhair longclannaigh;
a chnú ar gcraoibhe
's tú bhus caoimhe do-chonncamair.

11
Ger chaomh ar dtús
thú re figheadh th'fhuilt fhionnbhuadha
tug luach eich ort
do bheith fa fholt, a Fhionnghuala.

12
Áluinn fan fholt
th'aghaidh chorcra mar chéadshaimhghréin
th'fholt mar fhalaigh
ag tocht tar th'aghaidh n-éadainréidh.

13
Réidh an t-éadan
ar aghaidh th'fhuilt troim thaithneamhaigh
na gcleathrámh gcraobh
ós an ngealchlár gcaomh gcailceamhail.

14
Mailghe caola
ós chionn do cheathra gcraobhfhabhra
aonsduaim orra
dá chaolsduaidh dhonna dhaolamhla.

15
Tearc san chruinne
comhchaomh do rosg mall mongdhathta;
géagcruinn gruaidhe
dá réatlainn uaine ogradhta.

16
Gruaidhe donna
dá ndéantar dán saor sreathmholta
leaca as saor snuadh
le taobh do dá ghruadh ngealchorcra.

17
Béal dearg tana
tug dhuit Dia — déana a altoghadh —
a chrann cubhra,
a bharr mar ubhla ar n-abghughadh.

18
Deirge iná subh
snuadh do leacan re a lánfhaicsin
do bhráighe bhláith
i mbáine bhláith don bhrághaid-sin.

19
Cíghe troma
ós do thaobh tárraidh mochbhuadha;
ní fhuil fa ucht
a-muigh ar curp a gcomhchuanna.

20
Ucht mar eala
agad, a chall glan gealchoilleach;
slios caomh cladhach
do thaobh mar chanach [gCreamhchoilleach].

21
[Braine] mar bhláth
do bharr mar ór, crodh caomhuingeach;
folt clúmhraon gcam
ort, a ghlúnmhaol mhall mhaoluilleach.

22
Cuanna caomha
do dá cholbtha, a chraobh ghealthoirtheach;
beaga bhláthbhuinn
's iad seada sálchruinn seangthroightheach.

23
Milis do ghlór
a ghéag mhall Mhoighe Finnei-sin
. . .[1]

1. Line omitted in the MS.

24
Téighid sginge
do sgarlóid chorcra chorrtharaigh
th'ucht slimgheal saor,
a inghean chaomh Í Chonchobhair.

25
Do néimh th'aighthe
do áilnigh th'fholt cas claonbhuidhe
fionnNuadha Fáil
a Fhionnghuala Chláir Caonruighe.

26
Nuadha Fionn Fáil
fuair a cruth ríoghdha ronua-san
ó Nuadha a-nuas
ní chuala cluas a chomhuasal.

27
Ríoghradh Éireann
umut earla mar ghléidheaghór
go Conn na gcuan
is an drong uadh go hÉireamhón.

28
Níor fhás achd rígh
is ríoghna 'mod rosg ndeaghshádhal
callros fa chnuas
ó Mhaghnus suas go seanÁdhamh.

29
Cia [do] righeadh
riot, a ríoghan nach rosggruamdha,
cia ad-chluin nó ad-chí
go bhfuil i gclí do chomhsduamdha?

30
Comhsduamdha ód láimh,
a lacha áluinn aoigheadhach,
gach béas banda
eidir ghréas Ghallda is Ghaoidhealach.

31
Id bhruidhin bhric
bídh re béalaibh bhan lámhdhaidhe
fíon fuar finngheal
[ód] chuan, a inghean Árlaidhe.

32
A Fhionnghuala,
a ucht mar bhláth saor subhlosa,
a inghean ghlan mhall Mhaghnusa,
a chrann cumhra-sa.

33
Biaidh red reimhis,
a ríoghan Chruachna coillghile
— mar do bhaoi — bean
gan mhnaoi gan fhear 'ga hoirbhire.

34
Gnáth as dual dhuid
—is a dhéanamh ar dhánmholadh—
gan bheirt ar bhoin
gan [fheirc] ar ghroigh do ghrándoghadh.

35
Dual ót athair
a Fhionnghuala, a fholt maoithghleannach,
bheith ag díol dámh,
an fíon 's an dán do dhaoircheannach.

36
Dual dod bhais bhláith
bheith don aos dána ag druineachas
ceird cridhe ar crioth
gach file ar bioth dod bhuidheachas.

37
Dual duid dá mbeath
— ní budh beag d'fheidhm ná d'ordughadh —
Banbha ar do bhreith
mallbha agus eich ar mh'ordughadh.

38
Dual duid mé id thigh
ag toirbheart chliar gach chineadhaigh
d'fhoghluim ionnlais
ag comhruinn ionnmhais d'fhileadhaibh.

39
Th'ór is th'airgead
agam uaid ag a thiodhnacal,
gach ní fa nimh
dá mbí id thigh ar mo thiodhlacadh

40
Dual duid gach dámh
do dhol leam d'fhéachain th'fhinntighe
tú ag réir a rann
gan chléir ann achd ar mh'impidhe.

41
Dual duit gach magh
's gach móin go dtolchaibh tiormruadha
lán dod lacht-chrodh;
slán fat fhalcadh a Fhionnghuala.   SLÁN.

TRANSLATION

1
Hail to your bathing, serene, musical Fionnghuala, and to your hair: I dare say it will not go unnoticed!

2
Hail to your bathing and to the weaving of your wavy tresses; though you are crowned with youth as well, my first address is to your hair.

3
Hail to the straightening of the parting in your hair so smooth and long, stately sweet girl, head of bright tresses.

4
Hail to the combing of your flowing head, lovely to gaze at for ever. May it be smooth and shapely from that combing.

5
Easier for me to praise it fitly after its combing: every woven coil on your soft-piled head is smoothing out.

6
Each time you wash your ever lovelier hair, your lustre is as the warm sun from that washing.

7
Christ's cross about you! — goldenheads like you are rare. May you come to no grief on account of that golden hair.

8
Your hair causes dread — bewitches all who glance at it; fairest in body, your face is childlike beneath that hair.

9
The young face beneath the hair that is a bank of tresses — they are and ever will be becoming to her, and she lovable.

10
Lovable you are, ruling your farmed and marinered[1] land, nut of our branch, you are the fairest we have seen.

1. Irish *longclannaigh*, 'having many ships'.

11

Though fair from the outset, Fionnghuala, once you plaited it, being beneath your bright-beautiful hair added a steed's value to you.

12

Lovely as early summer sun is your ruddy face beneath your hair; it falls like a veil over your smooth brow.

13

Smooth the brow against your heavy, shining hair of undulating tresses over the bright, smooth, lime-white forehead.

14

Slender eye-brows over your four eye-lashes, equally fair are those two dark, beetle-black arches.

15

The eye in its niche — beautiful your slow, dark-lashed eye — like a jewel in the face is that green-blue star.

16

Bright-hued cheeks for which noble eulogy is made, cheekbones and colouring next your two bright-ruddy cheeks.

17

Subtle red mouth — God gave it to you — give thanks for it! O sweet-scented tree, O lip like ripened apples.

18

Redder than berry is the hue of your cheek, ever to be gazed at; your soft throat is amid fair whiteness.

19

Full breasts above your body which received early charms; no other body has as beautiful beneath bosom.

20

A swan's bosom you have, O pure bright-foliaged hazel, fair and curvaceous your side, a side like Creamhchoill's bog-cotton.

21

Like flowers your fringe, like gold your hair, a dowry of fair ingots, a head of flowing, wavy tresses, O soft-kneed, stately, lithe woman.

22

Fair and shapely are your two calves, O fair-fruited branch, small are your tender feet, slender, round-heeled, high-instepped.

23

Sweet your voice, O stately branch of yon Mag Finn[2] . . .[3]

24

Your pelisses of furbelowed scarlet warm your smooth-bright, noble bosom, O daughter fair of Ó Conchubhair.

25

Fair Nuadha[4] of Fál[5] with your face's light lovelified your wavy, golden hair, O Fionnghuala of Clár Caonraighe.[6]

26

It was fair Nuadha of Fál who procured her royal, summer-young form; no one has heard of its like from Nuadha onwards.

27

From Ireland's kings you got your hair like bright, true gold, from Conn[7] of the Harbours and the others, back to Éireamhón.[8]

28

From none but kings and queens did you get your noble, slow eye, a laden hazel-wood from Maghnus back to Old Adam.

29

Who was there to rival you, O queen who is never gloomy-eyed; who sees or hears tell of another mortal who is equally accomplished?

30

Equally accomplished from your hand, O lovely, hospitable duck, comes every womanly work, both foreign and Gaelic.

2. In Uí Mhaine territory, near Loch Ree.
3. Line omitted in MS.
4. A mythical king of the Túatha Dé Danann.
5. A poetic name for Ireland.
6. In southern Uí Mhaine territory.
7. Eponym of the Connachta.
8. Mythical ancestor of the Gaoidhil, who ruled in the Northern Half.

31

In your speckled palace, cool white wine from your harbour is set before women of hand-artistry, O daughter of Árlaidh.

32

O Fionnghuala, O bosom like wild strawberry's noble blossom, O pure, stately daughter of Maghnus, O perfumed tree.

33

As before, there will be — while you live, O queen of hazel-bright Cruachain[9] — one woman without reproach from man or woman.

34

One custom that is meet for you — and to stake your name on it — is that a cow should bear no burden and that a horse should have no whip lashing it.

35

It is meet for you, your father's daughter, O Fionnghuala, O soft-valleyed tresses, to be rewarding retinues, paying dear for wine and poetry.

36

It is meet for your soft hand to be embroidering

9. Rathcroghan, in County Roscommon, royal capital of Connacht.

for the *aos dána*, and every poet an artist with beating heart, from gratitude.

37

It would be meet for you — it would take little effort or arrangement — to have all Banbha at your disposal, to give grave cattle and horses into my trust.

38

It would be meet for you to have me in your house, rewarding the poet-bands of every kindred, learning lavishness while dividing riches with poets.

39

Your gold and silver given me by you for distribution, all things whatsoever that are in your house in my gift.

40

It would be meet for you that all poets should come with me to visit your fair house, you yourself giving reward for their poems, and no poet there except at my request.

41

It would be meet for you to have every plain and moor with dry-heathered hills covered with your own milch cows. Hail to your bathing, Fionnghuala.   HAIL!

CAOCH CEISE Ó CLÚMHÁIN

(*fl.* 1350)

BEAN FÁ EINEACH DO FHUAIR NIALL
(For Niall Mág Shamhradháin and Sadhbh, Daughter of Cathal Ó Conchobhair)
(*c.* 1350)

[The praise of this lord and lady turns on the complementary nature of their different roles. The poem seems to

idealize a rigid demarcation — 'Niall is on sea burning ships, Sadhbh at home arranging goblets' — except in the matter of giving patronage to poets. The real point is the call to lord and lady to co-operate in this activity, to the poet's benefit.

The fourteenth-century vellum manuscript in which the poem occurs is the earliest extant example of a *duanaire*. The Mág Shamhradháin *duanaire* was probably begun in the reign of Tomás Mág Shamhradháin (1303–43), Lord of Tullyhaw in County Cavan, but it incorporated poems concerning an earlier lord, Brian, and his wives and children. (For an address to one of Brian's wives, Fionnghuala (not derived from this *duanaire*), see the preceding poem in this anthology.) The Niall (d. 1362) addressed in the present poem was Tomás's successor in the lordship and the latest poems in the *duanaire*, or at least what remains of it (the last poem is incomplete), seem to have been added during his lifetime, or shortly afterwards. Three of these are especially concerned with his wife, Sadhbh (d. 1373); she is alluded to in a number of others. The three are the present poem, co-addressed to her and Niall, and two others which address her solely. A remarkable thing about the latter two poems is that they were composed before her marriage to Niall, when she was wife to Flaithbheartach Ó Ruairc (d. 1349), lord of neighbouring Bréifne. Sadhbh herself may have seen to the incorporation of these poems into the *duanaire* during her marriage to Niall. Indeed, given that it contains three poems to her, it is not unimaginable that it was she who commissioned all or many of the poems added to the *duanaire* in Niall's time.

The three poems to Sadhbh provide a composite picture. For example, the suggestion in the present poem of a sequestered wife is countered in another containing, for example, such quatrains as: 'She can turn the helm at the end of a boat, and can send her horse along at a gallop; her robe follows the altered line of her form; this means not decrease in health but pregnancy.' All poems in the *duanaire* were edited and translated by Lambert McKenna, *The Book of Magauran. Leabhar Méig Shamhradháin* (Dublin: Dublin Institute for Advanced Studies, 1947). Apart from minor changes in presentation, the following text and translation are as ibid., pp. 130–9; pp. 339–43. For the cited quatrain, see ibid., p. 328, and p. 101 (Irish). The Ó Clúmháin family from County Sligo supplied poets to the Ó hEadhra (O'Hara) lords in their home county, as well as to the Mág Shamhradháins.]

1
Bean fa eineach do fhuair Niall,
buaidh ar a n-eineach ar-aon:
do-ghéabhad uile ní ag Niall
tuile cliar gé thí re thaobh.

2
Fear fa heineach do fhuair Sadhbh,
deigheach ar a duain dá dhearbh;
dúthaigh dí car ar a charn
Sadhbh fa bhladh ar nach bí bearn.

3
Ní cruaidh an ghnaoisin do ghabh,
do fhuair an mnaoisin fa mhodh;
fa heinighidh do fhuair fhear
ní cruaidh bean deigheinigh Dhor.

4
Fear nochor smuain sise acht sé
sise fa bhuaidh gé do bhaoi;
ní fhuigheadh fear oile hí
bean Lí ar a goire don ghnaoi.

5
Céile fa teist a-tá ag Saidhbh
teist chéile na mná ní meirbh,
an dias tre dhíol na ndámh ndoirbh
sníomh soirbh a ndán ag a dheilbh.

6
Sadhbh 's a dámha ag díol na ndámh,
na dámha gá ndíon ag Niall,
mar ra-niad ní coimhshníomh caol,
siad ar-aon ag coimhdhíol chliar.

7
Lánamhain gan mhaitheas mion,
lánamhain chaitheas a cradh,
sgath gach cléire ag triall n-a dteagh,
Niall is bean Bhéirre fa bhladh.

8
Fearta féile a rath a-raon
— cá rath as réidhe re rádh?
maith dá díon a fear go fial,
Niall 's a bhean ag díol na ndámh.

9
Ionnmhas Néill chaitheas re clú
is léir ar mhaitheas na mná;
do-ríne mar chongol cnó
bronnadh bó an tíre i n-a dtá.

10
Cé théid ón daghmhnaoi gan díol?
an bhanghnaoi ní léig ar lár;
cia nach fuighe ní ó Niall?
do-ní riar duine gan dán.

11
Tug Niall fa bhuaidh is a bhean
gach a bhfuair gach cliar dá gcrudh;
ní ling rí an ghnaoisin do-ghabh
gan bhladh taoisigh dhí do dhul.

12
Niall féin nocho fear gan ghnaoi
acht gidh fial bean Néill fa ní;
's é luach ar a goire i ngnaoi
fuath le gach mnaoi oile hí.

13
Síodh 's na créachtaibh ó chleith Chál
dá mbeith i n-éantaigh ar-aon,
madh maith ag Dia gach fear fial,
do-sia Niall ar neamh na naomh.

14
Inghean Chathail ón glan gréas
ar gach bhfachain fa bhladh bhós;
nír chuir sí n-a cheann do chás,
acht a fhás teann do-ní a nós.

15
Slat mhórfháis ag sníomh na sluagh
mac Tómáis ag díol na ndámh,
biaidh fa bhladh mar ra bhaoi Brian;
do-ghabh Niall an ghnaoi ar a ghrádh.

16
Iomdha dámh re dtaoibh as-toigh
gá rádh ris an dá chraoibh chuir;
'Bhar nós gnáth ag gabháil libh
cách mar sin ag rabháidh ruibh'.

17
T'fhear i n-ágh ag corcradh chrann
nó ar an trágh ag locradh long,
dot ucht do chromadh a cheann
ag tolladh th'eang do lucht lom.

18
Do sgiath réidh, comhla na gcríoch,
a Néill, agud chomhdha ar chách;
gidh hí gá sgoltudh dod sgiath
is í an chliath ghontar do ghnáth.

19
Eang geal gá greanadh it ucht
dá bhar dtrealamh a bhean Bheart;
bláthoige gach ball id mhiocht,
sliocht do shnáthoide is cam ceart.

20
Ar son t'fhaithche núidhe, a Néill,
crodh na Búille a haithle th'áigh;
bha seach ód chathaibh do-chuaidh
creach n-a buaibh machaidh le mnáibh.

21
Éan balbh ar n-a dhéanaimh dhoit,
a Shadhbh, re fhéaghain is ait;
iomdha ealta it fháithim ghlic
im bláitheing mbric ngreanta id ghlaic.

22
Rabhudh ód mhnaoi a Néill, do neach
agat féin má do bhaoi brath;
dar leat is gonta dhí a dreach
mar do-chí th'each corcra ón chath.

23
Ríoghan Bhreagh ag déanamh dhealbh,
a fear ag féaghadh a cholbh,
Niall ar moir ag coinnleadh charbh
Sadhbh as-toigh ag coinnmheadh chorn.

24
Sádhal an bhean fholtghlan fhionn
is a fear ag folcadh reann;
do shnámh chuain chaiste nír chrom
an tonn bhaiste ó 'd-chuaidh ma chean.

25
Sadhbh is eang greanta ar a glún
nó gor ghearr leabtha n-a lár;
reanna na sleagh ar gurt ghliadh
re Niall 's a ucht geal re gádh.

26
Nír dhligh oige ar a mbiadh bearn;
Niall mar as oide don arm
díreach cruinne a chaoilearr ngorm,
is buime chorn saoireang Sadhbh.

27
Cá hionadh nach robha a rún?
siobhal na mara is dá mhian;
céim roimhe 's gan chéim ar gcúl
's do rún Néill i ngoire ghliadh.

28
Fiort as-tigh a-tá gá dheillbh,
na fir fa mhiocht na mná ag muirr;
do fhuair é i saoireing ag Saidhbh
ainm agus sé i gcaoileirr chuirn.

29
Bas an taoisigh nocho tim.
do chas chraoisigh as a heirr,
do chas chleith ndolámhaigh nduinn
do dhruim eich shodhánaigh sheing.

30
Ní ró don mhnaoisin a modh;
mó sa mhó an ghnaoisin do-ghabh,
sádhal ar mnaoi mBéirre i mbrugh
's a gnaoi ag dul don bhéinne bhan.

31

Ní dhingneam ceilt ar neart Néill,
ní imreann bheirt acht beart áigh,
Mág Amhradhán ó bhfill fóir,
glanbhranán óir a Cill Chláir.

32

Snaidhm gá nadhmadh gun mhín mheirbh
nachar snadhmadh i sídh Duilbh,
a chur nocho sníomh le Saidhbh
gach snaidhm dá mbíodh i mbrugh Bhuilbh.

33

Ón ghnaoisin do-chuaidh fa chrodh
geall gach thaoisigh fuair an fear;
géabhaidh an giall nachar ghabh,
béaraidh a bhladh Niall ar neamh.

34

Bean Mharr do chomhchabhair chléir
d'ibh Conchubhair an mhall mhín;
ó dtug géag Dhuibhe do dháimh
séad i láimh gach dhuine dhíbh.

35

Tuile cliar fa bhláth n-a bhrugh
fáth asa bhfuighe Niall neamh;
nocho cruaidh do chaith a chrodh
flaith Dor fa bhuaidh is a bhean. Bean

36

Ó Dubhda ní duine mion
ré cumhga dá bhfuighe an fear;
íoc i gceanaibh craoibhe Dor
crodh d'fhearaibh Baoille do bhean. Bean

TRANSLATION

1

'Twas by his generosity that Niall won his wife,
they both excell [*sic*] in it; though a flood of poets
surround Niall, they will all get something from
him.

2

'Twas by her generosity that Sadhbh won her
husband; a fine steed given for a poem is example
of this (generosity); Sadhbh's glory is undiminished; 'tis her nature to be ever adding to it.

3

Easily he won his fame for generosity; 'twas by
his character that he won his wife; easily did the
generous Princess of Dor get a husband bound
to her by bond of generosity.

4

Rich-gifted by nature, she set her heart on Niall
alone; Niall alone, so closely allied to glory could
have won the Lady of Lí.

5

'Twas owing to her fame that Sadhbh got her
husband, high too his fame; this pair, caring for
cranky poets — to compose poems for them is a
pleasant task.

6

Sadhbh's poet-bands safe-housed with Niall and
looking after poet-bands (that come on visit) — the
pair (Niall and Sadhbh) take equal care of them all,
practising therein a generous co-operation.

7

They are a couple who have great fortune and
who lavish their wealth; the flower of poets have
been to their house; Niall and the Lady of Béirre
are in glory.

8

Wonders of generosity make the fortune of them
both — and what fortune could be smoother?
Niall supports her in generous fashion, and he
and she support poets.

9

The wealth which Niall spends in winning fame
shows plainly in his wife's generous ways; she
thinks no more of giving away the kine of the
land where she dwells than of (playing at)
shooting with nuts!

10

Who comes away empty-handed from the noble
lady? She strives after a woman's true glory. Who
leaves Niall without being richer? He cares even
for those who have no poetic power!

11

The wealth got from them by poets has
established Niall and his wife in glory; the prince

gets none of his princely renown without a princely portion of it accruing to her.

12

Niall himself ever enjoys popularity, though generous is his wife also; the reward she gets for enjoying a favour nearly as great as his is that other ladies dislike her.

13

Were Niall, Prince of Gál, to pray pardon for all the wounds he has inflicted, if they were all piled up together (?), he would be granted his prayer in Heaven of the saints, for God loves a generous-hearted hero.

14

Cathal's daughter, who inspires every poem's beauty, is glorious too on every count; her renown waxes ever greater and she puts no check to its growth.

15

Niall, son of Tomás, constant support of poets, stout lath for weaving battle-ranks, will be for ever in glory as was Brian; he wins favour because he loves that glory.

16

Many the poets living with those two firm-planted branches and saying to them: 'May constant glory ever be with you, may all the world love you!'

17

The husband reddens lances in fight or makes ready (?) ships on shore; he would then (on coming home) bow his head in salutation before thee as thou art cutting thy cloth for the naked poor (?)

18

Thy smooth shield, O Niall, guards the approach to thy lands and defends thee from foe; 'tis the foes' rank which is always broken, split by thy shield (?)

19

Bright cloth for thy garment thou dost embroider on thy lap, O lady of Bearta; beautiful artistry is every part of thy coif; curving and symmetrical is every mark of thy needle.

20

For thy fresh lawn, O Niall, the cattle of the Búill are brought after thy fight; from each battle comes booty, a *creach*[1] of kine, milch-cows with their maids.

21

The silent bird thou depictest is lovely to see, O Sadhbh, and many herds find place on the neat border of the embroidered cloth which thou hast in hand.

22

By (the face of) thy wife, O Niall, one can tell if thou hast got word to set forth (?); thou findest her face flushed (with joy) on seeing thy bright steed return.

23

Breagha's Queen works figures (in tapestry), her husband examines his lance-shafts: Niall is on sea burning ships, Sadhbh at home arranging goblets.

24

The fair bright-haired lady rests comfortable at home while her spouse is wetting spears (with blood); never since the Baptismal wave flowed over his head has he bent before the current of the (foaming?) stream.[2]

25

Sadhbh kept the ornamental cloth on her lap till she had cut out[3] raised designs in the centre of it; Niall with his sharp lances is on the battlefield, his white breast facing danger.

26

No object of handicraft should be left in injured state; as Niall is a master in the use of arms, every crookedness in his pointed blue shafts is made straight, while Sadhbh gives a mother's care to the goblets with their fine carvings.

27

Whither has Niall's spirit not ventured? He loves to traverse the sea; when fight impends, his decision is to advance, never to retreat.

---

1. Irish for 'booty, prey'.
2. McKenna's note: i.e., crossing rivers when on raid.
3. McKenna's note: i.e., fashioned.

28
Men delight to look at the lady's coif, marvellous work made in the house; he (Niall) finds his name worked on Sadhbh's splendid tapestry and (cut) on his goblet's thin stem.

29
Strong is the captain's hand; he can brandish his spear (holding it) by its end, he can swing his cumbrous red lance as he sits on his graceful clever steed.

30
This lady will always have her graceful manners; ever greater the favour which Béirre's Princess gets and which rejoices her in her castle and flows forth on her retinue of ladies.

31
We shall proclaim Niall's power, every move he makes is a gallant one; Mág Samhradháin, terror of foes, is a golden chess-king from Ceall Cláir.

32
Stitches never made even in Dolbh's castle[4] are made by this gentle tender lady; no needle-work

wrought in Bodhbh's castle[5] gives Sadhbh any difficulty.

33
In the popularity which attached to his wealth this hero surpassed every other; the hostage he has not yet got he will get; he will bring his fame with him to Heaven.

34
The Lady of Marr, the gentle stately lady of the Í Chonchobhair, ever helps poets; owing to what this Branch from the Dubh[6] has given poets every man of them now holds a treasure in his hands.

35
The flood of famous poets in Niall's castle will earn Heaven for him; in no niggardly fashion has this gifted Prince of Dor — and his wife — spent treasure.

36
When time of stress comes on him, Ó Dubhda shows himself great; the way in which that Branch of Dor atoned for his faults was this — he raided the men of the Baoill!

4. McKenna treats Dolbh as a personal name, but it might equally be the noun *dolbh*, 'sorcery'; thus, *i sidh duilbh*, 'in a dwelling of sorcery'.

5. Bodhbh, of the Otherworld Túatha Dé Danann, is associated with Sid ar Femin (Slievenamon) in Munster.
6. The Blackwater river, which forms the western boundary of the barony of Tullyhaw.

GOFRAIDH FIONN Ó DÁLAIGH

(d. 1387)

MAIRG MHEALLAS MUIRN AN TSAOGHAIL
(A Child in Prison)
(14th century)

[These quatrains are excerpted from a poem on the vanity of the world, one of the most popular religious poems of our period. The theme is illustrated by the story of a child born in prison, taken from the *Gesta Romanorum*, a collection compiled in the fourteenth century, perhaps originally as a manual for preachers. Gofraidh Fionn Ó

Dálaigh seems to have been the first court poet to make use of material of this kind.
  The Annals of the Four Masters describe Gofraidh Fionn as chief *ollamh* of his time. His patrons included the McCarthys of Desmond (see pp. 276–7) and the Earls of Desmond, surnamed Mac Gearailt (Fitzgerald). One of his poems is a rhetorical address to a child of the 1st Earl, Muiris Mac Gearailt. In time, this child, named Gearóid, became himself an amateur poet and a patron to Gofraidh Fionn; the two poems following the present one are by him. Our text is from Láimhbheartach Mac Cionnaith (ed.), *Dioghluim Dána*, pp. 109–11. The translation by Thomas Kinsella is from his *New Oxford Book of Irish Verse*, pp. 107–9. The extended moral application (in quatrains 23–46) does not form part of this translation.]

1

Mairg mheallas muirn an tsaoghail
gearr bhíos buaidh a mhóraonaigh;
mairg nach róchaomhain é air
re ré an drochshaoghail deacraigh.

2

Flaitheamhnas mór ar mhuirn mbig,
beatha shíor ar sheal ngairid,
tréigean Dé is diombuaidh an dáil
ar ré ndiombuain an domhnáin.

3

Sógh na sochraide neamhdha
a-tá thuas mun dtighearna,
gach sódh fa nimh seacha sain
is beatha fhir i n-uamhaidh.

4

A dhaoine dá ndáiltear rath
leis nach beag méad a meadhrach
bhar sódh is uime as lór libh
gan sódh as uille d'fhaicsin.

5

Dá dhearbhadh sin ag so sgéal
bheanas ris do réir fíréan
— sgéal é ónab iontúir neamh —
gidh bé sgriobtúir ór sgaoileadh.

6

Bean torrach ag tuar broide
do bhí i bpríosún peannaide;
bearar do chead Dé na ndúl
lé leanabh beag san bhríosún.

7

Ar n-a bhreith do bhí an macámh
ag fás mar gach bhfochlachán
dá fhiadhnaibh mar budh eadh dhún
seal do bhliadhnaibh i mbríosún.

8

An inghean d'fhagháil bhroide
meanma an leinbh níor lughai-de
's í dá réir gé do bhaoi i mbraid
mar mhnaoi gan phéin gan pheannaid.

9

Do shoillse an laoi níor léir dhóibh
achd a bhfaicdís — fáth dobróin —

de dhruim iodhan an achaidh
tré ionadh thuill tarathair.

10

Mun n-orchra níor bh'ionann dál
dá máthair is don mhacámh;
do athruigh dealbh dá dreich ghil
is an leanbh ag breith bhisigh.

11

An leanbh dá oileamhain ann
do b'fheirr-de aige a fhulang;
níor léir don bharrthais óg úr
narbh fhód Parrthais an príosún.

12

Sei-sean ag breith ruag reabhraidh
si-se ag dul ar doimheanmain,
mairg thrá nach tiobhradh dá aoidh
ionramh na mná is a macaoimh.

13

Ar bhfaicsin déar re dreich ngil
ráidhis an leanbh lá éigin
'ó tharla a fhuigheall ar m'óidh
cluineam damhna do dhobróin.'

14

'Neimhiongnadh gé do-neinn maoith'
ar si-se 'a leinbh lánbhaoith'
'is rian chumhang nar dhleacht dún
teacht d'fhulang pian i bpríosún.'

15

'An bhfuil' ar sé, 'sódh eile
as aoibhne ná ar n-inmhei-ne
nó an bhfuil ní as soillse ná so
ó do-ní an toirse throm-so'.

16

'Dar linn' ar an leanabh óg
'gé taoi brónach, a bhean-ód,
is léir dhúin ar ndíol soillse;
ná bíodh ar th'úidh athtoirse.'

17

'A n-abhra ní hiongnadh dheit,'
ar an inghean, 'a óigmhic
dáigh treibhe an teagh do thaghais,
treabh eile ní fhacadhais.

18
'Dá bhfaictheá a bhfacaidh mei-se
re dteacht don toigh dhoirchei-se
do bhiadh doimheanma ort ann
id phort oileamhna, a anam.'

19
'Ós agad-sa as fhearr a dhearbh,
a inghean' ar an t-óigleanbh
'ná ceil foirn fionnachtain de
do mhoirn d'iomarcaidh oirn-ne.'

20
'Loise an tsaoghail mhóir-se a-muigh
is eadh tháirreas ó thosuigh;
mé i dtigh dhorcha 'n-a dheaghaidh,
a fhir chomtha, is cinneamhain.'

21
Le cleachtadh deacrachta dhe
's nach fuair sé sódh budh aoibhne
níor cheis a ghruadh ghríosúr ghlan
ar an bpríosún bhfuair bhfalamh.

22
Baramhail do-bhearthar dún:
an dream do bhaoi san bhríosún
lucht an bheatha ché an cúpla
a ré is beatha bhríosúnta.

TRANSLATION

Woe to him by this world enticed.
Short a success in its mighty lists.
Woe who bethinks him not of this
during a hard and evil life.

A mighty realm for a puny pleasure.
Eternal life for a tiny span.
Turning from God is a luckless thing
for the fleeting time of this little world.

The bliss of the hosts in Heaven
as they circle about the Lord,
all bliss under Heaven save that
is the life of a man in a cave.

You who have found good fortune
and pleasure that seems not slight
your happiness seems sufficient
because you have known no greater.

In proof of which, here is a tale
bears witness to that truth
— not in itself a claim on Heaven
though the Scripture is the source.

. . . .

A pregnant woman (sorrow's sign)
once there was, in painful prison.
The God of Elements let her bear
in prison there a little child.

The little boy, when he was born,
grew up like any other child
(plain as we could see him there)
for a space of years, in prison.

That the woman was a prisoner
did not lower the baby's spirits.
She minded him, though in prison,
like one without punishment or pain.

Nothing of the light of day
(O misery!) could they see
but the bright ridge of a field
through a hole someone had made.

Yet the loss was not the same
for the son as for the mother:
her face failed in form
while the baby gained in health.

The child, raised where he was,
grew better by his bondage,
not knowing in his fresh frail limbs
but prison was ground of Paradise.

He made little playful runs
while her spirits only deepened.
(Mark well, lest you regret,
these deeds of son and mother.)

He said one day, beholding
a tear on her lovely face:
'I see the signs of sadness;
now let me hear the cause.'

'No wonder that I mourn,
my foolish child,' said she.
'This cramped place is not our lot,
and suffering pain in prison.'

'Is there another place,' he said,
'lovelier than ours?
Is there brighter light than this
that your grief grows so heavy?'

'For I believe,' the young child said,
'mother, although you mourn,
we have our share of light.
Don't waste your thoughts in sorrow.'

'I do not wonder at what you say,
young son,' the girl replied.
'You think this is a hopeful place
because you have seen no other.

'If you knew what I have seen
before this dismal place
you would be downcast also
in your nursery here, my soul.'

'Since it is you know best, lady,'
the little child replied,

'hide from me no longer
what more it was you had.'

'A great outer world in glory
formerly was mine.
After that, beloved boy,
my fate is a darkened house.'

At home in all his hardships,
not knowing a happier state,
fresh-cheeked and bright, he did not grudge
the cold and desolate prison.

And so is the moral given:
the couple there in prison
are the people of this world,
imprisoned life is their span.

Compared with joy in the Son of God
in His everlasting realm
an earthly mansion is only grief,
prisoners all the living.

GEARÓID (IARLA) MAC GEARAILT

(1338–98)

MAIRG ADEIR OLC RIS NA MNÁIBH!
(Woe to Him Who Slanders Women)
(2nd half of 14th century)

[The first poet of Norman stock known to have composed in Irish, Gearóid Mac Gearailt, 3rd Earl of Desmond, is also the earliest recorded writer of courtly lyrics in the language. There are thirty-nine extant poems attributed to him. While they seem wholly native to the Gaelic world, they have features in common with the carols and lyrics of contemporary England and northern France.

The earliest copy of the present poem has a final quatrain which has been excluded from all editions to date. This copy is in a problematic version of phonetic script and, consequently, there is nothing to correspond to it in Thomas Kinsella's translation below. The following rendition of the quatrain in normalized spelling was suggested by William Gillies:

> Maith is spréidh an bheatha bheo
> ní fiú leo — a-déar a ndáil —
> muna éadtar colgtha an bod,
> mairg adeir olc ris na mnáibh.

It may be translated literally as: 'They reck the wealth and riches of the living world as nothing — I'll tell how it is with them — if the prick is not found rampant. Woe to him who slanders women.'

The text is from T.F. O'Rahilly, *Dánta Grádha: An Anthology of Irish Love Poetry (A.D. 1350–1750)*, 2nd ed. (Cork: Cork University Press, 1926), p. 4. Thomas Kinsella's translation is from *The New Oxford Book of Irish Verse*, p. 110.]

1

Mairg adeir olc ris na mnáibh!
 bheith dá n-éagnach ní dáil chruinn;
a bhfuaradar do ghuth riamh
 dom aithne ní hiad do thuill.

2

Binn a mbriathra, gasta a nglór,
 aicme rerab mór mo bháidh;
a gcáineadh is mairg nár loc;
 mairg adeir olc ris na mnáibh.

3

Ní tháinig fionghal ná feall,
 ná ní ar a mbeith grainc ná gráin;
ní sháraighid cill ná clog;
 mairg adeir olc ris na mnáibh.

4

Ní tháinig riamh acht ó mhnaoi
 easbag ná rí (dearbhtha an dáil),
ná príomhfháidh ar nách biadh locht;
 mairg adeir olc ris na mnáibh.

5

Agá gcroidhe bhíos a ngeall;
 ionmhain leó duine seang slán —
fada go ngeabhdaois a chol;
 mairg adeir olc ris na mnáibh.

6

Duine arsaidh leathan liath
 ní hé a mian dul 'na dháil;
annsa leó an buinneán óg bocht;
 mairg adeir olc ris na mnáibh!

TRANSLATION

Woe to him who slanders women.
 Scorning them is no right thing.
All the blame they've ever had
 is undeserved, of that I'm sure.

Sweet their speech and neat their voices.
 they are a sort I dearly love.
Woe to the reckless who revile them.
 Woe to him who slanders women.

Treason, killing, they won't commit
 nor any loathsome, hateful thing.
Church or bell they won't profane.
 Woe to him who slanders women.

But for women we would have,
 for certain, neither kings nor prelates,
prophets mighty, free from fault.
 Woe to him who slanders women.

They are the victims of their hearts.
 They love a sound and slender man
— nor soon do they dislike the same.
 Woe to him who slanders women.

Ancient persons, stout and grey,
 they will not choose for company,
but choose a juicy branch, though poor.
 Woe to him who slanders women!

AISLINGE DO-CHONARCSA
(On the Death of His Wife)
(1392)

[Eileanóir, daughter of Séamus Buitléir, Earl of Ormond, and Gearóid Mac Gearailt, Earl of Desmond, were married in 1358. She died in 1392. In a poem he wrote for Gearóid, the poet Gofraidh Fionn Ó Dálaigh addressed her as 'Countess of Desmond, ever indulgent to poets' (cf. Láimhbheartach Mac Cionnaith (ed.), *Dioghluim Dána*, pp. 338–44, at p. 344). Gearóid's poem says that love and faith prevent him from writing her elegy.
 The text reproduces, in normalized spelling, that published by Gearóid Mac Niocaill in 'Duanaire Ghearóid Iarla', *Studia Hibernica*, vol. 3 (1963), pp. 40–1, apart from a defective final verse in which the Virgin Mary and Saint Anne are invoked. It is here translated into English, for the first time, by Patrick Crotty.]

1

Aislinge do-chonarcsa
is mé gan chodladh rathrom:
damh níos shásadh codalta
mo cheirtleath do bhuain asam.

2

Atá aithbhear agamsa
ar Chríost ris nár chóir deabhaidh:
mar do scar sé mh'anamsa
riom féin, is mé im beathaidh.

3

Dó féin do ba éigcneasta
sinn do scaradh re chéile;
sinn riamh 'nar lucht éinleaptha
mar do chum an Flaith féine.

4

Ní dom dheoin mo dhealaghadh —
air seo is fiadha Rí nimhe;
gan againn cúis deaghalta
is mairg do dheaghail sinne.

5

Mairg do Mhac na fíorÓighe
rug an aoinbhean do thoghas
is go raibh 'gar dTríonóidne
mná na cruinne ar a chomas.

6

Ó nár leig Mac mórMhuire
dhi bheith níos sia 'nar n-iomdhaidh
go dtuga sé trócaire
dom anam is dom ionmhain.

7

Do-ghéanainn a marbhnaidhse
dá leigeadh a grádh damhsa,
dámadh fhearr dá hanmainse
ná guide ar son a hanma.

TRANSLATION

A vision I saw
in my fitful sleep,
I who have not rested
since the stealing of my soul.

Cause for complaint I have
against Christ the peerless
that He took my soul from me
and left me to live on.

Cruel was His sundering
of one from the other,
of bedfellows as spotless
as His sacrament ordained.

Unwilling was our parting:
the King of Heaven knows
We never would have parted.
Woe that He chose to part us.

Woe to the Virgin's Son
who took my chosen one
though the Trinity put all women
on earth at His command.

Since Great Mary's Son
turned her from our bed
may He grant mercy now
to my only love and soul.

I would compose her death poem
if my passion would permit it
and if that were better for her
than to pray that she be saved.

TADHG ÓG Ó hUIGINN

(d. 1448)

CIA DO-GHÉABHAINN GO GRÁINNE
(For Gráinne, Daughter of Ó Ceallaigh)
(early 15th century)

[Tadhg Óg Ó hUiginn was the outstanding poet of the fifteenth century. From c.1403 he was attached to Tadhg Ó Ceallaigh (d. 1410), chief of the O'Kellys, in Uí Mhaine in south-east Connacht. Ó Ceallaigh's sister, Gráinne (d. 1440), is the addressee of the following poem, in which the poet describes himself as her *ollamh*. He plays not only on her paternal ancestry in Uí Mhaine but also on her links through her mother with the line of Cathal Croibhdhearg (the 'Crobhdhonn'; d. 1224), ancestor of the O'Conors of Connacht, the epicentre of whose territory was Rathcroghan (Cruacha) in County Roscommon.

   The poem seems a genuine attempt to offer solace to Gráinne on the death of her son, Ruaidhrí. She had trovered a waif (*torchairthe*) from heaven and the Lord had chosen to reclaim him, but they will be reunited hereafter. The trope gestures to the opening quatrain of a poem written almost five hundred years earlier by another Connacht poet, Irard mac Coisse, for another grieving mother who was also, like Gráinne, of Connacht noble blood, but whose dignity was greater because she was

consort to the King of Tara (see pp. 305–7). Ó hUiginn's
poem gently links their fates. The earlier queen was called
Der Fáil, spelt Dearbháil in Early Modern Irish; Ó
hUiginn's wish is to assuage Gráinne's *dearbháile*, 'grief'
(quatrain 1). His long paraphrase of the earlier poem
details the *conghlonnacht*, 'analogy', between them
(quatrain 8), but also evokes *conghlonnacht* in its stylistic
sense — 'quatrain-linking through the repetition of the
closing word(s) of one with the opening word(s) of
another' — which in turn suggests the ebb and flow of life
to which she must be reconciled. Finally, he mentions two
extraordinary precedents for heeding a poet's request; a
third great honour will be shown to the poetic order if she
grants his request that she cease to mourn.

Apart from minor changes in presentation, the following
text and translation are as in: Lambert McKenna,
Aithdioghluim Dána, vol. 1, pp. 47–50; vol. 2, pp 29–31.]

1
Cia do-ghéabhainn go Gráinne
do bhacfadh dhí a dearbháile?
ar mo chomhairle an mbia an bhean?
mh'fhorfhuighle cia ó gcreidfeadh?

2
Más fhíor Gráinne i nglas chumhadh
nach urusa d'fhuasguladh
a-tá ormsa 'n-a eire
gobhang na mná Mainighe.

3
Biaidh mar shaoilim ó sho a-mach
ag ríoghain rátha Teamhrach
mo chéadfhuighle acht go gcluine
éagcuimhne ar a heolchuire.

4
Bás a meic gidh mór an crádh
do ríoghain Rosa Chomán
a fhearg do ba doilghe dhí
an Ceard do-roighne Ruaidhrí.

5
Dámadh hé a hadhbhar sgíse
sgaradh ria don Ruaidhríse,
ní hadhbhar sgís an sgaradh;
faghbhadh dís gan dealughadh.

6
Tuigeadh féin nach fáth tuirse
duilleabhar an domhainse
— gabhadh sé do Ghráinne greim —
is sgáile é nó is aisling.

7
Mar thorchuirthe tugadh dhí
nuachar na ríghe Ruaidhrí;
an Té rug é as a haithle
is É thug an torchairthe.

8
Do bhí ag mnaoi do mhnáibh Connacht
— is cubhaidh a gconghlonnacht —
mac mar sin do uair oighidh;
bir lat uaim dá hionnsoighidh.

9
Do chuir mar chuirim ba dheas
Mac Coise ceann na n-éigeas
go hinghin Taidhg uair oile
san aird thuaidh a theachtaire.

10
Teasda céadrogha an chuaine
rug do rígh na Craobhruaidhe;
an bhearn do-cháidh san chloinnse
Dearbh-áil nochar fhuluingse.

11
Nír bh'iongnadh éagcaoine a meic
d'inghin Taidhg an Eich oirrdhreic;
Rí Oiligh do b'é a athair
sé 'n-a oidhir d'Ultachaibh.

12
Aodh mhac Domhnaill Dúin Monaidh
ráith Oiligh 'n-a urchomhair;
dá mbeath d'ádh ar Oileach Néid
fa soidheach lán a leithéid.

13
'Ná bíodh uirre, aithnim dí,
cumha a meic' ar Mac Coise;
'abair dhamhsa re Dearbh-áil
gur sealbh fhallsa dá fhagháil.

14
'Ní tharla ar neach gus a-niogh
ní badh aoibhinn le haigneadh
nach cúis toirse i n-am oile;
sloinnse thall, a theachtoire.

15
'Mac ar iasacht má uair sin
ón Dúileamh aithidh éigin
abair re Dearbh-áil as m'ucht
nach sealbh do b'áil don iasucht'.

16
Searbh ar tús lé ga labhra
teagasg an fhir ealadhna;
gidh eadh do thráigh a tuirse
Dear-bháil leis na briathraibhse.

17
Tug do Dhia nach dingneadh sain
inghean ríogh Cruachan cumhaidh;
mairg nach dingneadh a ndearna
inghean Taidhg dá tighearna.

18
Déanadh a ndearna Dearbh-áil
do Dhia athair mar anáir;
ua an Chrobhdhuinn gá doilghe dhi
ná oidhre Domhnaill dise?

19
Sgar dhamh a cheo red chridhe,
— ar Ghráinne is é m'impidhe —
d'éis do mheic, a fhleasg leamhna,
gidh leasg dheit gan doimheanma.

20
Dias aile áiréamhas mé
tug dá honóir don éigse;
dá mbeath rún mh'éara agaibh
déana tnúdh le a dtugadair.

21
Bíodh ar th'úidh a aithris soin
a bhfuair Aithirne ó Eochaidh;
eochair dod chosg do chumhaidh
rosg Eochaidh don ollamhain.

22
Feadh bliadhna buan a loise
— sgéal ar a bhfuil fiadhnoise —
Maol Sheachluinn do-bhir Banbha
dom leathchuing fhir ealadhna.

23
Súil Eochaidh 'n-a honóir sain
ceannas Banbha re bliadhain
th'fhagháil as an gceas chumhadh
treas anáir na healadhan.

24
Fiarfoighidh do-ním a-nos
an fulang leat ar labhras?
munab cead ar chan t'ollamh
gá beag damh a ndubhromar.

25
Gabh chugad a gcanaim ruibh,
a ríoghain do fhréimh Ceallaigh,
— gá dás grádh ag duine dhí —
tuile agus trágh gach toice.   CIA.

TRANSLATION

1
Whom can I get to send to Gráinne to check her grief? Will she take my advice? What messenger could get her to believe my words?

2
Gráinne, I hear, is in chains of woe, and 'twill be hard to free her; the prison of the lady of Í Maine[1] oppresses me (too).

3
The grief of the queen of Teamhair Fort[2] will be felt no longer by her if she only hearken to my first words.

4
Though to the queen of Ros Comáin[3] her son's death is heavy affliction, yet she would find the anger of the Lord who created Ruaidhrí to be worse still.

5
If it be her separation from Ruaidhrí that casts her down, (let me tell her that) separation is no reason for being overwhelmed; let her find any two folk who are never separated!

6
Let her reflect that the (loss of) the world's glory is no cause of unhappiness; let this thought take hold of her; the world is a shadow or a dream.

7
Ruaidhrí was given a gift to her, spouse of the realm; He who took that gift away was He who gave it.

8
Another lady of the Connachta — I may aptly compare them — had a son who died like him; tell her that when thou goest to her.

1. Uí Mhaine.
2. In parish of Kiltoom, County Roscommon.
3. Roscommon.

9

Long ago Mac Coise, chief poet, sent, as I am now sending to Gráinne southward, a messenger to the daughter of Tadhg[4] in the North.

10

Of the children whom Dearbháil had borne to the lord of the Red Branch,[5] the choice one died; she could not bear the gap thus broken in her family.

11

No wonder that she, daughter of the famous Tadhg an Eich,[6] wept for her son; Oileach's[7] king was his father,[8] and he was heir to the men of Ulaidh.

12

To Aodh,[9] son of Domhnall of Dún Monaidh,[10] Oileach's Ráth was to come soon; a full vessel would have been Oileach of Néid had such a prince been vouchsafed it.

13

Mac Coise then spoke (to his messenger): 'I bid her not to grieve for her son; tell her from me that she had only an apparent ownership of him.

14

'No man ever yet had a thing which rejoiced his spirit but it caused him grief thereafter,' that is what thou art to say, O messenger.

15

'Tell her from me that, if she got a son on loan for a time, the loan was not meant to be a possession.'

16

Bitter at the first Dearbháil found the wise man's words, but they caused her grief to ebb.

17

The daughter of Cruacha's king agreed to God's wish that she grieve no more; 'twere a pity for any other lady not to do for her lord what Tadhg's daughter did.

18

Let her (Gráinne) do as Dearbháil to please God the Father; how was the scion of the Crobhdhonn[11] a bitterer loss to Gráinne than Domhnall's heir to Dearbháil?

19

Remove from thy heart, O princess of the Leamhain,[12] the mist of sorrow for him — this is what I beseech of Gráinne — even though thou art loth not to yield to dejection after his loss.

20

Of two others shall I speak who gave poetry its due honour; do thou imitate (them in giving) such honour (to me) if thou feelest inclined to reject my advice.

21

Take care to imitate the honour which was conferred on Aithirne by Eochaidh;[13] (the thought of) Eochaidh's eye given to the poet should stop thy lamenting.

22

For a whole year — the story is well attested — Maoilsheachlainn[14] entrusted Banbha to a poet like me; long shall the glory of it last.

23

Eochaidh's eye, the year's rule over Banbha, both given to honour poets — now thy rescue from grief shall be the third honour done the profession.

24

Canst thou, I ask thee now, bear to consider what I have said? If my words meet not with thy good will — well, at all events, I have said enough.

25

Take to heart what I tell thee, O queen of the stock of Ceallach;[15] every possession is a tide that ebbs; how can one love it?

4. i.e. Der Fáil (Dearbháil), daughter of Tadg mac Cathail (d. 956), King of Connacht.
5. A synonym for Ulster.
6. Tadhg *an Eich*, Tadhg 'of the Horse', alias Tadg mac Cathail.
7. Oileach (Aileach, alias the Grianán of Oileach (Grianán Oiligh), Oileach's Ráth (Ráth Oiligh), and Oileach of Néid (Oileach Néid)), is a massive stone fort four miles north-west of Derry city. It was royal capital of the Northern Uí Néill of Donegal, Derry and Tyrone.
8. i.e. Domnall úa Néill, King of Aileach, and King of Tara.
9. Dearbháil's son.
10. In Northern Uí Néill territory.
11. 'the Red Hand', i.e. Cathal Croibhdhearg, d. 1224.
12. In County Tyrone.
13. The legendary King Eochaidh took the eye out of his head for his poet Aithirne.
14. Maoilsheachlainn (d. 1022) son of Domhnall, King of Tara, who granted rule of Ireland to his poet.
15. Eponymous ancestor of the O'Kellys.

THOMAS SMYTH

(*fl.* 1561–91)

from:
INFORMATION FOR IRELAND (1561)

[The preceding selection of texts represents mainly the work of the upper echelons of professional poets. The lower orders of poets, and the diverse range of popular entertainers, troupers, healers and soothsayers, in whose ranks there were many women, are more difficult to trace. It would have been difficult to represent the performance aspect of their work in any case. In addition, their learned contemporaries had little interest in preserving their compositions. It is a tragic irony that they achieve a new visibility in the record for the sixteenth century during the Tudor conquest, when government policy threatened to annihilate them.

Thomas Smyth, an English apothecary living in Dublin, was acquainted with English officials and writers such as Edmund Spenser, Thomas Bryskett and Geoffrey Fenton. In 1566 he was granted an annual stipend, 'for that the greater part of this contray byrthe ar wonted to use the mynisterie of their leeches and such lyke; and neglecting the Apothecarie's science, the said Thomas therby hath been greatly hyndred, and in manner enforced to abandon that his faculty'. His account of 'Irish rhymers', addressed to the lords of the Queen's Privy Council, is ridden with prejudice, and perhaps professional jealousy. It is of great interest not only on that account, but also for the detail it preserves, much of it founded on fact. The most glaring distortion is his separation of the *aos dána* from the category of the *file*. These should properly be regarded as one category.

Smyth's account of the poets (dated 5 May 1561) was published by Herbert F. Hore in the *Ulster Journal of Archaeology*, vol. 6 (1858), pp. 165–7 and 202–12. The following excerpts are from ibid., pp. 166–7. The glosses in parentheses and round brackets are as in Hore's text.]

Their is in Irland four shepts[1] in maner all Rimers. The first of them is calleid the Brehounde,[2] which in English is calleid the Judge . . . The second sourte is the Shankee,[3] which is to saye in English, the petigrer.[4] They have also great plainty of cattell, wherewithall they do sucker[5] the rebells. They make the ignoraunt men of the country to belyve that they be discended of Alexander the Great, or of Darius, or of Cæsar, or of some other notable prince; which makes the ignorant people to run madde, and cerieth not what they do; the which is very hurtfull to the realme.

The thirde sorte is called the Æosdan,[6] which is to say in English, the bards, or the rimine[7] septes; and these people be very hurtfull to the comonwhealle,[8] for they chifflie mayntayne the rebells; and, further, they do cause them that would be true, to be rebelious theves, extorcioners, murtherers, ravners, yea and worse if it were possible. Their furst practisse is, if they se[9] anye younge man discended of the septs of *Ose* or *Max*,[10] and have halfe a dowsen[11] aboute him, then will they make him a Rime, wherein they will commend his father and his aunchetours,[12] nowmbrying howe many heades they have cut of, howe many townes they have burned, and howe many virgins they have defloured, howe many notable murthers they have done, and in the ende they will compare them to Aniball, or Scipio, or Hercules, or some other famous person; wherewithall the pore foole runs madde, and thinkes indede it is so. Then will he gather a sorte of rackells[13] [rake-hells] to him, and other he most geat him a Proficer [prophet], who shall tell him howe he shall spede (as he thinkes). Then will he geat him lurking to a syde of a woode, and ther keepith him close til morninge; and when it is day light, then will they go to the poore vilages, not sparinge to distroye young infants, aged people;

---

1. Septs.
2. For Irish *breitheamh*, 'judge'.
3. For Irish *seanchaidh*, 'historian'.
4. Pedigreer.
5. Succour.
6. For Irish *aos dána*, literally 'folk of art'; usually in reference to poets.
7. Rhyming.
8. Commonweal.
9. See.
10. For Irish *Ó* and *Mac* as first element in surnames.
11. Dozen.
12. Ancestors.
13. 'Rakell' is meant to translate Irish *ceithearn tighe*, a term usually anglicized as 'kerne'. The term *ceithearn tighe* was falsely etymologized in Irish as *cith Ifrinn*, 'shower of Hell', and this etymologizing is pointed up in 'rakell', as though from 'rake' and 'Hell'. See Alan Harrison, 'The Shower of Hell', *Éigse*, vol. 18, p. 305.

and if the women be ever so great withe childe, her they will kill; burninge the houses and corne, and ransakinge of the poore cottes [cottages]. They will then drive all the kine and plowe horses, with all other cattell, and drive them awaye. Then muste they have a bagpipe bloinge afore them; and if any of theis cattell fortune to waxe wearie or faynt, they will kill them, rather than it sholde do the honeur's [owners] goode. If they go by anye house of fryers[14] or relygious house, they will geave them 2 or 3 beifs [beeves,] and they will take them, and praie for them (yea) and prayes[15] their doings, and saye his father was accustomed so to do; wherein he will rejoise; and when he is in a safe place, they will fall to the devision of the spoile, according to the dyscresion of the captin. And the mesingers that goithe of their errants cleamith the gottes[16] for their parcell; — beycause it is an aunscient custome they will not break it. Now comes the Rymer that made the Ryme, with his Rakry.[17] The Rakry is he that shall utter the ryme; and the Rymer himselfe sitts by with the captain verie proudlye. He brings with him also his Harper, who please all the while that the raker[18] sings the ryme. Also he hath his Barde, which is a kinde of folise fellowe; who also must have a horse geven him; the harper must have a new safern [saffron-coloured] shurte, and a mantell, and a hacnaye;[19] and the rakry must have xx or xxx kine, and the Rymer himselfe horse and harness [suit of armour] with a nag to ride on, a silver goblett, a pair of bedes of corall, with buttons of silver; — and this, with more, they loke for to have, for reducinge distruxione of the Comenwealth, and to the blasfemye of God; and this is the best thinge that ye Rymers causith them to do.

The fourth sort of Rymers is called Fillis,[20] which is to say in English, a Poete. Theis men have great store of cattell, and use all the trades of the others, with an adicion of prophecies. Theis are great mayntayners of whitches[21] and other vile matters; to the great blasfemye of God, and to great impoverishinge of the comenwealthe. And, as I have saied of the foure secktes, ar

devided in all places of the fowre partes of Irland, as Ulster, Launster,[22] Munster, and Conet;[23] and some in Methe;[24] and some in the Ilands beyond Irland,[25] as the land of Sainctes,[26] the Ynce Bofine,[27] Ynce Tirke,[28] Ynce Mayne,[29] and Ynce Clere.[30] These Ilands are under the rule of Homaile,[31] and they are verie pleasaunt and fertile, plentie of woode, water, and arabell gronnd and pastur and fishe, and a very temperate ayer.

Their be many braunches belonging to the foure sortes; as the Gogathe,[32] which is to say in English, the glytayne,[33] for one of them will eate 2 or 3 galons of butter at a sitinge, halfe a mutton. And an other, called the Carruage;[34] he is much like the habram's man,[35] and comenlye he goeth nakid, and carise dise and cardes with him; and he will play the heare off his head, and his eares; and theis be mantained by the Rymers.

There is a sort of women that be calleid the goyng women;[36] they be great blasphemers of God; and they rune from contry to contry, soynge sedicione amongst the people. They are comen to all men; and if any of them happen to be with childe, she will say that it is the greatest Lorde adjoining, whereof the Lordes ar glad, and doth appoincte them to be nurysed.

Ther is one other sorte that is calleid the Mannigscoule.[37] Ther order is for to singe; and the chyfest of them most have but one eye, and he[38] is calleid Lucas; they do much harme.

Their is other towe sortes that goithe about withe the Bachell[39] of Jesus, as they call it. Theis run from contry to contry; and if they come to

14. Friars.
15. Praise.
16. From past participle of verb 'get'.
17. For Irish *reacaire*, 'declaimer [of poetry]'.
18. Ditto.
19. Hackney.
20. For Irish *file* (in singular, with English plural ending).
21. Witches.
22. Leinster.
23. Connacht.
24. Meath.
25. The five islands named are all west of Killary harbour and Clew Bay in County Mayo.
26. For Irish *Inis na Naomh* (literally 'Island of the Saints'), now called Caher Island.
27. Inishbofin.
28. Inishturk.
29. Inishmaine.
30. Clare Island.
31. Irish Ó Máille.
32. Possibly for Irish *cogantach*, 'masticator'.
33. Glutton.
34. For Irish *cearrbhach*, 'gambler; dice-player'.
35. i.e. 'Abraham-man' (beggar).
36. Probably a calque on Irish *techta*, 'messenger' (from the verb *téighid*, 'goes'), or on *ben tsiubhail* (plural *mná siubhail*): see next.
37. For Irish *mná siubhail* (later *mná siúil*), 'walking women' (from *siubhal*, 'walking').
38. *sic*.
39. For Irish *bachall*, 'crozier'.

any house wheir a woman is with child, they will putt the same about her, and, wither she will or no, causithe her to geave them money. They will undertake that she shall have good deilvery of her childe; to the great distruxione of the people conserninge ther soule's health. Others goith about with St. Patrike's croysur, and playse the like partes or worse; and no doubte as longe as theis bene usyed, the worde of God can never be knowne amongst them, nor the prince fearyed, nor the contry prosper.

For a reddresse theirof it might be esaly holpen[40] if your honours will geave eare ther

40. i.e. easily helped.

unto; and if it may stand with your pleasures that I should make any further sertifycate[41] how this nowghty[42] people may be ponyste,[43] and to cause them to leave their yle[44] facions, I will, if it be your pleasurs, showe by what mayne they may be redressed. And as concerninge the fostering of the Irishe men's children, it needed as muche redress as any other matter than can be movyed. The which I will showe your honours when it pleasith you.

41. Certificate.
42. Naughty.
43. Punished.
44. Vile.

ANONYMOUS

A COLD HOUSE OF CLAY: ANNALISTIC OBITUARIES AND NOTICES (900–1600)

[The Irish annals are not concerned exclusively with the deeds of men: they also contain a rich seam of notices about women, particularly death-notices. Some obituaries are formulaic, others are factual, many have both aspects. The characteristics for which a woman was most likely to be commended were generosity to the men of learning, charity to the poor, piety, and fidelity to her current partner; this last virtue was often equated with chastity. In the course of a lifetime, a noblewoman might contract a series of marriages, and far from evading the fact, her obituary may specify each of them (see, for example under 1327, 1421, 1493 and 1527 below). The remarkable nickname of one thrice-married woman (who also had other liaisons), 'Port of the three enemies', is invoked apparently as a badge of honour (1395).

It seems that numerous 'marriages' were endorsed as such by customary arrangements which did not necessarily include the sanction of church ceremonies. Indeed, the annals give honourable mention on occasion to the 'wives' and 'concubines' of clerics (for example, under 1419, 1427). However, a canonical marriage did not merely suggest Christian virtue but also had connotations of gentility and high character, and might be highlighted in an obituary by the use of terms such as *uxor* and *bean*

phósta, both meaning 'canonically recognized wife' (1239, 1527). Usually, however, the annals used the simple terms *bean*, 'woman; wife', or *inghean*, 'daughter', particular identity being fixed by reference to the woman's husband/partner, father or other male relative. As in the genealogies, so in the annals: the limited visibility women achieve is within a frame of patrilineal relations.

Not all unions were made peaceably. The fact that many aristocratic marriages were politically motivated increased the risk of intimidation or force being applied to women. It is impossible to determine how frequently women were handed over or abducted by their own kinsmen, who stood to gain by placing them in new unions; certainly, the notorious case of Derbforgaill, abducted with the help of her brother (see pp. 192–7) finds an echo, for example, in the case of Tadhg son of Cathal Croibhdhearg, who abducted his own mother to ransom himself (see under 1243). It is also difficult to establish what degree of violence was used against women in such cases. An annalistic notice will not disclose the full implications of an outrage. For example, not only is the rape of the Abbess of Kildare in 1132 (see below) described euphemistically, the motivation for it — to disqualify her from holding office in order to appropriate it for a kinswoman of her violators (as can be gathered from notices elsewhere in the annals) — is passed over. References to women's use of violence are few, but enough to show that it was not confined to the domestic sphere and that it won admiration on occasion (1305, 1315, 1316).

There was no ambivalence about the annalists' praise for women who dispensed largess, particularly to the men of learning, but there was more to this than male self-regard. Hereditary 'learned families' — of poets, historians, musicians and other artists — consisted of males and females, and no doubt the females, as much as the males, were conditioned to the belief that patronage of literature and other arts was praiseworthy. Women raised in this belief were likely to promote it very actively if they married into other learned families and especially if they became proprietors or co-proprietors of 'guest-houses' (1427, 1447, 1524). Yet women who were not related to poets and scholars also valued and invested much in learning and art, and some were disposed to remarkable acts of patronage (1451, 1540).

Broadly speaking, the obituaries show that one gained esteem in society in large part through giving gifts. This applied to bequests to the church, of moveable property (1157, 1167), and of land (1239, 1282), and to paying for the building of the monastery where one might be buried (1474, 1523). Burial in any prestigious monastery (1342, 1525, 1527) probably entailed large bequests before and after death. Charity to the poor and to strangers was the corollary of generosity to those who were 'deserving' of it. The piety of women is naturalized in the annals, with references such as those below to daily devotions (see notice of Máire daughter of Eoghan Ó Máille, who died in 1523), pilgrimage (1445), retirement from the world to a monastery (1437, 1447, 1477, 1528), and last rites (1327, 1395, 1527, 1542). The annals provide no account of women's funerals (but they were probably much like those of men of similar rank), and they rarely refer to the illnesses which caused death. An exception is the reference to a death from breast cancer (under 1451), perhaps the earliest such notice in Irish sources. Dismemberment and burial of parts of the corpse in different locations, for spiritual and temporal advantage, came into fashion among European royals and nobles in the twelfth century. This probably accounts for the reference to the separate burial of the body and relics (taisi) of Mór daughter of Ó Briain (under 1252).

Gaelic names are given in normalized spelling. Short titles are employed for the following publications (in order of appearance):

Annals of the Four Masters = John O'Donovan (ed.), *Annála Ríoghachta Éireann: the Annals of the Kingdom of Ireland by the Four Masters*, 7 vols (Dublin, 1848–51);

Annals of Loch Cé = William M. Hennessy (ed.), *The Annals of Loch Cé: A Chronicle of Irish Affairs from A.D. 1014 to A.D. 1590*, 2 vols (Dublin, 1871);

Annals of Innisfallen = Seán Mac Airt (ed.), *The Annals of Innisfallen (MS. Rawlinson B. 503)* (Dublin: Dublin Institute for Advanced Studies, 1951);

Annals of Clonmacnoise: = Denis Murphy (ed.), *The Annals of Clonmacnoise: Being Annals of Ireland from the Earliest Period to A.D. 1408* (Dublin: University Press, 1896);

Annals of Connacht = A. Martin Freeman (ed.), *Annála Connacht: The Annals of Connacht (A.D. 1224–1544)* (Dublin: Dublin Institute for Advanced Studies, 1944);

Annals of Ulster = W.M. Hennessy and B. Mac Carthy (eds.), *Annála Uladh: The Annals of Ulster,* 4 vols (Dublin, 1887, 1893, 1895, 1901);

Annals of Ireland = John O'Donovan (ed.), *The Annals of Ireland from the Year 1443 to 1468, Translated from the Irish by Duald Mac Firbis* (Dublin: Irish Archaeological Society, 1846).]

Díainim daughter of Dubgiolla

Dianimh, protection of our purity, is fettered
  by the power of the King of the elements;
Alas! that the long and beautiful person is
  in a cold house of clay.
[Annals of the Four Masters, *s.a.* 906]

Mór daughter of Congalach Úa Conchobair

An army was led by the son of Brian, i.e. Donnchad, and Conchobar Úa Máel Sechnaill, into Fine Gall;[1] and the men of Tethba,[2] i.e. the Sinnaig,[3] took many prisoners from the *Daimliag*[4] of Lusca;[5] and they carried off hostages from the son[6] of Máel na mBó, together with Mór, daughter of Congalach Úa Conchobair. Diarmait, son of Máel na mBó, and Gilla Pátraic, lord of Osraige,[7] went into Meath, whence they carried off captives and very great spoils, in revenge of the going of Mór daughter of Congalach Úa Conchobair, to Congalach Úa Máel Sechnaill, in violation of Gilla Pátraic,[8] and in revenge also of the cattle spoils which Úa Máel Sechnaill had carried off from Meath.
[Annals of the Four Masters, *s.a.* 1053]

The coarb of Saint Brigit

The abbot's house of Cill Dara[9] was captured by the Uí Cheinnselaig[10] against the coarb of Brigit, and burned, and a large part of the church was burned, and a great many were slain there; and

---

1. Area in north County Dublin, anglicized Fingall.
2. An area comprising most of Westmeath and part of County Longford.
3. 'Foxes', a term for the folk of Tethba,
4. 'Great stone church'.
5. Lusk, north County Dublin.
6. i.e. Diarmait, son of Máel na mBó.
7. Roughly coterminous with modern diocese of Ossory in the Midlands.
8. i.e. her husband.
9. Kildare.
10. Roughly coterminous with County Wexford and parts of counties Wicklow and Carlow.

the nun herself was carried off a prisoner, and put into a man's bed.
[Annals of Loch Cé, *s.a.* 1132]

Derbforgaill daughter of Murchad Úa Máil Shechnaill
A synod was convened by the clergy of Ireland, and some of the kings, at the monastery of Droichet Átha,[11] the church of the monks. There were present seventeen bishops, together with the Legate and the successor of Patrick; and the number of persons of every other degree was countless. Among the kings were Muirchertach Úa Lochlainn, Tigernán Úa Ruairc, Úa hEochada and Úa Cerbaill . . . Muirchertach Úa Lochlainn presented seven score cows, and three score ounces of gold, to God and to the clergy, as an offering for the health of his soul. He granted them also a townland at Droichet Átha, i.e. Finnabair na nIngen.[12] Ó Cerbaill also gave them three score ounces of gold; and the wife of Úa Ruairc, the daughter of Úa Máil Shechnaill, gave as much more, and a chalice of gold on the altar of Mary, and cloth for each of the nine other altars that were in the church.
[Annals of the Four Masters, *s.a.* 1157]

The Church of the Nuns at Cluain Mhic Nóis was finished by Derbforgaill, daughter of Murchad Úa Máil Shechnaill.
[Annals of the Four Masters, *s.a.* 1167]

Éadaoin daughter of Fínghin Mac Carthaigh
Tadhg, the son of Aodh, son of Cathal Croibhdhearg, was set at liberty by Ó Raghallaigh, and he came with his forces to the Abbey of Boyle,[13] and afterwards to the house of Mac Diarmada (Cormac, son of Tomaltach), whom he took prisoner, together with his wife, the daughter of Mac Carthaigh, (viz. Éadaoin, daughter of Fínghin), who was Tadhg's own mother, and gave her as wife to Cú Chonnacht Ó Raghallaigh, for his own ransom.
[Annals of the Four Masters, *s.a.* 1243]

Mór daughter of Conchobhar Ó Briain
Mór, daughter of Conchobhar son of Tairdelbach Ó Briain [and wife] of Cormac Mac Carthaigh,

— and there was no woman in her time better than she — rested in Christ at Cill Lonáin.[14] She was buried there, and her relics were brought to Lios na mBráthar.[15]
[Annals of Innisfallen, *s.a.* 1252]

Sláine daughter of Ó Briain
Sláine daughter of Ó Briain, abbess of Cill Eóin,[16] the most pious, the most charitable, and the most generous woman in all Munster, died. May the King of Heaven grant forgiveness to her soul.
[Annals of Innisfallen, *s.a.* 1259]

Christina daughter of Ó Neachtain
Christina, Ó Neachtain's daughter, the wife of Diarmaid Mídheach Mac Diarmada, a right exceeding beautifull woman, well limmed, bountifull in bestowing, chast of her body, and ingenious and witty deliverie of her mind, Devout in her prayers, and finallie she was Inferior to none other of her tyme for any good parts requisite in a noble Gentlewoman, and charitable towards the order of Grey Monks, died with good penance.
[Annals of Clonmacnoise, *s.a.* 1269]

Lasairfhíona daughter of Cathal Croibhdhearg Ó Conchobhair
Lasairfhíona, daughter of Cathal Croibhdhearg, *uxor*[17] of Ó Domhnaill, gave a half-bally[18] of her marriage portion, i.e. the half-bally of Ros Birn,[19] to Clarus Mac Maoilín, and the community of Canons of Trinity Island on Loch Cé,[20] in honour of the Trinity and Lady Mary, *in hoc anno.*[21]
[Annals of Loch Cé, *s.a.* 1239]

Lasairfhíona, daughter of Cathal Croibhdhearg Ó Conchobhair, wife of Domhnall Óg Ó Domhnaill, i.e. the most noble, and hospitable, and beautiful woman that was in Erinn in her own time, *quievit in Christo.*[22]
[Annals of Loch Cé, *s.a.* 1282]

11. Anglicized Drogheda; the monastery in question is Mellifont.
12. A townland in parish of Donore, County Meath.
13. In County Roscommon, a Cistercian abbey founded 1148.
14. Probably Killonan, in barony of Glenquin, County Limerick.
15. Probably near Limerick city.
16. Killone, in barony of Islands, County Clare.
17. i.e. 'married wife'.
18. 'Bally', from Irish *baile*, is a medieval territorial unit, of varying extent, depending on terrain and soil quality.
19. Rossborne, near mouth of Ballysadare river, County Sligo.
20. Lough Key, north-west of Carrick-on-Shannon, County Roscommon.
21. i.e. 'in this year'.
22. i.e. 'rested in Christ'.

In Ghaillseach Shacsanach[23] *wife of Piers Bermingham*
Muirchertach Ó Conchobhair Failghe, and An Calbhach his brother, were slain by Sir Piers Bermingham, after he had deceitfully and shamefully invited them and acted as god-father to [the child of] the latter and as co-sponsor with the other. Masir, the little child who was a son of the latter, and whom Piers himself had sponsored at confirmation, was thrown over [the battlements of] the castle,[24] and it was thus it died. And twenty-three or twenty-four of the followers of those men mentioned above, were slain, for *An Ghaillseach Shacsanach* (she was the wife of the same Piers) used to give warning from the top of the castle of any who went into hiding, so that many were slain as a result of those warnings. And woe to the Gaoidheal who puts trust in a king's peace or in foreigners after that!
[Annals of Innisfallen, *s.a.* 1305]

Dearbhforgaill daughter of Maghnus Ó Conchobhair
. . . Aodh Ó Domhnaill, king of Tír Conaill, came into Cairbre,[25] and all the territory of Cairbre was destroyed by him through the counsel of his wife, i.e. the daughter of Maghnus Ó Conchobhair; and she herself, together with all she found of the gallowglasses[26] and the Clann Mhuirchertaigh, attacked the churches of Druim Cliabh,[27] where several of the clerics and comarbs of Druim Cliabh were plundered by her, *in hoc anno*.
[Annals of Loch Cé, *s.a.* 1315]

Aodh Ó Domhnaill and all the Ceinéal Conaill mustered a large army and they came again into Cairbre, and went to Caisléan Conchobhair[28] on this occasion; and Ruaidhrí, son of Domhnall Ó Conchobhair, separated from his own brothers, and made peace with Ó Domhnaill, and gave him the lordship of Cairbre. And Derbhforgaill, daughter of Maghnus Ó Conchobhair, retained a band of gallowglasses, and gave them a reward for the killing of Ruaidhrí, son of Domhnall Ó Conchobhair, who was subsequently slain by

them in violation of the relics of Tír Conaill which had previously been pledged to him; and great depredations were committed by the Ceinéal Conaill on the inhabitants of the district of Cairbre.
[Annals of Loch Cé, *s.a.* 1316]

Gormlaith daughter of Mac Diarmada
Gormlaith, Mac Diarmada's daughter, for a while the wife of Maghnus, son of Domhnall Ó Conchobhair, tanist[29] of Connacht, and queen of the Uí Mhaine with Conchobhar Ó Ceallaigh, after Maghnus, and queen of Luighne[30] with Fearghal Ó hEadhra, (and who was the woman of greatest reputation, hospitality, and liberality of her own kindred), died after the triumph of penance.
[Annals of Loch Cé, *s.a.* 1327]

Dearbhfáil daughter of Aodh Ó Domhnaill
The wife of the Earl of Ulster's son, i.e. the daughter of Toirdhealbhach Ó Briain, was taken to wife by Toirdhealbhach Ó Conchobhair, King of Connacht, and Dearbhfáil, daughter of Aodh Ó Domhnaill, was abandoned by him, in this year.
[Annals of Loch Cé, *s.a.* 1339]

Dearbhfáil, daughter of Aodh Ó Domhnaill, came on a visit to Inis Doighre,[31] to Conchobhar Mac Diarmada, where her death sickness seized her; and she was afterwards interred in the monastery of the Búill.[32]
[Annals of Loch Cé, *s.a.* 1342]

Fionnghuala daughter of Mac Finghin
Fionnghuala, daughter of Mac Finghin, wife of Fearghal Ó Duibhgeannáin, the woman who was best that was in Ireland in her own sphere as the wife of a learned man, died that year.
[Annals of Ulster, *s.a.* 1347]

Cobhlaith daughter of Cathal Ó Conchubhair
Cobhlaith Mhór, daughter of Cathal, the son of Domhnall Ó Conchubhair, King of Connacht, a rich and affluent woman, of good hospitality,

23. 'The Saxon Foreigner'.
24. Castle Carbury, County Kildare.
25. Carbury, County Sligo.
26. From Irish *gallóglaigh*, 'foreign warriors': Scottish mercenaries who fought as heavily armed foot soldiers.
27. Drumcliff, County Sligo.
28. Castleconor, barony of Tireragh, County Sligo.

29. From Irish *tánis(t)e*, 'second': one second in command to the chief, heir apparent.
30. The territory of O'Hara (Ó hEadhra), County Sligo.
31. Inishterry, an island in the Boyle river, County Roscommon.
32. Boyle, County Roscommon.

died, after the victory of penance, and was interred in the monaster of Boyle. It was she who was commonly called 'Port of the Three Enemies'[33] for she was wife of Ó Domhnaill, i.e. Niall, Lord of Tír Chonaill; of Aodh Ó Ruairc, Lord of Bréifne;[34] and of Cathal, the son of Aodh Bréifneach Ó Conchubhair, *ríoghdhamhna*[35] of Connacht.
[Annals of the Four Masters, *s.a.* 1395]

Áine daughter of Éinrí Mac Cába
Áine, daughter of Éinrí Mac Cába, mother of the children of the Abbot of Lios Gabhail[36], that is, Thomas the abbot, namely, son of the Great Archdeacon [died this year].
[Annals of Ulster, *s.a.* 1419]

Mór daughter of Ó Briain
Mór, the daughter of Brian Ó Briain, and wife of Walter Búrc, and who had been married to Tadhg Ó Cearbhaill, the most distinguished woman in her time, in Leatha Mogha,[37] for knowledge, hospitality, good sense, and piety, died. She was usually called Mór Mumhan na Muimhneach 'the Mór Mumhan of Munster'.[38]
[Annals of the Four Masters, *s.a.* 1421]

Siobhán daughter of Mac Cathmhaoil
Siobhán, daughter of the Bishop Mac Cathmhaoil, wife of Muiris Mac Uidhir, that is, the Great Archdeacon, died on the 13th of the Kalends of February; one that maintained a guest-house[39] at Claoininis[40] and at Ros Oirthear[41] for six and fifty years reputably, humanely [and] charitably.
[Annals of Ulster, *s.a.* 1427]

Gormlaith daughter of Dáibhíoth Ó Duibhgeannáin
Gormlaith daughter of Dáibhíoth Ó Duibhgeannáin, wife of Brian Mac Aodhagáin, and ultimately an anchorite, entered into rest in the monastery of the Trinity on Loch Cé.
[Annals of Connacht, *s.a.* 1437]

Mairgréag daughter of Tadhg Ó Cearbhaill
Many of the Irish of Irland went towards the Citty of S. James ye Apostle to Spaine in that Summer, about Tomaltach Mac Diarmada King of Magh Luirg, and about Mairgréag, Ó Cearbhaill's daughter, Calbhach's[42] wife, and with Mac Eochagáin the Duke of Ceinéal Fiachach Mhic Néill,[43] and about Ó hEidrisceoil Óg, and many more noble and ignoble persons … Mac Diarmada, Mairgréag, and Mac Eochagáin returned safe and sound from Spaine to their own houses in Ireland after receuing the Indulgences of S. James. But Ó hEidrisceoil died on sea coming from Spaine, and Gearóid, the son's son of Thomas, one of the Momonian[44] Geraldines, died in Spaine, and Aibhilín daughter of Éamonn son of Tomás Ó Fearghail, mother to the sons of Piers d'Alton died in Spaine also.
[Annals of Ireland, *s.a.* 1445]

Mairgréag daughter of Tadhg Ó Cearbhaill
Mairgréag daughter of Tadhg Ó Cearbhaill King of Éile,[45] the best of the women of the Gaoidhil and the one who made most causeways, churches, books, chalices and all articles useful for the service of a church, and she who issued the two general invitations[46] in one year, at Cill Achaidh[47] at the feast of Da-Shincheall[48] and at Ráth Iomgháin[49] at the first festival of Mary,[50] died of a cancer in the breast this year.
[Annals of Connacht, *s.a.* 1451]

Fionnghuala daughter of Mairgréag daughter of Tadhg Ó Cearbhaill
Fionnghuala (daughter of Calbhach Ó Conchobhair and to Mairgréag, Ó Cearbhaill's daughter), Ó Domhnaill's wife first, and secondly Aodh Buidhe Ó Néill's wife, the fairest and most famous woman in all Ireland, besides her own

---

33. Irish, Port na dTrí Námhad.
34. Roughly co-extensive with modern counties Cavan and Leitrim.
35. i.e. 'the material of a king': one eligible for kingship.
36. Lisgoole Abbey, on Lough Erne, near Ennikillen, County Fermanagh.
37. 'Mogh's Half', i.e. 'The Southern Half' of Ireland.
38. Originally a goddess, historicized as a Queen of Munster, an epitome of royalty.
39. In Irish *teach oigheadh*.
40. Cleenish Island in River Erne, Clanawley barony, County Fermanagh.
41. Rossory, Clanawley barony, County Fermanagh.

42. i.e. Calbhach Ó Conchobhair Failghe. Failghe is anglicized as Offaly.
43. In counties Westmeath and Offaly.
44. Momonia, Munster.
45. Ely (Ely O'Carroll) was roughly coterminous with the modern baronies of Ballybrit and Clonlisk, County Offaly.
46. For a detailed account of the remarkable feastings which followed these invitations, see Volume v, pp. 622–3.
47. Killeigh, a monastery in the barony of Geashill, County Offaly, founded by Saint Da-Shincheall (alias Sincheall).
48. 26 March.
49. Rathangan, County Kildare.
50. i.e. the festival of the Assumption of the Blessed Virgin, on 15 August.

mother, renouncing all worldly vanityes, and terrestriall glorious pomps, embracing the Eternall glory which God reserues for his blessed Angels, virgins, blessed widdows, saints, with the rest of his chosen flock, betooke herselfe into an austere devoute life in the monastery of Cill Achaidh, and the blessings of guests and strangers, and poore and rich of both poete-philosophers and Archi-poet-philosophers of Irland be on her in that life.
[Annals of Ireland, *s.a.* 1447]

Sadhbh daughter of Uilliam Mac Branáin
Sara (i.e. Sadhbh) daughter of Uilliam son of Conchobhar Mac Branáin, Maoilín Ó Maolchonaire's wife, *banollamh*[51] of Síol Muireadhaigh Mhic Fhearghusa[52] and a nurse of all guests and strangers, and of all the learned men in Ireland, died on Wednesday next after the feast-day of St Catherine the Virgin, and is buried in St Patrick's church in Oil Finn,[53] and Lord God of St Patrick be propitious to her soul.
[Annals of Ireland, *s.a.* 1447]

Fionnghuala daughter of Ó Briain
The monastery of Dún na nGall[54] was commenced by the Ó Domhnaill, i.e. by Aodh Ruadh, son of Niall Garbh Ó Domhnaill, and his wife, Fionnghuala, the daughter of Ó Briain (Conchobhar *na sróna*, Conchobhar 'of the nose'), and was granted by them to God and the friars of St Francis for the prosperity of their own souls, and that the monastery might by a burial-place for themselves and their descendants; and they not only granted this, but also conferred many other gifts upon them.
[Annals of the Four Masters, *s.a.* 1474]

Ailbhe daughter of Aodh Mhág Uidhir
Ailbhe, the daughter of Aodh Mhág Uidhir, a woman who, a year before her death, had retired with all her fortune to the monastery of Lios Gabhail, died.
[Annals of the Four Masters, *s.a.* 1477]

Fionnghuala daughter of Ó Conchubhair Failghe
Fionnghuala, the daughter of Ó Conchubhair Failghe, i.e. Calbhach, the son of Murchadh, and

wife of Ó Domhnaill, i.e. Niall Garbh, son of Toirdhealbhach *an Fhíona*,[55] and who was afterwards the wife of Aodh Buidhe, son of Brian Ballach (Ó Néill), a woman who had preserved her widowhood for the period of forty-nine years after the death of these good men, had deported herself chastely, honourably, piously, and religiously, died on the 25th of July.
[Annals of the Four Masters, *s.a.* 1493]

Máire daughter of Eoghan Ó Máille

[This note occurs in Royal Irish Academy MS 24 P 25, a miscellany written in 1513–14 by Ciothruadh Mag Fhionnghaill for Máire, daughter of Eoghan Ó Máille and wife of Mac Suibhne of Fanad (in north-east County Donegal). It contains a mixture of saints' lives, religious tracts and pious tales. The Annals of the Four Masters note Máire's death *s.a.* 1523. From: Paul Walsh (ed.), *Leabhar Chlainne Suibhne* (Dublin: Dollard Printinghouse, 1920), pp. 67–9.]

[I]t was this Mac Suibhne who first built the castle of Ráith Maoláin,[56] and it was his wife, namely, Máire, daughter of Eoghan son of Diarmaid Bacach Ó Máille who erected the monastery of Ráith Maoláin. It was Mac Suibhne and this wife who brought to that monastery a community from the south, from Munster. The prior who introduced the community was Suibhne, son of Aodh, son of Donnsléibhe, of Clann Suibhne Chonnachtach. The year of the Lord when the monastery was founded was 1516. At the end of two years after his founding of the monastery Mac Suibhne died — he who was the constable of greatest name and fame, and who, of all that came in this latter age, bestowed most on poets and schools (he had been forty-six years in the chieftainship of his family, and was seventy-eight years of age when he died) — having gained victory over the devil and the world, in the habit of the Friars of Mary, in the monastery which he himself had founded in her honour, on the seventh day of the month of April, on the Wednesday between the two Easters, in his own seat of Ráith Maoláin.

And at the end of four years after that, his noble, lovable wife, the daughter of Ó Máille, the most generous and best mother, and the woman

51. Woman *ollamh*.
52. Roughly co-extensive with the modern County Roscommon.
53. Elphin, County Roscommon.
54. Donegal.
55. i.e. 'of the wine'.
56. Rathmullen, County Donegal.

of most fame in regard to faith and piety of all who lived in her time, died. This is the manner in which she passed her days: she used to hear Mass once each day, and sometimes more than once; and three days in each week she used to spend on bread and water fare, with Lenten fast, and winter fast, and the Golden Fridays. She also caused to be erected a great hall for the Friars Minors in Dún na nGall. Not only that, but many other churches we shall not here enumerate that woman caused to be built in the provinces of Ulster and Connacht. It was she also who had this book of piety above copied in her own house, and all affirm that in her time there was no woman who passed her life better than she. And the manner of her death, after victory over the devil and the world, was, in the habit of the Friars of Mary, in the monastery which she herself had founded.

The following were the children of that couple we have spoken of: Ruaidhrí Óg, son of Ruaidhrí, son of Maolmhuire (he was the elder son, and a noble, princely man was he; he travelled many of the countries of the world, and could speak all the common languages; he died in the town of Ráith Maoláin ten years before his father's death, and was buried in the church of Ráith Maoláin; his was the first body ever buried there, and it was mainly on account of it that the monastery was erected and completed . . .), and Toirdhealbhach was the second son of that famous couple we have spoken of, and he was Mac Suibhne Fanad . . .

Mór daughter of Ó Briain; Aibhilín daughter of Ó Donnchadha an Ghleanna
Ó Briain's daughter, i.e. Mór, daughter of Toirdhealbhach, son of Tadhg Ó Briain, a woman who kept a general house of hospitality, died *in hoc anno*. Aibhilín, daughter of the Knight of the Glen,[57] wife of Ó Conchobhair Ciarraidhe, a good, charitable, humane woman, died.
[Annals of Loch Cé, *s.a.* 1524]

Aodh Buidhe Ó Néill and Gormlaith daughter of Ó Domhnaill
[T]here came not of the Ceinéal Eoghain, during a long time, his equal in nobleness, in hospitality, and in reputation for defending his family, and one who less allowed his enemies to oppress him,

and who better defended his own native territory up to that hour: for he was the leader of his sept, and the true fountain of generosity, and the head guardian of the poetic order, and the flashing light-star of the race of Aodh Buidhe Ó Néill . . . Ó Domhnaill's daughter, i.e. Gormlaith, daughter of Aodh Ruadh, the wife of Aodh . . . i.e. a woman of general hospitality, and a protectress of wordly reputation, and the greatest benefactress to Orders and men of learning, died in the middle month of spring; and as this couple shared humanity and reputation with each other in the world, to the time of their decease, so may their souls share glory with each other in the kingdom of God.
[Annals of Loch Cé, *s.a.* 1524]

Caitirfhíona daughter of Ó Duibhgeannáin
The daughter of Ó Duibhgeannáin, i.e. Caitirfhíona, died after unction and penitence, on the festival of Colum Cille, and was honourably interred in the monastery of Dún na nGall.
[Annals of Loch Cé, *s.a.* 1525]

Mór daughter of Mac Cába
Mór, daughter of Maoleachlainn Mac Cába, *uxor* of Ó hAinlighe, i.e. the best woman that came into Ceinéal Dobhtha mhic Aonghusa[58] for a long time, the nurse of the learned and destitute of Erinn; the equal of Mór Mumhan in reputation, piety, and good will; the woman who gave most in offerings and alms of food and clothing to the poor, and to the orphans of the Lord, and to every one who would require to receive them, died in the middle of her own residence, in Port Locha Leise,[59] *et sepulta est*[60] in Oil Finn, under the protection of God and Patrick.
[Annals of Loch Cé, *s.a.* 1527]

Caitilín daughter of Ó Néill
Caitilín, daughter of Conn, son of Domhnall Ó Néill, a pious woman of good hospitality, who had been married to good men, viz. to Ó Raghallaigh at first, and to Ó Ruairc afterwards, died this year after unction and penitence.
[Annals of Loch Cé, *s.a.* 1527]

---

57. Glenflesk, County Kerry.

58. Doohy-Hanly, County Roscommon.
59. Unidentified.
60. i.e. 'and is she is buried'.

Fionnghuala daughter of Ó Briain
Ó Briain's daughter, i.e. Fionnghuala, daughter of Conchobhar, the woman who maintained the greatest reputation of all her contemporaries, as regards body and soul, died after spending her life and wealth at first in promoting hospitality and humanity, and after having been twenty-one years in the habit of the Third Order, performing devotion, clemency, and good works, on behalf of God and the world.
[Annals of Loch Cé, *s.a.* 1528]

Mairgréag daughter of Ó Conchobhair Failghe
The daughter of Ó Conchobhair Failghe, Mairgréag, went to England, relying on the number of her friends and relatives there, and on her knowledge of the English language, to request Queen Mary to restore her father to her; and on her appealing to her mercy, she obtained her father, and brought him home to Ireland; and other hostages were given up to the Lord Justice and the Council in his stead, namely, Ruaidhrí Ó Conchobhair, the eldest of his own sons, and other hostages along with him.
[Annals of the Four Masters, *s.a.* 1533]

Wife of Maghnus Buidhe Ó Duibhgeannáin
Maghnus Buidhe Ó Duibhgeannáin was strangled in the night by his own wife.
[Annals of the Four Masters, *s.a.* 1534]

Sadhbh daughter of Mac Uilliam Búrc
A school invitation was given by Ruaidhrí, son of Tadhg Mac Diarmada, and by his wedded wife, i.e. Mac Uilliam's daughter, i.e. Sadhbh Búrc daughter of Riocard Óg, the best woman of her own kindred, or of any other family of her time, (and she had not the palm from Ruaidhrí), for distributing various gifts to poets and *ollamh*s, and men of all other arts. And at this invitation Mac Diarmada came, i.e. Aodh, son of Cormac Mac Diarmada; and Ó Birn, i.e. Tadhg son of Cairbre; and Ó Flanagáin, i.e. Éamonn [son of] Uilliam; and Mac Diarmada Ruadh, i.e. Cathal[61] ... and many more that cannot be mentioned; for the poets and *ollamh*s of Erinn came to the seat of the hospitality and generosity of the province of Connacht, i.e. to the Rock[62] of the

smooth-flowing Loch Cé. And every one of them obtained the desire of his own mind and nature, according to his dignity and learning, on that illustrious, honourable festival, i.e. at Christmas. And let every one who reads this give a blessing on the souls of the humane couple we have mentioned above.
[Annals of Loch Cé, *s.a.* 1540]

The kalends of January on Sunday; the age of the Lord one thousand, five hundred, and forty-two years. Sadhbh, daughter of Riocard Óg, son of Uilleag Ruadh, son of Uilleag an Fhíona, i.e. the wedded wife of Mac Diarmada, i.e. of Ruaidhrí, the son of Tadhg, son of Ruaidhrí Óg, son of Ruaidhrí Caoch, and his children's mother, died on Carraig na Ríogh, i.e. the abode of the hospitality and dignity of the Clann Mhaolruanaidh; and it is doubtful if there ever came of the posterity of William the Conqueror a woman of her age better than she in hospitality and worth, in prudence and piety, in charity and liberality. On Maunday Thursday her soul and body separated from each other, after the triumph of unction and penitence ...
[Annals of Loch Cé, *s.a.* 1542]

Máire daughter of Calbhach Ó Domhnaill
Máire, the daughter of Calbhach, son of Mánus, son of Aodh Dubh Ó Domhnaill, and wife of Ó Néill (Seán), died of horror, loathing, grief, and deep anguish, in consequence of the severity of the imprisonment inflicted on her father, Calbhach, by Ó Néill, in her presence.
[Annals the Four Masters, *s.a.* 1561]

Medhbh daughter of Ó Conchobhair Sligigh
The great, regal, wedding feast of the Lord of the Rock,[63] and of his wife, i.e. Medhbh, the daughter of Domhnall Ó Conchobhair, i.e. Ó Conchobhair Sligigh, was celebrated together by Brian, son of Ruaidhrí Mac Diarmada, at which large quantities of all kinds of stock, and of all descriptions of treasures and valuables, were presented and dispensed, according to their wish, to every one of the men of Erinn and Alba that came to solicit them during that year.
[Annals of Loch Cé, *s.a.* 1582]

61. A long list of names found in the text is not reproduced here.
62. In Irish, Carraig na Ríogh or Carraig Mhic Dhiarmada, an island in Lough Key near Boyle.

63. i.e. Carraig Mhic Dhiarmada.

Beanmhumhan daughter of Ó Duibhgeannáin
Beanmhumhan Óg Ní Dhuibhgeannáin, daughter
of Maoleachlainn, son of Dubhthach Óg son of
Dubhthach Mór, erected the tomb of hewn stones
which is over the edge of the great well of the
Scrín,[64] for the soul of her husband, i.e. the Vicar
Mac Domhnaill; and Eoghan Mac Domhnaill was
the same vicar's name. And Mary, daughter of

Tadhg Dall Ó hUiginn, was born the aforesaid
year.[65] And God's blessing on those souls.
[A late addition to the Annals of Loch Cé, *s.a.*
1599]

65. The date is erroneous, as Tadhg Dall Ó hUiginn died in 1591. The
entries for two different years may have been run together.

Biographies/Bibliographies

For biographies and bibliographies, see 'Courts and Coteries II',
pp. 448–50.

64. Skreen, County Sligo.

AOIBHEANN NIC DHONNCHADHA, *Editor*

Irish Medical Writing, 1400–1600

Although medicine had been established as a distinct profession in Ireland by the eighth century at the latest, knowledge of its practice in pre-Norman times is almost exclusively dependent on references in law-tracts concerning legal liabilities for illnesses (on these, see pp. 31–3). In contrast, a wealth of medical literature, comprising mainly translations or adaptations from Latin, survives from the late medieval and early modern period. The texts, written in early modern Irish, the standard literary language used by the learned classes of Ireland and Gaelic Scotland, are preserved in more than one hundred manuscripts dating from the fifteenth century to the seventeenth. Throughout this period medicine was a hereditary profession, practised by particular learned families, many of whom maintained schools where training was provided for members of their own and other kindreds, and it is by members of this institutionally organized, cohesive and learned medical community that the texts were translated and transmitted.

Physicians enjoyed a high status in Gaelic society, and were supported by the hereditary tenure of lands granted to them by the landowning aristocracy in return for their professional services. Professional medicine was a male preserve. Women by virtue of their sex were excluded from Gaelic medical schools, as they were from university faculties of medicine on the Continent. They were thereby prevented from formally acquiring advanced medical education and from entry to the higher levels of the medical hierarchy. It may be presumed that there were women in Ireland who practised medicine outside of the niche occupied by academically trained physicians, but evidence of their activities is lacking.

There is a handful of references to female members of medical families in the manuscripts. One of the earliest is Donnchadh Ó Bolgaidhe's record of the death in 1474 of Sláine, daughter of Giolla Pádraig mac Diarmada, wife of Ó Bolgaidhe (National Library of Ireland MS G 11, p. 379b42). The Uí Bholgaidhe practised medicine in Leinster, but the identity of Sláine's husband is not known.

While in the early stages of copying a pharmacological treatise, which he completed on 6 November 1592, the physician Cathal Ó Duinnshléibhe (*fl.* 1592–1611) penned the following remark: 'Máirghréag, daughter of Donnchadh, it is ungracious of you not to make a string for our collar, and it would be good of you to do so' (*A Mairgreg ingen Donnchadh is lem duit gan srang do denamh dar gcoler 7 gur mait uait a denamh*, Trinity College Dublin MS 1437, p. 32.z). This Máirghréag is probably to be identified with the person of the same name Cathal mentioned some four years later in his colophon to a commentary on the *Prognostica* of Hippocrates: 'Finis. 1596, the 13 May. I am at Aghmacart now in the company of Donnchadh Óg Ó Conchubhair; and it is easy for me now to be sad because my friend and companion has left me, i.e. Máirghréag, daughter of Donnchadh, and upon my word I don't know what I shall do without her from now on' (*Finis anno domini 1596 an 13 la do Maius a nAchaidh mhic Airt damh an tansa a bfochair Dhonnchadh Óig Í Chonchubhair 7 is urusa dhamh anois bheith dobrónach oir adime mo charaid 7 mo chumpanach uaimh .i. Mairghrég inghen Donnchadh 7 dar an leabhar ní fes dam créd do dhén ina hégmuis fesda*, Royal Irish Academy MS 449 [23 N 16], f. 56r7–11). Máirghréag was evidently daughter to

Donnchadh Óg Ó Conchubhair (*fl.* 1581–1610), the physician Cathal mentions, who was described in 1590 by Risteard Ó Conchubhair (1561–1625), a student and kinsman of his, as 'the best of the physicians of Ireland in his own time' (*rogha legh Erenn ina aimsir fen*, Royal Irish Academy MS 439 [3 C 19], f. 234va23–4). He was chief physician to Fínghin Mac Giolla Pádraig (d. 1613), 3rd Baron of Upper Ossory, and head of a thriving medical school situated at Aghmacart (modern County Laois) in the Mac Giolla Pádraig lordship of Upper Ossory. His father, Donnchadh Liath Ó Conchubhair (d. 1562), his brother, Conchubhar (*fl.* 1566), and his son, Giolla Pádraig (*fl.* 1590), were also physicians. Of Máirghréag nothing further is known. On the basis of the latter colophon it has been suggested that she was Cathal's spouse: the deep affection for her evinced in the colophon, Cathal's lengthy association (1596–1610) with Donnchadh Óg's school, and the propensity of members of learned families to intermarry, might all be advanced in support of that suggestion.

Two unnamed female patients of his are mentioned by the physician Corc Óg Ó Cadhla (*fl.* 1577–83) in a colophon he wrote on 22 March 1578 to Book 3 of Bernard of Gordon's *Lilium Medicine*, a treatise in seven books or 'particles', which he had begun transcribing the previous year (now Royal Irish Academy MS 443 [24 P 14]). The colophon was written in 'Gráinseach na Manach', apparently Graiguenamanagh, County Kilkenny, in the house of Brian Caomhánach, head of an eminent sept of the Kavanagh family. Having acknowledged God's help in the work he had completed, and noted the date, Corc continued: 'and in Gráinseach na Manach in the company of Brian son of Cathaoir son of Art Caomhánach I completed it while treating his two daughters for a menstrual irregularity' (*7 a nGrainsigh na Manach a bhfocuir Briain mic Cathaoir mic Airt Caomhanaigh do crichnaigis e 7 me ag leges a deise ingen o hsecran fola mista*, p. 170a36–8). Colophons to other particles of the *Lilium* were written in Brian's residence at Tinnaranny, County Carlow, where, it appears, Corc was regularly based while writing the manuscript. In the Tinnaranny colophons Corc identifies Brian's wife as Isibél (*fl.* 1572–1608), daughter of Aodh Ó Broin; she was sister to the renowned Wicklow chieftain, Fiacha (mac Aodha) Ó Broin (d. 1597). The two women Corc treated in Graiguenamanagh were evidently daughters of hers.

The names of nine ladies of Leinster are recorded in a well-known colophon, translated below, which Risteard Ó Conchubhair wrote on 18 November 1590 to mark completion of the writing of Gordon's *Lilium* (now Royal Irish Academy MS 439 [3 C 19], ff. 1v–234v). Risteard, a student at the Aghmacart school, had begun writing the *Lilium* on 7 May that year, in Cullahill Castle, County Laois, principal residence of Fínghin Mac Giolla Pádraig. On 18 November, having completed Book 3 of the text, the last of the seven particles to be copied, he noted in his colophon, written in Courtstown, County Kilkenny, that he had transcribed the *Lilium* in places 'far distant from one another', and mostly in the houses of relatives or good friends. He went on to acknowledge the hospitality extended to him by the various couples he had visited while engaged in the work, his travels having taken him through the counties of Kildare, Kilkenny, Wexford, Carlow and Offaly. Of particular interest is his reference to the role played by his kinswoman, Gráinne, daughter of Brian Mac Giolla Pádraig, 1st Baron of Upper Ossory, and wife of Edmond Butler, 2nd Viscount Mountgarret, in promoting his education from the age of twelve onwards, when his father had died.

Several notes by physicians refer to women whose identities are not known. While transcribing Gordon's *Lilium* in 1578, Corc Óg Ó Cadhla made the following complaint against the woman who had deprived him of his comfortable bed-tick: 'It was bad of you to take the flock-bed from me, you harlot' (*Is olc do benuis an leabaidh fhlocuis dim a meretrix*, Royal Irish Academy MS 443 [24 P 14], p. 204bz). In the course of writing a commentary on the *Aphorismi* of Hippocrates, Cathal Ó Duinnshléibhe wryly remarked of a certain Cáit: 'O Mary Virgin! We have often complained to you, Cáit; and you have little regard for me today since you hear no coin in my purse' (*A Muiri a Chait as minic ar ngeran let 7 ni mor do chin orm aniudh o nac airighir aon bhonn am purs*, Royal Irish Academy MS 449 [23 N 16], f. 11vz). In another note, written while transcribing a text concerned with various foods, Cathal remarked to one Aodh, a colleague of his:

'That is for you Aodh; and in my opinion it is bad of Gráinne not to give us food' *(Sin duit a Aodh 7 go bfis dam is olc do ni Grainni gan biad do thabhairt duin,* Royal Irish Academy MS 467 [23 N 29], f. 96rz).

Medieval medicine was dominated by the teachings of the Greek physician Galen of Pergamum (129–*c.* 216), who had developed a comprehensive and coherent system of medicine based on the work of his predecessors and on his own major observations. A number of Galenic theories that were influential in shaping Irish physicians' beliefs about the female body may be briefly outlined here.

Central to Galen's physiology was the concept of innate heat, a doctrine based on the writings of Aristotle (384–322 BC), who held that the animal body and all its parts have a natural or innate heat which is necessary for the maintenance of life and whose source in sanguineous animals is the heart. Innate heat enables the body to concoct food into blood and so nourish itself; surplus nutriment undergoes a further concoction into residues, some of them useful, such as semen and menstrual fluid, others useless, such as the excrements. Females have less natural heat than males, and are therefore weaker and less perfect than they, being unable to concoct nutriment to the degree of development and perfection attained by the male. Semen in the man and menstrual blood in the woman differ only in their degree of development: the man, being warmer, can convert surplus nutriment into semen that has power to generate; the woman, being colder, is unable to effect this concoction and produces instead menstrual blood, which is devoid of generative power. In generation, the male semen contributes the form and the principle of movement required to generate an embryo, the female provides menstrual blood, the matter from which the embryo is created.

Galen accepted Aristotle's doctrine of innate heat, but being aware of the existence of the ovaries, which were unknown to Aristotle, took the view that females produced sperm; this he identified with the vaginal secretion that is produced during coition, a fluid that Aristotle had described as being not seminal. Galen held that because of the female's deficient innate heat her testes (modern 'ovaries') are smaller and less perfect than the male's, and that the sperm produced in them is scantier, colder and wetter than his; he believed, however, that the female sperm does contribute to the generation of the foetus, nourishing the male semen and contributing the material for the allantoid membrane.

As a further embellishment to Aristotle's thesis of woman's imperfection, Galen asserted that the female reproductive organs provide clear evidence of woman's coldness. Women, he argued, have all the generative parts that men have, but, because of lack of heat, the parts that are without in men are confined within the body in women. Galen proceeded to detail the anatomical symmetry that exists between men and women, noting that if the female apparatus were perfected so as to emerge on the outside, the uterus would become the scrotum with the female testes inside it. He was concerned to explain that the female's imperfection was not without a purpose: if she were perfectly warm she would disperse all her nutriment and be unable to produce menstrual fluid, which is the material that provides nourishment for the growing foetus.

In his anatomical work Galen was restricted to dissection of animals other than man, the practice of human dissection only gradually becoming a part of medical education from the early fourteenth century onwards. Despite this limitation he made outstanding contributions to knowledge of human anatomy, basing his descriptions on animals of many kinds, particularly apes. Application to humans of the anatomical features of animals gave rise, however, to a number of errors in his work, among them his description of the human uterus as being bicornuate, and as having two cavities, one in the right part, and another in the left, the two ending in a single neck common to both.

Galen also gave credence to the Hippocratic tradition that associated males with the right side of the uterus and females with the left, believing, erroneously, that the right male testis and the right side of the uterus are nourished by a more purified, and therefore warmer blood than that which nourishes their counterparts on the left. A man's right testis, he believed, manufactures warmer, male-producing sperm; his left, colder, female-producing sperm. Sperm from a dominant right testis falling into the right cavity of the uterus produces a male, that from a dominant left testis falling into the left cavity a female. The uterus, however, plays a decisive part in determining the sex of the foetus, for female-producing sperm warmed by the right uterus will produce a male foetus, and male-producing sperm chilled by the left uterus will produce a female foetus; this explains why male embryos are generally found in the right side of the uterus, and females in the left. (Galen held that the left uterus can sometimes be overcome by the heat in the male-producing semen that reaches it so that a male develops there, but that such cases are rare for they require a great excess of heat in the semen.) The precise role played by the woman's sperm in the process of generation remained unclear and gave rise to much discussion. Medieval authors who accepted Galen's two-seed theory, and who analysed the mechanics of reproduction and of sex determination, generally concluded that the determinative role belonged to the man's sperm.

Though Galen's theory of a two-cavity uterus was widely accepted, it did not prevent the doctrine of the seven-celled uterus, introduced into the West in the twelfth century, from gaining popularity amongst medical writers. According to this ancient concept, there are seven cells in the fundus of the human uterus, three on the right side developing males, three on the left developing females, and one in the middle reserved for hermaphrodites. The doctrine was accepted as fact by numerous writers, among them the anatomist Mondino de' Liuzzi (d. 1326), author of a famous textbook on dissection.

Galen explained the complex phenomena of menstruation and lactation as follows. A woman in her prime lacks sufficient heat to disperse all the nutriment she concocts in her body; so, through veins extending to the uterus, Nature evacuates each month in the form of menstrual blood whatever surplus has accumulated. Once conception has taken place, however, menstrual blood forms the nutriment for the growing embryo, any surplus not immediately required being diverted to the breasts, where it is transformed into milk in the course of gestation. When the child has been born all the menstrual blood flows to the breasts where it is transformed into milk to nourish the newborn infant. This, Galen explains, is the reason why 'the female cannot menstruate properly and give suck at the same time; for one part [i.e. either uterus or breasts] is always dried up when the blood turns toward the other' (*On the usefulness of the parts of the body*, Book 14.8).

The extent to which treatments prescribed in Irish medical treatises were actually implemented in practice is indeterminable. It is certain, however, that the theory expounded in the texts they studied profoundly influenced the way in which physicians understood the human body, diagnosed illness, and prescribed treatment. The Galenic concept of female anatomy and physiology outlined above, and illustrated in the texts translated below, informed all Irish discourse on female health, and was accepted by the medical profession as authoritative and essentially accurate.

RISTEARD Ó CONCHUBHAIR

(1561–1625)

A SCRIBE'S COLOPHON (1590)

[The following translation is taken from Reverend Paul Walsh, *Gleanings from Irish Manuscripts* (Dublin: At the Sign of the Three Candles, 1933, 2nd ed. with additions; 1st ed., 1918), pp. 129–32, the author's notes to the translation being synopsized here. For the background to the colophon, see the introductory essay above.]

There finished the third Particle of the *Lily* with the help of the Saviour, on the 18th November, and far distant from one another are the places in which this book was written. For none of my temporal lords remain,[1] and my parents, too, are

---

1. i.e. Risteard's father, or some of his immediate forebears, had lost their landed property.

dead, and I myself have neither wife nor home. All I could do when I was tired in one place was to transport myself to another. And, indeed, I did not write a week's work of it except in the house of a kinsman or kinswoman, or some great friend of my own.

In this way: I commenced it in Clann Fheoruis[2] at Cluain Each,[3] in the house of John Og Alye[4] and his wife Margaret Darcy.

From there I went to Baile an Fheadha,[5] and stayed with Calvagh,[6] son of O More, and his wife Margaret, daughter of Scurlock.[7]

And from there I went to Carraig Fheoruis[8] to Edward, son of Walter, son of John Mag Fheoruis [Birmingham], a true friend and a kinsman to me. His wife is Isabella Hussey, daughter of Meyler.

Then I went to Don Uabhair.[9] These are they who live there, namely, James, son of Gerald, son of John, son of William Og [son of William], son of Thomas (this William Og was grandson of Thomas Fitzgerald of Coill na Cuirte Duibhe[10]) and his wife Margaret, daughter of Redmond Og,[11] son of Thomas. This Redmond was the best nobleman of the descendants of John, son of the Earl, and also it is improbable that there was any of the Fitzgeralds of all Leinster in his own time comparable to him.

From there I went to Pollardstown[12] to the good heir of that good couple, namely, William, and that same son is my dearest friend in all the world except a few. The wife of William is Elinora, daughter of John Mac Valronta.[13]

And thence I went to Almhain Laighean[14] to Garret, son of Philip, son of Maurice. He is of the family of the Knight of Kerry, and I know not in the county of Kildare at this moment a head of a house more hospitable than he. His wife is Mabel, daughter of George Fitzgerald.

Next to Dun Muire.[15] There reside in that place, namely, Edward Hussey, son of Meyler of Mulhussey,[16] a gentleman pious and charitable according to his means, and his wife Mary, daughter of Calvagh,[17] son of Tadhg, son of Cathaoir O Connor, a kinswoman and a sponsor in baptism to me.

All these places we have mentioned are in the county of Kildare.

From there [Dun Muire], I went to the county of Kilkenny to visit Viscount Mountgarret, Edmund,[18] son of Richard, son of Piarus Earl of Ormond. His wife is Grainne, daughter of Brian,[19] son of Brian, son of Seán (namely, Mac Giollapadraig). Grainne's mother was the daughter of O Conchubhair by the Earl of Kildare's daughter.[20] The said Grainne was my temporal lady, and she, on her mother's side, was my near kinswoman. It was she who, after I had passed the age of twelve years, for the most part provided for my education. About the same age I lost my father. My years now are these: I shall be twenty-nine this next Christmas Eve.

And this portion of the book, the third Particle, was completed in Baile na Cuirte,[21] and it was written at a later time than the remainder, in the house of Grace, that is, Oliver, son of Robert, son of John, son of Oliver, a hospitable, noble and learned man. I do not mention here what was written of this book in Ossory in the house of Mac Giollapadraig[22] with his ollav, Donnchadh Og,[23] my teacher and my own kinsman; nor what was written of it in the county Wexford and in the county Carlow; nor the part of it which I wrote in the house of Thomas,[24] son

---

2. Country of the Birminghams, roughly co-extensive with the barony of Carbury, in the north-west of County Kildare.
3. Clonaugh, parish of Cadamstown, barony of Carbury.
4. An Englishman, he was granted Clonough in 1571; adept in the Irish language, he was official interpreter to Dublin Castle; d. 1612.
5. Ballina, parish of Cadamstown.
6. Son of Rury Caoch O More, chief of Leix; d. 1618.
7. He was of Frayne, County Meath.
8. Carrick, townland and parish, barony of Carbury, County Kildare.
9. Donore, parish of Carragh, barony of Clane, County Kildare.
10. 'Wood of the Black Court', probably now represented by 'Blackhall'; three places so named in County Kildare.
11. Redmond Og Fitzgerald of Rathangan, County Kildare.
12. Townland and parish, barony of East Offaly, County Kildare.
13. An Irish rendering of the English name Wesley, later Wellesley.
14. 'Allen of Leinster'; Allen, barony of Connell, County Kildare.

15. Dunmurry, townland and parish, barony of East Offaly.
16. Townland in parish of Kilclone, barony of Upper Deece, County Meath.
17. He was of Derrymullen, County Offaly; d. c. 1576.
18. Edmund Butler, 2nd Viscount Mountgarret, d. 1602. For a poem addressed to him and his wife, Gráinne, daughter of Brian Mac Giolla Pádraig, see pp. 382–4.
19. Brian Mac Giollapadraig, created (1st) Baron of Upper Ossory in 1541; d. 1575.
20. Brian Mac Giollapadraig's second wife was Elizabeth, daughter of Brian Ó Conchubhair Failghe by Mary, daughter of the Earl of Kildare and sister of Silken Thomas.
21. Courtstown, parish of Tullaroan, barony of Crannagh, County Kilkenny.
22. Finghin (Florence) Mac Giollapadraig, 3rd Baron of Upper Ossory, succeeded his brother, Brian Óg, in 1581.
23. Donnchadh Óg Ó Conchubhair (fl. 1581–1610), head of the medical school at Aghmacart, County Laois.
24. Thomas Fitzgerald of Clonbolg, parish of Clonsast, barony of Coolestown, County Offaly; d. 1590.

of Redmond, and his good wife, Sadhbh, daughter of Mac Giollapadraig; for I have spoken of these in another part of the book.

I am Richard, son of Muircheartach . . . who wrote [this], and I beseech the King of kings and the Creator of heaven and earth that He may assign and grant a Christian's share of His great merciful Principality to myself, and to every one of these good kindly couples which I have enumerated. And I put it as an obligation, for the sake of the God of heaven, on every one who shall read this to recite an earnest prayer for my own soul, and for their souls, and for the soul of every other Christian for whom we are obliged to pray by the wish of God and of the Church.

GUY DE CHAULIAC

(*c*. 1290–*c*. 1368)

from:
CHIRURGIA MAGNA
(Great Surgery) (1363)

[In this account of the anatomy of the uterus Guy de Chauliac endeavours to reconcile Galen's concept of a two-cavity organ, each hollow corresponding to the breast on its own side, with the doctrine of a seven-celled uterus, which had been accepted by the influential Mondino de' Liuzzi.

Guy de Chauliac's Latin text was translated into Irish by Cormac Mac Duinnshléibhe (*fl. c*. 1459). The Irish text is translated into English here from Trinity College Dublin MS 1436, p. 32b5-y, by the present editor.]

And after that for the sake of women let us speak of the uterus. And the uterus is the field of human generation, and it is for that reason it is a receptive organ. And its position is between the bladder and the intestine which is called *longaon*.[1] And its substance is membranous, composed of two tunics. And its form is round, with two horns or with two covered branches; and at the extremities of those there are small testes, planted in the upper part of them.[2] And it has a wide canal towards the front.

And this is how it is, like the penis reversed or placed inside, as Galen says in the fourteenth book of *De utilitate particularum*.[3] And there are two chambered branches above with testes like the scrotum; and there is a common cavity in its middle like the pectineal parts; and it has a cannulate neck[4] below like the penis; and it has an external opening which is called *vulva*, i.e. the vulva,[5] like the glans penis; and there is in the middle of that the member which is called *tentigo*,[6] like the prepuce; and the length of that neck is as the length of the penis, i.e. eight or nine inches.

And though only two cavities are obvious in it, like the number of breasts, yet there are three chambers in each chamber of those, and a single chamber in its middle, so that seven chambers are found in it according to Mondino.[7]

And it is connected to the brain, and to the heart, and to the liver, and to the stomach, and it is bound to the back. And there are veins between it and the breasts which are called *lactales*[8] and *menstruales*;[9] and it is through them the part of the menstrual blood from which breastmilk is made moves; and it is for that reason Hippocrates said that milk is a brother to menstrual blood; and it is for that reason it does not happen that the menstrual blood flows well and that a woman has milk at the same time.

---

1. Rectum.
2. The ovaries are attached to the uterine horns by the uterine tubes.
3. *On the usefulness of the parts of the body*, Book 14.6.
4. i.e. the vagina.
5. Irish *bandacht*, which translates Latin *vulva* in medical texts *passim*.
6. Clitoris.
7. Mondino de' Liuzzi (d. 1326), Italian anatomist, author of the *Anatomia* (1316), a famous manual of dissection.
8. 'Lacteal veins'.
9. 'Menstrual veins'.

ANONYMOUS

A DESCRIPTION OF THE UTERUS

(c. 1300)

[Aristotle believed that on account of the coldness of their nature female embryos are slower to develop than male ones, but that once born, females on account of their weakness are quicker than males to reach maturity and old age 'since inferior things all reach their end more quickly'.[1] Aristotle's dictum is echoed in this account of the uterus.

The text is translated into English, from an anonymous Irish translation (c. 1450) in Trinity College Dublin MS 1436, pp. 328b5–329a21, by the present editor.]

Let us speak now of the member which is called *matrix*, i.e. uterus. And it is said to be cold and dry. And it is made like the stomach, i.e. the upper part of it sinewy and the lower part fleshy. And it is composed of sinews and of villi.

And there are seven chambers in it, i.e. three in the right side, and three in the left side, and the seventh chamber in its middle. And the old physicians say that the form and figure of the human image is in each chamber of these.[2]

And they say also that sons are created in the three chambers that are in the right side of the uterus, and that daughters are created in the three chambers that are in the left side, and that fools are created in the middle chamber; and it is there *ermafrodisi*[3] are created, i.e. people who have both sexes simultaneously, which is abominable to God and to men.

Vulva, i.e. the vulva;[4] and this member is very perceptive and sensitive; and it is named from the word *volentuo*; and *volento*[5] means something which turns around, moving or springing towards sexual desire; and it is a part of the uterus.

Or it is named from this Latin word *valva*; and *valva* means door, for it acts as a door to the uterus, ministering to sexual desire, and closing and opening.

And sexual desire and appetite are in the mouth of the uterus,[6] and heat and digestion in its lower part to prepare the sperm for generation. And the mouth of the uterus is sinewy and thick to retain heat there, by which sexual desire is increased.

And Galen says that when the mouth of the uterus receives the male sperm that it closes so that the point of a needle would not enter it . . .

And Galen says that women more often, or more usually, get pleasure at the time of coition than men; and they eject their own sperm through the neck of the uterus[7] against the penis; and if the penis be short, it will not reach this path, and that is a cause of sterility.

And Averroes[8] says that pregnant women's desire for coition is greater than other women's desire.[9]

It is asked here why it is that a son grows better in his mother's womb than a daughter, and that a daughter grows better after her birth.

We reply to that according to Averroes, who says these words: *Herba mala cicius cresit quam bona,* i.e. a bad plant grows sooner than a good plant; and Averroes applies this analogy to the female: because of her badness she grows sooner than the male.

Another reason why a son moves sooner inside, i.e. because of the amount of heat he has in excess of a daughter, and every movement arises from its heat.

---

1. *Generation of Animals*, IV, vi, 775a4–23.
2. It is envisaged that the uterine chambers act like moulds, each conferring a distinctive shape on the foetus it houses.
3. Latin *hermafroditi*, hermaphrodites.
4. Irish *bandacht*. See note 5, p. 346.
5. Latin *volvendo*, from the verb *volvere*, 'to roll, turn about, turn around'.

6. i.e. the cervix of the uterus.
7. i.e. the vagina.
8. Latin name of the Arabic philosopher and physician, Ibn Rushd (d. 1198), author of the *Colliget*.
9. Aristotle held that menstrual fluid was unconcocted sperm. Pregnant woman do not normally menstruate, and an accumulation of unconcocted sperm increases their sexual desire.

TADDEO ALDEROTTI

(*c.* 1206–95)

from:
COMMENTARY ON THE
ISAGOGE OF JOHANNITIUS
(*c.* 1280)

[Medical writers frequently cast their views on a given topic into the form of a *questio* or disputed question, a method of exposition in which a problem is posed, and then discussed and solved on the basis of citations from authoritative sources. In the third of a series of seven such questions on generative power, the Italian physician and teacher Taddeo Alderotti asked: 'Do women have sperm or not?'

The text is translated into English, from an anonymous Irish translation (*c.* 1400) in Trinity College Dublin MS 1436, p. 61b13–34, by the present editor.]

I say to the third statement that it is perceived that women have sperm, for Aristotle says in *On animals*[1] that men emit sperm externally and women internally.

Item Aristotle says in the fourth book and in the fifth book of *On animals* that the foetus must be composed of the two sperms.

---

1. This title (Latin *De animalibus*) comprises the following treatises of Aristotle: *Historia animalium, De partibus animalium, De motu animalium, De incessu animalium* and *De generatione animalium.*

Item Constantinus[2] and Avicenna[3] and all authors say that women have sperm, for Constantinus says in the chapter on the embryo, and Aristotle says in the fourth chapter of *On animals* that women have a double pleasure, i.e. pleasure emitting their own sperm, and pleasure receiving the man's sperm.

The opposite to this is perceived according to Aristotle in the fifteenth book of *On animals,* for he says there that women do not have sperm since they have menstrual blood, which is sperm's matter, for if they were to have them both they could generate without a man.

And Aristotle says to this in *On animals* that sperm can be understood in common speech of every moisture that comes from the body of the man and of the woman at the time of coition; accordingly, if sperm were understood broadly as every moisture that comes at the time of coition, women would have sperm; however, if it be understood narrowly as the moisture which is sperm that is a residue of digestion and causes generation, according to that, women do not have sperm.

---

2. Constantinus Africanus (d. 1087), a monk of Monte Casino who translated medical works from Arabic into Latin, among them *Pantegni*, a medical encyclopaedia written by the Persian physician al-Majusi (d. 994).

3. Latin name of the Arabic physician Ibn Sina (d. 1037), author of the *Canon*, which was translated from Arabic into Latin in the twelfth century.

ANONYMOUS

from:
COMMENTARY ON THE
TEGNI OF GALEN (*c.* 1300)

[The following *questio* is based on the premiss that moderate coition is beneficial to both men and women, a view consistently held by physicians, who regarded it as

the most suitable way to expel sperm and to keep the generative organs healthy.

The text is translated into English, from an anonymous Irish translation (*c.* 1400) in Trinity College Dublin MS 1299, p. 25a28–b20, by the present editor.]

It is asked here if coition be performed properly whether it benefits women more or men more in the conservation of health.

It is perceived that it benefits the man more, for Avicenna says the sex that retention of sperm harms more, that is the sex its expulsion benefits more; and it is men its retention harms more, so its expulsion benefits them more than women in the conservation of health.

Item Avicenna says the sex that is more accustomed to emitting sperm, that is the sex that emission of sperm and its expulsion benefits more; and it is the male sex that is like that, therefore, it is it coition benefits in the conservation of health.

Item Avicenna says that the bad accidents that arise from retention of the male sperm for too long are greater and more furious than from retention of the female sperm; therefore, coition benefits men more in the conservation of health than women.

Item Galen says that corruption of the nobler instrument when it is changed harms more than corruption of the ignobler instrument; and the male sperm is nobler than the female sperm; therefore, its [sc. sperm's] excessive retention is more harmful, and its expulsion is more beneficial in men than in women.

This is disputed on the authority of Galen, who says that the sex in which repletion of sperm is more dominant, that that is the sex that retention of sperm harms more, and that its expulsion benefits more; and the female sex is more like that, i.e. with repletion of sperm, than the male sex; therefore, coition benefits the female sex more in the conservation of health than the male sex in the conservation of health.

Item Galen says the impurer the residue, the more its retention harms nature, and the more its expulsion benefits [it]; and the female sperm is impurer than the male sperm; therefore, coition benefits women more in the conservation of health than men.

Item Aristotle says the sex in which pleasure is greater at the time of coition, that that is the sex that coition benefits more; and women have greater pleasure and joy in coition than men, for the woman has pleasure expelling her own sperm, and pleasure receiving the man's sperm; therefore, coition benefits the woman more in the conservation of health than the man.[1]

We respond to that and we say that there are three things to be examined in sperm, i.e. consistency and quantity and quality. And we say as regards consistency and quantity that coition benefits women more, and that it benefits men more as regards quality.

It is asked here whether dark women have more sperm than fair women. It is seen that dark women have more, for darkness is one of the signs of heat, and sperm is increased by heat; therefore, sperm is more plentiful in dark women than in fair women.

Item Aristotle says that sperm is more plentiful in thin women than in fat women; and dark women are thinner than fair women; therefore, sperm is more plentiful in dark women than in fair women.

This is disputed on the authority of Aristotle; and he says that sperm is more plentiful in fair women, and that they emit more sperm at the time of coition than dark women emit.[2]

1. The theory of woman's double pleasure was first mooted in the *Pantegni* of Constantinus Africanus. Later authors compared man's single pleasure with woman's twofold one, and developed a doctrine that the woman's pleasure was greater in quantity, arising from a greater number of sources, but that the man's pleasure was greater in quality because of his more temperate complexion and his more perfect seed.
2. In reporting Aristotle's ideas, the commentator uses the word sperm in a general sense. Aristotle had argued that the moisture secreted by the woman in coition is not generative sperm.

MAGNINUS OF MILAN

(*fl.* 1326–36)

from:
REGIMEN SANITATIS
(Regimen of Health)
(*c.* 1334)

[Complexion, or temperament, was defined as a quality that arises from the mixture of the elemental qualities of hot, wet, cold and dry in the human body, which, like all other material substances, was said to be composed of the four elements, fire, air, water and earth. A body in which the four qualities were equally present was said to be of balanced or temperate complexion; one having them in unequal quantities was of unbalanced or intemperate complexion.

In the first of the following extracts Magninus explains that women's health regimen is distinct from men's because of difference in complexion, a difference that arises, in turn, from sex difference, men by virtue of their sex having a hotter and drier complexion than women.

An anonymous Irish translation of Magninus's text, dating from *c.* 1400, was edited by Séamus Ó Ceithearnaigh. The following extracts are translated into English by the present editor from his edition: *Regimen na Sláinte: Regimen Sanitatis Magnini Mediolanensis*, 3 vols (Baile Átha Cliath: Oifig an tSoláthair, 1942–4); vol. 1, (i) lines 388–436; (ii) lines 566–606; (iii) lines 2486–544; and (iv) lines 2656–83, respectively.]

(i)
Sicut diuerse complexiones indigent diuerso regimine, i.e. as the complexions differ they need a different regimen; and the sexes differ likewise, i.e. the different sex makes the complexion different. For males are hotter and drier, and longer-lived, and larger according to quantity, and stronger and more prudent than females in the human species, however they are in other species in which the female sex happens to be larger and stronger and hotter than the male sex, as is clear in animals of prey of whom we shall not speak now. I know from these facts then the things that are clear from the sayings of the wise, who say that males in the human species are hotter and drier than females, and that females are colder and wetter, and that their bodies are smaller than males' bodies. For man is hotter and

drier and more temperate than woman, and is more able to be temperate, therefore, consequently, they must have a different regimen to conserve them. Therefore, it is clear from those facts that the different sexes' different complexions require a different conserving and preserving regimen.

And this same thing is clear from the diversity of composition and of functions; for females have a different composition from males because females have many members that males do not have; for women have the uterus and the neck [of the uterus],[1] which men do not have, and men have the penis, and women do not. The breast is for producing milk, and it is not for that purpose only men have it, but for comeliness and to conserve the heat of the heart, and for that reason women's breasts are larger than men's breasts.[2] Moreover, i.e. women have pregnancy . . . and the evacuation of menstrual blood, and men do not. Moreover, women have the nursing of small infants. And because of that we require special different rules for the regimen of the female sex that are not required in the male sex. And we require also a conserving regimen for the uterus and its neck, and a preserving regimen in immoderate discharge and in immoderate retention of menstrual blood. And the breasts need a conserving and preserving regimen to produce milk in them. We need also a regimen to conserve pregnant women, and to assist in bringing forth their offspring, and to nurse infants, none of which is needed in men's regimen.

(ii)
[In the following passage Magninus outlines the health benefits of maternal nursing, but acknowledges that it is not always possible for mothers to nurse their own infants.]

---

1. i.e. the vagina.
2. Cf. 'Generally speaking, milk is not produced in any male animals, man included, but it is in some individuals . . . There are men from whom, after reaching puberty, a small amount can be squeezed out; some when milked have actually produced large quantities' (Aristotle, *History of Animals*, III, xx).

And when young they [sc. infants] need no other food save milk, for it takes the place of food and drink for them. And their mother's milk is the milk that is most suitable for infants; for that milk has been produced from blood very similar to the blood which was the matter from which the infant was generated and nourished. So, it is true to say that their mother's milk is very good nourishment for them; and this is how that is meant, provided the mother be healthy and following an appropriate regimen according as the act of nursing and the one nursed require.

And if it should happen that his mother were unable or unwilling to nurse him, let another healthy nurse be chosen for him who has a good complexion[3] and is of full age,[4] and is well-behaved, with her colour inclining towards darkness; and who has wide veins, and a thick neck, and a broad bosom, and breasts that are not very fleshy and that do not have a lot of slack veins, and let their milk be neither too thick nor too thin; . . . and who has good-tasting, good-smelling milk, which is not too near the time of giving birth or too removed from it. And if it be possible to get a nurse for the child who is similar in regimen and complexion to its mother, and who has these conditions we have mentioned, she is to be chosen as a nurse . . .

And in the first days after the child's birth it is not advisable that his mother nurse him for two reasons: the first reason, for the mother has been changed greatly by the birth; the second reason, because of the length the milk has stood in the breasts, for perchance it might be corrupt; and that is known from its colour and from its consistency. And for that reason French women, being suspicious of that milk, have a woman of low rank suck the milk from their breasts.

(iii)
[In the following passage Magninus sets out the physical and moral attributes that are to be sought in the wet nurse, since these will determine the quality and condition of her milk.]

Let us speak now of the nurses' regimen and we shall speak briefly about it. And we shall state firstly the nurse's conditions. And the first condition is derived from her age. And the appropriate age for her is when she has attained youth. And the period of youth is from twenty-five years to thirty-five years; for the milk should be perfect then because the members that are its origin are perfect.

The second condition, it is derived from figure and habit; for the woman who nourishes an infant should have a good body, and a thick neck, and a broad bosom and excellent muscles. And she should not be too thin or too fat but in between.

The third condition, it is derived from the breasts; for the breasts ought to be big, handsome and firm, and they should not be abnormally large, or be soft or flabby. And the tips of the breasts should not be too small for fear the infants might labour much to grasp them.

The fourth condition, it is derived from the nurse's conduct; for she should be well-behaved and praiseworthy so that she might not be easily changed by accidents of the soul,[5] namely fear, and sorrow, and anger and the like, for these things corrupt the milk's complexion. So, if she has been changed, let her not nurse the infant, for she is understood to have little concern about the infant then. Moreover, she ought not to be courting, or given to drink, for those corrupt the milk's complexion.

The fifth condition, it is derived from the milk's consistency, and quality, and quantity; for that reason the milk should be of medium consistency, neither runny nor thick, and not have different parts,[6] and not be foamy. For if a drop of it be put on the fingernail, and it disperses, that is a sign that it has a thin consistency, and if it does not disperse, it is a sign of thick consistency. And know that the cheesy parts and the watery parts of moderate milk are equal; and that is proven when a drop of the milk is put [in a vessel] and a drop of urine is added to it, and they are mixed together, and the wateriness and the cheesiness of the good milk will be obvious then. And the milk's colour should incline towards whiteness, and its taste towards sweetness. And the milk should not be salty, or sharp, or yellow-coloured or red-coloured.

3. i.e. temperament, physical constitution.
4. According to Magninus the body's members reach their full development about the twenty-fifth year; old age commences about the forty-fifth year.
5. i.e. the emotions.
6. i.e. it should be of a single consistency.

Moreover, the nurse should not be given to dreaming, or be a heavy sleeper; for nurses often let infants die of hunger because of the heaviness of their sleep, and they suffocate them other times sleeping on them.

And it is to be well understood that the milk is not to be too old, or too near the time of birth. So, let it be two months old, or a month and a half. And let her birth be natural, i.e. the woman is not to have given birth to a dead child.

(iv)

[In the following extract Magninus speaks of the health benefits that accrue to women from regular and moderate menstruation.]

And know that seeing the menstrual blood in proper quality and quantity and at the appropriate time according to custom in every period of time is a cause of conservation of health for the uterus and for the woman, and a cause of conservation from every harm; and it makes them chaste with little desire for coition. And the even measure for the menstrual discharge is that it should occur once in every month. And it need not be equally large or equally small in every woman. And it runs in the first quarter of the moon in girls, and in young women in the second quarter, and in women more mature than that in the third quarter, and in old women in the fourth quarter.[7] And the menstrual blood generally begins to flow in women after the fourteenth year, although it may flow earlier or later according to diversity of complexion and of habit, of regimen and of region, and the like. And that is how the menstrual discharge is finished, in some women early and in others late, according to diversity of the local causes we mentioned originally.

Item when the menstrual blood is changed from its own natural disposition that is a cause of weakness and of change of form for women, and that is a cause of scant conception and of a dead foetus. Therefore, let care be exerted that the menstrual blood does not change from its natural order.

7. See note 4.

BERNARD OF GORDON

(*c.* 1258–*c.* 1320)

from:
LILIUM MEDICINE (1305)

[In the first of the following extracts Gordon discusses obsessive love, an illness believed to be caused by a malfunctioning of the brain's estimative faculty, the power that regulates a person's judgement. The disease was thought to affect males primarily.

The extracts are translated from the Irish translation by Cormac Mac Duinnshléibhe (*fl. c.* 1459) in Royal Irish Academy MS 443 (24 P 14), (i) pp. 112b20–114b35; (ii) 304a24–y; (iii) 312a28–b2; and (iv) 312bx–313a33, respectively, by the present editor.]

(i)

Amor qui hereos dicitur est sollicitudo melancholica propter mulieris amorem, i.e. the love which is called hereos[1] is a pondering or melancholic anxiety on account of love for a woman.

Causes. The cause of this disease is a corruption of the faculty which is called *estimativa*[2] because a form and figure have been firmly fixed in it. And it is for that reason when one has been seized by love for a woman, it seizes his form, and his figure and his manner to this extent that he thinks and that he judges that she is the best, and most beautiful, and most worthy, and most esteemed, and most attractive, and the best as to natural gifts and manners of all women, and it is for that reason he desires her very greatly without limit or measure; and he judges that if he were

1. *Amor hereos* was the technical name given to the disease; *hereos* apparently derives ultimately from Greek *eros*, 'love'.
2. The estimative faculty.

able to achieve his aim, that that would be his happiness and his ultimate wealth. And the judgement of his reason is so polluted that he is constantly thinking about her, and that he abandons all his works, and if anyone speak to him that he hardly understands him. And since he is constantly pondering it is for that reason this disease is called a melancholic anxiety . . .

And their [*sc.* sufferers from this disease] judgement is corrupt, and it is for this reason the versifier said: *Omnis amans cecus, non est amor arbiter aequus. Nam deforme pecus iudicat esse decus*: For everyone who loves is blind, and love is not an equitable judge, for it judges the ugly beast to be beautiful or splendid. And he says in another place: *Quisquis amat ranam, ranam putat esse Deanam*: Whoever would love a frog would think that it was a goddess . . .

Symptoms. The symptoms of this disease are that these people go without sleep, and without food and without drink, and the whole body is made thin, save only the eyes; and they have hidden, deep thoughts with doleful sighing; and if they hear singing or a poem about love's separation, they begin to weep immediately, and to sorrow, and if they hear about its joining together, they begin to laugh and to rejoice immediately.

And they have an irregular, different pulse; however, it is fast, frequent and high if you say the name of the woman he loves, or if she walk into his presence. And this is how Galen recognized the disease of a young man who lay sorrowful and thin, and had an irregular, hidden pulse; and he [*sc.* the patient] did not wish to reveal his disease to him; and it happened by chance that the woman he loved came into his presence, and his pulse awoke powerfully immediately then, and when the woman went away the pulse returned to its own state again; and Galen recognized that he was lovesick; and he said to him: 'You have this disease,' he said, 'for you love this woman'; and the patient was amazed that the disease and the woman should be recognized like that. So, whoever wishes to know the name of the woman who is loved, let him say the names of many women, and when he says the name of the woman who is loved, the pulse will be raised, and that is she, and let him avoid her.

Prognostication. The prognosis of this disease is that if those suffering from hereos are not helped that they become manic or that they die.

[Various treatments for lovesickness are then prescribed; the patient's mind, for instance, is to be distracted by news, good or bad; he is to be kept from solitude and idleness; he is to be brought to distant lands to see various sights. The list of treatments concludes with a particularly spectacular cure.]

And finally, when we have no other advice, let us seek the counsel of old women to insult and defame her as much as they can; for they have a clever art for this more than men have . . .

So, let a very ugly old woman be sought out, with big teeth, and with a beard, and with unsightly attire; and let her have a cloth that has been dipped in menstrual blood in her bosom; and let her come into the presence of the lovesick man, and let her begin to revile his sweetheart, saying that she is mangy and given to drink, and that she wets the bed, and that she has epilepsy, and that she is unworthy, and that there are horrible scabs all over her body, that she has fetid breath, and other hateful things in which the old women themselves are skilled. And if he is unwilling to give her up at these urgings, let her draw out in his presence the bloodstained rag we mentioned, and let her shout: 'This is how your sweetheart is'; and if he does not give her up then he is not a man, but a devil incarnate, and let him have his own folly to harm him from that on.

[Having clarified four points that arose from the preceding discussion, Gordon continues.]

The fifth thing that should be made clear, i.e. that this disease occurs more frequently in men than in women because men, universally speaking, are hotter than women; and this is obvious in male brute animals who are driven with fury and frenzy to complete coition. So, since men are hotter, their pleasure at the time of coition is more intense. Women, moreover, their pleasure is greater, because they are delighted by their own sperm and by the man's sperm.

(ii)
[In the following extract Gordon describes the symptoms of menstrual retention, a disorder that was frequently discussed in medical texts, and lists the diseases that arise from it.]

Symptoms. If the menstrual blood be retained by a cold cause, the woman is then of a bad colour, or is pale and sleepy, with little thirst, and with a slow pulse, and with low urine,[3] and sometimes she expels viscuous residues through her intestines.

If it be from a hot cause, the woman is of a good colour and is thirsty, and with a quick pulse, and with high urine, and the other signs of heat are present.

Or we can know it in this way though it is not very becoming, i.e. let a clean narrow linen cloth be plunged into the menstrual blood, if it occur some time, and let it be dried; and let it be washed then; and if its colour incline towards redness, sanguine humour is the cause; and if it incline towards yellowness, choler; and if it incline towards whiteness, phlegm; and if it incline towards darkness, melancholy; and that is how the cause of retention and of the humour that is peccant is understood, and the cause of sterility, and the like . . .

Prognostication. If the menstrual blood be retained abnormally, the physician can predict one or many of these diseases, i.e. regarding the upper members, mania, and melancholia, and epilepsy, and dimsightedness, and the like; and regarding the spiritual members,[4] coughing, and phthisis and suffocation; and in so far as it pertains to diseases of the nutritive members, dropsy and nausea; and in so far as it pertains to diseases of the lower members, podagra and the like. Therefore, it is beneficial to provoke menstrual blood that is retained abnormally.

(iii)

[In the following extract Gordon describes the way in which coition should happen for it to be fruitful. Ideally, it should take place during the final stage of the body's digestive cycle when sperm is most plentiful, which, in those following a regular regimen, usually occurs between midnight and dawn. The coital position described in the text is that generally recommended by physicians as being the most suitable for conception. Violent movement by the woman after coition might dislodge the seed, and should be avoided.]

And this is the method of performing coition. For the man and the woman ought to be temperate, or inclining towards temperateness; and they ought to be temperate in their foods and in their drinks, and in the other non-

naturals.[5] And the food having been digested, and the residues having been expelled, after midnight and before day the man ought to excite and stimulate the woman to coition, conversing with her, and kissing her, and pressing her to him, and touching her breasts and her pubes and her perineum. And the reason all that is done is in order that the woman may be desirous for coition and that the sperms may come simultaneously; for women desire more slowly than men. And when the woman begins to stammer the man ought to unite with her and gently perform coition; and he ought to press greatly against her pubes so that air might not be able to enter. And the sperm having being emitted, he ought to remain on top of her without moving, and not arise from her immediately. And when he arises from her, the woman ought to stretch her legs and remain lying on her back; and let her sleep like that if she can, for that is very beneficial.[6] And let her not speak, and let her not cough, for all these things help greatly to retain the sperm. And for as long as she feels the sperm in her uterus let her lie down, and let her take only a gentle walk if it be necessary.

(iv)

[The signs of conception are enumerated in the following extract, three simple pregnancy tests are described, and a vivid account is given of the beneficial effects of a male conception.]

However, let us first consider the signs of pregnancy. For when a woman conceives, she feels horripilation in her pudenda, and the abdomen is narrowed about the navel, and the sperm and the menstrual blood are retained, and the desire for coition is lessened; and the urine is coloured, and contents like combed cotton are seen in it, and white contents move upwards and downwards in it; and the interior orifice of the uterus[7] is constricted so that a needle could not enter it, though there is no imposthume or hardness in it, and this is the surest sign of all; and it seems to the man that his penis after coition is dry. Then the

---

3. i.e. urine low in colour.
4. i.e. the organs associated with respiration.
5. The 'non-naturals' are six external factors that were held to affect health, namely, air, motion and rest, food and drink, sleeping and waking, evacuation and repletion, and 'accidents of the soul', that is, the emotions.
6. It was believed that sleep following coition would help to fix the sperm in the uterus and thereby assist conception.
7. i.e. the cervix of the uterus.

breasts being to thicken, and they crave various things,[8] and sometimes odious things; and their colour is changed and they have headache.

And we can know whether the woman has conceived or not, i.e. perform this test at night when she is about to go to bed, i.e. [let her] take mellicratum with rain water, and if she feel growling in her abdomen going to sleep, she is pregnant, and the opposite. And Avicenna says that that is true provided she was not accustomed to honey when in health.[9]

The second test: let her be suffumigated with goodsmelling things, and if she feel the vapour internally, she is not pregnant, and the opposite.[10]

8. Such craving (known as pica) was attributed to a humoral imbalance in the stomach, the predominant humour causing a desire for things that agree with it in colour and substance, melancholy or black bile, for instance, causing a desire for coals, clay, sloes and the like. On pica in some early medieval texts, see pp. 33–4.
9. The growling will be caused by flatulence temporarily trapped by the pressure of the pregnant uterus. The drink is given when the woman is going to bed because she will have eaten her fill then, and will be resting, both of which factors will combine to create flatulence. Had the woman used honey regularly 'in health', her body would be used to it, making the test less effective.
10. This and the following test are designed to ascertain whether the uterus is empty, or has closed about an embryo.

The third test, i.e. let the woman take a clove of garlic and let her put it under her[11] going to bed, and if she feel its taste in her mouth after sleep she is not pregnant, and the opposite.

Here are the signs of a male pregnancy, i.e. the woman who conceives a son, she is often of better countenance, and is swifter and lighter in her movements, and has a better appetite; and the right eye is more agile, and the right breast begins to thicken sooner and its colour to change; and there is a swelling in the right side of the abdomen, and movement comes there sooner; and if the woman be standing and be about to walk, it is the right foot she moves first; and if she be sitting and be about to rise, she puts her right hand on her right knee for support; and this pregnancy is moved sooner in the uterus, for it is moved within three months, and the female within four; and the milk is purer and thicker when it is a male, and the pulse is greater in the right side.

11. i.e. employ it as a pessary.

ANONYMOUS

from:
COMMENTARY ON GERALDUS DE SOLO'S PRACTICA SUPER NONO ALMANSORIS
(c. 1335)

[The following instruction regarding conception concludes with a strategy to ensure the sex of the resultant offspring.

The text is translated from the Irish translation (1400) by Tadhg Ó Cuinn in Royal Irish Academy MS 474 (24 P 26), p. 173.26–31, by the present editor.]

And know that when one wishes conception to occur that sperm should be increased by the man and by the woman for four days. And it is then it is appropriate to perform coition, after midnight, for it is then the body has been cleansed from its residues. And after emitting the sperm, let the man remain for a long time without rising from her, for fear that air should reach the uterus. And if she wishes to have a son, let her turn gently on her right side, and if a daughter, let her turn on the left side.

Biographies/Bibliographies

Risteard Ó Conchubhair

It was while he was attending the medical school run by his kinsman and teacher, Donnchadh Óg Ó Conchubhair (fl. 1581–1610), at Aghmacart, County Laois, that Risteard wrote in 1590 Royal Irish Academy MS 439 (3 C 19), a collection of medical texts that he transcribed, evidently for his own use, under Donnchadh Óg's supervision. Risteard was in his twenty-ninth year at the time of writing, having been born on Christmas Eve 1561. Of his career after 1590, little is known. On 7 June 1594, having completed transcribing in Ballybrittas, County Laois, the copy of the Irish translation of Valerius Cordus's (1515–44) *Dispensatorium pharmacorum omnium* (1535) that is found in National

Library of Ireland, MS G 414, pp. 181–473, the physician Eoghan Ó Beitheacháin (fl. 1594–1600) thanked Risteard for having loaned him the exemplar from which he had worked; this exemplar apparently does not survive. A later anonymous hand recorded the date of Risteard's death, 18 October 1625, in Royal Irish Academy 439, f. 234vb.

Guy de Chauliac

LIFE. Born about 1290 in the former village of Chauliac (Département Lozère), Guy de Chauliac studied medicine at Toulouse and Montpellier, and anatomy and surgery at Bologna. He was appointed physician to Pope Clement VI (1342–52) at Avignon and, after Clement's death, served two of his successors at the papal court there, Innocent VI (1352–62) and Urban V (1362–70). He died sometime between 1367 and 1370. His *Inventorium sive Collectorium in Parte Chirurgicali Medicine*, compiled at Avignon in 1363 and generally referred to as his *Chirurgia Magna*, is widely regarded as the culmination of medieval surgical literature. It comprises an introductory essay, prologue, and seven tractates or books. It appears that only its first book, that which deals with anatomy, was translated into Irish.

CHIEF WRITINGS. *Cyrurgia Guidonis de Cauliaco. Et Cyrurgia Bruni. Theodorici. Rogerii. Rolandi. Bertapalie. Lanfranci* (Venice: Bonetus Locatellus, 1498), ff. [1]–81.

BIOGRAPHY AND CRITICISM. George Sarton, *Introduction to the History of Science*, vol. 3 (Baltimore: [for Carnegie Institution of Washington] Williams and Wilkins, 1947–8), 1690–4; Bjorn Wallner, *The Middle English Translation of Guy de Chauliac's Anatomy, With Guy's Essay on the History of Medicine* (Lund: CWK Gleerup, 1964); Markwart Michler, 'Guy de Chauliac als Anatom', *Medizinische Monatsschrift*, vol. 18 (1964), pp. 306–11.

Cormac Mac Duinnshléibhe

LIFE. Cormac Mac Duinnshléibhe was descended from a royal family of Ulster, who were displaced by the Anglo-Norman invaders. A branch of the family migrated to Tir Conaill (modern County Donegal), where they became hereditary physicians to the O'Donnells. He held a baccalaureate in medicine, but the identity of the university from which he graduated is not recorded. He was an outstanding translator of medical texts from Latin into Irish, and nine of his works are extant, two of which have been published (see below). His translation of Gaulterus Agilon's *De Dosibus Medicinarum* had been completed by 29 March 1459. His floruit is established by reference to this. His longest and most famous work comprises a rendering of Bernard of Gordon's *Lilium Medicine* (1305).

CHIEF WRITINGS. Hugh Cameron Gillies, *Regimen Sanitatis: The Rule of Health: A Gaelic Medical Manuscript of the Early Sixteenth Century . . . from the Vade Mecum of the famous Macbeaths, Physicians to the Lords of the Isles and the Kings of Scotland for several Centuries* (Glasgow: University Press, 1911); Shawn Sheahan, *An Irish Version of Gaulterus De Dosibus* (Washington DC: Catholic University of America, 1938).

Taddeo Alderotti

LIFE. Taddeo Alderotti (alias Thaddeus Florentinus) was born sometime between 1206 and 1215 into a Florentine family. The details of his early life and education are obscure. His entire teaching career, begun by 1268, was spent at Bologna, where he became a celebrated professor of medicine, and where he maintained an extensive and lucrative medical practice. He died in 1295.

CHIEF WRITINGS. Joannis Baptista Nicollinus (ed.), *Thaddei Florentini Expositiones in Arduum Aphorismorum Ipocratis Volumen. In Divinum Pronosticorum Ipocratis librum. In Praeclarum Regiminis Acutorum Ipocratis Opus. In Subtilissimum Joannitii Isagogarum Libellum* (Venice: Luca Antonius, 1527).

BIOGRAPHY AND CRITICISM. Nancy G. Siraisi, *Taddeo Alderotti and His Pupils: Two Generations of Italian Medical Learning* (Princeton, New Jersey: Princeton University Press, 1981).

Galen

LIFE. Born in 129, Galen of Pergamum (now Bergama, Turkey) was the son of a wealthy architect and landowner. He studied medicine in Pergamum, and then in Smyrna on the west coast of Asia Minor, in Corinth, and in Alexandria. Pergamum was the site of a famous temple of the healing god Asclepius, and, on his return home in 157, Galen was appointed physician to its company of gladiators. He moved to Rome in 162, and practised there until 166, when he returned to Pergamum. His second stay in Rome began in 169, when he was appointed by the Emperor Marcus Aurelius as physician to Commodus, his son and successor. Specific details regarding the events of his later life are scant. He died about 216.

CHIEF WRITINGS. Carolus Gottlob Kühn (ed.), *Claudii Galeni Opera Omnia*, 20 vols (Leipzig: C. Cnobloch, 1821–33); Charles Mayo Goss, 'On the Anatomy of the Uterus', *Anatomical Record*, vol. 144 (1962), pp. 77–83; Margaret Tallmadge May (trans.), *Galen: On the Usefulness of the Parts of the Body*, 2 vols (Ithaca, New York: Cornell University Press, 1968).

BIOGRAPHY AND CRITICISM. George Sarton, *Galen of Pergamon* (Lawrence, Kansas: University of Kansas Press, 1954); Rudolph E. Siegel, *Galen's System of Physiology and Medicine: An Analysis of His Doctrine and Observations on Bloodflow, Respiration, Humors and Internal Diseases* (Basel and New York: S. Karger, 1968); Owsei Temkin, *Galenism: Rise and Decline of a Medical Philosophy* (Ithaca and London: Cornell University Press, 1973).

Magninus of Milan

LIFE. A physician and astrologer, Magninus Mediolanensis (alias Maino de' Maineri) was evidently a native of Milan. His name occurs in the chartulary of the University of Paris from 1326 to 1336. His *Regimen Sanitatis* was completed during the episcopate of Andrea of Florence (Andrea Ghini de' Malpighi) in the see of Arras (1331 to 1334), to whom Magninus was physician and to whom he dedicated the work. The *Regimen* was translated into Irish by an anonymous author sometime prior to 1469.

CHIEF WRITINGS. *Regimen Sanitatis* (Louvain: Joannes de Westfalia, 1482); Lynn Thorndike, 'A Mediaeval Sauce-book', *Speculum*, vol. 9 (1934), pp. 183–90; Terence Scully, 'The Opusculum de Saporibus of Magninus Mediolanensis', *Medium Aevum*, vol. 54 (1985), pp. 178–207.

BIOGRAPHY AND CRITICISM. L. Thorndike, op. cit.; T. Scully, op. cit.

Bernard of Gordon

LIFE. Probably a native of Gourdon in Quercy (Département Lot), Bernard was born about 1258. He began teaching in the medical faculty at Montpellier in 1283 where he was to spend his entire career, achieving renown as a writer, teacher and physician. He died about 1320.

CHIEF WRITINGS. *Practica Seu Lilium Medicine* (Naples: Franciscus de Tuppo, 1480).

BIOGRAPHY AND CRITICISM. Luke E. Demaitre, *Doctor Bernard de Gordon: Professor and Practitioner* (Toronto: Pontifical Institute of Mediaeval Studies, 1980).

Geraldus de Solo

LIFE. The details of Geraldus de Solo's life are obscure. A professor in the medical faculty at Montpellier, he is mentioned in the chartulary of that university as early as 1335. He died about 1360.

CHIEF WRITINGS. *Practica Geraldi de Solo Super Nono Almansoris. Introductorium Iuuenum. Tractatus de Gradibus. Libellus de Febribus Eiusdem* (Lyons: Francisus Fradin, 1504).

BIOGRAPHY AND CRITICISM. George Sarton, *Introduction to the History of Science*, vol. 3 (Baltimore: [for Carnegie Institution of Washington] Williams and Wilkins, 1947–8), pp. 876–7.

Tadhg Ó Cuinn

LIFE. Evidently a member of a branch of the Uí Chuinn kindred of Munster, Tadhg Ó Cuinn held a baccalaureate in medicine, but the identity of the university from which he graduated is not recorded. He was a translator of medical texts from Latin into Irish, and three of his works are extant, none of which has been published. His earliest-dated and longest translation, a rendering of an anonymous commentary on Geraldus de Solo's *Practica Super Nono Almansoris*, was completed on Spy Wednesday, 1400. His best-known work, a translation of an anonymous herbal, was completed on the Feast of Saint Luke, 18 October, 1415. His rendering of an anonymous commentary on the *Colliget* of Averroes (d. 1198) is undated.

CHIEF WRITINGS. See above.

BIOGRAPHY AND CRITICISM. Nessa Ní Shéaghdha, 'Notes on some Scribal Terms', in *Celtic Studies: Essays in Memory of Angus Matheson 1912–1961*, eds. James Carney and David Greene (London: Routledge and Kegan Paul, 1968); Tomás Ó Concheanainn, 'The Irish Astronomical Tract in RIA B II 1', *Celtica*, vol. 11 (1976), pp. 158–67.

MÁIRÍN NÍ DHONNCHADHA, *Editor*

Courts and Coteries II: c. 1500–1800

In this selection we encounter at last a body of Gaelic poems and songs composed by women who were literate or arguably so. Readers are nonetheless liable to be disappointed at the paucity of named female authors whose work is represented here: three from the seventeenth century, six from the eighteenth, and one from the turn of the nineteenth. This amounts to roughly half of the currently-known named women poets of Ireland's Gaelic tradition in the period 1500–1800. Much of their work is printed here for the first time, thanks to two scholars: Liam P. Ó Murchú who edited and translated early seventeenth-century elegies in *caoineadh*-metre by Fionnghuala Ní Bhriain (pp. 395–7) and Caitilín Dubh (pp. 399–405), and Pádraig A. Breatnach who edited and translated work by the eighteenth-century poets, Úna Nic Cruitín (p. 434), Eibhlín Ní Choillte (pp. 435–6), Máire Ní Dhonnagáin (p. 438–40) and Máire Ní Mhurchú (pp. 444–5). One may reasonably assume that women also composed some of the anonymous syllabic poems in the courtly love tradition (*dánta grádha*) which predominate in the first half of the selection.

Women are far more prominent in Scottish Gaelic than in Irish literary tradition of the early modern and modern periods. Almost two hundred poems and songs and over thirty named authors are known from the period up to 1750.[1] Indeed, Scotland can boast of surviving work by two women who composed in Gaelic in the fifteenth century: Aithbhreac inghean Coirceadail, wife of the warden of Castle Sween in Knapdale,

and Iseabail Ní Mheic Cailéin, probably Isabella Stewart, wife of Colin, first Earl of Argyll. As these women composed in syllabic metres and belonged to the aristocracy, the likelihood is that they were literate. Iseabail's poems are similar in form and theme to Ireland's *dánta grádha*. The plausible suggestion has been made that courtly love poetry reached Scotland from Ireland: for one thing, Gearóid Iarla, 3rd Earl of Desmond, was writing in this vein in the fourteenth century (see pp. 324–6). There has been much academic speculation regarding the origins of Ireland's Gaelic love.

A new code of courtesy reached Ireland within a century or two of the Anglo-Norman Invasion, probably through the medium of contacts which the Anglo-Normans helped establish with Wales and England on the one hand, and France on the other. Its arrestingly fresh and complex approaches and conventions effected a renovation of established ideas about love, particularly the idea of love as a sickness (cf. pp. 293–4, 352–3), and contributed to the emergence of new attitudes to friendship. The poems of Gearóid Iarla and Iseabail Ní Mheic Cailéin are a salutary reminder of how early the European phenomenon of courtly love was assimilated by Gaelic culture. Most of the recorded *dánta grádha* seem to date from the sixteenth and seventeenth centuries, by which time the impact on Gaelic literature of English poets such as Surrey and Sidney and a host of lesser figures was a distinct possibility, but many critics have noted the achieved artistry of particular *dánta grádha* which owe nothing to such influences.

Much of what was said in the Introduction to 'Courts and Coteries I, *c.* 900–1600' (pp. 293–303) is relevant to the contextualization

---

1. Anne C. Frater, 'The Gaelic Tradition up to 1750', in Douglas Gifford and Dorothy McMillan (ed.), *A History of Scottish Women's Writing* (Edinburgh: Edinburgh University Press, 1997), pp. 1–14 at p. 1.

of the poems which follow. To underline the continuity between the two selections, they have been made to overlap chronologically. Within both, long formal addresses to patrons alternate with shorter poems and the work of amateur poets is featured prominently, in an effort to imagine the circumstances in which women, as well as men, enjoyed and, on occasion, composed poetry. Conservative and apparently innovative forms appear side by side: two of the *caointe* of Caitilín Dubh, the earliest woman poet to have left a body of work in Irish, precede Tadhg Mac Bruaideadha's arrogant rebuke in *dán díreach* to a woman named Síle, daughter of Éamonn, who dared to question his historical knowledge (pp. 399–408). Ironically, one of Caitilín Dubh's *caointe* was in honour of Mac Bruaideadha's own patron, Donnchadh Ó Briain, 3rd Earl of Thomond, showing that even as Mac Bruaideadha blustered about his superior training in 'the smithies of Éire's sages' (*ceardcha ollamh Éirionn*), an approach to the aristocratic patron from another angle lay open to the female poet. It is suggested below that she may have been related by blood to the Earl's family.

Mac Bruaideadha's words rebuking Síle, daughter of Éamonn, have a deadly earnestness about them. If it is true that his poem was composed sometime before November 1580 (see headnote), then it is probably instinct with the memory of the hanging of a number of poets in 1572 by Conchobhar Ó Briain, father of the 4th Earl of Thomond. Ó Briain's action was regarded as a heinous attack on the poetic body and he was satirized and anathematized by many poets on account of it. Mac Bruaideadha's poem deals with a single woman's attack on the poetic body, represented by himself. Mac Bruaideadha was a supremely contentious poet. In fact, the great bardic contention known as *Iomarbhágh na bhFileadh* (The Contention of the Bards), which involved many of the leading Gaelic *literati* of North and South who between them contributed some thirty poems to it, originated with him in 1617. His address to Síle, daughter of Éamonn, might be seen as a mini-*iomarbhágh* against the forces for change in Gaelic culture. If this poem jars with those by Caitilín Dubh, that is all to the good: the search for female authors, the focus on female recipients and attention to gendering more broadly are bound to introduce discor-

dance into the received narrative of Gaelic tradition.

The degree to which formal bardic poetry is apostrophic has been remarked on already (p. 296). While many of the *dánta grádha* are also apostrophic, they seem destined from the beginning to be enjoyed by the unidentified reader, their status as artefacts reinforced by the lack of circumstantial detail. In an effort to allow the contemporary reader act as an independent arbiter in this matter, background information on the poems is supplied, where available. Such information reveals many blood-ties and other bonds from one generation to the next among the poets and the recipients of poems. For example, Maghnus Ó Domhnaill (d. 1563) of Donegal, the first named author in this selection, was grandfather to Rudhraighe Ó Domhnaill and to Nuala, both of whom also feature (pp. 370–1, 389–95). The couple addressed in 'Fuaras nóchar uaibhreach óigmhear' (pp. 382–4) were grand-parents to Eileanór Chaomhánach to whom Cearbhall Ó Dálaigh (*fl.* 1630) paid court (pp. 414–15). Pádraigín Haicéad, another author represented here (pp. 410–13), was an intimate friend of Ó Dálaigh's and exchanged poems with him.

As almost every poem below from the period before 1700 was authored by a castle-dwelling aristocrat, these bonds are hardly surprising: aristocracies tend to be close-knit. Eighteenth-century Gaelic poets, on the other hand, were typically middle-class. They also wrote for a larger public than their predecessors. Yet to say this is to generalize from male authors: the work of Gaelic female poets in the eighteenth century seems to have had a more limited circulation, a circumstance which must have contributed to a disproportionate loss of women's writing over time. With one exception (Máire Ní Mhurchú), all the female poets whose work is represented here can be shown to have had familial links to men associated with courts or literary coteries. What little we have of their work was almost certainly preserved on account of these links. Caitilín Dubh, Brighid, wife of Rudhraighe Ó Domhnaill, and Fionnghuala, daughter of Domhnall Ó Briain, cousin of the Earls of Thomond, were connected to aristocratic courts which were a magnet for literacy skills in the earlier period. Úna Nic Cruitín's father, Aodh

Buí Mac Cruitín, was a poet, a lexicographer and a scribe; the only extant copy of Caitilín Dubh's poems is in his hand. The husbands of Máire Ní Reachtagáin and Úna Ní Bhroin, Seán and Tadhg Ó Neachtain, were the leading figures in a Dublin circle of Gaelic scholars and poets. Úna was also a close relation, possibly a sister, of the archbishop of Dublin, Edmund Byrne. Máire Nic a Liondain's father, Pádraig Mac a Liondain, was a south-east Ulster poet who associated with Peadar Ó Doirnín, Séamas Mac Cuarta and other notable writers from this area. The family's interest in music brought them into contact with Toirdhealbhach Ó Cearbhalláin, Arthur O'Neill and Edward Bunting. Among Máire Ní Dhonnagáin's associates was Donnchadh Ruadh Mac Conmara, renowned as a teacher and poet; he wrote in Latin as well as Irish, and possibly also in English. Almost all that is known of Eibhlín Ní Choillte is that she came from Cathair Druinge, near Mitchelstown in County Cork. An early copy of her one recorded poem was made by Aindrias Mac Craith, a luminary of the *cúirt éigse* which met at Croom in neighbouring County Limerick; his interest in her work warns against taking his deprecation of scribbling women in the poem '*Éigsíní Ban agus Tae*' too seriously. The three poems commemorating Máire Ní Chrualaoich, the 'Sappho of Munster', were composed by men who were undoubtedly literate.

None of these women left any writing in her own hand; in fact, what appears to be the earliest existing Gaelic manuscript written by a woman dates from the 1820s. This is not to say that they were illiterate: most male poets who were literate left no proof of their competence either. While an element of doubt may always remain over some of these texts, particularly those that are the sole surviving examples of a woman's work, as a corpus they arrogate to women a small but significant place in Gaelic literary tradition.

Yet the more one engages with Gaelic tradition, the more problematic the compartmentalization of oral and written literature seems. The Cork poet, Máire Bhuidhe Ní Laoghaire, who died around 1849, the first female folk poet to have a volume of her work published (posthumously), was distantly related to Art Ó Laoghaire, keened so memorably by his wife, Eibhlín Dubh, nearly eighty years before

(pp. 288–90; pp. 1372–84). Points of difference in the poetry of these two women are more numerous than resemblances. The work of each is also markedly different to that of the early seventeenth-century poet, Caitilín Dubh. As things stand, one cannot show that any one of these three women was wholly illiterate in Irish, but equally it seems impossible to define the degree to which any of them was literate in that language. The fact that it is becoming more difficult to make generalizations about female poets' work is a healthy sign: for too long, the stereotype of the female poet as unlettered *bean chaointe* foreclosed on the search for other types.

* * *

Of all the poems presented here, the *dánta grádha* are those most likely to appeal to contemporary sensibilities. Their language is modern and simple, and many see their treatment of love as still meaningful. They have also been regarded with suspicion, however: some commentators have criticized them for reifying women while others see their courtliness as denaturing both men and women. To be sure, many of the *dánta grádha* concern male fantasies, and when women are given a voice, it is often to ridicule these fantasies. This sets the accessible, speaking woman against the more remote object of male desire, and works to undermine them both. Such binary thinking in relation to women and their bodies can take more gruesome form, as the cure recommended for lovesickness by Bernard of Gordon reminds us (see pp. 352–3 above).

Gaelic writing, unlike song, rarely represents women as losing themselves in fantasy; the rhapsodical lines spoken by Finnabair, daughter of Ailill and Medb, in the Old Irish tale *Táin Bó Fraích* (The Cattle-Raid of Fráech) as she watches her lover swimming are highly unusual. Consequently, the *dán grádha* might be seen as a form that facilitated female fantasy and its expression. The fact that some of the poems in women's voices which appear below are very slight pieces might even be taken as an argument for female authorship.

It may be that the representation of men as the primary sufferers of lovesickness helped to constrain, while simultaneously indulging, unruly erotic impulses (cf. pp. 169–70). If so, some male writers had their revenge on the socially controlling function of the *dán grádha*. For example, Mac Con Ó Cléirigh (d. 1595) wrote a vicious poem repudiating his wife, despite her claim to have a papal bull confirming their marriage. His poem is not a love-letter but a kind of *libellus repudii* (bill of divorce), echoing a husband's biblical prerogative to abandon his wife 'because she does not please him and because he finds something objectionable about her' (Deuteronomy 24:1–4; cp. pp. 10–11). To add to the insult, Ó Cléirigh claimed the Virgin herself was on his side (much as his contemporary, Domhnall Mac Carthaigh, called the Virgin to audit his more positive words above love: see pp. 371-2):

A mheirdreach labharthach lonn,
nách cruaidhe a hoiread d'iarann,
  créad rom-beir re mnaoi dod mheas?
  gan geir a-taoi, gan toirrcheas . . .

Gé nách beinn libhse ag lighe,
fóirfidh Mac na Maighdine;
  go mbeire mé a-nunn ar neamh
  an Té do chum an chéidbhean.

Whore of sound and fury —
Iron is not harder than you!
Why do I compare you to a woman —
You are dried up, void . . .

Though I may not lie with you
The Virgin's Son will save me;
May He who made the first woman
Bring me unto Heaven.

Poetry in the tradition and counter-tradition of courtly love has an abundance and variety scarcely hinted at in the following selection. Gearóid Iarla's poems (pp. 324–6) represent the first manifestation of the genre in Ireland, and there are some three hundred years between them and the latest *dánta grádha*. A new anthology of such poems might include long ones such as that composed by Piaras Feiritéar in honour of Meg Russell, daughter of the 4th Earl of Bedford, in 1629 or thereabouts ('*Tugas annsacht d'óigh Ghallda*'). In an unpublished paper, Máire Mhac an tSaoi and Máire Mhic

Chonghail showed that Feiritéar, whose landlord was Richard Boyle, Earl of Cork, almost certainly wrote this poem on the occasion of Boyle's visit to the Bedfords' home in Chiswick near London to seek Meg Russell's hand for his son, Richard; Meg Russell was eleven years old at the time. There are other examples of seventeenth-century poems in Irish which were written to mark the courtship and betrothal of nobles, and the trend ties in with practice elsewhere in Europe, in academic and court circles, to mark important occasions with specially commissioned works. For example, the arrival of the prince of Wales, the future Charles I, in Madrid in 1624 to court the Infanta was celebrated with a poem of welcome, written in Latin. A new anthology might also include some allegorical poems or poems with ingeniously extended metaphors such as '*Féuch féin an obair-si, a Áodh*' (pp. 419–22). It certainly should include some poems and songs in accentual metres, such as '*Dála an nóinín*' by Pádraigín Haicéad (pp. 410–11).

At present, there is only one anthology of *dánta grádha*, which its editor, Tomás Ó Rathile, published in two versions, the second one being a greatly expanded version of the first.[2] Every poem in the two versions is in a syllabic metre (a small number of them have a *ceangal* (final 'binding' stanza) in accentual metre). This conceals the fact that poets such as Piaras Feiritéar and Cearbhall Ó Dálaigh wrote both syllabic and accentual poems. The seventeenth century possibly saw more rapid change in Gaelic literary forms than any other. Accentual metres had long co-existed with syllabic ones, but had been regarded as aesthetically inferior. Now they began to displace the syllabic metres, as poets as accomplished as Feiritéar and Ó Dálaigh embraced them. What is particularly significant about these two poets is that they were musicians also: Ó Dálaigh was a renowned harper and Feiritéar appears to have been at very least a competent one (see p. 452). New compositions by harpers which were well suited to accentual metres may have done much to boost the popularity of these metres. Interestingly, the

2. Tomás Ó Rathile (ed.), *Dánta Grádha. An Anthology of Irish Love Poetry of the Sixteenth and Seventeenth Centuries* (Cork: Cork University Press, 1916); Idem., *Dánta Grádha. An Anthology of Irish Love Poetry (A.D. 1350–1750)* (Cork: Cork University Press, 1926).

earliest reliable information on Irish music in any quantity relates to the mid-seventeenth century. Furthermore, it is believed that some of the oldest known folk-songs, such as 'Eibhlín a rún', date back to the same period. This song is traditionally ascribed to Cearbhall Ó Dálaigh (see p. 414).

Pádraigín Haicéad was another transitional poet who was engrossed by music and harpers. He wrote this quatrain about a woman harper, Oileán Carrún:

> *Oiléan Carrún laglúb líomhtha léir,*
> *foiléim ainiúil teacht dúinn sínte lé;*
> *bruithshéis taidhiúir fhraischiúil chaoin a téad*
> *tug mé ag machtnughadh feadh chúig n-oidhche*
>   *ndéag.*

Helena Carron, soft-haired, polished, lucid,
I think of her near me and my mind takes
    flight;
The strains of her harp-strings' plaintive music
Have been my dream for all of fifteen nights.

References to women's musical accomplishments are scarce in formal bardic addresses but abound in *dánta grádha* of the sixteenth century and later. Most of the women in question were aristocrats or women in comfortable circumstances for whom music was a leisure activity, enjoyed at home. The poet Máire Nic a Liondain may have been one such (pp. 436–8). Female harpers who made their living from music are difficult to find in pre-eighteenth century sources, but the Memoirs of Arthur O'Neill (1734–1818), one of the last of the itinerant harpers, contain many references to female harpers whose paths crossed his as he travelled the country. Some, like him, were blind and travelled with a guide, but there is little explicit suggestion that their role as performers was circumscribed by their sex.

The first poem below was chosen to suggest a link between the *dánta grádha* and amatory letters. There are striking similarities between the two types of writing. Both love-poem and love-letter stand in for the lover whose desire is for physical intimacy. The poem or letter touches the other whom the writer desires to touch, and reveals what s/he dare not say in person. These conventions spill over even into business letters.

For example, a letter written by Lady Offaly to the Earl of March in 1623, regarding family lands in county Wexford, is signed 'Your Lordship's very affectionat frend to serve you, Letice Offaly' and has as postscript: 'Pray, my Lord, sufur this paper to kiss my Lady's fayr hands and to present my love and servis to her Ladyship'.

During the Renaissance, there was a surge of interest in letter-writing and new manuals of style were produced to cater for it. The full extent of the links between Irish epistolary conventions and the *dánta grádha* has yet to be explored. In other countries, the conventions of letter-writing promoted an emotionally expressive mode usually associated with women. Letters written by men to women conveyed desire femininely — openly and intensely. The formulations and emotional pitch were not essentially different in letters addressed by men to men. Letter-writing helped assimilate friendship between men to love between man and woman and this, in turn, promoted letters as signs of homoerotic as well as heteroerotic desire.[3]

The bardic poem, the *dán grádha* and the personal letter are apostrophic forms in which friendship is usually assimilated to love, and sometimes charged with eroticism. Of course, the conveying of erotic love was the primary function of the *dán grádha* and a predominant function of the letter. The way in which the text of the *dán grádha* seeks to bring the lovers together, and figures the desired bodily engagement, is eminently clear in Cearbhall Ó Dálaigh's poem for Eileanór Chaomhánach, '*Do mhúscail mé tar éis luí araoir go sámh*'. In praising her writing skills, his last lines seem to leap to bridge the space between them:

> *I gcúirt níl téxa Béarla nach bí aici a sháith*
> *Is dar liúmsa léighidh Gaedhalg mar shaoithibh*
>   *Fáil.*
> *Is dlúth tiubh géar glé a scríbhinn bhláith,*
> *Conclúision: 'Éist! adéaram — is fínit spás'.*

At court she can master any English text with
    wit.
She reads Irish like the sages of Inis Fáil.

3. See David M. Bergeron, *King James and Letters of Homoerotic Desire* (Iowa: University of Iowa Press, 1999), pp. 3–31.

Her script is lovely and clear, thick and
  close-knit.
Conclusion: 'Quiet! I say, space *finit*.'

(Translation: Seamus Deane)

Robin Flower wrote an introduction to each of
the two versions of Tomás Ó Rathile's anthology,
Dánta Grádha. Both Flower and Ó Rathile took
it for granted that the *dánta grádha* were the work
of a mixed group of professional and amateur
poets; the subject, of course, made amateurs of
them all. Flower and Ó Rathile seem not to have
registered the possibility that any of these poems
might be same-sex love-poems. Indeed, they
almost overlooked the fact that some of the
poems were written by women or as though by
women. Flower made a fleeting reference to
Iseabail Ní Mheic Cailéin and Ó Rathile
included one of her poems but for both men, the
dán grádha was essentially a love-poem written
by a heterosexual man for or about a woman. Ó
Rathile gallantly dedicated the anthology *Do
Bhantracht na hÉireann ós ortha atá na mná is
fearr san domhan* ('To the Women of Ireland since
they include the best women in the world').

For Ó Rathile, and possibly for Flower, the
only kind of orderly desire seems to have been
heteroerotic desire. They were perhaps unaware
of a propensity in Gaelic culture to represent
homoerotic desire as orderly, a propensity one
can find in man-to-man bardic poetry. It has
been argued already that, in the early modern
period, homoeroticism is particularly marked in
Gaelic texts dealing with friendship between
literary males, especially poets (pp. 296–8). Such
men were the typical authors of what Ó Rathile
and Flower understood to be *dánta grádha*. A
more comprehensive definition — or anthology
— of the courtly love-poems of the early modern
period would also encompass the poems of love
and friendship which these men exchanged with
each other.

From the sixteenth century onwards, there is
evidence of an explicit assimilation of love
between men to that between man and woman.
For example, Tadhg Ó Cobhthaigh (d. 1554),
who apparently tutored Maghnus Ó Domhnaill
of Donegal and who is described in his annalistic
obituary as 'Ireland's and Scotland's leading
tutor in poetry', has the following lines in a poem

he wrote as a *séad suirghe* 'love token' for
Ó Domhnaill:

*Mo thoil d'airdrígh chinidh Chuinn
mar thoil mná 'na meidh chomhthruim.*

My desire for the high-king of Conn's race
is as a woman's, measure for measure.

A fine poem by Piaras Feiritéar (d. 1653) on
the arms of love, addressed to a woman, is given
below (pp. 409–10). He also wrote many love
poems for men. The following quatrains are from
one he composed in honour of his friend,
Richard Hussey:

*A mhná uaisle an iongnadh libh
nach bean rom-mheall uair éigin,
nach stuagh gheal gan fheirg gan an,
acht fear gan cheilg dom chealgadh?*

*Dámadh aithnidh díbhse a dháil,
tréithe ionganta an ógáin,
ní bhiadh sibh gan suirghe ris —
mil a fhuighle re n-aithris.*

Ladies, why the surprise
That, for once, it is not a woman —
Fair, kind, of faultless form —
Beguiles me, but a guileless man?

If his ways were known to you,
The boy's amazing qualities,
You couldn't help but love him:
Just to praise him is honey-sweet.

Given the small number of recorded poems in
the female voice, it is not surprising that woman-
to-woman poems of love or friendship are
extremely rare. There is only one in this selection
and previous anthologizers, it must be said,
regarded it as a poem on the Dance of Death
(p. 252). Readers may judge for themselves
whether the present contextualization offers
support for an alternative interpretation.

* * *

One sometimes finds courtly love poems and
bardic poems represented as opposite kinds of
poetry. Bardic poetry may be portrayed as the
dull native product which was easily outshone by

the witty, ironic lyric that supposedly originated with urbane non-Gaels. Medieval-minded men wrote bardic poems, Renaissance men and women wrote *dánta grádha*. Although the more progressive Gaels took up this kind of poetry, the non-Gaels — call them 'Anglo-Irish' or 'Old English' or *Gaill* — continued to excel in it: their ethnic identity, cultural formation and more extensive use of the English language better equipped them to handle it. Or so it is suggested.

The idea that the *dánta grádha* were not quite as authentically Irish as bardic poems has led to an oddly acute interest in the ethnic identity of the authors. Much has been made of the fact that some of the most talented authors of *dánta grádha* had non-Gaelic surnames — writers such as Piaras Feiritéar, Pádraigín Haicéad and Séathrún Céitinn. But was the question of ethnic identity of any great moment to these writers when they wrote love poems? It seems unlikely, since writers, like Nennius, tend to make a heap of all they can find. It seems equally unlikely that authors with Gaelic surnames regarded the *dánta grádha* as being in any way counter-cultural; after all, they seem to have written most of them.

The suggestion of two cultures moving apart, one of them far less capable of change, is strong in many accounts of Irish literary history. In part, this is because two kinds of sources have had a privileged hearing: sixteenth- and early seventeenth-century Gaelic poems in which the poets figured their personal loss of patronage and privilege as the ruin of civilization, and New English writings which sought to justify the destruction of the power of Gaelic rulers and their corrupting influence. Over-attention to these sources can obscure the fact that Gaelic literature had long lain itself open to English-language cultural influences, and had a demonstrated capacity to assimilate them.

It is in the fifteenth century that one first sees significant evidence of English literary influences. Translations into Irish from English begin to appear in some number, although Latin texts continue to be more important. Adaptation of English sources coincides with new access to printed texts. Uilliam Mac an Leagha translated the Life of Mary of Egypt from an unidentified English source (cf. pp. 143–8). He is also credited with the only known copy of the Irish translation of Caxton's *The recuyell of the historyes*

of Troye, and it is likely that he was not merely the scribe but also the translator. The Irish translation was made very soon after Caxton's text was printed in 1474. Fínghin Ó Mathghamhna, a Gaelic chieftain in south-west Cork, far from the English Pale, translated both The Book of Sir Marco Polo, and The Book of John Maundeville into Irish. Translation from English also inspired original compositions: twenty new *dánta grádha* were intercalated into the Irish translation of the tale of William of Palerne, for example (for one of them, see pp. 369–70). This confidently creative approach to literature in English is characteristic of early modern Gaelic culture. It is worth remembering that many Gaelic writers of the sixteenth and seventeenth centuries had English, although they chose to write (or write primarily) in Irish. Indeed, many of the Irish elite, both Gaelic and Old English, knew Latin as well as English, and sometimes also French.

Two surviving lists show that there was a good library of books and manuscripts in English, Latin, French and Irish in the house of Gearóid Mac Gearailt (1451–1513), 8th Earl of Kildare, to which the 9th Earl added significantly. While men and women of such Old English families may have had access to more books, they were not a race apart from those of Gaelic extraction when it came to cultural influences. The Book of Lismore is one of a number of fifteenth-century Gaelic manuscripts compiled for lay-patrons; in earlier centuries, manuscripts were compiled mainly for use by professional scholars or monastery-libraries. It contains a poem for a couple who have been identified as Fínghin Mac Carthaigh (d. 1505), Lord of Cairbre in County Cork, and his wife, Caitilín (d. 1506), daughter of the 8th Earl of Desmond. It is probable but not certain that the codex was compiled for them. It contains mostly traditional Gaelic material, yet one can imagine that this couple may have also been interested in, and possibly the possessors of, books in English, Latin, or French. Yet another fifteenth-century manuscript contains a copy of *Cath Finntrágha* (The Battle of Ventry) written for Sadhbh, daughter of Tadhg Ó Máille (?died 1467) A colophon describes her as *saí mhná ar ghaís agus ar eineach agus gheanmnaigheacht*, 'a woman-sage as regards wisdom, honour and chastity'. She was probably related to Máire, daughter of Eoghan Ó Máille, whose 'book of piety' containing translations from Latin of the Lives of Saints Margaret and Catherine has been referred to above (p. 56).

There is abundant evidence of interest in other literatures and languages on the part of Irish speakers from the fifteenth century onwards. Attitudes towards the English language were complex, and became increasingly so in the course of the turbulent sixteenth century. However, recent work argues that the confidence of Irish speakers and the attractiveness of their culture to the Old English have been downplayed. Far from being hostile to Gaelic culture, many of the Old English participated in it to a degree that went far beyond the utilitarian. Their attitudes were fundamentally different to those of Elizabethan writers who had no knowledge of Irish and had to resort to construing it as a sign, 'an index of difference in a context of polarised conflict'. For the latter, Irish was not so much a language as 'the dissidence and contrariness it encoded', a rebel tongue, a papist tongue, the language of degeneracy.[4]

It is difficult to gauge how these attitudes affected Ireland's monolinguals and bilinguals but, clearly, dual competence was often a source of pride. Networks of personal contacts between writers of Old English and Gaelic descent provide telling evidence of a bilingual elite. One such network involved the Nugent (Nuinseann) family of Delvin, County Westmeath. Christopher Nugent (d. 1602), 9th Baron of Delvin, was educated at Cambridge where he prepared a Primer of Irish for Elizabeth I, in which he commended 'the desyer your Highnes hath to understande the language of your people'. Poems in Irish by his Oxford-educated younger brother, William (d. 1625), are still extant. In his *Description of Ireland*, Richard Stanihurst, overlooking this aspect of William's output, described him as 'a proper gentleman, and of a singular good wit; he wrote in the English toong diverse sonets'. Giolla Brighde Ó hEodhasa (d. 1614), who had been court poet to Aodh Mág Uidhir of Fermanagh, wrote poems for the Nugents, including one for William. Ó hEodhasa abandoned his family's hereditary calling, trained as a priest on the continent and became Guardian of the Franciscan College at Louvain. In his poem for William, Ó hEodhasa describes him as 'one who was the sun of my intellect, the meadow where my affection grazed' (*grian m'inntleachta úair oile,/clúain inghealta m'ionmhuine'*. Ó hEodhasa's *Teagasc Críosdaidhe* (Antwerp, 1611; Louvain, 1614) was the first Irish-language book from the Catholic side to be published. In 1604 William Nugent's cousin, Richard Nugent, published *Cynthia*, a collection 'containing direful sonnets, Madrigalls and passionate intercourses describing his repudiate affections expressed in love's own language'. Giolla Brighde was cousin to Eochaidh Ó hEodhasa (d. 1612), arguably the finest Irish-language poet of his generation and certainly one of the most innovative. The poem he wrote in the name of Cú Chonnacht Mág Uidhir to Brighid, teenage wife of Rudhraighe Ó Domhnaill, Earl of Tír Conaill, and her reply, are below (pp. 384–8).

The Nugent network points up many of the factors which made Irish-language writing at the turn of the seventeenth century exceptionally dynamic. The cultivation of Irish in the interests of religious reform became acceptable under Elizabeth I. Her decision to have the Bible translated into Irish resulted in the provision of type and a press to print it. Counter-Reformation writers adapted the technology to their own purposes. Print gave them easier access to the resources of other languages. Many who went abroad and became adept in continental languages devoted considerable energy to developing Irish as an effective medium for Counter-Reformation teaching, and to translating doctrinal and devotional works for an Irish readership. Writers of Irish who remained at home were energized by a zeal for translation which reflected the neoclassical aesthetic of the Renaissance along with the persuasive imperative of the Reformation and its aftermath. English interest in the resources of other literatures, sharpened by territorial and linguistic expansionism, also helped to broaden Irish literary horizons.

Classical traditions and apologues became a signal influence for change in Irish-language poetry. One effect they had was to displace the professional poet's conventional representation of himself as his lord's favourite or bed-fellow. Older, European conceits which allowed the poet to represent himself as the female partner in a

4. Patricia Palmer, *Language and Conquest in Early Modern Ireland: English Renaissance literature and Elizabethan imperial expansion* (Cambridge, Cambridge University Press, 2001), pp. 91, 95, and passim.

heterosexual relationship come to the fore at the end of the sixteenth century. For example, in a poem addressed to Maol Mórdha Ó Raghallaigh, a Cavan noble, Eochaidh Ó hEodhasa adapted the story of the triumvirate of Pompey, Caesar and Crassus to contemporary circumstances in the aftermath of the Nine Years War. In his poem, Caesar is the English power. Pompey stands for Aodh Ruadh Ó Domhnaill and Crassus for Aodh Mág Uidhir, two of Ó hEodhasa's former patrons who died during the War. He himself is Cornelia, who was married first to Crassus (a slight distortion of history here) and later to Pompey, and who now fears for the future of Ó Raghallaigh, should he too become Ó hEodhasa's 'spouse' or patron.

Some of Ó hEodhasa's contemporaries also innovated by figuring themselves as Diana, Venus, or Minerva. While classical tropes have an obvious intrinsic appeal, their use was given further impetus by the ideology of companionate marriage which ran against the traditional bardic valorization of male companionship. The deployment of 'sodomy' as a political category to stigmatize various groups as disorderly in the early modern period rendered figurative and actual homoeroticism less acceptable. Clerics, and especially Catholic clerics, were often charged with sodomy. In his *Image of Ireland* (1581), John Derricke, who characterized the Irish as irredeemably depraved, described Ireland as 'the devil's arse, a peak where rebels most embrace'. His notorious woodcut of the feast of the 'Macke Swine, a barbarous ofspring come from that nation, which mai be perceved by their hoggishe fashion' depicts various guests, including two bare-buttocked men. While these are usually construed as professional 'bum-crackers', the suspicion that Derricke was intent on suggesting sodomitical acts is difficult to avoid. The metaphor of Circe's Cup may underlie the unjustified implication that the name 'Mac Suibhne' (Macke Swine) is etymologically related to 'swine' (cf. 'hoggishe'). Indeed the metaphor of (English)men transformed into swine through intercourse with a demoralizing (Irish) female was pivotal in the rhetoric of English writing about Ireland. Derricke was possibly using the metaphor antithetically, suggesting that Irishmen's worst degradation was wrought not by intercourse with females but by intercourse with each other.

Ethnographic rhetoric aside, a predilection for Ovidian metaphors of erotic conflict and transformation is evident in seventeenth-century Gaelic poetry. The poem beginning '*Féuch féin an obair-si, a Áodh*' (pp. 419–22) is a superbly extended metaphor of marital sexuality disrupted by male homoerotic desire. The lyric flatters two patrons by hinting broadly that they provoke homoerotic desire: they are to the poet as Ganymede is to Jupiter (though the relation is sometimes reversed), and the names of seductively handsome Gaelic gods (Manannán, Óenghus, etc.) are invoked to drive the point home.

The network associated with the Nugents has many later parallels. Male and female writers who were involved in some of the foremost of them are encountered below, from Thomond, Ormond, Dublin, Oirghialla, and an extensive Limerick-Cork network. Traditional historiography encouraged one to view such networks as isolated constellations flaring briefly in the darkness which had awaited the Gael since the end of Nine Years War. The complex energies of even the most important of them, however, have perhaps yet to be understood. What is clear is that cultural continuity was maintained, from aristocratic court to *cúirt éigse*, and beyond.

Eighteenth-century poetry is pervaded by Jacobite ideology. Although not an exclusively Catholic phenomenon, the Jacobite dream of restoration — of rightful king, religious and ancestral privilege, and exiled aristocracy — consolidated the political identity of Irish Catholics (cf. pp. 273–6). The phenomenon of great families spreading outwards, their former clients overtaking them and some of their own offshoots sliding into obscurity was a constant in Irish history. Recalling one's ancestry was crucial to the project of re-ascent. Identifying the exiled Stuarts as their legitimate rulers allowed oppressed Catholics to view themselves as a kind of reduced aristocracy who might expect better days. Central to the promise of deliverance was the figure of the daughter of Zion, inflected through Mary, the female saints and a host of legendary and historical figures, down to her last manifestation here as '*ainnir na míne*' of Old Cill Chais who 'followed the prince of the Gaels'. Thus the *aisling* of Irish Jacobitism re-asserted a heterosexually constructed social vision.

ANONYMOUS

AOIBHINN, A LEABHRÁIN, DO THRIALL
(To the Lady with a Book)

[Text: T.F. Ó Rathile, *Dánta Grádha: An Anthology of Irish Love Poetry (A.D. 1350–1750)* (Cork: Cork University Press, 1926), pp. 1–2. Translation: Frank O'Connor, *Kings, Lords and Commons* (New York: Knopf, 1959), p. 71.]

Aoibhinn, a leabhráin, do thriall
   i gceann ainnre na gciabh gcam;
truagh gan tusa im riocht i bpéin
   is mise féin ag dul ann.

A leabhráin bhig, aoibhinn duit
   ag triall mar a bhfuil mo ghrádh;
an béal loinneardha mar chrú
   do-chífe tú, 's an déad bán.

Do-chífe tusa an rosg glas,
   do-chífir fós an bhas tláith;
biaidh tú, 's ni bhiad-sa, far-raor!
   taobh ar thaobh 's an choimhgheal bhláith.

Do-chífe tú an mhala chaol
   's an bhráighe shaor sholas shéimh,
's an ghruaidh dhrithleannach mar ghrís
   do chonnarc i bhfís a-réir.

An com sneachtaidhe seang slán
   dá dtug mise grádh gan chéill,
's an troigh mhéirgheal fhadúr bhán
   do-chífe tú lán do sgéimh.

An glór taidhiúir síthe séimh
   do chuir mise i bpéin gach laoi
Cluinfir, is ba haoibhinn duid;
   uch gan mo chuid bheith mar taoi!

TRANSLATION

Pleasant journey, little book
   To that gay gold foolish head!
Though I wish that you remained
   And I travelled in your stead.

Gentle book, 'tis well for you,
   Hastening where my darling rests;
You will see the crimson lips,
   You will touch the throbbing breasts.

You will see the dear grey eye.
   On you will that hand alight —
Ah, my grief 'tis you not I
   Will rest beside her warm at night.

You will see the slender brows
   And the white nape's candle-gleam,
And the fond flickering cheeks of youth
   That I saw last night in dream.

And the waist my arms would clasp
   And the long legs and stately feet
That pace between my sleep and me
   With their magic you will meet.

And the soft pensive sleepy voice
   Whose echoes murmur in my brain
Will bring you rest — 'tis well for you!
   When shall I hear that voice again?

NÍ BHFUIGHE MISE BÁS DUIT
(O Woman Shapely as the Swan)

[Text: T.F. Ó Rathile, *Dánta Grádha*, pp. 132–3. Translation: Padraic Colum, in John Montague, *The Faber Book of Irish Verse* (London: Faber and Faber, 1978), pp. 105–6).]

Ní bhfuighe mise bás duit,
   a bhean úd an chuirp mar ghéis;
daoine leamha ar mharbhais riam,
   ní hionann iad is mé féin.

Créad umá rachainn-se d'éag
   don bhéal dearg, don déad mar bhláth?
an crobh míolla, an t-ucht mar aol,
   an dáibh do-gheabhainn féin bás?

Do mhéin aobhdha, th'aigneadh saor,
　a bhas thana, a thaobh mar chuip,
a rosg gorm, a brágha bhán, —
　ní bhfuighe mise bás duit.

Do chíocha corra, a chneas úr,
　do ghruaidh chorcra, do chúl fiar, —
go deimhin ní bhfuighead bás
　dóibh sin go madh háil le Dia.

Do mhala chaol, t'fholt mar ór,
　do rún geanmnaidh, do ghlór leasg,
do shál chruinn, do cholpa réidh, —
　ní mhuirbhfeadh siad ach duine leamh.

A bhean úd an chuirp mar ghéis,
　do hoileadh mé ag duine glic;
aithne dhamh mar bhíd na mná;
　ní bhfuighe mise bás duit!

TRANSLATION

O woman, shapely as the swan,
On your account I shall not die:
The men you've slain — a trivial clan —
Were less than I.

I ask me shall I die for these —
For blossom teeth and scarlet lips —
And shall that delicate swan-shape
Bring me eclipse?

Well-shaped the breasts and smooth the skin,
The cheeks are fair, the tresses free —
And yet I shall not suffer death,
God over me!

Those even brows, that hair like gold,
Those languorous tones, that virgin way,
The flowing limbs, the rounded heel
Slight men betray!

Thy spirit keen through radiant mien,
Thy shining throat and smiling eye,
Thy little palm, thy side like foam —
I cannot die!

O woman, shapely as the swan,
In a cunning house hard-reared was I:
O bosom white, O well-shaped palm,
I shall not die!

A BHEAN FUAIR AN FALACHÁN
(The Dispraise of Absalom)

[Text: T.F. Ó Rathile, *Dánta Grádha*, p. 17. Translation: Robin Flower, *Poems and Translations* (Dublin: Lilliput Press, 1994), p. 133.]

A bhean fuair an falachán,
　do-chiú ar fud do chiabh snáithmhín
ní as a bhfuighthear achmhasán
　d'fholt Absolóin mhic Dháivídh.

Atá ar do chéibh chleachtsholais
　ealta chuach i gceas naoidhean;
ní labhraid an ealta-soin
　's do bhuaidhir sí gach aoinfhear.

Do bharr fáinneach fionnfhada
　roichidh fád rosgaibh áille,
na ruisg corra criostalta
　go mbíd 'na gclochaibh fáinne.

Maise nua do thógbhais-se,
　gibé tír as a dtáinig, —
do lámh gan idh órdaighthe
　is céad fáinne fád bhráighid.

Do chas an cúl tláthbhuidhe
　timcheall an mhuinéil dírigh:
iomdha idh fón mbrághaid-sin, —
　is brágha í dá-ríribh!

TRANSLATION

Veiled in that light amazing,
Lady, your hair soft-wavèd
Has cast into dispraising
Absalom son of David.

Your golden locks close-clinging,
Like bird-flocks of strange seeming,
Silent with no sweet singing
Draw all men into dreaming.

That bright hair idly flowing
Over the keen eyes' brightness.
Like gold rings set with glowing
Jewels of crystal lightness.

Strange loveliness that lingers
From lands that hear the Siren;
No ring enclasps your fingers,
Gold rings your neck environ.

Gold chains of hair that cluster
Round the neck straight and slender,
Which to that shining muster
Yields in a sweet surrender.

MAIRG ATÁ SAN
MBEATHAIDH-SE!
(Accursed this Life)

[Presented as an independent text in T.F. Ó Rathile, *Dánta Grádha*, pp. 75–7, this poem in fact derives from *Eachtra Uilliam*, an Irish translation of *William of Palerne*. The English prose-version on which the Irish was based was of a type printed in the first half of the sixteenth century. The Irish translator followed it closely but intercalated twenty syllabic poems in which the preceding speech or dialogue is epitomized. In this one, Melior, daughter of the Emperor of Rome, speaks of her new-found love for William. This new translation: Eiléan Ní Chuilleanáin.]

Mairg atá san mbeathaidh-se!
    furtacht uaithi ní fhuigeabh;
leath nó trian mo pheannaide
    ní fhéadann teanga a thuireamh.

Óm ghrádh don nua naoidheanta
    mo dháil cá dáil is deacra?
acht gidh olc an fhaoilbheatha,
    is measa go mór mo bheatha.

Gidh beag é dom ghalar-sa,
    coimhthe re grís mo chneas-sa;
tig arís im fharradh-sa
    fuacht i ndeaghaidh an teasa.

Cuairt i measg an bhanchuire
    beag fhurtaigheas dom bhuaidhreadh;
cuid eile dom amhghaire,
    ní fearr théid damh an t-uaigneas.

An chúis fa dtám roidheacrach,
    gion go n-admhaim mun am-sa,
an croidhe duairc doibheartach
    isé ro theagaisg dhamhsa.

Ón teidhm-se do tiocfaidhe
    dá mbeith an rosg gan radharc;
ní hé an croidhe is ciontaighe,
    acht an tsúil do-ní an t-amharc.

Ag diomdha go hinfheadhma
    ní bhiú ar an rosg fám róghrádh;
bheith umhal dá thighearna
    iseadh dhligheas gach óglách.

An croidhe go huilidhe
    isé chongmhas gach aonlá
grádh tachartha is tuilidhe
    do bheith againn gan chlaochládh.

An ghnúis álainn ainglidhe
    do mhéadaigh adhbhar m'osnaidh,
iongnadh go madh ainbhfine;
    ní deilbh dhaonna is cosmhail.

An folt dualach druimfhiar-sa,
    ós dó tugas mo chéidshearc,
dá bhfaghmais an tUilliam-sa,
    ní chuirfeadh oirn ar n-éigean.

A ghrádh sgríobhtha im chridhe-se
    m'aigneadh gach laoi do lomairg;
mar tá mé dá innisin,
    is mairg é agus is romhairg.

TRANSLATION

Accursed this life,
Pain that's never eased;
The half or third part
No tongue could relate.

I love a stranger,
That is my hard case:
The battered seagull's
Life's better than mine.

In my distemper
Flaming my skin burns,
Then come cold shivers
After the burning.

Women's company
Does me no good, but
Solitary life
Suits me no better.

Though I may never
Declare what caused it,
The heart grown savage
Caused me to suffer.

If the eye were blind
I'd escape this pain;
The heart's not guilty
But sight that showed me.

Yet I can't blame eyes
For showing me love,
A servant's duty
Is to the master.

Those angel's features
Make my sighs deeper;

Stranger he may be,
No face is like his.

The heart holds fast its
Unchanging passion,
An unknown foundling,
A nameless orphan.

To the boy's curled head
I gave my first love;
If I had William
He need not force me.

Love has tortured me
Writing in my heart.
Life, I declare it,
Is cursed, again cursed.

MAGHNUS Ó DOMHNAILL

(*c.* 1490–1563)

GOIRT ANOCHT DEREADH MO SGÉAL!
(A Famished End to My Tale This Night)

[It has been suggested that this, and the next poem, may be love elegies for Ó Domhnaill's first wife, Siobhán, sister of Conn Bacach Ó Néill; she died in 1535. One hesitates to accept this suggestion, as Ó Domhnaill contracted three further marriage alliances, and a second wife predeceased him in 1544. Text: T.F. Ó Rathile, *Dánta Grádha*, p. 74. Translation: Thomas Kinsella, *The New Oxford Book of Irish Verse*, p. 139.]

Goirt anocht dereadh mo sgéal, —
    annamh tréan nách dteagthar ris;
is dearbh dá maireadh Dian Céacht
    nách leigheósadh créacht mo chnis.

Ar mo thuirse ní théid trágh,
    mar mhuir lán ós ceannaibh port;
a bhfuair mé do dhochar pian
    níor chás rium riamh gus a-nocht.

Tarla a dheimhin damh, fa-ríor!
    gurb annamh fíon bhíos gan moirt;
is géar an fhobhairt é an brón, —
    dar liom féin is mó ná goirt.

TRANSLATION

A famished end to my tale this night.
    It is seldom a strong man will not cure,
but if Dian Cecht[1] were alive today
    this wound in my side he could not heal.

No ebb at all in my weariness,
    like an ocean full at the harbour mouth.
Such hard pains as I suffer now
    before this night I never knew.

Alas that I have found this truth:
    rare is the wine without its dregs,
and nothing tempers hard as grief,
    worse, I think, than any famine.

1. A mythical physician associated with the Túatha Dé Danann.

CRIDHE LÁN DE SMUAINTIGHTHIBH
(A Heart Made Full of Thought)

[See preceding headnote. Text: T.F. Ó Rathile, *Dánta Grádha*, p. 73. Translation: Thomas Kinsella, *The New Oxford Book of Irish Verse*, p. 139.]

Cridhe lán do smuaintighthibh
  tarla dhúinne ré n-imtheacht;
caidhe neach dá uaibhrighe
  ris nách sgar bean a intleacht?

Brón mar fhás na fíneamhna
  tarla oram re haimsir;
ní guth dhamhsa mímheanma
  tré a bhfaicthear dúinn do thaidhbhsibh.

Sgaradh eóin re fíoruisge,
  nó is múchadh gréine gile,

mo sgaradh re sníomhthuirse
  tar éis mo chompáin chridhe.

TRANSLATION

A heart made full of thought
  I had, before you left.
What man, however prideful,
  but lost his perfect love?

Grief like a growing vine
  came with time upon me.
Yet it is not through despair
  I see your image still.

A bird lifting from clear water,
  a bright sun put out
— such my parting, in troubled tiredness,
  from the partner of my heart.

DOMHNALL MAC CARTHAIGH
(1518–97)

OCH! OCH! A MHUIRE BHÚIDH
(The Body's Speech)

[Domhnall Mac Carthaigh, of the line of the Mac Carthaigh Mór kings of Desmond, was created Earl of Clancare in 1565. Text: T.F. Ó Rathile, *Dánta Grádha*, pp. 38–9. Translation: Frank O'Connor, *Kings, Lords and Commons*, p. 69. O'Connor's quatrain 6 conveys the substance of the original's quatrains 6 and 7.]

Och! och! A Mhuire bhúidh,
  a Bhuime Dé,
tugas grádh m'anma do mhnaoi
  ler marbhadh mé.

Atá an toil, a Mhuire mhór,
  'na tuile thréin;
do mharbh sin do láthair mé,
  a Mháthair Dé.

Tugas grádh m'anma do mhnaoi,
  ach! a Dhé,
's ní ráinig liom a innsin dí
  gur milleadh mé.

Grádh dá geilchígh is gile gné,
  mar lile ar lí,
's dá folt dualach druimneach dlúth
  is ualach dí.

Grádh dá gealghnúis chriostail mar rós,
  nár chiontaigh re haon,
's dá dhá gealghlaic leabhra lúith
  ler mealladh mé.

Rug a haolchorp sleamhain slán
  mo mheabhair uaim;
milseacht a gotha 's a glóir,
  mé im othar uaidh.

Atáim 'na diaidh, ochán , och!
  im bhochtán bhocht;
truagh gan an sluagh-sa ar mo leacht
  ag cruachadh cloch.

Truagh gan bráithre ag mianán orm
  re siansán salm,
ó tharla mé, a Mhuire mheirbh,
  im dhuine mharbh.

Amhrán a béil, bile mar rós,
  milis mar thúis,
do chuir mé ar buile báis, —
  cá cruinne cúis?

Fóir mé, ós féidir leat,
  a ghéag gan locht;
fóir mé le comhrádh do chuirp,
  ochán, och!

TRANSLATION

My grief, my grief, maid without sin,
  Mother of God's Son,
Because of one I cannot win
  My peace is gone.

Mortal love, a raging flood,
  O Mother Maid,
Runs like a fever through my blood,
  Ruins heart and head.

How can I tell her of my fear,
  My wild desire,
When words I speak for my own ear
  Turn me to fire?

I dream of breasts so lilylike,
  Without a fleck,
And hair that, bundled up from her back,
  Burdens her neck.

And praise the cheeks where flames arise
  That shame the rose,
And the soft hands at whose touch flees
  All my repose.

Since I have seen her I am lost,
  A man possessed,
Better to feel the world gone past,
  Earth on my breast;

And from my tomb to hear the choir,
  the hum of prayer;
Without her while her place is here,
  My peace is there.

I am a ghost upon your path,
  A wasting death,
But you must know one word of truth
  Gives a ghost breath —

In language beyond learning's touch
  Passion can teach —
Speak in that speech beyond reproach
  The body's speech.

ANONYMOUS

MOLADH MNÁ RÉ N-A FEAR TAR ÉIS A THRÉIGBHEÁLA
(He Praises His Wife when She has Gone from Him)

[Text: Robin Flower, in T.F. Ó Rathile, *Dánta Grádha*, pp. xxiv–v. Translation: Robin Flower, *Poems and Translations*, p. 154.]

Dá ghealghlaic laga leabhra,
troighthe seada sítheamhla,
  dá ghlún nach gile sneachta, —
  rún mo chridhe an chuideachta.

Trillse drithleacha ar lonnradh,
taobh seang mar sról . . .[1]
  braoithe mar ruainne rónda,
  gruaidhe naoidhe neamhónda.

1. The MS is faulty here.

Ní thig díom a chur i gcéill
díol molta dá dreach shoiléir,
   stuagh leanbhdha mhaordha mhálla
   mheardha aobhdha éadána.

D'éis gach radhairc dá bhfuair sinn
do mhearaigh go mór m'intinn
   ná raibhe suan i ndán damh;
   is truagh mo dhál im dhúsgadh.

Dob usa gan éirghe dhamh
d'fhéachaint an tighe im thiomchal;
   ní bhfuair sinn a sompla ó shoin,
   inn fá dhorcha 'na deaghaidh.

TRANSLATION

White hands of languorous grace,
Fair feet of stately pace
And snowy-shining knees —
My love was made of these.

Stars glimmered in her hair,
Slim was she, satin-fair;
Dark like seal's fur her brows
Shadowed her cheeks' fresh rose.

What words can match its worth,
That beauty closed in earth,
That courteous, stately air
Winsome and shy and fair!

To have known all this and be
Tortured with memory
— Curse on this waking breath —
Makes me in love with death.

Better to sleep than see
This house now dark to me
A lonely shell in place
Of that unrivalled grace.

A CHOMPÁIN, SEACHOIN SINNE!
(Avoid Me, My Dear)

[Text (here with minor changes) and translation are from: Pádraig Ó Fiannachta, 'Two Love-poems', *Ériu*, vol. 21 (1969), pp. 115–21, at pp. 118–21.]

A chompáin, seachoin sinne!
ná lean dh'áilgheas th'inntinne
ciodh rolonn, mo léan, do lot,
ná féach oram is ní fhéachfot.

Gabh thoram, ná taobhaigh mé,
's ní tháoibheóchad thú choidhche;
gidh bé mían fá deara dhúnn
cíall ar gceana do chlaochlúdh.

Atáid cách dár ccur a suim —
ná sill ós íseal oruinn;
síad ag dul dár ndáorbhrath dhe,
báoghloch ar ccor ré chéile.

'S gan acht féachoin soir nó síar
ní léigid lucht na sáoibhchíall,
gan ar n-annsa ar ccúl do chur
gér bhfallsa dhúnn a dhéanamh.

Ná leanuidh, a Dháibhíoth, dhe;
beannocht leat, do loc doighre;
iononn tairthe a chnead 's a chruth;
gér bheag, ní mhairfe amáruch.

Ó nach sámh linn rádh na leabhar sáer
gan láinteacht tar mhnáibh na malach ccáel,
ó táid cách fár ngrádh dár mbrath ar áen
A Dháibhe, ciodh crádh liom, seachoin mé.

TRANSLATION

Avoid me, my dear; follow not your mind's desire. Bitter, alas, though your wound is, we must gaze upon each other no more.

Pass me by, come not close to me, and neither shall I ever come close to you — whatever our motive for altering the meaning of our love.

Everybody is taking notice of us; steal no secret look at me. It is dangerous that we should be connected; folk are judging us harshly because of it.

The perverse-minded ones allow us to look only to the east or the west, unless we set aside our love — though we would be false to ourselves in doing so.

Give it up, David! Farewell, passion (?) has failed; its sighs and pretensions all come to the same thing. Enough! It will be dead tomorrow.

Since we enjoy not what the noble books say because they deal not completely with the slender-browed women, oh David, avoid me — though it grieves me — seeing that everybody is betraying us concerning our love.

A CHOMPÁIN, CUIMHNIGH MEISE
(Dear Friend, Remember Me)

[Edited and translated from the seventeenth-century manuscript, Dublin, Royal Irish Academy Library, MS No. 23 D 4, p. 213.]

A chompáin, cuimhnigh meise,
cuir mo chumann id' chroidhe-se,
   a roghrádh do thúr mh'annsa,
   's gur tú is iomrádh agam-sa.

Ná tréig is ní thréigeabh sibh
ar mo shamhail féin do dhaoinibh;
   tabhair do dhíleas fán am-sa,
   's ná tabhair mímheas orm-sa.

I gcéin uaibh nó i ngar daoibh
cuimhnigh oram, a mhacaoimh,
   's go bhfuil deirgchneidh ón ghreith ghráidh
   dom sheirgne anois, a chompáin.

TRANSLATION

Dear friend, remember me,
keep me in your heart,
love who drew forth love
you are all I mind.

Forsake me not and I'll not you
for another of my kind,
pledge yourself soon
and do not have me scorned.

Whether near you or afar,
young man, keep me in mind,
for a red wound of fervid love
is wasting me, dear friend.

?RIOCARD DE BÚRC

FIR NA FÓDLA AR NDUL D'ÉAG
(Women)

[More copies are extant of this *dán grádha* than of any other. Variously attributed to Riocard de Búrc, Ó Dálaigh, and Muiris mac Dháibhí Dhuibh Mhic Gearailt (?*c.* 1565–*c.* 1635), de Búrc's name is given precedence here only because it appears in the earliest manuscript. The name Riocard was popular among the Búrc (Burke) nobles of Upper and Lower Connacht. Text: T.F. Ó Rathile, *Dánta Grádha*, pp. 5–7. Translation: Frank O'Connor, *The Little Monasteries* (Dublin: Dolmen Press, 1976), pp. 25–7.]

Fir na Fódla ar ndul d'éag
   do ghean ar ghné na rosg nglas,
muna raibh eire óir ar a folt,
   dar leo féin is olc an dath.

Ní hionann iad is mé féin;
   dar liomsa ní clé an chiall,
ní fearr liom dath dá mbia ar a súil
   ná an dath bhíos ar chlúmh na bhfiach.

Ní iarraim iomad don rós
   'na haghaidh, ná ór 'na gruaig;
ait liom lí cailce ar a corp,
   is a folt ar dhath an ghuail.

Dubh do bhí máthar na mná
   tréar cuiradh ar lár an Trae,
's do bhí a hinghean mhaiseach mhór
   go ndeallradh óir ar a céibh.

Cé do bhí an dias bhéildearg bhinn
   bean díobh fionn agus bean dubh,
níor bhfeas d'aon dá bhfacaidh iad
   cé don dias do b'áille cruth.

Péarla croinn ar n-a cheangal d'ór,
   do mhnaoi bhig is mór mo ghean;
beag do hórdaigheadh ar dtúis
   an t-each, an chú, 's an bhean.

Do-ghéan m'fhaoisidin ós árd,
   inneósad do chách mo chaoi,
cuid is mó dá ndearna d'olc
   nách faicthear dam locht ar mhnaoi!

Ní locht liom uirthi a beith beag,
   ní misde leam a beith mór;
sáith ríogh ar leabaidh 's ar láimh
   gach inghean árd álainn óg.

Muna raibh a cneas mar chuip.
   nó mar shneachta cnuic gan clódh,
ní locht liom uirthi a beith ciar,
   geanamhail iad ó bheith crón.

Cuma liom a beith 'na siair
   nó a beith ó iaith Inse Craobh,
acht amháin gur dúbalta an grádh
   ag na mnáibh ó bheith 'na ngaol.

Ní do na mnáibh glioca a-mháin
   do-bheirim fós grádh nó gnaoi;
aithne an bhiolair tar an bhféar
   níor bheag liom do chéill ag mnaoi.

Ionmhain liom (maith do-ním)
   'na baintreabhaigh í is 'na hóigh;
gidh maith anmhain ris an aois,
   is maiseach í ó bheith óg.

Maith bean i n-eaglais na naomh,
   tromdha ar tulaigh, caomh 'na teach;
romhaith liom í lán do lúth
   nuair is éigean dúinn bheith leamh.

Ní bhfaghaim locht — bríogh mo sgéil —
   ar mhnaoi fán ngréin acht bheith sean;
is óg ar dhá fhichid iad, —
   's léigthear a mhian do gach fear.

TRANSLATION

Every man in Ireland caught
   By some girl with eyes of blue
Dolefully laments his lot
   Unless her hair be golden too.

What has this to do with me?
   No fanaticism I share
For blue or black in someone's eye
   Or the colour of her hair.

Golden mane or rosy grace
   Can never be my whole delight.
Dusky be the woman's face
   And her hair as black as night.

Black was the dam of her who brought
   Troy into the dust of old,
And the girl for whom they fought,
   Helen, was all white and gold.

Beautiful surely were the two
   Though one was dark and one was fair.
No one who ever saw them knew
   Which was the lovelier of the pair.

In little shells it may befall
   The loveliest of pearls is found,
And God created three things small —
   The horse, the woman and the hound.

Public confession suits my case,
   And all may hear what I would say —
In women, such is my disgrace,
   I never found a thing astray.

Though some are small I like them neat
   And some are tall of them I sing;
Two long legs to grace the sheet
   Are satisfaction for a king.

Foam may be brighter than her skin
   Or snow upon the mountain cold,
I'll take what pack I find her in
   And think her sweeter for being old.

Nor should I slight a relative
   For someone from outside the state;
Though novelty keep love alive
   Kinsmen love at double rate.

Nor do I ask for intellect:
    A little scholarship will pass;
All that of women I expect
    Is to know water-cress from grass.

I don't require them cold or warm;
    Widows have knowledge and good sense
But there is still a certain charm
    In a young girl's inexperience.

I like them in church, demure and slow,
    Solemn without, relaxed at home;
I like them full of push and go
    When love has left me overcome.

I find no fault in them, by God,
    But being old and gone to waste
Who still are girls at forty odd —
    And every man may suit his taste.

ANONYMOUS

SGÉAL AR DHIAMHAIR NA SUIRGHE
(A History of Love)

[Text: T.F. Ó Rathile, *Dánta Grádha*, pp. 8–9. Translation:
Frank O'Connor, *The Little Monasteries*, pp. 28–9.]

Sgéal ar dhiamhair na suirghe
    inneósad duibhse go frosach,
ós damh is cóir a sheóladh
    mar do rónadh í ar dtosach.

Mac ríogh ó Chorca Dhuibhne,
    Diarmaid na bruinne báine,
an céidfhear ar ar fionnadh
    ionga thabhairt do Ghráinne.

Macaomh eile tug annsacht
    do mhnaoi do bhantracht na Gréige,
Cú-chulainn na gcleas n-iongnadh,
    is leis do rinneadh an sméideadh.

Lá dhá raibh i ndiaidh seilge
    go bhfuair Deirdre ag dul 'na brógaibh,
Naoise, an fear fial fosaidh,
    isé do thosaigh na póga.

Uaithne mac Conaill Chearnaigh,
    seabhac na sealga sirthe,
ar an suirghe chuir cumaoin,
    claonadh an mhuiníl do righne.

Ábhartach ón tsídh bhallaigh
    nách gabhadh cumha ó ghallsmacht,
le hubhlaibh na gcrann gcaithne
    is leis do caitheadh an bhantracht.

Céadach mac Rí na dTolach,
    fear nár throdach i dtigh óla,
is leis do croitheadh an t-uisge
    ar mhnáibh cnisgheala Fódla.

Aonghas ó Bhrugh na Bóinne,
    mac an Óig an bhruit chorcra,
ar inghin ghruagaigh na sithleadh
    is leis do righneadh an folcadh.

Glas mac Aoinchearda Béarra,
    'gá bhfaghthaoi sgéala suarca,
is leis do léigeadh an osnadh
    ar bhruach locha na Luachra.

Silleadh súl, gearradh feadáin,
    suirghe Mhongáin mhic Fhiachra;
guth caoin do chur le téadaibh
    maith do bhréagfadh bean fhiata.

Mise féin — móide an donas —
    d'osgail doras an éada
's nár dhruid é go tapaidh;
    ag sin agaibh mo sgéala!

TRANSLATION

This is Love's history
  And how it all began:
As an authórity
  I am your foremost man.

Diarmuid the bold and gay,
  Chief of the warrior bands,
With Grania one day
  Invented holding hands.

While Ulster's Hound as well,
  When a Greek girl went by,
Falling beneath her spell,
  Was first with the glad eye.

Naisi, home from the chase,
  Weary, inspired with bliss,
Seeing Deirdre don her trews,
  Endowed us with the kiss.

The son of Conall met
  Their challenges with grace
And left us in his debt
  By figuring the long embrace.

Avartach, king of the fairies,
  Following in their track,
With his arbutus berries
  Put a girl upon her back.

Ceadach, master of trades,
  Seeing them still unversed —
Those white-skinned Irish maids —
  Made women of them first.

And Angus as they say —
  Lord of the Sacred Hill —
First took their clothes away,
  And gave them perfect skill.

Learning that hearts can break
  Under Love's miseries
Beside a Munster lake
  Glas filled the air with sighs.

Lamenting to soft strings
  And moans upon the pipe
Were Mongan's offerings
  To woo some timid wife.

But I, for my own grief,
  First opened Jealousy's door —
This is my tale in brief —
  And now it shuts no more.

ABAIR LEIS NÁ DÉANADH ÉAD
(A Learned Mistress)

[Text: T.F. Ó Rathile, *Dánta Grádha*, pp. 103–4.
Translation: Frank O'Connor, *Kings, Lords and Commons*, p. 57.]

Abair leis ná déanadh éad,
  's gur bréag an sgéal do cuireadh faoi;
is aige féin atá mo ghrádh,
  is m'fhuath do ghnáth agá mhnaoi.

Má marbhann sé mé tré éad,
  rachaidh a bhean d'éag dom dhíth;
éagfaidh féin do chumha na mná
  is tiucfaidh mar sin bás an trír.

Gach maith ó neamh go lár
  chum na mná agá bhfuil m'fhuath,
's an fear agá bhfuil mo ghrádh
  go bhfagha sé bás go luath!

TRANSLATION

Tell him it's all a lie;
  I love him as much as my life;
He needn't be jealous of me —
  I love him and loathe his wife.

If he kill me through jealousy now
  His wife will perish of spite,
He'll die of grief for his wife —
  Three of us dead in a night.

All blessings from heaven and earth
  On the head of the woman I hate,
And the man I love as my life,
  Sudden death be his fate.

A FHIR DO-NÍ AN TÉAD
(A Jealous Man)

[Text: T.F. Ó Rathile, *Dánta Grádha*, pp. 126–7. Translation: Frank O'Connor, *Kings, Lords and Commons*, p. 64.]

A fhir do-ní an t-éad
  binn an sgéal do chor;
ní tuilltear é uait,
  is iongnadh gruaim ort.

Bean dhoidhealbhtha dhuairc
  minic nach bhfuair gean;
gidh iongnadh leat é,
  is leat féin do bhean!

A ghiolla na rún.
  is ait dúinn do chor,
ag coimhéad do mhná, —
  sin an fál gan ghort!

Aon do chéad do chách
  atá slán mar taoi;
ní fáth eagla dhuit
  teanga i bpluic fád mhnaoi.

Ná creid neach dá mair
  ort dá brath go héag;
ná fágaibh-se an tír
  a fhir do-ní an t-éad!

TRANSLATION

Listen jealous man
  What they say of you
That you watch your wife
  Surely isn't true?

Such an ugly face
  The light loves disown;
Much to your surprise
  Your wife is all your own.

Other men must watch
  Who have wives to shield.
Why should you put up
  A fence without a field?

In a hundred none
  Is as safe as you
Nobody could think
  Such a thing was true.

Men cry when they're hurt
  Your cry's out of place,
Who do you think would want
  Such an ugly face?

CUMANN FALLSA GRÁDH NA BHFEAR!
(Men's Loving is a False Affection)

[Text: T.F. Ó Rathile, *Dánta Grádha*, pp. 106–7. Translation: Thomas Kinsella, *The New Oxford Book of Irish Verse*, pp. 137–8.]

Cumann fallsa grádh na bhfear!
  is mairg bean do-ní a réir;
gidh milis a gcomhrádh ceart,
  is fada is-teach bhíos a méin.

Ná creid a gcogar 's a rún,
ná creid glacadh dlúth a lámh,
ná creid a bpóg ar a mbia blas, —
  ó n-a searc ní bhfuilim slán.

Ná creid, is ní chreidfe mé,
  fear ar domhan tar éis cháich;
do chuala mé sgéal ó 'né,
  och, a Dhé! is géar rom-chráidh.

Do bhéardaois airgead is ór,
  do bhéardaois fós agus maoin,
do bhéardaois pósadh is ceart
  do mhnaoi, nó go teacht an laoi.

Ní mise amháin do mheall siad,
  is iomdha bean riamh do chealg
grádh an fhir nách bia go buan, —
  och, is mairg do chuaidh rem cheird.

TRANSLATION

Men's loving is a false affection.
  Woe to the woman does their will.
Though sweet their converse and correct
  their thoughts are hidden deep within.

Never trust their whispered secret,
  never trust their handclasp firm,
never trust their tasty kiss
  — such love as theirs has cost my health.

Never give, no more than I,
  your trust to any man on earth,
for yesterday I heard a tale
  that caused me anguish, O my God!

Gold and silver they will offer;
  wealth they will offer you as well;
law and marriage they will offer
  womanfolk, till break of day.

Not me alone have they deceived:
  many's the woman they have wronged.
The love of man will never last
  God help who follow in my footsteps.

Dar an Airdrígh marthanach
  bheireas na breatha cruaidhe,
roimpe riamh ní fhacamar
  ag mnaoi aigneadh ba luaithe.

TRANSLATION

Swifter than greyhound that none e'er outran
Is the will of my mistress to bed with a man.
Swifter than starling her heart is afire
  With inconstant desire.

Swifter than gales in the cold time of spring,
Around the hard crags ceaselessly ravaging,
Is the lust of a heart that is empty and dry,
  And a hungry green eye.

By the Lord of Hard Judgment that lives
  evermore!
By the High King of Heaven, there never before
Was her like among women, for who was afire
  With so swift a desire?

A SHLÁINE INGHEAN FHLANNAGÁIN
(Piece Work)

[The ordinariness of the name Sláine Inghean Fhlannagáin suggests that this is an address to a real woman. Irish *baincheann an uird chrábhaidh* (literally, 'female head of the holy order'), like English 'abbess', is slang for 'madam, brothel-mistress'. As the god Manannán is associated with the Otherworld of eternal youth and uncircumscribed sex, the description of the addressee's abode as Dún Manannáin, 'Manannán's Fort', conjures a place of similar promise. The poem is transcribed and translated from the seventeenth-century manuscript, Dublin, Royal Irish Academy Library, MS No. 5, pp. 92–3.]

A Shláine Inghean Fhlannagáin,
  déanam súsa go sármhaith
nach bia 'na ghreas amaláin
  dá mhalairt a measg mhargaidh.

Fearsad bhuidhe agamsa,
  ní maith súsa gan síoga,
iolar na ndath agadsa,
  dubh agus dearg id' íorna.

LUAITHE CÚ NÁ A CUIDEACHTA
(Swift Love)

[Text: T.F. Ó Rathile, *Dánta Grádha*, p. 103. Translation: the Earl of Longford, *Poems from the Irish* (Dublin: Hodges, Figgis; Oxford: B.H. Blackwell, 1945), p. 25.]

Luaithe cú ná a cuideachta, —
  tosach luighe dom leannán;
luaithe ná gach truidealta
  aigneadh géige an dá gheallámh.

Luaithe ná gaoth earrchamhail
  ag buain fá bheannaibh cruaidhe,
aigneadh baoth nách banamhail
  ag inghin an ruisg uaine.

Curthar m'fhearsad bhuidhesi
'na seasamh ansa tsúsa
's dá ngannuidhe aicesi
    léigthear mo cheirtlighe chúithe.

Mo dhá cheirtle odharghlas,
    's a síneadh ris na síogaibh,
bú suaitheantas an t-abharas,
    's a ccur re ciomhais ciordhuibh.

Déana an deilbh mar dubhramar,
    is biaidh misi, dhá bhféadar,
ag síorchur sa tsúsasa
    is dá úcadh a n-éinfheacht.

A Shláine inghean Fhlannagáin,
    a bhaincheann an úird chrábhaidh,
a bhean ó Dhún Manannáin,
    déanam súsa go sármhaith.

TRANSLATION

O Sláine Inghean Fhlannagáin
let's make a piece right well —
not the work of an innocent, mind!
to barter or to sell.

I've a tawny spindle.
A piece without twists isn't good:
you've the many colours,
in your skein there's black and red.

Stand the tawny spindle
in the piece side on
and should it want for wool
move the balls along.

With my two dun balls
bonding with the twists
the strick will be amazing,
next a trim of black.

Make the frame like I said
and while I'm in vigour
I'll full the piece and fuller it
over and over.

O Sláine Inghean Fhlannagáin,
O holy church abbess,
O dame from Dún Manannáin,
let's make a right good piece.

TADHG DALL Ó hUIGINN

(c. 1550–91)

AN tIM
(A Present of Butter)

[Most of Tadhg Dall's poems are praise-poems addressed to men. One formal address to a female patron has survived, as well as two poems describing a beautiful woman seen in an *aisling* which very possibly were personal love-poems. The present poem describes relations with a woman rather more impolitely. Lord Longford's translation is perhaps shy of the sexual connotations of the last line, 'an t-im 'na fheóil fuaras féin', literally, 'the butter I got that was flesh'.]

Text: Eleanor Knott, *The Bardic Poems of Tadhg Dall Ó hUiginn*, 2 vols (London: Irish Texts Society, 1922, 1926), vol. 1, pp. 260–1. Translation: the Earl of Longford, *The Dove in the Castle* (Dublin: Hodges and Figgis, 1946), pp. 152–3.]

1
Fuaras féin im maith ó mhnaoi:
    an t-im maith — mása maith é —
dóigh linn nách fa bhoin do bhí,
    an ní dá bhfoil do mhill mé.

2

Do bhí féasóg ar bhfás air —
  ná rab slán d'fhéasóig an fhir;
súgh as nách neimhnighe neimh
  geir go mblas seirbhdhighe sin.

3

Da ba bhreac, fa hodhar é;
  ní fa ghobhar bhleacht do bhaoi;
fada ó im i n-aisgidh é,
  'sa ghné d'fhaicsin linn gach laoi.

4

A ghíomh leabhar mar fholt eich,
  uch ní fríoth sgeana ro-sgoith;
fada is tinn an tí ro-s-caith,
  an t-im maith ro bhí 'nar mboith.

5

Brat eisréide fan ngréis ngoirt
  mar eisléine d'éis a chuirp;
dob airdhe déisdin le deirc
  an cheirt d'fhéiscin d'aidhbhle a huilc.

6

Do bhí ar an fearsoin túth trom
  do mhúch is do mhearuigh ionn;
tarfás dúinn gach aondath ann,
  barr craobhach clúimh ós a chionn.

7

Ní fhaca sé an salann riamh,
  ní fhaca an salann é acht uadh;
ní léigfe a chuimhne sinn slán,
  im bán is guirme iná an gual.

8

Do bhí an ghréis ann, 'sní hí amháin,
  do bhí gach re mball don chéir;
beag d'im do-uadhus 'na dheóigh —
  an t-im 'na fheóil fuaras féin.

TRANSLATION

A woman gave me butter now,
  Good butter too it claimed to be.
I don't think it was from a cow,
  And if it was it finished me.

A beard was growing on the stuff,
  A beastly beard without a doubt,
The taste was sickly, sour and rough,
  With poison juices seeping out.

The stuff had spots, the stuff was grey,
  I doubt if any goat produced it.
I had to face it every day,
  And how I wish I had refused it!

This splendid butter had a mane,
  The glory of my humble home.
No knife could cut it down again,
  It made me sick for weeks to come.

This nasty grease a wrapping had
  Like a discarded winding sheet.
Its very aspect was so bad,
  I scarcely had the nerve to eat.

This horror had a heavy stink
  That left one fuddled, stunned and dead.
'Twas rainbow-hued, with what you'd think
  A crest of plumes above its head.

The salt's a thing it hardly knew,
  In fact I think they'd barely met.
It was not white, but rather blue.
  I am not quite recovered yet.

'Twas made of grease and wax and fat,
  O thoughts too horrible to utter!
You may be sure that after that,
  I rather lost my taste for butter.

ANONYMOUS

from:
FUARAS NÓCHAR UAIBHREACH ÓIGMHEAR
(For Éamonn, Viscount Mountgarret, and Gráinne, His Wife) (*c.* 1600)

[This rare example of a bardic praise-poem written in *amhrán* metre is also remarkable for its vivid description of cultural life at the Butler castle at Mountgarret (alias Ballyragget, near New Ross, County Wexford). Most of its twenty-one stanzas concern Éamonn (d. 1602), 2nd Viscount Mountgarret. The two stanzas preceding the closing stanza or *ceangal* are for his wife, Gráinne, daughter of Brian Óg Mac Giolla Pádraig, Lord of Upper Ossory (Osraí). For a complimentary tribute to this couple by a medical scribe, see p. 245 The poet Cearbhall Ó Dálaigh was later to pay court to their grand-daughter: see below at pp. 414–5. The present poem's account of the ranks of entertainers is unconventionally inclusive, and its frank praise for Gráinne in her role as procuress is particularly noteworthy.
    Text: James Carney, *Poems on the Butlers of Ormond, Cahir, and Dunboyne* (Dublin: Dublin Institute for Advanced Studies, 1945), pp. 94–100, at pp. 94, 98–100. This new translation: Aogán Ó Muircheartaigh.]

1
Fuaras nóchar uaibhreach óigmhear
    d'uaislibh Fódla fóirne áille;
leannán cabhra cliar is cearrbhach
    iatha Banbha bórdbhláithe;
céile caithmheach éasgaidh aisdreach
    réidhghlan reachtmhar róghrádhmhor;
codhnach caoineach foghlach fíochmhur
    bronntach buidhneach bótháinteach.

2
Cuid dom shonus mar do thoghas
    tar Leath Mogha mórdhálaigh
deaghmhac Risdeird, fear gan tuirse
    re cléir thuigsigh thóghbhálaigh;
Bíocunt meanmnach fíochdha feardha
    gríobhdha gearamnach gleóláidir.
Níor airg tearmann, nír airg anbhfann,
    nír airg eagluis, órchrábhaidh . . .

15
Iomdha óinmhid bhíos 'na ósda,
    iomdha geócach glór-ráidhteach;
iomdha réidhbhean mhaiseach mhaordha
    ghasda dhéidgheal ghlórmhálla;
iomdha óigbhean nach tug eólas
    d'fhior gan phósadh ar phógámhailtigh,
agus biatach bailteach biadhmhar
    nár thuill riamh a rócháineadh.

16
Iomdha cearrbhach fuachtmhur feannaidioch
    uallach aistrioch ós táiplis,
agus dailtín bruighneach beaduighe
    cíocrach creatchríon crónmhásach;
iomdha gaghar déanta duilleach
    saothrach sirtheach srónálach,
agus fearchú thaidhbhseach thacúil
    dhaighnirt deaghchlúmhach dhó-áruigh.

17
Mar bhíd tonna uatha is chuca
    a ccuantaibh cruinne comhlána
tigid dámha ina ttáintibh
    go triath fáilteach Feóire áille;
is mar chuirid éisg a muirear
    ar an muir ttonnaigh dtórmánaigh
do-ní Éamonn ar an ngné sin
    d'éigsibh Éireann óglachus.

18
Gnúis gan éara ré dúil dhaonna
    as é súd Éamonn ógághmhar,
triath is séimhe, triath is féle,
    triath le [a] n-éistear órdhánta,
triath is úire, triath gan cuimhge,
    triath is cumhra comhráidhte,
triath is treise, triath gan teibe
    ara lia treise ag tórdhámhuibh.

19
Créad nach molfuidhe an bhé bhogchroidheach
    don réim Osruighigh óguasail?
daighbhean deighfhir bean a hinnmhe,
    bean as mionca mórdhuasa;
dona dámhuibh ghabhus táirse
    as námha Gráinne ghlórshuaimhneach;
ríoghan shuilbhir bhíos a' suirghe
    ris gach cruitire ceól-luaimhneach.

20
Bean gach file, bean gach duine.
  bean gach druinge don órd uallach,
bean an chleasuidhe do-ní paistím
  's a' bhaird bheadaighe bheólruathair;
re díol cléire, re díol méirdreach
  bhíos go taobhnocht tónluaimneach,
re díol éigse Innsi hÉibhir
  as í séidche as mó fuarus.

21
Iomdha stéad áluinn néamhárd is fearachoin
  laoich
is méar fáinneach créachtgheárrtha ó tharrang
  ngad righin,
éadáil mhná déadbháine ar leabaidh 'na luighe
do-ghéabhthá-sa a mBéal Átha Ragad a-rír.

TRANSLATION

1
Young, fleet and proud, you are my spouse,
A nobleman of Fodla's;
In Banba's lush and fertile fields,
You please the gamblers and the poets;
Undefiled and Solomon-wise,
Gallant companion, easy and free;
Winner of spoils, rich in kine,
A leader genial, most gregarious.

2
Great my joy that I have chosen
From the heroes in the southern half,
Richard's son who never wearies
Of sharp, astute and touchy bards;
A viscount vigorous, fierce and manly,
Griffin-like, and peeled for action;
No refuge shattered, no weakling battered,
No gilded chapel laid to waste . . .

15
Many buffoons frequent his court,
Many loud-mouthed jokers,
Many comely gentle ladies
With pearly teeth and seductive tones;
Many maidens who never shared
With unmarried men the kissing games,
And many food-giving men of means
Who never earned derision.

16
Many gamblers, frozen, cold,
Fickle at backgammon, full of bombast;
Many rowdy, little upstarts,
Decrepit grabbers with pitch-black arses;
Splendid dogs with lustrous hair,
Guard-dogs, pointers, Irish setters,
And countless hounds of noble strain —
In the canine world you'll find none better.

17
As the sea-waves wash to and fro
In deep and sheltered coves,
The rhymesters gather in their droves
Fêted by Éamonn, Lord of the Nore;
As fish lay their seed o'er the foam
That thunders and plays on the shores,
Just the same, my Éamonn the brave
Shapes verses for master-poets.

18
My lord, he has a heart of gold,
My youthful, valiant Éamonn,
My lord most gentle, my lord most bold,
My lord who savours golden lays;
My lord most tender, my upright sage,
My lord of words melodious,
My lord most virile who never fails,
Ever-bested by the grasping hordes.

19
There's naught but praise for the kindly dame
Of Osraí's young and noble strain,
A good man's good wife, lady of means,
Bestowing gifts like you'd broadcast seed;
Soft-voiced Gráinne is a daunting test
Of poets who would leave her court,
A gentle queen who is wont to flirt
With every nimble-fingered harper.

20
Woman to all, poet or no,
Woman to the droves of the boasting class;
Woman to jugglers who'll pass the time
And every raunchy, lip-blowing bard;
No dearer friend have I ever found
Than she who pays the bards and harlots
With naked thighs and swaying arses,
And rewards the poets of Éibhear's isle.

21
In their masses last night in Ballyragget —
Pure-blooded hounds and thoroughbred steeds —

Their ring-bedecked fingers with bowmen's
 scars,
Each warrior bold a fit mate for a queen.

EOCHAIDH Ó hEODHASA

(*c.* 1565–1612)

NÍ MÉ BHÚR nAITHNE,
A AOS GRÁIDH
(You Do Not Know Me)
(*c.* 1607)

[Much attention has been paid to this poem, and the following one, which constitute an exchange. One of the three extant copies of 'Ní mé bhúr n-aithne, a aos gráidh' (all seventeenth-century) attributes it to Eochaidh Ó hEodhasa, while a prefatory remark in another states that 'Cú Chonnacht Óg Mág Uidhir sent this in his own name to Brighid, daughter of the Earl of Kildare'. Scholars have concluded that the ascription to Ó hEodhasa is trustworthy and that he ghost-wrote the poem on behalf of Cú Chonnacht. Its recipient has been identified as Brighid, daughter of Éinrí Mac Gearailt (Henry Fitzgerald), 12th Earl of Kildare. Cú Chonnacht received from her, in response, the second poem below, 'A mhacaoimh dhealbhas an dán'. Its one surviving copy, written in 1645, is headed 'Brighid daughter of the Earl of Kildare composed this, so it is said' ('Brighid inghean Iarla Chille Dara cecinit más fíor'). While the words 'más fíor' introduce a suggestion of doubt, they also imply the attribution's plausibility. Some scholars saw a more serious argument against Brighid's authorship in her apparent declaration of inadequacy in the Irish language in a letter she wrote to Chichester. This letter is printed below, after 'A mhacaoimh dhealbhas an dán', where its evidential value is disputed.

Ó hEodhasa's poem is a playful yet brilliant deployment of the conceit that the speaker is a changeling, his real self having died of love, although his interlocutors are quite unaware a substitution has been made. It is in flawless *deibhí* metre. Brighid's wittily honest response is written in an amateur *óglácha* metre. She is not misled by Ó hEodhasa's riddling of Cú Chonnacht's name into his final quatrain (*sadh* 'hound' + *ciall* 'sense' + *gan fholach* 'no hiding-place' = *cú* 'hound' + *conn* 'sense' + *nocht* 'naked' = Cú Chonnacht). Although capable of applying the con-

vention in her own final quatrain, she is adamant that only one such as Ó hEodhasa himself could have crafted the more complex poem.

Brighid was married when Cú Chonnacht solicited Ó hEodhasa to write the poem on his behalf, sometime before September 1607. She had married Rudhraighe Ó Domhnaill when she was thirteen or fourteen years old, soon after his investiture as Earl of Tír Conaill on 29 September 1603. She was heavily pregnant with their second child and staying in the house of her paternal grandmother at Maynooth when he left Ireland in September 1607 in what became known as the Flight of the Earls, in the company of Cú Chonnacht. Rudhraighe died at Rome on 28 July 1608; Cú Chonnacht died of fever at Genoa on 12 August of the same year.

If Brighid had a literary sensibility, so did Rudhraighe. Ó hEodhasa, the outstanding Gaelic poet of his generation, describes him as one of his most exacting critics (in his poem 'Ionmholta malairt bhisigh': see *Irish Bardic Poetry . . . by Osborn Bergin*, compiled and edited by David Greene and Fergus Kelly (Dublin Institute for Advanced Studies, 1970), pp. 127–9; translation ibid., pp. 270–1). As for Cú Chonnacht, he had been on intimate terms with Ó hEodhasa since childhood, as Ó hEodhasa was *ollamh* to his father (also named Cú Chonnacht). Later, Ó hEodhasa was *ollamh* to Cú Chonnacht's brother, Aodh. His poems for Aodh include that made famous by Mangan as 'O'Hussey's Ode to the Maguire' (see Volume I, pp. 278–9; Volume II, pp. 28–9). The friendship between Cú Chonnacht and Ó hEodhasa continued after Aodh's death near Cork in March 1600, as did their traffic in poetry.

Edition (with translation and discussion): Cathal Ó Háinle, 'Flattery Rejected: Two Seventeenth-Century Irish Poems', *Hermathena*, vol. 138 (summer 1985), pp. 5–27, at pp. 11–13. This new translation is by Patrick Crotty.]

Ní mé bhur n-aithne, a aos gráidh,
ná sceinnidh re scáth seachráin;
fuar dár seise im' ionad ionn,
spiorad meise nach maireann.

An dóigh libh a los m'fhéaghtha
nach taidhbhse i dtruaill aiéartha,
nó spiorad anma fhallsa
tarla im' ionad agamsa?

A aithne is éidir damhsa
sibh gan fhiacha oramsa;
dá mbeth cás fám' éag oraibh,
mo bhás créad nach gcualabhair?

Truagh sin, a dhaoine dona;
do claochlódh bhúr gcéadfadha;
is eadh tharla im' ainm-se ann
taidhbhse anma gan anam.

Ní mise an duine is dóich libh;
adhradh damh is díth creidimh;
taidhbhse buile gan aird inn;
a Mhuire! is mairg do mhillfinn.

Dá bhféachtaoi fir na cruinne
annamh fuair dúil daonnaidhe
dá ré ar an saoghal acht sinn;
do naomhadh mé, má mhairim.

Gibé a-déaradh nach deachadh,
ní fhuil ann acht aimseachadh;
ní tráth damhsa a rádha riom,
cára almsa rem' anam.

Creidim féin go bhfuaras bás —
cumhain liom an lá theasdás
ar son a mhéada mhaireas
ag cor m'éaga i n-amhaireas.

Ní hanbhuain, ní hiomlat mbáis
rom-mharbh-sa, acht meisce shóláis;
ní scís meanma — gá mó broid? —
ní ró teadhma ná treabhlaid.

Más dúil do dhúilibh nimhe
tug le taidhbhreadh n-ainglidhe
goid m'anma gan iodhna báis,
iongna damhna mo dhóláis.

A radharc ó ráinig sinn,
uch, a Chríost, créad fá mairfinn?
dúil do mharbh an uile fhear,
is duine marbh nach muirfeadh.

Ní tonn líonmhar leanna duibh,
ní neamhghrádh neith ar talmhain,
ní hannsa duine — gá dtás? —
rom-mharbhsa uile acht uathbhás.

Ar n-éirghe as an riocht reimhe
(creididh sinn go simplidhe,
do mharbh sé don uamhain inn)
do chualaidh mé go mairim.

A héagosc ní fhidir mé,
ní fhéad súil silleadh uirthe;
a hamharc gion gur fhéad sinn,
a radharc do fhéag m'intinn.

Ós siabhradh meallta meise
gan dúil éirghe ón ainceis-si,
nár ria súil anduine í,
an dúil challaidhe ad-chíthí.

Ar dtaithbheoadh suil tí di,
Dia dár n-anacal uirthi;
ní tharla cás roimhe rinn,
an bás oile 'nar n-oirchill.

Ciall mh'anma an uair do mhaireas
tearc eolach 'na amhaireas:
sadh 'gá mbí ciall agus cruth
iar, agus í gan fholach.

TRANSLATION

You do not know me, dearest friends
— Don't recoil so in false alarm —
Cold in place of my counterpart
A spirit I am, that lives not.

Does it seem on looking closer
I'm a wraith, with body ethereal,
A false deceiving spirit
Occupying the space that's mine?

I recognise there's nothing
I owe you in the least —
If my death would have grieved you
You'd surely have heard of it.

What a pity, you creatures,
That you lost your faculties —
What animates my name
Is ghostly, not truly alive.

I am not what you think
— See me but do not believe —
I'm a poor distracted ghost:
Woe to him, Mary, I'd destroy!

Think of all who've ever lived
How few of them have had
Two terms on earth like me.
A saint I am — if I am at all!

No honest man could claim
That I haven't passed away:
It's not the time to tell me that
But to make offerings for my soul.

I believe myself I died —
I remember the day it happened
Despite those many doubters
Who insist I am alive.

No accident, no grievous wound
Killed me, but a bout of joy;
No sinking spirits — what worse ill? —
No sickness or sadness laid me low.

If by a creature from Heaven
In an angelic vision
My soul was gently sundered
My sorrowing now is strange.

Once I had glimpsed her, Christ,
How could I go on living?
From a creature who kills all men
Only the dead are safe.

No tidal wave of melancholy,
No hate for earthly thing,
Nor no love for anyone
Killed me — in fact — but terror.

On rising from my former state
— Simply believe that dread
It was that killed me —
I heard that I still lived.

I do not know her features,
Eye cannot gaze on her; yet
Though I could not look upon her
In my mind her image lingered.

Since I'm an enchanted changeling
At home in perplexity,
Let the eye of no evil person
See the human frame you see.

May God protect me from her
In case she restore me to life —
What I've been through is nothing
To the thought of a second death.

The meaning of my name when I lived
The scholars do not dispute:
For a hound with grace and sense
Ask, who has no hiding-place.

BRIGHID, DAUGHTER OF ÉINRÍ MAC GEARAILT (BRIGHID CHILL DARA)

(1589–1682)

A MHACAOIMH DHEALBHAS AN DÁN
(Young Man Who Fashions the Poem)
(c. 1607)

[See preceding headnote. Edition (with translation and discussion): C. Ó Háinle, 'Flattery Rejected: Two Seventeenth-Century Irish Poems', pp. 17–18. This new translation is by Patrick Crotty.]

A mhacaoimh dhealbhas an dán
tig aníos ar scáth na scol;
an dán lér chuiris do chlú,
maith a dhéanamh, is tú id' thocht.

Na roinn-se do-rinne sibh,
adéarthaoi rinn, a fhir ghráidh,
nach tú do dhlighfeadh an duas
dá dteagmhadh a luach 'nar láimh.

An dán do ghabhais fa seach —
go bhfios damhsa ní breath cham —
is d'fhior a ndéanta, más fíor,
dobudh tugtha díol na rann.

Beagán dána 'na dhán cheart;
maith a dhéanamh, a dhearc mhall;
is gan tusa it' adhbhar suadh,
iongnadh linne cruas na rann.

Ní chuirfinn i n-iongnadh ort
do dhán go holc gibé fáth;
gidh eadh as ró-iongnadh linn
sibhse do bhreith gill ar dhán.

Dar do láimh, a dhuine ghrinn,
is tú féin do mhill bhur modh
mar nach tángais fear-mar-chách
ar cuairt chugam le dán bog.

Mac Con Midhe, Fearghal Óg,
Ó Dálaigh Fionn, rómh na scol —
leo do cumadh an gréas glic,
más fior dom' aithne, a mhic Con.

Ó hEoghasa, oide na suadh —
fear a ndéanta go luath maith —
is é do rinne na roinn,
nó neach éigin do Chloinn Chraith.

Ach gibé acu sin saoi
lé ndearnadh an laoi gan locht,
ní mheasaim nach mór an slad
a chlú do bheith ar mhac Con.

Ní inneosad ainm an fhir
do dhuine ar bith gibé fáth:
is cuma liomsa cia hé
ach nadh deachadh dh'éag dom' ghrádh.

Mo shloinneadh ní chluinfe cách
uaimsi go dtile an lá inné;
atá mh'ainm, gibé lérb áil,
ar mhnaoi do mhnáibh fhlaithis Dé.

TRANSLATION

Young man who fashions the poem
Emerge from the shade of the schoolmen;
The poem you spread your fame by
Speaks well while you are silent.

These verses that you made
I'd say, dear man, don't call
For a poet's prize for you
— If I had that gift in my hand.

The poem you recited so featly
— And this is no crooked judgement —
Should win poetic payment
For the man who crafted it.

Flawless poems are rare;
Yours is trim, dark gazer
— Not even an apprentice, yet
The complexity of your verse is amazing.

I might have well expected
Your poem to be ill-made;
But to find it a prize poem
— That really is amazing.

I swear, dear chap, it was you
Yourself who spoiled your act
By not coming like a commoner
To present a slipshod poem.

Mac Con Midhe, Fearghal Óg,
Ó Dálaigh Fionn, lord of poets —
By one such, son of Cú,
Was this witty work composed.

Ó hEoghasa, the poets' teacher
Who makes swift quatrains well
— It was he who fashioned those verses
Or one of the clan Mac Craith.

Yet whichever man of learning
Composed that faultless lay
I will think it a great theft
If the son of Cú takes the credit.

I won't disclose the name
To anyone, for any reason,
I do not care whose name it is:
He would not die for my love.

My surname will not be heard
Until yesterday returns;
My forename, all may know,
Is borne by a woman in Heaven.

LETTER TO LORD DEPUTY ARTHUR CHICHESTER (1607)

[An immediate effect of the departure of the northern earls and their followers from Donegal to the Continent in September 1607 was the break-up of numerous families. Brighid, wife of Rudhraighe Ó Domhnaill, remained at Maynooth to await the birth of their child, while their son,

Aodh, a little under a year old, was taken abroad by Rudhraighe (see p. 384). Not long afterwards, Rudhraighe arranged with Eoghan Gruama Mac Craith (Owen Groome Maccrâ), deputy provincial of the Irish Franciscans, that eighty-one pieces of gold be delivered to Brighid at Maynooth, to pay for her journey abroad. Mac Craith twice visited Brighid, accompanied by another Franciscan named Thomas Fitzgerald (and not Denis O'Morcan, as suggested by Brighid below). Letters between the friars and Brighid were intercepted and Lord Deputy Arthur Chichester wrote to Brighid, charging her to reveal what she knew of Rudhraighe's departure. The reply he received from her on 1 October is given here (from *Calendar of State Papers of Ireland* 1606–8, pp. 296–7).

Brighid dissembled rather obviously in this letter. To feign ignorance of her husband's whereabouts, she implied that his messengers had not advised that she join him nor had they revealed when he might return. To make this dubious claim sound more credible, she intimated that her Irish and the messengers' English were such that she may not have fully comprehended all that was said.

It is extremely difficult to believe that Brighid was not completely fluent in Irish by 1607. Whether her upbringing at Maynooth left her with only rudimentary Irish is a moot point, but four years of life with Rudhraighe Ó Domhnaill almost certainly made good any deficit. Rudhraighe himself was obliged to employ a bilingual secretary in his transactions with the government, 'having great use of his pen and of his English tongue' (ibid., 1603–6, pp. 567–8, 12 September 1606).

In any case, when Thomas Fitzgerald was examined at Dublin Castle on 3 October, his statement flatly contradicted the substance of Brighid's letter. He related that Mac Craith and he had made detailed arrangements to enable Brighid to follow her husband. Her first wish had been to procure a passage to France or Spain, but later she 'resolved to go first into England' (ibid., 1606–8, p. 298). Brighid was never to see Rudhraighe (d. 1608) or their son, Aodh (d. 1642), again. Around 1617, she married Sir Nicholas Barnewall (created 1st Viscount Kingsland in 1645) of Turvey, near Donabate, County Dublin, by whom she had five sons and four daughters. The child to whom she gave birth soon after Rudhraighe's departure, a daughter, named Máire Stíobhard (Mary Stuart) in honour of the king, led a colourful and turbulent life. The latest record of her dates from 1639, when she was living in Rome.]

Bridgett Countess of Tirconnell to the Lord Deputy.

Right Honourable,

I have received your Lordship's letter by my cousin Bowrcher, and to satisfy your Lordship's request concerning my knowledge of my Lord's sudden departure, which I vow to your Lordship upon my honour I never had the least notice of his intent in that unfortunate journey; but, as near as I can remember, on the 16th of September last one Owen Groome Maccrâ (Magrath) sent to me to speak with him; unto whom I came, finding him accompanied with one Denis O'Morcan (I think), a priest, from whence we walked into Moyglare garden. I sent for Mr. Brian to come thither; but, a little before Bryan came, Denis O'Morcan went from us and left the friar and me, who (when he came, or soon after) delivered me the gold. Owen Maccrâ used these speeches at our first meeting, which Denis O'Morcan did interpret to me; — that my Lord had sent me that gold as a token, and wished me not to be grieved at anything; but the friar, seeing me lament, for that my Lord did leave me behind him, which I thought was for want of love, thereupon used these speeches; he thought that, if my Lord had known sooner of his going, he would have taken me with him. Upon Mr Bryan's coming to me, the friar uttered some words which (as near as Bryan in his broken English could interpret) was to wish me not to be grieved, but if I had a mind to go to my Lord, wished me to take counsel of my nearest friends; and for my Lord's return, I vow to God I have no knowledge thereof; but I pray God send him a fair death before he undergo so wicked an enterprize as to rebel against his prince. And for my conversing with priests, I would not willingly restrain myself from them; but if there shall be any notice come to me of my Lord's intent, I do protest I will acquaint your Lordship thereof, for they shall never make me to conceal anything that should tend unto His Majesty's service. I hold myself much bound unto your Lordship for your honourable advice, which I do kindly embrace, and do ever intend to observe it and will ever remain, though unfortunate yet, your Lordship's truly thankful.

Lady Tirconnell

EOGHAN RUADH MAC AN BHAIRD

(?1570–?1630)

A BHEAN FUAIR FAILL AR AN BhFEART
(Mac an Bhaird's Elegy on the Ulster Lords)
(1608)

[Nuala, sister or half-sister to Rudhraighe (Rury) Ó Domhnaill (see preceding three texts), and the Donegal poet Eoghan Ruadh Mac an Bhaird, were among those who left Ireland with the northern earls in September 1607. The Ó Domhnaill family had been patrons to Eoghan Ruadh's father as well as to himself, and he was particularly close to Rudhraighe and his siblings. Eoghan Ruadh travelled as far as Louvain but remained there when circumstances brought Rudhraighe and others on to Rome. From Louvain, the poet sent morale-boosting poems to the emigrés. One he composed on hearing that Rudhraighe had fallen ill may not have reached Rome before his death on 28 July 1608, which was soon followed by that of his brother, Cathbarr, on 15 September 1608. Their nephew, Aodh Ó Néill, also died at Rome, on 23 September 1609. All three were buried at San Pietro in Montario, in Rome.

In their elegies the poets often commanded the keening women to move back from the graveside as they claimed the right to stand closest and to speak first. Here, in Eoghan Ruadh's elegy for Nuala's three kinsmen, all is changed. He foregrounds her lonely vigil and solitary weeping at their grave in Rome against the Irish funeral clamour she can not have in this new reality, much as the poem attempts to evoke it. Nor has the crisis passed. He asks Nuala to pray that those surviving may yet escape 'the whelming wave' of God's wrath against the Irish, whose pride shipwrecked their people. She must turn her mind from useless sorrow to expiating the sins of her own kindred and assuaging divine anger.

As James Clarence Mangan's masterful translation, 'O Woman of the Piercing Wail', is well known, that given here is the scholarly translation made by Eleanor Knott to accompany her edition: 'Mac an Bhaird's Elegy on the Ulster Lords', *Celtica*, vol. 5 (1960), pp. 161–71.]

1

A bhean fuair faill ar an bhfeart,
truagh liom a bhfaghthaoi d'éisdeacht;
dá mbeath fian Ghaoidheal ad ghar
do bhiadh gud chaoineadh congnamh.

2

As fada go bhfuighthi an fhaill
dá mbeath thiar a dTír Chonaill
láimh re sluagh mBoirche dá mbeath,
ní foighthe an uagh go huaigneach.

3

A nDoire, a nDruim Chliabh na gcros,
a nArd Mhacha as mór cádhos,
ní foighthe lá an feart ar faill
gan mhná do theachd fa thuaraim.

4

Ná a nDún na nGall fan mín muir,
ná a n-áras Easbuig Eóghuin,
an cnoc 'nar crochadh Peador;
ná a nEas Ruaidh as séimhe sáil
ní bhudh réidhe an uain d'fhagháil.

5

Tiocfadh ad chombáigh chaoinidh
bean ón Éirne iolmhaoinigh,
bean ó shlios bhinnshreabh Banna,
inghean ó Lios Liathdroma.

6

Tiocfadh an bhean ón Mháigh mhoill,
ó Bhearbha, ó Shiúir, ó Shionainn;
an bhean ó Chruachuin na gcath,
'san bhean ó Thuathaibh Theamhrach.

7

Do hísleaghtha ó ingnibh sgor
an cnoc 'nar crochadh Peador;
ní bhiadh an teach gan gháir nguil
dá mbeath láimh re Fiadh bhFionntuin.

8

Ní bhiadh láimh risna leagoibh
cead suaimhnis ná sailmcheadoil;
ní bhiadh bearna gan bhróin mban,
na dearna im nóin gan niamhadh.

9

Dá mhac ríogh don fhréimhsin Chuinn
atá ar gach ttaobh d'Ú Dhomhnuill;

na trí cuirp ré a síneann sibh —
fírearr ar n-uilc a n-oighidh!

10

An dá chloichsin ósa gcionn
dá bhfaicdís ógbhuidh Éirionn,
ar aoi a líneadh do léaghadh
caoi ar míleadh do mhoisgéaladh.

11

Dias don triursoin tarla asttigh
clann Aodha, ardfhlaith Sligigh;
ua don Aodhsoin duine díobh,
cuire d'aostoigh na n-airdríogh.

12

Ua t'athar ar aoi a mháthar,
maraon red' dís ndearbbráthar:
ní guth dhuit gan chéill ad chaoi,
a bhfuil nó a méin dá meastaoi.

13

D'éis Í Dhomhnuill Dúna ós Sáimh,
dá dtánuig tús bhar dtocráidh,
ní guth truime do thuirsi,
uille iná t'uch t'adhbhuirsi.

14

Triath Modhuirne, Mac Í Néill,
dá bhféaghthaoi a chraobha cinéil,
a chruth, a airdhe oile —
ní guth aidhbhle t'eólchuire.

15

Dá bhféaghthaoi gach aonmhaith ann,
mac ríogh ó gConaill, Cathbharr,
a los ghnaoi, nó ghníomh ngoile,
ga díol caoi bhudh chosmhuile.

16

Ní bhiadh baile ó thuinn go tuinn,
dá dtuitdís so a gClár Chriomhthuinn,
gan gháir bhfaoilte nó gáir ghuil
le gáir gcaointe nó chosguir.

17

'Sna cathaibh do cuireadh linn
ag cosnamh Chríche Féilim,
dá dtuiteadh duine díobh soin
robadh sníomh uile d'Ulltoibh.

18
Lá oirdhearc Átha Buidhe,
inar ládh leacht sochuidhe,
dá dtuiteadh uainn Aodh Ó Néill
don taobh thuaidh robadh tuirléim.

19
Lá a mbéal Bhealaigh an Mhaighre
dá dtuiteadh triath Modhuirne,
bheith réidh dob aimhréidh d'iarruidh
ar dhaighfhréimh Néill Naoighialluigh.

20
A ló mhadhma an Mhullaigh bhric
ní géabhthaoi a nAodh mar éiric
na cairn d'éachtuibh muin ar mhuin
san mhaidhm ó éachdfhuil Eóghuin.

21
Laithe dóibh ag gabháil ghiall
ar sluagh a Mumhuin Mhaicniadh,
cionnas do géabhthaoi ag crú Chuinn
dá sgéarthaoi an chnú re a crobhuing.

22
Lá catha an Bhealuigh Bhuidhe
dá sgarthaoi rinn Rudhruighe,
do bhiadh gáir fhaoilte gach fhir
'na gáir chaointe aga chluinsin.

23
Dá dtuiteadh sé ón tír thall
a ló fhillte fian n-eachdrann
lá dob áille a nÁth Seanuigh
nír fháth gáire ag Gaoidhealaibh.

24
Lá a Leithbhior 'nar loiteadh sin,
lá ag Luimneach nó lá ag Gaillimh,
do-géabhtha mná caoine í Chuinn
lá Baoille nó an lá ag Liathdruim.

25
Dá dtíosadh a thuiteam dhe,
an lá do lingeadh Baile
Átha an Ríogh, a fhian Éirne,
ní bhiadh bhar síodh soidhéinmhe

26
Lá a nDoire 'nar dhearbh a láimh,
dá dtuctha leacht laoich Iomgháin,

do bhiadh t'éanghul 'na gháir ghuil
iar dtéarnamh dáibh ón deabhuidh.

27
Dá dtuiteadh sé re Síol gCais
lá troda re taobh bhForghais,
leis an sluagh ag teachta asteach
buadh na heachtra dob aithreach.

28
Lá a ndeabhuidh fa Dhún na nGall,
da bhfaicthi fuil re Cathbharr,
ba lór d'urbhuidh ar fhéaghadh,
slógh Murbhaigh do mhoithéaghadh.

29
Do ruaimnéaghtha ruisg ar niadh
dá dtuctha a leachd lá ar Coirrshlíabh;
dá dtuctha a leachd lá Sligigh
nír lá budh eachd d'fhoighidin.

30
Nír bheag an léan ar Leith Cuinn
bás Aodha, oidhidh Cathbhuirr,
sgaradh do Rudhruighe rinn
rabhadh urbhuidhe d'Éirinn.

31
Cia an Gaoidheal nach guilfeadh libh
bláth fréimhe maicne Mílidh?
bhar n-oire cia ar nach cuirfeadh?
cia an croidhe nach criothnuighfeadh?

32
Díbir ar Dhia an dtuirsi dtruim
uait, a Inghean Í Dhomhnuill;
gearr go dtéighe ar séad mar soin,
féag na céime fad' chomhair.

33
A láimh gcriadh ná cuir do dhóigh,
tuicthear libh, lór do sheanmóir,
do réir thagha an Tí ó bhfuil
go ragha gach ní, a Nualuidh.

34
Smuain an gcroich atá red' thaoibh,
a n-áit do dhuilghis díomhaoin;
tóguibh don uaighsi t'uille,
fógair uaibhsi t'eólchuire.

35

Cuir, a Dhé, budh deasda an dtuinn
tar fhuighleach n-áir chrú Conuill;
ar chás ar loingbhrisidh luigh,
bás na foirneisin féachuidh!

36

Tóguibh láimh, a Mheic Muire,
le taighdeadh do thrócuire,
a n-aghaidh na tuinne a dtám,
do chabhair luinge ar leanbán!

37

Bíodh an t-uchd ga n-altrom so,
bíodh an lámh uaibh, a Íosa,
ag taltoghadh a dtaobh soin,
glantoradh ar gcraobh gcnuasaigh!

38

A ríoghain fhréimhe Dáluigh,
tánuig ón tuinn iombádhuigh,
nach rabh ní as sia a fherg ret' fhuil
fagh ó Dhia, an Ceard rod chruthuigh.

39

Do shaoileamar, do shaoil sibh
dál cabhra ag clannuibh Mílidh
tréasan dtriar tarla san uaigh
ag triall ó Bhanbha bheannfhuair.

TRANSLATION

1

O woman that hast found the tomb unguarded, pitiful to me the number thou findest to listen; were the soldiery of the Gaels at thy side there would be help with thy keening.

2

Not soon would it be so unguarded were it west in Tirconnell; were it beside the host of Boirche the grave had ne'er been found lonely.

3

In Derry, in Drumcliff of the crosses, in Armagh great in sanctity, not one day would the tomb be found unwatched, without women coming to seek it.

4

Nor in Donegal, where the sea is gentle, or at the home of Bishop Eoghan, or in Asseroe of mildest brackishness, would it be easier to find an opportunity.

5

There would come in sympathy with thy wailing a woman from the many-treasured Erne, a woman from the shore of the sweetly-flowing Bann, a maiden from Leitrim's rampart.

6

A woman would come from the sluggish Maigue, from the Barrow, the Suir, the Shannon; a woman from Croghan of the battalions, and a woman from the Tribes of Tara.

7

Were it beside the Wood of Fionntan, the mound whereon Peter was crucified would be trampled down by horses' hooves; there would be no house without a cry of lamentation.

8

Beside the pillars there would be no leave for repose or for psalm-chanting; there would be no gap without a crown of women, no palm by noon that did not glisten.

9

Two king's sons of that seed of Conn lie beside O'Donnell, the three bodies by which thou art prostrate — their destruction is the very culmination of our woe.

10

Did the fighting men of Erin see those two stones above (the grave), the reading of their inscriptions would awaken the grief of our soldiers.

11

Two of those three within (the tomb) are the children of Aodh, high prince of Sligo, and one is grandson to that Aodh; a company of the ancient house of the high kings.

12

The grandson of thy father through his mother, together with thy two blood-brothers — it is no blame to thee that thy grief passes reason, were their family or their bearing considered.

13

After O'Donnell of Dún ós Sáimh,[1] from whom came the first of thy sorrow, no reproach is the weight of thy sadness, greater than thy sobbing is thy cause.

14

The lord of Mourne, O'Neill's son, were his kindred's branches considered, his beauty, his other traits, no reproach is the greatness of thy grieving.

15

Were every good in Cathbharr, son of the king of Conall's line, considered, for gentleness, for deeds of valour, what more likely mark for mourning?

16

There would not be a homestead from wave to wave had these fallen in Criomhthann's land, without a shout of joy or a shout of lamentation, with (also) shout of mourning or of triumph.

17

In the battles waged by us in contention for the land of Felim, had one of them fallen it had been an affliction for all Ulster.

18

On the famous day of the Yellow Ford,[2] where the graves of a multitude were made, had Aodh Ó Néill fallen it would have been an overthrow for the northern side.

19

On the day in the mouth of Bealach an Mhaighre[3] had the lord of Mourne fallen, it would not have been easy to ask the noble line of Niall the nine-hostaged to be calm.

20

The day of the defeat at Mullach Breac[4] the heaped mounds of those slain in the rout would not have been accepted as eric[5] for Aodh by Eoghan's warlike kin.

21

The day that our army was taking hostages in Munster[6] of Maicnia; how would the blood of

Conn have behaved were the nut parted from its cluster?

22

The day of the battle of Bealach Buidhe,[7] had Rury been parted from us each man's shout of joy had become a shout of wailing on hearing it.

23

Had he fallen from yonder shore the day foreign troops turned back, the finest day in Ballyshannon[8] had been no cause of exultation for the Gaels.

24

The day in Lifford,[9] where he was wounded, the day at Limerick or the day at Galway, women would have been found keening for Conn's descendants, the day of Boyle[10] (also) or the day at Leitrim.

25

Had his fall come about from the fighting the day Athenry[11] was stormed, O soldiers of the Erne, you had not been easily pacified.

26

That day in Derry when he proved his arm had the hero of Iomghán[12] found his grave, thy lonely cry would have been a shout of mourning when they had returned from the fight.

27

Had he fallen by the seed of Cas[13] that day of battle beside the Fergus,[14] the triumph would have been regretful for the returning host.

2. At the Battle of the Yellow Ford, near Armagh, in 1598, the English forces were routed.
3. The Moyry Pass, Killeavy parish, County Armagh. This may refer to an engagement between Aodh Ó Néill and Mountjoy in September 1600.
4. Mullaghbrack parish, near Armagh.
5. Irish *éraic*, 'body-fine, fixed penalty for homicide'.
6. Aodh Ó Néill's expedition to Munster was in 1600.
7. Near Ballinafod, County Sligo.
8. In County Donegal; August 1597.
9. In County Donegal; 1600.
10. In County Roscommon.
11. Athenry, County Galway, was taken by O'Donnell's troops in 1597.
12. The place-name Iomghán, also found in Dún Iomgháin, Dunamon, County Roscommon, is frequently used in epithets of the O'Donnells.
13. The Dál gCais in Thomond.
14. A river in County Clare. This possibly refers to O'Donnell's foray into Clare, in Thomond, in 1600.

1. Unidentified.

28

The day of the fight by Donegal had a wound been seen on Cathbharr, the host of Murbhach[15] would perceive it (to be) full calamity when considered.

29

The eyes of our champions would have been reddened had his grave been found the day on Coirrshliabh;[16] had it been found that day of Sligo that had not been afterwards a day for patience.

30

Not small the sorrow to Leth Cuinn, the death of Aodh, the tragic death of Cathbharr; Rudhraighe's parting from us is a warning of disaster for Erin.

31

Who is the Gael that would not weep with thee for the flower of the race of Míl's sons? On whom (of them) would thy burden not weigh? Whose heart that would not quiver?

32

Dismiss from thee for the sake of God that weighing sorrow, O daughter of O'Donnell; shortly though shalt go on the same path, behold the steps before thee!

33

In hand of clay set not thy hope; be it understood by thee, sermon enough, that according to the will of Him from whom it is shall everything take its course, O Nuala.

34

Ponder on the Cross by thy side, rather than on thy fruitless sorrow; lift thine elbow from the grave, banish from thee thy yearning.

35

Send now, O God, the wave past those survivors from war of Conall's blood; subdue the trouble of our shipwreck; consider the death of that company.

36

Lift up Thy hand, O Son of Mary, with the guidance of Thy mercy, against the wave in which we are (engulfed), to rescue the ship of our babes!

37

Let thy bosom nourish these, let Thy hand, O Jesus, give them comfort, pure produce of our fruit-laden branches!

38

O queen of Dálach's line, that hast escaped from the whelming wave, that His wrath against thy kindred continue no longer, obtain from God, the Artificer who fashioned thee.

39

We thought, as didst thou, that the Children of Míl had a prospect of help through those three in the tomb when they set forth from the cold peaks of Banbha.

IONMHUIN SGRÍBHIONN SGAOILTEAR SONN
(Great News) (1613)

[At around one year of age, Aodh Ó Domhnaill, son of Rudhraighe, Earl of Tír Conaill, and Brighid, daughter of the Earl of Kildare, was perhaps the youngest to leave Ireland in the Flight of the Earls in 1607 (see preceding headnote). He was given into the care of his aunt, Nuala, Rudhraighe's sister, and after Rudhraighe's death, she oversaw the education he received at the convent of the Dames Blanches and at the College of the Irish Franciscans in Louvain, where she eventually settled. Eoghan Ruadh's earliest composition in honour of Aodh, the Earl's heir, was written in Donegal, soon after the child's birth. He wrote the following poem on the occasion of receiving a letter from Aodh when he was seven. He may have hoped it would raise a smile from Nuala as much as Aodh.

Tradition has it that Nuala was an amateur poet and a simple lyric celebrating Donegal's natural beauty is attributed to her. If she did compose it, it seems that its present semi-accentual form replaced an original syllabic one, as often happened when a syllabic poem remained popular in folk tradition.

Aodh became colonel of an Irish regiment in the Spanish service, and died in Spain not long before September 1642. He was recognized on the Continent as the Earl of Tír Conaill (see Volume V, p. 29). Nuala's date of death is unknown. She was buried in the chapel of the Irish Franciscan College at Louvain.

Text: Paul Walsh, *Irish Men of Learning* (Dublin: At the Sign of the Three Candles, 1947), p. 184. This new translation is by Patrick Crotty.]

---

15. Murvagh in County Donegal.
16. The Curlew Hills in County Sligo: the Battle of the Curlews was in 1599.

Ionmhuin sgríbhionn sgaoiltear sonn
mór mbeadhgadh do bhean asom
    saor a Dhé ar aithleónadh inn
    aithbheódhadh é dom intinn.

Da mairdís a ffaca féin
duaislibh Gaoidheal guirt rígNéill
    do bheith fáth faoilte don dreim
    a ttráth sgaoilte don sgribheinn.

An naoidhe táinicc tar tuinn
bíodh nach beith na Ua Domhnaill
    díol é gach muirne da mhét
    go mbé ar cCoimdhe ag a choimét.

Aodh O Domhnuill ga ttám do
gan daois sunn acht seacht mbliadhno
    damhna mo ríogh robháidh linn
    sgoláir rod sgríobh in sgribhinn.

Dear the letter unbound here
That took my breath on opening it
    — God keep us from fresh harms —
    It has restored my mind.

Had those Gaels lived, those nobles
I knew at the court of Niall,
    They would have started for joy
    The instant the letter was opened.

The child that's come over the sea
Though not yet the Ó Domhnaill
    Deserves our greatest love: —
    May God protect him forever.

Aodh Ó Domhnaill, my treasure
Still just seven years old
    Heir to my king, my dear one,
    A scholar wrote when you wrote this.

FIONNGHUALA, DAUGHTER OF DOMHNALL Ó BRIAIN

(*c.* 1557–?)

A NAINM AN SPIORAID NAOIMH H'IMRÍGHE, 'UAITHNE
(On the Death of Her Husband, Uaithne) (1617)

[Fionnghuala, daughter of Domhnall Ó Briain ('Donal's daughter'), was aged about fifty-nine when her second husband, Uaithne Ó Lochlainn, died. She and Uaithne belonged to aristocratic Thomond families. Her paternal uncle, Donnchadh, was 2nd Earl of Thomond, and she was a first cousin to the 3rd Earl, Conchobhar (d. 1581), and a second cousin to the 4th Earl, Donnchadh (d. 1624). Uaithne ruled the Burren in Clare.

When Uaithne died, Fionnghuala lost more than a husband. In accordance with Irish custom, she was entitled only to the repayment of the dowry she had brought to the marriage. Any hopes she may have had of retaining rights over his property, including residence rights to their home

in Seanmhuicinis (Shanmuckinish) Castle, near Ballyvaughan, County Clare, would have been greatly undermined by the fact that he left no heir by her. In the event, two of Uaithne's kinswomen were named as his co-heiresses in an inquisition taken at Sixmilebridge in County Clare on 10 January 1625, and Fionnghuala was obliged to leave Seanmhuicinis (see headnote to the next succeeding poem).

In her *caoineadh*, Fionnghuala's fears for the future almost overtake her grief at Uaithne's death. While he is moving to heaven's 'big house', she stands to lose her own. She calls to mind that the man who acted as her 'protector' at a much earlier stage in her life, when her future also seemed bleak, is now dead (lines 27–33). As Liam P. Ó Murchú has shown, these lines almost certainly refer to the following circumstances. Fionnghuala's first husband, Tomás Mac Muiris, Lord of Lixnaw (County Kerry), had repudiated her and married her half-sister, Onóra, in December 1579. Some time later, Fionnghuala married Uaithne. As her father had been dead since October 1579, it was quite possibly her kinsman Conchobhar Ó Briain, 3rd Earl of Thomond, who brokered her marriage to this neighbouring lord. This would account both for the indebtedness she expresses to this Earl of Thomond and for her recollection of it at the time of her second husband's death.

Fionnghuala's praise for the 3rd Earl is also a call to the 4th to protect her interests, now that she is alone once more. In view of Fionnghuala's age, perhaps lines 40–3 should be understood as an appeal to him to ensure that she, as 'senior', is given precedence over her husband's co-heiresses. If so, there may be some grounds for regarding this *caoineadh* as a Gaelic parallel to the petitions addressed to the monarch or the London privy council, 'the most common form of public writing by women in the sixteenth century' (see Volume v, pp. 6–12). Adoption of the voice of a woman keening as though for the newly deceased is not unusual in *caointe* composed some time after death had occurred.

Text and translation (with detailed discussion, on which this headnote is based): Liam P. Ó Murchú, 'Caoineadh ar Uaithne Mór Ó Lochlainn, 1617', *Éigse*, vol. 27 (1993), pp. 67–79.]

Fionnghuala inghean Domhnaill Uí Bhriain
cecinit.

A nainm an Spioraid Naoimh h'imríghe,
    'Uaithne,
is triall ó thigh bhig go tigh mhuar sibh;
béara an t-áirdrígh dá láinbhrígh suas tu
don ádhbhadh ann nách fuighir gábhadh ná
    guasacht.

Biaidh mórmhac na hóighe gan ghruaim riot
do bhrígh tú bheith sgaoilteach fá a bhfuarais
's nach raibh stór cófra ná guais ort,
eaglais is aos ealadhan gan ghruaim riot.

D'inneosainn beagán beagán dot dhualgus:
cúig rígh fhichiot do bhí uaitse
ar Éirinn nár bhféidir a ruagadh,
deich rígh is fiche rígh gan truailleadh

do rígheadh cóigiodh, gér mhór attuairisg,
do churadhaibh lé ccurthaoi gach cruaidhthreas.
Muna leor so dot eolas uaimse
do gheabhthar sgeol ort a leabhur na suadha
's gur libh an céadlaoi dá nduantaibh.

Nár agra an t-airdrígh atá thuas ort
gur sibh féin do réigh so uatha
gur fhortabhair an tromdháimh trí huaire
is fir Éirionn dá léirsgris uatha.

Is mun bheith mur tharrla mé a ngruaim riot
do bheadh mac do mháthar dom buaidhriodh,
ó do síneadh gaois go luaith leat
is réidhteach ar sgéaltaibh badh muaircheisd,

do dhaonnacht gan aonbhuille cruais ann.
Sgéal fábhaill atá dom buaidhriodh:
atáim cráidhte ó bhás Iarla Tuadhmhun,
mo chré chúil, do bhrúghaidh go muar me,

árdfhlaith aga mbíodh cás im chruadhtan
ó bhfuighinn fáilte ghrádhmhar shuaimhneach
is fuighle badh binn liom am chluasaibh
is cáta tar alán do mhnáibh uaisle.

Ní oile is iongnadh go muar liom:
cé a nÉirinn éinneach do luaidhfiodh
tús na slíghe do bhreith uaimse
ó chuaidh tréine Uí Néill ar buaidhriodh,

Síol Eoghain dár chóir bheith uasal,
'sgur eadruibh féin do bhí an mhuardhacht.
San sgéal so ní faighthior bréaga uaimse,
gur bhé dlíghe na ttréinfhear gan truailleadh,

gidh bé díobh budh sinnsior an uair sin
an dís oile do stríocadh anuas dho.
A Éire atá taomannach buaidhiortha
ní buan do ré d'éinneach dár dhual tu;

's a mhéirdreach, ó thréigise h'uaisle
is cuma liom féin cia an té fá mbuailfir.
Is é do bhás tar chách do bhuaidhir me
'sa nainm an Spioraid Naoimh h'imrídhe,
    'Uaithne.

TRANSLATION

Fionnnghuala daughter of Domhnall Ó Briain composed this.

May your journey, Uaithne, be in the name of the Holy Spirit, you move from a small to a big house; the Supreme King in his omnipotence will bring you to the abode where you will encounter neither peril nor anxiety.

The great son of the Virgin will meet you in no surly fashion since you were lavish with what you got, and since the hoarding of coffered wealth cannot possibly be imputed to you, (as) the church and men of art (were) not disappointed with you.

I would briefly relate a little of your heredity: before you were twenty-five Kings over Ireland that could not be displaced, thirty uncorrupted kings who ruled a province, though their fame was great, warriors by whom each tough conflict was fought. If this knowledge I give of you is insufficient your story can be found in the book of the poets' considering that to you belongs the first poem of their compositions.

May the Supreme King on high not bring against you that you obtained this from them, that you thrice succoured the oppressive company of poets when the men of Ireland were extirpating them.

And were it not that I have been mourning for you, I would (still) be troubled by (you being) your mother's son, since wisdom was associated with you early on, as was the solving of grave affairs, your kindliness held not the slightest harshness.

Another affair troubles me much: I am grieved

since the death of my protector the Earl of Thomond, which (death) oppressed me greatly, a great lord who concerned himself with my hardship, from whom I got loving, soothing salutation, and speech which was sweet to my ears and honour above many noble ladies.

Another matter that I find quite surprising: where in Ireland is anyone who would cite my loss of precedence considering that the might of Ó Néill has dissipated, the race of Eoghan to whom it would have been proper to behave nobly; and greatness was shared by each of you.

In this matter I do not lie, (I say) that it was the unbroken rule of the mighty ones, to whichever one of you was superior then, that the other two would bow down.

Ireland, restless and tormented, no lasting reign has he who has proper claim to you; and, harlot, since you deserted your nobles I don't care to whom you attach yourself. Your death, beyond everyone, has oppressed me, and may your journey be in the name of the Holy Spirit, Uaithne.

ANONYMOUS

TUAR GUIL, A CHOLAIM, DO CHEÓL!
(The Dove in the Castle)
(c. 1617)

[After the death of Uaithne Ó Lochlainn in 1617, his childless widow, Fionnghuala, daughter of Domhnall Ó Briain was obliged to vacate the Ó Lochlainn castle at Seanmhuicinis (see preceding text). This anonymous poem mourns her going and catalogues the beloved sounds that are heard no more. The final 'binding' verse in *amhrán* metre, omitted by Lord Longford, is translated as follows in Seán Ó Tuama's and Thomas Kinsella's *An Duanaire 1600–1900: Poems of the Dispossessed* (Mountrath: Dolmen Press, 1981), p. 23:

Dove of the doleful music there on the fortress, sad is that splendid Rome powerless below you: stately Tulach Uí Róigh, of towering walls, without ale or the music of sails or blades flexing.

Texts: S. Ó Tuama and T. Kinsella, ibid., pp. 20, 22. Translation: the Earl of Longford, *The Dove in the Castle*, pp. 132–4.]

Tuar guil, a cholaim, do cheol!
    mo chroidhe ní beó dá bhíth;
do bhréagais mo dheor óm rosc;
    is truagh nách id thost do bhís.

A fhágbháil 'na aonar fúibh,
    iostadh fairsing múir uí Róigh,
an é do-bheir meanma ort
    ag nách éidir cosc do ghlóir?

Nó an í an chumha dod chrádh,
   a cholaim cheannsa, is fáth dhaoibh,
ó nách faice an úrbhas fhial
   do chleachtais dod riar gach laoi?

Cosmhail nách den tírse thú,
   a cholaim bhúidh thig ón Spáinn,
i n-ionad ar thárbhaidh dhúin
   nach faiceam acht tú a-mháin.

An múr 'na aonar a-nocht
   'na gcluininn gáir chrot is chliar,
gáir na bhflaith bhfairsing fó fhíon,
   gáir bhrughadh ag díol a bhfiach.

Gáir laoch ag líomhadh a n-arm,
   gáir na stoc i n-am na gcean,
gáir rámhadh isteach san gcuan,
   gáir fhaoileann i n-uaimh na sreabh.

Gáir fithcheall dá gcur i luas,
   gáir na suadh as leabhraibh sean,
gáir bhionnfhoclach na mban séimh,
   dream do thuigeadh céill ar gceast.

Inghean Domhnaill do mhear mé
   's do chuir mo chéill ar mo mhuin;
a beith gan oighre, gan ua,
   cá beag dhamh-sa mar thuar guil?

A chuilim an cheóil bhrónaig san dúna thall,
   Is duilibh an róimh nósmhar so fúibh go fann;
Tulach Uí Róigh mhórga na múrtha mbeann,
   Gan chuirm, gan cheol seolta ná lúbadh lann!

TRANSLATION

Why did you break that silence, dove? Ah why?
   A deathly grief that slept you seem to wake.
Your coos have coaxed the river from my eye.

How could you tell what havoc you would
   make?

Perhaps some echo of an ancient joy
   Stirs in your throat possessed and sing you
   must,
Some lingering phantom of the race of Roigh
   Moans in their halls amid the lonely dust.

Or mourn you, gentle bird, for one sweet friend
   Who comes no more, her foot that's fled away,
Her hand that would its pretty pigeon tend,
   Upon whose kindly palm you'd sit each day?

Perhaps, mild dove, you are not of this land,
   Some Spaniard, knowing nought of what is
   gone!
To-night for all O Lochlainn's pride you stand,
   Glory is fallen! You remain alone!

To-night this lonely mansion hears no more
   The chant of bards and harpers sweetly blent,
Lords riotous with wine, the table's roar,
   The clattering tenants bringing in the rent.

The din of warriors polishing their swords,
   The splash of oars as into port they ply,
The bellowing cattle, and the shouted words,
   While o'er the water comes the sea-gull's cry.

The tramp of chessmen as they march to fight,
   The drone of sages over ancient books,
The soft and tuneful talk of ladies bright,
   Tribe wise of mind for all their youthful
   looks.

My grief for Donal's daughter maddens me,
   My senses fail! Ah, would that I might die!
She without heir, without posterity!
   Why did you break that silence, dove?
   Ah, why?

CAITILÍN DUBH

(*fl.* 1624–9)

DO CHUALA TÁSC DO CHRÁIDH FIR ÉIREANN
(On Donnchadh Ó Briain, Earl of Thomond) (1624)

[Caitilín Dubh is the earliest Gaelic woman poet with a significant body of work still extant: five long poems attributed to her survive in a single manuscript. Yet almost nothing is known about her, apart from what may be gleaned from the poems. All five are elegies, in long-lined *caoineadh* metre, with an irregular number of stresses in the lines. Their subjects were among the leading nobles of Thomond: Donnchadh Ó Briain, 4th Earl of Thomond, who died in 1624; his sister, Máire, whose date of death is unknown; her husband, Toirdhealbhach Ruadh Mac Mathghamhna of Cluain Idir Dhá Lá (Clonderlaw), who died in 1629, subject of two elegies; and Diarmaid Ó Briain, 5th Baron Inchiquin, who died in 1624. The poems presented here are the first and last of these, and they present an interesting contrast.

The confident way in which Caitilín Dubh speaks of these nobles suggests that her background was also one of privilege. Since three of the poems concern one couple, she may have had a special place in their household. Perhaps her detailed knowledge of the 4th Earl's military campaigns was acquired as an intimate of his circle, maybe even a blood relation of the O'Briens (it is not known whether 'Dubh' is an epithet or a surname). The fact that she uses only *caoineadh* metre suggests she was not a schooled poet, but this is not to rule out the possibility that she was a professional. Yet if only an amateur, Caitilín Dubh seems to have been a regular practitioner, and was well-versed in the conventions of Gaelic poetry.

Donnchadh Ó Briain, a Protestant, was educated at the court of Elizabeth I and remained loyal to the crown throughout his career. He acted decisively during the Nine Years War (April 1593–March 1603) to put down Tyrone's rebellion. His opponents included his brother, Tadhg, who rallied to the cause of Tyrone, invaded Thomond, and claimed the title of Ó Briain for himself. The Earl took part in Essex's southward march after the rout of the Queen's forces at the Battle of the Yellow Ford in 1598 and he fought with Mountjoy at Kinsale in 1601.

Only the first thirty-six and the last nine lines of the following poem on the death of Donnchadh Ó Briain are manifestly elegiac. The remainder might be construed as the *caithréim* or 'battle roll' of Ó Briain during the Nine Years War. The fact that the poem refers to no event thereafter suggests Caitilín Dubh may have incorporated

materials from an earlier praise-poem into her elegy, as professional poets were also wont to do.

Her words convey no sense of a significant divide between Protestant and Catholic, or between crown forces and the 'natives', both Irish and Old English. For her, the Protestant Earl is 'guardian of the whole land of Fódla', a descendant of the great Irish heroes of legend, and a subject whose death will be mourned by James I and his court. The enemy is the rebel element within, Tyrone and his allies who, unlike Ó Briain, will never be of account with the royal houses of Europe. The elegy is distant and formal in tone, more intent on honouring the Earl than on expressing a personal loss.

Text (from Maynooth, St Patrick's College Library, MS M 107, pp. 193–7) and translation are provided by Liam P. Ó Murchú, whose edition of the complete poems is forthcoming. All data in the preceding headnote are derived from his work.]

Caitilín Dubh cecenit iar n-éag Dhonnchaidh
Iarla Tuadhmhumhan

Do chuala tásc do chráidh fir Éireann
do chuir a mnáibh tar bharr a gcéille
d'fhág a n-ughdair bruighte tréithlag
's do chuir an chliar fá chiaich in éinfheacht,
bás an iarla Uí Bhriain na dtréinbheart.

Gliadhaire do cheap fiadhghort Féidhlim,
do chuir a riaghail ar na séimhfhir,
talltóir i gcoigcríochaibh baogail,
feathmhóir sreabh lér sleasadh Éire,

caiptín sluaghchruaidhte na mbéimeann,
geinearál na harmála badh tréine,
buachaill bó Chláir Fódla in éinfheacht,
an gadhar luirg lér sriosadh na faolchoin.
Má tháinig deimhniughadh ar do scéala

's a gcur go Lonndain dá n-éisteacht
do chuir súd mórghruaim ar rígh Séamus
's ar onóir na bprionnsuidhe le chéile
ar dhiúicidhibh 's ar ghiúistísíbh tréana.

A rúin chroidhe 's na condaoisidhe ag géarghul,
is lucht gúnuidhe dá n-umhluigheadh an béarla.
Creach na n-óg thu is creach na n-aosta,

creach na nGall is creach na nGaedhal tu
's is foghtha atá Clár Cobhthaigh i t'éagmais
gan suan go sámh gan dán dá éisteacht
gan ceól gan cuirm gan cuireadh dá réidhteach,

gan buannuidhibh borba dá bhfostadh chum
  laochais,
gan bronnadh each, gan gean ar éigse,
gan iomad barc ag teacht go saothrach
i ndeóidh do bháis do chráidh gan éinneach.

Ón ló thionnscain Conn an céad cath,
ó marbhadh Cairbre i gcath na mbéimeann,
Eóghan mór i gcath Mhaigh Léana
is Eóghan oile do thuitim le Béinne,

ó thuit Brian is Murchadh in éinfheacht
níl éacht ós do chionn ar fhéachain,
a choileáin lér griosáladh Éire
tug cloidheamh is teine do Chúige Uladh ar
  éigin,

do chuaidh go Dún na nGall dá réabadh
's go Dún Geanainn gér neartmhar an céimsin,
go hEas Aodha Ruaidh ag bualadh do scéithe,
ar an Sraith mBáin is láimh le hEirne.

Ba maith Donnchadh Ó Briain mar léadar
's a bhaiclí dá leataoibh go fraochda
bhalasót ag fógradh dá chéile
a shróill ag preabadh le crannaibh 's ag séideadh.

I mBealach an Díre rín tú éachta
d'fhág tú Mac Uilliam go céimleasc
do bhain tú an spor 's a chos ón bpréimh dhe
is Fearaibh Manach do lasais ar éigin,

na tuatha 's na cluantaibh in éinfheacht,
An Cabhán ar cheartlár an lae ghil,
le triath Sligigh níor chumais bheith réigh leat
nó le Ó Ruairc gér mhuar a ghaol leat.

Fear Muighe Luirg do chuiris i ngéibheann,
Síol gConchobhair do rín tú do léirscrios,
do bhádar na cóigidhibh fád ghéarsmacht
is as súd go Tír Briúin an Bhéarla.

Do bhádar Fir Mhidhe fá dhíon do scéithe
is tugadar Laighnigh a mbraighdibh féin duit.

Créad b'áil liom dá n-áireamh ré chéile
's nach bhfuil ceann baile, bealaigh ná sléibhe

nach raibh aithne ar bhrataibh an tréinfhir.
Do bhádhais lá fada i mbun Banda ag déanamh
  éachta
is as súd siar go hiarthar Béarra.

Cidh bhí Donn Seón go lór dho thréine
dob éigean do umhlughadh go réidh dhuit;
tug sé a mhóid is fós a bhréithir
dá léightheá don Spáinn é ar chás éigin

nach tiocfadh chút ar úir na hÉireann.
Maith do fuair badh muar an baoghal do
nuair churthá do sconnsuidhe lena éadan
's t'fhearchoin daingne ar gach taobh dhe.

'S an uair do shanntaigh an giúistís éirghe
do dhúnais do champuidhe ina chéile.
Is maith do cuireadh plána ar Chlár Céin duit
a mhic ríogh Táil dár dáileadh Éire.

Leanfadsa d'eachtra do phréimhe
's gur as Teagh na Haustria do théarnais,
a bhráthair ríogh Lonndan na gcéad gcath,
ríogh stádmhar na Spáinne tréine,

ríogh Póland na Coróna nár claonadh
is ríogh Franc atá teann san éileamh.
A ghaoil ríogh uasail na Bohéime
a bhráthair Charoluis is tSéasair,

is Páras tug lánchath san Trae amuigh
's an impire lér tionnscnadh an féasta
tug ríogha an domhain mhóir dá chéile.
A bhráthair gach ardfhlaith dá aeirde,

má chuir an bás 'na tháille féin tu
súd Clár Banba feasta gan céile,
tug sí malairt ar atharrach scéimhe
do ghabh sí duibhe ar fhaicsin ghléigil.

Tá sí dall, do chaill sí a héisteacht,
do briseadh a cos, do stopadh a céimibh
i ndeóidh an fhir dá dtug sí a haonta
is truagh 's is deacair bhur scaradh ré chéile.

Do chuala tásc do chráidh fir Éireann.

TRANSLATION

Caitilín Dubh composed this on the death of
Donnchadh, the Earl of Thomond.

I have heard tidings that have tormented the
men of Ireland,
that have deranged their womenfolk,
that have left their authors bruised and
debilitated,
the poetic community in gloom —
this is the death of the Earl Ó Briain of great
deeds;

a warrior who checked the wild Land of
Feidhlim,[1]
imposing his rule upon her nobles,
a raider in dangerous territories,
a watcher of rivers who encompassed Ireland,

the blow-striking captain hardened through
encounters with hosts,
an army general most powerful,
guardian of the whole land of Fódla,
the tracker dog by whom the wolves were
extirpated.
If these tidings of you have been confirmed

and have gone to be heard in London,
then King James[2] has suffered great dejection
as have the honourable princes,
dukes and powerful magistrates.

His secret loves and countesses are crying bitterly
as are those, adorned in gowns, in whose
presence voices were wont to be lowered.
Your death is a ruinous loss to young and old,

to the foreigners and to the Irish
and the Plain of Cobhthach[3] is despoiled
through your death,
soothing sleep is not enjoyed, no poem is
listened to,
music, festiveness and feasting are neglected,

rough fighting men are not engaged to perform
heroic feats,
steeds are not bestowed, poetry is unloved,

boats in numbers no longer ply to shore
in the wake of your death which has tormented
all.

Since Conn[4] initiated the hundred battles,
since Cairbre[5] was killed in the battle of the
blows,
since Eóghan Mór[6] was killed in the battle of
Magh Léana
and since the other Eóghan[7] fell to Béinne,

since Brian and Murchadh[8] fell together in battle,
no death, it seems, exceeds your demise,
scion who provoked the whole of Ireland,
who visited sword and fire forcefully on Ulster,[9]

who went to Donegal in order to destroy it
and to Dungannon, a vigorous move,
to Assaroe beating your shield,
to Strabane and nearby the River Erne.

Donnchadh Ó Briain proved himself to be a
leader
when his fighting bands stormed beside him,
with his artillerymen shouting out to one another
and his battle standards blowing and bouncing
off their poles.

In Bealach an Díthrimh[10] you performed a feat,
you left Mac Uilliam[11] incapacitated
when you severed both leg and spur together
and Fermanagh you forcefully burned,

buildings and meadows together, in like manner
and Cavan in bright daylight;
you were not content to allow the Lord of Sligo
escape you,
nor Ó Ruairc[12] though he was closely related to
you.

4. Conn Céadchathach, a legendary battle-hardened king.
5. Cairbre Lifeachair, fictional High-King of Ireland.
6. Mythical ancestor of the Eoghanachta, the dominant sept in early
   medieval Munster.
7. Eoghan son of Oilill, beheaded by Béinne Brit in the legendary
   Battle of Mag Muccrama.
8. Brian Bórumha and his son, Murchadh, fell in the Battle of
   Clontarf, in 1014.
9. Lines 37–76 allude to various episodes in the Nine Years War and
   the places in which they occurred.
10. Thus in Annals of the Four Masters, *s.a.* 1590; near Windygap,
    barony of Tirawley, County Mayo.
11. Exceptionally, the allusion here is to an incident which occurred
    before the Nine Years War, in which Mac Uilliam Búrc of Connacht
    lost a foot.
12. Lord of Bréifne, who ruled an area corresponding to modern
    County Leitrim.

1. A kenning for Ireland.
2. James I (1566–1625), successor to Elizabeth I and ruler of the three
   realms of England, Scotland and Ireland.
3. A kenning for Ireland.

The chief of Moylurg[13] you made a prisoner of,
you destroyed Ó Conchubhair,[14]
all the provinces were under your control,
and thence to Tír Briúin[15] of the English.[16]

The men of Meath came under your protection
and the Leinstermen delivered up to you their
    own hostages.
Why should I enumerate these
since, into every town and highway and moor,

knowledge of the standards of this champion
    had reached?
You spent a long day in the mouth of the
    Bandon River[17] fighting
and from there you went to the west of Beare.[18]

Though Don Juan[19] had sufficient military
    strength
he was forced to surrender to you meekly;
he gave an oath and his word
that, if you allowed him to return in dire straits
    to Spain,

he would never show his face to you again in
    Ireland.
He did well in this for he was in great danger
as you put your defence works against him
and placed your eager soldiers on his every side.

When the Lord Deputy[20] was minded to raise
    the siege
you encamped your forces in one place.
Well was the land of Cian[21] smoothed over for
    you,
O son of the kings descended from Tál[22] to
    whom Ireland was given.

I shall again take up the story of your ancestry:[23]
you are of the line of the House of Austria,[24]
a kinsman of the battle-inured king in London[25]
and of the stately king of mighty Spain,[26]

of the king of Poland[27] whose crown was not
    brought low
and of the king of the French,[28] so stout in his
    demands.
Kinsman of the noble king of Bohemia,[29]
of Charlemagne[30] and of Caesar,[31]

and of Paris[32] who fought the prolonged battle
    in Troy,
of the emperor who started the feast[33]
and who gave the kings of the entire world to
    each other.[34]
Kinsman of every other exalted noble.

if death has claimed you as part of his fee
Banba is now without a spouse,
her visage has altered,
she has put on a black in place of a bright
    countenance.

She is blind, she hears not,
she is lamed and incapacitated
in the wake of him with whom she made union,
your separation from each other is pitiful and
    harsh.

I have heard tidings that have tormented the
    men of Ireland.

13. Lord of the Mac Diarmada territory of Magh Luirg in County Roscommon.
14. Of the lordship of Ó Conchubhair Sligigh (O'Conor Sligo).
15. Reading 'Tír' for MS 'Tor'. Tír Briúin (na Sionna) is in north-eastern County Roscommon.
16. Perhaps in the sense 'as said in English', referring to some English form of the name in vogue at that time.
17. In County Cork.
18. An area in West Cork.
19. Don Juan del Aguila, commander of the Spanish forces at the Battle of Kinsale in 1601.
20. Lord Mountjoy, commander of the English forces at Kinsale. That Mountjoy was about to raise the siege but was dissuaded by Donnchadh Ó Briain — if that is the import of these lines — is not recorded elsewhere.
21. A kenning for Ireland.
22. An early ancestor of the O'Briens and of other Thomond families.
23. Some of the following claims for Ó Briain's consanguinity may have been consciously vague.
24. The House of Hapsburg, which provided the emperors of the Holy Roman Empire.
25. James I, King of England, Scotland and Ireland.
26. Philip IV who reigned 1621–65.
27. Sigismund III who reigned 1587–1632.
28. Louis XIII who reigned 1610–43.
29. Frederick (the 'Winter King') reigned 1619–20. A son-in-law of James I (see footnote 25), he was routed by the Emperor Ferdinand II in 1620, but lived on until 1632.
30. Alias Charles the Great (*c.* 742–814), acclaimed and crowned as Emperor of the West.
31. The outstanding Roman general, dictator and statesman, Gaius Julius Caesar (*c.* 100–44 BC).
32. Paris's flight with Helen, wife of Menelaus of Sparta, led to the legendary Battle of Troy.
33. A reference perhaps to the Emperor of Rome and the account of the wedding feast found in the Early Modern Irish version of the romance of William of Palerne (*Eachtra Uilliam*).
34. Or perhaps 'which brought the kings of the world together'.

SEAL DÁ RABHAS GAN FHONN GAN AOIBHNEAS
(On Diarmaid Ó Briain, Baron Inchiquin) (1624)

[Caitlín Dubh's elegy for Diarmaid Ó Briain is quite different to that she composed for his more august kinsman the 4th Earl (see preceding text). This one is more pensive, setting a melancholy scene for the arrival of Aoibheall, Thomond's pre-eminent *bean sí* (see pp. 242–9) and a cipher for the poet in her role as *bean chaointe*, 'keening woman'. Its effort to produce a providentialist moral also suggests Diarmaid's death was keenly felt. His youthfulness, sensitivity, physical attractiveness and generous nature are all noted but the attention paid to his probity and honourableness is what really stands out.

Text (from Maynooth, St Patrick's College Library, MS M 107, pp. 198–200) and translation are provided, as before, by Liam P. Ó Murchú.]

Caitlín Dubh cecenit do Dhiarmaid Ó Bhriain
.i. An Barún.

Seal dá rabhas gan fhonn gan aoibhneas
ag féachain cuain fhuairghil na bhfaoileann
treathuidhe tonn ag teacht chum tíre
's gothaibh ciach ag tiacht chum tíre,

gáir na n-eón tráthnóna ag scaoileadh;
súil dá dtugas ag amharc im thimchioll
do chonnarc chúm go tuirseach Aoibheall,
an bhean cheannsa sheanda shíodha.

Do shuidh im fhochair do labhair go caoin liom
d'fhiafraigh do bhriathraibh dhíomsa:
'Ó, a Dhia, an raibh bean riamh mar taoimse
ag siubhal chnoc 's ag gabháil gaoithe,

ag téigheadh mo bhos 's ag dortadh mo
    chaomhchruith,
ar choill na ndos gan neach dom dhídean,
ag siubhal na sreabh gan bharc gan slighe agum?'
Adubhartsa léi 's níor bhréag dhamh innsin

gur seacht fearr a cás ná mar bhímse
gur bhris an chumhaidh lúdrach mo chroidhe
    ionnam,
d'imthigh mo lúth chum siubhail níl brígh
    ionnam
ní aithnighim an lá seach an oidhche,

mar tá Éire d'éis a claoidhte,
do bhuail sí an béim, níl feidhm a caoineadh,
tá sí leónte breóidhte taobhlag
i ndiaidh na foirne do mhóirshliocht Mhíleadh.

Adubhairt Béibhionn na dtromscoth
    ndlaoitheach:
'Ná bídh leó ní cóir a gcaoineadh
seanfhocal é atá ag Cáto scríobhtha
ní thig grian gan athrughadh síne.

Gnáthach doilbheas i ndeóidh aoibhnis
tig an tráigh d'éis láin na taoide
mar átá an clársa i ndeaghaidh na ríoghmhac.'
An t-iarla triaithbheartach daoineach,

an Barún badh tacamhail fuighle,
mac Uí Bhriain dá ngialladh mílte
is Diarmaid do chuir ciachbhruid ar dhaoine,
is diachair fá chliathaibh a gcroidhe isteach.

Lán beóil do chuir brón ar dhaoine
spéacláir na mbocht, scoth na ríoghmhac
lionnán dearmhuid d'fhág gach rígh aguinn
críoch iúil na n-óg chloinne Míleadh.

Cearchaill chliar Innse an Laoigh thu
aontsúil dot shórt san ord diadhachta
daltán is Manannán na ndraoithe
planda séimh do phréimh na ríoghradh,

péarla don déamond badh daoire
siansa bainfhiadhadh 's a mbrígh thu.
Is iomdha meirdreach bhaoth dot chaoineadh
is cearrbhach taobhnocht ó phlé an dísle,

mnáibh méirgheala ag tréigean a ndlaothfholt
ag maothughadh a néamhrosc gach laoi umat,
táid mnáibh aosta i ngéarbhruid chnaoidhte
is táid baird Éireann béaltais claoidhte.

Gach cléireach dá léaghadh an Bíobla
ní léir dho éinlitir síos de,
ó t'éagsa chlaonadar fiodhbha
ní réabaid éisc shrotha a líonta.

Ní léimeann réidhdhamh tar slighe amach
ní fhéadann cú béalfhada síneadh air,
ní éirghid na réalta san oidhche
táid spéarthaibh an aedhair ar aoinchrith

ó th'éagsa a lámh dhéanta na daonnacht
nár ob éigse fá spréidh do shíneadh
nach tug méinn do shéadaibh saoghalta
ná fuath chéile a dhéanamh ar aoinneach,

acht searc don mhaith is ceas re cinnteacht,
nár char bean tar cheart a caoimhthigh
nár ghlac breab ar bhreath do chlaonadh
nár bhain don lag ceart a shinnsear,

acht fáilte don tsean is maith do dhéanamh.
Mo ghrádhsa an fhlaith do mhaicne Mhíleadh,
do shliocht Chais nár thais le biodhbhaibh,
Éibhir is Éilim mic Críomhthainn,

is Chormaic mhic Airt tug cath Mídhe,
Ghearailt Ghréagaigh is Néill naomhtha
is Fhearghuis neartmhair do sheasaimh san innse.
Más mar éiric do ghlac Críost tu

ina ndéanadh na tréinfhirse 'dhíomas,
do chuir an leac san bhfeart mar dhíon ort,
d'fhág súd cnead faoi chreataibh laochradh.
Scéal do leath ar feadh na críche –
go ndéanadh bean gan neart a gcuibhreach!
uch! mo chreach! níl neart gan innsin.

TRANSLATION

Caitilín Dubh composed this for Diarmaid
Ó Briain, the Baron.

Once, when I was dejected and joyless,
gazing at the gull-filled cool bright harbour,
as stormy waves hit the land
and grief laden voices were heard,

and as the evening birds released their cries,
casting an eye about me
I saw Aoibheall approach me wearily,
the gentle, ancient fairy woman.

She sat next to me and addressed me gently
and enquired of me in these words:
'O, God, was any woman ever like me,
traversing wind-swept mountains,

'beating my palms and marring my looks
in thick woods where no one shelters me,
crossing streams boatless and directionless?'
I replied to her truthfully,

saying she was seven times better off than I was
since sorrow has broken my heart,
I have lost my vigour, I cannot walk,
I do not distinguish day from night,

for Ireland has been worsted,
she has lost her balance, it is no good to mourn
   for her,
she is broken, sick and weak in body
after that band of the great line of Míle.[1]

Béibhionn[2] of the heavy ringlets said:
'Do not heed them, it is not right to keen them,
an old saying written by Cato[3] has it
that there is no sunshine without a weather-
   change.

'Sadness follows every joy,
the ebb follows the full tide,
so this land is in the wake of the royal sons.'
The great-hosted earl of lordly deeds,

and the Baron of encouraging words —
the son of Ó Briain[4] to whom thousands
   submitted,
and Diarmaid[5] — have enslaved men to sorrow
and have sent a pang through the ribs to their
   hearts.

A man ever praised has plunged people into
   sorrow,
guiding light of the poor, the flower of princes,
the potion of forgetfulness bestowed on us by
   kings,
the paragon of knowledge for the youth of the
   line of Míle.

Support of the men of art of Inishloe,[6]
you were the one hope for your class in the eyes
   of the church,
a pupil and a very Manannán[7] to the poets,
an affable scion of the descent of kings,

1. Míle Easpáine was regarded as ancestor of the Irish.
2. A fairy woman, and harbinger of death.
3. Roman poet and grammarian, fl. 1st century BC.
4. i.e. Donnchadh, the 4th Earl, son of Conchobhar, the 3rd Earl.
5. The Baron, Diarmaid Ó Briain.
6. An island in barony of Clonderlaw, County Clare.
7. A god associated with exposition of occult knowledge, and with poets.

A jewel of diamond most precious,
sweet melody of ladies and their strength.
Many the foolish harlot keens for you
as does the gambler, threadbare from throwing
  the dice;

white-fingered ladies are abandoning their
  coiffed hair
and every day their eyes flow for you,
elderly matrons are in bitter, wasting misery,
bards have become soft-spoken and subdued.

Every clerk who was wont to read the Bible
cannot now distinguish one letter of it,
since your death woods have declined,
fish in streams no longer rend the nets.

The sleek deer does not leap across the
  pathway,
the long snouted hound does not run in pursuit,
the stars no longer rise by night,
the ethereal skies are a quaking mass

since your death, O hand that dispensed charity,
who did not snub men of art in distributing
  wealth,
who did not covet worldly goods,
who did not cause any man to despise his wife,

but who loved the good and who met
  miserliness with excess,
who loved no woman beyond the rights of her
  lover,

who could not be bribed in order to pervert a
  judgement,
who did not deny the weak their ancestral rights,

but who took delight in welcoming the old and
  in doing good.
Bravo the nobleman of the sons of Míle,
of the line of Cas[8] who was not soft with enemies,
of Éibhear[9] and Féidhlim son of Críomhthann,[10]

of Cormac mac Airt[11] who fought the Battle of
  Mídhe,[12]
of Gerald the Greek,[13] of Niall the devout[14]
and of mighty Fearghus[15] who defended in the
  island.
If Christ has taken you in retribution

for the arrogance of those warriors
and has placed a tombstone over you,
that has caused such a pain in the hearts of
  warriors
that a strengthless woman could bind them.
The tidings have spread throughout the land,
woe is me! — they must be told.

8. Cas, alias Cormac Cas, was eponym of the Dál gCais, from whom
    the O'Briens claimed descent.
9. One of the sons of Mile.
10. A ninth-century king of Munster.
11. Legendary king of Ireland.
12. Probably refers to Cormac's taking of Tara (in Midhe) from the
    usurper Mac Con.
13. Ancestor of the Irish Geraldines who boasted Greek ancestry.
14. Niall of the Nine Hostages, who brought Patrick to Ireland.
15. An eminent Ulster warrior.

TADHG (MAC DÁIRE) MAC BRUAIDEADHA

(c. 1550–post 1624)

DO B'FHEARR MO SHEACHNA, A SHÍLE
(For Síle, Daughter of Éamonn)
(c. 1580?)

[Arrogance was a trademark of the poets. This poem works hard to suggest that Mac Bruaideadha's indignation with the addressee is less shocking than the fact that she challenged him on a point of learning (ironically, his main patron was Donnchadh Ó Briain, for whom an elegy by the *female* poet Caitilín Dubh appears above). Her transgression against gender is weighed against his claim that 'even if we had . . . had the same training, I should have a superiority over thee'. He stops just short of threatening her with physical disfigurement, which he claims to be able to inflict through satirizing. Conclusive evidence is lacking, but it is possible that the addressee was of the Búrc sept of Castleconnell in County Limerick, and was the wife of Sir Seaán (son of Oilivéar son of Seaán) Mac

Uilliam Búrc of Lower Connacht (County Mayo), who
died in November 1580. If so, Sir Seaán is probably the
'Mac Uilliam' referred to in the final quatrain. Sir Seaán
Mac Uilliam was regarded as peaceable and courteous, by
English and Irish alike. The Lord Deputy, Sir Henry
Sidney, gave this account of him to the council in 1576: 'I
founde McWilliam very sensible: though wanting the
English tongue, yet understanddinge the lattin; a louer of
quiett and cyvilitie' (cf. Standish Hayes O'Grady,
Catalogue of Irish Manuscripts in the British Museum, vol. 1
[London: British Museum, 1926], pp. 404, 426). One can
only speculate as to his attitude to this dispute.

Text and translation: Lambert McKenna (ed.),
Aithdioghluim Dána, 2 vols (Dublin: Irish Texts Society,
1939, 1940), vol. 1, pp. 168–71; vol. 2, pp. 100–2.]

1

Do b'fhearr mo sheachna, a Shíle,
fiú ar fhéachas d'iúl sheinlíne,
a throigh náir chéimiodhan chorr,
nar cháir éilioghadh orom.

2

Dom dhearbhadhsa, a dhreach mhálla,
fuair tú nó ar tí teagmhála
ceisd cheilge nar dhiamhair dhún
nó is d'iarraidh m'fheirge d'fhadúdh.

3

Narbh fhiú liom labhra chorrach
tug mé ar th'aghaidh urromach
re hucht [coimhrighe], a chúl slim,
is rú oirbhire im inntinn.

4

Do bhádar adhbhair eile
liom bhós fa bheith céilleidhe
sinn éadána ar th'fhabhra mall
damhna th'éagcára d'fhulang.

5

Níor chuir mé i n-iongna oruibh
— cuid eile dom adhbhoruibh —
gan bheith fortuill i bhfoghluim
dod dhreich fholttruim abhramhuill.

6

Ní [tú] as cionntach, a chiabh lag,
'n-a bhfuil d'aineolas orad,
a chunn sídh bhoigInnse Breagh;
bídh ar th'oidibhse a aithbhear.

7

[Céillidh th'aitheasg], a fholt tiogh,
séaghuinn osgailte th'aigneadh
lucht foghluimthe acht nach fuair sibh,
a ghruaidh dhonnghairthe dhílligh.

8

Do faighreadh — feirrde m'aigneadh —
meise, a bhaisréidh bhrághaidghgeal,
nach mealltair go hollamh ionn
i gceardchaibh ollamh Éirionn.

9

Dámadh ionann — mar nach eadh —
oideas dúinn, a dhreach áilghean,
ná [hiongantaigh], a chiabh cham,
go mbiadh [th'iomarcaidh] agam.

10

Dall cách i gceird ar-oile;
cur riom, a rosg seabhcoidhe,
i gcroiniceacht níor chéim dhuit,
a shéimh fhuighilcheart ordhruic.
11

Ní hionann sinne is sibh féin;
ní chuirfinn, a chruth soiléir,
geall ar ghníomh ríoghnamhuil ruibh
do dhíol d'fhíormhodhuibh ionnuibh.

12

Níor bh'fhíor, a inghean Éamoinn,
— dámadh fhíor ní aibéaroinn
red dhreich seing mbairrleabhair mbinn —
go mbeinn d'airrdheanaibh inghill.

13

Ní hinghill — ní hiongna liom —
leat meise ar mhaille gcéimeann
ná ar ghlór mín i n-uair annuimh
ná ar fhuaim shídh do shaorchlannuibh.

14

Ná ar dhuasaibh móra mionca
ná ar fhoisdine n-aigionta
ná ar chruth gcaomh mbonnbhán mbanda
ná ar chomhrádh saor séaghanda.

15

Ní mar sin duitse, a dhearc-mhall;
do-rinnis d'éagcóir oram
cur ghill na [foghluime] féin
linn mar [fhoghlaime aigbhéil].

16
Do bheanais — níor bheanta dhuit —
a bhaincheann chríche Cormuic
— bheith réidh ní héadóigh uime —
béim san éagcóir oruinne.

17
Feirrde an rún do-rinne sinn
dámadh áil liom nach léigfinn
led chneas nglainrighin ngéag dtrom
méad bhur n-aindlighidh orom.

18
Ar son nar bh'fhíor a rád ruibh
ní budh iomnár let aghaidh
clár finnleargan do ghruadh ngeal
d'imdheargadh uam do b'éidear.

19
Do ghealfadh mé an malaigh nduibh
's do-ghéanuinn dubh 'n-a dheaghuidh
do thaobh chneasaolta mar chailc
do thaobh mh'easaonta d'adhaint.

20
Na ruisg gorma ar ghné an oighridh
do dheargfuinn iad d'fhorfhoighlibh
gríosadh th'aighthe acht nar dhual damh
['s do ghruadh] gairthe do ghormadh.

21
Gan chrithir m'fheirge d'fhiuchadh
fa ndearnais orm d'éiliuchadh
dod chéibh bharrúrthais shaoir shing
do thaoibh andúthchais fhuilgim.

22
Saoth liom nach do mhnáibh Muimhneach
tusa, a bhanda bhionnfhuighleach,
feadh do bhaoghlaighthe im bhuain ruinn,
a ghruaidh shaorghairthe shéaghuinn.

23
Dámadh d'Íbh Briain do bharr slim
ní fhuighthea a n-uarais d'uirim
nó d'Íbh Carthaigh Chuain Innse
— marthain uaim don fhuirinnse.

24
Fuil Cholladh fad chneas mar thuinn
lá na feirge dá bhfeasuinn
nó fuil mhaithmheach chaoin ó gCais
dob aithreach dhaoibh a ndearnais.

25
Duach mhac Briain do bheith umad
ó 'd-chuala, a chúl bachullag,
an aicmeise fad ghnúis ghluin
budh cúis mh'aintreise oruibh.

26
Breitheamh córach Clár na Niall
go bhfaice mé Mac Uilliam;
ní am aghaidh as cóir a dhul,
cóir im fhalaidh ní iarrobh.

TRANSLATION

1
It had been better to leave me alone, O Síle; my knowledge of your ancestry was such that I should not have been challenged on it, O smooth, modest, guileless foot.

2
'Twas to test or attack or anger me that thou, O gentle face, didst ask me that guileful question — no puzzling one for me.

3
My not caring for rough controversy made me indulgent to thee, O graceful curls, rather than quarrel with thee, feeling an impulse in my heart to revile thee.

4
There were other reasons, too, for my restraint; my respect for thy noble brow made me bear with thy injustice.

5
I was not surprised — this was another of my reasons — that thy heavy-haired noble-browed head was weak in lore.

6
Thou art not to blame for thy ignorance; thy teachers bear the blame, O waving hair, queen of peace in the Breagha's soft Isle.

7
Sensible is thy speech, vigorous and frank thy judgement, but thou hast not known learned men, O thick hair and bright brown graceful cheek.

8

I was trained in the smithies of Eire's sages; that has perfected my mind so that I do not easily make blunders, O smooth hand and fair bosom.

9

Think it not strange, O gentle eye, that, even if we had — as we have not — had the same training, I should have a superiority over thee.

10

Everyone is blind in his neighbour's art; 'twas foolish of thee to strive with me in history, O hawk-eye, gentle, fair-spoken, renowned lady.

11

We are different from each other, O fair form; I could not compete with thee in any queenly deed which would match thy fair manners.

12

It would not be true, O daughter of Éamonn — even if it were I would not say it — that I could rival in qualities thy shapely, fair, delicate, sweet face.

13

I am unequal to thee — naturally — in majesty of gait, in gentle rare-spoken voice, or, in reconciling nobles;

14

In giving many goodly gifts, in steadiness of purpose, in fair white-footed queenly form, in noble courteous speech.

15

Thy conduct to me was different (from mine to thee), O soft eye; thou hast, unjustly to me, challenged lore, a dangerous lake as thou now learnest.

16

Thou hast struck at me — thou shouldst not have done so — an unfair blow, O princess of Cormac's Land; but reconcilement is to be hoped for.

17

Good was the resolve I had made, that, even if I felt inclined to do so, I would not let thy fair stately full-limbed form go unpunished for thy great injustice to me.

18

Though it might not have been right to say aught to thee to shame thy face, I could have reddened the fair surface of thy bright cheeks.

19

I could have whitened thy dark eye-brow, and then have blackened thy lime-white skin owing to my anger being enkindled.

20

By my words I could have reddened thy ice-blue eyes, but I thought it not right to burn thy face and disfigure thy bright cheek.

21

I suffer thy challenge to me and I let not the flame of my anger burn, only because thou art of a foreign race, O noble graceful soft fresh hair.

22

When thou didst venture to attack me, I was sorry thou wert not a woman of Mumha,[1] O sweet-voiced gentle lady, bright and noble majestic cheek.

23

Had thy graceful head belonged to the Í Bhriain or the Í Charthaigh of Cuan Innse[2] — all hail to that stock! — thou wouldst not have been so gently treated.

24

When I was in wrath, had I learned that the Collas' blood flowed neath thy skin or the tender noble blood of Í Chais, thou wouldst have rued thy deed.

25

But when I heard, O soft-tressed hair, that Duach son of Brian was thy ancestor his blood in thy noble face caused my gentleness to thee.

26

May Mac Uilliam, just judge of the Nialls' Plain, look with favour on me; he has no cause to attack me; I shall not be asking pardon for a crime.

1. Munster.
2. A harbour in Munster, perhaps near Dunboy in west Cork.

PIARAS FEIRITÉAR

(d. 1653)

LÉIG DHÍOT TH'AIRM, A MHACAOIMH MNÁ
(Lay Your Weapons Down, Young Lady)

[As an experienced soldier as well as a poet, Piaras Feiritéar's appreciation of military conceits was likely to be keen. The heading 'Captaen Piaras Feiritear *cecinit* 1547' precedes this poem in one manuscript, the date perhaps in error for 1647.

The image of a dangerously armed woman is dramatically sustained. Her assailant's threats of royal restraint are useless in the face of her silent weapons: it is he who will surrender. The addressee is named obliquely in the final quatrain. Text and translation: S. Ó Tuama and T. Kinsella, *An Duanaire 1600–1900: Poems of the Dispossessed*, pp. 96–101.]

Léig dhíot th'airm, a mhacaoimh mná,
    muna fearr leat cách do lot;
muna léige th'airm-se dhíot,
    cuirfead bannaidhe ón rígh ort.

Má chuireann tú th'airm ar gcúl,
    folaigh feasta do chúl cas,
ná léig leis do bhráighe bhán
    nár léig duine de chách as.

Má shaoileann tú féin, a bhean,
    nár mharbhais aon theas ná thuaidh,
do mharbh silleadh do shúl mín
    cách uile gan scín gan tuaigh.

Dar leat féin gé maol do ghlún,
    dar fós acht gé húr do ghlac,
do loit gach aon — tuig a chiall —
    ní fearra dhuit scian nó ga.

Folaigh orthu an t-ucht mar aol,
    ná faiceadh siad do thaobh bog;
ar ghrádh Chríost ná faiceadh cách
    do chíoch roigheal mar bhláth dos.

Folaigh orthu do rosg liath,
    má théid ar mharbhais riamh leat;

ar ghrádh th'anma dún do bhéal,
    ná faiceadh siad do dhéad gheal.

Ní beag dhuit ar chuiris d'éag.
    cé shaoile nach cré do chorp;
folaighthear leat th'airm go cóir —
    ná déana níos mó de lot.

Más lór leat ar chuiris tim,
    sula gcuirthear sinn i gcré,
a bhean atá rem ro-chloí,
    na hairmsin díotsa léig.

Do shloinneadh, a mhacaoimh mná,
    ní beag liom ar chách mar cheist:
do chuirfeadh soin th'ainm i gcéilll
    dá mbeith a agus é leis.

TRANSLATION

Lay your weapons down, young lady.
    Do you want to ruin us all?
Lay your weapons down, or else
    I'll have you under royal restraint.

These weapons put behind you:
    hide henceforth your curling hair;
do not bare that white breast
    that spares no living man.

Lady, do you believe
    you've never killed, to North or South?
Your mild eye-glance has killed at large
    without the need of knife or axe.

You may think your knee's not sharp
    and think your palm is soft:
to wound a man, believe me,
    you need no knife or spear!

Hide your lime-white bosom,
    show not your tender flank.
For love of Christ let no one see
    your gleaming breast, a tuft in bloom.

Conceal those eyes of grey
  if you'd go free for all you've killed.
Close your lips, to save your soul;
  let your bright teeth not be seen.

Not few you have done to death:
  do you think you're not mortal clay?
In justice, put your weapons down
  and let us have no further ruin.

If you've terrified all you want,
  lady who seek my downfall,
now — before I'm buried in earth —
  your weapons, lay them down.

What your surname is, young lady,
  I leave to puzzle the world.
But add an 'a' or an 'é'
  and it gives your Christian name away . . .

PÁDRAIGÍN HAICÉAD

(*c.* 1604–54)

DÁLA AN NÓINÍN
(To Mary Tobin)
(*c.* 1625?)

[This is one of two extant poems by Pádraigín Haicéad, poet and Dominican priest, for Máire Tóibín; the second was composed after her death (see Volume I, p. 284). It has been suggested that he wrote them before taking holy orders but the evidence to prove this is lacking.

Two different English poems have been mooted as Haicéad's source for 'Dála an Nóinín', one by the Elizabethan poet Thomas Watson (*c.* 1557–92), and the other by his less well-known and younger contemporary Charles Best (*c.* 1570–1627). The Petrarchan conceit of the mistress as the sun and the lover as a humble flower devotedly turning in her light is found in all three, but the English poems' punning on 'marigold' as the type of the heliotrope is impossible with Irish *nóinín*, 'daisy'. Haicéad's poem also differs in not being constrained into Watson's and Best's 'sonnet' form. The possibility that Haicéad drew on an entirely different source is not to be discounted; he was fluent in Latin and various continental languages.

Text: Máire Ní Cheallacháin, *Filíocht Phádraigín Haicéad* (Baile Átha Cliath: An Clóchomhar, 1962), pp. 3–4. Translation: Michael Hartnett, *Haicéad* (Loughcrew: Gallery Press, 1993), pp. 17–18.]

Dála an nóinín — (ó' d-chí soilse i ngréin
is gearr go gcomhsgaoil clóilíon trilseach géag,
is tráth um nóin laoi, ar dtós dí i gcoim na
   néall,
fáisgidh fóichnín pórdhlaoi chruinn a craobh) —

Mo dháil le hóigín óirnidhe is milse méin,
Máire Tóibín, lóithnín lingthe laoch,
ghrádhmhar ghlóirfhíor ghnóchaoin ghrinnghlic
   ghaoth;
tálaim óm chlí sódh sídhe is sinn lairé,

'S mar fhágbhas m'óighbhríd gcóirchíogh
   gcoimseach mé,
ní fhághaim óm chroidhe comhnaidhe i gcuing
   go gcéill,
acht trácht, ar nós tsíor-nóinín fhinn na raon,
rem bháthadh i mbrónchaoi ghleódhaoir
   ghoilseach ghéir.

Má tá nach dóigh shíl tóraidhe i ndruim a dlaodh,
táinig cróch buidhe i gcoróin naoi a cinn gan
   chré,
fánar cóirigheadh borddhlaoi choinnleach
   chlaon
do tháin na n-eón bhíos ó shín gheimhridh tréith.

Ní táire fóisgríob chló chaoilphinn go ngléas
ná a dhá córrbhraoi ar shnó an daoil
   chionnduibh chéir,
ós ardaibh bórrbhlaoisg mhórdhaidhe a
   lionnruisg léith,
láimh re sómplaíbh róis trí fhionn 'na gné.

Cáidh 's is cóir í a sróinín; slim a taobh;
breághdha a beól caoin; cróichíor chruinn a
   déad;
álainn óghshnoighe a meóir mhín trilseas gréas,
is sgáil a sgornaighe fó mbíonn sgim ar aol.

Ní sáimhe ceól sídhe i bhfóidtír inse Néill,
's i gcáil ní glóraighe geóin tsaoi sheinnte téad,
ná rádha róchaoin bheóilín bhinn na bé,
sás ler thóg sí an ceó bhí ar m'intinn féin.

Cé tharla slóighlíon d'óigshíol Ghoill is
        Ghaoidheal,
i gcásaibh cróilighe ó a ghrís tinnsheirc tréimhs',
i n-áitibh óglaoich an ngeóbha sí sbreill mar mé?
Ní fearr mo bheó, 's ní móide í sinn iar n-éag.

TRANSLATION

Like the daisy when first it sees the sun
and its interlocking petals loosen all at once
or in the evening at the first cloud's cover
when its seedhead by a leaf is sheltered over:

so I, when this sweet distinguished friend —
Mary Tobin, breath of air, that storms the
        fighting men;
my true-voiced love who moves with gentle
        ease —
when I'm with her my heart pours out a gentle
        peace;

and if she leaves, my virgin of the perfect breasts,
my heart does not allow me sensibly to rest
but moves like the white eternal daisy of the
        field
and drowns me in the clamour of a bitter grief.

Though fruits do not seed on the crown of her
        head
yet the crocus comes forth, where there is no
        earth
and around goes a plait, glittering, in the form
of a birdflock tired from a winter storm.

A stroke from a sharpened quill is not more slim
than her eyebrows black as the beetle's wing
above her eyes — two spheres of liquid grey —
the archetypal rose is in the whiteness of her
        face;

her fine and smooth and well-proportioned nose,
her gentle lips that well-shaped teeth enclose —
lovely her holy hand fashioning needlework,
lovely her throat's hue beside which lime seems
        dull.

Entrancing music in our land gives not more
        peaceful sound,
the expert harpist's air has no more eloquence
than the smallest saying of her sweet mouth
that lifts the fog that clouds up all my sense.

Many young men come, all of Norman-Irish
        seed,
unmanned in the embers of their aching need;
instead of these, to choose such a wretch as I?
No better than death my life: no richer she that
        I die.

CHUM MO CHARAD ÓN BHFRAINC GO hÉIRINN
(To My Friend, from France to Ireland)
(*c.* 1635)

[Pádraigín Haicéad knew Éamonn Mac Piarais Buitléar, 3rd Baron Dunboyne, since childhood: Haicéad's mother was related to the Dunboyne branch of the Butlers of Ormond and he may have been fostered at Éamonn's home in Kiltinan Castle, near Fethard in County Tipperary. At any rate, Haicéad's affection for Éamonn was profound and lasting. In his moving elegy on Éamonn's death in 1640, one of the earliest extant in regular *caoineadh* metre, Haicéad says he has more reason to grieve than all the multitudes who keen him.

Having joined the Dominican Order in Ireland in 1625, Haicéad lived for some time in Louvain (*c.* 1628–34), Rennes (*c.* 1634–5) and Paris (*c.* 1635), before returning home in 1638. The following poem, addressed to Éamonn from France, is packed with terms for love: *tnúth, annsa, gean, muirnín, dúthracht, fonn*. Its pun on *toil*, 'will; passion; semen', recalls other Elizabethan puns on 'spirit' as both 'soul' and 'semen', or 'will (Will Shakespeare)' as 'will' and 'penis'. It plays daringly with grammatical and social gender to suggest the fluidity of the latter. Inevitably, this aspect loses in translation, even in Michael Hartnett's sympathetic version.

Text: Máire Ní Cheallacháin (ed.), *Filíocht Phádraigín Haicéad*, pp. 10–12. Translation: Michael Hartnett, *Haicéad*, pp. 28–30.]

Mór mo thnúth-sa lem Thoil féin,
ó thánag tar tuinn n-aigéin;
ise mar a bhfuil a fonn,
is mise fá oil eachtrann.

Ise i n-Éirinn na ríogh,
is mise i bhFrainc na bhfiairbhríogh;
ise i n-iathaibh a síthe,
is mise i gcliathaibh coigcríche.

Ó do fhághbhas Inis Fáil
mo Thoil níor chinn im chomhdháil;
fuair fear oile ar a annsa
gean mo Thoile thoram-sa.

Tar m'éis tsiar ó shoin i le
níor sgar leis lá ná oidhche,
ó ghríbh shéaghain na gciabh gcam,
aniar gan fhéaghain oram.

Leis do mealladh mo Thoil te,
triath daoineach Dhúna Búinne,
Éamann an chuirnín chasda,
muirnín gnéadhonn gníomhghasda.

Isin gcuradh 'na gcruth féin
tréithe gach saoi fa shoiléir,
aisde gach céime i gcalmacht,
gaisge, féile is flathamhlacht.

Gníomhaidh greagha, grádhaidh ceól,
díolaidh dán, dia do chineól!
bronnaidh ionar, ór is eadh,
go n-ól ag siobhal síorfhleadh.

Leanaidh connradh, corcraidh lann,
snoighidh céis croidhe a dhearnann;
feadh na raide sonnaidh sleagh,
maide mullaigh na míleadh.

Mo chean do tar gach nduine
d'fhoirnibh oirir Iughaine,
fear súlmhór is sáimhe reacht,
úrlón dáimhe is dílleacht.

Fear cothaighthe clú Bhanbha,
oirdhearcach na hathardha,
seangán seanachadh na bhFionn,
leannán ealathan Éireann.

Cú Chulainn chóige Dáire,
cú bheirtha gach bhanbháire,
cú fíochdha feithimh na bhfonn,
beithir líomhtha na lánghlonn.

Ón mBriotáin chum an éin fhinn
beannacht uaim-se go hÉirinn;

do ní lingthe an bheannacht bhocht,
beannacht dingthe do dhúthracht.

Ní sámh seasamh ná suidhe
go n-imgheam dá ionnsuidhe;
an laoch d'amharc sonn ba sódh;
m'fhonn dá radharc is ró-mhór.

TRANSLATION

Much I envy my own will
since I went ocean-travelling:
from her desire she never goes
while I'm the butt of foreign jokes;

she in royal Ireland stays,
I, in France of the crooked ways:
she is in her land at peace
and I among foreign phalanges.

When I left the Irish shore
my will's will was to stay at home,
another man, to her most dear,
received her love instead of me.

Left way behind me ever since
his side she never quits;
from her hero, curly-haired
a look she never throws my way.

My ardent will, she was beguiled
by the leader of Dunboyne —
Éamonn of the curling hair
beloved, noblefeatured, brave.

Clearly in his fighter's face
appear the traits of every sage;
the pattern of the brave is here,
skill and generosity.

Music-lover, stallion-rider,
pays for poems: bless his kindness!
bestowing tunics, gold and rings
and drink at endless feastings;

keeps his promise, bloodies blades,
the small carved harp his hand has made;
to the hilt he thrusts his spear,
poets' and orphans' provisioner.

He maintains his country's fame
splendid in his native place,
slim hero of this ancient land,
lover of our Irish arts.

A new Cúchulainn, Munster's hound,
victorious in every bout:
territorial watchdog he,
licked bear of total bravery.

To that white bird, from Brittany
a blessing on Ireland comes from me:
he should not shrink from my poor prayer
packed as it is with loving grace.

Sitting or standing, uneasy till
I go home to visit him:
even to have him here would please me
so very great is my need to see him.

ANONYMOUS

CONGAIBH ORT, A MHACAOIMH MNÁ
(Hold On, Young Girl)

[Robin Flower titled his translation of this poem 'Death
and the Lady' (*Poems and Translations*, p. 135), Frank
O'Connor called his 'Death and the Maiden' (*Kings, Lords
and Commons*, p. 63), and the text has been discussed
under the rubric of the *danse macabre*, with the speaker
regarded as Death himself. The translation by the present
editor, more literal than Flower's and O'Connor's,
interprets the poem quite differently and aims to bring out
a perceived homoeroticism. Text: T.F. Ó Rathile, *Dánta
Grádha*, p. 138.]

Congaibh ort, a mhacaoimh mná,
    gabh mo theagasg madh áil leat:
congaibh h'intinn go fóill,
    cuimhnigh oram, ná pós fear!

Gion go ngeabhthá teagasg uaim
    a stuaigh mhíolla na ngruaidh ngeal,
(ní haithnidh dhuit mé go fóill),
    cuimhnigh oram, ná pós fear!

Má tá nách aithnidh dhuit féin
    an corp seang nách léir do neach,
nó an chíoch chruinn ceiltear le sról,
    cuimhnigh oram, ná pós fear!

Ná braitear do ghrádh ná t'fhuath,
    ná nocht h'intinn go luath leamh,
ceil do rún, taisigh do phóg,
    cuimhnigh oram, ná pós fear!

Cuimhnigh oram, ná pós fear,
    tiocfa mise, an mar tá,
dot fhéachain gidh deacair tocht;
    congaibh ort, a mhacaoimh mná.

TRANSLATION

Hold on, young girl,
Heed my words if you will;
Don't be drawn for a while,
Think of me, wed no man.

If you won't hear me out
(You don't know me yet),
Then, lady of the bright brow,
Think of me, wed no man.

Even if you don't know
Your slender body seen by none
And the full breast hid in satin,
Think of me, wed no man.

Neither love nor loathing show,
Leave your inner thoughts unsaid,
Keep your secret, save your kiss,
Think of me, wed no man.

Think of me, wed no man,
I *will* come — stay as you are —
To pay you court, no matter what;
Young girl, hold on.

CEARBHALL Ó DÁLAIGH

(*fl.* 1630?)

FADA AR gCOTHROM Ó CHÉILE
(Far from Equal are We Two)
(*c.* 1630?)

[Cearbhall Ó Dálaigh may or may not have composed the well-known song 'Eibhlín a rún' (for which, see Volume I, pp. 307–8) but there is no reason to doubt the attribution to him of this syllabic poem or the one in *amhrán* metre that follows it. The *amhrán* occurs in a manuscript dated 1679, where it is titled 'Cearbhall Ó Dálaigh, for Eileanór, Daughter of Sir Murchadh Caomhánach' (Kavanagh). The syllabic poem is elsewhere headed 'A little love-lay addressed by Cearbhall Ó Dálaigh to his lady-love, Eileanór Chaomhánach'. His home was at Pallice, hers at Clonmullen Castle, both in County Wexford. The earliest source for the story of their elopement is Joseph Cooper Walker's *Historical Memory of the Irish Bards* (1786). According to Walker, Ó Dálaigh, disguised as an itinerant harper, won her heart when he sang 'Eibhlín a rún' to the harp. A poem addressed to Ó Dálaigh by his contemporary Pádraigín Haicéad gives confirmation of his reputation as poet and musician. Far more eloquent, however, are Ó Dálaigh's own words in praise of Eileanór's talent for music and writing, in the second poem below.
Text: T.F. Ó Rathile, *Dánta Grádha*, pp. 78–9. This new translation is by Seamus Deane.]

Fada ar gcothrom ó chéile,
mise is mo chéile chumainn, —
mise go ndíoghrais uimpi,
's gan í go suilbhir umainn.

Go dtréigfeadh mise ar shaibhreas
níl ann acht ainbhfios céille,
's nach tréigfinn mo bhean chumainn
's a teacht chugainn 'na léine.

Aici-se is ualach éadrom
a searc, is tréantrom oram,
's nach déanann goimh dom ghalar, —
ó chéile is fada ar gcothrom.

TRANSLATION

Far from equal are we two,
For I love her to the full
And 'tis pity, but 'tis true
To me she's noticeably cool.

She's daft enough to think wealth
Sufficient excuse to leave me.
Were she left standing in her pelt
I'd stay with her, believe me.

Though love's no burden for her — she
Bears it lightly, while its weight
Hangs on me — even this inequality
Does not twist my love to hate.

DO MHÚSCAIL MÉ TAR ÉIS LUÍ ARAOIR GO SÁIMH
(To Eleanor Kavanagh)
(*c.* 1630?)

[See preceding headnote. The text is based on copies in Dublin, Trinity College Library, MS 1399, fo. 189b, and MS 1367, p. 118; and London, British Library, MS Egerton 127, fo. 30b. The translation is by Seamus Deane.]

Do mhúscail mé tar éis luí araoir go sámh,
'S do-chiú rem thaobh aon bhruinneall mhín
    tais mhná
ba múinte méin mhaorga 's ba críonna cáil
d'úrfhuil réidh déithe nó ríthe d'fhás.

Ar dtús do léig séaghainn na mbraoithe dtáir
Go lúfar léir scaoth do ghaethaibh Chupído im'
    dháil,
Is túirseach tréith tréanlag tug mo chroí 'na
    chneáibh
Tré úrlainn ghéir chaol-nimhe shoighde an ghrá.

A-dúirt an ghéag shaor leabhair shíthe sháimh
Re múisic shéimh tar éis mise dhí do chrá:
'Biaidh tú red' ré i ngéibheann' ar sí, 's i bpáis
go smuainfir cé an té chuir na gaoithe grá.'

Do shiúlas féin Éire fo thrí 'na deaghaidh,
go ciúin-Locha Cé éigneach, Eas Craoibhe 's
   Máigh,
Go múr Locha Léin léigim arís mo stáid,
'S níor thúisce mé ag Éirne nó ag rí-Loch
   nEá'ach.

Go Plúto téim d'fhéachain Chasíotas láich,
I múrbhrog aolta Aonghais do fríodh mo thásc,
Ba siúlach mé ar Dheirdre is ar Aoibheall fáidh,
Ar rúnChraig Léith re chéile, 's ar Chlíona
   cháidh.

Do smuaineas féin tar éis iomad críoch do
   thrácht
Gur chúis leamhbhaoth éadrom gan bhrí mo
   dháil
'S nach dúil don fhréimh dhaonna bhí dom'
   chrá,
Acht Iúnó thréan, Vénus nó Mínervá.

Is lúfar léir caolchrobh an ríbheangáin
Ar liút, ar ghléas shaor-chruite, 's ar vírginál,
Is cumhra séis chaomhghutha a caoin-ghoib
   cháidh
re múisic shéimh shéaghanta chaoin-orgáin.

I gcúirt níl téxa Béarla nach bí aici a sháith
Is dar liúmsa léighidh Gaedhalg mar shaoithibh
   Fáil.
Is dlúth tiubh géar glé a scríbhinn bhláith,
Conclúision: 'Éist! adéaram — is fínit spás.'

TRANSLATION

I woke last night from a deep sleep and by my
   side
I see a young woman, tender and fair, finely-bred
As though from gods or kings, intelligent and
   wise.

From under her jet-black brows a smart rain
Of Cupid's arrows flew, skewered my heart,
Left me slack with their love-envenomed pain.
The fairy scion, music breathing in her voice,
To assuage my pain, said 'You will live in bondage
All your life until you know who made you her
   choice.'

I walked Ireland three times, pursuing her.
   Loch Key[1]
With its harboured salmon, by Eascreeve[2] and
   the Maigue,[3]
Loch Lene's castle[4] twice, the Erne, royal Lough
   Neagh.

Down to Pluto[5] to ask courteous Cassotis I go,
To the white fort of Newgrange, to Deirdre,
   Aoibheall,
I ranged all over arcane Cratloe,[6] to Clíona of
   Mallow.

After much travel I decided my suit, my pursuit
Was a lost and foolish cause. My love was a
   goddess,
Juno, Venus or Minerva, none sprung from
   human root.

This regal woman's little hand is nimble-sharp
On the lute, the soft harpstring, the virginal,
Her voice in her soft mouth is like music of the
   harp.

At court she can master any English text with
   wit.
She reads Irish like the sages of Inis Fáil.
Her script is lovely and clear, thick and close-
   knit.

Conclusion: 'Quiet! I say, space *finit*.'

1. In County Roscommon.
2. On the Bann river, near Coleraine, County Derry.
3. A river in County Limerick.
4. Probably Ross Castle on Loch Lene, County Kerry.
5. The Underworld.
6. Near Kilalloe, County Clare; reputed home of Aoibheall, *bean sí* of
   Thomond.

SÉATHRÚN CÉITINN (GEOFFREY KEATING)

(*c.* 1580–*c.* 1644)

A BHEAN LÁN DE STUAIM
(Woman Full of Guile)
(*c.* 1630?)

[This poem has been anthologized a number of times. English translations almost invariably overlook the last eight lines. In the Irish, their natural-stress metre underlines the way they undo the refusal of love in the strict syllabic quatrains. The Birth of Venus was a classic Renaissance figuration of erotic love.

Text: Pádraig de Brún, Breandán Ó Buachalla, Tomás Ó Concheanainn (eds), *Nua-Dhuanaire 1* (Baile Átha Cliath: Institiúid ArdLéinn Bhaile Átha Cliath, 1971), pp. 15–16. This new translation is by Seamus Deane.]

A fhinnebhean tséimh shéaghanta shárchaoin tsuairc
na muirearfholt réidh raonfholtach fá a ndíol gcuach,
is iongnadh an ghné thaomannach fhásaíos uait;
gé doiligh an scéal, tréig mé agus táig dhíom suas.

Do-bheirimse fém bhréithir dá mbáití an slua
san tuile do léig Vénus 'na táclaí anuas,
a bhurraiceach-bhé mhéarlag na mbánchíoch gcruaidh,
gur tusa mar aon céidbhean do fágfaí im chuan.

TRANSLATION

A bhean lán de stuaim
  coingibh uaim do lámh;
ní fear gníomha sinn,
  cé taoi tinn dar ngrádh.

Féach ar liath dem fholt,
  féach mo chorp gan lúth,
féach ar thraoch dem fhuil —
  créad re bhfuil do thnúth?

Ná saoil mé go saobh,
  arís ná claon do cheann;
bíodh ar ngrádh gan ghníomh
  go bráth, a shíodh sheang.

Druid do bhéal óm bhéal —
  doiligh an scéal do chor —
ná bíom cneas re cneas:
  tig ón teas an tol.

Do chúl craobhach cas,
  do rosc glas mar dhrúcht,
do chíoch chruinngheal bhláith,
  tharraingeas mian súl.

Gach gníomh acht gníomh cuirp
  is luighe id chuilt shuain
do-ghéan féin tréd ghrádh,
  a bhean lán de stuaim.

Woman full of guile,
Refrain. Stay your hand
Love-sick you may be
But I must take my stand.

Look. My hair is grey;
My body's defect
Plain; my blood is thin.
What do you expect?

Do not think I'm open
To your charms. Don't bend
Your head so. O sylph
Not lovers, but friends

Is our role. Your mouth
Is close, but this fire
Of touch, near-touch
Only arouses desire.

Your curling ringlets,
Green, lucent eyes,
Your tender breasts
Win praise in men's eyes.

What wouldn't I do
Short of lying with you?
O knowing woman,
Anything for love of you.

Fluent, fragrant, fascinating woman,
With your coils and ramparts of hair,
You disturb me deeply, intricately,
Release me from this painful snare.

But I swear if the whole world drowned
In those waves which Venus bestrode,
That you, full-bosomed, delicate of hand,
Would find harbour here, in my love's abode.

TADHG Ó RUAIRC

(*fl.* 1684)

GOINIM THÚ, A NAOÍDH BHEG SHÍAR
(A Game of Cards and Dice)
(*c.* 1650?)

[Games such as 'tables' and backgammon frequently figured — and preceded — the pursuits of love. It has not been possible to identify Bláthnat/Blánaid (quatrain 15), but Port Láirge 'Port of Thighs' and Lios Gabhuil 'Groin Fort' (quatrain 7) are to be found on the map of Ireland as Waterford and Lisgoole (cf. 'The Dindshenchas of Port Láirge' at pp. 270–1).
Text: David Greene, '*Un Joc Grossier* in Irish and Provençal', *Ériu*, vol. 17 (1955), pp. 7–15, at pp. 10–11. This new translation is by Derek Mahon.]

Goinim thú, a naoídh bheg shíar
  na bhfolt bfiar ar lí an óir;
s gach dúal díobh go fada fann
  nach gann do shín go barr feóir.

Na rosg líath, na bhféachan mall
  na maladh ngann mar sgríb phinn,
na ngrúadh ngeal, acht corcrós thríodh
  — ochón is tríod ataoím tinn!

An beól corcair ar snúadh cáor,
  s an déad cailce sáor gan mhéid,
an tsrón ndes, an smig nach mór,
  s an píob geal bhen snódh don ghéis.

An tenga bhlasda mhall bhfíor,
  is binne síons no guth téad;
ar chláirsigh, orgáin is liút,
  ní fríth riamh siúd mar ghléas.

Na ngéag úr, na ngeallamh ngeal,
  na meór lag, na niongan ndonn,
do ní gach ceól sithbhinn síor
  bláth ro sgríobh faoilionn fionn.

An uicht mar aól, na ccíoch ccruinn
  ariamh fós nar fhoirnigh fer;
an cuirp shéimhsheing, an táoibh báin,
  — ní seanuim dháoibh dáil mo sherc.

Trúagh gan mise astoigh fo ghlas
  ag mnaoi na mbas mbarrgheal mbúidh;
a bPuirt Láirge na slios ngeal,
  no a Lios Gabhuil na sreabh cciúin!

Do lairge caomh, do ghlún maol,
  do cholpa sáor, do thrácht glan,
do throigh mínbhán, mar uan tonn
  — dighbháil throm a bfaicsin damh.

Do ghoinis mé don taobh astigh,
  le saighdibh géara gráidh ón toil;
imrim ort, is daor romchráidh,
  shúas ar do láimh cuirim goin.

Aón is dó iarruim ort
  — a ghnúis ettrocht, coisg mo bhrón! —
ná mill mo dhísle a ttáobh, a bhen,
  caithfead áon go cert is dó.

Fear gonta od shaighdibh gráidh
  a chongmháil shuas ní dáil ghrinn;
gan caladh uaid dfosgladh dhó,
  más taiplios mhór imrir linn.

Mas tioc díreach no tioc cam
  no maadh gemonn nach mall bhíos;
laingmhír chóir no brannamh cert,
  is trúagh nach léigir mfersa síos.

Ar tí a do, no a ccaladh shíar,
   tabhair ionadh go dían, a shiúr;
don fhior ghonta ro cráidhis féin
   — ní iarruim é acht do thriúr.

Mo dhá dhisle, a naoidh bheg shíar,
   caithim ort go dían a ngrádh;
áon is dó ro chaitheas féin
   ar do sgéimh, a raod bheg mná.

Ós tu Bláthnat, rún mo chléibh,
   aonghrádh cumhra séimh gan ghoimh,
saoilim, óm lot lé do ghrádh,
   nach olc leat mo lámh do ghoin.

Druid um fharradhsa, a ainner na bfiarndlaoi
   nocht,
Cuir lámh tharum, a bhaisgheal na liathriginn
   rosg,
Sguir mh'anshocair, a thaisbhen fhíalmhín bog,
Guin is anacal ar leaba a seadh iarrmáoid ort.

TRANSLATION

I 'take' you, gorgeous adversary,
   you of the wavy gold chevelure,
each curl long and provocative
   reaching down to the forest floor.

Crazy about you, as you know,
   your grey eyes and lingering looks,
your bright cheeks where roses glow,
   the eyebrows like twin pen-strokes,

I watch your lips, so rowan-red,
   the neat nose, the rounded chin,
your fine teeth as white as chalk,
   the swan-white neck that shames the swan.

I listen to the languorous voice
   where your superior nature sings,
a finer sound than organ-pipe
   or lute, sweeter than harp-strings,

and gaze at your clean limbs, shy hands,
   the soft fingers and pink nails
designed to pluck a tremulous note
   or draw ink from quivering quills;

the perfect, opalescent breast
   no knight or rook has made his own,

the slim body, slender waist:
   I yield my heart to you alone.

High time you cornered me, admired
   woman of the skilful palms,
in glistening-sided 'Port of Thighs'
   or 'Groin Fort' of the quiet streams.

I've had my chips if I should glimpse
   a flash of knee or naked side,
the noble ankle, pale instep,
   foot creamy as the incoming tide.

You penetrate my weak defence,
   teasing me with anxious love.
I know the score; my turn to play,
   against your side I make my move.

So put your cards on the table now —
   shuffle the deck, ingenuous face,
and let the dice fall as they will;
   I sacrifice both deuce and ace.

It beats me you can leave erect
   a knight so stricken by desire
unless you're going to let him through:
   it's high stakes we play for here.

Be it tic-tac crooked or tic-tac straight,
   backgammon, checkers, chess, bezique,
strip poker, scrabble, bingo, snap,
   high time you had my man in check.

Above board or in a secret slot,
   sister, quickly make a space
for the poor pawn with whom you toy:
   relieve my vulnerable piece.

Importunately, my darling girl,
   I'm flinging down my double dice
before your beauty, heart and soul,
   aiming at you both ace and deuce.

Blánaid, my dear, my favourite one,
   gentle, fragrant, guileless love,
it's time for you to trump my man
   and 'take' me with a daring move.

Come sit beside me, woman of the wavy hair;
embrace me, bright branch of the cool grey eyes;
resolve my torment, generous-gentle woman,
and 'take' me quickly to your merciful bed.

ANONYMOUS

FÉUCH FÉIN AN OBAIR-SI, A ÁODH
(O Rourke's Wife and Thomas Costello) (*c.* 1650?)

[Frequently translated, this poem generated what became known as 'The *Féuch féin* controversy' (see James Carney, *Studies in Irish Literature and History* (Dublin: Dublin Institute for Advanced Studies, 1955), pp. 243–75). Broadly speaking, two readings of it have been proposed. At first, it was interpreted as a dramatic lyric spoken by a wife, wavering between love for her husband, Aodh Ó Ruairc (Hugh O Rourke), and for Tomás Ó Coisdealbha (Thomas, son of Siurtan, Costello), who is courting her assiduously in Ó Ruairc's absence. Carney identified the named characters as historical: Aodh Ó Ruairc, holder of extensive lands in Dromahaire, County Leitrim, whose death is recorded for 1684, and Tomás Ó Coistealbha, a contemporary Connacht poet. This led him to reject the early interpretation: 'one cannot imagine . . . an Irish poet whose function and profession is to praise his aristocratic patrons, entering into the mind of O'Rourke's wife and publicising her dilemma'. He argued that the poem was an unconventional eulogy in praise of two men. The poet 'speaks as if he were O'Rourke's wife, who is sorely tempted to love Costello. He finally chooses O'Rourke (who is very rich and doubtless his patron) but he does so in a way that Costello will find not unflattering. The whole thing is a conceit . . .' (ibid., pp. 258–9).
    Text: E.J. Gwynn, 'Tomás Costelloe and O'Rourke's Wife', *Ériu*, vol. 9 (1921–3 [1974]), pp. 1–11, at pp. 2–10. Translation: the Earl of Longford, *More Poems from the Irish* (Dublin: Hodges Figgis; Oxford: B.H. Blackwell, 1945), pp. 23–7.]

Féuch féin an obair-si, a Áodh,
a mhic Bhríain, a bhláth fhionn-chráobh,
a ghéucc amhra, is úaisle d'fhás,
sa n-úair-se tharla ar Thomás.

Lúathaigh ort, ainic misi,
má tá tú lé'r ttairsi:
ag so síodh-ruire brúaigh Bhreagh
úaibh dom fhíor-ghuide ós ísiol.

A mheic Bhríain, a bhrath m'éiccsi,
má's díth leat mo leithéid-si,

dom chabhair, a cháomh-shlat ghráidh,
labhair re sáor-mhac Siúrtáin.

Innis dó, le gcur na cenn,
nach mór d'éiccsibh na h-Éirenn,
mur ghné sheisi ó chráoibh Charadh,
meisi dháoibh do dheónughadh.

Ar mo thí an tráth-sa ó tharla
mealtóir an uird ealadhna,
bíodh go ngeallfadh sé mur sin
nach meallfadh mé, ná measaigh.

Dá measda, ní measdar leam
gaduighe fhileadh Éireann,
béd-leomhan do thúar mo thoil
nach éigneochadh úam mh'áontaidh.

Dá mealltáoi ar áoi n-annsa,
na háith, a Áodh, oram-sa:
le brath soibheart chúaine Cuinn
toighiocht úaidhe ní fhédaim.

Minic ticc ar tí ar mbréugtha
Tomás a ttlacht úathmhélta,
do cheilt ar sáoir-eachtra sonn,
a mbeirt dhraoidheachta um dhochum.

Minicc ticc athaidh oile
le m'ais, d'eitil sheabhcaidhe,
a measg cáigh d'fhúadach mh'annsa
'na ghrúagach cáidh chugam-sa.

Mur mhnáoi tháidhe a ttuighin m'fhir
minic ticc sé d'ar soighin
le briocht drúadh, le díamhair ndán,
dom íarraidh úam ar éládh.

Ticc a ndeilbh dháonna dhuine,
ticc fós a ffoirm shíodhuighe,
ticc úair a n-ionnus taidhbhsi:
cionnus úaidh dofhanfainn-si?

A gcéin ar chogadh Clann Néill
gluaister; is cuid dom chaithréim:
sinn ar óigh, derbhtha dhe,
a ndóigh go meallfa mise.

At eccosg-sa, a Áodh úi Rúairc,
minic ticc sonn ar sáor-chúairt
draig ciún-tláith, ór doilghe dul,
oighre Siúrtáin d'ar síabhradh.

Ticc dá theacht 'na Thomás féin
mo chur sechum ar sáobh-chéill,
no gur sguch mh'annsa dha halt,
dam-sa ni guth a ghlúasacht.

Muna ffuil inntleacht éigin
agaib d'fhurtacht m'fhoiréigin,
a sheise, a shengadh ar ngráidh,
do mealladh meisi, a mhacáimh.

Mh'iomlad eadraibh níor fhéd sinn:
do tshearc-sa, a Áodh, um intinn:
ar áoi gur híarnadh na tshás
dom shíabhradh atáoi Tomás.

Da mbeth sochar ruibh a rádh,
coisg dhínn, a dhegh-mhic Siúrtáin,
a rún cáigh, gan chláon n-irsi,
ná cráidh Áodh fam aithghin-si.

A Thomáis, a thocht mheanmnach,
a bhraighe ghill Ghoisdealbhach,
sguir dhínn, ní fheallam ar bfear,
sín ar mhealladh na maighdion.

Ní hionann mé is mná málla
mhealltáoi, a óig andána,
mo shíabhradh ní dóigh dhuit-si,
a ghrían-ghal sháimhshamhraidh-si.

Ná creid cách, ní meirdreach mé,
óg fúarus fios mo chéile:
fada ó tharla Áodh orm-sa,
h'abhra ná cláon chugam-sa.

Bhur bfé fía, ní feárrde dhuit,
aithnim thú d'aimhdheóin th'iomluitt:
a bhraduire, ná mill mé,
fill, a ghaduighe an gháire.

Coscc th'alguis úaim ní bfhuighe,
a bhradín, a bhréccuire:
led úaisli ná meraigh mé,
búail-si um cheanuibh gach críche.

A sháor-mheic Shiúrtáin bhuidhe,
a bhláth choilleadh cumhraidhe,
ar gháol, ar chrodh, nó ar choimsi,
dol ó Áodh ní fhédaim-si.

Ar n-áonta ó nach úair tusa
crum ar do cheird dhúthchusa,
móruigh brígh an chráoi-si Chuinn,
a Náoisi ó n-Ír ar fhoghluim.

A Mhanannáin mhúir Logha,
a Óenghus an fhíor-bhrogha,
a Shíodhmhaill na cceard ccuimsi,
a Fhionnbhairr chealg cugairsi.

A eagna Chorbmaic í Chuinn,
a fháith-chíall oighre Chumhaill,
a sheinm cor, a cherd Ghúaire,
a fhergc Con na Cráoibhrúaidhe.

A thúairgnidh choitchinn chatha,
a mhéduighthóir mhór-ratha,
a linn na n-uile ana,
a chinn uidhe an engnamha.

A chrann sesmhach seóil troide,
a rún díobhuigh dhochroide,
a bhrúcht buinne, a bhedhg nimhe,
a fhercc thuinne tairpidhe.

A theanchuir ghríosaigh an ghráidh,
a ghlór le mbréuccthar ban-dáil,
a phosd gáidh chagaidh d'íbh Cuinn,
ma táim agaibh, ní admhaim.

A Thomáis, d'aithle m'ionnlaigh,
a chuingidh chrú Ghoisdealbhaigh,
atá ar ccridhe da rádh rinn
do ghrádh d'ibhe, dhá n-ibhinn.

Mo bhennacht leat óm lán-toil,
a dhegh-úa dil Dubhaltaigh,
a bhúidh bharr-ghlain, ná brécc mé,
ná damnaigh d'éd ar n-áidh-ne.

Sgarthain so, gidh túar tuirsi,
ag so Áodh dom fhéchain-si:
lúathaigh thoram, trúagh an airc,
mo núar, oram ná hamhairc.

TRANSLATION

O son of Brian, noble Hugh,
O fairest flower that ever blew,
Behold, O branch of grandest tree,
What Thomas now would do with me!
If still my love is dear to you,
Come quickly, help me, keep me true.
The fairies of the mounds of Breagh
Keep gently whispering 'Come away!'
If ever, subject of my art,
The like of me could keep your heart,
Sweet husband, lest you find me gone,
I'd have you speak with Siurtan's son.
Go now to Thomas Costello,
And tell him — for he may not know —
You cannot give me out of hand
To one of Ireland's poet band.
Since from that learned order came
A coaxing thief to steal my fame,
Let him not think my spoils to take,
Whatever promises he make.
I swear the thing is past belief,
That he, this ravening poet-thief,
This beast of prey, should force consent,
And I to his desire be bent.
But blame me not for grievous wrong,
If treacherous art be yet too strong,
And love assume some flattering shape
Too soft and wily to escape.
He often comes to work me hard
In magic form of dire alarm,
He comes with tricks of druidry
To vanquish thoughts of chastity.
And oft beside me he'll appear
A swooping hawk in full career,
My love by dreadful wizardry
In view of all to snatch from me.
Or privately in man's attire
He cometh often to conspire
With secret spell and rhyme obscure
My flight and ruin to assure.
As mortal man he visits me,
In fairy shape as readily.
And then he cometh like a ghost,
And I must flee him or be lost.
Now see him ride to battles far,
And I'm the booty of his war:
And now he woos some provèd maid,
That I may be the more betrayed.
And Hugh O Rourke, he comes to me

In your own shape, as bold and free,
And like a stealthy dragon charms
The wife into the lover's arms:
And then like Thomas Costello
With passion doth my wits o'erthrow.
And then so far in love am I
That I've no strength to move or cry.
Unless you swiftly plan aright
To save me from my desperate plight,
My husband, comrade, love of old,
By Thomas' arts am I cajoled.
My struggling heart is lost between
My love that hath so constant been
For Hugh, and that which now I know,
O crafty wizard Costello!
If I could say what best would be,
Good son of Siurtan, go from me!
To treason you did ne'er incline:
Pierce not Hugh's heart in winning mine.
My glorious captive, Costello,
That did your captor's wits o'erthrow,
Use not O Rourke so treacherously,
Make free with girls and not with me.
Some women love to be cajoled,
Not I. You're young and overbold:
Tho' all the summer's in your face,
Don't hope to charm me to disgrace.
I am no whore, believe not so, —
I met my husband long ago:
When I was young my love was he:
So do not bend those eyes to me.
For all your tricks, your name I'll tell.
Your changes shall not serve you well.
You smiling cheat, you thief, begone,
Or she you courted is undone.
Of me you ne'er shall have your will,
You lying rogue, I know you still:
I'd have you seek another's arms,
Nor try to inflame me with your charms.
Sweet son of yellow Siurtan's race,
With flowering forests in your face,
For love or wealth, in gold or kind,
I cannot leave O Rourke behind.
Then since you find me not your friend,
Your passion on your craft expend,
And magnify our country's fame:
For you I'll call by Naoise's name,[1]
Or Manannan in castle grand,
Or Aonghus prince of fairyland

---

1. Naoise son of Uisneach was the lover of Deirdre.

Or Sioghmall of the cunning arts,
Or Finnbar,[2] whispering bane of hearts.
O wisdom learnt in Cormac's school,[3]
Clear image of the son of Cumhall,[4]
With Guaire's[5] song and crafts profound,
In wrath the match of Ulster's Hound:[6]
O valiant in the clash of war,
Augmenter of abounding store,
O fountain of prosperity,
O swordsman of dexterity,
O mast unbroken by battle's breath,
O secret Lord of wounds and death,
O blast of venom, furious flood,

O wave that never man withstood,
O tongs that stir love's sleeping fire,
O traitor's voice that lures desire,
O prop of all in stress of war:
If I am yours, I say no more.
When I in water dip my face,
O Thomas, champion of your race,
My heart is whispering, I think:
'Oh, drink his love, if you would drink.'
So take my blessing and begone,
Dear offspring of Dubháltach's son,[7]
My gentle friend, delude not me,
Lest Hugh be damned thro' jealousy.
To part with you doth presage grief —
My husband sees me, so be brief! —
Ah, woe! the hunger and the pain! —
And never look at me again.

2. Manannan (Irish, Manannán), Aonghus Sioghmall and Finnbar (Irish, Finnbhearr) were deities, often associated with love.
3. Cormac mac Airt, legendary king and law-giver.
4. Irish, Fionn mac Cumhaill.
5. Guaire, King of Connacht, d. 666.
6. Cú Chulainn.

7. Ancestor of Thomas Costello.

ÚNA NÍ BHROIN

(d. 1706/7)

Ó THUGAS MO GHRÁ DHUIT, MO LÁMH IS MO GHEALLADH
(Since I Gave You My Love)
(*c.* 1670?)

[This poem was apparently composed by Úna Ní Bhroin in response to one by the man she married, the poet and scholar Seán Ó Neachtain, beginning 'Rachainn fón choill leat a mhaighdean na n-órfholt'; for his, see Volume I, p. 291. No other poem by her is known to be extant.

The text is edited from Dublin, Royal Irish Academy Library, MS 23 o 35, p. 49. The translation is by Louis de Paor.]

Ó thugas mo ghrá dhuit, mo lámh is mo
  ghealladh,
Aon uair amháin duit, a Sheáin óig Uí Neachtain,
ar chomhairle mo chairde mo pháirt leat ní
  scarfad,
mar b'fhearr liomsa láimh leat ná i n-áras na
  n-aingeal.

A stórach, bheinn beo, 'sé mo dhóigh, go ceann
  bliana
gan dadamh a ól ná lón ar bith d'iarraidh,
mo bhéal ar do bhéal-sa 's mo dhóid ar do
  chliabh-sa,
ag éisteacht do ghlóir ghlic do thóigfeadh mo
  phianta.

Rachaidh mé féin leat gan éaradh go súgach
ag féachain 's ag éisteacht na n-éan beag ag
  súgradh,
céad fearr liom féin sin ná féasta na cúirte,
a dhianghrá 's a théagair, so mé leat gan
  diúltadh.

TRANSLATION

Since I gave you my love, my hand and my word
Once and for all, young Seán Ó Neachtain,
I'll never leave you in spite of my friends
For I'd rather be with you than dwell with the
  angels.

I could live for a year, I know, my love
Not asking for food or drinking a drop,
With my mouth on yours, my hand on your
    heart,
Hearing your small talk would heal my hurt.

I'd make no delay but go with you gladly
Watching and hearing the small birds at play,
— A hundred times better than courtly
    banquets —
My one love, my strength, I could never refuse.

EOGHAN Ó CAOIMH

(1656–1726)

MO CHÁS CUMHA, MO CHUMHGACH, MO CHOGADH, MO CHREACH
(On the Death of His Wife, Eileanóir)
(1707)

[Although adept in syllabic metres, Eoghan Ó Caoimh chose an *amhrán* metre to lament Eileanóir de Nógla, his wife of twenty-seven years. His autograph-copy has this note: 'I know of course the form appropriate to an elegy [*marbhna*] and the rules the poets apply, but I will give myself leave not to keen my companion in such fashion since I feel her loss so grievously and am bereft without her.' Edition: from Dublin, Royal Irish Academy Library, MS 24, p. 608, and MS 726, pp. 309–10. The translation is by Seamus Deane.]

Mo chás cumha, mo chumhgach, mo chogadh,
    mo chreach,
is m'fháth túirse gan chuntas thug srothach mo
    dhearc,
lá spiúnta mo dhubhachais, dom' chosnamh i
    gceas,
a bhláth mhúinte is tu dlúth-churtha ar
    Bhrosnaigh i bhfeart.

Mo chrá an úir iompaithe ar ghorm do dhearc,
is do ráite rúin cúl riom, nár chogair tar cheart,
do bhrá mar chúr dúnta faoi chlochaibh, is feas,
d'fhág mé ciúin cúthail gan soirbheas seal.

Do lámh gan lúth d'ionsmaigh a hobair go deas,
is do bhánchorp úr ionraic dár bhronnas mo
    shearc —
ag táintibh dubha dúra dá dtochailt i gclais,
d'fhág mé i bpúir brúite go follas ag meath.

Ó ráinig tú i n-úir curtha, a chogair gan chealt,
i gcáil chúnta nár iompaigh ó bhochtaibh do
    dhearc,
go bráth do ghnúis dlúth liom nach cosmhail do
    theacht,
lá cuntais an Dúilimh go roichir 'na theach.

Gráin chúige ort, a thrú liosta is duibhe ar bith
    dath,
a ghráig ghiúngaigh ghlún-fhada is miste mo
    rath,
a bháis bhrúid-smeartha thúrnas gach nduine
    go prap,
plá chughat ó dhlúth-scarais mise is mo bhean

An Ceangal

Go teach na bpian ná i ndiachair bhroide i
    ngéibheann,
i measc na ngiall, a Dhia, ná cuir mo chéile,
maith is mian is diagacht Mhuire an AoinMhic,
ó threabh na bpiast gan diamhair sirim saor í.

Saor í ar fhíoch na ndeamhan ndubh
    nduaibhseach,
créacht an chinn, an chroí, agus cnea na gualann,
ón éiric-ghníomh a clí má d'fhan i nguasaibh,
daonnacht Chríost gan mhoill go Neamh dá
    fuascailt!

TRANSLATION

Source of my ruin, root of my grief, ground of
    my woe,
That fatal day, thief of my joy, — how my
    eyes
Flow for my girl, who died this day and lies
    below,
Buried in Brosna,[1] while I break down in cries.

Your blue eyes drowned in clay, your sighs of
    love gone
From me, your flawless speech, your cries,
Your foam-white breast, extinct under stone.
I am mute, marooned, without friends or allies.

To think of your hand, needle-deft in its motion,
That sweet, white body that I loved now dead,
Tormented mid the bestial commotion
Of the monsters of the pit, afflicts me with dread.

Stifled in clay, you, my eternal love, who never
In your kindness ignored or forgot the poor,

1. In County Kerry, near Abbeyfeale.

Since I will not see your face again, not ever,
May God, on the Last Day, open to you his door.

May the blackest loathing of the whole region's
Hatred afflict you, shrivelled death, you
    importunate
Wretch, who scythes down the living in legions,
Took my wife, left me desolate, unfortunate.

The Knot

O God, I beg you do not condemn my wife
To the house of torment — give her eternal life.
Nor abandon her among the captive hosts
Of those reefed in pain. Through Mary's most
Precious desire, save her from the bestial fate
Of the damned. Keep her free, immaculate.

Release her from the fury of the demonic dead,
Save her from wound of shoulder, heart, or
    head.
If she must pay a ransom for a misdeed,
Let it be paid swiftly and with speed.
May the clemency of Christ come to her aid
And bring her into bliss, her ransom paid.

MÁIRE NÍ REACHTAGÁIN

(d. 1733)

IS MISE CHAILL AN PLANDA DÍLIS
(On the Death of Her Brother, Seoirse) (1725)

[In 1717 Máire Ní Reachtagáin married Tadhg Ó Neachtain who, like his father, Seán Ó Neachtain, was a leading figure in Dublin's circle of Gaelic poets, scribes and scholars. She was his third wife; the deaths of his earlier wives came close together. Poetry was not a male preserve in the Ó Neachtain family, even before she joined it: for a poem attributed to her mother-in-law, Úna Ní Bhroin, see pp. 422–3 above.

Surviving correspondence shows that the death of her brother, Seoirse, on 15 November 1725, was a cruel blow to the Ó Reachtagáin family, and deeply felt also by the

Ó Neachtain relations. Máire's elegy renders the conventions of the oral *caoineadh* in literary form and its mood is reflective, unlike extempore keening.

A second poem poem by Máire is known, one she wrote to welcome a friend to Dublin. It is a simple, personal address, probably intended for limited circulation, and survives only in a copy made by her husband.

The edition is based on texts in Dublin, Royal Irish Academy Library, MS 23 I 23, pp. 66–71, and National Library of Ireland, MS 132, pp. 111–15. The translation is by Biddy Jenkinson.]

Is mise chaill an planda dílis,
fear nár ghann in am na daoirse,
fear do chanadh ceart is fíre,
fear do thóigeadh brón do dhaoirsibh.

Ochón ochón ochón mo ghéarghoin!
Ochón ochón ochón mo théagair!
Ochón ochón ochón go n-éagad!
A Sheoirse Uí Reachtagáin, m'anacair ghéar
   thu.

Fear na ngéag chum déirc' do shíneadh,
fear ba scáth do chairde is dídean,
fear do ghéill do chléirchibh Íosa,
fear nár chrap a ghlac ón daonnacht.
   Ochón, ochón, etc.

Fear nár iata a chliabh ar dhísleacht,
fear ba dána lá na bruíne,
fear ar chlár ba tláithe míne,
fear gan scléip ós méad a mhaoine.
   Ochón, ochón, etc.

Fear ba gléigeal gné is braoithe,¹
fear do thóigeadh brón do dhaoine,
fear ba stuama ar ghuaillibh saoithe
fear don lag ba leaba scíse.
   Ochón, ochón, etc.

Fear gan toirse ag bronnadh díola,
fear gan fhuath, gan chruas, gan chríne,
fear ba hard is do chanadh ísleacht,
fear nár shantaigh clampar síobtha.
   Ochón, ochón, etc.

Fear nár dhearc ar ais go fiamhach,
fear nár cáineadh ó fhás go fínit,
is fear nár leor leis bord na scríbe
acht bord farsainn i searc 's i ndísleacht.
   Ochón, ochón, etc.

Bha a bhord gan fhios is go bhfios do ghaolta,
bord dó féin is don gcléir in aoinfheacht
ar ghrá caidrimh is teagaisc naofa
is bord don fhuar ar bhruach na gríosaí
   Ochón, ochón, etc.

Bord ar leith is fleidh don chnaíteach
is bord don tseanóir dearóil aosta,
searc na lag is a dteach díona
teach na mbocht — uch! anocht fó liaga.
   Ochón, ochón, etc.

B'aithne dhamhsa ar m'amhra síthe
ar dhíobháil suain is buairt na hoíche

nárbh fhada uaimse buaidhreadh sífe
bhíos dom ghoin go fuin mo chríche.
   Ochón, ochón, etc.

Do mo chairde is ábhar íonaidh
mo bheith beo i ndeoidh mo dhíograis
is nach dearna gealt nó spiorad díomsa
tré bhás an fhir a bhris mo chroí istigh.
   Ochón, ochón, etc.

M'ábhar bróin go deo na díle
mo gharbhráthair catach dílis,
Seoirse, stór is lón mo mhiangais,
Reachtagáin nár cháin acht daoithe.
   Ochón, ochón, etc.

Uch! a bháis do chráigh na mílte,
do roinne buacais shuaite dhíomsa,
saoth rug uaim don uaigh do shíor leis
sult is greann is m'ansacht fíre
   Ochón, ochón, etc.

is d'fhág 'na mhalrait agam choíche
leann go leor nach beoir na díoghla
acht leann le hairc do shlad na mílte
is leann dobróin is eol do chnaítibh.
   Ochón, ochón, etc.

Tré a bhás is cráite cloíte
bhíos mise ag ól i mbrón gan fhaoiseamh
go gcríochnaí mé mo laethaibh daonna
im' fhuachaid chráite chásmhar dhítheach
   Ochón, ochón, etc.

bhíos go bás mar táim ag caoineadh,
mac mo mháthar fáth mo scíse,
fáth mo mhire, meisce is íota,
fáth mo chantail 's m'angair choíche.
   Ochón, ochón, etc.

Ní mise amháin do fágadh thíos leis
acht a chlann i nganntan aoise,
's a máthair bhocht 'na bhfochair pianta,
Tomás fós mo scóladh i n-aoineacht
   Ochón, ochón, etc.

gan dearbráir lá na bruíne
ná fear trua i nguais má bhíonn san
isteach san uaigh ó chuaigh a thaoiseach
gan súil aisig feasta choíche.
   ochón, ochón, etc.

1. Reading *braoith*e for MSS *bruíghle*.

Damhsa is ceart atá gar i ngaol leis
ceart don bhocht don nocht 's don aosta,
's is ceart na gceart ár mbeannacht íogair
a chur leis go hiostas Íosa.
    Ochón, ochón, *etc.*[2]

Och! a Sheoirse, a stóir 's a ghrá mo chléibh,
och! mura spóirt leat brón do Mháire féin
atá lag id' dheoidh gan tsó gan ádh gan fhéidhm,
tara, fóir, is tóig go Parrthas mé.
    Áiméan.

2. 7 lines found in the MSS are omitted here as a missing 8th line
   occludes their meaning.

TRANSLATION

It is I who have lost my hero,
a generous man when times were evil,
one who sang of right and freedom,
lifting fear from oppressed people.
    Mourn, mourn, my heart is breaking!
    Mourn, mourn, sorrow's wakening!
    Mourn, mourn, till death takes me!
    Seoirse Ó Reachtagáin I blame you.

A man whose hands stretched to the needy,
strength of his friends, fold of the fearful,
a man who honoured Christ's own clergy,
never loosed his grip on mercy.
    Mourn mourn, *etc.*

A man whose heart was open, faithful,
a bold man in the day of danger,
in company most kind and gracious,
not inclined to ostentation.
    Mourn, mourn, *etc.*

A man most fair of countenance,
a man to cheer the saddest heart,
he was the sage at sages' shoulders.
The weak leaned on him, their supporter.
    Mourn, mourn, *etc.*

Untiring in bestowing favour,
free of hate and petty failings,
a noble, modest in demeanour,
a man who shunned loud disputation.
    Mourn, mourn, *etc.*

He never cast a cruel glance,
was never in his life reviled,
didn't keep a skimpy table
but a laden one with love set wide.
    Mourn, mourn, *etc.*

He was generous far beyond our knowing,
for the clergy he kept open board,
for love of company and learning, holy.
At his fireside, space for the poor and the cold.
    Mourn, mourn, *etc.*

Place at the feast for weak and wasted,
place for the needy bedraggled ancient,
roof of the wretched he was, poverty's favourite.
Tonight the poorhouse is devastated.
    Mourn, mourn, *etc.*

I knew, because of eerie dreams,
sleepless and tormented nights,
that endless suffering lay in wait
to plague me till the end of life.
    Mourn, mourn, *etc.*

To friends it is a cause of wonder
that I, so far, survive my dear,
that death, in breaking my heart asunder,
has not left me shrieking mad, for life.
    Mourn, mourn, *etc.*

The root of my sorrow from this day forwards,
my noble, loving brother's death.
Seoirse, shrine of all my longings,
Ó Reachtagáin by fools alone contemned.
    Mourn, mourn, *etc.*

Death you left a thousand aching.
You left me, a dry wick, forsaken.
Grief has carried to the graveyard
my life, my love, my joy, my gaiety.
    Mourn, mourn, *etc.*

leaving me to drink till doomsday
a bitter draft that brings no easing,
a draft of thirst that slays the people,
black sorrow's draft known to the needy.
    Mourn, mourn, *etc.*

I drink in sadness, in pain unceasing
because of his death, my gloom unyielding,

I'll end my days in rags and ravings,
an ugly, wailing, needy scarecrow.
  Mourn, mourn, *etc.*

I'll go to death forever keening,
my mother's son my cause of grieving,
my cause of anger, thirst and raging,
Of crossness and debilitation.
  Mourn, mourn, *etc.*

Not I alone have suffered loss,
his children are all young and small,
their mother bound with them in pain.
To think of Tomás[1] scalds hearts once again.
  Mourn, mourn, *etc.*

1. Seoirse's son.

Tomás has now no brother in a fight,
no henchman by his side when troubles rise,
since his chieftain went from him into the clay,
to the everlasting, unrelenting grave.
  Mourn, mourn, *etc.*

It is proper that I, being close in blood,
fitting that the poor, the naked, the old
should send, as is right, a sad salute
to him in the Residence of Christ.
  Mourn, mourn, *etc.*

Och! my Seoirse, my darling and love of my life
Och! if you're not making fun of your own
    Máire's plight
— for she's weak with regretting you, restless,
    luckless, no use —
Come, help me, carry me straight off to Paradise.

TOIRDHEALBHACH Ó CEARBHALLÁIN (TURLOUGH CAROLAN)

(1670–1738)

MÁIBLE SHÉIMH NÍ CHEALLAIGH
(Mabel Kelly)
(*c.* 1720?)

[Toirdhealbhach Ó Cearbhalláin, the most famous of the Irish harper-composers, was also highly regarded as a poet in his own lifetime, though the accolade is largely undeserved. Yet one should not be too critical: the words of his songs were ancillary to the music and the songs should be judged on their combined effects.

Ó Cearbhalláin had numerous patrons and was unlikely to have had a close personal relationship with the majority of them. Many of his most memorable song-airs were composed for female patrons and their daughters. In the following songs, the first for an unmarried, and the second for a married, woman, he draws on the language of traditional *amhráin ghrá*. Austin Clarke transposes them to a more intimate key.

Máible Ní Cheallaigh has been identified as the only daughter and heiress of Lochlainn Ó Ceallaigh of Lismoyle, County Roscommon. She died unmarried on 22 December 1745. James Hardiman's Irish text is given here, despite its irregular and occasionally incorrect orthography, as it was the basis for Clarke's translation. See: James Hardiman, *Irish Minstrelsy*, 2 vols (Shannon: Irish University Press, 1971), vol. 1, pp. 60, 62; Austin Clarke, *Selected Poems*, edited by Hugh Maxton (Dublin: Lilliput Press, 1991), pp. 53–4. The airs to this and the next song are well known.]

Cia b'é bh-fuil sé a n-dán do,
    A lámh-dheas bheith faoí na ceann,
Is deimhin nach eagal bás do,
    Go bráth ná 'n a bheódh bheith tinn,
A chúil dheis na m-bachall bh-fáinneach,
    bh-fionn,
    A chuim mar an Ealla ag snámhadh air an
    d-toínn,
Grádh 'gus spéis gach gasraidh, Máible shéimh
    n-í Cheallaigh,
Déud is deise leagadh ann arus a céinn.

Ní'l ceól d'á bhinne fós d'ar seinneadh,
    Ná'r bh'eólghach dhi-si thuigsin 's a rádh ann
    gach céim
A gruadh mar rós ag drithleadh, is buan 'n a
    g-cómharsa an lile,

A rosg is míne, glaise 'ná bláith na g-cráebh:
'S é deir olldhamh mollta chláir shíl Néill,
　Go g-cuirfeadh na corradha chodla le sár-
　　ghuith a béil,
Ní'l amhrus ann a súil bhreágh, lonnach,
　Acht óltar línn go grínn do shláinte mhaith
　　féin.

O d'éagadar na mná mánla
　Air a d-tráchdadaoís an domhain go léir,
Measaim nach bh-fuil 'n a n-áit aguinn
　Acht Máible le clú ann gach céim.
Annsacht gach duine a g-cáilídheacht 's a
　g-céill; —
　Is ághmhar do'n bh-filidh a fághail d'á n-déis,
Cúl na g-cráebh is finne, lúb na d-téud is binne,
　Snuadh na géise gile, a brághaid a's a táebh.

Ní'l aén d'á bh-feiceann an t-saoí-bhean
　mhaiseach,
　Nach éirghídheann mar na geiltibh, a
　　m-barradhaibh na g-craébh,
A's an t-é nach léur do an choingeal, lán de
　sbéis an leinbh,
　Is fearr tréighthe a's tuigsin dhe náisiún
　　Gáedhal; —
Is sí is deise cos, bas, lámh agus búel,
　Péighre rosg, a's folt ag fás léi go féur,
Tá an bháire-si línn ag sárúghadh luchd greínn,
　Fá rádh go bh-fuair mé an fhaíll, is ághmhar
　　liom é.

TRANSLATION

Lucky the husband
Who puts his hand beneath her head
　They kiss without scandal
Happiest two near feather-bed.
He sees the tumble of brown hair
Unplait, the breasts, pointed and bare
　When nightdress shows
　From dimple to toe-nail,
All Mabel glowing in it, here, there, everywhere.

　Music might listen
　To her least whisper,
Learn every note, for all are true.
　While she is speaking,
　Her voice goes sweetly
To charm the herons in their musing.
Her eyes are modest, blue, their darkness

Small rooms of thought, but when they sparkle
　Upon a feast-day
　Glasses are meeting,
Each raised to Mabel Kelly, our toast and darling.

Gone now are many Irish ladies
Who kissed and fondled, their very pet-names
Forgotten, their tibia degraded.
She takes their sky. Her smile is famed.
Her praise is scored by quill and pencil.
　Harp and spinet
　Are in her debt
And when she plays or sings, melody is content.

　No man who sees her
　Will feel uneasy.
He goes his way, head high, however tired.
　Lamp loses light
　When placed beside her.
She is the pearl and being of all Ireland
Foot, hand, eye, mouth, breast, thigh and
　instep, all that we desire.
Tresses that pass small curls as if to touch the
　ground;
　So many prizes
　Are not divided.
Her beauty is her own and she is not proud.

MÁRGHAIRIAD INGHIN SHEOIRSE BRÚN
(Peggy Browne)
(*c.* 1720?)

[See previous headnote. Márghairiad (Margaret) Brún
was identifed by James Hardiman as 'the daughter of
George Browne, the hospitable owner of Brownstown, in
the county of Mayo': see his *Irish Minstrelsy*, vol. 2, p. 125.
For his edition of this poem, see ibid., vol. 2, pp. 66, 68.
Translation: Austin Clarke, *Selected Poems*, p. 55.]

A Mhárghairiad Brún, is dúbhach do fhágbhais
　mé,
　Mo luíghe 'san uaigh 's gan cúmhdach mná
　　orm féin,
Fuil 'g a sgaoíleadh dhamh-sa a d-túis a's a
　n-deireadh gach láe,
　A's a Inghín Mheic Suíbhne, a rúin dhil,
　　tárthaigh mé.

Ghluaiseas 'núnn dar liom fá 'n tráth-so a n-dé,
    Fá'n g-coíll chroím, go cínnte b'árd mo léim;
Mo leabhrán grínn ag ínnsin fáth gach sgéil,
    Is eagal liom gur mhíll do ghrádh-sa me.

'S í Már'iad an aindear shéimh is caoíne glór,
    Is binne a béul 'ná guth na d-téud a's ná na
        síghcheóil,
Is gile taobh ná an eala shéimh théidheann air
    linn gach ló,
    'Gus a mhaiseach, bhéusach, ghasta,
        thréidhtheach ná diúltaidh mé.

Dul eadar an dair 'sa croiceann, 'sé mheasaim
    gur cruadh an céim,
    Dul eadar mé agus rúin-shearc agus grádh
        mo chléibh,
Air chur mo lámh tháirsi air maidin le
    bánúghadh an láe
    Fuair mé an staraídhe dubh ag
        gleacaídheacht le grádh mo chuím.

TRANSLATION

The dark-haired girl, who holds my thought
    entirely
Yet keeps me from her arms and what I desire,
Will never take my word for she is proud
And none may have his way with Peggy Browne.

Often I dream that I am in the woods
At Westport House. She strays alone, blue-hooded,
Then lifts her flounces, hurries from a shower,
But sunlight stays all day with Peggy Browne.

Her voice is music, every little echo
My pleasure and O her shapely breasts, I know,
Are white as her own milk, when taffeta gown
Is let out, inch by inch, for Peggy Browne.

A lawless dream comes to me in the night-time,
That we are stretching together side by side,
Nothing I want to do can make her frown.
I wake alone, sighing for Peggy Browne.

AODH BUÍ MAC CRUITÍN

(c. 1680–1755)

A GHÉIS GHARTHA GHLÉIGEAL
(O Swan of Bright Plumage)
(1718)

[Aodh Buí Mac Cruitín's career and writings were bound up with the Stuart cause and the expectations of Irish Catholics, but equally with the nobility of Thomond, especially the Uí Bhriain (O'Briens), not all of whom were Jacobite sympathizers or Catholics. He wrote the following poem in 1718 to celebrate the marriage of Isibéal Ní Bhriain, daughter of Criostóir Ó Briain of Ennistymon, to Somhairle Mac Domhnaill of Kilkee. Somhairle Mac Domhnaill inherited part of the attainted estate of the 3rd Lord Clare, who had raised a regiment for James II, and Isibéal Ní Bhriain converted to Protestantism shortly after her marriage. Nevertheless, they were important sources of patronage for Mac Cruitín throughout his life, and it was to them that he turned for help in the aftermath of the terrible famine of 1740–1.

The text, here in modernized spelling, is from: Brian O'Looney, *A Collection of Poems Written on Different Occasions by the Clare Bards* (Dublin: O'Daly, 1863), p. 2. The translation, ibid., p. 3, is by James Clarence Mangan.]

A ghéis ghartha ghléigeal, a bhéith mhaiseach
    bhéasach,
    A chraobh chneasda chéimleas do mhaithibh
        síol Táil;
A aonlasair sgéimhe na n-aolbhan le chéile,
    A bhéaltana an déid ghil na labhartha sámh.

Is tréan teacht do thréithe le féidhm mhaith na
    féile,
    'S t'aolchrobh le daonnacht is tabharthach
        tásg,
Don taisteallach tréith-lag, don aimid gan
    éifeacht,
    Don lagar le haostacht is tú a gcabhair 's a
        scáth.

Mar bharr ar gach léanlot do mheabhradh mo
   chéadfa,
     'S d'fhág dealbh gan chéill me im' mheathach
     mar 'táim,
Gur chailleas-sa laochra ba chabhair dom'
   éigean,
     Fearachoin éachtach' Chaisil 's Chláir.

Do cheanglais le nuachar, flaith ceannsa den
   chuainne,
     Ó Aontraim na nguaisbheart 's ó Albain aird;
Don chlainn sin Cholla Uais mhir, fuair
   Teamhair 's Tuamhain,
     A ndán sin 's a ndualgas na n-aithreach ór
     fhás.

Créad damhsa ná luafainn an lannmharcach
   uasal,
     An crann cathais cnuasach gan casadh ar a
     láimh;
Gan fann-bheart, gan truailleadh, acht
   ceannsacht le cuallacht,
     An planda do suathadh tre chaise d'fhuil Táil.

TRANSLATION

O, swan of bright plumage! O, maiden who
   bearest
     The stamp on thy brow of Dalcassia's high
     race,

With mouth of rich pearl-teeth, and features the
   fairest,
     And speech of a sweetness for music to trace!

O! how shall I praise thee, thou lovely, thou
   noble!
     Thou prop of the feeble, thou light of the
     blind!
Thou solace and succour of wretches in trouble,
     As beauteous in body as bounteous in mind!

Alas! these are woes from which nought can
   defend me,
     My bosom is loaded with sorrow and care,
Since I lost the great men who were prompt to
   befriend me,
     The heroes, the princes of Cashel and Clare!

But glory and honour to thee! — thou hast
   wedded
     A chieftain from Antrim, of chivalrous worth,
Of the great *Colla-Uais*[1] the Swift — they who
   headed
     So proudly the conquering tribes of the North!

To that bold cavalier hast thou plighted thy duty,
     And *he* is a hero whom none can surpass —
His valour alone was the meed of thy beauty,
     Thou Rose of the Garden of golden *Dal-Cas*!

---

1.   One of three brothers, all named Colla, who were mythical
     ancestors of tribes in Ulster.

AOGÁN Ó RATHAILLE

(*c.* 1670–*c.* 1728)

EPITALAMIUM DO THIGHEARNA CHINN MARA (The Star of Kilkenny) (1720)

[This joyful epithalamium was written to celebrate the marriage of Vailintín Brún (Valentine Browne), Lord Kenmare, to Onóra, daughter of Colonel Thomas Butler and his wife, Lady Iveagh, of Cill Chais in 1720 (on Cill Chais (Kilcash) see below, pp. 446–7). It renovates the trope of the sacral marriage of sovereignty goddess and rightful king. The promise of this marriage manifests not just terrestrially but astrally. Nor will this goddess fade from view: she will remain among her people as a shining star. For Ó Rathaille, the marriage is also a renewal of hope in the ultimate victory of '*an t-aon cóir*', the Stuart 'ace' (8th verse of the Irish).

The Brownes, descendants of early Elizabethan planters, were Catholics and Jacobite sympathisers. The world-view, aesthetics and ethics of Ó Rathaille's poetry are all to be understood in terms of Jacobitism. When he was growing up, near Killarney, the Brownes owned vast estates in Kerry and neighbouring counties. These were confiscated after the Battle of the Boyne because of their allegiance to the defeated King James. The expectation was that Sir Nicholas Browne's confiscated lands would revert to his eldest son, Vailintín, on his death. Ó Rathaille cannot but have looked forward to this event, anticipating that it would lead to the restoration of the social order he desired. Sir Nicholas died in 1720 and, six months later, Sir Vailintín married Onóra Butler.

Text: Patrick S. Dineen and Tadhg O'Donoghue (eds), *Dánta Aodhagáin Uí Rathaille. The Poems of Egan O'Rahilly* (London: Irish Texts Society, 1911), pp. 172, 174. Translation: James Clarence Mangan, from C.P. Meehan (ed.), *The Poets and Poetry of Munster*, 5th edition (Dublin: James Duffy [n.d.]), pp. 111, 113. The translation has nothing to correspond to the last four lines of the original.]

Atáid éisc ar an srúillibh ag léimrigh go
    lúthmhar,
    Tán an t-éclips gan fiúntar ag imtheacht;
Tá Phoebus ag múscailt, 's an t-éasca go
    ciuinghlan,
    Is éanlaith na cúige go soithimh.

Táid scaoth bheach ag túirling ar ghéagaibh is
    úrghlas,
    Tá féar agus drúcht ar na mongaibh
Ó's céile dhon mBrúnach í Réilteann na
    Mumhan
    'S gaol gar dhon Diuic ó Chill Choinnigh

Tá bíodhgadh i ngach támhlag, is
    groidhechnuic go láidir,
    'San ngeimhreadh tig bláth ar gach bile;
Cill Chais ó thárlaigh i gcuibhreach go
    grádhmhar
    Le Rígh Chille hÁirne ar gCuradh.

Ní'l éagcóir dá luadh aguinn, tá faothódh age
    truaghaibh,
    Ón scéal nódh so luaidhtear le drongaibh,
Ar an bpéarla óg mná uaisle (A Dhé, Ó, tabhair
    buaidh dhi!)
    Den chraeibh órdha is uaisle ó Chill
    Choinnigh.

Tá an Rífhlaith n-a ghárdaibh ar íslibh 's ar
    ardaibh,
    'S na mílte dá bhfáiltiughadh le muirinn;

Tá an taoidhe go hádhbharach, is coill ghlas ag
    fás ann,
    Is gnaoi ag teacht ar bhántaibh gan milleadh.

Táid cuanta, ba ghnáthach fá bhuanstuirm
    ghránna,
    Go suaimhneach ó thárlaidh an
    snuidhmeadh,
Tá cnuastar ar tráigh 'guinn ná luascann an
    sáile,
    Ruacain is báirnigh is duileasc.

Táid uaisle Chill Áirne go suairc ag ól sláintidhe
    Is buanbhith na na lánamhan i gcumann;
Táid suanphuirt na ndánta dá mbualadh ar
    chláirsigh,
    Gach suanphort ar áilleacht 's ar bhinneacht.

Tá claochlódh ar chruaidhcheist, 's an t-aon
    chóir ag buadhchant;
    Tá gné nódh ar ghruadhnaibh gach nduine;
Tá an spéir mhór ar fuaimint, 's an rae fós go
    suaimhneach,
    Gan caocheó gan duartan, gan tuile.

Tá scéimh ar gach ruaidhteach nach féidir do
    ruadhchan,
    Ó Léinloch go bruach Cille Choinnigh
Fá'n saorfhlaith dhul uainne do théacht as gach
    cruaidhcheist;
    N-a réim chirt gura buan a bhéas againn.

TRANSLATION

The fish in the streamlets are leaping and
    springing,
    All clouds for a time have rolled over;
The bright sun is shining; the sweet birds are
    singing,
    And joy lights the brow of the lover.
The gay bees are swarming, so golden and
    many,
    And with corn are our meadows embrowned,
Since she, the fair niece[1] of the Duke of
    Kilkenny,
    Is wedded to Browne, the renow'd.

1. Here in the sense 'kinswoman'.

The hills are all green that of late looked so
  blighted;
  Men laugh who for long lay in trouble,
For Kilcash is, thank Heaven, in friendship
  united
  With Browne of Killarney, our Noble!
Our poor have grown rich — none are wronged
  or o'er-laden,
  The serf and the slave least of any,
Since she came among us, this noble young
  maiden,
  The Rose and the Star of Kilkenny!
Her Lord, the proud Prince, gives to all his
  protection,
  But most to the Poor and the Stranger,
And all the land round pays him back with
  affection —
  As now they may do without Danger!

The ocean is calm, and the greenwoods are
  blooming,
  As bards of antiquity sung us,
And not even one sable cloud seems a-looming,
  Since he we so love came among us!

The Lords of Killarney, who knows what the
  wrongful
  Effects of misrule are, quaff healths to the
  pair —
And the minstrels, delighted, breathe out their
  deep songful
  Emotions each hour in some ever-new air.
The sun and the moon day and night keep
  a-shining;
  New hopes appear born in the bosoms of men,
And the ancient despair and the olden repining
  Are gone, to return to us never again.

SEÁN DE HÓRA

(*c.* 1714–80)

IS GÉAG DEN BHILE GHLÓRMHAR AN DEORAÍ SO I GCILL BHRIOCÁIN
(On the Birth of Séarlas Mac Domhnaill)
(1736)

[Aodh Buí Mac Cruitín wrote a genethliacon (see pp. 429–30) to celebrate the birth of a son, Séarlas, apparently their first, to Isibéal Ní Bhriain and her husband, Somhairle Mac Domhnaill, in 1736. So too did the less eminent Clare poet Seán de hÓra. This is the earliest of de hÓra's dated poems. He wrote many others for Isibéal and Somhairle's family, but their daughter, Máire, an older sister of the baby whose arrival is celebrated here, was his special patron. In 1750 or thereabouts, she married Muircheartach Mac Mathghamhna of Cluainíneach (Clooneena), near Doonbeg in south County Clare, and the poet went to work for them as a blacksmith. Mac Mathghamhna died prematurely but the poet's close relationship with Máire continued and carried over into subsequent generations: a poem celebrating the marriage of her daughter, Éilís, and another celebrating the birth of Éilís's first son, are extant. An early nineteenth-century manuscript containing the latter poem states Éilís was 'an excellent Irish scholar'.

The composition of genethliacons was apparently one of the duties incumbent on the bardic poet, although the earliest extant examples go back no further than the early seventeenth century. No doubt de hÓra saw himself as composing within an established tradition. His genethliacon, although intimate and personal, is also full of broad hints of Jacobite optimism.

The text, here in modernized spelling, is from: B. O'Looney, *A Collection of Poems . . . by the Clare Bards*, pp. 41, 42. The translation is by Moya Cannon.]

Is géag den bhile ghlórmhar an deoraí so i gCill
  Bhriocáin,
Do chuir mac Dé inár mbóthar le comhachta ó
  Rí na nGrás,
Is beannaithe an bhean óg í inar fórmaíodh ina
  broinn an bháb,
Craobh na finne Fódhla ag ól srotha cíocha Táil.

Bíonn *Huzza* is míle in éineacht ag saorchlanna
  saoithe ag ól,
Dá gcur i nglinnte spéartha roimh Shéarlas,
  mac maith mo leoin,
Bíonn *Punch* is fíon dá dtraochain re chéile agus
  díol den bheoir,
Cnámh na dtinte craorag go haerach ina soillse
  reomhainn.

Cuir i gcliabhán óir é, tabhair póg do agus lacht
  do chíoch,
Suigh is gabh huiseó dho go ceolmhar 's go
  blasda binn;
Racht ná léig go deo air ná deoir lena dhearca
  síos,
Bráthair ceart Bhriain Bhóirmhe 'chuir Fódhla
  faoi smacht a dhlí.

Is bráthair Bhriain Mhic Bhruadair i n-uaisle na
  sean do bhí;
Is bráthair d'Iarla Tuamhan é — san uair seo
  Inse Uí Chuinn;
Bráthair chliar an tsuaircis 's an ghruagaich, an
  flaith ón nDabhaich,
Thug barr an tiarnais uaibhse 'chuaidh uainne
  go harm Laoighis.

TRANSLATION

This newcomer to Kilbrickan[1] is a limb of the
  glorious tree,
God's Son sent him our way with gifts from the
  King of Grace,

Blessed is that young woman in whose womb
  the baby grew,
Fódhla's bright branch is nourished by a stream
  from the breast of Tál.[2]

Huzzas, one and a thousand, to heaven's glens
  are raised,
As noble clans of wise men drink to Charles,
  my lion's heir,
Both punch and wine are drained down and a
  share of ale as well,
While bonfires, bright and blood-red, before us
  gaily blaze.

Lay him in a gold cradle, kiss him, give him
  milk from your breast,
Sit and sing him a hushaby, tender music to
  bring him rest,
Don't let a tear wet his cheek, don't leave him
  to cry in distress,
True kinsman of Brian Bóirimhe[3] who ruled
  Fódhla from east to west.

He's kin to Brian Mac Bruadair of the nobles of
  old,
And kin to the Earl of Thomond — Inchiquin
  as now known,
He's kin to the merry poets and the long-haired
  Lord of Dough,[4]
The chief among you chieftains who left for the
  armies of Louis.

1. Kilbrickan, one of the residences of the Mac Domhnaill family, was
   located between Ennis and Quin, in County Clare.

2. A legendary ancestor of the people of Clare.
3. Eponym of the Uí Bhriain (O'Briens), the most successful of all
   early Irish monarchs, died in the Battle of Clontarf in 1014.
4. The castle at Dough (Caisleán na Daibhche), near Lahinch,
   County Clare, was an Ó Briain residence.

ÚNA NIC CRUITÍN

(*c.* 1740?)

A BHUIME DEN BHRÓD MHÓRDHA BA RATHAMHAIL RÉIM

(An Appeal to Isibéal Ní Bhriain)

(*c.* 1740?)

[Aodh Buí Mac Cruitín, the well-known lexicographer, father of the author of this poem, died in 1755. Members of Clann Chruitín served as hereditary poets and historians to the Uí Bhriain of Thomond, and Aodh Buí was among the last representatives of his class to spend a part of his life at least living on the practice of the profession into which he was born. A good number of his panegyrical compositions addressed to various members of the Ó Briain, Mac Domhnaill and Ó Lochlainn families of Clare has survived. These include two poems addressed to Isibéal Ní Bhriain, wife of Somhairle Mac Domhnaill; for one of them, see above, pp. 429–30.

To judge from the present verses, Aodh Buí's daughter, Úna Nic Cruitín, saw herself as a poet in the professional tradition also. The patronage she is seeking from Isibéal Ní Bhriain she claims as of right. In that sense her composition is of unique interest — no other of its kind is known to me. Unfortunately, it is also the sole surviving specimen of the poetry of Úna Nic Cruitín. My edition is based on Maynooth, Library of St Patrick's College, MS C 15, p. 132. For this edition and discussion (in Irish only), see my article: 'Togha na hÉigse 1700–1800', *Éigse*, vol. 28 (1994–5), pp. 135–7. The following translation is also by the present writer, Pádraig A. Breatnach.]

Úna iníon Mhic Cruitín *cecinit* do Eisibéal Ní Bhriain

A bhuime den bhród mhórdha ba rathamhail
réim
Is de chruithneacht na slógh sróillgheal ba
sleachtamhail saor

Ba coimirce mhór d'ordaibh 's ba ceanamhail
céim
Cá duine dem shórt beo anois gan mearughadh
i méin?

A bhan-ua na rithe is a bhruinneal den
mhórchraoibh thréan
Lér buadh an t-oineach gan time tar chóigíbh
Néid,
Ós dualgas duitse mo choimirce, tóg faoid scéith,
Fuasgail meise is ná fuiling i mbrón díth mé.

TRANSLATION

Úna, daughter of Mac Cruitín, sang this for Eisibéal Ní Bhriain

O lady of the highborn line whose rule prospered, sprung from the pick of the bright-satined, noble and prolific heroes, who were protective of the clergy and were ever kindly disposed: — where is there any of my kind to be found living now who is not distracted?

O heiress of kings, fair lady descended from the mighty kindred who won honour bravely throughout Néid's[1] provinces, as my protection is a duty incumbent upon you, shield me, relieve me, and let me not suffer the sorrow of indigence.

---

1. Néid: name of an ancient Irish war god.

EIBHLÍN NÍ CHOILLTE

(fl. 1745)

STADAIDH BHUR NGÉARGHOL, A GHASRA CHAOMHDHA
(Expelling Seán Buí)
(c. 1745)

[A version of the song-air known in Irish tradition as 'Seán Buí' first appeared in print bearing the title 'Over the Water to Charlie' in a Scottish publication dated 1752. It seems that 'Seán Buí' was an epithet originally applied to the followers of William III. Its use was extended to give the Irish equivalent of 'John Bull', in which sense it occurs in the following poem, and in more than a dozen others to the same tune that have survived from the eighteenth century. Perhaps the earliest is one by the poet, Fr. Uilliam Inglis, said to have been composed in 1742, in which Ireland's sufferings are lamented and Prince Charles Stuart is looked to for deliverance from the tyrant 'Seán Buí'.

To judge from the uniformly despondent view they take of Ireland's fortunes, past and future, most other poems to the tune seem much later than that by Inglis. The following one, however, is full of buoyant optimism for the future of the Stuart cause. This suggests it may have been composed in answer to Inglis (whose composition it mirrors closely), possibly in the atmosphere that followed the Scottish Rising of 1745 when expectations of a French-backed Stuart intervention in Ireland were raised, only to be finally laid to rest in 1748 with the peace of Aix-la-Chapelle which concluded the Austrian War of Succession (1740–8).

It survives in more than twenty copies, an indication that it was remarkably popular. These name the author as either Eibhlín Ní Choillte or Eibhlín Ní Eachiarainn. As the former appears in a more diverse cross-section of manuscripts, it seems deserving of greater credence. The poet Aindrias Mac Craith (see p. 456) is among the authorities supporting it. The only information tradition has preserved about Eibhlín Ní Choillte is that she came from Cathair Druinge (Caherdrinny), near Mitchelstown, County Cork. If this is to be trusted, then 'an chathair' in line 20 presumably applies to Cork city. The opinion given by James Hardiman, in his *Irish Minstrelsy*, p. 149, that Eibhlín Ní Choillte ('Ellen Quilty') was 'probably a nom-de-guerre, assumed by some bard to avoid detection', seems groundless.

The edition is based primarily on Dublin, Royal Irish Academy Library, MS 23 B 38, p. 231, with occasional readings from MS 24 C 55, p. 262, and MS 24 B 33, p. 184, in the same location. It and the translation are by the present writer, Pádraig A. Breatnach.]

Stadaidh bhur ngéarghol, a ghasra chaomhdha,
　Ná scaipidh bhur ndéara, ní gá dhíbh,
Táid fearchoin laochta na Banba aosta
　Go bagrach baolach ag gardaíocht,
An aicme seo an Bhéarla atá i gceannas na hÉireann
　Do cheangail ár gcléir bhocht faoi ardchíos —
Beid feasta fá dhaorbhruid ag freastal do Ghaelaibh
　Is gan acfainn a saortha ag Seán Buí.

Casfaid na Séamais le feartaibh an Aonmhic
　Is stadfaidh go héasca bhur n-ardchaoi,
Cé fada go faon sibh ag tarraing na cléithe
　Is bhur mbailte ag méirligh gan fáil dlí;
Níl spreallaire craosach lér spalpadh an t-éitheach
　Nach gcaithfeas de léim dul i mbarr claí
Le heagla Shéarlais an faraire tréitheach
　Is glanfar as Éirinn leis Seán Buí.

Beidh gairm ag Gaelaibh go fairsing 'na dhéidh sin
　Is Gallaibh dá dtraochadh mar táthaoi,
Beidh preabaire Gaelach 'na scafaire méara
　Is an chathair faoi féin is ní cás linn;
Beidh aifrinn naofa i gceallaibh na hÉireann
　Is beidh cantain ag éigse go hardbhinn
Is ar mh'fhallaing go mbéadsa is céad ainnir mar aon liom
　Ag magadh gan traochadh faoi Sheán Buí.

TRANSLATION

Cease bitter weeping, good friends, scatter not your tears, there is no need; old Banba's valiant champions are standing by with fearsome threat: the English-speaking contingent ruling Ireland who have placed high exactions on our poor clergy are destined to be in subjection answering orders from the Gael, and Seán Buí will have no power to free them.

The Jameses will return by a miracle of His Only Son, and your loud wailing will cease of itself. For although you have long languished and pulled the load while tyrants own your towns in which your rights are denied, yet there is not one gluttonous upstart stuffed full of lies but will be forced to scale a fence for fear of the versatile hero, Charles, and by him will Seán Buí be expelled out of Ireland.

After that Gaels will assemble from every side and the English will be beaten down as you are; an Irish champion will take charge as mayor and the city he will have for his own, and we welcome that. Holy masses will be read in the chapels of Ireland and poets will be singing loudly, and by my cloak! I with a hundred other maidens will be mocking Seán Buí without ceasing.

MÁIRE NIC A LIONDAIN

(*fl.* 1771)

COILLTE GLASA AN TRIÚCHA
(The Green Woods of Triúch)
(*c.* 1750?)

[Many poems by Máire Nic a Liondain seem to have been lost, and an inferior composition of his own was attributed to her by a later poet, but there is no reason to doubt the ascription to her of two long poems: a poem of welcome to one Joseph Plunkett to her home neighbourhood near 'Úrchnoc Céin Mhic Cáinte', north of Dundalk, County Louth, and an elegy of 248 lines on his death in 1771. The former is in *amhrán* metre, the latter in *caoineadh* metre.

Máire's father, Pádraig Mac a Liondain (*c.* 1665–1733), a landed gentleman who kept open house for Gaelic poets, was himself a poet and a harper. It is quite possible that her brother, Pádraig Mac a Liondain, was the harper of that name from whom Edward Bunting (1773–1843) collected some airs in 1802. 'Coillte Glasa an Triúcha' was named by the harper Arthur O'Neill (*c.* 1734–1816) as the air he played in competition at two grand balls held at Granard, County Longford, in 1781 and 1782, and again at the great Belfast Harp Festival of 1792. One of the houses mentioned by O'Neill as among those he visited on his countrywide tours was that of Joseph Plunkett's son.

There are many versions of the words of 'Coillte Glasa an Triúcha' but, excluding the ones that have borrowed no more than the title, the range of variation is such as one would find in a frequently sung song. The song is attributed to Máire's father, and once to another local poet named Niall Mac Canna, but it is her name that is most frequently associated with it. Her authorship would fit with the preceding details, and the song's occasional assonantal irregularites are mirrored in her two long poems. One is left to wonder whether she also composed the air. There is at least one source which says she played the harp.

The text, in modernized orthography, is based on Énri Ó Muirgheasa, *Céad de Cheoltaibh Uladh* (Baile Átha Cliath: Mac Giolla agus a Mhac, 1915), pp. 133–5. A few readings have been adopted from Dublin, Royal Irish Academy Library, MS 23 B 19, p. 89, and MS 23 E 12, pp. 355–6. The translation is by Moya Cannon.]

Dar mo láimh duit, a chailín, má ghluaisfir chun
    bealaigh
  Go bhfuighidh tú an uile shúgradh,
Céim, ól agus imirt, pléisiúr go deimhin
  Is féachaint mara agus cuain liom;
Níl traona nó truideog, smaolach nó fuiseog,
  Nó cuach bhinn bhlasta chumhra,
Nach mbeidh dhuit i gceiliúr, is téada dá seinm
  Fa choilltibh glasa an Triúcha.

Ó Pharrthas ní aithin damh aon áit insan
    chruinne
  Is áilne is is deise cúirtibh —
Fonn agus fearann, coill agus abhaill,
  Toradh trom, piorraí is úlla;
Caora ar chrannaibh, cná buí ar choillibh,
  Ag dortadh le ceathaibh cnuasaigh,
An chóisir inár gcoinne, is na céadtaí dár
    gcineadh
  Fa choilltibh glasa an Triúcha.

(An Cailín)
Aidmhím gan scáth gur maith a bhfuil tú a' rá
  Fá thorthaibh is fá bhláth cnuasaigh;
'S gurb aoibhinn an áit atá againn le fáil
  Is nach eagal dúinn go bráth cumha ann.
Acht dá mbeadh seinm na ndán is gach éan dá
    rabh san airc
  Ag ceiliúr go bráth dúinne,

Char mhiste dhúinn cáil den arán a bheith i
   láthair
   I gcoilltibh glasa an Triúcha.

(Eisean)
Tuig-se, a ghrá, iar gcruthú do Ádhamh,
   Nach arán a bhí i ndáil dúinne;
Cé go bhfuair sé gan spás compánach mná
   Is go ndeachaidh sé go Parrthas nua léi.
Acht dá gcongbhaidís a lámh ó aon úll amháin
   Ba é ár n-oiliúin cáil cnuasaigh,
Acht ní heagal dúinn cáin na haithne sin go bráth
   Fá choilltibh glasa an Triúcha.

Gheobhaimíd araon tigheadas dúinn féin
   Ar ealta an aeir san Triúcha,
Is ceatha dlúith' éisc ar easaibh go séimh,
   Is níorbh eagal dúinn ár mbeatha bheith
      dubhchroíoch.
Beidh duilliúr na gcraobh dár bhfolach ón
   ghréin,
   Agus ceiliúr na n-éan dár ndúisgeadh,
Uallghuth na ngadhar 'san bhforaois lenár
   dtaobh
   Agus an eilit ar a léim lúith leo.

(An Cailín)
A ógánaigh chaoimh, más deimhin gur fíor
   An méid sin a chuir tú i n-iúl damh,
Ar thorthaibh na gcraobh, 's ar áilne gach ní,
   Fán aird seo thíos don chúige,
Spré nó maoin ní ghabhfainn mar bhríb,
   Nó saibhreas ar rí mar chúitiú,
Gan bliain agus mí a chaitheamh do mo shaol
   Fa choilltibh glasa an Triúcha.

(Eisean)
A ainnir chiúin tséimh, is aithne damh féin
   Gach ní dá bhfuil do dhúil ann,
An saibhreas is fearr d'fhág mé mo dheaghaidh
   I n-oiliúin d'aireamh dhúchais.
Chífir cruithneacht mhaol, coirce geal na
   gcraobh,
   Is eorna ar gach taobh go dlúth ann,
Ná ceasnaigh go mbéir gan arán de phlúr déis
   Fá choillte glasa an Triúcha.

A spéirbhean bhreasnaí an déid ghil chailce
   Triall is bí ag teacht chun an Triúcha,
Is ní baol duit easbhaidh is mise ar mo mheisnigh
   Nó ar léim dhá chos go lúfar;

Nuair a bheas céad bean go tuirseach beidh
   mise agus tusa
   Le pléisiúr ag baint na n-úll ann,
Gheobhair mil ar gach cuiseog is líon geal 'na
   shliseog
   Fá choillte glasa an Triúcha.

TRANSLATION

If you come with me, girl, I give you my word
   You'll have every kind of diversion,
Dance, drink and sport, pleasure of all sorts
   And viewing of bays and oceans.
There's no stare[1] or corncrake, no thrush or lark
   Or clear-tuned, musical cuckoo
But will join in chorus when strings are struck
   Under the green woods of Triúch.

No place in the firmament save Paradise itself
   Has houses so fine and handsome —
Farms of good land, orchard and woodland
   Weighed down with pears and apples;
Berries on the branch, yellow nuts in the woods,
   Bowed low under clustered bounty,
A party out to greet us, our kin soon gathered,
   Under the green woods of Triúch.

(The Young Woman)
I'll admit straight away it is fine what you say
   About fruit and fruiting blossom;
That place we might have is pleasant for sure
   And there we would never fear sorrow.
Yet if the music of all arts and all the birds in
   the ark
   For us were singing in tune,
We would still have to have a little bread to hand
   Under the green woods of Triúch.

(The Young Man)
Oh, understand, dear, after Adam's creation,
   Bread was never intended as our share;
Though he was soon granted a female companion
   And they gained a new Paradise together.
But from that fated apple had they stayed their
   hands
   We would still be nourished on wild fruit,
Yet the weight of that command will not fall on us
   Under the green woods of Triúch.

1. Starling.

Together we'll gain wherewithal for ourselves
    From the flocks of the air in Triúch.
Weirs will yield up dense showers of fish
    And there's no fear we'll ever face hardship.
The leaves of the trees will shield us from sun
    And the chorus of birds will rouse us,
There'll be baying of hounds in the forest nearby
    With the light leaping doe out before them.

(The Young Woman)
Oh, gentle young man, if it's true for sure,
    All of what you tell me
Of fruit on the branch and beauty all around
    In that place in the south of the province,
I'll accept no bribe of dowry or wealth
    Or the riches of a king in lieu,
But a month and a year of my life I will spend
    Under the green woods of Triúch.

(The Young Man)
Oh mild, tender girl, I know full well
    Everything you desire now,

I turned my back on the finest wealth
    To serve my time as a ploughman.
You'll see bread wheat,[2] bright branching oats
    And barley on every side of you,
You'll never complain of lack of bread or grain
    Around the green woods of Triúch.

Oh, witty lady of the pearly teeth
    Come on away with me now,
You'll want for nothing for I have vigour
    And two limber legs for leaping;
Though a hundred women tire, you and I with
    pleasure
    Will still pluck apples together,
You'll have honey in hives and flax in sleighs[3]
    Around the green woods of Triúch.

2. *Cruithneacht mhaol*: (literally 'bald wheat') awnless wheat, commonly known as 'bread wheat'.
3. *Sliseog*: an oblong stack in which flax was built after being taken from the dam and dried.

MÁIRE NÍ DHONNAGÁIN

(*fl.* 1760)

AN PEACACH
(The Sinner)
(*c.* 1760?)

[The most precise statement on the identity of Máire Ní Dhonnagáin known at present is that which precedes this poem. It is confirmed by internal evidence in a second poem attributed to her, an elegy on the death of her brother of which part was composed at Dungarvan, in County Waterford, where he was waked, sometime in the mid-eighteenth century. Although she is said to have been prolific, these are the only poems by her known to have survived.

The heading tells that she composed the poem 'when the Church declined to admit her to confession' but her words shed no light on the reason for the refusal. The theme of repentance is well represented in Irish-language poetry since the seventeenth century. The poet suggests her expectation of salvation by identifying with the penitent Mary Magdalen, and with Israel, and she expresses the hope that she may be included in Mary's train of women.

The edition is based primarily on Dublin, Royal Irish Academy Library, MS 12 E 24, p. 153; MS 23 M 8, p. 264; and MS 23 C 13, p. 39. It and the translation are by the present writer, Pádraig A. Breatnach.]

Máire Ní Dhonnagáin *cecinit* ag admháil a peacaí do Dhia an tan do dhiúltaigh an Eaglais a glacadh chum faoistine. Do chónaigh an bhean-fhile seo i Sliabh gCua i gContae Phort Láirge insa mbliain 1760 nó i dtimpeall na haimsire sin agus ba fhile líofa í.

Mo fhaoisidín glan go pras don chléir chirt
In ainm an Athar, agus an Mhic agus an
    Spioraid Naofa:
I bpeaca an uabhair ba bhuanna tréan mé,
I bpeaca na sainte a bhfaighinn do chéilinn,
I bpeaca na drúise dar mo chúis! níor shaor mé,

I bpeaca an chraois do ghnínn nuair fhéadainn,
I bpeaca na feirge mo dheifir, bhínn traochta,
I bpeaca an fhormaid mo dhochar! ba léir mé,
I bpeaca na leisce ní cheilim ar aon chor
M'urnaithe chum Críosd go faillítheach do
    dhéininn
Is ba ró-annamh chum aifreann Dé mé.
Acht anois ó chím gur chloígh an saol mé
Gur lagaigh mo chaint, mo radharc, 's m'éiseacht,
Fóir agus leighis mé, a Dhia-Mhic naofa
Agus roinn cheart don aithrí mar Dháibhí léig
    liom.

Is maith do chím mo ghníomhartha saolta,
Laghad m'aoibhnis bídh agus éadaigh!
Monuar! ní chaoinim ar Chríost fuair daorchrois
Ná an t-allas fola a doirteadh dá éadan
Insa ngáirdín is gárdaí géara air.
Do tharraing an slua monuar! an Dé-Mhac
Go halla Philate a bhfeighil a dhaortha,
Do tháinig an chine Iúdaí i ndlúthdhlí dhaor air,
Níor chuireadar láimh i bpáirt a shaortha,
Do chaith sé an oíche agus daoirse dhaor air,
Arna mháireach níor bhfearr a scéalta,
Dia hAoine do bhí chúig mhíle daorlot
Ar a chorp séimh seang nár thionscain aon olc
'Dul tar mo cheann-sa i gcrann na péine
Agus san gan amhras d'fhonn mé shaoradh.
Tarraingeadh a chlí gan scíth ó chéile,
Cuireadh tairní 'na dhearnaí naofa,
An tsleá thríd ón dtaoibh go chéile,
Fáisgeadh pionna 'na throithe le faobhar,
'S an deoch dhomlais d'ibhis mar mhéile í.

Ní plát ná talamh ná flaitheas an tsaoil seo
Do thóg tú de rogha ach an chlann úd Éabha;
Seo mar dhíolas-sa an cíos in éiric
Fuil do chroí do sgaoileadh ar dhaorchrois:
Saint is díomas, baois is bréaga,
Móide móra, uabhar is éitheach,
Fuath is faillí is taithí chlaonta,
Agus fós níor thaithíos an aithrí a dhéanamh.

A rí do rin grása ar Mháire Magdaléna
Is ar an bpuibliocánach an uair do iarr air,
Do rin ród glan díreach tríd an dtréanmhuir
Do chlann Israoil dá ndíon ón méirleach,
Go bhfuascla tú mo chrua-ghlasa in éineacht
Is go leige tú suas ar shluagha Mhic Dé mé!
Nó ar bhantracht Muire má thitim ní baol dom.
A rí na n-aingeal fuair peannaid is péin-bhroid,

Do chuaigh go fada 's go gearra dár saoradh,
Do thug sealad i dtalamh na hÉigipt',
Do thobhaigh na hapstail chum teagasc do
    dhéanamh —
As ucht gach turais do thugais dár saoradh,
As ucht na croise 'na rineadh tú a chéasadh,
As ucht do bhuime bhí tuirseach ad fhéachaint
Saor-sa mise ó ifreann péineach!

Mo chrá croí nach fáiltíonn Mac Dé dhom
Fáiltí im pháirtíocht uair éigin,
Nó mar ard-chíos in áit mo ghníomhartha saolta
An áithrí mar Dháibhí do dhéanamh.

TRANSLATION

Máire Ní Dhonnagáin sang this, acknowledging her sins before God when the Church declined to admit her to confession. This poetess lived in Sliabh gCua in Co. Waterford in the year 1760 or about that time and she was a prolific poet.

(Here is) my full and ready confession to the good clergy in the name of the Father, and the Son and the Holy Spirit. In the sin of pride I was a practised champion, in the sin of covetousness I used to hide whatever I got; in the sin of adultery, by faith, I was not free of stain; and the sin of gluttony I practised whenever I could; from the sin of anger, alas, I was ever tired; as for the sin of envy, my guilt alas! was clear; as for the sin of sloth I hide not at all that I was remiss in my prayers to Christ, and too infrequently attended God's mass. But now, seeing that the world has overcome me, that my speech has failed, (and also) my sight, my hearing, assist and heal me, O Holy Son of God, and grant to me like David a proper portion of contrition.

I well behold my worldly deeds, my dearth of joy, of food and clothing. Alas, I do not keen for Christ and his passion on the cross, or the bloodsweat that spilled from his brow in the garden when keen guards surrounded him. The crowd alas! dragged the God-Son to Pilate's hall to condemn him (and) the Jewish race bore down upon him with a strict and cruel code; they raised no hand to free him; he passed the night in cruel bondage. On the morrow his lot was no better. On Friday five thousand cruel wounds were on the smooth fair flesh of him who did no wrong as he went to be hung on the cross of suffering on my behalf, and, of course, in order that I might be redeemed. His body was torn relentlessly apart, nails were put in his holy palms, and a spear from one side through to the other. A sharpened peg was put through his feet, and You drank of the gall as a potion.

You chose not plate nor land nor wordly power, but the race of Eve. Here is how I settled my obligation for the spilling of Your heart's blood on the cross of the passion: with greed, and spite, folly, and lies, great oaths, pride, and mendacity, hate, and laxity, and by yielding to temptation, and still I did not practise contrition.

O King who bestowed grace on Mary Magdalen and on the publican when he sought it, who made a clear straight road through the mighty sea for the children of Israel protecting them from slaughter, may You loosen my hard bonds together and may You allow me up to join the followers of the Son of God, or if I fall among the train of Mary's women, there I will be out of danger.

O King of the angels who suffered pain and torture, who went to every extremity to redeem us, who sojourned in the land of Egypt, who chose the apostles to give instruction, for the sake of every journey that you made in order to deliver us, for the sake of the cross upon which you were tortured, for the sake of your mother who sorrowed at seeing you, deliver me from hell's punishment.

Alas! that the Son of God does not receive me to welcome my devotion at some time or, as recompense for my worldly deeds, to confess my sins as David did.

AINDRIAS MAC CRAITH

(*c.* 1709–95)

ÉIGSÍNÍ BAN AGUS TAE
(On Tay-Drinking Poetesses)
(18th century)

Text and translation are from: Criostoir O'Flynn, *The Maigue Poets: Filí na Máighe* (Dublin: Obelisk Books, 1995), pp. 119–20.]

[One of the functions of the eighteenth-century *cúirt filíochta*, 'court of poetry', was to maintain high stylistic and formal standards among the poets and to decry shoddy verse-making by amateurs. Aindrias Mac Craith was one of the two leading figures at the *cúirt filíochta* which gathered at Croom in County Limerick (on the other, Seán Ó Tuama an Ghrinn, see p. 442). Although he earned his living, in part at least, as a teacher, he was nicknamed 'An Mangaire Súgach', usually translated 'The Merry Pedlar'. This poem does seem to suggest he was a monger of some kind (particularly if *cumaisc* in line 16 refers to 'compounds'). His image of the female scribbler may also owe something to experience, although simultaneously a construct. Since the *cúirt filíochta* was an exclusive club, perhaps aspiring women writers in the Croom district provided their own encouragement at another kind of venue.

Is cráite an scéal sa taobh so chluinim
Ag dáimh is cléir is éigse is uile,
Stráill gan bhéasa ach Béarla briste
Ón Mháigh go Féile de réir mar thuigim;
Má tá aici réal don tsaol nó scilling
Nach áil gan téa tug gaoth tar uisce;
Bíonn cába daor ar phéist an phruisle
Is lása fé go néata aici-se;
Bíonn lámhaing is créip is réidh-bhruit eile
'S go bráth an téa dá gléas mar thuilleamh;
Seo an fáth bheir Gaeil gan séan gan uirrim,
Gan stát gan séad gan spré gan spionnadh,
Fá cháim gach lae dá dtraochadh ag foirinn,
'S gan fáil 'na ngaor go téacht don duine;

Seo an fáth bheir mé gan chéim gan chiste
Gach lá, mo léan, ag plé le cumaisc;
Go bráth lem ré ag réabadh dlithe
I bpáirt na méirleach méithe buile;
Gach sár-fhear séimh ó Mhéin go Cuilinn,
Idir bhaird is éigse is saor-fhlaith cliste,
Is cás na nGael 's a gcléir fá thuirse
Is mnáibh an téa ag scríobh véarsa is fiche;
A lucht an téa, is trua bhur dtoisc-se,
Is bocht bhur scéal, is buartha bhur gcor-sa;
Is cathach le sealad mé 's is fraochmhar dreóil
Is d'atharraigh ar mhalairt cruith mo ghné 's
    mo shnódh,
Tá an ainnise go dearfa mar aon im dhóid
Ó scaras leis an ngasra nár chlaon i ngleo;
Is eatarthu do chaitheas-sa mo shaol go sóch
I gcarrabhas ag reacaireacht 's ag déanamh spóirt,
An baraille gan dearmad dá thaoscadh ar bhord
Is dramanna in aice sin le héigean póit.

TRANSLATION

The news that's reached me here upsets me:
Scholars, clergy and poets tell me
That uncouth streels with their broken English
From Maigue to Feale — it's hard to credit —
Come sixpence or a shilling in their way
Must order some of this foreign tay.
Each slimy slobberer in a costly cape
With lace beneath all nice and nate,
Gloves and crepe and fine soft wraps,
Must have her tay-cup in her lap.
No wonder our race is so dispirited,
Deprived and landless, sore afflicted,
Daily oppressed by a foreign class
Until that Person comes at last.
No wonder I'm left an outcast pauper
Depending, alas, on mongrels haughty,
Driven to lawless ways of living
Consorting with fat and foolish villains.
I call every true man in this land,
All cultured minds, each poet and bard,
To consider the state of country and clergy
And the tay-drinking women scribbling verses.
And you lovers of tay, your notions I pity,
Sad is your state, your values all twisted.
Regretful and angry, in spirit laid low,
My shape and my features despondency show;
In misery now I'm doomed to stay
From valiant comrades sent far away.
How pleasant it was when with them I sat
For our merry reciting and playing at cards,
The barrel to empty when we gathered round,
The glasses well filled with drink strong and
    sound.

SEÁN Ó MURCHADHA NA RÁITHÍNEACH

(1700–1762)

AR MHÁIRE NÍ CHRUALAOICH, SÁPPHÓ NA MUMHAN
(On Máire Ní Chrualaoich, the Sappho of Munster)
(1761)

[Not a word of Máire Ní Chrualaoich's poetry is thought to survive, nor any information about her except that she was known as 'Sápphó na Mumhan' and died in 1761. These short poems by three of her contemporaries must speak for her. Tadhg Gaelach's lines do not have the final foot found in the lines of the other poems, but otherwise the metre in all three is the same: clearly, the poets were intent on echoing each other. Tadhg Gaelach invokes the virginity trope when he says that Máire Ní Chrualaoich was assumed into heaven, and she is described as 'ógh', 'virgin', in Seán Ó Murchadha's poem. Perhaps she was an uncloistered vowed virgin, as Máire Lawless of *Párliament na mBan* seems to have been (cf. pp. 159–61). This speculation needs weighed in relation to the force of her epithet, 'Sappho'.

The Irish texts, here in normalized orthography, are from: Pádraig Úa Duinnín (ed.), *Filidhe na Máighe* (Baile Átha Cliath: Gill agus a Mhac, 1906), pp. 78-9. All three translations are by Biddy Jenkinson.]

An bláth is buacaí ghluais puinn eadrainn beo
  — in Éirinn,
Bás cé fuair sí, a huaislíocht mairfidh go deo —
  déanach,
Sápphó sua-ghníomhach nduan mbinn, startha
  agus comhad — nGaeilge,
Máire shuairc Ní Chrualaoich, eala 'gus óigh —
  's Phoenics.

The fairest flower that held sway here in Ireland
Was snatched by Death yet lives, her fame eternal.
Wise-acting Sappho of metres, couplets, sweet
  songs,
Dear Máire Ní Chrualaoich, phoenix, virgin
  and swan.

SEÁN Ó TUAMA AN GHRINN

(c. 1707–75)

AR MHÁIRE NÍ CHRUALAOICH, SÁPPHÓ NA MUMHAN
(On Máire Ní Chrualaoich,
Sappho of Munster)
(1761)

[See preceding headnote. Translation: Biddy Jenkinson.]

Seo an bás le ruaig nimhe bhuaidhir sinn,
  easnamh is mó — méala,
An bás im thrua-chlí chuir crua-shaighead is
  bearanna bróin — baogail,
An bháin-chnis d'fhuasclaíodh uaim ríomh
  ranna agus cló — daornod,
'S ní bás do fuair sí acht nua-shlí in amharc na
  nOrd — naofa.

Don dáimh is uaill í is crua-shnaidhm ceangail
  ar chló — céadfa,
An bás lér fuadaíodh uainn grinn greanadh san
  gcomhar — gcléire,

Máire an stua shníomhadh cnuas cruinn eagna
  is eoil — éigeas,
I dtámh mar chuaidh sí is uaigníocht easnaimh
  ar fód — Éireann.

TRANSLATION

This death in its cruel onslaught has left us
  anguished, aching,
Has put shafts of sorrow through my breast,
  sharp arrows fearful.
The fair one who solved for me dark riddles of
  verse making
Has left on a new course in the company of
  angels.

That death snatched from the poetic company
  its keen engraver
Has left our senses bound in black knots, has
  caused a cry of lamentation.
Máire, the stately one, weaver of wisdom and
  poets' learning,
In dying has bereaved the land of Ireland.

TADHG GAELACH Ó SÚILLEABHÁIN

(c. 1715–95)

AR MHÁIRE NÍ CHRUALAOICH, SÁPPHÓ NA MUMHAN
(On Máire Ní Chrualaoich, the Sappho of Munster)
(1761)

[See headnote on p. 441. Translation: Biddy Jenkinson.]

Ní bás do fuair sí ach guaillíocht aingeal is ord,
Is fáil go suairc síoch i gcuan dín Athar na
    gcumhacht,
Grá na slua í i n-uaim ghrinn ranna 'gus
    comhad,
'S í Máire luaim Ní Chrualaoich neartaigh mo
    bhrón.

Tá gáir is uall-chaí ag slua sí i bhfearannaibh
    Eoghain,
Cois Má is Ruachtaí, bruach Laoi is Life go
    Feoir,
Más cáil d'uaislíos do bhuaidh sí pearsa 'gus
    cló,
Máire Ní Chrualaoich is trua linn marbh faoin
    bhfód.

Ba bhinne ná cuach í, slua sí, is téada ceoil,
Ba shamhail le Nuaga í is bhuaidh sí ar Aonghas
    Óg,
Cuisle na ndrua í, tuar dín éigse is ord,
Is mo mhilleadh go cruaidh í i n-uaigh thíos
    faon ar feo.

Seacht gcéad déag is aon 'na chuim,
Is trí fichid mar áirím,
Ó fhulaing Chríost dhiaga an rí,
Go bás Mháire Ní Chrualaoich.

TRANSLATION

Not death, this carrying off shoulder-high by
    ranks of angels,
This joyous lodging in the Lord's safe haven.
Darling of all in her keen crafting of polished
    verses,
Máire Ní Chrualaoich has left me in sorrow
    past bearing.

Keening and wailing are the Shee of the land of
    Eoghan,
From Máigh and Ruachtach, by Laoi and Life
    to Feoir,[1]
Fame and form and grace itself, laid low
Máire Ní Chrualaoich, dead in her grave, our
    woe.

Sweeter than cuckoo call, sweeter than
    harp-strings, her song.
Compare her to Nuaga.[2] Aonghas Óg[3] she
    outshone.
Pulse of the poets, refuge of wisdom and worth
My destruction, my grief, that she withers away
    in the earth.

Máire Ní Chrualaoich died
Seventeen hundred and sixty one AD

1. This, and the preceding four names, denote rivers which flow
   largely through counties Limerick, Kerry, Cork, Dublin and
   Kilkenny.
2. Alias Nuadha, a mythical king of the Túatha Dé Danann.
3. A mythical chief of the Túatha Dé Danann, son of the Daghda.

MÁIRE NÍ MHURCHÚ

(*fl.* 1802)

AR MHINISTIR A THUG ANBHÁS DÓ FÉIN
(On a Minister Who Killed Himself) (1802)

[The various copies of this poem name its author as Máire
Ní Mhurchú and tell that it was composed in 1802. The poet
is otherwise unknown. The subject, a Protestant minister
who, according to the text, cut his own throat, is unidentified. The words *crosara an mhuilinn* in the first line may
represent an unidentified place-name. The language of the
poem is that of Munster, but its district is undetermined.

The opening verses praise the dead man for his virtues,
but praise soon gives way to invective. His good qualities
can bring him no benefit due to the error of his religion,
and so all that awaits him in the afterlife is to be received
by the devil in hell. A mixture of biblical, classical and
fiannaíocht traditions combine to give the character of
hell's torments. The final part of the poem looks forward
to a time when the mass is the only service in Ireland's
churches, and the followers of Calvin and Luther with
their ministers are gathered together in hell.

The metre is a popular variety of *amhrán* with lax
assonance and without isosyllabism, indicating that the
author may have been unpractised.

The edition is based on texts in Dublin, Royal Irish
Academy Library, MS 23 M 11, p. 228, and MS 24 M 4,
p. 271, and National Library of Ireland, MS G 218, p. 166.
It and the translation are by the present writer, Pádraig A.
Breatnach.]

Máire Ní Mhurchú *cct* 1802 ar mhinistir do
  thug anbhás dó féin.

Ag crosara an mhuilinn do bhí againn ministir
  Is ba ghrámhar, soineanta, an chomharsa é;
Do bhí ró-thuicseanach don fhánaí dhona
  Do bhíodh gan costas an bhóthair;
Do mhná is do leinbh do chíodh i n-uireaspa,
  Is deimhin go bpiocadh sé a phóca,
'S an t-éadach go dtugadh dá chnámha mar
  fhothain
  Don té bhíodh ar uireaspa córach.

Ní rinne a charthanacht ná a dhéirc aon tairbhe
  Mar ná raibh a theagasc ar fónamh

An tan nár baisteadh i dteampall Pheadair é
  De ghein ón Spiorad bheannaithe
  chomhachtach;
'Dul ar tarmann réaltan Pharthais
  Níor bhaol go ngearrfadh sé a scórnach,
Mar is mór é a caradas leis na trí pearsanaibh
  Is aoirde i gcathair na glóire.

Síol ní thigeann ar gheamhar na hiothlann
  Nuair ná cuirthear é ar fónamh,
Is chum trócaire ní thugann a dhéirc an ministir
  Nuair ná leanann sé an bóthar;
As iompar na croise tá súil againne
  Le dul go flaitheas na glóire
Mar is í sompla is teagasc do sheol an Leanbh í
  Tháinig ar an dtalamh dár bhfóirthin.

Uabhar is iomarca do dhíbir Lucifer
  'S a bhuíon ó chathair na glóire,
'S gur le sméideadh ón Athair do bhí Ifreann
  damanta
  Déanta ar lasadh 'na gcomhair sin;
Nuair dhruid an uireaspa leis an ministir
  Ansin do ghearraigh sé a scórnach,
Mar bhí an diabhal ag siosma 's ag síorthabhairt
  cuireadh dhó
  Gonuig an bpoll nárbh uras a thón d'fháil.

Nuair ghluais an ministir anuas go hIfreann
  Bhí Sátan 'cur tine 'na chomhair síos,
Bhí Charon 's a choite aige ar an abhainn ag
  feitheamh leis
  Go dtabharfadh dó caladh gan feoirlinn;
Níorbh é sin an donas acht an áit 'na raibh
  Oscar
  Ar chúlaibh an dorais 'na chomhair sin
Gur bhuail sé liobar dá shúist fé fhuinneamh
  air,
  Ní rinne a ghúna a bheith casta air a thóin dó.

Do bhí ár gcreideamh 'na sheasamh ó aimsir
  Pheadair,
  Bhí soilse ar lasadh le dóchas;
Is iad ár sagairt do gheibheadh an deachú,
  Bhíodh toradh agus rath ar an dtórramh,
Go dtí Seán Cailbhin is Mártan mallaithe
  An dís do mhaslaigh an t-ord ceart,

’S an uair d’éirigh eatarthu de dhroim na
  heasmailte
  Do ghaibh gach duine acu atharrach bóthair.

Is uathu a shíolraigh grathain an choimheascair
  Do chuir eaglais Chríost faoi dhaorsmacht,
Gach nduine mar thíodh ag baint a *thext* as an
  mBíobla
  Bhí go hacrach scríofa i mBéarla;
Do bhriseadar Aoine agus Cátuir Thímpir
  ’S ní choinneochdaois saoire ar aon chor,
’S ní raibh in Muire de bhrí acu acht an oiread
  le mnaoi ar bith
  Is í banaltra an Rí do shaor sinn.

Go bhfeiceam-na an t-am go mbeith aifreann,
  cantaireacht,
  Is easbarta i dteampaill Éireann,
Go dtiocfaidh scaipeadh agus scannradh ar
  shliocht Chailbhin an chlampair
  Do rinne oruinne feall is éirleach;
Gach ministir cíordhubh do bhriseann an Aoine
  ’S ná géillfeadh do shaoire na Naomh ngeal
In Ifreann suíte is an deachú dá díol leis
  ag Oscar is a mhaoil dá phléascadh.

TRANSLATION

Máire Ní Mhurchú said this in 1802 concerning
a minister who killed himself.

At the mill cross we had a minister, a kind well-
intentioned neighbour full of understanding
towards the poor wayfarer who had not the price
of the road, and ever sure to put his hand in his
pocket for women and children he saw in need;
he gave the clothes from his back to shelter
whoever wanted.

Neither his charity nor his alms were of benefit
for his teaching was false as he had not been
baptised in the church of Peter that sprang from
the holy powerful Spirit. Had he sought the
protection of the Star of Paradise there is no fear
that he would have cut his throat, for great is her
friendship with the three persons that are most
high in the City of Glory.

No seed comes from the springing corn when it
is not properly sown, and his alms do not lead the

minister to mercy when he does not follow the
road. From the carrying of the cross we hope to
go to heaven's glory because that is the example
and teaching that sent the Child who came on
earth to help us.

Pride and excess banished Lucifer and his
followers from the City of Glory, and by gesture
from the Father hell of damnation was made ready
and lit for them. When indigence came upon the
minister he cut his throat then because the devil
was sowing dissension and ever inviting him to the
pit whose bottom it was not easy to find.

When the minister set off down into hell Satan
was setting a fire for him, Charon[1] with his hounds
was waiting on the river to give him passage at not
a farthing's cost. That was not the worst, but
where Oscar[2] was waiting for him behind the door
he swung his flail at him with force, his cloak being
tied around him did not save him (?).

Our faith stood from the time of Peter, lights were
lit with hope. It was our priests who used get the
tithe, the harvest was fruitful and prosperous,
until there came John Calvin and wicked Martin
[Luther], the pair who insulted the true order.
And when they disagreed as a consequence of the
insult, each of them took a different road.

From them descended the contentious swarm who
put Christ's church in thrall, every one of them
taking his text from the Bible conveniently written
in English. They ignored Friday, and Ember Days,
and respected not Holidays at all, and for them
Mary who is the nurse of the King, who delivered
us, was no more than just any woman.

May we see the time that the mass, chant, and
vespers will be in the churches of Ireland, that
dispersal and fear may descend upon the seed of
acrimonious Calvin who betrayed and persecuted us, that every black minister who ignores
Friday and does not respect the Holidays of the
bright saints may be seated in hell and the tithe
paid to him by Oscar flailing the top of his head.

1. The ferryman who conveys souls across the Styx to Hades.
2. Tradition has it that Oscar, like others of the Fianna, was consigned
   to hell. Saint Patrick petitioned for some relief for him from his
   torments. God responded by equipping Oscar with a flail.

ANONYMOUS

CILL CHAIS
(Kilcash)
(*c.* 1802)

[The story of Old Cill Chais ends a few years after the death of John Butler (Seán Buitléir), 18th Earl of Ormond, in 1795. The castle, on a slope of Slievnamon in south Tipperary, had been in Butler hands since about 1540; it may have been a church site as early as the sixth century. John was the last of the Butlers to be buried there. If the poem encompasses three generations of the family, the presiding spirit is that of Lady Iveagh, wife of Thomas Butler (Tomás Buitléir, d. 1734).

Margaret (Mairghréad), Lady Iveagh, was a daughter of Mac Uilliam Búrc, 7th Earl of Clanrickard, County Galway. Her first husband, Brian Mag Aonghusa (Magenis) of Iveagh, County Down, died in 1696 and she married Colonel Thomas Butler in the same year; both men had fought against William III. Colonel Butler was pardoned for his role in the Battle of Aughrim in 1691 but remained a Jacobite sympathizer. Lady Margaret's brother, Lord Galway, died at Aughrim. Her sister, Onóra, married firstly Patrick Sarsfield, and secondly James Fitzjames, *maréchal* of France, a natural son of James II. These relations instance her more obvious ties of loyalty to the Stuart cause.

In Rome in 1712, her husband's brother, Christopher (d. 1757), was consecrated Archbishop of Cashel. His visits to Cill Chais were made as a fugitive from the Penal Laws and the professional priest-hunters. Lady Margaret was staunchly Catholic, and widely renowned for her personal piety and for harbouring and supporting Catholic clerics. Consequently, and especially as she outlived Thomas Butler by ten years, it is not surprising that the poem brackets her with Christopher Butler, the 'bishop' of the second verse.

Cruelly, two of her sons, and three of her daughters (including Onóra, on whom see above at pp. 430–32) predeceased her. Her remaining son, John, who converted to Protestantism, died in 1766, leaving no descendants as heirs. The castle passed to his first cousin Walter Butler (1703–83), *de jure* 16th Earl of Ormond (whose name has been eclipsed by that of his youngest daughter, Lady Eleanor Butler, one of the 'Ladies of Llangollen', on whom see pp. 1092–3). Walter Butler's only son, John (1740–95), 17th Earl of Ormond, also a convert to Protestantism, led a hectic, hard-drinking life which endeared him to many. His funeral was the last great social event at Cill Chais Castle. His son Walter, the 18th Earl, sold it 'for a trifling consideration' around 1800. The fine woods of oak, ash, beech and elm were sold in two lots, in 1797 and 1801. The 18th Earl, 'prionsa na nGael', and his Countess, 'ainnir na míne', went to live in England a few years later. They were among the first to leave Ireland after the Act of Union of 1800.

This version of the text was edited by Daithí Ó hÓgáin, and translated by Eiléan Ní Chuilleanáin. For text and translation, and for a detailed history of Cill Chais, see: John Flood and Phil Flood, *Kilcash 1190–1801* (Dublin: Geography Publications, 1999); cf. Eoghan Ó Néill, *Gleann an Óir* (Baile Átha Cliath: An Clóchomhar, 1988), pp. 178–83.]

Créad a dhéanfaimid feasta gan adhmad,
tá deireadh na gcoillte ar lár;
níl trácht ar Chill Chais ná a teaghlach,
is ní bainfear a cling go bráth;
an áit úd ina gcónaíodh an deighbhean
a fuair gradam is meidhir tar mhná,
bhíodh iarlaí ag tarraing tar toinn ann,
is an tAifreann binn á rá.

Is é mo chreach fhada is mo léan goirt
do gheataí breá néata ar lár,
an *avenue* ghreanta faoi shaothar
is gan foscadh ar aon taobh den *walk*,
an chúirt bhreá a sileadh an braon di
is an ghasra shéimh go tláith,
is in leabhar na marbh do léitear
an tEaspag is *Lady Iveagh*!

Ní chluinim fuaim lacha ná gé ann
ná fiolair ag déanadh aeir cois cuain,
ná fiú na mbeacha chum saothair
a thabharfadh mil agus céir don tslua,
níl ceol binn milis na n-éan ann
le hamharc an lae a dhul uainn,
ná an chuaichín i mbarra na ngéag ann,
— ó, 'sí chuirfeadh an saol chum suain!

Nuair a thigeann na poic faoi na sléibhte
is an gunna lena dtaobh is an líon
féachann siad anuas le léan ar
an mbaile a fuair *sway* in gach tír;
an fhaiche bhreá aoibhinn ina réabacha
is gan foscadh ar aon taobh ón tsín,
páirc an p*haddock* ina *dairy*
mar a mbíodh an eilit ag déanadh a scíth'!

Tá ceo ag titim ar chraobhaibh ann
ná glanann le grian ná lá,
tá smúit ag titim ón spéir ann,
is a cuid uisce go léir ag trá;
níl coll, níl cuileann, níl caora ann,
ach clocha agus maolchlocháin;
páirc na foraoise gan chraobh ann,
is d'imigh an *game* chum fáin!

Anois mar bharr ar gach mí-ghreann
chuaigh prionsa na nGael tar sáil,
anonn le hainnir na míne
fuair gairm sa bhFrainc is sa Spáinn —
anois tá a cuallacht á caoineadh,
gheibheadh airgead buí agus bán,
's ná tógfadh seilbh na ndaoine,
acht caraid na bhfíorbhochtán.

Aitím ar Mhuire is ar Íosa
go dtaga sí arís chughainn slán,
go mbeidh rincí fada ag gabháil timpeall,
ceol veidhlín is tinte cnámh,
go dtógfar an baile seo ár sinsear
Cill Chais bhreá arís go hard,
is go brách nó go dtiocfaidh an díleann
ní fheicfear í arís ar lár!

TRANSLATION

What will we do now for timber
With the last of the woods laid low —
No word of Kilcash nor its household,
Their bell is silenced now,
Where the lady lived with such honour,
No woman so heaped with praise,
Earls came across oceans to see her
And heard the sweet words of Mass.

It's the cause of my long affliction
To see your neat gates knocked down,
The long walks affording no shade now
And the avenue overgrown,
The fine house that kept out the weather,
Its people depressed and tamed;
And their names with the faithful departed,
The Bishop and Lady Iveagh!

The geese and the duck's commotion,
The eagle's shout are no more,
The roar of the bees gone silent,
Their wax and their honey store
Deserted. Now at evening
The musical birds are stilled
And the cuckoo is dumb in the treetops
That sang lullaby to the world.

Even the deer and the hunters
That follow the mountain way
Look down upon us with pity,
The house that was famed in its day;
The smooth wide lawn is all broken,
No shelter from wind and rain;
The paddock has turned to a dairy
Where the fine creatures grazed.

Mist hangs low on the branches
No sunlight can sweep aside,
Darkness falls among daylight
And the streams are all run dry;
No hazel, no holly or berry,
Bare naked rocks and cold;
The forest park is leafless
And all the game gone wild.

And now the worst of our troubles,
She has followed the prince of the Gaels —
He has borne off the gentle maiden,
Summoned to France and to Spain
Her company laments her
That she fed with silver and gold:
One who never preyed on the people
But was the poor souls' friend.

My prayer to Mary and Jesus
She may come safe home to us here
To dancing and rejoicing
To fiddling and bonfire
That our ancestors' house will rise up,
Kilcash built up anew
And from now to the end of the story
May it never again be laid low.

Biographies/Bibliographies

Cormac mac Cuilennáin

LIFE. King-bishop and scholar-poet, Cormac belonged to the Eóganacht Chaisil, and ruled as King of Munster from 902 until his death in 908. Combination of ecclesiastical and secular office was common practice in Munster since the mid-ninth century. Cormac's work is the first prominent exemplification of an ecclesiastic's interest in secular literature. According to the Fragmentary Annals, he was educated at the Leinster monastery of Dísert Diarmata (Castledermot, County Kildare). His best-known work is the Irish-language *Sanas Cormaic* (*Cormac's Glossary*), perhaps the earliest etymological dictionary in a vernacular European language. It makes comparative links with other vernaculars and with Latin, Greek and Hebrew. Its lengthier citations constitute texts in themselves. He allegedly compiled the lost *Saltair Chaisil* (*Psalter of Cashel*), a miscellany which included genealogies, tribal lore and an origin legend for the Eóganacht of Munster; some of its contents survive in the fifteenth-century manuscript, Laud Miscellany 610 (Bodleian Library, Oxford). Various secular and religious poems are attributed to him, often spuriously. Two verse-texts attributed to him which are roughly contemporaneous are 'Cormac's Rule', a rule for Christian life, and 'A Poem Attributed to Cormac mac Cuilennáin' (below), a metrical list of the kings of Munster.

His attempt to exert his influence beyond Munster in the Northern Half led ultimately to his death in the Battle of Belach Mugna (Ballaghmoon, County Kildare) in 908. He was a celibate, and was revered after his death as a saint, whose feast was celebrated on 15 September.

CHIEF WRITINGS. For details on the various editions of *Sanas Cormaic*, see R.I. Best, *Bibliography of Irish Philology and of Printed Irish Literature to 1912* (Dublin: National Library of Ireland, 1913), pp. 6–7, and *Bibliography of Irish Philology and Manuscript Literature: Publication 1913–1941*, pp. 3–4. On the poems attributed to him see Best, *Bibliography . . . to 1912*, pp. 145, 148 and 155; Best, *Bibliography . . . 1913–1941*, pp. 103, 109 and 113; John Strachan, 'Cormac's Rule', *Ériu*, vol. 2 (1905), pp. 62–8; Proinsias Mac Cana, 'A Poem Attributed to Cormac mac Cuilennáin', *Celtica*, vol. 5 (1960), pp. 207–17.

BIOGRAPHY AND CRITICISM. James F. Kenney, *The Sources for the Early History of Ireland: Ecclesiastical* (New York: Columbia University Press, 1929), *passim*; F.J. Byrne, *Irish Kings and High-Kings* (London: B.T. Batsford, 1973), *passim*; Paul Russell, 'The Sounds of a Silence: The Growth of Cormac's Glossary', *Cambridge Medieval Celtic Studies*, no. 15 (summer 1988), pp. 1–30; Pádraig Ó Riain, 'The Psalter of Cashel: A Provisional List of Contents', *Éigse*, vol. 23 (1989), pp. 107–30; Máirín Ní Dhonnchadha, 'On Gormfhlaith Daughter of Flann Sinna and the Lure of the Sovereignty Goddess', in *Seanchas: Studies in Early and Medieval Irish Archaeology, History and Literature in Honour of Francis J. Byrne*, ed. Alfred P. Smyth (Dublin: Four Courts Press, 2000), pp. 225–37.

Irard mac Coisse

LIFE. From Mag mBriúin, a plain between Galway and Tuam (County Galway), which was ruled by the Connacht dynasty of Uí Bhriúin Seóla. His annalistic obituaries for 990 describe him as 'Ireland's chief poet' (*priméices*) and 'Ireland's great chronicler' (*ardchroinicidh*). His known patrons were seculars. There are indications that Tadg mac Cathail of Uí Briúin Aí, who was King of Connacht from 925 until his death in 956, was an early patron. A poem he composed for Tadg's daughter, Der Fáil, on the death of her son is still extant (printed above at pp. 305–7). At the time, Der Fáil was married to Domnall úa Néill, King of Cenél nEógain, who established himself as King of Tara in 956. The internal evidence of the long prosimetrum text *Airec Menman Iraird maic Coisse* (*The Strategem of Irard mac Coisse*) indicates that it too was composed by Irard. It seems he wrote this allegorical tale to pressurize Domnall úa

Néill and Der Fáil into ensuring that he received compensation for an attack made on his house by Domnall's kinsmen, the Cenél nEógain, *c.* 956. At the time of the attack, Irard lived at Clártha, close to the power base of Clann Cholmáin Mide at Dún na Scíath (modern Doon) on Lough Ennell (County Westmeath). The location suggests that the Clann Cholmáin, too, had become patrons of his by 956 at the latest.

CHIEF WRITINGS. 'Apair damsa re Der Fáil / On my behalf tell Der Fáil', above at pp. 305–7; 'Airec Menman Uraird Maic Coisse', in *Anecdota from Irish Manuscripts*, eds O.J. Bergin, R.I. Best. Kuno Meyer, and J.G. O'Keefe, 5 vols (Halle: Max Niemeyer; Dublin: Hodges Figgis, 1908), vol. 2, pp. 42–76.

BIOGRAPHY AND CRITICISM. Proinsias Mac Cana, *The Learned Tales of Medieval Ireland* (Dublin: Dublin Institute for Advanced Studies, 1980), pp. 33–8.

Scandlán Mór

Nothing is known of this putative author apart from the attribution on pp. 307–8.

Giolla Brighde Mac Con Midhe

LIFE. His surviving work indicates that Giolla Brighde Mac Con Midhe flourished in the middle and in the second half of the thirteenth century. The Mac Con Midhe family were hereditary poets who held land in what is now Ardstraw parish, County Tyrone, in return for their services. His mother was of Ceinéal Conaill, in modern County Donegal, and Giolla Brighde was the first Mac Con Midhe poet to have a professional relationship with the Uí Dhomhnaill (O'Donnells) of Ceinéal Conaill. Other patrons were the Uí Néill (the O'Neills of County Tyrone), and the Uí Ghairmleadhaigh (O'Gormleys) of Ceinéal Muáin, in the Strabane area (County Tyrone). He died during the lifetime of Domhnall Óg Ó Domhnaill, whose death in 1281 fixes the upper limit for Giolla Brighde's span. The Ó Gairmleadhaigh kin buried him, and he is described as their own poet. Giolla Brighde was married, and had children who died young.

Of the surviving poems attributed to Giolla Brighde, at least twenty were composed by him. As only one of these is addressed to a member of the Ó Gairmleadhaigh kin, it may be concluded that much of his work has perished. Eleven others are addressed to members of the Ó Domhnaill kin, and one to a member of the Ó Néill kin.

CHIEF WRITINGS. N.J.A. Williams (ed.), *The Poems of Giolla Brighde Mac Con Midhe* (Dublin: Irish Texts Society, 1980).

BIOGRAPHY AND CRITICISM. N.J.A. Williams (ed.), *The Poems of Giolla Brighde Mac Con Midhe* (Dublin: Irish Texts Society, 1980), pp. 1–5; P.A. Breatnach, 'Léirmheas', *Éigse*, vol. 19, pt 2 (1983), pp. 411–26.

Tadhg Mór Ó hUiginn

LIFE. The Connacht branch of the Ó hUiginn family were celebrated poets and teachers of poetry from the fourteenth century onwards. The reputation seems to have originated with Tadhg Mór, who is described in his death-notice in the Annals of Loch Cé under the year 1315 as 'a man generally eminent in all arts pertaining to poetry' (*sói choitchenn gacha cerde dá mbenann re filidhecht*). Almost nothing is known about his life. In a poem which he addressed to Maghnus Ó Conchobhair (?–1293), King of Connacht, he depicts himself as Maghnus's former tutor and current *ollamh*. A poem by him to Maghnus's daughter, Fionnghuala, also survives (see pp. 311–16). Her marriage to Brian Mág Shamhradháin, Lord of Tullyhaw, County Cavan, probably brought Tadhg Mór the patronage which resulted in the three poems surviving which he composed for members of that family.

CHIEF WRITINGS. Láimhbheartach Mac Cionnaith (Lambert McKenna) (ed.), *Dioghluim Dána* (Baile Átha Cliath: Oifig an tSoláthair, 1939), pp. 325–30; pp. 394–8; Lambert McKenna (ed.), *The Book of Magauran: Leabhar Méig Shamhradháin* (Dublin: Dublin Institute for Advanced Studies), pp. 30–41, pp. 6–21 (a poem attributed to 'Tadg O hUigind'), pp. 258–69 (a poem attributed to 'Tadhg').

BIOGRAPHY AND CRITICISM. Standish Hayes O'Grady, *Catalogue of Irish Manuscripts in the British Museum*, vol. 1 (London: British Museum, 1926), pp. 487–90; Eleanor Knott, [*A bhFuil Aguinn Dár Chum*] *Tadhg Dall Ó hUiginn: The Bardic Poems of Tadhg Dall Ó hUiginn (1550–91)*, 2 vols (London: Irish Texts Society, 1922 and 1926), vol. 2, p. 321.

Caoch Ceise Ó Clúmháin

LIFE. The Ó Clúmháin family were poets in Connacht since the twelfth century: the Annals of the Four Masters record the death of Giolla Aonghuis, *'ollamh* of Connacht in poetry', in the year 1143. During the next three centuries, the family provided poets to the lordships of Ó Conchobhair in County Roscommon, Ó hEadhra in County Sligo, and Mág Shamhradháin in County Cavan. Nothing is known of Caoch Ceise's work apart from the poem anthologized above (see pp. 316–21). His floruit is established by reference to his addressees.

Gofraidh Fionn Ó Dálaigh

For biography and bibliography, p. 392.

Gearóid (Iarla) Mac Gearailt

LIFE. Born in 1338, Gearóid belonged to the Munster branch of the Geraldines (Fitzgeralds), the most powerful Norman family in late medieval Ireland. His father, Muiris, was 1st Earl of Desmond. After his brother's death by drowning in 1358, he succeeded as 3rd Earl. In the same year, he married Eileanóir, daughter of Séamus Buitléir (James Butler), Earl of Ormond. He administered extensive estates in counties Kerry, Cork, Waterford and Tipperary. He served two periods as Chief Justiciar, between 1367 and 1369, and held a series of government appointments into the 1390s. His wife died in 1392; he died in 1398.

His obituary in the Annals of the Four Masters describes him as 'a gracious and refined man who excelled the Normans of Ireland and many of the Gaelic Irish in knowledge, Gaelic learning, poetry, *seanchas*, and every other science in which he was adept'. Gearóid is the earliest recorded writer of courtly love-lyrics in Irish, and a body of work by him survives. The mainly fifteenth-century Book of Fermoy contains thirty syllabic poems attributed to him, and a further eight are found in the sixteenth-century Scottish Book of the Dean of Lismore. His immediate family was keenly interested in poetry. His father is credited with some fragments of verse in Old French, and was a patron of Gofraidh Fionn Ó Dálaigh, the most highly regarded poet of the day, as was Gearóid's older brother, Muiris, the 2nd Earl. The interest was probably shared also by Diarmaid Mac Carthaigh (McCarthy), Lord of Muskerry (d. 1381), with whom Gearóid was on intimate terms; his poems contain many references to their friendship. Gearóid himself was a patron of poets, including Gofraidh Fionn, and of other learned classes. He became an important figure in popular legend. An interest in medicine may account for some of the many tales which represent him as an adept in magic.

CHIEF WRITINGS. Gearóid Mac Niocaill, 'Duanaire Ghearóid Iarla', *Studia Hibernica*, vol. 3 (1963), pp. 7–59; Tomás Ó Rathile, *Dánta Grádha: An Anthology of Irish Love Poetry (A.D. 1350–1750)* (Cork: Cork University Press, 1926), p. 4.

BIOGRAPHY AND CRITICISM. 'G.E.C.', *The Complete Peerage*, vol. 4 (London, 1916), pp. 238–44; Gearóid Mac Niocaill, 'Duanaire

Ghearóid Iarla', *Studia Hibernica*, vol. 3 (1963), pp. 6–11; William Gillies, 'Courtly and Satiric Poems in the Book of the Dean of Lismore', *Scottish Studies*, vol. 21 (1975), pp. 35–53, at pp. 43–4; Séamus M. Mac Ateer, 'Gearóid Iarla, poète Irlandais du XIVᵉ S. D'origine Normande et son œuvre', *Études Celtique*, vol. 15 (1976–8), pp. 576–98; Cathal Ó Háinle, *Promhadh Pinn* (Ma Nuad: An Sagart, 1978), pp. 10–18; Seán Ó Tuama, 'Gearóid Iarla — "The First Recorded Practitioner"?', in *Féilscríbhinn Thomáis de Bhaldraithe*, ed. Seosamh Watson (Baile Átha Cliath: Coiste Fhéilscríbhinn Thomáis de Bhaldraithe, An Coláiste Ollscoile, 1986), pp. 79–85; Micheál Mac Craith, *Lorg na hIasachta ar na Dánta Grá* (Baile Átha Cliath: An Clóchomhar, 1989), pp. 42–61; Daithi O hOgain, *Myth, Legend and Romance: An Encyclopaedia of the Irish Folk Tradition* (New York: Prentice Hall, 1991), pp. 227–30; Seán Ó Tuama, *Repossessions: Selected Essays on the Irish Literary Heritage* (Cork: Cork University Press, 1995), pp. 168–9.

Tadhg Óg Ó hUiginn

LIFE. Born in the second half of the fourteenth century, Tadhg Óg seems to have been the outstanding Gaelic poet of the fifteenth. His death-notice in the Annals of the Four Masters *s.a.* 1448 describes him as the 'Chief Teacher' (*Príomhoide*) of the *aos dána* of Ireland and Scotland. Throughout his career, he had patronage from the Uí Cheallaigh (O'Kellys) of Uí Mhaine in Connacht, and his poems tell that he was reared in their territory. He was trained, in part at least, by his older brother, Fearghal Ruadh, probably at Cill Chluaine (Kilclony), where the family had a school. He died at Cill Chonla (Kilconla), and he was buried at the monastery of Áth Leathan (Athlahan). These three places lie close together, a few miles north of Tuam, County Galway.

At the beginning of his career, Tadhg Óg professed poetry for the house of Ó Conchobhair Cairbre (O'Conor Sligo). From *c.* 1403 he was attached to the house of Tadhg Ó Ceallaigh, Lord of Uí Mhaine. His latest datable poem was an elegy written in 1444 for this man's sister, Gráinne, and her husband. His extant work includes poems for a remarkably wide range of other noble families: Ó Néill of Tyrone, Ó Domhnaill of Donegal, Mac Domhnaill of Islay, the Burkes of Upper and Lower Connacht, Mac Diarmuda of Roscommon, Mág Uidhir of Fermanagh, Ó Conchobhair Ciarraidhe (O'Conor Kerry), the Earl of Ormond, the Earl of Desmond, and Ó Cearbhaill of Éile (Ely O'Carroll).

At least forty-five of his poems survive. Almost twenty of these are on religious themes. A total of forty-one are preserved in an Ó hUiginn *duanaire*, a lavishly decorated manuscript written in 1473, perhaps for the Ó hUiginn school of poetry which Tadhg Óg had helped to found in his day. This also contains fifteen poems by other Ó hUiginn poets. It now forms part of the composite manuscript known as the Yellow Book of Lecan. There are many citations from his work in the grammatical and metrical tracts which were composed for teaching purposes. He was married. Three sons' names are known: Maol Muire (d. 1488), Giolla na Naomh, and Domhnall.

CHIEF WRITINGS. Eleanor Knott (ed.), *Irish Syllabic Poetry 1200–1600* (Dublin: Dublin Institute for Advanced Studies, 1974), pp. 47–8; T.F. O'Rahilly (ed.), *Measgra Dánta: Miscellaneous Irish Poems* (Cork: Cork University Press, 1927, 1970), pp. 29–30; *Irish Bardic Poetry . . . by Osborn Bergin*, compiled and edited by David Greene and Fergus Kelly (Dublin: Dublin Institute for Advanced Studies, 1970), pp. 61–3, 147–50; L. Mac Cionnaith, *Dioghluim Dána*, pp. 16–19, 241–6, 312–4; Lambert McKenna (ed.), *Aithdioghluim Dána*, 2 vols (London: Irish Texts Society, 1939, 1940), vol. 1, pp. 35–9, 294–9; Lambert McKenna (ed.), *Dán Dé: The Poems of Donnchadh Mór Ó Dálaigh, and the Religious Poems in the Duanaire of the Yellow Book of Lecan* (Dublin: Educational Company, [1922]), pp. 1–3, 4–31, 69–99.

BIOGRAPHY AND CRITICISM. S.H. O'Grady, *Catalogue of Irish Manuscripts in the British Museum*, vol. 1, pp. 363–6; E.C. Quiggin, 'Prolegomena to the Study of the Later Irish Bards 1200–1500', *Proceedings of the British Academy*, vol. 5 (1911–12), pp. 89–143, at 103–4; L. McKenna (ed.), *Aithdioghluim Dána*, vol. 1, p. xxxv; E. Knott [*A bhFuil Aguinn Dár Chum*] *Tadhg Dall*, vol. 2, p. 321.

Thomas Smyth

LIFE. Thomas Smyth was an English medical man and apothecary living in Dublin. Sheriff of Dublin in 1576, and Mayor of Dublin in 1591. Allegedly a brother of John 'Bottle Smyth' who attempted to assassinate the Ulster leader Seaán Ó Néill with poison. Named, along with Edmund Spenser, as an interlocutor in Ludowick Bryskett's *A Discourse of Civill Life*, written *c.* 1580. Herbert F. Hore made the plausible suggestion that he may have been a relative of the English intellectual and politician Sir Thomas Smyth (1513–77), whose early career as professor of civil law at Cambridge was followed by periods as ambassador to France, privy councillor and secretary of state. Sir Thomas Smyth was an influential theorist of colonization. As part of his venture to establish a colony in the north of Ireland, in Clandeboy (Clann Aodha Buidhe) and the Ards peninsula (in Counties Antrim and Down) in 1572–5, he took the novel course of publishing a promotional broadsheet and pamphlet. The ideas expressed in them, which may be related to his more general political theory as found in his *Discourse of the Commonweal of this Realm of England* (1549), may also be related to those expressed in his namesake's account of the Gaelic poets and their retinues.

CHIEF WRITINGS. 'Information for Ireland, 1561' is apparently all that is extant of the writings of Thomas Smyth.

BIOGRAPHY AND CRITICISM. Herbert F. Hore, 'Irish Bardism in 1561', *Ulster Journal of Archaeology*, vol. 6 (1858), pp. 165–7, 202–12; Nicholas Canny, *Making Ireland British 1580-1650* (Oxford: Oxford University Press, 2001), pp. 1–2.

Maghnus Ó Domhnaill

LIFE. Maghnus, the eldest son of Aodh Dubh Mac Domhnaill, Lord of Tír Conaill, was born *c.* 1490. The Lords of Tír Conaill held sway over an area coextensive with County Donegal, together with parts of counties Derry, Fermanagh and Tyrone, and also claimed the lordship of northern Connacht. Maghnus was deputizing for his father by *c.* 1510, and gave him his support for the next twenty years, but from the early 1530s he was an aspirant to the lordship and his father's opponent. In 1537, after his father's death, he was inaugurated at Kilmacrenan, in Donegal.

With Conn Ó Néill he formed the alliance known as the Geraldine League, Ireland's first organized resistance to the Tudor state. When the league was defeated at Bellahoe in 1539, he opened negotiations with Dublin, and was one of the first lords to bow to the policy of 'surrender and regrant'. He was deposed by his son, Calbhach, in 1555 and he died in 1563. He was buried in the Franciscan Friary at Donegal. Brendan Bradshaw has contended that Maghnus may be described as a Renaissance prince — a political entrepreneur in the Machiavellian manner, but also an enthusiastic lay scholar, a humanist and an aesthete. In addition to composing *dánta grádha*, he is renowned for having 'authored' a new Life of Saint Colum Cille. The work was carried out in his castle at Port na dTrí Námhad at Lifford. Although he is identified in the Life as the actual author, his real role seems to have been that of supervisor, with the compiling and writing being undertaken by scholars, at least some of whom are likely to have been Franciscans; he strongly supported the order's renewal of religion. None the less, use of the vernacular and a superbly accessible prose style suggest his influence. The Life was translated into Latin by John Colgan in 1645.

CHIEF WRITINGS. A.O'Kelleher and G. Schoepperle (eds), *Betha Colaim Chille: Life of Columcille* (Dublin: Dublin Institute for Advanced Studies, 1994); Tomás Ó Rathile (ed.), *Dánta Grádha* (Cork: Cork University Press, 1926), pp. 70–4.

BIOGRAPHY AND CRITICISM. Brendan Bradshaw, 'Manus "The Magnificent": O'Donnell as Renaissance Prince', in *Studies in Irish History Presented to R. Dudley Edwards*, eds Art Cosgrove and Donal

McCartney (Dublin: University College Dublin, 1979), pp. 15–37; Darren Mac Eiteagáin, 'The Renaissance and the Late Medieval Lordship of Tír Chonaill 1461–1555', in *Donegal History and Society: Interdisciplinary Essays on the History of an Irish County*, eds William Nolan, Liam Ronayne and Máiréad Dunleavy (Dublin: Geography Publications, 1985); Seán Ó Tuama, 'Love in the Medieval Irish Literary Lyric', in *Repossessions: Selected Essays on the Irish Literary Heritage* (Cork: Cork University Press, 1995), pp. 1164–95; Máire Ní Mhurchú and Diarmuid Breatnach, *1580–1781 Beathaisnéis* (Baile Átha Cliath: An Clóchomhar, 2001), pp. 128–31.

Domhnall Mac Carthaigh

LIFE. Born in 1518, into the line of Mac Carthaigh Mór kings of Desmond in Munster, Domhnall Mac Carthaigh was a loyalist, created 1st Earl of Clancare (Clancarthy) in 1565, in a revival of the policy of 'surrender and regrant'. His illegitimate son, Domhnall, claimed the title of Mac Carthaigh Mór. A praise-poem for him, and various elegies on his death in 1597, are extant.

CHIEF WRITINGS. Two love-poems are his only known compositions: that above at p. 371–2 and 'Aisling thruagh do mhear mise', published in T. Ó Rathile, *Dánta Grádha*, p. 63.

BIOGRAPHY AND CRITICISM. S.H. O'Grady, *Catalogue of Irish Manuscripts in the British Museum*, vol. 1, pp. 377–9, 542–3.

Riocard de Búrc

None of the many bearers of this name can be identified with certainty as the author of the poem above, at pp. 374–6.

Tadhg Dall Ó hUiginn

LIFE. From the fourteenth century onwards, the Uí Uiginn of Connacht were celebrated as distinguished poets and teachers of poetry (see p. 448 and p. 449). Tadhg Dall was born about 1550, probably in Luighne (barony of Leyney), in County Sligo, and was fostered in Tír Conaill (Donegal), but it is not known where he received his professional training. There is no evidence that he was blind, despite his sobriquet 'Dall'. One of his earliest patrons was Domhnall, chief of the Ó Conchobhair Sligigh (O'Conor Sligo) family, but the patron with whom he was most closely identified was Riocard Mac Uilliam Búrc in Mayo, who shared his interest in poetry and *seanchas*.

Tadhg Dall also wrote for the Uí Néill (O'Neills) of Tyrone, the Méig Uidhir (Maguires) of Fermanagh, the Uí Ruairc (O'Rourkes) of Bréifne, Clann tSuibhne (the MacSweeneys) of Fánad, and the Uí Eadhra (O'Haras) of Sligo. Almost fifty of his poems survive, most of which are conventional panegyric, but it is likely that these represent only a fraction of his output. Among his best known is that beginning 'Tógaibh eadrad is Éire', for which see Volume I, pp. 51–4.

His career was prosperous in the main. At his death, on 31 March 1591, he held nine quarters of land, between Tubbercurry and Coolany, in the barony of Leyney. He is said to have been murdered by six of the O'Haras on account of a satire he wrote about them. In an inquisition in Sligo on 30 June 1617, six people, including five named O'Hara, were attainted of having murdered 'one Teige Dall O Higgen his wife and childe'. It is possible that the phrase 'Teige Dall . . . his wife and childe' referred to 'Tadhg Dall's wife and child' and not to all three. His son Tadhg Óg, born in 1582, was also a poet; he died sometime before 1641. The birth of a daughter, Máire (Mary), is noted in the Annals of Loch Cé (see p. 340).

CHIEF WRITINGS. Eleanor Knott (ed.), *[A bhFuil Aguinn Dár Chum] Tadhg Dall Ó hUiginn: The Bardic Poems of Tadhg Dall Ó hUiginn (1550–1591)*, 2 vols (London: Irish Texts Society, 1922 and 1926; rpr. 1996, with new preface by Pádraig A. Breatnach).

BIOGRAPHY AND CRITICISM. E. Knott [*A bhFuil Aguinn dár Chum*] *Tadhg Dall Ó hUiginn*, pp. xii–xxxii; S.H. O'Grady, *Catalogue of Irish Manuscripts in the British Museum*, vol. 1, pp. 407–42; Cathal Ó Háinle, 'D'fhior Chogaidh Comhailtear Síothcháin', *Léachtaí Cholm Cille*, vol. 2 (1971), pp. 51–73; Art Ó Beoláin, *Merriman agus Filí Eile* (Baile Átha Cliath: An Clóchomhar, 1985), pp. 24–37; Pádraig Ó Macháin, 'Tadhg Dall Ó hUiginn: Foinse dá Shaothar', *Léachtaí Cholm Cille*, vol. 24 (1994), pp. 77–113; Máire Ní Mhurchú and Diarmuid Breatnach, *1580–1781 Beathaisnéis* (Baile Átha Cliath: An Clóchomhar, 2001), pp. 151–3.

Eochaidh Ó hEodhasa

For biography, see Volume I, p. 325. See also pp. 299, 365–6 above.

CHIEF WRITINGS. Listed in P.A. Breatnach, 'Eochaidh Ó hEódhusa (*c.* 1560–1612)', *Éigse*, vol. 27 (1993), p. 129.

BIOGRAPHY AND CRITICISM. S.H. O'Grady, *Catalogue of Irish Manuscripts in the British Museum*, vol. 1, pp. 448–81; James Carney, *The Irish Bardic Poet* (Dublin: Dolmen Press, 1967); P.A. Breatnach, 'Eochaidh Ó hEódhusa (*c.* 1560–1612)', *Éigse*, vol. 27 (1993), pp. 127–9; Máire Ní Mhurchú and Diarmuid Breatnach, *1580–1781 Beathaisnéis* (Baile Átha Cliath: An Clóchomhar, 2001), pp. 146–7.

Brighid, Daughter of Éinrí Mac Gearailt (Brighid Chill Dara)

LIFE. Brighid, daughter of Éinrí Mac Gearailt (Henry Fitzgerald), 12th Earl of Kildare, was born around 1589. Her mother was Lady Frances Howard, daughter of Charles, Earl of Nottingham, who became Lord High Admiral of England. Her paternal grandmother was also English: she was Mabel, daughter of Sir Anthony Brown, Knight of the Garter and Master of the Horse to Edward VI. Brighid's father died in 1597. Her mother then married Henry Brooke, Lord Cobham, and Brighid's home until the time of her own marriage seems to have been Mabel Fitzgerald's dower house at Maynooth, County Kildare.

Brighid married Rudhraighe Ó Domhnaill soon after his investiture as Earl of Tír Conaill in 1603 and presumably spent much of the time thereafter in Donegal. Their first child, Aodh, was born in autumn 1606. She was at Maynooth, not long before the birth of their second child, when Rudhraighe left Ireland abruptly on 14 September 1607 in what became known to history as the Flight of the Earls. The indications are that the couple expected to be reunited on the Continent once Brighid had been safely delivered, but their immediate plans for Brighid to sail from Ireland were foiled by agents of the crown. Brighid went instead to England, from where she probably intended to sail for Europe. Her second child, a daughter, was born there. It is often said that a rift developed between Brighid and Rudhraighe but the evidence does not support this. That they were never reunited is probably explained by his early death, from fever in Rome on 12 August 1608. A poem written by Eoghan Ruadh Mac an Bhaird in 1608 ('Truagh do chor, a chroidhe tim') relates that he has received disturbing news of Rudhraighe falling ill after loss of an arm; the fatal fever is likely to have had the same cause. A final quatrain in this poem tells that Brighid ('inghean iarla fhóid Mhaighe', 'the daughter of the Earl of Maynooth') will start in alarm if she hears the worrying news the poet has heard — something which hardly indicates a rift.

Among the many other poems that Mac an Bhaird wrote for the Ó Domhnaill household is a genethliacon on the birth of Rudhraighe's and Brighid's first child, Aodh (*Cia re bhfáiltigh fian Eirne*). Other Gaelic poets, including Eochaidh Ó hEodhasa, were intimates of this household. Clearly, Brighid's connections were such that she might have felt entitled to claim both English and Gaelic literary traditions as her own.

James I was sympathetic to Brighid. He granted her a pension of £200 from the revenues of Rudhraighe's escheated estates. Her daughter was put under royal protection and was henceforth known as Mary Stuart. Brighid returned to Ireland in 1609. Around 1617 she remarried. Her husband was Sir Nicholas Barnewall, an Old English lawyer and a member of the Irish parliament, of Turvey, County Dublin. She bore him nine children. She and her second husband lived through the turbulent wars of the mid-century. He died in 1663, she died at a ripe old age in 1682.

CHIEF WRITINGS. 'A mhacaoimh dhealbhas an dán', pp. 387–8.

BIOGRAPHY AND CRITICISM. Cathal G. Ó Háinle, 'Flattery Rejected: Two Seventeenth-Century Irish Poems', *Hermathena*, vol. 138 (summer 1985), pp. 5–27; Jerrold Casway, 'Mary Stuart O'Donnell', *Donegal Annual*, no. 39 (1987), pp. 28–38.

Eoghan Ruadh Mac an Bhaird

LIFE. The original Mac an Bhaird stock were hereditary poets to the Uí Cheallaigh (O'Kellys) of Uí Mhaine in Connacht, and are recorded as associated with Cúl an Urtain (Coolorta[n]), in the parish of Knockmoy, County Galway, in the fifteenth and sixteenth centuries. The branch to which Eoghan Ruadh belonged are known to have lived in Donegal since the fifteenth century and to have professed poetry for the Uí Dhomhnaill (O'Donnells) of Donegal since the sixteenth. Three poems for Aodh son of Maghnus Ó Domhnaill by Eoghan Ruadh's father, Uilliam Óg (d. 1576), are extant, and Eoghan Ruadh's grand-uncle, Conchubhar Ruadh (d. 1541), was *ollamh* to Ó Domhnaill.

Most of Eoghan Ruadh's extant poems are addressed to the Uí Dhomhnaill, and may be used, in the absence of precise information on his dates of birth and death, to determine his floruit. 'Rob soruidh th'eachtra, a Aodh Ruaidh', on the departure of Aodh Ruadh Ó Domhnaill to Spain after the Battle of Kinsale, and 'Teasda Éire san Easbáinn', on Aodh Ruadh's death there in 1602, are among his earliest datable extant poems. He composed 'Dána an turas trialltar sunn' in September 1603, when Aodh Ruadh's brother, Rudhraighe, went to London, where his submission to the crown was rewarded with his investiture as Earl of Tír Conaill. Eoghan Ruadh accompanied Rudhraighe and some of his family to the Continent when they left Ireland in the Flight of the Earls in September 1607, and he settled initially in Louvain. After Rudhraighe's death in 1608, he went to Rome where he became the confidant of Aodh Ó Néill, the exiled Earl of Tír Eoghain. After Ó Néill's death in 1616, the poet focused his attention on Rudhraighe's son, Aodh, who had been brought to Europe in the Flight as an infant. Eoghan Ruadh's earliest poem for this heir of Rudhraighe's was composed in Ireland, soon after Aodh's birth in October 1606: 'Cia re bhfáiltigh fian Eirne'. The translation of a military handbook which he made for Aodh in 1626 is not extant, but the dedicatory poem which accompanied it, 'A leabhráin ainmnighthear dh'Aodh', is. This is his latest datable poem. It is not known when or where he died. His brother, Uilliam Óg, who was also a poet, was still living in 1641.

Throughout his time on the Continent, Eoghan Ruadh seems to have been very close to Rudhraighe's sister, Nuala, who was Aodh's guardian at Louvain. The manuscript known as *Leabhar Inghine Uí Dhomhnaill* (The Book of O'Donnell's Daughter), which most likely belonged to her (rather than to one of her sisters), contains fifteen poems attributed to Eoghan Ruadh, including one which he himself inscribed in the manuscript.

CHIEF WRITINGS. His known poems are edited, and translated into English, in Tomás Ó Raghallaigh, *Dánta Eoghain Ruaidh Mhic an Bhaird* (Gaillimh: Ó Gormáin, 1930).

BIOGRAPHY AND CRITICISM. T. Ó Raghallaigh, *ibid.*, pp. 11–55; Paul Walsh, *Irish Men of Learning* (Dublin: At the Sign of the Three Candles, 1947), pp. 151–9 ('The Learned Family of Mac an Bhaird'), pp. 179–205 ('The Book of O Donnell's Daughter'); Joep Leerssen, *Mere Irish and Fíor-Ghael: Studies in the Idea of Irish Nationality, Its Development and Literary Expression Prior to the Nineteenth Century*

(Cork: Cork University Press in association with Field Day, 1996), *passim*; Marc Caball, *Poets and Politics: Reaction and Continuity in Irish Poetry, 1558–1625* (Cork University Press in association with Field Day, 1998), *passim*.

Fionnghuala, Daughter of Domhnall Ó Briain

LIFE. Born *c.* 1557, Fionnghuala was the sixth child of Domhnall Ó Briain and his wife, Sláine (d. 1569). Fionnghuala's paternal uncle was Donnchadh Ó Briain, 2nd Earl of Thomond. Fionnghuala's first husband was Tomás Mac Muiris, Lord of Lixnaw, County Kerry, to whom she was related through her mother. He repudiated her and married her half-sister, Onóra, in December 1579. Some time later, Fionnghuala married Uaithne Ó Lochlainn, who ruled the Burren, in north County Clare. Uaithne died in 1617, leaving no heir, and Fionnghuala was obliged to leave their home in Seanmhuicinis Castle, some three miles north-east of Ballyvaughan, County Clare.

CHIEF WRITINGS. 'A nAinm an Spioraid Naoimh h'Imríghe, Uaithne', at pp. 395–7.

BIOGRAPHY AND CRITICISM. Liam P. Ó Murchú, 'Caoineadh ar Uaithne Mór Ó Lochlainn, 1617', *Éigse*, vol. 27 (1993), pp. 67–79; P.I.D. O'Brien, 'The O'Briens of Dough and Ennistymon', *Irish Genealogist*, vol. 6, no. 5 (November 1984), pp. 556–64.

Caitilín Dubh

LIFE. Almost everything that is know about this Clare poet, including her floruit of *c.* 1624–9, derives from her five surviving poems. These she wrote for male and female members of the extended family of the 4th Earl of Thomond, Donnchadh Ó Briain. It seems she was an intimate of this group, perhaps a relation, by blood or marriage. She is an intriguing case: a woman poet, who wrote long elegies which in substance resemble the work of professional bardic poets, while written in an accentual metre associated with non-professional poets. It is not clear whether she was in receipt or in need of material patronage. Her poems survive in a manuscript written for Sir Donnchadh Ó Briain (1642–1717), mainly by Aodh Buí Mac Cruitín (q.v.). An edition of them by Liam P. Ó Murchú is forthcoming.

There are nineteenth-century folkloric representations of her as a witch or charmer, associated with west County Clare, who pits her powers against famous *mná sí* of Munster such as Aoibheall of Craig Liath and Clíona of Carraig Chlíona. One account gives her full name as 'Caitileen Dubh Keating'. Such accounts credit her with a daughter, also with supernatural powers, named Caitilín Óg.

CHIEF WRITINGS. '*Do chuala tásc do chráidh fir Éireann*', pp. 399–402; '*Seal dá rabhas gan fhonn gan aoibhneas*', pp. 403–5; Library of the National University of Ireland, Maynooth, MS 107 in the Murphy Collection, pp. 193–211.

BIOGRAPHY AND CRITICISM. Brian Ó Cuív, 'Deascán ó Chúige Mumhan: Clíona agus Iníon Chaitlín Dubh', *Béaloideas*, vol. 22 (1953 [1954]), pp. 102–11.

Tadhg (Mac Dáire) Mac Bruaideadha

LIFE. Born the eldest child of Dáire Mac Bruaideadha (Mac Brody) *c.* 1550, Tadhg is recorded as 'gent.', resident, in 1586 and in 1602, in the parish of Kilmurry, barony of Uí Bhreacáin (Ibrekan), County Clare. He succeeded his father as proprietor of the family estate at Cnoc an Albanaigh (Knockalban) and was in turn succeeded by his son, Séamus. The Mac Bruaideadha family had been hereditary chroniclers to the Uí Bhriain (O'Briens) of Thomond since the mid-sixteenth century. Tadhg had a long-lasting and close relationship with Donnchadh Ó Briain, 4th Earl of Thomond (1581–1624) and President

of Munster (1615–24). The theologian Anthony Brody (Bruodinus), Tadhg's grand-nephew, states that Donnchadh Ó Briain was fostered by Tadhg's sister, had his early education under Tadhg's supervision, and was accompanied by Tadhg when he went for further education to the court of Elizabeth I in 1577. Tadhg married Áine, daughter of Tadhg Ó Mathghamhna. Four daughters and two sons are recorded.

Ó Briain, to whom five of Mac Bruaideadha's extant poems were addressed, was a Protestant, was closely associated with Sir George Carew during the Elizabethan Wars in Ireland and was loyal to the crown throughout his career. Mac Bruaideadha celebrated Ó Briain's support for the crown and did not engage with the issue of his religion. With others, the poet was often combative, even vengeful. In 'Fuiridh mo leisge, a Leath Chuinn', he threatened to satirize Aodh Ruadh Ó Domhnaill and his allies who had attacked Thomond in 1599, carrying off some of the poet's cattle in the process. A poem he wrote in 1616 instigated an acrimonious debate — to which he contributed nine poems in all — between the poets of the Northern Half and the Southern Half ('Iomarbhágh na bhFileadh/The Contention of the Bards'). In a thorough reassessment, Joep Leerssen argued that Tadhg's contribution to the *Iomarbhágh* translated the traditional rivalry between the two Halves into a conflict between rebellious, backward-looking, Gaelic Northerners and peaceable, modernizing Southerners — best exemplified by the Uí Bhriain — who were capable of adapting to the new pro-English order.

The latest datable poem by Tadhg is his elegy for Donnchadh Ó Briain who died in 1624, and his floruit is derived from that. The story that the poet was killed by a Cromwellian soldier who threw him over a cliff, saying *abair do rann anois a fhir bhig*, 'say your rann now, my little man', sounds like a romantic fiction.

CHIEF WRITINGS. Theophilus O'Flanagan, 'Advice to a Prince, by Thaddy Mac Brody, or Mac Brodin, son of Dary', *Transactions of the Gaelic Society* (Dublin, 1808); Lambert McKenna, *Iomarbhágh na bhFileadh*, 2 vols (London: Irish Texts Society, 1918); L. Mac Cionnaith, *Dioghluim Dána* (Baile Átha Cliath: Oifig an tSoláthair, 1938), Poem Nos 2, 17, 51, 95; Colm Ó Lochlainn, 'A Poem by Tadhg Mac Dáire Mhic Bhruaidheadha', *Éigse*, vol. 1, pt 1 (spring 1939), pp. 2–6; Brian Ó Cuív, 'An Elegy on Donnchadh Ó Briain', *Celtica*, vol. 16 (1984), pp. 87–105; Pádraig A. Breatnach, 'Litir ó Thadhg Mac Bruaidheadha', *Éigse*, vol. 28 (1994-5), pp. 97–9.

BIOGRAPHY AND CRITICISM. S.H. O'Grady, *Catalogue of Irish Manuscripts in the British Museum*, pp. 388–92; Cuthbert McGrath, 'Materials for a History of Clann Bhruaideadha', *Éigse* 4, pt 1 (summer 1943), pp. 47–66; Thomas Wall, 'Bards and Broudins', in *Father Luke Wadding Commemorative Volume*, eds The Franciscan Fathers (Dublin: Clonmore and Reynolds, 1957), pp. 438–62; Brian Ó Cuív, 'The Earl of Thomond and the Poets', *Celtica*, vol. 12 (1977), pp. 125–45; Joep Leerssen, *The Contention of the Bards (Iomarbhágh na bhFileadh and its Place in Irish Political History)* (Irish Texts Society Subsidiary Series 2) (Dublin 1994); Diarmuid Ó Murchadha, 'The Origins of Clann Bhruaideadha', *Éigse*, vol. 31 (1999), pp. 121–30.

Piaras Feiritéar

LIFE. The Feiritéar family, who were of Norman stock, settled in Corca Dhuibhne (on the Dingle peninsula) in West Kerry before the end of the thirteenth century, and their presence there is still reflected in many place-names. Piaras Feiritéar is regarded as one of the best poets of his remarkably accomplished generation. His date of birth is unknown. The tradition that he was also a skilful musician may be based in fact: an air he is reputed to have composed on his wife's death is extant and one of his compositions is a poem of thanks for the gift of a harp. He was fluent in English and, according to the *Commentarius Rinnucianus* (1661–6), he composed poetry in English. None of it has survived. His facility for syllabic metres indicates that he had a formal training in Gaelic poetry; he also handled the newly fashionable *amhrán* metres with flair. He was adept in the courtly lyric, but also wrote long praise-poems for men and women of Gaelic and Anglo-Irish noble families. One of his longest was written for Meg Russell, a relation of Sir William Russell, Lord Lieutenant in Ireland in 1594. By 1640 he was *taoiseach*, or chief, of his name.

At the outset of the rising of 1641, Pádraigín Mac Muiris, Lord Kerry and governor of the county, appointed him captain of the royalist force which was raised in Corca Dhuibhne to crush the rebels. Feiritéar switched his allegiance to the Catholic Confederation, joining forces with Finghin Mac Carthaigh. They captured Castlemaine Castle and laid siege to Tralee Castle. They eventually surrendered in late June 1653, and came to make peace at Castlemaine. Feiritéar was arrested as he returned to his home, and was hanged in Killarney on 15 October 1653. He is an important figure in folklore to this day.

CHIEF WRITINGS. Pádraig Ua Duinnín, *Dánta Phiarais Feiritéir* (Baile Átha Cliath: Oifig Díolta Foilseacháin Rialtais, 1934); Pádraig de Brún, Breandán Ó Buachalla, Tomás Ó Concheanainn (eds), *Nua-Dhuanaire I* (Baile Átha Cliath: Institiúid ArdLéinn Bhaile Átha Cliath, 1971), pp. 24–30; Pat Muldowney (ed.), *Dánta Phiarais Feiritéir. With Translations by Pat Muldowney* (Millstreet, County Cork: Aubane Historical Society, 1999).

BIOGRAPHY AND CRITICISM. P. Ua Duinnín, *Dánta Phiarais Feiritéir*, pp. 11–62; Art Ó Beoláin, *Merriman agus Filí Eile* (Baile Átha Cliath: An Clóchomhar, 1985), pp. 38–49; Mícheál S. Mac Craith, *Lorg na hIasachta ar na Dánta Grádha* (Baile Átha Cliath: An Clóchomhar, 1989), pp. 176–84; Seán Ó Tuama, *Repossessions: Selected Essays on the Irish Literary Heritage* (Cork: Cork University Press, 1995), pp. 176–7; Máire Ní Mhurchú and Diarmuid Breatnach, *1580–1781 Beathaisnéis* (Baile Átha Cliath: An Clóchomhar, 2001), pp. 34–6.

Pádraigín Haicéad

For biography, see Volume I, p. 325. See also:

CHIEF WRITINGS. Tadhg Ó Donnchadha (Torna) (ed.), *Saothar Filidheachta an Athar Pádraigín Haicéad* (Baile Átha Cliath: M.H. Gill, 1916); Máire Ní Cheallacháin (ed.), *Filíocht Phádraigín Haicéad* (Baile Átha Cliath: An Clóchomhar, 1962); Michael Hartnett (trans.), *Haicéad* (Loughcrew: Gallery Press, 1993).

BIOGRAPHY AND CRITICISM. Art Ó Beoláin, *Merriman agus Filí Eile* (Baile Átha Cliath: An Clóchomhar, 1985); Seán Ó Tuama, 'Ceathrúna Phádraigín Haicéad', *Irish Review* (winter 1998), pp. 1–23; Máire Ní Mhurchú and Diarmuid Breatnach, *1580–1781 Beathaisnéis* (Baile Átha Cliath: An Clóchomhar, 2001), pp. 38–40.

Cearbhall Ó Dálaigh

LIFE. 'Carrol O Dale, of Pallice', County Wexford, and 'Carroyle boye [*buidhe* 'fair'] O Dalie', of an unspecified place in County Wexford, are mentioned in Elizabethan Fiants for 14 November 1597 and 15 May 1601 respectively. T.F. O'Rahilly has argued plausibly that this man was either the poet, or more likely, the father of the poet, known in Irish as 'Cearbhall Ó Dálaigh'. The legend that he eloped with Eileanór, daughter of Sir Murchadh Caomhánach, is based on fact of some kind: it is likely that they were lovers or that they married. Gaelic manuscripts attribute many poems to Cearbhall Ó Dálaigh but, as yet, no attempt has been made to separate the spurious attributions from the rest. There are many accounts of him in folklore, representing him as a skilful and ingenious versifier, musician and lover.

CHIEF WRITINGS. P. de Brún, B. Ó Buachalla, T. Ó Concheanainn, *Nua-Dhuanaire I*, pp. 8, 30, 64–5.

BIOGRAPHY AND CRITICISM. T.F. O'Rahilly, 'Irish Poets, Historians and Judges in English Documents, 1538–1615', *Proceedings of the Royal Irish Academy*, series C, vol. 36 (1922), pp. 100–2; P. de Brún, B. Ó Buachalla, T. Ó Concheanainn, *Nua-Dhuanaire I*, p. 161;

Daithí O hOgain, *Myth, Legend and Romance: An Encyclopaedia of Irish Folk Tradition* (New York and London: Prentice Hall, 1991), pp. 334–7; Máire Ní Mhurchú and Diarmuid Breatnach, *1580–1781 Beathaisnéis* (Baile Átha Cliath: An Clóchomhar, 2001), pp. 124–5.

Séathrún Céitinn (Geoffrey Keating)

For biography and bibliography, see Volume I, p. 272, and Volume IV, p. 249.

Tadhg Ó Ruairc

LIFE. The outline of Tadhg Ó Ruairc's life remains conjectural, although the details cited in support of it are documented. James Carney identified the seventeenth-century Connacht poet of the name Tadhg Ó Ruairc with the son and heir of Aodh Ó Ruairc, described in the census of 1659 as 'titulado' of extensive lands in the barony of Dromahaire, County Leitrim. Aodh died in 1684, leaving as heir his son, Tadhg. Both James Carney and Robin Flower identified Tadhg as the recipient of a praise-poem from the contemporary poet Tomás Ó Coisdealbha, which begins 'A phór na Rudhraigheach, a chrú chroidhe rathmhar na Rúarc'. Flower, in addition, identified Tadhg as the author of 'Goinim thú, a naoidh bheag shíar' (printed above, at pp. 417–8), and suggested that he was the author of another poem, beginning 'Beir beannacht uaim siar tar h'ais'. It is clear from the latter poem that its author, named as Tadhg Ó Ruairc, was then a refugee on his way to Spain, bemoaning his lot, but saying it was less harsh than that of a priest of Ceall Fraoich who was cruelly separated from the bountiful Tadhg Ó hUiginn of Coolavin, County Sligo. This may have been the poet Tadhg Óg Ó hUiginn, son of Tadhg Dall (q.v.), who died some time before 1641.

CHIEF WRITINGS. 'Goinim thú, a naoídh bheg shíar', pp. 417–8; 'Beir beannacht uaim siar tar h'ais', in *Dán na mBráthar Mionúr*, ed. Cuthbert Mhág Craith, 2 vols (Baile Átha Cliath: Institiúid Ard Léinn Bhaile Átha Cliath, 1967, 1980), vol. 1, pp. 257–61; Robin Flower, *Poems and Translations* (Dublin: Lilliput Press, 1994), pp. 171–3 (translation only).

BIOGRAPHY AND CRITICISM. Robin Flower, *Catalogue of Irish Manuscripts in the British Museum II*, pp. 62, 169, 362; James Carney, '"Thomas Costello and O'Rourke's Wife"', *Celtica*, vol. 1, pt 2 (1950), pp. 280–4, at pp. 283–4.

Úna Ní Bhroin

LIFE. Úna Ní Bhroin is known to literary history as the wife of the poet and scholar Seán Ó Neachtain (*c.* 1640–1729). The date of their marriage may be conjectured by reference to the date of their first child's birth, in 1671. The child was Tadhg, the future poet. They had two more children, Lúcás and Anna. They lived in the Liberties in Dublin, in the vicinity of Thomas Street.

While her marriage undoubtedly gave her access to the significant group of Gaelic writers and scholars who gathered in Dublin around Tadhg, it may have been her own literary interests which led ultimately to marriage to Ó Neachtain. As Robin Flower suggested, Úna may have been related to Edmond Byrne (Ó Broin), Archbishop of Dublin 1707–23, whose death was lamented in a series of poems by Ó Neachtain and his circle. If so, she is likely to have had a solid education.

The only poem attributed to her which has come to light so far is that printed above at pp. 422–3. There is a complication in relation to this: in a copy of the verse-dialogue found in an eighteenth-century manuscript written in County Galway (Dublin, Royal Irish Academy Library, MS 23 O 35), the poem in response to Ó Neachtain's poem is attributed to Winifred Nogle, rather than Úna Ní Bhroin, and she is said to have married Ó Neachtain. However, this tradition is probably spurious as Winifred Nogle and her putative marriage to Ó Neachtain are otherwise unknown. Úna Ní Bhroin died on 5 February 1706/7. Two elegies on her death by Seán Ó Neachtain have survived. 'A théagair, is é m'éagsa is mé beo do bhás' is published in Breandán Ó Buachalla (ed.), *Nua-Dhuanaire II* (Baile Átha Cliath: Institiúid ArdLéinn Bhaile Átha Cliath, 1976), p. 8. The second elegy, beginning 'Thug mé searc mo chléibh' is mo ghrádh', is found in Dublin, Royal Irish Academy Library, MS 23 Q 2.

BIOGRAPHY AND CRITICISM. May H. Risk, 'Seán Ó Neachtuin: An Eighteenth-Century Irish Writer', *Studia Hibernica*, vol. 15 (1975), pp. 47–60; Cathal Ó Háinle, 'Neighbours in Eighteenth Century Dublin: Jonathan Swift and Seán Ó Neachtain', *Éire-Ireland*, vol. 21, pt 4 (1986), pp. 106–21; Alan Harrison, *Ag Cruinniú Meala* (Baile Átha Cliath: An Clóchomhar, 1988); Nessa Ní Shéaghdha, 'Irish Scholars and Scribes in Eighteenth-Century Dublin', *Eighteenth-Century Ireland. Iris an Dá Chultúr*, vol. 4 (1989), pp. 40–54.

Eoghan Ó Caoimh

LIFE. Born in 1656, John O'Daly gives Glenville (Gleann an Phreacháin), County Cork, as Eoghan Ó Caoimh's native place. He was schooled in Irish, Latin and English. He wrote poetry in both syllabic and *amhrán* metres. His earliest known poem was an elegy for Conn Ó Caoimh, perhaps a kinsman, who died in 1680. He engaged in verse-dialogue with various poets, including Liam Mac Cairteáin and Dáibhidh Ó Bruadair, and, in bitter vein, with Seán Clárach Mac Domhnaill. For a time he was president of the *cúirt éigse* at Charleville. He wrote, or translated from Latin or English, a number of short prose-texts. He also transcribed manuscripts of Gaelic lore in counties Cork, Kerry and Limerick. He was closely associated with a variety of Cork patrons, especially Dr Eoin Baiste Mac Sleighne, Catholic Bishop of Cork, Cloyne and Ross.

In 1681 he married Eileanóir de Nógla. They had four sons and three daughters. She died on 6 October 1707. Their eldest son, Art, a young poet and a seminarian at La Rochelle in France, died in 1709. Eoghan took orders and became parish priest of Doneraile, County Cork, where he died on 5 April 1726. He is buried nearby, in Oldcourt graveyard.

CHIEF WRITINGS. Tadhg Ó Donnchadha, 'An tAthair Eoghan Ó Caoimh: A Bheatha agus a Shaothar', *Gadelica*, vol. 1 (1912–13), pp. 3–9, 101–11, 163–70, 251–9; Máirtín Ó Murchadha, 'Dán le hEón Ó Caoimh', *Éigse* , vol. 10, pt 1 (autumn 1961), pp. 19–25.

BIOGRAPHY AND CRITICISM. John O'Daly, *The Poets and Poetry of Munster*, 3rd ed. (Dublin, 1851), p. 38; Tadhg Ó Donnchadha, art. cit.; Breandán Ó Conchúir, *Scríobhaithe Chorcaí 1700–1850* (Baile Átha Cliath: An Clóchomhar, 1982); Máire Ní Mhurchú and Diarmuid Breatnach, *1580–1781 Beathaisnéis* (Baile Átha Cliath: An Clóchomhar, 2001), pp. 106–7.

Máire Ní Reachtagáin

LIFE. Information on Máire Ní Reachtagáin derives mainly from notes inscribed in manuscripts written by her husband, Tadhg Ó Neachtain (*c.* 1671–1749). She was his third wife; they married in February 1717, and she died on 11 April 1733. Tadhg's previous wives were Caitríona Nic Fheoiris (Caitríona Bermingham), who died in 1714, and Máire Ní Chomáin, who died in 1715, three days after the birth of their child, Pádraig. He married again soon after Máire Ní Reachtagáin's death, on 3 November 1733. His fourth wife, Isibéal Ní Láithrín, died on 23 July 1745.

Tadhg was forty-six years of age at the time of his marriage to Máire. They do not appear to have had children of their own. By the standards of the time, their circumstances were comfortable. Máire may have been acquainted with Úna Ní Bhroin (q.v.), who was married to Tadhg's father, Seán Ó Neachtain. Like her, she would have found that being a member of the Ó Neachtain family brought her into contact with a large group of poets, scholars and scribes, including Aodh Buí Mac Cruitín

(q.v.), Dermot O'Conor, translator of Céitinn, Charles O'Conor of Belanagare, Charles Lynegar, who taught Irish at Trinity College Dublin, and Anthony Raymond, friend of Swift. If she did not know Úna Nic Cruitín (q.v.), she would undoubtedly have heard of her.

Her elegy for her brother, Seoirse, is not her only known poem. One she wrote to welcome one Father Proinsias Laighneach, a family friend to Dublin, is also extant. This is written in the new form known as *trí rainn agus amhrán* (three syllabic quatrains followed by one in stress metre) which was associated particularly with the Leinster–Ulster border area.

Máire's elegy for Seoirse survives in two copies. In one it is headed 'Máire Ní Reachtagáin's Sorrow-Poem on the Death of her Brother' ('Dolchuire Mháire nui Reachtagan air mbas a Dearbrathar Seorsa Ó Reachtagan': Dublin, Royal Irish Academy Library, MS 23 I 23, fo. 66m). The heading in the other is ambiguous: 'Tuireadh do reir Sheain ui Neachtuin' (Dublin, National Library of Ireland, MS 132, fo. 111). Given the existence of a second poem attributed to Máire, it seems safe to interpret this as 'Elegy according to Seán Ó Neachtain', the salient point being that Ó Neachtain made *a copy* of the elegy composed by Máire, perhaps from memory, but also possibly from another manuscript, with unconscious or deliberate changes. As her brother died in 1725 and Seán lived until 1729, there is no apparent difficult in crediting this interpretation. Tadhg composed an elegy on Máire's death, which begins 'Och! gan mo cheann ina linn déara'. In it, he asks the *mná sidhe* of Meath to assist him in keening her, which suggests that Máire may have been born or raised there.

BIOGRAPHY AND CRITICISM. C.G. Ó Háinle, 'Neighbours in Eighteenth Century Dublin: Jonathan Swift and Seán Ó Neachtain', *Éire-Ireland*, vol. 21, pt 4 (1986), pp. 106–21; C.G. Ó Háinle, 'A Life in Eighteenth Century Dublin: Tadhg Ó Neachtain', in *Féile Zozímus 1991*, ed. Vivian Uíbh Eachach (Baile Átha Cliath: Gael-Linn, 1992), pp. 10–27.

CHIEF WRITINGS. 'Is mise chaill an planda dílis', pp. 424–7; Tomás Ó Cléirigh, 'Leaves from a Dublin Manuscript', *Éigse*, vol. 1, pt 3 (autumn 1939), pp. 196–209.

Toirdhealbhach Ó Cearbhalláin (Turlough Carolan)

LIFE. Toirdhealbhach Ó Cearbhalláin was born in 1670 and lived near Nobber in County Meath until he was about fourteen years of age. His father was a farmer and a blacksmith. The family moved firstly to Carrick-on-Shannon, County Leitrim, but settled at Kilronan, County Roscommon, where the Mac Diarmada Rua (Mac Dermott Roe) family had an ironworks at Ballyfarnon. Ó Cearbhalláin owed his education to Máire Mhic Dhiarmada Rua (Máire Mac Dermott Roe). At eighteen, he caught smallpox and lost his sight. His subsequent education as a harper was at Máire Mhic Dhiarmada Rua's expense, and she also gave him a harp, a horse and provided for a guide to accompany him on his travels. He built up an extensive network of aristocratic patrons throughout Connacht, Ulster, six Leinster counties, and County Clare. He married Máire Mháguidhir from Fermanagh; they had one son and seven daughters. Their home was a farm at Mohill, County Leitrim, but Ó Cearbhalláin continued his itineraries to his patrons throughout his life. His wife died in 1733; he died on 25 March 1738. He was buried at Kilronan, and his funeral, which drew an enormous crowd including many notable harpers, lasted for four days. His fame, during his lifetime and after his death, derived in large part from the breadth of his contacts with notable scholars, poets and musicians; his songs did not survive in oral tradition as did those of folk-poets such as Raiftearaí.

He was by no means the best Gaelic poet of his day but he was the best known. He also provided one of the last great instances of the close relationship between praise-poetry and the harp. It was chiefly the music that was memorable; it, and the status of his patrons, ensured the preservation of the words he added to the airs after their composition. Almost all of his verse is ancillary to the music and he is best judged as a song-writer rather than as a poet.

Already, during his lifetime, he was used to figure an ancient and almost extinct civilization, and he came to embody the definitive idea of Irish music as it developed in the course of the eighteenth century. The first account of his life, by Oliver Goldsmith, was published in 1760, and a selection of his poems was published in 1786 by Joseph Cooper Walker: see Volume I, pp. 408–9, 410, 667–8, 962, 963, 976–7, 981.

CHIEF WRITINGS. Tomás Ó Máille, *Amhráin Chearbhalláin: The Poems of Carolan* (London: Irish Texts Society, 1916).

BIOGRAPHY AND CRITICISM. Donal O'Sullivan, *Carolan: The Life, Times and Music of an Irish Harper* (Cork: Ossian Publications, 2001); Harry White, *The Keeper's Recital: Music and Cultural History in Ireland, 1770–1970* (Cork: Cork University Press in association with Field Day, 1998); Máire Ní Mhurchú and Diarmuid Breatnach, *1580–1781 Beathaisnéis* (Baile Átha Cliath: An Clóchomhar, 2001), pp. 107–9.

Aodh Buí Mac Cruitín

LIFE. Aodh Buí Mac Cruitín was born *c.* 1680 in Kilmacreehy (Cill Mhic Críthe) near Liscannor, County Clare; his family professed *seanchas* for the leading families of Thomond in the fourteenth and fifteenth centuries, especially the Uí Bhriain, but were associated primarily with poetry by the seventeenth century. He is reputed to have been tutored by his kinsman, Aindrias Mac Cruitín (on whom, see p. 249). He was a prolific poet, whose patrons included the Mac Domhnaill and Ó Lochlainn families, as well as the Uí Bhriain. Some of his poems, including ones that were overtly Jacobite in sympathy, are aimed at a wider audience. He moved to Dublin around 1713, where he was closely involved with Seán and Tadhg Ó Neachtain, who shared his Jacobite politics, and their circle of scholars in Dublin. He served a term in prison for writing *A Brief Discourse in Vindication of the Antiquity of Ireland*, published in Dublin in 1717, the first history of Ireland in the English language written from a Gaelic perspective. While in prison, he wrote a grammar, published as *The Elements of the Irish Language Grammatically Explained in English* in Louvain in 1728. In the same year, at the age of fifty, he joined Lord Clare's regiment in Flanders, but left the following year. He remained on the Continent, mainly at Louvain and Paris, until 1736, where the poetry he wrote reflected the Jacobite aspirations of the Irish émigrés. He helped Conchobhar Ó Beaglaoich compile *The English Irish Dictionary. An Foclóir Bearla Gaoidheilge*, published in Paris in 1732. He returned to County Clare in 1736 where he worked as a teacher and scribe, survived the famine of 1740–1, and died in 1755.

CHIEF WRITINGS. For details of his published and unpublished writings, see Morley, below.

BIOGRAPHY AND CRITICISM. Vincent Morley, *An Crann Os Coill: Aodh Buí Mac Cruitín, c. 1680–1755* (Baile Átha Cliath: Coiscéim, 1995); Máire Ní Mhurchú and Diarmuid Breatnach, *1580–1781 Beathaisnéis* (Baile Átha Cliath: An Clóchomhar, 2001), pp. 71–2.

Aogán Ó Rathaille

For biography, see Volume I, p. 325, and Volume IV, p. 292.

Seán de hÓra

LIFE. Seán de hÓra was born around 1715. It is believed that he was originally from County Cork, and moved to Kilkee in County Clare to work as a blacksmith for Somhairle Mac Domhnaill. Mac Domhnaill had extensive lands, and both he and his wife, Isibéal Ní Bhriain, gave generous patronage to Gaelic poets. She was the eldest daughter of Criostóir Ó Briain, head of the branch of the O'Briens who were located at Dough and Ennistymon castles. Somhairle's and Isibéal's daughter, Máire Bhán, eloped with and subsequently married Muircheartach Mac

Mathghamhna of Cluainíneach. De hÓra moved to Cluainíneach at their invitation in 1750 or thereabouts. Almost half of de hÓra's extant poems were written for Criostóir and Isibéal's family, over a three-generation span. When Máire Bhán died in 1766, de hÓra returned to live at Dún Átha, near Kilkee.

It has been suggested that de hÓra was unlettered, but Mac Cumhghaill, who edited his poetry, argued that he was well versed in Irish history and classical literature, and also knew English. He is believed to have known Brian Merriman and he associated with other Clare poets and scholars, including Eoghan Mór Ó Comhraí, Peadar Ó Conaill, Tomás Ó Míocháin, and Seámas Mac Consaidín; the last-named composed two elegies on his death. It is also said that he visited the hostelry of Seán Ó Tuama (q.v.) in Croom.

His surviving poems include, in addition to those written for the Mac Domhnaill family, Jacobite poems, religious poems, and a mock warrant (*barántas*). His 'Aithrí Sheáin de hÓra' ('Seán de hÓra's Repentance') remained popular in the oral tradition of County Clare until the last century.

CHIEF WRITINGS. Brian Mac Cumhghaill (ed.), *Seán de hÓra* (Baile Átha Cliath: Oifig an tSoláthair, 1956).

BIOGRAPHY AND CRITICISM. R. Flower, *Catalogue of Irish Manuscripts in the British Museum II*, p. 196; Mac Cumhghaill, *Seán de hÓra*, pp. 11–23; Máire Ní Mhurchú and Diarmuid Breatnach, *1580–1781 Beathaisnéis* (Baile Átha Cliath: An Clóchomhar, 2001), pp. 32–3.

Úna Nic Cruitín

No further information is available.

Eibhlín Ní Choillte

LIFE. Eibhlín Ní Choillte, who flourished *c.* 1745, came from Cathair Druinge (Caherdrinny), near Mitchelstown, County Cork. The poem on pp. 435–6 is the only work known to be attributed to her.

Máire Nic a Liondain

LIFE. The surname 'Mac a Liodain' may be a modernized version of Mac Giolla Fhiontain. The principal sources for information on Máire Nic a Liondain's life are the nineteenth-century scholars Nioclás Ó Cearnaigh (Nicholas Kearney) and Matthew Moore Graham. Neither is entirely trustworthy, and Ó Cearnaigh was notorious for distorting and inventing as he pleased. Yet much of what is known about the work and the lives of the poets of Oirghialla — including Séamas Dall Mac Cuarta, Peadar Ó Doirnín, Art Mac Cumhaigh, and Pádraig Mac a Liondain (1665–1733), who was Máire's father — derives from their industry.

Her father's poetry, and poems written about him, supply certain facts and probabilities relevant to Máire's life. He lived in the area known as the Fews in south Armagh, probably in the townland of Lisleitrim in the parish of Lower Creggan, and he was buried in Creggan churchyard. His mother, Siobhán Nic Ardail, was a poet and a historian, and there were poets also in earlier generations of her family. It was held that Pádraig's interest in poetry derived from her. His poetry was marked by the transition from syllabic metres to stressed ones: he wrote poems of both kinds, and he also wrote in the newly favoured form of *trí rainn agus amhrán*. He and Mac Cuarta were close friends, and he was acquainted with Toirdhealbhach Ó Cearbhalláin, Peadar Ó Doirnín, Pádraig Ó Prontaigh, and many other notable poets and scholars, to whom hospitality was liberally dispensed at his home. He was renowned among this company for his harp-playing.

Additional detail may be gleaned from other sources. Pádraig had a son, also named Pádraig, whose poetic talent was slight. It has been conjectured that he was the harper of that name from whom Edward

Bunting collected airs in 1802 in Newtownhamilton. Nioclás Ó Cearnaigh compared Pádraig junior unfavourably with his sister, Máire: 'Patrick Lindon died in April 1733 in the 58th year of his age, leaving a son, Patrick the Younger, who though a learned man never came near his father in merit; and one daughter, Miss Mary Lindon, or as she was usually called Mailigh Nic a Liondain, who was a woman of great talent, and composed many sweet songs, among which as [*sic*] admired "Coillte glasa an Triucha. The Green Woods of Triuch", "Jospeh Plunkett Esq. of Sleeve" and "Deálradh an Lae. The Dawning of the Day"' (Dublin, Royal Irish Academy Library, MS 23 N 33, p. 50). Elsewhere, Ó Cearnaigh disputes her authorship of 'Coillte Glasa an Triúcha' but admits that that was the 'prevalent tradition' (Dublin, Royal Irish Academy Library, MS 23 E 12, p. 355). An unidentified scribe of a manuscript in the same holding says of this song that it 'was composed by Molly Lindon under the name of her brother Patrick the Younger, and addressed to a young woman named Mac Bride of Thornfield, to whom he paid his addresses' (MS 23 B 19, p. 89). An additional note in Ó Cearnaigh's hand states: 'The above note is correct, NKearney.'

There is no reason to doubt Máire Nic a Liondain's authorship of the poem of welcome to, and the elegy for, Joseph Plunkett. However, it seems that 'Dealradh an Lae. The Dawning of the Day' was one of Ó Cearnaigh's own compositions which he passed off on some occasions as hers, on others as Peadar Ó Doirnín's. Mangan, who translated this poem quite faithfully into English, was given to understand that it was by Ó Doirnín (see Volume II, p. 33). Versions of a verse-dialogue between Máire and Ó Doirnín also survive. In one published by Dubhghlas de hÍde in his *Abhráin Ghrádha Chúige Chonnacht (The Love Songs of Connacht)*, Máire is presented as competing with Ó Doirnín not only in versifying but also in harp-playing. De hÍde altered Peadar Ó Doirnín's name to 'Tadhg Ó Doirnín', and gave Máire's surname variously as 'Luinín' and 'Lindon', presumably to obscure his appropriation of Ulster poetry for Connacht.

Máire's poem of welcome to Joseph Plunkett is written from, or as though from, Cnoc Céin Mhic Cáinte (in English, 'Killen Hill'). This suggests she had moved from her home in Lisleitrim to the area of this hill, about two miles north-west of Dundalk. According to Ó Cearnaigh, after their father's death, 'Lindon's children felt a change of fortune . . . they were obliged to leave their native sod, and take refuge among their relatives in the County Louth' (MS 23 N 33, p. 50).

An advertisement in *Irisleabhar na Gaedhilge. The Gaelic Journal*, vol. 14 (1904–5), p. 768, stated that 'the poetical works of Miss Mary Lindon and of Doctor James Woods', comprising a full volume of the projected seven-volume *Bardic Remains of Louth*, 'will be published at any time that proper encouragement is given and will contain much useful and pleasant information'. One can only hope that some of Máire's work remains to be rediscovered in uncatalogued manuscripts.

CHIEF WRITINGS. Éinrí Ó Muirgheasa, 'The Modern Irish Poets of Oriel, Breffni and Omeath: "Fáilte Maighistir Ió Pluinceat"', *Journal of the County Louth Archaeological Society*, vol. 3 (1915), pp. 388–93; Dubhghlas de hÍde, *Abhráin Ghrádh Chúige Chonnacht* (Baile Átha Cliath: Oifig Díolta Foilseacháin Rialtais, 1931), pp. 60–2; Éamonn Ó Tuathail, 'Dánta de Chuid Uladh', *An tUltach* (November 1951), pp. 9–11; *An tUltach* (January 1952), pp. 10–11, (February 1952), pp. 11–12.

BIOGRAPHY AND CRITICISM. Seosamh Mag Uidhir, *Pádraig Mac a Liondain* (Baile Átha Cliath: An Clóchomhar, 1977); Seán Ó Dufaigh, Diarmaid Ó Doibhlin, *Nioclás Ó Cearnaigh: Beatha agus Saothar* (Baile Átha Cliath: An Clóchomhar, 1989), pp. 115, 133.

Máire Ní Dhonnagáin

LIFE. The poem printed above at pp. 438–40 survives also in an incomplete version, which is preceded by the following note: 'Maire Ni Dhonagainn [*sic*] was Waterford's greatest poetess. She was a contemporary and friend of William O'Moran [dates unknown] and Donnchadh Ruadh [1715–1810], and is buried in Knockboy

Churchyard in Sliabh gCua': see *Irisleabhar na Gaedhilge. The Gaelic Journal*, vol. 14 (1904), p. 729. John O'Daly, in *The Poets and Poetry of Munster* (Dublin: John O'Daly, 1860), pp. 211–12, also provides information on her, as follows: 'A poetess named Maire Ní Dhonogáin [*sic*] was contemporaneous with Moran, and resided in this parish also [= Sliabh gCua]. Her compositions are not so numerous as those of Moran's, but such of them as we have seen prove her to have been of the highest order among the bards of her time; and Munster at this period yielded a large crop of those gifted men . . . There was also another poetess named Lucas, who was no less gifted than Donogan, but her muse was entirely devoted to *keening* at wakes, of which she made a regular profession, and earned a sufficient livelihood by it. The compositions of these poetesses must be traditionally retained in the parish; and if any one would take the trouble of their collection, an opportunity may offer of leaving them on record, instead of dying away as they are now likely to do.' Nothing further is known of Máire Ní Dhonnagáin at this time.

CHIEF WRITINGS. 'Mo fhaoisidín glan go pras don chléir chirt', pp. 438–40; 'A dhearbhráthair ó mo mhile dith thú', *Irisleabhar na Gaedhilge. The Gaelic Journal*, vol. 3 (1887–9), pp. 104–5; vol. 4 (1889–94), p. 29.

Aindrias Mac Craith

LIFE. Aindrias Mac Craith is believed to have been born around 1709 in Fantstown (Baile an Fhantaigh), near Kilmallock, County Limerick, and to have been educated at a hedge-school in the vicinity, together with another future poet, Seán Ó Tuama (q.v.). He and Ó Tuama were the luminaries of the Maigue school of poets, who gathered *cois Máighe* — 'by the Maigue river' — in the barony of Coshma, County Limerick. Mac Craith moved to Croom, also in County Limerick, sometime after 1734, perhaps to replace Ó Tuama, who apparently quit his teaching post around this time in order to run a hostelry. It has been suggested that the poet and Franciscan priest Nioclás Ó Domhnaill was involved in the foundation of this school. Mac Craith played the rake throughout his life. His fondness for drink led him into many scrapes, and some serious disputes, and he may have been ousted from his post at Croom on account of his lifestyle. Dáithí Ó hÓgáin has argued that his most famous song, 'Slán is céad ón dtaobh so uaim', was written when his proposal to a woman in Croom was refused, after which he went to live in Ballineety. Ó Tuama's refusal to help him in his efforts to open a school in 1747 resulted in a sequence of bitter poems against his old friend. He is known to have lived and taught at various places in Limerick in subsequent years, including Ballingarry, Bruff and Grange. He married in the 1750s and had one daughter, with whom he lived in his old age. He wrote a wide range of poems: drinking-songs, satires, love-songs, political poems and prophecies of Stuart restoration, poems to honour friends, and mock warrants. He died in 1795.

CHIEF WRITINGS. Pádraig Ua Duinnín (ed.), *Filidhe na Máighe* (Baile Átha Cliath: Oifig an tSoláthair, 1916); Fiachra Éilgeach (ed.), *Éigse na Máighe* (Baile Átha Cliath: Oifig an tSoláthair, 1952); Máire Comer-Bruen, Dáithí Ó hÓgáin, *An Mangaire Súgach: Beatha agus Saothar* (Baile Átha Cliath, 1996).

BIOGRAPHY AND CRITICISM. Máire Comer-Bruen, Dáithí Ó hÓgáin, *An Mangaire Súgach: Beatha agus Saothar* (Baile Átha Cliath, 1996), pp. 5–41; Robert Welch (ed.), *The Oxford Companion to Irish Literature* (Oxford: Clarendon Press, 1996), pp. 330–1; Máire Ní Mhurchú and Diarmuid Breatnach, *1782–1881 Beathaisnéis* (Baile Átha Cliath: An Clóchomhar, 1999), pp. 63–4.

Seán Ó Murchadha na Ráithíneach

LIFE. This prolific poet and scribe was born in March 1700. His parents' farm was in the vicinity of Carrignavar (Carraig na bhFear), near Cork city. His paternal grandfather had moved to the area from

Ráithín, a townland in the parish of Knockavilla, east of Bandon, County Cork, hence the distinguishing epithet, 'na Ráithíneach'. During the poet's lifetime, Gaelic tradition and culture were cultivated and fostered in Carrignavar, in significant part because of the active interest of the Mac Carthaigh Spáinneach family, the local branch of the MacCarthys of Múscraí. The poet became literate in Irish and acquired a knowledge of English from a local schoolmaster, Seán Ó Macháin, who was employed by Cormac Spáinneach Mac Carthaigh. His earliest extant poem is an elegy on the death of his only brother in 1719. He married in 1725, and he and his wife, whose name is not recorded, had six daughters and one son.

From early adulthood, he was acquainted with many of the leading Gaelic poets of Munster. He was closely involved with the Cork poets Conchubhar Mac Cairteáin, Liam Mac Cairteáin, and Liam Rua Mac Coitir. Liam Rua Mac Coitir (c. 1690–1738) succeeded Liam Mac Cairteáin (c. 1668–1724) as ceannfhile, 'head poet', of the cúirt éigse held at Carrignavar, and was succeeded in turn by Seán Ó Murchadha. Cormac Spáinneach Mac Carthaigh occasionally presided as 'Justice' of the cúirt éigse during the period it was headed by Ó Murchadha. From 1739 until 1742, Ó Murchadha was employed as a clerk in the official court at Glanmire. Torna, who edited his poetry, suggested that he left this employment due to criticism from his confrères in the Gaelic 'court' (cúirt éigse). He died in 1762. Almost two hundred of his poems are extant. They have been praised for the detailed picture they provide of social, economic and cultural life, but have yet to receive an adequate critical evaluation. His work as a scribe has been detailed by Breandán Ó Conchúir.

CHIEF WRITINGS. Torna [= Tadhg Ó Donnchadha] (ed.), Seán na Ráithíneach (Baile Átha Cliath: Oifig an tSoláthair, 1954).

BIOGRAPHY AND CRITICISM. Torna, Seán na Ráithíneach, pp. v–xxxiv; Breandán Ó Conchúir, Scríobhaithe Chorcaí 1700–1850 (Baile Átha Cliath: An Clóchomhar, 1982), pp. 167–72 and passim; Robert Welch (ed.), The Oxford Companion to Irish Literature, p. 447; Máire Ní Mhurchú and Diarmuid Breatnach, 1580–1781 Beathaisnéis (Baile Átha Cliath: An Clóchomhar, 2001), pp. 159–61.

Seán Ó Tuama an Ghrinn

LIFE. If Seán Ó Tuama an Ghrinn was not born in Fantstown, near Kilmallock, County Limerick, it is likely that his mother's family were from there, judging from references in his poetry. The year of his birth was 1707 or 1708. In youth, Ó Tuama attended the same school as Aindrias Mac Craith (q.v.). For a time, Ó Tuama ran his own school at Croom (Cromadh an tSubhachais, 'Croom of the Merriment'), County Limerick, for students preparing for entrance to Trinity College Dublin. Later, he and his wife, Muireann, opened a hostelry in Croom. By the 1730s, this had become the location of a cúirt éigse. The poet Seán Clárach Mac Domhnaill was in attendance around 1735. The poet and Franciscan priest Nioclás Mac Domhnaill presided as judge for a period, as did Ó Tuama himself, and mock warrants were issued to brother-poets in Ó Tuama's name, from both Croom and Fantstown. Later in life, he moved to Limerick, where he opened another hostelry in Mungret Street. He died on 30 August 1775, and was buried in the old churchyard at Croom. Aindrias Mac Craith was only one of many poets who elegized him.

Ó Tuama's geniality, attested in his sobriquet — 'an Ghrinn', 'of the Merriment' — also shines through his poetry. Many of his extant poems are warm addresses to fellow poets or Catholic priests. Others are disputatious, occasionally in serious vein. Quite a few are calls for support for the Stuart cause, or fantasies of a glorious Stuart regime, while others register the bleak mood after the collapse of the Scottish Rising of 1745.

CHIEF WRITINGS. Pádraig Ua Duinnín (ed.), Filidhe na Máighe; Fiachra Éilgeach (ed.), Éigse na Máighe (Baile Átha Cliath: Oifig an tSoláthair, 1952).

BIOGRAPHY AND CRITICISM. Fiachra Éilgeach, Éigse na Máighe, pp. 35–70; Robert Welch (ed.), The Oxford Companion to Irish Literature, p. 462; Breandán Ó Conchobhair, 'Na Cúirteanna Éigse i gCúige Mumhan', in Saoi na hÉigse. Aistí in Ómós do Sheán Ó Tuama, eds Pádraigín Riggs, Breandán Ó Conchúir, Seán Ó Coileáin (Baile Átha Cliath: An Clóchomhar, 2000), pp. 55–82; Máire Ní Mhurchú and Diarmuid Breatnach, 1580–1781 Beathaisnéis (Baile Átha Cliath: An Clóchomhar, 2001), pp. 172–3.

Tadhg Gaelach Ó Súilleabháin

LIFE. Tadhg Gaelach was born around 1715 in Míntín Eoghain, in the parish of Kileedy near Toornafola, County Limerick. He left this area about 1740 and went to live in County Cork. Places in east Cork — Midleton, Carrignavar, Cove, Castlelyons — and Cork city itself figure repeatedly in the poems he wrote over the next thirty years. These poems were mainly on secular themes. For a time he was a Jacobite supporter and at one stage he was imprisoned for raising a Jacobite toast. Later, he was to achieve renown as a religious poet. It has been suggested that he received a clerical education, and his acquaintances included Bishop Seán Ó Briain and the Dominican priest and poet Uilliam Inglis. He espoused an ascetic life from around 1767, and this change coincided with a move to Dungarvan, County Waterford. From then on, he wrote only religious verse. In his old age he went to live in Waterford, where he died on 22 April 1795. A collection of twenty-five of his religious songs was first published in 1802 in Clonmel, under the title Timothy O'Sullivan's Irish Pious Miscellany: To which is Added a Poem on the Passion of Our Saviour, by the Rev. Dr Coyle, Roman Catholic Bishop of Raphoe. Eighteen or more editions were published between 1802 and 1850, and it became the most frequently printed book in the Irish language before the twentieth century.

The individual songs circulated orally and in manuscripts during Ó Súilleabháin's lifetime. Niall Ó Cíosáin has described the printed collection as paralleling collections produced in mid-seventeenth-century France as part of the 'Catholic Reformation' drive to inculcate more orthodox belief and practice. Similar collections appeared in the other Celtic languages. Two of the most frequently printed texts in Breton and Scottish Gaelic were Cantiquou Spirituel (first printed in 1642 and reprinted continuously until 1821) and Laoidhe Spioradail (first printed in 1767, and running to twenty-one editions by 1850).

CHIEF WRITINGS. Risteard Ó Foghludha, Tadhg Gaelach: Atheagar ar a Dhuana Diadha agus ar a Chuid Amhrán, Maille re Mórán Nuadh-Eolais ar a Bheatha (Baile Átha Cliath: Muinntir C.S. Ó Fallamhain, 1929); Úna Nic Éinrí, An Cantaire Siúlach: Tadhg Gaelach (Baile Átha Cliath: An Clóchomhar, 2001).

BIOGRAPHY AND CRITICISM. R. Ó Foghludha, Tadhg Gaelach, pp. 1–26; Niall Ó Cíosáin, Print and Popular Culture in Ireland, 1750–1850 (London: Macmillan, 1997); Ú. Nic Éinrí, An Cantaire Siúlach, passim; Máire Ní Mhurchú and Diarmuid Breatnach, 1782–1881 Beathaisnéis (Baile Átha Cliath: An Clóchomhar, 1999), pp. 136–7.

Máire Ní Mhurchú

No further information is available.

MARGARET MAC CURTAIN, *Editor*

Religion, Science, Theology and Ethics, 1500–2000

In this section we hear and interpret the words of women through the diverse themes of a multi-cultured religious experience over the past five hundred years in a country where settler and native met and exchanged in a variety of mediums. The subject of women and religion in Ireland began to find its voice confidently in the last quarter of the twentieth century, with the growth of women's studies in higher education. Feminist consciousness has given to research and writing in the areas of theology and ethics the tools to critique church structures in relation to women's subordination, and to offer alternative hermeneutics and theological reflection.

According to Gerda Lerner in her book *The Creation of Feminist Consciousness: From the Middle Ages to Eighteen-Seventy,* one of the greatest problems that women have faced concerns the basis on which they claim authority. Resistance to church patriarchy is complicated by the nature of religious authority, which makes patriarchy seem the way life is ordered. Consequently, she argues, any resistance appears 'ludicrous', even mad. Lerner identifies several sources of authority for women: themselves, mysticism, motherhood, creativity, knowledge and community. Each of these, she argues, offered women a particular point of departure and each places obstacles in the path of women writing themselves into the past.[1]

The key issue for women in the early modern period was the conflict between the authority of church leaders and the commandments of God

in the age of religious Reformation. The women whose religious choices influenced their society came from the nobility or ruling strata. For women of all classes, and this generalization holds up for succeeding generations, religion provided the most powerful incentive for experiencing autonomy and for independent action. In the early modern period the Reformation and the Catholic Counter-Reformation were designed by male hierarchies and controlled by them. The clerical state was male and church leadership of the different Christian denominations was in the hands of men. God was addressed as 'He' and the interpretation of the Bible apportioned a subordinate and serving role to women. In all spheres of public and domestic life church authority upheld male authority. Saint Paul's admonition to the Corinthians, 'Let your women keep silence in the churches' (I Corinthians 14.34–5), was given an application in this period as never before.

The Tudor conquest of Ireland and the introduction of plantations and resettlement of the native people were inextricably woven with the Protestant Reformation into the politics of the country. In the late sixteenth century and through the seventeenth century Ireland experienced the introduction of new Protestant groupings, notably the Puritans, the Presbyterians and the Quakers. Acceptance of or resistance to religious changes on the part of groups and individuals remains obscure until the middle years of Elizabeth's reign. Unlike Germany and England, women's activity in religious affairs in Ireland did not emerge until the 1570s. Women's writings in the early part of the Tudor religious

---

1. Gerda Lerner, *The Creation of Feminist Consciousness: From the Middle Ages to Eighteen-Seventy* (New York: Oxford University Press, 1993), p. 9.

459

Reformation, if they appear at all, take the form of letters, such as that of Margaret Fitzgerald, Countess of Ormond and Ossory in 1540, and conceal the real opinions of the writer. How much the scant evidence of women's involvement through pamphleteering and propaganda tracts is affected by the problem of determining literacy levels among women whose vernacular was the English and Irish languages remains indeterminate. The surviving evidence of women's religious writings makes it virtually impossible to determine how representative is what has been discovered.

Seventeenth-century Ireland found women participating in all manner of religious discourse. First, chronologically, came personal diaries and narratives such as Mother Browne's account of the beginnings of the Poor Clare foundations of nuns. After the mid-century, the works of Nonconformist women appeared, often in published form. Possibly the lifting of restrictions on printing presses at the beginning of the English Civil War in the 1640s gave women an opportunity to write their memoirs and testimonies for publication. To date, however, little attempt has been made to identify women born in Ireland among the extant writers that Elaine Hobby has researched in her study, *Virtue of Necessity: English Women's Writings 1646–1668*.[2] Lady Eleanor Douglas is a case in point. She was one of the early prophetic writers who had sixty of her works in print by the end of that period. Claiming to be a 'She-Counsellor . . . made like unto the Son of God', she makes use of dense biblical references, using the Book of Revelations to claim that a female deity and creator will end oppressive religion.[3] It would be an audacious act of reappropriation to claim her as 'Irish', yet she was the daughter of a Munster settler, Sir George Touchett, and her first marriage was to Sir John Davies, Attorney General for Ireland in the reign of James I. It would appear that she was born in Ireland and lived there during her early years.

Phil Kilroy, in selecting a group of Nonconformist women writers, situates them in seventeenth-century Ireland and uses 'witness'

literature of Quaker women to explore a hidden theme in their lives as settler wives and single women: belief in Jesus Christ in the midst of persecution. On their own admission they experienced religious doubt before finding people of similar religious convictions. John Rogers' Independent Congregation in Dublin offered them a haven of gender equality and a free space to talk about their religious conversion. One of the requirements of joining an Independent Congregation was the rendering of an autobiographical narrative in which the applicant presented her reasons for believing herself to be among the elect. Mary Rich's *Autobiography* springs from her conversion experience when she adopted the tenets of Puritanism wholeheartedly on her marriage to Charles Rich. Tutored by her father-in-law, the Earl of Warwick, in the practice of self-examination recommended by the Puritan spiritual guides, her diaries record the pattern of her devotions, her love of meditation and the growth of her spiritual understanding. The new self she constructed for herself allowed her to record the fluctuations of her states of mind and, at times, the turmoil of her feelings. In her almost daily entries for twelve years she established a routine of recording her thoughts as a device for making sense of a life of duty, in which her marriage became increasingly difficult to sustain.

Writings by women in the Irish vernacular still elude the hopeful researcher. The veiled references to mystical experience in the Bethlehem Poor Clare community of nuns, mentioned by Helena Concannon in her history of the Poor Clares which is anthologized in this section, raise expectations of lost treasures. The Irish translation of the Rule of Saint Clare, an early seventeenth-century document transcribed for that community by Brother Michael O'Cleary, chief annalist of the Annals of the Four Masters, is a document of rare interest that deserves more than a passing reference here. Likewise, Dubhaltach Ma Firbisigh's translations into Irish of devotional literature of the Saint Clare and Saint Colette tradition conceal a story of asceticism which remains uncoded. Among the tracts translated for the nuns of Bethlehem, who used Irish as their language of devotion, can be found: 'The Obligations of the Rule of Saint Clare As Regards Mortal Sin'; 'Praise of the

2. Elaine Hobby, *Virtue of Necessity: English Women's Writings, 1646–1668* (London, Virago Press, 1988).
3. Theodore Spencer, 'The History of an Unfortunate Lady', in *Harvard Studies and Notes in Philosophy and Literature*, 20 (Boston: Harvard University Press, 1938), pp. 1–15.

Rule'; 'An Examen of Conscience for Religious'; 'The Twelve Evils that Come by Venial Sin'; 'The Nine Ways by which We Participate in the Sins of Others'; Twelve Evangelical Counsels; 'The Maledictions of Saint Francis'. Their inaccessibility, and that of similar documents, becomes a metaphor of women's silent efforts to prolong a different experience of an older tradition of asceticism and spiritual formation.

What seventeenth-century texts provide are insights into the approaches women took in mapping out the paths of personal faith in a period when religion and politics were about power. Women's voices were muted. Their scene of religious experience was domestic and their writings concern themselves with doubt leading to conversion, sinfulness and salvation. The respective worlds of Roman Catholic and Protestant women remained sealed off from each other and survival in a harsh world of colonial settlement and forced plantation wove loss and death into spiritual considerations, and their faith-world remained enclosed in their religious affiliations.

The seventeenth century slid imperceptibly into the following one and despite the imposition of a Penal Code of diminished civil and religious rights for Roman Catholics and Nonconformists, in particular the Presbyterian community, for women there was little change in their status; they remained subjects, not citizens, yet curiously free to carry out practices of devotion and even works of charity. Religion for women was privatized but paradoxically presented them with opportunities for independent action in the sphere of philanthropy. Rosemary Raughter argues persuasively and convincingly that eighteenth-century Ireland offered Roman Catholic women scope for presiding over home-based religious practices, such as the house mass, instruction in catechesis, the reading of prayers and use of the rosary beads. Extrapolating from P.J. Corish's findings, Raughter considers Nano Nagle's founding of the Society of the Charitable Instruction (1775) — later to become the Presentation Order — as 'the high point' of this feminine period, which also heralded 'the close of the matriarchal era within Irish Catholicism'.

A somewhat similar phenomenon occurred in the Protestant minorities which flourished within mainstream Protestantism: the Quakers, Moravians and Methodists. The Quakers placed great reliance on inner truth rather than on received doctrine and gave women leadership roles. But perhaps the most significant and visible expression of the Protestant minorities was the prominence accorded to the laity. Women, drawn from the settler communities, were attracted by the prospect of an active involvement in the organized structure of these sects and by the concern of Methodism to reach out to the sick, the poor and the aged among them. C.H. Crookshank's *History of Methodism* gives many examples of women's initiatives in familiarizing the small towns and villages with Methodist practices. They made rooms available for preachers and became good preachers themselves. John Wesley advised Alice Cambridge: 'I would advise you not to speak at any place where a preacher is speaking near you at the same time, lest you should draw away his hearers.' Crookshank recounts how Alice Cambridge drew crowds 'amounting to eight or ten thousand persons' during a tour of Ulster at the beginning of the nineteenth century.

By the third quarter of the eighteenth century religion was providing a public role for women. The educational needs of the underprivileged, missionary zeal for the spread of Christianity, and religion-inspired philanthropy motivated women to enter the public arena. Rosemary Raughter argues that it was practical rather than theoretical in its approach. Women demonstrated their concern through their involvement in a multiplicity of benevolent ventures, both private and public. Roman Catholic and Protestant women alike took leadership in the charity school and voluntary hospital movements. Lady Arbella Denny founded the Magdalen Asylum in Dublin in 1766. Teresa Mulally established a school and orphanage in George's Hill in Dublin in the same year, both along denominational lines of Protestant and Catholic intake. Religious zeal was the primary underlying motivation. The remarkable parallels in the growth of philanthropic endeavour among Roman Catholic and Protestant women in the final decades of the eighteenth century suggest similar influences: for Protestant women, evangelicalism; for Catholic women, the institutional attraction of organized projects. The charities were confessional, rarely was there an interchange. The willingness of women to seize opportunities for active initiatives in philanthropy spurred them to imitate and even to compete with each other's enterprises and unwittingly prepared the climate for sectarian rivalries in the next century.

One of the generally accepted tenets of nineteenth-century religious behaviour was that women were more naturally fitted for religion than men. Women seemed to be present everywhere in the churches in the nineteenth century except on the altars. They were hymn-writers, catechists, writers of tracts. For Catholic women the new teaching and nursing orders offered lives full of usefulness and even adventure as the religious orders followed the flag of empire and spread to the ends of the earth. For Protestantism there was ambivalence about the boundaries of women's participation in the public sphere of church life. Janice Holmes's examination of women in the Ulster Revival of 1859 reveals that only during a period of religious upheaval and intense emotional confusion did women find voices that were recorded. With growing clarity women in this century perceived that the central issue for them was winning the power to direct their lives and achieve goals of their own choosing. 'Protest' literature, accounts of conversion, manuals of spiritual guidance, prayer books proliferate throughout a century when women expressed their determination to obtain the vote, to enter universities and to participate actively in politics.

Women's religious writings reflected the energy and high ambitions of this period. The foundresses of Catholic religious orders wrote reams of letters because writing was the standard form of communication in the age of the post office and the telegram. They were risk-takers whose faith and decisiveness gave their leadership a vitality that was rooted in personal charism. Often at odds with episcopal authority and sometimes with civic powers, like Margaret Aylward accused before the courts of proselytism, they had to struggle with innate prejudices entrenched in the Catholic perception of women as intellectually inferior and morally weaker than their male guardians, the bishops and priests who allowed the Sisters into their dioceses and parishes. Spirited, resourceful women sometimes lost the battle in their efforts to win the war. Catherine McAuley, foundress of the Mercy Order who never wanted her Sisters to be

cloistered nuns, had to bow to Rome and submit to the law of enclosure within the convent precincts. Margaret Anna Cusack, foundress of the Sisters of Peace, was continually embattled with members of the Catholic hierarchy. The legacy of their writings resides in convent archives and is gradually being rescued from obscurity with the new appreciation of women's religious writings.

Janice Holmes explores the range of religious and spiritual experience that Protestant women recorded. She retrieves the women involved in the great Ulster Revival of 1859. Mill girls were credited with possessing low characters but the Ulster Revival awakened them and one by one they testified their 'conviction' about the Spirit of God. Illiterate women longed to be able to read and they began to enjoy complex doctrinal sermons. Sharing testimonies during meetings, later to be published in local newspapers, empowered them. Irish Protestant mill girls in Ulster wrote their souls out for the world to read.

The nineteenth century was one of devotional hymn-writing in the English language. Cecil Frances Alexander is an integral part of Victorian hymnody, beloved or reviled with changing fashions. Charles Gounod, the great French religious composer of the celebrated 'Ave Maria', remarked that her words seemed to set themselves to music. The simple charm of hymns such as 'There is a Green Hill Far Away' and 'Once in Royal David's City' gives her compositions a popularity that has not waned since they were set to music one hundred and fifty years ago. Eleanor Hull with her skilful translations from Old Irish has added to the repertoire of hymns in the English language with the beautiful 'Be Thou My Vision' and 'It Were My Soul's Desire'.

Passing on to the twentieth century the historically dominant form of religious experience was the Catholic one. The Catholic hierarchy as authority, the Catholic school and the boarding-school filled with the presence of nuns, the stifling religiosity of the home, these were the memories of novelists such as Kate O'Brien, Norah Hoult and Edna O'Brien. *The Bell*, in the short stories it published, caught other facets of Catholic culture, subversive ways of dealing with repression and control. 'If I go in,' said Mother Mary Aloysius, 'it will be a mortal sin.' Thus she entered the house she had left to enter the convent fifty years before. Wherever the reader turns until well after the mid-century Irish women were writing about their memories of Catholicism, telling their stories, enhancing them, as Mary Lavin, the superb storyteller, did, relinquishing dead memories by narrating them, but always Catholicism, in some form or other, was at the core.

Women in twentieth-century Ireland were also struggling with identity problems and religion was one of the troubling elements. Even before the shared action and collective workshops of the activist seventies, women were exchanging their experiences with each other, wanting to know what other women believed in, how they came to be part of the same journey. Lucy Kingston's lucid exposition of Quakerism is a debt paid to the tradition of Quakerism in Ireland. Violet Disney's reflection on why she is still a practising member of the Church of Ireland needed to be heard by Roman Catholic people. Ronit Lentin's spiritual journey as a Jewish woman in twentieth-century Ireland is a lonely voice. Maura O'Halloran's voice was silenced by death in her twenties but her spiritual quest for Zen enlightenment is with us through her journals. Sister Stanislaus Kennedy reflects on her spiritual journey and why she was drawn to the poor. The Reverend Ginnie Kennerley pauses at an important moment in her life and in the lives of Irish women as she preaches before ordination to the priesthood in the Church of Ireland. Edel Quinn affords us glimpses of the inner life of a lay missionary in East Africa in the 1930s.

The poetry women wrote in twentieth-century Ireland about spiritual and religious matters is personal and authentic. This is most true of poetry written after the mid-century when women began to reclaim their voices with a growing confidence and articulateness. Often the voice comes out of isolation or takes up the older form of lament and uses it in a fresh setting. The women poets write with sureness in English and in Irish, sometimes merging pre-Christian with the Christian, and both with the contemporary. The cry of the outcast, the elegy for the dead hero find a new setting in poems crafted by women. Familiar sacred objects are turned upside down not in a spirit of irreverence but to see a different truth.

The small subsection on women's writing on

scientific matters was designed originally to explore the nature of doubt, even of atheism. In selecting astronomy, the editor, Maire Rodgers, reasons that it is the branch of science most closely connected with religion. Her three exemplars, Mary Ward, Agnes Clerke and Susan McKenna-Lawlor, have, as Rodgers suggests, offered us glimpses of 'the cosmic vision which fuels and is fed by the struggle to make sense of the observed universe'. They also span a time-scale which covers three visits of Halley's Comet, not merely to the skies of planet Earth but 'to the inner reaches of the solar system', and each has advanced observational technology in different ways.

For Kathleen Lonsdale the cosmic vision was threatened when nuclear warfare was introduced into the Second World War with the bombing of the Japanese cities Hiroshima and Nagasaki in 1945. Lonsdale (1903–71), crystallographer and chemist, spelt out for her generation of scientists in the decades after the Second World War the dangers of nuclear weapons, and the consequences for the planet of adopting nuclear power as a source of energy. Reared in a strict Baptist home, she found an alternative spiritual home as an adult in the Society of Friends. Her conversion to Quakerism in 1935 confirmed her as a pacifist, and deepened her concerns about militarism and the responsibilities of scientific research.

This section closes with Mary Condren's cluster of theological, ethical and philosophical writings by women scholars. Condren is the leading exponent of feminist hermeneutics in Ireland, challenging traditional interpretations not just of the Scriptures but of the myths that constitute early Irish literature, the four Cycles. She brings together a rich sample of writings that deal with feminist issues in religion. The pluralism of religious experience in the lives of women in Ireland has been examined and, in this final subsection, has been strongly affirmed by the scholarship and authority which characterize the writings selected by Mary Condren.

Perhaps no single volume can embrace the diversity of religious experience that marks five centuries of Irish women's writings. The desire to record their experiences, their ideals and, latterly, their theological arguments creates a narrative whose variety and depth are given their first exposure in this section.

MARGARET Mac CURTAIN, *Editor*

Women and the Religious Reformation in Early Modern Ireland

The religious Reformation, which Irish society experienced from the mid-1530s onwards, changed the denominational composition of the small population of the country significantly. At first sight it seemed an act of state, imposed upon a section of the island to which the Tudor King of England laid claim in the 1530s. In similar fashion, European crowned heads were favouring alternative modes of religious Reformation in their realms in this, the age of Martin Luther, John Calvin and the Council of Trent. The establishment of the Church of Ireland, following the Anglican model, was, in the main, the work of the Tudor monarchs Henry VIII, his son, Edward VI, and his daughter, Elizabeth I. By the middle of the seventeenth century, the Reformation had claimed different constituencies on the island. The government élites gave their allegiance to the established church, the Church of Ireland. The majority of the inhabitants, then estimated variously at under a million, declared for a renewed Roman Catholicism, rejuvenated by the decrees of the Council of Trent and mediated to Ireland through a European-educated clergy and hierarchy. Yet a third group who had come to Ireland during these formative centuries of the early modern period were settlers, different from the medieval Viking, Norman, or later English adventurers, who had formed the core of English administration in Dublin and its surrounding area, the Pale. As colonizers, the settlers of early modern Ireland had the support of the monarchy. Mainly interested in land investment, their general religious configuration was

Protestant. Within that classification were contained lines of religious demarcation. Elizabethan settlers, with a few noteworthy exceptions, belonged to the Church of Ireland. Scottish settlers came in significant numbers to designated areas of Ulster in the Jacobean period. Presbyterians, with the characteristics of the Lowland Scot, their religious identity was rooted in the Calvinism of John Knox.

How did the position and status of women change throughout the Reformation centuries? Did reformed Christianity address itself to the religious needs of women? Is it possible to trace the links that connect pre-Reformation expressions of religion which emerged in the refounding of Catholic religious life for women in eighteenth-century Ireland? In the prevailing vision of Ireland's past, a fissure of discontinuity separates the long and shared cultural perceptions of early and medieval Irish society from the genuinely historical changes that characterize the transitional nature of early modern Ireland.

All historians are seduced by the persuasiveness of a master narrative which neatly divides the medieval world from the modern by a chronology which situates all the significant changes in the contemporary world of a hypothetical but real period designated as 'early modern'. It was 'then' that western civilization encountered humanism. It was 'then' that reformed Christianity shattered the unity of Christendom. The discovery of the New World occurred during that period and, with it, the rise

464

of capitalism, nation states and national monarchies. For Ireland there was the added experience of incorporation into the British Empire, with the Tudor expansion accompanying a colonial experiment of settlement from the neighbouring countries of England, Scotland and Wales. In subscribing to a master narrative, historians section off the medieval world, isolating it so that its society and culture belong to a past extraneous to what follows. Historians of early modern Ireland succumb to the attraction of a great transition, but uncertainty prevails over the beginning and ending of the traditional periodization. Does the historian include the era of the Penal Code in the first half of the eighteenth century? Or was a new canon established in 1976, by giving the magisterial volume three of *A New History of Ireland* an end date with the final victory of the Williamite forces and the consolidation of the land settlement in favour of settlers?

There is consensus about the starting point for early modern Ireland. It is the Fall of the House of Kildare, with the liquidation of its leading members in the 1530s. Attempts to shift the emphasis back have not altered the master narrative. It is convenient for historians to establish a canonicity around the centuries that designate early modern Ireland. It privileges scholarship and offers compartmentalized sanctuary for medievalists as well as for early modern historians. In this arrangement, the distinction between the condition of medieval women and of early modern women carries with it pejorative assumptions. Women's lives worsened in the early modern period. Women lost ground in sixteenth-century Ireland and women's status and choices were drastically curtailed in the following century. Thus the notion of a major transition for women between the medieval and early modern centuries persists as integral to the master narrative instead of challenging it.

The historiography of early modern Ireland retains the configuration of an emerging political map. The traditional issues of historical investigation, such as the visible political developments, military events, and the impact of religious changes which received a major reinforcement of research in the 1960s with the study of the ruling élites, have remained the

longue durée of sixteenth- and seventeenth-century Ireland. Intersections between racial, ethnic, gendered and class identities attracted little research and the methods of the new 'social' history developed in the 1970s, such as quantitative analysis (borrowed from economics), the interpretation of symbols, such as the role of the poet or *file* (from anthropology), and the study of gender, using the tools of gender analysis, are conspicuous by their absence. The important theoretical models that have been built around women as gendered historical change-objects have not been addressed by mainstream historians of early modern Ireland. Certainly the perception of a categorical, dramatic change in women's lives between 1534 and 1691, wherever it is tested, holds up to scrutiny, but the uncritical assumption of a negative transition for women is a forceful and compelling paradigm in the developing field of Irish women's history. Like the model of a medieval and early modern divide, this secondary model of (liberated) medieval, (oppressed) early modern women fits into the master narrative because the areas tested are women, law and property, extrapolating too rapidly from that experience of diminishment of women's rights to an over-generalized picture of, and extinguishing of, women's presence in early modern Ireland.

Did the experience of women in the Reformation century go from bad to worse? How did women regard their religious experience in a reformed Christianity?

The most powerful and, in many respects, most independent women in the late medieval church in Ireland remain hidden from historical scrutiny. There are no mystical writings from the period, either before or after the Black Death, such as the English anchoress Julian of Norwich produced. There is no Catherine of Siena, doctor of the church and patroness of Italy, to recall the Irish church to its sense of mission, no Bridget of Sweden, who is credited with the vision of Ireland where she saw souls fall into hell like leaves in wintry weather. In point of fact there are no Irish women saints in this long period of medieval Ireland, when Rome gradually assumed control of who should be 'raised to the altars of the church'.

Of the major monasteries that were dissolved in the first distribution, 1536–7, during the reign of Henry VIII, two out of the seventeen monasteries dissolved by Crown Commissioners were nunneries: Graine, County Kilkenny, and Hogges Lane in Dublin. In the second distribution, 1539–46, a number of other nunneries are listed, of which Kilculliheen abbey and its abbess are the most frequently cited as evidence of moral decay. Citations from the document 'An Instrument Concerning Elicie Butler', here translated in full for the first time, have presented a picture of unmitigated decadence on the eve of the Reformation. The text in its entirety tells a different story. It is clear from the final section of the document that Elicie Butler and the abbey properties of Kilculliheen were victims of the rival jurisdictional claims of two neighbouring bishops. Deposed the following year, Elicie Butler retained a privileged position in her abbey and was awarded a pension at the dissolution of Kilculliheen.

Alison White was the spirited abbess of Grace Dieu, the most renowned Augustinian monastery and girls' school within Ireland when one of the commissioners for the dissolution, Patrick Barnewall, evicted her and her community, and adapted the buildings for his family mansion. Visitation records of Grace Dieu exist from the previous century and give a picture of a well-run establishment, where the 'divine offices are duly celebrated'. Studies of these sixteenth-century women, who administered large properties and had jurisdiction over many subjects, have yet to come. The aged Countess of Ormond, who died in 1542, was representative of a generation of propertied women of the ruling class and both she and Margaret Ball afford a glimpse of how women of their class carried out their religious duties. In the following century, Honor Fitzmaurice, Lady Kerry, conveys poignantly the sense of being obedient to a higher authority when law and order had broken down.

With the religious changes in sixteenth-century Ireland, the nunneries and their lively occupants disappear and information begins to flow about the reformed women. Their lives were difficult, particularly for the wives of the first reform bishops. Bishop John Bale of Ossory split his diocese asunder when he married. Archbishop Loftus of Armagh dismayed his subjects by marrying a local woman, and her sister married his successor. Nine of the first generation of reform bishops married: a new role for women had been created, the clergyman's wife. The Protestant idealization of motherhood, propelled by Luther's theology of the family, in turn influenced the Council of Trent's regulations on marriage. The history of marriage in this century suggests evidence of an improved status for women. Loss of property was continuous throughout the period but the miseries of clandestine marriages, abandonment and the injustices that beset the ordinary woman in the late Middle Ages, which we find in the filings of the Armagh registers, in the Gormanston records and in Archbishop May's registers, do not surface in the Irish Chancery Court after 1570. By that time extensive legislation relating to marriage had been enacted both in the civil and ecclesiastical courts. The Council of Trent restored marriage as a sacrament. The Book of Common Prayer introduced a splendid marriage liturgy, and the dispensations from the impediments of consanguinity and affinity were allowed for annulment purposes in Rome. Gone was the earlier reckless wife-swapping atmosphere of the 1530s; instead the Elizabethan church settlement made divorce difficult.

The paradigm of a diminishment in women's status in the post-Reformation era does not hold, despite an intensification and reinforcement of a patriarchal model of authority. In the following century the incidence of women writing about their religious experience, together with the feminization of domestic religion within the home, testify to the spiritual vigour that women discovered in their chosen religious affiliations. The diary of Mary Rich, née Boyle, deserves serious scholarly attention. Through its pages the reader is introduced to the intimacy of the Puritan female mind and discovers a clear exposition of the Puritan doctrine of daughterly obedience. By then, women of Quaker affiliation had entered Irish society. Their non-aristocratic background, their ability to take their own space in their assemblies, preaching, discussing, even interrupting sermons, testify to the spiritual freedom of Nonconformist women. Rediscovering the religious voices of women in the age of Reformation challenges the master narrative. Religious history is developing significant interconnections and parallels with other branches of the new 'social' history. The readiness to acknowledge the importance of unordained ministry and to examine the changing constructs of hagiography is a sign of that change. Possibly the most courageous leap forward that the new feminist religious history has made in the field of historical practice is its preparedness to adopt the techniques of qualitative analysis, to look at frameworks derived from feminist theology and biblical research, and to uncover the implications of the ongoing patriarchal control of organized religion for society in general and for the lives of men and women.

AN INSTRUMENT CONCERNING ELICIE BUTLER OF KILCULLIHEEN (1532)

[How Elicie Butler was removed from the office of abbess of Kilculliheen, situated outside Waterford city, on the evidence supplied by the nuns she governed, forms the subject matter of a deposition pronounced in St Canice's cathedral, Kilkenny, on 4 October 1532. The document brought the most serious charges against the abbess's government of the nunnery, and its state of dilapidation, as well as making shocking allegations about her personal character. Prepared by the nuns, the document gives no hint of how Elicie Butler was made a pawn in a game of politics between the Bishop of Waterford, the Bishop of Ossory and the rival claims of the Dublin and Cashel archdioceses. Subsequently, Elicie Butler succeeded in getting a pardon, which freed her from the penalties imposed upon her by the medieval statutes of provisions and praemunire (though her papal provisions were disallowed). She retained a privileged position in the abbey she had ruled. She received a pension from the state when the abbey was dissolved in 1539. The kernel of truth in the document is to be found not in the defamation of the abbess's character but in how the prevailing concerns with territorial rights are revealed. The original document in Latin is printed in B. Newport White (ed.), *Irish Monastic and Episcopal Deeds A.D. 1200–1600* (Dublin: Stationery Office, 1936), pp. 178–85. The translation is by John Higgins, a visiting scholar at the Dublin Institute for Advanced Studies.]

To all the sons of the nurturing mother the Church who shall see, hear or read this letter, containing in it trial and sentence, whom the underwritten matter concerns or might in whatever way concern in the future; and especially to the most reverend father and Lord in Christ, John, by divine permission and the grace of the apostolic see, bishop of Dublin, Primate of Ireland, and also to each and every one of the bishops, abbots, deans, priors of churches and also chapters of cathedrals, secular priests, provosts, rectors, vicars, chaplains and other ministers of the church to whose attention and notice these letters may come, MILO, by divine permission bishop of Ossory, sends greeting; eternal salvation in the Lord.

You have learned what has come to our hearing concerning the divers crimes and sins and excesses of Elicie Butler abbess of Kilculliheen, otherwise Fairport[1] in the diocese of Ossory, from the lamentable complaint of the entire convent of nuns that the monastery (for it being brought to our attention not only by public rumour and clamorous insinuation); (that is) that the aforesaid Elicie, abbess, did not shrink from dilapidating, consuming, dissipating and converting to her own profane and nefarious uses, the diverse goods, fruits, property, renders and income and the ecclesiastical benefices of that monastery, without seeking the consent of that same convent of nuns; and that she also permitted that monastery to fall prodigiously into ruin, nearly irreparable, even in respect of its walls, structures, windows, gate, roof, halls, outhouses, and edifices; and she has also wrongly and impiously seized from that convent the portion granted to them from the sentences, decrees, and composition of the ordinaries, and of other good men (and by the express consent of that same abbess interceding to this end); because of which, she compelled those nuns to go outside the cloister and the monastery through the court of powerful lords and other patrons, contrary to their regular observance, or to remain there in penury and poverty, without food and clothing; and she has perpetrated diverse other outrageous, vicious crimes and sins; by which she has rendered herself deservedly unworthy of the rule and administration of the aforesaid monastery; therefore the said nuns supplicated Us that We should quickly deign to provide for the best remedy for those nuns and the calamities of the monastery.

1. 'Elicie Butler, abbess of Kilkylhyn, otherwise Belliportu'.

Wishing to defend,[2] and to view diligently whether the said abbess had indeed done what we had heard, we decreed that the said monastery, in its head as much as in its members, should be subject to a visitation and reformed; and we cited and ordered to be called to judgement the said abbess and the entire convent of nuns of the same monastery, at a certain day and place (viz. at the 17th inst of September; viz., A.D. 1532, in the said monastery), transmitting our summons of a certain and accustomed tenor by our public herald; the tenor of which summons under our authentic seal clearly appears among the acts.

When the aforesaid term had arrived, and We were sitting in judgement in the aforesaid place and time as assigned, and when the aforesaid parties, viz., the abbess and convent of Fairport had been summoned and had appeared in person, the advocate of the aforesaid nuns, who were moving the inquest against the abbess, rose in the middle (of the court) and delivered a certain petition to us described in order against the aforesaid abbess, for the removal and deposition of the same abbess on account of the causes written below; from which petition he extracted and read aloud certain accusations, described and in order; the same advocate demanding immediately that We ought, having first imposed an oath about speaking the truth, and after the preliminaries had been disposed of, to admonish and order the same abbess to respond to these accusations through the word(s) 'Credo', 'Non credo', the tenor of which accusations follows these words.

'In the first place, the party of the entire convent of nuns of Kilculliheen, otherwise Fairport, puts it to you, the aforesaid Elicie, asserted abbess of the same monastery, in virtue of your oath, and if you deny, intends to prove, that you notoriously and incestuously have fornicated with a certain professed of the same religious order, openly bearing a child of his paternity; it accuses you conjointly and separately, and however you will.

'Again, the same party as above accuses you, and intends to prove if you should deny it that

you have consumed diverse goods, benefices, fruits, and incomes of the same monastery by senseless destruction; it accuses you conjointly and separately, and however you will.

'Again the aforesaid party of the aforesaid nuns accuses you, the aforesaid mistress Elicie, and intends to prove it if you deny it, that you have gadded about, wandering through the courts of the powerful and of secular lords; it accuses as above, conjointly and separately and however you will.

'Again, the party as above accuses you that you have done this to the damage of the aforesaid monastery, with no licence asked or obtained from any superior of yours; and accuses you as above.

'Again, the party as above accuses you, and intends to prove it if you deny, that, when you were bound by the chains of the major excommunication through letters patent of the reverend father in Christ, Oliver, sometime bishop of Ossory, for certain and reasonable causes, you celebrated as before the divine office(s) by participation and attendance,[3] involving yourself reprehensibly in the snare of canonical disqualification and accuses you conjointly and separately, as above.

'Again, it accuses you, Elicie Butler, asserted abbess of Kilculliheen, that you were bound by the chains of major excommunication for and because of this; that you cast violent hands even to the effusion of blood, by the persuasion of the devil (in person) on several of the professed nuns of the said monastery, viz., Anne Cleary, Elicie Gall and Katherine Mothyng, and still celebrated the divine office(s), involving yourself in the snare of canonical disqualification.

'(Again) the same party accuses you the said pretend abbess, and if (you deny) intends to prove that you have permitted the aforesaid monastery of Fairport, otherwise Kilculliheen, by the evident omission of regular upkeep to fall into enormous ruin in its walls, gates, windows, roofs, rooms, outhouses, halls and edifices, nearly irreparable, unless it is fixed by speedy repair; it accuses you conjointly and individually and however you wish.

'Again, the party as above accuses you, and if you deny intends to prove, that you have

---

2. The Latin edition of the text indicates 'Parchment holed'; perhaps the missing words are 'wishing to defend the Church', or 'the monastery'.

3. *active & passive* in Latin text.

mutilated a certain youth, viz., John McHugh,[4] servant of one Manus Fuscus,[5] by injury to his limb; and incurring the snare of canonical disqualification by this as well, from which you refused to be absolved by any but the apostolic see; it accuses you conjointly and individually and however you wish.

'Again, the aforesaid party of the nuns accuses you, Elicie Butler, that you had from the beginning a blameworthy entry into the habit and religious life and the monastery itself in which you are, just as you have up to now, since you illicitly received the habit of religion from the bishop of Waterford; outside the monastery, by an alien bishop, outside the diocese, without the licence of the then abbess of that monastery and of all the nuns of that monastery; it accuses you conjointly and separately and however you wish.

'Again, the party as above accuses you that after your pretended election to that abbacy of Kilculliheen was effected, you intrusively seized in the name of that same dignity the fruits, renders and proceeds of that same monastery through days and years; the party as above accuses you conjointly and separately and however you wish.

'Again it accuses you, and if you deny intends to prove that public rumour and scandal labours on all the preceding.'

When all the accusations had been read out in the courtroom, the said advocate immediately petitioned that We should command the said Elicie, asserted to be the abbess, to respond to the said accusations, upon her oath, through the word(s) 'Credo' or 'Non credo', according to the requirements of the law; and if she should contumaciously refuse to respond to them at our command, that these accusations — since the evidence had been presented that was earlier to be presented — ought to be held to have been confessed by that fact.

Finally then, when, after holding sufficient and mature deliberation, We ordered the abbess to respond to the accusation, she openly refused to respond to them, spurning our command; and contumaciously departed from Our presence. We assigned the following day in the same place for the adjudication for the matters set out above, to which day and place we peremptorily ordered the nuns and the abbess herself; and we continued the case.

The aforementioned day having arrived, when We sat in the judgement there, viz., in the place assigned, the nuns obeyed by their personal presence as well as by their advocate; the party of the abbess contumaciously refused to obey although expressly warned, cited and required. Then the advocate of the nuns instantly petitioned, because of the various testimony that had been alleged under oath, not only that the accusations should be held confessed by the contumacy of the abbess: but he also petitioned that all and single fruits, property, renders and incomes and tithes, of the said abbatial dignity should be sequestered on the account of the contumacy of the party of the abbess and because of the imminent loss of these fruits. And We, after taking into account the things that had to be considered, and after holding mature deliberation with the lawyers then assisting Us, decreed that all and single fruits and tithes of that monastery, because of the manifest contumacy of the abbess and because of the fear of dilapidation apparently imminent, from the next day should be brought to Our hands for sequestration, and We sequestered them, deputing as the trustees of Our sequester the lords Dennis Higgins and Dennis Leary, chaplains, and James Walsh. We decreed moreover that all the accusations of the nuns, because of the contumacy of the abbess at Our command, would be held confessed by that fact.

Finally, then, the said advocate converted those accusations, confessed that is in full, into articles, and petitioned that he be admitted to the proof of them as long as they had been permitted (to be so) by the interpretation of law. We, assenting to his petition for the greater declaration of his case, allowed him to convert those accusations into articles to be proved; whence he then brought into the way of proof, the common knowledge of the established fact; that is from the ruin of the monastery and the dilapidation of the fruits, the fornication, incest and procreation of issue, and the well-known seizure of the portion of what had been owed and was to be owed to the nuns for food and clothing; and beyond the common knowledge of all and singular of the preceding, he named and took

---

4. Johannem McOdo; might be Sean or Eoin or Jean, McAedh or Hughes or McKay.
5. Magoni Fusci; perhaps Manus O'Dubhda, black, Dark. rel. sim.

care that We should be examined Ourselves, and the *officialis* of Ossory and the lord precentor of the church of Ossory as well, who deposed under oath that all the preceding contained, as far as their better belief, truth; rendering as the cause of their knowledge that they knew, saw and understood all the preceding, because they were present (when?) all the preceding had been carried out and done, &c. as they now openly aver. Then finally the same advocate petitioned for a sufficient time for himself for the second producing of witnesses concerning the other articles, expositions and deductions to be proven, viz. concerning the articles of divers kind, of excommunication, canonical disqualification, usurpation and the mutilation of limbs, to be assigned at a convenient place and time. We assigned then the Monday nearest to that for the production of witnesses concerning the aforesaid articles, in the parish church of Dunfart of the diocese of Ossory; to which day and place we cited the parties peremptorily, and we continued the case &c.

When the day had arrived, and we were sitting in judgement there, the party of the nuns obeyed by their personal appearance as well as through their advocate: the party of the abbess remained in their accustomed contumacy. We then, having heard certain allegations of the party of the nuns for the conviction of the abbess's malice and hoping for her gracious advent, fixed and assigned, under the same desire, the Wednesday next following after the feast of St Michael the Archangel in the current year in the cathedral church of St Canice[6] in Kilkenny; to which day and place we cited the parties peremptorily, and we continued the case, &c.

When the proposed term also had arrived, and We were sitting in judgement in the place assigned, and when the parties had been called, the party of the nuns obeyed by their personal appearance as well as through their advocate; the party of the abbess remained in their accustomed contumacy. Finally the aforesaid advocate accusing the contumacy of the abbess, produced certain witnesses for proving that the aforesaid abbess was many times bound with the chains of major excommunication, the testimonies of which witnesses follows, &c.

William Comerford, dean of Ossory, the first witness, produced and diligently examined in form of law, deposed on his oath that he saw and read through the letters of the reverend father Oliver of good memory, sometime bishop of Ossory, sealed with his seal, directed against the abbess Elicie Butler, concerning the things in the articles and accusations, because of the nonpayment of a certain annual pension owed by that monastery to the cathedral church of St Canice; and he said that never did the abbess pay that pension up to now; and he said that up to now, as best he knew and understood, she was excommunicated, and which is common knowledge, that she celebrated and made to be celebrated before her, the divine office incurring from thence the stain of canonical disqualification. Master William Vale and Master Dennis Higgins, chaplains, similarly examined and sworn, agreed in everything and through everything with the last witness. Anastasia Cantwell, Elicie Gall, Katherine Mothyng and Anne Cleary, professed nuns of the same monastery, examined in form of law, deposed that the aforesaid abbess cast violent hand with effusion of blood on the persons of those nuns, viz., Elicie Gall and Anne Cleary, and without the effusion of blood on the person of Katherine Mothyng; asked whether she did this by way of correction, they said that she did not, but in quarrel and injury; they say that often after this she celebrated and caused to be celebrated, &c.

These witnesses having been heard thus according to law, and their testimonies having been published at the petition of the nuns because of the danger to their souls and the longtime abandonment of the said monastery, We fixed and assigned the next day, after the mature deliberation over what had taken place and over the future, in the same place, for the definitive sentence to be given in the case at issue, to which day and place, &c.

When that day had come, and We were sitting in judgement in the assigned place, the party of the nuns obeyed, and the party of the abbess remained in the accustomed contumacy. We proceeded to the delivering of a definitive sentence in the business aforesaid, the tenor of which follows, thus:

'We, MILO, by divine permission bishop of Ossory, do proceed with ordinary authority by

---

6. i.e. Sancti Kanici.

right, in the case of a certain inquisition moved against Elicie Butler, abbess of Kilculliheen, at the instance of the entire convent of nuns of that monastery, the nuns of the same monastery prosecuting the same case.

'SINCE we have found by understanding and seeing the merits of the aforesaid case, that all the articles proposed and administered through the same nuns who moved the inquisition against the oft-mentioned abbess are true, and proven legitimately before Us; viz., that the abbess committed the crime of fornication, dilapidation and incest, and We also find that she is incorrigible in all the vices, sins, crimes, excesses and other defects above-written, of which it has been articulated;

'THEREFORE, by invocation of the Name of Christ, by this Our definitive sentence, which We bear and promulgate in these writings, We deprive and remove the aforesaid abbess of the aforesaid abbacy of Kilculliheen, on account of the aforementioned crimes and sins, proved sufficiently before Us, and We show, discern and declare that she was deprived and removed from that dignity by her own faults, that is, her very many crimes, sins and excesses.'

This sentence was read and promulgated in this year, place, month and day as above, these witnesses being present: Master Nicholas Mothyng, chancellor of the church of Ossory, Tadg O'Hennessy, lawyer, Donatius McCathmell, cleric, John Doyle, Patrick Young, and many others. Moreover, in all and each part of this and in the whole trial, We, the afore-mentioned reverend father bishop, did instantly command the service of master Donatus Cathmyll, notary public, who was present then and through the whole trial, to reduce this to the form in which it is sent into public, &c.

These things were done as written above and recited, anno Domini of the fifth indiction in the pontificate,[7] places and days as above, under the testimony of our seal.

7. i.e. episcopacy.

MARGARET FITZGERALD, COUNTESS OF ORMOND AND OSSORY

(1458?–1542)

from:
LETTER TO HENRY VIII (1540)

[Margaret Fitzgerald was the daughter of Alison Eustace, wife of Gerald, 8th Earl of Kildare. In 1485 Margaret married Piers, 8th Earl of Ormond, and she was largely responsible for the restoration of the Butler fortunes. A great builder of castles, she was regarded as one of the most remarkable women of her age. Known as the 'Great Countess', she often signed documents with the Irish form of her name, Mairgréad Gearóid. She survived Piers by three years. According to the near-contemporary *Pedigree of the House of Ormonde*, 'during that small remainder of her life she lived most godly in contemplation and prayer, giving alms bountifully unto poor and needy people; and (at her proper costs and changes) built a schoolhouse near the churchyard of St Kenny's church'. In her letter to Henry VIII, two years before her death, the signature is written with the trembling hand of extreme old age. The unfeigned piety and veiled forgiveness give this letter of gentle affability a subtlety for which she was renowned. Modernized in spelling, the original is in the State Papers Henry VIII, vol. 3, part 3, p. 222.]

Please it Your Most excellent Highness to be advertised, that like as my Lord my husband, whose soul Jesu rest, at times delighted to provide such pleasures in this land, as should be acceptable to Your Majesty, as, in semblable wise, do I recognise myself much bounden to declare my heart and duty towards Your Grace of like sort and disposition.[1] And having sent unto Your Highness, by this bearer, two goshawks, to be delivered unto Your Majesty as of my poor gift, for lack of any

convenient time, at this time, being in my disposition to be presented to Your Grace; in most humble wise I beseech Your Highness to accept the same in good part. And thus the Blessed Trinity preserve your most Royal Person long and triumphantly to reign with much victory. Written at Your Highness City of Waterford the 8th of July.

Your Graces most humble bounden subject

M of Ormond & Oss.

1. Margaret had much to forgive Henry VIII. Her Fitzgerald nephew, Thomas, and six of his uncles had been executed with the king's consent in 1536. Previously, Henry VIII had snubbed her husband, Piers, a friend of Cardinal Wolsey, by bestowing his title of Ormond on the father of Anne Boleyn.

JOHN HOWLIN

(15??–1599)

from:
PERBREVE COMPENDIUM
(c. 1590)

[The chief sources of the consideration of Margaret Ball née Bermingham (fl. 1515–84) as a martyr in the canonical sense are John Howlin's Perbreve Compendium and David Rothe's De processu martyriali. Margaret Ball, daughter of Nicholas Bermingham of Corballis in the barony of Skreen, County Meath, and Catherine, daughter of Richard De La Hyde of Drogheda, County Louth, was the mother of Alderman Nicholas (Walter?) Ball. During his mayoralty, embarrassed by his mother's open recusancy, he had her arrested, dragged through the streets of Dublin on a hurdle, and thrown into prison. Conditions in prison were such as to constitute a sentence of slow death. She survived for three years before she died of ill health and hardship, c. 1584. The intolerant behaviour of Ball towards his mother was associated with her commitment to Catholicism and her memory rapidly assumed the proportions of fama martyrii, enshrined in the martyrological writings of the seventeenth century. In February 1915 Margaret Ball, née Bermingham, was one of 257 named martyrs for the introduction of whose cause for beatification permission was granted. Her case finally went forward with a number of others deemed worthy of martyrdom in 1988. She was beatified in Rome in September 1993. The following text is taken from John Howlin, Perbreve Compendium, printed with some inaccuracies in P.F. Moran, Spicilegium Ossoriense, vol. 1,

pp. 86–7. The original is in St Patrick's College, Maynooth, Salamanca MSS, legajo XI, no. 4. The translation is by John M. Cunningham OP.]

There was a noble widow in Dublin by the name of Matron Ball, a mother, hostess and receiver of Catholics, and also an instructress of Christian doctrine, for the servants and maids who left her house for other posts or who were given by her to some noble persons who asked for them went out like expert scholars from the finest school and won for Christ not only their fellow servants and maids but also sometimes and indeed very often their masters and mistresses. This widow had an heretical son for whose conversion she poured forth tearful prayers almost continuously. She was wont to invite many Catholic Bishops, priests and other learned men to her home secretly and with due care, and afterwards, she used to invite her son to dine in their company, so that at least by their company, prayers, and especially by their discussions (like another Monica) she might recall her son from heresy. (Of this I am a witness.) But his heart was hardened, he remained incapable of instruction. However his mother did not cease to pray for him and to get others to pray for him as well and on that account she always had a Catholic priest in her house, who for herself and for the conversion of her son used to offer sacrifice daily to the eternal Father. For that reason she was often accused and seized by the heretics, sometimes she was even apprehended during mass together with the priest who was saying it; and with him, vested in the priestly robes, she was led publicly through the streets to prison. And although in this way she lost several chalices and vestments (released from public custody by money and the help of noble persons), she did not omit to obtain other vestments afterwards and to secretly hear mass every day. At length her son about whom mention was made above, made mayor or governor of the city, had his own mother, infirm,

weak with old age and unable to walk, dragged from her house because she persevered in her holy custom and in the profession of the faith. And he saw to it that she was shamefully carried to prison on a device like a bier by the attendants of the heretics, where the unvanquished soul of the woman, fortified with faith and hope in Jesus Christ, patiently endured everything to the end. In the squalor of prison and worn out by the afflictions of hardship and infirmity, leaving an example of a truly Christian and Catholic woman, she died in the Lord about 1584 AD.

DAVID ROTHE

(1573–1650)

from:
THE ANALECTA OF DAVID ROTHE, BISHOP OF OSSORY (1884)

[This extract on Margaret Ball, née Bermingham, is from David Rothe, *De processu martyriali* . . . (Cologne, 1619), reprinted in P.F. Moran (ed.), *The Analecta of David Rothe, Bishop of Ossory* (Dublin, 1884), pp. 505–9. The translation is by John M. Cunningham OP, a classical scholar studying theology in the Angelicum University in Rome in 1994.]

A noble widow lived in Dublin, by the name of Eleanor[1] Bermingham, the widow of Bartholomew Baal.[2] And this lady was worthy of honour, from the opinion of Saint Paul ordering respect to widows who truly are widows; who learned first to govern their own homes, and to make some return to their parents; those who truly are widows and alone hope in God and continue in prayers and supplications night and

day. And such was this widow of ours; for she who is self-indulgent is dead while she lives; and this was not the case with her, but she was irreprehensible, managing the care of her own family and especially of her domestics. Indeed she had witness in her good works; she raised her sons, she tended those suffering trials; she followed after every good work, so that no one could have denied she was truly a widow.[3] And now in a few words let me relate how carefully and seriously she did all of these things.

Throughout her widowhood and desolation trusting so earnestly in the Lord she gave herself to prayer and supplication, from which one can suppose, that besides her morning and evening load (of prayers or of duties), never neglected by her; she willingly spent the other hours she had free from the management of the house, and from the occupations of Martha in Prayer cards, the penitential psalms, with Litanies and other Prayers; on feast days and even on ordinary days when it was licit she considered it a fault in some way not to hear mass; and so that she might be the more certain in fulfilling her devotions, and so as not to miss the daily sacrifice she always

1. Margaret Bermingham seems to be referred to as 'Eleanor' and also as 'Eleanora'.
2. For 'Ball'.

3. 1 Timothy 5:3–10.

kept at her house a Catholic priest (although the times were hostile since those who persecuted Catholics were in power) to whom she supplied food, clothing and a room, and in addition she supplied an annual stipend to another priest so that she would always have one who would celebrate and administer the sacraments, and would offer prayers to God for herself and for her son and her family.

On account of which she was often accused in the Council of the Realm. At length when public guards and attendants were sent while she was at mass in her house, hand was laid upon her and at the same time on the priest who was standing and celebrating mass at the altar. Both were seized by force, and by an armed division of soldiers were brought to appear before the Viceroy and the Chancellor and others from the inner Senate; and this with such speed and force so that assistance might not be given to the Priest to lay aside the sacred vestments; and thus he clothed in the vestments and she weakened by old age were dragged off violently by waggon to prison; and so that the arrest and abduction of the Priest might be more opprobrious he was brought through the streets in his vestments as a public spectacle. But although the spectacle caused the Protestants to laugh, however it confirmed the orthodox all the more in their religion and moved the Roman Catholics to piety and constancy; just as Marius, Martha and Audifax when their hands were cut off and tied at their neck were led through the centre of the city when Claudius was emperor.[4]

On that occasion the pious matron endured the plundering of her sacred furnishings, chalice, paten and all the priestly vestments, with other appendages upon which those plunderers of sacred things seized, and which the fanatical officers, who have all things in common use, turned to profane use. She also suffered the hardship of prison for an interval of time until money cleared the way and the solicitation and importunity of several Nobles softened the hearts of the Royal Ministers, she was dismissed from custody and allowed to return home.

What did she do after her liberation except the very thing which she had been doing before her imprisonment? She was vigilant at her devotions and other pious exercises; she took time and saw how sweet the Lord is; and she relieved the needs of the poor; and now she did those things with greater care and attention just as freedom is more pleasing after imprisonment, serenity after the storm, health after infirmity, food after hunger, good company after solitude, the known walls of home after the squalor of prison.

In her home she was an example of purity and chastity, piety and innocence, modesty and virtue, for her servants, for strangers, for those near and for those far away, for young women she was an example of celibacy, for widows an example of vidual continence; for young men and women a mistress of good conduct; for the aged a support for honesty; for the old an example of modesty, for all a lamp of faith, religion and holiness.

And as if to a house of piety and workshop of virtue so to her house it was that the more noble women desired to send their daughters from near and far alike to be educated by her, women for whom care was great about obtaining a holy and noble instruction for their daughters. These girls given into her hands and training she so disposed to virtue so that what Blessed Basil[5] wrote to the Neocaesarians about his grandmother Saint Macrina, how he called her his nurse in the faith because he had been imbued with sacred teachings by her when he was a young child; and how he gloried in the fact that he retained the same faith which he had once gulped from her breast as pure milk; this many in Ireland could say without pretence, many in whom the brave matron had instilled the dew of piety in first education, or even the old upon whom she had poured afresh dew with renewed infusion.

But the unseasonable harshness of her first born son Walter Baal who from association with the Reformers drank deeply the faeces of new teachings, afflicted her heart; she strove in every way to cleanse him from the yeast of wickedness; she prayed secretly and publicly, she implored and entreated the divine goodness, for the cleansing of his iniquity; she associated others with herself for that purpose; there was no Priest either regular or secular, no Bishop, no other man distinguished by title for sound doctrine and

4. While visiting Rome, Marius, a Persian, with his wife Martha and their sons Audifax and Abachum, gathered up and buried the relics of the martyrs. Arrested themselves, they were put to death *c.* 260, though not in the reign of Claudius.

5. Basil *c.* 358 settled as a hermit near neo-Caesarea.

piety, whom she when the opportunity arose did not beseech to assist and aid in the matter of his conversion. You would say Saint Monica was alive again and her concern about Saint Augustine straying beyond the orthodox rule, on account of which there was nothing which she did not attempt in order to bring him back. But Monica was happier who at length obtained her prayer and gained a Catholic son, who afterwards became a vigorous preacher and defender of the true faith; but the wicked son of our good mother Eleanor son of Belial escaped the yoke, served Baal and adored him;[6] and became 'Nabal stupid according to his name'[7] and he brought his

6. A play on the biblical word Baal, a cult which provided the greatest threat to the development of an exclusive Yahweh worship within ancient Israel.
7. Nabal was a biblical sheep- and goat-owner who refused help to David.

stupidity to the grave, although many others turned from their errors through the labour of this matron, he however hardened his heart and in his blindness died obstinately.

This was the height of his wickedness, that not content to soil himself in the filth of his errors, he pursued with hostility his mother so as to cover her with the same filth. For made Mayor of the city of Dublin he was so heartless and viperish towards the womb that bore him that he forced his aged mother, no longer able to walk due to weakness, into a chair like a bier and carried her to prison, when all else had failed to drag her to share his teachings.

This she patiently endured and with the most pleasing odour of her constancy, perseverance and undiminished faith remaining, in the confinement of prison she died happily about 1584 AD.

HELENA CONCANNON

(1878–1952)

from:
THE POOR CLARES IN IRELAND (A.D. 1629–A.D. 1929) (1929)

[Helena Concannon used Mother Bonaventura Browne's contemporary account of the beginnings of the Poor Clare foundations in seventeenth-century Ireland when writing her history *The Poor Clares in Ireland (A.D. 1629–A.D. 1929)*, published in 1929. The original text is in the convent archives at Nun's Island in Galway. The extract is taken from chapter three, 'Bethlehem', pp. 20–5, and reflects the commemorative, descriptive approach to archival records in vogue at that time.]

Hardly was the monastery of 'Bethlehem' established, when postulants presented themselves in great numbers. In a very short time, as we shall see, the Community numbered

sixty. Several of them were nieces of Mother Cicely Dillon — four being daughters of her sister, Elizabeth, wife of Thomas Fitzgerald of Newcastle, Co Longford; Ellen, Cicely, Ann and Brigid Fitzgerald. Two others were daughters of her brother, Sir Christopher Dillon, and his wife, Lady Jane Dillon, daughter of the first Earl of Roscommon: Elizabeth and Mary Dillon.[1]

Mother Cicely acted as Abbess practically all the time of this monastery's existence, having been elected no less than five times, according to Mother Bonaventure. The only other Abbess of whom the latter speaks is Mother Margaret

1. Lodge's *Peerage of Ireland*, vol. 4, p. 136. The Order of Poor Clares seems to have had a remarkable attraction for the Dillons and their kin. A note in the *Harold's Cross Annals* informs us that 'there were six descendants of the Viscount Dillon in North King St Convent, Dublin; one or two in Dorset St; seven grandchildren of the first Viscount Dillon, two of his daughters and one of his nieces, at Athlone'. The 'six descendants of the Dillons' in North King Street were Margaret O'Kelly, Mary Cruise and four Fitzgeralds.

Evangelist Moore. Sir Henry Piers of Trisgernaglish, in his *Description of Westmeath* (written about 1682) describes the last Abbess of 'Bethlehem' as 'a daughter of Sir Edward Tuite of Tuitestown'. But it is plain that he meant Mother Cicely — and was only mistaken in making her a daughter, instead of a grand-daughter, of Sir Edward Tuite.

Galway girls were numerous and prominent among the postulants. The first of these we can trace is Sister Catherine Francis Browne, daughter of James Browne of Galway, who was examined for Profession by Father Patrick Plunkett, OFM, Guardian of Athlone, on 29th January, 1632. In the course of that year she was followed to 'Bethlehem' by three townswomen of hers, who were destined to play great roles in the story we are now unfolding. One was Helen (Nell) Martyn, Sister Mary Gabriel, who was clothed in the holy habit of the Order on the Eve of the Annunciation, 1632 — and after the statutory 'year and a day' was professed on the Feast of the Annunciation, 1633. She was, eight years later, to be the first Abbess of the historic Convent of her Order in Galway, and about forty years later (1672) to be laid in that tomb in the graveyard attached to the Franciscan Abbey, Galway, which we can still identify. There she awaits the Resurrection — under a slab 'shewing forth' Our Lady receiving Gabriel's Message while a nun kneels at her feet — a touching and beautiful reference to the Feast of the Annunciation, which witnessed her Clothing and Profession, and inspired the choice of her religious name, Gabriel.

The other two postulants were two sisters, daughters of Alderman Andrew Browne, that sturdy champion of the Faith, of whose refusal of the Sheriff's office, for conscience' sake, we have already heard. One of these sisters — both of whom entered in 1632 and were professed in 1633 — took the name in religion of Sister Catherine Bernard: the other was our friend, Sister Mary Bonaventure. Her account of the life and work and spirit of 'Bethlehem' is, therefore, that of an eyewitness.

Having related the events connected with the closing down by the Lords Justices of the Poor Clares' Monastery in Dublin, and the refusal of the novices to avail themselves of their freedom to return to 'their sumptuous houses and dainty tables', preferring 'for the great love of God to go with the rest to a remote country village to live in great austerity amongst unknown people', Concannon goes on:

'Being out of the city they divided themselves in three companies among some noble country friends of theirs, who charitably harboured them until a poor house was built for their habitation in a solitary neck of land without inhabitants, near a great lake called Loughrie (which in English may be termed the King's Lake) not daring any more to settle themselves in any great town, city or popular place, and founded there a convent which they instituted [i.e. called] Bethlehem. And it was situated in such a low and shadowed bog that the physicians wondered how such tender creatures (very delicately bred) could live therein: for in wet and rainy weather the water would not only fall over them through the roof of the house, but also in several places came up under the ground; besides that all their houses were so low that their cells and all other rooms (except only the choir) were upon the ground.

'In this convent they increased to the number of three score, where might be seen the golden age in many religious, meanly apparelled, who employed themselves in the lowest offices and ate the grossest meats, though they were choice and noble persons in the world; none of them excused to labour, as in drawing of turf or wood with things necessary to the building of their house (when they were thrown into the Grate) as also to brew, bake, wash dishes, serve in the kitchen and the like. They prayed continually, for while they laboured by their hands, they used to be many times saying some kind of prayer in common, answering one another quirewise. They observed such silence that midday seemed midnight; they had mutual charity to help and comfort one another; rose continually at midnight to say Matins, and never ate fleshe meat, nor wore socks, shoes, or stockings, but contented themselves with wooden soles or patens under their feet, having a list nailed about to hold them on, and observed all other things ordained by the first rule of St Clare with the strict statutes made by St Colette upon said rule.'

The story of the austerities practised by these high-born, delicately-reared ladies, and the novelty of an enclosed Order, attracted many visitors to the 'Grille' or 'Grating' of the Poor Clares at 'Bethlehem'. Among the 'great personages who came from afar to see them, and were edified by their holy conversation', were Lady Wentworth, the wife of the Lord Deputy, and the famous Duchess of Buckingham, who after the death of the Duke had married as her second husband the Earl of Antrim. We can understand what brought the latter, apart from that natural feminine curiosity which, as we know from other incidents of her residence in Ireland, was not omitted from her 'make-up'. She was a connection by marriage of Mother Cicely Dillon's[2] — her sister-in-law, Lady Mary MacDonnell, having married Mother Cicely's nephew, Lucas, second Viscount Dillon. Mother Bonaventura recounts this visit in the usual vivid style:

'The fame of their virtuous life being spread abroad, it was cause that many great personages came to see them from far off, and were edified by their holy conversation; amongst the rest the Lord Wentworth's wife (who at that season was Deputy of Ireland) took such a desire to see them that she obtained leave from her husband to come along from Dublin (being sixty miles from thence) to visit them as did likewise the Duchess of Buckingham, and having enjoyed their delightful conversation; and the Lady Deputy with other ladies that were in her company told them that it was noted how those who persecuted them out of Dublin, did never after prosper well.'

A visitor to 'Bethlehem' whose name stirs us more than that of any 'Lady Deputy' or Duchess, came to the Monastery in these years and left a permanent memorial of his passing. Brother Michael O'Clery, almost straight from the completion of his enormous labours on the *Annals of the Kingdom of Ireland*,[3] and in collaboration with Father O'Raghailigh and Father Seumas O'Siaghail made, for the use of the Sisters, a translation into Irish of the First Rule of St Clare, and the Bull of Approbation of Innocent IV. Many of the nuns must, therefore, have been Irish-speakers, as well as Mother Bonaventura herself, who is praised in the Galway Annals as 'prudent, wise and well-spoken in English, Irish and Spanish', and was, as we know, a prolific author in Irish. Her interest in Irish was later demonstrated during her period in office as Abbess in Galway, when she employed the famous scholar, Duald MacFirbis, then living in the College, to translate into Irish the Testament and Blessing of St Clare, the Constitution of St Colette, and various other items concerning the rule.[4]

---

2. Lady Wentworth was also a connection by marriage of Mother Cicely's. Her husband's sister was married to one of the Dillons. Their son was the famous English poet, Wentworth Dillon, Earl of Roscommon, who translated into English the *Dies Irae*, and was so highly commended by Alexander Pope.

3. The Annals of the Four Masters were completed on 10 August, 1636.
4. MS DI 2, in Royal Irish Academy.

HONOR FITZMAURICE, LADY KERRY

(d. 1668)

LETTER TO PIERSE FERRITER (1641)

[Honor Fitzmaurice was the wife of the 19th Lord of Kerry, Patrick Fitzmaurice, whose family were the quintessential Geraldine survivors in Kerry. Patrick and Honor married in the early 1630s and the apparent peace in north Kerry in those years left them ill-prepared for the rebellion of 1641. The defection of the poet Pierse Ferriter was a bitter blow; he was a family friend, and he absconded to the rebels with the arms and supplies provided by Patrick for use against them. Honor's letter to Ferriter, dissuading him from joining the rebellion, betrays her incredulity, bewilderment and bitterness as she watched the country drift into violent conflict. Her husband's reaction was to flee, and they saw out the war in

London; in doing so, they avoided the confiscations of the Cromwellian period, allowing Honor and her children to return to Kerry in 1660 after Patrick's death and the restoration of the monarchy. Honor's letter never reached Ferriter, as it was intercepted, and Ferriter was later captured and hanged. Honor Fitzmaurice made a copy of the letter, which is preserved among the Kerry family papers. It appears in full in 'The Siege of Tralee Castle', in *Kerry Archaeological Magazine*, April 1915, pp. 79–80. The text was prepared by Helen O'Carroll, former research director of the Lixnaw Heritage Project.]

To my very loving friend, Mr. Pierse Ferriter, at Ferriter's Towne in Kerry:–
Theese —
Honest Pierse. (And I hope I shall never have reason to call you otherwise), this very daie is one coming out of Kerry unto me, that by chance fell into the companie of Florence MacFineen, and the rest of that rebellious crue, ye very daie yet they robbed Haly, who tells me yt you promised (as he heard Florence say) to be with them the week following, and to bring a piece of ordnance with you from the Dingell, and join with them to take the Castell of Tralee; but, and I hope in God it is far from your thoughts for you that had ever been observed to stand upon reputation on smaller matters, I trust will not now be tained [*sic*] with so foule and offensive a crime to God and Man — nor give your adversaries yet just cause of rejoicing, and just way for them to avenge themselves on you, not us that are your friends, that just cause of discontent that would make us curse the date that ever we saw you. But I cannot believe any such thing of you, knowing that you want not wit nor understanding enough to conceive and apprehend ye danger and punishment justlie due to such offenders: and therefore doubt not of God's mercies, in giving you grace to avoyd them, which none can more earnestly wish and praie for than your loving friend.

Honor Kerry
Corke, ye last of June, 1641.

Here I am settled and doe intend to staie, until the time grows quieter, which i hope in God will be ere long, for here is certaine newes of a mightee armie preparing in England to come over.

Biographies/Bibliographies

Margaret Fitzgerald, Countess of Ormond and Ossory

LIFE. Daughter of Alison Eustace and Gerald Fitzgerald, 8th Earl of Kildare, her mother was the daughter and co-heir of Sir Roland Eustace, Baron of Portlester, County Kildare, and was the first wife of Gerald Fitzgerald. Margaret was one of six daughters and married Piers Butler, 8th Earl of Ormond. She, more than her ambitious husband, was credited with restoring the Butler fortunes. A builder of castles, she was known as 'the Great Countess', and signed herself 'the Countess of Ormond and Ossory', or in the Irish form of her name, Mairgréad Gearóid, the latter as a reminder of her Fitzgerald lineage. She lived through the rebellion of her nephew Thomas Fitzgerald, Lord Offaly, against Henry VIII and his Irish Deputy, Sir William Skeffington, and the subsequent execution of Thomas and his five uncles, her half brothers. She survived her husband, Piers, by three years.

BIOGRAPHY AND CRITICISM. For general background, Steven Ellis, *Tudor Ireland: Crown, Community and the Conflict of Cultures, 1470–1603* (London and New York: Longman Group, 1984).

John Howlin

LIFE. The first of the Counter-Reformation martyrologists, John Howlin SJ was an Irish Jesuit who went into exile in Lisbon, Portugal, in the late 1580s, and was instrumental in founding the Irish College there. He was probably present at the executions of several of those who died for their religious beliefs. A meticulous chronicler of the forty-five victims of religious persecution in Ireland in the last decades of the sixteenth century, he knew Margaret Ball personally. He attested, as an eyewitness, to the several attempts she made to have him reconciled to the Catholic faith he had abandoned. In Lisbon he continued to collect information about Irish men and women who were executed for their religious beliefs. He died, a victim of plague, in Lisbon in 1599.

CHIEF WRITINGS. *Perbreve Compendium* ... now in Maynooth College, County Kildare, Salamanca MSS, legajo XI, no. 4. Printed in P.F. Moran, *Spicilegium Ossoriense*, 3 vols (Dublin: 1874–84), vol. 1, pp. 82–109.

BIOGRAPHY AND CRITICISM. Colm Lennon, *An Irish Prisoner of Conscience, Archbishop Richard Creagh of Armagh, 1529–1586* (Dublin: Four Courts Press, 2000); Francis Finnegan, *The Jesuit Mission in Ireland in the Sixteenth Century* (Dublin: Jesuit Publication, *c.* 1950).

David Rothe

LIFE. Regarded by his contemporaries, and in the judgement of later historians, as the leading architect of Catholic reorganization following the period of religious persecution which marked the last decades of the Elizabethan conquest of Ireland. Rothe was born in 1573 and educated for the priesthood in his native city of Kilkenny in Ireland and at Douai Irish College in the Spanish Netherlands (Belgium). Peter Lombard, Catholic Archbishop of Armagh, who was in exile in Rome, sent him to Ireland as vice-primate *c.* 1605. As one of his pastoral concerns Rothe gathered information about the Irish men and women who suffered death for their religious beliefs in the recent persecutions. His book, written in Latin, *De processu martyriali*, was the result of his researches and was regarded as the definitive study of the Irish martyrs. Appointed Catholic Bishop of Ossory in 1620, he remained at his post until his death in 1650, living through the Confederate wars of the 1640s and the capture of Kilkenny city by Oliver Cromwell's army. Over his lifetime he corresponded with leading scholars in Ireland, James Ussher the leading antiquarian, and in Europe with the Franciscan Luke Wadding and the Salamanca Irish scholars in Spain.

CHIEF WRITINGS. *Analecta sacra nova et mira,* of which *De processu martyriali* is volume 2 (Cologne, 1617–19).

BIOGRAPHY AND CRITICISM. *A New History of Ireland III: Early Modern Ireland 1534–1691,* eds T.W. Moody, F.X. Martin, F.J. Byrne (Oxford: Clarendon Press, 1976)

Helena Concannon

LIFE. Born Helena Walsh in Maghera, County Derry, in 1878. She was educated at Loreto convents in Coleraine and Dublin and at the Royal University of Ireland. She married Thomas Concannon, a national health inspector, in 1906 and went to live in Galway. She was a prominent member of the Gaelic League. Under pressure from Eamon de Valera, she became one of the National University's representatives in Dáil Éireann, 1933–7, and a member of the senate of the National University in 1938. She supported the Fianna Fáil Party. She published extensively on Irish history, partiuclarly the history of women, and died in 1952.

CHIEF WRITINGS. *A Garden of Girls, Or, Famous Schoolgirls of Former Times* (London: Longmans, Green, 1914); *Women of 'Ninety-eight* (Dublin: M.H. Gill, 1919); *Daughters of Banba* (Dublin: M.H. Gill, 1922); *Defenders of the Ford: Pages from the Annals of the Boys of Ireland from the Earliest Ages Down to 1798* (Dublin: M.H. Gill, 1925); *The Poor Clares in Ireland (A.D. 1629–A.D. 1929)* (Dublin: M.H. Gill, 1929); *Irish Nuns in Penal Days* (London: Sands, 1931); *The Queen of Ireland: An Historical Account of Ireland's Devotion to the Blessed Virgin* (Dublin: M.H. Gill, 1938).

BIOGRAPHY AND CRITICISM. Mary M. Macken, 'Musings and Memories: Helena Concannon, M.A., D.Litt.', *Studies,* vol. 42 (1953), pp. 90–7.

Honor Fitzmaurice, Lady Kerry

LIFE. Daughter of Sir Edmund Fitzgerald of Cloyne and Ballymaloe in County Cork, she married Patrick Fitzmaurice, Lord Kerry and Baron of Lixnaw, County Kerry, sometime in the 1630s. Lixnaw Castle being in ruins, the couple built a mansion in Ardfert, County Kerry. With the outbreak of rebellion in 1641, Fitzmaurice was appointed governor of military affairs in County Kerry. Embarrassed by the involvement of his half-brothers on the rebels' side, and by the defection of his friend the poet Pierse Ferriter (Piaras Feiritéar), whom he had empowered to raise six hundred men for the government side, the Fitzmaurices fled to Cork, and thence to England. By doing do they avoided the confiscation of their property in 1654 following on Oliver Cromwell's conquest of Ireland. Their lives in England were poverty-stricken, as the petitions of Fitzmaurice to the government of the time attested. He died in 1660 in England and Honor, Lady Kerry, returned to Ireland. She arranged for Ardfert cathedral to be rebuilt with stonework from her husband's castle at Lixnaw and she was buried in 1668 in a new tomb in the north-east chantry. She had three daughters and two sons, all of whom survived her.

BIOGRAPHY AND CRITICISM. Helen O'Carroll, *The Fitzmaurices of Kerry and Barons of Lixnaw* (Lixnaw, County Kerry: Lixnaw Heritage Group, 1993), pp. 43–4.

PHIL KILROY, *Editor*

Memoirs and Testimonies: Nonconformist Women in Seventeenth-Century Ireland

The memoirs and testimonies included in this subsection come from women who were born into the Reformation tradition. Taken in this context, and especially within their specific religious tradition, these women formulated and lived out their own response to events and experiences. At least five of them seem to have come from financially secure backgrounds, which ensured adequate education and the possibility of recording, or having recorded, significant aspects of their lives.

The Independent church in Dublin in the mid-seventeenth century required declarations of conversion from the congregation. The fact that the minister of that church published such declarations ensured that testimonies from several women were recorded. The Quaker practice of recording the lives of Friends moved William Wright to write a short biography of Anne Wright, his wife. Through leaving a legacy to the Presbyterian church in Ireland, Martha Magee's memory was preserved and insight into

her experience of widowhood gained. Perhaps Mrs Hackett and Mrs Cole might have preferred to remain unrecorded. Whatever the case, their acts and intents are well documented and serve to show independent spirits at work, filling gaps in church leadership, whereby they made a corrupt system work for them. Mary Rich, Countess of Warwick, used her diary to record her spiritual journey and the events of her life; in this way she came to terms with unrelenting stress. Ann Fowkes's *Memoir*, written over many years, was part autobiography, part family history, which she intended for her descendants.

Both Mary Rich's diary and Ann Fowkes's memoir are very much in the tradition of religious writings, which flowered especially from the mid-seventeenth century onwards. Indeed, it is evident from the several texts presented here that all these women exercised a great deal of independence, felt in charge of their lives and adequate to the seemingly daunting and overwhelming tasks they had to accomplish.

ELIZABETH CHAMBERS (*fl. c.* 1641), FRANCES CURTIS (*fl. c.* 1650), MARY TURRANT (*fl. c.* 1645)

from:
OHEL OR BETH-SHEMESH
(1653)

[During Cromwellian times in Ireland several Independent congregations were established both in

Dublin and in the garrison towns. Two congregations were particularly strong in Dublin, one in St Nicholas-Within-the-Walls and the other in Christ Church. While he did not accept the possibility of women as ministers, John Rogers maintained that they should be given the right to participate in church affairs: 'we plead . . . for the common ordinary liberty due to them as members of the church, viz. to speak, object, offer, or vote with the rest'.[1] 'The Covenant of the Church in Dublin' required a declaration of conversion and faith, either through the medium of dreams, inner experiences or sermons; these were seen as confirmation of election by God. After such testimonies were given individuals were welcomed into the congregation. Records show that many women gave witness in a variety of ways.[2] No details remain of the lives of Elizabeth Chambers, Frances Curtis, or Mary Turrant. Evidently they lived in Ireland prior to the rebellion in 1641. The testimonies of Rogers's congregation in Christ Church in 1650 provide the sole record found of several women at this time in Ireland.]

Experience of Elizabeth Chambers

When the Rebellion broke out here in Ireland, I went over with my husband into England, and at Bristol there were a poor despised people that met together and had some communion, but they were made a mere off-scorn and disdained by all almost . . . But being afterwards to return hither, when I was come over, I went to hear at Katherine's Church (so called) in Dublin; but I could not well hear the minister, and when I did he railed so bitterly against the godly people that I could not edify anything by him: but I heard Mr Briscoe[3] and was much moved by him, but yet I was without assurance, and had no clear and full satisfaction all this while.

Until the Lord . . . sent over Mr Rogers from the Council to us . . . He did show that unless Christ were revealed in us he was veiled in us . . . and he showed that unless Christ be in us, no salvation to us . . . Now after I had heard him on this I was much cast down, for I could not find Christ but corruptions and sins in me . . . My friends were much troubled to see me and questioned much with me; but yet being cast down and undone thus . . . went to bed with my heart full, and head full, and eyes full, and all afflicted. At length I slept and dreamed that unless Christ were in me I was damned, a reprobate, undone and lost forever.

When I awoke my heart ached, ready to break. I rose up and wept sore and with sighs and tears took the Bible and looked for Christ there; and looked out and turned to the proofs that Master Rogers mentioned and examined them and then I examined my own heart and searched. But all this while I was at a loss and lamenting. I told a gentlewoman my condition and she did what she could to comfort me but to no purpose. The next day I hasted away to hear him again and there I found comfort, for he was now upon certain signs whereby we might (likely) judge of Christ within, revealed in us and know it . . . by all of which I was much raised up and went home with joy and was sure I had found Christ now.[4]

Experience of Frances Curtis

I cannot but condemn myself before I speak. I am so unworthy of this mercy. I have lived wantonly in my youth, forgetting God, doing no good, but all evil, till God's hand was heavy upon me for about eleven years; and when in my outward state I began to mend, still in my inward I was much troubled, and wished that God had taken me away by my former afflictions; these inward were so great, and a troubled spirit, who can bear? But afterwards I was much comforted again.

In these wars I was stripped by the rebels (being abroad) and came home so, through sad tempests, and since have [been] through great troubles, and very many. A while after I heard that my husband was killed by the rebels, which I feared was by my sins, and so my troubles were renewed; and then the enemies came upon us, the cannon-bullets flew over my head; and in a few days I was turned out of doors, with my child in my arms. I cannot express what God has done for me in saving my life, and my husband's, in hearing my prayers and tears; and have now the testimony within of God's love to me, which makes so unfainedly to love him and his ways, and desire to be a member of his people, in his Church.[5]

Experience of Mary Turrant

I lived till my twenty-third year, and knew not God; but after that I came to religious people and received some good, and soon after was brought to the sight of myself, and then I despaired of

1. John Rogers, *Ohel or Beth-shemesh* (London, 1653), vol. 2, ch. 7, p. 475.
2. Ibid., pp. 403–19.
3. T.C. Barnard, *Cromwellian Ireland: English Government in Ireland 1649–1660* (Oxford: O.U.P. 1975), pp. 136n, 137, 141.
4. *Ohel or Beth-shemesh*, pp. 406–8.
5. Ibid., pp. 10–11.

mercy, and thought I was damned and none of God's a great while, but was at last comforted by good ministers and the Word of God. But I was in such a place and condition that for seven years I do not know that I saw as much as a religious man. My children were murdered by the rebels and I lost my husband by the sickness, and yet the Lord has spared me in mine old age; and now

I see why. That I may enjoy this great mercy, which I never looked for, to comfort me in my old age.

I have received great comforts by Master Rogers and I must needs say that I serve my God with a cheerful heart.[6]

6. Ibid., p. 11.

WILLIAM WRIGHT

(*fl.* 1670)

from:
A BRIEF AND TRUE RELATION OF ANNE, WIFE OF WILLIAM WRIGHT OF CASTLEDERMOT, IN THE COUNTY OF KILDARE IN IRELAND, WHO DECEASED THE 1ST DAY OF DECEMBER 1670 (1823)

[Founded in England in 1652, the Quakers came to Ireland as early as 1655, and their influence spread rapidly throughout the country. They were a totally new group within the Protestant tradition, very outspoken, openly critical of all religious sects in Ireland, and remarkable by virtue of the number of men and women who travelled and preached in Ireland. Accounts of the women who travelled the length and breadth of the country are extensive, as well as of women whose homes became meeting houses for Quakers at this time. Women endured the hardships of prison and persecution along with men as consequences of their actions: preaching in market places, interrupting sermons in churches, questioning doctrine as well as places and practices of worship, criticizing outward behaviour and dress. On their own evidence, the treatment meted out to Quakers was both severe and relentless and included imprisonment and beatings, disruption of Quaker meetings, severe fines, confiscation of goods. For a period after the Restoration, some Quakers continued to feel called to preach or speak out in public. Anne Wright of County Kildare pursued her calling in this regard.

She was born in England in 1623, and grew up in Kendal in Westmorland and in Great Yarmouth in Norfolk. She came to Dublin during the Cromwellian period and by 1647 had settled in Kildare. She showed an interest in the Quakers but was influenced by Dr Samuel Winter (Independent minister and provost of Trinity College Dublin) not to become a Quaker. Nevertheless, she continued to read Quaker literature and admired their way of life. She became convinced in June 1669, and died in December of the following year. Anne Wright left no writings of her own. The account of her life, convincement and travels as a Quaker was written by her husband, William Wright, and was published by Mary Leadbeater, *Biographical Notes of Friends in Ireland* (London: Harvey and Darton, 1823).]

I, William Wright, of Castledermot . . . being well-known in the counties of Kildare, Carlow, Wicklow, and city of Dublin, do hereby truly and faithfully certify and testify these things following, concerning my dear wife, Anne Wright:[1]

Towards April, 1670, she had a strong motion or command from God, as she said, to go to Dublin, into some cathedral there, in sackcloth and ashes . . . So she went, and on the 17th of April she went to Patrick's cathedral in Dublin in the time of their singing and common prayer, in black sackcloth of hair, and ashes upon her head and there stood till all was ended, and then told them. That was not the worship that God delighted in. But no man lifted a hand against her, but bade her depart in peace, which she did; and some said she was a mad woman, and some one thing and some another; but within two or three days after, she came home rejoicing and was very merry and pleasant with me . . .

1. Mary Leadbeater, *Biographical Notes of Friends in Ireland* (London: Harvey and Darton, 1823), pp. 52–78.

But she had not been long at home till she was strongly moved or commanded to go through the streets of the City of Cork in like manner . . . So upon the 1st of June, 1670, she took journey with Thomas Moore who rode before her on his own horse to Cork and she went through that city in sackcloth and ashes; and afterwards went to the mayor of Cork to reprove him, as I suppose, for his cruelty and bitterness in the persecuting of those people; who threatened to have her whipped through the city as a vagabond and an idle person, and was sending her away to the jail by an officer, had not one John Hammond stepped into the mayor and desired him not to do it, for she was no such woman, but the very contrary and that he knew her husband to be an honest and sufficient man. So the mayor asked her if she had her husband's consent. She said her husband did condescend . . .

. . . Soon in August a friend told me that he feared that she was not yet satisfied . . . but when she could hide it no longer, but that the time grew nigh that she must needs go through London, as she had done in Cork . . . she bought a Bible, a Testament and divers good books and other things . . . I ordered a man and horse to go to the ship which was at Passage West, near Waterford . . . her friends of the church being met together would not suffer her to go without the company of a woman. So Mary, the wife of Major Bennett, being strongly moved to go along with her, and Thomas Moore along with them by a general consent . . . I did ask her a little before we parted . . . whether she had any call or command to go to the king . . . which afterwards it appears she had . . . for . . . it was revealed to her one morning that she should speak to the king that day. And she made haste and went to a friend's house near St James's Park; and she was told that the king would walk in the park about such an hour. At the time appointed . . . she having on a gown of black hair-cloth and ashes upon her head but her riding-hood over it . . . she steps towards the king, as he came near, and throwing off her riding-hood to the little maid, and in her doleful habit of sackcloth and ashes she reached a paper to the king, with the ensuing words written therein: 'Received from the great and mighty God, in fear and trembling, in Ireland'. . . And when he had read it, he turned back and said 'What art thou, woman? A Quaker?' She answered and said 'O king, in obedience to the great God of heaven and earth, and to clear my conscience to thy immortal soul, I am here before thee this day.' So the king walked away and she left him.

MARY RICH, COUNTESS OF WARWICK

(1624–78)

from:
THE DIARY OF MARY RICH, COUNTESS OF WARWICK, 1666–78

[Mary Rich, née Boyle, Countess of Warwick, was the youngest daughter of the 1st Earl of Cork, and was born at Youghal in 1624. She had an independent spirit, expressed in her refusal to accept her father's wish that she marry Lord Clandeboy. For such a stance she was sent away 'until his fury was in some measure over'. Mary stood her ground and later accepted the offer of marriage from Charles Rich, younger son of the Earl of Warwick. They were married on 21 July 1641. She began keeping her diary in 1666, following her father's example, and continued until her death in 1678. She walked two hours each day, spending the period in meditation, calling it 'time in the wilderness', and recorded this daily reflection in her diary. Her entries show her running her household, dealing with society and family, while all the time struggling with a marriage that became progressively more difficult. The structure of her faith enabled her finally to come to terms with her situation. Mary Rich's complete diary is to be found in the British Library, Add. MSS 27. T.F. Crofton Croker published part of it as *Autobiography of Mary Rich* (London: Percy Society, vol. 22, 1848).]

9 October 1667
In the morning my lord was passionate with me without any occasion and shot out his arrows, even bitter words at which I was much troubled.[1]

9 October 1668
... As I returned home my lord without any occasion given me fell into a very insolent passion with me, speaking most bitter words, the suddenness and unexpectedness of it did much terrify and surprise me, and though I bless God I was enabled to forbear saying one word to him yet I find myself much more than ordinary surprised and troubled at it and was not able to forbear when I was retired weeping most passionately and bitterly though I much strove against doing it.[2]

12 November 1668
Spent the whole afternoon till evening in catechising my maids and instructing them and I did all the awakening and moving arguments I could use endeavour to stir them up to a serious diligence in the matters of religion. God was pleased to make some of them much moved.[3]

12 September 1671
God was pleased to break my heart for my disobedience to my dead father, this sin I did bemoan with great plenty of tears. [Note in ink: Her husband being often in violent passion with her and she forced her father's consent to her marriage, by declaring she would be married to none other but to Mr Rich, for so he was when she married him, his eldest brother, Lord Rich, being then living.][4]

25 January 1672
I returned to meditate, finding still upon myself a great and very oppressing burden of melancholy, having not yet been able to get off the grief that my husband's unkindness about 4 or 5 days ago had given me [when her lord was very passionate with her, sent her a very angry message] ... My undutifulness to my father in my youth ... and my loving my husband at so high a rate as made me give him more of my

heart than I did to God, and make me care to please him than to please my God: and my not mourning of late so much for my lord's sins as formerly and my being of late more backward to speak to him about his soul for fear of offending him.[5]

8 November 1675 [her birthday]
Meditated on the mercies of God from my infancy which did make me to weep much, these mercies which in an especial manner I was thankful for were God's great care of me in my infancy, in which time though he took away by death my own mother from me yet he provided for me a careful good lady who nourished me as her own;[6] for by his providence to me bringing me into England and then by my marriage settling me in a religious family where I had good examples to be good and good encouragement to be so and powerful awakening preaching to all in my home ... and for letting me find sensible disappointment from all persons and things from which I expected my happiness and for them (by my afflictions) bringing me to look for my happiness in Himself.[7]

8 November 1676
Whilst I was doing it [meditation] so it pleased God to give me such an overcoming prospect of his constant wisdom and goodness to me in the whole course of my forepast life as did much melt and inflame my heart with love to him which I found made great work in my breast. I was then ... able to justify God in his proceedings with me through the whole course of my life which I was reviewing I found was filled with chequerwork, black and white, but I still saw that though in the whole course of my life I had often smart afflictions yet I did then justify God in bringing them upon me and saw there not one I could have been without.[8]

11 December 1676
The sins which in an especial manner I grieved for were — my original defilement, the great

1. British Library, Add. MSS 27,351, f. 124.
2. Ibid., f. 247.
3. Ibid., f. 258 v.
4. British Library, Add. MSS 27,352, f. 226. The note in the text was by Reverend Thomas Woodroffe, chaplain to the Earl of Warwick.
5. British Library, Add. MSS 27,358, f. 63 v.
6. Mary Boyle was sent to be fostered in the home of Sir Randal and Lady Clayton at Mallow, until 1638 when she returned to Lismore.
7. British Library, Add. MSS 27,354, ff. 82–82 v.
8. British Library, Add. MSS 27,355, ff. 34–34 v. A similar meditation is recorded on 8 November 1677. Ibid., f. 209.

pride and vanity of my youth, and my great expense in time in curious dressing and in playing at cards and in seeing and reading plays and romances, and my disobedience to my father, these transgressions I did with sigh and tears bewail.[9]

9. British Library Add MSS, 27,358, f. 99.

THEIR MAJESTIES ROYAL COMMISSIONERS

from:
AN ABSTRACT OF THE ARTICLES EXHIBITED AGAINST THE BISHOP OF DOWN AND CONNOR UPON WHICH HE WAS DEPRIVED BY THEIR MAJESTIES ECCLESIASTICAL COMMISSIONERS AND THE DEPOSITIONS THEREUPON WITH THE ABSTRACTS OF THE SAID BISHOP OF DOWN AND CONNOR'S ANSWER TO THE SAID ARTICLES (1692)

[Thomas Hackett was Bishop of Down and Connor from 1672 to 1694. For the first ten years of his episcopate Hackett resided in Down and Connor. After that time he moved to London, living at Holland House in Kensington and in Hammersmith. He pleaded poor health and continually postponed his return to the diocese. During his absence both Lord Lieutenants Ormond and Clarendon expressed concern about the effect such absence was having in the diocese, though they refused to appoint a coadjutor bishop, fearing it would prevent Hackett's return. When he did come back to the diocese in 1692, Hackett was called before the Royal Commissioners and charged with absenteeism and simony. The charge of simony was based on the influence which Mrs Catherine Hackett and Mrs Mary Cole exerted on appointments in the diocese. The Royal Commissioners examined Bishop Hackett and presented him with fifteen testimonies against him, several of which dealt in particular with the role and influence of Mrs Cole. He was deprived of his diocese in 1694.[1]]

You have committed the care and custody of your episcopal seal[2] both in England and Ireland and much of the management of your church and ecclesiastical affairs in and of your said diocese to Mrs Mary Cole, widow, by whom many of your clergy were hindered from access to your lordship . . . that for all or a very great part of the said time you directed or at least permitted all instruments to which the said seal was to be affixed to be sealed by her or her order, and that you have also for a great part of the said time permitted most of your episcopal acts of collation, institution and letters of curacy and whatever required an episcopal seal to be managed by the said Mrs Cole, and blank licences for marriages with[out?] any bonds or usual oaths.

When John McNeale, Dean of Down, asked for the bishop's seal, Mrs Cole:

replied with an observation that neither the said bishop nor his deponent should have the said seal because she did not know what use might be made on it in her absence and that she had it given to her charge and that she would keep it. To which the bishop said to his deponent: 'you see how I am used, that I cannot command my seal'; which answer of Mrs Cole this deponent resenting, the said bishop said that Mrs Cole was placed by his

1. Henry Cotton, *Fasti Ecclesiae Hibernicae*, 6 vols (Dublin, 1845–78), vol. 3, pp. 208, 232; vol. 5, p. 235; vol. 1, pp. 240, 466.
2. Bodleian Library Oxford, Rawlinson MSS c. 926.

wife[3] and that he did not know what jumbling there was between them, but the said Mrs Cole was a necessary woman and did a great deal of business for him and therefore he must bear with her.

Another testimony declared:

that the said Mrs Cole did many things contrary to the said bishop of Down and Connor's mind and intention and when the said bishop would not comply with her she reviled him and called him an old rogue and several other ill names; that sometimes around the last assizes at Carrickfergus this deponent was sent into the said bishop to get

him to sign a certificate drawn by Mrs Cole's order, which certificate the said bishop signed but before he signed it he said these words: '. . . take notice that I sign this certificate against my conscience, but I must do it or else I shall have no quiet with this woman (meaning Mrs Cole) whom my wife has set over me . . .' In August last he heard the said bishop declare in the presence of the bishop of Derry and several other persons that his . . . wife had placed the said Mrs Cole over him and that she was her Deputy and he could not but do whatever she pleased . . . the said bishop often complain[ed] of the said Mrs Cole's management of his affairs And said to the said Cole 'meddle not with my ecclesiastical affairs for they do not concern you'; to which the said Mrs Cole replied 'You will neither do your own business nor let anybody else do it.'

3. Both Mrs Hackett and Mrs Cole had been involved with appointments to the diocese since at least 1686. When Charles Lesley and George Lovell sought appointments in the diocese it was understood that gifts were expected by Mrs Hackett, such as 'a handsome present to your lady', or 'a good purse of gold'. Rawlinson MSS c. 926, pt ii, ff. 20–23.

ANN FOWKES

(1692–1774)

from:

A MEMOIR OF MISTRESS ANN FOWKES NÉE GEALE DIED AGED 82 YEARS, WITH SOME RECOLLECTIONS OF HER FAMILY A.D. 1642–1774. WRITTEN BY HERSELF (1892)

[Baptists came to Ireland during the Cromwellian period mainly through the army and through ministers sent over by parliament. They quickly rose to power and influence and by 1655 Baptist officers governed twelve of the towns and cities of Ireland and many officers in the army were Baptist.[1] Baptist ministers were active in the country and, though few in number, they entered into controversy with other

Protestant traditions in Ireland. John Rogers' Independent Congregation in Christ Church, Dublin, became so divided on the issue of adult baptism that it dissolved in favour of the Baptists.[2] This whirlwind influence did not last after the Restoration and the Baptists became a small dissenting church, present in the country, but with the significant exception of Richard Lawrence, not politically involved. Lawrence's granddaughter Ann Fowkes wrote her memoirs, which give insight into the Baptist tradition in Ireland over several generations. She herself lived 'while eight crown'd heads since [James II] appeared in England'. She spent most of her life in Ireland, and although she suffered greatly through the deaths of seven of her nine children, she ran a business to support her family and her husband's ministry. The memoir traces her own spiritual journey, tells the life stories of her grandparents and close friends, discusses the preaching quality of ministers, meditates on the loneliness of widowhood (when Samuel Fowkes died in 1745), but most of all she follows the growth and development of her two children with great detail and satisfaction. The memoir was published in Dublin in 1892.]

1. Thomas Birch (ed.), *A Collection of the State Papers of John Thurloe*, 7 vols (London, 1742), vol. 4, p. 91; T.C. Barnard, *Cromwellian Ireland: English Government and Reform in Ireland 1649–1660* (Oxford, 1975), pp. 100–6.

2. St John D. Seymour, *The Puritans in Ireland 1649–1661* (Oxford, 1969 ed.), pp. 22–4, 59.

I was born in the city of Kilkenny, the 2nd January 1692, just as the storm was blown over which James the Second raised in Ireland and England ... My father's parents I well remember, who were the chief support of the Baptist Church in Kilkenny since I can remember ... My grandfather's name was John Geale; he came from the Saxons and was as I can remember in the county of Essex. He might have lived comfortably with his parents but being a little wild he chose the army and was of Cromwell's party ... he met with my grandmother somewhere in England ... she was an orphan ... with an independent fortune ... her maiden name was Mary Earwalker. My grandfather brought her ... to Ireland, where he first farmed and then bought land, was successful and much by his wife's means ... he lived many years in a town called Freshford, near Kilkenny, where he built a good house and carried on a variety of business. I think it was there he purchased three estates and his wife gave him her private purse to purchase one for my father which now my brother enjoys.

Since I can remember my grandfather paid the rent of the meetinghouse in Kilkenny in order to have it close to his own house for my grandmother's conveniency, who did not dare for so many years before she died to venture into the street so susceptible was she of cold. They kept two or three rooms furnished for the conveniency of travelling ministers and other Christian friends on their journeys where they were always entertained with hospitality. My grandmother died some years before her husband, though she was the youngest; and he having lost his old and beloved companion, broke up housekeeping and spent the rest of his days at my father's in the country, at a place called Golden Fields, where he died full of days and with a good character.

The 16 of June, 1712, and in the 20 year of my age, I was married to Mr Fowkes. About two months after my husband had a call from the Church of Waterford, where he went to reside, and we lived together there above thirty years. The 29 April, 1713, and in the 21 year of my age, I was delivered of a son, who we called Joseph, after my father. I had a dangerous lying in, was very weak near 4 months; but having youth and summer on my side ... I recovered. 26 September, 1714, I had another son, who we called Lawrence, after my mother's father. I had a far more difficult time than before; from September to March my life was in suspense, or rather dispair'd of ... no mother ever suffered more, I believe, for two children ... 15 June, 1716, I was delivered of a daughter, who we called Hannah, after my husband's mother ... but God fit to deprive me of her when she was one year and quarter old ... I had after her 4 sons and 2 daughters, who all died young ... My constitution was so broke and ruined with my two first, that none of the rest lived to be above two year old ... Yet I was obliged, with that shattered constitution to encounter a great deal of fatigue in journeys and voyages to buy my goods for my shop, and work I hard night and day to support my family yet God has been pleased to preserve me hitherto almost thro' a scene of miracles, blessed by His name. In the year 1717 I crost the seas with my husband, who went to England to see and take final leave of his relations, for so indeed, it prov'd we were, thro' the goodness of God, not only preserv'd from the danger of the sea, but also from the danger of being sunk by a large East Indie vessel, who, coming by us in a dark night, was very near striking against our little vessel and sinking it, but we escap'd, tho' narrowly, blessed by God. June, 1718, after I return'd home, I heard the Rev Mr Cook preach from them words, 2 Rev 4.5 [sic]: 'Nevertheless, I have somewhat against thee, because thou hast left thy first love' — which was a very affecting sermon to me. 1 Dec, 1720. I heard the Rev Mr Pettit preach on Ps 63, 1st verse: 'O God, thou art my God; early will I seek thee.' The Lord help me to experience that blessed propriety in God he then describ'd ...

July the 9, My dear mother exchang'd this wearisom life for a better. Her death was no small trial to me, she having been an indulgent, good and tender mother. The 19 of this instant, July, I had like to have lost the hope of my family, my two eldest children, who going down to the quay, one gave the other a little push, not considering where he stood, which was on the brink of the river, with the tide full in; he fell over into the river, and in his fall laid hold of his brother's leg and drag'd him in with him, and they had both been lost in all likelihood, had not a sailer, who was order'd by Providence, I don't doubt, standing at a distance with his back to them, and hearing them flump into the water, turn'd about and saw one of their heads rise out of the water; but before he got to them they sank again; he threw himself on his belly, and reach'd out his hat towards the eldest, who he saw rising again, and the child laid hold on the rim, by which the man gently wafted them both to shore, for the younger was all this while under the water, but kept the grip of his brother's leg; and when he pull'd them out they were almost dead, especially him who lay so long buried under water. His life was dispair'd of for some time. They were taken into a house, stript, and put to bed before I heard anything on't; and their father was out of town. The Lord help me to retain a grateful sense of His goodness on that account, and may I never, never forget what a present help He was in that time of need; for in the mount of straits He was seen: blessed be His holy name for ever. Amen . . .

April 15 [1724], I was deprived of my dear Nancy, the delight of my eyes, who but a little before was a most desireable enjoyment. She was aged about two years, and was, for her age, one of the most engaging babies I ever saw; but He who knew how foolishly fond I was, thought fit to remove her to a happier clime and better company. Oh! where shall I learn wisdom, if not from such trying providences? and since the Lord has been pleas'd to touch me in so sensible a part, may He thereby bring me to a right sense of my duty, and learn for the future wisely to fix my affections, and oh, that my God may grant me, instead of her, a more durable and abiding good; for tho' with the profoundest humility I would express it, I will not be put off with the world for my portion: give it to whom Thou pleasest, but give me Thyself.

All sublunary things uncertain be:
I ask them not — some better thing I see . . .

1728, January 2. — I am now in my 36th year of my age; and that my life shud be lengthen'd to such a date, considering my unprofitableness, is matter of surprise to me: when so many in my view whose lives, to all appearance, might have been much more useful, have been cut off, and some in their bloom. There has been near fifty persons in my own relations, and none of them very remote, who have slid off the stage of life, since I made my appearance on it: and I, worthless I, still keep my standing. 'Surely goodness and mercy have follow'd me all the days of my life.'[3] May I be so aided by Thy grace and Spirit, that if I should pass the approaching year, it may all be spent to Thy glory, or if it shud prove my last, that I may ascent to Thee.

3. Psalm 22.

Biographies/Bibliographies

Elizabeth Chambers, Frances Curtis, Mary Turrant

LIFE. No details remain of Elizabeth Chambers, Frances Curtis or Mary Turrant. Evidently they lived in Ireland prior to the rebellion in 1641. The testimonies of Rogers's congregation in Christ Church in 1650 provide the sole record found of several women at this time in Ireland.

CHIEF WRITINGS. The recorded testimonies are the only extant writing of these women.

BIOGRAPHY AND CRITICISM. See other testimonies in Rogers's work, *Ohel or Beth-shemesh*, pp. 403–19; Edward Rogers, *Life and Opinion of a Fifth Monarchy Man* (London, 1867); P.G. Rogers, *The Fifth Monarchy Men* (London, 1966); O.C. Watkins, *The Puritan Experience* (New York, 1972); Charles Lloyd Cohen, *God's Caress: The Psychology of Puritan Religious Experience* (New York, 1986).

William Wright

No information discovered.

Mary Rich, Countess of Warwick

LIFE. Mary Boyle was born in 1624, the youngest daughter of the Earl of Cork. After her marriage she lived in Leighs Priory, Felsted, in England. She took up her father's habit of keeping a diary, and records of this daily reflection date from 1666 until her death in 1678. She also wrote some pious poetry and meditation which are preserved in the British Library. She died on 12 April 1678.

CHIEF WRITINGS. Diary of Mary, wife of Charles Rich, 4th Earl of Warwick, and daughter of Richard Boyle, 1st Earl of Cork, 1667–77. With notes and alterations in the hand of Rev. T. Woodroofe, chaplain to the Earl of Warwick (British Library, Add. MSS 27, 351–5); Occasional Meditations of Lady Warwick, 1663–1677 (BL Add. MSS 27, 356); Collections out of my Lady Warwick's diaries, meditation etc. by R.T. Woodroofe (BL Add. MSS 37, 358).

BIOGRAPHY AND CRITICISM. Anthony Walker, *The Virtuous Women Found: Her Loss Bewailed and Character Exemplified in a Sermon Preached at Felstad in Essex, April 30, 1678* (London, 1678); *Lismore Papers*, ed. A.B. Grosart (10 vols., London, 1886–8); Charlotte Fell Smith, *Mary Rich, Countess of Warwick 1625–1678, Her Family and Friends* (London, 1901); Mary Prior (ed.), *Women in English Society 1500–1800* (London, 1985); Antonia Fraser, *The Weaker Vessel* (London, 1984).

Ann Fowkes

LIFE. Ann Fowkes was born in 1692 in Kilkenny towards the end of the Williamite Wars. She spent most of her life in Ireland, first in Kilkenny and, after her marriage to Samuel Fowkes, in Waterford. Only two of the nine children she gave birth to survived, and by her own account she had a 'shattered constitution'. Nevertheless she ran a business and helped support both her family and her husband's ministry. She died in 1774.

CHIEF WRITINGS. Ann Fowkes's *Memoir* was her significant work.

BIOGRAPHY AND CRITICISM. Thomas Patient, *The Doctrine of Baptism and the Distinction of the Covenants or a Plain Treatise, wherein the Four Essentials of Baptism . . . are Diligently Handled. By Thomas Patient, a Labourer in the Church of Christ at Dublin* (London, 1654); Kevin Herlihy, 'The Irish Baptists, 1650–1780' (unpublished Ph.D. thesis, Trinity College Dublin, 1992), and 'The Early Eighteenth Century Irish Baptists: Two Letters', *Irish Economic and History Review,* vol. 19 (1992), pp. 71–6; St John D. Seymour, *The Puritans in Ireland 1647–1660* (Oxford, 1921); T.C. Barnard, *Cromwellian Ireland: English Government and Reform in Ireland 1649–1660* (Oxford, 1975); B.R. White, *The English Baptists of the 17th Century* (London, 1895); J.F. McGregor, 'The Baptists: Font of All Heresy', in *Radical Religion in the English Revolution,* eds. J.F. McGregor and Barry Reay (Oxford, 1985).

ROSEMARY RAUGHTER, *Editor*

Eighteenth-Century Catholic and Protestant Women

Women in the Eighteenth-Century Catholic Community

Maureen Wall's pioneering work on the effect of the Penal Laws on the Irish Catholic community, written more than forty years ago, remains the classic treatment of this topic, and while it does not deal specifically with the female role in eighteenth-century Irish Catholicism, it does establish the basis upon which her successors in this field have recently begun to build in retrieving the story of Irish women's history at this period.[1] This process has to date largely concentrated on identifying topics for future research, but already it is clear that while Catholic women were on one level disadvantaged members of a disadvantaged sector, their actual status was considerably more complex, and that for them, as for women in a number of separatist Protestant sects at the same time, disruption brought its own compensation in the form of greater independence and opportunities for action.

On the other hand, the experience of discrimination should not be understated. Catholic women were as affected as their male counterparts by the penal legislation of the decades following the Williamite victory, and if the denial of access to political life and to the professions, and the restrictions on landholding, had little application to them as individuals, they suffered equally the social and material implications of such measures. They felt also, both as members of the laity and as religious, the disruption of diocesan and parochial organization. While a few of the female religious orders did remain in existence during this period, and while nuns were never proscribed as were Catholic bishops and unregistered clergy, they were not immune from interference; thus, in 1718 the Poor Clare convent in North King Street, Dublin, was raided and the sisters briefly held for questioning. In general, however, the orders were allowed to survive unmolested, though they were dogged by a shortage of recruits and by poverty.

Convents received support from aristocratic patrons such as the Duchess of Tyrconnell and the Countess of Fingall, while the Dominicans and the Carmelites ran boarding-schools in Dublin for the daughters of the Catholic nobility and gentry. Many more girls from this class were sent abroad for education, chiefly to convent schools in France, Spain and the Low Countries: Nano Nagle herself was educated in France, her cousin, Marie Ann Nagle, attended the celebrated girls' school of Saint-Cyr, near Versailles, and in 1778 Nano's nieces in their turn embarked for France, probably also bound for Saint-Cyr. The great majority of young women, however, lacked any access to education, since Catholic parish or pay schools, when they did begin to be established, catered exclusively for boys. Not until the mid-1750s did Nagle establish her first girls' schools in Cork, predating by just a few years Teresa Mulally's

1. Maureen Wall, *The Penal Laws 1691–1760* (Dundalk: Dundealgan Press, 1961), and 'The Rise of a Catholic Middle Class in Eighteenth-Century Ireland', *Irish Historical Studies*, vol. 11, no. 42 (September 1958). For discussion of women's role in the Catholic community, see Patrick J. Corish, 'Women and Religious Practice', in Margaret Mac Curtain and Mary O'Dowd (eds), *Women in Early Modern Ireland* (Dublin: Wolfhound Press, 1991), pp. 212–20; also Kevin Whelan, 'The Catholic Community in Eighteenth-Century County Wexford', in T.P. Power and Kevin Whelan (eds), *Endurance and Emergence: Catholics in Ireland in the Eighteenth Century* (Dublin: Wolfhound Press, 1990).

foundation of the first Catholic charity school for girls in Dublin.

However, if Catholic women, no less than men, were subject to the disadvantages imposed by the penal legislation, there are also indications that the peculiar circumstances of Irish Catholicism at this period offered women a degree of freedom and opportunity which was to be sharply curtailed within the resurgent church of the next century. Throughout western Europe, indeed, women's response to the spirit and teachings of the Counter-Reformation had been evident in their participation in the more strictly regulated and parochially based practices of religion, in their membership of a variety of new lay devotional and charitable associations, and in demands by pious laywomen and by female religious for a more active apostolate, most notably in the fields of education and philanthropy. The response of the institutional church to these female initiatives was decidedly ambivalent; while acknowledging the usefulness of women's contribution, churchmen reacted with disquiet to any activism which they regarded as challenging their own authority, or as serving, however tentatively, to enhance women's autonomy in the church or in secular society. Thus, in sixteenth- and seventeenth-century Europe, the structures envisaged by innovators such as Angela Merici, Jeanne de Chantal and Mary Ward, and the functions which their groups were intended to fulfil, were modified or countermanded by the ecclesiastical authorities, in accordance with prevailing perceptions of womanhood and of the female role in society and religion.

As Counter-Reformation influences penetrated Irish Catholicism in the course of the seventeenth and eighteenth centuries, Irish women reacted to them in a broadly similar way to their European counterparts. Their experience, however, was also a distinctive one, at once more disadvantaged and more privileged than that of Catholic women elsewhere. The penal legislation, while limiting the rights of all Catholics in relation to education, religious practice and property-holding, also produced a church whose organizational structures and lines of authority, despite gradual recovery, remained weak. In consequence, churchmen lacked both the means and the will to fully control the initiatives of more assertive female members, whose work they regarded in any case as a valuable adjunct to their own efforts to catechize and instruct the great mass of the Irish Catholic population. Under these conditions, the female laity enjoyed a centrality in the life of the Catholic community, and in religious practice, unattainable in those areas where parochial organization and ecclesiastical authority were more fully established, while a small minority of pious women were enabled to initiate action on a range of fronts and to effect a far-reaching transformation in the character of the female religious life.

John Bossy, in his study of English Catholicism, has noted the vital role played by women, especially but not exclusively as wives, in the preservation of the faith, and has gone so far as to describe the Elizabethan and Jacobean periods as a 'matriarchal era', ending in about 1620 with the decline in the implementation of the recusancy laws and an increasing tendency to spiritual uniformity and patriarchal authority within the household.[2] In Ireland, however, the intensification of discrimination from the 1690s created a comparable environment well into the eighteenth century. Thus, in both kingdoms, but at different times, repression had the effect of concentrating religious teaching and practice in the home rather than in the parish church, and of thereby producing a 'domestic' religion which, as Patrick J. Corish has pointed out, 'must be . . . very much influenced by women and especially by wives'.[3] On the mistress of the household rested the responsibility of ensuring that Catholic regulations on fasting and abstinence were observed, that all members attended daily prayers and that children and servants were instructed in the tenets of religion. The importance of this role is conveyed in texts such as Richard Challoner's *Considerations upon Christian Truths*, which, in its meditation on the feast of St Anne, the mother of the Virgin, reflects the currently approved version of Catholic womanhood,[4] and in contemporary biographical accounts, which cite the crucial part played by

2. John Bossy, *The English Catholic Community 1570–1850* (London: Darton, Longman and Todd, 1975), pp. 153, 158–9.
3. P.J. Corish, 'Women and Religious Practice', p. 214.
4. Dr Richard Challoner, *Considerations upon Christian Truths and Christian Duties* (Cork: William Flynn, 1773), pp. 60–1.

mothers and other female relatives in the subject's spiritual and moral training. Thus, Nano Nagle received from 'her pious mother . . . the earliest lessons of the female decorum', Teresa Mulally recalled her mother's benevolence as an example to be followed in her own life, while Mary Aikenhead, baptized in her father's Protestant faith, was sufficiently impressed by her Catholic mother, maternal grandmother and aunt to become a convert at the age of sixteen.[5]

The vital contribution of women to the maintenance and transmission of the faith was acknowledged in those gentry and middle-class families in which the husband conformed to the Established Church in order to inherit property or to practise a profession, while the wife remained Catholic and passed on elements of Catholic teaching to their offspring. This tendency was noted as early as 1729 by the Anglican Archbishop Boulter, who complained about the considerable number of lawyers who had converted, and who 'have a papist wife who has Mass said in the family and the children are brought up as papists'. The Burke family provide just one example of this pattern, operating throughout the eighteenth century; thus, while Richard Burke, an attorney, conformed in 1722, his wife, Mary Nagle, remained a Catholic; their son, Edmund, though baptized a Protestant, lived for a number of years with his Catholic maternal relatives in County Cork, and in his own marriage, his wife, Jane, remained a practising Catholic throughout her life.

Women's influence and their religious zeal were, however, not confined to the home but were increasingly applied within the wider Catholic community. While the philanthropic and educational ventures of pioneers such as Nagle and Mulally required an exceptional level of enterprise and commitment, for growing numbers of pious women, membership of a confraternity offered an opportunity for involvement in charitable works and in catechesis, as

well as for association with other like-minded individuals. In Ireland, as in Counter-Reformation Europe, women were eager recruits to these new devotional organizations. Thus, of the 681 members of the Wexford Confraternity of the Cord of St Francis for the period 1763–89, 609 were female.[6] Women were also admitted to the Sodality of the Blessed Virgin Mary, which had branches at Waterford, Cork and Dublin, while the Confraternity of Christian Doctrine, active in Wexford and in St Michan's parish in Dublin in the late eighteenth century, appears to have had a high proportion of female members, with all of the ninety-six teachers listed for St Michan's parish for the years 1799–1800 being women. In the following year, however, in a move symptomatic of the reviving church's tendency to assert its control over the activities of its women members, the parish priest, Father Wade, and his curate, Father Blake, took over and reorganized Christian doctrine teaching in the parish; male members were admitted to the congregation and separate branches created for boys and girls.

The charitable and educational work of pious eighteenth-century laywomen was undertaken in the absence of any significant activity in these areas by the female religious orders currently operating in the country. Factors inhibiting such activity included not only the penal legislation but also the rule of enclosure, to which all of the orders currently operating in Ireland subscribed. In consequence, those women who felt themselves to have a vocation to an active apostolate had no alternative but to establish their own initiatives. Initially, and of necessity, they did so as laywomen and with the assistance of lay colleagues. However, the benefits of placing these projects under ecclesiastical protection were clear; funds and new workers would be more easily attracted, and the survival of existing structures more definitely assured. In 1771, therefore, Nagle introduced the Ursulines into Cork, where in the following year they opened a boarding-school for the daughters of wealthy Catholics. However, the order's rule of enclosure prevented its members from taking over supervision of the poor schools, prompting Nagle in 1775 to establish her own congregation, the

5. Dr William Coppinger, 'The Life of Miss Nano Nagle, 1794', in T.J. Walsh, *Nano Nagle and the Presentation Sisters* (Dublin: M.H. Gill and Son, 1959), pp. 384–95; Professor Alfred O'Rahilly, 'A Letter about Miss Mulally and Nano Nagle', *Irish Ecclesiastical Record*, vol. 40 (July–December 1932), 5th series, pp. 474–81, 619–24, 620–1; S. Atkinson, *Mary Aikenhead: Her Life, Her Work and Her Friends* (Dublin: M.H. Gill, 1879), pp. 71–2, 80–3, 87.

6. Register of the Confraternity of the Cord of St Francis, Wexford 1763–1834, MS C342, Franciscan Library, Killiney.

Society of the Charitable Instruction, which, as a non-enclosed sisterhood, was able to pursue an active apostolate within the wider community. Twenty years later, the society took over the running of Mulally's school in Dublin, and by 1800 had houses at Killarney, Waterford and Kilkenny, as well as a second convent in Cork. Moreover, as an unenclosed and socially active sisterhood, the Presentation Order, as it later became, set the pattern which was to be followed to remarkable effect by female religious in nineteenth-century Ireland.[7]

Nagle's foundation, however, like that of Mary Ward in England a century and a half earlier, marked the high point, and heralded the close of the 'matriarchal era' within Irish Catholicism. In establishing her own congregation, Nagle placed herself and her sisterhood under the control of the ecclesiastical authorities, and the effect of this surrender of autonomy was apparent in the apostolic brief of 1805, which imposed on the Presentation Sisters a rule of enclosure which greatly restricted their ability to perform the active social role which Nagle herself had envisaged for them. As Clear has shown, female religious in nineteenth-century Ireland found their independence curtailed within an increasingly powerful and authoritarian church. Laywomen, too, experienced a loss of autonomy, with the transfer of catechesis from the domestic sphere to the parish clergy, and with the virtual monopolization by nuns of philanthropic and educational work.[8] If the Catholic mother continued to enjoy a high standing inside her own home, and if the 'domestic' nature of Irish Catholicism was never entirely obliterated, it is none the less clear that the options available to the female members of the laity were considerably diminished in the decades after the dismantling of the penal legislation. By their own notable contribution to the Catholic resurgence of this period, women helped to re-establish the traditional power structures of the church, and thereby to confirm the subordinate status of its female members, both lay and religious.

Women and Methodism

In 1747 Ireland became one of the chief areas of Methodist missionary endeavour when John Wesley made the first of twenty-one visits to the country. By 1767 Irish membership numbered 2,801, rising to 19,292 in 1800, and not the least of the factors contributing to the movement's growth was its strong female support base.

Methodism has been described as 'a woman's faith',[9] and the specific nature of its appeal has been the subject of much speculation by historians. It has been suggested that the more emotionally charged and 'hysterical' aspects of some separatist Protestant sects were especially congenial to women.[10] However, the latitude which early Methodism permitted to the individual believer may provide a more tangible reason for its success. Lacking its own clergy and places of worship, the movement relied on the initiative, zeal and generosity of its adherents, both male and female, and this dependence was reflected in its organizational structures, within which the laity enjoyed a greater influence than was allowed by any of the mainstream Christian denominations. The content of Wesley's message holds a further clue to the movement's advance. As O. Hufton has pointed out, Methodism equipped women with a realistic recipe for survival in an imperfect world.[11] The moral values which it promoted — such as industry, cleanliness, thrift and self-control — were qualities which, while far from heroic, nevertheless enhanced a girl's chances of making an advantageous marriage, and enabled her, as wife and mother, to advance both the moral and material welfare of her family. In addition, of course, women were influenced by the same factors which drew men to Methodism, among which have been cited Wesley's claims of 'special providences', offering assurance of protection in a hostile environment, and the shifting social, economic and political patterns of the period, in the face of which Methodism offered a sense of

7. For a more detailed discussion of eighteenth-century Catholic philanthropy, see Rosemary Raughter, 'Female Charity as an Aspect of the Catholic Resurgence', *Pages: Arts Postgraduate Research in Progress*, vol. 1 (1994), pp. 17–36; on female religious post-1800, see Caitriona Clear, *Nuns in Nineteenth-Century Ireland* (Dublin: Gill and Macmillan, 1987).
8. Caitriona Clear, 'The Limits of Female Autonomy: Nuns in Nineteenth-Century Ireland', in Maria Luddy and Cliona Murphy (eds), *Women Surviving* (Dublin: Poolbeg Press, 1990), pp. 15–50.
9. Olwen Hufton, *The Prospect Before Her: A History of Women in Western Europe, 1500–1800* (London: Harper Collins, 1995), p. 357.
10. Max Weber, *Sociology of Religion* (London: Methuen, 1966).
11. O. Hufton, *The Prospect Before Her*, p. 415.

certainty and of solidarity, as well as the assurance of ultimate victory.[12]

While the reasons for women's attraction may have been complex, the importance of their contribution is clear, and the view that they probably accounted for a majority of the early membership is supported by surviving membership figures for societies in both Britain and America.[13] In relation to the Irish movement, C.H. Crookshank's *History of Methodism* and his biographical studies of its 'memorable women', as well as the recent researches of David Hempton and Myrtle Hill, have confirmed the very significant part played by women in its consolidation and expansion during its first half century.

12. Ibid., pp. 415–16. For discussion for the reasons for Methodism's success, see David Hempton and Myrtle Hill, 'Women and Protestant Minorities in Eighteenth-Century Ireland', in *Women in Early Modern Ireland*, eds Margaret Mac Curtain and Mary O'Dowd, pp. 197–211, and David Hempton, 'Methodism in Irish Society, 1770–1830', pp. 119–25, 128–33.

13. E.K. Brown, 'Women in Mr Wesley's Methodism', *Studies in Women and Religion*, vol. 2 (New York, 1983), quoted in D. Hempton and M. Hill, 'Women and Protestant Minorities', p. 197; Malmgreen, 'Domestic discords', pp. 57–8; David Hempton, *Methodism and Politics in British Society, 1750-1850* (London: Hutchinson, 1984), p. 13.

MAUREEN WALL

(1918–72)

from:
CATHOLIC IRELAND IN THE EIGHTEENTH CENTURY: COLLECTED ESSAYS OF MAUREEN WALL (1989)

[With Maureen Wall's 1950s work on the Irish Penal Law experience, a more enlightened and objective study of an emotive subject was set in train. Her work remains important because she analysed the interaction of the Catholic community with other groups in society, and she established criteria for dealing with the issue of civic disabilities in eighteenth-century society, which had hitherto been clouded by sectarian interpretations, see Vol. v, p. 678–9.]

THE PENAL LAWS, 1691–1760

From the reign of Queen Elizabeth (1558–1603) until the treaty of Limerick, religion took second place to politics in the Irish policies of successive English rulers. Rebellion must first be crushed and plantations firmly secured before an all-out effort could be undertaken to spread the doctrines of the Reformation in Ireland. By the beginning of the eighteenth century it seemed that, politically, Catholic Ireland had been finally subdued; Protestant ascendancy was firmly entrenched and the time had arrived, it seemed, for embarking on a programme for protestantising the population of Ireland. But at no time during the whole of that century could the Established Church in Ireland be called a missionary church.

The Act of Uniformity, passed in 1560, had made attendance at the state church on Sundays compulsory for all, on pain of a fine of one shilling, but this section of the Act had fallen completely into disuse by the end of the seventeenth century. No attempt was made to compel attendance at the state churches, nor to collect recusancy fines, during the whole of the eighteenth century, although the law of 1560 remained unchanged until the passing of the Catholic Relief Act of 1793.

From the time of Henry VIII and Elizabeth it had been realised that the setting up of parochial and diocesan schools was essential for the spread both of the new religious ideas and of the English language, and many Acts had been passed making provision for the setting up of such schools, where free education would be provided for all. But the carrying out of these schemes and the financing of them was left to the bishops and clergy of the Established Church, and since few of these, however wealthy, were willing to provide funds for this purpose, the statutes were largely a dead letter. Such diocesan schools as were founded, and they were few, rapidly ceased to be free schools, and since a system of parish schools for the native population was never provided, little progress was made either in anglicising or protestantising by means of schools. It was not until the nineteenth century, when the State began to assume responsibility for the education of the masses, that such a policy could hope to achieve success, and by that time the Catholic Church was in a position to defeat the State-aided missionary effort undertaken by various Protestant organisations . . .

The missionary zeal evinced by British and Irish Protestants towards the end of the eighteenth century was the direct result of the great evangelical revival in England at that time, but at the beginning of the century this spirit had been lacking in Protestantism. After Cromwell, a reaction had set in in England, and the reign of Charles II had seen the rapid growth of indifferentism in matters of religion on the part of government and people, and ushered in what is sometimes called the 'ice age' in English Protestantism. Then too the overthrow of James II — the divinely-appointed head of the church — dealt a severe blow to church authority. The new king, who was also head of the church, was appointed by parliament, and from that time on parliament continued to interfere more and more in church affairs. The old position of autonomy enjoyed by the Established Church was weakened and this was particularly true of Ireland. From 1613 the church had been governed by its own convocation, which met in Dublin when parliament was in session. It resembled parliament, having an upper house in which the bishops sat and a lower house where the clergy met. But during the reign of William III (1688–1702) convocation was not summoned and although it met during the reign of Anne, it was never summoned again from her death in 1714 until 1869, when circumstances made it necessary to convene it in order to wind up the affairs of the church, which was then about to be disestablished. During the whole of the eighteenth century the Irish House of Commons was opposed to the assembling of convocation, as it was determined that no other body in the country would be allowed to challenge its own authority.

Relations between the Established Church and the House of Commons were far from being harmonious during the early part of the eighteenth century, the time when it might have been expected that church and state would be co-operating to bring about the long-delayed conversion of the Irish population to Protestantism. Appointments of all Irish Protestant bishops and appointments to many of the most coveted livings in Ireland were vested in the Crown, and it was the English ministry and not the Irish parliament which advised the Crown in the matter of Irish church appointments. Many of the bishops appointed were Englishmen and this was hugely resented by Irish Protestants. The tendency was to appoint bishops on grounds of political and party allegiance, rather than for their learning, piety, or zeal for souls. From 1702 until the Union all the Protestant Primates of Armagh were Englishmen. Three of them, Hugh Boulter (1724–41), John Hoadley (1742–46), and George Stone (1746–64), were so preoccupied with political activities — they acted as lords justices and were the mainstay of the English interest in Ireland in the absence of the Lord Lieutenant — that they had little time to devote to church affairs. Even George Berkeley, Protestant bishop of Cloyne (1734–53), who was deeply interested in the social reform of the Irish peasantry, does not seem to have considered undertaking the task of winning them from Catholicism.

The chief clash of interests between the Established Church and the House of Commons occurred on the question of the payment of tithes. This tenth part of the produce of the soil was claimed by the church from members of all religious groups in the country, and was bitterly resented by Catholics and Dissenters, who had to maintain their own churches and clergy as well. But they were not alone in their opposition to this demand, for the rich landowning members of the Established Church itself kept trying to whittle down the rights of the church in the matter, especially by insisting that pasture land should be free from tithe. The dispute was frequently brought into the law courts, but the Protestant landowning class collected funds and organised themselves to fight the cases there, and finally in 1735 a series of resolutions was passed in the House of Commons, declaring, in effect, that pasture land was free from tithe. These resolutions could not be embodied in an Act of Parliament because the Protestant bishops sat in the House of Lords and would have opposed the measure strongly there and at the English Court; nevertheless, they were regarded as having the validity of an Act of Parliament for the whole of the eighteenth century and from 1735 on the tithe was refused on pasture land throughout Ireland. It was this struggle, among others, between church and parliament, which led Dean Swift to make such violent attacks on the Irish House of Commons in his writings.

During the course of the struggle on the tithe question the members of the House of Commons intimidated the churchmen by threatening to set up a parliamentary examination into abuses in the church in Ireland, and at the time the church would have fared badly at the hands of a hostile commission of enquiry. Plurality — one person drawing the income from two or more benefices — was common, as was also non-residence. During the wars of the confederation and Cromwellian period many churches had been destroyed and had never been rebuilt. Often there was no glebe house for a parson's residence. In many parishes there were few or no Protestants and the parson who had no desire to bury himself in some out-of-the-way Irish parish contented himself with drawing the income from the parish and, if necessary, paid a curate a small salary to carry out the spiritual duties. The statutes regarding the erection of parish and diocesan schools had been disregarded, and in many other particulars the Established Church would have reason to avoid, if possible, any detailed enquiry into church affairs. Without first reforming itself it was clear that the Established Church was in no position to undertake missionary work among the Catholic population. Money would have been required if schools, churches, and glebe houses were to be built, and many more clergymen appointed, and the bishops were unlikely to provide the money for such a purpose, and little help was to be expected from the House of Commons . . .

Another great obstacle to the spread of Protestantism was the fact that Protestants were divided among themselves. Apart from the cities and towns the only place where Protestantism was strongly entrenched was Ulster, and here the problem of nonconformity complicated the issue. Although members of the Established

Church and nonconformists had united and presented a solid front to the Jacobites, the members of the Established Church were not prepared, once the danger was over, to accord equality to any form of Protestantism which differed from their own. There was a good deal of friction between the clergy of the Established Church and the Dissenters and, although the Dissenters were granted a grudging toleration from 1719 on, they remained second-class citizens, and were subjected to many disabilities, and any attempt by them to spread their own forms of Protestantism was sternly discouraged. The Dissenters comprised Quakers, French Huguenots, Baptists, etc. but the great majority of them were Presbyterians. These, like the Catholics, were compelled by law to pay tithes to the Established Church, but there was little sympathy between Catholics and Dissenters during the period under review (1691–1760), and Protestantism was greatly weakened by the emigration of large numbers of Presbyterians to America during the course of the eighteenth century.

The truth is, of course, that the spirit of monopoly and exclusiveness was stronger by far in the members of the Irish Protestant ascendancy than the desire to spread what they considered to be the true faith among the people in general. Protestant ascendancy, as applied to a small privileged group, must disappear if the whole population were to become Protestant. The religious bar operated to exclude the Catholic majority from all positions of importance in the country — from the professions, from parliament, and from the ownership of property — in the same way as the colour bar has operated to ensure white ascendancy in African countries in recent times, and it was to the material advantage of Protestants to maintain the *status quo* . . .

Though the Established Church showed little zeal for spreading Protestantism, it could be argued that there was a determination to prevent Catholics from making converts among the members of that church. This was, as we have seen, one of Boulter's aims in setting up the charter schools. The laws passed to prevent inter-marriage between Catholics and Protestants were very severe, as were also the penalties against persons lapsing into popery. But the fact that the marriage laws had to be re-enacted and amended, time and again, shows that they were being constantly evaded, and one is forced to the conclusion that this legislation represents an anxiety concerning property rather than souls. What Boulter calls 'Protestants of the meaner sort', as was to be expected, fell away. It was difficult for isolated Protestant families to maintain their religion in many parts of rural Ireland, considering the non-residence of many of the parochial clergy of the Established Church, and the fact that they were surrounded by Catholic neighbours. Even large colonies like the Palatines in Limerick and Kerry tended to fall away from Protestantism, and there is no evidence, so far as I know, that they suffered penalties as a result. Instances can be cited, however, in which determined efforts were made to deprive Protestants of their property when they contracted marriages with Catholics.

Since landed property was the basis of political power in the eighteenth century, the Government was most anxious to bring about the conformity of the few remaining Catholic landowners, and in this policy it was eminently successful. Sometimes the change of religion was brought about by the law requiring Protestant guardians to be appointed to Catholic minors, but many landowners conformed in order to save their estates, or because they could no longer endure the social and political exclusion which would be their lot if they remained Catholics. With regard to the religion of the masses of the Catholic population, the Irish parliament was content to demonstrate its zeal for the Protestant interest by passing a series of statutes, which, had they been enforced or enforceable, would have extirpated Catholicism in Ireland in a generation.

Like so much of the legislation of the Irish parliament in the eighteenth century, the popery laws were copied from laws already passed in England, though the Irish laws were not so severe as those passed against English Catholics. Such laws were out of date in an age when persecution on grounds of religious belief had been abandoned in most western European countries. The Protestant ruler of Holland and the Protestant princes of Germany, including the elector of Hanover, who became King of Great Britain and Ireland in 1714, had already granted religious toleration to their Catholic subjects. Defenders of the popery laws could, however, point to France, where Protestants had first been persecuted, and then expelled by the revocation of the Edict of Nantes in 1685, and to the persecution of persons who differed from the established religion in Spain and in the Empire. But these examples had one feature in common. The persecution was aimed at a minority of the population. In Ireland it was directed against the majority. These laws were placed on the statute book in Ireland in order to give a sense of security and power to the Protestant minority which ruled the country, but their enforcement at any given time depended on political rather than religious considerations. As far as the English government was concerned, its attitude was based on expediency, for, on religious as on so many other issues, there was no planned policy for Ireland.

RICHARD CHALLONER

(1691–1781)

from:
CONSIDERATIONS UPON CHRISTIAN TRUTHS AND CHRISTIAN DUTIES (1753)

[Dr Challoner's *Considerations upon Christian Truths and Christian Duties*, first published in 1753 and much reprinted during the eighteenth century, became a standard work of English-speaking Catholicism. This meditation for the feast of St Anne reflects the currently approved version of Catholic lay womanhood. The text is Proverbs 31.]

Consider . . . the properties of a *valiant*, that is, of a wise and virtuous woman, as all perfectly agreeing to this great Saint: particularly, her perpetual attention to do *good, and not evil, all the days of her life*; her unwearied industry in acquiring the spiritual riches of all virtues, and storing up a treasure for eternity; her diligence in the exercise of the works of mercy and charity; &c. *Strength and beauty are her clothing . . . She hath opened her mouth to wisdom, and the law of clemency is on her tongue . . . She hath looked well to the paths of her house, and hath not eaten her bread idle:* (by a serious application to keep herself always well employed, and to see that all under her charge are orderly). Such was St Anne, such ought all Christian matrons to be: of such as these the Spirit of God adds in the conclusion of the chapter. *Favour is deceitful, and beauty is vain: the woman that feareth the Lord shall be praised. Give her of the fruit of her hands: and let her works praise her in the gates.* Yes, the Lord himself shall give her the eternal reward of the fruit of her hands: and the gates of the Heavenly Sion shall resound with her praises for ever.

NANO NAGLE

(1718–84)

from:
LETTERS TO TERESA MULALLY (1776, 1780)

[The first letter, written in 1776 and addressed to the Dublin philanthropist Teresa Mulally, announces the establishment of Nagle's religious society, the Sisters of the Charitable Instruction, and expresses her hopes for the congregation's future expansion. The second letter, written nearly four years later in the aftermath of the anti-Catholic Gordon riots, describes the sisters' move from their first makeshift home to their new Cork convent. Apprehensive of hostile demonstrations on the model of the London disturbances, 'we stole like thieves,' Nagle reported, telling nobody of their intentions and leaving their old house at dawn. Although Nagle's fears on this occasion were unrealized, they were not without foundation, given that the early part of her mission coincided with an upsurge of sectarian animosity in the Cork region, and that she herself was acting in defiance of the law prohibiting Catholic education. Her habitual discretion is proof that the penal legislation had a psychological as well as an actual impact well into the eighteenth century. At the same time, her achievement is evidence of the extent to which the laws could be circumvented, while her history provides an insight into the part played by women, both lay and religious, within the eighteenth-century Irish Catholic community, and in that community's revival in the final decades of the century. These letters are included in T.J. Walsh, *Nano Nagle and the Presentation Sisters* (Dublin: M. H. Gill and Son, 1959), pp. 357, 364. The originals are in the Presentation Convent, George's Hill, Dublin.]

28 September 1776

This is a pleasure I have longed this some time past for: which was to acquaint you that, what Dr Moylan[1] mentioned to you about two years ago, that I had a desire some establishment should be made to keep up the schools for the poor children. Not finding any person here inclined to undertake such an affair, made me at last consent to the Doctor's request; and last Christmas I took in three persons to join me in this good work. What made me defer all this time was finding myself so improper a person to undertake it. The Almighty makes use of the weakest means to bring about His works.

I am to send two out of the small number we have to Dr Moylan, as he is very impatient to have them; and in my opinion they are very proper to make a foundation in Kerry, as they have great talents and every virtue proper for it.

I send you the rule which they follow — it's called The Sisters of the Charitable Instruction of the Sacred Heart of Jesus — by this most respectable clergyman, Mr Shortall,[2] who is most zealous for its success and will give you a particular account about it. I could wish that we may unite in this Society, and am confident that the great God will direct you to what is most to His glory.

1. Dr Francis Moylan (1735–1815), ordained in France, parish priest of St Finbarr's, Cork, and a strong supporter of Nagle's work. Bishop of Kerry 1775–87, and of Cork 1787–1815.
2. Father Patrick Shortall s.j., chaplain to the Cork Ursulines, 1771–6.

29 July 1780

I believe my long silence has surprised you. Be assured it was not for want of a sincere love and respect. The delay was owing to my waiting to give an account that we were fixed in the new house, which I thought we would have been there at Christmas. [It] was prevented by part of the wall of our yard being broken down to make room for cars to come in to bring stones to make the garden wall for the Ladies — which if I prevented, must have cost them a vast deal on this. I did [not] leave my old habitation, as I could not have the back part of our house exposed . . .[1]

Then when the disturbances broke out in London, I was afraid to venture, imagining the same contagious frenzy may break out in this kingdom. So [I] waited till the times seemed quite peaceful, yet notwithstanding we stole like thieves. I got up before three in the morning [and] had all our beds taken down and sent to the house, before any was up in the street. [I] begged of the Ladies not to say a word about it to anyone of their company that would come to see them. Nor did [I] not let any person know it in the town of my friends, as I was sure [that by] acting in this manner the good work could be carried on much better than in making any noise about it. We removed [on the] 15 [July], so were there on the festival of our Blessed Lady, under whose protection we are. I hope she will preserve us from our visible and invisible enemies and make this house prosper and others of the same Charitable Institution in time.

1. Nagle and her helpers Mary Fouhy, Elizabeth Burke and Mary Ann Collins were first housed in Nagle's cottage, close to the Ursuline convent which she had set up in 1771. The new convent of the Sisters of the Charitable Instruction was also in Cove Lane.

DAVID HEMPTON AND MYRTLE HILL

(1952–   )   (1950–   )

from:
WOMEN IN EARLY MODERN IRELAND (1991)

[In this extract, the authors David Hempton and Myrtle Hill examine the religious commitment and practice of Protestant women in eighteenth-century Ireland. 'Zealous expressions of piety, excessive spirituality and emotional responses to evangelical sermons, were common to both men and women in this period.' The authors examine the Quaker movement and the impact of Methodism. They conclude that 'while women were to some extent able to extend their influence and range of activities within popular Protestant minorities, they neither sought nor were offered a fundamental shift in their relations with men'. Their religion offered Protestant women domestic piety and opportunities for philanthropy and service to the community.]

WOMEN AND PROTESTANT MINORITIES IN EIGHTEENTH-CENTURY IRELAND

The social and ecclesiastical turbulence of the English civil wars and the more general emergence of pietist communities throughout seventeenth- and eighteenth-century Europe resulted in many new versions of popular Protestantism in both Britain and Ireland. Although they exhibited considerable theological and organisational diversity, it is possible to identify some common attributes. Their concern to separate themselves from the 'ungodly', for example, even if only as a prelude to a renewed assault on Satan's kingdoms, determined many of their most prominent features. Since their very existence was a form of protest against the wider world, both secular and religious, it was imperative that they asserted their distinctiveness. This was most evident in the enforcement of strict discipline in matters of morality, appearance and general behaviour. Moreover, in their forms of worship there was more emphasis on emotion and experience than on tradition and formality. With greater reliance placed on inner truth than on received dogma, the role of a mediatorial clergy was undermined as that of the laity was simultaneously enhanced. New organisational structures and, in the early stages at least, the lack of suitable meeting places outside the home, encouraged a degree of flexibility which gave women easier access to a range of religious activities.

Thus, Keith Thomas states that 'women were numerically extremely prominent among the separatists' of the English civil war period, and that Quakers had 'more women than men among their recognised ministers'.[1] Similarly, Earl Kent Brown states that women were in a majority, 'perhaps a substantial majority', within eighteenth-century Methodism, an assessment confirmed by recent statistical surveys.[2] Surviving class membership lists of the Moravian community in Dublin in the 1740s tell a similar tale.[3] The purpose of this essay then is to offer some preliminary observations on the role of women within these three religious communities, the Methodists, Quakers and Moravians; and secondly to show how women achieved a temporary position of influence in the early stages of the evangelical revival which was not sustained into the nineteenth century when male ministers, trustees and administrators regained full control. Equally revealing of social and religious attitudes in the eighteenth century are the boundaries within which women's influence was permitted, and while these were stretched for essentially pragmatic reasons, they were neither redrawn nor discarded.

Without having accurate information on the proportions of men and women within the established Protestant denominations in this period it is impossible to be certain that by comparison women were substantially over-represented within the smaller sects, but their presence was undoubtedly more visible. Various interpretations have been offered to explain the importance of women in such movements. While eighteenth- and nineteenth-century com-mentators shared the underlying assumptions of Max Weber's statement that women were especially receptive to 'religious movements with orgiastic emotion or hysterical aspects to them',[4] recent studies have drawn attention to more tangible considerations. Some have suggested that women were attracted into the new sects by the wider scope of activity offered to them by the concept of spiritual equality, while others have shown how the moral values of the new religious movements, including temperance, frugality, fidelity and self-improvement, had a daily relevance to women who were concerned for the physical and moral welfare of their families. Moreover, the search for motivation must also distinguish between characteristics based on wider cultural patterns and those specific to gender. For example, although accepted notions of what constituted 'natural' female behaviour helped to perpetuate ideal stereotypes, the characteristics upon which they were built, including zealous expressions of piety, excessive spirituality and emotional responses to evangelical sermons, were common to both men and women in this period. In addition, women are no more a cohesive social entity than men, and a shared gender does not in itself produce a common experience. Criteria such as social status, age and personal circumstances shape religious behaviour as they do other areas of life.

At the topmost level of society, aristocratic patronage and benevolence made an important contribution to the support and diffusion of evangelical principles both inside and outside the churches. Wives, widows and heiresses held strong positions of influence in their own locality — an influence frequently exercised on behalf of a strongly held personal faith. Their considerable financial and social advantages were frequently employed on behalf of their favourite religious organisations. The will of Lady Sophia Ward, whose conversion led to conflict with her father, the Viscount of Bangor, reflected her religious commitment, with nearly her whole property being left to religious and charitable purposes.[5] The financing of new churches or chapels of ease was an equally important outlet for aristocratic piety. Lady Arabella Denny founded the Magdalene Chapel in Dublin in 1773 which was frequented by persons of the highest social rank. For some years this chapel provided an important venue for preachers connected to Selina, Countess of Huntingdon, one of the most prominent early patrons of Calvinistic

1. K. Thomas, 'Women and the Civil War Sects', *Past and Present*, no. 13 (April 1958), pp. 42–62.
2. E.K. Brown, *Women of Mr Wesley's Methodism*, vol. 2 (Lewiston, New York: Edwin Mellen, 1984).
3. Transcript of the journal of John Cennick, Bristol Archives, Moravian Church House, London.
4. Max Weber, *Sociology of Religion* (London: Kegan Paul, 1966).
5. C.H. Crookshank, *Memorable Women of Irish Methodism in the Last Century*, 3 vols (London: Wesleyan Methodist Bookroom, 1882), pp. 151–60.

Methodism. Converted during a serious illness, the Countess joined with a 'select circle of women of high station' in prayer and scripture-reading meetings, appointed George Whitefield as her chaplain, and utilised her resources to send 'popular preachers' on evangelistic trips throughout the country. Determining that 'poor wicked Ireland' should have 'a Gospel day', she enlisted popular British evangelical preachers in the Irish cause, sending probationers as well as ministers when the supply outran the demand. She also founded a chapel in Plunkett Street in Dublin as a centre for evangelical preaching . . .

An even tighter set of social relations, based on a common ethnic identity, was evident in the Quaker movement. Although these seventeenth-century immigrants interacted widely with the wider Irish community — particularly in matters of commerce — their cultural assimilation did not extend to intermarriage. Their distinctiveness was reinforced by strict rules of dress and behaviour, with an emphasis on simplicity often taken to extremes. One young Quaker, for example, noted that her mother's objection to decoration extended to the display of images on china. Some Quakers did live in humble circumstances, and concern for the welfare of their poor was a central and recurring theme in monthly meetings, but their emphasis on literacy and education, the simplicity of their life style, and their renowned independence and industry characterised them as an upwardly mobile community which made 'a profound contribution to every aspect of commercial life in modern Ireland'.[6] The papers of Mary Leadbeater, poet, author, and daughter of a Quaker schoolmaster, reveal a social, intellectual and religious network stretching across Britain, and extending to North America. The religious visits of travelling ministers, granted certificates of 'unity and concurrence' by their local meeting, kept these groups in contact with each other. Such ministers could be of either sex, and Quaker women were also given their own separate spheres in other areas, with women's meetings at monthly, quarterly and provincial level paralleling those of the men.[7] However,

while women dealt with social and disciplinary manners concerning their own sex including the relief of the poor, widows and orphans, the good behaviour, marriage plans and dress of women and girls, the men's meeting alone had executive authority. Nevertheless, interaction between meetings and the idea of spiritual, if not executive, equality gave women important roles to play in this distinctive community.

At all levels of society, women, either individually or as part of a wider network, played a significant part in establishing links between religious groups and the communities in which they were situated. In the early days of a new religious movement, for example, success or failure was often determined by specifically practical considerations, and this was an area in which respectable, pious and independent women were especially useful. Itinerant preachers needed an introduction into the community, and a place to rest and hold meetings on their long and arduous circuits. Crookshank's *History of Methodism* abounds with examples of the support given and initiatives taken by women in introducing Methodism into the towns and villages of Ireland. In Belturbet, in 1782, Mrs Alice Dawes, a widow, the principal support of Methodism in the town, received the preachers and fitted up a room for their accommodation; the first preaching place in Armagh was rented by Mrs Russell, Mrs Isabella Maxwell and Mrs Jane Justice in 1762, and there are many examples of women inviting preachers to make use of their homes. Such women gave moral support and encouragement as well as practical aid to preachers. They also served as links between rural societies and the Methodist central leadership. Some corresponded with Wesley, for example, to comment and advise on individual preachers. In 1769, Mrs Bennis's request to Conference for the appointment of a specific itinerant to Limerick was noted by Crookshank as 'the earliest instance on record of the voice of the people being heard in connection with a preaching appointment'.

Methodism's concern to draw in those on the periphery of society, the sick, the aged and the distressed, gave official recognition to traditional female duties, and endowed them with a more tangible moral authority. Piety and respectability were more important attributes for sick visitors

6. D.H. Hempton, 'Religious Minorities', in P. Loughrey (ed.), *The People of Ireland* (Belfast: Appletree/BBC, 1988), pp. 155–68, 164.
7. Quaker Records, Public Record Office of Northern Ireland, Mic. 16.

and class leaders than finance, property or social status. The dynamics of female classes, which often seemed more durable than their male counterparts, provoked comment from many visiting itinerants, and kept the impetus going when initial enthusiasm had died down. Female prayer meetings were also noted as particularly successful examples of piety and devotion.

One Methodist historian suggests that it was as class teachers and even preachers that women really 'transcended the stereotypical roles' of attendants and listeners to become active participants,[8] and it was as preachers that their activities proved most controversial ... The concept of spiritual equality was given most expression by the Quakers, with women appearing as the first Quaker preachers in London, in the universities, in Dublin and in the American colonies. Quakers were however an ethnically distinct community. It was with the advent of Methodism that the phenomenon of women's preaching became more socially visible. Since most early Methodist preachers were not ordained, there was no official ban or prohibitive qualifications to deter female enthusiasts. Methodism's flexible structure and overriding concern to spread the gospel message gave rise to a pragmatism which deployed all methods in the interests of moral reformation. This was reflected

in Wesley's advice to aspiring female preachers which was cautious, but no different in essence from that given to men.[9] He advised Alice Cambridge, when dealing with critics, to

> Give them all honour, and obey them in all things, as far as conscience permits. But it will not permit you to be silent when God commands you to speak; yet I would have you give as little offence as possible; and therefore I would advise you not to speak at any place where a preacher is speaking near you at the same time, lest you should draw away his hearers. Also avoid the first appearance of pride or magnifying yourself.[10]

Women, like men, were therefore regarded as instruments of divine providence to meet exceptional circumstances, an interpretation confirmed by their popularity. Blind and emotional Margaret Davidson drew large crowds with the 'fervour and fluency of her witness',[11] and Alice Cambridge attracted numbers 'amounting to eight or ten thousand persons' on a tour of Ulster at the beginning of the nineteenth century.[1]

8. E.K. Brown, 'Women of Mr Wesley's Methodism'.

9. E.K. Brown, 'Women of the Word', in *Women in New Worlds*, eds H.E. Thomas and R. Skinner, 2 vols (Nashville, Tenn.: Abington Press, 1981, 1983), vol. 1, pp. 65–87.
10. C.H. Crookshank, *History of Methodism*, 3 vols (London: Woolmer, 1885–88), vol. 2, p. 31.
11. E. Smyth, *The Extraordinary Life and Christian Experience of Margaret Davidson* (Dublin, 1782).
12. C.H. Crookshank, *Memorable Women*, pp. 191–203.

MARY LEADBEATER

(1758–1826)

from:
THE ANNALS OF BALLITORE
(1766)

[The journals kept by Mary Leadbeater, née Shackleton, from 1766 to the end of her life are a detailed and vivid record of the happenings in an Irish village and Quaker settlement. Edited by her niece, Elizabeth, as *The Leadbeater Papers*, 2 vols (London: Bell and Daldy, 1862), they were subtitled *The Annals of Ballitore*. In this early record, Mary Shackleton gives a memorable picture of her aunt and of the virtues associated with Quaker piety — simplicity, concern for the welfare of the poor, frugality and independence of spirit. The undemonstrative practice of religion by the Quakers of Ballitore contrasts with the lofty and moralizing tone of the meditation, 'An Essay on Self-complacency', which is lodged in the Ballitore papers in the National Library of Ireland, MS n. 1937–9, pp. 1469–71.]

My aunt Carleton was fourteen years older than my mother, of a very lively, cheerful temper. In her youth she had been much admired, though her nose had a flatness at the upper part. Some of her neighbours being inclined to criticise, remarked that 'Debby Carleton would be a very pretty girl, but for her nose.' She happened to overhear them, and bolted upon them with the retort, 'She would be much worse without it.' The voice of envy unjustly accused her of sleeping in iron stays; for her figure was taper and shapely — 'fine by degrees and beautifully less'. The remains of her fine figure and her blooming complexion were still visible as I first remember her, and time could not destroy the animation, benevolence, and sensibility of her countenance. From early youth she was subject to ill-health, and to a nervous headache which often attacked her, confining her one day to her bed, or two if she struggled against it. When more dangerous illnesses visited her, we welcomed this headache as a sign of her recovery to usual health. But no interruption of this kind could lessen her filial attention to her aged mother. Her life had been much devoted to the care of the aged and infirm, and she frequently remarked that it seemed to be prolonged for that purpose.

She also enjoyed the happiness of saving several persons from impending death. One of these was a woman whose brutal husband in a fit of drunkenness and rage held a razor to her throat. My aunt heard her cries as she lay in bed; she ran to the window, and so effectually employed that power of persuasion which she eminently possessed, as to save the life of the unfortunate woman. Subsequently, as she was walking in Dublin, she was advised to turn back, as there was in her way a drunken woman maddened by the insults of the rabble, and throwing dirt and stones at all who came near her. My aunt, however, went on, and quickly perceived that this wretched woman was the same whom she had rescued from the fury of her husband. Calling to her by her name, she reproved her conduct, and commanded her instantly to return home. Gratitude overpowered every other emotion in the distracted creature; she dropt on her knees in the channel; imploring a blessing on her benefactress; then, rising, directly obeyed her. She saved another life by thrusting her hand into the mouth of an enraged mastiff who had seized a boy by the throat. The animal, knowing and loving her, quitted his grasp of his victim in order to avoid hurting her.

If her cares were precious to the aged, they were more so to the youth. In the science of education I never saw her surpassed. She had the happy art of nourishing confidence with restraint. She won our hearts and they were laid open to her. She made every proper allowance, granted every proper indulgence, yet she possessed much penetration, would quickly discern danger, and vigilantly guard against it. Her company and converse were as pleasing as profitable, and it is a proof of this that the young men who boarded at my father's, and who generally called her 'aunt', used to prefer sitting with her on First-day evenings while we were at meeting, which her poor health seldom permitted her to attend, to amusing themselves in other ways at a time when they were free from observation. After one of these visits I remember my aunt remarking the emotion with which Henry Leslie read to her the lamentation of Esau on being supplanted by Jacob. Henry wept and sobbed, and I'll warrant my aunt did so too, for seldom has there throbbed a more sympathizing heart.

Her limited circumstances, it would appear, forbade her indulging her natural benevolence, but she contrived to unite the pious offices of humanity with that strict economy which it behoved her to practise. She seemed to possess the gift of healing. The country resorted to her for advice. She kept a large assortment of drugs, she distilled simples, she sold to those who could afford to pay, and dispensed gratis to those who could not. In her rides she called to see or enquire for her patients. She was firm as well as tender, resisted imposition, and her foresight and presence of mind seldom deserted her. When a young woman, while out walking in Dublin with a friend of her own age, they were surprised by the appearance of a wild tumultuous mob, which they found it impossible to avoid. Her companion was ready to faint, and my aunt's terrors were perhaps little less, but she exerted herself to suppress them, and in a loud and animated tone encouraged her friend to come on; 'for,' added she, 'they are our own Liberty boys, and will not hurt us!' A huzza instantly followed this expression of confidence from the pleased multitude, who made a lane for the fortunate damsels to pass through.

My aunt got little out to religious meetings, or to meetings for discipline; her ill health and her care of the aged and youth might plead an excuse, but I never heard her plead any. Religion assumes not the same form in every character; some are called upon to fulfil its more active duties; others in retirement fulfil what is required of them. 'Let her alone,' said Elizabeth Robinson, in a meeting held at my aunt's house, 'she hath done what she could.' She commended and recommended decent pride, by which she meant abstaining from low or mean actions or company. She was not so strict in matters of dress as my mother, though she carefully avoided counter-acting her plans.

My worthy mother, cautious not to grant more liberty to her own children than to those of her husband's first wife, really granted us less; for at the time when particular distinguishing marks of plainness were put upon them, they were also put upon us, though we were several years younger than they were; and our youth rendered these distinctions much more remarkable. Our sisters as well as our aunt wished our mother to relax a little towards us in this respect, but this was a point not to be disputed, and whether it was that our situation was secluded so much from the world, or that our tastes did not yet lie in that direction, her intent was accomplished, and the fondness for dress so natural to youth was pretty much starved; nay, it became, perhaps, a matter of too much indifference to my sister and me. Yet to Friends, who profess simplicity, certainly simplicity in dress ought to belong; it is a kind of fence, and where a manifest disregard of our customs in this respect is evinced, it invites to associations inconsistent with our education, and betrays an attachment to an object unworthy to engross a rational mind.

In reading, also, my aunt was less severe than my mother. There were few if any books at that time calculated for children which combined entertainment with instruction, and there was great danger of our flying to stolen gratifications in this way without judgement or discrimination, had not my mother possessed a fondness for history, which she encouraged in us, and had not my aunt indulged us now and then with books of entertainment. The worst of this was, that the book was clapped under the cushion of her chair when my mother appeared. I had, by my aunt's permission, a collection of ballads containing 'The Babes in the Wood', 'Chevy Chase', 'Pennyworth of Wit', and others of equal respectability — but the very word ballad was a word of disgrace. At one time I stood at my aunt Fuller's gate with this favourite volume in my hand, when I saw my mother approaching; I ran in terrified to hide my book, and my mother rebuked me afterwards for not running to meet her.

My aunt kept her house neat, and was active in her domestic concerns. Being well skilled in the science of cookery, her little dinners were very comfortable. She perfectly understood the roasting of a pig or a hare. My father was always invited on these occasions (my mother made it a point not to dine abroad) and his conviviality and enjoyment of the little repast heightened the general satisfaction. My aunt's patients frequently brought her a present of a hare; this she concealed lest they should incur the aspersion of poaching, and it became a standing joke that my father asked who was the donor, and my aunt refused to tell. On one of these occasions my sister Margaret, his eldest daughter, delighted him by a remark which was frequently quoted afterwards, 'Here are the hare and many friends.'

AN ESSAY ON SELF-COMPLACENCY

The high opinion which we may entertain of ourselves is so seldom corroborated by that of the world in general, that we should do well to seek out surer sources of gratification; for self sets a bar between us and that kindly intercourse which naturally attracts man to man.

Children delight in the company of children and it is generally by the example of their seniors that these passions are strengthened which loosen the sacred bond of affection and teach them to give in to their own wills and wishes.

Let us permit our hearts to overflow with love to our fellow creatures, beholding them with ourselves destined to a terminable existence in this life and subject to the trials which attend our short sojourn here. Let love be the principle of our actions. God is love, and those that dwell in him dwell in love. We sadly deceive ourselves if our religion is not founded on this basis. Religion has no other foundation. We are only happy while we cherish this feeling, unhappy only when we renounce it.

It is our support through the trials of this life — our surest hope of a better, it is the firmest armour against temptation, it destroys self-complacency. It teaches us to do unto others as we would that they should unto us. He who is thus disposed neither envies nor despises the lot of another; the gifts bestowed upon him he receives as benefits, not as rewards; he submits to trials as to the chastisements of him who doth not afflict willingly and feels it incumbent on him to promote the welfare of all within his influence. How sweetly flows the cement of such a life. How pure the stream and how gloriously does it unite with the ocean of eternal rest.

LADY ANNE DAWSON

(1733–69)

from:
LETTER TO LADY LOUISA CLAYTON (1769)

[This is the last letter of Lady Anne Dawson, written to her sister, Lady Louisa Clayton, on 13 February 1769. Lady Anne died two weeks later, on 1 March 1769. According to her sister, Lady Anne's 'piety was exemplary, even from her earliest youth', and was manifested in her charities and in her resignation in the face of her daughter's death, as well as in outward observances such as regular fasting. The Townley Hall papers are lodged in the National Library of Ireland, NLI MS 11,886. This letter and Lady Clayton's account of her sister's death are located on pp. 48–61.]

13 February 1769

I have, my dearest, been declining the whole winter and now believe I am not very far from being removed out of this world, and I trust in the mercies of my gracious God, thro' the mediation of my dear Redeemer, to everlasting happiness with him. But my dearest, join with me in praises for his gentle and most merciful manner of withdrawing me, and consider the blessing of the change. You have my constant prayers, that it may not hurt you, nor the dear child.[1] Oh my dear, if in those blessed regions, where I trust I am going, I meet my darling child,[2] and that we are permitted to do so, sure we shall (according to your request) attend to watch over you, and our dear friends here . . . And now my dearest sister, adieu, may every happiness attend you and yours, particularly the peace of God, to guide you in the ways of his holy religion, that so you may be prepared for the time I am now come to, and find it an easy and comfortable passage, as blessed by his infinite goodness, I have hitherto done, and Oh! God, grant (that once over) we may have a joyful and glorious meeting never to part again. My own unworthiness, I have the deepest sense of, but my hope is pardon from my God, thro' the mediation of my dear Redeemer, and I trust firmly in his merits I shall receive it, which enables me to look forward with most pleasing and glorious expectations; all this is the gift of my good God, for which all praise and glory be to him. Adieu once more my dearest sister and friend. Oh, love God to whom in the unity of the ever blessed Trinity be all honor, glory, love and obedience now and for ever more.

1. Her son, Richard.
2. Her daughter, Henrietta, who died c. 1767 at the age of eleven.

LADY ELIZABETH FOWNES

(d. 1778)

from:
LETTER TO SIR WILLIAM
FOWNES (*c.* 1778)

[The letter quoted below was addressed by Lady Elizabeth (Betty) Fownes to her husband, Sir William Fownes of Woodstock, County Kilkenny. It is undated, but was possibly written in 1778, the year in which Lady Betty's niece, Sarah Ponsonby, who had been living at Woodstock, ran away with Lady Eleanor Butler. Their elopement precipitated a family crisis, during which it emerged that Sir William, in anticipation of his wife's death, had made improper advances to his niece. In fact, Lady Betty survived her husband, but only by a short time; he died in June 1778, and Lady Betty three weeks later. This letter, in the possession of Miss Katharine Kenyon, is reproduced in Elizabeth Mavor, *The Ladies of Llangollen* (Harmondsworth, Middlesex: Penguin Books, 1973), p. 37.]

My dear Sir Wm, the greatest grief I have in leaving this world is parting with you and the thoughts of your sorrow for me. Don't grieve my dear Sir Wm, I am, I trust in God, going to be happy. You have my sincere prayers and thanks for your tenderness to me and good behaviour to my dear child. May God grant you happiness in her. If you marry again, I wish you much happiness. If I ever offended you forgive me, I have never meant any offence. I have always meant to be a good wife and mother and hope you think me so. As to my funeral, I hope you'll allow me to be buried as I like, which is this: when the women about me are sure I am dead, I would be carried to the church and kept out of ground two days and nights, four women to sit up with me, to each woman give five pound. I would have twenty pound laid out in clothes for the poor people, in all forty. Nobody to be at my funeral but my own poor, who I think will be sorry for me. If Nelly be with me at the time of my death, give her fifty pound, she deserves it much. Take care of yourself (live and do all the good you can) and may God almighty give you as peaceful and happy an end as I think I shall have.

THEODOSIA BLACHFORD

(1744–1817)

from:
AN ACCOUNT OF MRS
BLACHFORD COPIED FROM
A MANUSCRIPT IN HER OWN
HANDWRITING (*c.* 1777)

[As an intelligent and serious-minded young woman, Theodosia Tighe took little pleasure in the fashionable Dublin society in which her family moved. Deeply religious, at the age of nineteen she experienced what she regarded as a spiritual awakening, after which she resolved to dedicate her life to piety and good works. In 1770, reluctantly, according to herself, she married Reverend William Blachford. Following his death in 1773, she devoted herself to the upbringing of her two children and to philanthropic projects, such as the Female Orphan House and a House of Refuge for unemployed and homeless young women. She joined the Methodist Society in about 1777, becoming one of the leading figures in the Irish organization; she was described by John Wesley as 'one of our jewels'. This account of her discovery of Methodism is from a manuscript in her own handwriting, found among her papers after her death. The Wicklow papers are lodged in the National Library of Ireland, NLI MS 4810.]

When death separated me from my poor husband, my hopes were animated that I would now indeed devote myself to God, and the happy state in which I saw him die, I considered not only as an unspeakable mercy on account of my affection towards him, but as a token that God did indeed regard the supplication of my heart. But alas! I was soon convinced how evil and bitter a thing it is to depart from God, and felt the horrors of being deprived of all temporal, and unqualified for spiritual consolations. Months and years passed away and I only found my corruptions gaining strength and my hopes of peace disappointed. My natural evil tempers of passion, pride and impatience showed themselves in dreadful forms, yet still I held fast my hope in Christ, tho' I could see so little fruit of my faith, that I knew I had good reason to question the reality of it. In this state of mind I fell in with the Methodists. Their hymns were adapted to my heart, tho' their lives did not tally with my ideas of Christian morality, yet when I looked on the hourly transgressions of my life I did not dare to indulge my disposition to censure them. Mr Brooke's[1] friendship has proved an almost daily relief and a precious balm to my soul, yet has often been embittered, principally owing to my own jealous suspicions and the eager desire of consolation and indulgence, as well as spiritual profit from his friendship. This makes me easily offended at any instances of his disregard and still more hurt by anything that I consider a defect in him. I *cannot* doubt, but that God, in much mercy, raised him up to me as a friend and a guide, and indeed before I ever saw his face it was for months impressed upon my mind that he would be a blessing to me. My connection with him, and thro' him, with the Methodists, I daily feel to be such, yet not in the degree I might

1. Probably Henry Brooke (d. 1806), a prominent member of the Dublin Methodist Society.

hope. This indeed is certain, that that violence of temper which, in the commencement of it was my besetting sin, and had daily effects on my conduct, as well as my peace, has been in a great measure subdued and it so often mocked my strength and repeated resolutions, that I should be very unbelieving not to attribute this to the power of God. Besides that for these last two months, I plainly feel on those occasions that most excite its impetuosity, God has enabled me, by a power evidently not my own, to fall from it. The eagerness of my spirit has also, within the last two months in some degree subsided, yet still affords me perpetual cause of lamentation and often carried me away (seemingly) in spite of myself thro' my own unwatchfulness. Yet on the whole, I bless God, for the comparative tranquillity of my spirit and find happy fruits of it in all my avocations. My chief distress, at present, is, the general barrenness of my prayers and inability to pour out my soul to God as I would wish, my imagination at such times, being occupied, most commonly, with the veriest trifles. Forms of prayer I have long laid aside and though I cannot bring myself to reassume them I sometimes doubt whether I have done well in rejecting them. In the avocations of the day I find that my heart retains a general sense of the presence of God and a desire to please him and I find his loving spirit ever ready to admonish me of evil. I deceive myself if I deliberately seek felicity but in conforming to the will of God, or indulge myself in any consolations but those which appear to lead to him — as in the performance of my duty and my intercourse with those I believe to be his children, yet in both of these I find a mingling of all my natural tempers, which often brings me into condemnation. When conscious of transgressing the law of truth and love I am always pained, tho' not so sensibly or deeply as I would wish, which shows me the lamentable hardness of my heart.

CHARLOTTE BROOKE

(1740–93)

from:
RELIQUES OF IRISH POETRY
(1816)

[Charlotte Brooke was devoted to her father, the author Henry Brooke, who encouraged her interest in Celtic antiquities, as well as her study of Irish literature and language, which led to her great work, *Reliques of Irish Poetry* (1789). Henry Brooke was sympathetic to Methodism, and Charlotte, too, was clearly drawn to the movement, although not herself a member. In these extracts from letters to an unidentified friend, Miss T——, Brooke describes the impact on her of her father's death and of other trials in her life, and the comfort which she finds in religion. In the final extract, while denying any tendency to mysticism, she lists the devotional works on which she depends for spiritual sustenance, particularly William Law's 'incomparable treatise on . . . the spirit of prayer' which 'I have just now finished (for, I suppose, the tenth or twelfth time)'.[1] The extracts are located in the 'Memoir' by Aaron Crossly Seymour, prefixed to the 1816 edition of *Reliques of Irish Poetry.*]

LETTERS TO MISS T——

15 May 1792

I have ever lived but for my father . . . Oh, may we never be divided! — May we roll together to that sea 'from whence we never have return'! In life, my Soul is his — in death I trust it shall join him! . . . I am indeed incapable of any other love — my heart was *intended* for that alone, and nature has not nor ever will have *room* for any other one. I see none on earth who resemble him, and therefore heaven alone can become his rival in my breast.

---

1. William Law (1686–1761), author and philanthropist. His works included *A Serious Call to a Devout and Holy Life* and *The Grounds and Reasons of Christian Regeneration.*

[Undated]

The remembrance of my own sorrows — of my own escape from despair, enables me, with

peculiar interest, to feel and to tremble for your situation. — Deprived of my father, of my brother, of my fortune, and of my health; disappointed in friendship, and betrayed in trust — my affairs ruined by those in whom I most confided,[1] and the best and dearest affections of my heart torn up, as it were, by the very roots! — My mind, like your own, was, for a time too much pressed down by anguish to lift itself to God, and when it *did* rise, alas, it was only to murmur, and to vent the complaints of distraction and despair. — Like you, I thought myself singled out for suffering, and that, not to despond would be not to feel. On this brink (I do believe) of madness, did the Divine Hand arrest me! — showed me the precipice into which my soul was plunging, and gave me, in resignation, an asylum from woe . . . My father, my brother, are as much lost to me now, as when I mourned them with such distraction: the ingratitude and treachery of those in whom I trusted, has not proved an illusion: it is still the same in itself and in its effects upon my fortune, as it was when it tore every fibre of my heart. My health, though not as bad as formerly, is in a fragile state; and my fortune, though not utterly lost, is still no more than what others would account as nothing. — Yet, notwithstanding this, I am happy! — Yes, O my gracious God! with humble and joyful gratitude, I own that I am blest as this earth can make me! — that if a sigh heaves, or a tear flows from me now, it is only from the grief that others are not equally happy with myself.

---

1. Brooke is referring to problems associated with the publication of her late father's *Works.*

[Undated]

You fear to be a mystic. — My friend, this is as groundless a fear, as that of a girl learning to spell, apprehending she should thereby become a *learned lady*. I have been reading Mr Law these fifteen years; and I am *not* a mystic, nor perhaps ever shall be. That knowledge which is 'too wonderful and excellent for me', I leave with women, untouched; and concern myself only with such as I find to be level to my comprehension, and necessary to my state. The mystic writers lead more directly to Christ than any other; and therefore it is that I read them: they place the reader with Mary, at the foot of Jesus, and make his divine language be heard in its own genuine truth and efficacy.

MARY TIGHE

(1772–1810)

from:
JOURNAL (1787–1802)

[Brought up by her mother, Theodosia Blachford, as a Methodist, Mary Tighe was trained from childhood to the relentless self-examination demanded by evangelical religion, and was deeply troubled by the conflict between the strict dictates of her faith and her desire for worldly success. In 1793 she married her cousin Henry Tighe and moved with him to London. The publication in 1795 of her poem *Psyche* brought critical acclaim, but her journal for this period reveals deep unhappiness, a sense of spiritual emptiness, and a preoccupation with, even a wish for, death, contrasting with the conventional piety of the earlier entries. The failure of her marriage and the apparent incompatibility between her religion and her way of life clearly contributed to her depression, but her state of mind was probably also affected by the consumption from which she was already suffering, and which led to her death in 1810. A copy of her journal, containing occasional entries for the period 1787–1802, is located in the Wicklow papers, NLI MS 4810.]

16 February 1787
When I look back and consider my past life (short as it has been), I see in it such an astonishing medley as causes me at times not to know what to think. Some part of my life I have been immersed in sin, and as I may say in the very jaws of the wicked one, at others rejoicing in the belief that I was in the favour of God and certainly whether I was in that deceived or not, it was the happiest part of my life. At other periods, I have been in a state which I cannot otherwise describe than by saying that I was asleep . . .

21 August 1790
A year has now elapsed since I have written anything here. It would indeed be impossible to relate how my heart has been since affected, but this to my eternal shame I must own, that thou, oh my God, hast not been in all my thoughts, and indeed scarcely in any . . . Sometimes my heart has been distracted by vain pleasures, false hopes, foolish disappointments, idle pursuits, trifling sorrows, useless alarms and childish vexations. Alas, my thoughts are more intent upon worldly knowledge, worldly fame and worldly pleasure than upon that knowledge which can alone be useful to my immortal soul. But Lord! shall I live ever thus? Return unto thyself my heart.

4 October 1793
My soul draws back with terror and awe at the idea of the event which is to take place tomorrow.[1] Oh my God! let it not be unattended with thy blessing.

4 January 1794
Unhappy in myself, offensive to others, desponding in my heart. I could have wished to have escaped from scenes my soul is weary of. Aye, but to die and go we know not where. There is the rub. Solitude at least is preferable.

25 March 1796
I have many serious thoughts this day, and indeed for some time past, about my way of life, or rather state of mind. I begin clearly to discern that I cannot serve God and Mammon. That the latter is my idol, can I deny to myself? What remains is alarming, and what is the consequence of not serving God? Yet I still cling to pleasure which I perceive gliding delusively from my

1. Mary Blachford married Henry Tighe on 5 October 1793.

grasp, and I seek to persuade the accusing spirit within me that God is surely too just to punish with eternal death the weakness of a being he has not created strong, but in vain. The torments I endure are at times terrible, and I have not power to pray. Oh why was I created?

28 March 1798
How long shall my soul be agitated by vain dreams? What is it that captivates my better judgement and thus subjects me to the cruel stings of disappointed hopes — hopes empty as vanity itself? What is it I desire, or what illusion is it I regret? Oh! that my hopes were fixed where true joy only is to be found. Shepherd of Israel, dost thou sleep and suffer thy wandering sheep to be devoured by the wolves of the forest? Wilt thou not have compassion on the flock of thy pasture and go in search of the one unhappy stray lamb?

26 March 1800
The finest day that ever shone and my heart felt some of that delirious sensibility which it is the property of spring alone to bestow. But how deadened all my sensations are. Within these two years, I am scarce the same being which once hailed with animation the pleasures of life.

28 April 1800
I spent a miserable morning. Gloomy thoughts oppressed me and I vainly sought for refuge in philosophy or in my feeble attempts at devotion. How often in the gloom of my soul did I say, how blest are they who sleep to wake no more! Oh my God! how often have I desired to be as the insensible dust and asked my Creator why I was called into existence if I have not the power of obeying his supreme will? Oh no, I feel that his love is beyond my thoughts!

DOROTHEA JOHNSON

(1732–1817)

from:
THE MEMOIRS OF MRS D. JOHNSON (1818)

[Dorothea Johnson converted to Methodism in 1757 and became a prominent figure in the Methodist Society in Dublin. In 1784 she moved with her husband, John Johnson, a Methodist preacher, to Lisburn, County Antrim. Both in Dublin and in Lisburn she had charge of several classes and bands, and helped to promote Methodist growth, and when John Wesley visited Lisburn in 1785 he noted the liveliness of the local congregation, 'owing chiefly to the good providence of God in bringing sister Johnson here'. Her *Memoirs*, including a journal which she began in 1771 and kept intermittently until her death in 1817, make clear the importance of female fellowship within early Methodism. In the following letter to Miss A—— S—— Donaghadee, County Down, dated August 1803, Johnson describes a meeting.]

M—— B—— said she was happy, E—— J—— had power to believe, widow W——n rejoiced in saving faith, and A—— McM——, who had long attended preaching and had latterly joined our class with deep solemnity, declared she had found peace . . . Betty S—— forgot her crutch, through the joy of her soul, went some way without it; is not this the dawn of a revival?

[Johnson's journal was intended primarily as a record of her spiritual state and repeatedly stresses the centrality of her faith and its superiority to all earthly affections.]

Jan. 5, 1790: Numberless instances of divine love and favour do I neglect to note; they are repeated every day. Since last I wrote, all is sunshine from him that makes my day. The first of this year, I renewed my covenant, with many others, in the Preaching-House, it was a solemn hour. Once more I gave myself unreservedly to him, in marriage covenant, humbly depending on his Almighty arm for assistance to fulfil my solemn vow, and believe it was ratified in Heaven.

[The following, the final entry in Johnson's journal, was written six months before her death on 23 July 1817.]

19 January 1817: I would render unfeigned thanks and praise to the adorable trinity, my *ever* gracious God, who hath blessed me with mercies without number. The 15th of last month, I was 84 years in my pilgrimage. I am blessed with the full enjoyment of all my faculties. Jesus my *all in all,* I am always blessed with his *peaceful presence*; my victory over satan is daily more and more complete, he keeps me in my sleep from that grand adversary, who pursued me with mortal hatred, he has shut the door of my heart against his fiery darts, he gives me peace in my family, protection from the wicked, a great measure of health, a competency of this world's treasure, and best of all, a constant witness of his indwelling spirit, that I am his child. I feel no inward corruption, and I have strong confidence that he will, through the blood and righteousness of my Redeemer, bring me where he is, his hand graciously holding me up in death — to him be all the glory, Amen.

[Johnson wrote a number of short poems on religious topics, among them the following, which refers to the concept, central to Methodist teaching, of a second birth.]

Ye must be born again

Say heaven born muse what means the second
   birth,
Through which we pass, nor taste the second
   death?
The holy spirit sows the seed, it grows,
And brings forth fruit, thro' many painful throws.
New-born the child can Abba Father call,
The heart is love and God is all in all.

ELIZA BENNIS

(1725–1802)

from:
DIARY, 1764–79

[Following her conversion to Methodism in 1749, Eliza Bennis played a leading part in the Methodist Society in her native Limerick and later in Waterford. She carried on a lengthy correspondence with John Wesley, to whom she conveyed the wishes of the membership, justifying her 'officiousness' by citing her ardour for the faith. Wesley, for his part, relied on her judgement and authorized her interventions in the affairs of local congregations. 'Be not idle,' he encouraged her, 'neither give way to voluntary humility . . . You were not sent to Waterford for nothing, but to "strengthen the things that remain".' In the following extract from her diary, Bennis describes her first encounter with Methodism and subsequent spiritual development. The letter to John Wesley dated 11 March 1766 describes her reasons for drawing up this 'experience in writing' and the results of doing so. This letter and Bennis's diary can be found in St George's Methodist Archives, Philadelphia.]

16 October 1765
I was very young when the spirit of God began to strive in me. In my childhood I had many drawings which then pass'd unheed'd by me. When I was about ten or eleven years old, I threw aside the forms of prayer which I had learn'd and pray'd extempore when alone . . . I was often given to see myself a sinner and to tremble under the wrath of God, but these convictions were not lasting . . . I was very fond of reading and wou'd sometimes read books of divinity for want of others . . . I was I believe about thirteen or fourteen years old when Mr Allen's Alarm came to my hands, this was the first alarm my conscience got . . .[1] I have often thought how comfortable a thing a Christian friend wou'd be to whom I might declare all that pass'd in my heart . . . but did not then ever expect to meet with such. In a little time my father died, and I married. I had still continual stings of conscience. I saw I was not right, yet saw that I was not as bad as many . . . [In 1749 Robert Swindells, the first Methodist preacher to visit Limerick, passed by

1. Joseph Alleine (1634–68) was a Puritan author and evangelist, associated with John Wesley's grandfather, and persecuted for his beliefs. His *Alarm to the Unconverted*, first published in 1672, was hugely popular.

Bennis's house on his way to the Castle Gate, where he was to preach.] I saw Mr Swindel . . . pass by my door with a great mob after him. Upon my enquiring who he was, they told me he was one of the people called Swadler, of whome I had heard some [? random] accounts, but had no desire or interest to hear him preach, being tenatious of my own church . . . This was the 17th day of March 1749, and the first time that any of those preachers had come here . . . in the morning about ten o'clock. I did not go to hear him, nor would my pride suffer me to mix with such a rabble, but afterward hearing a great account of the sermon I resolv'd to go in the evening . . . which I did and was much affected . . . and was determin'd I wou'd not miss another sermon whilst he staid in town, which was about three days . . . in about a month after another preacher came to town, and finding many here willing to receive the word, they soon establish'd a Society of which I was determin'd to be one . . . I was one of the first that joyn'd. Indeed I did it in much fear and trembling being perplex'd by various reports . . . concerning the wickedness and cunning of these men. But I had set a resolution that I wou'd not believe any report, but wou'd hear and see for my self . . . I was as a sparrow upon the house top, not one of all my family or relations seeing the necessity of being born again, therefore was obliged to suffer much on this account. [However, Bennis continued to experience doubt and uneasiness,] till in the year 1762 Mr Wesley came to this town, and again reviv'd the doctrine of holiness of heart . . . I found power to wrestle and strive with God in prayer, and in a few weeks after whilst I was at prayer the Lord did heal my back slidings, giving me power to believe in him, and a steadfast assurance of my acceptance through Christ.

from:
LETTER TO JOHN WESLEY, 11 MARCH 1766

Revd and dear sir,

It is not indeed want of love that hinder'd me from writing to you before now but upon an impartial enquiry I think it appears to be in truth want of simplicity but hope it shall not be so for the future.

When you were last in Limerick, my state was a mixture of happiness and distress. I found an entire deliverance from that natural propensity to evil which for many years before had made me miserable. I had the clear testimony of my heart being cleans'd from sin. But finding many things in my self which I did not expect in that state, I gave way to fearfulness and unbelief (not wilfully, but ignorantly) till God withdrew this evidence from me, but did not withdraw his grace. His work on my heart was still the same and sometimes shone by its own light, but then cou'd not satisfie. I was often under a painfull uncertainty concerning my state which was very grivious to me. This I say was my state when you were last here. I was indeed happy. Yet the fear of sin being still lurking in my heart pain'd my very soul. I now saw and bemoan'd my loss, cou'd not be satisfied till I had again receiv'd the testimony of God's spirit that my heart was cleans'd from sin. Yet my ignorance and my carnal understanding often block'd up my way. At this time I came acquainted with the master of a Dutch vessel which then lay waiting for a cargo. He was a Godly man and had a deep work of grace wrought on his heart. The Lord did often bless us together and gave me much light in speaking to him. After some time he requested that I wou'd give him my experience in writing, which I was backward in for two reasons. First, least I through my ignorance shou'd only darken what I wou'd attempt to explain. Secondly, if I wrote my experience I must do it honestly and must confess that I had lost the witness of my sanctification, and this might appear to him (who was not clear concerning this work) as tho' I had only deceiv'd my selfe in this matter, and lessen the work in his [? eyes]. These considerations kept me back for some time, till he repeated his request which I was afraid to refuse least I shou'd offend God, not knowing what he might intend by this, yet not forward in doing it for the above reasons, tho' making it a matter of prayer. I spoke to a Christian friend concerning it who advis'd me to write, saying perhaps God may approve of your doing it by restoring the witness of his spirit before you have done. I then determin'd to do it in such a manner as God shou'd enable me, laving the event to him, and found my self more than ever simple in his hands, yet earnestly wrestling for the witness, when on the 30 of September last, whilst I was reading a letter I had receiv'd from Brother Dillon, I was struck with a sentence in the letter and enabled to believe and found in that moment the testimony of God's spirit, that my heart was cleans'd. Satan did strive to rob me of it, but the Lord did enable me to keep my hold. Indeed, it was oft times with strong graplings and many fears, but blessed be my God, he does support my feebleness and causes me to rest in him. Since then God has enabled me more than ever to renounce my own wisdom and attend more simply to the teachings of his spirit, and in doing so I find my way wonderfully clear'd, many dificulties solv'd and the nature of this work made more intelligible to me, so that I am enabled to go on more steadily and more comfortably.

JOHN WESLEY AND ELIZA BENNIS
(1703–91)   (1725–1802)

from:
CHRISTIAN CORRESPONDENCE: A COLLECTION OF LETTERS WRITTEN BY THE LATE REV JOHN WESLEY, AND SEVERAL METHODIST PREACHERS IN CONNEXION WITH HIM, TO THE LATE MRS ELIZA BENNIS, WITH HER ANSWERS (1842)

[The following exchange of letters between Bennis and John Wesley demonstrates Bennis's active and assertive role within Munster Methodism during its formative years. From *Christian Correspondence* (Dublin, 1842), letters XV–XXI, pp. 30–43.]

John Wesley to Eliza Bennis, Whitehaven, 12 April 1770
How does the work of God go on at Limerick? Does the select society meet constantly: and do you speak freely to each other? What preachers are with you *now*? Do *you* converse frankly and openly with them, without any shyness or reserve? Do you find your own soul prosper?

Eliza Bennis to John Wesley, Waterford, 20 May 1770
Brother Saunderson[1] is now in Limerick; the select band meet regular, and a few have been lately added to it: they meet openly and freely, but mostly in a complaining state ... Brother Bourke[2] is on this circuit, the people here go on at a poor rate, not do I think it is likely to be otherwise until they have a stationed preacher; they desired me to mention this.

1. Hugh Saunderson was sent to Ireland by Wesley in 1768 and after serving in the north was appointed to Limerick in 1770.
2. Richard Bourke became a preacher in 1765, visited Limerick in 1769 and was appointed there in 1770.

John Wesley to Eliza Bennis, Yarm, 13 June 1770
How is this with respect to Waterford? They would, and they would not. I sent two preachers to that circuit — why did they not keep them? WL wrote word that there was neither employment nor maintenance for two, and therefore wished leave to return to England. Let me hear more from *you* on this matter. If you can guard brother S against pride, and the applause of *well-meaning* people, he will be a happy man, and a useful labourer. I hope brother M has not grown cold. Stir up the gift of God which is in you!

Eliza Bennis to John Wesley, Limerick,
8 July 1770
The people [at Waterford] are poor, and think the
expense of a preacher's horse and family more
than they can well bear; but if it were possible to
let them have a single preacher resident in the
city, or even to exchange monthly with the circuit
preacher . . . I think it might answer a good end.
As yet the circuit is best able to bear expenses;
indeed I feel much for the city society — a
handful of poor simple souls, that need every
support and encouragement. Dear Sir, I hope you
will not think me too presumptuous in dictating,
but I find my soul knit to these poor sheep. Sister
Ann S—— is lately married to brother L—— of
Clonmel. Brother Bourke and I made up this
match, and I think it is the Lord's doing: she is as
usual all alive to God, and I trust will be a means
of saving his soul. Brother Bourke, at my request,
has taken Clonmel into the circuit . . . I have to
request your forgiveness for my officiousness. If
you disapprove, it can be re-altered.

John Wesley to Eliza Bennis, Ashby,
27 July 1770
Will you ever find in yourself any thing but
unfitness? Otherwise, your salvation would be of
works, not of grace . . . If the preachers on
Waterford circuit had punctually adhered to the
plan which I fixed, the horse [for the preacher]
would have been no burden; but the misfortune
is, every dunce is wiser than me: however, at your
desire I will send a second preacher in to the
circuit after Conference; but the preachers must
change regularly . . . your alteration of the
circuit, so as to take in poor dead Clonmel, I
much approve, and hope sister L—— will be
made a blessing to the few there.

Eliza Bennis to John Wesley, Waterford,
7 May 1771
I just now received a satisfactory letter from
brother S. He says he wrote to you. The Lord has
begun a great revival in Dublin, and I trust he
will carry it on . . . Since you left this, brother C
has preached regularly . . . The day you left town,
I met the women's bands; the Lord did
wonderfully bless us together, and I find my
heart closely united to them. Last Monday I went
to the room, but none of them came; I do find it
a heavy cross.

John Wesley to Eliza Bennis, Limerick,
15 May 1771
If your sisters miss you any more, there is but one
way — *you must go or send after them*. Be not idle,
neither give way to voluntary humility. You were
not sent to Waterford for nothing; but to
'strengthen the things that remain'.

Biographies/Bibliographies

Maureen Wall

LIFE. Maureen McGeehin was born on 27 June 1918 in Seacor,
Glenswilly, County Donegal. She received her early education in
Treankeel school near Breenagh, where her parents were teachers.
There, with her seven sisters and one surviving brother, she was
introduced to local history and song through the teaching of her father,
Peader McGeehin, a native Irish-speaker. At thirteen she went to an all-
Irish college, Colaiste Brighde, Falcarragh, as a boarder, and from there
to Carysfort Training College in Dublin. She studied for her degree in
history and Irish in University College Dublin, and eventually
completed her Master's thesis in eighteenth-century Irish history,
concentrating on the 1770s and the relaxation of the Penal Laws. Her
health had suffered from a long bout of tuberculosis, and she began
working in the Folklore Commission in Dublin as a secretary–typist.
She married a colleague, the Folklore Commission's librarian, Tom
Wall. Invited to join the staff of the history department in University
College Dublin, she rapidly established herself as a foremost lecturer
and researcher. The importance of her contribution to eighteenth-
century Irish history was immediately recognized. She also wrote and
taught on a wide variety of topics in nineteenth- and twentieth-century
Irish history. She died suddenly in June 1972.

CHIEF WRITINGS. *The Penal Laws* (Dundalk: Dundealgan Press,
1961); 'The Catholics of the Towns and the Quarterage Dispute in
Eighteenth-Century Ireland', *Irish Historical Studies*, 1952; 'The Rise of
a Catholic Middle Class in Eighteenth-Century Ireland', *Irish Historical
Studies*, 1958; 'The Catholic Merchants, Manufacturers and Traders of
Dublin, 1778–1782', *Reportorium Novum*, 1960; 'The United Irish
Movement', in J.L. McCracken (ed.), *Historical Studies*, vol. 5 (London:
Routledge and Kegan Paul, 1966); 'The Age of the Penal Laws
(1691–1778)', in T. W. Moody and F. X. Martin (eds), *The Course of
Irish History* (Cork: Mercier Press, 1967); 'Catholics in Economic Life',
in L.M. Cullen (ed.), *The Formation of the Irish Economy* (Cork: Mercier
Press, 1968); 'The Background to the Rising: From 1914 until the Issue
of the Countermanding Order on Easter Saturday, 1916', in
K.B. Nowlan (ed.), *The Making of 1916* (Dublin: Stationery Office,
1969); 'The Plans and the Countermand: The Country and Dublin', in
ibid.; B. O'Cuiv (ed.), *The Doctrine of the Irish Language* (Dublin:
Stationery Office, 1969); 'County Donegal in 1845', *Donegal Annual*,
vol. 9, no. 2; J.T. Gilbert (ed.), *Documents Relating to Ireland, 1795–1804*,
Introduction by Maureen Wall (Shannon: Irish University Press, 1970,
rpr. of 1st edition of 1893); 'Glenswilly', a talk on her native glen given
by Maureen Wall on 17 June 1969, for the first Glenswilly Festival (150
copies printed for private circulation, 1973); 'The Whiteboys', in
T.D. Williams (ed.), *Secret Societies in Ireland* (Dublin: Gill and
Macmillan, 1973).

BIOGRAPHY AND CRITICISM. *Catholic Ireland in the Eighteenth
Century: Collected Essays of Maureen Wall*, edited by George O'Brien,
with a memoir by Tom Dunne (Dublin: Geography Publications,
1989).

Richard Challoner

LIFE. Born at Lewes, Sussex, in 1691, Challoner became a Catholic at the age of thirteen. He was educated at the English College in Douai, where he was ordained and taught for a number of years before joining the London mission in 1730. A noted preacher, controversialist and prolific author, Challoner was appointed Bishop of London in 1758, and on a number of occasions was threatened with prosecution under the penal legislation. He died in London on 12 January 1781.

CHIEF WRITINGS. *The Catholick Christian* (1737); *The Garden of the Soul* (c. 1740); *Memoirs of Missionary Priests* (1741–2); *The Rheims New Testament and the Douay Bible with Annotations*, 5 vols. (1749–50); *Considerations upon Christian Truths and Christian Duties* (1753); *The Life of St Theresa* (1757); *The Devotion of Catholicks to the Blessed Virgin* (1764).

Nano Nagle

LIFE. Honora (Nano) Nagle was born at Ballygriffin near Mallow in County Cork in 1718, the eldest of seven children of Garret Nagle and his wife Anne Matthew. Nagle's family were wealthy and well connected. While young she was sent to France to be educated in a convent and returned to Ireland on the death of her father in 1746. She lived in Dublin for a while and then went back to France with the intention of entering a convent. However, instead she was advised to return to Ireland and in about 1854 she opened her first poor school in Cork city. By 1786 she had opened seven schools using money supplied to her by a wealthy uncle. She invited the French Ursuline Order to take over her schools in Cork which they did from 1771. However, the Ursulines followed the rule of enclosure and could not venture into the Cork streets to attend to the poor schools Nagle had established. Between 1771 and 1775 Nagle moved towards setting up her own religious congregation to educate the poor. The new sisterhood was called the Sisters of the Charitable Instruction of the Sacred Heart of Jesus, later to become the Presentation Order. Nagle died in Cork on 26 April 1784.

BIOGRAPHY AND CRITICISM. Rev. W. Hutch DD, *Nano Nagle: Her Life and Labours* (Dublin: McGlashan and Gill, 1875); T.J. Walsh, *Nano Nagle and the Presentation Sisters* (Dublin: M. H. Gill and Son, 1959); M. Raphael Consedine PBVM, *Listening Journey* (Victoria, Australia: Presentation Sisters, 1983).

David Hempton

LIFE. Born in Belfast in 1952. Educated at Sullivan Upper in Hollywood, County Down, at Queen's University Belfast, and at St Andrew's Univesity, Scotlans. Professor of modern history in Queen's University Belfast 1997–2001, he is currently professor of biblical and historical studies and church history at Boston University, Chestnut Hill, Massachussets.

CHIEF WRITINGS. (with Myrtle Hill) *Evangelical Protestants in Ulster Society, 1740–1890* (London: Routledge, 1992); *Religion and Political Culture in Britain and Ireland* (Cambridge: Cambridge University Press, 1996).

Myrtle Hill

LIFE. Born in Belfast in 1950. Graduate of Queen's University Belfast and was junior research fellow at Institute of Irish Studies, Queen's University Belfast, 1986–7; awarded Ph.D. in history in 1987 and appointed to university staff in 1992 in Queen's University; currently director of the Centre for Women's Studies in the School of Sociology and Social Policy.

CHIEF WRITINGS. (with David Hempton) *Evangelical Protestants in Ulster Society, 1740–1890* (London: Routledge, 1992); (editor with Raymond Gillespie) *Sources and Resources in Local History* (Belfast: Institute of Irish Studies, 1998); (with Vivienne Pollock) *Women of Ireland: Image and Experience, c. 1880–1920* (Belfast: Blackstaff Press, 1993; rpr. 1999).

Mary Leadbeater

LIFE. Born Mary Shackleton in the Quaker community of Ballintore, County Kildare, in December 1758, daughter of Richard Shackleton and his second wife, Elizabeth Carleton. Her grandfather Abraham Shackleton had founded a school in the village at which Edmund Burke and two of his brothers were pupils. Abraham's son Richard, Mary's father, was also a pupil at the time, and became a life-long friend of Burke's. Mary was brought up in Ballitore and carefully educated by her father, who continued to run the school. She was able to read at four, and as a young woman wrote poetry, some of which was published in *Poems* (1808). After her death two volumes of manuscript poems were sold at the Malcolmson Sale in Dublin (1892). In 1784 her father took her to England where she was introduced to Edmund Burke, with whom she afterwards corresponded. On this visit she also met Sir Joshua Reynolds and George Crabbe. In June 1791, at the age of thirty-three, Mary Shackleton married William Leadbeater, descendant of a Huguenot family with some land at Ballitore, where she lived for the rest of her life, eventually becoming post-mistress. They had several children, including two daughters who were given a classical education. For a time she assisted in the school started by her friend Mrs Trench in 1808. She kept a journal for most of her life, and included in it a daily account of events in Ballitore during the 1798 United Irishmen Rising. This was not published until after her death, as *The Annals of Ballitore*, included in *The Leadbeater Papers* (1862). She wrote under the initials M.L. or M.S. in the magazines associated with her family's school, *Juvenile Magazine* (1814) and the *Ballitore Magazine* (1820–1). Her other writings were all inspired by the desire to instruct, from the early *Anecdotes Taken from Real Life for the Improvement of Children*, which was popular with children in spite of the title, to her famous *Cottage Dialogues Among the Irish Peasantry*, written when she was in her fifties. She died on 27 June 1826, and is buried in the Quaker burial ground at Ballitore.

CHIEF WRITINGS. *Extracts and Original Anecdotes for the Improvement of Youth* (Dublin: Jackson, 1794); *Poems* (Dublin: Keene, 1808); *Cottage Dialogues Among the Irish Peasantry* (Dublin: Carrick, 1811); *Cottage Dialogues Part Second,* with 'Glossary and Notes for the Use of the English Reader' (Dublin: Cumming, 1813); *The Landlord's Friend, Intended as a Sequel to Cottage Dialogues* (Dublin: Cumming, 1813); *Tales for Cottagers, Accommodated to the Present Condition of the Irish Peasantry,* with Elizabeth Shackleton, including a play, *Honesty is the Best Policy* (Dublin: Cumming, 1814); *Cottage Biography, Being a Collection of Lives of the Irish Peasantry* (Dublin: Bentham, 1822); *Memoirs and Letters of Richard and Elizabeth Shackleton late of Ballitore, Ireland, compiled by their daughter* (London: Harvey and Darton, 1822); *Biographical Notices of Members of the Society of Friends, Who Were Resident in Ireland* (London: Harvey and Darton, 1823); *The Pedlars: A Tale* (Dublin: Bentham and Harvey, 1826); *Cottage Dialogues, Third Series,* with twenty extra dialogues (Dublin: Kennedy, 1841); *The Leadbeater Papers* comprising *The Annals of Ballitore* and *Correspondence,* 2 vols (London: Bell and Daldy, 1862); *The Annals of Ballitore, 1766–1824,* ed. John McKenna (Athy: Stephen Scoop Press, 1986).

BIOGRAPHY AND CRITICISM. Ballitore in XCVIII, From the unpublished memoirs of the Late Mary Leadbeater, Citizen 2 (1840), pp. 418–30, includes a biographical sketch; *Memoir* of Mary Leadbeater by her niece Elizabeth Shackleton and some of her correspondence published in *The Leadbeater Papers* (London: Bell and Daldy, 1862); J. Hagan, 'An Irish Quaker Village and its Annalist', *New Ireland Review*, vol. 19 (1903), pp. 257–77; Catherine Hamilton, *Notable Irishwomen* (Dublin: Sealy, Bryers and Walter, 1904), pp. 45–57; Margaret Ferrier

Young, 'Ballitore and Its Institutions, Correspondence Between Mary Leadbeater and the Keatings of Narraghmore, 1811–1813', *Journal of the County Kildare Archaeological Society*, vol. 8 (1916), pp. 167–79; Olive C. Goodbody, 'Letters of Mary and Sarah Shackleton, 1767–1775', *Journal of the County Kildare Archaeological Society*, 14, no. 4 (1969), pp. 415–39; Clara I. Gandy, 'The Condition and Character of the Irish Peasantry as Seen in the Annals and Cottage Dialogues of Mary Leadbeater', *Women and Literature*, vol. 3 (spring 1975), pp. 28–38.

Lady Anne Dawson

LIFE. Born in 1733, Lady Anne was the sixth daughter of the Earl and Countess of Pomfret. She married Thomas Dawson of Dawson Grove, County Monaghan, in 1754, and died at Dawson Grove on 1 March 1769.

Lady Elizabeth Fownes

LIFE. Lady Elizabeth (Betty) Ponsonby, daughter of Sarah, née Margetson, and Brabazon Ponsonby, Earl of Bessborough, married Sir William Fownes of Woodstock, Inistioge, County Kilkenny, in 1739. Noted for her various charities, which included a lace-making school for local girls at Inistioge. She died at Rossana, County Wicklow, the home of her daughter, Mrs Sarah Tighe, in 1778.

Theodosia Blachford

LIFE. Theodosia Blachford, née Tighe, was born in 1744. She married the Reverend William Blachford in 1770 and was widowed in 1773. She was present at the inaugural meeting of the Friends of the Female Orphan House in 1790. She founded the House of Refuge, Baggot Street, in 1802. She was prominent in the Methodist movement and author of a number of tracts. She died in 1817.

Charlotte Brooke

For biography and bibliography, see Volume I, p. 1008. See also Volume V, pp. 811–12, 831.

Mary Tighe

LIFE. The poet was born in Dublin in 1772, the daughter of Methodist leader Theodosia (Tighe) and her husband, the Reverend William Blachford, a librarian, who died in her infancy. She had a strict religious education from her mother and began to write poetry as a child. In 1793 she married her cousin Henry Tighe. The couple lived a social and literary life in London. Her six-canto Spenserian allegory, *Psyche*, was privately printed in 1805. Tighe was already ill with consumption. She spent her last years in Duboin and Rosanna, County Wicklow. She died in 1810.

CHIEF WRITINGS. *Psyche; Or, The Legend of Love* (London: printed for the author, 1805); *Psyche: With Other Poems* (London: Longman, 1811); *The Work of Mary Tighe, Published and Unpublished*, ed. Patrick Henchy (Dublin: Bibliographical Society of Ireland, 1957); *Selena* (MS novel, National Library of Ireland); *Mary: A Series of Reflections During 20 Years* (1811).

BIOGRAPHY AND CRITICISM. Patrick Henchy, *The Works of Mary Tighe, Published and Unpublished* (Dublin: Bibliographical Society of Ireland, 1957); Earle Vonard Weller, *Keats and Mary Tighe. The Poems of Mary Tighe, with Parallel Passages from the Work of John Keats* (New York: Century, 1928); Marlon Ross, *The Contours of Masculine Desire: Romanticism and the Rise of Women's Poetry* (New York: Oxford University Press, 1989); James Chandler, *England in 1819: The Politics of Literary Culture and the Case of Romantic Historicism* (Chicago: University of Chicago Press, 1998).

Dorothea Johnson

LIFE. Born in Dublin in 1732 and converted to Methodism in 1757. In 1784 she married John Johnson, a Methodist preacher, and moved with him to Lisburn, County Antrim, where she took particular responsibility for the female members of the congregation. Widowed in 1803, she died in Lisburn in 1817.

CHIEF WRITINGS. *The Memoirs of Mrs D. Johnson, late of Lisburn. Extracted from Her Journals and Other Papers, Found after Her Decease, and Arranged by the Rev Adam Averell* (Cavan: J. O'Brien, 1818).

Eliza Bennis

LIFE. Born in Limerick in 1725, Bennis was converted to Methodism in 1749 and became one of the leading figures in the Methodist Society in Limerick and in Waterford. She emigrated to North America during the 1790s and died in 1802 in Philadelphia.

CHIEF WRITINGS. John Wesley, *Christian Correspondence: A Collection of Letters Written by the late Rev John Wesley, and Several Methodist Preachers in Connexion with Him, to the late Mrs Eliza Bennis, with her answers* (Dublin: Martin Keene, 1824).

John Wesley

LIFE. John Wesley was born in 1703, the son of an English clergyman. He was the founder of Methodism, which became a worldwide family of independent Christian churches after his death. A renowned preacher, he visited Ireland twenty-one times and made many converts to Methodism. His works contain valuable references to the state of the country and the people who came to hear him preach.

CHIEF WRITINGS. *The Works of John Wesley*, ed. Frank Baker (Oxford: Oxford University Press, 1975–83).

BIOGRAPHY. Vivian H.H. Green, *John Weslely* (London, 1964); C.H. Crookshank, *History of Methodism*, 3 vols (London: Woolmer, 1885–8).

CAITRIONA CLEAR, *Editor*

The Re-emergence of Nuns and Convents, 1800–1962

There were so many women entering convents in nineteenth-century Ireland that one convent chronicler commented in the 1890s: 'The labourers are many but the harvest is lacking'; her congregation's resources were hard put to find work for all those who clamoured for admittance.[1] The slow but steady increase in the number of convents and congregations since the late eighteenth century accelerated from about 1840. By 1900 there were 368 convents in the country (compared to 12 a century earlier), 53 religious congregations, and eight times more female religious than there had been in 1841. Nuns greatly outnumbered priests and brothers. With their schools, hospitals, workhouses, sick-visiting and many other projects female religious were, without doubt, the most effective arm of the Catholic church in nineteenth-century Ireland.

The religious life was attractive to Catholic Irish women for many reasons. The nineteenth century was a highly evangelical age all over the western world. Vigorous promotion of the everyday practices of religion among all social classes was part of the inculcation of a new social discipline believed by middle- and upper-class people to be necessary in a rapidly changing world. These tendencies were reinforced in Ireland by a Catholicism which, emerging from the oppression of the Penal Laws, identified strongly with political and social reform. The re-organization and centralization of the Catholic church which took place in nineteenth-century Ireland was partly dictated by Rome, but it would

not have been so successful nor would it have entrenched itself so deeply there had it not been for the strong undertow of native co-operation and initiative. Women religious, or nuns as they were popularly called, spearheaded this initiative, and almost all of the socially active female congregations were founded before Catholic emancipation was won in 1829. From the setting-up of Nano Nagle's Sisters of the Charitable Instruction in Cork in 1776 (recognized by the Vatican in 1805 as the Presentation Nuns) to the foundation of the Sisters of Mercy in 1828, Irish Catholic women of means were identifying social problems, setting up projects with strong religious motivations, and, often, living informally in a community under private vows before being approved by Rome. Nagle ran free schools in Cork city from the 1750s along the lines of the French work-schools, with which she was familiar from her French education. In the early years of her projects she broke the laws against Catholics running schools; most civil disabilities against Catholics had been removed by the time Catherine McAuley set up her first House of Mercy in 1828. Other new female congregations at this stage were the Brigidines, founded in 1807, the Irish Sisters of Charity (1815), and the Loreto nuns (1821), while older religious orders like the Carmelites and the Poor Clares were running schools, orphanages and other projects in response to the new wave of activity.

Catholic women from the middle classes were the main recruits to convents. It was quite common for siblings to enter the religious life, and often the same convent; three daughters of a County

1. Typewritten synopsis of annals, Good Shepherd Convent, Limerick.

Limerick magistrate entered the Limerick Mercy Convent in 1865, 1867 and 1871 respectively; 22.8 per cent of entrants to the Limerick Good Shepherd Convent between 1861 and 1900 also had a sibling or siblings who entered; 9 out of 12 daughters of a Newmarket-on-Fergus, County Clare, farmer became nuns, most of them in the Presentation order, between 1887 and 1905.[2] This could indicate the closeness that existed between women in families, and the influence which they had over each other. Becoming a nun was not a cut-price option for parents eager to get their daughters off their hands; dowries were always required. James Hardiman reports that intending Presentation nuns in Galway in 1823 had to bring five hundred pounds each with them.[3] In the early days before convents had established themselves as part of the Irish scene, donations would have been fewer and dowry requirements therefore high. The average dowry of women professed in the Galway Mercy Convent from 1840 to 1857 was 375 pounds, and the lowest sum was 200 pounds. This kind of money was out of the reach of women from working/labouring-class backgrounds, but there was a place for these women in most convents as lay sisters. Lay sisters were cooks, portresses, gardeners, cleaners — to all intents and purposes, servants who took religious vows. Most came from small farming, artisan and labouring backgrounds. They rarely, if ever, took part in the apostolic work (that is, teaching, nursing, etcetera) of the convent. While the choir nuns (as the majority, who were not lay sisters, were known) were carrying out an extension of women's nurturing functions in the larger community — teaching, nursing, sick-visiting, running orphanages, hostels and refuges — lay sisters were performing the vital under-pinning maintenance work — also traditionally women's work — without which life cannot continue.

A survey of the ages at entry into three convents between 1851 and 1900 shows that the average age was 23.3 throughout the period. At no time did it fall below 20. Critics who depicted convents as sinister institutions where young girls were cajoled or coerced into spending their lives did not realize, or chose to ignore, that women entering convents were adults, and in view of the dowries required, women who would probably have had the option of marriage. What they might not have had, in 'the world', was the option of work, and the religious life guaranteed challenging work, with no loss of social status. Nuns were the largest group of white-collar women workers in nineteenth-century Ireland.[4] On a day-to-day basis convents were free of male authority figures. Superiors (heads of individual houses), often called Reverend Mothers, were elected by secret ballot of all the choir nuns. Lay sisters did not usually have a vote in these elections. Once elected, superiors held office for a fixed term, usually three years. Critics of convent life often fastened on what they saw to be the potential for despotism in this structure, but professed nuns had certain rights which overrode those of superiors. The former could not be dismissed without the consent of the local bishop, and had the right to apply to the Holy See in the event of unfair dismissal. Tyranny and abuse of power no doubt existed in convents, as it does in all hierarchical working communities; there is also much evidence of co-operation and mutual respect.

As professed religious in the most long-lasting male-dominated institution in the western world, nuns had to make compromises with patriarchal authority. The two biggest and most widely distributed congregations in the country, the Presentation and the Mercy, were under the direct authority of the local bishop wherever they set up convents. Bishops and priests were wary of congregations which were centralized, with organizational ties to a mother-house and Mother-General (elected head of congregations); such congregations were either forced to cut links with their mother-house, as were the Loreto nuns in Navan, Fermoy, Letterkenny, Omagh and Killarney, settled from the mother-house in Dublin between 1833 and 1861, or else they did not make many new foundations. The Irish Sisters of Charity, founded in 1815 by Mary Aikenhead, were encouraged by Archbishop Daniel Murray to be a strongly centralized congregation. Consequently it made far fewer foundations throughout the century than did the

2. Register of entrants, Mercy Convent, Limerick, and census MSS 1901, National Archives; register of entrants, Good Shepherd Convent, Limerick; 'Nine Daughters Nuns' (*Limerick Leader*, 10 April 1943).
3. James Hardiman, *History of Galway* (Galway: W. Folds, 1820; rpr. Connacht Tribune, 1926).
4. Entry registers, Good Shepherd Convent, Limerick; Mercy Convent, Limerick; Dominican Convent, Taylor's Hill, Galway. See also occupational tables in censuses 1851–1901.

Presentation, despite the fact that the latter, being enclosed, were not at all as versatile as the Sisters of Charity. Congregations from abroad which set up convents in Ireland (and twenty did so between 1771 and 1900) were particularly at risk of being cut off from their central headquarters. This is what happened to the Sisters of St Louis in Monaghan in 1861, to name but one.

Because rapidly growing, socially active congregations of women, whether enclosed or not, were something of a novelty in nineteenth-century Ireland, bishops, priests and even nuns themselves were often uncertain about the extent of autonomy which a community, or even a congregation, could exercise. This gave rise to widely varying interpretations of the nature and extent of episcopal and clerical authority over nuns. The Good Shepherd sisters, a French congregation which settled in Limerick city in 1848, were forced by the bishop to stop sending their novices (religious in training) to France in 1861, while the Faithful Companions of Jesus, another French congregation which came to Limerick in 1845, were allowed to keep up this practice until well into the twentieth century. Both congregations had centralized structures and Mothers-General so there was no structural reason why one was subjected to interference and the other was not. It seems, however, that some of the parents of Good Shepherd novices put pressure on the bishop to stop their daughters being sent so far away.[5]

5. Good Shepherd Convent, Limerick (synopsis of annals); for a full discussion of the relationship between convents and bishops and priests, see Caitriona Clear, *Nuns in Nineteenth-Century Ireland* (Dublin: Gill and Macmillan, 1987), pp. 53–68.

Convents were not inviolate, isolated, cut off from the wider community of Catholics, lay and ecclesiastical, but very much part of it, and dependent upon it not only for recruits but for financial and moral support. Catherine McAuley was crisply realistic about what she saw to be the dangers of the convents' social milieu when she warned: 'No one should be able to say, when repeating a piece of towntalk or gossip, "I heard it in the convent parlour of the Sisters of Mercy".' Kate O'Brien's book about her two maternal aunts in the Presentation Convent in Limerick city towards the end of the nineteenth century, and her family's close relationship with them, vividly evokes Limerick middle-class life at that time.[6]

'The nuns are the best support to religion,' Archbishop, later Cardinal, Cullen (1803–78) admitted in 1852; usually credited with having almost single-handedly disciplined and modernized the Catholic church in nineteenth-century Ireland, he was in a position to recognize the nuns' vital agency in the spread of modern Catholic practice and the presentation of the church's caring face to the poor, the sick, the young, females, and other relatively powerless groups. Caught up in the ongoing crusade of a reorganizing Catholic church, and consigned irrevocably to the lowest reaches of the ecclesiastical hierarchy, nuns often found the independence of their own institutions undermined, virtually trampled in the headlong rush for expansion and consolidation.

6. Kate O'Brien, *Presentation Parlour* (London: Heinemann, 1963).

ELLEN MARIA LEAHY

(1803–74)

from:
THE ANNALS OF SOUTH PRESENTATION CONVENT, CORK (1981)

[Nano Nagle came from a Catholic landowning family in Ballygriffin, County Cork. Educated in France like most Catholics of her class, she lived in Paris for about a decade,

returning to Ireland in 1746. A brief spell in a French convent convinced her that the religious life was not for her and she returned to Ireland, setting up the first of six 'poor schools' in Cork city in or about 1757, in defiance of the Penal Laws which forbade Catholics from operating schools. Deciding that a convent was needed to place the schools on a permanent footing, Nagle invited the Ursulines to Cork. They set up their convent in 1771, but their practice of enclosure meant that they could operate only one of the six schools. In her disappointment, Nagle set up her own religious congregation, the Sisters of the Charitable Instruction of the Sacred Heart of Jesus in 1776, intending that this sisterhood would be free to go outside the convent and to visit the sick and the poor, as well as running schools. This congregation was formally instituted by the Sacred Congregation for the Propagation of the Faith as the Sisters of the Presentation of the Blessed Virgin Mary in 1805. Known as the Presentation nuns or sisters, this order practised enclosure and, contrary to Nagle's founding intention, confined itself to the running of schools. This extract, written by the first annalist, Ellen Maria Leahy (Mother de Pazzi), is typical of the style in which internal convent annals were written. South Presentation Convent, Cork, was the original founding house of the Presentation Sisters. The text was prepared by Caitriona Clear from a published version contained in *Presentation Roots* (Monasterevin: Presentation Publications, 1981), pp. 5–6, and can be found in the Original Annals, p. 99, in South Presentation Convent Archives.]

August 18 [1803]: Sister Mary Baptist McGrath pronounced her simple vows today, and received the Black Veil.

September 15 [1803]: At length, and not until our patience was well tried by want and other inconveniences, an arrangement has been made between Mr Joseph Nagle (the brother of, and executor to the Will of, our revered Foundress) and us.[1] He has signed a deed, which ensures to us the payment of the portion of property left us by his Sister: and had he continued to leave our affairs in their present unsettled state for a longer time, the result, of necessity would be, either that of our being reduced to beggary, or the total destruction of our Convent. The sum of L.2150, left us by the Will of Venerable Mother Nagle, and the interest which has been arising from it, since her death in 1784, we now hope to have promptly paid us. Mother Nagle's income was 600 pounds per annum. Her private expenses were so inconsiderable as scarcely to have infringed on this sum: she was therefore enabled to support her little Community and to build up our present Convent, as well as two small houses for our neighbours:— the 'Ursulines'. By her strict economy and assisted by a few charitable donations, she also continued to lay aside L.800 which she invested in the Irish Funds (Irish

government bonds) intending with it to enlarge our present inconvenient and miserable schools, and to build us a Chapel. Her Almshouse was built by means of a small sum which she wisely put together out of certain donations by pious wealthy ladies of acquaintance.

When she withdrew from the Ursulines to enter upon the foundation of our Institute (1776), she promised to give them L.2000 as a means of establishing with security their newly opened Convent — of this sum she paid the 1100 pounds, long before she died — the remaining 900 pounds she bequeathed in the Will to their Superioress Mrs Kavanagh. Altogether her legacies amounted to L.10,000 — and still how strange to tell, that at her death, she possessed of this world's wealth, but the small sum of one Guinea and a half — a proof this, how little was her heart fixed on money; and by it, how liberally and unostentatiously she must have contributed to the Comforts, as well as relieved the wants, of others.

Besides the money left us in her Will, as already specified, the residue of her property (when her charities were cleared off) she told Mother Angela Collins, she intended to give to us. In this respect her intentions were not carried out — this fund of whatever it consisted, was distributed to others, not any of it to this house, which she said, she knew would want it. We are also entitled to receive the one fourth of her Uncle's property — concerning which, a law suit is now pending, but no hope have we, that a pound of it will ever be ours — it consists of L.1000 ... Mother Nagle did not forget the Almshouse. She willing to her poor women there, the sum of 200 pounds — and when dying she begged Mother Angela Collins would expend for her, 80 pounds in small charities, which has ever been fully and scrupulously done.

Our community consists at present of ten Sisters, five of whom have means sufficient for their own support and nothing more — the other five with two servants have only to calculate upon Providence and uncertain resources in the way of presents or donations to provide for their wants.

Our Chapel is in a most miserable condition, quite unworthy of Him, who dwells therein — nor have we the means of rendering it less so.

Our Convent is so small and inconvenient, as scarcely to be calculated for the accommodation of ourselves, who are unaccustomed to anything

---

1. It was not until Joseph Nagle's death in 1813 that the nuns received all that was due to them, see T.J. Walsh, *Nano Nagle and the Presentation Sisters* (Dublin: M. H. Gill and Son, 1959), pp. 145–6.

that can be called comfort, and quite unpresentable to those, who wishing to sacrifice for God the conveniences of ordinary life, present themselves for admittance as willing workers in the vineyard of the Lord, the 'instruction' of His forgotten, neglected children — 'the Poor'.

Our schools are small, dingy and damp: and consequently, unwholesome and unpleasant —

Still neither resources nor means have we, to render things more decent or appropriate. Satisfied we are, and may be: for we have God our Hope. If our schools were larger our attendance of children would be most numerous. During this year we have been only able to add 148 children, to our usual numbers, which forms usually an average of about 600.

'MARY'

(fl. 1803)

from:
A LETTER ABOUT MISS MULALLY AND NANO NAGLE (1803–4)

[This extract from a memoir written in 1803–4 by an unknown writer named 'Mary' was addressed to Mother Ignatius Doran, Reverend Mother of George's Hill Presentation Convent, Dublin. The memoir gives many personal details of Teresa Mulally, who founded the convent at George's Hill in 1789 and died there in February 1803. Here 'Mary' recounts how Mulally, an important founding personality, met Nano Nagle and joined her fledgling religious order. The extract is contained in the transcripts preserved in George's Hill Convent archives, which were prepared for publication by Alfred O'Rahilly and appeared in full under the title 'A Letter about Miss Mulally and Nano Nagle' in *Irish Ecclesiastical Record*, 5th series, vol. 40 (July–December 1932), pp. 474–81; 619–24.]

She also informed me in the course of our conversation that she was then, in 1778, fifty years of age — which made her just eight years elder than I. [She said] that she had her school established for fourteen years,[1] in which she taught every day herself. [She also said] that after the death of her parents, as soon as she could realise thirty pounds a year she resolved to retire [from the millinery business], weary of adminis-

tering to the wants of them [her customers], while her own plain dress was no strong recommendation to a world that was at that time improving fast in frippery.

When she had accomplished her wishes, she had thoughts of becoming a nun; and each community of that kind in Dublin strove to win her to itself. While she was imploring the light of heaven how to dispose of her future life, she had heard of the celebrated Miss Nagle, a lady of family and fortune, who had founded the Ursuline Convent in Cork,[2] and had [previously] opened both male and female charity schools in the different quarters of that city, and to this lady she was strongly inclined to go and unite her labours. They corresponded, they were kindred souls and knew each other at a distance. On this important subject she consulted the reverend, wise and good Mr Mulcaile,[3] her director and steady friend through life. He answered [that] she had a field large enough at home and that the poor of Dublin were as dear to God as those of Cork. This determined her.

She took a little place in Mary's Lane, where she invited the children of the poor to come to her for instruction — which, I believe, was the first institution of the kind ever thought of in this city

---

1. This would date the starting of Mulally's school in Dublin in 1764; the exact date is 1765.

2. Nano Nagle founded the Ursuline convent in Cork in September 1771. On 24 December 1775 she started the Institute of 'the Sisters of the Charitable Instructions, called the Sisters of the Sacred Heart of Jesus'. Owing to Protestant and Jansenistic prejudice, the name of the institute was afterwards changed to that of the Presentation Order.

3. James Philip Mulcaile S.J. (1727–1801).

[Dublin]. When she had got a few subscribers, some of the children she boarded, some [she] clothed, and to others [she] gave breakfast according to her means and their necessities. I was told by clergymen that, after spending three hours of the morning in the chapel, she went to her school and taught herself until dinner time, and during the summer months [she] sent home her scholars for the afternoon. She set her house, reserving one room, where I had first the pleasure of introducing myself to her; and a neat apartment it was, as clean as her heart. Here she intended to pass all her leisure hours from her school, without mixing with the world. But she was pursued to her retreat by many who thought much of her. She assured me [that] nothing but to make friends for the charity could tempt her to dine abroad.

A life so uniform and sanctified cannot afford many events for entertainment, but that the most trivial circumstances relative to her must be dear to those who venerate her memory. We spent about three weeks in Cork, some of which time we waited for a returned carriage. But I could never persuade her to walk out with me to take a view of anything worth seeing in the city or in the environs. 'No,' said she, 'that is only dissipation, vain curiosity and loss of time.' But I rambled about while she was at her devotions.

One morning she asked the Chaplain of the convent to breakfast with us, the Rev Mr [Teahan], a holy and good man who since died a bishop.[4] Being then tolerably active, Miss Mulally desired me to make the tea. The gentleman and I were getting through our meal before she had finished one cup. At length I cried, 'Why, madam, you are very slow; whenever I set out on the road to heaven, I'll beat you!' The priest smiled, 'No,' said he, 'but I will tell you

what: you will set off in such a hurry [that] you'll fatigue yourself, puff and blow and be obliged to sit down and take breath, while she, quiet and easy, will get [there] before you.' No inspired man could more justly define my character. For a few years after, all zeal, I proposed joining Miss Mulally, and she encouraged it. But I was dissuaded from it; and so it was that the world prevailed — which I have since often and deeply regretted. Ah me! Ah me! But I'll be silent, as I am not here bound to confession.

The first morning after our arrival in Cork, there came a rap at our chamber door at six o'clock. Miss Mulally was putting on her clothes — for it could not be called dressing — when [there] entered a little elderly woman with a shabby silk cloak, an old hat turned up, a soiled dark cotton gown, and a coarse black petticoat, drabbled halfway and dripping wet — for it had rained heavily.[5] When she announced her name to be Nagle, they embraced for the first time with hearts congenial. She stayed but a few minutes to welcome her friend, but returned at nine. I was still in bed, taking boiled milk for my wretched stomach; but Miss Mulally introduced me to her. I asked her was she not afraid of taking cold. 'No,' she replied. 'I was once susceptible enough of it, but now I feel nothing.' It really confounded me to see myself such an animal among saints, with a trunk full of gay things to figure away in Cork, when a woman of her ample fortune made such a humble appearance. This lady, after founding a convent [of the Ursulines], not thinking the nuns attentive enough to poor children, established four charity schools, two for boys [and] two for girls; and I was told [that] in hail, rain and snow, she divided her days between them, and, I suppose, like Miss Mulally, devoted a great part of her nights to prayer.

4. Dr Gerald Teahan became chaplain to the Ursulines in 1776, and died as Bishop of Kerry in 1797.

5. This is the only contemporary description of Nano Nagle's appearance.

CATHERINE McAULEY

(1778–1841)

from:
LEAVES FROM THE ANNALS
OF THE SISTERS OF MERCY
(1881)

[Like Nano Nagle, Catherine McAuley was heir to a large fortune, and like Mary Aikenhead she had many Protestant relatives. The Sisters of Mercy originated as the Institute of the House of Mercy in Baggot Street, Dublin, a group of women led by McAuley, who lived together praying and devoting themselves to charitable works, notably the running of hostels for unemployed young women. McAuley was persuaded to set up a religious congregation by Archbishop Daniel Murray; papal approbation for the Sisters of Mercy was given in 1831. Like the Sisters of Charity, these sisters were free to go outside the convents and to carry out a variety of activities; like the Presentation, each convent was subject to the bishop of the diocese wherever it settled. By the time of McAuley's death in 1841 the young congregation had branches in all ecclesiastical provinces and in most of the major towns and cities. The excerpt describes the founding of the Galway convent of the Sisters of Mercy in 1840. It contains Catherine McAuley's letter referring to the Galway foundation and an amusing poem she wrote on her visit to the Carmelite monastery in Loughrea, County Galway. The text was prepared by Caitriona Clear and the original is in *Leaves from the Annals of the Sisters of Mercy* (New York: Mercy Publications, 1881), pp. 373–9.]

Although Galway was exceptionally well-provided with nuns,[1] yet there was ample room for the Sisters of Mercy and great need of them. The sick and destitute, the prisoner, and the almost equally unfortunate inmates of the bleak, said 'poorhouse' invented by Protestantism to keep the poor of Jesus Christ apart from its respectability, could not be aided by the cloistered nuns otherwise than by prayers. The zealous bishop desired to supplement the religious bodies already existing in his diocese by nuns who could visit his people in their affliction, and relieve their wants. He saw, and the

foundress saw, that it might not be easy to maintain a seventh [*sic*] community, which, as professing to perform the work of mercy, required some share of public support; for, in truth, the vulgar aristocracy of wealth was rarer among the 'Tribes' than the aristocracy of birth or intellect. Besides, she had scarcely any members to spare from the 'poor old mother-house'.[2] But after much prayer and some consultation it became evident that God willed her to undertake the work, and she prepared to do so with her usual reliance on His providence. While the preparations were in progress God took to Himself one of her most valued subjects, Sister M Frances Marmion, one of three Sisters called by their friends 'The Three Graces' on account of their personal loveliness, amiability and accomplishments, who were among her early children.

[Mother McAuley] says: 'Our beloved and edifying Sister M Frances did not speak again as I expected — expired without any struggle. This is a season of sorrow with us, thank God!' It was truly a season of sorrow; in March 1840, St Joseph called home three of her dearest and most efficient Sisters — RIP.[3] Whenever a foundation was accepted one member or more died, that it might have, as the Sisters were wont to say, intercessors in heaven.

A letter to Mother M Vincent Hartnett, Limerick, about this time, refers to the Galway foundation:

> I never for one moment forgot you or ceased to feel the most sincere interest and affection: so forgive all my past neglect, and I will atone in due season. A thousand thanks for the articles you contributed to the bazaar ... A letter from Birmingham informs us that we are to have five postulants this week or next, accompanied by a clergyman who is to bring plans of a convent to be shown to me. This unavoidably puts

---

1. There were, in 1840, five houses of female religious in Galway city: the Presentation nuns, the Dominicans, the Poor Clares, the Augustinians and, for a brief period, the Ursulines.

2. Baggot Street, Dublin foundation.
3. RIP: literally, *requiescat in pace*, 'rest in peace', sometimes placed in Catholic devotional practice after the name of a dead person.

me under arrest, though the Monday after Low Sunday was named by Rev Mr Daly [an important Galway priest] for Galway. Immediately after the bazaar and the arrival of our new Sisters we will start for Galway, go by Tullamore, and proceed to Limerick with our whole heart ... A new child [postulant] enters here on Thursday — our third since the last ceremony; and if five come from England we shall have a nice lot again, just when I thought we were retiring from business. God bless you, my own child and dear Sister! Give my fondest love to all, and pray for your affectionate

M C McAuley

Early in May 1840 the foundation set out for Galway, visiting Tullamore and Loughrea en route. During this pleasant excursion across the country, at the most delightful season of the year, she lodged with the Carmelite nuns in Loughrea. She wrote a rhyming chronicle for them:

Stopped at Mount Carmel on the way,
And passed a most delightful day.
Dear, simple nuns!

Had lamb and salad for our dinner,
Far, far too good for any sinner
At tea, hot buns.

Got use of the superior's cell
And slept all night extremely well
On my soft pillow.
When lying down on my soft bed
I thought how very soon this head
Must wear the willow.

Next morning we had Mass in choir,
And, to our very heart's desire,
Our own dear Father,
Then we had breakfast warm and neat
Both tea and coffee, eggs and meat,
Whiche'er we'd rather.

Although the foundress 'got use of the superior's cell', she takes care to inform them that a nice bed and a soft pillow were provided by the considerate though ascetic hostess. She was at that time in such wretched health that her appearance had shocked her Tullamore children, with whom she had rested the day before. She died the following year.

MARY CLARE AUGUSTINE MOORE

(1808–80)

from:
A MEMOIR OF THE FOUNDRESS OF THE SISTERS OF MERCY IN IRELAND (1864)

[Mary Clare Moore joined the Sisters of Mercy in Baggot Street, Dublin, in 1837. She wrote an invaluable memoir of Catherine McAuley, whom she had met in 1829. A fine artist, in this extract she describes Catherine McAuley's appearance in 1829 and provides a precise verbal portrait of her; there is no painted portrait of McAuley from life. She underestimated McAuley's age by some ten years. The memoir has been edited by Mary C. Sullivan, *Catherine McAuley and the Tradition of Mercy* (Notre Dame, Indiana: University of Notre Dame Press, 1995; Dublin: Four Courts Press, 2000), see p. 202 for extract.]

A very few days after [her brother-in-law's] death [in January 1829] I saw our foundress for the first time. My brother took me to introduce me. She was sitting in the little parlor on the right side of the hall as you enter. She was then upwards of 40 but looked at least 10 years younger. She was very fair with a brilliant color on her cheeks, still not too red. Her face was a short oval but the contour was perfect. Her lips were thin and her mouth rather wide, yet there was so much play and expression about it that I remarked it as the next agreeable feature in [her] face. Her eyes were light blue and remarkably round with the brows and lashes colorless but they spoke. In repose they had a melancholy beseeching look; then it would light up expressive of really hearty fun, or if she disapproved of anything they could tell that too. Sometimes they had the strange expression of reading your thoughts, which made you feel that even your mind was in her power, and that you could not hide anything from her. Her nose was straight but thick. She wore bands made from her own back hair which were so well managed as to be quite free from the disagreeable look bands of the kind usually give. The color was pale golden not in the least sandy, very fine and silky. She was dressed in black British merino which according to the fashion of the time fitted tight to her shape. She was remarkably well made, round but not in the least heavy. She had a good carriage, her hands were remarkably white but very clumsy, very large with broad square tips to the fingers and short square nails.

SARAH ATKINSON

(1823–93)

from:
MARY AIKENHEAD: HER LIFE, HER WORK AND HER FRIENDS (1879)

[This vivid and colourful account of the life of Mother Mary Aikenhead (1787–1858), who founded the Irish Sisters of Charity in 1815, is based on interviews, letters and personal reminiscences. Nuns were often at this time given the courtesy title Mrs and their surnames, when being spoken to, or of, by seculars, an indication of their social standing. The extract is from Sarah Atkinson's narrative, *Mary Aikenhead: Her Life, Her Work and Her Friends* (Dublin: M.H. Gill, 1879), pp. 373–8.]

From this date [1848] . . . Mrs Aikenhead lived on, struggling against an accumulation of infirmities, yet with a mind ever actively working, a hand from which the pen was seldom suffered to drop. She was now about sixty-five years of age — an old woman, certainly, yet full of intellectual vitality and mental power. One of her children (in religion), whose acquaintance with the Mother-General of the Sisters of Charity began at this time, has kindly, at our request, noted down her recollections of Mrs Aikenhead . . .

'When the religious vocation first began to make itself felt in me I certainly was not much in love with nuns. I had an idea they must be rather weak people. One day I thought I should like to have a look at one of them, and on some pretence or another I went to the Gardiner-street convent and knocked at the door. The sister who received me struck me as totally different from what I expected. She seemed a frank, reliable sort of person, who had a clear intelligence and knew how to use it. Soon after this, meeting a reverend friend who knew what were my views and wishes, I told him that I had seen a Sister of Charity, and that she looked as if she had the mind of a man . . . that there was a strength of character and an intellectual power in the appearance and manner of the Sister of Charity, though she was far from unfeminine, which particularly impressed me. "Ah," said he, "this comes from the great old mother — she puts her stamp on them!"

'By-and-by I got over some of my own difficulties about giving up my liberty and my friends, but there still remained many obstacles to be surmounted. I had little hope of getting easily away from home. However, it was necessary for me to go and speak to Mrs Aikenhead and see whether she would allow me to try to be a Sister of Charity, in case I found it possible to arrange matters so that I could enter the noviceship.[1] When I first went to her on this errand she was able to walk a little. So she came downstairs assisted by a lay-sister; leaning on a stick; and attended by a very plebeian black dog, which leaped up beside her when she sat down, and made one of the party. "This is Dandy," she said, "my faithful dog." I took greatly to the idea

---

1. Noviceship refers to the period of formation, usually from three to six years, before a religious sister is finally professed. It can also designate the part of the convent set apart for the novices.

of the dog, and thought there was a promise of kindness in the fact of his being admitted to the friendship of the Mother of the congregation. She struck me as a magnificent old woman, with — I cannot say the remains of great beauty, but — a beauty remarkable of its kind. There was a grandeur in the outline of the features and in their expression; and there were certain curves about the mouth and cheeks which I do not remember to have seen so marked in any other face. Her large, well-set eyes, which looked soft enough to melt when she was moved, and were so heavenly when a holy chord was touched, had also much humour in them at times, and could give full expression to a majestic severity when it was necessary to defend a just cause. Her soul shone through them.

'. . . People who were introduced to her in her sitting-room were likely enough to find their angry feelings, if they had them, mollified, and their unworthy ideas dispersed, in the presence of the woman who sat there like an old empress — yet all the mother too. I remember my father having to go to her one time, when he was far from reconciled to my retirement to a convent, and therefore not in the best dispositions. Rev Mother was afraid there would be much difficulty about the necessary arrangements; and I having left her and her visitor together, retired in no small anxiety. On my return what was my surprise to find them engaged in the most cordial conversation; my father with his best manners on — quite courtly — and all things settled satisfactorily. Much the same thing happened in the case of another father of a family, two of whose daughters had set their hearts on entering Mrs Aikenhead's congregation. The old gentleman was in a state of considerable irritation when he came to the convent to speak to the superior. Before he left, however, he knelt down and asked her blessing. "Oh," said she, "to think of a patriarch asking my blessing!"

'The first time I was admitted to Rev Mother's private sitting room, that is, the room in which her later years were almost entirely spent. I was much struck by its fitness to the grand old form, so motherly yet so majestic that sat there. Not that the apartment was grand in any sense: but there was something about it that harmonised with the mother herself: it was a good frame for a good picture. It expressed the common sense (not common-place) spirit of the institute she founded. It was not an austere-looking chamber by any means; for there she received her friends and persons who wanted to see her on special business . . . Rev Mother's constant attendant at this time was a lay-sister[2] named Monica. When not in the room she was sure to be within call, either waiting on the landing that looks out on the green fields, or in her own little cell just behind the apartment corresponding with Reverend Mother's, and called Mother Mary Lucy's room. Monica was an original character. She had not got much education, and though interested in what was going on, was not always able to follow the conversation which she heard when Rev Mother's visitors touched on topics of the day, or entered into questions of vital importance to Church and State. When the Peel ministry[3] went out of office, Sister heard the subject discussed and judging from the surprise and interest excited by the news, that something of the highest importance had occurred, ran off to one of the sisters, exclaiming "Sure Peel is out!" "Out of what?" inquired the sister. "Faith I don't know," returned Monica, "out of prison I suppose." Sister Monica, however, had very decided opinions on some subjects, and not only held to them firmly but expressed them in strong language on occasions.

2. Lay sisters took simple vows in religious communities that had solemn vows and were responsible for the running and upkeep of the convent. They could not vote or hold office and, in general, they came from a family background that was unable to provide a dowry. Their canonical status dates from the Middle Ages and began to disappear with the recognition of religious communities which took only simple vows in the late nineteenth century.

3. Robert Peel became Prime Minister of Great Britain and Ireland in 1841 and his ministry lasted until 1846.

LADIES OF CHARITY OF ST VINCENT DE PAUL

from:
ANNUAL REPORTS (1852–85)

[The following extracts are from the published reports of the charities established by Margaret Aylward (1810–89) in Dublin from 1851. The public meetings convened for the launch of each report provided a platform from which she outlined the philosophy, organization, progress and future possibilities for the charities, and the current financial and membership position, and called publicly for support. The occasions were used to alert the public to the extent of spiritual and material destitution in the city slums, including eyewitness accounts and case studies. They were also the means of relentlessly and provocatively exposing the activities of the proselytizing mission agents among the city's poor. Reports of the Ladies of Charity of St Vincent de Paul were published 1852–62: the first reports of St Bridget's Orphanage, 1857–8, were published as appendices to the Ladies of Charity reports, but from 1859 were published independently. In 1861 school reports were included with the orphanage reports, and the spelling was changed from Bridget to Brigid. John Gowan CM, spiritual director and adviser, collaborated in the production of several of the reports, as did another key co-worker and friend, Ada Allingham. The text was prepared by Jacinta Prunty.]

from:
FOURTH ANNUAL REPORT OF THE LADIES OF CHARITY OF ST VINCENT DE PAUL, 1855

Our visiting staff[1] would be more numerous still, were educated Catholics alive to the advantages arising both to rich and poor from constant mutual intercourse. The sorrows of the necessitous frequently paralyse their energy, and without it how can they escape the perils of destitution? And oh! how quickly are temptations strown upon the path of the very poor! The

1. The active members or lady visitors were the wives and daughters of professional and merchant families, and were themselves resident in the north city parishes of St Mary's and St Michan's, where they visited; in 1856 they numbered 148 (Ladies of Charity, Fifth Report, 1856, p. 4).

snares of the proselytiser[2] are spread under their feet: and if the love of Divine truth still glows within their breasts, and preserves them for a while, the fatal spirit shop presents a stimulus to their cold, and weak, and scantily-clad frame. To avert such evils from the Poor is the aim of the Association of St Vincent.

Not by money alone do the Associates labour to effect their object: their counsel, their care, is even more valuable than the pecuniary relief bestowed. It is not by lavishing large alms the Poor are to be lastingly or materially served: it is by teaching them their own dignity, the dignity of children of God: by instilling into them high principles of morality, habits of industry and order, and by teaching them the practice of true confidence in God, namely, an unbounded reliance on Him, whilst using every possible exertion on their own part.

The poor will not understand nor practise these lessons in a moment: patient, earnest, gentle perseverance, is necessary on the part of those who for God's sake engage themselves in their service. We must prove to them that we are their true friends, that we seek their eternal, much more than their temporal, welfare.

2. The establishment in 1847 of the society of Irish Church Missions marked an aggressive new wave of English Protestant missionary activity in Ireland. While the western missions were regarded as the most successful, much attention was devoted to Dublin (minutes of *Irish Church Missions*, 9 June 1859). Its use of material assistance to attract destitute 'inquiring Roman Catholics' to attend its services and (from 1852) the associated Smyly schools and homes led to bitter accusations of proselytism, which were countered by claims that the Roman Catholic poor schools operated similarly.

from:
SEVENTH ANNUAL REPORT OF ST BRIGID'S ORPHANAGE, 1873

It will be remembered that St Brigid's children are reared in family — one or two and sometimes three being located in a farmer's house.[1] There

1. The Act for the Effectual Relief of the Poor in Ireland, 1838, provided for the care of destitute, orphaned, deserted or illegitimate children within the workhouse only; in promoting the care of such children among rural families Margaret Aylward sought to demonstrate that supervised 'boarding out' was in every way preferable, and could be justified financially when the 'true' costs to society of the workhouse regime were considered.

are, undoubtedly, some disadvantages in having the children thus dispersed; but each year lessens these, and, on the other hand, brings out more clearly the advantages of the system. In the first place we beg to call attention to the low rate of mortality among the children. During the past year seven of our Orphans have died, and during the seven years of the existence of the Orphanage but thirty-eight of the four hundred and sixty children have died. This, taken in connexion with two other facts, namely, that there is no selection of healthy children, and that no child is returned to its guardians because of its being sickly, shows an almost miraculously-high sanitary state. In the poor-house there is a mortality among children during their first seven years of about sixty per cent . . . while in St Brigid's it is under twelve per cent. To state this properly, St Brigid's Orphanage has been the means of saving the lives of upwards of one hundred children, that is, if our four hundred and sixty Orphans had been placed in the poor-house or been left in the city, one hundred or more of them that are now alive would have died. If any one of our Subscribers had plunged into the stream and drawn out a drowning infant, or if, like St John of God, he had rushed into the flames of a burning house and taken from its cradle a babe hushed in perilous sleep, he would be looked upon as a hero of charity; and yet as truly and effectually has he saved many such little ones by upholding this institution. In the next place, the health of the children is greatly promoted by placing them in the country.[2] There are at present, with the exception of four who were presented to the Orphanage with broken spines, but five or six delicate children. If our children had remained in the city or been shut up in the poor-house, how many would be afflicted with scrofula, ophthalmia, and pulmonary complaints! There is no sadder sight than a little girl or little boy in his early boyhood, burdened with chronic disease, spiritless, dwarfed, and prematurely old, sitting upon some hall-door step, or with diseased eyes, listlessly bent over his task in the poor-house; and on the other hand, how charming to see them playing and bounding in the green field — the limbs lithe, the chest expanded, and the rose on

the cheek. Besides, St Brigid's Orphan has a home and a fireside, and calls its foster-parents by the dear names of father and mother. He becomes engrafted on the family-stock, and all the branches are become his kindred, his aunts and his uncles, his brothers and sisters. His heart learns to throb in their sorrows and to vibrate to their joys, and in one word, instead of a lone outcast, he becomes a member of a family.

from:

TWENTY-EIGHTH ANNUAL REPORT OF ST BRIGID'S ORPHANAGE, 1885

It is commonly supposed that the very poor children of Dublin, who run half-naked about the streets, are corrupt and almost irreclaimable, and that the only way to reform and civilise them is to commit them to the reformatory or Industrial School.[1]

No doubt there are subjects among them for both places. But most of them require only care and instruction, for they are naturally intelligent, quick, and amenable to discipline. It would be a blunder as well as a sin to seize poor children and deprive them of their liberty for five or seven years without a crime on their part, on the pretext of reforming them. Men are seldom reformed by coercion. In the ordinary providence of God, human beings are made good by enlightening the mind and directing the will. It is quite right to reform those who, by their misdeeds, have forfeited their liberty. But it is a totally different thing to take away liberty lest a bad use should be made of it. Experience proves the evil consequences of such experiments. Hence the surest and least expensive way of making Christian men and women of these poor hungry children, is to entice them to good schools by a little food and clothing.[2] If the

---

2. The children were grouped among neighbouring foster families in counties Dublin, Kildare, Carlow and Wicklow, to facilitate the twice annual and other inspections.

1. The establishment of both reformatory (from 1858) and industrial schools (1869) was undertaken by many religious communities as a very useful way of caring for large numbers of delinquent and destitute children, with full denominational control, and backed with government funds. It suited the state as the only expense to the ratepayers was the maintenance rate for each child; it did not have to staff or build the institutions.
2. Margaret Aylward opened a network of free Catholic schools, providing instruction, food and clothing, in the Dublin slums: Crow Street in 1861 (moved to Clarendon Street in 1870); Great Strand Street in 1863 and Jervis Street in 1870 (moved to Little Strand Street in 1888); West Park Street in 1865 (moved to Coombe in 1887).

charitable public only knew how kindly these poor children take to learning their prayers and their catechism, how willingly they prepare for and go to confession, they would not only support the few schools open but would endow a food-giving school in every parish of the city.

MARGARET ANNA CUSACK

(1832–99)

from:
THE NUN OF KENMARE: AN AUTOBIOGRAPHY (1889)

[This extract tells part of the tortuous tale of Margaret Anna Cusack's attempts to be transferred from one diocese to another when she endeavoured to found a new congregation, the Sisters of Peace, in Knock, County Mayo. Eventually the Archbishop of Tuam, Dr John MacEvilly (1816–1902), gave her permission to settle in Knock and to set up her convent, but her position there was never secure, and she left for America with her congregation. According to her own account, she met with further persecution and harassment until she resigned the leadership of her congregation in 1889. She died ten years later. The excerpt was selected by Caitriona Clear and is from Cusack's published book, *The Nun of Kenmare: An Autobiography* (London: Hodder and Stoughton, 1889). The story begins as Cusack arrives in Knock.]

I do not intend to enter into what I may call the spiritual part of my life at Knock or elsewhere. My present work concerns only the circumstances which obliged me to abandon my work for Ireland, and I may say the work for religion, which I had hoped to carry out there, and the work which I was authorised to do by the present Pope.

By Father Cavanagh's advice, I arranged to stop in Knock until I received a letter from Archbishop MacEvilly. My restoration to health made Father Cavanagh still more anxious that I should found a convent here. But in all such cases the rules of the Catholic Church very properly require that the consent of the bishop should be obtained, as well as the consent of the parish priest. There was no delay in this, for I received the next day the following letter from the Archbishop of Tuam:

Tuam, Nov 13 1881

MY DEAR MOTHER CLARE. — I intended leaving here next week, but as you promise to favour us with a visit, I shall remain here on Monday and Tuesday to see you, and I shall promise you the hospitality of the good nuns here [the Presentation] during your stay.

The idea you have in your mind, and wish to carry out [to set up a training-school for intending female emigrants] is admirable, and worthy of a religious soul, and I am sure it is one that must commend itself to every one that has the salvation of souls at heart. If it had the effect of encouraging emigration, I could not for a moment have anything to say to it. There is plenty of room and to spare for all our people at home, if things were well managed ... Still regarded from your point of view, considering people will emigrate, I think your scheme entitled to every consideration and practicable encouragement. It has for its object to mitigate a necessary evil, and save souls that might otherwise have been lost forever. As such, I cannot but encourage it.

Very faithfully yours,
John MacEvilly, Archbishop of Tuam.

I also had the following letter from Father Cavanagh:

Knock, Nov 16 1881

DEAR SISTER MARY FRANCES CLARE. — It is my highest ambition and most ardent desire to see a convent established at Knock, as I am convinced that it would prove productive of incalculable good, and the source of numerous blessings to the people, not only of the locality, but to the many pious pilgrims who resort here from America, and so many other countries.

I trust you will, by the merciful designs of God, become the founder of the religious community so earnestly longed for, as I am satisfied that under your benign care the good work would prosper and succeed.

I trust that nothing will deter you from complying with my request.

I remain, dear Sister Clare,
Yours faithfully in Jesus Christ,
B. Cavanagh, PP Archdeacon.

I was, in fact, if possible overcautious in taking care that I should have the usual episcopal, not only permission, but even approbation, for what I did. If I had foreseen my future troubles I could scarcely have acted more judiciously; but I was to learn, all too soon, that neither prudence nor justice nor the most exact observance of religious discipline would avail, where ecclesiastics, who should have been the first to protect a woman and a sister, were determined to ruin her as far as they could do so.

. . . Now as all the charges which have been made against me, both in England and America, are founded on the false statements circulated first by Cardinal McCabe, and instigated by the Kenmare Sisters and bishop Higgins [then Vicar-Capitular of Kerry], I ask careful attention to the following points, though they are a repetition of what has already been said.

It will be remembered that I had arranged to return to Newry Convent from Kenmare; that I had obtained permission to visit Knock on my way; that it was known to my superiors why I wished to go there, (1) out of devotion to the place, (2) to see if I should found a convent there for the special purpose which had been so long in my mind, and which I knew could only be carried out in an institution for the purpose.

I had all the canonical permission necessary, and I acted throughout in accordance with the rules of the church to which I belonged.

. . . I was very kindly received in the Presentation convent in Tuam, and had an interview with the archbishop the next morning. He asked me to remain with them for the present, and they cordially seconded his wish. My first desire was to get the written permission of the archbishop for the foundation at Knock. Dr MacEvilly assured me many times that 'his

word' was quite sufficient, and seemed to think it unreasonable that I should ask for a written authorisation, and I know not why I was so persistent . . .

[The bishop writes her a letter of permission to build her convent, conditional on funds and security being provided for the sisters, and insists that his approval in no way condones or approves of the 'alleged apparitions' at Knock.]

Full of hope and joy, I at once sent out appeals for help, and found encouragement on every side. The dear and good reverend mother of the Presentation convent handed me $25.00 [sic], a large gift from their poverty, that she might have the honour of giving the first donation for the work at Knock.

I wrote at once, both to Newry and Kenmare, and received encouraging replies from both places, and this should be noted in view of subsequent events.

I wrote to Bishop Higgins also, but it cost me a great deal to do so; still, it seemed the right thing to do, yet doing right, in my case at least, has not always brought its own reward. I wrote also, at once to Bishop Leahy of Dromore [Newry] diocese.

[She receives a letter from Bishop Higgins in which he draws her attention to the following points.]

Now it should be noted here that Bishop Higgins states clearly (1) I had his permission to leave Kenmare; (2) that he had no jurisdiction over me after I left it; and (3) that he did not object to my making the foundation at Knock. This letter, it will be observed, was written on the eighth of December.

I had also written to Newry to Bishop Leahy. In fact I had done all that was necessary, and more than was necessary, and Bishop Higgins's letter, with its protestations of non-interference and professions of kindness, so completely deceived me that I did not suppose it possible, whatever his feelings against me might be, that he was actually destroying my happiness for life, and bringing me unmerited reproach and suffering, from which nothing now can ever relieve me.

As I was anxious to return to Knock for a few days, I obtained leave from Archbishop MacEvilly to do so, and he very willingly granted me the permission. On my return to Tuam the storm burst. On, I think, the thirteenth of December, Archbishop MacEvilly sent for me to see him in the convent parlour, the reverend mother of the Presentation convent said he was very angry about something, she knew not what. I went, wondering what could be the trouble, and I was soon told. The archbishop held an open letter in his hand, and said he had very unpleasant news, that he feared I had done something wrong, he would not even tell me what; in fact he was greatly excited and greatly vexed . . .

I could only reply that as his grace would not tell me what I was accused of, nor who were my accusers, I could say nothing. Certainly nothing could have been more unjust; and it is precisely this unfortunate policy of condemning people without allowing them any chance of being heard, or of knowing who are their accusers, which brings such discredit on the Roman church.

. . . But to return to my own troubles. Archbishop MacEvilly was very decided; he said, 'I will not let you go, but you had better go to Newry, see Bishop Leahy, and get from him a written transfer to my diocese, and when you come back with it, I will receive you with open arms.'

It was fearful winter weather, heavy snow and frost, and I had spent several years in Kenmare, where I had never been in any way exposed to severe cold, and to travel now was at the risk of my life.

I had already received a very kind telegram from Bishop Leahy, who was quite satisfied with all the arrangements, and this should have been sufficient for Dr MacEvilly. I asked Archbishop MacEvilly could I not write to him for this document. 'No,' he said, 'you must go and get it.' Then I offered him three times to give up the Knock foundation; could I have done more? I am glad I did so, for however I have been made to suffer, my conscience at least has been clear.

The archbishop said he could not decide positively that day, but the next day he came to the convent early and gave me just an hour's notice to take the steam cars for Dublin. Shall I ever forget that terrible day and that weary journey? It is a miracle that I lived through it all; let it be remembered that I had suffered for years from acute rheumatism and a very serious internal complaint, besides general delicacy of constitution, and that I had not for years been exposed to the weather; so the risk I ran could hardly be over-estimated.

[Cusack goes to Dublin, en route for Newry, and receives a warm welcome from the Poor Clares in Harold's Cross, where she decides to stay for a few days, consulting doctors about her health. She makes a day-trip to Newry on 16 December.]

I was received with the greatest affection by the sisters at Newry, after my many years of absence there were many changes, but there was no change in their love for me. They were very anxious that I should remain some days with them, and I was equally anxious to do so myself, but still I felt that duty called me to my work elsewhere, and I resisted all their kind entreaties.

The dear reverend mother had been my mistress of novices, and she knew from others besides myself the treatment which I had to bear in Kenmare, and she had written more than one indignant letter on the subject to the reverend mother and sisters there.

My object was, to see the bishop who had professed me there, the Right Rev Dr Leahy, and to obtain from him personally, the document of transfer to the Tuam diocese, for which Archbishop MacEvilly had sent me.

Bishop Leahy received me with the greatest kindness, fully approved what I wished to do, and gave me the subjoined document, than which nothing could be more explicit.

Convent of St Clare, Newry, Dec 16 1881

MY DEAR LORD BISHOP, — I release Sr M Frances Clare Cusack from whatever canonical obedience she owes to me as Bishop of Dromore, and I hereby transfer that obedience to your Grace.

With sincere esteem,
Your Grace's obedient brother in Christ,
Brother John Pius Leahy OP
Bishop of Dromore

TO MOST REV DR JOHN MacEVILLY, Lord bishop of Tuam.

All this writing, however, was quite unnecessary, as I had received a despatch to this effect and shown it to Dr MacEvilly before I left Tuam. But he had to express dissatisfaction, to get me out of his diocese, when he hoped to keep me out.

So rejoiced was I, that had there been any way of going to Tuam across Ireland, even by travelling by day and night, without going through Dublin, I think I should have gone. All was settled now, and it seemed as if nothing more was needed to begin the great work for poor Irish girls, on which my heart had been so long set.

. . . I arrived in Dublin late at night, and hastened to Harold's Cross Convent. I saw that the sisters were greatly disturbed and distressed, but I could not imagine the cause; in fact they knew not how to break the terrible news to me. At last I was told everything. Cardinal McCabe, who had not been in the convent I think for four years, had called there early with his chaplain, and given orders that I was to be put out into the streets of Dublin.

The sisters were greatly distressed and asked what I had done to receive such treatment. His eminence refused any information, but to relieve them, he sent his chaplain to the nearest telegraph office, with orders to send a telegram after me, to forbid my ever entering his diocese again. This telegram I never received, and what is still more remarkable I could never get any trace of it from the post-office authorities. I therefore returned, as I have said, to the convent. One dear sister, so far kept her presence of mind and allowed her charity to overcome her fear of ecclesiastical censure, as to implore the cardinal, on her knees, to allow me that one night's shelter, as they knew I could not return till late, and it was a bitter night. His eminence granted her request, but only on one condition, that I should be put out on the streets of Dublin at daybreak next morning. I had

nowhere to go, and the sisters did not fail to remind his eminence of this. All my relations and friends are Protestants. If I had gone to any of them they would indeed have received me kindly, but I knew not how I could bring myself to tell them that I had been put out of a convent of my own order, on the streets of Dublin, without a word of explanation. The sisters wrote to me a year after, to say how they had wondered at my calmness, or that I could have borne the blow as patiently as I did, but I said, 'well, it is a great trial, but I can return to Tuam tomorrow,' and thought how much pleased the archbishop would be to receive such a document. He had sent me for it, he had declared he would receive me 'with open arms' when I came back; all would be well, and God would enable me to bear the great fatigue and excitement. How could I for a moment imagine that he had sent me for a document which he did not intend to accept.

But a short time only had passed when I was handed a despatch from Archbishop MacEvilly, which is now before me as I write.

[from the Archbishop of Tuam]

TO SISTER MARY FRANCES CLARE CUSACK, Harold's Cross, Dublin, —

Don't come to the diocese till consent is given by me in writing, and I judge first if the letter be satisfactory.

I soon saw that all had been carefully pre-arranged; for shortly after, I received a despatch from the Reverend Mother of the Presentation Convent in Tuam, saying the archbishop had 'commanded' her not to receive me into her convent again.

MOTHER KEVIN KEARNEY

(1875–1957)

LETTER TO COLLEAGUE (1953)

[Mother Kevin, born Teresa Kearney, was one of the great founding figures of modern mission times, establishing her

own missionary congregation of Franciscan Sisters, and setting up dispensaries, clinics and hospitals in Uganda as well as a Midwifery Training School there in 1921, thus beginning a long campaign with the Vatican to lift the prohibition forbidding religious women from training in and practising obstetrics. Not until 1936 was the prohibition lifted but, undeterred, Mother Kevin in her hospitals in Uganda and elsewhere pioneered new and better medical facilities. Before she died she had established an Institute for African Sisters as well as putting on a firm footing her earlier foundation which was titled the Congregation of Our Lady of Africa. A warm, informal letter-writer, she wrote as she travelled and the following samples, the first to her Franciscan colleague in England and the second to her family in Wicklow, display her practical and affectionate temperament.]

Dabarii-Busia P.O. E.P. Uganda Dec 23 1953
Deus det nobis suam pacem (God gives us His Peace)

My dearest Mary of the Trinity,

Oh my dear how often you have been in my thoughts! We reached Nairobi from London Nov. 26th since then I have visited every mission but never slept twice in the same bed!! We just came up to Karule where we are now for council meetings etc etc etc. There will be many changes. Sr Alcantra returns to London Jan 6th with Sr Cecilia for the film showing — Sr Stephen and Michael will leave sometime in February with Little Sister Aquinas and Carolina to go to Liverpool to Sr Vianney — to learn the Brail — the blind school in Liverpool!

You will be delighted to hear this — Feb 1st we are going to a new mission of the Kiltegan Fathers 12 miles from Kitali it will be a new vicariate. They got part of the Mill Hill Fathers two years ago — they are Irish and very nice — I am glad to help them — 3rd week Feb we go to Kokstad to Bishop McBride D.V. If only we had more Sisters — I'm not returning to Europe 1954. Too much work to do over here, but probably Sr Jacoba and Sr Amata will go to Holland and help with the Film. Its good to be back again, but have not had a minute to move about or write. There will be many changes I'm sure, we want to get *all* finished before Retreat — we go into Retreat Jan 4th. My dear dear love to M. Prioress you know you are the child of my heart — Poor Sr Jude's brother Finbar died Dec 13th — do pray for him R.I.P.

I just want to thank M. Prioress and you for your kindness and prayers for us out here and especially for myself. 4th to 11th pray much that all may be as God wishes. A very happy New Year and always.

Yours lovingly in XT
M. Kevin

LETTER TO HER COUSIN
(1954)

as from 628 Hope St.
Kokstad, EG S Africa
March 14th '54

My dearest Sarah, P and all,

Thanks for letters received — At the moment we are on 'Durban Castle' sailing to Durban where 'Bishop's Evangelist' will meet us, to take us to Kokstad. I am delighted to go to Franciscans 'Minors' to help the Africans. I hope to see Father Colbert Byrne in Durban. The heat is terrific here in 'Darasalam' where we are today but they tell us Durban will be very cold.

We opened the Mission with Kiltegan Fathers February 2nd '54! Maggie will be delighted. 'Our Lady and S. Bridgid' it's a lovely place, schools etc not much, but little convent is very nice, simple, chapel poor but very clean. Three sisters are there and are very happy. We here promised to open another convent for them in Nakuru for (for Goans). Maggie must keep Father McGrath up to his promise of trying to get us postulants. I am so glad you all saw the film. I am sure you liked it, its very interesting and very true.

Since my return I have been very busy one way and another and have no chance of going back this year but I just want *you all* to know how truly delighted to have even a little time with you all and dear P. How is Nora? You must miss her in many ways. I do thank God for his loving kindness to allow me to meet you all. I have written and told Anna Mary all about it, she will be very glad, she is over 80 years now. Sister Elizabeth is still in our convent, Foster St. Boston but her heart is in Uganda, I do hope one day she will return, after six years I expect.

The Mau Mau are pretty bad in Kenya, in Uganda also there is much unrest but sure it's all over the world, and all we can do is to carry on and try to do our best and trust in God.

Sarah do tell dear P I'll write to him and Breda in a few days, but my dear I hate writing any time.

My dear love to each dear one, not forgetting my namesake 'Tessie' and very much to your own dear self.

Affectionately yours,
M Kevin

MARIE MARTIN

(1892–1975)

from:
THE CONSTITUTIONS OF THE MEDICAL MISSIONARIES OF MARY (1962)

[From the last quarter of the nineteenth century Christian missionaries had gone to remote parts of the world, building churches, setting up Christian schools and introducing Western medical practices. After intense lobbying over many years, the Vatican, through the Sacred Congregation of Propaganda Fide in Rome, issued the Instruction on Medical Work *Constans ac Sedula* 11 February 1936. The decree gave new religious institutes of women permission to engage in medical work and especially in maternity work. Marie Martin had been preparing for that recognition for fifteen years and immediately put in train her plans for a Congregation of Medical Missionaries. The *Constitutions of the Medical Missionaries of Mary,* on which she worked assiduously all her life, was finally approved in draft form in February 1962. The following excerpt is the opening preamble.]

Art. 1. — The Congregation is called the 'Medical Missionaries of Mary', because it was founded primarily to help the foreign missions by means of medical work and has consecrated itself and its labour especially to Mary, Mother of God, Mediatrix of Grace.

Art. 2. — The general end of the Congregation is to glorify God, by the sanctification of its members and the salvation of souls; their perfection will be rooted and founded in Charity, and will be attained by the observance of the Simple Vows of Poverty, Chastity and Obedience and of these Constitutions, and by their apostolic work.

Art. 3. — The special end of the Congregation consists in the dedication of the Medical Missionaries of Mary to a life of sacrifice and apostleship to the extent of their power, for the Church and souls. At the wish of the Holy See and the Ordinaries they will go to any Mission and be ready to undertake any branch of medical science, to ease bodily misery, and open the way for the grace of redemption.

Art. 4. — While all branches of medical work are within the scope of the Congregation its special work will be to attend to the health of mothers and infants; to the formation of Christian women; and to the ultimate formation of a native Sisterhood especially in pagan countries. The Congregation will also be ready at the request of the Ordinaries to teach in any Mission Station. The Congregation will combine the Contemplative Spirit with the active life of love and sacrifice, imitating Mary our Mother at the Annunciation and the Visitation.

Art. 5. — The spirit, therefore, which should animate the Sisters of the Medical Missionaries of Mary is the spirit of Christ. He will be the centre and the model of their lives. They will strive daily to acquire His interior spirit and imitate His exterior life. So that with them, as with Him, their interior and active life may be perfectly blended together and thus their apostleship may be fruitful and their lives a perfect expression of the love of God and souls.

Art. 6. — Next to Christ their Model will be Our Lady. The Sisters will imitate the virtues she manifested at the Annunciation, the Visitation and the Nativity, above all her love for God and for souls, her humility and her simplicity.

[Marie Martin spent thirty-seven years developing missionary work along medical lines and membership of her congregation grew rapidly. Though she encouraged her sisters to keep up with the latest developments in medical science, she took a close personal interest in the spiritual formation of novices preparing for Final Profession which made them full members of the Congregation of the Medical Missionaries of Mary. Here Mother Mary Martin, as she was known, elaborates on the meaning of the Vow of Poverty.]

Poverty is best seen in the Nativity. We are not called to a very destitute state of poverty, but love God in everything: joys and worries. Think not so much of yourselves but more of God and you will go much faster. The crucifixion was God's greatest act of poverty — he sacrificed himself. We will not be crucified but we may contract leprosy, but love Him in that.

Never grumble no matter what happens, dear children. Unite yourself to Jesus in His poverty. That is living prayer. That is the life of Prayer. We are not perturbed at what happens. Not that we don't feel it. But after the first reaction, see what Our Lord would do now? Even though people around us are grumbling. Never mind. God will never, never let us down. Gold and silver I have not, you may say; but you should have the grace of God to give, pray for them, and maybe some rich man passing will give the 'gold and silver' for you. You give the prayer of your heart.

'All things common to all'; If you loose [sic] a handkerchief you don't get a new one but go and look for it, and find it in a spirit of poverty. It may have gone down the sluice and be lost forever; well, find that out and then you may ask for another.

'Sisters are not to murmur and complain . . .' that is the devil and a very bad spirit of poverty. Be a big person in a little space. 'Not to buy or sell anything.' Must ask permission. Do you go for every tittle tattle? No. Write it in the order book and give to the Secretary. 'Take care of all things': have a sense of responsibility in all things under your care. Run things well, efficiently but always practising poverty.

This is a thing I heard and which I see creeping — accepting personal gifts. We don't work for personal reward — we work for God. Let patients see quite clearly that you accept nothing for yourself. If you are embarrassed invite them to give something for the missions or the Congregation. Say to patients: 'we are not allowed to accept gifts'. Let them see quite clearly that you do not accept it for yourself.

Think supernaturally: From God's point of view.

Biographies/Bibliographies

Ellen Maria Leahy

LIFE. Born in Mallow, County Cork, in 1803, Ellen Mary Leahy entered the Presentation Order in South Presentation Convent, Cork, and was professed as a member of the order in 1834. Known as Mother di Pazzi, she compiled the first domestic Annals, a manuscript volume. Entries in her handwriting ceased after 17 January 1853. She died in 1874.

CHIEF WRITINGS. The domestic Annals of South Presentation Cork, which she compiled from various sources to cover the founding years of Nano Nagle's life and immediately after her death, 1771–1853.

Spiritual reflections incorporated into the *Directory* of the Presentation Order, 1850.

BIOGRAPHY AND CRITICISM. Mary Pius O'Farrell, *Nano Nagle, Woman of the Gospel* (Monasterevin: Presentation Generalate, 1996).

'Mary'

No information available.

Catherine McAuley

LIFE. Born at Stormanstown House, Dublin, 29 September 1778. Her parents died when she was young and at eighteen she was adopted by Mr and Mrs Callahan of Coolock House. She converted them both to Catholicism, and on his death in 1822, Callaghan left her his large fortune. She bought a site in Lower Baggot Street, and in 1827 built a school for poor children and a residence for working women, called the House of Our Blessed Lady of Mercy. In 1829, with two others, she entered the Presentation Convent at George's Hill, Dublin, and when they took simple vows of poverty, chastity and obedience on 12 December 1831, the Sisters of Mercy came into existence. Archbishop Murray supported her aims 'to educate poor little girls, to lodge and maintain poor young ladies who are in danger, that they may be provided for in a proper manner, and to visit the sick poor'. Her rule was approved by Pope Gregory XVI on 24 March 1835 and given final confirmation by him in June 1841. The order became the largest religious congregation ever founded in the English-speaking world, with houses in England, New Zealand and the United States. She died on 10 November 1841 and is buried at the convent in Baggot Street.

CHIEF WRITINGS. *The Correspondence of Catherine McAuley*, ed. Angela Bolster (Cork: Sisters of Mercy Publications, 1989); Angela Bolster, *Catherine McAuley in Her Own Words* (Dublin: Diocesan Office for Causes, 1979).

BIOGRAPHY AND CRITICISM. Angela Bolster, *Documentary Study for the Canonization Process of the Servant of God Catherine McAuley, Founder of the Congregation of Sisters of Mercy, 1778–1841: Positio Super Virtutibus*, 2 vols (Rome: Sacred Congregation for the Causes of Saints, 1985); Roland Burke Savage, *Catherine McAuley: The First Sister of Mercy* (Dublin: M.H. Gill, 1949); Mary C. Sullivan, *Catherine McAuley and the Tradition of Mercy* (Notre Dame, Indiana: University of Notre Dame Press, 1995; Dublin: Four Courts Press, 2000).

Mary Clare Augustine Moore

LIFE. Born in Dublin on 1 August 1808, Mary Clare Moore entered the Sisters of Mercy in Baggot Street in 1837 and was professed in 1840, taking the name Augustine. She met Catherine McAuley in 1829 and recalled her appearance years later. Possessed of artistic talents, she prepared an illuminated Register of the Dublin Community of the Sisters of Mercy and an illuminated copy of the Rule of the Sisters of Mercy. She taught in the school in Goldenbridge near Dublin and became supervisor of the Refuge for Women Prisoners there in 1870. Three years after the death of Catherine McAuley, Moore began to compile the long narrative, known as the Dublin Manuscript, and began her own *Memoir of the Foundress of the Sisters of Mercy in Ireland* probably in 1844; she completed it in 1864. She died in Dublin on 7 October 1880.

CHIEF WRITINGS. *A Memoir of the Foundress of the Sisters of Mercy in Ireland*, in Mary C. Sullivan (ed.), *Catherine McAuley and the Tradition of Mercy* (Notre Dame, Indiana: University of Notre Dame Press, 1995; Dublin: Four Courts Press, 2000), pp. 198–216; Autograph Manuscript (The Dublin Manuscript) in Archives Sisters of Mercy, Baggot Street, Dublin.

Sarah Atkinson

LIFE. Born Sarah Gaynot in 1823 in Athlone. She moved to Dublin when she was about fifteen years of age and married George Atkinson, a medical doctor, when she was about twenty-five. They had one child who died at the age of four. Thereafter Atkinson devoted much of her life to charitable work in Dublin. She campaigned successfully to have the Dublin Union Workhouse opened to visitors and in 1861 she read a paper to the Social Science Congress, which met in Dublin, on the evils of the workhouse and the need for industrial training. She wrote many anonymous articles on a variety of topical, religious and historical subjects in journals such as the *Irish Monthly, Irish Quarterly Review, Duffy's Hibernian Magazine* and the *Nation*. Her most substantial publication was her biography of Mary Aikenhead. She died in 1893 in Dublin.

CHIEF WRITINGS. Her journal articles are listed in 'Mrs Sarah Atkinson: A Few Notes in Remembrance', *Irish Monthly,* vol. 21 (1893), pp. 601–11); *Mary Aikenhead: Her Life, Her Work and Her Friends, Giving a History of the Foundation of the Congregation of the Irish Sisters of Charity* (Dublin: M.H. Gill, 1875; London: Burns and Oates, 1875). A collection of her essays was published posthumously as *Essays* (Dublin: M.H. Gill, 1895).

BIOGRAPHY AND CRITICISM. K.H., 'In Memory of a Noble Irishwoman', *Irish Monthly,* vol. 21 (1893), pp. 464–9; 'Mrs Sarah Atkinson: A Few Notes in Remembrance', ibid., pp. 601–11.

Margaret Anna Cusack

LIFE. Born in Dublin in 1832, the eldest of two children of Dr Samuel Cusack, a dispensary doctor, and his wife Sarah Stoney. Both parents came from a long tradition of Protestantism. When her parents separated, she went with her brother to live with her great-aunt Baker in Exeter, Devonshire, and joined the Plymouth Brethren. On the death of her fiancé, Charles Holmes, Cusack enrolled in the Sennonite Sisterhood of Doctor Pusey but converted to Roman Catholicism in 1858. She returned to Ireland and entered the Poor Clare convent in Newry, County Down, in 1859. For the following eleven years she enjoyed peace and fame, writing and publishing on a variety of subjects. In all, Cusack wrote about fifty books. After a period spent working in the famine-stricken regions of Kenmare, County Kerry, she encountered opposition from clergy and bishops in Kenmare and in Knock, County Mayo, where she built a convent and two schools. On the advice of Cardinal Manning she moved to England and founded her new Order of Peace in Nottingham. In 1884 Cusack went to Rome to apply for a dispensation from her vows as a Poor Clare. In Rome to some she was an excellent religious; to others her actions were incomprehensible and her fitness to found an order suspect. Two years later, instructed by Bishop Bagshaw of Nottingham, Cusack went to the United States to raise money and to open houses of the Order of Peace. In 1889 her autobiography, *The Nun of Kenmare*, was published. Convinced that her order would not prosper while she was the object of ecclesiastical disapproval, she left her religious community in 1895. Her final conversion was to Methodism and her last writings were hostile to the Catholic church. She returned to England and died in Remington Spa, Warwickshire, in June 1899. Eccentric and wilful, she never abandoned her pursuit of justice. In 1974 she was officially recognized by Rome as the founder of the Sisters of Saint Joseph of Peace.

CHIEF WRITINGS. *The Nun of Kenmare: An Autobiography* (London: Hodder and Stoughton, 1889); *The Patriot's History of Ireland* (Kenmare, 1869); *The Case of Ireland Plainly Stated: A Plea for My People and My Race* (New York, 1881); *Advice to Irish Girls in America* (New York, 1872).

BIOGRAPHY AND CRITICISM. Irene ffrench Eager, *Margaret Anna Cusack: A Biography* (Dublin: Arlen House, 1979); Jo Ann Kay McNamara, *Sisters in Arms* (Cambridge: Harvard University Press, 1996).

Mother Kevin Kearney

LIFE. Mother Kevin was born Teresa Kearney in Arklow, County Wicklow, in 1875, shortly after the death of her father. Her mother died when she was ten and she was raised by her grandmother. She worked for several years as a teacher before entering the Franciscan order at St Mary's Abbey, Mill Hill, London, in 1895. In 1904 she was sent to Uganda, with five other sisters, to assist in the establishment of the Catholic missions. She devoted the rest of her life to that cause and to Africa, building schools, convents and hospitals wherever she went. Mother Kevin founded two religious orders, the Franciscan Missionary Sisters for Africa and the Little Sisters of St Francis, the latter an order for African women. She received both an MBE and an OBE for her work, and her name has entered several African languages, where a 'kevina' means an act of service or generosity. She died in New York in 1957, and although her body was initially buried at Mount St Oliver, the mother-house of the Franciscan Sisters for Africa, it was later brought back to Uganda at the insistence of the people among whom she had worked.]

BIOGRAPHY AND CRITICISM. Mary Louis, *Love is the Answer* (Dublin: Franciscan Publications, 1964); Edmund Hogan, *The Irish Missionary Movement: A Historical Survey 1830–1980* (Dublin: Gill and Macmillan, 1990).

Marie Martin

LIFE. Born in Dublin, 25 April 1892, educated Sacred Heart Convent, Leeson Street, Dublin, Holy Child College, Harrogate, and finishing school in Bonn. Worked as voluntary aid nurse in England, France and Malta during First World War. Returned to Dublin in 1918 to train as midwife at National Maternity Hospital. Motivated to set up religious order of women to operate clinics and hospitals after seeing appalling conditions in Nigeria, 1921. Matron of Glenstal, 1923. Professed as nun 1937 and founded Medical Missionaries of Mary. Received Florence Nightingale Medal from International Red Cross, 1963. First woman to be awarded Honorary Fellowship of RCSI (1966). Received Freedom of Drogheda, June 1966. Died in Drogheda in 1975.

CHIEF WRITINGS. *The Constitutions of Medical Missionaries of Mary* (Drogheda: Medical Missionaries of Mary Publication, 1962).

BIOGRAPHY AND CRITICISM. Mary Purcell, *To Africa with Love: Life of Mother Mary Martin* (Dublin: Gill and Macmillan, 1987).

JANICE HOLMES, *Editor*

The Century of Religious Zeal, 1800–74

Much of what we know about female religious experience in nineteenth-century Ireland is based on a study of Catholicism. The role of nuns in Irish society, for example, and their impact on education, the care of the poor and work among prostitutes, is by now well documented.[1] Protestant women, however, have yet to receive the same level of attention. Of the research which has been done, much of it has focused on the outward manifestations of belief, such as women's denominational activities and their charitable work.[2] The reason for this emphasis is obvious: discussion, by women, of their internal religious beliefs is much harder to find. The extracts listed here, therefore, will serve as a welcome addition to our knowledge of the female experience of Irish Protestantism, primarily because they are concerned, for the most part, with the personal dimension of religious belief rather than with its social manifestations. Although there is mention of charitable bequests, school visiting and meetings among the poor, the primary focus of these documents is to recount, usually for general edification, the internal experience of vital religion. The involvement of Irish women in philanthropic work is considered elsewhere.[3]

Of the Protestant women represented here, the majority experienced religion of an evangelical variety. Evangelicalism was a movement of religious vitality which emerged out of the European pietism of the early eighteenth century. Through the efforts of individuals such as John Wesley, the founder of Methodism, and John Cennick, a Moravian evangelist, evangelical ideas spread amongst the existing Protestant communities of Ireland and led to the formation of Methodism. In the early years of the nineteenth century, evangelical ideas were responsible for initiating a reform movement within the Church of Ireland and instigating a 'purge' of theological liberals within the Presbyterian church.[4] The accounts of these Irish women, therefore, reflect the concerns, preoccupations and symbols which were common to many eighteenth- and nineteenth-century evangelicals.

At the outset, two points should be made. Firstly, not all Protestant women in early nineteenth-century Ireland were of an evangelical bent. Within the Church of Ireland, for example, although evangelicalism had made substantial headway among its clergy and adherents by the 1830s, the Established Church was not overwhelmingly evangelical in tone until the late 1860s.[5] Within Presbyterianism, the increasing

1. The main sources in this area include Caitriona Clear, *Nuns in Nineteenth-Century Ireland* (Dublin: Gill and Macmillan, 1987); Tony Faney, 'Nuns in the Catholic Church in Ireland in the Nineteenth Century', in Mary Cullen (ed.), *Girls Don't Do Honours* (Dublin: Women's Education Bureau, 1987), pp. 7–30; Maria Luddy, *Women and Philanthropy in Nineteenth-Century Ireland* (Cambridge: Cambridge University Press, 1995); Mary Peckham Magray, *The Transforming Power of Nuns: Women, Religion and Cultural Change in Ireland 1750–1900* (New York: Oxford University Press, 1998).
2. See subsections 'Philanthropy in Nineteenth-Century Ireland', Vol. v, pp. 691–704, and 'Education in Nineteenth-Century Ireland', Vol. v, pp. 619–76.
3. See subsection 'Philanthropy in Nineteenth-Century Ireland'.

4. For an account of the progress of evangelicalism within the Protestant communities of Ireland, see David Hempton and Myrtle Hill, *Evangelical Protestantism in Ulster Society, 1740–1890* (London: Routledge, 1991), chs 1–3; D.H. Akenson, *The Church of Ireland: Ecclesiastical Reform and Revolution, 1800–85* (New Haven and London: Yale University Press, 1971); R.F.G. Holmes, *Henry Cooke* (Belfast: Christian Journals, 1981).
5. David Hempton, 'Evangelicalism in English and Irish Society, 1780–1840', in Mark Noll, David Bebbington and George Rawlyk (eds), *Evangelicalism: Comparative Studies of Popular Protestantism in North America, the British Isles, and Beyond, 1700–1900* (Oxford: Oxford University Press, 1994), p. 171; D.H. Akenson, *Church of Ireland*, p. 132.

dominance of evangelical theology was a long, drawn-out process. During the 'subscription controversy' of the 1820s, conservative ministers in the Synod of Ulster were surprisingly reluctant to exclude their more liberal colleagues for refusing to 'subscribe' to the Westminster Confession of Faith. The synod finally did expel the non-subscribers in 1829, and only then did the expansion of evangelical influence become an inevitability.[6] As a result, Protestant women from within these two traditions would not necessarily have been evangelical in outlook.

Secondly, for those women who were influenced by evangelicalism, it is important to realize that they saw themselves not only as Irish, but also as part of a larger religious community, one that included evangelicals in Scotland, England and America. Many women would have been familiar with far-flung religious events through the publicity organs of sermons, devotional magazines and special services. In 1859, news of a revival movement in America, which had started in 1857, was avidly consumed at lectures and sermons throughout Ulster's churches.[7] Of the women selected for this collection, several had close denominational or familial connections to England. Two of them were born in England, although they spent extensive periods in Ireland and were closely linked to the Irish evangelical scene. In this respect, religious allegiances superseded national boundaries. And as a result, the experiences which these women relate are not distinctly 'Irish' in tone. They reflect the characteristics of a wider, transatlantic evangelical community, of which Ireland was a well established member.

For evangelicals, the most important experience in an individual's spiritual life was that of conversion: a conscious turning away from a life of sin and a deliberate turning towards a life lived for the glory of God.[8] For eighteenth-

and early nineteenth-century evangelicals this process often involved an intense conviction of sin which could last for several days, even weeks. Following this period of guilt and remorse, a spiritual encounter with God, along with an act of confession, led to the eventual achievement of peace. This process was an intensely private one, which could only be experienced on an individual level. Charlotte Elizabeth Tonna's conversion was preceded by several weeks of agonized soul-searching, the details of which she kept to herself. She later wrote, '[o]utwardly I was calm and even cheerful, but within reigned the very blackness of darkness'.

The actual means of conversion, however, could vary from person to person. Evangelicals placed a great deal of emphasis on 'preaching the gospel', which explains their commitment to evangelism and revival services. Other methods could be equally effective. Significant passages from the Bible, the words of a well-loved hymn, or a providential occurrence could often provoke thoughts of conversion. Tonna was, in her account, deeply influenced by a devotional book a Dublin friend had sent her. Alice Cambridge, a Methodist preacher and class leader, was moved by the testimony of a female friend with whom she met on a regular basis.

The experience of conversion, by its very nature, involved a process of intense self-examination which emphasized feelings of guilt and remorse. Under the influence of such strong emotions, individuals often exhibited their feelings in very physical ways, like moaning, sobbing, shaking and falling to the ground. The frequency of such behaviour among eighteenth-century Methodists earned them the appellations of 'Ranter' and 'Shaker' by their critics. While such manifestations could take place within the confines of a regular church service, they were more characteristic of religious revivals, a common feature of early evangelicalism. In the eighteenth century, revivals were spontaneous outbursts of religious excitement, where numerous individuals over a wide geographical area experienced conviction of sin and conversion often in unusual ways. In Ireland, the Presbyterian community experienced a regional revival in 1625, where the religious enthusiasm in evidence at monthly meetings was translated into numerous conversions. Irish Methodism

---

6. R.F.G. Holmes, 'Controversy and Schism in the Synod of Ulster in the 1820s', in J.L.M. Haire (ed.), *Challenge and Conflict: Essays in Presbyterian History and Doctrine* (Antrim: W. and G. Baird, 1981), p. 122; Peter Brooke, *Ulster Presbyterianism: The Historical Perspective, 1610–1970* (Dublin: Gill and Macmillan; New York: St Martin's Press, 1987), p. 153.

7. For an example of one such meeting, see 'Extraordinary Religious Excitement at Ahoghill', *Ballymena Observer*, 26 March 1859, p. 1.

8. A good summary of the major characteristics of evangelicalism, including conversion and an emphasis on the Bible, can be found in David Bebbington, *Evangelicalism in Modern Britain: A History from the 1730s to the 1980s* (London: Unwin Hyman, 1989), ch. 1.

expanded dramatically in size in the late eighteenth century through a series of emotional revivals.[9]

Revivals, with their fervent preaching and crowded meetings, traditionally upset conventional religious norms. For women, therefore, revivals could be extremely liberating events, temporarily lowering the barriers to their public participation in religious practice and allowing them opportunities to express their religious attitudes in previously unauthorized ways. Nowhere is this more true than in the Ulster revival of 1859. Between March and October of that year, a powerful religious movement shook the Protestant community of Ulster and filled the churches with earnest inquirers after salvation. Church meetings were long, crowded and frequent. The proceedings were often disrupted as members of the congregation cried out and fell to the ground under conviction of sin. Such manifestations were soon supplanted by the appearance of even more unusual phenomena, such as visions, trances, clairvoyance and stigmata-like markings.

Even a cursory glance at the contemporary sources generates the assumption that it was women who most frequently experienced these ecstatic phenomena. These women tended to come from the poorer segments of society. In rural areas they were employed as weavers and labourers. Critics of revival enthusiasm have argued that it was women's natural excitability and feminine weakness which made them more susceptible to fits of religious hysteria.[10] A closer examination of such behaviour, however, can tell us a great deal about female religious experience at a grassroots level, a group notoriously difficult to make assumptions about. An examination of the content of these visions, several of which are reproduced in the selection below, offers a path into female perceptions of religion and what women found to be meaningful forms of religious expression. Visions of heaven, of hell, of the Bible, all indicate that these working-class women had a fairly conventional view of Christian precepts, no doubt influenced by the sermons they heard on Sunday. Other visions, of women in beautiful clothes, of women convers-

ing with Jesus, could indicate a desire for status and recognition within the local community. The 'sleeping cases', where women predicted when they would fall into a trance, lacked a significant religious purpose, although they attracted enormous attention from the press, local ministers and the surrounding neighbourhood. According to one commentator, 'there was a crowd assembled outside the house [of a woman who had claimed to be marked by the Holy Spirit] extending to the centre of the street, and the ingress and egress of visitors reminded me of May's Market on the forenoon of the same day'. Despite the criticism of numerous clergymen, it was obvious that the crowds considered these women recipients of a special religious blessing. As a result, they gained a certain level of authority within their communities. They also achieved a degree of independence. These visions, involving as they did a direct, spiritual encounter with God, bypassed the clergy and other male mediators of religious practice. However, when revival excitement began to fade, so did the mandate for such feminine authority. Once established religious patterns were re-established, women retreated into their former positions, as the stereotype of women as meek, modest and submissive was only temporarily abandoned.

The extremely physical and public nature of women's conversions during the revival of 1859 offers a tantalizing glimpse of Protestant women's attitudes to their religion. But conversion is really only the beginning of the story. Once 'saved', new converts were expected to exhibit the 'fruits' of conversion in their daily lives. Thoughts, decisions, opinions and actions were all meant to be regulated according to biblical principles. Evangelicals, therefore, expected that those who had been 'saved' would read the Bible regularly, that they would conduct daily prayers, both in private and on a family basis, that their outward behaviour would seek to emulate the example of Christ, and that they would be diligent in speaking to others of their need for Him. The documents in this collection well illustrate this sort of constant self-regulation. In Anne Jocelyn's diary, she subjects her daily life to an intense scrutiny. Anne's accusations of pride ('at breakfast very proud towards one in heart'), vanity ('my dress has been a great snare

9. D. Hempton and M. Hill, *Evangelical Protestantism*, pp. 30–7, 148.
10. For one such assessment, see *Belfast Daily Mercury*, 27 September 1859, p. 2.

to me'), and sloth ('I was too long at the garden today. I was unprofitable'), reflect evangelical concerns to avoid 'worldliness' and to use time to its best advantage, that is, in the promotion of the gospel. Anne's feelings of unworthiness come from her perceived failure at achieving the unspoken ideal of total dependence on God. She constantly desired 'to give up all to the Lord' and that 'Christ must be my all in all'. Marie Fry, a young evangelical Irish woman, believed she needed to be 'moment by moment depending on our living Christ'.

Despite this emphasis on weakness and reliance, the personal faith of the evangelical women in this collection is anything but insipid. Their writings indicate a faith well grounded in scriptural knowledge and theological concepts. One of the most important characteristics of evangelicalism is its emphasis on the Bible as the sole source of truth.[11] Evangelicals believed that the Bible was inspired by God and that it contained all the guidance necessary to lead a Christian life. They were, therefore, encouraged to read it daily and to study its pages. At times of stress, the Bible was often a source of comfort. Alice Cambridge, at a particularly fraught moment in her religious life, held her Bible between her hands and prayed to God for a passage of scripture which would comfort her. Providentially, she was directed to the Song of Solomon, which, while not appearing to be a particularly relevant verse, 'overpowered' Alice with a 'sense of the divine favour'.

Long years of Bible study, devotional reading and attendance at Sunday church services gave many women an in-depth knowledge of biblical stories and examples which they used frequently in their own writing. In one instance, Marie Fry, whose mission was writing to soldiers about spiritual matters, managed to squeeze ten quotations from the Bible into a single letter. Fanny Grattan Guinness's spirited defence of female preaching revealed a high degree of biblical and theological knowledge. She relied not only on arguments from history (that women in the past had preached), but also on complicated expositions of the relevant biblical texts from both the Old and New Testaments. Her explanations included a knowledge of Greek and a familiarity with the standard evangelical biblical commentaries.

While most denominations would not have allowed Fanny to preach such a theological treatise from their pulpits, she was essentially fulfilling that very function, only in print. In this manner, the contradictory position which women occupied in nineteenth-century evangelicalism becomes more apparent. Female leadership was acceptable, but only within certain prescribed channels. Marie Fry's campaign to convert soldiers was considered appropriate feminine behaviour because she conducted it from within the privacy of her own home. The security of a domestic environment legitimated what was, in the words of her biographer, a position of 'preaching by post'.[12] Likewise, Fanny Grattan Guinness, in the course of her defence of female preaching, felt compelled to situate such behaviour in reference to women's domestic roles. At one point she argued that '*home* is woman's proper sphere . . . that it is her only really happy sphere (as, if her God-appointed one, it of course must be)'. Female preaching, Fanny averred, was only ever an exception to the general rule. Although the evangelical experience of religion could be a liberating one, as for the women in the 1859 revival, it could also be quite restricting. Women were often forced to confine their aspirations within the stereotypes of dependence and domesticity.

Despite their difference of denomination, class, nationality and time, the women represented in this collection testify to the commonality which can be found in an evangelical experience of religion. The centrality of conversion, the desire to lead a godly life and a devotion to the Bible were characteristics which evangelicals, be they in Ireland, England or America, would have recognized. The emotions and actions which these women have recorded also reflect an important paradox in the feminine experience of religion. As Gail Malmgreen has so astutely observed, the experience of female spirituality is a 'complex tension between religion as an "opiate" and as an embodiment of ideological and institutional sexism, and religion as a transcendent and

11. D. Bebbington, *Evangelicalism*, pp. 12–14.

12. Fanny Grattan Guinness (ed.), *Selections from the Correspondence of the late Marie Fry (of Dublin), with a Brief Biographical Notice* (2nd ed., London: S.W. Partridge [1874?]), p. 93.

liberating force'.[13] These Irish women viewed themselves very much in domestic and submissive terms. At the same time, they often used their religious behaviour to push at the boundaries of biblical prohibition, social expectation, church regulation and personal inhibition, even if those boundaries were never entirely eliminated.

13. Gail Malmgreen (ed.), *Religion in the Lives of English Women, 1760–1930* (London: Croom Helm, 1986), pp. 6–7.

ALICE CAMBRIDGE

(1762–1829)

from:
MEMOIR OF MISS A. CAMBRIDGE (1832)

[Alice Cambridge was a member of the Society of Methodists, an evangelical group which emerged in the early eighteenth century under the influence of the Reverend John Wesley, a minister in the Church of England. Methodists stressed the importance of a spiritual 'conversion' and claimed that individuals could have the assurance of salvation, a theological position known as Arminianism. In its early years Methodism was promoted by a group of travelling preachers, many of whom were laymen. More unusually, a substantial minority were women. Alice Cambridge was one of the few Irish women known to preach and she soon became very popular. In her memoirs she recounts the moment of her conversion. The providential discovery of a Bible verse as the trigger for her conversion is a common trope in many evangelical conversion accounts, as is the role which her female friends played in supporting and encouraging her efforts.]

I was meeting in band with Mrs. Strickett, my cousin Mary Norris, and I think Mrs. Magee, for they used to meet also; it was on a Saturday evening, on the gallery in the old preaching-house in Bandon . . . Mrs. Strickett was telling her experience of the gracious dealings of God towards her, and while she was thus delightfully speaking good of His name, He lifted upon me the light of His countenance; my mourning was turned into joy; I felt a change, which until that glad moment I had been a stranger to, and I rejoiced with joy unspeakable and full of glory. My dear friends rejoiced with me, and my loved Mrs. Strickett sung the following verses coming down from the gallery where we met, and where my God had so peculiarly blessed me:—

> What hath the world to equal this;—
> The solid peace the heavenly bliss,
> The joys immortal, love Divine,
> The love of Jesus ever mine?
> Greater joys I'm born to know,
> From terrestrial to celestial,
> When I up to Jesus go.

Mrs. Strickett was no stranger to what I experienced that evening — but it was new to me altogether . . . I went home to my father's house glorifying the Lord, and on my knees I bowed with a gladdened heart at the throne of grace to thank him for his great love manifested to me in Christ Jesus . . .

My thirst after holiness increasing, I longed for closer communion with God — to be made more like him, and to be set apart or consecrated to His service entirely; for this I was led most earnestly to supplicate at the thrones of grace, my Heavenly Father surely heard me, and often visited me with his soul cheering presence; but one day at that early period of my journeying to Canaan's happy land, the plenitude of heavenly light and love, which he poured into my soul, was such that I should not omit mentioning it . . . I was kneeling by my bed-side, drawn out I may truly say in vehement desire and supplication to be filled with all the fulness [*sic*] of God. I held my Bible closed between my hands, and prayed that some passage from the sacred volume might be applied to my heart, on which by faith I might lay hold — I was (I trust divinely) influenced to address the Almighty with all the earnestness of prayer that has a tendency to weaken the body, so that I found the mortal part nearly exhausted. When I took my hands from the Bible, it opened on the fifth chapter of Solomon's Song, the first verse of which caught my eye,[1] and was so powerfully applied to my heart, that I was almost overpowered with a sense of the divine favour, and for the space of eighteen or twenty minutes, I could neither read nor pray any more; it appeared almost as if prayer was lost for the world, no, not even for its lawful business and pursuits, all seemed to recede and disappear: I stood as on the verge of heaven, and my hope seemed full of immortality.

1. Song of Solomon 5:1: 'I have come into my garden, my sister, my bride; I have gathered my myrrh with my spice. I have eaten my honeycomb and my honey; I have drunk my wine and my milk. Eat, O friends, and drink; drink your fill, O lovers.'

CHARLOTTE ELIZABETH TONNA

(1790–1846)

from:
PERSONAL RECOLLECTIONS
(1854)

['Charlotte Elizabeth', as she was more commonly known, was a famous English tract-writer and well-known opponent of Catholicism. When about eighteen, she married an Irish man, Captain George Phelan, and between 1819 and 1824 lived on his small estate in County Kilkenny. Charlotte was clearly a woman of high spirits and her marriage to Phelan was not happy. He spent most of his time in Dublin, while she, horrified by the treatment of the local tenantry, retreated to the seclusion of her garden where she lived in virtual isolation. It was at this stage that she began to pursue a religious life and eventually experienced a conversion to evangelical Christianity. Her account reflects the importance of 'grace' as a mechanism within the conversion process. According to evangelicals, it was only possible to achieve salvation through the acceptance, by faith, of Christ's death on the cross. Although Charlotte tries to work her way to salvation, it is only when she recognizes that Christ's sacrifice applies to her, despite her sinfulness, that she finds peace.]

I came to the resolution of being a perfect devotee of religion: I thought myself marvellously good; but something of a monastic mania seized me. I determined to emulate the recluses of whom I had often read; to become a sort of Protestant nun; and to fancy my garden, with its high stone-walls, and little thicket of apple-trees, a convent-enclosure. I also settled it with myself to pray three or four times every day, instead of twice; and with great alacrity entered upon this new routine of devotion.

Here God met with, and arrested me. When I kneeled down to pray, the strangest alarms took hold of my mind. He to whom I had been accustomed to prate with flippant volubility in a set form of heartless words, seemed to my startled mind so exceedingly terrible in unapproachable majesty, and so very angry with me in particular, that I became paralyzed with fear. I strove against this, with characteristic pertinacity: I called to mind all the common-place assurances respecting the sufficiency of a good intention, and magnified alike my doings and my sufferings. I persuaded myself it was only a holy awe, the effect of distinguished piety and rare humility, and that I was really an object of the divine complacency in no ordinary degree. Again I essayed to pray, but in vain; I dared not. Then I attributed it to a nervous state of feeling which would wear away by a little abstraction from the subject; but this would not do. To leave off praying was impossible, yet to pray seemed equally so. I well remember that the character in which I chiefly viewed the Lord God was that of an Avenger, going forth to smite the first-born of Egypt; and I somehow identified myself with the condemned number. Often, after kneeling a long time, I have laid my face upon my arms, and wept most bitterly because I could not, dared not pray.

It was not in my nature to be driven back easily from any path I had entered on; and here the

Lord wrought upon me to persevere resolutely. I began to examine myself, in order to discover *why* I was afraid, and taking as my rule the ten commandments, I found myself sadly deficient on some points. The tenth affected me as it never had done before. 'I had not known lust', because I had not understood the law when it said 'Thou shalt not covet'. A casual glance at the declaration of St. James, 'Whosoever shall keep the whole law, and yet offend in one point, he is guilty of all', alarmed me exceedingly; and on a sudden it occurred to me, that not only the ten commandments, but all the precepts of the New Testament, were binding on a Christian; and I trembled more than ever.

What was to be done? To reform myself, certainly, and become obedient to the whole law. Accordingly I went to work, transcribed all the commands that I felt myself most in the habit of neglecting, and pinned up a dozen or two of texts round my room. It required no small effort to enter this apartment and walk round it, reading my mementos. That active schoolmaster, the law, had got me fairly under his rod, and dreadful were the writhings of the convicted culprit! I soon, however, took down my texts, fearing lest any one else might see them, and not knowing they were for myself, be exasperated. I then made a little book, wrote down a list of offences, and commenced making a dot over against each, whenever I detected myself in the commission of one. I had become very watchful over my thoughts, and was honest in recording all evil; so my book became a mass of black dots; and the reflection that occurred to me of omissions also being sins, completed the panic of my mind. I flung my book into the fire, and sank into an abyss of gloomy despair.

How long this miserable state of mind lasted, I do not exactly remember; I think about two weeks. I could not pray. I dared not read the Bible, it bore so very hard upon me. Outwardly I was calm and even cheerful, but within reigned the very blackness of darkness. Death, with which I had so often sported, appeared in my eyes so terrible, that the slightest feeling of illness filled my soul with dismay. I saw no way of escape: I had God's perfect law before my eyes, and a full conviction of my own past sinfulness and present helplessness, leaving me wholly without hope. Hitherto I had never known a

day's illness for years; one of God's rich mercies to me consisted in uninterrupted health, and a wonderful freedom from all nervous affections. I knew as almost little of the sensation of a headache as I did of that of tight lacing; and now a violent cold, with sore throat, aggravated into fever by the state of my mind, completely prostrated me. I laid myself down on the sofa one morning, and waited to see how my earthly miseries would terminate; too well knowing what must follow the close of a sinner's life.

I had not lain long, when a neighbour, hearing I was ill, sent me some books, just received from Dublin, as a loan, hoping I might find some amusement in them. Listlessly, wretchedly, mechanically, I opened one — it was the memoir of a departed son, written by his father. I read a page, describing the approach of death, and was arrested by the youth's expressions of self-condemnation, his humble acknowledgement of having deserved at the Lord's hand nothing but eternal death. 'Ah, poor fellow,' said I, 'he was like me. How dreadful his end must have been! I will see what he said at last, when on the brink of the bottomless pit.' I resumed the book; and found him in continuation glorifying God that though *he* was so guilty and so vile, there was One able to save to the uttermost, who had borne his sins, satisfied divine justice for him, opened the gates of heaven, and now waited to receive his ransomed soul.

The book dropped from my hands. 'Oh, what is this? This is what I want: this would save me — Who did this for him? Jesus Christ, certainly; and it must be written in the New Testament.' I tried to jump up and reach my Bible, but was overpowered by the emotion of my mind. I clasped my hands over my eyes, and then the blessed effects of having even a literal knowledge of Scripture was apparent. Memory brought before me, and the Holy Spirit directed it, not here and there a detached text, but whole chapters, as they had long been committed to its safe, but hitherto unprofitable keeping. The veil was removed from my heart; and Jesus Christ, as the Alpha and Omega, the sum and substance of every thing, shone out upon me just as He is set forth in the everlasting Gospel. It was the same as if I had been reading, because I knew it so well by rote, only much more rapid, as thought always is. In this there was nothing uncommon; but in the *opening of the understanding, that I might UNDERSTAND the Scriptures,* was the mighty miracle of grace and truth. There I lay, still as death, my hands still folded over my eyes, my very soul basking in the pure, calm, holy light that streamed into it through the appointed channel of God's word. Rapture was not what I felt; excitement, enthusiasm, agitation, there was none. I was like a person long enclosed in a dark dungeon, the walls of which had now fallen down, and I looked round on a sunny landscape of calm and glorious beauty. I well remember that the Lord Jesus, in the character of a shepherd, of a star, and, above all, as the pearl of great price, seemed revealed to me most beautifully; that he could save every body, I at once saw; that he would save me, never even took the form of a question. Those who have received the Gospel by man's preaching may doubt and cavil: I took it simply from the Bible, in the words that God's wisdom teacheth, and thus I argued:— 'Jesus Christ came into the world to save sinners: I am a sinner: I want to be saved: he will save me.' There is no presumption in taking God at his word: not to do so is very impertinent: I did it, and I was happy.

THOMAS SMYTH

(1808–73)

from:
AUTOBIOGRAPHICAL NOTES, LETTERS AND REFLECTIONS (1914)

[Thomas Smyth was born in Belfast, where his father was a grocer and tobacconist. Raised a Congregationalist, he went on to become a minister in the American Presbyterian Church, spending his entire career in Charleston, South Carolina. Smyth was related through his mother to Martha Magee. She was his aunt by marriage and he maintained regular contact with her until her death in 1846. By all accounts she was a cultured woman with an independent mind and spirit, although she had led a difficult and tragic life. She was widowed at a young age and had witnessed the deaths of both of her sons and her two brothers. The latter were not married and so she inherited their substantial fortunes. She then used her wealth to patronize a number of charitable causes and when she died, her will stipulated that at least £60,000 should go to the Presbyterian Church in Ireland. In particular, she left £20,000 as an endowment for the establishment of a Presbyterian college in Ireland, a college which would eventually bear her name. In the mid-nineteenth century, Irish Presbyterians were keen to educate their ministers at home, rather than at Scottish universities. While the bequest furthered this aim, the decision of the trustees to base the college in Londonderry and not Belfast caused division within the denomination for many years.]

My Mother's brother was the pastor of the Presbyterian Church in Lurgan, County Armagh in Ulster Ireland. He was the only husband of Mrs. Magee who so largely endowed the Presbyterian Ch. in Ireland . . . He left Mrs. Magee a widow. She was a Miss Stuart descended from a Scotch Royalist family who on account of their connection with the Pretender were obliged to leave and forfeit their estate. She had one brother a General, and the other a Colonel in the army in India. Both served full time and retired on full pay. Both remained unmarried and died intestate. The general lived longest and had sent for a lawyer to make his will, sending Mrs. Magee to visit a friend — (they lived together in Lurgan, where they spent the Winter — travelling during the Summer) — when he was seized with apoplexy and never spoke. Mrs. M. became therefore sole heir which she would not have been by will, as both brothers were irreligious and probably infidel. She then removed to Dublin and became a member of the Rev. Mr. Richard Dill's church[1] and a most liberal patron to him and his church and to every good cause. She principally erected and endowed

1. In fact, Magee attended another Presbyterian church and an Episcopal church before joining Mr Dill's congregation. The Reverend Richard Dill of Tandragee, County Armagh, was the minister of Ormond Quay Presbyterian Church in Dublin from 1835 until his death in 1858.

the Schools of the present handsome Ormond Quay Church — gave $2,500 to the Free Church Fund and left to Mr. Dill — besides unknown bounty while alive, to Dr. Henry, her physician, and to Mr. Greer, her counsellor, $25,000, besides large living benefactions — left $100,000 and upwards to found the Magee College at Derry, and several hundred thousand dollars to The Home and Foreign Missions of the Presbyterian Church.[2]

She made a yearly visit to my father's house, and was very partial to my mother. She called me her favourite, as resembling one of her two sons (and only children) who died in the army. James, the eldest, left our house to prosecute his voyage to India (Bengal) as an army Surgeon. I remember him well as a most noble hearted young man. He died there of hydrophobia, from the bite of his own dog.[3] She was thus left childless and very much broken in heart, though a woman of unbounded energy and self-countroul. The Diary of her son's sickness and death as kept by a brother Physician, came unintentionally to her knowledge and possession and was very frequently perused in lonely grief. She was a great reader, exceedingly smart and witty, equally proud and sensitive and full of hospitable generosity. I frequently spent part of vacation with her while a boy.

In 1844 I visited her at Dublin and spent six weeks in her house and was, I think, instrumental in deciding her to endow a Presbyterian College. She was very liberal and kind to me and urged me much to remain in Dublin, where the Adelaide St. Church was vacant, and would, she thought, and others said, no doubt have called me. My organ, which cost $750 altogether, was originally her gift. Had I done this, I might have inherited largely, as she seemed to doat upon me. But this I could not do. Some considerable time after and under various influences, she made her will and being made to believe I would not survive her, she left me only $10,000. When she became ill, however, she wrote for me, and I was

in Edinburgh on the way to see her, when at breakfast, at Dr. Chalmer's, with Drs. Candlish and others, I heard incidentally she was dead. She is buried at Harold's Cross Cemetery, where she pointed out to me her intended grave, and where, near to her, the Rev. Mr. Dill has since been buried.

AUTHENTIC REPORT OF THE PROCEEDINGS OF THE GENERAL ASSEMBLY, RELATIVE TO THE BEQUESTS OF THE LATE MRS. MAGEE (1846)[4]

Mr. Dill (Dublin) intimated that he had an important communication to make to the house, having reference both to their College and their missions ... After some conversation, it was agreed that Mr. Dill should be heard now.

... It will be generally understood that I refer to the subject of the late Mrs. Magee's bequests ... Altogether she has left above £60,000 to purposes connected with this Church. I think it will be felt that on the occasion of announcing to this Assembly the most munificent bequests which this Church has ever received, it becomes me, as the pastor, the friend, and one of the executors of the testatrix, to make a few observations regarding her. She was a native of Lurgan, and belonged to an ancient and respectable family of the name of Stewart, now almost extinct. She became the wife of the Rev. William Magee, Presbyterian minister at Lurgan, who died, leaving her with two sons, and with very limited means for their education and support. As she could not endure the idea of obligation or dependence, she lived in the most retired manner, and with the most exact economy. By her own unaided exertions both her sons entered the army, one as an ensign and the other as a surgeon. She lived for her sons. It pleased God, however, to bereave her of them both in the flower of their youth ... Sometime after their decease, her two brothers, both officers of the army, high in rank, died, leaving her the mistress of a princely fortune, but almost alone in the world — almost the last of her race.

2. Full details of her benefactions can be found in her will, dated 11 July 1845. It was extensively reproduced within Presbyterian circles and a copy can be found in Thomas Smyth, *Autobiographical Notes, Letters and Reflections*. Edited by his granddaughter Louisa Cheves Stoney (Charleston, South Carolina: Walker, Evans and Cogswell, 1914), pp. 409–12.

3. Her second son died 'in consequence of a fall'. The Reverend R. Dill quoted in T. Smyth, *Autobiographical Notes*, p. 423.

4. This meeting took place on 11 July 1846 and is quoted in full in T. Smyth, *Autobiographical Notes*, pp. 422–7.

She removed to Dublin for the easier management of her affairs, and joined one of our Presbyterian Churches. She subsequently joined the Episcopal Church in the vicinity of her abode. It was at this time I became acquainted with her, and sometime after she became a member of my congregation. She lived in Dublin, as she had done in Lurgan, with the utmost plainness. The sudden accession of great wealth made little change in her mode of life. She viewed the pomps and luxuries of the world not only with indifference but with contempt. She saw little society, and spent most of her time in reading. She possessed an intellect naturally of a high order, and which she had improved by the diligent culture of a long life . . . It was, however, for the qualities of her heart that she was most distinguished. Her warmth of affection, her munificent generosity of disposition and her nobleness of nature were her chief characteristics. Her friendships were widely different from those of the generality of the world. They were ardent, enthusiastic and devoted . . . Such princely liberality as her's must be considered the more extraordinary that she had been accustomed, during the greater part of her life, to an exceedingly limited expenditure, and still continued to exercise the strictest economy in the management of her own expenses. How few can abandon the habits of a life, and enlarge their spirit with the increase of their fortune; but, in her case, it would seem that her princely spirit only awaited the arrival of a princely fortune to exhibit itself, for her hand and her heart expanded at one to the full measure of her ample means.

LADY ANNE JOCELYN

(1795–1822)

from:
DIARY, 1822

[Anne Jocelyn was a member of a family which was prominent in the early nineteenth-century evangelical movement within the Church of Ireland. Her diary, in the National Library of Ireland, is transcribed and in three sections. The first, from 9 September 1810 to 10 November 1812, is written by a seventeen-year-old girl, possibly one of Anne's sisters. The second diary is a record kept by Anne of two separate trips to Europe with her sister Fanny and her husband, Richard Wingfield, Lord Powerscourt. The third diary and the one from which these extracts are taken, covers the period 21 June 1822 to 20 September 1822, when Anne was apparently living with her brother, Lord Roden, and his wife, Maria.]

1822
Fri., 21 June

Gave way to great sloth this morning, so had no profitable reading. My prayers too very indifferent and comfortless and family ones so full of pride and vanity. My dress is a great snare to me and has been all along. Reading after breakfast this morning, with Edward and Mr. Hore, and dearest R,[1] very delightful, though my poor body comes in the way, for I had a great headache. It was the 6th of Galations, but I have many sinful feelings to mourn over in it. Afterwards I wasted my time greatly and spoke too strong to Mr. Hore, and had hypocrisy with R talking of my dearest love's future prospects, felt very desolate, as if I had no one now, this led to prayer, evidently now I should bless the Lord for this chastening. Did not sing with the servants with any grace in my heart, only thinking of how to show off and this at family prayers too! At the School[2] not doing all to Xt. and for Christ, and I do not wish Him in sincerity to have all the glory. I was so inclined to pick a hole in God's people this evening, so full of sin, and allowed it particularly with regard to personal vanity. We went out this evening to

1. Robert Jocelyn, Earl of Roden (1788–1870), Anne's brother.
2. A local establishment, perhaps a Charter school, which Anne visited regularly.

Pigley's Cottage. I was with Louisa[3] in the little car, might have been trying to get more good from her. At night Edward expounded on the 3rd of John. How often had that been sounded in my ears without effect. Lord, grant that now it may not. Inclined to be affronted today. Had an unkind letter today from poor Mama,[4] which made me feel wretched indeed, looking all around me I feel standing alone in the world. Oh Lord, be Thou mine, and what matters for the rest, only subdue me unto Thee and be with me ever more, wretch that I am.

3. Louisa Jocelyn (d. 1874), daughter of George Jocelyn (1764–98) and Thomasine, née Cole Bowen (d. 1818). George Jocelyn was Anne's uncle, making Louisa her cousin.
4. Anne's stepmother, Juliana Anne Orde (c. 1774–1856).

Tues., 8th [July]

Up early, happy in my mind, sang my dear little hymn with great pleasure, but prayed dead and as through a film, strove a little against dress, but very little, afterwards gave way to it, and now at breakfast very proud towards one in heart and had high aspiring thoughts. Perhaps this is the reason I have been wretched and dead and dull all day. I read the Crucifixion and I was able to feel a drop at the Lord's Prayer, but how soon it has gone. I was so discontented and dull all day, so wishing for a friend to open one's heart to and despising the best and dearest of friends. Oh, horrible. Oh Lord, what need indeed have I of a change in heart. Oh, keep me from wishing for anything but the light of Thy countenance. This place brought so many sad thoughts to my mind, then Mr. P[1] and all the sisters being together, and I only a poor lone, solitary branch in the midst of them, this filled me with envy and jealousy, and yet Thou has spared me. Oh, I do trust it is to do some work for Thy glory. I was too long at the garden today. I was unprofitable. I spoke to Waugh about his sons but not earnestly at all. I had unkind thoughts in my heart against him and many others, at dinner talking and showing off. Grieved a little at dear M's[2] great formality makes [sic] such a difference between me and her

1. Here the transcriber has inserted a note: 'Pakenham I think'.
2. Anne's sister-in-law, Maria née Stapleton (1794–1861), daughter of Lord Le Despencer and a noted beauty.

sisters, not indeed in kindness for nothing can be more so, but it is all *civilities* not affection, but it is all my own fault, when I look back on my past conduct towards her, no wonder she has no affection for me and perhaps the Lord wants to show me I have literally nothing but Him. Oh Lord, make me to say *and that is everything*. I walked up to the village this evening and talked to Mrs. Millar, the old woman, and felt great comfort in it, she must be in my poor prayers. Prayers bad, and family do., thought scorningly of it and of some. I wasted a great deal of time today and had not any increased pleasure in my Bible. I believe it is my pride that had made me so discontented to be prayed against.

Tues., July 23rd

I have passed two unhappy days and all from not giving up all to the Lord. I have indeed been completely wretched. Oh, what a wretch I am! I fear all my religious and happy feeling was nothing, when I can't give Him up *all*. My dress has cost me a great deal, I must strive more against it in the Lord's strength. I have been so far off from Him, and after enjoying such sweet Communion with Him it is dreadful. I feel as if there is a cloud between me and my Lord, I can't get at Him, I have had great times[1] now and then, and then hypocritical, spoke to others, and felt I was acting so wrong myself. Wasted my morning, wished for vain things, had some very envious thoughts, Lord help a poor wretch, I can't pray with any comfort. This is my state and my only happy moments are when I am crying over myself before the Lord. Oh, what He has been to me in my trial, and that I should so grieve His Holy Spirit. The Pakenhams still here, I like him better, they are all very kind to me. Read this evening the dairy man's daughter[2] [sic] to 14 poor women, and we prayed after, that part happier, but wretched enough. Heard today that the Lord had settled for R that he was to have ample compensation for his situation . . .

1. The transcriber has inserted a query at this point.
2. Anne is referring to the extremely popular evangelical tract by the Reverend Legh Richmond entitled *The Dairyman's Daughter*, which was first published sometime prior to 1805 and was extensively reprinted throughout the nineteenth century. In it Richmond recounts the inspirational story of Elizabeth Wallbridge, a deeply spiritual farm girl from Arreton, Isle of Wight, who dies of consumption.

Thursday, 1st [August]

Up late again, prayers very bad, reading also. I was so ill in body but this should have driven me closer to my Rock. I fear I am getting some inward complaint, I never felt more ill. I went down to bathe, in the hopes it may be of some use to me. We sung some hymns on the way and read, my heart too full of man's praise for it. Oh, so wretched when I got home, I had proud and carnal feelings, but I got a check — I heard from dear Richard[1] telling me of his marriage on Monday last, the Lord look upon each, and bless them. I wrote to them and felt a bad feeling about one thing, and that, I would not give up the Lord. I fear my heart is not *single* with Him yet. In reading Bible which I have so neglected, was reading the 5th of 2 Cor. and these two days, that Christ must be my all in all. It is quite wonderful how He supports me and enables me to bear this trial, so that I can think of another bearing that dear name my angel did, with great calmness, so at times indeed it is so better, but

1. Anne is referring to her brother-in-law, Richard Wingfield, 7th Viscount Powerscourt (1790–1823), who had married her sister Frances Theodosia on 6 February 1813. She died on 10 May 1820 while on board a passenger boat leaving Madeira. Wingfield then married Anne's cousin Theodosia Howard (d. 1836) on 29 June 1822.

then it is, it humbles me [*sic*].[2] Have been given some few precious glimpses of my dear Lord and only hope, but cannot glorify Him. Oh, how sad to think how I prefer everything to Him, and His word, neglecting it for other books; at dinner selfish, seeking my own aims and ends, not promoting the happiness of others. Family prayers dreadful . . .

Friday, Sept. 20

Since I last wrote, I have been very ill and am so still. The Lord's hand has been upon me, and I may say, I have been like a bullock under the yoke. Oh, what evil tempers, what capricious fancies and turning every way but the right way to my Saviour. Last night my Lord enabled me to read a little and think of Him and put death before me. Oh, what lumps of sin, particularly hypocrisy, did he show me. It was very sweet to think the Blood of Jesus cleanses from all sin, but at night again my enemy came and I could not [words omitted] thinking of my Lord filled with sinful unkind thoughts towards one and this morning. Oh, how he comes on me with sloth.

2. Anne had been very close to her sister Frances and had nursed her during her final illness. She seems from this and other entries to have resented this second marriage.

WOMEN IN THE ULSTER REVIVAL OF 1859

[The Ulster revival was an extraordinary outburst of religious fervour that shook the Protestant community in the north of Ireland during the summer months of 1859. The number of church services, open-air gatherings and prayer meetings increased dramatically, as did their level of religious enthusiasm. Often in these meetings, men and women became 'convicted' of their sins in dramatic ways. Excessive crying, falling down and total physical prostration, followed by a 'conversion' experience in which the individual achieved peace with God, was a common occurrence. Some accounts, as printed in the local newspaper extracts below, were even more extreme and seem to have occurred primarily among women. As part of their conversions, women experienced elaborate visions, ecstatic trances and clairvoyant powers. The first extract is from the *Ballymena Observer*, 31 May 1859.]

from:
BALLYMENA OBSERVER
(31 May 1859)

The religious revivals

This remarkable movement respecting which, as exhibited at Connor and Ahoghill, we have heretofore published a variety of highly interesting communications, is now extending throughout the town and neighbourhood of Ballymena with the most astonishing celerity, accompanied by symptoms, and followed by results, for which none are able to account upon any established theory — whether of bodily suffering in its action upon the mind, or of mental operation in its influences upon the body. The prevailing opinion is that the movement is attributable to the supernatural actions of the Holy Spirit — that it is God's work upon the heart, producing an instantaneous conviction of sin, accompanied by an appalling sense of impending danger, and resulting in a thorough conversion to a life of faith, and works of corresponding holiness . . .

It is already known that the movement originated at Connor, became strongly developed at Ahoghill, and from thence spread along a broad tract including the entire line of country from Toome to Rasharkin. The first decided appearance of the prevailing sensations, northward of Ballymena, happened at Laymore, in the parish of Kilconriola, about two miles from this town, on the evening of Sunday the 17th ult. On that occasion a deputation of the converted, from Ahoghill, conducted open air services of prayer and exhortation at an immense assemblage of the neighbouring people, and in the course of these services some of the audience were very suddenly and remarkably impressed. Before the following morning ten persons who had attended the meeting exhibited all the symptoms heretofore described as peculiar to the visitation — they were suddenly 'struck' with great pain and weakness of body, nervous twitching or quivering of the muscles, fearful agony of mind, and a torturing sense of sin — as indicated by loud impulsive cries for pardon, and earnest supplications for reconciliation with God. The duration of this paroxysm is more or less lengthened — in some cases it extends over three days, but is always succeeded by peace of mind and reformation of character. The external symptoms in one case has been minutely described to us. The person affected was a married woman of middle age. She appeared to be greatly excited, and feverish; her pulse was quick, there was a hectic tinge upon the cheeks, her eyes were partially closed and bloodshot and her face was streaming with perspiration. Her appetite was entirely gone, and for the space of fifty-six hours she was unable to taste anything but water. After the first four hours of racking pain, and incessant cries for mercy, she became more composed, but remained prostrate for nearly three days in the condition which we have described. During the prostration of this woman her home was visited by hundreds of the neighbouring people. She had never been taught to read or pray and was unable to distinguish one letter of the alphabet from another, yet she prayed with intense fervency, and exhorted the people to repentence with the most astonishing fluency and accuracy of speech. This case, like many others, was accompanied by visionary scenes — illusions certainly, but of a very extraordinary character. Among other things she maintained that a bible, traced in characters of light, was open before her; and that, although unable to read, a spiritual power had endowed her with capacity to comprehend the meaning of every word in it. It is an undoubted fact that she repeated with literal accuracy, and as if reading from the volume, a very large number of quotations from the old and new testament — applying them in an appropriate manner in connection with the prayers and exhortations wherein she was incessantly engaged; but these perceptions gradually faded in her progress towards recovery, and entirely disappeared on restoration to her ordinary health.

[This account is taken from a letter from the Reverend F.F. Trench, a Church of Ireland minister from Kells, County Meath, to the *Daily Express*, a London newspaper. It was reprinted in the *Belfast News-Letter* on 15 June 1859. Having heard of the extraordinary religious awakening going on in Ulster, Trench had visited the area to see for himself. While in Belfast he and Mr H——, an Independent minister, visited Sandy Row, a working-class Protestant area which had been deeply affected by the recent revival.]

from:
BELFAST NEWS-LETTER
(15 June 1859)

The revival movement in Belfast

Having learned that there were many converts in Sandy Row, I proceeded thither to visit from house to house . . . The first house we entered in the neighbourhood of Sandy Row was that of William M'F——, a sawyer. We found there a young woman very yellow, lying on her back in bed, in a dull, heavy state, but quite sensible, uttering short sentences such as 'My sins! Jesus! Jesus!' Her father and mother told me that on Friday evening last, June 3rd, at Rev. Mr. H.'s meeting-house,[1] she had been struck, and had been carried home on a car. From that time till this morning, June 8, she had gradually recovered and thought herself well enough to go and work at the mill, but that when at work this morning she fell again, was carried home, and had since been in the state I saw her. Her two sisters and a married sister-in-law who were present had experienced the same kind of bodily affection, and were now 'rejoicing in Christ Jesus' . . . The next house we were conducted to was that of Eliza D——. Her house was a small shop where herrings were sold. She was in bed. She had been affected while weaving, and had this morning been carried home . . . Mrs. C—— has been one of the most striking cases I have seen, her bodily affection was very severe, she screamed, as I was told, so as to be heard a quarter of a mile off; she said 'She had felt heavy for some days, and had to hold up her heart' (putting her hands to her stomach). 'While she went about to hear a bit of singing and praying,' describing how she felt, she said that she thought that she saw a great black mountain, or black cloud, coming slowly towards her, about to cover her. She then began 'to pray to Jesus that He would show her as much as the back of her nail of the hem of His garment.' [I give the exact expression here, though Mrs. C.'s own statement was much more eloquently expressed than I can now repeat.] She further said that 'She prayed that a drop of His blood, even if it were no more than would fill the eye of a small cambric needle, might fall upon her soul. Then she saw a bright light come between her and the black mountain, and beyond it a narrow path, white as snow, no broader than would lead up through a field to a gentleman's house, and that of this path to glory she could not see the end.' She was still in a very weak state. Her husband, who had been a man of very bad character, had been converted also, but was now able to return to his work, and spent all his spare time in trying to convert others.

1. Trench is referring to the Reverend Hugh Hanna, the Presbyterian minister in charge of Berry Street church. Berry Street was located close to the city's numerous linen mills and, as a result, had a predominantly working-class congregation.

[The following is an extract from a Ballymena correspondent, who witnessed the startling experiences of M.J.C., an 18-year-old girl who lived with her parents in Ballymena. Unable to transcribe all the details of her utterances, the writer returned the next day and recorded the following interview with her.]

from:
COLERAINE CHRONICLE
(16 July 1859)

Ballymena

I called next day, and had a long interesting interview, which I hope I will never forget. She then most willingly and confidentially opened her mind to me, and said that during the prayer she was quite conscious of being in the body, and during part of the prayer felt an attack from Satan, which she explained. She prayed to be delivered from the temptation. Then she said two angels came down and lifted her up to the immediate presence of the Saviour, who immediately stretched forth his hand and welcomed her. 'I saw him,' she said, 'sitting on his beautiful white throne, but not the highest that was there, with a number of children around him, and he made me sit down beside Him. Then my joys commenced, He then took us round about the throne, where there was beautiful green walks. When we began to sing hymns, and enjoy the pleasures of Heaven — joys no tongue could explain. He still led us onwards and upwards, as we went round about the throne, and the glory and beauty always increasing. He went before us moving His finger to follow Him, when we immediately found we had beautiful white wings. Then we all began to fly, and followed Jesus as He was flying before us, and I imagined it might be about an hour before we reached another throne of glory higher up and more beautiful. When we reached the second throne Jesus said to us, "Look unto me all ye ends of the earth and be ye saved." Then He Lifted His robes and showed us his five wounds and made me sorry to look at them. Then He showed us how He bore the cross, bowing under it, with a crown of thorns on His head, to give us a crown of glory. He said "O come and drink of the water of life freely — I died that you might live." I then said to Him, "nothing in my hand I bring, simply to the cross I cling." Then He said, "blessed are they that mourn, for they shall be comforted." Then I said "how sweet the name of Jesus sounds in a believer's ear, it sooths [*sic*] his sorrows, heals his wounds and drives away his fears." I then saw Jesus pointing with his finger to a pool of blood, saying "there's plenty here for you and all." I then said "O its [*sic*] not near done, its [*sic*] clearing nice, there was never any sin in it." I then saw the blessed Jesus dip His finger in the blood and stroke all my sins out of the book, then I said, "That wee taste has cleaned a' that out." When we reached a third throne higher up, Jesus took the beautiful white robes and the wings off me, and he showed them to me, and offered to lay them by for me. I said to him, "lay it by, it fits me nice — ah there's plenty more. I will tell them to come for them. I will go a good bit to tell them." I saw the book of God's remembrance, and I said "that's a good book, there was a heap of sin in it," and then said "put a wee drap on it, and draw mine out too". I saw the pool of blood at the Saviour's side. He signified with His finger to tell everybody. I said, "I will tell my father and mother." I thought the Saviour was to depart, and prayed him not to depart, but plead with His Father that none should perish, but all should have eternal life. I said "I will have great pleasure reading the Bible now" ... When this vision closed, the Saviour shook hands and said, "Peace, peace!" and then I opened my eyes on earth again.'

from:
PORTADOWN WEEKLY NEWS
(23 July 1859)

The revival in Portadown

It is our privilege to report the rapid progress of this wonderful religious movement, the decided commencement of which we recorded last week. The public services held since have been exceedingly numerous, and in all cases of which we have heard, have been remarkably well attended . . . The cases of physical prostration which have occurred during the week both in town and in various parts of the country have been exceedingly numerous. Amongst them have been the young and the comparatively old, both of men and women . . . To commence to give an account of the state and feelings of those that

have been prostrated would fill columns. We give two that came under our own notice.

R.N. was stricken when at work in Messrs. Watson & Armstrong's factory. She said she found relief in thinking on a text of Scripture learned five years ago at the Sunday school — 'Believe on the Lord Jesus Christ, and thou shalt be saved.' During her indisposition hell was presented to her mind as a mountain of flame, but our Lord as a loving Saviour. In her recovery she prayed for every sinner — particularly for the scoffer.

A.S. convinced at a prayer-meeting at same place as last girl. She said she felt her heart extremely hard; and described hell as a burning lake, and that as she was passing it by, the gates flew open, and she beheld burning mountains of fire — the road leading to it was very dark and slippery, but Jesus was standing waiting to deliver her from the devil who was struggling hard to get at her, but Christ set her feet on a narrow path, on which she was continually slipping, but espying a little gate she entered and the view was transporting. She frequently repeated the following lines:—

> Lord, at thy feet how shamed I lie,
>   Upward I dare not look;
> Pardon my sins before I die,
>   And blot them from thy book.

She said she did not get time to see much of heaven; angels were there; she saw Jesus, all she wished to see, wearing a crown of dazzling brightness, and that his look was indescribable. She expressed herself very sorrowfully as having to come back to earth 'to bring sinners to God'. The time was she loved nobody, but now she loves everybody, and invites them all to come to Jesus, and 'taste the riches of His grace'.

from:
BALLYMENA OBSERVER
(13 August 1859)

The religious revival

We have already recorded various cases of very mysterious phenomena connected with the religious movement. — At present the most ordinary phase of such developments is a temporary loss of speech, hearing, and power of motion — many of the parties so affected having previously indicated the exact moment at which the use of these faculties would be restored. A very remarkable case of this description occurred last week. It was witnessed by several hundred people of the neighbourhood; and, amongst others, by most respectable gentlemen, at whose request we present the following as a perfectly authentic record of the leading facts. Mary Ann H. is now in the eighteenth year of her age, and is the daughter of Presbyterian parents resident at Tamlaght in the parish of Drummaul, about four miles from Ballymena. She is able to read, and was in the habit of regular attendance at a Sabbath school. On the morning of Sunday the 5th of June last, whilst in the act of passing through the door of her father's house, on her way to the school, she was unexpectedly 'stricken', and instantly fell prostrate and senseless upon the threshold. In falling, she caught the bolt staple of the lock, and clenched her hand upon it in such a manner that it was found impossible to loosen her grasp; the other hand quivered incessantly — and in this position she remained for about ten minutes. On regaining the faculty of speech she clasped her hands, raised them towards heaven, and fervently exclaimed, 'Oh Lord, be merciful to me, a sinner!' — 'Oh, pour the spirit of the living and true God into my heart!' — 'Lord Jesus, save me, or I perish!' Since that period, although able to work, she has never thoroughly regained her ordinary strength of body, and has repeatedly been subjected to like recurrences. Her demeanour has been exemplary; she prays repeatedly and earnestly; reads her bible diligently; and her example has exercised a powerful influence upon the conduct and character of her own parents. On the night of Saturday the 30th ult., she retired to rest in her usual health, and at the ordinary hour; but, towards midnight, she suddenly started from the bed, exclaiming 'The Lord has desired me to pray!' She remained on her knees in fervent prayer for half an hour — her attitude indicating the deep intensity of her devotions. Towards the close of her prayer, her eyes being directed upward in a steady gaze, she exclaimed, 'I know that I will be deprived of sight, speech, and hearing, till twelve o'clock tomorrow; but, Oh God, Thou wilt be with me! — Thou wilt never leave me! — Thou wilt pour Thy grace into my heart!' She then explained to her parents that she would have the power of speech only for a few minutes on Sunday (the following day) at twelve o'clock, after which she would remain blind and dumb, as before, till six o'clock on Monday morning. Immediately after giving this intimation her eyes closed, her teeth went together with an audible snap, and she was found motionless! In that state she remained till exactly twelve o'clock on Sunday. She then awoke to consciousness; but, regardless of all around her, engaged in prayer for a few minutes, and then fell back into the same trance-like state. Hundreds of the neighbouring people, and some strangers from a distance of several miles, on hearing of the strangely abnormal condition of this person, came to look at her. Some of them tried to insert the blade of a penknife between her teeth, but found it impossible. Her eyelids were fast closed, and *stiffened*. — Her lips were bloodless, and the colour of her face resembled that of a corpse, with the exception of a red spot about the size of a shilling upon the centre of each cheek. Many of the visitors expressed their opinion that she would never rise again; others waited patiently to watch the event in the expectation that, if she recovered speech, she would relate *what she had seen* — for all concluded that she was rapt in a vision of things pertaining to spiritual existence. The house was crowded to excess all night. There were more than twenty watches in it, all carefully regulated to the railway time. As six o'clock approached, the anxiety among the spectators became intense — but, up till within a minute of the time, the young woman remained insensible and motionless — not a muscle indicated that a spark of life remained within her body. Precisely at six o'clock, and when the gaze of all present was riveted upon her pallid countenance, her eyes opened; within a dozen seconds afterwards her jaws relaxed, her tongue was loosened, and, as before, she instantly engaged in prayer. She blessed God for his faithfulness — 'I knew,' she ejaculated, 'that even as Thou laidst me down, Thou wouldst raise me up again!' and then proceeded with a prayer for continued grace and mercy, and that the Holy Spirit would 'Touch the heart of all sinners.' People crowded about her bed to ask if she had *seen anything*. Her manner was a rebuke to their curiosity, for she made no reply . . .

Now, it is not unlikely that some persons may feel disposed to ask, *Cui bono?* What is the meaning or purpose of all this phenomena in connexion with a religious movement? We decline the responsibility of a reply. Our business is limited to a relation of *facts* — explanation or commentary we leave to others.

[In September the physical manifestations of the revival took on a distinctly sensationalist character, when some women in Belfast claimed that they had been 'marked' by the Holy Spirit. Most observers were sceptical of this spiritual origin, especially when it emerged that some of the marks had been misspelled, or could be rubbed off. Evidence of admission fees to see the marks fuelled further accusations of delusion and imposture. Other commentators, however, were willing to give these women the benefit of the doubt. Both opinions are represented in the following two excerpts.]

from:
BANNER OF ULSTER
(13 September 1859)

Extraordinary and delusive physical phenomena

Sir, — I can understand why many well-meaning people may have mistaken much in connexion with the present 'revival movement', for the work of the Spirit of Christ, but I cannot understand why so many notorious cases of imposture should have been permitted to be carried on in Belfast, and elsewhere, without one single Presbyterian minister coming forward to lift his voice in public against them. One of the grossest cases I have met is that of a girl, a mill-worker, who resides in B—— Street. It appears that, some twelve weeks ago, this girl attended a revival prayer-meeting in Kent Street, at which an address was delivered by a convert, and while there she was seized with a fit of crying and screaming, which continued an hour, after which she became insensible, and remained in that state for some time. On recovering, she was dumb, but indicated by signs that she would speak at a certain hour, at which hour she spoke accordingly. Since that time she has had several fits, and been sometimes dumb, sometimes deaf, sometimes blind, and occasionally deaf and dumb, or deaf, dumb and blind at the same time. She has had several communications from heaven; has been forewarned of all the various states through which she is to pass; and has been enabled to prove the reality of the work now going on, by foretelling the deprivations she has undergone, and is to undergo. For a length of time she found, even in her humble circle, sceptical people, who asked troublesome questions — 'who had not imported sufficient faith into their speculations, and had not learned to believe rather than philosophise' — and, to silence these foolish people, and convince all gainsayers, a most glorious miracle was performed upon her on Wednesday morning last. By heavenly agency the word 'JESUS' was imprinted on her bosom, and a cross on one of her arms. Several revivalists, who had inspected her told me they cried for joy, screamed aloud, when they beheld these signs and wonders, feeling assured that henceforth there would be an end to all unbelief regarding the revival. When I visited her on Friday evening, there was a crowd assembled outside the house extending to the centre of the street, and the ingress and egress of visitors reminded me of May's Market on the forenoon of the same day. When it is known that these visitors almost all paid sixpence each for the gratification of their curiosity, it will be perceived that the miracle has not been a profitless one. If any of your readers should desire to know, in a cheaper way, how the marks were imprinted on the girl's skin, I am happy to be able to tell them that they were scratched on with the point of a needle or a pin; and the attempt at forming the letters was most clumsy, the style of the operator resembling that in which Jack Sheppard cut his name on the beam in Newgate.

Mr. Editor, this is not a solitary case. I am sorry to say I could point to many others, almost equally bad — for example, in Grattan Street, M'Tier Street, Christopher Street, Ewart's Row, Shankill Road, Sandy Row, &c., &c; but I refrain for the present, in the hope that some person of influence in the Christian community will come forward and bear public testimony against scenes of delusion and imposture, before which winking madonnas and liquifying blood, Joe Smith and Mormonism may hide their diminished heads. —

Your obedient servant,
A TRUE PRESBYTERIAN
September 12, 1859.

from:
PORTADOWN WEEKLY NEWS
(18 October 1859)

Dear Sir, — Having met with a friend on Saturday last who told me he had no doubt of the reality of two extraordinary cases towards Scotch-street with marks upon their arms, I made an appointment with him to go and see her on Monday morning. We went first to Mrs. Annesley's, of Kingarve, where we saw Sarah Oliver, on whose left arm was the letters, GOD, and also MAN, with a half moon and a crown; these last letters had been visible for some time, but were now nearly obliterated. She informed me she would be stricken at four o'clock and remain so until eight in the evening. When we returned we saw her in that state upon the bed, and remained with her a considerable time; and she sometimes sang and prayed out aloud. We also proceeded to the house of Wm. M'Donnell, of Timakeel, and saw Sarah Gray, who had marks upon both arms; on the right arm the letter K, the word GOD, and a cross; on the left arm the letters B O, a half moon, a crown with four stars, five distinct spots, and the figure of a child. She had also the letter O upon her breast. While I was sitting beside her she was stricken, and in that state she had books handed to her — one of which was a hymn-book. A hymn she pointed out as her own experience; another, as one that they were singing in heaven; another, as belonging peculiarly to a person near at hand. She got a Testament, and pointed to 'neither do I condemn thee, go and sin no more', as what her Saviour said to her; told us of persons coming up the lane to the house; of the number present; and many other things too numerous to mention, but which impressed the minds of all in the apartment as being most extraordinary indeed. She said that on next Sunday, at four o'clock in the evening, she would be again stricken, that the old marks would then pass away, and new ones appear. I would recommend all interested in the matter to attend at that hour, and satisfy themselves respecting these things. I had an opportunity of conversing with a minister of the Established Church as I was going to see these parties, and found that he was well acquainted with them and their conversion to God. He told me that he was present when these marks began first to appear on one of them, and he had no doubt of their reality and genuineness. He said he could account for them in no other way than that the state of the mind might produce these effects upon the body. He acknowledged that he had no precedent in history for the idea, except that it was well known agony of spirit had made the hair white in the course of a single night. I have now given a faithful and correct statement of these extraordinary matters for which I pledge myself. — But now that I say nothing further, I am not responsible for anything more. Let the people go and judge for themselves as I did. The parties appear to have no hesitation in allowing their arms to be examined and themselves to be questioned, and they would be greatly displeased were any who visit them to offer money.

D'ARCY SINNAMON[1]

1. Sinnamon was an Anglican clergyman in the Portadown region.

WILLIAM GIBSON
(1808–67)

from:
THE YEAR OF GRACE: A HISTORY OF THE ULSTER REVIVAL OF 1859 (1860)

[After the excitement of the revival had faded away, supporters were keen to establish its social benefits. They pointed out the increase in church attendance, the greater attention to family prayers and Bible study. They also credited the revival with reducing the crime rate and the levels of alcohol consumption. Another favoured improvement was the increased desire for education on the part of the working classes. Numerous Sunday schools and evening schools had been set up with the intention of improving literacy, so the newly converted could read the Bible. The Reverend William Gibson was the minister of

Rosemary Street Presbyterian Church in Belfast and in 1859 he was also moderator of the General Assembly. He was a staunch supporter of the revival. In 1860 he published what became one of the most popular accounts of events in Ulster, entitled *The Year of Grace*. Although he accepted the physical prostrations as a work of God, he was also keen to show that the revival was having a permanent impact on society. In an extract from his work, Gibson recounts the establishment of a school for mill girls in Ewart's Row, a street in the heart of Belfast's textile industry.]

Not to dwell longer, however, on individual instances, I shall here introduce an interesting communication respecting the work in another district in the outskirts of the town. The place is called Ewart's Row, and is inhabited altogether by mill-workers. The proprietors of the mill, the principal of whom is our present excellent chief magistrate, lent every facility to their work-people to avail themselves of the opportunities of religious instruction which were so abundantly enjoyed, and have had their reward in the improved habits of their little community. The writer of the subjoined statement is a young female, the daughter [of] a respectable trades-man, whose own spiritual history is deeply interesting. Up to the 29th of June she was altogether frivolous in her tastes, and fond of gaiety and worldly amusements. She had, however, been importuned by a friend to attend a meeting in the Rev. Hugh Hanna's church, on the evening of the day in question, and very reluctantly complied. In the course of the service, a young woman fell down by her side, and in the act of rising, to follow and render her assistance, she herself was similarly seized. Having been removed to her own home, she was for several days subjected to extreme bodily weakness, her mind, however, all the while in 'perfect peace'. On her recovery, finding that a walk of usefulness was opened up to her, and under the prompting of an earnest desire to do good to others, she opened a class for the instruction of her sisters in the 'Row', so many of whom had been

themselves the subjects of the merciful visitation. Although in the subjoined statement she makes no reference to herself, it is well known that the enterprise owes its success mainly to her devoted labours:—

'Ewart's Row is a manufacturing suburb of Belfast, on the north side of the town, having a population of about fifteen hundred souls. It was visited by the grace of God at an early period of the revival. Many were brought to a saving knowledge of Jesus in a very remarkable way. The change that was thus manifested, and the earnest entreaties and fervent prayers of the converts for the salvation of their friends and neighbours, by the Divine blessing, awakened the whole locality. There was no district of Belfast so deeply moved. The whole population crowded to prayer-meetings and open-air preachings, evincing the deepest seriousness and concern about eternal things. Every one betook himself to the prayerful reading of the Bible. Those who could read but imperfectly or not at all, bewailed their inability; every one became eager for instruction in the Word of God. At this crisis the Ewart's Row school was opened by the district visitors connected with the Berry Street Church. Christian friends from other congregations joined in the good work, and the Lord has crowned their labour with abundant success. The average attendance on three evenings during the week is about one hundred and fifty. Many of the girls who could read but very imperfectly at the opening of the school, in three months had committed the whole of the Shorter Catechism; others, the greater portion of the book of Psalms; and many, portions of the Scriptures. Their memories are stored with the Word of God. Their hearts fondly cherish it, and their lives are beautifully regulated by its requirements. Useful branches of instruction have been introduced. Many of the poor girls now write a beautiful hand. Some have advanced considerably in arithmetic. Industrial occupations have engaged the time of others, who will shortly be better fitted for domestic duties.'

MARIE FRY

(1849–73)

from:
SELECTIONS FROM THE CORRESPONDENCE OF THE LATE MARIE FRY (OF DUBLIN) WITH A BRIEF BIOGRAPHICAL NOTICE
(c. 1874)

[Maria Margaret (Marie) and her family were active within the nineteenth-century Dublin evangelical community and attended Merrion Hall, a church which had been established in the wake of the Ulster revival of 1859 and which eventually became associated with the Brethren movement. One of the many outreach services which the hall sponsored was special services for the British army soldiers who were stationed in the Dublin garrison. Marie became involved in this work, particularly in the form of letter-writing to those soldiers who were now stationed elsewhere. When she died at the young age of twenty-four, her letters were gathered together by a close family friend, Mrs Henry (Fanny) Grattan Guinness, and published for the edification of other evangelicals, as well as with the intention of provoking a conversion within the unsaved reader. In them Marie exhibits some of the hallmarks of Victorian evangelicalism: an overriding concern for the salavation of souls; a close interrogation into lifestyle habits; and strong exhortations against 'backsliding'.]

Dublin, February 11, 1872

Dear M'M——,

I am very glad indeed to receive your letter, and to know that the Lord is keeping you and your wife close to Himself, for though I have not been able to write lately, I pray all the more for you. How blessed to know the Lord cleaves to us, and that our eternal security depends on His hold of us, so that Satan can never rob us of eternal life. Yet must we remember that if we are not moment by moment depending on our living Christ — looking up to Him for strength, asking His guidance, telling Him every secret feeling of our hearts (or, if we fail in these things, confessing it to Him) — Satan will surely rob us of our peace

and joy in Jesus. Have you not found it so, dear M'M——? The Lord desires to have us happy. 'Rejoice in the Lord always, and again I say, rejoice.' Each day I feel increasingly that the great secret of going on happily is to make a practice of confession. The moment we are conscious of a shortcoming, or feel that Satan has tripped us, we ought to go to Jesus and tell Him all about it. What a comfort it is to be able during the noise and conflict of the day, to look up often to our Advocate; His intercession for us is continuous. Seeing, then, that we have such an advocate and such a friend as our precious Jesus, 'let us come boldly unto the throne of grace, that we may find grace to help in time of need'. We are not to forget what we once were without Him; it says, 'Ye were sometimes darkness, but now are ye light in the Lord; walk as children of light.' How often we look down into our own hearts to find some good thing, and forget that God says they are only evil — 'darkness'. It is in Christ that He knows us as light — 'light in the Lord' — a light in which no darkness can mingle, because His light; we are 'partakers of the Divine nature', born again by the incorruptible seed of the Word; therefore He says to us, 'Walk as children of light.' How easy, how blessed, how natural to behave as what we are! But here, dear M'M——, we fail: we forget all we have and all we are in Christ! Well, we have a patient, gracious Saviour, who delights to restore the soul.

The Lord abundantly bless you and your wife, and lead you into a deeper knowledge of all the blessings which are yours in Christ Jesus, and teach you more of the exceeding riches of His grace. You will be glad to hear we have had some truly blessed meetings in the Hall. Mr. V—— has been preaching there, and God has given us much cause for praise in the salvation of many precious souls.

Last Thursday we had 500 soldiers in the Hall, and several found 'peace in believing'. The Lord is doing a good work amongst the Guards, and there is a little band of Christians amongst them. The corporal in the drums, too, has been saved, and we have good hopes of many of the lads.

They are good boys, and are always willing to hear the truth. I never hear anything of the drummers of the 1st Battalion. Corporals L—— and A—— sometimes write, but we can look forward to that day when the Hearer and Answer of Prayer shall gather together His precious jewels, and when we shall go out no more from His presence; then we shall rest and rejoice together for ever. I have not heard anything of your father for a long time. It is sad that you do not hear from him; but let us not grow weary of bringing him continually before the Lord in prayer, and 'leave it all with Jesus'.

We are all well, and join in kind Christian love for you and your wife. I hope soon to be able to get about as usual, but the Lord has been so kind and tender that I am satisfied with His will.

May you and your wife be often cheered by His own presence!

Believe me your true friend,
MARIE FRY

FANNY GRATTAN GUINNESS

(1831?–98)

from:

'SHE SPAKE OF HIM', BEING RECOLLECTIONS OF THE LOVING LABOURS AND EARLY DEATH OF THE LATE MRS. HENRY DENING (1873)

[Within nineteenth-century evangelical circles, public roles for women were rare. They were denied access to ministerial positions and were largely excluded from the financial and administrative aspects of running a church. There were, however, some exceptions. Throughout the century, particularly in England, there was a small but regular occurrence of female preaching. Initially supported by the various Methodist denominations, it occurred largely outside denominational structures before becoming institutionalized within the ranks of the Salvation Army. In the 1860s a group of middle-class female preachers emerged out of the evangelical wing of the Church of England. One of the most popular of such women was Geraldine Hooper. Born in Paris on 30 March 1841, she was raised in Bath and encouraged in her public preaching efforts by her local curate. By the mid-1860s she was preaching to audiences of over one thousand, mainly in south-west England. In 1868 she married Henry Dening, a large farmer, who accompanied her on her speaking engagements. She died on 12 August 1873 at the age of thirty-one.

Obviously, this activity was highly unusual for a woman of her social status and she and others like her attracted a great deal of criticism. Thus, Mrs Henry (Fanny) Grattan Guinness, a full-time mission worker and herself a one-time public preacher, in her biography of Dening, felt obliged to put forward the case for female preaching. Her arguments illustrate her desire to defend the practice of women's public preaching, not simply on the basis of its success in winning souls, but on the basis of justification by Scripture. That said, Guinness ultimately qualified her support for female preaching, thus reflecting the ambivalence which even its supporters had towards women occupying such public religious roles.]

That the subject of this Memoir was an evangelist few will deny; the foregoing facts prove that she had as good a right to the title as most that bear it . . . She was a true and very successful evangelist, and yet — she was a woman! a member of that sex excluded by custom, and many suppose by Scripture, from the duty and privilege of preaching Christ and Him crucified. We can hardly therefore close this sketch without a brief consideration of the subject of women's ministry in the Gospel.

It will not do to argue — *In this case the results were good, the practice must therefore be a right and Scriptural one.* To take such ground would be illogical, for God often overrules evil for good. What have been the results of the Crucifixion of Christ? And yet what was the deed itself? We assert rather, *the practice is right and Scriptural, and therefore the results in this and other cases are* glorious. And yet in a modified form there may be something in the other argument also. An evil tree does not bring forth good fruit, and God would not, could not, pour His blessing for ten or twelve years consecutively on a course of disobedience and sin. Though He overrules evil for good, He does not reward evil-doers for their evil deeds; but it is written: 'They that turn many to righteousness shall shine as the stars for ever and ever.'

Large and long-continued success of the highest kind in the work of God proves him who enjoys it to be a 'fellow-worker with God'. Under the old dispensation the Lord did, it is true, employ as instruments men who as regards the general tenor of their lives were in sinful opposition to Him and to His laws; but under the Gospel economy He acts very differently. His messengers are inspired by an *indwelling* Holy Ghost. The words of an ungodly man may occasionally be applied with saving effect, but it were little short of blasphemy to assert that a succession of cases of conversion such as is here recorded *could* occur as the result of a career of rebellion and sin. If God had desired to mark His *approval* of woman's ministry in the Gospel, how could He do it more evidently than by thus crowning a woman's labours with a blessing richer than that which He vouchsafes to the labours of most men? Though therefore we do not justify the practice because it is successful, we hold that it would not be successful were it not justifiable.

Nor would we maintain that women are *equally* called to the work with men: we believe, on the contrary, that the rule is men — the *exception* only, women; and that, as always, the exception only proves the rule. Nature, revelation, and experience alike indicate men as the proper occupants of public spheres, and women of private ones. But it does not follow that every man must shun private work simply because it is private, nor that every woman must shun public work simply because it is public. The rule is general and universal, but, like every other such rule it admits of exceptions. Beyond a doubt few, *very few*, are called to a path of service similar to that trodden by Mrs. Dening; *but a few are*, as her case and some others prove.

Superficial opponents sometimes say, But suppose every woman were to do so? We reply unhesitatingly, *It would be awful confusion;* but there is no danger! Suppose every minister were to follow the example of David Brainerd[1] or of William Burns,[2] and devote themselves to the good of the heathen? The Church would be left pastorless — the results would be most disastrous! But there is no danger! and their singular devotion was not sin; their course, though exceptional, was justifiable, and, perhaps, peculiarly 'well-pleasing to God'.

We go further, and admit freely, that it *may* be, if things were in a right and normal state, if every professed minister of Christ were actually accomplishing his Master's business, women would not be called of God to public ministry. And yet, we make this admission with a doubt, for Pentecostal power and apostolic order did not exclude 'daughters' that prophesied. Paul tarried many days in the house of an evangelist, whose four daughters were all what, in modern phraseology, would be called 'lady preachers', and we do not hear that he rebuked either them or their father.

But the Church is not in Pentecostal power, alas, now! And that which was admissible even then, is far more than admissible now, it is desirable. In days of delusion, disorder, and deadness, — in days when labourers are few, and fields white, when summer is nearly over, and harvest all but ended, we need not wonder if, in the merciful providence of God, exceptional cases multiply. Women are often called to work the pumps in a shipwreck, though when danger does not press the duty falls to the share of men . . . When so many ministers of the stronger and wiser sex are useless or worse than useless in the work of soul saving, and preach for years without being instrumental in a single conversion, is there not a cause for woman's ministry? . . .

Very much has been written and said on this subject, which is not much to the point, and strong prejudice has been raised by unwise

---

1. David Brainerd (1718–47), born in Hatham, Connecticut. He became one of the earliest evangelical missionaries when he started a mission work to convert Native Americans to Christianity. Although he died young, his published diary influenced many of the pioneers of the modern missionary movement in Britain, such as William Carey and Robert Murray McCheyne.
2. William Chalmers Burns (1815–68), a minister in the Church of Scotland. Deeply influenced by the Scottish revival of the 1840s, in 1847 he sailed to China to begin a missionary career. He died at the port of New Chwang in 1868.

advocacy. It is a question not of 'women's rights', but of women's responsibilities; and can be decided of course only by Scripture. Those who take opposite views of it, can each allege passages apparently in their favour. When challenged to justify her course, Mrs. Dening, for instance, could say, 'Women may preach and pray in public, for St. Paul directs them how to dress when they are doing so, speaks of those women who laboured with him in the Gospel, and saluted in the 14th of Romans more women fellow-labourers than men.' Those who disapproved her course could reply, 'But St. Paul distinctly says, "Let your women keep silence", and "I suffer not a woman to teach".' Both have a show of Scripture authority, but both cannot be right: the alleged contradiction must be only apparent. If both would give their full and fair weight to the passages that oppose their own view, the controversy would soon be settled by a compromise.

Space forbids anything but the briefest possible summary of the leading arguments that seem to justify, at any rate, an exceptional Gospel ministry of women . . .

We conclude, therefore, on grounds of deliberate judgment, what most who heard her concluded by intuitive perception — that Mrs. Dening's course was a right, though an exceptional one; and that it would not have been well-pleasing to God had she resisted the call of which she was conscious, and which she *alone* could hear; buried the talents Christ had committed to her; confined herself to a private sphere of action, and spent her life in the quiet domestic duties which befit most Christian women. We do not hold up her career as a model which all Christian women should strive to follow. Far, far from that. To any one similarly gifted, similarly guided, and similarly circumstanced, we would say, 'Go and do likewise'; and remember, she proved her vocation and her gift by years of patient continuance in well-doing in a secluded sphere, and amid much sorrow, 'ere she was fitted to fill the public sphere she afterwards did. But to Christian women in general we would say, 'Try to catch the *spirit* of her life, seek not to copy its form: *that* was essential, *this* accidental. Be loving, be zealous, be unremitting in your diligence, whatever be your work; so shall you be equally well-pleasing to Him, who accepts

"according to what a man hath, and not according to what he hath not", to Him who said *"she hath done what she could."* ' . . .

To all who would coldly criticise a course they could not take, and cannot understand; who can esteem ordinary piety, and approve the expenditure of the 'three hundred pence' on 'the poor', but who dislike and disapprove extraordinary exhibitions of love to Christ, we would say in His own words, *'Let her alone, she hath done what she could: it shall be spoken of for a memorial of her'*, and we would add: 'Judge nothing before the time, until the Lord come who will make manifest the counsels of the hearts', and give every one his due word of praise; but pray, oh 'pray ye the Lord of the harvest, that He would send forth labourers into His harvest'; and remember, that, 'God hath chosen the foolish things of the world to confound the wise, and the weak things of the world to confound the mighty; that no flesh should glory in His presence, but that he who glories should glory in the Lord?'

Biographies/Bibliographies

Alice Cambridge

LIFE. Alice Cambridge was born in 1762 at Bandon, County Cork. Her mother was a Presbyterian, her father a member of the Church of Ireland, and Alice was brought up in the Established Church. She left school early, despite a 'wish to learn, and . . . a degree of capacity'. Her mother, to whom she was much attached, died in 1780, and in her grief Alice started going to the Methodist preaching house. Influenced by some women, wives and relatives of soldiers quartered in the town, who were already Methodists, she experienced a conversion. When she joined the society she broke off her engagement to a young man, 'sincerely wishing him all happiness, and having no other fault to find that I recollect, but that his mind did not bend heavenward; that indeed was enough'. She began to preach publicly to mixed audiences and went on to establish a number of meetings throughout Munster, despite criticism from 'Christian friends' who included 'some of the Methodist preachers'. However, John Wesley, in a letter to Alice dated 31 January 1791, defended her right to preach, advising her to give the ministers 'all honour, and obey them in all things as far as conscience permits; but it will not permit you to be silent when God commands you to speak'. In 1802, the Irish Conference, the Methodists' governing body, however, refused to accept Alice's right to speak in public and voted to expel her from the society. Nevertheless, Alice continued to hold meetings and to speak in public throughout Ireland, although now most of her services were conducted in front of all-female audiences. When her health failed in about 1823, she retired to the home of a sympathizer in Nenagh, County Tipperary, where she died in 1829.

CHIEF WRITINGS. John J. McGregor (ed.), *Memoir of Miss Alice Cambridge* (Dublin: M. Keene, 1832).

BIOGRAPHY AND CRITICISM. C.H. Crookshank, *History of Methodism in Ireland*, 3 vols (London: T. Woolmer, 1885–8), and

Memorable Women of Irish Methodism in the Last Century (London: Wesleyan Methodist Book Room, 1882).

Charlotte Elizabeth Tonna

LIFE. Charlotte Elizabeth Browne was born in Norwich on 1 October 1790, the only daughter of the Reverend Michael Browne, the rector of St Giles' Church and a minor canon of Norwich Cathedral. By the age of ten she had suffered a bout of temporary blindness and had become totally deaf. For the rest of her life she communicated by 'finger alphabet'. After the death of her father, when she was about eighteen, she, along with her mother and brother, moved to London, where she met and soon before George Phelan, a minor member of the Anglo-Irish gentry and a captain in the 60th Rifle Corps. He had served with her brother in the Napoleonic Wars. After several years stationed in Nova Scotia and in England, she moved with her husband to Ireland, a place she 'hated . . . most cordially'. Here she lived on Phelan's Kilkenny estate in virtual seclusion and experienced her conversion to evangelical Christianity. It was also at this time that she began her writing career, publishing a series of stories and twopenny books for the Dublin Tract Society. The aim of this literature was conversionist, so the content was often sentimental and tragic. Charlotte Elizabeth also wrote a good deal of material which aimed to refute the errors of the Roman Catholic church. Catholicism was her nemesis. She called it 'the Babylon of the Apocalypse' and claimed it was an abomination. She viewed the passage of the act of Catholic emancipation in 1829 as a national apostasy and a time for collective mourning. Despite an abiding hatred of 'this dreadful perversion', as she called it, Charlotte Elizabeth soon fell in love with Ireland and the Irish, calling them 'the most loving and loveable race under the sun' and maintaining a lifelong interest in the country and its people.

Charlotte Elizabeth's marriage to Phelan had been an unhappy one. By about 1821 she records, 'I became chiefly dependent on my own exertions' and by 1824 the two had separated. She returned to England and lived in London with her brother's family. Her husband died in 1837 and in 1841 she married Lewis Tonna (1812–57), a tract writer twenty-two years her junior. This marriage was extremely happy. She seems to have maintained her own residence and to have continued her writing career. She wrote extensively in defence of Protestantism, publishing a series of books and contributing to a number of periodicals, including the *Protestant Magazine,* which she also edited. She also wrote on women's issues. She edited the *Christian Lady's Magazine* (1834–46) and published *The Wrongs of Woman* in 1843. In the latter she argues that while women are 'the weaker vessel', their lack of proper education has only exacerbated this position. For working-class girls in the textile and metallurgical industries this had led to exploitation, which should be prevented. She was involved in numerous efforts to convert the Irish in London and several of her hymns were adopted by the Orange Order. In 1844 she contracted cancer and died in Ramsgate in 1846.

CHIEF WRITINGS. *Derry: A Tale of the Revolution* (London: James Nisbet, 1867); *The English Martyrology. Abridged from Foxe,* 2 vols (London: R.B. Seeley and W. Burnside, 1837); *Letters from Ireland 1837* (London: R.B. Seeley and W. Burnside, 1838); *The Wrongs of Woman,* 4 pts (London: W.H. Dalton, 1843).

BIOGRAPHY AND CRITICISM. Clara Lucas Balfour, *A Sketch of Charlotte Elizabeth* (London: W. and F.G. Cash, 1854).

Thomas Smyth

LIFE. Thomas Smith was born in Belfast on 14 June 1808, one of twelve children of Samuel Smith and Ann Magee. Smyth adopted the spelling of his name with a 'y' in 1837. Raised a Congregationalist, he trained for the ministry first at the Royal Belfast Academical Institution and then at Highbury College, the Congregational seminary in London. After being implicated in an episode of theatre-going with a fellow student, he decided to emigrate to America with his parents. Upon arrival he joined the Presbyterian Church and entered Princeton Seminary. By 1832 he had received a call to 2nd Presbyterian Church, Charleston, South Carolina, a charge he held until his death. By 1832 he had also married Margaret Adger, the daughter of a wealthy Charleston family and pillar of the church. They had nine children, three of whom died in infancy. Smyth was strictly evangelical in his theology and conservative in his politics. He was opposed to 'prelacy' and to the abolitionist arguments concerning the legitimacy of slavery. He supported the South's seccession from the Union during the American Civil War. He was an avid scholar, publishing over 100 books and articles and amassing a library of over 12,000 volumes. He seems to have maintained a relationship with his mother's sister-in-law, Martha Magee, and to have visited her on several of his trips to Britain and Ireland in the 1840s. In her will she left him £2,000, although he suggests she might have left him more had she not been persuaded that he would predecease her. Smyth had always suffered from poor health and on several occasions had been attacked with partial paralysis. He was eventually forced to resign from active duty in 1870 and after a period of failing health died on 20 August 1873.

CHIEF WRITINGS. *Autobiographical Notes, Letters and Reflections.* Edited by his granddaughter Louisa Cheves Stoney (Charleston, South Carolina: Walker, Evans and Cogswell, 1914); J. William Flinn (ed.), *Complete Works of Rev. Thomas Smyth, DD. New Edition, with Brief Notes and Prefaces. Biographical Sketch in Last Volume,* 10 vols (Columbia, South Carolina, ???? 1908–12).

Lady Anne Jocelyn

LIFE. Lady Anne Jocelyn was born in 1795 to Robert Jocelyn, 2nd Earl of Roden (1756–1820), and Frances Theodosia, née Bligh (d. 1802). The Rodens were prominent members of the Irish landed gentry with extensive estates in counties Down, Louth, Essex and Hertfordshire. They were also part of a tightly knit group of aristocratic families which adhered to evangelical Christianity, including the Farnhams, Mandevilles and Mountcashels. Anne's sister Frances had married Richard Wingfield, 7th Viscount Powerscourt (1790–1823), and Anne spent much of her time at their residence in County Wicklow, nursing her sister through her final illness. Anne's brother Robert, the 3rd Earl of Roden (1788–1870), was a noted evangelical. He was an active supporter of a number of religious societies and was directly involved in the 'moral management' of his tenants' spiritual lives. He regularly conducted public religious services in the chapel at Tollymore Park, his seat in County Down. In political terms he was 'an ardent conservative' and Grand Master of the Orange Order. In 1849, after a serious clash between Orangemen and Catholics at Dolly's Brae, near Castlewellan, County Down, he was deprived of a government position as punishment for his irresponsible conduct. Little is known about Anne's life in particular. Clearly, she was raised in a deeply religious environment. Under her brother's influence 'an atmosphere of stern and uncompromising piety brooded over the house; the Sabbath was strictly kept'. From her diary, she seems to have conducted herself like many other women of her social class. She read, worked in the garden, visited with the local tenantry and helped out in the local school. She attended church and participated in family worship. She seems to have lived mainly with her brother and sister's families until her early death at the age of twenty-seven in 1822.

William Gibson

LIFE. William Gibson was born on 8 May 1808 in Ballymena, County Antrim. His father, James Gibson, was a merchant. He attended school first in Ballymena and later at The Royal Belfast Academical Institution, where he took the medal for classics in 1829. He then trained for the Presbyterian ministry, first in Belfast and then in Edinburgh. He was licensed in 1833 and ordained in 1834 as minister of First Ballybay, County Monaghan. In 1840 he was called to assist the Reverend Samuel Hanna in the charge of Rosemary Street Presbyterian Church, one of the oldest and most prestigious congregations in Belfast. He remained minister there until the end of his career. His interests soon took him down several different paths. In the early 1840s he was the driving force behind the establishment of the *Banner of Ulster*, a newspaper which reflected Presbyterian interests. In 1847 he was appointed professor of Christian Ethics in the Presbyterian church's ministerial training college and seems to have devoted much of his time to teaching and examining. At this time he requested an assistant at Rosemary Street to help him with his pastoral responsibilities. In 1859 he was elected moderator of the General Assembly and in this role travelled to America to investigate reports of a revival taking place in New York city. When similar events began occurring in mid-Antrim, Gibson began to compile an account of events which he eventually published as *The Year of Grace* (1860). This work, which viewed the many outbreaks of ecstatic behaviour throughout 1859 as a work of the Holy Spirit, attracted criticism from more conservative elements within the Presbyterian church. He was most notably challenged in his interpretation by the Reverend Isaac Nelson in his series of pamphlets entitled *The Year of Delusion*. The two men reflected the evangelical and liberal wings of the denomination. Gibson died suddenly in June 1867.

CHIEF WRITINGS. *The Year of Grace: A History of the Ulster Revival of 1859* (2nd ed., Edinburgh: Andrew Elliot, 1860).

Marie Fry

LIFE. Maria Margaret (Marie) was born in 1849, the daughter of William and Elizabeth Fry, of 13 Lower Mount Street, Dublin. As an infant she survived a mild bout of cholera. Her family was associated with the Dublin evangelical community and Marie was converted around the time of the Ulster revival of 1859. Throughout her teenage years, Marie's family attended Merrion Hall, an evangelical church which had been established in the wake of the revival and which had leanings towards Brethrenism. Marie was an extremely serious girl and is said to have had few friends. She was very active in a variety of evangelical pursuits, such as tract distribution and conducting children's Bible classes. She was also involved in a special outreach, run by Merrion Hall, to British army soldiers stationed at the Dublin garrison. In 1872 she became ill and died on 27 July 1873.

CHIEF WRITINGS. Fanny Grattan Guinness (ed.), *Selections from the Correspondence of the Late Marie Fry (of Dublin), with a Brief Biographical Notice* (Dublin: S.W. Partridge, [1874?]).

Fanny Grattan Guinness

LIFE. Fanny Emma Fitzgerald was born in London around 1831, the second child of Major Edward Marlborough Fitzgerald and Mabel Stopford, both of whom were from prominent Irish Protestant families. When she was very young her mother died of tuberculosis and her father committed suicide, so she was raised by the family solicitor, Arthur West, who was a Quaker. They lived in Exmouth and Dublin and eventually Bath, where, after West committed suicide, she worked as a teacher to support her foster mother and became associated with a group of Brethren. In 1860 she met Henry Grattan Guinness while on holiday in Ilfracombe. Guinness was a member of the famous Irish brewing family but had spent much of his childhood in Cheltenham. He was already prominent within evangelical circles for his preaching ability and had conducted preaching tours of France, Switzerland, Wales, Scotland and Ireland. Fanny and he were married in October 1860 and began a life of ceaseless evangelistic and missionary activity. The first year of their marriage was spent travelling throughout America and Canada, conducting evangelistic services. In 1872, after living for brief periods in Dublin, Bath and Paris, the Guinnesses and their six children moved to the East End of London and established a training college for lay missionaries called the East London Institute for Home and Foreign Missions. This work eventually moved to Cliff House, Derbyshire, as the Regions Beyond Missionary Union (RBMU). Fanny had always been an active partner to her husband. During their American tour, she had preached publicly to mixed audiences and continued to do so throughout the 1860s. She was the one who was responsible for the day-to-day administration and management of the institute, as well as writing its annual reports. She also wrote numerous books, including accounts of the RBMU, and several handbooks of biblical prophecy. In 1885 Fanny suffered an attack of Bell's palsy, which left her with facial paralysis. In 1892 she had a stroke, which forced her to give up her work and retire to Cliff House. She died on 3 November 1898 and was buried in nearby Baslow Church cemetery.

CHIEF WRITINGS. *'She Spake of Him', Being Recollections of the Loving Labours and Early Death of the Late Mrs. Henry Dening* (Bristol and London: W. Mack, [1872]); *Sitwana's Story* (London: n.p. [1882]); *The Wide World and Our Work in It; Or, The Story of the East London Institute for Home and Foreign Missions* (London: Hodder and Stoughton, [1886]). With Henry Grattan Guinness: *Hymns of the Cross, Selected and Arranged, with Introductory Meditations* (London and Norwich: n.p., 1864); *Light for the Last Days: A Study Historic and Prophetic* (London: Hodder and Stoughton, 1886).

BIOGRAPHY AND CRITICISM. Michele Guinness, *The Guinness Legend* (London: Hodder and Stoughton, 1990).

SARAH MacDONALD, *Editor*

Hymns and Hymn-Writers, 1850–1930

This subsection examines the contribution of Cecil Frances (Fanny) Alexander to Victorian hymn-writing. Victorian worship was characterized by congregational hymn-singing and Fanny Alexander wrote hymns for children as well as adults. From the end of the eighteenth century, there had been an upsurge of interest in writing for children. This may have been due to the emphasis which the evangelicals put on the moral development of children and their spiritual formation. Also the influence of the Oxford Movement and of John Keble, author of a collection of religious verse, *The Christian Year,* 1827, is evident in Alexander's early work: she based her first publication, *Verses for Holy Seasons,* 1846, on Keble's *Christian Year,* but hers was intended specifically for children. Keble prefaced her second collection, *Hymns for Little Children,* 1848, published with the instruction of children in the Apostles' Creed in mind.

Motherhood was a central theme in Alexander's hymns for children and Katharine Tynan also wrote about that topic and, like Alexander, was influenced by the Victorian love of nature and human interaction with natural events and the seasons of the year. Though Alexander's 'There is a Green Hill Far Away' was written for children, it deals poignantly with Christ's crucifixion and contrasts in an interesting way with Susan Mitchell's sacred poem 'Light of Lights', rarely performed musically.

The Gaelic revival saw the emergence of an academic interest in the Irish language, which led to a number of translations of ancient Irish prayers and literature into English. Translations such as Susan Mitchell's version of an old Irish poem, 'Amergin', and Eleanor Hull's 'Be Thou My Vision' have had an enduring popularity. Alexander's adaptation of the Lorica (St Patrick's Breastplate), 'I bind unto myself to-day', using the prose version of the scholar Whitley Stokes (1830–1909), has become a classic because of Alexander's use of rhythm and sensitivity of language and sentiment.

CECIL FRANCES ALEXANDER

(1818–95)

from:
HYMNS FOR LITTLE
CHILDREN (1848)

[In seeking to explain the tenet 'suffered under Pontius Pilate, was crucified, died and was buried', Alexander sought to illuminate the Gospel teaching regarding the plan of salvation, expounding the idea that the essential doctrine on which the Christian's salvation hangs is the doctrine of the Cross.]

There is a Green Hill Far Away

There is a green hill far away,
 Without a city wall,
Where the dear Lord was crucified
 Who died to save us all.

We may not know, we cannot tell
  What pains He had to bear,
But we believe it was for us
  He hung and suffered there.

He died that we might be forgiven,
  He died to make us good,
That we might go at last to Heaven,
  Saved by His precious Blood.

There was no other good enough
  To pay the price of sin;
He only could unlock the gate
  Of Heaven, and let us in.

Oh, dearly, dearly, has He loved,
  And we must love Him too,
And trust in His redeeming Blood,
  And try His works to do.

He was little, weak, and helpless,
  Tears and smiles like us He knew;
So He feeleth for our sadness,
So He shareth in our gladness.

And our eyes at last shall see Him,
  Through His own redeeming love
For that Child, so dear and gentle,
  Is our Lord in heaven above;
And He leads His children on
To the place where He is gone.

Not in that poor, lowly stable
  With the oxen standing by
We shall see Him; but in Heaven,
  Sat at God's right hand on high;
When like stars His children crowned
All in white shall wait around.

[Alexander's words seemed to set themselves to music, hence the perennial appeal of this Christmas hymn, which explains the words of the Apostles' Creed, 'born of the Virgin Mary'.]

Christmas

Once in royal David's city
  Stood a lowly cattle-shed,
Where a Mother laid her Baby
  In a manger for His bed;
Mary was that Mother mild,
Jesus Christ her little Child.

He came down to earth from Heaven
  Who is God and Lord of all,
Yet His shelter was a stable,
  And His cradle was a stall;
With the poor and mean and lowly
Lived on earth our Saviour holy.

And through all his wondrous childhood
  He would honour and obey,
Love, and watch the lowly Maiden,
  In whose gentle arms He lay;
Christian children all must be
Mild, obedient, good as He.

For He is our childhood's pattern
  Day by day like us He grew,

[In this hymn Alexander set out to list God's wonderful works of creation. She has been criticized for her seeming acceptance of the unequal distribution of wealth and privilege in the verse beginning: 'The rich man in his castle'. This was probably not intentional; Alexander was endeavouring to explain the tenet 'Maker of Heaven and Earth', and she seemed to accept the inequalities between rich and poor.]

All Things Bright and Beautiful

All things bright and beautiful,
  All creatures great and small,
All things wise and wonderful,
  The Lord God made them all.

Each little flower that opens,
  Each little bird that sings,
He made their glowing colours,
  He made their tiny wings.

The rich man in his castle,
  The poor man at his gate,
God made them high and lowly,
  And ordered their estate.

The purple-headed mountain,
  The river running by,
The sunset, and the morning,
  That brightens up the sky;

The cold wind in the winter,
  The pleasant summer sun,
The ripe fruits in the garden —
  He made them every one;

The tall trees in the greenwood,
  The meadows where we play,
The rushes by the water
  We gather every day —

He gave us eyes to see them,
  And lips that we might tell,
How great is God Almighty,
  Who has made all things well.

from:
POEMS ON SUBJECTS IN THE OLD TESTAMENT (1854)

[Alexander's measured emotion and careful employment of rhythm and rhyming schemes allowed for oral recitation. This poem was a popular choice for public recitations.]

The Burial of Moses

'And he buried him in a valley in the land of Moab over against Beth-peor, but no man knoweth of his sepulchre unto this day.'
                    Deuteronomy 34:6

By Nebo's lonely mountain,
  On this side Jordan's wave
In a vale in the land of Moab
  There lies a lonely grave
And no man knows that sepulchre,
  And no man saw it e'er.
For the angels of God upturned the sod,
  And laid the dead man there.

That was the grandest funeral
  That ever passed on earth;
But no man heard the trampling;
  Or saw the train go forth —
Noiselessly as the daylight
  Comes back when night is done,
And the crimson streak on ocean's cheek
  Grows into the great sun;

Noiselessly as the spring-time
  Her crown of verdure weaves
And all the trees on all the hills
  Open their thousand leaves;
So without sound of music,
  Or voice of them that wept,
Silently down from the mountain's crown
  The great procession swept.

Perchance the bald old eagle
  On grey Beth-Peor's height
Out of his lonely eyrie
  Look'd on the wondrous sight;
Perchance the lion stalking
  Still shuns the hallow'd spot,
For beast and bird have seen and heard
  That which man knoweth not.

But when the warrior dieth,
  His comrades in the war,
With arms reversed and muffled drum,
  Follow his funeral car;
They show the banners taken,
  They tell his battles won,
And after him lead his masterless steed,
  While peals the minute gun.

Amid the noblest of the land,
  We lay the sage to rest,
And give the bard an honoured place
  With costly marble drest
In the great minster transept
  Where lights like glories fall,
And the organ rings, and sweet choir sings
  Along the emblazoned wall.

This was the truest warrior
  That ever buckled sword;
This the most gifted poet
  That ever breath'd a word;
And never earth's philosopher
  Traced with his golden pen
On the deathless page truths half so sage
  As he wrote down for men.

And had he not high honour —
  The hillside for a pall,
To lie in state while angels wait,
  With stars for tapers tall,
And the dark rock pines like tossing plumes
  Over his bier to wave,
And God's own hand in that lonely land
  To lay him in the grave?

In that strange grave without a name,
    Whence his uncoffined clay
Shall break again, O wondrous thought!
    Before the Judgement Day,
And stand with glory wrapped around
    On the hills he never trod,
And speak of the strife that won our life
    With the Incarnate Son of God.

O lonely grave in Moab's land!
    O dark Beth-Peor's hill!
Speak to these curious hearts of ours,
    And teach them to be still.
God hath His mysteries of grace,
    Ways that we cannot tell,
He hides them deep, like the hidden sleep
    Of him He loved so well.

from:
HYMNS ANCIENT AND MODERN (1875)

[Written for Good Friday and based on words uttered by Christ on the Cross, this credal hymn is a fine example of Alexander's ability to combine theology and devotion.]

His are the Thousand Sparkling Rills

His are the thousand sparkling rills
    That from a thousand fountains burst,
And fill with music all the hills;
    And yet He saith, 'I thirst.'

All fiery pangs on battle-fields,
    On fever beds where sick men toss,
Are in that human cry He yields
    To anguish on the cross.

But more than pains that racked Him then
    Was the deep longing thirst Divine
That thirsted for the souls of men:
    Dear Lord! and one was mine.

O Love most patient, give me grace;
    Make all my soul athirst for Thee;
That parch'd dry Lip, that fading Face,
    That Thirst were all for me.

from:
IRISH CHURCH HYMNAL (1891)

[The Lorica, or Breastplate, of Saint Patrick was a lyrical rendering of Patrick's Christian faith. Patrick was, according to tradition, on his way to the court at Tara and facing death for his attempt to convert the local people to Christianity, when he composed this prayer. Alexander's version was based on a prose translation of the Lorica by Dr Whitley Stokes.]

The Lorica (Breastplate) of Saint Patrick

I bind unto myself to-day
    The strong Name of the Trinity.
By invocation of the same,
    The Three in One and One in Three.

I bind this day to me for ever.
    By pow'r of faith, Christ's Incarnation;
His baptism in Jordan river;
    His death on Cross for my salvation;
His bursting from the spiced tomb;
    His riding up the Heav'nly way;
His coming at the day of doom:
    I bind unto myself to-day.

I bind unto myself the power
    Of the great love of Cherubim;
The sweet 'Well done' in judgment hour;
    The service of the Seraphim,
Confessors' faith, Apostles' word,
    The Patriarchs' prayers, the Prophets' scrolls,
All good deeds done unto the Lord,
    And purity of virgin souls.

I bind unto myself to-day
    The virtues of the star-lit heaven.
The glorious sun's life-giving ray,
    The whiteness of the moon at even.
The flashing of the lightning free,
    The whirling wind's tempestuous shocks,
The stable earth, the deep salt sea,
    Around the old eternal rocks.

I bind unto myself to-day
    The pow'r of God to hold, and lead,
His eye to watch, His might to stay,
    His ear to hearken to my need.

The wisdom of my God to teach.
His hand to guide, His shield to ward;
The word of God to give me speech;
His heavenly host to be my guard.

Against the demon snares of sin,
The vice that gives temptation force,
The natural lusts that war within,
The hostile men that mar my course;
Or few or many, far or nigh,
In every place, and in all hours,
Against their fierce hostility,
I bind to me these holy powers.

Against all Satan's spells and wiles,
Against false words of heresy,
Against the knowledge that defiles,
Against the heart's idolatry,
Against the wizard's evil craft,
Against the death-wound and the burning,

The choking wave, the poisoned shaft,
Protect me, Christ, till Thy returning.

Christ be with me, Christ within me,
Christ behind me, Christ before me,
Christ beside me, Christ to win me,
Christ to comfort and restore me
Christ beneath me, Christ above me,
Christ in quiet, Christ in danger,
Christ in hearts of all that love me,
Christ in mouth of friend and stranger.

I bind unto myself the Name
The strong Name of the Trinity;
By invocation of the same,
The Three in One, and One in Three,
Of Whom all nature hath creation;
Eternal Father, Spirit, Word;
Praise to the Lord of my salvation,
Salvation is of Christ the Lord.

ELEANOR HULL

(1860-1935)

from:
THE POEM-BOOK OF THE
GAEL (1913)

[Besides being a noted scholar of Old Irish texts, Eleanor
Hull was a skilled translator and editor of medieval texts.
The anonymous, ninth-century poem she translated from
Old Irish as 'A Prayer' rapidly assumed the status of a
hymn for congregational singing at church services. Her
translation of the eleventh-century anonymous poem
which she titled 'The Soul's Desire' also made its way into
church liturgy.]

A Prayer

Be thou my vision, O Lord of my heart,
Naught is all else to me, save that Thou art.

Thou my best thought by day and by night,
Waking or sleeping, Thy presence my light.

Be thou my wisdom, Thou my true word;
I ever with Thee, Thou with me, Lord.

Thou my great father, I Thy dear son;
Thou in me dwelling, I with Thee one.

Be Thou my battle-shield, sword for the fight,
Be Thou my dignity, Thou my delight.

Thou my soul's shelter, Thou my high tower;
Raise Thou me heavenward, power of my power.

Riches I heed not, nor man's empty praise,
Thou mine inheritance now and always.

Thou, and Thou only, first in my heart,
High King of heaven, my treasure Thou art.

King of the seven heavens, grant me for dole,
Thy love in my heart, Thy light in my soul.

Thy light from my soul, Thy love from my heart,
King of the seven heavens, may they never depart.

With the high king of heaven, after victory won,
May I reach heaven's joys, O bright heaven's sun!

Heart of my own heart, whatever befall,
Still be my vision, O Ruler of all.

The Soul's Desire

It were my soul's desire
To see the face of God;
It were my soul's desire
To rest in His abode.

It were my soul's desire
To study zealously;
This, too, my soul's desire,
A clear rule set for me.

It were my soul's desire
A spirit free from gloom;
It were my soul's desire
New life beyond the Doom.

It were my soul's desire
To shun the chills of Hell;
It were my soul's desire
Within His house to dwell.

It were my soul's desire
To imitate my King,
It were my soul's desire
His ceaseless praise to sing.

It were my soul's desire
When heaven's gate is won
To find my soul's desire
Clear shining like the sun.

Grant, Lord, my soul's desire,
Deep waves of cleansing sighs;
Grant, Lord, my soul's desire
From earthly cares to rise.

This still my soul's desire
Whatever life afford —
To gain my soul's desire
And see Thy face, O Lord.

KATHARINE TYNAN

(1861–1931)

from:
TWENTY-ONE POEMS (1907)

[A prolific writer of prose and verse, Katharine Tynan was
a poet whose themes and lyrical quality established her as
a prominent figure in the Literary Revival and as a friend
of W.B. Yeats. Her first volume of poetry, *Shamrocks*, was
published in 1885, to be followed by *Irish Love Songs*
(1892), *The Wind Among the Trees* (1898), considered her
best collection, *Flower of Youth* (1915), and *The Holy War*
(1926). 'Sheep and Lambs' is Tynan's best-known hymn,
revealing her religious sensibility and her personal love of
nature. It was arranged by Hugh S. Roberton, composer
and musical publisher, for Mrs Bourke and the Barrow
Choir in 1911, and it has remained a firm favourite with
choirs and church congregations.]

Sheep and Lambs

All in the April evening,
    April airs were abroad;
The sheep with their little lambs
    Passed me by on the road.

The sheep with their little lambs
    Passed me by on the road;
All in an April evening
    I thought on the Lamb of God.

The lambs were weary, and crying
    With a weak human cry,
I thought on the Lamb of God
    Going meekly to die.

Up in the blue, blue mountains
  Dewy pastures are sweet;
Rest for the little bodies,
  Rest for the little feet.

But for the Lamb of God
  Up on the hill-top green,

Only a cross of shame
  Two stark crosses between.

All in the April evening,
  April airs were abroad;
I saw the sheep and their lambs
  And thought on the Lamb of God.

SUSAN MITCHELL

(1866–1926)

from:
THE LIVING CHALICE AND OTHER POEMS (1908)

[The title poem, 'The Living Chalice', is a spiritual meditation on the place of pain and suffering in the pursuit of communing with the Divine. Strictly speaking, this poem never passed into popular usage as a hymn, though music and singing were an integral part of Susan Mitchell's literary life.]

The Living Chalice

The Mother sent me on the holy quest
Timid and proud and curiously dressed
In vestures by her hand wrought wondrously;
An eager burning heart she gave to me,
The Bridegroom's Feast was set and I drew
    nigh —
Master of Life, Thy Cup has passed me by.

Before new-dresses I from the Mother came,
In dreams I saw the wondrous Cup of Flame;
Ah, Divine Chalice, how my heart drank deep,
Waking I sought the Love I knew asleep.
The Feast of Life was set and I drew nigh —
Master of Life, Thy Cup has passed me by.

Eyes of the Soul, awake, awake and see
Growing within the Ruby Radiant Tree,
Sharp pain hath wrung the Clusters of my Vine;
My heart is rose-red with its brimmed wine.
Thou has new-set the Feast and I draw nigh,
Master of Life take me, Thy Cup am I.

Biographies/Bibliographies

Cecil Frances Alexander

LIFE. Born in Dublin in 1818, the second daughter of Major John and Elizabeth Humphreys. In 1825 Major Humphreys became the land agent for the Duke of Wicklow and the family moved to Ballykeane. Friendship between the young Cecil Frances and the Duke's daughter, Lady Harriet Howard, evolved from their religious convictions and mutual interest in the principles of the Oxford Movement. It was at this time that she first began to display her ability to write verse, a talent she employed to promote her religious beliefs. She published her first book of hymns, *Verses for Holy Seasons,* in 1846, based on Keble's *The Christian Year.* She was later to meet Keble, Pusey and many other prominent members of the movement through her uncle Sir Thomas Reed. In 1847 she published an allegorical prose story for children, *The Lord of the Forest and His Vassals,* but as poetry rather than prose was the medium in which she excelled, she thereafter concentrated her talents in the area of hymn-writing and sacred poetry. In 1848 she published *Hymns for Little Children,* which contained three hymns for which she subsequently became renowned: 'All Things Bright and Beautiful', 'There is a Green Hill Far Away' and 'Once in Royal David's City'. In 1865 she edited and contributed to *The Sunday Book of Poetry.* Her selection of contributors indicates her own personal sense of the catholicity of Anglicanism, showing her synthesis of both the ideals of the Oxford Movement and, at the same time, her strong evangelical sympathies. In 1850 she married William Alexander, who became Bishop of Derry (1867) and later Archbishop of Armagh (1896). Although she had earlier managed to maintain her writing while raising four children and assisting her husband in his parish social work, her output diminished considerably following her husband's advancement. She died in Derry in 1895.

CHIEF WRITINGS. Poems and hymns: *Verses for Holy Seasons* (London: F. and J. Rivington, 1846); *Hymns for Little Children* (London: Joseph Masters, 1848); *Moral Songs* (London: Joseph Masters, 1849); *Narrative Hymns for Village Schools,* 5th ed. (London: Joseph Masters, 1859); *Poems on Subjects in the Old Testament* (London: Joseph Masters, 1854); *Hymns Descriptive and Devotional. For the Use of Schools* (London: Joseph Masters, 1858); *The Legend of the Golden Prayers and Other Poems* (London: Bell and Daldy, 1859); *The Sunday Book of Poetry,* selected and arranged by C.F.A. (London and Cambridge: Macmillan, 1864); 'St. Patrick's Breastplate', *Irish Church Hymnal,* 1891, Appendix; *Poems,* ed. W. Alexander (London: Macmillan, 1896); *Selected Poems of William Alexander and Cecil Frances Alexander,* ed. A.P. Graves (London: Society for Promoting Christian Knowledge, 1930). Fiction: *The Lord of the Forest and His Vassals: An Allegory* (London: Joseph Masters, 1848); *The Baron's Little Daughter and Other Tales* (London: Joseph Masters, 1848).

Religious work: *Easy Questions on the Life of Our Lord* (London: Griffith and Farran, 1891).

BIOGRAPHY AND CRITICISM. Valerie Wallace, *Mrs Alexander: A Life of the Hymn-Writer Cecil Frances Alexander, 1818–1895* (Dublin: Lilliput Press, 1995).

Eleanor Hull

LIFE. Born in Manchester in 1860, she was educated at Alexandra College in Dublin, where her father, Edward Hull, worked as a professor of geology in the Royal College. Her mother's surname was Cooke and she came from Cheltenham in England. Eleanor studied Irish with Kuno Meyer and Standish O'Grady. She subsequently went to live in London, where she founded the Irish Texts Society in 1899 and acted as its secretary for over thirty years. She was also an active member of the London Irish Literary Society. She died in 1935.

CHIEF WRITINGS. *The Cuchullin Saga in Irish Literature* (London: David Nutt, 1898); *Epochs of Irish History 1. Pagan Ireland* (London: David Nutt; Dublin: M.H. Gill, 1904); *Epochs of Irish History 2. Early Christian Ireland* (London: David Nutt; Dublin: M.H. Gill, 1905); *A Textbook of Irish Literature*, 2 parts (London: David Nutt; Dublin: M.H. Gill, 1906–8; rpr., New York: AMS Press, 1974); *A History of Ireland and Her People to the Close of the Tudor Period*, 2 vols (London: G.G. Harrap, 1926; rpr., New York: Books for Libraries Press, 1972).

BIOGRAPHY AND CRITICISM. Diarmuid Breathnach and Máire Ní Mhurchú, *1882–1982 Beathaisnéis a hAon* (Dublin: An Clóchomhar Íta, 1986), pp. 33–4.

Katharine Tynan

LIFE. Born into a prosperous Catholic farming family in County Dublin on 23 January 1861 and educated at a Dominican Convent school in Drogheda. Kate lived in Clondalkin as her father's favourite daughter until her marriage to Henry Albert Hinkson in 1893, after which she lived for the most part in England, except when her husband was resident magistrate for County Mayo (1911–19). In 1878 she joined the Ladies' Land League and she was a fervent Parnellite before and after the 'split'. Her first volume, *Louise de la Valliere and Other Poems* (1885), was very successful, and she went on to become a friend and associate of the young writers who inaugurated the Irish Literary Revival, especially Yeats. However, this nationalist phase was only one period in her long career as a full-time professional writer and even then she was a religious as well as a patriotic poet. After her marriage she turned to familial and maternal themes in both poetry and fiction. A prolific novelist, who wrote to support her family, she was interested in women's roles but tended to represent the views and mores of conservative English women of her own class in her highly popular fiction. In all, she published over 160 volumes of prose, fiction and poetry. Her poetry, on which her reputation now chiefly rests, was not marred by class prejudice, and here she often writes as an Oedipal mother, the emotional pivot of the family drama. She also edited *The Cabinet of Irish Literature*, the fore-mother of the *Field Day Anthology of Irish Writing*. She appears to have found women more interesting than men; *Memories* (1924) and her other memoirs (see below) include portraits of the many contemporary women writers with whom she was on friendly terms. She enjoyed her widowhood from 1919, travelling extensively with her daughter, Pamela, and continuing to publish almost until her death after a brief illness on 2 April 1931.

CHIEF WRITINGS. (Poems) *Louise de la Valliere and Other Poems* (London: Kegan Paul, 1885); *Shamrocks* (London: Kegan Paul, 1887); *Ballads and Lyrics* (London: Kegan Paul, 1891); *Irish Love-Songs* (London: T.F. Unwin, 1892); *Poems* (London: Lawrence and Bullen, 1901); *Twenty-one Poems* (Dundrum: Dun Emer Press, 1907); *New Poems* (London: Sidgwick and Jackson, 1911); (memoirs) *Twenty-Five Years* (London: Elder Smith, 1913); *The Middle Years* (London: Constable, 1916); *The Years of the Shadow* (Boston: Houghton-Mifflin, 1919); *The Wandering Years* (London: Constable, 1922); *Memories* (London: Nash and Grayson, 1924); *The Playground* (novel) (London: Ward, Lock, 1930); *Collected Poems* (London: Macmillan, 1930).

BIOGRAPHY AND CRITICISM. Marilyn Gaddis Rose, *Katharine Tynan* (Lewisburg: Bucknell University Press, 1974); Herbert Sussman, *Katharine Tynan* (Boston: Twayne, 1979).

See also Volume III, pp. 557–8.

Susan Mitchell

LIFE. Born in Carrick-on-Shannon, County Leitrim, in 1866. On the death of her father, Michael, her mother, Kate (Cullen), arranged for Susan to be adopted by her aunts, Michael's sisters, in Dublin, where she grew up. In 1900 she stayed with the family of John B. Yeats in London and was drawn into the Literary Revival circle, becoming assistant editor to George Moore at the *Irish Homestead*. Later she became sub-editor of the *Irish Statesman*, and remained a lifelong friend of Moore, publishing a valuable study of him in 1916. She published four collections of her poetry: *The Living Chalice and Other Poems*, 1902, in the Tower Press series, and *Frankincense and Myrrh*, 1912, in the Cuala Press, the frontispiece hand-coloured by Jack B. Yeats. A supporter of Charles Stewart Parnell, she joined the Irish Franchise League, and later, after the 1916 Easter Rising in Dublin, developed strong republican sympathies. Witty, satirical, she was a keen observer of events during the civil war and she was respected as a leading journalist whose objectivity never faltered. She died suddenly in 1926 and lies buried with her beloved aunts in Mount Jerome cemetery in Dublin.

CHIEF WRITINGS. *Aids to the Immortality of Certain Persons in Ireland: Charitably Administered* (Dublin: The New Nation, 1908; with additions, Dublin: Maunsel, 1913); *The Living Chalice and Other Poems* (London: Maunsel, 1908); *Frankincense and Myrrh* (Dublin: Cuala Press, 1912); *George Moore* (Dublin: Maunsel, 1916; New York: Dodd, Mead, 1916); *Secret Springs of Dublin Songs* (Dublin: Talbot Press, 1918).

BIOGRAPHY AND CRITICISM. Hilary Pyle, *Red-Headed Rebel, Susan L. Mitchell* (Dublin: Woodfield Press, 1998); Richard M. Kain, *Susan L. Mitchell* (Lewisburgh, Pennsylvania: Bucknell University Press, 1972); George W. Russell (AE), 'The Poetry of Susan Mitchell', *Irish Statesman*, 27 March 1926; Robert Skelton, 'Aide to Immortality: The Satirical Writings of Susan L. Mitchell', in *The World of W.B. Yeats: Essays in Perspective*, ed. Robert Skelton and Anne Saddlemeyer (Dublin: Dolmen Press, 1965).

MARGARET Mac CURTAIN, *Editor*

Recollections of Catholicism, 1906–1960[1]

The writings of this section recall the experiences of women raised in the Catholic culture of a church which remained long in the ascendant during the twentieth century. The role of the Catholic church, and its contribution to Irish society, still await definitive analysis, but there is no shortage of interpretative studies and convincing explanations of the unique position it held in twentieth-century Ireland. Tom Inglis in his book *Moral Monopoly: The Catholic Church in Modern Irish Society* examines the power the Catholic church exercised over the lives of its members through its domination of Irish education and its systems of moral discipline and social control. He argues that the church's influence on family life was mediated through a construction of Irish motherhood shaped by Catholic practices, under the moral guidance of priests and nuns.[2] J.J. Lee, historian of twentieth-century Ireland, profiles the characteristics of Irish society in this period. Resistance to change and to new ideas, a performance ethic directed to the goal of security, are among the factors Lee examines as causing the social and economic backwardness of the Irish state. Lee, however, identifies the Catholic church in the decades before the Second Vatican Council (1962–5) as an institution of vitality, attracting recruits of talent and becoming the main bulkwark of civic culture.[3]

It is worth noting that women writing from the 1970s to the 1990s, that is, from a perspective of a late-twentieth-century vantage point, take a backward look at the Catholicism of their youth to recall a lost innocence and to settle old scores with austere convent schools, whereas writers of previous generations critique the authoritarian patterns of family and social behaviour mediated by church teaching, which relegated women to a passive and subservient station in life.

Norah Hoult's novel *Holy Ireland* is set at the turn of the century and underscores the subordination of women in a middle-class Dublin family where conformity to the dictates of a tyrannical and nagging father are demanded in the name of Catholicism. Patrick O'Neill buttresses his paternalism with rituals of Catholic devotion. He manipulates the family rosary and the retreat sermon to stifle any intellectual conversation in his home. Margaret, the protagonist of the novel, in turn learns to be subversive and secretive. Kate O'Brien's memories of early childhood in a convent boarding-school in the first decade of the twentieth century possess the charm of looking back from a perspective of old age. In her *Memories of a Catholic Girlhood* she identifies for the reader the setting of her novel *The Land of Spices* (1942), and the figure of Mère Marie-Helene, the central character in the novel, as well as the atmosphere of the school, Laurel Hill convent in Limerick, where O'Brien spent her schooldays. The extracts from *As Music and Splendour* reveal the conflict between Catholic moral training and the acknowledgement of an intimate lesbian relationship. Clare, the heroine, in admitting her love for Luisa, regards herself as sinful and therefore not in a state of grace as a practising Catholic.

Sara Hyland, a Dundrum woman from greater Dublin, who spent summers in the 1920s

---

1. Although a number of the texts gathered here were written after 1960, they refer to pre-Vatican II.
2. Tom Inglis, *Moral Monopoly: The Catholic Church in Modern Irish Society* (Dublin: Gill and Macmillan, 1987).
3. J.J. Lee, *Ireland, 1912–1985, Politics and Society* (Cambridge: Cambridge University Press, 1989), pp. 390–6, 528.

in Connemara, describes a local wake and its attendant ceremonials, reminding the reader of another Ireland, where a priest knew his place and respected local customs. Hyland recalls her anxiety when she attended the funeral of her friend the 'Bun Lady' in a Church of Ireland ceremony in Dublin and how, despite the assurances of her employer, Lily Yeats, that she would not jeopardize her Catholic faith, she fretted that she would 'lose her religion'. The withholding of opportunity to share in common worship by Catholic bishops was a control mechanism in a period of increasing intolerance. Hyland charts the growing triumphalism of the Catholic church in her simple account of the celebration in 1929 of the centenary of Catholic emancipation and shows how the event became another step in the institutionalization of relations between the Catholic church and the ethos of the Free State.

Una Troy's story 'The Apple', published in Sean O'Faolain's journal *The Bell* in 1942, exposes the legalism of convent regulations in the early twentieth century. In Troy's story a nun transgresses the canonical rule of enclosure by re-entering and exploring the rooms of her old home. She comes out unrepentant, 'but she did not realize how precious and how terrible was the price she paid for it'. Some of the social snobberies attached to having a daughter a nun appear in the musings of Mrs Latimer, the narrator of Mary Lavin's story 'A Nun's Mother'. The merits of celibacy, the rejection of the world, are weighed against the responsibility of childbearing and Mrs Latimer recognizes in herself an ambivalence towards her own feelings as a mother.

Of the many accounts of being raised Catholic in the Free State, Clarissa A. Woods's essay 'Woman Kneeling' is a poignant gloss on the Censorship of Publications Act, 1929, which prohibited books and written information that advocated or gave instruction on methods of birth control, and the subsequent prohibition of the sale or importation of contraceptives by civil law in 1935. Fear of unwanted pregnancy and the bleak denial by the state of family planning rights dominated the childbearing years of many women's lives. Alice Taylor nostalgically evokes Irish rural life in the same period, giving an idyllic picture of the Christmas customs of a farming household in 'A Country Child's Christmas', from *To School Through the Fields.*

At the core of most women's memories of Catholicism in the Free State are the numerous accounts of their education at the hands of the nuns. Gráinne O'Flynn's account 'Our Age of Innocence' provides a context for an educational system designed to produce the wives and mothers enshrined in Article 41 of the 1937 Irish constitution, and another generation of women for Irish convents and mission life abroad. Such an educational system, with its emphasis on obedience, diligence, self-sacrifice and the celebrated religious counsel 'offer it up', answers the question why women in the Free State remained subordinate in a state they had helped create. Edna O'Brien's schooling in a convent boarding-school at Loughrea, County Galway, is characterized predictably by its savage asceticism and sense of being colonized and bound into an alien culture. Nuala O'Faolain, writing in *Religious Life Review*, a journal for women and men in religious vows, looks back ambivalently on her school-days, and her experience of being educated by four different orders of nuns. She acknowledges that she received a proper education, 'they gave me my chance in life', but her reflections are full of inconsolable grief and hurt and a sense of being dislocated in 'a special place, a convent' which she did not understand.

In a realistic setting, Dublin's inner city, Dinah Rooney and Catherine Waldron remember the ritual of 'churching', the blessing of a woman after childbirth by a priest. It was a cleansing ritual and was intended by the church to release women from any uncleanness associated with childbirth. It became obsolete in the 1950s.

Catholic culture in the first half of the twentieth century had to wait for the language and methodology of feminist theology to critique a patriarchal and gendered church. Irish feminist writing has brought to the surface an awareness of the silencing, the dispossession, the invisibility of Irish women in the life of the Catholic church for the greater part of the twentieth century. That is one of the benefits of hindsight. Telling the story, searching for the muted voice, finding and understanding the idiom that describes the loss of trust, the betrayal of faith, or the experience of spiritual anguish are complementary to the feminist analysis. They supply the texts.

KATE O'BRIEN

(1897–1974)

from:
MEMORIES OF A CATHOLIC
GIRLHOOD (1976)

[Shortly before her death, Kate O'Brien wrote but did not complete the autobiographical memoir from which the *Tablet* published a section on 4 December 1976. O'Brien spent her childhood from the age of six to eighteen in the boarding-school of Laurel Hill Convent in Limerick city. In this essay she supplied valuable information on the early childhood education of a creative writer, whose books about the inner conflicts of young women reaching adulthood in Ireland were banned by the Irish Censorship Board in the 1930s and 1940s.]

At the extreme end of the sixties, that is to say, as I write at this hour, within about 18 months of the span of three score and ten, one lives entirely alone. I do, in ordinary fact. I have lived alone always — even when I have been closely associated with other lives. I have always been split — as I imagine many intelligent people know themselves to be.

Loneliness is a condition of human life which one begins to understand, or rather to confront than understand, in adolescence. Childhood is for the more or less lucky child, at least, a season of curiosity and intake. In childhood we assemble ourselves. At the end of childhood we are the armoured or the wounded or the enlightened being, who has to draw breath, take decisions, and go ahead into that shadowy or glittering journey of adult life, which brings us to the inescapable other darkness. Out of the darkness we came — and suddenly we find ourselves on the cold brink of the other. Bede's wild bird we remember flying in and out . . .

Going back

The other day I walked over the gravel stretch that separates the high grey façade of Laurel Hill from its lawns and playgrounds. It was a June evening: the Shannon flowed peacefully seaward below, and the hills of Clare smudged in the well-remembered blue shadow. The silence and order of the place did not surprise me as they might have done, since this convent school is now closely pressed about by a thriving and almost noisy modern city; but they did knock at my breast in a sharp message of admonition.

The young member of the teaching staff who walked with me followed my glance up to the long row of windows of the first floor.

'Yes, they're all up there, at study now. Do you remember the study hall, Miss O'Brien?'

I could have described it to her in exact detail.

'How many of them?'

'Just over 90.'

In my time we were never more that 50 boarders; often under 40. And the last of those twelve Junes which I had spent under the authority of the Study Hall was now exactly 50 Junes ago. They must be crowded in that vast room. Surely they could not ruin it by trying to fit in 90 of our green-baize-covered desks?

But we were crowded too. A restless, changeful, puzzling and eccentric crowd of girls — varied and renewed in mixture from year to year, from term to term: and living for at least nine months out of every twelve under the guidance and in the society of a restless, changeful, puzzling and eccentric crowd of nuns, who were varied or renewed hardly at all — and then for the most part by a death in the community. That was always a red-letter event. A death of any one of the nuns was exciting: the requiem and the funeral procession to the little graveyard at the end of the kitchen garden were beautiful, whether in sunshine, or through wind or rain. The nuns' veils whirling, candles going out; confused Latin murmurs; and sometimes one was awestruck to see some nun crying as she walked behind a coffin. And of course there could be no lessons on such a morning, which injected a great secret gaiety into our voluptuous enjoyment of *De profundis*[1] and *Dies irae*.[2]

---

1. Psalm 12A is associated with rituals of death and burial in the Christian tradition.
2. *Dies irae* is one of the canonical sequences for the Catholic requiem in the Latin mass.

A few skulls lie in that graveyard that once were vessels of great intelligence to us. No Yoricks[3] but brains to which I owe a gratitude I cannot measure; yet I do not mean by that immeasurable. These few nuns were not geniuses. They were very modest people. And I think that all five or six of them, could they read me now, would rise in disgust against the description — modest people. For they were arrogant — to a nun. And that is why, given their brains, they were such good teachers. And I have to admit that they were all aristocrats. But Mother Maria — probably the most gifted of them — could be roused into hysterics if, in history class, one managed to suggest that her family came to its title by accepting the Act of Union 1800.[4] We always exercised ingenuity in history class to get her blazing about that. 'My family took its barony in the 18th century,' she used to hiss. 'I don't know why. But certainly long before the ignoble Act of Union.'

Mother Maria

Mother Maria was tall and thin and nervous. She taught history and mathematics to senior grade — the equivalent of sixth form in English schools. She had not the specific teaching qualities that other members of the community had, but she was truly intelligent, so honourable in argument that one was fortunate to be her pupil. Mother Maria never pretended to know what she did not know; and when I used to plague her to tell me what a logarithm was, and how it was arrived at, she would smile and say: 'I cannot do that, Kathy. The logarithm table is a given thing. I am not a mathematician. I accept this that the mathematicians give us — and so must you.' I did not accept it. And when I found the quadratic equation unsatisfactory, she laughed again, but with confidence. She was at ease with that equation, and because I found it unsatisfactory she was amused.

'Accept it, child, that you are not a mathematician. It is a defect in you, this block — not in the principle of the argument.'

3. Reference to Hamlet's meditation to Yorick's skull in the graveyard scene in Shakespeare's play.
4. Act of Irish parliament uniting it to the Westminster parliament in London.

It was great fun, learning either modern history or mathematics with Mother Maria. Later in life I was often to be reminded of her when I met English female dons — she was their prototype, and a curious thing about her was that, without beauty or coquetry or any kind of outgoing vanity, she inspired in my school an extraordinary amount of hysterical devotion, *Schwärmerei*. And that not all from her pupils — she taught only a few handpicked honours seniors. Her adorers, and they were many and troublesome, came from a group called Junior Pass. These were girls from 14 to 19 years, who would never be presented for the Intermediate Board examinations. But many of them adored Mother Maria; and some used to arrange to faint at Mass, so that she, who was usually on duty in chapel, would have to carry them out, and, one supposes, sponge their brows and generally restore them. I suspect the old awkward slyboots of having enjoyed all that nonsense. But it is curious that the sentimental tributes never came from those few of us whom she taught so brilliantly, but only from frivolous duffers who would never reach her honours senior classroom.

Lady Aberdeen

To go back some years from honours senior and Mother Maria — I first met pomp and circumstance when I was still not six years old. I presented a bouquet to Lady Aberdeen. Lord Aberdeen was then the viceroy, and his lady made herself earnest in touring about the country. I believe that her agitation against tuberculosis was in fact useful — but that her general approach to us all was disliked. However, our Reverend Mother was passionately and by birth English, and she revered castle government — so it seems that on one of her tours Lady Aberdeen was invited to visit Laurel Hill. And I, as the baby of the school, had to hand her the traditional bunch of flowers. I remember the immense glitter and fuss of the occasion — out on the lawn in strong sunlight, and with plumed horses attached to great carriages, champing about. It was alarming; but someone led me to where I had to bow. And now I remember three things from that surprising hour — 1. the big, doughy face of the old lady to whom I bowed and gave the flowers, 2. the beautiful, fair man to whom old doughy said 'See that she gets her present, Ronnie,' and 3. Reverend Mother's clawhand on my shoulder as she pulled me aside and said 'good child!'

I knew that my present would be a silver thimble, and nothing could have attracted me less. But anyway I never got it. And it was common understanding in Ireland that no promised Aberdeen present was ever given, not any photograph either. Certainly that day our Vicereine took innumerable snapshots of us all at Laurel Hill but the prints no more turned up than did my silver thimble . . .

Reverend Mother

Reverend Mother was not just English; she was late Victorian upper-class English almost one might have said (but wrongly) to the point of caricature. Unfortunately in appearance she suggested Queen Victoria in miniature. She was aquiline and neatly rotund and very small. And her eyes surprisingly blue when you got a straight look from them — were not protuberant like the Queen's but hooded; a bird's eyes. She was in her quiet way an almost fanatical instructor in behaviour, or deportment, on the obligation in a lady to move quietly, to hold her back straight, to open and close doors correctly, and *to sit still*. She aimed to teach us total outer command of our bodies; yet in the twelve years in which I watched her with respectful attention and grew most affectionately interested in her, I never saw her in command of her little claw hands. She was a tiny and disconcerting pillar of control and reserve; yet those ugly little hands were never still. Except, conceivably, when she slept. I hope they rested then. But when she prayed they fidgeted and fought together while all the rest of her was statue-still.

Over the long view one has seen how absurd it was that that little Englishwoman, that one especially, should have been in charge of the education of Irish girls of the Catholic middle class in the years so quickly leading up to 1916. Indeed, quite early in the century a Dublin weekly called *The Leader,* which seems to have been more socially than nationalistically *avant garde*, in an article assaulting the absurdities of education in Ireland, called out Laurel Hill convent by name and accused it of educating Irish girls to be suitable wives for bank managers and British colonial governors. If this charge was brought to Reverend Mother's attention and almost certainly it was — she might have winced about the bank managers, as they would have been a very low social target; but that we should be made fit to partner British colonial governors — that, by all means, she would have accepted as fair description of the product she aimed at.

I left Laurel Hill and said goodbye to Reverend Mother in June 1916. No more than 90 per cent of my fellow countrymen had I understood the curious event of Easter Week. And for Reverend Mother certainly it was no more than another sad little piece of Irish foolishness. For her, who was to die very soon, the climatic date had been August 14; she had to weep and pray for the sons and brothers of many of her dear daughters, boys fallen at Mons, Ypres and Gallipoli. And she had indeed kept us all busy knitting mufflers for Munster Fusiliers.

The little nun had a very hard role in the Ireland of my childhood. She was cold, nervous, inexpressive, and non-intellectual. She was hidebound English; her father, uncles, nephews were lawyers, doctors, judges. Yorkshire bred and Stonyhurst men. But she had grown up in London, off Park Lane. She held to all the clap-trap, standards that went with the 'season' and Church Parade and shopping with your maid, in Bond Street; and Her Majesty's Court and all the lot. She did not exactly talk of these social fixtures . . . No, it was simply that in Reverend Mother's 'politeness lessons', which took place on the evenings of Monday and Thursday, this background and its standards had to come through . . .

She was, from an Irish viewpoint, unprepossessing. She had no charm; she took no interest at all in the Gaelic Revival, which was deeply infecting a few of the more intelligent of her nuns; she resented the visits to these nuns of Limerick's very intelligent and arrogant bishop, Edward Thomas O'Dwyer. These two were indeed in dramatic terms well met. The Bishop of Limerick had no authority over this French foundation of Laurel Hill; all that was required of the community was courtesy and general conformity, which indeed were not withheld. But the Bishop had a habit of authority, and he took a very great interest in the Latin and the Irish teaching of certain excellent nuns in Laurel Hill, whom he visited with regularity. And he regarded himself as an authority on trees, and on roses. So when he did occasionally meet Reverend Mother, as he paced the grounds, talking in Latin, with Mother Thecla or Mother Lelia, he always had kind advice to give to this little Englishwoman, about the roses, or about the trees. He was a very handsome, aristocratic-looking man, Edward Thomas. Very deaf, with the piercing, tiring voice of a deaf man. He used to yell at Reverend Mother that she must cut down the elm trees that shaded the Visitors' Walk. It was clear from her courteous acknowledgments of these shouts, clear even to him, that she would never do so.

Gaelic Revival

The Gaelic Revival was sweeping in, and three or four of her most gifted teaching nuns — led by Mother Lelia Ferguson, the chief Latinist — were insisting on the study of Irish. Without any sympathy for the movement, this cold little Englishwoman allowed them evening classes and all the books they wanted and allowed them to receive teaching and directions from such cranks as Douglas Hyde and Lord Ashbourne. (It is admissibly arguable that she was influenced if puzzled by the fact that these gentlemen belonged to the ascendancy class; as indeed did the two or three nuns of her community who were pursuing this new study.) . . . I know, because I was one of its addicts, under the brilliant teaching of Mother Lelia, how frequently Reverend Mother reflected in wonder, and distaste, about the revivalist passion. She used to ask me about it: 'Do you like this language?' 'Very much, I find. It's very difficult — but so is Latin.' 'Ah yes. But Latin is important.' I think she was remarkably wise and considerate, as a passive authority, in a climate of thought which she could not enter. But then she did not enter climates of thought. From outside them, I think she watched with an attention of sensibility which only those could measure whose confidence, in distress, she would force. She forced mine, as I suppose she knew she could, after twelve years of love. And she forgave me then for all this after-life, which has been an insult to her simple ideals. I told her a lie on that day when she forced me to speak about my non-

belief and my private sins; and she accepted my lie and said she expected it and went on talking as if I had not uttered it. She never smiled; she said none of the bright things that one came to read later from English Catholics. She spoke, I think, in grief — and I was not able to help her. And she knew that. I was never to see her again after that painful conversation under the elms on the Visitors' Walk. After twelve years I was going out from her house an unbeliever — my silly lie had been of no avail.

During Lent or Advent, we usually gave up sugar in our tea or coffee. Reverend Mother always breakfasted in our refectory, at the Table of Honour. That was, if you like, High Table. It was on a dais and the Senior Honours people sat there. Let me recall, as I pass, what I owe to that refectory. It carried on its walls a complete series of really beautiful colour-prints of the Raphael cartoons. Twelve years' day-in, day-out association with those reproductions, hung at eye-level and for a child to stare at when she was in despair about finishing the fish-pie on her plate — that was accidental soaked-in experience for which I am far more grateful than for all the Piranesis of the playrooms. But pardon the aside — I was recalling breakfast with Reverend Mother. She sat always at the centre of the table, under the ugly engraving of the very boring Mother Foundress. And sometimes when we came in from Mass she was in her place before us. Grace was said — and then I or Marie Bagott or whoever was directly opposite her began to pour the coffee. And ah, that coffee! Not for nothing were the lay sisters in the kitchen still French! I can smell it now as we came half-fainting from Mass!

Well, in Lent or Advent there was in our general intention no sugar. But often, if Reverend Mother was there before us, you found when you drank your coffee that there was sugar at the bottom of the cup. So you protested, delightedly. And she used to say in her cold little voice that the Holy Ghost had told her that we needed, she thought, some sugar for just that day . . .

Mother Lelia and her younger sister Mother Sabina were Fergusons. I believe they were nieces of Sir Samuel Ferguson, the distinguished scholar-poet. Their father was a judge. They had been brought up in intellectual circles; both were very intelligent, and the elder of them, Mother

Lelia, was a natural and vivid intellectual. They two and Mother Maria (who was a ffrench with her two small fs) and Mother Thecla (who was a Patterson) were all, although near-aristocrats, what the Americans call cradle Catholics. That means that none of them owed their cultivated minds to England, although their families took their comfortable status in Ireland, no doubt, from their acceptance by the Castle and the Viceroy. But in my hindsight now — I did not notice political moods or gradings in my youth — every one of those four nuns stands out as her own kind of rebel — anarchists all four, I'd say. And each of them, on her own grounds, entirely contemptuous of English rule in Ireland.

This, because Reverend Mother was a controlled and just and eccentric governor, did not make difficulties for these four unusual nuns. Yet, characteristically and anarchistically no one of the four liked that Englishwoman. I would swear that not one of them, mature and witty women, understood her or admired her as I did, a mere child.

from:
AS MUSIC AND SPLENDOUR
(1958)

[The extract from *As Music and Splendour* (London: Heinemann, 1958) develops the theme of conflict between Catholic moral teaching and the possibility of lesbian love.]

'I can't understand that split in you.'

'Split? How do you mean, Thomas?'

'I mean, pet — sit down, don't look so furious — I mean, this unlucky *schwärm* you have for Luisa —'

'*Schwärm*?'

'Don't get cross. Wait. *Schwärm* is a good German word — *Schwärmerei* — for the manias girls get for each other or for their teachers — in school age. Your development has been delayed, and you are having a *schwärm* now for Luisa —'

'Oh Thomas, stop! Please stop. How dare you? Because I told you truly that I love Luisa you must not bring your clever talk against something you know nothing about.'

'No clever talk. Sit down.'

'Here I sit down. What now?'

'I know plenty about love, Clare.'

'In some ways you may, Thomas. And I have observed you, and I know your actions — but I appreciate your good manners. Still — I think you are amoral.'

'Amoral? But you, Clare? I take you to be serious and grown-up, in your own conception, when you say you are in love with Luisa?'

'Yes — Thomas.'

'Then — you are totally amoral.'

'No. I am, I suppose, a sinner — certainly I am a sinner in the argument of my Church. But so would I be if I were your lover. So is Rose a sinner — and she knows it — in reference to our education and faith. You, who come out of Baptist chapels, don't know how clear our instruction is. Rose and I know perfectly well what we're doing. We are so well instructed that we can decide for ourselves. There's no vagueness in Catholic instruction.'

'But there's a lot of disturbance.'

'That sounds witty. What disturbance have you encountered?'

'Well, love — the disturbance *you* create.'

Clare stood up. Standing she looked down on the weary, dusty young man whom she liked greatly, and to whose vivid intelligence and friendship she owed so much . . .

It was Sunday and hot noon, but Clare had not got up to go to Mass; and Luisa smiled when she reproached herself for this. The two, in their nightgowns, were loafing over coffee and fruit by an open window.

'Do you like to go?'

'I always have gone — until once or twice lately.'

'But — dearest — considering . . .' Luisa smiled teasingly.

'Considering that I'm not in the state of grace?'

'Well, yes.'

'Oh, it's a discipline. I think things over at Mass, and I read my Missal, and I wonder if Grandmother still prays for me —'

'You can be sure she does.'

'Well, anyway, at Mass I'm always sharply reminded that being happy isn't what we're here for!' She laughed and kissed Luisa's outstretched hand. 'Much good that does me!'

'Thank God!'

'More coffee? Shall I heat it up?'

This room which they loved and had shared for their last days together before Luisa sailed away in October, was two rooms in one, with a wide half-draped archway dividing it. Lofty, dusty and very shabby, the whole 'suite', as Mamma Lucia, the landlady, called it, was furnished in Neapolitan 1860 style. Velvet and chipped gilt, whatnots and bronze statues, and some very old and peculiar potted palms — but a few haphazard excellences too; a great, clean bed, a powder closet for the washstand, and in this outer part a cupboard with cups and plates, and a small oil-burning stove.

When Clare and Luisa had first sung together at San Carlo they had been directed to lodge with Mamma Lucia, and had occupied two small rooms on lower floors; but when they returned in October she had given them the 'suite', and Clare had made sure to have it when she came back alone to sing in Naples. She had done so because Luisa, in letters, begged her to be in the 'suite' for her return. And lived in by the two, with all their flowers and books and follies scattered, with the wine and fruit and bread they bought for supper and for breakfast, with windows open to the sky and noise of Naples in May weather, it was indeed a habitable place.

Clare re-heated the coffee.

'I'll peel us two more peaches,' said Luisa.

SARA HYLAND

(1893–1972)

from:
I CALL TO THE EYE OF THE MIND (1996)

[Sara Hyland's memoir of her years in the embroidery room of Lily Yeats at the Cuala Industries in Dun Emer is a narrative brimming with observations of childhood, work, politics, religion and her delight in learning the Irish language at Cois Farraige in Connemara, County Galway. Her narrative centres on village life in Dundrum outside Dublin city. There she grew up and worked in nearby Dun Emer. She describes rather than evokes past times, and her memories of childhood events and Connemara wake customs rely on careful observations of people and folkways. The manuscript was prepared for publication by Maureen Murphy (Dublin: Attic Press, 1996). The title, chosen by Hyland, is the first line of W.B. Yeats's poem 'At the Hawk's Well'. Where Yeats summoned up an image of desolation, Sara brings to the eye of her imagination lively accounts of past events.]

We Catholic children often envied our Protestant neighbours because their school had a large hall for concerts and other activities. We felt it was unfair to have such benefits in our country and that all Protestants should live in England. Didn't they wear Union Jacks and sing the English national anthem? When any of us tried to get in to one of their concerts, we were met with stiff resistance from the younger folk who knew we would get up from our seats so as not to be there for 'God Save the Queen'. They always sang it with great fervour . . .

My friend the 'Bun Lady' died in 1908. I did not see her corpse and never knew just what caused her death. My father took me and an elderly person to Mount Jerome Cemetery where she was buried after a Church of Ireland service. I was so bewildered at having to take part in the funeral, practically on my own, that I did not see where I was going until I heard or felt the church doors close behind me. I was almost distraught with fear that I would lose my religion and that when I came out of the church, people would see a difference in me. I tried in vain to repeat the Lord's Prayer as I felt it would help me, but I kept getting it all mixed up. I was fifteen and ought to have had more sense. Miss Lily must have often been amused at my attitude toward religion. She often smiled and said, 'Sara, In my Father's house, there are many mansions.'[1] She was so tolerant and understanding.

---

1. John 14:1. Lily Yeats reassured Sara with an ecumenical reading of the lines from the Gospel of St John.

The following year Dublin city was the centre of activity when the Catholic Church celebrated the centenary of its emancipation. Services were held in every church throughout the country and these culminated in a Sunday afternoon ceremony on O'Connell Bridge that was attended by thousands. General Eoin O'Duffy won acclaim for his organising skills and the press played its part by publishing details of assembly points for parishes and instructions for people planning to attend. Details were also given regarding the hymn singing, prayers and manner of departure. Everything went like clockwork, with suitable decorum, and those taking part felt that they had been re-baptised and that a bright future lay before them.

One afternoon on my way back from school (in the Connemara Gaeltacht) the *bean a'tighe* met me on the main boreen to take me with her to a wake and funeral. The house of the deceased neighbour was a short distance from us on *Bóthar na Trá*. When we reached the house, the men were seated in groups on the low stone walls surrounding the house and the women were gathered in the large kitchen where the corpse was 'waked' in her coffin in a very spectacular way.

The coffin rested on a heavily-draped table under a niche or window recess that was also heavily curtained with white material to form a pelmet which looped in the centre with full side pieces falling to the ground. The whole effect was that of a crib or a shrine. The corpse, very small and dainty, was clothed in white with a filled mob-cap that showed up her waxen face and grey hair. A few small white posies and some lighted candles had been placed on the table.

The neighbouring women were seated closely against the walls while the younger ones squatted on the floor in front of them. A neighbour woman helping the bereaved family handed around some snuff on tea plates and each woman took a pinch of snuff which she liberally applied to each nostril. Later the women were each served a drink of poteen from a large, narrow jug. It was poured into a cup or glass which was passed from person to person to drink as much or as little as they liked. When the glass was nearly empty, the dregs were tossed back into the jug and the glass was refilled to serve the next person until all the mourners had taken some of the poteen.

When the parish priest was seen approaching, a great silence fell on the house. We all stood when he entered with his usual blessing to all present. After speaking some words of condolence with the family, he recited some prayers and left the house accompanied by one of the members who had arranged a table and some chairs in the yard.

Now I learned the meaning of 'making a wake' in these remote parts of Ireland. The priest stood at the table with the son of the house and thanked each individual as he came forward to place his money offering on the table, each giving as much as he could afford. The money, so given, was for the benefit of the priest as there was not a collection at Sunday Masses. I don't know what other collections were made for the support of the clergy.

The wake in the house having concluded, the funeral procession got under way to the burial ground. On leaving the house, each member of the family, in order of seniority, contributed a loud wailing lamentation, a 'keen for the dead', giving a list of the successes and valiant deeds of the departed one now sadly missed. The dirge continued, without any repetition of deeds accomplished by the deceased, all the way in the slow-moving procession until we reached the graveyard, a stony spot almost on the seashore, enclosed by cement-built walls and an iron gateway. The coffin was laid in a grave which consisted of stones, stones, and still more stones.

NORAH HOULT

(1898–1984)

from:
HOLY IRELAND (1935)

[The central character of *Holy Ireland*, set in turn-of-the-century Dublin, is the rebellious and intellectual Margaret who defies her tyrannical and bigoted father by marrying an English Protestant, forsaking her Catholic religion for the Irish theosophism of the time. Patrick O'Neill's despotic bigotry is exercised in his home and is fuelled by his slavish rigidity to the legalism of his religion. As a domestic novel, *Holy Ireland* is, according to critic Janet Madden-Simpson in her preface to the 1985 edition (Dublin: Arlen House), 'unequalled in the canon of Anglo-Irish literature. No other novel reveals to us so painstakingly and with so much obvious compassion and regret, the condition of family life when it is dominated, rather than influenced, by dogma.' In this extract Hoult uses the familiar ritual of the family rosary to expose the underlying tensions of the O'Neill household.]

Bridget, the maid, had come in, and they were all kneeling down in the warm close room saying the Rosary. Patrick O'Neill's deep voice, quickened now, led his family in the words that were the most familiar to them of all words:

'*Hail Mary full of Grace, the Lord is with Thee. Blessed art Thou among women, and blessed is the fruit of Thy womb, Jesus*'; and half sigh and half gabble came the response, '*Holy Mary, Mother of God, pray for us sinners, now and at the hour of our death.*' As her beads slipped through her fingers, Margaret contemplated with detachment the familiar repetition. For long enough she had closed herself against what seemed an inevitable though irksome formula. All good Catholics said the Rosary every evening; she had been brought up in a good Catholic family: it was just something that had to be done like going to Mass regularly, but even duller, because it was difficult to concentrate on the gabble, gabble, gabble that went on and on almost interminably it sometimes seemed. She remembered the time Clem had walked in on them staring blankly before quietly withdrawing. She and Charlie had choked laughing: it was like someone who opened a bathroom door at the wrong time. She had

explained to him after, and he had said something about it being wrong to use vain repetitions as the heathen did. But they were not heathen she had told him, they were Catholics . . . there was the evening when she had knelt silently. But, of course, her father had missed her voice. 'Why was it you weren't praying tonight, Margaret?' he'd asked as soon as they rose from their knees, and the impossibility of really explaining to him had crushed all idea of active rebellion. Father wouldn't understand; he'd just blame Clem, and have a priest in to talk holy pie to her. Everything she did or didn't do he noticed; Lucy now, and he'd hardly give a feather off him.

'*As it was in the beginning, is now, and ever shall be,*' she murmured rapidly. Thank God. Another decade over.

When she got married, there'd be no Rosary, no Rosary. And no fish on Friday; she could eat what she dashed well chose. Yes, she would marry Clem. '*. . . and lead us not into temptation, but deliver us from evil.*' There was something happening. Yes, Johnnie had untied Bridget's apron strings. And Charlie had seen, and was cramming his handkerchief in his mouth. It was a shame for him encouraging Johnnie in his badness. She cocked an eye towards her mother: '*. . . hour of our death.*' No: Julia was deep in it.

It would have taken a bigger disturbance to have aroused Julia from her prayers, from the images she evoked as her fingers gently caressed and then departed tenderly from each bead. Her heart was now bowed in tenderness and worship before the Infant Christ lying in the manger among the beasts: she saw them: there was a cow, a sheep and a donkey, the donkey half turned down sniffing at the hay, arrested by the great happenings around; now the Holy Child was standing in the temple, and his poor mother distracted finding Him . . .

Now they passed to the Five Sorrowful Mysteries, and she bowed herself in contemplation of the cruelty of man, seeing with a never-fading sense of sorrow the anguish on the face of Our Saviour. The nightly religious exercise never lacked her imagination and sympathy; always she came with relief to the happy ending: The Glorious Mysteries, seeing the wonder and glory of Paradise opening first to the crucified Christ, then to His Blessed Mother. Oh, indeed she wouldn't have missed the saying of the Rosary, yet she never thought of herself as religious, knowing that in comparison with her husband something escaped her, something that weighed upon his heart, and made him impatient of her as if she failed him.

They blessed themselves and rose from their knees. Bridie was turning an indignant glare on Johnnie who looked phenomenally innocent. 'I'll be telling the master on yous so I will,' she whispered threateningly, her hands fumbling behind her back as she went to the door.

'Wait, your apron's undone,' said Charlie following her. 'I'll tie it for you.' He followed her into the hall quickly, but her giggle was overheard by Patrick who called, 'What are you doing there, Charlie?'

Before that voice sharp with suspicion, Charlie thought it well to return to the room.

'Nothing. Did you want me?'

'What were you at?'

'Nothing at all.'

The laughter went from Charlie's face. He hung his head, and shuffled his feet. The knowledge flashed sharply into his mind, 'he thought I was after kissing her'; he put the thought away as a schoolboy might put back in his pocket a forbidden sweet.

'Don't be fooling round now. D'ye hear what I'm saying?'

'Yes, *father.*'

'Yes, father.'

Patrick turned away. The momentary tension was relaxed. Charlie slouched down on the sofa, and took up *The Dowry of Mary*[1] in which he pretended to be deeply immersed. Johnnie and Lucy came forward to say good night to their father: they had to go to bed immediately after Rosary. Margaret and Charlie were allowed an extra while.

'Good night, my child. God bless you.' Patrick kissed Lucy, and shook hands with Johnnie. 'Mind you haven't to be called in the morning now.'

Julia fussed out of the room after them. 'You'll want another candle, Lucy. Wait a moment.'

Patrick overheard. Margaret sitting down opposite him took up a book quickly. But he turned to her.

'Is it that you're burning the candle too long at night, Margaret? Why else should it burn down on you that quick? It was only Wednesday you had a fresh one.'

'Was it Wednesday? I don't remember.'

'It was Wednesday, because I happen to remember you making a job with the candlesticks that night when I was after coming in.'

'I forget,' said Margaret with apparent unconcern. She turned over a page. It was not a well-considered action.

'It looks to me as if one of you is reading in bed at night. And I won't have that. It's dangerous. You'll be burning the house down on us one night. Do you read in bed?'

She hesitated between the truth and a lie. If she said she didn't there was the candle to explain. Why couldn't her mother have got a new candle without making a song about it?

'Well, I do for a bit of a while, now and then.'

'You're not to read at all. Put out the candle as soon as you've said your prayers. Don't you know that well? Have I to be telling you all over again?'

Margaret said nothing. She felt she hated her father. Clem was right. He *was* an ignorant ass.

'What is it you're so fond of reading? Is it a love story or what?'

'It is not then.'

As a matter of fact it was the *Origin of Species*[2] which Clem had given to her. Intellectual pride made her voice indignant.

'What is it then? Is it a book of devotions, or what is it at all?'

Margaret murmured 'No.' She wasn't going to be such a hypocrite as to say that.

'Well?'

'I forget. Ah, the other night I was just reading a bit of *The Mill on the Floss.*'[3]

The Mill on the Floss! Wasn't that what was called a classic? There mightn't be any harm in it. All the same, there were queer things in some of those books, things that weren't really fit and proper reading for a young girl. It might give her bad notions.

'Isn't that by a writer who was no Catholic?'

---

1. A popular book of devotion for Catholics.

2. Charles Darwin, *The Origin of Species.*
3. George Eliot, *The Mill on the Floss.*

'George Eliot? No, I don't think she was a Catholic. Well, father, you'd have hardly any books at all if they'd all to be by Catholic writers.'

She spoke a little contemptuously. Julia came in and they both turned to her. Margaret said quickly: 'Listen, mother, father seems to think we shouldn't read any books except they're written by Catholics. Sure, what could you read at all? You couldn't read Dickens, you couldn't read Scott. And you, mother, you couldn't read Ouida.'[4]

Julia looked guilty. She made a comical little grimace. Then, she said meditatively, as she settled by the fire, 'Ah, well, I often do be thinking that the best writers are really Catholic at heart.'

Patrick tried to think of a reply to this. His wife was always saying things that he felt distrustful about. But he had the unread man's inferiority before those who can read books with ease. He felt, too, that in those ways Julia might know better than he did. He retreated to safer ground.

'What I was after saying to Margaret here is this: she herself gives it away that she's been reading in bed, and burning the candle. And I told her, as I've told them all before — are you listening now, Charlie?'

'Sure, I don't read in bed.'

'Mind me all the same. After you've said your prayers and committed yourselves to your guardian angel's keeping, put out the light, lie still with your hands by your sides, and go off to sleep. Any other way is bad. And it would have been a sorry judgment on you, Margaret, if you'd been roasted alive, and had the whole house burned with you. It's easy happening. You fall asleep, and the candle drops on the bed, and in a minute the flames are speeding up and you choking with them before you can wake yourself.'

'God save us,' said Julia mildly. She was wishing she hadn't said anything about the new candle.

'Do you hear now what I'm saying, Margaret? And give heed to me now.'

'Yes, father.'

'No more reading in bed.'

'All right, father.'

'A priest was after telling us a terrible story in one retreat I was making,' continued Patrick.

4. A popular romantic novelist of the day.

'There was a man once, a good enough fellow in his way but he had grown neglectful of his religious duties. The priest went to him and spoke to him. He was always promising he'd go to confession, and take the Sacrament, but never was he to be seen at the altar rails. Again the priest went to him. "I'll do it soon, I'll promise you, Father," says he. "But last Saturday I was tired. And then I overslept." Ah, he'd always have some excuse on the tip of his tongue. "I warn you," says the priest, "you'll maybe leave it too late." And that very same night, mark you, he went to sleep in the chair with a book in front of him and the window was open, and a gust of wind blew in and heeled the lamp over. The flames spread like a sheet of lightning. And there he was burnt to death, for not a living soul in the house knew what was happening till the flames and smoke came roaring out and around them. Well, they saved themselves. But he was charred to a cinder, not a breath of life in him when they got him out.'

'God help him, the poor man!' said Julia. Margaret stared into the fire. She wasn't to be impressed by that sort of thing any longer she told herself! But in his seat Charlie uncrossed one leg.

'And there he was suddenly hurled into the presence of his maker without a chance of making even an Act of Contrition, with all his sins black on him,' concluded Patrick.

Margaret saw a picture of a poor burnt-out piece of flesh. Wouldn't God be sorry for him? Wouldn't He send angels to bear him gently after such an awful death?

'What priest told you that story?' enquired Julia in a voice of lively interest. 'Sure I remember hearing Father O'Brien, the Dominican, telling something very similar. He was preaching from the text, "Thou fool, this night shall thy soul be required of thee." O God, he has us all murdered. There were women fainting on all sides the way he was going on.'

'I heard Father O'Brien too. He took a retreat for us when I was at school. I couldn't stand him. He was always on at tortures, and God knows what.'

'That's the very same man, well, well. I wonder where he is now? He was a thick short man with a bull neck.'

Patrick slumped down in his seat. Vaguely he felt that it was no good talking to women. They always made everything into a gossip. What matter what priest had told the story? It was a true story, and it was an awful and terrible warning.

He sat motionless, his arms hanging loosely, head forward, looking into the fire. In its red heart he saw a faint transient image of hell: its hissing flames, its horrid tortures; and over this he brooded as one broods over a queer indecipherable dream. The sounds of Margaret's voice, Julia's voice, came to his ears divested of meaning and significance. Once he turned his head and saw Charlie crouched over his paper, by himself on the sofa; his gaze saw and dismissed the good-looking irresolute face of youth turning doubtfully into manhood, and returned to the fire.

But precisely at half-nine, his long fingers removed his watch from his pocket, and dangling it from its chain as he compared it with the clock, he said:

'Go on now, you two children. It's your bedtime.'

The old familiar irritation stirred in Margaret. She, nineteen years of age, to be called a child and sent to bed like that. Indeed, it was well for her that she had had a proposal of marriage, and was not considered by other people to be a child. The knowledge gave her support, and rising from her chair with an affectation of indifference she went up to her father to say good night.

His hand went out and gripped her arm. He stared into her face.

'No more reading in bed now, Margaret.'

'Very well, father. I won't.'

She said the words, while for consolation her heart repeated Clem's 'Ignorant ass.' No, she really didn't love her father.

Her lips brushed his cheek; and she turned and walked swiftly to the door. Julia called out, 'I'll be looking in, Mamie.' Charlie followed her; he wasn't sorry to be going to bed; his father had put odd thoughts into his head and he looked forward to savouring them.

Margaret groped her way to the candlestick on the little table which was between her bed and Lucy's. She struck a match, and the bedroom quivered from darkness into a faint streaked light with the furniture throwing shadows, and her own form monstrously enlarged on the wall and ceiling.

UNA TROY

(1913–)

THE APPLE (1942)

[Novelist and playwright Una Troy (Elizabeth Connor) wrote this story of an Irish nun who succumbs to the temptation to revisit her old home, even though the Rule of her convent does not permit such irregularities. Published by *The Bell* (vol. 5, no. 1, October 1942), it was republished in *Woman's Part: An Anthology of Short Fiction By and About Irish Women 1890–1960*, ed. Janet Madden-Simpson (Dublin: Arlen House, 1984). Troy, best known for her humorous, entertaining novels of small-town life, captures the innocent, childish life of nuns in the early years of the twentieth century when strict adherence to the Rule and Vows of religious life were the central preoccupation of convent life.]

She had never used her mind for thinking, only for recording the thoughts of others. She was happy.

She had always been happy. Walking now in the convent garden, her fingers straying automatically at the big, smooth beads of the Rosary that hung from her waist, her habit brushing on the bright June grass hedging the flower beds, she thanked God, with a simple, unsearching happiness, because the sky was blue, because the sun shone; she thanked Him, most fervently, for making this day, of all days, so fine and lovely, with no shadow of a cloud.

She was not afraid of being happy; she was used to it.

Reverend Mother was coming down the path towards her. She was smiling as she came.

'Are you very excited, child?'

Mother Mary Aloysius blushed.

'A little, Reverend Mother.'

Reverend Mother laughed.

'You're not the only one! They're like a pack of babies inside. I declare I've almost forgotten myself what the sea looks like.'

Forgotten the sea! Oh, but you couldn't! Even if you only saw it once in your life, you could never forget the sea. To-day, it was blue — pale, pale blue, with no horizon but a misty curve far off where it sloped up to meet the sloping sky. I can see it, flowing over the roses there by the wall and the gulls' crying is loud above the blackbird's song . . .

'It's fifty years since I've seen it,' said Reverend Mother, and there was a gleam in her old eyes.

Mother Mary Aloysius saw that gleam and she kept her face tight and hard so that it wouldn't smile. Because Reverend Mother hadn't wanted to go at all — and now she was as bad as any of them. When the Bishop had altered the strict rule that forbade any member of the Order to set foot outside the Convent grounds, Reverend Mother had been very angry. 'What was good enough for me when I entered,' she said, 'is good enough for me now', and she didn't speak at all kindly of the Bishop, who was only doing his best, poor man. 'I won't budge,' she said, and she didn't. She sent her nuns off on visits to the Convents at Michelstown, at Fermoy, at Kilkenny, and received them back with a sympathetic consciousness of her own firm virtue. But this year the Bishop himself had come and tackled her, like a brave man. She wasn't looking well, he said; the doctor prescribed a change; she needed the sea air. She was to take herself and four of her nuns off to the new house the Order had bought at Youghal and she was to stay there for a month, too. So of course Reverend Mother had to say 'yes' because Obedience was one of the Vows, but Mother Mary Aloysius had prayed for weeks that she would be one of the chosen. Oh, not because she wanted to be in Youghal — but because, if she went, they would travel the road by her own sea, her own rocks and cliffs, her own shining strand, her own home. 'Oh, please God,' she prayed, hoping hard it wasn't wrong to pray such a

worldly prayer and telling Him, if it was, not to grant it, 'please, God, let Reverend Mother take me', and God let her be taken, so everything was all right.

'It's thirty years since I saw the sea,' said Mother Mary Aloysius and kept on watching it flow beside her feet.

'Is it now, child? Well, well, how time does go, to be sure! Who'd think it was that length since you came to us! It seems only the other day you were going around in your postulant's cap. It makes me feel an old woman,' said Reverend Mother, indignantly, glaring at her seventy odd years. 'Sure, you must be near fifty now?'

'Forty-nine,' said Mother Mary Aloysius.

Reverend Mother opened her mouth to speak and snapped it shut again with a click of her teeth. It was a disconcerting habit but Mother Mary Aloysius knew it. She waited.

'I was thinking —,' said Reverend Mother.

'Yes?' said Mother Mary Aloysius.

'We'll pass by your old home this evening, won't we?'

'Yes, Reverend Mother.'

'Hm! I heard you talking about it in the Refectory. I was thinking — Would you like, now, if we stopped and you went and had a look at it? You know we still can't go inside any house, or even any other convents but our own Order's, but you could,' said Reverend Mother, 'you could walk around outside and you could,' said Reverend Mother, suddenly, 'you could look in through the windows.'

Mother Mary Aloysius gaped at her.

'Oh, Reverend Mother!' she said at last.

'Yes, child, yes,' said Reverend Mother.

'Oh, Reverend Mother!' said Mother Mary Aloysius.

'Yes. Well — we'll be leaving in half-an-hour,' said Reverend Mother, briskly, and was gone.

Mother Mary Aloysius hardly spoke at all in the car. She sat very straight and stiff between Sister Peter and Mother Mary Assumpta. She said yes, it would be very nice to see her home again after thirty years, and she said yes, that was a pretty view by those trees, and she said yes, that must be Waterford in the distance. And once Reverend Mother turned around from the front seat and smiled at her and Mother Mary Aloysius smiled back, but she smiled right through Reverend Mother.

She rode home from the hayfield on Susie, holding on to Susie's mane, because her legs were very short and Susie was very fat. Her father walked beside her; his hat was pushed on the back of his head and he carried a sprong over his shoulder. She dipped her fingers in the milk and held them out to teach the sucky-calves how to drink; she felt their rough, unaccustomed tongues drag at her hand. She scattered meal to the chickens and they came running. *Chuck-chuck-chuck-chuck!* She turned the wheel and blew the fire until it shone red on all their faces. She watched her mother put the cake in the pot-oven; it was special soda bread, with currants, because it was her birthday. Tom and Mollie and Joe and she played hide-and-seek; the haggard was 'home'.

'Be a good girl and say your prayers and you'll be happy,' her mother said. 'Early to bed and early to rise,' said her father. 'That's my own girl,' said her mother, proudly, when she brought back the *Extracts from Literature* that she won at school. 'I declare to God, she's nearly as big as yourself, ma'am,' said Father O'Shea.

'It's a grand thing to be a nun,' her mother said. 'Such a happy life — and a person hasn't a care or trouble in the world. I'd be easy in my mind — of course, 'tisn't everyone that God gives the call to.'

All the same, her mother cried when she was leaving and the first weeks at the Convent were lonely ones. But they weren't unhappy — and the weeks after that, and all the weeks since, were happy as her mother had said they would be. Every hour was mapped out for you and you could see right onto the end, where God would take you to Himself and you'd meet Father and Mother again — and Moll that got a cold on the lungs — and the others that might be there before you — and you'd be there waiting to welcome the ones that were yet to come. They'd be all home together, loving one another like they used to be, and it would be home for ever and ever then . . .

She saw a familiar curving line of mountain distance. With a jerk of the heart, she came back from yesterday and to-morrow to the living moment. She was looking out eagerly now, with wide hungry eyes. All at once, the road twisted to the left and beyond a field of young wheat was the sea.

'We're not so far now,' said Reverend Mother.

'Five miles,' she said. 'I know every inch of the way from here on. I used come as far as this in the horse and trap to see my cousins.'

'Do they know at home you're passing?' Sister Peter asked and the look she gave at Mother Mary Aloysius had a lot of envy in it.

'No. There's only Paddy left at the farm. There used be — ten of us it is that was in it, long ago.'

There was an ache in her eyes, that were looking and looking at so much; there was loving and grasping at all that she saw.

'Here's the village!' she said, and now she began to chatter because it helped to dull that odd feeling in her breast. 'That's Biddy Casey's — oh! of course she must be dead long ago — and there's a new name over the Post Office — Paddy didn't tell me — and that's old Mrs. Graney's where I used to spend my penny on sweets. Pink ones I always bought. Isn't it queer how you remember things?'

Reverend Mother said gently: 'Maybe it is.'

She saw it. The car stopped. They were there. Her heart wasn't big enough to hold it all — Paddy standing by the car, and the thatch and the pink walls, and the chip off the left hand pier of the gate. Everything the same — perhaps not so trim as it used to be but still just the same. It was crowding out her heart and hurting it. She must have a very small heart.

'Go around now, child, and have a look at things,' Reverend Mother said.

She looked in through the front windows. Everything was the same; Paddy had altered nothing. If he had a wife, she would have made changes. She was glad, until she stopped herself, that he hadn't a wife. She was at the back of the house now, and alone. She couldn't even hear the voices at the gate. She laid her hand on the walls; she stroked them. She looked through the windows. The same — all the same. The back door was open; she looked through into the kitchen. The blue plates were on the dresser; the clock ticked on the wall; the fire was a smoulder of turf on the hearth. She looked up and, under the strawy eaves, saw the tiny window of her own room. So often she would kneel at that window and see, out beyond the fields, the sea under the sun or under the moon. The beams curved up oddly in the ceiling of that room; her bed was in the corner; on a shelf by the door were her books. Maybe they were still there . . .

'I wish —' she said softly. 'If I had a ladder —' and then laughed to imagine Mother Mary Aloysius climbing a ladder with her black skirts flapping around her, Mother Mary Aloysius perched on top, peering in through a little window at a little room.

The back door was open. There was one green pane of glass in the four cramped panes of that crooked window. When you looked through it, you looked into a new world where the sea had come in and covered everything and you were living safely, a mermaid on the sea-floor. There was a picture of a dog and a child hanging above your bed. The back door was open. A board was loose by the window; it squeaked when you stood on it; you could press it up and down with your foot and frighten yourself by pretending there was a mouse in the room. You weren't really frightened of that mouse. It was a pet one; its name was Florrie. The back door was open. There were three nails where your clothes hung . . . The back door was open.

'If I go in,' said Mother Mary Aloysius, 'it will be a mortal sin.' She stood there rigidly.

'A mortal sin,' said Mother Mary Aloysius firmly, and went in.

She went through every room in the house. Last of all, and longest of all, she knelt by the window of her own little bedroom and gazed across the pasture land and the gold cliff-tops at her own sea. The sun shone on it, and the moon; the frosty stars hung low over it; the sea-mist and the night hid it from all eyes but hers. When she came climbing down the narrow attic stair, her habit clutched high in one hand, she carried the little room and all that was to be seen from it, safely in her heart. Her heart was so small that was all it could hold; and that fitted exactly into it as the egg to its shell.

'And now,' Mother Mary Aloysius said, as she stepped out into the sunshine, 'I am in mortal sin.'

The delicate blades of grass growing through the crevices of the stones by the door were silver with light; two swallows crossed the sun; a gull went calling towards the tide.

'My soul is black,' she said.

A poppy swayed at her from the hedge over the bohereen; a soft wind blew about her; her treasure, loveliest of all the loveliness of the day, was warm in her breast.

'Black . . .' she said.

But the poppy nodded; the breeze went rustling along; the grass grew and the birds flew into the sun.

And suddenly a dreadful thing happened to her. She could not understand it; she fought against it; 'But they told me so,' she said. 'They told me thus — and thus — and thus. They are right — they are always right.' She gripped at the beads of her Rosary; they slid from her blind fingers.

The world fell away from her, the world that others had fashioned for her with loving minds; and now she must strive for ever to refashion out of chaos the world of her own mind.

'It was no sin,' she said.

Her mind worked, quicker and yet more quickly, as she hurried back to the car. As she ran she held her hand to her breast as if to keep her treasure secure but she did not yet realize how precious and how terrible was the price she had paid for it.

CLARISSA A. WOODS

(*fl.* 1949)

WOMAN KNEELING (1949)

[Little is known about Clarissa A. Woods. Her essay appeared in the first issue of the monthly review *Envoy*, which replaced *The Bell* in December 1949. Founded and edited by John Ryan (1925–), who described its role in his memoir, *Remembering How We Stood* (Dublin: Gill and Macmillan, 1975), *Envoy* ran from 1949 to 1951 encouraged critical essays as well as stories. 'Woman Kneeling' is a poignant commentary on the predicament of many Irish women of that era, fearing pregnancy and without recourse to forms of contraception condemned by the Catholic church. Paradoxically many women had recourse to prayer, hoping for a divine reprieve from yet another pregnancy.]

She knelt, and the bend of her head spelled devotion. Her still-slender fingers moved among her beads with the restlessness of wind-teased branches. The fat curate, on his way to the confessional, observed her. A saintly woman, he thought. And he sighed.

But the thoughts in her heart were black thoughts and there was no faith in her. Let it not be another. Holy Mother, not another. And the latest not creeping yet. With himself off to the pub at sundown every blessed day, and me hard put to save a penny from him for the butcher. Back at midnight, breath stinking of the pub, forever waking me out of my first sleep. And no — this can't be, oh Lord. But in her heart she knew her prayer would not be answered. She had prayed such prayers before.

Once, long ago, prayer and God had been for her the only reality. Marriage, poverty, and the rapidly successive arrival of children had tarnished her faith in God and man. Though she clung to the habits and ritual of her religion (indeed, I don't see that it does any harm and who knows but what it might be a good thing in the Hereafter) she had long since ceased to believe that God or His angels or His saints took any interest in what happened on earth. When she told her children of guardian angels and of the miraculous deeds of saints, she recited in the strong legend-spirit of her race, just as she would have told them fairy tales, had she known any.

Her children brought her no joy, nor could she see that they ever would. Dirty little chislers, always snivelling, hard on shoes, and the boys picking up every dirty word they can lay ear to. And them growing up half wild, what with himself that would never lay a hand on them and me too weak to do it. And Sean, my eldest, him that should be a comfort to his mother, in and out of two jobs already and forever running after the girls. Sure, it's a hard row you've given me, oh Lord.

She muttered her prayers, unthinking. Holy Mary . . . you know what it is, but it was only one with you, and Him a joy and a glory. Knowing her prayers went no further than the curved dome of her skull, she prayed on. The church was quiet, a tiny island of peace. The children were safe under the eye of Mrs Dugan, from across the way. And her without a single child, after wanting them so bad. Now, wouldn't that be the proof of it? If prayers would have it, she'd have mine.

Decent in black (it's better to go about in it always and be spared the expense when someone dies), she prayed on. In the name of the Father . . .

Over the dim altar, before which the sacramental light glowed richly and votive candles made small nervous flowers of brightness, a white bird flew from the direction of the sacristy, circled, wheeled, hovered for a moment over the darkly gleaming tabernacle, white wings dripping light, then disappeared. Hypnotized by the mindless repetition of religious formula, she stared at it with dull, unwondering eyes. 'A death in this house,' dark superstition warned her. 'No, this is a church; it doesn't count.' Light triumphed.

Then the great bell began to peal, deeper than sound, shaking the dust of the dim air, pealing, pealing, till all the church was wrapped up in it, till stones, floor, walls, altar, the flickering candles became a part of the great joyous shouting of the bell, swinging with the clapper, metal striking metal, stone, flesh, going forth with each cry of it.

Her rosary finished, without the extras at the end, for the bell sound distracted her, she left the church, feeling through her feet the sound of the bell. As her hand touched the water in the font, water rippling with vibration, she felt an interior constriction and a release, sensation which she recognised with joy. She crossed herself. In the churchyard she was sure. 'Praise be to God,' she muttered, turning on to the broad bare street, ''twas the ringing of the bell that done it.' Lightening her steps, she hurried towards home, her thoughts fixed on the children's tea.

Behind her the bell still sounded, now dull and defeated, like a dirge.

MARY LAVIN

(1912–96)

A NUN'S MOTHER (1974)

[The seeming inconsequence of Mary Lavin's narrative conceals the skill which reveals character and personality. Drawing on the use of monologue and using rapid transitions of speech, Lavin's insight into an Irish mother's mind and heart in 'A Nun's Mother' uncovers the layers of feeling in a mother's musings to herself on the journey home after her daughter's entry into religious life. A relentless critic of her own work, Lavin considered 'A Nun's Mother' one of her best-constructed short stories. It appears in *The Stories of Mary Lavin*, vol. 2 (London: Constable, 1974).]

Supposing just for a moment that she had managed to corner Angela and had blurted out her question. What do you know, Angela, about human love? Physical love? The love of a man for a woman? Supposing — just supposing — she'd got that out! And supposing — just supposing — Angela had taken it from her — what then? Supposing the girl had admitted she knew nothing? And asked to be told? Good God! What would she have said then? Not that love was noble. Not that it was kind. Generous? No. Gentle? No. Dignified? (That was laughable!) In short, love was nothing that could be described in a way that would have an appeal for an idealistic young girl whose head was full of poetry. Why even the poets themselves hadn't been able to describe it. *There had fallen a splendid tear from the passion tree at the gate.* Lines like that might convey something to one when one was a bit older and understood the underlying suggestion — but at Angela's age it only added to the idealism — the unreality. Yet, Luke thought it could be done with a word. *Did you have a word with her?* Fool! She changed her position to shake off his hand, but not obviously — not hurtfully — or so she hoped. Then she returned to her thoughts. Even if love could be described with a word — or twenty words for that matter — would it have been right to interfere with what, after all, one was supposed to consider a Divine call? The fact that she herself never had much faith in the idea of a voice from Above speaking directly to one soul in a million (one in a million million if one wanted to be more

exact) her disbelief did not necessarily mean that the thing was altogether impossible. It was all a great mystery. Life itself, she meant. Hadn't she heard of cases where interference with a so-called vocation had been disastrous? Only recently she had heard about a girl who was determined to be a nun, and whose parents tried to prevent her. And what happened? One night the poor girl climbed out a skylight on to the roof in her night-dress with a crucifix in her hands. They managed to coax her down but she had to be sent to a mental home. And never came out again either. That was certainly worse than going into a convent, no matter what way you looked at it.

If she and Luke had attempted to baulk Angela in this, they might have regretted it bitterly in time to come. How could they have assumed such a heavy responsibility?

But here Mrs Latimer detected a trace of insincerity in herself. Hadn't they long ago accepted responsibility for Angela — when they brought her into the world? Indeed she herself had accepted it eighteen years ago when the child was conceived. As soon as she'd become aware she was pregnant she'd felt the weight of that responsibility. And immediately after her birth, when Luke had gone out of the room and the nurse had fixed her up and drawn the curtains, leaving her to rest, her joy as she lay in the darkened room had been tempered by a vague feeling of apprehension for the fate of the child she had just borne. To this day she could remember the strange thought that came into her mind, it was almost a vision. Lying there and looking down the years ahead, she had seen herself as a portal from which not only her child had come out, but the child of her child, and then that child's child and on — until a great multitude of people spread out over the world — a horde of human beings — who all, all had issued forth from her. She thought of them — *saw* them like people coming out of a cinema, singly at first, then forming into pairs, and then when they reached the street merging into threes and fours until they were soon spreading out over the whole city, the whole world in an ever-widening wedge.

And — this was the awful part — all those people — those strangers — had her features and they were looking back at her over their shoulders with looks of reproach — looks of accusation. Only for you we would never have been born, they seemed to say. Because in her physically depleted state it had seemed that one and all the lives of these unborn people would be dark, tragic — even evil. Better far, it would seem, for them never to have been brought into this wicked world.

Later, of course, when she was rested and felt stronger and when the flowers and telegrams began to arrive — above all when they'd brought back the baby and put it into her arms (ah — the anguish now to think that infant was Angela) — then of course she felt differently. Yet here, now, in the taxi at this moment, she shuddered. Why had she herself not gone away one summer day like Angela, her face washed clean with honest soap and water, her body shrouded in black, with flat-heeled shoes on her feet?

For Angela would never sit like this in a taxi, an old woman — well, say an ageing woman — shrinking from the thought of something long done and utterly irrevocable. With Angela life would come to an end, like a flower fallen into a stream and carried under the water before its seed had time to ripen and bear fruit.

But here Mrs Latimer sat up straight as she woke to a new significance in her daughter's rejection of the world. By taking this vow of chastity Angela was freeing her, too, from the future — and from her fear of it, whether foolish or not. A great sigh escaped her. The seed of her seed would be forever barren. And viewed in this light suddenly the attitude of other women — at which she had so lately sneered — seemed different, seemed more acceptable to her. For the first time in the dismal days, weeks, months that had passed she began to see that God might indeed have conferred a great grace upon her. And upon Luke. Perhaps in His infinite wisdom He looked mercifully on them and instead of impoverishing them He had bestowed His bounty upon them. All at once Mrs Latimer felt more carefree than she had felt for years. And into her heart — like when she was young — there flew a bluebird of happiness — to make its nest there again and — of this she felt sure — to dwell there now for ever. And like she had always done she wanted to share her happiness with Luke — to open her eyes and let her happiness fly forth into his in a flutter of smiles.

But just as she was about to turn towards him, Mrs Latimer hesitated. Could it be possible that she, who had always prided herself on knowing exactly what she felt, even deep down (although she had never gone along with all that probing into the subconscious that had become a mania with some of her friends), could it be that, all the same, deep down somewhere inside her, that old fear of responsibility had continued to lurk? Dear God — had it perhaps shown in her face? What about the day Angela had given her the list she'd got from the novice-mistress — the list of things she had to get? Angela's manner that day had been so antagonistic. She'd held out the piece of paper. 'Here is the list of what I've got to get,' she'd said almost brutally. That list had made everything so final, and in any case within a week the job of finding all those ridiculous, those crazy, items, had both of them flattened out and quite incapable then of talking about anything. They didn't get time — not once — for a cup of tea or coffee — much less to slip into a cinema, as was their normal pattern after a day's shopping in town.

EDNA O'BRIEN

(?1930–)

from:
MOTHER IRELAND (1976)

[Edna O'Brien rapidly established herself as the delineator of the hypocritical and puritan society of mid-twentieth-century Catholic Ireland with her first three books, *The Country Girls* (1960); *The Lonely Girl* (1962), reprinted as *The Girl with the Green Eyes*; and *Girls in Their Married Bliss* (1963). Critics hailed her earlier works as fresh and untutored but in the 1970s she became a deliberate stylist. 'The Convent' is an extract from her iconoclastic exploration of her country and society *Mother Ireland* (London: Weidenfeld and Nicolson, 1976). It echoes her portrayal of the convent culture of her schooldays: what she describes as 'the actual bleakness of the convent and the regimented life'.]

THE CONVENT

The convent was forty miles away and situated at the foot of a lake into which, legend said, a former hedonist city had been plunged and swallowed up. The town was grey and somewhat seedy and time seemed to pass slowly and without event. To go through the gateway and then hear the hasp being shut by the stooped gatekeeper was to take a step from which one could not retreat for five long years. The parents lingered in the reception hall talking to a nun and certain mechanical courtesies were exchanged. Then you were handed over, and the snivelling was dismissed by the nun with brusque and off-putting optimism.

Big spaces from now on — recreation hall, classrooms and refectory, rules for everything and name tapes on all one's belongings. The only escape came at dawn three mornings a week when we went to attend Mass in the Augustinian church and there one sometimes caught sight of the 'lovely priest', lost to us in his beautiful vestments and his mysterious Latin. Otherwise it was a world of women — nuns, lay nuns and little postulants and one was always seeing veils and starched headgear that framed the face and out of which eyes and nose peered as if out of a burrow. To see a nun's eyebrow was as wicked and as bewitching as Keats felt when he saw the ungloved hand of the woman he loved as she walked over Vauxhall Bridge.

Sins got committed by the hour, sins of thought, word, deed and omission, the sin of eating, nay devouring an illicit jam tart snatched from the cookery kitchen, the sin of smiling at a nun and having bad 'thoughts' about her such as brushing against her hand, the sin of sprinkling castor sugar onto the palm of one's hand and licking it to one's heart's content, the dreaded sin of consulting the mirror and then hawing on it to give oneself a dreamier look.

Once a year we were allowed out to the local show but there was about it a sort of unexpressed lethargy and disappointment, what with the muddied field, the winds (it was always October when the winds were said to lament), the men in their great coats, the women in their flat hats, the fillies and mares whinnying and rearing, the precarious showjumps and the spartan amusements (it was wartime) so that nothing quite lived up to anyone's expectations.

One of the vexations of later life is how carelessly we treat our elders. There is no regaining that time. There was the couple who had had a made match, who still kept the top tier of the wedding cake for the offspring that was not forthcoming. The wife was a distance away under an umbrella with a group of ladies, murmuring. He winked at me and said I was growing into a fine woman, then winked with the other eye, then nothing more. Standing there sucking the fibres of her scarf was a 'peculiar' lady who at times would burst into laughter and at other times accused people of laddering her viyella stockings with their diamond engagement rings. Except that there was not a diamond ring in sight, only the brown felt hats, the flecked tweed costumes, and brooches with lifelike similarity to beetles or spiders, brooches that were in vogue that year. The peculiar lady was just back from Lourdes and complained how everyone had to bathe in the same water, how it was not hygienic. Then she buried her face like a little girl in her fur collar, basked in it. I saw her twenty years later in a mental hospital, whereupon she asked me for a 'ciggy' and was playful as she had not been that day on the hill, when a horse bolted and the women became as hysterical as the children they were trying to protect. The odd toff had binoculars or a walking stick and one man with a black beard distinguished himself by wearing a faded green cape.

For refreshments we had lemonade, apples, and coffee-flavoured biscuits with a coffee icing. These biscuits required the accompaniment of hot tea to melt the icing slightly in the mouth so that the two extractions of coffee could be properly sampled and united. The apples smelt of nothing in particular out of doors, but back in the convent and just prior to Hallowe'en the parcels would pour in, be kept in the nun's little parlour, and to walk by there was to see them dimly through the frosted glass of the door and at once to imagine oneself in the ripest of orchards. Every girl's parcel contained a barmbrack and apples regardless of other treats and for a few days the convent acquired another smell and hence another atmosphere, whereby prayer and discipline and wax polish took mere second place and gorging was lauded.

Once after a nosebleed, when I had been laid on the red tiled floor and had keys and bunches of keys put all over my person, I was subsequently brought into that little parlour and told that I was a good girl, and given as reward a glass of lukewarm milk, which I hated. When the nun hurried out of the room to stop someone playing the piano in the recreation hall, I repaired to the vicinity of the three potted plants — a castor oil, a maiden hair and a bizzie lizzie, and doused each of them with the lukewarm stuff. I was still toying with the contents in the end of the glass when out of the corner of my eye I saw the milky liquid seep through the bottom of the terra cotta pots to the little saucers provided. Would she notice it?

'Have you thought of what you are going to be?' she asked with a certain coyness. Almost flirtatious was she. Oh to please her and win one's way into her hard heart and be invited to do little favours for her, like carrying her books, or opening or closing a window or cleaning the blackboards, oh oh to be her slave!

'A nun,' I said, quicker and more soulfully than I had ever said aught. The thought of a vocation danced before me; like a banner, the word waved and with it the vision of a young

postulant with a see-through veil, one foot in the world and the other sinking deeper and deeper into the mists of spirituality, towards the 'never to be forgotten day' when one would take final vows and be cut off from the world outside, from family, from pleasure, from men, from earthly love, from buses and shops and cafeterias, from life.

'A nun,' she said, swollen with pride. Meanwhile I was brimming with tears that were as thick as glycerine, though not so nourishing.

From then on there was subtle understanding I would become a nun and thus devolved on me extra duties such as to walk softly, to talk softly, to stay in the chapel after the others — the motley — had trooped out, to deny myself jam on Sunday, to drag my hair back severely from the forehead and therefore give no reign to quiffs or prettiness, to drink the senna tea without making a face, to read no delectable love story in the magazine that some day-girls brought in, to write a letter home only when one was permitted and to keep one's mind on such things as the visions of St Margaret Mary and the mortifications of the saints.

Parents seemed to exist no longer, or rather they had receded into being people who had given birth to one and about whom one had certain fossilised feelings, just as one day these nuns — the next instalment of parents — would recede and be replaced by another authority and yet another.

GRÁINNE O'FLYNN

(1938–2001)

from:
OUR AGE OF INNOCENCE
(1987)

[In an essay that examines the historical background of her Catholic education in the 1940s, Gráinne O'Flynn argues that the denominational division between Catholic and Protestant schoolchildren was reinforced by socialization strategies which did not encourage women to be active participants in social and political life. O'Flynn examines the influence of the religious educators on the Irish Department of Education, in particular the annual Conference of Convent Secondary Schools which she considered a powerful control mechanism for regulating the moral behaviour of Irish society. The essay was published in *Girls Don't Do Honours*, edited by Mary Cullen (Dublin: Women's Education Bureau, 1987), and concludes with a reflection that the church's idealism of innocence as an acceptable moulding block of woman's character is at base misogynistic.]

My Education and Upbringing

My parents had married in the late 1930s. They went to live in a new suburb in Dublin. They had two children. Our family was small in comparison with the rest of the families in the suburb, except for Protestant families. Protestant families were not a large component of the population — about five per cent — but by the age of six I was aware of the difference between us. Originally, awareness came from a myth — fortified to a degree by an accident of geography — that all Protestants lived only on the north side of roads. The second and most pervasive aspect of difference related to school attendance, church attendance and patterns of social activity.

Catholic church activity impinged greatly on our lives. Parish priests and curates concerned themselves with families and schools. Separate women's and men's sodalities were set up, as were committees to raise funds to pay off church debts. For many women the sodalities and the committees became focal social centres. There was an obvious competitiveness between members. This arose from the production of goods for church sales and also from interest in entertaining local clergy. We children could point out houses which were visited by clergy and where crustless sandwiches and sugar-dusted Victoria sponge cakes were served to them on wedding-present china. The visits led to increased standing for the hostesses in the neighbourhood and also to status for their children in local schools if they were picked out with kindness by visiting priests.

Catholic schools were new in the area and they were run by orders of nuns. Boys came to school with girls until they reached what was called 'the age of reason', but really the age of seven. More pervasively, our institutional socialisation into what it meant to be Catholic women began there. At first, probably because they looked so strange, we looked on nuns as being apart from the rest of humanity. Although we grew used to how they looked, we grew more convinced of their remoteness. They did not live in ordinary houses; they had to be accompanied by other females when they walked in the streets; they had exotic names; they were 'brides of Christ'. The other-worldliness which enveloped their lives added a mysterious and forceful

dimension to their statements. Occasionally some of us were cheeky to nuns, but we knew from an early age that to argue with a nun would be a most grievous transgression.

Young nuns often taught the infant and senior infant classes. We sometimes caught glimpses of favouritism directed by them at beautiful little girls and engaging little boys. Was this a long-suppressed desire for an ideal child which had got momentarily out of control? We hadn't the wit to form the question, but we were affected by the behaviour because the criteria by which we were judged were clear: engaging little boys were articulate little boys; beautiful little girls were clean, curly, docile and silent. From our first days at school we were sexually segregated in our classrooms. Commingling was represented to us as shameful. Often punishment procedures involved a blushing walk across the room to sit among members of the opposite sex. Energetic, exuberant little girls went to the boys' side: boys who wept were sent among the girls. We accepted the procedures without question and carried ideas of suitable female/male behaviour with us beyond the gates of the school.

Protestant friends attended different schools. They were not taught by nuns; their school principal was a man. Girls and boys stayed together in the national school until their final year. Their church involvement percolated more formally into their social lives than ours did. Whereas Protestant clergy did not need to involve the women of the parish in fund-raising activities to the same degree as Catholic clergy — their church was an old one — they did concentrate on youth organisations more than their Catholic counterparts. They had Sunday school, but what we envied most was the Girls' Brigade. The brigade sanctioned exciting physical sports. Members had uniforms; they were arranged in troops; they had secret codes; they had an *esprit de corps*. It all appeared to be daringly physical and independent. At the brigade's annual display our Protestant friends were awarded badges and medals for gymnastic feats which were prohibited to us by our parents and teachers. They centred on rope-climbing, high-jumping and vaulting. And, envy of envies, shorts were an approved part of their gym uniforms. Some nuns at our school had told us that Our Lady wept when girls wore shorts or trousers.

As we grew older and our social lives moved beyond the confines of our immediate area, the differences between our socialisation as Catholic women and that of our friends as Protestant women became more noticeable. During our middle years at secondary school, my Catholic school friends and I became expert at plotting the routes to and from school which held the maximum possibility for meeting with boys. It was possible on my bicycle journeys to cross roads leading to four boys' schools. The immediate objective was encounter and banter, but the general aspiration was to become a member of a 'mixed' group. Occasionally, some of us were invited by boys to the local cinema on Sunday afternoon. The meetings were arranged and took place without any parental consent.

Our Protestant friends did not become involved in our adolescent adventures. Firstly, there were no Protestant schools for boys on the way to their secondary schools. Secondly, it would have been entirely outside their terms of reference, and ours, if they, even at that age, had shown interest in Catholic boys. Thirdly, and perhaps most importantly, their parents approved of male/female relationships for young people long before ours did. Family outings and church outings were organised by their elders from about the age of fourteen. Although as children we had participated with our Protestant friends in birthday parties and other celebrations, as our interests positively shifted from jelly to men, the Catholic parties ceased and the Protestant ones became denominationally selective.

Without having more than naming knowledge of *Ne Temere* (the Catholic prohibition on mixed marriages unless there is an express promise to bring up the children as Catholic), I accepted this situation albeit reluctantly. The reluctance was many-faceted. I was annoyed at what appeared, even then, to be irrational bias; I was envious of parental approval of 'mixed parties'; I was dying to meet people called Hedley, Clive or Alan. I was convinced that I would be devastatingly witty in conversation with them. Hadn't my entire diet of extra-school reading centred on their prototypes in the *Girls Crystal* and the Abbey and Chalet School books? Hadn't my illicit cinema-going made me conscious of the type of articulate woman who would attract

them? They would call me 'old thing'; the friendship would deepen into inseparable companionship; this would (after some minor misunderstandings) blossom into love. From the wealth of experience which I had built up, this appeared infinitely more acceptable than being called 'stretch' or 'Yeats' (I was five foot nine and into poetry) by Brendans and Seáns.

With hindsight, it is possible to isolate some factors which contributed to the tension which grew between the images of our expectations and the reality of our existence. The images were those of innocents. They emanated from our educators, from fiction and from unreal, romantic aspirations of parents and teachers. They had little basis in reality, but reality, which had been avoided in our development process, was what we had to cope with. Before we perceived the dichotomy, some of us imagined that the reality we experienced was a localised distortion and that true life was to be found beyond our Dublin suburb.

By some circuitous reasoning process, plus an unarticulated revolt against tradition, a friend and I decided that men in Trinity College held the key to our realization as companionable women. We were seventeen, still at school, and we concentrated on an immediate possibility — entrance to a dance in the Dixon Hall in Trinity — rather than a long-term improbability — entrance to a degree course.

We planned with some determination to achieve our goal. We had to find out how to get in and how to get out. We knew no one who was or who had been a student there. We were aware of memories of British troops in Trinity's College Park in 1916 and of a flying Union Jack in our lifetime. We were also aware of an episcopal ban. We argued ourselves out of the ban. After all, going to a dance was quite different from attending a course of lectures. We did a daylight topographical survey from the college's Front Gate to the Lincoln Place Gate. We quashed the memories. At the dance we met two students who invited us for tea in their rooms on the following morning. The civilised nature of the invitation recompensed for a major disappointment — their names were Michael and Johnny — and a minor one — they couldn't pronounce ours. On the following morning we wore gloves and appeared at 11 am. We were given mugs, which we though very chic, and a rather uneasy conversation began. It centred on who we were and who they were. When we discovered that they were both sons of clergymen our courage collapsed, the folk memories revived and we left trailing uneasy excuses. Unlike other adventures, this one was never recounted to our friends. We realised that we had gone beyond the bounds of any imaginable limits. There was also the danger that some one might change the name of the beverage to soup.

In spite of the fact that we generally enjoyed our illicit activities, most of us experienced periods of guilt. We were fearful of the shadows of sin which appeared to surround the area of male/female relationships. We didn't talk to our parents because our parents didn't know what we were doing. Their references to sex were usually limited to vague talk about seeds and mysterious implantations. Because of this vague home atmosphere, the school 'retreat' (a period of withdrawal, usually involving religious lectures and conducted by visiting priests) became a focal point for questions about sex. In our school, the two senior classes were given what was called a 'special' session and written anonymous questions to the retreat director were allowed. What we all wanted to know was, was it a sin to kiss?

The replies had a pattern. First, we were warned about 'the world'. Then we were warned about our sex. The warnings were couched in obscure language and delivered in dramatic tones which thrilled but did not enlighten us. References were made to the arousal of passion, provocative female dress, perfume and 'challenging talk'. Since neither biology nor any science was taught to us, and since our reading was extremely limited, we were quite vague about what arousal meant. We did realise, however, that our normal dress — tightly tied navy gymslips, lisle stockings and gabardine coats — was highly unlikely to be provocative. Perfume as a stimulus to wild male response seemed interesting, though unviable at a distance, and what was 'challenging talk'? However, at the end of 'special' sessions one thing was very clear to us: we were potentially dangerous. The very female form was a source of evil. The best ways to rid ourselves of its encumbrances were to pray, be modest, adopt low vocal tones and become non-argumentative. To most of us the main difficulty of imple-menting the advice lay in the low vocal tones and non-argumentative enjoinders. We were develop-ing a desire for some kind of intellectual excite-ment and an interest in debate. Strangely perhaps, one of our intellectual stimuli came from our religious class. We studied Sheehan's *Apologetics* and Kavanagh's *Social Ethics*. Were we being asked to refrain from argument even in the sphere of faith?

Two of us met what we recognised as a real live communist when we were selling flags for the St Vincent de Paul Society in O'Connell Street. He argued that voluntary aid for the poor was a sop to radical political intervention aimed at eliminating all the divisions between the rich and the poor. We experienced thrills of anticipation during his lengthy discourse. We knew that we could reply with answers from Sheehan and Kavanagh. We knew that communists favoured state interference with the natural order. We knew such interference was morally wrong. We knew how to combat communism by an argu-ment using analogies of trees fulfilling their natural potential. We knew that our final telling phrase would be 'The family was there before the state'. But we remembered the prescriptive enjoinders about low vocal tones and non-argumentativeness and remained silent and went, rather sadly, to rattle our flag boxes under the noses of other people in the cinema queue.

When we left school we tried to kick against constraining mores in an ineffectual way. We began to smoke; we wore stiletto heels, we drank expresso coffee in coffee bars. We got jobs which were terminable on marriage and none of us encountered women in positions of decision making. We found no stimulus to argumentative discourse and we reserved whatever remaining tendencies we had for debate for the confron-tations we had with our parents when we stayed out late.

Everyone expected us to get married. We learned the significant pattern. He asked you out with increasing frequency. You met him at Clery's or the Metropole. One Sunday you brought him home. He gave you the watch for Christmas. You knew the next was the ring. Parents watched for the signs with some kind of hope. When the pattern had been established, they were relieved. Often their hopes were conveyed to neighbouring friends and relatives.

When I first went to University College Dublin, I met a male engineering student. He shared digs, a duffle coat and a hat with three others. He had ten shillings a week for pocket money. He knew about Sheehan and Kavanagh. He, like me, had 'done' the odd numbers in English prose and poetry for the leaving Certificate. We could recite bits of Hayden and Noonan's history off by heart together. We met frequently in the centre of O'Connell Street under the third angel flanking the centre of O'Connell's statue. He shouted things like 'Good night MISS and THANKS', along the main road of the suburb when he left me home. He gave me a tin of Libby's fruit cocktail and *Portrait of the Artist as a Young Man* for my birthday. The situation was viewed with some alarm by parents and peers.

Tensions which had developed between us and our parents, particularly between us and our mothers during the years between adolescence and marriage, generally disappeared on marriage. After marriage the old mother/child relationship appeared to be reactivated. There appeared to be a common ground — management of a household, husband and children. The role of mentor for our mothers seemed to be revitalised.

There are historical reasons peculiar to Ireland why our socialisation was shaped in this way. Our parents had lived through the political and social devastation of the 1920s. They had faced a new situation of near devastation during the second world war. As a result, they were deeply concerned with establishing stability in their lives. To a marked degree, the desire for stability was basic to their attempts to mould us in a way so that our futures would contain no elements of risk.

Our fathers had clerical jobs and were in many cases the first generation of their own families to have had these kind of jobs. Each one, consciously or unconsciously, wanted to maintain and increase his standing as a middle-class respectable citizen. The desire encompassed family life as well as work life. A family in which, for instance, a wife worked would have been regarded as one which was economically insecure.

For us, as their children, education was accepted as an important component of respectability. It was a passport to security, but perhaps more importantly, there was a significant class relationship between tolerance of time spent in the education system and social standing. In retrospect, perhaps the most important aspect of education was that the tolerance and sacrifice was sexist. Our parents did make sacrifices to send us to second-level schools. They had to pay fees and defer increases in family income while we were there. But the deferment period for girls in the system, in our suburb, was considerably less than it was for boys. It was accepted, without question, that if boys had a certain amount of talent, particularly in an area relevant to a future profession, and further, if they wanted to continue their education in a university, this would be sanctioned. The simple argument was that they, not the girls, would be the future breadwinners. For most girls who had completed second-level education, the next four or five years were regarded as a period in which they should be occupied in a 'nice' job until they got married.

NUALA O'FAOLAIN

(1940–)

MY MEMORIES OF NUNS
(1992)

[In this sombre piece written for *Religious Life Review*, no. 153 (March–April 1992), edited by A. Flannery, Nuala O'Faolain presents a picture of her school-days in the fifties. It was the decade when Senator Owen Sheehy Skeffington began his campaign in the Senate of the Oireachtas against the administration of corporal punishment in Irish schools, sanctioned by popular attitudes in society. A ruthlessly honest journalist, O'Faolain does not flinch from expressing what was her reality during three years in a convent boarding-school in this period.]

I left boarding-school with a veneer of piousness. On the day I left, Mother Dorothea took me aside and advised me with great earnestness that when I found myself in difficulties in later life, I was to think what the Virgin Mary would have done, and do likewise. At the time, this formula made some kind of sense to me. We talked that kind of language in the convent.

I joined the Legion of Mary in Dublin. I went back and back to the Pioneers, every time I had a drink. I went to Mass. I fell in love with an upright man — a Welsh Catholic who actually loved his faith. But this was only part of me. I was always simultaneously in love with sexy, thoughtless men. I drank more and more. I began to know anti-clerical socialists. I went to a talk one day, in U.C.D. [University College Dublin], about religions in the Mediterranean basin around the time of Christ. I'd never known before that you could compare religions, and that they would have features of their myths in common. The talk changed everything for me. Before, I was a bad Catholic. After, I considered myself not a Catholic at all. I was about 18 then.

I'd been educated by the Sisters of Charity, the Holy Faith Sisters, the Loreto Sisters and the Sisters of St Louis. I'd learnt to read and write, to get honours in school subjects, to get scholarships. But the thing that meant most to my educators — the thing that justified their educational role — had lasted about a year. Not one hour of all my schooling passed without some reference to the Catholic religion. We were soaked in its imagery. Yet so monolithic was it that it was vulnerable to the slightest questioning. And God had been used as an instrument of control. Every aspect of behaviour had been referred to His supposed approval or disapproval, often quite blatantly in the interests of the nuns! So I — and, I'm sure, many of my generation — had no notion of God's love persisting even if we behaved 'badly'. Mary was used even more trivially. She was used to stop us speaking loudly, or whistling, or putting our hands in our pockets. The 'Mary', then, whom Mother Dorothea had sent me into the world with, had not enough depth to survive even the first of the dilemmas that occurred.

For me, as a girl in Ireland in the 'forties and 'fifties, the nuns were the representatives of God in my life. I never spoke to a priest except in confession, and you wouldn't call that 'speaking'. In my first nuns' school I was the Angel Gabriel in a Christmas tableau, but I spoiled everything by waving my wings. The nun beat me very hard afterwards with the leg of a chair. In my second nuns' school, they wore leather straps as part of their habit. They had a special double strap in a cupboard, and I was often beaten with that. I'm a middle aged woman now, and I'm still appalled that they used pain to enforce their will over children.

Secondary schools didn't use corporal punishment then. But they had a rich repertoire of other punishments, especially in the line of emotional deprivation. I won a national prize once, and it was announced in front of the school. But none of the nuns would talk to me afterwards. It had been observed, I was eventually told, that I hadn't gone to the school chapel at once to thank God for my good fortune. That's what I'd done wrong. It is a miracle, and perhaps an argument for the existence of God, that I do, now, these days, thank Him for what I've got. I survived the method of instruction. Other episodes — like kneeling in front of the assembled school to apologise for stealing bread — I look on as less harmful.

Several sisters from my boarding school have talked to me in later life in various states of hurt and bewilderment at the blackness of my memories. 'But don't you remember the good times?' they say. 'Don't you remember all the joy and laughter?' Unfortunately, the truth is that I hardly do. Then they point out that they did a lot for me. They understood that I was a troubled child, and made allowances for me that I never knew about. They made special efforts for me — one in particular teaching me things far outside the syllabus. And if it comes to that, they taught the syllabus very well indeed. Their school was famous for its results.

It is true that they gave me my chance in life. They got me into college. I would otherwise have been — I *wanted* to be — a shop assistant. I owe to them the satisfactions of education and of rewarding jobs afterwards. They took me in when I'd been expelled from another school. They put up with my lies and my dramatics. They coped with my parents not paying their fees. Some of them cared about me. They made me work. I know what I owe them.

So you would think that I could be on easy, grown-up terms with them. They are not responsible for the Irish educational system in the 1950s. They're not responsible for the world which shaped them. You would think that I could think of boarding school now, without emotion.

But the past retains its power. Thirty years after I left boarding school, I was going through the town it was in. It's a day-school now, and in part of the old buildings the sisters have opened a museum about their order and the history of the school. I decided to take the chance of going in to the museum, even though I dreaded meeting anyone. But I wanted to see the courtyards again, the walls, the paths; huge, swirling things happened to me in that place. It could never seem ordinary to me. And if I was afraid of meeting somebody, it was more from a powerful and inexplicable guilt I feel about the nuns, than from fear of them.

I sneaked in. A nun came flying down a fire-escape. 'Nuala, Nuala!' she called. Imagine to be somewhere where I was remembered, recognised, after thirty years! 'Welcome, welcome!' I went around the museum with her. I was taken in to the parlour. The kind of tea that only priests got was offered to me. The apocalyptic figure of Mother Dorothea came in — a tiny benevolent, shuffling old lady. She leaned on me and we went slowly into the chapel. We said a prayer. Or — she said a prayer; I tried to control the weeping that was waiting to burst in me. What about? About their ordinariness and powerlessness, now? I don't know. I couldn't drive afterwards. I pulled into the side of the road and wept.

They persist even more than my family, those nuns. My parents are dead, so all that part of things can never be examined again. But nowadays a nun who taught me in that school had turned up in my life again, and she's told me about what the order is doing now (community renewal, prison visiting, all kinds of post-educational things) and again I can't just put school behind me.

It is as if it insists on being understood. This nun and I have had some awkward conversations about school. She mentions things that I think are meant to give me some perspective. She's proud of the history of the order, for instance — of those French nuns coming to Ireland after the famine and literally saving the girl children of unprivileged people. I do find that helpful. I wish I'd known then — I wish I'd been able to place the sisters and myself and the building in some history that made sense. I never knew why the school or I were there. Or, this nun tells me — when I point out that some of the teaching nuns were very strange people — that nuns themselves in those days had no choice. They were told to be nurses or mathematicians or whatever. She shows me how the order had utterly changed and diversified. Above all, in the tolerant, perceptive kindness with which she talks about the sisters and the girls we knew, she gives me an example of how to remember positively.

Yet still, even after being with her, even though I see that not for a minute did anyone ever wish me any harm — I still want to cry out 'you wounded me! All of you, you wounded me!' I don't forgive. I know it was no one's fault but I don't forgive. I feel I was got at. I feel God was got at. I can hardly make sense of it. After all, I was only in a convent boarding-school for three years. It shouldn't matter so much. Certainly, it shouldn't matter that the place was run by nuns. Wouldn't I have been just as troubled in a secular school?

But it does matter that they were nuns. That they each had felt and were living a special call from God. Because I saw social snobbery, terrible deference to bishops and priests, anti-intellectualism, bad art, sentimentality, favouritism, propaganda, and those would have been just part of the world, but that we weren't in the world. We were in a special place, a convent. I never found an authentic, truthful relationship to the nuns then. I still can't. I sense that they think I'm insincere: which I was, and am with them. I don't understand the rules they've made for themselves and others. I just don't understand.

ALICE TAYLOR

(1938–   )

from:
TO SCHOOL THROUGH THE FIELDS (1988)

[Alice Taylor's vignettes of family life on a farm in rural Ireland during the 1940s continue to attract readers of all ages. Her three volumes of memories of a childhood spent in the Irish countryside recall a way of life that is past. 'We were reared as free birds, growing up in a world of simplicity untouched by outside influences,' she writes in *To School Through the Fields*, her first volume of memories (Dingle: Brandon, 1988; New York: St Martin's Press, 1990; London: Century Publishers, 1991). Her second book, *Quench the Lamp* (Dingle: Brandon, 1990) was equally successful and was followed in 1992 by *The Village* (Dingle: Brandon, 1992). Although the narrative takes the reader through the year's events, each section is an entity. This extract is from the first volume, pp. 146–51.]

A COUNTRY CHILD'S CHRISTMAS

Christmas in our house was always magical and for weeks beforehand my toes would tingle at the thought of it. The first inkling of its reality was Santa's picture in the *Cork Examiner*: we pored over him, loving every wrinkle in his benevolent face. At first his was a small face peeping from an obscure corner, but as Christmas drew nearer his presence became more reassuringly felt as he filled a larger space on the page.

The first step in the preparations in our home was the plucking of the geese, not only for our own family but also for all our relations. A night in early December was set aside for killing and plucking; home work had to be completed quickly after school that day and when the cows had been milked and supper finished the kitchen was cleared for the undertaking. I never witnessed the actual killing because my mother performed this ritual away from the eyes of us children, but when she brought the geese still slightly flapping and warm into the kitchen I always felt that she, who was gentle by nature, had been through some sacrificial fire which but for necessity she would have avoided.

Each member of the family with arms strong enough sat on a *súgán* chair with a warm goose across their knee. My father, however, washed his hands of all this crazy carry-on and, after imparting a lecture about relations providing their own Christmas dinner, he set out across the fields roving to a neighbour's house where 'sanity' prevailed. Strong feathers were eased off first and put into a big box and then the pure down was stowed in a smaller one. As the night wore on our arms ached and our noses itched with downy fluff, but my mother coaxed and cajoled until half a dozen geese lay starkers on the floor. With our mission accomplished we viewed each other with great merriment, our white downy heads and eyebrows lending us the appearance of white-haired gnomes. We tidied everything up then and gathered together with cups of cocoa around the fire, where my father would join us with perfect timing, bringing with him the tang of night air and frost glittering on his high boots.

During the weeks that followed the outside walls of the farmyard were whitewashed or cement washed and all the yards and passageways were brushed. Inside the house itself was washed and polished, but first the wide chimney was brushed. Standing close to our fire and peering up the chimney you could see the sky: it was a perfect Santa chimney. The kitchen floor was scrubbed, as were two tables and the chairs used to seat the lot of us. Our household seldom numbered less than ten: my parents, six of us children, a man who helped my father, a girl who helped my mother, and invariably one or two others, either miscellaneous relations or extra helpers.

The next step was 'bringing of the Christmas', as we called it. My father and mother would set out early one morning for the nearest town to buy everything that was needed for Christmas. At this stage we usually had our holidays from school and we waited expectantly all day for the homecoming; usually night had fallen by the time we heard the pony's hooves in the yard. Bubbling with excitement we watched the succession of interesting boxes being carried in and stored away in the parlour and glimpsed bottles of lemonade sparkling amidst red and white Christmas candles which foretold their own story. Other goodies were skilfully obscured from our prying fingers and inquisitive eyes.

At last, Christmas Eve dawned. We brought in the holly which we had collected from the wood the previous Sunday and in a short time holly branches were growing from behind every picture — everywhere but around the clock, which was my father's sanctum and could not be touched. Then the Christmas tree. Our house was surrounded by trees: my father planted them all his life and he loved every one of them. At Christmas he suffered deciding which of his little ones had to be sacrificed. We usually ended up with a lop-sided branch instead of a full tree, but when it was dancing with Christmas cards and balloons it always seemed a beauty. We ran streamers across the kitchen and did everything our way while my mother made the stuffing and ignored the bedlam.

A big turnip was cleaned and a hole bored in it for the candle; this was decorated with red berried holly and placed in the window. That night no blinds would be drawn so that the light would shine out to light the way for Joseph and Mary. Before supper the Christmas log was brought in and placed behind the fire in the open hearth. Banked around with sods of turf it soon sent out a glow of warmth to make the toast that was part of our Christmas supper tradition. But before anything could be eaten the Christmas candle had to be lit. We all gathered round and my father lit the candle and my mother sprinkled us with holy water. Then we sat around the kitchen table, my father at the top with my mother on his right and each of us in our place. I feasted my eyes on the white iced cake, the seed loaf and barm brack, but most of all I gazed at the mountain of golden toast streaming with yellow butter. After supper we had lemonade and biscuits and the ecstasy of the gassy lemonade bubbling down my nose remains a memory that is Christmas for me.

Our gramophone was normally kept safe in the parlour but at Christmas it took its chance in the kitchen. Every Christmas my father bought new records and we played them non-stop. Silence was restored for the news on the radio but we young ones had no interest in the news; to us there was no world outside our own. After the news we all got on our knees for the rosary, something I never enjoyed usually, but on Christmas night it became real: this was the actual birthday of the baby. Looking out the window into the dark night, thinking that the same stars had shone on him so many years before, in my imagination I saw the cave and the animals in the warm straw and heard the angels singing. On that far-off Christmas night I was there in my child's mind.

Off our knees my father performed the usual ritual of winding the clock. Then, standing at the foot of the stairs, his last words to my mother were: 'Len, come to bed before morning.' My mother, a night person who always got a second wind facing midnight, had jelly to make, stockings to darn, underwear to air around the fire. We hung our stockings on the old-fashioned crane convenient for Santa as he came down the chimney, and then mother ushered us all off to bed, the more responsible ones with a scone and candle.

Ours was a large room with two beds and an iron cot with shiny brass railings and knobs. If the night was very cold we had a fire which cast mystic shadows along the low timber ceiling while the moon shone fingers of light across the floor. Anything seemed possible. Try as I might to keep my eyes open to see Santa appear out of the shadows, I was soon carried into the world of nod and awoke to the excruciating pleasure of sensing that Santa had been. No sensation in later life could compare with the boundless joy of those early Christmas mornings when Santa was an unquestioned reality. The gifts in the stockings were always simple and indeed often of a very practical nature but the mystique of the whole occasion gave them an added glow.

Having woken mother and father to display for them Santa's benevolence, those of us going to first Mass set out in the early dawn to walk the three miles to the church. Candles glowed from the farmhouses in the surrounding valley, making this morning very different. The lighted church welcomed us, but it was the crib rather than the Mass that was special to me, to whom these were no plaster dummies; they were the real thing. Afterwards we either walked home or got a lift from a neighbouring horse and trap. Breakfast was always baked ham, after which the remainder of the family went into the second Mass of the day. Before leaving for Mass my mother placed the stuffed goose in a bastable over the fire with layers of hot coals on the cover. There it slowly roasted, filling the kitchen with a mouth-watering aroma.

The clattering of the pony's hooves heralded the family's arrival home and finally after much ado we were all seated around the table for the Christmas dinner. Was anything ever again to taste so good? My mother's potato stuffing was in a class of its own. We finished our dinner as the King's speech began on the radio. My father had Protestant roots and always instilled in us an appreciation of things British as well as Irish. My mother listened to the Pope, my father to the King of England, and to us they were both as much a part of Christmas as Santa. Our new records were played again and again, and toys were savoured to the full until after supper exhaustion finally won the day and we dragged our small, weary feet upstairs to bed.

It was all over for another year, but each year was another page in the book of childhood.

DINAH ROONEY AND CATHERINE WALDRON

(*fl.* 1940)   (*fl.* 1940)

from:
LIVING IN THE CITY (1992)

[The North Inner City Folklore Project in Dublin grew out of community groups in the late 1980s. It was made possible by enthusiastic participation of local community groups in Sheriff Street, Sean McDermott Street, and North Strand: in short, all those places where, according to Alexis Moulder in his Introduction, the city 'wakes to the pungent aroma of stout brewing, drifting down the river from St James's Gate' (*Living in the City*, Dublin: Mount Salus Press, 1992). In this talkative urban setting memory was passed on by oral history. Dinah Rooney, a local midwife from Sheriff Street, and Catherine Waldron, mother of twelve children, recall the ritual of 'churching', or the blessing of purification in the church after childbirth.]

Churching

Dinah Rooney (midwife)
Sometimes the baby would be kept until the mother would be ready to go out for the baby to be christened. We'd carry the baby to the chapel, and the Godmother wouldn't take that baby until we would go into the chapel, when the child was about to be christened, the Godmother would be given the baby. The Godmother held the baby which I think is right. Now the father and mother is holding the child and the Godmother is standing beside. I don't think that's right, if the person is going to be Godmother and Godfather they held the child in the church. Now after the christening the mothers would be churched, after the babies would be all christened. The mother would be kneeling, all the mothers would kneel in the front seat, and they would have their candles, it wasn't just one candle going from one to the other, all the mothers had their candles. They were lit and the priest would say a prayer over them, put his hand over them each on the top of heads, and they were churched. Well as far back as I can remember with say my grandmother and her mother, it seemed when woman was exposed delivering, she was exposed to a different man, and that you were classed as 'the beast in the field' now that was the meaning of being churched.

Catherine Waldron (mother)
Well you got a candle, you lit a candle, and the priest prayed over you, it was more or less like you were thanking God. It had nothing to do with anything else. Now at that time, people would say now if you weren't churched, and you went out before you were churched, they'd say 'you wouldn't have luck meeting her, oh she's unlucky', now that was always said. A girl was after having a baby in the Rotunda, and they had to keep the baby in the central home, and the

nurse said 'will you come back up tomorrow and look at the baby?' and she said 'I couldn't come without being churched'. 'Oh, don't be ridiculous,' said the nurse. An awful lot of people now if they met you and you weren't churched, they just said, it's unlucky to meet her, they'd all say that, it isn't right for her to come out before she was churched. It stopped, some time ago, a priest gave a sermon out in the Lourdes church, he said, no such thing, it hadn't nothing to do with luck, bad luck, good luck or anything else. The reason you go to church to be churched after a babe, you were just going to thank God for the baby he sent you, and for strengthening you after the birth, that the churching had nothing else to do, it was only just thanking God, so it stopped then. At that time you could get the baby christened, Monday, Wednesday and Friday, well now you're waiting, you have to make an appointment, it is ridiculous, yeah, you have to make an appointment, Godmothers don't have to say the prayers now, one time when you would be standing for a child, if you didn't know the prayer the priest wouldn't let you stand for it.

Biographies/Bibliographies

Kate O'Brien

For biography and bibliography, see Vol. II, p. 1221 and Vol. V, p. 680.

Sara Hyland

LIFE. Born at 10 Pembroke Cottages in Dundrum village, then outside Dublin city, on 12 March 1893, Sara Hyland was the eldest child in a family of seven. Her father, James, was a coachman, who worked from Dundrum station on the old Harcourt Street railway line; her mother, Annie Kernan, did hand laundry at home. In 1908 Sara went to work for Lily Yeats in the embroidery workshop of the Dun Emer, later Cuala Industries. Her recollections of growing up in Dundrum at the turn of the century and her years with the Yeats sisters offer insights into many aspects of life at that time, including the working of the Cuala Industries, the writers and artists of the Irish Literary Revival and the Irish struggle for political independence. She died in 1972.

CHIEF WRITINGS. 'A Memoir', in I Call to the Eye of the Mind, ed. Maureen Murphy (Dublin: Attic Press, 1996).

BIOGRAPHY AND CRITICISM. Introduction by Maureen Murphy in I Call to the Eye of the Mind, pp. 11–17.

Norah Hoult

LIFE. Norah Hoult was born in Dublin in 1898. Educated in England, she worked on the editorial staff of the Sheffield Daily Telegraph, and later for Pearson's Magazines in London. Later she became active as a free-lance journalist and wrote fiction. She returned to Ireland from 1931 to 1937. Her first book of short stories, Poor Women! (1928), was widely acclaimed and often reprinted. She died in Ireland in 1984.

CHIEF WRITINGS. Poor Woman! (London: Scholartis Press, 1928); Closing Hour (New York and London: Harper and Brothers, 1930); Time Gentlemen! Time! (London: W. Heinemann, 1930); Violet Ryder (London: Elkin Mathews and Marot, 1930); Apartments to Let (London: W. Heinemann, 1931; New York and London: Harper and Brothers, 1932); Youth Can't Be Served (London: W. Heinemann, 1933; New York and London: Harper and Brothers, 1934); Holy Ireland (London: W. Heinemann, 1935; New York: Raynal and Hitchcock, 1936); Coming From the Fair (London: W. Heinemann, 1937; New York: Covici, Friede, 1937); Nine Years is a Long Time (London: W. Heinemann, 1938); Four Women Grow Up (London: W. Heinemann, 1940); Smilin' on the Vine (London: W. Heinemann, 1941); Augusta Steps Out (London: W. Heinemann, 1942); Scene for Death (London: W. Heinemann, 1943); There Were No Windows (London: W. Heinemann, 1941); House Under Mars (London: W. Heinemann, 1946; New York: Didier, 1947); Selected Stories (London and Dublin: M. Fridberg, 1946); Farewell Happy Fields (London: W. Heinemann, 1948); Cocktail Bar (London: W. Heinemann, 1950); Frozen Ground (London: W. Heinemann, 1952); Sister Mavis (London: W. Heinemann, 1953); A Death Occurred (London: Hutchinson, 1954); Journey into Print (London: Hutchinson, 1954); Father Hone and the Television Set (London: Hutchinson, 1956); Father and Daughter (London: Hutchinson, 1957); Husband and Wife (London: Hutchinson, 1959); The Last Days of Miss Jenkinson (London: Hutchinson, 1962); A Poet's Pilgrimage (London: Hutchinson, 1966); Not for Our Sins Alone (London: Hutchinson, 1972).

Una Troy

LIFE. Elizabeth Connor and Una Troy were names used by Una Walsh, who was born in 1913 in Fermoy, County Cork. She received her schooling at Loreto College, Dublin.

CHIEF WRITINGS. Her first two novels, Mount Prospect (1936) and Dead Man's Light (1938), were written under the pseudonym 'Elizabeth Connor', as were her plays for the Abbey Theatre, Swans and Geese (1941) and The Dark Road (1947), which can be found in Abbey Theatre archives. She subsequently published novels under her own name, of which We Are Seven (London: Heinemann, 1955) is her best known.

BIOGRAPHY AND CRITICISM. Ann Owens Weekes, Unveiling Treasures: The Attic Guide to the Published Works of Irish Women Literary Writers (Dublin: Attic Press, 1993), pp. 345–6; The Oxford Companion to Irish Literature, ed. Robert Welch (Oxford: Clarendon Press, 1996), p. 572.

Clarissa A. Woods

No information available.

Mary Lavin

For biography and bibliography, see Volume III, p. 1222.

BIOGRAPHY AND CRITICISM. Thomas J. Murray, 'Mary Lavin's World: Lovers and Strangers', Eire-Ireland, vol. 7, no. 2 (summer 1972); Catherine A. Murphy, 'The Ironic Vision of Mary Lavin', Mosaic, vol. 12 (spring 1979); Richard Peterson, 'Mary Lavin', Eire-Ireland, vol. 16, no. 3 (fall 1981), pp. 150–2; Patricia Meszaros, 'Woman as Artist: The Fiction of Mary Lavin'. Critique: Studies in Contemporary Fiction, vol. 24, no. 1 (fall 1982), pp. 39–54; Janet Dunleavy, 'Mary Lavin, Elizabeth Bowen, and a New Generation: The Irish Short Story at Midcentury,' in The Irish Short Story: A Critical History, ed. James Kilroy (Boston: Twayne, 1984), pp. 145–68; Susan Asbee, 'In Mary Lavin's "The

Becker Wives": Narrative Strategy and Reader Response', Journal of the Short Story in English, vol. 8 (spring 1987), pp. 93–101; Maria Gottwald, 'Narrative Strategies in the Selected Stories of Mary Lavin', in *Anglo-Irish and Irish Literature: Aspects of Language and Culture*, ed. Birgit Bramsback (Uppsala: Uppsala University Press, 1988), pp. 288–73; Masako Kameyama, 'Mary Lavin: As the Writer Sees Herself', *Journal of Kyoritsu Women's Junior College*, vol. 35 (February 1992), pp. 13–14; Martha Vertreace, 'The Goddess Resurrected in Mary Lavin's Short Fiction', in *The Anna Book: Searching for Anna in Literary History*, ed. Mickey Pearlman (Westport, CT: Greenwood Press, 1992), pp. 1992), pp. 159–66; Sarah Briggs, 'Mary Lavin: Questions of Identity', *Irish Studies Review*, vol. 15 (summer 1996), pp. 10–15; Robert L. Stevens and Sylvia Stevens, 'An Interview with Mary Lavin', *Studies: An Irish Quarterly Review*, vol. 86, no. 341 (spring 1997), pp. 43–50; Jeanette Shumaker, 'Sacrificial Women in Short Stories by Mary Lavin and Edna O'Brien', *Studies in Short Fiction*, vol. 32, no. 2 (spring 1995), pp. 185–97; Maurice Harmon, 'From Conversations with Mary Lavin', *Irish University Review*, vol. 27, no. 2 (autumn–winter 1997), pp. 287–94; Leah Levenson, *The Four Seasons of Mary Lavin* (Dublin: Mercier, 1998); Eileen Fauset, 'Studies in the fiction of Jennifer Johnston and Mary Lavin', *Working Papers in Irish Studies: 98* (Ft. Lauderdale (FL), Nova University, 1998).

Edna O'Brien

For biography and bibliography, see Volume III, p. 1134, and below for additional references.

ADDITIONAL WRITINGS. *Time and Tide* (London: Viking; New York: Farrar, Straus, Giroux, 1992); *House of Splendid Isolation* (London: Weidenfeld and Nicolson; New York: Farrar, Straus, Giroux, 1994); *Down by the River* (London: Weidenfeld and Nicolson; New York: Farrar, Straus, Giroux, 1996); *Tales of the Telling* (London: Pavilion, 1997); *Lives: James Joyce* (London: Orion, 1999); *Wild December* (London: Weidenfeld and Nicolson, 1999).

BIOGRAPHY AND CRITICISM. Darcy O'Brien, 'Edna O'Brien: A Kind of Irish Childhood', in *Twentieth-Century Women Novelists*, ed. Thomas Staley (Totowa, New Jersey: Barnes and Noble, 1982), pp. 179–90; Lynette Carpenter, 'Tragedies of Remembrance, Comedies of Endurance: The Novels of Edna O'Brien', in *Essays on the Contemporary British Novel*, ed. Hedwig Bock (Munich: Max Hueber, 1986), pp. 263–81; Kitti Carriker, 'Edna O'Brien's "The Doll": A Narrative of Abjection', *Notes on Modern Irish Literature*, vol. 1 (1989), pp. 6–13; Karen Ellen Buckley, 'Homeomorphic Patterns in the Fiction of Edna O'Brien', DAI, vol. 52, no. 5 (November 1991); Kiera O'Hara, 'Love Objects: Love and Obsession in the Stories of Edna O'Brien', *Studies in Short Fiction*, vol. 30, no. 3 (summer 1993), pp. 317–25; Rebecca Pelan, 'Edna O'Brien's "Stage-Irish" Persona: An "Act" of Resistance', *Canadian Journal of Irish Studies*, vol. 19, no. 1 (July 1993), pp. 67–78; Amanda Graham, '"The Lovely Substance of the Mother": Food, Gender and Nation in the Works of Edna O'Brien', *Irish Studies Review*, vol. 15 (summer 1996), pp. 16–20; Adrienne L. Friedlander, *Edna O'Brien: An Annotated Secondary Bibliography (1980–1995)* (Florida: Fort Lauderdale, 1997); Michael Patrick Gillespie, '(S)he was too Scrupulous Always: Edna O'Brien and the Comic Tradition', in *The Comic Tradition in Irish Women Writers*, ed. Theresa O'Connor (Gainesville: University of Florida Press, 1996), pp. 108–23; Jeanette Shumaker, 'Sacrificial Women in Short Stories by Mary Lavin and Edna O'Brien', *Studies in Short Fiction*, vol. 32, no. 2 (spring 1995), pp. 185–97; James Cahalan, 'Female and Male Perpectives on Growing Up Irish in Edna O'Brien, John McGahern and Brian Moore', in *Double Visions: Women and Men in Contemporary and Modern Irish Fiction* (Syracuse: University of Syracuse Press, 1999); Katie Gramich, 'God, Word and Nation: Language

and Religion in Works by V.S. Naipaul, Edna O'Brien and Emyr Humphreys', *Swansea Review* (1994), pp. 229–42.

Gráinne O'Flynn

LIFE. Born in 1938 in Dublin, Gráinne O'Flynn was educated in Holy Faith schools in Glasnevin and later at University College Dublin. She was attached to the Education Department of Trinity College Dublin from 1973 to 1980. She completed a three-year project for the Irish Council of Churches in association with the Department of Foreign Affairs. She was Education Officer with the Teachers' Union of Ireland, 1984–95. She died, after a short illness, in 2001.

CHIEF WRITINGS. *World Survival* (Dublin: O'Brien Press, 1984). Specialist articles and reports for TUI Education and Research Unit. 'The Education of Women', *Capuchin Annual*, Dublin 1976.

Nuala O'Faolain

LIFE. Nuala O'Faolain was born in Dublin in 1940 and was educated in Dublin, Hull and Oxford. She was a lecturer in the English Department at University College Dublin and then a television producer in London for the BBC/Open University. She worked throughout Europe, the United States, in Israel and in Iran as an occasional lecturer and reviewer. In recent years, she has been a producer of women's and other programs with RTÉ television, a lecturer in media studies at Dublin City University, and a journalist and opinion columnist with the *Irish Times*. She won the Jacob's Award for television in 1987 and the A.T. Cross Award for Woman Journalist of the Year in 1988. Her memoir, *Are You Somebody?*, was a best-seller in Ireland, Australia and the United States.

CHIEF WRITINGS. *Are You Somebody?* (Dublin: New Island Books, 1996); *My Dream of You* (London: Michael Joseph, 2001).

BIOGRAPHY AND CRITICISM. Máirín Johnston in conversation with Nuala O'Faolain, 'Nuala O'Faolain', in *Dublin Belles* (Dublin: Attic Press, 1988), pp. 59–65; Terry O'Faolain, 'Oh My Aunt', *Sunday Tribune*, 28 August 1988; Helen Callanan, 'The Loneliness of Emerging from Mother's Shadow', *Sunday Tribune,* 20 October 1966; Pamela Weaver, 'Yes, I am Somebody', *Examiner*, 14 February 1998.

Alice Taylor

LIFE. Born in 1938 in County Cork, where she still lives, Alice Taylor has written three books on Irish country life, which are based on her own childhood and upbringing.

CHIEF WRITINGS. *To School Through the Fields* (Dingle: Brandon, 1988); *Quench the Lamp* (Dingle: Brandon, 1990); *The Village* (Dingle: Brandon, 1992).

Dinah Rooney

No additional information available.

Catherine Waldron

No additional information available.

MARGARET Mac CURTAIN, *Editor*

Religious Conviction: Women's Voices, 1900–2000

The intensity of the bond between women and religion lasted well into the twentieth century. Nineteenth-century forms of religion with their emphasis on duty, reliance on discipline and law, and the accretions of pious customs and devotions, old and new, accompanied women into the new century in Ireland. The fervour of private prayer increased and though no Irish hymn-writer comparable to Fanny Alexander appeared, sacred choirs and religious processions to the shrine of the Blessed Virgin Mary were popular expressions of women's interest and investment in religious culture. Family prayer and the reading of Holy Scripture reinforced the influence of the mother who assumed iconic stature with her identification as the Mother of Sorrows in Patrick Pearse's poem dedicated to his own mother and written on the eve of his execution after the Easter Rising of 1916. The great wave of religious conviction, coming from a culture of faith which had been nourished and shaped by the calamity of the Great Famine, continued to engulf all the Christian denominations. Loss of husbands, brothers, sweethearts and nurses in the First World War, the Easter Rising and the subsequent War of Independence and civil war strengthened women's belief in a divine providence. It filled them, too, with an *angst* associated with deserved retribution from a God more feared and obeyed than loved.

Protestant women had come to a new understanding of women's place in society through their participation in the revival movements in the nineteenth century and their involvement in women's missionary society work. Irish Methodist and Presbyterian women were appointed by their denominations to be missionaries and went to foreign missions with a mandate from their churches to evangelize and enlarge their churches' missionary programmes. During and after the 1846–52 Famine, Quaker women's philanthropic efforts brought them into the sphere of social reform and from there into the area of women's rights. Their leadership in demanding constitutional changes such as women's enfranchisement was rooted in their religious acceptance of the equality of women with men. Lucy Kingston, reared in the Church of Ireland, attended the Friends' meetings in Rathmines as part of her suffragist activities in Dublin. Drawn to pacifism during the First World War, she joined the Society of Friends in the early twenties and poured her energies into the peace movements through her membership of the International League for Peace and Freedom.

Within the Church of Ireland the new century offered women what Violet Disney called 'a goodly heritage' in the security of being a religious minority with an ingrained respect for tradition, continuity and antiquity. She testified that 'a critical and independent mind was encouraged' as a female member of the Church of Ireland. As a student in Trinity College Dublin, she engaged in dialogue and discussion with members of other churches. The 1897 Lambeth Conference recognized the revived office of deaconess in the Church of England, a procedure which slowly opened the debate on the ordination of women to the priesthood. It was closely monitored by women within the 'Anglican Communion' to which the Church of Ireland belonged. The ordination of Ginnie Kennerley in 1991 in Christchurch Cathedral

Dublin was the culmination of a long divisive debate which she acknowledged honestly in her pre-ordination sermon. Throughout the twentieth century the Congregational Union, the Baptist Union, the Methodist Conference, the Church of Scotland and the Presbyterian Church of England admitted women to the ministry.

For Catholic women the century between the papal Dogma of the Immaculate Conception of the Virgin Mary, 1854, and that of her Assumption into Heaven, in 1950, placed the cult of Mary at the centre of their devotional practices. With the introduction of mass-produced goods for an expanding market, illustrated prayer books, small 'holy pictures' to be used as bookmarks, medals struck in honour of the Blessed Virgin or some saint remained the staple devotional diet of Irish schoolgirls and women until well beyond the half-century. Convent boarding-schools flourished and with them vocations to the religious life, which remained startlingly high until the early seventies.

For Protestant women the goal of equalizing male–female relationships inspired by nineteenth-century exegesis of the Bible continued to imbue their religious convictions with a social mission. Activists and leaders on a number of fronts, notably the suffrage movement, they included on their agenda the right of women to ordained ministry. There was a perceptible Jewish presence in Ireland in the early twentieth century and the writings of Jewish women of that period have yet to be researched and published. Given the variations of the Jewish diaspora between 1881 and 1924, their religious testimony will supply for that period what the spiritual journey narrated by Ronit Lentin reflects for a later period, the 1960s; the stories of Jewish women who came to Ireland after the Jewish Holocaust of the Second World War.

Despite the seeming unchangingness of the religious landscape, there were radical alterations in religious attitudes among large sections of women. The virulent religious sectarianism, which Elizabeth Grant Smith records in her *Irish Journals* (1840–50), supplies clues about its nature and how fiercely the antagonism and bigotry on both sides, Protestant and Catholic, raged. For twentieth-century women there were bondings across culture and faith in the Gaelic League, founded in 1893, in the shared humiliations of demanding women's suffrage, and in the nationalist struggle. It was no accident that the Women's International League for Peace and Freedom established a branch in Ireland within a decade of its foundation in 1915 and hosted an international conference in Dublin in 1926. A women-based, non-sectarian peace movement in twentieth-century Irish public life has been a small insistent voice bringing together women from diverse religious backgrounds. In the earlier part of the century women like Lucy Olive Kingston, with her readiness to discuss the theology of the Society of Friends, and Violet Disney, writing in *The Bell,* explaining her affection for and loyalty to the Church of Ireland, prepared the climate for the ecumenism which marked the new relationships between the Christian churches in the 1970s.

The Women's Liberation Movement of the seventies, the so-called second wave, opened new worlds to women disheartened by the patriarchal inter-connections between religion, politics and their own personal experiences. The combination of the new theological criticism and feminism in the seventies brought an influential number of women to the realization that they were marginal to their churches and religious affiliations. The ordination of Ginnie Kennerley to the priesthood of the Church of Ireland in 1991 was an important gesture towards women on the part of the historically significant Church of Ireland. Its effect on church attendance and the signal it gave to women, did not have an immediate dramatic result in encouraging the disaffected. By the 1990s women were drifting away from Church attendance. For some there was a search for roots in Celtic spirituality. Mary Condren's work and her book *The Serpent and the Goddess* (San Francisco: Harper and Row, 1989) have been instrumental in opening up alternative visions of the Goddess religion and Creation spirituality. Maura 'Soshin' O'Halloran's journey took her into Zen training and becoming a Zen monk in Japan before she was killed in a bus accident in her late twenties. Her search bears some similarities to that of Dungannon-born Margaret Noble, who embraced Hinduism in India and wrote extensively about the Hindu religion at the beginning of the twentieth century.

Women in the twentieth century found solace in organized religion and will most likely continue to do so, but the last quarter of the century is untypical in its religious configuration. Church attendance and sacramental practices have dropped. So also have vocations to religious life. Christian marriage is competing with civil registration and state divorce. Gender issues, the alienation of lesbian women from their churches, in particular the Roman Catholic church, and their search for an inclusive spirituality, are part of the diversity that marked the religious concerns of women in Ireland at the end of the twentieth century.

LUCY OLIVE KINGSTON

(1892–1969)

from:
WOMEN'S DEBT TO
QUAKERISM (*c.* 1930)

[A confident Society of Friends entered the twentieth century in Ireland. The Quaker community, about 2,600, was a small one, consisting of closely related families with a mix of young and old. Concern for foreign missions and a strong opposition to war were characteristics of the Irish Quaker community. In matters of faith, there was a developed theology of the Fatherhood of God as Creator of the Universe. Lucy Olive Kingston's essay is undated and was reprinted as a leaflet from the *Wayfarer*, the in-house journal of the Society of Friends at Friends' House, London.]

'Encourage all the women that are convinced in mind and virtue . . . that they may come into God's service . . . Let the creation have its liberty,' said George Fox.[1]

One of the most interesting studies in the history of Quakerism is the liberalism of George Fox where the equality of women is concerned, and how much ahead of his generation he was in this respect. Modern women Friends, especially those who have formerly belonged to other sects of the Christian Church, can best appreciate what this spiritual liberty means. 'To enter into worship in the Quaker way,' said one of these, 'is to feel oneself stretch spiritually.'

The era into which Fox was born was in no special way a kind one to women; and it has never been fully explained how he so entirely escaped the influence of a time which relegated them to a place considerably lower than the angels in Christian thought.

We are told that his first interruption in a religious service was made in defence of a woman who had quite legitimately asked a question of the minister, and had been silenced on grounds of her sex.

One may say that this recognition of women's spiritual equality was implicit in the pure teaching of Jesus; but was it implicit in the current teaching of Fox's early childhood, overlaid as that was with errors? Fox's realisation of the value and importance of the individual — the great central part of Christ's teaching — was intuitive and mystical rather than intellectual. He was, after all, an unlettered man and no scholar. We are indeed told that to the close of his life the writing of a letter was a journey on uncharted seas. Was it the ability to resist the wrong beliefs of a superstitious age that constituted the greatness of Fox? Is one led to the thought that one of the attributes of greatness is the power to resist ideas as well as the power to absorb them?

Be that as it may, women, with the coming of Quakerism, took up a position of equals and co-workers together in Christ. In the matter of testifying they came without ostentation or fanfare to the fore and continued there through trials and persecutions, with no reaction or weakening. Little as the Christian Church might know it — or even the women themselves — it was little short of a revolution within the religious field.

Criticism was naturally expressed at such a radical change; but it is noteworthy that the

1. George Fox (1624–91), founder of the Society of Friends; visited Ireland in 1669.

spectacle of the woman preacher lost something of what we now call 'notoriety value' from the fact that Friends were making such a general challenge to established religious practices. In the general disapprobation aroused amongst the orthodox by this sect, of whom no irrational behaviour was too great to be believed, the conduct of Quaker women was included. Just in the same way, at a later date, a writer on Calvinistic Puritanism remarked: 'In the disgrace which had overtaken music, painting, and every pleasant thing, woman was involved.'

The doctrine of women's complete equality in spiritual concerns was not argued; in the whole of Barclay's *Apology*[2] only one page is devoted to this matter. It was rather demonstrated by day-to-day experience which put it beyond all controversy. The earliest records of the work of women Friends show us that they ignored the restrictions of custom, travelling extensively in a time of difficult travel, giving a literal interpretation to the injunctions of Christ in leaving father, mother, home and family to take up the work of the Master in hazardous enterprise, in toil, in brave endurance. The words of W. Kay were never truer than when he said: 'Truth does not mean the acceptance of a casket handed down to us, but rather the risking in action that our beliefs are true.'

The story of the many women who took this risk is vividly told by M.R. Brailsford in her book *Quaker Women, 1650–90*.[3] Her tale is not only of the figures well known to all inheritors of Quaker traditions, but also of the lesser known. Looking on some of these indomitable characters portrayed in her book, and thinking of how much they must have meant to the advancement of the Society in their day, one finds it hard to understand the attitude of the Churches of to-day to the question of women's ministry.

2. Robert Barclay's *Apology for the True Christian Divinity* (1675) was the most influential of the early Quaker writings.

3. M.R. Brailsford, *Quaker Women, 1650–90* (London: Duckworth Press, 1915).

VIOLET DISNEY

(1889–1972)

WHY I AM 'CHURCH OF IRELAND' (1944)

[From July 1944 *The Bell* ran a series of essays on the subject of religious belief inviting selected contributors to present a personal reflection on the religion of their affiliation. According to *The Bell*, Violet Disney's essay 'describes the Faith of many of our fellow Irishmen, the Faith of many of our greatest historical figures — Parnell, Smith O'Brien, Butt, Thomas Davis, Lord Edward, Emmet, Yeats, Childers, and such living figures as an t-Uachtarán, Dr Dúbhglas de hÍde', vol. 8, no. 5 (1944), p. 379.]

It is impossible to put down facts about one's Religious Views and one's allegiance to a special denomination without using terms which are open to misunderstanding and variety of interpretation. Even in stating that I am a member of the 'church of Ireland' I make use of a name which does not seem to be in accordance with fact, and which, to those unaware of the reasons why it is so called, may give offence. However, in making this statement, I do not want to give offence, I wish to claim membership of that religious Body in Ireland which is in full Communion with the Church of England (Ecclesia Anglican), and all the other self-governing, indigenous Churches all over the world which are also in full Communion with that Church.

The Church of England, the Church of Ireland and these other Churches constitute the 'Anglican Communion'. Their Bishops come from all parts of the world, from India, China, and Japan, from North and South America, from Africa, Australasia and Melanesia to meet every ten years in London at the 'Lambeth Conference,' under the Chairmanship of the Archbishop of Canterbury. War has interfered with the holding of this Conference — it should have met in 1940; but as soon as circumstances permit, it will meet again. When it does, there will be amongst those Bishops a far greater proportion of brown, black and yellow faces than ever before; more and more the native races are assuming responsibility and rising to leadership in their Churches.

In the following paragraphs, I am going to try to answer two questions:—

1. What difference has it made to me personally that my family has for generations on both sides belonged to the Anglican Communion?
2. Why, having received a Liberal Education, and in the light of mature reflection, am I still a practising member of the Anglican Communion?

To answer the first question I rely on my memory of childhood's experiences and on the external acquaintance I have with the experiences of people nurtured in different traditions and allegiances. As I was born and brought up in Ireland, very early in life I became aware that I belonged to a different Communion from many of those I met every day. Both my parents had liberal and enlightened minds, neither of them was bigoted, but they were particular that their children should receive Religious Education only from themselves or from other members of the same denomination. In what did such education consist?

Long before I was able to read fluently, I was the possessor of a copy of the book of 'Common Prayer', to be carried proudly to Church, which from an early age I attended regularly with the rest of the family. I can still remember the shame and sorrow I felt when, on one occasion, my prayer book was taken gently out of my hands, because it was quite clear that I was only pretending to follow the canticle which was being sung (I think it was the Benedictus). This first prayerbook of mine was beautifully bound in red leather in one volume with a copy of 'Hymns Ancient and Modern': it was the gift of an aunt who lived in England and who had not realised that another hymn book was generally used in the Church of Ireland. The possession of that little book, visits to England, and the visits to our house of relatives from England, taught me that

there were some differences in the services of our own Church and those which I attended when I was in England — but the Prayer Book was common to them all. (This refers to a time before the last revision of the Irish Prayer Book, but with some slight modifications it holds good today.) I thus came to find out for myself that the importance of the Prayer Book in our Services was much greater and quite apart from that of the hymn book — the 'Church Hymnal'. Some pages of this little volume became grimy with use as they were held and turned Sunday after Sunday by my hot little fingers. Some of them were never turned at all.

The Book of Common Prayer contains a great deal which the ordinary layman seldom reads and some material that he never reads. Several prefaces: occasional services: all kinds of notes and instructions, the Canons of the Church of Ireland: but it also embodies the daily offices, the regular Services of our Church; the Collects, Epistles and Gospels for every Sunday and Holy Day throughout the year, the Psalter and the Church Catechism — all in the magnificent yet homely English of the 16th and 17th centuries. With this book, anyone who attends Church regularly grows more and more familiar. The language, the mental attitude of the Prayer Book are part of the background of his life — to a much greater extent probably than he is generally aware.

It was not only in Church that my knowledge of the Prayer Book was acquired. Every Sunday, I had to commit to memory the Collect and repeat it to my father who explained the difficulties. I can remember that I did not find the task at all an easy one. Every day, except Sunday, father or mother (in his absence) conducted family prayers. These opened with the Collect for the 2nd Sunday in Advent which begins 'Blessed Lord, Who hast caused all Holy Scripture to be written for our learning . . .' Then followed the reading of a passage from the Bible and some short prayers or part of the Litany from the Prayer Book.

Another book which was early placed in my hands was the Authorised Version of the Bible. This book was treated with the greatest possible respect; no other book or article was to be put on it. If a pile of books containing a Bible was placed on the table, the Bible must always be on top. To this day, I do not like to see anything placed on top of a Bible.

I received daily instruction in the Scriptures, or the Catechism, learning passages by heart. At first, I was taught at home by a governess, but later I attended a small school. When I was old enough to go so far with only an elder sister for escort, I went regularly to Sunday School which met in a hall adjoining the Church before the mid-day Service. There, too, we studied the Bible and the Prayer Book.

About the time I started going to Sunday School, a Children's Service was instituted which took place on Sunday afternoons, at which instruction was given by one of the Clergy, and a very simple form of worship offered. At this service, children formed the choir and we all learned to take our proper share in making responses. We loved the 'Children's Service' and hated having to miss it if illness or anything else prevented our attending it.

Now that I was growing up, 'Morning Prayer' following Sunday School, often seemed tedious and boring. The sermon might be long or above my head. We sometimes avoided attending it by going home a different route from that by which our parents generally came to Church. I do not remember any penal consequences when we succeeded in escaping; nor do I remember any compulsion to attend Church except that of example and custom.

One of the results of the comparatively small congregations which are normal in the Church of Ireland over most of the country, is the intimacy of the relations between the Minister and his flock. To him they became persons when they are baptised. This is of great significance when the time for confirmation approaches. The age for this varies considerably according to the views and wishes of the priest, the parents or teachers, and the candidates themselves. Boys and girls are seldom confirmed before 13 or after 18. Classes for Preparation are formed some months before the appointed date. This affords a wonderful opportunity for a clergyman to understand the young people and help them at a very difficult stage in their careers. Candidates for Confirmation attended the classes, held by our clergyman, for two successive years, though usually children attend such classes during one session only. Our clergyman, Dr Paterson Smyth,

who later went to Montreal, was a true pastor and lover of souls. Even our crude minds could appreciate that it was a great privilege to come in contact with him in this way and receive his teaching. Confirmation marks an important stage in the Religious life of Anglicans — they then become full members of the Church and are admitted to Holy Communion. I now could accompany my parents when they went to 'Early Service', hitherto a sealed mystery to me. We were instructed and encouraged to come to Communion regularly at least once a month, preferably early in the morning but, if not, to the Celebration after 'Morning Prayer'.

What difference then did this nurture in the 'Anglican Tradition' make; what kind of character did it tend to produce?

I grew up convinced that all who 'profess and call themselves Christians' should strive by the Grace of God to attain to a Christian standard of morals; that the individual is responsible before God to find out what this means in any given situation. To help him, he has the Bible; his instruction in his Faith; and the counsel of anyone in whom he has confidence. Truthfulness and sincerity were the most important virtues — the account of Ananias and Sapphira was one of the passages of Scripture with which I was very familiar. A promise must be kept at almost any cost. Not very long ago a group of girls aged about 16 expressed the opinion that, having got himself into the difficulty, there was no other course for Herod to pursue than to proceed with the murder of St John Baptist!

As a member of a Religious Minority, a critical and independent attitude was encouraged; but also a respect for Tradition, Continuity, Antiquity.

Loyalty to the British Crown and to the British Connection was taken for granted by these with whom I came much in contact in my childhood. It was a special instance of 'My Duty towards my neighbour'. At the time in question that was the political bias of the vast majority of Church of Ireland people. That is one of the causes for the depletion in our ranks and the flight from Ireland of the young and the strongest amongst us. Our Church is trying to adjust herself to the changed conditions. On her success, her survival as a factor in Eire largely depends.

To answer the first of my two questions, I have thus had but to draw on the storehouse of a retentive memory. To answer the second, i.e., why I still, in the light of mature reflection, am a member of the Church of Ireland, is a much more difficult undertaking. The issues involved are so important, and the problems so intricate, that it would strain the powers of a trained theologian to make a satisfactory answer within the compass of an article of this nature. However, it is possible to give some reason for the Faith that is in me and some account of the soul's journey to her present abode.

Until I was nearly grown up the social political arrangements which so nearly corresponded to some of the religious cleavages were taken for granted as part of the natural, proper ordering of my life. Then, at the age of 16, I was sent to the Alexandra College, Dublin, and later I entered T.C.D. [Trinity College Dublin]. In these institutions, I met and made friends with members of many other Communions: I joined societies and discussion groups and learnt about the experiences of people whose training and upbringing had been very different from my own. From that time onwards I have made close friendships with representatives of all the larger denominations to be found in Ireland. Here I had my first religious discussions, but in these our differences did not come into prominence. We were more concerned with the ethical aspect of religion; the shortcomings of a so-called Christian Society and such like topics. Christian denominations do not differ much about what constitutes right behaviour and the duty of man to man.

It was more through my studies, however, that I found cause for mental conflict. To everyone who tries really to think there comes a time when all that has hitherto been taken for granted, accepted from authority has to be examined, explained, tested. A different attitude of mind gradually develops. All one's standards, customs, shibboleths come under the microscope. They must either be justified or discarded. The question for me then was not: 'Why am I a member of the Church of Ireland?'; but: 'Why am I a Christian at all? And do I accept a Theistic account of the Universe?'

To those who are privileged to continue their education at a University, especially if their reading is concerned with Philosophy and kindred subjects — the time comes earlier than to those who are not so privileged. It would be difficult for me to determine exactly when this inner conflict began — when the books which I read began to assume more than 'Subject-for-Examination' importance — but I know that they did so and that an intellectually satisfying solution to my problem was not reached until many years after my college days were over. The whole process was gradual and other factors besides intellectual doubts were at work.

At no time, did I feel compelled to give up practising my own religion. Perhaps from timidity or because of 'wishful thinking' I gave Christianity the benefit of the doubt and remained an outwardly faithful member of my Church. But I had not really for myself answered the question 'What think ye of Christ?' Gradually, however, life with its problems and sorrows — in the years after 1914 — brought the vital need for a vital religion. There could be no rest in a half-way house. The fact that my original doubts were so profound and so far-reaching made it easier in the end than it might otherwise have been to accept wholeheartedly the orthodox Christian position. To summarise a long and painful process, for me the question became, 'Can I believe in a Beneficent Almighty God?' And I answered, 'Yes' to that — if Christianity be true: that is, I could not believe in a Beneficent God unless I also believed in the Incarnation. In such matters, logical proof cannot be attained, but Faith can and conviction that in Christ we have the highest revelation of the nature of God. Having arrived at such a conclusion, the return to the Religion of my childhood was not very difficult. In these few lines, I have, of course, tried to condense the outcome of the thought and reading of many years. They deal with the individual personal side of my religion.

Here I return to the specific question of why I remained in the Church of Ireland. Christianity is not only an individual personal matter. One is a member of a worshipping community as well as a soul seeking to find God. I am a member of the Church of Ireland rather than of some other denomination, first, because it was through her that I became 'a member of Christ, the child of God and an inheritor of the Kingdom of Heaven'; we come to conscious life as members of a family, a nation, a Church; when we come to maturity, we can repudiate any or all of these communities; but the reasons for doing so would have to be very compelling.

And I believe, secondly, that the Church of Ireland has, through her ministry, her sacraments and her doctrine, preserved continuity with the Church which began in the Jerusalem Upper Room at Pentecost. Like all organisations which depend on human agents, she has not always been true to her best nature. She has many imperfections; she has no monopoly of Truth; but I believe her to be a true branch of that Church — the spiritual Israel which took the place of the chosen race when they rejected their Messiah.

Thirdly, my Church has given me, in my mother tongue, the Scriptures; and the 'Book of Common Prayer' with all that it means of ordered, dignified worship in which I have my own share and function, and its provision for my spiritual needs through all 'the changes and chances of this mortal life'.

I feel that if we, her children, are faithful and try to realise and carry out God's purpose for her, we will make our contribution to that Catholic Church which is to be when holy charity shall have bound up the wounds of Christendom and healed her divisions. It is my conviction that a member of the Church of Ireland can say: 'Yea, I have a goodly heritage'; and again: 'Thou hast set my feet in a large room.'

LEON-JOSEPH SUENENS

(1904–96)

from:
EDEL QUINN, ENVOY OF THE LEGION OF MARY TO AFRICA
(1953)

[Edel Quinn, missionary lay-woman, left over two hundred letters giving an account of her missionary endeavours in East Africa in the 1930s and 1940s, and her first biographer, Cardinal Leon-Joseph Suenens, Archbishop of Malines-Brussels, included extracts from her correspondence in his highly acclaimed book, which appeared eight years after her death. Recognized officially by the Roman process for beatification, Quinn managed to infuse her last years, spent in East Africa, with a lively sense of adventure, though she was dying of tuberculosis. Despite failing health, she maintained a life of prayer remarkable for its sincerity and unobtrusiveness. Quinn wrote every week to the headquarters of the Catholic lay-organization the Legion of Mary, founded by Frank Duff in 1921. Amid a storm of controversy (because of her precarious tubercular condition), Duff selected Quinn as Legion Envoy to East Africa, there to work alongside missionary bishops, establishing the Legion of Mary. In the selected extracts Edel Quinn describes her work in East Africa just before the outbreak of the Second World War, when it was a British protectorate. Her itinerary indicates long journeys under harsh conditions and gives a vivid impression of Catholic missionary life in the late thirties. The account of her departure from Mauritius in 1940 marks the beginning of the last phase of her illness. She died of a heart attack brought on by extreme exhaustion and weakness on 12 May 1944 in the thirty-seventh year of her life. The accounts are in the English edition of Leon-Joseph Suenens, Edel Quinn, Envoy of the Legion of Mary to Africa (Dublin: Cahill, 1953), pp. 151–5, 178–9.]

At the end of December, 1938, she was preparing to embark for Mauritius when an attack of malaria obliged her to remain in bed. It was the first serious break in the health of the semi-invalid. The doctor decided that she was not in a fit state to set out for Mauritius and insisted that she wait till April, that is, till the cool season. For the first time in her letters to Dublin she admitted to being ill in bed with fever, but she begged that no one would be anxious on her account and that her attack should not be made generally known.

The authorities who knew on what a paradox of medical diagnosis this heroic missionary vocation rested, asked her to tell them exactly, without keeping anything back, what was her physical condition. In obedience to their injunctions, and against her deliberate custom, she faced up to this subject of health which she would have preferred to disregard.

Here is her letter of Christmas, 1938, dated from Kampala.[1]

'I am glad you realise why I didn't want the news of my little breakdown broadcast. It is so common out here. Only now and then does one get a *good* dose of malaria. The spasms last two days as a rule. Now you can take it for granted that I have not the slightest intention of issuing a bulletin every time I get a cold or something like that. I have never done it in my life, even when at home with the family, and I am too old to change my habits!

'If I am laid up for a considerable time, say for two weeks, I shall certainly let you know. I did so in regard to my 'cold' last June and now for this malaria. You can rely on this and therefore you need not worry, thinking that I might be seriously ill without telling you. If I got ill to the extent of being unable to carry on my Legion work in the way it should be done, or at the proper speed of a healthy Legionary,[2] I would say so straight off. Then we could so present things that my return would seem to be in the ordinary course. As this is my third year now, no one could charge you with rashness for having sent me out originally, nor could one find anything strange in my coming back. If I had had to go home in the first, or even in the second year, there would surely have been cries of 'I told you so!' But now the time factor puts that out of question altogether. Not that I want a bit to go home; I am enjoying myself thoroughly and am glad to be able to go on as long as there is work here to be done. I should have hated to be ill during the first or even the second year. But even if the fact of this malaria leaked out now, it would not be the sort of sensation which it would have been in the first year. To safeguard you from ever thinking that I am hiding something from you, I declare that this is the one point on which I would be really scrupulous. Let this afford you consolation. If I thought the work was suffering from my state of health, much as I enjoy doing it, I would not hesitate a moment in coming home. Or even, I would get a job out here, work

for the Legion locally, and give up the wider extension work. Now do not think I have taken up anything you have said as suggesting such a thing. I know too how 'touchy' you are on the score of my health; how apprehensive of a collapse in regard to which I would not have given warning in time. Out here, as elsewhere, the work is too important to be held up by personal considerations. With the present trend of things all over the world, I would regard — as you do, I am sure — the time factor as being decisive. Things are happening so quickly everywhere, and always against the Church. So much for health. What a subject for a Christmas Eve letter!'

And she concludes:

'Christmas time and all, I would not willingly change places with anyone at home this minute. One gets great happiness in the work.'

Better than an elaborate analysis, this letter reveals Edel's delicacy and tact. She speaks of her health for the sole purpose of preventing others from being anxious or feeling remorse at having sent her to Africa. The reasons she gives show how entirely she effaces herself in the interests of her mission. She intends to make way for another the moment her health become an impediment. But so long as God does not ask this sacrifice of her, she rejoices — more than ever on this Christmas night — at being allowed to hasten the spiritual birth of Jesus in the land of Africa. Christmas Eve is full of intense and dear memories of home and friends; but she would not exchange the joy of voluntary exile for any human happiness.

The letter shows, too, her extreme fear of alarming Dublin in regard to her health. Fr Reidy, a missionary, tells of the extraordinary precautions she would take to avoid inconvenient publicity. One day, he recalls, she ran a high temperature, but determined not to call attention to her condition by going to bed, she took the evening train for Nairobi, more than 300 miles away. In order to avoid indiscreet curiosity, she telephoned to two friends in Nairobi to meet her at an intermediate station and to drive her to a convent some 40 miles from Nairobi. She was so delighted at having escaped meeting anybody who would spread the news of her illness that she forgot how very ill she was! The same witness tells also of Edel's mischievous glee when shortly after this bout of fever, her photograph appeared

1. Probably addressed to the Legion of Mary headquarters in Dublin, to Jack Nagle, anchor man, and to Frank Duff, the founder of the organization.
2. Title given to active member of the Legion of Mary.

in *Maria Legionis*.[3] It was a snapshot in which she appeared to be in excellent health and she was delighted at the favourable impression it was sure to produce.

Fortunately, this time again, the attack of malaria passed off. At once Edel took up where she left off. At the end of January, 1939, she visited the Mission of Nyenga. Here the primitive simplicity of the inhabitants provided certain obstacles, though they were not lacking in goodwill and generosity. 'They have seven women members,' she writes, 'none of whom can read or write. These were being taught the prayers, and it took the majority of them nearly four months to learn the Catena.'[4]

There were other difficulties besides those arising from defective memories; there were unready pens. It was not simple to find a secretary. The easy way out would be to confide this task to the Spiritual Director. But the Legion distrusts easy ways and will not compromise on the functions of officers. The Legion is a lay association and must remain such. Responsibility has an educative value, it must not be measured out in pretty doses. If an increased output of energy, imagination and tenacity is needed for the putting of the Legionary principles into practice, then that extra output must be forthcoming.

In one of the Mission stations (Soroti Mission), Edel had another hard problem to solve:

'It is,' she wrote, 'the language question. The Praesidium[5] is Teso. There is one member, a Muganda, who knows English, Luganda and Swahili, and who can take notes perfectly. But if he writes the Minutes in any one of these languages, there will be members who will not understand. Now we have found a Mu-teso who can make a fair shot at note-taking in Teso, and he has a knowledge of Swahili. So we have two secretaries. The better one takes the notes in English, as given to him by his Teso partner, and then helps him to get it down properly in Teso during the week. This will at any rate give them the sense of responsibility for the Minutes (Feb. 15 1939).'

In the same letter, Edel announced that she was going to visit the Prefecture of Meru, under the care of the Italian Consolata Fathers, and that she would spend another fortnight in the Vicariate of Kisumu. In the Vicariate of Meru, under Bishop Nepote, the Legion had started some months before, without any help from Edel. It was important that she should get in touch with them to ensure that from the first every step would be in conformity with the rules. The Italian Fathers possessed only an English *Handbook*.[6] This situation drew her to go to Meru in preference to Mauritius. An additional reason led her to delay a little longer the visit to Mauritius promised to Mgr. Leen. Dublin had just announced that the French translation of the *Handbook* was in the press. The *Handbook* would be indispensable for her work in Mauritius; so she decided to defer the visit to Mauritius for a few months so that she would come to the island armed with French *Handbooks*.

The visit to Meru was free from difficulty. Before she came, the Missionaries had worked out for her an itinerary which took in the nine more accessible Missions. Departing, her task finished, Edel left six Praesidia in full operation.

From the moment that she was put in possession of 'Rolls Royce', her capacity to move about was greatly increased. Ever after, she continued full of praises for her car. Now she gives us a glimpse of her new driver.

'My driver,' she writes on September 26, 1939, 'recently turned out in immaculate white trousers and shirt, with a belt of zebra skin. But on the front of his shirt, he had written his name, Anselmo, in capital letters with a copying-ink pencil. What will happen when it goes to the wash remains to be seen.'

Meanwhile the state of the roads was a veritable nightmare to her and to Anselmo; she reports seven punctures in two days:

'I have had to survive a lot of leg-pulling here at the Mission Headquarters on my return from a recent trip. I was doing some Mission contacting with some odd jobs en route. Also I brought a C.S.Sp. [Congregation of Holy Ghost] Brother back from one Mission. I had not noticed that my front tyre was pretty worn. The

---

3. The in-house printed journal of the world-wide Legion of Mary.
4. Prayer recited by members of Legion of Mary.
5. Local group of Legion of Mary. Frank Duff gave Latin titles to his organization and its functions.

6. Frank Duff wrote a manual for the members of the Legion of Mary, an important source book for lay-spirituality.

tube burst. We put in another which held for a few miles. To cut a long story short, seven punctures were mended by the Brother and the driver during our two days on the road! The Brother took a day off when he got back here — the Bishop said he had well earned it!'

There is a special providence looking after motorists, as everybody knows. Edel was to have practical experience of the fact a few months later!

'The Legion car,' she writes, 'has had another adventure that may amuse you. We had only done about 11 miles of the road to Dar-es-Salaam, when three leaves of the front spring snapped. Such had never happened before, and my first thought was that we were caught in the mud. The driver put forth all his strength, and by using a log as a lever we succeeded in lifting the car. Next we had to bind the broken spring with cord, the branch of a tree serving as a splint. Then we started off, moving very slowly in case of further accident. It was nearly 7.30 p.m. when we arrived, which means that it was pitch dark. However I found out Father McCarthy's flat and he took me to the Mission house and the Bishop said: "I will see to that in the morning for you. I know a bit about cars." Next morning at 8 a.m., the Bishop appeared in overalls in the Mission garage, and from that till lunch he worked at the car. Twice I went in, but he was on the ground underneath it, so I left him in peace. That evening at 6 p.m. the job was finished, and he had also put clamps to keep the battery more firmly in place. He had to get one new leaf and he moulded two other leaves to fit. It seems he is a real artist with regard to cars, and takes pleasure in putting them in order. It is his way of relaxing. I went over next day to see him and to thank him, but he made nothing of it, just as if it were all in the day's work. If it was up country or out in the bush, I would not mind, but there are lots of garages in Dar-es-Salaam, and he could easily have let me take it to one of them. It seemed so funny to land into a place — and to see the Bishop spend every minute of the next day under your car repairing it!'

This event was more than sufficient to make Edel's 'Rolls Royce' famous. It was the subject of jokes in every Mission station, and Edel herself joined heartily in the fun.

STANISLAUS KENNEDY

(1939–   )

from:
SPIRITUAL JOURNEYS (1997)

[Stanislaus Kennedy, Religious Sister of Charity, has been at the cutting edge of justice and issues of structural poverty for the homeless and poor over several decades. In this essay, published in *Spiritual Journeys* (Dublin: Veritas, 1997), pp. 85–90, she traces the early impulses that influenced her. Her feminist consciousness was awakened during the closing decades of the twentieth century as she and a group of women in Dublin developed the shape and character of Focus Point Ireland (1994–   ), a dynamic agency concerned with the needs of Dublin's deprived citizens.]

MOMENTS OF GRACE

I was born Treasa Kennedy during the Second World War on the Dingle Peninsula, between Holy Mount Brandon and the Atlantic Ocean. I was one of five children and my childhood was a traditional one, lived among fishermen and farmers, the caretakers of a peasant tradition. In my early childhood, there was story-telling and card-playing in place of radio, cinema, television. It was a life of mystery, beauty and simplicity. The pattern of the day, the night, the year, and even life itself was lived unselfconsciously in the presence of God. The life of the people was deeply incarnational, whether saving the hay, telling the time from the sun and the tide, catching trout and salmon, going to stations, wakes, funerals, marriages, walking under hedges dripping fuchsia — which we called 'deora Dé' (God's tears) — cutting and footing the turf or bringing tea to the fields or the bog. But it was not all joy. We also knew hardship through the Depression and the War, with its food rationing. Hard times drove many from their land. But we were a close and neighbourly community. As the local writer Peig Sayers (whom I knew) put it:

> We all helped each other, living in the shelter of each other. Everything that was coming dark upon us we would disclose . . . Friendship is the fast root in my heart; it is like a white rose in the wilderness.

I went to Secondary school in Dingle, three miles away. Heading out the gate each day for school on my bike, the child was stealing out to me. It was a new world, dominated by nuns where everything was correct and proper, and one was expected to be polite, in place and on time. I did well at school. I enjoyed the camaraderie of my friends, and I was often involved in mischief and escapades. But I was lonely at times too, lonely, unhappy, rebellious, moody.

As I grew up, I read that there were children who were neglected and poor in the bigger towns and cities, and I wanted to help them, but I didn't know how to go about it. (There were no training courses in social work in those days.) Then I heard of nuns in Dublin who worked with the poor. I did not particularly want to be a nun, but it seemed to be the only way that I could work directly with the poor. That was how I stumbled upon the Sisters of Charity. What I didn't realise was that this was God's way of calling me to walk with him and with the poor.

A pre-Vatican II noviceship of rules, regulations, prayers and practices followed. It came as a shock to my youthful exuberance, but the companionship of the other novices, the deep spirituality of those who guided us, the serenity of some of the older sisters, the deep respect in which the sisters held the poor, and the idea that I would soon be working with the poor, in whom God resided in a special way, kept me going. Moments of grace.

After my noviceship, I went to work in a training school, laundry and youth club, at Stanhope Street Convent in Dublin, in the early 1960s. It was a new experience, sharing the hardship and humour of the poor of Dublin.

Then my life took an unexpected turn. A young bishop was appointed to the Diocese of Ossory, in Kilkenny. He was a man who had a great love for the poor, and he invited the Sisters of Charity to help him to establish social services in Kilkenny. This was the sort of work I was longing to do, but, as it happened, it wasn't I who made the decision. I was sent to join him. Moments of grace.

Bishop Birch was already being seen as different, a man ahead of his time. Treading new ground, he set out to build a domestic Church, where everyone was gift, bishop and clergy were servants of the people of God, and the poor and the marginalised were at the centre. Inspired by the bishop, it was the ideal for which I also worked, prayed, struggled and suffered for nearly two decades in Kilkenny, interrupted only by my undergraduate and postgraduate studies.

Together we were always discovering new ideas, new ways, new images, new visions, new needs, new services, new experiments. The young and the old, the rich and the poor, the able and the disabled, the sick and the well, the learned and the unlearned, the homed and the unhomed all had a place and a gift. Bringing the periphery into the centre, creating services, activities and communities, touching the hearts of the rich and poor alike, consoling the poor and disquieting the rich with the good news of the Gospel, we set out to build a new model of Church, vibrant, exciting, always changing, renewing, seeking, listening, searching, reading, waiting, speaking, campaigning, never satisfied. We invited new ideas, thoughts and people from all over the globe. Poets, artists, prophets and saints moved in and out of Kilkenny, many of them friends for life. Moments of grace.

National conferences on poverty and national programmes to combat poverty were all part of the 1970s. I was learning that we had to suffer with and for the poor. Living with insecurity and ambiguity, being understood and being mis-understood were part and parcel of living and working with the poor.

From Peter Birch's example, I learned to have a great sense of myself and a great sense of God. I learned to know where I began and where I left off, what area of myself I could yield to the encroachment of my enemies and what to the encroachment of those I loved. I learned to draw my inspiration from the Gospels and from my time alone, from nature and from music, literature and all forms of art, and from loving relationships with men and women.

Through Peter Birch, I met people I might never have met, dreamt dreams I might never have dreamt, and discovered gifts and talents in myself and others I might never have dared to. Above all I discovered the great gift and beauty those people who have been rejected by society can bring us if we can only stop and look, see and receive, and that the greatest temptation was not to look and see and act. Bishop Birch helped me to realise that what makes the Christian life worth living is a risky business, and that, despite the risks, we are all God's work of art. From him I learned that bit by bit, step by step, we become that work of art, if we allow our hearts to open and to unfold. Other seeds were being planted which would later come to fruition for me.

Bishop Birch's sudden and untimely death in 1981 came like a bolt from the blue. My soul was filled with a grief and a sorrow that I had never known before. His death seemed unbearable for a time. As well as a dear friend, I had lost the person who was the source of my inspiration. But sad though my loss was at the time, it was a beginning as well as an ending, the beginning of a new phase of life. I had many friends to comfort me, but I knew I had to discover for myself where God was drawing me. Moments of grace.

Later that year, Jean Vanier, founder of L'Arche,[1] whom I had met through Peter Birch some years earlier, came to visit, and with his visit the clouds began to lift. I had always been influenced by Jean's work and his commitment, but now he became my soul-guide and my inspiration. Living the Gospel in the L'Arche fraternity, committed totally to the restoration of a broken universe and acknowledging the special place of handicapped people in that restoration, he sustained, encouraged, inspired and guided me in the way of God's love, as my spiritual director and through the annual eight-day

retreats that he led, to find my strength in my weaknesses in the bright and dark days and years of the 1980s and 1990s. Moments of grace.

I left Kilkenny and the people I loved for Dublin in 1983, in sadness and sorrow, but with trust in God, not knowing where I was being led or drawn. Attending the general chapter of the Sisters of Charity that summer opened new windows of hope. Reflecting on the spirit of Mary Aikenhead, founder of the religious Sisters of Charity, we challenged each other again to listen to the cry of the poor and break the walls of prejudice and fear that protect our security and limit our vision.

By October of that year I was a senior research fellow at University College Dublin, with eight research assistants, among them Rachel Collier. We set out, using a variety of research methods, to discover more about homeless women in Dublin — who they were, where they were, and what they thought about their situation. Rachel took the risk of forfeiting a promising career in journalism and voluntarily embarked on this mission without knowing where it would lead us, and still works closely with me. We discovered the hidden homeless — women who were without homes and hidden away — and we challenged the popular belief that there were few if any homeless women in Dublin.

Inspired by the women and with a donation of £5,000 from the Religious Sisters of Charity, Rachel and I rented the top floor of an inner-city building. We spent the following year with eight young women who had been homeless and whom we had met during the previous year's research. It was a year of exploring, examining, understanding and discovering the deeper meaning of being out of home. Eating, listening, reading, writing, crying, and laughing, we shared our songs, poems, plays, joys and sorrows, hopes and fears, pains and struggles, the secrets of our souls. I came to realise in a deeper way that everyone who had been deeply hurt has the right to be sure that they are loved, that we all need a comforting presence to bring peace, hope and love, and that we all need and have a right to a place called home. During that year I learned in a very special way the wisdom of the excluded people, the rejected people, the women out of home, and I learned to let that wisdom guide me in a way I knew not . . .

1. Jean Vanier, a Catholic layman, is the founder of the L'Arche community for people with mental disabilities, which started in France after the Second World War and has over a hundred communities world-wide.

During that year a new movement was being conceived, almost without our knowing it. As we set about identifying a name for the new organisation, I knew that I too needed a 'focus', a groundedness. As we named the values that would underpin 'Focus Point', I too, with the women, named hospitality, safety, security, structure, compassion, equality, respect and dignity. We discovered how alike we all were in our common humanity, our giftedness, the frailty at the root of our creaturehood. That year had a profound effect on my life. I was helped to move into a sense of deep gratitude to and reverence for these women for all they taught me about myself, about humanity and about society, and gratitude to God for drawing me close to them and to him through them.

RONIT LENTIN

(1944–   )

from:
'WHERE DID THE JOURNEY BEGIN?' (1987)

[In this essay Ronit Lentin explores her spiritual journey through the lives of her ancestral women folk across four generations. Her meditation reflects her years of research into her family roots in central Europe and her ongoing research into the daughters of Holocaust survivors. Having lived in Ireland since 1969, she has been engaged in teaching and developing the theory and practice of feminist studies. She brings her feminist insight to bear on her Jewish identity. The essay appeared in *Womanspirit*, Journal of Irish Feminist Spirituality (autumn 1987), pp. 4–5.]

Where did the journey begin? Did it begin in 1984, standing at the edge of a small village cemetery in Vatra Dornei, mother's birthplace in Northern Romania, reading a tomb stone dedicated to the soap made from Jewish corpses?

Did it begin a few days earlier as the night train sped north from Bucharest, passing name places of towns where grandmother's, grandfather's, father's and mother's lives began?

Or did it begin in Czernowitz, today the Ukranian city of Chernovtsy, when I stood in the rococo style railway station, where mother and her parents bid goodbye to 1941 Europe on their way to Palestine?

Did it perhaps begin much earlier, going with grandfather Yossl to the synagogue yard in Tel Aviv to boil silver before Passover to make it kosher for that week when Jews are only allowed to eat unleavened bread? Or when, during my school years, Judaism and Zionism were so closely intertwined, that you could not separate religion from secularity, as holidays were celebrated nationally, with the deeply religious Day of Atonement as prominently marked as the secular celebration of Independence Day?

Or did it begin when I came to Ireland and became part of a religious minority? A new experience, which sharpened my sense of being Jewish and sent me in search of formal religion, a search which left me longing for the holiness of my beloved, forsaken Jerusalem, where simply to be in the gold evening light, is to experience the proximity to Shekhina, a Hebrew word in the female form, meaning divine presence.

Where did the journey begin?

There is much distress linking post-Holocaust Jewry. Like Isaac Deutscher,[1] I believe I am a Jew not because I am religious — I am not a practising Jew. Nor because I am a nationalist — I consider myself an internationalist. But because of the shared fate with all other Jews, and the sense of the tragedy linking all Jews.

The journey began there. Perhaps during my final year at school, when the Eichmann trial[2] was broadcast on radio and I was brought face to

1. Isaac Deutscher (1907–67), a Jewish Marxist, who wrote: 'I am a Jew by force of my unconditional solidarity with the persecuted and exterminated. I am a Jew because I feel the Jewish tragedy as my own tragedy.' From 'Who is a Jew?', in *The Non-Jewish Jew and Other Essays* (Oxford: Oxford University Press, 1968), p. 51.
2. In 1961 the state of Israel prosecuted Adolf Eichmann, chief, under Reinhard Heydrich and Heinrich Himmler, of the Jewish Affairs Bureau of the SS, executive arm of the Nazi Final Solution.

face with what happened. And the constant thought — it could have been me: if it was me, would I have survived?

That year was perhaps the first time when I realised that being Israeli did not exclude being Jewish, as our parents, who had just escaped the burning bush, wanted us to believe. 'I want you never to experience anti-semitism,' father said. He did not figure on my living in Ireland, where anti-semitism is deeply rooted in most Catholics, particularly those who have not worked out their anti-semitic feelings.

So I was Jewish. But it took many years to know I was. And many more to figure a space where I could be a Jewish woman, free of the exclusively male rituals, free of format rituals altogether, free of having to pray to 'our father, our king' because I could not get beyond the punitive, vengeful, yet all-forgiving god, who forgives and loves his people only and pours out his wrath upon all other nations, who do not know him.

But I digress. I was Jewish. Yet not knowing how to pray, not observing the 613 dos and don'ts which include praying every morning thanking god for having made me as he wished (while men thank him for not having made them a woman).

I was Jewish. Yet I rarely participated in communal rituals, rarely prayed. Not praying. Not praying. Not praying.

Why do I stress it? Is it because of the male language so many Jewish feminists rage against? Has it really ever bothered me? Or is it simply that for me, being Jewish has always been a completely secular experience?

I don't know where that journey began. I have always been journeying to the centre of what it means to be Jewish. It's hard to define the station of that night journey to the centre. But one thing has come clear to me over the last few years: I have always been journeying to become the women who made me.

I am Yetti, my emaciated great grandmother, who, at seventy, say, shrunken, long days on the veranda, asking every hour what time it was. Having lost her sense of time after long years in Transnistria, a camp in Northern Romania, where Jews were not exterminated, but where hunger, cold, typhoid and hard labour killed eighty per cent of all Jewish exiled there during the war.

I am Charlotte, my beautiful maternal grand-mother, who left in time, leaving her own mother behind, her mother being a member of the local bourgeoisie who refused to leave, believing that things could only improve. Charlotte, who cried in her sleep, never absolving herself of the guilt of having saved her skin and leaving her parents in the hell from which her father was not to return. Charlotte, who, once a lady of the manor, spent the rest of her life in a two-roomed apartment in the harsh climate of Tel Aviv, seeing Yossl, her gentle husband, slowly breaking his heart in Israel, the land of his dreams, which could not sustain him. Charlotte, who reigned supreme over her family, who slowly found their way to Israel, after years at the camp and of journeying laboriously from deserted railway station to deserted railway station.

(I cry as I write this. For them and for me, knowing all the time I could have been them. I was them.)

I am Rebecca, my great aunt, limping, shapeless, who lost her husband and her baby daughter in the camp, and who lives alone in Tel Aviv, her only son having preferred the fleshpots of Germany, heavy, ill, dreaming of better days.

I am Bertha, my paternal grandmother, who, at 45, was ashamed to discover that she was carrying my father. Bertha, who, having followed her scholarly, but utterly unworldly husband to the dusty Jerusalem of the mid-twenties, was to spend her last years shunted from daughter-in-law to daughter-in-law, penniless, her only asset a carved silver candlestick, which now stands in my Dublin living-room, a million miles from her dreams.

And I am Lia, my golden-haired mother, still facing day bravely in Haifa, my home town, strong, tight-lipped, brave Lia, who now cried in her sleep too. Calling Charlotte? Calling Miki, my father? Calling me, who is too far to give her enough time to let herself go and release the guilt, the unspent memories?

There is much more. There is my husband's family, refugees from Lithuanian pogroms, left in Ireland by greedy ship masters, who promised that Cobh harbour was their destination, America.[3]

---

3. Most of Ireland's Jews arrived from Lithuania in the 1880s. They embarked liners destined for America but were told, at Cobh, that this was their destination. One of them was Kalman, whose original name we are not sure of, and who changed his name to Lentin.

There is so much more in that sense of shared fate, those stations in the endless journey.

But as I cry for the women who made me, I keep thinking of the command that 'in every generation, a Jew must regard himself as having personally got out of Egypt, of the house of bondage', which we say every year on Passover around a laden family table, re-telling the story of the Exodus from Egypt. This is the other side of the distress coin, the other thing linking all Jews: liberation, the journey to the centre, the knowledge that I, and my daughter Alana, and my son Miki, are part of a whole, part of a nation striving together for freedom.

Part of that freedom is making my own boundaries. 'Every Jew makes his own Sabbath,' grandfather Yossl used to say, meaning that no Jew can justifiably claim to fulfil all 613 edicts. One can only strive. My boundaries have been set with the knowledge that a religion which does not allow me to lead, which excludes me from ritual domestic and communal, that speaks for me in an aggressive, male language, is not for me.

Yet, and this is always difficult to explain to Jew and non-Jew alike, I am completely Jewish, completely part of that journey to the centre, completely partner to seeing myself personally going forth from Egypt, from the house of bondage, every minute of every day.

Where does the journey begin? It begins every day, every morning. Every day, without lighting memorial candles as we are bound to do for dead parents, I think of Miki, my father, of grandmother Charlotte. Every day, without words, I think about 'there', about that soap tombstone in Vatra Dornei.

Every day as I go about my business, write, attend meetings, answer the telephone, prepare meals, shop, clean, I think about 'there'. Every day is a station in my journey to be freed from the house of bondage, from my personal Egypt.

Every day as I get closer into line with my women, I negate that vengeful, aggressive male deity. Every day I get closer to Shekhina,[4] that ever-present female divinity, to whom I don't have to pray because she knows I am journeying to her centre. Because she knows I am on my way.

4. From the Hebrew verb 'to dwell', Old Testament, meaning 'God dwells'; later use, 'the temple of God'.

MAURA 'SOSHIN' O'HALLORAN

(1955–82)

from:
PURE HEART, ENLIGHTENED MIND: THE ZEN JOURNAL AND LETTERS OF AN IRISH WOMAN IN JAPAN (1994)

[The Zen journal and letters of Maura O'Halloran were prepared for publication by her mother, Ruth O'Halloran, after a bus accident ended Maura's life at the age of twenty-seven. Though Maura never intended her journals to be published, her writings have been compared to the autobiography of Thérèse of Lisieux, the Roman Catholic Carmelite saint who also died in her twenties. Determined to become a Zen monk in Japan, O'Halloran left Ireland after her studies and underwent a three-year course in Zen training in Tokyo and Iwate in northern Japan, being given the Buddhist name of Soshin-san. In the following extracts the reader is admitted to O'Halloran's inner thoughts about her experience of studying Zen in a Japanese Buddhist monastery.]

Toshoji, Tokyo

February 21, 1980
Yesterday I bought books. I read about mu, read that mu is not a mantra, don't just repeat mu but struggle with What is mu? I went upstairs to zendo mu. I am mu. I am nothing, nothing nothingness. I do not exist (though I do). But nothing, absolutely nothing. Something trembled near my eyes. I wept, lay down on the tatami[1] and wept huge, heaving tears. I was nothing, my dreams my hopes, my conceits were nothing. I cried funeral tears. I was at my own funeral and

1. A mat.

no one else had come. I was crying and crying and crying and . . .

Downstairs, it was time to make toast. Tetsuro-san asked what was wrong. I am nothing, and it's very hard and very sad and tears pricked. 'Honto? You are near enlightenment. You must go to dokusan.'[2] I know I'm not near enlightenment but I would like to go to dokusan. I do mu, a deep total mu. Afterwards my vocal cords hurt. Roshi[3] says keep with mu 'til *sesshin/an intensive week of zazen/*and then I will attain enlightenment. (As for that 'will' — try 'may'.)

After dinner, Roshi says, 'Put an ad in the paper for a new cook.' He doesn't like my cooking. The fish was too hard (two weeks old, I scraped off the mould), the salad too hearty. It was true. I wasn't put out. It was true. Though I liked cooking, wished it had been good. I felt too drained to really react, to be really hurt. After all the tears, I had heard the shock of Tekkan-san's possible dismissal by the people of Morioka. There seemed to be an enormous web of conflicting saying and thinking. Morioka people had seemed so warm, generous, and appreciative of Tekkan-san, yet the dear little old ladies deftly stabbed him through the heart. Roshi dismisses us; the others say they're always hungry but grumble about too much food. I am tired, little sleep, and I am nothing — exhausted, spent. And Jiko-san says, 'You are too simple and too honest.' And for that time he is right. I can scarcely even feel bewildered, only wash the dishes and go to bed.

You must struggle with a koan,[4] fight with it and for it. My energy in mu is renewed asking. What is it? Getting up in the morning is one of the hardest things for me. So I will get up even earlier and go to the hondo[5] and sit.

2. Interview with one's teacher about one's practice.
3. Her teacher, Master Roshi.
4. A challenging bit of narrative that points to ultimate truth.
5. Meditation corner.

February 22 [1980]
    I was not born
    will not die
    for I am
    nothing
    but please do not
    stand on my
    toe.

If mu is mind, consciousness, it is nothing. I am always changing — not a thing. I am not the same person as ten years ago, or a moment ago, yet I am. But then where is I? A fish has the consciousness of a fish. I have the consciousness of a twentieth-century woman and no one before has had my consciousness. Where is rebirth? Consciousness changes. If reborn as a fish, I am a fish, not Maura, but a fish. Consciousness changes. Action and reaction, like a seal stamped on sand. Nothing is transferred, but the processes continue. Energy cannot be created or destroyed, only transformed. What is dead, and what is alive? He said, first and last thoughts. Makes sense. Plants and animals think. Has a stone consciousness? Is it conscious? If consciousness is energy, all form is, not has, consciousness. If we all are not havemind . . . huh? . . . what? . . . hmmm. Are things *mu/nothing/* and *u/something/*? Waves on the ocean are separate but the same. When the wave subsides it doesn't disappear, cease to exist, but does. It is no longer the wave but the ocean which is what it was anyway. Isn't that death? And mu is u and Joshu can say the dog has no Buddha nature.

Dinner was almost a fiasco. Jiko-san, at the last moment, added sauce and soothed my laments.

Does the first thought mean the beginning of a new life because thought is separation?

Roshi asked Jiko-san to place the ad [for a new cook]. He keeps changing his mind. He apologized and asked us to cook for a while, saying it's good to have cultivators in *tenzo* [*kitchen, or cook*], then changes. Jiko and I were sitting eating the brown rice glue that we have dubbed jiko-mochi and that I love, I saying the only thing I like more that tenzo is the garden. I didn't look forward to the hours of dusting the clean altars I had dusted the day before. Then Tessan-san tells me my new job will be the garden. I can't believe it; I'm overjoyed.

March 7 [1980]
The day before yesterday some psychologists came to test our skin potential, resistance, and breathing during meditation. Jiko was first. He came downstairs and told me how twice during meditation he had left his body and the researchers will be very surprised. I thought about my own meditations, how they are often so

sloppy. In the afternoon I went up. A wire from my ear, two around my waist and five in my left arm. I really felt like a laboratory rat. I might have been peevish (as I was a bit for the news interviewer), this 'probing a freak' bit, but the researcher does zazen[1] himself so I wanted to cooperate. My meditation was deep. I was one with everyone and everything, including them. I felt strong love for them. At one stage I was their machine, and its rotations were my heartbeat. At the beginning and end we just sat naturally. They rechecked the apparatus and kept telling me to just be at ease. I thought I must be nervous and it was showing up.

At the end they came over, extremely excited. '*Subarashii, subarashii* [*splendid, splendid*].' 'This is very rare data,' they said. 'We have tested many monks, 40–60 but this is very rare ... Your natural state is thirteen breaths a minute and in meditation three or four a minute; normally a good meditation is three to five.' They want to test me again next week. I was very pleased, and it was hard for me not to tell the others everything they said, but I don't want the thing to seem competitive. I needed encouragement and it came. However, the things they are measuring are only by-products; they have nothing to do with my understanding, and it is that I want.

I have been meditating now consistently for three months. (They couldn't believe that —

thought it must be a year and three months.) I can perceive subtle changes. My posture is different, composure better. I'm more quiet. I remember finding Sean's silences unbearable and needed constant chatter and once had to stop myself from begging him to talk about just anything. I'm no longer compulsive in eating and drinking. If I do something, I like to do it properly, and I care less about others' opinions of me. I can even serve a bad dinner, feel sorry that it was bad, but not be upset to the core and watching each expression. I'm much better disciplined, but I don't know how permanent any of these changes are. So I am a bit afraid to go back to the 'real world'.

Mum sent a letter saying she was sad I had given up the idea of a Ph.D. at the Sorbonne (which of course I haven't) and appealing to me to help her sell her Dublin house in the summer. But I am finally doing what I have wanted and needed to do all my life and am afraid to break. I consider Buddhism my 'religion', if it can be called that. On the other hand, I do want to continue with my outside life at some stage and finish the koans.[2] So maybe I should find a suitable temple and get on with it, as I'll have to break from here sooner or later. I love, respect and trust Roshi completely, yet I shouldn't be attached even to him.

1. Sitting meditation.

2. Many koans have been handed down from teachers in early Chinese Zen Buddhist periods.

GINNIE KENNERLEY

(1950?–   )

from:
PRE-ORDINATION SERMON
1991

[Ginnie Kennerley, a journalist, was the first woman to be ordained to the priesthood of the Church of Ireland, 21 October 1991, in Christchurch Cathedral Dublin. In this sermon delivered four days before her ordination in the chapel of the Church of Ireland Theological College, where she taught theology, she probes the notion of change in the context of the ordination of women. The original is in the archives of the Church of Ireland Theological College, Braemor Road, Dublin.]

Change is something that human beings don't like very much. Our brains — so incredibly complex that no computer could ever approach their sensitivity and potential — nonetheless develop in such a way that habits of thought and action are formed which become increasingly hard to change as we grow older.

Yet as Christians we are constantly called to change: to self-knowledge, repentance, and transformation. Like Abraham, we are called to walk by faith towards a promised land whose reality we can barely glimpse, leaving old ways and old captivities behind, risking past security for future fulfilment. And after responding to our first call, like Abraham and his father Terah, like the children of Israel in the wilderness, we are always liable to decide to settle down prematurely.

We are made in such a way that the familiar is what we feel comfortable with — which is just as well sometimes. But we are made also with a desire to uncover the truth — and more, fuller truth — and with a thirst for the transcendent, for the absolute good and fulfilment which lies beyond our sight. These two tendencies in us — will always be in tension within us. That is how God has made us. It may make life difficult, but at least it isn't dull!

Some of us can get very impatient with those who refuse the new, who cannot or will not accept new insights or adopt new ways of doing things which we consider are bringing the church closer to where God wants us to be at this time. Others get very distressed in the face of change. Our liturgical renewal over the past decades has shown us this; now, the ordination of women to the priesthood is causing more difficulty between those in favour of reform and those who consider that what was right for previous generations must be right for us, that the church does not need to evolve in response to the world we live in now — at least in this regard.

It's not a very comfortable position I find myself in — in the middle of the debate! But it helps to remember that fact about change and the human brain. It helps because it makes the issue less personal; makes us aware that every change, every call to conversion, will be harder for some of us than for others, through no fault of our own.

Yet we know we are called to transformation; that the reformed church is constantly in need of reform. We must always be on the alert for our tendency to get bogged down in the imperfect place in which we feel comfortable.

Hans Kung,[1] when he was here a few years ago, pointed out in a masterly lecture in Trinity[2] that Christianity has developed from New Testament times not in a smooth line of progress but through a series of troublesome paradigm shifts — times which caused dissension and difficulty precisely because many people were not able to distinguish their traditionalism, their comfortable presuppositions, from the heart of Christian tradition — which lies, in the words of today's collect, in loving what God commands and desiring what he promised in and through Christ, fixing our attention not on the law but on the spirit, not on the foreground but on the horizon, on the coming dawn.

The paradigm shifts — or changes of thought pattern — which Kung referred to include those of the first century Christians' opening to the Gentiles, of the Constantinian period, of Aquinas and scholasticism, of the Reformation, and of the Enlightenment. Each of these shifts gave rise to its own traditionalism, its own handed down habits of thought.

It is not suggested that in these shifts the right was ever all on one side; rather that the excesses accompanying each new thought pattern fell away in time, so that its key insight, its truth, eventually became acceptable to a much broader consensus. For example the great insights of the Reformation have largely become accepted in Roman Catholic theology today.

Hans Kung, often considered an 'honorary Anglican', also points out that we are in the middle of a new paradigm shift today. Part of that shift lies in our developing openness to the insights of other great world religions; part of it in our new awareness of the value of Christian traditions other than our own; part in our acceptance of Christ's call to work for justice and peace in this world as well as a share of glory in the next. The part we're most concerned with at this time and place is the shift from patriarchal modes of thought and feeling, in which the male dominates and dictates, to a pattern in which male and female are equally valued and accepted, both within ourselves, within God, and in our varying roles in society.

1. Hans Kung (1928–), German Roman Catholic theologian, leading ecumenical writer and professor of theology at Tübingen University in Germany.
2. Trinity College Dublin.

The shift is easier for some of us than for others; so I hope we will all be able to keep loving and praying for each other through it, judging no one but ourselves and always keeping our hearts 'where true joys are to be found', striving to live always in the presence of God, remembering that none of us have arrived. We're all still, with the whole church universal, on pilgrimage towards the eternal city; by slightly different routes maybe, but aiming together for the same oneness in Christ Jesus.

We can only hope to progress towards our goal through God's grace. Only grace enables us to change habits of thought and action by suddenly showing us how radically inadequate they have been. Whatever our opinion on this particular issue, there will be areas of our life still in need of new vision and transformation. May God keep us together in mutual acceptance as fellow pilgrims on the way. That is my prayer for us all tonight. I hope you can share it with me.

And now to God, who through his power at work within us is able to do exceeding abundantly more than we ask or think, to God be the glory in the church and in Christ Jesus, now and always. Amen.

Biographies/Bibliographies

Lucy Olive Kingston

LIFE. Born 1 June 1892 at Ballinakill near Glenealy, County Wicklow, to Sarah Anne and Robert Lawrenson. Active in the suffrage movement in Dublin, and after 1914 in the Irish Women's Reform League. A frequent contributor to the *Irish Citizen*. Joined the Religious Society of Friends (Quakers) in the early 1920s and began a life-long involvement with the Women's International League for Peace and Freedom and later with the Council of the Irish Campaign for Nuclear Disarmament. A prominent member of the Irish Housewives' Association. She died on 23 December 1969 in Dr Eustace's Home at Hampstead in Dublin.

CHIEF WRITINGS. *Emerging from the Shadow: The Lives of Sarah Anne Lawrence and Lucy Olive Kingston*, ed. Daisy Lawrence Swanton (Dublin: Attic Press, 1994); Essays, *Irish Citizen*, 1912–22.

Violet Disney

LIFE. Violet Patience Disney was the second of four children born to Henry Evans Disney, solicitor, of Dublin and his wife and first cousin, Emma Packenham Evans. Born 15 April 1889, at age sixteen she became a pupil of Alexandra College and, later, a graduate of Trinity College Dublin in 1911. She was a schoolteacher, but it is not known where she taught. She lived for much of her life with her brother, Tom, at Rock Lodge, Killiney, County Dublin, and after 1949 until her death on 25 December 1972 at 63 Park Avenue, Sandymount. She did not marry and was believed to be the last member of the family in Ireland.

CHIEF WRITINGS. 'Why I am "Church of Ireland"', *The Bell*, vol. 8, no. 5 (1944), p. 379.

Leon-Joseph Suenens

LIFE. Born in Brussels, 16 July 1904; ordained a Catholic priest in 1927; appointed Auxiliary Bishop of Malines-Brussels, 1945; became Archbishop of Malines-Brussels and Primate of Belgium in 1961. Made a cardinal in 1962, he was chosen by Pope John XXIII to be the overall moderator of the Second Vatican Council, 1962–5. He died 6 May 1996.

CHIEF WRITINGS. *Theology of the Apostolate of the Legion of Mary* (Cork: Mercier Press, 1951); *Edel Quinn, Envoy of the Legion of Mary to Africa* (Dublin: Cahill, 1953).

Stanislaus Kennedy

LIFE. Born Treasa Kennedy in 1939 in Dingle, County Kerry, she was educated at Presentation Convent, Dingle, and at University College Dublin, taking her MA in social policy at Manchester University. She joined the Sisters of Charity in 1958 and in 1964 was sent to Kilkenny Social Services Group, working with the Catholic Bishop of the diocese, Peter Birch. She went to Dublin in 1983. Created Focus Point, an active agency for the deprived of Dublin city. Focus Housing followed in 1989 and the national research, development and public awareness project, Focus Ireland, in 1994. Chairperson of the National Committee to Combat Poverty, 1974–80. Member of Council of State to the President of Ireland, 1997.

CHIEF WRITINGS. *Who Should Care?* (Dublin: Veritas, 1981); *One Million Poor* (Dublin: Veritas, 1981); *But Where Can I Go?* (Dublin: Focus Point, 1985); *Spiritual Journeys* (Dublin: Veritas, 1997).

Ronit Lentin

LIFE. Born 25 October 1944 in Haifa, Israel, attended Reali School in Haifa and the Hebrew University in Jerusalem. She has lived in Ireland since 1969, completed her MA in philosophy in women's studies in 1991, and has completed a doctorate in sociology/women's studies in Trinity College Dublin. She has worked as a freelance writer, published novels in Hebrew and English, and has had plays broadcast by Israeli and Irish radio. Co-ordinator of ethnic studies in TCD 1999–   . Married to Louis Lentin, a television and theatre producer; they have two children.

CHIEF WRITINGS. Novels: *Stone of Claims* (Tel Aviv: Simon Kria, 1975); *Like a Blondman* (Tel Aviv: Somon Dria, 1977); *Tea with Mrs Klein* (Dublin: Attic Press, 1989; Pittsburgh: Cleis Press, 1990). Reference: *Who is Minding the Children?* co-authored with Geraldine Niland (Dublin: Arlen House, 1981). Interviews: *Conversations with Palestinian Women* (Jerusalem: Mifras, 1982); *Songs on the Death of Children* (Dublin: Poolbeg Press, 1996).

Maura 'Soshin' O'Halloran

LIFE. Born 24 May 1955 in Boston, Massachussetts, the eldest of six children. Her father, Fionan, was a native of County Kerry; her mother a native of Maine. The family moved to Ireland when Maura was four and she was educated at Loreto convent schools in County Dublin. She attended Trinity College Dublin, where she completed joint degrees in mathematical economics/statistics and sociology. Marked by a rare spiritual insight as a student, she involved herself in volunteer social work with drug addicts and with the marginalized in Dublin. She intentionally lived a life of strict poverty. She travelled extensively as a student. Her interest in meditation led her to Japan, where she embarked on three years' training in Zen at Toshoji Temple in Tokyo and Kannonji Temple in Iwate Prefecture, Japan, 1979–82. She completed one thousand days of continuous Zen practice. Her daily practice included three hours sleeping in the gagen position and twenty hours of devotion to her studies, in order to attain salvation not only for herself but also for all people. On 7 August 1982 she was conferred an authorized certificate of 'Enlightenment Achieved'. On her way back to Ireland at Chiang Mai, Thailand, a traffic accident ended her life in 1982 at the age of twenty-seven. She was given the posthumous name of 'Great Enlightened Lady, of the same heart and mind as the Great Teacher Buddha', and there is a statue dedicated to her at Kannonji Temple.

CHIEF WRITINGS. *Pure Heart, Enlightened Mind: The Zen Journal and Letters of an Irish Woman in Japan*, Introduction by Ruth O'Halloran (Boston: Tuttle, 1994).

Ginnie Kennerley

LIFE. The Reverend Ginnie Kennerley was the first woman to be ordained a priest in the Church of Ireland, 21 October 1991. Previously she had worked as a journalist with the Independent Newspapers. She studied theology, taking a degree in Trinity College Dublin and her D.Min. in Princeton Theological Seminary. She lectured in the Church of Ireland Theological College in Dublin. After ordination, she was given the parish of Narraghmore and Timolin with Castledermot and Kinneagh in the Diocese of Dublin and Glendalough. In 1996 she was appointed canon in Christchurch Cathedral in Dublin.

CHIEF WRITINGS. Katherine V. Kennerley, 'The Use of Indigenous Sacred Literature and Theological Concepts in Christian Eucharistic Liturgy', *Studia Liturgica*, vol. 19, no. 2 (1982).

Poetry of the Spirit, 1900–95

The outstanding achievement of Irish women's poetry in the twentieth century is the emergence of authentic women's voices. Their nineteenth-century predecessors' devotional and mystical poems speak from female *personae*, and the voices tend to be depersonalized; often the speaker is a child or childlike (Ella Young, 'The Virgin Mother', Moira O'Neill, 'Grace for Light', Susan L. Mitchell, 'The Living Chalice' and 'The Descent of the Child'). The later twentieth-century poets reclaim distinct women's voices, mythological and historical, as well as the voices of ordinary women. The price of the authentic voice is often isolation: the self-imposed exile of a religious vocation like the Irish nun speaker in Eiléan Ní Chuilleanáin's 'J'ai mal à nos dents' or the woman outcast of Caitlín Maude's untitled poem that begins 'Idir an Paidrín Páirteach' ('Between the family rosary').

Other poems speak to the distinct spirituality of historical religious women. While these women do not speak for themselves in the canonical texts, poets turn to apocryphal legends or to imaginative reconstructions of their lives to give them voice. In two poems we hear the voices of women who have transgressed: Lot's wife who looks back and is turned to a pillar of salt and Mary Magdalene, the archetypal fallen woman. In Roz Cowman's poem Lot's wife is not punished for her curiosity — she escapes her patriarchal prophet husband, 'God's loud-speaker'; in 'St Mary Magdalene Preaching at Marseilles', Eiléan Ní Chuilleanáin draws on the tradition that the saint evangelized Provence with her own sermons, her own voice.

While Nuala Ní Dhomhnaill's 'Scéala' ('News') — one of her three Annunciation poems — begins with traditional iconography and ends with a parody of the familiar Roman Catholic prayer of Marian devotion 'The Memorare', the poem challenges conventional orthodoxy with its account of the Virgin who is impregnated by a Divine male lover, not by the holy spirit, and who leaves, perhaps forgetting the conceived child much as Zeus drops Leda 'from his indifferent beak'.

Some twentieth-century women poets, particularly those who write in the Irish language, have contributed to the literature of the lament. They have taken elements from the *caoine* and transformed them into contemporary elegies. Máire Mhac an tSaoi's vision of death as irrevocable loss is reflected in her elegy for the piper Séamus Ennis. In Irish fairy legend, a mortal piper is often abducted by the music-loving *sídhe*; however, in Mhac an tSaoi's lament, Ennis is taken from the supernatural as well as the mortal and natural worlds and together all keen the king of Irish pipers. A mixture of Celtic and classical allusions abounds: Donn, the old Irish god of death, spreads the word; Orpheus is evoked for the magical power of his music to transform stone, but Ennis, the mortal piper, is silenced (see Volume IV, pp. 1399–1420).

Caitlín Maude's untitled elegy for Bobby Sands, the Westminster MP for Fermanagh–South Tyrone who died on hunger strike in Long Kesh in 1981, reveals in its evocation of Sands, her sympathy and compassion for the outsider, which is informed by her own experience of being twice an outsider: as a woman and as a poet.

Twentieth-century women share with their menfolk a distinct Irish spirituality that often fused pre-Christian elements with Christian practices. A feature of Irish spirituality is an appreciation of the Divine in the natural world. Bríd Dáibhís's poem 'Wait for Me, God' expresses the orthodoxy of her faith in a celebration of nature: the coming of summer, which acknowledges aspects of both the Celtic festival of Bealtaine and the Marian May devotion with which it has been synchronized.

The Western tradition of the pilgrimage pre-dates the Christian era. A feature of early Irish Christianity from the seventh century was its appropriation of a number of Irish sites considered sacred. While twenty-first century Irish people in search of miracles are likely to travel to the Continent — to Lourdes and to Medjugorje — the medieval sick make the rounds of places associated with cures. Joan Sweetman's 'High Cross' offers spiritual rather than transforming powers of faith. Anne Le Marquand Hartigan's 'Path of Enduring Knowledge' sets her pilgrimage not in the Irish but in the Maori holy way.

Nuala Ní Dhomhnaill's 'Féar Suaithinseach' ('Miraculous Grass') offers a cure located in traditional spirituality for the anorexic young woman of the poem, suggesting, as she does in 'Turas Chaitríona', that there are illnesses of the spirit that remain outside the powers of conventional medicine.

The rounds at holy wells and other traditional sites are among the most enduring of popular devotions of rural Ireland. Moya Cannon celebrates the survival of an ancient sacred space in Irish folklife in 'Holy Well'. These devotions often include elements of Celtic survivals that existed alongside the orthodox Catholic rituals of the post-Famine period: benediction, the stations, retreats and Christmas cribs. Máire

Mhac an tSaoi's 'Oíche Nollag' ('Christmas Eve') tenderly describes the folk tradition of the Irish countryside — the candle in the window to welcome the Virgin and Child.

Roz Cowman's 'Medea Ireland' fuses paganism and religious and political experience to critique an Irish nationalism that demands the sacrifice of its youth.

Some twentieth-century women poets, writing in the metaphysical tradition of John Donne and George Herbert, construct metaphors that link the matters of ordinary life with the life of the spirit. Bríd Dáibhís's sheep pen is a metaphor for the enclosed life of a member of a religious community who waits with other Christians for healing in the waters of salvation. The speaker in Caitlín Maude's 'Caoineadh na Mná Tí' ('The Housewife's Keen') addresses a ruined house, a metaphor for all that suffer from neglect; Maude promises that peace and light await the poor in spirit. Joan Sweetman's 'Butterfly' sees in an electrical fault the unity of science and faith in the butterfly effect that acknowledges the significance of the individual act. Blanaid Salkeld's robust 'Leave us Religion' stands apart, theological in its argument, nostalgic in its mood, catching in its images the shadings of women's religious experience, and, like Paula Meehan's statue at Granard, speaks of the reality of many women's desire to give a human face to a harsh church. Ruth Hooley's 'The Fall' is an enigmatic meditation on the legacy of Christianity for women in late twentieth-century Ireland.

BLANAID SALKELD

(1880–1959)

from:
. . . THE ENGINE IS STILL RUNNING (1937)

[Salkeld calls for religion to be an individual rather than an institutional experience in this poem. Tethered to the church from birth with saints' names, tainted with the guilt of Original Sin, Salkeld charts an uncertain spiritual course, and her use of slant rhyme adds to the poem's density. Some references and use of words date the poem to the Catholic church before the Second Vatican Council. Philomena is no longer in the Calendar of Saints on the grounds of non-existence. Salkeld's description of the Church as 'gay' would be inappropriate in contemporary usage.]

Leave Us Religion

Leave us religion.
We have all been given
Saints' names. Whether you call Bernadette,[1]
Philomena,[2] or Margaret,[3]
And the rest —
Some pure unpressed
String echoes, under her palm,
Through an Angel's psalm,
In that still, calm,
Illuminated Region —
So we are linked up with Heaven.

Man, less significant
Than the ant
With its plan of campaign —
Thinks to sting Heaven with his pain.
'Pity!' we cry, and think to rive[4] and raid
Its golden forests with our pestilent storms:
Adulteries and deceits, the shifting forms
Of fear and hope — our follies, legion.
Yet we are starred from baptism . . . though the
        taints
Of infidelities divert us,
Patrons shall convert us.
We are all called after the saints;
We shall find, having left the years,
That untouched of tiredness, tears,
And flesh, Religion.

A spoiled child's insurrection —
Kept from the wild flutes of our lips' election,
Dumbed like a brute,
We would refute
Authority, and bite the mother's hands,
However, she understands.

Ignorant above day's indecision
And night's derision —
Leave us religion.
Trivial flower lifts sunward chin.
Higher than tree-tip, over dust and din.
The stony finger gold-thorned for sun-polish —
If hordes demolish,
Rebuild more loftily what signals higher
Than polar spire,
To sun-superior, light-surviving Region.
Leave us religion.
An escape? Why not. The Church is gay.
Escape, from pleasure — to nurse lepers
The face shines plain:
Can you explain?
Successful seekers have found pleasure out;
And the escape from love, of lechers
Is a lame rout;
Dead their gaze, no inner ray.
The warning proud borne off in stretchers;
All fugitives, we should be wary steppers.

Through leafless trees, this dreary day,
Blooms at the monastery steps,
Blue and unfading, the Virgin's dress —
In every weather, clear and gay.
For no new-fangledness
Will I turn away.

We have drunk fire and eaten dirt.
Given candid beauty much hurt;
Scrawled blasphemies on city walls;
Drawn coarse jests out with bitter drawls;
Our charity was curt.

In naked celerity,[5] remorse
Plunges out of its course,
Like a white frightened horse;
Our sins are legion.
Leave us religion.

1. Bernadette Soubirous (1844–79) experienced visions of the Virgin
   Mary at Lourdes. She was canonized in 1933.
2. Philomena, venerated as an early Roman virgin and martyr, was
   removed from the Calendar of Saints in 1963.
3. Margaret is the name of several saints.
4. 'To rive': to tear apart by pulling or tugging.

5. i.e. speed or swiftness.

JOAN SWEETMAN

(1909–   )

from:
POEMS (1986)

[Raymond Murray observed in the Foreword to *Poems* that Joan Sweetman takes as her themes the circumstances of her life: an electricity cut in a school study-hall, the baker's man at the convent kitchen door, and for her 'all circumstance is wafted into eternity'. Her poems reflect her life as a teaching Sister of the Society of the Sacred Heart in Ireland. 'Butterfly' was inspired by 'Butterfly Effect', an article in the *Tablet* (February 1991).]

Butterfly

The butterfly that stirred the air
In Peking yesterday
Can cause enormous turbulence
Tomorrow in Bombay.[1]

So speak the 'Chaos' scientists —[2]
Of morphic resonance,[3]
And tiny unpredictables
Around the cosmic dance.

Look closer at their antic steps.
Cry 'Chaos' not too soon.
Perhaps their leaps are keeping time
To an out-of-earshot tune.[4]

And quarky atoms floating free[5]
On some supernal breath
Can boost a global turning-point
Where life wins over death.

1. In H.G. Wells's *The Time Machine* a theory is proposed that if a butterfly flaps its wings it can set in motion a chain of events which, however small, can lead eventually to cataclysmic results.
2. 'Chaos' scientists such as Andrei Linde and Stephen Hawking argue that the universe could have arisen from a number of different configurations.
3. Sympathetic vibration in response to external stimulus.
4. This may be a reference in response to Henry David Thoreau's 'If a man does not keep pace with his companions, perhaps it is because he heard a different drummer. Let him step to the music which he hears, however measured or far away.'
5. A quark is the set of subatomic particles which most theorists believe is the fundamental constituent of the protons and neutrons that make up every atom. A line from Joyce's *Finnegans Wake*, 'Three quarkes for Muster Mark', gave Murray Gell-Mann the name for the phenomenon.

So never say you're powerless
Before these giant ills;
For all is process . . . Drop by drop
The elixir distills.

And your small effort, seen as slight
As Peking butterfly
Can be the straw that breaks the back
Of all that's gone a-wry.

And surely small is beautiful,
And multiplied has might
To draw the rainbow web of things
Into the Point of Light.

High Cross

[The reference to Daniel in the lions' den suggests that the high cross of the poem is the Moone Cross (County Kildare), where the Daniel panel appears on the east face of the base of the cross. In her notes on 'High Cross', Sweetman reflects on the various suggested uses of high crosses, among them the supposition that the terminally ill go there 'to steady themselves in the last testing' by contemplating the different themes on the stone panels.]

I see you, Aengus,[1] creeping to the Cross,
Excruciated, to the Crucified.
This twenty feet of carven comforting[2]
Must get through the endless summertide
Of terminal distress, its bad to worse,
Who have no smooth syringe of last recourse.

You settle in the grass and match your plight
With Daniel's — rigid in the lions' den.[3]
And woefully expect, in mounting flame,
The all-out rescue of the Three Young Men.[4]

1. Aengus (Aonghus, Oenghus) was the son of the Daghdha, chief god of the Tuatha Dé Danaan, and Boann (Bóinn), who gives her name to the Boyne, the river enshrined in Irish mythology and history. Aengus is often described as the Celtic god of love.
2. The Moone Cross is taller and narrower than other high crosses in Ireland.
3. Daniel 6:1–22. The Moone panel depicts the figure of Daniel with three lions on his right and four lions on his left.
4. The three young men were Shadrach, Meshach and Abednego. Daniel 3:12–30.

With Abraham and Isaac,[5] you admit
The death of hope, as this world reckons it.

Your eyes are weary, man, with looking up
To where the pierced Heart mulls each
    proffered grief.[6]
No scandal if along the ribboned base
You seek a milder, shallower relief;
A household cat, a huntsman with his deer,
Profane, made holy by the eyes they cheer.

5. God called on Abraham to sacrifice his young son Isaac, but He
   spared him as He spared the righteous Daniel and Shadrach,
   Meshach and Abednego.
6. Along with the panels of Daniel and of Abraham and Isaac, there is
   a panel depicting the crucifixion on the east face of the Moone Cross.

Joan cried out for the cross when faggots spat;[7]
A friar raised it in that northern town
In Cromwell's time;[8] but saints before and since
Have Lent on beauty as the night came down
'Tis said the dying ears of God on earth
Were soothed by bird-song from a neighbouring
    garth.[9]

7. Witnesses to Joan's execution describe her asking to have the cross
   from the church held before her eyes as the flames engulfed her.
   Shaw uses the episode in Scene VI of *Saint Joan*, demonstrating the
   transforming power of Joan's faith.
8. A reference to the siege of Drogheda, September 1649, under
   Oliver Cromwell, commander of the English military forces.
9. garth: enclosed ground.

MÁIRE MHAC AN tSAOI

(1922–   )

from:
AN CRANN FAOI BLÁTH/THE FLOWERING TREE (1991)

[Poetry came naturally to Máire Mhac an tSaoi; there are poets on both sides of her family. She cannot remember 'not having an absolute facility for metrical form'. Her spare, compressed poems have been praised for their sense of craft and their erudition. In 'Oíche Nollag', translated here by Gabriel Fitzmaurice, there is a formality and tenderness reminiscent of medieval Latin church lyrics. The poem alludes to the custom of putting a candle in the window on Christmas Eve to show Mary and Joseph that they would find welcome in the house. Mhac an tSaoi's contemporary Máirtín Ó Direáin wrote two Aran poems on the same theme: 'Coinnle ar Lasadh' and 'Cuireadh do Mhuire.']

Oíche Nollag

Le coinnle na n-aingeal tá an spéir amuigh
    breactha,
Tá fiacail an tseaca sa ghaoith ón gcnoc,
Adaigh an tine is téir chun na leapan,
Luífidh Mac Dé ins an tigh so anocht.

Fágaidh an doras ar leathadh ina coinne,
An mhaighdean a thiocfaidh is a naí ar a hucht,

Deonaigh scíth an bhóthair a ligint, a Mhuire,
Luíodh Mac Dé ins an tigh so anocht.

Bhí soilse ar lasadh i dtigh sin na haoíchta,
Cóiriú gan caoile, bia agus deoch,
Do cheannaithe olla, do cheannaithe síoda,
Ach luífidh Mac Dé ins an tigh so anocht.

Christmas Eve

With candles of angels the sky is now dappled
The frost on the wind from the hills has a bite
Kindle the fire and go to your slumber.
Jesus will lie in this household tonight.

Leave all the doors wide open before her
The Virgin who'll come with the child on her
    breast
Grant that you'll stop here tonight, Holy Mary,
That Jesus tonight in this household may rest.

The lights are all lighting in that little hostel,
There were generous servings of victuals and
    wine
For merchants of silk, for merchants of woollens
But Jesus will lie in this household tonight.

[In fairy legends, a mortal piper is frequently abducted by the music-loving *sídhe*, or people of the fairies; however, in Mhac an tSaoi's lament, Séamus Ennis is taken from the supernatural as well as from the natural world and all mourn the great uilleann piper who died in 1984. The poem draws on Mhac an tSaoi's immense learning and her technical knowledge of classical Irish poetry. The translation by the author is an elaboration of a first draft by Canon Coslett Quinn.]

Sunt Lacrimae Rerum[1]

I nDílchuimhne ar Shéamus Ennis

Sianaíl ag síofraí, geimhreata an gheon;
Caoighol ag símhná í bhfogus is fós
Siar go roinn duimhche: a Dhoinn, scaoil an
   sceol.

Súiste í uaill an droma mhóir —
   Tarraing go tréan;
Dlúigh le gach buille ina chóir,
   Tuargan an léin;
Taoiseach, iarr' ídeach don gceol,
   Gabhann chun an chré.

Ruaig ar lucht leasa agus brogha, mashlua an
   aeir;
Gruagaigh na scairte i luísheol, chucu an chíréip;
Grianáras Aonghusa ar Bóinn spéirling do réab.

Fásach gan cláirseach
   Fad tharla an Teamhair 'na féar,
Go hanois áfach
   Téanamh ón léan
Níor chuaigh dar n-áireamh —
   Feasta tám tréith.

Tocht broinne an aithrígh bheir bláth ar
   bhachall droighin;
De shians chroit Oirféis, an gallán cloiche rinnc;
Ach, a ríphíobaire Éireann, clos duit ní dán
   arís —

                    Choíche!

---

1. 'Here are the tears of things'. Virgil, *Aeneid*, 1, 462.

Lament

For Séamus Ennis, late Champion Piper of Ireland (Slow Air)

Shee-people[1] wheening,[2] wintry their wail;
Fairy wives keening[3] near and away
West to the dune's edge Donn,[4] spread the tale.

Make the drum's roar a flail —
   Lay on great strokes,
Redoubling each in train,
   Hammers of woe;
This prince, the music waned,
   Seeks his clay home.

Wizards of liss[5] and fort,[6] hosts of the air,[7]
Panicked and routed go, each from his lair;
Boyne's[8] airy pleasure-dome, rainstorm lays
   bare.

Desert and harpless,
   Tara[9] is grass;
Yet we had argued
   Each such pass
No mortal harm meant —
   No more, alas!

White flowers of repentance the barren staff
   knew;
The pillar-stones danced to hear Orpheus'
   tunes;[10]
But, King-piper of Ireland, voice is withheld
   from you —

                    Ever!

---

1. Fairy people.
2. Whining or whingeing.
3. Lamenting.
4. Donn of the Dune, the old Irish god of death.
5. *lios*, a ring fort of the early Christian era. Also a fairy mound.
6. Iron Age habitation sites.
7. People believed that the *sídhe* travelled in crowds or hosts and they were often called the 'hosts of the air'.
8. The prehistoric tombs in the Boyne valley were believed to be the palaces of the old gods.
9. The Hill of Tara in County Meath was the inauguration site of the kings of Ireland. It also has associations with Irish mythology and folklore.
10. Given the lyre by Apollo, Orpheus was the Greeks' mythic musician who could move trees and rocks with his songs.

ANNE LE MARQUAND HARTIGAN

(1929–   )

from:
IMMORTAL SINS (1993)

[The path of pilgrimage is the theme of 'Path of Enduring
Knowledge', the Maori name for 'holy way', where the
water bubbles up in blue hot springs.]

Path of Enduring Knowledge

On the Waimangu Thermal Valley, Rotorua,
New Zealand
for Michael Coady

It is the path we are all on:
we cannot change it,
whatever way you step
knowledge keeps knocking you.

There is no way to avoid it,
so travel easy
take care
safe journey.

We need these benedictions
a wave of water is
incense to celebrate.

If you stood immobile
at the sink all day
you are still on it.
Shutting the eyes is useless,
I know all this
and know nothing, but

the old ways of pilgrimage
have sound founding, and
our ancestors are waving to us
up through the ever bubbling spring,
in the warm stones underfoot, and,
in that startle of azure water,
that white rock.[1]

---

1. The Waimangu Cauldron in the Waimangu Thermal Valley occupies
    a crater which is the bed of a pale blue steaming lake that overflows
    periodically revealing the stark white walls of the crater.

BRÍD DÁIBHÍS

(1930–   )

from:
COSÁN NA GRÉINE/THE
SUN'S PATH (1989)

[Bríd Dáibhís, whose interests embrace poetry in modern
Irish as well as English, would like to see more traditional
music and native hymns in the Irish liturgy. In her poems,
Dáibhís expresses spiritual longings through images of
nature. They are poems waiting for musical settings. The
translations are by Margaret Mac Curtain.]

Fan Liom, A Dhia

Lig liom, a Thiarna,
Go ngabhfaidh mé
Draíocht na Bealtaine.

Róluath a bheas
Buí na nduillí
Ina ghlaise;
Róluath a bheas
Nuachair ag éanlaith
Agus tost sa chlaí.

Tá bláthanna na gcraobh
Mífhoighdeach;
Táthar á ngairm,
Á mealladh uainn.

Tá siosarnach shíodúil
Sa bhfeá;
Scairdeann an lon
A chuid braonacha aitis
Mar chuimilt méire
Ar scuaibín fiacal,
Is tá an ré
Ina fhinné órtha
Don fhlaithiúlacht.

Fan liom, a Dhia;
Fan, go mblaisfidh mé
Ód' mhéis,
Cuir stop le clog
Na Bealtaine,
Is maith dom
Mo chuid bréige:
Óir ní blaiseadh atá uaim
Ach béile beo do m'anam.

Wait for Me, God

Permit me, O Lord
To savour
The magic of May.[1]

Too soon the tender leaves
Will merge into green.
Too soon the birds will mate
And fall silent.

The flowers on the branches
Are impatient,
Being summoned,
Being called from our midst.

A silky whisper in the beechtree.
The blackbird whirrs a pleasant sound
Like a finger sweeping the top of a toothbrush.
Over them all a dazzling plenitude.

---

1. While Dáibhís refers to the magic of spring, she also alludes to the old Celtic celebration to welcome the first day of summer, a celebration which included the gathering of fresh flowers.

Wait for me, God
Wait till I taste
At your table.
Put a halt to the clock of May.
Forgive me my deceptions.
It is not a taste I desire
But living food for my soul.

from:
TRÁITHNÍN SEIRCE/STRAWS OF LOVE (1999)

[The practice of herding sheep into an enclosure so that they can be dipped to cure them of worms is Dáibhís's metaphor for her spiritual course, in this context the yearly nine days of withdrawal from worldly concerns, which is termed a 'spiritual retreat'.]

Lá Níocháin

Glaonn na huain go daonna, sioraí,
Glaonn na caoirigh in ard a gcinn
Ritheann siad síos an bóthar,
A gcrúbanna mar dhuirling á suaitheadh
Agus a sceoin féin ortha uile.

Glaonn Dia orm agus cuirim díom
Go malltriallach isteach sa bhfásach,
M'aigne mar dhuirling á suaitheadh.
Smaointe troma cré atá cruaite
Le casadh na mblian.

Beidh na caoirigh á ní inniu
Le hiomad fústair,
Le callóid is le hachasán
Don ghasúr nár stop an chaora siúd
Beidh gleo ós cionn an tobáin
Agus slad marbh ar 'chuile chnuimh.

Táthar am thiomsú ar an gcúrsa seo;
Beidh orm féin na bearnaí a bhaint
Agus bearnaí nua a oscailt.
A Aoire na gnúise gile,
Bí liom ar thóir na cnuimhe.
Druidse na geataí romham
Ar eagla go mba uaitse a d'éalóinn,
Óir is é mo mhiansa
Luí síos id' mhóinéar choíche.

Washing Day

The lambs cry like humans constantly.
The sheep bleat loudly, insistently.
They clatter down the road
Their hooves a pebbled sound.
I sense their fright each and all.

God calls me and I make towards
The wilderness reluctantly.
My mind swirling like a pebble.
Heavy earthy thoughts knotted
Around the turning years.

The sheep will be dipped today.
Lots of fuss.
Commotion, scolding the lad

Who let that sheep escape
Much bleating at the tub,
And slaughter on the worms.

I am being groomed for this course,
I must close the gaps
And open new ones.
O Shepherd of the Kindly Face
Stay with me in the pursuit of worms.
Let you shut the open gates
Lest I flee from you;
Because it is my true desire
To lie down
In your pleasant meadow forever.[1]

1. Psalm 23:1–2.

CAITLÍN MAUDE

(1941–82)

from:
DÁNTA (1984)

[In an interview with Siobhán McSweeney, Caitlín Maude described poetry as 'a function of the imagination and of the soul ... some contemporary poetry is over-intellectualized although poetry in itself is not a function of the intellect ... poetry changes one's understanding or should — we all long for unity'. Social and political issues were often the subject of Maude's muse. She was a strong sympathizer for the republicans on hunger strike in Long Kesh in 1981, and the first poem is her elegy for Bobby Sands (1954–81), which speaks in Sands's own voice. Although she was reluctant to have her poetry translated into English during her lifetime, some of her poems have been translated posthumously. The English version of the two poems selected are by Maureen Murphy.]

Gan Teideal

I m'áit dhúchais ó thuaidh
solaoid ar an mbeatha í an tsíon,
báisteach níos minicí ná gréin,
ach scal an ghrian ar mo chliabhán féin

is níor ghéill m'fhuinneoigín riamh don spéir dhubh.
Féach mé
nach bhfuair scíth i mo thír féin,
nár naomh ar bith
ach chomh maith le chuile dhailtín
ag smiochadh cloch
gur thuigeas nár chluiche sráide é
ar chor ar bith
agus gur mise an tIndiach.

Untitled

In my own place in the North
life is like the stormy weather
far more rain than sun.
But there was a sun-burst over my cot,
and I never gave in to the dark skies.
Look at me —
not able to find rest in my own country,
nor could any saint.
I walloped stones
along with every schoolboy,
understanding that it wasn't a street game at all —
and I was the Indian.

[Maude's sympathy for the outsider is reflected in this poem of the outcast woman who, like Christ, took the lonely way.]

Gan Teideal

Idir an Paidrín Páirteach
agus na deich n-acra fhichead
thit péarla do chreidimh
ar thír gan rath.
Cér chás
ach ba bheag do mheas
ar an mnaoi úd
a thug an ruaig
ab éigean di.
Ní raibh meas comharsan
moladh na gcarad
ná ola na sacraiméad
á cumhdach,
'Nós Chríosta
thriall sí an bóthar uaigneach.

Untitled

Between the family rosary
And the thirty acres
The pearl of your faith
Fell on stony ground
What odds
Except your lack of respect
For that woman
Who took the only way out.
She had neither neighbours' esteem
Nor the acclaim of friends
Not even sacramental oil for protection

Like Christ
She took a lonely way.

[Maude addresses a ruined house in the Irish countryside, a metaphor for all that is destroyed by neglect; however, the poem promises hope in a consolation that echoes the Beatitudes.]

Caoineadh na Mná Tí

A theach bhoicht
i do fhothrach
ceal lámh
a shlíocfadh do dheann
fulaingíonn tusa freisin
fís
Tugann tú dídean do throscán sí
ag fanacht leis an lá
go spíonfaidh an loinnir fhiáin
ina solas sámh

The Housewife's Keen

Poor house
in your ruin
wanting a hand
smoothing your sting
also suffering your
vision.
You shelter your fairy furnishings
waiting for the day
that the wild radiance will be teased
into a peaceful light.

ROZ COWMAN

(1942–   )

from:
THE GOOSE HERD (1989)

[Humour shot through with the insight of life's experience gives Lot's wife a voice that explains her preference, as

Cowman notes in *The Goose Herd*, for 'her oily kitchen' over the biblical Lot's 'back to Nature' strategy. Cowman's witty retelling of Genesis 19:1–26 from the point of view of Lot's wife ends not with her transformation to a pillar of salt but with her emancipation. She leaves Lot, 'God's loudspeaker', to take her chances in the city on the plain.]

Lot's Wife

What else could she do, when that old fool,
picked in prudence, holier than she,
God's loudspeaker, forced her to climb
up out of the plain, start again with him,
housewife to a tribe, getting back
to Nature as he called it, milking
his camels, hoarding their dung
for fuel, hearing him talk to his dreadful god
while the stars hummed like bees
in the white nights of the desert.

She was used to her oily kitchen
on the brawling street, the panniered donkeys,
dust-devils at corners, hawkers of fried cakes,
women with cures and curses,
littered courtyards, glossy young merchants
and soldiers in the market for discreet
invitations, suppers at twilight
on long terraces, with her
bawdy, middle aged companions.

Of course she paused, there,
at the head of the pass, at sunset,
looked back, longingly, thinking
it over, then retraced her steps.
He, to save face, shouted some imprecation
about fiery rain, pillars of salt . . .
But she, uncaring, walked back
down to the great plain,
and smoke of little cities on the evening air.

[Cowman mixed Greek myth with the legend of Saint Patrick in this poem which suggests Ireland/Medea sacrifices her children.]

Medea[1] Ireland

Snake-mother at the psyche's core,
she uncoiled for him;

and by what power could she then
mate and breed
with one, who shook the island
with hell-thunderings from his book,

and with his lore of God's love
dying between thief and thief [2]
and God's love living in a triple leaf [3]
spread madness with his seed?

The rime of death on children's bodies still
delays his pursuit of her flight through time.

1. Medea helped Jason steal the golden fleece from her father's kingdom and fled with him to Greece. Later, when Jason deserted her, she took her revenge by murdering their children, destroying his young wife, and escaping to Athens in a chariot drawn by winged dragons.
2. Matthew 27:38.
3. Saint Patrick was said to have used the shamrock to explain the Trinity.

EILÉAN NÍ CHUILLEANÁIN
(1942–   )

from:
THE MAGDALENE SERMON AND EARLIER POEMS (1991)

[Women speakers and subjects are the focus of Ní Chuilleanáin's *The Magdalene Sermon*, a collection of poems that gives voice to women by drawing on figures from mythology and from ordinary life. In 'J'ai mal à nos dents', she catches a moment in history when a twentieth-century Irish nun, in voluntary exile in a French convent, returns to Ireland to die at seventy-eight years of age.]

J'ai mal à nos dents

In memory of Anna Cullinane
(Sister Mary Antony)

The Holy Father gave her leave
To return to her father's house
At seventy-eight years of age.

When young in the Franciscan House at Calais
She complained to the dentist, *I have a pain in our teeth*

— Her body dissolving out of her first mother,
Her five sisters aching at home.

Her brother listened to news
Five times in a morning on Radio Éireann
In Cork, as the Germans entered Calais.[1]
Her name lay under the surface, he could not
     see her
Working all day with the sisters,
Stripping the hospital, loading the sick on
     lorries,
While Reverend Mother walked the wards and
     nourished them
With jugs of wine to hold their strength.
J'étais à moitié saoûle.[2] It was done,
They lifted the old sisters on to the pig-cart
And the young walked out on the road to
     Desvres,
The wine still buzzing and the planes over their
     heads.

Je mangerai les pissenlits par les racines.[3]
A year before she died she lost her French
     accent
Going home in her habit to care for her sister
     Nora
(*Une malade à soigner une malade*).[4]
They handed her back her body,
Its voices and its death.

1. General Heinz Guderian's 19th Panzer Corp surrounded Calais on
   24 May 1940. A city that the Germans used as a port for the
   planned invasion of England, Calais was bombed and shelled by the
   British.
2. I was half drunk.
3. An idiom meaning, I'll be pushing up the daisies.
4. 'A sick woman looking after a sick woman'.

[The solitary woman of the Christian scriptures, Mary
Magdalene, is glimpsed, with her long red hair covering
her body, preaching in Marseilles. Ní Chuilleanáin's poem
animates the legend.]

St Mary Magdalene Preaching at Marseilles

Now at the end of her life she is all hair —
A cataract flowing and freezing — and a voice
Breaking loose from the loose red hair,
The secret shroud of her skin:
A voice glittering in the wilderness.
She preaches in the city, she wanders
Late in the evening through shaded squares.

The hairs on the back of her wrists begin to lie
     down
And she breathes evenly, her elbows leaning
On a smooth wall. Down there in the piazza,
The boys are skimming on toy carts, warped
On their stomachs, like breathless fish.[1]

She tucks her hair around her,
Looking beyond the game
To the suburban marshes.

Out there a shining traps the sun,
The waters are still clear,
Not a hook or a comma of ice
Holding them, the water-weeds
Lying collapsed like hair
At the turn of the tide;

They wait for the right time, then
Flip all together their thousands of sepia feet.

1. The fish is a symbol associated with Christ.

NUALA NÍ DHOMHNAILL

(1952–   )

from:
SELECTED POEMS/ROGHA DÁNTA (1988)

[A measure of Nuala Ní Dhomhnaill's pre-eminence as a poet of her generation is the number of poems that have been translated brilliantly by Ireland's leading poets writing in English. 'Scéala' is one of three Ní Dhomhnaill Annunciation poems which include 'The Visitor' and 'Parthenogenesis'. In a 1987 interview with Lucy McDiarmid and Michael Durkan for the *Irish Literary Supplement*, Ní Dhomhnaill said, 'I never get over my fascination with the Annunciation, the virgin birth and parthenogenesis. When I write a poem, I have experienced inspiration and that is being impregnated by the divine. There is no other explanation.' The translation is by Michael Hartnett.]

Scéala

Do chuimhnigh sí
go deireadh thiar
ar scáil an aingil
sa teampall,
cleitearnach sciathán
ina timpeall;
is dúiseacht le dord colúr
is stealladh ga gréine
ar fhallaí aolcloch
an lá a fuair sí an scéala.

É siúd
d'imigh
is n'fheadar ar chuimhnigh riamh
ar cad a d'eascair
óna cheathrúna,
dhá mhíle bliain
d'iompar croise
de dhóiteán is deatach,
de chlampar chomh hard
le spící na Vatacáine.

Ó, a mhaighdean rócheansa,
nár chuala trácht ar éinne riamh
ag teacht chughat sa doircheacht
cosnocht, déadgheal
is a shúile lán de rógaireacht.

Annunciations

She remembered to the very end
the angelic vision
in the temple:
the flutter of wings
about her —
noting the noise of doves,
sun-rays raining
on lime-white walls —
the day she got the tidings.[1]

He —
he went away
and perhaps forgot
what grew from his loins —
two thousand years
of carrying a cross
two thousand years
of smoke and fire
of rows that reached a greater span
than all the spires of the Vatican.

Remember
O most tender virgin Mary
that never was it known[2]
that a man came to you
in the darkness alone,
his bare feet, his teeth white
and roguery swelling in his eyes.

---

1. Ní Dhomhnaill uses elements from the traditional Christian iconography that depicts the Annunciation.
2. These lines allude to the first lines of the popular Catholic prayer 'The Memorare'.

from:
FÉAR SUAITHINSEACH (1984)

[Based on a folktale from Dingle about a girl who drops the sacred host at communion and goes into a decline, Ní Dhomhnaill explores with great delicacy the metaphor of illness when love has mortally wounded. The poem is full of layered meanings and draws on Gaelic and folkloristic traditions around the *féar suaithinseach* (miraculous grass), the priest set apart at Mass and the cure of the 'sacred wafer'. Translated by Seamus Heaney in *Pharaoh's Daughter* (1990), the poem repays many readings in both Irish and English.]

Féar Suaithinseach

Nuair a bhís i do shagart naofa
i lár an Aifrinn, faoi do róbaí corcra
t'fhallaing lín, do stól, do chasal,
do chonnaicís m'aghaidh-se ins an slua
a bhí ag teacht chun comaoineach chughat
is thit uait an abhlainn bheannaithe.

Mise, ní dúrt aon ní ina thaobh.
Bhí náire orm.
Bhí glas ar mo bhéal.
Ach fós do luigh sé ar mo chroí
mar dhealg láibe, gur dhein sé slí
dó fhéin istigh i m'ae is im' lár
gur dhóbair go bhfaighinn bás dá bharr.

Ní fada nó gur thiteas 'on leabaidh;
oideasaí leighis do triaileadh ina gcéadtaibh,
do tháinig chugham dochtúirí, sagairt is bráithre
is n'fhéadadar mé a thabhairt chun sláinte
ach thugadar suas i seilbh bháis mé.

Is téigí amach, a fheara,
tugaíg libh rámhainn is speala
corráin, grafáin is sluaiste.
Réabaig an seanafhothrach,
bearraíg na seacha, glanaíg an luifearnach,
an slámas fáis, an brus, an ainnise
a fhás ar thalamh bán mo thubaiste.

Is ins an ionad inar thit
an chomaoine naofa féach go mbeidh
i lár an bhiorlamais istigh
toirtín d'fhéar suaithinseach.

Tagadh an sagart is lena mhéireanna
beireadh sé go haiclí ar an gcomaoine naofa
is tugtar chugham í, ar mo theanga
leáfaidh sí, is éireod aniar sa leaba
chomh slán folláin is a bhíos is mé i mo leanbh.

Miraculous Grass

There you were in your purple vestments
half-way through the Mass, an ordained priest
under your linen alb and chasuble and stole:
and when you saw my face in the crowd
for Holy Communion
the consecrated host fell from your fingers.

I felt shame, I never
mentioned it once,
my lips were sealed.
But still it lurked in my heart
like a thorn under mud, and it
worked itself in so deep and sheer
it nearly killed me.

Next thing then, I was laid up in bed.
Consultants came in their hundreds,
doctors and brothers and priests,
but I baffled them all: I was
incurable, they left me for dead.

So out you go, men,
out with the spades and scythes,
the hooks and shovels and hoes.
Tackle the rubble,
cut back the bushes, clear off the rubbish,
the sappy growth, the whole straggle and mess
that infests my green unfortunate field.

And there where the sacred wafer fell
you will discover
in the middle of the shooting weeds
a clump of miraculous grass.

The priest will have to come then
with his delicate fingers, and lift the host
and bring it to me and put it on my tongue.
Where it will melt, and I will rise in the bed
as fit and well as the youngster I used to be.

PAULA MEEHAN

(1955–   )

from:
THE MAN WHO WAS
MARKED BY WINTER (1991)

[Every town in Ireland has a grotto built around the statue of Mary, the Virgin Mother of God. In this poem, the statue of Mary at Granard, County Longford, gives voice to the sorrow of witnessing a fifteen-year-old girl, Ann Lovett, who 'lay down alone at my feet' on a cold winter's night to deliver the baby no one knew she carried. The statue watches as the young girl lies dying beside the dead baby, unable or unwilling to help her. See Vol. V, pp. 1435–9.]

The Statue of the Virgin at Granard Speaks

It can be bitter here at times like this,
November wind sweeping across the border.
Its seeds of ice would cut you to the quick.
The whole town tucked up safe and dreaming,
even wild things gone to earth, and I
stuck up here in this grotto, without as much as
star or planet to ease my vigil.

The howling won't let up. Trees
cavort in agony as if they would be free
and take off — ghost voyagers
on the wind that carries intimations
of garrison towns, walled cities, ghetto lanes
where men hunt each other and invoke
the various names of God as blessing
on their death tactics, their night manoeuvres.
Closer to home the wind sails over
dying lakes. I hear the fish drowning.
I taste the stagnant water mingled
with turf smoke from outlying farms.

They call me Mary — Blessed, Holy, Virgin.
They fit me to a myth of a man crucified:
the scourging and the falling, and the falling
    again,
the thorny crown, the hammer blow of iron
into wrist and ankle, the sacred bleeding heart.
They name me Mother of all this grief
though mated to no mortal man.

They kneel before me and their prayers
fly up like sparks from a bonfire
that blaze a moment, then wink out.

It can be lovely here at times. Springtime,
early summer. Girls in Communion frocks
pale rivals to the riot in the hedgerows
of cow parsley and haw blossom, the perfume
from every rushy acre that's left for hay
when the light swings longer with the sun's push
    north.

Or the grace of a midsummer wedding
when the earth herself calls out for coupling
and I would break loose of my stony robes,
pure blue, pure white, as if they had robbed
a child's sky for their colour. My being
cries out to be incarnate,[1] incarnate,
maculate[2] and tousled in a honeyed bed.

Even an autumn burial can work its own
    pageantry.
The hedges heavy with the burden of fruiting
crab, sloe, berry, hip; clouds scud east
pear scented, windfalls secret in long
orchard grasses, and some old soul is lowered
to his kin. Death is just another harvest
scripted to the season's play.

But on this All Souls' Night[3] there is
no respite from the keening of the wind.[4]
I would not be amazed if every corpse came risen
from the graveyard to join in exaltation with the
    gale,
a cacophony of bone imploring sky for judgement
and release from being the conscience of the
    town.

On a night like this I remember the child
who came with fifteen summers to her name,
and she lay down alone at my feet
without midwife or doctor or friend to hold her
    hand

1. Invested in bodily form.
2. Stain, soil.
3. All Souls' Night, 2 November, commemorates the souls of the faithful departed and special prayers are said for the dead.
4. Lamenting.

and she pushed her secret out into the night,
far from the town tucked up in little scandals,
bargains struck, words broken, prayers, promises,
and though she cried out to me in extremis
I did not move,
I didn't lift a finger to help her,
I didn't intercede[5] with heaven,
nor whisper the charmed word in God's ear.

5. Refers to the belief that saints and especially the Blessed Virgin
Mary have the power to intervene on behalf of the petitioner.

On a night like this I number the days to the
    solstice
and the turn back to the light.
                                    O sun,
centre of our foolish dance,
burning heart of stone,[6]
molten mother of us all,
hear me and have pity.

6. Perhaps an allusion to Juno's curtain speech in Sean O'Casey's *Juno
and the Paycock*, 'Sacred Heart o' Jesus, take away our hearts o'
stone, and give us hearts o' flesh!'

MOYA CANNON

(1956–   )

from:
OAR (1990)

[Moya Cannon's poetry is grounded in the western
mountains and lakes and the 'moody Atlantic' seascape of
the Burren in County Clare. Here she traces the presence
of water trapped in wells and pools in the porous
limestone of the Burren and the ancient fertility rites
associated with holy wells, suggesting, perhaps, that the
miracle of blessing and healing is nature itself.]

Holy Well[1]

Water returns, hard and bright,
out of the faulted hills.

Rain that flowed
down through the limestone's pores
until dark streams hit bedrock,
now finds a way back,

1. Many wells in rural Ireland are believed to have extraordinary
powers, especially to cure certain ailments.

past the roots of the ash,
to a hillside pen
of stones and statues.

Images of old fertilities
testify to nothing more, perhaps,
than the necessary miracle
of water trapped and stored
in a valley where water is fugitive.

A chipped and tilted Mary
grows green among rags and sticks.[2]
Her trade dwindles —
bad chests, rheumatic pains,
the supplications, mostly, and the confidences of
    old age.
        Yet sometimes,
        swimming out in waters
        that were blessed in the hill's labyrinthine
        heart
        the eel flashes past.

2. There is a custom of leaving tokens or offerings at the holy well.
Frequently bits of cloth were tied to a tree or bush near the well.

RUTH HOOLEY

(1953–   )

from:
SLEEPING WITH MONSTERS: CONVERSATIONS WITH SCOTTISH AND IRISH WOMEN POETS (1990)

[In an interview with Rebecca E. Wilson, Ruth Hooley (later Carr) said, 'I'm writing primarily from a woman's perspective. With a lot of my poems the gender of the poet wouldn't matter, but knowing the gender of the poet does make a difference. It comes across in the imagery'. 'The Fall' contrasts the plight of Irish women in the 1980s with the promise offered to them at the coming of Christianity in cryptic comments.]

The Fall

The coming of Christianity to Ireland

I

In the beginning[1] it was almost a blessing.
(The Word you spread among us more than
    bread — it fed our dignity.)

II

But in the end it brought the curse on every
    female head —
Granard, Kerry babies,[2] closed down clinics,
the boat to Liverpool[3] that we don't talk about,
homilies on condoms and the guilt . . .

III

Where there are women there's sin —
St Kevin's creed,[4]
bedrock of the Church that fears my sex.
But where there is sin there's the serpent
God made, that took even Patrick in.

---

1. Genesis 1:1.
2. Granard and the Kerry babies refer to two tragic incidents in the 1980s involving unwanted pregnancies. See Paula Meehan, 'The Statue of the Virgin of Granard Speaks', p. 637.
3. A reference to Irish women who go to England to have their pregnancies terminated.
4. A legend of Saint Kevin (d. 618), founder abbot of Glendalough, County Wicklow, describes a young woman coming to Kevin's cell only to be thrown into the lake by the hermit saint.

Biographies/Bibliographies

Blanaid Salkeld

LIFE. Blanaid ffrench Mullen was born on 10 August 1880 in Chittagong, India (now Pakistan), where her father was in the Indian medical service. After a childhood in Ireland, she married an Englishman, Henry Lyde Salkeld, in the Indian Civil Service stationed in Bombay. A young widow, she returned to Ireland with her children in 1908 and became involved in the nationalist movement, in the Gaelic League and in the Abbey Theatre, where she appeared in a number of plays in 1912 under the name of Nell Byrne. She wrote verse plays as well as poetry in Irish and English; *Scarecrow over the Corn* was produced by the Dublin Drama League in 1941. She started the Gayfield Press in 1937 with her son, the artist Cecil ffrench Salkeld. She died in Dublin in 1959.

CHIEF WRITINGS. *Hello Eternity!* (London: Elkins Mathew and Marot, 1933); *The Fox's Covert* (London: J.M. Dent, 1935); . . . *The Engine is Still Running* (Dublin: Gayfield Press, 1937); *A Dubliner* (Dublin: Gayfield Press, 1943); *Experiment in Error* (Aldington: Hand and Flower Press, 1955).

BIOGRAPHY AND CRITICISM. Devin A. Garrity (ed.), 'Notes on the Poets', in *New Irish Poets* (New York: Devine-Adair, 1948); Robert Hogan (ed.), *Dictionary of Irish Literature* (Westport: Greenwood Press, 1979); Ann Owens Weekes, *Unveiling Treasures* (Dublin: Attic Press, 1993), pp. 315–16.

Joan Sweetman

LIFE. Born in Dublin in 1909 and grew up in Glendalough in County Wicklow. She entered the noviceship of the Society of the Sacred Heart in 1929 at Mount Anville, Dublin, where she had received her schooling as a boarder. She later studied at University College Dublin, obtaining the degrees of BA and MA. During the following years she taught in the schools of the Sacred Heart at Armagh, Dublin and Roscrea. She also gave parish service in Seville Place, Dublin, and worked in the office of the Irish Commission for Justice and Peace in Dublin.

CHIEF WRITINGS. *Poems* (Dublin: Sacred Heart Printing, 1986).

Máire Mhac an tSaoi

LIFE. For biography and bibliography, see Vol. III, p. 935 and additional references, Vol. V, p. 1229.

Anne Le Marquand Hartigan

LIFE. Anne Le Marquand Hartigan was born in England in 1929 to an Irish mother and a Jersey (Channel Islands) father. She was educated in England, at St Joseph's Convent in Reading and at the Convent of the Sacred Heart in Tunbridge Wells. She studied painting at the University of Reading before she married Tim Hartigan and settled in Ireland to farm in County Louth. Her plays *Beds* and *La Corbière* were featured in the Dublin Theatre Festival in 1982 and 1989; they were a theatrical innovation in the way Hartigan combined music, dance and mime. She is a short-story writer as well as a poet, and her work has been translated into German and Russian. In recent years, she returned to her art to illustrate *Now is a Moveable Feast*.

CHIEF WRITINGS. *Long Tongue* (Dublin: Beaver Row, 1982); *Return Single* (Dublin: Beaver Row, 1986); *Now is a Moveable Feast* (Galway: Salmon, 1991); *Clearing the Space: The Why of Writing* (Galway: Salmon, 1992); *Immortal Sins* (Galway: Salmon, 1993).

BIOGRAPHY AND CRITICISM. Ann Owens Weekes, *Unveiling Treasures* (Dublin: Attic Press, 1993), pp. 140–2.

Bríd Dáibhís

LIFE. Born in old Ballybrittan, County Laois, in 1930, Bríd Dáibhís was educated in Killenard National School and the Presentation College in Mountmellick, County Laois. She trained as a primary teacher in Carysfort Training College, Dublin, and took her Diploma in Irish Literature at Maynooth College. She entered the Presentation Novitiate in Killenard, County Laois, in 1947 and on profession, she was assigned to Kilcock Presentation Convent, where she taught primary classes. She chaired the local Irish-language organization, Glór na nGael, and was a founder member of Comhaltas Ceoltóirí Éireann, an association for the promotion of Irish music, dance and song. Dáibhís writes in both Irish and English. Her poem 'An Gineadh' won the 1916 Commemoration Prize in 1966 and she has been awarded prizes in the Oireachtas competition. She was short-listed for the Hennessy Award, and was a short-story winner in the Maxwell House Women's Writing Competition, c. 1982.

CHIEF WRITINGS. *Ceol a Pháid* (Baile Átha Cliath: Fallons, 1960); *Corrán Gealaí* (Baile Átha Cliath: An Clóchomhar, 1978); *Cosán na Gréine* (Baile Átha Cliath: Coiscéim, 1989); *Tráithnín Seirce* (Baile Átha Cliath: Coiscéim, 1999).

BIOGRAPHY AND CRITICISM. Ann Owens Weekes, *Unveiling Treasures* (Dublin: Attic Press, 1993), pp. 93–4.

Caitlín Maude

LIFE. Caitlín Maude, born in Doiriú, Casla, in the Connemara Gaeltacht on 22 May 1941, traced her gift of poetry to her mother Máire Nic an Iomaire's side of the family. Maude was educated at Coláiste Chroí Mhuire in Spiddal and at University College Galway, where she studied Irish, English, French and mathematics. Like her mother, Maude became a teacher. While she was an undergraduate, she was active in the college drama society and in Galway's Taibhdhearc Theatre. She won international acclaim for her role in Máiréad Ní Ghráda's *An Triail* in the 1964 Dublin Theatre Festival. A playwright as well as an actress, Maude collaborated with Micheál Ó hAirtnéide (Michael Hartnett) on *An Lasair Choille*. She was also an accomplished *sean nós* singer, whose album *Caitlín* was produced by Gael-Linn in 1975. After her marriage to Cathal O'Luain in 1969, she worked with him to establish an Irish school in Tallaght. Maude died of cancer in Dublin in June 1982.

CHIEF WRITINGS. Ciarán Ó Coigligh (ed.), *Caitlín Maude, Dánta* (Baile Átha Cliath: Coiscéim, 1984) and *Drámaíocht agus Prós. Caitlín Maude* (Baile Átha Cliath: Coiscéim, 1988).

BIOGRAPHY AND CRITICISM. Máiréad Ní Ghráda, *Breithiúnas* (Baile Átha Cliath: Oifig an tSoláthair, 1978); Ciarán Ó Coigligh, 'Brollach' *Caitlín Maude, Dánta* (Baile Átha Cliath: Coiscéim, 1984); A.A. Kelly (ed.), *Pillar of the House* (Dublin: Wolfhound, 1988), pp. 129–30; Maureen Murphy, 'The Elegaic Tradition in the Poetry of Máire Mhac an tSaoi, Caitlín Maude and Nuala Ní Dhomhnaill', in James Brophy and Eamon Grennan (eds), *New Irish Writing* (New York: Twayne, 1989), pp. 141–51; Ann Owens Weekes, *Unveiling Treasures* (Dublin: Attic Press, 1993), pp. 221–2.

Roz Cowman

LIFE. Roz Cowman was born in Cork in 1942. She took her BA in French and her Diploma in Higher Education at University College Cork. She has taught in Ireland and abroad. She won the Patrick Kavanagh Award for Poetry in 1985.

CHIEF WRITINGS. *The Goose Herd* (Galway: Salmon, 1989).

BIOGRAPHY AND CRITICISM. Ann Owens Weekes, *Unveiling Treasures* (Dublin: Attic Press, 1993), pp. 81–3.

Eiléan Ní Chuilleanáin

For biography and bibliography, see Volume III, p. 1434.

ADDITIONAL WRITINGS. (Poems) *The Magdalene Sermon and Earlier Poems* (Winston-Salem: Wake Forest University Press, 1991); *The Second Voyage* (rev. ed.) (Winston-Salem: Wake Forest University Press, 1991); *The Brazen Serpent* (Oldcastle: Gallery Press, 1994).

BIOGRAPHY AND CRITICISM. Deborah Sarbin, '"Out of Myth into History": The Poetry of Eavan Boland and Eiléan Ní Chuilleanáin', *Canadian Journal of Irish Studies*, vol. 19, no. 1 (July 1993), pp. 86–96; Deborah McWilliams Consalvo, 'Interview with Eiléan Ní Chuilleanáin', *Irish Literary Supplement*, vol. 12 (fall 1993), pp. 5–7; Peter Sirr, '"How Things Begin to Happen": Notes on Eiléan Ní Chuilleanáin and Medbh McGuckian', *Southern Review*, vol. 31, no. 3 (summer 1995), pp. 450–67; Patricia Boyle Haberstroh, 'Eiléan Ní Chuilleanáin', in *Women Creating Women: Contemporary Irish Women Poets* (Dublin: Attic Press, 1996), pp. 92–121; Kevin Ray, 'Interview with Eiléan Ní Chuilleanáin', *Éire-Ireland*, vol. 31, nos 1–2 (spring–summer 1996), pp. 62–73; Dillon Johnston, 'Our Bodies' Eyes and Writing Hands: Secrecy and Sensuality in Ní Chuilleanáin's Baroque Art', in *Gender and Sexuality in Modern Ireland*, ed. Anthony Bradley (Amherst: University of Massachusetts Press, 1997), pp. 187–211; Leslie Williams, '"The Stone Recalls Its Quarry": An Interview with Eiléan Ní Chuilleanáin', in *Representing Ireland: Gender, Class, Nationality*, ed. Susan Shaw Sailer (Gainesville: University Press of Florida, 1997), pp. 29–44.

Nuala Ní Dhomhnaill

For biography and bibliography, see Volume III, p. 936.

ADDITIONAL WRITINGS. (Poems) (various translators) *Pharaoh's Daughter* (Oldcastle: Gallery Press, 1990); *Feis* (Maynooth: An Sagart, 1991); (translations by Paul Muldoon) *The Astrakhan Cloak* (Oldcastle: Gallery Press, 1992); (with trans. by Medbh McGuckian and Eiléan Ní Chuilleanáin) *The Waterhorse* (Oldcastle: Gallery Press, 1999).

BIOGRAPHY AND CRITICISM. Padraigin Ní Cheallaigh, 'An Nuala Rua is Dual . . .', *Comhar*, vol. 51, no. 5 (May 1992), pp. 211–13; Máire de Brit, 'An Slanu i Filíocht Nuala Ní Dhomhnaill', *Irisleabhar Mha Nuad* (1993), pp. 168–86; M. Louise Canon, 'The Extraordinary with the Ordinary: The Poetry of Eavan Boland and Nuala Ní Dhomhnaill', *South Atlantic Review*, vol. 60, no. 2 (May 1995), pp. 31–46; Deborah McWilliams Consalvo, 'The Lingual Ideal in the Poetry of Nuala Ní Dhomhnaill', *Éire-Ireland*, vol. 30, no. 2 (summer 1995), pp. 148–61; Patricia Boyle Haberstroh, 'Nuala Ní Dhomhnaill', *Women Creating Women: Contemporary Irish Women Poets* (Dublin: Attic Press, 1996), pp. 160–95; Mary O'Connor, 'Lashings of the Mother Tongue: Nuala Ní Dhomhnaill's Anarchic Laughter', in *The Comic Tradition in Irish Women Writers*, ed. Theresa O'Connor (Gainesville: University Press of Florida, 1996), pp. 149–70; Angela Bourke, 'Fairies and Anorexia: Nuala Ní Dhomhnaill's "Amazing Grass"', *Proceedings of the Harvard Celtic Colloquium*, 13, pp. 25–38.

Paula Meehan

LIFE. Paula Meehan was born in Dublin's inner city in 1955. She was educated at Whitehall House Senior Girls' School, at Trinity College Dublin, where she took her BA degree in English, history and classical civilization, and at Eastern Washington State University, where she received her Master in Fine Arts degree in poetry in 1983. Meehan had Irish Arts Council bursaries in 1987 and in 1990; she has read under its auspices in the former Soviet Union and in Europe. In 1988 she was a Fellow of the Robert Frost House in New Hampshire. Meehan has taught extensively in Ireland: at Trinity, at University College Dublin and at writing workshops in Ireland, including those for women prisoners in Mountjoy and Portlaoise prisons.

CHIEF WRITINGS. *Return and No Blame* (Dublin: Beaver Row, 1984); *Reading the Sky* (Dublin: Beaver Row, 1986); *The Man Who Was Marked By Winter* (Dublin: Gallery Press, 1991; Cheney: Eastern Washington State University Press, 1994); *Pillow Talk* (Dublin: Gallery Press, 1994).

BIOGRAPHY AND CRITICISM. Ann Owens Weekes, *Unveiling Treasures* (Dublin: Attic Press, 1993), pp. 224–6.

Moya Cannon

LIFE. Moya Cannon was born in Dunfanaghy, County Donegal, in 1956. She was educated at University College Dublin, where she studied history and politics, and at Corpus Christi College of Cambridge University. She won the Brendan Behan Prize for a first book of poetry in 1990. Her poems have been published in Ireland and abroad and some have been set to music by contemporary composers. She lives in County Galway, where she teaches Traveller children.

CHIEF WRITINGS. *Oar* (Galway: Salmon, 1990); *The Parchment Boat* (Oldcastle: Gallery Press, 1997).

BIOGRAPHY AND CRITICISM. Ann Owens Weekes, *Unveiling Treasures* (Dublin: Attic Press, 1993), pp. 68–70.

Ruth Hooley

LIFE. Ruth Carr, formerly Hooley, was born in Belfast in 1953. She edited *The Female Line* (1985), an anthology of poetry and fiction by Northern Irish women writers, and is currently associate editor of *HU* poetry magazine. A founder member of the Word of Mouth poetry collective, she works as a tutor in adult education and her first collection, *There is a House,* was published by Summer Palace Press (1999).

CHIEF WRITINGS. (ed.), *The Female Line: Northern Irish Women Writers* (Belfast: Northern Ireland Women's Rights Movement, 1985).

BIOGRAPHY AND CRITICISM. 'Interview with Rebecca E. Wilson', in Gillean Somerville-Arjat and Rebecca E. Wilson (eds), *Sleeping With Monsters: Conversations with Scottish and Irish Women Poets* (Dublin: Wolfhound Press, 1990).

MAIRE RODGERS, *Editor*

Expanding Boundaries:
Faith and Science, 1850–1990

Of all the branches of science, astronomy has been the one most closely associated with religion, from the earliest times when its development was largely in the hands of the priestly classes of ancient cultures, through to the Middle Ages when it was not clearly distinguished from astrology. The seventeenth century saw the beginning of the separation of science and philosophy and religion, and by the end of the nineteenth century little evidence of the personal beliefs of scientists was evident in their writings. However, in the writings of astronomers, in particular, one sometimes glimpses the cosmic vision which fuels and is fed by the struggle to make sense of the observed universe. In the extracts from the writings of the three Irish women astronomers selected here one senses the awe and excitement that accompanies this search.

Ireland has made a significant contribution to astronomy, not only on the purely scientific side, but also in the development of the technologies which have made the scientific observation and analysis possible.[1] Mary Ward, Agnes Clerke and Susan McKenna-Lawlor span a timescale which covers three visits of Halley's Comet to the inner reaches of the solar system and three different areas in terms of observational technology.

Mary Ward would have seen the comet pass when she was seven years old in 1834, at a time when the most advanced instrument of observation was the telescope. She witnessed the building of the world's largest telescope by her cousin Lord Rosse, at Birr Castle in 1845. Her own observations were largely made with a two-inch telescope. Agnes Clerke, who died just three years before the next transit of Halley's Comet in 1910, was writing at the time when spectroscopic analysis of the light from stars and nebulae was revolutionizing astronomical research. She herself made and published some spectroscopic observations during her short sojourn at the Cape Observatory in South Africa.[2] Susan McKenna-Lawlor was on the leading edge of the international collaboration which enabled Earth for the first time to visit Halley's Comet on its most recent fly-past in 1986. A new era of research was heralded when GIOTTO, the first European spacecraft to leave Earth's gravity, flew through the comet's coma and close enough to the nucleus to obtain information about the comet's composition and the physical processes that take place in its various layers. McKenna-Lawlor continues to be on the forefront of technological creativity.

While Mary Ward and Agnes Clerke communicated with astronomers and other scientists of international repute, their research and writings were largely solo efforts. A major difference in Susan McKenna-Lawlor's work is that both the research and the writing are of necessity group endeavours which cross major political boundaries, including those between East and West.

Although these women have excelled in what is still largely a male preserve, they are not alone in expanding the frontiers of knowledge through scientific endeavour. Irish-born Kathleen Lonsdale became a leading scientist in the field of crystallography and the structure of organic

---

1. See S.M.P. McKenna-Lawlor (ed.), *Whatever Shines Should be Observed* (Dublin: Samton, 1998).

2. See M. Bruck, *Agnes Mary Clerke, Chronicler of Astronomy* (1994).

crystals. Her understanding of the perils of using nuclear energy irresponsibly gave immense credibility to the cause of world peace and international co-operation. Unsung women have featured in almost every branch of science and some of their stories are now being brought to light.[3] When Halley's Comet returns in 2062 how will the boundaries for women stand?

3. See P. Phillips, *The Scientific Lady: A Social History of Women's Scientific Interests 1520–1918* (London: Weidenfeld and Nicolson; New York: St Martin's Press, 1990), and S.M.P. McKenna-Lawlor, *Whatever Shines Should be Observed.*

MARY WARD

(1827–69)

from:
TELESCOPE TEACHINGS
(1859)

[Mary Ward's popular book, *Telescope Teachings*, was based on her own knowledge and on the observations in astronomy gathered on visits to the great telescope at Birr Castle, County Offaly, home of her cousin William Parsons, 3rd Earl of Rosse. The extract is from chapter 1, 'The Observer's Apparatus, and What to Observe'. The author begins with a discussion of the tools of the amateur observer (a set of maps of the stars, an almanac, and a telescope), and goes on to explain how the stars appear to move.]

We will suppose, reader, that with regard to the movements of the heavenly bodies, you know but one fact with absolute clearness and certainty, namely, that the Sun rises every day in the east, glorious and glowing from behind the horizon, and travels southwards in a sloping direction till about noon, and that, as the day goes on, he evidently travels downwards, and at last sinks behind the western horizon, leaving only radiant clouds to tell of his brightness; and that the twilight gives way to night, and again, after some hours, night to twilight, and the Sun rises again. Nay, dear reader, be not offended at this low estimate of your knowledge; we speak only of what you know with absolute clearness and certainty, and what you have had so many more opportunities of observing than you are likely to have enjoyed with regard to the fixed stars. For how few have followed in the track of the Chaldean shepherds,[1] they who were among the earliest to collect and hand down to succeeding ages the facts of astronomy!

Did our usual occupations, like theirs, call us to spend the *whole night* under the blue vault of heaven, we should soon see for ourselves, and thoroughly comprehend, that even as the Sun rises in the east, travels upwards to the south, and descends in the west, so do all the stars which we can see as we sit to watch them, facing the south, the direction where the Sun was at noon.

All the night through we should observe that there are stars rising above the horizon at our left, others drifting slowly along opposite to us, others sinking at our right. We might also perceive that those which rise but a little way eastward of the south point which we are facing, remain but a short time in our view, never rise to any great height, and set but a little way west of the southern point of the horizon, and then remain invisible for many hours. Whereas those which rise so far to the east that we must look exactly over our left shoulder to see them emerge above the horizon, rise to a great height overhead, set far to the west, and remain so long in sight (namely, twelve hours), that the morning twilight has almost come before they have sunk at our right hand.

1. The Chaldean astronomers made accurate and systematic observations over long periods which enabled them to predict events such as the apparent motion of the planets, stars and lunar eclipses. R. Grant, in his Introduction to *History of Physical Astronomy from the Earliest Ages to the Middle of the Nineteenth Century* (London: Robert Baldwin, 1852), p. ii, notes the observational emphasis of the Chaldeans in contrast to the more theoretical and speculative approach of the Grecian philosophers; this was one of a number of books Mary would have read on the history of astronomy.

The stars still further removed from the south quarter of the horizon, what of them? They are still longer above the horizon, and a shorter time below than those which rise in the east. Turning our eyes completely away from the southern to the northern horizon, what do we see? Stars which merely descend for a brief interval, and again ascend; and above them, stars which never set at all, but slowly revolve round the almost stationary Pole Star.

But neither our present business, or we might say, the business of this little book, is with these northern stars, which indeed revolve like the others, but cannot be said to rise or set, as they are perpetually in sight on every cloudless night. We again turn our eyes to the south, and endeavour to impress on the reader that if he spend the whole of one clear night in the open air, he would see stars rising and setting, as he sees the Sun do by day. Or, without rivalling the Chaldean astronomers by actually watching all night, he may prove the same thing by observing the rising of some striking constellation, and tracing its progress occasionally

during the night. Let him fix on one which is not too near the southern horizon, and remains a considerable time in sight, and let him view it from an east window of his house at the time of its rising, say seven o'clock in the evening, in December. He may watch it now and then till eleven o'clock, when it will have gone so much to his right that he will now find it easier to see it from the south side of the house.

He chances to wake at one o'clock, and now the constellation is opposite the window which looks to the south, and is higher up than the observer has previously seen it. He now closes his shutters on the calm cold stars, but, true to his undertaking, seeks his constellation again in the faint grey of the morning, shortly before seven o'clock. It is then opposite a west window, and slowly disappearing below the horizon.

Such is the progress of a constellation during one night. We need hardly remind our readers than this apparent movement of the starry heavens is entirely caused by the real movement of the earth on its own axis.

AGNES CLERKE

(1842–1907)

from:
MODERN COSMOGONIES
(1905)

[Agnes Clerke developed a lifelong interest in astronomy. Educated by her parents in Skibbereen, County Cork, she later became a writer of scientific essays, contributing many articles to the 11th edition of the *Encyclopaedia Britannica* (1911). This extract comes towards the end of chapter VIII, 'Cosmogony in the Twentieth Century', in which the author discusses the latest far-reaching speculations about the origins of the universe arising from astronomical discoveries made possible by the development of photographic and spectroscopic methods of observation.]

The world of nebulae[1] confronts us with entire cycles of evolutionary problems, which can no longer be treated in the offhand manner perforce

adopted by Herschel.[2] The objects in question are of bewildering variety; yet we can trace, amid their fantastic irregularities, the underlying uniformity of one constructive thought. Nearly all show, more or less markedly, a spiral conformation,[3] and a spiral conformation intimates the action of known or discoverable laws. Their investigation must, indeed, be slow and toilsome; its progress may long be impeded by the interposition of novel questions, both in physics and mechanics; nevertheless, the lines prescribed for it seem definite enough to give hope of its leading finally to a clear issue. And when at last something has

---

1. Nebulae are bright or dark objects with a diffuse appearance.

2. Sir William Herschel (1738–1822), regarded by the author and others as 'The Founder of Sidereal Astronomy' (*A Popular History of Astronomy During the Nineteenth Century* [4th ed. 1902], p. 9). He was the first to build large telescopes and along with his sister, Caroline, made observations of thousands of stars and nebulae. He speculated that nebulae were possibly the raw materials from which stars evolved.

3. The spiral nature of nebulae had been discovered by William Parsons, 3rd Earl of Rosse, in 1848, with the 72-inch telescope he built at Birr Castle.

been fairly well ascertained regarding the past and future of nebulous spirals, no contemptible inroad will have been made on the stupendous enigma of sidereal relationships.

Its aspect, if we venture to look at it in its entirety, is vast and formidable. Not now, as in former times, with a mere fragment of creation — a single star and its puny client globes, one of which happens to be the temporary abode of the human race — but with the undivided, abysmal cosmos,[4] the science of origin and destiny concerns itself. The obscure and immeasurable uncertainties of galactic history invite or compel attention. We know just enough to whet our desire to know a great deal more. The distribution of stars and nebulae is easily seen to be the outcome of design.[5] By what means, we cannot but ask ourselves, was the design executed? How were things ordered when those means began to be employed? How will they be ordered when all is done? For an ultimate condition has, presumably, not yet been reached. And if not, agencies must be at work for the perfecting of the supreme purpose, which are not, perhaps, too subtle for our apprehension.

Meanwhile, facts bearing on sidereal construction are being diligently collected and sifted, and we shall do well to suspend speculation until their larger import is made known.

The inquisitions of science do not cease here. They strive to penetrate a deeper mystery than that of the scattering in space of stars and nebulae. What are they made of? is the further question that presents itself. What is the nature of the primal world-stuff?[6] Whence did it obtain heat? By what means was motion imparted to it? If it be urged that such-like topics elude the grasp of finite intelligence and belong to the secrets of creative power, we may reply that we are not entitled, nor are we able, to draw an arbitrary line, not to be transgressed by our vagrant thoughts. The world has been, by express decree, thrown wide to their excursions, and it is not for us to restrict their freedom. We need not fear getting too near the heart of the mystery; there is no terminus in the unknown to which we can travel by express; in a sense, we are always starting, and never getting near to our destination. But that is because it retreats before us. We do, in truth, advance; and as we advance the mists clear, and we see glimpses beyond of imperishable order, of impenetrable splendour. Our inquiries need not then be abandoned in despair at the far-reaching character they have spontaneously assumed.

4. In *Problems in Astrophysics* (1903), Agnes writes, 'The Milky Way is an integral part of the great sidereal system. It marks the equatorial girdle of a sphere containing stars and nebulae variously scattered and aggregated. The whole material creation is, to our apprehension, enclosed within this sphere' (p. 538). This view of the universe as confined to our galaxy was common at the time.
5. The distribution of different classes of stars and nebulae is also referred to in *Problems in Astrophysics* (p. 539): 'the distribution of sidereal, as of animal species, is the outcome of their history, a test of their longevity, and index to their nature. They are *where* they are, because they are *what* they are.'

6. The phenomenon of radioactive emission from some elements was already being investigated at this time but it was not until 1911 that Ernest Rutherford discovered the nucleus of the atom. In the next chapter, the author discusses the nature of the 'primal world-stuff', termed 'protyle'.

SUSAN M.P. McKENNA-LAWLOR

(*c.* 1950–   )

from:
THE EPONA INSTRUMENT ON THE GIOTTO MISSION — A PERSONAL REMINISCENCE (1990)

[Susan McKenna-Lawlor is internationally known for her contribution to research in cosmonautics. The recipient of many honours for her participation in the GIOTTO Extended Mission (1992), she was elected a member of the International Academy of Astronautics in 1993. This text is chapter 2 in N. Longdon (ed.), *Some Personal Reminiscences — The ESRO-ESA Space Science Story, Twenty-Five Years of European Co-operation*, in which seven scientists detail personal stories and reflections about the work of the European Space Research Organisation (ESRA) and its development after the merger with the European Launcher Development Organisation (ELDO) into the European Space Agency (ESA).]

The wonderful adventure which culminated in the encounter of an instrument from Ireland with comet Halley began very unexpectedly, far from the Emerald Island itself, when I arrived in mid-1980 to present an invited talk at the STIP[1] meeting in Smolenicie, Czechoslovakia. It had been very difficult to get there. Last-minute visa problems and tortuous connections had raised between Smolenicie and myself a series of obstacles which might well have deterred a less determined traveller. But now, with my presentation over and a pleasant evening in a fairy-tale-like castle stretching ahead, I turned to get to know the Conference participant who was to dine at my right hand.

'I am Rudegar Reinhard, Project Scientist for the GIOTTO Mission,' he told me and later remarked 'Ireland is now a full member of the European Space Agency, why is there no Irish experiment proposed to go to the Comet?'

There are moments in life for all of us which are of supreme significance. Moments when the inspiration provided by a startlingly important question can release the imagination to fly amid perspectives of previously undreamed-of possibilities. There were many logical reasons to explain why no one proposed an Irish experiment for the Comet. The special clean rooms, the environmental testing equipment, the particle accelerators, all of the special hardware that I personally knew from experience working with NASA would be required to construct an experiment that could go to and function in the cometary environment were, at that time, unavailable in Ireland. And yet, in the inspiration of the moment, I could look at my companion and say 'we have not so far proposed an experiment for GIOTTO from our country but — why not?'

The very beginning is, they say, a very good place to start and so it was with this project. At the suggestion of Rudegar Reinhard I went to meet Professor Ian Axford, Director of the Max Planck Institute at Lindau, Germany, and together we discussed what the Irish experiment might be.

Since my background was in studying solar cosmic rays, it appeared very suitable, and timely, to propose an instrument that would at first monitor flare particles during the approximately eight month cruise phase and then investigate the behaviour of energetic cometary ions in the close environment of Halley.

As the discussions proceeded apace, it became clear to both of us that such an instrument from Ireland, with a lady PI,[2] would very soon be proposed to the Agency and Professor Axford said, 'You need a name for the experiment that will be representative of Ireland; what will you call it?' My mind raced. 'It is,' I said, 'a device that measures energetic particles, the onset of energetic particles', and the letters EPONA (Energetic Particle Onset Admonitor) formed in my head, an acronym but also the name of the beautiful and mysterious Epona, a Celtic Goddess associated with the commencement of the Solar Year.[3] The experiment now had a name which would have a special resonance at home while linking our ancient culture with the new age of deep space exploration just then dawning in Europe.

Professor Axford generously promised that, should the EPONA instrument be successfully selected for the mission, he would provide access to the Lindau specialist laboratories for my engineers until I could install at my own University the kind of in-house facilities required to build flight-qualified instrumentation.

The next step was to gather together a team to formulate a proposal to the Agency and, if successful in the selection stage, to implement the experiment. Winning through to selection was not an easy task. Everyone in Europe, it seemed, wanted an instrument aboard the historic GIOTTO Mission and it was necessary to defend the EPONA Proposal like a thesis before specialist referees.

The instrument suggested was a lightweight single particle telescope (only 480g were available for the device) and it was a joyous day for our group when it was finally selected as one of the ten experiments on the mission. Soon after this acceptance however, I became aware that a somewhat larger GIOTTO spacecraft would have to be built than had been originally foreseen, to accommodate extra hydrazine for necessary mid-course corrections. The possibility to increase

---

1.   STIP: Study of Travelling Interplanetary Phenomena.

2.   PI: Principal Investigator.
3.   Epona is also known as the 'Horse Goddess'. See P. McCana, *Celtic Mythology* (London: Hamlyn, 1970).

significantly the mass allocation for EPONA and fly a sophisticated triple telescope on the mission thus began to suggest itself.

There were tough related negotiating sessions before this could be achieved since other experimenters who wanted to upgrade their designs were also in competition for the newly available resources. However, in the end, that triple telescope with its high spatial (8 sectors) and temporal (0.5s) resolution made it through the second-step selection process.

The months that followed were filled with activity. Ireland owes a deep debt of gratitude to the personnel at the Lindau Institute who so generously gave of their time and expertise to advise those of our team directly engaged in instrument construction and testing. By the time the design of the Engineering Model had been fully developed and verified, up-to-date laboratories had been installed at Maynooth wherein electronics for the Flight Model could be built, and the media flocked to the College to photograph these facilities and to hear about EPONA.

At last the time came for the launch campaign and I travelled to French Guiana to supervise the final tests before launch and sign the protocols that transferred the instrument, for the first time in five years, from my personal custody to that of the Agency. Experiment switch-on was to be on August 12, 1985, and it was a serious moment to sit in the big chair at ESOC,[4] Darmstadt, while the command EPONA ON was uplinked to the spacecraft.

The instrument, however, answered very sweetly indeed. Interplanetary space was, on that day, particularly quiet, and it was clear that EPONA's performance equalled the very best we had observed in the laboratory.

As the period of encounter approached, the historic importance of what was about to happen became increasingly manifest to all. People gathered in droves around the tracking station to try somehow to get closer to what they perceived to be an event of great significance. I had not gone back to my hotel for two days, preferring to stay at the data monitor, and a red hat that I had placed on my head about 30 hours before, stayed forgotten in place.

As we flew within about 7.5 million km of Halley it was clear that the instrument had already detected cometary ions. Then, as we crossed the Bow Shock[5] and flew close to the comet, a most dramatic signature indicated that we were recording ions of energies considerably greater than those attributable to the pick-up process acting alone. Remembering that I had promised TV presenter Patrick Moore to let him know if anything 'exciting' should happen within the experiment, I rushed into the BBC studios and showed on camera the wonderful record EPONA had sent us. All eyes apparently flew from the record to my red hat, and, by morning, I was a celebrity since the viewing public had not at all expected to see a lady PI, least of all one so attired.

Meanwhile, 'closest approach' was coming. A large screen in the laboratory showed a stream of updating pictures coming from the Halley Multicolour Camera and it was clear that we were flying into a most hazardous dust environment. Then, someone from the DIDSY[6] Team yelled 'we have penetration' as a large dust grain hit the spacecraft and set it into nutation.

During this period, every time the antenna pointed towards the Earth EPONA transmitted a burst of data and I knew that if the instrument could but survive until the nutation dampers worked, we might well continue to receive 'outbound' records.

At this critical interval, when the spacecraft was at closest approach, the instrument was recording a most remarkable enhancement in particular fluxes, and I feared that each transmission that came might be the last and that we would miss the end of the event.

Sufficient data to provide the overall profile however came through and, after about 32 minutes, the telecommunications link with Earth was fully restored. EPONA then transmitted a steady stream of beautiful data, indicating, as time progressed, that the outbound energetic particle signatures were significantly different from those obtained inbound.[7]

---

4. ESOC: European Space Operations Centre in Germany.

5. The interface formed as the fast-moving comet encounters the solar wind.

6. DIDSY: the Dust Impact Detection System on GIOTTO.

7. The 'inbound' records are those received as the spacecraft travelled into the balloon-like comet and the 'outbound' those recorded as it left the other side of the balloon.

As the night wore on, with the help of a young engineer from my group, I continuously printed and pasted together the records coming in and an enormously long trace charting the complete flyby was formed. When morning came, there was a noise in the corridor and the Director General of the Agency, Professor Lust, stopped at the door to see who was still burning lights in that part of the building. 'Come in, come in,' I said, 'see what I have to show you, a complete encounter with the Comet.' He took one look and then called to Professor Bonnet to come too to share the joy of the data-take.

Perhaps only scientists understand what such moments can mean, when, through the medium of an instrument, we seek to ask of Nature a question and receive in return a majestic response, revealing things that are wonderful and new, with intimations of hidden depths about which we had previously not even guessed.

A major press conference was planned for the media that afternoon and each of the PIS was asked to present 'first results'. I brought along my big chart and instructed the projectionist to feed it through the projector when I gave the word. 'Gentlemen,' I told the Press when my turn came, 'I invite you to fly through the comet with me,' and, as the chart moved along, I took them through all of the beautiful phenomena EPONA had recorded from the inbound bow shock to the latest piece of data that had been received.

The instrument continued to record spectacular traces until 3 am on March 15 when the mission was deemed by the Agency to be complete and telemetry coverage was discontinued. At that time, only the magnetometer and EPONA were still transmitting data and, in the enormous control centre which had previously so buzzed with life, only four people, two representatives of MAG,[8] my Chief Engineer, and myself, were still present. First the MAG screen went blank, then I heard a voice over the headphones say, 'in one minute EPONA will be switched off'.

In the darkened laboratory tears rolled unbidden down my face as I waited for the data stream to disappear. It was as if a life were being terminated.

At the present time, all of us who have been privileged to take part in the remarkable GIOTTO Mission look to the possibility that the spacecraft may yet be commanded to encounter another comet. While it is not yet certain at this time if such an expedition will really be implemented, the spacecraft and its payload are scheduled to be thoroughly checked by the Agency to see if such a mission is achievable and we will, at that time, attempt to re-activate EPONA.

It is nice to think that perhaps our Celtic Goddess is presently but sleeping and will fly again through interplanetary space, gathering further beautiful data to provide to those on Earth insights into mysteries as old as time.[9]

8. MAG: the magnetometer experiment on GIOTTO.
9. See biographical note, p. 654, for the subsequent reactivation and use of EPONA.

KATHLEEN LONSDALE

(1903–71)

from:
IS PEACE POSSIBLE? (1957)

[As a pacifist during the years of the Cold War, Lonsdale continued to campaign for disarmament and international co-operation, serving as president of the Women's International League for Peace and Freedom and as a member of the East–West Committee of the Society of Friends. In 1951 she visited Russia, as part of a delegation of Friends which met representatives of the Soviet Peace Committee, leaders of the Baptist and Orthodox churches, and Jacob Malik, Deputy Foreign Minister of the Soviet Union. In 1952 she edited the report of this delegation and in 1957 produced her own justification of pacifism. *Is Peace Possible?* was aimed at a general audience, warned of the dangers of nuclear weapons and sought total disarmament and the establishment of 'an impartial and objective World Court of Justice as a body to which all international disputes or grievances involving nations or governments can be referred'. Citing Martin Luther King's civil rights campaign, she demonstrated the power of non-violent protest and the ability of individuals to resist community evil by such methods. She also identified population growth as a major threat to world peace, as well as to health and living standards, while admitting the necessity of allowing countries such as China to develop their own response to this problem and pressing for increased aid from the developed nations to disadvantaged areas in order to improve agricultural methods and increase food supply. In this section, chapter 2, pp. 13–20, Lonsdale discusses the hazards of producing power from nuclear fuel. She suggests that the problems associated with radioactive waste disposal have implications globally if nuclear power stations are established on a large scale, even greater than the amounts that would be let loose, deliberately and devastatingly, in a nuclear war. The text was prepared by Rosemary Raughter.]

The one subject I do know something about is science. Let me begin with that. Is science friend or fiend? Forty years ago, when I began to study science at school, we had gas, but no electricity in our house. My brother worked in one of the first radio stations in the south-west of Ireland, but radio in the home was a thing of the future. Television was a fantastic dream. I had been born in the year in which the Wright brothers built and flew the first successful heavier-than-air machine, and years later Blériot had flown across the English Channel, but in 1916 the bombs that fell on our London suburb were dropped not from aeroplanes but from unwieldy and suicidal gas-filled Zeppelins. We sometimes watched them being shot down in flames and my mother cried, because she had read that some of the German crews were boys of sixteen. Somehow this seemed to have very little connexion with the science I was learning, but it may have had something to do with my own growing feeling that war was utterly wrong.

When I became a research student, training under Sir William Bragg in the very place where Sir Humphrey Davy, Michael Faraday, John Tyndall, Sir James Dewar, and other world-famous scientists had carried out their researches, the war was over and, as we thought, won. We genuinely hoped for a peace settlement that would end all war. Terrible things had happened, but we believed that there were plenty of good Germans, and that they would now have

a chance to come out on top. Terrible things had happened and were perhaps still happening in Russia, but other countries, America and France, for instance, had had pretty ghastly revolutions too, and then settled down. It might take time. Meanwhile my work was fun. I often ran the last few yards to the laboratory. Later on I took my mathematical calculations with me to the nursing-home where my babies were born: it was exciting to find out new facts.

Now science seems to have become something of a Frankenstein. Chunks of it have become secret; slightly indecent, as it were. For a time, indeed, during the war and for a few years after, secrecy became a disease. If a discovery had any practical value at all, it must be kept secret. If good, it must not be shared with our enemies or competitors. If bad, they must not be allowed to copy it or discover the antidote. What does this enmity and competition involve?

Scientific discoveries of any kind are certainly a power and a responsibility. The world's resources are very unevenly distributed. If a new use is found for some raw material that is the monopoly of one or a few nations, those nations may become wealthy overnight, or they may become a prey to more powerful neighbours. That was brought home to me very forcibly after World War II. I had gone to give lectures in Paris. My husband went to a scientific congress in Brussels. The shortages of food and of almost all other commodities were still acute in France. Not so, apparently, in Belgium. Why? Both had suffered during the war. But Belgium now had uranium to sell, from rich mines in the Belgian Congo. France was obliged to export her dairy produce. The uranium from Belgium was going to the USA for dollars, and some of it was sold to Britain.

Where was the Soviet Union to get uranium? No doubt she had some, and was busy prospecting to find more. There was some in Poland, too. But there were also rich uranium mines in Czechoslovakia. It was rather important not to let that go West, if the Soviet Union were eventually to compete on equal terms in the making of nuclear weapons and the production of power from nuclear fuel. There was a strong communist minority in Czechoslovakia, too, strong enough to seize power, with Soviet backing just around the corner. In fact, the Czechoslovakian *coup d'état* of 1948, which shocked and alarmed the West, and which has poisoned East–West international relations ever since, was an almost inevitable consequence of the dropping of the first two atomic bombs on Hiroshima and Nagasaki. It might have been expected. It could hardly have shocked intelligent politicians.

Of course it was deplorable. Although conditions have improved recently, no-one visiting Prague can pretend that this is a light-hearted, happy city. But I simply do not see how a nation such as Britain that believes in the policies of 'Peace through strength' and of 'Negotiation from strength', that holds on to unwilling colonies because they are important strategic bases or because they have important raw materials, could really have expected the Soviet Union to behave any differently. They are no better than we are. Why should they be? They believe in 'Negotiation from strength' too.

The enormous speed of scientific development during the past fifty years has meant a revolution in means of transport and communications, the mechanization of factories and homes, and the production of hideously destructive scientific weapons of war. Two developments are bound to follow. The first is that the next fifty or one hundred years are certain to bring other spectacular advances. The second is that some, at least, of the countries that are at present technically under-developed will undoubtedly catch up with the West, as the Soviet Union is now doing.

The material prosperity and military power of any nation is dependent upon its possession of raw materials and on its scientific and technical development. Those countries which as yet have few scientists, technologists, and technicians and have not built roads, railways, and power stations are technically under-developed even though they may have a long and honourable history and a high degree of culture. Whether they can become technically developed depends upon their possession of raw materials that can be traded for revenue, or upon the assistance of wealthier nations, or upon their having some means of attracting investment capital from their own or other people. There is no reason whatever why they should not, with expert help, be able to produce scientists, though of course it will take time. Japan did it. China is training scientists and

technicians at a great rate, many of whom are ploughed back into teaching. Iraq is planning to spend some millions of her oil revenue on the building of roads. Egypt has failed to attract the capital she needs for the construction of the Aswan High Dam, although without technical development and irrigation, plus good government of course, it is impossible for the mass of her people to live at anything more than a sub-human level.

In general, the lack of technical development means that the majority of the country's inhabitants do live miserably poor lives. Sometimes, if the weather is good and the soil rich, as in parts of Thailand, so that clothes and shelter, apart from shade, are unimportant, and food is fairly easily come by, life may not be too unendurable, provided that one's wants are few. But in places like China, where it can be very cold, very hot, or very wet, where floods and drought alternate and the population is too large for the amount of agricultural land available, the conditions under which many people have had to live are so ghastly that they must be seen to be believed. In such a case it is absolutely essential that the power consumption per man — the general availability of electrical and mechanical power — should be increased. Besides, the Asians are beginning to want bicycles, radios, refrigerators, and good drainage systems too.

Britain, with some 2 per cent of the world's population, is using some 10 per cent of the world's power.

India, with over 17 per cent of the world's population, is using only $1\frac{1}{2}$ per cent of the world's power.

This is the main reason for the difference in the standards of living in these two countries.

In China one can still see groups of men, women, and children working a kind of treadmill in order to raise water from the streams to the level of the fields. They have to work hard for hours to irrigate an acre. No wonder that the collective farms that have been able to acquire a mechanical pump can get bigger yields for less effort. We must not forget that many of the man-made wonders of the past — the Pyramids of Egypt, the Taj Mahal of India, the Temple of Heaven of Peking, the wonders of Greek and Roman architecture — were built by men who were either slaves or no better off than slaves.

Power is not something that need necessarily continue in short supply, but fuel is not evenly distributed, and it can be used up. Britain has been fortunate in having had ample supplies of coal and iron, but her coal is running out. Less easily mined seams are now being worked. The industry has been nationalized partly because although essential it was beginning not to pay. The best coal had been creamed off. Governments must look ahead in terms of centuries, and our coal will not last more than another couple of centuries even at its present rate of consumption, which must increase if we are to compete in the world's markets and maintain our own standards of living too.

What other sources are there? The sun? It may be possible to harness the energy of the sun, and even perhaps to store it, in those countries that get enough sunshine; but Britain does not. It is certainly very desirable indeed, from the point of view of the power-hungry countries, that research, guided and financed internationally perhaps, shall investigate the practical possibilities of utilizing solar energy.

Wind? We have had windmills for many centuries, but the quantities of power that can be generated in this way are too small for modern requirements: but again, research into new methods of utilization needs stimulating and encouraging. Tides? We have those in Britain, but (according to the late Sir Francis Simon) the maximum saving to be gained by harnessing the tides would be only about 2 per cent of our coal consumption at a cost of some £200 million. We could, if we wanted to, save up to 20 per cent at a cost of under £10 million, by getting rid of our open grates and installing closed stoves. This would still not solve our power problem.

We do not, in Britain, have the mountainous catchment areas that would provide us with sufficient hydro-electric power for our needs, although if capital were available some really enormous schemes of this kind could be put into operation in some of the technically backward areas. One such, suggested by Dr Hans Thirring, by harnessing the waters of the Tsangpo River, in Eastern Tibet, could provide up to 333,000 million kilowatt-hours of electricity annually.

We in Britain are importing oil to supplement our coal, mostly from the Arab States. Coal and oil are essential not only for our power supplies but also as source materials for our chemical and metallurgical industries: and they need to be conserved for that purpose. But imported goods are precarious.

The consumption of Europe as a whole in 1975 is likely to be over 1,000 million tons of coal. In order to replace coal gradually and to supplement it as our supplies run short, we plan to use power from nuclear fuel. We are building and putting into operation nuclear power stations. This is a considered decision involving large sums of public money and there is no doubt that nuclear power has come to stay. It brings with it hideous problems, problems of which both scientists and politicians are aware. Risks can be minimized and of course are being minimized, but they exist. What are they?

Well, there are the scientific risks. Nuclear fission is the break-down of the nuclei of certain heavy elements with the release of primary and secondary energy in the form of heat, light, and pressure waves. In addition, large quantities of special kinds of high-energy radiation are generated and these will include two or three neutrons violently ejected from each atom broken up, and the highly radioactive fragments — the fission products — of the divided nuclei. The ejected neutrons can act as projectiles causing a chain of further similar fission processes, and this chain reaction can be either controlled, as in the nuclear pile, or catastrophic, as in the atom bomb.

The risk of a nuclear pile, used for power production, accidentally getting out of control is very small indeed, smaller than the risk that a coal mine may become ignited, but both risks exist. It is a tragedy when coal miners lose their lives through an accident, but the effect of the vaporization of the material of a nuclear reactor in a highly populated area would be much more terrible. Even if it were not a highly populated area, many people would be killed, and a large area contaminated for a long time, with devastating effects on agricultural production.

Then there is the disposal of the radioactive waste from the atomic energy industrial processes.

In a nuclear power station it is heat that is used to generate useful electrical or mechanical energy, through the medium of a heat engine. The by-products, in the form of high-energy radiation and fission products, must be used or disposed of somehow. Some of the particles can be absorbed in order to breed new fissile material, some can be used to provide isotopes and radioactive substances of various kinds for research, for all sorts of useful medical and industrial purposes. But one pound of uranium gives long-lived radioactivity comparable with that from about half a ton of radium: and four ounces of radium are sufficient to treat several thousand patients every year.

As with strawberries and cream, too much of a good thing is an embarrassment. Some by-products of a nuclear power plant can be exported and used for beneficial purposes by other countries that have no nuclear piles of their own. The new fissile material could be used as fresh fuel for the power station. Unfortunately it can also be stockpiled for the making of nuclear weapons. But even then there is still an enormous quantity of dangerous waste material to be got rid of. When all the electrical power in Britain comes from heat generated by the fission of uranium, the radiation to be disposed of somehow will be as much as that from about a million tons of radium. Or, to put it another way, there will be several million gallons of highly dangerous waste materials to be dumped somewhere even within the next twenty-five years,[1] and there are gaseous fission products which must be either reduced to liquid or solid form, or released under very carefully controlled conditions.

These problems are being faced by all the countries that are now developing or proposing to develop power from nuclear fuel. The effects of radiation on crops, on animals, on marine life and on man himself are being studied and research in these fields will and must be stepped up, because we still have to admit ignorance in many very important respects. The last four sentences in a Report to the Public on *The Biological Effects of Atomic Radiation* published in 1956 by the US National Academy of Sciences are as follows:

> Obviously, it will not do to let nuclear plants spring up *ad lib* over the earth. The

development of atomic energy is a matter for careful, integrated planning. A large part of the information that is needed to make intelligent plans is not yet at hand. There is not much time left to acquire it.

At present, radioactive waste products are being stored in tanks or pits in the ground, carried out to sea in containers and dumped, or discharged into large river systems. In England we are piping them into the Irish Sea. Probably no serious damage has yet been done to marine life. The sea is vast and deep. But as nuclear power production is stepped up, the processes of isolation and dispersion of these dangerous materials will certainly have to be made the subject of international agreement.

Every country with a coast-line is surrounded by coastal waters over which there is a large measure of national jurisdiction. But the one thing no Government can prevent is the gradual inter-change of surface waters and the movement of plant and animal life in the sea. This can be proved by anyone with a bath and a fountain pen. If a drop of ink is deposited at one end of the bath, even in such stagnant water it will soon be dispersed so as slightly to colour the whole.

Measurements were carried out after the test explosions of nuclear weapons in the Pacific Ocean in 1954. There is always a certain small amount of natural radioactivity in the sea, mostly due to a radioactive form of the element potassium. Two days after the tests the radioactivity of the surface waters near Bikini was a million times greater than normal. Ocean currents, about which we still know far too little, helped to spread the contaminated water and four months later waters 1,500 miles from Bikini had three times as much radioactivity as their usual value.

All this time the radioactivity itself would be dying away — decaying — much as the hotness of a bath decays while we lie in it. Some kinds of atoms lose their radioactivity very quickly indeed, others more slowly. One of the most dangerous of the fission products, radioactive strontium, has a comparatively long life. It loses half its activity in 10,000 days. So that while the contaminated water moved away from the test area, the radiation itself would be decreasing, fast at first and then more slowly. Yet thirteen months later the water 3,500 miles away showed a small,

1. The US report (National Academy of Sciences) on *Disposal and Dispersal of Radioactive Wastes* gives the total as 200 million gallons by 1980 and 2,400 million gallons by the year 2000. Some concentration would be possible but very expensive.

but definite rise of radioactivity. It is not possible to say how much marine life may have suffered in the neighbourhood of the area or what degree of radioactivity is necessary before. immediately or genetically harmful effects result. But what does seem certain is that the total amounts of radioactive waste that will eventually have to be disposed of, as safely as possible, when there are nuclear power stations all over the world, will be even greater than the amounts that would be let loose, deliberately and devastatingly, in a nuclear war.

Biographies/Bibliographies

Mary Ward

LIFE. Born in 1827, the youngest child of the Reverend Henry King and Harriet Lloyd, Mary was brought up on her parents' estate at Ballylin near Ferbane, not far from Birr Castle, home of her cousin William Parsons, the 3rd Earl of Rosse, whom she frequently visited and who was influential in encouraging her early observations in astronomy. Like her two sisters, Mary was taught at home by a governess while her brother attended school and university. By the age of eighteen, when she had acquired the microscope with which she made a lifetime's observations, she was already noted for her skills as an artist and naturalist. In 1854 she married Henry W.C. Ward and from 1857 onwards lived at various locations in and around Dublin. She combined the raising of eight children and running a household (at times under reduced financial circumstances) with an avid pursuit of scientific study and writing. She wrote under the name the Hon. Mrs Ward and is best known for her beautifully illustrated popular books, *Telescope Teachings* (1859) and *Microscope Teachings* (1864). Sir David Brewster FRS, one of the eminent scientists she got to know through her connection with Lord Rosse, included some of her illustrations in his publications. In 1859 at the request of one of her many correspondents, Sir William Rowan Hamilton, she began to receive the monthly notices from the Royal Astronomical Society, and in 1862 she was allowed to visit the strictly all-male preserve of the Royal Observatory at Greenwich. Her untimely death in 1869 was the result of an accident while on a visit to the family of her late cousin at Birr Castle. Mary was riding with her husband and two of the Parsons on a steam locomotive (built by Lord Rosse) when she was thrown from the carriage and was killed immediately. Her telescope, microscope, paintings, books and some other effects are held on exhibition in Castle Ward, County Down.

CHIEF WRITINGS. *Sketches with the Microscope* (Parsonstown: Shields, 1857, limited ed., privately printed), republished as *A World of Wonders Revealed by the Microscope* (London: Groombridge, 1858); *Telescope Teachings* (London: Groombridge, 1859); (with Lady Mahon) *Entomology in Sport, and Entomology in Earnest* (London: Paul Jerrard, 1859); *Microscope Teachings* (London: Groombridge, 1864); 'Toads in Ireland', *Intellectual Observer* (May 1864), repr. in *Irish Times*, 6 May 1864; 'The November Shooting Star', *Intellectual Observer* (January 1867), pp. 449–58.

BIOGRAPHY AND CRITICISM. O.G. Harry, 'The Hon. Mrs. Ward (1827–1869), Artist, Naturalist, Astronomer and Ireland's First Lady of the Microscope', *Irish Naturalists' Journal*, vol. 21 (1984), pp. 193–200; O.G. Harry, 'The Hon. Mrs. Ward and 'Windfall for the Microscope' of 1856 and 1864', *Annals of Science*, vol. 41 (1984), pp. 471–82; O.G. Harry, 'The Hon. Mrs. Ward (1827–1869): A Wife, Mother,

Microscopist and Astronomer in Ireland 1854–1869', in *Science in Ireland 1800–1930: Tradition and Reform, Proceedings of an International Symposium held at Trinity College Dublin, March 1986*, eds J.R. Nudds, N.D. McMillan, D.L. Weaire, S.M.P. McKenna-Lawlor (Dublin: Trinity College, 1988), pp. 187–97; O.G. Harry, 'Mary Ward, Microscopist, Astronomer, Naturalist, Artist', in *Some People and Places in Irish Science and Technology*, eds. C. Mollan, W. Davis, B. Finucane (Dublin: Royal Irish Academy, 1985), pp. 52–3.

Agnes Clerke

LIFE. Agnes Mary Clerke was born in County Cork in 1842 to John William Clerke, a bank manager with expertise in chemistry and astronomy, and Catherine Deasy, a well-educated woman with considerable musical ability. Agnes was brought up in Skibbereen with her elder sister and lifelong companion, Ellen, and her younger brother, Aubrey. All three were later to become successful writers in their own fields and while Aubrey attended St Patrick's College, Carlow, and Trinity College in Dublin, Agnes and Ellen received an extraordinarily rich education (including science, classics, music and several European languages) from their parents and by self-directed study. From childhood Agnes developed her twin life interests in astronomy and music. The family moved to Dublin in 1861 and finally settled in London in 1877. From 1867 until 1877 Agnes and Ellen spent several winters and a continuous period of four years in Italy, where they studied extensively in the libraries of Florence. Between 1877 and her death in 1907, Agnes published fifty-three scientific and literary articles in the *Edinburgh Review*, wrote biographical essays on scientists for the 9th edition of the *Encyclopaedia Britannica* (1875–1902), contributed almost all of the biographies of astronomers for the *Dictionary of National Biography* (1885–1901), and wrote regularly for the scientific journals *Nature*, *Knowledge*, the *Observatory* and a number of magazines in Britain and the us. Her article on the history of astronomy and many biographies of astronomers were published posthumously in the 11th edition of the *Encyclopaedia Britannica* (1911). She is best known, however, for the first of three major books on astronomy, *A Popular History of Astronomy during the Nineteenth Century* (1885), which is still regarded as the most authoritative account of the subject. The international acclaim which this generated gave her access to the scientific and social network of astronomers such as William and Margaret Huggins (London), Edward Holden (California) and Sir David Gill of the Royal Observatory at the Cape of Good Hope. She spent some months in 1888 developing her practical astronomical skills at the Cape Observatory and went on to publish *The System of the Stars* (1890), and *Problems in Astrophysics* (1903). These technical books, along with her last book, *Modern Cosmogonies* (1905), show not only her comprehensive grasp of the latest research and theories about the origin and development of the universe, but also her understanding of the limits of these theories and her ability to speculate about directions for further research to expand the boundaries of knowledge about the cosmos. She was an elected member of the Astronomical Society of the Pacific (1889), member of the Council of the British Astronomical Association (1890), winner of the Actonian Prize of the Royal Institution (1892) and an honorary member (along with Lady Huggins) of the Royal Astronomical Society (1903). Like her sister and brother, Agnes remained unmarried throughout her life and had no children.

CHIEF WRITINGS. *A Popular History of Astronomy during the Nineteenth Century* (London: Adam and Charles Black, 1885; 2nd ed., 1887; 3rd ed., 1893; 4th ed., 1902); *The System of the Stars* (London: Longmans, Green, 1890; 2nd ed., 1905); *Familiar Studies in Homer* (London: Longmans, 1892); *The Herschels and Modern Astronomy* (London: Cassell, 1895); (with A. Fowler and G.E. Gore, ed. A.H. Miles) *Astronomy* (1 of 4 vols 1897–1914 in *The Concise Knowledge Library* (London: Hutchinson, 1898); *Low Temperature Research at the Royal Institution of Great Britain* (London: W. Clowes, 1901); *Problems in Astrophysics* (London: Adam and Charles Black, 1903); *Modern Cosmogonies* (London: Adam and Charles Black, 1905); 'History of Astronomy', in *Encyclopaedia Britannica* (New York: Encyclopaedia

Britannica, 11th ed., 1910), pp. 808–19; also in same edition, entries under Galileo (pp. 406–11), Laplace (pp. 200–3), Brahe (pp. 377–8), Copernicus (pp. 100–1), Flamsteed (pp. 477–8), Halley (pp. 856–7), Huygens (pp. 21–2), Kepler (pp. 749–51), Zodiac (pp. 993–8) and others.

BIOGRAPHY AND CRITICISM. S. Lee (ed.), *Dictionary of National Biography*, Supplement Jan. 1901–Dec. 1911 (London: Smith, Elder, 1912; rpr. Oxford University Press, 1920, 1966), 1966 rpr. pp. 371–2; *Who Was Who*, vol. 1, 1897–1916 (London: Adam and Charles Black, 5th ed. 1967), p. 142; *M.L. Huggins, Agnes Mary Clerke and Ellen Mary Clerke, an Appreciation* (London: 1907, privately printed); M.T. Brück, 'Companions in Astronomy, Margaret Lindsay Murray and Agnes Mary Clerke', *Irish Astronomical Journal*, vol. 20, no. 2 (1991), pp. 70–7; M.T. Brück, 'Ellen and Agnes Clerke of Skibbereen, Scholars and Writers', *Seanchas Chairbre*, no. 3 (1993), pp. 23–43; M.T. Brück, 'Agnes Mary Clerke, Chronicler of Astronomy', *Quarterly Journal of the Royal Astronomical Society*, vol. 35, no. 1 (1994), pp. 59–79.

Susan M.P. McKenna-Lawlor

LIFE. Susan McKenna was born in Dublin, *c.* 1950, and educated at the Convent of the Sacred Heart, Leeson Street, at University College Dublin, and at the University of Michigan, Ann Arbor, where she completed her Ph.D. research on solar flare phenomena and their effects at the Earth. She was awarded a post-graduate research scholarship to the Dublin Institute for Advanced Studies, and following work at Dunsink Observatory, Dublin, the San Fernando Observatory, California, and Culgoora Observatory, Australia, she soon gained world renown as she became increasingly active in international research work carried out using instrumentation flown aboard spacecraft of the US, European and Soviet Space Agencies (NASA, ESA, Intercosmos). In 1976 she participated in the 'Solar Flares' project of NASA's SKYLAB Space Mission which resulted in 1979 in the publication of a seminal book on Solar Flare phenomena. In 1980 she was appointed Guest Investigator for NASA's Solar Maximum Mission. She next formed and led the international teams which designed and constructed the (highly successful) first Irish instruments to be flown on an ESA spacecraft (the EPONA experiment on the 1985–6 GIOTTO Mission to Halley's Comet), and on a Russian spacecraft (the SLED instrument on the 1988–9 Phobos Mission to Mars and its Moons). Under her leadership, the EPONA instrument was subsequently reactivated aboard GIOTTO to secure historic data during Earth Flyby in 1990 and at comet Grigg-Skjellerup in 1992. She has taken a leading role in many collaborative international projects including participation in building four scientific instruments for the 1994–6 Russian Mission to Mars and various other such instruments for ESA's SOHO and CLUSTER and for NASA's WIND spacecraft. The international esteem in which she is held is reflected in her appointments: by ESA to a team compiling 'Space Horizon 2000' (a policy document which identifies future study targets for the agency); by Intercosmos to an International Initiative Group which planned the Mars-94 Mission and by the SOLTIP Solar Project of the International Council of Scientific Unions as a World Co-ordinator of the June 1980 Flare Campaign and of the World Interval covering the 1994 impact of comet Shoemaker–Levy 9 with Jupiter. She was winner of an Irish Person of the Year award award for scientific achievement (1986), presented with the Russian Tsiolkovsky Gold Medal for outstanding contributions to cosmonautics (1988), made an Honorary Citizen (for technological achievement) of San Jose, Silicon Valley, USA (1991), honoured with a personal presentation by ESA for her contribution to the GIOTTO Extended Mission (1992), and elected a member, in recognition of her outstanding space research work, of the prestigious International Academy of Astronautics (1993). She is co-founder and chief executive of a high-tech company, Space Technology Ireland, which designs, constructs and tests instrumentation for space and applies spin-off technologies to ground-based applications. She is also a professor in the Department of Experimental Physics at St Patrick's

College, Maynooth. Her prodigious output of writing largely concerns the analysis of scientific data recorded in space in the close environment of planets and comets and in the inter-planetary medium. She has published multiple papers in international refereed journals, in special publications of ESA, and in the proceedings of international conferences on space research. The list given here is only indicative of her output. She is author/co-author of several scientific books and has written a number of texts on Irish contributions to the history of astronomy. In 1968 she married Dr Micheal J. Lawlor, an international specialist in animal nutrition.

CHIEF WRITINGS. *A Detailed Study of Phenomena Attending the Disk Passage of an Exceptionally Active Solar Region, July 7–21, 1959* (Dublin: University College Dublin, 1969); *Irish Participation in Space Science* (Dublin: Royal Irish Academy, 1982); 'Planned Investigation of Energetic Particle Populations (20–500 ke V) in the Close Martian Environment', *Advanced Space Reviews*, vol. 15, no. 4 (1995), pp. 159–62; 'Particle Fluxes Observed in the Magnetic Pileup Regions of Comets Halley and Grigg-Skjellerup', *Advanced Space Reviews*, vol. 16, no. 4 (1995), pp. 29–34; 'COSTEP – Comprehensive Superthermal and Energetic Particle Analyses', *Solar Physics*, vol. 164 (1995), pp. 483–504; 'Dust Flux Analyses Experiment for the Rosetta Mission', *Advanced Space Reviews*, vol. 17, no. 12 (1996), pp. 137–40; 'Observation of Interplanetary Particles in a Corotating Interaction Region and of Energetic Water Group Ions from Comet Grigg-Skjellerup', *Planetary and Space Science*, vol. 45, no. 9 (1997), pp. 1105–17; 'Rapid: The Imaging Energetic Particle Spectrometer on Cluster', *Space Science Reviews*, vol. 79 (1997), pp. 399–473; 'Characteristic Boundaries of the Hermean Magnetosphere and Energetic Particles Close to the Planet', *Planetary and Space Science*, vol. 45, no. 1 (1997), pp. 167–80; 'Characteristic Boundary Transitions in Energetic Particle Data, Recorded at Comets P/Grigg-Skjellerup and P/Halley by the Epona instrument on Giotto', *Planetary and Space Science*, vol. 45, no. 9 (1997), pp. 1119–42; 'Interplanetary Variability in Particle Fluxes Recorded by the Low Energy Charged Particle Detector Ion (40 Kev–6 Mev) on the Soho Spacecraft During Its Cruise Phase of the L1 Point', *Advanced Space Reviews*, vol. 20, no. 1 (1997), pp. 99–102; *Whatever Shines Should be Observed* (Dublin: Samton, 1998).

Kathleen Lonsdale

LIFE. Born in 1903 in Newbridge, County Kildare, of an English father and a Scottish mother, Kathleen Yardley was the youngest of ten children. This, she said, may be the reason why she thought about problems of population in relation to peace. Working her way by means of scholarships to London University, she finally took her D.Sc. in physics, only to be appointed eventually as a professor of chemistry in University College, London, 1949–68. In the meantime she married a fellow student, Thomas Lonsdale, had three children, and joined the Society of Friends (Quakers). Other important events in her life occurred in 1943 when she went to prison as a conscientious objector to registration for civil defence duties, in 1945 when she was one of the first two women to be elected a fellow of the Royal Society, and in 1956 when she became a DBE and a grandmother almost simultaneously. She travelled widely and lectured about science or peace or both in nineteen countries, including the USA, the USSR, Spain, Australia, India, Japan and China. She also wrote and edited papers and books on both subjects. In 1968 she was elected president of the British Association for the Advancement of Science. She died in 1971.

CHIEF WRITINGS. *Simplified Structure Factor and Electron Density Formulae* (London: G. Bell, 1936); *Crystals and X-rays* (London: G. Bell, 1948); *International Tables for X-ray Crystallography*, vol. 1 (London: London University College, 1952), vol. 2 (1959), vol. 3 (1962); *Removing the Cause of War* (London: Allen and Unwin, 1953); *Is Peace Possible?* (Harmondsworth, Middlesex: Penguin, 1957); *I Believe* (Cambridge: Cambridge University Press, 1964).

MARY CONDREN, *Editor*

Theology and Ethics: The Twentieth Century

With one exception, the writings in this section span a mere thirty-two years. They could be said to encapsulate vividly aspects of the feminist movement of the late twentieth century, but equally, they could be said to represent much more: the hopes and the dashing of hopes; the innocence and the betrayal of innocence; the relative powerlessness and the abuse of power that has been women's lot throughout recorded history.

If *women's work is never done* in the cultural realm, it is because women, like Sisyphus, seem condemned to continually roll the stone up the mountain — all the time waiting for the lava to erupt and condemn them to oblivion.

Consider the fate of one woman: in 1923, a theological study was published in London. Based on St John's Gospel, and undaunted by the intellectual challenges posed by Marx, Darwin, or Freud, *A Psychological and Poetic Approach to the Study of Christ in the Fourth Gospel* was a highly sophisticated interpretative approach to the Bible.[1] The author, Eva Gore-Booth, proposed an imaginative approach to the text and developed from the evidence an ethic of non-violence.

Given the times, the aftermath of the First World War, and the Irish Easter Rising, the approach might not have been popular. But no mere differences of interpretation, no mere quibbles about the author's theological training or linguistic capabilities, could possibly justify the historical consignment of this book, the first major Irish feminist theological work, to almost

total oblivion. Today, the work will not be found on the reading lists of any Irish theological course, and outside the confines of some English literature departments, it has effectively been consigned to obscurity.

Eva Gore-Booth, suffragist, political activist and mystic, had emigrated to England, dedicating her life toward the alleviation of the plight of millworkers, flower-sellers and other victims of disadvantage. She developed her ideas in a series of other works, most of which await feminist theological scholarly analysis. She died in 1926.

The fate of this major work, written by a member of one of the most distinguished Irish families at that time, speaks volumes about the general fate of women's intellectual and theological work, and about the selective processes of *remembering* that constitute *his-story*.

A famous feminist article once asked: 'What if Shakespeare had a sister?' Eva Gore-Booth had, and when the history of those times was written, she herself was relegated to being a mere afterthought to her more famous sibling. For Irish schoolchildren, her sister was their role model: Constance Markievicz — the sole woman to appear, complete with military weapons, in the iconography of Irish revolution.

Eva Gore-Booth appears (one can never be sure) to have been a lone voice in the early modern systematic development of an Irish feminist theology. For the next forty or fifty years there is relative silence. Indeed, developing a feminist approach to theology would have been extremely difficult, especially for those in the Roman Catholic tradition, for whom religion was the largely uncritical, and often misogynistic,

---

1. Eva Gore-Booth, *A Psychological and Poetic Approach to the Study of Christ in the Fourth Gospel* (London: Longmans, Green, 1923).

vehicle of Irish independent nationalism as Ireland struggled to break free from seven hundred years of English colonization.

However, the emphasis on Ireland's anti-colonial political struggle obscured another layer of colonization in Ireland: that of Irish women to Irish men. Scholars throughout the world now document a historical revolution as important as any transition from Stone to Iron Age: the transition from matri-focal to patriarchal societies.

Archaeological evidence is overwhelming: Newgrange, Knowth, Dowth, Faughart and dozens of other major sites throughout Ireland (only now being interpreted) — all speak of an archaeo-mythological system in tune with the rhythms of women's bodies, the sun, moon and stars.

Mythology provides evidence of the rise of patriarchal thinking and theology, analysed in Mary Condren's *The Serpent and the Goddess: Women, Religion, and Power in Celtic Ireland*.[2] Celtics myths and sagas document the rationale underlying the denigration of a matri-centred world-view based on the essential mystery at the heart of life. In the Great Chain of Being maintained through links with one's mother, inevitable social conflicts could not ultimately be resolved and, like those of the Greeks, were resolved, or left unresolved in the form of paradox, honouring the essential mystery at the heart of life.

In the warrior Celtic society, this tragic vision was suppressed in favour of a triumphalist, linear-thinking and patriarchal way of life. The rule of force — the valour of the warrior and his capacity for death and death defiance — super-seded matri-centred ethics. The cry of the goddess Macha, documented in the texts of the Ulster cycle, 'a mother bore each one of you, help me in my hour of need' — a cry at once universalist and particular — was ignored at the very moment patriarchal society was born.

Not even the revelation of God in the person of Jesus Christ significantly arrested the development of patriarchal society and the further colonization of women. Indeed, despite Jesus' own views on the matter, his male disciples, from the Early Fathers onwards, have provided some of the most blatant treatises on misogyny, and prevented, to this day, the full participation or support of women in theological study, decision-making processes, or sacramental officiation.

After Eva Gore-Booth, it would be 1968 before the next major theological work by an Irishwoman appeared. The work appeared under the name of Sister Vincent Hannon, a sister of La Sainte Union. As she would now herself acknowledge, the compulsory taking of the male name 'Vincent' bespoke the other layer of colonization, that of Irish women, religious and lay, to Irish men.

For many women, religious life offered the only possible opportunity of education or independence. But if religious women often gained privileges within the patriarchal system, this would not ultimately protect them. Rita Hannon experienced a devastating backlash to her work, the most painful of which came from other women, including religious sisters. In a colonial system, 'divide and conquer' was the *modus operandi*. Emigrating to Africa, she spent the rest of her working life with women in Tanzania. She has now retired back to Ireland.

Rita Hannon had been at the forefront of the contemporary women's movement that unleashed what appeared to be an unstoppable dam. In the 1970s a series of pamphlets, edited by Mary Condren and published in Britain and Ireland, emerged from the Student Christian Movement. 'Toward a Theology of Sexual Politics', 'For the Banished Children of Eve', 'Abortion: The Tragic Dilemma', 'Why Men Priests?' were just some of the titles. The last was prepared for the Anglican Lambeth Synod of 1977, where the ordination of women to the Anglican priesthood was under discussion. It met with fierce reaction on the part of Anglican clerics.

By the mid-1980s, however, the tide had apparently begun to turn. Katherine Zappone, an American doctoral student who emigrated to Ireland, offered courses in Milltown Park, a theological institute run by a consortium of male religious orders. Her courses attracted huge numbers of women every night. Abruptly dis-continued after two years, the courses had, nevertheless, succeeded in bursting the dam, and women, refusing to take 'no' for an answer, were knocking at the doors of the theological establishments for admission as students.

2. Mary Condren, *The Serpent and the Goddess: Women, Religion, and Power in Celtic Ireland* (San Francisco: Harper and Row, 1989).

Women, although welcomed in large numbers to the study of religious education to prepare for careers as teachers (apart from a select few religious), until the late 1970s were not admitted to the study of theology in Irish seminaries or colleges. Faced with rapidly declining numbers of male candidates studying toward the priesthood and the closure of several seminaries, all this was to change.

By the late 1980s and early 1990s, several women had completed higher degrees in biblical study, ethics, religious education, spirituality and theology. By the late 1990s, women accounted for almost half the number of all theological students in Ireland. However, their willingness to study theology and related disciplines went unacknowledged by the Roman Catholic church's willingness to employ such women, let alone *ordain* them as full ministerial equals.

If Rita Hannon had set out innocently in 1968 to plead that women's full giftedness be used in service to her church, by the late 1990s such innocence was shattered by the reaction of the Vatican to women even *discussing* the question of their ordination. In 1995, Carmel McEnroy, an Irish Sister of Mercy, was fired from her tenured teaching position in the United States precisely on those grounds. Her story is told last in this section.

Carmel McEnroy's experience was unique only in that it was so public; it was public only because she assumed that the American system of tenure would protect her. Many other comparable stories will eventually be told of women's treatment in Irish theological institutions, especially those of women who do not enjoy the ambivalent *protection* afforded by the relative power of their religious congregations.

Irish-American philosopher and theologian Mary Daly once said: 'You get into as much trouble for being a little bit of a feminist as you do for going the whole way. So you might as well go the whole way.'[3] The history of the last thirty years of Irish women theologians bears this out.

The movement began humbly, tentatively, and yet hopeful that women would at last be included as equals around the banquet table. By the end of the century, those hopes were dashed. Yes, women could study theology, provided they left undisturbed the main tenets of a tradition they

had no part in creating, and indeed, one that was built, theologically and symbolically, on the backs of their exclusion. The dual fate of Eva Gore-Booth and Carmel McEnroy serves as a sharp reminder of the old adage: 'the powerful will only ever give up as much power as it takes to keep themselves in power'.

If women were begrudgingly accepted into the study of theology, fewer blatant obstacles appear to have been placed in the way of those pursuing philosophy. In addition to women theologians, Ireland has also produced significant feminist ethicists capable of deconstructing the mindsets of power and the secular mythologies supporting them.

Dublin-born Iris Murdoch, based in Oxford, produced an extraordinary collection of philosophical treatises and novels. Much of her work took the form of novels, a deliberate strategy that enabled her to achieve her goal: that of making the abstractions of philosophers accessible to a wider public. In her major systematic philosophical work, *Metaphysics as a Guide to Morals* (1992),[4] her views receive their definitive formulation.

Like Eva Gore-Booth, Iris Murdoch was of Anglo-Irish descent. Whereas Roman Catholicism had revelled and thrived on the power of imagination, Reformation thinkers had opted for what had increasingly come to be viewed as advanced rationalism that appeared to serve mechanistic, technocratic and alienating political economies. Gore-Booth and Murdoch were actively searching for the means to surmount the hermeneutic circle or dead end offered by such philosophies to the modern age. In particular, they sought to establish the possibility of the basis for ethics given the petrification of Christian doctrine (Gore-Booth), or a rapidly changing world-view (Murdoch).

The work of these two women anticipated Audre Lorde's dictum: 'the master's tools will never dismantle the master's house'. The challenge of deconstructing political mythologies, analysing our implications in the global process, and subverting the contemporary form of patriarchal dualisms is too important to be left to traditional methods. If women's inclusion into the realms of theology and ethics is to make a difference, the

---

3. In conversation with the author.

4. Iris Murdoch, *Metaphysics as a Guide to Morals* (Harmondsworth, Middlesex: Penguin, 1992).

philosophical pre-occupation with logic, consciousness and reason must be enhanced by an inclusive philosophia honouring diverse ways of knowing, emotional intelligence, richness of the unconscious and the power of imagination.

Traditional theological and philosophical methodologies are simply inadequate to the task that lies ahead. Phyllis Rooney here critiques the *maleness of reason*; Anne Thurston and Mary Malone both comment on ingredients missing in constructing culture; Katherine Zappone's essay on ritual indicates one of the possibilities for counter cultural forms of empowerment; while Attracta Ingram and Dolores Dooley caution against the dangers of positing *women's way of knowing*, or of arguing from difference to special treatment, given the conditions under which such *ways of knowing* have been developed. Citizenship, rather than gender identity, they argue, provides a more fruitful way forward.

Theologians and ethicists cannot confine themselves to studying the jealously guarded, well-picked and dried old bones that constitute the traditional canons of theological or philosophical texts. As the example of Eva Gore-Booth and Iris Murdoch reminds us, we cannot be content with simply replicating such work in its own terms. Canon formation is itself a strategy of power. What texts were included, excluded, and in whose interests?

Feminist theologians and ethicists in Ireland are today faced with a dual task. Celtic, Christian and philosophical sources need to be revised, and interpreted afresh with feminist hermeneutics of suspicion, a suspicion that must extend to translation, canon-formation and interpretation. This revisionist work is vitally necessary, immersed as we are in history, culture, symbolism and thought-patterns. By reinserting the role of imagination in hermeneutics (a perspective developed here by Ann Louise Gilligan), by delighting both in imagination, lucid thinking, and in the essential contingency of all thought, we can build bridges between the disciplines of theology, philosophy and art.

Indeed, if the task of elaborating an Irish feminist theological and philosophical project is to be developed, the old petrified distinction between symbols and words (exactly paralleling the Catholic and Protestant divides) will have to be surmounted.

Here we come full circle. In the pre-Celtic tragic vision, the world of either/or gives way to both/and: the sacred and profane dichotomies upon which religious patriarchal power is based are challenged by an ecological world-view, the basis of which is reverence for the earth, the tangible, physical and beautiful expression of the presence of the divine (see Anne Primavesi and Celine Mangan here). We return to those sources, not to find pristine or archaic *origins* uncorrupted by the weight of history, but to look afresh at Irish wisdom traditions for what they might have to offer us today.

And this work was never so important. Many women today consider themselves immune to, or beyond the grasp of such naked expressions of power as those experienced by women such as Carmel McEnroy. In Ireland's clichéd Celtic tiger economy, women enjoy political, sexual and economic *rights* undreamed of in their mothers' day. The late-twentieth-century revelations of abusiveness and deception practised under the auspices of religious institutions have apparently shattered the power of Irish clericalism, often considered to be co-extensive with Irish patriarchy.

Looking at Europe today, however, where war and the threat of war is the dominant grammar of human relationships, it would be naïve in the extreme to equate clericalism with patriarchy itself. Although religion often provides the symbolic superstructure or sacred canopy of oppressive social systems, its apparent demise must alert conscious women to identify the shifting goalposts of power.

While Irish women have benefited greatly from American feminism, our work must also be furthered by full participation in the European intellectual feminist community, where new importance is placed on the unconscious logic and underpinning of contemporary political and religious mythologies. Regardless of the truth claims of particular religious traditions, European theorists analyse such claims for their political and social effects.

Politically and spiritually, they argue, we have lived under the auspices of a 'sacrificial social order'. By this is meant that the very structures of thought are based on an exclusion, primarily that of our messy bodily origins (the religious and intellectual strategies of purification), but derivatively, on the exclusion of women and anyone else who represents our own *Otherness,* all that we try to repudiate as a condition of consciousness. In other words, our identities are sacrificially achieved at someone else's expense.

At the start of the twenty-first century, therefore, those engaged in theological or religious studies must develop a sophisticated approach that encompasses, not only the formal institutions of religion, but also other agencies responsible for generating contemporary systems of representation. Otherwise, we run the risk of self-deception, collusion, or amnesia for several reasons.

First, although Irish women may be doubly colonized as Irish and as women, in turn, insofar as we belong to one of the world's major European economies, we too are colonizers in the globalization process of the Superpowers. As such, we are deeply implicated (we manufacture and sell armaments) in the impoverishment of the Two Thirds World where war, famine and starvation are endemic. Linda Hogan warns us here against the dangers of false innocence, while Onora O'Neill critiques the language of *rights* for ignoring or subordinating that of *responsibility.*

Second, given that the last thirty years of feminism coincided with thirty years of extreme violence in Northern Ireland, no one in Ireland, male or female, can claim innocence in relation to the political mythologies that govern our lives and make such violence — and our silence or indifference — possible. In years to come, perhaps future generations will wonder — as young German children do today — what kind of worldview made such atrocities possible. Geraldine Smyth reminds us that the politics of identity can often conceal or sanitize naked quests for power that must be continually deconstructed.

Lastly, since *those who forget their history are doomed to repeat it* we should not forget that a Europe whose sign was once *the Christ who died for all* now meets under the sign of the Unknown Soldier *who gave his life for all.* While Western Europe might enjoy relative peace, the irredentist nationalisms of Eastern Europe have brought havoc to those countries in the last ten years. The goalposts have certainly been repainted but the underlying mentality seems unchanged.

The Hebrew prophets and Jesus Christ constantly cried out: 'I desire mercy, not sacrifice.' Throughout recorded history, the power of priests and warriors has been maintained by jealously guarding their exclusive rights to sacrifice, on the altars or on the battlefields, and by enjoying the religious and political structures established in their wake.

If today's cultural warriors — artists, poets, ethicists, theologians, and ritual makers — are to make a difference, they must challenge the sacrificial social order, develop new ways to nurture themselves and not fall into the trap of self-sacrifice, and carefully deconstruct the great Either/Or of social polity. Perhaps only then, as we enter fully into the twenty-first century, the denizens of sacrifice might finally be exposed and the challenge of mercy realized.

EVA GORE-BOOTH

(1870–1926)

from:
A PSYCHOLOGICAL AND POETIC APPROACH TO THE STUDY OF CHRIST IN THE FOURTH GOSPEL (1923)

[Eva Gore-Booth anticipated many themes only now being explored by contemporary feminist theory and theology regarding the politics of interpretation, the psychic underpinning of religion, the role of imagination, the critique of sacrifice, the ethic of non-violence, and even the Gaian hypothesis — the divine infusing nature. Because she was writing in the wake of the devastation of the First World War and the Irish Rising of 1916, and given the role played by religion in both these events, Eva Gore-Booth's approach to theology was poetic and mystical rather than dogmatic. The following extracts are taken from *A Psychological and Poetic Approach to the Study of Christ in the Fourth Gospel* (1923).]

[Eva Gore-Booth anticipated some concerns of contemporary feminist scripture scholars on the relationship between power and knowledge.]

[R]ecorders were not always impartial or strictly honest. Even as early as A.D. 170 we find Dionysius Bishop of Corinth, writing a letter to Bishop Soter of Rome complaining of people who tampered with and falsified the sacred writings, 'the writings of the Lord'. This means certainly the Gospels, but may also be the Pauline Epistles. In considering the motives for such falsification, there is a factor that must not be forgotten. This is the struggle that there was in the earliest ages between orthodox people and heretics over the texts of scripture. Both sides incessantly accuse the other of garbling and changing words to suit their views. Once, at all events, the text was avowedly altered and corrected by officially appointed 'correctors' to bring it into line with orthodox dogma. Thus the scriptures as we know them bear witness to the bitter struggle between opposing schools of thought in the first few centuries after Christ. [p. x]

It seems that we cannot doubt that the texts of scripture have been garbled and altered at different times by different people according to the religious tenets and doctrines of different schools. Indeed these considerations might fill our minds with confusions and despair, if we did not base our beliefs beyond all texts on an inner living knowledge of Christ. [p. xi]

Thus to anyone who believes in the universal Infinite love of God in Christ, any saying attributed to him that is not in harmony with Universal Infinite Love is, by the nature of it, incredible. [p. xi]

The reader is asked to look on this book as the result of that experience that friends call a concern, on the part of the writer, to offer to others certain personal intuitions and ideas, that have no claim to scholarship, but are the result of a study of the New Testament, prayer, and experience . . . those who have found thoughts that are precious and revealing to themselves must always offer them to others, in case someone else may be sensitive to receive them. [p. xii]

Christ's aim is to make people see truth, not to try and prove it. And for this reason he puts it before them, under the symbols of easily understood and familiar objects. Thus his every metaphor is like his life, a sort of incarnation of truth.

We value poetry for its vision, not its arguments, and all the greatest poetry is an attempt, however feeble, to speak in the manner of Christ, from an inner light, with a direct appeal to the power of vision in others.

Bread and wine, the growing corn, the harvest, the life of the vine, shepherds and sheep, eating and drinking, wind, fire, and water — all the ordinary facts and experiences of a simple outdoor life become, at his touch, something greater than themselves, images radiant with the Divine poetry of eternal things. [p. xiv]

But perhaps the deepest reason why Christ did not express his Logos in terms of abstract philosophy is to be found in the inner nature of his knowledge of God. Truth for him was one with and inseparable from Life and Love. Any philosophy that separates truth from Life and Love must lose touch with reality, and reality is the only wisdom. Therefore no thought is really true unless it is lived, and unless it is in essence, love. For (in Christ), Love, Truth and Life were and are for ever one God. [p. xv]

To the same causes, the action of a rising organisation, with tremendous powers, bent on the suppression of 'heresy' through persecution and education, we can trace the loss of the spiritual meaning of the word (ekklesia) translated officially as 'Church'. For such a spiritual meaning must, of course, be detrimental to the powers of any outside authority in spiritual matters.

The claim of the orthodox dogma that has come down to us, was only very gradually established, through much persecutions of 'heretical' opinions (the opinions of 'others'), and through the power of the state.

And here we must remember the orthodox 'corrections' of the text of the New Testament, spoken of by Epiphanius (A.D. 367); and also the way in which early interpretations, afterwards thought heretical, were suppressed. [p. 136]

[In this extract, Gore-Booth provides a precise rejoinder to the debates, sparked off by Darwin and Freud, concerning the priority of religion or science.]

Our mental life seems to them to be built out of the sensations that respond to these instincts. These instincts are the ego instinct, the herd instinct, the sex instinct. All our activities of thought, word and deed are, it is often asserted, nothing but the working out of energy, inherent in these instincts. Religion is the result of the herd instinct (the influence of society on the individual), or the ego instinct (the reaction of the individual against the tyranny of society), and all the different forms can be accounted for by a clash between the instincts.

Now the idea of these three instincts in the deeps of our being has, through the ages, been familiar to religious people, as the three root causes of what theologians have called original sin. But they have always looked upon them as the roots of evil in our nature, to be steadily controlled and transcended by anyone trying to be a Christian.

The names they gave them were not so polite as the definition of our modern scientific Calvinists. They called them the World, the Flesh, and the Devil. The world was, of course, the 'herd instinct', the flesh was the sex instinct. Quite distinct from these was the Devil, under which rather strange heading were classed all the sins not attributable to the influence of the world, or to the temptations of any form of sensuality, but such things as anger and pride and contempt, the direct results of the swollen ego instinct (the sin by which the Devil fell in the old theology was always pride).

But in this primary foundation region they found forces to the existence of which our modern investigators are blind. For in the psychic region, the foundation of our being is the word or Logos of God, and there, if anywhere in our nature we find the Divine living vibrations, the vibrations of the very being of God, Love, Truth and Life.

The proof of their existence is the same proof that we have of the existence of the 'three great instincts'. It lies in our power of responding to them in conscious life. Anyone who has ever felt the sheer passion for impersonal Truth will find it reasonable to think that this passion has its cause deep down in some vibration in the very roots of our being, just as much as a person, obsessed by sex, seeks his tormentor among the forces in the primary unconscious.

It is possible for any man to stop responding to the clamour of animal instinct, and listen to the voice of absolute truth, and universal love, in his inner being.

By these substitutions a man is 'born again', not of blood, nor of the will of the flesh nor of the will of man (the ego instinct, the sex instinct or the herd instinct) 'but of God'. [pp. 6–7]

[Gore-Booth, in the face of some feminist capitulations to the nationalisms of the First World War, espoused and practised non-violence, an ethic intimately grounded in her theories of knowledge that she characterized as 'imaginative pity' (see below).]

For those who begin prostrating themselves before the earth psyche, always end by despising it, in its weaker manifestations. For the life that is wholly sensation holds no pity, no mercy, for the defeated.

Pity is a wholly intellectual virtue; it is quite alien to the animal world of sensation; it is the result of the light of impersonal thought thrown on the ruthlessness of the psychic struggle, and it is the first link between the animal desire and repulsion, and the impersonality of divine love. For the psychic outlook, untouched by the Divine light of mind, is the narrow personal outlook of wholly animal life. [p. 69]

If we think that truth is God, and mind is a response to truth, we can have no doubt that life with mind is a greater thing than life without mind, though, of course, the force of life, or universal psyche itself poured out through all living things, must compel all men's admiration. [pp. 69–70]

The man who tries to know himself as the beginning of wisdom is, then, at first confronted with a chaos of mutually destructive vibrations. It is no wonder if the first result of such an attempt is to puzzle, bewilder and even shake people's faith in any possible divine harmony or peace. But anyone who does not despair, but perseveres using love or self-identification as a method of understanding others, will find in the practice of the method itself, the key to the solution of the problem on his own. [p. 111]

[Although untrained in the science of Scripture, Gore-Booth did not hesitate to offer positive interpretations of scriptural texts to support women's emancipation.]

There is a small point in the circumstantial story (The Wedding Feast at Cana) that should not be overlooked. The fact that Christ called his mother 'woman', instead of 'mother', added to the seeming snub of 'what have I to do with thee?' has been a stumbling block to some people. But if the words really mean 'what is mine is thine, woman' (or, 'what should separate our interests, woman?') the substitution of the impersonal word 'woman' for the personal 'mother' only implies the ignoring of a mere physical relation, in the presence of real spiritual nearness. His mother, like any other woman or man, was his friend, to whom he would give all that he had. This point of view seems to rule out the attempt of some critics to prove some kind of nearer relation between Christ and his men disciples, than that which existed between him and his women disciples. Westcott, indeed, remarks of this sentence, 'What have I to do with thee, woman?' that it shows that Christ could not take a suggestion even from a woman, even if that woman was his mother.[1] This is an important point, because ideas like this must always tend to feed the subconscious vanity in persons of one sex, and the laziness in persons of the other. And vanity and laziness are human qualities that lead away from Truth and Life and Love. In external things they are the deep subconscious justification in people's minds for the extraordinary exclusion of women from celebrating the Eucharist and preaching, an exclusion none the less materialistic and extraordinary because for many years unquestioned. In Christ there is neither male nor female, and it is a striking thought that Christ spoke to all women through his mother, breaking down for ever the ancient sensual and materialistic idea of sex in spiritual things, by saying simply, 'What is mine is thine, woman.' [p. 169]

[Eva Gore-Booth, using her ethic of non-violence, prophetically critiqued traditional interpretations of biblical incidents, asserting the priority of mercy over sacrifice.]

Is it possible that while Christ protested against buying and bargaining in the holy place, he had no word of condemnation for the far more real defilement of cruelty, the outrage on Love which is God, involved in the cruel destruction of life for sacrifice?

Never did Christ set stones and marble above mercy and love. To formulate such a statement is to disbelieve in its possibility. Nor could he ever have taught that you could please the living God by destroying any living being. [pp. 171–2]

To separate knowledge from Love is impossible, because Truth is Love, and in so far as one's knowledge is separated from Love it becomes a knowledge of falsehood or mirage. Neither can Truth and Love be separated from Life. This is the meaning of Eternity.

Thus the idea of this 'Trinity in Unity', seems to be the foundation of all Christ's teaching. And this explains that no knowledge arrived at through cruelty is to be trusted. [p. 228]

[Gore-Booth on Imaginative Pity]

It is only love that brings life, as it is only love that brings truth. The real helper, the Truth and the Life, must be let in by the porter, the conscious self, through the Door, Love, or the Love of God in Christ.[2] This Love is active intellectual sympathy, not passive emotion. It is the strongest exercise of the imagination, by which one knows another person by identifying one's self with them, and living, as it were from the centre of lives outside one's own. As self-love is the first response to the Love of God that makes animal life, so imaginative Love makes Eternal life, the full response to God. To live like this from Christ's centre, (the love of Christ) is to have in one the life of God, and to live from the centre of every other life in the world. This is real knowledge and Eternal life. For to know Christ is Eternal life. The Love of God is the door to all Love, the Love that is God. The simple test that shows the difference between the shepherds of falsehood and truth can be applied to all life, 'external' as well as 'internal'. The thieves and robbers who control people's minds, through a wrong approach to them, lead

1. B.F. Westcott, *The Gospel According to St John* (London: Murray, 1908).

2. John 10:3.

always to death and destruction. 'The thief cometh not, but to kill and destroy,'[3] applies to many a great leader of men, from the days of the Pharaohs to the present time. [p. 238]

True 'Christian love' then, is something much more than goodwill, or even affection. Its mental side, the truth that is love, is what we call imagination. It is the power of projecting oneself into other people's lives so that one feels their suffering as one's own. Where there is imagination there can be no cruelty or unkindness. It is not that the imaginative person thinks it wrong to make another suffer, it is that when another suffers he suffers himself. A soldier in times of war, with a little imagination, is a miserable thing. A soldier, with a universal imagination, would not be able to kill another person of any nationality whatever. Everybody has a certain amount of imagination, but it is a question whether anyone on earth has ever really, perfectly fulfilled Christ's law of absolutely universal love or imagination, which is the love or imagination of God in Christ. This love we can in the end attain to, through loving Christ and identifying ourselves with him, living in his life of universal love and imagination, and thus perhaps even sharing the creative will or love of God. [p. 319]

The Poet's God

'What is God?' men said in the West,
The Lord of Good and Ill,
Rewarders of the blest,
Judge of the evil will.

'What is God?' men said in the East,
The Universal soul
In man, and bird, and beast,
The self of the great whole.

I saw a primrose flower
Rise out of the green sod,
In majesty and power,
And I said, 'There is Love, there is God.'[4]

[Eva Gore-Booth's critique of churches and power.]

The tragedy of Christ's life to me is far greater to-day than it was during the few terrible last hours of suffering. For every church and every sect is but an organisation of thoughtless and well-meaning people trained in thought and controlled by juntas of priests and clergy who are used to doing all the things that Christ would have most disliked. And yet I don't know how this can be avoided, for without organisation Christ would be quite forgotten, and all organisation seems in the end to go the same road: and if it does not go in for graft and power it just fizzles out. That is what is wrong too with all public bodies and governments, and what the world has got to think out is some scheme by which power can be evenly distributed over every person in the world and by which the foolish and uneducated can no longer be grouped in unthinking battalions dependent on the few pushers, self-seekers and crooks and made slaves of and exploited.[5]

3. Ibid., 10:8.

4. Eva Gore-Booth, quoted in *Prison Letters of Constance Markievicz*, ed. Esther Roper (London: Virago, 1987), p. 131.
5. Ibid., p. 303.

MARY CONDREN

(1947–   )

from:
THE SERPENT AND THE GODDESS: WOMEN, RELIGION AND POWER IN CELTIC IRELAND (1989)

[*The Serpent and the Goddess* is located within and inspired by the international feminist theological movement that followed the belated twentieth-century admission of women into theological study. Initially grateful, women soon realized the deeply distorted theological and philosophical assumptions developed during the centuries of their exclusion. Focusing on biblical, mythological and historical narratives, many turned their attention to the history, causes, effects and structures generated by such exclusion in the clear understanding that history had been written by the winners about the losers. As man's Other, women are uniquely positioned to deconstruct the Othering processes in biblical, mythological and literary sources, and to use these insights to provide fresh interpretations of privileged texts.

Drawing on the rich, multi-levelled heritage of pre-Celtic, Celtic and early Christian legacy of myth, poetry and *dindshenchas* (place lore) materials, the book traces the overthrow of Irish matri-focal society — its structure, ethics and deities — in favour of male-dominated patriarchal social forms.

The image of Brigit, goddess, saint and folklore figure, is central. Like the Furies in Greece, she was sent culturally underground, but her spirit constantly promises to erupt, inspiring contemporary women's struggle for justice and authentic agency. This extract is taken from the chapter 'The Curse of Macha' in *The Serpent and the Goddess: Women, Religion, and Power in Celtic Ireland* (San Francisco: Harper and Row, 1989). Footnotes are by the author, see also Volume IV, p. 173–4.]

The Goddess Macha was one of the most important Goddesses in ancient Ireland. She gave her name to the present day Armagh, *Ard Mhacha,* and to the ancient fort of Ulster, *Emhain Mhacha.* An image of Macha is preserved in Armagh Cathedral to this day. At least four different accounts are given as to how the name Macha was bestowed upon these ancient sites. Studying these stories enables us to see the various transitions in status that the Goddesses underwent in the course of their history. The story of the overthrow of Macha could be described as the foundation myth of Irish patriarchal culture: the story of the Irish *Fall.*

The first of these stories is that Macha was the wife of Nemed, son of Agnoman, one of the earliest Irish invaders. Macha was the name of the twelfth plain that Nemed cleared, and according to the story Nemed bestowed the plain upon his wife so that it might bear her name. Macha had died tragically, her heart *broke within her,* when in a vision she had seen the forthcoming destruction caused by the *Táin Bó Cuailnge,* the *Cattle-Raid of Cooley,* Ireland's equivalent to the Greek heroic warrior-epics.[1] This story, although it links Macha with very ancient Irish history, is not the most revealing source of her early significance and is probably not the earliest story, since her importance is gained through her husband.[2]

The second, more colourful story indicates a more ancient source. There were three Ulster kings who agreed that they each should be seven years in the kingship. As guarantees of this agreement, they appointed seven druids, seven poets, and seven captains. Three conditions were laid down as proof of the justice of each reign. Should any of these conditions fail to be met, the reigning king would be overthrown: the mast (crops) should appear faithfully every year; there should be no failure of dyestuff (dyeing was a woman's art); and no woman should die in childbirth. The proof of the justice of their reign would be that those traditional areas of women's creativity should prosper.

Things went well until one of them, Aed the Red, died. Aed left only one daughter, Macha of the Ruddy Hair, who demanded that she take her father's place in the succession. The other two kings refused to let this happen on the grounds that they would not surrender the kingship to a

---

1. 'Edinburgh Dindshenchas', ed. Whitley Stokes, *Folklore*, vol. 4 (1893), pp. 471–97, 480.
2. 'The Prose Tales in the Rennes Dindshenchas', ed. Whitley Stokes, *Revue Celtique*, vol. 15 (1894), pp. 273–336, 418–84; vol. 16 (1895), pp. 31–83, 134–67, 269–312. No. 94.

woman, so Macha fought and beat them. After seven years she then refused to give up the kingship, because she had won the kingship in a battle rather than through the original agreement. Since they had broken the agreement, she argued, it no longer had validity. The sons of the second king, Dithorba, who had been killed in the first battle, fought with her again. Again she triumphed and banished them into the Connaught deserts. At this point she took the third king, Cimbaeth, to be her husband and to lead her armies.

Macha still was not satisfied. After her marriage she went off in search of Dithorba's sons in the form of a lepress, having rubbed rye-dough and red bog stuff all over herself. She found the men in the woods whereupon one of them said: 'Beautiful is the hag's eye! let us lie with her.' Macha let him carry her off to the woods. Once there she overcame him and bound him up. Then she went back to the men around the fire who asked where their brother was. 'He is ashamed to come to you after lying with a lepress,' she told them. The men declared that this was no shame, and each in turn carried her off and were tied up by Macha. She then took them with her to Ulster.

Upon reaching Ulster, the Ulstermen wanted to kill the captives; but Macha had better ideas: 'Nay,' she said, 'since it would be for me a violation of a prince's truth. But let them slave in slavery, and dig a *rath* (ring-fort) around me, so that it may be Ulster's chief city for ever.' She then marked out the fortress with her brooch *eó* of gold that was at her neck *muin*. Hence, Emuin, the *EÓ* that was at Macha's *muin*.[3]

In this story we can see that not only would Macha not tolerate discrimination against women in the matter of political leadership, but also in choosing her husband Cimbaeth, she was clearly taking the initiative in sexual relations. In addition, she rejected killing for its own sake and preferred non-violent (and purposeful) forms of punishment.

The third account of how Armagh got its name brings us even closer to her true identity:

And men say that she was Grían Banchure, 'the Sun of Womanfolk', daughter of Mider

of Brí Léith. And after this she died, and her tomb was raised on Ard Macha, and her lamentation was made, and her gravestone was planted. Whence *Ard Machae* 'Macha's height'.[4]

Macha may originally have been a sun-Goddess, and one of the common images of the sun-Goddess was that of a horse.[5] The horse was a particularly fitting symbol for the sun, since the sun travelled the sky at great speed and the horse was the fastest animal then known. Macha was, therefore, the Ulster Epona, the horse Goddess. It is in this context that we can begin to see the significance of the fourth story of how Macha stamped her name eternally on this Ulster city.

The story is usually called *The Debility of the Ulstermen* and is part of the preamble to Ireland's epic saga the *Táin*. The story begins with a rich man, Crunnchu mac Agnoman. His wife had died, and he was very lonely until one day a stately young woman came to him. She sat down by the hearth of the fire, stirring the embers without saying a word to anyone. Later she milked the cow and baked bread, still without speaking. In all her actions, however, she was careful to 'turn right' following the direction of the sun, a clue as to her identity. When night fell, she crept into Crunnchu's bed and made love to him.

Everything went well for a time, and we are told that 'his handsome appearance was delightful to her'. His wealth increased, and he enjoyed prosperity in every respect, but trouble was soon to follow. The annual assembly of the Ulstermen was due to start in the near future and Crunnchu wanted to attend. Macha pleaded with him to stay at home, since his going to the assembly could only cause trouble for her. Crunnchu insisted, and finally Macha permitted him to go only after he had promised not to speak a word to anyone of their union, since only harm could come of that. Crunnchu duly promised and set off.

This annual assembly was a great occasion, and people came from all over Ireland. One of

---

3. 'Rennes Dindshenchas', no. 161.

4. 'Rennes Dindshenchas', no. 94.
5. Marie Louise Sjoestedt, *Gods and Heroes of the Celts*, trans. Myles Dillon (Berkeley, California: Turtle Island Foundation, 1982), p. 30; EIHM, pp. 293–4; RAC, pp. 43, 188; Sjoestedt, *Gods and Heroes*, p. 30; Ross, *Pagan Celtic Britain*, pp. 224, 247, 324–6.

the main events was the horse-racing competition. Although many competed, the horses belonging to the king and queen defeated all before them. At the end of the games everyone assembled praised the monarchs. The people were heard to say: 'Never before have two such horses been seen at the festival as these two horses of the king: in all Ireland there is not a swifter pair.' Hearing this, Crunnchu could not resist. He cried out to the assembled people: 'My wife runs quicker than these two horses.' Furious, the king ordered him to be tied up until his wife could be brought to the contest to race against his horses.

Messengers were sent out to Macha, telling her to come urgently to the games. Macha was reluctant to go as she was pregnant and about to deliver, but upon being told that her husband would otherwise be killed, she agreed and set forth. When she arrived, they told her that she must race against two horses of the king. Hearing this, she grew pale and turned to the assembled people with a wrenching plea that would echo in Ireland down the centuries: 'Help me,' she cried to the bystanders, 'for a mother bore each one of you. Give me, O King, but a short delay, until I am delivered.'

Macha appealed to those assembled, not on the basis of an abstract system of ethics or for mercy: she appealed to them on the basis of their relationship to their mothers: 'A Mother Bore Each One of You.' Childbirth was a supremely sacred activity, and the needs of a pregnant woman had hitherto overruled the demands of any egotistical king. But the king refused to delay the race, impatient as he was to demonstrate his own superiority. Finally, Macha threatened that a severe curse would fall upon Ulster. 'What is your name?' asked the king, and Macha replied in ominous tones: 'My name and the name of that which I shall bear, will forever cleave to the place of this assembly. I am Macha, daughter of Sainreth mac in Botha (Strange son of Ocean).'

The horses were brought up and the race began. Macha won the race easily and before the king's horses had even reached the winning post, she gave birth to twins, a son and a daughter who, in turn, gave their names to Emhain Mhacha (The Twins of Macha). But suddenly, all the men assembled were seized with weakness and 'had no more strength than a woman in her pain', for at the moment of her tragic victory Macha pronounced a curse on the men of Ulster:

> From this hour the ignominy that you have inflicted upon me will redound to the shame of each one of you. When a time of oppression falls upon you, each one of you who dwells in this province will be overcome with weakness, as the weakness of a woman in child-birth, and this will remain upon you for five days and four nights; to the ninth generation it shall be so.[6]

The 'Pangs of the Men of Ulster', as Macha's curse was called, was said to affect all the men of Ulster but excluded women and children.

There are various interpretations as to what the curse of the Ulstermen actually meant. Some interpret it as simple taboo against indulging in warfare at particular times, especially during the holiday period of the Ulster games.[7] There is a long tradition that interprets the 'Pangs of the Men of Ulster' as a form of *couvade*, that is to say, a practice whereby men imitate the pains of childbirth during their period of initiation into warrior status.[8] A further interpretation is that in this initiatory period men, by imitating the pains of childbirth, hoped to draw on the help of the Mother Goddess as they went forth in their warrior bands. Apparently, they believed that if they imitated the movements of a woman in labour, the Goddess could be persuaded to give them the same help as she gave to women in childbirth.[9]

As we can see from these conflicting theories there is no agreement among Celtic scholars as to what this story actually means. Like all great myths there is probably a wealth of meaning in

6. All quotations taken from the version of the story in *Ancient Irish Tales*, ed. T.P. Cross and C.H. Slover (New York: Barnes and Noble, 1969), pp. 208–10.

7. Frank O'Connor, *A Backward Look* (London: Macmillan, 1967), p. 16.

8. Cf. Alwyn and Brinley Rees, *Celtic Heritage* (London: Thames and Hudson, 1978), p. 58; Sjoestedt, *Gods and Heroes*, pp. 40–2.

9. Sjoestedt, *Gods and Heroes*, p. 41. A more recent interpretation of the story is that it is the myth behind an ancient vegetation rite, the kouros or male fertility rite, in which the young king, having proved his heroism, takes over from the old-king, marries the goddess, but in turn has to surrender the title after a year. Cf. Tomás O'Broin, 'What is the Debility of the Ulstermen?' *Éigse*, vol. 10 (1963), pp. 286–99. According to one scholar the rites resemble those of the Phyrgian god in hibernation. Cf. John Rhys, *Lectures on the Origin and Growth of Religion as Illustrated by Celtic Heathendom* (London: 1898; New York: AMS Press, 1979), p. 632.

the story, and any one interpretation does not exhaust its richness. In that spirit, we can explore another interpretation, one that draws on elements of all of the previous theories and helps to explain the radical change in status that the Goddess in Ireland went through with the rise of the patriarchal warrior cult.

In one of the stories about Macha the kings had to provide three sureties as proof of the justice of their reign: that no woman should die in childbirth, that there should be no failure of dyestuff, and that mast should grow plentifully every year. 'Mast' was a general term for food, but it could also mean the nuts and acorns that fed the animals sacred to the Goddess, the deer and the boar.[10] Dyeing was also a woman's art and there are stories in which it was believed that if a man should come into the area where dyeing was taking place the dyes would not take effect.[11] The king's sureties in the early stages of kingship were intimately related to the needs and concerns of women and unless the king could be seen to take care of the cultural and fertility needs of the clan, symbolized by these women's activities, he would be overthrown. However, when next we come across the 'taboos of the kings of Ulster' there is no mention of childbirth, dyeing, or the fertility of the crops.[12]

When the king forced Macha to take part in a race just as she was about to deliver it would seem that he violated the conditions of his kingship. It was an unjust request that would rebound back on his reputation for justice, and this unjust request was bound to be punished. He also forced Macha to give birth in a public place. The implication from the story would seem to be that Macha died in the act of giving birth, but this would be the least of the offenses:

childbirth was a sacred occasion, and, indeed, some of the earliest religious centres were those in which women gave birth. For men to look upon the act of giving birth would be sacrilege of the highest order and in this case a sacrilege that also wrested power from the Goddess by exposing her ultimate act of creativity to the world.

Forcing Macha to give birth publicly was to force her to hand over her secrets to the watching bystanders. Thereafter, by imitating her movements in childbirth and by finding ways to give birth themselves, men could call upon the help of the Goddess in their warrior pursuits thus bringing her sacred power to bear upon their enterprises. They would imitate the Goddess through the hysterical pregnancies, birth mimes, and physical mutilations that are performed in the initiation rites of young men.[13]

There are numerous parallels throughout the ancient world for this interpretation. Many patriarchal rites celebrate the drama of the mother's death and the seizing of her power.[14] Some scholars hold that the foundation of patriarchal culture itself is the killing of the mother (matricide).[15]

The Macha story had even further reaching implications. Not only would men imitate Macha in her act of giving birth: birth and fertility themselves were being re-defined to suit the needs of the warrior society. The heads of those taken in battle by the Celtic warriors came to be known as the 'masts of Macha', as though Macha delighted in making a head collection just as she had once delighted in providing fruits and grains for her hungry people. This view of Macha is in

10. Cf. Proinsias Ní Chatháin, 'Swineherds, Seers and Druids', *Studia Celtica*, vols 14–15 (1979–80), pp. 200–11; J.G. McKay, 'The Deer-Goddess: Cult of the Ancient Caledonians', *Folklore*, vol. 43, no. 2 (1932), pp. 144–74. Boars, 'swineherds' and deer appear throughout the Lives of Irish saints and Irish mythology. For full references, cf. *The Motif Index of Irish Literature*, ed. T.P. Cross (Indiana University Publications: Folklore Series 7, 1952), which is a supplement to the Stith Thomson, *Motif Index of Folk Literature*, 6 vols (Copenhagen, 1932–58). Cf. also Howard Schlossman, 'The Role of Swine in Myth and Religion', *American Imago*, vol. 40, no. 1 (1983), pp. 35–49.
11. Cf. *Vitae Sanctorum Hiberniae*, ed. Charles Plummer, 2 vols (Oxford University Press, 1910), vol. 1, p. ci.
12. Cf. Myles Dillon, 'The Taboos of the Kings of Ireland', *Proceedings of the Royal Irish Academy* A 54 sect. C (1951), pp. 1–36, 19.

13. For details of the hysterical pregnancies, birth rituals and other forms of male imitation of women's generative powers, cf. Mircea Eliade, *Rites and Symbols of Initiation* (New York: Harper and Row, 1975); Bruno Bettelheim, *Symbolic Wounds: Puberty Rites of the Envious Male* (New York: Collier Books, 1954).
14. Macha had a counterpart in Cyprus, the goddess Artemis, who died in childbirth. On her festival a young man imitated her labour pains. Cf. O'Broin, 'What is the Debility of the Ulstermen?' *Éigse*, vol. 10 (1963), p. 298.
15. Cf. Erich Neumann, *The Origins and History of Consciousness*, trans. R.F.C. Hull (New York: Pantheon Books, 1949): Luce Irigaray, cited in Domna Stanton, 'Difference on Trial', in *Poetics of Gender*, ed. Nancy K. Miller (New York: Colombia University Press, 1986), pp. 157–82, 160. Irigaray claims that it is the murder of the mother rather than the murder of the father, as Freud would have it, that lies at the heart of Western culture. Cf. the theme of matricide in Aeschylus' *Eumenides* as being the foundation for the establishment of the judicial system, represented by the goddess Athena, born full-blown from the head of Zeus.

sharp contrast with her role in those stories where she appears as a character in her own right. For instance, as wife of Nemed, she died of heartbreak when she foresaw the destruction that would come in the *Táin Bó Cuailnge,* Ireland's great epic saga.[16] In the second story, where she defeated the opposition in her insistence that women, too, could be political leaders, she had no interest in executing her captives but put them to work at the fruitful task of building her fort. In the third story, where she curses the men of Ulster and gives them her 'Pangs', once again, she had no wish to go into competition and, indeed, cursed the men for forcing her to do so since this was the only way she could save the life of her husband. In all these actions she is clearly anxious to save life rather than take it needlessly, and yet she has become known as one of the bloodiest women in Celtic mythology: a War-Goddess.

Thus we can see a steady and ominous change taking place in the image and activities of Macha. In the stories where Macha is most active in her own right as the Mother Goddess she appears as Grían, the 'Sun of Womanfolk',[17] or 'bright Grían and pure Macha'.[18] When she next appears as wife of Nemed, she stands by helplessly while he clears the plains and is powerless to prevent the carnage that she foresees in the coming *Táin.*[19] Finally, Macha has become part of the trio of 'war Goddesses', Macha, Badb, and Mórrígan. In this capacity she is the daughter of Delbaeth son of Neid.[20] Her status has declined from Mother Goddess, to consort, to daughter. It is tempting to speculate that she became a war-Goddess only when she had been displaced from her previous position of power and importance. The society in which Macha had flourished had been overthrown and now her best efforts were directed towards undermining the activities of the warriors.[21]

The idea of a 'war-Goddess' is itself a reflection of the distorted perspective of patriarchal scholarship.[22] Scholars are agreed that the so-called 'Goddesses of War' do not 'themselves participate in battle'. Instead they usually try to undermine the male armies, to demoralize them or otherwise trick them into fulfilling their will. In some cases they will even confuse the armies into killing their own people rather than inflicting hurt on the opposition. Unlike the male gods who delight in the description of their weapons, the 'war Goddesses' use magical means to undermine the armies: weapons are not their province.[23]

The symbols of the Goddess were likewise opposed to battle. The blackbird of the 'Nuns of Tuam' (probably priestesses of the Goddess) eased the pain of warrior wounds and those of pregnant women.[24] The milk from the sacred cow acted as an antidote to the poison of weapons. Rather than being called 'war-Goddesses', they

and Bride Stealing: The Goddess in Indo-European Heroic Literature', *Religion*, vol. 14 (1984), p. 119. In some myths the goddesses turn vicious only after their children have been killed. Cf. discussion of the Babylonian Goddess Tiamat in Neumann, *Great Mother: An Analysis of the Archetype*, p. 214.

22. For the 'goddess of war' cf. Wm. Hennessy, 'The Ancient Irish Goddess of War', *RC*, vol. 1 (1870), pp. 32–55. Amendments to this article appear in Wh. Stokes, 'The Ancient Irish Goddess of War', *RC*, vol. 2 (1873–5), pp. 489–92; Charles Donahue, 'The Valkyries and the Irish War-Goddess', *Proceedings of the Modern Language Association*, vol. 56 (1941), pp. 1–12; John Carey, 'Notes on the Irish War-Goddess', *Éigse*, vol. 19, no. 2 (1983), pp. 263–76.

23. For instance, in the story of the death of Cúchulainn both the Morrígan and the Gray of Macha attempt to prevent him going into his final battle. Cf. 'The Death of Cúchulainn', ed. Wh. Stokes, *Revue Celtique*, vol. 3 (1876–8), pp. 175–85, 175. Cf. also 'Morrígan's Warning to Donn Cuailnge', ed. Garreth Olmsted, *Etudes Celtique*, vol. 19 (1982), pp. 165–71; Charles Bowen, 'Great Bladdered Medb', *Éire-Ireland*, vol. 10 (1975), pp. 14–34, 23. As Anne Ross points out, the goddess Medb in *The Táin* (a classic Irish epic saga) is the only exception to the rule that 'war-goddesses do not take up arms'. Cf. Anne Ross, *Pagan Celtic Britain* (New York: Columbia University Press, 1967), p. 223. *The Táin*, however, is essentially a satire, one of whose functions was to denigrate the goddesses and exalt the virtues of male-bonding. Cf. especially where the 'heroes' at the end of the battle strike at the Triple Mounds in Ath Luain (the Ford of the Moon) and at Newgrange. The heroes strike alternately at the mounds in each other's locality and the entire episode is punctuated by an incident symbolizing the incompatibility of war and menstruation. The goddess Medb, just as she had rounded up her armies ready for the final onslaught, got her 'gush of blood'. In the act of 'relieving herself' she caused several great channels to appear, thereafter called 'Medb's Foul Place', *The Táin*, ed. T. Kinsella (Oxford: Oxford University Press, 1969), pp. 248–51.

24. Cf. Professor Connellan, 'The Proceedings of the Great Bardic Institution', *Transactions of the Ossianic Society*, vol. 5 (1857), reprinted (New York, 1972), 59.

16. 'Edinburgh Dindshenchas', *Folklore*, vol. 4, p. 480.
17. 'Rennes Dindshenchas', no. 94.
18. 'Metrical Dindshenchas', vol. 4, p. 127.
19. 'Edinburgh Dindshenchas', *Folklore*, vol. 4, p. 480.
20. MacFirbis, *Genealogy*, p. 79. Cited in Wm. Hennessy, 'The Ancient Irish Goddess of War', *Revue Celtique* (1870), pp. 332–55.
21. For similar themes in Indo-European Literature cf. A.L. Frothingham, 'Medusa, Apollo and the Great Mother', *AJA*, vol. 15 (1911), pp. 349–77, and 'Medusa 11', *AJA*, vol. 9 (1915), pp. 13–23; Mary Beard, *Woman as a Force in History* (New York: Macmillan, 1946), p. 287; Ruby Rohrlich, 'State Formation in Sumer and the Subjugation of Women', *Feminist Studies*, vol. 5 (1980), pp. 76–102, 86–91; Ruth Katz Arabagian, 'Cattle Raiding

might more properly have been known as 'those responsible for turning back the streams of war', a title given to the early Irish abbesses of Kildare.[25]

Macha's transition from Mother-Goddess to War-Goddess reflects the new concerns of patriarchal consciousness. We saw how the Triple Goddess often appeared in abstract form in the form of a Triple Spiral. The triple male Gods, in contrast, are usually depicted as three-faced heads.[26] The head, rather than the body, was now the location of creativity. The 'masts of Macha', the severed heads of warriors slain in battle, indicate the increased importance given to the 'word' over 'fertility', a trend also in the Genesis stories. The warriors who developed the head-cult took possession of the heads of those whom they conquered believing that they were, thereby, controlling the spirit of the person since the head symbolized the 'very essence of being'.[27] The 'masts of Macha', which previously meant the nuts fed to the sacred pigs, are now 'Machae's mast-feeding', i.e. the 'heads of men that have been slaughtered'.[28] The foods sacred to the Goddess would no longer be enough for the warrior: divine food would be the conquered heads he had taken in war.

At night, after a hard day's battle, the warriors would place the head of whoever they had slain in battle between their legs.[29] This was a very serious ritual and, in one incident, in order to show his respect for his defeated opponent, the warrior Fland kissed Cormac's head, rather than press it between his thighs.[30] One warrior was said never to have 'slept without a Connaughtman's

head under his knee'.[31] Placing the head under the thigh was the ultimate symbol of conquest. The conquered head between the legs of the warrior dramatizes vividly the nature of the event. The warrior has given birth through killing his opponent; bloody skulls, rather than little infants, were the symbols of the new social life, where the warrior would be responsible for ensuring the 'life' of the tribe and would reign supreme. 'Life' now enters the world through death, a mentality which persists to this day and which is celebrated in the military rituals throughout the world.[32]

Like the Goddess Tlachtga, who had been gang-raped, Macha was also effectively violated at the feasts of *Samhain* held in Ulster where she had reigned. *Samhain* had been primarily a harvest feast celebrating the successful growth and gathering of the 'fruits' of the past year. Now the warriors came, conquered heads on their belts, and gave accounts of their deeds of valour, the new 'fruits' and 'harvest' of a warrior society.[33]

The cult of the warrior and hero would replace that of female creativity, with widescale repercussions for the future of humanity. For, whereas female creativity took place with regard to life, which included respect for death, male creativity had become inextricably bound up with the defiance of death . . .

In a warrior society, motherhood was no longer a source of strength, but a handicap, preventing one sex from participation or representation in the prestigious culture of the warriors. From now on whenever the warriors wanted to ridicule a weakling or fallen warrior, they would say with all the contempt of the triumphant philosophy: 'he was as weak as a woman in childbirth'.[34]

25. Cf. Donncha Ó Corráin, 'Woman in Early Irish Society', in *Women in Irish Society*, ed. Donncha Ó Corráin and Margaret Mac Curtain (Dublin: Arlen House, 1978), pp. 1–3, 10.
26. Pamela Berger, 'Many Shaped: Art, Archaeology and the Táin', *Éire-Ireland*, vol. 17, no. 4 (1982), p. 11. Cf. also Pierre Lambrechts, *L'exaltation de la tête dans la pensée et dans l'art des Celtes* (Brugge: De Lempel, 1954).
27. Berger, 'Many Shaped', p. 14. For a general discussion of the role of scalp-taking cf. Sanday, *Female Power and Male Dominance*, p. 107 ff. Sanday argues that in some societies men took scalps as their 'children'. She argues that this was not an expression of womb-envy but was an attempt to establish a balance between life-giving and life-taking forces in society. She also argues that in some societies it was believed that scalp-taking resulted in an increase in food (p. 44). Sanday also makes the interesting observation that there are more menstrual taboos in societies where scalping is actively pursued by men.
28. *Three Irish Glossaries*, ed. Wh. Stokes (London: Williams and Norgate, 1862), p. xxxv.
29. Cf. *Fragmentary Annals of Ireland*, ed. and trans. Joan Radner (Dublin: Institute for Advanced Studies, 1978), p. 159.
30. *Three Irish Glossaries*, ed. Wh. Stokes, p. xi.
31. 'Tidings of Conchobor MacNessa', ed. Wh. Stokes, *Ériu*, vol. 4, no. 1 (1908), pp. 18–38, 29.
32. For further elaboration on this theme cf. Mary Condren, 'Patriarchy and Death', in *Womanspirit Bonding*, eds Janet Kalven and Mary Buckley (New York: Pilgrim Press, 1984), pp. 173–89; Carol Cohn, 'Sex and Death in the Rational World of Defense Intellectuals', *Signs*, vol. 12, no. 4 (1987), pp. 687–718.
33. *Three Irish Glossaries*, p. xxxv. Cf. also *Ancient Irish Tales*, p. 176, where it is claimed that the men carried the tips of the tongues of those men whom they had slaughtered in their pouches to the harvest festival.
34. Cf. 'Death of Muircertach Mac Erca', *Ancient Irish Tales*, p. 517; 'The Burning of Finn's House', ed. E.J. Gwynn, *Ériu*, vol. 1 (1904), pp. 13–37, 25; cf. Ruth Katz Arabagian, 'Cattle-Raiding and Bride Stealing', pp. 107–42.

Death and birth are at polar opposites and as Simone de Beauvoir has argued, effectively accepting the premises upon which this philosophy is based: 'it is not in giving life but in taking life that mankind is raised above the animals. That is why superiority has been accorded in humanity, not to the sex which brings forth but to that which kills.'[35]

Macha's cry, 'a mother bore each one of you', was possibly the last symbolic attempt to appeal to motherhood as the basis for social ethics. The Triple Goddess whose spiral imagery represented life, death and the cycle of eternal return has been torn apart once and for all. The ambiguity and integration of the complex elements of matri-centered religion, as represented by the Serpent/Goddess in the form of a Triple Spiral, would be overcome and replaced eventually by the Sign of the Cross. Cyclical regeneration would give way to linear history and the cycle of eternal return would be replaced by the quest for personal immortality.

Men no longer need the Goddess in her life-giving form, yet the Goddess of death is still active, seeking out their destruction. A major change has taken place: she has suffered a subtle transformation from the Goddess of death into the Goddess of war. In patriarchal culture, in fact, the only Goddess who is tolerated is the Goddess of war: she is the only one with any real part to play, whether her name be Mother Ireland, the Motherland, or Britannia. She is the one against whom, or on whose behalf, men must constantly pit their wits and their strength, and if they fail in the attempt they can say (as we said in Ireland of the leaders of the failed 'Easter Rising' of 1916) that they died for her sake.[36]

And yet in the Macha story, the Irish warriors saw their period of hibernation in their 'Pangs' as a curse, just as the fall from grace in the Garden of Eden has led to the curse of Yahweh. They were aware that the overthrow of the Great Mother meant the end of their idyllic existence in the clan. The life of the warrior, under the rule of the king rather than the clan collective, would be bloody and brutal. They were indeed cursed and cast out of the Garden of Paradise but this time the curse came directly from the woman, the Great Mother Goddess Macha who clearly recognized the downward spiral of destruction into which humanity would be plunged if its political and religious foundations rested on the suppression and control of women.

The Irish story has, therefore, preserved for us the true nature of the event: the matricide that lies at the heart of patriarchal culture and the Fall into patriarchal time and space that would have devastating consequences for the banished children of Eve.

35. Simone de Beauvoir, *The Second Sex* (New York: 1961), pp. 58–9.

36. Cf. Augustine Martin, 'To Make a Right Rose-Tree', *Studies* (1966), pp. 38–50; G.F. Dalton, 'The Tradition of Blood-Sacrifice to the Goddess', *Studies* (1974), pp. 343–54; Francis Shaw, S.J., 'The Canon of Irish History: A Challenge', *Studies*, vol. 61, no. 242 (1972), pp. 114–53. For a contemporary study of the effects of this mentality today cf. Richard Kearney, 'Myth and Motherland', Field Day Pamphlet 5 (Derry, 1984).

RITA HANNON

(1935–   )

from:
THE EMANCIPATION OF WOMEN AND THE CHURCH (1971)

[While there is abundant evidence of women studying theology in the first twelve centuries of Christianity, following church reforms in the twelfth century and the continental reformations of the Middle Ages, women were virtually excluded and effectively silenced.

Following the second wave of the women's liberation movement, in the late 1960s, several works appeared in Europe and the United States. Women religious and some carefully chosen lay women (such as Mary Daly in the US) had just been admitted to the study of theology. Partly inspired by Simone de Beauvoir's *The Second Sex*, and delighted at the notion of equality, these works tentatively began to consider the possibility of women's admission to the priesthood. But their theological training had not prepared these women for the vicious backlash their works provoked from the ecclesiastical authorities and, even more painfully, from other women.

Irish-American Mary Daly in her later work radically critiqued her first tentative steps into print, producing several new versions of her book *The Church and the Second Sex*. Rita Hannon (then tellingly called Sister *Vincent* Hannon) emigrated to Tanzania where she spent the rest of her professional life working with poor women and children. This article poignantly reminds us of the innocence of those early days when women sought equality in a church determined to keep them in their place. In 1977, the Vatican published its definitive statement on women priests: *Declaration on the Question of the Admission of Women to the Ministerial Priesthood*. Alarmed as it was by the monstrous regiments of women entering theological study, several more documents would follow, forbidding even the discussion of women's ordination.

This extract is taken from 'The Emancipation of Women and the Church', published in the *Religious Life Review* (winter 1971). Footnotes are by the author.]

I suppose it can be presumed that to ask whether women, 'prey of the species', have a contribution to make to the revitalization of the Church is superfluous. Furthermore we can take it for granted that it is equally superfluous to ask if the Church needs their contribution. I'll not comment on what the Church seemingly wants from its women. Even in this twentieth century one hears such comments as 'let women keep to their place' and that could be anything from docile wives to ecclesiastical chars. If we think that the Church doesn't need the full participation of its women let me say that it could do worse than take a cue from the writings of a saintly Hindu and a committed Communist. Of his country Gandhi said: 'India's salvation depends on the sacrifice and enlightenment of its women.' And Lenin too could say: 'No revolution is successful without the participation of women.' How I wish that a pope had said these words! Back in the twelfth century a great German nun, Hildegarde von Bingen, diagnosed the malaise in the medieval Church and society as due to the conspicuous failure then to harness the potential of women. The conditions in both Church and society that necessitated the calling of Vatican II were to a great extent due to the non-use by the Church of women's total gifts — one half of its human potential. This is not to say, of course,

that the *ecclesia semper reformanda* would cease to need reform if women were admitted to full partnership in the Church. If the present effort at renewal is to be taken seriously the Church cannot continue to ignore the female half of its members and exclude them from real partnership with men in revitalizing its every cell . . .

A number of steps . . . suggest themselves and what follows are some immodest proposals!

1. Even at this late hour I would see some real value in a church document specifically aimed at eradicating entrenched sex-prejudice: a passing reference as in the *Constitution on the Church in the Modern World* is not very convincing.[1] Or, if not this, at least one would expect full backing from the Church for the U.N. Declaration on the Elimination of Discrimination against Women. Something more than a reluctant going along with the amelioration of their legal status by secular authority is needed.

2. I would also like to witness an official admission and repudiation of its discriminate treatment of women similar to that made by Pope Paul for the part which the Roman Church played in the Eastern schism.[2] Something more courageous in any case is needed than the belated conferral of the title Doctor on two of its great women.

3. A follow-up to these in terms of actual practice where the real work of exorcism takes place would be the only touchstone of a real determination to humanize the condition of women in the Church. For a start,

(a) the removal of offensive references to women from the liturgy. Pope John's removal from Good Friday's liturgical text of 'perfidious' as descriptive of Jews gave a much-needed lead towards better relations between them and Catholics. Or is it contended that the Church's record of anti-feminism is really less evil than its former anti-semitism?

---

1. This was one of the documents produced by the Second Vatican Council.
2. The Eastern Schism refers to the split between the Eastern and Western churches that culminated in the twelfth century. The conflict concerned the basis of papal authority and questions relating to the status of the Holy Spirit.

(b) The elimination of all hints of sex-discrimination from its revised code of canon law and the appointment of competent women to the commission engaged in this work.

(c) The unequivocal opening up to women of all offices and functions within the Church which at present laymen may hold or exercise would especially prove a change of heart. In regard to women religious one hopes that they will be trusted with autonomy not only theoretically but *de facto* in the renewal of their orders, congregations and institutes. That is, an autonomy at least equal to that enjoyed by men religious and in keeping with the principles of subsidiarity and the co-responsibility of all adult members of the Church for the spread of God's kingdom. It is intolerable that women religious should not have a voice in the policy-making decisions of the Church especially in those affecting their lives. It is also intolerable that Catholic women in general should not be allowed a share in determining the life and future of the Church . . .

Complaisant Women

It would, of course, be wrong to suggest that all obstacles come from ecclesiastical authorities. Men's rejection of women never comes without women having their share of responsibility for it. I agree with those in the Women's Liberation Front who hold men responsible for the second-class treatment given to women, but the passivity that women have shown in the face of intolerable situations is lamentable. Whatever the official Church does to emancipate them would be of no avail if women themselves do not now begin to utilize every opportunity to promote their status and overcome the obstacles to contributing their energies to the building up of the kingdom. Of course, there are women who take the easy way out by repeating ad nauseam that such and such an office or work is not for women. These are probably the same women who like to be dominated and reckon it virtue! This was a quality not unknown in slaves even after their emancipation! Shaw said somewhere that it is easier to put chains on men than to remove them if the chains confer benefits! The diffidence of

women in a Church which they knew to be antifeminist was understandable if not wholly pardonable. Only exceptional women by any standards had the stamina or courage of a St Catherine of Siena or a St Teresa of Avila to be themselves in a male-dominated Church. The former complained as follows when Christ commanded her in a vision to add action to her contemplation:

> It is all very well for men, but where and how can I, a wretched woman, be useful to others? Also it is not fitting for women to teach and preach; men have no esteem for them and moreover it is unseemly for a woman to have to do with men.[3]

St Teresa likewise realized the disadvantage of being a woman in a man's world and hints at this several times in her writings. In fact, it is embarrassing to read the way she almost apologizes so frequently for her existence. This was prompted not just by fear of the Inquisition but was the only passport that even a woman of her greatness had to movement in the intellectual and religious spheres of sixteenth century Spain. 'The very thought that I am a woman is enough to make my wings droop,' she lamented. Both women, however, transcended even their times . . .

Nuns Have Opted Out

There is a sense in which sisters over the centuries have betrayed their vocation. All religious whether male or female, active or contemplative, are eunuchs for the sake of the kingdom of God and they especially are the heralds or forerunners of the end of time. But forerunners, in the words of Gabriel Moran, do not sit at home waiting for the parousia. The vow of chastity is meant to have a liberating effect, to give more freedom for the sake of greater service. Women religious engaged in what is called the active apostolate, unhampered by the ties of family and domestic life should be ideally mobile, flexible and free for their mission as heralds. Not being wives and mothers they should have a certain transcendence even in a

3. A. Levasti, *My Servant Catherine* (London: Blackfriars, 1954), p. 50.

male dominated Church and society. Religious sisters do not receive their worth and importance from husbands and families, but from themselves. They are symbols of the worth of a human being; they who stand on their own feet should have convinced the Church and society of the dignity and sacredness in particular of women which has only begun to take place in reality. In the past they should have provided the pathfinders which the Church like every great body whether army, industrial plant, or government cannot afford to do without. Today more than perhaps ever this role is in need of dramatic fulfilment. It is no wonder that the great body which the Church is refrains from committing itself to vanguard action where great commitment is needed when its vanguard has fallen behind.

Religious are the ones that should have been piloting the movements for the elimination of all kinds of oppression and discrimination, provided blue-prints for reform and sponsored the cause of justice and freedom both within the Church and society at large. Instead, women religious failed the Church and betrayed their vocation in this regard. Instead of grasping and exercising the freedom inherent in their state, they settled for second-rate treatment from a paternalistic clergy. Indeed they even co-operated wittingly or unwittingly with the half deliberate and fully blameworthy efforts to subject or worse still to neutralize them! The assumption by women religious of men's names is only one example of this and has, of course, a deep psychological significance. It was part of that same process by which in a sense their womanhood was denied or held suspect and their personalities dwarfed. This involved a process closely akin to St Jerome's open recommendation that woman 'when she wishes to serve Christ more than the world (she) will cease to be a woman and will be called man (vir)'.[4] If their taking men's names was as artful and as beneficial to the Church as was Mary Ann Evan's pseudonym of George Eliot to the literary world, then the practice could be justified! In one of her books, Virginia Woolf rather good-humouredly takes women to task for keeping to the passive condition imposed upon them by men. 'Women have served all these centuries as

looking-glasses possessing the magic and delicious power of reflecting the figure of man at twice its natural size.'[5] In a sense nuns have played this role within the Church for the clergy with consequent damage to both. That men, fooled into believing they are superior, dominate women in the Church is not a good arrangement for women: it is no better an arrangement for men.

Regarding the movement towards the emancipation of women, nuns remained foreigners; their secular sisters instead executing their betrayed role. Instead of being the vanguard of the kingdom, they were an uncertain and uninspiring rearguard. Instead of being leaders, they were slavish adherents to conformity; their vow of obedience negating the liberty inherent in their virginity. The nun, instead of being out in front, was/is the precise symbol of backwardness and out of touchness. The causes of such betrayal are only all too understandable. It is more comfortable to settle into traditions and routine than to live the demanding life of an operative faith which relies not on customs and regulations but has absolute trust in God for the actions and risks taken for the sake of the kingdom . . .

Supposing that by the combined effort of the official Church and women themselves, especially religious, the female potential of the Church is opened up, what then? If I were a follower of the fixed-nature school I should proceed to argue how the typical qualities of women would come into full use in the building up of the kingdom. But, of course, if the stereotyped female image is not eliminated then their emancipation cannot take place because women would still have to be subject to a slavish symbol or else threatened with loss of sex-membership and no human gift is strong enough to flower fully in a person who is threatened with that. I do not, as does Von Fort[6] for example, argue that women are self-sacrificing, personal, spiritual, loving, generous, etc. What I do envisage is that when women are truly emancipated; when they are allowed, *helped and encouraged* to cultivate their gifts; when their contribution and influence are welcomed equally with men's, then we must

4. St Jerome, *Commentary on Epistles to the Romans.*

5. Virginia Woolf, *A Room of One's Own* (Harmondsworth, Middlesex: Penguin, 1967), p. 35.
6. Gertrude Von Fort, a forerunner of Germany's trained professional theologians.

inevitably have an enriched Church, better for not having excluded one half of its human potential. Although it is obvious what a mess men have made of the Church and secular society, I do not claim that women would have done any better. They could hardly have done worse! I do not wish for a Church or society dominated by any one sex but authority composed of, guided and supported by both women and men. Upon this principle of partnership depends the vitality of any community. When this situation obtains in the Church then will it have redeemed its past, shed one further remnant of its pagan legacy and advanced one great step closer to the fulfilment and freedom envisaged in the parousia. Only then will it be able to truly preach that it is 'neither male nor female . . . for we are all one in Christ'.

MARY MALONE

(1938–   )

from:
WOMEN AND CHRISTIANITY
(2000)

[In the short space of thirty years of access to theological study, women underwent a theological revolution equivalent to that of the time of the Reformations. Carefully guarded clerical zones of knowledge were exposed to the light of reason and justice from women's perspective. The following extract provides a very useful overview of this development and is taken from Mary Malone's *Women and Christianity: The First Thousand Years* (Dublin: Columba Press, 2000), pp. 17–28.]

Reading Women into History

In all of Jesus' teaching, as well as in his behaviour, one can find nothing which reflects the discrimination against women prevalent in his day.
(John Paul II, *Mulieris Dignitatem*, 13, 1988)[1]

The church too, both consciously and unconsciously, has been guilty of prejudicial action, practices and policies against women. Many women relate how often they feel patronised, undervalued and trivialised by church leaders.
(Bishop Howard Hubbard, Albany, 1990)[2]

When God is male, the male is God.
(Mary Daly)

That is why we can never ignore the fact that Christ is a man.
(*Declaration on the Question of the Admission of Women to the Ministerial Priesthood*, Paul VI, 1976)[3]

The history of Christianity shows great ambivalence towards women. On the one hand, women have been included, called, graced, inspired and canonised by Christianity throughout the centuries. On the other, as the quotation above from Bishop Hubbard's 1990 pastoral letter indicates, women have not always felt appreciated within the Christian tradition and indeed have often felt excluded and oppressed by church leaders. It is this ambivalence towards women that characterises the whole of Christian history.

The 'good news' for women rediscovered in the gospels forms the bedrock of the Christian tradition — some would say that this is one of its most radical innovations — and this 'good news' is rooted in the gospel portrait of the relationships between Jesus and women. From biblical times to the present, however, this gospel message for women has been variously interpreted, and, it must be admitted, during

1. See *Origins*, October 6, 1988, vol. 18: no. 17.
2. See *Origins*, November 15, 1990, vol. 20: no. 23.

3. The text of the document is published in *Women Priests: A Catholic Commentary on the Vatican Declaration*, eds Leonard Swidler and Arlene Swidler (New York: Paulist Press, 1977), pp. 37–49.

most of Christian history, it was presented to women as a negative message of exclusion, trivialisation and often quite astonishing hostility on the part of the clergy. This is what Bishop Hubbard alludes to, but it is not at all difficult to find in the pages of Christian history comments on women that make his allusions seem very tame by comparison.

Here I will mention just two of these comments. The first is from an eleventh century saint, Peter Damian, who was assisting Pope Leo IX in the task of cleaning up the image and role of the clergy. It is a shocking diatribe but it is not at all exceptional in the writings of church leaders about women. The fact that he is primarily addressing priests' wives as part of his celibacy programme does nothing to mitigate the utter nastiness of his comments:

> I speak to you, O charmers of the clergy, appetising flesh of the devil, that castaway from Paradise, poison of the minds, death of souls, companions of the very stuff of sin, the cause of our ruin. You, I say, I exhort you women of the ancient enemy, you bitches, sows, screech-owls, night-owls, blood-suckers, she-wolves . . . come now, hear me harlots, prostitutes, with your lascivious kisses, you wallowing places for fat pigs, couches for unclean spirits . . .[4]

And so it goes on for pages and pages. This form of discourse represents a kind of Christian 'road-rage' against women, appearing at particular crisis points in the tradition, and in fact was not as damaging in the long run as some more reflective comments. The second introductory comment sums up a tradition which, in its very thoughtfulness and careful reference to scripture, has been much more influential in perpetuating negative attitudes towards women. It is taken from a sermon of Pope Pius XII to newly-weds, preached on September 10, 1941, right in the midst of the Second World War.[5] The Pope speaks of the man and woman entering marriage on a 'perfectly equal footing' because of their equal creation by God, but then goes on to accentuate the position of the husband as the head of this new *visible* society called the family. The Pope stresses the need for such a male head as a result of the sin of Eve. The Pope then moves to the New Testament as follows:

> In holiness, by means of grace, both spouses are equally and immediately united to Christ. In fact, St Paul said that as many as have been baptised in Christ and who have put on Christ, are all sons (*sic*) of God; there is neither male nor female, because all are one in Christ Jesus. Not so, however, in the church and in the family, which are visible societies . . .

Notice the ambivalence in the Pope's presentation. He announces the 'perfect' equality of women and men, both in their equal creation and in their equal baptism, and then seems to cancel out that equality by invoking the necessary arrangements of the *visible* societies of family and church. This sermon illustrates perfectly the 'give and take' quality of women's position in Christianity, but it also illustrates, as Peter Damian's outburst does not, the inescapability of the scriptural witness to women. This biblical testimony can be explained away, re-interpreted according to the needs of the author, or quite simply forgotten, but it cannot be removed from the record.

Re-reading the 'Good News'

It is our first task, then, to look once again at this 'good news' for women as it appears in the whole biblical *corpus*, both canonical and apocryphal. A later and more extensive task will be to trace the historical development of this 'good news' throughout the Christian tradition. In both cases, our reading will be a gendered reading, that is we will explore and attempt to understand the multiple cultural and religious conclusions drawn from the biological fact of the division of the sexes into male and female. This will involve looking at the relationships between women and Jesus during the ministry period, and also the very diverse testimony to women in the earliest decades of Christianity and beyond. Since one of our operating definitions of history will be a

4. Anne Llewellyn Barstow, *Married Priests and the Reforming Papacy: The Eleventh Century Debates* (New York: Edwin Mellen Press, 1982), p. 60.
5. *The Woman in the Modern World*, arranged and edited by the Monks of Solesmes (St Paul Editions, 1959).

'fusion of horizons', this will also involve alternating our attention between biblical and historical times and the contemporary situation.

One of the major foci will be on the silencing of women and the ways in which the Christian tradition has succeeded in making women virtually invisible. We must also, then, ask questions about the blindness of women themselves in failing to see what was before our eyes in the biblical texts. Each century and each group of Christians have dialogued with the scriptures according to their own needs and faith experiences, so that when women today explore the scriptures from their own perspective, they are not doing anything novel. On the other hand, however, this contemporary search is a revolutionary act for women, or at least it was seen as such in the sixties and seventies of our century. For this was one of the very few times when women claimed the right to read and interpret the scriptures for themselves, and it is this initial re-reading that will be presented here, in order to share with contemporary readers the intense exhilaration of this first feminist re-reading. Since the sixties, there has been an explosion of biblical re-interpretation on every front, including very important feminist readings . . .

First, the decades of the sixties and seventies must briefly occupy our attention. What kind of time was it that gave birth to such a momentous turn of events for women believers?

The Sixties and Seventies

Nobody seems to be able to speak of the sixties without passion. Both chronologically and in a socio-religious sense, it was the century's turning point. Here, our focus will be on the Roman Catholic experience of the sixties, and from a fascinating canvas, we will highlight four points of greatest relevance to our present purposes. These are, first, the new global perspective; secondly, the personalist emphasis in the psycho-social field; thirdly, the second wave of Christian feminism; and fourthly, the radically new Roman Catholic approach to the scriptures initiated by the Second Vatican Council.

For the Roman Catholic — and indeed the whole Christian — tradition, the Second Vatican Council (1962–65) was a watershed. A whole generation of people still speaks of 'before' and

'after' the council when situating themselves and their faith. The council crept on the church quietly but as soon as the panoply of church-leaders assembled and began their discussions, the global significance of the event became clear. For the first time the news media became enraptured with the doings of the Roman Catholic Church. Perhaps what first became obvious was the new realisation of the global dimensions of the church. Bishops from all over the world with their diverse views and problems were featured daily in news reports. For many western Christians, this was a revelation, their assumption having been that there was absolute similarity among Roman Catholics all over the world. There were inevitable coincidences with world politics. Many bishops represented countries seeking liberation, whether from colonial or racial exploitation, indigenous war-lords, or what was then called the western military-industrial complex. The bishops took stands for justice on behalf of their people and this raised many questions for Catholics of all stripes. The emphasis in Christianity seemed to move from private devotion to global justice almost overnight. Besides, the great world religions seemed to be grappling with exactly the same issues as Christianity, sometimes more effectively. Judaism, Buddhism, Hinduism and Islam came onto the agenda as dialogue partners for the first time for centuries.[6]

Needless to say, many did not like this one bit. The supposedly once uniform message of Christianity looked as if it were being stretched beyond endurance. And in another stretching experience, personalist psychology influenced the deliberations of the Council in ways not perceptible before in Roman Catholic discourse. The Christian faith was portrayed as changing in emphasis depending on whether one was adult or child, first or third world, male or female, lay or ordained. There was a new quest for a relevant faith that responded to the needs and aspirations of contemporary believers. Sociologists pointed out that the old communities we all took for granted were losing their cohesion. Attention was turning to the internal dynamics of personal faith

---

6. The Decree on Ecumenism, *Unitatis Redintegratio*, was published on November 21, 1964, to be followed in 1965 by the Declaration on the Relation of the Church to Non-Christian Religions, *Nostra Aetate*.

rather than the external hold of traditional religious life. Church leaders hastened to assure their 'flocks' that the faith had not changed, but believers were discovering that reading the gospel in a different context was, in a sense, reading a new gospel.

One of the key characteristics of the sixties for women was the birth of the second wave of the Christian feminist movement.[7] For the first time for centuries, the specific voices of women believers were heard in the churches. Indeed, since most women had been quite unaware of the first wave of feminism, this was an entirely new experience. Second wave Christian feminism, in the spirit of the times, focused particularly on the struggle of women for human rights in many spheres. Among the rights that were sought by Christian women was the right to be considered for the ministry, particularly the ordained ministry. This feminist quest coincided with a decline in male priestly vocations and the actual abandonment of the ministry by hundreds of ordained men. A similar movement was perceptible among the ranks of religious women. Seminaries, monasteries and convents were forced to consider their survival as membership fell dramatically. In a rather ironic turn of events, many of these institutions were saved from extinction by the arrival of hundreds of lay women and men thirsting to explore the theological and historical foundations of their faith. Within a very short time, these new theological consumers were experiencing at first hand the clash between traditional ministry and theology patterns and the needs of the contemporary churches. For women theology students, in particular, the ambivalence of Christianity about women became glaringly obvious, both in theory and practice. Women from the various Christian traditions turned to each other in an effort both to learn and to share these new experiences. Besides, the so-called 'sexual

revolution' often stretched the relationships between women and their churches to breaking point and put the issues of women's personal sexual responsibility on the churches' agenda for decades, perhaps centuries to come.

Biblical Renewal Movement

One of the more dramatic changes in Christian life for many people was provided by the conciliar and post-conciliar deliberations on the scriptures, which created entirely new avenues of entry to biblical study. Among the last conciliar documents was the monumental *Dei Verbum* which opened the scriptures to Catholics with an urgency unheard of in previous centuries. Many Roman Catholics were not familiar with the Bible, seeing it as intrinsically related to the origins of Protestantism and the ongoing life of those so-called 'separated brethren'. It was assumed within the Catholic community, even if never actually taught in so many words, that the teaching and even the very existence of the Roman Catholic magisterium made scripture reading unnecessary for the Catholic faithful. This attitude rested partly on the assumption that scripture reading was too dangerous for the average lay person. Of course, it is quite true that the scriptures are revolutionary documents. As historians point out continually, every re-reading of the scriptures has led to a revolution in church life . . .

What was the new conciliar teaching on scripture? In a word, it was invitational: Roman Catholics were invited to make the scriptures their own, to study them, reflect on them and share their insights with one another. Scholars were invited to study the scriptures and share their findings with the community. The result was, at least in some circles, an outburst of enthusiasm. This was especially so with many women. They gathered in ecumenical groups, feminist groups, study groups, prayer groups and charismatic groups and revelled in the newly-discovered biblical vision of inclusion, healing, compassion, call, and challenge. More particularly, the conciliar teaching directed Catholics away from a literal reading of the gospels and pointed them in the direction taken by many Protestant scripture scholars for decades. These scholars had come to the realisation that the

---

7. The first wave of the feminist movement is associated with the mid-nineteenth century search for women's rights culminating in the demand for suffrage. Protestant Christian women, in their study of the scriptures, found no support for the religious and cultural restrictions on women, and began to challenge many facets of conventional living arrangements, from the use of 'masculine' language to the exclusion of women from political and religious leadership. The normative marital arrangement of male headship and female silence and submission was particularly challenged. With the achievement of the vote and the advent of the two world wars, much of this debate had been forgotten.

Bible was like a library with many kinds of literature, many different authors (most of whom were unknown), and many different literary genres. This suggested to believers new questions to put to the scriptures, and, above all, new ways of grounding their faith in a biblical spiritual vision.

In the mid-sixties, the Pontifical Biblical Commission pointed Catholics toward the realisation that the gospels were complex documents and much more diverse in their message and intention than a mere literal reading would indicate.[8] The commission pointed out that there were three stages to be taken into account in reading the gospels. In the intervening decades there has been a veritable mountain of research on these stages, and the volume of writing does not seem to be diminishing. Here, only an elementary account of the stages will be given.

The first stage refers to the gospel texts as we have received them, and as they are presented to us today. None of the gospels is an eye-witness account of the events it narrates and it appears that none of the named evangelists was an actual follower of the historical Jesus. Each writes from his own church context some forty to seventy years after the death of Jesus. Mark, for example, writes for a church enduring persecution in the early seventies of the Christian era, and so his main interest is writing an account of the sufferings of Jesus that will help his church to persevere. The vast majority of scholarly writing notes Mark's as the earliest gospel. Matthew and Luke follow some twenty years later, writing to their respective communities of convert Jews and Gentiles. These three are named 'synoptic' because of the obvious similarity of sources and narratives. John's gospel is dated another twenty years later and addresses a community whose needs are both more practical and more mystical. He also offers a corrective to some synoptic themes, and as an example of this, scholars point to his intentional placing of women at the core of the transmission of the good news. The Samaritan woman, Mary of Magdala and Martha take their place in this illustrious gallery.

The second stage in the composition of the gospels points to the period of oral transmission, when the stories and message of Jesus were passed on in the early communities, from the thirties to the sixties, in the context of liturgy and life. No actual written text remains from this period, though scholars are increasingly able to point out how the stories were selected and shaped. This is one of the most mysterious stages of the Christian story, when ministries and institutions were still fluid, and when women seem to have participated with full equality in the life of the young church. Much current research is focused on these earliest decades of Christianity, which seem at once so familiar and so strange to us. This was a time before dogma had been articulated and before the ministry had assumed the form we know today. It continues to be a time of utter fascination to women believers because, through the letters of Paul and the Acts of the Apostles, we meet women who are central to the mission and life of the young church. We know the names of many women who were co-workers and missionaries with Paul and who, in fact, preceded Paul in the Church's mission . . .

The final stage in the transmission of the gospels, that is the stage furthest from us, is the stage portraying the actual words and deeds of Jesus. A literal reading of the gospels has hardened our imagination about this period, as we have become accustomed to asking only questions of literal truth: did Jesus actually do this or say that? The recognition of the complex composition of the gospels, however, compels us to ask different questions. We wonder about the context of the preaching of Jesus and about the actual message of Jesus that lies behind several different versions of the same story. A good example of this is the story of the woman who anointed the head of Jesus. Each gospel treats the story differently for its own purposes, and so we are entitled to enquire about this purpose, and about the original intention of this woman's action and the response of Jesus, and even about whether or not the story has a historical base.

Enough has been said to show how the conciliar teaching on the scriptures opened up new avenues of study for believers and, coming as it did, in synchronicity with the feminist movement, it opened doors for women to discover new resources and challenges for their faith.

---

8. The Pontifical Biblical Commission was founded by Leo XIII at the beginning of the twentieth century to oversee proper biblical interpretation. One of its most influential documents was the 1964 *Instruction on the Historical Truth of the Gospels.*

Good News for Women

It is now time to ask what the women were finding as they read the scriptures in a completely new historical situation and with new literary tools. Many felt as if they had returned to the period of the first Christians. They read in the gospels a message of inclusion and call that they had not heard before. They read that they were a new creation, and in the reading, many actually experienced a newness in their relationship with God and with Jesus. They discovered that the gospel values totally reversed both contemporary secular values, and also the valuing of women that had been presented as traditional church teaching. They discovered that women and men had been equally called to discipleship, and even to apostleship. And they met a glorious array of women, some of whose names had been familiar, but who now seemed to take on personalities and to accompany them in their faith life as closely as their best friends.

It is also clear that there never was a debate about the initial inclusion of women in Christianity. Women have always been admitted to baptism and are, therefore, included as *imago dei*, the image and likeness of the creating God, as well as *imago Christi*, the image of Christ, crucified, buried and raised. The pre-Pauline understanding of baptism in Galatians goes on to denounce all exclusions or oppressions on the basis of sex, race or class (Galatians 3:27–28). This baptismal faith is rooted in the teaching of Jesus about the reign (or kin-dom) of God, which paints a vision of a community rooted in truth, love, justice and peace. This vision called all believers to a new ethic, a new way of life, where the first were last and the last first, where the mighty are cast down and the lowly raised up. This prophetic critique of a disordered society has always been seen as central to the Christian vision. The personal words and deeds of Jesus put flesh and colour on this vision, and his life is seen as a model for all, especially in its reversal of 'business as usual'.

Women Silenced

Within this overall vision, women are held up again and again as exemplars of the life of discipleship through their faith and courage. Their fidelity is painted against the backdrop of male infidelity; their presence right to the end is deliberately written into the text in contrast with the cowardice and desertion of the male followers. Women began to read the scriptures with a new sense of their place within this 'good news'. But unfortunately, this is not the whole story. Despite the good news of the gospels, the actual fruits for women show a pitifully meagre harvest. Women are, in no sense, central to these texts, and often feel as if they are clutching at straws in texts that are thoroughly patriarchal. The earliest piece of Christian writing known to us — Paul's first letter to the Thessalonians — is written as though the Christian community were composed entirely of men. As the first century progresses, the prescriptions for the silencing and exclusion of women become more vociferous. The resulting invisibility of women has become part of our imaginative self-identity as women believers, and the silencing of women has been taken for granted in all subsequent teaching and theology. This does not mean that women were absent from Christianity, but that their voice, insight, experience, wisdom, and faith were considered unnecessary to the understanding of the tradition. This constitutes an unimaginable loss for believers, and when one adds the loss of women's contribution as leaders of Christian worship and proclaimers of the gospel, one can understand the demands for inclusion at every level that have rocked the churches in recent times.

In the final texts of the New Testament canon patriarchal marriage, with all its strictures about the headship of the husband and the obedience and submission of the wife, is adopted as the normative Christian social relationship. This had practical consequences for the seclusion and relegation of women to a kind of second-class Christian membership. The espousal of Eve in the Pastoral Letters, as theological justification for the natural and necessary obedience of women, led very soon to the vilification of women as the source of all evil. In the case of women (though not only in their case), Christianity found itself to be practically incapable of incorporating the prophetic dimension of the message of Jesus.

All this has deprived women of a continuous story of public Christian activity. Women remain practically without models from the earliest periods, except for the women of the Apocryphal literature, who were very quickly assigned heretical status as a result of their struggles for full inclusion in the community. Another consequence of the exclusion has been the stereotyping of God-imagery and God-language. God has been overwhelmingly imaged in the light of his male spokespersons, and the language of theology, history, and liturgy continued for centuries to have a predominating masculine tone. Finally, today, as the voice of women is being heard as exegetes, preachers and teachers in some churches, a little light is beginning to be shed on solutions to some of these problems. At the close of the twentieth century, the presence of women does not have to be assumed, or tagged on as a footnote. Women are finding ways to voice their concerns and to begin to celebrate their journey towards full inclusion in the Christian community.

LINDA HOGAN

(1964–   )

from:

OCCUPYING A PRECARIOUS POSITION: WOMEN IN CULTURE AND CHURCH IN IRELAND (2000)

[In the 1970s and 1980s, feminist theological reflection flourished. As with all revolutionary movements, women began to occupy the high moral ground, pleading for women's way of knowing, or equating victimhood with innocence. Soon, however, dissident voices began to be heard: working-class, black, lesbian, disabled, or women who otherwise were excluded, erased, or taken for granted challenged feminist theorists. The category of experience was central to feminist theorizing, but now the experience of women who were doubly or triply marginalized needed to be taken into account. The category, Woman, also needed to be deconstructed to reveal the interconnected layers of class, racial, or sexual oppression. In this article, Linda Hogan outlines both the possibilities and limitations of feminism, given the multiple positions of power women occupy in the social order. This extract is taken from her article in *New Century New Society*, edited by Dermot Lane (Dublin: Columba Press, 2000). The footnotes are by the author unless otherwise stated.]

In her prose memoir *Object Lessons* Eavan Boland warns that we should not substitute the easy answer for the long haul. 'I see no redemption whatsoever,' she says, 'in moving from one simplification to the other.' She is referring here to an overly simplistic feminist reading of the history of women's exclusion from the poetic tradition; however, her caution has wider purchase beyond the realm of poetry and the arts. In the context of feminist analyses of Christianity, and, in particular, Roman Catholicism, her admonition is especially pertinent. It reminds one that the past cannot be read as one continuous patriarchal betrayal of women by men. Moreover, it suggests that a future cannot be imagined without confronting the reality that women as well as men have colluded in and extended patterns of oppression and violence.

In contemplating recent decades of feminist critique of the Christian tradition what strikes me most is that although feminism has given us a partial understanding of the structures of domination, we are still struggling to comprehend the complexities of power and the way it infuses all our relationships and institutions. Women and men both have occupied ambiguous and often precarious positions within patriarchy. However, feminist theorists must take care to avoid construing women primarily as victims and men as victors. This is especially the case in relation to the Roman Catholic church.

Of course, I do a disservice to feminism in suggesting that it is not sufficiently aware of the complexities of power relations and the role of women in their perpetuation of which feminism has long been cognisant. However, it has also been guilty of speaking in clichés, portraying women only as victims and promoting the facile hope that if women had a greater role to play society would be more just and caring. In fact, feminism's own past points to a far more intricate and subtle relationship between women, men and power.

The reality of feminist politics, both in the late nineteenth and twentieth centuries, suggests that women are not the great innocents of history and that relationships between women do not necessarily proceed on the basis of mutuality and care. Women, too, struggle to embody such values in our relationships, both personal and political. Indeed, it is my firm conviction that if feminism is to flourish in the next century it will need to divest itself of the myth of female victimhood and of a simplistic vision of global sisterhood.

In Ireland, women's position with regard to both church and society embodies many of these ambiguities. One reading of the political history of both church and state would relegate women to the periphery, would regard women to be 'outside history'. In many respects, women could be said to be absent from the collective public memory of our history, and when they are present it is often as tokens, interlopers or oddities. Our understanding of the true extent of women's involvement in the creation of contemporary Ireland is in some measure corrected by the retrieval of the memory of the politically and religiously significant women who have been written out of history.

Feminist scholars have highlighted the significance of women like Anne Devlin, compatriot of Robert Emmet, Countess Markievicz, Eva Gore-Booth, Catherine McAuley and Margaret Aylward, who in their different ways were politically influential.[1]

Similarly the heritage of Irish women artists, poets and intellectuals is being recovered. The

fragile worlds of the astronomer and microscopist Mary Ward, of the novelist Maria Edgeworth, and of artists Mary Delany and Mainie Jellet, who pursued their craft against the tide of history and social convention, suggest an account of women's involvement in the shaping of modern Ireland that cannot be understood as merely passive.

Yet it is fair to say that, on balance, women have been, and continue to be excluded from the centres of decision-making and influence. Undoubtedly, women have made significant strides in some fields. In medicine, in politics and in the financial sector women are present in far greater numbers than ever before. It must be acknowledged, however, that even in these arenas women continue to be under-represented in their higher echelons.

Women's contribution to the renaissance in the arts too is an indication of their growing public presence. However, beyond the professional lives of some women it is questionable whether the lot of women, especially of poor women, has improved substantially. True, there are fewer instances of overt discrimination. Women can now play their part as full citizens of the republic, can serve on juries, can continue in their jobs after marriage and are treated as adults by the bureaucratic arm of the state. There is also less tolerance of domestic violence and of abuse of various kinds. Yet the devastating poverty and violence that characterises the lives of many women, men and children stands as a corrective to the optimistic story of untrammelled progress which often goes unchallenged.

The feminist critique of the Christian tradition

In the 1960s, feminist challenges to the political system began to emerge. Eventually these began to be felt within religious traditions also. This is true of all the major world religions, but is especially true of Christianity in the western world. Mirroring feminism's interaction with other fields, feminist theology arose out of the recognition that the Christian tradition has radically excluded the experiences of women from the articulation of its beliefs, values and practices.

---

1. Anne Devlin was a young Irish woman who became involved in the revolutionary movement in Dublin in the late seventeenth century. Both Countess Markievicz and Eva Gore-Booth were significant players in the fields of social and political reform in the early twentieth century. Catherine McAuley and Margaret Aylward each founded women's religious orders dedicated to the education of the poor and the alleviation of their poverty.

From the 1960s on, a number of Christian women began to identify and critique the many ways in which the Christian tradition created and perpetuated the marginality of women, both in the churches and in society. Kari Borressen, Mary Daly and Rosemary Radford Ruether were among the most influential of the first wave of feminist theologians. Their critique involved a gendered analysis of biblical and theological texts in order to reveal the misogynistic assumptions beneath many of the doctrines and traditions of Christianity.

The study of what Phyllis Trible[2] called the 'texts of terror', those texts in which women are vilified, cursed, shunned and degraded, has formed an important part of feminist theological reflection. Accounts of woman as 'the devil's gateway' (Tertullian), as 'a misbegotten male' (Aquinas — taken from Aristotle), or as 'not the image of God save in her capacity as helpmeet' (Augustine) abound in the classic texts of the Christian tradition. And although they may now be rejected as unimportant vestiges of an age long past, feminists have insisted that their legacies endure in the institutionalised sexism of the contemporary Christian churches.

The Catholic church's refusal to recognise that women as well as men may have a vocation to the ministerial priesthood is a potent symbol of this persistent sexism. This sexism is seen also in the fact that virtually all the teaching offices of the Catholic church are occupied by men, even though the formal teaching offices need not necessarily be held by clerics.

The downgrading of female images for God, images that are evident in the symbolic tradition of Catholicism, is yet another instance of institutionalised sexism. The predominance of the father image in the contemporary God-language of Christianity also creates the false impression that the Christian God can be adequately and exclusively understood as male. This focus on just one of the many images used in the biblical texts has led to the exclusion of the rich and potent symbolism of biblical, patristic and medieval theology and spirituality from our contemporary religious consciousness. These and many other deeply ingrained patterns of

thought and practice contribute to the sense that many women and men have that Christianity in its many forms is inherently sexist and patriarchal.

Much of the initial scrutiny of the Christian tradition through the lens of gender occurred in the United States and in Britain. Once they had access to theological training and scholarship many women became conscious of the sexism that is part of the tradition. The Christian churches in Ireland have also been subject to similar, if not identical, criticisms and theologians working in Ireland have been to the fore in drawing attention to these problems. Indeed this growth in feminist consciousness among women and men has truly transformed the shape of theological scholarship in this country over the past two decades.

Influential thinkers and practitioners, such as Mary Condren, Katherine Zappone, Ann-Louise Gilligan, Ben Kimmerling, Anne Thurston, Enda McDonagh and Dermot Lane[3] to mention just a few, have given voice to the deep alienation generated by participation in destructive structures of thought and practice. But their analysis has not ended with critique. They and many others have also contributed to the discussion about alternative, liberative ways of being spiritual persons within a community of believers.

The critique of Christianity's sexist past has occasioned many debates about the ethical viability of Christianity and about whether women's spiritual future should lie within or outside the borders of traditional religion. Many women have joined Mary Daly in her exodus from patriarchal religion,[4] and have understood it as an exodus from alienated relationship. Others

2. Phyllis Trible, *Texts of Terror: Literary Feminist Readings of Biblical Narratives* (London: SCM Press, 1992).

3. Mary Condren is a feminist theologian and theorist. Katherine Zappone and Ann-Louise Gilligan are both theologians who have also founded The Shanty educational project in Dublin, which seeks to empower individuals trapped in poverty. Ben Kimmerling is a feminist theologian and community activist, working in the west of Ireland. Anne Thurston is a theologian, writer and broadcaster. Enda McDonagh is a moral theologian who has had a significant impact on Irish religious life over the past thirty years. Dermot Lane is also a theologian and president of Mater Dei Institute of Education in Dublin.

4. In 1971 the theologian and philosopher of religion Mary Daly preached a famous sermon during a Sunday service at Harvard University. During her sermon she invited the women and men present to join her in an exodus from the church, which many did. They enacted it symbolically that day by pouring out into Harvard Yard, thus making history.

have been similarly determined to journey from alienated relationship, but believe that this can be done within the church, through the transformation of the institutional patterns that deform the spirit of Christianity.

Those feminists who have remained (marginally) within the tradition have been adamant that no less than a complete paradigm shift is necessary if Christianity is to be a vehicle of spiritual growth and liberation for both women and men. Indeed much of the work of feminist theology since the 1960s, both in the academy and in the wider community, has been focused on identifying the elements that will facilitate a change of consciousness and effect this paradigm shift.

Women's experience as a source of religious insight

One of the most subversive aspects of feminist theology has been its insistence on writing women's experience into the centre of theological reflection. This has involved drawing on women's experience both as a source of religious understanding as well as an important component in the evaluation of the spiritual value of the tradition. Undoubtedly this has been a source of controversy, with opponents of feminist theology insisting that feminists import an inappropriate subjectivism and politicism into religion. However, as Rosemary Radford Ruether argues in her *Sexism and God-Talk*, those elements that have been called the objective sources of theology, that is Scripture and tradition, are themselves codified collective human experience.[5] Religion, according to Ruether, is constituted in a hermeneutical circle of past and present experiences, with Scripture and tradition being the expression and memory of the past. Religious traditions begin to be shaped when the community appropriates these revelatory experiences. These experiences are then categorised, invested with authority and ultimately mediated through narratives, symbols and rituals. What makes feminist theology distinctive in Ruether's eyes, is not that it imports a subjective element into the interpretation of

religious meaning (because all religion does this), but that it imports the experience of those whose voice has long been silenced, that is, of women. This understanding of the nature of religious traditions does not deny the significance of revelatory experiences; however, it insists that all revelatory experiences are mediated through past cultural symbols and traditions, which, in turn, are experiences that have been collectively moulded by a formative group.

The formative groups through history have tended to be the religious elites, those teachers, preachers and functionaries who have had access to scholarship and learning. Thus the construction and interpretation of church doctrines, the articulation of ethical frameworks, the crafting of symbol systems, in fact all that constitutes the substance of religion, all of this emerges out of the dialectic of collective religious experience. This way of understanding religious traditions is not specifically feminist, but it does explain the absence of a female voice in the shaping of Christianity as well as indicate a future role for women's experience in the articulation of that tradition.

Feminist theology's insistence that women's experience should be central to the interpretative process that constitutes religion is highly significant because it resituates religious authority and suggests a different model of power. As a result, religion is no longer conceived in terms of an almighty God revealing himself to a chosen few but in terms of the experience of the divine infusing one's religious imagination and thereby shaping the community's collective life and worship.

This process of imagining an alternative religious consciousness, one that is rooted in the texts and traditions of Christianity but understood in a different register, has been the major work of feminist theology in the last three decades. Of course, there were glimpses of such alternative visions in earlier centuries; however, this process has gained momentum in recent decades. The legitimacy of forging different symbol systems and ethical frameworks is underwritten by this recognition that existing patterns of thought are the product of interpreted experience.

Such a perspective allows for the possibility that at certain times inherited patterns of thought and symbolic practices may no longer illuminate contemporary religious experience.

5. Rosemary Radford Ruether, *Sexism and God-Talk Towards a Feminist Theology* (London: SCM Press, 1983), p. 12.

684 THEOLOGY AND ETHICS: THE TWENTIETH CENTURY

Indeed, this is precisely what has happened within the Christian tradition in the past three or four decades. Many women and men recognised that there is a contradiction between received images, interpretations and values on the one hand, and their experiences of grace and redemption on the other. And it is in this gap between received interpretations of religious truth that the sacred is currently being refigured.

The limitations of women's experience

Yet, even as Christian feminist women were protesting at the exclusionary practices of the institutional church and the absence of women's voices, feminists themselves were coming under attack from women whose perspective was not represented by feminism. Thus began a long and painful learning process in which many feminists recognised that they had replicated one of the most oppressive features of patriarchal thought, in assuming that all women share a common experience and in presuming to speak for all women.

African-American women were initially to the fore in reminding white middle-class women that they had essentially whitewashed women's experience and been blind to the racism and poverty that shapes the experiences of many women. Feminists have thus come to recognise that women's experience is extremely varied and fractured and that women do not share a uniform material reality. Furthermore, feminism world-wide has begun to acknowledge that there are serious inequalities of power between women, with many women making 'bargains' with the powerful institutions and thus benefiting from belonging to a particular racial, ethnic or economic group.

The politics of feminism in South Africa since the 1960s highlights the complex and often fraught nature of the power that women wield. Moreover, it suggests that a simple gender analysis is inadequate to the task of truly coming to terms with the nature and extent of patriarchal power in society.

Women and power

In both the secular and religious contexts in Ireland there is still a tendency to promote the kind of analysis which ignores the extent of the power and influence that women actually hold and which disregards the conflicts that exist between women. In the United States these issues have been frequently debated and much of the analysis is particularly instructive.

Since the beginning of the feminist movement in the nineteenth century in the United States the history of white women's participation in the culture of slavery has been a contentious issue. The fact that hundreds of thousands of white women colluded with and worked for the enforcement of the savagery of slavery challenges received ideas of women as innocent onlookers in a political system not of their making. Whereas it is true that women did not have a direct role in constructing and maintaining the political machinery of slavery, they did play a significant part in its perpetuation. One example of the numerous ways in which white women co-operated in this is recorded by Stanley Feldstein who tells of an incident in which a plantation owner was discovered raping a thirteen-year-old slave girl. His wife's rage was directed at the child who was flogged daily for several weeks.[6] Moreover, the realisation that white women benefited directly from the brutalisation and demonisation of black women further complicates the picture.

A number of the slave narratives of the nineteenth century record the 'patriarchal bargain' which white women made during the years of slavery. In addition, the fiction of many contemporary African-Americans like Toni Morrison help to unravel the complex manner in which gender and race intersect.

In Ireland we do not live directly with the heritage of slavery but the dynamics of power and the various positions of women within the web of unequal relationships which slavery reveals is relevant in this context also. One only has to think of the rigidly stratified society of Ireland in the 1950s to recognise the deep divisions that existed among women and the way in which the respectability of some women was bought at the expense of others. For example, the attitude to and treatment of unmarried mothers reveals a great deal about both the powerlessness of some women and the powerfulness of others.

---

6. Recounted in Bell Hooks's *Ain't I a Woman: Black Women and Feminism* (Boston: South End Press, 1981), p. 37.

In her novel *Down by the River*,[7] Edna O'Brien has a wonderfully revealing vignette in which this is explored. Here she lays bare the various mechanisms by which the virtuous women in any society perpetuate elements of the misogyny for self-interest and the way in which they throw in their lot with the patriarchy. It paints a picture of the patriarchal bargain in which women's own gendered subjectivities together with their investment in particular relationships, work to maintain a delicate balance of power and to safeguard spheres of autonomy they already control.

We see the complex nature of women and power played out in many situations, but there is none more challenging than the role of religious women in running institutions in which children were abused and brutalised. It is here that we come face to face with the inadequacy of simplistic analyses of patriarchy in which women are always cast as the powerless, voiceless victims. There is no doubt that women's collusion in deeply damaging practices can, in part, be explained by the internalisation of patriarchal values and by the attractions of the rewards that accrued to dutiful daughters. In the case of religious women the years of formation in the virtues of modesty, passivity and self-abnegation have certainly taken their toll. However, talk of colonisation and the internalisation of the patriarchal system cannot explain this away. In many respects women gained in direct proportion to the support they gave to these institutions.

In my view, this situation can be best understood as an instance of structural sin. This phrase refers to the fact that we live in a social environment that bears the marks of failure. Our social, cultural and religious context often functions to obscure value and to hinder our moral development. Our sense of value is tied up with the community to which we belong and the social context in which we live. This context often functions in a negative manner, hiding values, giving priority to inessentials or desensitising us to particular injustices. The fact that these biases are hidden in ideologies and reinforced in many different cultural assumptions and patterns of behaviour means that we are often unaware of our participation in social sin. As a result, the biases and blindness of the prevailing cultural ethos limit the extent to which one can make personal moral decisions.

However, although we may be caught in the web of structural sin and of systemic failure, we can never avoid the issue of personal responsibility. The Christian tradition is built on the assumption that although social and cultural practices play an important role in shaping our sense of morality, they do not determine it. We do have a sort of freedom that enables us to evaluate, and then either reject or endorse the dominant culture. Social embodiment is important, but not decisive, in the individual's pursuit of good.

Refiguring the dynamics of power

The history of Catholicism in twentieth century Ireland has been radically rewritten in the 1990s with the truth about the church's role in maintaining such a brutal system being told. Indeed, this changes completely and forever our received understandings and interpretations of 'Catholic Ireland'. The relentless revelations of abuse indicate that our theological and religious heritage needs to be re-evaluated. The degree to which women as well as men invested themselves in these institutions requires us to rethink the religious and moral formation that underlay and sustained such practices. We desperately need a systematic analysis of the various positions that men and women, religious and lay adopted together with an investigation of the underlying theology. The truth will inevitably be ambiguous and multi-layered, with prevarication and accommodation as well as resistance being part of the story. What is clear, however, is that an overly monolithic conception of male dominance will obfuscate rather than reveal the complex dynamics of power that characterises human relationships.

Feminist theology has long been critical of the destructive models of power together with the over-spiritualisation of persons and values that enabled these institutions and practices to flourish. Although it did focus initially on issues of women's exclusion, feminist theology has expanded both its analysis and its horizons in order to respond to all forms of dominance. In

7. Edna O'Brien, *Down By the River* (London: Phoenix Press, 1997).

this, feminist theology has been part of a collective determination on the part of many Christians to transform our received understandings of the tradition.

The centre of gravity of feminist theology is changing, with attention being given to the complex web of violence and domination that is suffused through social and cultural life. Gender is not unimportant, but the gendered construction of social roles and symbolic practices is but one of a number of factors that create systems of oppression. The church's response to the situation of women cannot be seen apart from its day to day struggle to enact the values of the gospel and to embody the Christian vision and vocation in the social context.

There are many people within the Christian tradition in Ireland who are working to create a new religious space and who are part of a fragile and somewhat haphazard coalition for renewal. Feminist theological analysis has contributed significantly to this process and continues to do so as its sense of the dynamics of power evolves and becomes more subtle. If the church is to have a future then it will need to contribute to our sense of human flourishing, facilitate the promotion of relationships of mutuality and trust and partake of the collective endeavour to envision and enact institutions of co-responsibility. The insights of feminist theology are vital to this task, not as an addendum, but as an integral component of both the critique and the reconstruction.

ANNE THURSTON

(1950–)

from:
BECAUSE OF HER
TESTIMONY (1995)

[Within the patriarchal system, the options for women were carefully circumscribed. Almost without exception, the only women to be made saints in the history of Christianity were virgins, widows or martyrs. The dualisms between body and soul, earth and heaven, women and men acutely affected sexually active women, even those fully complying with the marriage laws of the churches. Mothers were placed on a pedestal and idealized, but the messiness of their bodies was carefully excluded from the sanctuaries. Likewise, the apparent messiness of their thinking processes — their groundedness in care for the vulnerable, rather than the great Master Schemes of history or theology — until recently, excluded them from the study of theology. Even after such admission, a further struggle ensued: that of having their experiences as mothers, wives or lovers taken seriously, not to mention theorized as the basis of an holistic theology. This article was originally published in Anne Thurston, *Because of Her Testimony: The Word in Female Experience* (Dublin: Gill and Macmillan, 1995), pp. 23–38. Footnotes are by the author. See pp. 45–57.]

In Birth

You created my inmost self,
knit me together in my mother's womb.
For so many marvels I thank you;
a wonder am I, and all your works are wonders.

(Psalm 139:13–14)

The God who created the earth, the sea and the sky, the God who created the mountains and valleys is found here in the most intimate and hidden place — within the womb. The creative activity of God takes place in the weaving and 'knitting together' in the womb. This is the God who gives birth to creation, who gives birth to us. Birthing mothers image the birthing God. We are not all mothers but we are all born from the womb of mothers. We have all shared the experience of birth; we will all know death. We are connected by our beginning and by our end.

Why is it that there is so little theological reflection on birth? Is it perhaps because wombs belong to the female, and female metaphors and experience have not been thought appropriate for imaging the divine? We have indeed forgotten 'the Rock which begot us, the God who gave us birth' (Deuteronomy 32:18). We have truly forgotten the birthing God. The *Jerusalem Bible* translates that same verse as 'You forgot the Rock who fathered you, The God who made you, you no longer remember.' The translation totally obscures the female birthing imagery and insists on the male generative process. The rock has hardened and refuses to yield to the birthing womb.

Despite the sanitising of birth in our culture and the treatment of birthing mothers as patients in hospitals it seems to me that there remains within women themselves some sense that giving birth is indeed a sacred act. Despite the cultural conditioning which reduces the creative process to the banal 'What did you have?' we have touched mystery. We learn at this moment that life is ultimately meaningful. We know at this moment of total body awareness that we are part of the cycle of creation.

Knowing what it means to bring forth life we will be unwilling to destroy life. There is a strong urge in us to tell our story. Doing so we would be reclaiming a very old wisdom. Stories about birth, which are now exceptional and marginal, made up a large part of the stories which formed us. The Hebrew scriptures are full of stories about the births of babies. In such a tradition of celebrating birth it would not have occurred to people to imagine that they were self-sufficient. They recognised the breath of life as God's gift and celebrated the fragile vulnerable wonder of new life.

Contemporary culture regards births and babies as the business of mothers but Israel's wisdom suggests that births belong to the creative process of God. Biblical theologian Phyllis Trible draws the implications even further when she shows that the Hebrew plural for the word 'womb' is the same as the word for 'compassion'.[1] This organ which is unique to the female becomes a metaphor to express the compassion and the love of God. The God in whom we live and move and have our being is a God of womb-like love — a God who will hold

us close, and who, in love will withdraw, will contract her womb and give birth to us.

Our culture and indeed our theology is fascinated by death, by eschatology and paradoxically oddly disinterested in birth. Yet birth is so like death, and we have experienced birth, and birth-givers are among us. We haven't attended to them or listened to their experience. Thus we have missed the birthing imagery for God or concealed by the use of male imagery:

> Listen to me, O house of Jacob,
> all the remnant of the house of Israel,
> who have been borne by me from the womb,
> carried by me from the womb,
> even to your old age I am *he*
> and to grey hairs I will carry you,
> I have made, and I will bear,
> I will carry, and I will save.
>
> (Isaiah 46:3–4)

If ever a pronoun called to be changed from male to female it is surely here: 'I am *she*'.

In order to allow this imagery and the accompanying wisdom to permeate our theology women need to reclaim the experiences which have been defined as their punishment: 'In pain you shall bring forth children.' Childbirth as punishment, or at the very least as justification for the pleasures of sexuality, has dominated the tradition. But there are alternative stories of birth — stories of rejoicing with Sarah, with Hannah, with Mary. These stories have to be set alongside the Genesis text and woven into the actual birth experiences of women.

Giving birth provides us with a unique insight into creative, creating pain, into life coming out of death, into the boundaries which must be negotiated when we move into new life. Birthing mothers image the creative activity of God and provide us with an appropriate metaphor for the Divine. Yet these rich possibilities for nourishing our language about God have been suppressed. We have truly forgotten the God who gave us birth, who knit us together in our mothers' wombs.

Even when we come to reflect on the birth of Jesus we discover that it has been so interpreted as to remove it utterly from the realms of human experience. Yet the profundity of the phrase 'the Word was made flesh' lies in that last word 'flesh'

---

1. Phyllis Trible, *God and the Rhetoric of Sexuality* (London: SCM Press, 1993), Chapter 2.

— become like us. It may seem facile to suggest that only a patriarchal theology could have so impoverished this event or to ask whether women might have brought a different understanding to the mystery of that birth.

Is it not worth observing that while blood, sweat and tears are hallowed in the final event of the life and death of Jesus they are excised from his birth? But then perhaps the awareness that death is prefigured at birth is a wisdom only available to women! My reflection here will draw on embodied knowledge because, during pregnancy and birth, body knowledge is heightened to an extraordinary degree. We turn inwards tuning in to the messages from our bodies and from the child growing in the womb. In these months perhaps we come closest to an understanding of the meaning of creation as we become partners in the process of transmitting life. We embody new life. When it comes to the moment of giving birth, as we open to allow the child to pass through we are opened to wisdom.

Women attempting to articulate this experience cannot relate to the birthing mother Mary who seems to have been removed from the pain of childbirth and the total physical involvement entailed in giving birth. In suggesting that Mary by-passes this physical process are we not diminishing rather than increasing her holiness? Are we not also diminishing the power of the Incarnation? To obliterate the pain and tears at the beginning of the life of Jesus seems to me to be as little justified as the fallacious belief that Jesus did not actually suffer physical pain on the cross. In both instances we are talking about pain which has a purpose, pain which is a necessary prelude to glory. Can we not imagine that Jesus suffered that pain of separation when he emerged into the world which would reject him? It is here that birth and death meet as thresholds to new life. It is here that the cry from the cross, and the cry from the womb yield to life, to resurrection.

My sense is that the sanitising of the birth of Jesus by removing all physical and sexual connotations, has closed off whole areas of possible theological reflection. It seems that in the attempt to focus on the miraculous, on the mystery, the very depths of that mystery have been ignored. It is as if the spiritual dimension is grafted on to the physical and different language is required to describe 'the higher sphere'. It is

this dichotomy which leads to a kind of spiritual schizophrenia enabling us to speak of Mary as 'Virgin Mother'. We need to restore wholeness arriving thereby at a new understanding of holiness as a dimension of depth within the event itself, and not as some sort of supernatural annex.

As I come now to focus directly on my personal experience of giving birth I want to suggest that it raises some questions about our understanding and interpretation of the 'other birth'. The fact that not all women experience birth in the way I describe does not invalidate the reflection. I am simply suggesting the potential, offering a way of looking at birth which links it directly to God's goodness, God's creation and Incarnation, in such a way as to make a negative view of its physical dimension impossible.

It is difficult to believe that I will ever again have an experience so intensely physical, so deeply mystical as that of giving birth. It is an experience so profoundly moving that all attempts by the medical and clerical professions, usually male, to sanitise and institutionalise it are ultimately defied. Unfortunately, rigid moral codes have, in the past, so often led to the repression of woman's sexuality leading her to regard all bodily functions as somehow unclean. She was thereby prevented from entering fully into the event, blocked in a literal and metaphorical sense. Women who experience this repression may impede both their child's entry into the world and their own awareness of that entry.

The sanitised virgin birth is an impossible model. How can a woman immersed in the very physical act of giving birth, the very real pain of labour, identify with or model herself on one so thoroughly anaesthetised from all that physical impurity? It almost goes without saying that many women were inhibited by the virgin image from entering into that second most miraculous, most natural of events — that of breast-feeding their babies. The taboos surrounding this are so ingrained: breasts belonging to the fallen Eve rather than to the Virgin Mary.

If we just consider the phrase 'giving birth', we can sense its significance. By definition this cannot be a passive act (except of course sadly in the case of necessary Caesarean section). This act means giving, and such total giving — a literal emptying of oneself. It fulfils the paradox of mystery: the more one gives oneself over to the event the more strength one receives and the easier it becomes. The more one empties oneself of one's own preoccupations and attempts to home in on what is actually happening within, the more one is able to participate in that most creative of acts. You die a little death yourself in order that your child may live.

The dark side is very much there. You reach a point which is almost despair: 'Why hast thou forsaken me?' That very moment is the point of no return. There will be a birth. From then onwards the pain has a tangible purpose; the mother bears down and every fibre of her being is drawn into the effort of helping her child towards its new life — its own life. The triumphant cry of those around proclaims the 'crowning' of the head. The task is almost accomplished. Into your hands you take a slimy, bloodied, crumpled, living being. You have helped to give life to this life, you have shared in creation, you are overwhelmed with feelings of love, of joy, of an irrepressible urge to praise. At this moment the mother is truly 'full of grace'.

This reflection could lead us to a richer understanding, not merely of the motherhood of Mary, but also of her virginity. I am rejecting a narrow biological definition of that term reflecting instead on virginity as a 'state of grace', as radical holiness, as readiness to receive the word of God, to co-operate with the gifts of grace. Only with this kind of symbolic understanding do I feel able to speak of Mary as both virgin and mother.

This reflection does not simply open up a new way for women to relate to Mary but for women to relate to the birthing God. The female experience of the creative pain of birth becomes an appropriate analogy for divine love. This love is nurturing, caring, freeing, sustaining, unutterably tender and poignant as in these verses from the prophet Hosea:

Yet it was I who taught Ephraim to walk
I took them up in my arms;
but they did not know that I healed them.
I led them with cords of compassion,
with the bands of love,
I was to them like those
who lift infants to their cheeks.
I bent down to them and fed them.

(Hosea 11:3-4)

This evocative image is very far removed from the detached distant God of classical theism. Here is a God intimately bound up with the world. The image of God bent over the world comes directly from the female experience of feeding the child at the breast. It is very close to an image used by Jesus in Luke's Gospel: 'O Jerusalem, Jerusalem, how often would I have gathered your children together as a hen gathers her brood under her wings, but you would not' (Luke 13:34). Compassionate, womb-like love surpasses the imperfect love of actual mothers because even if the unthinkable should happen and mothers forget the children of their wombs 'Yet I will not forget you' (Isaiah 49:15).

Not all the maternal imagery is gentle, far from it: there is the fierce anger of the mother bear if someone attacks her cubs (Hosea 13:8), and the strength of the eagle spreading out her wings to protect her young (Deut. 32:11). The fiercely protective love testifies to the real experiences of actual mothers. Giving birth to a child also gives birth to the urge to protect that child. There seems to be a moral imperative to nurture the life which we have helped to produce.

The images from the scriptures are reflected in the strong and angry love of the mothers of the disappeared in Argentina, of the mothers who nurse children dying of Aids, of the mothers who go hungry so that their children can eat, of the mothers who watch over sick children, of mothers who demand justice and jobs for their children. There is a very strong, embodied sense of living no longer just for oneself but of one's life from the moment of giving birth onwards of being inextricably bound up with others. One discovers a self which is a self in relationship. Concern for the children of the womb opens out into a wider concern for justice.

The question which we must address now is whether in establishing motherhood as a suitable metaphor for God, we are binding women even more closely to a role which is not only determined by the needs of society but is now further underpinned by divine analogy. If women as mothers image God, then women as mothers fulfil their most sacred purpose. Have we simply succeeded in glorifying the trap, in making biology not merely the social but also the spiritual destiny of women? If the source of oppression for many women has been their physiological capacity to bear children then that same capacity cannot be the source of liberation. If women traditionally have been assigned to the roles of caring for children, church and kitchen — as the German phrase has it — then the first stage in the struggle for liberation surely has to do with freeing them from those roles.

However, a second stage must lead to a re-evaluation of those experiences, otherwise we will find ourselves once again denying the felt and lived experiences of many, though clearly not all, women. To give birth, to bring new life into the world, to nurture and sustain such life must be described and valued by women and for men and women. This is our wisdom — let us now name it and claim it.

One way out of this trap is to recognise that when male experience was reflected upon, it was considered normative for all human beings. Is it possible to take the female wisdom learnt through female bodies and allow it to permeate our total understanding of what it means to be human? In this way the wisdom claimed and named by women becomes not only relevant but imperative for all humanity.

The first wisdom or grace is mediated while the child is still in the womb; it is, as all grace must be, by definition, gratuitous. In the symbiotic relationship of pregnancy the mother experiences in her body what it means to be human. She learns that to be human is necessarily to relate, indeed that relationship is constitutive of the person. The myth of the Cartesian rational man, the human person described in terms of the solitary rational autonomous individual *Cogito, ergo sum*, is challenged by womb-knowledge. During pregnancy we carry a child in our womb who is both a part of us and yet separate from us. The child is dependent on our body to feed and nourish it and we are dependent on the environment outside the womb to feed and nourish us.

We can see this cycle of dependence through its negative effects by observing what happens to the unborn child when the mother is affected by radiation as in Chernobyl, or by war, or by drugs, or by smoking, or by excessive alcohol. The child in the womb forces changes on us even when we do not desire them. The heavily pregnant woman sits listening to music or watching a television programme, or even listening to a theological lecture, when quite unexpectedly she receives a kick in the ribs! 'Here I am.' She is not alone. The unborn child is already a presence, a person who affects and is affected by her.

Many women expecting a second child introduce their first child to its future sister or brother by allowing the child to lay its head on the mother's body and feel the movements of the baby — bodily experience communicating so much more effectively than mere words. As the pregnancy progresses the child can feel the shape of the head and the limbs and so is not shocked by the sudden and unexpected appearance of a 'new baby' from the hospital or the gooseberry bush! The child outside and the child inside have already begun a relationship. If the male whose sperm has fertilized the ovum disappears, abdicating responsibility, he has also lost the opportunity to learn in the most intimate way what being human is about. We are persons who live in the shelter of one another; to be is to be in relationship. The child in the womb shows us this. We begin our lives within another. And this is the first grace, the first wisdom that women must name.

The fact that motherhood was and to a very large extent still is for many women a role which confines and limits them, which results in economic dependency and a low social status, makes it problematic for feminists to use it positively as a resource for theology. Yet this is what we must do if we are to take the experience of women as givers and sustainers of life seriously.

I experience deep personal ambivalence around this whole area and perhaps it would be helpful to describe some of my personal paradoxes in the hope that this may help other women struggling in similarly muddied waters.

Wherever we are we find ourselves bound in by certain limitations — mine are domestic ones which spill over and into my work-space: it is here that I do my theology. It seems to me that I have the choice either to distance myself from my surroundings, abstract myself from them and produce appropriately cerebral theology or to immerse myself in my space and draw from its depths. Poet Eavan Boland seems to have this facility of homing in on the domestic detail until it becomes an epiphany:

But there's a way of life
that is its own witness.[2]

The domestic context as much or as little as any other limited space in which we find ourselves can be source of insight, a resource for theology. But at this time in the history of women it is a particularly ambivalent place to be. I ask myself constantly, have I chosen this, or did it seem my destiny? I ask whether I would make the same choices again. I am caught in a bind here. On the one hand, I recognise that choices made fifteen years ago when my first child was born have meant that I closed the door on certain career opportunities; on the other hand, those same choices have also given me the resources for a theology, born out of this experience. The opportunity of participating in the closest possible way in the emergence of new human life in pregnancy and in birth and the opportunity of watching the unfolding personhood of three distinct human beings has been an extraordinarily rich one.

Here is where I am caught: for the most part I cannot imagine that there is any work more fascinating than being part of this nurturing of life but caught into that are the boring, mundane, routine and mindless tasks of the everyday. But I do not want to see the nurturing of life either reduced to those boring tasks and thus relegated to the lowest rung in the social pecking order, or glorified and sanctified as 'the vocation of motherhood'.

The briefest of biographical details would quickly reveal how 'muddling through' rather than 'perfect mothering' has characterised my role. But that is not what matters here. I am not remotely interested in any romantic concept of motherhood, yet I need to say that mediating life matters, that children matter. They matter in a way which extends far beyond the private domestic sphere. They say something to us about the future, about survival, about life on this planet, about our own mortality, about relationship, about loving. We need to rethink what parenthood is about and it must be about more than the most efficient management of children until they reach independence.

2. Eavan Boland, 'Dedication', in *Nightfeed* (Dublin: Arlen House, 1982).

I feel that there is a mutuality in the relationship which is being missed. This is where I think that those who have been biologically involved in the bearing of children and traditionally involved in the caring for them should be the ones to interpret that experience and include it in our understanding of what it means to be human. So part of my theology — and quite a considerable part — will draw on what I have learnt in living with this community of growing children. This explains my ambivalence: the domestic 'trap' has paradoxically opened to insight. It is the knowledge gained along the margins and intensified by being devalued which now insists on being heard.

Perhaps the most critical issue is to re-evaluate the concept of parenting and recognise its community dimension. It is somewhat strange that 'Pro-Life' placards so fervently displayed when unborn life is threatened disappear after birth as if 'the life' which was so urgently protected is now once more a private concern — a mother's concern. Does the Christian community as a whole not share the commitment to mother new and vulnerable life? If we find womb-like love in our image of God, should such nurturing love not be the concern of all people, of male and female? The giving and sustaining of life affects the whole community yet the isolation of women and the privatisation of the nurturing and caring of children has made an issue of universal concern into a series of 'women's problems'. There is a resulting enormous gap between pronouncements made by agencies of church and state about the value of motherhood and the absence of real and adequate supports for those who care for children.

To care for new and vulnerable life is a moral imperative for all of us. To that extent one might argue that mothering must be extended across the gender boundary and re-formulated as community-supported parenting. Listening to the wisdom of those intimately involved with the care of fragile life, the institutions of society which are presently experienced as unfriendly to women and children will have to be adjusted. With the value of the person as a self constituted by relationship firmly in place, the autonomous individualistic egos are dethroned and the patriarchal structures begin to crumble. An ethic of the rights of the individual alters in favour of an ethic of relationship.

When this wisdom about our essential inter-relationship is confined to the private sphere then the excessive demands on women lead to a loss in their sense of self. Self-sacrifice does indeed become a sacrifice of the woman's self. The woman becomes 'their mother', 'his wife'. This distortion or perversion of the concept of relationship is as dangerous for the female as the excessive stress on the autonomous ego is for the male. If the wisdom of 'self-in-relationship' is shared then it provides us with the context in which the community as a whole can make the moral decisions which will allow for responsible attention to the needs of the weaker vulnerable members of society.

Feminist theologians talk about an ethic of care replacing an ethic of rights.[3] The call to 'mother' fragile life is a requirement not just for biological mothers nor for women generally but for the whole Christian community. It is in this context that decisions about the care of the handicapped, the old and the sick need to be made. The burden of responsibility for such members of society has generally fallen on women, usually without adequate support. If we extend the caring relational ethic then all persons male and female are called into responsibility for one another. This seems to fit not just with the image of the womb-like compassion of God but also with the particular concern of Jesus for the weak and the marginalised.

The call out of oneself towards the other who is and who is not like us is an experience learnt in giving birth. If we could exploit the birthing grace of fierce and tender love then there could be no more war. We need to release this wisdom from the domestic confines and allow the insight to transform the ideology of militarism with the cry 'These are all my sons, these are all my daughters.' Although there is a ready lapse back into egotism whether extended by two or even three, I feel that there is a birthing grace which momentarily pushes out the boundaries so that the love which one feels for the child of one's womb is extended to all fragile life. What we experience in an imperfect and temporary way is what we predicate of God 'with everlasting love I will have compassion on you' (Isaiah 54:8).

If we heed the wisdom of birthing women and allow the mothering, nurturing, sustaining values to permeate the community and to be appropriated by male and female who together image God, then we will begin the process of transforming our society.

To give priority to the bringing forth of life, caring for it and sustaining it, will have repercussions not just for human survival but for the continuing of all life on the planet. The crying out and panting of the woman in labour is reflected in the birth pangs of all creation, dying into life. The embodied knowledge of women testifying to our essential relatedness with one another calls us out of ourselves and into community.

I have taken the female experience of birthing and shown how, when the waters are broken, it floods us with vision and is an image for divine activity; and how the concept of the God of womb-like love can draw us all, male and female, into compassionate and freeing love for one another.

3. See Lisa Sowle Cahill, 'Feminism and Christian Ethics', in *Freeing Theology: The Essentials of Theology in Feminist Perspective*, ed. Catherine Mowry LaCugna (San Francisco: Harper, 1993), pp. 211–31.

CELINE MANGAN

(1938–)

from:
THE BIBLE AND ECOLOGY
(1993)

[From the outset, feminist religious scholarship has been grounded as much in the search for truth as in the concern with truth effects. All sources, biblical, literary, or historical, are interrogated in relation to their liberatory or oppressive potential.

Central to this exploration is the question of patriarchal dualisms, that is, the splits developed between body and soul, nature and spirit, the world and God, women and men. In the late twentieth century the threat posed to life itself on our planet by environmental pollution, nuclear warfare and human greed stimulated creation-centred spirituality. Biblical scholar Celine Mangan extends her textual analysis to nature and argues that animal and plant life are integral parts of God's creation. This extract is taken from *Milltown Studies*, vol. 32 (1993), pp. 110–22. Footnotes are by the author.]

The way the God of the Bible has been portrayed down the centuries has contributed to the present ecological crisis. The misuse of the text 'have dominion over . . .' (*Genesis* 1:28) to legitimize whole-scale exploitation is a glaring example of how human greed has led to global pollution and extinction of species.[1] Likewise, the overemphasis on a salvific and otherworldly theology in recent centuries has led to the demise of the centrality of creation for a proper understanding of our relationship to God. It could be argued, as well, that 'Christianity's orientation towards the future, and its emphasis on the new heaven and new earth at the end of history, has been transformed, in secular culture, into a dangerous myth of endless economic progress'.[2]

However, if it is true that the Bible has contributed to the ecological malaise at the present time, it can also be said that a better understanding of it will help towards a solution . . .[3]

The two creation accounts in *Genesis* (1:1–2:4a and 2:4b-25) are very different in intent and design, immediately alerting us to the fact that there is no one definitive understanding of creation in the Bible. The majestic, priestly account in *Genesis* 1:1–2:4a orders creation by means of a schema of seven days. The creation of human beings on the sixth day has, down the centuries, been taken as the apex of God's intention in creating the world. But a look again at the structure of those six days shows that they are presented in a circular form rather than in the pyramid fashion in which we have for so long interpreted them: the creation of the lights in the firmament of day four matches the creation of light on day one; birds of the air and fish of the

sea on day five; people the firmament above and the waters below of day two; while the animals and human beings on day six inhabit the earth created on day three.

Interpreters down the centuries have made efforts to upset the order here in Genesis so as to make human beings more prominent: the apocalyptic text of 2 *Enoch,* for example, puts the animals back with the fish and birds on day five in order to leave human beings a day all to themselves, thus ensuring their place at the apex of creation.[4] In the original *Genesis* reading, however, human beings are solidly within the circle of creation rather than at the pinnacle of it. This calls us today to see ourselves as interdependent within the circle of created things rather than totally apart and not beholden to other species . . .

The phrase which has caused most difficulty in the first creation account of *Genesis* from an ecological viewpoint is, of course, God's injunction to human beings to 'be fruitful and multiply, and fill the earth and subdue it; and have dominion over . . .' (*Genesis* 1:28). Nowhere is it more important to know the 'world behind the text' than here. The words, *rdh*, translated as 'dominion' and *kbs*, 'subdue' were part of the technical language of kingship (see *Kings* 5:5; *Psalms* 72:8). But as ideally exercised in Israel, kingship implied responsibility and caring especially for the poor and the weak in society (see *Isaiah* 11:1–5).[5] What is involved in relating these words to the non-human world in *Genesis*, therefore, is an attitude of stewarding and shepherding: 'This means in modern terms, a rational, sensible, humane, intelligent and thoughtful ordering of God's ordered world . . . a challenge to responsibility and the duty to make right prevail' . . .[6]

'Dust from the Ground'

The 'world behind' the second account of creation is a world where, it would appear, not

1. See D. Senor, 'The Earth Story: Where does the Bible Fit in?', in *Thomas Berry and the New Cosmology*, eds A.C. Lonergan and C. Richards (Mystic, Conn.: Twenty-Third Publications, 1987), p. 48, n. 1.
2. D. Edwards, *Creation, Humanity, Community* (Dublin: Gill and Macmillan, 1992), pp. 8–9, n. 10.
3. M. Dowd, *The Meaning of Life in the 1990's* (Ohio: Living Earth Christian Fellowship, 1990), p. 29.

4. 2 Enoch 30: see F.I. Andersen, '2 (Slavonic Acopocalypse of) Enoch', in *The Old Testament Pseudepigrapha*, ed. J.H. Charlesworth, 2 vols (London: Darton, Longman and Todd, 1983), vol. 1, p. 150.
5. See T. F. Dailey, 'Creation and Ecology', *Irish Theological Quarterly*, vol. 58 (1992), p. 5; A. Ganoczy, 'Ecological Perspectives in the Christian Doctrine of Creation', *Concilium* (1991), p. 45.
6. B. Vawter, *On Genesis: A New Reading* (London: Chapman, 1977), p. 59.

only human beings but also God is still within the circle of creation.[7] While the first account of creation depicts a transcendent God creating by command, the second account suggests a much more imminent God creating out of material to hand, breathing life, walking in the garden in the cool of the evening, sewing clothes for human beings. The realization that the Yahwist[8] 'is not intent upon depicting the divinely ordained separation of heaven and earth as two distinct realms'[9] is of paramount importance for ecology because it is such a separation which has in recent centuries not only put God outside nature but also human beings.[10]

The second account of creation ties us firmly to earth, formed from the same 'ground' (*Genesis* 2:7) as were the animals (*Genesis* 2:19). The word, '*pr*, literally means 'dust', the kind of dust that accumulates on books and not 'clay' which is often given as the translation. As one of my students pointed out, dust is very fragile indeed and so our hold on the earth is actually very tenuous: the world existed for millions of years before us; will it do without us again?

Chapters three to eleven of *Genesis* show, in the context of increasing sinfulness, the progression away from the close contact with the earth that 'dust from the earth' implies, first of all by the use of clothes (3:21), then by the cultivation of land (4) and finally by the building of cities (11:4). The placing of barriers between ourselves and nature has, on the one hand, led to the rightful growth of civilization and culture but, on the other, to the deterioration of relationships, not only between humans and the earth but also between humans and God . . .

'Wisdom as Bonding'

Walking in the countryside recently I tried my best to think of myself within the chain of being, one with the stone-chats chattering on the ditches, the wind whipping my face, the ground on which I walked, and I found it extremely difficult to even begin to know myself as part of the whole. Looking again at the wisdom texts is one step for me in the direction of seeing my close inter-dependence with the whole of reality.

Wisdom (Sophia) in the Bible is a much more pragmatic, down to earth word than the more intellectual concept of it which we in the West have inherited from Greek philosophical thinking. Wisdom could be as much in the hands as in the head; for example, those who were engaged in the making of clothes for the tent of meeting were 'filled . . . with the ability to do every sort of work done by a craftsperson or by a designer or by an embroiderer in blue, purple and scarlet stuff and fine twined linen . . .' (*Exodus* 35:35). As with Solomon (see 1 *Kings* 4:33–34) the world around was the place from which to learn wisdom: 'Go to the ant, O sluggard; consider her ways, and be wise' (*Proverbs* 6:6; see Job 38, 39, *Psalms* 104).

In some strands of the Wisdom Literature wisdom is personified as a feminine presence to the world. In *Proverbs* 8:22–31, for example, wisdom is beside God in creating and relating to the world as an '*mn* (8:30), a word usually translated in the sense of a craftsperson acting beside God in the creation of the world. Work on the textual variants of the word would suggest other meanings such as 'beloved child',[11] or 'faithful disciple'.[12] However, the word is probably better translated with the meaning of 'to bind' or 'to unite', yielding the translation: 'Then I was at God's side, *a living link*',[13] separate from God but forming a link between God and creation . . .

It is no accident that many feminists posit a link between the rape of the earth in which the Western world, in particular, is engaged at present and the almost complete absence of

7. See R.A. Di Vito, 'The Demarcation of Divine and Human Realms in Gen 2–11', in *Creation in the Biblical Traditions*, eds R.J. Clifford and J.J. Collins, 'Mono Series 24' (Washington, DC: Catholic Biblical Association of America, 1992), n. 16, pp. 39–56.

8. I am not entering here into the debate on Pentateuchal sources: see S. McEvenue, *Interpreting the Pentateuch*, 'Old Testament Studies 4' (Collegeville, Minnesota: Glazier/Liturgical Press, 1990).

9. R.A. Di Vito, 'Demarcation of Divine and Human Realms', p. 56, n. 7.

10. Barbara Ward, *Gifts of Peace: Spirituality and Ecology* (London: Pax Christi, 1989), in considering the way we raise our hands at polluting power stations and at farmers destroying the crops with fertilizers, asks: 'Which of you can cast the first stone at the power stations when you demand electricity at the flick of a switch' and 'demand food at the cheapest possible prices, all year round, with infinite variety, without blemish . . . ?', p. 7.

11. See G. A. Yee, 'The Theology of Creation in Proverbs 8:22–31', in *Creation in the Biblical Traditions*, eds R.J. Clifford and J.J. Collins, pp. 85–96.

12. *New Jerusalem Bible* (977, n. i).

13. See R.B.Y. Scott, 'Wisdom in Creation; The ámôn of Proverbs VIII 30', *Vetus Testamentum*, vol. 10 (1960), p. 222.

women in the public domain up until recent times. Katherine Zappone in her book, *The Hope for Wholeness*,[14] calls for the use of the earth-human relationship. For too long, she points out, the home has been the safe haven provided by women for men when they returned from their exploits and where a private morality could be practised that had nothing to do with life outside. The doors of our homes have to be thrown wide open.

14. K. Zappone, *The Hope for Wholeness* (Mystic, Conn.: Twenty-Third Publications, 1991), pp. 113–45; see H.M. Luke, *Woman Earth and Spirit* (New York: Crossroad, 1990), pp. 79–92.

ANNE PRIMAVESI

(1934–)

THEOLOGY AND EARTH SYSTEM SCIENCE (2000)

This essay is taken from *Challenging Women's Orthodoxies in the Context of Faith*, ed. Susan F. Parsons (Aldershot: Ashgate Press, 2000). Footnotes are by the author unless otherwise stated.]

[Behind all feminist religious scholarship lies the question of God. For some women the old man in the sky was often replaced with a Wise Woman in the Sky — the Goddess. Others referred to God as Verb, as Process, as liberatory impulse. Whatever the image or its verbal expression, feminist scholars usually agree that God is the name we give to that which gives us life, sets us free, and calls us to integrity. Some women go further than that. God is not outside, over or above, but integral to the foundation of our being. God is to be found, not in metaphysical abstraction or ontological truth, but in the very essence of being and of life, in what the ancient Irish called the *gnéart* or lifeforce.

In the light of the contemporary global ecological crisis, the ethno-centricity of Christianity — that God was revealed to a particular people, at a particular place, at a particular time (not to mention exclusively in a certain sex) — must be challenged. The revelation of God is effected not just through words but is immanent in the interactions of all living beings within earth's systems. Evolutionary theory, which throws light on the emergence of all species including our own, also demonstrates their radical interdependence. If we isolate our relationship with God from that enjoyed by others, its all-embracing character is lost. Limits placed on revelation (whose revelation counts?) serve the purposes of human power and hierarchy but radically limit our understanding of ongoing revelation. The holy or the sacred are presumed to be extra-terrestrial: heaven is opposed to earth; the spirit to the body. Such patriarchal dualisms must now, in the light of our awareness of their effects on attitudes to women and the earth, be replaced with systemic under-standing of our interdependence, and an holistic understanding of the ground of our being.

In February 1998, Gaia, the Society for Research and Education in Earth System Science, was founded 'to promote an integrated under-standing of the Earth system through research and education'. At the inaugural meeting I asked myself what kinds of understanding were to be integrated. Did they include theological understanding? The scientists there had already taken James Lovelock's Gaia theory as a framework for ongoing research projects and as a subject for scientific syllabuses. It is, after all, a scientific systems analysis of the structures and dynamics present in the chemical and physical evolution of the Earth system, and as one member of the Society wrote later, 'this systems-analytic approach becomes unavoidable once we perceive our planet as one unique entity driven by multiple internal and external forces towards ever higher degrees of complexity'. He sees the advancement within science of such a holistic perception as one of the great achievements of Lovelock and those who have worked with his presuppositions.[1]

Mary Midgley, who spoke at the Society's inaugural meeting, is also quite clear about the benefits for philosophy of pursuing a Gaian approach. The notion of the Earth system as an

1. H.J. Schellnhuber, 'Earth System Analysis: Integrating the Human Factor into Geophysiology', *Gaia Circular*, vol. 2, issue 3, pp. 12–13.

enclosing whole corrects, she says, a large and disastrous blind spot in our contemporary worldview. It reminds us that we are not separate, independent, autonomous entities. Since the Enlightenment, the deepest moral efforts of our culture have gone to establishing our freedom as individuals, and as a result, we have carefully excluded everything non-human from our value system and reduced that system to terms of individual self-interest. 'We are mystified — as surely no other set of people would be — about how to recognize the claims of the larger whole that surrounds us: the material world of which we are a part.' The idea of Gaia, therefore, 'is not a gratuitous, semi-mystical fantasy', but a cure for distortions in our current world view.[2]

This is not a new perception on her part. In 1983 she had written about the need for an environmental ethics which is not human-centred by re-examining the philosophical question of whether or not, when he was alone on his island, Robinson Crusoe had any duties. She pointed to various fallacies in the presupposition that duties only obtain as quasi-contractual relations between symmetrical pairs of rational human agents, concluding that while we have duties *as* farmers, parents, consumers etc, it is the business of each of us not to forget our transitory and dependent position, the rich gifts we have received and the tiny part we play in a vast, irreplaceable and fragile whole.[3]

The concept of non-human-centred duties is indeed a late arrival on the philosophical scene, for since Socrates to the present day, orthodox views of duties or ethics have assumed that moral concern only extends to human–human relations. But over the past thirty years or so, notably since Arne Naess published his classic statement of the distinction between human-centred and non-human-centred ethics, although the latter obviously take cognizance of human interests and concerns, the discussion has moved beyond the boundaries of the former.[4] Briefly, this move results from philosophical reflection on the natural environment as displayed to us by science, our relationship with it and our effect upon it.

I was left, however, with my question of what an holistic worldview arising from Earth system science might mean for theology. I offer some provisional answers in my book *Sacred Gaia: Holistic Theology and Earth System Science*. My question here centres on what it means for our theological self-perception to situate our relationship with God within rather than outside of Earth's history. Surely this accords with our linking the coming of the Messiah to an earth which shall be 'full of the knowledge of the Lord' (Isaiah 11:9). The refusal to endorse this belief has resulted in a potentially disastrous 'blind spot' in our theological perspective, one which remains as long as Christianity continues to function as a self-referential religious system where communication with the sacred is reduced to two forms: revelation based on written texts and personal or communal prayer. 'Nature' is presumed ignorant of and silent before God. So we relate to the non-human world as, at best, an object of pleasure but more and more, as an object for exploitation.[5] The scientific progress and technological innovation which followed the Enlightenment did not have to initiate the secularization of 'the environment' in order to exploit or devastate it. Science merely built on previous Christian secularization of the non-human world.

Today, theologians as well as philosophers and scientists live in a culture where our horizons of knowledge about the world are continually being widened through the application of scientific method. Most notably, we now have a view of the Earth from space which, while it calls for urgent research into key interactions between the Sun, the atmosphere, oceans, ice, land, marine and terrestrial ecosystems, does so in the context of the planet as an entity. Within that entity, as some scientists note, there have been and are significant interactions between all these systems and human societal, political and religious systems which have had significant effects on the Earth system as a whole. Some of these effects are quantifiable. Others are not. Another member of the Gaia Society, Chris Rapley, who heads the British Antarctic Survey, notes that

2. Personal communication.
3. Reprinted in *Environmental Ethics*, ed. Robert Elliot (Oxford University Press, 1995).
4. Arne Naess, 'The Shallow and the Deep, Long Range Ecology Movements: A Summary', *Inquiry*, vol. 16 (1973), pp. 95–100.
5. Niklas Luhmann, *Essays on Self-Reference* (New York: Columbia University Press, 1990), p. 153.

roughly half the planet's land area has been transformed by us, principally through agricultural and forestry systems. This has changed the surface reflexivity and flows of wind and water, with major impact on nutrient flows, soil degradation and biodiversity worldwide. But how do we measure the effects of theological anthropocentricity? How does a human-centred religious system validate our increasingly deleterious impact on marine and terrestrial ecosystems, and how do we move beyond it to a geocentric worldview?

Freedom to Develop Theologically

In a benchmark article in 1964 entitled *The Problem of Religious Freedom*, John Courtney Murray defined the theological task as tracing the stages of growth of a tradition as it makes its way through history. The further task, he said, is discerning the 'growing end' of the tradition. This is usually indicated by the new question that is taking shape under the impact of the historical moment.[6] On this premise, such questions, and the search for answers to them, would themselves become part of that 'growing end'. In this way historical consciousness, which is the ability to discern what is of moment at a particular stage in our history, in some measure constitutes and also acts as a necessary spur to the exercise of theological freedom. Therefore, the evolution of human history, recorded as change in human societies through time, is constitutive of the evolution of theological tradition, of its development through time. 'Stages of growth' within theology correspond in some measure to those discerned within history.

The historical theological moment for Courtney Murray was the Second Vatican Council and in particular its 'Declaration on Religious Freedom', not least because by recognizing the historic legal principle of religious freedom it also sanctioned the development of doctrine. The Declaration establishes the right of members of the Catholic Church, as well as those of other religions, to the free exercise of their religion. This right, it is argued, is based on persons' growing awareness of their own dignity

and of their active participation in society. The opening words of the Declaration, *Dignitatis humanae personae*, translate as 'the sense of the dignity of the human person', and it is this sense which is invoked as justifying the demand that we should act on our own judgment, 'enjoying and making use of a responsible freedom, not driven by coercion but motivated by a sense of duty'.[7]

However, the demand made by the Vatican document is for 'the right of the person and of communities to *social and civil freedom* in matters religious' (my italics). It is assumed that in regard to society they have demonstrated their capacity to handle the responsibilities of freedom. If this were paralleled in theological freedom, it would establish the right of theologians, on the basis of their human dignity and of their being active members of society, to demonstrate their capacity to handle the responsibilities of their freedom to theologize. It would assume religious freedom in the sense I am arguing for: freedom to respond theologically to the stages of growth within history; to the widening of the horizons of understanding through scientific research so that 'the growing end' of the theological tradition might be shaped by the concrete exigencies of contemporary personal, scientific and political consciousness.[8]

It is now, I believe, also being shaped by a particular consciousness of ourselves as belonging to a global rather than a geographic or ethnic community, situating us within the known range of emergent species on Earth and, as comparative latecomers, dependent on those which emerged before us. At the personal level, this self-perception is most visibly created/symbolized by the Internet. Access to it is still largely confined to those in the 'First' world, but we are all, potentially at least, 'worldwidewebbers'. At the global level, scientific space exploration and technology discloses the evolution of the physical, chemical and material earth systems which underpin our planetary interdependence and, through an ambitious satellite mapping programme, brings us brilliant pictures of our personal and planetary environments. The marvels revealed by the Hubble telescope offer

---

6. John Courtney Murray, 'The Problem of Religious Freedom', *Theological Studies*, vol. 25 (1964), p. 569.

7. Walter M. Abbott (ed.), *Vatican Documents* (London: Geoffrey Chapman, 1966), pp. 673, 675.

8. Murray, *op. cit.*, pp. 505, 523.

differing and elusive perspectives on the evolution of our universe and the knowledge that in a certain sense 'we are stardust'. All of which not only widens our scientific horizons but changes our self-perception — which change is itself part of the 'growing end' of contemporary theological consciousness.

Systemic Consciousness

This means that, since he wrote, the religious freedom argued for by Courtney Murray is now set within a changed, because expanded, historical consciousness. For our history is now situated within the history of the whole Earth household. This new historical setting also changes moral consciousness, for our necessary acknowledgement of human dependence on the other members of Earth's household is at the same time an acknowledgement of their intrinsic value to the ecosystems which sustain both us and them. In an historic twist in self-perception, as we come to know more and more about the complexity and diversity of those systems, our own intrinsic value to them is increasingly put in question. Rapley's sober statistics about agriculture and forestry make the point, as does the following fact. Our year-on-year global economic expansion, and the resultant increase in carbon emissions (around 200 tons of carbon burnt to produce $1,000 income), has affected world climate so adversely that most governments have agreed to the Kyoto Protocol. This international agreement would legally bind their countries to cut greenhouse gas emissions. Those involved realize that it doesn't make sense if our economic growth causes more damage than benefit: damage not only to ourselves, but also to the planet which has to sustain that growth. There are no extra-terrestrial resources available to us, and projects mooted for finding them, such as terra-forming Mars, would only use up even more of this planet's resource base.

The negative impact of our economic infrastructure and consumerist lifestyles undermines theological arguments for our supreme dignity and for its theological corollary, our God-given right to dominate the Earth household. Our dysfunctional behaviour within that household ill accords with the responsible use of freedom that would reasonably accord with that dignity. Can we honestly argue that we are worth more than any other creature and that a planetary household created and sustained over billions of years exists for our sole use and benefit? Can we claim a divine mandate for our species' increase in numbers to such an extent that we consume a totally disproportionate amount of the household's resources? Can we invoke a 'God-given' right to exploit and abuse other species by claiming that human communities alone, and their relationships with one another, are all that 'count' before God? In other words, can we make a convincing claim to our right to destroy our own life-support systems? Not unless, earth system science says, we are compiling the longest suicide note in history. And making God countersign it.

Systemically, all our interrelationships, and those with whom we share them, count as part of an interconnected physical and moral order. We can no longer see our wellbeing or our dignity as divorced in any real sense from that of the whole Earth household. How we live affects all its members, and measured along different axes and timescales, their lives affect ours. This growing ecological consciousness reflects a shift in western historical consciousness evident in legal/political foundations, in government ministries and programmes devoted to 'the environment', and in listings for university courses and school curricula which now include courses on environmental law, environmental health, environmental ethics and environmental justice movements worldwide.

Theological listings, however, remain almost exclusively focused on 'human-only' concerns, as do undergraduate and further education courses targeted on clergy and religious communities. Why so? Briefly, in traditional theology geocentricity only emerges as anthropocentricity, and the change in self-perception required by ecological consciousness requires a revolution away from anthropocentricity. And in the course of that revolution, the traditional theological centre cannot hold. The fears inspired by the loss of this theological anthropocentricity, or even the suspicion of its loss, explains the absence of ecology from theological syllabuses. But if this continues, what happens to theological relevance in an ecologically conscious society? What happens to any organism, person or tradition which refuses to grow, which refuses to evolve?

Evolutionary History

The ecosystems within which all living organisms interact with their environments have evolved over many millions of years. The term evolution, whether applied to physical, environmental, communal or social entities, is generally understood as meaning change through time, change through which new life forms and environments gradually emerge and healthy ecosystems are sustained which nourish the life potential of the whole Earth household. After Darwin, evolution usually focuses on a scientific description of the processes whereby organisms and their environments come into being and pass away. No species, including ours, can live outside these coevolutionary processes or fail to contribute to them, positively or negatively. The widespread use of the term evolution and evidence of its concrete exigencies in, for example, developments in genetics and biotechnologies, constitutes, literally and figuratively, one of the most visible 'growing ends' in contemporary consciousness.

However, for many Christians today, Darwin and his theories constitute as great a threat to human dignity as did Copernicus or Galileo. For the facts of evolution in relation to all species — that is, that all of them now living, including our own, may and do evolve from and into other species — signal the loss of the biblical notion that we are special because there is a sharp distinction between our creation by God (in God's image) and that of all other beings. And since our God-given supremacy over other beings rests on that distinction, to lose it is to lose our supremacy. So in 1999, in a decision forced through by Christian religious conservatives and supported by Roman Catholic bishops, the state of Kansas voted to remove most references to the theory of evolution from its new standards for science education from kindergarten through to high school.

This particular denial of our inclusion in an expanded Earth household and its moral order is unusually public. It usually takes the form of denial by omission. A quick glance at the indexes of most theological manuals will find no references to ecological and/or evolutionary consciousness, and those which do discuss the evolution of life in the universe do so as if nothing new has been discovered about it.

Noting this, Karl Schmitz-Moormann accounts for it by pointing to the change in perspective required if theologians take evolution seriously. The importance of the biblical text changes, he says, from absolute to relative, since knowing what the first man and woman did (as if we did know!) does not tell us much about human beings today. Our evolving universe is marked by the slow but constant emergence of new realities, and the new cannot be deduced from the old. 'Nobody who studies the earliest stages of the universe could write an algorithm that would lead with certainty to the existence of humans.'[9] There are, of course, those who claim that God did write such an algorithm, but then that leaves us facing another set of problems about freewill, contingency and determinism.

All this is unsettling enough, but for traditional theology there is a greater challenge still. Darwin moved the timescale inferred for the evolution of our species back beyond any individual 'Adam' to a shadowy and uncertain past where we, as one species among others, cannot point, in any strict sense, to a precise starting point for our own. 'Adam' ('earthling') was not, however much we might want to believe otherwise, put into the Earth household by God at a particular moment in time, in a pre-specified form and subject to specific rules of conduct. Yet western Christian theology and its cultural descendants have remained focused on the antithetical relationship postulated between this putative individual and Christ. The range of theological enquiry has been reduced to whatever has been deduced, imagined, interpreted, defined and taught about the relationship between them and its import for the whole of human history. Theology has officially and effectively been reduced to salvation history with all that has meant for Church life, order, teaching and authority. But, evolution asks, salvation from what? And for whom?

Anthropocentricity and Salvation

We are, we are told, saved by Christ from the bodily inheritance (sin) bequeathed us by Adam. His sin marked and marred every human being

9. Karl Schmitz-Moormann, *Theology of Creation in an Evolutionary World* (Cleveland: Pilgrim Press, 1997), pp. 1–26.

born after him, and left us lacking the ability to rescue ourselves from its effects, the most notable, it is averred, being death. Since the time of Augustine, mainstream Christianity has held that without Adam's sin, there would be no death.[10] But because Adam sinned and left us prey to the power of death, we need a saviour, Christ. The 'anthropo-logic' implies, indeed states, that we human beings were distinguished from all others by being created by God to live forever. Our salvation by Christ means that God's purpose stands, and that we alone, out of all species, are to be exempt from death.

However, our bodies die. So a further logical move is necessary. It is our souls which Christ rescues from death. They are the 'immortal' element in the human being, the element which distinguishes us absolutely from every other species. Our souls, reunited with our bodies, will live forever with God in an unearthly realm we call heaven. In this Platonic universe Christ saves us, ultimately, from being what we are: members of the whole Earth household.

Those other members who do not (according to us) share the distinction of having souls are nevertheless, we say, inextricably, and negatively bound by our history. They are condemned to eternal death because of what one member of our species did. In a fundamentalist version of this traditional doctrine, their condemnation is shared by the majority of our own species, since Christ saves only those who believe in him. All those who lived before him and those who live after him and who, for reasons of space and time, have no opportunity to believe in him, are not saved either. They are condemned to living death in the unearthly realm called hell.

This is the merest outline of a central Christian doctrine, and would, I know, be hotly disputed in regard to some of its features by representatives of different theological schools. But its centrality rests on an undisputed exclusive claim: that we are saved from death by Christ. The claim is validated by locking it into the claim to human dignity, one based on our being created in the image of God. That image, we are told, is centred in the human soul. As no other species is ensouled, we are distinguished from all others.

These claims interlock with and are used to validate our claim to be the centre of creation.

However as I argued in *From Apocalypse to Genesis*, a close reading of the biblical texts on which this claim is based (the first three chapters of Genesis) reveals no apple, no 'Fall', no use of the word 'sin'.[11] The tradition of reading these last two concepts back into the text has become so much part of Christianity as to be apparently unassailable. It remains so because it appears to answer some of our deepest questions, and indeed fears, about the nature of life and death, about human weakness and evil-doing, about our experience of suffering and our role in inflicting it. We find answers which are summed up eventually in Christ as *the* answer, as the one who saves us from weakness, evil-doing, suffering and above all, death.

Revelation and Earth System Science

There is another major change in western cultural perception of our origins which has, potentially at least, altered historical and ecological consciousness of the landscape within which Christian theology is set. Earth system science moves the timescale of our evolution back still further: beyond our species to the evolution of the first living organisms on the planet. There, ultimately, lie the days of our infancy, days so far removed from us in time and in emergent processes as to distance us almost completely from those life forms from which we originated. These processes continue to regulate the temperature and composition of the Earth's surface, keeping it comfortable for life. They are driven by free energy available from sunlight, and this fact, once intuited and now increasingly understood through modern scientific technologies, makes us all, whether we like it or not, heliocentric. We share and depend on this energy in all its forms, and constantly metabolize it for ourselves and for each other.[12]

The evolution of life on the planet over a vast timescale (*c.* 4.6 billion years) presupposes theologically that God's relationship with those

10. See my discussion of this in *From Apocalypse to Genesis: Ecology, Feminism and Christianity* (Burns and Oates, 1991), pp. 226–8.

11. Ibid., chapters 11 and 12.

12. Anne Primavesi, 'The Recovery of Wisdom: Gaia Theory and Environmental Policy', in *Spirit of the Environment: Religion, Value and Environmental Concern*, eds David Cooper and Joy Palmer (London: Routledge, 1998), pp. 73–85.

who emerged to form the Earth household is commensurate with the same period. God did not wait to form this relationship until we emerged, nor did we dictate the form it took. We relate to God from within and as part of the 'growing end' of an existing bond. It is continuous with the long, variegated lineages within the Earth household, and we share enough of our habits, needs and abilities with other species there to reveal our common life source, contemporary kinship and interdependence. Stardust we may be, but star trekking is not for us. We cannot survive naturally outside the world-mothering air of our planetary home.

Refocusing our self-perception in this way realigns our focus on the concept of revelation. Franz Rozenzweig's insight into the Genesis text shows the sequence of revelation following this pattern:

God spoke. That came third.
It was not the first thing.
The first thing was: God created.
God created the earth and the skies. That was the first thing.

The breath of God moved over the face of the waters:
over the darkness covering the face of the deep.
That was the second thing.

Then came the third thing.
God spoke.[13]

Taking this sequence seriously, one common to the biblical and Gaian accounts, we realize that we have long understood that God was not first revealed through speech. From 'the beginning' God was and is revealed through the processes of creating, through the evolution of the planet, its atmosphere, its life, its species. Here, in Rozenzweig's phrase, 'the shell of the mystery breaks'. And as it breaks, God's self is expressed, revealed throughout the processes we call evolution.

To whom, or to what is God's self revealed? To every living creature which emerges through coevolutionary process and which responds to God 'according to its kind'. But not with words. The morning stars sang together, the heavens recited the glory of God, but *no speech, no words, no voice was heard* (Psalms 19: 3. My italics).

This humbling recognition of the nature of revelation and of every living being's response to it has been obscured, if not totally discounted, by theological traditions that elevate the human soul to the cosmic place of honour, as the only one capable of receiving God's self expression and responding to it. Furthermore, they presuppose that God's self is expressed only in human words, and that that self was not revealed until someone spoke in God's name: until there was a human voice to utter and a human ear to hear; until there was a human intelligence to interpret and a human hand to record; until there was a human response to the mystery of God's self-expression.

Jesus is credited with an alternative view:

If they tell you,
Look! This presence is in the skies!
remember,
the birds who fly the skies have known this all along.

If they say,
It is in the seas!
remember,
the dolphins and fish have always known it.
It is not apart from you.
It wells up within each and surrounds all.[14]

Revelation within Christianity, however, has been consistently limited to human speech in such categorical statements as: *in many and various ways God spoke of old to our fathers by the prophets; but in these last days he has spoken to us by a Son* (Hebrews 1: 1–2). In the eponymous text, *Revelation*, it becomes 'the revelation of Jesus Christ', in which Jesus, a man, is the 'full' revelation of God, a 'fullness' made problematic since it is in fact confined by time, place, species, race and gender and defined as and in human male presence and language.[15]

---

13. Franz Rozenzweig, *The Star of Redemption*, trans. William Hallo (Indiana: Notre Dame Press, 1985), p. 112 f.

14. Gospel of Thomas 3 (Mark Primavesi's translation).
15. Anne Primavesi, 'The Spirit of Genesis', in *Upptäckter i Kontexten*, eds Sigurd Bergmann and Göran Eidevall (Lund: Institutet för kontextuell teologi, 1995), pp. 103–16.

Earth system science, however, appeals to us to exercise our theological freedom responsibly by recognizing God's continuous revelation to the whole Earth household and positing a response from each creature within it. This does not exclude revelation in Jesus, nor make it less precious to those to whom it is offered. But it does humble us, in the positive medieval sense of containing us within our limits (*virtus humilitatis in hoc consistit ut aliquis infra suos terminos se contineat*).[16] So contained, we do not extend ourselves into those things beyond our capacity. The ultimate arrogance in traditional views of revelation consists in the fact that by placing no limits on our own capacity to receive the full revelation of God, not only do we place limits on others' capacities and responses, but we have also (in intent if not in effect) limited God's capacity to reveal to our capacity to receive. We have forgotten Job's instructions to Zophar:

> But ask the beasts, and they will teach you;
> the birds of the air, and they will tell you;
> or the plants of the earth, and they will
>   teach you;
> and the fish of the sea will declare to you.
> Who among all these does not know that
>   the hand of the Lord has done this?

16. 'The virtue of humility consists in this, that someone contains himself within his limits.' Thomas Aquinas quoted in Heiko Oberman, *The Dawn of the Reformation* (Edinburgh: T. and T. Clarke, 1986), p. 187, n. 21.

> In God's hand is the life of every living thing
> and the breath of all humankind.
>
> (Job 12:7)

I am not saying that the mystery we call God has not been revealed to us through human language, nor that what has been revealed in and by the life of Jesus is not central for Christians. I am saying that we cannot reduce the whole of that revelation to what has been expressed to us, or by us; nor indeed can we reduce that to what has been said by or to a particular group of human beings at any particular time or place.

I am also saying that contemporary earth system science's appeal to us to develop the doctrine of revelation is at the same time an appeal to recognize the dignity of every living creature. All life forms that emerged, flourished and died in the billions of years before our emergence were worthy of knowing God according to their kind. Does recognizing their dignity diminish ours? Is it not rather the case that by exercising our freedom to accord them their own dignity, the dignity of the whole Earth household is enhanced? By respecting the limits of our own freedom, we respect the freedom of other creatures to exist in dignity, without coercion or exploitation. And by learning the interdependence of our own and others' dignity, we develop our capacity to live with them in noncoercive relationships. Which would be a positive contribution to the 'growing end' of scientific and theological tradition.

ANN LOUISE GILLIGAN

(1945–   )

from:
FEMINIST THEOLOGY AND IMAGINATION (1991)

[Patriarchal theology has proceeded historically along linear lines. The more we progressed, the clearer, the more rational and certain our knowledge of truth would become, and the less we would need to rely on imagery, symbols or imagination. The Protestant Reformations, in particular, attempted to eliminate imagery entirely in favour of the *Word*, as mediated through the accounts of salvation history in the Bible. Now, however, women ask such questions as *Whose salvation? Whose experience? Whose words?* Inevitably the answers reveal new levels of silencing, erasure or dismissal of women. In this article, Ann Louise Gilligan explores the importance of imagination, experience and imagery for holistic theologizing. This extract is taken from *Womanspirit*, vol. 5, no. 2 (October 1991).]

The starting point for the exploration of the connection between feminist theology and imagination is women's experience. Immediately we are reminded that life experience has theological significance. Indeed all theology through time has been rooted in the socio-political milieu of its time. That is to say, all theology is contextual, enhanced and limited by its day and age. What is new in the theological forum is that women's experience is now given voice. Women are no longer the objects of theological reflection but subjects doing theology. The incorporation of women's experience is affecting the transformation of theology; the absolutes of male normativity are melting as new humbler articulations of truth are being lisped . . .

To believe that women's experience is distinctive and worthy of attention is something that women themselves must be the first to claim. For women to name their experience and ultimately their own identity they must peel back layers of false imagery imposed upon them by patriarchal projection and then gradually construct their own self-image which reflects their experience of becoming woman. As Nellie Morton in that beautiful book *The Journey is Home* so accurately argues: 'Deep in the experience itself is the source of new imaging.'[1]

Image Breaking: A Feminist Theological Concern

The symbolic devaluing of women is one of the founding metaphors of Western civilization. Within the framework of early Greek philosophy 4th century BCE reality is understood hierarchically and imaged in dualisms. The male rational world is elevated as having the potential to image the divine and the female affective world is denigrated as defective in this regard. Consistent with this process, imagination is viewed over against reason and falls on the negative side of the divide.

The feminist imagination challenges the sexist assumptions underpinning this heritage. It is my contention that what Plato and Aristotle feared in the imagination is precisely what we ought to value; namely, the capacity of the imagination to

overcome dualisms, to destabilize hierarchies and to weave an integration between difference. If we continue to devalue the imagination then we are devaluing precisely what is most feared by those who keep us oppressed. As long as we live out of a world view that is hierarchical, imagination will be deprecated. As long as our framework is dualistic, rationality rather than creativity will be acclaimed. Put simply, imagination is feared, then as now, because of its potential to empower each of our lives.

For women to journey towards self-realization, towards a naming of our own identity out of our own self-understanding, the initial steps must involve exposing 'Women the myth' which is a projection of an exclusively male imagination and a patriarchal artifact. Women's lives have been encrusted with stereotypes and many women have spent their existence seeking to fulfil the projection of men's expectations of who they ought to be. Myths of the 'eternal feminine' must be demythologized. Universal images of women as 'other', as 'closer to nature', as 'passive', as 'feminine' must be recognized as false imagery and exorcised as demeaning of women. The exposure and the rejection of such imagery is vital if the dichotomies which pervade our lives are to be eroded . . .

Image-Making: A Feminist Theological Challenge

To reclaim our identity as women is to proclaim a new understanding of rationality. Rationality now holds intellect, emotion and imagination in a mutual embrace. The dichotomized relegation of feeling and imagination as lesser faculties which belong to the private sphere is no longer acceptable. Reclaiming the imagination as a midwife in women's rebirth of self is not a straightforward journey. Nor is it linear. Rather, it cycles and spirals forwards and backwards through layers of complexity listening acutely for whispers that could be amplified into imagery that heals and inspires. This voyage or rediscovery of women's true self is best undertaken with other women. The conversation of shared stories is honoured by attentive listening. Having come from a world where the dialectic of discourse is war-like debate, where 'proving one's point' and 'winning the argument' is the order of

1. Nellie Morton, *The Journey is Home* (Boston: Beacon Press, 1985), p. 127.

the day, listening is honoured as sacred. Such listening encourages radical truthfulness. Having bathed in our lies for so long, especially the lie of the imagination, women must now be faithful to the truth of their stories, if new images, new metaphors for woman's true self are to emerge.

The restoration of imagination as a central faculty, which shapes public discourse, broadens the boundaries of what is accepted as knowledge from criteria of 'absolute objectivity' and 'pure fact' to include intuitions and imaginings of the possible. Women must name and claim their images of new possibility as insight. In a word, broadening the horizon of knowledge to include imagination brings women's ways of knowing, especially intuitive knowing, into the public discourse.

This journey from colonized to creative imagination is a profoundly emotional one. The rage and the anger that erupts with the recognition of the pernicious imagery that has controlled our lives can gradually fuel a motivation to move beyond such enslavement. As Mary Daly correctly reminds us: 'Rage is not a stage. It is transformative focusing Force that awakens transcendent E-motion.'[2]

It is imagination that will sustain the struggle for new ways of being. Vivid imaginings of new possibility coupled with lively passion is a necessary partnership if motivation to struggle forward is to be sustained. Those who image vividly feel deeply . . .

Religious Imagery: Empowerment or Oppression?

The place of religious imagery in shaping women's self-image must never be underestimated. Long before our ability to conceptualise develops, imagery shapes our conscious and unconscious lives. Indeed images predate and post-date our linguistic lives as we are reminded in Christa Wolf's tale of Cassandra: as Cassandra approaches death words evaporate but images last to the end. 'The last thing in my life will be a picture, not a word. Words die before pictures.'[3]

Images are more powerful than concepts, and religious imagery has a capacity to free-wheel through our lives evoking memories from the past and startling us in the present with thoughts and feelings we believe that we have long outgrown. If, as I have called for earlier, we should raise critical awareness about the images which envelop our lives, this is even more pertinent when it comes to religious imagery. Through the ages the Churches have formed our common religious imagination with images and stories contained in Scripture and Tradition. There is no need here to rehearse or to demonstrate the diatribe of demeaning imagery of women that we have inherited from the Church Fathers. We are all too familiar with this legacy which imaged women as 'the devil's gateway', as Eve's co-conspirators. 'You are the devil's gateway . . .' The cacophonous sound of Tertullian's words could be orchestrated with many examples. However, while it is vital to know our heritage, it is even more important to examine whether sedimentations of this perspective linger in our midst.

Our concentration on language and the analysis of text has often led to a neglect of an equally important form of discourse, namely visual imagery. Our search to annotate history has taken us through the written documents that have survived, but an equal and at times more insightful reading of religious history can be undertaken by a critical evaluation of religious art in all its manifestations. Often the more popular theology of a period can be more adequately gleaned by the visual account.

Margaret Miles, historical theologian, engaging in a hermeneutics of the image in history, argues that because our inheritance of religious art is by and large the production of the male imagination this heritage is also androcentric. However, imagery is more expressive of the affective and catches up with the respondent in a relationship of feeling that is often absent in the narrative of the word. The image can take on a life of its own as it seeps through history bearing tidings unintended by its originator. Therefore, it is simplistic to condemn as unhelpful to women in the past all religious imagery. The least we must concede is that this is an extremely complex inheritance. For example, depictions of the Virgin Mary, Mother of God, can be critiqued as images

2. Mary Daly, *New Intergalactic Introduction to Gyn/Ecology* (Boston: Beacon Press, 1990), p. xxxi.
3. Cited in Mary Grey, 'Claiming Power in Relation: Exploring the Ethics of Connection', *Journal of Feminist Studies in Religion* (spring 1991), pp. 7–18.

of the impossible, frustrating the aspirations of ordinary women and depleting their strength . . . But such imagery could also have enabled women to identify the divine within and empowered women towards spiritual growth . . .

My main anxiety is not with the past but with the quality of religious imagery in our churches, schools and homes today. When the history of our post Vatican II Church is written, I fear we will be accused of being a profoundly verbal Church, a Church which neglected visual discourse. Good religious imagery that reflects present religious consciousness rooted in current experience is extremely difficult to find. Serious attempts to reflect religiously the mutuality of women and

men as created in the divine image are rare indeed. This great neglect of Church art, coupled with the continued presence of some dreadful plastic art representing the piety of an out dated era, will be something that we will live to regret.

Deep religious insight has been lost by the repression or neglect of creative imagery. As women journey towards full womanhood by exploring and naming the depths of their own experience and as they challenge the world of imagery to reflect the reality of their lives, they must also enter the womb of their imaginations and bring to birth images of the sacred, insights into the holy, which resonate with our divine potential.

IRIS MURDOCH

(1919–99)

from:
METAPHYSICS AS A GUIDE
TO MORALS (1992)

[Iris Murdoch was preoccupied throughout her life with the following questions: What are the connections between art, religion, morality and philosophy? How do we progress our thinking beyond 'uncriticised assumptions or unconscious drives and patterns' (p. 201). What is the route between knowledge and virtue? Deeply committed to making philosophical concepts accessible and intelligible for everyone, she addressed these issues through novels, plays, poetry and philosophy.

In her last major formal work, Murdoch marshalled the combined forces of her philosophical training. Against the post-modern collapse into relativism, the certainty of dogmatic rationalism or atheism, or the attempts to concretize or petrify intelligence through various psychoanalytic or philosophical forms of the collective unconscious, Murdoch stresses the need to combine logic, intuition and imagination. Whereas philosophy often focused on the question of God, in Murdoch's terms, the word 'God' now translates as 'absolute value, the unconditioned, the reality of good'. In *Metaphysics as a Guide to Morals*, she holds out for the possibility of deep structures through which we can discern in our common efforts 'a sense of reality, an orientation' (p. 239). However awkward, however tentative, however provisional, such

deep structures ground the search for meaning and ultimately, virtue, in an otherwise anarchic universe. This extract is from *Metaphysics as a Guide to Morals* (Harmondsworth, Middlesex: Penguin, 1992), pp. 235–9. Footnotes are by the author unless otherwise stated.]

These problems about 'deep structure' may prompt an outsider (including the outsider who dwells inside every philosopher) to ask whether there is any deep structure. Of course we recognise that our very small number of philosophical geniuses have suggested structures which have dominated and guided centuries of thought not only inside philosophy but in science, in theology, in morality, and in the most general sorts of world-view held by unreflective people. Philosophy, it may be said, collects and formalises new ideas which, at various times, for various often mysterious reasons, are hanging about in the air, sensed by thinkers of all kinds.

The 'universal' role of philosophy has led to it being thought of as a sovereign discipline. Since Hegel this mystery too, the *Zeitgeist*, has been a subject for metaphysical theorising. But after it all, and in spite of the undoubted influence of philosophical pictures, does anybody really believe, in any close or even quasi-literal sense, in

Kant's system or Hegel's system? Is Kant's 'machinery' supposed, even by Kantians, to be *really there* 'in the mind', what would it be like to believe this? Do we think that all these operations are taking place now? This may be considered a very naive question which, if pressed, might seem like an attempt to dismiss philosophy altogether; as philosophy is in fact, for just such considerations, dismissed by many people who know only a little about it.

Of course the 'outsider' received various sophisticated answers, of which one may be derived from Plato who, in the midst of hard detailed discussion and the use of innumerable examples, presents fundamental ideas metaphysically in the form of myths. You have to work hard to understand, and then throw away the ladder (*Tractatus* 6.54).[1] The *work* must be understood in relation to a conclusion which is not to be thought of as 'containing' it. Learning philosophy is learning a particular kind of intuitive understanding. Doubtless learning anything difficult may be said to involve what may be called intuition; and the idea will be less than enlightening unless one can suggest where it is and what it does. Plato's myths 'cover' and (often) clarify intuitive leaps which in other philosophers are also required but not (for better or worse) similarly adorned. The term 'intuition' often opposed to 'reason', is perhaps a dangerous one to use. It may be said that an 'intuitive leap' must be either a wild guess or a piece of unusually fast reasoning! What I mean to indicate here is that what is 'deep' in philosophy is not something literal or quasi-factual or quasi-scientific. A careful explicit use of metaphor, often instinctive, is in place. This may seem to leave the final utterance open to a degree of (carefully situated) ambiguity: which may in itself be a philosophical position. Formal philosophy can come only so far, and after that can only point; Plato's *Seventh Letter* suggests something like this. This is not mysticism but a recognition of a difficulty.

Philosophers who feel able to dispel all ambiguity also have to explain that a philosophical scheme is not like a literal account of the functioning of an engine, but is a special *method of explanation*, not easy to understand, but having its own traditional standards of clarification and truthfulness. Discussions and arguments proceeding from here are also philosophy, and philosophers, in the British and American empiricist school for example, have been much concerned with them. The continual demand for what has been called 'the case value' of abstract philosophical statements represents this very proper unease. This can also go too far in the direction of literalism, as when difficult concepts which cannot easily be explained in simple terms are classified as 'emotive' or dismissed as meaningless. In general, empiricism is one essential aspect of good philosophy, just as utilitarianism is one essential aspect of good moral philosophy. It represents what must not be ignored. It remembers the contingent. There is also, in the down-to-earth or anti-metaphysical style, the attitude, sometimes expressed by Wittgenstein, that the philosopher has no positive role, but is to sit at home until particular problems are brought to his attention (see 'the right method of philosophy', *Tractatus* 6.53). If Wittgenstein was preaching this, he certainly did not practice it, and it would be a difficult programme for a gifted philosophical thinker to carry out. Well, is there, discoverable by *philosophy*, deep structure, and if we assume (as of course we may not) that (somehow) there is or must be, what mode of philosophical speech can deal with it? Is it, initially, something psychological, or physical, or moral, which philosophy may comment upon, and set out in a formal manner in philosophy of mind, or philosophy of science, or moral philosophy, or philosophy of religion?

I hope in what follows to 'talk around' some of these questions. Such 'talking' may constitute or indicate answers. If we see why a certain kind of explanation must fail this will help us to see what to do next. Husserlian phenomenology and some of its descendants or (in similar style) rivals seem to me to constitute a philosophical dead end, because the chosen method of description or analysis of consciousness is too abstract, too rigid, inappropriately specialised, is at the wrong level, misses the nature of what it is attempting to explain. The detailed mobility of consciousness, its polymorphous complexity and the inherence

---

1. Ludwig Wittgenstein, *Tractatus Logico-Philosophicus*. Murdoch cited two editions: C.K. Ogden's translation of 1922 and D.F. Pears's and B.F. McGuinness's translation of 1961. [MC]

in it of constant evaluation, is lost. Such theorising fails because it aims at a kind of scientific status, mixes philosophy with over-simplified psychology, or attempts to offer a 'neutral' analysis which ignores morality (value) or treats it as a small special subject; whereas the inherence of evaluation of moral atmosphere, pressure, concepts, presuppositions, in consciousness, constitutes the main problem and its importance. The charm of Hegel is that he accepted this aspect of consciousness as fundamental. At the other end of the spectrum those who share Husserl's approach will be saying: but if morality is to be put into an account of mind we shall have nothing but confusion. States of mind are too mixed and complex, subject to various modes of continuity, and coloured by presupposition and evaluation for classification in terms of desires, beliefs, etc. to be useful. Hegel observes this in the quotation given earlier from the *Phenomenology*[2] where he speaks of mental concerns so sorted as constituting a ragbag. Of course the mind is like a ragbag, full of amazing incoherent oddments. This must be set as part of the philosophical problem of finding ways of talking about fundamental matters. Hegel so sets it, but in the context of a solution which obliterates the picture of individual people in an accidental world.

There may seem to be some awkwardness in continuing to pose the question of consciousness in the context of such heterogeneous theories, but it is an awkwardness which must be maintained. Looking at a variety of other views and metaphors may help, through understanding of what seems unsatisfactory, toward a grasp of something essential. At intervals one must stand back and ask: Well, what am I worried about, what do I want, what am I after, what is supposed to be missing? Here one tries, roughly and metaphorically, to delineate an impression. There are 'moral judgements', which may in some ways resemble judgments in law courts, or which take place at stated times and initiate visible new courses of action or the embryos of new dispositions. But there are also ways and states in which value inheres in consciousness, morality

colours an outlook, light penetrates a darkness. We have senses of direction and absolute checks. There are qualities of consciousness. Perhaps a purified consciousness might be able to do the sort of thing which Husserl wanted? After all, do I not wish to connect morality with knowledge? With truth, *ergo* with knowledge? The Cartesian movement, in Husserl's use and understanding of it, is not regarded as a moral movement or achievement. Is it then so simple and so easy? Descartes and Husserl *appeal* to consciousness and do so with certain ends in view; the consciousness of consciousness is to reveal the foundations of knowledge. (Do we all somehow believe in the possibility of such a revelation?) Descartes also says that in the pure separated (inner non-transcendent) consciousness we also discover God. We intuitively, and with certainty, know of God when with this particular movement of intensity of reflection we shift from the natural standpoint into the mind. This does not just mean that when we think about God, instead of thinking about the stove, we intuit God's existence. Descartes means that any pure certainty *includes* (is internally related to) an intuition of God. God is the light of truth. *Dominus illuminatio mea*. We might here translate 'God' into absolute value, the unconditioned, the reality of good.

Are there 'deep structures' in the mind, or in the soul? How is one to deny the claim, in the sense in which Thrasymachus for instance meant it, that there is nothing deep? Should philosophical approaches to the problem recognise the omnipresence of a moral sense in thinking and knowing? There is a point at which reflection, however beset, must stand firm and be prepared to go on circling round an essential point which remains obscure. As in the working of a ratchet, one must hold anything which seems like an advance, while seeking a method of producing the next movement. The contrast between the *cogitatio* of Husserl and that of Descartes offers a point from which to prospect. Descartes does not suggest that it is extremely difficult, though of course it implies some ability to reflect, to enact *cogito ergo sum*. He thinks (with the thought of his time and which unites him to Anselm) that the idea of God and the sense of God's presence is close, or potentially close, or integrally close, to any man. A modern formulation might suggest

2. G.W.F. Hegel, *Phenomenology of Mind*, trans. J.B. Baille (London, Macmillan, revised edition 1931), p. 332.

that the idea of good, of value, of truth, is thus close. This insight combines with, is one with, the ability to examine or arrest a momentary non-transcendent experience or instant of consciousness, as part of an argument which justifies our confidence in our forms of knowledge and our conception of the world. Husserl does not maintain that the movement to, or from, his

cogitatio or 'essence' has anything to do with value or moral insight, or with any specialised expertise except that of sustained introspection; whereas Descartes believes that by discovering God, and in the light of truth, in an exercise of reflection we discover our ability to know the realities of our world. What is discovered is a sense of reality, an orientation.

PHYLLIS ROONEY

(1953–   )

THE 'MALENESS' OF REASON
(1994)

[In the early days of this recent wave of feminism, women aspired to equality with men. The categories of both woman and man were apparently unproblematic and male philosophical strictures regarding deficiencies in women's reasoning ability were opposed, very much on their own terms. At the end of the twentieth century, however, none of these terms — man, woman, or indeed, reason — remains unchallenged. Phyllis Rooney explores the pressures now brought to bear from within and outside the philosophical tradition. This extract is from *American Philosophical Quarterly*, vol. 31, no. 1 (January 1994).]

Women are capable of education, but they are not made for activities which demand a universal faculty such as the more advanced sciences, philosophy and certain forms of artistic production . . . women regulate their actions not by the demands of universality but by arbitrary inclinations and opinions . . .
                    Georg Friedrich Hegel[1]

What are we to make of the fact that the Hegel remark above is all too familiar to any student of Western philosophy: the fact that women (or 'the feminine') have been *physically, literally, and metaphorically* excluded from the excellence of reason as that has been traditionally conceived? The 'physical' exclusion operated in the prohibition or discouragement of women from

the academy, from the halls of government, law, and commerce, realms which were typically seen to maintain the development and exercise of reason. The 'metaphorical' exclusion involves the persistent use of gender imagery, and sometimes race imagery, to 'explicate' the relationship between 'male' reason and 'feminine' unreason.[2] The 'literal' exclusion, on the other hand, refers to philosophers' frequent claims that women and people of 'inferior' races are (in some literal sense) less rational. The persistence of these various interrelated exclusions in our philosophical history presents us with a compelling picture that demands further analysis. Typically, the physical exclusion was argued on the basis of the literal one, and the slide between the literal and metaphorical exclusions has been a lot more slippery than we may have suspected. Our concern here is not just with the intellectual and discursive climate such exclusions have created for women and for men from traditionally less privileged groups, but also with the impact they might have had on our philosophical conceptualizations of reason and rationality.

While philosophers have generally insisted on a universal human faculty of reason, many have been equally insistent that such a faculty admits of degrees, in many cases degrees marked by gender and race. It is not clear, however, how we are to understand what is involved in a distinct nonphysical human faculty that admits of such degrees. Aristotle's view in this regard is more

1. G.W.F. Hegel, *Philosophy of Right*, trans. T.M. Knox (New York: Oxford University Press, 1973), p. 263.

2. Phyllis Rooney, 'Gendered Reason: Sex Metaphor and Conceptions of Reason', *Hypatia*, vol. 6, no. 2 (1991), pp. 77–103.

developed than that of many other philosophers. He distinguishes degrees of authority that the deliberative capacity in the rational part of the soul has over the irrational part, and the degrees were different for free men, for free women, and for slave women and men. As Elizabeth Spelman points out in her discussion of Aristotle: 'nature tossed [women and slaves] a dash of reason — enough to make them members of the same species as male citizens — but clearly not the kind of reason found in the souls of their natural rulers'.[3] Such 'abstract and dispassionate' insights into the nature and function of reason reveal little more than rationalizations of class and gender divisions needed to preserve specific structures in the social and political status quo.

Mary Briody Mahowald[4] provides selections from many philosophers in our tradition which illustrate very effectively the persistent discrepancies between conceptions of 'human nature' and conceptions of 'woman'. Many of these discrepancies acquire the status of inconsistencies. With quotations from Kant, Fichte, Rousseau, and Schopenhauer, Carol C. Gould[5] illustrates the difficulty many philosophers had, on the one hand, admitting women as human, yet, on the other hand, wanting to distance women from essential and necessary human characteristics like reason and freedom. Such examples, Gould claims,

> . . . suggest that human nature or essence, whether it be construed as freedom or reason or in some other way, is a sex-linked characteristic, since it is found only or truly in men and not women; or at the very least, that this nature is actualized only by men . . . these philosophers' views regarding universal human nature are simply contradicted by their views of concrete individuality in the case of women . . .[6]

Gould's suspicion that the 'criterion of abstract universality' chooses properties, roles, or

functions explicitly or implicitly identified as male can be underscored by insights that emerge from Genevieve Lloyd's work.[7] With an analysis that remains sensitive to historical shifts in conceptions of reason, Lloyd brings to the surface 'the implicit maleness' of the ideals of reason developed by many of those considered the major thinkers in our tradition — a maleness that, she argues, goes well beyond a superficial linguistic bias. Philosophical understandings of the force, the path, the power of reason have almost always involved some form of denigration, control, or transcendence of 'the feminine,' and in a way that is inherently incompatible with long-standing attempts to circumscribe a *'dispassionate'* reason. Thus, to take but a small (though representative) sampling, the Alexandrian Philo writes: 'The rational which belongs to the mind and reason is of the masculine gender, the irrational, the province of sense, is of the feminine.' Later, Augustine distinguishes between 'that part of reason which is turned aside to regulate temporal things [which] could be properly symbolized by [woman's] corporeal veil' and 'that part of the mind [which] clings to the contemplation and consideration of the eternal reasons'.[8] In this latter example the symbolic association of the female is with the lesser, practical kind of reason.

While it can be argued that many of these gender associations are symbolic or metaphoric rather than literal, recent work in the philosophical analysis of metaphor precludes our simply dismissing such metaphors as 'mere' stylistic embellishment, as I argue elsewhere.[9] One of the most distinguishing characteristics of French theorist Luce Irigaray's work is her central concern with making visible the impact of this persistent gender imagery in the delineation of the rational and the irrational in our western discourses of reason, though she sometimes does this in a style that can be somewhat formidable for anyone not familiar with Lacanian psychoanalytic theory.[10] Irigaray's strategy of mimicry, or

3. Elizabeth V. Spelman, *Inessential Woman: Problems of Exclusion in Feminist Thought* (Boston: Beacon Press, 1988), p. 45.
4. Mary Briody Mahowald, *Philosophy of Woman: Classical to Current Concepts* (Indianapolis, Ind.: Hackett, 1978).
5. Carol C. Gould (ed.), 'The Woman Question: Philosophy of Liberation and the Liberation of Philosophy', in *Women and Philosophy: Toward a Theory of Liberation*, eds Carol C. Gould and Marx W. Wartofsky (New York: Putnam, 1976), pp. 18–19.
6. Ibid., p. 20.

7. Genevieve Lloyd, *The Man of Reason: 'Male' and 'Female' in Western Philosophy* (Minneapolis: University of Minnesota Press, 1984).
8. Ibid., pp. 27, 31.
9. P. Rooney, 'Gendered Reason'.
10. Luce Irigaray, *Speculum of the Other Woman*, trans. Gillian C. Gill (Ithaca, N.Y.: Cornell University Press, 1985), and *This Sex Which is Not One*, trans. Catherine Porter and Carolyn Burke (Ithaca, N.Y.: Cornell University Press, 1985).

'mimesis', is a discursive strategy designed to have a disruptive impact on our 'regular' reading of traditional texts. She seeks to show how (in such traditional discourses) the 'man of reason' emerges as unitary, as absolutist and determinate, as undifferentiated presence, *through an explicit contrast with* the female as the site of instability, indeterminateness, fluidity, multiplicity, and difference. She sets out 'to try to locate the place of [woman's] exploitation by discourse . . . so as to make "visible," by an effect of playful repetition, what was supposed to remain invisible: recovering a possible operation of the feminine in language'.[11] Irigaray's position cannot be readily categorized as 'essentialist' (as some have claimed) in that she isn't simply positing or valorizing the operation of a 'feminine' in language. Gatens argues that by speaking from the position of 'the feminine' as the repressed in language, in philosophy, and in culture, Irigaray and fellow French theorist Hélène Cixous have as their aim not simply a reversal of the hierarchy between masculine and feminine 'but rather involves challenging and unsettling the coherence of the opposition itself . . . The point is rather to reveal the conditions for the functioning of phallocentrism: specifically the repression of difference and of femininity'.[12] Margaret Whitford has undertaken helpful expositions and analyses of Irigaray's work.[13] She also counters what may initially appear (from a feminist perspective) to be a 'symbolically retrograde move' in Irigaray's work: Whitford stresses that the male and female imaginary(s) as they are presented in that work should be seen as symbolic and cultural categories with a political dimension, rather than simply as essentialist or psychoanalytic categories. Whitford adds: 'I interpret the description of the female imaginary, for example, not as an essentialist description of what women are really like, but as a description of the female as she appears in, and is symbolized by, the Western cultural imaginary.'[14] It cannot be said

that Irigaray is simply creating or valorizing a link between conceptualizations of rationality and conceptualizations of sexual difference: she is hoping to make visible what she would claim has been there all along in our western discourses of reason.

Many feminist theorists thus draw upon the theoretical frameworks of psychoanalytic theory and deconstruction, and upon Foucault's (poststructuralist) analysis of the social and discursive manifestations of power to explore these dimensions of the gendering of reason. Though not explicitly presupposing any one such theoretical framework, Andrea Nye[15] develops a feminist analysis of the languages of logic (and especially the language used to explain and promote advances in logic) in terms of an analysis of 'words of power'. Susan Hekman[16] utilizes many of these 'postmodern' critiques in her feminist discussion of subjectivity, language, and rationality, arguing, in particular, for the theoretical possibilities of a conversation between postmodernism and feminism. Elizabeth Grosz[17] draws in part on Foucault's understanding of *bodies* as sites of social control, surveillance, and manipulation to argue for a feminist conceptualization of the body as the site of social associations and inscriptions (often marked by power structures) rather than simply as the locus of 'internal' biological and psychological formations. (One has only to note, for example, the many ways in which our various cultural mediums differently inscribe male and female bodies, particularly as sexed bodies.) Grosz argues that this kind of analysis helps us better understand how the projection of reason as disembodied, pure and uncontaminated was facilitated by having 'women take on the function of representing *the body, the irrational, the natural,* or other epistemologically devalued binary terms'.[18]

Much of this work draws us to a recurring question: could the 'man of reason' have been compellingly projected as the universal,

11. L. Irigaray, *This Sex Which is Not One*, p. 76; Margaret Whitford, *Luce Irigaray: Philosophy in the Feminine* (New York: Routledge, 1991), p. 71.

12. Moira Gatens, *Feminism and Philosophy: Perspectives on Difference and Equality* (Bloomington: Indiana University Press, 1991), pp. 113–14.

13. Margaret Whitford, 'Luce Irigaray's Critique of Rationality', in *Feminist Perspectives in Philosophy*, eds Morwenna Griffiths and Margaret Whitford (London: Macmillan, 1988), pp. 109–30, and *Luce Irigaray*.

14. M. Whitford, *Luce Irigaray*, p. 60, and 'Luce Irigaray's Critique of Rationality', p. 114.

15. Andrea Nye, *Words of Power: A Feminist Reading of the History of Logic* (New York: Routledge, 1990).

16. Susan J. Hekman, *Gender and Knowledge: Elements of a Postmodern Feminism* (Boston: Northeastern University Press, 1990).

17. Elizabeth Grosz, 'Bodies and Knowledges: Feminism and the Crisis of Reason', in *Feminist Epistemologies*, eds Linda Alcoff and Elizabeth Potter (New York: Routledge, 1993).

18. Ibid., p. 209.

objective, and generic subject if philosophers did not have such ready access to 'woman' as a persistent cultural and linguistic category upon which/whom to displace the particularity and subjectivity of bodily interest and location? The upshot of many of these discussions is the realization that there is a complex working of gender symbolism in the development of conception of reason, as Lloyd argues in a more recent paper.[19] The gender issue with reason is one that cannot be easily dismissed, nor can it be easily explicated or resolved: 'the operations of the male and female as symbols . . . interact, of course, with gender division and with the social formation of gender identity. Masculine socialization influences which symbols . . . influence in turn the social formation of gender identity.'[20]

Where does all of this leave us with respect to the long-standing attempt to postulate and develop a 'universal' or 'sovereign' reason? At least three summary points should be noted. First, we now see that the feminist correction must involve more than gaining admittance to all institutions of action and influence for those historically excluded, and treating philosophers' claims about women's lesser rationality (and other misogynistic comments) as bracketable aberrations due to historically limited under-standings of women and women's roles. We begin to suspect, as Michèle Le Doeuff does, that philosophers' 'stupid utterances made about women . . . are pertinent at a level different from the one at which they appear to have meaning'.[21] Second, any attempt to simply revalorize the traditionally denigrated 'feminine' can be problematic for, as Lloyd stresses:

> The idea that women have their own distinctive kind of intellectual or moral character has itself been partly formed within the philosophical tradition to which it may now appear to be a reaction . . . The affirmation of the value and importance of

'the feminine' cannot of itself be expected to shake the underlying normative structures, for, ironically, it will occur in a space already prepared for it by the intellectual tradition it seeks to reject.[22]

While acknowledging that much of the feminist work has made it apparent that 'hegemonic ideals of reason are constructed out of symbolisms, qualities, and modes of thought that map accurately onto, and are mirrored by, hegemonic ideals of masculinity',[23] Code details the complex balancing acts that feminists must undertake when they address this issue yet also want to steer clear of the false essentialism about female and male ways of being and knowing that can be seen, in part, to be a consequence of this same tradition.[24]

This brings us to a third consideration. This discussion draws into critical focus the whole notion of a universal, ideal, unitary, or sovereign Reason. Claims about degrees of reason have certainly emerged as politically suspect, but we must also ask to what extent the ideal of a sovereign reason has also functioned as a political requirement rather than a straightforwardly epistemological one. The 'universal' in many such contexts is theorized as that which in some sense transcends the particular, yet, as we have seen, it turns out that particular particulars are especially suspect: those that are literally or symbolically theorized as female, rendering the 'non-femaleness' of the flight of reason as something more than stylistic embellishment. Yet, because of this, concerns can also be raised about wholesale feminist dismissals of reason as masculine, since these can be seen to draw upon aspects of a *unitary,* sovereign Reason that are at the heart of the problem. This is a central concern in Le Doeuff's discussion,[25] and cap-tured most pointedly in her comment: '"Rationality" (or knowledge, or whatever) appears as a whole, and as a distinct or clearly defined reality only when it is associated with an exclusion ("what is beyond women's reach") or a

19. Genevieve Lloyd, 'Maleness, Metaphor, and the "Crisis" of Reason', in *A Mind of One's Own: Feminist Essays on Reason and Objectivity*, eds Louise M. Antony and Charlotte Witt (Boulder, Col.: Westview Press, 1993).
20. Ibid., p. 71.
21. Michèle Le Doeuff, *Hipparchia's Choice: An Essay Concerning Women, Philosophy, Etc.*, trans. Trista Selous (Cambridge, Mass.: Basil Blackwell, 1991), p. 13.

22. G. Lloyd, *Man of Reason*, p. 105.
23. Lorraine Code, *What Can She Know? Feminist Theory and the Construction of Knowledge* (Ithaca, N.Y.: Cornell University Press, 1991), p. 119.
24. Ibid., pp. 110–72.
25. Michèle Le Doeuff, 'Women, Reason, Etc.', *Differences*, vol. 2, no. 3 (1990).

rejection ("what, as a woman, I do not want for myself nor for any woman") in short with a personification.'[26] She suggests a shift in terminology that may facilitate better articulation of the feminist issues: 'in my opinion, the illusion of total rationality is linked, not with masculinity itself, but with masculinism — not with men themselves, but with the position of power they have or may assume'.[27]

Lloyd is somewhat optimistic about salvaging something of 'the ideal of a Reason that knows no sex': while philosophy has defined ideals of reason through exclusions of 'the feminine', she thinks that 'it also contains within it the resources for critical reflection on those ideals and on its own aspirations'.[28] Di Stefano[29] and Scheman[30] suggest that Lloyd may have underestimated the implications of her analysis. Di Stefano wonders what 'Reason' or 'Philosophy' is stripped of its androcentric content and associations.[31] Scheman wonders whether there will come to be interests and projects (like perhaps the continuation of life on the planet), which will 'in different ways genuinely engage all human beings and give us, for the first time in history, human philosophy, rather than the philosophy of man'.[32] This idea of drawing attention to the interests, practices, and projects around which reason and rationality are conceptualized and articulated may well provide the most productive path forward here ... Not only does it bring into clearer view the particular social and historical interests and practices that have informed traditional conceptions of reason, but it also provides interesting insights into the ways in which such conceptions start to change with a shift from one set of socially constructed and culturally informed practices to other such sets.

It may not be particularly constructive at this point to speculate about what a 'final' feminist judgement about universal Reason should be. Despite this, some important insights into our philosophical history are surely coming into clearer focus. We can now better explain curious yet persistent historical puzzles. While the 'great' philosophers were influential precisely because they could generally see beyond inherited prejudices in all sorts of areas, with some notable exceptions because so few (Plato and Mill, for instance, though there are definite limits to their feminist insights)[33] they seemed characteristically unable to see beyond inherited prejudices about women, and especially about women and reason. While sometimes obsessive in their claims about women's lesser rationality, they themselves seemed characteristically unable to reason well (by their own standards) about possible connections between women's confinement to specific roles with lack of educational opportunities and their purported deficiencies in reasoning abilities that by these philosophers' own accounts required educational training and exercise. We thus need to be as diligent in our examinations of assumptions deeply embedded within conceptions of reason as we are in our reassessments of women's achievements. The very notion of a sovereign Reason — regularly theorized as a kind of ultimate arbiter against ideology — must be examined anew in light of the critical awareness that this ideal persisted for so long so comfortably harbouring pockets of inconsistency and ideology about women.

26. Ibid., p. 7.
27. Ibid., p. 8.
28. G. Lloyd, *Man of Reason*, p. 109.
29. Christine Di Stefano, 'Dilemmas of Difference: Feminism, Modernity, and Postmodernism', in *Feminism/Postmodernism*, ed. Linda Nicholson (New York and London: Routledge, 1990), pp. 63–82.
30. Naomi Scheman, 'The Force of Reason', *Women's Review of Books*, vol. 3, no. 1 (October 1985), pp. 15–16.
31. C. Di Stefano, 'Dilemmas of Difference', p. 72.
32. N. Scheman, 'The Force of Reason', p. 16.
33. Linda Nicholson, 'Women's Work: Views from the History of Philosophy', in *'Femininity', 'Masculinity', and 'Androgyny'*, ed. Mary Vetterling-Braggin (Totowa, N.J.: Rowman and Allenheld, 1982).

ATTRACTA INGRAM

(1945–   )

from:
THE PERILS OF LOVE:
WHY WOMEN NEED RIGHTS
(1988–90)

[In the early 1980s, a succession of major works extolled women's way of knowing, women's distinct moral voice, or the inadequacy of rights theory in relation to women's ethics of care. The 1990s produced an extensive critique of this school of thought, claiming that it did not respect wide divergence in women's social or ethnic positioning; it appeared to valorize ethical thinking derived under conditions where women had been relegated to the private sphere; and it did not take account of the dialectical relationship between the public and private worlds. Attracta Ingram's article represents a timely reminder of the perils of love in a rights based legal system. This article is extracted from 'The Perils of Love: Why Women Need Rights', *Philosophical Studies*, vol. 32 (1988–90). Footnotes are by the author.]

Recently there has been a revival of interest in the communitarian ethics of love as an alternative to rights-based moral theory.[1] This paper offers a perspective on that revival from the standpoint of women and argues that women should think in terms of rights as well as love when contemplating a communitarian romance.

For communitarians morality is based on personal attachments and loves, social connections and loyalties born of the shared understandings of communities of which we are a part. The communities favoured in the literature are our 'given' communities: the family, neighbourhood, clan, tribe, nation and so on.[2] These are said to form our social identities and generate moral relationships, expectations and debts that

we inherit rather than make.[3] At its best, a community constitutes a social self that is imbued with communal values of care, nurturance, and interdependence, so the natural moral motive for the responses members make to each other is mutual affection.

Since women in our culture are taken to have a primary interest in love and intimacy values there is a natural point of contact between communitarianism and feminism and we would expect that to be reflected in the writings of women scholars. Yet a notable feature of communitarian revivalism is that its leading advocates are men. Of course, to some extent, women moral philosophers are reflecting and developing an ethics of love.[4] But they are not prominent in the larger theoretical project of re-creating and validating communitarianism.[5] Women scholars, while making strong contributions to modern moral philosophy, have avoided the impulse to grand theory that gives rise to such systematic diagnoses and prescriptions as those of Alasdair MacIntyre or Roberto Unger. As Annette Baier has observed, none of the contributions to moral philosophy by women count as moral theory in the sense of systematic theory built on a key concept or grounding *motif* and dealing in a fairly comprehensive way with a large area of morality. Baier hypothesises that if reflective women were to set themselves to produce such moral theory they would produce an ethics of love 'expressive mainly of women's insights and concerns'[6] . . .

Women are wary of communitarianism for several reasons. First, its 'male-stream' history (to borrow Mary O'Brien's term)[7] does not

1. Communitarian revivalists include: Roberto Unger, *Law in Modern Society* (New York: Free Press, 1976); Charles Taylor, 'Atomism', in A. Kontos (ed.), *Power, Possessions and Freedom: Essays in Honour of C. B. Macpherson* (Toronto: University of Toronto Press, 1979); Alasdair MacIntyre, *After Virtue* (London: Duckworth, 1981), and *Whose Justice? Which Rationality?* (London: Duckworth, 1988); Michael Sandel, *Liberalism and the Limits of Justice* (Cambridge: Cambridge University Press, 1982), and (ed.), *Liberalism and its Critics* (Oxford: Basil Blackwell, 1984).
2. See MacIntyre, *After Virtue*, pp. 204–5, and Sandel, *Liberalism and the Limits of Justice*, p. 179.
3. MacIntyre, *After Virtue*, p. 205.
4. See, for example, the literature cited by Annette C. Baier in 'What Do Women Want in a Moral Theory?', *Nous*, vol. 19 (1985), pp. 53–63.
5. However, see Marilyn Friedman's recent contribution to developing communitarian thought toward communities of choice in her 'Feminism and Modern Friendship: Dislocating the Community', *Ethics*, vol. 99 (1989), pp. 275–90. See also Jean C. Tronto, 'Beyond Gender Difference to a Theory of Care', *Signs: Journal of Women in Culture and Society*, vol. 12 (1987), pp. 644–63.
6. Baier, 'What Do Women Want in a Moral Theory?', p. 55.
7. See Mary O'Brien, *The Politics of Reproduction* (London: Routledge and Kegan Paul, 1981).

predispose women to believe that an ethics of love and the caring virtues automatically embodies an understanding of these that is sensitive to the development of a mutuality in which women as well as men receive what is due to them as persons. Women's communitarian experiences have been of subordinate status in patriarchal hierarchies. Women are the ones with first-hand knowledge of how the values of caring, sharing, and self-sacrifice are warped by gender-based power relations within intimate communities and the family.

A second and related reason for women's wariness of communitarianism is that questions of gender justice do not appear on its current agenda. The prominent communitarian writers simply do not address the disparities between the sexes of social status, wealth, education, and opportunities.[8]

Third, social and political power has rarely escaped male hands, and until that hegemony is broken, many women see a need to exploit current legal and social recognitions of an ethic of justice and rights, much as women and low-status men have in the past . . .

Women's fight against subordination necessarily employs the ethical resources of the political culture in which they find themselves and those resources include the historically potent terms of liberation: rights, justice, and autonomy. Mary Wollstonecraft's *A Vindication of the Rights of Women* is a model of the language and form of argument women have learned to deploy with success in their pursuit of equality.[9] The partial successes of their resistance to subordination have been in claiming autonomy rights to the vote, to property, to equal opportunities of education and work. Their failures have been in getting recognition, both personal and political, for attachment values of care, nurture and affection.

Autonomy values have been highly instrumental for women's liberation. Nevertheless, they are found and felt by many women to be abstract, formal and legalistic. The ethic of justice as a system of rules for treating like cases

alike is false to their experience that focusing on the likeness of different cases often masks their morally relevant differences.

One reason for this experience is that in our society the social task of maintaining and nurturing relationships has devolved on women. So women have typically been the ones who have responded to the needs of 'this particular' child, relative, friend or stranger. Their experience is of concrete needs and of the importance of being able to make the fine discriminations of relevant features that make for equitable responses to those varying needs. The natural expression of such experience is George Eliot's view that moral judgements 'must remain false and hollow unless they are checked and enlightened by a perpetual reference to the special circumstances that mark the individual lot'.[10]

So, women may find themselves in two minds about an ethics that expresses their concerns and insights. In one mind they favour the formal rule-based ethic of justice and rights because it has been a highly effective weapon against two kinds of traditional defence of patriarchy: theories of natural hierarchy which subordinate women on the alleged ground of their natural inferiority to men; and theories which mark out separate spheres of male (public) and female (domestic) activities. In their other mind women have to set against a rights-based ethic the fact that in our society they are usually the primary carers and their experiences and moral development may be better captured in a radically particularist ethic of love. For women, achievement turns on being able to expand and defend equality interests by appealing to rights while relationships turn on care as expressed in an ethics of love. So women end up divided in their concerns and about what they want their ethics to be . . .

Women need an ethics of justice and rights, at least as a background to their attachments, for three main reasons that I now develop.[11]

The first is that things go radically wrong in relationships and families. Notoriously, affections

8. As Marilyn Friedman points out, neither MacIntyre nor Sandel mentions sex or gender as constituting one's identity. 'Feminism and Modern Friendship', pp. 278–9.

9. Mary Wollstonecraft, *A Vindication of the Rights of Women 1792* (New York: W.W. Norton, 1967).

10. *The Mill on the Floss* (Harmondsworth: Penguin, 1979), p. 510. Carol Gilligan drew attention to the passage from which this quotation is taken in her book *In a Different Voice: Psychological Theory and Women's Development* (Cambridge, Mass.: Harvard University Press, 1982), p. 148.

11. In agreement with Tronto's point that feminists must situate the ethic of care in the context of rights/community debates, 'Beyond Gender Difference', p. 662.

fail. When they do, a structure of rights acts as a safety net for individuals who may be precipitated out of their previous roles and identities, or, simply neglected.[12] The role of rights here is to provide some protection for those whose existence and identities are otherwise wholly dependent on the contingent affection of others. Women and children need rights because affections fail in marriage, parent-child, and other love-based arrangements. When love fails, women who are full-time unpaid carers may find themselves without alternative material resources and often too without moral resources to reconstruct their identities for they have constituted themselves in terms of their relationships as daughters, wives, lovers, mothers and so on. This is why, while contract cannot be the essential basis of marriage or other intimate relationships, it can be the default position, the legal shell that the parties fall back on if attachments fail.[13]

The second reason why women should think in terms of rights is that they are important for women's self-inclusion in the web of care. Gilligan has drawn attention to women's identification of morality with giving and selflessness. That identification operates to exclude as selfish what are in fact entirely appropriate concerns of women for their own individual well-being. So they fail to include themselves in the web of care, a failure that seems to me to be tied to a lack of self-esteem . . .

To constitute themselves as worthy of self-love and inclusion in the web of care women need to embrace a conception of self as authoritative originator of view-points, claims and interpretations. That is the conception of selves as autonomous. As moral ideal, autonomy honours our natural capacities to identify for ourselves the character of a just social order and a worthwhile individual and social life. Recognition and exercise of autonomy is highly instrumental for cultivating a sense of individual worth, capacities for self-love and creative interpretation as well as criticism and re-definition of our traditions and communities. If women eschew autonomy values in the name of avoiding social disconnection, the prescription they take disempowers them to create either their own identities or social formations which respect their equality as persons. They are blocked from pursuit of the ideal of forming their own ideas and so forming themselves in conditions of their own choosing.

So, women need to have the conception of themselves as autonomous in order to see themselves as proper subjects of care. But autonomy can be exercised only if there are limits to the constraints set by intimate personal and community relationships . . .

Rights stake out the claims of women on the social goods women need for personal growth and self-direction. They are claims for themselves as individuals, naturally, but women should not be reduced by the jibe that such claims are individualistic and selfish. It is as individual women that they suffer discrimination, violence and disrespect. To claim rights not to have these harms inflicted is necessarily to call upon a moral concern for individuals, one that is already part of our moral culture . . .

I want now to turn to a third consideration, one which looks forward to new social relationships, rather than backwards to the conditions for emancipated engagement in, and reformation of, existing relationships.

Boldly stated, rights permit us to withdraw from existing communal roles, lifestyles, and attachments to try what Mill called 'experiments in living'.[14] What ways of life are feasible and productive of happiness cannot be decided in advance of experience. They have to be found in living. A society that discourages experimentation in the name, perhaps, of stability, limits the possibilities of human good to the scheme of ends described by its dominant morality. Such a society diminishes not only autonomy, but also the enhancement of human well-being that participation in a richly diverse social union brings . . .[15]

---

12. The image of the net (under the tightrope act!) is used by John Hardwig, 'Should Women Think in Terms of Rights?', *Ethics* (April 1984), pp. 441–55. Hardwig claims that rights are destructive of intimate personal relationships although he grants that they are part of the public system of impersonal relations. My view is that rights sensitize us to forms of forbearance and cherishing appropriate to respectful love. So rights contribute, in our culture at any rate, to the development of caring personal as well as public relationships.

13. For an excellent elaboration of this point, see Waldron's own essay 'Nonsense Upon Stilts? — A Reply', in *Nonsense Upon Stilts*, ed. Jeremy Waldron (London: Methuen, 1987), pp. 189–90.

14. See J.S. Mill, *On Liberty*, Fontana collection, ed. M. Warnock (Glasgow: Fontana, 1962), p. 185.

15. For the idea of social union, see John Rawls, *A Theory of Justice*, p. 520 ff.

An ethics of love cannot of itself prevent the partialities that corrupt community. Indeed, it is an inbuilt source of the fragility of communal bonds. There are three salient reasons for fragility. The first is that the institution of the family, which is central to much communitarianism, is a forum of intimate ties more commanding than our community attachments. In any situation of conflict, we will naturally prefer to advance the interests of our close kin over those of less loved friends and neighbours. So as long as the institution of the family exists, the political is under constant threat from the personal priority of family. If we would rather live with that personal–political tension than abolish the family, communal bonds will remain fragile.

Secondly, even without the family the fragility of political community might exist in any case if Aristotle is correct in observing that limits of time and the intensity of love preclude loving many persons in the same way.[16] Love among friends consumes emotional energy; it requires an appreciation of the same things; and it takes time to engage in the common pursuits and honour the responsibilities of friendship. So human emotional capacities, value orientations, and physical energies set limits to the number of close friendships a person can sustain. If love must exist within the bounds of our natural capacities, it seems psychologically difficult and even undesirable to put loyalty to the community ahead of loyalty to our closer friends.

16. Aristotle, *The Nichomachean Ethics*, trans. J.A.K. Thomson (Harmondsworth: Penguin, 1953), book 9, chap. 10.

In modern states there is a third source of fragility in the existence of philosophical, religious, and moral differences about the nature of human well-being. Part of what a philosophical, religious or moral view is for us is a source of deep commitments which may well lead us into serious conflict with others. Such differences seem bound to continue as long as human inspiration or creativity hold out. So a politics of care, while favoured by just institutions would seem to be contingent on our having political mechanisms for dealing with the conflicts that the limits of love and the size of modern political communities conspire to assure. That is why, finally, as citizens we need the assurance of institutions that underwrite our mutual trust in one another's integrity. We must be able to defend ourselves and our political community from the tendencies of private interests to subordinate public interests. That requires an internal guarantee in the form of a system of rights against the state. In sum, conflicting loves call for a background structure of rights under communitarian politics so we cannot expect rights to disappear on the installation of caring values . . .

Attachment to autonomy is not incompatible with an ethics or politics of care. Indeed rights devised to secure autonomy interests presuppose a fundamental mutual concern and identification. And women, in whose psyches is reproduced the current cleavage between love and rights, may be in the best position to unite both concerns by building communities that understand caring to include the respectful love that comes of acknowledging autonomy.

ONORA O'NEILL

(1941–   )

WOMEN'S RIGHTS: WHOSE OBLIGATIONS? (1996)

[The concern for equal rights on a par with men in the recent wave of feminism was quickly superseded by the notion of a distinct women's moral voice and distinct ethical standpoint. For some feminisms, *rights talk* quickly became the province of adversarial patriarchal discourse. Onora O'Neill takes issue with this position on several grounds. She distinguishes between various forms of rights, asks about the corresponding forms of *obligations*, critiques the notion that women are or should remain primarily in the private sphere, and questions the existence of a *Real Patriarchy* in this day and age.

Women's concerns and needs may be distinctive but as long as women bear primary responsibility for the socially vulnerable — children, elderly, the sick — and as long as they have fewer resources to do so, their interests are best served by a sophisticated approach to human rights and corresponding obligations. Originally published in Alison Jeffries (ed.), *Women's Voices, Women's Rights: Oxford Amnesty Lectures* (Colorado: Westview Press, 1996), pp. 57–69. Footnotes are by the author.]

Contemporary rhetoric about justice celebrates human rights, and justice for women is supposed to celebrate women's rights. Yet rights are mere pretence unless others have obligations to respect them. Why then do we now talk so relentlessly about rights, and so little about obligations? Does this show that we take rights seriously?

A Martian, or a Venusian, listening to the public rhetoric of our day, just to the ordinary pronouncements of politicians and the ordinary reports of the media, might conclude that we take rights very seriously indeed, even that we are obsessed by them. She might even conclude that we take the rights of women very seriously indeed. Women's rights may have seemed shocking when Mary Wollstonecraft chose the title of *A Vindication of the Rights of Woman* in 1790; now they are part of the rhetoric both of the established order and of its critics. They elicit more yawns and inattention than hostility, although there is still a bit of that.

Taking the rhetoric seriously is one thing; taking the substance seriously another. One of the main uses of this rhetoric is to point out how often human rights, and with them women's rights, are violated. No doubt a gap between rhetoric and reality is unsurprising; but this gap is more than evidence of failure to practise what we preach. Putting the matter starkly: if we think about justice primarily in terms of rights we are more or less bound to find not only that we do not or cannot live up to it, but also that we cannot work out what we are trying to live up to. The rhetoric of rights is not only deceptively easy to promulgate, but deeply evasive. Most of the difficulty of thinking about women's rights grows out of this general evasiveness of thought about rights, so it is to this pervasive difficulty rather than to battles about the rights women should have that I shall turn first.

1. Rights and Obligations

In speaking of the rhetoric of rights as evasive I do not mean to suggest that human rights, or women's rights, are unimportant, or that securing them is an unimportant political goal. My concern is rather that talking as if rights were the *core* of justice, and rights for women the *core* of justice for women, is a lazy way of talking and of thinking, which systematically obscures what we would most need to think about and to do if we were to take rights seriously.

We often talk of *having* rights. This gives rights a nice substantial feel, as though they were bits of hardware that could be touched and traded, purloined or protected. This way of talking misleads. Talking of rights and of obligations are both ways of talking about action, not about items that can be possessed. Moreover, most important rights are intrinsically relational in that they are *claim rights*, which mirror certain sorts of obligation: both claim rights and the corresponding obligations are a matter of required types of action, or of omission.[1] When we talk of such rights we look at the required action from the perspective of the claimant or right-holder; when we talk of obligations we look at required action from the perspective of the obligation-bearer, of the one who is to act. So it is clear enough that there will be no claim rights unless others have obligations. If anyone is to have a right of free association, then everyone must have an obligation not to obstruct free association. If anyone is to have a right to information about family planning, then someone, or perhaps a number of people, must have an obligation to make that information available. If anyone is to have a right of access to children with whom they do not live, others must have obligations to allow that access and to ensure that it is not thwarted. If anyone is to have a right to a free or even to an affordable nursery place for her pre-school children then somebody, and probably many people, must have obligations to contribute to providing that nursery place.

---

1. The only exceptions are those unprotected rights sometimes spoken of as *mere liberties*. For example, I may have a right which is a mere liberty to pick up a coin from the pavement, and so may you. Neither of us will have an obligation to let the other exercise the right: finders keepers. This is quite different from my having a *claim right* to pick up the coin, which you have an obligation to respect — even if you find the coin first. The rights that are most important to justice are not mere liberties but claim rights with corresponding obligations.

So far, so commonplace. In a way, the fact that there are no claim rights without obligations is so obvious and well known that it is embarrassing to bring the matter up. Yet I believe that a great deal of discussion of rights, including of women's rights, continually misstates the ways in which and the extent to which rights and obligations correspond to one another, and hence fails to see how much it matters whether discussion of justice emphasizes rights or obligations.

There are two very general reasons why starting with rights is a lop-sided way of thinking about ethics, and even about justice. The first and the more general, to which I shall return, is that while claim rights are mirror images of obligations, not all obligations have mirror images. If there are obligations without corresponding rights it will evidently impoverish moral thinking if one starts with the rights and leaves aside those obligations not mirrored by any rights. This thought by itself is reason enough to *begin* with obligations and not with rights. To do otherwise is about as sensible as trying to count the adult population of a country by counting all the parents, so overlooking all childless persons. However, for the moment I shall leave aside this large reason for starting with the obligations rather than the rights, and consider why the rhetoric of rights has such great capacities to dash the very hopes of justice that it raises.

The second very general reason why the rhetoric of rights creates problems is not that it is blind to obligations without counterpart rights, but that it obscures what is really at stake by focusing on the rights rather than the obligations. The obscurity arises because claim rights are easy to proclaim without paying much attention to the obligations which are their counterparts. This deceptive convenience is due, at least in large measure, to the fact that it is so easy to slide between discussion of positive (institutional, customary) rights and of moral (natural, human) rights. Everybody acknowledges that positive claim rights must have well-defined corresponding obligations: to speak of them as *positive* is just to speak of them as institutionalised, and we are evidently speaking of one and the same set of institutionalized requirements for action (or forbearance) when we speak of positive claim rights and of their corresponding obligations.

However, the point of appealing to human rights, or to women's rights, is not to endorse the positive rights embedded in existing institutions. The point is often to challenge existing positive rights (or their absence) and, of course, existing positive obligations (or their absence), or to justify different rights and different corollary obligations. What would be the point of appealing to human rights if they were no more than the institutionalised rights of some social order, or the various vestigially institutionalized 'manifesto rights' promulgated in Charters and Declarations, however august?[2] The rhetoric of rights supposedly appeals to fundamental moral principles, and aspires to justify or to condemn institutional and positive rights, and indeed to justify or to condemn the claims of the grand Declarations and Charters, so cannot coherently presuppose them.

But once we start talking about moral (human, natural) rights, and however we think they are to be justified, it becomes easy to let questions about obligations drift out of sight. The Rights of Man have much more immediate charm than the Duties of Man; and equally the Rights of Women can have much more immediate charm than the Duties of Women — let alone than the duties that correspond to the Rights of Women.

It is easy to succumb to the charm of rights, and delightful to think about claiming them. Claiming that one has a right, whether to certain liberties or to security, or to goods or services, perhaps to welfare, can be heady stuff. It is a matter of thinking about what one ought to get or to have done for one, and about what others (but which others?) ought to do or provide for one. Of course, claims are not likely to be effective unless somebody ought to meet those claims, and often they will be ineffective unless the claims are not merely allocated to some agent or agency, but accepted and enforceable. But the actual claiming can go on loudly and confidently, with panache and bravado, without establishing who should deliver whatever is claimed. It is even possible to claim what nobody can deliver as a right: I was once publicly admonished for asking who holds the obligations that correspond to an

---

2. Manifesto rights can provide indicators for institution building. Too often, however, their normative force is an illusion because they are neither principles of justice for which arguments are provided, nor institutionally anchored normative requirements.

alleged right to health (not merely to a right to health-care!) on the grounds that health is too important to human beings not to be the object of a right.

Moreover, there can be political and rhetorical advantage as well as charm in being vague about obligations. Claims about rights need only assert what right-holders are entitled to; only the curmudgeonly will object. Others may be animated and have their hopes raised. But claims about obligations have to specify not only what is to be accorded, but which obligation-bearers are going to have to do what for whom and at what cost. This is a much less charming topic. Unsurprisingly the rhetoric of obligations and duties has an unsavoury reputation, and those on whom burdens may fall often object.

Yet strangely the rhetoric of rights is often praised for taking human agents and their dignity seriously. When we think of others as right-holders it is, of course, true that we no longer think of them as mere subjects, who plead abjectly for better treatment. We think of right-holders as full persons, as citizens or citizens-to-be. Yet when claimants point to others' duties (which others' duties?) they do not have to take much action, and may even wrap themselves passively in a cloak of grievance or of resentment. They do not need to work out who will have to do what for whom at what cost, let alone what they themselves will have to do at what costs to themselves. In short, the rhetoric of rights, although *more* active than a rhetoric of dependent pleading, of mere subjects, is still a rhetoric of recipience rather than of action. It still takes the perspective of the claimant rather than of the contributor, of the consumer rather than the producer, of the passive rather than of the active citizen.

2. Liberty and Welfare

Of course, these points are hardly novel. They have surfaced repeatedly in the truly enormous contemporary literature on theories of justice. Much of this literature argues for rights and assumes that *if* claim rights can be established, then obligations will follow calmly in their wake. This theoretical literature may lack the full charm and bravado, let alone the political bite, of more public uses of the rhetoric of rights, but much of it shares the intellectual failings of claims to rights, in that it takes obligations less seriously than rights.

These failings cropped up repeatedly in the prolific disputes about justice throughout the last part of the twentieth century. The most enduring dispute has been between more or less libertarian thinkers and advocates of various conceptions of social justice. Libertarians have argued that all universal claim rights are liberty rights with corollary obligations not to interfere. The advocates of social justice have argued that there are also universal claim rights to certain goods or services, and in particular to welfare, with corollary obligations to deliver the goods.

All advocates of rights are agreed that *if* there are universal claim rights to liberty, then the corollary obligations must also be universal. For example, a right not to be raped, or a right to compete with others for employment will be marred if it is a right against some but not against all others. If there were some others who have no obligation to refrain from raping, or no obligation to let others compete in the market place, then nobody would have unrestricted rights of either sort. Mere liberties apart, universal liberty rights require corresponding universal obligations.

Libertarian advocates of rights insist also that universal claim rights *must* be liberty rights, and that universal rights to goods or services, hence to welfare, are incoherent. Goods and services have to be delivered at particular times and places, hence by particular agents and agencies. They cannot be delivered by everybody rushing in everywhere and treading on one another's toes. There can be no universal obligations to provide goods and services that correspond to universal rights to goods and services *in the same way that universal obligations to respect others' liberties correspond to universal liberty rights*. It follows, they conclude, that there cannot be universal rights to goods and services, hence that there can be no universal economic, social or cultural rights, and that the august Charters and Declarations make incoherent claims, which can indeed be put to rhetorical use, but can only disappoint those who take them seriously.

This libertarian line of thought is often extended with the claim that since there can be no universal rights to goods and services, any such rights must be not universal but 'special' rights, to which the 'special' obligations of specified parties correspond. In short, rights to goods and services and obligations to provide them are inevitably not moral or human rights at all. They are only the institutionalised or positive rights of a specific social order or reflections of a specific contractual arrangement or social role.

The implications of this line of thought can bite hard. For example, libertarians will agree that the staff of a maternity ward may have an obligation of care — a special obligation — to those patients who have been appropriately admitted, and those patients may have a special right to care from that staff. But they will deny that the staff have any more general obligations to provide care, or pregnant women a more general right to claim care. This line of thought accepts that all rights to goods and services are special rights that presuppose the specific relationships that may be established, for example, by legislation or by contract, by custom or by practice. Which sorts of special rights to goods or services and which sorts of special obligations are to be established is left entirely open. Special obligations to provide and rights to receive medical care and attention from the staff of a maternity ward may be on a footing with special obligations to shackle women prisoners even when in labour and special rights to be protected from the threat of women in labour absconding.[3] On this account, rights to goods and services are not human or moral rights at all; they are no more than instances of the very sorts of institutional rights which the rhetoric of rights aspires to criticise.

But the argument is not sound. All that follows from the convincing thought that universal rights to goods and services cannot be matched by universally delivered obligations to provide at all relevant times and places is that *if* there are universal rights to goods and services, then aspects of the corresponding obligations which have to do with delivery will have to take a different form. There is no intrinsic problem here. While it is true that a right not to be raped, or a right to compete for employment, is marred unless the counterpart obligation is universally held, this is not true of rights to goods and services. If, for example, persons with dependent children have a right to adequate housing, then the right can be fully met if *somebody* — or *some body* — provides each such person who lacks housing with adequate housing. It is not necessary that everyone contribute to provision, and wholly counter-productive, not to say impossible, if everyone attempts to be the provider on all occasions. Or if women have a right to ante-natal medical care, then it will be enough if *some* medically qualified persons provide that care to each woman — and downright dangerous, not to mention exhausting, and ultimately impossible, if everybody medically qualified tries to do so for each or all women.

In short, the obligations that correspond to rights to goods and services *must* differ in form from at least some of the obligations that correspond to liberty rights. Universal rights to goods and services are quite coherent,[4] provided that those aspects of the counterpart obligations which have to do with delivery are *distributed* or *allocated* to specific agents and agencies. On the other hand, those aspects of the counterpart obligations which have to do with *determining a scheme of delivery*, or with *refraining from obstructing delivery*, or with *contributing proportionally to costs* can quite well be universally held obligations.

Evidently, a universal right to some good or service is not taken seriously unless specific obligations to deliver the relevant good or service are established, so ensuring that the right is secured for each, so for all, right-holders. We are quite familiar with the thought that universal rights can be met *distributively*, and can point to many cases where universal welfare rights have been established within the domain of certain states by distributing obligations to provide welfare to cover each, hence all, right-holders. Those who established such welfare rights did not miraculously work out how everybody within those states could be omnipresent, forever fulfilling obligations to deliver food or medical care or housing to each and so to all, or even to all in need. What they did was hard enough, but it wasn't physically impossible.

---

3. Regulations requiring prison staff in the UK to shackle pregnant prisoners when in labour were rescinded after public outcry during the winter of 1995-6.

4. This argument to show that universal rights to goods or services are coherent is intended only to dispose of libertarian allegations that there cannot be such rights, and not to justify any specific rights to goods or services.

There are then, as libertarians insist, certain clear disanalogies between universal liberty rights and universal rights to goods and services. However, the libertarian claim that universal rights to goods and services are incoherent has not been established. The disanalogy might be summarised as follows: the conclusion of libertarian arguments is a *political agenda* of securing a particular list of liberty rights and their corresponding universal obligations, but no rights to goods or services. The conclusion of a social justice line of thought combines parts of the libertarian agenda — a rather more restricted set of liberty rights is to be secured — with an open *political debate* premised on the thought that there are obligations to support those in need, that a scheme for fulfilling these obligations must be established, and that, once established, all those in need will have acquired special obligations to specific goods and services. Universal rights to goods and services are to be secured by establishing any one of many possible schemes which distribute obligations to deliver those rights for each and so for all.

Social justice liberals have often queried this disanalogy.[5] They suggest that there are no serious differences between universal liberty rights and universal rights to goods and services. They point out, for example, that even impeccable liberty rights with well-defined counterpart obligations — a right not to be tortured, a right not to be raped — cannot be secured without complex institutions which will adjudicate cases and enforce rights. Liberty rights and their corresponding obligations may need police, courts, and many other forms of accountability if they are to be enforced; institutions of enforcement too have to distribute obligations for specific aspects of enforcement according to one or another scheme. So liberty rights too are amorphous until one or another institutional scheme has been established, which determines who bears the counterpart obligations.

However, there are deeper discrepancies between liberty rights and rights to goods and services than this attempt to yoke them allows. To be sure, the *enforcement* of liberty rights, or rather of their corresponding obligations, needs

5. An early and strongly argued version of the query can be found in Henry Shue, *Basic Rights: Subsistence, Affluence and U.S. Foreign Policy* (Princeton, New Jersey: Princeton University Press, 1980).

institutions. This is hardly news. However, the correspondence of universal liberty rights to universal obligations is relatively well-defined even when institutions are missing or weak. For example, a violation of a right not to be raped or of a right not to be tortured may be clear enough, and the perpetrator may even be identifiable, even when institutions for enforcement are lamentably weak. But the correspondence of universal rights to goods and services to obligations to *provide or deliver* remains entirely amorphous when institutions are missing or weak. Somebody who receives no maternity care may no doubt *assert* that her rights have been violated. But unless obligations to deliver that care have been established and distributed, she will not know where to press her claim, and it will be systematically obscure whether there is any perpetrator, or who has neglected or violated her rights.

Rights to goods and services can be thought of only in the hazy way which the rhetoric of rights favours and allows until they are at least partly institutionalized. It may be possible to state *what* ought to be provided or delivered, but it will be impossible to state *who* ought to do the providing or delivering. *Who* can be called to account when deliveries are botched, or nothing is delivered, unless there are established institutions and well-defined special relationships? Rights to goods and services are easy to proclaim, but until there are effective institutions their proclamation may seem bitter mockery to those who most need them.

Liberty rights, however, are different because far more is determined even when institutions are missing or weak: as soon as it is possible to state what ought to be provided — non-interference — it will also be possible to state who ought to provide: everyone and all institutions ought to do so. Institutions come into the picture subsequently for purposes of enforcement. By contrast, when we discuss obligations, of whatever sort, we immediately have to consider *whose* obligations we have in mind and so will define *against whom* rights-holders may lodge their claims.

3. Women's Rights

How does this matter for women, and for women's rights? A small, and once again embarrassingly commonplace, reminder may be helpful here. In speaking of women's rights, most people have meant to speak of rights that men have, which women should have as well. They have not generally meant to speak of any distinctive rights which women should have and men should not. The exception — not without controversy or importance — lies in rights that are quite specifically connected to differences of sex and reproduction. Rights to maternity services would properly be women's rights and not men's. But men too may have rights not be raped, as women too may have rights to vote and rights of association.

However, it is evident that the sorts of rights to goods and services on which women and men may rely most frequently can often differ. For example, as long as women still carry more of the real work of caring for true dependants (children, those who are ill, the elderly) and as long as they have fewer resources with which to do so, they will need rights to financial support and to relevant social services more often. Equally, as long as a disproportionate amount of juvenile crime is committed by boys and young men, their need for rights of due process and for other relevant social services will be greater than that of girls and women of like age. However, such differences in (average) situation do not show that women's rights should differ from men's rights outside the areas of maternity care and the like. It is not surprising that for most of its history the women's movement has been a movement that claimed for women the *same* rights as were claimed for men — from rights to hold property, to the franchise, to rights to enter all lines of employment.

Yet from the 1980s parts of the women's movement took quite another turn. Many influential feminists stressed not the similarities of men and women, and their entitlement to the same rights, but their differences, opening the door to the thought that their ethical claims might differ. Yet surprisingly, the emphasis on differences has not, on the whole, been used to develop alternative accounts of the rights of women. One reason for this has been that those who affirm the ways in which women are different from men also often stress that they differ in their moral categories or 'voice'.[6] The

way was open not for a traditional feminist claim that women have been denied their due rights, or even for a revisionary claim that they should have some alternative set of rights, but for a more radical claim that any focus on justice — whether centred on obligations or on rights — uses a strident and inappropriate ethical register, and may even be seen as an aspect of the oppression rather than the liberation of women. An increasing amount of radical feminist writing of the 80s and 90s criticized concern with justice, hence with rights, as an abstract, adversarial, 'male' concern, and put forward conceptions of ethical life that centre on certain 'female' virtues of care and concern, of responsibility and affiliation. Some of this writing suggested that we must choose between these ethical voices or stances; that we must choose between justice (and with it obligations and rights) and care and concern; in short, that justice and the virtues are the focus of antagonistic rather than of complementary visions of human life.[7]

The worry that we will be forced to this painful choice has a number of sources. One is a lurking belief (mentioned earlier), that just as all rights need corresponding obligations, so all obligations need corresponding rights. If all obligations were the counterparts of rights, then it seems that no discussion of obligations *could* have anything to say about the virtues, about care and concern and the other matters which so many feminists, and so many virtue ethicists, have properly insisted are ethically important: for these can surely not be claimed as matters of right.

But why should one look at things in this way? While there may be many obligations to which rights correspond, why should there not be other significant obligations to which no rights correspond? The traditional distinction between *perfect* or *complete* obligations with counterpart rights, and *imperfect* or *incomplete* obligations without counterpart rights of any sort reminds us that many historically important discussions of human obligations have not restricted themselves to the domain of obligations to which rights are

6. See in particular Carol Gilligan's *In a Different Voice: Psychological Theory and Women's Dependence* (Cambridge, Mass.: Harvard University Press, 1982), 2nd edition 1983.

7. An enormous literature on 'the ethics of care' and related virtues appeared in the wake of Gilligan's book. For reasons for thinking that justice and virtue are complementary rather than antagonistic see Onora O'Neill, *Towards Justice and Virtue: A Constructive Account of Practical Reasoning* (Cambridge University Press, 1996).

supposed to correspond.[8] There may, for example, be obligations to show others care and concern whose recipients are not specified, and which are to be met by showing *some* others *some* appropriate form of care and concern. Such obligations could not be a matter of providing all possible care and concern to all others, which is impossible. They are inevitably selective. If on the other hand, like so much writing on justice, we treat rights as the basic ethical category, then obligations without rights may simply be overlooked, and it may seem that all virtues must be wholly optional excellences.[9]

However, the fact that obligations with rights may not be the whole story does not mean that they are unimportant, or specifically that they are unimportant for women. To neglect obligations with corollary rights in a discussion of women's issues is no mere oversight. In a world in which women, like men, act and are acted on by the multiple complex institutions and systems of institutions, and by many distant strangers, a pretence that their significant ethical relations are entirely face-to-face, entirely a matter of virtuous relationships, of personal attachments and commitments, of care and concern, and never a matter of required action, of obligations or of rights, is both illusory and dangerous.

The danger is perhaps readily overlooked because the vision of women as using a distinct ethical 'voice' or register, which stresses care rather than justice, virtues rather than rights, is coupled with a (sometimes tacit) assumption that women still, at any rate more than men, lead their lives in a 'private' sphere whose central ethical categories are appropriately those of virtue rather than of justice. This assumption is false for two distinct reasons. First, it is straightforwardly false of many women, particularly in the more developed world, that many, let alone all, aspects of their lives are lived in anything that could be called a private sphere. Labour-force participation rates, voting patterns and dependence on publicly provided support systems all show that women's lives are no longer ensconced, either cosily or uncomfortably, in any private domain. The second reason why the assumption that women's lives are not insulated from the public sphere is false is that *no* supposedly private sphere is wholly insulated from the impact of public forces and activities. Economic, political and social forces shape and often grind all private spheres. Economic forces sustain or impoverish families and communities; political realities destroy or enable intimate and personal relationships. This is as true of undeveloped as of developed societies. The only worlds in which it may not have been true are those archaic (or at any rate obsolescent) worlds, which lack any clear distinction between public and private domains — the worlds of true *Gemeinschaft* (primitive community). In the worlds in which we now live women may have somewhat different lives from men, but often the difference is simply that they have more sustained real responsibility for real dependants — for children, for the seriously ill, for the elderly — although they remain economically and socially less powerful.[10] In such worlds it is mere fantasy to think that a private sphere provides a protective retreat which makes ordinary, mundane rights redundant.

4. Real Patriarchy?

Yet the image of a sheltered space within which domestic and personal life can be insulated from the pressures of the public domain, and the virtues can flourish, has deep appeal. Perhaps its appeal has increased as the economic, social, political and cultural forces which bear on our lives are increasingly globalized. If we imagine a world in which this sheltered space is peculiarly the domain of women, in which men shelter women from the ravages of the public domain, we are drawn less to the image of *Gemeinschaft* than to the image of *Real Patriarchy*.

The proponents of women's distinctive ethical voice are not, of course, keen on patriarchy of any sort. Yet only patriarchy offers women any

---

8. For an account of traditional, especially early modern, views on justice and virtue that brings out these points see J.B. Schneewind, 'The Misfortunes of Virtue', *Ethics*, vol. 101 (1990), pp. 42–63.

9. In fact there is no reason to expect that all virtues will be of one kind. Some might be a matter of requirement, even if not owed either to all or to some, hence without counterpart rights. Other virtues might be those of certain roles, relationships or traditions. Yet others might be entirely optional, hence in no way obligatory, *a fortiori* not claimable as a matter of right.

10. For an account of women's lives and especially of mothering which acknowledges these stark realities, see Sara Ruddick, *Maternal Thinking: Towards a Politics of Peace* (Boston, Mass.: Beacon Press, 1987).

prospect of the very insulation from public forces whose attractions seem so persistent to some of those who over-emphasize the distinctiveness of women's moral voice and vision, and who aspire to fit all of morality into an ethic of care. Real patriarchy should at least then be taken seriously, if only because real patriarchs have, or at least had, real obligations, which could provide something worth having — if at a cost. However, all that remains of patriarchy (at least in the developed world) are remnants of patriarchal sentiment and rhetoric without much in the way of patriarchal obligations. The evidence that there isn't much real patriarchy around in the developed world can be readily assembled by any woman who demands that her male relatives shoulder the obligations of patriarchy, for example by providing her with a suitable husband or life-long subsistence, or by forcing an erring husband back onto the straight and narrow. Since these fruits of real patriarchy are rarely on offer, the private sphere is unlikely to offer women the securities that supposedly make justice dispensable. Even those who cling to the rhetoric of patriarchy do not now often care to shoulder its obligations; if they try to, they are likely to find that the powers and protected spaces by which and in which those obligations could be discharged are no longer available. Would-be patriarchs are almost bound to be frustrated; and probably a bit touchy. Even the remnant patriarchs who survive in less developed corners of the world are increasingly powerless to protect women under their sway from larger economic, political and social forces; soon they too may find themselves with too little power to fulfil what they take to be the obligations of patriarchy.

Yet it surely cannot be a matter for serious regret that there are now no well-insulated private spheres, that real patriarchy is no longer an option, and hence that there is nowhere for women to cultivate their gardens and the virtues without concerning themselves with the obligations and rights of justice. If the remnant patriarchs are impotent, the rights and above all the obligations of the public domain can hardly be irrelevant to women; and if they are powerful, but unaccountably so, they will present other dangers, and once again the rights and above all the obligations of the public domain can hardly be irrelevant to women. In either case, reasons for thinking that rights are irrelevant to women or that men and women should have fundamentally different sets of rights are lacking.

If women's rights are not redundant in our world, we need to ask what it would be to take them seriously. I have argued that taking them seriously is pre-eminently a matter of taking the obligations that are their counterparts seriously. Since rights may be of various sorts, so too may obligations. The obligations that correspond to liberty rights fall on all, and so on women as much as on men, on men as much as on women. By contrast some of the obligations which correspond to rights to goods and services remain amorphous until one or another institutional scheme is established. What matters for women is that the allocation of those obligations to provide goods and services should itself take account of the real resources and responsibilities, of the real capabilities and vulnerabilities, of those who are to bear the obligations. As long as some people, and today it is often (but by no means always) women, and especially poor women in poor economies, have fewer resources and carry higher burdens of others' dependence, as long as they are vulnerable in ways in which others are not, a case may be made for allocations of obligations which fall more on those who have more resources or carry lower burdens of others' dependence and consequently have greater capabilities. This, however, is not a case for differential rights for women, except in the area of maternity services and the like. It is a case for allocations of obligations to deliver goods and services that take account of the realities of different sorts of lives.[11]

11. See 'Justice, Gender and International Boundaries', in *British Journal of Political Science*, vol. 20 (1990), pp. 439–59.

DOLORES DOOLEY

(1940–   )

GENDERED CITIZENSHIP IN THE IRISH CONSTITUTION (1998)

[The question of difference, especially those differences between men and women, has been fundamental to recent feminist theorizing. Given the history of discrimination against women, can or should we argue from those differences for special treatment? Are differences innate or culturally constructed? If we acknowledge difference, can we argue for equal rights, and, if so, on what basis? In this article, Dolores Dooley argues that citizenship, rather than gender identity, should be the grounds for full equality before the law, a position that has widespread potential repercussions for reproductive rights. (See also Vol. v, section 'Politics, 1500–2000', especially the subsections by Alpha Connelly, 'The Law and Private Life in the Republic of Ireland', and Frances Gardiner, 'The Women's Movement and Women Politicians in the Republic 1980–2000'.) From: *Ireland's Evolving Constitution, 1937–97: Collected Essays*, eds Tim Murphy and Patrick Twomey (Oxford: Hart Publishing, 1998). Footnotes are by the author.]

Citizenship is alive and well in Ireland today as it has seldom been since the early twentieth century suffragettes[1] or even earlier since 1825 when a radical Irish text on gendered citizenship was published, *Appeal of One Half the Human Race*.[2] The text, authored by the Cork political economist and feminist philosopher of the British Co-operative Movement, William Thompson (1775–1833), is a detailed discussion of the benefits of political rights in citizenship. The *Appeal* was damning in its indictment of women's categorical exclusion from citizenship in James Mill's treatise, *On Government,* published first in 1819.[3] But the *Appeal* speaks to modern concerns

about citizenship in unravelling the concept of political citizenship to show how skills of self-government and self-respect are best developed by exercising full rights of democratic participation. To the extent that women's citizenship became an issue, men, holding the power in institutions, were necessarily implicated. The text has been largely invisible in Irish history.

Today there is a resurgence of writing on the concept of citizenship. Political theorists are aware that this renewed interest in citizenship is filtering down to grass-roots community projects where there is a growing awareness of a need to discover or define social and political identity. Multicultural groups within nation states, minority groups (religious, cultural, sexual), women and the economically oppressed question whether their citizenship has any meaning or power which might improve the quality of their lives.[4] Irish citizens have begun envisaging a European citizen identity that can both integrate and expand their sense of political participation.

In Western Europe the increasing economic, legal and political integration of the European Community is beginning to challenge national sovereignty and citizenship . . . it is also beginning to involve the creation of a new trans-national European level and sphere of citizens' rights, institutions and community.[5]

A scepticism among socially marginalised groups voices the suspicion that their citizenship is somehow subordinate to citizens of dominant social groups within Irish society.[6] Against this

---

1. Louise Ryan, *Irish Feminism and the Vote* (Dublin: Folens, 1996), p. 15.
2. The full title of William Thompson's text is *Appeal of one Half the Human Race, Women, against the Pretensions of the Other Half, Men, to Retain them in Political and thence in Civil and Domestic Slavery*. This text is abbreviated as *Appeal*. In an introductory letter in this text, William Thompson acknowledges the collaboration of Mrs Anna Doyle Wheeler from County Tipperary. She is the muse, the source of a woman's experience to clarify the arguments for women's inclusion in citizenship. William Thompson, *Appeal [1825]*, ed. Dolores Dooley (Cork: Cork University Press, 1997, see Vol. v, pp. 63–4).
3. James Mill, *An Essay On Government* (Cambridge: Cambridge University Press, 1937).

4. Will Kymlicka and Wayne Norman, 'Return of the Citizen: A Survey of Recent Work on Citizenship Theory', *Ethics*, vol. 104 (January 1994), pp. 352–81. See further for radical reconceptualisations of citizenship Paul Barry Clarke, *Deep Citizenship* (London, Pluto Press, 1996); Anne Phillips, *Engendering Democracy* (Cambridge: Polity Press, 1991); Susan Moller Okin, *Women in Western Political Thought* (Princeton: Princeton University Press, 1979), and Carole Pateman's now classical studies of social contract theory in *The Sexual Contract* (Cambridge: Polity Press, 1988) and *The Disorder of Women* (Cambridge: Polity Press, 1989).
5. Maurice Roche, *Rethinking Citizenship* (Cambridge: Polity Press, 1992), p. 1.
6. See Sean J. Healy and Brigid Reynolds, *Ireland Today* (Dublin: Justice Office of the Conference of Major Religious Superiors, 1985). See also Gerry Whyte, 'Marginalised Groups Deserve Constitutional Protection', in the *Irish Times*, 8 July 1996.

backdrop of history and current events, a review of the Constitutions of 1922 and 1937 as they pertain to women is overdue. Women's citizenship, as it is ideologically framed in the Constitution, is a case study of gender-differentiated and 'second-class citizenship'.[7] The Constitution of 1937 was a retrograde step from the non-gendered document of 1922. The question is whether women today can any longer give credence to the Constitutional 'social contract' endorsed in 1937.

Free State Constitution: 1922

Liberal politics seems to have won the day when, in Article 3 of the Irish Free State Constitution of 1922, the following rights were conceded to women: to vote, to hold office on equal terms with men and to enjoy all the privileges of such citizenship. Unlike the successor Constitution of 1937, the Constitution of 1922 gives no code of behaviour for women in living out their citizenship. Nevertheless, if the Constitution of 1922 seemed distinctly liberal towards women's political participation, this constitutional guarantee was almost immediately undermined by subsequent legislation that effectively denied a full political identity to Irish women. By 1937, women's political, economic, and reproductive rights had been so severely curtailed that women were explicitly barred from claiming for themselves a public identity.[8]

Gendered legislation between 1922 and 1937 prepared the way for the ideology of woman that would pervade the new Constitution. The Civil Service Act of 1924 restricted civil service examinations according to sex. While the Act was amended in 1925, the Civil Service (Amendment) Act still allowed the government to limit examinations for positions in the Civil Service on the basis of sex. During the Civil service debate, the fact that determined the decision was that women married.[9] Given a presumption that women would leave work on marriage, positions appropriate to women and not wasteful of too much training time would be those of typists, stenographers and other lower grades in the Civil Service.[10] The operative assumption was that the highest Civil Service positions would be held by men. Accordingly, even though not all women would, in fact, marry, discrimination along the lines of sex was the admitted and unapologetic practice. The sanctity and indissolubility of marriage was reinforced, civil divorce being ruled out by a Dáil motion of 1925.

The Juries Bill 1927 was another legal marker that the 1922 Constitution's generous spirit of equality was under review. Concessions of equality might not guarantee the behaviour from citizens that is considered appropriate or necessary to achieve the social ideals and the common good of the State. The law on jury service was convoluted but virtually excluded women from jury service since only citizens who were rate-payers or property owners could serve. Women had to apply for jury service. They would not be automatically invited.

Feminists saw the Juries Bill as discriminatory and subtly excluding women from the public forum. They were not far off the mark of the intent. In the Juries Bill debate, the Minister for Justice, Kevin O'Higgins, stated, as if a matter of eternal truth: 'It is the normal and natural function of women to have children. It still is the normal and natural function of women to have charge of households.'[11] The statement makes transparent the government's increasing reliance on a Natural Law philosophy which shows unwarranted confidence in reading from nature and the voice of inner reason what is 'normal and natural' and, by implication, what is moral. This Natural Law philosophy becomes more overt in the constitutional Articles discussed below. O'Higgins defended himself and the Irish

---

7. Iris Marion Young, 'Polity and Group Difference: A Critique of the Ideal of Universal Citizenship', *Ethics*, vol. 99, no. 2 (January 1989), pp. 250–74. Young defends the concept of 'differentiated citizenship' as the best way to realize the inclusion, empowering and participation of everyone in full citizenship. My own analysis here agrees with her general point but argues that the Constitution of a State is not the place for congealing citizenship debates.

8. Maryann Valiulis, 'Power, Gender, and Identity in the Irish Free State', in *Irish Women's Voices Past and Present*, eds Joan Hoff and Moureen Coulter, a publication of the *Journal of Women's History*, vol. 6, no. 4/vol. 7, no. 1 (Blooomington: Indiana University Press, 1995). pp. 117–36. See in this same volume, Mary E. Daly, 'Women in the Irish Free State, 1922–39: The Interaction between Economics and Ideology', pp. 99–116. Daly has an alternative reading of the 1937 Constitution as it pertains to women than that offered in this essay.

9. Valiulis, 'Power, Gender and Identity', p. 123.

10. As documented in ibid., *Seanad* Debates, 17 Dec. 1925, vol. 6, cols 247–8, and *Dáil* Debates, 18 Nov. 1925, vol. 13, col. 504.

11. *Dáil* Debates, 23 Feb. 1927, vol. 18, col. 766, as cited in Valiulis (1995), p. 134.

Government with unblushing paternalism for the provisions on Jury service:

> [we] . . . are preventing people getting something which they pretend they want, and which would not be good for them . . . In this matter I am really the champion of women in the State, but I never expect to get any gratitude for that.[12]

It was not until 1975 in *De Burca and Anderson v. Attorney General*[13] that women were called to give service using the same criteria as applied to men but allowing opportunities for either sex to apply for exemption.[14]

By the early 1930s the legal, philosophical and religious foundations were firmly in place for the ideology of women's citizenship that appears in the Constitution of 1937. A profoundly relevant yet predictable fact which makes one sceptical of the shared and equal 'contractual character' of the Irish Constitution is that women had no part in framing Bunreacht na hÈireann. Not one woman took part in drafting it.[15] The plebiscite that approved the Irish Constitution on 1 July, 1937 'agreed' to a number of rules and ideals contained in its Articles: rules which include the structures and offices of the emerging Government, stipulations defining the terms of citizenship and ideals spelling out goals to promote a State of equal civil freedom among Irish citizens. The margin of win was narrow enough: 685,105 votes to 526,945. The contract was conceptualised and written, in the main, by the then Head of State, Eamon de Valera, and Roman Catholic churchmen, most notably John Charles McQuaid and the Jesuit Edward Cahill.[16]

The shapers of the Constitution created a document that embodied the aspirations, ideals and social values of a Roman Catholic State. It was a constitution that pleased the Vatican.

Women and the social contract of 1937

The Constitution of 1937 is complex in its ideological rendering of woman's identity, her proper nature and moral responsibilities to promote the stability of the Irish State. The evolution of unenumerated rights in the Constitution has enabled women to progress in spite of the Articles analysed in this essay. Contemporary feminist theorising would have a field day with this Constitution. It embodies in a few explicit articles the central disputed concepts in feminist theory: the false universal 'woman', the public-private divide, family, mothering, and reproductive rights for women. Similarly noted is a radical asymmetry in only stipulating role assignments for women. The provision of particulars defining women's role as citizen has no equivalent for male citizens though there are implications for men in the provisions about women. An explanation of relevant articles on marriage, family and reproduction gives a glimpse of aspirations for women's identity and duties that are still in place though vigorously under re-assessment by Irish women.

Legal and 'thick' citizenship

Article 9.1.3 in the 1937 Constitution ensures that 'no person may be excluded from Irish nationality and citizenship by reason of the sex of such person'. What is conceded in Article 9.1.3 is the *legal status* of citizenship in the particular political community of the Irish State. This legal entitlement should be differentiated from citizenship-as-desirable-activity or 'thick citizenship', where what is debated is the complex normative view of what is meant by 'good citizenship'.[17] The normative view of 'good citizen' remains deeply debated in political theory today. It is no less important that the understanding of 'good woman citizen' in the Irish Constitution needs to be seriously contested.

12. *Seanad* Debates, 30 Mar. 1927, vol. 8, col. 691, as cited in Valiulis (1995), p. 135.

13. [1976] IR 38.

14. This concern about taking women from their homes to serve on juries was not solely an Irish one. For the United States debate on the issue of jury duty for women, see Susan Moller Okin, *Women in Western Political Thought* (Princeton: Princeton University Press, 1979), pp. 260–4.

15. Dr Yvonne Scannell, 'The Constitution and the Role of Women', in Brian Farrell (ed.), *De Valera's Constitution and Ours* (Dublin: Gill and Macmillan, 1988), p. 123. See also Alpha Connelly, 'The Constitution', in *Gender and the Law in Ireland*, ed. Alpha Connelly (Dublin: Oak Tree Press, 1993), pp. 4–27.

16. Dermot Keogh, *Ireland and the Vatican, 1922–1960* (Cork: Cork University Press, 1995), especially pp. 132–40. See also by the same author, 'Church, State and Society', in *De Valera's Constitution and Ours*, ed. Brian Farrell (Dublin: Gill and Macmillan, 1988), pp. 103–22.

17. The distinction is clarified and expanded in Will Kymlicka and Wm Norman, 'Return of the Citizen'.

The equality of citizenship conferred in Article 40.1 of the Irish Constitution anticipates what looks like a surprisingly modern and feminist view of human persons as *equal but different*.

> All citizens shall, as human persons, be held equal before the law. This shall not be held to mean that the State shall not in its enactments have due regard to differences of capacity, physical and moral, and of social function.

Article 40.1 combines the values of equality and affirmation of differences, an apparent move away from false universals of 'human citizens' where 'human' reads male. However, this liberality is only apparent. We are handed the proverbial two-edged sword. To know how sharp the sword might be one needs to ask what understanding of human persons supports the social contract ideal of equality with difference contained in article 40.1.

Feminist theorists are divided in their analysis of contract theories.[18] Some are sharply critical, in that the traditional models of such theory are deeply patriarchal, in assuming the universal male as norm: the citizen is the worker in the public domain, the bread-winner, the politician and lawmaker and the economic head of households. Other feminists see greater potential in properly analysed contract theory especially views in sympathy with the ideas of the German philosopher Immanuel Kant, who see a conception of human worth in citizen identity as non-negotiable.[19] The important insight in Kant's concept of person is that people have intrinsic, non-instrumental value. Human persons should never be treated as means but always as ends in themselves. Respecting the worth of human persons cannot be essentially derivative on the functions they perform towards servicing the State or its institutions. If a concept of respect for human persons is not to be exploitative and is to value persons for their intrinsic worth, such

respect needs to acknowledge the liberty of persons to explore, to learn and to choose their own defined interests and central concerns. The imaging of women in the Irish Constitution, the identity, ideals and moral norms given to women betrays an underlying functionalist mode of thought which does not respect women for their choices of identity for themselves. Rather, the underlying instrumentalist philosophy of person permits rationalisations of inequality using the rhetoric of equality. A functionalist conceptualisation of women underlies the apparently benign affirmation of her 'differences'. Article 40.1 logically prepares the reader for the relevant sections defining woman's differences in her physical and moral capacities and her attributed social functions. The multiple *differences* of woman are ones she executes with superior skill within the presumed private sphere of the family. Her differences of reproductive capacity and domestic nurturing of others distinguish her by sex; such differences make her *other* and morally more responsible than men for promoting the prominent ideals of the State: the common good, public order and morality. The implications are negative for men who would see in their own identity qualities of nurturing, parenting and fathering. Nowhere in the Irish Constitution is parenting in the plural mentioned. Fathering is outside the conceptual framework of Natural Law's deliverances for women.

Family: Defining Woman's Sphere

It is impossible to overstate the importance of the family as institution within the Constitution. Correlated with this pre-eminence of family, is woman's prominent positioning within this social unit. Article 41.1.1 defines the family in the following terms:

> The State recognises the Family as the natural primary and fundamental unit group of Society, and as a moral institution possessing inalienable and imprescriptible rights, antecedent and superior to all positive law.

Natural law theory is again implicit here in seeing family as *natural* and *fundamental* and as a *moral institution*. The natural is deemed moral. The

18. See, for example, S. Mullally, 'Equality Guarantees in Irish Constitutional Law: The Myth of Constitutionalism and the "Neutral" State', in *Ireland's Evolving Constitution*, eds Tim Murphy and Patrick Twomey (Oxford: Hart Publishing, 1998), pp. 147–62.
19. Jean Hampton, 'Feminist Contractarianism', in *A Mind of One's Own*, eds Louise M. Antony and Charlotte Witt (Boulder, Colorado: Westview Press, 1993), pp. 227–55.

strength of commitment to the normal conceptualisation of family and the moral role it is to
play is evident in being given imprescriptible
rights, *antecedent and superior to all positive law*. It
is the only correct understanding of family, as
designed according to laws of nature. Thus, the
implied description of this *natural* moral unit was
clearly intended to be that of legalised heterosexual marriages. Today these constricting terms
of reference for the concept of family would be
greatly contested. Many look for inclusion under
the concept of family the reality of single parent
families (men or women) who never married, or
who are now separated, the partnerships of gay
or lesbian couples who choose means to have
children which they then parent. Neither
women's nor men's roles as citizen was ever
envisaged in such *unnatural* units. The
unnaturalness of such alternative family compositions made the experience of social ostracisa-
tion and deviance a painful reality for persons
with sexual orientations other than the heterosexual. Article 41.1.2 further emphasises the
naturally and properly ordained parameters of
family: 'The State, therefore, guarantees to
protect the Family in its constitution and
authority, as the necessary basis of social order
and as indispensable to the welfare of the Nation
and State.'

It is the home which harbours the family
woman's designated *proper* and *natural* place. An
uncritical acceptance of Natural Law analyses
and the certainty of insights derived from that
philosophy determines the definitions and moral
boundaries of family.[20] Conclusions are suited to
the concern with control and sexual order in the
ethos of the Constitution. With Article 41.2.1
there is little ambiguity about the ideal place for
woman to live and develop her citizen identity:
'In particular, the State recognises that by her life
within the home, woman gives to the State a
support without which the common good cannot
be achieved.'

In this article, the Constitution adopts most
explicitly a dualism of private and public spheres
with women's citizenship mandated for the realm
of domestic management, nurturing, education
of young and a plethora of complex and

demanding tasks. Woman's *life* is in her home and
a strong implication can be drawn that this is
where her primary citizen commitments should
be contained. If the reality of women working
caused distress to the politicians and husbands in
early Ireland, the 1937 Constitution tries to
consolidate an ideal for women to approximate.
The life given to important realities of home and
family may not be the choice of some women.
Where is their diversity valued in the universalis-
ing thrust of the reference to *woman*? Are these
diverse women who choose not to marry, not to
mother, either legitimated or valued under the
normative simplicity in the concept *woman*?

In a striking *non sequitur*, Article 41.2.2 conflates a false universal 'woman' with the role of
mother: 'The State shall, therefore, endeavour to
ensure that mothers shall not be obliged by
economic necessity to engage in labour to the
neglect of their duties in the home.' This is the
strongest statement of expectations that women
will give their full energies in fulfilling duties in
the home. It is seldom detailed what those duties
are though we are supposed to assume they are
all, as duties, essential and praiseworthy.
However, it is important to remember that one
fundamental duty of women, often clarified by
tradition in the Roman Catholic Church is
women's *sexual duty*: making herself available for
sexual relations virtually on demand. The
reasoning is that this is inherent in the *constitution
and authority of marriage*. It is a sexual imperative
for women to help prevent male extra-marital
liaisons.

While feminist theory critiques the implications of women's economic dependence on men
so defended by this Article, many women home-
makers resent feminism's apparent under-
valuing of the life of women in the home. It is a
fair reminder of the need for vigilance in feminist
theory so as to avoid undermining the importance of diversity of women's choice. A
sympathetic reading of the Irish Constitution
might see these Articles about women's duties in
the home as implying that the private sphere has
been validated and positively valued as women's
contribution to the body politic. This reading has
legitimacy within limits. If the private sphere of
domestic management, human nurturing and
educational work is valued, this is progressive.
But the role of home-maker is exclusive and

20. See Desmond M. Clarke, *Church and State* (Cork: Cork University
Press, 1984), especially chapter 2, 'Natural Law'.

defining of woman's citizen role. It includes praise but excludes provisions for her to be economically independent. The defining of woman's role in the home constitutionally endorses her radical dependency on the bread-winner who traditionally has been male. Two points need to be made to indicate that article 41.2.2 was taken seriously by State legislators. Because work outside the home for married women was regarded as a selfish distraction from home duties, the Civil Service Regulation Act, 1956 provided that women employed in the civil service, other than those employed in certain excluded non-pensionable posts, were required to resign on marriage.[21] If economic indepen-dence of women was valued, the State would have put money forward as economic endow-ments — indeed inducements — to continue the valued work in the home. But economic independence for women permits latent power to lose its grip. The power and the ultimate family *authority* is often vested in the income earner.[22] One is left with little evidence to believe the Government was committed to providing for economic independence for women, even by modest domestic endowment.

Marriage and the sexual contract

William Thompson and Anna Wheeler could have enlightened the prelates who accompanied Eamon de Valera to the Vatican and expanded their imaginations about lived marriages. Marriage is depicted in the *Appeal* of 1825 as little more than an opportunity for unrestrained exercise of power by husbands over women. Clearly the benign and flourishing relationships of marriage were evident but the opportunity for power in the marriage institution was little discussed, though clearly experienced, in 1937. Well-wrought articles on marriage consolidated its legal indissolubility for almost sixty years to come. Article 41.3.1 gives the full backing of the State's institutions to ensure family solidarity: 'The State pledges itself to guard with special care the institution of Marriage, on which the Family is founded, and to protect it against attack.'

The military metaphor of *attack* suggests that the Irish Government envisaged an onslaught of paganism from foreign shores reminiscent of the days of Brehon laws when women cohabited with more than one man. The pledge of special care is coupled with a legal ultimatum that would leave little discretion to subsequent judiciaries to alter the status of marriage. In Article 41.3.2 we read, *No law shall be enacted providing for the grant of a dissolution of marriage.* The shapers of family and marriage ideology in the Constitution either failed to recognise the extent to which women's dependence and submission are encapsulated in the institution of marriage or, having recognised it, assume that this dependence and submission are natural and so morally obligatory. The State has, for long, refused to accept evidence which challenges the adequacy of their marriage proposals, the fact that marriage relationships irretrievably break down. If they do acknowledge this reality and still hold firm to the indissolubility of marriage then the metaphysical conception of idealised marriage exercises a tyranny over citizens' opportunities to build new relationships.

Increasing public awareness of domestic violence and family sexual abuse cannot be dismissed; it is a painful and not infrequent dimension of married, family life, especially for women whose economic dependency is a major factor in restraining them from possible exits. The economically powerless home-maker was for years denied access to free legal aid even though they were faithfully fulfilling the Constitutional duties of upholding the stability of the State.

The articles on family and marriage are clearly concessions to the teachings of social encyclicals of the Catholic Church. The universal abstrac-tions of marriage and family are typical of metaphysical abstractions which one does not test against the concrete realities of people's lives. Women's voices have brought the metaphysics of these ideals down to earth with stories of lived realities within these rarefied social institutions.[23]

21. Yvonne Scannell, 'The Constitution and the Role of Women' (1988), p. 126.
22. See Gisela Bock and Susan James (eds), *Beyond Equality & Difference: Citizenship, Feminist Politics and Female Subjectivity* (London: Routledge, 1992).
23. Linda Connolly, 'The Women's Movement in Ireland 1970–1995: a Social Movement's Analysis', *Irish Journal of Feminist Studies*, vol. 1, no. 1 (March 1996), pp. 43–77.

The articles on family and marriage are symptomatic of a State that has been fearful of the uncontrollable power that might be unleashed if the concession of sexual equality of citizenship were realised in action. Apprehensions of a *liberalism of fear* are not wide of the mark. The democratic order is vulnerable to the subversive dynamic of equality and the Irish Constitution's affirmation of woman's difference, her designation as sexual *other* in the private sphere is:

> an institutional fixation of sexual difference in the hierarchical marriage . . . to protect democratic society against an understanding of equality that would break down all distinctions and meaningful differences . . . The task at hand is to construe a power that will secure the unity of marriage, as well as the tranquillity of civil society, against the adverse consequences of a wife's independence of will . . . and to ensure the sexual fidelity of a wife.[24]

A divorce referendum in 1986 was defeated by almost 66% of the electorate. In 1996 a referendum to change the Constitution and allow the introduction of legislation for divorce was passed but only barely. Contrary to the growing data on marriage breakdown, the specifically religious ideal of the Constitution, mandating permanence in marriage, seems still to be upheld by many citizens, though clearly for a diversity of complex reasons. Not the least of these are adherence to one's Church beliefs on marriage *and* concern about the distribution of property in the event of divorce.

Reproduction

No power of women has been more protected and constrained in Ireland than her capacity for reproduction. Choosing not to be a mother has never been a legitimate option under the cultural ideology of the Irish State. The containment of women's sexuality has been the single obsession of the Roman Catholic Church and successive Irish governments who refused to implement conditions for diverse women to have liberty of choice about reproduction.[25] Under the Criminal Law (Amendment) Act, 1935, it was a criminal offence for any person to sell or to import for sale any contraceptive. It was 1974 in *McGee v. Attorney General*[26] before the legal sale and use of contraceptives was permitted, and even then within the context of *bona fide* marriage relationships.

The Catholic Church has always taught that voluntary sterilisation of reproductive capacities is intrinsically wrong. Sterilisation is seen as the antithesis of the obligations within marriage to populate the State with new citizens or to abstain from sexual intercourse. This moral prohibition on sterilisation was clearly evident until the 1980s; there were no more than two hospitals in the State which rather freely provided female sterilisation. The control was effectively implemented through the religious control of hospitals in the State. Even public-run hospitals were effectively governed by the Catholic ethos prohibiting sterilisation. As a result, if a woman desired a tubal ligation because a further pregnancy was either undesired or even risky to health, it was either flatly refused or a request had to be put by the consultant gynaecologist before an established ethics committee to hear the case. Because of the red tape, the practice sometimes chosen was to recommend hysterectomy for women for contraceptive purposes. In giving reasons, one can always cite numerous reasons for hysterectomies and the contraceptive motivations need never be publicised.

Ethics committees with ex-officio membership of Catholic and Protestant clergymen were standard for consultation on this issue. It was a moral tribunal to ensure as much as possible that the religious ethos would be a force in determining women's decisions about reproduction. The annoyance of medical consultants about the intrusion into their doctor-patient relationships has altered this situation to a great extent. There is an anomaly in the Irish State that proportionately many more men than women have been sterilised. The explanation is greatly in the institutional structures: women need to be in-patients in hospitals governed often by a denominational

24. Ursula Vogel, 'Marriage and the Boundaries of Citizenship', in *The Condition of Citizenship*, ed. Bart van Steenbergen (London: Sage Publications, 1994), p. 84.

25. See Dolores Dooley, 'Expanding an Island Ethic', in *Ireland: Towards a Sense of Place*, ed. Joseph Lee (Cork: Cork University Press, 1985), pp. 47–65.

26. [1974] IR 284.

ethos; men can be sterilised as an out-patient procedure in family planning clinics after due counselling and necessary partner consent. Such constraints on reproductive choice are consistent with women's mandates in the Constitution. Such constraints are also partial evidence for my interpretation that fear of women's liberty, equality and sexuality has been an almost obsessive concern of the Irish State and has led to the adoption of severely controlling practices regarding women's reproductive choices.

Abortion has been an ethical hornets' nest for Irish citizens. The limits of patience in deliberative democracy have been sorely tested with emotive rhetoric and damning judgments about fascism surfacing on various sides of the debate.[27] This moral question has virtually dominated social, ethical debate since 1983, when a national referendum put in place the constitutional amendment 40.3.3: 'The State acknowledges the right to life of the unborn and, with due regard to the equal right to life of the mother, guarantees in its laws to respect, and, as far as practicable, by its laws to defend and vindicate that right.'

This amendment is placed under the articles on citizenship, thus making the unborn a citizen of the Irish State. The conceptual difficulties in attempting to spell out the conceivable duties and responsibilities of the *unborn citizen* have not yet been faced. However, by inserting this Article in the Constitution, the citizens of the State declared that a human foetus is to be considered a constitutional person. In *Life's Dominion*, Ronald Dworkin explains that the decision to make the human foetus a constitutional person is often anything but benign, especially to women and their liberty to make reproductive decisions. Such creation of the category of *unborn citizen* assumes that the Irish State

> can curtail constitutional rights by adding new persons to the constitutional population, to the list of those whose constitutional rights are competitive with one another.[28]

This was, of course, the intent in seeking an amendment. But in the case of the Irish Constitution where women's right to abortion was not clearly decided by any judicial decision, the creation of citizenship status for the unborn was pre-emptive curtailment of possible moves of the much feared *liberal* populus. Presently, abortion is legal in highly specified circumstances as determined in the Supreme Court decision of *Attorney General vs. X and Others*.[29] But the reality of Irish women's diverse choices reveals approximately 7,000 Irish women going to England each year to procure abortions. The efforts to contain and constrain women's powers in controlling their sexuality is most clearly demonstrated in the abortion debate. A strong pro-natal philosophy governs this debate which simplifies to distortion the complex realities of women's lives that lead them to choose abortion. The respect for the unborn, voiced from all perspectives in the debate, is never thought compatible with the endorsement of abortion as essentially a woman's choice.

Conclusions

The Irish Constitution of 1937 purports to be a liberal social contract. To the extent that it is dependent on a liberal political philosophy it has also adopted the framework of dividing the state into the public and private domains where women are expected as citizen-actors dominantly in the latter. The implication is that women's fullest participation in *both private and public life* has been pre-empted. Only women's resistance and determination has made wider public participation a reality. Few women in 1937 would ever have envisaged a woman in the Presidency.

To the extent that the Constitution is meant to be a co-operative contract based on consent, the implied *respect* for the person inherent in legitimate contracts is lacking. Rather a functionalist representation of women is provided. Her duties to the State are her reason for being. The *respect for persons* required for a legitimated social contract would call for liberties of choice and participation in the deliberative democracy — as much to encourage a development of women's

27. See Dolores Dooley, 'Abortion and the Law', in *Morality and the Law*, ed. Desmond M. Clarke (Cork: Mercier Press, 1982), pp. 31–47. For recent discussions relevant to the Irish abortion debate in the 1990s, see Ailbhe Smyth (ed.), *The Abortion Papers Ireland* (Dublin: Attic Press, 1992).

28. Ronald Dworkin, *Life's Dominion* (London: Harper Collins, 1995), p. 113.

29. [1992] 1IR 1.

person as to provide public contexts for diversity of women's voices and experience. Hearing these voices will help challenge the adequacy of both the public and private spaces of her society. Some writers might argue that the Articles I have looked at here from the Constitution of 1937 are not circumscribing or stereotyping women in Irish society but rather that they positively and primarily credit women's special qualities.

They [the Articles] should perhaps be seen as reflecting the lives of most Irish women in the 1930s. At that time the overwhelming majority of Irish women — married, widowed, and single — were based within the home. On this basis the Constitution can be viewed as acknowledging the importance of women's lives and work within the home giving status to many members of Irish society who were otherwise ignored.[30]

But, the document of a Constitution needs to be carefully wrought so that gender roles and norms are not specified today, only to become desperately outmoded tomorrow. Gender-norms in the Irish Constitution were not simply reflecting the way things were. Rather, the gender ideology achieved for many decades a containment and circumscription in women's citizenship; this ideology resulted in mechanisms to control the power of her sexuality. The Constitution's ideology of *woman* was perpetuated with a complex cultural dynamic with a history of its own.

An understanding of the history and social origin of the Constitution cannot blind us to the profound underlying patriarchy of Church and

State that determined the 1937 document. The document was a grand gesture of male political power. The *citizen differentiation* I have read from the Irish Constitution of 1937 is not a constructive and liberty-affirming endorsement of women's special qualities. We do not need to be suspicious or cynical about affirmations of special differences that women are credited with. We do need to be very cautious that the affirmation does not conceal an autocracy of intent in harbouring those differences for ends which women, in their diversity, might not choose for themselves.

The question which remains is how the Irish Constitution of 1937, with its Articles designating the sexual differences of woman, can continue to win consent from the diversity of women and men in Ireland. The radical changes in Irish society since 1937 must produce scepticism that this Constitution has anything of legitimacy in its presumed *contractual* features. The gendering of citizenship in the Irish Constitution provides a case study in what a Constitution should never aspire to: to gender-differentiated citizenship premised on a socially precarious and uncritical ideology supporting, not the interests of women, but patriarchal interests of Church and State. The meanings of citizenship, what it means to develop skills for *good citizenship,* need to be debated in the many local and national contexts of deliberative democracy. A State's constitution is not the place to copper-fasten sexual identities or attempt to determine constraints on women's diverse choices for full participation in the power dynamics of the closely interrelated private and public spheres of the State.

30. Mary E. Daly, 'Women in the Irish Free State, 1922–39', pp. 111–12.

GERALDINE SMYTH

(1948–　)

from:

ENVISAGING A NEW IDENTITY AND A COMMON HOME: SEEKING PEACE ON OUR BORDERS (2000)

[The first thirty years of the second wave of feminism overlapped with a time in Ireland in which over three and a half thousand people were violently killed; many thousands more were left wounded, mutilated, orphaned, or widowed. Apart from rarefied academic settings, in Ireland the optimism and innocence of many other feminisms were virtually impossible. The category 'Woman' seldom appeared without other communal or class labels attached. Indeed, the currency of all labels — republican, feminist, Christian, or dissenter — was radically debased.

In her role as director of the Irish School of Ecumenics, theologian Geraldine Marie Smyth attempted to forge linkages between debates on identity politics in feminist theory and similar debates in Northern Ireland and to relate these to theological renewal. This extract is taken from her article, 'Envisaging a New Identity and a Common Home: Seeking Peace on our Borders', *Milltown Studies* (winter 2000), pp. 58–84. Footnotes are by the author.]

> That ethnic differences should
> lead men into a darkling wood
> stained with internecine blood
> is to be mourned
> when there is so much beatitude
> within our bourne
>
> Iain Crichton Smith

Probing the Boundaries and Dynamics of Identity

In her Booker prize-winning novel, Arundhati Roy depicts how a community was trapped into a rejection of life and change by a corrupted religion and a primordial cultural tradition.[1]

1. Arundhati Roy, *The God of Small Things* (London: Flamingo, Harper Collins, 1997).

These latter are portrayed as a way of escaping the messiness of communication and compassion, of refusing the bonds of social responsibility. The story charts the corruption of an effete, high caste household, inheritors and imitators of a spent colonialism. A meta-narrative to the story of the actual house and family is presented in terms of the shadowy workings of the 'History House'. Although full of decay, and presided over by hungry ghosts, this house operates by intractable laws and is served by its own minions, who continue to re-inscribe it with a myth-like destructive power. Its hidden forces are set to crush those who would transgress the boundaries laid down by dogmatism of ethnicity and religion, in a bid for personal freedom or some private happiness. The house has its agents of destruction and its hapless victims.

There is no small irony that the novel's anti-hero, who is religiously and morally infantile, still clings, aged 80, to the pet-name Baby. Her fierce self-absorption and cult of the sentimental disguise from nobody but herself the reality that she is a heartless purveyor of suffering and destruction. As guardian-in-chief of the History House she cossets herself against anyone who might need anything from her, and seals the windows of her own house against the outside air, lest it expose her to the winds of life or change.

Set in post-colonial India, this novel speaks to our condition in Ireland, North and South, as we experience the conflicting reactions to the dismantling of our own 'History House' with all its embattled history, its mythic fascination and its restless train of never-satisfied ghosts. For those with a neurotic craving for order and security, nesting inside the 'History House', warmed by the influence of totalitarian politics, 'communalist' culture, or fundamentalist religious constructions can feel normal. The sealing off of the system against other or 'opposite' groups is viewed as a condition of survival, and the rage for security creates its own irrevocable norms. Dissidence from within must be quelled.

In such a situation, there will be little interest in the politics of equality or human rights for all. The focus is rather on a politics of identity — and of identity skewed towards preserving difference rather than equality.

Turning to the older social scientific literature of group identity, we detect two main streams of thought. Those who argue from the primacy of 'primordial affinities and attachments', and emphasise 'the identity made up of what a person is born with or acquires at birth' can be termed primordialists.[2] Such legacies of biology, and 'in the beginning' logic, impose a mythological weight, particularly in relation to one's political group as dominating or dominated. Thus, one can trace a trajectory of collective myth, historic event and folk culture into repeated stances and patterns of ethnic, political or religious behaviour, and recognise the sense of collective identity and self-esteem which these confer.[3]

The other school of thought claims that identity is not so much a given as a chosen reality. It is not the symbolic-structural objects of ethnicity that are stressed. What is emphasised rather is their structural significance which can and does change, reflecting greater plurality and a complexity of influences. Also underlined is the factor of self-conscious and strategic choice, as well as the role of social and political construction. Thus, [Daniel] Bell has demonstrated that in the context of the break-up of imperialism, ethnicity is to be understood, '*not* as a primordial phenomenon in which deeply held identities have to reemerge, but as a strategic choice by individuals who, in other circumstances, would choose other group memberships as a means of gaining some power and privilege'.[4] He also notes that 'the strength of primordial attachment is that emotional cohesion derives not only from some inner "consciousness of kind", but from some external definition of an adversary as well'[5] . . .

Vamik Volkan, the notable theorist on conflict transformation, has spoken of the way ethnic groups develop out of their shared cultural narratives a 'canopy of identity' to provide a sense of protective belonging, and a banner to signal the boundary between insider and outsider. In the context of the Judaeo-Christian tradition, one recalls the cultural-religious significance for 'Chosen People' journeying for forty years towards the holy mountain, of the symbols of the pillar of fire by night and of the cloud by day — the *Shekinah*. These served as a canopy of identity for the people, rallying them when they were faint-hearted, offering visible and felt reminders of God's unfailing promise and election.

But one should note the *provisional* dimensions of these symbolizations, suggesting more a promise than a guarantee that God's presence would accompany the people on their *pilgrim* journey. Too often, in ethnic and religious contexts, the canopy becomes a fortress with thick walls cemented by fundamentalist versions of history and tradition, and with guards to fight off perceived attack from without or defection from within.

One chilling example of the deadly effect of a primordialist view of identity is given by Volkan in relation to the behaviour of Armenian victims of the 1988 earthquake which devastated their country. He relates that as the death-toll mounted, and numbers of injured rose to 25,000, the Soviets collected blood to meet the overwhelming demand. In a humanitarian gesture, the Azerbaijanis (the historic enemy of Armenia) also sent blood supplies. But the Armenians refused it. To accept it would be to contaminate their blood-line. Seventy years of Soviet solidarity were as nothing against the

2. Harold R. Isaacs, 'Basic Group Identity', in *Ethnicity: Theory and Experience*, eds Nathan Glazer and Daniel P. Moynihan (Cambridge, Mass.: Harvard University Press, 1975), p. 29.

3. Isaacs explains the new preoccupation with ethnic identity in terms of a 'massive retribalisation', in reaction against the 'present pervasive condition of group fragmentation in all our current politics, post-colonial, post-imperial, post-revolutionary . . .' (ibid., pp. 29–30).

4. Daniel Bell, 'Identity and Social Change', in *Ethnicity: Theory and Experience*, pp. 170–1.

5. Bell, ibid., p. 174. A much more inflected discourse of comparative ethnicity has developed since this 1970s collection. There is of course a dynamic interplay between these two broad interpretative approaches to identity, and this reflects the reflexive nature of the interplay between culture and political interests in identity formation. For present purposes, however, these two approaches still offer a useful lens and interpretative point of departure in making sense of the conflicting interpretations of ethnic identity and political interests in Northern Ireland at the present time. Particularly significant sociological works include Benedict Anderson, *Imagined Communities* (London: Verso Press, 1991); Anthony Smith, 'The Ethnic Sources of Nationalism', *Survival*, vol. 35, no. 1 (1993); and Bill McSweeney, *Security, Identity and National Interests: A Sociology of International Relations* (Cambridge: Cambridge University Press, 1999), pp. 8–9, 180–95, 213–14.

claims of ancient faith and ancient blood. Death was preferable. Death was election — death by purity.[6]

Deterrence Relations Within a Majority–Minority Political Paradigm

In the battle for minds and hearts in Northern Ireland at the present time, it would be folly to ignore the magnetic force of primordial belonging. Cultural identity, as a kind of History House, encloses Nationalists and Unionists alike. Against this one must expose the politically constructed dimensions of such ethnic belonging, and argue the possibility and the necessity of change. No house is without doors and windows that open to some wider reality. It is by passaging between the inner and outer worlds that one can hear counter-voices and discover alternative dimensions to one's original identity. We cannot overestimate the need to sustain the internal critique within both Unionism and Nationalism, which stresses identity as a *chosen* form of identification, and argues for a dynamic of dialogue and negotiation in the process of identity formation and transformation.

It is nonetheless vital to understand the peculiar dynamics of intercommunal deterrence in regard to ethnic, cultural and religious identity in Northern Ireland. Frank Wright's exposé of this dynamic is illuminating. Wright classifies Northern Ireland as an 'ethnic frontier society' in which relationships of antagonism are structural.[7] The establishment of the border and thereby of the Northern Ireland state, evoked equal and opposite attitudes to the legitimacy of that state in the dominant majority and large minority community. This is accompanied by conflicting approaches to politics, society and the criminal justice system, and socio-economic access. Within the contested space, relationships are governed by the mutual threat of violence, vigilance against violence, defiance actions and retaliation from official and rebel sources, all of which operated *in a systemic way*.

Rivalry and violence, both veiled and unveiled, are at the core of this system, which can, at best, set limits to violence, whether by political defiance or political decree. At best, the system offers a 'tranquillity of communal deterrence'. It has no power within itself to generate peace, and it cannot be understood as a normal democratic society. In this paradigm it becomes clearer why such events as the Civil Rights Campaign of 1969, Internment without Trial, respective rationales for paramilitary Republican and Loyalist campaigns of violence, the Hunger strikes, and the Anglo Irish agreement have been viewed with a radically different hermeneutic by each community. It also becomes clearer why the Good Friday Agreement may represent the beginning of the end of the old order, in its conception of a future based on relationships and political systems of interdependence.

It is, of course, increasingly true that wherever cultural particularity is threatened — whether, for example, by colonisation or globalisation, the fight to preserve cultural difference can be a resilient manifestation of life. Resistance to assimilation becomes a way of surviving. In ethnic frontier societies, however, the pattern is both intensified and distorted by the dynamics of communal deterrence. Driven by the mimetic pattern of desire and rivalry, each group's expectations of victory rise and fall and everyone loses. For the 'tranquillity of mutual deterrence' to be changed, its driving ideology must be unmasked, and its mimetic symbols, language games and behaviour patterns interrupted. For the peace process in Ireland to have real substance or hope, the hostile ethnic groups will need to extend the spaces that are open to one another; to develop common agendas within civil society; and together imagine

6. Vamik Volkan, *Bloodlines: From Ethnic Pride to Ethnic Terrorism* (Boulder, Col.: Westview Press, 1997*)*, p. 5. Certainly too, the boundary lines between Unionist and Nationalist areas run deep. Under pressure of threat and violence, the ethnic divisions of urban geography once constructed by gerrymandering, have hardened along cultural and forever religious fault-lines configured around fear and ignorance of the other. The problem deepens when the legitimate claims of different cultures for parity of esteem is reduced to a mega-game of snakes and ladders, that is doomed to go on without end.

7. Frank Wright, *Northern Ireland: A Comparative Analysis* (Dublin: Gill and Macmillan, 1992). Wright adduces the analysis of René Girard on violence, culture and religion, to good effect, in his exposition of such systemic dynamics as mutual deterrence, mimetic desire, mimetic rivalry, blaming and scapegoating, for example, cf. pp. 19, 11–20, 122, 210–11 and *passim*.

a shared lifeworld beyond the old deterrence system of threat and fear.[8]

Beyond Single Identity: 'Withdrawal for the Sake of the Return'

It is against this background that I believe it necessary to probe the current fascination in Northern Ireland with the preservation of ethnic and cultural identity systems, whether of Unionist or Nationalist, Protestant or Roman Catholic hue. In general terms the contention is made that before people can engage in the work of reconciliation, each group must first develop a self-conscious confidence in its identity as autonomous and different. In situations where segregation is preferred to mixing, and where words such as 'reconciliation' and 'ecumenism' are suspect, one needs to question the organized massaging of group identity through the over-emphasis on minor differences. This process, ironically, increases a kind of mirror-image sameness, rather than allowing authentic difference to emerge, and that where it is most likely to emerge, in the act of recognition by the other, in and through encounter. As the darling of funding bodies, 'Single Identity Work' has, in recent years, enjoyed a certain *cachet*. By encouraging a cult of small differences as an end in itself, the process is more likely in fact to thwart the well-being of both groups. 'Single Identity Work' is a contradiction in terms.[9]

This is in no way to deny the relative value, for limited purposes and times, for groups to with-draw, to reflect on their internal cultural narrative as shaping their identity, and to venture fresh and freeing articulations of that narrative *vis à vis* their purpose and direction. The problem arises when the group, in its self-conscious withdrawal, puts itself beyond the critique and, indeed, the affirmation that emerge in dialogue, and without which one is captive to a self-referential system. Withdrawal can play an important critical function in identity formation, and to frustrate the need for the moment of distance is to increase the likelihood of alienation. John Macmurray reminds us in his philosophical reflection on psychological develop-ment, that the act of withdrawing is *the necessary negative* phase of personal relation. But, withdrawal is not for its own sake:

> To be negatively motivated is to be con-cerned for oneself in relation to the Other. The relation cannot be annulled; and the reference to the Other, since it is constitutive for the personal, cannot be evaded. We need the Other in order to be ourselves.[10]

Any attention to identity needs intentionally both to keep the Other in view and to remember that withdrawal is always for the sake of the return. Otherwise, far from providing a panacea for groups chasing after identity, the process is more likely to collude in the refusal (reflecting at times the inability) to see beyond a group's particular cultural narrative. In a setting of separateness, exclusive ritual and selective memory will more thoughtlessly be tied to ideology. With the cultivation of small dif-ferences, and the re-inscribing of the selective historic memory of the 'chosen trauma' or of the 'chosen glory' as mainstays of identity,[11] the

---

8. It is interesting to chart the contrasting course of the spoken Irish language North and South over the past fifty years. Irish has at last attained recognized status in the North, implying a formal and overdue recognition of the human rights of people of the minority culture. With predictable mimetic rivalry, however, there has been a resurgence of moribund aspects of the Planter tradition, via a populist re-inscribing of the rhetoric of civil and religious liberties, in regard to the demand that Scots Gallic (spoken by the tiniest minority of Unionists in County Antrim) be accorded equal status with Irish — a matching demand for government documents, public signs and street names to be given in the Scots Gallic form. Cf. John Darby, *Scorpions in a Bottle: Conflicting Cultures in Northern Ireland* (London: Minority Rights Publications, 1997).

9. Michael Ignatieff, *The Warrior's Honour: Ethnic War and the Modern Conscience* (London: Chatto and Windus, 1998), pp. 34–71. In this chapter, entitled 'The Narcissism of Minor Differences', the author reasserts the liberal as something to live by rather than as an epistemological outlook. He calls for the exercise of moral imagination in the holding of the paradox of a 'polity based on equal rights with the full incorporation of all available human differences' (p. 69) and of a liberal society whose function 'is not merely to teach the noble fiction of human universality, but to create individuals, sufficiently robust in their own identity, to live by that fiction' (p. 71).

10. John Macmurray, *Persons in Relation* (London: Faber and Faber, 1961), pp. 86–105, 94. In this work, Macmurray demonstrates in a number of reflective moves that the 'idea of an isolated agent is self-contradictory. The agent is necessarily in relation to the Other. Apart from this essential relation, he does not exist. But, further, the Other in this constitutive relation must itself be personal. Persons, therefore, are constituted by their mutual relations to one another. "I" exist only as one element in the complex "You and I"' (p. 24).

11. Volkan, ibid. On the phenomena of 'chosen trauma' and 'chosen glory', cf. pp. 48–9, 81–2. Volkan adduces Freud's work on the 'narcissism of minor differences' in explaining how the cultivation of such differences increases cohesion within one's own group, but he takes it further in explaining how 'potential collective anxiety over the loss of a group's identity' can lead that group, under certain stressful conditions, to invest hugely in the upholding of such minor differences (pp. 108–9). The different pronunciations of the letter 'H' might be the classic case among certain Unionists and Nationalists in Northern Ireland.

separatist illusion and tendentious quest for single identity begins again and again and again.

We are all familiar with how this works in Ireland. The Siege of Derry, the Cromwellian massacres, the 1916 Easter Rising or the Hunger Strikes of the early 1980s set pulses rushing as if they happened yesterday and have the power to inflame instant resentment or pride in mythic proportions. Thus, the prevailing myths of martyrdom or siege are recycled, and function as a lens through which to interpret and allocate blame for whatever current injustice or political impasse. Thus, the Other continues to be a source of fear or resentment; change is felt as threatening to identity; and every gain of the other group is construed automatically as loss to one's own. This is the calculus of the 'zero sum game', where any gain by the other group is reckoned as trespass against one's own group, necessitating a *quid pro quo*.

In the contested interpretations and implementation of the Good Friday Agreement, the sequencing of 'moves' on the part of Sinn Fein and the Unionist Party has had to be skilfully choreographed. But in the end it was demonstrated that choreography will not create peace so much as self-limiting action rooted in a recognition of the Other's needs and claims. In negative terms, this will require of each group a hermeneutic of suspicion towards their own cultural story, a reading of history against the ethnic grain, and the acceptance of John Berger's adage that never again will a single story be told as though it's the only one. More creatively, it challenges each group to begin to think 'convivially', and to believe that the flourishing of one's own ethnic and religious tradition is inextricably bound up with that of the other group.

Peace-making calls for a holding together of political ethics with an ethics of life in community, and a recognition that both within and between communities, people share in a range of overlapping identities — family, work and professional associations, interest groups. Adjacent ethnic groups inhabit each other's memories, stories, and histories. Again, in the words of Macmurray, 'in discriminating myself from the Other, it is always as belonging to the Other . . . We are part of that from which we distinguish ourselves and to which, as agents,

we oppose ourselves.' There is no identity apart from difference — ordered to relationship. The flourishing of all demands that each group actually assumes some responsibility for freeing the Other. It is through the risk and vulnerability of responsibility, that one's own identity can be at once inhabited and transcended.

The work of Seyla Benhabib is à propos in the context of self–other relations. Pushing further the work of writers like Levinas and Habermas to reflect both postmodern and feminist critique of the unencumbered self and of the autonomous subject, Benhabib insists on the need to speak not simply of some 'generalised other', but of a 'particularised other'. Within the paradigm of a communicative (as distinct from a communal) ethic, she argues the necessity of recognition of the particularised other, but without relinquishing a universal horizon. Thus she calls for an

> interactive universalism [which] regards difference as a starting point for reflection and action. In this sense, 'universality' is a regulative ideal that does not deny our embodied and embedded identity, but aims at . . . encouraging political transformations that can yield a point of view acceptable to all [through] the struggle of concrete, embodied selves, striving for autonomy.[12]

Reflecting on the recent political dynamics in the North of Ireland, one gets the distinct impression that Unionists and Nationalists have

12. Seyla Benhabib, *Situating the Self: Gender, Community and Postmodernism in Contemporary Ethics* (Cambridge: Polity Press, 1992), p. 153. While calling for a redefining of moral theory in gender terms, Benhabib is not seeking either a moral or political theory consonant with the standpoint of the concrete other (e.g., female), but rather to 'develop a universalistic moral theory that defines the 'moral point of view' in light of the reversibility of perspectives and an 'enlarged mentality' (p. 164). The universalism is developed through interaction. In this she recognizes 'the dignity of the generalized other through an acknowledgement of the moral identity of the particularized other' (p. 164). Benhabib's comments throw interesting light on the failure in Northern Ireland within formal politics with its ideological discourse to see political reality from a number of concrete perspectives. We can, however, find positive evidence for her thesis within civil society, and in the new political parties that had their origins in the community or indeed in prisons, where discourse has been narratively shaped — through sharing stories and embodied experiences of grief, anger and struggle to find an alternative to what went before. Here we find notable embodiments of a capacity to see political life from the point of view of another's experience — Benhabib's 'reversibility of perspectives' creating an 'enlarged mentality' and the real possibility of political agreement.

largely failed to recognise the reality of the other group as concretely different from their own. The tendency is to move *tout court* from the perspectives of one's own group to a totalising of political identity on the basis of expecting the other group to adopt one's own perspective. The discourse of peace is shared only in the words used. Words, like 'peace', 'justice' or 'security' are contested. They break apart into two meaning systems, influenced by significantly different approaches to the state, to law and order, to violence, and to the dynamics of democracy.

It is often claimed that Unionists fundamentally fear Nationalists and the violence from within the Nationalist community. And so, security, law and order have always been paramount in Unionist thinking. The fundamental Nationalist reaction to Unionists is resentment at the experience of violent suppression and exclusion from political and civic influence. And so for Nationalists, the withholding of full assent to the state and its structures was deemed a necessary step on the path to freedom and equal recognition of their rights and culture.[13] The Unionists make it all sound so difficult, so great is the fear and mistrust. The Republicans make it sound too glib and easy, disguising their mistrust, as they smoothly pour the language of agreement over the troubled waters of a difference that refuses to be assimilated or persuaded away. The attempted compromise of the Good Friday Agreement in its approach to the when and wherefore of decommissioning failed to bridge the chasm of different meaning systems in the wider community. There remains an inability to envisage peace as a new experience of right relationship, rooted in new experiences of encounter — in theological terms, as a New Creation.

The moot point is often couched in terms of 'face-to-face talks'. The Nationalists see this as the only way forward to 'Agreement' — all very unthreatening and straightforward. But for the Loyal Orange Orders, such 'face-to-face talks'

are a doomed road ending in surrender, compounding their intrinsic difficulty of sitting down to sup with those who have maimed and murdered their people and still have the capability of doing so. Levinas's metaphor of the 'face to face', I would suggest, holds a challenge to both parties — Loyalists not to over-estimate, and Republicans not to under-estimate the costs and responsibility that will be demanded. For the 'face-to-face' encounter implies a summons to the responsibility of relationship: 'the face to face [is] the irreducible and ultimate "relation"'.[14] For Levinas, 'The Other remains infinitely transcendent, infinitely foreign; his face in which his epiphany is produced . . . breaks with the world that is common to us . . . Speech proceeds from absolute difference.'[15] In the Irish context of head to head claims for rights and liberties, Levinas's words on the limits to freedom are also apposite. In this regard, he posits the will as subordinated to responsibility, language and reason. Thus, one's free will is not an absolute beginning: it always finds itself already summoned, obliged to responsibility before the other. The 'imperialism of the same' is thus disrupted by conversation. And the face to face is 'a calling into question of oneself, a critical attitude which is itself produced in the face of the other and under his (*sic*) authority . . . The face to face remains an ultimate situation'[16] . . .

From a Political Ethics to an Ethics of Life

Within the political arena, relationships are under the control of the 'social contract'. The political structure and legal system have at their disposal the language of human rights and contractual obligation, as a means of resolving conflict. These offer a model of political ethics developed to ensure minimum laws, codes and charters of protection *against* infringements of the individual's security, freedom, and economic

13. In addition to Frank Wright's work cited above, cf. 'An Interchurch Group on Faith and Politics', *Doing Unto Others: Parity of Esteem in a Contested Space* (Belfast, 1997), which examines this asymmetry in regard to this conflict of interpretations and how these are played out currently in terms of 'parity of esteem', cultural symbols, emblems and rituals, and the need for an inclusive approach to the bi-national identity claims of people in Northern Ireland.

14. Emmanuel Levinas, *Totality and Infinity: An Essay on Exteriority* (Pittsburg: Duquesne University Press, 1969), pp. 194-201, 291.

15. Levinas, ibid, p. 200. The significant correlationship made here between the transcendent and the ethical is portrayed in the concrete interplay of the face's revelation and the expressions of speech: 'This attestation of oneself is possible only as a face, that is, as speech' (p. 201). Self-understanding is thus conditioned by and honed through the intelligibilities of conversation and in the face to face encounter with the Other.

16. Levinas, ibid., p. 81.

justice. It also protects a person in respect of her ethnic entitlements and claims to cultural or religious distinctiveness.

Where there are competing claims to goods and rights, citizens must depend on this negatively based model of political ethics functioning to protect them by putting social and contractual constraints on violence and oppression. In any post-conflict situation, however, people need ways that also take human *needs* into account, opening up new spaces for relationship; ways of developing that space, not simply by relying on arbitration over conflicts, but by summoning up the as yet untried capacity for communication. Michael Ignatieff reminds us that rights language, while offering a protection for the individual against the collectivity, is relatively impoverished as a means of expressing *individuals' needs for the collectivity*: — 'We are more than rights-bearing creatures and there is more to respect in a person than [his or her] rights.'[17]

In the North, communities are coming back to life after thirty years existing within a culture of death. Many are still numb or angry or grief-stricken, as their personal and communal suffering is finally given public recognition. Many are still testing ways of negotiating relationships outside the shadow of violence. Discovering how to live creatively and peacefully with the Other is exercising communities in quite a different way than that required in surviving conflict. Thus, in addition to a political ethic, we need an ethics of life. To engage in this life ethic as the necessary correlative to our political ethic, requires that we strengthen the capacity for trust, imagination and risk. In strengthening such capacities, people come more and more to recognise the needs of strangers, and to expect that the stranger may have new and different gifts to share.

This alternative ethics of life is rooted in particular spaces in Northern Ireland, and has been expressed and developed by community groups, women's associations, neighbourhood

and inter-neighbourhood bodies and uncentralised ecumenical groups and peace movements. They operate, not simply through formal procedures bent on reducing conflict and violence, but by processes that generate life within and across communities, enabling people to discover and express their potential as bearers of life and witnesses of hope.

Through small circles and quiet processes of people on the margins — bereaved families or unemployed youth, for example — or through women's development projects, or initiatives in interchurch reconciliation, new opportunities have been created to reach across borders or address common concerns with the strength of different perspectives. By so doing people have come to a fuller understanding and confidence in who they are and that they need not be wholly subject to state-driven policies. Such groups are most often actively non-violent and committed to furthering participation and new consensus, but without relinquishing robust expressions of diversity. They have been life-bringers and sustainers of life.[18]

Operating with the faith that the North can be re-created as a common home, such people have been shaping a vital alternative to the dead hand of the 'History House'. They have been building if we might extrapolate from *I Peter* — a 'Household of Life'. This 'Household of Life' is grounded in peacefulness and in the capacity to practise new ways of living together, respecting differences, but open to the demands of reconciliation. Catalysts for this change of paradigm have varied — anger, pain, defiance, hope. But more and more discernably, one notes in recent years a newly awakened responsibility within the wider community to the children, and new-

17. Michael Ignatieff, *The Needs of Strangers* (London: Hogarth Press, 1984), p. 13. Ignatieff's later volume, *Blood and Belonging: Journeys into the New Nationalisms* (London: BBC Books and Chatto and Windus, 1993), offers some interesting comparative analysis and also offers the helpful distinction between 'ethnic nationalism' and 'civic nationalism' (pp. 3–9).

18. For a wide-ranging portrayal and analysis of such contributions within the 'lifeworld' of civil society, cf. Andy Pollak, ed., *A Citizens' Inquiry: The Opsahl Report on Northern Ireland* (Dublin: Lilliput Press, 1993). For further comment on the socio-theological dimensions of the significance of the contributions of such groups and movements (particularly those in which women's influence has been substantial), cf. Geraldine Smyth, 'Sabbath and Jubilee', in *The Jubilee Challenge: Utopia or Possibility — Jewish and Christian Insights*, ed. Hans Ucko (Geneva: World Council of Churches Publications, 1997), pp. 59–76. Clearly what is needed is an expansion and redefining of the understanding of politics in relation to such community life concerns. Locally based research to back this claim is not wanting. Cf. R. Miller, R. Wilford and F. Donoghue, *Women and Political Participation in Northern Ireland* (Aldershott: Avesbury, 1996).

awakened hopes of parents who themselves lost out on their youth, and who are determined that their children and grandchildren will 'have a life'. By crying out, 'Enough!' these parents and elders have generated a renewed faith that people who desire peace can find peace and ways of living in peace to sustain life for the next generation . . .

Stewart Parker's play *Pentecost* is set in Belfast during the grim days of the Ulster Workers' Strike in 1974. In the closing scene four characters — at once friends and strangers — argue and quarrel together, each locked into old and bitter resentments towards one another, each striving to escape pain and despair, yet incapable of hope. Everything in their separate lives is at the point of collapse. Suddenly, at mention that Pentecost is near, it is as if the Spirit descends in flames of fire, and Marian is given a kind of revelation which powerfully releases her from the emotional numbness which has gripped her since her baby's death, many years before.

Her words express something of the desperate hope I experienced at the funerals, just after the Omagh bomb, of three Buncrana school boys — James, Sean and Odhran. A few rows in front of me stood David Trimble beside the President of Ireland, Mary McAleese. I wondered if those words echoed something of what was in their minds too:

I want to live now. I want this house to live. We have committed sacrilege enough on life,

in this place, in these times. We don't just owe it to ourselves, we owe it to our dead too . . . our innocent dead. They're not our masters, they're only our creditors, for the life they never knew. We owe them at least that — the fullest life for which they could ever have hoped, we carry those ghosts within us, to betray those hopes is the real sin against the Christ, and I for one cannot commit it a day longer.[19]

At the end of the funeral Mass, Bishop Hegarty thanked David Trimble and said how deeply the people appreciated his presence among them in Buncrana in the Republic of Ireland. As he wished David Trimble a fair wind in his new role as first minister, the congregation broke into applause. There, in front of the three coffins, the people applauded, and it was no sacrilege. It was rather a sacramental moment where old and narrow identities were utterly transcended. It was part of what we owed to our innocent dead — a pledge to continue to reach across the old barriers for 'the fullest life for which they could ever have hoped'. We carry their ghosts to remind us. If people could transcend identity's narrow ground at the gravesides of Buncrana or Omagh, there is an unquenchable hope that we can find peace on our borders and find it together.

19. Stewart Parker, *Pentecost: Three Plays for Ireland* (Derry: Field Day, 1987), p. 208.

KATHERINE ZAPPONE

(1953–   )

from:
THE HOPE FOR WHOLENESS:
A SPIRITUALITY FOR
FEMINISTS (1991)

[While feminist scholars eagerly engage in the discourses of philosophy, theology and ethics, ritual has always been more problematic, an apparent remnant of a medieval world-view that secular, rationalist, contemporary women should avoid. Ritual practices are often seen simply as tools of domination, disciplinary practices used to colonize vulnerable minds and bodies. Women scholars of religion know, however, that rituals can empower as well as oppress; that bodies can be liberated as well as subjugated, and that art, symbolism, poetry and music are as essential as food, air and water to integrate the human body and spirit. This extract is from *The Hope for Wholeness: A Spirituality for Feminists* (Mystic, Conn.: Twenty-Third Publications, 1991). Footnotes are by the author.]

Because I was raised in the Roman Catholic tradition, I was bequeathed a deep love of ritual. One of my favourite memories from an early childhood is accompanying my parents to benediction. I can still smell the incense, see the Blessed Sacrament exposed in gold, hear the hushed sounds of silence and sense the awe in the air. At its best, this experience enabled me to feel wholly the presence of the sacred. The benediction ritual provided a rhythmic form and special space to meet the transcendent God. The sacrament of Eucharist also bestowed this possibility. Frequent attendance at the ritual of the Eucharist solidified belief, touched my soul, and drew me into a sacred presence that nourished a lifestyle guided by Christian faith.

Lex orandi, lex credendi: 'The way we pray is the way we believe.' To put it another way, 'the way we pray determines what we believe and what we do'.[1] This is the heart of ritual's power at the personal level. But it is also the crux of why feminists have had to distance themselves from the rituals that maintain the patriarchal essence of religions. The rituals of the fathers not only exclude women's experience, they reinforce dualistic beliefs and sacralise the superiority of maleness. Since embarking on the feminist spiritual journey, I, along with countless other feminists, have realised and felt that the rituals of our childhood negate the spiritual insights and practices of living interdependently. Consequently, to continue to seek nourishment and sacred presence within the rhythm of patriarchal ritual is dangerous to our health.

Something else is going on, though, in addition to the personal impact of ritual. Anthropologists tell us that there exists a dialectical relationship between ritual and culture. The symbols, dreams, and values of a culture shape the structure, themes, and meaning of religious ritual. Likewise, sacred ceremonies sanctify the patterns of valuing, knowing, and behaving within a particular culture. Traditional Jewish and Christian rituals have celebrated and maintained the worldview, symbols, and values of Western patriarchal culture. Ritual's power extends beyond the personal to the political. The

central and ongoing objective of feminism is to fashion a culture that takes us beyond the vision and activities of patriarchy. The practitioners of feminist spiritualities are keenly aware of the constructive role that ritual can play in this dynamic. The vision, symbols, and values of a feminist culture require that religious ritual be re-created.

I am fully aware of the pain, fear, and confusion that is part of this process. Before feminism there was so much security and familiarity with the rituals; our very relationship with God depended upon them. We knew how and where we could encounter the divine. The formulas were crafted very carefully over centuries. No one ever taught us how to fashion our own; we were the passive recipients of others' power to mediate access to the sacred. This spiritual dependency paralysed our own ability to imagine language and symbols that could express our experience of the sacred. I am also cognizant of the radical nature of the invitation to re-create religious ritual. It means far more than putting together a 'para-liturgy'. The sanctuary has been opened regardless of ordained or non-ordained status. The sacred space is no longer restricted to one particular place or a specified set of actions. This, however, is a necessary and vital part of embodying the feminist hope for wholeness.

What is Feminist Ritual?

One of the most remarkable signs of the health of the feminist spirituality movement is the celebration of rituals by people coming together from different backgrounds and religious traditions. The conversational character of a spirituality for feminists is embodied through the creation of rituals that respect the diversity and interdependence of its participants. This phenomenon, I believe, gives witness to the hope for wholeness that is at the heart of the spirituality paradigm throughout this book. It also directs my choice for the word 'ritual' as the most inclusive term for describing what is happening.[2] Though 'liturgy', 'worship', and 'prayer service' are terms also in use, these

---

1. Martha Ann Kirk, in *Liberating Liturgies*, compiled by members of the Women's Ordination Conference (Fairfax, Virginia: Women's Ordination Conference, 1989), p. 10.

2. See the discussion in *Women's Spirit Bonding*, eds Janet Kalven and Mary Buckley (New York: Pilgrim Press, 1984), that identifies their reasons for choosing 'ritual' as the most inclusive term, pp. 345–6.

surface primarily in Jewish and Christian feminist spiritualities, and are employed interchangeably with ritual. By choosing 'ritual' I want to indicate a significant part of the common language in a spirituality for feminists. Its use is meant to represent two things:

1. that feminists are and ought to continue celebrating rituals with others from varied traditions and
2. that feminists are and ought to continue creating rituals within their own traditions.

In these ways we publicly express the truths that exist in our own traditions and the courage to have those truths enriched or confronted by the spiritual journeys of other feminists.

So, what is feminist ritual? Having participated in various kinds and having examined a number of authors, I offer the following as an effort to identify common threads in diverse tapestries. First, a definition: *Feminist ritual is imaginative symbolic expression of the sacred movement of life, death, and rebirth.* It is 'corporate symbolic action'[3] that expresses the interdependence of self, the sacred, others, and the earth in artistic form. It is symbolic activity that is above all a revelatory experience. Ritual enables us to reveal our present effort to move toward wholeness through and with the sacred. Ritual reveals sacred presence within ourselves, our activities, and relationships with one another and the earth. This process, as Starhawk says, 'sustains us as it marks the cycles of birth, growth, decay, and renewal that sustains our lives'.[4] The structure of rituals vary from something as simple as opening prayer, meditative music, sharing our imagery of sacred presence, closing prayer to a larger communal gathering that expresses the specific memories and hopes of a group that has been with one another over a certain period of time.

Many feminists also practise personal rituals. These are moments set aside for individuals to focus on the interior process of deepening self-integrity or personal power. Starhawk, Hallie

Iglehart, and Dianne Mariechild offer several examples of ritual-work that nourish individual needs and assist the process of integrating body and spirit, sexuality and spirituality, emotion and intellect.[5] The greater number of feminist rituals, though, are practised within a communal context. Christian feminist base communities, Jewish feminist communities, covens, and women's spirituality groups provide a supportive setting for the public expression of self-love, mutuality in diversity, reverence for the earth, and sensing sacred presence. In community, feminists ritualise their experiences of relationship and their search for justice, love, and peace. Through diverse structures and different traditions feminist ritual enacts communal faith in and hope for wholeness.

Feminist Ritual: Artistic, Creative, Imaginative

There is an infinite number of ways to ritualise the feminist spiritual journey. It is up to each participant to draw on her or his creative ability to image the symbols, words, movement, and music that will express the particular focus of each ritual. For many, this is one of the most difficult challenges of feminist ritual. Not only is it plain, hard work; very few of us have been taught to 'tap our own inner imagery'.[6] It is true that some will be more naturally gifted than others, yet the richness and effectiveness of ritual will depend on everyone making some effort to contribute. Simple guidelines that facilitate this process include: 1. spend some time individually through silence and/or guided meditation to identify appropriate symbols and images; 2. bring together a number of resources for prayer, music, poetry, sacred text, and/or body movement; 3. as Diann Neu says, 'Discover who the artists are: dancers, musicians, mimists, storytellers, creators of environment, poets, organisers, and invite them to use their talents in the celebration'[7] and 4. select from the resources inside and outside the group.

3. The definition offered by Linda Clark, Marian Ronan and Eleanor Walker in *Image Breaking/Image Building: A Handbook for Creative Worship with Women of Christian Tradition* (New York: Pilgrim Press, 1981), pp. 33–4.
4. Starhawk, *Truth or Dare* (San Francisco: Harper and Row, 1988), p. 99.
5. See, for example, Starhawk's *The Spiral Dance* (Harper and Row, 1979); *Dreaming the Dark* (Boston: Beacon Press, 1982); and *Truth or Dare*.
6. A phrase often used by the authors of *Image Breaking/Image Building*.
7. Diann Neu, *Women and the Gospel Traditions: Feminist Celebrations* (Silver Spring, Maryland: Waterworks Press: The Women's Alliance for Theology, Ethics, and Ritual, 1989), p. ii.

Shared creativity is an integral dimension of becoming active participants in the ritual-making process. It also accentuates the equal value of individuals and the nourishing character of interdependent activity. Yet the importance of imagination in feminist ritual travels deeper than this. Much of the deadness in patriarchal religious ritual arises from not calling on the arts. Theological discourse encapsulated in rigid prayer forms emphasises the superiority of reason over imagination. Feminist ritual attempts to shatter this expression of dualism by becoming 'more than words'.[8] In describing what they wanted their rituals to accomplish, the authors of *Women's Spirit Bonding* identified the centrality of 'enabling individuals to draw upon their physical, emotional, and imaginative powers as well as their analytic skills'.[9] The art of individual and collective imagination symbolises and deepens the wholeness that we seek.

Feminist Ritual: Sensual

Imaginative symbolic expression engages our whole body-spirits. The sacred space of feminist ritual creates boundaries wherein we can sense the depth of spiritual experience. The light of candles and the colour of our symbols and environment invite a renewed sense of sight. Incense and flowers enliven smell. Body-movement, even such simple gestures as a handshake or blessing on the forehead of another, bring forth a different way of knowing our connections with one another. Telling stories and making music raise quiet energy through hearing. Many rituals incorporate a time for feasting, signifying that 'eating food together is a holy action, a necessary luxury'.[10] This process of 'coming to our senses' offers whole forms of healing. It integrates diverse ways of knowing where we have been and what we ought to do. It reminds us that our participation in the sacred movement of life, death and rebirth is an embodied one . . .

It is through feelings as well as thoughts that we discover self-integrity and healthy forms of interrelatedness. Together, emotion and rationality enable self-determination and a lifestyle of interdependence. Ritual supports the integration, not suppression, of feelings. It does this not only through serious and solemn moments. Feminist ritual extends its boundaries to incorporate time for spontaneity, laughter, and play. It is all right to laugh within the sacred space. Why? Starhawk says, 'The elements of laughter and play keep us from getting stuck on one level of power or developing an inflated sense of self-importance. Humour keeps kicking us onward, to go deeper . . .'[11]

Feminist Ritual: Repetitive

Repetition has always been a fundamental characteristic of ritual. We often name activities or events 'rituals' if we engage in them frequently. Birthday celebrations, having a cup of tea or coffee at a certain time each day, and opening a football game with the national anthem are all examples of what we might designate as 'rituals'. Religious rituals such as the Seder meal or the sacrament of baptism comprise prayers, blessings, and stories that are repeated each time the rite takes place. Repetition provides a sense of familiarity and security; it roots participants in their cultural, familial, and religious heritages.

One of the earliest critiques that feminists raised regarding the rituals of their religious traditions, however, was the absence of women's directives in formulating the rites. Furthermore, repetition of men's formulas left little room for the inclusion of women's contemporary experiences. In fact, as they are practised in many communities today, Jewish and Christian rituals value the past more than the present precisely through the rigid repetition of outdated formulas and prayers. What has this meant for feminist ritual? Initially we veered away from any kind of repetition, especially by creating prayer services and liturgies that were completely outside of sacramental or Sabbath settings. Or, even as Christian feminists followed the basic structure of sacramental rites we consistently created different prayers, creeds, and blessings. As time has passed, though, I think that we are beginning to reclaim the value of repetition in ritual . . .

8. The full title of this resource is *More Than Words: Prayer and Ritual for Inclusive Communities*, by Janet Schraffran and Pat Kozak (Oak Park, Illinois: Meyer Stone Books, 1988).

9. *Women's Spirit Bonding*, p. 345.

10. Diann Neu, *Women and the Gospel Traditions*, p. ii.

11. Starhawk, 'Ritual as Bonding: Action as Ritual', in *Weaving the Visions*, eds Judith Plaskow and Carol Christ (San Francisco: Harper and Row, 1989), pp. 326–7. Barbara Walker echoes these sentiments by declaring that 'laughter is not hostile to spirituality, play can have profound resonances in human psychology'. See her *Women's Rituals: A Sourcebook* (New York: Harper and Row, 1990), p. 7.

What is Feminist Ritual for?

Ritual should transform its participants. It should heal us so that we can partake in the world's healing. What most feminists find, though, is that ritual's effectiveness for healing is integrally linked to the communal setting that bodies it forth. There must be some form of community, some kind of trust or practice of mutual relationships in order for ritual to work. Healing does not take place without some shared vision or in an atmosphere of distrust. Consequently, ongoing feminist communities and/or gatherings of feminists with a common purpose provide the most effective context for ritual. There is another side to this reality: feminists have discovered over the years that they need spiritual communities wherein the practice of rituals forms an integral part. Feminist spiritual communities offer sustenance and support especially through opportunities for ritual-making. Likewise, ritual is a very effective medium for building and maintaining a community's vitality . . .[12]

Another central purpose of Christian feminist ritual is to remember and reform the tradition. Members of Protestant denominations create new prayers, blessings, and creeds that are used within traditional prayer services and liturgies. They incorporate biblical stories retold from a feminist perspective. They use a multiplicity of symbols and metaphoric language to celebrate an inclusive God and to lift up the revelatory character of women's experience. Implicit in their ritual-making is the rejection of churchmen's exclusive control of Christian worship. They refuse to be excluded any longer from creating symbolic expression of the sacred movement of life. The same is true for Roman Catholic feminists. The women-church movement in the United States is a prime example of women and men locating ritual and 'sacramental power in the community rather than in ordained representatives'.[13] They no longer wait for the reforms of churchmen; they create their own rituals — both inside and outside of sacramental settings. They believe that each ritual 'effects what it signifies' (the traditional understanding of sacramental power), thus providing the spiritual nourishment necessary to remain in dialogue with the institutions of Christianity.

Feminist ritual, as it is practised today, embodies the hope for wholeness in diverse ways. Yet, as I have also tried to indicate, common features exist in each kind of feminist spirituality. This furnishes the extraordinary opportunity to ritualise our own experiences of relationship, and to be healed by the ritual activities of others. This, I believe will deepen like nothing else our consciousness of interdependence and prompt action toward the health of all creation.

12. See Martha Acklesberg's description of the various conflicts and rewards of creating ritual within a Jewish feminist community, in her article 'Spirituality, Community and Politics: B'not Esh and the Feminist Reconstruction of Judaism,' *Journal of Feminist Studies in Religion*, vol. 2, no. 2 (Fall 1986), pp. 109–20.

13. Mary Jo Weaver, *New Catholic Women: A Contemporary Challenge to Traditional Religious Authority* (San Francisco: Harper and Row, 1986), p. 257, n. 32. See also Marjorie Proctor-Smith, *In Her Own Rite: Constructing Feminist Liturgical Tradition* (Nashville: Abingdon Press, 1990).

CARMEL McENROY

(1936–   )

from:
GUESTS IN THEIR OWN HOUSE: THE WOMEN OF VATICAN II (1996)

[This final selection in this section serves as a sharp reminder as to just how vulnerable and tenuous is the hold on the ground that women have claimed for the past thirty years. Carmel McEnroy taught systematic theology at St Meinrad School of Theology, Indiana, for fourteen years; she was tenured in 1992. Following her public support for women's ordination, with less than two weeks' notice and the offer of six months' salary, in May 1995 she was fired from her tenured teaching position. The extract is from her 'Postscript' to her book, *Guests in Their Own House: The Women of Vatican II* (New York: Crossroads, 1996). Footnotes are by the author.]

POSTSCRIPT

My editor and concerned friends urged me to conclude with an autobiographical note that they saw as particularly relevant and indeed poignant, given the topic and thrust of my book . . .

The charge brought against me was 'public dissent' from magisterial teaching in regard to women's ordination. In May 1994, Pope John Paul II published an open letter, saying that the question of women's ordination was definitively closed. In October 1994, the Women's Ordination Conference responded in kind with an open letter to the Pope and U.S. Bishops, which I and about two thousand other people signed, respectfully requesting that the discussion be continued. The letter was published in the *National Catholic Reporter* (11/4/1994). In accordance with my rights as a citizen and private person (guaranteed by my contract), I did not indicate my professional affiliation with St Meinrad School of Theology, nor did I use the initials of the Congregation of the Sisters of Mercy of Ireland and South Africa.

On April 26, 1995, I received a letter from Archabbot Timothy Sweeney, OSB, stating that he was asking President-Rector Eugene Hensell, OSB, to terminate my contract at the end of the semester, allegedly because asking that the discussion continue on women's ordination made me 'seriously deficient in my duty', in his interpretation of Canon 253 (although it does not mention 'dissent'). On May 9, my last teaching day, I received a letter from Hensell (who signed my tenured contract in 1992) informing me of my termination.[1]

All of this was in stark contrast to my evaluations over the years. Daniel Buechlein, then President-Rector, hired me in 1981, knowing my views on women's ordination. During my interview I told him I had no personal sense of vocation to priesthood. He said that because of his position he was not actively working for women's ordination. In reply to my question as to how structures changed if there was no help from within, he said, 'By hiring people like you.' When reappointing me for a

seven year term in 1983, Buechlein wrote, 'I was pleased by the positive report which was presented by the Personnel Committee and I concur with the specific commendations . . . In a very short time, you have become a valuable member of our faculty and have won the genuine respect of our students.' In 1984, he wrote, 'I'm delighted to grant your sabbatical request for . . . 1985 . . . May I take this opportunity to congratulate you for your marvellous contribution to our life and work here. We value your presence as well as your various and substantial contributions as a colleague. Thank you!'

In 1988, the middle of my first seven-year contract, President-Rector Hensell responded to my faculty evaluation. 'Your teaching ability is clearly appreciated by our students and your presence on the faculty over these past years has been an asset to the school. During these years of transition in the church, I realize that it is not easy being a woman theology teacher in a seminary . . . I encourage you to feel "at home" on our faculty. You have manifested your ability as a faculty member and therefore you are encouraged to enjoy this very important work with a sense of confidence and a spirit of relaxation . . . It is an important time for women in our church. Solid scholarly contributions to the area of theology by women are very important. We will support your efforts to the best of our ability. I want to thank you for your work and presence at St Meinrad. I look forward to working with you in the years to come.'

In approving my 1993 sabbatical to work on the Women of Vatican II, Hensell stated, 'I think it has a great deal of significance for the Church . . . I wish you well in this project. Its completion will be a credit to you and a benefit to our school' (March 2, 1992). Two months later he granted me Continuing Appointment (tenure) and added: 'Your faculty review was very positive and clear recognition was given to the gifts you bring to the School especially in the area of your teaching. As you are well aware, these are very challenging times for schools of theology. Our students will continue to need solid grounding in systematic theology in order that they be able to provide the kind of ministry and leadership the Church needs and deserves. Your proven ability as a teacher will be a very important asset for our school, our students, and the Church in the years ahead.

---

1. All of this was in clear violation of the terms of my contract, the procedures spelled out in the *Faculty Handbook*, and the school's endorsement of the American Association of University Professors' Statement on Academic Freedom.

Congratulations on achieving this important step in your teaching career.' Four days later, Academic Dean Walters wrote: 'I want to take this opportunity to formally say "Congratulations" on your Continuing Appointment to the School of Theology. While Gene's comments echo mine, I want to add that you are also to be commended on your research regarding the women of Vatican II. Because of your intellectual curiosity and desire to push the boundaries of theological research, we are a better school.'

With that consistent type of commendation for my work over the years, I was not prepared for the accusation of being 'seriously deficient in my duty' in 1995. The first rumour I heard about my possible firing was on March 6, the morning after the arrival of the National Council of Catholic Bishops' Visitation Team, which consisted of Archbishop Elden Curtiss of Omaha, Bishop Seán O'Malley of Fall River, Rector Pat Brennan of Mt Angel, and Rector Pat Guidon of Oblate College, San Antonio. Curtiss, the Team's Chair, made it known publicly to students that he was there to carry out Archbishop Daniel Buechlein's wishes against feminism, including firing me, and homosexuality. Allegedly, according to Curtiss, because I signed the open letter to the Pope, I forfeited my right to teach in a seminary, and action had to be taken against me. Academic Dean Tom Walters called me into his office to tell me this shortly before Hensell presented the oral report to the faculty on March 8.

Two weeks prior to the Visitation, Bishop Slattery of Tulsa and his vocation director, Tim Davison, visited the seminary and showed administrators a copy of the NCR letter with my name highlighted. I was never officially informed of this.

A week prior to Slattery's visit, Archbishop Buechlein addressed the faculty at the invitation of President-Rector Hensell. When asked what the Visitation Team might be looking for, Buechlein said, among other things, 'they will be looking at individuals and why they are here'. No one questioned his cryptic remark, but some faculty later made the connection between this statement, Elden Curtiss's recommendation that I be fired, Timothy Sweeney's initiative against me, and Eugene Hensell's actualization of my termination. Hensell told me Buechlein had been trying to get rid of me for nine years because I

was a feminist theologian, although in Hensell's own estimation, I was a moderate one.

St Meinrad administrators totally ignored letters from the Leadership Team in my congregation, at the central, provincial, and individual level, as well as from members of my family, who tried to initiate discussion before I was terminated.

The administrators' precipitous unilateral action against me evidenced, at best, their ignorance of the nuanced understanding of 'dissent', which clearly distinguishes honest differences from those that are hostile and obstinate, as set forth in the Congregation for the Doctrine of the Faith (CDF) 1990's 'Instruction on the Ecclesial Vocation of the Theologian'.[2] They ignored the exhortation to bishops to initiate dialogue with theologians so as to create a climate of trust and offset major difficulties, 'to seek their solution in trustful dialogue', and to follow the proper procedures (40, 42). This magisterial document states that prior to removing a theologian's teaching mandate, the magisterium is required to carry out 'a thorough investigation conducted according to established procedures which afford the interested party the opportunity to clear up possible misunderstandings of his [her] thought' (37).

The procedural steps are further explicated in the 1975 Thesis set forth by the International Theological Commission,[3] which is clearly the parent document of the CDF's 1990 Instruction. For example, it states: 'When one party "unilaterally" takes over the whole field of the dialogue, he [sic] violates the rules of discussion. It is especially damaging to dialogue between the magisterium and theologians when the stage of discussion and debate is broken off prematurely, and measures of coercion, threat and sanction are employed all too soon.'[4] Furthermore, 'Before instituting any formal process about a question of doctrine, the competent authority should exhaust all the ordinary possibilities of reaching agreement through dialogue in order to clarify a questionable opinion (for example by discussing the matter in person or by corre-

---

2. The text appears in *Origins*, vol. 20, no. 8 (July 5, 1990).
3. All references here are taken from the International Theological Commission's text as it appears in Francis Sullivan's *Magisterium* (Ramsey, New Jersey: Paulist Press, 1983), pp. 174–218.
4. Ibid., Thesis 12.

spondence in which questions are asked and replies given). If no genuine agreement can be reached by such dialogical methods, the magisterium should employ a broad and flexible range of measures, beginning with various kinds of warnings, "verbal sanctions", etc. In the most serious kind of case, when all the methods of dialogue have been used to no avail, the magisterium, after consulting theologians of various schools, has no choice but to act in defence of the endangered truth and the faith of the believing people.'[5] Even Canon Law provides a process before action.

St Meinrad authorities' extreme action against me was diametrically opposed to the CDF's dialogical method and the spirit of trust it requires as the hallmark of those engaged in the collaborative pursuit of truth in the service of the church. While invoking magisterial teaching in defence of their action, they failed to honor even the doctrinal principle of 'hierarchy of truths' set forth at Vatican II.[6] Even more basically from a Christian perspective, was their neglect of the threefold biblical process for settling differences set forth in Mt 18:15. Presumably, a seminary committed to the education of future priests would be a place that could be expected to operate from a model of practical justice and charity.

On May 10, Dr Bridget Clare McKeever, SSL, tenured professor in Pastoral Care and Counseling, submitted a letter of resignation to Eugene Hensell. He never acknowledged it. McKeever wrote: 'The events of the past two months have raised serious questions regarding how and where I should devote the remaining years of my active ministry. The model of Church which the NCCB Visitation Committee exemplified and which, to my acute disappointment, St Meinrad School of Theology also displayed in its response, is one with which I cannot identify and which I cannot support. The circumventing of the faculty constitution and the terminating of Dr Carmel McEnroy's tenured contract without due process is, in my opinion, a breach of faith not only with Dr McEnroy, but also with the entire faculty. Regardless of how these actions are rationalized, they are unjustified and unjust.'

McKeever quoted from her community's Mission Statement, stating, 'Through all our ministries . . . we resolve to become agents of change in struggling to transform unjust structures and to promote reconciliation.' She added, 'I have believed in the good will and in the good faith of St Meinrad as long as I could. However, it is no longer possible for me to do so.'

In the cover letter she sent to her colleagues with a copy of her letter of resignation, she wrote: 'I believe I could have lived with the behavior and the report of the NCCB Visitation Committee, it being a hostile force outside St Meinrad. However, when Carmel's professional life and ministry was so obviously used by St Meinrad as a bargaining chip between ecclesiastical power brokers, I realized that my ethical boundaries were being stretched beyond their limits. I had no option but to resign.'

The Catholic Theological Society of America at its 1995 meeting in New York overwhelmingly endorsed a statement and two resolutions in my favour. It viewed my dismissal 'with dismay'. Furthermore, it stated: 'The absence of any process to deal with the charges against a tenured faculty member raises serious concern that after more than a decade of joint efforts by American bishops and scholars to formulate processes to insure fair treatment for Catholic scholars accused of doctrinal error, due process, even that guaranteed by contract, is often jettisoned. Dr McEnroy's is a case in point.' The society questioned the charge of dissent, asked that I be reinstated, since 'in the view of the society the demands of justice have not been met'. It testified that 'nothing has changed in the professional role of Dr Carmel McEnroy. She is a Catholic theologian in good standing.'[7] I was gratified by the CTSA's support, and I trust the judgment of this informed group of contemporary female and male *periti* (experts).

The outpouring of support I have received and continue to receive from men and women, many of whom I don't know, indicates the outrage of the people of God with the hierarchical abuse of power, symbolized by my unjust dismissal. They demand that the Spirit not be silenced in the

---

5. Ibid., Thesis 12.
6. These were set forth in the documents of the Second Vatican Council's *Unitatis Redintegratio* (Decree on Ecumenism).

7. The entire text of the CTSA's statement is published as an appendix in the *CTSA Proceedings of the Fiftieth Annual Convention*, ed. Paul Crowley (Santa Clara, California: Santa Clara University, 1995), pp. 326–9.

people's church. In my own situation I find parallels to Jesus' disciples and friends. Some betrayed him; some fled in fear; others came to him by night; still others remained faithful to the end; and complete strangers befriended him.

In its *Pastoral Constitution on the Church in the Modern World*, the church assembled in Vatican Council II recognized that while it had a message for the world, it could also learn from the secular world. It is time to implement the conciliar *Declaration on Religious Freedom* within the church's own structures. Since I have been denied my rights by St Meinrad School of Theology under the guise of 'church law', I have no option but to turn to the civil courts for justice. My lawyer filed a sex discrimination complaint with the Equal Employment Opportunity Commission, and he has received a permit to file the lawsuit in federal court. This will be done within a few weeks.[8]

In light of the contemporary backlash against theologians and women in particular within the wider retrenchment from Vatican II, it is more urgent than ever that the story of the conciliar women be told. May it empower many bent-over women with courage to stand up tall and claim their baptismal rights and dignity as human beings made in the image of God. May it validate the experience of courageous men, especially bishops and priests, who experience the cost of discipleship when they break ranks with their peers in the cause of justice and charity. May it challenge fearful women and men to dare to make a difference by declaring once and for all that the Auschwitz principle of blindly following orders is no substitute for responsible Christian action and human decency. I take the liberty of paraphrasing Pastor Niemoeller's painfully true reflection: 'They came for the homosexuals, and I didn't speak up because I wasn't a homosexual . . . They came for the women, and I didn't speak up because I wasn't a woman . . . Then they came for me, and there was no one left to speak up.'

August 2001. Postscript to 'Postscript': My case was filed unsuccessfully in the Evansville District court, the Spencer County Circuit Court, and the Indiana Court of appeals. Finally, I petitioned for a *Writ of Certiorari* in the Supreme Court of the

United States, but it was denied. No court would accept my case because of how St Meinrad wrongly labelled it as belonging under the separation of church and state. Isaac McDonald, a St Meinrad monk, gave a sworn affidavit stating what President Rector Eugene Hensell told him and others. Hensell's lawyers said it would be 'very messy' if he fired me because I was tenured, and he would have to answer under public scrutiny for everything in the *Faculty Constitution*. The President/Rector alone had the constitutional right to hire and fire. The 'cleanest' way to get rid of me was to call it 'church law' and have either the Archbishop of Indianapolis, Daniel Buechlin, or the Archabbot of the St Meinrad Monastery, Timothy Sweeney, dismiss me. The American Association of University Professors conducted a special on-site investigation of St Meinrad School of Theology and censured the School for its unlawful dismissal of a tenured professor and its failure to follow its own due process and the terms of the AAUP's Statement on Academic Freedom and Tenure which the School had freely endorsed and included as an Appendix in its *Faculty Handbook*.[9]

9. The full report and censure were published in *Academe* (July–August 1996), pp. 51–60. The AAUP's censure of St Meinrad came in 1997 and was published in *Academe* (July–August 1997).

Biographies/Bibliographies

Eva Gore-Booth

LIFE. Eva Selena Gore-Booth, sister of Constance Markievicz, was born at Lissadell, County Sligo, on 22 May 1870, and educated privately. Her family were paternalistic landlords. In 1897 she renounced her ascendancy inheritance and moved to Manchester to live with the working-class activist Esther Roper, and join with her in battling for the political and economic enfranchisement of women. From 1900 she became a leading figure in the Women's Trades Union movement and she edited its paper, the *Women's Labour News*. She campaigned tirelessly on behalf of working women, writing, speaking at large gatherings throughout England and organizing deputations to MPs and cabinet ministers. Unlike her sister Constance, who was a militant revolutionist, Eva was a pacifist, who was very active in the Women's Peace Crusade during the First World War. In spite of her strenuous political schedule, she was a prolific poet and verse dramatist. Though some of the poems in *The Egyptian Pillar* (1906) treat of her life in Manchester, she was regarded as a Literary Revival writer and she was one of the poets whose work was included by AE in the revivalist anthology *New Songs* of 1904. She frequently drew on Irish materials in her poems and plays, being particularly attracted by the Cú Chulainn saga, especially by the figure of Maeve whose grave was near her family home in Sligo. Her representations of Maeve reflect her own feminist and pacifist concerns. While she disapproved of violent revolution, she was deeply moved by the

1916 Easter Rising in which her sister Constance played a leading part and wrote many poems on this theme. Her concern over the fate of the 1916 leaders and Roger Casement coincided with her broader interest in prison reform and the abolition of capital punishment. Eva had shared in the Literary Revival interest in Celtic mysticism and theosophy but in later life she became a Christian mystic. Her later writings are almost all religious or mystical in orientation. From 1917 her health began to decline; cancer was diagnosed in 1925 and she died on 30 June 1926.

CHIEF WRITINGS. *Poems* (London: Longman, 1898); *The One and the Many* (London: Longman, 1904); *Unseen Kings* (London: Longman, 1904); *The Three Resurrections and the Triumph of Maeve* (London: Longman, 1904); *The Egyptian Pillar* (Dublin: Maunsel, 1907); *The Sorrowful Princess* (London: Longman, 1907); *The Agate Lamp* (London: Longman, 1912); *The Perilous Light* (London: Erskine MacDonald, 1915); *Broken Glory* (Dublin: Maunsel, 1917); *The Sword of Justice* (London, 1918); *A Psychological and Poetic Approach to the Study of Christ in the Fourth Gospel* (London: Longman, 1923); *The Shepherd of Eternity* (London: Longman, 1925); *The House of Three Windows* (London: Longman, 1926); *The Inner Kingdom* (London: Longman, 1926); *The World's Pilgrim* (London: Longman, 1927); Esther Roper (ed.), *Collected Poems*, with 'The Inner Life of a Child', Letters, and a Biographical Introduction (London: Longman, 1929); *The Buried Life of Deirdre* (London: Longman, 1930).

BIOGRAPHY AND CRITICISM. Gifford Lewis, *Eva Gore-Booth and Esther Roper: A Biography* (London: Pandora, 1988).

Mary Condren

LIFE. Born in Dublin in 1947, Mary Condren was educated at the University of Hull, in England, Boston College and Harvard University where she completed her doctorate in the area: religion, gender, and culture. Throughout the 1970s, she worked with the Student Christian Movement of Britain and Ireland as editor of *Movement*, a journal of theology and politics, where her early writings appear in edited and co-edited collections such as *Theology and Sexual Politics* (London, 1974); *Celtic Theology* (Dublin, 1975); *For the Banished Children of Eve* (Dublin, 1976); *Why Men Priests?* (Dublin, 1978); *Abortion: The Tragic Dilemma* (Dublin, 1978); *New Heaven New Earth* (Dublin, 1978). Co-founder and co-ordinator of the Women's Project of the World Student Christian Federation, Mary Condren has also been a research resource associate in women's studies at Harvard Divinity School; a lecturer in gender analysis at Mount Oliver Institute, Dundalk; and a lecturer in women's studies at University College Dublin. She is currently director of the Institute for Feminism and Religion in Ireland and a research associate in the Centre for Gender and Women's Studies at Trinity College Dublin. A founding editor of the *Irish Journal of Feminist Studies*, her current writing is on the complementary roles of women and men in war, founding the sacrificial social contract.

CHIEF WRITINGS. 'An Introduction to Feminist Theology', *Banshee, Journal of Irishwomen United*, vol. 1, no. 1 (1976); 'Power', in *Woman Power* (Geneva: World Student Christian Federation, 1981); 'Patriarchy and Death', in *Womanspirit Bonding*, eds Janet Kalven and Mary Buckley (New York: Pilgrim Press, 1984); 'To Bear Children for the Fatherland: Mothers and Militarism', *Concilium* (December 1989), and in *The Power of Naming*, ed. Elisabeth Schüssler Fiorenza (New York: Orbis Books, 1996); 'Women as a Colonised People', in *Womanspirit*, vol. 7, no. 2 (autumn 1993); *The Serpent and the Goddess: Women, Religion, and Power in Celtic Ireland* (San Francisco: Harper and Row, 1989); 'Women, Religion, and Northern Ireland', in *Papers from Women and Religion Conference* (Centre for Research on Women, University of Ulster, Jordanstown, 1992); 'Sacrifice and Political Legitimation: The Production of a Gendered Social Order', *Journal of Women's History* (spring 1995); 'Feminism, Religion, and Therapy', *Inside/Out: A Quarterly Publication for Humanistic and Integrative Psychotherapy*, vol. 23 (1995); 'Forgetting Our Divine Origins: The Warning of Dervogilla', in *From the Realm of the Ancestors: An Anthology in Honor of Marija Gimbutas*,

ed. Joan Marler (Manchester, Conn.: Knowledge, Ideas and Trends, 1997), also published in *Irish Journal of Feminist Studies*, vol. 2, no. 1 (1997), pp. 117–32; 'Mercy Not Sacrifice: Toward a Celtic Theology', *Feminist Theology*, no. 15 (May 1997); 'Von Menschenhand gemacht: Die gesellschaftliche Konstruktion heiliger Orte', in *Schlangenbrut: streitschrift für feministische und religiöös interessierte frauen*, Nr. 66 17. Jg. (1999), pp. 28–31; 'Women, Shame and Abjection: Reflections in the Light of Julia Kristeva', *Contact: The Interdisciplinary Journal of Pastoral Studies*, no. 130 (1999), pp. 10–19; 'The Theology of Sacrifice and the Non-Ordination of Women', in *Concilium: The Non-Ordination of Women and the Politics of Power*, ed. Elisabeth Schüssler Fiorenza and Hermann Haring, vol. 3 (London: SCM Press, 1999), pp. 50–7; 'The Uncreated Conscience of Our Race', in *Celtic Threads*, ed. Padraigin Clancy (Dublin: Veritas Books, 1999), pp. 1–11; 'Brigit: Soulsmith for the New Millennium', in *Concilium: In the Power of Wisdom*, eds María Pilar Aquino and Elisabeth Schüssler Fiorenza (London: SCM Press, 2000), pp. 107–19.

Rita Hannon

LIFE. Rita Hannon was born in County Sligo in 1935. She joined La Sainte Union Sisters in 1953 and became a teacher in 1959. She studied theology in Rome (Regina Mundi) and philosophy in King's College, London, and then taught at La Sainte Union College in Southampton and St Paul's College, Rugby. In 1978 she went to Africa (Burundi) and to Tanzania in 1980 as a secondary school teacher, where she also did voluntary work with women and the poor. She is now retired and living in Ireland.

CHIEF WRITINGS. *The Question of Women and the Priesthood: Can Women be Admitted to Holy Orders?* (Dublin: Geoffrey Chapman, 1967).

Mary Malone

LIFE. Mary T. Malone was born in Ballycanew, County Wexford, in 1938. After studies at University College Dublin (BA) and Victory University, Manchester (B.Ed.), she completed her early studies at the University of Toronto, gaining a Ph.D. in classical languages and literature (1970). She taught feminist theology and history at the Toronto School of Theology from 1974 to 1987 when she transferred to St Jerome's University, Waterloo, Ontario. In 1998 she retired as chair of the Department of Religious Studies and now lives in Wexford.

CHIEF WRITINGS. *Who is My Mother: Rediscovering the Mother of Jesus* (Dubuque, Iowa: Wm C. Brown, 1984); *Women Christians: New Vision* (Dubuque, Iowa: Wm C. Brown, 1985); 'Women and Religion: Aspects of a Conversation About God', *Vox Feminarum* (March 1996), pp. 26–38; 'Leaving Home: Finding a Voice', *Vox Feminarum* (July 1999), pp. 11–18; 'Women in Theology', *The Furrow* (April 1999), pp. 217–25; 'Living Without a Wiger Tree', *Doctrine and Life* (September 1999), pp. 398–404; 'A Preacher for the Celtic Tiger', *Doctrine and Life* (November 1999), pp. 516–23; *Women and Christianity: The First Thousand Years*, vol. 1 (Dublin: Columba Press, 2000).

Linda Hogan

LIFE. Linda Hogan, born 1964 in Callan, County Kilkenny, is a graduate of St Patrick's College, Maynooth, and Trinity College Dublin, where she gained her Ph.D. in 1993. She held the post of lecturer in gender, ethics and religion at the University of Leeds from 1995 to 2001. She is currently lecturer in international peace studies at the Irish School of Ecumenics, Trinity College Dublin.

CHIEF WRITINGS. *From Women's Experience to Feminist Theology* (Sheffield: Sheffield Academic Press, 1995); *Christian Perspectives on Development Education: Human Rights* (Dublin and London: Veritas/Trocaire/CAFOD, 1998); *Confronting the Truth: Conscience in the Catholic Tradition* (New York: Paulist Press, 2000).

Anne Thurston

LIFE. Born in Dublin in 1950, Anne Thurston studied English and German for her BA in University College Dublin, where she also completed her MA in German literature in 1973, and a Higher Diploma in Education in 1974. In 1975–6 she worked as an assistant lecturer in the German department at UCD. As a mature student, she studied theology in Trinity College Dublin and was awarded a BD in 1993. She has contributed to courses in several Dublin institutes including the Irish School of Ecumenics, the Church of Ireland Theological College, and Kimmage Institute. She is currently teaching a course in feminist theology on the Graduate Diploma in Humanities in All Hallows Dublin and in Marianella Pastoral Institute Dublin. She is a freelance writer and lecturer, and a frequent national broadcaster. Her current interests include feminist perspectives on Scripture and the interface between art and theology.

CHIEF WRITINGS. 'Living with Ambiguity: Divorce, Remarriage and the Eucharist', *Doctrine and Life*, vol. 44, no. 9 (November 1994), pp. 537–42; 'The Risk of the Human: Discerning the Body', *The Furrow*, vol. 50, no. 1 (January 1999), pp. 8–17; *Because of Her Testimony: The Word in Female Experience* (Dublin: Gill and Macmillan, 1995: New York: Crossroad, 1995); *Knowing Her Place: Gender and the Gospels* (Dublin: Gill and Macmillan, 1998; New York: Paulist Press, 1999).

Celine Mangan

LIFE. Born in Killorglin, County Kerry, in 1938, Celine Mangan is a Dominican Sister and lecturer in Scripture at the Milltown Institute of Philosophy and Theology, Dublin. Her MA in Semitic languages is from University College Dublin and she studied also at the École Biblique, Jerusalem. She received a Licentiate in Sacred Scripture from the Pontifical Commission, Rome. She has worked with many groups, especially as the Scriptures relate to women and ecology.

CHIEF WRITINGS. *I Am With You: Biblical Experiences of God* (Dublin: Veritas, 1975); *1 and 2 Chronicles, Ezra and Nehemiah*, Old Testament Message Series (Wilmington: Glazier, 1982); *Can We still Call God Father?* (Wilmington: Glazier, 1983); *Women in the New Testament*, Study programme for the Women's Study Group (Dublin: Irish Commission for Justice and Peace, 1994).

Anne Primavesi

LIFE. Anne Primavesi was born in Dublin in 1934. She took a BD degree at London University, followed by a doctorate in systematic theology. Primavesi was formerly research fellow in environmental theology at the Department of Theology and Religious Studies, University of Bristol. She is currently at the Centre for the Interdisciplinary Study of Religions, Birkbeck, University of London, and is a fellow of the Westar Institute, Santa Rosa, California.

CHIEF WRITINGS. *Our God Has No Favourites: A Liberation Theology of the Eucharist*, with J. Henderson (Tunbridge Wells: Burns and Oates; San Jose: Resources Publications, 1989); *From Apocalypse to Genesis: Ecology, Feminism and Christianity* (Tunbridge Wells: Burns and Oates; Minnesota: Fortress Press, 1991), German, Spanish, and Portuguese editions also available; 'A Tide in the Affairs of Women?', in *Ecotheology: Voices from South and North* (Geneva: Orbis Books; New York: WCC Publications, 1994), pp. 186–99; 'The Spirit of Genesis: Liberation and Environmental Theology', in *Upptäckter i Kontexten: Teologiska föreläsningar till minne av Per Frostin*, eds Sigurd Bergmann, Göran Eidevall (Lund: Institutet för Kontextuell Teologi, 1995), pp. 98–117; 'Faith in Creation', in *True to This Earth: Global Challenges and Transforming Faith*, eds Alan Race and Roger Williamson (Oxford: Oneworld Publications, 1995); 'A Just and Fruitful Creation', in *Industrial Mission in a Changing World*, ed. J. Rogerson (Sheffield:

Sheffield Academic Press, 1996), pp. 91–102; 'Accepting Diversity: Healing a Violent World', in *Pastoral Theology's and Pastoral Psychology's Contributions to Helping Heal a Violent World*, ed. M. Cordner (Surakarta, Indonesia: Dabara Publishers, 1996), pp. 11–20, 256–8; 'Earth the Original Ark', in *Passion for Critique: Essays in Honour of F.J. Laishley*, eds Herman Browne and Gwen Griffith-Dickson (Prague: The Ecumenical Publishing House, 1997), pp. 131–51; 'Biodiversity and Responsibility: A Basis for a Nonviolent Environmental Ethic', in *Faith and Praxis in a Postmodern Age*, ed. Ursula King (London and New York: Cassell, 1998), pp. 47–60; 'The Recovery of Wisdom: Gaia Theory and Environmental Policy', in *Spirit of the Environment*, eds David Cooper and Joy Palmer (London and New York: Routledge, 1998), pp. 73–86; 'The Christian Gene', *The Fourth R*, vol. 14, no. 3 (May–June 2001), pp. 3–8.

Ann Louise Gilligan

LIFE. Born in Dublin in 1945, Ann Louise Gilligan is a lecturer in the Department of Education and co-ordinator of the Centre for Educational Disadvantage, St Patrick's College, Drumcondra. She is chairperson of the National Educational Welfare Board, and co-founder of the Shanty Educational Project.

CHIEF WRITINGS. 'Returning for the First Time' in *Faith and the Intifada: Palestinian Christian Voices*, eds Naim S. Ateek, Marc H. Ellis and Rosemary Radford Ruether (New York: Orbis, 1992), pp. 188–92; 'Finding a Voice Where They Found a Vision: Feminist Theology and Spirituality in Ireland', in *Feminist Theology in a European Context*, eds Annette Esser and Louise Schottroff (Yearbook of the European Society for Women in Theological Research) (Kampen: Kok Pharos Publishing House, 1993); 'Lifestyle: Women's Community Education', *EcoTheology*, vol. 1 (July 1996), pp. 103–5; 'Education Towards a Feminist Imagination', in *Women and Education in Ireland*, vol. 1, eds Brid Connolly and Anne Bridget Ryan (Maynooth: MACE, 1999).

Iris Murdoch

LIFE. [Jean] Iris Murdoch was born in Dublin in 1919 of Anglo-Irish parents, spent her schooldays in London and Bristol and her childhood holidays in Ireland. She went to Oxford University and later to Cambridge as a student in philosophy. In 1942 she worked in the Treasury. After the end of the Second World War she went to Belgium and then Austria, where she worked in a Displaced Persons Camp. In 1948 she became a fellow of St Anne's College, Oxford, where she taught philosophy for many years, living in Oxford with her husband, Professor John Bayley. She received numerous honorary degrees from American and English universities, a CBE in 1976 and a DBE in 1987. Her literary successes include the James Tait Memorial Prize for *The Black Prince* (1973), the Whitbread Literary Award for *The Sacred and Profane Love Machine* (1974), and the Booker Prize for *The Sea, the Sea* (1978). Her novels have been translated into twenty-six languages and several have been adapted for television. Her portrait by Tom Philips was hung in the British National Gallery in 1987. She died in February 1999.

CHIEF WRITINGS. (Novels) *Under the Net* (1953); *The Flight from the Enchanter* (1956); *The Sandcastle* (1957); *The Bell* (1958); *A Severed Head* (1961); *An Unofficial Rose* (1962); *The Unicorn* (1963); *The Italian Girl* (1964); *The Red and the Green* (1965); *The Time of the Angels* (1966); *The Nice and the Good* (1968); *Bruno's Dream* (1969); *A Fairly Honourable Defeat* (1970); *An Accidental Man* (1971); *The Black Prince* (1973); *The Sacred and Profane Love Machine* (1974); *A Word Child* (1975); *Henry and Cato* (1976); *The Sea, the Sea* (1978); *Nuns and Soldiers* (1980); *The Philosopher's Pupil* (1983); *The Good Apprentice* (1985); *The Book and the Brotherhood* (1987); *A Message to the Planet* (1989); *The Green Knight* (1993); *Jackson's Dilemma* (1995). All published in London by Chatto and Windus. (Drama) with

J.B. Priestley, *A Severed Head* (London: French, 1964); with J. Saunders, *The Italian Girl* (London: French, 1968); *The Servants and the Snow and The Three Arrows* (London: Chatto and Windus, 1973); *Joanna, Joanna* (London: Colophon, 1994). (Poetry) *A Year of the Birds* (London: Chatto and Windus, 1984). (Non-fiction) *Sartre: Romantic Rationalist* (London: Bowes, 1953); *The Sovereignty of Good Over Other Concepts* (Cambridge: Cambridge University Press, 1967); *The Fire and the Sun: Why Plato Banished the Artists* (London: Clarendon, 1977); *Acastos: Two Platonic Dialogues* (London: Chatto and Windus, 1986); *Metaphysics as a Guide to Morals* (London: Chatto and Windus, 1992).

BIOGRAPHY AND CRITICISM. (Selected) A.S. Byatt, *Degrees of Freedom: The Novels of Iris Murdoch* (London: Chatto and Windus; New York: Barnes and Noble, 1965); Peter Wolfe, *The Disciplined Heart: Iris Murdoch and Her Novels* (Columbia: University of Missouri Press, 1966); Frank Baldanza, *Iris Murdoch* (New York: Twayne, 1974); Donna Gerstenberger, *Iris Murdoch* (Lewisburgh, Penn.: Bucknell University Press; London: Associated University Press, 1975); Rubin Rabinovitz, 'Iris Murdoch', in *Six Contemporary British Novelists* (ed.) G. Stade (New York: Columbia University Press, 1976); Jack I. Biles, 'Interview', *Studies in the Literary Imagination*, vol. 11, no. 2 (1978), pp. 115–25; Richard Todd, *Iris Murdoch: The Shakespearean Interest* (London: Vision; New York: Barnes and Noble, 1979); Elizabeth Dipple, *Iris Murdoch: Work for the Spirit* (London: Methuen: Chicago: University of Chicago Press, 1982); Richard Todd, *Iris Murdoch* (London and New York: Methuen, 1984); Harold Bloom (ed.), *Iris Murdoch* (New York: Chelsea, 1986); Peter J. Conradi, *Iris Murdoch: The Saint and the Artist* (New York: St Martin's Press, 1986); Kate Bagnal, *Iris Murdoch: A Reference Guide* (Boston: G.K. Hall, 1987); Richard Todd (ed.), *Encounters with Iris Murdoch* (Amsterdam: Free University Press, 1988); Sugana Ramanathan, *Iris Murdoch: Figures of Good* (New York: St Martin's Press, 1990); Darlene D. Mettler, *Sound and Sense: Musical Allusion and Imagery in the Novels of Iris Murdoch* (New York: Peter Lang, 1991); Jeffrey Meyers, 'An Interview with Iris Murdoch', *Denver Quarterly*, vol. 26, no. 1 (summer 1991), pp. 102–11; Diana Phillips, *Agencies of the Good in the Work of Iris Murdoch* (New York: Peter Lang, 1991); Lindsay Tucker (ed.), *Critical Essays on Iris Murdoch* (New York: G.K. Hall, 1992); Cheryl K. Bove, *Understanding Iris Murdoch* (Columbia: University of South Carolina Press, 1993); Jack Turner, *Murdoch vs. Freud: A Freudian Look at an Anti-Freudian* (New York: Peter Lang, 1993); David J. Gordon, *Iris Murdoch's Fables of Unselfing* (Columbia: University of Missouri Press, 1995); Maria Antonaccio and William Schweiker (eds), *Iris Murdoch and the Search for Human Goodness* (Chicago: University of Chicago Press, 1996).

Phyllis Rooney

LIFE. Born in 1953, Phyllis Rooney grew up in north Leitrim. She attended Ard Lughaidh, Bundoran, County Donegal, and Trinity College Dublin, and completed her Ph.D. in philosophy and logic at the University of California at Berkeley. She is now an associate professor of philosophy at Oakland University in Michigan. Her current work examines the philosophical impact of the persistent historical exclusion of women or the 'feminine' from ideals and domains of reason and argues for a rethinking of conceptions of reason in the light of such exclusions. She is now working on a book on reason and gender, and on an introductory text in feminist epistemology.

CHIEF WRITINGS. 'Gendered Reason: Sex Metaphor and Conceptions of Reason', *Hypatia*, vol. 6, no. 2 (summer 1991), pp. 77–103; 'A Different Voice: On the Feminist Challenge in Moral Theory', *Philosophical Forum*, vol. 22, no. 4 (1991), pp. 335–61; 'Recent Work in Feminist Discussions of Reason', *American Philosophical Quarterly*, vol. 31, no. 1 (1994), pp. 1–21; 'Rationality and the Politics of Gender Difference,' *Metaphilosophy*, vol. 26, nos 1 and 2 (1995), pp. 22–45; 'Putting Naturalized Epistemology to Work', in *Epistemology: The Big Questions*, ed. Linda Martin Alcoff (Oxford: Blackwell, 1998), pp. 285–305.

Attracta Ingram

LIFE. Born in County Offaly in 1945, Attracta Ingram studied philosophy at University College Dublin in the late 1960s and later obtained her Ph.D. from Trinity College Dublin. She has lived and studied in the UK, the US and Italy and is now associate professor of politics in UCD. Her research interests include rights theory, liberalism, pluralism, and citizenship and national identity.

CHIEF WRITINGS. 'Gender Cleansing Justice', *Feminist Legal Studies*, vol. 1, no. 2 (1993), pp. 209–14; *A Political Theory of Rights* (Oxford: Clarendon Press, 1994); co-editor, *Justice and Legal Theory in Ireland* (Dublin: Oaktree Press, 1995); 'Rawlsians, Pluralists, and Cosmopolitans', in *Pluralism and Philosophy*, ed. Dave Archard (Cambridge: Royal Institute of Philosophy and Cambridge University Press, 1996); 'Constitutional Patriotism', *Philosophy and Social Criticism*, vol. 22, no. 6 (1996), pp. 1–18; co-editor, *Questioning Ireland: Essays in Political Philosophy and Social Policy* (Dublin: Institute of Public Administration, 2000); joint editor, *Pluralism: The Philosophy and Politics of Diversity* (London: Routledge, 2000).

Onora O'Neill

LIFE. Onora O'Neill was born in 1941 in Aughafattern, Northern Ireland, and was educated at Oxford and Harvard University before beginning a teaching career in the United States and England. Formerly professor and head of the Philosophy Department at the University of Essex, she is principal of Newnham College, Cambridge. Internationally recognized for her contributions to philosophy, she has written widely on ethics and political philosophy, with particular interests in questions of international justice, and in the philosophy of Immanuel Kant. She has been president of the Aristotelian Society (1988–9), a member of the Animal Procedures (Scientific) Committee (1990–4) and of the Nuffield Council on Bioethics 1991–8 (chairman 1996–8). She was a member and later acting chairman of the Human Genetics Advisory Commission (1996–9). Currently chairman of the Nuffield Foundation, she was created a life peer in January 1999 and sits as a cross-bencher.

CHIEF WRITINGS. Published under the name Onora Nell, *Acting on Principle* (New York: Columbia University Press, 1975); editor, with William Ruddick, *Having Children: Legal and Philosophical Reflections on Parenthood* (New York: Oxford University Press, 1998); *Faces of Hunger: An Essay on Poverty, Development and Justice* (London: George Allen and Unwin, 1986), revised edition to be published by Cambridge University Press; *Constructions of Reason: Explorations of Kant's Practical Philosophy* (Cambridge: Cambridge University Press, 1989); *Towards Justice and Virtue: A Constructive Account of Practical Reasoning* (Cambridge: Cambridge University Press, 1996), German ed., *Tugend und Gerechtigkeit; Eine Konstruktive Darstellung des practischen Denkens* (Berlin: Akademie Verlag, 1996); *Bounds of Justice* (Cambridge: Cambridge University Press, 2000).

Dolores Dooley

LIFE. Dolores Dooley was born in 1940 and raised in Chicago, Illinois; she emigrated to Ireland in 1974 after marrying a Dubliner she met at the University of Notre Dame, where she completed her Ph.D. in ethics. She began lecturing at the National University of Ireland at Cork in 1975. She lectures in bioethics to nursing and medical students and was a founder team-member of the MA in women's studies at University College Cork. Her collaboration with colleagues in women's studies energized her research in co-operative socialist feminism of the nineteenth century, resulting in *Equality in Community* (1996) and in 1997 a student's edition of William Thompson's (1825) *Appeal on Behalf of One Half of the Human Race*. During the 1990s she worked in several European Union projects in bioethics and completed a text for health care practitioners, *Ethics in New Reproductive Technologies*. She was a founding editor of the *Irish Journal of Feminist Studies* and serves on the advisory board of the *Journal of Medical Ethics*.

CHIEF WRITINGS. 'Moral Disagreement and Abortion', in *The Abortion Papers Ireland*, ed. Ailbhe Smyth (Dublin: Attic Press, 1992), pp. 166–74; 'Anna Doyle Wheeler', in *Women, Power and Consciousness in Nineteenth Century Ireland*, eds Mary Cullen and Maria Luddy (Dublin: Attic Press, 1995), pp. 19–53; *Equality in Community: Sexual Equality in the Philosophy of William Thompson and Anna Doyle Wheeler* (Cork: Cork University Press, 1996); editor of William Thompson, *Appeal on Behalf of One Half the Human Race* [1825] (Cork: Cork University Press, 1997); 'Gendered Citizenship in the Irish Constitution,' in *Ireland's Evolving Constitution 1937–1997*, eds Tim Murphy and Patrick Twomey (Oxford: Hart Publications, 1998), pp. 121–33; 'Ethics and Genetic Screening in the Republic of Ireland,' in *The Ethics of Genetic Screening*, eds Ruth Chadwick et al. (Dordrecht, Netherlands: Kluwer Publishers, 1999), pp. 95–105, and 'Reconciling Liberty and the Common Good?', pp. 191–207; 'Assisted Procreation: The Pursuit of Consensus?', *Medico-Legal Journal of Ireland*, vol. 5, no. 2 (1999), pp. 65–9.

Geraldine Smyth

LIFE. Born in Belfast in 1948, Geraldine Smyth was educated in St Kevin's Primary School and St Dominic's High School, Falls Road, Belfast, and at the University of Ulster, Coleraine, County Derry, where she read English. After taking an MA programme in the Irish School of Ecumenics, she gained a Ph.D. in theology at Trinity College Dublin in 1993. Active in the ecumenical movement in Ireland and further afield, she was appointed director of the Irish School of Ecumenics and served from 1994 to 1999; she is currently on the staff at ISE, which is now integrated into Trinity College. A member of the Irish Dominican Congregation, Smyth was elected Congregation Prioress in 1998.

CHIEF WRITINGS. *A Way of Transformation: A Theological Evaluation of the Conciliar Process of Mutual Commitment to Justice, Peace, and the Integrity of Creation. World Council of Churches, 1983–91* (Berlin: New York: Peter Lang, 1995); 'Sectarianism: Theology Gone Wrong?', in *Sectarianism: Papers of the Corrymeela Ecumenical Conference*, eds. Alan Falconer and Trevor Williams (Dublin: Dominican Publications, Irish School of Ecumenics, 1995); 'Peace in Ireland? Grace Beyond Innocence', *Doctrine and Life*, vol. 46, no. 5 (May–June 1996); 'Sabbath and Jubilee', in *The Jubilee Challenge: Utopia or Possibility? Jewish and Christian Insights*, ed. Hans Ucko (Geneva: World Council of Churches Publishers, 1997); 'A Turning Point in Scotland and Ireland', in *A Turning Point in Ireland and Scotland: The Challenge to the Churches and Theology Today*, Occasional Paper no. 43 (Edinburgh: Centre for Theology and Public Issues, New College, University of Edinburgh, 1998); 'Envisaging a New Identity and a Common Home: Seeking Peace on our Borders,' *Milltown Studies* (winter 2000), pp. 58–84.

Katherine Zappone

LIFE. Katherine E. Zappone was born in Spokane, Washington, in 1953. She was educated at Seattle University (BA), Catholic University

Washington, DC (MA), University College Dublin (MBA), and Boston College (Ph.D.). She came to Ireland in 1983, and for the next nine years lectured on feminist theology and feminist spirituality throughout Ireland, including a number of years in practical theology and women's studies at Trinity College Dublin. In 1986 she co-founded and co-directed the Shanty Educational Project with Ann Louise Gilligan. She was a founding member and editor of *Womanspirit: The Irish Journal of Feminist Spirituality*. Former chief executive officer of the National Women's Council of Ireland, Katherine Zappone is now an independent social policy research consultant, a commissioner of the Irish Human Rights Commission.

CHIEF WRITINGS. *The Hope for Wholeness: A Spirituality for Feminists* (Mystic, Conn.: Twenty-Third Publications, 1991); 'Women's Special Nature: A Different Horizon for Theological Anthropology', *Concilium*, vol. 3 (1992), pp. 87–97; 'The Faith of Feminists: Charting New Territory', *Vox Feminarum: The Canadian Journal of Feminist Spirituality*, vol. 1, no. 1 (1996), pp. 5–18; 'Top-Down or Bottom-Up: The Involvement of the Community Sector in Partnership', in *In the Shadow of the Tiger: New Approaches to Combating Social Exclusion*, eds P. Kirby and D. Jacobsen (Dublin: Dublin City University Press, 1998); with Susan McNaughton, 'Should We Stay at the Table: Evaluating Social Partnership in Ireland', in *Social Partnership in a New Century*, eds Seán Healy and Brigid Reynolds (Dublin: Conference of Religious in Ireland, 1999).

Carmel McEnroy

LIFE. Carmel McEnroy was born in Ballinamore, County Leitrim, in 1936 and was educated by the Sisters of Mercy in Leitrim and Ballymahon, County Longford. She joined the order in 1955, volunteered for the US mission and went to teach in Columbia, Missouri, in 1961. She obtained her BA degree from Marillac College, St Louis, and her MA and Ph.D. in systematic theology from the University of St Michael's College, Toronto. She has taught in Ireland, Canada and the USA, including fourteen years at St Meinrad School of Theology, Indiana. She has been Visiting Lilly Professor at Berea College, Kentucky. She received the Catholic Press Association Book Award in History/Biography in 1997 for *Guests in Their Own House*. Carmel McEnroy is currently a part-time adjunct professor of Catholic studies at a Protestant seminary in Lexington, Kentucky. She is writing her legal story, *Monkey Business: The Miscarriage of Justice in McEnroy v. St Meinrad*.

CHIEF WRITINGS. 'Women of Vatican II: Recovering a Dangerous Memory', *The Church in the Nineties: Its Legacy, Its Future*, ed. Pierre Hegy (Minnesota: Liturgical Press, 1993), pp. 149–57; lead article for Symposium Review of Leonard Swidler's *Toward a Catholic Constitution* (New York: Crossroad, 1996) in *Horizons*, vol. 24, no. 1 (spring 1997), pp. 100–4; *Guests in Their Own House: The Women of Vatican II* (New York: Crossroad, 1996); 'Friends, What Have You Done to Me? The Crucified Woman Challenges the Gold-Crowned Jesus', *Toronto Journal of Theology*, vol. 16, no. 1 (2000), pp. 167–86.

SIOBHÁN KILFEATHER, *Editor*

Sexuality, 1685–2001

If I'd known we were going to cast our feelings into words, I'd have memorised the Song of Solomon.[1]

What have people in Ireland written about, when they have written about sexuality? It is a topic on which everyone might claim some expertise, yet it is also popularly believed to be the area of ourselves we understand least.

John McGahern has described one of the problems inherent in writing about sexuality:

> Yes, you almost can't write about sex, like you can't write about happiness, because in a way it's private and it's mechanical . . . Pornography is everything that sexuality is not: it's a fantasy, it's cruel, it's not real, and the other thing is frail, it's vulnerable, it's awkward, it's difficult, and actually, by putting a backdrop of pornography, is to see can one have a look at sexuality. That was the idea behind *The Pornographer*. It's like trying to follow the sun in the dusk rather than looking up at the sky.[2]

The question 'Can one have a look at sexuality?' might be followed by 'Can one say anything new about it?' Elaine Scarry has written of the 'unsharability' of another intimate physical experience, that of pain, an unsharability ensured 'through its resistance to language'. 'Physical pain does not simply resist language but actively destroys it, bringing about an immediate reversion to a state anterior to language, to the sounds and cries a human being makes before language

is learned.'[3] Something similar might be said about orgasm (which we tend to call physical pleasure) but with very different political implications of course. The relief of pain is almost universally understood to be 'good'. Scarry argues persuasively for the commitment of intellectual work to achieve this good. Towards the end of his influential *History of Sexuality: Volume One* Michel Foucault makes an appeal for a movement in discussion of sexuality towards 'bodies and pleasure'.[4] Judith Butler has questioned Foucault's maintenance of the existence of a body 'prior to its cultural inscription' as assuming a 'materiality prior to signification and form'.[5] For Butler a history of sexuality could not be a history of bodies, but a history of meanings. The issue of the materiality of bodies and how they can be understood to signify has particular resonance in an Irish context, since for much of the period since 1680 the Irish were governed by institutions that made no attempt to represent the majority of people, and in a language foreign to that majority. There is a strong temptation when discussing the famine for example, to let the crudest materiality — a body count — dominate interpretation.

Writing about sexuality can be an embarrassment to both author and readers and although such embarrassment may be effectively exploited within texts, it may also be part of the reason why literature on the subject so often turns to quotation and allusion. The tradition of writing about love and sex in Western European

1. Tom Reagan (Gabriel Byrne) to Verna (Marcia Gay Harden) in *Miller's Crossing* (written by Ethan Coen and Joel Coen, dir. by Joel Coen, USA, 1990).
2. Rosa Gonzales Casademont, 'An Interview with John McGahern', *Europen English Messenger*, vol. 4, no. 1 (spring 1995), pp. 19–20.
3. Elaine Scarry, *The Body in Pain* (New York: Oxford University Press, 1985) p. 4.
4. Michel Foucault, *The History of Sexuality*. Volume I: *An Introduction* (London: Penguin, 1979).
5. Judith Butler, *Gender Trouble: Feminism and the Subversion of Identity* (New York: Routledge, 1990), p. 130.

literatures is long established and some of the best known examples in that tradition raise important questions as to what writers are interested in when they contemplate sexuality as a subject. It could be argued of the most famous practitioners of love poetry, the Renaissance sonneteers including Petrarch, Sidney and Shakespeare, that the challenge for such writers is one of form. In Western literature 'The Song of Solomon', Ovid's *Amores* and *Metamorphoses,* the lyrics of Sappho, Plato's *Symposium,* the fidelity of Penelope and Deirdre, the jealousy of Emer, the rape of Philomel, the vengeance of Medea, the dance of Salome, the repentance of Mary Magdalen, the loss of Euridyce have been translated, adapted, transformed and alluded to by writers through the centuries, who have found that telling old stories in new tones or new contexts has enabled them to speak to both the deeply familiar, internal and yet shared experience of sexual feelings, and at the same time to register novelty and alienation. It has also allowed writers of each generation to test themselves against the standards set by their predecessors. Sexuality is a major theme not only in love poetry but in satire, and again one can see in satirists such as Jonathan Swift and Molly Keane the response to a literary tradition. Swift directed his critique of eighteenth-century society by way of Horace and other classical satirists, while Keane developed the novel of manners perfected by Frances Burney, Maria Edgeworth and Jane Austen to chronicle the 'domestic violence' of early twentieth-century Irish gentry living. Because of this interest in form, genre has been one of the central preoccupations in these pages.

In its original uses the term sexuality was concerned with organizing knowledge about plants and animals along lines of difference. In the modern period writing about sexuality has as one of its concerns a meditation on the relationship between biological (anatomical or chromosomal) sexual difference and gender difference, or the ways in which people learn to behave as male or female and how the performance of that difference influences the sense of self.

Whatever the foundation of sexual difference, its elaboration across the life of an individual is always enwrapped in other issues, other discourses. There is no such thing as an unmediated representation of sexual acts or sexual attitudes. Twentieth-century debates on the nature of sexuality tended to divide, though not always simply divide, between what are called essentialist and social constructionist theories of sexuality. Essentialist theories might briefly be characterized as those which propose that certain facts about bodies and desires are and always have been universally true — for example, that men and women are anatomically different, or that every child desires her/his mother until culture intervenes to regulate that desire.

Opposed to the essentialist arguments, which have been most strongly defended by physical scientists, have been the proponents of theories for the 'social construction' of sexuality. At its crudest, social constructionism sometimes seems to imply that sexuality is a 'learned' behaviour, while at its broadest it could be seen to argue that no utterance is free of context. Achilles and Patrocles, Abelard and Eloise, Diarmuid and Gráinne, Swift, Johnson and Vanhomrigh, Parnell and O'Shea, Yeats and Gonne, Wilde and Douglas, Somerville and Ross experienced desires, acted and uttered as they did within possibilities that were formed and amended by world views that included expectations about how people should feel about one another, their access to different kinds of freedom within institutions such as family, church and state, deep cultural taboos regarding endogamous and exogamous relationships. At different historical periods there have been various understandings of the right — if such a right exists — to self-determination, including the right freely to manage and dispose of one's body according to one's own needs and desires.

If the social construction of sexuality does not imply complete freedom of choice — since every person is formed within and acted upon by matrices of power and belief — there have been theorists who have seen certain deployments of sexuality as potentially radical political acts, just as normative sexual expression (marriage and reproduction) could be understood as conservative practises fostered by the state and proceeding in its interests. In the latter half of the twentieth century the idea that it is possible to represent fully or well a gender or sexual identity one has not experienced oneself came to be seen as more and more problematic. Male representations of female sexuality and straight representations of queer sexualities could be deconstructed as forms of stereotyping or expressions of phobia. Where the representations are telling, then often biographies of writers have been rewritten to explain the experiences (including the experiences of desires) that might have given rise to a particular insight.

A vocabulary of 'voice', 'experience', 'body', 'history' and 'identity' has been developed by theorists who assert the importance of recognizing essential differences between men and women, and there have also been proponents of essentialism in terms of sexual identities. The veneration of authenticity and the conviction that self-knowledge is possible were suspicious to other people who felt that it was possible to accept the slogan that the personal is political and yet still analyse experience and narrative. The women's movement of the 1960s and 1970s placed a high value on personal testimony and the grounding of political action in personal experience. While academic critics adopted some of these perspectives, they tended to do so within an analytic framework that interrogated ideas of authenticity and the formation of subjectivity. Journalism and other more popular forms of writing continued to favour personal testimony and confessional modes of address, to the extent that early twenty-first century Irish society might be described as dominated by confessional culture, whether in the personalisation of debates over divorce and abortion (see Vol. v, pp. 1409–15), the popularity of tabloid journalism, chat shows and scandal, the dominance of the 'memoir' across genres including autobiography, anthropology, fiction, drama, poetry, film and television, and the widespread interest in modes of remembrance. One of the most frequently reiterated criticisms of volumes I–III of *The Field Day Anthology* was that it failed to provide a narrative that could help to interpret events such as the death of Ann Lovett (see Vol. v, pp. 1409–15). Early discussions of volumes IV and V were inflected by the impetus to provide such narratives, but also by a deep distrust of the notion that an anthology could or should be representative. The material on sexuality is largely a collection of stories and at first glance it is largely a collection of examples of what Mary Wollstonecraft called the 'Wrongs of Woman', a

phrase used by Charlotte Elizabeth Tonna to title her history of women in 1843, see Vol. v, pp. 1435–9. There are stories of violence, poverty, coercion, children abused and murdered, women beaten, raped, abandoned, forced into unwanted sexual liaisons including marriage, traded, enslaved and exploited. There are also narratives of desire and of the affections, and examples of transgressive behaviour that defied or subverted the conventions of each period. The extracts have been chosen as much on the basis of form as of content, so that each piece might raise questions about the materiality of the body and how that takes shape in language.

Attempts to narrate histories of sexuality generally encompass the arenas of sexual behaviour and of sexual attitudes. We have two primary means of knowing about the history of sexual behaviour: the first is through a study of demography and the other is through personal description. The study of demography is complex for a number of reasons, the most obvious being that it depends on the analysis of imperfect records, and in making any claim about changes in population, for example shifts in age of first marriage, it must take account of a wide range of contingent factors. For example, was there less illegitimacy in eighteenth-century Ireland than in other European countries because there was less extra-marital sexual desire? or because people were more 'virtuous'? or because people were skilful at preventing conception? or because there were lower levels of fertility? or because women procured abortions, or committed infanticide before the births were detected? or because pregnant women were more likely to marry their lovers? Are the records accurate? Each of these questions needs to be weighed very carefully and examined in a local as well as a national context. Can personal description help to adjudicate amongst the possibilities thrown up by statistics and reveal what happened sexually in the past? Since this is an anthology of writings rather than a history of sexuality it is more concerned with attitudes than with behaviour and where it does concern itself with behaviour it places its emphasis on those personal descriptions which can easily be excerpted, read and interpreted without specialist historical skills.

Personal description also needs to be broken down into two categories: evidence generated by subjects about their sexuality, among which one might include letters, diaries, folk-tales, songs and other broadly autobiographical narratives including fiction; and evidence extracted from subjects by institutions which take an interest in sexual practices (the state, churches, aspects of scientific enquiry) including medical treatise, courtroom evidence, demographic and anthropological surveys, history, journalism, academic analysis, public opinion polls. The difficulty in distinguishing between demographic inquiry and a study of personal description is perhaps made most manifest in a document such as a census report, produced in order to enable statistical analysis but dependent upon an individual giving a personal description of her/his circumstances.

These methodological problems haunt any form of inquiry, but they present particular problems in relation to sexuality for two related reasons: in Western European society a significant number of sexual 'acts' are practised either alone, or with only two people present; and there is a long and deeply held belief in Western society that sexuality is not only part of 'private' rather than 'public' identity, but that it may even be the foundation of private identity. Part of the establishment of a distinction between public and private selves has been organized around what it is possible and appropriate to talk about or write about in public. It is because of the interest that the various governments of Ireland have taken in regulating sexuality, promoting some kinds of reproduction and discouraging others, that many intellectuals have insisted that there needs to be a debate about sexuality in Ireland.

For the purposes of the anthology it was necessary to think about the variety of times and places where sexuality *is part of* a discourse. Inevitably the boundaries of the anthology led to the question — does sexuality have national characteristics? Writing on Ireland suggests that it does, although the characteristics projected onto Ireland and to some extent internalized seem to have a great deal in common with those of other invaded territories with extended hostilities between a settler colony and indigenous populations. For some of the early settlers, including Edmund Spenser, the distinctive formation of Irish family life (as they understood it) with its emphasis on extended family and

particularly on fostering, threatened their sense of selfhood.

At the start of the twentieth century Horace Plunkett expressed his concern that excessive sexual surveillance by rural priests and older members of the community was driving people to emigration: 'In some parishes the Sunday cyclist will observe that strange phenomenon of a normally light-hearted peasantry marshalled in male and female groups along the road, eyeing one another in dull wonderment across the forbidden space . . .'[6] The notion of a to some extent self-imposed forbidden space — as the only place of possible communion — is a recurrent theme in writing about desire in Ireland. William Carleton's autobiographical account of his long unspoken love for Anne Duffy is eloquent on silence, as is Emily Lawless's novel *Grania*, and Dorothea Herbert's melancholy conclusion to her memoirs, in which she had developed the conviction that she was married to a neighbour with whom she was once romantically involved, at least in her own imagination:

> Here I conclude my History a long and Arduous Task Plann'd and Accomplish'd in my Melancholy Confinement — Some Years of my Life remain undetailed but I finish at the Year 1806 anxious to finish my work though my chief Solace in Solitude . . . Oh that I could fly where love and the Muses lead me — then should I hover over the dwelling of my Dear John Roe — Perhaps he would relent if he knew his Unfortunate Wife Dorothea Roe.[7]

The various resonances of the word 'knew' in that final sentence evoke the many implications for self-knowledge and self-esteem of the various possible constructions of sexual and affectionate relationships.

This section deals almost exclusively with material written in English because of its concern with sexuality and discourse. Máirín Ní Dhonnchadha and Angela Bourke examine very fully the ways in which female sexuality is

---

6. Horace Plunkett, *Ireland in the New Century* (London: John Murray, 1904).
7. *Retrospections of Dorothea Roe, 1770–1806* (Dublin: Town House, 1988), pp. 420–1.

articulated in the Irish language and in the oral traditions. In 'Medieval to Modern, 600–1900', Máirín Ní Dhonnchadha traces the cultural interest in 'virginity', for example, through hagiographic, literary and poetic texts. Angela Bourke presents aspects of women's life stories where they discuss their sexuality, but also shows how aspects of sexuality could be encoded in rich and varied ways in forms such as 'fairy legends', 'folktale' and 'song'. There is English language material from folklore, oral histories and ballad traditions in the following pages. The kind of knowledge about sexuality transmitted in oral traditions seems superficially to be less concerned with private self-construction and more obviously addressed to the place of individual choice in a community context. It is tempting to glamorize folklore as yielding a more authentic version of culture, and it has increasingly emerged as one of the most exciting and productive areas of feminist scholarship in Ireland, especially when expounded with the kind of sophisticated understanding of the formation of subjectivity provided, for example, in the work of Angela Bourke.[8]

Supported by the growing influence of post colonial critique, Irish feminists have begun to be more interested in uncovering indigenous modes of thought and activity as models for feminist practice. In the last ten years there has been a growth of interest in folklore and the oral tradition, in collecting and representing women's narratives, in facilitating groups which have had difficulty in gaining access to the public sphere — for example travellers, the economic under-classes, sex workers, survivors of violence, lone parents, asylum seekers — to develop and present their own needs and objectives. There has been more willingness to criticize feminist heroines such as Mary Robinson, and to demand more solidarity from feminists on issues such as race, class and sexual orientation.

Contemporary Irish feminism offers a fairly robust critique of the young urban professional post-feminist women who are most visible in the media — the ones who might be said to be most indebted to the changes of the 1980s and 1990s — and increasingly venerates the traditional knowledge and skills of an older generation of 'oppressed' women, celebrating the resourceful-ness with which they negotiated their captivity. The apparently rapid social changes that have come on the heels of recent economic change have left people in the Republic asking what responsibility feminism has to be inclusive, and how it can bridge the widening gap between privileged and underprivileged.

The appreciation of traditional stories and ballads is not only about nostalgia — with all the positive as well as suspect implications of that term — but reflects the development of an aesthetic preference for the eloquence and art of apparent simplicity. Narratives of promise, fulfilment, secrecy, betrayal and loss speak to common experience and a story stripped of particularity allows the reader/listener to fill in the absences and gaps in a text with her/his own understanding of the particular. Modern Irish writing is rich in examples of the ways in which memories can be triggered by traditional music. Popular ballads such as 'She Moved Through the Fair', 'The Lass of Aughrim', 'My Lagan Love' and 'If I was a Blackbird' provide a resource at times when feelings deprive people of words. Advertisers and film-makers frequently exploit these effects as a short-hand reference to memories which even when they are framed with irony have the power to move listeners.

> He promised to take me to Donnybrook fair
> To buy me red ribbons to bind up my hair.
> And when he'd return from the ocean so wide,
> He'd take me and make me his own loving bride.[9]

Whether the extracts that follow are as apparently artless as Nelly Salvy's gallows confession to the murder of her baby or as apparently obscure and challenging as Medbh McGuckian's oblique poem on Roger Casement, the major revelation about sexuality in Ireland is not what happened but how it was cast into words.

8. See Angela Bourke, *The Burning of Bridgit Cleary* (London: Pimlico, 2000).

9. Anonymous, 'If I was a Blackbird', Volume II, p. 102.

Note on Texts

Of the material originally published before 1900, most documents appeared in only one edition. Where subsequent editions did occur they were often pirated and without authorial imprimatur. It has been our practice wherever possible to take texts from the first edition, and where there are few extant copies of an individual text, the headnote will give the library location of the original. This applies mainly to seventeenth- and eighteenth-century material. In a few cases, such as that of Maria Edgeworth, where there were revised editions of a work in the author's lifetime, the text is taken from what the editor judges to be the most authoritative edition. After 1900 the first edition, where available, has usually been preferred. Any deviation from the first edition is explained in the headnote. Variants have not generally been noted but care has been taken to compare Irish with other imprints, since there are sometimes significant differences. Where publication appears to be simultaneous (as between Dublin and London, or later between London and America) preference in the selection of a copy text has been given to the Irish over the British edition and to the British over the American. Exceptions are noted in headnotes. Where material is newly edited from manuscript the headnote will indicate whether it is taken from an original manuscript or from a typescript held by the archive.

Spelling and punctuation generally follow the originals, except that the long 's' has been shortened and the '&' expanded to 'and'. Women writers were often criticized, particularly in the eighteenth and nineteenth centuries, for poor grammar and spelling and for a lack of classical education. The spelling and punctuation of a text often provide insights into the writer's level of literacy and creativity. Of course, the earlier the document the more likely that spelling, punctuation, capitalization and italics have been determined by the printer, but that information is also useful in helping to establish the implied audience for a text. Some egregious printers' errors — such as the frequent setting of letters upside down — have been silently corrected and ambiguities have been decided by the editors

rather than offered as variants. In the eighteenth century the spelling of proper names was not regularized and even the most educated men are not consistent in their spelling. Variant spellings of proper names have been left, with footnotes to elucidate any confusion as to identity.

A further editorial problem has arisen that is particular to Irish writing in English. A very high proportion of these texts attempt to represent Hiberno-English vocabulary and even accent through an irregular spelling of English words — for example, 'hwat', for 'what', 'darlint' for 'darling', 'ker' for 'car'. Were each of these 'distortions' to be annotaed the text would be overburdened with footnotes, so the editors have tried to reserve annotation for places where the meaning is unclear. This is not a scientific method and at times we will have erred on the side of the ludicrously obvious.

The frequent appearance in eighteenth-century texts of 'L' or 'l' before or after numerals indicates pounds sterling. Before the mid-nineteenth century the title 'Mrs' might be applied to married or unmarried women.

Definitions of words or phrases draw heavily on *The Oxford English Dictionary* (Oxford: Oxford University Press, 1971); E. Cobham Brewer, *A Dictionary of Phrase and Fable* (London: Cassell, n.d.); Michael Traynor, *The English Dialect of Donegal: A Glossary* (Dublin: Royal Irish Academy, 1953); Diarmaid Ó Muirithe, *A Dictionary of Anglo-Irish: Words and Phrases from Gaelic in the English of Ireland* (Dublin: Four Courts Press, 1996); Patrick S. Dinneen, *Foclóir Gaedhilge agus Béarla/An Irish-English Dictionary* (Dublin: Irish Texts Society, 1927). Dates of birth and death are chiefly drawn from *The Drennan-McTier Letters,* edited by Jean Agnew (Dublin: Irish Manuscripts Commission, 1999); *The Concise Dictionary of National Biography* (Oxford: Oxford University Press, 1992); Virginia Blain, Patricia Clements, Isobel Grundy, *The Feminist Companion to Literature in English: Women Writers from the Middle Ages to the Present* (London: B.T. Batsford, 1990); and *Horace Walpole's Correspondence: The Complete Index,* compiled by Warren Hunting Smith (Oxford: Oxford University Press, 1983).

SIOBHÁN KILFEATHER, *Editor*

Sexual Discourse in English Before the Act of Union: Prescription and Dissent, 1685–1801

Seventeenth- and eighteenth-century writing might be said to organize sexuality into two broad categories: approved and unapproved modes of sexual expression. The line between the approved and the unapproved roughly equates with the line between the legal and the illegal. Courtship, marriage, reproduction, family affection and mourning are all socially and legally approved modes of expression. Abduction, rape, infanticide, domestic violence, adultery and divorce are illegal (although the laws proscribing them are frequently ineffectual, and in the cases of adultery and divorce there is a process of legalization to manage what is recognized as a moral and social failure). Homosexuality, cross-dressing, bestiality, sex work and pornography are subject to legal censure, although each of these activities has modes of practice at the edges of the law that may or may not be either recognized or condemned.

Much of what we may suppose to be the unproblematically approved modes of sexual expression go unrecorded in the literature of the period. The English novelist Charlotte Lennox (1720–1804) has a character in her novel *The Female Quixote* (1752) who, when asked for the story of her life, replies:

> [W]hen I tell you . . . that I was born and christened, had a useful and proper education, received the addresses of my Lord ——, through the recommendation of my parents, and married him with their consents

and my own inclination, and that since we have lived in great harmony together, I have told you all the material pages of my life; which, upon inquiry, you will find differ very little from those of other women of the same rank, who have a moderate share of sense, prudence, and virtue.[1]

Or, as the Russian novelist Leo Tolstoy (1828–1910) was to put it in 1873, 'All happy families are alike'.[2] Maria Edgeworth made this claim about her own private life: 'As a woman, my life, wholly domestic, cannot afford anything interesting to the public.'[3] Women who placed a value on reputation and who desired the approval of their communities were unlikely to write about sex, even sex within marriage, for most of this period. Historians can gather information about what happened from records of birth, marriage and death, and from newspaper reports of crimes such as infanticide and rape (though all these records are far from complete or decisive), but it is more difficult to establish what women or men thought about their sexual lives. Many of the female-authored texts in this subsection are defences, attempts by women to redeem their

1. Charlotte Lennox, *The Female Quixote; Or, The Adventures of Arabella* (1st ed. London, 1752; London: Pandora, 1986), pp. 365–6.
2. Leo Tolstoy, *Anna Karenina* (1st ed. 1875–7), trans. Constance Garnett (New York: Frederick Gilles, 1917).
3. *Memoir of Maria Edgeworth with a Selection from Her Letters*, ed. Frances Edgeworth, vol. 3 (privately printed, 1867), p. 259.

reputations in the face of an already existing public narrative about their sexuality. Dorothea Du Bois reveals intimate secrets of her parents' marriage because they are already involved in a public scandal and she wishes to defend her mother. Sarah Colvill explains to a friend how she became caught up in an attempted abduction. Grace Maxwell is obliged to make public the failures in her marriage in order to secure a divorce and save her property. Margaret Leeson writes against the grain of the prejudice that prostitutes have no character to lose, explaining what drove her into sex work, and also asserting her rights to think and speak on other issues, such as patriotism. Leeson's *Memoirs* are a hinge between two notions of female self-representation in this subsection. While there are women such as Du Bois and Colvill, forced into the glare of publicity and choosing to explain themselves, the much more common type of text about female sexuality is one in which male writers ventriloquize a woman's position, in a variety of genres ranging from gallows confessions to sentimental fiction to pornography. The authors of the dying speeches of the infanticides Nelly Salvy and Ellinor Sils may be recording the women's speech, but these texts might also be invention. Hugh Kelly (see Volume I, pp. 656–7), was the author of a sentimental novel, *Memoirs of a Magdalen* (1767), indebted to Samuel Richardson (1689–1761) and Choderlos de Laclos (1741–1803), in which the heroine, Louisa Mildmay, describes her own seduction and betrayal; the narrative strategies of these sentimental fictions are close to the strategies of overtly pornographic texts, such as John Cleland's *Memoirs of a Woman of Pleasure* (1748).

Marriage

It is generally believed that in most classes of society, apart perhaps from the poorest, marriages were arranged; but what is an arranged marriage? Is it a marriage where parents choose a partner for their child regardless of her/his wishes? Clearly some parents forced unwilling children into marriages, or separated them from the objects of their desires, or forced them into religious orders, and many of these cases made a stir in the community, and were written about in letters, diaries, newspapers or fiction. The very fact that

they caused a stir might suggest that they were the exceptional cases. S.J. Connolly argues that

> A system in which all or most young couples submitted unwillingly to naked coercion could not have been maintained indefinitely: matchmaking remained a workable system only as long as the sort of rebellion represented by elopement remained a rarity . . . Personal inclination may occasionally have over-ridden other considerations, but in most cases it seems likely that the parties to an arranged marriage accepted the same system of priorities as the parents or other 'friends' who worked out the terms on their behalf.[4]

The early lives of Mary Delany and Eleanor Butler do, however, demonstrate that there were plenty of parents willing to terrify or beat their children into submission, and that elopement was usually only available as a form of rebellion for those with a little money and somewhere to go.[5] Generally, however, parents expected to love their children and have their best interests at heart, and when parents did act tyrannically communities sometimes voiced their disapproval and even offered partial support to rebellious children.

Fiction and non-fictional texts from the eighteenth century support Connolly's thesis that there was broad social consensus on the conduct of courtship and marriage, and that rural Ireland was also characterized by 'a strict code of sexual behaviour'.[6] But that is not the only story they tell. There may have been general consensus about the way of life that people accepted but poetry and fiction also reveal that women in particular yearned for something different, and the yearnings articulated in and fuelled by imaginative literature may have contributed to those exceptional cases — the elopements and abductions, seductions and betrayals — that feature so strongly in public

4. S.J. Connolly, 'Marriage in Pre-Famine Ireland', in *Marriage in Ireland*, ed. Art Cosgrove (Dublin: College Press, 1985), pp. 78–98, p. 87.
5. Mary Delany (née Granville) (1700–88) was at the age of seventeen forced by her father to marry his 59-year-old drunken, lecherous crony, Alexander Pendarves. Eleanor Butler (1739–1829) made several attempts to elope from her home at Kilkenny Castle with Sarah Ponsonby (1755–1831). When they were captured she suffered physical abuse from her family, who wished her to enter a convent.
6. S.J. Connolly, 'Marriage in Pre-Famine Ireland', p. 90.

discourse about sexuality and marriage. Women fantasized about strangers and escape, about people of a different (usually higher) social class, about the kinds of independence necessary to reject marriage.

Two commonplace observations about marriage in Ireland, particularly in the earlier part of this period, have been questioned by recent historians. Seventeenth-century visitors to Ireland, particularly British commentators hostile to native Irish culture, accused the Irish of a lax morality, exhibited most dramatically in widespread polygamy. A more general belief — one which persisted through the eighteenth and nineteenth centuries — was that the Irish married very young and had large families. The facts of these matters are dealt with elsewhere in this volume, but it is worth observing that the perception of Ireland as a site of wild, fertile, unregulated sexuality contributes on the one hand to the deployment of Irish figures in English pornography and humour, and on the other hand to a defensive strategy of patriotic writings in which the Irish are represented as exceptionally chaste and virtuous. By the early nineteenth century these positions strangely fused into a belief that native Irish culture had once been remarkably frank and bawdy, and that a healthy openness about sexuality was a feature of its (now lost) innocence. Readers familiar with Brian Merriman's *Cúirt an Mheón-Oiche* (*The Midnight Court*), *c.* 1780, translated by Dennis Woulfe in the 1820s (see Volume I, pp. 297–303), or with ballads such as 'The Country Wedding' which appeared in collections of polite literature, inclined to concur with Jonah Barrington's view in 1827 that prudery and shame were relatively new features in Irish life, and that 'there are few changes in the manners and customs of society in Ireland more observable than those relating to marriage . . . Formerly no damsel was *ashamed*, as it were, of being married. The celebration was joyous, public, and enlivened by every species of merriment and good cheer.'[7] And as Dympna McLoughlin has observed of the nineteenth century, 'Alongside the observations of the exceptional chastity of the Irish were parallel statements of shock at the ribaldry and sexual explicitness of the games meant for the mourners at wakes.'[8]

Sexuality Outside Marriage

In the absence of other evidence, the assumptions made about unauthorized sexual activity are inevitably coloured by experience documented in other times and other places. There is relatively little direct documentary evidence from Ireland about pre-marital sex, incest, bestiality, unwanted pregnancy or adultery in this period. One might infer that (with the exception of bestiality) these were less common in the countryside than in towns, where vulnerable young people might be working as apprentices or servants, far from family protection and surveillance. Or one might infer that in the countryside, surrounded by friends and neighbours, further from the reach of the law and the newspapers, a family might more successfully repress and cover up unapproved behaviour. Anne O'Connor is one scholar who has led the way in suggesting that one needs to be able to read folklore in conjunction with newspaper reports, legal documents and statistics to understand the dynamics of rural practice and belief.[9] The documentary evidence that has survived generally reflects the experience of the prosperous, or of women who end up in Dublin or London, characters on a public stage, close to printing presses. It is not surprising to find that servants were easy victims of abuse, as were motherless children, and the children of the urban or displaced poor. Compared to the close-knit rural areas, the cities seemed places of disguised origins and potential deception. Some women saw this as an opportunity, and a few — such as the actor Margaret Woffington, the female soldier Christian Davies, or the Lurgan prostitute turned fraudster Margaret Caroline Rudd — transformed themselves and put one over on their contemporaries, as least for a while. The more common narrative, however, is of women deceived — tricked into sex and work and tricked out of money and family.

7. Jonah Barrington, *Personal Sketches of His Own Time* (3 vols, London: Henry Colburn, 1827–32).

8. Dympna McLoughlin, 'Women and Sexuality in Nineteenth-Century Ireland', *Irish Journal of Psychology*, vol. 15, nos 2–3 (1994), pp. 266–75.

9. Anne O'Connor, *Child Murderess and Dead Child Traditions: A Comparative Study* (Helsinki: Suomalainen tiedeakatemia, 1991).

Sexual Violence

Historians of sexuality in eighteenth-century Ireland have been particularly interested in the phenomenon of heiress abduction because this was a practice regarded at the time as peculiarly common in Ireland, though not unknown elsewhere, and because the social prominence of the victims led to substantial documentation through newspaper reports, private letters and other accounts. It has been the subject of comprehensive overview investigation by A.W.P. Malcolmson and James Kelly,[10] and individual cases have been studied in some detail.[11] Kelly has demonstrated that perpetrators came mainly from groups on the cusp of social change, for example on the boundary between the strong farmer and the lower gentry, where the access to wealth through marriage could lead to significant social advancement. Such abductions usually involved the seizure of a young woman or child from her home by a gang of armed men who would carry her away to an isolated location where she might be beaten or terrorized into agreeing to some form of marriage and where she was raped either before or after the marriage. The use of the word 'abduction' to distinguish these cases from other kinds of rape should not occlude the fact that these were crimes involving serious sexual violence. Kelly has identified some cases where the victim was an older woman, and at least one case where the victim was an elderly man. Many abductions probably went unreported because the families eventually agreed to accept the marriage, or because there had been prior knowledge and collusion between the couple. This is the version of abduction popularized in nineteenth-century accounts such as those of Maxwell and Walsh,[12] but it seems more true of later eighteenth- and early nineteenth-century cases than of earlier examples. Where women and their families decided to prosecute, the perpe-

trators were frequently apprehended, convicted and executed. Most abductions were intra- rather than inter-religious (although naturally the exceptions attracted most controversy), and the majority of abductions therefore took place among Catholics, following the general demographic.

For English readers, the reports of abduction from Ireland suggested a general lawlessness operating particularly in the remote countryside, and also caused a wariness with regard to Irish men in England, who were frequently presumed to be fortune hunters or men-on-the-make (as, of course, some of them were). In 1742 a Dublin pamphlet provided *The Irish Register: Or a List of the Duchess Dowagers, Countesses, Widow Ladies, Maiden Ladies . . . and Misses of Large Fortune in England*, being a list of names and addresses. The Irish fortune hunter or gigolo is a staple of the eighteenth-century British novel. In the mid-eighteenth century the politician Robert Nugent (later Craggs) three times married rich widows, for which practice Horace Walpole invented the term 'Nugentize', and it was partly in a move against such opportunists that the Hardwick Marriage Act 1753 required public marriage in church. This act did not extend to Ireland.

Rape was probably a dramatically under-reported crime, as was incest. The disincentives for survivors to prosecute family members on whom they were economically as well as emotionally dependent, or to suffer public exposure in their communities, were probably even greater two hundred years ago than today. Newspaper reports and other accounts of the trials that did take place suggest that the more vulnerable, poorer classes — servants, the unlanded peasantry, sex workers, labourers and particularly orphans — were most likely to suffer stranger attacks. Perpetrators were usually from the same social class as victims and gang attacks, such as that suffered by Margaret Leeson, seem to have been common. Sex attacks on male victims, particularly young males, seem to have been most common in the army and navy.

Queer Lives

There has been almost no work on which, if any, spaces were frequented by gay men and women

10. A.W.P. Malcolmson, *The Pursuit of the Heiress: Aristocratic Marriage in Ireland, 1750–1820* (Belfast: Ulster Historical Foundation, 1982); James Kelly, 'The Abduction of Women of Fortune in Eighteenth-Century Ireland', *Eighteenth-Century Ireland/Iris an dá chultúr*, vol. 9 (1994), pp. 7–43.
11. See for example Toby Barnard, *The Abduction of a Limerick Heiress: Social and Political Relations in Mid-Eighteenth Century Ireland* (Dublin: Irish Academic Press, 1988).
12. W.H. Maxwell, *Wild Sports of the West* (London: Richard Bentley, 1832); J.E. Walsh, *Sketches of Ireland Sixty Years Ago* (Dublin: James McGlashan, 1847).

in eighteenth-century Ireland. Emma Donoghue has documented some of the attacks on Sapphic women in early eighteenth-century Dublin and evidence of homophobia towards men is reported in Barrington's *Sketches* as well as receiving passing references in several fictional works. On the other hand, examples have survived of people leading queer lives and surviving — the autobiography of Christian Davies may have fictional elements but the lives of the Ladies of Llangollen are well documented, and odd people appear incidentally in many texts, as with the appearance of the transvestite Miss Gore in Dorothea Herbert's *Retrospections*. The sentimental seduction narrative by Hugh Kelly, *Memoirs of a Magdalen,* has already been mentioned, and sexuality is a central theme in several other novels, notably in Frances Sheridan's *Memoirs of Miss Sydney Bidulph* (see Volume I, pp. 726–38) and Thomas Amory's *Life of John Buncle, Esq.* (see Volume I, pp. 694–704); the latter is the funniest Irish investigation of curious and medical discourse on the body.

Colonial Regulation — Post-Colonial Critique

The following selection of texts begins and ends with examples of the kind of interest the British government might take in Irish sexuality. Jonathan Swift's *A Modest Proposal* is the best-known satire on the projectors and analysts who attempted to describe and manipulate population size and modes of reproduction in the Gaelic/Catholic population. Projects to manage the economy were often interwoven with projects to manage dissent. There is a frequent sectarian inflection to the ruling class's understanding of how the population is reproducing both physically and culturally. The writings of Petty and Madden can read like the work of arch-manipulators, as they imagine governments making direct interventions into family life, insisting on pre-marital chastity, inspecting for venereal diseases, promoting breast-feeding. The more anxiety administrators display over sexual conduct, of course, the more attractive an anarchic, unregulated sexual freedom seemed to be.

WILLIAM PETTY

(1623–87)

from:
THE PETTY PAPERS: [SOME UNPUBLISHED WRITINGS OF SIR WILLIAM PETTY. EDITED FROM THE BOWOOD PAPERS BY THE MARQUIS OF LANSDOWNE] (1927)

[William Petty was a political economist who left MS notes and letters on a variety of projects to 'improve' society. His notes towards the regulation of marriage and reproduction in Ireland indicate a recognition that a colonial administration tends to make sexuality subject to public surveillance. There is an interest both in reproduction and in morality. Petty identifies five million as the ideal Protestant population for Ireland, and proposes his

scheme until that is achieved. These notes seem to have been composed *c.* 1685, subsidiary to a lost *Essay for Multiplication. The Petty Papers* were published in two volumes by Constable in 1927.]

OF MARRIAGES &c.[1]

1. That none copulate without a covenant.[2]
2. That no youth under 18, and girle under 16, meddle with each other.
3. That such [shall] produce a child once in 3 yeares whilst they are teeming,[3] under a penalty; except in case of sickness, loathsomness[4] &c.

1. Marquis of Lansdowne's note: The context shows that this was written as applying to Ireland.
2. A binding agreement.
3. Fertile.
4. Ill in such a way as to excite nausea in others.

4. That a covenant may bee disolved in 6 monthes, in case of no conception, to be provd by proper signes; otherwise to continue till the delivery of the woman.

5. That every woman between 18 and 45 pay an half penny per diem, and every man between 18 and 60 pay a penny per diem to the publicq.

6. That 50s. per annum bee allowd for keeping a child till full 7 yeares old, and 20s. for a woman lying in, to the publicq places or to each woman herselfe in particular.

7. That at 7 yeares old the children bee disposed for 14 yeares after, and bee then free, having been taught some Trade.

8. That every man and woman have a livelyhood *ut alibi.*[5]

9. That a woman is not bound to declare the father, but to the officer who was privy to the contract and *habet sub sigillo.*[6]

10. That this liberty for short marriages do not take away the present way, nor other covenants of cohabitation, estate, rewards &c.

11. That both parties shall swear they [are] free from any fowle disease.

12. That if either parent bee Protestant, the child shall be such; and the child that shall come into the hospitall, or the child of the mother who shall lye in the comon house, shall be a Protestant.

13. When Ireland hath above 5 millions of people, that this liberty may cease.

14. Women of above 45 yeares old may not use men, unless all under 45 be provided with men.

15. Q. Whether the parents of hospitall children shall be connected absolutely or in part?

16. None under covenant shall meddle with another.

17. English Protestant women shall bee exchanged for others, when the cabbins are reformed.

18. Incest shall extend but[7] to mother, daughter, and sister.

19. Women that can produce 3 children in 3 yeares shall have —— reward, for 10 children ——, for 15 children ——, and —— for 20, out of the public stock.[8]

20. The hospitall children to bee bred up without sucking, or with very little in speciall cases.

21. A method is to bee set down for the diett, clothes and lodging of the hospitall children and of their breeding.

22. The same for women who lye in the publicq houses.

---

5. As elsewhere.
6. Has [it] under seal.

7. Marquis of Lansdowne note: i.e., only.
8. Marquis of Lansdowne note: The rewards for prolific mothers are left blank in the original.

ANONYMOUS

from:
VERTUE REWARDED;
OR, THE IRISH PRINCESS
(1692)

[This is the first known novel in English by an Irish writer with an Irish setting. Set in the garrison town of Clonmel at the time of the siege of nearby Limerick, *Vertue Rewarded* describes the courtship by a Dutch prince in the

Williamite army of a young Protestant woman.[1] The historical and geographical accuracy of the text, with its descriptions of Clonmel and Limerick, and its knowledge about the siege, suggest if not a first-hand experience of the events, at least a very close source of information.

---

1. Limerick was held by supporters of James II, led by Patrick Sarsfield, Earl of Lucan. The siege of Limerick was the last major struggle of the war, and the fall of the town precipitated the departure of a large number of Irish Catholic gentry and nobility to continental Europe. This exile is usually referred to as 'the flight of the wild geese'.

Marinda and her community are engaged in identifying themselves with the Dutch and English interests and differentiating themselves from the enemy, the native Irish, but the fluid boundaries between the two Irish communities are repeatedly exposed as they are asserted.

The anonymous author shows some familiarity with Gaelic traditions, as well as with the Protestant community, and the analogy between the prince's courtship of Marinda and his part in the siege of Limerick is by no means unambiguous. The novel is set during the Prince of Orange's Irish campaign and, like that campaign, represents an argument over the rightful sovereignty of Ireland. In subtitling the story as that of 'The Irish Princess' the novel sets up a theme of Irish female sovereignty as a counterpoint to the growing Williamite hegemony. The structure of the romance between the invading foreign prince and the Irish woman is a familiar one in Irish history. The initial English colonization of Ireland is frequently narrated in terms of the romance between Strongbow and Aoife, a romance in which the latter betrays her country in order to secure for herself a Norman husband. In *Virtue Rewarded* the possibility of female sovereignty is recuperated through an antiquarian narrative about the well of Cluaneesha.[2] One day, soon after his arrival, the prince, who has been surveying the terrain, sits down to rest by a well on the outskirts of the town. At this point the narrator interjects a story told directly to the reader, which comes, s/he claims, from 'an ancient *Irish* chronicle'.

The story of the well breaks the narrative frame of the novel, for, unlike every other digression in the novel, it is not filtered through the voice or consciousness of any character, but is transmitted directly from narrator to reader. So far as we are told, neither the prince nor Marinda ever hears the story of the well. The story refers us back to an Ireland before foreign invasions and the planter community, an Ireland misrepresented as 'barbarous'. The narrator not only displays a knowledge of a hidden Gaelic history of Ireland, but also a familiarity with the impulse in Gaelic narrative towards *dinnseanchas*, a poetics of place, particularly of sacred places. The account of Ireland's degeneration in the colonial period at least calls into question the assumption that the novel is merely Protestant propaganda. The particular arrangement of this sub-text, with its suggestion that Irish women were once particularly chaste, and thus fit for sovereignty, but that they have since (the Norman invasion) been corrupted, calls into question the trajectory of the main plot in its movement towards the marriage of Marinda and the prince. That marriage, in turn, alludes to the marriage of William and Mary, with its invitation to the invasion of England and Ireland. The particular details of a princess plotted against by usurping relations, and suspected through a false pregnancy, must have called to mind the

2. See Máire Herbert, pp. 250–3; Máirín Nic Eoin, pp. 273–6.

accusations against the integrity of the former Queen Mary (James II's consort), and the incidents of the 'warming-pan plot'. It is by no means clear that this novel, published in London after the establishment of William and Mary, may not have Jacobite rather than Williamite impulses. The story of the well ends with the possibility that when, through disuse, the well lost its fame, then perhaps it lost its *virtue*; but the novel seems to refute that suggestion in its next move, for the prince, who has been resting by the well while the reader learns its story, suddenly hears the voice of Marinda confessing her virtuous love for him. The juxtaposition of the narrative of Cluaneesha (the ancient Irish princess) with that of Marinda (her modern counterpart) suggests that political virtue may be as much at stake as chastity at the siege of Limerick. No direct source for the story of Cluaneesha has been found, but there are some echoes of the legends associated with the local saint Íte (see pp. 242–9). The name Cluaneesha might be derived from Ítes Meadow. St Íte founded her community at Clúain Credail (Holy Meadow) later known as Cill Íte, anglicized Kileedy, Co. Limerick. *Virtue Rewarded* was published in London for Richard Bentley in volume 12 of a series called 'Modern Novels'. This text is taken from the British Library copy.]

Cluaneesha, the only child of *Machuain*, King of *Munster*, was accused of having been too familiar with one of her Father's Courtiers; the fact was attested by two Gentlemen that waited on the King's Person, and to confirm it, the Princess herself had such a swelling in her, that few doubted but that their Witness was true, and would soon be proved by her being brought to Bed: Her Father, being old and sickly, was desired, for the prevention of Civil Wars after his Death, to nominate a Successour: The People shewed their unanimous consent to confer the Crown on her Uncle, because they would not have a Strumpet for their Sovereign; So the old King was perswaded to proclaim his Brother Heir Apparent, and condemn his Daughter to a Cloister: The Courtier fled beyond Sea, and went a Pilgrimage to the Saint at *Poshanie*; the very night that he arrived there, one appeared to the Mother Abbess, in the form of a Nun glorified, and told her, that she was *Edith*, daughter formerly to King —— but now in happiness; that she loved Chastity and Innocence while she was on Earth, and therefore defended it still; that she was constrained to leave the seat of Bliss to protect Vertue, injured in the Person of *Cluaneesha*; that the Persons who swore against her were suborn'd; that the swelling of her Belly was but a Disease; and that if she and the witnesses would go and drink of a Well, which sprung out of a Hill near *Clonmell*, there she would convince all the Spectators, that what she now told her was true: The Abbess told this the next day to the King's Confessor, and he told it the King; the King ordered one who was Confessor to the two Witnesses, to enjoin them, for their next pennance, to drink no other Liquor, but the Water of this Well, for a Week together; they obey'd him, but it was their last, for it made them swell as if they were poisoned; in the meantime the Mother Abbess came down thither with her Royal Novice. She charged them with the Perjury, and they confessed publickly, that the King's Brother, taking advantage of that swelling, which he thought was but a Tympany,[3] suborned them to swear against her Chastity, expecting that either it would kill her, or at least it might deceive the People so long till the King was dead, and he in possession of the Crown: A certain Citizen of *Clonmell*, who came among the rest to see them dying, and heard the Confession, admiring the strange virtue of the Water, went immediately home to his Wife, and telling her that he was suspitious of her Honesty, and desired that, to satisfie his Jealousie, she would drink a draught of Water, and wish it might be her last, if she were unfaithful: She not yet having heard of the others punishment, and willing to clear her self, drank of it as he desired, but swell'd with it as the others did, and dyed soon after in great torment. When the Well had grown famous by the exemplary deaths of the Perjured Witnesses, and the Adulterate Citizen, the Princess declared she would drink of it too; and that the clearing of her self might be as publick as her accusation was, she sent up to the King, who was then at *Cork*, to desire that her Uncle himself might be present when she drank, to witness her innocence; he excused himself, and would not go, but a great many of the Court coming thither to see the Princess clear her self, she went in solemn Procession barefoot, from the City to the Well; and taking up a glass full of the Water, she protested her Innocence, and using the same imprecation with the others, if she did not speak the truth, drank it off; but instead of working the

same effect on her, it in a little time cured her of the Disease she had, recovered her Health, and with it brought so much Beauty, that all the neighbouring princes were Rivals for her: She had design'd to build a Nunnery by that Well, but her Father dying left her the cares of a Crown, which diverted her from it: But the Well was long after reverenced, and for the quality it had of discovering Unchastity, it was much resorted to; for the inhabitants of *Ireland* (how barbarous soever the partial chronicles of other Nations report 'em) were too nice in Amour to take a polluted wife to their Bed, as long as this Well would shew them which was a chast one; but the wickedness of after times grew too guilty to bear with such Tryals; thence by disuse this Well lost its Fame, and perhaps its Vertue.

A FULL AND TRUE ACCOUNT OF A BARBAROUS AND BLOODY MURDER COMMITTED BY NELLY SALVY, A COOK-MAID, WHO LIV'D IN A GENTLEMAN'S HOUSE THE OTHER END O' *CAPLE-STREET*, ON THE BODY OF HER OWN YOUNG CHILD JUST BORN, THE 25TH, OF THIS *INST*. JAN 1725 (1724 [*sic*])[1]

[Public executions had long been a source of narrative, particularly of popular ballads which mythologized the life, crimes and sufferings of the condemned, but at the start of the eighteenth century this genre was transformed through the relatively new medium of cheap printed flyers and pamphlets. The life stories of 'criminals' were collected from trial evidence, prison interviews and newspaper accounts and written up as 'dying words' or

---

3. Swelling of the abdomen, caused by gas or air.

1. Text dated 1724, presumably a printer's error.

'confessions', sold as single-page flyers in the days just before and after an execution. There are no other sources to corroborate the events described in the next two extracts, but Peter Linebaugh, using similar sources for his study of eighteenth-century executions in London, has discovered that these texts are usually factual as to names and events described, and has pointed out that they differ from ballads in 'the verifiability of time and place in each of the accounts', the pretension to history rather than fiction.[2]

There has been no thorough statistical analysis of infanticide in early eighteenth-century Ireland but it seems probable that approximately 10 per cent of women who were executed were convicted of infanticide. It has been observed that the enforcement of this law, at the level both of detection and conviction, fluctuated strikingly from decade to decade. It is more difficult to speculate on the rates of commission, but evidence from the nineteenth century would suggest the plausible theory that women were more likely to resort to infanticide in periods of extreme economic hardship.

The infanticides by Nelly Salvy and Ellinor Sils reveal the vulnerability of female servants, both to seduction and to surveillance by their employers. They ask us to think about how people recognized, disguised and interpreted the pregnant body. The mothers appear to wish to treat the babies' bodies as excrement, but those bodies return or become blockages and interruptions — their refusal to go away is reminiscent of the returning or transformed babies who appear in popular superstition. These confessions often accuse the male sexual partner of 'deluding' the woman, even when, as in Sils's case, she knew of his marriage. Their sensationalism calls on the image of the burnt bodies of the mothers as well as the murdered infants. The text on Salvy was published in Dublin in 1725 by C.C. Grierson; the text on Sils was published in Dublin in 1725 (publisher unknown); copies of both are held in the British Library.]

This Unhappy Wretch was got with Child by a fellow Servant of hers, and so continued for the space of eight Months and better, at last she grew so bigg, that she was afraid that it would be Discover'd tho' she us'd ways and means to hide her Condition, as by wearing large Hoop Petticoats, loose Dresses, and several other ways.

But at last it came to her Ladies Ears, and having a mistrust of her Maid before, she looking so bigg about the Body, the Lady call'd for the Cook-Maid, and closely examin'd her about her being with Child, who got it, and how it happen'd; whereupon she kneel'd down before her Lady, and us'd several rash and bitter Expressions, as, wishing that the Devil might rip her Bowels in Pieces, and several other Vile and wicked words, if she was with Child, or ever us'd any ways to have one, tho' 'tis said she had one before this, by all her Protestations, she over-perswaded her Lady that there was nothing in it, and she seem'd to be satisfy'd that it was so, and so it past off, for that time there was no more of it.

In a Night or two after this Examination, and her woful Expressions to the contrary, it happen'd so that hard Labour fell on her, (and as 'tis said) the Child came safe to the World, and it Crying, she cram'd her Handkerchief into the Mouth of it; but finding Life in it still, she immediately took a Case Knife[3] and stuck it in the left side of the Body, then taking a Rope, ty'd it about the Childs Neck, and so Convey'd it privately to the House of Office,[4] where she left it.

After she had committed that Cruel and bloody Fact,[5] she return'd, and was nothing concern'd at the Vile and bloody Action that she had so lately committed, but went to Bed as at other times, and she rising early the next Morning, as usual, minding her business, no doubt but this had pass'd for a while, had not the Gentleman's Shore[6] next Door been stopp'd by the means of her bloody Fact, for they could not get theirs clear with all their endeavours till they sent to the Gentleman's House where this Maid liv'd, so knocking at the Door the Gentleman himself appear'd, and they told him that his Shore being Stopt they could not clear theirs unless he would do something to his, on that he Order'd his Servant Man to go and use his Endeavours to it, with that the Man went and

2. Peter Linebaugh, 'The Ordinary of Newgate and His *Account*', in *Crime in England, 1550–1800*, ed. J.S. Cockburn (Princeton: Princeton University Press, 1977); Peter Linebaugh, *The London Hanged: Crime and Civil Society in the Eighteenth Century* (London: Penguin, 1990); Brian Henry, *Dublin Hanged: Crime, Law Enforcement and Punishment in Late Eighteenth-Century Dublin* (Dublin: Irish Academic Press, 1994); James Kelly, *Gallows Speeches from Eighteenth-Century Ireland* (Dublin: Four Courts Press, 2001); James Kelly, 'Infanticide in Eighteenth-Century Ireland', *Irish Economic and Social History*, vol. 19 (1992), pp. 5–26; A. O'Connor, *Child Murderess and Dead Child Tradition*, 1991.

3. Large kitchen knife.
4. Privy.
5. Evil deed or crime.
6. Sewer.

took a long pole with Crook at the end of it, and searching every corner of the House of Office he stuck the Crook in the *Body* of the Child, he brought it up, and said it was a Dogg or a Cat, but bringing it to the Light, found it to be a Child.

So having a mistrust of the aforesaid Cookmaid they had her Secur'd, and on Examination before a Justice of the Peace, she was Committed to Newgate, where she lies, 'tis Visible that the Great God will not suffer Murder for to go Unpunish'd long, for as soon as the Innocent Child was taken up, both Shores were Clear; 'tis said that she will be burnt at a [*blank*].

SPEECH AND DYING WORDS OF ELLINOR SILS, WHO IS TO BE BURN'T ALIVE THIS PRESENT WEDNESDAY BEING THE 19TH OF THIS INSTANT MAY 1725 FOR MURDERING HER OWN CHILD (1725)[1]

Good People,

At first I had no thought of making a Speech, had I not heard a false and scandalous Paper cry'd about, call'd my Speech, Printed by one *Brangan* but as I am since Inform'd, it was done by one *C——r* in *Fishamble-street*; the which was an Imposition on the Publick; therefore that causes me to make a Speech which is as follows (*viz.*)

I drew my first Breath at the Place call'd *Lisnaw* in the County of *Kerry*, of very honest Parents, (my Father having the Honour to be Coach-man to the Lord of the same) who brought me up very tenderly, 'till I was fit for Service, and I praise God for it, had always the good Fortune to get a Service among the best, and thro' my Industerous [*sic*] Care, Learned to be a Cook-Maid, and had the Honour to be among the best of People. Thus I continued for a long while, and kept myself free and Chast from all Men, till about this time three Years, that I was deluded, and got with Child, the which soon after Dy'd.

Then I made a firm Resolution never to have another, nor would I, had not one *Mc. Cormick* (that he and his Wife were my fellow Servants) deluded me, and got me with Child, which pass'd for a long Time undiscover'd, but drawing near my Time, my Mistress seeing me more large, and more unhealthy than usual taxed me about it, but I alas! poor wretch had no mind to have the Name of any such thing it deny'd to her, by Reason the Devil prompted me so to do, on purpose to back my shame; but my Mistress Insisted still it was so, but the more she said it the more I Curs'd and Swore it was not so.

Thus I continued under sensure of my Mistress, who kept a Watchful Eye over me, untill the unhappy Day came I was deliver'd, which Day I stuck more close to my Business, than I did for a Month before, in hopes there should be no Suspicion of me, but when Night came, I went to my Chamber, but being missed, my Mistress sent her waiting Maid up after me, but to no purpose, for I fast'ned the Door very well within side, and said I would not admit any one into the Room at all, for that I was Sweating, and would not get up.

Thus I spent the most part of the Night in great Sorrow, Grief and Pain untill I was Deliver'd, then I poor Wretch, having not the fear of God or Man in me, took my tender Babe in my Arms, and went down Stairs, and threw it into the Privy, in the Dead time of the Night, and the next Morning I got up and was as strong as if nothing ail'd me, but when my Mistress saw me, asked me how I was, and whether I was Delivered or no, I told her I was well, but as for being Delivered, I told her I had nothing to be Delivered off; upon which I was immediately Discharged.

About 3 or 4 Days after my poor Babe was found where my own Hands laid it, by the Servants of the House, who got one *Mackelroy* a Porter, to take it up, (and who was a very great Evidence against me at my Tryal) then serch was made after me untill I was taken, and now am made a Publick Example of to the whole World;

---

1. See also *The Whole Tryal and Examination of Oonagh Dun etc. Who were Try'd and Found Guilty this Day, being the 9th Instant May 1725* (no publication details; copy in the British Library): 'This Day Ellinor Sils was brought to the Bar in order to receive sentence, for barbarously Murdering her Child, by throwing it into a Privy, the Court ask'd her what she had to say for herself before sentence of Death was Awarded against her, then she pleaded her Belly, the Court told her that she shall be burnt alive.'

now I beg of God, that this my untimely Death may be a Warning to Young and Old, for realy the Sin of geting a Child by a deluding Man is enough, but far more greater in the Murdering of it.

Thus Christians have I given you a true Narative of my past Life and Conversation, likewise of my base and cruel Astions concerning the Murder of my Child, the which, I hope, will be a means to deter others of my Sex from doing the like.

Having no more to say, my Time being so short, but beg the Prayers of all good Christians, while I am alive. I fereely forgive both Judge and Jury, because they did nothing but according to what the Evidences swore. I also forgive my Prosecutor, but I can scarce forgive Mc. Cormick *who got me with Child, but as I am commanded to forgive my Enemies, I obedient to that Command, do freely forgive him also. I am now about 28 Years of Age, and am an unworthy member of the Church of England as by Law Established, and the Lord have Mercy on my Soul,* Amen.

A FULL AND TRUE ACCOUNT OF THE TAKING AND APPREHENDING OF MRS. ANNA MARIA LASONS, FOR THE BARBAROUS, INHUMAN AND BLOODY MURDER OF HER OWN SON, A YOUNG CHILD, WHICH SHE FIRST STAB'D AND THEN THREW IT IN THE HOUSE OF OFFICE, AT THE SIGN OF THE WATER-ENGINE IN DAMES STREET, WHICH WAS FOUND THE EIGHTH OF THIS INSTANT, OCTOBER 1725 (1725)

[This broadsheet account of the arrest for infanticide of Anna Maria Lasons is a slight variant of the gallows-speech genre. Amongst its notable features are the way in which the dead baby bleeds when Lasons touches it — it was a popular Irish superstition that murder victims would bleed anew at the approach of a killer — and the poignant naturalistic touch of the mother's breasts leaking milk, and thus betraying her, when she sees her child. Published in Dublin in 1725, publisher unknown. Text in British Library.]

It may be thought by some, needless to give the Publick a Particular Account of this Unfortunate young Creature, but however, take it as follows. She is out of England, of good People, tho' reduc'd, which made her come to Ireland, where she for three or 4 Years with good Credit, work'd for her Bread, but at length comming acquainted with a Girl, who belong'd to Madam Lorenzina, the famous Ropedancer, she got a light Character, upon which Account she fain would have gone to be a Rope Dancer, but her Mistress going away, she again betook herself to work Lace, which she continu'd to do for a good while, behaving herself very soberly, and she then went to Service at a Gentleman's House near the Colledge, and whilst she continu'd there, a young man, servant to a fellow Commoner, courted her and he not being in want, gain'd her good Will so far, that she was content to Marry him, but the young Fellow beforehand, so ingratiated himself with her that he got her with Child, and then forsook her, the Time of her being thus, she frequently went to see a young Woman, who Lodg'd at the Water Engine in Dames Street, and there being very free and knowing the House very well, she entertained Thoughts of getting rid of her Burthen there, and accordingly she watch'd her Opportunity, and one Night she went into the Privy House, (as a Woman living there reports, who heard her groaning) and falling in Labour there, and being deliver'd she inhumanly Murder'd it, and threw it down the Share, and immediately went to her Master's where she continued Sick for a considerable Time, but at length getting up, she came to see her old Acquaintance, in the House, which was the very Day the Child was found and drawn out.

Upon which she went down, and with Several young Women, was looking at the Child, but she was observ'd to alter strangely, and others putting their Hands on the Child, she with another touch'd it, upon which it was observ'd to bleed some drops at the Nose, which was wonder'd much at, but a Crowd gathering fast, it was not minded at that Time, but her Acquaintance, the young Woman who liv'd there, took particular Notice on't, and observing her nearer, she discover's her Shift stain'd as with Milk, and her Breasts grown very big, which she would fain have known the Reason of, but the other made a confus'd Excuse, and immediately went Home, and took her Things from her Master's telling, her Uncle had come from England, and had order'd her to come away with him, she then went out of Town and stayed in a Loding[1] near Kilmainham, where she being seen by some of her Acquaintance, and the above Circumstances being remembred [sic], she was soon apprehended, and committed, till she can be brought before a Justice, when there is no doubt but there will be a further Discovery made.

1. Lodging.

JONATHAN SWIFT

(1667–1745)

AN EXCELLENT NEW BALLAD; OR, THE TRUE EN——SH D——N TO BE HANG'D FOR A R-PE
(1730)

[The incident referred to in this poem followed the appointment, in January 1729, of an English clergyman, Thomas Sawbridge, as Dean of Ferns and Leighlin. In June 1730 Sawbridge was arraigned for 'forcibly and feloniously ravishing' Susannah Runcord. After two appearances in court, when no evidence was brought against him, Sawbridge was acquitted. Swift wrote to the Earl of Oxford, 'The plea he intended was his being drunk when he forced the woman; but he bought her off. He is a dean, and I mention him to your lordship, because I am confident you will hear of his being a bishop; for, in short, he is just the counterpart of Charteris, that continual favourite of ministers.'[1] This is one of many accounts of the case[2] and an example of Swift's indignation at the abuse of power by the English church in Ireland. There is a steadfast refusal of the language of seduction and a powerful reiteration of the violence of rape. The partial blanking of words, particularly the word 'rape', is a commentary on the Walpole[3] government's heavy deployment of censorship in the 1720s. Swift famously presented Ireland as an 'injured lady'[4] in her relations with England. The poem is edited from a copy in the British Library, on which there are no printer's marks. The annotations are indebted to previous editors of Swift's Poems: Harold Williams (ed.), *Poems of Jonathan Swift* (Oxford: Clarendon Press, 1958, 3v.); Herbert Davis (ed.), *Swift: Poetical Works* (London: Oxford University Press, 1967); Pat Rogers (ed.), *Jonathan Swift: The Complete Poems* (New Haven: Yale University Press, 1983).]

I

OUR Brethren of *E*——*nd* who love us so dear,
And in all they do for us so kindly do mean,
A Blessing upon them, have sent us this Year,
For the Good of our Church a true *En*——*sh D*——*n*.
A holier Priest ne'er was wrapt up in Crape,[5]
The worst you can say, he committed a R-pe.

II

In his Journey to *D-bl-n*, he lighted at *Ch-st-r*,
And there he grew fond of another Man's Wife,
Burst into her Chamber, and wou'd have Carest her,
But she valu'd her Honour much more than her Life.

1. *The Correspondence of Jonathan Swift*, 5v ed. Harold Williams (Oxford: Clarendon Press, 1963–68), Vol. 3, p. 405. Col. Francis Charteris (1675–1732) was an ex-army officer (he had been dismissed for cheating), a man of large fortune, and a notorious profligate, known by the soubriquet 'Rape-Master General of Great-Britain'. In 1730 he was convicted of rape, but pardoned.
2. *Dublin Weekly Journal*, 13, 16 June 1730; *The Case of Daniel Kimberley . . . to which is added an account of a rape committed on . . . Susannah Runcord by Dr. Sawbridge . . .* (Dublin, 1730).
3. Sir Robert Walpole (1676–1745), 1st Earl of Orford, Whig leader and several times Prime Minister of Great Britain.
4. See 'The Story of the Injured Lady' (1720).
5. Thin, worsted fabric from which clerical garments were made.

She bustled and strugled, and made her
      Escape,
To a Room full of Guests for fear of a R-pe.

III

The D——n he pursu'd to recover his Game,
And now to attack her again he prepares,
But the Company stood in Defence of the Dame,
They Cudgell'd, and Cuft him, and kick him
      down Stairs.
    His D——nship was now in a damnable
      Scrape,
And this was no Time for committing a R-pe.

IV

To *D-bl-n* he comes, to the *Bagnio*[6] he goes,
And orders the Landlord to bring him a Whore;
No Scruple came on him his Gown to expose,
'Twas what all his Life he had practis'd before.
    He had made himself Drunk with the Juice of
      the Grape,
And got a good *Clap*,[7] but committed no R-pe.

V

The D——n and his Landlord, a jolly
      Comrade,
Resolv'd for a Fortnight to Swim in Delight,
For why, they had both been brought up to the
      Trade
Of drinking all Day, and whoring all Night.
    My Landlord was ready his D——nship to Ape
In ev'ry Debauch, but committing a R-pe.

VI

This *Protestant* Zealot, this *En——sh* Divine
In Church and in State was of Principles sound,
Was truer than *Steele*[8] to the *Ha——ver*[9] Line,
And griev'd that a *Tory* should live above
      Ground.
    Shall a Subject so Loyal be hang'd by the
      Nape,
For no other Crime but committing a R-pe?

6. Brothel.
7. Gonorrhoea.
8. Richard Steele (1672–1729), author and Whig politician. In 1714
   he issued *The Crisis* in favour of a Hanoverian succession; Swift
   replied with *Public Spirit of the Whigs*.
9. George Lewis (1660–1727), Elector of Hanover, became King of
   Great Britain and Ireland in 1714.

VII

By old Popish Cannons,[10] as wise Men have
      Penn'd 'em,
Each Priest had a Concubine, *jure Ecclesiae*;[11]
For who would have *F——ns*[12] without a
      Commendum?[13]
And Precedents we can produce, if it please ye,
    Then, why should the D——n, when Whores
      are so cheap,
Be put to the Peril, and Toyl of a R-pe?

VIII

If fortune should please to take such a
      Crotchet,[14]
(To thee I apply great *Smedley's*[15] Successor)
To give thee *Lawn-Sleeves*[16] a *Mitre* and *Rotchet*,[17]
Whom would'st thou resemble? I leave thee a
      Guesser;
    But I only behold thee in *Atherton's*[18] Shape,
For *Sodomy* hang'd, as thou for a R-pe.

IX

Ah! dost thou not Envy the brave Colonel
      Chartres,
Condemn'd for thy Crime, at three score and
      ten?[19]
To hang him all *En——nd* would lend him their
      Garters;
Yet he lives, and is ready to ravish agen,
    Then Throttle thy self with an Ell[20] of strong
      Tape,
For thou hast not a Groat[21] to Attone for a R-pe.

10. Rules, laws or decrees of the church.
11. By the law of the church.
12. Ferns.
13. 'In commendum was an ancient manner of holding ecclesiastical
    benefices. On the vacancy of a benefice by the preferment of the
    holder it was *commended* by the Crown to another, frequently the
    bishop of a poorer see, until a new incumbent was appointed'
    (Harold Williams (ed.), *The Poems of Jonathan Swift* [Oxford:
    Clarendon Press, 1937], p. 303).
14. A perverse conceit, but Swift may also be playing with the closeness
    to 'crotch' and to 'crotchet' as a hook or fang, as forked instrument,
    and as instrument in obstetrics.
15. Jonathan Smedley (*fl.* 1689–1729), Dean of Clogher, exchanged
    libellous lampoons with Swift.
16. Bishops' sleeves were made of lawn, a fine linen.
17. Obscure form of 'rathchet' — meaning here unclear.
18. John Atherton (1598–1640), Bishop of Waterford and Lismore;
    hanged at Dublin for sodomy.
19. Actually, Charteris was fifty-five.
20. A measure of varying length, in England 45 inches.
21. A denomination of coin, worth approximately 4 pence, which
    ceased to be issued in 1662.

X

The D——n he was vext that his Whores
  were so willing,
He long'd for a Girl that would struggle and
  squal,
He ravish's her fairly, and sav'd a good Shilling;
But, here was to pay the Devil and all.
  His Troubles and Sorrows now come in a
  Heap,
And hang'd he must be for committing a R-pe.

XI

If Maidens are ravish'd, it is their own Choice,
Why are they so willful to struggle with Men?
If they would but lye quiet, and stifle their
  Voice,
No Devil nor D——n could Ravish 'em then,

Nor would there be need of a strong
  Hempen[22] Cape,[23]
Ty'd round the D——n's Neck, for committing
  a R-pe.

XII

Our Church and our State dear En——nd
  maintains,
For which all true Protestant Hearts should be
  glad;
She sends us our —— and —— and ——,[24]
And better would give us, if better she had;
  But, Lord how the Rabble will stare and will
  gape,
When the good En——sh D——n is hang'd up
  for a R-pe.

22. Made of rope, in common parlance, hangman's halter.
23. Short cloak, fitting round the neck.
24. 'Bishops and Judges and Deans'. Words first printed in full in
    Hawkesworth's edition of Swift's *Works*, 1755.

SAMUEL MADDEN

(1686–1765)

from:
REFLECTIONS AND RESOLUTIONS PROPER FOR THE GENTLEMEN OF IRELAND, AS TO THEIR CONDUCT FOR THE SERVICE OF THEIR COUNTRY, AS LANDLORDS, AS MASTERS OF FAMILIES, AS PROTESTANTS, AS DESCENDED FROM BRITISH ANCESTORS, AS COUNTRY GENTLEMEN AND FARMERS, AS JUSTICES OF THE PEACE, AS MERCHANTS, AS MEMBERS OF PARLIAMENT (1738)

[Samuel Madden devotes a substantial part of his reflection to a consideration of sexual morals, particularly as those morals affect reproduction and infant mortality. His tirade against upper class women who fail to breast-feed partly indicates a concern for the children, but is also inflected with a critique of luxury and a belief that motherhood is the most appropriate female role. His attack on whoredom suggests that both the prostitutes and their clients are 'corrupted'. Published in Dublin for R. Reilly, 1738. Text in the British Library.]

We resolve, as Members of Parliament, that we will promote such sumptuary Laws, as will be most conducive to reform the Manners of our People, by Fencing against Luxury and Vanity in the better sort, and securing Sobriety and Frugality in the lower . . . Let us add to all this, if it may be said without offence, that the Discipline of our Laws against Whoredom and Adultery, is not only extreamly Defective, but very much Relax'd, thro' the frequency of the Crime, and the Difficulty that attends their putting them in Execution. It is therefore highly requisite to enforce the laws in those Points, by adding to them severe Penalties and easier Remedies, and especially to make the Detection of Houses of Evil fame, and the Punishment of the Wretches, who consume and Debauch our Youth there, more easy to the Magistrate, and more Penal to the Offender. The debauching of young Women and the maintenance of Bastards, are two things, which there is little or no Provision made for by our present Laws, and what an influence this has on the corrupting our Morals, and peopling us with Wretches abandon'd by their Parents, and left to starve in their Infancy, or rob and steal if they grow up, will well deserve to be consider'd by those, whose Province it is to deliver us from such destructive Evils . . .

We resolve, as Members of Parliament, to remedy by all possible Ways and Means in our Power, that great Obstruction to the Prosperity of this Nation, the want of Hands. It is a self evident Truth that all Kingdoms, are more or less considerable in Proportion to the Numbers of their Subjects, and tho' Industry is a main Point to encrease their Value, yet where numerous Bodies of Men can be had, wise States will easily provide Means and Methods to secure their Industry, and their being Numerous is a mighty Help to it. We are very defective in both these particulars in *Ireland*, and it will want all our Care to find out proper Remedies for them . . . If therefore our small and few Manufactures decline, as without better Encouragement they are like to do, our Numbers, thin peopled as we are, must sink with them, and leave us every Day with fewer Hands than ever. And we see in Fact, this is so by the Crowds that of late Years, are gone off to our Colonies abroad; besides Numbers that go in search of Wages and Labour to *England*: Nor is this all the Evil, for of the few Hands we have,

at least Four-fifths are *Papists*, and this sad Disproportion is likely every Day rather to enlarge than lessen, for as I have formerly observ'd, our Protestants don't marry Young, but they wait for a tollerable Portion, and some Settlement to live easy on; whereas, the *Papists* are Careless as to Wealth and Portion, and will have Wives, let them be maintained how they will.

. . . [A]s to our Numbers, it would certainly encrease them if Celibacy were discountenanc'd, and Marriages were duly encourag'd, and Whoredoms and Adultery as we observ'd already, severely and exemplarily Punished by our Laws.

. . . And now I am upon the Subject of encreasing our Birth, I will mention another Particular, which will conduce extreamly to preserving their Lives, when they come into the World, and that is to Lay a Tax on all hir'd Nurses, of at least 21. *per Ann.* unless Oath be made by the Mother, that she is *bona fide* not capable of nursing her Child herself.

. . . There is another Article, which I am loath to add to this sad Account of things, because I know we are very seldom guilty of it, and that is the horrible Practise of Abortions. We see the famous Midwife who was put to death at Paris for this Crime, confest she had procur'd many hundreds to conceal unhappy Intreigues, but as we, I thank God, are Strangers to such Wickedness, I shall only say, that by Way of prevention, if our laws made such Practises Felony, our Posterity will neither be the fewer, nor the worse of it.[1]

1. The British legal commentator Sir William Blackstone (1723–80) discusses the question of whether abortion is an offence in Common Law in his *Commentaries on the Laws of England* (1765–9), and whether its criminality depends on 'quickening', but the issue was not firmly established in British and Irish Law until 1803, when abortion before quickening was made a felony, and abortion after quickening became a capital offence.

CHRISTIAN DAVIES

(1667–1739)

from:

THE LIFE AND ADVENTURES OF MRS. CHRISTIAN DAVIES, COMMONLY CALL'D MOTHER ROSS; WHO, IN SEVERAL CAMPAIGNS UNDER KING WILLIAM[1] AND THE LATE DUKE OF MARLBOROUGH,[2] IN THE QUALITY OF A FOOT-SOLDIER AND DRAGOON, GAVE MANY SIGNAL PROOFS OF AN UNPARALLELL'D COURAGE AND PERSONAL BRAVERY. TAKEN FROM HER OWN MOUTH WHEN A PENSIONER OF CHELSEA-HOSPITAL,[3] AND KNOWN TO BE TRUE BY MANY WHO WERE ENGAGED IN THOSE GREAT SCENES OF ACTION (1740)

[Many eighteenth-century women were frustrated by the restrictions on women's action, and a few people are known to have evaded those restrictions by cross-dressing. In her autobiography, Christian Davies describes herself as naturally boyish in her childhood. She first adopts men's clothes as an opportunity to travel in search of her husband, but she continues as a man after discovering him because she enjoys male freedom, including the possibility of indulging in some form of bisexuality. For an example of the female warrior ballad tradition in Ireland, see 'Willie

Taylor', pp. 1319–20. This extract published in London by R. Montagu, 1740. Text in the British Library. See also *The Dublin Tragedy, or the Unfortunate Merchant's Daughter* about a Belfast girl who dressed herself in men's clothes to follow her lover, an ensign in the army, and then went to America where she was taken at Saratoga (Dublin: Wholesale and Retail School Book Warehouse).]

I was born in *Dublin*, in the Year 1667, of Parents whose Probity acquired them that Respect from their Acquaintance, which they had no Claim to from their Birth. My Father was both a Malster and a Brewer; in which Business he employed at least twenty Servants, besides those under the Direction of my Mother, in a Farm he hired of *Arthur White*, of *Leslip*, Esq.; left entirely to her Care. My Father was remarkable for Industry and Vigilance in his Affairs, which employing his whole Time in Town, he never saw my Mother but on *Sundays*, except some extraordinary Business required his visiting the Farm, which, though of fourscore Pounds a Year, she managed with great Prudence and Œconomy. They were both very tender of me, and spared no Cost in my Education, though I did not make the best Use of their Care in this Article. I had Patience, indeed, to learn to read, and become a good Needle-woman, but I had too much Mercury[4] in me, to like a sedentary Life, the Reason that I was always at the Farm to assist my Mother; this I did as much thro' Inclination as Duty, being delighted with a Country Life, it indulging my Love of ramping,[5] and the Pleasure I took in manly Employments; for I was never better pleased than when I was following the Plough, or had a Rake, Flail, or Pitchfork in my Hand, which Implements I could handle with as much Strength and Dexterity, if not with more, than any of my Mother's Servants. I used to get astride upon the horses, and ride them bare-back'd about the Fields, leaped Hedges and Ditches, by which I once got a terrible Fall, and spoiled a grey Mare given to my Brother by our Grandfather. My Father never knew how this

1. William III (1650–1702), King of Great Britain and Ireland from 1689.
2. John Churchill (1650–1722), 1st Duke of Marlborough, English general, frequently commander-in-chief from 1690.
3. Chelsea Royal Hospital for Invalid Soldiers opened in 1694.

4. The volatile metal was an emblem of liveliness and inconstancy.
5. Romping.

Mischief happened, which brought me under Contribution to a Cowherd, who saw me tumble the Mare into a dry Ditch, and whose Secrecy I was obliged to purchase, by giving him, for a considerable Time, a Cup of Ale every Night. I shall pass by the wild, girlish Tricks I and my companions were constantly playing, as they can administer nothing entertaining, and mention one only, to show an odd curiosity in a Nobleman. I and four of my Companions, were rolling ourselves down a Hill, and turning Heels over Head, when the Earl of C——d was passing in his coach, drawn by six beautiful grey Horses, by the Road, divided from the Scene of our Diversion by a Quickset Hedge and a Ditch. He stopp'd his Coach to be a Spectator of our Gambols; but finding that we put an End to our Pastime on our perceiving him (for the eldest of us was seventeen and consequently had sense enough to think the shewing our naked tales not over decent), he called to us, and promising to give us a Crown apiece, if we would begin and pursue our Diversion; our Modesty gave way to our Avarice, we indulged his Lordship's Opticks, and he, having been amply satisfied by the Unreservedness of our Performance, kept his Word . . .

[Christian's father, though a Protestant, joins King James's army and is killed at the Battle of Aughrim. The government seizes all his effects. Christian is seduced or raped by her cousin. She moves to Dublin, to the home of an aunt who keeps a public house, which business she inherits at her aunt's death. She falls in love with her servant, Richard Welsh, and marries him. They have two children and are expecting a third when Richard is press-ganged. She learns that he is in the army in Flanders and decides to follow him.]

I was not long deliberating, after this Thought had possessed me; but immediately set about preparing what was necessary for my Ramble; and disposing of my Children, my eldest with my Mother, and that which was born after my Husband's Departure, with a Nurse, my second Son was dead; I told my Friends, *That I would go to* England *in search of my husband, and return with all possible Expedition after I had found him.* My Goods I left in the Hands of such Friends as had spare House-room, and my House I let to a Cooper.[6] Having thus ordered my Affairs, I cut off my Hair, and dressed me in a Sute of my Husband's, having had the Precaution to quilt the Waistcoat, to preserve my Breasts from hurt, which were not large enough to betray my Sex, and putting on the Wig and Hat I had prepared, I went out and bought me a Silver hilted Sword, and some Holland[7] Shirts: But was at a Loss how I should carry my Money with me, as it was contrary to Law to export above Five Pounds out of the Kingdom; I thought at last of quilting it in the Waist-band of my Breeches, and by this Method I carried with me Fifty Guineas without suspicion.

I had now nothing upon my Hands to prevent my setting out wherefore, that I might get as soon as possible to *Holland*, I went to the sign of the *Golden Last*, where Ensign *Herbert Laurence*, who was beating up for Recruits, kept his Rendezvous. He was in the House at the Time I got there, and I offered him my Service to go against the *French*, being desirous to show my Zeal for his Majesty King *William*, and my Country. The Hopes of soon meeting with my Husband, added a Sprightliness to my Looks, which made the Officer say, *I was a clever brisk young fellow*; and having recommended my Zeal, he gave me a Guinea enlisting Money, and a Crown to drink the King's Health, and ordered me to be enrolled . . .

I was in *Gorkham*, where my Grief for my Husband being drowned in the Hopes of finding him, I indulged to the natural Gaiety of my Temper, and lived very merrily. In my Frolicks, to kill Time, I made my Addresses to a Burgher's Daughter, who was young and pretty. As I had formerly had a great many fine Things said to myself, I was at no loss in the amorous Dialect; I ran over all the tender Nonsense (which I look upon as the Lovers heavy Canon, as it does the greatest Execution with raw girls) employed on such Attacks; I squeezed her Hand, whenever I could get an Opportunity: sighed often, when in her Company: looked foolishly, and practised upon her all the ridiculous Airs which I had often laughed at, when they were used as Snares against myself. When I afterwards reflected on this unjust Way of Amusement, I heartily repented it; for it

6. A craftsman who makes and repairs wooden vessels.
7. Linen fabric.

had an Effect I did not wish; the poor Girl grew really fond of me, and uneasy when I was absent: for which she never failed chiding me if it was for but half a Day. When I was with her, she always regaled me in the best Manner she could, and nothing was too good or too dear to treat me with, if she could compass it; but notwithstanding a declared Passion for me, I found her nicely virtuous; for when I pretended to take an indecent Freedom with her, she told me, *That she supposed her Tenderness for me was become Irksome, since I took a Method to change it into Hatred. It was true, that she did not scruple to own she loved me as her Life, because she thought her Inclination justifiable, as well as lawful; but then she loved her Virtue better than she did her Life. If I had dishonourable Designs upon her, I was not the Man she loved; she was mistaken, and had found the Ruffian, instead of the tender Husband she hoped in me.*

I own this Rebuff gained my Heart; and taking her in my Arms, I told her, *That she had heightened the Power of her Charms by her Virtue; for which I should hold her in greater esteem, but could not love her better, as she had already engrossed all my Tenderness;* and, indeed, I was now fond of the Girl, though mine, you know, could not go beyond a Platonick Love.

[A sergeant attempts to rape the burgher's daughter and Christian fights a duel on her behalf. The girl gratefully proposes marriage to Christian, but Christian uses the burgher's opposition to his daughter's marrying a common soldier as a means of extricating him/herself, and the regiment moves on.]

After the taking of *Namur,*[8] I went into Winter Quarters at the *Boss,* where a very odd Adventure befel me. I went with two of my Comrades to a House of civil Recreation,[9] where they made a Bargain for, and retired with, such Ware as they wanted, and I diverted myself with serenading them on the Tongs and Key.[10] A Lady of the civil Conversation, who was very big,[11] happened to take a Liking to me, and used all the common Methods of those virtuous Damsels to entice me; but finding they had no Effect, she swore she would revenge the Slight, which she soon after did, by swearing me the Father of her Child. Whether this was the Effect of her Revenge, or her Judgment, as I made a better Figure than any private Dragoon in our Regiment, and she thought me the best able to provide for her in her Month, and to take Care of her Bastard, is what I won't take upon me to determine; but I was so surprized and enraged at the impudent Perjury, that I was almost tempted to disprove her effectually, and give her up to the Law; but, on a mature Deliberation, I thought it better to defray the Charge, and keep the Child, which I did; but it died in a Month, and delivered me from that Expence, though it left me the Reputation of being a Father, till my Sex was discovered.

8. The Belgian town was captured by Louis XIV of France in 1692, and retaken by William III of Britain and Ireland in 1695.
9. Brothel.
10. Instruments in burlesque music.
11. Meaning big with child.

ANONYMOUS

from:

TEAGUE-ROOT DISPLAY'D: BEING SOME USEFUL AND IMPORTANT DISCOVERIES TENDING TO ILLUSTRATE THE DOCTRINE OF ELECTRICITY, IN A LETTER FROM PADDY STRONG-COCK, FELLOW OF DRURY LANE, AND PROFESSOR OF NATURAL PHILOSOPHY IN M. KING'S COLLEGE, COVENT-GARDEN, TO W—— M W——N, F.R.S. AUTHOR OF A LATE PAMPHLET ON THAT SUBJECT[1] (1746)

[This short text in the tradition of mid-eighteenth-century comic/pornographic pamphlets and novellas participates in the formation of a stereotype of the Irish gigolo, prevalent in drama and novels, and also draws on a racialization of Irish sexuality as sub-human. For example, the marriage of Edward Hussey, an Irish gentleman, to Isabella, Duchess of Manchester and co-heiress of the Duke of Montagu, in 1743, gave rise to numerous jeers and lampoons on Hussey's sexual prowess.[2] If the following extract seems neither particularly lewd nor particularly funny that may be because many of these texts depended on the specific local reference, here to William Watson. Collections of caricatures of prostitutes and punters, for example, were fairly common and are now difficult to read because of their dependence on a verbal circulation of gossip and scandal. Published in London in 1746 by W. Webb, a copy of the text is held in the British Library.]

1. Sir William Watson (1715–87), physician and naturalist, Fellow of the Royal Society in 1741; published notes on electrical experiments from 1745.
2. See A.W.P. Malcolmson, *The Pursuit of the Heiress*, p. 29. For an Irish satire on the stereotype of the Irish fortune-hunter, see *The Irish Register: Or, A List of the Duchess Dowagers, Countesses, Widow Ladies, Maiden Ladies . . . and Misses of Large Fortune in England* (Dublin, 1742).

It is a very kindly Root, and will grow in all Climates; but thrives best in our more Northern Countries. The warm Countries of *Spain* and *Italy* produce it in great Plenty; but it's too forward with them: it's suddenly ripe, and as soon rotten; and does not retain its Beauty, Vigour, nor Virtue, half as long as in Climates where the Heat is less intense.

I have seen it in most Countries of *Europe*; but I never met with any so good as in *Ireland*: There it arrives to the greatest Perfection, and is a strong, lusty, beautiful Root: In that Country, its lowest Growth is seven Inches, and it sometimes arrives to the Height of twelve, and is about two Inches over, three-corner'd, and a little bending; the Top of it is a beautiful Carnation-Colour, and softer than the softest Down: At the bottom of the Root issue two round Globes, that are pendulous in a Bag, where they seem to be loose, tho' bound to the stem of the Root, by small yielding Fibres: The outside of this Bag is wrinkly, and cover'd with a kind of Down, much resembling Hair, or the Beards of common Leeks.

There are two Kinds of this Root, the Male and the Female; the Male is that which I have now described, the Female is not so beautiful a Root; it's a broad Root with a Hole perforated thro' it, which will contract, or dilate itself upon Occasion, like the Mouth of a Purse: To look at some of them, you would imagine that you could not introduce a Straw, or a Goose-Quill; but, upon Tryal, they'll dilate so much, as to receive a Rolling-Pin: The Mouth of the Hole, and the whole Face of the Root is cover'd with a bushy Kind of Hair, which gives the Whole a very shocking Appearance; tho' I have known numbers of People doat upon this Root, and gaze upon them with the strangest Raptures that could be imagin'd: but that is to be ascrib'd to the wonderful Effects of Electricity, of which I shall have Occasion to take more Notice immediately . . .

I know a certain *Virtuoso*-Lady, that constantly imports a Cargoe of Male-Roots from *Ireland* to divert her, with a very vigorous Female-Root she has had these fifty Years and Upwards in daily

Use, and yet not a Whit decayed. She gives a great Price for them, and often makes Provision for Life for their Original Owners; and I believe now she may have her Grounds as well stock'd with strong and lusty Roots, as any one Person in *England*.

from:

THE IRISH MISCELLANY; OR, TEAGUELAND JESTS: BEING A COMPLEAT COLLECTION OF THE MOST PROFOUND PUNS, LEARNED BULLS, ELABORATE QUIBBLES, AMOROUS LETTERS, SUBLIME POETRY, AND WISE SAYINGS, OF THE NATIVES OF TEAGUELAND. BEING A SEQUEL TO JOE MILLER'S JESTS (1749)

[At least since the late sixteenth century, when the first extensive representations of spoken English in Ireland and Irish emigrants in England are available, the Irish were described as often unwitting jokers, who could not use the English language without some confusion of ideas or some strategy of evasion. Reports of Irish dialogue in *Captain Thomas Stukely* (1596–1605), *Sir John Oldcastle* (1599–1600), *Bog-Witticisms* (1687), *The Irish Hudibras* (1689), *The Irishman's Prayers* (1689), Barnabe Rich, *The Irish Hubbub; Or, The English Hue and Cry* (1617) and Jonathan Swift's *A Dialogue in the Hibernian Stile* (*c.* 1735) depend on the prevalence of this stereotype. From the seventeenth century there seem to have been chapbook collections of Irish jokes — as there were of English jokes — which often emphasized provincial ignorance and regional pronunciation.[1] It is difficult to establish an original date for *The Irish Miscellany*, which had several reprints, and its relation to joke collections published under the names Teddy O'Flannigan and Joe Miller. The first joke plays upon a stereotype of the Irish servant as both stupid and knowing; the second is an early example of an association between black people and the Irish. Both rely on crude and heavy-handed marking of dialect speech. The text is taken from the 3rd edition, published in London in 1749 for R. Adams, a copy of which is held in the British Library.]

Donnel was preferr'd from being a Skip,[2] to marry my Lady's Chambermaid, and receiv'd 50 Pounds in Consideration of a crack'd Pitcher,[3] which he took for her honest Portion: About three weeks after, the Bride was deliver'd of a Child; and, *Donnel* being at his Master's House, the Lady told him, She did not think him to have been such an active Man, to have a Child so soon: *Be me shawl, me dear Lawdy*, reply'd he, *and why should'st dee tink me such a Fumbler, when me owne Mother was brought to Bed of mee two Months before she was marry'd: In Fait noow, I shou'd have thought me Peggy had been barren, if she had not kidded[4] in three Weeks after* . . .

It is impossible to tell you the Surprize that *Mac-Clan* was in, when he had lain at a Bawdy-house all Night, and spent his Estate of four *Irish* Half-Crowns there, as they call them; when in the Morning he found a black Wench[5] in his Arms, instead of an Harlot of another Complexion; he started out of Bed, ran down the Stairs naked, crossing himself over and over; feeling for his Beads,[6] when he had never a Rag about him; and skipping up and down like one of the most frantick in *Bedlam*,[7] roaring and bellowing; *Whoo! whoo! boo! boo! vat vill I doe? be Chreesht mine owne Moder vill kill me for mauking Child upon the Dee'ls awne shelf: Vat vill I shay to mine Confesshor indede, ven I come for de Absholushion? I musht shay dat I pot — upon de Dee'l, indede. Whoo! whoo! boo! boo! Noow, de Dee'l tauke me Shoul, all de Holy Vater vill not mauke me shweet again,[8] be me Fait; I vill e'ne goe and put haung upon my shelf, or mauke some great Bonfire upon* Tyburn,[9] *and dere mauke burn upon mine*

2. Footman, lackey or manservant.
3. Crockery and china were frequent metaphors for chastity.
4. Given birth.
5. There was at least one well-known black prostitute working in London; see David Dabydeen, *Hogarth's Blacks: Images of Blacks in Eighteenth-Century English Art* (Manchester: Manchester University Press, 1987).
6. Rosary beads.
7. Applied to the Hospital of St Mary of Bethlehem in London, an asylum for the mentally ill.
8. Water blessed by a priest and used in devotional rites.
9. Place of public execution in London.

1. For a discussion of the stereotypes, see David Hayton, 'From Barbarian to Burlesque: English Images of the Irish *c.* 1660–1750', *Irish Economic and Social History*, vol. 15 (1988), pp. 5–31.

awne reprobated *P——. Whoo! whoo! boo!* What the Plague is the Matter, says the old Bawd, with this whining Son of a Whore? Who, but the Devil, or his Daughter, wou'd have to do with such a lousy, scabbed, Bog-trotting[10] Son of a Whore? I'll cure the Heat ——, you Whore's-bird, with a Vengeance; and so threw a full Pot of Chamber-lye upon him, which swill'd him out of the House.

10. Seventeenth- and eighteenth-century pejorative description for the Irish.

from:
THE CHARMS OF BEAUTY; OR, THE GRAND CONTEST BETWEEN THE FAIR *HIBERNIANS*; AND THE *ENGLISH* TOASTS, A POEM: OCCASIONED BY THE MARRIAGE OF HIS GRACE THE DUKE OF *HAMILTON*[1] WITH MISS *ELIZABETH GUNNING*,[2] AND THE EXPECTED MARRIAGE OF HER ELDER SISTER[3] WITH A CERTAIN NOBLE EARL[4] (1752)

[The Gunning sisters were among the most celebrated beauties of the eighteenth century. The deployment of that beauty in the achievement of apparently advantageous marriages drew cynicism from some commentators, but the following poem uses Elizabeth's marriage to the Duke of Hamilton as an opportunity to suggest that there has been a migration of virtue from the British metropolis to Ireland, and by implication suggests that this physical beauty may be a metaphor for political and social virtues.[5] First published by J. Gifford, London, in 1752, the text is taken from a copy held in the British Library.]

1. James, 6th Duke of Hamilton and Brandon (1724–58).
2. Elizabeth Gunning (1734–90), Duchess of Hamilton, and later, by her second marriage, Duchess of Argyll. She was the daughter of John Gunning of Castle Coote, County Roscommon, a barrister, and of his wife Bridget, a relatively poor aristocrat. Elizabeth and her sister Maria were famous for their beauty, and when they went to London at the ages of seventeen and eighteen, crowds would gather in the parks to see them pass. Clever management by their mother seems to have added to their celebrity and led to marriages that were considered quite brilliant in material terms.
3. Maria Gunning (1733–60), Countess of Coventry.
4. George William, 6th Earl of Coventry (1722–1809).

The *British* Ladies long unrivall'd stood,
And Beauty's Prize have claim'd in Right of
　Blood.
No foreign Tincture on the finest Skin,
By Nature painted with a Hand divine;
No Features, e'er so regular and true,
Can charm Mankind, the *British* Fair, but you;
At least our Complaisance to you have made
Our flattering Tongues the real Truth evade.
　Hibernian land, amidst its Bogs and Fens,
Has cultivated Beauty, Wit and Sense.
How widely have we erred from the Truth,
To call the *Irish* wild, and scorn their Youth?
They Nature's Dictates wisely do pursue,
Live by her Laws, and as she bids they do.
By foreign Fashions they are not disguis'd,
What Heaven gives, by them is choicely priz'd.
Their Sense is native, so their Beauties too,
And artless Love within their Bosoms glow.
　Such were the GUNNINGS on their native Soil,
And Thousands more within that happy Isle;
Who if reveal'd, and brought upon the Stage,
Would all Mankind in their Behalf engage.
These Two their Father as a Sample gives,
To shew that Beauty in *Hebernia*[6] thrives;
Brings them with Pleasure to the publick Tent,
And lets our Judgment on their Merit rent;
Bids us peruse them with a curious Eye,
And all their Faults impartially decry.
If none are found (tho' Malice be the Judge)
What gen'rous Mind can their due Praises
　grudge?
　No More, ye Ladies of this Island boast,
That you alone deserve the publick Toast,
Rivall'd you see you are, perhaps excell'd,
Which by your Wit can never be refell'd.
Our Eyes, now open'd, can discern the Truth,
And how, like Tricksters, you impose on Youth
Pleas'd if you can but keep them in the Dark,
And hedge the roving Deer within your Park.

5. Robert Jones, 'Such Strange Unwonted Softness to Excuse: Judgement and Indulgence in Joshua Reynold's Portrait of Elizabeth Gunning', *Oxford Art Journal*, vol. 18, no. 1 (spring 1995), pp. 29–43.
6. Pun.

With what Inveteracy do you exclaim
Against all Ladies of a foreign Name!
Ugly their faces, or ill-shaped they be,
Scarce one without some sad Deformity.
One has a pretty Face, 'tis such allow'd,
But then her Legs are bandy'd, or she's proud.
Another's praised for her easy Shapes,[7]
But her sad awkward dress proclaims her Trapes.[8]

How oft have we been arrogantly told,
That Perfect Beauty's cast in *English* Mould;
Forms so exact scarce Angels can excel,
Too perfect on this filthy Earth to dwell.

No more, ye Fair, on your Perfections stand,
For Beauty flourishes in every Land.
Ev'n Negroes, so distasteful to the Sight,
Produce their Beauties eminently bright.
Exactest Symmetry their Persons form,
And glowing Graces all their Features warm.
Wit and good sense are equally their Due,
Their Colour only differs them from you:
And what is Colour but a tinctur'd Skin,
Tho' black without, yet all is fair within;
'Tis *Virtue gives a Beauty to the Face,*
The fairest Form may be without a Grace;
The Rose and Lilly, now in fragrant Bloom,
Sickness or Age will wither and consume;
A pallid Colour will your Visage seize,
And leave you not a feature that can please.

7. Appearance.
8. Slovenliness.

from:
THE SECRET HISTORY OF BETTY IRELAND CONTAINING AN INTERESTING ACCOUNT OF HER UNFORTUNATE MARRIAGE AT THE AGE OF FOURTEEN . . .
(*c.* 1750)

[This is one of the earliest examples of Irish female sexuality being represented as essentially promiscuous and deceptive. The figure of the Irish prostitute, of her rapacious greed and sexual appetite, is a common one in eighteenth-century British writing, and also colours the many biographies and autobiographies of Irish female actors. Published in London *c.* 1750 for S. Lee, the text is taken from the British Library copy.]

It is a good family, says an old Proverb, *which has neither whore nor rogue in it*; for the sake therefore of the person from whom *Betty Ireland* is descended, I have avoided to make mention of her sur-name; in the room of which I have substituted that of the country wherein she was born.

Her grandfather was Physician to King Charles the Second, from whom he received the honor of knighthood; and while he attended that monarch in his exile, he married a German lady, whose fine house, and a very large town of which she was sole mistress, were unhappily reduced to ashes in the space of twelve hours. Nevertheless, her dowry, at the time of her marriage, amounted to upwards of ten thousand pounds, besides plate and jewels; and coming to England with her husband at the restoration, they did not continue long in this Kingdom, but went into Ireland, where they left behind them four sons and two daughters, and made a handsome provision for each of them.

The youngest was a captain of horse, at the revolution, and attended King William[1] in the wars of Ireland. Betty was the second daughter, and had been bred up under her grandmother, whose too indulgent nature she abused. As she was well shaped, had a fine mein, a large share of wit and sense, so she was wonderfully beautiful; to which were added the advantages of the best education. She had scarce arrived to her fourteenth year, when she became the reigning toast of all the city; crowds of lovers constantly attended her wherever she went; and at last a match was proposed between her and the Earl of M——: but he being old enough to be her grandfather, she could not be persuaded to comply, though he offered to settle a jointure upon her of a thousand pounds a year.

Her young blood began to circulate briskly, and having a strong inclination to be made a wife, and

1. William III (1650–1702), King of England, Scotland and Ireland, declared king in 1689, after the revolution which evicted his father-in-law, James II.

resolving to choose a husband, who was not many years older than herself, she unfortunately flung herself away upon a tradesman, who, by the contrivance and assistance of her maid, palmed himself upon her for a gentleman of a good family and a large estate. She quickly conceived, and in due time brought forth a daughter; she was cast off by her relations, and despised by those who admired her before: and her husband, being baulked in his expectations of a large fortune, used her (as she often declared) very roughly, and induced her at last to act on the stage, which business he then followed.

Her friends, judging rightly what would be the consequence of this scene of life, and what a disgrace it was to them, made application to the master of the play-house, who, at their request, discarded her from being an actress. Had they applied themselves sooner, they might probably have prevented what afterwards befel her; for as most gentlemen are fond of a young creature, upon her first appearance at a theatre, so Mr. M——, a gentleman of good address and fortune, found out an opportunity to seduce her, and kept company with her in private for the space of two years. She was delivered of a second daughter, but her husband could not be induced to believe that he was the father; and thereupon an uneasiness arising between them, and their jars continually increasing, she communicated her design to her new lover, who, providing handsome lodgings for her in a village, two miles distant from Dublin, received her into his arms the night that she eloped from her husband.

Here she lived for the space of twelve months, and wanted nothing that love or money could supply her with; her lover doated on her, and she had art and cunning enough to make him believe she was as fond of him, always pretending to be uneasy when he went away from her, and telling him how pensive and melancholy she sat during his absence. In a short time she informed him of her pregnant state, at which he professed great satisfaction, and the next time he returned to her, presented her with a rich piece of silk for a gown and petticoat, a gold watch, and a diamond ring, assuring her; that if she should be delivered of a boy, he would settle three hundred pounds a year upon him for ever, and give her five hundred guineas. Nature gratified both their desires, and the child was named Richard, after the father,

who faithfully performed his promise to both, and left the deed of settlement in the mother's hands, to whose care and management he left his spurious son. Betty growing weary of leading a retired life in the spring of her age, placed her child out to nurse, and took lodgings in Dublin, unknown to her kind keeper, for whom she sent a message the night she came into them. He was much surprised at this sudden change, and not thinking it proper to be seen with her in public, went to one of his acquaintance who had been privy to their intrigues, and desired her to let Betty know the reason of his not going to her that night, and how uneasy he was at the false step she had taken in coming to town; however, he would dine with her the next day at the Ring in Ring's End.[2] This message nettled Betty at first, but upon the remonstrances of her confidant, she was appeased, and they both lay together.

The next day about noon they went to the place appointed, where they met the gentleman, whose countenance was not altogether so pleasant as usual; nor did he receive Betty with his accustomed ardour. She looked upon this as a mark of contempt, or a slight at best, and could not refrain from bursting into tears. When this shower was over she asked him what she had done that could occasion him to treat her in such a cold manner? 'Is this the recompense you make me for having sacrificed my reputation for you, and given up myself to your embraces? Ungenerous man! I am justly punished for breaking my marriage vow, and for my folly in loving a man who does not merit my love. Say, false deceiver, are you not grown weary of me? Have you not cast your eyes upon some new face, which seems at present a more pleasing object to you, because it is new; but, remember that I tell you, she will never prove so constant and faithful to you as your Betty has been.'

The gentleman was so much astonished at this unexpected attack, that he remained speechless for some time; at last he recovered his senses, and taking courage, said: 'You have no reason, Betty, to call me ungenerous, for I have done more for you than you desired; I do not speak this in a boasting way, but 'tis what I am compelled to say in my own vindication; and yet had I done ten times more I own it would not be a sufficient

2. Area of central Dublin, then a harbour.

recompense for your love and fidelity to me. As to the other part of your charge, it has no other foundation than bare suggestion, and groundless jealousy, nor have I the least inclination to change one mistress for another. My reason for not coming to you last night was, that I did not judge it convenient; for as you have taken lodgings in a very public part of the town, and our love affairs have been hitherto kept secret, should I go thither, they would soon be blazed abroad, which might be attended with a bad consequence.'

Betty being convinced of the reasonableness of what he had spoke, a reconciliation was soon made by the good offices of the confidant. And, after they had dined, they took coach, and went to visit their son. She promised to go very speedily to her country lodgings, and he was so well pleased with the assurance she had given him that she would perform it, he made her a present of twenty guineas. When they returned to Dublin, she took her friend with her, and having continued there two nights, she pretended the air was too sharp for her constitution, and then removed; sending a letter to her spark,[3] to acquaint him with what she had done. Having approved her conduct herein, he came and stayed with her all night, and seldom failed either to visit or send to her every day for ten months. But she being naturally inclined to roving, could not bear this retired way of living any longer; and the next night that her lover came to her, he told her that he was obliged to go into the country for three or four days, and desired her to divert herself during that time in what manner soever was most agreeable to her. She embraced this opportunity, and coming the next evening to Dublin, she went to the play, where she was picked up by a handsome young gentleman, with whom she went to the tavern before the play was ended, and from thence to the bagnio. This was the second loose she had given to love, and was the cause of all the misfortunes that afterwards happened to her: for her new lover being in a pickled[4] condition, communicated the infection to her, who gave it to the person that had seduced her, before she was aware of it. This occasioned a separation, and being now entirely at her own liberty, she became in a little time so great a prostitute, that the vilest rake in the kingdom would not venture to touch her. When she reflected upon the lamentable case she was in, she sent for a very able surgeon, who undertook to cure her, which he performed effectually in as short a compass of time, as the nature of the disease would admit; and being now like a blown deer,[5] shunned by every one, she resolved to leave the kingdom, and try what fortune she might meet with in England, hoping she might pass there for a plumb, whose bloom was not worn off.[6] She therefore wrote a letter to her injured lover, wherein she acquainted him with her intentions, begging a thousand pardons for abusing his love and tenderness to her, and requesting him to take care of the child he had by her, and not let him suffer for the folly and imprudence of the mother. He was so sensibly touched when he read the letter that the tears ran down his cheeks; he promised to grant her request, and to manifest that he had still a tender concern for her, and pitied the misfortunes she had unhappily plunged herself into, sent her a bank note of fifty pounds, and wished her all the prosperity imaginable.

3. Lover.

4. Infected with a sexually transmissible disease.

5. Andrew Marvell (1621–78), *The Rehearsal Transpos'd* (1673): 'And chase the blown Deer out of their Heard', II, 33.

6. The bloom of the plum (or plumb) was often used proverbially as an image of freshness.

ROBERT NUGENT

(1730–after 1755)

from:

THE UNNATURAL FATHER; OR, THE PERSECUTED SON. BEING A CANDID NARRATIVE OF THE MOST UNPARRELLELLED SUFFERINGS OF ROBERT NUGENT, JUNR., BY THE MEANS AND PROCUREMENT OF HIS OWN FATHER. WRITTEN BY HIMSELF, AND EARNESTLY RECOMMENDED TO THE PERUSAL OF ALL THOSE WHOSE GOODNESS GIVES THEM THE INCLINATION TO ALLEVIATE THE DISTRESS OF THEIR FELLOW-CREATURES, AND ARE BLEST WITH THE MEANS (1755)

[Robert Nugent was the illegitimate offspring of an affair between two cousins, Robert Nugent[1] and Clare Nugent. Each subsequently married and one interesting feature of this text is the way in which the mother's transgression is overlooked within her community. Neither parent is willing to take full responsibility for the child (the narrator) and his father actively persecuted young Robert. The story has many parallels with Samuel Johnson's life of the poet Richard Savage,[2] although in Nugent's case it is the father rather than the mother who so relentlessly oppresses the illegitimate child. The text raises the problem of how paternity is established and there is an element of fear and threat in the way proper names are disguised and revealed. Published in London in 1755 'for the author and sufferer now a prisoner in the Fleet',[3] the text is from the 1st edition, held in the British Library.]

As to the melancholy Affair from whence I derived my Being, so fatal to the Honour of my Mother and her Family; so unpardonable in my Father; and so lamentable in its Consequences with Respect to myself, as it is too long as well as too mournful for a Son's Recital, over that let a Veil be drawn. Suffice it that I am the unfortunate Son of R——t N——t, Esq; M——r of P——t, etc. etc. by his first Cousin, Miss *Clare Nugent*, Daughter of a Gentleman in *Ireland*, of 2500l. *per Annum*, my Father afterwards married Lady *A——a Pl——tt*, Daughter of Lord *F——ll*,[4] by whom he has a Son now also living, (a Close Copier of my inhuman Oppressor, and of whom *remarkable* Mention will hereafter be made.) My father's present Lady was Sister of the late *S——y C——gs*,[5] who I must do that Justice to say, she possesses every amiable Quality, and to whom I must acknowledge myself under the greatest Obligations.

I was born in the Parish of St. *George's, Hanover-Square*, in the County of *Middlesex*, in the Year 1730, but as the Circumstances that attended my Infancy, are not very material to relate, nor being capable of rehearsing them from my own Knowledge, I shall proceed by observing, that I received part of my Education at Mr. *Fagen's* Academy in the city of *Dublin*, by my Father's Direction, and at his Expence; but the Distraction occasioned in my Mother's Family, by the ever to be lamented Misfortune,

1. Robert Nugent (later Craggs) (1709–88), Earl Nugent, politician and poet. Three times married rich widows, for which practice Horace Walpole invented the term 'Nugentize'. MP for St Mawes (his wife's property) 1741–54; Bristol 1754–74; St Mawes 1774–84.
2. Richard Savage (d. 1743), English poet, claimed to be the illegitimate son of Richard Savage, Earl Rivers (1660–1712), and Anne, Countess of Macclesfield. The latter treated him with great hostility, documented in the *Life of Savage* (1739) by his friend Samuel Johnson.
3. The Fleet prison was situated near the Fleet Ditch, now a covered sewer, which runs from Ludgate Circus to Fleet Street in London.
4. Anna Plunkett, daughter of the Irish Catholic peer, Lord Fingall.
5. Anna Craggs (c. 1697–1756), daughter of Secretary of State, James Craggs (1657–1721), twice widowed before her marriage to Nugent.

of which I am the unhappy Offspring, and the Resentment my Father had thereby drawn upon himself, giving just Reason to apprehend I might fall an innocent Sacrifice to the growing Animosity, when I was about twelve Years of Age, my Grandfather, Capt. *Michael N——t*, being no Stranger to my Father's Disposition, and looking with an Eye of Commiseration upon my truly precarious and pitiable Condition, became particularly solicitous for my future Welfare, and falling sick, and from the Nature of his Indisposition, much doubting his Recovery, he called upon my Father for Assurance that he would make a suitable Provision for me, otherwise he would do it himself; when my Father protesting in the most solemn Manner, that he would in every Respect answer his sanguine Inclinations, my Grandfather confided therein, and dying soon after, left me nothing . . .

Upon the Decease of my Grandfather and Grandmother, my Mother's Relations (by whom I had then been some Time supported) sent me over in the Year 1748, to my Father in *England*, to reap the Benefit of his solemn Engagements, but not knowing what Kind of Reception I might meet with, my Mother, who was then married to another Gentleman, furnished me with a Certificate to the following Effect.

I do hereby Certify, that Robert Nugent, *the Bearer, is the Real son of* R——t N——t, *Esq; of* Gos——ld *in the County of* Essex, *as witness my Hand.*
CLARE BRIEN
Witness *Elinor Dardis*

This Certificate my Mother signed as above, in the presence of the Witness mentioned, who was her Servant.

As soon as I came to *London*, I waited on my Father, flattering myself with a kind Reception; but how apt are Youth to err, when abandoned to their own Judgment unaided by cool Reason! I no sooner presented myself than I produced the Certificate, which in the greatest Rage he instantly tore from me and destroyed, and treated me with an Air of the greatest Indifference: At

length, he made me an Offer of going to Sea, though that very coolly, and with seeming Reluctance; this Proposal, however, coming from my Father, I thought it my Duty to accept with Cheerfulness, though it was to act in the mean Capacity of a Captain's Servant, in which Station I accordingly embarked on board his Majesty's Ship *Windsor*, Capt. *Thomas Hanway*, not in the least doubting from my Father's affluent Fortune, I should in all Respects be suitably equipped.

[He goes to sea. Father deprives him of his prize money.[6] Other relatives and friends help him and he sets up as a grocer in Dublin. Father has him arrested for debt. He is bailed by friends. Goes to Bristol to appeal to his brother, who has him arrested and reimprisoned. He is released at election time. He wishes to go to a maternal uncle in France but his father attempts to stop him.]

Writs were absolutely sued at and dispatched to all the Sea-Port Towns, to prevent my getting off. Such implacable Malice in a Father to his OWN SON, I believe was never before heard of. My Mother's family were so incensed at my Father's ungenerous Behaviour, they would not suffer her to countenance what they looked upon to be a living Monument of the Disgrace; and my Mother being since married to another Gentleman, it was the less to be expected, but my Father was under no such Restrictions; he was the Author of my Being, under God, and were the Consequences of his *own Act* ever so fatal, I was not to be blamed; nor can the Family Inveteracy be any Cause for attempting my Destruction! which is now too obvious was the Drift; or, Why was I not permitted to seek an honest Livelihood when in a Way to have done extremely well in *Dublin*? and why were all these Measures taken to obstruct my going to my Uncle? But it sufficiently appearing it was not my Father's Intention I should have *any Being*, I shall proceed to relate his further Conduct, and leave the World to form their Judgment from the Facts.

6. The booty from a captured ship was divided as prize money amongst the crew of the ship that captured it.

ANONYMOUS

from:
MEMOIRS OF THE CELEBRATED MRS. WOFFINGTON, INTERSPERSED WITH SEVERAL THEATRICAL ANECDOTES; THE AMOURS OF MANY PERSONS OF THE FIRST RANK; AND SOME INTERESTING CHARACTERS DRAWN FROM REAL LIFE (1760)

[Margaret Woffington was born in Dublin *c.* 1714, the daughter of a bricklayer. She began her acting career in Madame Violante's Lilliputian company in Dublin, and later worked at the Smock Alley theatre. In 1740 she moved to London, working at Covent Garden and Drury Lane. For some time she lived with the actor-manager David Garrick (1717–79), and generally had a reputation for promiscuity. She was one of the most celebrated actors of the century, best known for the breeches role of Sir Harry Wildair in *The Constant Couple* (1699) by George Farquhar (1678–1707), in which her legs were much commented on and admired. She attracted a number of mock biographies in verse and prose, most of which exploited the erotic potential of her story. The *Memoirs* is interesting for its acknowledgement of the sexual vulnerability of children, and the pornographic exploitation of that vulnerability.[1] Published in London in 1760, the text is from the 2nd edition, held in the British Library.]

Peggy Woffington was at her Father's Death no more than ten years of Age, and her Sister eight years younger than herself. Even at that tender Age, she discovered Beauties which surprized and enchanted. An irresistible Grace appeared in her minutest Actions, and over her Whole Frame was diffused such a pleasing *Je ne scais quois*, as struck the Spectators with Wonder and Delight. Her Eyes were black as Jet, and while they beamed with ineffable Lustre, at the same Time, revealed all the Sentiments of her Heart, and shewed that native good Sense, tho' improved by Education, resided in their fair Possessor . . . Her Cheeks were vermilioned with Nature's best *Rouge*, which, like the Lilies and Roses, blended in Sweet Conjunction, were striving for Preference, and outvied all the laboured Works of Art . . . Her Breasts, which just then began to pout, and declared the Woman, were ravishingly delicate and inexpressibly pleasing . . .

She was, however, sent to school to learn to read of an old Woman in the Neighbourhood, and continued at it from the age of Five 'till Ten, when she was taken from it to assist her Mother in her Business, and domestic Concerns. She used particularly to carry Home the Linen, which was given to her Mother to wash, and by her decent modest Carriage, so much attracted the Notice and Esteem of her Mother's Employers, that she was pointed out as an Example for other Children to follow . . .

She had often been seen by the well-known Mademoiselle VIOLANTE[2] in the mean Employment of fetching Water from the *Liffey* for her Mother's Use; who being at that Time Mistress of a Booth,[3] in *Dame Street*, and a Person of no small Penetration, thought she could read in PEGGY'S Features, a Mind worthy of better Employment . . .

It may easily be conceived, that a Young Creature not quite twelve Years of Age, without Education, without Practice, without Friends, should be greatly dismayed at the Thoughts of passing through the fiery Ordeal of a public Appearance. From the Time of VIOLANTE'S first Intimation of her being to act *Polly*,[4] she applied

---

1. See Kristina Straub, *Sexual Suspects: Eighteenth-Century Players and Sexual Ideology* (Princeton: Princeton University Press, 1992).

2. According to Austin Dobson (see n. 4 below), Violante was a French performer, a tumbler and tight-rope dancer who had built a booth at the back of a house close to College Green. From *c.* 1718 to 1728 she performed circus tricks using children and then founded a troupe of 'Lilliputian' child actors.

3. Covered stall or tent, in this case for performances.

4. One of the Lilliputians' most celebrated performances was of *The Beggar's Opera* (1728) by John Gay (1685–1732), in which Woffington made her début as Polly Peachum. It was so successful that they moved to a theatre in Rainsford Street. Austin Dobson, 'Introduction' to *Peg Woffington* by Charles Reade (London: George Allen, 1899).

with the most assiduous Industry to get the Character by Heart; and being by Nature blessed with excellent Retentive Faculties, she soon surmounted it: But then she was equally at a loss to express the different Passions of the Mind which are in that Character; and the Timidity, naturally attendant on Merit, which she could not help feeling, gave her no small Uneasiness, and represented the Light in which she should be viewed by the disgusted Audience and her estranged Patroness, in no agreeable a Manner . . .

Let us now leave our gallant Heroine toiling for Perfection in the dramatic Mines, and represent the frail Girl sinking into the arms of unbridled Lust.

BOB C——LL——S was in the Year 1722, a Lad of some Spirit, born of poor Parents, but possessed of true Hibernian Assurance. He had often seen PEGGY, but not with Impurity. Her charms subdu'd his Heart; and he longed, not like the Lovers of Romances, to throw himself at her Feet, but to press her to his Breast, clasp her yielding Waist, and shew the Vastness of his Love by the Ardor of his Kisses. He was a Neighbour's Son, and consequently, Opportunities of seeing his Charmer were not wanting. Peggy, while with M. Violante, constantly visited her Mother, and Bob took Care to call there at those Times he was sure of seeing her. He had long conceived a violent Affection for her, had poured out the Fulness of his Love, and had been well received; but whether it was owing to Inexperience, or Fear of offending, I know not, but he had never asked for the last Favour, 'till after his Charmer had been on the Stage about two months.

PEGGY was then within a fortnight of Eleven, and Imagination can scarcely conceive what a lovely Figure she was. BOB was robust, masculine and bold. His Age was seventeen, and his Desires violent. Having a most convenient Opportunity of addressing his Charmer, when her Mother had been gone to *Ringsend*, to carry home some Linen, he mentioned the love he had long borne her, and begged her to gratify his wishes. PEGGY frowned, and BOB iterated his Request. She darted a Look of Anger, mixed with Majesty; but what would split the strong-ribbed Oak, passes harmless o'er tender Shrubs; and what would terrify a Monarch or a Hero beyond Measure, is not felt by a Clown. BOB regarded not her Frowns, but imprinted a Kiss on her sweet Lips. The Kiss had some Effect: PEGGY gently pushed him from her, but grasped his hand at the Same Time. The Grasping of his Hand thrilled his very soul, and his Heart danced unusual Measures. Furious and wild he again invaded her Lips: Those Lips, sweeter than the Honey of *Hiblaen* Bees, became a Prey to the bold Invader. The Breast-work was next attacked. With manly Vigour he snatched her to his glowing Breast; while the poor, tender, innocent Girl, unable to resist so mighty a Champion, sank in his Arms, and gave him Kiss for Kiss, and sigh for sigh. Her breast now beat with tumultuous Throbbings. Her Eyes flashed Fire; her Knees knocked together; and her whole Frame was so agitated, she could not speak, nor had strength to resist. In that critical, that soft Moment, the vigorous BOB taking her in his Arms, threw her on the ★★★★★★★★★★★★★★★★★★★★★★★★★★★★★★★★★★★★★★ Oh happy Bob! ★★★★★★★★★★★★★

Hic MS. *est Valde deflendus.*[5]

Peggy now performed the highest of Characters, and was looked upon by everyone as the chief Support of Violante's House.

---

5. i.e. Here this manuscript is powerfully to be wept over.

ARCHDEACON HUGH HAMILTON

(1729–1805)

from:
LETTER TO EARL OF ABERCORN[1] (1761)

[John McNaghten/McNaughton (1724–61), one time Collector of the King's Duties at Coleraine, was a gambler and spendthrift who had wasted his fortune. When his first wife died in childbirth he tried to abduct and trick into marriage Mary Anne Knox, of Prehen, Londonderry, the sixteen-year-old daughter of Andrew Knox, MP for County Donegal, and heiress to £6,000. When his plot was thwarted he continued to insist that Knox was his wife, and Andrew Knox appealed to the ecclesiastical courts to prove that there was no marriage. In November 1761 Andrew Knox decided to move his family to Dublin to escape McNaughton's attention. McNaughton and a number of accomplices attacked the coach in which the family was travelling, close to Strabane. Mary Anne Knox was shot dead and a family servant was injured. McNaughton and his accomplice, David Dunlap, were captured and sentenced 'to be hanged, but not until dead, and then to have their bowels taken out and burned, and their heads erected on the gaol'. McNaughton attempted to thwart the dismemberment by leaping from the gibbet, but the rope broke, and the sentence was carried out at the second attempt. The general sympathy for rapists and abductors (except in cases such as the Cotter trial, where there is a clear sectarian issue) has not yet been sufficiently explained, although in many cases the public perception was that the abduction was consensual. A striking feature of McNaughton's case was the refusal of the general population to collaborate in the erection of the gibbet.[2] A typescript of the letter is held in the Public Record Office of Northern Ireland, D623/A/35/58, Abercorn papers.]

1st December 1761
Baron's Court

We have yet hardly recover'd ourselves from our consternation occasion'd by one of the most daring and inhuman act[s] of violence that I ever

1. James Hamilton (1712–89), 8th Earl of Abercorn.
2. See J.B. Cunningham, 'Sir James Caldwell and the Life of Half-Hanged McNaughton', *Donegal Annual*, vol. 13 (1980), pp. 549–58; A.P.W. Malcolmson, *Pursuit of the Heiress*; James Kelly, 'The Abduction of Women of Fortune in Eighteenth-Century Ireland', *Eighteenth-Century Ireland/Iris an dá chultúr*, vol. 9 (1994), pp. 7–43.

remember, I mean the murder of Miss Knox by Mr. McNaghten; I see by the English papers you have already had some account of it but as the particulars have never yet been truly given to the public and as your Lordship may possibly have some curiosity to know them. I will just mention some of the most remarkable ones which I had from Captain J. Hamilton and an other person who assisted in taking examinations. McNaghten has been lurking about this country in disguise for these five months past, and by his address found means to conciliate to his interest many persons, whom one wou'd hardly have suspected. They agreed with him that he was highly injured by having his wife detain'd from him and listen'd with pleasure to his declarations that he wou'd recover her by force, bind her father and mother and consummate the marriage in their presence; this scheme was applauded by many and in particular by several ladies whose knowledge of it will be proved and some of whose letters will be produced in court. It seems however that this was only a feint and that his real plan was to murder the whole family in the actual execution of which he had engaged three desperate assassins formerly his servants, whose names are known, and one of whom I hear is taken since the Proclamation, offering five hundred pounds reward for apprehending each of them. He had besides many spies and letters particularly two Irwins of Lisdivin within a few miles of Strabane, and one Winsley who I believe is your tenant. These persons procured information that Col Knox was to pass that way on Tuesday the 19th of this instant which was ascertained by a letter from Mr. Knox in answer to one from Mr. Hamilton of Dunamanna who desir'd a place in his coach to Dublin, falling into the hands of one of the Irwins, in what manner will be better known in a few days. It appears already from Mr. Hamilton's examination that he knew of McNaghten's being in that place with the Irwins for several days before, and though it is also proved he apprehended something dangerous was there contriving, he gave his friend Mr. Knox no account of it, but desir'd Mr. Tyrrel the collector of Strabane the very morning of the assassination to use his influence with the Irwins to drive McNaghten from their house. Now cou'd Mr. Hamilton who is their landlord stand in need of such influence? Sums of money have been discovered to have been lodged for the service of intelligence of Mr. Knox's motions, and some of his servants were actually bribed and one particularly now in prison, who was entrusted to load the arms and which he did in such a manner as to make them inoffensive, except the gun of one servant whose cowardice they thought made that precaution unnecessary. The 10th one of the Irwins set out upon the business of setting the coach, and when it had passed, rode after it looked into it and then went on briskly about a mile to the wood where McNaghten and his accomplices were posted, who upon the coach's coming up immediately rushed out on foot, as I believe they were all. The coachman was call'd upon to stop and fir'd at but without affect. Mr. Knox was attended by two persons on horseback, one with a Blunderbuss, the other with a gun; three shots were immediately fired at the former, as he was the only one they fear'd, though the servant I mention'd who was not in company had previously taken care to shake out the priming of the Blunderbuss, which he snapped twice upon their first coming up and must have prevented the whole mischief had it gone off; the poor fellow was totally disabled though not mortally wounded. McNaghten then stept'd up to the coach and with a long gun, shot Miss Knox in the side below her stays, who immediately cried out, I am killed; the other servant who was indeed timorous had retir'd behind a turf stack and fir'd at the very same instant and lodged three bullets in McNaghten's back whose position was such that they glanced up instead of going to his body as they must have done had he been standing upright. Mr. Knox snapp'd a pistol at him, which did not go off; he then ran round to the other side of the coach and two shots were immediately fired into it through the wooden blind which was drawn up but did no hurt. Mr. Knox then fir'd his second pistol close to him and was surprised

to find it had no effect. McNaghten finding himself weakn'd by the wounds he had receiv'd, thought proper to make his retreat and was assisted in getting over the brook and help'd upon his horse by the same Irwin who set the coach; he then went to Winsleys house and conceal'd himself in the hay loft not being able to ride any farther. Mr. Knox's son upon his sister's being wounded rode in all haste to Strabane and return'd in a very short time with Dr Law and a party of the light horse; a reward of a hundred guineas being offered to who ever shou'd take McNaghten, they separated and began the pursuit. The Corporal and Knox the innkeeper at Strabane went to Winsleys house and not seeing any horse began to despair finding him there, but Winsley's daughter passing them in the yard with a teapot in her hand, they question'd her what she had been doing with it, and not getting a satisfactory answer they renew'd their pursuit. The Corporal immediately rush'd up into the hay loft and having had two shots fir'd at him without effect, McNaghten apprehending a return surrendered himself and was tied upon a car and convey'd to Lifford Gaol; it was thought at first his wounds wou'd prove mortal, but he is in no danger from them. His design at present is to starve himself having refused to take any sort of food for these three days. Judge Scot and Baron Mountney are to be at Strabane on Saturday the 5th of December to try him and his accomplices there. As he has too many well wishers, it is thought necessary to keep a very strong guard over him. I forgot to mention that the poor young lady died about five hours after she receiv'd her wound. The trial will certainly be a remarkable one, as in the course of the evidences who are to be call'd, upon the connivance of many persons and not of the lower class, to McNaghten's first pretended scheme will be incontestably proved. I have most likely tired your Lordship with this long detail, as there is no other subject of discourse here at present, I enter'd upon it without intending to be so prolix. Mrs. Hamilton desires to join with me in best compliments to your Lordship and Lady Abercorn.

DOROTHEA DU BOIS

(1728–74)

from:

THE CASE OF ANN COUNTESS OF ANGLESEY, LATELY DECEASED; LAWFUL WIFE OF RICHARD ANNESLEY, LATE EARL OF ANGLESEY, AND OF HER THREE SURVIVING DAUGHTERS, LADY DOROTHEA, LADY CAROLINE, AND LADY ELIZABETH, BY THE SAID EARL (1766)

[Dorothea was the eldest of three daughters of Ann Simpson, herself the daughter of a Dublin merchant, and Richard Annesley, later Earl of Anglesey.[1] She was born in Dublin in 1728, and educated at boarding-school there. Annesley inherited his earldom in 1737, and in 1740 he declared his marriage to Simpson invalid, deserting her and her children in favour of his housekeeper, whom he later married. The countess charged him with cruelty and adultery and was awarded alimony in the Ecclesiastical Court in Dublin. Annesley refused to pay, and was excommunicated. In 1752 Dorothea married a French musician, Peter Du Bois, and they had six children. She wrote plays, poetry, a novel and an anthology to earn money and also to publicize her father's ill-treatment of his family. A number of her writings retell the scene of her attempted reconciliation with her father, when she travelled to Wexford to see him in 1760; she was attacked, held at gun point and beaten, apparently at the instigation of his new wife. This set of documents is particularly valuable because it demonstrates the effectiveness of various genres in narrating the same set of events, in particular in revealing how family violence can be presented to different audiences in different styles. It also indicates the complexities and contradictions of the relationship between a prosperous Protestant woman and her Catholic servants. Dorothea has an investment in believing that her mother was generous towards and beloved by tenants and servants. At the same time, the venom of her response to Annesley's mistress, Julian/a Donnovan (sometimes Donovan or O'Donovan), is coloured with racial, sectarian and class prejudices. Many passages in Du Bois are similar to narratives of slave-holding women in the nineteenth-century American South. The first selection is from Du Bois's Introduction. All the following texts are from copies in the British Library.]

In November 1760, I was informed my Father, *Richard*, the last Earl of *Anglesey*, lay dangerously ill; Nature wrought so powerfully in my Breast, as to determine my endeavouring to see that dear deluded Father, in hopes the Sight of a Child, he once dearly loved, might be a Means of recalling him to a Sense of his Duty, and a Desire of Reconciliation with his Family. It was certainly very great Rashness in me, to venture myself in the Hands of Enemies, with whom he was surrounded, whose inveterate Hatred I had before experienced, and particularly at a Time, when my Spirits and Strength were greatly impaired by Child-Birth, having lain-in about seven Weeks before of my sixth Child. With great Difficulty I prevailed on my Mother and my Husband, to consent to my taking this hazardous Step; but this Point gained, after recommending myself to the Protection of Almighty God, I set out for the Family Seat, at *Camolin-Park* in the County *of Wexford*, attended only by an old Man, and a Foot-boy of thirteen Years of Age, who rode before me. I lay that Night at a Town within two Miles of my Father's, and well convinced that, if

---

1. Richard Annesley (1694–1761), 6th Earl of Anglesey, succeeded his brother as 5th Baron Altham, 1727, and his cousin as 6th Earl of Anglesey, 7th Viscount Valentia, 7th Baron Mountnorris, and Baron Newport Pagnell in 1737. He seems to have married Ann Prest (or Prust/Phrust) (d. 1741) in 1715, and Ann Simpson (bigamously) in 1737; from 1741 he lived with Juliana Donnovan, whom he married in 1752. On his death both Simpson and Donnovan claimed the titles of Valentia and Mountnorris for their children. Donnovan won the case and her son Arthur Annesley succeeded, but he was unable to establish his claim to the Anglesey earldom. Richard Annesley's own claim to the earldom had been contested for many years by his brother's son James Annesley (1715–60). Richard Annesley notoriously succeeded in having this boy sent to America as a slave, but he returned to challenge for his inheritance. These were not the last members of the family to be associated with sexual scandal: in 1797 the 1st Earl Annesley, a childless widower, bigamously married Sophia O'Connor, the wife of his brother's gardener, who later became involved in lengthy litigation for his estate.

known, I should have no Chance of seeing him, I ordered Matters so, as to be there early the next Morning, when concealing my Face, and knowing the Situation of my Father's Bedchamber, I made my Way to it, without the least Difficulty or Obstruction, but alas! found a Female Companion with him, from whom I could hope for little Lenity. — She started when she saw me enter, and discover who I was, by throwing myself on my Knees at my poor Father's Bed-side, and, with Tears, implore his Blessing. — No one but such as have the same Feelings I have, can conceive the tender Agony that seized my Soul, on seeing the Change Time had wrought in the Author, under God, of my Being. — But who can describe my Astonishment and Grief, at hearing him utter the most shocking Imprecations against his Child; — a Child that loved him as her Life, and would have sacrificed it to his Preservation and Conversion. — How shall I repeat it? He called for his Pistols to shoot me! — Self preservation, they say, is the first Law of Nature — therefore, seeing Mrs. *Donovan* make towards a Closet where I formerly knew Fire-Arms hung, — I started to my Feet, and charged her, at her Peril, not to harm me, as she certainly would suffer for it, if she did, as many knew of my coming, and for what Purpose, which was no other than to obtain a Father's Blessing before he died. After a few more Altercations not worthy Repetition, she rang the Bell, when a number of ill-looking Wretches, who dishonoured the Name of Servants, appeared; Mrs. *Donovan* ordered those, her Ruffians, to seize and drag me out of the Room, vainly imagining that, if I could obtain a few Moments longer Stay in his Presence, my Father's Heart would relent, as his Anger seemed to subside; on finding myself thus attacked, I drew a small silver-mounted Pistol from my Pocket, which I blush to say was, with its Fellow, unloaded; and only meant to keep those Ruffians, I expected to meet, at a Distance. A Cry, equalling that they describe the wild *Indians* to give, was set up at the Sight of this formidable Weapon. Presenting the harmless Bugbear[2] alone at my ferocious Assailants, I bid them not lay Hands upon me, or expect the Consequences. At first they obeyed through Fear, but finding I did not fire, they pressed in upon me; three Men all

at once laid hold on it, and had Strength and Valour sufficient to wrest it out of the Hand of a weak Woman; but not without leaving that Hand in a gore of Blood. While those attacked me in Front, others endeavoured to strangle me behind my Back, by pulling my Cloak, and had effected their Intention, were I not under the Banner of an all-wise all-powerful Being! who ordered the Strings to break; I was again saved by the same Hand! who intimidated the Hand of Mrs. *Donovan's* Son from letting off a Pistol, which he courageously held cocked at the back of my Head, and occasioned his meeting with a severe Rebuke from an ignorant Pantry-boy, whom he desired to shoot me, the Boy telling him, '*you may do it yourself, I have no Mind for the Gallows*'. After this, they turned me down the Stairs into the Hall, took my other Pistol from me, but not before I unscrewed the Barrel, and shewed them there was nothing in it. Then it was my humble Lot to be obliged to sit in the Kitchen, where I was an Eye-witness to such Things as gave room for this Reflection, *that where Vice presided, Order, Regularity, and Plenty were banished.* My Servants were threatened with a Goal [sic], together with their unfortunate Mistress, they were pinioned like Thieves, and by the Order of the young Lord,[3] as they called Mrs. *Donovan's* Son, they inhumanly cut off the Ear of the innocent Horse I rode, though the poor Brute could not possibly be deemed an Accessary in my Offence, had my Intention even been Criminal . . .

[The following is taken from the body of the text.]

In the Year 1741, the said *Ann* Countess of *Anglesey*, being thus forlorn and totally destitute of any Subsistence, she by the Advice of Doctor *Boulter*,[4] the then worthy and virtuous Lord Primate of *Ireland*, with whose Family she was in great Intimacy, instituted her Suit in the Consistorial Court of the Diocese of *Dublin*,[5] against the said Earl *Richard*, for Cruelty and Adultery, with the said *Julian Donovan*; and upon Confession of his Marriage with the said

2. An imaginary terror.

3. Author's note: Who now stiles himself Earl of Anglesey, etc., etc.
4. Hugh Boulter (1672–1742), Archbishop of Armagh, frequently acted as Lord Justice in Ireland.
5. Ecclesiastical courts had jurisdiction over wills, marriage, sexual immorality, defamation, heresy, blasphemy and issues related to ecclesiastical fees.

Countess *Ann*, in his personal Sentence, she obtained an Order against him for an interim Alimony of Four Pounds a Week until a full Answer should be pronounced in the said Suit; and further, that the said Earl should pay her Costs to that Time, and her future Costs in the Cause.

The said Earl having been served with a Monition[6] to pay the said Order, and having declined to perform the same, Sentence of Excommunication was pronounced against him, and having still continued in his Obstinacy, he was, after all the due Forms had been used, declared an excommunicated Person, and so remained till his Death; and Application having been made to the then Lord Chancellor for a Writ, *de excommunicado capiendo*,[7] to take the said Earl into Custody, and the Chancellor having declined to grant it, on Account of his Privilege of Peerage, her Suit in that Respect proved ineffectual; and her sole Support, and that of her Children, from thence forward to her Death, which happened in *August* 1765 was a Pension of *200l.* a Year upon the *Irish Establishment*, which his late most excellent Majesty was graciously pleased to grant her, on the Representation of the Earl of *Chesterfield*,[8] then Lord Lieutenant of that Kingdom, of the Cruelty and Hardship of her Case.

The said Earl *Richard* and his Accomplices finding themselves defeated in their — Scheme of obtaining a Divorce, thought proper to try by some other Method. He therefore, in the course of the above-mentioned Proceedings in the consistorial Court, (having first in vain applied to his late Majesty for a *noli prosequi*[9] on account of Bigamy) set up another Marriage, *prior* to that of his Countess, with one *Ann Phrust* of the County of *Devon* in *England*, who died some short Time before, as appeared by one of his answers to the Libel of the said Countess of *Anglesey*, which was

the first Notice she ever had of any such Marriage; but, on the contrary, if the said Marriage had any real foundation, the same was all along concealed from her with the greatest Care and Secresy till that Time. And it is particularly to be observed with relation to that pretended Marriage, that some short Time after the said *Richard* became Earl of *Anglesey*, the above named *Ann Phrust*, who had never in the least claimed him as her Husband, or given the least Notice to Lady *Anglesey* of her *prior* Marriage, if any such was really solemnized, wrote him a Letter from *Biddeford* in *Devonshire* to *Ireland*, to claim an Alimony; and that his Lordship was so alarmed at this Letter, and so industrious to conceal it from his Countess, who by this Time had been introduced at the Lord Lieutenant's Court, and complimented by all the Nobility of the Kingdom as Countess of *Anglesey*, that he immediately wrote to one *William Henderson* his *English* Agent, a most pressing Letter, requesting him to go immediately to *Biddeford*, and silence that Woman let it cost what it would, lest her Pretensions should make a Noise, and come to Lady *Anglesey's* Ears.

. . . It is in like manner to be observed, that the Evidence given by *Ruth Coxon* in favour of Mr. *John Annesley*,[10] was so very material to disprove the pretended Marriage of the said *Julian Donovan* in *September* 1741, that they had no other way of avoiding the force of it, but by procuring a set of low lived illiterate Papists, most of whom are Persons of bad Character themselves, to make Affidavits tending to impeach hers; although what these people have sworn against her, is clearly repugnant to the offices she had been employed in about the said Earl's Family, and to the Trust reposed in her by him as well as by his Countess *Ann Simpson*, in committing the education of their Children to her Care in their early Infancy; and afterwards by the said Earl's sending her to *Bray*[11] in the year 1741, after he had abandoned his Countess and taken the said *Julian Donovan* into keeping as a Concubine, to be in his Family, and to instruct the said *Julian* how to dress and behave herself. Moreover, her Character would have been

6. Admonition, warning.
7. The ecclesiastical court could apply to the civil court to issue a writ *de excommunicado capiendo*, under which an excommunicated person could be committed to gaol until s/he submitted to the court's authority. Ordinary excommunication was thought to have little effect in Ireland, where the majority of the population was Catholic or Dissenter, since the real penalty of excommunication was not so much exclusion from the church as from the society of all its members.
8. Philip Dormer Stanhope (1694–1773), 4th Earl of Chesterfield, Irish Viceroy 1745–6.
9. *Nolle prosqui*: petition from a plaintiff to stay a suit.

10. John Annesley, heir-at-law to Earl Richard, successfully contested the legitimacy of Arthur Annesley, son of Richard and Donnovan.
11. Seaside resort, south of Dublin.

supported by several Persons of Worth and Veracity, particularly by the Evidence of the Clergyman of the parish of *Bray* where she resided, who not only voluntarily granted her a Certificate of her Sobriety and good Behaviour, in contradiction to the Affidavits sworn against her by those wretches, but would have given Evidence of the same, had not the said *John Annesley* by an inexcusable neglect of his own Interest omitted it, was well as many other material Things, which would have strengthened his Case, and invalidated that of his Adversary.

from:
THEODORA: A NOVEL (1770)

[*Theodora*, an anagram of Dorothea, is an auto-biographical novel which retells the story of the Annesleys' marriage. The first extract suggests that the ideal mother combines nurture of her child with domestic industry and shows a solidarity towards other women. The comparison between Theodora and the illegitimate child prefigures her later change in status. The baron's alienation from and anger towards his own illegitimate child is characteristic of the gulf in sympathy between landlord and peasant classes, also evidenced in the extract from Dorothea Herbert (pp. 815–17). The text is from the British Library copy, which has extensive MS annotation by Sir William Musgrave (1735–1800), the antiquarian scholar who was clearly familiar with the case.]

Tho' Lady *Altamont* was married very young, yet her knowledge, so far surpassed her years, that she was a perfect pattern of prudence and œconomy. She nursed her children; nay so indefatigable was she, in the duties of her houshold, that she has been known to spin very fine yarn, give suck to her child, and read at the same time. A thing which very few ladies would, or indeed could have done.

One day that she was thus employed, and Lord *Altamont* from home, a woman with a fine girl, of about a year and half old, came to the house, and enquired for Lady *Altamont*. The Baroness was sitting in the parlour, when the woman entered (for she was never denied by her own orders to the poor,) but was so intent on what she was about, that she did not perceive her. The woman was amazed at the way in which the Baroness was occupied; and could scarce believe her eyes. She gazed in silence for sometime, but at length awakened the attention of the Baroness, by crying out, Good God, is it possible! On which the Baroness started, and was like to have let fall her little daughter, *Theodora*. The woman fell on her knees, and intreated her pardon for having disturbed her in so abrupt a manner; but declared, that she could not avoid crying out; for she had never before seen so fine a sight. Lady *Altamont*, smiling, bid her rise, and assured her, that her pretty compliment more than compensated the surprize her exclamation had occasioned.

But what is your business, good woman? said the Baroness. I came, replied she, in order to make you my complaint, and to implore your ladyship's pardon and protection, which I was encouraged to do, from hearing what a sweet good Lady you were. Good woman, said the Baroness, if you knew how little I am pleased with flattery, you would not be so very prodigal of it; if I can serve you, I will. Whose fine child is that? The poor woman blushed, and held down her head. I suppose it is your own, continued the Baroness; pray, are you married? No, my Lady, replied the woman, Who is the father of the child? said the Baroness, with some emotion. 'Tis — 'tis — replied she, faultering, 'tis — Speak, said the Baroness, if any of my servants is the father, I may, perhaps, by my authority cause him to marry you. Oh! said the woman, falling on her knees, and bursting into tears, forgive me, my good Lady; I am a poor wretched woman, that was ruined by your Lord before he was married to you. I have nursed his child such as you see; living ever since upon my father and mother, who are unable to support us longer. I cannot consent to put my baby into the poor-house. — Yet, I know not what else to do. I have got people to write several petitions to your Lord; but I cannot obtain the smallest relief from him. Indeed, my good Lady, I am almost starved, and my little one is quite naked; for I borrowed the cloaths it has on, to make it fit to appear before you. The Baroness, touched with pity more than resentment, made the woman rise, and giving *Theodora* into her arms, took her child in her own, and kissing it said, she believed it was her husband's, for it resembled him. She held the child close up by *Theodora*, and asked the woman if she did not think it like her little darling.

She then ordered the woman some refreshment, and kept her child until she had finished her repast. She desired her to come the week following, and she would have some things ready for her child; and giving her a piece of money, with an assurance of a fresh supply, dismissed her unexpected visitant with a heart overcharged with gratitude.

The woman came at the time appointed, the Baroness dressed the child out very fine, and gave the mother several changes for it, together with the promised supply. This innocent intrigue was carried on for more than three months; the woman still taking care to come when the Baron was out. But unfortunately for her, the Baron's fondness for *Theodora*, who was then sick, made him return one day sooner than was expected: He met her coming out of the house, and immediately recollecting her, D——n you, said he, you w——e, what business have you and your bastard in my house? My Lady, answered She, has been good to me, though you never have; and it is a pity that an angel such as she, should fall into the hands of a brute.

His lordship immediately set his dogs at her, and turned into the house. The huntsman, very luckily, for the poor wretch, happened to be in the court-yard, who, as soon as he saw the Baron gone, called off the dogs. They had already rent her cloaths, while her fondness for her infant made her hold it over her head, to preserve it as long as she could from their fury. The Baron's first salute to his Lady, for an act which a grateful man would have admired, was D——n you —— you mean spirited little b——h, how dare you to notice or harbour my bastard? By G——d, if I ever find out, or hear, that you do the like again, I will make you repent it. Notwithstanding his menaces, she still found means to relieve the child, who did not very long enjoy the fruits of her charity; for the poor babe died soon after this notable adventure . . .

If to be universally beloved and esteemed, could make the Countess happy, she would now most certainly be so; but alas! the Earl began to give full indulgence to his inclinations. This the Countess one day remarked to him, when he was in one of his best humours, and said, that he was quite changed from the man he was some time before. You are mistaken, replied the Earl, I have been always the same, but different circumstances gave me different appearances. I was then unable to shew myself, but I am no longer necessitated to wear the mask; I had always the inclination but not the ability, and as they both now coincide, I shall for the future cast off all restraint. This the reader may imagine was no very pleasing prospect for the Countess.

She was now rendered extremely miserable by the unjust suspicions of her husband. Should a gentleman chance to look on her, it wakened his jealousy; or should her eyes happen to meet those of the person who viewed her, he was certain she was ogling him, and had some private intelligence with him. He would retire to bed at eight in the evening, and cause her to go with him, though the house was full of company, under the pretence of being taken suddenly ill. When in bed, he would often pinch and beat her, being certain that shame would prevent her from crying out. One time he followed her from room to room, with a cocked pistol in his hand, and frightened her almost to death. Another time in his own closet, after consulting with her on business of consequence, he took her on his knee, and drew his chair close to his bureau. She perceived him searching in his pocket for his key, which having found, he strove to unlock the bureau. The Countess, reading a malignity in his looks that terrified her, asked him, with some emotion, what he was about? I only want a razor, said he, holding her still closer. Not to cut my throat, I hope? cried the Countess. No, no, my dear, he replied, I would only scarify your face, which Iago[1] (who was the family surgeon) will soon heal. I shall not then be so unhappy as I am; for by G——d you are now so handsome, that every fellow who looks on you, is in love with you.

The Countess, on hearing this, and perceiving he had laid hold on a razor, gave a sudden spring and disengaged herself. She fled as fast as she was able, until she reached her dressing room, where her woman and some other of her attendants were. As soon as she entered the room, she dropped down in a fit.

The Earl hearing a great bustle in the house, and reading consternation in the looks of all the family, was ashamed of the unaccountable

---

1. John Ians. Musgrave's note: 'Mr. Ians — a surgeon in the Case of Ann, Countess of Anglesey.' Du Bois describes him as 'a Popish surgeon'. The name Iago identifies Ians with the villain of Shakespeare's *Othello*.

attempt he had made, called for *Theodora*, who generally mediated on those occasions, and told her he had vexed her mamma. He desired her to go, and endeavour to reconcile her to him, and to promise faithfully on his part, that he would never disoblige her for the future. *Theodora* succeeded in her embassy. The innocent caresses of the pleasing little flatterer, pleaded so strongly with the Countess, that she could not resist her.

[The following extract describes the attendance of a peasant midwife at the countess's lying-in.]

The poor woman, who had never seen a stair-case before, when the servants desired her to come up, looked quite scared, and cried out, Is it I go up that high place to break my neck? not I, by my troth; I know better things than that, though so great a fool as you may think me. Finding that they could not persuade her by any means to venture up, two of the footmen were obliged to lay hold on her. The old midwife, frighted out of her senses, began to kick and scream in a horrible manner. She then seemed greatly concerned to know how she should get down again; but the men, assuring her that they would take her down as safely as they had brought her up, prevailed on her to commit herself to the care of the women-servants.

Having led her through the different rooms, in each of which she expressed her wonder at the fine things she saw, they brought her at length to that where their Lady was in bed. This room was hung with tapestry, the figures as large as life. At the first view of them she started back, crying, By my own sweet soul, agrah, I won't go into a place where there is so many fine gentry. This caused the Baroness to laugh, notwithstanding the pain she was in. The servants eased her scruples with regard to the fine gentry, by putting her hand upon the tapestry. This again excited her wonder. Faith, honey, says she, I did not think they were dead people, I thought they were all alive. The woman hearing the Baroness laugh when near to the bed-side says, *O hone*[2] my dear joy if you can laugh so heartily, 'tis sign you are not after being so bad as they said you were. I don't believe but you sent for me to make your own game of me, honey. The Baroness now laughed so

immoderately, that the poor midwife was quite enraged; she squatted herself down on her haunches by the fire-side, pulled out of her bosom a tobacco-pipe of about two inches in length, black as jet, which she set fire to, and began to smoke so furiously, that she almost suffocated the poor Baroness. It had, however, a good effect upon her; for from that moment she grew better. The poor woman was handsomely rewarded for the mirth she had created, and went away well satisfied.

from:
POEMS ON SEVERAL OCCASIONS. BY A LADY OF QUALITY (1764)

[Du Bois's first writings are accounts in poetry, fiction and pamphlet of her own remarkable family history. Her personal experience of patriarchal tyranny makes her an advocate of certain women's rights. The text is from a copy owned and annotated by Sir William Musgrave, in the British Library. This work was published by subscription, and the 296 subscribers, all apparently Irish, included several aristocrats and bishops. 'A True Tale' retells the narrative of her life. This time Dorothea (Dorinda) attempts to visit her father on his deathbed but is driven away.]

from:
A True Tale

Sh'obtain'd the sight, so earnestly she sought,
But at the Hazard of her Life 'twas bought
The cruel Father imprecating lay,
Disowning Nature, order'd her away;
Tho' to Appearance, ready just to go,
And pay that Debt which all to Nature owe.
A num'rous Throng of Ruffians now surround
The sad *Dorinda*, prostrate on the Ground.
His base-born Son, a Pistol e'en presents,
Behind her Head; but watchful Heav'n prevents
The Fiend from executing his Intents.
They pull and drag her, tear her Hands and
    Cloak,
Nay dare uplift their own to give a Stroke:
Force her from Room to Room, then down the
    Stairs,
Nor heed her piteous Cries, nor flowing Tears.

2. *Ochón*, alas.

Some, more humane, now shook indeed their
    Head
As they pass'd her, but nothing still they said.
(Scarce two Months past a dang'rous Lying-in,
Such cruel Usage surely was a Sin.)
Now driven from the House, *Dorinda* sate
And humbly warm'd her at the Kitchen Grate.
While ev'ry Word, was followed by a Sigh,
Behold her Woes draw Tears from ev'ry Eye.
Her Servants now are ty'd, her Horse's Ear
Inhumanly cut off: 'tis much they spare
Dorinda's Life, whom thus they seem to hate
With Spleen, uncommonly inveterate.
Forc'd now to walk along the dirty Road,
Her Legs scarce able to support their Load;
They bring her Pris'ner to th'adjacent Town,
Where her unhappy Fate's no sooner known,
Than all lament the Usage she receiv'd,
They wept in Secret, and in Secret griev'd:
But none dare openly express their Grief,
Nor, tho' she fasting was, bestow Relief.
Faint, hungry, cold and comfortless she sate
The whole long Night, bemoaning of her Fate;
No Bed whereon to lay her weary'd Head,
By Grief and Sorrow she alone is fed.

The Amazonian[1] Gift

Is Courage in a Woman's Breast,
    Less pleasing than in Man?
And is a smiling Maid allow'd
    No Weapon but a Fan?[2]

'Tis true, her Tongue, I've heard 'em say,
    Is Woman's chief Defence;
And if you'll b'lieve me, gentle Youths,
    I have no Aid from thence.

And, some will say, that sparkling Eyes,
    More dang'rous are, than swords;
But I ne'er point my Eyes to kill,[3]
    Nor put I trust in Words.

1. An ancient race of female warriors, alleged by Herodotus to live in Scythia.
2. Fans for cooling the face have existed since ancient times. The folding fan was invented in Japan and transported from there to China and Europe. Fans became a common part of female dress in England from the sixteenth century, and British manufacturing began in the mid-seventeenth century.
3. 'Those eyes are made so killing' were the last words of Sir Fopling to Belinda in *The Rape of the Lock* (1712) by Alexander Pope (1688–1744).

Then, since the Arms that Women use,
    Successless are in me;
I'll take the Pistol, Sword or Gun,
    And thus equip'd live free.

The Pattern of the *Spartan* Dame,[4]
    I'll copy as I can;
To Man, degen'rate Man, I'll give
    That simple Thing, a *Fan*.

4. Sparta was the capital of the ancient Doric state of Laconia. Spartan women were characteristically careless of appearance as well as being simple, frugal and courageous.

On the Death of a Young Lady who was Inoculated for the Small-pox[1]

Did you, to save poor *Sally's* Beauty strive?
Have you destroy'd what might be still alive?
Where was a Mother's Fondness flown,
Or who'd inflict *Job's* torment[2] on their own?
Or wou'd presume to tempt the Lord on High,
Or his divine authority defy?
Audacious Mortals, see! how soon He can
Undo and frustrate the Attempts of Man.
Sweet *Sally* thanks thee, for thy unskill'd Pains;
Your's still be the Affliction, her's the Gains.
She, like a Rose misplac'd by Nature, sprung
From a coarse Bramble, on a heap of Dung;
But to her kindred Heaven, she is gone,
Have you her Equal with you? no not one.

Sally indeed, was lovely and discreet,
Mild in her temper, in her Nature sweet;
Innocently gay, civil yet sincere,
For *Sally* was, in short, above her Sphere.

1. Smallpox, or variola, is an acute infectious disease characterized by fever and by the appearance on the surface of the body of an eruption of pustules, which, after passing through various stages, dry up, leaving distinct, and often lasting, depressed scars. Inoculation, the introduction into the system of a mild dose of the virus, was extensively practised in Turkey in the early part of the eighteenth century, and was introduced to Britain largely through the letters of Mary Wortley Montagu. Although it made an impression on the rates of fatality from the disease, it was often unsuccessful, leading to serious disfigurement or death. In the 1790s inoculation began to be replaced by Jenner's discovery, vaccination. The dilemma of inoculation is treated in Elizabeth Griffith's novel, *The Delicate Distress* (1769).
2. In the Judaic testaments, the Book of Job describes how Yahweh permits Satan to test Job's faith by, among other things, covering him in a plague of ulcers (Job 2:7–8).

Ah! was it then the mere Effect of Pride?
And strove ye just to save a fair Outside?
Was not a Soul in such bright Robes array'd
Sufficiently attractive in the Maid?
Who wou'd the Mind's superior Beauties place
In Competition with a pretty Face?
And yet, where is the wise Mamma, or wiser
    Father,
Who if they had the Choice, wou'd not much
    rather

Have their sweet darling Babe a perfect Beauty,
Than just remarked for Piety and Duty?
The Sight attracted, quickly gains the Heart,
While Sense, but slowly does her Charms impart.
But, Thanks to Heav'n! who has given me
Sufficient Sense, to wait its wise Decree;
No Vanity of mine, shall make me dare
With its high Judgment e'er to interfere.
But to my lov'd Creator, I will still
Submit each Dictate of his Servant's will.

ANONYMOUS

from:
THE GENUINE MEMOIRS OF MISS FAULKNER; OTHERWISE MRS. D***L**N;[1] OR, COUNTESS OF H*****,[2] IN EXPECTANCY. CONTAINING, THE AMOURS AND INTRIGUES OF SEVERAL PERSONS OF HIGH DISTINCTION, AND REMARKABLE CHARACTERS: WITH SOME CURIOUS POLITICAL ANECDOTES, NEVER BEFORE PUBLISHED (1770)

[Mary Anne Faulkner (sometimes referred to as Anna Maria Faulkner) was born in Dublin, the niece of George Faulkner (1699–1755), bookseller and printer. According to many sources, her first husband was called 'Donnellan', although the editors of *Horace Walpole's Correspondence. Complete Index*, compiled by Warren Hunting Smith (Oxford: Oxford University Press, 1983), identify her first husband as William Donaldson (m. 1743) and mention a second marriage to Colonel Charles Lumm (m. 1784).

She was working as a singer at Drury Lane Theatre in London in the early 1750s when she was engaged by the widowed Earl of Halifax as governess to his three daughters. She became Halifax's mistress and they had two children, George (d. 1767) and Anna Maria (d. *c.* 1771). Faulkner returned to Ireland in 1761 when Halifax was created Lord Lieutenant. The advancement of her many relations during the Halifax regime led to her frequent caricature in cartoons and squibs.[3] This mock-autobiography is among the most pornographic examples of the genre, and seems to draw on the reputed exploits of the Hell-Fire Clubs in Ireland.[4] The text is taken from the British Library copy (London: William Bingley, 1770).]

She was somewhat above the middle size, but as exactly proportioned, as ever any goddess was drawn by the pencil of a *Guido*[5] or a *Titian*,[6] — her hair, which was as black as ebony, in flowing curls, covered the finest neck and skin in the universe; her eyes also were large and black, with all the *soft languishments of the blue*; and every turn of her face, discovered some new grace: add to all these natural charms, a voice that was perfectly transporting, assisted by all the powers of musick, and you may, perhaps, form some idea of what Miss Faulkner then appeared to her numerous train of admirers . . .

[Lord K——] after protesting, in the most solemn manner, that he never would marry the lady she spoke of, that, if she would condescend

1. Donnellan, or Donaldson.
2. George Montagu Dunk (1716–71), 2nd Earl of Halifax, was Lord Lieutenant of Ireland 1761–3.

3. The political background to this text is explored by Robert Blackey in 'A Politician in Ireland: The Lord Lieutenancy of the Earl of Halifax, 1761–63', *Éire-Ireland*, vol. 14, no. 4, pp. 65–82.
4. Name given to clubs of wild young men in the eighteenth century.
5. Guido Reni (1575–1642), Bolognese painter.
6. Tiziano Vecellio (?1488–1576), Venetian painter.

to go with him into the country, he would settle an ample fortune upon her for her life, and that, if he ever did marry, she should be his choice. He represented to her, that the consequence of her refusal would be his marrying the lady she mentioned, and that, if she remained with her uncle, she would in course be tied to some rude, low bred mechanic,[7] who would not only despise and abuse her lovely person, but keep her in a servile poor way, where she would languish out her life, without tasting those luxuriant pleasures and elegancies, to which her wit, beauty and accomplishments entitled her. Thus pressed by love on one side, by splendour, importunity and deceit on the other, Miss Faulkner was prevailed on, and did consent to elope with his Lordship into the country . . .

Lord K——'s father had expended upwards of sixty thousand pounds in building there one of the finest palaces in Europe, with suitable offices, and other conveniences.[8] It is situated in the middle of a most delightful country, and nature has been more profuse in her bounties to this enchanting spot, than to any other perhaps in the universe. Through the gardens runs a large river of the finest water, which discharges itself into a large lake, surrounded by several high hills, covered with pines, oak, and other woods, for several miles: which affords a prospect diversified and beautiful. The lake is several miles broad, and on it his Lordship has built two very elegant ships of war in miniature, and by art has raised an island or peninsula, the exact model of *Gibraltar*. In the summer season he frequently entertains his company on this fine sheet of water, and while the ships regularly besiege this little garrison, which is defended by a number of small pieces of cannon, which are very regularly and beautifully played off in it's [*sic*] defence, the musick, warlike instruments, fireworks, etc. form sounds and diversions that are perfectly inchanting.

To this *paradise* Lord K—— conveyed Miss Faulkner, and on her arrival introduced her to Lady *Valeria*, (which was the name of the foreign Lady already mentioned) who received her with every mark of respect and esteem, as from the great complaisance, which his Lordship showed to his fair stranger, this lady concluded Miss Faulkner was more than a common acquisition to the *number* of those unfortunate beauties, who had visited this mansion during her residence here.

You must not be surprized, gentle reader! at the mention of *numbers*, that had visited this mansion of seduction and prostitution; for numbers, indeed, of innocent pure virgins were here frequently sacrificed, and robbed of their innocence. For such was the unbridled passion of this unfortunate Nobleman, that he constantly kept in his pay a whole troop of abandoned, profligate old women, who travelled, in different disguises, through all parts of the kingdom, and wherever they saw any prey worthy his Lordship's appetite, they immediately began their plan of seduction and procuration, for which purpose they were constantly furnished with large sums of money, and never differed about the price; but if that failed, they reported their endeavours, with such a description of the object, when his Lordship either personally attended, or sent more proper or capable persons on the enterprize. By these means, and the fruits of his own industry, he never wanted a variety of these victims, who were seduced to this house, and there dressed in all the gaudy pomp that can dazzle the weak minds of such innocents.

And for the preparing of these unfortunates for his embraces, a like number of infernal matrons constantly attended in his house, who gave them such instructions and pious documents, that his Lordship had no more *trouble than he desired* in the accomplishment of his unbounded wishes; nor was it uncommon with him, *in one night*, to debauch two or three of these deluded wretches, who, from the treatment they at first received on their initiation, fine cloaths, delicacies, and the pleasures with which they were intoxicated, imagined they were landed in paradise.

Their pleasures were, however, of a very short duration; for his Lordship very seldom visited any of them a second night, unless it were an uncommon beauty indeed, and then the continuance of a week was an amazing proof of his constancy: such of them however, as were afraid or ashamed to return to their friends or parents, he sent to a *Seraglio*,[9] which he kept, for

7. Labourer, synonymous with vulgar or low.
8. Estate identified in text as Rockingham.

9. Harem.

that purpose, on the borders of the beautiful lake above mentioned. To others of them he gave considerable sums of money, so much at least as generally contented them *for what they had lost*; and many he had married to his servants and tenants, to whom he generally gave two or three hundred pounds as a portion, which, with his former knowledge of the bride, was an ample fortune.

It may be supposed that his Lordship kept his *Seraglio* for his own gratification, as it was supported at a prodigious expense. There seldom were less than fifty or sixty unfortunate girls contained in it; all of whom were attended and supplied, not only with all the necessaries, but all the luxuries of life; a number of women servants were kept to wait on them; and as the greatest part of them were generally pregnant, physicians, apothecaries, and midwives were also constantly employed; nor was the smallest necessary or convenience wanting to any of them. This is mentioned in common justice to his Lordship; for though he constantly visited and inspected into the management of this *Seraglio*, when in the country, he was seldom or never known to trespass on the sanctity of the place, or any of its inhabitants, after they had once taken up their Residence there.

What then, will the reader say, could induce him to keep up such an expensive establishment? It was really and truly for the accommodation of his friends. His Lordship spent the greatest part of the year in the country, and, besides a number of gentlemen that occasionally visited his house, he gave a public hunt once every month, and sometimes once every week in the season. His general rule was to invite every gentleman that hunted to dine with him, and consequently to sleep at his house; and as to those that he was more intimately acquainted with, or chose to compliment, he generally asked them if they chose a *bedfellow*, which being usually answered in the affirmative, a servant was ordered to attend his guest to the *Seraglio*, where he might chuse for himself; and when he had made his option, he returned to his Lordship, and the object of his choice was immediately conveyed to his Lordship's house; and when the gentleman retired, he found the Lady of his choice in bed, perhaps dreading, instead of impatiently expecting, his arrival: and according to his

Lordship's particular esteem, or as a distinguished mark of respect, every gentleman had a right of precedency in this visit to the *Seraglio*.

In further vindication of his Lordship's character, it will here be also necessary to observe, that none of those ladies durst, upon any account whatever, accept of the smallest favour, gratuity, or present, from any of his Lordship's guests on pain of immediate expulsion; unless any of his friends became enamoured of his bed-fellow, and desired to take her into keeping, which if the lady relished, his Lordship always consented to, and she was directly struck out of the books of the convent,[10] and sent to such quarters as her lover thought proper.

As to the results of those nocturnal embraces, his Lordship, as has been observed, employed every needful assistance; and the number of children, annually produced from this intercourse, were carefully sent to proper nurses, and maintained at his Lordship's expense, to the great benefit of the community, and the increase of his Majesty's subjects . . .

[Lord K—ngsb—r—gh elopes to Paris with another woman. Miss Faulkner goes to London. Lord K—— later tries to find her but fails and returns to Ireland, where he dies. Miss Faulkner appears as a singer in London. She marries Mr Donnellan and meets with cruel treatment from her husband. She meets Lord Halifax, who sends her husband to America and takes her into keeping. They have two children. She accompanies him to Ireland when he is made Lord Lieutenant.]

The necessary preparations being made, his Lordship[11] set out for his government, and took *her Excellency*[12] with him; but as he could not, with any propriety, take her to the usual place of residence of the *Vice Roys* of that kingdom, a certain courtier, (who was then heartily tired and ashamed of the very name he was born with, and therefore warmly sollicited for a title, which he has since obtained) having a delightful *villa*, within a few miles of the capital, made his court to our heroine, not doubting but it was the proper channel for preferment, and requested she would honour his seat with her residence, during her

10. It is a commonplace of eighteenth-century pornography to use convent imagery.
11. Halifax.
12. Faulkner.

Vice-Royship, which *was graciously accepted.* — The name of this place is Luttrelstown, where she kept a very brilliant court, and received as many addresses and memorials, as the first governor of that, or any other kingdom. She indeed filled her part of the administration with the greatest dignity and applause, and became as remarkable, and as universally respected for her generosity and compassion, as for her patriotism and profound skill in politics. She was, in short, the *Maintenon*[13] of the age . . .

On enquiry into her own family affairs, she found both her parents were dead, and had left a son unprovided for, who lived with a gentleman near the place of his nativity: this brother she sent for, and ordering him to be cloathed and properly dressed, he made his appearance at court, but a few degrees above *Peter the wild boy*.[14] He was, however, immediately put under the care of a tutor, to instruct him as well in letters as behaviour, and in a short time he could make a very decent bow, and return a civil answer to any question that was asked him.

13. Françoise D'Aubigné (1635–1719), Marquise de Maintenon, mistress, later second wife, of Louis XIV of France. Like Faulkner, Maintenon first came to her lover's attention as governess to his children, and was supposed to wield inappropriate political influence.

14. A boy found living in the woods of Hanover in 1725. Brought to England by order of George I, he was the object of great scientific and literary curiosity and lived until 1785.

SARAH COLVILL

(*c.* 1731–1835)

from:
LETTER TO
ROBERT COLVILL (1772)

[This letter provides one of the best documents of attempted heiress-abduction in the eighteenth century; it is particularly valuable since it is narrated by one of the female protagonists. She describes the attack in Longford, in 1772, by Thomas Johnston[1] on the heiress, Charlotte Newcomen,[2] fiancée of William Gleadowe,[3] Johnston's death and the subsequent court case. A typescript of the letter is held in the Public Record Office of Northern Ireland, D3196/L/5/1, Dunraven papers, 1772.[4] Most of the footnotes are indebted to insertions, apparently by Sarah Colvill, in the PRONI's copy of the letter; these are indicated by an asterisk. This edition may reproduce errors in the typescript, but since that remains the only source, it is taken as authoritative.]

1. Johnston, a recent graduate of Trinity College Dublin, was a member of the County Longford gentry.
2. Charlotte Newcomen of Carrickglass, County Longford, heiress to an estate of £4,000–5,000 per year; she married William Gleadowe, who took her name, and was created a peeress in 1800.
3. William Gleadowe of Killester, County Dublin, was a prominent Dublin banker. He took the name Gleadowe-Newcomen on his marriage, and was created baronet in 1791.
4. See also *Hibernian Journal*, 7 October 1772. This letter is discussed by A.P.W. Malcolmson, *Pursuit of the Heiress*.

This day twelve months I set off in Mr Gleadow's[5] postchaise and four to visit my friends in Longford. Mr Colvill accompanied me to Kinnegad, and returned next day. I've been long kindly pressed by my friends and Miss Newcomen[6] to take this jaunt, and Mr Gleadowe, who was soon to be married to Miss N., and then going to visit her, had promised them to take me with him. On Thursday we were to leave this, and on Tuesday he called on me to fix the hour. When I had so done, I told him I had had a letter from Miss N. and one from Miss Webster two days [ago] telling me that a large party of men had been seen in Miss Newcomen's avenue, who were put to flight by Mr Connell,[7] that the report was their intention was to carry her off, that she had been greatly frightened, had gone for some days to Mr Webster's at Longford, and was then returned to Carriglass[8] with her mother and Miss Webster, and that they believed it must be robbers, so kept armed men sitting up in the house all night, and neither Capt. Agnew or Mr Webster[9] slept in it.

5. *Afterwards Sir William Newcomen.
6. *Afterwards Lady Newcomen.
7. *Grandfather to the chaplain at the Royal Hospital.
8. *Then the seat of Miss N., later of Baron Lefroy.
9. *My great-grandfather.

They said they gave no credit to the report of a design to run away with her, and the gentleman who was suspected for that had left the country.

Mr Gleadowe asked, did I know his name, I at first said, no, but afterwards told him it was Johnston; on which he asked me many questions about him, which I answered. Mr G. had never seen or heard of him before. I had seen him here on visits to Miss Webster in winter, and knew he had only then a bow or curtsey acquaintance with Miss Newcomen, which I told Mr Gleadowe, and that it was impossible to believe a lad so young and gentle as he was could form such a thought. I guessed him to be about twenty-two, was either in, or had just left, College, seemed as modest as a lady, and I thought had too much good sense to make such a villainous attempt on a lady who was just going to be married to another, as he had nothing to expect but the gallows for his pains. Mr G., was vastly alarmed, and declared he would go off to Carriglass next day. I did all I could to laugh him out of this piece of 'night-errantry', as I called it, and really I thought it. He was three times with me that day, and told me the last time that his postchaise (and his own man to ride by it) should call on me on Thursday morning, but he would go off himself on horseback next day, that he had wrote that night to Miss N. that I would dine with her on Friday at Carriglass, and said I should meet some of my Longford friends there.

Wednesday he left Dublin, and Thursday I did. Friday the horses and servants delayed me long at breakfast. I knew Carriglass was three miles from Longford. Where I was to turn to it on the road, I knew not, but was out of patience at near 4 o'clock to find I was still on the Longford road. I thought my friends would be frightened at my stay, and was in the greatest confusion and surprise to find myself entering Longford town and set down at my Uncle Webster's door. A servant had been sent to prevent my going to Carriglass, but that was concealed from me. I was met at the door by Capt. Tom Webster[10] and May. They met me with open arms, but something in their looks alarmed me, and I was like to faint when they told me my coming there was no mistake, for Carriglass family was all in town. I tottered into the parlour, saw Mrs, Miss N., Mr Gleadowe and uncle's family all well and just done dinner. I drank a bumper of wine, and was told I must suspend my curiosity till I ate my dinner. That was soon dispatched. I begged again to know why I found them all there, and was told that the day before, Capt. Agnew and my Uncle Webster had both come in from Carriglass, as they knew Mr Gleadowe would be there before dinner and would take care of the ladies; but just as Mr Webster got to his own house, a man who wished to serve him came and told him that, as he had watched over Miss Newcomen for some time with great care, then was his time to save her, for that the same gentle Mr Tom Johnston had a party of between 40 and 50 men ready-armed to attack the house early that night, so no time was to be lost. Capt. Agnew and Mr Webster hurried back. The latter gave orders for the doors to be locked, and on no account to be opened that night, and got all the arms in the house charged, and placed armed men about it on the outside. Between 7 and 8 o'clock they were drinking tea in the dining room, when Mr Johnston and his party made a violent effort at both back and front doors at the same time, as if with sledges to burst them open. The doors was [sic] strong, and resisted, a gun went off (it's supposed by accident among themselves), but it alarmed them, and they ran off. They had undoubtedly friends within, and expected to find the doors open (for one maid would have the doors opened to go out for clothes that [were] bleaching), and when Mr Gleadowe ran upstairs for his pistols, which he had left charged in his room three hours before, he found the charge had been drawn. Miss Webster had been all along with Miss Newcomen, and Mrs Connell had come there to dinner, so they two, with Mrs and Miss N. (half dead with fear) hid in the cockloft,[11] and the gentlemen stood as sentinels at different parts of the house the whole night. As soon as it was day, they ordered the coach to the door, and drove off to Longford. Miss N.'s agent loved her father, and resolved to do everything in his power to serve her. There I found her, and was in no little terror to find that Johnston and his men had, on quitting the house, gone to Lord Annaly's,[12] expecting she would take shelter

10. *My grandfather.

11. Small loft at the top of a house above the garrett, often used for storage.
12. John Gore (1718–84), Baron Annaly, Irish judge, best known for the introduction of Mortgage Relief Bills in 1768, 1769 and 1771.

there, but on their being disappointed, they had resolved to attack Mr Webster's house in the night, and carry her off. This he was assured of by one he could depend on, so had all his windows nailed down, a good store of firearms charged, and several stout men, both within and out the house, well-armed.

It was a dreadful night of wind and rain, yet he went round all his neighbours to beg their assistance, should they hear any disturbance about his house, which they all readily promised. I was in a continual fit of trembling, yet could scarce think it possible that any man in their senses would dare to attempt the house of a man who I knew to be esteemed by all the gentlemen in the county, had lived forty years in the town, had always been called on to decide differences, and was, I may say, a father to the poor and a friend to everyone in distress.

Capt. Agnew laughed at our fears, but to oblige Mr. G., sat up all night with the gentlemen (for all sat up), but we females went to bed, [and] slept little, for every mouse alarmed us. Miss Webster lay down with me in her under-petticoats and bedgown, for fear of an alarm. She told me that the first she had got was on Thursday the 15 of September, when their family and Mrs and Miss Newcomen had dined at Capt. Agnew's in Longford, that she was to go with them to Carriglass, but when the coach came to the door, Miss Newcomen's servant called her out, entreated she would not go home that night, for he was assured by a person who made him take an oath not to reveal their name, that Mr Johnston had a party of above thirty men on the road to run away with her. This she thought so improbable that she ran laughing into the parlour and whispered it to Miss Agnew and Miss Webster, who joined in the laugh, and wondered who could raise such a report of the gentle Tom Johnston (as they called him), as the girls thought it a thing impossible. She would have gone to Carriglass, but the whisper went round, and the older ladies thought it best they should stay that night, and next morning they went home without the least fear. They were, after they got home, assured the report was true, and that he had a cabriole[t?] of Mr Hamilton's to carry her off in.

He then stayed at his Uncle Featherstone's of Whiterock, about two miles from Longford, and I believe about the same distance from Carriglass. It was thought remarkable that Mr Featherstone went into Longford about 8 o'clock that night and stayed all night — a thing he was never known to do before; and next day he went on a very foolish pretence to Miss N.'s and stayed dinner, though not asked, we now suppose to hear what would be said; but not a word passed about it, and a gentleman who dined there that day told me Miss N. scarce looked at him or gave him a civil answer (which was behaving very unlike herself). He was to go to Dublin next day. His housekeeper had lived eight years with him. She followed him out, told him the report, and begged he would for God's sake take Mr Johnston to Dublin with him, to save him from doing what he might be hanged for; but Mr Featherstone only laughed at her, left his nephew behind him, and a favourite servant who he was never known to leave before.

On the Sunday following, Mr and Mrs Connell (who is daughter to Capt. Agnew) dined at Carriglass. About 8 o'clock, as they were going away, Mr Connell showed [sic] a man pulling bushes out of a gap in Miss N.'s avenue. He called three times, 'Who is there?', but on getting no answer, he leapt the ditch and saw about a dozen men on horseback. He immediately recollected the report, and as he was sub-sheriff, called out as if he had a party behind him to follow him and [that] he would have the rogues in Longford jail before morning. This put them to flight, and he rode back to the house, and stayed all night; so did his poor wife, terrified to death. She rode behind a servant, and in her return to the house, met ten or twelve armed men walking slowly two-and-two. One had a crepe on his face, came close by her, and looked up at her. She dreaded they had killed her husband, and [was] happy to find him at the house before her. From this time, Miss N. had armed men sit up in the house all night. But she, her mother and Miss Webster went to Mr Webster's in the morning and stayed till Friday. They expected Mr Gleadowe every day in the county, so would not write to alarm him, and the lawyers who were drawing the settlements delayed him in town.

The 21st or 22nd of September, Mr Johnston went to Longford and sent the most artful letter was ever penned (a copy of which I will put to the end of these sheets [not found]) to Mrs N., and begged Mr Webster would go to him at the inn, that he might clear himself or so vile a slander. Mr Webster went, said he never saw a man in a greater passion, but thought nothing he said acquitted him. He pretended to go to Dublin with his brother, and that day his horses returned from Mullingar, went through Longford, and on Monday the 28th Miss N. got a letter from him with the Dublin stamp and freed by a Member, and in that he strove to clear himself, and begged her answer, enclosed to Mr Joseph Husbands, Darbey [sic] Square, Dublin; so we all thought Johnston there till the 1st of October, when he attacked the house. A man could then swear he knew his voice bidding 'Damn the men! Why did they not shoot through the doors and windows?' (it was his pistol that went off by accident).

Saturday October the 3rd. A beautiful morning dispelled the fears of us timorous females, and we met at breakfast in the parlour, happy in Miss Newcomen's safety, who believed herself in no danger. Capt. Agnew came in and declared he had stole away at break of day, as he would had been ashamed to have it known he sat up all day to guard such a man's house in the middle of the town, as the market is held just before Mr Webster's door. Miss N. and me were observing there was a vast number of people in town that day, and were laughing to see many of them standing on the palisades, staring in the window. I said it was to see her and Mr Gleadowe. The poor man was the only unhappy man in the house, and after breakfast did all that lay in his power to persuade Mrs and Miss N. to go to Lord Annaly's[13] but they were immoveable, and both declared they thought themselves as safe as in the Castle of Dublin. Poor Mr Webster laughed at his fears, said he had had Miss N. for many a night under his protection, and he thought it would be a stout fellow indeed who would attempt to force a lady out of his house, surrounded by good neighbours who were all ready and willing to assist him; that there could be no fear in daylight, and last night his house would have stood a siege; so, laying his hand on his breast, he bid Mr Gleadowe be easy, for he would answer for her with his life while she stayed in the house. I followed Mr Gleadowe upstairs, and bid him

remember Miss Mary Anne Know,[14] who was safe in her father's till he attempted taking her to Dublin. I told him that a dreadful scene presented itself to my imagination the moment he proposed to go to Lord Annaly's, and confidently believed, if he went, there would be bloody work, as Johnston was undoubtedly on the watch that road, so begged for God's sake he would not think of it. The sweet girl would have gone to oblige him, but her mother would not, which was happy for them all. Mr G. proposed to take Mrs or Miss Webster and Capt. Agnew and Mr Webster to accompany them. God knows if any of them would ever have returned.

About one o'clock Mr G. went to Castle Forbes to get Lord Granard[15] to go to Whiterock with a challenge to Mr Johnston, but none of Mr Webster's family knew his errand. After two o'clock I was laughing with Miss N. [about] the fright her money (she had £4,000 or £5,000 a year) had put us in the night before, for we should all have slept happy had she been the greatest beauty was ever framed. I went into my own room to fetch a newspaper, and had just got it into my hand when I heard a violent scream. I supposed the chimney or house was on fire, and ran to the room door (which joined the top of the stairs and dining room door), where I had just left Mrs Agnew, Mrs and Miss Newcomen and two children. I was met at the top of the stairs by two men — one had a blunderbuss, the other a pistol — crying out, 'Where is she? By God, we'll have her now.' I thought all I could do was to run and call for help, which I did, through a parcel of armed men, but, alas, no one would hear me. I tremble now at the writing it, twelve months after. I flew to the parlour, threw up the window, shrieked for help, but it was too heavy; it fell, and took a bit out of my elbow. I then ran into the street. A great big fellow laughed at me, swore he was a clever fellow, that he deserved her and would get her.

Mr Webster and his son were both in the office (one in the inside, the other in the outside, office) when these ruffians entered the house. Johnston rushed in with a pistol in one hand and a sword in the other, which he first clapped to Mr Tom

13. Tenlick — now Colonel White's.

14. A reference to the murder of Mary Anne Knox during an attempted abduction by John McNaughton in 1761 (see pp. 789–90).

15. George Forbes, 5th Earl of Granard (1740–80).

Webster's breast, and pressed so hard the mark was there for some days, swearing [at the] same time he would put him to death, did he make any resistance; then left him, and attacked his father in the inner office, swearing he would kill him if he attempted to oppose him. Mr Webster (though near sixty-six) wrested the sword out of his hand, set his foot on it, and would have got the pistol out of his hand too, but three of the party came in, seized his arms behind, held their pistols to his breast, and took such a hold of his throat he was black in the face when his maid servant came to his assistance, dragged off one man, and called in one Reynolds, who set him free. He and his son ran out crying 'fire and murder', but no one near would come, and those who would have assisted him were prevented hearing or seeing by the bustle and noise of the market. Miss Webster was the first above stairs that heard what was doing below. It was she that screamed. She was in a room near the dining-room, ran and locked it outside, and clapped the key in her pocket. The men I met ran from room to room, and clapped their pistols to the breasts of the two Misses Websters in different rooms. Miss Webster met Johnston as pale as death. 'Oh, Mr Johnston,' cried she, 'are you going to murder us?' He made no answer but burst in the dining-room door. The ladies within had in the first alarm run into the bedchamber and bolted the door, but he broke that lock also, and called to the two men with him, 'Seize her, she is my wife.' Mrs Newcomen caught him by the collar and said, 'You lie, you villain. She's not your wife.' He shook her off, and one of his men clapped a blunderbuss to her breast. Mr Thomas Webster came in, and they did the like to him, and Owen Dougherty (who was Mr Johnston's chief man) followed him from room to room swearing he would blow his brains out if he attempted to take a firearm or attempted to stop Miss Newcomen, who made all the resistance that woman could do. She was dragged down stairs. On the first flight Miss Webster met her and caught her in her arms; then both held fast by the banister of the stairs. Johnston, they say, cried out, 'Break their arms!' They were both dragged down together, Miss N.'s head foremost part of the way. Her cap fell off, her hair fell down, and she lost both her shoes in the street. William Edwards, on a horse of Mr Robert Featherstone's with a pillion

behind him, stood near Mr Webster's doorway ready to receive her. As Johnston came out of the door, a Miss Cornwell, niece to Mr Webster, who lived next door struck him on the head with an iron pin which fastened her window. He raised his sword, looked about, but said nothing till he got Miss Newcomen fairly out of the door; then he flourished his sword over his head, and huzzaed. Mr Featherstone's servant was one of those who guarded the doors with sword and pistol, but all now followed their leader, and formed a ring round Miss Newcomen, doing all in their power to put her on horseback behind Edwards. The poor soul cried to the Almighty, to Mr Webster and to everyone to help her, scratched Johnston's face, cuffed Edwards, tore his hair and kept herself so stiff by the help of an iron that was to the pillion, that they could not get her fixed to the horse, though they attempted many times and had got her almost to the bottom of the street. When they left the house, Mr Tom Webster called for the key of the press (into which the firearms had been put that morning). Miss Webster had run to her mother for it, and both met at the press. He ran out with a blunderbuss, and she ran out with as many pistols as she could carry, which he and her sister gave to Mr Gleadowe's servant and as many as they thought would fight in the cause. Mr W. had gone after Miss Newcomen down the street, but recollecting it was madness to go without some weapon of defence, he was returning for one when his daughter Mary, who had followed him, gave him a pistol. I said I was in the street calling for help, and turned into Miss Cornwell's, when I heard them shout in the street, 'He has got her.' I ran back to Mr Webster's door, and met Mrs Newcomen like a mad woman in the street shrieking, 'My child, my child!' We got her in. My good aunt (who was patience itself) and I did all we could to quieten her, while young Mrs Webster and my May, like two heroines, were distributing pistols, powder and shot. How few women, if they loved their friend ever so well, would have behaved with such courage, when the father and husband of one and the father and brother of the other were going (without a second charge of powder) to encounter between forty and fifty armed ruffians, headed by a rash young man who kept flourishing his sword and swearing he would cut anyone to pieces that came near him, so that he kept a circle clear, like a cockpit around her (whom they dragged barefoot through a street as dirty as possible, and in their attempts to put her on horseback, used her with as much roughness and as little delicacy as if she had been a common hussy). On seeing Mr Webster, she held out her arms and begged for assistance, but saw him fall, thought he was killed and she undone. A button of his coat saved him for being stabbed with a sword, but [he] was knocked down and for a minute insensible. The first object that met his recovered sight, was Johnston. His party called to him, there was Webster. He faced about, changed his pistol from his left to his right hand, and presented it at Mr Webster, who fired, and Johnston fell on his knees. Owen Dougherty at that instant would have stabbed Mr Webster with a sword, but before he made good his thrust, Mr Thomas Webster saved his father by shooting him with a blunderbuss; and here the hand of providence was visible, for it was loaded with about a dozen slugs, all of which lodged in his body, and no other creature hurt. (As young Mrs Webster said, God would preserve the innocent, so it happened.) They were pulling Miss N. on horseback when the shots went off. The horse started, and she fell. Mr Webster saw her fall, and thought her killed. One Mills and some other had come to his assistance. He ran to her, and with the assistance of an old woman (who had been a servant in her father's family), got her into Mr Barber's house, which was just by her. Although the street was full of men and women who heard her cry, no one had mercy on her but this poor woman, who stuck by her and endeavoured to keep down her petticoats, for which good office she was knocked down, but still persisted.

Johnston was mortally wounded in the breast [and] was carried into a house. Mr Tom Webster sent Mr Archer, the surgeon, to him. William Edwards galloped off, and the rest of the party ran as fast as they could (all but one Newman, a principal man, who [was] taken and lodged in jail). Some say Edwards snapped his pistol at Mr Tom Webster. Mr Featherstone's servant did make a thrust at him, but he twisted the sword out of his hand, wounded his arm in doing it, then broke the sword, which was afterwards claimed by Mr Hamilton of Kilnacana. I believe five minutes finished all transactions out of the house. We in it

heard the shots, but were soon made happy by hearing the sweet girl had escaped the ruin that threatened her, and her brave deliverers were safe and well. We were next distressed for Mr Gleadowe, who was to return the road the ruffians went. Young Mr Webster cried out, 'They will murder him', then ran to send people to warn him of his danger. We were all dreadfully shocked at Mills, who had gone to assist my uncle, coming in with his head and face all bloody, but it was but a light wound, which six guineas and a half from Mr Gleadowe helped to heal.

As soon as Miss N. got into Mr Barber's, the doors were locked and they prepared for an attack on the house, but all kept quiet, and Capt. Agnew, who went there to her, then Mr Websters [and] some more of her friends with cocked pistols guarded her to Mr Webster['s]. I need not say the joy this meeting gave us all. She was covered with a cloak, but when that was off, looked like a mad woman: her face bloated, her eyes looked ready to jump out, her hair hanging down, not a pin in the breast of her gown, it almost tore to pieces, and it and her petticoat covered with dirt, and her stockings so thick of [sic] dirt they could hardly be got of. She cried and shrieked most dreadfully as she embraced us, but in particular her deliverers (getting the dear good man and his son in my arms made my tears flow, which gave me great relief, for I was bursting).

One of the first things Miss N. asked when she came in was, 'Is Mr Gleadowe killed?' She would scarce believe he was not till he came in, which he did in a quarter of an hour after her. Lord Granard was at the other end of the bridge when Johnston was shot, heard the shots, saw them attempt at that instant to put her on horseback, and saw Edwards gallop off. He had nothing in his hand but a whip, so galloped back to tell Mr G. (who was following him in his carriage) what he had heard and seen, and that his mistress was safe. Mr G. mounted one of the servant's horses, and both galloped into town. Poor Miss Newcomen's plight had thrown off all reserve and the joy she expressed at seeing him showed how well she loved. He wanted her to rise off the bed and go with him directly to Lord Annaly's, but she was not able, and he afterwards owned (what we knew to be true) that he was quite mad for an hour. He begged pardon next day for what he had said then (on his knees) to young Mrs

Webster, who he said brought him to reason by asking him, would he go and leave the family who had saved Miss N. exposed to the insults of an enraged mob. He then vowed to leave them in safety or lose his life. Lord Granard sent to Castle Forbes for a Capt. Coates, who came directly and got [a] share of a spoiled dinner. But the stomachs that were to eat it were worse spoiled, so it was no matter.

Mr Archer was an intimate friend of Mr Johnston's, but was never let into this secret. When he dressed his wound, he came to tell us that it was mortal, and he thought he would scarce live till morning; said he and Mr Gardiner, the clergyman, had asked him, had he any encouragement from Miss N., and why he would undertake so rash an action. He said villainy, ambition and bad advice had prompted him to it (as her estate lay amongst his friends); that it was a base action; that he was sorry he had done it, and for a lying letter he had written to Miss N. to deceive her, which he would give anything to recall; declared Miss N. never gave him any encouragement or showed him any civility except what any gentleman might expect; said his father had charged him to drop all thought of her, and knew nothing of this attempt, but believed him in Dublin, and that he concealed it from Mr Archer lest he should dissuade him from it. Mr Webster, he said he did forgive him and everybody, that he deserved his fate and had no one to blame but himself. This was as it ought to be, and had the unhappy young man died that night, I should forever [have] had compassion on him. About eight o'clock at night Mr Gardiner or Mr Archer, I forget which, came with Mr Johnston's dying request that Mrs [and] Miss Newcomen and Mr Webster would pardon him before he died, and promise not to prosecute the poor wretches concerned with him, as he had bribed them to what they had done.

[PRONI note: 'Although there is no interruption in the typescript at this point, there clearly must have been a page, or pages missing in the original, since the narrative runs on to a subsequent court case brought by Johnston's friends and relations against the Websters and their associates.']

Oh the joy I sit down with to tell my dear Bob that the wished-for, dreaded day ended in triumph to our dear friends, and confusion to our enemies. All the bills were thrown out, except those for Uncle and Cousin Tom, who were in court from nine till nine (but were never in the dock), and were surrounded all day by the gentlemen. Lord Annaly sat on the bench (but not as a judge); Lord Granard has not left us night or day; Lord Longford, Mr Pakenham, Dean Harman, his nephew, Dean Ryder, Capt. Dobbs, Major Pepper, Capt. Enstree, Capt. Atkinson, Mr Beaty [sic], Mr Dobbs, all the Nesbitts, and in short, all the gentles of the county, attended here, and not a man of them took the least notice of Featherstone or Johnston, who paraded the streets by themselves. The first day, Featherstone strove to join several knots of gentlemen, while Mr Gleadowe, like a proud peacock, strutted after him and I may say hunted him from place to place. This delighted me, yet I feared it might produce a quarrel. In the middle of the street, Mr F. bowed to Lord Granard, who looked at him, raised his head half a foot higher, and passed him by. Was not that charming! My heart died within me when my dear uncle left the parlour and bid God Almighty be with us all. Every witness they called against him made as much for him as those on his own side. Poor creatures! Perjury would not stand the test of Counsellor Scott's cross-examination. (He really is a clever fellow.) Mr Archer's evidence, who was called on by Johnston to prove his brother's death, was so clear against Johnston that only a few were examined, for form's sake, on uncle's side. None of the ladies but Mrs Gleadowe [formerly Miss Newcomen] were called on, and she gave as clear and distinct evidence as could be given. They asked her but a very few questions. Mrs Connell, Webster, Miss Gleadowe, Agnew and Mary attended her. They were back again in less than half an hour. Capt[s] Anstree [sic] and Atkinson will give a better account of what remained than I can. The judge thought the jury might lawfully bring them in not guilty, which was done in three minutes. Oh the tumult of joy which rushed in here with the dear, honest man, and as many gentlemen as this house could hold.

One thing which added to our happiness was that, while the trial was going on, in the morning, Jeny [sic] was brought to confess that the impudent Pat. Dempsey was in the attack at Carriglass. He was then a marked man in court. A warrant was issued for him, but he got intelligence, and made his escape. This morning he sent word he would stand his trial; Newman too was to stand his; the jury was fixing; when Mr G. and uncle went into court and forgave both. The judge made a very handsome speech, thanked them for their generous, humane conduct, said he never saw a prosecution carried on with more injustice and rigour than that against them; said the young man had intended to die like a Christian, as he owned his crime and had begged forgiveness; [and] that the rancour

and malice came all from his wicked advisers (or words to that purpose). F. wept at this, whether for spite or remorse I leave you to judge. Many a rap on the knuckles he got from the lawyers during the trial . . .

This house is like a fair. Mr G., etc, came in to dinner on Thursday. A thousand people, I believe, ate and drank here this week, and all the fine people dine here today. I must go dress.

Your affectionate wife, S.C.

ANONYMOUS

from:
AUTHENTIC ANECDOTES OF THE LIFE AND TRANSACTIONS OF MRS. MARGARET RUDD: CONSISTING OF A VARIETY OF FACTS HITHERTO UNKNOWN TO THE PUBLIC. ADDRESSED IN A SERIES OF LETTERS TO THE (NOW BY A LATE ACT OF PARLIAMENT) MISS MARY LOVELL[1] (1776)

[Margaret Caroline Rudd (*c.* 1744–*c.* 1797), a sex worker and later confidence trickster, came to public prominence during the trial in London of the Perreau brothers,[2] who were convicted of fraud and hanged together. Her notoriety prompted a number of publications both attacking and defending her character. The following excerpt, concerning her early life in Lurgan, County Armagh, and Downpatrick, County Down, is taken from

a two-volume memoir in the British Library, originally published in London by J. Bew in 1776.]

Notwithstanding that much boasted *pedigree*, smuggled with some clandestine view, yet it is a fact, that she is descended from very mean and ignoble parents. Her father, whose name was Youngson, lived as an Apothecary at Lurgan, an obscure village in the North of Ireland; a person of little business or eminence in his profession.

If he had any property, it must have been inconsiderable, and upon his decease fell into the hands of the mortgagee. Her mother was a sister to Mr. John Stewart, who farms his own lands of fourscore pounds a-year, and has a contract to supply the linen manufactory in that part of the kingdom, with potash. The one died when Miss Youngson was an infant; and the other before she attained the age of eight years old.

Thus circumstanced, the charge of her education devolved upon her uncle Stewart; — who from motives of charity sent her to school at Downpatrick. But our heroine did not continue there any considerable time; — such being her genius at that early period for vicious practices and intrigue, that the parents, one and all threatened to take away their children, if one immodest girl was not immediately discarded. It would be too indelicate to relate the particulars of a criminal intercourse that happened between her and one of the servants belonging to the school. The fact, with all its aggravating circumstances, is well known in the town of Downpatrick.

---

1. Mary Lovell is described in the text as a friend of Rudd in 'prostitution, forgery and intrigue'.
2. The events of the trial have been the subject of two recent books: Donna T. Andrew and Randall McGowan, *The Perreaus and Mrs. Rudd: Forgery and Betrayal in Eighteenth-Century London* (California: University of California Press, 2001); Sarah Bakewell, *The Smart: The Story of Margaret Caroline Rudd and the Unfortunate Perreau Brothers* (London: Chatto and Windus, 2001).

Too many of our boarding schools for young ladies, even in the environs of this metropolis, are at best but nurseries for vice, and the contagion of bad example; — and where one scabby sheep may infect the whole flock. The domestic plan under the inspection of an exemplary parent, is generally the most safe, if not the most accomplished.

THE COUNTRY WEDDING (1776)

[This popular poem appears in many versions. Other examples are given by Andrew Carpenter in his anthology of eighteenth-century verse.[1] This ballad presumes that a robust, healthy and openly expressed sexuality is to be found in the peasant class. The use of Hiberno-English is common in eighteenth-century comic verse and may indicate bilingual authorship or readership, although poems by Jonathan Swift and others in this genre suggest that a poet could be interested in macaronic effects without great linguistic knowledge.[2] The erratic spelling makes it particularly hard to annotate, and some of the notes are guesswork. The text is from *The Charms of Melody. Being a Select Collection of the Newest and Most Approved Love and Sentimental Songs* (Dublin: John Colles, 1776), held in the National Library of Ireland.]

The Priest of the Parish rode his garene Bawn,[3]
And married young Phelim to his dear Shevaun,[4]
There was Padrig and Dermot, and ten score beside,
With long flails and pitch-forks to wait on the Bride.
CHORUS
You're welcome heartily, welcome Gramacree,[5]
Welcome all of you aye by my troath.

There was Eileen and Roseen[6] and dear Sheelah Wee,[7]

O hon[8] 'pon my soul she's the cushla ma cree,[9]
There were patties[10] and ratties[11] in long legged pan,
Sat boyling on Bohraons[12] as fast as they can.
    And your, etc.

There was tuff maddhy brishea[13] like gads[14] I may say,
And dipt rushes[15] platted burn'd brighter than day,
Rare victuals in platters were set in a row,
And neat wooden trenchers[16] far whiter than snow.
    And your, etc.

There were young cail[17] and nettles mixt with prassaugh-wee,[18]
Made the rearest callcannon[19] that e'er you did see,
There was maskans[20] of butter laid on not struans,[21]
And good Iskea-baha[22] serv'd up in quohans.[23]
    And your, etc.

Take away the dishes and platters Shaneen,[24]
Drink a health to the Bride and shudurth a voorneen,[25]
Then the pipers struck up, we danced all in a ring,
Each maiden a Queen, and each man a King.
    And your, etc.

When we fell a dancing each man gave a pogue,[26]
To his sweet-heart that smack'd like the dab of a progue,[27]

8. Irish *Ochón*, Alas.
9. Pulse of my heart.
10. Potato.
11. Hare.
12. Shallow domestic vessels, not normally used in cooking.
13. Broken drinking vessels.
14. Knots (in timber).
15. Rushes dipped in tallow and plaited were used as candles.
16. Plates, platters.
17. Cabbage.
18. *Praiseach bhuí*, wild cabbage.
19. Dish made from cabbage and potato.
20. *Meascán*, ball or pat of butter.
21. *Sruthán*, stream.
22. *Uisce beatha*, whiskey.
23. *Quirren*, a small pot.
24. Seáinín, from Seán.
25. A toast: *Seo dhuit, a mhúirnín*: Here's to your health, my darling.
26. *Póg*, kiss.
27. A blow from a spade.

1. Andrew Carpenter, *Verse in English from Eighteenth-Century Ireland* (Cork: Cork University Press, 1998).
2. Ibid. See also 'Anglo-Irish Verse 1675–1825', ed. Bryan Coleborne, volume I, pp. 395–657.
3. *Gearrán bán*, white nag.
4. Siobhán.
5. Term of endearment, from *grá mo chroí*, love of my heart.
6. Róisín.
7. *Síle Bhuí*, yellow (fair-haired) Síle).

We danced till we sweated, our buts they did
   smoak,
So strong the poor piper had like to be choak'd.
    And your, etc.

   When the Bride and the Bride-groom they
    pulled of their brogues,[28]
No person cou'd stand for the smell of their toes,
When the Bride and the Bride-groom were put
   into bed,
She pulled off her shift and put it under her head.
    And your, etc.

So when that was over and we then went to
   bed,
And lay head and points as if we all were dead,
Next day, when the Bride and the Bride-groom
   appear'd,
She look'd like an angel and he hung an ear.
    And your, etc.

   We kissed and we parted, each man took his
    leave,
The poor tired Bride-groom look'd wonderful
   grave,
So we all returned home contented and gay,
To our plows and our milk-pails 'till next holiday.
    Your welcome all of you welcome heartily,
    Welcome gramacree aye by my troath.

28. Shoes.

GRACE MAXWELL

(*fl.* 1776–9)

LETTER TO MR. STERLING (1776)

[Grace Corry was a wealthy widow with property in Fermanagh, Monaghan and Tyrone when she was courted by Colonel John Maxwell.[1] At their marriage in 1776 she settled her estate on their issue, with remainder to herself, but then found that he was unable to consummate the marriage and that he treated her unkindly. She was nevertheless sufficiently anxious to placate him that two years later she resettled her estate on him. A letter to a friend in the year of her marriage suggests that Grace was still willing to seek a reconciliation with her husband, had he been agreeable. Only the subsequent discovery that he had made a will leaving all her money to his nephews and nieces, leaving her nothing but 'a small island on the coast of North America . . . actually in the hands of the insurgents', seems to have provoked her to seek a divorce and have the settlement set aside. Despite the elaborate legal language, the anguish of impotency for both parties is apparent. The letter from Grace Maxwell to Mr Sterling, Sackville Street, Piccadilly, London, is held in the Public Record Office of Northern Ireland, D1556/17/4/2.]

Portsmouth, April 21st, 1776

Dr Sir

My compliments and best wishes wait upon you and Mrs Sterling hope you are both perfectly well — I return you my most sincere thanks for your friendly advice you was so kind to give me — I arrived here this day and had the happiness of seeing the Col he is well, though not so conceeding as I could wish altho I pursued the Dictates of my own better reason and your kind recommendation — you sir were so good repeatedly to offer your best services, you will effactually serve us both if you can Heal this unhappy breach, and restore peace Between us, and acte the part of the Good Samaritan[2] — perhaps it may not be Convenient to mention the Conversation between us in London further than that you understood there was some little Coolness between the Col and me, on account of some letters I wrote Him, and that you found me determined to come down and acknowledge my

1. John Maxwell, of Falkland, County Monaghan, later Governor of the Bahamas.

2. Luke 10:27–39.

Error in writing what had given him offense — This is Taxing your friendship highly but the freedom will convince you of the value I set on your mediation which I hope will excuse this trouble from —

Dear Sir your very sincere and obliged Humble servt

Grace Maxwell

The Col dont know I write you.

ANONYMOUS

from:
CASE FOR THE OPINION OF THE RIGHT HONOURABLE THE PRIME SERJEANT[1] (1779)

[A surviving manuscript in the Public Record Office of Northern Ireland (PRONI D1556/17/4/3) records the case presented on behalf of Grace Maxwell to the Prime Sergeant on 12 February 1779, but it has not been possible to trace any record of the opinion returned. In the manuscript John Maxwell appears as 'AB' and Grace Maxwell as 'CD'. Emphasis is placed on non-consummation and on John Maxwell's intention to deceive.]

AB: Having paid his addresses to CD: of the City of Dublin widow and being both of free age and Protestants of the Church of England a Marriage was agreed to be had between them . . .

The pursuance thereof the Marriage ceremony was perform'd between the said AB and CD: by a Clergyman of the Church of England duly Impowered by Licence, but the said AB being an Officer of Rank in the Army and his Regiment then in America Insisted upon the Marriage being kept a Secret — apprehending, as he sayed, the world might Censure him for neglect of his Military duty, and therefore the said Marriage Ceremony was performed privately in the house of EF a Mutual Friend of the partys and attorney for the said AB.

The said AB had taken much pains to gain the affections of the said CD: and had succeeded so Effectually therein, that she previous to the Marriage Ceremony, promised to settle upon him

all her Estates to take Effect, if there should be no Issue of the Marriage; and if he should survive her, to his own, absolute use forever, and this not yet being carried into [obscure] made the said AB assume a more attentive behaviour to the said CD than proceeded from his real Inclination, his only object being by the opportunitys which the Ceremony of a Marriage, he was not actually able to Consummate, would give him to secure to himself and his family the estate of the said CD as hereafter is mentioned.

On the night of the marriage of the said AB and CD: the Gentleman in whose house the Ceremony was performed requested the said AB and the said CD to stay that night, but to the surprize of all present the said AB declined and it was then with some difficulty and apparent reluctance the said AB consented that he would return to the said CD's lodgings to Consummate the Marriage.

When the usual time for the ladies to retire came, the said CD got up to go, as had been agreed on, to her own lodgings, and was followed to the Hall door by the said AB who in handing her to her Chair (her lodgings being at some distance from the house they were married in) put a small piece of paper into her hand, and on her arrival at her Lodgings, Instead of finding her husband along with her, as she expected, read on the said piece of paper these words 'I shall see you tomorrow at 12 o'clock.'

This treatment somewhat Chagrin'd the said CD; however on the next day the said AB came to her, at the appointed time, and Insisted then only Consummating the Marriage and by persuasion and threats upon the said CD, to acquiesce with his desire, but further disappointment was only added to the said CD's resentment by finding the said AB, after many Efforts, totally Impotent and Incapable of

---

1. Walter Hussey Burgh (1742–1783), Prime Sergeant at Law, represented the king in matters of law.

Consummating the Marriage, even this deficiency the said AB had the address to palliate assuring the said CD it was only the Effects of a Severe Cold and that he would soon be restored to his usual faculties.

Under this belief the said CD: in performance of her promise at the request of the said AB directed the said EF to prepare a deed to be Executed by her conveying her Estate to the said AB if he should SURVIVE her . . .

When the said AB's scheme of having the said Deed executed had taken Effect he no longer preserved any appearance of even civility to the said CD, but took every opportunity to distress her by neglect, bad Treatment, abuse and otherwise, and in short made her experience every distress which a bad malicious Temper of mind and a Total debility and Impotence of Body could Inflict.

from:
A SKETCH OF THE LIFE OF CATHERINE NETTERVILLE, THE CELEBRATED IRISH COURTEZAN, COMMONLY CALLED KITTY-CUT-A-DASH (1788)

[Catherine (Kitty) Netterville was one of the best-known prostitutes in late eighteenth-century Dublin. She died in poverty in Broadstone in 1787. While many prostitutes' memoirs are primarily salacious, this life of Netterville sets out to preach an exemplary lesson. More attention than usual is given to the characters of her 'keepers', particularly to the life of young K——, the mulatto whose position as an outsider parallels Kitty's own situation. The memoir, published in *Walker's Hibernian Magazine* in February 1788, is frank about domestic violence, although Kitty's beatings do not cause her prostitution, as they seem to do in the case of Margaret Leeson, for example (see pp. 819–21).]

As medicines are extracted from the most noxious weeds and poisonous drugs, so in the lives of the most vicious and profligate mortals may be found incidents, which by the influence of example, produce salutary effects.

It is as important to extirpate the wicked from society as it would be to free the world from reptiles. In those countries which we call barbarous, where arts and politeness are unknown, nature has this great advantage, that simplicity of manners often secures innocency of mind; and as virtue is not civilized, neither is vice refined. But in the politer parts of the world, where virtue excels by rules and discipline, vice also flourishes under instruction, and good qualities do not spring up alone, but, like the finest flowers in the richest soils, weeds will shoot with them and increase, unless continually watched and removed. Kitty was one of those weeds; but her ill qualities were the effect of the soil wherein she originally sprung, and the climate wherein she was nurtured; they were not hers by nature: had she in her early days been transplanted by some tender hand into a garden of virtue, she would not only have proved a beautiful but a wholesome flower, 'sweet to the scent and lovely to the eye'.[1]

Her parents were among the most indigent of the poor in Dublin; they were local beggars, and inhabited a cellar under a wretched alehouse in an obscure part of the town, called Lazer's hill.

Her first occupation was pot-girl[2] to this alehouse, in which situation she had not remained long till her beauty attracted the basilisk[3] eye of a prostitute, who, being nearly worn out by practices of infamy, resolved by the initiation of Kitty into the ways of vice, to procure sustenance by dividing the profits.

To accomplish this purpose, she seduced Kitty from her service at the alehouse, and engaged her in the capacity of fille de chambre[4] to attend her in a garret, situated near the university, the members of which occasionally visited her.

In such a situation it cannot be supposed that Kitty long retained her virtue: her mind, which from her infancy had been continually blotted and polluted by vulgar and coarse conception gradually corrupted, and it is probable in her early transgressions, she was unconscious of committing sin, for at the age of fourteen she was notoriously known upon the town, with the character of being a Good-natur'd Girl.

1. Unidentified.
2. Employed to serve and carry pots of ale.
3. A fabulous reptile whose look was fatal.
4. Chambermaid.

To follow her through the mazes of her indiscriminate amours from this period till she attained the age of sixteen, would be wading through a labyrinth of filth: for in this space of time she went through every degree of the university from the junior freshman to the senior fellow; she often frequently went the circuit,[5] and of course was well known from the attorney's clerk to the attorney-general; and from her repeated visits to the barracks there could be no doubt of her attachment to the military. She could boast favours from the drummer to the colonel, but was always constant to her regiment.

From this life of itinerant infamy and casual prostitution, she was taken by a gentleman named Netterville:[6] he was then a minor, entitled to a great estate, but rather weak in his intellects, and remarkably plain in his face and person. Mr. Netterville was undoubtedly fascinated by Kitty. He purchased her cloaths to a considerable amount, and every necessary to the paraphernalia of a fashionable woman. He took a house in a genteel street, furnished it with elegance, and, to complete his bounty, elevated her at once from her street-walking pattens[7] to a high phaeton,[8] in which he often appeared himself sitting by her side.

Kitty bore this sudden change in her situation with the utmost composure. She dropped all her former connections, and to the surprise of all who spoke with her, though she could neither read nor write, she conversed with ease; and gave orders to her servants with a dignified authority that commanded respect and enforced obedience.

Her person finely formed, and gracefully turned, was set off by her dress, in which she had an exquisite taste, to the utmost advantage; and though she bore the mark of a deep cut in her face, inflicted by the hand of a ruffian in a brothel, yet there was a condescending sweetness and amiability in her countenance that engaged the heart and prejudiced the mind in her favour on the first view.

The mental properties of Kitty were equal to her charms: to these, however, her friend paid no attention, nor could it be expected he should, his own understanding being barren. She, however, felt for the uncultivated state of her mind, and resolved to improve it; for which reason, she appropriated the money lavished upon her by her keeper to the retaining of masters, and in very short time not only acquired the art of reading and writing, but also a knowledge of music and dancing. By these means she improved her mind, and expanded her imagination, which now appeared with considerable lustre, and gained her the reputation of being a wit.

With Mr. Netterville she lived for some years, when, by the persuasions of his family, the connection was dissolved; but he acted generously, not only by making her very considerable presents, but giving her a small settlement.

Mr. C——,[9] a gentleman of small fortune, his father being living, had long solicited attention from Kitty. He was young and handsome, and though she never betrayed to him the confidence Mr. Netterville had placed in her by admitting him to a participation of the favours that gentleman paid for, and which he had warmly and repeatedly solicited, yet it is certain he had made an impression, and probably the first impression ever made upon her heart; for immediately after her separation from her first keeper, she admitted the visits of Mr. C——.

This connection was of but short duration: C—— was inconstant, and Kitty had spirit. An offer of great consideration was made to her, and she accepted it.

This offer came from a gentleman named K——,[10] at that time a minor, but entitled to a very considerable personal fortune, which his father, who had been a colonel in the company's service, had acquired in the East Indies, where he had married a native, immensely rich.

Young K—— had been sent to the university of Dublin for his education. His person was slender and well-made, but his skin discovered his origin, and having always a command of money, and a gay turn, he experienced a hearty welcome every where, especially among the bon vivants.

He was in this situation when Kitty struck his fancy, and his offers being profuse were soon

---

5. The journey of judges and other legal professionals to a succession of locations for the purpose of holding courts and assizes.
6. The Netterville family were Catholic aristocracy; the family seat was Dowth Hall, County Meath.
7. Shoes.
8. Light, four-wheeled, open carriage.

9. James Cavendish.
10. Alexander Kirkpatrick (sometimes given as Kilpatrick), known as 'the Nabob', later alderman and sheriff's peer of the city of Dublin.

accepted. He gave her an elegant house, furniture, and equipage; a complete set of jewels, an allowance in money sufficient to support her in the enjoyment of every public amusement and private luxury.

Her house was situated in Grafton Street and here Mr. K—— generally saw his friends, whom he entertained with all the elegance of Eastern dissipation. The chambers were fitted up for the large purpose of amorous intrigue, and as part of his entertainment his guests were always provided with partners, or were welcome to introduce their favourite fair.

We do not find that during this connection Kitty was ever detected in any act of infidelity, but it is certain she had her private favourites, who were occasionally admitted to participate in those joys which the Asiatic paid so highly for, and thought to monopolize; and as he was often jealous, poor Kitty frequently underwent very severe lessons of manual discipline, which she however returned with spirit: and those quarrels always tended to her pecuniary advantage, a diamond, a purse, or an order on a tradesman, being constantly called in as mediators.

Mr K——, after living several years in this disreputable manner, was at last persuaded by his friends to break the connection, and unite himself by marriage to a young lady named R——,[11] whose father was a barrister, nearly related to the Earl of B——,[12] and lived in a retired manner with a very large family on a very small fortune. This young lady possessed beauty, was well accomplished, and of a very amiable disposition; but to assist her family and procure a large settlement for herself, she after long entreaty, consented to sacrifice herself to the embraces of an East-Indian, devoid of learning, debilitated by debauchery, destitute of every mental attribute, and eminent for only one quality, which was good nature in forgiving offences. Soon after this marriage, Mr. K—— purchased a borough, and for the first time a Mulatto appeared in the character of a member of parliament. He did not, however, long survive his marriage, for returning to his excesses, he was in less than three years carried off by a fever.

from:
HIBERNIAN JOURNAL (1788)

[The assault on Mary Neal(e) was one of the more notorious criminal cases of the late eighteenth century. The difficulty in procuring corroborating evidence and the general reluctance to credit children meant that sexual abuse of children was rarely recognized. In this case the brutal physical injuries, the involvement of more than one assailant, and the presence of a female attacker contributed to sensationalize the case and Lewellin was demonized as an unnatural woman. Lewellin was sentenced to death, but pardoned by the Lord Lieutenant on the morning scheduled for the execution, possibly because her defence had produced evidence that the child, Neal, was herself an habitual sex worker.[1] These articles were published in the *Hibernian Journal*, vol. 20, on 2 and 7 July 1788.]

2 July

Maria Lewellin, found guilty on two indictments; one for aiding and abetting a man, name unknown, to commit a rape on the body of one Mary Neale, a child about twelve years of age; and the other indictment was for carrying away the said Mary Neale, with an intent to have her defiled, and for procuring and maintaining the said man, name unknown, to commit the said felony. It appeared by the evidence of the said procutrix, that she was decoyed into a house in Blackamore-yard, which was kept by the prisoner, and when she got into the house, she was pushed into a back room in the lower part of it, where she was detained for the space of three hours, during which time a man had carnal knowledge of her by force, and contrary to her will, though she made all the noise she possibly could to get extricated, but could not get away, the door of the room being locked on the outside. It also appeared by the evidence of a medical gentleman, that the child was very much injured. The said Maria Lewellin was also indicted on two other indictments, one for keeping a house of ill fame, and the other was for assaulting the said Mary Neale; but on these other indictments she was not given in charge to the jury.

---

11. Possibly Rochfort, since this is the family name of the Earl of Belvidere.
12. Robert Rochfort (1708–74), Earl of Belvidere (*c.* 1756).

1. See Leslie Hale, *John Philpot Curran: His Life and Times* (London: Jonathan Cape, 1958), pp. 73–4; Brian Henry, *Dublin Hanged* (Dublin: Irish Academic Press, 1994), pp. 42–3.

7 July

As a certain most atrocious malefactrix has been recommended to mercy by a sympathizing Jury, and is to suffer the punishment of her sentence on the 26th of November, that is *at the Greek Catends*, it is hoped her ladyship will not again be let loose, but consigned to some factor at Canada or Botany Bay.[2] Her crime, of which we may now speak freely, is of a nature that dishonours not only that sex whereof she is a most unworthy member, but might shock the feelings of a street-robber or highway-man; many of whom, without a grain more of real honesty, would abhor the commission of such a fact. A fellow of spirit, though abandoned in other respects, might endure the appellation of wicked *man*, but could never bear to be stigmatized with that of a *brute*.

2. Destinations for transported felons.

DOROTHEA HERBERT

(*c.* 1768–1829)

from:
RETROSPECTIONS OF DOROTHEA HERBERT, 1770–1806 (1929)

[What links the following selections from Herbert's diary is their concern with disguise, identity and reading the sexual body. The mother who mistakes a prostitute for her daughter, the family who 'adopt' the mysterious transvestite, the gentlewoman disguised as a seduced peasant girl all illustrate radical ambiguities within this culture about bodies and meanings. If language, class and gender can be so effectively mimicked, wherein reside authentic identities? There is also, of course a question about the fictiveness of Herbert's journal, clearly influenced by Gothic and sentimental fiction, which includes her own bizarre, sad claim to be John Roe's wife (see p. 824). The manuscript, which in the 1920s was in the possession of the Mandeville family, cannot now be traced. In this text, published in London in 1929 by Gerald Howe, Herbert's grammar, spelling and punctuation have been preserved. They give a flavour of the diary's immediacy, indicate the level of the author's literacy, and in some cases show her propensity to juxtaposition and sometimes odd conjunctions.]

1779

The Season now arrived when my Aunt resolved to treat her two Girls to an Evening at the Rotunda[1] — Great Preparations were made for our Debut, And My Cousin Grace[2] was all on the Alert making up her own and my finery — She was indeed a Charming well disposed good natured Pet with only a few little foibles arising from an affectation Natural to her Age and Situation being an Heiress of large fortune.

To the Rotunda then we went dress'd out at all Points . . . No other Event of importance Marked our debut in Public except an awkward Mistake of my Aunt Herberts[3] who joined us there She mistaking Kitty Cut-a-Dash[4] the famous Thais[5] of the Times for her Daughter Fanny (they being dress'd alike in White Lutestring[6]) made several Promenades leaning on her Arm and Conversing with another Thais her Companion whilst Kitty and her friend acted their Parts to a Miracle —.

1. The Rotunda was adjacent to Dublin's Lying-In Hospital, founded by Benjamin Mosse in 1745 and built (1751–7) on the site of a pleasure garden, opened by Mosse with a view to funding the new hospital. The hospital included a revenue-raising chapel and the gardens included an orchestra and coffee house. The garden was so successful that in 1767 the Rotunda building was erected to permit indoor entertainments and promenades.
2. Grace Cuffe, daughter of Dorothea's paternal aunt Thomasine and her husband Thomas Cuffe, was an heiress who later married the 4th Lord Maxwell.
3. Catherine Herbert, Dorothea's paternal aunt, was married to the Reverend Robert Herbert.
4. Catherine Netterville, see pp. 812–14.
5. A famous Athenian courtesan, who accompanied Alexander on his Asiatic conquests.
6. A glossy silk fabric.

1780

. . . About this time a Young Person appeard here dressed in Mens Cloaths who gave out that he was a Woman — He called himself Miss Gore — Said he had escaped from a Mad house where his Relations put him on Account of an Attachment they disapproved of — He said he was of a Genteel family but would not tell their Names — And what between his flightiness and reserve we could Never arrive at any Certainty either as to his Sex or Situation — He really had all the appearance of being long Confined — His shoulders seem'd to have been tied back his legs were crampd and he shriek'd at the Name of a Straight Waistcoat — His face was very handsome with the finest pair of black Eyes long Dark Eyelashes and arched Eyebrows possible — When dressed in Male Attire he appeard like a Woman — in womens Cloaths lookd Coarse and Masculine — He told such piteous Tales and sang such Melancholy Songs, that he quite soften'd all the Ladies hearts, so that they were always bestowing some charitable donation on him but he would Never take Money — Nice Cloaths he delighted in, and was soon equip'd from head to foot — My mother kept him in her house out of Pity, And he made himself so interesting that he often spent weeks at Castletown[7] and the different places about the Neighbourhood, In his lunatic fits he often absconded but was pursu'd and brought back — The Gentlemen laugh'd at the Ladies about him, but he was too great a favourite to be relinquish'd on their raillery — At length he found Means to Escape and we never heard more of him — Mrs Carshore[8] was then alive and bestowd much care and Attention on him though Mr Carshore often scolded her for encouraging so mysterious a Person — He sometimes made use of very illiterate Expressions but in general his Conversation was interesting, his Language high flown and his Manners extremely insinuating . . .

1785

. . . We were now at full Liberty to follow our Amusements — We had Many flaming Parties

this Summer, especially one Given by Mr Simon Osborne of Annfield (a Widower) to a Miss Dodd with whom he flirted, and who pestered him out of a Fete Champêtre[9] — Every one within twenty or thirty Miles was invited — We dined under Tents and Marquees in the Lawn — Nothing could exceed the Elegance of the Entertainment, and there was no counting the Company — But the chief heroines were two Miss Kennedys[10] both newly Married — They were just come from the assizes of Waterford[11] where they prosecuted to Conviction three Men who ran away with them a Month before from whom they were rescued by their present Bridegrooms — The Men were hanged and every one was disgusted at the Ladies appearing so soon in Public after so horrid a Business — The Eldest Sister at the Tryal fainted several Times and wished to evade the Prosecution, but was urged on to it by the Youngest who was hardened and inexorable — This fair Termagant[12] was a very fine handsome Woman and came to the Ball dressed in a great display of Bridal Finery — pure Virgin white, trimmed all over with Silver Coxcomb[13] whilst many cursed her Cruelty in hanging three very handsome young fellows of good Families Who treated her with Respect whilst she was with them. The Eldest a pretty Woman was more Moderately dressed in a brown Lustring quite plain.

1786

. . . They[14] had however Scarce vented their Laughter at Miss Howleys[15] Expence when I play'd them a Trick which though not so vexatious compleatly duped them — I dressed Myself as a raw Country Girl and went in one Night with a Letter which on rapping at the Door I delivered to Old James Meaker the Butlar and he presented to

7. Castletown Cox, County Kilkenny.
8. Mr Carshore was the local surgeon — he and his wife were among the Herberts' closest friends.

9. *Fête-champêtre*, outdoor entertainment.
10. See headnote to Battier extract, p. 817. Herbert's chronology is mistaken or misremembered; she assumes that the events here immediately succeed the executions, when they are in fact five years later.
11. In fact the trial and executions were at the Kilkenny assizes.
12. Name of an imaginary deity, of violent and overbearing temper, believed by medieval Christians to be worshipped by Muslims.
13. Lace, with edging like a cock's comb.
14. The Jephsons, neighbours to the Herberts.
15. The vain companion to Mrs Honora English, a widow living in Carrick-on-Suir; the previous episode narrated was a practical joke on Miss Howley.

his mistress — In it I complained that I was a poor Country Girl who had the Misfortune of having a Merry begotten Child, That I complained to Mr Cox the Magistrate[16] of the Young Man who had quitted Me — but that he order'd me to be turned out of his House and I threw myself on her Honours Mercy to speak to Mr Cox as I knew she was intimate with him, and he could refuse her Nothing she asked — It was a long Letter and so compleatly disguised in the Hibernian Dialect that She never once suspected the Forgery — Meanwhile James Meagher [*sic*] came to the Door and was very inquisitive to know what brought me there so late at Night — He questioned me so hard, and I made such pert Answers that he called Nurse Dwyer who advised him to kick me out of

the Hall — In a little time the Bell rang violently — and I heard Mrs Jephson in the greatest passion crying 'The Audacious Creature! How durst she presume to think I would speak to Mr Cox on such a Business' — Our family all drank Tea there on purpose to witness the Joke — When they had worked up Mrs Jephson sufficiently, the Boys came out to me and we had such a Sham Battle of ill Language that James, Nurse, and Mrs Jephson were compleatly transmogrified into Furies — they shook me and threatened Me with so many Grimaces that the Boys and Girls screech'd again with laughter — I was at last kicked out of the House and the Door clap'd in my Face — Mrs Jephson kept the Letter and shew'd it to the Gentlemen about — They offered a Reward for Apprehension and Not till a long time after did we inform Mrs Jephson who her Petitioner was.

16. Cox of Castletown Cox.

HENRIETTA BATTIER

(1751–1813)

from:
THE PROTECTED FUGITIVES: A COLLECTION OF MISCELLANEOUS POEMS. THE GENUINE PRODUCTIONS OF A LADY (1791)

[Catherine Kennedy (aged 15) and her sister Anne (aged 14), of Rathmeaden, County Waterford, were visiting friends at Graignuenamana on 12 April 1779 when they were abducted by 19-year-old James Strange, of Ullard, County Kilkenny, and 23-year-old Garret Byrne, of Ballyine, County Carlow. They were taken on horseback to Kilmacshane, where an irregular priest[1] married them to their abductors. They were then raped and taken on the run for five weeks, until they were discovered on board a ship near Wicklow. Strange and Byrne fled to Wales but were captured with Strange's brother Patrick, who had

assisted in the abduction, and they were tried at Kilkenny assizes in October 1780, before the attorney-general, John Scott. All three were found guilty and executed in December 1780. There was a surprising degree of sympathy for the abductors, perhaps from a general suspicion, articulated by Battier, that the Kennedy girls had known and colluded with their 'husbands'. (See, for example, Dorothea Herbert's mention of the case, p. 815.) This case has been credited with marking a turning-point in attitudes to abduction, particularly by Catholic 'middleman'. The number of abductions seems to have peaked in the decade up to 1780, but a marked decline in cases is only noticeable from the 1790s. Andrew Carpenter suggests that Battier may well have been paid to address the following petition to the MP for Kilkenny. This case is the subject of Margery Weiner's *Matters of Felony. A Reconstruction* (London: Heinemann, 1967).

The following lines addressed to the late Lord Clifden,[2] in behalf of the three young men, who ran away with the Miss Kennedy's, were written

1. Irregular priests were sometimes known as 'couple-begging' priests.

2. James Agar (1734–89), MP for Kilkenny, became Baron Clifden in 1776 and Viscount Clifden in 1781.

at the request of Miss Byrn, who was sister to one
of them, and a most amiable woman.

Oh! Thou in whom united virtues shine,
To Mercy's pleadings let thy heart incline,
Thy goodness oft prevented my request,
This is the last and grant it — 'tis the best;
A word from you, my honour'd friend, may save
Three wretched youths from an untimely grave,
What tho' offended Justice turns away,
From all their kindred or the world can say,
Yet thou wert made in Mercy's happier hour,
Nor vainly just, nor arrogant of power;
The clay was purcelain,[3] of which you were
    form'd,
And gentler passions have thy bosom warm'd,
And Mercy mark'd her character in vain
In Clifden's face, if blood those marks should
    stain.
Think not, my friend, I dare point out to you,
Where mercy most, or retribution's due;
But yet, in equity, you'll own, my Lord,
That greater crimes oft scape a just reward;
Had brutal force, preventing their escape,
Compell'd their persons to a marriage rape,
Then every honest, generous breast must own,
No death but CHRIST's could for the crime
    atone;
But think, my Lord, they were their willing
    wives,
And spare, oh! spare, their wretched husband's
    lives;

3. Porcelain.

Justice has past her sentence, now, my Lord,
Let Mercy sheath the all-avenging sword.
From the dark horrors of those dreadful cells,
Where dire Remorse, and black Conviction
    dwells
The sad triumvirate for mercy sue;
Their mothers, kinsmen, and a sister too,
Unhappy girl, oh! Clifden, had you seen
The wild distress, which mark'd her graceful
    mien,
The storms of sorrow that convulsed that
    breast,
Where all the friend and sister stood confest,
A mind, less amiably kind than yours
Would soothe the anguish that her soul endures.
Think then, my friend, when that all pleasing
    form,
Which Clifden owns, and many virtues warm,
Has past the pleasures of his youth and prime,
And waits the sure, tho' slow award of time,
When silver age has dim'd those speaking eyes,
And every joy must from reflection rise;
Think then, I say, how exquisitely great,
Beyond the glories of terrestrial state,
Will be the memory of an act like this,
That brings a foretaste of eternal bliss.
Oh! then, anticipate the dear delight
Of conscience telling you, you acted right!
For power's best charter, rightly understood,
Is the prerogative of doing good;
Think not presumption has inspir'd my pen,
Thou most benignant of the sons of men,
Nor let my noble generous friend refuse,
The meek intreaties of the suppliant Muse.

MARGARET LEESON

(1727–97)

from:

THE MEMOIRS OF MRS MARGARET LEESON, WRITTEN BY HERSELF; IN WHICH ARE GIVEN ANECDOTES, SKETCHES OF THE LIVES AND BON MOTS OF SOME OF THE MOST CELEBRATED CHARACTERS IN GREAT BRITAIN AND IRELAND, PARTICULARLY OF ALL THE FILLES DES JOYS AND MEN OF GALLANTRY WHICH HAVE USUALLY FREQUENTED HER CITHEREAN TEMPLE FOR THESE THIRTY YEARS PAST (1797)

[The pseudo-memoirs of prostitutes were a popular semi-pornographic genre of eighteenth-century writing. Among the best-known examples is John Cleland's *Memoirs of a Woman of Pleasure* (1748). It is a commonplace of these memoirs to include several Irish characters, the result of a conflation of stereotypes: first, that the Irish being less civilized are therefore less disciplined in their sexual practices; second, that Catholicism, and especially a convent education, produces licentious conduct in women — a convention partly inherited from French erotic fiction; and third, a suspicion that the Irish in England were an unknown quantity, adept at acting, masquerade and fortune-hunting. Leeson enters this genre and exploits some of its conventions, but the text is distinctively original in a number of ways, not least in that it seems to have been genuinely written by her. It begins with an account of how she was driven into prostitution by the experience of domestic violence — in Leeson's case the extreme brutality of her brother. Leeson is also unusual in that she presents prostitution as an unruly behaviour, one which *deliberately* flouts the law and subverts the state. She is decidedly pro-Catholic and seems to take particular pleasure in revealing the sexual foibles of Protestant clergymen. The naming of clients — or the playing with initials and descriptions which threaten to name them — is not so unusual, although Leeson makes heavier use than most of local detail. The identification of figures whose names are occluded in the text has been aided by the fact that the copy of the memoirs in the National Library of Ireland (one of only three surviving copies in public collections) has annotations to the third volume in a near-contemporary hand, and these annotations have been used by Mary Lyons in a table of identification to her 1995 reprint. The following text is taken from the copy in Columbia University Library.]

In about a fortnight after I had got good riddance of the *woman of Ireland*,[1] Miss Mc Pherson from Banbridge[2] called to see me; she looked wretchedly, and appeared in great distress, and upon impatiently enquiring into her story, she told me, she and her unfortunate sister had been seduced by the late and present M—— of D——, father and son,[3] that the present man had cruelly disordered her wretched sister, and afterwards suffered her to languish under the disease, without affording her the smallest relief, or medical assistance, till she died; that for her part, her fate was milder, for her *hoary old lecher* was extremely fond of her; had her picture drawn by the late Jos. Wilson of Belfast,[4] in various attitudes, dressed and naked; kept her in the most exalted stile, introduced her among his tenantry and dependants, at all the *Hillsborough*[5] *balls* and entertainments, and so thrust her down the throats of all the little country *squires*, squireens and squirts, and their ladies, in the vicinity of his residence; that she generally went by the title of the *Marchioness* of ——; that at length, her most *noble antiquarian* beginning to

1. A prostitute named Magee.
2. County Down.
3. Wills Hill (1718–93), succeeded as Viscount Hillsborough, 1742, created 1st Marquis of Downshire, 1789; Arthur Hill (1753–1801), 2nd Marquis of Downshire.
4. Joseph Wilson (d. 1793), Belfast portrait and landscape painter, *fl.* from 1770.
5. County Down.

tire of attempting what he was not by any means equal to, bestowed her fair hand upon a little inferior lowlived revenue officer, for whom he procured an employment in the revenue; that she had willing embraced the proposal, in order to get rid of her *old tormentor*, which was not the case, for by the permission of her mean-spirited and rascally husband, she was obliged to obey the mandates of her old teizing friend, who frequently sent for her to spend the night with him; that at last it pleased Providence to take her patron of fumbling memory from her, and shortly afterwards her *accommodating spouse*; in consequence of which the present M——s refusing to allow her the smallest support, and finding herself despised by those who in better days courted her acquaintance, she had ventured up to this city[6] in search of adventures, and begged my assistance to forward her in her amorous *career*; though I saw nothing in Mc P——n that could promise any emolument, yet as 'twas my constant study to alleviate the miseries of all the *woe-worn animals* who applied to me for relief, I heartily welcomed her to Pitt-street, lent her five guineas to get a change or two of linen, which she stood much in want of, and pushed her into company by the title of the cidevant[7] M——ss, which had the desired effect, and procured her a few gallants, who would never have noticed her as plain *Molly Mc Pherson*. While this lady was in the character of my *Protegée*, another sham Marchioness came to pay her a visit; she was a lady who had been in *high keeping* with the late worthy honest Marquis of A——,[8] who had no fault on earth, but too great an attachment to the brandy bottle, in which he'd indulge with any of his own servants, from the hour he rose in the morning, till he'd get so drunk as not to be able to walk through the streets; and many and many a time, has this most noble peer visited me in that state, — a state of utter stupefaction. Among other no less curious anecdotes which this lady amazed us with was an assurance, that though the Marquis had kept her in her coach for several years, she had in all that time no sort of connection with him; with astonishment, we both asked her in a breath, for what purpose had he

kept her? 'for merely the unspeakable pleasure' answered she archly, 'of picking, washing, and cleaning my pretty little toes, which he took great delight in, and in which pleasurable, innocent, and inoffensive pastime he often spent hours; 'twas the greatest gratification to him on earth, not did he (said she) indulge in any other, as in all the time we spent together, he was never rude enough even to give me a kiss; however I amply made up for the time I lost with this poor drunken *peerless Peer*, as the instant he left me, I sent for my poor friend Frank Mc G——, and with him enjoyed every *luxury of love*, — both laughing heartily at ——'s whimsical letch.' . . .

[The final passages of the memoir were apparently composed when Leeson was dying from venereal disease, contracted after she and her companion, Peggy Collins, were robbed and raped by group of men. Although prostitutes' memoirs conventionally end with death or repentance there is a robust independence in Leeson's account, even of violence and destitution, that distinguishes it from the generality of the genre.]

Peggy and I continued together in tollerable tranquillity for several months, untill one evening I took it into my head to take a walk towards Drumcondra, to see my old Poetical friend Mrs. H——,[9] and took poor Peggy with me as a safeguard; and on our return in the dusk of the evening, we were attacked by five ruffians, who dragged us into an adjoining field, and after stripping us of our shifts, and robbing us of what cash we had about us, actually compelled us by force to comply with their infamous desires, and otherwise used us most cruelly, as we made as much resistance as was in our power; particularly poor Mrs. Collins, who in her rage thrust her scissors, into one of the villains belly's at the very moment he was enjoying her, after they severally satiated their brutal appetites, they left us as I said before, stripped to our shifts, carrying off even our shoes and stockings, and indeed was it not for one of them, who had less ferocity than the others, they would have taken away our very *shifts*; — in this wretched situation we were obliged to return to Mrs. H——, who kindly procured for us from her friends Broadhead's,

---

6. Dublin.
7. Former.
8. John James Hamilton (1756–1818), created Marquis of Abercorn in 1790.

9. Mary Lyons suggests that this may be Mrs Robert Hill of Drumcondra (d. 1793).

shoes and stockings, with two old plaid cloaks; and in this miserable plight we arrived at our lodgings, very much cut and bruised, at about two o'clock in the morning: Mrs T——[10] was astonished when she saw us, and when we related the way we had been treated, she absolutely shed tears of compassion, and would not let us retire till she made us take some warm punch, at the same time giving us every consolation in her power. Poor Peggy and I went to bed, but not to rest, and what was a greater affliction to us than all, in a few days afterwards we found we were infected with the most wretched of disorders; in fact we were injured by the nefarious villains in the most virulent degree, and this in all my round of pollution was what I never experienced before; — almost frantic, and not knowing what to do; I was at first resolved to lye under the fould disease till it should terminate my wretched existence, but then on reflection I considered my poor Peggy's case, and at last determined to send for either Blind Billy J——ns[11] or Surgeon B——r,[12]

but in sending a note to the former, I found he had been for a considerable time, a *Sunday beau*, and the poor surgeon was to my great grief in durance vile,[13] for large sums of money; — I therefore applied to my worthy friend Mr. Brady, who was obliged, our diseases were so virulent and obstinate, to put us both in a salivation,[14] — in which we were for near three months, at the end of which time, we found ourselves reduced to skeletons, all our money exhausted, deeply involved with Mrs T——, our landlady, and our clothes in pawn: — A glorious situation for two miserable repentent sinners, who had not by any crime of their own, in any shape contributed to bring on these unheard of misfortunes; what to do we knew not, and what was still worse (as misfortune never comes alone) Mrs T——, and who could blame her, gave us warning to quit her home.

10. Leeson's landlady in Clarendon Street, Dublin.
11. William Lionel Jenkins, apothecary, of Dame Street.
12. Surgeon Charles Bolger of Suffolk Street.

13. Imprisoned.
14. The administration of mercury — a standard treatment for sexually transmitted diseases — caused an excessive production of saliva, resulting in discharge.

JOHN FITZGIBBON, 1ST EARL OF CLARE

(1749–1802)

from:
LETTER TO WILLIAM EDEN, 1ST LORD AUCKLAND[1]
(*c.* 1801)

[The following excerpt is from a letter to Auckland discussing Clare's bad relations with the new Irish administration. It is in the context of this critique that Clare cites the example of an apparent discrepancy in the administration of justice on abductions, which may lead to bad feeling in the populace. On 22 June 1797 Mary Pike,

1. William Eden (1744–1814), created 1st Baron Auckland (1789), statesman and diplomat, Postmaster-General 1798–1804.

a Cork Quaker heiress, was abducted by Sir Henry Browne Hayes of Vernon Mount, a Cork baronet of mercantile backgound, in want of money. Hayes married Pike at gun point, but was unable to consummate the marriage, apparently through impotence. Pike was rescued and, after a period on the run, Hayes was captured and tried at Cork, after a series of delays, in 1801. He was found guilty but because he had done Miss Pike 'no personal violence' the verdict came with a recommendation for mercy. The judge, Robert Day, commuted the usual death sentence to one of transportation to Botany Bay, Australia. Hayes was released from Botany Bay in 1812. In 1801 two other men, of much lower social standing, were executed for abduction. A typescript of the letter is held in the Public Record Office of Northern Ireland, T.3229/1/38, Sneyd papers. This seems to be copied from the Sneyd Muniments at Keele University (unexamined).]

19 Sep. [1801] Clare, Mount Shannon

This county has been more disturbed than any part of Ireland for the last two years, and Lord Cornwallis[2] did at my earnest recommendation, after a very minute enquiry into the state of the country, when he was here in the last Summer, give to Sir James Duff,[3] who commands at Limerick, a discretionary power to execute sentences of military tribunals for corporal punishment, without awaiting the confirmation of the Lord Lieutenant. This power has been revoked within the last week by Mr Abbot,[4] without the slightest communication with me, although it is notorious that the power was given to Sir James Duff at my recommendation, and that it has done more to restore quiet in this county than any measure taken since the disturbances broke out; and now Mr Abbot's orders are that no sentence shall be put in execution until it shall be transmitted to him, and he shall signify the Lord Lieutenant's[5] pleasure upon it.

He has, I am confident, induced Lord Hardwicke to make a very improper and disrespectful proposition to me, upon a probable vacancy on the bench, to which, however, I have given such an answer that I do not think a similar experiment will be again made on me. Lord H. originally desired me to recommend to him a proper person to succeed to the bench in case the vacancy took place. Afterwards, he wrote to me *on consideration* to return him the names of three persons, that he might select one of them: in other words, that Mr Abbot might scrutinise the return.

To one of our judges he has not acted with so much caution, as you will see by the correspondence which I enclose to you.[6] To the judge he gives positive orders how he is to discharge his duty on the bench. Sir Henry Hayes and Murphy were indicted and tried on the same statute, each for carrying off a woman by force with intent to marry her. Murphy succeeded in ravishing his lady, Sir Henry Hayes attempted to ravish his, but did not succeed, because the cock would not fight, and after standing out all legal process for five years, and bidding defiance to two proclamations offering a reward of five hundred pounds for apprehending him, he was at length brought to trial, found guilty, and respited by Mr Day, upon a silly doubt in his mind on a point of law. Poor Murphy has been hanged, and Sir Henry Hayes has been pardoned. Another poor wretch of the name of Lupton[7] was hanged almost at the same time upon the same statute. His crime was assisting a friend in carrying off a woman whom he wished to marry. And certainly, if ever any crime deserved capital punishment in a civilized country, Mr Murphy's, Sir Henry's and Mr Lupton's did merit it. But it will be difficult to persuade the lower orders of the people that equal justice has been administered to rich and poor. Burn the papers which I enclose to you after you have shown them to Hobart.[8] Of course, he will not quote me as the person from whom he has learned the contents of them. The correspondence upon the fate of Sir Henry Hayes was sent to me by Lord Hardwicke's desire, upon Cooke's[9] having stated to him my extreme surprise that a pardon should be granted to Sir Henry Hayes, and I took the liberty to state to his Excellency that the style of his Secretary was much too dictatorial.[10]

3. Sir James Duff (1752–1839), British commander of Limerick district from 1797.
4. Charles Abbott (1757–1829), 1st Baron Colchester (1816), Chief Secretary for Ireland 1801.
5. Philip Yorke (1757–1834), 3rd Earl of Hardwicke (1790), Lord Lieutenant of Ireland 1801–6.
6. According to the PRONI typescript, this enclosure has not been found.
7. Henry Lupton of Queen's County (now County Laois).
8. Robert Hobart (1760–1816), Baron Hobart, succeeded as 4th Earl of Buckinghamshire (1804); assisted Auckland (1799) in arranging details of Irish union; Secretary for War and the Colonies, 1801–4.
9. Edward Cooke (1755–1820), Under-Secretary in the Irish military department, 1789–95, and in the civil department, 1796–1801.
10. For further correspondence on the case see British Library Add.Ms 45,031/f32 (Kilwarden to Fitzgibbon 28 August 1801) and BL Add. Ms 33, 114/f36–37 (Kilwarden to Hardwicke 15 September 1801).

Biographies/Bibliographies

William Petty

For biography and bibliography, see Volume I, p. 955.

Jonathan Swift

For biography and bibliography, see Volume I, pp. 393–4.

Samuel Madden

LIFE. A writer and philanthropist, Samuel Madden was born in Dublin in 1686, the nephew of scientist and political writer William Molyneux (1656–98). Madden received his BA at Dublin in 1705 and his DD in 1723. He was ordained and held a position as rector of Drummully. He established premiums for the encouragement of learning at Trinity College Dublin and helped Thomas Prior (1681–1751) to found the Dublin Society in 1731. He was interested in the encouragement of Irish agriculture, manufacture and trade. He died in 1765.

CHIEF WRITINGS. *Memoirs of the Twentieth Century. Being Original Letters of State under George the Sixth, Relating to the Most Important Events in Britain and Europe* (London: Osborn, Longman and others, 1733); *Reflections and Resolutions Proper for the Gentlemen of Ireland* (Dublin: R. Reilly, 1738).

BIOGAPHY AND CRITICISM. D. Clarke, *Thomas Prior, 1681–1751: Founder of the Royal Dublin Society* (Dublin: Three Candles Press, 1951); Paul Alkon, 'Samuel Madden's Memoirs of the Twentieth Century', *Science-Fiction Studies*, vol. 12, no. 2 (1985), pp. 184–201; S.J. Connolly, *Religion, Law and Power: The Making of Protestant Ireland 1660–1760* (Oxford: Clarendon Press, 1992).

Christian Davies

LIFE. According to her autobiography, Christian Davies was born in Dublin in 1667 to a family named Cavenaugh. Her father was a brewer and her mother a farmer at Leixlip. Although Protestants, they supported James II, her father leading a troop in James's Irish army. The family lost considerable property after James's defeat. Cavenaugh inherited money from an aunt and she married her servant, Richard Welsh. Welsh was later coerced into travelling to Flanders and joining the army. After some time, his wife disguised herself in men's clothes and followed him. She had a long career in the army, returning to Dublin from time to time to see her children and look after her property. She eventually retired to Chester and then to the Chelsea hospital, where she and her husband were both pensioners. Davies died on 7 July 1739, and was interred in the Chelsea-Hospital Burial Ground, with military honours.

CHIEF WRITINGS. *The Life and Adventures of Mrs. Christian Davies, Commonly Call'd Mother Ross . . . Taken from her Own Mouth when a Pensioner of Chelsea-Hospital* (London: R. Montagu, 1740). There were numerous subsequent editions, including 1741 when the phrase 'the British Amazon' was added to the title, 1742, 1743, 1893, trans. into French 1934; it appeared in numerous collected editions of Daniel Defoe (to whom it was long attributed) including 1893 and 1928.

BIOGRAPHY AND CRITICISM. John Campbell Major, *The Role of Personal Memoirs in English Biography and Novel* (Philadelphia, 1935); Estelle C. Jelinek, 'Disguise Autobiographies: Women Masquerading as Men', *Women's Studies International Forum*, vol. 10, no. 1 (1987), pp. 53–62; Julie Wheelwright, '"Amazons and Military Maids": An Examination of Female Military Heroines in British Literature and the Changing Construction of Gender', *Women's Studies International*

Forum, vol. 10, no. 5 (1987), pp. 489–502; Fraser Easton, 'Plebianizing the Female Soldier: Radical Liberty and the Narrative of Christian Davies', *Eighteenth-Century Life* (forthcoming).

Robert Nugent

LIFE. The son of Robert Nugent, Earl Nugent, afterwards Craggs (1702–88), and his cousin Clare Nugent, later O'Brien. His autobiography records his birth in London in 1730, education in Dublin, career in the British navy, and later business as a grocer in Dublin, all of which endeavours were thwarted by the persecution of his father and half-brother. At the conclusion of the text he is imprisoned for debt in London.

CHIEF WRITINGS. *The Unnatural Father; Or, The Persecuted Son. Being a Candid Narrative of the most unparrallelled Sufferings of ROBERT NUGENT, Junr., by the Means and Procurement of his own Father* (London: printed for the author, 1755).

Archdeacon Hugh Hamilton

LIFE. Hugh Hamilton was born in 1729. He took his MA from Trinity College Dublin in 1750 and his DD in 1762. He was a fellow of Trinity College, 1751–64; Dean of Armagh, 1768–96; Bishop of Clonfert, 1796–9; Bishop of Ossory, 1799. He died in 1805.

CHIEF WRITINGS. *The Works of Hugh Hamilton Collected and Published, with some Alterations and Additions, from his Manuscripts, by A. Hamilton, His Son*, 2 vols (London, 1809).

Dorothea Du Bois

LIFE. Dorothea was the eldest of three daughters of Ann Simpson and Richard Annesley, later Earl of Anglesey. She was born in Dublin in 1728, and educated at boarding-school there. In 1767 Du Bois was trying to secure payment from the heir, Arthur Annesley, Earl of Anglesey, of jointures to her and her sisters (Lady Caroline White and Lady Elizabeth Hyde). Du Bois died destitute in Dublin in 1774.

CHIEF WRITINGS. *Poems on Several Occasions. By a Lady of Quality* (Dublin: printed for the author, 1764); *The Case of Ann Countess of Anglesey, Lately Deceased; Lawful Wife of Richard Annesley, Late Earl of Anglesey, and of Her Three Surviving Daughters, Lady Dorothea, Lady Caroline, and Lady Elizabeth, by the said Earl* (London, 1766); *Advertisement. A warning Against Arthur Annesley, calling himself Earl of Anglesey, Who is Trying to Sell Part of the Disputed Estate* (London, 1767); *Theodora. A Novel* (London: printed for the author by C. Kiernan, 1770); *The Magnet: A Musical Entertainment* (1771); *The Divorce. A Musical Entertainment* (1772); *The Lady's Polite Secretary; Or, New Female Letter Writer* (London, n.d.); 'The Haunted Grove, A Musical Piece' (not published).

Sarah Colvill

LIFE. Sarah Lennox was born *c.* 1731 in the North of Ireland. She married Robert Colvill of Newtownards, County Down. After his death she moved to Dublin. She was a cousin of William Drennan (1754–1820) and Martha McTier (1742–1837) and features in their correspondence. She died in 1835 at the age of 104.

Grace Maxwell

LIFE. Grace Corry was a landed widow with property in Fermanagh, Monaghan and Tyrone when she married Colonel John Maxwell in 1776. She attempted to divorce him in 1779; it is unclear whether she succeeded.

Dorothea Herbert

LIFE. Dorothea Herbert was born in Kilkenny around 1768, the eldest child of Reverend Nicholas Herbert (d. 1803) of Muckross, Killarney, and his wife Martha (Cuffe) (d. 1811), a daughter of John Cuffe, 1st Lord Desart of County Kilkenny. Her father held livings at Carrick-on-Suir and at Knockgrafton. In May 1789 the family moved from Carrick into the Parsonage House at Knockgrafton and became acquainted with their new neighbours, the Roes of Rockwell. Dorothea fell in love with John Roe, a son of the family. There is little evidence of any courtship between the two, but when John Roe married a Miss Sankey, Dorothea regarded it as a betrayal, and referred to herself as his true wife. She seems to have suffered from increasing mental illness and complains of great cruelty, including physical violence and confinement, from her mother and brother Nicholas, after the death of her favourite brother (1800) and of her father (1803). The Retrospections and other writings seem to have been composed from 1806, although Herbert claims they were partly based on earlier manuscripts. At her death in 1829 the manuscripts were inherited by her brother Nicholas and from Nicholas they passed into the family of his relations, the Mandevilles. When George Mandeville published Retrospections in 1929, it was the only manuscript volume he could find, and by 1988 it had been apparently lost.

CHIEF WRITINGS. Retrospections of Dorothea Herbert, 1770–1806 (London: Gerald Howe, 1929).

BIOGRAPHY AND CRITICISM. Benedict Kiely, 'All for Love', Ireland of the Welcomes, vol. 35, no. 1 (1986), pp. 3111–35; Louis Cullen, 'Historical Backdrop', Afterword to 1988 edition.

Henrietta Battier

LIFE. Henrietta Fleming was born in Staholmock, County Meath, in 1751 and in 1768 she married Major John Gaspard Battier (d. 1794), the son of a Huguenot banker in Dublin, and in 1769 they were with his regiment in Limerick. They later moved to Dublin. Battier is amongst the most nationalist of eighteenth-century women writers, and most of her work addresses public affairs. Her first poems were published under the pseudonym 'PATT. PINDAR'. There are passing references to her in many documents from the 1790s, and her wit is often mentioned, but there has so far been no systematic gathering of these references and very little is known of her life. She visited London in 1783–4 and acted briefly at Drury Lane. In London she sought subscribers for a collection of poetry and was helped by Samuel Johnson. She died in 1813.

CHIEF WRITINGS. An Address on the Subject of the Projected Union, to the Ill-Starred Stephen III, King of Dalkey, etc. (Dublin, 1790); The Protected Fugitives (Dublin, 1791); The Kirwinade (Dublin, 1791); The Gibbonade (Dublin, 1793–4); Marriage Ode, after the Manner of Dryden (Dublin, 1795); An Irregular Ode to Edward Byrne, of Mullinahack, On His Marriage with Miss Roe (Dublin, 1797); The Lemon (Dublin, 1797, 1798); Bitter Orange (Dublin, n.d.).

BIOGRAPHY AND CRITICISM. Janet Todd (ed.), A Dictionary of British and American Women Writers 1660–1800 (London: Methuen, 1984); Virginia Blain, Patricia Clements, Isobel Grundy (eds), The Feminist Companion to Literature in English: Women Writers from the Middle Ages to the Present (London: Batsford, 1990); Andrew Carpenter, Verse in English from Eighteenth-Century Ireland (Cork: Cork University Press, 1998).

Margaret Leeson

LIFE. Margaret Plunket was born at Killough, County Westmeath, in 1727, the daughter of Matthew Plunket, a landowner from near Corbet's-town, and his wife née O'Reilly. She was one of twenty-two children, of whom eight survived infancy. Two older sisters married prosperous tradesmen in Tullamore and Dublin. While Margaret was in her teens her mother and eldest brother died of fever. Her father was then a bereaved invalid and signed over the whole of his estate to his son Christopher. Christopher was a violent alcoholic who beat and starved his brother and sisters. One sister married well, against his will, leaving Margaret at home with a younger brother and sister and an ailing, distressed father, as well as Christopher. The sister died, a victim to cruelty and neglect according to Margaret, and she herself tried and failed to elope before she was finally assisted to escape by her father and younger brother, Garrett, who were frightened by the beatings she received. She moved to her sister in Arran-Street, Dublin, and soon after began an affair with a man named Dardis. When she became pregnant he persuaded her to move into lodgings in what subsequently turned out to be a brothel. After the birth of her daughter she separated from her lover, tried and failed to be reconciled with her family, became a 'kept woman' and eventually a prostitute and then a brothel-keeper. Her most famous establishment was in Wood-Street, Dublin. In her sixties she published the first two volumes of her memoirs, to pay her debts. She was later attacked by a gang, beaten and raped, and later died of a venereal disease in 1797. The third volume was posthumously published.

CHIEF WRITINGS. The Memoirs of Mrs Margaret Leeson, Written by Herself: In which are Given Anecdotes, Sketches of the Lives and Bon Mots of Some of the Most Celebrated Characters in Great Britain and Ireland, Particularly of all the Filles des Joys and Men of Gallantry which have usually Frequented her Citherean Temple for these Thirty Years Past (Dublin, 1797).

BIOGRAPHY AND CRITICISM. Terry Castle, Masquerade and Civilisation: The Carnivalesque in Eighteenth-Century English Culture and Fiction (Stanford: University of Stanford Press, 1986); Siobhán Kilfeather, 'Look Who's Talking: Sexual Scandal in Irish Memoirs', Irish Review, vol. 14, no. 1 (1993), pp. 40–9; Mary Lyons, 'Introduction' to The Memoirs of Mrs Leeson, Madam, 1727–1797, ed. Mary Lyons (Dublin: Lilliput Press, 1995).

John Fitzgibbon, 1st Earl of Clare

LIFE. Born in 1749, son of a convert from Catholicism to the Established Church; educated at Trinity College Dublin and Christ Church, Oxford; called to the Irish bar in 1772; Attorney General, 1783; MP for Dublin University, 1778–83, and for Killmallock, 1783–9; Lord Chancellor of Ireland, 1789–1801; created Baron Fitzgibbon, 1789, Viscount, 1793, Earl of Clare, 1795, UK peer, 1799. Orchestrated the passing of the Act of Union (1801); opposed Catholic relief. He died in 1802.

CHIEF WRITINGS. Letters Written in the Year 1788; Being a Correspondence Between a late Attorney General, then the Right Hon. John Fitzgibbon, Esq; and His Client, Joseph Henry Kearman (Dublin: Joseph K, 1790); Letters to a Young Chancellor; Or, A Letter from Mentor to Lord Jeffreys, Baron Petulant [i.e. J.F.] (Dublin, 1792); Paddy Whack [pseud. J.F.], No Union! but Unite and Fall. By P.W., of Dyott-Street, London; in a Loving Letter to His Dear Mother, Sheelah, of Dame-Street, Dublin . . ., 2nd ed. (London: W.J. and J. Richardson; J. Harding and H.D. Symonds, 1799).

BIOGRAPHY AND CRITICISM. Ann C. Kavanagh, John Fitzgibbon. Earl of Clare: A Study in Personality and Politics (Dublin: Irish Academic Press, 1997).

SIOBHÁN KILFEATHER, *Editor*

Sexual Expression and Genre, 1801–1917

The fact is, though it is difficult for an outsider to believe it, that the whole subject of love, of passion of any kind, especially from a girl and with regard to her own marriage, is such an utterly unheard-of one amongst Grania's class that the mere fact of giving utterance to a complaint on the subject gave her a sense not merely of having committed a hideous breach of common decency, but of having actually crossed the line that separates sanity from madness.[1]

As far as we know people went on having sexual and affectionate relations in much the same way after 1798 as they had done before, and patterns of behaviour underwent relatively minor changes up till the great trauma of the famine and the subsequent depopulation of Ireland in the 1840s and 1850s. There were however some changes in the aesthetics of representation which made an impact on how people thought about family life, romance and personal identity in the first half of the nineteenth century. Some of these changes in representation can be associated with the changes in sensibility, the increasing interest in individual subjectivity, the development of pity, the possibility of sympathy projected by observers onto the observed, the desire to represent the underclass, the obsession with children, a belief in the growth of the mind — in other words with the cluster of new ideas and practices called Romanticism. These changes affected the ways in which people thought about sexuality in several specific ways. For example, the figure of the

prostitute had traditionally appeared as a satiric vehicle in literary texts. When Jonathan Swift writes in 'A Beautiful Young Maiden Going to Bed' (1734), 'Corinna in the morning dizened, / Who sees will spew; who smells be poisoned', his business is to rebuke his readers, not to invite them into empathy. The ghosted memoirs of Mary Anne Faulkner and Margaret Woffington are essentially comic, as is Margaret Leeson's autobiography, albeit as fierce as Swift in its comedy. By the 1820s, however, *The Life and Transactions of a Female Prostitute* and the ballad of *The Wandering Girl* are absolute weepies, tales of innocence seduced and betrayed, the innocence so popular in contemporary fiction and best represented by Eily O'Connor, the betrayed and murdered heroine of Gerald Griffin's novel *The Collegians* (1829).

The year 1798 represents an important turning point in the representation of family life because of the ways in which both loyalist and rebel accounts of that year mobilized images of the family to evoke ideas both of suffering and of affiliation. Both sides build on Edmund Burke's metaphor of the 'little platoon' to make connections between private family life and public representation. From the beginning of the nineteenth century a happy and correct family life comes to be regarded as an expression of Christian piety amongst Catholics and Protestants, and there is an increase in didactic literature giving advice on how to manage marriage and children. Of course, as Dympna McLoughlin and others have observed, 'there was a spectacular range of sexual relationships in nineteenth-century Ireland, thus challenging the stereotype of a country of exceptional chastity

1. Emily Lawless, *Grania: The Story of an Island* (London, 1892), p. 249. See Volume v, pp. 980–5.

825

and prudery'.[2] It is interesting therefore that representations of sexuality become more strikingly polarized between versions of the authentic Ireland as a realm of purity and versions which insist that the true Irish character is ribald and promiscuous.

The violent abductions which were so prominent in representations of eighteenth-century Ireland either changed in character or were believed to have changed in character into something closer to convenient fictions to permit elopements, when families disapproved of marriage. The legal process, like other forms of narrative, seems to have moved towards a more sentimental reading of victim status within family disputes, although this did not alter the fact that women were still massively discriminated against when it came to rights to property, residence, custody of children, or protection against violence from husbands and other male relatives.

Common sense tells us that the Famine made a huge difference to individuals' sense of autonomy, to the choices open to sufferers, survivors and witnesses in every aspect of their lives. Families and communities were destroyed. The contexts for sexual expression and reproduction were profoundly changed, at least in the short term. It has, however, been difficult to isolate themes such as sexuality and study the impact of famine on them. David Fitzpatrick has pointed out that since events overwhelmed procedures of systematic record keeping, it is almost impossible even to establish the relative mortality of men and women during the period, never mind examining more precise differences in famine experience. Nevertheless, extrapolating from exemplary local studies he has suggested that women and men experienced the Famine differently, and that the possibilities for survival among women were dependent on age and marital status, but that 'if women were indeed the victims of systematic discrimination during the Irish famine, the evidence in support of that hypothesis has yet to be assembled'.[3] The post-

Famine anxiety over prostitution and venereal disease was not peculiar to Ireland, but the widespread guilt and the terror of infection may take a particular inflection in the Irish context from the memory of the Famine. Representation of the Famine itself had been prepared for in the 1820s and 1830s by the expanding genre of rural tours and tales of the Irish peasantry, in which the observer's experience was often pitted against or in support of the narrative produced by the Poor Law Commission.

Emily Lawless, in *Grania* (1892), tackles a problem that haunts much nineteenth-century Irish fiction: how to present the apparently inarticulate masses without merely re-presenting the stereotypes associated with stage-Irishry, the brogue and the Irish Bull. In her heroine, Grania O'Malley, named for an almost mythical figure in Irish women's history,[4] Lawless creates a subjectivity whose complexities are indicated by sense, feeling and intuition rather than articulation, a woman isolated from her community by a superior sensibility which she has no words to explain, even to herself. Grania never succeeds in telling her lover about her dissatisfactions and desires. The drama of their conflict depends on an interplay between free indirect discourse and an omniscient narrator to suggest to the reader the meaning of Grania's social, sexual and spiritual frustrations.

Terry Eagleton writes that in nineteenth-century Ireland 'the sexual culture of the nation belonged to a complex economy of land and inheritance, property and procreation. As far as sexuality goes, we are speaking less of the erotic or psychological than of dowries and matchmakers.'[5] At one level Emily Lawless's novel would seem to concur with the view that Irish sexuality is so materially located as to exclude expressions of desire and sensuality, even to make such expressions seem absurd or insane. At another level the very posing of the question of how to articulate desire within the novel suggests that the social or anthropological model for recording Irish sexualities is inadequate to the lived experience of those sexualities. Eagleton's description of the sociological model is true to

2. D. McLoughlin, 'Women and Sexuality in Nineteenth-Century Ireland', *Irish Journal of Psychology*, vol. 15, nos. 2–3 (1994), pp. 266–75; excerpted in *The Irish Women's History Reader*, ed. Alan Hayes and Diane Urquhart (London, 2000), pp. 81–6.

3. David Fitzpatrick, 'Women and the Great Famine', in *Gender Perspectives in Nineteenth-Century Ireland: Public and Private Spheres* ed. Margaret Kelleher and James H. Murphy (Dublin: Irish Academic Press, 1997), pp. 50–69.

4. See Vol. v, pp. 20–1.

5. Terry Eagleton, *Heathcliff and the Great Hunger: Studies in Irish Culture* (London: Verso, 1995), p. 227.

one dominant discursive mode of constructing Irish sexualities, the sketches of Irish life that run through those texts of political economy, travel writing, fiction, memoirs and journalism that seemed to look to a British or American as well as an Irish audience. Many of these include a homage to the possibility of some form of self-representation by the masses in so far as they include documentation such as interviews or testimonies presented in court, to journalists, or to officials such as census takers or Poor Law Commissioners. The following pages illustrate in the work of writers such as James Greenwood, Christian Johnstone and W.H. Maxwell a variety of modes of representing Irish lives.

James Greenwood was an English journalist who came to Ireland in the 1860s to write an exposé of prostitution and depravation around the military camp at the Curragh for his brother's periodical, the *Pall Mall Gazette*. In the nineteenth century journalism evolves into a fully developed genre particularly interested in uncovering secrets, and therefore drawn to represent, if not discuss, unapproved modes of sexual expression. Newspapers are not only a source to tell us what happened, for example in the case of the emigrant women travelling to America on the *City of Mobile* in 1857 (see pp. 859–60), but can be interpreted as a discourse actively involved in the production of conservative and normative versions of appropriate female behaviour. The sensational reporting of sex crimes, for example, while sometimes apparently sympathetic to the victims, tends to reinforce the idea that the middle-class home is a woman's only safe haven, and that any form of female adventure will be punished.

In the latter half of the nineteenth century a self-proclaimed feminist analysis of Irish life emerges, one that is heavily influenced by the social purity movement as well as by its links with a spectrum of anti-Unionist movements. British feminists such as Josephine Butler and Annie Besant identify Ireland as a feminist issue. In fiction the dominant motifs are at first Gothic and sensational, but a genre of 'new-woman' novels, represented here by the work of Sarah Grand, emerges. Gothic and sensational novels are a significant source of 'information' about sexual desire and fantasy because novels have a special ability to incorporate conflicting discourses without necessarily reconciling them. The Gothic is also amenable to the development of a 'camp' stylistics, as demonstrated in the work of Irish writers from Charles Robert Maturin, through James Clarence Mangan, Bram Stoker and Oscar Wilde. Prostitution and disease become the focus of journalistic and bureaucratic investigations, and some of the most sensational early twentieth-century Irish novels such as Amanda M'Kittrick Ros's *Helen Huddleson* (posthumously published in 1969), *The Story of Mary Dunne* (1913) by M.E. Francis and *The Tragedy of Chris* (1903) by Rosa Mulholland (see pp. 1104–5) concern the White slave trade. In the autobiographical writings of William Carleton, George Egerton, W.B. Yeats and Katharine O'Shea Parnell, one can trace an interest in the possibility that an emerging vocabulary drawn from international sources on psychoanalysis and the rediscovery (as was believed) of indigenous Irish writings and belief in the Revival might lead towards new forms of subjectivity and new ways of being public and private sexual beings. After 1916 a new romance of nation would place new demands on constructions of Irish sexuality.

WILLIAM M. MEDLAND AND CHARLES WEOBLY

(*fl.* 1803)   (*fl.* 1803)

from:
A COLLECTION OF REMARKABLE AND INTERESTING CRIMINAL TRIALS, ACTIONS AT LAW, ETC. TO WHICH IS PREFIXED, AN ESSAY ON REPRIEVE AND PARDON AND BIOGRAPHICAL SKETCHES OF JOHN LORD ELDON, AND MR. MINGAY (1803)

[Records of civil and criminal cases not only provide evidence of sexual practices, but their popularity as reading material, both in newspapers and in collections, indicates some of the narrative forms in which sexual lives are cast. They suggest the boundaries of men's and women's expectations in sexual and romantic relations. Crime reporting was to be an important source in the development of melodramatic and sensational drama and fiction in the nineteenth century. Published in London: John Badcock, 1803: copy in the British Library.]

BREACH OF PROMISE OF MARRIAGE

Tried in the Court of King's Bench, Dublin, May 25, 1803.

Kelly Against Brennan

This cause was tried at Nisi Prius,[1] before Lord Kilwarden.[2]

It was the case of a Miss Jane Arabella Kelly, against a Mr. Brennan, of the Merchant's-quay, Dublin, to obtain damages, which were laid at 2000l. for breach of a contract of marriage.

Mr. CURRAN[3] for the plaintiff, exerted a great portion of his unrivalled powers to contrast the innocence and the misfortunes of the plaintiff, with the odious, cruel, and triumphant profligacy of the defendant, her seducer.

The principal evidence was Mrs. M'Garry, sister to the plaintiff, who keeps a boarding-house in Queen-Street; which, at the period when the declaration stated this transaction to have taken place, went under the denomination of a boarding school, as exhibited by a brass plate on the door, kept by Mrs. Kelly. The actual mistress, however, was Miss Kelly, who succeeded her sister in the department of teaching females, but who since, according to her own testimony, was privately married to M'Garry, her present husband. Her direct and cross-examination, in a material degree illustrated the private history of the plaintiff's family as well as her own. From the first part of her depositions it was collected that her father, a Mr. Hubert Kelly, was a gentleman of some respectability and consideration, about twenty years since, or upwards, in the county of Meath, from whence he removed: that her mother, after having borne eleven children, eight of whom were females, had died much about the time of his removal, or some short time previous, to the King's county.[4] Though in habits of genteel life, and associating with the first company in the King's county, after his removal there, it would appear that his circumstances were not altogether affluent, as his daughter, Miss K. who died unmarried, had sought her bread in Dublin, in the character of a schoolmistress, in Queen-street, in the house where Mrs. M'G. after her decease, had succeeded her in the same capacity. It appeared by subsequent evidence that Mr. K. the father, had, after his emancipation from the trammels of matrimony, dedicated a great portion of his time and attention to amorous pursuits, and had actually, at an advanced period of life, kept a concubine, by whom he had children, in the same house with the plaintiff and her sister M'Garry.

---

1. 'The second statute of Westminster (1285) instituted judges of *nisi prius*, who were appointed to travel through the shires three times a year to hear civil causes' (*Brewer's Dictionary of Phrase and Fable*).
2. Arthur Wolfe (1739–1803); created Baron Kilwarden of Newlands (1798), 1st Viscount Kilwarden (1800); Attorney General and Irish privy councillor, 1789; Chief Justice of King's Bench, 1798; killed by rebels during the Emmet insurrection.
3. John Philpot Curran (1750–1817); called to the Irish Bar, 1775, Master of the Irish Rolls and privy councillor, 1806–14.
4. Nineteenth-century name for County Laois.

He had afterwards, it appeared, in the 75th year of his age, married a girl of the age of 20. The plaintiff, some time in the year 1801, came to visit her sister, Mrs. M'Garry, and remained with her for some time at her boarding school or house, in Queen-street, where gentlemen as well as ladies were, with equal complaisance and hospitality, entertained.

The plaintiff, on coming to her sister's house, met the defendant, who was a boarder there. After four days acquaintance, and dining at the common table, Mrs. M'Garry perceived such attentions from the defendant to her sister, the plaintiff, as induced her to suppose that he had no less than honourable views of matrimony towards her. The acquaintance and mutual attention of the parties to each other increased, and became more conspicuous in the course of a few months, a circumstance which at length induced Mrs. M'Garry to interrogate the plaintiff as to any declarations or proposals of matrimony, which she conceived it probable the defendant must have made her. Explanations on the subject succeeded, and Mrs. M'Garry swore positively to a formal promise, in three several instances, which the defendant had made, to marry the plaintiff; in one of which overtures of matrimony directly came from him, and the lady's reply was, that she had a father to consult. On this the defendant rejoined, that he would accompany her to her father's in the country, to ask his consent. During this negotiation however, the plaintiff became pregnant, as appeared by her communication to the defendant from her father's house in the country to which she retired but whither, after certain plausible excuses, the defendant declined to accompany her. The defendant's answer to this letter, which was read in court, occasioned a remark from Mr. Plunket,[5] that it was an heterogeneous compound of philosophy, vulgarity, sentiment, and duplicity. It set out with violent protestations of unceasing love and fidelity, hoping it was only her fears, her inexperience, and timidity, which caused apprehensions in her mind of consequences, which, under a variety of circumstances, must be distressing to him, consequently, which, in the transports he felt in her society, he did not find time to reflect on or anticipate: but, let the event be what it may, she might rely on his honour, his fidelity, and protection; at the same time, advising her, if her fears should be realized, and that she could ascertain the fact she apprehended, to make some excuse to come to town to her sister M'Garry, of whom, if all other expedients failed, it would be necessary to make a confidant. He attributed the commencement of a long projected reformation to her influence — he was no longer the gay, the gallant, and rattling Brennan, but a sober, melancholy man of business, and he would say, of sense, if modesty would permit him. Another fond letter or two succeeded, after arrangements had been made for the lady's secret *accouchement*,[6] under the management of her sister M'Garry; but previous to that event, love and sentiment seemed to have subsided. In one, or two subsequent letters, written to Mrs. M'Garry, he talked with all the method of a man of business, of sending the unfortunate young woman's child to the poor-house, being, he said, the proper receptacle for the illegitimate offspring of an unnatural mother.

The defendant, by his counsel, Serjeant Moore and Mr. Barrington,[7] set up his youth against the plaintiff, who, only on the testimony of one witness, appeared to be a few years older than he, alledging that she was the seducer, in concert with her sister M'Garry, whose character was attacked on the circumstance of her appearing pregnant at the same time with her sister, neither avowing marriage. On Mrs. M'Garry's testimony, however, it appeared, that at the time of her pregnancy, she had been privately married to her husband, and that family reasons compelled them to keep the marriage secret.

There are few cases on record where it was acknowledged by the Bench that greater ingenuity had been displayed by counsel on both sides; and his Lordship confessed that he felt his mind enlarged by many observations advanced at the bar.

Lord KILWARDEN, in his usual style of dispassionate perspicuity, charged the jury, who returned a verdict of 1000l. damages, and 6d. costs.

---

5. William Conygham Plunket (1764–1854); 1st Baron Plunket (1827), lawyer and politician, called to the Irish Bar 1787, Solicitor General from 1803.

6. Confinement.

7. Jonah Barrington (1760–1834); lawyer and writer, called to the Irish Bar 1788, knighted 1807.

THE TRIAL OF JAMES MURPHY, LATE OF PATRICK-STREET, DUBLIN. FOR CRUELLY ASSAULTING, IMPRISONING, AND STARVING HIS WIFE. AT THE DUBLIN SESSIONS, FEB. 21, 1803

A number of witnesses were examined on behalf of the prosecutrix, who generally deposed to her exemplary conduct, and the brutality of Mr. Murphy. Facts were sworn to, which would almost stagger belief, and which, for the sake of humanity, is sincerely to be wished had not been substantiated. An infant child, which the mother's miserable condition deprived of proper sustenance, died a few months before; and its wretched parent, oppressed by hunger, blows, and imprecations, was driven for redress to the Justice of her country.

By the evidence of the unfortunate Prosecutrix, corroborated by several of the most respectable witnesses, it appeared, that about two years ago she married the defendant, who keeps a porter-house,[1] in Patrick-street, Dublin, and brought him a portion of near 200l.: that a few days after their marriage they went to live at Lucan,[2] where they remained eleven months; that there, although permitted to dine at the table, she was treated with the utmost cruelty, frequently horse-whipped, once for stealing a morsel of chicken she longed for (being with child), which the defendant having discovered, brought a whip to the table the next day, at dinner, and horse-whipped her for the theft: at another time, for presuming to put her hand to a dish to chuse a good potatoe, his mother cut her in the elbow with a knife; and, at another time, for a like offence, she received a gash on one of her fingers, from her husband — the marks of both which she exhibited to the jury — They next removed to Mr. Andrews's in the Circular Road, where they lodged about a month: the family consisted of his mother, two young ladies, his sisters, a young gentleman, his brother, and his wife. Here the unhappy woman must have been great with child, for the lodgings were taken in June, and by the testimony of Miss Murphy, his sister, she was delivered on the 8th of August; yet, her *tender* mother, and her *affectionate* sisters-in-law, in the most taunting manner, made her scour[3] tubs, and carry to their apartments, up stairs, all the water they wanted for domestic use, although at this time, besides being so far advanced in her pregnancy, as to render it dangerous to carry such loads, she must have been extremely weak, for want of food. She was not only driven to the necessity of picking crumbs off a dunghill,[4] where Mr. Andrews's table-cloth had been shaken, but deprived the pigs, &c. in the farm-yard, of part of their food, by eating potatoes, which she took out of their trough; and, after Mr. Andrews's family had dined, she had put into her pocket, from his kitchen, the leaves of cauliflowers, and other offals,[5] that came from his table, to sustain life. It also appeared, that Mrs. Andrews and her maid had often given her food, when she complained of being hungry; but these were her halcyon days of wedlock! She was next removed to the porter-house, in Patrick-street; there she was confined to a closet,[6] in a back garret, where she was delivered. Until she recovered, after lying-in, she had a feather-bed, but then it was changed for a flock-bed,[7] and a pair of blankets, without a sheet, bolster, or pillow, or any other furniture, except an old chair and a box: she was even refused, although she frequently besought, a *certain utensil* peculiarly necessary for a bed-room.[8] In this apartment she nursed her child for six months. Her food, during that time, was, for breakfast, a thin slice of a sixpenny loaf, and water and sugar, without any flavour of tea; for dinner, the refuse of potatoes, with water to drink, but never at any time was she allowed sufficient to satisfy her hunger. Her child's allowance of bread and milk was equally scanty, for she was obliged to warm her own cold potatoes in her mouth to feed her infant. In this situation she remained for six months, in all which time, and during the whole winter, she had neither fire nor candle-light: she was obliged to wash for herself and her child, and her mode of drying her cloaths, was by hanging them on a line in her closet, and at the end of two days, she took the child's cloaths into bed, and

1. A house at which porter and other malt liquors are sold.
2. Spa town in the Liffey valley, west of Dublin.
3. To clean by hard rubbing.
4. A heap of refuse.
5. Refuse.
6. Small room.
7. Bed stuffed with coarse tufts and refuse of wool, cotton and other fabrics.
8. Chamber-pot.

completely dried them with the heat of her own body. She was ordered, by the women who attended her in her lying-in, to have some wine in her gruel,[9] but she never received any; and in place of gruel, they gave a sort of slop.[10] There were a few dozens of wine in an open room next to her closet, out of which she once stole a bottle, which she believed saved her life. At three months after her delivery, she lost all appearance of suck: her difficulty then encreased, to sustain either her own or her child's life; but on the 8th of February, past, the Almighty was pleased to take the latter to a better world; and on the 11th she was rescued from the gripe of death by her friends.

Sir HENRY JEBB, M.D. sworn. — He was called upon about a fortnight ago to visit the prosecutrix. — He perceived a scurf[11] upon her skin, and a kind of downy hair, that generally proceeds from famine; but, never having seen her before, he could not then positively determine; however, from her appearance this day, and the progress she has made in her flesh, and otherwise, he has not a doubt of the fact.

Mrs. ANDREWS, and her maid, corroborated the testimony of Mrs. Murphy, respecting her receiving, on asking for it, food for them at Sally Park. The maid proved that she saw the prosecutrix take a leaf from a cauliflower, and put it in her pocket, and pick some potatoes out of the water that had been boiled for pigs, which she also secreted and carried to her apartment.

Mr. BARRINGTON made an able defence for the defendant: a number of witnesses were produced, amongst whom, were a Mr. Byrne of Francis-street, woollen-draper; Miss Margaret Murphy, one of his sisters; a young gentleman, his brother; and Edward Swan, who lived with the defendant fourteen years. These witnesses flatly contradicted the whole of the evidence for the Crown. The chief object of the defence was, to prove the prosecutrix a drunkard, a thief, and other-wise improper in her conduct; in support of which Mr. Byrne swore he considered her a drunken woman, and in the habit of drinking spirits; but on the cross-examination he said, he never saw her drink spirits but once, which was a few days after her marriage, in a large company of most respectable persons, whose names he declined to mention, except Margaret Murphy's, and a gentleman then in court; he, himself, helped her to spirits, and to wine; though he helped her to spirits, he was her husband's particular friend, and her husband was present; her husband kept a hospitable house, gave plenty of wine, punch, and the best dinners he ever sat down to, that he often declined invitations from men of the first consequence about Lucan, to dine with Mr. Murphy, the traverser![12] He met the prosecutrix soon after her marriage, at her own door, about six o'clock in the morn., as he and two other gentlemen were going to shoot grouse: she looked so mean and dirty, that his friends were surprised at his having such an acquaintance; and, they talked so much about her appearance, that he quarrelled with them, and quitted their society; he returned, however, that morning, to her house, where he breakfasted and, at eleven o'clock, accompanied her to mass, returned, dined, and spent the whole day with her and her husband. In support of the charge of other crimes, he said she accompanied him, and one of the young ladies, her sister-in-law, twice to the parade in Lucan.

MARGARET MURPHY swore, that three months before the child died, the mother told her she would 'put it out of the way', and from thence she was fully convinced she intended to murder it. The day after she was married she shewed the witness her legs, all broke out with scurvy; and she had a desperate scurvy all over her body; she had the itch,[13] and her brother told her that was the reason he would not sleep with her at all, as she gave him the itch; she would not be allowed to go down stairs to the shop, as she had been detected stealing wine and spirits out of the cellar; she saw her stealing the spirits. On her cross-examination, she admitted, that although she, her mother and family, intended to murder her child, and although they knew her blood was so corrupted with scurvy that she was the most

---

9. A light, liquid food, oatmeal-based, but often including other ingredients, suitable for invalids.
10. Refuse liquid, including tea and coffee rinsings, and dishwater.
11. Incrustation.

12. One who denies a plea in court.
13. Scabies, a contagious skin disease.

unfit person in the world to nurse the child yet they not only allowed her to do it, but to keep it every night in the closet. She saw her once drink spirits; a large teacup full she gave her to rub her leg, she drank in her presence. She stole wine, for sure she found two empty bottles sewed up in the bed she lay on; to be sure she knew them by the marks on the sides, although she did not read the letters on them; her sister-in-law had the command of the house, so far as eating when she chose; but what had she to do with any thing else when her mother managed the business? Sure she had no right to interfere, where she could not hem a pocket-handkerchief for her husband; her sister-in-law would eat more than any man in the kingdom; she ate ten times every day! If her brother was convicted, and if it appeared she and her family were implicated in a conspiracy against his wife, she would not think it an imputation on her character; her brother was distracted when he saw the child dying, for he threw his hat about the floor.

Mr. MURPHY, brother to the defendant swore, that the mark of the cut of a knife on her elbow was the consequence of a fall, in his presence, soon after she was married; that she charged him at the time not to tell her husband, as she knew he would beat her. He never saw him strike her but once, and that was only a slap on her cheek.

EDWARD SWAN supported the whole of the evidence in the defence, adding, that the prosecutrix had always fire in her room. On his cross-examination, he said, he had no call to go into her room; but that he knew there was always fire in it, because he saw fire there on the night of the child's wake (burial).

Mr. M'NALLY asked him if he had heard all the witnesses give their testimony? He replied in the affirmative. He asked, 'Was not every word they swore false?' He replied 'It was.' — Swan also said, that on the night of the wake, the prosecutrix told him she was glad the child was dead, as she had then her liberty to go out when and where she pleased. The learned Judge, Johnson, summed up the evidence in a speech of considerable length and ability, remarking severely the unexampled perjuries on the trial. — 'In all my life, (he said), while at the bar, and since I have been on the bench, I never witnessed such shocking perjury as has appeared on this trial; although the Noble Lord who sits by me (Lord Kilwarden) and I presided at a trial, where such perjury was discovered, as we imagined never before was exhibited in this world.' The learned Judge also observed that a number of witnesses were examined on both sides: that they flatly contradicted each other; and it was for the Jury to determine between them.

The Jury in about forty minutes returned a verdict — *Guilty*, and the prisoner was instantly taken in charge by the Keeper of the Kilmainham gaol.

At the following sitting of the Court he was sentenced to be imprisoned two years, and fined 100l. Mr. M'Nally, as Counsel for the prosecutrix, addressed the Court, saying, that the unfortunate man confessed his crime, in its extent, and proposed making a settlement on his wife, if he was enabled so to do, by a remission of the fine, and a mitigation of a part of the punishment. The Court, replied that they would not entertain the subject until they were satisfied that a settlement was properly secured. It would then be time enough to take the matter into consideration. The unhappy man has written several letters to the friends of his wife, wherein he confesses his guilt, and offers every atonement in his power; he is willing to make her ample recompense, for all that is past, by taking a house for them both, and going into business, without having any thing more to do with any of his family, who (he says) brought all this miserable business on him.

ELIZABETH HAM

(1783–after 1852)

from:
ELIZABETH HAM BY
HERSELF, 1783–1820 (1945)

[Elizabeth Ham, like Dorothea Herbert, offers a record of middle-class rural Protestant life at the turn of the nineteenth century. Both diarists emphasize how boring rural life often seemed to women, and mention cross-dressing and practical jokes as one form of release. Ham's autobiography was edited and published by Eric Gillet in 1945. Gillet claims to have cut over 50,000 words from the text and to have searched for further evidence of Ham's life after 1820. He does not, however, reveal the source of his text — whether manuscript or printed copy — and I have been unable to trace any record of an earlier edition. This excerpt is taken from Gillet's edition published in London by Faber and Faber, 1945.]

Several Carlow people called on me, but I never took to any of them as I did to the Burrowses.[1] I might have learnt a lesson from my friend Ann, who owed a great deal of her popularity by being 'all things to all men'.[2] Among those with whom I might have been intimate had I so chosen, was the wife of a D.D., whose name I forget, and her sister Lucy Madden.[3] I was told an anecdote of this last which impressed her name on my memory. She was on a visit at the house of a friend, and among other guests was a certain Dr. Robinson of Tullow. There was a fair held in the neighbourhood to which they all repaired. The Ladies got home before Dr. Robinson and his man, who were on horseback. Lucy Madden and another girl thought it would be a good joke to waylay and rob the pair. They immediately disguised themselves in man's attire and armed with a brace of pistols hastened to conceal themselves in a place they were to pass. As soon as the men came up they both rushed out. Lucy Madden seized the bridle of the doctor's horse and presenting her pistol demanded his money.

'Oh, you wicked man!' began the Doctor, 'to rob a Divine! Don't you know me? I am Doctor Robinson of Tullow.' — 'And who the Devil cares for Doctor Robinson of Tullow! — your money or your life,' was the reply. Whilst they were engaged with his master, the man attempted to slip off, but was stopped by the other girl, who demanded *his* money. He began to beg for mercy, declaring that he was but a poor servant and hadn't a farthing in his pocket. 'You lie! you rascal,' said she, 'where is the five and eightpence you got in change with your new hat?' The money was given up, and the two girls with their booty, by means of a short cut, got home before them.

Dire was the tale of the highway robbery told by Dr. Robinson and his man, and they only waited to relate it before proceeding to lay an information before a magistrate. As nothing could persuade them to delay their intentions, it was necessary to inform the Doctor of the real state of the case. Nothing could exceed his rage; and it was weeks before he could be persuaded to give up his purpose of prosecuting them.

---

1. Mother and sisters of the Dublin Whig lawyer, Peter Burrowes (1753–1841).
2. Corinthians 9:22.
3. A relation of Samuel Madden, see p. 823.

AMELIA BRISTOW

(*fl.* 1810)

from:

THE MANIAC, A TALE; OR, A VIEW OF BETHLEM HOSPITAL: AND THE MERITS OF WOMEN, A POEM FROM THE FRENCH: WITH POETICAL PIECES ON VARIOUS SUBJECTS, ORIGINAL AND TRANSLATED (1810)

[Following the United Irishmen's Rising in 1798, a number of writers, chiefly loyalist, attempted to represent in a variety of genres what impact the rebellion had had not only in terms of the things that had been seen and experienced, but the fears that had been activated and that continued to haunt Ireland for many years. Amelia Bristow's narrative poem, 'The Maniac', begins with a prospect of a lunatic asylum and then goes on to explain how one of the inmates is a victim of the horrors of the rising. Whereas many of the loyalist women in the southern counties such as Wicklow and Wexford write about their alienation from and fear of their neighbours and servants, for Bristow — a northern Protestant — it is the internecine aspect of the conflict that is most terrifying. She attempts some distancing strategies, such as the deployment of names from Gothic fiction, and there is none of the local detail to be found in the witness statements, but she shares the common loyalist perspective that the rebellion (to which she is more sympathetic than many of her contemporaries) has fractured the organic relationship between 'family' and 'nation'.

The poem narrates the history of two childhood friends, Bernardo and Albert, Protestants living in the North of Ireland. When Bernardo marries Albert's sister, Emma, and Albert marries Matilda and each couple has a young family, they seem fixed in a happy prosperous existence. But Bernardo is an idealist who becomes involved with the United Irishmen. Published in London, by J. Hatchard, 1810. Copy in the National Library of Ireland.]

from: The Maniac, A Tale; or, A View of Bethlem Hospital

Now had Sedition, with her horrid brand,
Spread wide her baleful influence through the
 land:
In public, bade her mobs tumultuous rise;
In private, broke through Nature's dearest ties:
And, whilst mock patriotism brawled aloud,
Infus'd her venom through the insensate crowd.
 Bernardo's ardent soul with virtue glowed;
But, wrong directed, wide mistook her road.
Whilst Faction fierce declaimed, he caught the
 flame
Of *glorious Freedom*! prostituted name!
Nor deemed he that, beneath the insidious fire,
Lurked anarchy, foul rapine, murder dire!
Nor deemed he that the hackney'd word, *reform*,
Meant revolution's fiercest, deadliest storm.
From principle he acted; nor conceived
Th'enlighten'd mind could deviate; nor believed
Infernal passions could deform a plan,
Which seemed to him the noblest work of man.
To free a nation from oppression's yoke!
'Twas thus his generous indignation spoke.
Firmness, he hoped, might gain the wished
 redress;
And link all parties in the bond of peace.
But step by step led on, he left the shore
Of Moderation, which he touched no more;
Borne by the torrent meanest souls among,
His part once taken, to the cause he clung.
 So, when the whirlwind sweeps o'er regions
 vast,
Relentless Havoc rides upon the blast:
Its fury whelms, in one great sacrifice,
The hallowed temple and the den of vice;
The gorgeous palace, erst so proud which
 shewed,
Levels with squalid Penury's abode.
Awful memento to the human soul,
Its elements, fierce passions to control.
The rock-based fabric, sole, repels the shock:
True principle is 'founded as the rock.'
 Albert, with grief, beheld this first of friends,
A dupe to demagogues, and their base ends.
With oft renewed remonstrances, he tried

To win his reason to the better side.
That soothing eloquence which once could
   charm
His fiery passions, and their rage disarm,
Had now no influence; nothing could obtain:
With party spirit argument is vain!
Bernardo, grateful, felt his friend's warm zeal;
Still loved his brother, but his country's weal,
To his enthusiasm, soared far above
Ev'n sacred friendship, or fraternal love.
Albert, thus baffled, sighed; each hope resigned,
To move his friend's unalterable mind;
And lest suspicion should involve his name,
Was forced to shun whom he was forced to
   blame.
   With mental anguish, and with health
      impaired,
A brother, too, estranged, th'emotion shared,
The gentle Emma drooped, oppressed with
   grief.
Bernardo, now proclaimed a rebel chief;
Pursued by justice, driven from his blest home,
To skulk in caverns; or by night to roam,
With vile banditti, whom his soul despised:
Her feeling heart was torn, was agonized!
But when short intervals the chief restored
To her fond bosom, whom he still adored,
Her sweetness soothed his agitated breast,
She smoothed her brow, and every pang
   suppressed.
Their young Bernardo, too, with cherub smile,
His doating father's troubles would beguile.
   Now all the loyal youth were roused to arms,
And called, where danger loudest spread
   alarms.
Though no commotions, yet, the place had felt,
Where he and happiness so long had dwelt,
Albert, whose active spirit scorned repose,
His country thus rent by intestine foes,
Assumed the martial character; prepared
To join her standard, and her freedom guard.
A summons now, to a more distant scene,
Though prompt obeyed, called forth sensations
   keen.
To leave whom his fond soul adored — his wife!
The bliss and partner of his happy life!
How did the hours, with her in transport
   passed,
Those now to separation doomed, contrast!
For her pangs, too, his manly bosom swelled,
But duty called, and each fond thought repelled.

Matilda, too, from all complaint forbore;
She loved her Albert! but his honour more.[1]
She bade him go; whilst sorrow's starting tear,
And painful throb, spoke him — how fondly
   dear!
He cheered her spirits, clasped her to his breast;
Blessed his sweet babes; and flew where danger
   pressed.
   To Wicklow's plains his martial troop he led:
In Wicklow the first hostile blood was shed:
The contest there was short; 'midst guilt's
   alarms,
Whole dastard thousands soon laid down their
   arms.
Their leaders yielded up, their terms of grace:
By treachery's crime, rebellion's to efface!
Amongst the rest, Bernardo was resigned;
Betrayed by those to whom his sanguine mind
Had vowed to give, (or perish in the strife!)
Sweet liberty, that brightest gem of life!
   By summary justice, (so required the times,)
Their doom was fixed — death — to atone their
   crimes.
Unmoved, Bernardo saw the impending stroke;
His dauntless spirit by mean fears unbroke:
His soaring mind looked down on death and
   pain,
As what required no effort to sustain.
One sole emotion could the calm destroy;
His angel Emma's pangs, his darling boy!
His friend, his brother too! each tender tie
Rushed on his heart, else, well prepared to die!
But, short-lived is the pang his bosom rends;
An ignominious death the conflict ends:
His life, thus risked in foul rebellion's cause,
Fell forfeit to his country's outraged laws.
   Albert saw all with agonizing pain;
But interference was, he knew, in vain . . .

[Albert goes to his sister Emma to offer her comfort, but
she dies of grief, leaving her small son in his care. Albert
then decides to return home to live a life of domestic
retirement.]

The sight of home attained, his bosom glows
With all the ecstasy sweet hope bestows:
The precious objects of his love so near!
By absence rendered still more fondly dear.

1. Allusion to 'To Lucasta, Going to the Warres' by Richard Lovelace
(1618–1657).

His gates thrown wide, now met his wondering
    eye.
His heart beat quick — he feared — he knew
    not why.
No prompt domestics there, as wont, to meet
His wished return, and their loved master greet.
Proceeding onward, he began to trace
Marks of rude havoc nature's charms deface:
Approached his house, he saw a ruin frown;
Each window shattered and each door torn down:
His precious moveables all broken, strewed
The spacious grounds, and party rancour shewed.
But, of what import this? — not worth a thought!
Not these the objects his affections sought.
Where were his wife, his children? Heavenly
    Powers!
What cloud portentous o'er his fate now lours
    [*sic*]!
The attendant, who had reached the unhinged
    door,
Cried, 'Oh! my master!' but could add no more.
Each pulse wild throbbing, Albert darted
    through
The yawning entrance; there — soul-blasting
    view!
His beauteous infants, on the ensanguined
    ground,
Lay, sunk in death! deep pierced with many a
    wound!
A little farther on — racks, tortures, wheels!
Are bliss, are paradise, to what he feels!
Of ruffian violence the bleeding prey,
His soul's rich treasure, his Matilda lay!
Life's ebbing tide now nigh exhausted quite;
And her pure soul just winged to take its flight.
    'Matilda! oh! my love, my life!' he cried.
She raised a languid hand, looked up, and died!
Transfixed with horror, rooted to the ground!
The woe-struck Albert wildly glared around:
Then stooping, bent, as if intent to hear
The dulcet sounds that wont to charm his ear.

But all was hushed! no dulcet sounds no flow,
To charm his year [*sic*], or sooth his mighty
    woe!
Whilst deepest torturing pangs his heart assail,
The powers of memory begin to fail.
Fantastic forms thick crowd his maddening
    brain;
And reason fled, ne'er to return again.
    Loud frantic laughter spoke his o'er thrown
      mind.
Then, starting sudden, fleeter than the wind,
He flew those scenes, unknowing where he flew!
Each object flits before his vacant view:
In lifeless torpor each idea chained;
His mind a vacuum, no past trace retained.
But when short gleams of recollection brought
A retrospective view, a grief-winged thought,
Rage, torture, frenzy! all expression's vain,
To speak the whirling tumult of his brain!
His sorrowing friends each application tried
That skill could dictate and affection guide,
To heal his mind, lost reason to restore: —
In vain! the fugitive returned no more!
His malady, on which no new hope gleamed,
'*Incurable* and *dangerous*' was deemed:
And that lone cell received a wretch forlorn,
To brightest hopes and happiest prospects
    born . . .

[At the end of the poem Bristow has a coda in prose.]

Unfortunately, there is not much of exaggeration in this melancholy tale. Instances of insanity, from distress of mind, occurred during the late unhappy rebellion in Ireland: and scenes similar to that here represented, as having occasioned that catastrophe, were, alas, but too frequent, where activity opposed the popular ferment. The writer has only blended circumstances; scarcely heightened any.

MARIA EDGEWORTH

(1768–1849)

from:
MEMOIRS OF RICHARD LOVELL EDGEWORTH ESQ., BEGUN BY HIMSELF AND CONCLUDED BY HIS DAUGHTER MARIA EDGEWORTH (1820)

[Maria Edgeworth's account of her father's fourth marriage is an intimate account of a common phenomenon. With so many women dying in pregnancy and childbirth, or from the consequences of childbearing, a prosperous man such as Edgeworth might be widowed several times. The children of earlier marriages might reasonably fear the power of a stepmother, while the new wife could be intimidated both by comparison with her dead predecessor and by established family relations. Edgeworth presents her father's marriage as a romantic union, but one which also has a direct impact on many other lives. Moreover, she situates the marriage in the context of the 1798 disturbances, contrasting her father's chosen and essentially egalitarian union with the prospective Act of Union, which he had determined to oppose. Published in London in 1820 by R. Hunter, this extract is taken from a copy held in the British Library.]

My father was past fifty, when he was left a third time a widower, with a numerous family, by different wives: four sons and five daughters living with him; some of them grown up, others very young — the youngest but three years old — two of the daughters fourteen and sixteen, just at the age when a mother's care is of most importance. Besides his children, two sisters of the late Mrs. Edgeworth[1] had resided with us for several years. Though these had friends and near connexions in England, for whom they felt high esteem, they had remained in Ireland with us, and they formed part of this large family, attached to them by ties of kindred, and by feelings of gratitude and esteem. Those who knew him intimately, and all indeed who had

seen how much the felicity of his former life had depended upon conjugal affection, were aware, that he would not be happy unless he married again.

The life of every man, as it has well been observed, 'is a continual chain of incidents, each link of which hangs upon the former'. Even where no striking incidents appear, the chain of causation may often be traced to some habit, passion, or taste, of the individual; it is curious to observe how differently the fates of men are decided, some by the occurrence of accidental circumstances, others by internal causes, constantly recurring in their mind, and belonging to their characters: those governed by the will of others, these by their own decision.

After the first years of youth, my father's destiny in life was never decided by what is called accident; nor was he drawn against his better judgment by the persuasion of others. His own principles, his sense of duty, and the conviction of his understanding, appear to have determined constantly his course of life; his discrimination of character, and his tastes for literature and science, uniformly directed him in the choice of his friends; these, and not accident, led to his forming those nearer and dearer connexions, on which his uncommon domestic happiness depended.

In his own narrative, he has shewn how much his destiny was influenced by his predominant taste for mechanics, which introduced him to Dr. Darwin,[2] led him to Lichfield, and to his acquaintance with Miss Seward,[3] and with Honora Sneyd.[4] The same tastes, still prevailing, prepared and influenced in a similar manner his choice in another connexion, and decided his fate at a much later period of life.

1. Elizabeth (née Sneyd) (1753–1797).

2. Erasmus Darwin (1731–1802); physician, radical, freethinker and inventor. Edgeworth first sought him out at his home in Lichfield in Staffordshire, on account of an ingenious carriage Darwin had invented.
3. Anna Seward (1747–1809); poet and resident of Lichfield, Staffordshire. After the death of her sister in 1764, Seward's parents adopted Honora Sneyd, who, in 1773, became Richard Lovell Edgeworth's second wife.
4. See note 3.

Many years previous to this time, in the summer of 1774, when he was just married to Miss Honora Sneyd, in the bridal visit which they paid at Black Castle to my father's favourite sister, Mrs. Ruxton,[5] they met at her house Dr. Beaufort,[6] his wife, and daughter. Dr Beaufort's name is well known to the British public as the author of our best map of Ireland, and most valuable Memoir on the Topography, and Civil and Ecclesiastical State of this country. He is still better known in Ireland as an excellent clergyman, of a liberal spirit and conciliating manners, and as a man of taste and literature. My father was much pleased with him, and desired to cultivate his acquaintance. The daughter, who was with Dr. Beaufort on this visit, was a little child of six years old, in a white frock and pink sash: her image was fixed in my father's recollection by a question that occurred, whether her mother did or did not spoil her? He could little foresee how much influence this child was to have, years afterwards, on his happiness.

Dr. Beaufort and his family went to reside in England, and my father never saw him for many years. In 1785 their acquaintance was again renewed by meeting at the Royal Irish Academy, and at the house of Dr. Usher[7] (Professor of Astronomy to the University of Dublin). Dr. Beaufort had received from Edmund Burke[8] a commission to procure the skeleton of a moose deer; the bones of these deer were to be found in a lake near Edgeworth-Town,[9] and my father undertook the commission for the Doctor. This led to a slight correspondence, advancing their intimacy a degree or two. A year afterward Dr. Beaufort, in a progress through Ireland, to collect materials for his civil and ecclesiastical map, paid us a visit of a few days at Edgeworth-Town; but for subsequent years, living at a distance, we saw nothing of him. Meantime, Dr. Beaufort's little daughter grew up. My father's sister, Mrs. Ruxton, whose intimacy with the Beaufort family continued, was particularly fond of Miss Beaufort, and often spoke of her to us as a friend and companion peculiarly suited to her taste; still we never met. The acquaintance was renewed, when my father went to see his friend Mr. Foster,[10] at Collon, of which place Dr. Beaufort was vicar.

It happened that Miss Beaufort, who possessed uncommon talents for drawing, had, at the request of my aunt Ruxton, sketched some designs for 'The Parent's Assistant,'[11] which were shewn to my father, and which he criticised as freely, as though they had not been the work of a lady, and designed for his daughter. He was charmed with the temper and good sense, with which these criticisms were received. But this impression, however favourable, was but slight. They were again separated, and it was not till some time afterwards, when in a visit, which she, with her family, paid at Edgeworth-Town in 1798, my father had an opportunity of discerning, that she possessed exactly the temper, abilities, and disposition, which would ensure the happiness of his family as well as his own, if he could hope to win her affections.

The marked approbation of a man of distinguished abilities could not but be gratifying to the object of his attention. She had conversed with him with perfect freedom, admiring the various knowledge and genius, which appeared in his conversation; attentive to all that could improve her own understanding, or assist her taste for literature; listening to his counsels as to those of a friend, but obviously without a thought of him as a lover. The difference of their age prevented her suspecting his attachment, till a few hours before it was declared. The thought of his large family, more than any disparity of age, was the first and great objection. My father's estate, though considerable, was not sufficient to afford any settlement, that could have been a temptation in the Smithfield-bargain way of estimating things. If the lady's parents had not been far above such views, they could scarcely have been justified in advising the connexion. They neither pressed nor dissuaded, but left their daughter entirely to her own judgment and inclinations. When I first knew of this attachment, and before I was well acquainted with Miss

5. Margaret Ruxton.
6. Daniel Augustus Beaufort (1739–1829); Irish geographer, whose map of Ireland was published in 1792.
7. Henry Ussher (d. 1790). In 1783 he became the first Andrews Professor of Anatomy at the University of Dublin.
8. Edmund Burke (1729–97); politician and political philosopher.
9. The Edgeworth family home in County Longford.
10. John Foster (1740–1828); last Speaker of the Irish House of Commons.
11. *The Parent's Assistant* (2nd ed., 1800).

Beaufort, I own that I did not wish for the marriage. I had not my father's quick penetration into character; I did not at first see the superior abilities, or qualities, which he discovered; nor did I anticipate any of the happy consequences from this union, which he foresaw. All that I thought, I told him. With the most kind patience he bore with me, and instead of withdrawing his affection, honoured me the more with his confidence. He took me with him to Collon, threw open his whole mind to me — let me see all the changings and workings of his heart. I remember his once saying to me, 'I believe, that no human creature ever saw the heart of another more completely without disguise, than you have seen mine.' I can never, without the strongest emotions of affection and gratitude, recollect the infinite kindness he shewed me at this time, the solicitude he felt for my happiness at the moment when all his own was at stake, and while all his feelings were in the agony of suspense; the consequence was, that no daughter ever felt more sympathy with a father, than I felt for him; and assuredly the pains he took to make me fully acquainted with the character of the woman he loved, and to make mine known to her, were not thrown away. Both her inclination and judgment decided in his favor. His eloquent affection conquering her timidity, and inspiring her with the necessary and just confidence in her own abilities, she consented to undertake the great responsibility of becoming the mistress of that large family, of whose happiness she was now to take charge . . .

While my father's domestic happiness seemed preparing so smoothly, public affairs in Ireland wore a stormy aspect. This was in the year 1798 . . . [W]e heard, that a conspiracy had been discovered in Dublin, that the city was under arms, and its inhabitants in the greatest terror. Doctor Beaufort and his family were there. My father, who was at Edgeworth-Town, set out immediately to join them. On his way he met an intimate friend of his; one stage they travelled together, and a singular conversation passed. This friend, who as yet knew nothing of my father's intentions, began to speak, of the marriage of some other person, and to exclaim against the folly and imprudence of any man's marrying in such disturbed times, 'no man of honor, sense, or feeling would incumber himself

with a wife at such a time!' — My father urged, that this was just the time, when a man of honor, sense, and feeling, would wish, if he loved a woman, to unite his fate with hers, and to acquire the right of being her protector.

The conversation dropped there. But presently they talked of public affairs — of the important measure expected to be proposed of a union between England and Ireland — of what would probably be said and done in the next session of Parliament; my father, foreseeing that this important national question would probably come on, had just obtained a seat in Parliament.[12] His friend, not knowing or recollecting this, began to speak of the imprudence of commencing a political career late in life.

'No man, you know,' said he, 'but a fool, would venture to make a first speech in Parliament, or to marry, after he was fifty.'

My father laughed, and surrendering all title to wisdom, declared, that, though he was past fifty, he was actually going in a few days, as he hoped, to be married, and in a few months would probably make his 'first speech in Parliament.'

His friend made as good a retreat as the case would admit, by remarking, that his maxim could not apply to one who was not going either to be married or to speak in public for the first time. As fast as possible my father pursued his way to Dublin. He found the city as it had been described to him, under arms, in dreadful expectation. The timely apprehension of the heads of the conspiracy at this crisis prevented a revolution, and saved the capital. But the danger for the country seemed by no means over — insurrections, which were to have been general and simultaneous, broke out in different parts of the kingdom. The confessions of a conspirator, who had turned informer, and the papers seized and published, proved, that there existed in the country, a deep and widely spread spirit of rebellion. Though disconcerted by the present vigilance or good fortune of government, it was hardly to be doubted, that fresh attempts, in concert with foreign enemies, would be made in future. From different reasons, all parties thought the country in a dangerous situation, and foresaw, that there must be further commotions.

12. Author's note: He was elected for the borough of St. John's Town, County of Longford.

Instead of delaying his marriage, which some would have advised, my father urged for an immediate day. On the 31st of May he was married to Miss Beaufort, by her brother, the Rev. William Beaufort, at St. Anne's church, in Dublin. They came down to Edgeworth-Town immediately, through a part of the country that was in actual insurrection. Late in the evening they arrived safe at home, and my father presented his bride to his expecting, anxious family.

Of her first entrance and appearance that evening I can recollect only the general impression, that it was quite natural, without effort or pretension. The chief thing remarkable was, that she, of whom we were all thinking so much, seemed to think so little of herself.

A more trying situation for a wife could hardly be imagined, than that in which she was now placed. She knew, that in the minds of all who surrounded her — sons, daughters, and sisters-in-law, old associations and present feelings, though not averse to her individually, must be painfully affected by the first introduction of a new wife and mother. She was aware, that points of comparison must continually recur with those, who had been much beloved or highly admired. Love and sorrow for their late mother were still fresh in the minds of her own children; while ever present to the memory of others of the family, and of traditional power over the imagination, was the character of one highly gifted and graced with every personal and mental endowment the more than *celebrated*, the revered Honora! Knowing and feeling all this — and who could know or feel it more — my father seemed neither embarrassed nor anxious for his present wife; nor imprudently impatient to have her admired or beloved by his family.

Soon after this marriage, things and persons found themselves in their proper places; and the fear of change, which had perplexed numbers, was gradually dispelled. The sisters of the late Mrs. Edgeworth, those excellent aunts (Mrs. Mary and Charlotte Sneyd), instead of returning to their English friends and relations, remained at Edgeworth-Town. This was an auspicious omen to the common people in our neighbourhood, by whom they were universally beloved — it spoke well, they said, for the *new* lady. In his own family, the union and happiness she would secure was soon felt, but her superior qualities, her accurate knowledge, judgment, and abilities, in decision and in action, appeared only as occasion arose and called for them. She was found always equal to the occasion, and superior to the expectation. The power and measure of her efficient kindness could never be calculated, and was never fully known to each individual of her family, till by that individual it was most wanted.

This lady, thank God, is still living! — and, thank God, still living with us. No one can disdain flattery more that she does, or than I do. It is unworthy of her and of myself: She will see this before it is printed, and I am aware, that, though she will be certain that I think and feel what I say, she will at first wish, that this page should be suppressed: but I claim from her affection to my father the right to state opinions and facts necessary to do justice to his judgment and his character — essential to prove, that he did not late in life marry merely to please his own fancy, but that he chose a companion suited to himself, and a mother fit for his family. This, of all the blessings we owe to him, has proved the greatest.

ANONYMOUS

from:
THE CAVERN IN THE WICKLOW MOUNTAINS; OR, THE FATE OF THE O'BRIEN FAMILY; A TALE FOUNDED ON FACTS (1821)

[This anonymous novel tells the story of a Roman Catholic republican family in the years surrounding the United Irishman rebellion of 1798. The narrator of the following sequence is Gerald O'Brien, who has been captured and imprisoned in Dublin Castle, and is awaiting execution. His rescue by his sister interrogates assumptions about gender, patriotism and activism.[1] Printed in Dublin by James Charles for the author, 1821. Text is from the editor's copy.]

The gaoler had that morning informed me that I was to suffer the next day. I was sitting mournfully musing on my situation, and the dear inhabitants of the cavern forcibly striking on my imagination, I pictured to myself the grief, the inconsolable anguish they would feel, when my cruel and untimely fate became known to them. Those tender thoughts quite unmanned me; the idea of death became insufferably painful, when the door opened and my darling sister rushed into my arms; I wept, and was near fainting, which Harriet perceived, and seating herself, described her progress from the cavern to Dublin. Imperceptibly she stole from my mind part of its sadness; I listened with attentive pleasure to her story; but when she ceased, the thought, the dreadful thought, that to-morrow I should die; that the present was the last time her voice would charm my soul to forgetfulness, or her loved presence enliven my sad heart, wound my feelings to the highest pitch of torture.

She watched the varying changes of my countenance, and read my sorrowful ideas; with a smile playing round her lip, she took my hand

and pressing it between both her's, said, calm your mind, I have a plan, which if you put into execution we may still be happy; a plan! replied I, looking her full in the face, what does my Harriet mean? is it to cheat me into hope, where no hope is? But there is a hope, replied she with energy; listen, my dear Gerald, and oppose not what I say; you must change clothes with me, and at seven o'clock, the hour I am to leave this prison, go hence. The dress I have on, I got purposely for you; compose yourself, be steady and fear not. Well, Harriet, said I, suppose I should comply with your plan, what is to become of you in the event of my escape being known? Oh! replied she, with a smile of fond expectation, fear not for me, my life is in no danger, and leave the rest to Providence. I hesitated; I could not endure the idea of exposing her to the insults of the unfeeling monsters that surrounded the tower; but she importuned me with such warm affection and deep concern — so sweetly persuasive were her words, and the horror of death growing more and more intolerable, I at last consented.

Her dress was a long black habit, black hat, and long veil; she got very high heels to her boots, and being very tall, she thought the difference of our height would not be observed; with trembling apprehension I dressed myself in her clothes, and folding the habit round me, and throwing the veil over my face in the same manner she had it coming in, we were soon completely metamorphosed, and seating ourselves at the table, she laid her head on her hand, with her handkerchief to her face, when the gaoler came, and desired me to go, supposing I was Harriet. I thought my heart would have burst, and clung to my sister; she fearing my agitation would betray me, softly said, if you do not wish my death go, and disengaging herself from my embrace, I left the room. I really was weeping, and holding my handkerchief to my face, I walked out of the tower without the least suspicion. At a little distance from the gate the Abbé was waiting with a coach, in silence he shook my hand, and stepping into it we drove a few miles from Dublin, when the unprotected state of my sister coming powerfully into my mind, I insisted on returning to the city to wait the event of her

1. For a discussion of victim substitution, as a trope in writings on the French Revolution, see Richard Maxwell, Introduction and Appendices to *A Tale of Two Cities* by Charles Dickens (London: Penguin, 2000).

being discovered in my place, and if any bad consequence was likely to result, to give myself up and save her. The Abbé would not listen to my argument, but said I should not return, that we would proceed forward to the cavern, where my mother waited with fond anxiety to fold me to her maternal bosom, and added, do you Gerald by your folly want to undo what we have suffered so much to accomplish? be more reasonable; Harriet I hope is in no danger, but if she is, I know she possesses sufficient firmness of mind to meet the severest trial; such is the greatness of her soul, that she never sinks with misfortune, but rises superior to it. Rouse my dear fellow, from this weakness, or I will be inclined to think with your garb you changed your nature; resume the man and be yourself; the delicacy of your motives I know and feel, but we must not, to avoid a temporary deprivation, embitter by imprudence our future days. His words sunk deep into my heart; the praises he so lavishly bestowed on my angelic sister, gratified and quite subdued me. I wept, and for a short time he suffered me to give free vent to my tears, and when I became a little calm, he laid his hand on my arm, and in a tone of sympathetic kindness, said, let us alight and walk the rest of the way home.

[Harriet is released at the intervention of a sympathetic officer, but there is no happy ending, as the family is riven by guilt and insanity.]

from:
THE LIFE AND TRANSACTIONS OF A FEMALE PROSTITUTE . . .
(*c.* 1826)

[This penny chapbook was printed in Belfast and marks a change in the style and purpose of prostitutes' memoirs. All the enjoyment of illicit behaviour and rebellion disappears from accounts of prostitution and is replaced by relentless reports of misery, degradation, guilt and possible repentance. The woman is presented as an abject victim, and 'respectable' families are warned to protect their daughters. At the same time all specificity of location

has disappeared and, in contrast to eighteenth-century memoirs, no respectable men are named or implicated in her degradation. The cheap production and price suggests that a poorer audience is targeted for this pamphlet, perhaps a similar audience to that for ballads. Published *c.* 1826, the title continues 'For the last 20 years, wrote by herself and who died in an awful condition in Margaret-street, Belfast, this unfortunate victim of dissipation was born of respectable parents in Belfast, and received an education fitted to adorn her sex, but at last died in a common brothel. To which is added her solemn warning to her sister companions, who are running the same destructive course which caused her death.' I am indebted to Maria Luddy for pointing me towards this text. Luddy is currently completing a book length study of prostitution in Ireland.]

The above unfortunate woman was born in Belfast on the 25th of March 1790, of respectable parents, who gave her a liberal education, and did every thing in their power to keep her from the snares to which young women are exposed; but unluckily for them, and far worse for herself, the snare of the fowler was set, and she unhappily fell into it. At this time in the bloom of youth, she paid little heed to the matter till sad experience showed her the error she had committed; he who promised such great things for her now forsook her and left her a cast-away upon life's changing ocean. Grieved parents did every thing in their power to draw her back to the path of duty, but the golden chain was broken, and she resolved to follow the [dictates] of her own reason in preference to that of her parents, and falling in with one of these unfortunates who traverse our streets, her misfortunes then began. From one scene of dissipation to another, she ran with increasing avidity, undergoing all the pains of loathsome disease and sometimes punished by imprisonment, till worn out with the fatigues of a wicked and vicious life, she lay down on that fatal bed from whic[h] she knew she would never rise. In this state she continued for several weeks, and a few days before her death she wrote the following solemn warning to her wicked and thoughtless companions, that they might be induced to forsake their former evil practices.

'S—— O——[1] to her former wicked companions.

1. Four pages later the testimony is signed 'S—— G——'.

'Before you receive this, my final state will be determined by the judge of all the earth. In a few days at most, perhaps in a few hours, the inevitable sentence will be passed that shall raise me to the height of happiness, or sink me to the depths of misery. While you read these lines, I shall be either groaning under the agonies of absolute despair, or triumphing in fulness of joy.

'It is impossible for me to express the present disposition of my soul — the vast uncertainty I am struggling with! No words can paint the force and vivacity of my apprehensions. Every doubt wears the face of horror, and would almost overwhelm me, were it not for some faint beams of hope which dart across the tremendous gloom! who can utter the anguish of a soul suspended between the extremes of infinite joy and eternal misery? I am throwing my last stake for eternity, and tremble, and shudder for the important event . . .'

This woman died on the 17th March,[2] 1826, and was at one time qualified for very useful purpose, and she wrote this account for the benefit of young women, that they be not led astray at first by seducing men, who have no other end in view but their ruin, as my history fully exemplifies.

2. St Patrick's Day may have been selected as the date of death to emphasize the national problem of prostitution.

from:
A NEW SONG CALL'D THE WANDERING GIRL. TO WHICH ARE ADDED, THE SAILOR BOY, AND RACHELL M'LAUGHLIN'S LAMENTATION (1826)

[Popular ballads are exemplary narratives of a community's fantasies and fears. The following selection of ballads were printed in the 1820s and 1830s, though many of the ballads themselves may be older. 'The Wandering Girl' and 'The Sorrowful Lamentation of Rachell M'Laughlin' appeared in the same chapbook, which was obviously set by a printer with relatively poor literacy, at least in English.

As well as the 'errors' recorded here, a number of letters are set upside down and the spelling even of proper names is radically inconsistent. Who is the implied reader of such a production? Was the printed version to serve chiefly as a memory-aid to an audience already familiar with the ballad in the oral tradition? This might be true of 'The Wandering Girl', which tells a familiar story of seduction and abandonment, but 'Rachell M'Laughlin' seems much closer to the memorial verses that appeared in local newspapers throughout the nineteenth century (and are not unknown today). 'Now fair raceel is no more she is / Aughoghill mould' shows some of the verve later found in the work of Amanda M'Kittrick Ros (pp. 883–7). In contrast to these naïve pieces the remaining ballads show some sophistication of poetic diction and 'The Carlow Maid' (which has been frequently reprinted, some token of its popularity) plays with notions of decorum in both form and subject matter. Copies of the texts are held in the British Library. For a full discussion of contexts for the Song Tradition in Ireland, see pp. 1312–17. See also 'The Wandering Boy', Belfast, Joseph Smythe, 1826.]

The Wandering Girl

White was the meadows deep covered with snow,
And loud over the mountains the tempest did
  blow,
While Mary poor Mary with her bibe aloe,
Went wandering alone alass with out friend or a
  home,
Then loose hung her hair like loks of despair,
Her fancy as wild as the tirint did warble,
Saying Jonney did grieve me O why did you leve,
Your poor little babe and the wandering girl,
With the pledge of our love I now stand over
  heth
When nature is tuched with the figure of death,
While it draws at my boosom it forces a teer,
O hush my sweet babe your fathar is near,
O yes he is coming across the rood waves,
But not till poor mary is laid in her grave,
Then he may scorn me and then he may cry.
When the green turf shall cover my baba, and I,
My charms oft you persed then with many a
  smile,
You kissed and you pratted my heart to beguile,
I believed all was true but alas it was in vain,
For all my fond pleasures are turned to pain,
My Father and Mother dispised me for thee,
No straw covered cottage remain now for me,
Winters dread fury does some to encrease,
To lull me to sleep in amasition of peace

While thus then she spoke quite Francis
diderrem,
The lost spark of life on her eye bolls did beam,
Fo cold was the baby she held to her breast,
Anddeath closed the eye of poor mrey to rest,
No more shall she wander like tirents nor warble,
Shesfree from her woe lies cold in the snow,
The poor little baba and the wandering girl, [sic].

The Sorrowful Lamentation of Rachell M'Laughlin, who was Drowned at the Main Water[1]

The 12 day of october, last it being a
dismal day,
It was her fate one morning my love
was cast away,
The swelling floods the did combine it
was a fall of rain,
It was their fair Rachael lost her life all
in the river main,

When she sell into the water sb avese [sic]
a loud loud cry,
The wesving of her milk white hands
unto the heavns high,
She struggled long in Water deep,
thinking to reach the shore,
In deaths cold Arms she fell asleep her
sorrows were no more.

Her lovely corpse ehe float along, the
Waters bore them down,
Like a milk white swam may love she
swam past Cullybackey town,
Evry one as; the pass by this doleful
news to hear,
From evry heart it brought a sigh from
evry eye a tear.

Her cousin dear he lived near, with
grief was sore oppressed,
Sleeping or Walking its he could find
no Nest,
He says I will go find my love the
the [sic] powers will me guide,
There he found sweet Rochael fair on
the main Water side.

1. The river Main flows through Cullybackey, Co. Antrim.

Had yo seen her mother it would made
pour heart relent
Likewise her true love William unto her
Corpse he went,
Her ruby lips as cold as clap he kiss'd
o'er and o'er,
He says fare you well sweet Rachael
dear we part to meet no more.

Her cheeks they are a rosey red, her
skin was a milk White
There was none so foin in my view on
the main Water side,
Her was a lovely brown most curious
to behold,
Now fair raceel is no more she is
Aughoghill[2] mould.

2. Ahoghill is a nearby village.

from: WITHIN A MILE OF EDINBURGH. TOGETHER WITH THE WIFE CONTENDING FOR THE BREECHES. THE BEWILDERED MAID. THE SAILOR'S FAIRWELL TO HIS SWEET-HEART. THE BENIGHTED WATCHMAN. CURIOUS CONUNDRUMS (n.d.)

[From a chapbook published in Dublin by R. Grace, no date, copy in the British Library.]

The Wife's Contending for the Breeches

In summer you a wooing go,
And intend a wife to marry;
Marriage is not like foot-ball play,
Have a care you don't miscarry.

But if you should a wooing go,
To a lass with store of riches,
She may prove your overthrow,
And be striving for the breeches.

A woman that don't frown or scold,
Her lips are sweet like sugar-candy,
And if I had a hundred pound,
I would share it with such a dandy.

But such womenkind are hard to find,
Which makes me use dissembling speeches,
If all mankind were of my mind,
Women would never wear the breeches.

I would have you take advice,
And never doat upon her beauty,
For if you do she'll you despise,
And conclude it is your duty.

But love her for her own desert,
Tho' she does not abound in riches,
You may love your wife with all your heart,
But never let her wear the breeches.

Each day my passion's stronger,
When sprightly Nancy then did say,
You'll die dear sir, the Irish way,
    To live a little longer.

At length grown jealous, Venus[2] cries,
    This pride's beyond all bearing,
And quickly sent Mars[3] from the skies,
    In form of Captain Dearing;
        Then with a sigh
        'Twas Oh! I die!
As sprightly Nancy then did say,
You'll die dear sir, the Irish way,
    To live a little longer.

Like hero bold, well arm'd he press'd,
    And quickly saw by Nancy,
The snow was thaw'd within her breast
    A soldier caught her fancy;
        With down cast eye,
        She heav'd a sigh,
        She found her passion stronger,
And sprightly Nancy then did say,
I'll die myself the Irish way,
    To live a little longer.

2. Roman goddess of love.
3. Roman god of war, married to Venus.

from:
THE KING'S VISIT. DRUMION DUBH.[1] WHACK! FOR THE EMERALD ISLE. THE CARLOW MAID. IN A COTTAGE NEAR A WOOD (n.d.)

[From a chapbook published in Dublin by R. Grace, no date, copy in the British Library.]

The Carlow Maid

In Carlow town there lived a Maid,
    More sweet than flowers at daybreak,
Their vows contending lovers paid,
    But none of Marriage dar'd speak;
        Still with a sigh
        'Twas Oh! I die!

1. *Drumion dubh* means 'the white-backed black cow'. For the poem 'Ceann Dubh Dilis', see p. 1065.

from:
THE SONS OF THE EMERALD ISLE. TOGETHER WITH NO MORE COME TO WOO. THE BANKS OF INVARARY. WOMAN. NO TRICKS UPON TRAVELLERS (n.d.)

[From a chapbook printed and sold in Dublin by the Wholesale and Retail Book Warehouse, no date, copy in the British Library.]

No More Come to Woo

Ah think when you left,
Of all pleasure bereft,
    A girl who confided in you,

How keen were my pains,
They have broken Love's chains,
    Then I pr'ythee no more come to woo.

I was simple I own,
And should better have known,
    Than to trust such deceivers as you,
He that won't, when he may,
When he will, shall have nay,
    Then pray you no more come to woo.

from:
GUARDIAN AND CONSTITUTIONAL ADVOCATE (1828)

[From the early nineteenth century, newspapers become an important site of discourse about sexuality, particularly the eruption of sexuality into the public sphere through crime or scandal. This example of a domestic dispute, published in the Belfast newspaper on 12 September 1828, identifies the readers with the spectators in court, who laugh at M'Govern's cuckoldry.]

NEWRY PETIT SESSIONS

George Feran, of Newry, a porter, next presented himself to the notice of the Bench, and prayed their interference to restrain a *gentleman* of his own profession, named Alexander (alias *Belcher*) M'Govern, from offering further violence to his person and feelings, as also that of his family.
I. Glenny, Esq. — Pray what is it you complain of?
Why, your honour, when on my way home last Monday night, I saw a man and a woman in close conversation, and coming up, I found to my surprise, *Mr.* M'Govern with his arms in a very loving manner around my wife.
Mr G. — Well, how did she seem to enjoy *Mr.* M'Govern's embraces?
Your honour, she seemed quiet enough. (A laugh.)
Mr G. — What did you say?
Your honour, I thought it hard enough, and only said, Oh! I caught you at last. — (Continued laughter.)

Mr. G. — Have you anything further to say of *Mr. M'Govern*?
Your honour, the next day I met him in the streets, and *becase* I asked him what he was about, he struck me, *without saying one word.* (Great laughter.)
Bench —That was too bad: how has the peace of your family been disturbed?
Your honour, my wife and I have not seen one another since.
The Bench — Go and see your wife, make peace with her, and if *Mr.* M'Govern will not make you an ample apology before next Court day, come to us and we will issue our warrant against him for the assault.

from:
LONDONDERRY SENTINEL AND NORTH-WEST ADVERTISER (1833)

[A common space-filler in newspapers was the precursor of modern advice columns, a set of maxims or rules of conduct. These were usually copied from conduct books or other newspapers. 'Maxims for the Married' is an example of the 'double standard' often complained of by Victorian feminists. From vol. 4, no. 5, 24 August 1833.]

MAXIMS FOR THE MARRIED

Code of Instruction for Gentlemen

. . .
4. Be strictly moral in your conduct; how can you pretend to be a guide to your house, if you are not? Consider what you would think if your wife should become immoral in her conduct . . .

Code of Instruction for the Ladies

1. Let every wife be persuaded that there are two ways of governing a family; the first is by the expression of that which will belong to force; the second to the power of mildness, to which every strength will yield. One is the power of a husband; a wife should never employ any other arms than that of gentleness. When a woman

accustoms herself to say, I will, she deserves to lose her empire.

2. Avoid contradicting your husband. When we smell at a rose, it is to imbibe the sweets of its colour; we likewise look for everything that is amiable in woman. Whoever is often contradicted feels insensibly an aversion for the person that contradicts, which gains strength by time; and, whatever her good points, is not easily destroyed.

3. Occupy yourself only with household affairs; wait till your husband confides to you those of higher importance, and do not give your advice till he asks it.

4. Never take upon yourself to censor your husband's morals, and do not read lectures to him. Let your preaching be a good example, and practise virtue yourself to make him in love with it.

5. Command his attention by being always attentive to him; never exact anything and you will obtain much; appear always flattered by the little he does for you, which will excite him to perform more.

6. As men are vain, never wound this vanity, not even in the most trifling instances. A wife may have more sense than her husband, but she should never seem to know it.

7. When a man gives wrong council, never make him feel that he has done so; but lead him on by degrees to what is rational, with mildness and gentleness; when he is convinced, leave him to the merit of having found out what is just and reasonable.

8. When a husband is out of temper, behave obligingly to him; if he is abusive, never retort; and never prevail over him to humble him.

9. Choose well your friends, have but few, and be careful of following their advice in all matters.

10. Cherish neatness without luxury, and pleasure without excess; dress with taste, and particularly with modesty; vary the fashion of your dress, especially in regard to colours. It gives a change to the ideas and recalls pleasing recollections. — Such things may appear trifling, but they are of more importance than is imagined.

11. Never be curious to pry into your husband's concerns but obtain his confidence at all times, by that which you repose in him. Always preserve order and economy; by these means he will find his own house pleasanter than any other.

12. Seem always to obtain information from him, especially before company, though you may pass yourself for a simpleton. Never forget that a wife owes all her importance to that of her husband. Leave him entirely master of his own actions to go or come whenever he thinks fit. A wife ought to make her company amiable to her husband, that he will not be able to exist without it, then he will not seek for pleasure abroad if she do not partake of it with him.

CHRISTIAN JOHNSTONE

(1781–1857)

from:
TRUE TALES OF THE IRISH PEASANTRY, AS RELATED BY THEMSELVES, SELECTED FROM THE REPORT OF THE POOR LAW COMMISSIONERS[1] (1836)

[Johnstone was one of the first writers to identify and exploit the narrative possibilities offered by the Irish Poor

Law Commission. British radical writers had, at least since the 1790s, been concerned with the problem of representing the suffering of the masses as dramatically or effectively as the story of an individual, particularly of a literate, self-reflective individual. Feminists in Britain, many of whom offered powerful critiques of the family as a British institution, identified it as a site of resistance in Ireland.

1. The Commission of Inquiry into Poor Law in Ireland was established in 1833. The report found that there were 2,385,000 people in want for at least thirty weeks of the year. The commission did not recommend the extension of English Poor Law to Ireland, but after a second report by George Nicholls (1781–1865) in 1836–7 such an extension did in fact take place, in the Irish Poor-Law Act (1838–42), supervised by Nicholls.

(See Besant, pp. 875, and Butler, pp. 876–7.) In particular, they drew on the work of the Poor Law Commission to suggest that Irish chastity and domesticity were undermined by poverty and misgovernment. Johnstone and successive apologists for the Irish peasantry contributed to the production of a moral climate in which unruly, illegitimate sexuality became unrepresentable. This extract is taken from the 2nd edition, published in Edinburgh in 1836 by William Tait, in the British Library. I failed to locate the first edition.]

Advertisement

... So far as I am aware, I was the first, as I am still almost the only *light* writer — or a more proper word may be, *slight* writer — in this island, that ever endeavoured to awaken a just, and if a just, then a kindly feeling for the Irish among my own countrymen. I was then, and I am still convinced — that the actual condition of that singularly circumstanced and unfortunate kingdom, and the true character of the people, only required to be thoroughly understood in England, and especially in Scotland, to be warmly appreciated, and valued more highly than it has ever yet been. Since my early efforts in *Story-telling* about Ireland and the Irish[2] — valueless save in the motive — a host of eminent native fictionists have arisen, and made known the genius, and the true spirit and worth of their country. The admirable tales of Banim[3] and Carleton[4] have, I trust, paved the way for the success of the object of the TRUE STORIES of the Irish Peasantry told to the Poor-law Commissioners ...

Improvident Marriages

No fact is more fully established by this Report, than that early improvident marriages are the inevitable consequence of extreme poverty, and of the low standard of living which it has produced. The son of a small farmer is uniformly more cautious in contracting marriage than his father's labourer, working for from 6d. to 8d. a-day, when he can obtain work; and often without money to pay the priest the marriage fees. 'Sure we cannot be worse off than we are,' is the unvarying ultimate reason assigned. Then a wife is found useful to go about to beg for potatoes in times of distress; and children are looked to as a support against destitution in old age ...

In Kilfaroy parish, county Clare — M'Mahon says 'It is always the poorest man marries first, because he knows he cannot be worse off by it; it is better for him to marry early, than to seduce the girls, who are so poor and wretched that this would often happen. Besides, we poor people have a strange idea that it is a good thing to have children as soon as possible, in order to help and support us when we begin to grow old.'

In answer to the question, whether labourers became old and disabled before other people, M'Mahon replied, 'We are worked harder and worse treated than the slaves in the colonies; I understand they are taken care of by their masters when they are sick or old. When we are sick, we must die on the road, if the neighbours do not help us. When we are old, we must go out to beg, if the young ones cannot help us; and that will soon happen with us all. We are getting worse and worse every day, and the landlords are kicking us out of every little holding we have ...

'A labouring couple marries' says Mr. Vaughan, 'that whatever they have may be kept together, and because they are tired of living on another man's floor.' There were, however, many mechanics of the middle period of life who had remained single, and who say that they would be glad to marry if they could afford it. Mr. O'Brien remarks, 'A man is considered stale at 30 and a woman at 20.' ...

Conclusion

There is a class I would wish to interest in these TRUE STORIES about our next-door neighbours and fellow-subjects — our own people, if we would wisely and properly consider the relation — I mean those persons who have sympathies so unbounded as to comprehend all Hindostan, who cherish patriotism in Turkey and Spain, enthusiasm in Poland, and indulge in just indignation against the slaveholders of America. These are all excellent feelings; but why not include the Irish within this great circle of universal sympathy? When we reproach the

---

2. Johnstone's novel *Clan-Albin: A National Tale* (London: Longman, 1815) is set in Scotland and Ireland.
3. John Banim (1798–1842) and Michael Banim (1796–1874), Kilkenny brothers, wrote novels singly and in collaboration, sometimes as the O'Hara brothers.
4. William Carleton (1794–1869), novelist.

citizens of the United States with the condition of the black and coloured populations, are they not entitled to retort — 'Look you at home.

Remove the beam from your own eye. Ameliorate the condition of your starving Irish *serfs*, before you speak to us about our well-fed Africans.'

W.H. MAXWELL

(1792–1850)

from:
WILD SPORTS OF THE WEST, WITH LEGENDARY TALES AND LOCAL SKETCHES . . . (1832)

[Maxwell's account of Hennessey's elopement draws attention to the way in which a figure could become outcast in a rural community, and describes the traditional customs that accompanied country weddings. *Wild Sports of the West, with Legendary Tales and Local Sketches by the Author of 'Stories of Waterloo'* was published in 2 vols in London by R. Bentley in 1832. Editor's copy.]

LETTER XLI

Dull Evening — Memoir of Hennessey

We sat down to dinner *tête-à-tête*, and although both myself and my kinsman made an exertion to banish unpleasant reminiscences, the evening was the most sombre that I had yet passed. The happy party who once tenanted our 'merie home,' are never to meet again. The otter-killer 'sleeps the sleep that knows no breaking'[1] — the Colonel has retired to his winter quarters — the Priest's confessions call him from us for a season — and some secret intelligence which reached the lodge overnight, has caused Hennessey to disappear.

To gratify a strong expression of curiosity on my part respecting the latter, my cousin told me the following particulars of this singular personage:

'If ever man came into the world with the organ of destructiveness surcharged, it was my unhappy foster-brother. He was a lively and daring boy, and being a favourite with my late father, had opportunities of improvement afforded to him, which persons in his sphere seldom can obtain. But Hennessey showed little inclination for literary pursuits, the gun was more adapted to him than the pen — and at fifteen, when but a very indifferent scribe; he was admitted by the whole population to be the best shot of his years that "ever laid stock to shoulder." Encouraged by my father's partiality, from this period he led an idle careless life, and rambled over the country, breaking dogs, or amusing himself with the gun and fishing-rod.

'I was at the college when the first of his misfortunes occurred. He had imprudently ventured into a dancing-house, where a number of the *Sweenies* were assembled, with whom he had previously been at feud, and, as might have been anticipated, a quarrel quickly arose. Hennessey, too late, perceived his danger; but with that daring determination for which he has ever been remarkable, when the assault began, he made a sudden dash for the door, and overturning all that opposed him, succeeded in escaping. He was, however, closely pursued. From his uncommon activity, he far outstripped all but one of his enemies. He had nearly reached the river — but his enemy was close behind. Intending to disable his pursuer, Hennessey picked up a stone, and unfortunately threw it with such fatal precision, that the skull of his opponent was beaten in, and he expired on the spot.

'Well, this was an unfortunate affair, but it was homicide in self-defence. My father accommodated matters with the Sweenies, and my foster-brother was discharged without a prosecution.

---

1. Unidentified. Possibly an allusion to William Cowper (1731–1800), *The Task* (1803), Book v, line 669.

'A year passed, but the Sweenies had not forgotten or forgiven the death of their kinsman. Hennessey's rambling habits exposed him to frequent encounters with this clan: and one night, when returning late from the fair of Newport,[2] with two or three companions, he came into unexpected collision with a party of his ancient enemies. A scuffle ensued — in the struggle he wrested a loaded whip from his antagonist, and struck the unhappy wretch so heavily with his own weapon, that after lingering nearly a month, he died from the contusion.

'The second mishap occasioned us a deal of trouble; but Hennessey surrendered, was tried, and acquitted, and we all trusted that his misfortunes were at an end. He abjured the use of spirits, avoided late hours, and such meetings as might expose him to any collision with that clan who had been so unfortunate to him, and to whom he had been so unfortunate, and religiously determined to avoid every cause of quarrelling; but fate determined that it should be otherwise.

'Having been invited to a *dragging home*,[3] as the bridegroom was his near relative, Hennessey could not without giving offence decline attending on the happy occasion. He was then a remarkably handsome fellow — and you would vainly now seek in those gaunt and careworn features, the manly beauty which then caused many a rustic heart to beat. The bride's cousin accompanied her; she was remarkably pretty, and was, besides, reported to be the largest heiress in the barony. With such advantages, no wonder "of lovers she'd plenty,"[4] as the ballad says: — my foster-brother met her, danced with her, drank with her — loved her, and was beloved in turn. Every rival was double-distanced; but she was unfortunately betrothed by her father to a wealthy *Kearne*,[5] and although I, in person, interposed, and used my powerful influence, the old fellow her father was obstinate in refusing to break off the match.

'Hennessey was no man to see his handsome mistress consigned without her own consent to the arms of a rival. He made the usual arrange-

ments, and I encouraged him to carry her off. The evening came — he left the lodge in a boat, with six fine young peasants; and crossing the bay, landed by moonlight at a little distance from the village where his inamorata[6] dwelt.

'That very night a multitude of the Malleys had accompanied the accepted suitor to conclude all necessary preliminaries. The cabin of the heiress was crowded, and all within was noisy revelry. Hennessey, with one companion, stole to the back of the house.

'He knew the chamber of the bride elect, for he had more than once, "when all the world were dreaming,"[7] visited his pretty mistress. He looked through the little casement, and, sight of horror! there she was, seated on the side of the bed, and the Kearne's arm around her waist, with all the familiarity of a priveliged [sic] lover! There, too, was the priest of Inniskea, and divers elders of "both the houses"[8] — while the remainder of the company, for whose accommodation this grand chamber was insufficient, were indulging in the kitchen or dancing in the barn.

'Since the days of Lochinvar,[9] there never was a more daring suitor than my foster-brother; yet he did not consider it a prudent measure to enter the state apartment "'mong bridesmen, and kinsmen, and clansmen, and all,"[10] — but waited patiently at the window, to see what some lucky chance might do. Nor did he wait in vain. Kathleein turned her pretty eyes on the moonlit casement, and thought, poor girl! how often her young lover had stolen there in secret, and told his tale of passion. A tap, too light for any but the ear of love to detect, arrested her attention, and she saw the indistinct form of a human face outside; and whose could it be but her favoured youth? Seizing an early opportunity, she stole from the apartment; she soon was in her lover's arms; a few words, and a few kisses, — and all was settled; — while the Kearne, the priest, and the father, were regulating the exact quantities of cattle and plenishing,[11] that were to dower the

2. In County Mayo.
3. Bringing of the bride to her new home.
4. Unidentified.
5. Boor — derives from a derogatory term for the wild Irish. Author's note for Kearne *Anglice*, a rich vulgar clown.
6. Italian, meaning, 'loved one'.
7. Unidentified.
8. Allusion to William Shakespeare's *Romeo and Juliet*.
9. The story of Lochinvar, which dates from the Middle Ages, had been retold in 1808 by Walter Scott (1771–1832) as part of *Marmion: A Tale of Flodden Field*.
10. *Marmion*, canto v, line 326.
11. Author's note: *Plenishing*, means household furniture, beds, blankets, etc. etc.

handsome bride, Kathleein was hurrying to the shore with her young and daring suitor.

'An attempt so boldly and so fortunately begun, was, however, doomed to end unhappily. One of the Malleys had discovered the interview, and witnessed the elopement. Having silently observed the route of the fugitives, he apprized the parties within, that their negotiations were likely to become nugatory, and a fierce and vindictive pursuit was instantly commenced. The distance, however, to the beach was short: the companion of the bold abductor had run forward, the bride was won — the boat was launched — the oars were dipping in the water — when, alas! the rush of rapid footsteps was heard, and oaths and threats announced that the fugitives were closely followed. Two or three of the Malleys had far outstripped the rest; but a minute more, and pursuit would have been hopeless. One man had passed the others far, and on the brink of the tide he caught the fair runaway in his arms, while the companions of the gallant were actually pulling her on board. The chase was hard at hand — twenty feet were heard rushing over the loose shingle — not a moment was to be lost, or the bride was gone for ever. Like lightning Hennessey caught up a stretcher[12] from the bottom of the boat, discharged one murderous blow upon the man who held back his beloved mistress, a deep-drawn moan was heard, and the unhappy Kearne, for it was himself, sank upon the beach without life or motion! Off went the boat — off went the lady — and the athletic crew pulled through the sparkling water, little dreaming that their exulting leader was for *the third time* a homicide! Great God! I cannot tell you what I suffered next morning, when the tragical result of an attempt I had myself encouraged was told me. My first care was to look to the safety of my foster-brother and his bride; and until pursuit was over, I had them conveyed by Pattigo[13] in the hooker[14] to Innisboffin.[15] There they remained in safe concealment, and for six months it was not deemed prudent to permit them to return, as the clan of the deceased were numerous and vindictive.

'Time flew. They came back, and for some time remained here unmolested. Kathleein was near her confinement, when one day we received information that the Malleys had procured a warrant with a civil force to execute it, and were determined at every hazard to arrest my foster-brother. I, a magistrate myself, could not openly protect him; and that evening he left the lodge at nightfall, to shelter himself in the island of Innisbiggle[16] until the threatened danger passed. Kathleein unfortunately accompanied him; although we told her that there was but one poor family on the place, and its difficulty of approach, while favourable to the concealment of her husband, was unsuited to any female situated like her.

'On landing on the island, the solitary family, who generally resided in the single cabin it contained, were absent at the fair of Westport.[17] Hennessey and his wife took possession of the hut, lighted a fire, and made themselves as comfortable as the wretched hovel would admit. Even then he urged her to return to the lodge — but to leave him in perfect solitude on this desolate place was more than she could determine. Night came, and the weather, which had been squally all day, became worse momently, and at midnight blew a gale. The outlaw and his wife were now shut out from all the world, for a raging sea was roaring round the island, and all communication with the main was interrupted. Whether fear precipitated the dreaded event I know not; but in the middle of the night, while the elemental war was in its fury, symptoms of approaching travail were perceived by poor Kathleein, and the unhappy girl became more and more sensible of the terrible danger that was coming on. God of mercy! what was to be done? It wanted some hours of morning, and even were it light, until the tide fell no mortal could cross that stormy water. Poor wretch! with a withered heart, all that he could do to cheer his sinking companion was done; but every hour she became worse, and every moment her pain and danger were increasing. Driven to madness, at the first dawn of morning he rushed madly to the beach, and though the retiring tide rushed

---

12. Crosspiece placed between a boat's sides to keep them apart.
13. Servant.
14. One-masted fishing boat.
15. Island off the coast of County Galway.

16. Although it is only four hundred yards from Achill Island, County Mayo, Inishbiggle is a small, isolated island.
17. County Mayo.

between the island and the main with furious violence, he plunged into the boiling eddies, and with great strength and desperate courage made good his passage to the opposite shore.

'To obtain help was of course attended with delay; at last, however, it was accomplished, and the tide fell sufficiently to permit some females to cross the *farset*.[18] He, the unhappy husband, far outstripped them: like a deer he bounded over the beach that interposed between the cabin and the sands — he reached it — a groan of exquisite agony was heard from within — next moment he was stooping over his exhausted wife — a dead infant was pressed wildly to her bosom: she turned a dying look of love upon his face, and was a corpse within the arms of the ill-starred homicide!

'When the tidings of the melancholy fate of poor Kathleein were carried to the lodge, I got the hooker under weigh and stood over to the island. My unhappy foster-brother appeared paralyzed with sorrow, and incapable of any exertion. We brought him, with the bodies of the young mother and the dead babe, to the house, and the latter were in due season interred with every mark of sympathy and respect.

'For a time I dreaded that the unfortunate homicide would have sunk into hopeless idiotcy [*sic*]; but he suddenly appeared to rouse his torpid faculties; he became gloomy and morose — and, deaf to all my remonstrances, to the least of which formerly he would have paid the most marked regard, he wandered over the country and seemed to court an arrest, or rather an attempt at it; for, from his desperation, I am inclined to think he would have done some new deed of blood had his enemies ventured to assail him. All I could do to prevent mischief I did. I had the bullets drawn from his fire-arms when he slept; I kept him under constant espionnage, and retained him as much about my person as I could possibly contrive. Whether none would grapple with a desperate and well-armed man, or that some feeling for his sufferings softened the rancour of his enemies for a time, I know not, but he passed unmolested through the country; and the most daring of the Sweenies and Malleys left the road when they accidentally met my unhappy foster-brother. Time has gradually softened his distress, and the asperity of his temper has subsided; he has lost the fierce and savage look that lately no stranger could meet without being terror-stricken; and I shall endeavour to get the death of his miserable rival, which decidedly was unpremeditated and accidental, accommodated. Some intelligence has made it advisable for Hennessey to leave the lodge, although I hardly think any of his enemies would dare to seek him here; but still we cannot be too cautious, and to be placed in the power of his former foeman at this moment, would be to involve his life in imminent peril.

'His misfortunes have given me more distress than anything that has ever befallen myself personally. His attachment to me is so devoted, that I cannot but have brotherly feelings for this ill-starred fosterer. Although he would follow me the corners of the earth if I required, he would rather risk a trial than leave the country, which I have often and earnestly entreated him to do.'

I offered here to take Hennessey under my protection to England, but my kinsman shook his head.

'It is a kind intention, Frank, but he would not leave me. I am the last link that binds him to the world, and while life lasts, we must run our wild career in the same couples. Poor Hennessey! there are worse men than he, although misfortune has made him *thrice* a homicide.'

It was late; John brought oysters at the customary hour, and soon after we separated for the night.

18. Author's note: The strand communicating at low water between an island and the main.

CHARLOTTE ELIZABETH TONNA

(1790–1846)

MATERNAL MARTYRDOM. A FACT ILLUSTRATIVE OF THE IMPROVED SPIRIT OF POPERY, IN THE NINETEENTH CENTURY (1830?)

[This story has many elements familiar from other narratives of domestic violence — O'Neil's jealousy, the psychological manipulation, the murder of the child, the custody conflict — but what is particularly interesting is the way in which Tonna weaves her feminist interests with her passionate anti-Catholicism. From the mid-nineteenth century the 'mixed marriage' develops increasing significance as a site of domestic conflict that can function as a metaphor for national disharmony. This text is taken from a copy in the British Library. The Library catalogue suggests London[?] 1830[?] and it was published anonymously.]

If the circumstances now about to be related were swelled out to furnish the pages of a volume, it would be placed on the list of improbable romances: yet those circumstances are softened in the narration, through regard to feelings which wives and mothers will know how to appreciate. The leading fact has been brought forward in the newspapers of the day: we take not our statement from their columns — we give it from that source which a long personal intimacy with the sufferer has opened to us; and we pledge ourselves that the tale, though divested of many harrowing particulars, is, in all its points, so far as it goes, plain unvarnished truth.

It is needless to suppress or disguise names, which the proceedings of a court of justice have given to the world. Mrs. Elizabeth O'Neil is an Irish lady, educated in the sound principles of Protestantism. Her early years were clouded by sorrows neither few nor slight; but these we pass over to state, that, some eleven or twelve years ago, she became the wife of a Roman Catholic, a young man employed in the excise department, who won her affections, and, under the usual pretence of full toleration, prevailed on her to unite herself with him. She soon experienced what is the general lot of such confiding characters, that no peace must be hers, unless she surrendered the great bar to domestic happiness — the faith of the gospel. With a pertinacious zeal, putting to shame the lukewarmness of those who acknowledge a pure faith, did this devotee of Romish error labour for the perversion of his wife to what he verily believed to be the only true church. And if, in the progress of his endeavours, he used the harshest means for intimidation and coercion, where he could neither convince or persuade, what does it prove but his consistency? Is not persecution, even to the utmost extent of torture, wrenching asunder the bones and sinews of its victims, a living principle of the apostate church? Protected by the still existing laws of a Protestant government, our poor friend was indeed preserved from such extremity of bodily suffering; but when obliged to seek the shelter of those laws, from the perilous fanaticism of her poor husband, and to pray for a peace-warrant against the man to whom she had borne eight children, was the mental suffering less acute than what the body must have undergone, had the Popish inquisition enclosed the victim in its cells? Let the tender heart of woman answer.

Four of the children had been mercifully removed to the bosom of a loving Father in heaven. Somewhat of a veil must be drawn over what ensued in the last month. O'Neil, transported beyond all bounds by the firm resistance of his wife to all the varied efforts which he, under the direction of the neighbouring and notorious Popish College of Carlow, was daily making to draw or drive her from the Protestant faith — fired a pistol at her. The loveliest and best-loved of her children, a little girl of five years old, was present. How the deed affected the tender infant we cannot precisely say: but while the mother escaped, the child fell a victim to the terrors of that moment. Little Fanny died the next day.

In one fortnight, the wretched father was no more: and Eliza was laid on a bed of delirious suffering — a dreadful fever having been the consequence of this aggravated torture. A husband's hand raised against her life; her darling child the sacrifice; and that guilty but still beloved husband called away ... It is one of those cases where language utterly fails; and the sickened heart turns from it, unable to endure the contemplation.

O'Neil had a sister, a school-mistress, in the same town, Leighlin Bridge, near Carlow, who had never shewn any kindness to the heretic wife of her brother; but now, as if moved by those awful visitations, she came to the house of mourning, and proffered her help, to take care of the three surviving children. These were, a girl of ten years, a boy of eight, and another of three. They were, unsuspectingly, given up to her, by the perplexed attendants, and when Eliza, passing the crisis of her disorder, awoke to the terrible consciousness of her situation, and asked for her only earthly solace, her remaining little ones, they were brought to her for a short visit, and then taken away again, by Lucinda O'Neil: and no plea, no entreaty, no threat of the agonized mother, could extort any other communication than that they should be given up to her if she solemnly bound herself to educate them all in the popish religion: otherwise she would never see them more. Ascertaining that Miss O'Neil had conveyed them to the house of the popish priest, Keogh, Eliza sent a female friend to implore that he would allow even one of them to remain with her; he refused, on the alleged and most unfounded plea that she was incapable of taking care of them through mental imbecility. She was then told that if she went to Carlow for them, they would be given up to her: and there she twice dragged her harassed, debilitated frame: but the only result was a mocking reassurance that she should have them in the court-house, at the assizes. This feint was resorted to, in the hope of deluding her into a delay in applying for an *habeus corpus*; as term was nearly concluded. The matter was, however, brought into court, and for a time Miss O'Neil resisted the order: but on finding that imprisonment for life would be the sentence awarded, unless she restored them, they were sent back to the heartbroken mother.

But the actors in this infamous outrage had made good use of the many weeks during which they retained the children. The eldest boy had been unremittingly attended to by a student of the Carlow college, who has so successfully poisoned his tender mind, that all the fond love of a doating mother cannot succeed in removing the dark and hateful prejudice with which the little fellow has been taught to regard her. The girl is similarly perverted, through the same means: and to crown the whole matter Mrs O'Neil is exultingly assured, by the fearless emissaries of darkness, that, go where she may, they will follow her: and find means to counteract whatever of Christian principle she may be enabled to infuse into their minds. They know that she is utterly ruined, in temporal goods, by their flagitious [*sic*] proceedings. Poor O'Neil was a well-educated gentleman, formerly tutor in a nobleman's family; but as his whole income was latterly derived from an official situation in the revenue, of course all died with him. The heavy expences of two funerals, and her own severe illness, followed by those of repeated journies, and legal proceedings for the recovery of her children, have left the widow in such circumstances, that those wily serpents well know her only prospect is some obscure hovel, where she may vainly strive to hide her hunted little ones from their keen eyes and venomous tongues. But one question is yet to be solved — Will the mothers of Protestant England acquiesce in it? Will ANY Christian mother, as she glances from this to her own darlings, and from them to the blessed book whose page she can lay open before them, with none to make her afraid, withhold a little help from this poor, quiet sufferer; this maternal martyr? We know enough of her sentiments to be conscious that it was not without a bitter pang that she heard her last-born boy receive the baptismal name of O'CONNELL;[1] but she battled not for names — it for the awful reality she now strives.

Place the matter in one plain point of view: a mother has her children stolen from her, whilst lying helpless on a sick bed: she only recovers them by means of a legal process, after a delay of months. During this delay they are sedulously wrought upon, by all the powerful machinery of the most finished piece of infernal contrivance

---

1. Named after Daniel O'Connell (1775–1847) leader of the movement for Catholic emancipation.

that the world ever saw: their tender minds overawed — terrified — coerced into verily believing that the indulgence of one natural feeling towards their parent will be visited with everlasting perdition. Had she powerful friends, or ample means, she could at once place them beyond the reach of farther contamination, under the foistering [*sic*] care of some competent instructors: but she has no friends, she has no means. She has none to appeal to but the God of the widow: she has nothing to offer but the prayers of the destitute. It has been her lot from early childhood to find only thorns on the rose-bush of domestic life: its blossoming sweets never bloomed for her. A path of sorrow led her early to the rest that can only be found at the feet of Jesus: and she would not sell her Lord, even for the costly price of a beloved husband's answering love. Now, the hearts that are steeled against her are the hearts of her own children — the hands that are lifted to bar her fond caress,

are the little hands that used to clasp her neck, and innocently to wipe away the tears of bursting sorrow. Personal affection for the sufferer may, and does, plant a keener pang in our own heart wile recording the story: but it does not, for it cannot, add a single tint to the deep dye of the transaction. Who shall paint a blush on the gorgeous scarlet in which the mother of abominations here stands out, glaring in all the horrible splendour of her harlot pride!

The Lord, the righteous Judge, has made his glorious hand very conspicuous in the stedfastness [*sic*] of our poor friend, and the comparative rescue of the children. To Him we commit their cause; and to Him we appeal in their behalf. And in laying the matter before our dear country-women we have but one word to add — 'Judge the fatherless.'[2] C.E.

2. Isaiah 1:17.

R.R. MADDEN

(1798–1886)

from:
THE LITERARY LIFE AND CORRESPONDENCE OF THE COUNTESS OF BLESSINGTON (1855)

[The development of a discourse on the wrongs of women made it possible for women such as the Countess of Blessington to publicize their experience of domestic violence. Blessington was unable to marry her second husband until her first was dead, but there was a growing campaign for the liberalization of the divorce laws, especially for women trapped in violent marriages. Published in London in 1855 by T.C. Newby, the following excerpt is from Madden's Introduction.]

The particulars of this unhappy marriage had best be given in the words of Lady Blessington, and the following is an account of it furnished me by her Ladyship, on the 15th of October, 1853.

'Her father was in a ruined position at the time Lady Blessington was brought home from school, a mere child, and treated as such. Among his military friends, she then saw a Captain Farmer[1] for the first time; he appeared on very intimate terms with her father, but when she first met him, her father did not introduce her to him, in fact she was looked on then as a mere school-girl, whom it was not necessary to introduce to any stranger. In a day or two her father told her she was not to return to school, he had decided that she was to marry Captain Farmer. This intelligence astonished her; she burst out crying, and a scene ensued in which his menaces and her protestations against his determination terminated violently. Her mother unfortunately sided with her father, and eventually, by caressing entreaties and representations of the advantages her father looked forward to from this match with a man of Captain Farmer's affluence,

1. Captain Maurice Farmer (d. 1817).

she was persuaded to sacrifice herself and to marry a man for whom she felt the utmost repugnance.[2] She had not been long under her husband's roof when it became evident to her that her husband was subject to fits of insanity, and his own relatives informed her that her father had been acquainted by them, that Captain Farmer had been insane; but this information had been concealed from her by her father. She lived with him about three months, and during this time he frequently treated her with personal violence; he used to strike her on the face, pinch her till her arms were black and blue, lock her up whenever he went abroad, and often has left her without food till she felt almost famished. He was ordered to join his regiment, which was encamped at the Curragh of Kildare. Lady Blessington refused to accompany him there, and was permitted to remove to her father's house, to remain there during his absence. Captain Farmer joined his regiment, and had not been many days with it, when in a quarrel with his colonel, he drew his sword on the former, and the result of this insane act (for such it was allowed to be) was, that he was obliged to quit the service, being permitted to sell his commission. The friends[3] of Captain Farmer now prevailed on him to go to India (I think Lady Blessington said in the Company's[4] service); she, however, refused to go with him, and remained at her father's.'

Such is the account given to me by Lady Blessington, and for the accuracy of the above report of it I can vouch; though, of course, I can offer no opinion as to the justice of her conclusions in regard to the insanity of Captain Farmer.

2. In 1804.

3. 'Friends' include patrons and relations.
4. English East India Company (founded late sixteenth century), an incorporated company for the exploitation of trade with India.

DINAH GOFF

(*c.* 1784–after 1856)

from:
DIVINE PROTECTION THROUGH EXTRAORDINARY DANGERS; EXPERIENCED BY JACOB AND ELIZABETH GOFF AND THEIR FAMILY, DURING THE IRISH REBELLION IN 1798 (1857)

[After the United Irishmen's Rising in 1798 a number of accounts appeared in which individuals gave personal descriptions of their experiences during the rebellion. Some of these were solicited in the immediate aftermath for propaganda purposes by figures such as Sir Richard Musgrave, while others appeared for a variety of motives and audiences throughout the life spans of those who could remember the events of '98. The overwhelming majority of surviving testimonies are written from a loyalist perspective. This may be because the victors had easier access to publication, and because the memoir itself is in some ways a quintessentially Protestant form, emphasizing the providential and individual aspects of a life history. Catholics seem to have favoured poetry, ballads and anecdotes — more collective forms of memorial. Much Catholic response to the rebellion is, of course, in the Irish language. When republican accounts of the rising began to appear it was largely in the form of historical memoirs, rather than autobiographical witness statements. Goff's account is an interesting example of a loyalist statement because, as a Quaker, she elevates 'friendship' as a social and religious value. In many other testimonies the loyalists proclaim the value of family — and by extension, kinship, culture and race — while the United Irishmen stand for an enlightenment ideal of friendship. This text was published in both London and Philadelphia in 1857. There is no obvious way of determining which is the prior edition, and there are significant differences between them; given that Goff's last residence is Cornwall, I have preferred the London text, published by William and Frederick Cash. The Philadelphia text was published by The Tract Association of Friends. Goff's original MS is in the library at Trinity College Dublin, Ms 5116.]

It has often occurred to me that I ought to leave some little memorial of the preservation extended by our Heavenly Father to my beloved parents and the family, as well as of the remarkable faith and patience with which they were favoured, under circumstances of a very peculiar and distressing manner.

It was about the middle of the Fifth Month, 1798, that the county of Wexford, in Ireland, became a scene of open rebellion, headed by B—— H——,[1] a Protestant gentleman, and two Roman Catholic Priests, John Murphy and Philip Roche.[2] The aims of the insurgents were various; some were more cruelly disposed than others; all determined to liberate themselves by force of arms from the unequal yoke, as they believed it, of the British Government, and to become a free people; some to bring all Ireland to Catholicism, etc.

About ten days before the rebellion broke out, a Roman Catholic gentleman, who resided near, called on my father, and desired to speak to him in private. He then informed him that the county would, in the course of a few days, be in a state of general insurrection. My father replied that he could not credit it, for that he had frequently heard such rumours. The person assured him that he knew certainly it would be so, and that he had procured a vessel, now lying at Duncannon, to convey himself and family to Wales; and that, as a friend, he gladly offered accommodation to our household. My father thanked him for this act of friendship, but said that it felt to him a matter of great importance to remove from the position allotted him by Providence, yet that he would consider it of, and consult his wife. After having endeavoured to seek best wisdom, my dear parents concluded that it was right for them to remain at home, placing their dependence and confidence in Him who alone can protect, and who has promised to preserve those who put their trust in him.

The estate and spacious mansion, called Horetown, occupied by my parents, Jacob and Elizabeth Goff and the family, were situated about ten miles from each of the towns of Wexford and New Ross. The rebels formed two camps, at Carrickburn and Corbitt Hill, one on each side of the house, at distances of two and five miles from it. This central position caused a constant demand on us for provisions with which the insurgents were daily supplied, and they often said that they spared the lives of the family for that purpose . . .

Soon after the general rising and arming of the people in the county of Wexford,[3] we were roused one morning by the sound of cannon at a distance, and quickly heard that there had been an engagement at a place called the 'Three Rocks,' on the mountains of Forth, near Wexford, between the yeomanry and the rebels. After a severe conflict, the former were put to flight, with great loss of life; sixty or seventy were buried in one grave.

Two of my cousins named Heatly, whose mother had married out of our society, were officers in that corps, and escaped to our house under cover of the darkness of night. On their arrival, they found that their father and mother, and seven or eight little children, had been turned out of their comfortable home, and had also fled to my father's, where they were affectionately received. We had all retired to rest when these young officers arrived. The thankfulness of their parents, who had never expected to see them again, passes all description; they were much affected, and immediately returned thanks, on the bended knee, for the preservation of their children. For some days the two young men remained in the house, hiding from room to room, sometimes under the beds; as there was a frequent search for arms and Orangemen by the rebels. Some of the chiefs of these, having information of their being with us, called, demanding them to surrender, and offering them the United Irishmen's Oath. This, however, they absolutely refused, saying they had taken an oath of allegiance to their sovereign but a few days before, and would never perjure themselves. On

1. Beauchamp Bagenal Harvey (1762–98), commander-in-chief of the Wexford insurgents.
2. Author's footnote: Murphy was a chief instigator to cruelty and murder; he pretended to catch the flying bullets of the royalist troops, but was at last killed by a cannon ball. Roche, though more humane, was finally hung.
3. Author's note: Keightly remarks 'it was in the County of Wexford that the rebellion really raged — a county which would probably have remained at rest, had not the people been goaded into rebellion by the cruelties inflicted by the military and the self-styled loyalists. It was here only that priests appeared among the rebels, and that murders on a large scale were perpetrated by them' — History of England, Volume III. Thomas Keightly, The History of England (London: Whittaker and Co, 1839, 3 vols).

this, one of the rebels laid his hand on his sword, and in great irritation said, were it not for the respect they had for Mr. Goff, and that they did not wish to spill blood in his hall, their lives should be the forfeit of their refusal. At length, my cousins left our house by night, intending to make their way to Ross, and took shelter in the house of an old Roman Catholic nurse employed by the family, but by her they were betrayed, and handed over to the rebels, who took them prisoners to the camp. The lives of these interesting young men were, however, remarkably preserved, after they had endured much hardship in prison.

Two Roman Catholic men-servants in our family and lodging in the house, were compelled to join the rebels to save their lives; and were armed with pikes — the first we had seen. On my dear mother's hearing of their having brought these weapons, she sent to let them know she could not allow anything of the kind to be brought into her house; so each night they left them outside the door. They behaved quietly and respectfully throughout, generally returning home at the close of day.

The rebels set fire to the houses of many Protestants; and in the morning after the general rising, a Roman Catholic family, seven in number, came from Enniscorthy, apparently in great distress, saying they left the town on fire. They received shelter and hospitable entertainment from my dear parents, and remained with us the whole time. My mother often remarked, with reference to her large family, that provisions from day to day were so wonderfully granted that it seemed like the cruise of oil and the barrel of meat,[4] never-failing.

About twenty persons surrounded our dinner table each day, besides those in the kitchen, four of whom were members of our society; which my mother considered a great advantage at that awful period. She frequently said that 'hind's feet' appeared to be given her, in being enabled with extraordinary ease to get through the numerous household duties that then devolved upon her. Thus the gracious promise was verified in her experience: — 'As thy days so shall they strength be.'[5]

A rebel once enquired of her, 'Madam, do you think we shall gain the day?'

Feeling it to be a serious question, after a pause, she replied, 'The Almighty only knows.'

He answered, 'You are right, madam; not a *hair* of *your* head shall be hurt; but when this business is over, the Quakers are all to be driven down into Connaught, where the land is worth about two-pence an acre, and you will have to till *that*, and live on it as you can.' My mother smiled, and said, 'Give us a good portion, for we have a large family.'

Hannah and Arabella (afterwards Fennell), with Dinah W. Goff, aged about thirty, nineteen and fourteen, were the only daughters at home at this time. The two former usually walked three miles on First-days to the Meeting-House at Forrest, accompanied by two of the women servants, though they met with many interruptions on the way.

One day some of the people said, as they passed the Roman Catholic chapel, 'How they dare us by going through the streets! If they persist, they shall be taken and dragged to the altar of the chapel, and suffer the penalty of their obstinacy.' But my sisters passed quietly on. On one of these occasions, they remarked that a strange dog accompanied them: it followed them for some miles, and when they got safe home could not be induced to enter the house, but went away. This circumstance, though simple, seemed remarkable at the time. I fully believed that their minds were not resting on outward help, but on that Omnipotent arm which was mercifully underneath to sustain. They were enabled regularly to pursue their way, and to unite with the few Friends that were permitted to meet, remarking those opportunities as being peculiarly solemn. Our dear parents would gladly have joined them, but were unable, from the infirmities of age to walk so far, and had no horses left to draw a carriage . . .

A barn, about a mile and a half from us, belonging to a gentleman who lived at Scullabogue, was used as a prison, in which about 250 persons, chiefly Protestants, were confined — men, women, and children, some being infants in their mothers' arms. There they remained from Sixth until Third-day, without receiving any food, except some sheaves of wheat occasionally thrown in, that the rebels might have

4. I Kings 17:7–16.
5. Deuteronomy 33:25.

the amusement of seeing them scramble for the grains. On the day of the battle of New Ross, sixty or more of them were brought out on the lawn, and offered, one by one, life and liberty if they would change their religious profession; but they all refused. Some, after being half tortured to death, answered, 'No; give me more powder and ball first.'

Two of the prisoners, John and Samuel Jones, had attended our meeting, though not members; and their case was a particularly dreadful one. Samuel was kindly supported by his wife whilst he was unmercifully tortured; one limb after another being broken and each time the question repeated, 'Will you have the priest?' which he steadily refused: looking calmly at his faithful wife and saying, 'My dear, I am not hurt; I feel no pain.' His brother also bore his martyrdom with firmness, and was put to death by slow degrees in a similar way. The wife, with ample fortitude, stood between them when they were shot, and

held up a hand of each. She then implored the murderers to take her life also; but they refused, saying, 'They would not dishonour the Virgin Mary by killing a woman.' I saw her afterwards in deep affliction passing our gate as she sat in a cart with the remains of her husband and brother. On the same day, — viz. the 4th of Sixth month, — the barn was set on fire, and all the other prisoners (said to be 184) were consumed. Some of the poor women put their infants out through the windows, hoping to save them; but the ruffians took them up on their pikes, and threw them back into the flames. I saw the smoke of the barn and cannot now forget the strong and dreadful effluvium which was wafted from it to our lawn.[6]

6. Author's note: Yet Keightly remarks — 'We fear, if a fair balance were struck of the bloodshed, the cruelties, and the other enormities committed during these unhappy times, that the preponderance would be greatly on the side of the loyalists.'

ANONYMOUS

from:
SEA MONSTERS AND
IRISH VICTIMS (1857)

[In the 1850s the philanthropist Vere Foster[1] provided money to assist young Irish women to emigrate to America. In May 1857 a party of 120 girls travelled to America on a packet ship, *City of Mobile*. Foster himself travelled to New

1. Henry Lewis Vere Foster (1819–1900) was a member of a family settled in Ireland since the late seventeenth century. The separation of his grandmother Lady Elizabeth Foster from her husband and involvement in a *ménage à trois* with the Duke and Duchess of Devonshire had brought her children to England, and Vere Foster's father spent his career in the British foreign service. Vere Foster spent most of his childhood in Turin, was educated at Oxford, and worked at the Audit Office in London and the foreign service in Brazil, before making his first visit to his family's estate in County Louth in 1847. He was very much affected by his observations of famine and devoted much of the rest of his life to philanthropy in Ireland. From 1849 to 1857 he defrayed the expenses of 1,250 female emigrants and a much smaller number of men and children, spending approximately £10,000 on the project. For further information, see the subsection 'Women and Emigration from Ireland from the Seventeenth Century', edited by Maria Luddy and Dympna McLoughlin, Volume V, pp. 567–88.

York by steam, and was there when *City of Mobile* arrived. He discovered that some twenty-six of the girls had either left the ship to join relatives or become involved in sexual relations with crew members and disappeared from the ship. On 15 August 1857 the following letter appeared in a New York newspaper, the *Irish Vindicator*, drawing attention to these events and questioning the wisdom of emigration. The following month an article in the *Freeman's Journal* told the story of one of the alleged emigrants, Susan Smith, found wandering on Broadway: 'Her face was covered with bruises and her body with rags. She told a wild and pitiful story to the commissioners of emigration — that she came to New York in the *City of Mobile* under the care of a gentleman whom she afterwards requited with ingratitude — that she had since lived a life of crime and suffering, and was now a wanderer in a strange land without a home, friends or money.' The *Freeman's Journal* went on to claim sensationally that 'Out of 120 who left Ireland in safety, with their characters vouched for by their clergy, only twelve or so were uninfected, the rest having been ruined in the short space of one month.'[2] This story undermined the confidence of families and priests in Louth to this sponsored female emigration.]

2. *Freeman's Journal*, 5 September 1857.

A few weeks since the British Consul prosecuted an American Captain for corrupting an English girl, who had been committed to his charge as a passenger on board his ship. After a lengthened investigation, the charge was dismissed, on account of great levity on her part.

A case has just occurred, of such wholesale villainy, that public opinion ought to be invoked to brand with obloquy, and, if possible, visit with condign punishment, the infamous violators of innocence. As the victims of these cowardly outrages are Irish girls, we have no hope that the British Consul will stir in the matter, although the case is a far more grievous one than that which caused his indignation on a former occasion. The circumstances are these: Mr. De Vere Foster, a benevolent Irish landlord, sent out in an American packet ship, some time ago, about a hundred and twenty young women, selected on account of their irreproachable characters. These were testified to by the Priests and other influential and respectable persons, who had known them from childhood. In order to make proper arrangements, Mr. Foster came over here in advance. Upon the arrival of the vessel, he found that nearly twenty of these poor girls were either missing, or refused to remain any longer under his control, they having been seduced by the officers and crew during the voyage. They were hid in the vessel on their arrival here, and then smuggled ashore to some vile dens in Water street, where they were abandoned by these cowardly ruffians to a life of horror and shame.

As a specimen of the rapidity with which these poor creatures are hurled down the path of vice and death, let us give one instance. About a fortnight since a gentleman was attracted by the appearance of what seemed to be a bundle of rags, but which, on being roused, was really a girl of about eighteen. Her face was covered with bruises, given by some unmanly wretches, and she seemed as though her lingering humanity was flying from her for ever. He ascertained that this poor creature's name was Susan Smith, of County Meath; that she had left her native land in this accursed plague ship, and had been corrupted by some of these sea-wolves, the sailors, and left to die a dog's death, in that most pitiless of all places, New York.

This, of course, is the fate of hundreds of our poor countrywomen, who, driven by famine, and the oppression of the British Government at home, are sent to what they consider a Land of Promise, to find a shelter and a home. But alas! they have to pass the fiery ordeal of the sea passage, in these floating Pandemomiums [sic], called emigrant ships, manned by the vilest of God's creation! Better — far better — that the mothers had dashed, when babies, the brains out of these future victims to the lust and villainy of man. Better that Mr. De Vere Foster abandon his scheme, since the cost is so fearful. Better that the poor girls die, overworked and famished in old Ireland, so that they fill a virtuous, though a pauper's grave. Indeed, in one respect, this emigration, while it has been the making of America has been the destruction of Ireland.

The bone, muscle and valor which have made this Republic the boast of her sons, and the envy of the world, have drained Ireland of her vigor. The men who carried the Stars and Stripes through Mexico, were the men who should have achieved the independence of their own beloved Ireland.

But to return to the more immediate subject, the protection of these poor girls in emigrant vessels, and the sure punishment of the monsters who insult and defile them. This is a question which concerns not alone the honor of Ireland, but also that of America. We say that the treatment these poor Irish girls receive from the officers and crews of the passenger vessels, is a foul disgrace to our Republic, and, as an American citizen we declare it must be redressed.

Surely there are enough Irish ladies and gentlemen ... whose feelings remain true to their instincts of sympathy with their poorer countrywomen? Let them come forward and form a committee to protect our fair children, lest in their transit from the lovely land of their birth to the glorious one of their adoption, they become a grief and reproach to the name of both. We call for help in this matter, in the name of all that's sacred in the eyes of man and woman — the purity of our wives and daughters — which must be shielded at all hazards from such roving fiends as compose the crews of too many of our emigrant ships.

FRANCES BROWNE

(1816–79)

from:
THE HIDDEN SIN (1866)

[In the 1860s literary critics identified a new sub-genre in popular fiction, termed 'sensation novels'. Wilkie Collins and Mary Anne Braddon are among the best-known English practitioners; Frances Browne, Charlotte Riddell and J.S. Le Fanu[1] were the major Irish contributors to this new fashion. The sensationalists were apparently more concerned with crime and violence than with character and sentiment. Their readership was identified as largely female and the secrets at the heart of these novels was often the secret of women's anger, frustration and fantasy of escape from domestic imprisonment and suffocating relationships. Novels such as Wilkie Collins's *The Moonstone* (1863) are also preoccupied with crimes committed by British imperialists coming home to roost in the English country house. Finally, these novels came into vogue just at the time when there was widespread anxiety over a perceived explosion of syphilis and other sexually transmitted diseases. This anxiety led to the passing of a series of Contagious Diseases Acts,[2] regulating prostitutes in garrison towns, and to a feminist campaign for the repeal of these acts and a debate on marital sexuality. Frances Browne's novel combines these concerns with crime, empire and syphilis, giving them a specifically Irish dimension. The plot is necessarily complicated. In 1800 an Armagh family called La Touche[3] is in financial trouble. An elder son is sent to Dublin to collect money from their bank to settle debts. He disappears without trace. The family is disgraced, the home sold, and the children dispersed to relatives. Thirty years later the narrator, Lucien, returns from America, where he has been brought up, to London, where he contacts his father's old friend, a Scots Presbyterian, and gets a job as a clerk in a bank owned by Madame Palivezi, a woman of a certain, or rather uncertain, age, heiress to a Greek banking fortune, but the last of her line. Lucien, although engaged to a young woman he met in America, falls under the spell of Madame Palivezi, whom he calls his 'Gloriana.'[4] In the following excerpt, from Volume III, Chapter VII, she reveals to him her family secret.]

THE HISTORY OF THE PALIVEZI, AND THEIR DOOM

'My family were reckoned old and illustrious among the Greeks settled in Southern Russia, that corner of ancient Scythia,[5] to which Greece sent out her earliest colonies, the meeting-place of Europe's oldest civilisation and most ancient barbarism, where the creeds and customs of East and West still flourish side by side, and their races have dwelt for ages without mingling. We were not sprung from the early colonists, but of the Attic[6] stock; Archons of Athens[7] were among our ancestors; but, like many of the Greek patricians, we removed to Byzantium,[8] when Constantine the Great[9] made it his capital and founded the Eastern Empire.

'Ages after, when the Ottoman[10] Turks were becoming known on the Greek frontiers, and the Russians of the North were catching the lights of civilisation and Christianity from Constantinople, a dispute with the Patriarch[11] which began about Church dues, and ended in an accusation of worshipping Jupiter,[12] made us emigrate first to the flourishing city of Novgorod,[13] and afterwards to Kief,[14] still the holy place of the North, and then chosen by Saint Vladimir[15] as the capital of his new-christened kingdom.

---

1. Charlotte Riddell (1832–1906), novelist and ghost story writer; Joseph Sheridan Le Fanu (1814–73), novelist, author of *Uncle Silas* (1864).
2. The Contagious Diseases Acts (1866–9) allowed for the compulsory inspection of 'prostitutes' for venereal diseases in certain army camps in Britain and Ireland.
3. The real La Touches were a family of Huguenot merchants, who opened a bank in Dublin in the eighteenth century.
4. Gloriana is one of the names under which Queen Elizabeth I is known in Edmund Spenser's *The Faerie Queene* (1590, 1596).

5. A large country, whose boundaries were unknown in the ancient world, including modern-day Asian Russia, Siberia, Ukraine, Poland, Lithuania, northern Scandinavia and others. The Scythians were composed of several nations or tribes and were often represented as peculiarly barbarous.
6. Attica was the part of Greece which included Athens.
7. The Archontes were the chief magistrates of Athens.
8. Byzantium, a city on the Bosphorus, was renamed Constantinople (when Constantine made it his capital) and is now Istanbul.
9. Constantinus (d. AD 337), the Roman emperor, was on his way to battle when he saw a cross in the sky and consequently converted to Christianity. He removed part of the Roman senate to Constantinople, and soon after his death there was a separation of the eastern and western parts of the Roman empire.
10. Of the Turkish dynasty founded by Osman I, *c.* 1300.
11. Bishop of Constantinople.
12. Most powerful of the Roman gods.
13. Russian town, on the banks of the Volkhov.
14. The city of Kiev was site of the first Christian church in Russia.
15. Vladimir (*c.* 956–1015) was Grand Duke of Kiev. He converted to Christianity in 988, to marry the Roman princess Anna, and took her brother's name, Basil. He had the people of Kiev baptized in the River Dnieper.

'From that period the Palivezi lived and traded among the Greeks of Russia. Always of a patrician rank and good estate, they had become merchants and bankers as early as the Roman times; the Greek nobility gave example in this respect to those of Venice and other Italian cities. They carried their business with them to the North; Novgorod and Kief were the emporiums of European and Asiatic commerce; from the tenth to the fifteenth century, the Greeks monopolised its higher and more profitable branches, and the Palivezi were the most successful house among them. In spite of intestine wars and Tartar[16] invasions, which often passed over the land in those five hundred years, their mercantile prudence, enterprise, and honour — which, by the way, were equally proverbial — enabled them to gather and keep riches which no other firm in the north could boast. It was their wisdom and it proved their strength . . .

'When at length the northern torrent overwhelmed the land, they bribed barbarian prejudices, bought over favourites, and thus obtained good terms from the Tartar chiefs, with whom they treated on their own account as independent powers. They had similar dealings, warlike and pacific, with the Poles and the Teutonic knights; in short, with all the conquerors and troublers of those times.

'But Russia struggled back into national life. Vasilrewitsch[17] shook off the Tartar domination, and built the Kremlin[18] at Moscow, the cross[19] was established in the north, and the crescent[20] waned before it step by step, and year by year, till in the days of Ivan,[21] called by his own subjects the Terrible, and known in England as the Muscovite Czar who sent ambassadors to Queen Elizabeth,[22] and allowed her subjects to form a trading company at Archangel,[23] the kingdoms of Crimea and Kazan, to which his ancestors had paid tribute, were conquered and reduced to Russian rule, the whole South and East, as far as the frontiers of Poland and the Euxine Sea, became his dominions, and the Palivezi had to deal with an absolute and Christian Czar.

'They lent him money, as they had done to his predecessors; they bought over his ministers and favourites — for the terrible Ivan had some such — but Christian Russians were more expensive to bribe and buy than Mahometan Tartars. The conquering Czar could not be so well secured by loans as his tribute-paying ancestors had been; it was requisite to please and serve him too, if they would live and trade within his bounds, and about this time Ivan required a piece of special service.

'He had conquered the kingdom of Kazan; internal feuds and the chances of war and time had exterminated its royal house all to one old man, trembling on the verge of the grave, and his daughter, the last but undoubted heiress of the Tartar line. It was true that women counted for little among the Eastern and Moslem races, but the blood of Zingus[24] was in her veins; the Tartar chief who happened to marry her might claim the sovereignty of Kazan, in her right, and Ivan was determined to secure it to his posterity. The antipathies of race and religion were stronger in those days than they are now among the Russians. The absolute Czar, though he might set up wheels and gibbets for them, could not ask one of his Muscovite nobles to marry the Tartar princess, with any amount of dowry; but the head of the Greek banking house had an only son and heir, yet undisposed of in marriage, and Ivan fixed on him as a safe husband for the dangerous heiress . . .

'Now, Lucien, I am about to tell you one of those traditions which dignified historians ignore, and sensible biographers reason away, but which are nevertheless the truest part of national or family history. Yermiska, that was the Tartar name of the princess, though they baptized her Helena, in the newly-erected church dedicated to that saint[25] in Kazan, had formed an early attachment to a Calmuck chief, who had fought gallantly for his share of the Crimea, retired with his tribe before the advancing Russians, far eastward, and was said to have ultimately settled on the frontiers of China. His descent was held

16. Inhabitants of Central Asia.
17. Basil III (1505–33).
18. Fort in the centre of Moscow.
19. Christian symbol.
20. Muslim symbol.
21. Ivan IV (1530–84), Tsar of Russia from 1533.
22. Elizabeth I (1533–1603), Queen of England from 1558.
23. Russian town at the head of the Dvina river. The modern town dates from the visit of English voyager Richard Chancellor in 1533, and an English factory was built on the river soon afterwards.

24. Genghis Khan (1162–1227), Mongol emperor.
25. Helena (c. 247–c. 327), wife of Roman emperor Constantinus I Chlorus, mother of Constantine the Great.

inferior to her own; I believe the tribe were not orthodox Mahometans either; but there was a vow between them, and Yermiska would fain have retired eastward, too. But, the old chief, her father, would not leave the soil of Kazan and the stone coffins of his ancestors.

'For the sake of remaining there, he consented to her marriage with the Christian trader; the conquering Czar commanded it; the Palivezi, father and son — though solemnly warned of the bride's aversion, by her old confidential nurse, secretly sent to their house under shade of night — held on to the wedding which promised such advantages.

'Yermiska was a Tartar Moslema, accustomed to think of revenge, but never of revolt or disobedience; and the night before her marriage she deliberately drank a potion, prepared for her by a Calmuck sorceress, famous throughout the north, and known to journey as far as Khamtschtka in her search for plants of power. How, or of what that draught was compounded, the Powers of Darkness best know; but the Princess declared, and time has proved her statement true, that it would transmit hereditary and irremediable madness to the utmost generation of her descendants.

'You look incredulous, my friend. There are secrets in nature for which the boasted science of Europe has neither name nor place. Among the rank-growing weeds of her fens and marshes, among the wind-sown flowers of her woods and wilds, there are plants that draw occult influences down from the midnight moon, or up from the nether kingdom, to mingle with their juices, and furnish the skilful searcher with weapons against life and death, never yet matched by your chemists and anatomists. They were known three thousand years ago to necromancers, who sought them out on the plains of Thessaly[26] and the vales of Etruria.[27] Through them they changed men's natures and turned the course of their affections; the love philtres were not all fancies, neither were the tales of Caligula and Domitian.[28]

'From them the Egyptian embalmers drew the gums which fenced their dead against decay, while it fell on successive creeds and dynasties. That knowledge, like all the deeper and higher sorts, has no written records. It cannot be found in books; they contain but the husks and rinds of learning, being meant for the common eye and mind. It exists, nevertheless, among primitive and unlettered races; the African slave and the Hindoo pariah[29] have visited the sins of the fathers upon the Anglo-Saxon families by means similar to those which the unwilling bride employed against mine.

'Strange that such mysterious drugs should be far less powerful to save than to destroy; as it is thought because the plants that bear them grow so near the dead, for the graves of earth's first inhabitants are in her wastes and wilds. You cannot believe it — the subject is too new to you; we will talk of it hereafter, if there be time; but the night wears, and I must proceed with my weary tale.

'Eusebius Palivezi, one of the handsomest men of his time, and one of the wealthiest in Russia, though never able to supersede the Calmuck chief, espoused his Tartar bride, with a pomp which astonished all Kazan, in the church where she had been baptized on the previous day, brought her home to his house in Kief, with splendour and festivity befitting a wealthy Greek of the sixteenth century, and was henceforth established in the favour of the terrible Czar, and in the monopoly of Easter trade and banking.

'The Princess Helena, as people continued to call her, behaved like a dutiful and prudent wife — though she insisted on having her tirema, or harem apartments, kept strictly separate from the public rooms — wore a thicker veil than Greek ladies were accustomed to, and never went to church if she could help it. There was great peace, if nothing better, between her and her husband for full thirty years.

'They had three sons and two daughters; the house of Palivez had increased in riches as well as in numbers, when the great plague,[30] which devastated Eastern Europe at the end of the sixteenth century, found its way to Kief, entered their walls in spite of wealth and care, and first lighted on the Princess Helena. The Tartar woman was dying, and she knew it.

---

26. Northern Greece.
27. Northern Italy.
28. Caius Caligula (c. AD 12–41) and Titus Flavius Domitianus (AD 51–96), Roman emperors famous for cruel and outlandish behaviour.

29. Member of low caste.
30. Plague was common throughout Europe in the sixteenth century; a wave of plague said to have originated in Constantinople spread across eastern Europe in 1575.

'In the middle of the third night, a band of Greek monks stood round her bed; they had come to administer the last sacraments and see the soul won from Mahomet safe on its last journey; her husband and children stood at the chamber-door — they could venture no nearer the pestilence, though the black cross marked the door, and none might pass out or in. But the daughter of Zingus raised herself with a final effort, looked Eusebius Palivez in the face, and told him, in a tone which all the house could hear, what she had done for him and his posterity the night before her marriage; prayed that the Prophet in whom her fathers trusted, might hold the curse over them to their latest generation, struck the Eucharist out of the hand of a horrified monk, and, with a shout of fierce laughter, fell back and died.

'Eusebius Palivez lived to see his hundred and fifth birthday. He also lived to see the fearful intelligence of that midnight proved true; his eldest son, about the age of fifty, fell, as all the Palivez have, or would have, fallen, into strange and hopeless insanity. Up to that time he had been a man of clear intellects, sober, honest habits, and more than common understanding.

'There was no cause of accident or disease the doctors could discover for his madness. It began with an unaccountable loss of memory; Lucien, I hold that faculty to be the hinge on which both life and mind turn. Well, it went from him, as it were, piecemeal, for about six months; and then furious, raging frenzy was suddenly developed.

'I have heard that he killed three keepers within the first year; and the part of the house where they kept him had to be walled up, to prevent his getting out and destroying the entire family. After about seven years of that frantic state, he gradually sank into imbecility, so grovelling and degraded that the details could only produce disgust.

'I have heard them all, for this was the first case and example of our family misfortune; henceforth it was the sure inheritance of every succeeding Palivez, man or woman — somewhat modified in the latter, but the same in character and duration; for both there was no recovery — no interval; and it always came on at middle age, sooner or later, according to constitution, but never deferred beyond the fiftieth year. You will say it was hereditary in the Princess's Tartar family, derived, as it was, from barbarous warriors, whose lives had been full of wild excitement, and probably wilder excess.

'That would be a probable and sensible explanation; but I believe in the account handed down to us from Eusebius, her unlucky husband, and my unlucky ancestor. He left a doom hanging over every Palivez, which prudence could not ward off, or wealth bribe away — coming nearer to them year by year, as they grew out of youth into the business and importance of rich and wise men of the world; but there was brave blood among them.'

[Madame Palivezi goes on to explain the family's movement from Russia, to Amsterdam, and then to Dublin, and its suicide pact. She asks Lucien to be her killer when madness begins to afflict her.]

JAMES GREENWOOD

(1832–1929)

from:
THE WRENS OF THE CURRAGH (1867)

[The sensation fiction of the late nineteenth century was both inspired by and in its turn influenced sensationalism in other narratives. Newspaper reporting made much of sex scandals, murder, insanity and exploitation, particularly of the poor. James Greenwood, an English journalist, had contributed significantly to the success of his brother Frederick's new journal, the *Pall Mall Gazette*,[1] with the publication of three papers entitled 'A Night on

1. Frederick Greenwood (1830–1909) had succeeded Thackeray as editor of the *Cornhill* magazine; in 1865 he founded the *Pall Mall Gazette* with George Smith, an evening newspaper to be made up 'of original articles upon the many things which engage the thoughts, or employ the energies, or amuse the leisure of mankind'.

the Casual Ward' in 1866; in 1867 he travelled to Ireland to investigate stories about the miserable lives of prostitutes living near the army camp at the Curragh. These stories had particular resonance in the wake of the passing of the first Contagious Diseases Act (1866), allowing for the compulsory inspection for venereal disease of women at certain army camps in Britain and Ireland. The 'wrens', so-called because their makeshift huts appeared to be burrows in the earth, had been reported as a feature of the Curragh from the 1840s. Greenwood was a friend and colleague of English novelists such as Thackeray and Meredith,[2] and his reporting veers between comedy and pathos in a way that is typical of nineteenth-century British novelistic representations of the poor. The article appeared in the *Pall Mall Gazette* on 15 and 17 October 1867.]

For many a year mysterious little stories have wafted to England from the Curragh — hints and glimpses of a certain colony of poor wretches there who lived as nobody else in the three kingdoms lived, and died most like people who do come within the bills of mortality — tramps and others — when they happened to perish of cold, want, and whisky, upon that vast common. In these stories there was always something so shocking that comfortable people were glad to disbelieve them, and something so strange that it was reasonable enough to set them aside: they were not probable in an orderly, commonplace, police-regulated, Christian community like our own. Besides, one could not read those little stories — paragraphs in odd corners of news-papers in the great gooseberry season — without a knowing suspicion that if only half they told was true more must have been heard of them. This seemed all the more likely because the Curragh is not an unfrequented nook in some distant corner of the land, but a plain near a capital city — an encampment wherein thousands of Englishmen as well as thousands of Irishmen constantly live, gentle and simple both, and where scores of strangers, visitors who go there for no other purpose but to see what is to be seen, peer about every week of every summer season. It did not seem at all natural that things so very unlike what ought to happen in a nineteenth century as those little wandering paragraphs hinted at could go on from year to year without investigation and arrest. But our own observation is that the wildest circumstances and most incredible anomalies of life are those which lie open to every eye, and are stared at, and are not seen.

. . . Therefore we solicited some one to go to the camp, and find the wrens (if any), and visit their nests (if any), and spend time enough by day and night amongst them to let us know what peculiar people it is of which so many incredible hints have been given — and forgotten. What the nature of the task really was, and what additional knowledge it gives us of the world we live in, will appear from the following narrative: —

It was on an evening before September had cooled — three weeks ago and more — that I set out to investigate the manners and customs, the habits and habitat, of a bird not unknown indeed in England, not even in London, but reported to be on the Curragh of a seriously peculiar kind. Rumour had told us all we had heard of the species; Rumour is of ticklish veracity; but one thing may be said for her, that if she sometimes tells more lie than is tolerable, she sometimes tells more truth than it is convenient to believe . . . From London to Holyhead, from Holyhead to Kingstown, from Kingstown to Dublin — all this was within the limits of civilization . . . Dublin — yes, Dublin is a civilized city too: there is not courage enough in the world to deny it. But Kildare, county town though it be, one may be permitted to withhold from it the all-sufficing designation. To Kildare my steps were directed, for that town is nearer than any other to the Curragh camp: — thence could I most easily go a-nesting . . .

In the afternoon Jimmy Lynch — my carman on many little expeditions afterwards — a loud locquacious carman, whose adoration was given to horses and his respect to M. Donnelly who fought the great fight with Mr. Cooper in Donnelly's hollow — called to take me on my first visit to the Curragh. As we drove along Jimmy talked of his mare — there was never such a mare; of the fight — there was never such a fight; while I, half listening, looked away to the vast common where an army lives all the year round. 'How many men do you think, Jimmy?' I asked, breaking into his raptures about the 'Scottish Queen'. 'Well, thin, tin or twelve thousand, maybe! and a moighty foine toime

2. William Makepeace Thackeray (1811–63) and George Meredith (1828–1909).

they have of it!' 'Without their wives and sweethearts?' 'Widout their wives, shure, and hwat of that, yer hanner? But some of their wives is with them, I belave, good luck to them! though there's no sweethearts in the camp at all — divil a one! But over there,' pointing vaguely with his whip across the common, 'there's minny of them poor devils living in places made of furze inthirely. Winther and summer in a bit of a bush.' 'Wrens, don't you call them?' 'Wrins! That's the name ov 'em! Wrins! that's what they *do* call 'em, and a dridful life they lade. Most distrissing, belave me!' This exclamation was not priggish in Jimmy — it was only a note caught from the mouths of *other* intelligent tourists. A moment of silence and his mind sought relief in the virtues of his mare, while my eyes wandered over the common where many a furze bush was visible, but none which looked as if it could be inhabited by any creatures but birds of the air and beasts of the field . . .

When once a wren's nest is distinguished from the natural mounds of furze amidst which it is placed, after recognition is tolerably easy; though at a first glance it is so much like a mere bush that you might well pass by without dreaming that it was the habitation of human creatures. However, there are differences of course; and thus after I had looked for a few moments at my first nest, and glanced around and was in fact in the midst of a little village, with as many — homes shall I say? and as many inhabitants as some English hamlets whose names are well marked on the map. Dotted about to right, and left, and onward, at intervals varying from 20 to 100 yards, were other bushes, which bore not only certain signs of man's constructive skill, but of woman's occupancy. Suspended against the prickly sides of one of them was a petticoat, against another a crinoline; an article so bulky and intractable that it could not well be got inside. Indeed, the probability is that it never did get inside at all — never was inside; but was put on and taken off, as occasion required, at the hole that served for a door. How *could* three or four large-limbed women, crinolined accordingly, live in a space no bigger than the ox's crib or the horse's stall? Besides, that is exaggeration. To be particular, the nests have an interior space of about nine feet long by seven feet broad; and the roof is not more than four and a-half feet

from the ground. You crouch into them, as beasts crouch into cover; and there is no standing upright till you crawl out again. They are rough, misshapen domes of furze — like big, rude birds' nests compacted of harsh branches, and turned topsy-turvy upon the ground. The walls are some twenty inches thick, and they do get pretty well compacted — much more than would be imagined. There is no chimney — not even a hole in the roof, which generally slopes forward. The smoke of the turf fire which burns on the floor of the hut has to pass out at the door when the wind is favourable, and to reek slowly through the crannied walls when it is not . . .

[R]eady as Jimmy was to 'call' upon the energies of Scottish Queen, I insisted upon his going slowly through the bush village, and then I was enabled to see on a first visit that its inhabitants at any rate were all of one kind and looked all alike. In the first place every woman is Irish. There is not a single Englishwoman now in the nests, though there were two of our countrywomen there lately: these girls, however, went away with a regiment ordered elsewhere. Then the wrens are almost all young — the greater number of them being from seventeen to five and twenty years old. Then they almost all come out of cabins in country places, and seem still to enjoy — most of them — some remains of the fine strength and health they brought from those wretched cots. Then there was a common look, shocking to see, of hard depravity — the look of hopeless, miserable, but determined and defiant wickedness. Fine faces, and young ones too, were marred into something quite terrible by this look, and the spirit of it seemed to move in the lazy swing of their limbs, and was certainly heard in their voices. And lastly they are dressed alike. All day they lounge in a half-naked state, clothed simply in the one frieze petticoat, and another equally foul cast loosely over their shoulders, though towards evening they put on the decent attire of the first girl I met there. These bettermost clothes are kept clean and bright enough; the frequency with which they are seen displayed on the bushes to dry shows how often they are washed and how well. These observations apply to the cotton gown, the stockings, the white petticoat alone — frieze and flannel never know anything of soap and water at all apparently. The 'Curragh petticoat' is familiarly known for miles and miles around: its peculiarity seems to be that it is starched but not ironed. The difference in the appearance of these poor wretches when the gown and petticoat are donned and when they are taken off again (that is to say, the moment they come back from the 'hunting grounds') answers precisely to their language and demeanour when sober and when tipsy. In the one condition they are generally as well behaved and civil as any decent peasant women need be; in the other they are like raging savages, with more than a savage's *vileness* . . .

The communistic principle governs each nest, and in hard times one family readily helps another, or several help one; the deeps are not deaf to the voice of the lower deeps. None of the women have any money of their own. What each company get is thrown into a common purse, and the nest is provisioned out of it. What they get is little indeed; a few halfpence turned out of one pocket and another when the clean starched frocks are thrown off at night make up a daily income just enough to keep body and soul together. How that feat is accomplished at all in winter — in such winters as the last one — which was talked of only three weeks ago as a dreadful thing of yesterday and its recurrence dreaded as a horrible thing of to-morrow — is past my comprehension. It is an understanding that they take it in turns to do the marketing, and to keep house when the rest go wandering at night; though the girl whose dress is freshest generally performs the one duty, and the woman whose youth is not the freshest, whose good looks are quite gone, the other. And there are several wrens who have been eight or nine years on the Curragh — one or two who have been there as long as the camp itself . . .

Visiting the bushwomen of the Curragh in the daytime naturally seemed to be an incomplete way of ascertaining how they really lived. The wren is, of course, a night bird, and ought to be seen at night by any one who thinks it worth while to learn her real characteristics and the part she plays in the economy of the universe. Therefore I ventured on a journey to the bush one evening, making myself as safe as a man can be who goes into haunts of recklessness and crime with nothing about him to tempt cupidity, and with a stout stick for the casual purposes of defence. I did not suppose I should have any

extraordinary adventures, but the Curragh is a wide place, and very lonely, and such of the Queen's troops as consort with the bushwomen are often of a dangerous character, especially when they happen to be drunk . . .

No. 2 nest had also its turf fire burning, near the door; by the light of which I saw, as I approached it, one wretched figure alone. Crouched near the glowing turf, with her head resting upon her hands, was a woman whose age I could scarcely guess at, though I think by the masses of black hair that fell forward over her hands and backward over her bare shoulders that she must have been young. She was apparently dozing, and taking no heed of the pranks of the frisky little curly-headed boy of whom I have made mention before; he was playing on the floor. When I announced myself by rapping on the bit of corrugated iron which stood across the bottom of the doorway, the woman started in something like fright; but she knew me at a second glance, and in I went. 'Put back the iron if ye plaze,' said the wren, as I entered; 'the wind's blowing this way to-night, bad luck to it.' The familiar iron pot was handed to me to sit upon, my stick was delivered over to poor little Billy Carson, my whisky flask and my tobacco were laid out for consumption, and I laid *myself* out for as much talk as could be got from the watching wren. Billy Carson had not the splendid appearance he wore when I last saw him, in his Sunday frock. His clothes were rags, and they were few and foul. The face of the poor child was of the colour of the earth he sprawled upon; but there were his thick curly black locks and his great big eyes, so full of fun and sense, of innocence and spirit, as if he wasn't a wren's child at all. While I looked at this unfortunate little fellow, wondering what was likely to be the end of him, and what my own end might have been had I begun life as a wren's little boy, the woman still sat crouched near the fire, with her face hidden on her folded arms, in a very miserable and despairing attitude indeed. I asked her whether the boy was hers, by way of starting a conversation; she bluntly answered me without looking up that 'it wasn't, thank God.' I tried again. 'Have some whisky; you're cold.' 'Indade I am, but it's not whisky that will warm me this night,' said she. But next minute she jumped up, turned some whisky into a cup, tossed it off with a startlingly rapid jerk of hand and head, went to the looking glass (an irregular fragment as big as the palm of your hand), and wisped her hair up in a large handsome knot. Then the whisky began to operate; her tongue was loosed. She readily answered all the trifling questions I asked of her, meanwhile putting Billy to bed, who had got sleepy. I was very curious to see how this would be done when she proposed it to Billy, but there was nothing remarkable in the process to reward expectation. The straw was pulled from under the crockery shelf, and Billy was placed upon the heap dressed as he was, with an injunction to shut his eyes. He did so, and the operation was complete.

Of course I wanted to know how my wretched companion in this lonely, windy, comfortless hovel came from being a woman to be turned into a wren. The story began with 'no father nor mother,' an aunt who kept a whisky store in Cork, an artilleryman who came to the whisky store, and saw and seduced the girl. By-and-by his regiment was ordered to the Curragh. The girl followed him, being then with child. 'He blamed me for following him,' said she. 'He'd have nothing to do with me. He told me to come here and do like other women did. And what could I do? My child was born here, in this very place, and glad I was of the shelter, and glad I was when the child died — thank the blessed Mary! What could I do with a child? His father was sent away from here, and a good riddance. He used me very bad.' After a minute's silence the woman continued, a good deal to my surprise. 'I'll show you the likeness of a betther man, far away! — one that never said a cross word to me — blessed's the ground he treads upon!' And, fumbling in the pocket of her too scanty and too dingy petticoat, she produced a photographic portrait of a soldier, inclosed in a half a dozen greasy letters. 'He's a bandsman, sir, and a handsome man indade he is, and I believe he likes me too. But they have sent him to Malta for six years; I'll never see my darlint again.' And then this poor wretch, who was half crying as she spoke, told me how she walked to Dublin to see him just before he sailed, 'because the poor craythur wanted to see me onst more.' The letters she had in her pocket were from him; they were read and answered by the girl whose penmanship I have already celebrated, and who seems to be the only woman in the whole colony who can either read or write. I could not find another, at any rate.

From this woman, so strangely compounded, I learned, as I sat smoking over the turf fire — and the night was bitterly cold — much that I have already related. I also learned the horror the women have of the workhouse; and how, if they are found straying over the limits allotted to them, they have to appear at Naas to be fined for the offence (a half-crown seems to be the fine commonly inflicted), or to be sent for seven days to gaol. There, according to this woman, they get about a pint of 'stirabout' for breakfast, at two o'clock in the afternoon some more stirabout and about a pound of bread, and nothing more till breakfast time next day. I cannot but think this a false statement, and yet she spoke of the workhouse as a place still more unlovely. However, she had suffered so much privation last winter that she had made up her mind not to stay in the bush another such season. 'At the first fall of the snow I'll to the workhouse, that I will!' she said, in the tone of one who says that in such an event he is determined to cut his throat. 'Why, would you belave it, sir, last winter the snow would be up as high as our little house, and we had to cut a path through it to the min, or we'd be ruined intirely.' In this way she talked, and I listened, and heard how one of the inhabitants of the place I was in had been seduced at the age of thirteen years and four months by an officer in a rifle regiment — a circumstance of which my companion seemed to think there was some reason to be proud. 'A rale gentleman he was.' In some such spirit one woman declared to me, with a scornful air, 'It wasn't one man brought me here, but minny! and that's the truth, bedad!'

WILLIAM CARLETON

(1794–1869)

from:
'AUTOBIOGRAPHY' in
THE LIFE OF WILLIAM
CARLETON (1896)

[Carleton provides evidence that courtship was heavily codified in early nineteenth-century rural culture, and that community values were sufficiently internalized for people to police their own behaviour to a great extent. The extraordinary silence of his passionate love for Anne Duffy is an extreme example of the reticence, even shyness, between young people noted by other commentators such as the Halls. William Carleton's fragment of *Autobiography* was incorporated into D.J. Donoghue's *The Life of William Carleton*, 2 vols (London: Downey & Co., 1896).]

There was at that time a vocal choir of young men and women in the parish, who, in virtue of their office, were obliged to kneel around the altar, where they sang some very beautiful music. Among the females was one tall, elegant, and lady-like girl, whose voice was perfectly entrancing. Her name was Anne Duffy, daughter of George Duffy, the miller of Augher Mill.[1] She knelt that Sunday, and, in fact, every Sunday, on the left hand side of the priest, next the altar; while I, more by accident than anything else, placed myself in the same position on the other side, so that we were right opposite to each other. Whether it was the opportunity of having her before me, or her beauty, I cannot decide, probably it was both together — but I said no prayers that day. My eyes were never off her — they were riveted on her. I felt a new sensation, one of the most novel and overwhelming delight. After Mass I followed her as far as the cross-roads at Ned McKeown's. Ned's was a corner house, with two doors of entrance — one to the kitchen, and the other into a small grocery shop, kept by a man named Billy Fulton. It was a great convenience to the neighbourhood, especially to those who lived in the mountain districts, or what was termed the 'Mountain Bar'.

Before Mass, a great number of both sexes, but principally men, lingered about these cross-roads, engaged in chat upon the usual topics of the day: the most important, and that in which they felt the deepest interest, was the progress of the Peninsular War.[2] Bonaparte[3] was their favourite, and their hopes were not only that he would subdue England, but ultimately become monarch of Ireland. From what source they derived the incredible variety of personal anecdotes respecting him it is impossible to conjecture. One of the most remarkable, and which was narrated and heard with the most sincere belief in its truth was the fact of his being invulnerable. It mattered nothing whether he went into the thickest part of the battle or not, the bullets hopped harmlessly off him like hailstones from a window.

Now Anne Duffy's father was a great politician, and sometimes spent half an hour at the cross-roads, both before and after Mass, and Anne herself occasionally stopped a short time there, but very rarely. At all events I saw her there again, and our looks met. She appeared to be amused by my attention, which she seemed to receive agreeably, and with pleasure. Well, I went home a changed man — of fifteen years of age — wrapped up from the world and all external nature; the general powers of my mind concentrated into one thought, and fixed upon one image, Anne Duffy.

There has been much controversy upon the subject of love at first sight. I, however, am a proof of its truth. The appearance of the sun in the firmament is not more true. I went home, elated, entranced — like a man who had discovered a rich but hidden treasure. My existence became important. I had an interest in life — I was no longer a cipher. I had something to live for. I felt myself a portion of society and the world. How I spent the remainder of the day I scarcely remember, especially as to association with my companions on this festive occasion. All

1. Augher, County Tyrone.

2. Peninsular War, 1807–14; Britain was at war with Napoleon in Spain.
3. Napoleon Bonaparte (1769–1821), first Emperor of France.

I know is, that Anne Duffy was never for a single moment out of my head, and when I was asleep that night she appeared as distinctly before me as she did during the day; but with this difference, that her beauty was more exquisitely angelic and ideal, and seemed to bear a diviner stamp.

For nearly five years after this my passion for her increased with my age, although I thought when I first fell in love with her that nothing could have added a deeper power to it. For upwards of four years I knelt opposite her at the altar; for upwards of four years my eyes were never off her, and for upwards of four years I never once, while at Mass, offered up a single prayer to heaven.

As I grew up, she seemed to feel a deeper interest in me. The language of her eyes could not be misunderstood. Through the medium of that language, I felt that our hearts were intimately acquainted, precisely as if they had held many a loving and ecstatic communion. During the period of this extraordinary passion, I indulged in solitude a thousand times in order to brood over the image of her whom I loved. On returning home from Mass of a summer Sunday, I uniformly withdrew to the bottom of the glen behind our house and there, surrendered myself to the entrancing influence of what I felt. There in the solitude of that glen I felt a charm added to my existence which cannot be described. I knew — I felt — that she loved me. This habit of mine was so well known by my family that, when dinner was ready and they found that I was absent, they knew perfectly well where to call for me. After the first six months I could not rest satisfied with parting from her at the 'Forth'; so, for three years and a half, I walked after her, and never turned back until I left her at the town of Augher, at the turn which led by a side street to her father's mill; and this during the severity of winter and the heat of summer. Now this I am describing was my silent — my inner life; but the reader is not to imagine that it prevented me from entering into the sports and diversions of the day. I devoted myself to athletic exercises until I was without a rival — until, in fact, I had a local fame which spread far beyond the limits of my native parish. I was resolved to make myself talked of — to be distinguished by my excellence in these feats — and the ambition which I then felt owed its origin to my love for Anne Duffy. I remember well that when nineteen years of age, my appearance in fair or market caused crowds to follow the young fellow who stood unrivalled at every athletic sport which could be named. This fact is well known and remembered by some of the oldest inhabitants of my native parish to the present day.

The reader will consider it strange that during this long period of devoted and enthusiastic attachment, I never spoke to Anne or declared my passion. It is, however, a fact, that during the period I allude to, a single syllable of spoken language never passed between us. This, however, is easily accounted for. My father died in the early course of my passion, and then I began to feel with some bitterness the consequences of decline. Had I spoken to Anne, and gained her consent to marry me, I had no means of supporting her, and I could not bear the terrible idea of bringing her to distress and poverty, both of which she must have endured had she become my wife.

I was sitting before our kitchen fire one evening (in autumn, I think), thinking of her as usual, when my eldest brother came in, and after having taken a seat, communicated the following intelligence.

'Did you hear the news?' said he.

'No,' replied my mother, 'what is it?'

'Why, that the miller's daughter' (by this appellation she was generally known, and not by her Christian name) 'the miller's daughter was married this morning to M.M., of Ballyscally.'

The sensation I felt was as if something had paralysed my brain or my heart. I was instantly seized with a violent dizziness, and an utter prostration of bodily strength; an indescribable confusion seized upon me — thought for a moment abandoned me and I laboured under the impression that some terrible calamity had befallen me. So long as she remained unmarried, I still entertained a vague and almost hopeless hope that some event might occur which, by one of the extraordinary turnings of life, might put it in our power to marry. Even this faint hope was gone — my doom was irrevocably sealed, and the drapery of death hung between her and me. I rose from my chair with difficulty — I staggered out, and went into the barn, where I wept bitterly. My life had now lost its charm, and nothing but a cold cheerless gloom lay upon it and my hopes. During three or four months this miserable state of feeling lasted. I was, however, in the heyday of youth — just in that period of existence when sorrow seldom lasts long. The sensation gradually wore away, and after a lengthened interval I recovered my usual spirits. A short but interesting anecdote will now close this extraordinary history of my first love. I think it was in the year 1847 that I resolved to pay a visit to my native place. When I left it, many years before, it was with fixed resolution never to write a letter home, or to return to my friends, unless I had achieved some distinction which might reflect honour upon my name. Fortunately I was able to accomplish this strange determination; and what is, after all, not strange, I do assure my readers that Anne Duffy, though the wife of another, was a strong stimulus to my pursuit of fame, and in the early period of my literary life a powerful element in my ambition. She would hear of the distinction I had acquired, she would probably even read of the honourable position I had reached, by universal consent, in the literature of my country.

On paying this visit to the City of the Stone of Gold,[4] I went first to Lisburn, where my friend John Birney, the solicitor, resided. With him I stayed for a few days, when we started for Clogher, his native town; and it was rather singular that the very inn we stopped at had been during my boyhood the residence of his father, who was a most respectable magistrate, and a man deservedly loved by the people of all creeds and classes. It was to John Birney that I dedicated the first series of my *Traits and Stories of the Irish Peasantry*. He had a good property about Clogher, and on this occasion, as he was going there to collect his rents, we went together. I stayed at the inn, which had formerly been his father's house, and so did he. One day after, I had been about a week there, I received an invitation to breakfast with a gentleman who lived in a pretty, secluded spot, formerly called 'The Grange', but changed by its present proprietor into 'Ashfield', if I remember correctly. After breakfast, he proposed or I proposed, I forget which — to take a walk up to what was once Ballyscally, but which was now a scene of perfect

desolation. Out of seventy or eighty comfortable cottages the gentleman in question had not left one standing. Every unfortunate tenant had been evicted, driven out, to find a shelter for himself where he could. Ballyscally had, I think, been the property of the See of Clogher, but how it came into this person's possession I know not. Upon second thoughts, it must have been I who proposed the walk in that direction, and for this reason: there was but one house left standing in Ballyscally — certainly the best that ever was in the town — but that house, as I knew for many a long year, was the residence of the husband of Anne Duffy. We went up by Ballyscally, which had consisted of houses scattered over the top and side of an elevated hill, that commanded a distant view of a beautiful country to an extent of not less than fifty miles. The long depression of the land before you to the west and north under the hill constitutes that portion of the county known in ancient Irish history as the 'Valley of the Black Pig'. My companion brought me up to see an obelisk which he was building, on the top of a much higher hill than Ballyscally. It was nearly finished, but we reached the top with some difficulty, and after all saw very little more than we could see from its base. Like many other similar and useless structures it was called 'B——'s Folly'.

As we returned, I proposed that we should pay a visit to her husband's house, then, as I said, the only one in all Ballyscally. Up to this moment, she and I had never exchanged a word. What she might have expressed, had she known I was on my way to visit her, I do not know, but, notwithstanding every attempt to keep cool, I felt my heart palpitate as it had not done for years. We shook hands, and had some commonplace conversation, when after a few minutes her husband came in; and as he and I had known each other long before his marriage, we also shook hands as old acquaintances. After a little I looked at her, and then turning to him,

'Michael,' I said, 'there stands the only woman I ever loved beyond the power of language to express. She had my first affection, and I loved her beyond any woman that ever breathed, and strange to say, until this occasion we never exchanged a syllable.' 'Well,' she replied, 'I can say on my part — and I am not ashamed to say it — that I never loved man as I loved you; but

4. Clogher, County Tyrone. Carleton states earlier that he believes the derivation to be *Clogh-air*, 'golden stone'.

there was one thing clear, that it wasn't our fate ever to become man and wife. Had you married me it's not likely the world would have ever heard of you. As it is, I am very happily married, and lead a happy life with as good and as kind a husband as ever lived.'

Michael laughed, and appeared rather pleased and gratified than otherwise. We then shook hands again, I took my leave, and that was my first and last interview with her whose image made the pleasure of my whole youth for nearly five years.

ANONYMOUS

from:
MINUTES OF EVIDENCE TAKEN BEFORE THE SELECT COMMITTEE ON THE CONTAGIOUS DISEASES ACT (1881)

[In the 1860s increased anxiety among senior officials in the British army about the spread of venereal diseases led to the passing of the Contagious Diseases Acts (1866–9), allowing for the compulsory inspection of women believed to be prostitutes in certain garrison towns. These acts created a storm of protest and were objected to on several grounds: some protested that they represented an infringement of civil liberties, others that by regulating prostitution they actually represented a fostering of vice by the state. Many women objected that the acts, by inspecting women but not men, enshrined a sexual double standard. This last position gained strength as it emerged that the acts were being used to police the conduct of women in general, since some of the behaviour which could be used to justify police inspection included drunkenness, rowdiness, adultery and even appearing alone in public places. In 1869 Josephine Butler[1] founded the Ladies' National Association in England to campaign for repeal of the acts. In Ireland Isabella Tod and Anna Haslam[2] were involved in the foundation of branches of the LNA and in the repeal campaign (see Volume V, pp. 77–8). A select committee of the British parliament collected information on the operation of the acts over several years, hearing testimony from 'authorities' such as military officials, police, doctors and clergymen. the following extract reveals the increasing doubts of doctors, in particular, on the efficiency of the acts in preventing the spread of disease. The Contagious Diseases Acts were suspended in 1883 and repealed in 1886. Maria Luddy drew my attention to this text.]

27th June 1881

Mr. RAWTON MACNAMARA called in; and Examined.

Mr. *Osborne Morgan.*[3]
Q. I believe you are the Senior Surgeon of the Westmoreland Lock Hospital in Dublin?
A. Yes.

Q. How long have you been connected with the hospital?
A. Some six or seven years.

Q. As a surgeon, I presume?
A. Yes; I am surgeon also to the Meath Hospital and the County Dublin Infirmary, and I have had considerable experience with this class of patients by having been at the commencement of my career surgeon in rotation to almost every dispensary on the South side of Dublin; and then I had experience of these cases whilst serving my apprenticeship to the late Sir Philip Cramptom.[4]

Q. How is the Westmoreland Lock Hospital supported?
A. By a government grant; the grant at present being 2,600l. per annum . . .

1. Josephine Butler (1828–1906), campaigner for women's rights with a particular interest in prostitutes.
2. Isabella Maria Susan Tod (1836–96); Anna Haslam (1829–1922).

3. George Osborne Morgan (1826–97), created baronet 1892, lawyer and Liberal MP for Denbighshire and later East Denbighshire, judge advocate-general 1880–5.
4. Sir Philip Crampton FRS (1777–1858), surgeon to the Meath hospital in Dublin, later surgeon-in-ordinary to the Queen.

Q. What is the character of the patients; they are not all prostitutes?

A. We have married women, and I would not call them prostitutes, and girls that have been seduced and almost on the first act have been diseased; and then we have what are called first admissions, and then we have the *habituées*.

Q. Can you tell me what proportion the *habituées* would bear to the other classes?

A. I should think the professional prostitutes would number about 60 per cent.

Q. You have had great experience as to venereal disease in Dublin; can you give me any idea as to its character at present, whether the syphilis[5] is of a severe type?

A. We have a most extraordinary outbreak at the present moment of gonorrhoea;[6] I never saw gonorrhoea so virulent as it is in the female patients at the present time in the Lock hospital. We only admit women to the Lock hospital, amongst the private male patients who do me the honour of consulting me, I never saw anything so severe as the character of the gonorrhoea at the present moment prevalent in Dublin . . .

Q. May I take it that syphilis, as well as gonorrhoea, prevails in Dublin to a great extent, and is of a very severe type?

A. It does; I base my opinion as to that fact on the result of my experience in connection with the Lock hospital and the Meath Hospital, and also on this return which I wish to refer to, from which you see that more than one-third of the garrison of Dublin last year were invalided. (*The Return was put in.*)

Q. Would you allow me to read you a letter from the colonel commanding the 80th Regiment: 'Since the arrival of my regiment in Dublin, there have been the enormous number of 166 admissions to the hospital from men suffering from primary syphilis; and the admissions from gonorrhoea amount to 118. Thus during a period of 10 months, considerably over 43 per cent of the unmarried portion of my regiment have been incapacitated from duty.' Are you surprised to hear that?

A. I am not in the least surprised to hear it; but the same thing applies to every other regiment in the garrison . . .

Q. This syphilis that you speak of, would it be likely to be transmitted herediterally from parent to child?

A. It depends very much on how they have been treated; but even under the most apparently successful kinds of treatment syphilis is transmitted from parent to child in spite of the very best directed efforts . . .

Q. With regard to these women who are admitted into your hospital, in what condition are most of them?

A. Well, the practice which we know to be in existence is, that as long as they possibly can keep out of the hospital they do, and they are only driven in by very severe and urgent symptoms. They won't come in for trifling cases, though capable of communicating disease; and whilst able to stay out and to pursue their trade they will, until at last it comes to the state of that woman I alluded to, that I said, 'My God! What kept you out so long?'

Q. Are they most of them in an actively contagious state of disease?

A. That is what I tried to convey; that though perfectly capable of communicating disease, so long as they are able to stay out they will stay out, until really I am surprised how they could have stayed out so long . . .

Q. Let me ask you another question; does it not sometimes happen that a woman may be in an actively contagious state without knowing it?

A. It is not only possible for a woman to be in that state, but I have known men to be in that condition . . .

Q. Of course you have no means of compulsorily detaining women in your hospital?

A. No, that has annoyed me more than I can possibly describe. I get the woman in, and I am getting her on to a point of being well, and she claims her discharge and she goes out, I knowing thoroughly that she is going back to her trade and thoroughly aware that she is capable of diseasing anybody that comes into contact with her . . .

5. A disease communicated by sexual contact or by infection of the child *in utero*. In the early stages cankers appear on the infected part; later stages may include skin disease and infection of muscles, bones and brain.
6. An inflammatory discharge of mucus from the membrane of the urethra or vagina.

Q. Has any attempt been made to your knowledge to shut up the brothels in Dublin?

A. That has been a very old story in Dublin; almost all the houses of ill-fame were in a street called French-street, and another street called Clarendon-street; French-street is very close to the Square where I live, which is well-known to you all, St. Stephen's Green-park, and we did not like to have such people near us, and we were anxious to close it. Clarendon-street is the *locale* of a very beautiful chapel, and the priests did not like to have them there. The result was that police were put at the doors and took down the names of everyone who came; these were what we call the upper class, if there can be such a thing, of prostitutes, and the policemen took down the names of all the gentlemen going to enter, and that at once drove them out of that, and then they went to the banks of the canal. But they were moved from there and the result is that they are scattered in different outlying parts, Mecklenburgh-street; in fact, I do not know the *locale* of them now; but that occurred in Dublin to my own knowledge . . .

Q. You heard I think the evidence of the clergyman who was interviewed before you; he stated that he was unable to visit prostitutes in their homes in Cork; I suppose the same thing would apply in Dublin?

A. One of the advantages of having these poor women in such places as the Lock hospital is, that they come directly under the influence of the different ministers of their different religions; but the priests, I believe as a rule, object to visit the low places where these lowest class of prostitutes live; and I happen to know this, from my own personal knowledge. I was sent for to see a poor prostitute dying in a place called Bracken's-lane, a very low place, and, though a Protestant myself, I considered it my duty to to [*sic*] tell her to send for a priest, that she was dying. When I went to visit her next day, she was not in Bracken's-lane. I inquired where she was, and she had been removed in her dying state from Bracken's-lane to Townsend-street, and there in an upper room, I found her dying. I asked her why it was, that being in that state, she had been removed, and the answer was, that the priests had made it a rule not to go into Bracken's-lane in consequence of a most indecent assault on the last priest who went into it for the purpose of the administration of his religion.

Q. As an inhabitant of Dublin, can you give us any information as to the condition of the streets there?

A. The streets at night are always a source of very great worry to the fathers and mothers of families when their young lads go out to a party or anything of that kind.

Q. Is there much solicitation going on?

A. A great deal. Their audacity is such that I was sent for a short time ago to the Gresham hotel in Sackville-street, to see a patient, and when I came out of the hotel, after seeing my patient, I found a prostitute seated in the cab, and she said she would not get out until I paid her. She got in while I was in the house, and wanted to force her company on me in the cab.

Q. You say the condition of the streets is outrageous?

A. Yes.

Q. And a respectable man, much less a respectable woman, cannot go about at night?

A. No respectable young woman would dream of going out at night to walk across the town.

ANNIE BESANT

(1847–1933)

from:
COERCION IN IRELAND AND ITS RESULTS: A PLEA FOR JUSTICE (1882)

[Annie Besant is a British feminist best known in her early career for organizing women to protest against labour conditions and for pioneering work in advocating education about birth control; she converted to theosophy and from 1895 was active as a politician in India. Like many British radicals, she was sympathetic to the Irish Land-Leaguers and in this text she identifies a specifically feminist grievance of the Lady's Land-League — namely that it effectively denied to married women the right to independent political action. Printed in London in 1882 by Annie Besant and Charles Bradlaugh, the text is taken from a copy held in the British Library.]

The Coercion Act[1] is not the only coercive measure now being largely used in Ireland. By 34 Edw III., c. 1, justices of the peace are empowered to 'bind over to the good behaviour' 'all them that be not of good fame.' This statute is being utilised in the most cruel way in Ireland, more especially against women. If the accused person is unable, or refuses to enter into recognisances,[2] the justice can imprison. Now, it must be remembered that the justices belong to the landlord class, that the persons arraigned before them belong to the class now struggling to gain the right to live, and the 'justice' meted out will be readily understood. Thus, the other day, they ordered a married woman, Mrs. Moore, to

enter into recognisances, and committed her in default. A married woman is legally incapable of entering into recognisances, and Mrs. Moore was imprisoned because her legal incapacity made it impossible for her to come up with the required sureties. Miss Reynolds was the first lady imprisoned under this most evil law, which, in Ireland, puts the liberty of the workers at the mercy of persecuting landlords. She was prosecuted for advising a man not to pay his rent. I am informed that the following are the facts of the case: Patrick Murphy lived in a cottage bought by his father from the man who built; it stood on a plot of grass in the middle of cross-roads, and no rent and no taxes were paid for it during the more than twenty-one years since it came into the Murphys' hands. Rent for three years for this cottage was suddenly claimed by a landlord from whom Murphy held other land and to whom he was in debt. Murphy was advised that if he paid it, he would lose the right acquired by his long and undisturbed possession. Miss Reynolds apparently counselled him not to pay under these circumstances; she was sent to jail, and Murphy was turned out of his house . . .

Miss McCormick was sentenced by Major Lloyd — on the evidence of a policeman that he believed she had been going about inciting the people to discontent — to three months imprisonment in default of bail. The judges, on application, held that Miss McCormick's admission that she was a member of the Ladies' Land League was a proof of the truth of the charges. My informant complains that 'in Ireland the fact of being a member of the Ladies' Land League was held to be proof of her criminality, while in England, in the House of Commons, the Attorney-General cited the fact of her imprisonment as proof of the criminality of the League.'

1. Between 1800 and 1921 the Westminster parliament passed 105 Coercion Acts giving the Irish administration emergency powers during what where considered times of severe public unrest.
2. A bond or obligation recorded before a court or magistrate, for example to appear in court, to pay a debt, or to keep the peace.

JOSEPHINE E. BUTLER

(1828–1906)

from:
OUR CHRISTIANITY TESTED BY THE IRISH QUESTION
(1887)

[Josephine Butler, another English feminist whose reputation is mostly connected with her campaign to repeal the Contagious Diseases Act and her interest in 'Social Purity' feminisms, also writes against the Coercion laws, and harks back to Christian Johnstone (see pp. 847–9) in adding the arguments that the Irish are being treated worse than enslaved Americans and that Irish people are naturally more chaste and virtuous than other peoples. She concludes by considering the implications of Irish Home Rule for Scotland and Wales, using the analogy of marital relations, in which England stands as 'husband' to each of the other three. Published in London in 1887 by T. Fisher Unwin.]

Ireland Governed without Law

. . . During the greater part, then, of this century, the Irish have been reduced, by English rule, to a condition of slavery. I use the word, not sentimentally, but in a strictly legal sense. The definition of slavery is not mine; it is gathered from all our great Constitutional writers. Slavery means, say they, 'that condition in which an individual is not master of his own person'; and the condition of slavery is defined in Magna Carta by 'the omission of all slaves from the rights which that charter grants to everyone else.' Now that charter has been virtually repealed by the successive Acts of a coercive nature under which Ireland has been ruled during the greater part of this century . . .

Crowbar Brigades, Ropes and Pulleys

. . . We are probably all aware that, in spite of such misery, the family life of the poor of Ireland is worthy of admiration. Half-starved and half-naked, yet they have many virtues. Their purity of life contrasts favourably with that of England. They are chaste and moral — in their

own land, — and the affection between husbands and wives, parents and children, is strong and enduring. It stands the test of long separations. We all know how emigrant sons or daughters, fathers or husbands, stint themselves in order to send the unfailing little money-order to the starving family at home.

What must the wrongs be, then, what the sense of injustice, which can rouse a people of this natural gentleness to acts of violence? Mr. Tuke, in his work on 'Donegal and Connaught in 1880',[1] wrote: — 'It cannot be doubted that the political unrest and discord, the angry, defiant menace, the murderer's uplifted arm — all spring from one and the same source; and that that source is poverty.' Mr. Lecky says: — 'Infanticide, desertion, wife-murder, and other crimes indicating a low state of domestic morality have been much rarer among the Irish poor than among the corresponding classes in England . . . A proneness to crimes of combination has been one of the worst and most distinctive evils of modern Irish life.'[2] It is not only against 'crimes of combination,' but against combination itself — now sought to be made of itself to constitute a crime — that this latest, fiercest, and most merciless proposed Coercion Act is directed. The one sole, legal method that was left for this unjustly-treated and cruelly-suffering nation to employ, in order to obtain some redress, is taken out of their hands by this Act, an Act directed not so much against private offences, as against political combinations; and then, should such a proposal become law, what have the people of Ireland left to them, except the methods of the Nihilists[3] of Russia, and other repressed classes rendered voiceless and powerless? . . .

1. James Hack Tuke (1819–96), English Quaker philanthropist, who came to Ireland during the Famine to administer relief and returned in 1880 during famine in Connacht. Author of *Irish Distress and its Remedies* (1880). The quotation has not been precisely located.
2. William Edward Hartpole Lecky (1838–1903), historian and Liberal-Unionist politician. Quotation unlocated.
3. The Nihilists were Russian political activists who advocated anarchy and were active from the 1850s onwards, coming to international prominence from *c.* 1870.

If Ireland, why not Scotland and Wales?

. . . By way of illustration, we may take a supposed case. Mrs. A. desires a judicial separation from her husband, on the ground that she was married to him against her will; the union was brought about by a mixture of force and guile, and for a long period since that union she has had to complain of the ill-treatment of her husband. You reply to Mrs. A.: 'We cannot grant you this separation, because, if we do, we may also be required to grant judicial separations to Mrs. B. and Mrs. C., and we see no right which you have to ask for it which they do not equally possess.' Mrs. A.'s reply is as follows: 'But neither Mrs. B. nor Mrs. C. have asked for this separation, the union in both these cases is harmonious and accepted; no complaint is made.'

JANE FRANCESCA ELGEE (LADY WILDE)

(1821–96)

from:
ANCIENT LEGENDS, MYSTIC CHARMS, AND SUPERSTITIONS OF IRELAND. WITH SKETCHES ON THE IRISH PAST (1887)

[Popular superstition and folktales are texts which often encode social secrets and articulate social anxieties. Wilde's collection of superstitions suggests that hatred and revenge are as potent as love and reproduction in the construction of desire. Before psychoanalysis became a popularly known discipline, Wilde demonstrated the ways in which dreams are narratives of fantasy and wish-fulfilment. The presence of anthropomorphized animals in many of these tales hints at bestiality as a practice and at the interpretation of sexuality as bestial. *Ancient Legends, Mystic Charms, and Superstitions of Ireland. With Sketches of the Irish Past. To which is Appended a Chapter on 'The Ancient Race of Ireland', by the late Sir William Wilde*, 2 vols, was published in London in 1887 by Ward and Downey.]

The Demon Cat

There was a woman in Connemara, the wife of a fisherman, and as he always had very good luck, she had plenty of fish at all times stored away in the house ready for market. But to her great annoyance she found that a great cat used to come in at night and devour all the best and finest fish. So she kept a big stick by her and determined to watch.

One day, as she and a woman were spinning together, the house suddenly became quite dark; and the door was burst open as if by the blast of the tempest, when in walked a huge black cat, who went straight up to the fire, then turned round and growled at them.

'Why, surely this is the devil!' said a young girl, who was by, sorting the fish.

'I'll teach you how to call me names,' said the cat; and, jumping at her, he scratched her arm till the blood came. 'There now,' he said, 'you will be more civil another time when a gentleman comes to see you.' And with that he walked over to the door and shut it close to prevent any of them going out, for the poor young girl, while crying loudly from fright and pain, had made a desperate rush to get away.

Just then a man was going by, and hearing the cries he pushed open the door and tried to get in, but the cat stood on the threshold and would let no one pass. On this, the man attacked him with his stick, and gave him a sound blow; the cat, however, was more than his match in the fight, for it flew at him and tore his face and hands so badly that the man at last took to his heels and ran away as fast as he could.

'Now it's time for my dinner,' said the cat, going up to examine the fish that was laid out on the tables. 'I hope the fish is good to-day. Now don't disturb me or make a fuss; I can help myself.' With that he jumped up and began to devour all the best fish, while he growled at the woman.

'Away, out of this, you wicked beast!' she cried, giving it a blow with the tongs that would have broken its back, only it was a devil; 'out of this! No fish shall you have to-day.'

But the cat only grinned at her, and went on tearing and spoiling and devouring the fish, evidently not a bit worse for the blow. On this, both the women attacked it with sticks, and struck hard blows enough to kill it, on which the cat glared at them, and spit fire; then making a leap, it tore their hands and arms till the blood came, and the frightened women rushed shrieking from the house.

But presently the mistress returned, carrying with her a bottle of holy water,[1] and looking in, she saw the cat still devouring the fish, and not minding. So she crept over quietly and threw the holy water on it without a word. No sooner was this done than a dense black smoke filled the place, through which nothing was seen but the two red eyes of the cat, burning like coals of fire. Then the smoke gradually cleared away, and she saw the body of the creature burning slowly till it became shrivelled and black like a cinder, and finally disappeared. And from that time the fish remained untouched and safe from harm, for the power of the Evil One was broken, and the demon cat was seen no more . . .

To Win Love

'O Christ, by your five wounds,[2] by the nine orders of angels, if this woman is ordained for me, let me hold her hand now, and breathe her breath. O my love, I set a charm to the top of your head; to the sole of your foot; to each side of your breast, that you may not leave me nor forsake me. As a foal after the mare, as a child after the mother, may you follow and stay with me till death comes to part us asunder. AMEN.' . . .

Another

A charm of most desperate love, to be written with a raven's quill in the blood of the ring finger of the left hand.

'By the power that Christ brought from Heaven, mayest thou love me, woman! As the sun follows its course, mayest thou follow me. As light to the eye, as bread to the hungry, as joy to the heart, may thy presence be with me, O woman that I love, till death comes to part us asunder.' . . .

To Cause Hatred between Lovers

Take a handful of clay from a new-made grave, and shake it between them, saying —

'Hate ye one another! May ye be as hateful to each other as sin to Christ, as bread eaten without blessing is to God.' . . .

An Elixir of Potency
(From a manuscript of date 1770)

Two ounces of cochineal,[3] one ounce of gentian root,[4] two drachms[5] of saffron,[6] two drachms of snakeroot,[7] two drachms of salt of wormwood,[8] and the rind of ten oranges. The whole to be steeped in a quart of brandy, and kept for use . . .

Dreams

To dream of a hearse with white plumes is a wedding; but to dream of a wedding is grief, and death will follow.

To dream of a woman kissing you is deceit; but of a man, friendship; and to dream of a horse is exceedingly lucky.

1. Water blessed by a priest, found at the entrance to Catholic churches and to many Catholic homes.
2. The wounds to hands, feet and side received during the Crucifixion.
3. A scarlet dye-stuff made from the dried bodies of an insect.
4. *Gentiana lutea*: the root is used in medicine.
5. An apocatheries' weight, one-eighth of an ounce or 60 grains.
6. Dried crocus stigmas, which produce a vivid orange colouring in food or clothing dyes.
7. A name applied to several plants, in some cases because they resemble snakes, in others (mainly American) because they are thought to be antidotes to snake poison.
8. The plant *Artemisia absinthium*, whose leaves and tops have a variety of medicinal and household uses.

OSCAR WILDE

(1854–1900)

from:
SALOME (1893)

[The biblical figure of Salome[1] became an important cultural icon in Europe at the end of the nineteenth century. She was a quintessential *fin-de-siècle* emblem, figuring in literature, visual arts and performance, representing both the aggressive feminism of the 'new woman' and the perverse aesthetic of the decadents. Wilde's version of the story, first written in French under the influence of the avant-garde and symbolist theatre in Paris, was banned from public performance in the United Kingdom because it dealt with a biblical subject in blasphemous fashion. Through the dangerous phallic woman, Wilde, the homosexual artist, participates in the new woman's attack on patriarchy, at the same time as he registers a fear of the female energy unleashed in that attack. Headnote by Éibhear Walshe.]

SALOME: Jokanaan!

JOKANAAN: Who speaketh?

SALOME: Jokanaan, I am amorous of thy body! Thy body is white like the lillies of a field that the mower hath never mowed. Thy body is white like the snows that lie on the mountains, like the snows that lie on the mountains of Judaea, and come down into the valleys. The roses in the garden of the Queen of Arabia are not so white as thy body. Neither the roses in the garden of the Queen of Arabia, the perfumed garden of spices of the Queen of Arabia, nor the feet of the dawn when they light on the leaves, nor the breast of the moon when she lies on the breast of the sea . . . There is nothing in the world so white as thy body. Let me touch thy body.

JOKANAAN: Back! daughter of Babylon! By woman came evil into the world. Speak not to me. I will not listen to thee. I listen but to the voice of the Lord God.

SALOME: Thy body is hideous. It is like the body of a leper. It is like a plastered wall where vipers have crawled; like a plastered wall where the scorpions have made their nest. It is like a whitened sepulchre full of loathsome things. It is horrible, thy body is horrible. It is of thy hair that I am enamoured, Jokanaan. Thy hair is like clusters of grapes, like the clusters of black grapes that hang from the vine trees of Edom in the land of the Edomites. Thy hair is like the cedars of Lebanon, like the great cedars of Lebanon that give their shade to the lions and to the robbers who would hide themselves by day. The long black nights, when the moon hides her face, when the stars are afraid, are not so black. The silence that dwells in the forest is not so black. There is nothing so black as thy hair . . . Let me touch thy hair.

JOKANAAN: Back, daughter of Sodom! Touch me not. Profane not the temple of the Lord God.

SALOME: Thy hair is horrible. It is covered with mire and dust. It is like a crown of thorns which they have placed on thy forehead. It is like a knot of black serpents writhing round thy neck. I love not thy hair . . . It is thy mouth that I desire, Jokanaan. Thy mouth is like a band of scarlet on a tower of ivory. It is like a pomegranate cut with a knife of ivory. The pomegranate-flowers that blossom in the gardens of Tyre, and are redder than roses, are not so red. The red blasts of trumpets that herald the approach of kings, and make afraid the enemy, are not so red. Thy mouth is redder than the feet of those who tread the wine in the wine-press. Thy mouth is redder than the feet of the doves who haunt the temples and are fed by the priests. It is redder than the feet of him who cometh from a forest where he hath slain a lion, and seen gilded tigers. Thy mouth is like a branch of coral that fishers have found in the twilight of the sea, the coral that they keep for the kings! . . . It is like the vermilion that the Moabites find in the mines of Moab, the vermilion that the kings take from them. It is like the bow of the King of the Persians, that is painted with vermilion, and is tipped with coral. There is nothing in the world so red as thy mouth . . . Let me kiss thy mouth.

JOKANAAN: Never! daughter of Babylon! Daughter of Sodom! Never.

---

1. Matthew 14:1–12 describes how Herod's mistress Herodias, his brother's wife, hates John the Baptist for speaking against their union. During celebrations for Herod's birthday, Herodias's daughter dances for Herod and pleases him so much that he promises her any reward. Prompted by her mother, she asks for John's head on a dish. According to the historian Josephus, the girl's name is Salome.

SARAH GRAND

(1854–1943)

from:
THE HEAVENLY TWINS (1893)

[Grand's Irish background is most explicitly engaged with
in her autobiographical novel, *The Beth Book*, but the Irish
question haunts *The Heavenly Twins*, where it is a striking
marker of Evadne's dissent from the masculine, imperialist
society into which she deludedly marries, and with which
she attempts to make some honourable accommodation.
This is a quintessential 'new woman' novel, in which
several young women are tracked from girlhood to
womanhood and have to confront the extraordinary
difficulties in achieving independence and integrity within
a masculine, heterosexual economy.

George Bernard Shaw[1] makes several references to *The
Heavenly Twins* in his critical writings, indicating how far
Grand's novel was seen as a challenge to male patriarchal
dominance and the 'double standard': 'For my part I am a
man; and Madame Grand's solution fills me with dismay.
What I should like of course, would be the maintenance of
two distinct classes of women, the one polyandrous and
disreputable, the others monogamous and reputable. I
could then have my fill of polygamy among the polyandrous ones with the certainty that I could hand them over
to the police if they annoyed me after I had become tired
of them, at which date I could marry one of the
monogamous ones and live happily ever afterwards. But if
a woman were to say such a thing as this about men I
should be shocked; and of late years it has begun to dawn
on me that perhaps when men say it (or worse still, act on
it without confessing to it) women may be disgusted.'[2]

In the first of the following extracts Angelica discovers
that her friend Edith's romantic marriage has been a
dreadful error of judgement, not simply on the part of
Edith but of the bishop, her father, and her whole society
which colludes with promiscuity and double standards.
Edith and her baby are infected with syphilis.]

Angelica had never been in the same house with
a baby before, and she was all interest. Whatever
defects of character the new women may eventually acquire, lack of maternal affection will not
be one of them.

'Have you seen the baby?' she asked Elizabeth,
when the latter was brushing her hair for dinner.

---

1. George Bernard Shaw (1856–1950), Irish dramatist.
2. G.B. Shaw, review of four plays reprinted in *Our Theatre in the
Nineties* (London: Constable, 1932), vol. 3, pp. 49–50.

He had not been visible during the afternoon,
but Angelica had thought of him incessantly.

'Yes, Miss,' Elizabeth answered.

'Is he a pretty baby?' Angelica wanted to know.

Elizabeth pursed up her lips with an air of
reserve.

'You don't think so?' Angelica said — she had
seen the maid's face in the mirror before her.
'What is he like?'

'He's exactly like the bishop, Miss.'

Angelica broke into a broad smile at herself in
the glass.

'What! A little old man baby!' she exclaimed.

'Yes, Miss — with a cold in his head,' the maid
said seriously.

When she was dressed, Angelica went to make
his acquaintance. On the way she discovered her
particular friend, the bishop, going furtively in
the same direction, and slipped her hand through
his arm.

'We'll go together,' she said confidentially,
taking it for granted that his errand was the same
as her own.

The nurse was undressing the child when they
entered, and Edith sat watching her. She was
already dressed for the evening, and looked worse
in an elaborate toilet than she had done in her
morning dress. A stranger would have found it
hard to believe that only the year before she had
been radiantly healthy and beautiful. The puzzled,
pathetic expression was again in her eyes as she
watched the child. She had no smile for him and
uttered no baby words to him — nor had he a smile
for her. He was old, old already, and exhausted
with suffering, and as his gaze wandered from one
to the other it was easy to believe that he was asking
each dumbly why had he ever been born?

'Is *that* Edith's baby?' Angelica exclaimed in
her astonishment and horror under her breath,
slipping her hand from the bishop's arm.

She had seen enough in one momentary
glance, and she fled from the room.

[Angelica temporarily finds some freedom by dressing as a
man and masquerading as her twin brother. In this guise she
befriends the tenor in the cathedral choir. This discussion

follows his discovery of her true identity, and indicates the unacknowledged homoerotic dimension to ordinary male friendships and the importance of cross–dressing women as female role models. It is significant that the tenor sees cross-dressing as a mode of sexual adventure, while for Angelica it represents the release of career ambitions.]

'I kept my disguise a long time before I used it,' she began again, another morsel of the incident and motive recurring to her. 'I don't think I had any very distinct notion of what I should do with it when I got it. The pleasure of getting it had been everything for the moment, and having succeeded in that and tried the dress, I hid it away carefully and scarcely ever thought of it — never dreamt of wearing it certainly until one night — it was quite an impulse at last. That night, you know, the first time we met — it was such a beautiful night! I was by myself and had nothing to do as usual, and it tempted me sorely. I thought I should like to see the market-place by moonlight, and then all at once I thought I *would* see it by moonlight. That was my first weighty reason for changing my dress. But having once assumed the character, I began to love it; it came naturally; and the freedom from restraint, I mean the restraint of our tight uncomfortable clothing, was delicious. I tell you I was a genuine boy. I moved like a boy, I felt like a boy; I was my own brother in very truth. Mentally and morally I was exactly what your thought me, and there was little fear of your finding me out, although I used to like to play with the position and run the risk.'

'It was marvellous,' the Tenor said.

'Not at all,' she answered, 'not a bit more marvellous in real life than it would have been upon the stage — a mere exercise of the actor's faculty under the most favourable circumstances; and not a bit more marvellous than to create a character as an author does in a book; the process is analogous. But the same thing has been done before. George Sand,[3] for instance; don't you remember how often she went about dressed as a man, went to the theatres and was introduced to people, and was never found out by strangers? And there was that woman who was a doctor in the army for so long — until she was quite old. James Barry,[4] she called herself, and none of her brother officers, not even her own particular chum in the regiment she first belonged to, had any suspicion of her sex, and it was not discovered until after her death, when she had been Inspector General of the Army Medical Department for many years. And there have been women in the ranks too, and at sea. It was really not extraordinary that an unobservant and unsuspicious creature like yourself should have been deceived.'

This recalled the patronizing manner of the Boy at times, and the Tenor smiled.

3. George Sand (1804–76), b. Amandine-Aurore Lucille Dupin, French novelist who adopted a male pseudonym and male dress.
4. James Barry (1795–1865), niece of the painter James Barry (1741–1806), Inspector of the Army Medical Department, was revealed as a woman after her death.

GEORGE EGERTON

(1859–1945)

LETTER TO GOLDING BRIGHT (1901)

[George Egerton's fiction is best remembered for its treatment of sexual repression, sexual liberation and the 'new woman'; much of it is clearly autobiographical. Egerton had lived in Ireland, Chile, Scandinavia, Germany and Britain and had had several affairs and a failed marriage when she met her future husband, Reginald Golding Bright, in London. He was an American theatre critic,

fifteen years her junior. The following letter charts some of the anxieties of their courtship — both were involved with other people at the time. It reveals maternal aspects of Egerton's feeling for Bright and also her awareness of a conflict between sexuality and writing. Her willingness to debate her feelings and the style of that debate are both characteristic of her fiction. Like many of her contemporaries, Egerton is trying to establish an individual moral code and free herself and her friends from prejudice. The letter is reproduced in *A Leaf from the Yellow Book: The Correspondence of George Egerton*, ed. Terence de Vere White (London: Richards Press, 1958), pp. 58–62.]

February 21, 1901

Good little son, curious tangle of affection, I have read your long letter through twice. I am grateful to you, boy, for much kind dear thought of me in it, but in some ways you mistake. A mistake arising out of my too great reticence as to my own feelings. I have felt and feel a difficulty and if you had not overcome your dumbness enough to attack me as it were on this point, should not speak of it now. I know you do so because you care for me in a strange beautiful way, a way I care greatly to have. I have felt a strange shyness in speaking of my feelings towards Ole,[1] almost worthy of a girl of fifteen. I only did so at all because I was not sure of your real feelings for Miss Russell[2] and I wished to guard you from any possible mistake as to your feelings for me.

It is not really conceit because you had spoken of and resented my 'personal magnetism' and as I was not sure, I wished to protect you — from myself. I have felt almost disloyal to my little man up there in opening the door of the special room in which he lives in my heart to any other eyes. You are wrong in saying I am unwilling to belong to him. As far as I am personally concerned that is not so. I have never known such complete satisfaction as when with him but there are other factors which make me shrink from anything new. You write of love that is the love of a healthy-souled man and woman in a way to make me believe you have no idea of what love is.

To Ole loving me as he does no relationship other than wife would be possible, and rightly so. Love is something apart from platonics. You speak of the relationship of a man and a woman loving one another (as man and woman can when they believe they are the only two in the world for one another) as sensuality! I see that with different eyes. I can't word it in a letter to you. You will find it and all else I think of love in *Rosa Amorosa*.[3] Your attitude is born of solitude, of an almost morbid desire to protect and love without letting anything other than the spiritual side of affection dominate. Boy dear, you will know better some day when the right woman comes. If it is written that I am to go across the border, I could not be *me* as I wish to be

if I were not to go bravely, go true to myself, to what I believe is the right thing for me as *woman* — as artist, ah, that is a different matter. My art is of less importance to me than my life as a woman. My shrinking from this journey is rather something belonging to my physical weakness. I am very far from well, the few journeys I have had to town this week have torn my nerves to pieces. I am one cry of back-ache, so I dread the journey. I am anxious too. I feel — know — something is wrong there. He is either ill, or his father. Naturally I dread arriving not to find him there — I too dislike leaving Boy[4] — though he is happiest where he is. I dread the hours I shall be alone alien to everything and I do not know how anything will be arranged. I know one thing, no man could love a woman better than my boy there does, but he is no soft lad willing to sacrifice more than a man ought — If it were not a sacrilege you should see some letters of his and you would know better how great, how clean, how good a feeling he has for me. I have gipsy traits in me, am artist to the finger-tips, vagabond blood not a little — but I am a woman and I need love as few women. I have found no man to love me *long* platonically. Ole never did, how could he? when I am the woman, the one and only other for him — You are safeguarded by your care for another — and your need of my motherliness, yet you miss me after the few times I have been with you. You let me play a part in your thought disproportionate to your feeling for me. You try to anticipate my wishes, you trouble more about me than I trouble over myself, you torture yourself with doubts, fears concerning me. You cry at the very thought of my death. My dear, good little son, I have no fear. I am impersonal even in thinking of myself. I have let you do more for me than I have ever let anyone do, because I believe it is good for you to come out of that place of despondency in which you were sitting in the dark. I could make you laugh and rejoice and think life good if I were to see you oftener. That I came in when I did is written for some purpose. I would not be patient with your weakness long, I have sharp angles, hardnesses too, and you have too good, too big a heart to fossilise as you are doing. I shall expect much from you — not for myself or in relationship to myself — but for *yourself*. Your care for others might only

1. Egerton's Norwegian lover.
2. Annie Russell, American comedy actor.
3. Egerton's letters to Ole were published in the novel *Rosa Amorosa: The Love-Letters of a Woman* (London: Grant Richards, 1901).

4. Her son.

produce weakness in them. I no longer believe in abnegation nor renunciation. All my sacrifices have been useless — harmful often, destructive of the forces I might have held in reserve to help others wisely — one pamperizes and demoralizes others. I now try to help others to *help* themselves. Ole and I are alike in our egoism. As he once said: 'We two, complete egoists as we are, are happy with another from an egoistic starting point and seek to become one complete individual only by the complete preservation of our separate individualities.' Do not fret or trouble about me. I dree my weird.[5] You have been a dear son to me and I am grateful for what I have taken from you because I feel you loved to give it to me. I shall always keep the *Imitation*[6] next my bed. If you want anything from me, ask, or I shall feel hurt. What I said to you I meant as long as I am here below, come to me as often as you will. Realize I have no fear of anything. I have two boys in England instead of one. I have missed you today. There is a confession.

I come up 10.6[7] on Saturday. If you care to you can help me to get my things to Liverpool Street[8] and I am grateful to you for coming to Harwich. There is no one I care more to have. I lunch with my sister and have a call to make if you care to have me later on until it is time to go. Unless you have anyone there Sunday afternoon, I shall be pleased to spend my last hours in your tidy prim restful room. I have hardly thanked you for all your pretty thought of me, your flowers and books and tender care but believe I am none the less grateful. You ask me to pray for you. My dear good boy, I rarely pray actually and never for myself. I try to live rightly from my point of view. I am glad to help, glad I have made you anxious to do something, be something for yourself without reference to others. That is the real strength, all other is spurious. I care greatly now what happens to you.

I am very tired and in great pain, have still much to do. I feel like a little child that has been set too hard a sum to solve. I hope you get my note to the office, good kind little son of mine. Cook will send my ticket to you. Keep it for me. You can get me some ammoniated quinine. There is a standard prescription. Perhaps I shall hear from you before Saturday. I believe I am right about Mlle H. That would have been fateful for you and a *great, great wrong to her. Rosa Amorosa* is going to tell you things good for you to hear. A letter posted early in the day reaches here at 6 p.m. Dear glad hopeful good boy, life has much in it. Don't fret over the little mother, she has always gone her own gait. Don't fancy she is going to leave you awhile. There is more to her to do. She bids you good morning, comes to your side and stoops down and rubs out all the wrinkles and hopes you are not tired and tells you to be strong and sensible and glad, above all glad. Her kind boy! Shut your eyes and I will smooth my hands over your hair, your little Mother.

5. I endure my fate.
6. Thomas à Kempis (*c.* 1380–1471), *Of the Imitation of Christ*.
7. Presumably, 10.06 a.m. train.
8. Railway terminus in London.

AMANDA M'KITTRICK ROS

(1860–1939)

from:
DELINA DELANEY (1898)

[Although Ros situates her work within the genres of popular romantic fiction, it would be a mistake to read her as representative of that fiction. She described herself as 'the personality who has disturbed the bowels of the millions' but she is better known as a cult author and perhaps unconscious humorist than as a women's writer.

Like Frances Browne and Joseph Sheridan Le Fanu, she writes 'sensation fiction', and the following scene from *Delina Delaney* owes something to Mrs Henry Wood's celebrated popular novel *East Lynne* (1861), where a disfigured, adulterous wife reappears in disguise as her children's nurse and governess.[1] Ros is not in command of the metaphorical resonances in national or feminist

1. Ellen Wood (1814–87), better known as Mrs Henry Wood, had a huge popular success with her first novel, *East Lynne*.

politics of plots such as *Lady Audley's Secret*, *The Hidden Sin* or *Uncle Silas*.[2] It would be almost impossible to read Ros for the plot. It is more useful to think of her as a reader than a writer, a woman in modest provincial life whose fantasies were shaped by the ingredients of popular fiction and who found an outlet for those fantasies in vanity publishing. The writing has extraordinary linguistic power, and inherits from earlier writers such as Le Fanu and the Brontës a cast of characters and set of situations in which arbitrary violence can erupt. It has been pointed out that Ros, like the writers of the *Nation*, is obsessed with blood and with the disintegration of the body. Her most lurid sexual fantasies, not accidentally interwoven with her hatred of Gothic Catholicism, come in the Belfast brothel scenes in *Helen Huddleson* (posthumously published in 1969), but *Delina Delaney* has more connection to the romantic sexual fantasies of more successful women writers. The plot concerns Delina, the orphan child of a Connemara fisherman, who has married Lord Gifford, a local aristocrat. His evil cousin, Mattie Maynard, disguised as the sinister French governess Madam-de-Maine, has driven Delina from their house in London, and reduced Gifford to a sick, drunken stupor. Dr Norton appoints a nurse to care for Gifford, and she turns out to be Delina, whose one ally in the house is a servant, old Joss Danvers. The following excerpt is from Chapter 19.]

MURDER OF JOSS DANVERS

Nurse Delaney saluted him with a graceful bow. He made an effort to raise himself on his elbow, an act he utterly failed to accomplish, and gasped in a low, painful voice:

'Never — never! It cannot be — it cannot be!' at the same time holding out his hot, feverish hands. He could no longer mistake the fact that this was his own darling that was lost and found, about whom he grieved so much, and almost ruined his existence.

Dr. Norton, whose chief concentration was upon her, stood puzzled and baffled at their meeting.

Often girls are quick to detect interest in themselves, promoted often by the opposite sex; but Nurse Delaney was too wholly engrossed just now with the dashing force of Fate to notice a slight quiver on the doctor's lip, or the quick heaving of his breast.

2. *Lady Audley's Secret* (1862) by M.E. Braddon, *The Hidden Sin* (1866) by Frances Browne (see pp. 861–4), and *Uncle Silas* (1864) by J. Sheridan Le Fanu were celebrated sensation novels.

Dr. Norton was always reckoned a self-possessed man, somewhat reserved and slightly shy: but the handsome face of Nurse Delaney, outlined in girlish innocence, had so figured its fairness on his heart that he shook under the merest look that would tend to win her affection. He was aware she was only a girl, her pores incapable yet of the tiniest stream of love, he thought, to trickle through them; and with the strong nerve of one labouring beneath a load of hope, he immediately checked the tenderness of his passion, that leaped within him, blinding her against the shock his emotion had sustained, and donned again that nature he knew before he met her. Controlling the tremor of his deep passion, he said to Nurse Delaney, who sat bathed in tears:

'You know your patient, then, nurse?'

'I — have met him — before,' she stammered.

'Oh!' returned the doctor, totally puzzled, pulling rather unmercifully the ends of his silver moustache. Having some professional calls to make, he thought the sooner he now performed them the better for all concerned. After carefully instructing her how to treat Lord Gifford, and dwelling emphatically on the words, 'On no account allow Madam-de-Maine to offer him anything without my express permission,' he left Clapham Hall to listen to the childish complaints of a mother whose boy had got his finger slightly burned; to sympathise with the feverish father, and prescribe for him the usual remedies; to administer a soothing draught to the maid charged with a lingering consumption; and, after performing these duties to his entire satisfaction, to enter his home and brood over the current events of the day. There are stillnesses more awful than words of tender recollection — ghastly images more heart-rending than death.

Nurse Delaney sat terror-bound, after the doctor's exit, at the tied-up forehead and lip, the deathly glare of his dark eyes, the awful pallor of the visible portions of his face, the thin, hot hands that still clasped hers with forced grasp, and the shattered, slim frame of the robust lover she not so long ago had known.

He lay back, exhausted with the overpowering stroke of joy, of which he had lost all hopes. All his doubts now had fled as mist before a sunray; his brain rolled; he violently shook. Silence claimed him; sorrow disowned him. At times he lay apparently lifeless and motionless; at others breathing heavily, and tumbling to and fro. The recollection of her departure cast him senseless; the exultant leap of her recovery blurred his understanding.

She threw her tender arms around him, weeping copiously; she kissed his cheek and hands, stroked the bandage on his painful brow, whispering words of courage to soothe him in an hour of which Nature seemed to rob him; she fondled and caressed him as if a helpless infant; every spark of sympathetic tenderness was alive in her at the grasp of his suffering.

He opened his eyes of deadly flare, and closed them, not conscious who stood watching over him.

'Ah, my own Lord Gifford,' she said, leaning over the emaciated body, 'don't you know me? Don't you know Delina Delaney, you used to love?' She flung herself across the bed, hiding herself from another terrible and painful stare.

'He will never get better — never!' she groaned, sobbing aloud.

He lay as noticeless of her dreadful agony as he was unconscious of his own.

She rose, bent over him again and again, saying: 'I love you, I love you, dear Lord Gifford! Delina loves you still!'

Not a muscle moved. He lay now still, as if in a slumber. She resolved not to disturb him for a goodly time, earnestly praying that out of this form of rest he'd awake, conscious that she was with him at last to succour and strengthen him in his hour of distress.

The hollow-hearted are numerous; the genuine-hearted rare. Scarce, whom Nature honestly leadeth; plentiful, who falsifies her endeavours.

Still slumbering, Nurse Delaney let him rest. She thought the pain had ceased, mentally and bodily, and bore up her strength with the hope that quietness would shorten the journey of pain.

Moving to the window, her attention was drawn to the tall figure of a woman making across the road towards the gate that led to Clapham Hall. As she passed lightly along, walking on tip-toe, anxious to gain the door unobserved in a measure, which, so far, she had not done. It was Madam-de-Maine — no mistake whatever about it. Her very shadow ran through Nurse Delaney like a stream of icy water. She dreaded meeting her in her present capacity, and, in fact, at almost any risk. She loathed, with terror dancing on every feature, meeting this woman, through whose rough usage she was obliged to bend the yoke that once bound her in faith to her lover. Many a pang of sorrow rent her young heart since then.

Instantly Madam-de-Maine entered her first inquiries were about the doctor's visit.

'Was he accompanied by anyone?' she smartly demanded.

'By a nurse,' the maid replied.

'Hang the old puppy!' she vociferated, bit her lip with an intensity not usual, and smartly tripping towards the patient's room, she had an encounter with old Joss, whom she chanced to meet in the lobby.

'Now, mae wumman,' said Joss, with a certain amount of bravo in his tone, 'Oi've fixed ye! Gwin dthere,' pointing with his short, rough finger, 'an' ye'll mibby see what 'ill sittle ye. Ye'll nat git doin' is ye loike now — pity ye shud! Mae good masther's sleepin', dthe noice wee attindint tills me, an' it's maeself dthat's wearyin' ta hiv 'im an his feet agane.'

A smart slap on the ear was the only practical reply Joss received from Madam-de-Maine, as she rushed into the sick room, not forgetting to turn the key, lest Joss would follow her. A hasty glance at Nurse Delaney woke within her old remembrances. She grew first a mahogany colour, then, as if magically, a ghastly white swept over every feature. Despite all previously-conceived efforts, Nurse Delaney sat as if glued to her chair. Viewing her with eyes of flashing fire, sickening sparks shooting from their intense sheen, she concluded that something more than sympathy for her patient lay closeted in her beating breast.

'Back again to Clapham Hall?' she said, with a sort of cynical sneer.

'Back again,' Nurse Delaney softly replied.

'For what length of time, pray?'

'Lord Gifford will, I presume, decide that matter.'

'You look fancy, to be sure, in nurses' garb! Mockery, by heavens, mockery, and the height of it!' she loudly exclaimed, making for the bedside of the slumbering patient. Peacefully he seemed to rest, to her gross vexation. She rushed to the door, unfastened it, closed it after her, muttering along the corridor:

'Devil take that little fisherwoman! Never mind, I'll make it hot for the urchin — that I will!'

Standing concealed behind a heavy portière, old Joss listened, with every nerve unstrung, for her return. As these last words died on her lips, he popped out triumphantly from his place of ambush.

'An' so ye'll make it hat fur dthe orchin, will ye? 'Dade, in be hivins, Oi'll make it as hat fur yerself, fur Oi'll watch fur dthe dacther ta-marra, an' till 'im ivery word ye sade; Oi'll put 'im an dthe thrack iv watchin' ye. It's dthe divil' loife ye give till aal iv is, an' now ye want till taurmint dthf very sowl iv innacence dthat Oi wus dthe manes iv procurlin' fur the ristorashun iv mae good masther's hilth. Ta hill wid ye fur iver an' iver!' accompanying his remarks with a stout blow of his hard old fist.

Madam-de-Maine reeled and fell, while Joss tripped away as if nothing had happened. She hadn't assumed this position long until she felt it acutely. Half afraid to draw upon her Joss's tongue again, or the weight of his fist, she formed a resolution of revenge that held within its howling hollow the nature of a savage race. The shock brought her keenly to a sense of self, as she straightened her slim figure before the orbs of anyone would be upon her. She walked, with eyes of evil, to her room, shut herself in to brew over the future and her encounters bordering on the near past. Her strength of thought, formed in moments of daring passion, was afterwards carried out with fearless and dauntless remorse.

Night came gently on, darkened by a heavy sky.

Delina being shown to a little room, by order of Madam-de-Marine, in which stood a small bed and a sprinkling of furniture and toilet requisites, she bathed her face and hands, brushed the elegant coils of hair, some of which hung daintily on brow and neck; changed her cotton gown to one of a newer, fresher shade, and hurried to perform the duties of night-nurse. She felt sleep would never again claim place until her lover was free from danger. Her senses were stuped in anxious thought, robbing them of all Nature's demands.

Ten o'clock struck, and still Lord Gifford never awoke. His breathing became quicker as the long, weary hours rolled by; his face appeared flushed and hot, remaining in this sick state until the doctor arrived early next morning.

Madam-de-Maine sat in her room caressing her rage at the course of events. She cursed old Joss in her heart for being the instigation of all that had taken place, for being the means of Lord Gifford's state becoming known to Dr. Norton so soon, and, worse than all, the return of Delina Delaney, whose existence she had learned to well-nigh forget.

As the timid movements of Delina along the polished corridor to her little room were delicately performed, an ear of burning strain to catch them welcomed their faint echo. Rising hastily, Madam-de-Maine made for Lord Gifford's room, not to inquire after his wants or health, but for an object hideous, horrifying, and revolting. Clasping steadily the murderous weapon that glittered beyond Lord Gifford's head, she glided triumphantly out of the room, enveloping it with her silken shawl. An adept in the art of handling deadly weapons, she satisfied herself it was fully charged. She sat on, without any cognizance of the flight of time, until the deep, ringing tones that escaped from the face of an adjacent church convinced her that eleven of its deep, sweet strokes proclaimed, in sober solemnity, night was steadily advancing.

Joss, who pattered about doing little odds and ends; after the servants had retired for the night, entered the stable to examine his master's favourite pony before he, too, sought sleep. This act was the finale of his everyday duties.

Madam-de-Maine's breath came and went as she heard his heavy footsteps die below. She walked into the stillness of the night, and stood for a time face to face with coal-black surroundings. Lightly moving in the direction of the stable, she heard the familiar voice of old Joss heaping praises on the dumbness of his charge. She stopped at the half-open door, looked with devilish intensity, and observed her foe stroke the silken mane with his wrinkled, rough hand, and, muttering a few words of parting pathos, turned to come away. He held in his hand a lantern, exposing his exact position. A loud report, a sudden flash, a dense smoke, and poor old Joss staggered and fell lifeless on the stable's pavement. She wrested from his hand the lantern he still firmly clutched, set it a considerable distance apart from the blood-steeped corpse of her victim. She closed his hands round the deadly weapon, with mouth upwards, — to establish the fact that fiction claimed to be a case of suicide, — hummed the following lines before she closed the stable door, with a voice strong and courageous:

> Lie still, thou devil I take thy rest;
> Sleep on, thou imp of Erin, sleep,
> Steeped in the blood I've done my best
> To scatter at thy mistress' feet.
> True to thy master here on earth,
> False to her who hath stayed thy might;
> Lie still, old Joss, for now no more
> Thou'lt threaten her — good-night —
> good-night.

Breathing an air of freedom, she stood in the night's dead darkness. The stillness was broken by a miserable wail from a neighbouring bird that haunted the churchyard trees. She had now reached the hall door that opened so lately to the touch of a fully-fledged mass of mischievous tyranny: closed to the force of a clouded murderess. The light from the yellow-shaded lamp in her room shone over her. Now and then a deep-drawn sigh escaped from her lips. Her frame sometimes shook to chorus a thirsty sob, as if she were again contemplating a similar ordeal. Eventually, however, the signs of nervousness, that now had visited her, died and withered away, and a miraculous peace, sometimes seen on the marbled faces of Roman statuary, that exhibit strongly the polished calm of revengeful rulers, rested on her features. Her thin hands she tightly clasped, as they lay in her lap, stained with the blood of her savage bravery.

The dog now barked and whined. She quickly rose, undressed, and, burying herself in the manufacture of deft hands, whether to sleep or not she best knew.

DORA SIGERSON SHORTER

(1866–1918)

from:
COLLECTED POEMS OF DORA SIGERSON SHORTER
(1907)

[Unhappy marriage is a major theme of late-nineteenth-century women poets and their contemporaries, the 'new woman' novelists. *Collected Poems* was published in London in 1907 by Hodder and Stoughton with an introduction by George Meredith.]

The Skeleton in the Cupboard

Just this one day in all the year
Let all be one, let all be dear;
Wife, husband, child in fond embrace,
And thrust the phantom from its place.
No bitter words, no frowning brow,
Disturb the Christmas festal, now
The skeleton's behind the door.

Nor let the child, with looks askance,
Find out its sad inheritance
From souls that held no happiness
Of home, where love is seldom guest;
But in his coming years retain
This one sweet night that had no pain;
The skeleton's behind the door.

In vain you raise the wassail bowl,
And pledge your passion, soul to soul
You hear the sweet bells ring in rhyme,
You wreath the room for Christmas-time
In vain. The solemn silence falls,
The death-watch ticks within the walls;
The skeleton taps on the door.

Then let him back into his place,
Let us sit out the old disgrace;
Nor seek the phantom now to lay
That haunted us through every day;
For plainer is the ghost; useless
Is this pretence of happiness;
The skeleton taps on the door.

[For a discussion of Gormlaith and how she has been traditionally represented in Irish literature, see Máirín Ní Dhonnachda, p. 133–9. Dora Sigerson Shorter takes part in a revivalist project to allegorize Ireland as a heroic and haunting female victim.]

Death of Gormlaith

Gormlaith, wife of Niall Glundu,
  Happy was your dream that night,
  Dreamt you woke in sudden fright,
Niall of Ulster stood by you.

Niall of Ulster, dead and gone,
  Many a year had come again,
  Him who was in battle slain
Now your glad eyes rest upon.

Well your gaze caressed him o'er,
  His dark head you loved so well,
  Where the coulin[1] curled and fell
On the clever brow he bore.

1. coulin: forlock

Those brave shoulders wide and strong,
  Many a Dane had quaked to see,
  Never phantom fair as he, —
Wife of Glundu, gazed so long.

Glad Queen Gormlaith, at the dawn,
  Up you sprang to draw him near,
  Ah! the grey cock loud and clear
Crew, and then the Ghost was gone.

Stretched your arms in vain request,
  Slipped and fell, and wounded sore
  Called his name, then spake no more,
For the bed-stick pierced your breast.

Queen, your smiling lips were dumb
  With that last dear name you cried,
  Yet some had it, ere you died,
Niall of Ulster whispered, 'come'.

ROBERT WILSON

(*fl.* 1906)

from:
MINUTES OF EVIDENCE TAKEN BEFORE THE VICE-REGAL COMMISSION ON POOR LAW REFORM IN IRELAND (1906)

[A Vice-Regal Commission in 1906 discovered that workhouses throughout Ireland had changed their function since their establishment — they had become institutions for children, the old and the infirm, particularly lunatics. In 1853, 38 per cent of the inhabitants of the Belfast workhouse were able-bodied men and women; by 1905 this had fallen to 8 per cent. Belfast differed from most other areas in the resistance shown by the Board of Guardians to outdoor relief. The text is from Michael Farrell, *The Poor Law and the Workhouse in Belfast, 1838–1948* (Belfast: PRONI, 1978), quoting Volume III, pp. 388–9.]

Evidence from Robert Wilson[1]

During the twelve months until March 1903, 153 illegitimate children were born in the Workhouse Maternity Hospital. Of this number as far as could be ascertained 140 were first cases and 13 not. Thirty-seven of the mothers, with their children, subsequently drifted into the nursery departments of the workhouse. On inquiry, I have found that there is, at any one time, an average of fifty women with their children being maintained there by the Guardians, or over 100 persons in all.

I have long felt that if the Local Government Board[2] could see their way to order and authorise a Ladies' Committee, that such a committee could quietly and unostentatiously assist these

1. Master of the Belfast workhouse.
2. The Local Government Board, established in 1872, took over responsibility for the Poor Law from the Poor Law Commissioners.

women to obtain suitable employment, and in addition, if the Guardians were empowered to have their children looked after in properly equipped day nurseries, many of them would be saved from ruin, the children's lives in many cases saved, and the Poor Law expenditure considerably reduced. I have, in my own experience, found such to be the case in those cases which the lady members of the Board have taken in hands [sic] at my request. I tried to trace what became of these first cases afterwards. One case, M.J., born 10th April, 1902, went out within fourteen days, was readmitted, with the mother and child 5th November 1902, died 3rd December 1902. Another case, born 19th of May, readmitted 28th June; child died shortly after that. I have had many consultations with the Deputy Coroner of the city, and we really don't know what to do with them. He has informed me that the number of infant children on whom he has had to hold inquests is abnormal in the city of Belfast . . .

These girls very often come into the workhouse in the dead of night; apparently they don't want anyone to know where they are going. I have made it a rule to receive them; in fact, I have had one or two object lessons to teach me to do that. One respectable girl from whom I had an application told me, after I had decided to admit her, that it was just as well I had done so, for had she been turned away she would have thrown herself into the river. Belfast is peculiarly situated with regard to this matter, owing to the fact that there are a considerable number of young girls from the adjoining counties, employed as servants, factory and wareroom workers, &c., in the city, whose parents are in the country, and with whom almost invariably the girls refuse to communicate when they are obliged to seek shelter in the workhouse for confinement or after confinement. I can assure the Commission with the greatest respect, that I have often watched those girls going out with their children on to the streets of the city when they were discharged at their own request, and having told me, in reply to my enquiries, that they did not know what they might do or where they were going, and I have been disgusted to think that the state of the Poor Law permitted such a thing without protection.

KATHARINE PARNELL

(1845–1921)

from:
CHARLES STEWART PARNELL, HIS LOVE STORY AND POLITICAL LIFE (1914)

[When Katharine Parnell published this memoir it was both widely read and widely criticized. Those who wished to defend Parnell's memory suggested that it had been largely written by Gerard O'Shea, son of Katharine and William O'Shea. Katharine was described by reviewers as a modern Delilah, recounting the destruction of her Samson (see R.F. Foster for discussion of the publication).[1] One could equally argue, however, that Katharine Parnell writes against her reputation as a scandalous and adulterous woman, and attempts to refigure her relationship with Parnell within the domestic. By emphasizing quotidian intimacies, she defuses some of the disruptive and radical potential of female sexuality and bolsters up 'marriage'. While making safe Parnell's relation to herself, however, she eroticizes in quite interesting ways his relationship to the Irish people. Her rhetoric repeatedly asks her audience to remember him as chief; the souvenirs in his pockets recall 'the deft, modest fingers' of blushing 'sweet-faced nuns', the bullets, the noose, the handiwork of colleens and 'herself', drawing attention to the desire of the masses centred on the body of this hero.]

When Parnell came home from Ireland after these meetings he would sit smoking and watching me as I went through the pockets of the coats he had worn while away. It was a most interesting game, and he enjoyed it as much as I when I brought out a new trophy from the depths of the deepest and most obvious side-pocket. It was a point of honour that he should not 'feel or look' till he got home to

1. R.F. Foster, 'Love, Politics and Textual Corruption: Mrs Katharine Parnell', in *Paddy and Mr Punch: Connections in Irish and English History* (London: Penguin, 1995), pp. 123–38.

me, and I have a dear little collection of souvenirs now from these pockets — little medals with the images of various saints, scapulars[2] and badges, slipped in by the deft, modest fingers of sweet-faced nuns, in the crowds, whose startled, deprecating blushes when he turned and caught the delinquent in the act always won a courteous bow and smile from the heretic 'Chief' whose conversion their patriotic hearts so ardently desired. I found also odds and ends pressed upon him by the hero-worshipping peasants, some gruesome scrap of the rope that had hanged some unknown scamp and hero, so 'aising to the bone-pains, an' his riv'rance not looking, a bit of a twisht roun' yer honour's arrm!' or perhaps a flattened old bullet that had gained some fancied power in its evil journey through a man's heart. Then there were the brand-new kerchiefs of most vivid green, most beautifully embroidered by the clever fingers of 'herself,' and so many four-leaved, and therefore 'lucky,' shamrocks from the 'colleens,' who went singing all the year if they thereby earned a smile from the Chief. Even the little children used to make sudden, shy offerings to their hero; a 'quare bit ave a stone,' a 'farden[3] me mither[4] give me,' or some uneasy looking fragment of what might once have been a bird's egg. Of sticks, blackthorns[5] and others, I once had an enormous collection brought back to me at various times by Parnell, but these, together with the two riding-whips I had myself given him, were stolen from me some ten years ago, when I was moving from one house to another. The two riding-whips I prized very highly, for Parnell was so pleased when I gave them to him. One was gold-mounted, the other silver-mounted, and each had 'C.S.P.' engraved upon it.

Among my stick collection was one made of horn — a curious thing, carved and inlaid with ivory, sent him by some unknown American admirer. He used this stick on his last journey upstairs from the sitting-room to the bed where he died.

In January of 1881, Willie, who had rooms then in Charles Street, Haymarket,[6] came down to Eltham[7] suddenly, very angry indeed with me because he had seen some men watching his lodgings, and imagined that I had engaged a detective to do so. As I had never had an idea of doing anything of the sort I was extremely annoyed, and a violent quarrel was the result. As a matter of fact the men were watching the upper floor, where a friend of Willie's lived, and this friend's wife afterwards divorced him.

All these months, since my first meeting with Mr. Parnell, Willie knew at least that I frequently met him at the House. He had invited him to Eltham himself, though when the visit was first proposed I said my house was too shabby, the children would worry so nervous a man, and we had better not break the routine of our (Willie's and my) life (which by then was tacitly accepted as a formal separation of a friendly sort), giving any and every excuse, because of the danger I knew I was not able to withstand.

But Willie was blind to the existence of the fierce, bewildering force that was rising within me in answer to the call of those passion-haunted eyes, that waking or sleeping never left me. Willie then, as always, was content that what was his, was *his* for good or ill. He knew that men, in our past life together, had admired me, even that some had loved me; but that was to their own undoing, an impertinence that had very properly recoiled upon their own heads. *His* wife could not love anyone but himself; perhaps unfortunately she did not even do that, but after all 'love' was only a relative term — a little vulgar even, after girlhood had passed, and the mild affection of his own feelings towards her were no doubt reciprocated, in spite of the unfortunate temperamental differences that made constant companionship impossible.

So Parnell came, having in his gentle, insistent way urged his invitation, and from Willie. And now Willie and I were quarrelling because he, my lawful husband, had come down without the invitation that was now (for some years) understood as due to the courtesy of friends, and because he had become vaguely suspicious. Flying rumours had perhaps reached his ears; and now it was too late, for he dared not formulate them, they were too vague; too late, for I had been swept into

2. An article of devotion comprising two small pieces of woollen cloth fastened together by strings, worn around the shoulders.
3. Farthing.
4. Mother.
5. A walking stick made from the blackthorn bush.
6. Central London.

7. Before her marriage to Parnell, Katharine O'Shea lived with her children at the home of her wealthy aunt, Mrs Benjamin Wood, at Wonersh Lodge, Eltham.

the avalanche of Parnell's love; too late, for I possessed the husband of my heart for all eternity.

I had fought against our love; but Parnell would not fight, and I was alone. I had urged my children and his work; but he answered me: 'For good or ill, I am your husband, your lover, your children, your all. And I will give my life to Ireland, but to you I give my love, whether it be your heaven or your hell. It is destiny. When I first looked into your eyes I knew.'

When Willie arrived so suddenly at Eltham Mr. Parnell was not there, but Willie went into his room, and finding his portmanteau,[8] sent it to London, and left my house, declaring he would challenge Parnell to fight a duel and would shoot him.

'My dear Mrs. O'Shea,' wrote Parnell from London on the 7th of January, 'will you kindly ask Captain O'Shea where he left my luggage? I inquired at both parcel office, cloak-room, and this hotel at Charing Cross to-day, and they were not to be found.'

Willie later challenged Parnell, sending The O'Gorman Mahon[9] to him as his second; but the duel was not fought. My sister, Mrs. Steele, came down to see me, and patched up a peace between myself and Willie; and Mr. Parnell, while making arrangements to go abroad to meet Willie, explained to him that he (Parnell) must have a medium of communication between the Government and himself, that Mrs. O'Shea had kindly undertaken the office for him, and, as this would render negotiations possible and safe, he trusted that Willie would make no objection to his meeting her after the duel.

'I replied to Captain O'Shea's note yesterday,' writes Parnell, 'and sent my reply by a careful messenger to the Salisbury Club; and it must be waiting him there.

'He has just written me a very insulting letter, and I shall be obliged to send a friend to him if I do not have a satisfactory reply to a second note I have just sent him.'

Willie then thought he had been too hasty in his action, and, knowing I had become immersed in the Irish cause, merely made the condition that Mr. Parnell should not stay at Eltham.

From the date of this bitter quarrel Parnell and I were one, without further scruple, without fear, and without remorse.

8. Suitcase.
9. Charles James Patrick Mahon (1800–91), adventurer, politician and famous duellist.

PATRICK PEARSE

(1879–1916)

from:
COLLECTED WORKS OF
P.H. PEARSE
(1917)

[Post-colonial distrust of the 'unmanly' homosexual resulted in a complete obliteration of the homoerotic from within nationalist discourse (despite the palpable presence of same-sex desire in the writings of two key figures in republican agitation, Patrick Pearse and Roger Casement), much as James Connolly's socialism and Eva Gore-Booth's feminism became subaltern in the New Ireland. This poem is from vol. 3 *Plays, Stories, Poems* of the *Collected Works*. Headnote by Éibhear Walshe.]

Little Lad of the Tricks

Little lad of the tricks,
Full well I know
That you have been in mischief:
Confess your fault truly.

I forgive you, child
Of the soft red mouth:
I will not condemn anyone
For a sin not understood.

Raise your comely head
Till I kiss your mouth:
If either of us is the better of that
I am the better of it.

There is a fragrance in your kiss
That I have not found yet
In the kisses of women
Or in the honey of their bodies.

Lad of the grey eyes
That flush in thy cheek
Would be white with dread of me
Could you read my secrets.

He who has my secrets
Is not fit to touch you:
Is not that a pitiful thing,
Little lad of the tricks?

Biographies/Bibliographies

William M. Medland and Charles Weobly

LIVES. No information discovered.

CHIEF WRITINGS. W.M. Medland and Charles Weobly, *A Collection of Remarkable and Interesting Criminal Trials, Actions at Law, etc. To Which is Prefixed, An Essay on Reprieve and Pardon and Biographical Sketches of John Lord Eldon, and Mr. Mingay* (London: John Badcock, 1803).

Elizabeth Ham

LIFE. Elizabeth Ham, autobiographer, poet and novelist, was born in 1783 at North Perrott, Somerset, to a farming family. The family lived in Ireland from 1804 to 1809, a period recollected by Ham in the autobiography she wrote more than forty years later. On her return to England she attempted several careers, including school-keeping, millinery, magazine journalism, and novel-writing. Date of death unknown.

CHIEF WRITINGS. *Elgiva; Or, The Monks* (London: Baldwin, Craddock and Joy, 1824); *Infants' Grammar* (Dorchester, 1820–2); *The Ford Family in Ireland* (London: T.C. Newby, 1845); *Elizabeth Ham by Herself, 1783–1820*, ed. Eric Gillett (London: Faber and Faber, 1945).

Amelia Bristow

LIFE. Amelia Bristow is known only by a single publication, which gives some indication as to her background and connections, but is not decisive. She is not the 'Amelia Bristow' who at the same period was writing novels in England, many on Jewish themes, although certain catalogues and reference works naturally confuse the two. From the list of subscribers to *The Maniac*, a Miss Bristow from Birchill, County Antrim, took eight copies and it seems likely that this was the author. A Reverend Charles Bristow and a Miss Bristow of Belfast are probably relatives, and they may all be related to Reverend William Bristow (1736–1808), vicar of Belfast. A high proportion of subscribers are from Belfast and the northern counties. There are also quite a number of Dublin subscribers, and some from London and Kent. There are several aristocrats, including the Duke of Leinster and Lord William Fitzgerald, whose inscribed copy is the one now in the National Library of Ireland. Other well-known subscribers are Martha M'Tier, Narcissus Batt, Isaac Corry, Lord John Russell, and Francis Turnly.

CHIEF WRITINGS. *The Maniac, The Merits of Women, and Other Poems* (London, 1810).

Maria Edgeworth

For biography and bibliography, see Volume I, pp. 1051–2.

CHIEF WRITINGS. *The Novels and Selected Works of Maria Edgeworth*, 12 Volumes, general editors: Marilyn Butler and Mitzi Myers, Consulting Editor: W.J. McCormack (London: Pickering and Chatto 1999-2003)

BIOGRAPHY AND CRITICISM. Elizabeth Kowaleski-Wallace, *"Their Fathers' Daughters": Hannah More, Maria Edgeworth and Patriarchal Complicity* (New York: Oxford University Press, 1991); Brian Hollingsworth, *Maria Edgeworth's Irish Writing: language, history, politics* (Basingstoke: Macmillan, 1997)

Christian Johnstone

LIFE. Christian Isobel Johnstone was born in Fife in 1781 (birth name unknown). She was divorced from a Mr McLeish and married John Johnstone, a teacher, c. 1812. Her first and most popular novel, *Clan-Albin,* was published in 1815, followed by other novels, domestic manuals and literature for children. With her husband she edited the *Inverness Courier,* then the *Edinburgh Chronicle* and the *Schoolmaster and Edinburgh Weekly Magazine,* which became *Johnstone's Edinburgh Magazine* in 1833. She died in 1857.

CHIEF WRITINGS. *Clan-Albin: A National Tale* (London: Longman, 1815); *The Cook and Housewife's Manual* (1826); *The Students; Or, Biography of Grecian Philosophers* (London: John Harris, 1827); *Elizabeth De Bruce* (1828); *Scenes of Industry* (London: John Harris, 1829); *Nights of the Round Table; Or, Stories of Aunt Jane and Her Friends* (1832); *True Tales of the Irish Peasantry, As Related by Themselves, Selected from the Report of the Poor Law Commissioners,* 2nd ed. (Edinburgh, 1836); (editor) *Rational Reading Lessons* (Edinburgh, 1842).

W.H. Maxwell

LIFE. William Hamilton Maxwell was born in Newry, County Down, in 1792 and was educated at Trinity College Dublin. He served as a soldier in the Peninsular War and at Waterloo. He later became a Church of Ireland clergyman and went to a living at Ballagh in Connemara in 1820. He published almost a book a year from 1825, writing popular fiction, sporting books, military history and memoirs. He died at Musslburgh near Edinburgh on 29 December 1850.

CHIEF WRITINGS. *O'Hara; Or, 1798* (London: J. Andrews, 1825); *Stories of Waterloo and Other Tales* (London: H. Colburn 1829); *Wild Sports of the West* (London: Richard Bentley, 1832); *The Dark Lady of Doona* (London: Smith, Elder, 1834); *My Life* (London: Richard Bentley, 1835); *History of the Irish Rebellion in 1798* (London: Bailey Brothers, 1845); *Brian O'Linn; Or, Luck is Everything* (London: Richard Bentley, 1848); *Erin Go Bragh; Or, Irish Life Pictures* (London: Richard Bentley, 1859).

Charlotte Elizabeth Tonna

For biography and bibliography, see p. 560.

R.R. Madden

LIFE. Richard Robert Madden was born on 22 August 1798. He was educated at a school in Dublin and studied medicine in Paris, Naples and London. In the 1820s he travelled in the Near East. In 1853 he went to Jamaica, where he served as one of the special magistrates appointed to superintend the statute abolishing slavery. He became a strong advocate of the liberated slaves. He later worked in Havana, Cuba, in Africa, and for aboriginal rights in Australia. In 1845 he returned to Ireland. From 1850 to 1880 he was secretary to the Loan Fund Board, Dublin Castle. In 1828 he married Harriet Elmslie of Jamaica, and they had three sons. He died at Booterstown on 5 February 1886.

CHIEF WRITINGS. *The United Irishmen, Their Lives and Times* (London, 1842–6); *The Life and Times of Robert Emmet Esq* (Dublin: James Duffy, 1847); *The Literary Life and Correspondence of the Countess of Blessington* (London: T.C. Newby, 1855); *Literary Remains of the United Irishmen of 1798, and Selections from Other Popular Lyrics of Their Times, with an Essay on the Authorship of 'the Exile of Erin'*, collected and edited by R.R. Madden (Dublin: James Duffy, 1887); *The Memoirs — Chiefly Autobiographical, — from 1798–1886 of R.R. Madden*, edited by his son T.M. Madden (London: Ward and Downey, 1891).

Dinah Goff

LIFE. Born *c.* 1784, Dinah Goff was the youngest daughter of Jacob Goff and his wife Elizabeth (née Wilson), of Horetown House, near Foulkesmills, County Wexford. The family remained relatively neutral during 1798, though with an obvious prejudice in favour of the previous *status quo.* They were offered compensation for damage to their property after the rebellion but, according to Dinah, her father felt that 'as a member of the Society of Friends, and not taking up arms in defence of government . . . he could not accept it'. After her father's death Dinah and her mother moved to Dublin. Dinah Goff eventually moved to Penzance in Cornwall, where she dated her testimony in 1856. Her date of death is unknown.

CHIEF WRITINGS. *Divine Protection through Extraordinary Dangers During the Irish Rebellion in 1798* (Philadelphia: Tract Association of Friends, 1856).

BIOGRAPHY AND CRITICISM. John D. Beatty, 'Protestant Women of County Wexford and Their Narratives of the Rebellion of 1798', in *The Women of 1798*, eds Dáire Keogh and Nicholas Furlong (Dublin: Four Courts Press, 1998), pp. 113–36.

Frances Browne

LIFE. Frances Browne was born in Stranrolar, County Donegal, on January 16, 1816, where her father Samuel was village postmaster and her parents members of the local Presbyterian church. The seventh child in a family of twelve, she lost her eyesight following an attack of smallpox at the age of eighteen months. As Browne later recounted, she educated herself by 'listening attentively to my young brothers and sisters reading over the tasks required at the village school' and later by borrowing books from 'the few acquaintances I had' to be read to her by her young relatives. Among the works which influenced her most were the novels of Walter Scott, Pope's translation of *The Illiad* and Byron's *Childe Harold.* Her first published poems appeared in the short-lived *Irish Penny Journal* and later in the *Athenaeum, Hood's Magazine* and *The Keepsake*, edited by Countess Blessington. In 1844, a volume of poems entitled *The Star of Attéghéi* was published, and included a memoir of her early life. A portion of the money received from her publications was used to employ her younger sister as her amanuensis. In 1847, following an award from the Royal Bounty Fund of £20, she and her sister moved to Edinburgh where they lived for five years; during this period, her 'legends of Ulster' appeared in *Fraser's Magazine* and *Tait's Edinburgh Magazine.* In 1852 Frances moved to London where she resided until her death. In 1861 she published her first three-volume novel entitled *My Share of the World*; in 1866 her novel *The Hidden Sin* appeared anonymously. Known to many of her contemporaries as 'the blind poetess of Donegal', she received a pension of £100 from the civil list in 1863. She died from apoplexy at Richmond, Surrey, on August 21 1879.

CHIEF WRITINGS. *The Star of Attéghéi; The Vision of Schwartz; and Other Poems* (London: Moxon, 1844); *Lyrics and Miscellaneous Poems* (Edinburgh: Sutherland and Knox, 1848); *The Ericksons; The Clever Boy; or Consider Another* (Edinburgh: Paton and Richie, 1852); *Pictures and Songs of Home* (London: Nelson, 1856); *Granny's Wonderful Chair and Its Tales of Fairy Times* (1856; London: Griffith and Farran, 1857); *Our Uncle the Traveller's Stories* (London: Kent, 1859); *The Orphans of Elfholm* (1860; London: Groombridge, 1862); *The Young Foresters* (1860; London: Groombridge, 1864); *My Share of the World: An Autobiography*, 3 vols (London: Hurst and Blackett, 1861); *The Castleford Case*, 3 vols (London: Hurst and Blackett, 1862); *The Hidden Sin: A Novel*, 3 vols (London: Bentley, 1866); *The Exile's Trust and Other Stories* (London: Leisure Hour, 1869); *The Nearest Neighbour and Other Stories* (London: Religious Tracts Society, 1875); *The Dangerous Guest: A Story of 1745* (London: R.T.S., 1886); *The Foundling of the Fens* (London: R.T.S., 1886); *The First of the African Diamonds* (London: R.T.S., 1887).

BIOGRAPHY AND CRITICISM. 'The Life and Writings of Miss Browne, the Blind Poetess', *Dublin Review*, XVII (1844), pp. 517–60; Review of *My Share of the World, Chambers' Journal*, 35 (1861), pp. 281–4; Charles A. Read and T.P. O'Connor's (eds), *The Cabinet Irish Literature: Selections from the Works of the Chief Poets, Orators, and Prose Writers of Ireland. With Biographical Sketches and Literary Notices*, 4 vols (London, Glasgow, Edinburgh and Dublin: Blackie, 1879–80), new ed. by Katharine Tynan Hinkson (London: Gresham, 1902–3); 'Our Poets: No. 29 Frances Browne (sic)', *Irish Monthly*, 24 (1896), pp. 262–8; Justin McCarthy, Charles Welsh et al. (eds), *Irish Literature: Irish Authors and Their Writings*, 10 vols (Philadelphia: Morris, 1904); Frances Hodgson Burnett, 'The Story of the Lost Fairy Book', introduction to *Granny's Wonderful Chair* by Frances Browne (London, New York: McClure, Phillips, 1904); Dollie Radford, 'Preface', *Granny's Wonderful Chair and Its Tales of Fairy Times*, Everyman's Library (London: Dent, 1906); Gillian Avery, 'Frances Browne', *Dictionary of National Biography: Missing Persons*, ed. C.S. Nicholls (Oxford: OUP, 1993).

James Greenwood

LIFE. James Greenwood, journalist and novelist, was born in London in 1832, the son of a coachman. He was the brother of Frederick Greenwood (1830–1909) founder in 1865 of the *Pall Mall Gazette.* James's journalism contributed to the journal's success, particularly with the publication of three papers entitled 'A Night on the Casual Ward' in 1866. He died in 1929.

CHIEF WRITINGS. (with Frederick Greenwood) *Under a Cloud. A Novel* (London: 1860); *Wild Sports of the World, A Boy's Book of Natural History and Adventure* (London: S.O. Beeton, 1862); *Curiosities of Savage Life* (London: S.O. Beeton, 1863); *The Purgatory of Peter the Cruel* (London: George Routledge, 1868); *The Seven Curses of London* (Boston Fields: Osgood and Co, 1869); *Wilds of London* (London: Chatto and Windus, 1874).

William Carleton

For biography and bibliography, see Volume II, pp. 205–6.

Annie Besant

LIFE. Annie Besant was the daughter of William Wood and Emily Morris and was born in 1847. After the death of her father, a doctor, when she was five, Annie was brought up by Ellen Marryat while her mother worked at the English public school Harrow. At the age of nineteen Annie married a clergyman, Frank Besant, and had two children. She separated from her husband and took one of her children to live in London, where she joined the Secular Society in 1874. She developed a relationship with Charles Bradlaugh, editor of the *National Reformer* and began to write on women's issues for that journal. In 1877 she was charged with Bradlaugh for publishing 'an obscene libel' — a book by Charles Knowlton on birth control. In the 1880s Besant started her own campaigning newspaper, *The Link*, and on 23rd June 1888 she published in issue 21 an article 'White Slavery in London', which was an attack on the employment conditions for women at the Bryant and May match factory. She joined the Fabian Society and in the 1890s became a supporter of theosophy. This led to her emigration to India, where she joined the Indian Home Rule movement. She died in India in 1933.

CHIEF WRITINGS. *My Path to Atheism* (London: Freethought Publishing, 1877); *Beauties of Islam* (Adyar: Theosophical Publishing House, 1932); *England, India and Afghanistan* and *The Story of Afghanistan; or, Why the Tory Government Gags the Indian Press* (Madras: Theosophical Publishing House, 1931); *The Law of Population: Its Consequences, and Its Bearing upon Human Conduct and Morals* (London: Freethought Publishing, 1877); *Coercin in Ireland and Its Results: A Plea for Justice* (London: A. Besant and C. Bradlaugh, 1882).

BIOGRAPHY AND CRITICISM. Olivia Bennett, *Annie Besant* (London: Hamilton, 1988); Rosemary Dinnage, *Annie Besant* (Harmondsworth, Middlesex: Penguin, 1986); Anne Taylor, *Annie Besant. A Biography* (Oxford: Oxford University Press, 1992).

Josephine E. Butler

LIFE. Josephine Butler, the daughter of John Grey and Hannah Annett, was born in 1828. Her father was a wealthy landowner, social reformer, and cousin of Earl Grey, British Prime Minister 1830–4. In 1852 she married George Butler and they had four children, living first in Oxford, later in Cheltenham, and finally in Liverpool. The death of her only daughter in an accident in 1863 had a profound effect on Butler, who subsequently devoted her life to philanthropy and protest. Among her wide range of political activities, she is chiefly remembered for her campaigns to increase women's access to higher education and her campaign for the repeal of the Contagious Diseases Acts. She died in 1906.

CHIEF WRITINGS. *The Education and Employment of Women* (London: Macmillan, 1868); *Women's Work and Women's Culture* (London: Macmillan, 1869); *Recollections of George Butler* (Bristol: J.W. Arrowsmith, 1892); *Personal Reminiscences of a Great Crusade* (London: H. Marshall, 1896).

BIOGRAPHY AND CRITICISM. Jane Jordan, *Josephine Butler* (London: John Murray, 2001).

Jane Francesca Elgee (Lady Wilde)

LIFE. Jane Elgee was born into a Protestant middle-class family in Dublin on 27 December 1826. There are conflicting accounts of her conversion to nationalism. She began submitting poems and poetic translations to the *Nation* in February 1846 under the name 'Speranza', at first concealing her gender by accompanying her contributions with letters signed John Fanshaw Ellis. She contributed numerous poems between 1846 and 1848, patriotic ballads, poems on the theme of famine and emigration, poetic translations from six different languages. As Speranza, she became a household name in Ireland. While Charles Gavan Duffy, the *Nation*'s editor, was imprisoned to await trial for sedition, she wrote inflammatory leaders for two successive issues of the paper, 'The Hour of Destiny', 22 July 1848, and a week later 'Jacta Alea Est' ('The Die is Cast'), articles which were deemed highly seditious and attributed to Duffy. The story that she bravely claimed the authorship of these articles in court during Duffy's trial is apparently apocryphal. Discouraged by the failure of the abortive 1848 uprising, she virtually gave up her political writing and turned to prose translation. She married Sir William Wilde, an eminent medical specialist and scholar, on 14 November 1851. They had two sons, William and Oscar, and a daughter Isola who died young. As an intellectual and affluent couple the Wildes enjoyed a brilliant social life.

Sir William's death in April 1876 left Lady Wilde in straitened circumstances and she moved to London on 7 May 1879. She was also freed to lead a literary life and among the books she wrote in London were two important collections of folklore based on her husband's papers. When Oscar toured the US in 1881–2, he was welcomed by Irish-Americans as Speranza's son. Her last year was wracked by illness, poverty and sadness at Oscar's imprisonment. She died on 3 February 1896 and was buried next day in Kensal Green cemetery.

CHIEF WRITINGS. *Poems* (Dublin: James Duffy, 1864); *Poems: Second Series: Translations* (Dublin: James Duffy, 1867); *Poems* (Glasgow: Cameron and Ferguson, 1871 and 1883; Dublin: M.H. Gill, 1907); *Driftwood from Scandinavia* (London: Richard Bentley and Son, 1884); *Ancient Legends, Mystic Charms, and Superstitions of Ireland* (London: Ward and Downey, 1888); *Ancient Cures, Charms, and Usages of Ireland* (London: Ward and Downey, 1890); *Notes on Men, Women, and Books* (London: Ward and Downey, 1891); *Social Studies* (London: Ward and Downey, 1893). Translations: William Meinhold, *Sidonia the Sorceress* (London: The Parlour Library, 1849; Kelmscott Press, 1893; Reeves and Turner, 2 vols, 1894); Alphonse de Lamartine, *Pictures of the First French Revolution* (London: Simms and McIntyre, 1850) and *The Wanderer and His Home* (London: Simms and McIntyre, 1851); Alexander Dumas, *père*, *The Glacier Land* (London: Simms and McIntyre, 1852); M. Schwab, *The First Temptation or 'Eritis Sicut Deus'* (London: T. Cautley Newby, 1863).

BIOGRAPHY AND CRITICISM. Horace Wyndham, *Speranza* (London: T.V. Boardman, 1951); Terence de Vere White, *The Parents of Oscar Wilde* (London: Hodder and Stoughton, 1967); Joy Melville, *Mother of Oscar: The Life of Jane Francesca Wilde* (London: John Murray, 1994).

Oscar Wilde

For biography and bibliography, see Volume II, p. 514. See also:

BIOGRAPHY AND CRITICISM. Lucy McDiarmid, 'Oscar Wilde's Speech from the Dock', *Textual Practice* 15:3 (Winter 2001) pp. 447–468; Neil McKenna, *The Secret Life of Oscar Wilde* (London: Macmillan, forthcoming).

Sarah Grand

LIFE. Frances Elizabeth Clarke was born at Donaghadee, County Down, in 1854, the daughter of Margaret Bell (Sherwood) and Edward John Bellenden Clarke, a naval officer and coastguard. Her father died when Frances was seven, and the family moved to Yorkshire. She was educated at boarding school. At sixteen she married army Surgeon-Major David MacFall. They travelled to Hong Kong and the Far East, later settling in Norwich and then Warrington. Under the name of Sarah Grand, she began publishing stories in magazines and the success of her first novel, *Ideala*, in 1888, gave her enough money to leave her husband and move to London. She was highly active in the Women's Suffrage Society, the Women Writers' Suffrage League, and the National Council of Women. In later years she lived in Bath, where she was mayoress for six years. She died in 1943.

CHIEF WRITINGS. *Two Dear Little Feet* (London: Jarrolds, 1873); *Ideala: A Study from Life* (London: E.W. Allen, 1888); *A Domestic Experiment* (Edinburgh: Blackwoods, 1891); *The Heavenly Twins* (London: Heinemann, 1893; with an introduction by Carol A. Senf, University of Michigan Press, 1992); *Singularly Deluded* (Edinburgh: Blackwoods, 1893); *Our Manifold Nature* (London: Heinemann, 1894); *The Beth Book* (London: Heinemann, 1897; with an introduction by Elaine Showalter, London: Virago Press, 1983); *The Modern Man and Maid* (London: H. Marshall, 1898); *The Tenor and the Boy* (London: Heinemann, 1899); *The Human Quest: Being Some Thoughts in Contribution to the Subject of the Art of Happiness* (London: Heinemann, 1900); *Babs the Impossible* (London: Heinemann, 1901); *Emotional Moments* (London: Hurst and Blackett, 1908); *Adnam's Orchard* (London: Heinemann, 1912); *The Winged Victory* (London: Heinemann, 1916); *Variety* (London: Heinemann, 1922); *The Breath of Life* (privately printed, 1933).

BIOGRAPHY AND CRITICISM. Elaine Showalter, *A Literature of Their Own* (London: Virago Press, 1977); Joan Huddleston, *Sarah Grand, A Bibliography* (University of Queensland, 1979); Gillian Kersley, *Darling Madame: Sarah Grand and Devoted Friend* (London: Virago Press, 1983); Joseph Allen Boone, 'Wedlock as Deadlock and Beyond: Closure and the Victorian Marriage Ideal', in *'For Better or Worse': Attitudes Toward Marriage in Literature,* ed. E. Hinz (Winnipeg: University of Manitoba Press, 1985), pp. 65–82; John Sutherland, *The Stanford Companion to Victorian Fiction* (Stanford: Stanford University Press, 1989).

George Egerton

LIFE. Mary Chavelita Dunne was born to a Welsh mother and an Irish father in Australia in 1859, and brought up in Ireland and Chile. After working in Germany, New York, Dublin and London, she moved to Norway, then came back to Ireland in 1891, and published four volumes of stories under the name of George Egerton. She also published translations and biographies of her contemporaries, and wrote four plays, three of which were staged in the United States. Egerton died in 1945.

CHIEF WRITINGS. *Keynotes* (London: E. Mathews and J. Lane, 1893); *Discords* (London: J. Lane, 1894) (the two reprinted together London: Virago Press, 1983); *Symphonies* (London: J. Lane, 1897) and *Fantasias* (London: J. Lane, 1898). Her novels are the semi-autobiographical *The Wheel of God* (London: Grant Richards, 1898); *Rosa Amorosa: The Love-Letters of a Woman* (London: Grant Richards, 1901); and *Flies in Amber* (London: Hutchinson, 1905); *A Leaf from the Yellow Book: The Correspondence of George Egerton,* ed. Terence de Vere White (London: Richards Press, 1958).

BIOGRAPHY AND CRITICISM. Ernst Foerster, *Die Frauenfiage* in den Romanen enghscher Schrifstellerinnen den Gegenenwart (George Egerton, Mana Caird, Sarah Grand) Marburg: 1907.

Amanda M'Kittrick Ros

LIFE. The writer and (perhaps unconscious) humorist was born 8 December 1860 near Ballynahinch, County Down, daughter of head teacher Edward Amlane M'Kittrick. Educated at Marlborough Training College, Dublin, she became a teacher at Larne, County Antrim. She married Andrew Ross, Larne stationmaster, in 1887 (d. 1917), and Thomas Rodgers, farmer, in 1922 (d. 1934). She published her own novels and poems, in which she attacked critics (notably Barry Pain) and other enemies. Her extraordinary linguistic inventiveness, which veers between regional brusqueness and an almost parodic sentimentality, has made her a cult figure. In contemplation of dead literary predecessors she wrote 'Some rare bits of brain lie here / Mortal loads of beef and beer'. She died in 1939.

CHIEF WRITINGS. *Irene Iddesleigh* (Belfast: W. and G. Baird, 1897); *Delina Delaney* (Belfast: R. Aicken, 1898); *Fumes of Formation* (Belfast: R. Carswell, 1933); *Donald Dudley, The Bastard Critic* (Thames Ditton: Merle Press, 1954); *Helen Huddleson* (London: Chatto and Windus, 1969).

BIOGRAPHY AND CRITICISM. J. Loudan, *O Rare Amanda! The Life of Amanda McKittrick Ros* (London: Chatto and Windus, 1954); F. Ormsby, *Thine in Storm and Calm: An Amanda McKittrick Ros Reader* (Belfast: Blackstaff Press, 1988).

Dora Sigerson Shorter

LIFE. Dora Mary Sigerson was born in Dublin in 1866, daughter of the historian and translator George Sigerson (1836–1925) and his wife Hester Varian, a poet and novelist. In 1895 Dora married the English critic Clement Shorter (1857–1926), editor of the *Illustrated London News,* and they lived in London. She died on 6 January 1918.

CHIEF WRITINGS. *Verses* (London: E. Stock, 1893); *The Fairy Changeling and Other Poems* (London: J. Lane, 1898); *Ballads and Poems* (London: J. Bowden, 1899); *The Father Confessor, Stories of Danger and Death* (London: Ward, Lock, 1900); *The Woman Who Went to Hell, and Other Ballads and Lyrics* (London: De La Mare, 1902); *As the Sparks Fly Upward* (London: Alexander Moring, 1906); *The Country-House Party* (London: Hodder and Stoughton, 1905); *The Story and Song of Black Roderick* (London: Alexander Moring, 1906); *The Collected Poems of Dora Sigerson Shorter* (London: Hodder and Stoughton, 1907); *Through Wintry Terrors* (London: Cassell, 1907); *The Troubadour and Other Poems* (London: Hodder and Stoughton, 1910); *New Poems* (Dublin: Maunsel, 1912); *Do-Well and Do-Little* (London: Cassell, 1913); *Love of Ireland, Poems and Ballads* (Dublin: Maunsel, 1916); *Madge Linsey and Other Poems* (Dublin: Maunsel, 1916); *Sad Years and Other Poems* (London: Constable, 1918); *A Legend of Glendalough and Other Ballads* (Dublin: Maunsel, 1919); *A Dull Day in London, and Other Sketches* (London: Eveleigh Nash, 1920); *The Tricolour* (Dublin: Maunsel and Roberts, 1922); *Twenty-one Poems* (London: Ernest Benn, 1926).

Robert Wilson

LIFE. Master of the Belfast workhouse c. 1906. No other information discovered.

Katharine Parnell

LIFE. Katharine Wood was born at Rivenhall in Essex in 1845. She married Captain William O'Shea (1840–1905), Irish politician, in 1867. Financial hardship led her to live with a rich aunt, Mrs Benjamin Wood, in Eltham, outside London. The O'Sheas were effectively separated when Katharine met Charles Stewart Parnell (1846–91), leader of the Irish Parliamentary Party, in 1880. She continued to support her husband's political career and he seems to have acquiesced in her affair with Parnell, which began in the early 1880s. She had three daughters by Parnell, as well as older children by O'Shea. William O'Shea and Charles Stewart Parnell became increasingly hostile to one another through the 1880s, and when Mrs Wood died in 1889, leaving Katharine £145,000, Captain O'Shea sued for divorce, citing Parnell as co-respondent. The divorce scandal ruined Parnell's career, and led to a split in the Irish Parliamentary Party. Katharine married Parnell in June 1891 and they moved to Brighton, where he died in October of the same year. She lost custody of her children (including Parnell's daughters) and some of her inheritance to her former husband. She died in 1921.

CHIEF WRITINGS. *Charles Stewart Parnell, His Love Story and Political Life* (London and Toronto: Cassell, 1914).

BIOGRAPHY AND CRITICISM. Joyce Marlow, *The Uncrowned Queen of Ireland: The Life of 'Kitty' O'Shea* (London: Weidenfeld and Nicolson, 1975); Mary Rose Callaghan, *'Kitty O'Shea': A Life of Katharine Parnell* (London: Pandora, 1989); R.F. Foster, 'Love, Politics and Textual Corruption: Mrs O'Shea's Parnell', in *Paddy and Mr Punch: Connections in Irish and English History* (London: Penguin, 1995), pp. 123–38.

Patrick Pearse

For biography and bibliography, see Volume II, p. 561. See also:

BIOGRAPHY AND CRITICISM. Vincent Quinn, 'Fostering the Nation: Patrick Pearse and Pedagogy', *New Formations,* vol. 42 (winter 2001), pp. 71–84.

JO MURPHY LAWLESS, *Editor*

Childbirth, 1742–1955

In 1671 James Wolveridge, a man midwife, as he called himself, based in Cork, published the *Speculum Matricis; Or, The Expert Midwives Handmaid*, in which he described Irish women as those

> whose fruitfulness is such that there is scarce one barren among them and whose hardiness, and facility in bringing forth, is generally such as neither requires the nice Attendance of diligent, vigilant Nurse-keepers, or the Art of expert Anatomists or the unwearied pains and skills of dexterous midwives.[1]

In March 1745 the following report appeared in *Faulkner's Dublin Journal*:

> On Friday, the 15th instant, was opened an hospital for poor lying-in women in George's Lane, facing Fade Street; and the same evening Judith Rochford was received into the said hospital, recommended by the minister, churchwardens, and a great number of the principal parishioners of St. Andrew's parish, as a very great object of charity; and on Wednesday last she was safely delivered of a son.[2]

Between these two dates, a new way of thinking about pregnancy and birth, about women's bodies and about their caretakers during labour and birth emerged. Wolveridge was the first midwife to write

of childbirth in Ireland as a scientific matter. Judith Rochford was the first woman to give birth in a building designed exclusively for lying-in women. Wolveridge was followed by thousands of men who made this their special discipline; she was the first of countless numbers of women whose pregnancies would be defined and affected by that discipline. By 1745, Irish women were no longer written about as hardy in giving birth, and as for women midwives, in Ireland as elsewhere in Europe, their reputation for dexterity, skill and dedication had vanished beneath a torrent of male medical invective and disavowal.

Before men midwives introduced themselves in the latter half of the seventeenth century, barber surgeons came to the bedside to perform instrumental deliveries for women midwives when the latter were unable to deliver a baby, most often because the birth passage was obstructed. Iron hooks and crochets were used in 'destructive operations' when the foetal body or head had to be shattered in an effort to free the obstruction and save the mother's life. Later, forceps were used to try and free a baby. However, midwifery was exclusively a female domain.[3]

The rise of the man midwife was an invasion of this domain in the name of science. First with his scientific discourses and then with the lying-in hospitals he set up, the man midwife legitimated his work as a special discipline necessary to women's well-being and therefore to society, and vastly superior to the work of women midwives. Thus Frederick Jebb, later to become fourth master of the Rotunda Hospital in Dublin, wrote in 1772:

1. James Wolveridge, 'The author to the reader', *Speculum Matricis; Or, The Expert Midwives Handmaid* (London: E. Okes, 1671). The originality of Wolveridge's manuscript relates entirely to his preface in which he discourses on the birth practices of Irish women. The rest of the manuscript is plagiarized from the work of William Harvey (1578–1657), the English scientist.
2. *Faulkner's Dublin Journal*, 23–26 March 1745.

3. See Jean Donnison, *Midwives and Medical Men* (London: Heinemann Educational, 1977).

From the moment that the practice of midwifery became the object of men of science and sagacity, we find the history of that art dates its commencement. Everything before the period concerning it, is wrapt up in the ignorance and superstition of the persons who professed it nor can there be urged in my opinion, any argument against Females meddling in science of greater weight than . . . from the beginning of time . . . down to the seventeenth century, the art of midwifery (for which women surely qualified if for any branch of science) was exercised almost exclusively by females.[4]

At first, this scientific breed relied on a familiar word and described themselves as 'men midwives', but they also called themselves operators, *accoucheurs* (the stylish French term), and eventually, towards the end of the nineteenth century, obstetricians.

The dyad of the 'poor suffering woman', who was unable to withstand the pain of childbirth, and the heroic man midwife, who claimed to be able to relieve her helplessness, equipped with his scientific approach, was invented during this period:

the Course of Anxiety, Pain and Danger which Women undergo, from the Time of Pregnancy till some time after the Birth, is very considerable, even when it is most successful. How extraordinary then must the Danger be, when Nature is interrupted in her usual Progress towards a happy Conclusion of this grand Undertaking?[5]

The volume of medical writing on childbirth increased dramatically in the early eighteenth century and it also changed in tone, often becoming inflated with self-importance.[6] This development was followed by the rise of lying-in

hospitals, institutions which served complex purposes. The Dublin Lying-in Hospital in Great Britain Street, later known as the Rotunda, was the first such institution in the British Isles. It was founded by Bartholomew Mosse to extend and replace his private charity, the George's Lane Lying-in Hospital, where Judith Rochford had given birth. Mosse was reputed to have said of those Dublin women living in poverty:

Their lodgings are generally cold garrets open to every wind, or in damp cellars subject to flash floods from excessive rains, themselves destitute of attendance, medicine, and often proper foods, by which hundreds perish with their little infants and the community is at once robbed of both mother and child.[7]

Poor women were now seen to need help in greater numbers than well-off women, but the latter could pay for their care, whereas the former were dependent on charity. Building a specific institution for poor lying-in women provided men midwives with a constant and large source of clinical material whereby they could extend their science. It also offered possibilities of more closely controlling and monitoring the actions of lower class families; of easing pressures on the parish's public purse by preventing the disruption of a family's economic activity during and just after birth; of encouraging an increase in the population of labourers, soldiers and sailors; and of preventing infanticide.[8] Thus the expanded public charity of the Great Britain Street Lying-in Hospital neatly fitted a number of disparate goals which are cited in the Royal Charter, issued in 1756.

The rationale men midwives were advancing about women's delicacy and feebleness in birth represented only part of the vast project of the Enlightenment period, redefining society and individual units within that society, a project which Foucault has referred to as 'bio-politics'.[9]

4. Frederick Jebb, 'Of an Haemorrhage Occasioned by the Adhesion of the Placenta to the os uteri', *Transactions, Medical and Philosophical Memoirs*, vol. 3 (Dublin, 1772), p. 45.
5. Ibid., p. 70. See also Jo Murphy Lawless, 'Images of "Poor" Women in the Writing of Irish Men Midwives', in *Women in Early Modern Ireland*, eds Margaret MacCurtain and Mary O'Dowd (Edinburgh: Edinburgh University Press, 1991), pp. 291–303.
6. See Robert Erickson, 'The "Books of Generation": Some Observations on the Style of the British Midwife Books 1671–1764' in *Sexuality in Eighteenth Century Britain*, ed. Paul-Gabriel Boucé (Manchester: University of Manchester Press, 1982), pp. 74–94.

7. See William Wilde, 'Illustrious Physicians and Surgeons in Ireland. No. II: Bartholomew Mosse, founder of the Dublin Lying-in Hospital', *Dublin Quarterly Journal of Medical Science* (November 1846), p. 569.
8. Ibid., p. 577. See also Rev. John Lawson, 'A Sermon Intended to have been Preached at the Publick Opening of the chappel of the Lying-in Hospital in Great-Britain-Street' (Dublin: George Faulkner, 1759).
9. See Michel Foucault, *The History of Sexuality, Volume One: An Introduction* (Harmondsworth, Middlesex: Penguin Books, 1981).

Tracts on women and their role as mothers dating from this period reveal the discovery of the importance of maternal behaviour to the state and how important the issue of controlling women and defining their social role was becoming.

Establishing obstetrics as a clinical discipline did not diminish the attacks on male midwives made by men. The most common description of them continued to be that they were ignorant. Ludmilla Jordanova[10] has argued that medical science worked with gendered meanings about men's and women's presumed innate capacities which were deeply contradictory definitions but which none the less tended to be contained in seemingly universal categorizations. For example, she points to a consistently strong association between women, nature, superstition and the countryside in eighteenth- and nineteenth-century medical and scientific writing. Equally, the association between men, science and civilization, thinking, and city could have both good and bad connotations. They were, however, gendered connotations which operated to exclude and constrain women in the intellectual domain. For women midwives, these gendered meanings operated very curiously. Their practices differed little from those of men midwives, yet they were castigated for the damage they did to women in labour, whereas male medical efforts were seen as building a science. On the other hand, their reputation for putting the pains of labour on a man, most usually when he behaved cruelly, or when she cockolded him; or employing charms and spells to cure barrenness or make a man love-sick were written of as important cultural manifestations of the Irish peasantry. Their role in subverting the male order as matchmakers and spellbinders on behalf of women was clearly considerable and respected in the countryside.[11]

The medical men wrote with condescending dismissiveness of midwives' superstitious practices yet there was an unconscious irony in their so doing. Practices employed in Connacht to secure a safe delivery by hanging a ribbon, band or scarf upon a hedge during the night, or sometimes round the woman's body, were less injurious than the mid-nineteenth-century hospital practice of binders pulled tightly around a woman's uterus while she was in labour.[12] Medical science's uneven stumbling progression towards its definitions of the female body in pregnancy and birth more often than not paralleled the midwives's efforts. But the former could legitimate its use of violence, lacerating the vagina and cervix with forceps for example, while the latter were condemned for their use of the medoag.[13]

It remained a highly contradictory process. Midwives were seen as necessary and important in specific contexts. The Royal Charter for the Rotunda in 1756 had cited the need to have trained women midwives for those parts of the country without the benefit of male doctors. The lack of male doctors was still viewed as a significant problem in the late 1830s, when the Poor Law Commission on the dispensary system detailed the many unions across the country where doctors were not attending midwifery cases. They recommended that there should be a system of midwives to do this work in such instances.[14] Truly positive accounts of women midwives are rare. The impetus to constrain midwives within the medical hierarchy gathered pace in the early twentieth century and they finally became an accepted, if completely subordinated, part of the medical team.

Despite the continuing high mortality rates for childbearing women, medicine refused to acknowledge the connection between risk of illness and death through pregnancy and uncontrolled fertility. Indeed, the high birth rates in Ireland were cited as evidence 'that in this matter at least the poorest Irish peasants are

10. Ludmilla Jordanova, *Sexual Visions: Images of Gender in Science and Medicine between the Eighteenth and Twentieth Centuries* (London: Harvester Wheatsheaf, 1989).

11. William Carleton, *Tales and Sketches Illustrating the Character . . . of the Irish Peasantry* (Dublin: James Dotty, 1849; London: Garland, 1980), p. 115; Sean O'Suilleabhain, *Irish Folk Custom and Belief* (Dublin: Three Candles, 1967), pp. 43–4; William Wilde, 'A Short Account of the Superstitions and Popular Practices Relating to Midwifery, and Some of the Diseases of Women and Children in Ireland', *Monthly Journal of Medical Science*, vol. 35 (May 1849), p. 722; Lady Augusta Gregory, *Visions and Beliefs in the West of Ireland* (Gerrards Cross: Colin Smythe, 1976), p. 161.

12. W. Wilde, 'A Short Account', pp. 722–3; Thomas Beatty, 'First Report of the New Lying-in Hospital, Dublin for the Year 1834', *Dublin Journal of Medical Science*, vol. 8, no. 22 (1835), pp. 69–96.

13. *Meadóg*: Irish, meaning 'short knife'.

14. Poor Law Commission, *Report of the Poor Law Commissioners on Medical Charities, Ireland Pursuant to the 46th Section of the Act 1 & 2 Victoria, C. 56. With Appendices and an Index* (Dublin, 1841), Appendix B, No. 12, p. 157.

richer than the people of England' and therefore that the neo-Malthusian demand for a brake on expanding populations could be rejected as nonsense.[15] The fact that women were still dying was often attributed to their not seeking medical help in time and they were criticized for 'that apathetic and somewhat heroic attitude of many poor and other mothers concerning the sicknesses suffered with childbearing'.[16] But the woman was also praised for her role as child-bearer and home-maker. Bethel Solomons urged his fellow medics not to ignore the care of the woman who had had several pregnancies and who was therefore more at risk of illness and death in pregnancy than the first-time mother. He wrote that 'the multipara is probably more important to the State than the primigravida, and demands equal care. She is the more skilled housekeeper and she knows the weaknesses of her husband; she is the mother of one or more children, and it may be taken as an axiom that mothers cannot be replaced.'[17]

But it was also Solomons who wrote that women with heart disease 'should not marry, and if they do, they should not become pregnant or they will surely die'. The conservative ethos of the medical profession unable to confront the image of unregulated female sexuality was many years coming to terms with women's active practices compared with the passive formula of abstention and denial Solomons recommended.[18] Controlling her own fertility through abortion or effective contraceptive control remained a huge issue and there is an arresting series of images of what this meant for many thousands of women down to the 1970s. The interests of medicine in controlling women's bodies is just as strong a theme in the early twentieth century for Irish women as it is in the eighteenth- and nineteenth-century documents.

15. Halliday Sutherland, *Birth Control: A Statement of Christian Doctrine against the Neo-Malthusians* (London: Hardy and Moore, 1922), p. 40. Sutherland practised as an obstetrician in the Rotunda Hospital.
16. John A. Musgrave, 'The Role of the Midwife in the Public Health Service', *Irish Journal of Medical Science* (1932), p. 204.
17. Bethel Solomons, 'The Dangerous Multipara', *Lancet* (7 July 1934), p. 8.
18. Bethel Solomons, 'The Prevention of Maternal Morbidity and Mortality', *Irish Journal of Medical Science* (April 1933), p. 175.

FIELDING OULD

(1710–89)

from:
A TREATISE OF MIDWIFRY IN THREE PARTS (1742)

[Fielding Ould, who published his book on midwifery in Dublin in 1742, gives us a portrait of the intrepid man midwife, battling against ignorance and death to save the poor suffering woman. But he also inadvertently provides us with an account of childbirth as a deeply contested arena of life. There were the woman, her 'friends', the woman midwife, and other men midwifes, all voicing their opinions. Irish women in the eighteenth century gave birth in various postures, according to Ould: 'on their Back, Side, Knees, standing, and sitting on a perforated Stool'. Ould preferred to have women lie on their side for the actual moment of birth, not least because 'as the Operator and Standers by, are by this Means behind her Back, she is less subject to be disturbed by their Remarks and Whispers'. We get the sense of a well-populated room during childbirth, one in which the principal dramatis personae are the woman and those who know her well. But it also conveys a reshaping of the birth drama in which the woman is easily unsettled and in which the 'Operator', or man midwife, has the major role to play opposite hers.

Ould indicates the growing competition amongst men midwives in Dublin in the 1730s with a story that criticizes his competitors while promoting his own skills. This case history is a typically dramatic scene of a woman in danger of bleeding to death because the placenta, which has lain across the mouth of her womb, preventing the birth of her baby, has been manipulated, precipitating a haemorrhage. Note that the woman, while in the course of this crisis, intervenes and rejects forcibly the use of forceps, the 'clashing' of which alerts her to the man midwife's intentions.]

Here I hope the Reader will not take amiss, the Relation of a Case which shews the Necessity of this Practice, even when the Patient is come to her full Time: I was sent for to the Wife of one TILBURY, a Constable, living in the Earl of *Meath's Liberty*, who had been for two Days in Labour, and was then ready to expire by a violent Flooding, which I was convinced of by seeing her; by inquiring what had been done for her Relief, I was told by her Friends, that finding her very weak, and not likely to be delivered, after two Days Labour, they thought it necessary to send that Morning (it being now about Noon) for the Assistance of a Man-Midwife, who, according to their Phrase, had worked at her near an Hour, upon which ensued the above-mentioned Flooding; at length, the miserable Patient, after the Operation of his Hands had ceased, heard the clashing of Irons against each other, which terrified her prodigiously; and asking him what he was then going to do, he told her, that without having Recourse to the Help of Instruments, her Life was inevitably lost; which she absolutely declared she would not submit to, but chose rather to die, whereupon this worthy Operator in a violent Passion went away, and swore she would not live five Minutes; whereupon her distressed Friends, unwilling to believe him, sent for me; I found this unhappy Woman in the most imminent Danger, being seized with Faintings, Hiccup, having her Face pale and Hippocratic; upon Examination, I found the Placenta presented to the Orifice of the Womb, which I immediately extracted, and though the Head was far advanced in the Passage, yet I put it back into the Womb, and taking hold of the Feet, brought a living, though very weak Child into the World; the Mother also recovered, though with much difficulty, and is now living, and ready to testify to the Truth of what is here related.

From considering the Circumstances of the above History, it is evident, in the first Place, that there was no extraordinary Obstacle to the Delivery of this poor Woman; but that this Monster of a Man thought it necessary, I suppose, for his own Credit, that he should deliver her instantly, by main Force; imagining, be the Event what it would, that the ignorant Spectators would judge of his Merit, according to the excess of his Labour, which is too often the Case, though here Providence ordered it otherwise; it is also certain, that by his Ignorance, and the violent Action of his Hands in the Womb, he separated the Placenta, which occasioned the Flooding; here in all likelihood, he thought he had effectually destroyed her, and that there was nothing left to save her, but his pretended Application of Instruments, whereby he might Appeal to the deluded Spectators, that notwithstanding the Help of Instruments she wasn't to be saved. Every thinking Person will immediately be convinced that there was no necessity for, nor possibility of the Appliance of Instruments for the Extraction of the Placenta, it being a soft pliant body, easily taken hold of by the Hand, the same may be said in respect of the Child, from the Method whereby it was brought forth.

Here I cannot avoid expressing my Concern that in so great and flourishing a City as this of *Dublin*, there is no Method of hindering such Impostors, from committing these outrageous Villainies on the Public, who in this respect are so liable to be deceived. It is true, the better Sort of People are cautious whom they imploy; but the poorer, who are by much the greater Number, and most subject to Misfortunes in Child-bearing, are glad to get the Assistance of any kind of Man in their Extremity, without farther Inquiry. I am the more imboldened, to enter into this Digression, as I am convinced, that the Person concerned in the above History, is no more intitled by his Education, to Practice Midwifry, or any other Branch of Surgery, than a Carpenter or Shoemaker; this I am obliged to declare, to free Gentlemen of Merit from Censure.

THOMAS SOUTHWELL

(*fl.* 1742)

from:
REMARKS ON SOME ERRORS BOTH IN ANATOMY AND PRACTICE IN A LATE TREATISE OF MIDWIFERY BY FIELDING OULD (1742)

[In his critique of Ould's work, Southwell, a man midwife practising near Kildare, has no praise for women midwives: 'As to the female professors of the art, for whose use this Treatise was chiefly designed, they are generally speaking, incapable of forming any judgment of the truth or falsehood of the Doctrine laid down or the practice recommended to them in that treatise' (p. 2). However, he disagreed strenuously with Ould's position on the Caesarean. Ould had written that the operation was an 'unparalleled Piece of Barbarity' attributable to the 'Principle among Roman-Catholics, that the Soul of every Child that is not baptised, is annihilated'.[1] Thus the Caesarean would be performed, he argued, in hopeless cases of obstructed labour to baptize the infant at the expense of the mother's life. In favouring the potential of the Caesarean to save mothers' lives, Southwell was led to quote the first known case of a successful Caesarean in the British Isles, where the mother lived. The practitioner happened to be a woman midwife.]

One Alice O Neal aged about 33 years, wife to a poor farmer near Charlemont,[2] and mother of several children, in Jan 1738–9 took labour but could not be delivered tho' several women attempted it. She remained in this condition twelve days, till Mary Donally, an illiterate woman performed the Caesarean operation with a razzor: at the aperture she took out the infant and the secondaries, and held the lips of the wound together, till one went a mile for silk and common needles, with which she stitched the wound, and dressed it with white of eggs; the cure was completed with salves[3] of the midwife's own compounding; in about 27 days, the Patient walked a mile on foot and came to me, she frequently walks to the Market of this town, which is six miles distant from her house.

1. F. Ould, *A Treatise on Midwifry*, p. 198.

2. An estate on the outskirts of Dublin.
3. Healing ointments.

ANONYMOUS

from:
A COPY OF HIS MAJESTY'S ROYAL CHARTER FOR INCORPORATING THE GOVERNORS AND GUARDIANS OF THE HOSPITAL FOR THE RELIEF OF POOR LYING-IN-WOMEN, IN DUBLIN (1756)

[The Royal Charter, granted by George II to what became known as the Rotunda Hospital in Dublin, drew together arguments about preserving infant life, preventing infanticide, and providing a basis for the training of Irish men midwives there. The charter is dated 2 December 1756, and the extract has been taken from a copy held in the British Library.]

That such Hospital, when established will be a means not only of preserving the lives and relieving the Miseries of numberless Lying-in Women, but also of preventing that most unnatural (though too frequent) Practice of abandoning, or perhaps murdering, new born Infants. And that it may prevent such Gentlemen as intend to practise Midwifery in our said Kingdom, from going Abroad for Instruction.

That by admitting and instructing in such Hospital, Women, who, after some time spent there, being duly Qualified, may settle in such Parts of our said Kingdom, as most stand in need of such Persons, it will be a Means of preventing the unhappy Effects owing to the Ignorance of the generality of Country Midwives. That by preserving the Lives of so many Infants, who, in all probability must otherwise Perish, it will increase the number of our Subjects, in our said Kingdom.

from:

A WORD TO MOTHERS, FROM A BLUNT CITIZEN, WHICH MAY PRESERVE THE LIVES OF MANY THOUSAND CHILDREN EVERY YEAR (1762)

[The emphasis on the importance of the preservation of infant life and the need to police women as mothers to reduce untoward occurrences, like abandonment, was the impulse behind two articles that appeared in *Faulkner's Dublin Journal*, 31 July–3 August 1762. The title of this article points to this bio-political agenda.[1] The anonymous author attacks women for abandoning their children to wet nurses while pursuing 'pleasure' and paints a terrifying picture of the fate of swaddled infants.]

These tender Mothers having thus got rid of the amiable but laborious Offices of maternal Affection, run without Moderation or Restraint, in the wild Career of Amusement and Pleasure. But while they are thus gaily killing the Hours, do they know the Treatment which their poor, captive, swaddled Infant is receiving in the Village from his hireling Nurse? Do they know that when the least Hurry of Business overtakes this fictitious Mother, she suspends the helpless Child on a Peg, as one would do a Bundle of Cloaths, and lets it remain in this State of Crucifixion while she is following her own private Business, with as little Concern as if she had nothing else to mind. The Children that have been found in this Situation, had their Faces covered with a bluish Colour resembling that of a Violet; and no Wonder indeed! Since the violent compression of the Breast stopping the Circulation of the blood, it was forced to return back to the Head, and fix itself there; while the poor Infant was supposed to be in a State of Security and Ease, because suffocated in this cruel manner, it had not the Strength to put forth its Lamentations, nor to express its Anguish.

1. See Elizabeth Badinter, *Mother Love: Myth and Reality* (London: Macmillan 1981) for a discussion of how and why women in the eighteenth century used wet-nurses, and the strident male opposition to what was perceived as 'maternal indifference'. Maria Edgeworth treats this issue in her novel *Belinda* (1801).

JOSEPH CLARKE

(1758–1834)

from:

ABSTRACT OF A REGISTRY KEPT FOR SOME YEARS IN THE LYING-IN HOSPITAL IN DUBLIN (1817)

[In this passage, Clarke is discussing a 'cross presentation', that is, when the baby lies across the uterus. His attack on women midwives for their work in general and specifically how they deal with this presentation provides insight into the problems women in labour and their care-givers confronted. The article was published in *Transactions of the Association of Fellows and Licentiaries of the King and Queen's College of Physicians* in 1817.]

In cross presentations, our practice in the hospital must appear unsuccessful, but much of this is to be attributed to injudicious attempts to turn, and sometimes to pull away, the foetus by the presenting arm[1] before the admission of the patient. Midwives in this city and its environs, are in general, ignorant, self-sufficient, and prone to drunkenness. I have no doubt they destroy many of those entrusted to their care; nor have we any law, either to prohibit or punish them; I have good reason to think that three of the six patients who died of cross births, fell a sacrifice to their ignorance by lacerations of the vagina.[2] No instance of the spontaneous evolution of the foetus, as described by Denman[3] occurred in the hospital, one excepted, of which I am not altogether certain. One of my assistants in the

hospital was sent for in the middle of the night, by the attending midwife, to turn a child; when he arrived in a few minutes after, he found the breech in the passage. Whether the midwife was correct in her examination and report I cannot pretend to determine. In two instances foetuses nearly full grown and putrid[4] were expelled double, when on the authority of Denman, I expected the breech to come foremost; both however were cases much mismanaged in the commencement. Among the lower orders of women in this city many of such mismanaged cases occur, and I have lately heard of several patients who lost their lives by practitioners of good repute insisting on turning the foetus, although evidently putrid.

1. Turning the baby externally was done to prevent its shoulder being the first part to present at the birth outlet, which held grave risks for the baby.
2. He refers to cutting perineal tissue to make the birth outlet larger.
3. Denman was a British midwife of the period.

4. The foetuses had died in the uterus before birth and were decomposing.

ANONYMOUS

from:
REPORT OF THE POOR LAW COMMISSIONERS ON MEDICAL CHARITIES IN IRELAND (1841)

[Despite consistently adverse accounts about midwives' practices from medical practitioners, they themselves were by no means as available in cases where operative skills were necessary as they might like the situation to be portrayed. Amongst the many problems with the way local dispensary systems were organized, their absence in difficult childbirth cases was deemed to put women in danger, as this extract, one of many similar reports, indicates.]

The surgeon of the Balintra[1] dispensary is not expected to attend dangerous Midwifery cases which is the more to be regretted as it is said that no other Medical Man in the District is qualified to do so and the more surprising as on the occasion of an impending election for a Medical officer, the subscribers passed a resolution that no one would be elected unless he possessed a Midwifery Certificate. It is however certain that under the circumstances provision ought to be made for attendance on such cases for nothing can be more horrifying than the death of a poor woman in child-birth whose friends provide the assistance of a midwife but who are unable to provide for Medical aid when the danger is such as to require it.

1. County Donegal.

JOSEPH CLARKE

(1758–1834)

from:
COLLECTED ESSAYS ON PUERPERAL FEVER (1849)

[In this extract, Clarke describes the third major epidemic of puerperal fever in the Rotunda since its inception. With the help of detailed clinical notes, he is attempting to isolate and scientifically analyse the condition and all possible factors contributing to its spread, including the state of the wards. He himself was probably contributing to the epidemic, carrying infection from the dissecting rooms in Trinity College Dublin, where he lectured in anatomy. The *Essays* were edited originally by Fleetwood Churchill.]

20. During spring, 1787, the temperature of the air was in general very cold, with sharp winds from the east and north-east. Inflammatory diseases were more prevalent among our patients than usual; particularly acute rheumatism. Some were affected with severe pains in the thorax, and difficult respiration. In consequence of these complaints, we were obliged to have recourse to venesection more frequently, during February and March of this year, than during the preceding twelve months.[1]

21. It was a general observation, that our patients recovered slowly; or, to use the language of the nurses, it was much more difficult to get them out of bed than usual. This was peculiarly distressing, as the admission of poor women was now very numerous, probably on account of the severity of the weather. Contrary to our established custom, we were sometimes obliged to put two in a bed, rather than refuse admittance to those who solicited at our gates.[2]

22. As a considerable time had elapsed since our wards had been painted and whitewashed, I thought it probable that these circumstances might contribute to the slow recovery of our patients. Application was therefore made, in the month of February, to a board of the governors of the hospital, for an order to have the wards repaired. It was apprehended that the expense might be considerable; and the funds of the charity being then low, the secretary was desired to give notice, that he would receive proposals for doing the business by contract.

23. While we were thus waiting in expectation of repairs, the puerperal fever began to make its first appearance, and in a very treacherous manner. The first woman was attacked on the 18th of March, and the second not until the 31st; the third on the 3rd of April; the fourth, on the 7th; the fifth, on the 10th; the sixth on the 11th; on the 14th two; on the 15th, two more; and one on the 17th. It was not, then till the middle of April that its progress began to be rapid, and its nature as an epidemic clearly ascertained.

24. The symptoms of this fever corresponded so nearly with what Dr. Hulme has well described, that a very few remarks will suffice on this subject. It always began with a distinct chilliness or shivering. The pain in the cavity of the abdomen was not more frequent in on part than another, nor was the tenderness so great as to be much affected by such trifling causes as the pressure of the bedclothes. Little or no vomiting appeared in any stage of the disease, no delirium, no unequivocal marks of putrescency in any part of the system. The pulse, in general, beat from 120 to 140 strokes in a minute. The lochial discharge and secretion of milk were not subject to any general law. Sometimes they continued regular for a short time, and sometimes were suppressed from the beginning. They have never appeared to me more deranged in this, than in other disorders where the circulation of the blood is equally disturbed.

25. The appearance, on dissection, of the bodies of six patients who died of this fever, were not materially different from what have been described by writers who have seen the disease in

---

1. This was the practice of blood-letting using leeches or by cutting a surface vein to remove 'bad blood' from the body.
2. Clarke disapproved of this practice, suspecting it led to the spread of diseases. In the instance of puerperal fever, it would have done so.

hospitals. In all our subjects, the omentum appeared inflamed, and wasted in substance, but in no instance mortified. I am inclined to think, from numerous observations, that those writers who have described mortification of the omentum, and some other parts of the abdominal viscera, allowed the dead bodies to remain too long after death before they inspected them. In all our dissections, the peritoneum appeared everywhere unusually vascular and inflamed. Next to the omentum, the broad ligaments of the uterus, the caecum, and sigmoid flexure of the colon seemed to suffer most by inflammation. We always met with more or less a turbid yellow, and sometimes fetid fluid floating among the intestines; coagulated purulent-like masses, adhesive inflammation, glueing the intestines to each other, &c. In no instance did the appearances of inflammation seem to penetrate deeper than the peritoneal coat, on any of the viscera of the abdomen or pelvis . . .

27. Most of our patients attacked in the year 1787 were admitted in a weakly state, or had tedious and fatiguing labours. Four of those who died, were cases of first children. Two appeared to be ill during labour, and continued so, without intermission, after delivery. One of them died in thirty-six hours, and the other lived till the sixth day. Three were attacked on the second day after

delivery, and died on the seventh, or of five days' illness. One was attacked on the fourth, and died on the tenth. One was very distinctly attacked on the ninth day, as she was sitting by a good fire, and died on the twelfth. Notwithstanding the short duration of this patient's disease, from five to six pounds of a yellow fetid fluid were found floating in the cavity of the abdomen, and a great deal of adhesive inflammation.

28. The attic story of our hospital, on which all our patients are delivered, is separated into four great divisions, each consisting of a great ward, and two small ones. The former contain seven, and the latter two beds each. To each division a maid-servant and nurse-tender are allotted. I mention these circumstances, in order to render a remarkable fact intelligible, viz. one of these divisions did not lose a single patient by the puerperal fever, whereas the mortality among the other three was nearly equal, though, upon the whole, there was a greater number of women sick in two of these divisions, which have a southern aspect.

29. Such partial distribution of disease, joined to circumstances already mentioned (21, 22) rendered it probable that this fever derived its origin from local contagion, and not from anything noxious in the atmosphere.

WILLIAM WILDE

(1815–76)

from:
A SHORT ACCOUNT OF THE SUPERSTITIONS AND POPULAR PRACTICES RELATING TO MIDWIFERY, AND SOME OF THE DISEASES OF WOMEN AND CHILDREN IN IRELAND (1849)

[Wilde, writing about women midwives at the end of the Famine period, was doing so because 'the present

condition of this country, the total disorganization of society, extending from the poorest to the highest, the ravages lately made by famine and pestilence, and the enormous emigration which has been and is still going forward' were obliterating the old customs. On difficult labours, Wilde records the following midwifery practices. The article from which these extracts are taken was published in the *Monthly Journal of Medical Science*, vol. 35 (May 1849), p. 712.]

It is boasted that the Irish midwives were acquainted with the efficacy of spurred rye, or smitted corn, long before the ergot was made use of by regular practitioners.[1] But in cases of want of uterine action, several other substances were employed, some of rather a disgusting nature. Among the rest the husband's urine was regarded as highly efficacious. To promote labour the country midwives sometimes placed the parturient woman with her hips directly opposite a roasting fire, as is the common practice in several parts of India. In some localities it was not in former times uncommon, when the labour was very tedious, to get two or three stout men to shake the unhappy patient backwards and forwards in her bed with great violence; and for some reason, which I am unable to account for, a ploughman was more frequently chosen for such purposes than any other person; but, to prove efficacious, he should be taken direct from the plough. Owing, however, to the number of country midwives that have of late years been educated at our different lying-in hospitals, practices such as those related are seldom had recourse to now.

[Wilde also critically describes other labour practices to indicate how ignorant women midwives were.]

The rude interference of some of the country midwives, particularly in the province of Connaught, caused frightful consequences in former times. I have heard my father, who was in extensive practice in that part of the country, say that he had known midwives constantly attempt forcible extraction of the foetus, with the hook of an ouncel or steel bar; and I am informed by practitioners residing in the county of Galway still, that some years ago, when any difficulty or delay occurred in the child's head passing through the external parts, the midwives used to cut or lacerate the perinaeum with a sort of curved knife called a 'medoag', formed out of the point of an old reaping-hook.

[The problem of a retained placenta, after the baby's birth, with the consequent threats of infection and haemorrhage, produced in the texts of male midwives, techniques such as pushing a finger down the woman's throat, pulling on the 'navel string', removing the placenta manually, and squeezing the uterus, driving it downwards towards the small of the pelvis. These legitimated institutional medical practices are little different to those Wilde is decrying.]

MANAGEMENT OF THE PLACENTA. — In cases of retention of the after-birth, it is even still a practice to force a piece of mould candle down the patient's throat. It is possible that, by inducing vomiting, it may prove efficacious in causing the uterus to expel its contents. But in almost all instances among the lower orders in the remote districts, where the placenta has been retained for an unusual length of time, the cord is either tied to the patient's thigh, or held fast by one of the attendants. I remember having been sent to a case of this description in a distant part of the country; I found the midwife on her knees at the bed side with a firm grip of the funis in her hand, which she exultingly displayed to me, observing, 'Doctor I never let it out these five hours.' It is a popular belief that if the funis was let go, it might slip back into the uterus and be for ever lost sight of. I have known more than one instance in which eversion of the uterus was produced by the midwife forcibly dragging the funis.

[The following document discusses fertility and risk. The feminist argument that unregulated fertility and unwanted pregnancies threaten women's lives and well-being is a very recent discourse, which none the less reflects the accumulated experience and struggles of women over many centuries, to control their reproduction. Abortion is one aspect of this struggle, infanticide another.[2] Wilde recorded some mid-nineteenth-century Irish practices on abortion. Note his designation of the midwife as a 'she-quack'.]

Abortion. — Next in order we should consider procured abortion, instances of which frequently come under the cognizance of the medical man and the magistrate. Here as in the former case,[3] the she-quack is generally referred to, and besides the inculcation of certain mystic ceremonies and Pagan rites, of which the foregoing may be taken as the type, she administers the most drastic purgatives and emmenagogues, of which aloes

---

1. This was not an idle boast. Women midwives throughout early modern Europe are recorded as using rye affected by the fungus called ergot and infected corn to deal with insufficient uterine action. See Edward Shorter, *A History of Women's Bodies* (London: Allen Lane, 1982), p. 38.

2. See Anne O'Connor, 'Women in Irish Folklore: The Testimony Regarding Illegitimacy, Abortion and Infanticide', in M. MacCurtain and M. O'Dowd, *Women in Early Modern Ireland*, pp. 307–17.

3. Wilde has just been describing, in the previous section, love charms and philtres and their use as part of mystic rites.

and gomboge are the chief ingredients.[4] Certain herbs and plants, particularly rue and savine, pulled in a particular manner, which I shall describe upon another occasion, are believed by the country people to effect a like end. Whether medicinal substances or herbs are employed, a certain ceremonial is likewise enjoined. Can we wonder at the ignorant Irish girl wishing to conceal her shame by the destruction of her offspring, in a country acknowledged to be one of the most moral in Europe, and where caste is more certainly lost by circumstance of pregnancy before or without marriage, when, in other lands boasted to be the most civilized, induced abortion, even among married females, in the upper ranks of life, is spoken of in society without reserve.

4. Bitter juice or gum resin is obtained from trees of the genus *Garcinia*.

EDWARD SINCLAIR AND GEORGE JOHNSTON

(1824–82) (1814–89)

from:
PRACTICAL MIDWIFERY: COMPRISING AN ACCOUNT OF 13,748 DELIVERIES WHICH OCCURRED IN THE DUBLIN LYING-IN HOSPITAL, DURING A PERIOD OF SEVEN YEARS, COMMENCING NOVEMBER, 1847 (1858)

[This is the most detailed account of the routine established for women in labour by the mid-nineteenth century in the Rotunda Hospital in Dublin. Note the authors' irritation with women for not staying in hospital the full length of the designated lying-in period. *Practical Midwifery* was published in London in 1858 by John Churchill.]

Admission was obtained by means of tickets . . . this form was almost always gone through some considerable time before full term, and the ticket was generally kept about the person so that at any moment the woman could avail herself of it.

As soon as possible after the entrance of a patient into the labour ward, her condition was inquired into by one of the Assistants . . . When she was found to be in the second stage of labour, she was undressed, and placed upon a small, low narrow bed having curtains open at the top and situated at one side of the fire-place called 'the couch' upon which, when practicable, all patients were delivered. She was then permitted to remain, for an hour after her delivery, on this couch, and at the expiration of that time, should there have been no contra-indication, such as a tendency to hemorrhage, etc etc, she was carried horizontally to her bed, which was fresh and dry for her reception. The child which had in the meantime been washed and dressed was placed beside her provided it was quiet and unlikely to disturb her.

For the first three days, the patient was kept upon spoon diet, viz., whey and gruel *ad libitum*, and about eleven ounces of bread each day. Upon the fourth day (if fit for the change) she was placed upon broth diet. Extras, of any kind whatever, at the discretion of the medical officers, were permitted; and it was found that a considerable number of those under treatment required them, not only on account of delicacy, but also because of the meagre dietary of the hospital. Primiparous women were not permitted to rise till the fifth day; otherwise, they were allowed to be dressed, and to lie outside their bed, on the fourth; and on the eighth day they were discharged, if well enough, and if, as before mentioned, they desired it. They were generally removed to their homes in a covered vehicle. It may be here stated that, as a general rule, it was with the greatest difficulty patients could be prevailed upon to remain in hospital even so long as the eighth day, and numbers, to our knowledge, have insisted upon being discharged before the ordinary time. The general desire of these women to leave the hospital as soon as possible we could only attribute to their intense dislike to discipline and control; however, it must also be mentioned, that this impatience had in many cases been induced from the fact of their husbands and children being deprived of their assistance, and their houses of their supervision, during their sojourn with us.

GEORGE JOHNSTON

(1814–89)

from: CLINICAL REPORT OF THE ROTUNDA LYING-IN HOSPITAL FOR THE YEAR 1872 (1873)

[Johnston is defending the Rotunda from charges of endangering women by exposing large numbers to the risk of puerperal fever by pointing to the weakened physical and emotional condition women are in when they present themselves for admission The article was published in the *Dublin Quarterly Journal of Medical Science* (1873).]

The victim of seduction, the houseless stranger, the famished wretch all seeking admission may enter at any hour, night or day, without either note or ticket of recommendation, their only requirements being that they stand in need of our assistance, a circumstance which, so far as I am aware, is peculiar to this institution. The modest girl, who, having been led astray, and acutely sensitive of her fallen state, flying from the observation of her family and friends, in order to avoid the scandal and opprobrium that she would be exposed to were she to remain in her own home or neighbourhood, seeks the shelter of the Rotunda, where unknown, among the multitude, she hopes to elude observation.

Women deserted by their husbands, or who have been left destitute by their partners having fallen victims to the many diseases always so prevalent in large cities, but particularly within the past year, leaving the widow in a state of mind often bordering on distraction, themselves and families being in a state of penury, not knowing where to look for succour.

[Women's emotional instability was presumed to reach a peak during pregnancy, labour and the immediate period after birth and was used to account for the appearance of 'mania', which in reality was the result of fever, stemming from a violent uterine infection carried into her bloodstream. But the label of 'mania' as distinct from the diagnosis of puerperal fever had tragic consequences, as the next excerpt and those concerning Ellen Owens show.]

E.R., aged 24, 1st pregnancy; had to be delivered with forceps in consequence of the narrowing of the pubic arch, went on well till the 4th day, when she was attacked with violent mania (having been disappointed at her mother not coming to see her); had to keep her under chloroform almost continuously for 6 hours before she could be calmed; had a rigor at midnight, under treatment pulse fell from 140 to 92, weak. On the 2nd day the suffusion of her eyes became more intense; great sickness of stomach; gradually became comatose and died of apoplexy.

C.D., aged 33, 1st pregnancy; seduced; labour difficult owing to early rupture of the membranes and disproportion, had to be delivered with the forceps; no P.P.H. 30; she was very silent from the commencement; found great difficulty in getting her to answer questions; became quite maniacal on the 4th day, sent her to the Asylum on the 14th.

CHIEF SECRETARY'S OFFICE

from:
REGISTERED PAPERS (1891)

[This document deals with the fate of Ellen Owens, committed as a lunatic in 1891. The papers begin on 24 August 1891, when a warrant was sworn for the woman's arrest and appearance before the court and medical officers. The complainant was listed as her husband, James Owens. The original papers can be found in Registered Papers, 1891/23052, National Archives, Dublin.]

The Defendant, Ellen Owens is astray in her mind, and has been so for the last three weeks. That on the 23 and 24 days of August 1891 at Ballysnod in the county of Antrim she threatened to kill herself and James Owens, and on said days attempted to assault James Owens but was prevented from doing so, and the said James Owens is of opinion that if she be not confined she will do serious bodily injury to herself and others.

[Two magistrates who heard the case and the report of the Medical Officer, Dr. J.M. Killen, signed the Committal Warrant of a Dangerous Lunatic. The information on the medical certificate accompanying this warrant tells us that Ellen Owens was thirty-nine years old, a Presbyterian married to James Owens, himself a labourer, with no independent means of her own. She had children. No near relative had been known to suffer from insanity and her 'Habits of life' prior to the onset of puerperal fever had been 'Temperate'. She could read and write. She had been 'violent' for three weeks and the 'Probable Cause of Derangement' was 'Puerperal', the principal symptoms being 'violence and threats'. She was afflicted with the 'Bodily Disease of Phlegmasia dolens'.[1] The 'Facts indicating that the Patient is a Dangerous Lunatic' are these: 'she tried to kill herself by beating her head against wall, threatened to kill her husband'. The next document is a report from the Coroner's Court, 25 August 1891, which states that 'the said Ellen Owens on Monday the 24th day of August 1891 died at Greencastle Parish of Shankill and county of Antrim from Exhaustion the result of Puerperal Fever and Phlegmasia dolens'. This is accompanied by a report from Constable W. Reeves on the 'Sudden death of Ellen Owens a lunatic prisoner'.]

I have to report that as Ellen Owens a lunatic prisoner was being conveyed on 24th inst: in a covered car by Police Escort from Larne to the Belfast lunatic Asylum — Act:Supt. T.H. Weathered 40999 in charge — she became very ill when passing through Whitewell and on arriving at Kane's public house on the Antrim road in the Sub Dist. of Greencastle she died as the Police were carrying her into the house. When passing through Whitewell, the Acting Sergeant stopped at the Police Barrack and tried to get a doctor, but there was not one to be had and he then thought that the best course was to drive on to Belfast and obtain the nearest doctor there, but the woman got rapidly worse and the escort had to stop when they arrived at Kane's public house.

An inquest was held there yesterday at which I attended and the jury returned the annexed verdict. I enquired closely into all circumstances of the case and am quite satisfied that no blame whatever can be attributed to the escort. The prisoner was very violent at times during the journey and I believe the Acting Sergeant and Const. R Fitzgerald 41231 who was with him did all they possibly could for the unfortunate woman. She was the wife of a respectable farmer residing at Ballysnod near Larne.

[The next document, a typewritten one, is dated 5 September 1891, after an inquiry was launched into Ellen's death with queries about the circumstances surrounding her committal and whether she had shown signs of insanity prior to her contracting puerperal fever.]

In reply to reference No 22302 of the 3rd Instant, it appears that the woman at the time of her committal as a Dangerous Lunatic was suffering from 'childbed fever', complicated with a disease known as 'milk-leg', which is a clotting of blood in the vessels of the leg. The removal of a patient in this condition, and a fortiori, a long journey in a jolting vehicle, would be necessarily dangerous, as any sudden or rough movement is liable to loosen and carry to the heart a portion of the blood clot, and thus lead to quick or sudden death. It is not improbable that this is what happened in this particular case.

---

1. Referring to the absence of any post-partum haemorrhage.

The points which suggest themselves to us for further inquiry are:—

(1) Date of patient's confinement
(2) Did Medical Officer certify her as fit for removal?
(3) Why was she moved by car, not by train, from Larne to Belfast (a distance of about 25 miles)?
(4) Did a woman form part of the escort in accordance with Police Regulations?

[These questions produced the replies that Ellen had given birth on the 21 July 1891 and that the medical officer had certified it as necessary to secure her 'speedy admission into Belfast Lunatic Asylum'. The replies to the third and fourth queries produced the following information.]

(3) She was removed by car by order of the committing magistrates. The car which was a covered one, went by Ballymore, the distance by that route to Belfast being 18 miles. It was alleged that owing to the Violent Conduct of the prisoner, a covered car by road would be much more suitable than sending her by train in which a great commotion would probably be caused.

(4) No, a woman did not form part of the Escort. Mrs. Owens' husband told the Magistrates he would go with her but at the last moment as the car was starting he refused to accompany her. The conduct of Mrs Owens when being first brought to the Barrack here was very violent and it was as much as two Police could do to restrain her. She was very violent again while on her way to Belfast and I believe that a female attendant would only have been in the way and practically of no use.

I have seen Dr Killen the Medical Officer and he informs me that after he had examined Mrs Owens he saw no other course but to give the certificate as annexed. She could not be kept in her own house without great danger to herself her husband and her children and there was no other place but the lunatic Asylum to which she could be sent.

[The final document, signed by Deputy Inspector W. Reeves, was issued on 26 September 1891.]

We consider that in this case a Medical Certificate of the patient's fitness to undertake the journey to Belfast should have been obtained previous to her removal. The Medical Officer it is true signed the form that the patient was 'a fit subject for speedy admission in to the Belfast Asylum' but that statement does not necessarily imply that she was fit to undertake a road journey of eighteen miles, and the event shows that she was not so.

A violent patient could, we think, be more safely controlled in a railway carriage than in a jolting covered car and it therefore seems to us a matter of regret that the Magistrates should have ordered her removal by road instead of train.

In all such cases, the regulations requiring a patient to be accompanied by a female escort should be observed in our opinion.

LADY GREGORY

(1852–1932)

from:
VISIONS AND BELIEFS IN THE WEST OF IRELAND COLLECTED AND ARRANGED BY LADY GREGORY: WITH TWO ESSAYS AND NOTES BY W.B. YEATS (1920)

[Lady Gregory included several stories about midwives in her folklore collection from the West of Ireland, published in 1920, which showed that the custom of couvade was a strong tradition. 'Couvade' usually means treating the man as if he were carrying the pains of labour rather than the woman, often even putting him to bed. However, in these instances pain was imposed by the midwife on a man as a punishment for ill-treatment of his wife. Published in 2 volumes in London in 1920 by G. Putnam.]

Mrs. Halloran: 'Did I know the pain could be put on a man? Sure I seen my own mother that was a midwife do it. He was such a Molly of an old man, and he had no compassion at all on his wife. He was as if making out she had no pain at all. So my mother gave her a drink, and with that he was on the floor and around the floor crying and roaring. "The devil take you," says he, and the pain upon him; but while he had it, it went away from his wife. It did him no harm after, and my mother would not have done it but for him being so covetous. He wanted to make out that she wasn't sick.'

JOHN A. MUSGRAVE

(1892–1948)

from:
THE ROLE OF THE MIDWIFE IN THE PUBLIC HEALTH SERVICE (1932)

[In the wake of independence, the regulations of the 1902 Midwives Act were modified by the Central Midwives Board Order No. 9 of 1923. Despite the fact that doctors with inadequate training and procedures were directly implicated themselves in the continued loss of maternal life, midwives still carried the brunt of criticism by the profession.[1] In this extract, the Medical Officer of Health for County Louth, discoursing on the 1923 regulations, presents an account of midwifery in which medicine is glorified and midwives are put down. Note his emphasis on the need to have a controlled corps of women midwives. The article from which this extract is taken was published in the *Irish Journal of Medical Science* (1932).]

Rule D, which I have purposely placed last, is a series of regulations, which every midwife should, if she be efficient, know in every detail. That any midwife should plead ignorance of any paragraph, clause or direction of this rule seems incomprehensible. That any midwife should be found on inspection to have no copy of this rule is still more incomprehensible.

The final results of ignorance of this rule may be disastrous both to the patient and to the midwife. In order to appreciate the necessity for the strict code laid down in Rule D it is informative to consider the general significance of the history of midwifery.

It has been stated that the practice of midwifery may be divided into historical stages,

1. See H. Jellett, 'The Teaching of Practical Midwifery in the Past and Present Time', *Dublin Journal of Medical Science*, vol. cxxviii (1909), p. 436; B. Solomons, 'The Prevention of Maternal Morbidity and Mortality, *Irish Journal of Medical Science* (April 1933), p. 176.

every one of which is well defined by a marked decrease in maternal mortality.

The first period, starting with the dawn of medical history, finishes in the middle of the eighteenth century, the maternal mortality being generally assessed at 23 per 1,000 births or more.

Then, with the better training of medical men, perhaps, and with an undoubted increase in the number of cases conducted by medical practitioners, and (I have read) owing to an increasing knowledge of forceps, the second stage developed and lasted till the beginning of the nineteenth century, when the maternal mortality was about 9 per 1,000.

The general advance of the scientific study of midwifery marks the third stage, which reduced maternal mortality to somewhere about 5 per 1,000.

The passing of the Midwives Act launched a fourth stage, for then appeared on the scene the subject of this paper, the trained controlled midwife service.

In 1931, the rate for deaths from puerperal conditions in Saorst tEireann was 4 per 1,000 births, and for puerperal sepsis 1.1 per 1,000 births. These figures indicate that there is ample opportunity for good work and continuous effort ahead. Further, these figures, if considered in alignment with the history of midwifery, emphasise the obvious, viz., that the main part in the public health scheme, which the efficient midwife fulfils, is the reduction of maternal and infantile mortality.

BETHEL SOLOMONS

(1885–1965)

from:
THE WORK OF THE MIDWIFE (1932)

from:
REPORT OF THE ROTUNDA HOSPITAL (1933)

[The midwife, once controlled, could be praised for her work, albeit alongside the presumption that she had been responsible for her own bad reputation. Hence the reference to Charles Dickens's scurrilous characterization of a midwife, Mrs Gamp, in this next extract. The irony that it was the medical profession which had the power to legitimate the evidence on sepsis and asepsis and had failed to do so, was usually lost on its members. The article from which this extract is taken was published in the *Irish Journal of Medical Science* (May 1932).]

The midwife fills a want in the nation; she has been maligned and has lived it down. The days of Mrs Gamp are gone, and the clean aseptic midwife with a knowledge of her work continues, and will continue to be a help to mothers and babies and a help in combating the appalling maternal mortality and morbidity which beset the world.

[A woman attempting her own abortion could not be certain of the reaction of the medical establishment to her plight. Solomons, in his discussion of Caesarean sections, included case notes on the death of such a woman and, with characteristic honesty, admitted to 'warped judgment'. The article from which this extract is taken was published in the *Irish Journal of Medical Science* (August 1933).]

The third case was that of a woman of 25 who was admitted with a history of vomiting and of having taken a large quantity of abortifacients. The vomiting cleared up on 3 days. She was admitted 23 days later about 16–20 weeks pregnant looking ill, although the general conditions were fair. The Fouchet test was positive, and the vomiting was continuous. The next day she improved, but the following day she was not so well, and intravenous glucose was given. Soon after icturus[1] appeared the patient got a sudden and complete collapse. Hyperglycaemia was diagnosed, but in spite of insulin and restoratives there was very little improvement.

1. Another term for jaundice.

With the idea of saving her life a minor section was done and she was better. She became suddenly ill six hours later and died despite all treatment. This woman might have been saved by an earlier minor section, but her desire for abortion rather cloaked the gravity of her case and probably warped judgment.

J.K. FEENEY

(1912–?)

from:
THE GRAND MULTIPARA: TRAUMA OF LABOUR (1955)

[As late as 1955, an article on women with many pregnancies could still be written without a single reference to their need to regulate their fertility. The article from which this extract is taken was published in the *Journal of the Irish Medical Association*. It brilliantly details the cumulative strains for women, while declining to make any suggestions about preventing pregnancy.]

1. The grand multipara is likely to suffer from certain social and domestic deficiencies and disadvantages. Anaemia and malnutrition are common as a result of the high cost of essential foodstuffs, faulty diet habits, lack of cooking facilities in tenement rooms, undeveloped sense of thrift, sacrifice of choice pieces to husband and children, unemployment, poverty, defective physical constitution, very hard work within and outside the home, nausea and vomiting, dental caries, rapidly succeeding pregnancies, etc. She may, indeed, be ill-fitted to withstand the stresses and strains of pregnancy, labour, the puerperium and of lactation.

Biographies/Bibliographies

Fielding Ould

LIFE. Fielding Ould was born in County Galway in 1710 and was a graduate of Trinity College Dublin. He later trained at the famous Hôtel-Dieu in Paris, the lying-in hospital for training women midwives;

he is the author of *A Treatise of Midwifry in Three Parts* (1742). He contributed observations on the rotation of the baby's head in the birth canal and on the operation of episiotomy to the annals of male midwifery. Second Master of the Rotunda, 1759–66, he died in 1789.

Thomas Southwell

LIFE. Thomas Southwell was a man-midwife, trained in Paris and based in Kildare. Author of *Remarks on some Errors both in Anatomy and Practice in a late Treatise of Midwifery by Fielding Ould* (1742). No other information.

Joseph Clarke

LIFE. Joseph Clarke was born on 8 April 1758 in the parish of Desertlin, County Louth, the second son of James Clarke, an agriculturalist. Clarke studied in Glascow and Edinburgh. He was elected Master of Physicians at the Dublin Lying-in Hospital in 1786, serving until 1793. In 1786 he married a niece of Dr Cleghorn, founder of the anatomical school at Trinity College. Clarke rigorously attacked the problem of puerperal fever in the hospital and published the first medical report on the hospital. He died in 1834.

CHIEF WRITINGS. 'Observations on the Puerperal Fever', *Edinburgh Medical Commentaries*, vol. 15 (1790), pp. 299 ff; 'Remarks on the Causes and Cures of Some Diseases of Infancy', *Transactions of the Royal Irish Academy*, vol. 6.

BIOGRAPHY AND CRITICISM. Collins, *Sketch of the Life and Writings of Joseph Clarke, M.D., with the Results of His Private Practice*.

William Wilde

LIFE. William Robert Wills Wilde was born in Castlerea, County Roscommon, in 1815. He was first apprenticed to a surgeon at Dr Steeven's Hospital in Dublin in 1832. He then studied midwifery in the Rotunda but later practised as an eye and ear specialist, establishing his own Eye and Ear Hospital. He travelled widely in Europe and the Middle East and wrote copiously on medical, historical and archaeological matters. He married the poet Jane Francesca Elgee (see p. 894) and was the father of Oscar Wilde (see Vol. II, p. 514). He died in Dublin on 19 April 1876.

CHIEF WRITINGS. *Biographical Memoir of Robert J. Graves* (Dublin: McGlashon and Gill, 1864); *An Essay on the Unmanufactured Animal*

Remains in the Royal Irish Academy: Illustrative of the Ancient Animals of Ireland (Dublin: M.H. Gill, 1860); *Irish Popular Superstitions* (Dublin, 1852; rpr. Shannon: Irish University Press, 1972).

Edward Sinclair

LIFE. Born in 1824 and educated at Trinity College Dublin, Edward Sinclair was Assistant Master of the Rotunda Hospital (*c.* 1847–58), and he founded a school of army midwives in Dublin. He died in 1882.

CHIEF WRITINGS. With George Johnston, *Practical Midwifery* (London: John Churchill, 1858).

George Johnston

LIFE. Born on 12 August 1814 in Dublin, son of an eminent surgeon, George Johnston was educated at Trinity College Dublin, became a member of the Royal College of Surgeons in England in 1837, and studied further in Paris and Edinburgh. He was appointed Assistant Physician at the Dublin Lying-in Hospital in 1848. He became the seventeenth Master of the Rotunda, 1868–75, at the beginning of which period there was an intense debate as to whether the hospital should be closed to prevent the spread of puerperal fever. He and his wife Henrietta had six children. Johnston died on 7 March 1889.

CHIEF WRITINGS. With Edward Sinclair, *Practical Midwifery* (London: John Churchill, 1858).

Lady Gregory

LIFE. Lady Gregory was born Isabella Augusta Persse on 15 March 1852, the twelfth daughter of an ascendancy family at Roxborough in County Galway. The family nurse, Mary Sheridan, was a storehouse of folklore and introduced the child to Fenianism. She lived quietly at home for the most part until her marriage at twenty-eight to the elderly Sir William Gregory of Coole, County Galway, a cultivated gentleman and ex-governor of Ceylon. With him she travelled to India, Ceylon, Egypt, Spain and Italy and spent much of her time in London. Their only son, Robert, was born in May 1881. Widowed in February 1892, she turned to writing, at first editing her husband's papers. Influenced by Hyde's *Love Songs of Connacht* (1893), she learned Irish and was soon proficient enough to collect the folklore published in such books as *A Book of Saints and Wonders* and *Visions and Beliefs in the West of Ireland*. She popularized the old Irish mythological cycles in *Cuchulain of Muirthemne* and *Gods and Fighting Men*. These had wide public appeal (4 editions before 1914) and also served as a resource for the dramatists of the Literary Revival. Her house at Coole became a centre for the revival, visited by most of its writers and frequented by W.B. Yeats, with whom she collaborated in writing plays. The extent of her contribution to such plays as *Kathleen ni Houlihan* has only recently received widespread scholarly recognition. She was one of the three co-founders and original directors of the Abbey Theatre in 1904 (the other two being W.B. Yeats and J.M. Synge) and she maintained her interest in Abbey policy and administration until 1930. Lady Gregory was one of the early Abbey's most talented and versatile dramatists. Her comedy *Spreading the News* played on its opening night became a comic classic. Though she scored her most popular success with *The Rising of the Moon*, a nationalist comedy, she revealed a remarkable talent for tragic irony and poignancy in *Dervorgilla* and *The Gaol Gate*. Lady Gregory's plays tend to be noted for their Hiberno-English dialogue (Kiltartanese), but she also excelled in dramatic construction. Much of her energy in her declining years was spent on an unsuccessful attempt to have her nephew Hugh Lane's collection of Impressionist paintings moved from the Tate Gallery to Dublin. She died on 22 May 1932.

CHIEF WRITINGS. *Arabi and His Household* (London: privately pub., 1882); *Over the River* (London: privately pub., 1888; 1893); *A Phantom's Pilgrimage; Or, Home Ruin* (anon.) (London: Ridgeway, 1893); ed. *The Autobiography of Sir William Gregory* (London: John Murray, 1894); ed. *Mr Gregory's Letter Box, 1813–1830* (London: Smith, Elder, 1898); ed. *Ideals in Ireland* (London: Unicorn, 1901); *Cuchulain of Muirthemne* (London: John Murray, 1902); *Gods and Fighting Men* (London: John Murray, 1904); *A Book of Saints and Wonders* (Dundrum: Dun Emer Press, 1906); *The Kiltartan History Book* (Dublin: Maunsel, 1909); *Seven Short Plays* (Dublin: Maunsel, 1909); *The Kiltartan Molière* (Dublin: Maunsel, 1910); *The Kiltartan Wonder Book* (Dublin: Maunsel, 1910); *Irish Folk History Plays*, 1st series (London: Putnam, 1912); *Irish Folk History Plays*, 2nd series (London: Putnam, 1912); *New Comedies* (New York and London: Putnam, 1913); *Our Irish Theatre* (London: Putnam, 1913); *The Golden Apple* (London: John Murray, 1916); *The Kiltartan Poetry Book*, Translations from the Irish (London: Putnam, 1919); *Visions and Beliefs in the West of Ireland* (London: Putnam, 1920); *Hugh Lane's Life and Achievement* (London: John Murray, 1921); *The Image and Other Plays* (London: Putnam, 1922); *Three Wonder Plays* (London: Putnam, 1923); 'The Old Woman Remembers', *Irish Statesman* (22 March 1924); *The Story Brought by Brigit* (London: Putnam, 1924); *A Case for the Return of Sir Hugh Lane's Pictures to Dublin* (Dublin: Talbot, 1926); *On the Racecourse* (London: Putnam, 1926); *Three Last Plays* (London: Putnam, 1928); *My First Play, Colman and Guaire* (London: Elkin Mathews and Marot, 1930); *Coole* (Dublin: Cuala, 1931); Lennox Robinson (ed.), *Lady Gregory's Journals, 1916–1930* (London: Putnam, 1946); T.R. Henn and Colin Smythe (eds), *Seventy Years: 1852–1922: Being the Autobiography of Lady Gregory* (Oxford: Oxford University Press, 1974); Daniel Murphy (ed.), *Lady Gregory's Journals*: vol. 1, Books 1–29, 10 October 1916–24 February 1925 (Gerrards Cross: Colin Smythe, 1978); vol. 2, Books 30–44: 24 February 1925–9 May 1932 (Gerrards Cross: Colin Smythe, 1987; Lucy McDiarmid and Maureen Waters (eds), *Selected Writings* (Harmondsworth: Penguin, 1995).

BIOGRAPHY AND CRITICISM. Elizabeth Coxhead, *Lady Gregory: A Literary Portrait* (London: Secker and Warburg, 1966); Anne Gregory, *Me and Nu: Childhood at Coole* (Gerrards Cross: Colin Smythe, 1966); Ann Saddlemyer, *In Defence of Lady Gregory, Playwright* (Dublin: Dolmen, 1966); Hazard Adams, *Lady Gregory* (Lewisburg: Bucknell University Press, 1973); E.H. Mikhail, *Lady Gregory: Interviews and Recollections* (London: Macmillan, 1977); Mary Lou Kohfeldt, *Lady Gregory: The Woman Behind the Irish Renaissance* (London: André Deutsch, 1985); Ann Saddlemyer and Colin Smythe (eds), *Lady Gregory, Fifty Years After* (Gerrards Cross: Colin Smythe, 1987).

See also Volume II, p. 560.

John A. Musgrave

LIFE. John Aloysious Musgrave was born in 1892. He gained his licentiate from the College of Physicians in 1915, and was Medical Officer of Health for County Louth. He died in 1948.

Bethel Solomons

LIFE. Bethel Solomons was born in 1885. He was a graduate of Trinity College Dublin and also studied in Paris, Vienna, Berlin, Leipzig, Dresden and Munich. He was Master of the Rotunda Hospital, Dublin, 1926–33. A distinguished gynaecologist, he contributed extensively to medical journals on obstetrics and gynaecology. He died in 1965.

John K. Feeney

LIFE. John K. Feeney was born in 1912. He was Master of the Coombe Lying-in Hospital, 1949–56, and has written extensively on trauma in labour and problems of high parity.

DYMPNA McLOUGHLIN, *Editor*

Infanticide in
Nineteenth-Century Ireland

It is very difficult to quantify the extent of infanticide in nineteenth-century Ireland, as only a small number of culpable mothers were actually sent for trial. Most studies of infanticide to date have concentrated on the cases of women convicted for this crime, without acknowledging that these were a minority. Too close a concentration on judicial records and official proceedings reveals little of the fate of the majority who got through the official net. The Irish judicial statistics reveal that the number of infanticide cases reported to the police was minuscule. In 1865, for example, only forty-one cases were brought before the courts as a result of coroners' inquests. In a return of criminals tried at Armagh district court from 1887 to 1897 not one woman was charged with infanticide, whilst four were charged with attempting to procure an abortion, and three with concealment of birth.[1]

Considering the very low numbers of women convicted of infanticide it is helpful to attempt an international comparison. In 1868, 47 Irish women faced trials on infanticide charges, in real terms a rate of 0.85 per cent per 100,000 of population, this compared with 222 in France (0.58 per cent per 100,000 of population) in 1867 and 15 in Belgium (0.32 per cent per 100,000 of population) in 1860.[2] Despite the various filtering out processes which reduced the numbers of culpable women charged with infanticide, this is a significant figure, and suggests that infanticide was not uncommon in nineteenth-century Ireland. Only a small number

of infanticide cases ever came before the courts and there was a high rate of acquittal. Generally there was some degree of public sympathy for pregnant women, most especially those who had become pregnant as a result of coercion or rape. There was also an understanding of the absolute nature of contemporary poverty and the hard choices a woman might have to make, including the destruction of a new-born, in times of sickness, destitution or famine. There was such a problem with deserted and orphan children that ratepayers, who made up the juries, had a vested interest in the quick demise of unwanted infants.[3] Foundlings remained social outcasts. Considering the high levels of sickness and high child mortality, there was little official interest in following up every case of suspicious infant death. Patriarchal officialdom only became interested in cases of attempted concealment of births, where a 'brazen' woman was caught or suspected of trying to hide the evidence of her 'sexual sin'. It was commonly perceived that these were 'evil' women who were not willing to face up to the repercussions of their actions and therefore had to be punished in the severest manner.

Social commentators in both Britain and Ireland either ignored or underestimated the frequency of infanticide. The killing of babies and young children was believed to be found only in barbarous countries not yet incorporated into the empire. Yet British and Irish jurists, coroners, medical practitioners and most ordinary individuals were aware of infanticide as

---

1. Irish Judicial Statistics, 1865; Return of Criminals Armagh, 1887–97 (Public Record Office of Northern Ireland).
2. Return dated 9 October 1869, British Library, Gladstone papers, Add. MSS 44798, f. 118.
3. Ratepayers had to pay for the upkeep of the deserted child by either paying a wet-nurse or by placing the child in the workhouse and thus adding to the burden of the poor rate.

a common enough occurrence. There was, however, a huge contemporary difficulty in actually admitting that infanticide existed in their 'civilized' world. The unwillingness to name the practice in Ireland was significant since if it was not named then in reality it did not exist. Instead these children 'perished before they were discovered' or were 'unsuccessfully deserted'. Women who publicly and deliberately rid themselves of their unwanted infants were considered to have been unhinged by the traumatic birth process and to have gone against their maternal instinct. They could not be responsible for their actions and were in consequence considered mentally ill. Those 'evil' women who deliberately killed their children and tried to conceal their crime by burying the body faced either execution or transportation.

Women with means and resources could easily dispose of a child without public knowledge. Poorer women, especially domestic servants, found it harder to dispose of the body without the complicity of other women. In the majority of cases local women, when interrogated by the police, held their tongues. The poor were generally wary of officialdom, feeling they had little to gain from the direct interference of the state into their lives. Women were in an excellent position to shield female suspects, should they be moved to do so, by obscuring evidence, or by their reluctance to offer important details. By the same token they could quickly deliver up suspects and bring forth damning information against those women for whom they had little empathy or respect. In most cases it was only when they were directly implicated in the crime that neighbours volunteered any information.

The child itself was not of particular interest to the prosecuting authorities. There was no emotive outpouring of sorrow at the fate of these unwanted infants. The focus instead was on the 'unnatural' mother who had killed them. These women had to be shown to be the exception to the majority of women. It was assumed that 'normal' mothers could not reject their child in such a manner. The most obvious explanation for such a horrendous crime was to believe that these women were evil. A more convincing, and less threatening, explanation emerged by way of the medical profession. In rejecting the central tenet of their feminine role such women were

deemed to be mentally unstable or insane. Once categorized as sick, they could be treated against their will. Adopting a medical approach meant that explanations of infanticide lay at the level of individual deviance, thus muting any potential critique of the prevailing rigid concept of the maternal.

From the 1830s the popular press began to cover infanticide cases in detail for a public both alarmed and interested in the sensational and gruesome. The fact that accused women were, most often, unmarried and poor, confirmed middle-class suspicions of the criminality of this class. Furthermore, the publicity given to infanticide cases implicitly urged the constant patriarchal surveillance of women, especially since the most cunning of them were apt to try and conceal the fruits of their sexual laxity.

Apart from making an example out of the few culpable women, public officials deliberately played down the extent of infanticide in Ireland. Property owners, in particular, interpreted the practice in a most remarkable way. Each case of infanticide became a case of an 'unsuccessfully deserted child'. A belief in the essential maternal nature of all women was articulated with every instance of infant death. The widespread evidence to the contrary, instead of challenging this illusion, was carefully reworded and reinterpreted to strengthen, rather than undermine, the association of the feminine with the maternal. Indeed, according to this discourse whilst erring women might try in an impulsive moment of weakness to desert their children, they were incapable of infanticide. Effectively then, for commentators, the reality of what was happening in their own parishes and the reality of women's lives was denied.

In the records of the 1836 Poor Law Inquiry, one of the few sources to record the attitudes and activities of ordinary men and women as well as the more influential community members, there are few documented cases of infanticide, but several of children 'perishing before they were discovered'. These infants were not seen as the victims of infanticide, instead they were unfortunate in not surviving the trials of exposure. The mother was not publicly acknowledged as culpable.

Neither was it contemplated that there might be situations and circumstances where a child might be unwanted: if it was the result of rape, for example, or if the mother had not the means to feed another mouth. It is worth remembering that individuals died from exhaustion and starvation, and their associated illnesses, in times other than the Famine of 1845–9. Subsistence was a way of life, especially for women who were frequently deserted by their men, or, if more fortunate, spent six months of the year maintaining their children alone while their men travelled independently as seasonal labourers to the midlands of Ireland, as well as to Scotland and England. These women knew the dangers and difficulties in trying to care for infants in hard times. A new-born was often not allowed to jeopardize the physical and economic survival of the mother and the larger 'family unit'.

The all embracing belief in maternity can be witnessed in accounts of child desertion. It was believed that women were not indifferent to their child even when abandoning it. Every act of desertion took on a benign character where the caring qualities of the mother were still in evidence. In the Poor Law Inquiry reports for Kilkee and Moone, for example, it was noted that the mother generally placed the child 'in some conspicuous and much frequented place very frequently at the door of some parish priest'.[4] There was also the frequently articulated belief that 'few mothers will desert their children if there is any chance they will not be taken care of'.[5] Along with benign desertions, the motivations ascribed to a woman's actions were either a wicked and impulsive moment of weakness, after which the child was invariably reclaimed, or, again, the desertion was evidence of a long-term strategy of care in that resources had to be gathered in the interim so as to maintain the child.

Generally, the abandoning of a child was not interpreted as killing it, but rather as a means of shirking responsibility for its upkeep and maintenance. The women who had deserted their children lacked fortitude and moral fibre in failing to provide for them. These women had therefore to be coerced into their 'natural' maternal duties. Jailing was attempted in some cases. Punishing the mother by jailing her was not a deterrent and neither did it solve the problem of

'unnatural' mothers who persisted in abandoning their children often with fatal results. Far more effective was community scrutiny and gossip. Each foundling raised the poor rate and placed a financial burden on propertied community members. Community pressure had thus to be brought to bear on women to force them to take responsibility for a child, whatever their own feelings, state of health or material circumstances. All women then had to be carefully watched and scrutinized and if a pregnancy was detected greater surveillance was needed to ensure that the woman was forced into child-rearing. In Massareen in 1836, for example, it was noted that a night watchman had been established 'to curb the practice of desertion',[6] and in Toome ominous-sounding 'inspectors' were appointed to seek out the mothers of deserted children.[7] Generally, all parishioners became vigilant and the result of this vigilance, it was claimed, ensured that 'a mother is now afraid to expose her child as detection now almost always follows'.[8]

Infanticide was not a straightforward crime. In most cases of suspected infanticide the child was not violently killed. Whilst violent deaths got most publicity, they represent only a fraction of children who were unwanted and allowed to die. By far the greatest number of infant deaths were caused by neglect, ignorance and the absence of vital care in the infant's first few hours of life. The omission, it is suggested here, was often deliberate; the mother being unable or unwilling to take care of the child. By letting the child die through neglect, the mother could argue that she gave birth unattended, was ignorant of the essential techniques necessary for the child's survival, or was in physical distress and unable to carry them out. She, therefore, had a strong defence if the criminal charge of infanticide was brought against her. The bodies of these children, given birth to in secret, were usually concealed in shallow graves and their whereabouts only discovered by accident. If a few weeks had gone by then there was little hope of identifying the putative mother. Public officials assumed that many of these were stillborn and rudimentary

4. See *First Report of H.M. Commissioners of the Poorer Classes in Ireland*, App. A, H.C. 1835, xxxii, Baronies of Oughteray, Kenaught and the parish of Banagher [hereafter Poor Inquiry].
5. Poor Inquiry, App. A. Parish of Castledermot.
6. Ibid., parishes of Aughadowey, Templemore and Tomfinloe.
7. Ibid., parish of Lisburn.
8. Ibid., parish of Ahoghill.

medical tests were carried out on some of them to confirm this. Considering the difficulties involved in ascertaining the true fate of the child, and in the absence of the mother, many of these children were recorded as stillborn and quietly buried.

Another indirect way of letting an unwanted child die without much public notice was death by omission — that is, a failure to nourish the child. Breast milk was essential to the survival of infants in the nineteenth century. Whenever food substitutes were used, such as bread and cow's milk, arrowroot, sugar and water, or cornflour, they served ultimately to reduce the child's chances of survival. Those who were unwilling or unable to feed the child themselves paid a neighbour or friend to wet-nurse it for them. Whilst some women made sporadic attempts to feed their children, others never exerted themselves at all, suggesting that they had little interest in the survival of the child. However, in most cases where a child was unwanted, the mother often made sure that she could not be legally implicated in the child's death. In cases of new-born infants dying suddenly, or failing to thrive, the onus was on the mother to give physical evidence that she wanted the child. This was usually achieved through the production of garments for the baby, which proved that she wanted the child to live, or from testimonies of her neighbours that she had looked after the child and had not violently mistreated it.

About one-third of the children examined by the coroner in cases of sudden death were judged to have been accidentally overlain. This accidental smothering of infants usually occurred in the first two months of life but could extend up to six months. Usually the mother claimed that she had fallen asleep whilst nursing the child, thus depriving it of essential oxygen. Such cases may seem very straightforward, yet there is implicit in many inquests an uneasy sense that all is not as it should be, and more than a lingering suspicion on the part of jurors that at least some of these deaths were deliberate and linked to the fact that many of these young children were insured. Many exhausted women did accidentally roll over upon their sleeping infants and suffocate them. Some also died during the night of unaccounted causes. Bearing all this in mind, public officials were much more suspicious of children who were accidentally overlain than children who had died by any other means.

Pauper women had their children with them whilst begging, on their travels, on admittance to such institutions as jails and workhouses and whilst they were out in public drinking houses late at night. Wet roads, winter journeys, late night hours and the seemingly arbitrary leaving of infants with young children who minded them on the streets, all entered middle-class minds as carelessness, neglect and, in many instances, as exposure. Pauper women associated with their young in quite a different manner from the respectable citizens who condemned and, on occasion, prosecuted them for what, in terms of the dominant and law-enforcing culture, was interpreted as neglect. In this respect pauper women were prosecuted for their poverty and their lifestyle. Were the deaths of the children of the poor due to carelessness, neglect or the variety of childhood ills resulting from lack of adequate food, clothing and shelter? It is difficult to say with certainty that these children were deliberately killed, and yet, at the same time, contemporary reports that deal with the circumstances of the mother's life leave no doubt that many of these children were unwanted.

Deserted children were looked upon with much odium and were seen both as the living fruits of gross immorality and a burden on the pockets of the respectable people of the community. Few were willing to support them and they were not generally perceived to be deserving of public charity. That there was no public interest in their fate is revealed by the inability of public officials to account for children deserted in their own parish. If a child was aged over twelve months at the time of its desertion, it was not given to a wet nurse. At this tender age it had to make its own way in the world, usually by begging and scrounging from the neighbours, until it was old enough to work and maintain itself. At about three or four years of age these children became independent workers and were tolerated in the local community. However, they retained the stigma of foundling throughout their lives. Whilst a man could redeem his name by hard work, and marry into the small farming community, such was not the case for abandoned female children, who remained outcast for their entire lives.

As the nineteenth-century progressed, society became increasingly less hospitable to women who deserted or abandoned their children. Women who did not conform to the dominant patriarchal notions of acceptable feminine behaviour for mothers were sought out, institutionalised and punished. These women, usually unmarried, had their children permanently removed from them by the state and its institutions. The motivation and personal circumstances of women's lives were rarely alluded to. When the reality of women's lives was ignored it became easier to exclude from contemporary consciousness the dramatic actions of women who resorted to infanticide, and eventually to almost obliterate them from the historical record. In twentieth-century Ireland mothering was supposed to be a privilege for respectable mothers of legitimate children.

ANONYMOUS

from:
KERRY EVENING POST (1835)

[The following three extracts relate the case of Catherine Harrington, accused of burying her infant alive.]

25 April 1835

Committed to the county jail, under the warrant of Thomas Ponsonby, Esq., Catherine Harrington, charged on the oath of George Burson, with having, on the evening of the 21st instant, buried her child alive, which caused death.

The circumstances of this most extraordinary case, we are informed, are as follows:— On the evening of Tuesday last, the unfortunate woman above mentioned brought a female infant to the churchyard of Kilflyn, and laid it by the side of a wall, while she went to a neighbouring field, where some people were at work planting potatoes, and requested the loan of a spade to dig a grave for a little child. The man to whom she applied asked her whether she had any one to assist her, and on answering in the negative, he gave the spade to his son (a little boy) with directions to dig the grave: it was done accordingly, and when the woman took up the child from the side of the wall, it screamed, upon which the boy in astonishment, exclaimed, 'Sure that child is not dead?'. The mother answered, 'It is the same thing — it soon will', and having laid it in the grave, covered it up with earth and heavy stones. The boy, frightened, ran away and told the circumstances to his father, who immediately hastened to the churchyard, and on his approach, saw the woman still employed in covering up the grave. The man instantly disinterred the poor child, which was found quite dead; though only a few minutes in its cold prison. We understand the only excuse this wretched woman offers for her savage and unnatural conduct, is 'that the child was rickety and sickly!!!, and that she wanted to get rid of it'. A more appropriate apology could not have been offered by a New Zealand Cannibal. An inquest was held on the body, by James McGillycuddy, Esq., Coroner, and a verdict returned accordingly . . .

25 July 1835

. . . [T]he spade was laid on the wall . . . for the prisoner's use, and in a few minutes after, John Benson, still seeing the spade on the wall, said to the little boy, his son, 'perhaps the poor woman is not able to dig the grave, go and dig it for her'; on which the witness got over the wall into the churchyard, and saw the child, wrapped in a bundle of rags, lying at a distance from him, (about twenty yards), and close to the wall; he dug the grave accordingly, it was, in depth, not more than the length of the iron part of the spade; up to this time he did not hear the child make any noise, but when the grave was ready the woman took up the child from the side of the wall, and while she was bringing it towards the hole he heard a 'weak cry', which it repeated as she was bringing it along; the witness then said, with fear and astonishment, 'are you going to bury the child alive!', the prisoner replied, 'Oh, it is a weak child and won't be long alive!'. She then laid the child in the grave, and, while doing so, it again uttered a feeble cry, and she then commenced filling up the hole with earth and stones; on seeing this the witness fled, in terror and dismay, to look for his father, who he found in about half an hour after, and told him the horrible tale. The father said, 'it is too late to save the child's life now'; and it was left in the grave until the following day, when it was disinterred at the coroner's inquest . . .

Mary Mullowney sworn . . . was with her brother on the road the evening the child was buried; saw the prisoner that evening on the road leading to the church with the child in her arms; saw the prisoner dandling the child, as if it were alive; heard the child cry. The prisoner was then walking towards the church; heard nothing more about the child until the next morning.

Judith Stack a decent farmer's wife, sworn — Knows the prisoner; she came to the house of witness on the 20th of April (Easter Monday), while the witness was at mass; on the witness's return home she found the prisoner, who had a child in her arms; it was a newborn female infant; she asked the prisoner when it was born; prisoner replied it was born the previous Friday; witness expressed her surprise that prisoner said 'she could not help it'; witness took compassion [on] her, and kept her in [the] house for that day and night, and saw her frequently suckle the child; the prisoner left after breakfast (about 12 o'clock), on Easter Tuesday, the 21st of April, (the day laid in the indictment), the child was then alive.

Maurice O Conner, Esq. M.D. sworn — Attended the Coroner's Inquest at Kilflyn, on the 22d of April — saw the child disinterred — opened the body — there were no external marks of violence, nor internal appearances of disease — a child, of that age, might have been buried alive and, on a post mortem examination exhibit none of those appearances . . .

Thomas Ponsonby, Esq. sworn — Is a Magistrate for this county — heard of the circumstances of the infanticide on the 22d of April — sent the police in pursuit of the prisoner —

went himself in pursuit — saw the prisoner running along a ditch, pursued and arrested her, and she attempted to escape — saw the child disinterred and it was opened by the medical gentleman in attendance.

Thomas Power (the father of the murdered child) was next examined, he appeared to be a savage as civilised as a cannibal of New Zealand. — He swore that the prisoner lived with him as a servant maid — they had another illegitimate child, aged three years — the prisoner brought the infant to his house on Easter Monday, and said, 'here is your child' — it was then dead — she said 'I must wash it and put a clean shirt on it!!!' — and she did so, and then carried it away to bury it. (Mark — the child was alive at 12 o'clock on the day following in the house of Judith Stack). This fellow swore that he was so poor that he could not support himself, his mother, or his illegitimate children, and that he was obliged to live on the charity of some friends — he came on the table half drunk, and no one believed a word he swore . . .

29 July 1835

The wretched woman Catherine Harrington, on whom sentence of death was passed on Friday last, and who was ordered for execution on Monday, has been respited until the 5th of October next, on a memorial presented to the humane Judge, Baron Foster, by the jury on whose verdict she was found guilty. We are happy that this act of mercy has been extended to this miserable object, for we think it impossible that any sane being, whose reason was not clouded by ignorance more gloomy, and less useful for self preservation than that portion of instinct which the Almighty has granted to the beasts of the field, could be so egregiously foolish as to call people to witness so atrocious an act of murder as that [of] burying her own child alive.

[The *Kerry Evening Post* of 19 September 1835 reported that Catherine Harrington had been removed to Cork and was awaiting transportation.]

from:
FIRST REPORT FROM H.M. COMMISSIONERS OF INQUIRY INTO THE CONDITION OF THE POORER CLASSES IN IRELAND (1835)

[This extract from the Poor Inquiry reveals common attitudes towards illegitimate and deserted children. The evidence comes from the parish of Kilnmore Erris, in the barony of Erris. Amongst those giving evidence were small farmers, a number of widows and labourers, a stipendiary magistrate, a parish priest, a chief constable of police and a schoolmaster.]

No children have been deserted in this parish within the recollection of any of the witnesses. There have been a few cases of infanticide, in which the children have been invariably believed illegitimate: two such cases have happened within the last two years, both supposed to have been caused by the father's refusal to support the child. In one case, the mother was turned out of doors by her parents, partly for the disgrace she brought on them, partly from their inability to support any increase of family; under these circumstances, and being unable to support the child by any industry of her own, she was driven to the commission of the crime. There was a great number of orphan children through the villages, their number being greatly increased since cholera visited this district; they lived mostly by begging, their relatives being for the most part too poor to undertake the support of them. Many of them between the ages of 12 and 18 hire with the small farmers, perhaps for one quarter, and beg the next. During spring and harvest they may obtain some casual employment, but in winter and summer begging is their only resource. This applies only to orphans above 12 years, below that age they must beg through the whole year; the elder beg for the younger children; and if any be old enough to marry, all the others fall in upon them for support . . .

from:
FREEMAN'S JOURNAL (1860)

[Although a number of witnesses are recorded as testifying against Ellen Murphy, a publican's daughter, she is acquitted by the jury. Significant features in the report are the absence of the men on the day of the birth, the mother's objectifying of the baby — 'take that thing' — and the apparently gratuitous information that the chief witness is herself a single mother. A significant factor is that the acquittal may have been on account of the fact that Ellen Murphy, unlike Catherine Harrington, offered the jury a plausible alternative narrative: the baby died when s/he was born onto the stable floor, and in any case Murphy would have too weak to have killed him/her.]

Ellen Murphy (daughter of a publican residing at Clogheen) was placed at the bar, charged with the wilful murder of her illegitimate child on the 19th of September last. The prisoner pleaded not guilty.

Catherine Flynn examined by Mr. Wale Q.C. — Was in the service of Mr. John Murphy of Clogheen; recollects the fair day of Cahir, last September; her master and his son went to the fair; prisoner eat [sic] her breakfast with a woman named Catherine Keeffe; prisoner then went out into the stable; witness went up to her work to wash out a room; in about three quarters of an hour Catherine Keeffe called her down to go out into the stable, and see what Ellen was doing; witness went into the stable; saw prisoner standing there, with a bundle in her hand — something wrapped in a calico petticoat; prisoner threw the bundle on the ground, and a child cried out of the bundle; she said. 'Will you take that thing out of that and bury it'; witness said she would not have anything to do with it; prisoner again asked her to take it and bury it; after a quarter of an hour witness returned to the stable; found prisoner still there, heard the child moaning, as if dying; said to her 'O! Ellen, you've committed murder'; she said, 'what's that to you, it's I that will have to suffer for it; it's better for me to do that than to shame my father'; witness said, 'Very well, you have it now and keep it'; witness had a child herself, is not married; is trying to rear her child; prisoner asked her to bring her a spade, and she would bury it herself; witness went in and brought out a spade;

prisoner said she was not able to bury it; asked witness again to do so, which she declined saying, she was afraid the police would catch her; she asked witness to bring her water to wash her face and hands; witness did so; there was blood on her face and hands, which she washed off; the bundle was left in the manger, and both came in together; witness then by her direction brought in the bundle, and locked it up in the prisoner's box [trunk], the child was dead and cold; prisoner came down and said to her stepmother 'Thank god, I have made a liar of all those who were belying me'; she submitted herself to her stepmother for examination, who replied, 'Thank god, you have, my child'.

. . . Catherine Keeffe, an elderly woman in employment of prisoner's father, proved that she scolded prisoner for denying that she had been in the family way, and asked her what she had done with the child, when she said that she had it in her box.

Ellen Brien proved that she buried the child by prisoner's direction in the garden; had no spade, and covered it with rubbish; Prisoner told her that the child was dead born.

Jeremiah Sullivan proved that he found the child in the garden of prisoner's father.

Doctor Walsh proved that on the 10th October he made a post-mortem examination on the body of the child, which was in a very far advanced state of decomposition; found a fracture of the head; that fracture must have been occasioned by violence — either a blow or a fall. Cross examined by Mr Rolleston — In an unassisted birth the child might have fallen on the stable pavement which would have occasioned the fracture.

Catherine Keeffe was recalled . . . deposed that prisoner had an attack of paralysis, from which she was dead on one side, and has ever since been very weak and delicate . . .

The jury, who, after deliberating for about twenty minutes, acquitted the prisoner.

MARJORIE HOWES, *Editor*

Public Discourse, Private Reflection, 1916–70

The year 1916 roughly marks the beginning of the period when the southern twenty-six counties of Ireland could pursue a national policy of their own with regard to sexuality. Twentieth-century Ireland became famous for its determined and multi-faceted repression of sexuality. But the fact that post-independence Irish culture treated sexuality with nearly equal parts of anxiety and fascination indicates more a set of post-colonial problems than the standard prurience of the puritan. In a nation seeking to define and assert its own unique voice, sexuality was an unmentionable subject that lurked beneath every conversation. In a society preoccupied with establishing and maintaining order, sexuality constituted a principle of chaos. In a culture struggling to redefine community and its relation to the individual, sexuality provided a window onto disturbing truths about human relationships and a means of plumbing the depths of the self. Obviously, there is far more to sexuality than just sex, either as an act or as an attribute. Many complex forces help organize the sexual desires and activities of individuals and their imaginative and emotional relations to their desires and activities. The selections here have been chosen in part to emphasize sexuality's intimate connections with a wide range of issues — religious, social, national, economic and cultural.

Irish culture has long had, for better or worse, a keen sense of the public determinants and consequences of the apparently private realm of sexuality. This sense manifests itself in a tension between emphatic attention to sexuality and equally emphatic reticence about it. On the one hand, from Parnell to the *Playboy* riots[1] to debates over censorship, contraception, divorce and abortion, sexuality has been a subject for public scrutiny and debate. On the other hand, nothing testifies more eloquently to sexuality's central symbolic importance than Ireland's various official and unofficial injunctions against public displays or discussions of many aspects of sexuality. Some Irish writers have responded with a lyric nostalgia for a truly private and genuine sexual world, unmolested by 'external' events and pressures; one finds traces of this structure of feeling in Maura Laverty, Anne Crone and Temple Lane. Others have reacted with public-spirited calls for greater social openness and tolerance concerning sexuality, as have Dorine Rohan, Nuala Fennell and, in a different way, Edna O'Brien (see pp. 1047–51).

Since independence, sexuality has been an important, if somewhat confusing, marker of Irish national difference. The establishment of the Free State did not eliminate the need for government and society to define the Irishness of the Irish nation; on the contrary, such efforts continued vigorously and anxiously, especially as it became clear that independence had brought few economic and social changes. One method of

1. Charles Stewart Parnell (1846–91) was Leader of the Irish Parliamentary party (1880–90) until the party was split by the revelation of his affair with Katharine O'Shea (see pp. 889–91); in 1907 an Abbey Theatre production of *The Playboy of the Western World* by John Millington Synge (1871–1909) provoked riots over its representation of Irish peasant society.

defining and asserting the national character that enjoyed wide popular support, accorded with the Free State's now legendary social and economic conservatism and marked a clearly visible difference between Ireland and England was the formal and informal enforcement of Catholic social teachings, particularly in the area of sexual morality. During the 1920s and 1930s, the Free State established censorship of films, books and magazines, outlawed contraception, established stricter regulations for dance halls, banned married women from a number of jobs, and produced a constitution that prohibited divorce and designated the home and motherhood as a woman's true place and mission in society. Various Irish women's groups protested the 1937 constitution vigorously,[2] but in general it and the new legislation met with little resistance. Such measures complicated the issue of partition, as they meant that, at least theoretically, women in the North of Ireland enjoyed opportunities and freedoms not available to women in the Free State. Whether or not Northern women took advantage of them is another question; in general, they appear not to have done so. While this introduction focuses on the twenty-six counties, the sexual culture of the North had a great deal in common with that of the new Irish state.

For the great majority of the population, North and South, sexuality meant married, reproductive heterosexuality. Bisexual and gay women were virtually invisible until very recently. The dominant Irish culture and the Catholic church equated sex with procreation rather than passion, and sanctioned it only within marriage. While significant sections of the population have periodically defied church teachings on issues relating to nationalism, large-scale violation of church doctrine on sexual issues was much rarer until relatively recently. The anthropologists Arensberg and Kimball reported that the rural folk culture of small farmers prized the 'good long family', praised and valued married women for their fecundity, and heaped varying degrees of contempt, disapproval and pity on the unmarried, the

childless and the ill-matched.[3] Illegitimacy rates are not an ideal index for measuring how widespread sexual activity outside marriage may have been in Ireland, given practices like hastily arranged weddings after conception, the emigration (voluntary or forced, temporary or permanent) of pregnant unmarried women, abortion and infanticide. What the low rates of reported illegitimacy measure most reliably is the heavy social stigma attached to it, especially in rural areas. However, most scholars agree that the available evidence suggests that, compared to people in other countries, relatively few Irish violated the taboo on extra-marital sex.[4]

One important reason why such social norms remained dominant (though they did not go completely unchallenged) as long as they did was that Ireland's high rates of emigration acted as a kind of safety-valve. While 'Irish-style marriage' was symbolically central, David Fitzpatrick observes that in practice it was 'a minority experience for the Irish people after the famine'.[5] The people most likely to rebel against or chafe under Ireland's sexual culture were also often those most likely emigrate. The Irish who stayed in the country appeared to be uniquely abstemious sexually. Ireland had the highest rates of postponed marriage and permanent celibacy of any western European country that kept such records. In 1926, 72 per cent of Irish men between the ages of 25 and 34 were unmarried, as were 53 per cent of Irish women of that age.[6] In 1936 censuses showed that one quarter of Irish women never married, and 25 per cent of Irish men remained permanently celibate.[7] These trends did not change substantially until the 1950s. A number of factors encouraged late marriages and permanent celibacy. For Catholics, a late marriage was one of the few available methods of controlling family size, and many women may have resisted marriage because while it was quite acceptable for single

---

2. Rosemary Cullen Owens, *Smashing Times: A History of the Irish Women's Suffrage Movement 1889–1922* (Dublin: Attic Press, 1984), p. 132.

3. Conrad Arensberg and Solon T. Kimball, *Family and Community in Ireland* (Cambridge, Mass: Harvard University Press, 1968), chs 7 and 11.

4. K.H. Connell, *Irish Peasant Society* (Oxford: Clarendon Press, 1968), p. 119.

5. David Fitzpatrick, 'Marriage in Post-Famine Ireland', in *Marriage in Ireland*, ed. Art Cosgrove (Dublin: College Press, 1985), p. 116.

6. Robert E. Kennedy, jun., *The Irish: Emigration, Marriage, and Fertility* (Berkeley: University of California Press, 1973), p. 143.

7. Ibid., p. 144.

women to work, social custom generally forbade married women to do so. Other possible reasons included the indissolubility of marriage and increasing desires for a higher standard of living.

This apparent reluctance to marry was particularly characteristic of small farmers, and was shaped by a set of economic and social structures that Arensberg and Kimball called familism.[8] Under this system, landowners did not subdivide their holdings among their children, as they had often done, with disastrous results, before the Famine; instead they usually dowered one daughter and left the farm to one son. Without money or property, the other children had little chance of marrying within their own class. They could emigrate, enter the church, learn a trade (though this was much easier for men than for women) or remain in the country — celibate, and often as poor dependants or unpaid helpers on family farms.

Those marriages that did take place were organized with economic as well as romantic considerations in mind, and in the 1920s and 1930s arranged matches were still fairly common in rural areas. A farmer's son usually could not marry until his parents retired and turned control of the farm over to him, but often this did not happen until he was in his forties or even older. For the landowning classes in the Irish countryside, access to licensed sexuality went along with other kinds of access — to money, to land, to partners whose material contributions would be commensurate with theirs. It was not age but marriage that conferred social status. A married woman, no matter how young, was accorded respect, rights and privileges denied to an unmarried woman; a single woman of fifty was still referred to as a 'girl' and treated accordingly.[9]

The sexual mores associated with familism were profoundly middle class, and were less prevalent among landless labourers in the countryside. Because they were not tied to parcels of land, labourers often had greater mobility; they could travel to find a spouse or to escape the social repercussions of sexual transgressions. Labourers were also likely to marry earlier and

with less attention to the financial standing of prospective mates than landowners. In rural areas an immense social chasm separated the two classes. Farmers who married propertyless labourers were thought to have 'married down' substantially, and risked being disinherited by angry parents. Landowners often viewed the labouring classes with a combination of sexual suspicion and class resentment. While urban dwellers married slightly earlier and more often than the rural Irish, steady rural-urban emigration ensured that familistic values and behaviours appeared to some degree among the middle classes in cities as well.

The mainstream Catholic church, Ireland's major arbiter of sexual morality, exhorted the large proportions of unmarried people to chastity. While before the First World War the hierarchy had been particularly concerned over Irish rates of alcoholism, denunciations of creeping sexual corruption — illustrated in dancing, company-keeping, obscene books, periodicals and films, and revealing clothing — became increasingly common in the decades after 1922.[10] The hierarchy had always policed the sexual morality of the faithful, but now their pronouncements were intertwined with the post-revolutionary quest for national self-definition. They often cast sexual immorality as English or, more generally, foreign, and sexual purity as naturally and genuinely Irish. Sex replaced drink as the nation's chief evil during this period largely because it was difficult to blame Irish intemperance on British rule or continued influence. A 1925 government study revealed that Ireland maintained, in proportion to its population, twice as many licensed houses as England.[11] However, most of the texts, dances and fashions against which the church warned did come from England or elsewhere abroad, and could be cast as threats to national as well as sexual character. The Lenten Pastorals of 1924 encouraged the Irish to condemn the 'cross-channel unclean press'[12] and a 1927 archbishop's speech claimed, 'In recent years the dangerous

8. Conrad Arensberg, *The Irish Countryman* (Garden City, New Jersey: Natural History Press, 1968 [1937]), and C. Arensberg and S.T. Kimball, *Family and Community in Ireland*.

9. Caoimhim O'Danachair, 'Marriage in Irish Folk Tradition', in *Marriage in Ireland*, p. 100.

10. J.H. Whyte, *Church and State in Modern Ireland 1923–1970* (New York: Barnes and Noble, 1971), pp. 27–8.

11. Terence Brown, *Ireland: A Social and Cultural History 1922–1985* (London: Fontana, 1985), p. 43.

12. Michael Adams, *Censorship: The Irish Experience* (Dublin: Scepter Books, 1968), p. 17.

occasions of sin had been multiplied. The old Irish dances had been discarded for foreign importations which, according to all accounts, lent themselves not so much to rhythm as to low sensuality.'[13]

The church jealously defended its position as moral guardian and resisted anything it perceived as an effort to encroach on its control of the Irish educational system. In 1951, Dr Noel Browne, the Minister for Health, proposed the Mother and Child Health Scheme, which would have provided free pre-natal care and education about maternity for mothers, and health care for children, regardless of means. The hierarchy objected strenuously, and a controversy ensued (see Volume v, pp. 170–1). The government, hesitant to defy the church, failed to support Dr Browne, and he resigned. The hierarchy had several objections; an important one was that the scheme would empower doctors to educate women 'in regard to the sacred and delicate subjects of sex, chastity, marriage, child birth and family life'.[14] The church was anxious to reserve this power for itself, and the incident provoked a lively debate about church–state relations in Ireland.

It would be a mistake to attribute too much of Ireland's sexual culture to Catholicism, however. The church was most successful in enforcing its doctrines when other factors, like the familistic structure of rural life, also encouraged conformity. Many priests encouraged early and universal marriage and were ignored. Irish Catholicism's emphasis on chastity and sexual morality, which became woven into post-revolutionary efforts to define and assert the national character, was more the result than the cause of Irish rural bourgeois values.[15] In addition, just how far the Catholic church should be held responsible for the kind of Irish puritanism that led to the removal of all the nudes from the Municipal Gallery or the banning of Kate O'Brien's *Land of Spices* on the basis of a single indecorous sentence is debatable, as the contrast between the essays by Rohan and Josephine O'Brien indicates. Joseph J.

Lee points out that while in Maynooth 'sex was equated, for all practical purposes, with sin', post-Famine Protestant clergies were also notoriously puritanical, and that 'Trinity College Divinity School, influenced by the evangelical revival, produced clergy who suspected sex and Catholicism with equal fervour.'[16] Several historians have also argued that in important ways Ireland's sexual conservatism reflected the colonial imposition of British Victorian prudery onto Irish Catholicism.[17]

Some observers of Irish sexual culture thought the Irish uniquely, laudably chaste, others sensed corruption and exhorted them to be more chaste, and, somewhat later, still others worried that they were excessively, unnaturally chaste. Beginning in the late 1940s, some commentators claimed the unusual celibacy of the Irish encouraged emigration and warped the social and sexual relations between the sexes. J.H. Whyte observes that 'almost every area of the country has its folklore about local puritans'.[18] In 1953 Sean O'Faolain lamented continuing emigration and Irish reluctance to marry, and blamed the sexual culture fostered by church and state: 'Since my boyhood I have heard my elders fulminating about keeping company, night courting, dancing at the crossroads, V necks, silk stockings, late dances, drinking at dances, mixed bathing, advertisements for feminine underwear, jitterbugging, girls who take part in immodest sports (such as jumping or hurdling), English and American books and magazines, short frocks, Bikinis, cycling shorts, and even waltzing, which I have heard elegantly described as "belly-to-belly dancing".'[19] By 1970 a strand of earnest self-examination had emerged as a well-established, though still marginalized, discourse on Irish sexual identities and activities.

One thing most observers of Irish sexual culture, liberal and conservative, shared during this period was an acute sense of Irish sexual

13. J.H. Whyte, *Church and State in Modern Ireland*, p. 25.
14. Speech by Bishop Browne of Galway at Salthill, quoted in ibid., p. 257.
15. See K.H. Connell, *Irish Peasant Society*, and R.E. Kennedy, *The Irish: Emigration, Marriage and Fertility*.
16. Joseph. J. Lee, 'Women and the Church Since the Famine', in *Women in Irish Society: The Historical Dimension*, eds Margaret MacCurtain and Donncha O'Corrain (Westport, Connecticut: Greenwood Press, 1979), p. 40.
17. See for example, Tom Inglis, *Moral Monopoly: The Catholic Church in Modern Irish Society* (Dublin: Gill and Macmillan, 1987).
18. J.H. Whyte, *Church and State in Modern Ireland*, p. 28.
19. Sean O'Faolain, 'Love Among the Irish', in *The Vanishing Irish: The Enigma of the Modern World*, ed. John A. O'Brien (New York: McGraw-Hill, 1953), p. 121.

uniqueness. Over time, the meaning of that uniqueness became increasingly unclear and worrisome, but the sense that the Irish were sexually isolated persisted. In fact, Irish sexual culture was almost certainly more diverse and less isolated than many commentators thought. The available written materials do not represent all aspects of Irish sexual culture and behaviour adequately. Marginalized intellectuals are over-represented, while the sexual ideologies and activities of Travellers, landless labourers and the urban poor are under-represented. An exaggerated sense of Irish difference and isolation was as seductive to Irish intellectuals who were intent on defining Irish culture and literature as it was to the clergy anxious to purge Irish morality of foreign influences. What neither of these groups wanted to acknowledge was the extent to which British and American popular culture had already permeated Ireland and begun to alter its sexual culture.

Irish rural life was also changing. Rural life was being modernized gradually, and was becoming more closely connected to urban life. The rise to power of the middle-class Catholic landowner meant that the Victorian sexual mores of the British middle classes began to displace those of Irish folk culture. Irish folk culture's production and enforcement of sexual norms favoured humour over reticence and displayed a different and more relaxed vision of human bodies and bodily functions. After the late 1930s, and especially after the Second World War, the bourgeois ideals of love and romance, more common in urban areas, began to permeate the countryside. The expectations and aspirations of people in rural Ireland began to change. Rural populations began to decline, and more and more people began to reject the social and moral values, as well as the low material standard of living, associated with rural life. Increasingly, familism came to be seen as a way of organizing sexuality that left something to be desired. Countless Irish texts depict conflicts between a younger generation who have begun to dream about and demand more romance and less common sense in their sexual lives, and an older generation who view the new idealization of love with suspicion and insist that other things are more important in the making of a successful marriage.

Ireland remained a predominantly rural nation until the 1950s, but the symbolic significance of the countryside far outstripped its material importance. Irish culture at large often ignored the harshness of Irish rural life, as well as the ways in which that life was changing, and idealized rural Ireland as a static source of national identity and virtue. Eamon de Valera, in particular, was famous for his pastoralist pronouncements about the virtues of Irish rural life. One of the most salient features of the counter-revival in Irish writing is its determination to subject the idealized portrait of rural Ireland to the withering glare of the grim social realities of the Irish countryside. Most of the writers here, even those who write out of a deep appreciation for rural life, are at pains to contest the sunny misrepresentations that were common during this period. The sexual poverty of Irish rural living was perhaps most famously depicted in Patrick Kavanagh's *The Great Hunger* (1942). But while Kavanagh focuses on the debilities and frustrations of bachelorhood, many women writers emphasize a different kind of sexual famine: the sexual poverty of a loveless marriage. Rural women had fewer options than men, and were more likely to marry out of economic desperation. Laverty's description of the disgust Johnny Dunne's revolting body and personal habits provokes in his wife offers a particularly graphic example of what sexuality could mean as a repulsive and forced presence rather than an absence.

The world of the Irish countryside was not only a harsh world; it was also a man's world, so that for Irish women writers the counter-revival often involved an examination of how the dismal realities of rural life were distributed unequally between the sexes. Margaret Barrington's extravagant portrayal of these inequalities in 'Village Without Men . . .' is symbolically apt, if not sociologically entirely realistic. In fact, rural life was so much harder for women than for men, particularly in the decades before the 1940s, that as a result women suffered from increased mortality rates.[20] Many young, single Irish women viewed both celibacy and rural marriage as unattractive alternatives. From the late

20. R.E. Kennedy, *The Irish: Emigration, Marriage and Fertility*, pp. 51–65.

nineteenth century onwards, more Irish women than men emigrated to cities inside Ireland or abroad, in contrast to most other European countries. Despite the high rates of celibacy, they did not go, in general, merely to find husbands. As late as the 1960s, while women outnumbered men in cities, bachelors outnumbered marriageable women in rural areas, often by a substantial margin. As Robert Kennedy observes, 'If young Irish women were emigrating simply to find a husband, they were going in the wrong direction.'[21] Instead, such women left to find work, achieve a higher standard of living, and attain greater sexual and social freedom. Particularly after the Second World War, most women who left the country were not seeking the kind of sexual life rural marriage offered them; they were rejecting it in favour of another kind of sexual life.

Emigration carried connotations of sexual freedom and adventure, as well as sexual danger and loss. Away from the scrutiny of families, local priests and small communities, Irish women could test or violate the sexual boundaries they had been raised on, with less risk of social repercussions than at home (see Maria Luddy and Dympna McLoughlin, 'Emigration from Ireland from the Seventeenth Century', Volume V, pp. 567–88). The prevailing stress on women's place in the home, the fact that economically and socially women had fewer opportunities for travel than men, the way children drastically diminished the mobility of married women, and the common practice of going away to have an illegitimate child or an abortion meant that for women the very concept of geographical mobility was often bound up with a complex set of ideas about sexual freedom, transgression and punishment. In addition, a large proportion of female emigrants to Dublin, London and the United States became domestic servants, a position that entailed considerable sexual vulnerability and often brought inexperienced young women into startling contact with a new and confusing sexual culture.

Once married, Irish couples had the highest rate of marital fertility in Europe,[22] which reinforced the cultural equation of sexuality, especially female sexuality, with reproduction. While Katharine Tynan's work frequently celebrates that equation, many other women writers explore the damage done by it. Crone's *My Heart and I* chronicles the life of a woman who gives up her own sexual and romantic happiness in order to better fulfil her ideal of motherhood. A number of commentators echoed Mary Francis Keating, speculating that Irish women in unhappy and unfulfilling marriages lavished affection on their children, especially their sons, to compensate for the affection their husbands withheld. Laverty wondered, 'Do Irishwomen lavish this inordinate love on their sons in an effort to compensate themselves for inadequate husbands?'[23] In addition, for married women, however devoted to their children they might be, sexuality often initiated a steady and exhausting series of more pregnancies than they really wanted or could cope with. And, of course, for unmarried women like Norah Hoult's Bridget Kiernan, an unwanted pregnancy was the potential punishment for the crime of sex. For the women writers of this period, the significance of pregnancy as the ever present, ever possible consequence of sex can hardly be overestimated.

Beginning in the 1960s some women defied church doctrine by going on the pill, which sympathetic doctors could prescribe for 'medical' reasons. This trend continued even after Pope Paul's 1968 encyclical reaffirming the church ban on so-called unnatural contraception. Contraception was not made legal until 1980, and then only for married couples who obtained a doctor's prescription to use it for 'legitimate family planning purposes'.[24] The most significant change near the end of this period, however, was not the greater availability of birth control, which the discreet and determined had been able to obtain through mail order or travel for decades. Rather, it was the greater willingness to use it.

Irish literary censorship was about sexuality more than anything else. The initial draft of the 1929 Censorship of Publications Act equated

---

21. Ibid., p. 72.
22. Ibid., p. 176.

23. Mary Francis Keating, 'Marriage-shy Irishmen' and Maura Laverty, 'Women-Shy Irishmen', *The Vanishing Irish: The Enigma of the Modern World*, ed. John A. O'Brien (New York: McGraw Hill, 1953); Laverty, p. 57. For Katherine Tynan, see p. 569.
24. See section 'Politics, 1500–2000', Volume V, especially the subsections edited by June Levine, Frances Gardiner and Alpha Connelly, pp. 177–226; 227–319; 320–52.

sexual passion with sexual immorality by defining the word 'indecent' as 'including calculated to excite sexual passion, or to suggest or incite to sexual immorality, or in any other way to corrupt or deprave'. After debate in the Dáil and public controversy in the press, legislators amended the bill so that the wording which became law did not include 'calculated to excite sexual passion'.[25] The Censorship Board, however, often appeared to operate under the assumption that sexual passion itself was immoral and should not be represented or aroused. In its zeal the board often violated the very terms of the Censorship Act, which stated that a book must be 'in its general tendency indecent or obscene' (as opposed to containing an indecent passage or two) in order to be banned. The other major target of Irish censor-ship was literature relating to or advocating 'the unnatural prevention of conception or the procurement of abortion or miscarriage'.

From its inception, the Irish censorship was roundly criticized, without much effect, for a variety of reasons: the bill's vague wording, the general severity of the Censorship Board's enforcement, individual decisions, and the prac-tice of accepting books for review from citizens or vigilance societies who had underlined offen-sive passages. As a rule, the critiques of and debates about censorship did not extend to the ban on literature relating to contraception and abortion. The censorship law was liberalized twice; in 1948, an appeal board was established, and in 1967 the period for which a book could be banned was limited to twelve years, so several thousand books automatically became unbanned. This last change did not apply to literature about contraception, for which the ban remained permanent. The Censorship Board's authority to ban books on contraception (though not on abortion) was removed in 1979.

Nearly all western nations had some form of censorship at this time, but the severity of Ireland's censorship in practice and the fact that so many contemporary Irish writers were banned made censorship loom especially large in the Irish literary imagination, if not in the imagination of the population as a whole. There were several consequences for representations of

sexuality. In the literature of this period sexuality is often represented in indirect and coded form, and is allied with secrecy and silence. At the same time, explicitness as such becomes an important issue, on both a formal and a psychological level, particularly in prose works. For most of the writers selected here, the relationship between directness and indirectness is more complicated than a simple contrast between healthy honesty and damaging repression, though of course such contrasts do appear in a number of important ways. In one version of this relationship, Mary Lavin's deliberately understated and encoded representations of sexuality embody the sexual repression which shapes the lives of many of her characters. But this is not because Lavin chose indirectness as the appropriate vehicle for portraying repression and sublimation. Rather, sexuality subtly saturates her descriptions of ordinary actions and scenes because in Lavin's world that is how sexuality, repressed or otherwise, operates. In another version, Edna O'Brien's famously explicit characters are often volubly inarticulate about their sexuality; their directness constitutes a search for sexual freedom and self-knowledge, rather than its achievement.

Censorship has also encouraged much Irish writing to cast sexuality as an issue of individual freedom versus societal constraint. A few writers figure this conflict as a clash between a rebellious individual and external controlling forces. But many others emphasize self-censorship and the internalization of social constraints. The most common sexual tragedy in these selections is the tragedy of a character who voluntarily renounces sexual happiness or is unable to embrace it when it is offered. Censorship, both official and unofficial, meant that especially before the 1960s, many Irish people grew up surrounded by a palpable dearth of open discussion and information about sexuality. As a result, sexuality in Irish culture is often figured as a matter of ignorance versus knowledge. To be sexually active is not just to do something, it is to know something, something both important and unspecified. In Lavin's story, a single woman's horrified efforts to understand her father's erotic relationship to Annie Bowles take the form of a failed quest for a secret knowledge from which she is excluded. This conception of sexuality as knowledge is also apparent in the Catholic

25. M. Adams, *Censorship: The Irish Experience*, pp. 47–51.

church's steadfast objection to any kind of sex education, which assumes that the mere possession of knowledge will inevitably lead to sin.

While novels and short stories often organized their representations of sexuality around constructions of knowledge, silence and disclosure, these tropes were somewhat less important to most women poets of this period. They drew on the greater directness about intense passion and intense regret available in Irish folk ballads and the mature Yeats. The poets selected here were not particularly interested in formal innovation. Mary Devenport O'Neill is one of the few who seem to have been significantly influenced by Anglo-American modernists other than Yeats. Most of them favoured and were most successful at short poems and lyrics. Some, like May Morton and Winifred Letts, borrow the sacramental and devotional languages of religion to express sexual feeling. In general the women writers of this period were more interested in the erotics of religion than their male counterparts, who, as Terence Brown observes, tended to cast religious issues as 'the struggle of the individual against the constraining nets of an all-encompassing religious authority and its demands'.[26]

The 1960s was something of a watershed decade for Irish sexuality; it set in motion a number of changes which prepared the ground for the profound alterations of the 1970s and 1980s. Economic revival and increased urbanization brought rural and urban areas into closer touch with each other. Under Sean Lemass, economic nationalism, isolationism and provincialism gave way to an emphasis on economic growth, membership in a larger community of nations, and a more outward-

looking view of Irish culture. The 'outside influences' which had been finding their way into Ireland for years were no longer as threatening as they had been. Beginning in the early 1950s, many parts of the Irish Republic (including Dublin) could receive British television signals that spilled over from Northern Ireland, and the Irish national television service was established in 1962. Censorship laws were liberalized, and enforcement became less stringent. The Catholic social movement began to focus on issues of social welfare as well as social morality, and people even began to criticize the church of the 1930s and 1940s. The family values of rural Ireland had virtually disappeared. Increasing numbers of lay people began to defy the church quietly (and a few not so quietly) in matters of sexual morality and contraception. After 1967, when abortion was legalized in England, it became easier than ever to go abroad to obtain an abortion, and in 1969 the first family planning clinic opened in Dublin. It circumvented the ban on selling contraceptives by giving them away and asking for 'donations'.

A number of important developments lay just ahead. By the 1970s a strong feminist movement had emerged and had begun a campaign for reproductive rights. The early 1970s saw the contraception train, on which women publicly defied the Republic's ban on contraceptives by bringing them from Belfast to Dublin, the Commission on the Status of Women (see Volume v, pp. 188–91), and the Supreme Court decision that the ban on contraception was unconstitutional. Also ahead, in the 1980s, were the referendums on divorce and abortion, and several controversial and well-publicized cases involving teenage pregnancy, infanticide and abortion, as sexuality in Ireland became more hotly and more openly debated than ever before.

26. Terence Brown, *Ireland's Literature: Selected Essays* (Totawa, New Jersey: Barnes and Noble, 1988), p. 50.

WINIFRED LETTS

(1882–1972)

from:
THE SPIRES OF OXFORD
AND OTHER POEMS (1917)

['Home' explores the complex attitude of middle-class reformers towards the poor. This attitude combines kindness, progressive social intervention, condescension and bourgeois disgust, and the poem embodies these tensions in competing definitions of 'home'.]

Home

(In Dublin)

I gave her bread and bid her lead me home,
For kilt she was with standing in the cold,
An' she, the creature, not turned eight years
    old.
She went before me on her small bare feet,
Clutching some papers not yet sold,
Down Westland Row and up Great Brunswick
    Street.
Sometimes she'd turn and peer
Into my face with eyes of fear.
She'd hunch her rags in hope to find some heat,
And stare at shops where they sold things to eat.
Then suddenly she turned,
And where a street lamp burned
Led me along a narrow, dirty lane;
Dim glass and broken pane
Stood for the windows. Every shadowed door
Held children of the poor.
That sheltered from the rain.
Through one dark door she slipped and bid me
    come
For this was home.
A narrow stair we had to climb
To reach the topmost floor.
A hundred years of grime
Clung to the walls, and time
Had worked its will. Tenants the like o' these
The landlords don't be planning how they'll
    please.
A smell was in it made you hold your breath:
These dirty houses pay the tax to death

In babies' lives. But sure they swarm like bees,
Who'd wonder at disease?
The room held little but a depth o' dark;
A woman stirred and spoke the young one's
    name.
The fire showed no spark,
But presently there came
A slipeen of a girl who made a flame
By burning paper, holding it torch-fashion,
Thinking, maybe, the place would stir
    compassion.
A dirty mattress and a lidless chest
That served for cradle; near it stood
A table of dark painted wood;
Foreninist[1] the grate a chair
With three legs good.
The place was bare
Of any sign of food.
The light burnt out. The young one found more
    paper
And kindled it for taper,
This time I saw above the bed
Our Lady in a robe of blue,
A picture of our Saviour's head,
Thorn-crowned. The light fell too
On the child's frightened face,
The wretched dirty place.
And so I spoke of what the priests might do,
Of them that help in such a case.
They'd send the child to some good Home,
And never let her roam
About the streets, half-dead
With cold and hunger.
They'd teach her and befriend her,
Wash her and mend her,
They'd see her clothed and fed,
And in a decent bed.
She'd have her brush and comb.
From every sort of hurt
They would defend her.
All this I said,
And paused to let them speak.
The child had caught her mother's skirt
And pressed her cheek

---

1. 'foreninist': opposite, directly in front of.

Against her arm,
As if she feared some harm.
So, clasping her, the mother shook her head.
'You have a right,' said she,
'To leave her here with me.
Heart-broke in such a place she'd be —
The creature loves her home.'

from:
MORE SONGS FROM
LEINSTER (1926)

[Letts favours the ballad form, and like 'A Girl of the
Glens to Her Careless Lover', many of her ballads
resemble translations of Irish ballads.]

A Girl of the Glens to her Careless Lover

I THOUGHT I had forgotten you and found
      peace at last;
   I had so busied myself with this and that,
In making griddle cake and soda bread,
   In working linen on a little frame.
And all the time I sang lest anyone
   Should pierce my thoughts with your name.

I thought I had forgotten you and grown so
      steadfast
   That I could walk the hills with a careless step
And see the mountainy young lambs at play
   And laugh at them having left you behind:
But as I stood above the Glen Imaal¹
   Your name was breathed by the wind.

I thought I had forgotten you so that the spring
      time
   Would never repeat your promises again,
But all night long the corncrake shouted them,
   And the full moon remembered how we met,
Even the white sweet hawthorn at the door
   Remembered. Could I forget?

True, I had not forgotten you. I shared my secret
   With whispering reeds round Lough
      Nahanagan.²

1. A spectacular glen in the Wicklow mountains.
2. Near the Wicklow Gap.

The cuckoo in the woods near Kevin's bed³
   Called to us both the livelong day. The scent
Of every whin bush held lost happiness:
   It was vain to seek content.

I would pay golden guineas to win forgetfulness.
   But no mountain lough would be deep enough
To hide from you, nor Lugnaquilla's⁴ crests
   Be far enough away. The heather's breath
Would bring you to my thoughts. I doubt myself
   I shall forget you in death.

3. Saint Kevin, the sixth-century hermit, founded a monastery at
   Glendalough in County Wicklow. A narrow cave, in which he is
   reputed to have spent the early days of his solitary life, is known as
   Kevin's Bed.
4. The highest mountain in the Wicklows.

[In 'Tin Gods' Letts criticizes Irish artists for making a
virtue of their estrangement from the religious codes,
sexual morality and ordinary people of the Irish Free
State.]

Tin Gods

I hate, —
Although my speech is mild and temperate,
I hate with hidden and yet deep disgust
The small tin gods that sit and prate
About themselves the livelong day,
Shouting like corncrakes, 'Great, Great, Great
We are the people. Bow to us!
Let the old gods be swept away,
We are the hierarchy of tin.
The olden gods you loved of late,
The golden gods are out of date.
Greater than law we sit in state
Singing of decadence and lust,
We mock at righteousness and sin.'
The small tin gods they prattle thus.

I hate them,
Windy in the head,
Who for the sake of some small art
Disdain to sweat for daily bread,
And live apart
Upon their fellows' honest toil
By desk and counter, mine and soil.
Shaggy of head and slack of tie,
They babble in the market-place,

'Behold us, all ye passers-by,
We rule the world by right and grace.
The old-world gods are long since dead
And we, the new gods, rule instead.'

I hate them and the creed they teach,
But being mild of look and speech
I hide my hatred in my heart.

NORAH HOULT

(1898–1984)

BRIDGET KIERNAN (1928)

['Bridget Kiernan' was published in Norah Hoult's first volume of stories, *Poor Women!*, her best-known and most widely admired work. Hoult's work often investigates the relationship between gender, sexuality and economic forces in situations ranging from marriage to prostitution to domestic service. One of her strengths as a writer lies in her ability to create characters whose thoughts and language inspire both the reader's sympathy and a sharp awareness of their limitations without direct authorial comment. The text is from the 1st edition, published in London by the Scholartis Press in 1928.]

'BRIDGET! Bridget!'

Bridget Kiernan answered before she was fully awake, some automatic impulse propelling her.

'Yes, ma'am.'

'Are you getting up?'

'Yes, ma'am. I'll be down in a minute.'

'Well, be quick. It's twenty past seven. You ought to have been ready long ago.'

Bridget raised herself reluctantly, and, sitting on the side of the bed, reached for her stockings. Listening, she heard Mrs. Fitzroy's door close. Isn't that the devil's own luck now, she thought. That one would be as cross as two sticks all day because she had had to shout to her to get up. It was queer she hadn't heard the alarum: she must have been sleeping very heavy.

Merciful Jesus! For the moment she had forgotten . . .

Bridget stood still, holding her vest in her hand. Full consciousness gripped her with a cold squeeze. Jim! Jim had gone. And what was worse, she was beginning to be afraid she might be going to have a child. Nothing had happened yet.

And she had been awake half the night with the worry of it.

Well, there was no time to think about it now. Pull on her clothes quick to keep out the creeping November cold. She'd have to hurry or there'd be no breakfast for the master. But all the same it was nearly dead she was for want of sleep.

'Bridget! I thought you said you were nearly ready.'

The mistress again!

'Yes, ma'am. I won't be a moment, ma'am. I'm coming now.'

'Why *don't* you come then? Half-past seven, and not a sign of you. It's disgraceful.'

With fingers made fumbling with haste, Bridget twisted up her hair into a knot, and stuck in two hair-pins. There was certainly no time to wash; anyway it was too cold. There wouldn't be time either for her to kneel down and say a mite of a prayer. But she remembered to cross herself hastily and murmur, 'Jesus, Mary and Joseph, I give you my heart and soul,' before she opened her door. SHE was waiting with her bedroom door open. SHE'd be shouting at her again in another minute. It was terrible the way that hard, thin voice made her lose her poor head altogether.

As she came out of her attic bedroom, she felt a little dizzy with cold, excitement and haste. But there was no time to stop and collect herself. Just keep on walking down the narrow stairs, holding the balustrade for support. As she passed the front bedroom, Mrs. Fitzroy poked her head out. 'That's right, Bridget,' she said with bitter sarcasm. 'Take your time. It's only getting on for eight.'

Bridget quickened her steps without replying. She was in the kitchen now, and the first thing to do was to rake out the fire. If only she'd done it the night before. But she had felt too tired and bothered, small blame to her.

How cold it was! She felt her body trembling with cold. And her hands hadn't any feeling in them at all. The air being full of dust and ashes made it all the colder. Cold and dirty. Just shove the cinders into the grate and leave them. No time to take them away now.

She eased herself and rubbed her hands together for warmth. Now she had to go down to the cellar to bring up coal and sticks. It was colder than ever in the cellar, and dark and ghostly. Wasn't that a rat she heard scurrying in the corner? Perhaps only a mouse. Never pay any heed. Shovel the coal into the bucket and bring it up. It would be better when she had got the fire set and lit.

The sound of the sticks crackling and the look of the flames as they tried to push their way up comforted her. Nothing was so bad after the fire had been lit, and you were sure it was going. And it was going well to-day. Who knew but that this mightn't be a good sign for herself. She mightn't be going to have a baby after all. Sure, it was only a few days over the time. No need to fret herself yet.

She went into the scullery to get the breakfast things. She ought, she knew, by rights sweep out the kitchen and the kitchen passage first. But it would be just like Mrs. Fitzroy, the old devil — 'God forgive me,' murmured Bridget under her breath as she heard the bad word come — it would be just like herself to hurry up with her dressing and come running down post-haste to have the satisfaction of saying, 'And the table not laid yet, Bridget!'

Well, she wouldn't give her that pleasure anyway.

The dining-room was very mournful-looking with the yellow blinds still down. It hadn't woken up yet, and it didn't want to be woken yet. But the Fitzroys got up so early! Much earlier than the Gallaghers in Dublin, where her sister was. You wouldn't think the gentry would want to get up so early. But you wouldn't call the Fitzroys gentry. No style about them at all, there wasn't.

Those white cups and saucers and plates on the white tablecloth were terrible chilly-looking. Why wouldn't she have a few flowers on her cups, something a little bright? Bridget let her mind survey disapprovingly all Mrs. Fitzroy's

crockery. So little there was of it, too! Why wouldn't she be after having a fire in the dining-room in this bitter cold? It wasn't much comfort for the master setting off on a morning the like of this. Not that she minded. It would make much more work for her, and that was the truth. Carrying up coals. And before breakfast. But it was hard on the master never to have a proper warm before he went off. And it just showed the meanness of her.

She ran down to see to the fire, and then reloaded her tray, thinking of Mr. Fitzroy. A nice, quiet man, he was. One who'd always pass the time of the day with her when the mistress wasn't by to hear. A little stiff, perhaps, but that was the way Englishmen were.

If he heard she was going to have a baby how would he behave? Pass her by with eyes turned down, most likely. Pretend not to have seen her at all. That was what another man would do, if he had proper feelings, and wasn't the kind that would be encouraged immediately to think he could do the same with her.

Stop thinking, now, about that! Herself would be down and in the devil's own tantrams at finding no kettle on. She ran downstairs again, and her quick arrival in the kitchen gave her the impression that she was getting on rapidly with her work: she took the bread out of the bin, and banged the lid down, pleasantly conscious of the bustle she was making. What about making some toast? Wouldn't that be a way of getting the mistress into a good temper? Ah, but the fire was not good for toast yet. And it was ten past eight, a bit after. She'd better be cutting the rind off the bacon for frying.

Bridget jabbed at the white fat with an over blunt kitchen knife, and once again questioned her mistress's ideas. What was in her head, now, that she made her cut the rind off before frying it in the pan? Because wouldn't anyone know that it was much easier to cut it when it was cooked, that is if you were so particular, and couldn't cut it off when it was on your plate.

That was Mr. Fitzroy in the bathroom. SHE'd be down any moment now fussing round, and chattering about how late it was. For God's sake! Wasn't that her step?

No! It was all right. There was no one. But she'd better be quick and get the rinds shoved into the dust-bin in the yard, or else she'd be complaining that she'd cut off too much of the rasher with them.

She returned from the back door with a relieved feeling. Three eggs, for himself, herself, and Miss Paula. They wouldn't spare one for her, of course, only bacon! Did anyone ever hear the like? Eggs regarded as though they might be a great luxury, and held away from the servant!

There! She was calling out to Miss Paula. Now she was on the stairs.

Bridget rushed for the frying-pan, and was laying the rashers in with an intent face when Mrs. Fitzroy came in. She was interrupted by a cry of horror from her mistress.

'Bridget! For Heaven's sake!'

Bridget was confounded. What was it she was doing wrong?

'Your filthy black hands, all over coal dust, Bridget. Touching the food we are going to eat. How *can* you?'

Bridget was still perplexed. What was it that she was meant to do then? She looked at her hands, and then at the pieces of bacon.

'Use a fork, girl, can't you? And look at the fire! Nothing but smoke. How can you expect to fry anything on that? And there's no good leaving the kettle on.' She removed it with a firm hand. 'It would take an hour to boil like that. Can't you see?'

Bridget couldn't. She was conscious that she knew nothing, and that since the appearance of Mrs. Fitzroy the cooking of the breakfast had become surrounded by immense difficulties.

'Don't stand there doing nothing. Get a newspaper; there's one in the sitting-room, under the armchair cushion; and hold it in front of the fire.'

For twenty minutes the atmosphere was heavily charged with vexation and turmoil. Bridget no longer thought. She became merely what she appeared to Mrs. Fitzroy to be — an evil-doer, who had made breakfast late, and was far too stupid to be capable of atoning for her transgressions. She had done so many things wrong that now Mrs. Fitzroy was standing in front of the fire cooking the bacon herself, and only occasionally uttering a command, or asking in a carefully restrained voice that denoted the pitch of fury at which she had arrived, some question which revealed all the things Bridget had left undone. There were one or two terrible

moments when Bridget was left standing with idle hands. She dare not remain still, yet there was nothing, she felt, she dare do. Her guilt, symbolised in the figure of Mrs. Fitzroy cooking her own breakfast, seemed then too heavy to be borne.

To avert disgraceful tears, she went over to the kitchen table, and began to lay her own cloth. Anything was better than standing like a fool. But Mrs. Fitzroy, watching her out of the corner of an eye, reflected bitterly: 'That's all she's thinking about. Her own breakfast. I've a good mind to throw her piece of bacon into the fire.'

But she did not go so far. She only disassociated it from the rest by thrusting it viciously into the side of the pan, where only a minor degree of heat could reach it. Then triumphantly she noticed an omission.

'If you can spare a minute, Bridget' — Bridget, startled, turned apprehensively — 'get me the bacon dish cover. You have only got the plates and dish warming here.'

Bridget went hastily to the pantry. She wasn't supposed to be setting her own breakfast, then. What she ought to have done, perhaps, was to go upstairs, and give the sitting-room a dust? But it was too late now. Would she ever do anything right for that one, with her face like a thunderstorm?

Paula came running into the kitchen. She was a pale child of seven, with fair, bobbed hair, heavy cheeks, and hard, staring, light-grey eyes. 'Mummy, I'm ready. So's Daddy. He wants his breakfast.'

Mrs. Fitzroy turned from the fire, and spoke with the terrible calm of the martyr. 'Tell Daddy, breakfast is just coming. I'm cooking it myself.'

At last it was over. The tea had been mashed, and taken up, and Bridget was free to get her own breakfast. She gave another turn to her rasher. There wasn't any dip left. Well, thanks to the mistress being in such a temper, she had lost all her appetite. A cup of good, strong tea was what she wanted, and she wasn't going to spare the tea either.

As she was washing up her own cup and plate in the scullery, she heard the front door bang. That was the master gone. A minute later, Mrs. Fitzroy bore down like an avenging angel.

'You can clear, Bridget. Your master hasn't been able to have a proper breakfast because it was so late. Do you see now all the trouble you cause by not getting up in time?'

'Yes, ma'am.'

The two women stood facing each other. Bridget saw through downcast lids a tall, thin woman wearing an old skirt, and yellow-brown cardigan. Mrs. Fitzroy never dressed properly till after breakfast; and her brown hair, badly shingled,[1] had a greasy, matted appearance. Her rather large nose was reddened at the tip by the hot tea she had been drinking, and she wore a fretted expression. She was a woman who always gave the impression that she was only in her present place for a few moments, and that it was not worth while to unbend and settle herself comfortably. But to Bridget at the moment her appearance resolved itself into a matter of cold, blue, accusing eyes, and an ugly red nose; while she listened to the precise English accent which made her feel she was dealing with someone she could never approach as an ordinary human being; one who must be an inhabitant of a quite different world from herself.

And Mrs. Fitzroy viewed Bridget with an equal distaste. She saw an exceedingly slatternly servant girl with a dirty, pale face and untidy dark hair that was always falling over her face. It was true, she had previously admitted, that the young woman mightn't be so bad looking if she would only keep herself clean and tidy. She had large, clear eyes, and thick black lashes — if she only had not had such a disconcerting habit of dropping them, which gave her a deceitful air. But then her mouth was always a little open, a thing which always irritated Mrs. Fitzroy in anybody. 'Makes the girl look half-witted,' she decided. But it wasn't so much her appearance as her way of dragging herself about as if there was no such thing as time in the world which annoyed Mrs. Fitzroy. 'And she looks,' reflected Mrs. Fitzroy again, 'as if she has been crying. That seems her usual occupation. Though I'm sure she gives me far more to cry about than ever I do her.'

Leaving instructions, Mrs. Fitzroy went away to get dressed in a spirit of acute dissatisfaction. It was a reflection on the house, she thought, to have such an untidy, depressed-looking girl about as Bridget. And Irish people were supposed to be

bright and witty! Sooner or later she'd have to give her notice, and start the search all over again. Or move into a flat with a gas stove, and manage herself with a day girl. This servant problem was really driving responsible women like herself mad.

Bridget cleared the upstairs table, and washed up. Then she laid a fire in the study, where Paula had her morning lessons from a visiting governess. As she dusted the room, Paula sat on a chair, looking at a book. She kept calling Bridget to show her pictures and to tell her about the story they illustrated. Bridget went on saying, 'Is that so?' and 'Yes, Miss Paula,' with mechanical regularity. It was hard to keep her attention alert that morning, but alert it had to be while Mrs. Fitzroy was still in the house. For you never knew when she'd be coming in with some question or other, just an excuse, of course, to see what you were after doing. And if you were taken by surprise, as well you might with her flopping softly round in bedroom slippers, and started, then she'd say, 'Dreaming again, Bridget,' or 'Looks very suspicious,' as if she thought you had stolen something.

So Bridget kept listening all the while she was turning out the dining-room. The dirt rose from the carpet and settled in her hair and all about her. Her hands were swollen and purple, and she felt stifled for want of a breath of clean, fresh air. She wished she was back home, back where the air was soft, and people moved slowly.

At last Mrs. Fitzroy went out to do her shopping, and Bridget came thankfully back to the kitchen fire for a comfortable warm before going up to do the bedrooms. She disliked doing the big room, because she always felt the mistress didn't really care for her being in there at all. It was the most unfriendly room in the whole house to her, and her eyelids were downcast when she entered it. Yet all the same you couldn't help being impressed by it in a way. All those silver things on the dressing-table, and the lovely blue eiderdown that was so rich looking. And the big, real mahogany wardrobe, must have cost something, that must have. Then there was that picture of a lady in evening dress, real evening dress, that showed a bit of her bosom like grand ladies did when they were off to a ball of an evening. A bit like the mistress this lady was, only lashings better looking. A sister, it might be, who

---

1. Cut in layers, to resemble roof shingles.

had married a richer man than the master, and had a motor-car, and lived in the real London you read about in books, the London where there was a real gay life, not like this Ealing place![2] Sure, Dublin was a hundred times as lively.

Now there were the potatoes to peel in the scullery. It was work that gave her a few minutes to think of herself before Mrs. Fitzroy came back, and there was the usual set-to about getting the bite she called lunch.

Well, here she was, Bridget Mary Kiernan, aged twenty-five, in a pretty plight, and she might as well face it here and now. She had committed a mortal sin, fornication, and unless she had a piece of luck she might be going to have a baby. All because of that good-for-nothing fellow, Jim — Jim, with his lovely blue suit, and smart figure, and wavy fair hair, and laughing blue eyes. And his warm lips that held yours till they seemed to draw you out of yourself into a great fire and confusion. Stop now! That was no way to be thinking. Where was her pride? A likely-looking lad enough, maybe, but he had gone now and left her for ever. Deserted her! Deserted — that was the word they called it.

And there was no way of speaking to him, a boy that she'd met in the pictures three months gone, and had never got to know anything about, though he had met her regular every Thursday evening up to four weeks ago. No, three weeks. It was a month now that *that* had happened between them, God forgive her . . . She ought to have know the sort of fellow his lordship was when he had started hinting. But there it was. It was her own fault in a way, because she hadn't chosen to take heed of his style of talking. She had liked the feel of his arms about her in the pictures too much to frighten him off with being prim and proper. And there was an ache in her all the time till he was with her again, and she felt him touch her. Sure, no one with a heart could blame her too much. Wasn't he the only friend she had in London? And everybody wanted a bit of fun now and again.

She hadn't really known, before God she hadn't, what he meant when he suggested going to a restaurant instead of to the pictures that Thursday. And she had felt shy even in her best clothes, and glad to know that it was in what was

called a private room they were going to have dinner, where there'd only be the two of them.

It was true she had felt there was something wrong when he was muttering so long with the waiter. And it was such an odd, dirty place, not like a proper restaurant at all. She had felt all queer when she saw the big sofa. But all the same she was dying to know what he was going to do. And he must have spent some money to get the room all to themselves. Half a bottle of expensive wine, too. She had laughed a lot. Wine always made her laugh a lot. But afterwards, in his arms . . . it just didn't seem to matter at all. Give him his way . . . She couldn't really see now that it was such a terrible thing as the way in which people talked about it. But, of course, it was badness, and she'd been bad, she had so.

All the same it was difficult to understand anything one way or another, and all that a poor, ignorant girl the like of herself could do was to be good and leave the matters to the priests and learned people to settle. She had done wrong, and there was no use her trying to get out of it. Her mother would be terribly upset when she heard about it — that was if she had to hear — and there was no one at all to help her.

She ought to go and make her confession. Who would she go to? She had never been to confession the whole year long she had been in England, not the five months she had been in the Isle of Man, nor the six months, as it nearly was, that she had been with Mrs. Fitzroy. It was so different here, where no one seemed to have any religion at all. Even Mass sounded different, and had different things in it. And she never been very particular about religion. Perhaps it was a pity she hadn't.

Jim had no religion, any more than that fellow she had gone out with in the Isle of Man — Frank — had. Perhaps if Jim had had religion, been a Catholic, he'd have behaved different. He had thought light enough of what they had done. Just laughed when she said they had been wicked, and then got cross when she wouldn't let him kiss her. Walking away like that in the street when she had told him what she thought of him. She was an Irish girl , and wasn't going to put up with being treated any way. Walking away and leaving her like that in the street! She'd never forgive him for that, never. Ah, well, no good exciting herself with thinking of that all over

2. West London.

again. But she had her pride, and even if he wanted to marry her she wouldn't. No one might believe it, but she wouldn't, not if he went down on his bended knees.

The potatoes were finished now. She carried them into the kitchen, and at the same moment she heard the latch of the front door turn. Her High and Mightyship was back. There'd be no peace now for a while.

Mrs. Fitzroy brought down the parcels she had been carrying. 'Here, Bridget, is the chop I got for your dinner. And the potatoes are in the basket. Those are tomatoes that I've got for to-morrow to fry with the bacon. We've got eggs, haven't we? Miss Rowbotham and Miss Paula and I are having scrambled eggs. And coffee. Can you do the eggs?'

'Yes, ma'am.'

'You ought to, considering the number of times I've had to stand over you to show you. Have you laid the table?'

'No, ma'am.'

'Well, go and do it now. It's twenty to one. And I don't want lunch later than one because of Miss Rowbotham.'

Miss Rowbotham came out of the nursery as Bridget passed on her way to the dining-room. She had curly brown hair, a small, round face and bright brown eyes that peered over her plump little body with an air of being willing to meet everybody half way.

'Good morning, Bridget,' she said with an air of cheerful benevolence. You always have to be so careful with the servants, was one of Miss Rowbotham's maxims.

'Good morning, Miss.'

The girl seems respectful enough, thought Miss Rowbotham, and, by way of rewarding her, she gave a little shiver and said, 'Isn't it cold?', in a little upward rush of words.

'Indeed it is, Miss.'

They parted, and Bridget, laying the cloth, thought: 'The English are always saying, "Good morning," or "Good afternoon," or something like that. And that teacher will be washing her hands again before her dinner. Is it to please Mrs. F. or to suit herself that she's so particular? I wouldn't be surprised but that she's scared stiff of her, like the master, and every blessed one in this house.'

Paula came silently in, thrusting her under lip forward as was her habit when she was in a bad temper, and stood watching Bridget arranging the knives and forks. 'You do look dirty and horrid, Bridget,' she remarked after a thoughtful pause.

Bridget made no reply. 'Mother says you are the dirtiest girl she has ever had, but that all Irish people are dirty. Is that true?'

Bridget thought it politic to refrain from uttering a direct denial. She'd only be making trouble with her mother, the little brat, she thought.

'The dirty Irish, the dirty Irish!' cried Paula in sudden excitement, dancing up and down, and then pulling Bridget's apron-strings loose before springing away.

'Ah, go away now, Miss Paula, and leave me alone,' said Bridget, the blood mounting to her cheeks.

'Shan't, shan't. The dirty Irish!'

Bridget felt an angry despair surging up. They were all against her, shouting at her and mocking at her. Very well, she'd stick up for herself. She had some spirit left in her, thank God. She turned round smartly on Paula.

'Do you hear what I say? Go out from here. This minute.'

'Don't speak to me like that. Or I'll tell my mother of you.'

For a moment the two stood confronting each other: Paula, pouting and lowering, Bridget with flashing eyes, and a look on her face new to the child. After a moment Paula, discomfited, ran out of the room, turning at the door to make a last thrust: 'I hate you, you horrid girl.'

Bridget stood still for a moment with a hand pressed to her rapidly beating heart, and then went on setting the table. But when she went back to the kitchen, Mrs. Fitzroy observed on her face what she described as her mulish look, and deemed it better to postpone a complaint that too many potatoes had been peeled till later.

'You go on making the toast, Bridget. I've beaten up the eggs.'

The task of getting lunch proceeded silently, the two women ignoring each other's presence as far as possible. At last it was done, and taken up, and Bridget was left to fry her own chop.

She ate absent-mindedly, occupied with the new feelings which Paula's attack had aroused in her. Now they'd got her blood up she wouldn't care what she did, and she wouldn't be asking help from nobody either. If she was going to have a baby, what need was there for any great to-do? They'd have to take her in at the workhouse anyway, and then she'd go on the streets . . . steal. Get put in prison. What matter? . . .

There was Margaret Callaghan of Carrickmore,[3] that the priest had sent away out of the parish because she wouldn't tell him the name of the fellow that was after giving her a child. And she had just sailed off as cool as you please to Dublin, and, so they said, was seen walking down Grafton Street,[4] dressed up to kill, with not a feather off her. Well, those girls might be bad, she wouldn't say they weren't, but didn't they have a better time than sticking on toiling and moiling day after day with no thanks from anybody? . . .

The great thing was not to get in a stew or to be put on by anybody. If there wasn't anyone to help her, there wasn't anyone, and there was an end of that. And hadn't many another girl had her trouble, and got through it, and nobody a penny the wiser?

She washed the dishes, with her thoughts repeating themselves in gestures of defiance, and she became almost happy in her new boldness. Now she could think of Jim with indifference and even contempt. A poor, ordinary, skulking fellow he was, doing an ordinary, mean sort of thing, and then afraid to face the band. In love with him? Not a bit of it! A bit of a fancy perhaps, but she was well out of it and over it now, thanks be to God.

It was as if she had suddenly grown a year older, having come to read things aright that an hour or two ago had been confused and dark. She went about the house, finishing her work with a determination that perplexed Mrs. Fitzroy, and made her suspicious. 'It's not her afternoon and evening off,' she pondered. 'What's she up to now, I wonder?'

It was almost strange to Bridget, so conscious was she of this change in her outlook, to find that the streets outside looked just the same when she went out to take Paula for her walk.

She went up the long stretch of Pitshanger Road, staring with unwonted curiosity about her. It was, she thought to herself, as if in the usual way you went along never looking up to take

more than a penny-worth of notice of anything about you, and thinking your own thoughts about the things that had happened to you, and the things that might happen to you, and then one day you got a shove when you weren't expecting it, and you were startled into taking heed of things that had been there all the while only you hadn't bothered your head about them.

Those houses now, big and dark and silent, frowning away there they were, as if the devil himself had taken possession of them. Sure, no one would know who and what lived in a house the like of that one there unless you went up and knocked and were shown in. And the cracks in the pavement stones, streaks of black amid grey, hadn't they a queer way of shooting up into your eyes, so that having noticed them you had to go on noticing them. And in front the wide, hard road stretching on and on with an errand boy bicycling down. There was the red 150 'bus just turning the corner; and, coming towards them, a white dog rooting along with its nose to the pavement. A nice garden that one was, with its yellow chrysanths.; and there was a woman in blue with dark hair sitting by the window. More cheerful-looking than the other houses it was, and she did right to be proud of her garden as surely she would be. Then, if you looked up, there was the still, grey wintry-looking sky over everything . . . no change in it as far as your eyes could stretch.

Bridget puckered her brows, feeling suddenly tired.

What did these things stand for? What sense was there, after all, in them? They were things that went on, and would always go on whatever misfortune happened to a girl like herself, but what meaning was to be got out of them it would take a wiser girl than she was to find out.

Paula, who had been walking on a little in front to make Bridget think that she didn't choose to own her, or have anything to do with her, got tired of her own company, and decided to talk.

'Bridget, did you see that lady with the red face and the fur coat who went by on the opposite side? Mother knows her. She's Lady, Lady . . . something, I forget what. That's a very important thing to be, you know,' she added condescendingly.

'Yes, Miss,' said Bridget dreamily.

---

3. A common parish or townland name in Ireland, meaning big rock.
4. A major street in the shopping district of downtown Dublin.

'Do you have ladies in Ireland? Like Lady Jane Grey and Lady Duff Gordon. And Lady Astor.[5] You don't, do you?'

'Ah, sure every country has them. You read about them in the papers.'

'Not every country. You *are* ignorant, Bridget. You couldn't have them in France, because in France they talk a different language. They talk French. I learn French with Miss Rowbotham. But you're too stupid to understand things like that.'

'Haven't I told you not to speak that way to me, Miss Paula?'

'Mother does.'

'Aren't you brought up the way you know how to speak nicely?'

'Yes, if I want to.'

There was a silence. Bridget thought without resentment that it was a pity Paula wanted so much pleasing, and was so unfriendly. But there was no use taking to heart what a child would be saying. A spoilt little madam she was, and no mistake. But then she was an only child, which was an unnatural thing for a child to be.

As she turned home the melancholy of gathering dusk took possession of her. Paula, who had chattered more than usual, disturbing Bridget with her questions and comments, and achieving a triumph in being the one to remember they had forgotten to buy more eggs, was now quiet; and Bridget realised that in her growing weariness something had escaped from her. This was the time when most she was put in mind of her own country with its creeping mists that counselled resignation. She heard the doleful cries of the grey birds that would be wheeling in from the mountains, and saw the tree in the middle of the field at the back of her mother's cottage. It would be bare-looking now standing lonely against the sky. Inside, there would be a warm fire, making the red patchwork rug look gay and snug. And the little statue of Our Lady smiling down from her niche on the wall. Her mother would be chatting, maybe, to Mrs. Connolly over a cup of tea, bragging, for all that she knew to the contrary, about one of her children or another. Bridget herself perhaps it would be, who had a grand post as a help in London, where everyone was rich and there were more people than anywhere else in the whole wide world. Except perhaps New York, in America, where Kevin was. Ah, well, her mother was an old woman now, and she ought to be allowed her bit of romancing.

It was queer and lonesome when you got thinking of home. It was a pity in one way that she had crossed the water, though two fortune-tellers had told her that that would be her fate, and that she would marry a handsome, fair man, and keep her own servant. Well, there was a laugh to be got out of that bit. She had certainly thought Jim might be her fate when she met him. She had never been very partial to the one in the Isle of Man; and he was dark and small, but Jim had really been the spit of the fortune-teller's description. Well, she had had her wish to travel, and now she was landed with one of the crossest women you could ever meet, a bold, forward child, and nothing but cross words, however much she killed herself with trying to do work in new ways that no one had ever heard of before.

She sighed gently, and raising her eyes murmured under her breath, 'Blessed Virgin, help me. Sacred Heart of Jesus, have pity on me!' It was no use her getting worked up. There was nothing she could do. That was a certainty. She hadn't the price of her fare home till the end of the month. And home was no place to go to anyway if it was a child of badness she was bringing with her. Bringing scandal into the parish and disgrace on her poor mother. Ah, well, what did they say? That there was no use crossing a river before you came to it.

That policeman was taking a good look at her. The cheek of him! Now he was turning his head to stare after her. She knew it without looking round. Would there be any harm in her glancing back casual-like and giving him a bit of a smile? Better not. Paula might notice and then come out with it. She was cute[6] enough to watch her even

---

5. Lady Jane Grey (1537–54) was a puppet in her father-in-law's scheme to prevent Mary Tudor from ascending the throne. She was Queen of England for nine days, until his plan failed. She and her husband were executed. Lady Lucile Duff-Gordon (1821–69) was an author and translator best known for her *Letters from Egypt 1863–5* (1865) and *Last Letters from Egypt* (1875), written in Egypt, where she settled permanently for the sake of her health in 1862. Lady Nancy Astor (1879–1964) was the first woman to sit in the British parliament: when her husband, Lord Waldorf Astor, entered the House of Lords, she was elected to his seat in the House of Commons.

6. Acute.

when she seemed to be seeing nothing at all. But, all the same, the knowledge of the policeman's interest pleased her, as if a sore place had received balm, and as they turned in at the house, she said cheerfully to Paula, 'Here we are. Now you'll get your tea that you've been wanting.'

There was a light in the kitchen! That meant the mistress was down there. It would be just like her if she had been prying into the drawer where she kept her paper-backed Smart Novels. Three of them, Bridget remembered, there were. She might even have thrown them out as rubbish. And she hadn't finished 'When Love Flies in at the Window.'[7]

Mrs. Fitzroy said nothing to her maid, but welcomed Paula expansively, 'Well, darling. Had a nice walk?'

'No,' said Paula. 'Just ordinary. Up to the shops. And Bridget forgot to get the eggs till I reminded her. So we had to turn and go all the way back when we got to the Underground.'

'That was my clever little girl to remember for mother.'

Bridget carefully deposited the parcels on the table. She didn't like to say anything to the mistress unless she was spoken to. Mrs. Fitzroy was so different from Mrs. Reynolds, who had kept the Isle of Man boarding-house, and who was always ready for a chat. She might as well go upstairs and take off her things. But when she was half through the door, Mrs. Fitzroy called her back: 'Oh Bridget! Put on the kettle before you go up. And when you come down make some buttered toast. Three rounds. I've laid the table.'

Bridget put on the kettle ungraciously. 'Why, I wonder, couldn't she have done a little thing like that without calling me?' she asked herself. But when she came downstairs again she found the kitchen empty, and kneeling in front of the fire she looked round and took pleasure from the warmth and familiarity of the scene. She liked the room best in the evening, when Mrs. Fitzroy only came in for a few moments just to see if her dinner was going all right. Then each item became definitely hers. The light shining on the plates on the dresser, and the firelight warming the blue and red tiles; the clean-scrubbed, yellow

deal table. Oh, it was a pleasant enough room when the little red curtains were drawn across the window. Quite friendly like. She liked looking, too, at the shiny red bread-bin with its big black letters; and the tin tea-caddy that stood by its side with its picture of an Irish girl and an English girl and a Scotch girl all joining hands. And there was the old basket chair that she would be able to give herself a rest in later.

The day was getting through, thank God for it; and the furniture and crockery and tins that had been pushed and banged about were now given a moment of peace, so that they took on a quiet and solid look that was never theirs in the morning, but which was the one natural to them.

Look at that now! She'd been and burnt the toast. Smoking away in blackness. No good doing anything with it. SHE would turn up her nose at it, however much it was scraped. She'd best hide it behind the clock on the mantlepiece, and do another piece. Perhaps she'd have it for her own tea. Or else throw it in the dust-bin when the mistress was off out of the way.

Mrs. Fitzroy was already in the dining-room when Bridget took up the tray. 'You've been a long time, Bridget. I suppose you burnt the toast or something. I thought there was a smell.'

'No, I did not, ma'am.'

'Why have you been so long then?'

'Was I long, ma'am?'

Mrs. Fitzroy made an impatient movement, and then lifted the tea-pot towards her.

'Is there anything else you're wanting, ma'am?'

'No. Oh, yes. Bring up the biscuits I bought, please. They're in the pantry. And put them in the biscuit-jar first.'

Bridget enjoyed her tea. She made herself more toast, and buttered it generously. It wasn't as if she had had much to eat that day, she thought to herself, noticing her appetite approvingly. And she wouldn't be having anything for her supper beyond a cupful of cocoa. Mrs. F. was very close with food for the kitchen, and the meat didn't taste like good Irish meat at all, it didn't. She'd probably be having a good look at that loaf, the old skinflint. It couldn't be helped. Didn't she have to keep up her strength some way? And she wasn't going to be treated much worse than a dog . . . even if that one expected her to find nourishment out of the smell of what was cooking for herself and the master.

---

7. Possibly *When Love Flies Out O' The Window* by Leonard Merrick (1864-1939) (London: Pearson, 1902), reprinted frequently up to the 1940s.

That put her in mind. She pulled out the drawer in the table. No, the three of them were there safe. If they hadn't been, she'd have asked straight to her face, so she would: 'I see you've borrowed a book of mine, Mrs. Fitzroy.' Or, 'Might I trouble you to give me my book back, ma'am.' 'I think you have interfered with my property, ma'am. Might I ask why?' Quite easy and polite, but enough to show that she wasn't intimidated by HER. That she knew her legal rights, which she did. There was the bell! Ah, she could wait. She wasn't going up till she had finished her tea comfortably. Wasn't she ever to be allowed a bite of food quietly?

When she was washing up the tea things, she heard Mrs. Fitzroy go into the kitchen, and she also heard the bread-bin being ransacked. A moment later her mistress came into the scullery wearing her gravest face.

'Bridget, I'm not sure that there'll be enough bread to last us till the baker comes to-morrow. When you have finished you'd better run out to Paley's and get another loaf.'

'Yes, ma'am.'

'There ought to have been sufficient, but it seems to have gone very fast to-day.' There was a note of interrogation and disapproval in her voice, which Bridget ignored.

Mrs. Fitzroy sighed. 'When you've got your things on, tell me, and I'll give you the money.'

Bridget hurried up. It was a pleasure to go out by herself in the evening, even if only to post a letter, and ponder over the recipient. Now she shut the door behind her with alacrity, and it seemed to her that the lamps to her right and left threw a friendly regard her way. There were two young men standing at the corner as she passed, and one raised his hat, and said 'Good evening.'

Of course she didn't reply, but hurried on, her heart beating faster. The nerve of that one! But it was very gentlemanlike the way he raised his hat. Better-class than when they just coughed. Not that she cared that much for any of them! Weren't all the men the same? A few soft words to wheedle you, 'What wonderful eyes you've got!' and that sort of light chat, and then away, chasing after someone fresh. Oh, she knew them, the sort they were.

Still it cheered her up being out of the house on her own, and feeling the keen air against her face. And the little lighted shops looked gay.

Would you believe it — the Christmas cards were out already! When she had got the bread she was loth to leave them, and sauntered slowly, looking in the windows.

How pretty the red apples and yellow oranges looked all piled up together in that tasty way! Those writing-pads at threepence each were very cheap. A real bargain! Then the array of magazines and papers with their bright red and blue and yellow covers adorned with pictures of smiling girls and illustrations of frocks and cami-knickers (some with patterns to be given away) held her eyes. That was a notion! She'd treat herself to 'Home Notes'[8] that evening. Sure, the way things were, didn't she need something to take her mind out of herself?

The woman inside was friendly, and said it was a lovely evening, very seasonable. 'Indeed it is,' replied Bridget heartily, and went out feeling really light-hearted.

As she had come so far she might as well slip along and have a look to see what was on at the cinema. It was only a minute away; no one at all would be the wiser.

She walked fast now, feeling a little guilty; but when she got to the entrance she lingered fascinated. 'The Sins Ye Do,'[9] the big film was called; and there was a huge picture, at the side, of a beautiful girl standing outside a great palace of a house with a baby in her arms. She wouldn't be married, because she was poorly dressed, and looked desperately miserable. That would be where her mother and father were living, and they wouldn't have anything to do with her any more. Staring big blue eyes the girl had.

It would be a tragic film. Wasn't it a pity now she couldn't see it, for how did she know but that she wasn't going to be the same way as that young lady. And she might have got a hint or two from the film what to do. But, of course, that girl was extra beautiful, so that she'd be sure to meet someone after a bit who'd fall really in love with her, and forgive her everything. There'd be a fade-out with a man in evening dress kissing her over a cradle with the baby in it, and saying that he'd never hold it against her.

---

8. *Home Notes* was founded as a penny monthly woman's magazine in the 1890s; it merged with *Woman's Own* in 1957.
9. Possibly based on Emmeline Morrison, *The Sins Ye Do* (London and Edinburgh: John Long, 1923). I haven't discovered a film by this name.

Or if it were a really tragic film the girl would die a beautiful death with everyone sorry and weeping that they'd been so unkind, and hadn't known that she was more sinned against than sinning. Or something. Anyway, it would be lovely to see it. It was after six and people were just starting to go in. She watched a young man clink money down while his girl stood waiting. They'd have a grand time inside with the orchestra playing, sitting so comfortable on the red velvet seats, with the warm darkness wrapping them round. And after a while she'd put her head on his shoulder . . . Well, no use standing there.

She found she had lost her light-heartedness as she walked quickly back. The picture had come as a sharp reminder of something she had almost forgotten. But she felt a little important, too, because the picture's subject had brought her the assurance that many people would regard her as a sad victim of man's wickedness. 'She gave her all and he left her to pay the price.' The sentence came into her head, and she muttered it to herself with a sort of satisfaction. She, Bridget Kiernan, was one of that sort of woman, more shame to the man.

She was so deep in her thoughts that she was taken aback when she heard the sharp edge of Mrs. Fitzroy's voice: 'Here you are at last. You've been long enough to buy out the whole shop.'

'They were sold out at Paley's, so I had to go along to Bowen's,' said Bridget glibly, and admired herself for the way she had found on the spur of the moment a feasible explanation. She'll hardly take the trouble to go out to Paley's and see, she assured herself.

Mrs. Fitzroy looked disbelieving. 'That's queer. I've hardly ever known Paley's sold out before. They always keep a few loaves for the next day. Some of their customers only like it when it's a day old. And in any case, I couldn't have thought it took half an hour even to go to Bowen's.'

Bridget was silent. She had said her say, and if Mrs. F. didn't like it she could lump it. She noticed that her mistress had changed into her brown crêpe de chine frock, and powdered her face. You could well see where the powder ended on her nose. If she only knew she needn't think it improved her, because it didn't. She was a plain-looking woman, and a cross woman, and she wasn't going to demean herself by answering her for all her disagreeableness and innuendos.

Mrs. Fitzroy turned angry. 'Understand this, Bridget, when I send you out for bread, I don't mean you to go for a walk. This isn't your evening off, you know. Be quick now, please. I want some coals taken up to the study.'

Bridget went upstairs to her room without a word, and banged the door behind her. She sat down on the bed and thought murderously of Mrs. Fitzroy. She imagined her in hell, and the flames scorching her that she screeched out for mercy. But there wasn't one would have mercy on her. Wasn't it true that they said all Protestants had to go to hell? And it might be so. Certainly it would be true for a woman with a temper the like of hers. And meanness! And ugliness! And sneakiness! And her thin, pinched voice!

She mimicked it to herself. 'Understand, please, I don't want you to go for a walk. It's not your evening off.'

'I'll walk out of here, anyway, Mrs. Fitzroy. And I'll have my wages, if you please!' That would have been a great thing to have answered her with. And she'd say it, too, if there was much more of her impudence. Sure a black or a slave would get more decently spoke to. They would so.

She pulled off her hat and coat, and went down with a feeling of going into mortal combat. No one in the kitchen. SHE'd be up in the study with Paula. What was the time? Twenty after six. A bit more, for the clock was slow. Into the dirty cellar again, and yet was expected to keep as clean as a shining angel in Paradise.

She clattered about, and after a while her rage wore down. The joint was cold; that was a mercy. Potatoes on to boil. She'd brought in a cauliflower. When Mrs. Fitzroy came down to make what she called a sweet, Bridget went upstairs to lay the table. Mr. Fitzroy had returned, and was in the dining-room, measuring out a whisky and soda.

'Good evening, Bridget.'

'Good evening, sir.'

That was a nice smile he had given her! But it made her feel shy like, being there all alone with him.

Mr. Fitzroy observed Bridget without appearing to do so. She seemed a bit down in the mouth, he thought. Not bad-looking. Pretty hair, and good eyes. Irish, she was. Cheer her up a bit. No harm in a friendly word.

'Well, Bridget, how do you like London?'

Bridget knew she didn't know. She'd only been up to London proper twice. Once with Jim, for THAT! And then when she had had tea in a Lyons,[10] near Oxford Circus, and been terrified of getting lost. Still he wouldn't expect her to say all that piece.

'I like it well enough, sir.'

'I suppose it strikes you as very big and noisy after the country. So much traffic, and all that.'

'Oh, indeed, you're right, sir. Very big . . . And very smelly,' she added thoughtfully, remembering her first impression on arriving at Euston.[11]

Mr. Fitzroy was a little puzzled by the last word. But at the same time he thought he heard a sound on the stairs. 'You'll soon get used to it,' he said hastily; and went thoughtfully out of the room. It wouldn't do for Dorothy to hear him talking to the maid. She was always so suspicious. And he didn't want her to know he was having an appetiser. Women always called it, 'Drinking again!'

Bridget knew why the master had gone out so suddenly. She could have told him the mistress was safely away for a few minutes. Ah, well, the poor man had a good heart, and you could only pity him, seeing the sort of woman he was married to.

Sadness came upon her as she smoothed the tablecloth. The room looked pretty now with the pink shade over the electric light. And the rose-coloured chrysanths on the white tablecloth, and the glittering silver on the mahogany sideboard. But it didn't belong to her. It wasn't intended for her. There didn't seem anything that belonged to her in the whole wide world.

She went to the window to draw the curtains. The sitting-room of the house opposite was lit up, and a piano was tinkling out a tune. It was meant to be gay; yes, 'Where's my sweetie hiding?'[12] That was it. They played it at the pictures. But it was mournful sounding all the same, coming across the dark, quiet road. The more the person playing banged it out, the more it caught at your heart-strings, because of the lonesome way the notes flowed into the silence.

There she was, playing the fool again! Standing, dreaming! Bridget pulled the curtains to with a determined hand, and went back to the kitchen.

Mrs. Fitzroy looked up from the table at which she was standing.

'Don't you think, Bridget,' she said in a voice that sounded strained in her effort to speak pleasantly when she was moved by a spasm of sharp irritation, 'that you might give your face a wash? There's a clean towel on the roller in the scullery.'

Bridget did not trust herself to speak. She would have burst into tears if she had. And she couldn't disobey the old beast without saying one word. She put the tray down, and, glad to get her back turned, went into the scullery.

'Oh, God, can't she die? Kill her! Kill her! Kill her!' she prayed violently as she splashed a little water on her face down which tears of anger and mortification came rolling fast. 'Bad luck to her in her life and in her dying and in her death. Oh, kill her, kill her, kill her, and may she suffer the tortures of the damned, the eternally damned!'

She choked a sob in the towel. To be after humiliated that way! To be spoken to like that! Told to wash! She, Bridget Kiernan! An Irish girl! She'd get her own back somehow, she would so.

She stood for a moment getting her breath under control. Paula came running downstairs and into the kitchen. Bridget turned back to the basin, and washed her hands noisily. Anything to give herself a few seconds more out of the sight of the mistress. She wouldn't give the old bitch — she didn't care; that was the right name for her — she wouldn't give the old bitch the chance to see she'd been crying.

She went back with the water-jug filled. The mistress didn't turn round from the fire, but Paula stared at her, and said in her shrill voice: 'You *have* got a red face, Bridget. You look as if you'd been crying.'

'Run upstairs, Paula, till you're called to have your cocoa,' said Mrs. Fitzroy firmly; and Paula, running after Bridget, pushed past her so that Bridget nearly stumbled. 'Will you look where you're going, and don't push,' said the girl so sharply that Paula was surprised into saying, 'Sorry.'

Ah, but the dining-room had a blessed coolness with no one in it. If she could only lock the door, and stand there for ever by herself.

10. Lyons was the name of a chain of British cafés, particularly popular with women.
11. London train station, terminus for the boat train from Ireland.
12. Recorded by Isham Jones and his Orchestra, Chicago, Brunswick label, November 1924.

The piano across the road was still playing. She listened to it awhile, her lips apart and a dreamy look in her eyes. She and the pain inside her, and the little song in the night, and the silence that surrounded them were all part of one another, or seemed so in some queer fashion that brought its soothing message. After a while she stirred herself, and gave a little thoughtful nod. That was the way things were, God pity us all!

When dinner had been taken upstairs there was Paula to be seen to, and the cocoa made for them both. When they were drinking it the bell rang, and Bridget took up the pudding and clean plates on a tray. As soon as she got in the room she knew they had been talking about her because of the sudden conscious silence into which they were immediately plunged. She held her head high as she went out of the room.

Then Paula was sent for to say good night; and Bridget had to prepare her bath. She felt a sudden impulse to be determined and hasten things along.

'Will you come on now, Miss Paula,' she called irritably from the bathroom.

Paula came running in with just her little vest on. 'Didn't your mother say you were to wear your slippers and put on your dressing-gown?' Bridget demanded mechanically.

Paula disdained reply. She put her fingers in the water. 'It's too cold, turn some more hot on.'

Bridget obeyed, testing the water with her hand meanwhile. Paula decided to be naughty. 'I don't like you putting your dirty red hands into my bath water,' she said, wrinkling her nose with disgust.

Bridget turned off the tap with a jerk. Then she brought her face close to Paula.

'You don't speak to me like that. Do you hear me now? You don't speak to me like that.'

There was so much passion behind her words that Paula, abashed, got into the bath without replying. She meditated bursting into tears, for she knew that in the ordinary way it was just because Bridget, like the previous maids, was afraid of her crying and bringing up her mother that she got her own way. But Bridget was different to-night. Perhaps it wasn't worth it.

Going back to get Paula's nightgown and slippers, Bridget looked at herself in the wardrobe glass. She had a vague impression of a queer-faced girl with a lot of dark hair, eyes that seemed all black pupils, and a white apron over a black dress. It was strange and queer that that should be herself, Bridget Kiernan!

Paula was put into bed and left with her picture-book till her mother should come and put out the light. Bridget went down, and cleared away the dinner things. Her brain had stopped registering anything; she felt very tired, and her back ached; only a dull hate burned within her.

As she cleaned the knives she heard voices in the hall. Were they after going out? Please God, they were! She stopped and listened attentively.

Someone had gone upstairs. She'd take the silver up to the dining-room; that would give her a chance to see what was going on. Returning, she saw Mrs. Fitzroy come down the stairs with her hat and coat on. 'Oh, Bridget, I'm going out. Have you washed up?'

'I have, ma'am.'

'Wait a minute then.'

She went into the study and lifted the coal-box lid. 'You'd better bring up some more coals.' When Bridget came back, she found Mrs. Fitzroy still in the room. Mr. Fitzroy was sitting reading the evening paper. So *he* wasn't going out.

'If anyone calls, Bridget, tell them I'm out, but that Mr. Fitzroy is in.'

'Yes, I will, ma'am.'

No one had ever called since Bridget had been there, except the mistress's brother. And once the master had brought home a friend. But SHE always told her to say that. She had told her to bring up more coal when it wasn't wanted, because she didn't want her to come in the room with the master there by himself. She saw through her well enough.

Bridget returned to the kitchen, and stood waiting till she heard the front door slam. There it was! She relaxed. The old devil was out of the house for a while. Thanks be to God for it!

'Isn't it a pity she hasn't taken herself off for good?' she muttered to herself. 'Begob,[13] she's the worst vixen in the world; and it wouldn't hurt me at all to know that she'd fallen down where she stood and died. Not at all it wouldn't.'

She shook her head, the sense of all her wrongs coming uppermost to her mind. Then she sat down in the easy chair, and buried her head in her arms. Soon she found herself shaken by sobs,

13. By God, an exclamation.

the sobs that had been pent up within her for the last hour or two. They grew more and more unrestrained till she recollected herself in a fright, and with her hand pressed to her mouth got up and closed the kitchen door. The master mustn't be let hear.

Now for a good cry. It would relieve her feelings. She sniffed and whimpered and gasped, while her nose became swollen, and her eyes grew small as they disappeared under her puffy eyelids. Sometimes her grief would slacken in its expression for a moment; but then the remembrance of one or another of her troubles and resentments would surge up again, and she would renew her sobs. It was a shame for her! A shame! And no one cared a tither.

At last she cried herself out. At first she was conscious of nothing but that her skin seemed pressed tightly over the top of her head, and that her body was giving little uncontrollable shivers. She poked up the fire and turned her chair round to it. For some while she sat thus, smoothing out the pain at the back of her forehead with her fingers.

Slowly odd fragments of thoughts began to drift to and fro in her mind. The delf was still in the scullery, she'd have to put it away. Wasn't it very still? You couldn't hear a sound . . . it was twenty to nine . . . the big picture would about be on at the cinema, what would happen to the girl in it? Anyway there'd likely be a happy ending . . . There was her 'Home Notes,' and she didn't feel like reading it at all . . . she'd had all her pleasure spoilt . . . would those two fellows have picked up two girls? . . . were they having a good time? . . . It was a shame the way she was put on by the mistress . . .

'Bridget!'

My God! Was that someone calling? Bridget went quickly to the door and opened it. It was Mr. Fitzroy. He was standing at the top of the kitchen stairs.

'Yes, sir.'

'Are you there, Bridget? I thought you might like to look at the evening paper?'

Bridget went quickly upstairs, feeling the perplexity suggested by her temperament. Did he mean her to take the paper or not? He might be depriving himself.

'Ah, sure, it's all right, sir,' she said hesitatingly.

'I've finished with it.'

'Thank you very much, sir.'

She took the newspaper and turned her back as quickly as possible, leaving Mr. Fitzroy to return to his chair disturbed. The girl had been crying. There was no doubt about it. Poor little soul! It seemed a bit thick for her to be crying down there in the kitchen while he sat there. Was she homesick? Her home was a long way away, and the Irish, of course, were very patriotic. Or Dorothy might have been sharp with her? She had been complaining at dinner about her being stupid and dirty.

He went into the dining-room, and poured himself out a whisky. It was a pity he couldn't go down to the kitchen and comfort the girl. But too dangerous. He'd never forget Dorothy catching him out kissing that girl — what was her name? Alice — they had had a couple of years ago. Never gave him a chance to forget it, she didn't. Ah, well!

He returned to the fire. Dorothy would be back soon. He'd speak to her about it. Or better not. Women were the devil to one another. The girl wasn't bad-looking either. Something soft and appealing about her. The way she spoke perhaps.

No good letting his mind run on women.

Bridget had carefully spread the paper out on the table. She stood for a moment, looking at it unseeingly, and feeling warmed by the kindness shown her. 'That's a decent one,' she thought to herself. 'He deserves a better one for his marriage bed. Wouldn't it be grand now if I could get a place with a man by himself, as his housekeeper. Someone who'd know how to treat a girl polite?'

She moved into the scullery and restored the crockery to its right place. Then she sat down again.

Well, she felt better now that she'd had her cry out. She wouldn't have minded a bit of a read. Nothing like a good story to take your mind off things. Only she ought to think of her position really seriously like. Suppose she really was going to have a baby? She'd give herself another week, and then, God help her, if she didn't come on, she'd be sure she was in the way.

The terrible part of it all was that there wasn't a creature she could talk it over with. Now these London girls would be sure to be up to all sorts of tricks for stopping things. There was the girl next door that she'd passed the time of day with. But could she go and say to her . . . ah, of course she couldn't. It wouldn't be decent.

There was her mother. 'My dear mother, I take my pen in my hand to tell you I have bad news for you. There was a fellow I met, and I am sorry to say he has got me into trouble . . .'

Oh, Holy Mary! What would her mother say, and she reading a letter with news the like of that? Oh, didn't it sound terrible when you came to put it into words. A disgrace to her poor mother she was, and a disgrace to herself . . .

Tears were unloosened again, but her mind was no longer still. It seemed to her she was weeping for remorse at her wickedness, and the thought vaguely comforted her. The first thing she must do was to repent. Wasn't there the Blessed Mary Magdalene?[14] She'd pray for her intercession. And she'd say an Act of Contrition[15] as if it were to the priest himself. First she'd confess.

Bridget knelt down on the floor and with folded hands repeated the Confiteor.[16] When she came to the words, 'I have sinned exceedingly in thought and word and deed, through my fault, through my fault, through my most grievous fault,' she had to pause for sobbing. The magnitude of her sin overwhelmed her, and it seemed to her that she had been hard and unashamed up to now.

Then she repeated the Act of Contrition. That was better. Sure, God would forgive her if she truly repented and offended Him no more. And she did truly repent. Perhaps He'd let her off having a baby. Now a Hail Mary. 'Hail Mary, full of grace, the Lord is with thee: blessed art thou among women, and blessed is the fruit of thy womb, Jesus. Holy Mary, Mother of God, pray for us sinners, now and at the hour of our death.'

The familiar words soothed Bridget. There's nothing so comforting as a Hail Mary when deep troubles come upon you, she reflected, and repeated the invocation several times. Then she said the 'Hail Holy Queen',[17] and then a Paternoster.[18] And then she turned back once more to the words which gave her the most healing, 'Holy Mary, Mother of God, pray for us sinners, now and at the hour of our death.'

Hadn't Father Reilly once preached a sermon — she remembered the time well, because she had been wondering if it would be right to pray for a bit of money so that she could get herself the new cute hat in Murphy's — hadn't he said then that the Blessed Virgin never denied her intercession to those who approached her in sorrow and contrition?

That was true. There were the words, 'A contrite and humble heart, O God, Thou wilt not despise.'[19]

She blessed herself and rose. She felt tired, but there was a sort of happiness with her all the same. There was great help in saying a few prayers, and no one could say else. She had been brought up badly, and that was the truth. It was her father's blame. For ever cursing and swearing at the priests and saying they were the bane of the country. God forgive him! Well, he was dead and knew better now. God spare him and deliver him from distress and torments. 'Deliver him, O Lord, from eternal death.'[20]

In a fashion it was due to him and the way he'd never set an example that she'd lost her beads which Father Reilly had blessed. In the Isle of Man she'd never given a hoot. Well, indeed and indeed, it would be different from this time on. She'd be chaste and pure; she'd put away all thoughts of badness, kissing and such-like. She'd buy a new Rosary as soon as she got her money; she'd go to Mass every Sunday; she'd go to confession . . . .

But that last wasn't too pleasant to think about. What would the priest be after saying at all? Would he tell her to confide in her mistress? She wouldn't do that. Never. After all, the mistress was a Protestant. Would he let her off if she told him that? He might.

You could never tell what an English priest would do. He might be poking his nose in her affairs all the time. Hadn't her father always said they were the meddlesome fellows, making trouble and bringing ill-luck wherever they went.

What was she thinking? Ah, nothing! Nothing at all. (She crossed herself quickly.) She wasn't meaning any harm. But it was difficult. The more you thought the more troublesome everything was.

14. Disciple of Jesus, traditionally figured as repentant for her promiscuity.
15. Part of the Roman Catholic rite of confession.
16. The confessional prayer.
17. Prayer beginning, 'Hail Holy Queen, Mother of Mercy'.
18. The 'Our Father' (Matthew 6:9–13).
19. Reportedly the dying words of St Teresa of Avila quoting Isaiah 66.2 and the Psalms.
20. From a payer by St Cyprian (d. 258).

A red bank of cinders broke and fell to the bottom of the grate. Bridget roused herself, and gave the fire a poke. Watching the flames dart swiftly upwards, she meditated whether she would put some more coal on. Better not. SHE'd march in, stare hard at the fire, as if she'd never seen such a thing in all her life before, and say something about wasting coals at night-time. What was the time? Half nine. She must mind not forget she had the shoes to clean. Would she want hot milk when she got in? Another saucepan to clean. Never cared what trouble she gave.

Her evening off to-morrow. Nobody to meet. It might be a good thing to go up to the Church, and see if she could find anything out about a priest. Somebody might be giving her a tip about getting hold of the decentest one; someone with a bit of sympathy in him. Ah, there was no call yet. There mightn't be anything in it after all. And she worrying herself to flitters with no need. It was the thinking and worrying that had you driven distracted.

A wind blew up, murmured, complained, and sank down. Bridget heard and shivered. You never knew your luck, of course, and it was a queer world to be in. Anything might happen to anyone at any time. God help us all!

It wouldn't hurt her at all to die at this moment. It would be a way out of it all. No more getting dog's abuse from morning to night. No more cleaning out the grates. Eternal rest. She couldn't kill herself or else she'd go to hell maybe. 'The horrid darkness, the hissing flames, and the excruciating tortures.' Ah, no! But to die quietly as she was sitting there. Heart failure. And then people would be sorry. Mrs. Fitz. would be shown up for what she was. Her mother and the neighbours would be weeping and crying when they heard the news. 'Is it Bridget?' they would say. 'Is it Bridget Kiernan?' 'She that went to the Isle of Man and London?' 'Poor Bridget's gone.' 'Is she now?' 'That's bad.'

Was that the front door? Bridget sat up alertly. Yes, a key was turning in the lock. It was the mistress back. If she came down, she'd better look as if she'd been reading the paper. Oh, she'd gone in the room to the master. Better go and get the shoes done.

As she was knocking off the dry dirt into the coalbucket, she heard Mrs. Fitzroy call:

'Bring me up a cup of hot milk, please.'

'Yes, ma'am.'

She filled the saucepan and brought it to the fire. There was only a little fire left. What'd she'd best do was to hold a paper in front. The paper on the table would do well enough. The master had said he'd done with it. Unthinkingly, she held the newspaper to the fire, her heart heavy again with apprehension. There was no happiness possible when that one was about.

A flame singed the edge of the sheet, and Bridget was only just in time to prevent it catching fire. The fire would do now. But the milk wasn't near boiling. She tested it with her finger. Only tepid. Had she better go up, and tell the mistress that the fire was nearly out? But it was like taking poison to go near her. And she didn't like speaking in front of the master.

Her predicament was decided by the study bell going.

That was terrible. Mrs. Fitz. didn't often ring the bell, at least not so late in the evening. It meant she must be in one of her tantrums again: would it be that she'd get herself scolded in front of the master for being so slow with the milk?

When she opened the door of the room, Mrs. Fitzroy was sitting on the couch, looking very solemn, while Mr. Fitzroy appeared to be reading some book intently. 'Oh, Bridget, I should like to see the evening paper if you've finished with it. And isn't the milk ready?'

'Yes, ma'am. I'll bring it up, ma'am. The milk's nearly ready, ma'am, but the fire isn't very grand.'

'I suppose you mean there's no fire at all. Why didn't you say so before? Well, bring up the saucepan here, and I'll see to it on this fire. And a cup and saucer. On a tray. *On* a tray, remember.'

'I will, ma'am.'

Bridget went downstairs with her cheeks burning. She hated it when Mrs. Fitzroy put on that thin voice with no sort of expression in it at all. As if she were speaking to a piece of furniture, and as if she, Bridget, wasn't really flesh and blood, and couldn't be expected to understand things like other people. Those English airs!

She fetched the tray and pondered for a moment on the question of putting the saucepan on it as well as the cup and saucer. Perhaps not, because it would make a dirty mark. But if she didn't it would be wrong . . . And then the paper that was burnt! Arrange it so as not to show the singed place. Sure, she'd probably never look at it. She went upstairs again.

Mrs. Fitzroy nodded. 'All right, I'll see to it. Give me the saucepan, and leave the tray on the desk. That's right. You'd better get off to bed now. It's after ten. Is your alarm clock working correctly?'

'It is, ma'am.'

'And you've cleaned the shoes?'

'Yes, ma'am.'

Mrs. Fitzroy dismissed her with a nod. Mr. Fitzroy turned over another page.

She went back to the kitchen feeling guilty and yet triumphant. She had got out of that all right, so long as the mistress didn't take it into her head to walk into the kitchen and see the shoes only half done. Ah, well, it wouldn't take her long to polish them off. It was no use telling her that she hadn't finished them, and give her a chance to be disagreeable in front of the master.

Upstairs, Mrs. Fitzroy poured out the milk and then started to read the paper. As she turned it over she noticed the burnt place. 'With all respect, Harry,' she said suddenly, 'I don't think Bridget does much newspaper reading. I am quite sure she has never looked at this the whole evening — just used it to get the fire going. Look! Newspapers are not in Bridget's line. She keeps incredibly dirty-looking paper novelettes for her reading purposes.'

'Sorry, my dear. I won't give it her again.'

Dorothy Fitzroy was unable to control a grimace of irritation. Men were so stupid; answering you as if you had said things you never had.

'It isn't that. I'm sure I should be only too glad if she showed an intelligent interest in anything. I don't want her not to get every consideration. But she's an absolute fool. And a liar. That's what I object to most.'

Her voice grew shriller, and her husband didn't reply. Usually he was more sympathetic than this. 'You think I'm hard on her? Well, just take today. At twenty past seven there was not a sign of her, and I had to get out of my bed, and go and call her. That meant that I had to cook the breakfast myself so as to get you off in time. You ought to have seen her standing gaping at me, incapable of doing a thing. Just the same with luncheon; she's always wriggling out of doing things, so that it's simpler to get them done myself. And it makes me feel ill, positively ill, in

any case, to see her dirty hands — she never washes unless she's told, and I *did* tell her this evening, unless, of course, she's going out for the evening, and then she's dressed up and powdered — well, it makes me sick to see her hands poking into the food we're going to eat.'

Mr. Fitzroy murmured agreement.

'It's the same with errands. She forgot to get the eggs this afternoon when she was out with Paula, until the child reminded her. And after tea, when I sent her to get some more bread — there's nothing wrong with her appetite, I'm always having to get extra bread and tea and potatoes in, and butter — she took over half an hour over it. And then pretended they were sold out at Paley's and she had had to go just a few doors further on to Bowen's. What do you think of that for a story? A child could see through her. Walking up and down staring at the shops as cool as a cucumber of course. And the way she throws food away. After all we're not millionaires. When she was out I found in the dust-bin a huge piece of toast she had thrown away. Burnt it, you see, and then sneaked it away, thinking I should never see. She's always burning bread. And she throws away half the potatoes with the peel.

'If she was only willing to learn, I'd never say a word. But she's not. She lets you do anything rather than do it herself. Just stands by and stares at you, without raising a finger. And if you speak a word to her, then she goes away and cries. Or else looks like a thunderstorm. I really sometimes think she can't be all there the way she goes on.'

She paused, and Mr. Fitzroy saw a reply was expected. He moved uneasily, remembering Bridget's swollen, tear-stained face. 'Perhaps she's homesick?'

'If she hasn't got over that by now, she ought to. She came to me of her own free will, didn't she? And she'd been in the Isle of Man before that. Though she's obviously never been properly trained. You don't seem to bother about me, but I can tell you it's not very pleasant having a girl going about the house all day looking like a sick cow. As if she might burst into tears at any moment.

'And she hasn't gone up to bed now. I told her to go off, because I was determined she shouldn't have any excuse for not getting up to-morrow. But she calmly disobeys me. It's waste of time saying anything to her. But I believe I know what's she doing.'

Dorothy got up suddenly and went to the door, opening it very quietly. She went a few steps along the passage, and then listened. Presently she returned and closed the door.

'As I thought,' she said triumphantly. 'She's cleaning the shoes. You heard her say, didn't you, that she had done them?'

Mr Fitzroy pursed his lips gloomily, and nodded.

'Another lie! Then she was afraid I'd find her out. So she sneaks down, and does them on the quiet. That's the sort of thing I'm always having to put up with. You see for yourself now?'

'Why don't you dismiss her then if you're not satisfied?'

'I expect it'll come to that. But it's no joke getting girls in these days. They're nearly all as bad. Or unkind to Paula.'

Mr. Fitzroy let his eyes return to his book. He wished Dorothy would go to bed so that he could have another whisky.

Mrs. Fitzroy observed him with resentment. He was not really sympathetic. You worked from morning to night to see that the house was run properly, and got no thanks for it. People seemed to think you *liked* being disagreeable. As if it wouldn't be far easier to let the maids do as they liked and not give a button, like some women. The house would be dirty, and bills run up, but it wouldn't matter to them. Or apparently it wouldn't. Just give Harry the chance to see how uncomfortable he would be if she didn't look after things. It would make him sing a different tune then . . .

But she was tired to death of it all. You wore yourself out coping with dirty, ignorant, lying sluts, and no one cared . . . no one cared.

Bridget passed the door, and though she was going softly, Mrs. Fitzroy, who had been waiting for the sound, heard her. There the girl was, she thought, creeping up to bed like a thief. Well, if she had any more trouble getting her up in the morning she'd give her notice. She'd made up her mind to that!

She turned her attention to the leading article headed 'More Efficiency,' and read it with approval. It comforted her, for it secured to her the feeling that she was in the right. Cleanliness, speaking the truth, punctuality, capability, were things that mattered. The whole country would be in the work-house otherwise. And she and Henry would be in the workhouse, if she took her hands off the household helm (something like that the paper said, and very rightly). It was the individual's contribution that mattered. Well, she would go on doing her share, whether she got any sympathy or not!

Upstairs, Bridget was lying in bed wrapped round in a blissful feeling of security. She had made a discovery. She was safe after all. No baby on the way! Wasn't that the great mercy? God had answered her prayers. The Blessed Virgin had not interceded in vain. After this you couldn't say but that there was a great deal in religion. Oh, she'd keep her word to Our Blessed Lord, and be a good girl for keeps. Wait till marriage after this scare! It was she was the happy girl, with the relief of it. The mistress didn't matter, not at all she didn't. She'd give her notice one day soon, see if she didn't. It wouldn't be difficult to get another job. There was a great shortage of domestic servants, so the papers were always setting forth. A job now where she'd see a bit more life would suit her grand. She must mind and remember to get the beads all the same. Sure, God was good, and it wasn't a bad world, if a queer up and down one at that.

KATHLEEN COYLE

(1886–1952)

from:
LIV (1928)

[*Liv* was first published with an introduction by the English feminist writer and intellectual Rebecca West (1892–1983), who had known Coyle from her early days in London. West praises *Liv* as a novel in which Coyle has finally found appropriate subject matter, a critique of the self-indulgent dislocatedness of Paris intellectuals in the 1920s. Coyle had herself lived in Paris, where she had known Nora and James Joyce and their circle, but her object is the modernist evasions of more minor talents. Rebecca West had named herself after the heroine of Henrik Ibsen's *Rosmersholm*, and like much Irish work of the period *Liv* shows the influence of Ibsen, not least in the Scandinavian origins of the eponymous heroine. Liv goes to Paris to discover some kind of fulfilment, falls in love, but decides to leave her lover to return to her home. The following extract is the final passage of the novel. *Liv* was first published in London by Jonathan Cape in 1928. The text here is from the first edition.   S.K.]

It seemed ages to Liv before Sonja came. She sat on the edge of Olaf's tumbled bed and buttoned and rebuttoned the linen cover of the eiderdown, grinding out her thoughts like a mill: 'I am here. I am here and he is alone. I have left him alone. I have deserted him.' He had expected her and she had not come. Now that the panic of her escape was settling, it seemed the grossest betrayal. She was a coward. She was abased before him and before her own conscience. Barbra had greater courage. She felt proud of Barbra's spirit, understanding her, as she sat on Olaf's bed teasing his eiderdown. Her humiliation was so great that it was a torture to her. She went over to the window twisting her hands. Behind the grey-blue of the trees Trangfoss fell. The water fell in a great powerful flow, no weakness in it, no wavering. The surf edged it like flowers. The summer had gone. Everything had that cold grey look to which only the snows brought redemption. She would write to Per Malom to tell him that she was here, here with Aunt Sonja, about whom she had spoken. She would explain nothing of her flight. It was

beyond explanation. If she could tell him anything it would only be that she was so unhappy, that she had had to come. She had made up her mind in a moment, hearing names she loved, in the midst of a crowd of writhing, clutching people. Fascinating — like serpents. Per Malom had had a strange look in his eyes when she had mentioned Aunt Sonja, and he had said: 'That means there will be nothing to tell.' She remembered perfectly. It was direct of him, prophetic. It fastened her contract with him. Well! There was nothing to tell. There was only this terrible revelation within her own being that would make her different as long as she lived.

Immediately she had yielded to the impulse to return it obsessed her, blinded her to its full meaning. It was only now, when she had actually arrived, when it was clear beyond doubt that he was *there* and she was *here* that she began to take in the significance of what she had done. She had come back. Yes, she had come back. She had never, she realised now, meant to stay — not from that moment on Stortoppen when she had so valiantly declared her desire to go and had been granted such sudden permission. Some germ in her blood, some instinct as in a migratory bird had cried out to go and had been appeased by the liberty of going. She had taken the voyage, and at the end of the journey she found Per Malon. She had found Love. He remained for her, in the midst of automata who would vanish, and he created her in his image. He was hers and she was his . . . and utterly beyond possession. He would never be obliterated. In that brief spell she had reached his life — his childhood, his frustrated mother, his love for his father, his passion for the dark girl with the rose in her hair, his crazy wife and the baby that had never been born . . . and all the others. The others Sasha had warned her about . . .

Aunt Sonja stood in the doorway. She saw the girl's locked hands, and the locked expression in her eyes as she turned and found her. She entered and shut the door. She, too, had stood like that. It took her clear to her own spell of madness and the savagery of the longing that had been unabatable. It had abated. The years, the inexorable years, had gone over it. Out of it she had learned to pick up trifles. One is bent under the storm to count the grains of dust on the roadway. One learns to know trifles for trifles and see beyond them to the sum of human motives. People, she had discovered, failed one out of the aridity of their own natures, never for anything you had done. And it was only the small mind that sat in judgment, only the little defeated souls who caught at the weakness of the strong as proofs of equality. 'Liv,' she said gently, 'tell me only what you want to tell me, but there is no need to tell me. I know. I . . .' she broke the dumb years that had gone over it and showed her own agony. 'I also . . . we are like each other.' She felt the tremor go through Liv and pretended not to be aware. 'I felt it at once. It made me hard to you. I did not feel hard — as I must have seemed to you. The hardness was for myself, not for you.' There was silence between them like a spear, sharp with a wound fresh on it. 'I know, Liv. We are so swept down there. And when we are young, oh, my dear, it is impossible not to feel, not to . . . I can't put it clearly.' She was clasping her hands very tight, keeping an outward calmness that levelled her voice and bestowed peace on the girl at her side. 'It descends upon us . . . It is not of our choosing . . .'

'Oh, it isn't of our choosing!' the girl cried, putting out her hands and drawing them swiftly back again. 'Aunt Sonja, I feel as though my heart would break.' She turned away again towards the window.

Sonja moved closer without touching her. She did not do anything that would tear the girl's reserve. 'In that short time. It seems only like yesterday since you went away, since you were here.'

'Yes, yes.' It was only a few weeks. It was only, actually, for her, two days. Two days with Per Malom. Two days in eternity. Two days in heaven and hell. Two days in which she had run out from all shelter into the ruck of life; the battle and the hardness, racket and emergency, where men and women loved and died. They took the fine things, as Barbra took them, and enamelled them in bright hard colours to disguise them so that they would no longer be ashamed to possess them. Barbra was twisted in the hardness. She painted everything that reminded her of Norway

grotesquely as a flag upon the restlessness. Cut off from it as she was now, she wondered what it was all worth — this play of life? Something was missing. But what? What a fool she was to run away from it. She said it aloud. 'I have behaved like a fool.'

Sonja was reminded that it had been her own point of view. It was a minute or two before she spoke. 'No, Liv, it isn't being a fool. It is . . . taking things too deeply. I did.'

There was another pause in which their eyes met and read each other. 'I did not,' Liv said at last, slowly, 'run away, Aunt Sonja, from the depth . . . it was from the others.'

'Oh!' Sonja laughed sharply, 'they are the masquerade. Don't tell me, Liv, and expect me to believe, that you were afraid of them?'

'Oh, no!'

'Well, then?'

She had nothing to say. She thought absurdly of Jacob Fuller's rams and Barbra's little red foxes. Faces out of Mina Fuller's crowd flashed before her. While she had been there, amongst them, it was herself whom she had pitied. It was she who had seemed the one to be pitied, who lacked the right quality. And now she reversed it. She spilled them all out like a cup of water and they were lost in her own fjords. Only Per Malom remained. He would remain to the end. She wondered, the wonder darted through her if he would come up here to seek her in these solitudes, to find her. What would she do then? She turned to Aunt Sonja as though asking the question, and was filled with quiet. There would be no mockery, no cheating, no pretence — for either of them, if he came. All the same, she said: 'I feel as if I had been cut in two.'

Sonja said nothing. It was true. She had never really grown together again. Her sons had come to fill the gap in her being, to possess her with some of that measure which women need. When they would cease to possess her, if they ever did, the sense of wholeness would vanish again. She would disintegrate . . . She pushed her thoughts away, and put her arm round Liv and drew her towards her.

'There is something wrong with us in this Northland, Liv. We have become like the earth we inhabit. Our natures are white as the driven snow outside and full of dark passion beneath. It is all right for us here. Here we . . . we preserve our pride. When we go south, into warmer lands, we lose something of ourselves. We thaw, we flood over. We are not to blame. We have to be born down there to know how to deal with it.'

'You mean not to get broken?'

'We are too easily hurt,' she answered.

'But what are we to do?'

Sonja listened to Trangfoss, storing the music in her mind. She thought vaguely of Harald Christensen, he was only a name to her, and wondered what he could do for Liv. She let him go again. She remembered the morning of her own marriage in Trondjem. These things had nothing at all to do with Liv, for whom nothing had, in that short time, been consummated. She did not know what to say to Liv, and she said — more to herself than to the girl — with Trangfoss ringing against their ears: 'It is better, I think, to stay where we belong . . . where even the trees know us . . .'

MARY DEVENPORT O'NEILL

(1879–1967)

from:
PROMETHEUS AND OTHER POEMS (1929)

[Mary Devenport O'Neill is one of many Revival poets to draw on the Irish ballad tradition in her love poetry. 'The Queen's Song' alludes to the recurring tension between the demands of property — in this case of the land itself — and those of desire.]

The Queen's Song

Irish refrain: *Nach iad na fir maithe a phasas na mna gan spre.*[1]

1. Aren't they the great men who marry the dowryless women?

There is a glen where garlic grows:
'Tis good men marry women without money.
There fern grows too and spicy thyme,
And all the branches of the trees
Are hanging low with heavy bees,
With bees made opulent with loaded honey:
'Tis good men marry women without money.

Through all the glen a long stream flows:
'Tis good men marry women without lands.
A lengthy water muttering rhyme.
While through its shallows one by one
Throughout the day the red trout run,
Sun-drunken salmon lie in drowsy bands:
'Tis good men marry women without lands.

MARIE STOPES

(1880–1958)

from:
DEAR DR. STOPES: SEX IN THE 1920s (1978)

[Marie Stopes's much-publicized work on birth control brought her a large correspondence from people seeking advice. The following letters indicate that Irish people felt particularly far removed from medical help with reproductive control. From the first year of the Irish Censorship Board,[1] Stopes's writings, especially *Married Love*, featured prominently on the list of banned books. Edited by Ruth Hall and published in London by André Deutsch in 1978.   S.K.]

1. The Censorship Board, consisting of five members appointed by the Minister of Justice, began operations in 1930, under the Censorship of Publications Act (1929).

August 8, 1918, Belfast: Mr WA to MCS

My wife and I have read your articles in this and last week's *Sunday Chronicle* with very deep interest inasmuch as our case is a tragic example of the need for reforms you advocate.

We had been married 17 months and our ages are 25 and 24 respectively. A month or so before we married my wife had a very nasty sore on her lip. As it did not disappear with ordinary home treatment she went to a Manchester doctor about it, who gave her medicine saying that 'her blood was out of order and that she must continue to attend him'. In a week or so the sore disappeared, and as the doctor's remarks had not led her to believe there was anything very serious wrong with her, she discontinued to attend him. Shortly afterwards we were married, and about two months after that date her throat became very sore and small painful sores appeared on the private parts of her body. She accordingly went to a doctor here in Belfast, who after examining her and learning of the sore she had had on her lip, stated that she was suffering from syphilis and that she had got it by kissing some syphilitic person, or from a teacup etc. We were naturally astounded and much troubled to learn this, because by this time my wife had conceived — I made it my business to visit the doctor and asked him if in view of the circumstances he would not do anything to prevent her bringing into the world such a child. Needless to say the reply he gave was decidedly negative. She was put under mercurial treatment (3 grams a day) and has remained under it ever since.

Seven months ago our child was born. At birth he weighed 3½ lbs and in spite of all treatment, today he weighs a little over nine pounds, does not notice, is ruptured and in consequence of all the trouble we are having with him, our lives are a misery.

Added to all this my wife is now a week late with her menstruation, we fear she has conceived again and we are faced with the dreadful probability of having another child like the present one. Needless to say, if we knew how to prevent it, we could not have the slightest hesitation in doing so, for I consider it would be a lesser sin than to allow another child to be born . . .

August 21, 1918: MCS in reply

In reply to your letter, I must first express my sympathy with your case which seems an extremely hard one . . . As regards your present anxiety about your wife, I fear very little can be done. She must on no account take the various quack drugs that are on the market. The only thing I can suggest is that she should two or three days before the next menstruation is due, take several good doses of epsom salts and the very hottest baths she can stand. Operations for abortion are illegal you know and though in your case I am sure it would be justifiable I really do not know any doctor who would do it for her. Let her take plenty of good iron pills, every day (Widow Welch's are the best) and then try the hot baths at every menstruation period. I think there is a reasonable hope that you need not fear a birth . . .

February 3, 1919, Dublin: Dr LD to MCS

. . . I was wondering if you have published any book or leaflet embodying your theories that would be suitable for distributing amongst the labouring classes. Because here there seems to be a tremendous need. My work as helper and visitor in Baby Welfare work brings me into contact with many of these poor families and my heart bleeds to see the overburdened mothers struggling on under the strain of a far too rapidly increasing family. I am one of a great many others who have tried in all the first class chemists in Dublin for the appliances you recommend and have been met with an indignant denial of stocking any such things (in the very best chemists in Dublin I was told that they were not allowed to stock anything of the sort) . . .

February 6, 1919: MCS in reply

. . . As regards your question about a leaflet for the labouring classes, I have all along been conscious that that was the most urgent and necessary part of my work, and I have delayed publishing it only in order more securely to establish my general propaganda first . . . You confirm my general impression of Ireland when you tell me how particularly urgent it is in that country. As regards your difficulty in obtaining the pessaries, I am interested and surprised at the treatment you receive in Ireland. I should be very glad if you would let me have the names and addresses of the firms that told you they were not allowed to stock anything of the sort. I have already had more than half a suspicion that the authorities, who dared not attack me openly, are trying to counter the result of my propaganda in this way . . .

December 28, 1923, No address: Anonymous letter to the Mother's Clinic

If a married woman named Kennedy (Irish and slightly Irish accent) age 28–30, slightly below average height, slim, black hair, small face, from Camden Town area, brings to you an Irish girl (unmarried) named Miss MD (native of Co. Clare) age 22–24, average height, fairly plump, fair hair, full and round fresh-complexioned face, for the purpose of fitting your rubber cap on Miss D's womb, you will know that it is for an improper purpose. As the woman Kennedy is au fait with your procedure and knows that you take precautions as far as you can against abuse of the purposes of your Clinic it is of course certain that the single girl will pose as a married woman. A fictitious name will of course be used by the single girl who has a pronounced Irish accent but the married woman may or may not use a fictitious name. I am writing as one who thinks your Clinic is a boon for proper purposes and as one who knows that you guard as far as you can against its abuse for purposes of prostitution.

HELEN WADDELL

(1889–1965)

from: PETER ABELARD (1933)

[Helen Waddell's novel retells the story of Peter Abelard (1079–1142), the French scholastic philosopher and teacher, and his relationship with his pupil Heloise. It is a meditation on the erotics of teacher–student friendships and intellectual companionship, and of the heightening of passion in an atmosphere of secrecy, disguise, repression and frustration. In the following scene from Book III, Abelard turns from his work on the *Sic et Non*, a collection of unreconciled contradictory statements by the church fathers on such topics as priesthood and celibacy, to his last meeting with Heloise before he is attacked and castrated by her family and his philosophic enemies. S.K.]

Paris
July–October 1118

'It is our custom in our daily speech,' wrote Abelard, 'to speak of things as they appear to our bodily senses, rather than as they are in actual fact. So, judging by the sight of our eyes, we say it is a starry sky, or not, or that the sun is hot, or has no heat at all, or that the moon is shining more, or less, or even not at all, when these things, however variable they show to us, are ever in one stay. Is it any wonder, then, that some things have been stated by the Fathers, rather from opinion than from the truth? Moreover, many a controversy would find a swift solution if we could be on our guard against the same word used in different senses by different authors.'

The wheels drove heavily. He set down his pen and yawned. The first discovery of argument in one's own mind had always a glory about it: one could recapture something of it, watching it strike fire from the right audience: but this arguing at two removes, with a goose quill instead of the human voice, was a dry business. The preface to the *Sic et Non* must be written: it must lay down the principles for all judicious reading, whether of Holy Writ or of the Fathers: yet when he wrote, he rattled dry peas in the bladder that was his brain. It was a sullen day: there was no sun shining, and the gutters stank most vilely. He had spent most of it indoors, this Octave of St. Peter and St. Paul. He had gone to Mass that morning, in the hope that he might see Heloise, but she was not there, nor Fulbert. The

Schools were empty, for the men had gone a week ago, on the 29th of June, and there was nothing to take him out.

He yawned again and came back to his manuscript, turning the pages idly. Whether Adam was created inside Paradise or out: whether Eve alone was seduced or Adam also: whether James, brother of Our Lord, was first Bishop of Jerusalem or not: whether one already baptised may be baptised again or not: whether sin was remitted in the Baptism of John, or not.[1] He scowled as he read. He knew that these had served his purpose well enough, that they proved the contradictory authority of the Fathers: he knew too that he had dealt with weightier things: but none of them, on this perverse day, would meet his eye. Here were pages on virginity, whether it be prescribed or not: whether any human copulation can be without sin: whether the married priest is to be rejected by his parishioners or not. Undoubtedly he was being happily guided in his *sortes*.[2] '*Whether it is ever lawful for a man to marry her with whom he hath committed fornication.*' It caught him fair between the eyes. Well, what had they to say about it? He settled down to read sardonically. St. Ambrose: for any Christian to enter upon marriage with her whom he hath stained with unlawful defilement, was even as the sin of incest. Augustine,[3] on the other hand, that legitimate marriage with good intent may well follow an illicit union, and that true marriage may follow even adultery, if the husband of the first marriage be dead. Gregory the Great,[4] as grim as Ambrose. Council of Châlons,[5] against. Council of Aix-la-Chapelle,[6] against. Ivo of Chartres: that on the whole the Fathers, concerned for the honour of marriage, denounce it: but others, regarding the weakness and folly of their fellows with an instinct of compassion, would fain temper the rigour of the canon.[7] *And between their opinions seems to me just such a distance as lies between justice and mercy.* Abelard thrust the manuscript from him and was on his feet, snarling in sudden ungovernable fury.

Regarding the weakness and folly of their fellows . . . between justice and mercy . . . Let them keep their mercy till they were asked for it. Let them turn their backs like good old bilious Gregory and walk off holding their noses as from the sin of incest. Anything was more tolerable than this insufferable patronage of the saints.

'*Neither do I condemn thee: go and sin no more.*' He stopped his trampling up and down the room. He did not know where the words had come from; he had been in no humour to call them to his mind, and suddenly they were in him, like a memory in the blood. His rage dropped from him, though a pulse was still beating in his cheek. He sat down, utterly exhausted, and dropped his head on his hands. 'And because He would not condemn me,' he thought, 'I could lay my head in the dust.'

He sat there, thinking not at all, breathing slowly. The anger that had swept through him was like a heather fire: for a while it had left no life in him. The bell began ringing for Compline,[8] and in a little while he heard, far off and faint, the chant from the choir. It brought to him the memory, not of the evening office, but of that morning's mass for the octave of St. Peter and St. Paul, and the gradual.[9] Was there any so beautiful in all the circuit of the year? '*The souls of the just are in the hand of God, and the torment of malice shall not touch them: In the sight of the unwise they seemed to die, but they are in peace.*'

He sat still, the remembered chant stealing like a river through the chambers of his brain. The *torment of malice*: there was strange wisdom in the liturgy that could dare to bring that hissing serpent of a word into its requiem, secure that it could not shake its peace. *The souls of the just are in the hand of God.* He got to his feet, with a quick sigh. He was far from that yet.

Standing there, saddened as he was, a sudden wave of tenderness swept over him for Heloise. He could do so little for her, body or soul. Had he done right to bring her from Denise and her kind fostering, and her little son, and Hugh the Stranger, and all that gentle countryside, to these rank gutters and that dark house? *The torment of malice* — he put it from him quickly. There was

1. A series of scholastic controversies.
2. Excursions.
3. Augustine (354–430), one of the fathers of the Latin church.
4. Pope Gregory I (*c.* 540–604).
5. Châlons-sur-Saône, a town in east-central France.
6. Aix-La-Chapelle, better known by its German name, Aachen.
7. Church law.

8. The last service of the day.
9. Antiphon sung between the Epistle and Gospel at the Eucharist.

no hint of that. She had assured him, over and over, that Fulbert was kind with her, even tender, sometimes. She had looked white and cold, almost like a dead thing, at their secret marriage in St. Aignan's, but he and she had both spent the night in vigil in the church, and it was no wonder if she seemed ill and strained at dawn. As for Fulbert, he was another man. Every day seemed to fill out the little figure to its old comfortable roundness, the grease stains were gone from his cassock, and he crossed the Parvis[10] with his old jaunty step, nodding a little, like the more important of the pigeons. To Abelard himself he was even effusive. Once only, when he brought Heloise for the first time into the old man's presence, had he seen any trace of the old rancour. At first Fulbert had had eyes only for her. He had stood, holding her in his arms, shaking, half crying, his head buried on her shoulder. Then when he righted himself and turned to greet Abelard, there had been — or had Abelard imagined it? — the merest suggestion of a flicker in his eye, the flash of an adder into the long grass. Even if it were, thought Abelard, it would have been natural enough. And since then he had been complaisance itself.

Too complaisant. Abelard scowled at divers memories. Could the man not behave like her guardian and her uncle, instead of fawning on him like a gratified father-in-law, or worse still, leering like a pimp? Whatever ailed him, Abelard felt guiltier now in his rare visits to Heloise, than when he had been at his wits' end to contrive a meeting with her. And Heloise too seemed sometimes subdued. They laughed less, he thought sadly, yet from no weariness. Their passion was no less, but it had taken to itself a quality of tenderness that made it more poignant, less easily slaked: sometimes as she clung to him, he could feel her tears salt on his lips and could not question them, for they stung in his own eyes.

Well, he would go and see her. It was five days since he had been to the house, though he had written to her every day, and she to him. Fulbert had not been at Mass: it would be something if a touch of fever, or bile, had him in bed. Cheered even at the ghost of the possibility, he took his hood and went down the well of the stairs, and

out into the dead air of the July dusk. At Le Palais they would have nearly finished cutting the hay. He had smelt new-mown hay from the fields across the river, yesterday, but there was no wind to bring it to-night, or to carry off the smell that hung about the tanneries. That seemed able to cross the river at any time. Among the cobble stones at his feet a fish's eye from its decapitated head looked up at him with a kind of white malevolence. Of such, he said to himself, are the evening primroses of Paris.

He had to stand for a while on the doorstep, after knocking. The door was never open now: that was one change from the old days of unsuspecting intimacy that had persisted, even in the new understanding, and it never failed to irk him. For unless Heloise was watching for him, it meant that he must see Grizzel, and for Grizzel, reason with himself as he might that she was only an ancient bristled sow, he had a repugnance that was more than physical. He was superstitious about meeting her. It could spoil his eagerness, as the ugly chatter of a single magpie could jar into a spring day. She had never been more than civil with him: his first coming had made more work in the house, and only his careless lavishness had kept her spite from overflowing her greed. Moreover, of late it had gone against the grain with him to give her money: it seemed to him that he was placating a bawd. He gave it to Heloise for her, instead, bidding her not to say it was from him.

Had she guessed it was he at the door? The minutes seemed interminable. He was about to knock again, when he heard her grunting approach. She was watching him through the lattice of the grille, he knew, but he deliberately kept his back turned. At last he heard the bolts drawn, and the door creaked open. She looked up at him silently. More than ever the evil eye to-night, he thought. As a rule he asked for her master, but some obstinacy made him change his mind.

'Is your mistress within?'

Her lips curled back like an old bitch's snarl. 'Aye, *your* mistress is,' said she, then suddenly cringed. He had not struck her, but the eyes had a glance like a levin[11] bolt and her knees gave under her.

'It was a slip o' the tongue,' she mumbled, retreating against the wall. 'She's in her room, sir.

---

10. The enclosed area in front of a building, particularly a church.

11. Lightning.

Not with the master. You'd better not go near the master,' she cried after him, with a sudden return of the snarl.

Abelard stopped on his way to the stairs.

'Is your master ill?'

'Aye.' She looked at him, powerless and malevolent. 'God blast the pair of ye, that brought him to it,' she said very slowly. There was a sincerity in it that in some curious way robbed it of any offence. Abelard turned on his heel and went on up the familiar stairs, past Fulbert's room, the door closed, and on to the great room that had been his. As he climbed the next flight, and the step gave under him with its remembered groan, he heard her door open. He could almost feel the strained expectancy with which she would be listening.

'It is I, beloved,' he said, very low.

She said nothing, but he heard her take her breath. She had gone back into the room, and as he came through the door she closed it behind him and caught him. Neither of them spoke. That some cruel thing ailed her, he knew, without a word from her: knew too that all she wanted for the moment was the silent holding of his arms.

In a little while she sighed and held him away from her. 'Now nothing matters,' she said, with a ghost of a laugh in her voice. 'I have seen you again.'

She drew him over to the settle and sat down, still holding him away from her. She was very white and panting a little. In spite of the closeness of the night, she had a wrap muffled about her throat.

'Child,' he said, forgetful of Grizzel's news, 'you are not ill? Have these stinking gutters caught you in the throat?'

'No, no. At least,' she hesitated, 'it is a little sore. But nothing that matters. I have wrapped it up. Nothing matters, now that I have seen you.'

He looked at her, thoroughly uneasy.

'Is it swollen?'

She shook her head. 'It is nothing. It will be well again in the morning. No —' she drew the scarf closer round it and moved away from his outstretched hand. 'Please, Peter. At least, not just now. Let me talk to you a little first.'

She was more like herself now, and he thought it best to humour her.

'I was vexed,' she went on, 'that I did not hear you, to let you in. Was it Grizzel?'

'It was,' he said grimly. 'And in a good mood too. But tell me,' he suddenly remembered the news of Fulbert, 'she said your uncle was ill?'

Heloise nodded. 'I think,' she said quietly, 'he has had another stroke. Simon Trivet came and bled him.[12] He is sleeping now.'

Abelard was dumb for a moment. The memory of the first stroke, in this very room, was upon him. What had brought the second? He could hardly bear to question her, yet she was looking at him as if she would gladly speak, and could not bring herself to it.

'Were you with him? Was he in his own house?'

She nodded. 'It was before Vespers.[13] Geoffrey of Chartres was here. And,' her voice changed, 'Alberic of Rheims.'

Abelard uttered a stifled exclamation. 'Together? Did they come together?'

'No. Geoffrey came first, with a message from Gilles. You know the book of Ivo's letters that I have been copying for Gilles. Geoffrey was anxious to see it, because of some trouble he is having with the Count of Chartres. Gilles says he will be a great bishop, Peter.'

'Geoffrey? It is as wise a brain as there is in France.' He saw that she was eager to speak of indifferent things, and went on talking of Geoffrey and his brother Hugh, the Seigneur de Lèves. He would be a better successor to Ivo than either Bernard or his brother Thierry, he said, for Bernard cared too much for Virgil, and Thierry for mathematics, to have the charge of a great diocese, above all with a ruffian like Count Thibault to keep in his place. Besides, the De Lèves were as good blood as the Counts of Chartres, and that was always a help. 'Had you much talk with him?'

Heloise shook her head. 'He had hardly told my uncle his errand when Alberic came in. I had never seen him before. Very fat, and small eyes peeping. He said to my uncle that he had long had a great desire to see his relic, you know, that bit of the spine of St. Évroul, and my uncle was all flattered and happy and took him to his oratory. I do not believe he came for that, I think it was only to spy. And when they came back, Alberic began talking to Geoffrey, praising the schools at

12. It was common practice in early medicine to cause bleeding in a patient in order to relieve the symptoms of an illness.
13. Evensong.

Chartres and making little of his own at Rheims. I do not know why it is so much worse for a fat man to fawn than a thin one. But Geoffrey only laughed, and said that Paris had overtopped them all, and that Chartres was become no better than a grammar school for it.'

Abelard smiled grimly. 'That would please Alberic.'

'All the time he was watching me sideways. And then he looked down his nose and said that he had understood it was under a cloud of late, and that Master Peter Abelard was said to be beginning to repeat himself.'

'Well? Had Geoffrey anything to say to that?'

The light leapt in Heloise's eyes. 'He laughed, you know that light amused laugh of his. "Don't listen to the cockroaches, Alberic," said he. "Do you know that I had a deal more consequence in Rome as friend to Peter Abelard than as Bishop-elect of Chartres? They call him the Socrates[14] of Gaul."'

Abelard was crimson with pleasure. 'Geoffrey always was a good fighter,' he said. 'They used to say he was better at attack than defence, for by the time he had begun the first, there was no need for the second.'

'There wasn't, here.' Her eyes were shining. Then they clouded. She looked down at her hands.

'Well, child?' said Abelard gently. 'Did it annoy your uncle to hear me praised?'

'No, oh no,' she cried. 'I wish it had.' She was scarlet with mortification. 'I could not look at him. He sat, looking from one to the other, rubbing his hands and beaming and making little noises, and when Geoffrey had finished he began about its being very gratifying for him. Geoffrey tried to interrupt (I think he felt that something was wrong, without divining what it was), and said that as a canon of Notre Dame he must be proud to own you, but my uncle could not be stopped. He said that he had more intimate cause than that to be proud of you, for he had always regarded this child here — and he pointed at me — as a daughter, and to know her married to so great a man —' She stopped. She could go no further.

Abelard's hand tightened on hers. It was for her reassurance, for he himself felt nothing. It had come, then. Well, what of it?

14. Athenian philosopher (469–399 BC).

'Well, child?' he asked, so tranquilly that she stole a glance at him and took courage.

'Geoffrey had got to his feet and was saying something very loud about having to sup with Gilles, and Alberic coming too. But Alberic sat leaning forward, with his eyes darting out of his head. "Married?" said he. "I do indeed congratulate you on your — son-in-law," and then he turned to me, "and you," said he, "on your — Socrates."' She paused again.

'My uncle stood there, babbling and smiling. And I said, "I am afraid, Master Alberic, that with my uncle the wish has begotten the thought. It is his delusion that I am married to Master Peter, but it is not true." My uncle stood staring at me. I think he hardly took in what I was saying. They all stared. And then Alberic thrust his face nearer mine and said in that pasty voice of his: "You are not then his wife?"'

Abelard had risen to his feet. 'And you said?'

She had risen, too, confronting him, and smiling. 'I said I was your mistress.'

Abelard drew a sharp breath. Her courage slashed him like a sword. He stood for a moment gazing at her, his pride in her overtopping even his wonder. Then he went on one knee before her, and kissed her hand.

'Beloved, it was magnificent. But —' he rose to his feet, in sudden comprehension, 'your uncle —?'

She turned away . 'My uncle —' She stopped. 'Ah, Peter, you can imagine it. He was shrieking and then . . . he fell.' She sat down, as if her story was finished and there was no more to say.

Abelard was looking down at her, mentally filling in the gaps.

'Did he touch you?'

'He — Ah, what does it matter? I told you he was mad.'

Abelard stooped and unwound the scarf from her throat. She did not struggle. He stood for a while looking at it.

'So he clawed you. Like a wild beast.'

He dropped on his knees beside her, his head on her lap. He had brought her to this, his darling to the power of the dog.

'Beloved, it was only for a moment. They both pulled him away. He was tearing at them, too. And then suddenly he fell, in a fit. Geoffrey stayed and helped to get him to bed. And Alberic went for Simon Trivet, to bleed him. Grizzel is minding him. It is better for him not to see me yet.'

Abelard got up and moved over to the window. 'He is not ever going to see you again,' he said briefly. 'Heloise, for God's sake do not try to spare me. How long have you been in dread?'

'Do you remember the night we came? It was the look in his eyes when he turned to you. A little red speck, like on a viper's back.'

'I saw it,' said Abelard. 'I hoped you had not.'

'I was afraid for you, after that, every time you came to the house. It was one reason why I would never have you eat or drink in the house, unless I had seen to it myself, even brought up the wine from the cellar.'

'But for yourself? Was he harsh with you?'

She shook her head. Then suddenly she dropped her head on her hands and began crying quietly. He came over to her then and held her. She thrust her head into the hollow of his arm.

'It was the nights,' she said. 'I used to waken in the dark, and know that he was standing at the foot of the bed. He would stand there, stooping forward, peering at me. And then after a long while he would go away. I couldn't bolt the door, for he had the bolt taken away after that night he found us together. I used to lie and watch it, till it began opening.'

He could say nothing. His self-reproach was too bitter. She soon was quiet, lying in his arms. In a little while she touched his cheek.

'Now that I have told you,' she said, 'I think I shall never be afraid again.'

He disengaged her then, and set her down beside him, his arm still about her shoulder.

'Listen, beloved. I shall stay with you tonight, and to-morrow you and I will ride back to Brittany.'

She shook her head.

'I knew you would say that,' she said, 'and I have been thinking, as soon as I came up here by myself, what I must do. I knew you would not let me stay here. I do not think I could. But if we go to Brittany, it will be confirmation of everything my uncle has said. As it is, I think it was well they

saw him in his madness. They will believe more easily, even Alberic, that what I said is true, that it is his delusion. And so I made up my mind that I would go, for a while anyhow, back to Argenteuil. I shall tell Reverend Mother everything. She would know it, anyhow. She is like Gilles, in that. And I am not afraid of her any more. It is odd how much I have been thinking of her, of late. She is not a good woman. I used to think that she was even wicked. But she is strong. And she would never give away anything one told her. Besides, she is Gilles's cousin.'

Abelard had risen and was leaning against the window, silent. Were they born with the wisdom of the ages, these women?

'I shall even ask her,' Heloise went on, 'if I may wear novice's dress. And everyone will be told that I am going to take the veil,[15] in a year or two. It will give the lie to anything my uncle may say or do. Even if he brings witnesses of our marriage, it will not matter. For even if we were married, it would annul it if I took the veil.'

She had grown very white. Abelard turned from the window to see the still face, the eyes that looked out at emptiness. He tried to come to her, but he could neither move nor speak. Grotesquely there came to him the memory of the clerk who set a ring on the finger of the statue of Venus in the market place, and found the marble image bedded between him and his young bride. She had gone on speaking, but he had ceased to take it in. At last he managed a kind of strangled croak.

'Heloise, have pity,' he said.

The unseeing eyes came to life, in a flash she was beside him, clinging to him, kissing his sad eyes, his trembling mouth.

'Beloved, beloved, as if any vows could take me from you.' For a while they stood, holding one another. He heard her murmur under her breath, 'The gates of hell shall not prevail against us.'[16]

15. Become a nun.
16. 'Thou art Peter, and upon this rock I will build my church; and the gates of hell shall not prevail against it' (Matthew 16:18).

EIBHLÍS NÍ SHÚILLEABHÁIN

(1911–71)

from:
LETTERS FROM THE GREAT BLASKET (1978)

[In 1931 George Chambers, an Englishman, visited the Great Blasket Island, off the coast of Kerry, and made friends with Eibhlís Ní Shúilleabháin, a native of the island, then a young woman of twenty. On his return to England the two corresponded and Chambers preserved the letters, which offer a brief record of the last decades of community on the island. In these extracts Eibhlís describes her marriage to Seán Ó Criomhthain, son of Tomás, 'the Islandman.'[1] She indicates the decline of marriage and reproduction on the island as well as the closeness of family and friends. In a particularly lyrical passage she paints a picture of herself and Seán returning to the island by boat on their wedding night. Eibhlís eventually left the island in 1942. Additional extracts from this text appear at Volume v, pp. 1059–60.   S.K.]

12.5.1933

Well friend I am home at present with my future husband John Crohan, Tomás Crohan's son. I was married with John last Saturday (May the sixth), my twenty-second birthday the day before it, in Ballyferriter by Rev. N. Brown, P.P. We had only two motorcars. We came from town there and then off again to Dingle Town after Mass, few Islanders attended because of the weather being far from fine. I was in my little island home then again at about nine o'clock on Saturday night, I mean in my new house, but not yet the house of my dreams but some day yet with God's help. Well friend just another few words on this subject, I love my husband and my home, all the world has changed to me, everything for the better. Let us all praise God in Heaven.

12.6.33

Well good friend, the details of the wedding are few, but anyway I'll make my best to tell you. Mary and myself went out Tuesday before. We walked it from Dunquin into town (about twelve miles). We rested in town for a few days and then we brought everything necessary for the wedding day, which was Saturday after, such as a blue dress with white collar and cuffs, a long one too, a pair of black shoes, and a new shawl, and we dressed the same though Mary was not my bridesmaid for John's niece came from Burnham College Dingle that morning — named Mary Malone — and she was the one, then Pádraig was John's best man.

Friday evening John (my husband), Pádraig, Seán and my uncle came to town. My husband John came in to see me that evening and showed me the ring and told me to wear it so he could see would it suit my finger. Well I tried it on and it fitted all right so he took it away until tomorrow morning.

They stayed in another house in town and early Saturday morning a motor stopped at Mrs Curran's house and someone was knocking at the door. We were ready and we went out, there were two motors there, I did not go in with John at all, because it is said around here in every place that it is unlucky to go with him in the motor to church. Is it like that in London?

At eight o'clock the ring was fitted rightly on my finger and Eibhlís of the island was Mrs Eibhlís of the Island and everything was changed for the better thank God.

We went to town again and had breakfast in Keane's house and done lots of messages there again. We had some dancing there too and Seán was playing the violin and we all enjoyed the evening until rather late. Then we got all parcels and luggage packed and we had then a good drive to Dunquin.

The night was lovely, there wasn't a stir in the air and the sea was like glass. The moon was just coming up and now and then a black cloud which was passing would darken the world but when that would pass it, the moon would come out again and was surely looking down on a small canoe with four men rowing and two women seated in its end. The man next to the younger of the two men was the husband, next to him was the bride, so calm and lovely with her dark brown eyes admiring the loveliness of the world.

So now dear friend I am a very happy bride with a dear husband and home in this Island.

---

1. Tomás Ó Criomhthain (Tomás Ó Crohan) (1855–1937) was author of a celebrated Gaelic autobiography, *An tOileánach* (*The Islandman*), published in 1929.

PATRICIA O'CONNOR

(1908–*after* 1950)

from:
MARY DOHERTY (1938)

[Mary Doherty is the young Catholic companion to an elderly Protestant woman in a small Ulster town. The local big farm is owned by the Scott family, and after a party at the Scotts' Mary is raped by David, the elder son and heir to the estate. David wishes to marry her but cannot contemplate Catholic children inheriting the land. Meanwhile Mary refuses to marry him, although she is obviously attracted to him despite her anger. In Belfast David is attacked and shot by her republican brother. Eventually the tensions of the novel are formally resolved when David's doctor brother, Allan, discovers that Mary is infertile. Patricia O'Connor's plays and novels all deal with sectarian and class division in small town Ulster society. The novels have something in common with those of Anne Crone, but O'Connor, while not so subtle in her treatment of character and landscape, is more robust in her attitude to sexuality and forges strange dystopian resolutions to her plots. Perhaps the most interesting aspect of the following extract is the matter-of-fact attitude to the rape. Published in London in 1938 by Sands.   S.K.]

David Scott avoided the gratitude in her eyes. He had an idea that he were stealing under false pretences. He had no claim on her gratitude.

'Mary, you mustn't say things like that, and you mustn't want to be like me or anyone else. You're much nicer as yourself.'

'But I don't want to be like you,' said Mary unflatteringly. 'You're a Protestant and an Ulsterman . . . I mean a Unionist . . .'

He shook her playfully.

'You young rebel! Aren't you beginning early?'

She put her hand in his pocket, extracted his cigarettes, lit one leisurely, and stood up with a little gesture of impatience.

The man watched her with interest. She had lost every trace of her old awkwardness. She wasn't merely pretty; she was beautiful. And she was completely unconscious of herself. The combination was as fascinating as it was unusual. Such natural breeding didn't come out in people . . . unless it were in them, away back somewhere. Yet the chances were that she was a little waif Miss Dowie had picked up in the slums of Belfast. Could it be that there were thousands like Mary, scorned, kept down, given no chance . . . while all the time they had that something in them that only needed a breath of fresh air to restore a battered self-respect? Could the system he admired so completely be guilty of unjust . . . no, unnatural tyranny . . . the cream on top; the mud at bottom . . . An inevitable rule couldn't be reversed . . . He checked his train of thought sharply and turned to Mary.

'What have you against Unionists?' he asked teasingly.

Mary Doherty stared out of the window.

'Everything,' she said tensely. 'Everything in the world. They've tortured Ireland; they've mutilated her. God, how I hate them.'

'Mary, Mary,' David was beside her, shocked by her display of venom. 'A girl of your age to be so bitter! And do you hate me also?' he asked, determined to turn her thoughts from whatever it was that obsessed her.

Mary Doherty dropped her bitterness quick as light, and laughed merrily.

'Indeed I don't. The very idea! But you're lots of things I couldn't be . . . and if I could, I wouldn't . . . ever. We belong to different worlds, and I'd rather have my own world.'

She had put into words what he would have been bound to express in some form or another before the flirtation he contemplated could have commenced with any fairness to her. He was spared an unpleasant task, but he was not grateful.

*   *   *   *   *

Mary Doherty enjoyed the party that evening. During the early part of the night she saw little of David, who was undertaking most of the duties as host, Allan and Kathleen Porter, in view of their recent engagement, having claimed the privilege of being guests.

Though she had little opportunity of speaking to him, Mary noticed that David was not his usual sober self. He was not by any means drunk. She could not imagine David drunk, but she suspected that he had been drinking. There was a gaiety and recklessness about his demeanour that had needed something stronger than the stimulation of the party to bring to the surface. Mary smiled. David was the kind of man who would have been displeased with himself if he could see himself like this. The engagement must be responsible. She watched him admiringly. He was rather a wonderful man. Nothing upset his balance very far. David Scott was incapable of looking foolish. She didn't want to belong to his world, but it would have been nice if he had been someone else . . . She was mad, mad. How amused he would be if he knew what she was thinking. The thought of his amusement made a different girl of her.

Towards the close of the evening David was at last free to enjoy himself, and he immediately went over to dance with Mary. As he guided her skilfully through the crowded room she knew that her suspicion was correct. Seeing that he was leading her towards the hall, Mary remonstrated.

'David, you're half drunk.'

He made no reply until he had achieved his purpose and closed the door.

'I believe you're not far out, but I can kiss you at last. I've been watching for an opportunity all night.'

The girl's further remonstrances were cut short. Unwilling to create a scene, Mary accepted his kisses in silence. He didn't mean anything, she told herself wildly. He'd forget to-morrow, and she wouldn't ever forget. She escaped and rushed blindly for her coat. She wanted to get away. She ought never to have come. David Scott meant nothing, nothing. He'd kissed her because he wasn't sober. She'd had the most ridiculous ideas all afternoon, just because he'd called in to see her. There was neither sense nor reason to them. David Scott was drunk.

By the time she had her coat on she was in a more normal state of mind. Other people came in to find their coats, and Mary found she was able to chat quite naturally. She decided she'd go down and say good-bye to Mrs. Scott, and then she could go home.

But Mrs. Scott was delighted with the success of her party, and in a mood to distribute favours.

'Now, Mary, you're not going home at this hour by yourself. David!' she called briskly to her son. 'You'll see Mary home, won't you?'

David smiled at Mary's almost undisguised horror.

'Of course. I was looking for her everywhere. Just wait ten minutes until I see the others off.'

Mary sat making mechanical replies to Mrs. Scott's conversation. It was nearly half-an-hour before David came for her.

As soon as they were away from the house she turned to him.

'I wish you'd go back. I don't want you to come with me.'

He shook his head.

'That's childish. You're angry with me?'

'I'm not. I ought to be. You'd no right to . . . kiss me. I know you didn't mean anything, but —'

He stopped her abruptly.

'Didn't mean anything! Mary, I love you. I've loved you always, ever since I first saw you.'

'You can't . . . You're a Protestant. You don't know what you're saying. Please be sensible. Go back. You're not yourself to-night.'

He hesitated. She was right. He wasn't quite himself. She really did want him to go back.

Before he had come to a decision a sharp shower of rain began.

'That settles it,' he said. 'I can't let you set out in this. You'd be soaked before you were half way. Let's take shelter until the shower passes.'

They had come out by the farm entrance, which was nearer the village. David turned back and Mary Doherty followed him reluctantly. She would have preferred to go home, in spite of the rain. He pushed open the door of the barn.

'Stand in here for a few minutes.'

Mary hesitated. From the moment that David had kissed her she had felt that he had established a new power over her. She had been dominated by a warning urgency that she must get away from him and root this new element out of her mind. It was not only stark folly, but, things being as they were, it was wrong. She had no right to imagine that she loved David Scott, and he had no right to say that he loved her. There were certain laid-down rules too obvious to be forgotten or ignored. Once she got away and was alone, she would be able to get back to where she had been that morning . . . before David came to see her. Yet in spite of her urgency to avoid him, Mary Doherty did not suspect that she was in actual danger. She admired David Scott, and drunk or sober she did not contemplate the possibility of his harming her.

Noticing her hesitation, the man pushed her inside. He was dimly surprised at the roughness of his action, but his slipping self-control was carrying with it much of the veneer that in his more sober moments was habitual with him. In a normal frame of mind, David's sense of chivalry would have been easily aroused. But he was far from a normal state of mind.

He put an arm around her and drew her further into the darkness. Her furious resistance did nothing to abate his ardour; it reminded him of her as he had first seen her.

If she had kept her head she might even then have avoided precipitating a situation that was rapidly becoming inevitable, but in her terror she forgot everything but her desire to escape. She broke away, and rushed towards the door. He dragged her back. The barn was fragrant with hay . . . A few glasses of brandy, a shower of rain, the smell of withered grass — little things that strip a man of a not too adhesive civilisation.

Her low heart-broken crying at last roused him to a realisation of his action. Every decent human instinct in him forced him to an immediate decision.

'Don't cry like that, Mary. We shall be married at once . . . you know I wouldn't ever let you down. Ah, hush little one. Everything is going to be all right.'

His tender, reassuring tone soothed her. She was like a frightened child seeking comfort.

'David, what shall I do? What shall I do?'

He drew her gently to her feet.

'There's not a bit of use saying I'm sorry. That's not going to help now. But don't worry. I'll come to see you to-morrow, and we'll arrange everything. I love you, Mary, and nothing is going to stand between us.'

He went for his car, and as he drove round from the garage he wondered if his mother would hear. If so, she would certainly be curious as to why he had taken the car out after apparently seeing Mary Doherty home. The whole situation appalled him, but behind his masculine distaste of the row that was now beyond his powers of averting he was inwardly jubilant. He could not get out of marrying Mary Doherty, come what might. It was nonsense to say that compulsion made a man unwilling to fulfil his obligations. The knowledge that he was compelled to marry Mary Doherty was the only

cheering issue in the whole bad business as far as he was concerned.

He had known that he had drunk too much to Allan's approaching wedding. That, he had no doubt, was responsible for his criminal madness. Well, Allan could drink to his now. His mother would not take it well, but if needs be she must know the truth. There would be endless disputes over religion . . . but these were little things. They could not separate him from Mary Doherty. He hoped that Mary would be reasonable. It would make everything much easier. She had said that they belonged to different worlds, but that was over now . . . it must be.

CHAPTER IV

The morning post brought David a letter from Mary Doherty. He picked it out from among the letters on the hall table. It was unstamped. Mary had evidently given it to the postman that morning. He looked at the unfamiliar writing. It seemed odd that Mary Doherty's writing was strange to him. He opened the letter after making sure that the morning-room was empty.

She wrote:

> Dillon House,
> Ballyhinlin,
> Saturday.

Dear David,

You said last night that you would talk things over to-day. I am writing to you because I don't want to talk anything over, and I don't want to see you again.

I'm tired of trying to think of something that would be right for us both, and there isn't anything. You wouldn't sell the Grange to a Catholic, much less leave it to a Catholic heir, and if I had any children they would have to be Catholics, so what's the good of talking about it.

I wish things had been different, but in any case your family would have objected.

> Yours sincerely,
> Mary.

The resigned finality of the letter roused all the obstinate Ulster blood in David Scott. Dimly he recognized the Celt, the tragic, lovely, shadow, that bound men's souls and imaginations and against which words or deeds, kindness or oppression, wealth or prestige, nothing, nothing, nothing, wise or sane men might try could avail them anything.

It was ridiculous. Resignation was no part of David Scott's creed. The girl had been overwrought. When she realized the seriousness of her situation she would listen to reason.

'Good morning, David.' Mrs. Scott entered the room in her usual brisk way. 'Reading a letter from your beloved?'

David put the letter in his pocket and sat down at the breakfast table.

'Curious, aren't you?' he teased.

'Very much so. What's her name?'

David regarded his mother with a smile.

'Have a guess?'

'But surely I don't know her?'

'You do.'

'Do I? I couldn't really guess.'

'Well, she's turned me down in the meantime so it does not matter.'

'Turned you down!' Mrs. Scott stared at her son in blank astonishment. 'You mean to say that you actually asked some girl in Ballyhinlin to marry you and she refused?'

'Exactly.'

'Who is the girl?' The woman's voice was sharp with curiosity and surprise.

'Mary Doherty.'

'David! Are you insane? Do you know that girl's reputed history? You do know that she is a Catholic, that she has no family, that she is little more than a servant girl. I presume this is your idea of a joke. If so, I consider it in very poor taste.'

David frowned.

'I assure you I was never more serious in my life. I am not interested in Mary's reputed history. I do know that her parents are dead, but Mary Doherty is hardly responsible for that. She is not the only girl of culture and refinement who has been compelled to earn her own living. The fact that she is a Catholic has not prevented my falling in love with her, and I have no intention of allowing it to prevent my marrying her.'

His mother's face went white.

'David, this is enough to make your father turn in his grave. I have always depended on you, been sure you were reliable and steady, with a sense of responsibility, a realization of what is due to yourself and your family. Have you no loyalties to all that makes you what you are? You are a Scott, David, an eldest son. This place belongs to you, but it carries obligations. Your forefathers have been here for generations. You cannot smirch a name like ours for a passing whim; you have not the right, David. You have not the right.'

David rose. He, too, was angry. He was finding the shackles of tradition more irksome than his obligation to Mary Doherty.

'That will do, Mother. You have no right to suggest that the entrance of Mary Doherty into this family is an insult to any Scott, living or dead. You have nothing against her but a pack of snobbish prejudices. But please understand nothing you can say will make any difference; I shall stop at nothing in order to persuade her to marry me.'

'Sit down a moment, David. This is a bad shock to me. Perhaps I spoke harshly. It has all been so sudden. Two days ago you spoke of Mary Doherty as if she meant nothing to you. Something must have happened to make you come to so sudden a decision. Why should she write to you when she saw you last night. David . . . you didn't . . . you can't —'

His silence answered her, refused her the contradiction her intuition would have rejected.

It was typical of the innate justice of the woman that she did not blame the girl. The cruel, relentless, honesty of her breeding denied her any false comfort. Be she what she may, Mary Doherty was no designing minx. David had used his knowledge of her childish admiration to persuade her . . . With a feeling of sick horror the woman remembered that for the first time in her life she had noticed that David had been under the influence of drink the evening before. There was no escape. Slowly a sense of relief came to her; her son was not lost to all decency. He was prepared to stand by his action. Another man might have lied or remained silent, but not her son. Good blood told, even in wrong-doing. It was hard, but it must be endured.

When she spoke again David knew she had accepted the inevitable.

'The girl must become a Protestant.'

David's voice was gentle.

'Mother, it is not for me to make terms. If Mary wishes to remain a Catholic she must do so.'

'But surely she must see —'

'Let us hope so. I shall talk to her later. By the way, I think I shall go up to Belfast this afternoon. I'll probably stay with Allan over the week and we will both come down on Saturday.'

'Very well. You wouldn't like me to call on Miss Dowie?'

'No. You can do that later. I'll write to Mary, I want to give her time to think the matter over.'

He bent and kissed his mother, a rather unusual action for the undemonstrative David. Mother and son had never admired one another as at that moment.

★   ★   ★   ★   ★

The Grange,
Newton Laughton,
Saturday.

My Dear Mary,

Your letter distressed me very much. In respect to your wishes, I am leaving to-day for the City, and shall be staying with Allan for the rest of the week. By then I hope that you will be willing to see me and discuss matters in a reasonable frame of mind.

I can hardly imagine that you thought the matter over very carefully, judging from your letter. In refusing to marry me you apparently do not consider that you may be compelled to do so. I hope I make myself perfectly clear. It is hardly a time for beating about the bush, and you will forgive me if I do not put the matter as tactfully as I might.

I ask you to be my wife, and I assure you your religion is, and always will be, a matter for yourself to decide. We must discuss more distant possibilities as they arise. Why make yourself unhappy over problems that are at the moment very indefinite? You will find that these difficulties have a habit of solving themselves. When we leave Ireland (we shall be going back to India immediately after the wedding) we shall leave behind all this stupid intolerance and bigotry.

I am afraid I sound very unromantic for a suitor. But, Mary dear, you know that I care for you deeply. I feared greatly that I had lost your affection by my own mad folly. Since that does not appear to be the case, I must regard any other barriers as trivial. There is no question of my family objecting; if they did, it would not matter;

but I have spoken to my mother, and she is perfectly ready to welcome you into the family.

Drop me a line to cheer my exile. You know Allan's address, and remember, I shall come to see you on Sunday, so don't argue.

Yours affectionately,
David.

Mary Doherty read David's reply several times. She was alone, with no one to advise her. Miss Dowie would be kind, but Mary realized that David's offer would influence her heavily. Whatever he had done, he could not be accused of refusing to abide by his folly. Little though she knew of the world, Mary Doherty knew with many men unsolicited support might not have been as readily forthcoming. Hurt and saddened though she was, she was grateful for his loyalty. Miss Dowie would fail to see the impossibility of accepting it. As a Protestant herself, she must in the last issue take David's side.

There was no one on whose sympathetic support she could depend. Would she be strong enough to stand out against everyone, when even her own heart was playing her false? She longed for the kindly wisdom of Father Murphy. He would have known how to strengthen her in the hour of need. Fears of the emergency at which David hinted had never been absent from her mind. So much of the fabric of her existence had been destroyed that no disaster seemed remote. Her contented, untroubled life had become terrifying and sinister. She sank to her knees and sobbed out her desperation to her God.

'Mary, whatever is the matter?' Miss Dowie's face was eloquent of her bewilderment. 'You have been moping about all morning. I insist that you tell me.'

Mary's tragic eyes frightened the older woman. There was more here than a passing fit of depression. Besides, Mary was never moody, and seldom ill. The child was in serious trouble.

'I am tired after the party. If you don't mind, I think I should like to go to bed. My head aches.'

Miss Dowie laid a hand on the girl's shoulder. 'You cannot put me off like this, Mary Doherty. While you are under my roof I am responsible for you. If you are in trouble you owe it to me to let me know. Won't you trust me, Mary?'

The girl rose wearily, and closed the door. She had decided that Miss Dowie was right. From

David's letter she surmised that his mother must be aware of the facts. She knew also that David would keep his word. He would not permit her to evade an interview, and sooner or later Miss Dowie would hear the story. She might as well get it over.

'You have noticed that David Scott has been very friendly. Last night he was not sober. After the party he was to take me home. It began to rain, and we took shelter. I don't think he was entirely responsible for what he did; in any case he did what he wanted. I was not able to stop him.'

Miss Dowie's fury was ugly, her enraged grief was a strange contrast to Mary Doherty's hopeless despair.

At first the woman could not speak. She held the girl in her arms, fiercely, protectingly.

'Don't fret, Mary. Men are all alike, cruel and wicked, indifferent to anything but their own selfish pleasures. It is my fault. I thought he was a good man, that he would respect your youth. But he will pay for this. My God, he will pay. He will regret the day he laid his foul hands on you. I will have him hounded out of the country. The Scotts indeed! We shall see if they can cover this up . . . I could kill him . . . kill him with these two hands.'

Mary was shocked by her violence.

'Hush, Miss Dowie, please. The maids will hear you. You must not speak so. David did wrong, but he is not as bad as you think.'

'Not as bad as I think? If he had a spark of manhood in his whole make up would he not come forward and shoulder his responsibility? Bah! A Protestant and an Ulsterman, forsooth!'

'He is willing to shoulder his responsibility, as you put it; but, Miss Dowie, I cannot marry him.'

'You cannot marry him! Did he ask you?'

'Yes.'

'When?'

'Last night and again to-day.'

'He was here this morning?'

'No. I sent him a letter. I had a reply this afternoon.'

'Let me see it.'

Mary handed over David's letter. Miss Dowie's face changed as she read it. This letter had not been written to calm a terrified girl. David Scott was in earnest. He was fond of Mary Doherty, and he would marry her. One could be too hasty judging people. An unwilling man

would have accepted the girl's refusal. David Scott went out of his way to satisfy her objections. He had apparently over-ridden even his mother's objections. An admirable young man, in spite of his scoundrelly behaviour.

'But, Mary, it seems to me that he could not do much more. It is that you do not care for him?'

'No, it's not that.'

'Well, dear, there is really no tragedy about it. He obviously cares for you. I can understand that you are naturally angry. So am I. Very angry. But what is done cannot be undone. There is not a trace of condescension or unwillingness in that letter. Under the circumstances you are very lucky. Don't worry any more about it.'

'You seem to forget the question of religion.'

'But David is willing to allow you to remain a Catholic.'

Mary shook her head drearily.

'I know . . . but there's more to it than that.'

Miss Dowie moved impatiently.

'Yes, yes, I understand. But there is no point in looking too far ahead. Do you think it is wise to create difficulties at this stage? He is doing his best, Mary. You must meet him half way. As he very wisely points out, you can arrange . . . other things later. These things are a matter for mutual give and take between your two selves.'

'No,' said the girl fiercely, for she was arguing with herself as well as with Miss Dowie.

'No. I'm not allowed to take chances like that. There are no hazy borders, no half-observed rules. My Church will not recognize my marriage with David unless he gives a written guarantee that all the children of the marriage be brought up in my Faith.'

Miss Dowie stifled the inclination to say 'Tosh!' with an unusual effort of self-restraint.

'And you would expect David Scott, with his traditions and upbringing, the heir to a fine old Ulster property, whose ancestors have through the generations been Protestants — sincere, God-fearing, religious men, who fought and died for their creed when the need arose . . . you expect him to give such a guarantee! Mary, be fair.'

'No,' said the girl quietly; 'I do not expect it. But I, too, have traditions . . . even an up-bringing of sorts. My people have fought and died for their creed. That is not a big thing to do for a creed. Men of all kinds have done it for creeds of all kinds. We have done . . . are doing something far more difficult and distasteful. We have sacrificed prestige, position, power; all that was and is our birthright.'

The woman gaped at her, flustered.

'Now, Mary, Father Murphy told you himself that you ought not to look backwards so often.'

'I'm not looking backwards. I'm looking right here, in this place, at this time, and as far into the future as any of us can imagine. Didn't you say yourself that Irish Catholics make the best servants? And they ought to! They've had plenty of training. What was the use of abolishing penal laws when they are stamped indelibly on the minds of almost every individual of the Ascendancy Party in our Province? I could not expect David Scott to condemn his children. He is an Ulsterman, and he knows too well what it would mean for them. Don't you see how impossible it is?'

Miss Dowie did not see, but she saw the girl was excited, and she decided to leave David to plead his own cause. She did not believe that Mary would hold out against him, and in the meantime it was better to let the matter rest.

'You must act as you think right, Mary,' she said. 'But I pray God that you two will be able to come to some agreement.'

*   *   *   *   *

Allan Scott was not surprised at his brother's casual remark that he was thinking of marrying Mary Doherty if she would have him. He had heard David returning for his car on the night of the party, and since his arrival in Belfast the young doctor was well aware that he had a good deal on his mind. Any doubts he may have hopefully retained were scattered by the reference to marriage. Well, rows or otherwise, he damned well ought to marry her. They'd get on fine, if they could ever live it down in this charity forsaken spot. The kid thought the world of David, and there had never been much doubt as to how he felt about her. It would work well enough if people didn't interfere. At heart David was a decent sort, even if he had been a bit of a swine. He was just the kind to go off the deep end properly, once he set his mind on anything. That was the worst of these steady, reliable, conventional fellows.

Allan went straight to the point.

'Going to be a Holy Roman?'

'No.'

'Think Mary Doherty will make a good Orangewoman?'

'Mary has expressed a wish to remain a Catholic. I shall not attempt to influence her.'

'No; on the whole I'm inclined to think it would be waste of energy. But two prayers under one blanket, as they say in the country, isn't terribly satisfactory.'

David laughed in spite of himself.

'Allan, you are an annoying devil.'

'What about the kids?'

'What kids?' said David blandly.

'A married couple have been known to have children before this.'

David raised his eyebrows in assumed amazement. Allan frequently irritated him exceedingly.

'Interesting that. It must be marvellous to be a doctor, so well informed, and all that sort of thing.'

'Aye, just so. Especially "that sort of thing." But see here, laddie, you're dodging the issue. Am I right in assuming . . . how shall I put it nicely to suit your fastidious tastes?'

'Is this the Church Catechism, by any chance?'

'No. Just idle curiosity.'

David was becoming exasperated, yet he wanted Allan's opinion.

'Cut it out, Allan; it's not a matter for jesting.' Allan nodded.

'Just as I thought. In that case, David old fellow, you've got to be highly improper and consider your unborn sons and daughters. I once nearly proposed to a little Catholic girl, but she was so taken up with her children she put me off. Catholics are like that. No sense of decency. Imagine asking a fellow about his kids before he's married — perfectly disgusting.'

David was following the argument much too well for his own peace of mind.

'Just what are you getting at?'

Allan Scott swung round and faced his brother as he occasionally faced a particularly criminal patient.

'See here, David, Mary Doherty is barely twenty — an orphan without a relation in the world. We have no sisters, but if we had one I shouldn't care to be the man who treated your sister as you have treated this girl.'

David showed no emotion.

'You missed your vocation badly, Allan old chap; you'd have made a grand preacher.'

'Maybe, but thank God I wouldn't make much of a hypocrite.'

'And where does the hypocrisy come in, may I ask?'

'You may, and you'll get answered, whether you like it or not. You're sitting there pretending to yourself and me, and probably the girl herself, that you intend to marry her, and you have no more notion of marrying her than I have.'

'That's a damn lie.'

'It's not, David, and well you know it. You know you do not intend your children to be Catholics. You know as well as I do that Mary Doherty's Church will not stand for anything less. You offer to marry her on conditions she cannot accept.'

David looked at him.

'Allan, you are a Scott no less than I. You know our record. It is unthinkable that one of us should strike the name such a blow.'

Allan poured his brother out a drink.

'You can hardly avert a blow of one sort or another. A bastard on the horizon isn't going to increase the family prestige.'

David realized why he had been given the drink. He winced at the savagery of his brother's honesty. In his own way poor old Allan was as tied up by these cursed traditions as he was himself.

'Aren't you rather looking for trouble?' he said quietly. Actually he was trying to soothe Allan, not himself. He would have welcomed any eventuality that might strengthen his case with Mary and break down her insane fatalism.

'Looking for trouble! I think one in the family on that particular job is more than enough. David, I could very cheerfully kill you.'

David rose. There was no sense in going on like this.

'I know, Allan. God only knows what came over me. Think what you like, I intend to marry the girl if I can. But if the worst comes to the worst, you will keep an eye on her and let me know?'

'Oh, go to hell,' said Allan violently.

* * * * *

Miss Dowie greeted David Scott without a trace of her usual manner. 'Mary has told you?' he asked. She nodded.

'I made her.'

'I'm glad you did. Is she fearfully upset?'

'No. But you must be careful. It is going to be very difficult, David. She's afraid of those priests.'

'Where is she?'

'In the dining-room. David, be kind to her. She's so young, she does not understand.'

David Scott smiled ruefully.

'She's got all the cards, Miss Dowie. I fancy it is Mary Doherty who is going to be unkind.'

They faced each other. The man was more nervous than the girl. He went to her and kissed her gently.

'You did not write to me,' he said reproachfully.

'No; you said you were coming, and I waited. There was nothing else to say.'

'Mary, tell me one thing. Are you afraid of me?'

'Yes, I think I am.'

'Don't you know I would be good to you? Won't you try to trust me again?'

'It's not that, David. It's really not you I am afraid of; it's myself. I know what I ought to do about this, but I'm not as strong as I ought to be. But if you know what is right you must do it, mustn't you?'

'But you surely do not think it is wrong to marry me?'

'But I do.'

'Why?'

'You read my letter. What is the use of going over the same ground again? You know the difficulty. We cannot pretend it does not exist. You cannot accept the conditions the Church lays down, therefore I cannot marry you.'

'You are putting me in an unbearable position.'

The girl's eyes filled with tears.

'Ah, no, David. Do not say that. I am not asking you to do anything, except to refrain from urging me to follow a course I cannot follow. I do not expect you to be disloyal to yourself. None of us is free. We do what we must do.'

David Scott took the girl in his arms.

'Mary Doherty, I love you. Neither of us will be really happy if you send me away. Surely love and happiness count for something. You cannot hurt yourself and me like this. I won't let you.'

Mary Doherty freed herself angrily.

'And who are you, David Scott, that you should imagine you can destroy my soul as you have destroyed my life? "If thine eye offend thee . . ."[1] aye, though that eye represents love and happiness. Do you think I would sell my God for anything that you can offer? I wouldn't dare. I'd be afraid, David . . . like Judas was. I expect he thought he could buy wonderful things with his silver . . . but he didn't. It was just used to purchase a grave-yard for the burial of strangers.'[2]

1. Mark 9:47.

2. Judas Iscariot betrayed Jesus to the chief priest for thirty pieces of silver. After the arrest Judas was remorseful and returned the money. The priests used it to buy a potter's field for the burial of foreigners. Matthew 26:14–16; 27:3–10.

BRENDA CHAMBERLAIN

(1912–71)

from:
THE DUBLIN MAGAZINE
(1942)

[The Welsh poet and artist Brenda Chamberlain drew heavily on the landscape, and particularly on the Irish Sea, in exploring a shared Celtic culture. She is especially interested in isolated fishing communities and how people and landscape mark one another.]

Song

Bone-aged is my white horse;
Blunted is the share;[1]
Broken the man who through sad land
Broods on the plough.

Bone-bright was my gelding once;
Burnished was the blade;
Beautiful the youth who in green Spring
Broke earth with song.

1. Ploughshare.

Lament

MY MAN IS A BONE RINGED WITH WEED

Thus it was on my bridal-night:
That the sea, risen to a green wall
At our window; quenching love's new delight;
Stood curved between me and the midnight call
Of him who said I was so fair
He could drown for joy in the salt of my hair.
We sail, he said,
Like the placid dead
Who have long forgotten the marriage-bed.

On my bridal night
Brine stung the window.
Alas, in every night since then
These eyes have rained
For him who made my heart sing
At the lifting of the latch;
For him who will not come again
Weary from the sea.

THE WAVE TORE HIS BRIGHT FLESH IN HER
 GREED:
MY MAN IS A BONE RINGED WITH WEED.

MAURA LAVERTY

(1907–66)

from:
ALONE WE EMBARK
(1943)

[*Touched by the Thorn*, the American title of Maura Laverty's novel, is taken from 'Oh! Think Not My Spirits are Always as Light', one of Thomas Moore's *Irish Melodies*: 'And the heart that is soonest awake to the flowers, / Is always the first to be touch'd by the thorns.'[1] Set mostly in rural Ireland between 1928 and the end of the Second World War, the novel portrays a harsh world in which kind, sensitive, honourable and loving people often suffer precisely because they have these qualities. However, Laverty draws all the characters so as to elicit a fleeting sympathy for even the most unlikeable. The novel, which was banned in Ireland, centres on Mary Sheehy, who throws over her true love Denis Doran to make an unwise love match and is widowed shortly after having a son. Destitute, Mary enters into a loveless, numbing marriage with Johnny Dunne, a wealthy, repulsive old man who blackmails her with the promise that he will keep her mother out of the squalid charity hospital. After a single sexual encounter with Denis, who has returned from America, Mary becomes pregnant.]

When he went in to tea, Peejay thought Jack must surely have been mistaken about his stepfather's bad humour. He had never seen the old man so chatty. Usually, Johnny gobbled his meals without a word to throw to a dog. This evening he had plenty to say. Unobservant though he was, Peejay was made uncomfortable by the geniality of the old man's voice and by the way he kept watching Mary out of the corners of his queerly smiling eyes.

They were an odd trio at the table in that stuffy little parlour behind the shop — the lovely woman, the ferretfaced old man and the bright-cheeked child.

In spite of the tired, strained look that sometimes came into her eyes, Mary had lost none of her beauty. The shape of her face had changed, maybe — become a little longer, a little less rounded — but

this took nothing from her loveliness. As she poured the tea and spread jam on her son's bread, the softness and warmth of her were as movingly present as when she was twenty. She had seemed to have lost these qualities in the long years after her mother's death. Often then she had wondered, when looking in the mirror, if that hard-eyed woman, bitter-mouthed with unhappiness, could be herself. Julia and Peejay had helped to make up to her for the high price she had had to pay for her mother's happy death, but even they could not have brought back the tenderness to her mouth and eyes. Denis Doran had done that. The comfort of knowing he was within a few miles of her, the joy of meeting him now and again; it was this that gave her a shield against Johnny Dunne.

Johnny had not improved since his second marriage. As year after year went by without bringing him the sons for whom he had bargained, his liking for Mary curdled to deep resentment, and he showed in a thousand ways his feeling that he had been cheated. His first big chance of retaliation came when one of the Nolans, from whom Johnny had seized Bohercille House, came with an offer to buy it back. The offer was good and Johnny accepted it. 'What would a man with no family be wanting with a place like that?' he taunted Mary. 'You and me and the young lad will have plenty of room over the shop.' Mary did not mind. A fine house could not lessen the trials of living with Johnny.

With the move back to the town, the old man had dropped any attempts at refinement which had been forced on him with his rise in the world. It was as if he had reverted deliberately to the habits of his wretched boyhood on realizing that through no son of his would he ever be compensated for his early hardships. It was difficult to get him to change his clothes, and he shaved only on Sundays. That revolting drop at the end of his nose was more persistent than ever, but Johnny never used a handkerchief to it now. When he thought of it, he rubbed it away with the back of his hand.

Meal-times would have been impossible for Mary had Peejay not been there to occupy her

---

1. Thomas Moore (1779–1852) published his *Irish Melodies* between 1808 and 1834; see Volume I, pp. 1053–69.

eyes and ears. The old man was being particularly trying this evening. He seemed to be doing
his disgusting best to provoke her. He scrabbled
in his plate of rashers and eggs with dirty fingers;
he sucked his dingy teeth and slugged his tea
from the saucer. A couple of times he cleared his
throat with a horrible hawking sound and spat
over his shoulder into the fireplace. Mary felt a
great relief when he brought the ordeal to an end
by pushing back his chair and belching loudly.

'Run and tell Moll Slevin to put on the water
for your bath, Peejay,' she told the child. 'And
clean your Sunday shoes for Mass in the
morning. I'll be down to wash your hair when
I've the table cleared.'

Peejay went off obediently, and Mary started
to pile the dishes onto the brown enamelled tray
that had *Player's Please*[2] written across it. She was
puzzled that Johnny showed no sign of hurrying
down to the shop. Most Saturday evenings, he
could barely wait to bolt the last mouthful before
rushing back to take in the money. This evening,
he remained sitting in his chair, eyeing her
sideways with that disturbing, knowledgeable
leer. There was something about him that made
her think a snake would look like that when
getting ready to strike, and her heart thumped a
little as she lifted the piled tray and turned
towards the door.

He stopped her before she could escape.

'Come back with your tray, Mary,' he said. 'I
want to talk to you.' Mary felt a sick, cold feeling
in the pit of her stomach. She put down the tray
and faced him. 'Musha,[3] Mary,' he began with a
wheedling softness that was frightening because
of the way the venom in his crafty eyes belied it
— 'Musha, Mary, who's the fellow you do be
meeting up the road?' Her eyes widened and the
back of her hand went to her mouth. 'You're not
denying it, are you, Mary? Because I happen to
know it's true. I had a letter from a friend this
morning telling me all about it. It's Denis Doran
you're meeting, isn't it, Mary?' His stubbled face
still had that venomous smile, his tone that
terrible playfulness.

When he stood up and came towards her she
backed to the wall, but Johnny pressed after her.

Suddenly his hand shot out and gripped her arm,
and she had to bite her lips to keep from
screaming as cruel fingers bit into soft flesh. He
thrust his mean jowl close to her face. 'Answer
me, you bitch!' The smile was gone and the
playfulness. 'Isn't it Doran, you whore?'

The epithet jerked her out of her fright. She
tore his hand from her arm and thrust him back.
'Keep your bad names to yourself, Johnny
Dunne!' she cried. 'There's no dirt here unless
for what's in your own dirty mind. Yes, it's Denis
Doran. Six times in two years I've spent an hour
up the road with him — and Father Carroll
himself could have seen what passed between
us.'

'Do you swear that?' Johnny asked quickly.

'Before God, I swear it.' The little red eyes
searched her face for perjury but found only
innocence and honesty.

'So much the better,' he said. Anger returned
to rout his relief. 'Whore or no whore, you're
after getting yourself talked about,' he said
thickly. 'Begod,[4] I could cut your throat! I took
your mother out of the Union[5] — I took you and
your brat when you hadn't a rag to your backs.
And the return I get for it is to have me name
dragged in the mud.' He eyed her with hatred.
'And to think I turned down a good match with
Tommy Heffernan's daughter for you!' he said
bitterly. 'To think I lost me chance of that fine
woman who's after having five children in eight
years for Tim Coffey!'

'You made a bad bargain, Johnny Dunne,'
Mary said quietly. 'But I'm glad I never had any
children for you — glad, glad! Marrying you cost
me enough without that.'

He looked at her in genuine amazement.
'Why, you poor deluded beggar, you!' he
stuttered. 'Didn't I lift you out of hardship into
the lap of luxury? Amn't I after supporting your
child for you? And now you have the gall to talk
of what marrying me cost you?'

'It cost me Denis Doran,' Mary said with
trembling lips. 'It cost me love. It cost me
happiness.'

Johnny's loose-lipped mouth was crooked
with contempt. 'Denis Doran, me backside! It
wasn't about Denis Doran you were thinking

2. An advertising slogan for Player's cigarettes.
3. From the Irish *maiseadh*, literally, 'if it is so', an exclamation of
surprise or exhortation.
4. By God; an exclamation.
5. The workhouse.

when you ran off with the Baltie. Love! Happiness! A body would only have to hear the things you say to know the kind of a cracked, flighty woman you are. But I'll put a stop to your gallop. Don't think I'm jealous of Denis Doran. I don't give a damn about the way he feels for you, or you for him. But I'm telling you now I won't have you making me name a byword in Tullynawlin. I've worked hard to make meself respected in this town, and neither you nor Doran is going to pull me down. I'll see you damned in hell first! I'll go to Father Carroll about you. I'll get Doran run out of the parish. I'll' — Johnny stopped suddenly, his little eyes narrowed, his foxy face full of cunning. 'No,' he said quietly. 'I won't. I won't make any scandal at all. I can do better than that. I know a grand way to keep you easy.'

Mary looked at him quickly. 'What is it?' she asked. 'What is it you're threatening?'

Johnny put his head to one side. 'You're very set on sending your son to school, aren't you, Mary?' The false, wheedling tone had returned to his voice. 'You're very anxious to make something out of him?'

'But you promised! That day coming home with my mother from Knockvilly you swore you'd educate him. You can't go back on it. You promised!'

'What's to prevent me going back on it? You can take it from me that he'll never see the inside of a college if I hear tell of you making little of yourself with Doran again. He'll be thirteen next August, and ready to leave the national school. You were thinking of sending him over to the Christian Brothers[6] in Kildare. Now listen well to what I'm telling you. If you don't behave yourself and show respect to my good name it isn't to the Christian Brothers he'll go but into the shop below, where I'll give him a taste of what I got meself. And that's as true as God is listening to me!'

Mary's eyes were fixed on her husband's greasy, egg-stained tie. But she was not seeing it. What she was seeing was Peejay growing to manhood in that cluttered, low-ceilinged shop, his boy's muscles straining at barrels of liquor and sacks of meal, his cheerfulness beaten out of him by Johnny's harshness. She saw him growing

up in ignorance, learning to toss off a quick, surreptitious half-one after the example of Tim, the poor drunken barman. She could not bear to see any more, and she made her decision. She would have to meet Denis just once, to explain why they must never hope for more than the words and glances that may be exchanged in the presence of others. After that, they would not meet again.

'Well?' Johnny demanded. 'Did you make up your mind?' Her sudden wilting and the bleakness of her face gave him his answer. 'Yes,' she said woodenly. 'You may set your mind at rest. Your good name will be safe from now on.'

Johnny nodded in satisfaction. 'Good,' he said. 'I'll be keeping an eye on you.'

Mary carried the tray out of the room. 'I'll manage a word with him coming out of second Mass tomorrow,' she planned. 'I'll arrange where I'll meet him.'

CHAPTER FOUR

Julia cut the madeira cake and drew in her breath with regret for its greyness. 'May God be with the days,' she sighed, filled with nostalgia for spacious pre-war times when cooks knew no handicaps.[7] She put the cake in the centre of the table and stood back to judge the effect. 'It could be worse,' she decided. It was true for her. Fresh scones, glazed and browned, a plate of pale pink ham slices, her prized dish of green pottery which Nora Higgins had once given her: two shallowly-cupped leaves joined by a stem that was bent to form a handle, one leaf holding golden twirls of butter, the other a big ruby of crab jelly. In spite of the offending madeira cake, the table could have looked worse.

Julia liked to greet Mary with a nicely set table when she came down on Sunday nights. Sometimes Biddy Blocks came in, but usually they had the place to themselves, for Molly Teeling always cycled home after Mass on Sundays to spend the day with her mother and father.

---

6. Roman Catholic religious order involved in education.

7. Although Ireland remained neutral during the Second World War, Britain's blockade regulations made it difficult to get British imports. Because of the resulting shortages, the Irish government imposed rationing on various items, including clothes, bread, sugar and tea.

Tonight all her trouble was wasted, for when Mary came in she refused tea, she would not even take off her coat. 'Maybe I'll have a cup when I come back, but I can't wait now. I must be off.'

There was a feverishness about her which Julia could not miss. She hesitated for a minute and then decided to speak. 'Stay, Mary,' she pleaded gently. 'If it's off to meet Denis Doran you are, don't go. Stay here with me, alanna.[8] You're a married woman and you do wrong to be meeting him. You can't get past that.' With her loving hand she stroked the sleeve of Mary's coat. 'I know you don't see him often. I know it's very hard on the two of you, and I know Johnny gives you plenty to put up with — no one knows that better than myself. Still and all, you shouldn't be meeting him. If you only let him put his arms around you you're making him commit a sin. Besides, people will start talking. If Johnny hears anything, where will you be?'

Mary caught the woman's hand. 'Will you hush, Aunt Julia? Hush, and listen to me.' The words tumbled quickly. 'He has heard. He taxed me with it yesterday evening. Told me he'd take Peejay from school next year and put him to work in the shop if I met Denis any more. I'm only seeing him this once. I couldn't let him go without a word, could I, Aunt Julia? After this, I promise you I'll never meet him alone again.' Mary's voice trembled. 'It was so little we had. Six times we met in two years, Aunt Julia. We didn't harm anyone — and nothing but a few kisses between us.'

'I know, Mary. I know. But God knows where it might end. You'll be wiser to put a finish to it.'

'Listen, Aunt Julia,' Mary's face was anxious and troubled. 'Will you do something for me? He has been watching me all day as a cat would watch a mouse. When I said this evening I was coming down here I thought by him he had his suspicions. I think he might even have come down with me to make sure, only the sergeant and a few others came in for a game of cards. He couldn't refuse the sergeant, and he had to stay back with them. But he looked fit to be tied, to see me coming out by myself.'

'What is it you want me to do, Mary?'

'I want you to tell a lie if he comes down looking for me while I'm gone. When I was

coming out they were all settled in the snug, but you could never tell what time the cards might stop. If he comes before I get back, say I'm out with Molly Teeling. Say anything, only don't let him guess. Please, Aunt Julia. I'll never ask you to do such a thing again.'

Julia had no liking for lies, but she nodded her head. 'I'll do it — seeing it's the last time. But don't delay, Mary. Hurry back.'

'God bless you!' With a quick kiss Mary was gone.

She kept close to the hedge, well out of the moonlight. But she was safe enough, for she met no one on the road but the Lamb Doyle and he was walking in another world and did not see her.

Denis stepped out from the hedge as she neared their trysting place. He was hatless and in the clear pale light his face showed tense with waiting.

'Mary!' he said, and the way he said it was all the love-poems in the world reduced to one word. 'I thought you were never coming.' He put his arms about her and she clung to him for a minute.

'We mustn't stay on the road,' she told him breathlessly. 'I mustn't be seen talking to you. Where can we go? I can't stay long.'

'We'll go into the grove,' he answered. 'The gate is only down the road. I left the bike there.'

In the security of the small copse they turned to each other again. The moon could not reach them as they stood there together, their bodies a blur against the blackness of thickly-growing tree trunks.

'What is it that's troubling you, little love?' Denis breathed the words against her lips. 'What did you want to say to me?'

The reminder silenced the singing in Mary's blood, and she drew back a little. 'He's found out, Denis,' she said shakily. 'I can't meet you like this again. He says he'll take it out on Peejay if I do. This has to be good-bye.'

Denis grew tense. 'Don't heed him, Mary! Don't mind him — he blackmailed you into this marriage and everyone knows a forced vow isn't binding.'

'Whisht, Denis love. Have sense,' Mary pleaded. 'There was no forcing. I married him of my own free will. And supposing I went against him? What would happen to Peejay?'

8. From the Irish *álainn*, meaning 'beautiful'; a term of endearment.

'Leave him, Mary. I'll look after the two of you. We'll go up to Dublin. Or maybe over to England, where no one would know us. I'd soon get a job there.' His arms were around her again, drawing her to him, but she put her hands against his chest and resisted. 'You're blathering, Denis. How could I do that to Peejay? And how would you leave your father and he needing you? He'd never manage without you now that times are so hard, with the compulsory tillage[9] and everything.' She put up her hand and fondled his cheek. 'You know there's nothing in the world I'd like better than to be with you. But I was selfish once before and look what came of it. We must think of the child and your father. And of poor Julia, too — 'twould break her heart if we did a thing like that.'

'Would you never think of me, Mary?' he asked with some bitterness. 'The torture it is for me to see you tied to the like of Johnny Dunne. And to think from now on we're not even to get a few minutes together! It was the only thing that kept me going, Mary — the chance of getting my arms around you for a little while.' The bitterness went out of him and he pleaded with her. 'Leave him, Mary. We'll go away together. We'll manage somehow.'

Mary's voice had in it her exhaustion at having to battle with him as well as herself. 'Why do you keep on like that when you know we can't do it? I am thinking of you, Denis. You'd never be happy — neither of us would be happy — to be living like that. Even our few kisses were wrong. We'd find it hard to admit there could be sin in the way we feel about each other, but it's wrong just the same. Be honest, Denis — haven't I been a cause of confession to you?'

'Maybe,' he admitted reluctantly. 'But I can't help wanting you — sure I'm only flesh and blood. Didn't I go to America to try to forget you? But I can never put you out of my mind. I'm a man, Mary — I'm going on for forty. I've wanted you too long to be able to stop now. You can't do this to me! If you won't come away with me, you'll have to let me see you now and again.'

'There's the child, Denis,' she reminded him quietly. 'We daren't meet again. I'm afraid of Johnny — he has eyes in the back of his head. For the child's sake, I mustn't meet you again.'

Denis was silent. When he spoke, his words were heavy with acceptance. 'Aye — the child,' he said. 'He changes everything. So we're not to meet after tonight?' She did not speak. 'Let me kiss you, then,' he said, almost roughly. He caught her to him and kissed as he had never kissed her before.

Suddenly he released her, and because of her weakness and dizziness she had to lean back against the tree. He was trembling. 'Mary — will you do something for me?'

She was on guard immediately. 'What, Denis? What do you want me to do?'

'Only a little thing, love. Sit down beside me for a minute.'

She hesitated. 'No, Denis! No. I should be going back.'

'Please, Mary. It is not much to ask. Only for a minute, darling. I only want to hold you near me.'

The wariness was still in her, but there was such pleading in his voice that pity welled up in her, sweeping away will and conscience.

They faced each other on the moonlit road. 'Are you mad at me, Mary?' he asked humbly.

'No, love. How could I be?' Later, her conscience would return to make her mad at herself, but at him, never.

She was afraid to let him walk back to the town with her. 'Say good-bye to me here,' she said. This time, their kiss was without roughness. It held pain and parting and the sad ghost of their ecstasy. Then she turned and almost ran from him and she was crying like a child as she hurried along the road.

CHAPTER ELEVEN

Johnny Dunne was feeling worried, so worried that good businessman though he was he paid little attention to Ber Higgins' conversation, and he served him automatically. He was worried about Mary and wishing she was home. At five o'clock she had come to him looking white and disturbed to say that Julia Dempsey had brought her bad news. That her aunt, Mrs. Teeling of the bog, had taken a bad turn and wanted her. He

---

9. During the 1930s, and especially during the Second World War, the Irish government took a number of steps to encourage increased Irish agricultural production. In 1940 the government mandated that one-eighth of the arable land in each holding be tilled. By 1943 the required proportion was as high as three-eighths.

had done his best to dissuade her from going. 'Are you out of your mind, woman?' he had demanded. ''Twould be the height of foolishness for you to go traipsing out all that way and you in delicate health. Do you want to make away with the child, or what?' 'I'll take it easy,' she had said. 'Didn't Dr. Mangan say only yesterday I'm not getting half enough exercise? Anyway, I'm going.' Her unexpected stubbornness and the look in her face had warned him not to try to insist. If the Button had not gone to Monasterevan with the car, he would have driven her out himself. But there it was. He had to stand back and see her start out on the long walk.

He felt she was being criminally unfair to him in taking such risks with his child. He fretted and fumed and took out his anxiousness on Tim until the distracted barman was thanking God that expectant fatherhood did not come often on his employer.

When Peejay came home, he sought out his stepfather in the bar. 'Can Paddy Gallagher have a lift in the car tomorrow morning?' he asked. 'He has to catch the train.'

Johnny jerked his thumb at Ber Higgins. 'There's the man who's paying for the hire of it,' he said sourly. 'You can ask him.'

Ber waved a genial hand. 'If he's a friend of yours, old son, he'll be more than welcome.' The porter he had been drinking all evening had irrigated his temper, making flowers of joviality and good humour spring up in florid luxuriance. He wanted to prove to all the world the generous, good-hearted fellow he was. Peejay's fishing-rod caught his eye. 'I believe you were out fishing with my daughter this evening.' He grinned beerily at Johnny and winked an eye. 'We'll have to watch these two, Mr. Dunne. I suppose the chiseller here will be wanting to be my son-in-law any of these days.' He laughed loudly and clapped Peejay on the back. To the child's relief, Ber drained his glass and moved to the door. 'Well, I suppose I'd better be going home to her. A father's heart you know. A father's heart.' He tapped his chest and sighed with heavy sentimentality. 'Good night all. At nine tomorrow I'll be expecting the car.' He went.

'You be off with yourself now and do your lessons,' Johnny said. 'I don't know how you ever expect to be able to earn your living if you do nothing but gallivant.'

'I'm going,' Peejay stopped at the door. 'Is my mother in the kitchen?'

'She's not, then,' Johnny snapped. 'She's gone traipsing out to Teelings' of the bog.'

'There! I knew the Lamb Doyle was raving.' The boy's eyes were full of gentle scorn. 'He said he saw her in the other direction altogether. Anyway, I knew my mother wouldn't be crying.'

Johnny took a dirty cloth from under the porter sump and started to mop up the counter. There was no alertness yet, for he was listening with only half of his mind. The other half was prodding and goading his irritation with Mary for not being safely at home. 'What the hell are you blathering about?' he asked impatiently.

'The Lamb Doyle. He had a queer notion about my mother. He was trying to make out he saw her down in the grove this evening when the Angelus[10] was ringing. He said she was crying. Isn't he getting very queer in the head, Mr. Dunne?'

New alertness came. Like the crack of a whip it came. Easy now — go easy, he warned himself. Wait till we get to the bottom of this. He dropped his eyes to the counter and the hand holding the duster started to mop up a porter ring with slow carefulness.

'Isn't poor Lamb Doyle getting very bad lately, Mr. Dunne?' the child repeated.

'He is to be sure.' The voice was very quiet. 'Very bad entirely he is. Tell me' — the duster moved very slowly, very stealthily — 'tell me, Peejay, did the poor eejit[11] have any other queer notions about your mother? Did he say anything else?'

'No. Only that. That she was crying in the grove. He said something about some man being with her. Some man who was sorry for her — I couldn't make head or tail of it. Will she soon be home from Teelings', Mr. Dunne?'

'Aye. Soon.' Johnny turned his back and started to rearrange the bottles on the shelves. Peejay went on into the kitchen.

Johnny was not seeing the bottles. He was seeing Mary's face, tense and strained and disturbed. Would Mrs. Teeling's illness have given her that look? Wouldn't she have waited till the

---

10. A devotional exercise said by Roman Catholics at morning, noon and sunset.
11. Idiot.

car had come home if it was only a case of going out to the Teelings'? Was this thing true, then? Was the bitch shameless enough to be meeting Doran and she heavy with his, Johnny Dunne's, child? Would she have the indecency to be bringing scandal on his name by carrying on in broad daylight?

His first impulse was to rush down to Julia and demand the truth. But he knew well that if Mary had deceived him, Julia would not give her away. And he knew — he had known it from the first — that he did not need confirmation from anyone. With sickening certainty he knew that the Lamb Doyle had not been raving. Fury rose in him, but he fought it back.

Easy, easy — keep cool, now. Keep your head, man. How are you going to know the best way to deal with this if you lose your head? Isn't she the streap,[12] though? Is there a woman in Ireland who'd do the like? There she is, the dirty trollop, out courting in the ditches, when she ought to be at home minding herself like any decent, respectable wife who'd be going to have a child. It's horsewhipped she ought to be for belittling her husband, for belittling his child. His child — His child?

He reared away from the suspicion in wild panic.

Oh, God, no! Not that! Wouldn't I go stone stark mad if I thought that? The child's mine — mine! It's nobody else's. It's my child that I've been waiting for all the days of my life — that I worked for and cadged[13] for and saved for. My grand, lovely little son that's going to grow up to full and plenty, that'll have a gentleman's education and a gentleman's life. My son, Doctor John Dunne — his reverence, young Father John — my son, John, the best solicitor in Ireland.

The terrible suspicion mocked Johnny's efforts to escape it. It pressed after him and forced him to turn and face it. He cast wildly around for weapons to vanquish it, but he could find none. He found instead a score of things which, at the time of their happening, he had refused to notice, but which had seeped past his complacency and now rose to taunt him: the stupefaction of Biddy Blocks on the day he had given her the five pounds — the strained, worried gaze of Mary when she had told him — her maddening refusal

to share in his jubilation or to join in his glad planning of the child's future.

But these things were not enough. He wanted more — he had to be certain! With the masochism of jealousy which craves for proof of what it fears, his mind ferretted about for further evidence. Would they have been writing to each other? Would there be anything in her room which would tell him what he wanted and dreaded to know?

He forced himself to take the stairs slowly and quietly, reminding himself at every step that he must not play into their hands by losing his head. He closed the bedroom door softly behind him and began his search. He started with the wardrobe. He went through the pockets of her clothes, but found nothing. It was the same with the chest of drawers, though he even lifted the paper with which the drawers were lined. He pulled out her trunk from under the bed but there was nothing in it but winter clothes and camphor balls. He was careful to leave everything as he found it. If he was mistaken, it would never do for her to know he had searched her things.

He closed the lid of the trunk and sent his crafty eyes around the room. Was there any other place where she'd be likely to hide letters? No place, except maybe that little wooden box of hers on the mantlepiece. But wasn't it only a few weeks since she had taken down the box to show Peejay the photographs? Hadn't she turned every bit of old rubbish that was in it out on the table? Still, he'd make sure. He took down the box, a light little box with a weak, simple lock. To break it open would be the easiest thing in the world, but again he imposed on himself that cunning caution. He took his bunch of keys from his pocket and selecting the smallest of them he tried them one by one on the small, vincible lock. The key of his tin cash box fitted. A little careful working, a slight, steady pressure and the key turned.

Under the old photographs and the odds and ends of trinkets which had belonged to Peg Sheehy, he found Denis's letter. It told him everything. When he had read it he put it back in its place, and he locked the box and returned it to the mantelpiece. Then he sat down quickly on the bed. For a minute he was afraid he was going to retch, but the nausea passed over him, leaving him trembling and weak. The old man rocked himself from side to side in an agony of grief. Ah, the cruel bitterness of it! There would be no child for him, no child at all. His bright, darling son was gone — the light of his eyes — his own heart's blood. His lips kept mumbling the little phrases from the caoin[14] as if he were in reality looking on the dead face of his only-born. When he bethought himself of the woman who had done this terrible thing to him his grief was ousted by a murderous anger, and his hands clawed at his knees in frenzied anticipation of the feel of her small, white neck. So she thought she could put the horns on him, did she? She thought she could father Doran's ill-begotten bastard onto her decent husband. But he'd show her now! He'd fling her out on the road. He'd make her the talk of the seven parishes. He'd drag her name in the mud. He'd —

The mad gallop of his vengeful planning was jerked to a sudden stop. Wait a minute, though — If there was scandal would she be the only one to suffer? Wouldn't the big mouths have something to say about him, too? After all his boasting of the past few months, wouldn't he be the laughing-stock of the world? Was he going to let that happen? Anything but that. He'd have to find some other way to pay her out.

He stood up and took a few turns about the room, his hands stroking each other behind his back, the mean, out-thrust head wagging to this thoughts. He had it — he knew what he'd do! There was no need for him to get his name in the papers by choking the rotten life out of her. No need at all to make a laughing-stock out of himself by letting people know the way she was after codding[15] him. There was a better way. He'd keep quiet — hadn't he always said the quiet way was the best? He wouldn't let on a word — not even to her. But he'd pay her out, never fear. He'd knock the high notions out of her. She'd find a change from now on. No college for the Baltie's brat, for a start. Not another mouthful of idle bread, but into the shop with him, and plenty of the hard knocks that decenter lads than him had had to put up with. And the same with Doran's bastard when the time would come. No more of their high living, either. No more of their rashers and eggs at every hand's turn, and their lawdydaw[16] puddens and their grandeur. He'd keep them on short rations — maybe that would cool them down. He'd make her go down on her knees to him for every penny. He'd get rid of Moll Slevin, too. Maybe if her ladyship had plenty of hard work to keep her going, her mind wouldn't be quite so full of romance. And, wouldn't he laugh inside himself when he'd see her out of her mind with wondering what was wrong — wondering if he knew? He'd never tell her — that would be the best of it. The bitch could wonder and worry and watch him out of the corners of her lying eyes, but he'd never tell her. Before he was finished with her, she'd be wishing herself at the bottom of the canal.

He smiled and nodded in gloating satisfaction. There was one thing he'd have to do immediately. He'd have to go over to Mr. Sweeney in Kildare and get him to change the will. Not that there was any fear of him dying — ha! She needn't be hoping she'd get out of it as easy as that. Hadn't the insurance doctor told him he'd live to be a hundred? But 'twould be as well to change it at once, just in case. He'd go do it in the morning. Instead of letting the Button go over with that Higgins fellow, he'd drive the car himself.

He looked around the bedroom to make sure everything was in order, and then went downstairs.

14. Lament.
15. Deceiving.

16. La-dee-da.

TEMPLE LANE

(1899–1978)

from:
FISHERMAN'S WAKE (1939)

[Temple Lane offers the paradox of lonely, isolated individuals who are at the same time oppressed with a sense of surveillance. The poems are from *Fisherman's Wake* and *Curlews*, published by Talbot Press in Dublin in 1939 and 1946 respectively.]

Circumspection

Within the round rath[1] where the thistle heads
  shake,
The grasses were bowed in the hollow we made.
But always I said — 'Wait, and speak low!
I heard a voice talking: did somebody move?'

There in the dip where the land falls away
A far house would peer at us, eyelids aslant.
And always I said — 'Wait, and keep still!
Someone is watching us, there through the
  blinds.'

How should they see, and they a mile off?
How should the dry dead uncoffined stand up?
But one and the other, the near and the far,
Kept us in terror till Love died of age.

1. Ringfort.

Maybe old prayers when the wild blood is
  screaming
Ring us with terror soul's peril to meet . . .
Only the grave-worm will ravish me now.
In the rath sunlessness warps the new flowers.

from:
CURLEWS (1946)

The Lonely Woman

I would like a settled place,
  A small place to be:
To watch the firelight touch one face
  And the seasons touch one tree.

I would like a steady fire
  And you at the hearth side,
With patient eyes that would not tire
  When my face was winter-dried.

I'd not fear the birth throe,
  A rest from mind's pain,
I'd like some place we two could go
  And never stir again.

JOSEPHINE O'BRIEN

(*fl.* 1944)

from:
SEX, SAINTS, AND CENSORS
(1944)

[Josephine O'Brien's article, published in *The Bell* in April 1944, contributes to the debate over censorship in Ireland by making a distinction between Irish Catholicism and Irish puritanism and arguing that puritanism, rather than Catholicism, is the moving spirit behind the Censorship Board's decisions.]

Somebody — was it Augustine Birrell?[1] — said that Jane Austen[2] was the only woman-writer he knew who 'could coolly and sensibly describe a

1. Augustine Birrell (1850–1933) wrote a number of books on literary and religious topics.
2. Jane Austen (1775–1817), English novelist.

man.' *Cool and sensible* is the best description of the average Irish priest's attitude towards sex. He neither puts women on a pedestal nor looks down upon them. He accepts without fuss their essential equality as human beings, while being extremely suspicious of any pretensions to such equality as would ignore what he considers the essential differences between the sexes. He praises and blames them according as they come up to, or fall short of, these standards. He likes and dislikes them according as they please or annoy him, all very much the same as he does with men. He is not likely to be embarrassed by the physical side of sex: he knows too much about it for that. It is true that a certain cynicism about its potential value to the human spirit, due to professional contact with its seamy side and to his own celibate experience of getting on all right without it, often gives him a blind-spot when dealing with those 'who love, not wisely, but too well.'[3] But his friendships with happily-married people generally go far to prevent this error from warping his general outlook on sex.

If all this is so, why, it may be reasonably asked, are not Irish priests more liberal in their outlook upon sex in literature? Mr. C.B. Murphy[4] gave one reason worth considering here. Having emphasised that Roman Catholic theological principles strongly support the freedom of literature to deal with sex, and repudiated the 'family circle' standard of literary decency,[5] he remarks: 'That part of the Irish mind which runs after sex, does not bother much about books, either to read or to write them; but in the few cases where it does, it manages to give the Victorians their needed excuse and unfortunately to swing to their side what should be one of the few sane and powerful forces in Ireland that make for objectivity about sex — Roman Catholicism.'

It is important to understand the reason for this, for if it is not understood, Irish writers and book-lovers may play into the hands of their enemies by alienating the clergy. A good priest is rightly concerned with the morals of his people rather than with their literary culture. That is his job, and it would be a blunder to find fault with him for doing his job as well as he can. Even if he overdoes it; if in his mistaken zeal he mixes up prudery with common decency and claims for prudery what decency only can claim, we have no need to take his words or acts as those of his Church. And it is only with the whole Church behind him that the priest has any lasting influence in Ireland.

Take the present position of the Literary Censorship. It is dead, as dead as ever was any institution, by law established, which had lost its hold on the public conscience. The Censorship depended upon the support of the Roman Catholic Church for its hold on the public conscience; it lost that support as soon as the public lost its belief that the Censorship was conducted on Catholic principles. The precise time when that belief was lost must have been when the daily papers published the fact that the Censorship Board had banned as being in its general tendency indecent a book which had been approved by the highest Roman Catholic authority in England. The public could not swallow that. The priests could not defend it on any Catholic principles, yet most of them felt it was just an unlucky blunder and that there must be some explanation for it. But the more it was debated, the more evident it became that the Censors were only acting on their usual policy when they banned Dr. Halliday Sutherland's *The Laws of Life*, and that it was not a mistake but the logical consequence of their policy.[6] Some Irish priests may still continue to support the Censorship's policy. They can give it not the support of their Church, only of their personal opinions.

The Censorship has been killed by Roman influence, working on Irish minds, just as it invaded us long ago, 'in a powerful and subtle manner through the Christian Church.' But Irish puritanism is not dead. It is kept alive by a fear of the standing threat of sex-attraction to the

---

3. William Shakespeare, *Othello*, Act v, Sc. 2, ii. 343–4.

4. C.B. Murphy's 'Sex, Censorship and the Church' appeared in *The Bell*, vol. 2, no. 6 (September 1941), pp. 65–75.

5. The principle, supposedly used by censors, that any book that could not be read aloud in the home to all members of the family should be banned.

6. The banning of Halliday Sutherland's *The Laws of Life* (London and New York: Sheed and Ward, 1936) in 1941 aroused considerable controversy. Sutherland (1882–1960) was a distinguished Catholic gynaecologist, and the book, which offered information about the 'safe period' or 'rhythm method' of birth control, the only form of contraception permitted by the Catholic church, had been approved by the Archdiocese of Westminster. Stranger still, the book was not banned for advocating birth control; it was banned as being indecent in its general tendency, a bizarre judgement by any stretch of the imagination.

established order of conduct. Nor is it an unreasonable thing to recognise that sex-attraction does often threaten orderly conduct, and to take precautions against disorder. It is only when this becomes a morbid fear, when it leads to the adoption of precautions that would smother all rational liberty, that it becomes a worse danger than the threat which it purported to counter. With a powerful native force, however, on the side of civilised thinking about sex — the common-sense of the average priest and his skill in social relationships — there is not much fear that puritanism will dominate us in the long run though it may, as we have seen, dominate us for a while. Some, who happen to have the ear of Rome, may even succeed in getting things said and done in Rome which appear to favour Irish puritanism. But until they succeed in changing Roman Catholic theology such expedients will fail, for Catholic reviews run by competent Catholic theologians will continue to disconcert the Irish Censorship by praising the books it bans.

It is most important, nevertheless, to remember that this conflict between the fear of sex-attraction and the need of the civilised mind to think and talk about sex in order to achieve a rational attitude towards life as a whole, is endemic in every human community. It is inherent in human nature, Irish, English, Latin, Teutonic, modern, medieval, ancient, pre-historic. There is no need at all for either side to call the other side names, suggesting that all who are in favour of rational liberty for writers to deal with sex are under 'foreign,' 'pagan' or unChristian influences, or that all who oppose this liberty are obscurantists. It is a conflict for each individual to resolve for himself, for it goes on in his own mind whether he knows it or not. The less cocksure we all feel about our own particular solution, and about the utter-rightness of the side on which we happen to be born, brought up in, or into, the more likely is the community to achieve the proper atmosphere for a rational solution of its own.

MARION BRENNAN

(*fl.* 1944)

CEILIDHE (1944)

[In the absence of any other information about Marion Brennan — which may be a pseudonym — it is impossible to categorize this piece as fiction or autobiography, but it throws light on the local dance hall as the scene of frustrated desire in de Valera's Ireland. Published in *The Bell* in 1944.   S.K.]

I had ten days' leave, and I felt as lost as only a native can feel in a native city. All day Sunday I had meandered aimlessly through the little lanes which are so numerous around Dundrum;[1] when evening came it looked as though the cinema was the only alternative to a boring evening. Then suddenly I thought of the Mansion House. I decided to go there and to spend the time dancing to Irish Music, though I confess that I

had for years harboured an undying resentment towards the Gaelic League and all its Siamsai.[2] This absurd attitude can only be explained by the fact that as a school-girl my vanity suffered at its hands. For, as a school-girl I revelled in ceilidhes, drama festivals, and so on, but never had any success at them. I remember, when I was about eight years old, my Mother dressed me carefully to go to a Ceilidhe; my meticulous toilette was brought to a glorious end by my own addition of 'Ashes of Roses'. I shall never forget my bitter despair and misery at the Ceilidhe as I stood by the wall all night and watched my friends dancing madly, while I stood there alone with my thoughts and my 'Ashes of Roses'.

My lack of success was not due to an excessive lack of good looks, or any of the other vulgar reasons which ostracise one socially. That has been proved adequately enough in later years. I believed

1. Dublin suburb.

2. Musical entertainments.

that it was due to the peculiar snobbery which members of the Gaelic League seem to revel in. I had the misfortune to be the daughter of a tradesman: my Father could never add delightfully Irish little noms-de-plume to his name: he could never boast of fighting in 1916. He did not even belong to the Civil Service or to the ranks of National Teachers: therefore — I concluded — I was unknown and undanced with, and my resentment had piled up through the years.

I am afraid that I went to the Mansion House that Sunday evening in a spirit of aggressive nonchalance. Perhaps that was why I made up heavily and professionally, with an extra amount of mascara thrown in for good luck. I am sure I looked like a slightly battered edition of Mata Hari[3] as I slid through the doors, my entrance slightly ruined by the fact that I tripped over the foot of a large man who looked as if he had just finished a day's ploughing. I sat down and watched the orchestra beginning to strike up the music. Soon the floor was crowded, and in a little while the dancing began. I looked around with interest and took stock of the girls. Most of them were cleanly scrubbed and plain. The others were well-fed brawny lassies. I saw with a feeling of warmth and companionship two lone, satin-clad, nicotine-stained girls who came over to me with a cigarette each in their hands and said hoarsely, 'Give us a light, love.'

The music was as heady and as lilting as only Irish music can be. If I were to associate music with colours, as I do sometimes, I should always think of Irish Dance Music in terms of green and gold. But it has a cold, soulless, brainy rhythm about it which is not conducive to any sort of sensual excess, and as I listened I began to realise how good this type of dancing must be for keeping the unruly passions of the young in check. American dance tunes on the other hand are like red satin, they have such a vital, live strain running through them. The boys at the Ceilidhe were boys in the true sense of the word; they were loose-jointed pale young fellows with tweed-suits and open-necked shirts. The average age was from thirteen to twenty. A few elderly men stood around with vacant faces; they wore shabby navy-

blue suits. With renewed despair, I felt the old wall-flower feeling creeping up on me again. None of the girls smoked except the two satin-clad damsels who puffed frantically and swore softly at all the 'big eejits' who wouldn't give them a dance.

The 'Fear a' Tighe'[4] spoke Gaelic with such a thick *blas*[5] that all his sentences sounded like wet muck. A few of the youths looked at me with a sterile cold gaze as if they were divesting me of all my make-up and were not quite satisfied with what they saw underneath. I longed for a few natural glances, even for a horrible leer or two, just to show that I was in the company of men — and human men at that.

Then, suddenly things looked a little brighter. A tweedy youth gave me a look which was alive with interest, and I praised God for the initiative and independent spirit which differentiated him from his fellow males. In a little while he asked me to dance, and soon I was in the midst of the sixteen-hand reel and my prejudices had flown with the gay sound of the music. My partner had been in England for quite a long while, which probably accounted for his unusual audacity. During the dance I received two hefty kicks on the ankle which made everything go black for a minute. When swinging I nearly had my arm torn from its socket, all done by the same stalwart who tripped me on my entry into the hall earlier in the evening. When it was all over I limped back to my place by the wall; my arm hung loosely by my side and my make-up was lost in perspiration.

I went out to the Ladies' Room to repair the damage. While I was powdering my nose I heard two damsels from Kerry talking quickly in Gaelic to one another. They rapidly discussed their jobs (they were both evidently Civil Servants), they also discussed the bad quality of the food they were getting, and kept going into raptures about their mothers' grand bacon and cabbage. I went back into the hall and made my way with a feeling of relief to my little haven of refuge by the wall. A dark, swarthy little fellow beside me looked at the dance which happened to be 'Port an Fhoghmhair'[6] and when he said with a gesture of disgust, 'Aw, I seen this dirty thing done before' my heart warmed to another kindred

---

3. Professional name of Gertrud Margarete Zelle (1876–1917), Dutch exotic dancer, turned spy for the Germans, who was executed by the French during the First World War.

4. 'Man of the house', in this case, a master of ceremonies.
5. Accent.
6. Harvest Air.

spirit. I found that, like my previous partner, he also had been in England for a few years. He then looked at the Mansion House floor and said, 'Wouldn't this make a lovely floor for Ballroom Dancing?' After a few moments' conversation we became very friendly, and soon he was telling me about the three hundred pounds he had won at the Phoenix Park Races the previous Saturday, he told me also the amount of money he had to spend to buy a decent suit on the Black Market.[7]

7. Although the Republic of Ireland was neutral during the Second World War, rationing and shortages led to a thriving black economy.

We did the 'Walls of Limerick' together. In this dance I was attacked again by an elbow in the stomach as the sprightly set of young boys rushed gaily under an arch made by our hands, so that when it was finished I decided I had had enough and bade my partner good-night. As I was walking towards the door I saw the stalwart at whose hands I had suffered the whole evening leaning over the balcony, as if he intended to fling a chair down on my innocent head as a fitting climax to the evening's fun. He smiled a toothless grin and I bowed gracefully and dodged out the door as quickly as I could.

RHODA COGHILL

(1903–2000)

from:
THE BRIGHT HILLSIDE
(1948)

[Chance and uncertainty dominate Coghill's representation of marriage in 'The Young Bride's Dream'. The speaker's anxious questions about married life find analogies in the difficulty of interpreting her dream and the ambiguities of the closing line.]

The Young Bride's Dream

I wonder will he still be gentle
When I am fastened safe to his side?
Will he buy grandeur to cover my beauty,
And shelter me like a bird that he'd hide
In a quiet nest, and show me great courtesies,
And make me queen of his body and all that he
    is?

Or curse me, use me like a chance woman,
A servant, a girl that he'd hire at a fair?
Bid me rip my fine gown to a hundred pieces,
Make rags of it then, for the floors and the stair?
I had warning, last night, in a dream without
    reason or rhyme;
But the words may be true ones: *'Obedience is
ice to the wine.'*

from:
TIME IS A SQUIRREL
(1956)

[In 'Flight' Coghill examines the aftermath of a lovers' quarrel within the confines of a small, rural community, linking the quarrel and the speaker's inability to avoid encountering her ex-lover to the rhythms of the working agricultural year.]

Flight

This is the road that since the summer — since
their parting — she shunned, for fear of meeting
    him.

Until the time of ripening their quarrel
lasted, and in September, when the harvest

was brimming in the fields, she went her way
by other paths. Through any opening gate

he suddenly might come, on a waggon loaded
with tousled grain; and when mists of a mild
    October

crawled on the sodden soil, he would be cutting
his straggled hedges, time-serving till the sullen

fallow land should harden with more than the
first
gossamer frost, and open to winter work.

But today she takes that road in the late afternoon
when already across the bloodshot sky the rooks

are blinking home. She is no longer afraid while
the year lasts, knowing the watchdog daylight

whines in November on a shortened leash.
She holds her scarf tightened along her cheek;

her worn shoes make no noise but a crisp soft
crushing of frozen grass and ivy and dock,

that keep her footsteps, still as a pattern in
damask.
She moves in the ditch of the drab lane, patched
with agate

ice-pools, dried after sharp showers by a long
sweeping wind. Her ears tell that beyond

the sheltering hedge two horses — a stubble-
dappled
roan, and a mare as red as springing sally

whips[1] or a burnt-out beech — are treading the
dead-branch
crumbling clay, that breaks against the metal

harrow's teeth . . . He shouts to make them turn;
behind him turns a cloud of white sea-birds . . .

She keeps to the near ditch; but the road
winding
and bending again shows a new-made breach in
the briars.

At the treacherous gap she stops. Oh! now to run,
to hide like a feathered frightened thing in the
dusk!

But she who thought to pass like a bird or a bat,
encountering only the hedge-high gulls, is
trapped:

for the too-familiar face, the known shape
walking the furrows, are seen . . . So it was vain

to shield evasive eyes, to discipline
rebellious feet: vain to her and to him

the fugitive pretence. For a proud pulse
beats in her brain like a startled wing; the blood

tramples its path in the stubborn heart's field
with the eightfold stamping hooves of a strong
team

of horses; and she feels, raking the flesh,
the harrow of love's remembered violence.

1. Sally (willow) shoots were often used as whips or canes.

J.H. COUSINS AND MARGARET E. COUSINS
(1873–1956)   (1878–1954)

from:
WE TWO TOGETHER (1950)

[James Cousins and Margaret Gillespie belonged to a group of intellectuals who were attempting to re-think relations between the sexes along with other projects to reform society in the late nineteenth century. Their autobiography is an interesting collaborative exercise. In the following extract they each recall their memories of their courtship and early marriage. Margaret Cousins seems to have experienced a revulsion at sexual intercourse which led her to advocate celibacy within marriage. A number of feminists saw celibacy as politically preferable, at least in the short term, although there were different reasons for this preference. The British suffragette leader Christabel Pankhurst (1880–1958) saw women's celibacy as a political response to men's corrupt sexual behaviour; others such as Beatrice Webb (1858–1943) advocated celibacy on medical, spiritual or ideological grounds. Published in Madras in 1950 by Ganesh.   S.K.]

(J.H.C.) In the dusk of April 8, 1903, a jaunting car conveyed a man on the verge of thirty across Dublin. The event was not unusual in what Lady Morgan,[1] a literary-minded society leader of a century or so earlier, had called 'The car-drivingest city' in the world. What was unusual was that the man, though quite sober (otherwise he could not have done what he was doing, though the doing of it might itself have suggested intoxication to the uninformed passer-by), was balancing a large mantelpiece clock perilously on his knees as the car swirled round corners and skidded in tram-tracks. I can vouch for his sobriety despite appearances, for I happened to be the said man, carrying an almost eleventh-hour wedding-present from a friend to complete the exhibition in a hotel where 'Miss Gillespie' and her mother, up from the west, were to stay over night; from which they would sally forth the next morning to the wedding of the eldest of a family of a dozen, divided equally between sons and daughters, to the eldest son of four brothers; and in which the wedding breakfast would be held. I was at Sandymount Methodist Church in good time. The day was Maundy Thursday.[2] My 'best man' was Harvey Pelissier, a musician who saw that I was all in order, including lavender gloves and ring in vest pocket for the decisive moment. The organist who was to play the bride to destiny was in his place, Tom Keohler, who brought poetry to the occasion, as Pelissier brought music — not to mention the musical bride and her singing sister Annie who was her bride's-maid, and the poetical bridegroom. The tall handsome father, on whose arm the bride came up the church aisle, may be added to the musical side of the event, not only as instigator and supporter of the bride's musical education, but as a technical aid by causing her, from an early age, to accompany his throaty baritone at local concerts, and as a chronic strummer on the banjo outside legal hours. And there was her tall goddess-like fourth sister who was to do things in painting. The Rev. J.W. Ballard, something of a poet, who had baptised me, officiated. At the wedding breakfast, the new 'Mrs. Cousins,' when the customary dainties fabricated from tortured

and murdered creatures began to be served, gently but conclusively announced, in presence of parents and relations and guests, that from that moment she joined her husband as a vegetarian. I had not asked, not even suggested, her doing so. I had not even hoped that my assurance to her of complete freedom in all our relationships would be met by any concession from her side. I had reached the conviction that only in such freedom, individual, collective, international, could the unity of spirit and feeling be engendered through which richness of character, benignity of action, sufficiency of substance, with their inevitable fruitage of peace and happiness, would grow. I had sensed her nobility of spirit, her natural idealism, her impulse to disinterested service seeking fulfilment through a clear mind and aesthetical temperament; and I had made up my own mind that our marriage would be, on my side, neither a racial expedient nor a personal satisfaction, but a high privilege and spiritual responsibility. Her voluntary determination to join me in the purification of our physical lives, in setting ourselves right with the creatures that shared life with us on the planet, was to me an invisible marriage, deeper and more binding than the ritual of conventional respectability through which we had just passed.

We left the hotel in a shower of rice. In one of the main city thoroughfares by which a cab took us towards the station for Killarney on the four-day honeymoon which was all my employers would give me, the cab pulled up, and Pelissier's face came fiercely through a window and hissed, 'Have you a knife?' I had not specially equipped myself in the Nietzschean[3] manner of not forgetting a whip, or its equivalent, when one went near a woman. But I did happen to have a knife among the odds and ends in a pocket. He cut a string at the back of the cab, and left a long line with an old shoe at its end for the first collector of wedding souvenirs who turned up before the official street cleaners. It was no sixpenny novelist's shy maiden who accompanied me on my honeymoon, but a free-minded young woman who saw no sense in being self-conscious on an occasion through which all the world and

1. Sydney Owenson, Lady Morgan (?1776–1859). See Volume II, pp. 867–73, Volume V, pp. 849–57, 1105–7.
2. The day before Good Friday, named after Christ's great mandate.
3. Friedrich Nietzsche (1844–1900), German philosopher, profoundly antagonistic to the 'new woman'.

his wife had gone, and would go for some millions of years to come, otherwise there would be no one left to keep count of the years. She carried her wedding bouquet from the station entrance to the carriage in full sight of the universe and stacked it on the parcel-rack with its festive ribbons dangling in the breeze.

The country through which we passed on that spring afternoon was new to us, and presented many natural and human features for exchange of reactions. In the dusk, hills loomed up with their customary suggestion of interested presences, and touches of silver indicated streams and lakelets. But knowledge of these had to await a new day. We arrived at Killarney in darkness, odorous, whispering, hill-haunted, star-strewn darkness, at the hotel managed by a lady bearing the ancient and geographical name of MacGillicuddy. But if she was a descendant of the chieftain after whom the range of mountains somewhere beyond present sight was called MacGillicuddy's Reeks,[4] she had not added dietetics to ancestry. We had sent word in advance that we did not use flesh-foods of any kind. Her brilliant idea of alternatives was a combination of cabbage, rhubarb and cheese; either of these in its own place would have served nature's purpose, but the three for a single meal were incongruous. Anyhow we had all life before us for making good temporary deficiencies in feeding, which was half a habit if half a necessity. There was a large slab of the wedding-cake that we had cut together at the breakfast in Dublin in her trunk to fall back on — and to share with the other visitors in the small hotel. And after a chapter of Maeterlinck's 'Wisdom and Destiny'[5] and a night's unruffled sleep, we awoke to Good Friday[6] fresh in body and mind and ready to take all we could out of our brief first visit to Killarney.

The holy day was given to a compendious view of the lakes and their surrounding mountains on a jaunting-car whose driver had a good story for every quarter mile. At twilight we walked to Ross Castle on a lake-side. A distinctive young man, who had left a cycle against a wall and was absorbing the mystic beauty of the hour and place, just had to relieve his feelings in conversation. When he left us we had acquired two new pieces of information; that he was a nephew of the King of Portugal (which he may have been for all we knew), and that cycles could be hired in Killarney town by the day, even as he had hired his. Next we were 'over the hills and far away'[7] on wheels, through scenes out of many an old song, and back by the barren but impressive Gap of Dunloe.[8] Sunday being Easter Day we went to church, or, more correctly, she felt she should go to church, and I felt I should go with her; and all I remember of the service was the falling of a quantity of rice out of the fallals[9] of a bridal hat on the floor of the pew as the bride knelt in prayer. As I had to be at my office desk on Tuesday morning at 9 to receive and pay-out other people's monies, we had to leave Killarney on Easter Monday afternoon. Pending the availability of a house we took up temporary lodgings in the home of a quaint middle-aged pair, the man of whom had attained the eminence of being a Poor Law Guardian.[10] A small parlour on the ground-floor gave us some preliminary experience in the life of cultural acquisition and scattering on which we were entering. We read together; and what we read we assimilated and gave out in occasional symposia of friends some of whose names became known in literature. Our bedroom was on the top floor under the slates; and if we could not see Dublin Bay, there being no side window, we could at least see stars through the skylight, when there were any stars to be seen.

CHAPTER VIII

Meeting Himself

(M.E.C.) Romance comes natural to me. Like any normal high-spirited girl of nineteen I liked the companionship of young men, and I met plenty of them in that first year of freedom in Dublin after four years of boarding-school life. I had a clear

---

4. A mountain range in County Kerry, including the highest summits in Ireland.
5. Maurice Maeterlinck (1862–1949), Belgian dramatist and poet, interested in mysticism.
6. Church feast remembering Christ's Crucifixion.
7. Refrain of a popular ballad by John Gay (1685–1732), *The Beggar's Opera* (1728), Act I, Scene 13, air xvi.
8. Beauty spot near Killarney.
9. Finery.
10. Each workhouse in Ireland was supervised by a Board of Guardians.

idea that it would be a tragic fate to become an old maid. I knew I would like to get married and enjoy a life-companionship with a man whom I would respect and love. I also had formulated my ideal quite vividly: he must be tall and dark, a professor with a beautiful voice. Contrary to my dreams, when he materialised he was small and fair, an accountant in a business concern, and, worst of all, possessed a marked North-of-Ireland accent which we of the South and West detested.

I did not fall in love. I had to be dragged up into it. Often I asked myself why it was that in that first year of knowing him I had such a dislike for him. I cried with disappointment the night after he proposed to me. But I knew he was good and clever and full of the highest ideals. Also I was queerly humble about myself and strangely worldly-wise. With three lovely younger sisters I thought this was probably my only chance of marriage. I must not rashly throw it away. I knew he was a poet; and I loved poetry. Perhaps a poet might work out as well as a professor. I decided to give him a trial. We often met at the house of a mutual friend. My interest was aroused in him by his poetry and later by his dramas, also by his love of all beautiful things. For six months I forced myself to suffer his company so that I might, as I told him, 'learn what he was really like.' But scandal began to wag its tongue about us. So I agreed to an engagement, but made the provision that I reserved the right to break it at any moment. Fortunately we had no money, and I had to finish my Mus. Bac. course.[11] So there was no temptation or forcing into marriage. In the three years following 1900 I was completely won over.

Looking back to those days, how simple and rusticated the world and life seem then to have been, and how young we ourselves were! Motor cars, electric trams, aeroplanes, were rare birds. There were no cinemas, no radios, no electric light; gas sufficed our needs. We had not awakened to problems of woman suffrage or slum work or child welfare schemes. Every weekend in the summer we took a Saturday afternoon trip to one of the pretty spots on the sea-coast north or south of Dublin. In the winter we visited the Botanical Gardens, the Parks, the Museum and National Gallery, or went to plays or concerts or lectures. Every Friday evening he

whom I then thought of as my Poet waited for me to see me home from a teaching engagement with a bunch of flowers in his hand; not many, but choice; a tree carnation, Parma violets, lilies of the valley; the writing of whose names recalls the wafture of their respective fragrances.

It was stimulating to listen to AE[12] expounding Indian philosophy, and art, and the idealism of the Irish Agricultural Organisation Society.[13] Harvey Pelissier I found piquant. Leslie Pielou attracted me by his suggestion of a knight of King Arthur's Round Table, always immaculate and courtly. In comparison with such contemporaries my wee North-man shrank as a personality. But I was learning to appreciate his depth and purity of thought, his genius in expression, his understanding of the need for every human being to have freedom to grow in their own way. And we explored together, and grew together, he in literature, I in music, and both in the fine art of co-operation.

Some time in 1901 I got one of the jolts of my life up till then. Books of the higher criticism, on rationalism and socialism, came my way. I read them with growing interest and knowledge — and before long the whole conventional religious edifice of belief crashed. My people, especially my father, had believed in the literal inspiration of the English Bible. My free reason refused to accept such credulity and the faith based on it. For two and a half years I was an entire but humble agnostic. My fiancee [sic] brought me to a lecture by Mrs. Annie Besant[14] some time during that period; but I was neither attracted nor impressed by either her subject-matter or her personality. Little children can feel superior to their elders; and I was still but a little child in wisdom.

When Paderewski[15] gave his first recital in Dublin I was raised to the seventh heaven of happiness. His playing of 'Reflects dans l'eau' was my first hearing of Debussy's[16] compositions.

11. Baccalaureate in music.

12. AE was the pseudonym of George Russell (1867–1935), poet, journalist and economist; from 1891 to 1897 he lived at the Theosophical Household.
13. Founded by Horace Plunkett (1854–1932) and associates from the Irish Co-operative Movement in 1894; AE edited its journal, the Irish Homestead, from 1905.
14. Annie (Wood) Besant (1847–1933), reformer, journalist, orator and Theosophist (see p. 893).
15. Ignacy Jan Paderewski (1860–1941), Polish pianist, composer and statesman; Prime Minister of Poland in 1919.
16. Claude Debussy (1862–1918), French composer.

It introduced me to a new world of tonal effects. I bought a copy of the piece next day. It took me a fortnight to read it, picking it out from bar to bar laboriously; but I rejoiced in its strangeness.

I worked hard at my musical subjects. Before being allowed to sit for examinations in the specialised aspects that I have already detailed, a thesis had to be accepted. For the final examination I set one of the Psalms to music for four voices, with full pipe-organ accompaniment, eight-part harmony in some sections. It was a miniature cantata; but somehow I never had pride in it then or later. I early realised that I was not a born composer though I had some skill in music-technique. In October 1902 I was qualified to receive the degree of Bachelor of Music of the Royal University of Ireland. My father and mother came up from our home town for the Convocation. It was a great day for my family, and for my ever helpful, and devoted fiancee who had often to stand my nerviness and tiredness during those years of study.

The six months previous to our marriage was a testing time for me. I had to leave Dublin and retire to the bosom of my family to be taught how to cook, to collect a trousseau, and learn household management. I was then the eldest of a dozen children. The three nearest me were away from home; but the home atmosphere had been for years one of continuous babies, growing parental friction, a queer mixture of autocracy, kindliness, love of music and beauty, an irrational kind of religious faith, a sense of congestion. One could see everywhere what a lottery marriage had been; how many blanks had been drawn. What was my guarantee for life-long happiness in such an inescapable close relationship? It had taken me half of our three year engagement to grow content with Fate's choice for me. The second half of the engagement had built up knowledge, respect, admiration and affection in me for a truly worthy man; and it had made us enjoy one another's companionship and dependence on little mutual services. In those first years I used to analyse my lack of emotional care whether he turned up or not as I continued my piano practice and he happened to be later than our time of appointment. And now, so near the fatal or heavenly day of marriage I still had some region of indifference or coldness or uncertainty about the future in me which I was rather ashamed of as being unworthy of him, and not the fictional sort of emotionalism that a bride is expected to have. Imagine then the effect on me of the question of an old friend of my mother's: 'With all these youngsters around you, Gretta, are you not afraid to be married?' Actually I was not afraid; but I had a clear knowledge of the uncertainty of circumstances, and how they could alter cases. In those engagement days we hinted at control of our future. Jim had once clearly promised, 'Anything about the coming of children will be entirely left to your choice.' I believed him. I knew nothing of the technique of sex, but I had utter trust in his knowledge, his will and his integrity. So the question of my mother's friend did not ruffle my feelings as much as it might. Even at that early date I had settled in my mind that every wife should have been so educated that she could earn her own living; so that economic helplessness should not tie her to marriage, and force her and her children to remain with a man or in conditions that were a hypocrisy, a degradation, or a bad influence on the children. Now that I had secured the unusual degree of Bachelor of Music I knew I could always earn my livelihood. But deeper than these Jim and I had realised that our surest unity was in our similar aspirations to build purity and beauty and harmony into our lives and into the world.

In our case the length of our engagement had given us time to gear into one another's ideas about things naturally and inevitably, not violently and not too many together and pell-mell. One of the first things that I disliked about this Mr. Cousins was his vegetarianism. Yet he did not draw attention to it or preach it. He simply didn't eat fish, flesh or fowl. Somehow he managed to get enough vegetables, fruit, nuts, cereals, to satisfy his hunger and keep him healthy. Although I argued against this food-faddism at first, and had no natural inclination towards it, I found certain points connected with it appealing to me. The Dublin Vegetarian Restaurant was a rendezvous for the literary set, of whom AE was the leader. We frequently joined these idealists for lunch, and later met a number of Hindu vegetarians who had come to Dublin on medical and legal studies. By these things the soil of my free-thinking mind was harrowed; and one day about six months before my final music examination I suddenly realised as in a blinding light of unarguable Truth: 'If it is not necessary for health that I should demand living creatures, small and large, to be slaughtered, and their flesh to be cooked for food for me, then it is murder, and a crime for me to be a party to such cruelty and wickedness, and as soon as I am free to order my own food I will be a vegetarian.' That vow was taken by my Spiritual Will to my Highest Self after a moment of illumination. From that decision I never went back. I had set the compass of my life to the pole star of determination to do all that in me lay not to violate the Law of the Sanctity of Life. Of course I told Jim, and the resolve and its reason made him deeply happy. It was like a betrothal of spirits. He never doubted that I would live up to my vision of a bloodless, slaughterless dietary, just as I never doubted that he would carry out his promise about sex-relationships. So we were very happy between ourselves, like wise children.

We were very Irish about money. We had reckoned that Jim's pay, as clerk in a coal and shipping office, would keep us in food and rent and needed recreation. Our wedding outfits would keep us in clothes for two years. Our furniture we would pay for on the hire-purchase system. Wedding presents would help considerably, and my father's wedding cheque would buy a piano. How simple it seemed; and how simply it worked out. Our desires for objects kept within the cash we could depend on. 'Miracles' happened now and then, and what they brought we quickly spent in 'extras', such as our first trip to London together, the same to Paris and Normandy, and so on in ever-widening range.

We were ready for starting the great adventure, the smallest kind of co-operative society, and the most fraught with unknown results from the most intimate and sustained mental and physical relationships possible to humanity. What an amazing driving force is that of Life! The 'life-force' was then a fashionable phrase, due perhaps to Bernard Shaw's virile use of it.[17] It had, as its allies, the 'glamour' that girls retained in the way of dressing their hair, a certain delicacy which called for protection; and its stronger ally was

undoubtedly the ignorance of girls as to the facts of sex.

The mutual happiness that Jim and I had in one another's company we brought to our wedding day in Dublin, April 9, 1903 (Holy Thursday), and we have not lost it in forty years (1943). The cynicism behind the phrase, 'How to be happy though married,' was displaced, in our case, by the affirmation, based on experience, that, begun in happiness, based on love, knowledge and spiritual aspiration, marriage is secondary, not primary. We learned how to be married though happy. At the wedding breakfast in a fashionable hotel I started being a vegetarian. The bride and bridegroom got little to eat compared with the other guests; but they were happy to look the animal kingdom innocently in the face, and depend on the wedding cake to keep them alive till they reached Killarney, where their full freedom began to make their lives according to their New Order of Peace on Earth and Universal Kinship . . .

Leslie Pielou, who was a vegetarian and had married my sister Annie, was my special collaborator in the development of my psychic gift in those years in Dublin, particularly when the evenings of my husband were engaged in literary activities. I would lie on our comfortable sofa, and Leslie would use magnetic passes to get me into such control of the restless automatic mind that I could hold it in a deliberate mirror-like receptivity to a condition of reinforced super-consciousness for an hour to an hour and a half. Later I recounted what I had seen and heard to Jim who recorded it in shorthand.

Naturally all these contacts with extensions of knowledge about occult explanations of the universe and about esoteric Christianity and other world religions and the continuance of personality after death and research into the psychic world, raised many problems and adjustments in our minds. These we discussed and argued about interminably, it seemed, in those first years of our joint life. Then about 1907 I realised that we had ceased speculating, that we had grown quiet. We had entered an ocean which was so full of new affirmations and new orientations towards the bases of life and thought that it gave us contentment and a working programme that lasted for many years without serious disruption or challenge.

---

17. George Bernard Shaw (1856–1950), dramatist, critic and Fabian socialist. His ideas on the 'Life Force' are most clearly articulated in *Man and Superman* (1905).

It was providential that there were so many interests claiming my attention in those first years. I remember that I grew white and thin during our first married year. People thought this was due to my being a vegetarian. But I knew it was due to the problems of adjustment to the revelation that marriage had brought me as to the physical basis of sex.

Every child I looked at called to my mind the shocking circumstance that brought about its existence. My new knowledge, though I was lovingly safeguarded from it, made me ashamed of humanity and ashamed for it. I found myself looking on men and women as degraded by this demand of nature. Something in me revolted then, and has ever since protested against, certain of the techniques of nature connected with sex. Nor will I and many men and women of like nature, including my husband, be satisfied, be purified and redeemed, life after life, until the evolution of form has substituted some more artistic way of continuance of the race.

MARY LAVIN

(1912–96)

A SINGLE LADY (1964)

[Mary Lavin is one of the few Irish women writers who have received relatively widespread attention and acclaim. Her short stories seldom represent sexuality explicitly, but they are often saturated with sexual significance and erotic tensions. In 'A Single Lady', the title story of a collection published in 1951 by Michael Joseph, a celibate woman confronts, or, more accurately, fails to confront, sexuality — her own and her father's. Isabel's conception of appropriate sexual relations, embodied in her parable and her disapproval of the age and class differences between her father and Annie, leads her to react with outrage and horror to her father's erotic relationship to a servant. But, as often happens in Lavin, Isabel's moral indignation, while not necessarily to be dismissed as false or wrong, also reveals her own sexual confusion and deprivation. Lavin revised the story by the time of its re-publication in *The Stories of Mary Lavin* (London: Constable, 1964) from which this text is taken.]

Apart from anything else he wasn't that kind of man; the reverse indeed; distant; cool in his manner. And as for his manner towards the servants, in her mother's time at least he used to treat them as if they were made of wood; as if they had no feelings whatever. Latterly, of course, things had changed so much that they both had to alter their attitude towards them. And when it came to having only the one wretched creature for all the drudgery of the great barrack of a house, there had been times when she herself had felt it necessary to be familiar. But even then, even when she had made concession after concession, it was a long time before he unbent to any degree. Was it any wonder, then, that she discredited people's hints and insinuations. At least in the beginning! What daughter in the world would have given any credence to them. And yet the remarks continued to be made.

Oh, but it all seemed so unreal; so impossible. At his age! Why! if he had any inclinations of that sort he could have satisfied them long ago in a manner compatible with his position. There had been nothing in the past fourteen years to prevent him from remarrying if he wished to do so. Up to quite recently he had kept his appearance fairly well, and with that and his first wife's fortune he stood a fairly good chance of marrying some person of suitability. Even five years ago he cut a passable figure. But this! This! Who could blame her for having refused credence to this! Her father! — and a common servant! If she were even that! but a wretched little slut. Yes! What was the use of denying it. Had she not, right from the start, been repulsed at the idea of having to have such a poor type of creature in the house? Isabel shuddered. Hadn't she been disgusted by the food? Hadn't she been afraid to look too closely at anything the creature handled? And as for the creature's room, in spite of the fact that she knew it was her duty to do so, she had never once gone into it. She knew so well what it would be like: smelly and close, the windows never opened, and the bedclothes bundled about like rags. A servant indeed! Too good a word for her!

To think that she, Isabel, was responsible for bringing the creature into the house! But what could she do? She was in such a quandary when poor old Mary Ellen was taken ill.

Such a quandary: for a moment a curiously soft, even stupid, expression came over Isabel's thin features, as she tried to recall how it had come about that she had hired the creature in the first place. Then her face sharpened again. It was for his sake; for her father's sake. It was out of consideration for him that she had done it. She didn't want him to suffer any inconvenience while she was endeavouring to find the proper kind of person. That, of course, had been her intention: to look around for a suitable person. And although she had to admit that after a day or two she had drifted into accepting the situation, it might not have been so easy to get anyone better. That was what she said to him when he had been so aghast at letting the like of her into the house.

'Only as a stop-gap, Father! Just to give me time to look around for someone proper.'

'But am I to understand that you are letting this person sleep here?' he demanded. 'Where are you going to put her? What room do you intend her to occupy? What bedclothes will you give her? And what condition will the room be in when you get a proper girl? Have you thought of that?'

He felt that at the very least the creature should come by the day and go home at night.

Isabel smiled bitterly.

It had been in order that he would have his early morning cup of tea that she had insisted on having the girl live with them. If she had only had her own comfort to consider it would have been a different matter. She wouldn't mind if she had had to go without her breakfast until the middle of the morning. Indeed, it was often the middle of the morning now before this impudent slut made any effort to give her anything. It was one excuse after another. First it was her father's early tea. Well, that was all right. But after that it was his shaving water. The kettle had to be filled again for that. And when that kettle was boiled there was certain to be another demand upon it.

'Is the kettle boiled yet for my tea?' One or two mornings, from sheer hunger and cold, she had to come down the passage and humiliate herself to the creature.

She never got any satisfaction.

'It's boiled all right. But what about the milking-pans?'

It seemed as if there was always an opportunity for the creature to appear in the right, and for her, the mistress, to appear in the wrong. The milking-pans had to be scalded. The herd could not be kept waiting about all morning in the kitchen. She knew that. But at the same time she knew that if it wasn't the milking-pans it would be something else! She was always being relegated to the kettle after the next!

And the cleverness of the creature. She was careful never to go too far. After the taunt came the sop.

'I'll fill it up again for you, Miss. You must be starving. It won't be a minute coming to the boil.'

Oh, the cleverness; the slyness. Next thing she'd do would be to jab a poker between the bars of the grate and rattle it until she had filled the kitchen with smoke and ashes, and shaken down all the red embers into the ash-pit. 'That is to say if any kettle could be got to boil on this fire.' That was her method; to taunt and placate, to placate and taunt; making things unpleasant all the time, but careful never to go beyond a certain limit. When there was hardly a spark of red left in the grate, she'd become agreeable enough. 'Wait a minute now, Miss. It's nearly out, but I'll bring it up again with a few sprigs of kindling.' But the sprigs were certain to be wet, or there would be too few of them. As likely as not it would be another hour after that before she got her tea. And such tea!

Once or twice she had thought of getting some kind of a small oil-burner and making her own tea in the breakfast-room, but she decided that it would look too much like giving up her authority in the house.

Her authority! Two hard-pressed tears came into Isabel's eyes and fell on to her white blouse, making the starch limp in spots. Authority was a thing of the past. What authority had she, for instance, in the kitchen? She hardly dared go into it. If she had any say at all would it be in the condition in which it was? Would the floor be coated with grease? Would the walls be yellowed with smoke? And would the tea towels be as they were?

Isabel thought miserably of the dirty grey dishcloths, always wet and slimy, and disgusting to handle. They were never put out on the clothes line. They were always hanging wetly over the backs of the chairs. Authority! The word was a joke.

For a long time Isabel sat in the badly-lit room that used to be so bright and gay when her mother had it for her boudoir, and as she sat sadly reflecting there, she stared into the fireplace, where a fair enough fire blazed between the unblackened bars of the grate, under the neglected and discoloured mantelpiece.

Oh, the neglect! The neglect everywhere, she thought. That mantelpiece used to be so white and glossy.

And to think that she didn't dare to say a word about it. She sat forward. How, how did this state of affairs come about? A frown of concentration came between her eyes. Why had she not seen how things were shaping? Why had she let them go so far? Why had she not put down her foot? But as she looked down at it, her narrow foot with the pointed shoe looked a weak and inadequate symbol of the power with which she was to have put down Annie Bowles.

Isabel felt her helplessness could hardly have been so great in the beginning. Surely there must have been some point at which she might have made a stand against the creature?

Just then, faintly, so faintly in fact it was remarkable that her ears should catch it, there was a sound from the kitchen; the sound of a wicker chair creaking.

Isabel tightened in every muscle. There! There was a point at which she could have made a stand. To think that she had said nothing when the wicker chairs were taken down from the bedrooms and brought into the kitchen to be warped and put out of shape by the heat and the damp. And not only one, but two. To think she had allowed the creature to bring down a second one. Oh, she was blind indeed.

At thought of that second wicker chair, Isabel's hands began to tremble. When it came to the bringing down of that second chair things had come to a nice pass. It was no wonder that people had begun to talk. It was no wonder there had been whispers and hints. The only wonder was

that she had been so slow to suspect anything.

Why, why, why had she not seen how the land lay? Against this, however, there was always the same answer. How could she have believed such a thing of her own father? Even now, at this moment, when she should have been accustomed to it, it was still almost unbelievable to her that he was down there in the kitchen, probably sitting on one of those wicker chairs, opposite the creature, looking at her, and making those foolish eyes at her.

There! Faintly, from the far region of the kitchen, came another dry creak of a wicker chair. She knew it; he was sitting down. She could fancy him lifting his long leg to cross it over its fellow. The osiers creaked again. How loudly this time the creaking sounded in the silence.

That was another thing that had baffled her at first; the silence. Even when she had begun to notice one or two things she did not like, even after she had become aware that he was always shuffling down the passage to the kitchen, even after she had taken note of how long he stayed down there, she had been foolishly reassured by that silence. Now, of course, she dreaded it. Now it confused her, put her nerves on edge, like the untidiness and dirt of the girl.

For there had been a time when, that too, she had regarded in a different light. If, she argued, the creature had designs upon him, the least one would expect would be that she would wash her face and keep her clothes together. Isabel smiled forlornly. For days she had fed on this gloomy hope. But as with the silence, she had come to feel there was something flauntingly evil in the disarray of her outer person. Those dirty greasy rags she wore; that ravelled red cardigan pulled across her bust with a safety pin; and those cracked old boots, with her feet showing through them! Had she no respect for how she looked; no shame; no modesty? Modesty? When Isabel went into the kitchen one night wasn't she busy with a needle and thread, there in front of the fire, patching and dragging together some filthy garment that was spread out on her lap. And when in spite of her distaste she had looked more closely at the thing, what was it but a filthy old corset; a corset!

At the thought of such indelicacy a feeling of bewilderment came over Isabel. What was the meaning of it? She flinched from the answer. But as if against her will she was being forced to face some issue, at that moment there came again from the kitchen the sound of the wicker chair creaking and protesting.

Protesting against what? What were they doing? Could it be possible that — ? Her mind for a moment gathered itself together and seemed ready to face whatever lay behind those questions, but as quickly again it shrank back from even a half-thought of such a revolting nature.

Not that she was so innocent! As if she was accused of ignorance, Isabel sat suddenly bolt upright. As a matter of fact, it had always been one of the things she resented most vehemently, the suggestion that a woman should be regarded as in any way ignorant of certain matters just because she was single.

Nothing exasperated her more than the way young married women regarded certain matters as sacrosanct, matters that large-minded people would not hesitate to discuss openly and frankly. In her own university days there was nothing, absolutely nothing, that was not discussed freely, and as often as not in mixed company as well. And then she was only in her twenties, whereas now, at forty, it seemed as if people supposed she knew nothing when it came to talking about certain things. Why! even this wretched slut in the kitchen had a curious look on her face at times, as if she too imagined that she had some hidden knowledge; some secret wisdom.

Isabel trembled with irritation, but after a minute she became calmer. She made a deliberate effort to be tolerant. For some people it was intellectually impossible to apprehend the nature of life. For them knowledge was only soluble in experience. It was so different for her with her university education, and her highly developed intellect.

Isabel felt the better for having recalled her own worldliness. Even this aberration of her father's, she thought, even this was nothing new. It was common enough for men of a certain age to display certain tendencies. It was common enough for them to be subject to peculiar physical disturbances. For a period they might even become unaccountable for their behaviour. It was nature manifesting itself as their bodies became subconsciously aware of the approach of

senility and impotence! That was it. There was nothing so dark or hidden about it. The climacteric; that was all.

Reassured somewhat, Isabel began to apply her wisdom to her sores. Yes, even on their last visit to the city she noticed the way he stared at young girls in the street, and on the tram cars, and once or twice in a restaurant when the waitress was giving him his change she fancied — Oh, but that was hardly fair. It was so difficult to take anything from another person's hand without one's fingers touching. And even if he had held the waitresses' hands, or made those foolish eyes at them, she wouldn't really have minded if it stopped at that; she would have put up with it.

Isabel sighed. She had been prepared to put up with so much! All at once another aspect of her misery came over her.

'After all the sacrifices I made for him!' and although those sacrifices were vague and unspecified, the thought of them filled her with new misery, and she stared dismally down at her feet. Abruptly then she stuck out one foot. Her feet hadn't always been as thin and narrow as that! She hadn't always worn such narrow, pointed shoes. The tears started into her eyes again. The dowdy habits of spinsterhood had crept insidiously upon her. But was it to be wondered at: living as she did in this bleak isolated place, never meeting anyone, never having anyone call. That, too, she had done for his sake; never leaving the place, never going away for a visit, however short, and never on any account staying away for the night. Not one night had she been away from the place in twelve solid years. They had gone away together, of course, upon little excursions. But that was not the same thing.

And yet, as she thought of those trips to London, to Southport, and once even to Ostend, her tears scalded her face. If only those times would come again how little she would count all the other sacrifices she had made. They used to be so happy. Only a year ago they had gone to London. It was less than two years since they had been in Ostend. And only a few months ago he was talking of another trip. What had happened since then? How had things altered? What had come over him that he had changed so much?

Desperately Isabel tried to go back over the

past to discover an answer to those agonized questions. Had it been her fault in any way? Could she have done anything to prevent things from taking the course they had taken? But her mind had no sooner fastened upon this last question than it grasped avidly at another. Could she do anything even now?

If she could make him come away with her — now — for a few weeks, it might break the spell that was over him. But she knew her hopes were idle. That creature wouldn't let him go. She had a hold over him: some hideous hold over him.

Oh! if only she could get rid of her!

Fallaciously Isabel fed herself with another desperate hope. Why didn't she? Supposing she stood up and walked down the passage and ordered her out of the house this minute?

So powerfully for a moment did she imagine herself bursting into the kitchen, Isabel sprang to her feet and began to walk up and down the floor. She put her hands to her face, it must be ablaze; and her eyes!

But as she strode across the floor for the fourth time Isabel caught sight of herself in the mottled and foggy mirror over the mantelpiece. She came to a stand. Where were the flaming cheeks, and the righteous, angry eyes? In the cold glass she saw only the same pale, harassed face with which she was daily familiar.

That face wouldn't help her much. She stared into the glass. It was hard to believe that the angry hurt of her heart should show so little. She sat down. There was one other thing she could do: go away and leave them to their own devices.

This latter step, drastic as it was, did not excite her greatly, however, for the simple reason that it wasn't the first time that such a thought had come into her head. Months ago this way of evasion had occurred to her, but it had seemed a cowardly and selfish step to take. Now it seemed there was nothing else to do.

Disconsolately Isabel looked around her. She hadn't the first idea of how to set about her departure. Where would she go? That, she supposed, was the first thing to settle. And then the question of money; that was another thing to be settled. In fact that, she supposed, should come before anything else. Briskly she went over to her desk and took out a sheet of paper on which to make the necessary calculations, but her feet lagged and her hands moved uncertainly

among her papers, because, with a chill, she was beginning to realize that here, too, the spectre of defeat would rise to confront her. She would have to speak to her father. It would be necessary for him to arrange about her investments, to convert them into money. There could be no question of leaving without his consent. Or could there? She tried to concentrate. There were those papers she had signed a few years ago. What had become of them? He had taken them away, hadn't he? Yes, he had locked them up somewhere, probably in the tin box he kept under his bed. She supposed she would have to have those papers to take to the bank if matters were to be arranged properly. If she had those papers it might be possible to let her have some money, there and then, on account. That would simplify matters. Dully, however, she felt that things could not be simplified so easily. Why had he taken the papers away? Why had he made her sign them in the first place? And what had she signed? Naturally she had not bothered to read them. If it had been a stranger who had asked her to sign something she would have been more prudent: more cautious. But her father! She tried to be sanguine, but gloomy forebodings settled upon her. It might not be so easy to settle matters. And she was so ignorant of financial affairs. It was a mistake; she saw that now. If she could only concentrate. She forced herself to do so. There had been two occasions when she had signed something. And her father had said something. What was it? What could it have been? Something about temporary accommodation, whatever that might be. Well, Isabel shrugged her shoulders, if, as she must suppose had happened, she had signed something which gave him a use of part, or even all of her money, that would undoubtedly entail a delay.

Then too, if he was irritated with her, as he might easily be, he could probably drag out the transactions. He could probably put her in an awkward position.

Isabel stared at the fire. It was getting low. In her lap her hands had fallen flaccidly apart. A frightened look came into her eyes. Supposing he was vindictive towards her? Supposing — she could hardly bear to think of it — but supposing that creature had a say in the matter? — supposing —

Oh! — Isabel's lids closed over her eyes and she was overpowered by a feeling of weakness, but after a few moments she pulled herself together. Perhaps she was worked up over nothing. After all, her father was her father. He might lose his head. He might make a laughing-stock of himself over this creature, but when it came to touching her money; hers! Isabel's! his daughter's! When it came to that! Isabel was ashamed to think that she had allowed even a shadow of distrust to fall across her mind. How could she have entertained such a thought for a moment? Nature was nature. Blood was thicker than water. Yet fast as those clichés flocked to her aid, a gnawing fear had fastened upon her and she could not shake it from her.

Hadn't he acted very oddly on the only occasion she had thrown out a remark upon the matter? She had merely made some remark about investments in general. She wasn't even thinking of her own investments, but she noticed at once the way he evaded the subject. Indeed, a peculiar glitter had come into his eyes, and a look, at first defensive, then prohibitive, as if warning her not to say anything further!

Thinking of that warning glitter, Isabel's heart, that had risen to no purpose so often, and fallen again, seemed finally to turn over. All the self-pity, all the repugnance, all the humiliation and all the wounded vanity she had suffered in the past twelve months was suddenly set at nothing, and the possibility of her own financial embarrassment was all that concerned her.

Oh, what had she done? Why had she been such a fool? Such a stupid, blind fool!

Another thought flashed into her mind, making her more miserable still. What would her mother say if she could see what a fool she had been; her mother who had so expressly bequeathed the money to her in her own right. The bewildered look came over her face again.

But as she rocked herself from side to side, there began to stir in her mind a vague memory of something her mother had once told her, when she was only a young girl, hardly listening indeed, hardly paying attention at all. It was a story about some servant girl that her mother had heard about long ago, but it seemed to have made an impression upon her. What was this it was? In spite of her preoccupation with her own distress, Isabel's mind kept turning upon the old story. This girl was working in the house of a small farmer. Yes, that was right, and there was

an old man living in the same neighbourhood, a kind of farmer too, she supposed, but he had a couple of hundred acres, and a big ramshackle three-storey house. The old fellow had been married twice and buried both of his wives. He was nearly seventy, bent almost double, and he was bow-legged into the bargain. But he had plenty of money. And the girl knew it.

Isabel sat upright. It was all coming back to her. But why should it come to her mind now? Why, indeed, had Mother told it to her in the first place? To what purpose had she told it? Supposing that she in turn were to tell it to her father?

Suddenly Isabel's mind was illuminated with a great flash. Supposing her mother, long ago, had perceived some merit in that story: some merit as a parable? For that was just what it seemed to be: a parable.

If I were to tell it to him, she thought with excitement, what would he think of it? What would he say? It would at least let him see that I knew what was going on behind my back. It would at least give him something to ponder upon.

And supposing she told it to the other creature? What effect would it have upon her? It would at least let her see that people weren't as blind as she took them to be all the time!

Isabel sprang to her feet again. Supposing she went down to the kitchen this minute and told them both together.

Would she?

Like an answer, there came from the kitchen a subdued sound of chuckling. That settled it. The next moment she was midway down the dark passage, groping her way with her hands.

'Who is this?'

It was her father who called out. Isabel shuddered. There was something detestable in the false note she detected in his voice, the more so since she could almost have sworn that he called out in order to cover some other sound for which her ear strained in vain as she stumbled down the passage.

But when she went into the kitchen, she felt foolish when she saw how innocently the old man was sitting with his feet up on the range. She felt an impulse of pity towards him. He looked so old; almost feeble, she thought.

Then suddenly she saw that he was in his stocking feet, and at the sight of his grey socks she felt her annoyance return. And when he opened his mouth she immediately caught the false note in his voice again.

'Oh, it's you, my dear! Did you let your fire go down!' He had hastily taken his feet down from the top of the stove when she came into the room and stuck them into his shoes. He put his hands on the arms of his chair, too, as if he was about to stand up, but casting a glance at the range he sank back in his seat while he reached for a sod of turf from the basket beside the chair. 'Not that our fire is so good,' he said. He looked across at the creature. 'What were we thinking about,' he said, 'to let our fire go so low?'

We! Ours!

Isabel stared at him with a cold hard stare, but he was busy poking the fire.

'Will you sit down, my dear?' he said then, setting about getting up again.

Sit down; in that chair; on that filthy cushion? Sit down opposite that slut? Isabel pressed her lips together and looked for the first time at Annie Bowles.

Annie Bowles, as a matter of fact, seemed to be almost asleep. She didn't appear to have moved a muscle since Isabel came into the kitchen, but sat, staring into the fire, her big face red with heat, and her big calves, that bulged out of her broken boots, so rosy-marbled from the fire that only an imbecile would continue to sit so close to the heat.

Isabel looked steadily at the gawky creature. Why she looked like a gom!¹ She looked back to her father. Was he doting? A half-wit peasant, and a doting old man. If she wasn't able to pit her wits against these two!

'No, thank you, Father!' She leant back against the edge of the table. 'I'm all right here.' She turned to the other creature. 'That's all right!' she said, making a deprecating gesture. 'Stay where you are!' she said. This, she felt, was a very tactful remark. It was not unfriendly, but it had the right element of patronage, because it went without saying that the ignorant lump hadn't made any effort to budge out of her chair.

All the same, after a moment, Isabel felt foolish standing there while the others sat, and so she sat up on the edge of the table. Compared with that sluggish lump in the wicker chair, she felt that there was something keen and alert about sitting

1. Simpleton.

on the edge of the table. She felt more confident; she felt altogether more capable of dealing with the situation.

There was only one obstacle; how to start?

'Oh!'

It was the first syllable the creature had uttered, and at the same time she drew back her feet with a start from the fire. For, as a sod fell from the grate, a shower of starry sparks had scattered into the air, glittering for a moment and then vanishing; but in their momentary voyage, travelling a fiery path towards Annie Bowles. 'Oh!' she cried again, 'oh!' and she drew back her chair still more.

The occupant of the second wicker chair, on the other hand, sat forward. To him the scattering of sparks was a welcome distraction from a situation that threatened to become awkward.

'Ah-ha!' he said, a roguish note in his voice that set Isabel's teeth on edge, 'Ah-ha, Annie, there's money coming to you!'

Was he mad? Isabel had forgotten this old superstition, but suddenly she remembered it. And then almost immediately she saw her chance of using it for her own ends.

'Money coming to you, Annie?' she said quickly. 'I hope it will bring you luck. Not like a girl I heard about!'

Her exclamation was so sudden, her voice so decisive, that the other two looked up with a surprise that approximated to interest.

'Yes,' she said maliciously, throwing a glance at her father, 'Mother told me the story.' But immediately she tried to disguise her malice. 'I forgot all about it until this minute,' she said nervously, falsely, 'I don't know what put it into my head!' Her voice was rapid, reckless. She laughed too, nervously and hysterically. All the same she knew what she was doing, and the way they were looking at her, stupidly and puzzled, was a help. Why! her father looked stupefied. As for Annie Bowles, she looked no more than a half-wit. There she sat, her legs apart, and her mouth open. 'Do you want to hear the story?' said Isabel brightly and briskly, but they had no chance to reply before she began it, turning from one to the other, but mostly towards her father.

'Not a bad kind of girl at all,' she said, 'came from a respectable home, I believe.' Here Isabel turned and threw a word, direct, to the servant girl. 'As a matter of fact her name was Annie too, as well as I remember,' she said. 'She was attractive, too, I suppose,' she said grudgingly, as her eyes lingered upon the real Annie, 'in a dumpy kind of way, I mean; with a big red face and big red cheeks.' Isabel stared harder at the real Annie, and, as if her imagination was feeding and fattening upon her, she piled detail on detail. 'Her neck was big and soft,' she said, 'I suppose some people might find that attractive, but it looks too much like goitre[2] for me.' Isabel shuddered and turned back to her father. She had begun to forget that her story was supposed to be hearsay. 'Anyway, she was big and strong, and I suppose there would have been plenty of young fellows of her own class willing enough to marry her and provide her bread and butter.' Here Isabel stopped and stared first at her father and then at the girl; they were both listening, although her father's interest was reluctant, and as if he was on his guard against something. 'But,' said Isabel relentlessly, 'it wasn't bread and butter she wanted!'

There was silence for a moment.

'Well, what did she want?' said the man at last.

All at once Isabel felt weak. She had come to the awkward part of the story. The next word, and unless he was a fool her father would have guessed her motive in telling the story. Out of the corner of her eye she felt that the old man was staring at her with a peculiar look.

'I'll tell you what she wanted,' she said, 'but first of all I must tell you there was an old fellow living outside the village,' jerkily she got out her words. She didn't dare to look at either of them now, but out of the corner of her eye she fancied her father was still staring peculiarily at her. 'He was about eighty,' she said, hoping to lessen the likeness between him and the old farmer. 'An old bachelor!' she lied. She was getting more and more nervous and not daring to raise her eyes she fastened them on his shoes. They were so well-cared and polished, so youngly fashioned, so dapper, indeed, for a man of his age, that looking at them Isabel suffered a curious sensation. She felt that his age had fallen away from him, and that he was the spruce and dapper man he had been when she was a child: the father before whom she had always been so cowed and docile. She stared at the shoes and her heart began to

beat violently. What wrath was she drawing down upon her foolish head? Where her thin black hair was parted in the middle she suddenly felt as if the skin was as fragile as silk. She wanted to put up her hand to it, and protect it. She even began to imagine that a pulse at that point was opening and shutting like the fontenelle in a new-born child.

But after a moment of staring dully at those dapper patent leather shoes her eye travelled upwards a few inches. Pah! Beyond the neat toecaps the shoes were unlatched, over them the old man's worsted socks were rumpled and untidy, while between the socks and the end of his trousers, his felted underwear showed. And she remembered the indignity in which she had surprised him with his stockinged feet on the range.

'The old fool!' she said, suddenly out loud, meaning at one and the same time the old man in front of her and the old fool in the story. 'The old fool,' she repeated. 'He could have married hundreds of times, but he never seemed to take any notice of any girl until he put his eye on this creature — this girl I was telling you about. I don't know how he first came into contact with her, but it wasn't long until the whole locality was talking about them. He was always finding opportunities for walking past the house where she worked, and when she went into the town he always managed to be in the town at the same time. Then he began to wait for her on the road, and walk home beside her. And after that the gossip started! But the old fellow didn't seem to mind. He didn't seem to care what people said, which was surprising, because he was a man who prided himself on his position, prided himself on his reputation and dignity. There was never anything' — Isabel hesitated — 'never anything —' she hesitated again. Ever since she had first given credence to the hints and whispers about this affair, there was one word above all others she longed to throw in his face; one word she wanted to hear herself utter, but before the enormity of such an utterance her spirit had failed. But now, now was her opportunity — 'nothing lecherous about him!' she said, and she sat rigid as death.

There was a lifetime of silence to be lived through in the instant after the enormous word had fallen upon them all. And then, as she began

2. An enlargement of the throat glands caused by a tumour.

to feel the throb in her head once more, Isabel got another curious sensation. She got the sensation that the others had not been listening to her at all. But how could that be? A moment before the old man's eyes had burned through her. Isabel was baffled. She lost her place in the story.

But they must have been listening after all because her father was able to prompt her.

'Well,' he said deliberately, but looking queerly at her, 'what did they say about him?'

'They said he was doting!' she said crudely, cruelly.

But her father only laughed. After a moment he spoke again.

'What did they say about her — about Annie?' he asked, and there was something shocking in his having the name right.

'They knew her kind,' she said shortly, 'and anyway, she made no secret of what she had in mind. Even in the start when people gave her a sly dig about the old fellow, she always had the same answer. "How badly off I'd be," she said, "if I had his money."'

There! She was beginning to touch him on the raw.

'The old fool,' she said again, exulting in the appellation. 'He thought she was marrying him for love. For love!' Isabel's voice rose. 'For love!' she said. 'Could you imagine anything more laughable!' She turned her head to look from one of them to the other, but just then again she got the same curious sensation as before that their attention had escaped her. She looked sharply at them. Did she imagine it or had they crossed glances quickly, furtively, under her very eyes? A vague feeling of misgiving came over her, and she began to doubt the wisdom of having begun such a story at all. As long as she had begun it, though, she had to end it. And the end was what mattered.

'They were the laughing-stock of the countryside,' she said. In her excitement once more she forgot that her story was supposed to be hearsay. 'You should see the way he looked at her,' she said. 'You should see him making sheep's eyes at her, and the killing part of it was he had hardly enough sight in his eyes to put one foot in front of the other.'

At this point, unexpectedly, Annie Bowles tittered.

Isabel looked sharply at her.

What made her laugh? She glanced back at her father. He was looking at Annie, but he looked back quickly.

'By all accounts he needed a wife,' he said.

Oh, so that was his attitude. Isabel drew herself up. Wait till he heard more.

'He got a nice one!' she said. 'Do you want to know what she said the night before the wedding? Well, I'll tell you. The house was full of people and she passed near someone in time to hear them saying something about the old fellow. "She'll bury him inside a year!" That's what she overheard. But wait a minute, what do you suppose she said?' Isabel looked straight ahead of her. 'She only gave a laugh. "I won't have to bury the money," she said.'

There! Did he hear that?

Isabel looked at her father. He heard her all right. He wasn't looking at the creature now; he was looking at her.

'How long did he live?' he said.

Isabel hesitated. She could say what she liked. She could make out that he paid for his passion: that he was dead in a few months! But some dissatisfaction with the effect she was making upon the man made her turn towards the other creature.

'He lived for sixteen years,' she said, her voice thick with satisfaction. 'He lived long enough to turn her from a young girl into a dull middle-aged woman, worn out from minding him, and lifting him from the bed to the fire, and from the fire to the bed, to say nothing of the way her heart was scalded with his jealousy and his doting. That's how long he lived,' she said.

But as she looked to see the effect of her words on Annie Bowles, she was in time unmistakably, to see them look at each other, and she knew that some meaning was passed between them in that look.

Isabel's heart faltered. What had gone wrong with her parable? It had only furthered them in their badness.

'Well!' Ignoring her, her father leaned forward towards Annie Bowles. 'Well,' he said provocatively, 'she got the money, didn't she? She got what she wanted?'

He was asking Annie Bowles. And Annie Bowles had an answer.

She gave it at first only with her eyes, and a ribald look at the old man. Then she tossed her head.

'Well!' she countered. 'He got what he wanted too, didn't he?'

And there and then, under her eyes, there passed between them another of those looks that she used to imagine only when she sat alone in the little boudoir, those looks so heavy with intimations beyond her understanding.

Isabel looked from one of them to the other, but it was no longer possible to see them separately. Something seemed to hold them bound together as one.

Oh, the ugliness; oh, the badness! Isabel pressed her lips together. She didn't want them to see what they had done to her. She got to her feet. She might as well go to bed and leave them to their devices.

'Good night,' she said abruptly and awkwardly. But they hadn't heard her. She went to the door but at the door she looked back at them. And she was struck by the brightness and glitter of her father's eyes. They burned upon Annie Bowles. And Annie Bowles? Isabel looked at her, but Annie's back was turned. She could not see her face, yet she knew the light that lit her eyes. And ugly or not, evil or not, Isabel knew its meaning was not discoverable to her.[3]

---

3. In 1951 the following two sentences (omitted by 1964) concluded the story: Among the many attributes of the intellect the power to fathom that glance was not numbered. Its import was for ever hidden from her; an educated, intellectual, and highly developed single lady.

MAY MORTON

(1876–1957)

from:
SUNG TO THE SPINNING WHEEL
(1952)

[In 'Fidelity' May Morton plays on romantic conventions of sexual fidelity and on Catholic doctrine, which casts faith as the foundation of all other virtues. The poems are from her collection published in Belfast in 1952 by Quota Press.]

Fidelity

Let me be true to all of those I love
Nor ever ask if they be true to me:
The faithful have their faith, it is the false
Who have most need of my fidelity.

To Her Last Love

Self-prisoned in the ruin of lost years
I set a flower beside each scattered stone
that I might make a garden of the tomb
where memory and I dwelt all alone.

Safe in the polished armour of a smile
(for smiles like roses grow on many a grave)
I bartered all the blossoms of my pain
and in my coat of mail I passed for brave.

But when you came I tore up by the roots
the gaudy blooms that hid the buried years
and gave you truth for truth. So wept no more
into my secret, useless well of tears.

I have rebuilt the temple of my soul:
Its jewelled windows paint the sunlit air
its quiet cloisters shelter healing peace
that you may come and find refreshment there.

And I have cleansed my heart of all its griefs
that I may dedicate myself anew
to tend my altar-flame of loving faith
and keep it burning day and night for you.

ANNE CRONE

(1915–72)

from:
BRIDIE STEEN (1948)

[In *Bridie Steen*, Anne Crone focuses on sectarian and class differences between Catholics and Protestants, and on the implications of these differences for inter-marriage. Bridie, the orphaned child of a mixed marriage, is raised by her severe, pious, Catholic aunt, but goes to live with her clannish Protestant grandmother at eighteen. She falls in love with her Protestant cousin, William Henry, but her desire to marry him and let her romantic loyalties supersede her religious ones is thwarted by the excruciating inner conflict it produces. The novel, published in New York in 1948 by Scribners, is set in the North of Ireland, near Lough Erne.]

'But I can't stay here, darling. You don't know the world. I'll come and see you every evening until we get married, and then we won't be separated any more.'

They were standing in the hall in the twilight. She looked out through the side-panes of the door at the grass in the patch of front garden where the rain was falling sullenly. The last funeral guest had gone, the last slice of ham and beef had been consumed, and there was nobody in the kitchen except Mrs. Blake. The house yawned with emptiness.

'We'll be married soon, little one, isn't that right? In a month. I'll get the licence. I can't leave you here alone any longer than that. Will that please you?' He held out his arms and she crept into them. 'Will that please you?'

She nodded.

'It's so lonely here to-night!'

'I know, but Mrs. Blake is going to stay with you. You can ask her to sleep with you, if you like.'

The idea of sleeping with Mrs. Blake did not appeal to Bridie.

'No.' She shook her head. 'I wouldn't be afraid if —'

'If what?'

'If — I had my beads.'[1] She raised her eyes in distress. 'I know it's very wrong of me now that grandma's dead. Her ghost would torment me if I looked at them. I haven't really ever looked at them since you — since that time in the car. I thought of you instead, but now I'm afraid.'

He was not at all angry, as she had expected he would be. He smiled kindly. 'Poor little Bridie! I know. You are hemmed in by fears. The habits of a lifetime are bound to rise up at a crisis. Look at your beads if you wish. You needn't worry about Aunt Lisha's ghost. She has no ghost, any more than the millions of human beings who have died before her, but' — he stooped and whispered — 'promise me one thing — that you won't say any prayers over them. When you have me always, you won't ever think of them again.'

'I promise.'

She let her head sink on his breast in an overflow of gratitude.

When he had gone, she went into the kitchen with some comfort in her heart. Mrs. Blake, wearied, was sitting on the bench contemplating Davy at the end of the table opposite her. Davy was no longer as the world had known him. This day had been a turning-point in his life. He had, in fact, created the sensation of the day.

'Where is Davy?' Bridie had asked William Henry when the men came back from the funeral.

'Davy? He must be somewhere. I didn't notice. Is he not outside?'

He was not outside, and the most exhausting of searches for him proved vain. In the memory of her own despair at Uncle James's death Bridie had divined what had befallen him.

'He has stayed with her! He is beside the grave!' she cried.

William Henry had driven his car to the graveyard to see, silhouetted against a sombre sky, Davy's figure, with raised shivering shoulders and drooping head, crouching upon the top of the grave. He had not wanted to come home. He had merely shaken his head with an air of total incomprehension. In this unwillingness there was not the smallest trace of violence. Apparently he

1. Rosary beads.

now fully recognised that his mistress was dead, but, without wishing to combat the thought, was overwhelmed by the futility of further existence. The power of reason was not in him as in his fellow-men to tell him that, suffer what he might, he must go on, must return home and feed the pigs and calves and milk the cows until his summons came as his mistress's had come. Since he had to live, he would live beside what had been she. He would stay there for ever and play with the stones and break the little lumps of earth that came in contact with his fingers. Only when William Henry, realising the depth of the abyss into which his wits had sunk, knelt down beside him and offered him the money from his pocket to play with, did he succeed in awakening response in him. He played with the money, dropping it from one hand to the other, listening to the clinking noise it made with the complete absorption of a child of two. Under the spell of the money and a few pencils which William Henry had in his pocket, he was brought home.

Thus it was a different Davy who sat in the kitchen that evening, playing with teaspoons, placing them in rows and piles and upsetting them to build them again. He seemed to remember nothing of what had been his duties in the farmyard, of the washing of dishes or the sweeping of the hearth. For him those things had vanished with Miss Lisha.

'Poor Davy,' murmured Mrs. Blake. 'It's terrible to see a human being like that.'

The thought, however, cannot have weighed too heavily on her for she fell asleep five minutes later.

Bridie sat watching Davy with compassion and an unconquerable sense of desolation. She almost wished that it was bedtime for the relief of being alone and handling her beads. Yet, when bedtime came and she stood in her bedroom before the drawer in which the beads lay, she hesitated. William Henry had allowed her to handle them. But her mind reverted to her grandmother's passionate appeal to her to turn[2] on the night when she had come back from Miss Anderson's. Her grandmother had hated these beads. She had come through that very parlour and found her unawares with them. She had pulled them from her with fingers that itched to

2. Become a Protestant.

break them. Her poor grandmother! Death would have been a horror to her, had it not been for her faith in Bridie's love for William Henry. Some loyalty to clan stirred in Bridie. She would not break faith with her. Telling herself that she would think of William Henry instead, she averted her eyes from the drawer and climbed into bed. Sleep was long in coming to her and the pleasant thought of William Henry was repeatedly marred by the memory of the glimpse of the coffin, the minister's voice, the picture of Davy playing with the spoons.

As the days passed, the impression of gloom and emptiness gradually faded. Mrs. Blake chattered incessantly and the kitchen was frequently invaded by the younger members of her family, now under the guardianship of Tessie, who no longer came to the farmhouse. They clustered round their mother and could only be prevailed upon to depart when they had been given hot potato-bread or apples. William Henry came each evening, bringing in his pockets trifles from the shop for the amusement of Davy, whom Bridie had persuaded to resume the task of feeding the hens. He always had to be reminded of this duty, but he seemed to like scattering the food.

So life stirred in the old house. At the end of a week Bridie began to think only of William Henry again. Their joy temporarily marred by the sadness of death, they became once more lovers, wholly absorbed in each other. Every evening before his car departed, she would run into the yard and cling to him there, wishing that it were already the next evening and that he were only coming.

'Do you look at your beads any more?' he once said playfully.

She shook her head confidently.

'No. I've forgotten about that because I think only of you.'

He talked much of their approaching marriage which he said would be just before Christmas, and became gayer than she had ever known him.

'Aunt Lisha would have liked us to be gay,' he said once, as if it had occurred to him that Bridie might think him heartless.

He had endless plans for the improvement of the house which, he declared, he and she would make young again together. He taxed his ingenuity in divining what gifts would best please her and drove several times to Enniskillen to buy her jewellery.

'Not that they could ever make you more beautiful to me, love,' he whispered, as he clasped a rope of pearls round her neck.

Into this happier world walked one morning a visitor, so unexpected that Bridie almost lost control of her limbs from surprise at the sight of her. It was Aunt Rose Anne, who descended from a hired car in the yard and came calmly through the kitchen doorway.

'Aunt Rose Anne!' cried Bridie from the pantry. Hesitating for a moment, she ran to embrace her. 'It's such a long time since I've seen you.'

'It is,' said Aunt Rose Anne. 'I'm thinking you're a bit too grand now for the likes of me.'

She sat down and looked round the kitchen, her eye taking in every detail with greedy curiosity. She had grown more placid. The restless feverish glint in her eyes had died, leaving a hard, critical stare. There was a sickly pallor in her cheeks.

'You don't look well, Aunt Rose Anne!' exclaimed Bridie. 'I'll make you tea.'

She set about the process with an extreme nervousness. There was nobody who could make her as nervous as Aunt Rose Anne.

'Thank you,' said Aunt Rose Anne, still looking round. 'I haven't been well lately. The nuns wanted me to stay in bed and get the doctor for me. But I never lay in bed in my life and I've no faith in doctors. I've always been used to hard work and I keep going while I can. You're very grand here. Mind you, I'm glad for your sake. I'm glad the old witch is dead. She lived too long.'

Bridie straightened herself. A hot impulse of loyalty to her grandmother made her open her lips to speak, but she restrained herself.

'Is it true,' said Aunt Rose Anne, fixing her eyes directly upon her, 'that she has left you all? They say it is so in Castlerivington.'

Bridie laid the dishes upon the table with jerky movements.

'It is true,' she said with a flash of pride. 'She was very fond of me.'

'There's no need to get hot about it. What a spitfire you've turned into! Money is giving us airs, even to them that reared us.' Aunt Rose Anne made a motion to wipe away a tear from her eye, which was, however, dry. 'I'd have thought you wouldn't have put on airs to me, Bridie. I know I'm poor and have to earn my living, and now you own six farms of land, but there was a time when you were glad of the shelter I could give you.'

Bridie was discomfited.

'I'm not putting on airs. I am grateful to you, Aunt Rose Anne. I've never forgotten you and I never will.'

Aunt Rose Anne moved to the table and sat down in preparation for her meal, then swung her chair round to face Bridie with determination.

'I'm glad to hear you say it, Bridie. It's only what I'd expect. But I want to hear you say more. That's why I'm here to-day. Now you've got what is your right, I hope you'll stand on your own feet and thank God that what was that spiteful old woman's has come into the hands of one of the faithful. Look here, Bridie.' Aunt Rose Anne got up and walked towards Bridie with a suspicion of the old glint in her eyes and something panther-like in her step. She grasped the front of her dress. 'You're a good Catholic, aren't you? They haven't weakened you? She couldn't put it out of you, could she? She couldn't put out what I put in? You're going to stay a Catholic, aren't you, with your six farms of land? Thank God something worth having in the neighbourhood's coming to Catholics, they that have been persecuted and downtrodden through the ages.' She stopped for breath. Bridie shivered, suddenly wishing she were dead.

'I wouldn't have been uneasy about it,' said Aunt Rose Anne, 'only that I heard a rumour in Castlerivington that you were going to marry that young Musgrave that works in Parks' of Innischree, and then it came on me like a flash that he might work on your mind to turn. Even if he didn't try that, you would be mad to marry him, because no mixed marriage ever comes to good and he'd make your children Protestants. He'd only want to get what you have out of your hands. You couldn't be such a fool. You're not going to marry him under any condition, are you? You're not going your mother's road?'

She shook her forcibly. Bridie had a feeling that her mind was being torn asunder as if it had been some physical part of her. She wrenched herself away from Aunt Rose Anne.

'I can't stand it! Leave me alone! I'll do what I like!'

Aunt Rose Anne breathed hard, looking steadily at her.

'So you're guilty,' she said deliberately and swung her hand like a sledgehammer with a resounding crack against Bridie's ear. 'You treacherous little brat! I curse the day your mother bore you! Her sin has stuck to you. You're deep in it. I couldn't keep you straight that worked and prayed for you. I hate you!' She breathed venom and wrestled with her hands as if she would have liked to twist and break Bridie's body.

Bridie had fallen back against the door into the hall.

'Tell me the truth!' shrieked Aunt Rose Anne, seizing her shoulders and shaking her again. 'Tell me the truth! Are you going to marry him? Are you going to turn?'

The fire of the Musgraves must have been slumbering somewhere in Bridie. She tore herself free and rushed to the other side of the kitchen, leaving Aunt Rose Anne to turn round and stare at her.

'I'm going to marry him and I'm going to follow whatever religion he tells me. You can call it turn, if you like. I'll be happier with him than I ever was in my life. I am the mistress of this house and I'm free and I'll do as I please!'

The words were enormous, final. Aunt Rose pulled her coat about her.

'I see,' she said with grim calm. 'That's my thanks. I tried to bring you up right when you were small. Now I came to try to save you at the last minute. For them that will go wrong there is no right. Have it your own way.' She walked to the door with flashing eyes and a mocking smile. In the doorway she stopped and turned. 'You can't blame me for telling the priest. It is my duty. You may talk to him as you talked to me, if you like. But for me, I've done with you. I can only say that I leave you my curses.'

She walked across the yard and climbed into the motor-car, which drove away.

Bridie was mentally crippled for the rest of the day. Complaining to Mrs. Blake, who fortunately had gone to pay a short visit to her home just before Aunt Rose Anne's arrival, that she had a headache, she lay down upon her bed. The sight of Aunt Rose Anne, apart from what she had said, had stirred up the past in her to such an extent that it struggled and jarred against the present in her brain. Certain parts of it rose before her with an insistent clarity; the visits to the chapel where she had experienced the

moments of mysterious pleasure; the little statue in Aunt Rose Anne's bedroom; the saints who blessed Uncle James, Aunt Rose Anne and herself; the comfort of holding her crucifix in bed at night; her confirmation; purgatory. They would not die. She could not forget them. Yet forget them she must since she would not go to the chapel any more. But would she ever really be able to forget them? Was it a sin to forget them? Were they not perhaps right? Perhaps they were not. But, even if they were not, there was always the fear that they might be. She shivered and pulled the old rug which covered her closer around her. Aunt Rose Anne had said she was deep in sin and cursed her. She was going her mother's way. It was uncanny. And now she was just the same as she had always been before William Henry had made her different — she was afraid. She stretched out her hand to the drawer where her beads were, but drew it back, remembering her grandmother and William Henry. William Henry stood opposed to this fear. He alone could drive it out, keep it away, banish it for ever. She loved him. He was her life. She had defied Aunt Rose Anne for him. His spirit must stand by her now in moments like these. 'It will stand by me, it will, it will,' she whispered to herself in a violent effort to stifle the thought that the priest would come to warn her. But the thought of the priest would not be stifled. Her awe of him was part of her flesh and blood and bones, something that she had acquired as she had acquired the teeth in her head, deeper even than love. He would come, and she would have to face him. Thus she tossed on the bed until late in the day, buffeted rudely from love to dread, from William Henry to the priest. When at last she rose, she was feverish. Her eyes glittered. Her hands were hot and trembling.

That evening she ran to meet William Henry with greedy affection, casting her arms round him and pressing him to her in a manner which surprised him.

'Darling!' he whispered and, since it was quite dark and there was no possibility of anybody's seeing, picked her up and carried her to the doorstep.

'You look pale, yet your hands are hot. What ails you, love?' he said later, when the two of them were sitting in the firelight and she was clutching and stroking his arm, as if it had been a buoy to which she was clinging to save herself from drowning in a stormy sea.

'Nothing,' she lied. 'I only love you, William Henry.'

She had determined not to mention Aunt Rose Anne's visit to him, lest by seeing symptoms of distress in her, he should doubt her love. He must never do that.

'Aunt Lisha's death has taken more out of you than I knew,' he said soothingly. 'It's rather unhealthy for you here alone all day. Once we are married, I shall take you away to Belfast for a while, and there you will forget.'

'The city!' she said with childlike wonder, Belfast always having appeared to her as a sphere of gold rising in misty sun-tinted splendour even above the awesomeness of Enniskillen.

'Yes, the city, where there are lights and tram-cars and buses and always crowds of people. It will fascinate you,' he said indulgently. 'I shall buy you something beautiful there, as a souvenir.'

'I can hardly believe that it will happen to me,' she said, shaking her head with a high-pitched laugh which was almost hysterical.

Would it happen to her? she asked herself in bed that night. Would not a nameless something, the sickening dread which ached in the pit of her stomach, prevent it? By an almost superhuman effort she resolved that the dread should die, and for a week lived in the glow of an agony of loving. She hung upon William Henry, never letting him out of her sight for a minute while he was in the house, kissed him with the fervour with which she used to kiss her crucifix, questioned him incessantly about how much he loved her with an insistence alien to her shy and reserved nature. He was a little surprised by this new demonstra-tiveness, but attributed it to the state of her nerves and talked of bringing their marriage still closer.

'Yes, yes, let it be soon,' she whispered.

The thought of its proximity was the only thing which steadied her anxiety. When the wedding day came, all fear would be lost in William Henry. He would always be there to drive the ghosts of fear away. Not even the priest would avail then. She would shut her eyes and hold to William Henry and not see him.

The priest, however, came before the wedding day. She was in Davy's room one morning, making his bed, when, looking through the window, she saw him cross the yard. He was a tall, robust, jovial man, popular throughout the parish, not in the least a symbolic representation of the significance he bore in Bridie's mind. Immediately she saw him, her brain registered one thought. She could not, would not face him. The rigour of death creeping over her, she stood motionless, staring. The priest knocked the door but obtained no answer. Mrs. Blake had gone home and Davy had wandered away on one of his now frequent meanderings by the lough. The priest knocked again with a slightly impatient air, as one who is used to being promptly and respectfully received. His nature did not brook ignoring. A sense of horror swept over Bridie. What was she doing? Was she defying God and the Blessed Virgin? She was on the way to hell. What had come over her? She scarcely knew herself. The priest held the key of heaven in his hand and she dared not meet him. William Henry's image floated before her. 'Heart's jewel,' he had whispered. Were they damnation, those sweet, unforgettable words that would haunt her to her life's end, the words that had made up for all her loneliness, that had coloured her life anew and brought back a hundredfold the love of Uncle James, that made living worth while? Almost in a swoon, she sank upon the bed and clutched the counterpane with weak fingers. How long she lay there she did not know. Whatever space of time it was, it was oblivion, eternity. When she rose and staggered to the window, the priest had gone.

She walked down the steps and out into the yard with legs that felt like stilts. She had done it, the dreadful thing. With a strange calm, which detached her for the time being from her situation, she saw the enormity of it. When the priest had been there, the question still hung in the balance, the struggle was in progress. Now it was over. Then she had not really known the meaning of it. Now she knew. She had let heaven go. Hell lay before her. Aunt Rose Anne's curse had come upon her. She was very tired and almost feelingless. In comparison with such an enormous act as that which she had committed nothing mattered, not even William Henry or her wedding day. There could be no wedding day, there never could have been one. After such an act, happy existence for her would be impossible. Her face was grim and haggard, her eyes sunken and leaden. Had Mrs. Blake been there to see her, she must have cried out. With a determination which came not from thought but from some deep instinct, she walked slowly through the kitchen, the hall and the parlour, to her bedroom where she took her beads out of the drawer. Then she walked back to the hall and weariedly put on her old coat. She was going away. She could never meet William Henry again, never look into those bright, kind eyes. Between her and them floated an intangible, all-powerful something which she did not understand and which was stronger than she. She did not know where she was going, but she knew it must be so. Without once looking round the kitchen, without thought either of Mrs. Blake or Davy, she let the latch fall gently behind her and walked down the lane. She was aware neither of the time of day nor of the old shoes and apron which she wore, nor of whom she might meet. She was outside herself and the life which she had known.

By the time she had reached the end of the lane one idea filled her mind. She would rest. She would lie down and forget. The convent! She would go to the convent. The calm, quiet nuns would open the door and forgive her and take her in. In the convent her sin would be washed away. Within its walls there was peace, the peace of the good Catholics whose souls were safe into eternity. The nuns would understand. They would protect her and pray for her. Their white-encircled faces would cluster round her like the heads of angels. It would be a peace like that of the bog beneath the stars on calm nights when she and Uncle James had strayed among the heather. The thought brought her a still greater yearning which, when it rises in the heart of the Irish peasant, quenches all lesser loves. In her mother's blood in her veins stirred the passionate, irreconcilable Celt, who in his distresses turns his eyes to the hills, the crags, the open spaces of his native soil. She would see the bog again. Nothing would prevent her. The bog came before the convent. She would walk to Corramore. How she was thus to divert her path and reach the convent before night did not occur to her. Time or distance mattered nothing. Instinct ruled. She must go there.

Now and then blinding flashes of William Henry illuminated her as she walked, making her writhe by their very brilliance. When they came, she had to stop upon the road. She loved him!

Tonight there would have been the joy of meeting him, to-night and many other nights, and ultimately the joy of being with him for ever. Again and again she almost turned back. Only one thought made her able to go on as fear told her she must go. That was the thought of the bog and its peace.

They sought her that evening and all next day.

from:
MY HEART AND I (1955)

[The title is taken from Elizabeth Barrett Browning's poem 'My Heart and I', which begins, 'Enough! we're tired, my heart and I' and laments the lonely world-weariness of the speaker. Irish sociologists have often speculated that Irish women who make loveless marriages lavish their affections on their children, especially their sons, to compensate. In *My Heart and I* Crone explores the implications of this pattern for Irish women. After her husband dies, Grace Lennox devotes her whole emotional and material life to her son, John, and to her plan that he acquire an education and become a doctor. For him she sacrifices not merely material comforts but also her personal happiness; she declines to marry a man she loves simply because John objects. John does become a doctor. When he marries, Grace finds the sacrifice of her life and heart forgotten, as John neglects her and his new wife actively strives to keep Grace out of John's affections and even out of his house. Published in London in 1955 by Heinemann.]

John and Christine were married about three months later in Belfast. Shyness and the dread of making a journey prevented Grace from attending the wedding.

'Don't ask me to go, John,' she pleaded. 'You'll understand how strange I'd feel there in the city among Christine's friends. And what would they think of me?'

'I don't see why you should feel at all strange or why you want to make yourself odd. You'd be the best-looking person of your age there, I'm sure. It's surprising that you don't *want* to come!'

'Ah, John, you know it's not that I don't want. I can't, I can't indeed. That's the truth. Sure I on'y went to Belfast once all the time you were there. You ought to know your own mother better than to think such things about her.'

He did know his mother very well, knew, beneath his protests, that her disinclination to go came from an invincible, constitutional sensibility, that such an ordeal would possibly mean several sleepless nights for her. In the end he agreed tranquilly enough that she should remain; and she sweetened his humour by repeated promises of preparations for his return with Christine a fortnight after the ceremony.

It was a wet evening in November when they returned. She heard them call to each other in the high wind as they climbed out of the car and extracted luggage from it. When she reached the doorstep, she stopped, uncertain whether she should go forward. An urgent desire to do what John would consider right had given her a nervous headache and two flushed patches upon her cheeks. Susan, in a new apron, hovering in the lighted hall behind her, involuntarily whispered, 'Wait, ma'am,' presumably indicating that it was more fitting for one of her age not to go forward. Nevertheless, go forward she did, as in final surrender to the future, determined that she should err on the side of generosity.

'Welcome home, Christine,' she murmured quickly, holding out her arms to embrace what she divined to be Christine's form in the darkness.

'Ah, Mrs. Lennox! Just a minute! My hands are full!' called Christine, stepping quickly forward to the patch of light upon the doorstep and into the hall, where she set down two small suitcases with a sigh of relief.

'What, Mother! You out in the dark!' whispered John, also laden, but setting down his burdens to kiss Grace, before they followed Christine to the door.

'Now that we can see each other, it will perhaps be better. Two for luck,' said Christine prettily, coming to lay a hand upon each of Grace's shoulders and kissing her first on one cheek, then on the other, while John looked on with a shy, pleased, and rather foolish air. 'No need to come up, Mrs. Lennox. John can show me,' she added brightly as she turned to run upstairs. 'Bring as much as you can, dear,' she called to John from the top of the staircase.

Left alone, Grace began to walk to and fro, between the dining-room and the kitchen, to make sure that the meal in preparation was well advanced and that nothing had been overlooked in the laying of the table. She had thought that John would come down again (as he usually did when he had been away) to follow her here and there with fragments of news about the journey and inquiries about what had happened in his absence. But he did not appear, and, after a time of restless flitting from room to room, she sat down by the fire in the dining-room to await the descent. The door of the couple's bedroom was closed, and she could hear a low murmur of voices. As she sat with her hands clasped upon her lap and her eyes fixed upon the face of the clock, her mind slid down one of the tunnels that lead to that underworld of half-thought and half-feeling in which realities have a wan, glassy look. Why was she sitting thus nervously in this little room, afraid to call her son, her own John, down to his meal as she had called him a thousand times? What was this unfamiliar dread among familiar objects? When at last John and Christine came, she shook herself out of a long shiver like an ague.

John and Christine came together. Perhaps Grace's impressions of the evening could have been most adequately summed up in that one word — together. Within an hour she understood that all mental preparation she had made to say and do kind things to welcome Christine had been vain. The fact that the pair were together effaced the need of it. It was a power, this being together; it emanated from Christine to Grace's feelings as clearly as the hum of bees from a hive to an ear. It was self-sufficient, proud, challenging. It had eyes and ears for nothing which did not pertain unto itself. 'Look at us,' it cried to whom it might concern. 'We are one. We are a phenomenon which you and the world must accept. You cannot approach one of us save through the other. The sooner you learn we are a two-headed being the better.'

During the meal talk was animated between the couple. It was stimulated by Christine, who recalled little incidents of the honeymoon, laughing to John about them in a way which invited him to laugh too, or at least, as he more often did, to smile. Grace was included in the conversation, but, as Christine related only a fragment of the amusing memory or alluded to some person or thing of whom Grace had no knowledge, it would have been impossible for her to take an active part in it. 'Oh, it was funny, Mrs. Lennox,' or 'You should have seen John,' Christine would say, turning towards Grace as though to solicit her amusement, then towards John to add, 'Don't you remember, darling?'

In Grace this produced a state verging upon bewilderment. Feeling that such gaiety was artificial, she could see no reason why it should be maintained. She was not without sense of humour, but her large and serious mind would at any time have been impatient of a conversation composed entirely of trivialities. And this day had immense significance for her. Yesterday she might have called it the most important in her life. She had prepared for it, seeing it as an occasion which would call forth the noblest that was in her, the power of sacrifice, the total width of her humanity. She had told herself she must seek and find some point of mental contact with Christine, must touch the spring which would awaken the understanding between them upon which happiness depended. She had intended to show her photographs of John when he was a boy, to tell her things he had said and done, to demonstrate her willingness to share him with her. And now this rising sickness in the pit of her stomach told her that that could never be, that Christine had taken John without in any sense waiting to receive him, that the overflow of her gaiety with him now was a fortification against an intruder like herself. Together. That was it. Together. And *she* was outside their life, having no part in it, no rights. She was a pale ghost, contemplating them. She and her memories of John were unwanted. He was reborn for Christine on the day of their meeting. The sharpness of these facts was increased by the abruptness of her comprehension of them. The palms of her hands grew hot and clammy. Her temples throbbed. In her head was a lightness which made it feel separate from her body. Then it began to ache with a new heaviness. When John passed his cup to her, her hand shook, and she poured out the tea with difficulty.

'Mother! Aren't you well? You're trembling.'

'I'm — very well. I always had a shaky hand.'

'You are flushed, Mrs. Lennox,' said Christine, looking at her with new seriousness. 'You must have been overdoing things. I hope you haven't gone to extra trouble on our account.' (Despite her agitation Grace noticed the word 'our' and wished that John could be allowed to express his own regret for any trouble his mother might have taken on his account.) 'And, John, how careless we've been! She's been eating nothing at all!'

'I never eat much at this time o' day.'

'You're over-tired, I think. Couldn't you go to bed now? Don't sit up for us.'

'I'm all right, thank you. I might not sleep if I went to bed so early.'

'But you could at least lie down. Isn't there a sofa upstairs in the drawing-room? I seem to remember one there. Couldn't you lie on it for a little while?'

To this Grace agreed, feeling a spurt of resentment that Christine should have assumed the right to prescribe for her instead of John. Relieved to be alone, she made her way to the drawing-room, where, in preparation for this important occasion, she had lighted a fire. But she did not lie down on the sofa as Christine had suggested. Probably with less care than ever before she sat down in one of the arm-chairs.

She knew now that she could do nothing for Christine. Christine did not need to be told; Christine knew. Christine did not want to be helped; Christine could. She had fancied that she would ask to see the house, that she would admire the tea-service, that she would possibly be nervous and a little ill at ease! She ought to have known better, ought to have foreseen that marriage could not thus alter one who before it had shown neither nervousness nor a tendency to be ill at ease. Christine's nature was in fact outside her power of imagining, one which was unlikely to allow any situation to take it unawares. And Christine had made one single plan of campaign which frustrated all her mother-in-law's smaller plans. Together — together — together.

On the following day Grace rose with the conviction that her feelings upon the previous evening had been exaggerated, that nerves had distorted her vision. She must try again. The ideal could not easily be relinquished. Christine might secretly have been as nervous as herself. She would not judge her rashly.

'Be good to Christine, Mother dear,' whispered John as he left them that morning at breakfast.

Notwithstanding her good intentions, Grace flushed. The whisper was audible to Christine, and she could not help feeling humiliated to be instructed by her son before his wife. Had he told Christine to be good to her, his mother? When she looked across the table at Christine, a certain firmness in the line of her lip and chin told her that he had not done so.

'Would you like to see the house, Christine?' she asked when they were alone.

'Oh — I forgot to say that John showed me most of it last night when we'd persuaded you to go to bed.'

'I — I hope you like it. It's comfortable, anyway.'

'Yes, I think it's pleasant. A little small for a doctor perhaps. It's a pity the surgery and the waiting-room have to be in it. But I suppose that has to be put up with in the meantime.'

Grace did not know what Christine meant by 'in the meantime'. She had accepted the fact that a large part of a doctor's house must be given up to his practice. 'It's always that way with a doctor, isn't it?'

'Not necessarily. A surgery can be built on so that the patients don't come near the dwelling-house. But I shouldn't encourage John to do such a thing here. There isn't enough room for expansion, and anyhow the house isn't big enough to justify the expense.'

Grace had assumed that John would always live in this house. Now the understanding flashed upon her that possibly she had not done enough for him, that the result of her effort was something poor and mean which Christine could tolerate only temporarily.

'I counted it a fairly big house,' she said in a loud, shaky whisper.

'Well — big enough for two or three adults, I suppose. But when you think of a growing family.'

Grace was dumbfounded. Her pain was for the moment forgotten in her surprise. She did not move freely enough in society to have become aware of the fashion which had developed since her youth of referring to families yet unborn in the same manner as to houses yet unbuilt. Deeply embarrassed, she could say nothing and looked at her lap, unable to raise her eyes to meet Christine's.

'Children need a lot of room,' Christine was saying. 'And you cannot have them on top of you all the time. There isn't a room here that could very well be made into a nursery, is there? In what direction does the back of the house face?'

'East — or near it.'

'No good, you see. Only the early morning sun. The afternoon is best for a child in winter if it can't be taken out.'

Grace could carry the conversation no further, but, since both had finished eating, began moving the dishes on the table in preparation for carrying them away. She longed for Susan to appear with the tray. Christine did not appear to be conscious of her embarrassment. Already Grace was beginning to learn that she was little affected by another person's presence.

'By the way,' she said suddenly so that Grace started, 'where did that curious old rocking-chair in our bedroom come from?'

The words brought relief. Here at least was something about which Grace could talk. 'It was my mother's. When I was married, it was the one thing I took with me from home. My father was able to spare it to me. I wanted something o' mother's. She had a hard life. We were poor — and she came through a great deal. I was never separated from her.'

'I see,' said Christine slowly. About to say more, she paused, causing Grace to look at her with new interest, in anticipation of some question about her mother or her past life.

However, Christine's thoughts were not with Grace's mother. 'The rest of the furniture in the bedroom is so modern that I was struck by the difference. And the chair kept creaking last night — because of the wind in the chimney, John said.'

'When we came here from the farm we bought most of the furniture. We hadn't much to suit this house. But we kept a few things here and there. I wanted something to remind me of old days. So did John, I think.' For the first time Grace felt distinct shyness in making a statement about her son. She suspected that Christine would consider it almost temerity on her part to know anything of his likes or dislikes.

Christine played with her teaspoon. 'I like modern furniture,' she said.

'There are plenty of new things in the house. Perhaps they're not as good as they might be, but they were all we could afford at the time.'

Christine scanned the room thoughtfully. 'Everything's new here but the sideboard, I believe. Did it come from the farmhouse?'

'Yes. It's a good one, and holds a lot. I did not like to part with it. Such good mahogany. You wouldn't get it now, John says. The Lennoxes had good things.' (In Christine's presence Grace was proud of the Lennoxes' good things.) 'See.' She rose and opened two doors of the sideboard to reveal an array of china. 'Good, roomy shelves. These are the two best tea-services.' She had been about to say 'my two best tea-services', but restrained herself.

'They are pretty,' said Christine a little languidly. 'Old-fashioned.' She turned the first cup proffered her, one of Andrew Lennox's mother's, slowly in her hand. The second, one of those which Grace had bought in her brief period of enthusiasm for beautifying the farmhouse, she did not raise from the table where Grace set it beside her. 'Do you mind if I go to my room to arrange my things? It was so late last night that we did next to nothing.'

She remained upstairs for most of the morning. As she dusted in the rooms on the ground floor, Grace could hear her tripping to and fro between her bedroom and the bathroom.

'When does John come in, Mrs. Lennox?' she called down once.

'Between one and two usually.'

Grace heard her breathe a mock sigh. 'What a long time to wait!'

She must have been watching from her bedroom window for the returning car, for when John arrived she rushed downstairs into the hall to meet him before he could turn his latchkey in the lock. Nor did her watchfulness decrease on the succeeding days. In fact, whether by intention or not, for the space of a month Grace did not exchange a word of converse alone with her son.

The following night John carried the rocking-chair on to the landing and left it where its creaking should not disturb his wife's sleep. Grace, who always rose first to waken Susan, emerged from her bedroom in the early morning to find it there. She stood for some instants rigid, contemplating the great, faded roses of its carpet-covered back. In the stillness of the sleeping house a more arresting comprehension of the issues involved in the lives of those within it broke upon her. She understood that everything she had felt until now had been more or less founded upon apprehension or suspicion. She *might* have been misjudging Christine. But *this* was tangible. Her mother's chair discarded! John, in whose room it had been for years, had carried it out! A sense of utter loneliness gripped her. John was gone. His thoughts, his feelings, his very preferences had been absorbed by a power which was indifferent, if not hostile, to her. Henceforth he could only smile at her wanly, as through dim glass. She was cheated, robbed of the common rights of her age, she who had worked so hard. Forgetting the cold and the thinness of her nightdress, she leaned against the door post of her bedroom, a violent dislike of Christine rising, rising, rising in her till it burst in silent rage in all her nerves, making her tremble. Something should, something must, be done. This was unjust. Mothers could not be treated so. People respected mothers. Was it not in the Bible? She had meant to be fair, had tried in every possible way. Somebody should take her part, somebody *must*.

Then, as the understanding came to her that there was nobody to do so, the perspiration which had burst from her turned cold. She was alone. She must help herself. Determinedly she opened the door of her bedroom to its fullest extent and gripped both arms of the chair. It was heavy and, possibly because extreme agitation had made her weak, she could not properly raise it. She was obliged to lower it abruptly with a gentle thud.

'Ma'am!'

Startled, she turned to behold Susan, round-eyed, flushed from sleep, standing in her nightdress upon the lower landing.

'Ma'am! What's wrong?'

'Ssh, Susan. Don't waken the doctor —' She paused with a nervous laugh, remembering that there was possibly something ridiculous in her present position, and ashamed before Susan.

'You'll get your death o' cold, ma'am. You look so pale and queer. What's the rocking-chair on the landing for?' Susan had mounted the few steps and now stood level with her mistress, scanning the haggard form in the long nightdress of striped grey flannel over which hung two plaits of black hair which had come loose at the ends.

'Ssh, ssh, you'll waken the others. Help me, will you? I want to get this chair into my own room.'

Despite her bewilderment, Susan obeyed. After much tugging and straining the object was achieved, and the chair was in Grace's little room.

'I don't right see how you'll move about with it here,' said Susan doubtfully. 'And the cleaning'll be hard. It was better in the doctor's big room where't stood out on the floor, and you could see the beauty of't and the carving on the rockers.'

Susan had always regarded the rocking-chair with reverence. Pieces of furniture similar to most objects in the doctor's house were to be seen at Rennick's store. Rocking-chairs like this one were not.

'Perhaps, but it'll do very well here for the present, Susan. You'd better go back and get dressed now.'

At the door Susan paused and, gaining courage because of the unusual circumstances, asked, 'Did she not want it?'

Grace had sat down in the rocking-chair. Her back was towards Susan, her head bowed. 'No.'

'The divil take her!' said Susan with a flash of temper, and, in spite of the necessity of not disturbing the repose of the doctor and his bride, slammed the door viciously as she went out.

Almost to her own surprise Grace laughed faintly. Susan was right. The divil take this woman who had cut right into her heart! The divil take her! With the thought of Susan's support came a temporary return of strength. Other people would feel like Susan. The whole world would see that she, Grace, was in the right.

Her exhilaration was brief. She remembered then that other people who might have supported her must not even know of her suffering, that their very support would be a humiliation. All this turmoil of feeling must be hidden deep, so deep that none must suspect it existed. The doctor's wife and mother must appear to agree, to be happy in each other's company. There could be no justice ever.

How badly she had begun! She should not have allowed Susan to speak thus of her son's wife. She had humiliated her son before a servant. She had been unforgivably weak. In future she must be strong.

With leaden limbs she began to dress.

'You are to be mistress here, Christine,' she said that morning, when they were left alone. 'I've had my day. The natural mistress of the house is John's wife, and I'd rather it was so.'

She spoke with effort, not because she had any wish to remain mistress of John's house, but because of regret for the past, for its pain as well as its sweetness, that was crying in her, and for the fact of being useless and in the way. Nevertheless there was pride in her words, a pride which rose up at the first warning of the approach of humiliation.

Christine gracefully demurred. 'I'm not sure that I like the word "mistress". In ways it's an ugly word. I would rather we could live like mother and daughter.'

Pretty words. Christine had a gift for pretty words, her mother-in-law was discovering.

She went to her bedroom early that evening in order to be alone, and sat long in the rocking-chair, thinking. The chair had been in her mind all day. She had fully expected either John or Christine to say why it had been put out and had been prepared to reply that it could stay in her room. But presumably they had forgotten about it, or else, noting its disappearance from the landing, thought it best to avoid an embarrassing subject.

She was now sufficiently calm to analyse her feelings of the morning. Not merely the sentimental value of the rocking-chair had caused her to bring it into her room. The question had been one of pride. The rocking-chair had ceased to be of wood and carpet and had become the symbol of her right to life and freedom. Its rejection was Christine's first challenge, the first clear proof that she cared nothing for her mother-in-law's feelings or her past, the first indication that a new order had begun and the old could only persist in so far as it was approved by the new. Grace's pride had been quick to accept the challenge, to make the first step in Christine's advance the first in her retreat. If the presence of Grace's mother's rocking-chair were irritating to Christine, Grace would make sure that the chair was removed. Whatever inconvenience its bulk caused in this little room, here it must, here it would, remain. Unless — how far might not the rule of Christine extend? Possibly even this room would have to meet with her approval. Did the rights of the lodger that Grace would henceforth be entitle her to choice in furniture? Perhaps only an appeal to John could ultimately keep the rocking-chair within the house. And Grace knew that she would not make such an appeal.

Dimly conscious that Christine had begun to play the piano in the drawing-room, she sat long in the rocking-chair. Her feet and hands became numb and her thoughts ever darker, losing themselves finally in shadows where her lonely heart, stripped of flesh and earthly trappings, lamented incessantly with the cry of a lost child.

EIGHTEEN

Christine's nature was, to some extent, moulded by circumstances of which Grace had no knowledge. From her adolescence she had planned that her life should bring her things which magazines, films and other girls implied that she ought to like and have. Except to attain her son's success Grace had never planned. Christine had aimed at making what she wanted out of living as she would have made a new dress out of a length of material. Grace had merely existed, letting the days carry her on, doing the duty which they made necessary. The lives of girls like Christine who lived in hostels and went out to work in organisations in daily contact with men would have abashed her. She could not know that Christine's self-assurance, her inability to be shy, her complete lack of sentiment, her indifference to the feelings of those with whom she came in contact, had developed from what she felt to be the necessity of upholding her rights among others, much in the way a superior strength of upper arm comes to people long-practised in the art of elbowing a way through crowds. She could not know that her desire to marry had been artificially stimulated by stories in magazines and even by advertisements which told her that the best way to achieve her end was to use a certain kind of toilet-soap, face-cream and hair-shampoo. She could not understand that from the great amount of information about woman's life available to Christine in the magazines she had fingered through daily, and in the cinemas she visited weekly, had emerged one central fact — that women must get the best out of living, that this best was only to be had through marriage, and that even in marriage a constant effort must be made to retain it. She could not know that in marrying John Christine was consciously building her 'life'. In short, she could not see Christine against the age of ready-made ideas to which she belonged.

To Grace as a conscious being Christine was blind. On coming to Williamsborough as John's wife, she felt no more emotion in meeting her mother-in-law than had the latter been (somewhat inconveniently) a boarder. Yet the aridity of her nature in this respect in no way diminished her understanding of what she had seen from the beginning, that John's mother would be likely to wield influence over him. She was much too clever to displease John by saying the most trifling thing which he might have interpreted as disrespectful to his mother. Her manner towards Grace always displayed the height of conventional consideration. If Grace had a headache, Christine would advise aspirin and rest, speaking melodiously and looking concerned, allowing the loving eyes of John to see her as a ministering angel. At the same time she would concede nothing in the matter of rights. John was hers: she would show no interest in him in any other aspect, in the faintest shadow of him as Grace's. She was prepared to receive him in no way as a gift from his mother. Marriage was a contract. You gave your life. You expected something in return which came to you by right, not as a favour. When you bought a house, it was indisputably yours to arrange as you thought fit. Likewise a husband.

These ideas could not be expressed to John. Christine had to maintain in some subtler way her ownership of him and her guidance of both their lives, had to wean him from lingering in the old life and rear him irrevocably in the new. Since John was very much in love, she had early and easily found the subtler way. She had disliked the rocking-chair. A plaintive whisper that she could not sleep, and — it was banished by John's strong arm. The possibility that Grace might have feelings about its ejection did not even occur to her.

She interposed herself continually between mother and son. Together. It was the only way. John must be made to need her, to find her above all other beings indispensable. If he were to slip back more or less into his old life, she, and not Grace, might become the superfluous one. This thought caused her to make a concentrated effort to monopolise her husband's attention. It seemed to her that the eyes of John's mother in the background disputed every moment of his life, that they were watching for a relaxation on her part in order to draw him away; and, like a mechanical toy wound up to perform in a certain way, she consciously and untiringly acted in a way to charm her husband.

Thus, living side by side, the two women watched each other in silence, every channel of communication between them sealed. Neither saw nor ever could see the sadness of the other.

ROBERTA HEWITT

(1904–75)

from:
DIARY (1948–72)

[When Roberta Hewitt died in 1975, her widower, the poet John Hewitt, gave a set of her papers to the Public Record Office of Northern Ireland.[1] Among these papers was an autobiographical fragment and a diary intermittently kept from the late 1940s. Roberta Hewitt is chiefly known as the spouse of the poet, although she also had a voluntary career in issues related to childcare and education, work made more poignant by her own experience of infertility. Her diary raises questions of public and private character for women, and of the relationship between creative writing and other forms of labour. The diary dramatizes a tension between self-deprecation and self-assertion played out in her possessive and defensive attitude to Hewitt's poetry and reputation. It offers a rich narrative description of life in Northern Ireland in the late 1940s and early 1950s; it includes reports of conversations with and observations about many well-known writers and artists; it is a moving account of the difficulties, including forms of self-denigration and lack of confidence, that often accompany the role of 'poet's wife'; it contains unique observations from a patient's viewpoint on the state of hospitals and the practices of gynaecology in this period, and illuminates the subject of infertility, which was so little discussed in mid-century.

A popular Freudianism influences her retelling of certain dreams — dreams she revisits when she returns to make marginal annotations in the diary in 1972. These dreams are important sites for her descriptions of anxiety in the face of the Cold War and possible nuclear holocaust, fears which provide their own context for and comment upon her passionate reach for an anti-sectarian liberalism in Northern Ireland. John Hewitt suggested that — 'How much of you is in my verse / another age deserves to say . . .' In a relationship analogous to that between Dorothy and William Wordsworth, Roberta Hewitt made many of the political observations and gestures that are interrogated as well as supported in her husband's poetry. The diaries help us to see that the process of creating a regional voice for Ulster poetry was concurrent with attempts to forge such a regional voice for 'private' experience. There is an implicit critique of Hewitt's work in his wife's diary that illuminates his acknowledgement of 'the hard bombardment of your love'. His decision to make that diary public indicates his recognition that her voice had been temporarily occluded by his reputation but that it might one day come into its own.   S.K.]

My name is Black. My father Robert Shepherd Black. He was a jeweller and worked for my uncle Jim Urquhard, mother's brother in a watch makers shop in York St . . . My mother, being deformed, went to work for Uncle Jim when she left school and became pregnant when she was 16. My father was 15 years older. The Urquahart family were horrified — got them married and mother went to live with my father's mother and sister. She had a bad time. Lizzie [later called Lilian] was born with curvature, which added to my mother's guilt. 11 months later Margaret later Peggy was born, an elder sister of my father's, Ellen Campbell, took Lilian to live with her until my father got a job in Larne, where I was born in October 30th 1904. We came to 48 Agnes St., Belfast where my father had a little shop on is [sic] own about 1907. Watch repair mainly. At some stage my father became an alcolic [sic] and we were in great poverty. He died about 1915 and my mother took a shop on Crumlin Rd and started in boots. Not a first rate business woman she struggled on — eventually marrying Samuel Somerset Reith about 193[?]. There was still no money but he gave her companionship and affection until he died. Lilian worked in shops generally and then opened the shop next door under Andy Millar's scheme of development much later until that was a failure.

Margaret, Peggy, went to office work and eventually became Head book-keeper in Blackstaff Spg. Co.[2] in Weaving office where she stayed till her marriage to Andrew Millar about 1930.

I went to office work at the age of 14 during the war I got into Flax Control Board. Then after war Blackstaff Spg. Co. with Peggy. Lilian opened a shop in Bangor[3] and took ill. I was taken from Blackstaff and put in shop a complete failure. Then Arnotts[4] at 7/6 per week where I left to emigrate to Canada from Saxone Boot Shop[5] in 1929, June. In the fall of 1930 to New York.

---

2. The spinning and weaving of flax was one of Belfast's major industries in the first half of the twentieth century.
3. Bangor, County Down.
4. Department store.
5. Major chain of shoe shops.

1. MS. PRONI Document D33838/4/4–5.

Home for a holiday in 1933 I remet Johnny and married in 1934.[6] Johnny was then in Art Gallery, Belfast and we married on £230 per year and paid £60 per year rent and rates for a flat in 45 Malone Rd. Mr Hewitt[7] was school master in Agnes St. Methodist School and he used to come into my father's shop. He called in to tell my father when Johnny was born. Then Mrs Hewitt[8] and my mother got friendly. I think she was being kind to this poor wee woman, my mother had very bad spine deformation and was about 4' tall: my fath [sic] 6' at least. Johnny has one sister Eileen[9] 5 years older than he is. I am 3 years older than he is: I feel he is still greatly under the influence of parents and Eileen . . .

1 May 1948

I wish I had more time to write some of Johnny's monologues to me. When he is really interested in something he expounds it to me in great earnestness, sometimes when I am rushed to death and trying to cook or think of what I am going to give our numerous callers to eat. I listen with one ear and then I get some rather wonderful thought from him and I feel a proper Martha[10] and know I should listen to him and remember. He must talk out what he is thinking and working at. He should have married a more intelligent woman and with money. It is sometimes too much for me to be the cook and cleaner, Literary confidant, wife and fan and then try to keep a person on the boards that is Roberta and not just Johnny's wife . . . Johnny is obviously nominated Bard. My job is to keep the wheels greased and remain a nonentity. But I can't remain quiet for if there is any conversation I am in it before I know.

Monday 13 September 1948

I write this account of our doings. For what? What good if atom bomb[11] plunks on old Belfast.

I had a dream Sat. night. I was seated on an aeroplane more like an open frame a driver in front of me who tucked my feet one on each side of him under his arms to keep me from blowing off. A man on one side and a woman on the other. I thought we were out in space and then we spotted the arch of the world like a large moon. I momentarily felt afraid of engine trouble and what would happen if we fell in space. But I put it from me and said 'this is lovely' and the world looked lovely there in front and below us and was getting larger and turning when I woke.[12]

1 July 1950

Coming home got a fit of the blues, I have a ghastly habit of reliving unhappy events and my misery of last Sunday's journey swept over me as living as ever. I wonder what I could do to get over this bad habit — Poor Johnny is punished many times for every mistake and I hate myself. I had a dream on Sat night or Sun A.M. It was a house, a two-story stone house — grey like basalt — it was solid and strong; with a square tower at right hand end and the white mortar showed very clearly between the dark stones — it did not appear to have a roof, certainly no visible one, I realised it was my house and I had built it but was unfinished; I don't know what part was not finished, and I remember saying to myself or thinking 'I wonder where I could find an architect who would help me finish my house.' The windows were long and more Georgian than this sketch.[13] Maybe my house has no roof and I allow the elements to have their way with me. I am alright in fine and sunny weather, but, rain and cloud and even wind come in and around me and I blame them for coming. It was a strong house and surely if I could build it, I could manage the final effort to roof it. Does it need more intellect to roof your house? People always talk of the house built on the rock and the rains come and the floods descended[14] — but what use the foundations if it had no roof. Wanted: an architect's plan to roof my house.

---

6. 7 May 1934, married in Belfast Registry Office.
7. Robert Telford Hewitt (1873–1945).
8. Elinor (Robinson) Hewitt (1877–1958).
9. Eileen (Hewitt) Todhunter (1902–75).
10. In the gospel story, Martha complains that she has to get on with housework while her sister Mary listens to Jesus (Luke 10: 38–42).
11. Before her marriage, Roberta had been secretary of the Belfast Peace League; when she moved to Coventry in 1957 she became active in the Campaign for Nuclear Disarmament.

12. Author's note: This dream has remained very clear: every service and when moon-landing go-on I feel I know the sensation of space. 1972.
13. A rough sketch appears here in the manuscript.
14. Matthew 7: 24–7.

Thursday 12 July 1951

Royal Victoria Hospital. Here I am in hospital on the *12th*.[15] Over a month of my 'life' unrecorded. And I haven't the old part with me to see where I left off.

Monday *11th*. Even I do say it twice was the day Prof. Baxter phoned J. to say that his M.A.[16] was to be awarded and we were most relieved and very happy, mamma Hewitt was very pleased and was most moved — she is just interested in the M.A. if J. had got it on research into boot-polish she would be equally pleased.

Tues. lunch at Purdysburn Fever[17] with Members of the Authority and a Party at Eileen's to drink J.'s health. Very nice but I feel now I have written all this.[18]

Sat 16th Opening of exhibition of painting and pottery in gallery[19] at 3 o'c. Prof. E. Evans[20] opened it but small attendance. It was well hung but a lot of poor stuff too. I was pleased that the pottery looked well as it was my suggestion to J. to include it. To opera at 5 o'c. Barber of Seville.[21] R.D. Boyd from Achill Island called in Evg.

Mon 18th Opening of Museum's Conference in Stranmillis and in Evening we had a Ceildhe(?) [sic] I did not enjoy it much, but I'm sure that was my fault.[22]

Tues 19th A Reception in City Hall at 8 o'c. I enjoyed this. I put on my 65/= frock and it looked quite well. Spoke to D. Allen of Edinburgh. J. Luke[23] was working away at his mural all the while and he came down the ladder about 10.30 when we were collecting to go home and J. started up an applause which everyone there took up. I had a waltz with George Thompson of the Museum which I enjoyed and he was kind enough to say he did too. He is a nice fellow and feels J. is a bit of an enigma, but says he keeps pegging away. J. hadn't told anyone in gallery he was doing his thesis so M.A. was a great surprise. J. always says 'Do they *have* to know before he tells much.' . . .

Wednesday 20th Tea at Queen's in Whitla Hall[24] we were at a small table with McHeael [Michael?] Quarnes and Richard Hayward[25] and I forget the two Englishman [sic]. R. Hayward never stopped telling slightly dirty stories some of them funny but he is a bit wearing as there cannot be any real conversation where he is. At the dinner in Grand Central[26] in the evening J. says he was just the same and some of the men were so disgusted with the dinner which J. said was poor and the speeches too long. Dame Dehra[27] spoke well but Brian Maginess[28] was awful. J. took a few, plus R. Hayward to the Arts' Club and R.H. told filthy stories all night till 2 o'c — the English men enjoyed it immensely. The bus and tram men went on strike today over the dismissal of a driver who had been in an accident — I don't know all the rights and wrongs of the case at all — I am inclined to think it was badly handled by the head ones — but I do know that many of the tram drivers are not very helpful and many of the conductors are not very civil.

Thursday 21st In Evg. we had a reception at Stormont[29] Dame Dehra Parker received us. The

---

15. Twelfth of July, anniversary of the Battle of the Boyne (1690), when Orangemen hold controversial marches through the North of Ireland.
16. On 10 July 1951 John Hewitt was awarded an MA by Queen's University Belfast for his thesis, 'Ulster Poets, 1800–1870'.
17. Purdysburn Fever Hospital, on the outskirts of Belfast, later specialized in treatment for the mentally ill.
18. She recorded these events as they happened.
19. Belfast Art Gallery.
20. Emyr Estyn Evans (1905–89) was a Welsh scholar who came to teach geography at Queen's University in 1928. He established scientific archaeology in Belfast, was chairman of the Ancient Monuments Council and helped found the Ulster Folk and Transport Museum. His books include *Irish Heritage* (1942) and *Mourne Country* (1951).
21. Opera by Gioacchino Rossini (1792–1868).
22. A later insert, probably 1972, adds 'I was ill and didn't realize'.
23. John Luke (1906–75) was a Belfast painter. John Hewitt put on a one-man exhibition of his work at the Ulster Museum in 1946 and in 1951 Luke was commissioned to commemorate the Festival of Britain by painting a large mural in the dome of Belfast City Hall.

His pencil portrait of Roberta Hewitt (1935) was part of the Roberta and John Hewitt bequest to the Ulster Museum in 1987.
24. The Sir William Whitla Hall at Queen's University was named after the professor of Materia medica and Pro-Chancellor of the University. Whitla (1851–1933) represented the university in parliament 1918–22 and left it an endowment.
25. Richard Hayward (1898–1964), Belfast dramatist specializing in Ulster dialect. He also wrote a travel series on Ireland and *The Story of the Irish Harp* (1954).
26. Hotel.
27. Dame Dehra Parker (1882–1963), Ulster Unionist politician; in 1949 she became the first woman cabinet minister in the Northern Ireland government, as Minister for Health. Two of her grandsons later became prime ministers in Northern Ireland: Terence O'Neill and James Chichester-Clark. See Volume v, p. 372.
28. William Brian Maginess (1901–67), Ulster Unionist politician, was Minister for Home Affairs in 1951.
29. Seat of the government of Northern Ireland from 1932.

Andrew Stewart's [*sic*] were there and all the conference people. Took Mr. Butler and Miss Evans to Odd Man Out pub.[30] . . . The strike continues and my bicycle is very useful.

Sunday. J. and I took a walk to the Ormeau Park where we hadn't been for years. Reading Zola's Lourdes.[31] It is terrific.

Monday To Olive Anderson[32] as I have had haemmorige [*sic*] since Thursday 31st and very tired — piles. Heard a good play 'The Nameless One' by Jas. Forsythe[33] on Radio . . .

Tues 3rd [July] Back to Dr Olive Anderson — she thought I should see Dr [or Mr?] H. Lowry.[34]

Wed 4th Andy and Peggy brought Mother and Pappy over in car to Castlereagh to the Festival Farm and Factory exhibition . . .

Thursday 5th Saw Lowry at 5.30. He says curette[35] and arranged for me to go into Royal Victoria Hospital.

Prof. Baxter came for supper at 7.30. He is very nice indeed and J. and he had quite a good chat. He was very nice about J.'s thesis and would like a Bibliography — J. would like it done but feels it would be a tedious job and he would rather be doing something more creative: J. left at 10.00 to do his Ulster Commentary broadcast — which as Mamma Hewitt said 'was a nice wee crock that anyone would understand'.

Friday 6th J's poem in Dublin magazine[36] and tonight is 'Ulster Names' again in repeated programme of this in N. Ireland. 'Ulster Names' has made more than almost the whole of his other poems to date with £8 each of 3 broadcasts and an overseas at £8.

Sat. 7th Ran over to see mother. We are very excited about the truce in Korea — pray heaven Wisdom will fall about them . . .

Sunday 8th Patrick's. Janet lovely. Maureen very kind nice day: Maureen said if I wasn't well after my operation I should come out and stay with them — was very pleased — it was really kind.

Tuesday 10th Graduation Day. Mamma came over and we went to Whitla Hall. It was a lovely ceremony. Johnny didn't like the thought of it at all. But it was nice to look down and see him sitting there in his little blue hood. His hair looked lovely and Mamma said 'His head is a nice shape today'! The robes were lovely and I enjoyed it very much. Poor old Lord Allenbrook stuttered and stammered thrice and pronounced Johnny a D. of Arts. The largest applause came from a young B.A. who is a Rugby player. A nice man got a Hon degree for developing the daffodil. And we brought John home a Master of Arts.

Mamma for lunch and we went to Garden party — undistinguished — .

Wed 11th Entered Royal Victoria Hospital at 2 o'c. Went up alone for preference. Got put into the side ward with a nice woman called Mrs. Moffat. Then life became beds — a bit hard, but they are buying dunlopillo mattresses for the new beds. And much better bed tables metal. Mine is a heavy zinc like they will the door opening the wrong way or the rail for the towel at the back — impossible for patient to reach: Food not bad. One bath — which a woman with cancer uses, whose legs are ulcers. Why will hospitals not have shower baths? The phone rings near by all the time from a central operator and it rings and rings — when surely one or two rings would do. All the washing up is done in kitchen just across the passage — a mistake dishes should be put in containers with rubber wheels and taken at least across the corridor. In fact it could be a large box or tank one side being moveable sink the other side plate racks. Boiling water could be let into tanks on side[37] drained off into a large grating, washed dishes put in racks

30. Author's note: Don't remember who they are 1970 Gt Victoria Street. The Crown Inn in Great Victoria Street is one of the settings for Carol Reed's Belfast film, *Odd Man Out* (1947).
31. *Lourdes* (1894) is the first of the trilogy, *Trois Villes*, by Emile Zola (1840–1902).
32. Gynaecologist.
33. Unidentified.
34. Charles Gibson Lowry (1880–1951) was consultant gynaecologist at the Royal Victoria Hospital and Pro-Chancellor and Emeritus Professor of Midwifery and Gynaecology at Queen's University Belfast.
35. Surgical procedure to scrape the womb.
36. Literary quarterly published 1923–58.
37. Author's note: 1972 dish washing machine in fact.

given a hose with boiling water and left to dry. — Wheeled back to kitchen — Cutlery would I suppose have to be drained unless — maybe hot air could be used. The noise of dishes and knives and forks and the natural gossip and loud talk of dish washers. Food being cooked for night nurses. Drs. coming from cups of tea. All good and necessary but spoils the rest and sleep at night. The nurses are all very nice indeed — grand little girls without exception. The Dr here Dr Hillman gave me and Mrs Moffat two sleeping pills which was wonderful. A lovely nights sleep after an enema? Tea and toast at six o'clock. Another shave for poor wee Fanny a wash down by myself and now the large white flannel nighty with linen buttons. [obscure], thick white knitted stockings and a nasty white plastic cap with elastic — with that minus my teeth I will be a beauty and no mistake and my other end doesn't look any more glamorous shaved. The matron yesterday when she came round and I told her I was J.'s wife spoke very highly of him and said he had a wonderful brain and how much she enjoyed his article in the book of the Arts in U.[38] Be that as it may the Sister was most impressed and tho' I had said before I was cold a bit, in two minutes a lovely warm blanket arrived with a nurse who said 'what is your name' I told J. his fame was at least good for a blanket for my cold feet. Well, here I wait for the theatre and the great man who can put God's poor handiwork to rights — I am not much worried as it is so slight and I feel in the best of health. I only hope I won't talk — can I will myself to say nothing under the anesthetic? [sic] and will I obey myself? — or is it wrong and just a sense of pride or fear of exposing some evil in me. Should I let out what's there. Dear me Roberta lie back and wait and don't be so self-important. Johnny couldn't get thro' the orangemen last night and was 20 minutes late and I was hurt and poor man he was in a fit and he gave me such a nice loving farewell kiss. I do love him very much. To be continued after my little death.

About 11 o'c. a.m. I was very sleepy when the nurses came for me but I climbed into the trolley and again onto the operating table. Dr Lowry came and smiled down at me — I remember getting an injection almost at once I could taste it in my mouth and I said so. Then I blinked and saw the lights in the roof — the day light and I thought I was still in the theatre and I wished they would get on with it I blinked again and there was Johnny standing there and it was after 3 o'c. I talked to him and went into little snoozes and at one point I was dreaming about a large piece of cheese partly covered with silver paper, with the cheese part on the ground and a large hand on it and as I wakened I asked J. to give me a piece of cheese. Then he was gone and someone told me it was five o'clock. A nurse came to take temperatures and pulses and then 3 nurses came and took my pulse and I heard one of them say it was 32. Then I woke up at about 7 o'c. I had been sick at intervals and so very thirsty the back of my throat seemed to be closing. But still I got a cup of tea about 9.30 and managed to keep it down. We were five of us pushed into the ward for the purpose, with tiled walls and floor easy to clean if we were sick. The others got sleeping pills but the Dr. would not give me one and he said I had managed to scare the nurses. I slept little — it was a long night but I was comfortable and not in pain and it passed. My bed was pulled back into the little side ward after breakfast. The nurses were most kind and attentive and we could not get better care . . .

Johnny came at 3 o'c today and brought my white asters and sweets. He had been at the cricket match this morning and the South Africans are playing and he was going back when he left here at 4.15 pm. Visiting hours are from 3 to 3.45. When I was coming in there was another girl coming in for an operation and I talked to her mother then the mother saw me in here one day and came in and said 'Hello'. I was operated the same day and when I came too [sic] I was beside the girl and her mother was with her. Today the mother came into the ward here and brought me 4 chocolate biscuits. I was so pleased. There is a Mrs McCluskey who sits up in bed smoking with large gold hoops of earrings in a dirty pink bed jacket. She moves around in the day time and tells us all about her insides — twenty years ago her overies [sic] were taken away. Now she says her womb and half of her pipes, and holding her hand at her navel she says 'Och dear, I'm empty (empy) from there down.'

---

38. *The Arts in Ulster: A Symposium*, eds S.H. Bell, Nesca A. Robb and John Hewitt (London: George G. Harrap, 1951).

Tuesday 12 February 1952

I felt awfully fed up with the flat when I got back — I suppose I was envious[39] — I got cross with J. and started a yap about him not allowing to buy a house ages ago — not being interested in furniture or where we lived. I behaved badly. We went to bed and our old hard bed had annoyed me more and I yapped on to silent John, which made me worse, then he got mad and got out of bed and went down stairs. Later he came up for his dressing gown and I said 'If you are being heroic take the eiderdown' but he ignored me. Then I got up and dressed and said 'I complain of the bed so you go back to it and I will go for a

walk.' He commanded me not to go but I could see he could hardly keep from laughing and I suppressed the desire to laugh myself and in the end we went back to bed and I had to take off my gloves and strip, feeling a small and dispicable [*sic*] unlovely creature and knowing I should have been given the cat o' nine tails — but the next day J. repaired the table that had been broken for ages. It was too bad of me knowing he is struggling with a new job in the gallery.

Thursday 14th Frederick Street committee. Busy. I am pleased to see the wee plants come up of cedar trees that I have in a pot. And I dreamt that a woman told me she had planted the same kind of seeds in a pot and said to me 'You wouldn't believe how they are growing' I wanted to tell her about mine but didn't.

39. She had just been to visit Estyn Evan's renovated Georgian house and commented 'I would like such a house'.

DORINE ROHAN

(*fl.* 1969)

from:
MARRIAGE IRISH STYLE
(1969)

[The social changes and debates of the 1960s brought greater openness about sexuality and greater awareness of the potentially damaging effects of repression and silence. Dorine Rohan's semi-sociological analysis, published in Cork in 1969 by Mercier Press, defines Irish sexual identity through the varieties of sexual dysfunction, inhibition and ignorance her interviews revealed. She attributes much of the damage done to the influence of the Catholic church. Her vigorously frank analysis is notable for its attention to the feelings and opinions of ordinary Irish citizens about sex.]

SEX IN IRISH MARRIAGE

'Whoever said you were supposed to enjoy sex? Sure, aren't we all here to suffer, and the more we suffer in this life, the better it will be for us in the next' — Irish mother of nine children.

'Would you ever tell me what *is* an orgasm? Do you see stars and that sort of thing? I've never had one as far as I know' — Irish mother married for fifteen years.

'We have had four children in five years, and we don't want any more for the moment — but my husband is very decent, he uses the withdrawal method.'

These are quotes from some of the women I interviewed on marriage.

The men and women whom I interviewed were very surprisingly frank about their views, and although most of them felt shy about talking about sex in front of their husbands or wives, on their own they were even eager to give their views and opinions. As all my interviews were strictly private, (unless husbands and wives wanted to talk together) and as I did not have their names recorded or written down, they felt free to give honest opinions. A group discussion on sex, certainly a social discussion, on the subject is rarely informative. Personally I have never heard an honest conversation on sex in Ireland. A psychiatrist commenting on this said, 'I'm not surprised. I don't think there is such a thing as an honest discussion on sex — between a group of people who have met socially that is — it is too personal a thing for one to be objective about it, and a person who initiates a conversation about sex is usually angling for something' — (probably sex). This probably puts it in a nutshell. The Irish on the whole have many inhibitions and complexes about sex. So deeply complex is the attitude of the majority, that they rarely overcome their inhibitions. Usually conversations on sex start with a wisecrack, followed by giggles, insinuations and inevitably ending with somebody feeling uncomfortable.

Nowhere is a man more sensitive than when his ability as a lover, or for a woman her attraction, is questioned. This reaction is not peculiar to the Irish man and woman, but here in Ireland there appears to be a peculiar hysteria very near to the surface on the subject of sex. This mostly manifests itself if one listens to what is called 'drink talk'.

I found that lovemaking was rarely a beautiful thing in Irish marriage. Donald S. Connery remarks in *The Irish*: 'His (the Irishman's) wife is a kingsized hot water bottle who also cooks his food and pays his bills and produces his heirs. In the intimate side of marriage he behaves as if he were slightly ashamed of having deserted his male friends and his bachelorhood. He takes what should be the happy, leisurely lovemaking of marriage like a silent connubial supper of cold rice pudding. A rapid sex routine is effected as if his wife is some stray creature with whom he is sinning and hopes he may never see again. Though many Irish wives are pre-conditioned to such behaviour, having seen its like in their own fathers and uncles, they resent it deeply. But as they turn from their husbands to lavish affection on their sons, and then, in later years, strive to "protect" them from scheming girls wishing to marry them, they carry on the vicious circle of maternal possessiveness and male selfishness.'[1] We have been called a 'sick society as regards sex', 'lousy lovers', 'indiscriminate breeders of unwanted children'. A curious thing is that nobody seems to

want to believe anyone else who claims to have an enjoyable sex life. I heard one woman expounding once how fabulous a lover her husband was, tender, loving, virile, wonderful, she could not possibly be interested in other men. —When she had left the company someone remarked 'Isn't she lucky with her Romeo between the sheets?' 'Rubbish,' somebody else replied, 'if it was like that she wouldn't be talking so much about it!' which goes to prove the futility of giving a personal and subjective opinion! The unfortunate thing is that sex appears to become a much more important factor in one's life if a satisfactory sex life is lacking. When a couple are compatible sexually, it does not seem to be a factor of such magnitude in their daily lives. Unfortunately in Ireland the compatible couple seem to be the exception rather than the rule. The extent of satisfaction for most couples appears to be of a rather negative quality. 'I'm lucky, I don't mind it' or 'He's very good, he doesn't want it very often' were remarks I heard frequently from women I spoke to. The men too were in many instances upset and disturbed about their sexual relations with their wives.

'But she never seems to want it, the only time she is in good humour with me in bed is the time of the month when we can't make love.'

'When I am making love to her she keeps telling me that she is bored and to hurry up.' From these views, one would not only deduce that 'the romance had gone out of the marriage' but that it had never been in it in the first place. Many saw sexual intercourse as nothing more than a biological function. 'We're all animals after all, aren't we?' one man said to me with a shrug. 'I don't believe in all this spirituality lark about sex.'

'Irish men don't make love, they copulate or mate, or whatever you like to call it, but love doesn't come into it,' said one Irish woman sadly.

It is sad how many Irish people do regard what should be making love as an animal desire to be ashamed of if not carried out with the express (!) intention of having children. It is indicative that so many Irish people feel only inclined to make love when they are alcoholically inebriated; as if the fact of being anaesthetised from drink took away from the awareness of their 'distasteful' behaviour. Here, indeed, there is little of the mutual satisfaction and joy which should be

1. Donald S. Connery, *The Irish* (London: Eyre and Spottiswoode, 1968; New York: Simon and Schuster, 1968), p. 200.

derived from the complete awareness of their bodies in physical union. If people think they are animals it would follow that they are quite likely to behave like animals. Sexual intercourse which consists of a grab in the dark followed by a 'five minute togetherness' does not deserve the name of making *love*. There is probably no greater emotional aloneness than that suffered where love is lacking in love-making.

Fear of pregnancy has been named as the commonest reason for the failure of Irish women to achieve orgasm in marital relations with their husbands. I would very much doubt this, as many of the women who say they have never had satisfactory intercourse certainly wanted the first child if not the first three or four. Of eighty four patients recently queried at a Dublin family planning clinic, twenty per cent said that they never achieved orgasm, and fifty eight per cent said that they always achieved orgasm. Twenty two per cent said they did sometimes. It was stated that those attending such a clinic however may not represent the incidence among the general married population. Of course there is always the question of what is an orgasm, as one psychiatrist said to me, 'No man knows what a woman's orgasms means, and vice versa, there is no way of measuring the feelings or reactions of people under such circumstances.' Probably the answer would be like Fats Waller's[2] reply to the question he was asked 'What is jazz?' 'If you don't know you ain't got it.' Similarly, with orgasms it might be said 'If you don't know, you ain't had one.'

More than any other factor in a marital relationship the sexual problem is probably the one most likely to drift, (where it is a problem) and if allowed to develop as a problem, it is likely in the vast majority of cases that neither party will do anything towards solving the problem. This is the case in many marriages where sex is not a definite physical problem, but rather where love and tenderness and sensitivity play no part in the 'love-making'. One of the most frequent complaints I heard from Irish wives was that their husbands were completely insensitive to them as lovers, and many husbands complained that Irish girls are frigid or not interested in the sexual side of marriage. To me it seems a more

positive problem than insensitivity and disinterest. The problem in fact is a very deep and complex one in many cases. For centuries the Roman Catholic Church, and indeed many other churches, (but we are primarily concerned with the influence of Roman Catholicism as it is the religion of the vast majority of Irish people and has been for hundreds of years) frowned on sex, and preached the rewards of a celibate or virginal way of life . . .

Sex in Irish marriage however is no longer looked upon as 'permission to sin', and the more progressive Fathers of the Church are favouring a far more liberal attitude to sexual relationships, probably in the light of what has been discovered by psychologists in the field of the importance of a healthy sex life.

It is one thing, nevertheless for the Church to acknowledge the necessity of a healthy and more enlightened attitude towards sexual relations in marriage, (as is recognised as necessary for the emotional and mental welfare of individuals) but it is another matter to try to undo the harm that has obviously been done by less enlightened generations in the way of repression and inhibitions which in a mild form manifests itself in a type of prudery, and in a more advanced form as I encountered in many cases a positive revulsion to the sex act. This revulsion I found not only in women, but some men I spoke with told me of their inhibitions which they felt would never be overcome. They performed the sex act as the result of an overpowering biological urge, (often as the result of alcohol) and afterwards in some cases felt ashamed. Many women spoke to me of their failure to overcome their inhibitions about sex.

'I'd like to have a better physical side to my marriage, but it's just hopeless. I was always taught that sex was dirty and sinful, and I have never been able to adjust. No, I haven't gone to see anyone about it. I feel it's too late, but I feel guilty for my husband's sake. I have six children and I hope to give them a better upbringing that way.' 'I dread it every time my husband wants to make love to me. He never satisfies me but I don't think that it is entirely his fault. I never tell him that I don't enjoy it. I think it's better that he doesn't know how I feel.' Altruistic as this attitude may seem it is indeed a sad thing that a couple can experience ten or twelve years of

2. Fats Waller (1904–43), a black American musician and composer, was a key figure in the development of jazz.

marital relations and a husband does not know or does not want to know that his wife is not satisfied or happy with their lovemaking.

It appears in many instances that the couple develop a mental block about their sex life and never discuss it or refer to it any time — probably lest the enormity of their sexual inhibitions should become too important if they are brought out into the open. And so they continue, with that side of their relationship, to which psychiatrists attribute 30%–50% of the importance of marriage success drifting into a dull, drab, uninteresting if not positively distressing, feature of their lives. It is understandable that a person who has been taught from early childhood that babies are found under gooseberry bushes, that one's genital organs are not to be looked at, thought about or discussed, and that physical contact of any sort with a member of the opposite sex is evil, should find it difficult to walk down the aisle from the altar rails thinking that sex is all-beautiful and rewarding.

'Sex is the only sin in Ireland,' one husband told me bitterly. 'You can go to confession and say you got drunk or were uncharitable and it doesn't matter. You are just "a hard man". But anything to do with sex, and the gates of hell are wide open for you.'

With the inhibitions, there is also in Ireland a considerable number of young people who have no idea even of the simple biological function of the sex act. Not only in their late teens but a number of young people getting married have come home from their honeymoon and sought the assistance of doctor, or gynaecologist or priest as to how to perform the marital act. And this in a country where the vast majority accept that a marriage is not consummated without the marital act having taken place! In many cases the only knowledge about the 'facts of life' consists of what has been picked up from dirty jokes from older friends, or pornographic literature, which is only read because it is forbidden. With this scanty knowledge, of doubtful assistance in their understanding of the 'facts of life', they pretend to or think they 'know all' until they reach the stage of marriage.

In many cases the ignorance has led to young girls ending up on the boat to England four or five months pregnant. Many of the girls in this unhappy position are genuinely amazed and horrified, having thought that, (as most five and six year olds think) 'you have to be married before God will give you a baby'.

However, as one doctor said to me, it is not the number whose only problem is ignorance, who have the greatest difficulty with their sexual relationships. They can be taught and instructed in a way that will benefit their relationship with each other, (and all the more so if both seek help and advice and not just the wife as happens in many cases) but of far greater concern is the person or couple who have a 'sick idea' and views on sex. It is particularly difficult to undo the damage that is caused when children are instilled from their earliest years with the idea that sex is evil. In many cases one finds that men consider women 'the unclean vessel' and women consider men 'dirty' and 'animalistic'. A shaky enough basis for a healthy marital life! . . .

There is also much ignorance on the part of Irish husbands as regards their wives' functions in procreation. Very many know nothing more than the four letter words for the female genital organs. Words such as vagina, ovary, hymen, are a foreign language to him. A senior nurse in a semi-state maternity home told me that a number of men (and even some women) do not know how or where a child is born when they first become parents — one woman's husband enquired 'with vague interest' how babies were born, after the birth of his fourth child! Most women are not particularly frightened at the thought of childbirth unless they have had a particularly bad time. Most men think it is a horrifying business, but natural to women, and one husband remarked to me, 'It's extraordinary with the advances that have been made in medicine and science, men landing on the moon etc., and women are still suffering terrible pain in childbirth as they have done for thousands of years.' 'Coitus interruptus' is a fairly widely used form of 'contraception' in Ireland, although doctors are worried about this and say that it is detrimental psychologically and physically to both partners. It is also a mortal sin. Due to its rather low rate of success the 'rhythm method', the only form of birth control permitted to date by the Roman Catholic Church, is not much relied upon, although a priest in the Catholic Marriage Advisory Council told me that 'for those who persevere with it, it is quite successful'. Apart from anything else it is quite a complicated business, and many appear to abandon it in the early stage for various reasons. Until recent years, even the rhythm method was not wholly approved of by the Church, and many women told me that the priest told them to abstain altogether. They said they never got round to finding out if it worked or not, as their husbands 'got fed up waiting'. (It takes at least three months to determine when (and if) regular ovulation occurs.) By this method, the woman must take a rectal temperature each morning before rising for at least two menstrual months. During ovulation there will be a rise in temperature which persists through ovulation and then descends to its previous level. When ovulation time has been determined for a few months, a menstrual calendar may be prepared for guidance. Even those who did persevere with

it, (whom I spoke to) said that they were nervous wrecks wondering whether they had 'got caught or not'.

The inhibitions and problems relating to sex in Ireland are not likely to disappear overnight as a result of recognizing that they are there. It will take probably not only a number of years, but a number of generations of 're-education' on the subject. As one priest said to me, 'The trouble is that most of those in charge of forming young people's minds are also a product of the "sick society" as regards sex in Ireland. There are many priests and parents who are strongly "anti-progress" in the field of a healthier education on personal relationships between men and women. For this reason it will take generations to undo the harm. It is not as if they all recognized the need for re-thinking. Consequently the problems are doubled.'

NUALA FENNELL

(1935–)

from:
IRISH MARRIAGE —
HOW ARE YOU!
(1974)

[Nuala Fennell's investigation of the links between sexuality, marriage and domestic violence in Ireland breaks an important taboo by discussing wife-beating and marital rape, and she exposes the legal system's failure to protect women or punish their attackers. Her well-intentioned efforts to be even-handed in her treatment of the sexes sometimes lead her to suggest that women can be the ones to blame for their own brutalization; her association of masochism with domestic violence is particularly unfortunate. The controversy as well as praise surrounding Roddy Doyle's television drama, *The Family*, and his subsequent novel, *The Woman Who Walked into Doors*, suggests that many of the problems for victims identified by Fennell in the 1970s were still operative in the 1990s.]

WIFE-BEATING — A HUSBAND'S PREROGATIVE?

Self-consciously her forefinger went up to a three inch scar beside her mouth. She explained it has been caused by a breadknife. 'If I lock the door he breaks his way in, and physically he is stronger than me. Neighbours cannot always be interfering to help, and short of having a policeman living in I can do nothing. I never refuse him a meal if I have the food in the house, even if it is only a packet of soup and tea. I know he will beat me if he has drink, so I take two sleeping pills and sleep in the bath if he is out late. The bathroom is the only place I can lock myself in. Once after he beat me I had him taken into custody and charged but when leave of appeal was granted and bail fixed, his mother went bailee[1] and got him out. It's not that I am hard

1. Guaranteed his bail money.

but I think jail would have been good for him. Mostly his problem is sexual, I am still a virgin, our marriage was never consummated. When he found intercourse impossible on our honeymoon I thought this would sort itself out with time and patience. It has only become worse and he is tortured by some terrible inadequacy.'

In dealing with the problem of wife brutality, the incidence of which is increasing both in Ireland and England, I am relating the cases as they came to us. Sometimes, as in the foregoing case it is easy to put a finger on a contributory cause of the problem, in later pages a psychiatric view is given.

Canon Law in years past accepted wife-beating as a fair means of keeping a spouse in order, a hundred years ago it was an unquestioned pattern in many families, due in part to the lack of status of a woman, and in part to their chattel value in a marriage.

In all fairness while women can be guilty of precipitating marital breakdown by their infidelity, alcoholism or desertion, when it comes to brutality by and large it is a one-way application, by a husband. One obvious factor to militate against a wife who has to contend with a violent husband is the lack of muscle and might, she is just not his physical equal, nor has she been conditioned or trained as he has been to take a physically offensive position on issues. Because it appears that wife-beating most often shows as an early pattern in marriage (normally passive husbands do not act so out of character) young wives, through shame, ignorance or loyalty, tolerate repeated beatings until they become a way of life for them. Brides are traditionally more romantic than wise.

There is despair and deep unhappiness in many of the letters under this heading, like this mother: 'For twelve years my husband has beaten me, and at the beginning (I was only seventeen when I married) I never questioned his right to do it, but I hated him for it. I was pregnant and had to get married, but that baby was the only one of my children conceived in affection, if not love. The others were a result of rape, and let no one tell me you cannot have that in marriage. My husband is fifteen years older than me and has a good standing in the community, they all think he has a dizzy young wife. For years I tried to tell people how I was suffering, but I only embar-rassed them because we have always lived in a country town. Often I wished I could hide one of those self-righteous pillars of the Church in a cupboard in my home, and let them hear a little of our Christian marriage. How I am sane I'll never know. I cannot leave, I have nowhere to go. I have no money and I adore my five children too much to walk out and leave them.' The sister of another victim of such brutality wrote from the country, 'The man has a tempestuous and violent character and I worry for them all, my sister has ten children, with two sets of twins. She is regularly brutally assaulted, and has fled to another sister who lives locally. But he would not allow her to take the younger children and they are very neglected. The husband has in the past been charged with attempted rape of his ten year old, at that time he was warned by the Guards[2] either to emigrate or go for trial, in the meantime with the present undesirable circumstances, no one wants to intervene.'

In so many cases it was a relative or friend who wrote to us, like this mother, 'Unfortunately from the start my daughter's marriage was a disaster. She had courted a boy for five years, and he was always kind, agreeable and appeared devoted to her. He was an only child and totally spoiled. His mother was anxious for the marriage, she thought I would give a big dowry, but I was cautious about giving it on her marriage. In any case she got pregnant straight away and the husband made her life unbearable, forcing her to live with his mother, aged grandfather, and workmen. The mother made her presence felt, she resented my daughter, and criticised everything she did. When she came home with her tiny baby her husband started rough tactics. He caught her by the hair and threatened to choke her, he hit her across the face several times. After one such night she came home to me all black and blue and in a state of nervous collapse. Now I know I must protect her and her child. I can support her, but her husband is saying if he can't kill her one way he will kill her another, as he will take her to the Courts and get the child. He has made no direct approach to his wife to effect reconciliation, apart from sending his Parish Priest over to talk to her.'

According to a Report brought out in 1972 by a group of law students (Free Legal Aid Centres)

2. The *gardaí*, the Irish police, Garda Síochána.

from their experience there are several recurring factors in marital disharmony, the chief factor seems to be violence, 80% usually brought on by drink. However they do point out that violence and drink are sometimes separate agents. The Report further states, 'The wife in difficulties with her marriage has several options open to her. Sadly none of these provides her with a complete solution to her problem. She may serve her husband with an assault summons if he has beaten her. Most wives are extremely reluctant to take their husbands to court on such a charge. Even when she is persuaded to take the step, there is no guarantee that it will improve her position. A short, often suspended prison term does not always help. In some cases, the husband becomes even more vicious towards the wife after she has taken this step. The Gardai rarely interfere in cases of family dispute.' . . .

Court action for brutality seldom resolves the real problem, but few end as tragically as the case of Ann, a mother of five and four months' pregnant. The morning she appeared in the District Court to give evidence of assault by her husband, she had been up all night, most of it spent sitting in her local police station where she had fled in terror when her husband, who was an alcoholic, had come in at 3 a.m. and attacked her. Charging him was a last resort for Ann. She knew he was dangerous to her, to their five children, and to himself, and she wanted him committed to a detention centre where he could get the treatment she felt he so badly needed.

She asked the judge to remand him in custody for a medical report, pleading that he be referred for treatment. She was told her request was out of order, this was not her privilege. It was implied that she was taking unfair advantage of her husband, who the Judge admitted, 'looks in bad shape and has obviously had a few drinks'. The case was adjourned for a week, the husband freed on his own surety, and over drinks later with friends he admitted that he 'lied to the judge like a gentleman'. But he was dead two days later, having jumped bail, borrowed money and gone to France where he was hit and killed by a lorry. His widow sent the following letter to the District Justice who heard the case:

'On the Sixth of last month I asked you to have my husband remanded in custody for a medical report due to his illness (alcoholism) that my life was in danger and that he was a danger to himself. You told me that I had no right to make the request even though the guard confirmed my evidence of his previous disposition and convictions for assault. Although I was in a distraught condition (in court) due to the treatment received from my husband, and a total lack of sleep, I endeavoured to make you aware of why I had to take him to court. You gave me little opportunity to inform you of the seriousness of my position. I left the court with the impression that you either did not want to hear my evidence or that you disbelieved me. My sole purpose in being in your court was for the protection of my husband, myself and my children, but within twenty-six hours of your decision, my husband was dead and my worse fears were realised. I write this letter in the interest of people who might in the future find themselves in my predicament. I would now have to carry less worry if you had given me the opportunity of a more patient and less aggressive hearing.'

Any woman who has not been a victim of a beating by her husband must regard the practice with total incomprehension, and wonder how the voluntary contract of marriage with a promise to honour, love and cherish could deteriorate all too quickly to a boot in the ribs or a fist in the eye. We can all surmise about influences that combine to make a wife-beater. In many cases there are strong mother-son relationships, which persist to the extent of the husband's mother showing a total lack of objectivity about his action, and giving him sanctuary or as we have seen going bailee. The surprising thing about such situations is that very often this mother may have suffered beatings from her own husband, but instead of, as one might expect, this giving her a special understanding and compassion for the young wife's ordeal, what appears to happen is that she will justify his behaviour. This type of mother has most likely over the years switched the love and allegiance she might have had for her husband on to her sons, with a consequent critical approach to any daughter-in-law. Another factor many feel could be responsible for brutality in marriage is our educational environment which accepts corporal punishment as a normal penalising procedure.

The psychiatrists to whom I spoke hadn't got a lot to say on the subject of wife brutality, and certainly were not in any way optimistic about a cure. There is apparently a strong aggressive need in men to identify with their traditional place in the family unit. He can have (generally unfounded) fears that for instance, because his wife is on the pill she may be unfaithful, or there may be jealousy of a successful career wife, though this may not be fully revealed. There is as little clinical evidence that wife-beaters are grown-up boyhood bullies, as there is to support the idea that they can be successfully treated and cured.

If a man is made of the stuff in which violence towards a weaker person is part of the behavioural pattern, nothing short of a real religious experience is going to change him. It is worth remembering that some people, like St Paul,[3] who were very violent, were changed through a religious experience.

There are three situations in which wife-beating most often occurs. They can be identified under the following (a) Provocation (b) Inadequate Man and (c) Problem Sex. Outlined under (a) are wrong attitudes of wives, the ones who nag incessantly and ask for retaliation, the hyper-critical wives who don't seem to like anything about their husbands because there was probably not the right basis for the marriage in the first place. Some are dirty, untidy, don't keep house properly nor care for the children adequately, they can be improvident and some even drink to excess. (b) The Inadequate Man is really an extension of the above, again relating to the wife. This situation, of which wife-beating can be an effect, is created when a husband's worth (as he sees it) is not recognised in his job (there are many good people who are never recognised in their lifetimes). If the wife of such a man does not show sympathy, understanding and the necessary loyalty to bolster his hurt ego and faltering morale, violent aggression may likely develop in that marriage. In this situation the violent assertion of a man in his home can come about because, whether through lack of influence or lack of ability, his aspirations to be boss in his job are not realised.

But (c) Sexual Problems is probably the most common cause. It could be considered a more important factor than the others because it is very often an unknown and unrecognisable one. The amount of impotence and partial impotence one psychiatrist admitted that he comes across is quite astounding. If there is male impotence very often the wife is a living rebuke to the sexual inadequacy and brings out violent frustrations in the man. But the sexual difficulty could be originating from the wife's attitude to sex, her inhibitions, even her frigidity, could in turn make him more aggressive in his treatment of her, if this is his behavioural pattern.

The major linkage with wife-beating found by psychiatrists in this country (and elsewhere) in clinical evidence has been sexual inadequacy or misunderstanding, which leads to masochism and sadism. There is some evidence that a woman may in fact enjoy the pain inflicted by the beatings and in this way get a measure of masochistic pleasure. Psychiatrists do not understand why this should be so, it is a feminine characteristic.

Sex as a main problem area is not so much a result of no formal sexual education, as it is typical of generally repressive public attitudes to things related to sex. Though this situation is changing in Ireland, the changes are not quick enough to cope with other environmental changes and not obvious in a reduction of clinical cases.

Violence is near the surface in most people, both sexes, and any manifestation of violence to-day must be taken in the context of the widespread acceptance of violence all over the world.

Women can be violent also, there are cases of husband bashing, admittedly these instances would not be as numerous, nor would the injuries be as severe as in wife-beating. Women show their aggression in different ways to men, maybe with equal or greater effect to hurt, mentally if not physically. Treatment of a violent husband is not easy, for they will refuse to come for treatment, to be examined or even to discuss the problem with a third party. Will the campaign of equality for women, which one hopes will lead to financial, intellectual, and social benefits for wives, also lead to further conflict in marriage? One would hope not. If it is to become the enriching dimension to married couples that is anticipated, it will need a tremendous amount of readjustment on the part of men towards their wives.

3. Acts of the Apostles 7–9.

SIOBHÁN NÍ SHÚILLEABHÁIN

(*fl.* 1883)

from:
LEGENDS FROM IRELAND
(1977)

[The increased scientific and sociological discourse about sexuality in the 1970s deployed interviews and reportage as important strategies for gaining access to the experiences of 'ordinary' people. Dorine Rohan and Nuala Fennell both record the kinds of embarrassment Irish people felt at discussing sexuality. Folklore remained an important way of expressing feelings about issues such as desire, violence, impotence and infidelity in metaphoric language. The matters are discussed fully by Angela Bourke in her General Introduction to 'Oral Traditions', pp. 1191–7, and in the introduction to 'Legends of the Supernatural', pp. 1284–6. The following entry illustrates the increasing representation of Irish folklore in popular anglophone writing in the twentieth century. This story, attributed to Siobhán Ní Shúilleabháin and translated by Sean O'Sullivan,[1] was recorded in Irish by Seosamh Ó Dálaigh, 14 September 1937, from Seán Ó Grífin, Cathair Boilg, parish of Ventry, County Kerry, who had heard it fifty years earlier from Ní Shúilleabháin, a woman of the same district. Irish Folklore Commission Ms. Volume 430: 109–15. It appears in *Legends from Ireland* (London: Batsford, 1977), collected, edited and, where necessary, translated by Sean O'Sullivan. The thematic ordering of the narratives in such collections emphasizes their place in 'world' folkculture. *Legends from Ireland* was published in a series of legends from different parts of the British Isles, including Devon, Cornwall, the Welsh Borders, and the Scottish Highlands.   S.K.]

DEAD COUPLE MARRY AFTER DEATH

Long ago there was a boy and a girl and they were in love with each other. They had been walking out together for five or six years and the boy had promised to marry her. That was all right until a second girl came home from America. She had a good lot of money, and didn't the boy turn

his back on the first girl and go about with the other. When the first girl saw what was happening, she became heart-broken and died. That was that. Before the day on which he was to marry the second girl came, some kind of sickness came on him and he died.

Seven years after that there was a wedding in the next townland, and all the local boys and girls went to it. A young man was on his way to the wedding at night, and his shoes needed mending. He went to the house of a shoemaker at the side of the street and asked him would he mend his shoes.

'I will. Take them off,' said the shoemaker.

He slipped off the shoes, and it was late at night by the time they were mended. He set out then for the wedding-house. He took a short-cut by the side of a hill. The night was fine and bright. He saw a white ghost coming down the hill towards him, and he stopped to look. When the ghost came near him at the other side of a fence, the young man asked him was he dead or alive.

'I'm dead,' said the ghost.

'What's wrong that you are like this?'

'I'll be like this forever until I marry the girl I promised to marry in this world,' said the ghost. 'I have been dead for seven years and have been going about like this ever since. I was engaged to a girl before I died but I broke my promise to her and went with another girl. The first girl died of a broken heart, and I died before I could marry the other one. I'll be going round like this forever unless I get someone from this world to stand sponsor for me at my marriage in the next world. Will you do that?'

'I will!'

The ghost left him and it wasn't long before a kind of sleep came over the young man beside the fence. He awoke to find himself at the edge of a cliff. He saw an island in the sea in front of him. Sleep came over him again and when he awoke he found himself on the island. He stood up and remembered his promise to stand sponsor at a wedding. He saw a chapel some distance away and he went towards it. He went in and sat on one of the seats. It wasn't long until a priest passed by

---

1. Sean O'Sullivan, also known as Seán Ó Súilleabháin (1903–96), was archivist to the Irish Folklore Commission and later to the Department of Folklore at University College Dublin. He is the author of several important reference works as well as the editor of more popular collections of Irish folktales.

him up along the chapel, and then he saw the white ghost following, with a girl at the other side. They didn't stop till they reached the altar. The priest went up on the altar, and the ghost and the girl went on their knees. The priest called out:

'Come up here, living man, and stand sponsor for these!'

He got up from the seat and went to the altar. The priest married them and then took them into a small room. The priest wrote down in a book that the pair were married, and the young man had to write with the pen that he had been sponsor.

'Now,' said the priest to the young man, 'when you go home, you must go to the parish priest and tell him that I have married such a couple in the other world. He won't believe you, but he will get it in his book!'

'I'm very thankful to you,' said the ghost. 'This is the girl I was to marry first, but we died. Your father knew this girl well.'

They left him. Sleep came over him once more, and he awoke at the foot of the hill where he had fallen asleep first. He stood up and went off towards the wedding-house, but it was almost over. He danced a little and took a drink and ate a bite; he was very hungry after the night. When he reached home, he told his father what had happened.

'Father,' he asked, 'was there a couple like that here who died?'

'There was. I knew them well.'

'I must go to the parish priest today to tell him that they are married,' said the son.

He went to the parish priest. The priest asked him what he wanted.

'This is what I want. Go to your book of marriages and see will you find the names of a certain couple in it.'

He told the priest their names.

'Don't be telling lies! It can't be true!' said the priest.

'It might be, father. I had to promise that I'd come to you to ask you to search your book for them.'

The priest got up and went to the marriage-book. He found their names there.

'You were right,' said he.

That's my story. If there's a lie in it, let it be! I heard it about fifty years ago from an old woman named Siobhan O'Sullivan, who lived in this townland. She was about fifty years old at that time.

MARGARET BARRINGTON

(1896–1982)

VILLAGE WITHOUT MEN . . .
(1982)

[In Margaret Barrington's story sexuality both drives rural depopulation and provides the bulwark against it. Her portrait of rural life in the west of Ireland as exotic, brutal, mythic and unchanging has more in common with the Irish Literary Revival than with the counter-revival. At the same time she emphasizes the sexual frustration and patriarchal social structures that encouraged young people, especially young women, to migrate to cities. She also represents the sexuality of the older women, once rekindled, as a primitive force for vitality and survival. Towards the end of her life Barrington's stories were collected for publication in book form. 'Village without Men . . .' appeared in *David's Daughter, Tamar* (Dublin: Wolfhound Press, 1982) just after her death.]

Weary and distraught the women listened to the storm as it raged around the houses. The wind screamed and howled. It drove suddenly against the doors with heavy lurchings. It tore at the straw ropes which anchored the thatched roofs to the ground. It rattled and shook the small windows. It sent the rain in narrow streams under the door, through the piled-up sacks, to form large puddles on the hard stamped earthen floors.

At times when the wind dropped for a moment to a low whistling whisper and nothing could be heard but the hammering of the sea against the face of Cahir Roe, the sudden release would be intolerable. Then one or another would raise her head and break into a prayer, stumbling words of supplication without continuity or meaning. Just for a moment a voice would be heard. Then the screaming wind would rise again in fury, roaring in the chimney and straining the roof-ropes, the voice would sink to a murmur and then to nothing as the women crouched again over the smouldering sods, never believing for a moment in the miracle they prayed for.

Dawn broke and the wind dropped for a while. The women wrapped their shawls tightly round them, knotted the ends behind them and tightened their headcloths. They slipped out through cautiously opened doors. The wind whipped their wide skirts so tightly to their bodies it was hard to move. They muttered to themselves as they clambered over the rocks or waded through the pools down to the foaming sea.

To the right Cahir Roe sloped upward, smothered in storm clouds, protecting the village from the outer sea. The ears of the women rang with the thunder of the ocean against its giant face. Salt foam flecked their faces, their clothes as they struggled along in knots of three or four, their heads turned from the wind as they searched the shore and looked out over the rolling water. But in all that grey-green expanse of churning sea, nothing. Not even an oar. All day long they wandered.

It was not until the turn of the tide on the second day that the bodies began to roll in, one now, another again, over and over in the water like dark, heavy logs. Now a face showed, now an outstretched hand rose clear of the water. John Boyle's face had been smashed on the rocks, yet his wife knew him as an incoming wave lifted his tall lean body to hurl it to shore.

For two days the women wandered until the ocean, now grown oily but still sullen with anger, gave up no more. Niel Boylan, Charley Friel and Dan Gallagher were never found.

The women rowed across the bay to the little town of Clonmullen for the priest. After the heavy rain the road across the bog was dangerous, and the village was cut off by land. The young curate, Father Twomey, came across. When he looked at the grey haggard faces of these women, all words of comfort deserted the young priest. His throat went dry and his eyes stung as if the salt sea had caught them. What comfort could words bring to women in their plight? He could with greater ease pray for the souls of the drowned than encourage the living to bear their sorrow in patience.

The women had opened the shallow graves in the sandy graveyard. They lowered the bodies and shovelled back the sand. Then for headstones, to mark the place where each man was laid before the restless sand should blot out every sign, they drove an oar which he had handled into each man's grave and dropped a stone there for every prayer they said. The wind blew the sand into the priest's vestments, into his shoes, into his well-oiled hair and into his book. It whirled the sand around the little heaps of stones.

As the women rowed him home across the bay, the priest looked back at the village. The oars in the graves stood out against the stormy winter sky like the masts of ships in harbour.

The midwife was the first to leave the village.

As they brought each dead man up from the sea, she stripped him and washed his body. For most of them she had done this first service. From early youth, first with her mother, then alone, she had plied her trade on this desolate spit of land. These same bodies which once warm, soft, tender and full of life, had struggled between her strong hands, now lay cold and rigid beneath them. She washed the cold sea-water from these limbs from which she had once washed the birth-slime. Silently she accomplished her task and retired to her cottage. Of what use was a midwife in a village without men?

She wrote to her married daughter in Letterkenny[1] who replied that there was work in plenty for her there. Then two weeks later when the hard frosts held the bog road, she loaded her goods on a cart and set out for Clonmullen from where she could get the train to Letterkenny. She took with her young Laurence Boyle, John Boyle's fourteen-year-old son, to bring back the donkey and cart.

The women watched her go. A few called Godspeed but the others, thin-lipped, uttered no word. Silently they went back to their houses and their daily tasks. From now on their bodies would be barren as fields in winter.

All winter the village lay dumb and still. The stores of potatoes and salt fish were eaten

1. Town in County Donegal.

sparingly. The fish might run in the bay now, followed by the screaming seagulls, but there were no men to put out the boats or draw in the gleaming nets. The children gathered mussels to feed the hens.

Then in the early spring days, the women rose from their hearths, and tightly knotted their headcloths and shawls. They took down the wicker creels from the lofts, the men's knives from the mantelshelves and went down to the rocks below Cahir Roe to cut the seawrack for the fields. The children spread it on the earth. Then with fork and spade the women turned the light sandy soil, planted their potatoes, oats and barley. The work was heavy and backbreaking but it had to be done. If they did not work now with all their strength, their children would be crying for food in the coming winter.

Driven, bone-tired, sick at heart, they rose early and worked all day, stopping at midday as their husbands had stopped, to rest in the shelter of a stone wall, to drink some milk or cold tea and to eat some oatbread the children brought to them in the fields. At night they dragged their bodies to bed. There was no joy, no relief to be got there now. Nothing but sleep, easing of weary muscles.

Their work in the house was neglected. The hearths went untended, their clothes unwashed. They no longer white-washed the walls of the cottages or tended the geraniums they grew in pots. They did not notice when the flowers died.

The next to leave the village was Sally Boyle. She was to have married young Dan Gallagher after the next Lent. There at the end of the straggling village was the half-built ruin of the house he had been getting ready with the help of the other men in the village. All winter she moped over the fire, only rousing herself when her mother's voice rose sharp and angry. Now in the spring she began to wander about restlessly. She would leave her work and climb the great headland of Cahir Roe, there to look out to where Tory[2] rose like a fortress from the sea — out there across the sea in which Dan Gallagher had been drowned, the sea which had refused to surrender what should have been hers. At night in bed she could not control the wildness of her body. She pitched from side to side, moaning and muttering. Her whole mind was darkened by the memory of soft kisses on warm autumn nights, of strong hands fondling her. She felt bereft, denied.

She slipped away one day and joined the lads and lasses in Clonmullen who were off to the hiring fair at Strabane.[3] Later her mother got a letter and a postal order for five shillings. Sally was now hired girl on a farm down in the Lagan.[4]

Then in ones and twos the young girls began to leave. With the coming of spring their eyes brightened, their steps grew lighter. They would stop and look over their shoulders hurriedly as if someone were behind. They would rush violently to work and then leave their tasks unfinished to stand and look out over the landscape, or out to sea from under a sheltering hand. They became irritable, quarrelsome and penitent by turns. Somewhere out there across the bog, across the sea, lay a world where men waited; men who could marry them, love them perhaps, give them homes and children.

The women objected to their going and pleaded with them. Every hand was needed now. The turf must be cut in the bog, turned and stacked for the coming winter. Surely they could go when the crops were gathered in. But tears and pleading were in vain. Nature fought against kindness in their young bodies. Here no men were left to promise these girls life, even the hazardous life of this country. They gathered their few garments together and departed, promising to send back what money they could. But their mothers knew that it was not to get money they left. It was the blood in their veins which drove them forth. And though the women lamented, they understood.

No use now to give a dance for the departing girls. There were no men with whom they could dance. No use to gather the neighbours into the house to sing. The voices of women are thin and shrill without men's voices to balance them.

Larry Boyle found himself the only lad in the village. The other boys were many years younger and those who were older had been lost with their fathers in the storm. The winter gloom, the silence of the women and his loneliness drove him to day-dreaming, to the creation of a fantasy world. He saw himself, in coming years, stronger

---

2. Tory Island, off the coast of Donegal.

3. Market town in County Tyrone.
4. Area of County Donegal.

and taller than any man, towering over humanity as Cahir Roe towered over the sea, impregnable, aloof. Boats, fields, cattle, houses, everything in the village would belong to him. For as yet the outside world meant nothing to him and women had no power over his dreams. They existed but to serve him.

At first the women paid no more attention to him than they did to the other children. He ate what food was set before him. Some potatoes, a piece of dried salt fish, a bowl of buttermilk. He performed such tasks as were set him, helping with the few cows, carrying the seawrack, heeling the turf. Indeed he was despised rather than otherwise, for the girls of his age were more nimble and less absent-minded than he. But slowly, as if in answer to his dreams, his position changed. In every house he entered he was welcomed and given the seat by the fire. He was never allowed to depart without food and drink. The older women baked and cooked for him, kept the best for him, gave him small presents from their hoard; a husband's knife; a son's trousers. They began to compliment him at every turn on his strength and growth. No one asked him to work.

Now he allowed his hair to grow like a man's. The stubby quiff vanished and a crop of thick, fair curls crowned his forehead, giving him the obstinate look of a fierce young ram. He became particular about the cleanliness of his shirt, refused to wear old patched trousers and coats. Gradually he dominated the whole village. Even the dogs owned him sole master, and snarled savagely at one another when he called them to heel. The young boys were his slaves, to fetch and carry for him. He scarcely noticed the girls of his own age, never called them by name, never spoke directly to them. Unlike them, he had no wish to leave the village.

A day came when Larry Boyle went from house to house and collected the fishing lines, hooks and spinners which had belonged to the drowned men. They were granted him as if by right. He took them to the rock behind the village where formerly the fish had been dried and where the men had then met in the summer evenings to talk, away from their women-folk. It was a day of shifting sun and shadow and the wind from the west broken by the headland.

He sang as he carefully tested, cut and spliced each line. He rubbed the hooks and spinners clean of rust with wet sand from the stream. He made a long line, tested each length and wound it in a coil between hand and elbow. He fastened the hooks and the lead weight. Then, satisfied, he went down to the shore to dig bait.

He swung his can of bait over his shoulder, picked up his line and made for Cahir Roe. He was going to fish for rock-fish.

A deep shelf ran round part of the headland and from this the men had fished in the drowsy heat of summer days when they could spare time from the fields. He clambered along the shelf and stood on the edge. The sea heaved and foamed beneath him. Far out, Tory rose, a castle against the white line of the horizon.

He fixed his bait carefully and placed the loose end of the line beneath his heel. Then, clear of the beetling rock behind, he swung the coil of line above his head and threw it far out. His body, balanced over the edge, seemed to follow it as his eye watched the untwisting of the cord, the drop of the lead towards the sea. He bent down and gathered up the end.

He could feel the movement as the length of line ran through the sea and the weight sank slowly through the heavy water. His hand knew what was happening down there beneath the surface of the water. He felt the lead strike the bottom. His fingers, born to a new delicacy, held the line firmly so that the bait should float free. He could feel the gentle nibbling of the fish at the bait, nibbling cautiously, daintily, as sheep nibble grass. Twice he drew in his line to rebait the hook. Then one struck.

Excited, breathing heavily, his eyes distended, he drew in the line slowly, letting it fall in careful coils at his feet. Then the fish left the water and the full weight hung on the line. It plunged about madly in the air, twisting and flapping. The cord rubbed against the edge of the shelf as it passed from hand to hand, dislodging small stones and dirt from the crumbling surface. He had to lean out to jerk the fish over the edge, at that moment unaware of everything but the twisting, flapping fish. He threw it well behind him so that it could not leap back into the water. It lay there, twisting and turning, its brilliant orange and green colouring coming and going, its belly heaving, its panting gills shining red. Then it lay still and from its open mouth the brick-red blood flowed over the stones. Another leap, another twitch. It was dead.

Larry passed the back of his hand across his forehead to wipe away the sweat. Before he stooped to disengage the hook from the jaws of the fish, he looked around him, at Tory on the far horizon, at the towering cliff above, the heaving sea beneath. For a moment his head reeled as he felt the turning of the world.

The women liked the new schoolmistress. They liked her modesty and reserve. Though young she knew how to keep the children in order, teach them their lessons and their manners. They looked after her with approval when they saw her walk precisely from the school to the cottage where she lived, her hands stiffly by her sides, her eyes lowered. They admired her round, rosy face, her light hair, her neat figure. She appeared so young and lovely to these women whose bodies were lean and tired from hard work and poor food.

She never stopped at the half-door for a chat, nor delayed for a moment to pass the time of day with a neighbour on the road. She never played with the younger children. She walked around encased in herself.

Every Saturday while the road held, she would mount her clean, well-oiled bicycle and cycle to Clonmullen. On the way she did not speak to anyone nor answer a greeting. With gaze fixed on the road before her, she pedalled furiously. In Clonmullen she would make one or two purchases, post her letters and cycle back home. All attempts at conversation were firmly repulsed. She did not even stop to have tea at the hotel.

She lived alone in a small cottage built on the rise of ground just beyond the village. For an hour at a time she would kneel in the shelter of the fuchsia hedge and gaze hungrily at the houses she did not wish to enter, at the women to whom she did not care to speak. She knew all their comings and goings, all the details of their daily life. She watched them at their work, in their conversation. She watched the children at play. She watched Larry Boyle as he wandered along the shore towards Cahir Roe to fish, or passed her cottage on his way to set rabbit snares in the burrows.

The July heat beat down on the earth and the blue-grey sea moved sleepily under a mist. He was returning home when he saw her, standing in the shelter of the bushes that grew over the gateway. She was looking at him with fierce intentness. He stood still and gazed back, his eyes wide and startled. The fear of unknown lands, of uncharted seas took hold of him. His mouth dropped open, his skin twitched. His throat hurt and there was a hammering in his ears like the heavy pounding of the surf on Cahir Roe. He could not move hand nor foot. With a sudden movement her hand darted out and caught his wrist. She drew him towards her, in the shelter of the thick fuchsia hedge. Frightened by her intent stare, her pale face, her quick uneven breathing, when she put out her other hand to fondle him, he pulled away and burst through the bushes. Quietly, with lowered eyes, she listened as his boots clattered over the rocky road. She sighed and turned back into her house.

But he came back. Furtively. He would steal into her kitchen when she was at school and leave some offering; a freshly caught fish, a rabbit, some rock pigeon's eggs. He had so little to give. She did not seem to notice. She did not stop him to thank him when they met. She passed without even a greeting, once again encased in her rigid calm. Then one evening, as darkness fell, he lifted the latch of her door. She was seated on her hearthrug, gazing at the glowing turf fire. He approached in silent desperation and with the same wild desperation she answered.

Such happenings do not long remain hidden in a small world. Without a word spoken, the women came to know. Primitive anger seized hold on them. They said nothing to Larry. Their belief in man's place in life and the fact that they had denied him nothing shut their mouths. All their rage turned against the young teacher whom they had thought so modest and gentle. They became as fierce as hawks at the theft of their darling.

They ceased work. They came together in groups, muttering. They buzzed like angry bees. Their lips spoke words to which their ears were long unaccustomed as they worked themselves into an ancient battle fury. They smoothed their hair back from their foreheads with damp and trembling hands. They drew their small shawls tightly round their shoulders.

From behind the fuchsia hedge the girl saw them coming like a flock of angry crows. Their wide dark skirts, caught by the light summer breeze, billowed out behind them. Their long, thin arms waved over their heads like sticks in the air. Their voices raised in some primitive battle cry, they surged up the road towards her.

Terrified of this living tidal wave, she rushed out. The uneven road caught her feet. It seemed to her that she made no headway as she ran, that the surging mass of women came ever nearer. Stones rattled at her heels. She ran on in blind panic, unaware of where she was going. Her chest began to ache, her throat to burn. A stone caught her shoulder but she scarcely felt the blow. Then another hit her on the back and she stumbled. Still she ran on, not daring to look back. A stone struck her head. She reeled and fell. Over the edge of the narrow bog road, down the bank towards the deep watery ditch. Briars caught her clothes. Her hands grasped wildly at the tufts of rough grass. There she lay, half in, half out of the water, too frightened to move or struggle.

When they saw her fall, the women stopped and stood there in the road, muttering. Then they turned back. They burst into her neat little cottage. They threw the furniture about, broke the delft, hurled the pots out of doors, tore the pretty clothes to ribbons. Then they left, still muttering threats, like the sea after storm.

Later, shivering, aching, sick, the girl dragged herself back onto the road. There was no one there now. The flock of crows had gone. She stood alone on the empty road. There was no sound but the lonely call of a moor bird overhead.

The next day Larry, too, left the village.

The war when it came meant little to these women. The explosions of mines on the rocks could not harm them now that there were no men to risk their lives on the water. The aeroplanes which from time to time circled over the coast seemed to them no more than strange birds, at first matter for wonder and then taken for granted. Sometimes the sea washed up an empty ship's boat, some timbers or empty wooden cases. One morning scores of oranges came dancing in on the waves. The children screamed with delight and, not knowing what they were, played ball with them. But since the oranges did not bounce they soon tired of them and left them along the shore to rot. The women only realized that the war could touch them when the supplies of Indian meal ran out.

All that winter storms lashed the coast. Snow whirled around the houses, blotting out the sight of the fierce sea which growled savagely against the headland of Cahir Roe day and night. Not once during the bitter months did the snow melt on the mountains beyond Clonmullen. The wind tore at the ropes which tethered the thatched roofs, rotting and grass-grown from neglect. The north-east wind drove under the doors, roared in the chimneys; it hardened the earth until it was like a stone.

Yet now it seemed that the silence was broken, that terrible silence they had kept in mourning for their dead. Now in the evenings they gathered round one another's firesides. They told stories, old Rabelaisian[5] tales heard when they were children from the old men of the village. Such tales as lie deep in the minds of people and are its true history. Tales of old wars, of great slaughter of men, of the survival of the women and children, of tricks to preserve the race. They told of the Danes and their love of the dark-haired Irishwomen. They laughed quietly and spoke in whispers of the great power of the Norsemen's bodies, of the fertility of their loins.

Over and over again they told the story of the women of Monastir, who, when widowed and alone, lured with false lights a ship to their shore. What matter that their victims were dark-skinned Turks. Their need was great.

The eyes of the women grew large and full of light as they repeated these tales over the dying embers of their fires. A new ferocity appeared in their faces. Their bodies took on a new grace, grew lithe and supple. As the body of the wild goat becomes sleek and lovely in the autumn.

Spring came suddenly. After the weeks of fierce winds and wild seas, followed days of mild breezes and scampering sunshine. The women threw open their doors and stepped out with light hearts. As they cut the seawrack for their fields, they called to one another and sang snatches of old songs. Sometimes one or another would stop in her work and look out over the water at the sea-swallows dipping and skimming over the surface of the water, at the black shags as they swam and dived, at old Leatherwing standing in his corner in wait. The older children laughed and shouted as they helped to spread out the wrack on the fields. The younger ones screamed as they ran along the shore

---

5. Rabelaisian has come to mean a literary style that is sexually explicit in a manner that is frank, grotesque, extravagant and often satirical, after the work of François Rabelais (1494?–1553).

and searched under the rocks for crabs. They called and clapped their hands at the sea-pies as they bobbed up and down on the waves.

On and on the children ran, their toes pink in the sea-water. They chattered together like pies[6] over each fresh discovery. They travelled along the shore until they found themselves out on the point of land beside Cahir Roe, facing the open sea. There they stood and looked out to sea from under sheltering hands.

For some minutes they stood and stared. Then in a body they turned and ran towards the women, shouting all together that out there, coming in closer every minute, was a strange boat.

The women straightened their backs and listened. Even before they understood what the children were shouting, they let down their petticoats and started for the point. There they stood in a group and stared, amazed that a boat should put in on that inhospitable shore. Close in now, with flapping sail, the boat came.

They could make out only one man and their eyes, used to long searching over water, could see that he was lying across the tiller. Was he alive or dead? Could he not see where he was going? If he did not change his course now he would fetch up on the reef below Cahir Roe. They rushed

6. Magpies.

forward to the water's edge and shouted. The man bent over the tiller did not move. They continued to shout. They waded into the sea until the water surged against their bodies and threatened to overbalance them. Their dark skirts swirled round them in the heavy sea as they shouted and waved their arms.

Then the man at the tiller slowly raised his head. He looked around him, at the sea, at the screaming women, at the great red granite face of Cahir Roe. With great effort he pulled his body upright and swung the tiller over. Then he fell forward again. Even before the keel had grounded on the gravel, the women had seized the boat and dragged it up onto the beach.

Six men lay huddled in the bottom of the boat. Great, strong men, now helpless. The women turned to the helmsman. He looked at them with dull, sunken eyes. He moved. He tried to speak. His grey face was stiff, his lips cracked.

'Scotland?' he asked, and his voice was hoarse.

The women shook their heads. Then the man slowly lifted one hand, pointed to the men at his feet and then to himself.

'Danes. Torpedoed. Ten days.'

The women cried aloud as they lifted the heavy bodies of the men. Their voices sang out in wild exultation.

The Danes. The Danes were come again.

DOROTHY HARRISON THERMAN

(1917–   )

from:
STORIES FROM
TORY ISLAND (1989)

[Popular anthropology, in the form of oral histories, is an increasingly common method of surveying 'ordinary lives' in Ireland. The Gaelic-speaking populations have been particularly subject to this form of investigation, because they seem to represent both a perceived survival of earlier rural lifestyles and an 'other' or primitive culture that can be analysed using methodologies honed by ethnographers of the developing world. Dorothy Harrison Therman's book about Tory Island, published in Dublin in 1989 by Country

House, foregrounds the potential for communication between a woman historian and female subjects. This excerpt highlights the economic and community context in which sexuality and reproduction were managed on Tory, with figures such as the priest and the district nurse variously representing authority generated from within the community, and authority as state interference.]

The recording on both sides of the tape went quickly with no interruptions. When I returned to Mary's house the next afternoon we continued with the story of her life. After her marriage to Pádraig McClafferty, she remained with her mother, a custom that was prevalent in those days. Mary explained, as had her brother Dan, that staying on in the family house was due in large part to the fact that there was no money for the newly married couple to build a house for themselves. But there were other reasons as well. Sometimes either the husband or the wife was quite content in the old house and did not want to leave. And there were women who wouldn't, or couldn't, live with their mothers-in-law. 'It was very hard to please people at that time. Ah, they wouldn't take you in.' One man married only for the dole his wife would bring; there was no need to live with her. And the intricacies of the inheritance of land no doubt caused some difficulties. Mary gave a litany of examples.

Aye. Look at Dan McClafferty. He was married to Kitty Doohan and *she* was at home all the time.

And Jimmy Doohan was married to Mary McClafferty, and *he* was at home.

And Johnny Doohan was married and he was at home. Three, in one house. That's true.

And the McGinleys over here now, next to Jimmy Antoin, there was a crowd there married: Mary was married to Dan Mooney,

and Nellie was married to Pat McClafferty,

and Pádraig was married to Bríd Duggan, Bríd Antoin,

and Dennis was married to Kitty Meenan . . .

But that's the way they were here. And, Dorothy, that's what left Tory without population. All of them that got married that time, they had no family. That generation left Tory without people.

And I had then to stay at home too, and I was working hard and I had to see to the child. I was six years at home before I came over down here with Patrick. And I had only John Joe at the time. John Joe was born in 1937 and Mary not born till 1942. If you would be married, at home, the old people — my mother and every other mother — they wouldn't allow you to have any more children. They had their own family and that was enough. And *far too* much sometimes; at that time there was six or seven of a family in every house.

Mary told me how hard the women had to work during their pregnancies. She herself, while pregnant, was 'working like a horse at the land': putting up hay on the carts in the harvest time;

digging limpets; putting out seaweed, filling the creels with it and loading it into the cart; and filling carts with manure and putting it on the land.

The labour, before the baby was delivered, was often long, but it was taken for granted. 'It *has* to be that way,' Mary's mother would tell her. 'It has to be.' After the birth only oatmeal porridge and oatmeal bread was allowed. 'No such thing as potatoes or meat,' Mary said. 'Oh! If anybody would go in with a cup of tea to you, with the home-made bread, my mother would murder them.'

It was Nurse McVeagh, one of a series of Public Health nurses on Tory, who delivered John Joe, Mary's oldest child, and many other children as well. She spent seventeen years on Tory and was remembered with great affection. 'She came to Tory round about 1936,' said Mary, 'when I got married. She was very old when she came here, the *créatúr*,[1] but still and all. Ah, she was very good, Nurse McVeagh. She was a nice woman, she would do her best, *a thaisce*,[2] that's the kind she was.' Bridget Doohan told me that Nurse McVeagh would arrive for a delivery carrying a black bag in which were a pair of old shoes and two pairs of rubber gloves. She would leave the gloves in the bag and throw the shoes under the bed for luck. 'All the same it went on grand,' as Bridget remarked of her own delivery. Gráinne Joe Rodgers said that Nurse McVeagh, after throwing the old shoes under the bed at the start, did nothing else but pray, holding her rosary beads hidden in her hand. All, however, were in agreement that she was 'great at cutting the cord'. Mary said: 'The best thing of all I seen her doing was the cord. She was very good at the cord and she was very good at the afterbirth. For I know that.' When Nurse McVeagh retired, a nurse of a different type — according to Mary — took her place

When Paidí [Mary's third child] was born, there was a nurse here.

Well, I'll tell you this story now.

This Sunday she came down to me, down here, that was the seventeenth of March. And the first thing she said to me — I was gutting fish, at the door — she said to me, 'Mary, isn't it funny,'

1. Creature, colloquially 'poor thing'.
2. My dear.

she says to me, 'the way the Tory people,' she says to me, 'keep their children a long time.'

'Isn't it funny, Mary,' *at the door,* she said this.

'Well,' I says to her, 'You have to wait anyhow.' Says I to her, 'Good Lord, nurse,' says I, 'we have to wait. Sure, *I* can't pull the child out of my stomach,' says I.

'Well,' she says, 'I notice that,' she says, 'the Tory people, the *way* they keep their children. And they're very slow, when they get sick as well.'

'Well,' says I, 'surely everybody has to wait here,' says I.

'Well,' she says, 'I hope you won't go over this day, anyhow.'

Sure I was only due. But let me tell you this.

This was on Sunday. And there was a drama over in this [building] — where the factory is, now — there was a drama there, *Paidí Michael Art.* It was a drama, Father McDyer had. And, God rest him, Pádraig was there too.

And, round about seven o'clock in the evening, I was in bed. But not a word out of me, you didn't say a *word.* There was no use in talking.

But that night, when the drama was over, Pádraig walked in, and I was in bed. 'Mary,' he says to me, 'are you not well?'

'No,' says I, 'but I'm all right,' says I, 'sure, I'm only starting. Maybe it will be morning,' says I, 'before this'll happen.'

And I had the old people that time [Padraig's parents] as well; the two of them, Barney, *his* father, and Nabla, his mother. And *she* was doting [senile], the woman.

But, he came in and this is what he said to me, 'Well,' he said to me, 'I'll let the priest know,' he says, 'about you.' And he says, 'He'll read you,' he says, 'an office anyhow, before you go to bed.'

I says, 'That will be all right.'

He went up to Father McDyer; and Father McDyer came in to me and I was out of bed again. And 'Mary,' he says — the old lady was talking, going strong in the room, she was doting — 'It will be all right, Mary,' he says. 'That child, Mary,' he says to me, 'will be born round about tomorrow morning,' he says, 'nine o'clock, when I'm reading Mass.'

'Well,' says I to myself; I didn't say that to the priest, but says I to myself, 'if I have to suffer until nine o'clock tomorrow morning . . .'

This is what he said, 'And don't worry, Mary,' he says, 'you'll be all right.'

But, Dorothy, the shape I was in. Paidí, he was born at nine o'clock in the morning as the priest said.

So the nurse come over around about eight or half eight, and do you know what? She nearly took my life. And do you know what she did?

The child was born and she wasn't able to do anything with the afterbirth.

And *the sea,* was *mad* high. And it was clear ten [force ten winds]. That was the seventeenth of March. She came in and she says to Pádraig, 'No trawler or nothing,' she says, 'will be able to come today?'

'Oh, no,' Pádraig says.

'I can't do nothing about this woman,' she says, 'I can't do nothing about her.'

Jennie Hughie, that time, she was August-born. And she got the doctor for *her.* The day was good . . .

She wasn't able to do anything.

So she said to me, *again,* 'It's funny, Mary,' she says — she had the child all right, and the cord, I done all the rest myself — 'it's funny how the Tory people,' she says, 'keep the afterbirth.' [Mary laughed.]

'But, good Lord, nurse,' says I to her and I was lying ill in bed, 'Good Lord, nurse,' says I, 'when Nurse McVeagh was here,' says I, 'and she was only an *old woman.* And she could get the afterbirth,' says I, 'just put her finger there,' says I, 'and the afterbirth would come. I suppose,' says I, 'you never done anything like this before?'

'Ah, no,' she says, 'it's the Tory people themselves,' she says, 'is the cause of this.'

But wait till I tell you *this.* That was all right.

'Well,' she says, 'wait,' she says, 'I'll go up home yet,' she says, 'and I'll get my husband's dinner,' she says, 'and when I come back again,' she says, 'you might be all right.'

Paidí was born at nine o'clock and this is two o'clock nearly. That was bad.

'Well,' says I, 'by the way you're going,' says I, 'I won't be all right today.'

She came over then when she gave him the dinner; she came over and she *must* have [had] a drink because she went over to me, and she couldn't do nothing.

She opened this case. And she took out a bottle about that size. And what was written on the bottle? 'Poison!'

That's true. And if there was a woman there

that wouldn't be able to read, she would be *dead*.

I'll tell you why she was going to do this. She knew rightly if that [afterbirth] wouldn't come that I would die. And, she thought to herself, 'I'll try this anyway. If she *dies, nobody* will *know* what happened.' That's true as God. I told that to Father McDyer too, when he came down.

She came over with the bottle, and she opened the door and she said to Pádraig, 'Have you an egg cup?'

The *créatúr*, he give her an egg cup, but still *I* was looking at the bottle. And she put *this* wee bottle, about that size, in the egg cup. 'Here, Mary,' she says to me, '*drink* this,' she says to me, 'it will do you all the good in the world.'

'Well, nurse,' says I, 'I never took poison in my life.' I was great too, Dorothy.

'I had *no* call, nurse,' says I, 'to take poison. Because,' says I, 'when Nurse McVeagh was here,' says I, 'she never gave me the like of that.'

'Well,' she says, 'you can have it,' she says to me, 'anyhow.'

'No,' says I, 'I won't. Put that back,' says I, 'where you got it.'

Well here, she put it back in the bottle again, she put on the top, she put it in the case, and away she goes, up to the priest. She never told the priest that she gave me this bottle, she told the priest that I wasn't well yet.

But he says to her — 'Leave that woman,' he says, 'alone for another hour. Don't go near her,' he says, 'that woman will be all right when I'll go down.'

He came down to me — Father McDyer, a big tall man — and he opened the door over. And I was as strong, that time, Dorothy, as a horse.

'Mary,' he says to me, 'congratulations.' This is the first time ever I hear 'congratulations'.

'Congratulations, Mary,' he says, 'you're all right, *a thaisce*.' He was very good to me. He could see the way I was going.

'But, Father,' says I, 'I'm not well yet at all,' says I.

'I know,' he says, 'you're not.'

'And wait till I tell you this,' says I. 'But sure,' says I, 'half an hour ago and the nurse took over a wee bottle here of poison and put it in an egg cup and giving it to *me*.'

'She *what*?' he says.

'I know rightly, Father, what happened. She

thought that I would die with this anyhow, with the complaint I had, and then if I would take that, Father, I would be dead now.'

'*Good Lord*,' he says to me, 'is that right?'

'Oh, yes, Father.'

'Well,' he says to me, — he went over on the bed with me, put his hand on my head [and made the sign of the cross] — he was very good that priest, too. And he said to me, 'You'll be all right now, Mary,' he says, 'in an hour's time.' But he says, 'If you'll get someone,' he says, 'that will be up in ages, they might know all about it.'

Fortunately for Mary, Nelly Rodgers Cormac came in. She heated a piece of flannel in the big pot of boiling water she brought to the bedside, and applied it to Mary's abdomen, repeating this treatment for half an hour.

That afterbirth, Dorothy, came with no bother. Well, I suppose that that did it, but the priest done his best for me.

And my mother that time was out on the road, *créatúr*. And they were saying that she was over and back and over and back, doing like this [Wringing her hands].

The day was rough.

Mary was married at twenty-two, but continued to live with her mother for six years. Then she moved into the house of her husband's parents.

Biographies/Bibliographies

Winifred M. Letts

LIFE. Born in 1882 and educated in St Anne's Abbots, Bromley, and at Alexandra College, Dublin. Two of her one-act plays were produced at the Abbey, *The Eyes of the Blind* (1907) and *The Challenge* (1909), and a three-act play, *Hamilton and Jones* (1941), was produced at the Gate. She also wrote short fiction and a novel. However, her reputation rests on her poetry and on her book of reminiscences, *Knockmaroon* (1933). (Knockmaroon was the name of her grandparents' house in County Dublin.) Her *Songs from Leinster* was reprinted six times between 1913 and 1928. She married W.H.F. Verschoyle and moved to Faversham in Kent. She died in 1972.

CHIEF WRITINGS. *The Mighty Army* (hagiography) (New York: F.A. Stokes, 1912); *Songs from Leinster* (London: John Murray, 1913); *Christina's Son* (novel) (London, 1915); *Halloween and Poems of the War* (London: Smith, Elder, 1916); *The Spires of Oxford and Other Poems* (New York: E.P. Dutton, 1917); *More Songs from Leinster* (London: John Murray; New York: E.P. Dutton, 1926); *St Patrick the Travelling Man* (London: J. Nicholson and Watson, 1932); *Knockmaroon* (London: John Murray, 1933).

Norah Hoult

For biography and bibliography, see p. 600.

Kathleen Coyle

LIFE. Kathleen Coyle was born in Derry in 1883. An accident in childhood left her foot permanently damaged. She was educated at home, first in Derry, later in Liverpool. She began to write at a very young age. Her first job was in a library in Liverpool. She later worked as an editorial assistant in London, before moving to Paris, Belgium and Dublin (where she was active in the Suffragettes and with the Labour Movement). She had early critical success but her work became neglected after her death in 1952.

CHIEF WRITINGS. *Piccadilly, etc.* (London: Jonathan Cape, 1923); *The Widow's House* (London: Jonathan Cape, 1924); *Youth in the Saddle* (London: Jonathan Cape, 1927); *Liv* (London: Jonathan Cape, 1928); *A Flock of Birds* (London: Jonathan Cape, 1930); *There is a Door* (Paris: Edward Titus, 1931); *Undue Fulfilment* (London: Ivor Nicholson and Watson, 1934). *The Magical Realm* (New York: E.P. Dalton 1943).

Mary Devenport O'Neill

LIFE. Mary Devenport O'Neill was born in Loughrea, Co. Galway in 1879 and educated at Eccles Street College and the National College of Art in Dublin. In 1908 she married the poet Joseph O'Neill. Her early interest was in combining ballet, acting and verse-speaking in the performance of verse plays. She knew Yeats and consulted with him while he was writing *A Vision*. She died in 1967.

CHIEF WRITINGS. 'Three Poems', *Irish Statesman*, vol. 4 (1 August 1926), p. 650; *Prometheus and Other Poems* (London: J. Cape, 1929). Plays: *Bluebeard* (produced 1933), and *Cain, Dublin Magazine*, vol. 13 (spring 1938), pp. 30–48, produced 1945; 'Dead in Wars and in Revolutions', *Dublin Magazine*, vol. 16 (winter 1941), p. 7; 'Scene-Shifter Death', *Dublin Magazine*, vol. 19 (spring 1944), p. 40; 'Valhalla', *Dublin Magazine*, vol. 22 (summer 1947), pp. 20–39; 'The Visiting Moon', *Dublin Magazine*, vol. 23 (spring 1948), pp. 35–46; 'Lost Legions', *Dublin Magazine*, vol. 24 (spring 1949), p. 16.

Marie Stopes

LIFE. Marie Stopes was born in Edinburgh in 1880, daughter of the feminist Charlotte Carmichael and a scientist, Henry Stopes. Marie studied botany at University College London and in 1905 she took her D.Sc., and became the country's youngest doctor of science. She became a member of the Women's Freedom League and she married Reginald Gates in 1911. They quarrelled over her feminist views and over sexual difficulties, and Stopes had the marriage annulled on grounds of non-consummation in 1914; they were divorced in 1916. She had difficulty finding a publisher for her first book, *Married Love*, but when it appeared in 1918 it was an instant best-seller. It was accused of obscenity and banned in the United States of America and Ireland. A meeting with the American birth-control campaigner Margaret Sanger led Stopes to take up the campaign in Britain. Her guide to contraception, *Wise Parenthood* (1918), outraged the churches. The Catholic church was particularly aggressive in its campaign against her work. In 1918 Stopes married a wealthy man, Humphry Roe, and with his help in 1921 she founded the Society for Constructive Birth Control and opened the first of her birth-control clinics in north London. Stopes spent the rest of her life working for a variety of feminist campaigns, and writing fiction and poetry. She died in 1958.

CHIEF WRITINGS. *Married Love* (London: A.C. Fifield, 1918); *Wise Parenthood* (London: A.C. Fifield, 1918); *Love's Creation* (London: J. Bale, 1928); *Love Songs for Young Lovers* (London: Heinemann, 1938).

BIOGRAPHY AND CRITICISM. *Dear Dr. Stopes: Sex in the 1920s*, ed. Ruth Hall (London: André Deutsch, 1978); June Rose, *Marie Stopes and the Sexual Revolution* (London: Faber and Faber, 1992); Greta Jones, 'Marie Stopes in Ireland — The Mother's Clinic in Belfast, 1936–47', *Social History of Medicine*, vol. 5, no. 2 (August 1992), pp. 255–76.

Helen Waddell

LIFE. Helen Jane Waddell, novelist, poet, translator and scholar, was born in Tokyo in 1889, where her father, Hugh Waddell, a Presbyterian minister, lectured at Imperial University. She was the youngest of ten children and her mother Jane (Martin), of County Down, died when Helen was three years old, having returned to Belfast with the children. Helen was educated in Belfast at Victoria School for Girls and at Queen's College. She is best known for popularizing the Middle Ages through her learned translations and novels. She had a long relationship with Otto Kyllmann (d. 1959). The last decade of her life was passed in a state of advanced senility and she died in London in 1965.

CHIEF WRITINGS. *The Abbé Prévost. A Play in a Prologue and Three Acts* (London: Constable, 1933); *Medieval Latin Lyrics* (London: Constable, 1929); *New York City, etc.* [sic] (Newtown: Greynog Press, 1935); *Peter Abelard. A Novel* (London: Constable, 1933); *Poetry in the Dark Ages. The Eighth W.P. Ker Memorial Lecture Delivered in the University of Glasgow 28 October 1947* (Glasgow: Jackson, 1948); *The Princess Splendour and Other Stories*, Retold by Helen Waddell, Ed., Eileen Colwell. Illustrated by Anne Knight (London: Longmans Young Books, 1969); *The Spoiled Buddha. A Play in Two Acts* (Dublin: Talbot Press, 1919); *Stories from Holy Writ* (London: Constable, 1949); *The Wandering Scholars* (London: Constable, 1927); *Lyrics from the Chinese* (London: Constable, 1913).

BIOGRAPHY AND CRITICISM. Monica Blackett, *The Mask of the Maker* (London: Constable, 1979). D. Felicitas Corrigan, *Helen Waddell: A Biography* (London: Victor Gollancz, 1986).

Eibhlís Ní Shúilleabháin

LIFE. Born in 1911 on the Great Blasket Island, County Kerry, Lís Ní Shúilleabháin was related by birth and by marriage to several of the island's Irish-language writers. In 1933 she married her cousin Seán Ó Criomhthain, son of Thomás Ó Criomhthain, author of *An tOileánach/The Islandman* (1929), and himself a writer. They had two daughters and in 1942 left the island to live on the mainland. Ní Shúilleabháin died on 12 September 1971. Seven years later *Letters* was published. It consists of letters she had written over a period of twenty years to an Englishman, George Chambers.

CHIEF WRITINGS. *Letters from the Great Blasket* (Dublin: Mercier Press, 1978).

BIOGRAPHY AND CRITICISM. Diarmuid Breathnach and Máire Ní Mhurchú, *1882–1982 Beathaisnéis a Cúig* (Baile Átha Cliath, 1997).

Patricia O'Connor

LIFE. Born in Donegal in 1908, Patricia O'Connor was educated at Collegiate School, Celbridge, and from the age of fourteen at Dunfermline High School. She trained as a teacher in Edinburgh. O'Connor was relatively prominent in the arts scene in the north of Ireland in the 1940s and 1950s but I have been unable to trace her subsequent career.

CHIEF WRITINGS. *Mary Doherty* (London: Sands, n.d. [1938]); *The Mill in the North* (Dublin: Talbot Press, 1938); *Highly Efficient* (Belfast: Quota Press, 1943); 'Choosing Teaching as a Career', *Lagan*, vol. 1 (1944), pp. 92–6; *Select Vestry. A Play* (Belfast: Quota Press, 1946); *Four*

New One Act Plays, selected and edited by Patricia O'Connor (Belfast: Quota Press, 1948); *Master Adams. A Play* (Belfast: H.R. Carter in association with Quota Press, 1950); *The Farmer Wants a Wife. A Comedy* (Belfast: H.R. Carter, 1955).

Brenda Chamberlain

LIFE. Brenda Chamberlain was born in Bangor, Wales, in 1912, of English, Irish and Manx extraction. She was educated privately in Bangor and then trained as a painter at the Royal Academy in London, where she met the painter and engraver John Petts, whom she married. They settled in Caernarvonshire and Chamberlain began to work as a poet as well as an artist. Her marriage ended in 1946 and she lived for a period in Germany. She returned to north Wales and from 1947 to 1961 she lived on Ynys Enlli (Bardsey Island) off the Lleyn peninsula. In 1961 she moved to the Greek island of Ydra but she left after the 1967 coup, returning to Bangor, where she died in 1971.

CHIEF WRITINGS. *Christmas Eve* (1950); *The Green Heart* (London: Oxford University Press, 1958); *Tide-race . . . With paintings and illustrations by the author* (London: Hodder and Stoughton, 1962; rpr. Bridgend: Seren, 1987); *A Rope of Vines: Journal from a Greek Island (with drawings by the author)* (London: Hodder and Stoughton, 1965); *Poems, with drawings* (London: Enitharmon Press, 1969).

BIOGRAPHY AND CRITICISM. Kate Holman, *Brenda Chamberlain* (Aberystwyth: University of Wales Press, 1997).

Maura Laverty

LIFE. Born Maura Kelly in Rathangan, a village in County Kildare, in 1907, Laverty was a novelist, playwright and author of children's books and popular cookbooks. She also worked as a journalist and broadcaster. Her first novel, *Never No More*, appeared in 1942. One of her subsequent novels, *Alone We Embark* (1943), although winner of the Irish Women Writers Award, was banned in Ireland. Her popular novel *Lift Up Your Gates* (1946), centred around the life of Chrissie Doyle, a fourteen-year-old from Dublin's slums, was adapted for the stage as *Liffey Lane*, and produced at the Gate Theatre in 1951. Her play *Tolka Row* opened at the Gaiety in 1950 and transferred to the Gate in 1951, and *A Tree in the Crescent* was produced there in 1952. Laverty died in 1966.

PUBLISHED WORKS. *Flour Economy* (Dublin: Browne and Nolan, 1941); *Never No More* (London and New York: Longmans, 1942; rpr. London: Virago, 1985, 1992); *Alone We Embark* (London: Longmans, 1943); *No More than Human* (London: Longmans, 1945; rpr. London: Virago, 1986); *Gold of Glenaree* (New York: Longmans, 1945); *The Cottage in the Bog* (Dublin: Browne and Nolan, 1946; rpr. Dublin: Town House, 1992); *Lift Up Your Gates* (London: Longmans, 1946), in the United States, *Liffey Lane* (New York: Longmans, 1947); *Maura Laverty's Cookbook* (London: Longmans, 1947; New York and Toronto: Longmans, 1947); *The Green Orchard* (London: Longmans, 1949); *Kind Cookin* (Dublin: Electricity Supply Board, 1955).

CRITICISM. Christopher Fitz-Simon, *The Irish Theatre* (London: Thames and Hudson, 1983), p. 179, and *The Boys* (Dublin: Gill and Macmillan, 1994), pp. 169–76.

Temple Lane

LIFE. Born Mary Isabel Leslie in Dublin in 1899, she spent her childhood mostly in Tipperary. She was educated in England and at Trinity College Dublin, where she won the Large Gold Medal in 1922 and later earned a doctorate in philosophy. *The Little Wood* won the Tailteann Gold Medal. As well as Temple Lane, she used the pseudonym Jean Herbert. She died in 1978.

CHIEF WRITINGS. *Burnt Bridges* (London: J. Long, 1925); *No Just Cause* (London: J. Langs, 1925); *Second Sight* (London: J. Long, 1927); *Watch the Wall* (London: J. Long, 1927); *The Bands of Orion* (London: Jarrolds, 1928); *The Little Wood: A Romance with Interruptions* (London: Jarrolds, 1930); *Blind Wedding* (London: Jarrolds, 1931); *Sinner Anthony* (London: Jarrolds, 1933); *Full Tide* (London: J. Heritage, 1932); *The Trains Go South* (London: Jarrolds, 1938); *Fisherman's Wake* (Dublin: Talbot Press, 1939); *Battle of the Warrior* (London: Jarrolds, 1940); *Friday's Well* (Dublin: Talbot Press, 1943); *House of My Pilgrimage* (Dublin: Talbot Press, 1944 [1941]; London: Frederick Muller, 1941); *Come Back!* (Dublin: Talbot Press, 1945); *Curlews* (Dublin: Talbot Press, 1946); 'The Dramatic Art of Teresa Deevy', *Dublin Magazine*, vol. 21, no. 4 (October–December 1946), pp. 35–42); *My Bonny's Away* (Dublin: Talbot Press, 1947).

Josephine O'Brien

No information discovered.

Marion Brennan

No information discovered.

Rhoda Coghill

LIFE. Born in Dublin in 1903, Rhoda Sinclair was the daughter of a Scotsman who had come to Ireland to manage the printing works of Eason and Son. She attended Alexandra College and then Trinity College Dublin, where she received a B.Mus. in 1922. After studying music in Berlin for a year, she returned to Dublin where she worked as a pianist. She played concertos with the Dublin Philharmonic Orchestra and later with the Radio Éireann Symphony Orchestra, taught at the Read Piano School, and became the station accompanist for Radio Éireann in 1939. Although she was most widely known and admired for her talents as a piano accompanist, she was also an accomplished composer and poet. Her chief hobby was translating poetry, particularly that of Rilke. She died on 9 February 2000.

CHIEF WRITINGS. *The Bright Hillside* (Dublin: Hodges, Figgis, 1948); *Time is a Squirrel* (Dublin: Dolmen Press, 1956).

Margaret E. and J.H. Cousins

LIFE. Margaret E. Gillespie was born at Boyle, County Roscommon, in 1878, and educated locally, then in Derry, and later at the Royal University of Ireland, where she took a degree in music. In 1903 she married James Cousins. She describes in their autobiography how she cried the night he proposed to her, but she thought she would not get another offer. She goes on to chart a gradual growth of attachment to James through admiration of his poetry and conversation. In 1908 she joined with Hanna Sheehy Skeffington in the foundation of the Irish Women's Franchise League, of which she became treasurer. She also helped to establish the suffrage newspaper, the *Irish Citizen*. She represented Ireland at the Parliament of Women in London in 1910, and was arrested and sentenced to six months in prison.

James Henry Sproull Cousins, poet and dramatist, was born in Belfast in 1873. He was educated in Belfast and began his career as a clerical worker. He moved to Dublin in 1897, where he met writers of the Literary Revival, and acted and wrote for the Irish National Theatre Society. In 1905 he became a schoolmaster at Harcourt Street. In 1908 he joined the Theosophical Society.

The Cousins left Ireland in 1913, going to Liverpool and then on to India. By 1916 Margaret was the first non-Indian member of the Indian Women's University at Poona. She became a founder member of the Indian Women's Association and was headmistress of the national Girls'

School at Bangalore. She was imprisoned for a year in India in 1932 after protesting against changes in the penal code. Margaret died in 1954, James in 1956.

CHIEF WRITINGS. They have a long list of pamphlet publications. Of most relevance to their Irish backgrounds are: JHC: *Ben Madigan and Other Poems* (Belfast: Marcus Ward, 1894); *The Voice of One* (London: T. Fisher Unwin, 1900); *The Quest* (Dublin: Maunsel, 1906); *The Awakening and Other Sonnets* (Dublin: Maunsel, 1907); *The Bell-Branch* (Dublin: Maunsel, 1908); *Etain the Beloved and Other Poems* (Dublin: Maunsel, 1912); *Collected Poems, 1894–1940* (Adyar [Madras]: Kalakshetra, 1940); JHC and MEC: *We Two Together* (Madras: Ganesh, 1950).

BIOGRAPHY AND CRITICISM. Alan Denson, *James H. Cousins and Margaret E. Cousins, a Bio-Bibliographical Survey* (Kendal: Alan Denson, 1967); Catherine Candy, 'Relating Feminisms, Nationalisms, and Imperialisms: Ireland, India and Margaret Cousins's Sexual Politics', *Women's History Review*, vol. 3, no. 4 (1994), pp. 581–94.

Mary Lavin

For biography and bibliography, see Volume II, p. 1222, and Volume IV, p. 600–01.

May Morton

LIFE. Born Mary Elizabeth Morton in County Limerick in 1876, she lived in Belfast from 1900 onwards. She became secretary and later chair of Belfast PEN, and was a founding member of the Young Ulster Society. She worked as vice-principal of the Girls' Model School until 1934. Her poetry was published in various periodicals and broadcast on the BBC and Radio Éireann. In 1951 her poem 'Spindle and Shuttle' won the Festival of Britain Northern Ireland Poetry Award. She died in 1957.

CHIEF WRITINGS. *Dawn and Afterglow* (Belfast: Quota Press, 1936); *Masque in Maytime* (Lisburn: Lisnagarvey Press, 1948); *Sung to the Spinning Wheel* (Belfast: Quota Press, 1952).

Anne Crone

LIFE. Born in Dublin in 1915, Anne Crone was educated in Belfast and Oxford, and became a teacher and a novelist. She died in Belfast of asthma in 1972.

CHIEF WRITINGS. *Bridie Steen* (New York: Charles Scribner's Sons, 1948; London: Heinemann, 1949; Belfast and Dublin: Blackstaff Press/Arlen House, 1984); *This Pleasant Lea* (New York: Charles Scribner's Sons, 1951; London: Heinemann, 1952); *My Heart and I* (London: Heinemann, 1955).

Roberta Hewitt

LIFE. Roberta Black was born in Larne, County Antrim, in 1904. Her father, Robert Shepherd Black, was a jeweller, who worked originally for her mother's family (the Urquhards) in York Street, Belfast. Robert Black had his own watchmakers in Agnes Street, Belfast, from about 1907. He died in 1915, and his widow ran a boot shop. Roberta started office work at the age of fourteen. She emigrated to Canada in 1929,

and then went to the USA. Home on holiday in 1933, she re-met the poet John Hewitt (1909–87), and they were married in 1934. Hewitt worked at the Belfast Museum and Art Gallery. When political bias led to Hewitt being passed over for the position of gallery director, they moved to Coventry in 1957. They retired to Belfast in 1972, and Roberta died from a sudden illness after a trip to the USSR in 1975.

CHIEF WRITINGS. Diary, 1948–72, MS PRONI document D33838/4/4–5. No page nos.

Dorine Rohan

LIFE. Dorine Rohan was born in Midleton, County Cork. She contributed to various newspapers and magazines. No further information has been discovered.

Nuala Fennell

LIFE. Born in Dublin in 1935, Nuala Fennell was educated at Dominican College, Dublin, and at the Public Relations Institute of Ireland. She has worked as a journalist and broadcaster and co-founded AIM, a family law reform lobby, in 1972 and ADAPT, a support group for deserted wives, in 1973. She also founded Women's Aid in 1975, which provides refuges for battered wives. She was a Fine Gael TD , 1981–7; 1989–92. She was appointed Minister of State at the Department of the Taoiseach and the Department of Justice with responsibility for women's affairs and family law reform in 1982, an office which she held until 1987. She was a member of the Council for the Status of Women.

CHIEF WRITINGS. *Irish Marriage — How Are You?* (Cork: Mercier Press, 1974); co-author with Deirdre McDevitt and Bernadette Quinn, *Can You Stay Married?* (Dublin: Kincora, 1980).

Siobhán Ní Shúilleabháin

No information discovered.

Margaret Barrington

LIFE. Born in Malin, County Donegal, in 1896, Margaret Barrington was educated in Dungannon, County Tyrone, and at Trinity College Dublin. She married Edmund Curtis, the historian, in 1918 or 1922; the marriage was later dissolved. In 1926 she married Liam O'Flaherty. They had one child, and were separated in 1932. During the 1930s she spent several years working and writing in England, where she was active in helping refugees from Nazi Germany. She died in 1982.

CHIEF WRITINGS. *My Cousin Justin* (1939); *David's Daughter, Tamar* (Dublin: Wolfhound Press, 1982).

Dorothy Harrison Therman

LIFE. Born in 1917 near Philadelphia, USA, Dorothy Harrison Therman 'discovered' Tory Island through an exhibition by its painters at an Edinburgh gallery in 1978. She made her first visit to the island in 1981. She has made many more visits, conducting taped interviews and taking photographs. She continues to live in Pennsylvania, in the house where she was born.

SIOBHÁN KILFEATHER AND ÉIBHEAR WALSHE, *Editors*

Contesting Ireland: The Erosion of Heterosexual Consensus, 1940–2001

Since the growth of second-wave feminism in the 1960s and 1970s sexuality has come to be recognized as a crucial topic for contemporary debate — so crucial, indeed, to an understanding of women's experience that substantial parts of the sections in this anthology edited by Mary O'Dowd and Clair Wills on contemporary politics and literature are devoted to sexuality. The following selection of texts focuses on a very specific aspect of contemporary sexuality — the way in which certain writers have attempted to contest a conservative, family-centred, monogamous, heterosexual vision of Ireland, shared and promoted by a variety of establishments from Fianna Fáil to the Democratic Unionist Party, upheld by churches and the education system. Maria Luddy looks at how institutions such as hospitals, prisons and Magdalen Asylums managed female sexuality, while Angela Bourke shows how it remains a powerful theme in the oral tradition. Marjorie Howes has written, in her introduction to the previous section, of the self-censorship in Irish society explored and often exhibited by women writers in the middle of the twentieth century, and the ways that this self-censorship becomes manifest in plot and characterization: 'The most common sexual tragedy in these selections is the tragedy of a character who voluntarily renounces sexual happiness or is unable to embrace it when it is offered'.

In describing nineteenth-century Ireland I have already argued that the stereotypes associated with

sexuality disguised a much greater variety of practices than were apparently allowed for in the ideology. In twentieth-century Ireland, as that ideology became in many ways more rigid, there were significant gestures of resistance to the normative. In this section there is a particular focus on 'queer' sexualities because of their defiance and critique of what it means to be Irish, because they have a history of self-representation in radical political movements, from Gay Liberation and Aids activism, to anti-nuclear, feminist and Green protest movements. Unlike Emma Donoghue's selection of literary representations of lesbian relationships, this section places more emphasis on theory than representation. The literary excerpts — poetry and fiction — have been chosen because of the ways in which they break new ground and assault certain kinds of taboo. Writing about gay and lesbian sexuality is not the only way in which this has been done. In the early 1960s, Edna O'Brien's novels presented female heterosexual desire, and particularly the sexual experience of young girls and women, in a way that was explosively original to Irish fiction.

It is impossible to begin to do justice to lesbian, gay and bi-sexual writings on sexuality without looking at work produced in the last three decades. This is not to say that queer writers, queer readers and queer identities have only recently emerged — one might offer queer readings of many of the texts in this anthology from 1700 onwards — but it is peculiarly true of queer writers that their work has been recognized and reinterpreted in very specifically new ways as the legal framework of censorship and punishment of lesbian and gay people in Ireland has begun to be dismantled.

Contemporary writers such as Mary Dorcey and Frank McGuinness have provoked Irish readers to re-examine ideas of identity and tradition. It is hardly novel to remember that Ireland has produced some famous queer intellectuals such as Oscar Wilde and Eva Gore-Booth, but it has been commonplace to suggest that Ireland itself was such an illiberal terrain that such writers could only become queer when they went into exile. It should be clear from reading previous excerpts that sexuality in Ireland has in fact, and for several centuries, involved more diverse practices and identities than are commonly recognized.

The assertion of a distinct, autonomous gay identity within Irish writing extends the process by which it is possible to trouble and challenge privileged formations of what traditionally constituted 'woman' and 'man' in Irish writing and, in particular, it troubles and complicates 'masculinist nationalism' in Irish cultural discourse. Historically, the primacy of a particular form of masculinist nationalism in Irish writing led, inevitably, to the suppression of a number of counter-discourses such as feminism, radical socialism, lesbianism and the homoerotic, and therefore, in reclaiming liminal and marginalized homoerotic narratives within Irish writing, a common ground for re-appropriation is being realized. The homosexual, usefully, unsettles and makes problematical established notions of 'manliness'. The first three volumes of *The Field Day Anthology* told us a great deal about what it might mean to aspire to be a heterosexual man in Ireland, and one might read many of the stories and poems included here as both complement and critique to the modes of masculinity presented in such disturbed pieces as Samuel Beckett's *Murphy*, Patrick Kavanagh's *The Great Hunger*, John McGahern's 'Korea', Paul Muldoon's 'Aisling', Michael Longley's 'The Adulterer' and Eugene McCabe's 'Cancer', all of which appear in Volume III. One would not have to look very far in the first three volumes of the anthology to assemble a narrative of Irish male identity that involves sexual self-loathing,

misogyny, homophobia and impotence, although that was not, of course, how the material was presented. Writers such as Beckett and Kavanagh offer a fully self-reflective representation of the failed ideology of Irish masculinity, but without the acknowledgement of work by women and queer writers that failure seems to leave only a hopeless stasis.

In the first three-quarters of the twentieth century Irish writing on homosexuality was characterized by indirection and oblique reference. In the past ten years or so an in-your-face gay aesthetic has emerged, for men and women, as exemplified in the interview with Emma Donoghue and the selection of writings by Tom Lennon, Keith Ridgway and Gerry Stembridge. A high premium in this selection has been placed on controversial ways of living, ways of writing and modes of dispute. There is danger, however, in forwarding the most brash, explicit and confessional writing as the most challenging. Some of the most direct statements here — such as those by Joni Crone and the Irish Council for Civil Liberties — are part of a rhetoric of political campaigning that places a high priority on reaching out and communicating through consciousness-raising narratives of experience. There are other writers, especially some of the younger generation who have been influenced by the problematizing of identity-based arguments in postmodernist critical theory, who prefer to register excess, disruption, alienation and fragmentation through form and style. Frank McGuinness and Medbh McGuckian are particularly alert to the possibilities of difference within the 'self', and to the linguistic magic through which the effect of a self is created in writing and performance. Gerry Stembridge and Tom Lennon are writers who confront their readers with explicit scenes of sexuality, and who do so with a certain stylistic verve and imagination.

Academic criticism within a range of disciplines has contributed to an increased awareness of Ireland as a 'queer space'. It is always difficult to excerpt from an essay without caricaturing the argument, but I have included four different direct theoretical statements on queer Irish identity, by Emma Donoghue, Éibhear Walshe, Vincent Quinn and Cherry Smyth. There are also two pieces of cultural criticism that are historicist in nature and involve attempts to reread major figures from the start of the twentieth century from a gay perspective. Lucy McDiarmid and Roz Cowman are not driven by a desire to present Roger Casement or Sommerville and Ross as gay icons, but rather to ask what difference it would make to view them from a gay perspective and what difference to their reputations has been made by various kinds of speculations about their sexuality. These extracts are included not to prove anything particular about their subjects but to suggest the productiveness of certain kinds of critique.

Excerpts from several influential mid-twentieth-century prose works open the selection: Forrest Reid's quiet account of a supernatural experience; Janet McNeill's subtle account of lesbian longing in the genteel Belfast middle classes; Brendan Behan's story of homoerotic attraction played against the backdrop of bereavement; and Kate O'Brien's elegant deployment of the conventions of exotic location and unfulfilled desire, with the single sentence that caused the banning of the book. The move towards sexual liberation in the 1960s is represented by excerpts from Edna O'Brien and Maurice Leitch.

Nell McCafferty's extraordinary court reports for the *Irish Times* in the 1970s offered a bleak picture of the human suffering consequent on legal penalties against free expression of gay lives and loves. Later campaigners for the removal of discriminatory laws and for changes in social attitude produced both coming-out narratives and human-rights-based arguments that describe the injustice under which gay people laboured and which is still a feature of unofficial modes of prejudice.

The homoerotic aspects of writings by such nationalist heroes as Patrick Pearse and Roger Casement were widely denied by their admirers for most of the twentieth century. The re-formation of anti-constitutional nationalisms in the North post- 1968 attracted lesbian and gay people who were more willing than their predecessors to demand that republicanism and loyalism should include a challenge to the oppression of homosexuality. Margo Gorman and Brendí McClenaghan try to explain how discrimination on grounds of sexual orientation could be construed as part of a neo-colonial legacy. The

anthropologist Begoña Aretxaga analyses the sexual dynamics of the dirty protests in Armagh prison. All three speak to some of the ways in which sexual drive is woven into struggles for power and domination. Almost every piece here traces some connection between sex and violence, as for example Joni Crone's discussion of lesbian fear of male violence, or the palpable tensions in the scenes set by Janet McNeill, Gerry Stembridge and Keith Ridgway.

An anthology of women's writing across the centuries gains some of its coherence from the fact that women have historically constituted the other against which patriarchal power and privilege is defined. Writing about sexuality is writing about difference and the desire produced by difference. For much of the last three hundred years writing about sexuality in Ireland has also been a mode of writing about binary oppositions — native and settler, English and Irish, nationalist and loyalist, Catholic and Protestant, man and woman, landed and landless, legal and illegal, old and young. Those oppositions have not dissolved in the last thirty years, but a confidence in essential differences has been shaken and while the oppressed — including many lesbian, bi-sexual and heterosexual women — continue to find a use for a strategic essentialism, there is also new awareness both of other previously overlooked binaries — straight and gay, Traveller and settled, for example — and of the ways in which people situate themselves in a variety of sometimes conflicting loyalties. The dissolution of the heterosexual family values enshrined in de Valera's constitution may be succeeded by the multiplication of objects and modes of desire. However such a multiplication evolves it is likely that at least one group of people so far radically under-represented in writing — the new Irish immigrants and asylum seekers — will come to play a significant role in the fantasy life of the nation.

All texts have been selected and edited by Éibhear Walshe except where the initials E.D. for Emma Donoghue, M.H. for Marjorie Howes, S.K. for Siobhán Kilfeather or C.W. for Clair Wills appear after the headnote, which initials also indicate attribution of the relevant biography.

[Siobhán Kilfeather]

FORREST REID

(1875–1947)

from:
PRIVATE ROAD (1940)

[In his autobiography, published in London in 1940 by Faber and Faber, Forrest Reid describes an encounter with the ghost of a small boy. Homosexuality is frequently represented by a ghost haunting realist texts. Reid, in particular, was intrigued by sexuality in young boys and this ghost echoes back to his own childhood. One might compare this to the contemporary uses of the supernatural in Elizabeth Bowen, in stories such as 'The Demon Lover'. S.K.]

I fear I have wandered from my subject: let me give, before finally abandoning it, one further and more positive experience, because this time I actually saw something.

During the years following the war I very often went on motor tours through England with Frank Workman[1] and his wife. They were really croquet tours, for we played in various tournaments, and on the occasion I have in mind we had wound up our trip at Eastbourne. At least half a dozen other players were stopping at the hotel where we put up, among them E.S. Luard, who no longer played, but was managing the tournament, a pretty big one and the last of the season. Of course everybody in the croquet world knew everybody else and I had often met Luard before. He told me casually that before the end of the tournament — which lasted for a fortnight — he expected a visit from his grandchildren and their parents; but I took no particular interest in the matter.

In fact I had forgotten all about it when, a few mornings later, on coming out of my bedroom, the door of which faced Luard's own room, I saw a small boy in the passage. He was about eight or nine, dressed in a blue jersey and shorts, and he had his back turned to me, so that I did not see his face. One of the grandchildren, I surmised, and I supposed he had been paying an early visit to his grandfather and was now going down to

1. Francis Workman (1856–1927), founder of Workman Clark, the Belfast ship-building company.

breakfast. I followed him along the passage with the intention of making myself known to him. He turned the corner, but instead of descending the flight of stairs leading to the ground floor, he continued on his way, and I continued too. He turned the next corner — the three passages being as three sides of a square — and I was now close on his heels. I also turned the corner, and found that the passage was empty.

The child, I decided, must with remarkable celerity have nipped into the first room on either the right or the left, so I retraced my steps, and this time went downstairs. The first person I saw in the dining-room was Luard himself, having breakfast.

'I see the grandchildren have arrived,' I remarked casually, but to my surprise he answered, 'They haven't; I don't expect them till next week.'

I said no more, for after all there was nothing to say; I had merely guessed that the little boy in the passage was one of the grandchildren, and now I found he wasn't Nevertheless, though I haven't a notion why, I felt puzzled. The child had vanished with astonishing quickness, and now I came to think of it, I had heard no sound of an opening or closing door. I continued to ponder, with the result that after breakfast I sought out the manager of the hotel. I approached the matter with circumspection, but none the less definitely. He was equally definite. There were no children staying in the hotel. Was he sure? He was absolutely sure. Could a little boy be there without his knowledge? He could not. Then of course he asked me 'Why?' I murmured something vague, and, hotel managers being adepts in the art of tact, the subject was dismissed.

Actually the only person to whom I spoke of this adventure was Mrs. Workman, but Mrs. Workman regarded me as a person to whom adventures readily happened, and wasn't so much impressed as I had expected. She even appeared to think it quite natural for me to meet in broad daylight a small boy who didn't exist, and that the only strange feature of the case was that he hadn't been accompanied by a phantom bulldog. Yet this story is true. I mean there is no vagueness, no uncertainty about it, no loophole for the entrance of imagination. I saw that little boy, pursued him, and lost him. I am not subject to hallucinations. I had no feeling of ghostliness; it was early morning; the sun was shining; and anything less ghostly than that up-to-date hotel would be difficult to conceive. I never saw my little boy again. I questioned the hall-porter and he was as positive as the manager. Moreover, what possible reason could they have for telling me lies? Perhaps there was some perfectly natural explanation, but I did not push my inquiries further. Somehow I did not want to. To drag that happy little ghost into the dubious atmosphere of psychic phenomena would have been like shutting a bird in a cage. I don't even believe he knew I was there. If he had known he would have waited for me.

But the experiences I have mentioned here were not those de Selincourt alludes to in his letters:[2] they happened later. And they left me — even that last queer little adventure — as they found me — half convinced, half doubtful, wholly unable to attach to them any positive significance. If actually I had been a seeker of the marvellous they would have been more understandable, but I wasn't, and I mistrusted those who were. Nor had they anything to do with what I really was seeking: at least I could trace no connection; they seemed to me no more relevant to that than would have been the pranks of a poltergeist.

2. Allusion untraced. Ernest de Selincourt had recently produced an edition of *The Letters of William and Dorothy Woodsworth* (Oxford: Oxford University Press, 1937), but it seems unlikely that these are the letters meant by Reid. The reference may be to Basil de Selincourt, critic on *The Observer*.

KATE O'BRIEN

(1897–1974)

from:
THE LAND OF SPICES (1941)

[Kate O'Brien's novel, published in London in 1941 by Heinemann, was banned by the Irish Censorship Board on the grounds of objections to the following passage in what was otherwise an admired book. Homosexuality, however obliquely invoked, threatened the whole decorum of the novel of manners. Helen, O'Brien's heroine, lives in Brussels with her father, and attends a convent boarding school.]

It was June and brilliant weather. Helen's last term as a border at Place des Ormes. At the end of July she was to go to Italy with her father and they would not return until mid-October, when his autumn classes, and her university studies, began.

One Saturday evening many of the girls who lived in Brussels had gone home for the week-end, and there was a pleasant sense of indolence through the convent. Helen, after having played some tennis, amused herself by helping Mère

Alphonsine to arrange the flowers for the chapel. The next day was the Sunday within the Octave of Corpus Christi and Mère Alphonsine was dissatisfied with the colours of the roses Soeur Josèphe had sent in from the garden. She wanted more red ones, she said, and Soeur Josèphe said she couldn't have what wasn't there and that she was never satisfied.

Helen said that unless Marie-Jeanne had taken them all to Malines that day, whither she had gone for her nephew's first communion, there were red roses in the garden at Rue Saint Isidore. Mère Alphonsine commanded her to go and fetch them.

She went very happily, as she was, hatless and in tennis shoes. Glad of the sun and the lovely evening, and the chance of a word with Daddy, if he was at home. The gate squeaked and let her in unwillingly, as usual. She never rang the front-door bell, even when Marie-Jeanne was at home to hear it; she always went straight through the garden to the ever-open kitchen door.

Her father's study was at the back of the house, above the kitchen. It had a long, wide balcony of wrought iron which ran full across a wall and ended in an iron staircase to the garden. This balcony made a pleasant, deep shade over the flagged space by the kitchen door, where Marie-Jeanne often sat to prepare vegetables, or to have a sleep. Traffic was free up and down these stairs; and Henry Archer was not formal about access to his study, even when he was working, even when he was having a silent and solitary mood.

Helen glanced in at the empty kitchen, scratched the cat behind the ears, and hoped that Marie-Jeanne wasn't getting too drunk at Malines. Then she ran up the iron stairs and along the balcony to the open room of her father's study.

She looked into the room.

Two people were there. But neither saw her; neither felt her shadow as it froze across the sun.

She turned and descended the stairs. She left the garden and went down the curve of Rue Saint Isidore.

She had no objective and no knowledge of what she was doing. She did not see external things. She saw Etienne and her father, in the embrace of love.

BRENDAN BEHAN

(1923–64)

AFTER THE WAKE (1981)

[This story, first published in *Points* in Paris in 1950, describes a world of subterfuge and encoded allusion as the narrator becomes emotionally and erotically entangled with a young married couple in Dublin. 'After the Wake' is the title story in a collection of prose writings by Behan, edited by Peter Fallon and published in Dublin in 1981 by O'Brien Press.]

When he sent to tell me she was dead, I thought that if the dead live on — which I don't believe they do — and know the minds of the living, she'd feel angry, not so much jealous as disgusted, certainly surprised.

For one time she had told me, quoting unconsciously from a book I'd lent him, 'A woman can always tell them — you kind of smell it on a man — like knowing when a cat is in a room.'

We often discussed things like that — he, always a little cultured, happy and proud to be so broadminded — she, with adolescent pride in the freedom of her married state to drink a bottle of stout and talk about anything with her husband and her husband's friend.

I genuinely liked them both. If I went a week without calling up to see them, he was down the stairs to our rooms, asking what they'd done on me, and I can't resist being liked. When I'd go in she'd stick a fag in my mouth and set to making tea for me.

I'd complimented them, individually and together on their being married to each other — and I meant it.

They were both twenty-one, tall and blond, with a sort of English blondness.

He, as I said, had pretensions to culture and was genuinely intelligent, but that was not the height of his attraction for me.

Once we went out to swim in a weir below the Dublin mountains. It was evening time and the last crowd of kids too shrimpish, small, neutral cold to take my interest — just finishing their bathe.

When they went off, we stripped and, watching him, I thought of Marlowe's lines which I can't remember properly: 'Youth with gold wet head, through water gleaming, gliding, and crowns of pearlets on his naked arms'.[1]

I haven't remembered it at all but only the sense of a Gaelic translation I've read.

When we came out we sat on his towel — our bare thighs touching, smoking and talking.

We talked of the inconvenience of tenement living. He said he'd hated most of all sleeping with his brothers — so had I, I'd felt their touch

---

1. Christopher Marlowe (1564–93), homoerotic poet; the quotation is an echo of lines from *Edward II*, Act I, Scene 1, lines 61 ff:
   Sometime a lovely boy in Dian's shape,
   With hair that gilds the water as it glides,
   Crownets of pearl about his naked arms,
   And in his sportful hands an olive-tree,
   To hide those parts which men delight to see.

incestuous — but most of all he hated sleeping with a man older than himself.

He'd refused to sleep with his father which hurt the old man very much, and when a seizure took his father in the night, it left him remorseful.

'I don't mind sleeping with a little child,' he said, 'the snug way they round themselves into you — and I don't mind a young fellow my own age.'

'The like of myself,' and I laughed as if it meant nothing. It didn't apparently, to him.

'No, I wouldn't mind you and it'd be company for me, if she went into hospital or anything,' he said.

Then he told me what she herself had told me sometime before, that there was something the matter with her, something left unattended since she was fourteen or so, and that soon she'd have to go into hospital for an operation.

From that night forward, I opened the campaign in jovial earnest.

The first step — to make him think it manly, ordinary to manly men, the British navy! 'Porthole Duff', 'Navy Cake', stories of the Hitler Youth in captivity, told me by Irish soldiers on leave from guarding them; to remove the taint of 'cissiness', effeminacy, how the German Army had encouraged it in Cadet Schools, to harden the boy-officers, making their love a muscular clasp of friendship, the British Public Schools, young boxers I'd known (most of it about the Boxers was true), that Lord Alfred Douglas[2] was son to the Marquess of Queensbury[3] and a good man to use his dukes[4] himself, Oscar Wilde throwing old 'Q' down the stairs and after him, his Ballyboy attendant.

On the other front, appealing to that hope of culture — Socrates,[5] Shakespeare,[6] Marlowe — lies, truth and half-truth.

I worked cautiously but steadily. Sometimes (on head of a local scandal) in conversation with them both.

After I'd lent him a book about an English schoolmaster, she'd made the remark about

2. Lord Alfred Bruce Douglas, 'Bosie' (1870–1945), Oscar Wilde's lover.
3. Sir John Sholto Douglas, 8th Marquess of Queensberry (1844–1900), established the rules for boxing, known as the 'Queensberry Rules'.
4. Slang for 'fists'.
5. Socrates (c. 470–399 BC), the Greek philosopher whose thoughts on pederasty are recorded in *The Symposium* by Plato (d. c. 347 BC).
6. William Shakespeare (1564–1616), whose sonnets are often read as homoerotic love poems.

women knowing, scenting them as she would a cat in the dark, otherwise empty room.

Quite undeliberately, I helped tangle her scents.

One night we'd been drinking together, he and I, fairly heavily up in their rooms.

I remember when he'd entered and spoken to her, he said to me: 'Your face lights up when you see her.' And why wouldn't it? Isn't a kindly welcome a warming to both faith and features?

I went over and told her what he'd said.

'And my face lights up when I see yours,' she said, smiling up at me in the charming way our women have with half-drunk men.

The following morning I was late for work with a sick head.

I thought I'd go upstairs to their rooms and see if there was a bottle of stout left that would cure me.

There wasn't and though she was in, he was out.

I stopped a while and she gave me a cup of tea, though I'd just finished my own down below in our place.

As I was going she asked me had I fags for the day. I said I had — so as not to steal her open store, as the saying has it — and went off to work.

She, or someone, told him I'd been in and he warned me about it the next time we were together. He didn't mind (and I believed him) but people talked, etc.

From that day forward I was cast as her unfortunate admirer, my jealousy of him sweetened by my friendship for them both.

She told me again about her operation and asked me to pray for her. When I protested my unsuitability as a pleader with God, she quoted the kindly, highly heretical Irish Catholicism about the prayers of the sinner being heard first.

The night before she went into hospital we had a good few drinks — the three of us together.

We were in a singing house on the Northside and got very sob-garbled between drinking whiskey and thinking of the operation.

I sang 'My Mary of the Curling Hair' and when we came to the Gaelic chorus, *siúl, a grá* (Walk, My Love), she broke down sobbing and said how he knew as well as she that it was to her I was singing, but that he didn't mind. He said that indeed he did not, and she said how fearful she was of the operation, that maybe she'd never come out of it. She was not sorry for herself, but for him, if anything happened to her and she died on him, aye, and sorry for me too, maybe, more sorry, 'Because, God help you,' she said to me, 'that never knew anything better than going down town half-drunk and dirty rotten bitches taking your last farthing.'

Next day was Monday and at four o'clock she went into the hospital. She was operated on Thursday morning and died the same evening at about nine o'clock. When the doctor talked about cancer, he felt consoled a little. He stopped his dry-eyed sobbing and came with me into a public house. When we meet his mother and hers and made arrangements to have her brought home and waked in her own place.

She was laid out in the front room on their spare single bed which was covered in linen for the purpose. Her habit was of blue satin and we heard afterwards that some old ones considered the colour wrong — her having been neither a virgin nor a member of the Children of Mary Sodality. The priest, a hearty man who read Chesterton[7] and drank pints, disposed of the objection by saying that we were all children of Mary since Christ introduced St. John to Our Lady at the foot of the Cross — Son, behold thy Mother; Mother belold Thy Son.[8]

It is a horrible thing how quickly death and disease can work on a body.

She didn't look like herself any more than the brown parchment-thin shell of a mummy looks like an Egyptian warrior; worse than the mummy, for he at least is dry and clean as dust. Her poor nostrils were plugged with cotton-wool and her mouth hadn't closed properly, but showed two front teeth, like a rabbit's. All in all, she looked no better than the corpse of her granny, or any other corpse for that matter.

There was a big crowd at the wake. They shook hands with him and told him they were sorry for his trouble; then they shook hands with his and her other relatives, and with me, giving me an understanding smile and licence to mourn my pure, unhappy love.

Indeed, one old one, far gone in Jameson,[9] said she was looking down on the two of us, expecting me to help bear him up.

Another old one, drunker still, got lost in the complications of what might have happened if he died instead of her, and only brought herself up at the tableau — I marrying her and he blessing the union from on high.

At about midnight, they began drifting away to their different rooms and houses and by three o'clock there was only his mother left with us, steadily drinking.

At last she got up a little shakily on her feet, and, proceeding to knock her people, said they'd left bloody early for blood relatives, but seeing as they'd given her bloody little in life it was the three of us were best entitled to sit waking — she included me and all.

When his mother went, he told me he felt very sore and very drunk and very much in need of sleep. He felt hardly able to undress himself.

I had to almost carry him to the big double bed in the inner room.

I first loosened his collar to relieve the flush on his smooth cheeks, took off his shoes and socks and pants and shirt, from the supply muscled thighs, the stomach flat as an altar boy's, and noted the golden smoothness of the blond hair on every part of his firm white flesh.

I went into the front room and sat by the fire till he called me.

'You must be nearly gone yourself,' he said, 'you might as well come in and get a bit of rest.'

I sat on the bed, undressing myself by the faint flickering of the candles from the front room.

I fancied her face looking up from the open coffin on the Americans who, having imported wakes from us, invented morticians themselves.[10]

7. G.K. Chesterton (1874–1936), English writer who converted to Roman Catholicism in 1922.
8. John, 19:26–27.
9. John Jameson, an Irish whiskey.
10. Allusion to the final line of Maria Edgeworth's *Castle Rackrent: An Hibernian Tale* (1801).

EDNA O'BRIEN

(1930?–   )

from:
THE LONELY GIRL (1962)

[Edna O'Brien's *Country Girls* trilogy, *The Country Girls* (1960), *The Lonely Girl* (1962) and *Girls in Their Married Bliss* (1964), chronicles the lives of two friends from a small village near Limerick. All three novels were banned by the Irish Censorship Board. Caithleen is an intelligent, sensitive, somewhat awkward woman with romantic ideals and vaguely defined literary talents. Baba (Bridgid) is a pert, cynical materialist. O'Brien once commented that 'Baba was sex and Cait was romance'.[1] Like many young, single Irish women, they migrate from the village to Dublin, and from there to London. Caithleen narrates this excerpt, which recounts her painful efforts to overcome the sexual shame and inhibitions her upbringing has instilled in her and lose her virginity. Later reprinted as *Girl with Green Eyes* (Harmondsworth, Middlesex: Penguin, 1964).   M.H.]

I went most Sundays after that, and then, one Sunday night I stayed.

I slept in the guest room, where the floor and woodwork had been newly varnished. Everything was a little sticky.

In fact I didn't sleep, I kept thinking of him. I could hear him whistling downstairs and moving around until after three o'clock. He had left me a magazine to read. It contained a lot of drawings — people with peaked noses and suitcases growing out of their ears — which I did not understand. I kept the light on because Anna said a woman had died in that room just before Eugene bought the house. A colonel's wife who took digitalis pills.

Toward morning I dozed, but the alarm clock went off at seven and I had to get up to go back to work.

'Did you sleep?' he asked. We met going down the stairs, and he yawned and pretended to stagger.

'No, not very well.'

'Nonsense, isn't it! Two people at opposite wings of the house lying awake. Next time we'll keep each other company and put a bolster in the bed between us, won't we?' he said as he kissed me. I looked away. I had been brought up to think of it as something unmentionable, which a woman had to pretend to like, to please a husband.

He brought a rug for my knees and a flask of tea, which I drank in the car, as there was no time for breakfast.

The next Sunday I stayed, and I still went to my own room. I did not want to sleep in his bed; he put it down to scruples, but actually I was afraid. Early the next morning he tapped on my door, and as I was awake I got up, and we went out for a stroll through the woods.

There are moments in our lives we can never forget: I remember that early morning and the white limbs of young birches in the early mist, and later the sun coming up behind the mountain in crimson splendour as if it were the first day of the world. I remember the sudden brightness of everything and the effect of suffused light as the sun came through the mist, and the dew lifted, and later the green of the grass showed forth very vividly, radiating energy in the forms of colour.

'I wish we could be together,' he said, his arm around my neck.

'Will we be?' I said.

'It seems so natural now, so inevitable, I was never one for necking in backs of cars, it strikes me as being so sick,' he said.

Kissing, or 'necking', as he called it, suited me nicely, but I could not tell him that.

But I could only postpone it until Christmastime.

He invited Baba, Joanna, and Gustav for Christmas dinner, so that I would feel at ease, as his friends terrified me. They were mostly people from other countries who told each other obscure jokes, and I felt that they looked on me as some sort of curiosity brought in for amusement.

It was a pleasant dinner, with red candles along the table and presents for everyone on the tree; Joanna was in her element, she got an old

1. Interview with Edna O'Brien, in *Banned in Ireland: Censorship and the Irish Writer*, ed. Julia Carlson (Athens, Georgia: University of Georgia Press, 1990), p. 71.

gilt frame to bring home and some logs for the dining-room grate. Baba waltzed with Eugene after dinner to gramophone music, and everybody had plenty to drink.

At midnight the guests went home, but I stayed. It looked quite respectable really, because Eugene's mother was also staying. She was frail, argumentative little woman, with a craggy face and a big forehead like his. She coughed a lot.

Eugene helped her upstairs to the guest room (the room I usually slept in) and brought her hot whiskey and a little mug for her teeth. Then he came down and we ate cold turkey and cream crackers.

'I hardly saw you all day, and you looked so pretty at dinner,' he said as we sat on the sheepskin rug in front of the fire, eating. He read to me, poems by Lorca,[2] which I didn't understand, but he read nicely. He wanted me to read one but I felt shy, sometimes I became very shy in his company. One side of my face got very hot, so I took off one of my red lantern earrings. Raising his eyes from the book, he saw the warm lobe blackened a little by the cheap tin of the earring clip, and he groaned.

'Your ears could go septic,' he said as he examined the red earrings which I had bought on Christmas Eve so that I would look glamorous for him.

'Made in Hong Kong!' he said as he threw them in the fire. I tried to rescue them with the tongs but it was too late; they had sunk into the red ashes.

I sulked for a bit, but he said that he would buy me a gold pair.

'If I didn't care about you I wouldn't worry about your ears,' he said. I laughed at that. His compliments were so odd.

'You soft, daft, wanton thing, you've got one mad eye,' he said, looking into my eyes, which he decided were green.

'Green eyes and copper hair, my mother wouldn't trust you,' he said. His mother had cold blue eyes which were very piercing and shrewd. A smell of eucalyptus oil surrounded her.

I lay back on the woolly rug, and he kissed my warmed face.

After a while he said, 'Will we go to bed, Miss Potts?' I was happy lying there, just kissing him; bed was too final for me, so I sat up and put my arms around my knees.

'It's too early,' I said. It was about two in the morning.

'We'll wash our teeth,' he said, so we went upstairs and washed our teeth. 'You're not washing your teeth properly, you should brush them up and down as well as back and forth.'

I think he just said that to put me at my ease. I had stopped talking and my eyes were owlish, as they always are when I am frightened. I knew that I was about to do something terrible. I believed in hell, in eternal torment by fire. But it could be postponed.

The bedroom was cold. Normally Anna lit a fire there, but in the excitement of dinner and presents she had forgotten about it.

He undressed quickly and put his clothes on a wing-backed armchair. I stood watching him, too self-conscious to move. My teeth chattered, from fear or cold.

'Hop in before you get cold,' he said as he got something out of the wall press. His long back had one vivid strawberry mark. Dark tufts of hair stuck out from under his arms, and in the lamplight the smooth parts of his body were a glowing honey colour.

He got into bed and propped his head on one fist while he waited for me.

'Don't look at me,' I asked.

He put his hand across his eyes; the fingers were spread out so that there were slits between them. While I undressed, he recited:

> Mrs. White had a fright
> In the middle of the night,
> Saw a ghost, eating toast
> Halfway up a lamp post . . .[3]

Then he asked me to unscrew the Tilley lamp. A trickle of paraffin flowed out from the metal cap and mingled with the toilet water which I had poured on my hands and wrists.

'You're such a nice plump girl,' he said as I came toward him. The light took a few seconds to fade out completely.

2. Federico García Lorca (1899–1936) was a well-known Spanish poet and dramatist. He was arrested and shot by the Francoists on the eve of the Spanish Civil War.

3. A children's street rhyme. For a selection of such rhymes, see Angela Bourke, 'Work and Play', pp. 1421–32.

I took off the coat which I had been using as a dressing gown, and he raised the covers up and gathered me in near him.

I shivered, but he thought it was with cold. He rubbed my skin briskly to warm it and said that my knees were like ice. He did everything to make me feel at ease.

'Have you fluff in your belly button?' he asked as he poked fun at it with his fingers. It was one thing I was very squeamish about, and instantly (I began to tighten with fear) my whole body stiffened.

'What's wrong?' he said as he kissed my closed lips. He noticed things very quickly. 'Are you filled with remorse?'

It was not remorse. Even if I had been married I would have been afraid.

'What is it, darling, little soft skin?' If he had not been so tender I might have been brave. I cried onto his bare shoulder.

'I don't know,' I said hopelessly. I felt such a fool crying in bed, especially as I laughed so much in the daytime and gave the impression of being thoughtlessly happy.

'Have you had some terrible traumatic experience?' he asked.

Traumatic? I had never heard that word before, I didn't know what to say.

'I don't know,' I said. 'I don't know' was the only sentence which formed itself in my crying brain.

He tried to assure me, to say that I need not worry, that there was nothing to be afraid of, that surely I was not afraid of him. He caressed me slowly and gently, and I was still afraid. Before that, on armchairs, in the motorcar, in restaurants, I touched his hands, kissed the hairs on his wrists, longed for the feel of his fingers on my soft secret flesh, but now everything had changed.

He said that I should talk about it, tell him what exactly appalled me, discuss it. But I couldn't do that. I just wanted to go to sleep and wake up, finding that it was all over, the way you wake up after an operation.

I lay in his arms crying, and he said that I must not cry and that we would do nothing but have a big, long sleep and wake up full of energy. He was a little quiet. He blamed himself for being so stupid, so unthinking, for not having known that I would be nervous and afraid.

Eventually he turned over on his other side to go to sleep. He took a sleeping pill with a glass of water.

'I'm sorry, Eugene . . . I do love you,' I said.

'That's all right, sweetling,' he said, patting my warm bottom with his hand. At least we had got warm.

'I won't be afraid tomorrow,' I said, knowing that I would.

'I know that,' he said. 'You're just tired; now go to sleep and don't worry about a thing.'

We joined hands. I wanted to blow my nose, as I could scarcely breathe from all that crying. I was ashamed to blow it, in case it was vulgar.

I went to sleep, mortified.

Sometime toward morning we must have come together again, because I woke up to find myself refusing his love.

Immediately afterward he got up and dressed. I apologized.

'Stop saying you're sorry,' he said as he drew his braces up. 'There's no need to be sorry, it's a perfectly natural thing,' he said. He sat on the armchair and put on his socks.

'Are you getting up?' he asked.

'Yes, I often get up at dawn when I don't sleep very well; I go out for a walk or do some work . . .'

'It's my fault.'

'Stop saying it's your fault, stop worrying,' he said. I was glad that it was too dark for me to see the expression on his face; I could not have looked at him.

He left the room, and later I heard his steps outside on the gravel.

I lay on, and wept. I had never felt so ashamed in my whole life; I felt certain now that he was finished with me because I had been so childish. When daylight came, about half past eight, there were a few stars left in the heavens. They looked wan and faint as stars do in the morning.

'Go home . . . vanish,' I said to the stars, or to myself, and I got up and dressed when I heard Anna poke the range downstairs. I did not know how I would face her, or Denis or his mother or him. My black, sequinned jumper, which I had thought so charming at the dinner table, seemed idiotic in the early morning. I wished that I could get out of the house and escape back to Joanna's without being seen. I looked in the mirror. My face was red, blotchy, swollen. Everyone would know!

It began to snow. It came very fast and sudden, and it fell slant-wise on the front field but did not lodge there. It melted as it touched the ground. I stuck my head out, hoping that the sleet might change my face, and then I went to the second guest room to toss the bed which I should have slept in. It seemed foolish and sad to have to do such a thing, but Anna was very observant and would have noticed. Under that divan bed I found a box of old toys and torn books.

This book belongs to Baby Elaine Gaillard, I read on the flyleaf of an animal book. I nearly died. He had never said that he had a child, but I ought to have wondered why he was so tender with Anna's baby. It made everything worse; I looked at the toys, torn and chewed, and cried over them. The sleet, my red, unslept cheeks, the silly sequinned jumper, the cold green porcelain of an unlit anthracite stove in the room, all seemed to multiply my sense of shame. I sat there, weeping, until Anna knocked on the door to say breakfast was ready.

Down in the kitchen I could not bring myself to look at him. I held my head down. He handed me a cup of tea and said, 'Did you sleep well, Miss Caithleen Brady?'

Anna was there, watching.

'Yes, thank you.'

He bent his head and looked sideways at my face, hung in shame. He was laughing.

'I'm very glad that you slept well,' he said as he brought me over to the table and buttered some toast for me.

Later his mother came down and we had breakfast together. She complained about the porridge being lumpy. She lived with a sister in Dublin, and said that there was one thing she could not stand and that was lumpy porridge.

He drove her back around noon and I thought I should go too, but he asked me to stay a while longer, as he said he wanted to talk to me. I stayed.

'See you again, dear,' his mother said as he helped her into the car. She had a shawl over her fur coat and a hot-water bottle for her knees. She looked rather happy, because he had given her whiskey and chocolates and white turkey meat wrapped in butter paper. She liked to be pampered; she was making up for all the years when she had worked as a waitress to rear her son. He was quite distant with her and she was sharp with him. But she liked it when he fussed over her.

When they had gone I went up to the woods. The sleet had stopped and now it rained mildly. I did not know whether I should risk staying another night or not. I was trying to decide — the gently falling rain made a background of vague soothing noise for my muddled thoughts. I thought of other woods, dampness, cowslips in a field of high grass, all the imaginary men I had ever talked to and into whose strong arms I had swooned in a moment of ecstatic reconciliation. But I could not decide; I had never made decisions in my life. My clothes had always been bought for me, my food decided on, even my outings were decided by Baba. I walked round and round, touching the damp trees, inhaling the wild smells of the damp wood.

When I heard the car come back I walked toward the house and then I heard him whistle as he came up to the woods to find me. He wore an old brown hat, which made him look rakish, and as he came toward me I knew that I would stay another night and risk making a fool of myself again.

'I'll stay,' I said instantly, and he was pleased. He said that I looked a lot better since I came out and that rain suited me and that I must always live in rainy country and wear my hair long, like that, and wear a dark mackintosh.

'And I won't be afraid,' I said as we ran down the wooded hill toward the yard in order to make some tea. He was dying for tea. I did not feel sleepy anymore. We spotted Anna looking at us through his field glasses.

'She'll break those glasses,' he said, but by the time he got in the house, she had restored them to their brown leather case, which hung on the end of the curtain pole in his study. When he complained, Anna said that he must have been seeing things. He prepared a turkey hash, while Anna and I chopped vegetables.

Before dinner he carried a white china lamp upstairs to the dressing table in his room so that I could make up my face. He stayed there, watching, while I applied pancake makeup with a damp sponge and spread it over my face evenly. It made me pale. In the mirror my face looked round and childlike.

'The old man and the girl,' he said to the spotted mirror, which was wedged at the right angle by a face-cream jar — one of Laura's no doubt. He debated whether or not he should shave.

'Am I likely to be kissing anybody?' he asked the mirror as he stroked the stubble on his chin.

I laughed.

'Well, am I?' he asked again. I loved kissing him. I thought, if only people just kissed, if all love stopped at that.

He picked up my hairbrush and began to brush my hair very slowly. I liked the slow, firm strokes of the brush on my scalp, and after a while I felt exhilarated from it. He smiled a lot at me in the mirror.

'I have too much chin and you have a shade too little. We should make perfectly chinned children,' he said. He expected me to laugh, but I didn't. There were some things which I was very touchy about: babies for instance. Babies terrified me. Then I remembered the box of toys; I had never forgotten it really, just postponed thinking about it.

'There is a box of toys in my room, under the bed,' I said.

'Yes, I know, they're mine. I had a child.'

'Oh.'

'I had a daughter, she's three now.' I thought his voice changed, but I could not be certain. I imagined him giving a little girl a pickaback,[4] and the thought stabbed me with jealous pain.

'Do you miss her?' I asked.

'I miss her very much, almost every minute of the day I think of her, or think that I'm hearing her. Once you've had a child you want to live with it and watch it grow.'

He went on brushing my hair, but it was not the same after that.

4. Piggy-back ride.

from:
BANNED IN IRELAND: CENSORSHIP AND THE IRISH WRITER (1990)

[Edna O'Brien was interviewed by Julia Carlson for the volume she edited for Article 19, the International Centre on Censorship, a human rights organization that campaigns for the right to freedom of expression worldwide. During the 1960s almost all O'Brien's fiction was banned in the Republic of Ireland, and she responded with public protests, including bringing the books across the border in defiance of the authorities. *Banned in Ireland: Censorship and the Irish Writer*, edited for Article 19 by Julia Carlson (London: Routledge, 1990).]

Do you think people were disturbed by your treatment of women?

I think so, yes. I think so because it was about the covert and the not-so-covert, rather foolish sexuality of two girls. It was their romance and their sexuality because Baba was sex and Cait was romance. I admitted their sexuality, also unhappy married life — a young girl yearning and, indeed, eventually having sex with a much older married man. *Girls in Their Married Bliss* horrified them completely. Indeed, it was very funny. When it was published, I was really savaged. They all said that I had lost my lyrical quality. In fact, now, twenty-five years later, *Girls in Their Married Bliss* stands up. It has some guts. But I did have a very rough time on two levels. On the public level, being banned, and on a more personal level.

Were you hurt in other ways when your books were banned — by your family or by the community in which you were reared?

Very much. You know, a bit of affirmation either from the family or the community helps a lot, especially when you start off. I had none. My own family, my mother and father, God rest them, were appalled. Everyone in the village was. I got anonymous letters about sewers and sewage and all that innuendo . . .

I think censorship was always more severe in rural Ireland.

Understandably. People know each other's lives. But to write it is taboo. Then if you write in a kind of personal tone, as I do, they assume without any shadow of doubt that everything in it happened to you. They don't understand that the soul of a book like *A Portrait of the Artist as a Young Man*[1] or even, to a lesser extent, *The Country Girls* springs from a fusion of fact, feeling and imagination . . .

What kind of damage do you think censorship has done in Ireland?

Closed the minds of the people. Frightened them. It's a fuckup, if you'll excuse the word. Ignorance and darkness and bigotry only lead to psychic sickness.

1. *A Portrait of the Artist as a Young Man* (1916) by James Joyce (1882–1941).

Who do you think is responsible for this damage?

The Church — it's the Church and the blind adherence of people — the Faithful . . .

You once said that you felt censorship was rooted in fear.[2] What kind of fear?

Fear of knowledge. Fear of communicating our desires, our secrets, our stream of consciousness.

Do you think that kind of fear lies behind censorship in Ireland?

It lies behind censorship everywhere — Ireland,

2. Michael Adams, *Censorship: The Irish Experience* (Dublin: Scepter Books, 1968), pp. 21–4.

South Africa, Russia. The Russians know it better than anyone, by putting their poets in exile, in labour camps, or killing them all off. It's a fear that thinking and openness will spread. Now the Russians and the Irish differ radically in their opinion of what is to be banned or what is censorable. The Russian censorship has always been political, and the Irish has always been religious. Sex is the factor here. The fear would be that the people would become libidinous, rampant. This makes me sad, really sad. Repression and ignorance is the biggest rot of all because from it springs sickness, insanity, schizophrenia, which as we know is very high in Ireland. By saying 'Thou shalt not', one opens the sluice gates to inner dilemma.

JANET McNEILL

(1907–?)

from:
THE MAIDEN DINOSAUR
(1964)

[This rather grim study of a group of middle-class Protestant Belfast friends has usually been read in terms of emotional sterility. But Sarah, the middle-aged, sex-phobic spinster of the title, has been in love with her friend Helen since their schooldays. Like several early lesbian novels (such as Mary Renault's *The Friendly Young Ladies*, 1945), this one has an unconvincing eleventh-hour 'happy ending' in which the heroine decides to try sleeping with a man. The following excerpt starts at the home they share in Belfast and then moves to the Northern Irish seaside town where Helen and Sarah holiday every year. The text is from the first edition, published in London in 1964 by Geoffrey Isles.   E.D.]

Back at Thronehill, she found Helen with her room littered and the suitcases still unfilled. 'I can't decide what to take — help me, Sarah!' She bullied Sarah into making decisions, then revoked them if it suited her and told Sarah what to pack. This was part of the ritual, the intro-

ductory movement to their closer association during the fortnight. Sarah, bruised by her failure with Kitty, succumbed to it and knew that Helen was pleased.

'My head aches. Nobody brushes my hair like you do, Sarah. Brush it for me.'

The rhythmic movement of the brush and the feeling of Helen's hair in her hands, fragrant and silky, roused an ecstasy of tenderness in her. Helen sat, with her head back, eyes closed, almost a girl's profile. 'Lovely, lovely.'

Felicity knocked and came in. 'I'm sorry.' She stood hesitantly in the doorway as if she intruded on an intimate scene.

Sarah put the brush down, feeling foolish. Helen said, 'Come in, child.'

Felicity looked untidy and exhausted. Her eyes were shadowed. She was wearing no make-up and a stained dressing gown with draggled frills.

'It's about the laundry, Mrs. Harris; you said you wanted me to send your parcel off when he called.'

'The laundry — how clever of you to remember. Just imagine — I'd forgotten all about it.' She smiled at the girl and shrugged, playing for sympathy — a mind like a sieve, be sorry for me — but the girl's heavy face was unresponsive.

'Isn't it lovely to be going off on holiday?' Helen demanded, 'we're so excited.'

Felicity pushed her hair back. 'I expect it is.'

'We've done this every year for ages, Sarah and I. To the same place, but it's always wonderful. When do you and Justin go?'

'I don't expect we do. I don't think we can afford it, and there's the baby.'

Helen smiled. 'Next year then; it's something to look forward to.'

'Unless there's another baby by then.'

'My dear —' Helen hesitated, unsure of her ground. Her face, framed in the long hair that lay over her shoulders, looked a little grotesque like something out of a pantomime.

'It must be nice for you I'm sure,' the girl said, unnecessarily loudly, 'I hope you have a lovely time.' She picked up the pile of laundry and went away.

They waited until the door had closed. Helen lifted the brush. 'I'll finish it myself. No, don't fuss, Sarah, I said I'd finish it. She's an odd child, I don't think she meant to be rude. They let themselves go, these young things, when they have a baby. What she'll do with two — surely they can plan nowadays. Pills are so much more civilised.' . . .

They walked into the village before dinner and bought postcards and an evening paper in the usual little shop where they were welcomed like friends. Helen was on top of her form; she had a gift for reclaiming acquaintance on a year-old thread. She went into the chemist's for a film. 'I have your number waiting for you,' the man said, 'knowing you'd be here.' The sailor with paralysed legs sitting on the chair at his cottage door greeted them. All down the steep street it was the same. Childishly Helen declared that dogs and cats remembered her, challenging Sarah to doubt it. 'And the same seagulls!' she cried.

They owned the place before they went on to the pier to see the lighthouse swing its first beam, as they always did on their first evening of the holiday. They stood under the massive wall listening to the suck of waves against it. Light had nearly gone. The sky was packed with clouds crowded together like driven sheep. A yacht bucked and creaked at its moorings.

Helen stretched her arms wide, laying her palms against the lighthouse wall, embracing it. She put her cheek against it. 'You can still feel the sun.' Then she looked up at the lantern. 'It won't be long now.'

I do not know how I can condone these theatricals and still love her. Loving Helen is the only deliberate dishonesty I allow myself, and I justify it because I admit I am being dishonest. We are not two absurd middle-aged ladies playing dolls. We are women performing a rite. We have come back to the primal things, sun, sand, sky and sea. Our faces in the bedroom mirror are a year older, but these things do not change. After a year that has offered us nothing but small things we have come back for comfort and assurance from ribbed sand, the pattern of breaking water as it runs over a rock, clouds assembling before the wind; things that have been the same since we were children and will be the same long after we are dead. And though our bodies leave no children who will enjoy these things after us these elements have still the power to move us. But they move us in different ways. Helen identifies them with herself and wears them as ornaments. I have become separated from the nondescript woman who stands here and is grateful she is not beautiful, and I am the seagull, the wave, the cloud. Where the bee sucks there suck I, and twelve stone of me waits in my unimaginative shoes until I am ready to occupy them again.

The light above their heads shone out strongly, startling them although they had been expecting it, and wheeled and swung. They remembered the rhythm of it at once. It lit the row of houses edging the harbour in unfamiliar detail, the church spire, the derelict castle, then it flashed out to sea, where the mist of it at once defined and limited its beam to a geometric form. Inland again, probing the sweet slope of the hill that rose behind the houses, curved like a woman's breast. Not my breast, Sarah thought, never mine.

'Home,' Helen said. They turned back in the direction of the Hotel. She tucked her arm into Sarah's.

MAURICE LEITCH

(1933–   )

from:
THE LIBERTY LAD (1965)

[Maurice Leitch is not the first twentieth-century novelist to write about gay male experience in Ireland — he was preceded, for example, by Forrest Reid and by Kenneth Martin's *Aubade* (1958) — but Leitch stands out for his self-conscious decision to employ fiction as a form of critique and to see 'gay' writing as part of that critique. Leitch's novel observes a diverse range of sexual identities from the perspective of protagonist Frank Glass. In the following passage Glass reflects on the charged homo-erotic relationship between himself and his openly gay friend, Terry, during a visit to the latter's bedroom. Both *The Liberty Lad* and another novel, *Poor Lazarus* (1969), were banned in the Republic of Ireland. *The Liberty Lad* was first published in Dublin by MacGibbon and Kee in 1965. The text is from the first edition.]

He was at his hair now proper, sleeking down his smooth, black, Valentino-type[1] mat with twin, pearl-handled brushes. You couldn't call him good-looking though because he's too thin and his teeth protrude slightly. Sometimes I tell him he's got an X-certificate look — lean and hungry with dark eyes and a sensual mouth — Count Dracula-ish.[2] He never knows whether to feel flattered or not because he's so conscious of his weight; he just can't get it above nine stone or so, which you must admit, looks ridiculous on a six-footer. I'm about five-eleven myself and I weigh twelve and a half.

'Darling, do you mind if I strip in front of you?'

He was fluttering his eyelashes again, so playing him at his own game, I drawled, 'Not at

1. Rudolph Valentino (1895–1926), Italian-American film star, the romantic idol of the 1920s.
2. Count Dracula is the eponymous hero/villain of the novel by Bram Stoker (1897). The allusion here is more probably to the most famous screen representation of Dracula, that of the actor Bela Lugosi (1882–1956) in *Dracula* (1930).

all, sweetie, go right ahead and do that very thing.'

His pyjamas were in blue and he had his monogram on the breast pocket. He pulled off the jacket and stood in front of the wardrobe full-length mirror sadly surveying his over-defined rib-cage.

'You, too, can have a body like mine—'

'— if you're not careful,' he finished it for me. 'Ha bloody ha!' Then he pulled at his pyjama string and he was in his buff.

We looked at each other for the briefest possible moment and then our eyes slid away. In that second our mood changed to seriousness and then back again to the old flippancy. I was being scrutinized with an almost painful intensity for my slightest reaction. I didn't like the feeling and I said heartily, 'Did no one ever explain to you the meaning of private parts?'

I remembered one hot, lazy, August afternoon on the sandy beach at the Lough. Boredom had sparked off a fit of horseplay on the spread rug and, after a few minutes sweaty tussle, we had both drawn back laughing, pointing mockingly at the bulges that had suddenly appeared in our trunks. And I suppose before that there must have been other times too when we fumbled innocently with each other. Just how *normal* was our relationship anyway? Most people would jump to one conclusion, only, if they could overhear most of the conversations we have, for most people, I have discovered, although they don't talk about it, are terrified of even thinking of *that* subject. I don't know if I have the same sort of fear myself deep down, because old Terry and I, we've talked about it so much and he's told me so much about *his* side of things, that it's hard to imagine what a 'normal' reaction is like. So that makes *me* not 'normal' . . . All this deep thought was beginning to give me a headache so I decided to pay attention instead to what the horny old goat was bubbling about, as he was putting in his cuff-links.

from:
BANNED IN IRELAND: CENSORSHIP AND THE IRISH WRITER (1990)

[Maurice Leitch was another writer interviewed by Julia Carlson for her book on Irish censorship.]

How do you feel about the fact that your books were banned in the Irish Republic?

I have to tell you that I'm very pleased in a way. I think that makes my books much stronger in many ways. I think that means they were hard-hitting and powerful and honest, those three adjectives, if they were banned. I think if a novelist was writing at that particular time about what was going on in his environment, if he was youngish and wasn't banned, there was something wrong somewhere because he was closing his eyes to what was going on around him.

Most of the writers banned in the Republic were harassed in various ways because of the contents of their books. Did that ever happen to you?

I did get a lot of backlash, particularly my first book.[1] Nothing to do with the job. I'm talking socially, not from my own immediate family, but from people who knew me socially and from the village I came from. It still affects certain people. It seemed terribly shocking that I would actually mention the fact that homosexuality existed, particularly in an Irish context, whether North or South. It just seemed a subject worthy of writing about because it was another extension of

1. *The Liberty Lad* (Dublin: MacGibbon and Kee, 1965).

repression. Ireland is sexually repressed; let's face it. It was also part of the fifties and sixties; that sort of repression was everywhere almost . . .

The kind of sexuality you describe in the novels, the stunted, twisted sexuality, do you think that's a particularly Irish problem?

Yes, there's no doubt about that. It's a fear of the sensual almost in any shape or form, which obviously comes from the church whether it's the Protestant tradition or the repressive Catholic tradition. There's no doubt about that.

So you think it crosses the divide?

We've got that in common. That's one reason why the border might disappear — about the only reason, I would imagine.

You mentioned that people were shocked by the homosexual content of The Liberty Lad. *Did they fix upon it, in particular, as being offensive?*

Yes. Also they thought that it was untrue: they felt I was doing this deliberately to create sales for my books. Some reviews in the North said that about my last book, *Silver's City* (1981). I remember very well how shattered I was. The first review I read was in Belfast. This man gave me the worst review I've ever had. He said that the book was a disgrace: it was a disgusting book; it wallowed in filth — all sorts of things like that. I was quite shattered. Then, of course, I went back to London, and suddenly I realized that the reviews here were ecstatic, and I won the Whitbread prize. But he was saying what they said about the first book. What he was really saying was, You've no right to put us in this light; what will other people think of us?

MARGO GORMAN

IRELAND: DILEMMAS AND STRUGGLES (1979)

[This article appeared in *Outcome: A Magazine of Sexual Politics Produced by Lesbian and Gay People* in Lancaster, England. In the 1970s there was almost no outlet for lesbian debate within the mainstream Irish press, and there is little written record of many of the most hotly debated issues. Gorman draws attention to the ways in which an identity politics forged in a lesbian context has complex repercussions for thinking about Irish identity. She also examines the relevance of party-political and sectarian arguments within Ireland to women in general, lesbians in particular.   S.K.]

Since I came out as a lesbian, I've found it easier to stand up for myself as an Irish woman. This may be a combination of increased resilience on my part to 'put downs'; increased contact with the indigenous population (before that most of my friends weren't English); perhaps even increased openness over the past few years to reassessing the Irish political situation. As someone who's been critical of the mainstream politics of Ireland on the left, I have often felt patronised or silenced by English 'comrades', let down or overridden by my compatriots, subjected to unconscious racism by other socialists and feminists. This oppression has been contributed to by my own confusion and inarticulacy, caused by the contradictions in Irish politics as well as by the prejudices, unconscious or otherwise, assumed by others. For example if you say something defending the interests of the Protestant working-class in Ulster, it is assumed you're from a 'Protestant' background and have no conception of the 'real' oppression suffered by Catholics. Criticise the tactics of the troops-out movement and you're likely to be seen as 'pro-British'. Many wrangles later, my politics are clearer and less defensive but there are still many dilemmas.

These dilemmas are most intense when considering sexual politics in Ireland. It is difficult to disentangle the influences of religious ideology, Nationalism, Loyalism, the development of capitalism, the connection with Britain etc. on the issues of sexual politics. The struggle to establish the right to practise the Catholic religion has meant Catholic ideology has become historically intertwined with opposition to British dominance. The demand for self-determination for Ireland as an island is portrayed as the only progressive response to the present-day connection with Britain. It is rarely attempted to relate such a demand to the present historical situation and to an overall political strategy which is progressive. The reasons behind the North/South split and Protestant–Catholic polarisation are rarely made clear. It is not enough to 'blame' that polarisation on British policies on Ireland. It needs also to be examined in the light of internal Irish politics, the development of capitalism in Ireland and the dominant ideologies.

The present situation of women and gays in Ireland is in many ways much worse than that here in England. In the North, in spite of the link with Britain, many reforms (including the Homosexual Law Reform Act of 1967) have never reached Northern Ireland. There is at least legal contraception but abortion is much more difficult to obtain than in England. In the South, the dominance of Catholic ideology means that any reform related to sexuality (e.g. introducing 'family planning' measures) meets considerable opposition.

In his article in *Gay Left* No. 7, Jeff Dudgeon[1] argues that gays should campaign for increased links with Britain so that we can benefit from the reforms and liberalisation that emanate from the central parliament at Westminster. Jeff gets entangled in the notion of Northern Ireland as a 'backward' province of Britain (with the implication that Eire is even more backward). It seems to me a mistake to attribute the reactionary influence of Catholic and Protestant ideology in Ulster to provincial backwardness. Jeff's arguments are also rather contradictory as he goes on to show how radically attitudes to homosexuality have changed in Ulster — claiming, quite rightly, some credit for that for the Northern Ireland Gay Rights Association (N.I.G.R.A.). N.I.G.R.A.

---

1. Jeff Dudgeon, Northern Irish gay rights activist, who took the British government to the European Court over its failure to extend the 1967 Act to Northern Ireland.

has fought gay oppression in Northern Ireland with strength, confidence and some success, in spite of the armed warfare all around them and a lack of support from other groupings. It is important that our struggle doesn't rest at accepting paltry reforms granted by the British government with every Irish gay dreaming of being part of the Great Gay Ghetto-TRB badges,[2] discos and all. Organic change in Northern Ireland politics and ideology must be rooted in Northern Ireland itself.

The analysis usually accepted by most socialists is that the war being waged in Northern Ireland is a war of 'national liberation' against the forces of British Imperialism. Other issues, like those raised by sexual politics for example, are usually seen as secondary or diversionary to that struggle. As well as disagreeing that the issues of feminism and gay liberation are a digression, I would challenge the notion that the present struggle is a national liberation struggle. Ireland fought against British Imperialism in 1916 and gained independence for the twenty-six counties. Northern Ireland chose to remain 'loyal' because of its closer economic and ideological links with Britain. The fact that it was correct strategy to support the 'national liberation' struggle in 1916 doesn't mean that the same strategy is correct to-day. The operation of imperialism has changed dramatically since then and supporting a united Ireland now is not necessarily any threat to the forces of imperialism that operate in Ireland to-day. A much more significant threat to imperialism would be the development of a united working class politics — a politics which would also pose a threat to the reactionary religious ideologies that inhibit the development of a progressive politics of sexuality.

All political movements in Ireland are forced to take some perspective on the war currently being waged in Ulster. N.I.G.R.A. ignores it as far as possible. Most other 'progressive' groups adopt an 'anti-imperialist' position — identifying British imperialism in the presence of the British troops rather than analysing the economic forces.

The limitations of such sloganistic politics means that there are many divisions and splits within progressive groups. The Women Against

Imperialism group in Belfast split from the Belfast Women's Action Group because they felt the group wasn't giving priority to the 'anti-imperialist struggle'. Feminist groups in Dublin have had many disagreements on the role they should play in relation to the war in Ulster. Even so, women's groups are often better than most. Among other groups there are as many differences as there are a lack of positive solutions. The major political parties are dominated by the ideologies of the respective camps. In Eire not one of the parties, Fianna Gael, Fianna Fáil or Labour would stand out openly against the Catholic Church. In Ulster the Social Democratic and Labour Party depends on the Catholic minority for support. The Provisional Irish Republican Army ('Provos') see all issues as secondary to the 'national liberation struggle'. Its members appear to be no less dominated by Catholic ideology than other nationalist groups e.g. prominent members have been known to declare abortion as murder. The Official Irish Republican Army ('Officials') split from the Provos mainly because they wished to adopt defensive tactics against the British Army and the security forces and aim for a political settlement. It does at least have a programme of women's rights (with no mention of lesbianism or the dreaded abortion issue of course). The rights are mainly employment centred. The Official I.R.A. is influenced by the Communist Party of Ireland which gives support to a women's rights movement in Northern Ireland — often criticised by feminists for its reformism. The Unionist groups — split many times over in the past ten years — are varying degrees of reactionary, with Enoch Powell[3] and Ian Paisley[4] as the vociferous spokespersons for the right. Ian Paisley instigated a 'Save Ulster from Sodomy' campaign in response to the demand for homosexual law reform. The Ulster Defence Association (U.D.A.), a Protestant paramilitary organisation, has no overall progressive politics. The Alliance Party attempts to be Ulster's

---

2. Tom Robinson Band, which produced the gay anthem 'Glad to be Gay'.

3. Enoch Powell (1912–88), English MP who in his later years became a spokesperson for a number of right-wing positions, including loyalism in Ulster. In 1974 he left the British Conservative party and stood as Unionist MP for South Down.

4. Ian Kyle Paisley (1926–   ), leader of the Democratic Unionist party since 1971 and a co-founder and Moderator of the fundamentalist Free Presbyterian Church of Ulster since 1951.

Liberal Party but is even more ineffectual than England's. Support for any of these seems to me, as a lesbian, a socialist, a feminist, a waste of time.

A class politics of Northern Ireland, which would 'dispel the mists of Irish patriotism' (to quote Connolly)[5] has yet to emerge. For a complex of historical and political reasons, Irish Nationalism and Catholic ideology, Ulster Loyalism and Protestant ideology are closely identified in Ireland. As women and as gays we

5. James Connolly (1868–1916), Republican socialist.

can help undermine the ideologies of both reactionary camps by giving support to the struggles for abortion, contraception, divorce and homosexual law reform. We can extend solidarity to Irish lesbians and gay men by exchanging information and support. Taking an interest in Irish culture and history helps undermine the racism of the English towards the Irish. We can combat the media censorship of Irish politics by seeking and circulating as much information as possible. We can raise the issues of sexuality and sexual politics in Ireland. We can challenge any political analysis which sees these issues as diversionary.

NELL McCAFFERTY

(1944–   )

from:
IN THE EYES OF THE LAW
(1981)

[Nell McCafferty's account of two men tried after a sexual encounter in a public toilet reveals that late-nineteenth-century stereotypes about gay male sexuality were still very much in play in the Irish legal system in the 1970s. The men are pathologized, represented as immature, recommended for medical treatment and publicly humiliated. The judge acknowledges and dismisses the fact that Ireland is regressive in its sexual attitudes compared with other European countries. *In the Eyes of the Law* was published in Dublin in 1981.   S.K.]

Consenting Males Bound Over

Dublin District Court 4 was cleared of the public. Two men entered the dock and sat apart, like strangers, before District Justice Ua Donnchadha. The wife of one of the men sat in a corner at the back of the court. Solicitors for both men said they would be pleading guilty.

As the result of a complaint, the prosecuting guard said, he had gone to the public toilets in a certain area. After waiting there a while, the door to one of the cubicles opened and one man came

out. The guard saw a second man still inside the cubicle.

He stopped both accused and spoke to them outside the toilets. At that time they denied everything. Later they admitted all. The guard proposed to read their statements.

'In view of the wife's presence in court, perhaps we need not hear the statements,' one solicitor delicately suggested.

'If the wife does not wish to hear she can go outside,' the justice said. 'This is a public court.'

The wife remained and listened to the two accounts of the men's sexual activities together in the toilet.

Neither had any previous convictions.

A psychiatrist for the younger man, aged 25, was called to testify. The defendant had been referred to him by a priest.

'He has been attending me regularly, five days a week, since this happened,' the doctor said. 'The conclusion I came to is that first he is very sincere . . . I am very slow to come to conclusions about cases which are pending in court.

'But in this case I am convinced of his sincerity. He did not think in fact that he could be treated, and was wrongly advised to this effect by a psychiatric nurse. Depending on his desire, he can be treated . . . with psycho-therapy . . . no medication is being used.'

Was it fair to suggest that he was sexually immature, the solicitor asked.

He was, the doctor agreed.

The justice interjected to wonder why men behaved in this manner. 'It's a completely unnatural performance,' the justice said. 'Normally at his age, young men are more interested in people of the opposite sex.'

There was a total pattern, involving the young man's background, which explained it, the doctor said. 'But he did have a girl-friend and he dreams about girls. However, he lacks self-confidence and feels inferior . . .'

'Would you say that he could have a fruitful relationship with a member of the opposite sex? That he could marry and have children?' the solicitor asked helpfully.

'Yes, indeed,' the doctor said.

The other solicitor went into the case history of the married man. He had married two years ago, and unfortunately his job entailed his being away from home very often. 'The only conclusion I can come to,' said the solicitor, 'is that he was suffering from depression.

'He'd had a few drinks on that evening . . . a conviction would result in the loss of his good job . . . on the strength of the job he and his wife had bought a house with heavy mortgage commitments.

'His wife says they are happily married. She is a very nice person obviously. So is he . . . I think I can assure you, justice, that there will be no repetition of this incident.'

The justice pointed out that the statements implied a prior association. 'They'll have to break up such associations,' the justice warned. 'It's extraordinary how these types seem to gravitate to each other. In other countries, I understand, this is not an offence between adult consenting males.'

'And no-one actually saw them do it,' the solicitor came in.

'Well,' said the justice finally. 'It's against the law here. The law's the law and they broke the law. One answer is prison obviously. If they had been dealt with before a jury they could have gotten penal servitude, strange as it seems to say. In the interest of justice, I will bind them in their own bonds to keep the peace for a year.

'It goes without saying that their association must break up and there must be no repetition of this.'

12 September 1975

DUBLIN LESBIAN AND GAY MEN'S COLLECTIVE

from:
OUT FOR OURSELVES: THE LIVES OF IRISH LESBIANS AND GAY MEN (1986)

[In 1986 the Dublin Lesbian and Gay Men's Collective published a collection of 'coming-out' stories. These constitute a political intervention in that they provide a narrative bridge between 'normative' Irish life and the world of the sexual outcast. Such narratives have been important consciousness-raising moments in many political movements. Published in Dublin by Women's Community Press, 1986.]

Some years ago I was in London with my brother, and went with him to an office where he had to meet someone to finish off some business. As we came out he said 'Sorry, he took hours, you must have been bored out of your mind.' 'Not at all,' I said, 'I was perfectly happy there, he was a gorgeous guy.' My brother, who knew I was gay, looked at me with surprise. 'You know, that's the first time I've understood what being gay is all about.'

Growing up gay is very hard, but more so if you happen to be growing up in rural Ireland. You have a very negative attitude all around you and many people would prefer to lose a gay family member rather than have to face the neighbours. The catholic religion is still a powerful force and because of it many people believe that homo-sexuality is immoral and wrong. I grew up on a farm in Kerry and homosexuality was something you did not discuss. People saw stereotypes and most articles which appeared in the papers helped to reinforce these stereotype images. Two of these that my family believed were that all gays were either screaming queens or else they were child molesters.

Because of my family's attitude towards homo-sexuality I grew up alone and wasn't very close to any of them. How could I love someone who would hate me if they knew the real me? I was always independent and made my mind up about everything. As a child I was very religious and for a while even considered becoming a priest but now I didn't even go to mass. In school I felt very out of place because all of the rest of my friends were interested in was football and I was interested in sex.

With the passage of time, I realised it was my life and if I wanted to be happy then I would have to live it my way. My parents never had great control over me and now they lost me altogether. Even though I wasn't yet eighteen and still at school I started having full sex and staying out all night long. Some Monday mornings I would go straight from my lover's bed to school. Once when I was togging out for P.E.,[1] my teacher and classmates noticed love-bites running from my neck down and disappearing inside the front of my trousers. Later the school principal came up and asked me where I was coming from at 8.00 am. I told him it was none of his business. He warned me about the 'danger of having sex with girls outside marriage' so I told him I'd stop.

1. Physical education.

FRANK McGUINNESS

(1953–)

from:
CARTHAGINIANS (1988)

[This one-act play, set in contemporary Northern Ireland, draws a parallel between Carthage, the ancient city destroyed by Rome, and Derry, a city threatened by sectarian violence. In the following extract we are introduced to Dido,[1] openly and subversively gay. In this text the gay man is explicitly cast as archetypal woman (Queen Dido). McGuinness draws on an interesting tradition of war literature that suggests that sexual intercourse with 'enemies' is a form of loyalty rather than betrayal, because it is a mode of subverting their morale. Romance or sexuality across party lines is one of the most common tropes of 'troubles' writing, but by figuring such encounters as perverse, McGuinness goes beyond the usual banality of the genre. *Carthaginians and Baglady* was published in

London by Faber and Faber in 1988. Carthaginians was first performed at the Peacock Theatre, Dublin in September 1988, directed by Sarah Pia Anderson.]

Characters

MAELA, *in her forties*
GRETA, *in her thirties*
SARAH, *in her thirties*
DIDO, *in his twenties*

Scene 1: . . . DIDO *enters, pushing a battered pram, wearing a pair of Doc Marten[2] boots, dyed pale blue, an 'Arm the Unemployed' T-shirt and a long pink scarf.*
    'Oh, seek the spot where I will be lying,
        And kneel and say an Ave[3] there for me.'[4]
(*Silence. The women look at him*)
        Yes, heads, still here?

1. According to Virgil and Ovid, Dido (Elissa), founder and ruler of Carthage, killed herself after the departure of her lover, Aeneas, founder of Rome. This was supposed to be the origin of the great antipathy between the rival empires. A long literary and antiquarian tradition traced Irish descent from Carthage, while the English were supposed to be descendants of Romans.

2. Heavy lace-up boots that were, in the 1980s, one of the badges of youth culture.
3. *Ave Maria*, Hail Mary.
4. He is singing 'Danny Boy', a ballad also known as 'The Londonderry Air', and as a semi-official anthem for Northern Ireland.

MAELA: Hello, Dido? How are you, son?

DIDO: Surviving, Maela. How are yous?

MAELA: Grand. Surviving.

SARAH: What's on your T-Shirt, Dido?

(DIDO *displays his chest*)

MAELA: 'Arm the Unemployed'.

DIDO: Solidarity, soul sister.

(DIDO *raises his fist*)

MAELA: You never did a day's work in your life.

DIDO: It's the thought that counts.

GRETA: Where the hell were you?

DIDO: What do you mean, 'where the hell was I'?

GRETA: You were supposed to be here at ten o'clock. It's now half-twelve. I ran out of fags an hour ago and Sarah's tongue is a mile long waiting for her coffee.

DIDO: Listen, wagon, I'm not running a charity service. Business, baby. I've got other commitments. Count yourself lucky I'm here. I had to fight my way to this graveyard through three army checkpoints. I could have been detained. There could have been an assault.

MAELA: What did they threaten to do to you, Dido?

DIDO: It was more what I threatened to do to them. No luck though. No score. I think they were on to me as a health hazard. One of them was nice. Blond. From Newcastle.[5] Interested in football.

GRETA: How can you chat up Brits?

DIDO: Greta, you know that my ambition in life is to corrupt every member of Her Majesty's forces serving in Northern Ireland.

GRETA: Jesus, that should be difficult.

DIDO: Mock on. It's my bit for the cause of Ireland's freedom. When the happy day of withdrawal comes, I'll be venerated as a national hero. They'll build a statue to me. I'm going to insist that it's in the nude with a blue plaque in front of my balls. (*He holds an imaginary plaque in front of himself*) This has been erected to the war effort of Dido Martin, patriot and poof.

5. Newcastle upon Tyne.

IRISH COUNCIL FOR CIVIL LIBERTIES

from:
EQUALITY NOW FOR LESBIANS AND GAY MEN
(1990)

[In January 1990 the Irish Council for Civil Liberties published a study calling for the decriminalization of homosexuality in the Republic of Ireland entitled *Equality Now for Lesbians and Gay Men*. The following is an extract from the section 'Prejudice in the Supreme Court of Ireland' and deals with the right to privacy for lesbians and gay men. The Norris case referred to is the action taken by the Dublin academic David Norris against the Irish government in 1984, contending that the criminalization of homosexuality was an infringement on his human rights. He lost his case at the Irish High Court and Supreme Court but won at the European Court of Human Rights (see Volume v, pp. 331–2, 332–3.]

Privacy, Freedom of Intimate Association and Self-Expression

The High Court and Supreme Court in *Norris* also failed to appreciate the plaintiff's arguments in relation to the right to privacy and freedom of association and expression in the sexual context. The right to privacy, as a constitutional civil liberty, was inferred by the Supreme Court in *McGee v Attorney General*.[1] There the Supreme Court upheld the right of a married couple to import contraceptives for use within their marriage. In *Norris*, both the High Court and a majority of the Supreme Court reject the claim that article 40.3 guaranteed a right to privacy encompassing gay sexual activity and the claim

1. See subsection 'The Law and Private Life in the Republic of Ireland', edited by Alpha Connelly, Volume v, pp. 335–8.

that the constitutional guarantees of expression and association fortified such a right.

The judges, we submit, missed the point that at the heart of the privacy doctrine developed by the Supreme Court in *McGee* lies a right to freedom of sexual autonomy, intimate association and self-expression, and that the implications of the values which give this liberty its most coherent sense cannot be stifled at the boundaries of formal marriage or procreational sex. The values involved include: the value of being intimately involved with another person; the value of caring for and being committed to another, recognising that to be human is to need to love and be loved; the value of intimacy, embodying the ideas of sanctuary, secrecy and enjoyment of friendship; and the value of self-identification or expression, involving the shaping of an individual's sense of his or her own identity. It is the autonomous choice to form and maintain an intimate association that allows one fully to realise the values that give substance to the right.

In our view the *McGee* decision should have been read by the *Norris* court as exemplifying the principle that every individual has the right, consistent with a like right or liberty for all, to be free from unwarranted interference with his or her decision on matters of sexual autonomy and intimate association. A mature person's choice of an adult sexual partner would seem clearly to be a matter of the utmost private and intimate concern.

BRENDÍ McCLENAGHAN

(*c.* 1958–   )

INVISIBLE COMRADES: GAYS AND LESBIANS IN THE STRUGGLE (1991)

[Brendí McClenaghan was sentenced to five life terms of imprisonment for republican offences in 1978. He wrote this piece while he was serving time in the Maze prison. In a letter to the editor of *An Glór Gafa* in 1994 he writes of himself: 'I am the second youngest of a family of nine children and I was brought up in an area of North Belfast called "Ardoyne". I have been a member of the Republican movement since I was nine, and I am now in the seventeenth year of imprisonment. I came out as a gay man in the mid 1980s, after many years of both knowing and hiding from others the fact that I was gay. I believe passionately that Republicans must recognise that the struggle for freedom of our people and our country must be inclusive to all people.' This article was published in the prisoner's magazine, *An Glór Gafa: The Captive Voice*, vol. 3, no. 3, in 1991.]

Gay men and lesbian women have been involved in the struggle for national liberation and independence as long as any other section of our people. You might claim that you have never known nor met a gay man or a lesbian woman but you have met one or more — today, last week, last year, 22 years ago — for they have been there among us, in struggle alongside you. The primary reason you have not noticed them is that the prevailing culture in our society in relation to sexuality in general and to homosexuality in particular, compels gays/lesbians to conform, thus their sexuality becomes invisible.

Women as a whole were once virtually invisible in the national struggle. In recent years, however, they have argued forcefully that women's liberation must be an integral part of the struggle. In order that the concept of women's liberation be recognised and accepted as an equal, valid component, women comrades confronted their male counterparts with the contradictions of sexist words and actions. While there is still a long way to go to overcome male chauvinism and sexism, at least today women have succeeded in putting feminist issues on the agenda of the anti-imperialist fight.

It is now time, indeed long past time, to open up debate among republicans on the issue of gays and lesbians, our oppression and its causes, and on our right to be visible equal partners. I believe that national liberation by its very nature incorporates gay/lesbian liberation, as an integral part, and it is only through open debate leading to an understanding of gay/lesbian experience that our equality in struggle can be made a reality.

Social and economic oppression is something the people in the whole of Ireland have suffered, and in the North the weight of British occupation is an added burden. As gays/lesbians we are doubly oppressed for we have had to endure further oppression within our families, local communities and within the Republican movement because of our sexuality. This manifests itself in many ways and affects every part of our lives.

The state's laws deny equality in marriage, education, social welfare, employment, adoption, life insurance . . . the list is endless. The state denies gay/lesbian relationships the same recognition as heterosexual relationships under the civil law. While British law allows for consensual relationships between men over 21 the position in the 26 counties remains that gay men of any age are liable to imprisonment because of their sexuality — and this in spite of the fact that the Dublin government has accepted, in theory, the ruling of the European Court of Human Rights that present legislation is in breach of the rights of gay men.[1] Both the British and Irish states have appalling records in the area of gay/lesbian rights, especially when compared to other countries in Europe. The legal age of consent, for example, is 16 in Portugal, Switzerland and Holland.

The legal status of gays/lesbians reflects attitudes in the wider society. All the Churches promote traditional, stereotypical views in relation to matters like contraception, abortion, sex education for young people and the rights of women in marriage. The Catholic Church in particular seeks to maintain its control over our lives and our sexuality, and it has spawned organisations such as Family Solidarity whose views on homosexuality range from the patronising and arrogant to the downright chilling:

'If homosexual acts are legalised, the likelihood is that this will be interpreted as a major reversal in social policy, as a recognition by society that for those who are so inclined, engaging in these unnatural, unhealthy and immoral acts is now to be seen as a right . . . [Legislative reform] would send shock waves through every part of society, the structure of marriage and the family would be interfered with, the rights of children and their parents violated, and the freedom and autonomy of religious institutions and schools would be seriously breached.' (*Family Solidarity News*, Spring 1991).

In short, the end of civilisation as we know it because of men loving men and women loving women! Such attitudes, which are based on intolerance, misinformation and fear, serve only to demonise gays and lesbians in the minds of the Irish people, evoking images of us as depraved men and women wreaking havoc throughout society.

While oppression from the state and the institutions of society adversely affects the quality of life for gays/lesbians, there are other forms of oppression which are as much, if not more, detrimental. Gays and lesbians face oppression daily from family, comrades, neighbours and friends due to the irrational fear of and deep prejudice against homosexuality.

The most direct expressions of such homophobia are insults, derision and threatened or actual violence. Indirect expressions are sometimes harder to pin down but are nonetheless just as offensive: the pressures to 'be what you are but keep it secret and don't rock the boat'. This is nothing short of moral blackmail as it is usually accompanied by comments like 'What will the family think?', or, 'It will harm the Movement/struggle.' Thus gays/lesbians are forced into invisibility within both the community and the Republican Movement, and consequently within the struggle.

This is a situation which must be confronted not only by gays and lesbians but by everyone who espouses the ideals of republicanism. 'We declare that we desire our country to be ruled with the principles of liberty, equality and justice for all,' states the 1919 Democratic Programme

---

1. In 1993 the Irish government finally responded to the ruling of the European Court of Human Rights with the Criminal Law (Sexual Offences) Act, which provided for equality between heterosexuals and homosexuals.

of Dáil Eireann. Republicans who have always been to the fore on the issues of justice and equality must begin to recognise the oppression of gays/lesbians and to identify with their needs. Republicans must acknowledge and resolve the contradictions in their attitude and behaviour which add to that oppression.

Our participation in the national liberation struggle is not a detraction from its nature and objectives; on the contrary, our involvement is a reinforcement that the struggle is indeed about the freedom and equality of all who are oppressed. No one should feel excluded. Gay men and lesbian women, especially gay/lesbian comrades within the Republican Movement, must begin the process of full integration and acceptance into the struggle by becoming more visible and making our voices heard on issues that affect us. The prejudices of others can be resolved only by confronting them and by exposing the oppression that those prejudices give rise to, with the resultant fear, isolation and violence. The experience of such feelings is not imaginary; they are a daily reality for gays and lesbians in the Bogside, Falls, Monaghan, Dungannon, Ardoyne, Ballymun, Crossmaglen and every other town and village in Ireland.

The key to gay/lesbian liberation lies in the success of the national liberation struggle. Gays and lesbians must be a visible part of that struggle so that everyone will recognise that we fought to end the oppression of all. This vital necessity is stressed by those involved in other wars of liberation.

Simon Nkoli, a gay activist involved in the Delmas treason trial in South Africa in 1986, has this to say:

'There are lots of gay activists involved in political organisations, but because of the pressure put upon the gay and lesbian community, we are afraid to come out.

"What will people think if they know I'm a gay person? I'd better fight against apartheid in a hidden way." The danger of that is that when South Africa is liberated we as gay people will seem never to have taken part in liberating our people. What will we say if people ask, "What did you do to bring about change in this country, where were you during the battle?" We'd have to come back to them and say, "we were with you but we didn't want you to know we were there." That would be a foolish answer.'

Gays and lesbians need to seek out the strength and support of each other, and of those around us who are receptive to the cause of our liberation. There is a need for gay/lesbian comrades to discuss together the issues that affect our lives and which retard participation in the national liberation struggle. In isolation we stand alone and remain invisible, continuing to be oppressed not only by the state but within our own communities.

Through mutual reinforcement and support we can break down the isolation that each feels and discard the cloak of invisibility that has for too long made a misery of, and destroyed, the lives of gays and lesbians. Together we can articulate the relevance of gay/lesbian liberation, confront the homophobia that faces us and attempt to resolve it through dialogue and discussion. This can only be based on logic and facts, not on the myths and mistruths deliberately fed to our people by those who seek to maintain control over every aspect of our lives: social, political, cultural, economic and sexual.

Everyone has a role to play in the struggle to end all oppression. Those who are themselves oppressed have an obligation to ensure that they do not contribute in any way to the oppression of others. To do otherwise is to deny the essence of the struggle for 'liberty, equality and justice for all'.

CATHAL Ó SEARCAIGH

(1956–)

from:
AN BEALACH 'NA BHAILE
(1993)

[Cathal Ó Searcaigh's love poems at once challenge the perceived conservatism of modern Gaelic culture and revive possible homoerotic traditions in Gaelic poetry. In 'Ceann Dubh Dílis', translated here by Gabriel Fitzmaurice, he sets up an explicit opposition between eroticism and religion, while in 'Laoi Cumainn', translated by Gabriel Rosenstock, he uses the figure of the hero Cú Chulainn, heavily if unselfconsciously eroticized during the Gaelic revival, as a figure through which to associate the sexual male body with the northern landscape (see Máirín Ní Dhonnchadha's Introduction to 'Courts and Coteries I, 900–1600', pp. 293–303). This latter move inverts a traditional association of the female body with the Irish landscape and therefore challenges some of the essentializing distinctions between male and female frequently made in Irish literature and criticism.]

IR Ceann Dubh Dílis

A cheann dubh dílis dílis dílis
d'fhoscail ár bpóga créachtaí Chríosta arís;
ach ná foscail do bhéal, ná sceith uait an scéal:
tá ár ngrá ar an taobh thuathal den tsoiscéal.

Tá cailíní na háite seo cráite agat, a ghrá,
's iad ag iarraidh thú a bhréagadh is a
    mhealladh gach lá;
ach b'fhearr leatsa bheith liomsa i mbéal an
    uaignis
'mo phógadh, 'mo chuachadh is mo thabhairt
    chun aoibhnis.

Is leag do cheann dílis dílis dílis,
leag do cheann dílis i m'ucht a dhíograis;
ní fhosclód mo bhéal, ní sceithfead an scéal
ar do shonsa shéanfainn gach soiscéal.

TR My Blackhaired Love

My blackhaired love, my dear, dear, dear,
Our kiss re-opens Christ's wounds here;
But close your mouth, don't spread the word:
We offend the Gospels with our love.

You plague the local belles, my sweet,
They attempt to coax you with deceit
But you'd prefer my lonely kiss,
You hugging me to bring to bliss.

Lay your head my dear, dear, dear,
Lay your head on my breast here;
I'll close my mouth, no detail break —
I'd deny the Gospels for your sake.

Laoi Cumainn

Anocht agus tú sínte síos le mo thaobh
a chaoin mhic an cheanna, do chorp
teann téagartha, aoibh na hóige ort,
    anseo tá mé sábhailte
cuachta go docht faoi scáth d'uchta:
sleánna cosanta do sciathán
    mo chrioslú go dlúth
óir is tusa mo laoch, an curadh caol cruaidh
a sheasann idir mé agus uaigneas tíoránta na
    hoíche.

Is tusa mo laoch, mo thréan is mo neart,
mo Chú na gCleas agus níl fhios agam i gceart
cé acu an luan laoich é seo
    atá ag teacht ó do chneas
nó gríos gréine. Ach is cuma. Tá mé buíoch as
    an teas,
as na dealraitheacha deasa ó do ghrua
    a ghealaíonn mo dhorchadas,
as an dóigh a ndéanann tú an t-uaigneas
a dhiongbháil domh le fíochmhaireacht do ghrá.

Anocht má tá cath le fearadh agat, a ghrá,
bíodh sé anseo i measc na bpiliúr:
Craith do sciath agus gread do shleá,
    beartaigh do chlaíomh
go beacht. Lig gáir churaidh as do bhráid.
Luífidh mé anseo ag baint sásamh súl
    as a bhfuil den fhear
ag bogadaí ionat, a dhúil, go ndéanfaidh tú do
    bhealach féin
a bhearnú chugam fríd pluid agus piliúr.

Agus is toil liom, a mhacaoimh óig
gurb anseo ar léana mo leapa
a dhéanfá le barr feabhais
   do mhacghníomhartha macnais,
gurb anseo i ngleannta is i gcluanta
mo cholla, a thiocfá i dteann is i dtreise
   is go mbeadh gach ball
do mo bhallaibh, ag síorthabairt grá duit
ar feadh síoraíocht na hoíche seo.

Anocht cead ag an domhan ciorclú
leis na beo is leis na mairbh:
Anso i dtearmann dlúth na bpóg
   tá an saol ina stad:
Anseo i ndún daingean do bhaclainne
tá cúl ar chlaochlú. I bhfad uainn
   mairgí móra na tsaoil:
na tíortha is na treabha a dhéanfadh cocstí
de cheithre creasa na cruinne lena gcuid
   cogaíochta.

Anocht, a mhacaoimh óig, bainimis fad saoil
as gach cogar, gach caoinamharc, gach cuimilt.
Amárach beidh muid gafa mar is gnáth
   i gcasadh cinniúnach ne beatha,
i gcealg is i gcluain na Cinniúna.
Amárach díolfar fiacha na fola is na feola
   ach anocht, a fhir óig álainn,
tá muid i gciorcal draíochta an ghrá.
Ní bhuafaidh codladh orainn ná crá.

Hound of Ulster[1]

Now, tonight, stretched by my side
delightful lad, your strong
sinewy limbs smile youthfully,
   here I'm safe a while
squirrelling up to your trunk:
your limbs are swift spears
   fending off the world
my champion, proud sleek warrior
you man the gap between me and night's tyranny.

My solace, my defence, my fortress,
Playful Hound, how can I tell

is it the valour-halo
   which emanates from your skin
or sun-glow? No matter, I'm grateful for the
   warmth,
those darting rays from your cheek
   that illuminate the obscurity;
how you match my wretchedness
with the savagery of your love.

Tonight, sweet soul, should you declare battle
let it be here among pillows:
let your shield shudder, aim your spear,
   let your sword be ready
and true. Shout aloud your war-cry.
Here I'll lie, my eyes entranced
   as your manliness
moves and — darling — I lie in the breach,
in the theatre of linen.

And how I desire, nimble Hound,
that here on this white plain
you should surpass yourself
   in thrust and swagger:
here in the recesses and glens
of my body come with your assault
   so that every rock and fern
cries out in sweetest anguish
the long night through.

Let the world on its axis turn
with all the living and the dead;
here in the sanctuary of lips
   our world ends.
Here in the citadel of your arms
time has run out. The world's misery
   an aeon away,
nations and tribes, fighting it out,
all day, every day.

Tonight, Hound of Ulster, let each whisper,
each glance, each touch be for ever.
Tomorrow we shall be, again, like all others,
   fulfilling our fateful rounds —
the deceit and treachery of it all!
Tomorrow the debt of flesh and blood must be
      paid,
   but tonight, my lone warrior,
the chalice is moist at the brim
And — miserable sleep! — stay away from him.

1. Cú Chulainn, hero of the early Irish Ulster cycle (see Volume I,
   pp. 1–59), whose name literally means 'hound of Culann', was also
   known as the hound of Ulster.

EMMA DONOGHUE

(1969–   )

from:
CAUSING A STIR: AN INTERVIEW BY LIAM FAY
(1994)

[Emma Donoghue represents a younger generation of Irish lesbian feminists who benefited from the women's liberation and gay liberation movements of the 1960s to 1980s and feel not only able to 'come out' but to speak about sexual desire and sexual practices more openly, if anything, than their straight contemporaries. This interview was published in *Hot Press* on 9 February 1994.   S.K.]

L.F.: In a recent *Sunday Times* interview . . . Camille Paglia[1] . . . launched a full-frontal attack on the act of lesbian love-making which she described as 'frustrating' and lacking in the 'wild', 'primitive' and 'brute animal quality' of heterosexual shagging. 'Bodies fit together in heterosexuality,' she asserted. 'It's so tiring, making love with women, it takes forever . . .'

'I think she's a nut case,' responds Emma Donoghue. '. . . If she thinks that all lesbian sex is slow and frustrating then she's not meeting the lesbians that I'm meeting . . .'

'Yes, heterosexual bodies fit together in the sense that you can put a penis in a vagina, but that doesn't achieve all that much on its own. I'm biased here (*laughs*) but in terms of the details of technique, lesbians are often very imaginative because there's no one thing they've been traditionally told to do. There tends to be a huge amount of variety and experimentation. We listen to each other's bodies more, I suppose, because we haven't been brought up to believe that sex is one particular act.

'Camille is also on record as saying that lesbians are sexually inert — I just don't know where she gets these ideas. She's peddling stereotypes, that gay men are exciting whereas gay women are hung up on their mothers all the time. That just doesn't connect with my experience at all. She makes these statements, like "Lesbians don't have one-night stands". *Rubbish!* Lots of them do. Maybe not as many of us as heterosexuals, but do we judge the excitement of sexuality in terms of how many one-night stands we have? I've met every variety of lesbian — the ones in long-term couples, the ones who are having one-night stands all the time, the ones who rarely have sex, the lot.' . . .

'I think we're more honest about the number of relationships we have[.]' . . . 'I think you might look at a heterosexual couple and see that they've been married for twenty years but you don't know all the affairs they've been having. Whereas we would tend to say, well, yes, I had a lover then and another lover then and another lover then. And also, we don't reproach people as much for having serial relationships. We don't see it as failure. If I break up after a couple of years with someone, I don't see it as a marriage that went wrong. I see it as a few good years with someone from which I learnt a lot and it was a good thing.

'There are pressures on us socially that make it hard to have very long-term relationships because we don't get things like tax benefits, all those things that heterosexual relationships get wound around. And again, we don't have that many role models. You see plenty of husbands and wives on chat shows but you don't see long-term couples in the media much.

'Anyway, I don't think that we necessarily want any equivalent of heterosexual marriage. And I feel it's quite healthy, this code of serial monogamy or serial relationships even. Quite a few lesbians don't even want to be monogamous. They say it's an unnatural life to try and only be sexual with one person in the entire world. I'd say it's serial monogamy is what actually appeals to me.'

---

1. Camille Paglia (1947–   ), a controversial American academic, journalist and broadcaster; although Paglia is a self-identified lesbian, she is noted for her critiques of lesbian and feminist culture and politics.

JONI CRONE

from:
LESBIANS: THE LAVENDER
WOMEN OF IRELAND (1995)

[Joni Crone argues for the maintenance of a firm distinction between the experiences of gay men and lesbians, as they are represented in political movements and in theoretical discussions. She describes how gay men have benefited hugely from the power and privilege of masculinity, even if they have in some areas of their lives experienced discrimination and repression. For Crone, it is important for lesbians in Ireland to align themselves with straight women. She writes as an activist for whom the frequent use of 'we' is empowering. This piece was published in *Lesbian and Gay Visions of Ireland: Towards the Twenty-first Century*, edited by Íde O'Carroll and Eoin Collins (London: Cassell, 1995).   S.K.]

Lesbian women have played a part in every liberation movement in Ireland over the past twenty years, but we have seldom been sung about, written about or given any kind of prominence. Our contributions have gone unrecognized because we have been content to work behind the scenes. As a native Irish lesbian who has loved through two decades of lesbian activism, I would like to bring our achievements out of the closet, to show why I can still say in the 1990s: 'I am Lesbian and I am proud.'

The lesbian movement in Ireland has suffered because our energies have been divided between the Women's Liberation Movement, the anti-nuclear Greenpeace movement and the gay movement. Gay men have mostly been active on their own behalf in relation to law reform . . . The story of liberation for lesbian women in Ireland, however, is very different. It is a story which has remained, of necessity, hidden from the public eye. A story of an underground minority, a subculture whose members have been unwilling or unable to court publicity, because to do so may have invited violence, rape, or even death. These are the hard facts of lesbian life in Ireland. They are not easy to live with but I believe it's time they were stated and acknowledged.

I have no wish to underplay the difficulty gay men encounter in 'coming out', or the suffering they have endured publicly and privately. What I want to emphasize is that the experience of coming out in Ireland is very different for a lesbian and for a gay man. There are times when our territories overlap, when we appear to have common ground — on law reform, for instance, or health issues or gay community centres — but the vast majority of lesbians and gay men experience life very differently. This is not due to any lack of solidarity but to our gender differences.

'Coming out' to ourselves as lesbians, to our friends and family is a complex process. Lesbians are not strange, extraordinary or exotic women. We are ordinary women, and as ordinary women, reared in heterosexual families, we have been socialized into a mothering role as helpers, assistants and carers. 'Coming out' as an Irish lesbian involves undoing much of our conditioning. It means recognizing the external and internal barriers which prevent us taking charge of our lives, and resolving to become autonomous human beings, independent human beings with a right to life, a right to love, a right to live free from harassment in our work and our homes, a right to choose who we love, how we love, and if or when we want to become parents.

These rights for men have been recognized for centuries. Heterosexual and gay men have created democratic institutions and interminable legal and political systems to protect their basic human rights. But women have had no part in framing the laws that oppress us or protect us because for centuries we were considered, in law, to be men's property. As wives and daughters we have been valued primarily for our capacity to be 'the vessels which carried the seed', as Aristotle[1] taught. We have been valued solely for our bodies, the means to ensure the reproduction of males.

The abortion debate is very much a 'live' issue in Ireland, after twenty years and more of political campaigning . . . The furore around granting women — heterosexual and lesbian women — the right to say no to pregnancy is so intense because it goes to the heart of the power relations of men over women.

---

1. Aristotle (384–322 BC), Greek philosopher, pupil of Plato.

GERRY STEMBRIDGE

(1959–   )

from:
THE GAY DETECTIVE (1996)

[The play is set in Dublin in 1993, the year that homo-sexuality was decriminalized in the Republic of Ireland. It examines the way in which sexuality functions as a secret in Irish society — and the consequent forms of blackmail thus engendered — and looks at state surveillance of sexuality. Stembridge is most provocative in his insistence that the homosexual is within society and its institutions — not an outsider to be either alienated or glamorized as a marginal figure. First produced at the Project Arts Centre, Dublin, in February 1996.]

Characters

PAT, *the gay detective*
SUPERINTENDENT BEAR, *a senior officer in the Gardaí*

Act 1

PAT *speaks the first line of the play in blackout. Then the lights snap on and we find him sitting on a bed holding* GINGER.

PAT: I am the Gay Detective. (*Lights snap on*) Remember it was you called me that. And as usual you were right. Even now, when it shouldn't matter any more, I'm still at it. Sifting. Turning facts and memories over and over in my head. Of course I'm hoping that my investigations will prove me innocent; that it was just events and pressures and . . . well the times we live in, drove me inevitably to do the things I did.

But instead all I ever see is one word hanging there in front of my eyes. Betrayal.

So — I was wondering — would you mind if I tell you the truth, love? Burden you? Not looking for forgiveness or anything, I know that's OK. But for me. So I can get used to it. Get in lots of practice. Because when you're gone — I'll need something to hold onto, won't I? (PAT *begins to put on his uniform.* SUPERINTENDENT BEAR *enters*) So . . . I'll try and tell you everything. Things you never knew before. I'll be as honest as I can I

promise. About the only thing I'm sure of is where to start. That's easy. That was memorable. The first time my work collided with my life. (*To* BEAR.) Superintendent Bear.

BEAR: Sergeant, how are you?

PAT: I'm fine sir.

BEAR: I'm sure you are, I'm sure you are. You're doing good work Sergeant, we've been watching. We've been impressed. Do you like the sound of that?

PAT: Impressed? — I definitely like the sound of that.

BEAR: Good, good. I'd have said now, you were the sort of fellow who'd be after promotion. Would you fancy that — promotion?

PAT: Yes. I do. I would.

BEAR: Well you're not there yet, but you're nearly. I wanted you to know that. That's why I gave you a shout to come here today. I wanted you to see that we're paying attention. I asked to see you to reassure you. Not that I'd say you were worried, you're not the worrying type are you?

PAT: No I'm not. I wasn't worried sir — I'm only at it two years.

BEAR: But you've made an impression. (*Looks at his file*) Logical . . . good concentration . . . stylish approach, that's an unusual one — that's not a comment I often hear about young Gardaí — stylish. I must check who made that one. Anyway so on and so forth, all very complimentary, so I decided I should give you a bit of a gee up — let you know that we think highly of you and see you going places, down the road, round the bend . . .

PAT: Thank you sir. That's . . . that's fantastic.

BEAR: Yes. Good. Now, do you know Detective Sergeant Cat?

PAT: No sir.

BEAR: Not his real name of course — he's one of our undercover lads, about the same age as yourself, a good enough lad in his way. Of course he wouldn't be around here very often.

PAT: (*Puzzled*) Ah . . . no.

BEAR: He was telling us he bumped into you.

PAT: Oh?

BEAR: He was working you see and he bumped into you — well as I understand it, you started talking to him, but he was busy keeping an eye on a certain party, so he didn't really have time to chew the fat with you. But he remembered you all right, which I suppose is a compliment of sorts.

PAT: I'm sorry sir — I don't remember this at all.

BEAR: You don't. I see. Well sure why should you, I've hardly given you enough information. So now . . . what's your next question Sergeant?

PAT: Sorry?

BEAR: Your next question — I've told you someone met you, and you can't recall it, so if you want more information you need to ask me more questions — so what's the next question?

PAT: Ah — did I speak with him for long?

BEAR: Arra Sergeant — You can do better than that.

PAT: Well — you see sir, I don't really know the point of the inquiry.

BEAR: You want promotion Sergeant. You want to be a detective. Show me your talent. Ask me the next logical question.

(*Pause.* PAT *is very nervous*)

PAT: Where . . . where did I meet him?

BEAR: Good. In a club. Go on.

PAT: What was the name of the club?

BEAR: Let me see. (*Checks his file*) Shaft. (*Pause*)

BEAR: The thing is Sergeant — he was there working, but you weren't. I also understand that you complimented him on his eyes. Do you remember this conversation now?

PAT: No sir. I honestly don't.

BEAR: So are you telling me it didn't happen?

PAT: No sir. It's just I would have had many such conversations. (*Sigh*) What can I say sir. It's true. I was in —

BEAR: Shh. I haven't asked you any more questions. You don't have to answer what you're not asked. Just be very, very careful Sergeant won't you? I do want to be able to promote you. So in the name of Jesus don't be doing anything that'll spoil that. You know the law don't you?

PAT: Yes.

BEAR: Well now even though we mightn't enforce it — it's still the law isn't it?

PAT: Yes.

BEAR: Grand. Good luck so. And remember — you're one of our young stars. I mean that.

ÉIBHEAR WALSHE

(1962–   )

from:
SEX, NATION AND DISSENT
IN IRISH WRITING (1997)

[The following extract comes from the introduction to the first collection of essays in literary criticism in Ireland from a 'queer' perspective, edited and introduced by Éibhear Walshe, who has been a leading figure in the development of queer theory in Ireland. There are revisionary essays on established figures such as Oscar Wilde, Eva Gore-Booth, Elizabeth Bowen, Molly Keane, Kate O'Brien and Cathal Ó Searcaigh, as well as essays on new themes in drama and cinema. Almost as important as the revisionary impulse in the collection is the question of how far sexual dissidence has informed and critiqued certain national projects. The book was published in Cork by Cork University Press in 1997. Footnotes are by the author.]

Post-colonial countries like Ireland have particular difficulty with the real presence of the homoerotic. Colonialism itself generates a gendered power relationship and, inevitably, casts the colonising power as masculine and dominant and the colonised as feminine and passive. One of the consequences of this resistance to the imperial was an increased unease with the shifting and 'unstable' nature of sexual difference, and so a narrowing of gender hierarchies ensues. In Irish cultural discourse, silencing sexual difference became imperative because of a supposed link between homosexuality and enfeebled, 'feminised' masculinity. The post-colonial struggle to escape the influence of the colonising power became a struggle to escape the gendered relation of male colonist to female colonised. Therefore the post-colonial culture could not permit any public, ideological acknowledgement of the actuality of the sexually 'other'. The post-colonial theorist Ashis Nandy, in his study *The Intimate Enemy*, argues convincingly that the colonial relation is inevitably and profoundly gendered.[1] In this particular context, his thesis could be extended in this manner: the homosexual is assumed to be a transgendered 'pretend' woman and the lesbian to be an unsexed 'pretend' man, and thus lesbian and gay identity is acutely threatening and unsettling within any post-colonial culture. For a nation 'coming of age' the lesbian and gay sensibility must be edited out, shut up.

Ireland provides a striking example of this kind of post-colonial censorship. (For a full historical account of gay law reform in Ireland see Kieran Rose's excellent *Diverse Communities: The Evolution of Lesbian and Gay Politics in Ireland.*[2]) In his study 'Homosexual People and the Christian Churches in Ireland', David Norris argues persuasively that the history of prosecution of same-sex desire in Ireland is intertwined with the history of colonisation.[3] The moment when homosexuality stopped being a sin and became a crime took place in 1510 under Henry VIII as part of a repressive Tudor policy of centralisation and colonisation. British law was responsible for the continued criminalisation of Irish gay men, but, ironically, it was de Valera's[4] pro-family, pro-Catholic Irish constitution of 1937 that allowed a court case to be taken by David Norris against the Irish government for discrimination on the grounds of sexual orientation.

A distrust of the 'unmanly' homosexual resulted in a complete obliteration of the homoerotic from within nationalist discourse. In much the same way, Connolly's[5] socialism and the Gore-Booths'[6] feminism became subaltern in the Irish Free State. The tenuous nature of national identity necessitated a denial of difference, with its incipient threat of dissidence, and thus same-sex desire continued to be criminalised in Ireland long after Britain had decriminalised homosexual acts between consenting adults.

1. Ashis Nandy, writer on post-colonialism, psychology and cricket, director of Delhi's Centre for the Study of Developing Societies. *The Intimate Enemy* (New Delhi: Oxford University Press, 1984).
2. Kieran Rose, *Diverse Communities: The Evolution of Lesbian and Gay Politics in Ireland* (Cork: Cork University Press, 1994).
3. David Norris, 'Homosexual People and the Christian Churches in Ireland', *Crane Bag*, vol. 5, no. 2 (1981).

4. Eamon de Valera (1882–1975), Irish Taoiseach and later President.
5. James Connolly (1868–1916), labour leader executed after the 1916 Easter Rising.
6. Eva Gore-Booth (1870–1926) and her sister Constance Markievicz (1868–1927); the former is associated with socialist feminism and worked with the industrial working class in Manchester, while the latter — the first woman elected to the Westminster parliament — channelled her feminism through Irish nationalism.

ROZ COWMAN

(1942–   )

from:
LOST TIME: THE SMELL AND TASTE OF CASTLE T. (1997)

[This is an extract from an essay on the writers Edith Œ. Somerville and Martin Ross which appeared in *Sex, Nation and Dissent in Irish Writing* (Cork: Cork University Press, 1997). Cowman is sceptical as to whether the partners had a physically erotic relationship, but she uses their letters to explore what the relationship meant to them in their terms and also to contextualize their friendship in terms of the material condition affecting women's lives in late-nineteenth-century Ireland. She goes on from this passage to develop a reading of the fiction in terms of a displacement of the erotic onto landscape and memory. Whether or not one agrees with Cowman's conclusion in the specific instance, her essay offers one model for how one might develop queer readings of pre-twentieth-century writers, while a later piece by Lucy McDiarmid on Roger Casement (pp. 1075–7) offers a very different strategy. Footnotes are by the author.   S.K.]

Because Somerville and Ross lived within a concentrated family network, and at the centre of a complex social system, we have to evaluate their relationship, their sense of self-definition and personal identity, in the context of their extended family and social circle . . .

If we examine the relationship from internal evidence, it can be seen that their way of life in nineteenth-century Anglo-Ireland would render unlikely any physical sexuality between them. There is a deep and exclusive love implicit in the letters, and also a series of uneasy references to sexuality, especially on Martin's part . . .

Martin's concept of sex as the central physical point of life isolates it from emotional, spiritual and erotic potential. She encourages Edith to be the judge of acceptable sexual references — referring to a countrywoman speaking of 'one child and the invoice of another,' she asks Edith: 'Is this very improper? I feel it is, but I'm not sure.'[1] In a letter written on 6 September 1889, a good example of the extraordinary physical toughness and sexual prudery peculiar to her, Martin describes a rare experience of horror:

> I looked through *Nana*, Zola's book.[2] I feel ashamed of having opened it . . . I am sure you despise me a good deal, and I certainly think it is not a book to read as there is no use in getting familiarised with bad things . . . I thought I should feel better if I told you.[3]

Then she goes on to describe the circumstances in which she has read the book:

> A very weird room — on the ground floor — with an earthy smell . . . a horrid long dark passage leading to the door and nothing else . . . in the top of the door glass put in . . . so the door and passage seem to stare with those square eyes . . . Mrs Persse assured me they [rats] couldn't get into the room but the noise they made was intolerable, and I slept very badly . . . I wasn't frightened, just bored by them.

> Neuralgia, the earth smell, and rats over the ceilings and down the walls . . . and Zola's dreadful facts streaming and reeking in one's mind.[4]

In this poignant letter we can see the strange contradictions — the noise of rats kept her awake, she is fully aware of the sinister aspect of the room, but it is the horror and the sexual shock of what she has read in Zola that leave her feeling brutalised, and needing to be reassured by Edith.

Apart from this internal evidence of a shunning of physical sexuality, we find Elizabeth Bowen, herself a member of the landed class and a contemporary, though not of their generation, referring to Edith and Martin's relationship: 'Nor was its nature — as it might be in these days — speculated upon . . . The upper class, the Anglo-Irish, were then non-physical — far from keen participants even, from what one hears of them, in the joys of marriage.'[5] Pat O'Connor, in *Friendships Between Women*, examining the forces that shape women's relationships, quotes Faderman: 'It was virtually impossible to study the correspondence of any nineteenth-century woman . . . and not uncover a passionate commitment to another woman, at some time in her life', although 'most of these relationships were not lesbian in the sense that they were genital.'[6] Both Edith and Martin were familiar with the legendary friendship between Maria Edgeworth and their grand-grandmother, Mrs Bushe. The form this friendship took was a lifetime of effusive letters from Miss Edgeworth and considerably calmer replies from Mrs Bushe, with rare meetings. Edith refers to this as Edgeworth's 'falling in love with Mrs B.' Edith and Martin were familiar also with the close family relationships usual among women of their class, with a sister or a cousin, in which they would support each other through the trials of marriage and family life. In other words, the intensity of their own relationship did not appear unusual to these women, nor to their contemporaries.

It is difficult to imagine nowadays the obstacles that existed to a friendship between two

1. *The Selected Letters of Somerville and Ross*, ed. Gifford Lewis (London: Faber and Faber, 1989), p. 132.
2. *Nana*, by Emile Zola (1840–1902), tells the story of a prostitute who dies of syphilis.
3. *The Selected Letters of Somerville and Ross*, ed. Gifford Lewis, p. 154.
4. Ibid., p. 154.
5. Elizabeth Bowen, *The Mulberry Tree: Selected Writings of Elizabeth Bowen*, ed. Hermione Lee (London: Virago Press, 1986), p. 186.
6. Pat O'Connor, *Friendship Between Women* (Hemel Hempstead: Harvester Wheatsheaf, 1992), p. 13.

women at the end of the nineteenth century. If we assume that shared interests, leisure, liberty, regular meetings, transport and money are some of the factors that underlie a modern friendship, it is sobering to realise that shared interests were the only factor available to Edith and Martin. We can see how their position as chatelaines in the landowning class both increased and diminished the possibilities of a partnership. It is significant that their meeting first took place when both were in their twenties. Since the degree of

cousinship was close, the delay in their meeting reminds us that over one hundred miles separated their homes. At that time such a journey would have taken at least eight hours by public transport. We read in the letters of Edith, when finances were troubled, offering to pay Martin's travel expenses so that they can work together on a book, and of paying for her keep when she visits Martin. This expense of time, effort and money in order to meet must be considered in contextualising their friendship.

BEGOÑA ARETXAGA

(1960–   )

from:
SHATTERING SILENCE: WOMEN, NATIONALISM AND POLITICAL SUBJECTIVITY IN NORTHERN IRELAND (1997)

[Begoña Aretxaga's feminist ethnography of the violence in Northern Ireland examines the role of nationalist women, particularly the deployment of tactics of popular resistance at the level of streets and small communities. Aretxaga's approach combines interpretative anthropology with post-structuralist feminist theory. In the following selection from her book she examines the way in which sexuality was a site of oppression and then, through the dirty protest, of reclamation and resistance for some women prisoners. An engagement in politically motivated violence led some women to challenge and reshape normative sexual decorums for Catholic women. Published by Princeton University Press, 1997. Footnotes are by the author.   S.K.]

SEXUALITY AND THE POLYVALENCE OF DOMINATION

The Catholic discourse in Ireland, North and South, has converted sexuality into a taboo subject. There is no sex education in schools and it is difficult for women to talk explicitly about

their sexuality.[1] Sexual matters, rarely discussed in the context of the family, are the object of much embarrassment when they are not safely disguised in joking. Many women commented, sometimes with resentment, about the painful process of learning from scratch about sex or childbearing. Modesty is deeply rooted among young girls and women in Ireland, and its transgression produces deep feelings of humiliation and shame. Remember the categoric refusal of an arrested woman to undergo a strip search . . . 'I wouldn't have done it for the doctor, you know.'[2]

The Armagh prisoners were very young women, many of them still teenagers. They were socialized in a strict Catholic morality that strongly emphasized modesty. The handling of women prisoners' bodies by male officers was deeply distressing. At least in one case, that of Rosemary Callaghan, the handling and beating was accompanied by exposure of the body as well as by moves highly evocative of sexual assault: 'I was suddenly pinned to the bed by a shield and the weight of a male screw on top of me,' and later 'during the course of my being dragged and hauled from the wing, both my breasts were exposed to the jeering and mocking eyes of the

1. Jenny Beale, *Women in Ireland* (Basingstoke, 1986); Eileen Fairweather, Roisin MacDonough, Melanie MacFayden, *Only the Rivers Run Free. Northern Ireland: The Women's War* (London, 1984).
2. Aretxaga, *Shattering Silence*, p. 60.

screws.' She was forcefully held in front of the prison governor with her breast still exposed; the episode being 'totally embarrassing and degrading.'[3]

The importance of disciplinary techniques of the body in the production and deployment of power, particularly visible in total institutions like the prison, has been extensively elaborated by Foucault.[4] Among the discourses and practices constituting the political economy of the body, sexuality, he argues, 'appears as an especially dense transfer point for relations of power, one endowed with the greatest instrumentality.'[5] Relying heavily on Foucault, Feldman has analysed the use of bodily techniques by male republican prisoners during the dirty protest.[6] Although Feldman does not comment on sexuality as a relevant dimension to the men's protest, it is crucial to the women's. Sexuality emerged in the eighteenth century as a (scientific) social construction playing a crucial role in describing power relations of various kinds: not only between men and women but also between social classes, 'races', and colonial others.[7]

Political practices articulated through an explicit or veiled sexual discourse, such as the military assault on the Armagh prisoners, are

undoubtedly power mechanisms. To interpret them *only* as disciplinary techniques that inscribe power relations in the body, however, is to miss the cultural and psychological dimensions that make their use possible in the first place. Practices such as sexual harassment during interrogation, strip searches, or male military assaults involve complex emotions around which the formation and transformation of subjectivity takes place. For Foucault it is precisely the formation of subjectivity (the construction of docile and unthreatening subjects) that constitutes the whole rationale of disciplinary and punishment techniques. It is the 'soul' not the body that is the target of disciplinary power. Yet if the transformation of subjectivity is what is at stake in the bodily disciplines of the prison, the directions that such transformations may take escape the panoptic control of the prison to hinge on a multiplicity of contingent cultural, historical, and personal circumstances. As Garland has argued, punishment cannot be understood solely in terms of power and rationality; the subjectivity of the actors must be seen not only as the product of rational techniques of control but also a crucial element in moulding any resistance to them.[8] For the women prisoners, unlike the men, the subjectivity of the dirty protest was inscribed within the permutations of gender and sexual difference.

Emotions and affects generated by manipulations of the body are always powerful components of social order. The narrative of Rosemary Callaghan, aimed at denouncing physical punishment as disciplinary mechanism, ends with feelings that 'it was most embarrassing and degrading.' Without attention to the feelings permeating the protest and their historical configuration it is difficult to grasp the meaning of thirty-two women living for more than a year without washing, surrounded by their own excreta and menstrual blood.

The male officers' assault can be interpreted as both an institutionalized attempt to discipline through punishment and an assertion of male dominance on the bodies of women. This latter is of course one of the most common forms of subduing women. The fact that after the initial

3. *Women Protest for Political Status in Armagh Gaol.* Report by Women Against Imperialism, April 9, 1980, p. 24. I confirmed the statements made by prisoners in interviews with them during my fieldwork.
4. Michel Foucault, *The History of Sexuality*, trans. Robert Hurley (New York: Pantheon Books, 1979); *Discipline and Punish* (New York: Vintage Books, 1980).
5. *Discipline and Punish*, p. 103.
6. Allen Feldman, *Formations of Violence: The Narrative Body and Political Terror in Northern Ireland* (Chicago: University of Chicago Press, 1991).
7. There is a growing body of scholarship on the discourse of sexuality and power. See, for example, Jean Comaroff and John Comaroff, *Of Revelation and Revolution: Christianity, Colonialism and Consciousness in South Africa, 1* (Chicago: University of Chicago Press, 1991); Ludmilla Jordanova, 'Natural Facts: A Historical Perspective on Science and Sexuality', in Carol MacCormack and Marilyn Stratheren (eds), *Nature, Culture and Gender* (New York: Cambridge University Press, 1980), pp. 42–69; Peter Stallybrass and Alison White, *The Poetics and Politics of Transgression* (Ithaca, NY: Cornell University Press, 1986); Ann Laura Stoler, 'Carnal Knowledge and Imperial Power: Gender, Race and Morality in Colonial Asia,' in Micaela De Leonardo (ed.), *Gender at the Crossroads of Knowledge: Feminist Anthropology in the Postmodern Era* (Berkeley: University of California Press, 1991), pp. 51–101; and Sara Suleri, *The Rhetoric of English India* (Chicago: University of Chicago Press, 1992). For more information on the sexualization of early colonial discourse in Ireland, see Ann Rosalind Jones and Peter Stallybrass, 'Dismantling Irena: The Sexualization of Ireland in Early Modern England', in Andrer Parker, Mary Russo, Doris Sommer and Patricia Yaeger (eds.), *Nationalisms and Sexualities* (New York: Routledge, 1992).
8. David Garland, *Punishment and Modern Society: A Study in Social Theory* (Chicago: University of Chicago Press, 1980), pp. 158–85.

blows the beatings and handling of women were done in a generally individualized fashion in the enclosed space of the cell by armed men perceived to be profoundly anti-Catholic was doubly humiliating and distressing. The women, Mairead Farrell reported to her family, 'were in a state of panic,' and it took a while to calm them down.[9] These women, who had taken pains to

9. Mairead Farrell (1957–1988). See Volume V, p. 1544. As reported in *Women Protest for Political Status in Armagh Gaol* (published by Women Against Imperialism) and Tim Pat Coogan, *On the Blanket: The H-Block Story* (Dublin: Ward River Press, 1980).

assert 'their difference' from the ordinary inmates and had taken pride in their political identity, needed some kind of action to relieve personal humiliation and regain political leverage. Thus, I suggest that at the level of consciousness the dirty protest was politically motivated, but it also involved a deeper level of personal motivation. Indeed, all former prisoners were quick in remarking to me that the morale among the women skyrocketed after they embarked on the dirty protest. And several observed that 'the anger kept us going.'

LUCY McDIARMID

(1947–   )

from:
THE POSTHUMOUS LIFE OF ROGER CASEMENT (1997)

[When Roger Casement joined the Gaelic League he was participating in a movement that was inventing a Gaelic tradition of pure, pre-colonial Irish masculinity, which could be resurrected through the Irish language, Irish music and dance, and Irish sports. The histories of pre-colonial Ireland, such as that by Casement's close friend Alice Stopford Green, with their emphasis on communal aspects of Brehon law, were utopian fantasies about the past that were often read as blueprints for a new Ireland. Part of this fantasy which appealed to feminists and socialists was a fantasy of communal property and of sexual liberation, fuelled also by the sympathetic account of Celtic practices offered in Engels's *Origin of the Family*.

Casement's diaries show him to be a writer fractured by competing styles, someone whose work challenges an opposition between public and private languages. Ernley Blackwell, legal advisor to the Home Office during Casement's trial, notoriously extrapolated from the diary his own phobic interpretation, that 'Of later years he seems to have completed the full cycle of sexual degeneracy and from a pervert has become an invert — a woman, or pathic, who derives his satisfaction from attracting men and inducing them to use him.'

The *News of the World* claimed in 1916 that no one who saw the contents of his diaries 'would ever mention Casement's name again without loathing and contempt'; but they also brought a 'staggering shock' to Casement's

close friends. If these contemporary responses to the diaries owe as much to the revelation of the fact of Roger Casement's sexuality, subsequent commentators have had difficulty in coming to terms with the language of the diaries. One of the most interesting questions raised by Casement's diaries is whether sexuality has specific national or racial formations.

The American academic critic Lucy McDiarmid has been an exemplary figure in terms of the introduction of theoretical perspectives from queer theory in Irish studies. As well as work on Oscar Wilde and Roger Casement, she has examined class anxieties and gender anxieties that have emerged in a variety of controversies in Irish literary history. Her work on Lady Gregory illuminated the creatively perverse aspects of the writer that had been previously ignored or dismissed The following extract is from the beginning of an essay on the posthumous reputation of Roger Casement, which appeared in a collection of essays, *Gender and Sexuality in Modern Ireland*, ed. Anthony Bradley and Maryann Gialanella Valiulis (Amherst: University of Masachusetts Press, 1997). McDiarmid is more interested in analysing the uses to which Casement's reputation has been put in various discursive practices than in arguing about the facts of his life or the 'forgery' case. Footnotes are by the author. S.K.]

. . . that dear Norwegian girl helped me stow away all the old hairpins . . . Now, when I saw Hibernia *on the caps of the men, I nearly kissed them . . .*[1]

1. Roger Casement, 28 October 1914, letter. The holograph copy of this letter is in the National Library of Ireland, NLI 13082–4. I am grateful to Patricia Donlon for permission to quote it.

The indeterminacy of Roger Casement's posthumous life no doubt began in the disguises of the living man, adopted to make his identity indeterminate. Within a few short weeks, in October 1914, eluding detection as he slipped into enemy territory — Germany — by way of New York and Norway, Casement became, in quick succession, Mr. R. Smythe of London (in New York); James E. Landy of New Jersey (on shipboard); his own, non-existent female American cousin (in a letter); and Mr. Hammond of New York (in Berlin). A life between accents, nationalities, allegiances, and genders, hybrid and subversive, was given local habitation in these aliases. No wonder fellow travellers assumed he was a spy. Casement had boarded the *Oskar II* as himself, but as a disguised, effeminized Sir Roger, having shaved off the famous beard and washed his face in buttermilk to lighten his complexion. As the ship sailed out of New York harbour he turned into James Landy — whose passport he carried — and openly joined Adler Christiansen, the Norwegian sailor he had picked up on Broadway and who accompanied him as his servant. When the ship was stopped by the British vessel *Hibernia*, Christiansen shaved Casement and discarded the razor blades ('all the old hairpins').

In an unmailed letter addressed 'Dear Sister', Casement described these events coyly, as if he and Christansen were girls. The camp locutions ('that dear Norwegian girl,' 'the dear, kind captain, such a nice Dane with a beard just like cousin Roger's') sound like MacNeice's 'Hetty to Nancy' in *Letters from Iceland*, the deliberately girlish utterances of a faux-homosexual voice. Patently comprehensible like all the codes Casement attempted, this one was intended to record his journey but deceive British agents, should they ever come across it. But at the same time as the letter hid treason, its style outed its author's sexual preference — or might have, to an alert reader. At the very least, the American, female persona allowed free expression to the writer's ambivalence about gender even as it obfuscated his political intentions.

The 'official' British outing of Casement was every bit as equivocal and evasive as this simpering, camp epistle. When Sir Ernly Blackwell recommended that Casement's private diaries, with their record of homosexual assignations, be 'given as much publicity as decency permits,' he was outing Casement covertly. Neither the Foreign Office, nor the Home Office, nor the Attorney General wanted to be known publicly to be giving the diaries publicity; so the publicity had to be private publicity, sub rosa but not red-handed. Like dirty books in a primary school, typed transcripts and photographed copies of pages were surreptitiously shown by one man to another. The private publicity was sanctioned by officials of state: 'Excellent,' Asquith observed to the American ambassador at a dinner party the night before Casement's execution, learning that he had seen the diaries, 'and you need not be particular about keeping it to yourself.'[2] Once leaked, the forgotten private records became international smut. These quasi-outings were followed by quasi-definitive proofs that the diaries were forged and apparently definitive assertions that they were authentic. And judgments about authenticity, or the lack of it, have been inseparable from judgments about militant nationalism and about homosexual behaviour — all issues which have not inspired unanimity of opinion at any moment during the past eighty years.

Nothing about Casement has ever been stable, definitive, determinate, 'official,' except the fact that he was hanged. Posthumous Casement, like living Casement, has endured in a blur of rumour, gossip, romance, and innuendo, public pronouncements and private uncertainty. 'Be a good patriot, shut your mouth. Lie down,' says the Cardinal to the dead hero in David Rudkin's play about Casement's funeral.[3] But by the time of de Valera's 1965 oration at the reinterment of the remains in Glasnevin, Casement had too long and complex a posthumous history to lie quiet. Even Parnell's posthumous life has been less volatile. Discourse about the problematic sexual lives of public figures — Parnell, Pearse, Eamonn Casey — has become a distinct Irish speech genre, one that tends to fit Luke Gibbons's binaristic analysis of rumour as a corrective to 'official' information in Irish public life, an 'alternative line of communication' opposed to those of 'political correspondents, public

2. Roy Jenkins, *Asquith* (London: Collins, 1964), p. 403.
3. David Rudkin, *Cries from Casement as His Bones are Brought to Dublin* (London: BBC, 1974), p. 76.

relations agencies and government information services.[4] Like the folk-histories that oppose official histories, rumour, Jean-Noël Kapferer has argued, 'constitutes a relation to authority . . . a counter power.' 'Rumours are necessarily unofficial . . . they challenge official reality by proposing other realities.'[5] Discourse about Casement is unique, however, because two governments are involved, and so there are two opposed 'official' views, and a host of unofficial views, not necessarily consonant with or directly opposing their own nation's ideology. Even the dominant Irish view that he was a revolutionary hero has been contested by those who thought he was a minor player ('a side-bird to the main event,' as a friend of mine called him); and that view has been countered by those who extol his international humanitarian contributions. There has always been a case to be made for every

4. Luke Gibbons, 'The Camel in the Koran: Rumour in Irish Politics,' *Irish Reporter*, vol. 5 (1992), p. 14.
5. Jean-Noël Kapferer, *Rumors: Uses, Interpretations, and Images* (New Brunswick and London: Transaction Publishers, 1990), pp. 215, 263. This book is cited in Gibbons's essay mentioned above.

permutation of opinion. The leakage of the diaries was done unofficially, of course, and so could only be opposed unofficially, by those who thought they were forged or by those who thought they were genuine but irrelevant. And Irish and English opinions, over the years, have been complexly distributed: some Irish people have quietly assumed Casement was homosexual, and some English have protested against the 'forgeries.' . . .

A man who was busy most of his life with secret activities of various kinds, a man around whom other people's secret activities circulated, makes an attractive hero for a society that privileges the hidden. Eighty years-worth of rumours and ballads issued from a people with a deep, traditional distrust of the official; and with a corollary faith that the hidden is true, or if not true, at least valuable in its opposition to what is public. This value is not linked with any particular content, but with the condition of hiddenness, especially when some secret — piety or impiety, purity or contamination — is hidden from outsiders and unknowable to them.

KEITH RIDGWAY

(1965–   )

from:
THE LONG FALLING (1998)

[Grace, an English woman living in Ireland, kills her abusive husband and flees her home to go and live in Dublin with her estranged gay son, Martin. This is one of the first Irish novels to deal with the 'bathhouse' scene in Dublin and to represent an alienated, promiscuous, drug-using, urban gay experience of the kind found in novels set in London, New York or San Francisco. Although the novel has a third-person narration, there is a radical shift in perspective, with each chapter using free indirect discourse to represent the point of view of a different character. The following extract centres on Martin. *The Long Falling* was published in London by Faber and Faber in 1998.]

Halfway down the lane there was a grey door lit from above, the entrance to the sauna club, the small way in to a large space. As he pushed open the door Martin glanced back. The cars passed by on George's Street. People scurried along the pavement in the distance, crossing the gap in an instant without looking down. In the shadows closer to him he could see the orange dot of light rising and falling, where the waiter stood and watched him.

Inside, everything was painted a battleship grey. The walls and ceiling of the stairwell as grey as sky. Cement sky. He thought it might have something to do with reassurance. This is a grey area. Leave your scruples at the door. Leave your panic and your guilt and your fear at the door. Pick them up on the way out. Martin's hiccups had stopped.

At the top of the stairs he paid the man and scrawled a name on the sheet of paper that was

thrust in front of him. He was given a locker key.
A buzzer sounded and he pushed open another,
heavier door with his shoulder.

There was a thick heat, and a sweet, vague
scent. Two men with towels held around their
waists looked down from the narrow stairs.
Martin glanced up at them and then ducked his
head and turned the corner into the changing-
room. It was empty and he breathed, breathed in
again, a muscle in his hand twitching, his feet
catching awkwardly on the thin dark carpet.

He was very drunk. The change in the
temperature had his head spinning. He sat on a
bench and scanned the lockers for his number.

Three times a week sometimes, in his first days
in Dublin. Then less and less as he had met more
people in the pubs. By the time he had met
Henry he had not been in six months or more.
And since then only that one time. Falling over in
the showers. Spilling a bottle of poppers[1] in one
of the tiny mattress rooms with two other men
about whom he could remember absolutely
nothing. Telling himself that it was despair when
it was not. It was less than that.

He had trouble getting the key into the lock
and then almost fell over while trying to untie his
shoelaces. He took a ragged, pale blue towel from
the locker and stuffed his coat into the small
space, patting it down and putting his shoes on
top of it. He took off his jumper and his shirt. He
stood for a moment in his jeans, running his
hand gently over his chest.

The temperature suited bare skin. The air
clung to him so that he could not feel it. He
swam in the heat. He took off his jeans, pulling
them inside out over the obstruction of his socks.
Then his socks. He slipped his underpants down
to his ankles and kicked them up into the air with
one foot and caught them.

'Cool,' he muttered, and saw a dripping man,
paunch, grey hair, rolling towards him with a
smile.

'There's a trick,' he said.

'Fuck off.'

He picked up his towel and slammed the
locker door and it bounced out again. He closed
it and locked it and scratched his head.

'Sorry,' he said, and touched the man's
shoulder in passing.

'That's all right.'

He walked unsteadily from the room and past
another room where men watched television.
There was the sound of gunfire and explosions.
One man was black. Another drank from a
plastic cup. He went into the next room where
the man who had let him in stood behind a
counter dispensing tea and coffee and
sandwiches and chocolate. Martin handed in his
key, saying the number in his head over and over,
glancing at a big bowl of condoms and a big bowl
of mints and at a man who sat on a stool reading
a newspaper. The black man came in and asked
for tea. Martin took two mints and brushed past
him and went out slowly, pulling his towel tight.
Carefully, one narrow foot after another, like the
long hands of a climber, he went upstairs.

It was crowded. All eyes. They were all ages,
walking to and fro, naked but for their towels,
some carrying keys, some cigarette boxes, all with
the same look. Just eyes. Martin smiled. They
looked like men given some terrible task. They
wanted it over with. They wanted it done right.

A line of towels hung on hooks outside the
steam room. As Martin passed the door it opened
and two young, good looking men emerged,
naked, their cocks sticking out from them like
arrows shot in. They took their towels and moved
awkwardly away, the one in front checking that
the other followed, towards the next flight of
stairs.

He thought of going in there but he put it off.
He thought of Henry and shook his head. His
towel slipped and he caught it. A blond guy who
looked too young smiled at him. He went to the
video room and stood in the doorway. The two
tiers of seats, just wide ledges really with thin
black-plastic mattresses, were full. In one corner
sat a fat boy with a bottle of poppers pressed to
his nostril. Beside him a bald man moved a hand
up and down beneath his towel. On the bottom
tier, in the corner, a man with a moustache, his
eyes half closed, his head lolling on his shoulders,
his towel on the floor, masturbated as if he'd
been doing it for days. An asylum scene. Martin
turned away.

On screen there was something happening in
what looked like an African hut, with reed mats
and a veiled bed and a fire in the middle of the

1. Amyl nitrite, commonly taken as a short-term stimulant to intensify sexual gratification.

floor. One black man and two white. Something was said and Martin thought there was something wrong with the sound until something else was said and he realised that they were speaking French. French. He turned away.

At the end of the corridor was a toilet and the showers. He watched a man washing his hair. He watched suds run over his back and tried to see his face but it was scrunched up and anyway, he decided, the body was just a little too good. He said 'overdressed' to himself and laughed. He stopped laughing when he felt the return of his hiccups. He bent over the sink outside the toilet and cupped his hands and drank tepid water and caught a bad smell and moved away, brushing slightly against the warm walls, stared at by an elderly man with hair like his father's.

He rubbed his eyes and saw parts of Henry spin around in front of him like branches broken off in a storm.

At the door to the steam room he hung his towel over another hook and glanced back up the corridor and saw the man from the shower look at him. Inside there were grey bodies piled in a corner and the smell of poppers was like a gas leak, and almost immediately his cock was in somebody's hand. He pushed him away, tried to get his bearings. Sweat started on his forehead. The man from the shower came in and stood beside him. Martin found the bench and sat down. The man sat down too, thigh against thigh. He put his hand on Martin's balls, very gently, and leaned in close as if to kiss him. Martin stood, turned, faced the guy, pointed his cock at him, tried to hold his head. Half heartedly, the man kissed Martin's stomach and Martin sighed as loudly as he could, and coughed, and went out.

Downstairs there was the type of telephone that allowed you to dial and wait until your call was answered before you had to put in any money. He poked at the numbers and heard the sound they made and heard the familiar clicks and the odd tone that he always mistook for engaged, but which was not engaged. It was like a hospital machine, tethered to a death-bed. He let it ring until it rang out.

Upstairs he decided to limit himself to men who had poppers.

TOM LENNON

from:
CRAZY LOVE (1999)

[The use of second-person narration, a relatively unusual narrative device — it was employed by Neil Jordan in *The Past* (1980) — is effective in the gay context because it attempts to move the reader from voyeur to subject. This extract looks at the pains of rejected love in a culture of secrecy and 'passing'. *Crazy Love* was published by O'Brien Press in 1999.]

Two weeks pass and there's no contact. You phone his house what seems like half a million times and leave half a million messages, but he doesn't return any of your calls. His younger brother and sister appear to live beside the phone. Two rings and one of them plucks it from its cradle. Most times they just say, Sorry, he's not in. Occasionally though, they holler his name out, and you hear it echo around that house you think about so often and your pulse begins to quicken, but they come back to the phone and say, Sorry, he's out at the moment, would you like to leave a message? It's embarrassing that the same two people keep answering. You can almost hear them think, Oh God, it's Baldy again, how'll I get rid of him this time. So you try to alter your voice, but this backfires when they ask if you'd like to leave a message and you have to give the same name that must be filling their phone-message pads by the score. You don't pursue them for further information on his whereabouts because you're sure that they either suspect your motives, or he's warned them not to give anything away.

So, for those two weeks, you do little else except think about what he could be doing. You never stray too far from your phone, and this leaves you constantly on edge, constantly waiting, constantly stressed. Now you see the benefits of a mobile. Whenever it gets really bad you take a stroll down to his old office, sit on his chair, dip into the drawers of his desk, take out old scribble pads and stare at any little snippet of his handwriting. They're full of nonsensical drawings and words, but you're sure it's just a matter of staring at them long enough to decipher some secret coded message.

A replacement is found for him, a twenty-four-year-old newly qualified accountant named Janet. She was one of the original interviewees, the one the Phantom thought ought to get the job, and naturally, the fact that choosing her is going to cause further irritation for Kevin Daniels is undoubtedly instrumental in your decision. She's a pleasant type, exceptionally bright and meticulous, but it somehow jars with you to see her sitting at Johnny's desk. Like the Vikings, you feel that his entire office should be set alight and pushed out to sea in a longboat.

There are memories of him everywhere, and each one inflicts a sharp stab of bleak pain. You feel like someone who has stayed behind in a holiday resort after the summer has ended, and all your friends have departed; the weather has turned cold and your desolation is amplified by all the lingering memories of those carnival times. Everywhere you go in the building you can recall things he said, things he did, the way he smiled, the easy way he stood with his arm resting on his hip.

By the Friday of the second week, you're almost frantic from the craving. You feel like you're going to die if you don't see him. If you thought it'd work, you know you'd take out a full page ad in a newspaper to arrange a date. Now you understand what people mean when they talk about the throes of addiction. If you see him just one more time, you tell yourself, that will be it. One more fix will satisfy you, you tell yourself, even though you know you're fooling yourself.

And that's when the tiniest chink of light appears from an unexpected source. Bernie arrives into the tearoom and announces that she bumped into the 'mad lad' on Dame Street. She's aiming her comments in your direction, and you're soaking up every word she says, while at the same time, you're pretending that you're listening to some other conversation. Andy has his sharp eyes upon you. One slip and he'll do his merciless impersonation. He once had the Phantom building a wooden artefact of Marcus in his bedroom.

'He said to say hello to you,' Bernie says when she catches your attention.

'Who's that?'

'You've forgotten poor old Johnny already.'

'Oh, Johnny,' you say, struggling to maintain that look of indifference, while inside, everything has gone into a mad spin. 'Has he found another job yet?'

Bernie laughs. 'Yeah, in the circus.'

The others laugh and the conversation steers away.

VINCENT QUINN

(1968–   )

from:
ON THE BORDERS OF ALLEGIANCE: IDENTITY POLITICS IN ULSTER (2000)

[This is the final section of an article that appeared in the collection *De-centring Sexualities: Politics and representation beyond the metropolis*, edited by Richard Phillips, David Shuttleton and Diane Watts (London and New York: Routledge, 2001). The essay begins with the question, 'If gay space exists what does it look like?' Quinn goes on to examine the asymmetry between metropolitan discussions of identity politics and the rather specific identity culture that pertains in Northern Ireland, focusing first on his native city Derry/Londonderry. A discussion of historic representations of Derry is followed by an analysis of the gendered metaphors in Seamus Heaney's poetry, 'a myth of creativity which makes a claim on universality while simultaneously suppressing the voices of gay men and lesbians'.   S.K.]

To summarize: so far I've been arguing that Irish history has usually been represented in terms of polarities rather than multiplicity or diversity. Combined with this is a tendency to invoke a male/female binary as a template for the supposed dichotomies of Irish culture. One of the many debilitating results of this is that same-sex stories have been consistently written out of Irish life. Now it's time to consider the spaces within which it might be possible to produce the new metaphors that I'm advocating. In particular I want to look at how 'coming out' represents a challenge to the received formations of Northern Irish life.

Utopian Sexualities?

'Coming out' is a contentious concept, one which Alan Sinfield[1] describes as quintessentially metropolitan. Moreover some queer writers have complained that the ideology of 'coming out' enacts and maintains the gay/straight divisions of identity politics. How, then, can 'coming out' undermine set categories? Well, for one thing, Ulster lesbian and gay identities are not exact replicas of the models circulating elsewhere in Britain and their difference ought to make us re-think the assumption that 'coming out' is a single mode. Moreover, 'coming out' in Northern Ireland creates identities which supplement and refigure sectarian loyalties: it forces a reconsideration (though not necessarily a rejection) of the Nationalist/Unionist map. The resulting selves are mixtures of gay and Republican, lesbian and Unionist; they can be seen as hybrid identities, unfixed categories.

Information and advice circulated by lesbian and gay groups in the North often have graphic representations of these inter-identifications. For example the letterhead of the Queen's University Belfast Lesbian, Gay and Bisexual Society has a rainbow flag alongside the University arms. The potentially alienating Red Hand of Ulster (which features in the University crest) is therefore re-inflected by being juxtaposed with a symbol of inclusion and alliance. The result is a space in which supposedly contrary identities are allowed

to co-exist, thus reconciling the ghettos with which I began this chapter. Similarly, the Foyle Friend Homepage is dominated by a huge rainbow flag carried aloft during a Pride Parade and the accompanying text refers to the group's location in the 'North West of Ireland' rather than in 'Derry' or 'Londonderry'. Besides avoiding disputed names, this places the city in a wider geographical context, thus undermining the border's power to enforce division. (That is, the 'North West' includes Co. Donegal, which is in the Republic, as well as Co. Londonderry, which is in the North.)

A slightly different approach is taken by Belfast's Queer Space Project, which aims to create

> a lesbian, gay, bisexual, transgender (LGBT) community space. It is for the promotion of LGBT visibility, resources, networking and communication within the community. Queer Space aims to form a collective, where participation by all members of the LGBT population is welcome on all levels, from administration of space to attendance in it. (*Queer Space*, 1998)

The project's website has a stylized picture of the group's meeting place: green walls with a purple easy-chair and well-stocked bookshelves. (The books are a mixture of colours, including green and orange, but shades of lavender predominate.) A rainbow flag hangs from the window. The accompanying policy statement rejects all forms of inequality — including discrimination on grounds of religion, nationality and ethnicity. It stresses the four principles of accessibility, communality, non-commercialism and non-judgementalism.

The language here is a striking mixture of old and new. Contemporary queerness (with its emphasis on inclusivity and multiplicity) meshes with concepts from 1970s identity politics (collectivity, community, economic self-sufficiency). Responsibility towards the group exists alongside individual subject positions, but no attempt is made to erase the *differences* between the project's various constituencies. Significantly, 'members of the community will not be asked to hide or change any element of their identity within *Queer Space*'. This recognition of multiple loyalties allows for diversity without imposing

---

1. Alan Sinfield (b. 1941), a leading British queer theorist and literary critic. See 'The production of gay and the return to power', *De-centering Sexualities*, pp. 21–36.

censorship. The resultant 'queer family space' supplements Ulster's 'two communities' and creates, at least in theory, a multicultural locale.

Like sectarianism, the Queer Space Project operates simultaneously on a discursive and a material level. Its rhetoric is obviously shaped in part by postmodernism — hence the use of queer terminology and spatial metaphors. But there's an obvious danger in placing too much faith in the virtual reality of Utopian postmodernism: crucially, a discourse of inclusion does not *in itself* create a 'safe space' even if it helps us to envisage one. This is in no way a criticism of the Belfast project (which seems exemplary); rather, it's a reminder that however much language shapes materiality discourse alone cannot change societies. Culture, after all, consists of competing and opposed discourses, and queer inclusivity cannot, alas, vanquish sectarian conflict in anything more than a fleeting (though none the less valuable) way. Therefore although the Ulster gay scene could be described as a Foucaldian heterotopia, we should be wary of attributing magical powers to it just because it's 'a space that is other'.[2] The cross-identifications of Northern Irish queer life also evoke Homi Bhabha's theory that hybridity is 'the third space' which 'displaces the histories that constitute it, and sets up new structures of authority, new political initiatives, which are inadequately understood through received wisdom'.[3] What could be more hybrid, one wonders, than queer Unionism or lesbian Catholicism? However, I share the scepticism that several commentators have shown towards theories of hybridity. Sally Munt writes that 'models such as Homi Bhabha's Third Space and hybridity have a tendency to be applied as though any kind of instability, like "difference", is an end in itself, and intrinsically progressive'.[4] Having made a similar point, Alan Sinfield remarks that 'it is easier than we once imagined to dislocate language and ideology; and harder to get such dislocations to make a practical difference'.[5]

'This is certainly apposite to Northern Ireland, where the recent cease-fires have been marred by an *increase* in violence towards gay men and lesbians.' All the same, if hybridity 'has to be addressed not in the abstract, but as social practice',[6] Ulster has lessons for the rest of Britain, if only because Northern Irish queer identities are hybrid in a conspicuous and *specific* way. In this context, one 'comes out' to a series of balancing acts rather than to a single, rigid, born-again self. The particularities of the Northern Irish situation in turn suggest that 'coming out' (even in a *metropolitan* location) is an ongoing transaction that continues to provoke reformulations of identity: it's a process, not a once-in-a-lifetime act.

'Coming out' clearly isn't the only way of unsettling sectarianism and nor is it always successful in doing so. (There are gay paramilitaries as well as gay moderates.) But the central point is that identities based on sexual oppression can counter-weigh religious or cultural grievances and create agendas which compete with ethnic identifications. And as a result it may be possible to evolve new narratives for and about life in Northern Ireland. Such an enterprise is inevitably utopian, with all the problems that utopianism brings. But even though the Belfast Queer Space Project is vulnerable to atttack (from its members as well as from outsiders) it's none the less an investment in the idea of *positive* change, as opposed to sectarian stagnation or the 'instability' as 'an end in itself' identified by Munt. Indeed even if such a space only existed on a metaphorical level (which is not the case), it would still countermand the gendered myths examined earlier in this chapter. Instead of claiming to be unified and natural, the Queer Space Project acknowledges its own diversity — and in doing so it reveals the excluding and constructed nature of Heaney's supposedly 'authentic' culture. This doesn't eliminate the existing myths of Irish and Ulster identity, but it allows several different subcultures to reimagine their relation to dominant ideologies.

One example of how this process might work is provided, ironically, by the border. This — the most contested line in Ireland — is the zone

2. Michael Foucault (1926–84), 'Of Other Spaces', trans. J. Miscowwiec, in *Diacritics* 16.
3. Homi Bhabha, 'The Third Space', in *Identity: Community, Culture, Difference*, ed. J. Rutherford (London: Lawrence and Wishart, 1990), p. 211.
4. Sally Munt, *Heroic Desire: Lesbian Identity and Cultural Space* (London: Cassell, 1998), pp. 170–1.
5. Alan Sinfield, *Gay and After* (London: Serpent's Tail, 1998), p. 34.
6. Ibid., p. 34.

which defines 'Northern Ireland' and keeps it in uneasy relation to 'the South'. (Until very recently the Republic's constitution has laid claim to the six counties, thus refusing the legitimacy of partition.) Contemporary Republicanism is structured around opposition to the border while Ulster Unionism is predicated on its maintenance. So the border is both a physical entity and a symbol of wider disputes. Moreover, by creating the political units that lie on either side of it, the border has been an agent of cultural production; the different routes taken by North and South since 1920 have arisen, to a large extent, from their contradictory responses to partition. As a result Ireland has been conditioned socially, as well as geographically, by the border.

Given that it is *literally* divisive, the border is hardly a promising place in which to look for ways forward. It could of course be redeemed through postmodernism: the liminal zone, like the twilight zone, might be a place where freaky things take place. Unfortunately, however, Ireland's border zone continues to be a site of violence rather than of playful inversion. A fake traffic sign saying 'Sniper at Work' may be witty (and semiologically sophisticated) but it is underpinned with the threat of concrete violence — a bullet in the brain would be rather less droll. Furthermore, living on the border does not in itself unfix rigid loyalties; if anything it strengthens them. Three-quarters of the Derry/ Londonderry secondary school Protestants interviewed by Desmond Bell in 1985 had either never crossed the border, or had only done so 'a few times'.[7] Mirroring this, Derry/ Londonderry Catholics tend to identify themselves with the land across the border in Donegal, rather than with the rest of Northern Ireland. The polarities encoded in Derry/ Londonderry's name are not, therefore, deconstructed through the city's borderline status.

This assumes, however, that all Nationalists and Loyalists feel the same way about the border — which is surely not the case. Subcultural groupings within Republicanism and Unionism are likely to have particular responses which may not tally with the responses of other Unionists and Republicans. In particular, what might happen if queer Irish people began to contemplate the border in a new way? In certain contexts it could be an enabling line rather than a dividing one.

Although this is partly a postmodern gambit, it's also based on social actualities. Take the recent (though incomplete) liberalisation of life in the Irish Republic. Interesting questions arise for a gay Unionist when one considers that between 1993 and 1998 the legal age of consent for homosexual sex was lower in the Irish Republic than in the North. And although the legal age of consent in the North is soon likely to become 16 (as opposed to 17 in the South),[8] the Irish Republic can still boast an array of anti-discrimination legislation that's singularly lacking in Britain. (Sexual orientation is included in the Republic's Unfair Dismissals Act and extremes of homophobic (and/or sectarian) rhetoric can be challenged under the Prohibition of Incitement to Hatred Act. Irish law does not recognize the category of 'gross indecency', and there is no ban on gay men and lesbians serving in the Irish armed forces.)

So how might these factors cut across existing cultural and religious suspicions? Do they represent a temptation to young gay Unionists? The question is rhetorical. Given my own identity as an expatriate lapsed Catholic, I'm hardly in a position to speak for Ulster Loyalists; in any case Jeff Dudgeon (whose action against the British Government brought the 1967 Homosexual Law Reform Act into force in Northern Ireland) is a committed Unionist.[9] Besides which, the Irish Republic is not yet as modern a state as is sometimes claimed. The improved position of gay men in the South is not matched by an equivalent advance in the status of women, whether gay or

---

7. Desmond Bell, *Acts of Union: Youth Culture and Sectarianism in Northern Ireland* (Basingstoke: Macmillan Education, 1990), p. 150.

8. Author's note: In 1993 the Irish government decriminalized homosexual acts and set a common age of consent for gay and straight sex. In 1994 the Westminster government lowered the age of consent for gay sex in mainland Britain from 21 to 18. The fact that Northern Ireland had been initially excluded, for tactical reasons, from this legislation did not prevent Ian Paisley (leader of the fundamentalist Democratic Unionist Party) from opposing the measure in the House of Commons. In June 1998 the British House of Commons voted to lower the age of consent to 16; so far, however, the House of Lords has failed to ratify this decision; reform of the Upper Chamber makes it likely, however, that the age of consent (at least in mainland Britain) will eventually be lowered to 16.

9. See G. Woolaston, 'The Green, the Orange, and the Pink', *Gay Times* (October 1991).

straight. Confronted by a Republican tradition that's ambivalent about homosexuality, and by a state that's still associated with a homophobic church, emigration to England, not the Republic, remains a compelling choice for many Northern Nationalists.

There's no reason why lesbian or gay Unionists should have to abandon their traditional allegiances in favour of a queer United Ireland. Nor should Nationalists have to leave the North to evade the homophobic attentions of the RUC. But the discrepancies between North and South provoke unique dilemmas for Irish gay men and lesbians. So much so that their identities represent a different sort of boundary. If living on the physical North/South border does not necessarily create plurality and fluidity, what about the psychic borderland of being gay *and* a Nationalist, or lesbian *and* a Unionist? This involves a stronger form of agency — it's a *choice* of identity (and a double one, at that) rather than the acceptance of a single, pre-ordained cultural category. Those inhabiting it are therefore ideally placed to produce new ways of thinking about nationality and sexuality. Like 'Ulster' itself — which is composed of nine counties, of which six are in the North and three in the South — this is a location which crosses boundaries and *need not* be subject to sectarian divisions, even if those divisions have hitherto structured political and cultural debate in Ireland.

CHERRY SMYTH

(1960–   )

from:
AREA OF DETAIL:
THE PERSISTENCE OF
HOMELAND AS INVOCATION
AND REPUDIATION (2001)

[This is an extract from a public lecture delivered by Cherry Smyth at the Centre for Migration Studies, Cork University, in 2001. Smyth reminds her audience that sexual repression in Ireland has driven many people to emigration, but she also welcomes the emergence of new hybrid, diasporic identities. It is a form of 'coming-out' narrative, but one that is very self-consciously theorized.   S.K.]

I took flight from Protestantism, from paramilitary violence, from a provincial town, from the family, from heterosexuality — in that order — but never stopped being Irish and circling a small area of detail on the Derry coast in the work of my imagination. Are displacement, diasporic pride and a global queer identity enough to compensate for generations of settled place and inherited culture?

As I wrote in the short story, 'Aristocrats in Asia': 'Geography is more than a small grey map in the newspaper. It is more than mountains and valleys and rivers and untarred roads and dense forest. It is whispers in another language, how far you live from the capital and running water, and to whom you say your prayers.'

Anger and repudiation fuelled my early departure from the North, more than the economic necessity, which has motivated most Irish emigration. I found it stifling, regressive, confusing, patriarchal, provincial and deeply conservative. To become who I wanted to be, I could only evolve beyond the narrow confines of Ulster, with its tight-knit community and culture of conformity. If I say nothing, I will belong. If it hadn't been for my deep love of Irish writers and literature, I might not have identified with Ireland so strongly and might have followed some of my more radical peers to universities in England, but I chose to go to Trinity College, Dublin, thinking I was following in the steps of James Joyce. It was only sometime after my arrival that I learnt that the sectarian divide had thrived until recently at the hallowed college. By choosing Trinity I'd merely reinforced generations of Protestant Ascendancy . . .

I sense that I have committed a double transgression by leaving Ireland and by betraying heterosexuality. There is more pressure to be the happy emigrant when the spectre of loneliness is invoked and stoked by homophobia. There is a 'you've made your bed in a strange land, with strange partners — now lie in it' attitude . . .

There have been times when I felt I couldn't be Irish enough because I was Protestant and then not Protestant enough because I was a lesbian. I gained legitimacy for my own Irish and Protestant writing through my writing . . .

If I chose self-banishment without knowing I was a lesbian, being gay has made my choice to live away from home easier to sustain. The cultural dislocation is offset by the communities and cultures of international queers who have gravitated to London to live more freely. My friends are Italian, Jewish Irish, Pakistani, American and English. The English I love hate the English I hate too. In England, I was politicised by feminism, peace activism and lesbianism and through those movements was able to be with Irish Republican and nationalist women in a way that I had not been able to in Ireland. Feminism and sexuality united us against a common enemy and it was then easier to be accepted as legitimately Irish and pro-nationalist.

Choosing a state of displacement has become more conscious latterly. In some ways, I thrive on the polarities of rootedness and displacement. This is also linked to my sexuality: I am female, look feminine, am perceived as heterosexual. Yet I want and desire women and operate outside heterosexuality and its privileges. Lack of fixity has become a post-modern model of how to be and opens up possibilities for fictions rather than closing them down. As some theorists have suggested, migration is not so much 'a mere interval between fixed points of departure and arrival, but a mode of being . . . For those who come from elsewhere and cannot go back, perhaps writing becomes a place to live.'[1]

1. R. King, Introduction to *Writing Across Worlds: Literature and Migration* (London: Routledge, 1995).

MEDBH McGUCKIAN

(1950–   )

from:
CAPTAIN LAVENDER (1994)

[Since the early 1980s Medbh McGuckian's densely literary and allusive poetry has confronted boundaries of gender and sexuality. She writes intricate, obliquely autobiographical poems, thick with sensuous imagery and an often complex private symbolism. Her early poems were centrally concerned with female experience — pregnancy and childbirth, and the process of self-definition of the woman, as writer and mother. Yet the constantly shifting pronouns emphasized the slippage of gender characteristic of her work, as she explored a female body parcelled out between male and female elements, inside and outside, individual and nation. In the last ten years McGuckian has increasingly focused on connections between sexuality and war, in the contexts of the 1798 United Irishmen rebellion, the 1916 Easter Rising, and the recent Northern troubles. The following poems are taken from her three most recent books: 'Captain Lavender' is the title poem of her 1994 volume, an extended elegy for her father who is imagined as both feminized and martial (Dublin: Gallery Press, 1994); this theme continues in 'The Feminine Christs' taken from her 1798 commemoration volume, *Shelmalier* (Dublin: Gallery Press, 1998). 'The Moses Room' is in part a poem in memory of Roger Casement, the republican leader accused of homosexuality in a whispering campaign at the time of his treason trial in 1916. Casement had family connections with Ballycastle in County Antrim, where McGuckian's father was born. 'The Moses Room' appears in *Drawing Ballerinas* (Dublin: Gallery Press, 2001).   C.W.]

Captain Lavender

Night-hours. The edge of a fuller moon
waits among the interlocking patterns
of a flier's sky.

Sperm names, ovum names, push inside
each other. We are half-taught
our real names, from other lives.

Emphasise your eyes. Be my flare-
path, my uncold begetter,
my air-minded bird-sense.

from:
SHELMALIER (1998)

The Feminine Christs

Christmas Day, 1996

Their pulses are differently timed, mule-
powered, safely poured in two directions
into time, into the collected object.

All their fingers are together, they are
tight-lipped, unwakeable mothers
embraced to the hilt and reconceived.

Whom persons, unwed, now identified
in marble, looking small enough
to take in one's western arms.

Wounded tables decorated with autumn
leaves, planked streets, desolately
curved roads, unhappy anythings.

Every star is an upper self
that half-hangs down out of the heated
audible blue behind them.

Their dreams churn in the midyears
from century to century, their bought
books are a sharp green hedge.

It would be better to turn round
and say 'The Spring', or any other
whole-hearted not sincerely.

If ever you wanted to buy a museum,
to see whether a gentle snowstorm
always filled with moving

could seem natural, turn to a new altar,
a stronger faith and a weaker life,
reach to the last drop your virtue.

from:
DRAWING BALLERINAS
(2001)

The Moses Room

I who have eyed the weather constantly
and wanted to call the sea back from its bed
am nobody's host and nobody's guest, in the
all-white snowclad living-room, in the curve
created by the road. The road is an invert,
a woman, the bachelor wind blows the colours
of the haphazard sailing-boats before her,
and I feel compelled to follow it to the end,
for R's sake, though it still rushes backwards
and forwards between the same two places;
still with the Englishness of a railway,
or a thin line of gold braid edging
the predominantly silver canal of my desire.

A rain is the picture of the year,
with two pianos back to back, an inscription
over the fireplace saying 'Two lovers
built this house'. And the gossip of all the girls
who danced there was the man who lunches
with me in London, who wore silver
where a diplomat wears gold. Like a swarm
of bees let loose upon visitors, he suddenly
swept the flowers off the table, as if
a secret wasp had sawn at his finger,
the only entry in my 'Who's Who'
not carried forward into 'Who was Who',
unseaworthy, more my lover than he knew.

You who have changed the name
of your third son, with four underlinings
and two different pens, because his name
meant a sum paid by a bridegroom
for a bride, reverse the name of 'Kingstown'.
The horses are wearing frost shoes
for the home-stretch, after three round trips
they became recusant, rough in their play:
the blot of rust mould discolouring his letter
like a leap-second salutes when the guns say.

Biographies/Bibliographies

Some of the following writers do not wish details of their life histories to be published. In other cases it has been difficult to trace information.

Forrest Reid

For biography and bibliography, see Volume II, pp. 1218–9.

Kate O'Brien

For biography and bibliography, see Volume II, p. 1221. Also Vol. V, p. 680.

Brendan Behan

For biography and bibliography, see Volume III, p. 232.

Edna O'Brien

For biography and bibliography, see Volume III, p. 1134, and Volume IV, p. 601.

Janet McNeill

For biography and bibliography, see Volume III, p. 1132.

Maurice Leitch

LIFE. Maurice Leitch was born in Muckamore, County Antrim, in 1933 and was educated in Belfast. In 1960 after some years as a teacher he joined the BBC as a radio features producer. He now lives in London. He has written novels, radio plays, short stories, television screenplays and documentaries. In 1981 *Silver's City* won the prestigious Whitbread Prize for Fiction.

CHIEF WRITINGS. *The Liberty Lad* (London: MacGibbon and Kee, 1965); *Poor Lazarus* (London: MacGibbon and Kee, 1969); *Stamping Ground* (London: Secker and Warburg, 1975); *The Hands of Cheryl Boyd, and Other Stories* (London: Hutchinson, 1989); *Silver's City* (London: Secker and Warburg, 1981); *The Smoke King* (London: Secker and Warburg, 1998).

Margo Gorman

LIFE. An Irish woman who lives and works in the north of England.

CHIEF WRITINGS. 'Ireland: Dilemmas and Struggles', *Outcome: A Magazine of Sexual Politics Produced by Lesbians and Gay Men* (spring 1979), pp. 14–15.

Nell McCafferty

LIFE. Nell McCafferty was born in Derry in 1944. She was educated at Queen's University, Belfast, and received an honorary Doctorate of Letters from Staffordshire University. She was Secretary of Derry Labour Party during the Northern Civil Rights Movement (1968–70), and a founding member of the Irish Women's Liberation Movement, Dublin (1970). An award-winning journalist and broadcaster with the *Irish Times*, the *Irish Press*, the *Sunday Tribune*, *Magill* magazine and RTÉ.

CHIEF WRITINGS. *In the Eyes of the Law* (Swords: Poolbeg Press, 1981); *The Armagh Women* (Dublin: Co-op Books, 1981); *The Best of Nell: A Selection of Writings over Fourteen Years* (Dublin: Attic Press, 1984; rpr. 1993); *A Woman to Blame: The Kerry Babies Case* (Dublin: Attic Press, 1985); *Goodnight Sisters, Selected Writings*, vol. 2 (Dublin: Attic Press, 1987); *Peggy Deery: A Derry Family at War* (Dublin: Attic Press, 1988).

Frank McGuinness

For biography and bibliography, see Volume III, p. 1307. See also:

CHIEF WRITINGS. *Someone Who'll Watch Over Me* (London: Faber, 1992); *Dolly West's Kitchen* (London: Faber and Faber, 1999).

Brendí McClenaghan

LIFE. Born *c.* 1958. In 1978 he received five life sentences for republican activity. He was released after seventeen and a half years. During the second half of his prison term he became increasingly prominent as a spokesperson for gay issues in the republican movement, and corresponded with many leading gay activists and theorists in Britain and Ireland.

Cathal Ó Searcaigh

For biography and bibliography, see Volume III, p. 936. See also:

CHIEF WRITINGS. *An Bealach 'na Bhaile/Homecoming*, ed. Gabriel Fitzmaurice (Conamara: Cló Iar-Chonnachta, 1993).

Emma Donoghue

LIFE. Born in Dublin in 1969, Emma Donoghue is a novelist, playwright and literary historian. She was educated at Mount Anvill National School, Muckross Park Convent, University College Dublin (BA 1990) and Cambridge (Ph.D. 1997). Her fiction includes the contemporary Dublin novels *Stir-fry* (1994) and *Hood* (1995, winner of the American Library Association's Gay and Lesbian Book Award), a sequence of fairy-tales, *Kissing the Witch* (1997), and a novel about an eighteenth-century murder, *Slammerkin* (2000). Her first two stage plays — *I Know My Own Heart* (1993) and *Ladies and Gentlemen* (1996) — were produced by Glasshouse Productions in Dublin, and her third, *Kissing the Witch* (adapted from her book), premièred at the Magic Theatre in San Francisco in 2000. She has also written plays for RTÉ and BBC. Donoghue's first book was the ground-breaking history *Passions Between Women: British Lesbian Culture 1668–1801* (1993), which she has followed up by editing anthologies of lesbian poetry and short stories, as well as writing a biography of two Victorian poets entitled *We are Michael Field* (1998). Her works have been translated into Dutch, German and Swedish. She now lives in Canada.

CHIEF WRITINGS. *Passions Between Women: British Lesbian Culture, 1668–1801* (London: Scarlett Press, 1993); *Stir-fry* (London: Hamish Hamilton, 1994); *Hood* (London: Hamish Hamilton, 1995); *Kissing the Witch* (London: Hamish Hamilton, 1997); (editor) *What Sappho Would Have Said: Four Centuries of Love Poems Between Women* (London: Hamish Hamilton, 1997); *We are Michael Field* (London: Absolute Press, 1998); *Ladies and Gentlemen* (Dublin: New Island Books, 1998); (editor) *The Mammoth Book of Lesbian Short Stories* (London: Robinson Publishing, 1999); *Slammerkin* (London: Virago Press, 2000).

Joni Crone

LIFE. Founder member of Dublin Lesbian Line, Liberation for Irish Lesbians, and the Lesbian Disco, where she was DJ (1977–90). She is a writer and community arts worker.

Gerry Stembridge

LIFE. Gerard Stembridge was born in Limerick in 1959. He is a theatre director, playwright, broadcaster and film-maker. He was scriptwriter for the 1990 RTÉ Radio series *Scrap Saturday*. He has directed *Guilt Trip* (1996), *Black Day at Black Rock* (RTÉ, 2001) and *About Adam* (2001). He lives in Dublin.

CHIEF WRITINGS. *The Gay Detective* (London: Nick Hearn, 1996); *Ordinary Decent Criminal* (London: Headline, 2000).

Éibhear Walshe

LIFE. Born in Waterford in 1962, Éibhear Walshe now lives in Cork, where he lectures in the English Department at University College Cork.

CHIEF WRITINGS. (editor) *Ordinary People Dancing: Essays on Kate O'Brien* (Cork: Cork University Press, 1993); (editor) *Sex, Nation and Dissent in Irish Writing* (Cork: Cork University Press, 1997); *Elizabeth Bowen Remembered* (Dublin, 1998); *Kate O'Brien: A Biography* (forthcoming).

Roz Cowman

For biography and bibliography, see p. 640.

Begoña Aretxaga

LIFE. Begoña Aretxaga was born on 23 February 1960 in San Sebastian, in the Basque country. She was educated at the University of the Basque Country and in the USA. While researching her Ph.D. in anthropology for Princeton she spent two years doing field work in west Belfast. She taught for six years at Harvard and now teaches in the Anthropology Department at the University of Texas at Austin.

CHIEF WRITINGS. *Los Funerales en el Nacionalismo Radical Vasco: Ensay Antropologico* (San Sebastian: Editorial Baroja, 1989); 'Striking with Hunger: Cultural Meanings of Political Violence in Northern Ireland', in *The Violence Within: Cultural and Political Opposition in Divided Nations*, ed. Kay B. Warren (Boulder, Colorado: Westview Press, 1993), pp. 219–56; *Shattering Silence: Women, Nationalism and Political Subjectivity in Northern Ireland* (Princeton: Princeton University Press, 1997); 'What the Border Hides: Partition and the Gender Politics of Irish Nationalism', *Social Analysis*, vol. 42, no. 1 (1998), pp. 16–32; 'Playing Terrorist: Ghastly Plots and the Ghostly State', *Journal of Spanish Cultural Studies*, vol. 1, no. 1 (2000), pp. 43–58.

Lucy McDiarmid

LIFE. Lucy McDiarmid is an American critic who teaches in the English Department of Villanova University, in Pennsylvania.

CHIEF WRITINGS. *Auden's Apologies for Poetry* (Princeton: Princeton University Press, 1990); 'Augusta Gregory, Bernard Shaw and the Shewing-Up of Dublin Castle', *PMLA*, vol. 109, no. 1 (January 1994), pp. 26–44; 'The Demotic Lady Gregory', in *High and Low Moderns: Literature and Culture 1889–1939*, ed. Maria DiBattista and Lucy McDiarmid (Oxford: Oxford University Press, 1996), pp. 212–34; Lady Gregory, *Selected Writings*, eds Lucy McDiarmid and Maureen Waters (London: Penguin Books, 1996); 'The Posthumous Life of Roger Casement', in *Gender and Sexuality in Modern Ireland*, eds Anthony Bradley and Maryann Valiulis (Amherst: University of Massachusetts Press, 1997); 'Oscar Wilde's Speech from the Dock', *Textual Practice*, vol. 15, no. 3 (Winter 2002) pp. 447–468; editor of 'Secular Relics' a special Irish issue of *Textual Practice* (Summer 2002).

Keith Ridgway

LIFE. Keith Ridgway was born in Dublin in 1965. He now lives in London. Some of his work can be found on his website.

CHIEF WRITINGS. *Horses* (London: Faber and Faber, 1997); *The Long Falling* (London: Faber and Faber, 1998); *Standard Time* (London: Faber and Faber, 2001).

Tom Lennon

LIFE. 'Tom Lennon' is a pseudonym. No other information is available.

CHIEF WRITINGS. *When Love Comes to Town* (Dublin: O'Brien Press, 1993); *Crazy Love* (Dublin: O'Brien Press, 1999).

Vincent Quinn

LIFE. Vincent Quinn was born in Derry in 1968, and educated at St Columb's College, Derry, and at Oxford and Cambridge. He has taught English at the University of Sussex since 1994.

CHIEF WRITINGS. *Luxurious Sexualities: Effeminacy, Consumption and the Body Politic in Eighteenth-Century Representation. A Textual Practice Special Issue*, ed. with an Introduction by Vincent Quinn and Mary Peace; 'Literary Criticism', in *Lesbian and Gay Studies: A Critical Introduction*, eds Andy Medhurst and Sally Munt (London: Cassell, 1997); 'Loose Reading? Sedgwick, Austen and Critical Practice', *Textual Practice*, vol. 14, no. 2 (2000); 'On the Borders of Allegiance: Identity Politics in Ulster', in *De-Centring Sexualities*, eds Richard Phillips, David Shuttleton and Diane Watt (London: Routledge, 2000); 'Fostering the Nation: Patrick Pearse and Pedagogy', *New Formations*, vol. 42 (2001), pp. 71–84.

Cherry Smyth

LIFE. Born in Portstewart, County Derry, in 1960, Cherry Smyth now lives in London, 'resisting assimilation'. She works as a journalist and film curator.

CHIEF WRITINGS. *Virago New Poets*, eds Melanie Silgaro and Janet Beck (London: Virago Press, 1993); *Lesbians Talk Queer Notions* (London: Scarlett Press, 1992); (with Laura Cottingham) *Bad Girls* (London: ICA Publications, 1996); Sally Munt and Cherry Smyth (photographer), *Butch/Femme: Inside Lesbian Gender* (London: Cassell, 1998). *When The Lights Go Up* (Belfast: Lagan Press, 2001).

Medbh McGuckian

For biography and bibliography, see Volume III, pp. 1435. See also:

CHIEF WRITINGS. (Poems) *Marconi's Cottage* (Oldcastle: Gallery Press, 1991); *Captain Lavender* (Oldcastle: Gallery Press, 1994); *The Flower Master and Other Poems* (Oldcastle: Gallery Press, 1994); *Shelmalier* (Oldcastle: Gallery Press, 1998); *Selected Poems* (Oldcastle: Gallery Press, 1997); *Drawing Ballerinas* (Oldcastle: Gallery Press, 2001).

BIOGRAPHY AND CRITICISM. Peggy O'Brien, 'Reading Medbh McGuckian: Admiring What We Cannot Understand', *Colby Quarterly*, vol. 28, no. 4 (December 1992), pp. 239–50; Clair Wills, 'Medbh McGuckian: The Intimate Sphere', *Improprieties, Politics and Sexuality in Northern Irish Poetry* (Oxford: Oxford University Press, 1993), pp. 159–93; Susan Shaw Sailer, 'An Interview with Medbh McGuckian', *Michigan Quarterly Review*, vol. 32, no. 1 (winter 1993), pp. 111–27; Eileen Cahill, '"Because I Never Garden": Medbh McGuckian's Solitary Way', *Irish University Review*, vol. 24, no. 2 (fall–winter 1994), pp. 264–71; Peter Sirr, '"How Things Begin To Happen": Notes on

Eiléan Ní Chuilleanáin and Medbh McGuckian', *Southern Review*, vol. 31, no. 3 (summer 1995), pp. 450–67; Mary O'Connor, '"Rising Out": Medbh McGuckian's Destabilizing Poetics', *Éire-Ireland*, vol. 30, no. 4 (winter 1996), pp. 154–72; Patricia Boyle Haberstroh, 'Medbh McGuckian', *Women Creating Women: Contemporary Irish Women Poets* (Dublin: Attic Press, 1996), pp. 122–59; Sarah Broom, 'McGuckian's Conversations with Rilke in *Marconi's Cottage*', *Irish University Review*, vol. 28, no. 1 (spring–summer 1998), pp. 133–50; Shane Murphy, '"You Took Away My Biography": The Poetry of Medbh McGuckian', *Irish University Review*, vol. 28, no. 1 (spring–summer 1998), pp. 110–32.

EMMA DONOGHUE, *Editor*

Lesbian Encounters, 1745–1997

Irish lesbians are beginning at last to step into the light. As we come out of our various closets and make ourselves visible in Irish culture, many of us face worse things than invisibility — violence, homelessness, the loss of jobs, the loss of children, to name but a few — but invisibility is perhaps the most debilitating. As Irish women who love women, we have been like faces looking into a mirror and seeing nothing, like voices shouting into a cave that swallows the sound.

It seems at first glance that when we have appeared at all in the records of Irish history and culture, it has been as spinsters, neurotics, eccentrics. Euphemism veils our characters, and the double standard of privacy ('husband' is a respectable public term but 'lover' is considered personal) writes our relationships out of the records. A survey of canonical texts suggests that Irish literature has little or nothing to say about women who love women.

I have been delighted to discover that this is not quite true. At least two dozen Irish writers, from the late eighteenth century to the late twentieth century, have touched on lesbian themes in their works.[1] If some of the names are familiar, few of the works are; fictions about love between women have remained on the margins of Irish literature as it is published and taught. To illustrate the surprising quantity and diversity of what has been written, and to increase the set of stories about lesbian existence in circulation, I have not chosen a handful of these writers to focus on, but have sewn together a patchwork of appetite-whetting passages: my priority has been

to open up this branch of Irish literature to readers.

These selections are mostly from novels, stories and poetry, along with memoirs and diaries. It is generally in the private sphere, in tales of homes and holidays and dinner parties, that we find representation of Irish lesbian experience. Our points of entry to culture are very different from those of gay men. Discussing the David Norris case for the decriminalization of anal sex between men, Justice O'Higgins claimed that the state was 'perfectly entitled to have regard to the difference between the sexes and to treat sexual conduct or gross indecency between males as requiring prohibitions because of the social problem which it creates, while at the same time looking at sexual conduct between females as being not only different but as posing no such social problems'.[2] Of course we are a 'social problem', as the justice would call it, since our lives and choices pose a threat to the dominant institution of the heterosexual family, but it is a threat traditionally faced by turning a blind eye. The justice's comment does not show tolerance of love between women, but simply that the Irish state is not inclined to make us visible even by mentioning us in its laws. This is an interesting anomaly in Irish culture, a sort of privacy traditionally offered to lesbians in exchange for our silence. It is a bargain that will not last.

These 'Lesbian Encounters' are lesbian in content, not necessarily in authorship. However, I have prioritized women writers whose lives revolved around attachments to women

1. Some others writing today are Aine Collins, Honour Molloy, Louise C. Callaghan, Claire Ní Measc, and Linda Cullen (author of *The Kiss* [Dublin: Attic Press, 1990]), as well as the excellent and prolific Anna Livia who has an Irish background.

2. Justice O'Higgins, quoted in John Kelly, *The Irish Constitution* (Dublin: Jurist, 1984), pp. 456–7.

(examples include Maria Edgeworth, Edith Somerville and Martin Ross, and Eva Gore-Booth), as well as those women writing today who are 'out' as lesbian or bi-sexual, because writers in both groups have an insider's perspective on love between women, and because their work has often gone unread or misread. Though I have looked for well written pieces, my first criterion has been: what meanings does this text add to a barely audible debate?

This section is structured to emphasize variety, and to prevent any one writer being taken as the voice of her or his era. Previous attempts by historians to chart the 'development' of lesbianism — for example, in a simple shift from innocent friendship to guilty sex in the late nineteenth century — leave out so many contradictory signals. In fact, the nineteenth-century pieces in this section are often explicitly erotic, and the modern pieces (for example, from June Levine's *A Season of Weddings*) often dwell on romantic friendship. The connection between same-sex desire and androgyny is one issue that crosses the centuries, being just as crucial to Maria Edgeworth as to Maeve Binchy. We find lesbianism continually associated with foreign countries and 'exotic' women, as much in a contemporary novel by Edna O'Brien as in Joseph Sheridan Le Fanu's early vampire tale.

As we embark on a new era in which more lesbian books will get written, published and distributed without censorship in Ireland, and (most importantly) reach a wide readership, it is useful to look back. Perhaps because we have been starved of images of ourselves in popular culture, our communities have always given a central place to lesbian authors; they pass through several of the texts included here. Eva Gore-Booth, for instance, haunts the landscape for Mary Bramley, whose speaker (unlike W.B. Yeats, whose poem Bramley echoes) feels she has 'no season here, / no privileged duality / and lack a myth that might protect me'. We may have no myth of our own, but our writers often re-fashion myths — Eva Gore-Booth's Niamh, Susan Connolly's banshee, Mary Dorcey's Virgin Mary.

What we do have is a rich history in literature, something I hope this section goes some way to show. And we are beginning to create a grammar of lesbian connection, complex yet clear enough to free us from the self-hatreds of the closeted past; as Nuala Archer describes it,

> & my tongue
> tonguing a language
> edging beyond destruction.

CHARLOTTE MacCARTHY

(*fl.* 1745–68)

from:
THE FAIR MORALIST; OR, LOVE AND VIRTUE. A NOVEL. BY A GENTLEWOMAN. TO WHICH IS ADDED SEVERAL POEMS BY THE SAME (1746)

[Charlotte MacCarthy's poems of idyllic, virtuous love between pairs of women are typical of a huge body of 'romantic friendship' literature written since the Renaissance, probably reaching its emotional peak in the late eighteenth century. The favourable contrast with male–female love in MacCarthy's first poem, and the pastoral landscape in the second, are both very common motifs.]

To the Same[1]

Tell me, ye Registers of Fate,
Why thus my Soul with *Chloe* moves;
  Why I abhor whom she must hate,
Or why I love whom *Chloe* loves.

---

1. Third in a sequence of poems to 'Chloe', also called Miss W——m.

Why when she frowns, my every Joy,
To dark Oblivion sinks away;
  Or why her Smiles my Cares destroy,
And adds new Sun-shine to my Day.

Were she (bright Nymph) some Shepherd
    Youth,
Then had I thought the little Loves
  Had bid me quit romantick Truth,
And only doat whilst Beauty moves.

Said Fortune most compleats our Bliss,
And Love with that flies swift away;
  That colds the Touch, that faint's the Kiss,
When Wealth and Beauty both decay.

But this is something more divine,
For tho' my *Chloe*'s Charms shou'd fade,
  Her Beauty still to me wou'd shine,
Still I'd adore the heavenly Maid.

Tho' Fortune shunn'd her every Hour,
More dear to me wou'd *Chloe* prove,
  Than if the Gods a golden Shower
Had sent to recompence my Love.

'Tis Friendship, noblest of the Mind,
'Tis that, that can this Difference make;
  The Links of that in Heaven are join'd,
Which Time, or Fortune, ne'er can break.

Contentment, to a Friend

This small Repast, with her I love,
By her dear Hand thus neatly dress'd,
  To me is more than if great *Jove*[1]
Had bid me to an heavenly Feast.

When e'er she fills the little Cup,
(Tho' from the Spring she brings the Treat)
  With eager Joy I drink it up,
And Nectar ne'er was half so sweet.

The Trencher[2] which she laid herself,
Tho' plain, and homely to behold,
  Is brighter than the Miser's Pelf,[3]
When form'd in Plates of shining Gold.

So where we love, the meanest Cell,
Is Peace, is Pleasure's rich Retreat;
  Whilst gilded Courts, where Monarchs dwell,
Are Dungeons black, with those we hate.

1. Jupiter, the supreme god of Roman mythology and a famous
    seducer or abductor of women.
2. Place setting for a meal.
3. Riches (in a bad sense).

ELEANOR BUTLER AND SARAH PONSONBY

(1739–1829)   (1755–1831)

from:
THE HAMWOOD PAPERS OF THE LADIES OF LLANGOLLEN AND CAROLINE HAMILTON (1930)

[In 1768 Sarah Ponsonby, a thirteen-year-old orphan, arrived at Miss Parke's boarding school in Kilkenny. She was soon befriended by Lady Eleanor Butler, sixteen years her senior, and in 1778 they left Ireland for Wales, in the company of a servant and friend, Mary Carryll. Butler, who was a Catholic and a member of the Ormond family, had been under pressure from her family to enter a convent. Ponsonby was subject to sexual harassment from her guardian. They had made previous attempts to get away together, including one elopement in men's clothing, but had been recaptured. Eventually their families reluctantly accepted their departure. They settled at a cottage in the Vale of Llangollen, where they passed the remainder of their lives, becoming famous for their 'romantic friendship'. They were visited by many celebrated figures of their period as well as by the extensive connections of their Irish families.

In July 1790 Butler and Ponsonby were distressed by a newspaper article in the *General Evening Post*, which carried the innuendo that they were lesbians. Entitled 'Extraordinary Female Affection,' it narrated their 'elopement' and described them as follows: 'Miss Bulter is tall and masculine, she wears always a riding habit, hangs her hat with the air of a sportsman in the hall, and appears in all respects as a young man, if we except the petticoats which she still retains. Miss Ponsonby, on the contrary, is polite and effeminate, fair and beautiful.' They wrote to Edmund Burke, asking for advice on how to respond, but although he was sympathetic, he could not suggest any legal remedy, promising instead to put personal pressure on the newspaper's proprietor.

In recent years Butler and Ponsonby have been regarded as key figures in histories of lesbian culture. Although they were diarists, and wrote extensively about their relationship, the extent of their self-awareness about their sexual identities remains unclear. Commentators have disagreed about whether their relationship would have been sexually consummated. The following extracts relate primarily to their attitudes to other social misfits, and demonstrate that however they may have understood their own lives, their general attitudes were if anything much less liberal than those of many of their bluestocking friends. *The Hamwood Papers . . .* was edited by Mrs. G.H. Bell (John Travers) and published in London in 1930 by Macmillan.]

from: Letter from Sarah Ponsonby to Mrs Tighe[1] 1785

February 7th
Mrs Herbert's[2] conduct has shock'd Us . . . My B[3] thinks that if all Ladies who are guilty of that Crime, were Branded, with its Initial, a Great A in the Forehead — it would be the most likely means to deter others, from following the example. Don't you think it a good idea?

from: Eleanor Butler's Diary 1788

Monday March 3rd
Rose at eight. Beautiful morning. Birds innumerable. Air rather cold and harsh. Nine till three reading, writing. The parish having sent a Warrant to Llandrdglee eight people came last night as witnesses against that unfortunate wretch who is suspected of having murdered her child.

Sunday March 9th
My beloved and I walked in the field before our cottage. Many decent orderly people hastening to Llansantiffraid. A Methodist preacher[4] there. The unfortunate wretch who was suspected of murdering her child taken up last night. The Body of the Infant being found by some persons who were in search of a Fox on the wildest part of the Merionethshire Mountain. The body was covered with sods under a great Rock. How shocking to Humanity!

Monday March 10th
Cold and gloomy. The Body of the poor Infant brought down the field in a basket. Three men and four women from the mountains with it as witnesses. The Inquest at this moment sitting over the Body in the Church . . . Letter from Miss Bridgeman.[5] Coachman taken ill last night which prevents their coming. Her regret sweetly and tenderly expressed. Wrote to her. Inquest pronounced Wilful murder — poor wretched creature to go to Ruthin Jail to-night. Bell tolling for the Infant, who is to be interred in the Church yard, having been baptised.

Tuesday March 11th
White sky, pale sun. The poor unfortunate wretch sent to Ruthin Jail last night, confessed the Infant was hers, but denied having mangled it in that shocking manner. May the Almighty in his infinite mercy give her grace to repent of this horrid deed. Writing, Drawing. Very cold and windy . . . our excellent Barretts fearing we should be unprovided sent a fine leg of Veal and a Calve's head with a letter written with their accustomed kindness . . . At half-past four a Rap at the Door. I was very agreeably surprised by seeing Monseigneur who is going to London to see his Brother, and our good Friend, poor Mr Butler of Ballyraggad, who is in a very dangerous state of health with water on his lungs.

---

1. Sarah Tighe, daughter of Sir William and Lady Betty Fownes, the cousins into whose care Sarah Ponsonby was placed when she was orphaned at the age of thirteen.
2. Elizabeth Herbert, daughter of Lord Sackville (1716–85), and wife of Henry Herbert of Muckross, County Kerry; an unsettled marriage, in which she had had a number of scandalous flirtations, ended in her elopement with a Scottish major.
3. Eleanor Butler.
4. Methodism was particularly influential in eighteenth-century Wales, where open-air preachers attracted large audiences.
5. Among their closest friends in the area were the family of Sir Henry Bridgeman, of Weston Park, on the Shropshire–Staffordshire border.

Thursday March 13th
Letter from Miss H. Bowdler[6] dated Portsmouth the 9th, from Mrs Tighe dated Harrow the 7th. Excellent thoughts on the Slave Trade in Mrs Tighe's Letter. Those who remain in their native country are treated worse than in the Islands, where, under most of their Masters, they meet with good treatment and are instructed by the Catholic and Moravian missionaries in the Christian religion. A reformation in the manner of bringing them over, and a general attention to their morals, manners and health afterwards, and having them well-instructed in Religion and after some years set free, appears better than the abolition of the Trade.

Tuesday March 18th
Letter from the unfortunate creature in Ruthin Gaol. What can we do for her? Reading, drawing . . . We then went the Home Circuit, told Richard we thought rolling four small Barrows full of gravel into the new kitchen garden was a very little morning's work. He gave us warning which (to his infinite surprise and evident regret) we immediately accepted, being determined never, while we retain our senses, to be imposed upon by a servant. Three dinner, boil'd Fowl, boiled mutton. Reading, writing. Richard sent in his keys. We sent out his wages. He went away with great reluctance. But not chusing to let our servants change place with us, We resolved when He gave Warning in the morning that he should take the consequence of it in the afternoon. Soft moist mild night . . . Nine till twelve in the Bedchamber reading. A day of sweetly enjoyed retirement, the little Fracas of Richard's sauciness not having disturbed us, as we think we acted with becoming calmness and presence of Mind.

Saturday March 22nd
Celestial glorious spring day. Through the Lenity of Pepper Arden[7] the girl acquitted of the murder of her Infant, which we are truly glad of, as had

the Judge enquired minutely into the particulars she must have been hanged this day on the green in this village.

Saturday May 3rd
Mr Woolham from Wrexham came with his bill. A very good sort of man, sensible and intelligent. Asked him many questions concerning Charlestown, South Carolina, where he resided some years. He gave us an account of the Rattle snake and the discovery which a Negro accidentally made of a Cure for the Bite, which before was thought Mortal. This man was bit in the woods and in the Anguish of mind and Body pulled up some leaves of American Plantain which grew near him; — he chewed their leaves and applied them to the Wound. He returned to his master and informed him of what had happened and prepared to die, which was always the consequence a few hours after the bite, but to the Surprise of every person the negro felt no inconvenience from the wound. Which attributing to the Virtue of the Plantain, he suffered himself to be twice bit by a Rattle Snake, and each time applying the leaves, as at first, felt no Pain from the Wound. This discovery was of so much importance, so many dying every year by the Rattle Snakes, that there was an assembly held, the negro was freed, fifty pound per annm. settled on him, and the cure has been every year published in the Almanacks of that Country.

1789

Tuesday March 10th
Gypsey came to the Door, wanted to tell fortunes. Dismissed her. Hate such people.

Saturday March 14th
Letter from Miss Shipley[8] dated Bolton St. Thurs. 12th. 'Dowager Lady Spencer[9] says she is wild to be acquainted with *Les Amies* and their lovely Cottage, and had Lord Spencer[10] gone to Ireland she had determined when she visited him to spend the day in the sweet Vale of Llangollen.'

6. Henrietta Maria (Harriet) Bowdler (1745–1830), sermon writer and novelist. Bowdler was attracted to the friends, and although she seems to have preferred Ponsonby, actually described herself as romantically involved with Butler, whom she described as a man.
7. Bell's note: Richard Pepper Arden (1745–1804). Became Baron Alvanely, 1776, judge on the South Wales Circuit. Later Solicitor-General, Attorney-General, Chief Justice of Chester, Master of the Rolls.
8. Sister of Jonathan Shipley (1714–88), Bishop of St Asaph, and friend of Edmund Burke; Miss Shipley was one of a group of intellectual women who met in Bath, often at the home of Anna Riggs Miller.
9. Widow of John, 1st Earl Spencer.
10. George John Spencer, 2nd Earl Spencer (1758–1834).

Friday March 20th

Sent for Mr Edwards of the Hand[11] about *very Particular business*. He came immediately and acted as we expected and indeed always experienced. Sent to invite the Vicar to coffee. I am so puzzled I scarce know what I write. The Vicar came to tea. Our Landlord came. Paid him his half year's Rent, which was due last November but we had not money. Now for the Cause of my Puzzle. Peggy, our undermaid, who has lived with us three years, was this day discharged our service. Unfortunate girl. Her pregnancy she could no longer conceal, nor could she plead in her excuse that she had been seduced by promises of marriage. Nine till twelve in the Dressing-room concerning that Poor Peggy Jones. Her father would not admit her to return to his House. We prevailed on the Weaver and his wife to receive her. What is to become of her?

11. Local inn.

Saturday March 21st

Lovely delicious day. The Vicar came. Mr Chambre's Clerk James Price, the Churchwardens John Ellis and John Jones ... The Certificate signed at last ... Peggy Jones went to Trevor Hall this morning and I fear perjured herself. The Person to whom she swore her pregnancy was due was not the man to whom she was attached. Ordered her to be dismissed from the Weaver's which was instantly done.

Sunday April 19th

Our good landlord came with a letter to us from that Price who was condemned for sheep stealing. His sentence was reserved and the judge promised to recommend him as an object of mercy and that he should be Transported. He writes to us, to entreat we will get him off from Transportation. Threw his letter in the fire as we cannot consider a noted Sheep Stealer entitled to much lenity even had we interest to get him off.

MARIA EDGEWORTH

(1768–1849)

from:
BELINDA (1801)

[This novel contrasts the passionate yet benevolent romantic friendship between Belinda Portman and Lady Delacour, with the unsettling flirtation offered by the cross-dressing villain, Mrs Harriot Freke. Edgeworth emphasizes gender rebellion rather than sexuality, but does mention that the symbolically named Mrs Freke has been known to lure young women away from home to live with her. In this scene, taken from a chapter entitled 'Rights of Woman', Harriot Freke has her first conversation with Belinda, and tries to drag her away from her gentle hosts, the Percivals. The text is taken from the 3rd edition, *Tales and Miscellaneous Pieces by Maria Edgeworth in Fourteen Volumes* (London: R. Hunter, 1825).]

Belinda was alone, and reading, when Mrs Freke dashed into the room.

'How do, dear creature?' cried she, stepping up to her, and shaking hands with her boisterously — 'How do? — Glad to see you, faith! — Been long here? — Tremendously hot to day!'

She flung herself upon the sofa beside Belinda, threw her hat upon the table, and then continued speaking.

'And how d'ye go on here, poor child? — Gad! I'm glad you're alone — expected to find you encompassed by a whole host of the righteous. Give me credit for my courage in coming to deliver you out of their hands. Luttridge and I had such compassion upon you, when we heard you were close prisoner here! I swore to set the distressed damsel free, in spite of all the dragons in Christendom; so let me carry you off in triumph in my unicorn,[1] and leave these good people to stare when they come home from their sober walk, and find you gone. There's nothing I like so much as to make good people stare — I hope you're of my way o' thinking — you don't

1. A carriage drawn by two horses abreast and one in front.

look as if you were, though; but I never mind young ladies' looks — always give the lie to their thoughts. Now we talk o' looks — never saw you look so well in my life — as handsome as an angel! And so much the better for me. Do you know, I've a bet of twenty guineas on your head — on your face, I mean. There's a young bride at Harrowgate, lady H——, they're all mad about her; the men swear she's the handsomest woman in England, and I swear I know one ten times as handsome. They've dared me to make good my word, and I've pledged myself to produce my beauty at the next ball, and to pit her against their belle for any money. — Most votes carry it. — I'm willing to double my bet since I've seen you again. — Come, had not we best be off? Now don't refuse me and make speeches — you know that's all nonsense — I'll take all the blame upon myself.'

Belinda, who had not been suffered to utter a word whilst Mrs Freke ran on in this strange manner, looked in unfeigned astonishment; but when she found herself seized and dragged towards the door, she drew back with a degree of gentle firmness that astonished Mrs Freke. With a smiling countenance, but a steady tone, she said, 'that she was sorry Mrs Freke's knight-errantry should not be exerted in a better cause, for that she was neither a prisoner, nor a distressed damsel.'

'And will you make me lose my bet?' cried Mrs Freke. 'O, at all events you must come to the ball! — I'm down for it. — But I'll not press it now, because you're frightened out of your poor little wits, I see, at the bare thoughts of doing any thing out of rule, by these good people. Well, well! it shall be managed for you — leave that to me. — I'm used to managing for cowards. — Pray tell me — you and lady Delacour are off, I understand? — Give ye joy! — She and I were once great friends; — that is to say, I had over her "that power which strong minds have over weak ones" — but she was too weak for me — one of those people that have neither courage to be good, nor to be bad.'

'The courage to be bad,' said Belinda, 'I believe, indeed, she does not possess.'

Mrs Freke stared. — 'Why, I heard you had quarrelled with her!'

'If I had,' said Belinda, 'I hope that I should still do justice to her merits. It is said that people are apt to suffer more by their friends than their

enemies. I hope that will never be the case with lady Delacour, as I confess that I have been one of her friends.'

'Gad, I like your spirit — you don't want courage, I see, to fight even for your enemies. You are just the kind of girl I admire — I see you've been prejudiced against me by lady Delacour. But whatever stories she may have trumped up, the truth of the matter is this; there's no living with her she's so jealous — so ridiculously jealous — of that lord of hers, for whom all the time she hasn't the impudence to pretend to care more than I do for the sole of my boot,' said Mrs Freke, striking it with her whip, 'but she hasn't the courage to give him tit for tat. — Now this is what I call weakness. Pray, how do she and Clarence Hervey go on together? — Are they out of the hornbook[2] of platonics yet?'

'Mr Hervey was not in town when I left it,' said Belinda.

'Was not he? — Ho! ho! — He's off then! — Ay, so I prophesied. She's not the thing for him. — He has some strength of mind — some soul — above vulgar prejudices. — So must a woman be to hold him. He was caught at first by her grace and beauty, and that sort of stuff; but I knew it could not last — knew she'd dilly dally with Clary, till he would turn upon his heel and leave her there.'

'I fancy that you are entirely mistaken both with respect to Mr Hervey and lady Delacour,' Belinda very seriously began to say; but Mrs Freke interrupted her, and ran on.

'No! no! no! I'm not mistaken; Clarence has found her out. — She's a *very* woman — *that* he could forgive her, and so could I. — But she's a *mere* woman — and that he can't forgive — no more can I.'

There was a kind of drollery about Mrs Freke, which, with some people, made the odd things she said pass for wit. Humour she really possessed; and when she chose it, she could be diverting to those who like buffoonery in women. She had set her heart upon winning Belinda over to her party. She began by flattery of her beauty; but as she saw that this had no effect, she next tried what could be done by insinuating that she had a high opinion of her understanding, by talking to her as an esprit fort.[3]

---

2. Small books made of horn were early readers for small children.
3. Strong spirit.

'For my part,' said she, 'I own I should like a strong devil better than a weak angel.'

'You forget,' said Belinda, 'that it is not Milton, but Satan, who says,

"Fallen spirit, to be weak is to be miserable".'[4]

'You read I see! — I did not know you were a reading girl. — So did I once! but I never read now. Books only spoil the originality of genius. Very well for those who can't think for themselves — but when one has made up one's opinions, there is no use in reading.'

'But to *make* them up,' replied Belinda, 'may it not be useful?'

'Of no use upon Earth to minds of a certain class. — You, who can think for yourself, should never read.'

'But I read that I may think for myself.'

'Only ruin your understanding, trust me. Books are full of trash — nonsense. Conversation is worth all the books in the world.'

'And is there never any nonsense in conversation?'

'What have you here?' continued Mrs Freke, who did not choose to attend to this question; exclaiming as she reviewed each of the books on the table in their turns, in the summary language of presumptuous ignorance. '"Smith's Theory of Moral Sentiments" — milk and water! "Moore's Travels" — hasty pudding! "La Bruyere" — nettle porridge! This is what you were at when I came in, was it not?' said she, taking up a book in which she saw Belinda's mark, '"Essay on the Inconsistency of Human Wishes."[5] Poor thing! who bored you with this task?'

'Mr Percival recommended it to me, as one of the best essays in the English language.'

'The devil! They seem to have put you in a course of the bitters[6] — a course of the woods might do your business better. Do you ever hunt? — Let me take you out with me some morning. — You'd be quite an angel on horseback; or let me drive you out some day in my unicorn.'

Belinda declined this invitation, and Mrs Freke strode away to the widow to conceal her mortification, threw up the sash, and called out to her groom,

'Walk those horses about, blockhead!' Mr Percival and Mr Vincent at this instant came into the room.

'Hail, fellow! well met,'[7] cried Mrs Freke, stretching out her hand to Mr Vincent.

It has been remarked, that an antipathy subsists between creatures, who, without being the same, have yet a strong external resemblance. Mr Percival saw this instinct rising in Mr Vincent, and smiled.

'Hail, fellow! well met, I say — shake hands and be friends, man! — Though I'm not in the habit of making apologies, if it will be any satisfaction to you, I beg your pardon for frightening your poor devil of a black.'

Then turning towards Mr Percival, she measured him with her eye, as a person whom she longed to attack. She thought, that if Belinda's opinion of the understanding of *these Percivals* could be lowered, she should rise in her opinion: accordingly, she determined to draw Mr Percival into an argument.

'I've been talking treason, I believe, to miss Portman,' cried she, 'for I've been opposing some of your opinions, Mr Percival.'

'If you opposed them all, madam,' said Mr Percival, 'I should not think it treason.'

'Vastly polite! — But I think all our politeness hypocrisy. What d'ye say to that?'

'You know that best, madam!'

'Then I'll go a step farther; for I'm determined you shall contradict me. — I think all virtue is hypocrisy.'

'I need not contradict you, madam,' said Mr Percival, 'for the terms which you make use of contradict themselves.'

'It is my system,' pursued Mrs Freke, 'that shame is always the cause of the vices of women.'

'It is sometimes the effect,' said Mr Percival; 'and, as cause and effect are reciprocal, perhaps you may, in some instances, be right.'

'O! I hate qualifying arguers. — Plump assertion or plump denial for me. — You shan't get off so — I say, shame is the cause of all women's vices.'

'False shame, I suppose you mean?' said Mr Percival.

4. John Milton, *Paradise Lost* (1667), vol. 1, p. 157.
5. Adam Smith, *The Theory of Moral Sentiments* (1759); John Moore, *A Journal During a Residence in France . . . 1792* (1793); Jean de la Bruyère, *The Characters, or Manners of the Age* (1699).
6. *Artemisia Absinthium*, wormwood. The leaves and tops were used as a tonic.
7. Common greeting, recorded in Jonathan Swift's 'My Lady's Lamentation'.

'Mere play upon words! — All shame is false shame. — We should be a great deal better without it. What say you, miss Portman? Silent — hey? Silence that speaks!'

'Miss Portman's blushes,' said Mr Vincent, 'speak *for* her.'

'*Against* her,' — said Mrs Freke — 'Women blush because they understand.'

'And you would have them understand without blushing?' said Mr Percival. 'So would I; for nothing can be more different than innocence and ignorance. Female delicacy —'

'This is just the way you men spoil women,' cried Mrs Freke, 'by talking to them of the *delicacy of their sex*, and such stuff. This *delicacy* enslaves the pretty delicate dears.'

'No; it enslaves us,' said Mr Vincent.

'I hate slavery! Vive la liberté!'[8] cried Mrs Freke, 'I'm a champion for the Rights of Women.'

'I am an advocate for their happiness,' said Mr Percival, 'and for their delicacy, as I think it conduces to their happiness.'

'I'm an enemy to their delicacy, as I am sure it conduces to their misery.'

'You speak from experience?' said Mr Percival.

'No, from observation. — Your most delicate women are always the greatest hypocrites; and, in my opinion, no hypocrite can or ought to be happy.'

'But you have not proved the hypocrisy,' said Belinda. 'Delicacy is not, I hope, an indisputable proof of it? — If you mean *false* delicacy —'

'To cut the matter short at once,' cried Mrs Freke, 'why, when a woman likes a man, does not she go and tell him so honestly?'

Belinda, surprised by this question from a woman, was too much abashed instantly to answer.

'Because she's a hypocrite. That is and must be the answer.'

'No,' said Mr Percival, 'because if she be a woman of sense, she knows that by such a step she would disgust the object of her affection.'

'Cunning! — cunning! — cunning! — the arms of the weakest.'

'Prudence! — prudence! — the arms of the strongest. Taking the best means to secure our own happiness without injuring that of others, is the best proof of sense and strength of mind,

whether in man or woman. Fortunately for society, the same conduct in ladies which best secures their happiness most increases ours.'

Mrs Freke beat the devil's tattoo[9] for some moments, and then exclaimed —

'You may say what you will, but the present system of society is radically wrong: whatever is, is wrong.'[10]

'How would you improve the state of society?' asked Mr Percival calmly.

'I'm not tinker general[11] to the world,' said she.

'I am glad of it,' said Mr Percival; 'for I have heard that tinkers often spoil more than they mend.'

'But if you want to know,' said Mrs Freke, 'what I would do to improve the world, I'll tell you: I'd have your sex taught to say, "Horns! horns!"[12] I defy you.'

'This would doubtless be a great improvement,' said Mr Percival; 'but you would not overturn society to attain it, would you? Should we find things much improved by tearing away what has been called the decent drapery of life?'

'Drapery, if you ask me my opinion,' cried Mrs Freke, 'drapery, whether wet or dry, is the most confoundedly indecent thing in the world.'

'That depends on *public* opinion, I allow,' said Mr Percival. 'The Lacedaemonian ladies,[13] who were veiled only in public opinion, were better covered from profane eyes, than some English ladies are in wet drapery.'

'I know nothing of the Lacedaemonian ladies, I took my leave of them when I was a schoolboy — girl — I should say. But, pray, what o'clock is it by you — I've sat till I'm cramped all over,' cried Mrs Freke, getting up and stretching herself so violently that some part of her habiliments gave way. 'Honi soit qui mal y pense!'[14] said she, bursting into a hoarse laugh.

Without sharing in any degree that confusion which Belinda felt for her, she strode out of the room, saying, 'Miss Portman, you understand these things better than I do; come and set me to rights.'

---

8. Long live liberty.

9. Tapping fingers or toes for an irritatingly long time.
10. Reversal of the aphorism by Alexander Pope (1688–1744) in *An Essay on Man* (1733–4): 'One truth is clear, Whatever is, is Right'.
11. i.e. not responsible for mending the world.
12. Emblem of cuckoldry.
13. Spartan women often went naked as part of the austerity of their regime.
14. Evil be to him who evil thinks.

When she was in Belinda's room, she threw herself into an arm chair, and laughed immoderately.

'How I have trimmed Percival this morning,' said she.

'I am glad you think so,' said Belinda; 'for I really was afraid he had been too severe upon you.'

'I only wish,' continued Mrs Freke, 'I only wish his wife had been by. Why the devil did not she make her appearance? — I suppose the prude was afraid of my demolishing and unrigging her.'

'There seems to have been more danger of that for you than for any body else,' said Belinda, as she assisted to set Mrs Freke's *rigging*, as she called it, to rights.

'I do, of all things, delight in hauling good people's opinions out of their musty drawers, and seeing how they look when they're all pulled to pieces before their faces. Pray, are those lady Anne's drawers or yours?' said Mrs Freke, pointing to a chest of drawers.

'Mine.'

'I'm sorry for it; for, if they were hers, to punish her for *shirking* me, by the Lord, I'd have every rag she has in the world out in the middle of the floor in ten minutes! You don't know me — I'm a terrible person when provoked — stop at nothing!'

As Mrs Freke saw no other chance left of gaining her point with Belinda, she tried what intimidating her would do.

'I stop at nothing,' repeated she, fixing her eyes upon miss Portman, to fascinate her by terrour. 'Friend or foe! Peace or war! Take your choice. Come to the ball at Harrowgate, I win my bet, and I'm your sworn friend. Stay away, I lose my bet, and am your sworn enemy.'

'It is not in my power, madam,' said Belinda calmly, 'to comply with your request.'

'Then you'll take the consequences,' cried Mrs Freke. She rushed past her, hurried down stairs, and called out,

'Bid my blockhead bring my unicorn.'

She, her unicorn, and her blockhead, were out of sight in a few minutes.

MARY TIGHE

(1772–1810)

from:
PSYCHE,
WITH OTHER POEMS (1811)

[Mary Tighe's address to pleasure attempts to represent the sensuousness of erotic passion in the language of romantic poetry. Tighe is often compared to John Keats; like Keats, she suffered from consumption, which fact may give to her poems the urgency both of sensuality and of guilt. The text is from the edition printed for Longman, Hurst, Rees, Orme and Brown, London, 1811.]

Pleasure

Ah, syren Pleasure! when thy flattering strains
Lured me to seek thee through thy flowery plains,
Taught from thy sparkling cup full joys to sip,
And suck sweet poison from thy velvet-lip,

Didst thou in opiate charms my virtue steep,
Was Reason silent, and did Conscience sleep?
How could I else enjoy thy faithless dreams,
And fancy day-light in thy meteor gleams;
Think all was happiness, that smiled like joy,
And with dear purchase seize each glittering
  toy?
Till roused at last, deep-rankling in my heart,
I felt the latent anguish of thy dart!
Oh, let the young and innocent beware,
Nor think uninjured to approach thy snare!
Their surest conquest is, the foe to shun,
By fight infected, and by truce undone.
Secure, at distance let her shores be past,
Whose sight can poison, and whose breath can
  blast.
Contentment blooms not on her glowing ground,
And round her splendid shrine no peace is
  found.

If once enchanted by her magic-charms,
They seek for bliss in Dissipation's arms:
If once they touch the limits of her realm,
Offended Principle resigns the helm,
Simplicity forsakes the treacherous shore,
And once discarded, she returns no more.
Thus the charmed mariner on every side
Of poisoned Senegal's ill-omened tide,
Eyes the rich carpet of the varied hue
And plains luxuriant opening to his view:
Now the steep banks with twenty forests
   crowned,
Clothed to the margin of the sloping ground;
Where with full foliage bending o'er the waves,
Its verdant arms the spreading Mangrove[1]
   laves;[2]
And now smooth, level lawns of deeper green
Betray the richness of the untrodden scene:
Between the opening groves such prospects
   glow,

1. Tropical tree.
2. Bathes.

As Art with mimic-hand can ne'er bestow,
While lavish Nature wild profusion yields,
And spreads, unbid, the rank uncultured fields;
Flings with fantastic hand in every gale
Ten thousand blossoms o'er each velvet-vale,
And bids unclasped their fragrant beauties die
Far from the painter's hand or sage's eye.
From cloudless sun perpetual lustre streams,
And swarms of insects glisten in their beams.
Near and more near the heedless sailors steer,
Spread all their canvass, and no warnings hear.
See, on the edge of the clear liquid glass
The wondering beasts survey them as they pass,
And fearless bounding o'er their native green,
Adorn the landscape and enrich the scene
Ah, fatal scene! the deadly vapours rise,
And swift the vegetable poison flies,
Putrescence loads the rank infected ground,
Deceitful calms deal subtle death around;
Even as they gaze their vital powers decay,
Their wasted health and vigour melt away;
Till quite extinct the animating fire,
Pale, ghastly victims, they at last expire.

JOSEPH SHERIDAN LE FANU

(1814–73)

from:
CARMILLA (1872)

[This early vampire tale shows the naïve narrator being drawn into an obscurely erotic bond with her evil friend Carmilla. It is not clear whether Le Fanu thought of their relationship as sexual, exactly, but today 'Carmilla' tends to be read as the first in an underground tradition of lesbian vampire stories. The following conversation takes place early in the girls' friendship. 'Carmilla' was first published in the short story collection *In a Glass Darkly* (London: R. Bentley, 1872).]

She used to place her pretty arms about my neck, draw me to her, and laying her cheek to mine, murmur with her lips near my ear, 'Dearest, your little heart is wounded; think me not cruel because I obey the irresistible law of my strength and weakness; if your dear heart is wounded, my

wild heart bleeds with yours. In the rapture of my enormous humiliation I live in your warm life, and you shall die — die, sweetly die — into mine. I cannot help it; as I draw near to you, you, in your turn, will draw near to others, and learn the rapture of that cruelty, which yet is love; so, for a while, seek to know no more of me and mine, but trust me with all your loving spirit.'

And when she had spoken such a rhapsody, she would press me more closely in her trembling embrace, and her lips in soft kisses gently glow upon my cheek.

Her agitations and her language were unintelligible to me.

From these foolish embraces, which were not of very frequent occurrence, I must allow, I used to wish to extricate myself; but my energies seemed to fail me. Her murmured words sounded like a lullaby in my ear, and soothed my resistance into a trance, from which I only seemed to recover myself when she withdrew her arms.

In these mysterious moods I did not like her. I experienced a strange tumultuous excitement that was pleasurable, ever and anon, mingled with a vague sense of fear and disgust. I had no distinct thoughts about her while such scenes lasted, but I was conscious of a love growing into adoration, and also of abhorrence. This I know is paradox, but I can make no other attempt to explain the feeling.

I now write, after an interval of more than ten years, with a trembling hand, with a confused and horrible recollection of certain occurrences and situations, in the ordeal through which I was unconsciously passing; though with a vivid and very sharp remembrance of the main current of my story. But, I suspect, in all lives there are certain emotional scenes, those in which our passions have been most wildly and terribly roused, that are of all others the most vaguely and dimly remembered.

Sometimes after an hour of apathy, my strange and beautiful companion would take my hand and hold it with a fond pressure, renewed again and again; blushing softly, gazing in my face with languid and burning eyes, and breathing so fast that her dress rose and fell with the tumultuous respiration. It was like the ardour of a lover, it embarrassed me; it was hateful and yet overpowering; and with gloating eyes she drew me to her, and her hot lips travelled along my cheek in kisses; and she would whisper, almost in sobs, 'You are mine, you *shall* be mine, you and I are one for ever.' Then she has thrown herself back in her chair, with her small hands over her eyes, leaving me trembling.

'Are we related,' I used to ask; 'what can you mean by all this? I remind you perhaps of some one whom you love; but you must not, I hate it; I don't know you — I don't know myself when you look so and talk so.'

She used to sigh at my vehemence, then turn away and drop my hand.

GEORGE MOORE

(1852–1933)

from:
A DRAMA IN MUSLIN.
A REALISTIC NOVEL (1887)

[This novel shows the influence of French naturalists such as Emile Zola (1840–1802), who often wrote about passionate love between women as something exotic and sinister. *A Drama in Muslin* deals with a group of Anglo-Irish girls leaving school and facing the humiliating marriage market. One who will take no part in it is Cecilia, who is in love with her friend Alice. The text is from the 1887 edition, published in London by Scott.]

She had just laid aside her pen and was waiting for Cecilia. Suddenly footsteps were heard in the corridor.

'Oh, Alice darling, how are you? I am delighted — I am so delighted to see you. Let me kiss you,

let me see you; I have been longing to see you for weeks — for months.'

Alice bent her face down, and Cecilia lay sobbing with joy upon her shoulder for some moments. Then, holding each other's hands, the girls stood looking through a deep and expressive silence into each other's eyes. Cecilia's eyes! — large, mellow depths of light, vague and melancholy with the yearning of the soul. You see the high shoulders, the chin and neck how curiously advanced. But little is seen but the eyes! the eyes of the deformed, deep, dreamy depths of brown, luminous with a strange weariness, that we who are normal, straight, and strong, can neither feel nor understand. The brown is now liquescent; it burns, and becomes golden with passion; it melts and softens to strange tenderness. The eyes of the deformed! — deep enigmatic eyes, never will your secret be revealed; there is a trouble that words cannot speak, but that eyes may sometimes suggest: — the melting questioning grief of the spaniel that would tell his master of his love. There was something dog-like in the lavish affection with which Cecilia welcomed her friend; and, like the dumb animal, she seemed to suffer from her inability to express her joys in words.

'I wish, Alice, I could tell you how glad I am to have you back: it seems like heaven to see you again. You look so nice, so true, so sweet, so perfect. There never was anyone so nice as you, Alice.'

'Cecilia, dear, you shouldn't talk to me like that; it is absurd. Indeed, I don't think it is quite right.'

'Not quite right,' repeated the cripple sadly; 'what do you mean? Why is it wrong — why should it be wrong for me to love you?'

'I don't mean to say that it is wrong; you misunderstand me; but — but . . . well, I don't know how to explain myself, but . . .'

'I know, I know, I know,' said Cecilia; and her nervous sensitivity revealed thoughts in Alice's mind — thoughts of which Alice herself was not distinctly conscious, just as a photograph exposes irregularities in the texture of a leaf that the naked eye would not perceive.

'If Harding were to speak to you so, you would not think it wrong.'

Alice coloured deeply, and she said, with a certain resoluteness in her voice, 'Cecilia, I wish you would not talk to me in this way. You give me great pain.'

'I am sorry if I do, but I cannot help it. I am jealous of the words that are spoken to you, of the air you breathe, of the ground you walk upon. How, then, can I help hating that man?'

The teeth gnawed at the lips, and the eyes were shot with strange flames. Alice trembled: she was obscurely troubled. At last she said:

'I do not wish to argue this point with you, Cecilia, nor am I sure that I understand it. There is no one I like better than you, dear, but that we should be jealous of each other is absurd.'

'For you perhaps, but not for me.'

GEORGE EGERTON

(1859–1945)

from:
THE SPELL OF THE WHITE ELF (1893)

[In her 'new woman' fiction, George Egerton (Mary Chavelita Dunne) often deals with passionate friendships between women; what is unique about this story is the characterization of one such woman as androgynous and seductive. The narrator is revisiting Norway, where her childhood sweetheart Hans promised that he would always be waiting to marry her. On the ship, her attention is caught by an English anthropologist who is said to have a stay-at-home husband. The story is from a collection, *Keynotes*, published in 1893 by E. Matthews and J. Lane.]

My compatriot is stretched in a big arm-chair reading. She is sitting comfortably with one leg crossed over the other, in the manner called 'shockingly unladylike' of my early lessons in deportment. The flame flickers over the patent leather of her neat low-heeled boot, and strikes a spark from the pin in her tie. There is something manlike about her. I don't know where it lies, but it is there. Her hair curls in grey flecked rings about her head; it has not a cut look, seems rather to grow short naturally. She has a charming tubbed look. Of course every lady is alike clean, but some men and women have an individual look of sweet cleanness that is a beauty of itself. She feels my gaze and looks up and smiles. She has a rare smile, it shows her white teeth and softens her features:

'The fire is cosy, isn't it? I hope we shall have an easy passage, so that it can be kept in.'

I answer something in English.

She has a trick of wrinkling her brows, she does it now as she says:

'A-ah, I should have said you were Norsk.[1] Are you not really? Surely you have a typical head, or eyes and hair at the least?'

'Half of me is Norsk, but I have lived a long time in England.'

'Father of course; case of "there was a sailor loved a lass",[2] was it not?'

I smile an assent and add: 'I lost them both when I was very young.'

A reflective look steals over her face. It is stern in repose, and as she seems lost in some train of thought of her own I go to my cabin and lie down; the rattling noises and the smell of paint makes me feel ill. I do not go out again. I wake next morning with a sense of fear at the stillness. There is no sound but a lapping wash of water at the side of the steamer, but it is delicious to lie quietly after the vibration of the screw and the sickening swing. I look at my watch; seven o'clock. I cannot make out why there is such a silence, as we only stop at Christiansand[3] long enough to take cargo and passengers. I dress and go out. The saloon is empty but the fire is burning brightly. I go to the pantry and ask the stewardess when we arrived? Early, she says; all the passengers for here are already gone on shore; and there is a thick fog outside, goodness knows how long we'll be kept. I go to the top of the stairs and look out; the prospect is uninviting and I come down again and turn over some books on the table; in Russian, I think. I feel sure they are hers.

'Good-morning!' comes her pleasant voice. How alert and bright-eyed she is! It is a pick-me-up to look at her.

1. Norwegian.
2. Traditional song.
3. Kristiansand, a port on the southern tip of Norway.

'You did not appear last night? Not given in already, I hope!'

She is kneeling on one knee before the fire, holding her palms to the glow, and with her figure hidden in her loose, fur-lined coat and the light showing up her strong face under the little tweed cap, she seems so like a clever-faced slight man, that I feel I am conventionally guilty in talking so freely to her. She looks at me with a deliberate critical air, and then springs up.

'Let me give you something for your head! Stewardess, a wine-glass!'

I should not dream of remonstrance — not if she were to compel me to drink sea-water; and I am not complaisant as a rule.

When she comes back I swallow it bravely, but I leave some powder in the glass; she shakes her head, and I finish this too. We sat and talked, or at least she talked and I listened. I don't remember what she said, I only know that she was making clear to me most of the things that had puzzled me for a long time; questions that arise in silent hours; that one speculates over, and to which one finds no answers in text-books. How she knew just the subjects that worked in me I knew not; some subtle intuitive sympathy, I suppose, enabled her to find it out . . .

I had been talking of myself and of Hans Jörgen.

'I like your Mr. Hans Jörgen', she said, 'he has a strong nature and knows what he wants; there is reliability in him. They are rarer qualities than one thinks in men, I have found through life that the average man is weaker than we are. It must be a good thing to have a stronger nature to lean to. I have never had that.'

There is a want in the tone of her voice as she ends, and I feel inclined to put out my hand and stroke hers — she has beautiful long hands — but I am afraid to do so.

ROSA MULHOLLAND

(1841–1921)

from:
THE TRAGEDY OF CHRIS
(1903)

[This novel is a late example of romantic friendship literature, and also of the 'social issue' fiction produced by such novelists as L.T. Meade, Sarah Grand and M.E. Francis. When Chris, a young Dublin flower-seller, saves Sheelia from beggary, they become devoted partners, living together and even fostering a child. Their relationship is the focus of the novel, but it is never presented as sexual or in any way deviant. Chris is kidnapped and sold into prostitution in London;[1] after an arduous hunt, Sheelia tracks her down and drags her away from her keeper. The following excerpt is from Chapter 24. Published in London in 1903 by Sands.]

'IT WENT AGAINST ME'

Sheelia turned the key in the door.

'Now, off with every stitch of clothes you have got on you,' she said; 'don't keep as much as a stockin' or a garter. I've enough to share with you, an' these must go back to the devil you got them from.'

Chris sat stupid and passive while Sheelia undressed her. The pretty boots, the elegant skirts, the decorated hat, were flung into a corner, and in a few minutes Chris appeared, clothed in one of Sheelia's clean cotton frocks and a pair of her well-worn, if small and shapely, shoes. Then she placed her sitting in an old cane chair, went on her knees beside her, and threw her arms around her.

'Oh, Chris, my darling, it's you at last! I've got you, my dear, after all these years of looking for you!'

Tears were running down Sheelia's face. Chris burst into an agony of weeping and shrank from her.

'You don't know anything about it,' she said. 'I'm not the same as I was before. I'm not fit for you to touch or to speak to.'

Sheelia seized the averted head and drew the shamed and miserable young face closer to her own.

'Yes, you are fit,' she said, kissing her with passion. 'You are fit for everything good. Nothing that happened to you was your fault, and now you've left if all behind you.'

Chris made no reply, except by yielding to the embrace and allowing her poor, thin face to be pressed and held close to Sheelia's womanly shoulder. Her tears coursed silently down the hollows where the dimples had been. No one but Sheelia herself could have recognised in this broken creature the dancing, joyous child of the Liberties,[2] gay in despite of hard living, and crowned with her daffodils.

'Chris, you must cheer up. You saved me long ago, and I'm going to save you now. We'll go away somewhere, home to our own country, some place where nobody will ever know what happened. And we'll live together and make friends for ourselves.'

A wild sob broke from Chris, and her tears poured down only the more plentifully.

[Sheelia returns to Ireland with Chris, whose mind has been deranged by her experience. Before the end of the novel Chris dies, leaving Sheelia free to marry.]

---

1. This section of the novel very much resembles M.E. Francis's sensational novel of the white slave trade, *The Story of Mary Dunn* (1913).

2. The area of inner-city Dublin where Chris and Sheelia worked.

EDITH Œ. SOMERVILLE AND MARTIN ROSS

(1858–1949)   (1862–1915)

from:
IRISH MEMORIES (1917)

[This memoir was written by Edith Somerville after the death of her partner and collaborator, Martin Ross (Violet Martin), but was published in both their names, as Somerville was convinced of their psychic communication. Though their love is described in confident terms, showing no shadow of the newly popularized theories about homosexuality as a congenital, pathological condition, Somerville does call it 'another way', making it clear that their choice marked them out from their marriageable friends. Published in London in 1917 by Longmans.]

WHEN FIRST SHE CAME

'Sure ye're always laughing! That ye may laugh in the sight of the Glory of Heaven!'

This benediction was bestowed upon Martin by a beggar-woman in Skibbereen,[1] and I hope, and believe, it has been fulfilled. Wherever she was, if a thing amused her she had to laugh. I can see her in such a case, the unpredictable thing that was to touch the spot, said or done, with streaming tears, helpless, almost agonised, much as one has seen a child writhe in the tortured ecstasy of being tickled. The large conventional jest had but small power over her; it was the trivial, subtle absurdity, the inversion of the expected, the sublimity getting a little above itself and failing to realise that it had taken that fatal step over the border; these were the things that felled her, and laid her, wherever she might be, in ruins.

In Richmond[2] Parish Church, on a summer Sunday, it happened to her and a friend to be obliged to stand in the aisle, awaiting the patronage of the pew-opener. The aisle was thronged, and Martin was tired. She essayed to lean against the end of a fully occupied pew, and not only fully occupied, but occupied by a row of such devout and splendid ladies as are only seen in perfection in smart suburban churches. I have said the aisle was thronged, and, as she leaned, the

pressure increased. Too late she knew that she had miscalculated her mark. Like Sisera, the son of Jabin,[3] she bowed (only she bowed backwards), she fell; where she fell, there she lay down, and where she lay down was along the laps of those devout and splendid ladies. These gazed down into her convulsed countenance with eyes that could not have expressed greater horror or surprise if she had been a boa constrictor; a smileless glance, terribly enhanced by gold-rimmed *pince-nez*. She thinks she must have extended over fully four of them. She never knew how she regained the aisle. She was herself quite powerless, and she thinks that with knee action, similar to that of a knife-grinder, they must have banged her on to her feet. It was enough for her to be beyond the power of those horrified and indignant and gold eye-glassed eyes, even though she knew that nothing could deliver her from the grip of the demon of laughter. She says she was given a seat, out of pity, I suppose, shortly afterwards, and there, on her knees and hidden under the brim of her hat, she wept, and uttered those faint insect squeaks that indicate the extremity of endurance, until the end of the service, when her unfortunate companion led her home.

It was, as it happens, in church that I saw her first; in our own church, in Castle Townshend.[4] That was on Sunday, January 17, 1886. I immediately commandeered her to sing in the choir, and from that day, little as she then knew it, she was fated to become one of its fundamental props and stays. A position than which few are more arduous and thankless.

I suppose some suggestion of what she looked like should here be given . . . She was of what was then considered 'medium height,' 5ft. 5½ in. Since then the standard has gone up, but in 1886 Martin was accustomed to assert that small men considered her 'a monstrous fine woman,' and big men said she was 'a dear little thing.' I find myself

1. Skibbereen, Co. Cork.
2. Richmond, Surrey.
3. Sisera, the captain of Jabin's army, killed by Jael who drove a tent peg into his head while he was sleeping; see Judges 4:17–21.
4. Castle Townsend, Co. Cork.

incapable of appraising her. Many drawings I have made of her, and, that spring of 1886, before I went to Paris, I attempted also a small sketch in oils, with a hope, that was futile, that colour might succeed where black and white had failed. I can only offer an inadequate catalogue.

Eyes: large, soft, and brown, with the charm of expression that is often one of the compensations of short sight. Hair: bright brown and waving, liable to come down riding, and on one such occasion described by an impressionable old general as 'a chestnut wealth,' a stigma that she was never able to live down. A colour like a wild rose — a simile that should be revered on account of its long service to mankind, and must be forgiven since none other meets the case — and a figure of the lightest and slightest, on which had been bestowed the great and capricious boon of smartness, which is a thing apart, and does not rely on mere anatomical considerations . . .

Martin's figure, good anywhere, looked its best in the saddle; she had the effect of having poised there without effort, as a bird poises on a spray; she looked even more of a feather-weight than she was, yet no horse that I have ever known, could, with his most malign capers, discompose the airy security of her seat, still less shake her nerve. Before I knew how extravagantly short-sighted she was, I did not appreciate the pluck that permitted her to accept any sort of mount, and to face any sort of a fence, blindfold, and that inspired her out hunting to charge what came in her way, with no more knowledge of what was to happen then Marcus Curtius[5] had when he leaped into the gulf.

It is trite, not to say stupid, to expatiate upon that January Sunday when I first met her; yet it has proved the hinge of my lie, the place where my fate, and hers, turned over, and new and unforeseen things began to happen to us. They did not happen at once. An idler, more good-for-nothing pack of 'blagyards' than we all were could not easily be found. I, alone, kept up a pretence of occupation; I was making drawings for the *Graphic* in those days and was in the habit of impounding my young friends as models . . .

It is perhaps noteworthy that on my second or third meeting with Martin I suggested to her that we should write a book together and that I should illustrate it . . .

In June I returned from Paris; 'pale and dwindled,' Martin's diary mentions, 'but fashionable,' which I find grafitying, though quite untrue. It was one of those perfect summers that come sometimes to the south of Ireland, when rain is not, and the sun is hot, but never too hot, and the gardens are a storm of flowers, flowers such as one does not see elsewhere, children of the south and the sun and the sea; tall delphiniums that have climbed to the sky and brought down its most heavenly blue; Japanese iris, with their pale and dappled lilac discs spread forth to the sun, like little plates and saucers at a high and honourable 'tea ceremony' in the land of Nippon;[6] peonies and poppies, arums and asphodel, every one of them three times as tall, and three times as brilliant, and three times as sweet as any of their English cousins, and all of them, and everything else as well, irradiated for me that happy year by a new 'Spirit of Delight.' It was, as I have said, though then we knew it only dimly, the beginning, for us, of a new era. For most boys and girls the varying, yet invariable, flirtations, and emotional episodes of youth, are resolved and composed by marriage. To Martin and to me was opened another way, and the flowering of both our lives was when we met each other.

If ever Ireland should become organised and systematised, and allotmented, I would put in a plea that the parish of Castle Haven[7] may be kept as a national reserve for idlers and artists and idealists. The memory comes back to me of those blue mornings of mid-June that Martin and I, with perhaps the saving pretence of a paint-box, used to spend, lying on the warm, short grass of the sheep fields on Drishane Side,[8] high over the harbour, listening to the curving cry of the curlews and the mewing of the sea-gulls, as they drifted in the blue over our heads; watching the sunlight waking dancing stars to life in the deeper blue firmament below, and criticising conde-scendingly the manoeuvres of the little white-

---

5. A Roman youth (*c.* 360 BC) who sacrificed himself by leaping on horseback into a gap that had opened in the forum — an oracle had decreed that the gap would close when Rome threw into it whatever was most precious — and the gap closed over his head.

6. The Japanese name for Japan, literally 'the great land of the rising sun'.

7. The bay area around Castle Townsend.

8. Drishane House, Castletownshend, the Somerville family home.

sailed racing yachts, as they strove and squeezed round their mark-buoys, or rushed emulously to the horizon and back again. Below us, by a hundred feet or so, other idlers bathed in the Dutchman's Cove, uttering those sea-bird screams that seem to be induced by the sea equally in girls as in gulls. But Martin and I, having taken high ground as artists and idealists, remained, roasting gloriously in the sun, at the top of the cliffs.

That summer was for all of us a time of extreme and excessive lawn tennis. Tournaments, formal and informal, were incessant, challenges and matches raged. Martin and I played an unforgettable match against two long-legged lads, whose handicap, consisting as it did in tight skirts, and highly-trimmed mushroom hats, pressed nearly as heavily on us as on them. My mother, and a female friend of like passions with herself, had backed us to win, and they kept up a wonderful and shameless *barrage* of abuse between the petticoated warriors and their game, and an equally staunch supporting fire of encouragement to us. When at last Martin and I triumphed, my mother and the female friend were voiceless from long screaming, but they rushed speechlessly into the middle of the court and there flung themselves into each other's arms . . .

When I try to recall that lovely summer and its successor, the year of the old Queen's First Jubilee, 1887,[9] I seem best to remember those magical evenings when two or three boat-loads of us would row 'up the river,' which is no river, but a narrow and winding sea-creek, of, as we hold, unparalleled beauty, between high hills, with trees on both its sides, drooping low over the water, and seaweed, instead of ivy, hanging from their branches. Nothing more enchanting than resting on one's oars in the heart of that dark mirror, with no sound but the sleepy chuckle of the herons in the tall trees on the hill-side, or the gurgle of the tide against the bows, until someone, perhaps, would start one of the glees that were being practised for the then concert — there was always one in the offing — and then Echo,[10] that dwells opposite Roger's Island, would wake from its sleep and join in, not more than half a minute behind the beat.

Or out at the mouth of the harbour, the boats rocking a little in the wide golden fields of moonlight, golden as sunlight, almost, in those August nights, and the lazy oars, paddling in what seemed a sea of opal oil, would drip with the pale flames of the phosphorous that seethed and whispered at their touch, when, as Martin has said,

'Land and sea lay in rapt accord, and the breast of the brimming tide was laid to the breast of the cliff, with a low and broken voice of joy.'

These are some of those Irish yesterdays, that came and went lightly, and were more memorable than Martin and I knew, that summer, when first she came.

9. Queen Victoria came to the British throne in 1837.

10. In Roman mythology, a nymph so in love with Narcissus that she pined away until only her voice remained.

EVA GORE-BOOTH

(1870–1926)

from:
POEMS (1929)

[Working in a time of uneasy transition between concepts of love between women as being lofty and pure or sick and unnatural, Eva Gore-Booth was always careful to write on the 'romantic friendship' side of the line. Her appropriation and 'lesbianizing' of Celtic myths is particularly interesting. These three poems characterize passion between women as, respectively, a matter of spiritual partnership, feminist solidarity, and pagan worship. The text is from *Poems of Eva Gore-Booth*, with a biographical introduction by Esther Roper (London: Longman, 1929).]

The Travellers
(to E.G.R.)[1]

Was it not strange that by the tideless sea
The jar and hurry of our lives should cease?
That under olive boughs we found our peace,
And all the world's great song in Italy?[2]

Is it not strange though Peace herself has wings
And long ago has gone her separate ways,
On through the tumult of our fretful days
From Life to Death the great song chimes and
        rings?

In that sad day shall then the singing fail,
Shall Life go down in silence at the end,
And in the darkness friend be lost to friend,
And all our love and dreams of no avail?

You whose Love's melody makes glad the gloom
Of a long labour and a patient strife,
Is not that music greater than our life?
Shall not a little song outlast that doom?

1. Esther Gertrude Roper (1868–1938), the half-Irish trade unionist,
   with whom Gore-Booth lived for the last three decades of her life.
2. Gore-Booth and Roper met when both were staying at the house of
   the writer George MacDonald in Italy in 1895.

Women's Rights

Down by Glencar Waterfall[1]
There's no winter left at all.

Every little flower that blows
Cold and darkness overthrows.

Every little thrush that sings
Quells the wild air with brave wings.

Every little stream that runs
Holds the light of brighter suns.

But where men in office sit
Winter holds the human wit.

In the dark and dreary town
Summer's green is trampled down.

Frozen, frozen everywhere
Are the springs of thought and prayer.

1. In County Sligo.

Rise with us and let us go
To where the living waters flow.

Oh, whatever men may say
Ours is the wide and open way.

Oh, whatever men may dream
We have the blue air and the stream.

Men have got their towers and walls,
We have cliffs and waterfalls.

Oh, whatever men may do
Ours is the gold air and the blue.

Men have got their pomp and pride —
All the green world is on our side.

The Vision of Niamh[1]

Life grows so clear, beneath the dreaming lamp,
I can see through the darkness of the grave,
How, long ago in her high mountain camp
The stars shone on the stormy soul of Maeve.[2]

And leaning from the shadow of a star
With hands outstretched to hold the hands of
        clay,
One looked into her spirit fairer far
Than sun or moon of any mortal day.

Oh Niamh, thou are child of the dim hours
Between the day and night, when Summer flings
A little flashing dew on the wild flowers,
And all the starlight glimmers in thy wings.

Thou sorrow of lost beauty, thou strange queen
Who calls to men's soul out of the twilight seas,
Whose white hands break the stars in silver sheen,
Whose voice is as the wind in the fir trees.

For thee Maeve left her kingdom and her throne,
And all the gilded wisdom of the wise,
And dwelt among the hazel trees alone
So that she might look into Niamh's eyes.

1. Irish fairy queen who rules Tir nOg, the land of eternal youth.
   Gore-Booth identifies her with Urania, the goddess of heavenly
   love.
2. Legendary Queen of Connacht, whose exploits are recorded in the
   Táin Bó Cuailgne.

No sorrow of lost battles any more
In her enchanted spirit could abide;
Straight she forgot the long and desolate war,
And how Fionavar[3] for pity died.

Ah, Niamh, still the starry lamp burns bright,
I can see through the darkness of the grave,
How long ago thy soul of starry light
Was very dear to the brave soul of Maeve.

3. Queen Maeve's daughter, who died of grief looking at the battlefield after her mother's victory.

ELIZABETH BOWEN

(1899–1973)

from:
THE HOTEL (1927)

[Throughout her work, Elizabeth Bowen presents a range of erotic relations between women, from the passionate sisters in 'The Happy Autumn Fields' (see Volume II, pp. 940–8) to a character named as 'a Lesbian' in *The Little Girls* (1963). More typical is the ambiguous, flirtatious kind of friendship found in *The Hotel* (1927). Staying at a seaside resort, Bowen's young heroine Sydney has become infatuated with the sophisticated Mrs Kerr. In this difficult conversation in a patisserie, Mrs Kerr has expressed her disappointment that Sydney and her visiting son Ronald have not become close. Published in London in 1927 by Constable.]

Mrs. Kerr's hand, that lay with casually spread-out fingers under Sydney's eyes along the edge of the table, had some vague connection with her personality, but neither seemed to have anything to do with what had been said. The amazed Sydney could not reconcile them. 'Do you mean what you've just been saying?' she said doubtfully. 'Do you really believe what you've just said? Did much really stand or fall on our making a success of things — I and Ronald?'

'So it did seem to me,' said Mrs. Kerr, also looking slightly bewildered, as though by all these questions Sydney were confusing the issue.

'Did you think you had helped us?'

'Only by . . . valuing both of you.'

'I suppose,' said Sydney, struck by this, 'you do in a kind of way value us?'

'Yes,' said Mrs. Kerr, 'and I've missed you very much. When I had to throw away your carnations this morning I was sorry; I didn't a bit want to.'

'Only this morning? Carnations do last a long time,' said Sydney, and considered the phenomenon gravely. 'One didn't want to intrude, you see,' she added.

'Intrude?' said Mrs. Kerr, repeating the rather middle-class word wonderingly. Her gentle, mystified air was not sympathetic. 'I think,' she said slowly, as though trying how best to express herself to an almost strange young woman, the school friend, as it might be, of a daughter, 'that you've been a little . . . over-important about it, perhaps, haven't you? I mean, how could your coming or not coming make any difference between me and Ronald? He would have been pleased, he was ready to be friendly; he knows just what you've been to me, and in his own tied-up sort of way he is ever so grateful. He likes me to have friends wherever I am. I don't think,' she concluded, with a smile of pity for the girl's inevitable incomprehension, 'that anybody could put things wrong between me and Ronald.'

'In fact, one seems to have taken too much for granted. Funny!' said Sydney and laughed.

'Oh, Sydney dear, no. Why? Don't be so bitter.'

'Why bitter? I see how tiresome a girl can be.'

'Never tiresome; you've been charming; more than unselfish — giving up so much of your time to me, giving me so much — I've accepted too much, I'm afraid.' Mrs. Kerr broke off with compunction.

'Why reproach yourself? Don't you find all your friends are the same?'

Mrs. Kerr sighed and looked down at her hands, allowing this to pass for an admission. With a smile of particular ruefulness that drew up the eyebrows tragically and brought the face to its fullest, profoundest expression of all of her, she confessed: 'But in your case I've been specially guilty. I begin now to guess you've expected much more of me, and that I've been taking and taking without so much as a glance ahead or a single suspicion of what you would want to have back. I'm afraid we've gone wrong through your not quite understanding. You see, I'm so fond of you, but —'

'But?'

'Well, simply but! I mean, there is nothing else there. It has always seemed to me simple to like people and right to be liked, but I can never feel that much more is involved — is it? I have a horror, I think, of not being, and of my friends not being, quite perfectly balanced. I think moderation in everything — but perhaps I am cold . . . Will you take my purse now — if you won't eat any more — and go in and pay for the cakes?'

To Sydney the cumulative effect of this succession of touches (especially the last: herself brandishing with commercial insistence a long bill that her bewildered debtor felt unable to meet) was of vulgarity. The attribution to herself of an irritable sex-consciousness *vis-à-vis* to Ronald did not hurt, but sharply offended. Mrs. Kerr, however, sitting there with her half-smile, her evident deprecation of the interlude, her invincible air of fastidiousness, had maintained her own plane, whereon 'vulgarity' would be meaningly. Sydney could only suppose that cruelty as supremely disinterested as art had, like art, its own

purity, which could transcend anything and consecrate the nearest material to its uses.

The friend sitting back to back with Mrs. Kerr had gone away minutes ago; the little blue tables one by one were deserted. The business of the Patisserie wilted temporarily before the approach of lunch-time. Surprised by this isolation, as though the trees of a wood had melted away from around them, the two left the shade of the awning and stood dazzled for a moment, looking vaguely up and down the street.

'Where now?' said Mrs. Kerr, and laid a hand on Sydney's sleeve in her anxiety to be directed.

Sydney could make no suggestion; she remembered they were on an edge of Europe and had an impulse in the still active top of her mind to suggest Prague, the Hook, or Rouen. The facility with which it would be possible for her to cover larger distances and her present complete inability to move from the curbstone presented themselves simultaneously. She could not command the few words, the few movements which should take her away from Mrs. Kerr, or imagine where, having escaped, she would find a mood, room, place, even country, to offer her sanctuary. Her own background, apart from which the crisis of today, of these last weeks, had produced itself, was seen very clearly at this distance away from it, but presented an impenetrable façade with no ingress. She could see her life very plainly, but there seemed no way into it; the whole thing might have been painted on canvas with a clever enough but not convincing appearance of reality.

She thought, 'So there is really nothing to go back to,' and said, gently drawing her arm away from Mrs Kerr: 'I think, if you don't mind, I really must go back to the Hotel.'

MOLLY KEANE

(1904–96)

from:
DEVOTED LADIES (1934)

[In several of Molly Keane's novels, women are bound together by infatuation and manipulation; this is the one in which such a relationship is most central. On a visit from England to Ireland, Jane's dominating friend Jessica finds herself confined to bed with a broken leg, and becomes increasingly irritated by her hostess Piggy, who has a romantic attachment to her married friend Joan. Keane creates wicked humour from the clash between these two competing (and mutually uncomprehending) versions of love between women, neither of which is presented explicitly as lesbian. *Devoted Ladies* was published under the pseudonym M.J. Farrell in 1934.]

Jessica was a hateful woman. He would like to inflict some more physical pain upon her. Sylvester was increasingly resolved in his plan to free Jane from her possession. Then he would bestow freedom on that poor thing, Jane, and inflict a crushing blow upon Jessica. Two good things to do.

In Jessica's room Jane was wondering drearily what to do about the next few hours. Jessica was well enough to-day to want to read to her. How much Jane wished that it could be one of Albert's duties to listen to Jessica reading aloud. But Jessica had a thing about reading to Jane. She derived from it an obscure sadistic pleasure. And this morning after so much pain she had no intention of denying herself anything.

So she read and read to Jane, saying at intervals: 'I do think that is *so* right,' or 'Pretty rude, don't you think so?' just in case Jane should be thinking quietly about something else, some dreary triviality such as the design of a new evening gown, and from such a state of absent coma Jessica's remarks would jolt her roughly enough.

The day outside was bright with the piercing excitement of an autumn morning. There was as though a ringing through the day, endless circles of sound such as come from a glass finger-bowl flipped by a thumb nail. Jane, sitting fidgeting on the window-seat of Jessica's room, was outside the day, but she ought to have belonged — it was unfair. She was a sad, weak creature but there was a shivered possibility within her, a quality that was not alien to the day — alien as Jessica was alien, lying there in her rich dressing-gown, reading on and on in her educated, affected voice.

'There's the doctor —'

A car stopped at the door; yes, its engine was switched off, but Jessica, paying no attention either to this or to Jane's interruption, read on to the end of a long, involved sentence. Then she said:

'He won't be long. There's really nothing for him to do.'

Hester's voice came calling up the stairs:

'Jane, Jane — *Could* you come down a moment?'

Jessica's face went dead. 'How *very* unnecessary,' she said. But Jane was gone, flying out of the room on long, light feet — escaping. It was a flight.

Jessica sat up in bed listening. She heard voices in the hall — a man's voice that was not Sylvester's or the doctor's voice. Odd. Very odd. Maddening. To be anchored by pain, her leg strapped in a wooden box — her helpless state overcame Jessica. She called:

'Jane! Jane!'

She was weaker than she thought. Such pain as she moved, scarcely stirred, in bed. They should not leave her alone. It was monstrous.

'*Jane!*'

She called again. They were laughing in the hall. They had not heard her. By God, she would ring the bell. A sharp jangling on that little brass bell would startle Jane back to her. Back she'd come, flying back. Jessica stretched out her hand for the bell. But the bell was not beside her. Away and far off upon the dressing table the bell was sitting beside that mammoth photograph of a silly woman and two gross boys with knees like elephant's feet.

The voices in the hall were silent. There was an emptiness of silence in the house. In a minute she heard them again out on the grass in front of the house and Jane's voice light and brittle saying: '*Fascinating*' — saying: 'Oh, you're horrible —'

3.269

Jessica moved herself again in bed, straining all her power to see out of the window, desolate and angry and now in some pain she called again and again. But Jane did not hear.

Piggy, who was seldom up and dressed before eleven in the morning, heard, and came bustling in, full of goodwill, her face freshly powdered, her hair newly released from its rows of curlers, her mauve kimono tightly folded about her body.

'Aren't we comfy?' she said. 'Can a Piggy be any help?'

Piggy in her day had ardently attended quite three Red Cross lectures before her enthusiasm for nursing left her. She shifted Jessica's leg and fastened it up in its box again, and tidied everything on the bed deftly out of reach in quite a professional way. Then she sat down, longing to have a little talk about herself. Jessica ground the teeth of her mind together and closed her eyes.

Piggy was saying: 'So, like most other people, you probably think I'm very lazy just because I don't get up before eleven; but I find going through life one can do ever so many quiet little jobs without any one knowing about them.'

'Yes.'

'For instance, last Thursday I tidied out the medicine cupboard. So I knew at once when the doctor came to look at your leg that there were no bandages in it and only three aspirins left in the bottle.'

'Oh.'

'And yet people will tell you I am lazy —' Piggy went fidgeting round the room, peering at her photographs as though she had never seen them before and longing for Jessica to ask her questions about them. At last she could contain herself no longer, so, picking up the photograph of Joan and the twins, she said in a voice full of feeling, which she vainly imagined to be entirely casual, 'Don't you think that's *rather* a lovely face?'

After this Jessica could no longer with decent politeness keep her eyes shut. Neither could she simply say No. Or, Oh. Neither would she say, Yes. She said instead:

'It depends on what you mean by lovely.'

'Most people think she's rather wonderful,' Piggy proceeded, undeterred by Jessica's lack of interest and determined that she should hear all a Piggy could tell of the Beauty and importance of a Piggy's friend. There was a burning enthusiasm in her to tell of Joan, a testament that would not be denied.

'— Of course you've probably seen masses of photographs of her in the *Tatler*,' Piggy wound up a lingering description of Joan's beauty. 'She's in it almost every week — Hates it simply — She and I are always dodging the camera at race meetings.'

'Oh. Are you a keen racing woman?' *Anything to get away from this dreary girl-friend*, Jessica thought.

'Oh, it's not really much in a Piggy's line, you know, but I do try to take an interest for Joan's sake. She so loves me to go to horse shows and race meetings with her.'

'Oh, yes.'

'Of course, with the poor old heart so wonky, I can't hunt, which is sad. Of course, as you probably know, Joan is the most brilliant woman to hounds in Ireland. No two opinions about it. She's a real *Crasher*.'

'How lovely.'

Piggy drew a deep breath. She was about to make her favourite remark about Joan —

'— And in spite of all this, you know, her beauty and her success and what I call "being Joan", if you know what I mean, all the time at heart she's *just a lovely child*. Just the youngest, most unspoilt *child*, that's what Joan is.'

'How too *frightening*.'

'Oh, you mustn't be frightened of her,' Piggy answered with literal reassurance. 'She's sometimes a little silent with people she doesn't know, and the silly asses think she's rude, but she's not — she's simply *shy*.'

'Oh, yes.'

'I'm longing for you to meet her,' Piggy proceeded heartily. 'Did Jane — you know we've decided to drop Mrs. and Miss, it's so formal, isn't it? — did Jane tell you Joan had asked me to bring her over to lunch at Castlequarter on Sunday?'

'No, Miss Browne, she did not.'

'Oh, you *mustn't* call me Miss Browne.'

'But I don't know what your Christian name is.'

'My real name is Viola, but everyone calls me Piggy.'

'Piggy? Of course, how fascinating!'

'I used to call myself Piggy when I was a little girl —'

'How quaint and whimsey of you —'

'— And now somehow the name has stuck to me ever since. I must have been a quaint, funny child as you say. I don't believe anyone *quite* understood me.'

'I daresay not.'

'I was rather a lonely little sprite I think, and you know — you *mustn't* laugh at me — I *really*

believed in fairies. I'm not sure there aren't moments when I still do. Do you?'

At this moment Albert popped his head round the door and Jessica, breathing a sigh of nearly rapturous relief, murmured: 'Sometimes — Almost — Albert, you promised I should have that drink by half-past eleven and now it's twenty-nine minutes past. Pretty good!'

KATE O'BRIEN
(1897–1974)

from:
MARY LAVELLE (1936)

[This novel is set among Irish governesses in Spain of the 1920s. On hearing that her beloved friend Mary Lavelle (who is secretly in love with a man) is about to go home, Agatha Conlan blurts out the secret of her 'absurd infatuation'. Though some elements of Agatha's characterization are very conventional — her androgyny, intensity and martyr role showing the influence of Radclyffe Hall's *The Well of Loneliness* (1928) — O'Brien is ahead of her time in presenting Agatha's unrequited love so seriously and sympathetically, and in having Mary react without homophobic panic. Published in London in 1936 by Heinemann.]

It was about a fortnight now since their conversation in the square of San Geronimo, and though they had met at least four times since then neither had referred to Agatha's confession of that night. But curiously enough, although she had, as she had expected, suffered very deep misery in the day or two which followed that conversation, her relationship with Mary had not suffered or been made painful. Instead, a certain relaxation, even an affectionate, unspoken peace had entered it. For Mary had not been frightened or repulsed. Perhaps Juanito was right in calling her a pagan and her face Aphrodite's; certainly, now that feeling consumed her for him, her understanding of feeling in others, as, for instance, in O'Toole and Pepe,[1] was immediate and natural. So,

though no word more of emotion was said between them, her voice and manner with Agatha had automatically become easier and more sisterly, not so much because Agatha fantastically and perversely loved *her* but because, like her, she was fantastically and perversely in love. Agatha felt this unuttered sympathy, and it made her reaction from her own confession less savage, easier to bear. It also made her sense of loss much deeper, and this afternoon's meeting of farewell a pain almost insupportable.

'You're really going to-morrow?'

'Yes. I'm really going.'

Agatha had never asked her why she had taken this decision, or what was the cause of her tears when they talked in the Plaza San Geronimo. She knew that Mary was not going home to marry, but merely to escape from Spain. Something had happened in these four months which she could not support. That was all that Agatha knew and she could understand it. She asked no teasing questions.

'Have you said good-bye to Pepe and O'Toole?'

'Yes. I was in there last evening. O'Toole says she'll see me at the train to-morrow.'

'She's dejected over your going.'

'You and she — you've been so good to me, both of you.'

'Ah — please!'

'Agatha — I've thought very much about what you said that night — about being fond of me.'

'Well — did it disgust you?'

'Please don't say that. You take one kind of impossible fancy, I take another.' There was a pause. Agatha sipped some tea carefully. Mary

1. Another of the Irish governesses, and the Spanish man she has become engaged to.

looked at the strained, fanatic's profile and felt great affection for this woman she was probably talking to for the last time.

'I hate to have made you unhappy,' she said. 'But it'll pass soon — won't it?'

'I hope not.'

'But —'

'It can't be such a ghastly crime to — to think about you.' She turned and smiled at Mary and said quite pleadingly: 'Have you got a photograph — a snapshot?'

'I — I'm afraid not.'

'Oh, but at home you must have. Will you send me one?'

'If you'd really like —'

'Oh, thank you. Don't forget.'

Mary looked about the ladies' alcove, and out past the Englishmen's tables at the frostily decorated mirrors.

'I feel as if I'd known this place a long time,' she said.

'Don't ever come back,' said Conlan. 'Don't ever come looking for me in the Alemán again.'[2]

'Why?'

'I'm going to settle into old age now.'

'What of that?'

'Well, Keogh always says that I'll be the sort of muttering hag children throw stones at!'

Mary reached for Agatha's hand, which was not given to her.

'And suppose you are, could I throw stones?'

'No. But don't come back. If you're going now, stay away. Truly, I beg you. You've — upset me very much. I'll pull myself together somehow

when you're gone, and become the sort of bitter pill I am. Only, stay away.'

'Will you never leave Spain?'

'Never. I can always get work. Although people don't like me, they know I teach English better than the others.'

'Will you ever write?'

'I don't think so. I'll write to thank you for the snapshot.'

'Why have you — liked me so much?'

'Ah!' Agatha smiled slowly, and looked out across the empty, quiet café. 'I'll never forget my first sight of you. You were sitting where you're sitting now — in a crowd of misses. And you had no hat on, any more than you have now. I had never known anything about attraction to other people or about the sensation of pleasure human beauty can give. If you had turned out to be a conceited mean little bore of a girl — you would have had to be tolerated — because of that first second. In gratitude. But — you were nice as well. So I fell into what my confessor calls the sin of Sodom.'

'They have queer names for things,' said Mary.

'They know their business. And hard cases make bad laws.'

'Will you come in here much? I'll be trying to imagine your life.'

'I come in most days, as you know. But you have to forget Spain — not remember.'

'That's true.'

Mary looked at her watch.

'Are you in a hurry?'

'I'm afraid I'm in a bit of one.' Mary spoke guiltily now. She was in fact in no hurry at all, but she had an odd desire to keep some part of this last evening to herself.

2. Their local café.

EDNA O'BRIEN

(?1930–   )

THE MOUTH OF THE CAVE
(1968)

[The combination of promise and threat suggested by this story's sexually symbolic title conveys the narrator's ambivalence about her homosexuality. 'The Mouth of the

Cave' was published in the collection *The Love Object* by Jonathan Cape in 1968.]

There were two routes to the village. I chose the rougher one to be beside the mountain rather than the sea. It is a dusty, ill-defined stretch of road littered with rocks. The rocks that have fallen from the cliff are a menacing shade of red once they have split open. On the surface the cliff appears to be grey. Here and there on its grey-and-red face there are small clumps of trees. Parched in summer, tormented by winds in winter, they nevertheless survive, getting no larger or no smaller.

In one such clump of green, just underneath the cliff, I saw a girl stand up. She began to tie her suspenders slowly. She had bad balance because when drawing her knickers on she lost her footing more than once. She put her skirt on by bringing it over her head and lastly her cardigan, which appeared to have several buttons. As I came closer she walked away. A young girl in a maroon cardigan and a black shirt. She was twenty or thereabouts. Suddenly and without anticipating it I turned toward home so as to give the impression that I'd simply been having a stroll. The ridiculousness of this hit me soon after and I turned round again and walked toward the scene of her secret. I was trembling, but these journeys have got to be accomplished.

What a shock to find that nothing lurked there, no man, no animal. The bushes had not risen from the weight of her body. I reckoned that she must have been lying for quite a time. Then I saw that she, too, was returning. Had she forgotten something? Did she want to ask me a favour? Why was she hurrying? I could not see her face, her head was down. I turned, and this time I ran towards the private road that led to my rented house. I thought, Why am I running, why am I trembling, why am I afraid? Because she is a woman and so am I. Because, because? I did not know.

When I got to the courtyard I asked the servant who had been fanning herself to unchain the dog. Then I sat out of doors and waited. The flowering tree looked particularly dramatic, its petals richly pink, its scent oppressively sweet. The only tree in flower. My servant had warned me about those particular flowers; she had even taken the trouble to get the dictionary to impress the word upon me — *Venodno*,[1] poison, poison petals. Nevertheless I had the table moved in order to be nearer that tree and we steadied it by putting folded cigarette cartons under two of its

legs. I told the servant to lay a place for two. I also decided what we would eat, though normally I don't, in order to give the days some element of surprise. I asked that both wines be put on table, and also those long, sugar-coated biscuits that can be dipped in white wine and sucked until the sweetness is drained from them and re-dipped and re-sucked, indefinitely.

She would like the house. It had simplicity despite its grandeur. A white house with green shutters and a fanlight of stone over each of the three downstairs entrances. A sundial, a well, a little chapel. The walls and the ceilings were a milky-blue and this, combined with the sea and sky, had a strange hallucinatory effect, as if sea and sky moved indoors. There were maps instead of pictures. Around the light bulbs pink shells that over the years had got a bit chipped, but this only added to the informality of the place.

We would take a long time over supper. Petals would drop from the tree, some might lodge on the stone table, festooning it. The figs, exquisitely chilled, would be served on a wide platter. We would test them with our fingers. We would know which ones when bitten into would prove to be satisfactory. She, being native, might be more expert at it than I. One or the other of us might bite too avidly and find that the seeds, wet and messy and runny and beautiful, spurted over our chins. I would wipe my chin with my hand. I would do everything to put her at ease. Get drunk if necessary. At first I would talk but later show hesitation in order to give her a chance.

I changed into an orange robe and put on a long necklace made of a variety of shells. The dog was still loose in order to warn me. At the first bark I would have him brought in and tied up at the back of the house where even his whimpering would be unheard.

I sat on the terrace. The sun was going down. I moved to another chair in order to get the benefit of it. The crickets had commenced their incessant near-mechanical din and the lizards began to appear from behind the maps. Something about their deft, stealthlike movements reminded me of her, but everything reminded me of her just then. There was such silence that the seconds appeared to record their own passing. There were only the crickets and, in the distance the sound of sheepbells, more dreamlike than a bleat. In the distance, too, the lighthouse, faithfully signalling.

---

1. This is close to the Spanish words for poison and poisonous — *veneno* and *venenoso* — but it is not actually a word, and is probably a typing error.

A pair of shorts hanging on a hook began to flutter in the first breeze and how I welcomed it, knowing that it heralded night. She was waiting for dark, the embracing dark, the sinner's dear accomplice.

My servant waited out of view. I could not see her but I was conscious of her the way one sometimes is of a prompter in the wings. It irritated me. I could hear her picking up or laying down a plate and I knew it was being done simply to engage my attention. I had also to battle with the smell of lentil soup. The smell though gratifying seemed nothing more than a bribe to hurry the proceedings and that was impossible. Because, according to my conjecture, once I began to eat the possibility of her coming was ruled out. I had to wait.

The hour that followed had an edgy, predictable and awful pattern — I walked, sat on various seats, lit cigarettes that I quickly discarded, kept adding to my drink. At moments I disremembered the cause of my agitation, but then recalling her in dark clothes and downcast eyes I thrilled again at the pleasure of receiving her. Across the bay the various settlements of lights came on, outlining towns or villages that are invisible in daylight. The perfection of the stars was loathsome.

Finally the dog's food was brought forth and he ate as he always does, at my feet. When the empty plate skated over the smooth cobbles — due to my clumsiness — and the full moon so near, so red, so oddly hospitable, appeared above the pines, I decided to begin, taking the napkin out of its ring and spreading it slowly and ceremoniously on my lap. I confess that in those few seconds my faith was overwhelming and my hope stronger than it had ever been.

The food was destroyed. I drank a lot.

Next day I set out for the village but took the sea road. I have not gone the cliff way ever since. I have often wanted to, especially after work when I know what my itinerary is going to be: I will collect the letters, have one Pernod in the bar where retired colonels play cards, sit and talk to them about nothing. We have long ago accepted our uselessness for each other. New people hardly ever come.

There was an Australian painter whom I invited to supper having decided that he was moderately attractive. He became offensive after a few drinks and kept telling me how misrepresented his countrymen were. It was sad rather than unpleasant and the servant and I had to link him home.[2]

On Sundays and feast days girls of about twenty go by, arms round each other, bodies lost inside dark commodious garments. Not one of them looks at me although by now I am known. She must know me. Yet she never gives me a sign as to which she is. I expect she is too frightened. In my more optimistic moments I like to think that she waits there expecting me to come and search her out. Yet I always find myself taking the sea road even though I most desperately desire to go the other way.

2. Walk arm in arm with him.

MAEVE BINCHY

(1940–   )

from:
HOLLAND PARK (1978)

[This story is set during a party given by a trendy London couple, Melissa and Malcolm, to which the narrator has brought her friend Alice. When their hosts invite them on a yachting holiday, the narrator begins to realize that she and Alice are being perceived as lovers. 'Holland Park' was published in the collection *Central Line, Stories of Big City Life* by Quartet Books in 1978.]

'Well, when the two of you make up your minds, do tell us,' she said. 'It would be great fun, and we have to let these guys know by the end of the month, apparently. They sound very nice actually. Jeremy and Jacky they're called, he makes jewellery and Jacky is an artist. They've lots of other friends going too, a couple of girls who work with Jeremy and their boy friends, I think. It's just Jeremy and Jacky who are . . . who are organising it all.'

Life a flash I saw it. Melissa thought Alice and I were lesbians. She was being her usual tolerant liberated self over it all. If you like people, what they do in bed is none of your business. HOW could she be so crass as to think that about Alice and myself? My face burned with rage. Slowly like heavy flowers falling off a tree came all the reasons. I was dressed so severely, I had asked could I bring a woman not a man to her party, I had been manless in Greece when she met me the first time, I had just put on this appalling show of spitely spiteful dikey jealousy about Alice's relationship with a man. Oh God. Oh God.

I knew little or nothing about lesbians. Except that they were different. I never was friendly with anyone who was one. I knew they didn't wear bowler hats, but I thought that they did go in for this aggressive sort of picking on one another in public. Oh God.

Alice was talking away about the boat with interest. How much would it cost? Who decided where and when they would stop? Did Jeremy and Jacky sound madly camp and would they drive everyone mad looking for sprigs of tarragon in case the pot au feu was ruined?

Everyone was laughing, and Malcolm was being liberated and tolerant and left-wing.

'Come on, Alice, nothing wrong with tarragon, nothing wrong with fussing about food, we all fuss about something. Anyway, they didn't say anything to make us think that they would fuss about food, stop typecasting.'

He said it in a knowing way. I felt with a sick dread that he could have gone on and said, 'After all, I don't typecast you and expect you to wear a hairnet and a military jacket.'

I looked at Alice, her thin white face all lit up laughing. Of course I felt strongly about her, she was my friend. She was very important to me, I didn't need to act with Alice. I resented the way the awful man with his alcoholic wife treated her, but was never jealous of him because Alice didn't really give her mind to him. And as for giving anything else . . . well I suppose they made a lot of love together but so did I and the unsatisfactory journalist. I didn't want Alice in that way. I mean that was madness, we wouldn't even know what to do. We would laugh ourselves silly.

Kiss Alice?

Run and lay my head on Alice's breast?

Have Alice stroke my hair?

That's what people who were in love did. We didn't do that.

Did Alice need me? Yes, of course she did. She often told me that I was the only bit of sanity in her life, that I was safe. I had known her for ten years, hardly anyone else she knew nowadays went back that far.

Malcolm filled my coffee cup.

'Do persuade her to come with us,' he said gently to me. 'She's marvellous really, and I know you'd both enjoy yourselves.'

I looked at him like a wild animal. I saw us fitting into their lives, another splendid liberal concept, slightly racy, perfectly acceptable. 'We went on holiday with this super gay couple, most marvellous company, terribly entertaining.' Which of us would he refer to as the He? Would there be awful things like leaving us alone together, or nodding tolerantly over our little rows?

The evening and not only the evening lay stretched ahead in horror. Alice had been laying into the wine, would she be able to drive? If not, oh God, would they offer us a double bed in some spare room in this mansion? Would they suggest a taxi home to Fulham since my place was nearer? Would they speculate afterwards why we kept two separate establishments in the first place?

Worse, would I ever be able to laugh with Alice about it or was it too important? I might disgust her, alarm her, turn her against me. I might unleash all kinds of love that she had for me deep down, and how would I handle that? Of course I love Alice, I just didn't realise it. But what lover, what poor unfortunate lover in the history of the whole damn thing, ever had the tragedy of Coming Out in Malcolm and Melissa's lovely home in Holland Park?

MAURA RICHARDS

(1939–   )

from:
INTERLUDE (1982)

[This, probably the first explicitly lesbian novel set in Ireland, is an example of how light fiction can be valuable for its content, especially to a readership starving for any representation of their lives. Two very different Irish women, Martha (married to an English man) and Sheila (a nun on a trial absence from her community), have become lovers and have left the stresses of Dublin behind for a peaceful cottage in Galway. In this scene, Sheila's conversation in Irish with Seán Óg, a local sheep farmer, leads to a crisis.]

'Have you a wife?' Sheila asked gently.

'I have not, no, there isn't a woman in County Galway would live in my little house, and with the old fellow as well.'

'But have you no woman? Have you nobody to love?'

'Yes, my dog, I have a great love for my dog.'

'That's good, but what do you do about love?'

Martha nearly jumped with surprise, Sheila had asked the question so simply, as if it was an everyday matter to ask a strange man what he did for a sex life. The answer was even more extraordinary, if Seán Óg's understanding of the question was the same as Martha's.

'My dog.' There was a long pause. Martha could just see Sheila's face which wasn't showing the slightest hint of surprise, just relaxed, sharing the silence with the man. Maybe she hadn't heard properly. Martha decided that her Irish was so bad that she was completely mixed up about what she was hearing.

'Yes, I have no love now but my dog, I have neither girl nor mother. I used to have a great hate for my father, but that is gone now, everything is gone now, all that's left is myself and my dog . . .'

The remnants of dried-up hope in his voice sent a shiver of pity through Martha; she wanted to gather him into her arms and breathe life into him.

'Why don't you go away from this place? You'd be able to go to the town, you'd find work, you'd earn money.' Sheila's voice was getting animated at the possibilities.

'It's too late altogether,' the weary voice answered her. And then, for the first time, he asked a question: 'Have you a husband yourself, and children?'

'I have no husband or child at all,' Sheila answered with a laugh.

'But I'm sure you have a man that you're in love with. Is he here with you?' Martha imagined that Seán Óg was looking around as if expecting the man to materialise.

'Yerra, I've no man at all, I've no love for men. My liking is for women; there's a woman with me, and I'm very fond of her . . .' Sheila's voice trailed away and Martha could see her face changing. Something electric was happening to the air. Martha could hear the rocking of the stool as Seán Óg got quickly to his feet, then there was a kind of hissing breath as he exclaimed, '*Aimn Dé*,'[1] and then he spat on the floor. 'Unnatural woman!' he shouted in English. Martha rushed to put her arms around Sheila, who seemed to be about to collapse. Seán Óg's huge form darkened the doorway. He wasn't half as old as Martha had imagined. He glared at the two women with such a look of hatred that her face went pale with fright; she was sure he was going to attack them physically. But he was making the sign of the cross over himself again and again, shouting at them:

'Work of the devil, you will burn in hell. You are not women at all!' And with one more spit, he strode out of the door, his faithful dog at his heels.

---

1. *Aimn Dé*: (in) the name of God.

MARY DORCEY

(1950–)

from:
MOVING INTO THE SPACE
CLEARED BY OUR MOTHERS
(1991)

[As a Rooney-prizewinning writer, and perhaps the first Irish lesbian feminist activist to come out publicly, Mary Dorcey has been a sort of watershed in Irish lesbian culture. Her poetry and prose are remarkable for their breadth of content — wife-battering and parent–child bonds, prison-wall protests and middle-class closets — as well as the startling lyricism of her style. The following three poems show how Dorcey manages to eroticize lesbian relationships without evading painful truths. Published in Galway in 1991 by Salmon Press.]

Beginning

She showered and scoured
her skin clear.
Dressed in fresh clothes,
cut her hair
and old friends.
Took up Aikido,[1] Celtic studies and Zen.
Tore up snapshots and letters,
painted all her walls white.
Smiled at each woman she passed
in the street.
And asked nobody home
who might find out
that for months
she still slept
in your blood stained
sheets.

1. A Japanese martial art.

Friendship

Although we had talked all night,
about rejection, hurt
and the bitterness of those
we had once most trusted,
lying in your arms, in a warm bed,

rummaging through our injuries
like two old drunken women on a bench,

It no longer mattered at all
— none of it.
Breast against breast
desiring nothing more than sleep,
loss was a once sharp blade
that had cut me loose
for this friendship.

Come Quietly or the Neighbours will Hear

Have you ever made love
with the t.v. on
— to spare the neighbours
landlady lord —
the embarrassment;
the joy undisguised
of two people;
especially women
(imagine the uproar!)
coming together?

Come quietly
or the neighbours will hear.

That year was the worst
an aching winter of it —
small minds and towns
rented rooms and narrow beds,
walled in by other people's
decencies
and at every sitting down
to table,
broadcast at breakfast
dinner and tea
the daily ration
of obscenity.
Have you ever
made love with the t.v. on?

Come quietly
or the neighbours will hear.

On a dark evening
autumn cloths spread for tea,
fires lit.
In the wet gardens
leaves falling
on a dark evening
at last alone
a space, hungry with wanting
waiting, a fire catching
we fell —
skin in firelight burning
fell the long fall
of grace, to the floor.
On a dark evening
night coming softly in the wet gardens.

Come quietly
or the neighbours will hear.

Mouth at my breast
hands ringing in my flesh
when the Angelus[1] rang
from the t.v. screen.
The angel of the lord
declared unto Mary
and she conceived of the Holy Ghost[2]
the earth, the sun and the seas.
Hail Mary   Holy Mary.
Be it done unto me according
to thy word[3]
Hail Mary, and oh —
the sweetness of your breath —
the breath of your sweetness.

Come quietly
or the neighbours will hear.

And the word was made flesh
and dwelt amongst us.
Hands   skin   mouth   thighs
in the bedrock of flesh
sounding,
fields flooded
blood uncoursed.

Blessed art thou
and blessed is the fruit
of thy womb.[4]
Bitter and sweet
earth opens stars collide.
Blessed and sweet,
the fruit
among women
Hail Mary   Holy Mary.

Come quietly
or the neighbours will hear.

When the six o'clock news
struck.
Into the fissures
of mind   and bone
the deadly tide
seeping.
The necessary,
daily litany.
Come quietly or the neighbours
will hear.

She was found
on a park bench   backstreet barn
dancehall   schoolyard   bedroom bar —
found with multiple stab wounds to
thighs breast and abdomen.
Come quietly   come quietly
or the neighbours . . .
hands tied behind her back,
no sign of
(mouth bound)
no sign of
sexual assault.

Come softly
or the neighbours will hear.

Your breast and belly,
your thighs,
your hands behind my back
my breath in yours.
No one heard her scream.
Your eyes wide.
Come quietly or the neighbours . . .

1. In this case, the recording of a bell played on television in Ireland at noon and 6 p.m. to invite Roman Catholics to say a devotional exercise known as the Angelus from its first words (in the Latin version) 'Angelus domini nuntiavit Mariae'.
2. These three lines are the opening (in English) of the Angelus.
3. A line in the Angelus based on Mary's response to God's choosing her as mother to his son; see Luke 1:38.

4. From the 'Hail Mary', a prayer repeated in the Angelus; this line is Elizabeth's blessing on her cousin Mary, see Luke 1:42.

She was found
at the dockside riverbank,
in the upstairs flat
his flat
wearing a loose . . .
Your mouth at my ear.

Come quietly
or the neighbours will hear.
Blood on the walls
and sheets,
a loose negligée
in her own flat,
stripped to the waist.
Come quietly, come quietly.
No one heard her scream —
come softly or the neighbours . . .
Did you ever make love
with the t.v. on?
— the neighbours heard nothing —
she was always —
no one would have thought —
always a quiet girl.

Stripped to the bone
blood on our thighs
my hands behind your back
come quietly, come,
legs tangled with the sheet
mouth to mouth
voices flung.

Come softly
or the neighbours will hear.

Did you ever make love
with the t.v. on?
to spare the neighbours
landlady lord
her cries in our ears
we came . . .
no one heard her scream
her blood on our hands.
Yes —
coming,

Not quietly —
beyond bearing;
in the face of the living
in the teeth of the dying
forgetting the uproar

the outrage —
(imagine —
the joy
undisguised
of two women
— especially
women —)
two women
together —
at last alone
night falling in the wet gardens
on a dark evening
with the t.v.
off.

Die quietly —
die quietly —
or the neighbours will hear.

from:
A COUNTRY DANCE (1989)

[The following story, published in *A Noise in the Woodshed* (London: Onlywomen Press, 1989), vividly evokes the disruptive effect of lesbian romance in a community where heterosexuality is as all-pervasive as alcohol. The thirty-year-old narrator and her nineteen-year-old friend have accepted a lift to a late-night disco in a country hotel.]

In the unlit carpark we find Peg's Fiat and pile in — Frank pulling me towards his knee: 'If you were the only girl in the world and I was the only boy.'[1] Rain slashes at the windscreen, one wiper stuck halfway across it. Peg seems to drive by ear. Wet fir trees arching over us make a black tunnel of the road. The road to God knows where.[2] I recognise none of it, letting myself be carried forward — lapsing into the heedless collective will. All needs converging in the simple drive for one more drink. 'Nothing else would matter in the world today . . .'[3] Frank's whiskey breath encircles us. We reach tall, silver gates, pass them,

1. Title of a song by Nat D. Ayer and Clifford Grey from the musical *The Bing Boys are Here* (1916). Recorded in 1917 by Henry Burr and in 1930 by Rudy Vallee.
2. Line from the traditional Irish song, 'On the One Road' popularised in a recording by the Wolf Tones.
3. Line from 'If you were the only girl in the world'.

and sluice through rain-filled craters in the drive, the wind snapping at our wheels. A furious night — clouds blown as fast as leaves across the sky. Lights ahead — the tall Georgian house bright in welcome. Braking almost on the front steps, Peg jumps out, leaving the door wide: 'I'll put in a word for you.' We follow, our faces lowered from the rain. In the hallway with the bouncer, her blonde head bent to his ear, she is confidential, explaining that we want only a takeaway — no admission. Solemn as a mother entrusting her daughters. Then she turns back to the car and her boys waiting outside. She throws a wicked grin at me over her shoulder — why? — 'Enjoy yourselves girls,' and she is off.

Out of the night — into a frenzy of light and sound. We push through the black swing doors. Red and purple light, great shafts of it, beat against the walls and floor. The music hammers through my chest, shivering my arms. A man and woman locked together, move in a tight circle at the centre of the room. In the corner, beside a giant speaker, two girls on stiletto heels dance an old-fashioned jive. We push through the wall of shoulders at the bar, country boys shy of dancing. 'Two large bottles of stout,' I order. The barman reaches for pint glasses and shoves them under the draught tap. 'Bottles — to take away,' I call across to him. But it is useless, he has already moved to the far end of the counter to measure out whiskey.

'We will just have to drink them here,' you say, putting your mouth close to my ear so that I feel the warmth of your breath. So be it — at least we are in from the rain for a while.

We choose a corner table, as far from the speakers as possible, but still I have to shout to make you hear me.

'It's easier if you whisper,' you say, bringing your lips to my ear once more, in demonstration.

'You are used to these places, I suppose.' It is years since I have sat like this. Though so little has altered. The lights and music more violent maybe, the rest unchanging. Nobody really wants to be here, it seems. Young women dressed for romance display themselves — bringing their own glamour. The men stand banded in council, shoulders raised as a barrier, until they have drunk enough. The faces are bored or angry. Each one resenting his need, grudging submission to this ritual fever.

You finish half your pint at one go and offer the glass to me. I down the remainder and together we start on the next, laughing. A rotating light on the ceiling spins a rainbow of colours: blue, red, gold, each thrust devouring the last. Smoke hangs in heavy green clouds about us. As though it were the fumes of marijuana, I breathe it deep into my lungs and feel suddenly a burst of dizzy gaiety . . . the absurdity of it all — that we should be here. And back to me come memories of years ago — adolescence, when it might have been the scene of passion, or was it even then absurd? The pace slows and three couples move to the centre of the floor. 'I don't want to talk about it — how you broke my heart.'[4] The voice of Rod Stewart rasps through the speakers in an old song. But a favourite of yours. We have danced to it once before — in the early hours of Clare's party two weeks ago, when Maeve had left without you. You stand beside me now and in pantomime stretch your hand. 'Will you dance with me?' You walk ahead on to the floor. Under the spotlight your white shirt is luminous — your eyes seem black. You rest your hands on your hips, at the centre of the room, waiting.

'If you stay here just a little bit longer — if you stay here — won't you listen to my heart . . .' We step into each other's arms. Our cheeks touch. I smell the scent of your shirt — the darkness of your hair. Your limbs are easy, assured against mine. Your hands familiar, hold me just below the waist. We turn the floor, elaborately slow, in one movement, as though continuing something interrupted. The music lapping thigh and shoulder. 'The stars in the sky don't mean nothing to you — they're a mirror.' Round we swing, round; closer in each widening circle. Lost to our private rhythm. The foolish words beating time in my blood.

I open my eyes. The music has stopped. Behind you I see a man standing; his eyes riveted to our bodies, his jaw dropped wide as though it had been punched. In his maddened stare I see reflected what I have refused to recognize through

4. In 1977 Rod Stewart had a hit single, 'I don't want to talk about it', written by Danny Whitten and first recorded by Danny Whitten and Crazy Horse in 1970. There are several quotations from this song in the bar scene: 'I can tell by your eyes that you've prob'ly been cryin' forever / And the stars in the sky don't mean nothing to you, they're a mirror / I don't want to talk about it how you broke my heart / If I stay here just a little bit longer / If I stay here won't you listen to my heart / Oh, oh, heart'.

all these weeks. Comfort, sympathy, a protective sister — who have I been deceiving? I see it now in his eyes. Familiar at once in its stark simplicity. Making one movement of past and future. I yield myself to it; humbled, self-mocking. Quick as a struck match.

As if I had spoken aloud, with a light pressure of my hand, you return to consciousness and walk from the floor.

I follow, my skin suddenly cold. I want as quickly as possible to be gone from the spotlight. I have remembered where we are: a Friday night country dance, surrounded by drunken males who have never before seen two women dance in each other's arms. All about the room they are standing still, watching. As we cross the empty space to our table no one moves. I notice for the first time Brid Keane from the post office: she is leaning against the wall, arms folded, her face contorted in a look of such disgust, it seems for a moment that she must be putting it on.

'Let's get out of here — as soon as you've finished your drink,' I whisper.

'What — do you want another drink?' Your voice rises high above the music that has begun again. I stare at you in amazement — is it possible that you haven't noticed, that you don't yet know what we've done? Can you be so naive or so drunk that you haven't realised whose territory we are on?

And then someone moves from the table behind and pushes into the seat opposite us. Squat, red-faced, his hair oiled across his forehead. He props an elbow on the table, and juts his head forward, struggling to focus his eyes. His pink nylon shirt is open, a white tie knotted about the neck.

'Fucking lesbians,' he says at last. 'Are you bent or what?' The breath gusting into my face is sour with whiskey. We look towards the dancers writhing under a strobe light and ignore him.

'Did you not hear me?' he asks, shoving his face so close to me, I see the sweat glisten on his upper lip. 'I said are you bent — queers?' He drives his elbow against mine so that the stout spills over my glass.

A familiar anger rips through me, making my legs tremble. I press my nails into the palm of my hand and say nothing. I will not satisfy him so easily.

'What were you saying about the music?' I throw you a smile.

'I asked you a question,' he says. 'Will you give me a bloody answer.' He runs the words together as though speed were his only hope of completing them.

'I said it's lousy,' you reply, 'about ten years out of date.'

He looks from me to you and back again with baffled irritation and his voice grows querulous. He asks: 'Look, would one of you lesbians give me a dance.'

A friend has joined him now, leaning over the back of your chair, a grin on his lips sly and lascivious.

'Will you not answer me?' the first one shouts, 'or are you fucking deaf?'

Drawing my shoulders up, I turn and for the first time look directly into his eyes. 'No,' I say with warning deliberation, 'we are not deaf, yes, we are lesbians and no, we will not give you a dance.'

He stares at us stupefied, then falls back into his seat, breath hissing from his chest as though a lung had burst. 'Jesus, fucking, Christ.'

You give a whoop of laughter, your eyes wide with delight. It seems you find him hugely amusing. Then you're on your feet and across the room in search of the toilet or God knows another drink.

I have my back turned to him when I feel the pink, sleeved arm nudging mine again. 'Hey, blondie — you've gorgeous hair,' he says, giving an ugly snigger. 'Did anyone ever tell you that?' It is a moment before I recognise the smell of singed hair. I reach my hand to the back of my head and a cigarette burns my fingertips. With a cry of pain, I grab hold of the oily lock across his forehead and wrench hard enough to pull it from the roots. He stretches his arm to catch hold of mine but I tear with all my force. 'You fucking cunt!' he screams.

Suddenly someone catches hold of us from behind and pulls us roughly apart. It's the bouncer — a big red-haired man in a grey suit. When he sees my face he steps back aghast. He had plainly not expected a woman.

'I don't know what you two want,' his voice is cold, contemptuous, 'but whatever it is you can settle it between you — outside.' He drops the hand on my shoulder, wheels round and walks back to his post at the door. At the sight of him my opponent is instantly subdued. He shrinks back into his seat as though he had been whipped, then slowly collapses on to the table, head in his arms.

You return carrying another drink. I wait until you are sitting down to whisper: 'We have got to get out of here, Cathy — they're half savage. That one just tried to set fire to my hair.'

'The little creep!' you exclaim, your eyes sparking with indignation. 'Oh, he's easily handled — but the rest of them, look.'

At the bar a group of six or seven are standing in a circle drinking. Big farm boys in tweed jackets — older than the others and more sober. Their gaze has not left us, I know, since we walked off the dance floor, yet they have made no move. This very calm is what frightens me. In their tense vigilance, I feel an aggression infinitely more threatening than the bluster of the two next to us. Hunters letting the hounds play before closing in?

'I think they might be planning something,' I say, and, as if in response to some prearranged signal, one of them breaks from the group and slowly makes his way to our table.

His pale, thin face stares into mine, he makes a deep bow and stretches out his hand. 'Would one of you ladies care to dance?'

I shake my head wearily. 'No, thanks.'

He gives a scornful shrug of the shoulders and walks back to his companions. A moment later another one sets out. When he reaches us, he drops to one knee before you and for the benefit of those watching, loudly repeats the request. When you refuse him he retreats with the same show of disdain.

'They can keep this going all night,' I say, 'building the pressure. With their mad egotism anything is better than being ignored.' And I know also what I do not say, that we have to put up with it. They have us cornered. Under all the theatrics lies the clear threat that if we dare to leave, they can follow, and once outside, alone in the dark, they will have no need for these elaborate games.

'What can we do?' you ask, twisting a strand of hair about your finger, your eyes attentive at last.

'I'll go off for a few minutes. Maybe if we separate, if they lose sight of us, they might get distracted.'

Five minutes later, pushing my way through the crowd to our table, I find you chatting with the one in the pink shirt and his mate, smoking and sharing their beer like old drinking pals.

How can you be so unconcerned? I feel a sudden furious irritation. But you look up at me and smile warningly. 'Humour them,' I read in the movement of your lips. And you may be right. They have turned penitent now, ingratiating: 'We never meant to insult you, honest, love. We only wanted to be friendly.' His head lolling back and forth, he stabs a finger to his chest: 'I'm Mick, and this is me mate Gerry.'

All right then, let us try patience. At least while we are seen talking to these two the others will hold off.

'You know, blondie, I think you're something really special,' with the deadly earnestness of the drunk, Mick addresses me. 'I noticed you the second you walked in. I said to Gerry — didn't I Gerry? Blondie, would you not give it a try with me? I know you're into women — your mate explained — and that's alright with me — honest — that's cool, you know what I mean? But you never know 'till you try, do you? Might change your life. Give us a chance, love.' He careens on through his monologue, long past noticing whether I answer or not. On the opposite side I hear Gerry, working on you with heavy flattery, admiring your eyes (glistening now — with drink or anger — dark as berries), praising the deep red of your lips — parted at the rim of your glass. And you are laughing into his face and drinking his beer. Your throat thrown back as you swallow, strong and naked.

Mick has collapsed, his head on the table drooping against my arm. 'Just one night,' he mutters into my sleeve, 'that's all I'm asking — just one night. Do yourself a favour.' His words seep through my brain, echoing weirdly, like water dripping in a cave. Drumming in monotonous background to the movements of your hands and face. Half turned from me, I do not hear what you answer Gerry, but I catch your tone; languorous, abstracted. I watch you draw in the split froth on the table. Your eyes lowered, the lashes black along your cheek, one finger traces the line of a half moon. Behind you I see the same group watching from the bar; patient, predatory. My blood pounds — fear and longing compete in my veins.

And then, all at once, the music stops. Everyone stands to attention, silent. The disc-jockey is making an announcement: the offer of a bottle of whiskey, a raffle, the buying of tickets — gripping them as the music and dance never could. This is our moment, with Gerry moving to the bar to buy cigarettes and Mick almost asleep, slumped backwards, his mouth dropped open. I grasp your hand beneath the table, squeezing it so that you may feel the urgency and no one else, and look towards the green exit sign. We are across the floor, stealthy and cautious as prisoners stepping between the lights of an armed camp. At the door at last, 'Fucking whoores — you needn't trouble yourselves to come back,' the bouncer restraining fury in the slam of the swing doors behind us.

And we are out.

Out in the wet darkness. The wind beating escape at our backs. I catch your hand. 'Run and don't stop.' Our feet scatter the black puddles, soaking our shins. The fir trees flapping at our sides beckon, opening our path to the gates. So much further now. The moon will not help — hidden from us by sheets of cloud — withholding its light. We run blind, my heart knocking at my ribs; following the track only by the sting of gravel through my thin soles. 'Come on — faster.' The gates spring towards us out of nowhere — caught in a yellow shaft of brightness. A car rounds the bend behind us, the water flung hissing from its tyres. We dodge under the trees, the drenched boughs smacking my cheek. The headlights are on us, devouring the path up to and beyond the open gates. The window rolled down, I hear the drunken chanting — like the baying of hounds: 'We're here because we're queer because we're here because we're . . .' 'Great fucking crack, lads . . .' Gone. Past us. Pitched forward in the delirium of the chase — seeing nothing to left or right. A trail of cigarette smoke in the air.

from:
A NOISE FROM THE WOODSHED (1989)

[This piece is from one of Mary Dorcey's best-known stories. In an experimental prose characterized by lists and word-association, she conjures up a pastoral landscape which acts as both a literal and a symbolic setting for her pair of lovers.]

You were walking along through the river — that is to say along the path that was flooded — a wild orange torrent of water, cascading. You had forgotten once again to wear galoshes — who in god's name ever remembers to wear galoshes these days? Certainly not women of your advanced thought and sophistication, not to say outlandish ways and habits. So there you were — are, but this is fiction and must remain consigned to the regions of certainty — stumbling on the stepping stones, submerged and slithering, up to your knees in trouble and water with cold feet again, when she came along. Like a warrior in white armour, did she come, gallant and fearless though double-breasted, come like an answer to prayer; a maiden's prayer — yours — though no maiden, and sweeping down from her white charger sweep you up and bear you across the river to sanctuary? Or did she come like a woman; unheralded, unassuming, a woman struggling to keep a footing, to make a living, to make a loving?

Yes, that was it, she came like a woman, with a woman's courage into your life, into the torrent and helped; with all the simple things — all the small everyday, do all over again things — like making the breakfast, doing the shopping, scrubbing the bath, remembering to turn on the blanket, washing up when you're too tired, and never being too tired; loving to love or be loved in any order and who's counting? listening, oh, yes, hours, weeks, years of listening and talking, knowing when to stop and give you a kick in the ass more literal than metaphorical; being the one you can ask if you look alright before going out to face them, being the one who asks you if she looks alright — and no need to ask — yes gorgeous, facing or not, in or out — being the one you can be all these things with, this or that, you now, she later, in any order and who's counting? Women do these things countless times, so fast and so often any one would lose count. It was men who started the whole business of counting: numbers and keeping a ledger. And how was it for you? Can you for one second imagine one lone woman asking another and how was it for you? Where has he been for the last three hours?

Anyway, she came along like a woman when you were standing there up to your neck in life and because she was wearing wellingtons (though she had never so much as heard of Baden Powell,[1]

---

1. Robert Stephenson Smyth, first Baron Baden Powell (1857–1941), British general, founder of the Boy Scout and Girl Guide movements.

much less his motto), and had kept her legs dry she said, climb up, I'll give you a picky-back. And you did, and she did, and she ferried you over the rushing brackish water, keeping her footing on the shifting sands, and high up on her back you kept your head and well above water, and when you gained the bank she set you down the way a woman does, not waiting for thanks, not noticing that she's done you a favour and that just for the moment she was better prepared than you. And all the way across the smell of her hair was in your nose — the earth warm, straw warm, jasmine sweet scent of her hair — and the curls of it tickling your cheek, and you were laughing like you were your own child being carried, and whipping her flanks as you used to when these rides were a regular occurrence, but you were promising yourself, feeling the lovely muscles of her flanks between your thighs, that the moment she set you down you were going to get very serious. And two grown women getting serious, looking into each other's eyes seriously; seeing one another entire, absolute and not as some stop-gap, mediator, sympathiser, counsellor in the doings of men, that look; that long, tasting, touching look is one of the most serious and the best things going. And who can keep it going without laughing? And that's another of the best things — that laughing that women are always doing; not the belly laugh, the guffaw, the snicker, the cracking a joke — no, this laughter in the joy of harmony, of doing something well together, at the same time, at the absurdity of managing the physical world (women being left mostly in charge of it), such as folding a sheet, or holding a ladder while the other climbs up, digging a bed for an apple tree, pulling socks onto a small child's feet that will not stop wriggling, covered in sand and itchy between the toes, composing a concerto before tea, dictating a letter to the press, rehearsing their maiden (that word again) speech, pushing the shopping trolley in the supermarket, playing bingo — that laughter you hear everywhere between women friends, sisters, mothers, daughters, lovers, doing some simple thing together — going with the thing instead of trying to get the better of it, and laughing at the absurdity of its going its own way. Well you promised yourself that when you got to the other side of the water, you would get very serious.

You were back in the house five days before either of you noticed the noise from the woodshed. The rain had been coming down like cats and dogs, and the dogs and cats had been coming down like rain, pit-patting, pat-pitting all over the house with wet ears and cold noses into rooms and out again; the gutters were leaking, emptying their cargo of drenched summer leaves, splashing onto the clothes blowing on the line; skirts and frocks and jeans and shirts and socks and hats that must have belonged to more than one person, you thought, and did. We should take the clothes in, she said. Yes, you said, biting her thigh, and the books were lying all around unread on the shelves, and the hens were squawking unfed in the yard, and the beaches, tossed by the sea, uncleaned, and the potatoes sprouting sprouts, unplanted, chaos ripening all about you, lost in wonder. It was small wonder you had not noticed the noise from the woodshed. Listen, she said, that noise! And you raised yourself for the first time in days, and listened. Was it a bird or a cat or the wind singing in the willows; willows weeping in a grove of tears below your feet?

But wait — what is this? Where have you taken us now? You are losing the run of the thing entirely, racing on regardless without description or report. You were last heard of crossing the river, ferried on the broad plane of her back, her flanks warm between your thighs, and promising yourself that the moment you reached the bank you would get serious. And you did, oh you did. You got as serious as two women can get without laughing. And you were not laughing then as you fell to your knees in the wild bright poppies, fell to your backs, to your shoulders, to your breasts, to your face, fell to your senses in the long green growing grass, her wellingtons still wet and muddy from the river and no time to remove them, and who cares, they were not in the way entirely, or not to begin with, attention being concentrated right then not on feet but on hands and mouths (but when you at last discovered her feet, you were glad of boots that had kept this last delight to last, and your feet naked and loved from the first, toe by toe). And there you were, fully serious, lying low on the low lying bank of the river, the orange water thrashing in its bed, its stones upturned, its ripples foaming. And isn't this just what you would expect from two women messing about in the country unchaperoned, unbridled by labour or conscience, fording streams, scaling mountains, running sylph-like through woods and green pastures, women of a certain persuasion with nothing better to do? And there was nothing better to do all the live-long day, lived long and hot and cool in the breeze of the river, in the length of the grasses, from the first stepping out of the gushing water to the very last — and what was last? — laughter or crying, hollering, rolling about in sun and wild poppies, half drowning in mouth to mouth resuscitation?

And when you stood up, you dressed for the world, following historical precedent in this much; you drew on your assemblage of garments: shirts and skirt, jeans and blouse, belts and socks, bracelets and rings and one pair of wellingtons. And she said, why don't you come home, for she had one and you being temporarily between homes, wandering vagrant and curious, and seeing

the shell that you carried like a world on your back; seeing how well it would fit with hers, she being temporarily fully equipped with the trappings of fittings and fixtures called home. Why don't you come back for something to eat, she said, and speaking of something to eat, she kissed your bruised, bitten neck, and the midges circled waiting their turn, and she said at your nape, why don't you come back. Home then you went and no need to ask, for as long as you needed it, or each other, as it always was, and you needed each other so long and so fast that you halted your journey three or four times, falling down to the earth that lay all around to receive you, birds startled from their nests to air, frogs croaking, dogs howling until, finally tired and exalted, you reached the house in the forest with the red tiled roof, the wide windows, the painted chairs, the open hearth.

MÁIGHRÉAD MEDBH

(1959–   )

from:
THE MAKING OF A PAGAN
(1990)

[Máighréad Medbh writes rhythmic, accessible poetry about childhood, sex, feminism, men and women; this poem celebrates 'the female whirl' of eroticism. Published in Belfast in 1990 by Blackstaff Press.]

Nights with Anne

nights with anne
and the headlights are on
and the alcohol flow
is rushing my head upriver
i'll escape this present
i'll fly to the moon and back

she has the pale brightest
pair of eyes so prophetic
that ever spoke spear
to my own dark horse

steal a saddle to another world
we are high-ho-thunder away

we are saved from
    the wolfing plastics
    the tin buttresses
    the right attitudes
    the feminine assent

strike a song there
for i and i am
in sudden ignition
my own bright key
my own fused force
propelled by me
not men not god
but the female whirl
is fuel to our moves
as we sing
raise cries
raise glasses
raise skirts
to the knee
to the waist
to the neck
to the head
to the
come on up baby
i'm home

SUSAN CONNOLLY

(1956–   )

from:
HOW HIGH THE MOON (1991)

['The Banshee' is a long poem, part of a sequence called
'Boann' which also includes 'Boann', 'Badh', 'Sheela na
gig' and 'Fedelm'. These are 'spirit-women' who reflect on
life, death, sex and fertility and generally have no male
equivalents. The first part of 'The Banshee' also appears in
Connolly's collection *For the Stranger* (Dublin: Daedalus,
1993). *How High the Moon,* which includes work by
Catherine Phil MacCarthy, was published in Dublin by
Poetry Ireland in 1991. See also pp. 1303–4.]

from: The Banshee

> *What*
> *a nightmare strangeness life is*
> *at death point.*[1]   Marina Tsvetaeva

White — like the full moon
outside my window
you waken me —
and I climb towards you
as if you were
my way out —
female voice
rising and falling
in hypnotic
bittersweet waves

You pace the dark hills
around this house
crying the tears
I feel too numb
to cry —
and I welcome you,
wanting to die

You point the way
to my house —
and I never felt
more alive,

tender towards
everyone.
Why do you love me?
Is it because
you alone hear
my outrageous
thoughts?

Three shrieks
make the valley
echo.
Tree-roots tremble
the sky shakes
I shake.
Three more shrieks
loud enough
to deafen anyone —
yet only I hear you
quieten again,
your lonely sound
calling me away

Your eyes are red
with centuries
of crying.
Mine are tired
and dry
from inward lament.
Both of us
so thin the wind
could break us.
You shiver violently
from cold and grief.
I am shaken
with longing
for someone
who doesn't exist

Are you the spirit
of a silent woman
who walked
the hills
above her village?
Sad ancestor
urging me
to say the words

---

1. This line is from 'The end of the Poem' in *Marina Tsvetayeva,*
   Selected Poems translated by Elaine Feinstein (Harmondsworth:
   Penguin Books, 1974), p. 97.

that set us free.
Your cry is the noise
of your comb
as you draw it
through
your waist-length
hair.
Threatening
alluring
forewarning
it goes on
and on and on —

half-way between
the spirit-world
and an ordinary woman
lamenting her death

White-Lady-of-Sorrow
Lady-of-Death
Woman-of-Peace
Spirit-of-the-Air —
let me rest my head
on your gaunt stomach
and cry death away

NUALA ARCHER

(1955–   )

from:
THE HOUR OF PAN/AMÁ
(1992)

[Nuala Archer's experimental poetry frequently focuses on the lesbian body; in this poem she fuses images of oral eroticism and oral language. Published in Galway in 1992 by Salmon Press.]

%%%%%%

wet sex
of you is
what I'm dreaming
how as in sorrow
I echo silence
then double back
to truth in a tremor
& my tongue
tonguing a language
edging beyond destruction
into an alert field
of fragrances where
I find your scentpurr-
scent stirring
our time's
grrrrr-
ace

JUNE LEVINE

(1931–   )

from:
A SEASON OF WEDDINGS
(1992)

[June Levine's thoughtful novel is an analysis of marriage across cultures, and touches on the emotional needs of women which marriage might not fulfil. Her husband having left her, Nora travels as a wedding guest to India.

She forms an intense, romantic friendship with Maya, the young mother of the bride, and gradually comes to wonder if she is 'bisexual' — a word that means nothing to Maya.]

She watched the ant wriggle into the fold of Nora's elbow and reaching out to take the pale arm, she brushed the insect away. 'It has not become brown,' she said.

Nora turned her arm over and placed it beside Maya's. 'Barely beige was all I hoped for,' she said, 'and yours has not become white.'

Maya stroked the golden down of Nora's forearm and leaned forward to caress her throat with the back of her forefinger. 'Everything is the way it is supposed to be,' she said. A balm of healing spread through Nora. Everything is the way it is supposed to be, she repeated to herself, and thought that she must keep telling herself that, hang on to it as she felt Maya's hair cool and smooth against her cheek, while Maya sighed at the feel of Nora's curls against her ear.

In the mirror Nora could see the silken pool of sari where it had slipped out of its folds onto the floor. Maya woke and moved back into the hollow of Nora's shoulder.

'I was sleeping?' she said, 'I left you alone?'

'I slept too,' she said, 'it is gone four in the morning, my favourite time in India when things stop . . .' She was interrupted by a blast from a transistor radio across the roof tops and they laughed. 'For a second or two,' Nora said.

'The earth wakes first, doesn't it?' she asked Maya.

'No,' Maya said, muffled against Nora's breast, 'the workers in the sugar cane are first. If you sit out there and listen, soon there will be sounds in the sugar field before the Muslims call, then maybe the earth and the insects.'

'I still can't hear that, it's too far away.'

'That is because you do not know for what you are listening.' They were silent for a moment before Maya spoke. 'I wish to tell you secret.'

'What secret?'

'Secret I have never said. No one is knowing this secret, but now I can tell. I had love like this in college. After my fiancé married other one, there was someone. A girl from my own village. We were so happy. Like now, while everyone is sleeping, no others in the world, just we two. She said we must go away together, maybe Calcutta, but this dream of hers is impossible, entirely not practical. How can we do such as thing? She came to my wedding. It was torture for her, but all her family members were invited so she must come. A match was found for her at my wedding. Often at weddings it happens like this. She was married one year and one half year later. I did not go to her wedding because mother-in-law was ill that time, so I always remember her at my wedding only. I see her now,' Maya rubbed her forehead with four fingers. 'She looks at me with such a look in her eyes. I was in the back of the bullock cart leaving my village, all my dowry things around me. I felt bad for so long knowing that she comes before husband in my heart. No, please, let me say all. I could not love husband like that. Like this. I used to wish he was woman. Foolishness. He is always husband. Not cruel husband, just husband. Good husband, it is only fair to say. For years I felt like, like . . .' Maya searched for a word. 'It must be like exile,' she concluded, pleased with having found the word. 'Exile,' she repeated and Nora held her closer.

PÁDRAIG STANDÚN

(1946–)

from:
CION MNÁ (1993)

home to Bridie. Published in Indreabhán, Conamara, in 1993 by Iar-Chonnachta.]

[This novel breaks new ground in its focus on converging issues of sexuality, privacy and ambition. Therese, a senior officer in Udarás na Gaeilge, employs Bridie, a mother escaping from a violent marriage, as her housekeeper. They become friends, make love one night and shy away from the consequences. After a meeting in which pressure is put on Therese to take voluntary retirement, she rushes

'Jesus,' arsa Bridie, nuair a chonaic sí ag teacht í. 'An tinn atá tú, nó céard tá ort? Tá dath an bháis ort.' Rith Therese isteadh ina gabháil, ar ballchrith. D'inis sí faoin méid a tharla agan gcruinniú.

'Cén fáth nach bhfuil siad in ann ligean do dhaoine a saol féin a bheith acu?' Chuimil Bridie a gruaig lena lámh. 'Tar éis an mhéid atá déanta agat don taobh seo tíre.'

'Is mó le rá acu céard a dhéanann duine ina leaba san oíche, ná saol na ndaoine a chur chun cinn.'

'Ach cá bhfios dóibh?' Sin é a bhí ag cur iontais ar Bhridie. 'Níor dhúirt mise tada, agus táim cinnte nár dhúirt tusa.'

'Thóg siad ina n-intinn bhrocach féin é. Tá a n-aird chomh dírithe sin acu ar a magairlí gur bagairt dóibh mná a bheith ag fanacht in éindí.'

'Muna bhfuil *peeping Tom* eicint ag breathnú tríd an bhfuinneog san oíche, cá bhfios dóibh rud ar bith?' arsa Bridie. 'Cén fhianaise atá acu?'

'Theastódh muineál an-fhada ó *pheeping Tom* ar bith a thiocfadh thart, muna mbeadh dréimire are bith a thiocfadh thart, muna mbeadh dréimire aige. Tá an garáiste faoi fhuinneog an tseomra codlata. Ní fheicfí rud ar bith trí na cuirtíní troma sin ar aon chaoi. Ní theastaíonn fianaise ar bith uathu sin le duine a dhamnú. Dhéanfaidís d'aonturas é. Chraith Therese a cloigeann. 'Níl a fhios agam céard ba cheart dom a dhéanamh.'

'Seas an fód.'

'Ar mhaithe le m'*ego* féin? Tá an scéal níos leithne ná sin. Tá tusa agus Caomhán[1] i gceist freisin. Tá do mhuintir ina gcónaí thart san áit.'

'Cén fáth nach gcuireann tú an dlí orthu?'

'Níl tada ráite go poiblí.'

'Ach nach bhfuil clúmhilleadh déanta ort? Nach bhfuil tuairisc an chruinnithe le fáil?'

'Tá rúndacht i gceist. Tá a fhios agam gur féidir ar dlí a chuir ar bhall a scaoileann rún, de réir Acht bunaithe an Udaráis. Scaoilfear an rún, ar ndóigh i chuile bheár sa nGaeltacht anocht, ach ní féidir breith ar an gcaint sin, breith ar rud eicint a d'fhéadfaí a chur faoi bhráid na cúirte. Agus tá run eile ann.'

'Céard é féin' a d'fhiafraigh Bridie.

'Tá na ráflaí fíor.'

'Níl aon ghá é sin a rá.'

'Ach sin é a chaithfí a rá dá mbeadh cás clúmhillte sa gcúirt.'

'Ní ligfinn leo ina dhiaigh sin.'

'Níl a fhios agam an fiú an tairbhe an trioblóid. Tá cathú orm glacadh leis an síneadh láimhe, leis an gcraitheadh lámh órga, mar a chuir an cathaoirleach é. D'fhéadaimís a bheith compoirteach go maith an chuid eile dár saol.'

D'fhéadfaí tionscal beag a chur ar bun. B'fhéidir gur fearr sin ná an *hassle* uilig.'

'Ach tá prionsabail i gceist.'

'Ní chuireann prionsabail feoil ar an bpláta.' Chuaigh Therese anonn chuig an gcófra ina raibh an t-ól. 'Beidh ceann agat?'

'Ní leigheas ar bith é an t-ól ar na rudaí seo.'

'Ceann leis na néarógaí a shuaimhniú, leis an gcreathadh a bhaint díom.' Líon sí branda an duine dóibh.

'Nach aisteach an ceann mise,' arsa Bridie, 'ag cur m'fhear den ól, agus mé féin tosaithe air i lár an lae.' Smaoinigh sí ar feadh nóiméid. 'Cén fáth nach dtarraingníonn muid amach, agus bailiú linn go Londain arís? Bheinnse i bhfad ó John,[2] agus bheifeása glan ar obair bhrocach sin an Udaráis.'

'Sin é an chéad smaoineamh a tháinig isteach i m'intinn inniu, nuair a thosaigh an rud seo. Is smaoineamh maith é, cinnte. Bheadh suaimhneas againn, suaimhneas de chineál éigin, cé nár thaitin sé chomh mór sin le ceachtar againn cheana.'

'Bheadh sé difriúil nuair a bheimís le chéile.'

'B'fhéidir. Níl a fhios agam an mbeifeá socair chomh fada sin ó do mhuintir, agus táim cinnte nár mhaith le do mháthair tú a fheiceáil ag imeacht.'

'Caithfimid cuimhneamh orainn féin freisin.'

'Agus an bhfuil tú ag iarraidh Caomhán a thógáil ansin?'

'B'fhearr é ná a bheith anseo agus gasúir eile na scoile a bheith ag déanamh ceap magaidh de sna blianta atá romhainn.'

'Tá a fhios agam sin, ach ar bhealach ní muide amháin atá i gceist anseo, ach mná uile na hÉireann, má théann sé go dtí sin. Dá ndíbreofaí mise mar gheall ar seo, bheadh mná uile na tíre thíos leis. Ní bheadh cos le seasamh uirthi ag bean ar bith a gcuirfí rud ina leith, fíor nó bréagach.'

'Cén fáth gur tusa a chaitfeas cás a throid do mhná na hEireann? Nach féidir é a fhágáil faoi dhuine eicínt eile an fód sin a sheasamh?'

'Sin é a dhéanann an iomarca daoine. Sin é an fáth a shiúltar orthu, mná go háirithe. Nach tú féin a dúirt liom ar ball an fód a sheasamh?'

'An gcríochnóidh an bheirt againn i dteach na ngealt mar gheall ar seo?'

'Má chríochnaíonn féin, cén dochar?' Bhí Therese ag fáil a misneach ar ais.

---

1. Mac óg Bhridie.

2. Fear céile Bhridie, ar mhaith leis athaontú.

from:
A WOMAN'S LOVE (1994)

[This English version by the author is not so much a translation as a toned-down rewrite, in which lines and arguments are often swapped between Bridie and Therese, who never make love, but simply cuddle.]

'You look like death,' was Bridie's greeting when Therese arrived home unexpectedly for her lunch. She normally ate with the Board members on days that there were meetings. She couldn't face them now.

'I'd get sick if I was to sit down to eat with that crowd.'

'What's wrong? What have they done?'

'Just hold me,' she said, before telling what had happened.

'Tell them where to stick their job,' Bridie said. 'You don't need them.'

'But where did the rumours come from?'

'Maybe there's some peeping Tom about.'

'He'd need a very long neck. The bedroom is over the garage.'

'Why don't you sue them?'

'They haven't put anything on the record,' Therese replied. 'And anyway, you and Caomhán would be dragged into it.'

'Don't give in to them.'

'The golden handshake is pretty tempting. We could have a nice quiet comfortable life, start a small industry, maybe.'

'It's a matter of principle.'

'Every principle has a price, Bridie.'

'I don't think you're that cynical.'

'Why don't the three of us just go away, to London, or someplace?' Therese went to the drinks cabinet and got out the bottle of brandy. 'I know that this isn't a great idea in the circumstances, but I want to settle my nerves before going back in there. Will you have a drop?'

'No, thanks, and I don't think we should run away either. That'd look very like an admission of guilt.'

'You'd be away from John, and I'd be free of all this hassle.'

'Do you think London is the place to rear Caomhán?'

'It'd be better than being here with the other children teasing him about us. Anyway, we could afford to get a place in the country.' Therese began to feel giddy after a couple of sips of brandy. 'I could fancy myself as part of the stockbroker belt.'

'I thought you came back because you wanted to spend your life in the Gaeltacht.' Bridie tried to bring her back to what she considered reality. 'And haven't you often said that you don't give a damn what anyone thinks?'

'Everybody says that until it's themselves that are involved.'

IDE O'CARROLL

(1958–   )

MNÁ I mBOSTON (c. 1990)

[It is impossible to appreciate the cultural prejudice against lesbian writers in Ireland without acknowledging that their work does not always circulate in mainstream cultural outlets. The next four poems were circulated in manuscript and read at poetry readings in the early 1990s. Ide O'Carroll's 'Mná i mBoston', translated here by Louisa C. Callaghan, captures the sense of lesbianism as discovery, a female 'awakening', rather than the lesbian as a distinct character type.]

Mná i mBoston

Bheith sáite im' bhaclainn.
Sin a theastaigh uaithi.
Is dúisithe díreach ar maidin,
bheith nochta liom.
Athbheochaint na maighdine.
Athbheochaint na mban,
óg, aosta,
páiste ó bhean,
beola ar bheola.

Eadrainn ceangal, fluich, ceolmhar
beogach, bainniúil.
Smior an tsaoil
inár mbéal.

Women in Boston

To be deep in my arms . . .
That's what she wanted:
Awoken in the morning,
Be naked with me.

The reawakening of virgins.
The reawakening of woman.
    The young, the old;
Child out of child
Woman out of woman
Lips on lips.
Between us this connection;
Wet, musical, lively,
A milkiness.
    And the marrow of life
    In our mouths.

MARY McDERMOTT

(1959–   )

FRONTIERS
(*c.* 1990)

[This poem probes some of the differences age can make
to matters of self-disclosure and moral judgement.]

I

At eighteen,
so easy, then, to tremble with pain
sweat the fear of exposure,
cut rough tracks to that first one
whose very face beaconed love.

So easy, the terror of being known
tell the tale
tell it all

it could all be said, then.

And in that ancient time
blood rushed
tumbled unknowing
over fresh turned soil
soaked the centre,
swamped the sloping sides
coursed from source to sea.

A new land;
scorched soul, searing skin
epiphanies of certain love
senses loyal to the end.

II

They say
the thirties are our prime,
we women who have
reached our clear eyed time.
Satiated, knowing,
echoing,
smooth words,
easy on the ear.
Too tired, really
to tell again,
no need, really.

Telling's not enough.

Who could recount
the jaded story
or think to let it go
after all
those *lesser, travelled,*
diverged roads we took
to that glory shore.

III

Though . . .
we speak too
in our own fashion,
with less certitude.
A slow knowing
recalls with care.

Tides turn, rise,
and fall,
set the heart
afloat

to ripple on the shingle,
lap each shore
with remembering ways.
The ragged jetsam line
our fragile skin.

Blood slow with baggage,
no innocent frontiers,
no absolutes,
no absolutions.

A mottled land.

CHERRY SMYTH

(1960–   )

from:
WHEN THE LIGHTS GO UP
(2001)

[Cherry Smyth's work investigates 'queer culture' with
humour, pain and raunchiness; this poem has been chosen
for its evocation of a brief encounter outside the
traditional framework of lesbian romance.]

Hotel Room

I didn't care that the lift was pitch
for her lips were light, her tongue a torch,
her hands a searchbeam under my mac,
that could not shine like our flesh.

London misses her,
that early evening fuck by the naked window.
The eyeful hotel opposite did not stop her
lifting the folds of my skirt,

bare bum above her, toes singing,
I didn't have time to surround her lust,
become its singular, constant source,
nor rifle her unruly suitcase,
for clues to her hopefulness,
her I-don't-give-a-damn nerve,
which may have narrated,
negotiated my way through the dark.

Her plane left at six.
There is nothing to claim, but you know,
when she knelt to fasten my underwear,
it was more intimate than licking,
tender and shameless as the mother,
who crouched over a tampon to show her how.

She'd laugh, lines dashing by her mouth,
if I said I'd been feeling old,
just a muscle doing its job,
till she quickened my skin,
made words strike like flints
on that narrow, unmade bed.

MARY BRANLEY

(1962–)

LISSADELL RETOLD
(c. 1990)

[Lissadell was the family home of Constance Gore-Booth (1868-1927) and her sister Eva (1870-1926) (see pp. 749–50). Lissadell features in the poem 'In Memory of Eva Gore Booth and Con Markiewicz' 1927 by W.B. Yeats (1865-1939).]

The barnacle geese in season
from October on, leave Greenland
on a southern curve, they navigate
the skies and stay all winter
at Lissadell
in sanctuary, they used to say
the geese began as fish
birthed by the barnacle
and then turned fowl.

I have no season here,
no privileged duality
and lack a myth that might protect me
hunkered down in the smell of the sea
at low tide
slipping fingers under moist

and matted wrack
picking mussels off a soft furred rock
their lips are sealed.

Telling the story of the 'big house'
I must recover the discarded ones
from the official line
Constance raced her chestnut mare
across the strand
Eva, a poet and a suffragette
picked mussels here with Ester,[1]
hand in salty hand, we watch the sunset
coaxing light into another time.

The house is falling slowly down
and the name will die,
Perhaps some shrewd immigrant
with dollars from New York
will snap it up and start a health spa.
The local maids will trudge along the corridors
glad of the work, saved from the ship,
It's summer now and the geese have gone.

1. Eva Gore-Booth (see pp. 749–50), who lived and worked all her adult life with her beloved companion Esther Roper.

EMMA DONOGHUE

(1969–)

THE TALE OF THE SHOE
(1997)

[This story is one of a collection in which traditional fairy tales are reworked from an overtly lesbian perspective — in this instance the story is on the Cinderella theme which appears in several different treatments in this anthology. The feminist revision of fairy tales has developed as a popular genre with women writers since the 1970s, but the lesbian perspective attempts to put a new twist in the tale. For another contemporary treatment of fairy tale motifs,

see Volume v, pp. 1203–14. Published in *Kissing the Witch* (London: Hamish Hamilton, 1997).]

Till she came it was all cold. Every word that came out of my mouth limped away like a toad. The bed felt hard as a stone floor. Everything I put on my back turned to sackcloth and chafed my skin. The days were like ash on my fingers.

I kept running to the door but there was never anyone there. Envelopes arrived with nothing in them.

Nobody made me do the things I did, nobody scolded me, nobody punished me, but me. The shrill voices were all in my head. I scrubbed and scoured and swept because there was nothing else to do. When everything that could be done was done for the day, I knelt on the hearth and looked into the cinders until my eyes swam. I was trying to picture a future.

Once, out of all the times when I ran to the door and there was nobody there, there was still nobody there, but she was behind me. I thought she must have come out of the fire. Her eyes had tiny flames in them, and her eyebrows were silvered with ash.

Thing was, she finished the sweeping when my back was tired. She took me into the garden and showed me a hazel tree that I had never seen before. I began to ask questions but she put her long finger over my mouth so we could hear a dove murmuring on the highest branch.

It turned out that she had known my mother, when my mother was alive. She said that was my mother's tree.

How can I begin to describe the trans-formations? My old dusty self was spun new. This woman sheathed my limbs in blue satin. I was dancing on points of clear glass.

And then, because I asked, she took me to the ball. Isn't that what girls are meant to ask for?

She took me as far as the palace steps. I knew just how I was meant to be; I had heard all the stories. I smiled ever so prettily when the great doors swung wide to announce me. I refused a canapé and kept my belly pulled in. I danced with all the elderly gentlemen under the thousand crystal lamps.

At ten to twelve I came down the steps and she swept me away. Had enough? she asked, lifting a hair off my satin glove.

Thing was, I thought she was old enough to be my mother. I was keeping one eye out for the prince. Take me back tomorrow night, I said.

So she appeared again just when the soup was boiling over, and let me put my feet up. Our fingers drew pictures in the ashes on the hearth. She showed me the sparkle in my eyes, how wide my skirt could spread, how to waltz without getting dizzy. I was lithe in green velvet now, my own mother would not have recognised me.

That night I got right into the swing of things. I tittered at the king's jokes; I accepted a single chicken wing and nibbled it daintily. I danced three times with the prince, who had very little to say but did not let that stop him. I said nothing but indeed and oh yes and do you think so?

At five to midnight when my feet were starting to ache I waited on the bottom step and she came for me. On the way home I leaned my head on her shoulder and she put one hand over my ear. Had enough? she asked.

Thing was, I felt sure the prince was going to pick me; that was how the story went. Take me back tomorrow night, I said.

So she came for me just when the small sounds of the mice were getting on my nerves, and she told me they were coachmen to drive us in state. She could always make me laugh. She said her finger was a magic wand, it could do spectacular things.

That night my new skin was red silk, shivering in the breeze. The prince hovered at my elbow like an autumn leaf ready to fall. The musicians played the same tune over and over. I danced like a clockwork ballerina and smiled till my face twisted. I swallowed a little of everything I was offered, then lent over the balcony and threw it all up in a napkin. I had barely time to wipe my mouth before the prince came to propose.

Out on the steps he led me, under the half-full moon, all very fairytale. But as soon as the words leaked out of his mouth, they formed a cloud in which I could see my future. What the prince proposed was white and effortless, comfortable as fog. The midnight bell began to toll out the long procession of years, palatial day by moonless night. And I leapt backwards down the steps, leaving one shoe behind.

The bushes tore my dress into the old rags. She was waiting for me in the shadows on the edge of the lawn. She didn't ask had I had enough.

Thing was, I hadn't noticed she was beautiful. I must have dropped all my words in the bushes. I reached for what I wanted.

What about the shoe? she asked.

It was digging into my heel.

What about the prince? she asked.

He'll find someone to fit, if he looks long enough.

What about me? she asked very low. I'm old enough to be your mother.

Her finger was spelling on the back of my neck.

You're not my mother, I told her. I'm old
enough to know that.

I threw the other shoe into the brambles,
where it hung, glinting.

So then she took me home, or I took her home,
or we were both somehow taken to the closest
thing.

Biographies/Bibliographies

Charlotte MacCarthy

LIFE. *Fl.* 1745–68. Appears to have grown up in Ireland. She refers to
her father as a 'gentleman', who died destitute after nearly fifty years of
government service. It seems likely that she came from a Catholic family
but was raised as a Protestant when she was orphaned. She describes
being frightened by Catholic children in her childhood, and later was
convinced that a Jesuit had attempted to poison her. She tried to publish
in Ireland, but was thwarted by the printers and by an unnatural
(presumably Catholic) relation, bigoted against her by religion. She
made her way to London, collecting subscriptions from tradespeople in
Liverpool, Chester, Manchester and London. *The Fair Moralist* was
successful enough to warrant a second edition. In 1749 she was selling
theatre tickets in Twickenham and Richmond. Her fate after her last
published piece in 1768 is unknown.

CHIEF WRITINGS. *The Fair Moralist; Or, Love and Virtue* (London,
printed for the author, 1745; 2nd ed. 1746; rpr. New York, 1974); *News
from Parnassus, or, Political Advice from the Nine Muses, to his Grace, the
D—— of B——D. A Poem* (Dublin, 1757); *The Author and Bookseller*
(London, 1765); *Justice and Reason, Faithful Guides to Truth. A Treatise
Under Thirty-Seven Heads. To Which are Added, Letters Moral and
Entertaining (Never Before Publish'd)* (London, 1767); *A Letter from a
Lady to the Bishop of London* (signed Prudentia Christiana) (London,
1768).

BIOGRAPHY AND CRITICISM. Emma Donoghue, *Passions Between
Women: British Lesbian Culture 1668–1801* (London: Scarlett Press,
1993).

Eleanor Butler

LIFE. Lady Eleanor Butler was born in 1739 at Cambrai in France,
youngest daughter of Walter Butler, who from 1766 was recognized as
16th Earl of Ormond. The family, who were Roman Catholics, had lost
part of their title and much of their estates during the Jacobite
disturbances of the 1740s. Eleanor was educated at a French convent
and later came home to live at Kilkenny Castle. Around 1768 she met
Sarah Ponsonby, then a thirteen-year-old boarder at a school in
Kilkenny. By the time Sarah left the school to return to her relations in
1773, Eleanor was coming under pressure from her mother to enter a
convent in Liege. In March 1778 Eleanor made her first attempt to
elope with Sarah, the two disguised in men's clothes, but they were
recaptured outside Waterford, and the Butler family intensified the
pressure on Eleanor to enter the convent. In April she escaped from her
brother-in-law's house at Borris, and was concealed by Sarah for
twenty-four hours at Woodstock, helped by a maid, Mary Caryll. After
weeks of negotiation the two families agreed to let Eleanor, Sarah and
Mary Caryll leave Ireland together. After touring Wales and the
Marches for some weeks they rented a house near Llangollen in Powys.
They became famous for their 'romantic friendship' and were visited by
Edmund Burke, William Wordsworth, Hester Piozzi, Anna Seward and
other well-known literary figures. Since Llangollen was easily accessible

to travellers between Britain and Ireland, who crossed from Holyhead
in Anglesey, they maintained a number of Irish friendships. Eleanor
Butler died at Llangollen in 1829.

CHIEF WORKS. Butler kept diaries of her time in Wales, and some of
her surviving manuscripts were published as *The Hamwood Papers of the
Ladies of Llangollen and Caroline Hamilton*, ed. Mrs. G.H. Bell (London:
Macmillan, 1930); a selection of the diaries appears in *A Year with the
Ladies of Llangollen*, ed. Elizabeth Mavor (London: Penguin Books,
1986).

BIOGRAPHY AND CRITICISM. Elizabeth Mavor, *The Ladies of
Llangollen* (London: Michael Joseph, 1971).

Sarah Ponsonby

LIFE. Sarah Ponsonby was born in 1755, the only child of Chambre
Brazabon Ponsonby and his wife Louisa Lyons. Her mother died when
she was three and her father married Mary Barker. Chambre Brazabon
Ponsonby died when Sarah was seven and Sarah's stepmother married
Sir Robert Staples. She had a half-brother, born after his father's death,
and two half-sisters. Lady Staples died when Sarah was thirteen, and
Sarah was placed in the care of her father's cousin, Lady Betty Fownes,
of Inistiogue, County Kilkenny, who sent her to Miss Parke's boarding-
school in Kilkenny town. Lady Betty had asked the Ormond family to
take notice of Sarah, and so her friendship with Eleanor Butler began.
In 1773 at the age of eighteen Sarah left school to live with Lady Betty
and Sir William Fownes at their estate, Woodstock, Inistiogue. Soon
after, Sir William began to subject Sarah to sexual harassment. In 1778,
after several attempted elopements, Sarah Ponsonby and her maid Mary
Caryll left Woodstock with Eleanor Butler, and moved to Llangollen in
Wales. She died in 1831.

Maria Edgeworth

For biography and bibliography, see Volume I, pp. 1051–2 and Volume
IV, p. 892.

Mary Tighe

For biography and bibliography, see p. 516.

Joseph Sheridan Le Fanu

For biography and bibliography, see Volume I, pp. 1298–9.

George Moore

For biography and bibliography, see Volume II, pp. 560–1.

George Egerton

For biography and bibliography, see p. 895.

Rosa Mulholland

LIFE. Rosa Mulholland was born in Belfast in 1841. Following the
death of her father, Dr Joseph Stevenson Mulholland, the family moved
to Letterfrack, County Galway. She at first intended to become an artist
and was an art student in South Kensington, London; at the age of 15
she sent comic sketches to *Punch* which were rejected. Her early literary
work was encouraged by Charles Dickens, who published her stories
and poems in *Household Words* and *All The Year Round*. Her first novel,

Dunmara (1864), was published under the pseudonym Ruth Murray; her first poem, published in the *Cornhill Magazine* under the pseudonym Ruth Millais, attracted the attention of the painter John Millais, who offered to take her as a pupil and illustrated some of her work. Her sister Clara also became a writer, primarily of stories for young girls, and her sister Ellen married Lord Charles Russell, Lord Chief Justice of England and brother of Matthew Russell SJ, editor of the *Irish Monthly*. In a literary career which spanned over fifty years, she wrote numerous novels and short stories, many of which appeared in the *Irish Monthly*, and published three collections of poetry. In 1891, W.B. Yeats described her as 'the novelist of contemporary Catholic Ireland'. In that year she married John Gilbert (1829–98), historian and antiquary, knighted in 1897; from 1891 she lived in Blackrock, County Dublin. Following a long illness, she died in 1921.

CHIEF WRITINGS. *Dunmara*, 3 vols (London: Smith, Elder, 1864); republished as *The Story of Ellen* (London: Burns and Oates, 1907); *Hester's History*, 2 vols (London: Chapman and Hall, 1869); *The Wicked Woods of Tobereevil*, 2 vols (London: Chapman and Hall, 1872); *Eldergowan; Or, Twelve Months of My Life, and Other Tales* (London and Belfast: Marcus Ward, 1874); *The Wild Birds of Killeevy: A Tale* (London: Burns and Oates, 1879); *Hetty Gray; Or, Nobody's Bairn* (London, Glasgow, Edinburgh and Dublin: Blackie, 1883); *The Walking Trees, and Other Tales* (Dublin: Gill, 1884); *Vagrant Verses* (London: Kegan Paul, Trench, 1886); *The Late Miss Hollingford* (London, Glasgow, Edinburgh and Dublin: Blackie, 1886); *Marcella Grace: An Irish Novel* (London: Kegan Paul, Trench, 1886; republished Washington DC: Maunsel, 2000); *A Fair Emigrant: A Novel* (London: Kegan Paul, Trench, 1888); *Gianetta: A Girl's Story of Herself* (London, Glasgow, Edinburgh and Dublin: Blackie, 1888); *The Haunted Organist of Hurly Burly, and Other Stories* (London: Hutchinson, 1891); *Nanno: A Daughter of the State* (London: Grant Richards, 1898); *Onora* (London: Grant Richards, 1900), republished as *Norah of Waterford* (London and Edinburgh: Sands; New York: P.J. Kenedy, 1915); *The Tragedy of Chris: The Story of a Dublin Flower-Girl* (London and Edinburgh: Sands, 1903); *Life of Sir John T. Gilbert* (London: Longmans Green, 1905); *Our Boycotting: A Miniature Comedy* (play) (Dublin: Gill, 1907); *Spirit and Dust* (poems) (London: Elkin Mathews, 1908); *Old School Friends: A Tale of Modern Life* (London, Glasgow, Edinburgh and Dublin: Blackie, 1913); *Narcissa's Ring: The Story of a Strange Quest* (London, Glasgow, Edinburgh and Dublin: Blackie, 1915); *O'Loghlin of Clare* (London and Edinburgh: Sands; New York: P.J. Kenedy, 1916); *Dreams and Realities* (poems) (London and Edinburgh: Sands, 1916).

BIOGRAPHY AND CRITICISM. Charles A. Read and T.P. O'Connor (eds), *The Cabinet of Irish Literature: Selections from the Works of the Chief Poets, Orators, and Prose Writers of Ireland. With Biographical Sketches and Literary Notices*, 4 vols (London, Glasgow, Edinburgh and Dublin: Blackie, 1879–80), new ed. by Katharine Tynan Hinkson (London: Gresham, 1902–3); Justin McCarthy, Charles Welsh, et al. (eds), *Irish Literature: Irish Authors and Their Writings*, 10 vols (Philadelphia: Morris, 1904); Matthew Russell SJ, 'The Literary Output of Three Irishwomen — Mrs Hinkson, Mrs. Blundell', *Irish Monthly*, vol. 38 (1910), p. 349; Stephen J. Brown SJ, *Ireland in Fiction: A Guide to Irish Novels, Tales, Romances and Folk-lore*, vol. 1 (1916; new ed. Dublin and London: Maunsel, 1919; 1919 ed. rpr. Shannon: Irish University Press, 1968); 'Obituary of Rosa Mulholland, Lady Gilbert', in John S. Crone (ed.), *Irish Book Lover*, vol. 13 (1921–2), pp. 21–2; Katharine Tynan, 'Rosa Muholland', in *Memories* (London: Everleigh Nash and Grayson, 1924); James H. Murphy, *Catholic Fiction and Social Reality in Ireland, 1873–1922* (Connecticut and London: Greenwood Press, 1997).

Edith Œ. Somerville and Martin Ross

For biography and bibliography, see Volume II, p. 1217.

Eva Gore-Booth

For biography and bibliography, see pP. 749–50

Elizabeth Bowen

For biography and bibliography, see Volume II, p. 949. See also:

BIOGRAPHY AND CRITICISM. Andrew Bennett and Nicholas Royle, *Elizabeth Bowen and the Dissolution of the Novel: Still Lives* (New York: St Martin's Press, 1994).

Molly Keane

LIFE. Molly Keane (Mary Nesta Skrine) was born in County Kildare in 1904, one of five children to Moira O'Neill, poet and virtual recluse. She grew up in 'a lovely country-house life' which later provided the material for her books. Between 1928 and 1956 (out of boredom and to supplement her meagre dress allowance) she wrote several plays and eleven novels under the pseudonym M.J. Farrell. (Admission of authorship would have incurred exclusion from the hunting society she enjoyed.) When her husband died suddenly, aged thirty-six, she was left to raise a young family on her own. Eventually she returned to writing in the seventies, but her black comedy, *Good Behaviour*, met initially with rejection until its merit was recognized and its publication in 1981 constituted a spectacular comeback for the author. It has been translated into several languages and, along with *Time After Time*, adapted for television. Many of Molly Keane's novels have been reprinted by Virago Press. She died in April 1996.

CHIEF WRITINGS. (Novels) *The Knight of Cheerful Countenance* (1926; rpr. London: Virago, 1993); *Young Entry* (1928; rpr. London: Virago, 1989); *Taking Chances* (1929; rpr. Middlesex: Penguin, 1987); *Mad Puppetstown* (1931; rpr. London: Virago, 1986); *Conversation Piece* (1932; rpr. London: Virago, 1991); with Snaffles, *Red Letter Days* (London: Collins; New York: Farrar and Rinehart, 1933; published in US as *Point-to-Point*); *Devoted Ladies* (1934; rpr. London: Virago, 1984); *Full House* (1935; rpr. London: Virago, 1986); *The Rising Tide* (1937; rpr. London: Virago, 1984); *Two Days in Aragon* (1941; rpr. London: Virago, 1985); *Loving Without Tears* (1951; rpr. London: Virago, 1988; published in US as *The Enchanting Witch*, New York: Cromwell, 1951); *Treasure Hunt* (1952; rpr. London: Virago, 1990); *Good Behaviour* (London; Deutsch, 1981; New York: Dutton, 1981); *Time After Time* (London: Deutsch, 1983; New York: Knopf, 1984); *Loving and Giving* (London: Deutsch, 1988; published in US as *Queen Lear*, New York: Dutton, 1989). (Plays) (All written with John Perry and directed by John Gielgud) *Spring Meeting* (London: Collins, 1938); *Ducks and Drakes* (London: Collins, 1942); *Treasure Hunt* (London: French, 1951); *Dazzling Prospect* (London: French, 1961). (Non-fiction) *Molly Keane's Nursery Cooking* (London: Macdonald, 1985); autobiographical chapter, *Portrait of the Artist as a Young Girl*, J. Quinn (ed.) (London: Methuen, 1986), pp. 63–78; (ed. with Sally Phipps) *Molly Keane's Ireland: An Anthology* (London: Harper Collins, 1993).

BIOGRAPHY AND CRITICISM. Bridget O'Toole, 'Three Writers of the Big House: Elizabeth Bowen, Molly Keane and Jennifer Johnston', in Gerald Dawe and Edna Longley (eds), *Across a Roaring Hill: The Protestant Imagination in Modern Ireland* (Belfast: Blackstaff Press, 1985), pp. 124–38; Vera Kreilkamp, 'The Persistent Pattern: Molly Keane's Recent Big House Fiction', *Massachusetts Review*, vol. 28 (autumn 1987), pp. 453–60; Katie Donovan, *Irish Women Writers: Marginalised by Whom?* (Dublin: Raven Arts, 1988), pp. 27–9; Maurice Elliot, 'Molly Keane's Big Houses', in Jacqueline Genet (ed.), *The Big House in Ireland* (Dingle: Brandon, 1991), pp. 191–208; Rüdiger Imhof, 'Molly Keane: *Good Behaviour, Time After Time* and *Loving and Giving*', in Otto Rauchbauer (ed.), *Ancestral Voices: The Big House in Anglo-Irish Literature* (Hildesheim: Georg Olms, 1992), pp. 195–203.

Kate O'Brien

For biography and bibliography, see Volume II, p. 1221.

Edna O'Brien

For biography and bibliography, see Volume III, p. 1134, and Volume IV, p. 601.

Maeve Binchy

LIFE. Born in Dalkey, County Dublin, in 1940. She was educated at the Convent of the Holy Child, Killiney, County Dublin, and University College Dublin, from which she graduated with a BA in history and French. She joined the *Irish Times* in 1968 and was an active supporter of the Irish Women's Liberation Movement. In 1973 she moved to the London office of the *Irish Times*. She subsequently became a very successful novel writer. Several of her novels have been adapted for television. She has also written a number of plays. She was awarded an honorary D.Litt. from the National University of Ireland in 1990. Several of Binchy's novels have been adapted for television and film. She is married to writer and broadcaster Gordon Snell.

CHIEF WRITINGS. *Maeve's Diary* (Dublin: Irish Times, 1979); *Central Line, Stories of Big City Life* (London: Quartet, 1978); *Victoria Line* (London: Quartet, 1980); *Dublin Four* (London: Century, 1982); *Light a Penny Candle* (London: Century, 1982); *London Transports* (London: Century, 1983); *The Lilac Bus* (Swords: Ward River Press, 1984); *Echoes* (London: Century, 1985); *Firefly Summer* (London: Century, 1987); *Silver Wedding* (London: Century, 1988); *The Storyteller* (London: Longman, 1990); *Circle of Friends* (London: Century, 1990); *The Copper Beech* (London: Orion, 1992); *The Glass Lake* (London: Orion, 1994); *Dear Maeve* (Dublin: Poolbeg, 1995); *Evening Class* (London: Orion, 1996); *Aches and Pains* (London: Orion, 1999).

Maura Richards

LIFE. Born in Mitchelstown, County Cork, in 1939, Maura O'Dea came to Dublin in 1968. She had a daughter in 1970, which inspired her semi-autobiographical novel about single motherhood. She was active in the 1970s in establishing Cherish, the self-help group for single mothers. *Single Issue* is an account of those years. Since 1977 Richards has lived in England, working as an administrator in the area of child protection.

CHIEF WRITINGS. *Two to Tango* (1981); *Interlude* (1982); *Single Issue* (Dublin: Poolbeg, 1998).

Mary Dorcey

LIFE. Born in Dublin in 1950, Dorcey has lived in France, Spain, England, America and Japan. She was a founder member of Irishwomen United and the Irish Gay Rights Movement. Her first collection of short stories, *A Noise from the Woodshed* (1989), was awarded the Rooney Prize for Literature. She received an Arts Council Bursary in 1991. Her poetry and stories have appeared in many anthologies, and have been read on RTÉ Radio and performed on stage.

CHIEF WRITINGS. *Kindling* (London: Onlywomen Press, 1982); *A Noise from the Woodshed* (London: Onlywomen Press, 1989); *Moving Into the Space Cleared by Our Mothers* (Galway: Salmon, 1991); *The River that Carries Me* (Galway: Salmon, 1995).

BIOGRAPHY AND CRITICISM. Antoinette Quinn 'Speaking of the Unspoken: The Poetry of Mary Dorcey' Colby Quarterly 28 (December 1992): 227–238.

Máighréad Medbh

LIFE. Born in Limerick in 1959. Lives in Dublin, where she works mostly as a performance poet. In 1998 she won Dublin's first Poetry Slam.

CHIEF WRITINGS. *The Making of a Pagan* (Belfast: Blackstaff Press, 1990); *Tenant* (County Clare: Salmon, 1999).

Susan Connolly

LIFE. Born Drogheda, County Louth, in 1956. She studied Music and Italian at University College, Dublin. She was awarded the Patrick and Katherine Kavanagh Fellowship in Poetry in 2001.

CHIEF WRITINGS. *How High the Moon* incorporates 'Boann and Other Poems' with Catherine Phil MacCarthy's 'Sanctuary' (Dublin: Poetry Ireland, 1991); *For the Stranger* (Dublin: Daedalus, 1993); *Stone and Tree Sheltering Water: A Exploration of Sacred and Secular Wells in County Louth* (with Anne Marie Moroney) (Drogheda: Flax Mill, 1998); *Race to the Sea* (Drogheda: Flax Mill, 1999); *Ogham: Ancestors Remembered in Stone* (with Anne Marie Moroney) (Drogheda; Flax Mill, 2000); *A Salmon in the Pool, the River Boyne from Source to Sea: A Map of Poetry and Place names* (Drogheda: Tearmann, 2001)

Nuala Archer

LIFE. Born in the United States in 1955, and brought up largely in Panama, where her parents (who had left Ireland in the 1950s as doctors) were Protestant missionaries. Spanish was her first language but a visit to Ireland led to a stay of years and a house in Dublin. In 1977–8 she studied Anglo-Irish literature at Trinity College Dublin, and later taught in Ireland and the United States while working at her Ph.D., which she received from the University of Wisconsin at Milwaukee. Although she left Ireland in 1983 and has lived since then in the United States and Israel, she has kept in touch with Irish writers. In 1986 she edited a special issue (no. 3, winter) of Irish Women's Writing for the *Midland Review* (Oklahoma State University Press). Her first volume of poems, *Whale on the Line* (1981), won the Patrick Kavanagh Award.

CHIEF WRITINGS. (Poems) *Whale on the Line* (Oldcastle: Gallery Press, 1981); (with Medbh McGuckian) *Two Women, Two Shores* (Galway: Salmon, 1989); *The Hour of Pan/amá* (Galway: Salmon, 1992); *Pan/amá, a chapbook* (New York: Red Dust, 1992); *From a Mobile Home* (Galway: Salmon, 1995).

BIOGRAPHY AND CRITICISM. Robin Becker, 'Nuala Archer (1955–)', in *Contemporary Lesbian Writers of the United States*, eds Sandra Pollack and Denise D. Knight (Westport: Greenwood, 1993), pp. 26–30.

June Levine

LIFE. Born in Dublin in 1931. She was educated at Zion School, the national school for Jewish children in Bloomfield Avenue, Dublin, which was then in the centre of the Dublin Jewish community. She began her journalistic career with the *Irish Times* as a cub reporter. She married a Canadian medical student in 1951 and emigrated to Canada with him and her two children in 1957. She worked there as a journalist and doctor's wife until she returned to Ireland in 1967 to rear two sons and a daughter on her own. In 1968 she joined the *Irishwoman's Journal*, a 'magazine for the thinking woman', of which she later became editor. She was a columnist with the *Sunday Independent*, 1969–72, and later joined the team of the *Late Late Show* on RTÉ. She has also worked on other television programmes. She lives in Dublin.

CHIEF WRITINGS. *Sisters: The Personal Story of an Irish Feminist* (Dublin: Ward River Press, 1982); co-author with Lyn Madden, *Lyn: A Story of Prostitution* (Dublin: Attic Press, 1987); *A Season of Weddings* (Dublin: New Island Books, 1992).

Pádraig Standún

LIFE. Pádraig Standún was born in 1946 and ordained to the priesthood in 1971. His first book *Súil le Breith* was published in 1983. It was translated into English as *Lovers* (1991) and filmed by Bob Quinn as *Budawanny*. He has worked as a curate in the Connemara and Aran Island Gaeltacht.

CHIEF WRITINGS. *Na hAntraipeologicals* (Indreabhán, Conamara: Cló Iar-Chonnachta, 1993); *Celibates* (Dublin: Poolbeg, 1993); *Cion mná* (Indreabhán, Conamara: Cló Iar-Chonnachta, 1993); *Ciorcas* (Indreabhán, Conamara: Cló Iar-Chonnachta, 1991); *Saoire* (Indreabhán, Conamara: Cló Iar-Chonnachta, 1997); *Stigmata* (Indreabhán, Conamara: Cló Iar-Chonnachta, 1994); *Stigmata*, English translation (Dingle: Brandon, 1995); *Súil le Breith* (Indreabhán, Conamara: Cló Iar-Chonnachta, 1983); *Lovers* (Swords, County Dublin: Poolbeg, 1991).

Ide O'Carroll

LIFE. Born in Tullaghmore, County Offaly, in 1958, where she grew up bilingual, Ide O'Carroll has worked as a secondary schoolteacher and a lecturer in Irish studies and women's studies; she holds Masters degrees from Northeastern and Harvard universities. She is currently on a number of research teams working on Travellers' needs, on Dublin women's history, and on lesbian and gay poverty. She spent five years in the United States, and was a founder of the Irish Women in Boston Group and of a media collective, Trasna na dTonnta. She has also published papers on women in the construction industry and 'queers in the quad', lesbians in a university context.

CHIEF WRITINGS. *Models for Movers: Irish Women's Emigration to America* (Dublin, 1990); (editor, with Eoin Collins) *Lesbian and Gay Visions of Ireland: Towards the Twenty-First Century* (London: Cassell, 1996).

Mary McDermott

LIFE. Born in Dublin, 1959, Mary McDermott is now researching feminist theory for a Ph.D. in women's studies at Trinity College Dublin.

Cherry Smyth

For biography and bibliography, see p. 1088.

Mary Branley

LIFE. Mary Branley was born in 1962 and brought up in Sligo. She lived for many years in the USA. Her first play, *Silk Kimonos,* was staged in Sligo during the 1995 Yeats summer school. She works as a teacher in London.

Emma Donoghue

For biography and bibliography, see p. 1087.

SIOBHÁN KILFEATHER, *Editor*

Explorations of Love and Desire in Writing for Children, 1791–1979

Much of the earliest printed literature for children, in the seventeenth and eighteenth centuries, was published anonymously and comes in the form of text books to aid in the teaching of reading and writing. Horn books were usually abcedarium, and at least until the end of the eighteenth century teaching the alphabet was strongly associated with religious instruction. The alphabet was followed by prayers and from the late seventeenth century a catechism was commonly included. Simple rhymes and fables were used with illustrations as literature for the nursery and schoolroom in the eighteenth century. Older children would have been expected to read their bibles or stories such as John Bunyan's *Pilgrim's Progress*. A number of early printed ballads would clearly have appealed to children and seem to be remembered by adults as part of their early childhood reading. In cabins and smaller farmhouses ballads and broadsheets were often pasted to the walls as decoration.

In 1827 Jonah Barrington describes his own childhood some fifty to sixty years previously:

> The library was a gloomy closet, and rather scantily furnished with everything but dust and cobwebs: there were neither chairs nor tables; but I cannot avoid recollecting many of the principal books, because I read such of them as I could comprehend, or as were amusing; and looked over all the prints in them a hundred times. While trying to copy these prints, they made an indelible impression upon me; and hence I feel

confident of the utility of embellishments in any book intended for the instruction of children. I possessed many of the books after my grandfather's death, and have some of them still. I had an insatiable passion for reading from my earliest days, and it has occupied the greater proportion of my later life. Gulliver's Travels, Robinson Crusoe, Fairy Tales, and the History of the Bible, all with numerous plates, were my favourite authors and constant amusements: I believed every word of them except the fairies, and was not entirely sceptical as to those good people neither.[1]

Like *Pilgrim's Progress*, Daniel Defoe's *Robinson Crusoe* and Jonathan Swift's *Gulliver's Travels* were books for adults that appealed to children's imaginations. As novels became increasingly popular it became clear that they could be employed for didactic and pedagogic ends. Rolf Loeber and Magda Stouthamer-Loeber have for some years been collecting material on early Irish children's literature, as part of their ongoing research into Irish fiction 1700–1900, and they have identified some of the earliest texts produced for girls. *The Polite Tutoress* (anonymous, Dublin, *c.* 1760) seems to have been intended for girls in boarding-schools. Maria Edgeworth and Charlotte Brooke wrote for children of either sex, and Edgeworth often represents boys and girls learning together at home or at school. There were

1. Jonah Barrington, *Personal Sketches of His Own Time* (London, 1827), volume 1, pp. 1005–6.

fewer dedicated children's writers in the nineteenth century than today, and more women who wrote stories for children as part of a career in writing. Harriet Beaufort, L.T. Meade, Kathleen Fitzpatrick and Patricia Lynch wrote almost exclusively for children, but most of the writers excerpted here are as well if not better known for work in other genres. Amongst many other children's writers included in the anthology are Mary Leadbeater, Anna Maria Hall, Rosa Mulholland, Emily Lawless and Lady Gregory. Two of the earliest girls' school stories are *Eda Morton and Her Cousins* by Mary Letitia Martin (1815–50) and *Nathalie: A Tale* by Julia Kavanagh (1824–77). In the latter half of the nineteenth century there was a huge expansion of fiction for older girls/young women, describing the transition from girlhood to adult life, and often including an idealized love story. There is an example here from Winifred Letts, and other specialists in this area were Clara Mulholland, Rosa Mulholland, Katharine Tynan, Margaret Hungerford, Elizabeth Lysaght and May Crommelin.

Ireland, of course, had a rich oral storytelling tradition and whilst Irish-speaking children would have had first-hand access to this tradition there is also evidence of its strong influence on the anglophone population. Here is a passage from Emily Lawless's *The Book of Gilly* (1906), where Gilly's parents discuss why the father wants his son to be raised in Ireland:

> 'It was your mother that put it in your head to think so much about Ireland, wasn't it?' Lady Dukerron asked. 'I have always heard she was devoted to it. It seems so odd, too, when she wasn't Irish herself. She liked being in Kerry better than anything, didn't she?'
>
> 'Yes.' There was an emphasis about the word that seemed greater than the occasion called for, as, with hands still behind his head, Gilly's father continued to stare out of the window at the swaying plane trees.
>
> 'When I look back,' he presently went on, — 'when I look back, and remember how her whole time used to be spent riding or walking about the hills there; in and out of all the cabins; sitting for hours at a time in the chimney corners; knowing every man, woman, and child in the place as well

as — in fact a lot better — than you know your own cousins. Remembering too how I used to scuttle round like a small dog at her heels; listening to the old people's stories, yes and believing in them, by Jove! lying out for hours at a time on the rocks, sniffing at the Atlantic; getting all sorts of notions into my stupid little head, and scraping acquaintance with everything and everybody, down to the very puffins; remembering all that, it makes me sick, Cynthia, nothing short of sick, to think of that unfortunate little Gilly-boy being stuck the whole time we are away in India with his nose in the machinery here.'[2]

These stories were not, from Lord Dunkerron's point of view, to make his son wholly Irish, someone who would reject the 'machinery', but were to provide a supplement to, rather than an overthrow of, reason and enlightenment. By the time the Celtic Revival was fully underway, however, a more subversive potential in folklore and mythology was to be identified. Writers such as Lady Gregory and Eleanor Hull turned to ancient Irish history and myth to school children in a pre-sectarian Irish history and to develop pride in a distinctive Irish tradition. Cú Chulainn was particularly popular for many reasons, but for children there was a special emphasis placed on his childhood exploits. The popular histories of royalty and imperial adventures common in Britain in the Edwardian period were replaced in the Irish Free State by narratives of the childhood of Irish saints or of heroes such as Hugh O'Neill or the United Irishmen. This was propaganda, of course, but then many of the early nineteenth-century anglophone texts for children had been texts overtly or implicitly promoting the use of the English language and proselytizing for Protestantism (and later, in reaction, for Catholic publishing projects). From the 1920s the Irish state sponsored Irish-language publication and one of the most sustained projects was the translation of suitable children's literature, from nursery rhymes to major novels, into Irish.

Writing for children was, like translation, for a long time an under-appreciated, under-rewarded

---

2. Emily Lawless, *The Book of Gilly* (London: Smith, Elder, 1906), p. 5.

literary career, and therefore largely populated by women writers. The implied author of fiction, particularly for younger children, was often the mother addressing her child. In the eighteenth and nineteenth centuries male writers were generally — though not exclusively — associated with writing either fantasy or adventure stories for children, leaving the domestic to women.

If sexuality is not usually explicitly addressed in children's writing, it has been recognized as one of the strongest implicit themes of the most successful stories. Children's writing is often at its most enthralling when it describes how a child first explores and decodes the secret knowledge of the adult world. Children fear adult power, and in that fear there is an element of sexual tension. They also long to progress to adulthood and suspect that there is some enchantment in adult desires. I do not know of a single Irish book that creates a stranger, more fearful and more thrilling atmosphere than *The Weans of Rowallan*. It maps out a place that is densely located in late-nineteenth-century County Down and yet is like no place in the world, and a family of children brilliantly, unsentimentally characterized and differentiated. Its terrors are unexplained and its griefs unresolved. It is a masterpiece, yet even in Ireland it is almost completely unknown.

CHARLOTTE BROOKE

(1740–93)

from:
THE SCHOOL FOR CHRISTIANS, IN DIALOGUES, FOR THE USE OF CHILDREN (1791)

[The Socratic dialogue, which underpins Charlotte Brooke's narrative strategy, fuses with the catechisms which were used as vehicles for both religious and secular education in eighteenth-century children's writing, in this text of religious instruction. It is a model for Protestant instructors to explain the explicit sexual material in Genesis, especially the connection between original sin and sexual knowledge, to very young children. Published Dublin: Bernard Dornin, 1791. The text is from a copy in the British Library.]

DIALOGUE I
Paternus, Filiolus

Filiolus. Good Morrow, papa.
Patern. Good morrow, my love, — what is the matter? your eyes look red.
Filio. Oh, papa! — that story you were telling me, out of the Bible, last night, made me so melancholy! — I could not help crying to think

what a pity it was of Adam and Eve, to grow so naughty, after God had made them so good! — I was thinking of it all night. — But, papa, why did God let them be so naughty, and do themselves so much harm? Sure he could have hindered them, if he pleased, from eating that nasty tree?
Pat. He could.
Fil. And why didn't he then?
Pat. Because he created them with a free will, my dear.
Fil. What's that, papa?
Pat. Why, he put it in their power to think of what they pleased, and have a mind to whatever they pleased.
Fil. But, why did he then? Why didn't he hinder them from having a mind to be naughty?
Pat. If God had given them no choice, they could not have chosen good any more than bad and could not more have loved or served God, or been capable of happiness, than this stupid stick. — Tell me, do you love this stick?
Fil. Oh! — papa, — you may make me laugh; — is it love a stick?
Pat. And why not?
Fil. Why, sure, because the stick can't love me.
Pat. Do you love your dog?
Fil. Oh yes, very much indeed.
Pat. And why?
Fil. Because he loves me in his heart, papa.

Pat. Have you any other reason, besides this, for loving him?

Fil. Oh yes, for he diverts me, and comes when I call him, and carries me about, and does everything that I bid him.

Pat. And are you not as much obliged to your stick? — You have it whenever you please, and you play with it, and ride upon it, as well as you do upon Pompey.

Fil. Aye, but no thanks to the stick, though: the stick does not care a pin for me; it won't come when I call it, like Pompey; I must go and fetch it, when I want it, papa: sure it is not out of good nature it carries me about, like Pompey! the stick can't help itself, or hinder me, but Pompey could hinder me, if he had a mind, and for all that he does everything that I bid him, out of his own good will, and because he loves me.

DIALOGUE IV

Pat. After they had transgressed, and began to perceive the effects of what they had done, God saw the misery of their situation, and he had compassion on them; and he called them out, from among the trees of the garden where they were striving to help themselves, foolishly forgetting that nothing can be hidden from the eyes of heaven; so, they came from behind the trees, trembling, and confused (as you will find in the Bible here) and alleged, in their excuse, that they found themselves naked, and not fit to appear in the presence of God: — they found themselves stripped of their pure and immortal bodies, and left in all the nakedness of a body of shame, and corruption. Now, God knew, as well as they did, everything that had befallen them; but he wanted to convict them, out of their own mouths; and he, therefore, asked them, who had told them that they were naked, or what was the sudden alteration which made them unfit to appear! They then confessed what they had done, but still strove to throw the blame from themselves; Adam laid the fault upon Eve's advice, and Eve laid the fault upon the serpent's advice; — but they were soon made sensible of the crime of minding the advice of any creature, more than the command of God: — God shewed them the guilt of their disobedience, and pointed out all the terrible consequences which that guilt would bring upon them, and upon all their children. — However, when he had convinced them of their crime, and saw them silenced in his presence, and overwhelmed with shame and despair; he then began to comfort and speak kindly to them.

ADELAIDE O'KEEFFE

(1776–1865)

from:
ORIGINAL POEMS FOR INFANT MINDS (1805)

[Adelaide O'Keeffe's children's verse appeared in an extremely popular poetry collection, *Original Poems for Infant Minds* (London: Darton and Harvey, 1805), in which most of the poems were by the sisters Jane Taylor (1783–1824) and Ann Taylor (1782–1866). The poems address perceived female vices such as exhibitionism, extravagance and dishonesty. The follies of children's behaviour are represented as a terrible predictor of future adult vice. This is a message found in many of Maria Edgeworth's *Early Lessons*. Mary's false alarms are heavy with sexual innuendo and the extraordinary mutilation she suffers in punishment hints at the anxiety provoked by a young girl's independence. 'False Alarms' is a precursor of such well-known cautionary tales as *Struwwelpeter* (1845) by Heinrich Hoffman (1809–94) and the story of 'Matilda' who meets a similar fate to Mary in *Cautionary Tales for Children* (1907) by Hilaire Belloc (1870–1953). From a copy in Birmingham Public Library.]

False Alarms

One day little Mary most loudly did call,
'Mamma! O mamma, pray come here,
A fall I have had, oh! a very sad fall.'
Mamma ran in haste and in fear.

Then Mary jumped up, and she laughed in
   great glee,
And cried, 'Why, how fast you can run!
No harm has befall'n, I assure you, to me,
My screaming was only in fun.'

Her mother was busy at work the next day,
She heard from without a loud cry:
'The great Dog had got me! O help me! O pray!
He tears me, he bites me, I die!'
Mamma, all in terror, quick to the court flew,
And there little Mary she found;
Who, laughing, said, 'Madam, pray how do you
   do?'
And curtseyed quite down to the ground.

That night little Mary was some time in bed,
When cries and loud shrieking were heard:
'I'm on fire, O mamma! O come up, or I'm
   dead!'
Mamma she believed not a word.
'Sleep, sleep, naughty child,' she called out from
   below,
'How often have I been deceived!
You are telling a story, you very well know:
Go to sleep, for you can't be believed.'

Yet still the child screamed: now the house filled
   with smoke:
That fire is above, Jane declares:
Alas! Mary's words they soon found were no
   joke,
When ev'ry one hastened up-stairs.
All burnt and all seamed is her once pretty face,
And terribly marked are her arms,
Her features all scarred, leave a lasting disgrace,
For giving mamma false alarms.

Sophia's Fool's-Cap[1]

Sophia was a little child,
Obliging, good, and very mild,
Yet lest of dress she should be vain,
Mamma still dressed her well, but plain.
Her parents, sensible and kind,
Wished only to adorn her mind;

No other dress, when good, had she,
But useful, neat simplicity.
Tho' seldom, yet when she was rude,
Or ever in a naughty mood,
Her punishment was this disgrace,
A large fine cap, adorned with lace,
With feathers and with ribbons too;
The work was neat, the fashion new,
Yet, as a fool's-cap was its name,
She dreaded much to wear the same.

A lady, fashionably gay,
Did to mamma a visit pay;
Sophia stared, then whisp'ring said,
'Why, dear mamma, look at her head!
To be so tall and wicked too,
The strangest thing I ever knew:
What naughty tricks, pray, has she done,
That they have put that fool's-cap on?'

from:
PATRIARCHAL TIMES; OR THE LAND OF CANAAN: A FIGURATIVE HISTORY, IN SEVEN BOOKS. COMPRISING INTERESTING EVENTS, INCIDENTS AND CHARACTERS, FOUNDED ON THE HOLY SCRIPTURES (1811)

[Historical novels, largely developed by women writers in the eighteenth century long before Walter Scott brought literary respectability to the genre, offered women an opportunity to re-imagine historical events as more influenced by women's actions than was emphasized in approved sources. A re-interpretation of biblical stories allows O'Keeffe to investigate assumptions about women's guilt in the Hebrew texts and offer a critique of patriarchal times. In re-telling the story of Abraham[1] she shifts

---

1. A cap of fantastic shape and decoration, worn by a court jester. This poem may be indebted to Mary Barber, 'A Letter Written for my Daughter, To a Lady Who Had Presented Her with a Cap', Volume v, p. 789.

1. Based on Genesis: 16–22. Abraham's wife Sarah is childless, so she gives him her Egyptian slave, Hagar, who bears him a son, Ishmael. When Ishmael is thirteen God intervenes to make Sarah bear a son, Isaac. When Sarah sees Ishmael play with Isaac she is jealous, and insists that Abraham exile the boy and his mother. Hagar believes that she and her son will die in the desert, but God once again intervenes to save them.

emphasis from Abraham's trial over the order to kill Isaac, to Hagar's trial when Abraham responds to Sarah's sexual jealously by exiling Hagar and her son Ishmael. Religious texts were also an opportunity to engage with racy material, which, when dealt with in sentimental novels by writers such as Mary Wollstonecraft, Elizabeth Inchbald and Amelia Opie, led to criticism of the author's morality. Published in London: Gale and Curtis, 1811, text taken from the editor's copy.]

Abraham, lifting up his hands, exclaimed with pious fervour, 'Blessed be her faith! — Now mark me, Hagar; the hour of trial is at hand — great must be thy anguish, but glorious thy reward.'

The bond-woman heard him not, her eyes being fixed upon Ishmael, whom she discerned afar, running down the slope of the hill. 'He comes!' she cried, and was going forward to meet him on his way, when Abraham rising, asked, 'What is he who approaches with such speed?' To which she replied, smiling, 'Our son, thy Ishmael — and now he is lost to my view in a grove of myrtles —'

'Hagar!' — 'My lord! — what means my lord? Thou art pale, O very pale! Said I not that the dews of the morning would bring on sickness? Enter the dwelling, and seek thy bed, so mayest thou sleep away this sudden chill — Most revered Abraham, wilt thou not hearken to the voice of thy servant? Why dost thou gaze on my face? — why trembles thy lip? Now verily such looks of anguish I never yet beheld — speak, Abraham, honoured lord, father of my child! O speak, or thy heart will break.'

The Patriarch strove to speak, but the sound died away — he turned from her, and took from beneath the bench whereon he had sat, a bottle of water and a loaf of bread; these he extended to Hagar, then laying them at her feet, pointed to the highway which led from his dwelling. His purpose, like lightning darting through the gloom of night, flashed upon the mind of the woman, and his words, 'turned forth to wander in wretchedness,' now struck upon her recollection like a tremendous sentence; cold dews burst from her forehead, dimness came over her sight — her heart sickened, and she sat down upon the bench.

Swift as the air-cutting eagle, graceful as the purple flax when waving in the wind, and wild as the roebuck of the mountains — thus lovely,

wild, and swift, young Ishmael rushed upon their presence. The fresh air of the morning had heightened the glow of his smiling cheeks, and as he ran, the breeze blew back the dark curls of his hair. On one arm, he carried a basket filled with flowers and balsamic herbs,[2] with new gathered fruits and mandrakes,[3] and in his hand he held a panting dove.

'I have climbed a tall tree,' he cried, as he came towards them, 'and have seized a woodpigeon on its nest. I will tame it for my brother Isaac, and it shall eat out of his hand, and nestle in his bosom.' But when he drew near, and beheld the face of his father — a face of agony, and the eyes of his mother closed as in death, a faintness came over him — his hands were relaxed — the basket fell to the ground, and the wood-pigeon flew back to its nest.

Approaching Hagar, he threw his arms around her, saying, 'Mother, art thou ill? — My father, say, what aileth my mother? Hath Sarah again spoken to her unkindly? or is thy anger kindled against me for having disposed of the she-ass and its burden to the forlorn Nehazi? In this I but followed thy counsel, my father, which hath ever been to me — "Succour the unfortunate, and console the mourner".'

The voice of the lad brought back life to Hagar's bosom, she folded her arm round his waist, and looking up to Abraham, said — 'My lord, father of this boy, if thou hast done this but to tempt me — the child is young — his limbs are tender — even the kite puts not her little ones from the nest ere they be fledged: — suffer us to lay our gifts before the eyes of Sarah — she will relent — we will humble ourselves in the dust — she will forget the past. Why dost thou shake thy head? do I not know that the heart of my mistress is kind and compassionate when her wishes are not opposed. Ishmael, my love, gather up thy fruits and flowers, and follow me; we will bow so low — never will we cease weeping on her feet until we are forgiven.'

She was entering the door, when the Patriarch, laying his hand upon her arm, said, in a solemn and determined voice, 'Hagar, thy doom is not from me; it hath passed the lips of God, and the fate of this child is written by his finger. Ye must

2. Aromatic herbs, with healing properties.
3. Medicinal plant.

go hence, and never again cross yon threshold. The Lord appeared to me this night in a vision, and hath required ye at my hands. Speak, wilt thou go forth under the protection of the Almighty, or by tarrying, here, call down his anger on thy head?' Hagar paused: she looked at Abraham, and then upon Ishmael. 'O put us not forth,' said Hagar, faintly. — 'It is not I that put thee forth,' replied he; 'it is the voice of God which calls both thee and thy son. — What were now thy words? saidst thou not, that on the Lord thy soul was fixed, and that no evil could befall thy child unless it was his will?'

'These were my words,' returned Hagar, 'spoken in the bosom of security: thus a man shall say, How easy is it to leap from yonder precipice! but let him approach the brink —'

On the Patriarch's reminding her, that in early youth she confided in the Eternal, when he bade her return and submit to the hands of her mistress; the bond-woman replied, 'O my Lord, it is easier to obey the voice which says, "Get thee from the wilderness to the house of comfort," than that saying, "Go thou and thy helpless child from the house of comfort, and perish in the wilderness." Be not offended, my lord, but hear me with patience, I beseech thee. — Ishmael has never hungered, neither knows he what is thirst; the damps of night have never chilled his blood, or the meridian sunbeam scorched his head; never has his neck been bent to the yoke, or his presence regarded as nought. Ere I was taken into thy service, I felt all these; therefore a change so great may not bring such bitterness to me. Behold there are merchantmen travelling daily from Mesopotamia to Egypt; I will join them, and return to Phatures, my native city, peradventure some of my kindred yet live; but thou wilt keep my child — Ishmael may stay with thee; may he not, my lord? Take him — take him, Abraham; he is thy son, thy once darling Ishmael — wilt thou not take his hand? — O Abraham! whither is flown that justice, that tenderness, that uprightness which made thee the favoured of the Most High, and the honoured among men? — Then thou wilt give us a camel, or some other beast of burden, and lade it with provisions, and send us with a guide, at least send Ishmael to thy brother Nahor, who dwells in Padan-aran; or to thy kinsman Lot, abiding on the banks of the Jordan — so shall the lad, though far from hence,

be safe, and Sarah contented. Say, my lord, shall it not be thus.'

'Hagar, hear me,' answered the Patriarch: 'the Almighty hath said, "Deliver thy son and his mother into my hands," and shall I say, "Nay, Lord, but into the hands of my kinsmen will I deliver them?" I repeat to thee once again, thou must away, and my son must also go.' — At these words, cold shiverings seized the limbs of Ishmael, and he exclaimed, whilst terror was in his face, and doubt in his eyes, 'Go! whither must I go? — from home? — leave my home! Art thou not my father? Thy house is my house. — I cannot go — I know not where to go. Say, my mother, what gave rise to this? — May we not stay? — why should we not stay? — I cannot go.'

The sufferings of Abraham became insupportable, and he could no longer suppress his tears, when he answered, 'Now God help thee, my beloved! but thou must, and speedily — yea, thou must not be here when Sarah shall rise; behold the sun appears above the hill. Hagar! — my Son! — O gracious Creator and Preserver of all things in heaven and on earth, into thy hands, and at thy command, I give my child and his mother, — feed, clothe, bless, and protect them! — Hagar, thou mayest judge by these sighs, these tears, this anguish of my soul, how severe this parting is to me; and yet I will kneel to thee, so thou wilt listen to my voice, and not tempt the anger of the Lord by further disobedience.'

He would have fallen at the feet of the woman, had she not prevented him — 'Beloved, gentle, and most virtuous Hagar!' continued he, folding her to his breast. — A long and mournful silence ensued; then, lifting her head from his shoulder, and casting up her eyes, in which was expressed the most extreme distress, she replied, 'I obey; but should Isaac die, then wilt thou think on Ishmael. I go — but in thy prayers to heaven, remember me, and this thy son. A little water, and a little bread, is then all the inheritance of my Ishmael! If thou thinkest we can live when these are spent, great is indeed thy faith. — Ishmael, give me thy hand.'

'Stay,' cried Abraham, and hesitated — 'I have not kissed him, let him receive my last kiss' — he stooped, but his embrace was not returned. The Patriarch threw his arms around the waist of Ishmael, who setting his hands against Abraham's breast thus held him back, and gazed upon his countenance.

'My father,' said the lad, 'what have I done that thou shouldest shut thy door against me? — keep me, O keep me! where should we sleep? — there are no beds in the fields — the wild beasts would hunt and devour us — my mother would die with hunger, and I should die — canst thou feed cows, and sheep, and dogs, and not feed me! Look, my mother, he smiles — he will not turn us away — he hath not the heart to do it — I said he would not turn us away — dear father — kind father — I love thee father.' Thus Ishmael continued to stroke his face, and kiss his beard, and eyes, and lips, until Abraham, no longer able to endure the scene, rose hastily, and with trembling hands placed the vessel of water and the bread on Hagar's shoulder.

'My Lord!' said Hagar — 'Father!' cried Ishmael, — and tears choked his voice — 'my father! O he is gone — he is gone, he hath shut the door against us.' — Then throwing himself on the ground, 'here will I die — my father to do this — my father whom I loved so much!' Hagar looked down upon him, she sighed, but could not weep.

'My child — treasure of mine eyes, and darling of my heart — my precious Ishmael — wilt thou too forsake me? must I wander forth alone — canst thou abandon thy wretched mother? — deprived of thee, then indeed am I destitute.' He raised his head and sobbing, answered — 'Forsake thee! never — open thy arms to me, beloved mother — yes, we wilt go, — we will — but my heart will break. O father — cruel — cruel father!'

She took his hand, and with slow and lingering steps they left the house, and wandered towards the wilderness.

MARIA EDGEWORTH

(1768–1849)

THE PURPLE JAR (1809)

[The hugely influential *History of Sandford and Merton, A Work Intended for the Use of Children* (1783–9) by Richard Lovell Edgeworth's friend, Thomas Day (1748-89), popularised the sophisticated cautionary tale[1] (that is to say, a tale embedded in a story with some plot and character development) as a means of both entertaining and educating children, and indeed the working classes, as can be seen, for example in *Cheap Repository Tracts* (1795–8) by Hannah More (1745–1833). Maria Edgeworth's children's stories demonstrate an excellent instinct for pitting the fallible and believable child against temptations scaled to her/his imagination. Rosamond, the protagonist of 'The Purple Jar', was, according to family history, based on Edgeworth herself, and the purple jar, like the bazaar, 'Araby', in the story by that name from *Dubliners* (1914) by James Joyce (1882–1941), conjures up a world of gaudy splendour and incipient desire, cut across by a brutal disappointment. The child's thwarted ambition and the deployment of a dialogue between adult and child over the moral of the tale became central features of nineteenth-century children's literature. Edgeworth had innumerable imitators, including Louisa May Alcott (1832–88), whose

Little Women (1868) uses some of Edgeworth's story titles as chapter headings. 'The Purple Jar' was first published in *The Parents Assistant* (1795) and transferred to *Early Lessons* (1801). In later editions the story of Rosamund was revised and expanded to several chapters and there are numerous editions through the nineteenth century. I have chosen the 1809 edition (a copy of which is in the British Library) for its extensive use of dashes and exclamation marks, and because Rosamund is less correct and more vivid in her speech than in later versions, where the emphasis shifts very slightly away from the child's yearning and disappointment to the adult's moral.]

Rosamond, a little girl of about seven years old, was walking with her mother in the streets of London. As she passed along, she looked in at the windows of several shops, and saw a great variety of different sorts of things, of which she did not know the use, or even the names. She wished to stop and look at them, but there was a great number of people in the streets, and a great many carts, and carriages, and wheelbarrows, and she was afraid to let go her mother's hand.

'O! mother, how happy I should be,' said she, as she passed a toy-shop, 'if I had all these pretty things!'

---

1. One of the earliest collections of warning tales in English is Elizabeth Newbery's *Vice in its Proper Shape* (c. 1774)

'What, all! Do you wish for them all, Rosamond?'

'Yes, mamma, all.'

As she spoke, they came to a milliner's shop; the windows were hung with ribands and lace, and festoons of artificial flowers.

'Oh, mamma, what beautiful roses! Won't you buy some of them?'

'No, my dear.'

'Why?'

'Because I don't want them, my dear.'

They went a little further, and came to another shop, which caught Rosamond's eye. It was a jeweller's shop, and there were a great many pretty baubles, ranged in drawers behind glass.

'Mamma, you'll buy some of these?'

'Which of them, Rosamond!'

'Which, — I don't know which; — but any of them , for they are all pretty.'

'Yes, they are all pretty; but what use would they be of to me?'

'Use! Oh, I am sure you could find some use or other for them if you would only buy them first.'

'But I would rather find out the use first.'

'Well, then, mamma, there are buckles: you know that buckles are useful things, very useful things.'

'I have a pair of buckles, I don't want another pair,' said her mother, and walked on. Rosamond was very sorry that her mother wanted nothing. Presently, however, they came to a shop, which appeared to her far more beautiful than the rest. It was a chemist's shop, but she did not know that.'

'Oh, mother! oh!' cried she, pulling her mother's hand; 'Look, look, blue, green, red, yellow, and purple! Oh, what beautiful things! Wont you buy some of these?'

Still her mother answered as before; 'Of what use would they be to me, Rosamond?'

'You might put flowers in them, mamma, and they would look so pretty on the chimney piece; — I wish I had one of them.'

'You have a flower-pot,' said her mother, 'and that is not a flower-pot.'

'But I could use it for a flower-pot, mamma, you know.'

'Perhaps if you were to see it nearer, if you were to examine it, you might be disappointed.'

'No, indeed, I'm sure I should not; I should like it exceedingly.'

Rosamond kept her head turned to look at the purple vase, till she could see it no longer.

'Then, mother,' said she, after a pause, 'perhaps you have no money.'

'Yes, I have.'

'Dear , if I had money I would buy roses, and boxes, and buckles, and purple flower-pots, and everything.' Rosamond was obliged to pause in the middle of her speech.

'Oh, mamma, would you stop a minute for me; I have got a stone in my shoe, it hurts me very much.'

'How comes there to be a stone in your shoe?'

'Because of this great hole, mamma — it comes in there; my shoes are quite worn out. I wish you'd be so very good as to give me another pair.'

'Nay, Rosamond, but I have not money enough to buy shoes, and flower-pots, and buckles, and boxes, and every thing.'

Rosamond thought that was a great pity. But now her foot, which had been hurt by the stone, began to give her so much pain that she was obliged to hop every other step, and she could think of nothing else. They came to a shoemaker's shop soon afterwards.

'There, there! mamma, there are shoes; there are little shoes that would just fit me, and you know shoes would be really of use to me.'

'Yes, so they would, Rosamond. Come in.' — She followed her mother into the shop.

Mr. Sole, the shoemaker, had a great many customers, and his shop was full, so they were obliged to wait.

'Well, Rosamond,' said her mother, 'you don't think this shop so pretty as the rest?'

'No, not nearly; it's black and dark, and there are nothing but shoes all round; and, besides, there's a very disagreeable smell.'

'That smell is the smell of new leather.'

'Is it? — Oh!' said Rosamond, looking round, 'there is a pair of little shoes; they'll just fit me, I'm sure.'

'perhaps they might; but you cannot be sure till you have tried them on, any more than you can be sure that you should like the purple vase *exceedingly*, till you have examined it more attentively.'

'Why I don't know about the shoes, certainly, till I've tried: but, mamma, I'm quite sure that I should like the flower-pot.'

'Well, which would you rather have, that jar, or a pair of shoes? I will buy either for you.'

'Dear mamma, thank you — but if you could buy both.'

'No, not both.'

'Then the jar, if you please.'

'But I should tell you, that I shall not give you another pair of shoes this month.'

'This month! — that's a very long time indeed! You can't think how these hurt me; I believe I'd better have the new shoes — but yet, that purple flower-pot. O, indeed, mamma, these shoes are not so very, very bad; I think I might wear them a little longer; and the month will soon be over. I can make them last till the end of the month; can't I? — Don't you think so, mamma?'

'Nay, my dear, I want you to think for yourself: you will have time enough to consider the matter, whilst I speak to Mr. Sole about my clogs.'

Mr. Sole was by this time at leisure; and whilst her mother was speaking to him, Rosamond stood in profound meditation, with one shoe on, and the other in her hand.'

'Well, my dear, have you decided?'

'Mamma! — yes, — I believe, — If you please, I should like to have the flower-pot; that is, if you won't think me very silly, mamma.'

'Why, as to that, I can't promise you, Rosamond; but, when you are to judge for yourself, you should choose what will make you happiest; and then it would not signify who thought you silly.'

'Then, mamma, if that's all, I'm sure the flower-pot would make me the happiest,' said she, putting on her old shoe again; 'so I choose the flower-pot.'

'Very well, you shall have it; clasp your shoe, and come home.'

Rosamond clasped her shoe and ran after her mother. It was not long before the shoe came down at the heel, and many times she was obliged to stop, to take the stones out of her shoe, and often was she obliged to hop with pain; but still the thoughts of the purple flower-pot prevailed, and she persisted in her choice.

When they came to the shop with the large window, 'Rosamond felt her joy redouble upon hearing her mother desire the servant, who was with them, to buy the purple jar, and bring it home. He had other commissions, so he did not return with them. Rosamond, as soon as she got

in, ran to gather all her own flowers, which she had in a corner of her mother's garden.

'I am afraid they'll be dead before the flower-pot comes, Rosamond, said her mother to her, when she was coming in with the flowers in her lap.

"No, indeed, mamma, it will come home very soon, I dare say — and shan't I be very happy putting them into the purple flower-pot?'

"I hope so, my dear.'

The servant was much longer returning than Rosamond had expected; but at length he came, and brought with him the long-wished-for jar. The moment it was set down upon the table, Rosamond ran up to it with an exclamation of joy: 'I may have it now, mamma?' — 'Yes, my dear, it is yours.' Rosamond poured the flowers from her lap upon the carpet, and seized the purple flower-pot.

'Oh, dear mother!' cried she, as soon as she had taken off the top, 'but there's something dark in it — it smells very disagreeably — what is it? I didn't want this black stuff.'

'Nor I, neither, my dear.'

'But what shall I do with it, mamma?'

'That I cannot tell.'

'But it will be of no use to me, mamma.'

'That I can't help.'

But I must pour it out, and fill the flower-pot with water.'

'That's as you please, my dear.'

'Will you lend me a bowl to pour it into, mamma?'

'That was more than I promised you, my dear; but I will lend you a bowl.'

The bowl was produced and Rosamond proceeded to empty the purple vase. But she experienced much surprise and disappointment, when it was entirely empty, to find that it was no longer a *purple* vase. It was a plain white glass jar, which had appeared to have that beautiful colour, merely from the liquor with which it had bee filled.

Little Rosamond burst into tears.

'Why should you cry, my dear?' said her mother; 'it will be of as much use to you now, as ever, for a flower-pot.

'But it wont look so pretty on the chimney-piece: I am sure, if I had known that it was not really purple, I should not have wished to have it so much.'

'But didn't I tell you that you had not examined it; and that perhaps you would be disappointed?'

'And so I am disappointed, indeed. I wish I had believed you before hand. Now I had much rather have the shoes: for I shall not be able to walk all this month: even walking home that little way hurt me exceedingly. Mamma, I will give you the flower-pot back again, and that purple stuff and all, if you'll only give me the shoes.'

'No, Rosamond, you must abide by your own choice, and now the best thing you can possibly do, is to bear your disappointment with good humour.'

'I will bear it as well as I can,' said Rosamond, wiping her eyes, and she began slowly and sorrowfully to fill the vase with flowers.

But Rosamond's disappointment did not end here, many were the difficulties and distresses into which her imprudent choice brought her, before the end of the month. Every day her shoes grew worse and worse, till at last she could neither run, dance, jump or walk in them. Whenever Rosamond was called to see any thing, she was detained pulling her shoes up at the heels, and was sure to be too late. Whenever her mother was going out to walk, she could not take Rosamond with her, for Rosamond had no soles to her shoes; and at length, on the very last day of the month, it happened that her father proposed to take her with her brother to a glasshouse, which she had long wished to see. She was very happy; but, when she was quite ready, had her hat and gloves on, and was making haste down stairs to her brother and her father, who were waiting for her at the hall-door, the shoe dropped off, she put it on again in a great hurry, but, as she was going across the hall, her father turned round. 'Why are you walking slip-shod? no one must walk slip-shod with me; why, Rosamond,' said he, looking at her shoes with disgust, 'I thought that you were always neat; go, I cannot take you with me.'

Rosamond coloured and retired. 'O, mamma,' said she, as she took off her hat, 'how I wish I had chosen the shoes — they would have been of so much more use to me than that jar: however, I am sure, no, not quite sure — but, I hope, I shall be wiser another time.'

CECIL FRANCES ALEXANDER

(1818–95)

[By the middle of the nineteenth century there is a perceptible crisis in middle-class marriage involving a resistance on the part of women to the double standard and a revulsion against forms of male sexuality. Women like Alexander became involved in social decency campaigns, particularly in rescue work among prostitutes. One reaction to a perceived syphilis epidemic is a campaign for celibacy within marriage (see Cousins, pp. 984–90). One way of reading the sensuous religious verse and hymns of the nineteenth century is as a displacement of erotic feeling onto the suffering body of Christ, frequently represented as a lover. It would be crude to suggest that this is the primary function of such poetry, but nineteenth-century novels are filled with women whose devotion to the church is in obvious conflict with other social relations. In writing for children Jesus often becomes an obscure object of desire or enthusiasm, offered in contrast to the escapist fantasies that dominate juvenile literature. Some of Alexander's best known hymns for children appear in Sarah MacDonald's section, 'Hymns and Hymn Writers', Volume IV, pp. 562–69.]

from:
VERSES FOR HOLY SEASONS; WITH QUESTIONS FOR EXAMINATION
(1846)

[The following hymn is a medium for instructing in and moralising from scripture. The disappointment attending the earthly wedding contrasts with the promise that Christ the bridegroom is approaching. Text from the second edition (London: Francis and John Rivington, 1846).]

The Twentieth Sunday after Trinity
And they all with one consent began to make excuse.

St Luke XIV. 18

'Go call my guests,' the monarch said,
'The ready board is richly spread,
  The rosy wine runs bright,
The bridegroom and the bride are here;
Go, let my hidden guests draw near,
And bid them taste our royal cheer,
  And grace the festal night.'

In vain the obedient servants speed;
They do not hear, they will not heed; -
  The busy cares of life
Have all their hearts so closely bound,
They cannot hear that gentle sound,
One seeks his oxen, one his ground,
  And one will wed a wife.

Oh sorrow! Is that royal board,
With costliest dainties richly stored,
  Untrusted left and bare?
Can these not cast their toils aside?
Can this not bring his wedded bride,
Alike accepted, at his side,
  To pay her homage there?

The glorious King of earth and sky
Has spread His marriage feast on high,
  And bids us come and share;
Still day by day, and year by year,
The sweet sounds linger in our ear,
GOD's chosen servants say, 'Draw near,
  For heaven your hearts prepare.'

If we, unheeding, turn away,
If worldly toil, or pleasant play,
  Fill all our foolish breasts.
So full, we have no time to pray,
To watch, to tread our Master's way, —
Then, sure we are as bad as they,
  The king's ungrateful guests.

Not thus, not thus, CHRIST's blessed band;
Come, take your loved ones by the hand,
  Obey the festive call;
Put on your wedding garments fair,
Ye know not, lost in worldly care,
How soon the Bridegroom will be there;
  Be ready, one and all.

from:
HYMNS FOR LITTLE CHILDREN (1850)

[Alexander attacks Mariology and condemns fantasies that are not Christ-centred. First American edition. Philadelphia: Herman Hooker, 1850.]

from:
The Third Promise. To keep God's Holy Will and Commandments, and walk in the same all the days of my life.
Of the Commandments.

II

There are strange countries far away
  Where GOD's Name is unknown,
Where children live who say their prayers
  To gods of wood and stone.

But Christian children go to Church
  They kneel at home in prayer;
And GOD, Who is a Spirit, hears
  And answers everywhere.

His ear is open to their call,
  In childhood, age, and youth,
And they must always worship Him
  In spirit and in truth.

They must not think of other things,
  Light toys, or merry play,
When they are listening to GOD's Word,
  Or kneeling down to pray.

For they who worship at GOD's throne,
  With hearts so dull and dim,
Make idols of their foolish thoughts,
  And love them more than Him.

They may not kneel to any form,
  Or picture that man paints,
Of CHRIST, or of his Mother dear,
  Or of his blessed saints.

They may not worship nor bow down
  To cross of stone or wood,
Though it be our redemption's sign, —
  Such worship is not good.

For we must pray to GOD alone,
  Who is in heaven on high,
Who is one earth with us unseen,
  Who always hears our cry.

HARRIET BEAUFORT

(1778–1865)

from:
THE HEIRESS IN HER MINORITY; OR, THE PROGRESS OF CHARACTER (1850)

[Harriet Beaufort, the author of *Dialogues on Botany for Young Persons* (1819), develops the Socratic dialogue as a means of instructing the young in such topics as history, geography and the natural sciences, with a richer fictional narrative than had existed in many earlier pedagogic novels. She uses the commonplace device of a travelogue in which the protagonist is instructed in the course of a tour of Ireland. Her subtitle is also crucial to understanding her project. Like her stepniece, Maria Edgeworth, Harriet Beaufort represents the acquisition of knowledge and the development of reason as educational projects that must be accompanied by, and are only valuable insofar as they contribute to the development of good principles and an affectionate heart. The heiress in question is Evelyn O'Brien, who has been brought up in England by her maternal grandfather. On his death she inherits a large fortune and is required to live for the remainder of her minority at Cromdarragh Castle, in the West of Ireland, under the guardianship of two English friends of her grandfather, Mr Driver and Mr. Stanley. Her father and stepmother, Mr and Mrs Desmond, are now made known to her, almost for the first time. She arrives in Ireland ignorant of the country and prejudiced against her step-mother. The following scene from early in the novel is an example of how information is put across in the context of dramatizing relationships between the characters. (London: John Murray, 1850). The text is taken from the British Library edition. This novel is almost always catalogued under the incorrect attribution to Jane Marcet.]

In the course of their walk through the gardens Mr. Desmond led the way to the stove, in which a few plants were still carefully cultivated by the gardener. Mrs. Desmond, smelling a pancratium lily, said it was a favourite of hers, for it was both fragrant and elegant.

'Yes,' said Mr. Desmond, 'but the golden pancratium is, I suppose, vastly superior to that, as it is considered of such importance in Peru, of which it is a native, that on some particular festivals, St. John's Day for instance, everyone is anxious to be decked with it. We ought to have had it on the joyful occasion of your return to your own country, Evelyn, as a suitable token of rejoicing.'

'Oh, Papa! You would not prefer a foreign lily to our shamrock — the most appropriate as well as the most abundant ornament I could have? But I never have heard of that lily; why is it so remarkable?'

'From its beauty and fragrance,' replied her father, 'and on great festivals the churches and houses in Peru are adorned with its festoons. It is called Amencaes in its own country; and is found in profusion in one valley in particular, which is named after it. The removal of the cattle on St. John's day to the cool valley from farmsteads is likewise a sort of festival; and on that day the inhabitants of Lima assemble on the grand Almeda or public walk, and thence proceed to the valley of the Amencaes. People of all ages and occupations meet there to join in the general rejoicing . . . But while talking of the plants of other countries, we are forgetting your intended improvements, my dear Evelyn. In laying out a garden we should try to ensure its beauty by arranging a succession of flowers to ornament it during as large a portion of the year as possible.'

'Certainly,' said Mrs. Desmond, looking towards Evelyn. 'Let us consider then what Evelyn should plant in this sunny place, so well sheltered from the north and east. Come, Mr. Desmond, what do you suggest?'

Just at that moment Mr. Stanley came to the gardener and Mr. Desmond, on introducing him, said they had been considering of improvements in the garden, and that, under Mrs. Desmond's direction, Evelyn might make it a charming spot — her taste would be such an advantage to Evelyn.

'No doubt,' said Mr. Stanley, glancing towards Evelyn, whose countenance however did not respond to the idea. He observed, as the colour mantled in her cheek, a strong expression of disdain and displeasure; but without noticing it he immediately entered into conversation with Mrs. Desmond, and found her refined and gentle manners very different from the notion he had formed of Irish ladies. Evelyn meanwhile, offended at the bare idea of Mrs. Desmond's directing her about her own garden, in her own demesne, where she was sole mistress, resolved to show her father that she would not submit to be directed or controlled by any stepmother in the world. During the walk she was silent, or, when spoken to, replied only by monosyllables. And anyone might have reasonably imagined that her good humour would not return while Mrs. Desmond was at Cromdarragh Castle.

CHARLOTTE ELIZABETH TONNA

(1790–1846)

from:
THE FORTUNE TELLER
(1829)

[Once again a dialogue between mother and daughter is the scene of instruction in this story, which has been included as an example of how ugly prejudices (in this case against nomads and Jews) were a commonplace feature of children's writing, and part of the formation of a certain kind of social consensus. This passage is from the opening of the story, which goes on to warn of the particular dangers of fortune-telling and other kinds of superstition which were believed to hold particular attraction for women, children and servants. The story was published in *Little Tales for Little Readers*. Dublin: J. and M. Porteus 1829. Text from British Library copy.]

The Gipsy woman was dressed in a short jacket of dark-blue cloth, the skirts of which hung down a little way over a petticoat of strange patchwork. Stuffs of all colours seemed to have been used to mend and piece out the old dirty dark green that still remained. Her hat was of black beaver, very much the worse for wear, and it was tied under her chin with a red cotton handkerchief. Fastened to her back in a sort of bag, she carried a little child, whose bright black eyes shone out like jet from beneath its tangled hair. Its face was dirty, even more so that its mother's, and so sun-burnt that it seemed never to have known the comfort of shade.[1]

Besides her baby, the Gipsy woman carried a wallet slung over one shoulder, and hanging at her side; and a tattered apron was gathered up, and knotted into a piece of cord that served her for a belt. Altogether, there was something so remarkable in their appearance, that little Jessy, who was running before her Mamma, in the shady green lane, stopped to look with surprise at the Gipsy woman; and then, rather frightened by the bold look of her piercing eyes, she turned back, and ran to her Mamma, taking hold of her hand, and keeping close beside her.

The Gipsy passed them, making a low curtsey to the lady, but not speaking a word; and Jessy looked round to observe the baby, for it had laughed and crowed when it saw her.

'I thought she had been a beggar woman, Mamma,' said Jessy, 'but she did not ask for anything. How black her eyes are, and the baby's too.'

'They are Gipsies, my dear,' said Mrs. Howes, 'and Gipsies do not often beg; but I am sorry to say that they cheat and steal, and do many other bad things.'

---

1. Author's note: The Gipsies are a wandering people; they are found in various parts of England and Scotland; they are, in their countenance, character, habits, a distinct people.

'Where do they live, Mamma?'

'They are wanderers over the earth, having no settled home, Jessy. They are found in most countries, and are very nearly the same everywhere. It is not known exactly from whence they came; but they are generally supposed to be what their name expresses, Egyptians. It was foretold by the prophets, that the mighty Egyptians should become the basest of all people; and that they should be scattered among all nations. We here see the threat of the Lord against them as exactly fulfilled as that against the Jews.'

'Oh, Mamma,' exclaimed Jessy, 'tell me more about them. I am so sorry for the Jews, because God loved them very much once, and now He is so angry with them. It is a terrible thing to have God angry with us, Mamma.'

'A terrible thing, indeed, my love!; and you know the Bible says, "God is angry with the wicked every day",[2] and all are wicked in God's sight who do not believe in His blessed Son, Jesus Christ, and pray continually to have their sins washed away in His most precious blood.'

'Do the Gipsies believe in the Lord Jesus, Mamma?'

'Oh no, my dear, they have no religion at all, even in name: they are the most ignorant and wretched people among us. Knowing nothing themselves, they cannot instruct their children; but they bring them up in idleness and vice, to lie and swear, steal and defraud — to impose on the charitable and to deceive the unwary.'

2. 'God is angry with the wicked every day', Psalms 7:11.

ANNA JAMESON

(1794–1860)

from:
LEGENDS OF THE MADONNA AS REPRESENTED IN THE FINE ARTS (1852)

[Although this book was not written specifically for children, Anna Jameson's criticism in it is clearly pedagogic and reflects a nineteenth-century interest in balancing moral and aesthetic considerations in making critical judgements. Her work is both explanatory and discriminatory and she makes debates in Western art available particularly to girls who had limited opportunities to travel and were less likely to know ancient or modern languages. See also pp. 45–59, where Máirín Ní Dhonnchadha discusses the beauty and modesty of the Virgin Mary. London: Longman, Brown, Green, and Longmans, 1852.]

THE MARRIAGE OF THE VIRGIN

This, as an artistic subject, is of great consequence from the beauty and celebrity of some of the representations, which, however, are unintelligible without the accompanying legends. And it is worth remarking, that while the incident is avoided in early Greek art, it became very popular with the Italian and German painters from the fourteenth century.

In the East, the prevalence of the monastic spirit, from the fourth century, had brought the marriage into disrepute; by many of the aesthetic writers of the West it was considered almost in the light of a necessary evil. This idea, that the primal and most sacred ordinance of God and nature was incompatible with the sanctity and purity acceptable to God, was the origin of the singular legends of the Marriage of the Virgin. One sees very clearly that, if possible, it would have been denied that Mary had ever been married at all; but, as the testimony of the Gospel was too direct and absolute to be set aside, it became necessary, in the narrative, to give to this distasteful marriage the most recondite motives, and, in art, to surround it with the most poetical and even miraculous accessories.

But now we enter on the treatment of the subject, it is necessary to say a few words on the character of Joseph, wonderfully selected to be the husband and guardian of the consecrated mother of Christ, and foster-father of the Redeemer; and so often introduced into all the pictures which refer to the childhood of our Lord.

From the gospels we learn nothing of him but that he was of the tribe of Judah and the lineage of David; that he was a *just* man; that he followed the trade of a carpenter, and dwelt in the little city of Nazareth. We infer from his conduct towards Mary that he was a mild, tender and pure-hearted, as well as an upright man. On his age and personal appearance nothing is said. These are the points on which the Church has not decided, and on which artists, left to their own devices, and led by various opinions, have differed considerably.

The very early painters deemed it right to represent Joseph as very old, almost decrepit with age, and supported by a crutch. According to some monkish authorities, he was a widower and eighty-four years old when he was espoused to Mary. On the other hand, it was argued, that such a marriage would have been quite contrary to the custom of the Jews; and that to defend Mary, and to provide for her celestial offspring, it was necessary that her husband should be a man of mature age, but still strong and robust and able to work at his trade; and thus, with more propriety and better taste, the later painters have represented him. In the best Italian and Spanish pictures of the Holy Family, he is a man of about forty or fifty, with a mild, benevolent countenance, brown hair, and a short curled beard: the crutch, or stick, however, is seldom omitted; it became a conventional attribute.

In the German pictures Joseph is not only old, but appears almost in a state of dotage, like a lean, wrinkled mendicant, with a bald head, a white beard, a feeble frame, and a sleepy or stupid countenance. Then again, the later Italian painters have erred as much on the other side; for I have seen pictures in which St. Joseph is not only a young man, not more than thirty, but bears a strong resemblance to the received heads of our Saviour.

FRANCES BROWNE

(1816–79)

THE STORY OF CHILDE CHARITY (1857)

[*Granny's Wonderful Chair*, from which this story is taken, was popular at the time of its original publication and revived later in the nineteenth century when Frances Hodgson Burnett (1849–1924) — author of her own remarkable orphan tales, *Little Lord Fauntleroy* (1886), *Sara Crewe* (1888), and *The Secret Garden* (1910) — who had owned and lost Browne's book in childhood, published her own version of one of the stories. When she was sent the original by an outraged reader, she sponsored its re-publication and wrote a Preface explaining why it had been her favourite children's book:

Other books always spoke of a time when people believed in fairies, but this one told of the days when fairies were in the world. So one had no need to doubt anything or think it was only a pretence. In all the stories the fairies were spoken of, not as if they were unreal creatures quite different from anyone else, but as if they were as real as birds and butterflies and little children. They made part of the crowds which went to festivities; they danced on the hilltops in countries they liked; they went away when people grew cross and their countries dull, and they came back to their old places, when everyone became happy and good-tempered and the countries were bright again. They went to fairs with other people quite comfortably and they sat spinning on silver spinning wheels at cottage firesides when everyone was asleep. They came and went and were part of the populace, and one felt one might meet one at any moment.[1]

Browne's story is a version of the Cinderella story popular throughout Europe and known in Ireland in several versions. See pp. 1214–18, 1247–52. There is also some mixture of the fairy-tale of Beauty and the Beast, and of the story of Patient Griselda, which had been re-

---

1. Frances Hodgson Burnett, Introduction to *Granny's Wonderful Chair* (London: Griffin, Farran, Brown, 1904).

presented and critiqued by Maria Edgeworth in her tale 'The Modern Griselda'. Charity's story is more clearly set in a prosperous farming community than some grander and less specific versions of the story. The peril of dependency was a popular subject for nineteenth-century children's writers, conscious of the peculiar vulnerability of orphans at a time when state and religious authorities took little interest in their welfare. Before Charity makes her fantastic escape to fairyland, she forms more plausible and poignant substitute family relations with a despised beggar woman and an ugly mongrel. The text is from the first edition of *Granny's Wonderful Chair, and Its Tales of Fairy Times*, published in London by Griffith and Farran, 1857, with illustrations by Kenny Meadows.]

Once upon a time there lived in the west country a little girl who had neither father nor mother; they both died when she was very young, and left their daughter to the care of her uncle, who was the richest farmer in all that country. He had houses and lands, flocks and herds, many servants to work about his house and fields, a wife who had brought him a great dowry, and two fair daughters. All their neighbours, being poor, looked up to the family — insomuch that they imagined themselves great people. The father and mother were as proud as peacocks; the daughters thought themselves the greatest beauties in the world, and not one of the family would speak civilly to anyone they thought low.

Now it happened that though she was their near relation, they had this opinion of the orphan girl, partly because she had no fortune, and partly because of her humble, kindly disposition. It was said that the more needy and despised any creature was, the more ready was she to befriend it: on which account the people of the west country called her Childe Charity, and if she had any other name, I never heard it. Childe Charity was thought very mean in that proud house. Her uncle would not own her for his niece; her cousins would not keep her company; and her aunt sent her to work in the dairy, and to sleep in the back garret, where they kept all sorts of lumber and dry herbs for the winter. All the servants learned the same tune, and Childe Charity had more work than rest among them. All the day she scoured pads, scrubbed dishes and washed crockery-ware; but every night she slept in the back garret as sound as a princess could in her palace chamber.

Her uncle's house was large and white, and stood among green meadows by a river's side. In

front it had a porch covered with a vine; behind, it had a farmyard and high granaries. Within there were two parlours for the rich, and two kitchens for the poor, which the neighbours thought wonderfully grand; and one day in the harvest season, when this rich farmer's corn had been all cut down and housed, he condescended so far as to invite them to a harvest supper. The west country people came in their holiday clothes and best behaviour. Such heaps of cake and cheese, such baskets of apples and barrels of ale, had never been at a feast before; and they were making merry in kitchen and parlour, when a poor old woman came to the back door, begging for broken victuals and a night's lodging. Her clothes were coarse and ragged; her hair was scanty and grey; her back was bent; her teeth were gone. She had a squinting eye, a clubbed foot, and crooked fingers. In short, she was the poorest and ugliest old woman that ever came begging. The first who saw her was the kitchen-maid, and she ordered her to be gone for an ugly witch. The next was the herd boy, and he threw a bone over his shoulder, but Childe Charity, hearing the noise, came out from her seat at the foot of the lowest table, and asked the old woman to take her share of the supper and sleep that night in her bed in the back garret. The old woman sat down without a word of thanks. All the company laughed at Childe Charity for giving her bed and her supper to a beggar. Her proud cousins said it was just like her mean spirit, but Childe Charity did not mind them. She scraped the pots for her supper that night and slept on a sack among the lumber, while the old woman rested in her warm bed; and next morning, before the little girl awoke, she was up and gone, without so much as saying 'Thank you' or 'Good morning'.

That day all the servants were sick after the feast, and mostly cross too — so you may judge how civil they were; when, at supper time, who should come to the back door but the old woman, again asking for broken victuals and a night's lodging. No one would listen to her or give her a morsel, till Childe Charity rose from her seat at the foot of the lowest table and kindly asked her to take her supper and sleep in her bed in the back garret. Again the old woman sat down without a word. Childe Charity scraped the pots for her supper and slept on the sack. In the morning the old woman was gone; but for six nights after, as sure as the supper was spread, there was she at the back door, and the little girl regularly asked her in.

Childe Charity's aunt said she would let her get enough of beggars. Her cousins made continual game of what they called her genteel visitor. Sometimes the old woman said, 'Child, why don't you make this bed softer? And why are your blankets so thin?' But she never gave her a word of thanks nor a civil 'Good morning'. At last, on the ninth night from her first coming, when Childe Charity was getting used to scraping the pots and sleeping on the sack, the old woman's accustomed knock came on the door, and there she stood with an ugly ashy-coloured dog, so stupid-looking and clumsy that no herd boy would keep him.

'Good evening, my little girl,' she said when Childe Charity opened the door. 'I will not have your supper and bed tonight — I am going on a long journey to see a friend; but here is a dog of mine, whom nobody in all the west country will keep for me. He is a little cross and not very handsome; but I leave him to your care till the shortest day in all the year. Then you and I will count for his keeping.'

When the old woman had said the last word, she set off with such speed that Childe Charity lost sight of her in a minute. The ugly dog began to fawn upon her, but he snarled at everyone else. The servants said he was a disgrace to the house. The proud cousins wanted him drowned, and it was with great trouble that Childe Charity got leave to keep him in an old ruined cowhouse. Ugly and cross as the dog was, he fawned on her, and the old woman had left him to her care. So the little girl gave him part of all her meals, and when the hard frost came took him privately to her own back garret, because the cowhouse was damp and cold in the long nights. The dog lay quietly on some straw in a corner. Childe Charity slept soundly, but every morning the servants would say to her:

'What great light and fine talking was that in your back garret?'

'There was no light but the moon shining in through the shutterless window, and no talk that I heard,' said Childe Charity, and she thought they must have been dreaming; but night after night, when any of them awoke in the dark and

silent hour that comes before the morning, they saw a light brighter and clearer than the Christmas fire, and heard voices like those of lords and ladies in the back garret.

Partly from fear, and partly from laziness, none of the servants would rise to see what might be there; till at length, when the winter nights were at the longest, the little parlour-maid, who did least work and got most favour because she gathered news for her mistress, crept out of bed when all the rest were sleeping and set herself to watch at the crevice of the door. She saw the dog lying quietly in the corner, Childe Charity sleeping soundly in her bed, and the moon shining through the shutterless window. But an hour before daybreak there came a glare of lights, and a sound of far-off bugles. The window opened, and in marched a troop of little men clothed in crimson and gold and bearing every man a torch, until the room looked bright as day. They marched up with great reverence to the dog, where he lay on the straw, and the most richly clothed among them said:

'Royal prince, we have prepared the banquet hall. What will your highness please that we do next?'

'You have done well,' said the dog. 'Now prepare the feast and see that all things be in our first fashion: for the princess and I mean to bring a stranger who never feasted in our halls before.'

'Your highness's command shall be obeyed,' said the little man, making another reverence; and he and his company passed out of the window. By and by there was another glare of lights, and a sound like far-off flutes. The window opened, and there came in a company of little ladies clad in rose-coloured velvet and carrying each a crystal lamp. They also walked with great reverence up to the dog, and the gayest among them said:

'Royal prince, we have prepared the tapestry. What will your highness please that we do next?'

'You have done well,' said the dog. 'Now prepare the robes and let all things be in our first fashion: for the princess and I will bring with us a stranger who never feasted in our halls before.'

'Your highness's commands shall be obeyed,' said the little lady, making a low curtsy; and she and her company passed out through the window, which closed quietly behind them. The dog stretched himself out upon the straw, the little girl turned in her sleep, and the moon shone in on the back garret. The parlour-maid was so much amazed and so eager to tell this great story to her mistress, that she could not close her eyes that night, and was up before cock-crow; but when she told it, her mistress called her a silly wench to have such foolish dreams, and scolded her so that the parlour-maid durst not mention what she had seen to the servants. Nevertheless Childe Charity's aunt thought there might be something in it worth knowing; so next night, when all the house were asleep, she crept out of bed and set herself to watch at the back garret door. There she saw exactly what the maid told her — the little men with the torches, and the little ladies with the crystal lamps, come in making reverence to the dog, and the same words pass, only he said to the one, 'Now prepare the presents,' and to the other, 'Prepare the jewels'; and when they were gone, the dog stretched himself on the straw, Childe Charity turned in her sleep and the moon shone in on the back garret.

The mistress could not close her eyes any more than the maid from eagerness to tell the story. She woke up Childe Charity's rich uncle before cock-crow; but when he heard it, he laughed at her for a foolish woman and advised her not to repeat the like before the neighbours, lest they should think she had lost her senses. The mistress could say no more, and the day passed; but that night the master thought he would like to see what went on in the back garret: so when all the house were asleep he slipped out of bed and set himself to watch at the crevice in the door. The same thing happened again that the maid and the mistress saw: the little men in crimson and their torches, and the little ladies in rose-coloured velvet with their lamps, came in at the window and made a humble reverence to the ugly dog, the one saying, 'Royal prince, we have prepared the presents,' and the other, 'Royal prince, we have prepared the jewels'; and the dog said to them all: 'You have done well. Tomorrow come and meet me and the princess with horses and chariots, and let all things be in our first fashion: for we will bring a stranger from this house who has never travelled with us nor feasted in our halls before.'

The little men and the little ladies said: 'Your highness's command shall be obeyed.' When they

had gone out through the window the ugly dog stretched himself out on the straw, Childe Charity turned in her sleep and the moon shone in on the back garret.

The master could not close his eyes any more than the maid or the mistress for thinking of this strange sight. He remembered to have heard his grandfather say that somewhere near his meadows there lay a path leading to the fairies' country, and the haymakers used to see it shining through the grey summer morning as the fairy bands went home. Nobody had heard or seen the like for many years; but the master concluded that the doings in his back garret must be fairy business and the ugly dog a person of great account. His chief wonder was, however, what visitors the fairies intended to take from his house; and after thinking the matter over he was sure it must be one of his daughters — they were so handsome and had such fine clothes.

Accordingly, Childe Charity's rich uncle made it his first business that morning to get ready a breakfast of roast mutton for the ugly dog, and carry it to him in the old cowhouse; but not a morsel would the dog taste. On the contrary, he snarled at the master, and would have bitten him if he had not run away with his mutton.

'The fairies have strange ways,' said the master to himself; but he called his daughters privately, bidding them dress themselves in their best, for they might be called into great company before nightfall. Childe Charity's proud cousins, hearing this, put on the richest of their silks and laces and strutted like peacocks from kitchen to parlour all day, waiting for the call their father spoke of, while the little girl scoured and scrubbed in the dairy. They were in very bad humour when night fell and nobody had come; but just as the family were sitting down to supper the ugly dog began to bark, and the old woman's knock was heard at the back door. Childe Charity opened it, and was going to offer her bed as usual, when the old woman said:

'This is the shortest day in all the year, and I am going home to hold a feast after my travels. I see you have taken good care of my dog, and now if you will come with me to my house, he and I will do our best to entertain you. Here is our company.'

As the old woman spoke there was a sound of far-off flutes and bugles, then a glare of lights;

and a great company, clad so grandly that they shone with gold and jewels, came in open chariots, covered with gilding and drawn by snow-white horses. The first and finest of the chariots was empty. The old woman led Childe Charity to it by the hand, and the ugly dog jumped in before her. The proud cousins in all their finery had by this time come to the door, but nobody wanted them; and no sooner were the old woman and her dog within the chariot than a marvellous change passed over them, for the ugly old woman turned at once to a beautiful young princess with long, yellow curls and a robe of green and gold, while the ugly old dog at her side started up a fair young prince, with nut-brown hair and a robe of purple and silver.

'We are,' said they, as the chariots drove on, and the little girl sat astonished, 'a prince and princess of Fairyland, and there was a wager between us whether or not there were good people still to be found in these false and greedy times. One said "Yes", and the other said "No"; and I have lost,' said the prince, 'and must pay for the feast and presents.'

Childe Charity never heard any more of that story. Some of the farmer's household who were looking after them through the moonlight night said the chariots had gone one way across the meadows, some said they had gone another, and till this day they cannot agree upon the direction. But Childe Charity went with that noble company into a country such as she had never seen — for primroses covered all the ground and the light was always like that of a summer evening. They took her to a royal palace, where there was nothing but feasting and dancing for seven days. She had robes of pale green velvet to wear and slept in a chamber inlaid with ivory. When the feast was done the princess gave her such heaps of gold and jewels that she could not carry them, but they gave her a chariot to go home in, drawn by six white horses; and on the seventh night, which happened to be Christmas time, when the farmer's family had settled in their own minds that she would never come back and were sitting down to supper, they heard the sound of her coachman's bugle, and saw her alight with all the jewels and gold at the very back door where she had brought in the ugly old woman. The fairy chariot drove away, and never came back to the farmhouse after. But Child Charity scrubbed and scoured no more, for she grew to be a great lady, even in the eyes of her proud cousins.

L. T. MEADE

(1844–1914)

from:
THE REBEL OF THE SCHOOL
(1902)

[The Great Shirley is a day school for girls set in a fictional English provincial town. It has been set up by a charitable foundation and is the premier school for female academic achievement in the area. About a quarter of the pupils come from poor families, pay no fees and are known as 'foundationers'. The other pupils are from genteel families of modest means — there are no rich girls or aristocrats at the school until the arrival of Kathleen O'Hara, a fabulously wealthy Anglo-Irish girl from a castle on the West Cork coast, whose mother had been educated at Great Shirley. Kathleen is very homesick and her only consolation is a passionate crush she develops on a slightly younger girl, Ruth Craven, who is a poor orphan, living with her grandparents. When Kathleen discovers that Ruth suffers some stigma as a foundationer, she decides to organize all the foundationers into a secret society called the 'Wild Irish Girls'; the girls meet outside school hours, wear heart-shaped silver badges beneath their uniforms, and refuse all communion with the fee-paying girls. Ruth is academically brilliant and when one of the fee-paying girls offers to share with her a private tutor so that they may compete for the school's two prestigious scholarships, Ruth decides that she owes it to her grandparents to take up the offer. She then feels honour bound to leave the Wild Irish Girls. In the scene that follows, Ruth is asked to betray her former associates to the school governors.

L.T. Meade was one of the earliest writers to develop the girls' school story into a distinct sub-genre, one which became hugely popular and influential not simply in Britain and Ireland but throughout the British Empire.

Meade was an extraordinarily prolific writer, working for a range of ages, but is now best remembered for her school stories, particularly *A World of Girls*, which clearly influenced such writers as Angela Brazil and Enid Blyton.

The Rebel of the School has many of the features most characteristic of the genre. The entry of two new girls temporarily disrupts the school, but the institution shows itself capable of responding and adapting to new needs, while the girls are to some extent interpellated into the school's ideology. Certain personality types are prominent in the cast of characters: the snob, the swot, the timid child, the poor child, the orphan, the enthusiast, the tomboy. Some girls make intense emotional investments in their peers — a massive 'crush' is at the centre of this story. Teachers are sympathetic observers but remain essentially distant from the girls' inner lives.

But *The Rebel of the School* is remarkable in as many ways as it is typical, and much that is remarkable about it has to do with the place of Ireland in the novel. Kathleen objects from the start to the school's patronizing liberal ethos, in which affection is to be measured and reasonable, contrasting it with what she sees as the virtue of Irish emotiveness and enthusiasm. When she realizes that the foundationers are second-class citizens in the school she intervenes explicitly on the grounds that the Irish always have a passion for social justice. In the house where she boards, she takes over much of the domestic work of the mother and the servants, whom she identifies as overworked and under-rewarded, and by so doing incidentally shames her classmate, Alice, whose good education was being purchased by the sacrifices of her family. Kathleen herself speaks at times in an almost ludicrous stage-Irishry, but what is interesting are the reactions she provokes in others, reactions based on her disruption both of political class allegiances and of the school's sexual economy. Many of the older girls have a crush on beautiful Ruth Craven, and there is a decorum for managing such feelings in the school culture; but when Kathleen first sees Ruth she bursts through a line of other girls, embraces her passionately (incidentally frightening Ruth and the other girls) and from then on bombards her with violent protestations of love. Kathleen's excess flushes out the excessive feelings of proprietorship and competition in other girls. Her club is perceived by the authorities as a sexual and a political threat. It is the teachers and governors who start employing the language of 'secret society', 'rebellion' and 'insurrection', as if Kathleen and her peers were Land Leaguers rather than young girls exchanging clothes and going out to tea. And when, after the scene excerpted below, Ruth explains her dilemma to her grandfather, he insists that she must not become a 'king's informant'. Almost all school stories celebrate the ethos of the school itself, but Meade rebels against the apparent liberalism of Great Shirley, exposing a mixture of hypocrisy, weakness and manipulation in its governance. London: W. and R. Chambers, 1902.]

THE GOVERNORS EXAMINE RUTH

It was the custom of the governors to meet four times a year as a matter of course, and as a matter of expediency they met about as many times again. But a sudden meeting to be convened within forty-eight hours' notice was almost unheard of in their experience.

When they were all seated round the table Miss Mackenzie, who was chairwoman, took out the agenda and read its contents aloud. These were brief enough:

'To inquire into the insurrection amongst the foundationers, and in particular to cause full investigation to be made with regard to the Irish girl, Kathleen O'Hara.'

'This is really very astonishing,' said Miss Mackenzie, turning to the other governors. 'An insurrection amongst the foundationers! Had we not better summon Miss Ravenscroft,[1] who will tell us what she means?'

A clerk who attended the meetings (also a woman) went away now to summon Miss Ravenscroft. She appeared in a few minutes, was asked to seat herself, and was requested to give a full explanation. This she did very briefly.

'At the beginning of the term,' she said, 'a girl of the name of Kathleen O'Hara joined our number. She was eccentric and untrained. She came from the south-west of Ireland. I had her examined, and found that she knew extremely little. We were forced to put her into much too low a class for her years and general appearance.'

'Well,' said Miss Smyth, 'that, after all, isn't a crime. I don't quite understand.'

'If you will kindly resume your story we shall be obliged, Miss Ravenscroft,' said Miss Mackenzie.

Miss Ravenscroft did resume it. She traced Kathleen's conduct from the first day of her arrival to the present hour. Short as the time was — not more than six weeks — she had worked havoc in the school. Her influence was altogether felt amongst the foundationers. They crowded round her at all hours; a glance from her eyes was sufficient to compel them to do exactly what she wished. They ceased to be attentive to their lessons; they were often discovered in school in a state of semi-drowsiness; they were rebellious

1. The headteacher.

and impertinent to their teachers — in short, they were in a state of insurrection.

'And you trace this disgraceful state of things to the advent of the Irish girl?' asked Miss Mackenzie.

'I am sorry to say, Miss Mackenzie, that I do. When I noticed that Kathleen O'Hara had a disturbing influence over the girls I caused further inquiries to be made, and I then made a discovery which distressed me very much. My eyes were first opened by the fact that one of our teachers picked up off the floor, just where a certain Clara Sawyer, one of the best and most promising of the foundationers was sitting, a small locket, evidently a badge. She brought it to me, and I now hand it to you ladies for inspection.'

The little silver heart-shaped badge was passed from one lady to another. The Misses Scott thought it pretty and quaint. Miss Jane Smyth murmured the words 'Wild Irish Girls'[2] under her breath. Mrs. Ross pushed it away as though it was beneath notice. Mrs. Naylor said:

'Very pretty; quite touching, isn't it? Heart-shaped. I always think that such a sweet emblem; don't you, Miss Mackenzie?'

But Miss Mackenzie, with a sniff, took up the little talisman and turned it from right to left.

'"Wild Irish Girls",' she said aloud. 'What can this mean?'

'I think I can throw some light on the subject, but not much,' said Miss Ravenscroft. 'It is quite evident that a society calling itself by this name exists, and that it has been instituted and formed altogether by Kathleen O'Hara, who has induced a great number — I should say fully half — of the foundationers to join her. They meet, as I have discovered, at night; their rendezvous being, up to the present, a certain quarry a short distance out of town. What they do at their meetings I cannot tell, but I believe they are very riotous, with singing and dancing and sports of all sorts. Of course, as you know, Miss Mackenzie, such proceedings are altogether prohibited in our school.'

'But this takes place out of school,' said Mrs. Naylor.

'Mrs. Naylor, I should be much obliged if you would allow Miss Ravenscroft to continue,' said Miss Mackenzie.

Miss Ravenscroft did continue.

'Putting aside that question,' she said, 'the effect on the girls is most disastrous. They are completely out of my control, and I know for a fact that they do not care to please anyone except Kathleen O'Hara.'

'Of course our duty is plain,' said Miss Mackenzie. 'We must get the ringleader into custody, so to speak, and either bind her over to break up the society, and so keep the peace, or expel her from the school.'

'She is a difficult girl to deal with,' said Miss Ravenscroft. 'She has a great deal that is good in her; she is handsome and rich, very affectionate, and full of spirit.'

'But what has a girl who is handsome and rich to do in a school like the Great Shirley?' asked Mrs. Ross.

'That is the curious part of it. Kathleen's mother was educated in this school, and she made up her mind that Kathleen should never go to any other. Kathleen lives with the Tennants. I should be sorry if she were expelled; there is so much that is good in her. It would be a pity to harden her or hold her up to public disgrace. I hope some other way may be found of bringing her to order.'

'You are quite right, Miss Ravenscroft,' said Miss Smyth. 'I never did hold with the severe hardening process.'

'Certainly in the case of Kathleen it would do no good,' said Miss Ravenscroft.

'But what do you propose to do, then?' said Miss Mackenzie. 'You have not come here without having some plan in your head.'

'The first thing to do is to get hold of all possible facts,' said Miss Ravenscroft. 'Now there is one girl in the school who could tell us, a charming girl, a new girl — for she also only joined this term — but in all respects the opposite of Kathleen O'Hara. She for a short time belonged to the rebels, as I must call the Wild Irish Girls, but she saw the folly of her conduct and left them. She could tell us all about them if she liked, and help us to bring the insurrection to an end.'

'Then that is capital,' said Miss Mackenzie in a tone of enjoyment. 'Have the girl summoned, please, Miss Ravenscroft.'

Miss Ravenscroft turned to the clerk, who went away at once in search of Ruth. Ruth came in looking very white, her face dogged, her usual beauty and charm of manner having quite

---

2. The society takes its name from the novel *The Wild Irish Girl* (1806) by Sydney Owenson (later Lady Morgan) (?1776–1859).

deserted her. She wore her little school-apron, and she kept folding it between her fingers as she stood in the presence of her judges.

'Your name?' said Miss Mackenzie.

'Ruth Craven.'

'Your age?'

'I am fourteen.'

'Where do you live?'

'In No. 2 Willow Cottages.'

'Oh, I know,' said Miss Mackenzie, looking with more approval at the child. 'I have often met your grandfather. You live with him and his wife, don't you?'

'Yes, madam.'

'And you've been admitted here as a foundationer?'

'Yes, madam.'

'In what class is Ruth Craven, Miss Ravenscroft?'

'Ruth is a very diligent pupil. She is in the third remove,' replied Miss Ravenscroft, looking with kindly eyes at the child.

Ruth just glanced at her teacher. Her beautiful little face was beginning to have its usual effect upon most of the ladies present. Some of the stony despair had left it; the colour came and went in her cheeks. She ceased to fiddle with her apron, and clasped her two little white hands tightly together.

'My child,' said Mrs. Naylor, 'your object in coming to school is doubtless the best object of all.'

Ruth raised inquiring eyes.

'I mean,' said the little old lady, 'that you want to learn all you can — to gain knowledge and wisdom, to learn goodness and forbearance and long-suffering and charity.'

'Oh yes,' said Ruth, her eyes dilating.

'If,' continued Miss Mackenzie, interrupting Mrs. Naylor, and speaking in a very firm tone — 'if, instead of these pleasant things happening, a little girl learns to join insurrectionists, to forget those to whom she is indebted for such advantages, then how do matters stand — eh, Ruth Craven?'

'I don't understand,' said Ruth.

Her trembling and fear had come back to her.

'The dear child is frightened, Miss Mackenzie,' said Mrs. Naylor.

'I hope not,' said Miss Mackenzie; 'but I as chairwoman am obliged to question her. — Ruth Craven, is it true that you became a member of a silly schoolgirl society called the Wild Irish Girls, and that you wore a badge like this?'

Ruth nodded.

'Don't nod to me. Speak.'

'It is true,' said Ruth.

'Are you now a member of that society?'

'No.'

'Why did you join it?'

'Because I loved Kathleen O'Hara.'

'She is the promoter, then?'

Ruth was silent.

'You have heard me?'

'Yes, madam.'

'Kathleen O'Hara is the promoter?'

Again Ruth was silent. Miss Mackenzie glanced at the other ladies. After a pause she continued:

'We will leave that matter for the present. Please write down, Miss Judson' — here she turned to the clerk — 'that Ruth Craven has refused to answer my question with regard to Kathleen O'Hara. We will return to that point later on. — Why did you leave the society?'

'I did so because I wanted to join a scheme proposed by a girl who was not a foundationer and not a member of the society. Her name is Cassandra Weldon.'

'One of our best and most promising pupils,' interrupted Miss Ravenscroft.

'I know her,' said Miss Mackenzie. 'We have every reason to be proud of Cassandra Weldon. — And so she, this charming and excellent Cassandra Weldon, is your friend, little Ruth Craven?'

'She has been extremely good to me, madam. She offered me the services of her own coach in order that I might work up for the Ayldice Scholarship.'

'And do you think you have a chance of getting it?'

'I don't know. I mean to try.'

Her dark-blue eyes flashed with intelligence and longing as she uttered these words.

'I think we are now in possession of the facts,' said Miss Mackenzie. 'Is that not so, Mrs. Ross? Ruth Craven was a member of the objectionable society; she very wisely left it, knowing that she would better herself by doing so. — Now then, Ruth, we expect you to tell us all about the society — where it meets, and as much as you know about its rules. And you must also acquaint us with the names of the girls who are members.'

Ruth was again silent, but now she held herself erect and looked full at Miss Mackenzie.

'You hear me, child. Speak. You can make your narrative brief. Where does the society meet? What does it do? What are its rules? Go on; you are not stupid, are you?'

'No, Miss Mackenzie,' said Ruth, 'I am not stupid; and I am very sorry indeed to seem rude, but I cannot answer your questions. You know that Kathleen's society exists; that fact I cannot hide from you, but you will not hear anything more from me. It would be a very terrible thing for me to be expelled from this school; it would mean great sorrow to my grandfather and grandmother; but I cannot betray my friend Kathleen, nor any of the other girls of the society.'

Miss Mackenzie was silent for quite a minute. The other ladies fidgeted as they sat. Ruth, having delivered her soul, looked down. After a long pause Miss Mackenzie said quite gently:

'Ruth Craven, you scarcely realise your own position. We cannot possibly let a little girl who is rebellious, who keeps secrets to herself which she ought to tell for the benefit of the school, continue in our midst. We will give you three days to think over this matter. If at the end of three days you are still obstinately silent, there is nothing whatever for it but that you should be expelled from the school. Do you understand what that means?'

'It means that I must go, that I shall lose all the advantages,' said Ruth.

'It means that and more. It means that in the presence of the whole school you are pronounced unworthy, that you leave the school publicly, being desired to do so by your teacher. It is an unpleasant ceremony, and one which you will never be able to forget; it will haunt you for life, Ruth Craven. I trust, however, my dear child, that such extreme measures will not be necessary. You think now that you are honourable in making yourself a martyr, but it is not so. We who are old must know more than you can possibly know, Ruth, with regards to the benefit of a great establishment like this. Insurrection must be put down with a firm hand. You will see for yourself how right we are, and how wrong and silly and childish you are. — Miss Ravenscroft, a special meeting of the governors will take place in this room on Saturday morning. This is Wednesday. Until then we hope that Ruth Craven will carefully consider her conduct, and be prepared to answer the very vital questions which will be put to her. — You can go, Ruth.'

Ruth left the room.

'An extraordinary child,' said Miss Mackenzie.

'A sweet child, I call her,' said Mrs. Naylor. 'What a beautiful face!'

'My dear Mrs. Naylor, does the beauty of Ruth Craven's face affect this question? She is, in my opinion, extremely silly, and a very naughty child. — Miss Ravenscroft, we leave it to you to bring the little girl to reason. I have known her grandfather ever since he kept a grocer's shop in the High Street. I have respected him more than any man I ever knew. This child in appearance is one of Nature's ladies, but we must get her to see things in the right light, and if necessary she must be made an example of. It will be very painful, but it must be done.'

KATHLEEN FITZPATRICK

(1872–?)

from:
THE WEANS AT ROWALLAN
(1905)

[The five Darragh children — Mick, Jane, Patsy, Fly and Honeybird — live at Rowallan, a decayed big house in the Mourne Mountains, County Down, at the end of the nineteenth century. Their English mother is deranged with bereavement from the murder of their father, who died on the night of Honeybird's birth, five years before the novel begins. The children are therefore being raised by elderly servants, Lull, Andy and Ould Davy, and they are able to roam the countryside freely. One of the novel's remarkable strengths is that not too much is revealed, so that the reader shares the children's sense of mystery. We are never told why the father — a liberal landowner — was murdered, other than that he was mistaken for his brother Neil, who — again mysteriously — is a convert to Roman Catholicism. When Neil in turn is murdered, we know who the killer is but not the clearly political motive for the killing. The date of the action is left vague, and there is no explanation for the children's odd names, or for the family's loss of fortune. The story begins and ends abruptly — the ending, in fact, is so abrupt that in the 1934 editions an extra chapter was added. The five children are brilliantly characterized and their desperate fears for their mother's health is quite haunting. The benign neglect in which the children are raised allows Fitzpatrick to explore the poetics of rural dialect, without being bound to represent too much of the labour and hardships of the poor. The following excerpt is from Chapter 13 of the first edition. When an elderly widower remarries, his crime is a combination of haste and a decision to look for a wife outside his own townland. The baiting of Jimmie by the villagers is consistent with various accounts by nineteenth-century commentators of 'rough music' accorded to unseemly marriages.[1] London: Methuen and Co., 1905.]

JIMMIE BURKE'S WEDDING

Jimmie Burke's wife had not been dead a month, when one morning Teressa brought the news that he was going to be married again.

'The haythen ould Morman!' said Lull.[2] 'God help the wemmen these days.'

At first the children could not believe it. The late Mrs. Burke had been a friend of theirs. They had walked to the village every Sunday afternoon, for the whole long year that she had been ill, with pudding and eggs for her. And they thought Jimmie was so fond of her. He was heartbroken when she died. When they went to the cottage the day before the funeral with a wreath of ivy leaves to put on the coffin, they found him sitting beside the corpse, crying, and wiping his eyes on a bit of newspaper. Even Jane, who, for some reason that she had not given the others, had always hated Jimmie, told Lull when they came home that she could not help thinking a pity of the man sitting there crying like a baby.

'It bates Banagher,'[3] said Teressa, sitting down by the fire with the cup of tea Lull had given her

'an' the woman not cowld in her coffin yet; sure, it's enough to make the dead walk.'

'Och, but the poor critter was glad to rest,' said Lull.

'An', mind ye, he's the impitent[4] ould skut,'[5] Teressa went on, stirring her tea with her finger; 'he come an' tould me last night himself. An' sez he: "The wife she left me under no obligations," sez he; "but sorra a woman is there about the place I'd luk at," sez he.'

'They'd be wantin' a man that tuk him,' said Lull. 'The first wife's well red a' him in glory.'

'When's the weddin', Teressa?' Fly asked.

'An' who's marryin' him?' said Lull.

'He's away this mornin' to be marriet. She's a lump of a girl up in Ballynahinch,' said Teressa. 'Troth, ay, he lost no time; he's bringing her home the night, the neighbours say.'

In the stable Andy Graham was even more indignant. 'Its the ondacentest[6] thing I iver heard tell of,' he told Mick; 'an' the woman be to be as ondacent as himself.'

But Andy's indignation was nothing as to what Jane felt. 'I knowed it,' she said to the others when they were together in the schoolroom; 'I knowed the ould boy was a bad ould baste.[7] Augh! he oughtn't to be let live.'

'Away ar that, Jane,' said Patsy; 'sure that's the fool talk. Where's the harm in him marrying again?'

'Harm!' Jane shouted. 'It's more than harm; it's a dirty insult. Ye ought always to wait a year after yer wife dies afore ye marry again; but him! — him! — he just ought to be hung.'

'It's a dirty trick, sure enough,' said Mick; 'but ye couldn't hang him unless he'd done a murder.'

'An' so he did,' said Jane sharply. 'Think I don't know? I tell ye he murdered her, as sure as I stand on this flure.'[8]

---

members to Parliament, and was . . . a famous pocket borough. When a member spoke of a family borough where every voter was a man employed by the lord, it was not unusual to reply, "Well, that beats Banagher." [Francis] Grose, however, gives another explanation. According to him Banagher (or Banaghan) was an Irish minstrel famous for telling wonderful stories.'

4. Possibly a play on the resemblances between 'impatient', 'impudent' and 'impotent'.

5. A disparaging term. According to Michael Traynor, *The English Dialect of Donegal* (Dublin: Royal Irish Academy, 1953), it is usually applied to women, but I believe it has a more general currency in the north-east.

6. Most indecent.

7. Beast.

8. Floor.

1. See S.J. Connolly, 'Marriage in Pre-Famine Ireland', in *Marriage in Ireland,* ed. Art Cosgrove (Dublin: College Press, 1985), pp. 78–98, p. 91 ff.

2. A reference to Mormon polygamy.

3. E.C. Brewer, *A Dictionary of Phrase and Fable:* 'That beats Banagher — wonderfully inconsistent and absurd — exceedingly ridiculous. Banagher is a town . . . on the Shannon . . . It formerly sent two

'Whist,[9] Jane,' said Mick; 'that's an awful thing to be sayin'.'

'An' I can prove it, too,' she went on, 'for I saw it with my own two eyes, not wanst but twiced, an' she let out he was always doing it. I promised her I wouldn't come over it, but there's no harm tellin' it now she's dead. Ye know them eggs Lull sent her?' The children nodded. 'Well, do you mean to say she iver eat them? For she just didn't; he ate ivery one himself, an' he eat the puddens, an' he drunk the milk. Augh, the ould baste, he'd eat the clothes off her bed if he could 'a' chewed them.'

'Who tould ye he eat them all?' said Patsy.

'Sure, I saw him doin' it myself, I tell ye. He come home drunk one day when I was there. He was that blind drunk he niver seen me. An' he began eatin' all he could lay han' on. He eat up the jelly; an' two raw eggs, an' drunk the taste a' milk she had by her in the cup, an' he even drunk the medicine out of the bottle, an' eat up the wee bunch a' flowers I'd tuk her, an' when he'd eat up ivery wee nip he could find, he lay down on the flure, an' went to sleep.'

'The dirty, greedy, mane ould divil,' said the others.

'An' she tould me he always done it,' Jane went on. 'An' I seen it was the truth, for he come in another day, an' done the same, an' he was that cross that he frightened her, an' she begun to spit blood, an' if it hadn't been for me I believe he'd 'a' kilt her; but I was that mad that I hit him a big dig in the stomach; an', mind ye, I hurted him, for he went to bed like a lamb, an' I tied him in with an ould shawl before I come away.'

The others could find no words to express their disgust. They agreed that Jane was right — such a man ought not to be allowed to live.

'If we tould Sergeant M'Gee he'd hang him,' said Fly.

'That'd be informin',' said Mick.

'Almighty God's sure to pay him out when he dies,' Honeybird said.

'I'd rather pay him out just now,' said Jane. At that moment there was a flash of lightning, and a crash of thunder overhead, and then a shower of hailstones rattled against the window.

'Mebby he'll be struck dead,' said Fly; 'Almighty God's sure to be awful angry with him.'

For three hours the rain poured in torrents. The children watched it from the schoolroom window splashing up on the path, and beating down the fuchsia bushes in the border.

But by dinner time it had cleared up, and the sky looked clean and blue, as though it had just been washed. When dinner was over they went off to the village, expecting to hear that Jimmie had been struck by lightning, or, as Fly thought would be more proper, killed by a thunderbolt.

Mrs M'Rea was standing at her door, with a ring of neighbours round her. As they came up the street they heard her say, 'There's the childer, an' they were the kin' friends to her when she was alive.'

'Good-mornin', Mrs M'Rea,' said Jane; 'has Jimmie been kilt?'

'Is it kilt?' said Mrs M'Rea; 'deed an' it's no more than he desarves — but we don't all get what we desarve in this world, glory be to God! Troth, no; it's marriet he is, an' comin' home the night in style on a ker,[10] all the way from Ballynahinch.'

'We thought Almighty God'd 'a' kilt him with a thunderbolt,' said Fly.

'Do you hear that?' said old Mrs Clay. 'The very childers turned agin him — an' small wonder, the ould ruffan; it's the quare woman would have him.'

'By all accounts she is that,' said Gordie O'Rorke, joining the group; 'they say she's six fut[11] in her stockin's an' as blackavised[12] as the ould boy himself.'

'We'll be givin' her the fine welcome the night,' said his granny; 'she'll be thinkin' she got to her long home.'[13]

'They say she's got the gran' clothes,' said Gordie, 'an' a silk dress an' a gowld watch an' chain; mebbe that's what tuk his fancy.'

'If she doesn't luk out he'll be eatin' it,' said Patsy. There was a roar of laughter.

'There's none knows better than yous what he could ate,' said Mrs M'Rea. 'Any bite or sup I tuk the woman I sat and seen it in her afore I come away.'

'He's stepped over his brogues this time,' said Gordie, 'for me uncle up in Ballynahinch is well

9. Hush.
10. Car.
11. Feet.
12. Swarthy-complexioned.
13. Grave.

acquainted with the woman, an' he says she's a heeler,[14] an' no mistake.'

'Well, well,' said ould Mrs Glover, 'I'm sayin' she'll not have her sorras[15] to seek.'

'No; nor Jimmie either,' said Mrs M'Rea. 'But where's the good a' talkin'? It's the lamentable thing entirely; but they're marriet now, an' God help both a' them.'

'Deed yis; they're marriet,' said Mrs O'Rorke, 'an' we'll not be forgettin' it the night. It's tar bar'ls[16] we'll be burnin' — they'll be expectin' it to be sure — an' a torchlight procession out to meet them forby.'

'Troth, then, they'll get more than they're expectin',' said Gordie.

'What time did ye say they'd be comin' back the night, Mrs M'Rea?' Mick asked.

'Ye know we'd like to come to the welcome,' said Jane.

'Och, it'd be late for the likes a' yous,' answered Mrs M'Rea. 'It'll be past ten, won't it Gordie?'

'Nearer eleven than ten,' said Gordie.

'You lave it to us, Miss Jane; niver fear but they'll get the right good welcome.'

Going home they were all very quiet. No one spoke until at last they came to the gates. Then Patsy said: 'Lull'll niver let us out at that time a' night.'

'We'll just have to dodge her,' said Jane; 'it'd be the wicked an' the wrong thing to let ould Jimmie off.'

'It'll be the quare fun,' said Patsy, dancing around.

'It won't be fun, Patsy; it'll be vengeance,' said Jane severely.

'Ye'll take me with ye, won't ye?' Honeybird begged.

'Deed, we'll take the sowl', said Mick; 'but ye'll be powerful tired.'

'What do I care about that?' she said. 'I just want to hit that bad ould man.'

Lull was surprised to see them go to bed so quietly that night. 'Ye niver know the minds a' childer' they heard her say as they left their mother's room after they had said good-night. 'I made sure they'd be wantin' to the village to see Jimmie Burke come home.' Honeybird sniggered, but Fly nipped her into silence.

The convent bell was ringing for Compline[17] when Lull tucked them into bed, but before the schoolroom clock struck ten they were on their way to the village. When they got to Jimmie's cottage the crowd was so great that they could see nothing. 'We'll have no han' in the welcome at all,' said Mick.

'An' it's that pitch dark we'll niver see them,' said Patsy.

'We'd better be goin' back a bit first along the road, an' give them the first welcome,' Jane said. 'Come on, quick,' she added, 'an' we can stand on the wall, an' paste them with mud as they come by.'

'Hould on a minute,' said Mick. 'I've got a plan: we'll stick my lantern on the wall, an' shout out they're home; they'll be that drunk they'll niver know the differs; that'll make them stop, an' we'll get a good shot at them.'

'Troth, we'll do better than that,' said Patsy, with a chuckle. 'They'll be blind drunk, I'm tellin' ye, an' it's into the ould pond we'll be welcomin' them. Yous three can stan' on the wall out a' the wet, an' me an' Mike'll assist the man an' his wife to step off the car.'

The pond was at the side of the road, not more than a hundred yards from the village, and the wall ran right through the middle of it. The children climbed on the wall, and crept along on their hands and knees till they came to the deepest part. The water was up to the top of the wall, so they had to sit with their legs doubled up to keep them out of the wet.

Soon they heard the wheels of the car coming along the road.

'Now, mind ye all screech at onst,' said Patsy as he dropped off the wall. 'Auch! but the water's cowld.'

The car came nearer. Jane held up the lantern. 'Hurrah, hurrah!' they shouted; 'here ye are at last. Hurrah!'

'This way, this way,' Mick shouted; 'drive up to the man's own dour.'

A stone from Patsy smashed the lamp on the car.

'Begorra, I can't see where I'm goin',' said the driver.

'Ye're all right,' Mick shouted; 'there's the lamp in the man's windy.'

'Home, shweet home,' said Jimmie; 'no plache like home.'

---

14. 'A sharp, prying, managing woman', Traynor, *The English Dialect of Donegal*.
15. Sorrows.
16. Barrels.

17. Last of the seven canonical hours in the Roman Catholic Church. Said around 8–9 p.m.

'Hurrah, hurrah!' they shouted as the horse splashed into the pond.

'Jump off, Mister Burke, there's a bit of a puddle by the step,' said Mick.

'Home, shweet home, me darlinsh,' said Jimmie; 'lemme shisht ye off kersh.'

'Come on, we'll help the wife off,' said Mick.

But Jimmie had taken his wife's arm, and as he jumped she jumped too. Splash they went into the pond, and at the same time a shower of stones came from the wall. The horse took fright, and started off, the driver shouting 'Murder!' as they raced down the road.

'In the name a' God, where am I?' shouted Mrs. Burke.

But she got no answer, for Jimmie, with the help of Mick and Patsy, was taking back ducks in the pond. Mrs. Burke splashed towards the light, going deeper every step.

'Ye ould villain, will ye come an' help me out?' she screamed. 'Sure, it's ruinin' me dress an' me new boots I am.'

Then the light went out, and a moment later there was a gurgling cry, followed by shrieks and cries of murder. In the middle of it all voices were heard coming along the road from the village, and the sound of the car coming back.

'Hist!' said Mick. 'Home.'

'Och, I'm wet to the skin,' said Patsy as they ran along the road, 'but ould Jimmie's far wetter.'

'He's as dry as the wife,' said Jane, 'for I ducked her three times; she went down awful easy.'

'It was me helpin' ye,' said Fly; 'I had her by the leg.'

'Wasn't it quare and good a' God to make the pond that deep?' said Honeybird. 'It must 'a been Him that put it into Patsy's head to duck them.'

'That's why He made it rain so hard this mornin',' said Jane, 'an' me thought there was no manin' in it.'

'It was the finest piece of vengeance I iver seen,' said Patsy. 'Ould Jimmie was as light as a cork, an' we soused him up and down till there wasn't a breath left in him.'

'I wonder what Lull'll say when she sees our clothes,' said Jane; 'me very shimmy's[18] wet.' But, to their surprise, when they woke next morning clean clothes had been put out for them, and when they came downstairs Lull only said:

'Have any of ye tuk a cold?'

'No, we haven't,' said Jane.

'Well, then, don't name it to yer mother,' Lull said, and left them wondering how she had found out.

Andy Graham called them into the stable after breakfast.

'Did ye hear the news?' he said.

'What news?' said Mick.

'The news about the weddin',' Andy said. 'Didn't Lull tell ye about it? Sure, the whole place is ringin' with it. Poor ould Jimmie Burke an' the wife were near kilt last night. A pack of ruffians stopped the ker at the ould pond, an' ducked both him an' the wife. He was that full a' watter they had to hould him up by the heels an' let it run out; an' the wife covered with black mud from head to fut.'

'Who done it?' said Patsy, looking Andy in the face.

'Who done it, do ye say?' said Andy — 'sure that's what I'd like to know myself. There wasn't wan out a' the village but what was waitin' at the man's own dour when the ker came up, and ne'ery a wan on it but the driver, shoutin' murder, an' when the neighbours went back along the road there was Jimmie an' the wife in the middle a' the pond, and niver a sowl else to be seen.'

Mick laughed. 'Ye're the fly ould boy, Andy,' he said; 'an' I must say ye done it right well, but didn't ye get awful wet when ye were duckin' them?'

Andy stared at him.

'It's all right, Andy; we'll niver name it,' said Patsy. 'An' I wouldn't 'a' blamed ye if ye'd 'a' drownded the both 'a them.'

Andy whistled. 'Ye've as much brass as would make a dour knocker,' he said. 'But, see here, the next time yous are on the war pad don't be lavin' circumstantial evidence behind ye.' He brought out from behind the door an old rag doll, soaking wet.

'Och a nee!' wailed Honeybird, 'it was me done that. I hadn't the heart to lave her at home,' she explained. 'She's Bloody Mary,[19] an' I thought she'd enjoy the vengeance.'

'I thought I knowed her when I seen her lyin' at the side a' the pond this mornin',' said Andy. 'An', mind ye, I'm not blamin' ye, an' I'm not

---

18. Chemise.

19. Honeybird's doll is named after Mary I (1516–58), Queen of England, whose persecution of Protestants earned her the epithet 'Bloody Mary'.

saying but what Jimmie an' the wife disarved it, but ye'd better keep a quiet tongue in yer heads. There's nobuddy but meself an' Lull knows who

done it, and nobuddy'll iver know. It's all very well for a wheen a' neighbours to do the like, but it's no work for quality to be doin'.'

LETITIA MacLINTOCK

(fl. 1869–84)

JAMIE FREEL AND THE YOUNG LADY (1909)

[From the mid-eighteenth century onwards there was a divergence in how writers chose to represent folk cultures and the oral traditions of Britain and Ireland in print, particularly when translations from the Scottish, Welsh, Irish and Ulster Scots were involved. Bardic material tended to be translated into highly mannered poetic diction, while folk material increasingly drew on dialect. Popular superstitions, folklore and ballads might be some of the languages in which ordinary people articulated the complexities of desire, and the inverted logic of dreams has a pronounced role in such articulations. From the publication of *Fairy Legends and Traditions of the South of Ireland* (1825–8) by Thomas Crofton Croker (1798–1854) there had been a growing interest in the publication of Irish fairy tales. 'The Fairies' (1850), a poem by the Ballyshannon poet William Allingham (1824–89), rapidly became a favourite in children's anthologies. In 1892 W.B. Yeats (1865–1939) published *Irish Fairy Tales* in T. Fisher Unwin's Children's Library series, and the end of the nineteenth century saw a huge expansion in such collections. *The Irish Fairy Book* (1909), from which this story is taken, was edited for T. Fisher Unwin by the poet Alfred Perceval Graves (1846–1931), with illustrations by George Denham. It is an anthology of material in verse and prose from such figures as Allingham, Crofton Croker, Yeats, Lady Gregory, James Clarence Mangan (1803–49), Eleanor Hull (1860–1935), Alfred Tennyson (1809–92), Standish James O'Grady (1846–1928), Douglas Hyde (1860–1949) and a dozen other writers. Letitia MacLintock's story of fairy abduction draws on a familiar trope from oral tradition (see, for example, 'Bean Óg a Tugadh sa mBruín / A Young Woman Taken by the Fairies' from Éamon a Búrc in the subsection 'Legends of the Supernatural' (pp. 1296–1303)), but it also has interesting echoes of eighteenth-century heiress abduction narratives, such as the Newcomen case as described by Sarah Colvill (pp. 801–8) and the 'Memoir of Hennessy' by W.H. Maxwell (pp. 849–52). The family's refusal to recognize the returning child could be read as a form of rejection and ostracism as well as a supernatural event.]

(Ulster Irish)

Down in Fannet,[1] in time gone by, lived Jamie Freel and his mother. Jamie was the widow's sole support; his strong arm worked for her untiringly, and as each Saturday night came round he poured his wages into her lap, thanking her dutifully for the halfpence which she returned him for tobacco.

He was extolled by his neighbours as the best son ever known or heard of. But he had neighbours of whose opinions he was ignorant — neighbours who lived pretty close to him, whom he had never seen, who are, indeed, rarely seen by mortals, except on May Eves and Halloweens.[2]

An old ruined castle, about a quarter of a mile from his cabin, was said to be the abode of the 'wee folk'. Every Halloween were the ancient windows lighted up, and passers-by saw little figures flitting to and fro inside the building, while they heard the music of flutes and pipes.

It was well known that fairy revels took place; but nobody had the courage to intrude on them.

Jamie had often watched the little figures from a distance and listened to the charming music, wondering what the inside of the castle was like; but one Halloween he got up, and took his cap, saying to his mother, 'I'm awa to the castle to seek my fortune.'

'What!' cried she. 'Would you venture there — you that's the widow's only son? Dinna be sae venturesome and foolitch, Jamie! They'll kill you, an' then what'll come o' me?'

'Never fear, mother; nae harm'll happen me, but I maun gae.'

He set out, and, as he crossed the potato field, came in sight of the castle, whose windows were ablaze with light that seemed to turn the russet

1. Fánaid (Fanad), County Donegal.
2. Traditionally these are times of major activities for supernatural beings.

leaves, still clinging to the crab-tree branches, into gold.

Halting in the grove at one side of the ruin, he listened to the elfin revelry, and the laughter and singing made him all the more determined to proceed.

Numbers of little people, the largest about the size of a child of five years old, were dancing to the music of flutes and fiddles, while others drank and feasted.

'Welcome, Jamie Freel! Welcome, welcome, Jamie!' cried the company, perceiving their visitor. The word 'Welcome' was caught up and repeated by every voice in the castle.

Time flew, and Jamie was enjoying himself very much, when his hosts said, 'We're going to ride to Dublin to-night to steal a young lady. Will you come too, Jamie Freel?'

'Ay, that I will,' cried the rash youth, thirsting for adventure.

A troop of horses stood at the door. Jamie mounted, and his steed rose with him into the air. He was presently flying over his mother's cottage, surrounded by the elfin troop, and on and on they went, over bold mountains, over little hills, over the deep Lough Swilley,[3] over towns and cottages, where people were burning nuts and eating apples and keeping merry Halloween. It seemed to Jamie that they flew all round Ireland before they got to Dublin.

'This is Derry,' said the fairies, flying over the cathedral spire; and what was said by one voice was repeated by all the rest, till fifty little voices were crying out, 'Derry! Derry! Derry!'

In like manner was Jamie informed as they passed over each town on the route, and at length he heard the silvery voices cry, 'Dublin! Dublin!'

It was no mean dwelling that was to be honoured by the fairy visit, but one of the finest houses in Stephen's Green.[4]

The troop dismounted near a window, and Jamie saw a beautiful face on a pillow in a splendid bed. He saw the young lady lifted and carried away, while the stick which was dropped in her place on the bed took her exact form.

The lady was placed before one rider and carried a short way, then given to another, and the names of the towns were cried as before.

They were approaching home. Jamie heard 'Rathmullan,' 'Milford,' 'Tamney,' and then he knew they were near his own house.

'You've all had your turn at carrying the young lady,' said he. 'Why wouldn't I get her for a wee piece?'

'Ay, Jamie,' replied they pleasantly, 'you may take your turn at carrying her, to be sure.'

Holding his prize very tightly he dropped down near his mother's door.

'Jamie Freel! Jamies Freel! is that the way you treat us?' cried they, and they, too, dropped down near the door.

Jamie held fast, though he knew not what he was holding, for the little folk turned the lady into all sorts of strange shapes. At one moment she was a black dog, barking and trying to bite; at another a glowing bar of iron, which yet had no heat; then again a sack of wool.

But still Jamie held her, and the baffled elves were turning away when a tiny woman, the smallest of the party, exclaimed, 'Jamie Freel has her awa frae us, but he shall nae hae gude of her, for I'll mak' her deaf and dumb,' and she threw something over the young girl.

While they rode off, disappointed, Jamie Freel lifted the latch and went in.

'Jamie, man!' cried his mother, 'you've been awa all night. What have they done to you?'

'Naething bad, mother, I hae the very best o' gude luck. Here's a beautiful young lady I hae brought you for company.'

'Bless us and save us!' exclaimed his mother; and for some minutes she was so astonished she could not think of anything else to say.

Jamie told the story of the night's adventure, ending by saying, 'Surely you wouldna have allowed me to let her gang with them to be lost for ever?'

'But a *lady*, Jamie! How can a lady eat we'er (our) poor diet and live in we'er poor way? I ax you that, you foolitch fellow!'

'Well, mother, sure it's better for her to be over here nor yonder,' and he pointed in the direction of the castle.

Meanwhile the deaf and dumb girl shivered in her light clothing, stepping close to the humble turf fire.

'Poor crathur, she's quare and handsome! Nae wonder they set their hearts on her,' said the old woman, gazing at their guest with pity and

---

3. Lough in County Donegal.
4. Fashionable square in central Dublin.

admiration. 'We maun dress her first; but what in the name o' fortune hae I fit for the likes of her to wear?'

She went to her press in 'the room' and took out her Sunday gown of brown drugget.[5] She then opened a drawer and drew forth a pair of white stockings, a long snowy garment of fine linen, and a cap, her 'dead dress', as she called it.

These articles of attire had long been ready for a certain triste ceremony, in which she would some day fill the chief part, and only saw the light occasionally when they were hung out to air; but she was willing to give even these to the fair trembling visitor, who was turning in dumb sorrow and wonder from her to Jamie, and from Jamie back to her. The poor girl suffered herself to be dressed, and then sat down on a 'creepie'[6] in the chimney corner and buried her face in her hands.

'What'll we do to keep up a lady like thou?' cried the old woman.

'I'll work for you both, mother,' replied the son.

'An' how could a lady live on we'er poor diet?' she repeated.

'I'll work for her,' was all Jamie's answer.

He kept his word. The young lady was very sad for a long time, and tears stole down her cheeks many an evening, while the old woman span by the fire and Jamie made salmon nets, an accomplishment acquired by him in hopes of adding to the comfort of their guest.

But she was always gentle, and tried to smile when she perceived them looking at her; and by degrees she adapted herself to their ways and mode of life. It was not very long before she began to feed the pig, mash potatoes and meal for the fowls, and knit blue worsted[7] socks.

So a year passed and Halloween came round again. 'Mother,' said Jamie, taking down his cap, 'I'm off to the ould castle to seek my fortune.'

'Are you mad, Jamie?' cried his mother in terror; 'sure they'll kill you this time for what you done on them last year.'

Jamie made light of her fears and went his way.

As he reached the crab-tree he saw bright lights in the castle windows as before, and heard loud talking. Creeping under the window he

heard the wee folk say, 'That was a poor trick Jamie Freel played us this night last year, when he stole the young lady from us.'

'Ay,' said the tiny woman, 'an' I punished him for it, for there she sits a dumb image by the hearth, but he does na' know that three drops out o' this glass that I hold in my hand wad gie her her hearing and speech back again.'

Jamie's heart beat fast as he entered the hall. Again he was greeted by a chorus of welcomes from the company — 'Here comes Jamie Freel! Welcome, welcome, Jamie!' As soon as the tumult subsided the little woman said, 'You be to drink our health, Jamie, out o' this glass in my hand.'

Jamie snatched the glass from her and darted to the door. He never knew how he reached his cabin, but he arrived there breathless and sank on a stove by the fire.

'You're kilt, surely, this time, my poor boy,' said his mother.

'No, indeed, better luck than ever this time!' and he gave the lady three drops of the liquid that still remained at the bottom of the glass, notwithstanding his mad race over the potato field.

The lady began to speak, and her first words were words of thanks to Jamie.

The three inmates of the cabin had so much to say to one another that, long after cock-crow, when the fairy music had quite ceased, they were talking round the fire.

'Jamie,' said the lady, 'be pleased to get me paper and pen and ink that I may write to my father and tell him what has become of me.'

She wrote, but weeks passed and she received no answer. Again and again she wrote, and still no answer.

At length she said, 'You must come with me to Dublin, Jamie, to find my father.'

'I hae no money to hire a car for you,' he answered; 'an' how can you travel to Dublin on your foot?'

But she implored him so much that he consented to set out with her and walk all the way from Fannet to Dublin. It was not as easy as the fairy journey; but at last they rang the bell at the door of the house in Stephen's Green.

'Tell my father that his daughter is here,' said she to the servant who opened the door.

'The gentleman that lives here has no daughter, my girl. He had one, but she died better nor a year ago.'

5. Coarse woollen material.
6. A low stool.
7. A particular style of spun wool.

'Do you not know me, Sullivan?'

'No, poor girl, I do not.'

'Let me see the gentleman. I only ask to see him.'

'Well, that's not much to ax. We'll see what can be done.' In a few moments the lady's father came to the door.

'How dare you call me your father?' cried the old gentleman angrily. 'You are an impostor. I have no daughter.'

'Look in my face, father, and surely you'll remember me.'

'My daughter is dead and buried. She died a long, long time ago.' The old gentleman's voice changed from anger to sorrow. 'You can go,' he concluded.

'Stop, dear father, till you look at this ring on my finger. Look at your name and mine engraved on it.'

'It certainly is my daughter's ring, but I do not know how you came by it. I fear in no honest way.'

'Call my mother — *she* will be sure to know me,' said the poor girl, who by this time was weeping bitterly.

'My poor wife is beginning to forget her sorrow. She seldom speaks of her daughter now. Why should I renew her grief by reminding her of her loss?'

But the young lady persevered till at last the mother was sent for.

'Mother,' she began, when the old lady came to the door, 'don't you know your daughter?'

'I have no daughter. My daughter died, and was buried a long, long time ago.'

'Only look in my face and surely you'll know me.'

The old lady shook her head.

'You have all forgotten me; but look at this mole on my neck.[8] Surely, mother, you know me now?'

'Yes, yes,' said her mother, 'my Gracie had a mole on her neck like that; but then I saw her in the coffin, and saw the lid shut down upon her.'

It became Jamie's turn to speak, and he gave the history of the fairy journey, of the theft of the young lady, of the figure he had seen laid in its place, of her life with his mother in Fannet, of last Halloween, and of the three drops that had released her from her enchantments.

She took up the story when he paused and told how kind the mother and son had been to her.

The parents could not make enought of Jamie. They treated him with every distinction, and when he expressed his wish to return to Fannet, said they did not know what to do to express their gratitude.

But an awkward complication arose. The daughter would not let him go without her. 'If Jamie goes, I'll go, too,' she said. 'He saved me from the fairies, and has worked for me ever since. If it had not been for him, dear father and mother, you would never have seen me again. If he goes, I'll go, too.'

This being her resolution, the old gentleman said that Jamie should become his son-in-law. The mother was brought from Fannet in a coach-and-four, and there was a splendid wedding.

They all lived together in the grand Dublin house, and Jamie was heir to untold wealth at his father-in-law's death.

---

8. For lost family members recognized by a mole, see William Shakespeare, *Twelfth Night*, Act v, Scene 1, lines 234–40; and Maria Edgeworth, *Belinda*, Chapter 27.

ELEANOR HULL

(1860–1935)

from:
CUCHULAIN. THE HOUND
OF ULSTER (1909)

[This is an example of the 'high style' in which many of the ancient Irish myths were presented to children during the Irish Literary Revival. One can trace the influence of *Le Morte d'Arthur* (1485) by Thomas Malory (d. 1471) as well as the influences of James Macpherson (1736–96) and Charlotte Brooke (1704–93). Text from *Cuchulain. The House of Ulster* (London: George G. Harrap, 1909).]

HOW CUCHULAIN WOOED HIS WIFE

[W]hen she saw him Emer knew that it was the man of whom she had dreamed. He wished a blessing to them, and her lovely face she lifted in reply. 'May God make smooth the path before thy feet,' she gently said. 'And thou, mayst thou be safe from every harm,' was his reply. 'Whence comes thou?' she asked; for he had alighted from his seat and stood beside her gazing on her face. 'From Conor's court we come,' he answered then; 'from Emain, kingliest of Ulster forts, and this the way we took. We drove between the Mountains of the Wood, along the High-road of the Plain, where once the sea had been; across the Marsh they call the Secret of the Gods, and to the Boyne's ford, named of old the Washing of the Horses of the Gods. And now at last, O maiden, we have come to the bright flowery Garden-grounds of Lugh. This is the story of myself, O maid; let me now hear of thee.' Then Emer said: 'Daughter am I to Forgall, whom men call the Wily Chief. Cunning his mind and strange his powers; for he is stronger than any labouring man, more learned than any Druid, more sharp and clever than any man of verse. Men say that thou art skilled in feats of war, but it will be more than all thy games to fight against Forgall himself; therefore be cautious what thou doest, for men cannot number the multitude of his warlike deeds nor the cunning and craft with which he works. He has given me as a bodyguard twenty valient men, their captain Con, son of Forgall, and my brother; therefore I am well protected and no man can come near me, but that Forgall knows of it. To-day he is gone from home on a warrior expedition, and those men are gone with him; else, had he been within, I trow he would have asked thee of thy business here.'

'Why, O maiden, dost thou talk thus to me? Dost thou not reckon me among the strong men, who know not fear?' 'If thy deeds were known to me,' she said, 'I then might reckon them; but hitherto I have not heard of all thy exploits.' 'Truly, I swear, O maiden,' said Cuchulain, 'that I will make my deeds to be recounted among the glories of the warrior-feats of heroes.' 'How do men reckon thee?' she said again. 'What then is thy strength?' 'This is my strength,' he said. 'When my might in fight is weakest, I can defend myself alone against twenty. I fear not by my own might to fight with forty. Under my protection a hundred are secure. From dread of me, strong warriors avoid my path, and come not against me in the battlefield. Hosts and multitudes and armed men fly before my name.'

'Thou seemest to boast,' said Emer, 'and truly for a tender boy those feats are very good; but they rank not with the deeds of chariot-chiefs. Who then were they who brought thee up in these deeds of which thou boastest?'

'Truly, O maiden, King Conor is himself my foster-father, and not as churl or common man was I brought up by him. Among chariot-chiefs and champions, among poets and learned men, among the lords and nobles of Ulster, have I been reared, and they have taught me courage and skill and manly gifts. In birth and bravery I am a match for any chariot-chief; I direct the counsels of Ulster, and at my own fort at Dun Dalgan they come to me for entertainment. Not as one of the common herd do I stand before thee here to-day, but as the favourite of the King and the darling of all the warriors of Ulster. Moreover, the god Lugh the Long-handed is my protector, for I am of the race of the great gods, and his especial foster-child. And now, O maiden, tell me of thyself; how in the sunny plains of Lugh hast thou been reared within thy father's fort?' 'That I will tell thee,' said the girl. 'I was brought up in noble behaviour as every queen is reared; in stateliness of form, in wise, calm speech, in comeliness of manner, so that to me is imputed every noble grace among the hosts of the women of Erin.'

'Good, indeed, are those virtues,' said the youth; 'and yet I see one excellence thou hast not noted in thy speech. Never before, until this day, among all the women with whom I have at times conversed, have I found one but thee to speak the mystic ancient language of the bards, which we are talking now for secrecy one with the other. And all these things are good, but one is best of all, and that is, that I love thee, and I think thou

lovest me. What hinders, then, that we should be betrothed?' But Emer would not hasten, but teasing him, she said, 'Perhaps thou hast already found a wife?' 'Not so,' said he, 'and by my right-hands valour here I vow, none but thyself shall ever be my wife.' 'A pity it were, indeed, thou shouldst not have a wife,' said Emer, playing with him still; 'see, here is Fiall, my elder sister, a clever girl and excellent in needlework. Make her thy wife, for well is it known to thee, a younger sister in Ireland may not marry before an elder. Take her! I'll call her hither.' Then Cuchulain was vexed because she seemed to play with him. 'Verily and indeed,' he said, 'not Fiall but thee, it is with whom I am in love; and if thou weddest me not, never will I, Cuchulain, wed at all.'

WINIFRED LETTS

(1882–1972)

from:
THE QUEST OF THE BLUE ROSE (1910)

[The period from 1880 to 1914 saw the publication of a large number of novels directed at girls on the threshold of adult life. Influenced by emerging feminists, they negotiate the challenge of apparently new freedoms for young women looking for education and a career. The typical heroine is orphaned, or alienated from her family, hard-working and ambitious to achieve something 'artistic' and has highly wrought romantic ideas about love. To say that *The Quest of the Blue Rose* is typical of a genre is not to be derogatory — as with the emergence of the female gothic at the turn of the previous century, it is possible to appreciate these popular novels as part of a wide cultural engagement with dramatic changes in the status of women. The following extract is from an early chapter in the book. As the newly orphaned Sylvia is on the verge of leaving home to make her way in the world she reflects on the importance to her girlhood dreams of a room of her own, with books, music and art. Published in London in 1910 by Henry Frowde, Hodder and Stoughton, and illustrated in colour by James Durden.]

She went home quickly and up to her pretty little room that looked out over the garden. What happy

hours that room had known! And how much it reflected its owner. It had been Sylvia's pride and the temple of that delightful privacy which is far from loneliness but rather an arbour in the social life of home. There were her favourite pictures on the wall, three or four old masters, the prints that had come from abroad, water-colours wrought by herself in a vain attempt to follow after Turner,[1] small copies of pictures by Millais, Rossetti and Burne-Jones, for who has reached twenty without the fine fervour of pre-Raphaelitism?[2] And then 'Love and Death' and two more by Watts[3] hung over her bookshelf, the bookshelf that Sylvia had enamelled a very aesthetic green. And because her bookshelf is likely to be a satisfactory index to her character, and because all bookshelves are interesting, its contents may be mentioned here. There was a shelf devoted to poets, and all these were rather well-worn, especially Keats, Tennyson,

1. Joseph Mallord William Turner (1775–1851), English painter.
2. The Pre-Raphaelite brotherhood was founded in 1848 by the painters Holman Hunt (1827–1910), John Everett Millais (1829–96), Dante Gabriel Rossetti (1828–82) and others, in rebellion against the grand style dominating English painting. They were particularly interested in colour and symbolism, and their influence, which extended to poetry and other arts, is a significant presence in *The Quest of the Blue Rose*.
3. George Frederick Watts (1817–1904), English painter and sculptor.

Rossetti and his famous sister.[4] Browning[5] lay on the table near her bed. And many shabby books of childhood occupied the next shelf — dearly-treasured Kate Greenaways, Caldecotts and Walter Cranes, Hans Andersen and the *Parables of Nature*, the Fairchild Family, Holiday House, Miss Edgeworth, and all Mrs. Ewing.[6] On the third shelf there were Dickens and Thackeray,[7] and by these two great ones sat *Little Women* and *Good Wives*,[8] and many other of a miscellaneous, much-prized collection, saved for, longed for, through the course of months. The second hand *Marcus the Epicurean*[9] — what a prize that had been. And how dear was the *Cranford* that sat next the *Life of Charlotte Brontë*.[10]

The books, like faithful friends, would go with her to the new home in the city where she had found an appointment, for she had been transferred to the post-office of Norchester, a big manufacturing Lancashire town. And in a few days she would leave the little house with all its sad and happy recollections, and go forth into the new world, where she would never be happy . . . never . . . never.

Above her little mantelpiece hung a Dresden china plate given to her once by an old godmother. Sylvia, young as she then was, had prized the plate exceedingly. Her mother had often wondered at the care lavished upon this treasure, its dustings and washings. But Sylvia had seen in it the gem of a possible collection. It represented to her an old-fashioned country house and a cool dining-room where one took fruit from Dresden plates and enjoyed to the full a drowsy calm where no telegraph machine ever clicked and where the letters G.P.O. did not haunt one's mind with the sense of an unending business.

The plate was adorned with a bird that sat upon an unknown tree whose leaves were sadly sparse. At intervals around the rim were placed a beetle, a potato flower, a butterfly, a nameless flower, and a blue rose. It was the blue rose that Sylvia loved. For what did that blue rose not signify? All the unattainable glorious things that the soul desires, the right to walk among the elect in meadows of asphodel, the right to look through the gates of Paradise, the right to say 'I have achieved.'

Now Sylvia stared at it, reflecting on the quest of the Blue Rose and on those who finding it have seemed to walk in gardens closed strictly to the general public. How did they feel, these happy ones who might go further than their fellows? How would it be to know oneself a Florence Nightingale, or a Miss Weston; to have written Cranford or Silas Marner or Jackanapes,[11] to realise that one really was Kate Greenaway or Miss Rose Barton,[12] or yet in another sphere Miss Ellen Terry; or looking in the glass to recognize oneself as a Christina Rossetti or Miss Ethel Clifford, whose *Songs of Dreams*[13] lay under the Browning by Sylvia's bed?

But she was none of these. Her eyes strayed to her own reflection in the wardrobe mirror. She saw a pale girl with fair hair, and eyes and nose red with tears. Certainly the picture was not inspiring. She did not look like a poet or an artist, or anything more than what she was, a fairly competent telegraphist earning a wage of fifteen shillings a week. No, the Blue Rose was not for her. She dried her eyes and sat down near to the window with Mark Twain's *Tramp Abroad*[14] to comfort this sad hour of waning daylight.

4. John Keats (1795–1821); Alfred, Lord Tennyson (1809–92); Christina Rossetti (1830–94).
5. Robert Browning (1812–89).
6. Kate Greenaway (1846–1901), Randolph Caldecott (1846–86) and Walter Crane (1845–1915), children's illustrators; Hans Christian Andersen (1805–75); *Parables from Nature* (1855–71), a series of children's stories by Margaret Gatty (1809–73); *The Fairchild Family* (first published 1818, with later additions) by Martha Mary Sherwood (1775–1851) was designed to show the benefits of religious education; *Holiday House* (1839) by Catherine Sinclair (1800–64); Maria Edgeworth (1768–1849); Juliana Horatia Ewing (1841–85).
7. Charles Dickens (1812–70); William Makepeace Thackeray (1811–63).
8. *Little Women* (1868) and its sequel *Good Wives* (1869) are novels for girls by the American novelist Louisa May Alcott (1832–88).
9. *Marcus the Epicurean* (1885), a philosophical romance by Walter Pater (1839–94).
10. *Cranford* (1851–3) is a novel and the *Life of Charlotte Brontë* (1857) a biography, both by Elizabeth Gaskell (1810–65).
11. Florence Nightingale (1820–1910), pioneering English nurse; Miss Weston, probably Agnes Elizabeth Weston (1840–1918), organizer of 'Sailors' Rests'. *Silas Marner* (1861) by George Eliot (1819–80); *Jackanapes* (1879) by Juliana Horatia Ewing.
12. Rose Barton, book illustrator for *Picturesque Dublin, Old and New* by Frances Gerrard (1898) and *Familiar London* (1904).
13. Ethel Clifford (no dates discovered), *Song of Dreams* (1903).
14. *A Tramp Abroad* (1880) is a travel narrative by the American novelist Mark Twain (1835–1910).

from:
NAUGHTY SOPHIA (1912)

[*Naughty Sophia* is a picaresque novel for younger children, relating the various adventures of the scampish heroine and her friend Hans, two German children from a world that borders fairyland and reality. It specializes in a light grotesque, and like many fairy stories has a great deal to imply about the fears of adult sexuality and abuse that may lie behind childhood terrors. In this chapter Sophia and Hans have been kidnapped by a robber baron, who gloats over his capture of the little girl, and to whom Sophia — like Scheherazade — must tell nightly stories to preserve her life. Published in London in 1912 by Grant Richards and illustrated by Ruby Lind.[1]]

HOW THE ROBBERS HAD HIGH TEA

All the robbers came to high tea. They were expected to wash their hands at the pump before they came in. If the Baron saw dirty hands he was much annoyed; and his punishments were so terrible that the robbers dared not disobey him.

He himself was most particular about his toilet. He always put on a clean collar before tea, and he brushed his hair with hair oil, the white sort that looks like cream. He wore a velvet coat, too, and an embroidered waistcoat and a diamond scarf-pin. He was very fond of jewellery. When he saw Sophia beautifully dressed, with her fair hair combed so nicely, he became more benevolent than ever. And he placed her at his right, and squeezed her hand under the tablecloth.

'I am *very* fond of little girls,' he said softly. 'I am sure we shall all be great friends.'

Then he offered her buttered toast, and he spread it with strawberry jam, though that, of course, was more generous than wise. Hans sat among the robbers, and he did not admire their manners at all; for they began at once upon the cake, and, as we all know, nicely behaved people begin tea with bread and butter, and work up to the jam stage, and finish up with cake. But the robbers began with cake, so as to be sure they got it, and finished up with cold pork and apple sauce.

Hans found their conversation very amusing, for they all talked about desperate adventures. When they shouted too loud, the Baron tapped the table with his knife-handle, and said, 'gently boys . . . a little quieter, if you please.' It was strange that though he spoke so kindly, the robbers all seemed to hold him in the greatest awe.

Once he looked down the table and called, 'Arabert, I want you.'

A robber with black hair and a hooked nose turned quite pale. But he pushed back his oak chair and came to the Baron's side. He was terribly frightened.

'Arabert, my dear fellow,' said the Baron gently, 'you have not cut your nails for a long time, I fear. You have not even cleaned them. Now, you know the punishment for that, don't you, Arabert?'

Arabert trembled and his eyes filled with tears.

'You must go to the torture chamber after tea,' said the Baron, 'and get them cut.'

Sophia was so very sorry for the poor robber that she cried, 'Oh do forgive him, please.'

The Baron beamed on her.

'Very well, as it's your first night, I'll forgive him this once. But if it happens again, I fear Arabert must get his punishment.'

The robber looked gratefully at Sophia, and went to his place. And a little while after they rose and left the table.

After tea they all sat round the fire, and the robbers sharpened their knives on scythe-stones, or dozed, or counted up their pocket-money. Hans was carving a funny pipe, and this amused them all, for they could not carve themselves. Sophia, who had not lost her knitting when they captured her in the woods, took out her ball and began to knit.

'What could be more charming,' cried the Baron, who was lolling in a big oak chair, 'than to see such industry in the young? It brings tears to the eyes to observe the play of the little girl's needles. Tell me, my pretty dear, can you knit socks?'

Now Sophia seized upon this as a possible chance in an hour of danger.

'Oh, yes,' she whispered; 'and I could knit your Excellency a fine pair of red socks with this new ball of wool, if you would allow me to do so.'

The Baron clapped his fat hands.

'Charming!' he exclaimed. 'I should like them of all things, and perhaps you could embroider

---

1. Ruby Lind (Lindsay) was a celebrated Australian book illustrator who died of consumption soon after emigrating to England. *Naughty Sophia* is her only major European work.

them with purple and green silk; I *do* like embroidered socks.'

'Yes, I could . . . purple flowers and green leaves.'

'Capital! Capital! Begin at once, my pet, and pray make them wide enough; my foot is a trifle broad.'

He made Sophia sit on a high footstool quite close to him, where he could see his socks being knitted.

A great silence fell upon them all, for some were sleepy, and few had much to say, and the Baron began to feel bored.

'It is really a pity,' he said regretfully, 'that I killed my jester yesterday. I saw him looking into the well, and I thought it would be such a joke to push him in . . . poor, dear fellow! He'd made so many jokes at my expense that I thought I'd make one at his. I always enjoy a practical joke, don't you?'

Sophia looked doubtful.

'It just depends,' she said.

'Why so it does, my pet, so it does. I never knew if the poor fellow saw the joke, for, of course, he couldn't tell me, for his head was in the bottom of the well. He made such a fine splash as he went in. I like splashes, don't you?'

'Well, that depends too,' said Sophia.

'Of course it does . . . how wise you are, you dear little pet! But now I quite miss the poor fellow, for he told us stories in the evening, and that passed the time.'

'I can tell you stories too,' said Sophia. 'Hans and I can invent them during the day, and I will tell them at night. But Hans must help me, so you mustn't play a practical joke on him.'

'Oh, very well; we shall love to hear your stories, but they must have lots of adventure in them . . and only quite a little moral. And don't make any little orphans die in the snow, for we're so soft-hearted we can't bear that. Do begin — right away, my little friend. We'll give you till we count ten to think it out, and then off you go.'

They all counted ten in a loud voice, and then Sophia began, for she had invented lots of stories before she went to sleep on those summer nights on the Wunderberg. The story was full of adventures: there was a buried treasure, or an earthquake, or a fire, or a burglary, or a mad bull almost every five minutes. But her voice soothed the robbers so much, and they lived such a tiring life, that by nine o'clock they were nearly all asleep. Then Aunt Hildegarde rose and lit a candle; the candlestick was solid silver embossed with dragons.

'You had better come to bed,' she remarked; 'you are going to sleep with me.'

'Where will Hans sleep?' asked Sophia.

'Oh, he'll sleep down there by the fire with the rest of them.'

'Do they never go to bed?'

'Dear me, no! Why, you don't think we could afford clean sheets and pillow-cases for all that lot, do you? Besides, they'd go to bed in their boots and spurs, and that would tear the bed-clothes.'

'Do you promise me that Hans will be safe?'

'Oh, yes. Your stories have pleased my grand-nephew very much, and he'll keep you whilst you can think of new adventures. The worst is that he tires very soon of all amusements, and then he starts his little practical jokes; and then — well, I can't answer for your safety.'

Hans got up and kissed Sophia good night. All the robbers were snoring round the fire. Robbers always do snore, you know, and that is why they never really hide under your bed, though you may think they do. For if they snored, then your father would find them out and give them over to the police.

Up in Aunt Hildegarde's room the floor was flooded with moonlight. Sophia stood on a chair to look out of the narrow window. Below her lay the moonlit waters of a mountain-lake. The lake was like a steel shield, so cold and shining. 'Does he ever throw people in there?' asked Sophia, with bated breath.

'Oh, yes, and one never sees them again. It is so deep that no plummet can touch the bottom.'

Aunt Hildegarde would not talk any more. She got into bed and closed her eyes. Then Sophia said her prayers. And when she prayed for Johann and Babina, and for kind Kaiser and Mein Herr the cat, tears came flowing down her cheeks to think of how far she was from those she loved. Then she heard a rustle at the door, and this terrified her greatly. She crept to the door and tried to peep through the keyhole.

'Who's there?' she whispered.

'Only me,' whispered Hans, and though this was not good grammar, Sophia did not mind at all.

'I'm going to sleep at the door and guard you,' whispered Hans.

'Oh, dear Hans, I do think you're a nice boy.'

'Stuff!' said Hans.

He had to say that because he was a boy. But perhaps he was really pleased for all that.

HELENA CONCANNON

(1878–1952)

from:
A GARDEN OF GIRLS; OR, FAMOUS SCHOOLGIRLS OF FORMER TIMES (1914)

[Helena Concannon produced a number of imaginative historical texts for children, many on Irish themes. *A Garden of Girls* sits in a tradition established by nineteenth-century critics of extending imaginative sympathy with historical or fictional characters by inventing their childhood personae. One of the best-known examples of this kind of writing is Mary Cowden Clarke's *The Girlhood of Shakespeare's Heroines* (1850–2), and from the 1880s onwards non-fiction as well as fiction began to be addressed specifically to 'girls'. As well as a chapter on Lady Pamela Fitzgerald, this collection of stories has chapters on 'Darlugdacha. A Little Schoolgirl of St. Brigid' and St Elizabeth, Cecilia Gonzaga, Margaret More, Marie Jeanne D'Aumale, Hélène Massalski, Anna Green Winslow and Marjorie Fleming. Five of the sketches appeared in the *Irish Rosary* in 1912. *A Garden of Girls* was published in London by Longmans, Green and Co. in 1914. For an example of Concannon's feminist history writing, see Volume V, pp. 1113–15.]

INTRODUCTION

I offer this little book (which aims at a reconstruction as faithful and accurate as careful research could achieve, of the real school-life and education of real little girls in many ages, and in many lands) to all those interested in the education of the Irish Girls of To-day — the women of a great and splendid To-morrow.

If it be true, as Cardinal Logue[1] reminds us, that 'A Nation is what its Women make its Men,'

at no time was the question of the Education of her Girls of more importance to Ireland than it is now.

Is all well with that Education? By what tests shall Ireland prove it?

As I write these words, there comes before me a memory of a wonderful little room, at the end of a Dresden Gallery, where the Sistine Madonna[2] hangs beautiful and alone. Here, generation after generation of artists have come to gaze on that Miracle of Loveliness, and to test their own art by its perfection.

So, a little apart in the Gallery of the Scriptures, hangs the immortal picture of the 'Valiant Woman'.[3] And it seemed to me, as I was writing of the Little Girls in my book, that I could see each age and each country coming to that picture as to a shrine, and trying to copy, each in its own medium, its untold perfection.

Do those who have charge of the Education of the Irish Girls of To-day stand often before that picture of the 'Valiant Woman', and do they try to reproduce her image?

If so, all is well with the Education of Ireland Girls — and all will be well with Ireland, the Nation.

---

1. Michael Logue (1839–1924), Cardinal, Archbishop of Armagh and Roman Catholic Primate of All-Ireland 1887–1924.

2. The Sistine Madonna (1512–14) is a painting by Raphael.
3. 'The Gemäldegalerie in Dresden cannot identify a 'Gallery of the Scriptures' or a picture entitled the 'valiant woman' as having been hung anywhere in the gallery in this period. One possibility is that Concannon mistranslated labels in the gallery. Near to the Sistine Madonna was a print gallery which would probably have had a print of Raphael's 'Donna Velata', a painting often compared to the Sistine Madonna. Deborah, Judith, Ruth, Rachel and other old testament heroines were often referred to as 'valiant women'. Gemäldegalerie has a striking picture of Judith, who would certainly be a provocative exemplar for young Irish girls in 1914, but there is not enough evidence to make such an identification with confidence.

from:
PAMELA AT BELLECHASSE: THE SCHOOLDAYS OF LADY EDWARD FITZGERALD

'Pale, pretty Pamela!' So charming a picture she makes, in her husband's letters to his mother, as she sits in the window of the garden of Kildare Lodge, daintily stitching for her baby; or out in the garden (while *he* sits in the window) 'busy in her little American jacket planting sweet pea and mignonette'; or in stately Leinster House,[4] making for him a point of light in its gloom, of comfort in its loneliness, with her baby in her arms, 'her sweet, pale, delicate face bending over it, and the pretty look she gives it,' that our hearts are hers for all time. Even the sordid story of after years cannot alienate them from her. For us, in Ireland, whatever France may have done with her in the hard and pitiless 'twenties' of the nineteenth century, she lives for ever, set by husband's love in an atmosphere of eternal youth, of eternal romance — lovely and pale, and sweet — Lord Edward's girl-wife . . .

The children had a chemist and a botanist among their teachers, a Monsieur Alyon, who accompanied them in all their walks, made them pick flowers, and taught them Botany. M. Alyon gave them, every summer too, a practical course in Chemistry, at which Madame de Genlis[5] made a point of being present. A Pole, called Merys, who was very clever at black-and-white drawing, and water-colours, and had executed many commissions for the Duchess, was employed by Madame to prepare slides for an historical magic lantern. Four different sets of slides were painted by him, from written descriptions made by Madame, and in this attractive way the children learned their Bible History, Ancient History, Roman History, and History of China and Japan. The youngsters, we learn, took their turn week about lecturing with the lantern. Can anything be more modern?

4. Leinster House (architect Richard Castle) was built from 1745 as the Dublin residence of James, Earl of Kildare (later the first Duke of Leinster), the father of Lord Edward Fitzgerald.

5. Stéphanie Félicité Duncres de Saint-Aubin, Comtesse de Genlis (1746–1830), author of works on education, was Pamela's mother.

PATRICIA LYNCH

(1898–1972)

from:
FIDDLER'S QUEST (1941)

[The novel opens when Miles Cadogan, a happy-go-lucky figure about to emigrate to America, leaves his only child Ethne on a boat bound from Liverpool to Dublin, with instructions to go to a shop on the Quays where she'll be looked after and sent on to the west of Ireland, to her grandfather's home. When Ethne arrives penniless at Andy Dolan's shop it turns out that no arrangement has been made and he is too poor and too henpecked by his termagant sister to help Ethne. The child is taken in by the 'Widow' Rafferty, not literally a widow but a woman whose husband left her and his five children to go to America, and has never been heard from again. The Raffertys are very poor and Ethne does the housework and works in a shop while waiting for a reply to a letter she has sent to her grandfather in the West. Ethne is a great fiddler and entertains the tenement with her music. It is 1916 and Eamon, Mrs Rafferty's eldest son, has become involved with a rebel leader, Nial Desmond. Published during the emergency, *Fiddler's Quest* reminds readers of an earlier war and thematizes issues of secrecy, isolation and surveillance also to be found in the work of other Second World War writers such as Elizabeth Bowen (1899–1973). Eventually Ethne and the Raffertys flee Dublin with a wounded Nial Desmond, the Rafferty children are reunited with their father and Ethne finds her grandfather and his island, but the brutal and mysterious disappearance of Miles Cadogan, with which the novel opened, has no resolution. In the following passage Ethne first recognizes her attraction to the rebel.]

NIAL DESMOND

When Mrs. Rafferty came back from her work with the dinner in a big market bag she found the rooms swept, the crocks washed and dried, the fire blazing. She looked forward to reaching home and, instead of the empty desolate rooms, finding Ethne there with her fiddle and the cat and dog stretched at ease before the hearth.

'Sure I'll miss the child terrible when she goes,' she told herself. And she couldn't understand Miles for leaving her behind and the grandfather for not coming across Ireland himself to welcome his granddaughter.

She told Ethne all about Tim Rafferty, who went to America and never came back.

'If we'd stayed in Knockbarra 'twould never have happened,' she said sadly. 'But we'd heard such gran tales of Dublin. We thought we'd only to find our way here an we'd be rich in next to no time. We were terrible poor but sure we never knew hardship till we left Knockbarra. Yet I wouldn't go back. Still an all Dublin's a fine city, a darlin city.'

'Maybe Eamon or Nono will go back one day and you can visit them,' Ethne told her.

'There's many come into the city, but mighty few ever leaves it,' declared the widow. 'Nono thinks she'd love to be in Knockbarra, but she wants the streams an the the mountains an gas an water laid on too. She's no notion of the privation there does be in the country.'

Ethne looked at her in wonder. She thought Bishop's Court a kind place, but she had never known there were such poor homes, yet Mrs. Rafferty was looking about her with pride shining in her eyes.

Now Ethne was alone. The widow had gone out murmuring about Christmas presents. Nono was working late. Eily and Ger were in with old Billy Regan. Patsy had vanished silently with Flitters while his mother was putting on her coat. Eamon had rushed off from breakfast, a slice of bread in his hand. He hadn't been in to dinner and a saucepan of thick soup simmered on the hob, its pungent smell steaming into the room.

Ethne propped her music on the table against a tin box, but it was too low down, so she fixed it on the mantelpiece. She had packed all the music she could, but she grieved over the pile she had left behind.

'Still, if I practise the scales and get these exercises perfect, I'll not be too bad,' she told herself.

There was a looking glass on the mantelpiece and she watched her hands in that as she played.

She could see her serious face and tumbled hair and suddenly she smiled. Something had happened to her playing since she came to the courtyard. The stiffness and doubt had gone from it. She could hear the violin singing to her as she cuddled it against the velvet pad beneath her chin.

The light faded in the room before it was dark in the yard outside, but the fire sent up a red glow so that she had no need to light the gas.

'This is better than getting up at six o'clock in the morning to practise in a cold music room,' she thought with satisfaction, looking back on her schooldays which seemed so far away.

The fire was dying down and, as she turned to reach for one of the paper spills Nono kept folded in a jar on the mantel, she thought the door closed softly.

She had not heard it open, nor had she heard footsteps on the cobbles. Who came so noiselessly? Mrs. Rafferty's strong, solid boots could easily be heard, Eamon marched with a determined tramp, Nono's feet, in their high-heeled city shoes, tapped as if she danced along the streets. But the young ones came and went without sound, even in the new books Eamon had bought them, for when he had money he was generous.

'Is that you, Eily?' asked Ethne. 'Come over to the fire. I'll make it up.'

Ethne spoke in a whisper for she was frightened. There was no answer and, thrusting a spill into the fire, she held its comforting flare up so that she could see across the room.

The door was shut, she was alone, but now the sound of a lorry stopping at the gateway startled her, so that she forgot the other noise.

Lorries passed continually on their way to the North Wall, but Ethne had never heard one stop before. She had seen lorries crowded with soldiers, rifles on their knees, thundering through the streets, where the people watched with hostile or anxious looks.

Sometimes they pulled up outside a house. If the door did not open at once to their knocks, the soldiers burst it in. Then came shouts and cries, the smashing of pictures and furniture and often, when the soldiers came out again, they dragged with them a struggling prisoner.

Could this be one of the military lorries with soldiers coming to search the courtyard? Who could they be seeking?

Footsteps tramped through the gateway. Ethne heard the beating of fists on doors and the sound of Billy Regan's high-pitched voice as he scolded the intruders.

'What ails yez? Haven't yez anythin better to do than to come scarin dacent people out of their wits and terrifyin innocent childer? Sure tis the bad old days come agin!'

Ethne, still holding her violin, stepped towards the door. Before she reached it, it was flung open. A group of soldiers peered in and an officer marched up to her.

'All alone, Miss?' he said, striking a match and lighting the gas.

Ethne nodded.

'Don't be frightened. We're looking for a murdering rebel — Nial Desmond. Has he been this way?'

She shook her head.

'Did you hear anyone running?' the officer asked. 'Did you hear a shot fired? He was seen coming into this yard.'

Ethne remembered that faint closing of a door before the lorry drove up.

'I was playing,' she said. 'I mightn't hear unless there was a big noise.'

He stared about him, smiled as if satisfied, then turned away.

'That's O.K. he must have kept on. Down to the quays by now. But we'll catch him. Take my advice, Miss. Keep that door locked. You never know who may come bursting in. We might come back for a tune.'

They went off laughing. At once the door was pushed slowly ajar and Ger's face was poked round, his eyes wide open with excitement.

'Were you afeared, Ethne?' he whispered. 'Billy ses will you come an have a cup of tay? He has a big bag of ginger cakes.'

'Not now,' said Ethne. 'Thank him very much, but say I mustn't leave the place empty.'

Ger nodded, his face puckered with sympathy. Once more the door closed.

The mumbling of the lorry had grown faint, the excited voices of the neighbours had grown quiet, when the door of Eamon's room opened and the big tabby cat walked out.

'Draw the curtains,' said a gentle voice.

She obeyed and Nial Desmond stepped into the room.

'Did they frighten you?' he asked curiously.

She shook her head.

'That's the girl. I was dead beat,' he said, 'or I wouldn't have come in here. But I had the window open. I'd have got away at the back. They wouldn't have found me. I try not to bring trouble on me friends.'

He smiled and Ethne, who had been feeling very indignant with him, smiled back. Then she frowned.

'You've brought trouble enough to the Raffertys!' she told him severely.

He dropped on the stool by the fire and looked up startled. Laery jumped on the young man's knee and rubbed and purred into his waistcoat.

'What's wrong? Has anything happened?' asked Nial.

'You're worrying Mrs. Rafferty to death the way you're leading Eamon,' Ethne told him. 'She wants him to be a carpenter and he's always running messages for you. She pretends she thinks he's down at the boats, but she knows what he's doing, so does Nono, so do I, so do Patsy and the children.'

'Anyone else?' he asked, looking up at her with a rueful grin.

'Mebbe,' replied Ethne.

Already she regretted finding fault with him, but she hoped she had been right.

He laughed, picked up the steaming saucepan from the hob and tried to drink the soup, but it was too hot. Ethne brought him a spoon and stood watching as he gulped it down.

'There's eating and drinking,' he declared. 'That woman can cook. Was that for you?'

'No, for Eamon.'

'He won't mind,' said Nial laughing.

He stood up and stretched himself.

'A snug little home,' he murmured. 'Don't worry. I won't let harm come to Eamon. He's a great lad. Oh, how I wish I could lie down and sleep.'

His face was lined with weariness. His eyes were closing as he stood swaying on his heels.

'Lie down on Eamon's bed,' urged Ethne. 'I'll keep watch.'

'One day,' he said, 'I'll ask you to play for me, Ethne Cadogan. But now I'm on the run. Don't mind, child. I'll find a corner out in the wind's way and, if I can get as far as Kilmashogue, there's a little hut I know, with a bed and wood and a kettle and a shelf of books. Oh, don't I wish

I were there now. Well, I'll be going.'

He went to the door, looked back and smiled.

'Don't forget, to-day you saved me liberty, or maybe it was only me life.'

He nodded, opened the door, and was gone.

Ethne rubbed her eyes. Had she been dreaming? There was only the empty saucepan with the spoon in it to show that someone had rested on the creepy and talked to her. Laery was carefully cleaning out the saucepan, purring with pleasure.

'I can't blame Eamon,' she thought. 'I wanted to watch for him, and I wish he'd let me take his messages. Mebbe if Mrs. Rafferty knew him she wouldn't mind so much. After all, he is a hero, like Robert Emmet or Michael Dwyer!'[1]

She was standing there gazing at herself in the looking glass, when Mrs. Rafferty came in.

1. Robert Emmet (1778–1803) and Michael Dwyer (1771–1815), United Irishmen.

GRACE ABRAHAM, ELEANOR CAVANAGH, STELLA DONNAN

from:
UNDER THE MOON, OVER THE STARS: YOUNG PEOPLE'S WRITING FROM ULSTER (1971)

[The increased access to education after the Second World War brought a change in teaching strategies and a new interest in children as writers as well as readers. Children's work as creators and transmitters of oral poetry and song is mentioned by Angela Bourke in 'Work and Play', p. 1421. These three poems by children were published in a collection edited by the poet Michael Longley (b. 1939), then literature director of the Arts Council of Northern Ireland, which had solicited children's poems through schools and which published the anthology. Many similar projects have been carried out in Ireland and Britain since the 1970s.]

Grace Abraham (aged nine)

My Dream

Last night
As I lay sleeping
I dreamt
I was a man.
I was big, broad and ugly,
And awful strong.
I could lift

A mountain into a valley,
Houses onto the hills.
When I woke
I found
I was the same little girl.

Eleanor Cavanagh (aged seven)

The Ghost

I'm a ghost,
A little white ghost.
I am very scared of people.
When there are only two,
I think it's a crowd.

Stella Donnan (aged fifteen)

The Dreamer

My two yellow candles
Make love
In my world.
Outside is a sky,
An ink-black sky.
In my world
Of mellow-yellow
My yellow candles
Make love.

JOAN LINGARD

(1932–)

from:
ACROSS THE BARRICADES
(1972)

[Joan Lingard's children's novel about the troubles in Northern Ireland, *The Twelfth Day of July* (1972), charted the relationship between two working-class children — the Protestant Sadie Jackson and the Catholic Kevin McCoy — who live along the peace line in Belfast and who change from enemies to friends in the fortnight leading up to the annual Twelfth celebrations. *Across the Barricades* is the first sequel in what became a sequence of novels about Kevin and Sadie. It begins three years after the first novel, when the protagonists have left school and have not seen one another since the eventful summer when they became friends. Sadie works in a department store and Kevin for a scrap merchant. When they accidentally meet on the street they decide to go for a walk at the top of the local Cave Hill. In many ways the novel follows the commonplace 'Romeo and Juliet' structure found in many novels about the North — see, for example, Patricia O'Connor's *Mary Doherty* and Anne Crone's *Bridie Steen*. Lingard, like Bernard McLaverty in *Cal*, reverses the stereotype by making the female lover a Protestant, and it is in the characterization of Sadie that the novel's greatest strength is found. The series is particularly popular in Britain, where it might be seen to offer a simple but vivid and apparently only mildly politicized account of life for children in the troubles. There are of course disingenuous aspects to Lingard's apparently non-sectarian liberalism — the implied reader of the novels and the normative values against which Belfast in the troubles is to be judged, are definitely those of the United Kingdom rather than the Republic of Ireland.]

Sadie and Kevin sat on the top of Cave Hill with the city spread out below them. They looked down at the great sprawl of factories, offices and houses that were gradually eating further and further into the green countryside beyond. Into the midst of the town came Belfast Lough. It was blue this evening, under a blue, nearly cloudless sky, speckled with ships and spiked with shipyard gantries.

'I like looking down on the town,' said Kevin.

'Me too,' said Sadie. 'It looks so peaceful. I wish it were!'

It was peaceful up there on the hill with the wind playing round their faces and tousling their hair.

Sadie sat with her knees up to her chin, hugging her legs. She felt at ease with Kevin, though of course it was seldom she felt ill-at-ease with anybody, but she also felt a kind of contentment that she was unused to.

'It's funny,' she began.

'What?' He turned on one elbow to look at her.

'I was just thinking a place looks better if you've got somebody with you.'

'Two pairs of eyeballs are better than one. As long as they're the right two pairs of course.'

He has a sweet tongue on him, she thought. He was gazing back down at the city again. She stole a look at him. His face was not very broad but it was firm and had a suggestion of strength about it; it was also deeply tanned with the look of one who was seldom indoors. He probably went home only to sleep. She understood the feeling of restlessness in him. She had it herself.

He pointed down at the ships.

'Have you ever been in a boat, Sadie? A proper one?'

'No. Only a row boat at Bangor.'

They both laughed.

'We'll go to Bangor one day again, will we?' said Kevin. 'And I'll take you out in a row boat. I'll row you across the sea to Scotland. How would you like that?'

'I'd like it fine.'

'You've devil enough in you for it, haven't you?'

Her eyes glinted. 'My mother says I go out of the way to avoid the easy way round.'

'If our mothers were to get together they would probably be saying the same things.'

The words silenced them, for they realized the impossibility of their mothers ever getting together.

'Well,' said Kevin lightly, jumping to his feet, 'will we go?' He held out his hand to her.

They walked down the hill close together but not touching. Lights were springing up in houses, the blue in the sky was deepening and changing. Every moment it looked different; new colours and shades merged and infiltrated the blue: pinks, yellow, turquoise, red.

'Look at the sky,' said Sadie. She felt she had never seen a sky before.

They stopped to look at it and Kevin rested a hand on her shoulder. His hand was warm and she liked the feel of it.

'It's a fair sight,' said Kevin. 'You never see it properly from the street.'

He held her hand as they descended the last part of the hill and kept hold of it once they had reached the bottom.

'Would you like some chips?' he asked. 'My stomach feels in need of something tasty.'

They walked along the main road towards the centre of the city. He told her of some of the funny things they turned up in the scrap business, and she recounted some amusing tales of the women who shopped in the hat department.

He put his hand out to touch her silky fair hair briefly. 'I can't imagine you with a hat on your head.'

They saw a Coca-Cola[1] sign shining ahead and smelt the chips before they reached the café. They went inside. It was warm and bright and a juke box was playing. She sat down at an empty table, he went to the counter to get their order.

She glanced around her. The customers were nearly all teenagers sitting over cups of coffee and Coca-Cola. At the other side of the room she saw two girls she recognized; they worked in the same store. At the moment she saw them, they saw her too.

They got up and came across to her.

'Hi ya, Sadie. What are you doing round here?'

'I've been up the Cave Hill.'

'On your lone?'

'No.' She nodded towards Kevin where he stood in the queue.

They looked him over carefully and rolled their eyes in approval.

'Handsome looking fella. Where did you pick him up?'

'I didn't pick him up. I've known him a long time.'

They examined him again with curiosity. The girls in the shop liked to spend their breaks talking about their boyfriends. Sadie seldom joined in for such talk bored her. They all had one thought in their minds: to get married as soon as possible.

Kevin came back carrying two plates of fish and chips. He set them down on the table. Sadie introduced him reluctantly to the girls who flashed bright smiles at him, but as soon as she said his name she could see their thoughts ticking over. Kevin McCoy. A Catholic name, unmistakably Catholic. Sadie stared them hard in the eyes, daring them to show anything they were thinking.

'Well, we'd better be getting along. See you the morn, Sadie.'

They took another long look at Kevin before they went out. They would be waiting for her in the cloakroom in the morning bursting with questions that she would not answer. There was no one better than Sadie Jackson at telling people to mind their own business.

Sadie laughed.

'What is it?' asked Kevin.

'Them two. They've got something to talk about all the rest of the way home.'

'People have little to talk about,' he said with disgust. 'Come on, eat your fish and chips before they get cold.'

Sadie discovered she was hungry after the fresh air up on the hillside. They ate quickly and then relaxed to drink their coffee. She asked him about the rest of his family.

'How many brothers and sisters do you have now?' she said. 'I don't remember.'

'There's eight of us altogether. One more than when I last saw you and there'll be another next month.'

'Nine,' she said in horror. 'What a life for your mother!'

'She's happy enough,' he said shortly.

'Oh Kevin, don't be daft, what woman wants to wear herself out bringing up a load of kids like that?'

His face closed. He shrugged. He did not want to pursue it any further but she would not let it die. She knew she was bad that way: often when it would be better to let something slide she went on determinedly.

'How can you ever expect to have a decent life if you go on having all those numbers of kids? I don't know why the Pope has to make you do it.'

'You're talking rot.' He was angry now. 'The Pope doesn't make us. You Prods are all the same. You haven't the faintest idea what you're talking about.'

---

1. An American soft drink manufacturer often referenced in late twentieth-century writing to emblematize the triumph of global capitalism over local political concerns.

They glared at one another across the table, then let their eyes fall. They did not want to fight, as they once had. Sadie swallowed hard before she spoke. She always found it difficult to withdraw.

'I'm sorry,' she said. 'I didn't really mean it like that.'

'That's all right.'

It was the first time since their meeting that evening that there was any unease between them. Kevin's brow was creased and his eyes were dark. Sadie fiddled with the spoon in her saucer.

'I wouldn't have nine kids myself, mind you,' he said.

'No?'

'No. I couldn't feed them.' He stood up. 'Come on, I'll leave you home.'

'You don't have to.'

'I don't have to do anything. I never do anything I don't want to do. You should know that about me, Sadie Jackson.'

She laughed and jumped up. 'I know that. But it might be asking for trouble coming into my street.'

'I'll leave you at the head of it, I won't come to your door. I wouldn't want to give your ma a heart attack.'

They were friends again. They walked, hand in hand, through the streets, skirting the areas that were strung with barbed-wire barricades, or that they knew might be troublesome. Once they had to take shelter in a door-way to get out of the path of two men. The men were running, feet clattering on the pavement, their breath gushing out in loud rasps. As they passed, Sadie and Kevin saw the look of the hunted in their faces. Seconds later four soldiers thundered by. When the noise of their feet had faded Sadie and Kevin went on their way. They walked with a feeling of closeness for they knew that they were inviting trouble walking together at all.

ANONYMOUS

from:
SONGS OF BELFAST
(1978)

[*Songs of Belfast* is a collection of ballads and street songs edited by the singer and broadcaster David Hammond, and published in Dublin by Gilbert Dalton in 1978. The best introduction to the following songs is Hammond's own comments in the book on children playing: 'Like children everywhere, the children of Belfast possess their own store of tradition, a symphony of jingles, tongue-twisters, macabre rhymes, vulgar verses, songs of ceremony and custom exploring notions of love, birth, death, courtship, innocence and change. This lore has nothing to do with the world of the nursery rhyme, but is passed on from child to child and is remote from the world of adults, a kind of underground movement' (p. 8). See John Buckley's discussion of children's street rhymes and how they deal with romantic encounters, pp. 1427–9.]

The Wee Falorie Man[1]

I am the wee falorie man
A rattling roving Irishman.
I can do all that ever you can
For I am the wee falorie man.

I have a sister Mary Ann
She washes her face in the frying pan
And out she goes to hunt for a man
I have a sister Mary Ann.

I am a good old working man
Each day I carry a wee tin can
A large penny bap and a clipe of ham
I am a good old working man.

1. Hammond's note: Falorie-man is an odd fellow, a mystery man, perhaps a form of forlorn. Here he is a bit of a braggart, related to the English 'Gable 'oary Man' — the Gabriel, Holy Man.

I'll Tell My Ma
A skipping game

I'll tell my ma when I go home,
The boys won't let the girls alone,
They tossed my hair, they broke my comb,
So that's all right till I go home.
She is handsome, she is pretty;
She is the belle of Belfast City.
She is a-courting one, two, three,
Please can you tell me who is he?

Albert Mooney says he loves her
All the boys are fighting for her.
They rap at the door and ring at the bell
And say, 'My true love, are you well?'

Out she comes, as white as snow,
With rings on her fingers, and bells on each toe.
Oh, Jenny Murray says she'll die
If she doesn't get a fellow with a rolling eye.

Let the wind and the rain and the hail blow
     high;
The snow comes falling from the sky;
Jenny Murray says she'll die
If she doesn't get a fellow with a rolling eye.
One young man is fighting for her,
All the rest, they swear they'll have her.
Let them all say as they will,
Albert Mooney loves her still.

JOANNE FARMER, ADRIAN LEONARD, GILLIAN McCONNELL

from:
THE SCRAKE OF DAWN
(1979)

[In 1979 the poet Paul Muldoon (b. 1951) made a selection of children's poems for the Arts Council of Northern Ireland, to celebrate the International Year of the Child.]

Joanne Farmer (aged five)

The King Went to Visit

The king went to visit
the princess in the castle
and they had a party
and fell in love
and got married
and went to live in Drumbreda.

Adrian Leonard (aged eleven)

Fat Poof

One day I was walking home from school and all I heard was 'Fat Poof' from the other side of the road.
There was a small lad on a bicycle. He was about eight years old. He repeated this gesture again and again. I got fed up and walked over onto the same side of the road as him and digged him in the arm. A sudden cry of pain came from him and he said 'Fat Poof' again. He was holding his bicycle in front of him. I pushed down on the pedal and he jerked forward and fell down on the top of his bicycle. I walked off and left him there.
I was really proud of what I had done. When I got home I told Dad. He said 'Quick thinking Batman'.

Gillian McConnell (aged eleven)

Paradise Island

Maybe you've been to Timbuktoo,
Or maybe you've been to Waterloo,
But I've been to a place where no one has gone,
I've been to Paradise Island at the scrake of
dawn.

The sea is silver
The sand is gold
The food is exotic
And the tall trees are bold.
There's music playing,
And dancers swaying,
On Paradise Island at the scrake of dawn.

Biographies/Bibliographies

Charlotte Brooke

For biography and bibliography, see Volume I, p. 1008.

Adelaide O'Keeffe

LIFE. Adelaide O'Keeffe was born in 1776, the daughter of two Dublin actors, the Protestant Mary (Heaphy) and the Catholic John O'Keeffe. Her father took the children to London when his marriage broke down and then sent Adelaide to be educated in a convent. From the age of twelve she worked as an amanuensis to her near-blind father, a popular dramatist. Her novels are mainly historical and were praised by other women writers; she was even better known for her children's verse, published in Jane and Ann Taylor's *Original Poems for Infant Minds* (1804–5). There is a memoir of her father (d. 1833) in her edition of his poems, O*'Keeffe's Legacy to His Daughter* (1834). She lived in poverty for most of her life, dying in 1865.

CHIEF WRITINGS. *Llewellin* (1797); *Original Poems for Infant Minds* (1804–5); *Patriarchal Times* (1811); *Zenobia, Queen of Palmyra* (London, 1814); *National Characters Exhibited in Forty Geographical Poems* (London: Darton and Harvey, 1818); *Dudley* (London, 1819); *O'Keeffe's Legacy to His Daughter* (1834); *The Broken Sword: Or, A Soldier's Honour* (London, 1854).

Maria Edgeworth

For biography and bibliography, see Volume I, pp. 1051–2.

Cecil Frances Alexander

For biography and bibliography, see pp. 568–9.

Harriet Beaufort

LIFE. Henrietta (Harriet) Beaufort was born at Allenstown, County Meath, in 1778. She was the daughter of Reverend Dr Daniel Augustus Beaufort and his wife Mary Waller (of Allenstown). The family mainly lived at Collon, County Louth, where Dr Beaufort was vicar. As well as being a clergyman, Dr Beaufort was an architect, cartographer and horticulturalist. From 1779 to 1785 Harriet was brought up by her grandparents at Allenstown, while her parents were in exile in England, escaping their creditors. Later in life she returned to reside with her grandparents. In 1798 her eldest sister, Frances Anne (1769–1865), married Richard Lovell Edgeworth and became stepmother to Maria Edgeworth. Some of Harriet's publications have not survived, but in 1819 she published *Dialogues on Botany, for the Use of Young Persons*. In 1830 she published (anonymously) *Bertha's Visit to Her Uncle in England*, in which Bertha Montague is sent from Rio de Janeiro to live with her uncle in England, and keeps a journal for her mother. *The Heiress in her Minority* (1850) is set in Ireland and was much less popular than *Bertha's Visit*, which went into a number of editions. Most bibliographies and library catalogues ascribe these last two books to Jane Marcet (1769–1858), another children's writer. Another of Harriet's sisters, Louisa Beaufort (1781–1867), also wrote for children and in 1819 she published a companion to *Dialogues on Botany* called *Dialogues on Entomology, in which the Forms and Habit of Insects are Familiarly Explained*, published by R. Hunter. Harriet and Louisa ended their days living together. Harriet died in 1865.

CHIEF WRITINGS. *Dialogues on Botany, for the Use of Young Persons: Explaining the Structure of Plants, and the Progress of Vegetation* (London, ??????, 1819); *Bertha's Visit to Her Uncle in England*, 3 vols (London, John Murray, 1830); *The Heiress in Her Minority; Or, The Progress of Character*, 2 vols (London, John Murray 1850).

Charlotte Elizabeth Tonna

For biography and bibliography, see p. 560.

Anna Jameson

LIFE. Anna Brownell Murphy was born in Dublin in 1794, the eldest of five daughters of Denis Brownell Murphy, a miniature painter. The family moved to England and Anna was educated at home, becoming a governess. In 1825 she married Robert Jameson, a lawyer. In 1836 Robert and Anna moved to Canada but she returned after a short time alone. She became a full-time writer, supporting her parents through journalism, travel writing, fiction and especially literary and art criticism. In each genre she focused on women as writers, artists, historical figures, and as readers. From 1851 she received a Civil List pension. She died in 1860.

CHIEF WRITINGS. *Diary of an Ennuyée* (London: Henry Colburn, 1826); *The Loves of the Poets* (London: Henry Colburn, 1829); *Characteristics of Women, Moral, Poetical, and Historical* (London: Saunders and Otley, 1832); *Sacred and Legendary Art* (London: Longman, Green, Brown et al., 1848); *Legends of the Monastic Orders as Represented in the Fine Arts* (London: Longman, 1852, enlarged second edition); *Legends of the Madonna as Represented in the Fine Arts* (London, Longman, Brown, Green, and Longmans, 1852).

Frances Browne

For biography and bibliography, see p. 893.

L.T. Meade

LIFE. Elizabeth Thomasina Meade was born in Bandon, County Cork, in 1844, the daugher of the Reverend Richard Thomas Meade and his wife Sarah Lane. Her father was rector of Nohaval near Kinsale, where she grew up. She died in 1914.

CHIEF WRITINGS. L.T. Meade has been credited as the author of around three hundred titles. It has proved difficult to establish the chronology and publication details of her works, but the following list includes most of the books of specific Irish interest as well as her other best known writings: *Lettie's Last Home* (London: 1875); *The Angel of Love* (London: Hodder and Stoughton, 1875); *Great St. Benedict's. A Tale* (London: 1876), reprinted as *Dorothy's Story; The Children's Kingdom: The Story of a Great Endeavour* (London: [1878]); *Water Gipsies; or, The Adventures of Rag, Tag, and Bobtail* (London: 1879); *The World of Girls* (London: 1886); *Polly: A New-fashioned Girl* (London: 1889); *The Home of Silence* (London: [1890]); *The Cleverest Woman in England* (London: 1898); *Light O'The Morning. The Story of an Irish Girl* (London: [1899]); *The Rebel of the School* (London: 1902); *The Stormy Petrol* (London: 1909).

Kathleen Fitzpatrick

LIFE. No information discovered, other than birth date, 1872.

CHIEF WRITINGS. *The Weans at Rowallan* (London: Methuen, 1905; rpr. as *They Lived in County Down,* with an Introduction by Walter De La Mare and an additional final chapter — authorship unclear — London and New York: 1937).

Letitia MacLintock

LIFE. No information has been found, although Stephen Brown suggests that she may be connected to the County Louth Maclintocks (*A Reader's Guide to Irish Fiction*). In some catalogues her name appears as MacClintock.

CHIEF WRITINGS. *The Cottagers of Glencarran* (Edinburgh, 1869); *Fred and His Friends, and the Wisdom He Learned* (Edinburgh, 1870); *The Story of the Mice: and of Rover and Puss* (Edinburgh, 1870); *Sir Spangle and the Dingy Hen* (London, 1876); *A Boycotted Household* (London, Smith Elder, 1881); *Alice's Pupil* (London, Nizbet and Co. 1883); *Fritz's Experiment; Or, The Poor Salamander. A German Story* (London, 1884); *The March of Loyalty* (London, Tinsley Brothers, 1884); *A Little Candle* (London: T. Nelson, 1886).

Eleanor Hull

For biography and bibliography, see p. 569.

Winifred Letts

For biography and bibliography, see p. 1035.

Helena Concannon

For biography and bibliography, see p. 479.

Patricia Lynch

LIFE. Patricia Nora Lynch was born in Cork on 7 June 1898. She was educated at convent schools in Ireland, England and Belgium. She married the historian R.M. Fox in 1922. Her first book appeared in 1925 and her first work for children in 1932. Her work was hugely popular in Ireland and widely translated. She published over fifty books, her best-known works being *The Turf-Cutter's Donkey, Strangers at the Fair, Fiddler's Quest* and *The Bookshop on the Quay.* In 1947 she published the autobiographical *A Storyteller's Childhood.* She died in Dublin on 1 September 1972.

CHIEF WRITINGS. (Pamphlet) *Scenes from the Irish Rebellion,* repr. in *Rebel Ireland* (London: Workers' Socialist Federation, *c.* 1920). (Children's books); *The Cobbler's Apprentice* (Dublin: Talbot Press, 1930); *The Turf-Cutter's Donkey* (London: Dent, 1934); *King of the Tinkers* (London: Dent, 1938); *Fiddler's Quest* (London: Dent, 1941); *Long Ears* (London: Dent, 1943); *Strangers at the Fair, and Other Stories* (Dublin: Browne and Nolan, 1945); *A Storyteller's Childhood* (London: Dent, 1947); *Orla of the Burren* (London: Dent, 1954); *The Bookshop on the Quay* (London: Dent, 1956); *Fiona Leaps the Bonfire* (London: Dent, 1957); *The Kerry Caravan* (London: Dent, 1967).

Grace Abraham, Eleanor Cavanagh, Stella Donnan

Since these writers were children at the time of publication and were entered for that publication by their schools, it seemed inappropriate to look for biographical information beyond that which appeared in the volume.

Joan Lingard

LIFE. Joan Lingard was born in Edinburgh in 1932. She lived in Belfast from the age of two until she was eighteen. She has lived for many years in Edinburgh.

CHIEF WRITINGS. Novels: *Liam's Daughter* (London: Hodder, 1963); *The Prevailing Wind* (London: Hodder, 1964); *The Tide Comes In* (London: Hodder, 1966); *The Headmaster* (London: Hodder, 1967); *A Sort of Freedom* (London: Hodder, 1968); *The Lord on Our Side* (London: Hodder, 1970); *The Second Flowering of Emily Mountjoy* (London: Paul Harris, 1979); *Greenyards* (London: Hamish Hamilton, 1981); *Sisters by Rite* (London: Hamish Hamilton, 1986); *Reasonable Doubts* (London: Hamish Hamilton, 1986); *The Women's House* (London: Hamish Hamilton, 1989); *After Colette* (London: Sinclair-Stevenson, 1993); *Dreams of Love and Modest Glory* (London: Sinclair-Stevenson, 1995); The Kevin and Sadie Quintet: *The Twelfth Day of July* (London: Hamish Hamilton, 1970); *Across the Barricades* (London: Hamish Hamilton, 1972); *Into Exile* (London: Hamish Hamilton, 1973); *A Proper Place* (London: Hamish Hamilton, 1975); *Hostages to Fortune* (London: Hamish Hamilton, 1976). Other Children's Novels: *Dark Shadows* (London: Hamish Hamilton, 1998); *The File on Fraulein Berg* (London: Julie MacRae, 1980); *The Clearance* (London: Hamish Hamilton, 1973); *The Resettling* (London: Hamish Hamilton, 1975); *The Pilgrimage* (London: Hamish Hamilton, 1976); *The Reunion* (London: Hamish Hamilton, 1977); *Tug of War* (London: Hamish Hamilton, 1989); *Between Two Worlds* (London: Hamish Hamilton, 1991); *Night Fires* (London: Hamish Hamilton, 1993); *Natasha's Will* (London: Hamish Hamilton, 2000); *Rags and Riches* (London: Hamish Hamilton, 1988); *Glad Rags* (London: Hamish Hamilton, 1990); *Lizzie's Leaving* (London: Hamish Hamilton, 1995); *A Secret Place* (London, Hodder, 1998); *The Freedom Machine* (London: Hamish Hamilton, 1986); *The Guilty Party* (London: Hamish Hamilton, 1987); *The Winter Visitor* (London: Hamish Hamilton, 1983); *Strangers in the House* (London: Hamish Hamilton, 1981); *The Gooseberry* (London: Hamish Hamilton, 1978), re-issued as *Odd Girl Out* (London: Hodder, 2000); *Snake Among the Sunflowers* (London: Hamish Hamilton, 1977); *Hands Off Our School* (London: Hamish Hamilton, 1992); *Frying as Usual* (London: Hamish Hamilton, 1971); *Secrets and Surprises* (London: Macmillan, 1991); *Clever Clive and Loopy Lucy* (London: Macmillan, 1993); *Slo Flo and Boomerang Bill* (London: Macmillan, 1994); *Sulky*

Suzy and Jittery Jack (London: Macmillan, 1995); *Tom and the Tree House* (London: Hodder, 1998); *The Egg Thieves* (London: Hodder, 1999); *River Eyes* (London: Hodder, 2000). Picture Books: *Can You Find Sammy the Hamster?* (London: Walker Books, 1990), illustrated by Jan Lewis; *Morag and the Lamb* (London: Walker Books, 1991), illustrated by Patricia Casey; *The Same Only Different* (London: Glowworm, 2001), illustrated by Olwyn Whelan.

BIOGRAPHY AND CRITICISM. Joe Cleary, *Literature, Partition, and the Nation-State: Culture and Conflict in Ireland, Israel and Palestine* (Cambridge: Cambridge University Press, 2002).

Joanne Farmer, Adrian Leonard, Gillian McConnell

Since these writers were children at the time of publication and were entered for that publication by their schools, it seemed inappropriate to look for biographical information beyond that which appeared in the volume. In 1979 Joanne Farmer was a pupil at St Patrick's Primary School, Armagh; Adrian Leonard was a pupil at Stranmillis Primary School, Belfast; Gillian McConnell was a pupil at Olderfleet Primary School, Larne.

ANGELA BOURKE, *Editor*

Oral Traditions

Not all important ideas are found in books. Before writing began, law, history, genealogy, poetry, stories, records of title to land — everything comprised by the idea of 'documents' — was transmitted orally. Even today, among people who do not write, or write much, oral culture persists as an important medium of creative expression and, to a lesser extent, of record-keeping. Humans have developed elaborate verbal art forms through which to arrange knowledge and ideas in patterns, partly in order to conserve and transmit them with maximum efficiency, partly for the aesthetic pleasure of such patterning. Like needlework, painting, dance, cooking and other arts, oral verbal art offers ways of thinking and knowing which can be independent of the linear modes of writing and print. Like any art, it offers individuals and communities ways of constructing and maintaining identity, often against considerable external pressure.

It is perhaps at first sight anomalous to include oral traditions in an anthology consisting primarily of Irish *writing*: the texts presented under this heading are for the most part precisely those which were not written by their composers, but were spoken, recited, chanted or sung. As other sections in volumes IV and V attest, however, women's relation to the written word has never been simple, while women's access to literacy has often been different from men's. This section serves in part as background to the others, some of which represent mediations of oral tradition through writing; in itself, however, it presents material without which no representation of women's relation to the word in Ireland could be comprehensive, much less complete.

Writing was introduced to Ireland along with Christianity in the early Middle Ages, but until relatively recently, the ability to read and write was confined to a minority, most of whom were men, while oral culture continued as the medium through which the majority expressed themselves. Story and song were the principal forms they used, backed up by proverbs, riddles and other genres: age-old devices through which performers negotiate for the attention of an audience and frame a moment of time as separate from the continuing present. Stories and songs were performed in many contexts, but featured prominently on occasions when people gathered in groups: at weddings and wakes, at 'patterns', as local pilgrimages to holy wells or other sacred sites were called, and at the *meitheal*,[1] or communal work-party.

In the nineteenth century, a profound change overtook the lives of ordinary people in Ireland, one aspect of which was a dramatic increase in literacy following the establishment of the national schools in the 1830s. After the Great Famine of 1845–9, as the wealth and prestige of the Catholic church increased, and many of the landlord class retreated to England, the propertied Catholic middle class, from which most of the clergy and religious were drawn, came to dominate public life, gradually distancing itself from the rural poor. The middle class was literate and English-speaking, with clearly defined ideas about gender and a rigid decorum of sexuality and marriage. Many of the poor were Irish-speaking, and most were illiterate. Dying of starvation or fever, or emigrating in order to survive, over a million of them became victims of the Famine. Meanwhile, the interests which came to dominate Irish life systematically devalued their culture, and wakes, 'patterns', and the *meitheal* became less common.

1. See Anne O'Dowd, *Meitheal: A Study of Co-operative Labour in Rural Ireland* (Baile Átha Cliath: Comhairle Bhéaloideas Éireann, 1981).

Songs continued to be sung, however, stories told and riddles asked, in the social gatherings which were still part of people's lives, urban as well as rural. New works of verbal art were created, and old ones adapted to changing circumstances. Individual women and men continued to weave and repair a fabric of shared reference that was too useful and aesthetically rewarding to be discarded. Literacy advanced gradually, and unevenly. Written productions like political ballads, intended for popular consumption, were constructed according to the conventions of oral composition, and adopted into their repertoire by oral performers, while some genres — notably jokes, riddles and children's games — are still transmitted orally, even among the highly literate. Irish continues to be spoken as the language of daily use in several areas called Gaeltacht, chiefly along the west and south coasts, and in individual homes and workplaces all over Ireland, but until recently, advancing literacy meant literacy in English only, so in Gaeltacht areas the status of oral poetry and storytelling remained high, even as it declined elsewhere.

By the end of the twentieth century, the revolution in global communications and a huge increase in migration in and out of Ireland had made the concept of Gaeltacht as a distinct geographical area problematic. Less Irish was being spoken in the designated areas; more elsewhere.[2] Learners of Irish all over the world found language classes and websites through which to connect to a 'virtual' Gaeltacht, while electronic media and telecommunications led to what Walter Ong has called 'secondary orality': an abandonment of the written word in favour of the spoken. A strong sense of regional identity remains, however, and the new media industries which flourish in Gaeltacht areas draw much of their inspiration from indigenous traditions of storytelling and music-making. All the five, long, complex stories in the subsection 'International Folktales' were collected in Gaeltacht areas, and all are given here in the original Irish, with English translation. Half the thirty songs in 'The Song Tradition' (see pp. 1312–1364) are in Irish

too, reflecting the rich singing tradition in that language. 'Legends of the Supernatural' are found in both Irish and English: the system they articulate, of referring to and dealing with the unknown and the ambiguous, was so fundamental to Irish culture at the time of language change, and so intimately mapped onto the physical and social landscape, that it survived to some extent in all areas.

Traveller traditions are a special case, at once part of and apart from the wider currents of song and story in Ireland. Irish Travellers' lives traditionally include extended periods of nomadism, both in and outside Ireland, so that their access to schooling was minimal until recently; literacy levels remained low, and the prestige of oral tradition correspondingly high. John Reilly's 'The Well Below the Valley', which he sang for Tom Munnelly in 1967, two years before his death, is an international ballad found in early collections, but this and a couple of fragmentary texts collected by Munnelly remain the only sound recordings of this ballad from oral tradition. 'The Well Below the Valley' appears in 'The Song Tradition' (see p. 1335), while 'Storytelling Traditions of the Irish Travellers' includes examples of both the international folktale and the legend, all told in English.

The Irish language, with its ancient literature and vibrant oral traditions, was an important rallying point for the nationalist movements of the nineteenth and early twentieth centuries. Members of the metropolitan middle class, like their counterparts elsewhere in Europe, became increasingly interested in rural traditions at the same time as they romanticized wild, remote landscape. Both seemed to embody national character, as much for those who sought to see Ireland as exotically 'other', as for revivalists within the country, where opposing factions fought for control of new literary expression in Irish. Debate raged about whether a new literature should draw exclusively from 'native', often oral sources, or respond to contemporary movements elsewhere.[3] Revivalist periodicals regularly published items of oral tradition submitted by readers, especially from Gaeltacht

---

2. For an informed discussion of Irish as a world language see James McCloskey's bilingual *Guthanna in Éag: An Mairfidh an Ghaeilge Beo? / Voices Silenced: Has Irish a Future?* (Baile Átha Cliath: Cois Life, 2001).

3. See Philip O'Leary, *The Prose Literature of the Gaelic Revival 1881–1921: Ideology and Innovation* (Philadelphia: Pennsylvania State University Press, 1994).

areas. Oireachtas na Gaeilge, with its literary and singing competitions, was founded in 1897. Apart from a fifteen-year gap in the 1920s and 1930s, it has been held every year since, offering a platform especially for *sean-nós* (old style) singing in Irish. Although some would argue that its focus on competition led to a sanitization and dilution of the singing tradition, it undoubtedly lent prestige to the art of *sean-nós* at times when it might otherwise have died out, and many of the singers whose performances are documented here have been prizewinners.

With the foundation of the independent Irish state, a policy of cultural recovery was instituted, which gave new prominence, and state funding, to the revival of the Irish language and to the collecting, archiving and preservation of oral traditions, particularly those of the Gaeltacht. The Irish word *béaloideas*, literally, 'oral teaching', was chosen as the name for that which would be preserved and studied. As in other English-speaking countries, the term 'folklore', coined in England in 1846 by William Thoms, was accepted also and given academic standing, despite its self-consciously archaic and romantic overtones. The Folklore of Ireland Society (An Cumann le Béaloideas Éireann) was founded in 1926, and began publication of its journal, *Béaloideas*, edited by James H. Delargy (Séamus Ó Duilearga, 1899–1980), the following year. In 1930, with government support, the Irish Folklore Institute was founded, succeeded in 1935 by the Irish Folklore Commission (Coimisiún Béaloideasa Éireann). Delargy was appointed director and a state grant of £3,200 was provided, representing £100 for the collecting and cataloguing of oral traditions from each county of Ireland, north and south. At first, most collectors worked with pen and paper, but before the advent of the tape recorder the Commission's full-time collectors also had the use of the Ediphone recording machine, invented by Thomas Edison in the late nineteenth century. Sound was recorded on wax-covered cylinders and could be played back through the tube into which the informant spoke or sang. Very few of these Ediphone recordings survive, however, as collectors were forced to economize, especially during the war, by reusing the expensive cylinders after transcribing them.

The official importance given to Irish oral traditions had two results. On the one hand, like Finland and some other emerging nation-states, but quite unlike the established world powers of the twentieth century, Ireland accumulated an enormously rich folklore archive, and built extensive scholarly expertise in vernacular culture. On the other, as the Irish language and its oral traditions were consistently invoked by the most conservative elements of a conservative society as unchanging expressions of censorious authority or as officially sanctioned entertainment, both came to be identified in the minds of many with the prescriptions of authoritarian patriarchal nationalism. The shawled, sharp-eyed, benign image of Peig Sayers appears in all manner of tourist iconography, especially in the Gaeltacht of west Kerry, where she lived and died. She was a magnificent storyteller, whom scholars travelled from all over Europe to visit at her home on the Great Blasket Island, and her Irish-language autobiography, *Peig*, written down by her son from her oral account of her own life, was a familiar feature of the school curriculum from shortly after its publication in 1936, until 1995. It was embraced by the educators of the newly independent state as a document of indigenous, uncorrupted values, and cordially disliked by many who studied it for the same reason, but it tells much about the social and economic, as well as the imaginative and spiritual, dimensions of a woman's life at the westernmost edge of Europe early in the twentieth century. Since it ceased to be a required text for schools, *Peig* has acquired enthusiastic new readers in Irish and in translation.

The Italian socialist thinker Antonio Gramsci (1891–1937) presented oral traditions as the subversive, pluralist, unruly, and potentially revolutionary expressions of a subaltern class, but his and subsequent ideas were not applied to the Irish situation until the 1980s and had relatively little influence.[4] James Delargy was appointed Professor of Irish Folklore at University College Dublin in 1946, a post he held until 1969. As Honorary Director of the Irish Folklore Commission, however, he was released from professorial responsibilities to concentrate on the collection, preservation,

---

4. For fully documented discussion of these issues, published while this volume was in preparation, see Diarmaid Ó Giolláin, *Locating Irish Folklore* (Cork: Cork University Press, 2000).

indexing and publishing of Irish Folklore: the Commission's brief did not include teaching. Folklore was first offered as a subject to students when the Commission moved from its headquarters in St Stephen's Green to the new university campus at Belfield in 1971. The Irish Folklore Commission changed its name to the Department of Irish Folklore, UCD, and so began a new era of the study of oral traditions in Ireland.

Often poorly understood within the world of literacy, oral culture is sometimes regarded as a lower, inferior stage on a ladder of cultural evolution. In this it occupies the same side of a polarized pair as Irish does in relation to English, female in relation to male, or, as Bairbre Ní Fhloinn points out in her introduction to 'Storytelling Traditions of the Irish Travellers', as nomadic peoples do in relation to settled communities. As the unstandardized, uncentralized expressions of ordinary people, however, oral traditions live alongside writing and print culture and interact with them as well as with each other. They are not one, but many, and offer a record of eloquence and a reservoir of ideas which constitute a valuable, and sometimes a dissident, counterpart to the dominant discourses found in print. Like the handcrafted and the homemade in other areas of human creativity, they range from the merely useful, economical or amusing to the highly polished and unique.

As artists do in perhaps all media, oral performers offer entertainment, but the space within the frame they establish may also be used to contemplate and convey information about almost anything, from the trivial to the deadly serious. Oral verbal arts need live audiences for their transmission, but the music and metre of songs and the highly patterned shapes of oral stories mean that the solitary individual can also remember, rehearse and contemplate them. The most notable performances come from people who have thought long and deeply about their material. Such artists do not function in a vacuum, however, and depend on their audiences not just for attention, but for critical discrimination and validation. Repertoire is a mesh of songs, or a network of stories. A storyteller always knows more than one story; a singer more than one song, and many of the most celebrated know hundreds. Stories, songs, proverbs, riddles, local history,

place-names and place-lore, and the system of classification which underlies much traditional practice, are all interconnected and cross-referenced in individual and shared memory.

As Ríonach uí Ógáin and Tom Munnelly remark below, much of the repertoire of oral verbal art was common to women and men. Some is anonymous, but many songs in particular are attributed to individual composer-singers. Hugh Shields makes an important distinction between '"makers" ... local song-makers who are usually themselves singers [and] "poets" ... other poets whose written words have been set to traditional airs'.[5] Songs are often accompanied by stories of their composition and transmission, giving a picture of life in Ireland which is independent of and far removed from the centralized discourses of print and other media. This is not to say that print did not play a role in the dissemination of oral verbal art: many songs were learned from broadsheets and songbooks; but the performers of oral tradition are also its critics: discerning selectors of material which has value and relevance for them and for their audiences. Songs and stories whose strength derives from living human voices, male as well as female, are presented here in print as a window on the intellectual, emotional and aesthetic life of women in Ireland.

It is illuminating to look at women in Irish oral tradition from at least three perspectives. First we may observe the individual performer as an active artist, balancing her expression of self with the concerns of the audience and of the wider society; second, we may examine the material of oral traditions: the story- and song-themes and the repeated phrases and formulae which the singer or storyteller uses as the grammar and vocabulary, or recipe and ingredients, of a finished performance; third come the collectors, archivists, editors and scholars who have shepherded oral traditions into the world of books. Their objectives have varied over time, as has the degree to which they have attempted to communicate, or succeeded in conveying, the flavour of oral performance. They represent an important element in a series of debates about cultural identity and gender in Ireland.

5. Hugh Shields, *Narrative Singing in Ireland: Lays, Ballads, Come-All-Yes and Other Songs* (Dublin: Irish Academic Press, 1993), p. 251.

Women turn up as artists of memory and performance in Irish oral traditions, and as the subject of innumerable stories, songs, proverbs, jokes, riddles and sayings. Some of the earliest collectors and publishers of these texts were women — or ladies, as they were known — but when the collection of folklore was professionalized in the 1930s, it became for a time an exclusively male pursuit. Patricia Lysaght describes the early collectors and collections of folklore in her introduction to 'Writing Oral Traditions', while Éilís Ní Dhuibhne assesses the effect of gender on both the telling and the collecting of stories in 'International Folktales'.

Oral performance allows individuals to earn prestige and respect, often over a wide area and many generations, and to convey their understanding of life to their peers and to younger people. While this is true for both women and men, women's traditional oral performance in any culture offers information about their role in society — often more active and influential than outside observers acknowledge — and about specifically female concerns and attitudes. Studying women's oral performance in Ireland, we find vividly expressive personalities and talented artists, fully acknowledged as such, although they may be almost unknown in the written record. Meanwhile, sometimes in unexpected ways, their material illuminates social issues better known to readers through history and literature.

When women are the subjects of oral narrative, song or other genre, the performer may be either a man or a woman, the representation sympathetic or not. But every oral performance represents an interplay between communal, or received, values and the will of the individual, so that 'communal' values are constantly being renegotiated. Oral traditions contain a great many gender stereotypes, but these are by no means homogeneous, and the very art forms which convey them are also frequently used to challenge and subvert them. Folklore scholars are keenly aware of the feminist potential of the oral poetry and narrative they study, but others have been slow to discard the view of oral tradition as a reservoir of demeaning anti-feminist stereotype.[6]

The texts which follow are both familiar and strange. Writing, in Walter Ong's words, restructures consciousness.[7] The thought processes we bring to our reading of new material have been formed by our familiarity with printed and handwritten text and are currently being reshaped by electronic media; our learning is structured by the availability of reference books, lists, charts and tables, in ways that are utterly foreign to members of purely oral cultures. Without writing, memory is everything: a sentence once spoken, or a difficult formulation finally arrived at, are gone forever unless someone — and preferably many people — can remember them. So oral culture abounds in repetitions and mnemonics; in alliterations, rhymes, and formulaic closures. The concept in biology of the gene pool provides a useful analogy for the way an oral tradition works: just as an animal or plant species, in order to evolve over generations, must have many features among which to 'choose' those which will best adapt it to new circumstances, so oral tradition must operate on a principle of redundancy and surplus: there must be poor singers as well as good singers in order that there may be wonderful singers, and there must be tellings of stories which are gapped, inconsistent or otherwise unsatisfactory, at least to the reader of transcribed text, so that the truly talented storyteller may have an audience and an incentive to excel. Excellence in oral verbal art is achieved not through drafts revised and discarded, or through footage left on a cutting-room floor, but through a multiplicity of performances, in the course of which an aesthetic is developed, refined and transmitted.

For readers of English, a 'folktale', 'legend' or 'ballad' is most often a text in a book, suitable, perhaps, for reading to children. One offshoot of the Romantic movement in Europe was the rush by educated people to collect and publish 'popular antiquities': the oral poetry and storytelling which were still the major verbal art of rural, and especially of remote, areas. This paralleled the movement to seek out wild plants, found also in the wild landscapes preferred by the Romantics, and bring them into cultivation

---

6. See Joan N. Radner (ed.), *Feminist Messages: Coding in Women's Folk Culture* (Chicago: University of Illinois Press, 1993).

7. Walter Ong, *Orality and Literacy: The Technologizing of the Word* (London and New York: Methuen, 1982), p. 78.

in botanic gardens. The Grimm brothers in Germany and Francis James Child at Harvard University were scientists. They collected and published texts which were anthologized again and again, becoming part of that monolith known as 'English literature'. Fairytales and ballads were presented as though written directly from the lips of singers and storytellers, but in fact had usually been edited to render them suitable for drawing-room and nursery and to give them the coherence and continuity demanded of written text.

The question of authorship is not straightforward in any oral tradition, for performance is at least as important as composition, and in fact is often part of the same event, as Albert B. Lord pointed out in his groundbreaking study of oral epic, *The Singer of Tales*, in 1960.[8] Folktales in particular, although their basic structure may be found over several continents and many centuries, gain all their flavour and much of their meaning from the artistry of the person telling them and from their context. As Éilís Ní Dhuibhne points out in her essay on 'International Folktales', 'It would be surprising if a version of "Cinderella" told in Galway in 1937 carried the same coded messages as a version written down in France in 1695, or told in Germany in 1800' (see p. 1216). In the case of songs, too, although some are attributed to named authors, performance, not text, is what is remembered and discussed. Attributing such songs to 'Anonymous' is to misrepresent how they are known and heard, for their singing, usually among people known to one another, is anything but anonymous. As an actor 'creates' a role written by someone else, the talented traditional singer may be said to 'create' a song, and is often granted an informal but exclusive right to perform it. 'Traditional' in this context does not mean sternly conservative or resistant to change; nor does it imply anything about the singer's ancestry, for there have been fine traditional singers who learned this music as adults. A 'traditional singer' as the term is used at the beginning of the twenty-first century, is one who possesses a particular combination of musical, lyrical and personal sensibilities,

recognized by other singers and by the audience. While other sections of this anthology head each extract with the name of its *writer*, therefore, the names given in the headings of extracts here are those of the storytellers and singers from whom they were collected. An exception has been made in the case of the highly personalized eighteenth- and nineteenth-century texts in 'Lamenting the Dead', where the names given are those of the probable composers.

Much of the material given here comes from the manuscripts and sound recordings of the Irish Folklore Collection (IFC), housed in the Department of Irish Folklore at UCD; other items have come from printed sources and commercial recordings, from other manuscripts, and from recordings made by the Irish and British broadcasting services, Radio Telifís Éireann (RTÉ) and the British Broadcasting Corporation (BBC). Irish-language material is given in the original and in translation, and since the chief object of the anthology is to provide readable texts in English, Irish-language texts have not been standardized beyond a minimal silent editing where necessary for comprehension. In general, Gaeltacht placenames are given in Irish, in the form used by An Post, the postal service. Other forms of some names are in common use, however, and will sometimes be found in quoted material: Rann na Feirsde for Rinn na Feirste, for instance. Personal names may also present some problems, especially when encountered in books or on record labels. In Gaeltacht areas, the custom of women taking their husbands' surnames was not widely adopted, although most dealings with the world of officialdom required it. In addition, many storytellers and singers are known by nicknames or patronymics, and by names in both Irish and English. Storyteller Anna Nic an Luain was born Anna Nic an Bhaird, but generally known in her home area as Anna John Chiot; Peig Sayers, whose husband was Peatsaí 'Flint' Ó Gaoithín, kept the same surname throughout her life, but was sometimes known as Peig Mhór: Big Peig; Mrs Elizabeth Cronin, traditional singer, was known as Bess, but also as Éilís Bean Uí Chróinín, while Seosamh Ó hÉanaí was also called Joe Éinniú and Joe Heaney.

Professional folklore collectors go to considerable lengths to transcribe accurately what

8. Albert B. Lord, *The Singer of Tales* (Cambridge, Mass.: Harvard University Press, 1960), *passim*.

they hear — writing *those couple they got married*, for instance, rather than 'correcting' it to *that couple* — so texts in both English and Irish will be found sometimes to depart quite dramatically from the written standard. Placenames, personal names and other details often alter as songs and stories travel, and may end up garbled. Such variation serves two purposes: it can give valuable information about dialect, and, by clearly distinguishing those texts transcribed as heard from those copied from books, it testifies to their oral provenance. Warranties like this are important in mapping the distribution of stories, ballads, and other items, many of which have been in circulation for centuries, across oceans and language barriers. They enable scholars to trace innovation and creativity across a given genre, and remind us as readers that the songs and stories in question were learned not from books, but by listening.

Folklorists classify folktales, legends and ballads using a number of international cataloguing systems: these have been included in the material below, but have been kept to a minimum.

Unlike other sections of this anthology, the subsections in 'Oral Traditions' are not dated, although individual items are, where possible. Starting and finishing dates are not appropriate to the presentation of material whose appearance in print may come many years after its performance, while the performance itself may have been only one in a series lasting almost a lifetime. It is true to say, as Lord did in *The Singer of Tales*, that 'in a very real sense, every performance is a separate song',[9] but part of the interest of the songs and stories of oral tradition lies in the way they combine what has been learned from others with what an individual seeks to express on a given occasion.

Much more could have been included in this section, had space allowed, and many different selections could have been made and defended; the oral tradition is not dead, although it is greatly changed, and it continues to generate new stories and new songs. The requirements of an anthology such as this one are different from those of an archive or cataloguing system, and my concern has been to offer as wide a range as possible of the material which shows women defining themselves in performance, and being defined by others. This has meant choosing some items for the talent of the performer, and others for the sake of comprehensiveness — if not completeness — in representing genre; seeking out texts which would represent cities and towns as well as rural areas; the English language as well as Irish; children and 'minor' performers as well as those widely celebrated. It has led to a division of the material into nine subsections, beginning with 'Life Stories' and ending with 'Writing Oral Traditions'. Some subsections, such as 'International Folktales' and 'The Song Tradition', have had to be long, simply in order to give a sense of their range. Others contain an element of overlap, so that 'Storytelling Traditions of the Irish Travellers' includes both international folktales and legends of the supernatural, while songs appear in 'Lamenting the Dead' and 'Work and Play', as well as in 'The Song Tradition'. 'Lamenting the Dead', 'Spirituality and Religion in Oral Tradition' and 'Work and Play' have been allotted separate subsections as three distinct areas in which women's participation has been crucial. 'Writing Oral Traditions', dealing as it does with women's contribution to folklore scholarship before and after the founding of the Irish Folklore Commission in 1935, contains a variety of material, including several legends. Six editors have contributed the material presented here, and work by Patricia Lysaght, Éilís Ní Dhuibhne and Angela Bourke will be found in more than one subsection. Each subsection is identified as the selection made by one or two editors; in the latter case, introductions, headnotes and translations are individually initialled.

9. A.B. Lord, *The Singer of Tales*, p. 4.

ANGELA BOURKE and PATRICIA LYSAGHT, *Editors*

Life Stories

All of the three women whose stories are excerpted here have been literate, but they have also excelled in oral verbal art. They have been assisted into print by others, sufficiently impressed by the fluency of their verbal memories to want to write them down for publication. In the case of Peig Sayers, the writing of her story in Irish in the 1930s, when a Fianna Fáil government was in power for the first time, was an important event in Irish cultural politics and was instigated by visitors from Dublin to the Great Blasket Island; the publication of Nan Joyce's book in 1985 was part of a wider movement to assist Travellers' civil rights, while Leland Bardwell interviewed Rosaleen Ferguson for *Force 10*, a magazine whose innovative approach is characteristic of regional cultural initiatives at the end of the twentieth century.

These life stories differ from much of what follows in this section in that each is unique to its teller, rather than representing an individual's interpretation of a shared tradition. They emerge from that shared tradition, however, and show women narrators taking responsibility for maintaining communal as well as individual memory. Speakers place their own lives within a network of relationships, and situate them in landscapes in which the things that surprise the individual serve to frame the familiar. Contrasts drawn between past and present risk being dismissed as nostalgia, or even as sentimentality, but they are the markers of oral social history, lending authority to the narrative and to its teller, defining a space in which she may express her individual voice and vision, and aiding her memory. Unlike many of those interviewed for modern oral histories, the women whose words appear here have told their stories repeatedly and, in the cases of Peig Sayers and Nan Joyce at least, for attentive audiences.

The women represented here have fashioned over years an oral memoir form which owes much to the skills of formal storytelling. Their accounts are larded with references to folk beliefs and practices, those of Peig Sayers, in particular, showing the currency of proverbs and of traditional prayers and blessings in the everyday language of Irish-speakers, together with the care taken by a skilled verbal artist in constructing a narrative of adherence to social norms. Motherhood is a recurring theme, but the women who tell their life stories also insist on the subjectivity of the girls they have been.

ANGELA BOURKE

PEIG SAYERS

(1873–1958)

from:
PEIG .i. A SCÉAL FÉIN (1936)

[Educated essentially through the medium of English, Peig Sayers's genius in her adult life was her command of the spoken Irish language, which was recognized by the many eminent scholars and students of modern Irish who visited her in her island home. Among them was the English scholar Robin Flower (1881–1946) who spent a considerable amount of time on the Great Blasket between 1910 and 1930. In *The Western Island or The Great*

Blasket (1944, p. 49) he specifically mentions Peig's mastery of language as follows: 'For Big Peg — Peig Mhór — is one of the finest speakers on the island; she has so clean and finished a style of speech that you can follow all the nicest articulations of the language on her lips without any effort; she is a natural orator with so keen a sense of the turn of phrase and the lifting rhythm appropriate to Irish that the words could be written down as they leave her lips, and they would have the effect of literature with no savour of the artificiality of composition.'

Peig's years on the island (1892–1942) encompassed a period of intense cultural and political activity in Ireland. The west of Ireland, especially the Gaeltacht or Irish-language areas and particularly the islands, had special cultural and symbolic significance for cultural nationalists and those involved in the fight for independence. From the 1930s this interest was largely translated into a movement to learn the Irish language, and the Great Blasket became a focal point for those so engaged.[1] It was during this period that Peig Sayers became acquainted with two women visitors to the island from Dublin — Máire Ní Chinnéide and Léan Ní Chonnalláin — who persuaded her (as other scholars and visitors from outwith the island had encouraged Tomás Ó Criomthain and Muiris Ó Súilleabáin[2]), to dictate her life story to her son Micheál Ó Gaoithín (Ó Guithín), recently returned to the island from the USA. Edited by Máire Ní Chinnéide, one book appeared in 1936 under the title *Peig .i. A Scéal Féin* and a further volume, *Machtnamh Seana-Mhná*, was published in 1939.

Peig Sayers had spent more than forty years living on the Great Blasket when these works appeared. They are important contributions to the descriptions of life on the island from a woman's perspective. The social effects on the island families of economic decline resulting in emigration and falling birthrate are graphically portrayed. The high incidence and heartbreak of child mortality is another striking feature of her account of island life. Of the ten children born to her Peig says 'death swept three of my family in their infancy and then the measles took Siobhán,

a fine bouncer of a girl eight years old'. Her son Tomás was killed in a fall from a cliff on the island in 1920. Four of her remaining children emigrated permanently to the USA; the fifth, Micheál Ó Gaoithín (Maidhc File, 1904–74), returned to the Great Blasket from Boston when his health failed.

Peig's attitude to the sea emerges as an important element in her relationship with the island. Although she became integrated into the life of the island and spoke about it as an insider, she could, and did, also assess it from the point of view of the mainlander that she was: Peig Sayers, in fact, remained a reluctant 'Island woman'. Her works are clouded by a sense of confinement, isolation, adversity and the frugality which the island life entailed. Speaking to her son Muiris as he is about to emigrate she says: ''Twould be a bad place that wouldn't be better for you than this dreadful rock . . . All around me I can see nothing on which a man can earn a living, for here there's neither land nor property. I wouldn't like to make a cormorant of you, my son.' Fear of the sea on which the island economy was so largely dependent is ever present in her accounts. Shortly after coming to the island on her marriage she declared: 'I think that this is a very confined place with the sea out there to terrorize me . . . and it's out on that sea my husband will spend half his life from this day forward.' She was also terrified that her children would drown in the sea because 'the breed of the sea was in them', and she would smash their toy boats in an effort to keep them away from the shore. Acutely aware that the islanders were at the mercy of the winter storms she talks about 'the great sea coming on top of us and the storm force of the wind helping it'. Right through her island days, Eagle Mountain (*Sliabh an Iolair*) on the mainland remained a powerful symbol of joy and happiness for her; she regretted that she was separated from it by 'the big watery sea', and that it was no longer the smell of heather which surrounded her but the smell of the sea ('but I've only the smell of the sea since I left you').

Peig Sayers married into the Great Blasket Island on the eve of her nineteenth birthday in 1892. Hers was an arranged marriage, and according to the following extract from her autobiography, she had never met her future husband prior to the occasion of their matchmaking.[3]

1. This significant role of the Great Blasket and the fruitful interaction of the islanders and the scholar visitors is further discussed in Patricia Lysaght, 'Change and Transition in the Folk Narrative Environment in Ireland in the Nineteenth and Twentieth Centuries', in G. Hirschfelder, D. Schell, A Schrutka-Rechtenstamm (eds), *Kulturen, Sprachen, Übergänge*. Festschrift für H.L. Cox zum 65. Geburtstag (Köln, Weimar, Wein: Böhlau Verlag, 2000), pp. 61–83 (here pp. 71–80).

2. Brian Ó Ceallaigh from Killarney, County Kerry, encouraged Tomás Ó Criomhthain to write a sketchbook of daily life on the Great Blasket Island (*Allagar na hInise*), (ed.) An Seabhac (Baile Átha Cliath: C.S. Ó Fallúin i gcomhair le hOifig an tSoláthair, 1928), and variant (ed.) Tim Enright as Tomás O'Crohan, *Island Cross-Talk* (Oxford: Oxford University Press, 1986), and his autobiography, *An tOileánach* (ed.) An Seabhac (Baile Átha Cliath: C.S. Ó Fallúin i gcomhair le hOifig an tSoláthair, 1929); translated by Robin Flower as Tomás O'Crohan, *The Islandman* (Dublin: Talbot Press; London: Chatto and Windus, 1937).

3. W.R. Rodgers, in his Introduction to Peig Sayers, *An Old Woman's Reflections* (London: Oxford University Press, 1962), p. x, also states that Peig told him she had never met her husband prior to marriage (this is repeated by R. MacCullagh in *The Irish Currach Folk* (Dublin: Wolfhound Press, 1992), p. 129: 'I never met my husband till the day I married him,' she told me, 'but it was a love-match till the day he died. And why shouldn't I, for he was a fine big man.' A variant account stating that Peig and her mother had, by chance, met and socialized with Peig's future husband and two other island men, prior to the matchmaking occasion, appears in *Beatha Pheig Sayers* (Baile Átha Cliath: Foilseacháin Náisiúnta Tta, 1970), pp. 18, 20–1, another description of her life, published by her son Micheál Ó Gaoithín more than a decade after her death.

Matchmaking was an important social institution in rural Ireland as the match (marriage) involved both a transfer of economic control and an advance to adult status. Social and economic parity between the contracting parties was considered desirable and matchmaking, a highly ritualized process involving a series of negotiations related to the economic and social standing of the parties concerned, was designed to achieve this. As a bargaining mechanism, especially in relation to the dowry of the bride-to-be, matchmaking was ostensibly a male institution, but women also played a vital, though less formal, role. Usually also the prospective bride's consent to the marriage was obtained, and in many instances the matchmaker's role, as an independent third party, was essentially to facilitate the creation of a formal marriage contract from an existing informal understanding between a couple. A significant aspect of Peig's description of the matchmaking session and the arrangement of her marriage is that no dowry was negotiated. The fact that a woman did not need a dowry to marry into the Blasket Island was a measure of her own not very prosperous economic standing and social status, as well as that of the island community into which she was marrying.

The traditional time for weddings in rural Ireland was just before the penitential season of Lent — during which the solemn celebration of marriage was prohibited — with Shrove Tuesday the most popular day for weddings in many parts of the country.

Further extracts from the autobiography of Peig Sayers appear in the 'Women in Irish Society' section in Volume v (pp. 598–99) and the 'Women and Writing' section, Volume v (pp. 1055–58). A passage from her *Machtnamh Seana-Mhná* (*An Old Woman's Reflections*) appears in this volume, pp. 1401–1404, and her telling of the 'Cinderella' story appears on pp. 1253–1261. *Peig* was published in English in 1973, translation by Bryan MacMahon.[4]   P.L.]

4. Peig Sayers, *Peig: The Autobiography of Peig Sayers of the Great Blasket Island,* translated into English by Bryan MacMahon (Dublin: Talbot Press, 1974, repr. 1983).

from: CAIBIDIL A XVIII
CLEAMHNAS IS PÓSADH

Lá Sathairn i dtosach na hInide bhí Seán sa Daingean, is tar éis teacht abhaile, dúirt sé liom go raibh scéal nua aige.

'Cad é an scéal é?' arsa mise.

'Scéala cleamhnais, a chailín!' ar seisean.

'A Dhia na bhFeart! cé hé an fear?' arsa mise.

'Fear ón Oileán,' ar seisean. 'Buachaill mín macánta, agus fear maith, leis. Tá súil agam go ndéanfaidh tú rud orm. Beidh siad ag teacht chughainn oíche éigin.'

Is amhlaidh mar bhí an scéal agamsa maidir le mo dhearthár, Seán, san am sin, dá ndéarfadh sé liom dul ag taoscadh na farraige dhéanfainn rud air. Ní raibh duine eile ar an saol seo san am sin ba mheasa liomsa ná Seán.

Trí oíche ina dhiaidh sin bhuail triúr fear an doras isteach. Fáiltíodh rompu gan dabht. Ní raibh aon fhios ag m'athair iad a bheith ag teacht ach bhí fhios aige go maith cad a thug iad ansin. I gceann tamaillín tharraing duine acu píobaire buidéil as a phóca. Lean píobaire agus píobaire eile é sa tslí go raibh a ndóthain go maith ólta acu, agus gan aon cheal cainte orainn. Ní raibh focal asam féin ach mé ag gliúcaíocht fé m'fhabhraí ar na fir óga. Bhí sé ag teip orm a dhéanamh amach cé acu den triúr a bhí do mo lorg féin, mar ní raibh aithne agam ar aon duine acu. Níorbh fhéidir liom rogha ná díogh a bhaint astu. Bhí gach duine acu ró-mhaith d'fhear domsa dá mbeinn seacht n-uaire níos fearr ná mar bhíos.

Níor mhór an mhoill an cleamhnas úd a dhéanamh, faraoir! Ní raibh aon ní ann ach 'Téanam' agus 'Táim sásta.' Tháinig m'athair chugham anall.

'Tóg suas do cheann!' ar seisean. 'An raghaidh tú don Oileán?'

Dheineas machtnamh, mar bhí rogha de dhá chrann ar mo bhois agam, is é sin pósadh nó dul in aimsir arís. Bhíos cortha go maith ag an aimsir chéanna, is smaoiníos gurbh fhearr dom fear cúil agus garda cosanta, agus tigh, a bheith agam féin go mbeadh neart agam suí i bhfeighil mo shuaimhnis nuair a bheinn cortha.

Labhair m'athair arís.

'Cad tá le rá agat?' ar seisean

'Níl aithne ná eolas agam ar mhuintir an Oileáin,' arsa mise, 'ach tá aithne agus eolas maith agatsa orthu, agus an rud is maith leatsa is é is maith liomsa. Raghad pé áit a déarfaidh tú liom.'

'Dia leat!' ar seisean.

Bhí an margadh déanta is bhíos-sa agus Pádraig Ó Guithín le pósadh i gceann cúpla lá. Dé Sathairn an lá spriocáilte. Ní raibh gluaisteán ná cóistí san am sin ann murab ionann is anois. Nuair a bhíomar ullamh an mhaidin sin ghabh Seán an capall is chuaigh scata againn isteach sa chairt. Nuair a shroicheamar an Buailtín, bhí dath dubh ar an áit le daoine. Bhí seacht bpósadh ann an lá sin, is ba mhór an t-uafás an méid daoine a bhí ann.

Nuair a fhágamar an Séipéal bhí ciarláil agus dul-trí-chéile ann, ceol agus rince ag na daoine óga, amhráin agus ól ag na daoine aosta. Bhí tamall maith den lá caite acu ar an gcuma sin. Bhí sé in am ag gach aon duine bheith ag baint an tí amach nuair a tháinig Seán ag glaoch orm féin. D'imíos féin is a thuilleadh cailíní lena chois abhaile. B'é nós na haimsire sin, gach duine a bheadh ar an bpósadh a theacht go dtí tigh na bainise. Bhíodh fear ag teacht ó am go ham go dtí go mbímis go léir bailithe ar ócáid phósta. Ansin thosaíodh an rí-rá.

Ach nuair a thángamar-na abhaile, ní raibh aon scéal fónta romhainn, mar bhí corránach iníne le mo dhearthár, Seán, le béal an bháis. Ní raibh aon choinne againn leis an scéal sin, mar is amhlaidh a tháinig taom obann uirthi, agus fuair sí bás an oíche chéanna.

Fé mar a bhíodh fear ag teacht shuíodh sé go ciúin gan gíog as. Is mór go léir an bháúlacht a bhí ag mo dheartháirse le muintir an Oileáin riamh ina dhiaidh sin — a fheabhas mar a dheineadar comhbhrón leis an oíche úd. Bhí bainis agus tórramh in éineacht againn. Sin é mar d'imigh ar mo bhainis bhochtsa!

Dé Máirt a bhí chugainn is ea bheartaíodar ar dhul abhaile. Ghabh Seán an capall, is buaileadh isteach inti dhá bhairille den lionn dubh is crúsca uisce-beatha is a thuilleadh gréithe d'fhan gan chaitheamh toisc bháis an linbh. Ansin bhogamar linn síos chun Barra na hAille. Bhí mo dheirfiúr Máire le mo chois, agus Cáit, bean mo dhearthár.

Nuair a shroicheamar an caladh, buaileadh ar snámh ceithre naomhóg. Cuireadh na bairillí agus na gréithe eile i gceann acu. Bhí ceathrar fear i ngach naomhóig. Shuíos féin isteach i ndeireadh na naomhóige a raibh m'fhear céile inti. B'é sin an chéad uair riamh ar an bhfarraige agamsa. Is mé a bhí go scanraithe.

Bhí an tráthnóna go hálainn is an fharraige go ciúin, is iad ag bosáil leo isteach nó gur shroicheamar caladh an Oileáin. Bhí oiread ionadh ormsa an tráthnóna úd, is dá mba ag dul go cathair Londain isteach a bheinn.

Nuair a dhruideamar isteach, bhí dath dubh ar an áit ag daoine, beag agus mór, ag fáiltiú romhainn. Dheineas mo shlí tríothú chomh maith is ab fhéidir liom.

Bhíos ag cuimhneamh conas a chuirfinn suas lena leithéid de bhaile, gan gaol, gan cairde in

aice liom. Ní raibh aithne agam ar aon duine acu a bhí ag croitheadh lámh liom. 'N'fheadar,' a deirim liom féin, 'an dtiocfaidh an lá go deo go ligfead mo chroí leo, nó an ndéanfaidh mé chomh dána ina measc is dhéanfainn i measc muintir Bhaile Bhiocáire? Ó, ní bheidh siad go deo, dar liom, chomh deas le muintir Bhaile Bhiocáire! Mo shlán beo chugat, a Cháit Jim! Nach leat a bhí an t-ádh! Beidh lán do chos den talamh míntíreach agat, pé scéal é. Ní mar sin domsa! Is uaigneach atáim anseo ar oileán mara, gan le cloisint feasta agam ach glór na dtonnta á radadh féin ar ghaineamh na trá! Ach tá aon sólás amháin agam — fear breá dathúil, agus fé mar a thuigim ón gcogar mogar seo ar siúl, ní mise an chéad bhean a bhí ag caitheamh na spor air. Ach is agamsa atá sé anois, agus nára maith acu sin déanamh á cheal! Tá cairde mo dhóthain ar an Oileán seo agam a fhad a fhágfaidh Dia agam é. Nach breá pearsanta an chuma atá air! Agus an t-eolas atá aige ar ghnóthaí farraige! Ba dhóigh liom ná beadh aon bhaol báite go deo orm a fhaid a bheadh sé in aon bhád liom.'

D'fhanas ansin nó gur tháinig sé chugham, is bhuaileamar suas chun an tí le cois a chéile, agus scata de pháistí an bhaile inár ndiaidh. Ag tnúthán le milseáin a bhíodar, na rudaí bochta. Bhí scaimh orthu chucu!

Bhí seandaoine an bhaile istigh romham, agus is orm a bhí an cheist agus an ceann fé toisc gan aithne a bheith agam ar aon duine acu. Ach ní fada gur chroitheas suas mé féin. Labhair Seán-Mhicí Ó Guithín, athair mo chéile, liom. Lúbaire righin láidir ba ea é, ach bhí an t-aos á leagadh síos. 'Flint' an leasainm a bhí air.

'Céad míle fáilte romhat, a Pheigí!' ar seisean.

'Go maire tú slán beo!' arsa mise, agus mo cheann cromtha agam le sórt támáilteacht.

'Bain díot do bhrat, agus croch anuas é, a dhalta,' arsa Máire Ní Shúilleabháin, máthair mo chéile, a bhí ina céad chuid timpeall orm. 'Ná bac leis! déanfad féin é. Tá tú cortha.'

Bhaineas díom mo bhrat agus chroch sí anuas é ar chipín a bhí sáite isteach sa bhfalla.

'Is maith an mháthair chéile tú agus is tláith,' arsa mise i m'aigne féin, 'agus is maith an rud gur ghlacas le dea-chomhairle mo dhearthár, Seán.'

Bhí fhios agam go maith nach spreasán ab fhonn le mo dhearthár a cheangal liom agus, dá bhrí sin, níor chuireas ina choinne an oíche úd a bhí an cleamhnas á dhéanamh.

from: CHAPTER XVIII
MATCH AND MARRIAGE

One Saturday in the beginning of Shrove, Seán was in Dingle; when he came home he told me that he had news for me.

'What news?' I asked him.

'News of a match, my girl!'

'God above! Who's the man?'

'An Islandman,' he said. 'An even-tempered, honest boy and a good man as well, so I hope you'll take my advice. They'll be coming to visit us some night soon.'

The way matters then stood between my brother Seán and myself, if he ordered me to go and bail the ocean I'd obey him, for no one in the world stood higher in my affections than did Seán.

Three nights after this, three men walked in the door. They got a hearty welcome. My father had no idea that they were coming but then he realized fully what had brought them. After a little while one of the men produced from his pocket a bottle with a long neck; bottle followed bottle until they had a fair share of drink taken and then we had no shortage of talk! I didn't open my mouth, but I was peeping from under my eyelashes at the young men. I couldn't decide which of the three was asking for me because I knew none of them. I could neither choose one nor bar any. Each one of them was too good a man for me even if I were seven times a better woman than I was.

Oh dear, that match didn't take long to make! There was little more to it than 'Come along' and 'I'm satisfied.' My father came over to me.

'Raise up your head!' he said. 'Will you go to the Island?'

I considered for a while for I had two choices in the palm of my hand — to marry or go into service again.[1] I was sick and tired of that same service and I thought it would be better for me to have a man to my back and someone to protect me, and to own a house too, where I could sit down at my ease whenever I'd be weary.

My father spoke again: 'What have you to say?' he asked.

'I know nothing at all about the Island people,' I said, 'but you know them through and through.

Whatever pleases you pleases me and I'll go wherever you tell me.'

'God be with you,' my father said.

The bargain was made; Peats[2] Guiheen and myself were to be married in a few days' time.

Saturday was the day appointed. There were neither motor-cars nor side-cars there at that time — it's a different story altogether nowadays. When we were ready that morning Seán tackled the horse and a crowd of us sat into the cart. When we got to Ballyferriter, the place was black with people for there were seven weddings there that day and there was a great throng of people present.

When we left the chapel there was right tip-of-the-reel and hullabaloo; the young people had music and dancing and the older people were singing and drinking. A good part of the day was spent like this; when Seán called for me it was time for everyone to be moving towards the house, so some other girls and myself went off home with him. It was customary at that time for everyone who attended the ceremony to go to the house for the wedding reception. The men would arrive later in ones until at last we were all together. Then the revelry would begin.

But when we got home there was no good news to greet us but word that a fine big daughter of my brother Seán was at death's door. We never expected news like that for the fit had come on her all of a sudden. She died that same night.

So, according as each man arrived at the house he'd sit down quietly without speaking a word. Ever afterwards my brother had great affection for the Island people because of the fine manner in which they had sympathized with him that night.

We had a wedding-feast and a wake at one and the same time. That's the way my poor wedding went.

The Islanders had decided to go home on the following Tuesday. Seán tackled the horse; then two barrels of porter, a jar of whiskey and the eatables that hadn't been consumed because of the girl's death, were loaded onto the cart. Then we moved off down to Barra na hAille — the cliff top. My sister Máire was with me, as was Cáit, my brother's wife. When we reached the creek

---

1. Peig had by this time spent two long periods as a maidservant, in households some miles from her home.

2. Pronounced 'Pats'.

four currachs[3] were launched on the water and the barrels and other goods were loaded into one. There were four men to each currach. I sat into the stern of the currach in which my husband was and as this was my first time ever on the sea I was terrified out of my wits.

The evening was beautiful and the sea was calm and the men were rowing easily until at last we reached the Island haven. I was as amazed that evening as if I were entering the city of London. When we moved close to the Island the place was black with people big and small all gathered there to welcome us. I made my way through the crowds as best I could and all the while I was turning over in my mind how I'd come to accept this kind of home without a relation or a friend near me. I didn't know one person among all those who were shaking hands with me and I kept asking myself if the day would ever dawn when I'd open my heart to these people or make as bold among them as I would among the people of Vicarstown. Oh, never, never, I told myself, could they be as kind as the people of Vicarstown. The blessing of God be with you, Cáit-Jim, I said in my own mind, you were the lucky one! Whatever happens, your feet will be planted on mainland clay. Not so with me! How lonely I am on this island in the ocean with nothing to be heard forever more but the thunder of the waves hurling themselves on the beach. But I have one consolation — a fine handsome man, and as I can gather from the whispering going on around me I'm not the first woman who cocked her cap at him! But he's mine now, and no thanks to them to do without him! I'll have friends aplenty on this island as long as God leaves him to me. And hasn't he a fine presentable appearance! And his knowledge of the ways of the sea! I thought I would never be in danger of drowning if he and I were in the same currach.

I stayed where I was until my husband came to me and then, side by side, we walked upwards to the house with a crowd of the village children following us. They were wild for sweets, the poor things, and their mouths were working at the thoughts of them.

The old people of the place had gathered into the house to welcome me. I was shy and backward because I knew none of them, but before long I pulled myself together. Then Old Micí Guiheen, my father-in-law, addressed me; he was a rough strong hardy man but age was catching up on him. 'Flint' was his nickname.

'Welcome a hundred thousand times, Peig,' he said.

'That you may live long in the whole of your health,' I answered and my head was bent with a sort of shyness.

'Take your shawl and hang it up there, child,' said Máire O'Sullivan, my mother-in-law. She was, as the saying goes, all about me! Then: 'Never mind! I'll do it myself as you're exhausted,' she added.

I took off my shawl and she hung it on a little peg that was driven into the wall.

'You're a good mother-in-law and a gentle one too,' I told myself, 'and it's a great blessing that I took the sound advice of my brother Seán.'

I knew well that Seán didn't want to tie me to a good-for-nothing, so I didn't go against him the night my match was being made.

[Peig Sayers's first child, a son named Muiris, was born on the mainland. Shortly before the birth, with the encouragement of her island mother-in-law, Máire Ní Shúilleabháin (O'Sullivan), Peig went home to Vicarstown where her son was born with the assistance of Neil Pheig, the 'handywoman' or midwife. Within two days of his birth, her baby son was baptized in the church in Ballyferriter. Peig was not present. Consulted by her husband about a name for the child, she wished to name him after her brother Pat, but yielded to her husband's preference for Muiris, a traditional name in his family. Her husband was one of the party which brought the child to the church for baptism, but we are not told who the godparents were.

Six weeks after her son's birth Peig and her husband brought him home to the Great Blasket amid scenes of community and family welcome and celebration. The old women's scrutiny and comments on the child mentioned by Peig were not malicious; they served rather to identify him as a member of a particular family and thus to incorporate him into the island community.   P.L.]

from: CAIBIDIL A XXI
MO SHAOL SAN OILEÁN

Nuair a bhí sé seachtaine caite agam i mBaile Bhiocáire, ba mhithid, dar liom, teacht abhaile; ach bé an ceann ab fhearr den scéal mé féin agus

---

3. Light keel-less rowing boats made of tarred canvas stretched on a wooden frame.

mo leanbh a bheith ag teacht abhaile fé mhaise agus fé áthas.

Dé Domhnaigh a bhí beartaithe agam chun teacht abhaile. Tháinig Pádraig agus a dheartháir Mícheál, agus beirt eile i naomhóig ón Oileán fé mo bhráid. Nuair a bhíomar ullamh chun gluaiseacht labhair mo mháthair sa chúinne.

'Tabhair dom i leith an linbhín,' ar sise, 'go bhfágfad an slán déanach aige!'

Thóg sí chúichí ina baclainn é agus phóg sí go dil dúthrachtach é.

'Go ndéana Dia fear mór maith díot a stóirín!' ar sise, 'agus slán agus beannacht leat go dtí an tOileán! Ní fheicfeadsa go deo arís tú!'

Ní fhaca leis, mar ní fada ina dhiaidh sin gur cailleadh í.

Shín sí chugam an leanbh, agus dúirt: 'Gura slán as gach láimh tú, agus as mo láimhse, leis!' agus ansin bhogamar linn.

Bhí an tráthnóna go hálainn is an fharraige go ciúin, is ní rabhamar i bhfad ag teacht abhaile. Ar m'fhocal, a léitheoir, gurb' shin é an lá is meidhrí agus is croíúla a chaitheas-sa roimhe sin riamh ná ó shin anuas.

Nuair a thángamar isteach ar an gcaladh, bhí mo sheanchara, Cáit Ní Bhriain, agus Máire Ní Chearna, agus sean-Mháire Ní Shúilleabháin féin romham ar an gcaladh. Sciob Máire Ní Shúilleabháin léi an leanbh mar a sciobfadh iolar uan óg. Bhí an bhean bhocht aosta ag pocléimnigh den talamh.

'Mo ghrá deoil m'ainglín bán!' ar sise.

D'fhan Cáit Ní Bhriain liom féin, agus tháinig sí le mo chois go dtí an tigh.

Bhí a lán de na seanmhná istigh romham. Béas é sin a bhíonn ag seanmhná, agus dá bhrí sin ní raibh seanmhná an Oileáin saor ón seanbhéas céanna.

Bhí gach aon duine agus a mheas féin aige ar an leanbh. Bhíodh an locht seo nó an locht úd air, dar le duine acu — an tsrón beagáinín rómhór, na súile beag, na cluasa gan iad a bheith cruthanta a ndóthain, agus mar sin de. Fé dheireadh labhair Micí, an t-athair críonna, a bhí ina shuí le hais na tine:

'Mhuise, dalladh is caochadh oraibh!' ar seisean, 'mura deacair d'aon duine aon mháchaill a bheith air gan fhios díbh is mura agaibh atá ag gliúcaíocht ar an leanbh! Nach mó craiceann a chuireann an óige di?'

'Mhuise, is fíor duit,' arsa Cáit Ní Bhriain, á

fhreagairt, 'ach is dóigh liom go ndéanann gach aon duine nath den chéad duine, a Mhicí.'

'Ar mh'anamsa,' arsa Micí, 'gur mar a chéile an chéad duine agus an duine déanach, agus is minic gurb é 'scríobadh an chrúiscín' an duine is measa leat.'

'Am briathar mhuise,' arsa Máire Ní Chearna á corraí féin suas ar an stól, 'gurb é an duine déanach ba mheasa duit, mar gur minic a thóg bean bhocht ál maith clainne, is gurbh é an duine déanach is fearr d'fóirfeadh uirthi.'

'Is minic a thitfeadh rud den sórt sin amach,' arsa Micí; 'ach caithimis uainn é mar scéal, agus déantar an tae.'

Ba ghearr ansin go raibh scaipeadh ag dul ar na seanmhná. Níor fhan gan imeacht ach Cáit Ní Bhriain.

'Chuiris an ruaig orthu, a Mhicí,' ar sise.

'Nach bhfuil 'fhios agatsa, a Cháit Ní Bhriain,' arsa Micí, 'nárbh fhearrde Parthas Dé na mná sin a bheith ann. Ní thógfadh sé ló go n-oíche uathu Neamh a chur trí chéile!'

from: CHAPTER XXI
MY LIFE ON THE ISLAND

After I had spent six weeks in Vicarstown I thought it time to return home; the best part of my story was that myself and my child were returning well and happy.

Sunday was the day I had decided upon to return. Peats, his brother Mícheál, and two others came for me from the Island in a currach. When we were ready to leave, my mother spoke up from the corner.

'Bring me the infant,' she said, 'until I bid him my last good-bye!'

She took the child in her arms and kissed him lovingly and tenderly.

'May God make you a fine big man some day, my little one,' she said. 'Good-bye now and my blessing go with you to the Island. I shall never see you again.'

She didn't either, for she died soon afterwards.

She held out the child to me and said: 'May you prosper by the hand of everyone and by my hand too.' Then we set off.

The evening was delightful; the ocean was calm and it didn't take us long to get home. I can tell you, dear reader, that that was the happiest and most heartwarming day I have ever spent before or since.

When we reached the landing-slip, my old friend Cáit O'Brien, and Máire Kearney, and even old Máire O'Sullivan herself, were before me on the shore. Máire O'Sullivan snatched the child away as an eagle snatches a young lamb. The poor old woman was beside herself with glee.

'My suckling dearie! My little white angel!' she kept repeating.

Cáit O'Brien stayed with me and accompanied me to the house.

There was a good number of the old women inside before me; that's a custom old women have everywhere and one to which the old Islandwomen weren't immune.

Each one delivered her own summing-up on the child. According to one, he had this fault and that fault: the nose was a little too big, the eyes were small, the ears weren't exactly perfect and so on. At last the grandfather, Mící, who had been sitting by the fire raised his voice.

'May blindness and shortsightedness overtake ye!' he said. ''Tis hard for anyone to have a flaw unknown to ye. And all that peering ye have at the child! Doesn't youth go through many a change!'

'True, indeed,' said Cáit O'Brien in reply. 'But I daresay everyone takes a lot of notice of the first child.'

'My word!' Mící answered. 'It's all the same whether it's the first child or the last. Often it's "the scraping of the skillet" is the one you'd like the most.'

'With that I agree!' said Máire Kearney stirring herself on the stool. 'The last child might matter most to you; indeed 'tis often an unfortunate woman reared a fine clutch of a family and the last child of all would turn out to be the best head to her.'[1]

'That often happened!' Mící said. 'But forget it for a story and make the tea.'

Before long the old women began to scatter and then the only one left was Cáit O'Brien.

'You ran 'em, Mící!' she said.

'You know well, Cáit,' Mící replied, 'that God's Paradise won't be any the better of having those women inside its gates for it won't take them twenty-four hours to upset heaven.'

1. i.e. 'who would treat her best'.

NAN JOYCE

(1940–   )

from:
TRAVELLER: AN AUTOBIOGRAPHY (1985)

[Traveller activist and spokesperson Nan Joyce has written a manifesto of Travellers' needs, one of the first such documents to be taken up by the media. She has also written poetry, but she dictated her autobiography on tape to editor Anna Farmar, and prefaced it with this note: 'It's an awful sad thing to have no education. If I knew how to write properly and had good spelling I wouldn't have done this book on tape. Anna Farmar recorded it and wrote it out for me — if I wrote a book by myself whoever published it would need a medal for bravery!'

Nan Joyce's account of her family history and early childhood shows the importance of orally preserved genealogy. Her idyllic description of the Travellers' summer life up to the end of World War II contrasts sharply with the conditions in which most Travellers now live year-round on the outskirts of towns and cities. A further extract from *Traveller* appears in 'Women and Irish Society' (Volume V, pp. 605–6). For more on Travellers' culture, see 'Storytelling Traditions of the Irish Travellers' (pp. 1263–1283).   A.B.]

from: CHAPTER 1
A DIFFERENT-SPEAKING PEOPLE

When I was a child we were hunted from place to place and we never could have friends to be always going to school with. The little settled children would run past our camps — they were afeared of the travellers. Other people had a sort of romantic idea about us, because of the horses and the colourful wagons. They would ask us did we come from some place special like the gypsies you see on the films. They thought that the travellers had no worries and that we didn't feel pain, or hunger or cold. The truth is that we're people like everybody else but we're a different-speaking people with our own traditions and our own way of life and this is the way we should be treated, like the Gaeltachts, not like dirt or drop-outs from the settled community.

Some of my ancestors went on the road in the Famine but more of them have been travelling for hundreds of years — we're not drop-outs like some people think. The travellers have been in Ireland since St Patrick's time, there's a lot of history behind them though there's not much written down — it's what you get from your grandfather and what he got from his grandfather.

The original travellers were tinsmiths and musicians and they were great carpenters, they made all their own musical instruments and the wagons and carts. Over the years they mixed in with travellers from other countries, like the Spanish who came to Ireland four or five hundred years ago. You can see the Spanish blood coming out today in our family: my mother and her brothers were completely dark. My mother's mother was from Roscrea,[1] she was one of the Doyles and they're very dark beautiful people with big black eyes and shiny black hair.

My other granny's name was Power, that's a Norman name.[2] Her people would have been English travellers who came here years and years ago and married in with the Irish travellers.

Then there were the settled people who took to the road for various reasons and mixed in with the travellers. One of my great-grandfathers, going back six or seven grannies, was a Protestant minister. His son married in with the Joyces, a tribe from Galway. Other people were burned out during the Famine. The travellers were used to coping with cold and hardship and hunger, they could survive anywhere because they had their own way of working and their own culture.

But the settled people weren't used to managing on their own, they slept in old sheds and barns and did a sort of slave work on the farms. Some of them married in with travellers.

The various tribes have different beliefs and ways of going on. Some of them are strong fighting people because for hundreds of years they had to fight to survive, it wasn't that they were bad. You can tell what tribe a person is from by just looking at them. If I saw a group of travellers and there was one there from every part of the country I could pick out where each came from without even asking. The Wexford tribes are mostly red-haired and they have freckles though some of them are fair-haired. The Galway tribes are very dark and good-looking. My father's people, the O'Donoghues, came from County Longford and they had snow-white hair and very blue eyes and then there were Donoghues from Dublin who were very dark.

My father's name was John O'Donoghue and my mother's name was Nan McCann. They were married in 1937. I was born in 1940 in Clogheen, a little place not far from Ballyporeen in County Tipperary. My sister Kathleen is the oldest in the family, she's two years older than me, my brother Willie was born two years after me and the other children followed on like steps in a stair with just a year or so between them. I had eight or nine brothers and sisters.

When I was three or four we went down to Belfast to the Bog Meadows. It's a tiny place with little red-brick houses and a factory. All the wagons were piled in on top of one another and there was no privacy. Just like we are today we had no water or toilet. Even as a child I was the sort of person who could see what was going on; the way the travelling people were hunted from place to place and they never got to settle down.

Ireland was very poor then, especially the Free State,[3] you couldn't get copper or brass or tin or anything like that so the travellers used to smuggle it in their wagons. They'd bring it into the Free State in big hundredweight bales and they'd make tins and pots and lovely copper ornaments and buckets. In those days travellers were different; they were a very proud people

1. County Tipperary.
2. See storyteller Nora 'Oney' Power in the subsection 'Storytelling Traditions of the Irish Travellers', pp. 1271–1279.

3. Following partition, the Irish state was officially known as the Irish Free State (1922–37).

with their own way of life that was precious to them. Some of them had to beg to survive but more of them could sell their wares and do various things to keep themselves going.

Some people gave us a welcome. If they were living on the side of a mountain, or in a real lonely place, they mightn't get to the town for six months and they loved to see the travellers coming so that they could get their pots and kettles mended and buy little things. In those days the half-doors would all be open. You'd look in across the door to ask the woman did she want anything and she'd ask you in to have a cup of tea. She'd say, 'Now, tell us all the news. What's happening in Belfast?'

So we were sort of newspapers and radio as well as everything else. And we were trusted: the woman of the house would go out the back or upstairs and she'd leave her money and know well no-one would touch it whereas today people are told to be afeared of the travellers.

In the summer we'd go travelling. We'd leave up the heavy wagons because it was easier on the horses, they just had to pull the car, and we'd sleep in tents. They were made from green covers with hazel branches for wattles. In the mornings we'd roll up the sides, and fold the bedding, fresh air would get in and the place would be cleaned up spotless.

Mother and Father had this thing for cleanness. Even though we only had an old wagon or tents in the summer everything had to be shining. The mugs might be washed perfectly clean but still a kettle of water would be boiled and thrown over them before father would drink the tea. Mother was always bathing us and washing our hair. The old shampoo we had years ago was a powder and it had to be mixed with water. There was a picture of a lovely blondy-haired girl on the packet. Mother would mix the powder and water in a bottle and throw it on our heads. Our hair used to be glittering.

When we were leaving a camp father would break so many pieces of thorny bushes and tie them together on the end of a long stick to make a broom and he'd sweep up all the camp. He'd even cover the marks of the fire with sods of grass so you'd never think there was anyone camping there. The only thing left would be the marks of the horses: the ground would be trampled where they were tied.

from: CHAPTER 9
'GO! MOVE! SHIFT!'

[A series of episodes from her adult life shows Nan Joyce's increasing political awareness, as well as a considerable generosity of spirit in her interactions with the settled community.   A.B.]

The day before Elizabeth was born we pulled into a little green space in Finglas;[1] it was the middle of winter and it was freezing cold. I was in labour all the next day but the Corporation[2] sent men along to shift us and the bulldozer pulled us out. We had to shift whether we liked it or not. We moved down beside Cardiff Bridge, there are new houses built in that space now. Everything was upside-down: when you move a caravan you can't have a fire in it so the little ones were freezing. I had to go into hospital to have the baby but all I was worried about was leaving the rest of the children. I went to St James's[3] again and the sisters and nurses were really great — they've always been good to the travellers up there.

When I came out of hospital Elizabeth was christened and we moved over to Rathfarnham.[4] We kept getting moved and after about a year we came back to Finglas and camped along by the side of the road near the football grounds. Then the guards[5] started harassing us.

If you're a traveller you're not supposed to have nice things but I've always loved beautiful things. Years ago down on the quays in Dublin you could go into the antique shops with a few shillings and you'd pick something up. Maybe it'd be all dirty and dusty but you'd bring it home and wash it and it'd be really lovely. I love old things — a little piece of old china is part of the past. I have china from every place we travelled in England and Scotland and the North and I have a silver kettle on a stand and a silver punchbowl. I got them for a few pounds before I had any children.

---

1. Finglas, a village in north County Dublin, whose population increased dramatically in the 1950s with the building of large local authority housing estates, making it part of Dublin city.
2. Dublin Corporation: the local authority.
3. One of Dublin's major hospitals.
4. A suburb on the south side of Dublin. Like Finglas, it was originally a country village.
5. Garda Síochána: police.

One night the men went off to have a pint and I was alone with the children. The guards came over from Ballyfermot[6] and started searching the place. We had some money saved up to buy a mobile caravan and when they looked in the drawer they saw it. 'Where did you get that?' they said. 'It's our own money,' I said, 'we're saving up to buy a mobile caravan.' The guards took all the money out of the drawer and they took my silver kettle and the dish and they brought me off to the barracks, to a little back room in Finglas police station. When John came back about eleven o'clock I was missing but when he came up to the barracks the guard in the office didn't know we were in the back room. He said, 'There's no-one here, there's no Nan Joyce here.' I was nearly getting into a bad row about it because some men get very nasty if you're not there at night-time.

The guards counted the money — you know the way you throw money into a drawer without counting it, I didn't know exactly how much there was. They gave me back the money in the end but they took my silver things over to Ballyfermot police station and threw them into a cardboard box. A few days later they put them on the television, on *Garda Patrol*,[7] asking the owner to come along and claim them. I went over to Ballyfermot police station but they wouldn't believe me. One of the guards, a detective, was real cheeky and he kept shoving me out and saying, 'Where would you get them things? They're not yours.' So we had no chance of getting our things back because they didn't believe the travellers should have anything. In the end a settled man we knew went over and told the guards that he knew John for so long and that we had the things in the trailer for years and years. So they gave them back to us. But we'd never have got them back by ourselves.

About nine years ago, just before Richard was born, we were staying over in Ballymun[8] and every second morning the guards were in at us before I was up out of bed. I don't know what they were looking for or what they were up to because my husband wouldn't steal a match and I would never steal anything now. When I was a child I often stole food, I admit it, but that time you had to steal to survive but since I got married I've never stolen anything. But the guards don't believe this and when they didn't find anything they never apologised.

Sometimes when I'd be in bed in the morning I'd waken up and see them all in the caravan. I'd say to them, 'Could you wait outside till I get my clothes on, please?' I'd try to keep myself covered with all these strange men in the trailer but they'd come out with these funny remarks, 'Oh don't mind us, we've wives of our own.' Just because they're married they think they have the right to see women getting dressed in the morning. Sometimes they would show a warrant and more times they wouldn't. They were detectives, they weren't in uniform so I couldn't even take their number.

I got really tormented with them. They'd turn out every drawer and every press, they even took all the food out of the cupboards. They'd take the children out of bed in the night and turn the mattresses over. We'd been there a long time and we wanted to stay because the children were going to school but I got so fed up I told John to move. It was the guards made us move not the Corporation, if it wasn't one person it was another.

I grew up with a fear of the guards but now I'm a middle-aged woman I'm not against them and I really believe in law and order. The way we live we've no phone or address and if we need an ambulance or a doctor in a hurry, the first place we'll go is the garda barracks and they will do it all and be very good at it. Guards can be nice people and understanding and still not neglect their duty. But in Dublin for the last ten years it's been awful, some of them are going around like Hitler's men. I don't think the Minister for Justice knows about it because you have to be with people the whole time to know what they're up to. When you have a flock of dogs one dog will be like a saint when you're looking at him but when he's out of the noose he's eating sheep.

6. A western suburb of Dublin, extensively developed with local authority housing in the 1950s.
7. A weekly television programme on RTÉ, 1964–91, in which members of the Garda Síochána appealed to the public for help in solving crimes.
8. A suburb on the north side of Dublin, where low-cost, high-rise residential tower blocks were built in the 1960s, even as similar buildings were being demolished in Britain.

ROSALEEN FERGUSON

(1929–   )

from:
FORCE 10 (1991)

[In an interview with Leland Bardwell, published in the innovative regional magazine *Force 10: A Journal of the Northwest*, no. 3 (1991), pp. 84–9,[1] Rosaleen Ferguson spoke of her childhood on tiny Coney Island in Sligo Bay, where her father was a lighthouse keeper. She described her family's way of life, the impact of World War II, her life with her grandmother and Aunt Katie Haran, and her aunt's vivid and assertive personality. Her account includes several references to folk beliefs and practices, such as the widely held ideas that possession of part of the caul of a newborn child offers protection against drowning, and that certain 'wise women' could cure sprains and other ailments. Her memory of the visits of travelling tinsmiths corroborates Nan Joyce's account (p. 1207), while her experience of the silence and solitude of island life, and her appreciation of the natural environment, recall the words of Peig Sayers. The light-houses around the Irish coast are now all maintained automatically, without resident lightkeepers.   A.B.]

[T]he thing my grandmother never forgot was that I was born with a lucky cap on. What must have happened was I could have maybe drowned because my mother's waters hadn't broken, so grandma said. And that's the reason it was called a lucky cap because if sailors took it they never drowned, so my grandmother treasured this lucky cap and she'd give parts of it to seafarers.

My cousin Jim Leyden had a bit. He was in the Merchant Navy during the war and was torpedoed on the *Iron Door Star*. He was on a raft for a fortnight before he was saved, and the reason he thought he didn't drown was that he had a piece of my lucky cap!

. . . I remember we stayed on Oyster Island[2] for a bit. And we also went to Fanad Head[3] and Black Sod.[4] And that was a lot of upheaval. My father had a roll of linoleum and I can still see it rolled up. There was hardly time to put it down

on the floor. It all depended on how long my father was needed.

My father was an A[ssistant] K[eeper]. An AK was an assistant but a P[rincipal] K[eeper] was the man in charge. The AKs were always on the move. It was hard for the women. All those places were so inaccessible. Often no roads to the lightkeepers' houses. The houses were supplied by Irish Lights. When my father was stationed at Island Magee near Larne,[5] he had to do Rock Duty. That meant going out to the Maidens.[6]

I think he was three months on and two weeks off. I always came down here for my holidays while my mother stayed with the rest of them on the Isle of Magee. I was put on a train and I got off at Clones[7] and got another train to Sligo and [my uncle] Josie used to meet me there. I always remember there was a cafe there called the Cafe Cairo which had the most beautiful hams. My uncle met me in this cafe and then brought me over to the island by boat from the Point.[8] He was a contractor for the Irish Lights in this area so they gave him a boat. He used to have a sort of taxi service for the keepers and their wives on Oyster. After my holidays were over I'd make the same journey back up to Larne by myself.

In bad weather the rock boat couldn't go out to relieve the lighthouse keeper on the Maidens. A hard life. They had to be tremendously strong people. They had no access to public houses, betting shops, no barbers, nothing. They just lived by the sea. It wasn't so bad for my mother. She had other lighthouse-keepers' wives and her children. But my father. I don't know how any man could have stuck it. Especially in the winter. He'd say sometimes the waves used to crash right up to the windows. Imagine the sound of that. And then these men were totally self-sufficient.

They did their own baking, cooking, sewing. He was a kind man, my father, gentle. Quiet. I don't think he was cut out to be a lighthouse keeper. In those days they went into the

---

1. The magazine has a policy of publishing photographs, original artwork and interviews, along with new writing.
2. Between Coney Island and Rosses Point, in Sligo Bay.
3. County Donegal.
4. County Mayo.
5. A port in County Antrim.
6. A series of exposed rocks north of Island Magee.
7. County Monaghan.
8. Rosses Point, County Sligo.

lighthouses — we called them the Lights — and your wage was guaranteed. My oldest uncle Hugh was a lighthouse keeper so it ran in the family. And Jim Leyden, after he left the sea, also. It seemed to be that kind of a way.

But I often think of my father. These rocks! He used to semaphore to us. He'd send messages by flags. We'd semaphore back. But I think he was too far out to see our flags. Even on Oyster Island. When they wanted Packie to come out for them — if one of the lights needed servicing and they had to be taken to the rocks below the Point — they'd semaphore the message to the island and Packie would come out for them.

They didn't live on the rock but it had to be serviced. Lit with carbide. That was a great thing here.

There were two lighthouses on Coney Island, unoccupied. Just lights. They're gone now. And they used to bring the carbide over from Oyster. And we'd go down to the pier in an ass and cart and haul it up to the lights. But there was a great throw back from it. A lovely white sort of lime fell down into a sort of pit below the lights and we used to paint all the houses with it. Stables also. It made everything look so clean. Everybody on the island had the use of it.

There was always a 'rock basket' for the keepers. A wicker hamper and that had to be filled up once a month, I think. The basics were flour, condensed milk and corned beef. And maybe syrup, sugar etc. And my father turned his condensed milk and syrup into beautiful toffee and used to send it back to us children in empty corned beef tins. We used to wait for the rock boat coming back with all this haul!

Then there was the tragedy of the birds. The birds that were migrating from Africa or whatever, at night especially if they ran into a storm, they'd make for the lights. But sadly what happened was that they battered themselves and their legs got broken against the lantern and the men used to pick them up in the mornings and mend their legs and wings with match sticks. All those birds hopping around! Amazing when you think about it. The great thing about these people is they didn't require speech. And they had to get on together. And they did. They all did different things. Some men carved wood, others made tapestry, embroidery. If one got sick they had to semaphore. And if the sea was bad the boat often

couldn't get them off. The lights were built on treacherous rocks so often the boats couldn't get near them. The keepers would wait down at the little jetty but if the boat couldn't come in it would just return to the mainland. When my father was on Tory,[9] they had to come in by boat. When my cousin Jim Leyden went there were helicopters. Very different from my father's time!

. . . So then when my father was gone I stayed on the island with my younger brother and sister. That was about 1938. I always remember Franco.[10] People on the island were interested in the Spanish Civil War. Some of them wanted to run away and fight Franco. I used to wonder who was Franco.

People did actually get up and make their way to the war. Then the next thing was a man called Hitler.[11] And Johnny Conway, a nice man, used to call him Helter. So who was Helter who was starting another war? We had no wireless then. My mother was the first to bring a wireless to the island. My father was fanatical about the radio and he made a crystal set. But that was later.

My grandmother and Katie were the only ones with glasses. So when Ward took the newspaper, the *Irish Independent*, out to the island, everyone was waiting for the news. Uncle Packie was the postman so we used to get the paper. You've no idea the excitement. Most people on the island came to read it. Katie used to read the news to us all. Although we were not over-educated we could all read and write, but when the paper came in Katie would read it out in the lamplight. She had a lovely pair of pince-nez. She was very vain. She had a chain over the ear. She was real ladylike.

. . . It was hilarious when we saw a boat coming. Katie had a telescope. Since we had about fourteen dogs and none of them were licensed Katie would warn us when she saw the guards and we'd hide the dogs under the rocks. The dogs were kept for hunting rabbits. We'd eat the flesh and during the war sell the skins to England for lining gloves and boots. A man would come and collect them and give us a halfpenny a skin! Rabbit was our only meat in the winter.

9. A Gaeltacht island nine miles off the coast of Donegal.
10. General Francisco Franco (1892–1975) led Nationalists against the Republican government in the Spanish Civil War, 1936–9.
11. Adolf Hitler (1889–1945) became chancellor of Germany, 1933.

There used to be pigs but they died off the island. Grandma said they were too much trouble. They are like human beings. They die in the heat and die in the cold. I do remember the lovely trotters and pigs' cheeks. But then we grew our own wheat and barley and bartered it for the grinding on the mainland. We had the Golden Drop for our breakfast, this was porridge made from Indian Corn bought off the boat. Our own oats were kept for the animals.

We salted pollock for the winter and ate the mackerel fresh. And shlug, the seaweed.[12] We'd scrape that off the rocks. We'd wash and wash it to get the salt out. Then we'd put it in a big iron pot and pound it. When the lodgers came in the summer they'd have seaweed baths for the rheumatism and the goitre. The iodine was supposed to cure it. Then we had cockles, mussels, and winkles. Katie raged when they built the Marina at the Point. She said it would ruin the beaches with the changing of the channel. There was a woman we called the Shlug Woman who regularly came in from Sligo. She'd walk across the strand with a sack and fill it and walk all the way back to Sligo.[13] The shlug kept away the cholesterol; there were few, if any, heart attacks on the island.

Some years the tinsmiths would come and go round the houses to ask what was needed. They'd make the ponjers[14] for us. They were polite people. And they also made muzzlers for the calves to keep them from suckling.

. . . I came very close to Katie. Everybody used to say she was a terrible 'read out'[15] and I suppose she was. She'd read everybody out. She raged against a lot of things and for a lot of things. She had a war against barbed wire. She bombarded Sligo Council about the state of the roads on the island, the state of the pier. She sent letters off to the Dáil.[16] She had no fear of officials of any kind.

She carved out her own private wars with almost everyone on the island and off it. She couldn't stand injustice and what she called ignorant people telling her what to do. She would even lecture the bishops about the way the church was run.

She had plenty of chances to get married. It is said she was in love with a Black-and-Tan soldier — they were billeted everywhere in the Troubles.[17] But of course she was a strong Republican so that love came to nothing. She always said: 'Men are nuisances of nuisances.' Her father used to say no man could put up with her with her fiery temper. She was a great campaigner during the Sixteen Rising.[18] And later for the hunger-strikers.[19] She was invited as her cousin's last relative to go to the unveiling of a monument to him on Ben Bulben[20] — he had been shot in the Troubles. She always took causes for or against something. When she was young she was a great one for dances, especially at the Point.

We kept a foot in both camps — the pagan and the Christian. For instance we gathered primroses in the spring and threw them on the roof for luck and plenty.[21] And there was 'the thread'.[22] Willie Brown sprained his ankle and of course there was no such thing as a doctor unless you were near death so Katie said to me: 'You'll have to go to the wise woman in the Rosses.' She

---

12. Irish *sleabhac*, an edible seaweed, possibly *Porphyra umbilicaulis*; also anglicized as 'sloke': laver, laver-bread. Diarmuid Ó Muirithe, *A Dictionary of Anglo-Irish: Words and Phrases from Gaelic in the English of Ireland* (Dublin: Four Courts Press, 1996), p. 179, suggests *Porphyra laciniata*. See also P.W. Joyce, *English as We Speak it in Ireland* (1910) (new ed., with an Introduction by Terence Dolan, Dublin: Wolfhound Press, 1979), pp. 327–8): 'Sloke, a table delicacy . . . seen in all the Dublin fish shops . . . [its] name known all over the Three Kingdoms'.

13. Coney Island is accessible on foot from the mainland at low tide.

14. Porringers: originally vessels from which oatmeal porridge was eaten.

15. A sharp-tongued person.

16. The parliament in Dublin.

17. The Black and Tans were ex-soldiers and sailors recruited from January 1920 to reinforce the Royal Irish Constabulary during the Anglo-Irish War (the 'Troubles') of 1919–22. They were inadequately trained and notorious for their undisciplined violence, and their nickname came from their *ad hoc* uniform of army trousers and police tunics.

18. The Easter Rising of 1916.

19. The most famous hunger-striker was Terence MacSwiney (1879–1920), republican Mayor of Cork, who died on 25 October 1920 after seventy-four days on hunger strike in prison.

20. A conspicuous mountain in County Sligo, mentioned frequently in oral tradition and in the poetry of W.B. Yeats.

21. A common May Eve and May Day custom in Ireland, where the flowers were sometimes said to protect the house from fairies. See Kevin Danaher, *The Year in Ireland* (Cork: Mercier Press, 1972), pp. 88–9; Mary Carbery, *The Farm by Lough Gur* (Cork: Mercier Press, 1973 [1937]), p. 158; Patricia Lysaght, 'Maytime Verdure Customs and their Distribution in Ireland', in *International Folklore Review* (London, 1991), pp. 75–82.

22. A folk cure, whose efficacy would depend on the scrupulous carrying out of instructions. *Ortha an Leona*, the charm for a sprain, is a rhyme found in many Indo-European languages, including Irish and English (for more on charms, see the introduction to subsection 'Spirituality and Religion in Oral Tradition', pp. 1399–1401.). The healer usually ties a thread around the affected part while saying the words. Scepticism about such cures is not unusual.

lived near Lissadell.[23] Katie gave me a thread to take with me. But I was not to ask anyone when I left the house for directions.

Packie rowed me across. So I came to this little hamlet. Not even a street,[24] all sand. A man was sitting outside his half door. So I went to the house across from his and this woman appeared. You have no idea! She was a gypsy with earrings and a headband. There were all manner of herbs, dried lavender and stuff hanging. Again I said not a word. The idea was to exchange threads. So we exchanged threads. Then she disappeared behind a bead curtain. I was terrified. I came all the way back.

So they tied the thread around Willie's ankle and believe it or not the swelling came down. Katie was mad because Willie kept scorning her. It was amazing how I found my way, though. All around and beyond Dulmore strand. Then there was a magical stone for curing horses' legs. More thread. You were sent to this stone and you'd leave one piece and take another and and come back and wind it round the animals' legs. The stone was out near Strandhill.[25]

Being reared out on the island gave me two great things which have lived with me all my life. Patience and a love of solitude. When your life is ruled by the weather and the tide you have patience and when you have a lot of tasks to do, that have to be done alone, you learn solitude. I love people, and love to be with them, but I also love solitude.

23. Lissadell House, on the northern shore of Drumcliff Bay, County Sligo, was the home of the Gore-Booth sisters, Eva (1870–1926) and Constance, later Countess Markievicz (1884–1927).
24. The 'street' is the paved area immediately outside the front door of a house, even in the country. The 'yard' is at the back of the house.
25. A seaside village on the southern shore of Sligo Bay.

Biographies/Bibliographies

Peig Sayers

LIFE. Peig Sayers was born in Baile Bhiocáire (Vicarstown), Dún Chaoin (Dunquin), County Kerry, in 1873, the youngest of a family several of whose children had died. Thus she grew up in a household of adults, as did many children who were to become important bearers of oral tradition. As a young girl, she worked as a maidservant, first for a shopkeeper's family in Dingle, later on a farm a few miles on the other side of that town, until she married Pádraig Ó Gaoithín ('Patsy Flint') at nineteen and went to live with his family on the Great Blasket Island. She gave birth to ten children, of whom six survived childhood. Patsy Flint died in 1923. Peig's autobiography tells of her pride and pleasure in learning to read English as a child at school; however, in adult life she excelled at oral storytelling, remembering and reinterpreting long, colourful folktales, legends and narratives of local history, many of which she had heard from her father, for listeners who crowded into her house night after night. Widowed at fifty, she became famous when international scholars sought her out, studying the Irish language with her expert aid, and transcribing her stories. Máire Ní Chinnéide convinced her to commit her own life story to writing, and the result was two books, dictated to her son Maidhc and edited by Ní Chinnéide. In 1942 Peig Sayers moved back to the mainland with Maidhc, and settled in Baile Bhiocáire. She spent the last ten years of her life in Dingle hospital, where she died on 8 December 1958. She is buried in Dún Chaoin. Maidhc died in 1974.

Máire ('Molly') Ní Chinnéide was born in Dublin in 1878 to a prosperous middle-class family. She belonged to the generation of women who studied in private colleges for the examinations of the Royal University, which would not admit them to lectures. She attended the Dominican-run Ardscoil Mhuire, Merrion Square [St Mary's University College], and graduated BA in modern literature, 1901. From 1903 until her marriage to Seán Mac Gearailt in 1906, she was professor of Irish at Ardscoil Mhuire in Donnybrook, Dublin. She was active in the work of Conradh na Gaeilge, the Gaelic League, and in Oireachtas na Gaeilge, the annual Irish-language cultural festival, writing and publishing plays in Irish, among them Gleann na Sidheog (1902) and An Dúthchas: Dráma éin-ghníomha (1908). In 1903 her efforts led to the founding by Conradh na Gaeilge of the first-ever camogie club. Her only daughter, Niamh (b. 1909), was well known as an actor in Irish-language plays, but died in 1939. Máire Ní Chinnéide died in 1967. See Diarmuid Breathnach and Máire Ní Mhurchú, 1882–1992: Beathaisnéis a Dó (Dublin: An Clóchomhar, 1990), pp. 79–81.

CHIEF WRITINGS. Peig. i. A Scéal Féin do Scríobh Peig Sayers (ed.) Máire Ní Chinnéide (Dublin: Talbot Press, 1936); Peig Sayers, Peig: The Autobiography of Peig Sayers of the Great Blasket Island, translated into English by Bryan MacMahon (Dublin: Talbot Press, 1974, repr. 1983); Machtnamh Seana-Mhná (ed.) Máire Ní Chinnéide (Baile Átha Cliath: Oifig an tSoláthair, 1939); new ed., P. Ua Maoileoin (Dublin: Oifig an tSoláthair, 1980); trans., Séamus Ennis, An Old Woman's Reflections, with an Introduction by W.R. Rodgers (London: Oxford University Press, 1962); (ed.) Kenneth Jackson, Scéalta ón mBlascaod (Dublin: An Cumann le Béaloideas Éireann, 1998 [1938, 1968]); Peig. A Scéal Féin (eds) Máire Ní Mhainnín, Liam P. Ó Murchú (An Daingean: An Sagart, 1998).

BIOGRAPHY AND CRITICISM. Micheál Ó Guithín [Ó Gaoithín], Beatha Pheig Sayers (Dublin: Foilseacháin Náisiúnta Tta, 1970); Máire Ní Chéilleachair, Peig Sayers Scéalaí, 1873–1958 [Ceiliúradh an Bhlascaoid 3] (Dublin: Coiscéim, 1999); R. MacCullagh, The Irish Currach Folk (Dublin: Wolfhound Press, 1992); (ed. and trans.) Seán O'Sullivan, Folktales of Ireland (London: Routledge and Kegan Paul, 1966), nos 14, 24, 36; Joan N. Radner, '"The Woman Who Went to Hell": Coded Values in Irish Folk Narrative', Midwestern Folklore (Journal of the Hoosier Folklore Society), vol. 15, no. 2 (1989), pp. 109–117; Eibhlín Ní Mhurchú, 'Peig Sayers', in Aogán Ó Muircheartaigh (ed.), Oidhreacht an Bhlascaoid (Dublin: Coiscéim, 1989), pp. 238–52; Cathal Ó Háinle, 'Peig, Aonghus Ó Dálaigh agus Macbeth', ibid., pp. 253–69; Diarmuid Breathnach and Máire Ní Mhurchú, 1882–1992: Beathaisnéis a Cúig (Dublin: An Clóchomhar, 1997), pp. 265–7; Muiris Mac Conghail, The Blaskets. People and Literature (Dublin: Country House, 1994 [1987]), pp. 156–61; Patricia Lysaght, 'Traditional Storytelling in Ireland in the Twentieth Century', in Traditional Storytelling Today (ed.) Margaret Read MacDonald (Chicago and London: Fitzroy Dearbon, 1999), pp. 264–72 (here pp. 267–8).

Nan Joyce

LIFE. Born Ann O'Donoghue, in Clogheen, County Tipperary, in 1940, Nan Joyce had five brothers and four sisters, one of whom is Chrissie Ward, (see 'Storytelling Traditions of the Irish Travellers', p. 1282). Her parents were John O'Donoghue and Nan, née McCann; her grandparents John O'Donoghue and Sarah Power, and Richard McCann and Nan Doyle. Most of her childhood was spent in Belfast, but she spent two years in England and Scotland with her family from age nine to eleven. At sixteen she married John Joyce, another Traveller, in Donnybrook church in Dublin. They had eleven children. Later she was a founder member of the Travellers' Rights Committee, and stood as an Independent candidate in the 1982 general election. In the 1990s she moved to a house in Coolock, in north Dublin, where she still lives. A new edition of her autobiography appeared in 2000.

CHIEF WRITINGS. *Traveller: An Autobiography by Nan Joyce* (ed.) Anna Farmar (Dublin: Gill and Macmillan, 1985); republished, with a new Afterword by Anna Farmar, as *My Life on The Road* (Dublin: A. and A. Farmar, 2000).

Rosaleen Ferguson

LIFE. Daughter of a lighthouse-keeper, Rosaleen Ferguson was born Rosaleen Hilary Doyle on Coney Island, in Sligo Bay, County Sligo, 30 December 1929, third eldest of eight children. She grew up in lighthouse communities around the Irish coast, going back and forth to Coney until the age of eight, when she went to live there with her grandmother and aunt. When she was almost fourteen, she moved to Edinburgh to join her mother, and has lived in Scotland since. She went to work in Jenners, in Prince's Street, and later worked in Boots, the chemists. In November 1953 she married Preston Ferguson. They had three sons and two daughters, one of whom, Eileen Ferguson, is an artist, living in County Monaghan. They lived mostly in Edinburgh, with one period spent as owner-managers of a small country hotel. They also kept racing pigeons and bred dogs. Since her husband's death in 1994, Rosaleen Ferguson has lived in Edinburgh, reading, walking, gardening, and seeing her family and friends.

CHIEF WRITINGS. Interview with Leland Bardwell, *Force 10: A Journal of the Northwest*, no. 3 (1991), pp. 84–9, and 'Memoir', *Force 10: A Journal of the Northwest*, no. 8 (n.d., *c.* 1996), pp. 31–3.

ÉILÍS NÍ DHUIBHNE, *Editor*

International Folktales

In *The Western Island*,[1] Robin Flower translates a version of a long fairytale, 'Purty Deas Squarey', as told to him by Gobnait Ní Chinnéide on the Great Blasket Island, County Kerry. Gobnait told the story while she was sewing at a kitchen fireside, making a dress for a child. The audience consisted of the child Máirín and her grandfather Seán Ó Duinnlé, Robin Flower and a few others. Gobnait, 'a strongly built woman of forty', was reluctant to tell the story, which she considered only fit for children. However, she was persuaded. Flower describes the scene when she finished:

> 'Well, well, well,' broke in Seán, 'it's a good tale enough, but we wouldn't have called it a tale at all in the old times. Devil take my soul, it's long before I'd put a tale like that in comparison with the long Fenian[2] stories we used to tell. It was only the other day that I had all the old tales in my mind, and I could have spent the night telling them to you without a word out of its place in any tale. But now I couldn't tell a tale of them. And do you know what has driven them out of my head?'
>
> 'Well, I suppose you're losing your memory,' I said.
>
> 'No, it isn't that, for my memory is as good as ever it was for other things. But it's Tomás has done it, for he has books and newspapers and he reads them to me, and the little tales one after another, day after

day, in the books and the newspapers, have driven the old stories out. But maybe I'm little the worse for losing them.'

Here, I thought, was the clash of two traditions, the oral and the printed, vividly present in the figure of that heroic old man.[3]

This vignette throws light on a number of aspects of Irish oral storytelling in this century. Flower noted the clash of oral and post-oral cultures, but a clash between the masculine and the feminine traditions is also clearly apparent. Seán is scornful of Gobnait's story. It is a fairytale, one of the great genres of oral narrative, mainly told by men in Ireland, but a tale of a particularly feminine kind: a version of 'Cinderella',[4] a story of particular appeal to women. Seán compares it to the 'Fenian' tales or *Fiannaíocht*, epic tales of adventure, told by men in the traditional society. Women were discouraged from telling these stories. He indicates that the good old days, when men told them, are over, and that only insignificant tales, which even a woman can tell, are to be heard now.

The storytelling community in Ireland was never gender-exclusive, as it was in some cultures, where the narrative context was usually in an all-male establishment, such as the coffee houses of Yugoslavia,[5] which women simply did not attend.[6] In Ireland, stories were usually told in the kitchens of dwelling houses. Girls and women, as well as boys and men, could hear them, and learn them if they had a wish to do so. As far as we know, boys and men were encouraged by tradition to learn

1. Robin Flower, *The Western Island* (Oxford: Oxford University Press, 1944), p. 60 ff. Flower, who was deputy keeper of manuscripts in the British Museum, London, 1929–44, visited the island regularly between 1910 and 1930.
2. In Irish, *Fiannaíocht*: stories of Fionn mac Cumhaill and his band of warrior-hunters. See James H. Delargy, 'The Gaelic Storyteller', Sir John Rhŷs Memorial Lecture 1945, Proceedings of the British Academy, vol. 31 (rpr., Chicago: University of Chicago Press, 1969).

3. R. Flower, *Western Island*, p. 17.
4. AT 510 'Cinderella'.
5. Described by Albert B. Lord in *The Singer of Tales* (Cambridge, Mass.: Harvard University Press, 1960).
6. The public houses in Irish country towns, formerly almost exclusively male establishments, were not venues for storytelling.

stories, while girls and women were apparently not encouraged to learn or tell the most public forms of tale. Neither did they have as much freedom as boys and men did, to go visiting neighbours' houses, and would therefore have had a more limited access to storytelling sessions. In spite of these restrictions, some women did learn and tell stories, including the longest and most demanding forms.

The word 'folktale' has a variety of connotations in popular parlance, but within the discipline of folkloristics it has a specific meaning. Folktales are fictitious stories, formal in structure and making limited concessions to realism. The term is wide enough to include many of the most basic forms of oral narrative, such as the joke or the animal fable, as well as the most complex and highly developed, such as the fairytale. Folktales are usually defined by distinction with the legend, which is, in general, more realistic and more closely knitted into the fabric of everyday life.[7] The folktale, on the other hand, can often be perceived as floating free of its sociological and historical context. The texts which follow are examples of the international folktale, categorized in the classic Aarne-Thompson index as *Märchen* or fairytales.[8]

No genre of oral narrative, or any kind of oral tradition, can be totally free of social context. Piotr Bogatyrev and Roman Jakobson point out that an essential difference between literature and folklore is that the latter is entirely dependent on social support for its survival: if a folklore item ceases to have relevance to society, it ceases to exist, since it depends for its existence on being listened to by groups of people.[9] The

stories which survived in oral tradition (as opposed to writing) did so because they were of interest to people, and were in some kind of vibrant and essential interaction with social values, attitudes and mores. In folktales, this interaction tends to be of a predominantly metaphorical or symbolical kind. Folktales carry information about attitudes, manners and mores, but fairytales, in particular, are less rich in other kinds of sociological detail than are legends. Narrators have probably always understood, however, that the fantastic characters, plots and images of the tales can carry deeper meanings and are not simply entertainments.

The fairytale is the the most interesting and complex form of oral narrative from an artistic and psychological point of view, and the question of how women have related to it is of overwhelming significance to our understanding of the history of women as narrators, or indeed as artists of any kind, in Ireland. Fairytales are stories of quest and adventure, peopled by beautiful girls and handsome boys, who encounter hags, ogres, dragons and giants, fly on eagles' wings, climb glass mountains, eat from magical tablecloths, and finally marry beautiful rich partners and live happily ever after. Such tales have been found all over the world; many crop up in literary sources from the Middle Ages onwards, and some occur in ancient literary sources.[10]

The theme of all fairytales is the quest for love and marriage; they begin with the break-up of one family and end with the establishment of another.[11] The greater part of the plot is concerned with how the protagonist successfully completes this transition from childhood to married adult life. Like other kinds of oral narrative, fairytales can be used to transmit many kinds of information about social and sexual mores and behaviour, including messages about the acceptable behaviour of women and men in various situations.

One of the best studies of the hidden meanings and messages of fairytales is by Bengt Holbek, who limits his interpretation to texts collected in a particular place at a particular time, insisting

7. For legends, see the subsection 'Legends of the Supernatural', pp. 1284–1311.
8. Antti Aarne and Stith Thompson, *The Types of the Folktale* (Folklore Fellows Communications, No. 184) (Helsinki: Academia Scientiarum Fennica, 1961). Folktales are conventionally referred to by the numbers assigned in this index, prefixed with the letters AT. A useful outline of the kinds of folktale found in Ireland is Seán Ó Súilleabháin, *Storytelling in Irish Tradition* (Cork: Mercier Press [for the Cultural Relations Committee of Ireland], 1973). The index of Irish folktales by Seán Ó Súilleabháin and Reidar Christiansen, *The Types of the Irish Folktale* (Folklore Fellows Communications, No. 188) (Helsinki: Academia Scientiarum Fennica, 1963), provides a full list of all international tales found in Ireland.
9. See Piotr Bogatyrev and Roman Jakobson, 'Die Folklore als eine besondere Form des Schaffens', *Verzameling van opstellen door oud-leerlingen en bevriende vakgenooten opgedragen aan mgr. Prof. Dr. Jos. Schrijnen (Donum natalicum Schrijnen)* (Nijmegen/Utrecht, 1929), pp. 900–13.
10. See Stith Thompson, *The Folktale* (Berkeley, Los Angeles, London: University of California Press, 1946).
11. Max Lüthi, *Das europäische Volksmärchen: Form und Wesen* (Bern: A. Francke, 1947).

that the meaning of the tales depends upon their immediate sociological context and is not necessarily universal.[12] He also insists on trying to interpret the meaning of the tales as understood by the tellers, arguing that to understand the subtext of the story, it is necessary to relate it to the experiences of the teller and to the social setting in which it is told. It would be surprising if a version of 'Cinderella' told in Galway in 1937 carried the same coded messages as a version written down in France in 1695, or told in Germany in 1800.

Ireland has more versions of fairytales collected from oral tradition than any other country, but these have been relatively little studied, despite a wealth of scholarship on the international fairytale.[13] In fact, Irish fairytales are not markedly different from the same tales collected in other parts of the Indo-European tradition zone (given that variation in motifs and choice of episodes occurs everywhere). They are sometimes said to be longer, perhaps as a result of better collecting techniques in Ireland than in other countries, at a time when storytellers still remembered fairytales. The rhetorical 'runs' used by some Irish narrators to embellish their fairytales are borrowed from the tale tradition of *Fiannaíocht*. In general though, rather than being unique or unusual, the telling of fairytales in Ireland is part of an international tradition.

Fairytales can be categorized as 'masculine' or 'feminine', depending on the focus of the tale on a hero or a heroine. We might perhaps expect women to favour those tales which have a female protagonist and deal with love from the female point of view, although most fairytale types in the international corpus are not of this kind, but are masculine in orientation.[14] 'Feminine' fairytales include AT 313 'The Girl as Helper in the Hero's Flight', AT 510 'Cinderella', and AT 425 'The Quest for the Lost Husband', all of which have been very popular in Ireland and samples of which are presented here.

Disconcertingly, the Irish records do not indicate that women prefer these to other, masculine, tales, but suggest that men and women tell both masculine and feminine fairytales in equal numbers. The context in which most of our texts were collected may have affected the pattern here, as men may have told tales to collectors which they might not have told under normal circumstances. Women interested in narrating had little choice in any circumstances but to tell at least some stories with a masculine emphasis, since these were in the vast majority. Storytellers like Peig Sayers or Sorcha Mhic Ghrianna, who had large repertoires, simply knew practically all the fairytales current in their neighbourhoods. Individual or gender orientation may have influenced the way they told the stories, but not their actual choice of tale. Máire Mhic Fhionnlaoich, on the other hand, seems to have known a good proportion of tales which have a feminine orientation, and to have preferred such stories.

Most of the stories folklorists in Ireland deal with were collected during a period of transition from one kind of culture to another, so that the narrators who told them were not necessarily representative of those who would have shone in the primary oral community. The impression that women were in the minority among storytellers has been encouraged, if not largely inspired, by one of the few survey articles ever published on storytelling in Ireland: James H. Delargy's 'The Gaelic Storyteller'. There he refers to the traditional prohibition on the telling of hero-tales or *Fiannaíocht* by women, and indicates that fairytales also were mainly told by men. Women, he says, in an often-quoted passage, specialized in other forms of tradition:

Seanchas, genealogical lore, music, folkprayers, were, as a rule, associated with women; at any rate they excelled the men in these branches of tradition. While women do not take part in the storytelling, not a word of the tale escapes them, and if their relatives or close friends make any slip or hesitate in their recital, it is no uncommon experience of mine to hear the

12. See Bengt Holbek, *The Interpretation of Fairytales: Danish Folklore in a European Perspective* (Folklore Fellows Communications, No. 239) (Helsinki: Academia Scientiarum Fennica, 1987), p. 157.
13. See for example Reidar Christiansen's *Studies in Irish and Scandinavian Folktales* (Copenhagen: Rosenkilde and Bagger [for Coimisiún Béaloideasa Éireann], 1959). For references in passing, see J. H. Delargy, 'The Gaelic Storyteller'; S. Ó Súilleabháin, *Storytelling in Irish Tradition: Folktales of Ireland*; Alan Bruford, *Gaelic Folktales and Medieval Romances: A Study of the Early Modern Irish 'Romantic Tales' and Their Oral Derivatives* (Dublin: Folklore of Ireland Society, 1959).
14. See B. Holbek, *Interpretation of Fairytales*, p. 161.

listening women interrupt and correct the speaker.[15]

Delargy goes on to mention a few exceptions to the general rule, and to name some women who knew hero-tales.

This comment, which has had much more far-reaching influence than its author could have anticipated, is quoted on almost all occasions when the question of women's role as narrators is discussed.

Irish collectors of folklore in the past have been accused of having neglected to collect from women.[16] For many years all the full-time collectors of the Irish Folklore Commission (IFC) were men. Most of them were born in the early years of this century; all were Catholic; all were brought up in a society and at a time which were essentially masculinist. We can safely assume that men like Seosamh Ó Dálaigh, Seán Ó hEochaidh, Ciarán Báiréad, born in the Gaeltacht regions of Kerry, Donegal and Galway, regions still not notable for their gender egalitarianism, were probably not feminist in outlook. Nevertheless, a cursory check of informants' names in the IFC archive indicates that somewhere between a quarter and one-third of the names are those of women; investigations of particular folktale types have suggested that about one-third of their narrators are women.

Field diaries kept by full-time collectors do not indicate any prejudice against women as informants. During his first year, 1936-7, Seosamh Ó Dálaigh collected extensively from Máire Ruiséal, from her sister Cáit, and from Méiní Uí Dhuinnlé, to mention but a few of the women narrators in his collections. He was later responsible for recording from Peig Sayers the largest body of oral narrative ever collected from any Irish storyteller. Seán Ó hEochaidh visited and recorded from half a dozen women story-tellers during 1938. More of his informants during that year were men, but there is no evidence in his diary that he even considered neglecting women informants.

The difference in gender between collector and informant may have affected the nature of the material collected: we would not expect

much information on menstrual habits, for instance (and it might not have been collected in the Ireland of the 1930s even had collectors been women), but the male–female juxtaposition could benefit the collecting relationship. The mildly sexual nature of the encounter between informant and collector — usually muted, remote and subtle, especially in the early days, when the male collectors were all aged about twenty and their female informants in their seventies and eighties — would not have been entirely negative. While the fact that all the full-time collectors of Irish folk narrative for several decades were men must have had some effect on the documentation of women's folklore, there is no evidence that they seriously neglected to collect from female narrators. Since the Department of Irish Folklore at University College Dublin took over the work of the IFC in 1971, a high proportion of collectors and folklorists have been women.

What of Delargy's general impression, that the majority of storytellers telling the large, public genres, were men, while women had a relatively 'passive' knowledge of complex forms such as the fairytale and hero tale, but were active tellers of legends and other kinds of lore which were told in smaller and more private situations than the long stories? It is likely that both men and women who would have been passive, rather than active, tradition bearers in the primary oral community would have been able to remember and tell stories to collectors. Bengt Holbek, in his study of fairytales collected by Evald Tang Kristensen in nineteenth-century Jutland, found that the proportion of female to male narrators increased as the tradition declined: women continued to tell stories to children when they had ceased to be an important adult form of entertainment; they also told them to collectors.[17] It seems probable that a similar situation obtained in Ireland, where all the indications are that men dominated as narrators of the main story genres when storytelling was a living tradition.

When the tradition was in decline, women co-operated with collectors by telling them the stories they remembered, but might not have had a chance to perform when storytelling was an

15. J. H. Delargy, 'The Gaelic Storyteller', p. 7.
16. See for example Clodagh Harvey, *Irish Times*, 4 November 1993.

17. B. Holbek, *Interpretation of Fairytales*, p. 167.

important form of entertainment in the adult community: the significance of shyness, unwillingness to appear unfeminine or forward, and social pressure to conform to the traditional stereotype, should not be underestimated. It is not difficult to imagine that it would have been much easier for a woman to tell stories to a folklore collector on a one-to-one basis, than to sit in front of a gathering of twenty or thirty neighbours, and do the same thing. The difference is between public performance and a private chat. It is probably no exaggeration to say that for most Irishwomen the latter has traditionally been, and to some extent still is, the more acceptable context for performance of any kind. In any case, women in country households were so occupied with house and farm work that they had limited opportunities for any kind of leisure activity. Collectors' memories and diaries indicate that it was difficult to collect from women: they were always jumping up to do something in the kitchen.

Preliminary examination of the repertoires of some women storytellers in Kerry shows that Máire Ruiséal knew several international folktales, including many of the great classic fairytales, and about an equal number of legends.[18] Her sister, Cáit Ruiséal, was more interested in religious tales and legends. Peig Sayers knew huge quantities of folktales of all kinds. Cáit (Bab) Feirtéar, granddaughter of Cáit Ruiséal, two of whose stories appear in the subsection 'Spirituality and Religion in Oral Tradition,' pp. 1416–1420, knows very many folktales, has a fondness among them for religious tales, and also knows a great number of legends. Individual knowledge, taste, and the relationship between the narrator and the narrators who influenced her, must be taken into account. Máire Ruiséal usually cites her father as her source; Bab Feirtéar often cites her uncle. The connection between men and women storytellers is very intricate. Micheál Ó Gaoithín learned many of his tales from his mother, Peig Sayers, who, in turn, had learned stories from her father and uncle.[19]

18. Unpublished work by Bo Almqvist.
19. Bo Almqvist, 'Beirt Scéalaithe i Scáthan Scéil: Insintí Pheig Sayers agus Mhichíl Uí Ghaoithín ar eachtra nua-aimseartha (AT 821B, "Chickens from Boiled Eggs")', in *Féilscríbhinn Thomáis de Bhaldraithe*, ed. Seosamh Watson (Baile Átha Cliath: Coiste Fhéilscríbhinn Thomáis de Bhaldraithe, An Coláiste Ollscoile, 1986), pp. 134–52.

Little is known about the Donegal storyteller Anna Uí Shighil, but Seán Ó hÉochaidh collected enough local lore and legends from her to fill some four hundred handwritten pages, along with a number of folktales, one of which is given below.

The two most significant influences on a storyteller's style seem to be the traditional style of narrators in the community where she or he lives and her or his own personality. In the fairytales presented here, Sorcha Mhic Ghrianna and Máire Mhic Fhionnlaoich, from the Rinn na Feirste–Gaoth Dobhair (Rannafast–Gweedore) region of County Donegal, exhibit very clearly the formal stylistic features common to men and women in that area. Máire Ruiséal, on the other hand, has the freer and more individualistic style found among all narrators in the Dingle, Co. Kerry, area and elsewhere in Ireland. Almost all of the narrators presented use the rhetorical 'runs' which are characteristic of male narrative style.

The stories allow for considerable individual input in terms of emphasis, attitude to the events and to the characters, as well as choice of vocabulary and motifs. Gender seems not to have had much effect on the selection of the last two elements, but does seem to affect narrators' attitudes to the events of the tales. Thus, Sorcha Mhic Ghrianna is sensitive to the emotional strain placed on the hero of her story, 'Rí na Fásaighe Duibhe', 'The King of the Black Desert', while he is waiting for the eagle to return to him: 'He sat there then for a very long time, as it seemed to him, sometimes thinking, sometimes staring up at the skies, and all the time waiting to see the eagle returning to him.' This concern with the minutiae of emotion is unusual in fairytales, where the characters typically exhibit only the most basic feelings, such as love, hate and hunger. Even physical pain is never described. It may be regarded as evidence of Sorcha Mhic Ghrianna's femininity — although it could equally well reflect her personal, rather literary, cast of mind. Similarly, Máire Mhic Fhionnlaoich's emphasis on the mother's role and her sympathy with her point of view in her version of 'Bluebeard' seems very feminine and maternal. Máire Ruiséal also seems feminine in her understanding of the love of her heroine for her husband in her 'Sceal an Ghabhairín Bháin', 'The Story of the Little White Goat'.

MÁIRE RUISÉAL

(1856–*c.* 1945)

from:
IRISH FOLKLORE
COLLECTION MS NO. 243 (1936)

[This is a version of the story told in antiquity about Cupid and Psyche, and known in children's literature as 'Beauty and the Beast'. It has been told and collected in many parts of Ireland, where the animal husband is usually a dog, or a wolf, rather than a goat, as in this version.[1] Seosamh Ó Dálaigh recorded it in Dún Chaoin, 5 September 1936, his second day working as a full-time collector of folklore. Máire Ruiséal had heard stories from her father when she was a girl, and cited him as her source for 'Scéal an Ghabhairín Bháin', which suggests that she could have first heard it in the 1860s. She was eighty-one when it was collected. This was probably the first story she had ever told to someone using a mechanical recording device; it may have made her nervous, as she becomes slightly confused in places. Nevertheless, this is one of the greatest examples available of a 'feminine fairytale'. Among all the fairytales, it is the best tale of a woman's obsessive love for a man and has one of the most active, stubborn and assertive heroines one could encounter. The narrator indicates that she understands entirely the heroine's desire for her husband and has every sympathy with her. (A story like this may let us know more about the storyteller's character than the bald facts of her biography, which do not suggest much concern for romantic love.) She unhesitatingly and skilfully uses the rhetorical 'run' describing nightfall ('and dewfall and night came upon her . . .', etc.), testimony that women narrators do not always avoid these rhetorical figures, as is sometimes suggested. Her sense of humour is evident in her treatment of the episode involving the Scabby Crow's efforts to elicit information about her 'sod of death' from the old hag which is a version of AT 425, 'The Search for the Lost Husband'. From IFC 243: 161–207. The translation has been silently emended for ease of reading in places where the storyteller appears to have confused pronouns and other details. Translation and headnote by E. Ní D.]

SCÉAL AN GHABHAIRÍN BHÁIN

Do bhí feirmeoir ann tamall do bhlianta ó shin, agus aon iníon amháin do bhí aige. Sea. Bhíodh gabhar bán ag teacht go[2] dtí béal an doiris nach aon lá insa tseachtain chúiche. Agus faoi dheire thiar thall do thit sí i ngrá leis an ngabhar.

Agus dh'imigh sé chun siúil agus do dh'imigh sí sin ina dhiaidh, agus má dh'imigh do lean sí é riamh agus choíche.

Do chuadar isteach i gcúirt bhreá. Do labhair sé léi ansan.

'Mhuise, sea anois,' ar seisean. 'Cé acu is fearr leatsa anois,' ar seisean, 'mise bheith mar ghabhar istoíche nó mar fhear istoíche agus im ghabhar isló?'

'Ó go deimhin,' ar sise, 'is fearr liom cuideachta na hoíche — tú bheith mar fhear istoíche agus id ghabhar isló.'

Mar sin do bhí.

Do thiteadar féin lena chéile tamall. I gceann bliana do rángaigh leanbh mic aici. Agus dúirt sé léi gan deoir do ghol ná shileadh anuas as a súile má dh'imeodh aon rud nó íde ar an leanbh san, nó má dhéanfadh sí aon deoir do ligint anuas ná beadh sé féin aici. Go gcaithfeadh sé imeacht uaithi.

Sea! Nuair a saolaoídh an leanbh ní mhór na laethanta a bhí an leanbh bailithe uaithi as an leabaigh. Agus do tháinig saghas tocht agus rud uirthi, ach chuimhnigh sí ná raibh aon ghnó aici aon deoir do shileadh.

Agus nuair a tháinig sé chúichi —

'Tá do leainbhín bailithe uait,' ar seisean, 'ach má tá,' ar seisean, 'ní haon ní é sin,' ar seisean, ''fhaid a bheadsa agat,' ar seisean, 'mar chuideachta.'

Mar sin do bhí.

Bliain ón lá san arís do saolaíodh leanbh eile mic di. Agus dúirt sé léi gan deoir do ligean anuas as a súile má dh'imeodh aon íde nó rud ar an leanbh, nó má dhéanfadh sí aon deoir do shileadh ná beadh sé féin ina teannta.

---

1. 275 versions of it are listed in S. Ó Súilleabháin and R. Christiansen, *The Types of the Irish Folktale*. The word *gadhar*, meaning 'dog', closely resembles *gabhar*, 'goat'.

2. MS has *do* throughout. This has been emended to *go* where appropriate, while *dur* has been emended to *gur*.

D'imigh an leanbh uaithi. Árdaíodh uaithi as an leabaigh é. Agus do tháinig tocht uirthi. Agus má sea féinig do chuimhnigh sí uirthi féinig ná raibh aon ghnó aici aon deoir do ligean anuas agus níor lig. Bliain eile ón lá san do saolaíodh leanbh eile mic di agus dúirt sé léi gan aon deoir do ligean anuas má dh'imeodh aon ní uirthi nó ar an leanbh san. Má dh'imeodh sé uaithi bheith sásta leis, nó mara mbeadh ná beadh sé féin aici.

Do mhachnaigh sí. Agus nuair a dh'imigh an leanbh uaithi, n'fhéad sí é, gan deoir do ligeant anuas as a súil. Agus do bhuail sí suas seáilín póca lena súile chun ná cífeadh sé sin fliuch iad. Agus is mar sin a bhí.

Nuair a tháinig sé chúichi.

'Sea anois,' ar seisean, 'ní bhead-sa agat,' ar seisean, 'aon lá eile. Dá mb'áil leat,' ar seisean, 'do shúil a choinneáil tirim, ní móide gur ghanntar duit iad a fhliuchadh go deo arís, ach níl aon dul anois agat' ar seisean, 'ar mise bheith agat,' ar seisean, 'caithfead bailiú uait.'

'Má dh'imíonn tusa,' ar sise, 'imeodsa id dhiaidh.'

'Níl aon ghnó agat imeacht,' ar seisean, 'mar ná fuil aon dul agatsa orm.'

D'imigh sé agus d'éirigh sí agus do dh'imigh sí ina dhiaidh.

I gcaitheamh an lae siar bhí sí stolta stracaithe aiges na sceacha, agus é sin ag imeacht roimpi. Ach do bhíodh sí ag iarraidh radharc do choinneáil air i gcónaí, go mbeadh solas aici air.

Nuair a tháinig drúcht agus deireadh an lae uirthi, do bhí an madra gearra dul ar scáth na cupóige, agus an chupóg ag teitheadh uaidh, agus an madra rua ag dul ina phluaisín féinig.[3]

Do tháinig an oíche uirthi, agus shuigh sé síos ar thurtóg, agus d'fhan sé léi. Mar sin a bhí.

'Ní mór an gnó athá agat ag rith im dhiaidh-sa,' ar seisean.

'Níl leigheas agam air,' ar sise. 'Leanfad trí uisce agus trí thine tú,' ar sise.

'Sin thíos tig,' ar seisean, 'agus téire síos ann, agus loirg bheith istigh go maidin,' ar seisean. 'Mara mbeidh tú á dh'fháil,' ar seisean, 'loirg ar shon an ghabhairín bháin slí na hoíche.'

Mar sin a bhí.

'Agus an bhfanfaidh tusa liom?' ar sise, 'go maidean.'

'Fanfaidh mé anso leat,' ar seisean, 'go maidin.'

Chuaigh sí síos agus do loirg sí bheith istigh go maidin agus ní raibh sí á dh'fháil.

'Mhuise,' ar sise, 'má b'é do thoil,' ar sise, 'lóistín na hoíche a thabhairt dom,' ar sise, 'ar son an ghabhairín bháin?'

'Gheobhair agus míle fáilte ar a shon san,' ar sise, 'suigh síos,' ar sise.

Shuigh sí síos. Fuair sí bia agus deoch, leaba chodlata, agus bricfeasta ar maidin. Agus nuair a bhí sí ag imeacht uaithi ar maidin ansan thug sí cíor di go gcíorfadh sí a ceann agus go dtiocfadh an ghruaig is breátha a bhí ar chailín óg riamh uirthi.

D'imigh sí léi agus bhí sé roimpe ansan phaiste céanna.

'Ní mór an gnó athá agat ag rith im dhiaidh-sa,' ar seisean léi.

'Níl leigheas agam air!' ar sise. 'Leanfaidh mé thú,' ar sise.

'Ní leanfaidh tú mise,' ar seisean, 'mar ná beidh a fhios agat,' ar seisean, 'b'fhearra dhuit filleadh abhaile,' ar seisean, 'agus dul abhaile go dtí t'athair.'

'Á, níl aon ghnó agamsa abhaile go dtí m'athair,' ar sise, 'agus teacht ag triall ortsa, agus leanfaidh mé thusa.'

Dh'imigh sí uirthi ina dhiaidh, is d'imigh sé sin agus do ghaibheadh sé trí's nach aon achrann agus trí's nach aon sceacha d'fhonn agus go bhfillfeadh sí agus í stollta stracaithe aiges na sceacha go dtí gur *tháinig drúcht agus deireanaí na hoíche uirthi, an madra gearra dul ar scáth na cupóige agus an chupóg ag teitheadh uaidh, agus an madra rua ag dul ina phluaisín féin, ní ná locht ar an madra macánta.* Do shuigh sé síos ar thurtóg agus do d'fhan sé léi.

'Tán tú marbh tráite,' ar sé, 'agus is beag an maitheas duit,' ar sé, 'bheith ag rith im dhiaidhse,' ar sé. 'Bheadh sé chomh maith agat,' ar sé, 'filleadh abhaile: sin thíos tig,' ar sé, 'agus téir síos,' arsa seisean, 'agus loirg do lóistín go maidin ann,' ar seisean, 'agus fanfadsa ansan go dtiocfa tú. Mara mbeir á d'fháil,' ar seisean, 'loirg é,' ar seisean, 'ar son an ghabhairín bháin,' ar seisean, 'is gheobhair.'

Mar sin a bhí. Loirg sí lóistín na hoíche, agus ní raibh sí mór-fháilteach roimpe.

'Ó, má b'é do thoil é,' ar sise, 'an dtabharfá dhom lóistín na hoíche,' ar sise, 'ar son an ghabhairín bháin!'

'Gheobhair agus fáilte,' ar sise, 'ar a shon san.'

Fuair sí bia agus deoch, leaba chodlata agus nuair a dh'éirí sí ar maidin, do fuair sí a bricfeasta. Agus nuair a bhí sí ag bailiú léi, do thug sí sisiúirín di.

'Seo sisiúirín duit,' ar sise, 'agus nuair a bhearrfaidh tú na giobail athá ort,' ar sise, 'tiocfaidh an t-éadach is breátha a bhí ar chailín óg riamh ort.'

Mar sin a bhí. Do dh'imigh sí agus do bhí sé roimpe. Agus do bhí sé roimpe sa phaiste chéanna. B'shin é an tarna lá.

'Sea anois,' ar seisean, 'b'fhearra dhuit,' ar seisean, 'filleadh abhaile, agus dein rud orm anois,' ar seisean, 'agus fill abhaile agus téir abhaile,' ar seisean, 'go dtí tig t'athar agus do mháthar.'

'Níl aon dul agamsa ar m'athair ná ar mo mháthair,' ar sise, 'agus níl aon radharc le fáil agam orthu go deo,' ar sise, 'ó leanas tusa. Leanfaidh mé thusa,' ar sise, 'pé áit do raghaidh tú.'

'Ní bheidh aon dul agat ormsa,' ar seisean, 'ach inniu. Ní bheidh aon dul agat orm,' ar seisean, 'aon lá eile.'

D'imigh sí ina dhiaidh agus do ghaibheadh sé trí's nach aon achrann agus trí's nach aon ghleannta agus trí's nach aon sceacha d'fhonn agus go gcaithfeadh sí filleadh — í stollta stracaithe, *agus bhí drúcht agus deireanaí an tráthnóna agus na hoíche ag teacht uirthi, an madra gearra ag dul ar scáth na cupóige, an chupóg ag teitheadh uaidh, agus an madra rua ag dul ina phluaisín féin, ní ná locht ar an madra macánta.* Do shuigh sé síos ar thurtóg agus d'fhan sé léi, agus dúirt sé léi —

'Dá mbeadh ciall agat,' ar seisean, 'do dh'fhillfeá abhaile,' ar seisean, 'an chéad lá a leanais mise,' ar seisean.

'Ní dh'fhillfead abhaile anois leis, mhuis,' ar sise.

'Sin thíos tig anois,' ar seisean, 'agus téir síos go maidin ann agus sin a bhfuil do mhaith dhuit,' ar seisean, 'agus loirg a bheith istigh,' ar seisean, 'ar shon an ghabhairín bháin go maidin. Fanfadsa anseo go dtiocfair,' ar seisean, 'ach má dh'fhanann,' ar seisean, 'sin a mbeidh agat.'

D'imigh sí síos agus do loirg sí bheith istigh ar shon an ghabhairín bháin. Fuair agus céad agus míle fáilte, bia agus deoch agus leaba chodlata. Agus nuair a dh'éirí sí ar maidin do chonaic sí triúr beag leanbh ar fud an tí. Agus bhí sí ag cuir a dá shúil tríd an dtriúr leanbh.

'Cad é an fhéachaint atá agat?' arsa bean a tí 'ar na leanaí beaga san?'

'Mhuise, níl aon fhéachaint agamsa ar na leanaí beaga san,' ar sise, 'mar ná feadar cé hiad, ach is deas liom iad,' ar sise, 'agus is maith liom a bheith ag féachaint orthu,' ar sise. 'Ní mar gheall ar aon ní atháimse ag féachaint orthusan.'

'Bíodh deireadh agat leis,' a dúirt sí, 'bheith ag féachaint ar an dtriúr leanbh san,' ar sise.

Thug sí éadach cláir dhi. Nuair a leathfadh sí amach an t-éadach cláir go dtiocfadh nach aon tsaghas bídh chuici ar an éadach chun a dóthain dh'ithe agus dh'ól. Agus do bhailigh sí léi.[4]

Nuair a tháinig sí chuige —

'Sea anois,' ar seisean. 'Níl aon mhaith dhuit anois,' ar seisean, 'bheith ag treabhadh im dhiaidh-sa. Agus tá sé chomh maith anois agat filleadh abhaile,' ar seisean. 'Níl aon dul agat go mbeadsa romhat aon tráthnóna eile, ach an tráthnóna aréir,' ar seisean, 'chun aon fhóirthint a dhéanamh ort. Agus fill abhaile.'

'Á, ní dh'fhillfeadsa in aon chor abhaile,' ar sise, 'ach is cuma liom,' ar sise, 'leanfaidh mé thusa.'

'Cad é an maitheas duit,' ar seisean, 'a leanúint an té,' ar seisean, 'ná chífir ón nóimint seo go bráth aríst?'

'Is cuma liom,' ar sise. 'Leanfaidh mé thú,' ar sise, 'trí thine, trí uisce, trí ghleannta, trí nach aon achrann go dtí go mbeidh staidéar éigin i dteannta a chéile againn.'

Mar sin a bhí. D'imigh sé roimpi, agus do dh'imigh sí sin ina dhiaidh, agus ní raibh sé ag fanacht socair in aon chor i rith an lae faoi mar a bhíodh sé nach aon lá eile, ach ag géarú air i gcónaí. Agus do bhí sí traochta, marbh ag iarraidh go gcoinneodh sí radharc air go mbeadh a fhios aici cad é an áit do stadfadh sé. Agus do bhí sí ag faire i gcónaí, agus í ag géarú léi go bhfaca sí é ag stad ar bharra faille. Ó chonaic sí ag stad é, ní fheadair sí do thalamh Dé an domhain cad é an áit a shlog é. Ach do choinnibh sí radharc ar an bpaiste go bhfaca sí stadaithe é. Do tháinig sí go dtí an bpaiste sin agus nuair ná faca sí aon tsaghas dealramh air chun dul síos nó suas, soir nó siar ann, ach an paiste glas ar bharra na faille, do shuigh sí síos. Do chrom sí ar ghol agus ar bhéicigh.

---

4. End of cyclinder (on which the story was originally recorded). Repetition in narration, omitted in this edition.

'Cad tá le déanamh anois agam?' ar sise. 'Nó cad é an áit do rachaidh mé nó cad a dhéanfad?'

Do bhuail fear chuici, agus dh'fhiafraigh an fear di cad a bhí uirthi nó cad é an chúrsaí goil a bhí aici.

'Ó, ní fhéadfainn mo chás do dh'innsint duit,' ar sise.

Chrom sí ar a bheith ag eachtraí dó, agus ansin do stad sé.

'Raghadsa abhaile. Tabharfaidh mé liom ramhainn agus beidh a fhios agam duit,' ar seisean, 'an bhfuil aon dul agat,' ar seisean, 'ar ghabháilt síos nó suas ann.'

Dh'imigh sé abhaile agus do thug sé leis ramhainn, agus chrom sé ar a bheith ag taighde, ag taighde leis i gcónaí. Agus ar an dtaighde dho, do bhuail leac mhór ghroí chloiche leis. Do thóg sé in airde an leac, agus do chonaic sé uaidh síos na staighrí ag dul síos an fhaid a bhí radharc aige orthu.

'Sin staighrí,' ar seisean, 'athá ag dul i dtaobh éigin,' arsa an fear léi.

'Mhuise, b'fhéidir le Dia san,' ar sise. 'Geobhaidh mé iontu síos,' ar sise.

'Is féidir leat,' ar seisean, 'má bhaineann tú aon talamh amach thíos ann.'

'Bainfidh mé amach áit éigin,' ar sise, 'le cúnamh Dé.'

D'imigh sí uirthi trí's na staighrí síos, agus bhí sí ar na staighrí dhi, agus ná feadair sí an mbuailfeadh aon talamh go deo léi. Faoi dheireadh thiar thall do chuaigh sí síos agus do bhuail áit léi. Agus do dh'imigh sí ar fud na háite, agus do bhuail bothán beag léi, agus chuaigh sí isteach ann. Agus do bhí lánúin chríonna roimpi istigh ann, agus do bheannaigh sí dhóibh agus do bheannaíodar di. Agus do dh'fhiafraíodar di conas do bhí aon dul aici ar theacht anseo.

'Ó, n'fheadar,' ar sise, 'ach go bhfuilim tagaithe ann,' ar sise, 'agus ná feadar,' ar sise, 'cé ngeobhaidh mé soir nó siar anois.'

Shuigh sí síos i dteannta an lánúin chríonna agus d'inis sí dhóibh ó thús go deireadh conas mar a bhí an scéal aici.

'Mo ghraidhin thú, a chailín bhoicht,' a dúirt an fear críonna, 'is mór an trua thú. Fan fada leat féin,' ar seisean, 'agus gheobhair bia agus deoch uainne.'

'Á mhuise,' ar sise, 'ní gá dhomsa,' ar sise, 'bheith ag brath oraibhse,' ar sise, 'chun bia nó deoch a thabhairt dom. Gura míle, míle maith

agaibh,' ar sise. 'Tá bia agus deoch ar iompar agamsa,' ar sise, 'mo dhóthain, agus bhúr ndóthainse leis,' ag leathadh an éadaigh chláir amach.

Do tháinig nach aon tsaghas bídh chuca ar an éadach cláir. Agus do shuíodar i dteannta a chéile, triúr acu, agus do chromadar ar a bheith ag ithe. Agus dá mbeidís ag ithe ó shin, ní dh'fholamhóidís an t-éadach.

'Tá rud maith fachta agat i gcomhair do shaoil,' arsa an seanduine.

'Mhuise,' ar sise, 'b'fhearr liomsa,' ar sise, 'mo ghabhairín bán ná an méid a leanann an t-éadach san,' ar sise.

'Gabh amach amáireach,' ar seisean, 'agus b'fhéidir,' ar seisean, 'tá an tseana-chailleach faoi dhraíocht thiar, sa chúirt athá thiar, ansan thiar,' ar seisean léi. 'Agus tá iníon don seana-chailleach' ar seisean, 'sea an Cara Ghearbach. Mac don seana-chailleach,' ar seisean, 'is ea an gabhairín bán, agus,' ar seisean, 'tá triúr iníon aici, aige an seana-chailleach,' ar seisean, 'ina dteannta san go bhfuairis an t-éadach cláir ó dhuine acu.[5] Iníon di sin, agus thug sí di an t-éadach cláir, an sisiúr, an cíor. Dá gcíorfadh sí a ceann go dtiocfadh gruaig bhreá chomh breá agus bheadh ar aon chailín óg riamh.

Mar sin a bhí. Dhúradar sin léi é sin, an seanduine agus an tseana-bhean, agus gabháilt amach amáireach, agus go mb'fhéidir go gcífeadh sí an Chara Ghearbach agus go ndéanfadh sí aon fhóirithint a thabhairt uirthi.

Bhuail sí amach amáireach, ag balcaeracht di féin ar fud na háite go brónach, agus chonaic sí uaithi an Chara Ghearbach. Agus do chrom sí ar a bheith ag baint na ngiobal a bhí uirthi leis an sisiúr, agus do chonaic an Chara Ghearbach an t-éadach breá ag teacht uirthi in ionad na ngiobal. Agus do rith sí chuici.

'Mhuise,' ar sise, 'an dtabharfá dhomsa an sisiúr sin?'

'Do thabharfainn, mhuise,' ar sise, 'agus míle fáilte, ar an oíche anocht dh'fháilt i dteannta an ghabhairín bháin.'

'Á, ní agamsa tá é sin do dhéanamh duit,' ar sise, 'ach dhéanfainn mo dhícheall duit chuige, ach aige an seana-chailligh,' ar sise.

'Ní thabharfadsa dhuitse an sisiúr,' ar sise, 'go mbeidh sé sin fachta agam,' ar sise.

---

5. End of cylinder. Repetition in narration, omitted in this edition.

D'imigh sí uirthi an Chara Ghearbach siar go dtí an gcailligh, agus dúirt sí lei go bhfaigheadh sí sisiúr a bhí ag an gcailín.

'Nuair a bhearraigh sí di na giobail gur tháinig culaith bhreá éadaigh uirthi, agus dúirt sí liom go dtabharfadh sí dhom é,' ar sise, 'ach an oíche anocht a dh'fháilt i dteannta an ghabhairín bháin.'

'Abair léi go bhfaighidh,' ar sise.

Mar sin a bhí. Thainig sí chuici, agus do fuair sí an sisiúr, agus nuair a tháinig an oíche do dh'imigh sí uirthi faoi dhéin na cúirte, agus thug an tseana-chailleach ordú dhi dul don tseomra sin go mbeadh sé sin ann ina teannta go maidin. Chuaigh sí don tseomra agus chuaigh sí a chodladh, agus nuair a tháinig an gabhairín bán chun an tí, do fuair sé bia agus deoch ón seana-chailligh, agus do thug sí dho deoch a chodlata. Agus nuair a chuaigh sé a chodladh n'fheadair sé bean nó fear nó éinne bhí insa leabaigh. N'fheadair sé aon ní mar gheall uirthi, agus í d'iarraidh cainte do bhaint as i gcónaí i rith na hoíche, agus gan aon tor aige á thabhairt uirthi.

Nuair a dh'éirí sí ar maidin bhí sí dubhach brónach ag imeacht amach as an gcúirt, chomh dubach, chomh brónach agus bhí sí ag teacht isteach. Agus do tháinig sí go dtí an mbothán go dtí an seanduine agus go dtí an seana-bhean agus duirt sí leis an seana-bhean agus leis an seanduine go raibh sí chomh brónach ag teacht agus bhí sí ag imeacht.

'Á, tá rud éigint á dhéanamh ag an léir-mheirdrigh sin,' arsan seanduine, ar sé. 'Fán fada ar an seana-bhean san,' ar sé, 'ar an gcailligh ghránna. Sin é mar thá aici,' ar sé. 'Gaibh amach amáireach arís,' adúirt an seanduine, 'agus buailfidh an Chara Ghearbach leat, agus beir leat an chírín sin agat,' ar sé.

Ghaibh sí amach, agus do chonaic sí amach uaithi an Chara Ghearbach, agus do chuaigh sí faoina bráid agus do thairrig sí chuici an chíor. Agus bhí sí ag cíora a cinn, agus an cúl breá gruaige a tháinig uirthi nuair a chíor sí a ceann.

'Mhuis,' arsan Chara Ghearbach, ar sise, 'an dtabharfá dhomsa í sin?'

'Do thabharfainn,' ar sise, 'agus fáilte,' ar sise, 'ar son an oíche anocht a dh'fháilt i dteannta an ghabhairín bháin.'

'Beidh fios agam duit,' ar sise.

D'imigh sí uirthi agus chuaigh sí dtí an gcúirt agus dúirt sí leis an seana-chailligh go bhfaigheadh sí an chíor a bhí aici, an chíor bhreá a bhí ag an gcailín. Agus go bhfaigheadh sí í ar shon an oíche anocht a dh'fháilt i dteannta an ghabhairín bháin.

'Abair léi go bhfaighidh,' ar sise.

D'imigh sí uirthi, agus do fuair sí an chíor, agus nuair a tháinig an oíche do tháinig an cailín bocht go dtí an gcúirt agus do thug an tseana-chailleach ordú di dul don tseomra a chodladh. Agus nuair a chuaigh sí don leabaigh, nuair a tháinig an gabhairín bán, do fuair sé bia agus deoch ón seana-chailligh, agus do fuair sé deoch a chodlata. Agus nuair a chuaigh sé don leabaigh n'fheadair sé fear nó bean a bheith ann. Bhí sí ag priocadh, ag priocadh, ag priocadh air i rith na hoíche, agus ag caint leis, agus ag gabháil air agus ná féadfadh sí aon fhocal riamh a bhaint as. Bhí sí chomh dubhach, chomh brónach ar maidin agus do chrom sí ar ghol. Agus do tháinig sí go dtí an mbothán go raibh an seanduine agus an tseanabhean.

'Mhuise, is ainnis é mo scéalsa,' ar sise.

'Is dócha é, a chailín bhoicht,' a dúirt an seanduine. 'Sin é mar tá ag an gcailligh sin,' ar seisean. 'Amáireach anois,' ar seisean, an seanduine, léi, 'Ní haon mhaith dhuit,' ar seisean, 'bheith ag gabháil di nó ag tabhairt aon ní dhi,' ar seisean, 'mara mbainfidh tú an méid seo amach as an gCara Ghearbach.'

'Abair léi a rá leis na buachaillí go bhfuil a leithéid sin de chailín ag teacht don leaba nach aon oíche chuig an ghabhairín bháin; go raibh an bhean phósta a bhí aige, go raibh sí insa leabaigh nach aon oíche ina theannta le dhá oíche agus de réir dealraimh ná feadair sé ann ná as í, agus go bhfaigheann sé deoch a chodlata ón seana-chailligh, agus nuair a gheobhaidh sé anocht í, í a dhorta agus a ligeant air go mbeadh sí ólta aige, go raibh an cailín bocht san in ana-thrioblóide, agus gur mhór an trua í agus go raibh sí le dhá oíche ina theannta, agus ná feadair sé ann nó as í. Abair léi é sin do rá agus dá neosfá dó é, go mbeadh seans éigint agat,' arsan seanduine léi.

Ghaibh sí amach agus do bhuail sí chuice a héadach cláir, agus do ghaibh an Chara Ghearbach chuice, agus an t-éadach cláir oscailte amach aici, agus nach aon tsaghas bidh a dh'iarrfadh do bhéal ná a dhéanfá a chaitheamh ar an éadach cláir. Agus do tháinig iontas uirthi nuair a chonaic sí an t-éadach breá a bhí ag an gcailín sin, agus nach aon tsaghas bídh ar an éadach cláir.

'Mhuise,' ar sise, 'an dtabharfá dhomsa é sin?' ar sise.

'Do thabharfainnse dhuitse é sin,' ar sise, 'ar shon dul i dteannta an ghabhairín bháin anocht. Agus ní haon mhaitheas domsa,' ar sise, 'bheith ag dul nó ag tabhairt aon ní duitse,' ar sise, 'chun dul go dtí an ngabhairín bháin,' ar sise, 'mar n'fheadair an fear bocht,' ar sise, 'ann nó as mé. Ach mara raghaidh tusa,' ar sise, 'go dtí's na buachaillí atá ag obair ar an ngort, agus a rá leo go bhfaigheann sé deoch an chodlata ón seana-chailligh, agus nuair a gheobhaidh sé í anocht, í sin do dhortadh agus go raibh a bhean phósta roimis sa seomra, sa leabaigh. Agus go raibh sí ann le dhá oíche roimhe sin, agus ná feadair sé ann nó as í.'

'Déanfadsa san duit,' a dúirt an Chara Ghearbach,' agus míle fáilte,' ar sise, 'agus is é tá uaim,' ar sise, 'é sin do dhéanamh duit,' ar sise.

'Sea gheobhair-se uaimse,' ar sise, 'an t-éadach cláir mar sin.'

D'imigh sí agus chuaigh sí dtí an gcailligh, agus d'fhiafraigh sí di an bhfaigheadh an cailín teacht go dtí an gabhairín bán anocht, go raibh éadach breá cláir aici, agus nach aon tsaghas bídh do dh'iarrfadh do bhéal go rabhadar air.

'Abair léi go bhfaighidh,' ar sise.

Tháinig sí chuici.

'Sea anois,' ar sise, 'an bhfuileann tusa ag geallúint dom?' ar sise. 'Táimse á gheallúint duitse, an bhfuileann tusa ag geallúint dom,' ar sise, 'go ndéarfair an méid sin leis na buachaillí, a rá leis an ngabhairín bán?'

'Ó admhaím duit,' ar sise, 'óm chroí amach,' ar sise, 'go raghad féin chucu,' ar sise, 'anocht, agus go ndéarfad leo é.'

D'imigh sí uaithi agus thug sí dhi an t-éadach cláir. Nuair a tháinig an oíche, d'imigh sí faoi dhéin na cúirte, agus do chuaigh sí go dtí an gcúirt.

'Téir don tseomra a chodladh dhuit féin,' arsa an seana-chailleach léi.

Ní bia ná deoch a thug sí di. Chuaigh sí a chodladh, agus bhí sí insa leabaigh nuair a tháinig an gabhairín bán. Do fuair sé bia agus deoch ón seana-chailligh, agus ní dhein sé aon tsaghas ach í a chaitheamh síos ar an urlár, an deoch chodlata, agus dul a chodladh. Agus do rug sé isteach lomabharróg ar an gcailín ansan, agus do dh'fhiafraigh sé di conas a dh'fhéad sí teacht.

'Do bhí seans éigint i do bhóthar,' ar sé, 'agus a rá go bhfuairis amach mise,' ar seisean, 'ar an gcuma do bhíos agus do thána anseo agus tusa dom leanúint,' ar seisean, 'agus gan aon dul agat orm.'

'Ach féach,' ar sise, 'go raibh dul agam ort,' ar sise, 'mar bhí Dia ag cabhrú liom chun teacht chugat.'

'Ó, bíonn san mar sin,' ar seisean, 'ach tá nach aon ní,' ar seisean, 'chomh hainnis fós,' ar seisean, 'agus do bhí riamh, mara bhféadfa tusa anois,' ar seisean, 'a bhaint amach as an gCara Ghearbach conas,' ar seisean, 'atá aon dul,' ar seisean, 'ar an gcailleach san a chur chun báis. Mara bhfaghfar amach é sin,' ar seisean, 'go bhfuil aon dul ar an seana-chailligh a chur chun báis,' ar seisean, 'tá an draíocht orainne fós. Agus sinn go léir faoi dhraíocht aige an seana-chailligh sin,' ar seisean. 'Ach má tá aon léith mór aige an gCara Ghearbach leatsa, tabharfaidh sí an méid sin cuntais go bhféadfadh sí baint amach as an seana-chailligh sin cá bhfuil fód a báis. Agus abair léi é sin agus go mbeidh tú féin go maith dhi fós.'

Mar sin a bhí. D'imigh sí léi go dtí an mbothán go raibh an lánúin chríonna ann ar maidin, agus pé ní is mar dhein sí inné roimhe sin, ní raibh bia ná deoch aici le ligint amach mar bhí an t-éadach cláir tugaithe aici uaithi, ach más ea féin, do bhí beagán bídh aige an lánúin chríonna, go bhfuair sí bia uathu le tabhairt di, agus dúirt sí leo. D'inis sí dóibh tríd agus tríd go b'shin é mar bhí.

'Déanfaidh an Chara Ghearbach,' arsa an seanduine, 'a dícheall duitse,' ar seisean, 'mar bhís go maith dhi, agus beidh sí ag priocadh bhuaithe. Ach a ngeobhaidh sí chugat amáireach, glaoigh leat í agus abair léi go ndéanfá ionad aon deirfiúr nó dearthár di go bráth, ach é a bhaint amach as an gcailligh conas do thá fód a báis chun í a chur chun báis.'

'Déanfad mo dhícheall duit,' arsa an Chara Ghearbach.

Agus do bhí san go maith. Agus lá ar na mhárach dúirt sí leis an seana-chailligh: 'Tá ana-scanradh ormsa, a Mháthair,' ar sise, an Chara Ghearbach. 'Tá ana-scanradh ormsa, a Mháthair,' ar sí, 'go bhfuileann tusa ag dul chun deire,' ar sise, 'is cad tá agamsa le déanamh ansan,' ar sise, 'cé bheidh im chúnamh?'

'A ghrá gil,' a dúirt an tseana-chailleach. 'A ghrá gil,' ar sise, 'ní baol duit,' ar sise, 'go bhfuil aon dul agamsa bheith ag fáil bháis,' ar sise, 'mar na fuil aon rud chun mé chur chun báis.'

'Ó, an bhfuil aon rud in aon chorach,' a dúirt an Chara Ghearbach, 'nó an bhfanfaidh tú mar sin go bráth?' ar sise. 'Sin é tá uaim.'

'Tá,' ar sise, 'ach,' ar sise, 'ina dhiaidh san,' ar sise, 'tá mo bhás istigh sa bhloc san amuigh,' ar sise, 'agus níl aon tsaol go mbrisfidh éinne go deo,' ar sise, 'an bloc san.'

Lá arna mháireach arís do chrom an Chara Ghearbach ar a bheith ag cur *posies* agus rudaí ar an mbloc, á ní agus á ghlanadh, agus ag cur nach aon tsaghas péinte agus rudaí faoin mbloc do ligfeadh sí uirthi gurb ann a bheadh fód a báis, a máthar, an tseana-chailleach.

'Ó, mo thrua mhór tú,' arsa an tseana-chailleach. 'Mo thrua mhór thú,' ar sise. 'Ní ansan atá mo bhás,' ar sise, 'agus ná bí ina cúram.'

'Agus cá bhfuil do bhás mar sin? ' ar sise. 'Caithfeadsa bheith ina chúram,' ar sise, 'mar tá scanradh ag teacht orm. Tá tú ag druidim leis an saol a bheith caite,' ar sise, 'agus tá scanradh orm,' ar sise, 'chun a rá ná beinn á shocrú suas, ach inis dom,' ar sise, 'cá bhfuil do mharú, muna bhfuil aon dul air go deo,' ar sise, 'mar sé tá uaim gan a bheith.'

'Níl,' ar sise, 'aon dul aige aon duine,' ar sise, 'ar mise a chur chun báis, agus na bíodh aon eagla ort. Sa ghort,' ar sise, 'go bhfuil na buachaillí ag obair, sin é an áit,' ar sise, 'go bhfuil mo bhás-sa,' ar sise, 'is níl aon dul air go deo. Tá leac mhór chloiche ansan,' ar sise, 'agus níor mhór ceathrar fear,' ar sise, 'chun na lice sin a thógaint. 'Agus tá molt thíos ansan,' ar sise, 'agus do dh'éireodh an molt aníos. Do chaitheadh an molt uaidh lacha, agus do chaitheadh an lacha uaithi an t-ubh. Agus cá bhfuil an té a gheobhadh an t-ubh san chun é a ghabháilt túisce a chaitheadh an lacha uaithi é, agus é a bhualadh, agus féach,' ar sise, 'an ball dubh san,' ar sise, 'atá i mo chliathán deas,' ar sise, 'agus é sin a bhualadh isteach leis. Cé dheanfaidh é sin go deo?' ar sise. 'Níl aon dul air, agus ná bíodh aon eagla ort.'

'Á, shin é thá uaim,' ar sise.

Chrom sí ar a bheith á ní agus á glanadh ansan, go gcífeadh sí i gceart cad é an áit go mbeadh an ball. Bíodh sí á ní nach aon lá, agus do chuaigh sí go dtí's na buachaillí agus dúirt sí leis na buachaillí go ndéanfadh sí aon rud dóibh

go deo, agus an áit sin, taighde, agus go bhfaighdís amach an leac. Agus dúirt sí:

'Is insa ghort go bhfuilean sibhse ag obair,' ar sise, 'atá an leac sin,' ar sise, 'agus í a thógaint in airde agus déanfad aon rud díbh go deo,' ar sise, 'má dhéanann sibh é sin,' ar sise, 'agus nuair a dh'eireoidh an molt aníos, caithfidh an molt uaidh an lacha, agus caithfidh an lacha uaithi an t-ubh, agus dá bhféadfadh sibhse an t-ubh a ghabháilt agus a thabhairt chugamsa.'

Mar sin a bhí. Dúradar go ndéanfaidís a ndícheall agus do dheineadar. Agus do thugadar chuici an t-ubh, agus do bhuail sí an t-ubh isteach leis an mball dubh a bhí ina cliathán, agus do dhein cnapán mór salainn di. Agus d'fhan sí ansan.

Sea. Bhí san go maith, agus d'fhágas im' dhiaidh í.

Do phrioc sí uaithi roime sin cén áit go raibh an dul ar an ndraíocht do bhaint dóibh féin, agus d'inis sí dóibh.

'Níl,' ar sise, 'tar éis mo bháis-se agus is fada é sin, 'tá slaitín draíochta,' ar sise, 'faoi bhun an churpaid, agus trí bhuille den slaitín draíochta sin,' ar sise, 'a thabhart don ghabhairín bán, agus déanfaidh fear mór breá dho,' ar sise. 'Agus an trí bhuille céanna a thabhairt duitse,' ar sise, 'agus déanfaidh cailín mór breá duit. Agus na trí bhuille céanna,' ar sise, 'a thabhairt dos nach éinne dod' triúr deirfiúr' — sin iad na mná seo — 'agus ansan beidh an draíocht bainte dhóibh,' ar sise. 'Ach anois,' ar sise, 'níl aon dul ar sin,' ar sise, 'mar ná caillfear choíche mé.'

Cailleadh í. Dhein cnapán salainn di, ach tá sé ráite againn cheana. B'fhearra dhom é a rá arís.

Bhí san go maith. Agus nuair a deineadh cnapán salainn di féin, do tháinig áthas agus móráil uirthi bheith mar scéal nua roimis an ngabhairín bhán nuair a thiocfadh sé abhaile i gcomhair na hoíche. Agus nuair a tháinig an gabhairín dúirt sí leis:

'Sea, a dheartháirín,' ar sise. 'Tá neart agam anois,' ar sise, 'deartháir a thabhart ort,' ar sise. 'Tá seans faighte agat anois,' ar sise. 'Tabhair leat anois,' ar sise, 'chugamsa an tslaitín draíochta,' ar sise, 'tá istigh faoi bhun an churpaid, agus tabhair dom im dhorn é.'

D'imigh sé go háthasach. Agus do thug sé dhi ina dorn í, agus do thug sí trí bhuille den slaitín draíochta dhon ngabhairín bán, agus dhein buachaill mór breá dho.

'Tabhair-se dhomsa a dheartháir anois,' ar sise. 'Trí bhuille eile dhi, agus ní bhead im Chara Ghearbach,' ar sise, 'faoi mar a bhíodh.'

Do thug, agus do dhein cailín mór breá dhi. Agus níor tháinig gearb ná eile dá raibh tríthe cheana. Níor thánadar tríthe amach thar n-ais, agus do bhí sí ina bean mhór bhreá. Agus do bhíodar mar sin go háthasach ansan i dteannta a chéile ar feadh tamaill. Agus dúirt an gabhairín bán.

'Sea, tá nach aon ní go maith anois,' ar seisean, 'buíochas le Dia,' ar seisean, 'agus sid í anseo faoi ndeara dhúinn an méid sin tabharthas a dh'fháilt,' ar seisean. 'Do bhí sé ceapaithe dhi. Do fuair sí smúit maith dho na dhua. Is mó sceach agus gleann do chuir sí dhi ag rith im dhiaidhse, ach féach anois,' ar seisean, 'buíochas le Dia go bhfuilim aici. Sea, raighimid anois,' ar seisean, 'agus bainfeam an draíocht dár dtriúr deirfiúr agus do mo thriúr leanbh. Agus tá mo thriúr leanbh, ar seisean, go maith romham agus aon ní amháin, ar seisean, go bhfuil an tsúil bainte as ceann acu agus is mór an scrupall é.

'Á níl,' adeir sí sin. 'Tá sí anso agamsa,' ar sí, im' haincisiúir póca, gur ghaibheas í, ar sise, nuair a ligeas anuas an deoir,' ar sise, 'le heagla romhatsa, le heagla romhatsa, go n-imeofá uaim. Do ghaibheas im' haincisiúir póca í agus tá sí istigh fós ann.

Do ghluaiseadar orthu. Thug sé an Chara Ghearbach do cheann de na buachaillí le pósadh agus do bhronn sé an chúirt orthu agus na hollmhaitheasaí go léir a bhí ann, agus do dhein sé slí mhaith a thabhairt don seanduine. Bhíodar san leis fén draíocht. Bhain sé an draíocht dóibh agus do bhíodar go lán sásta as san amach.

Do tháinig sé go dtí na triúr deirféir, agus do thug sé leis abhaile a thriúr leanbh. Agus do mhair sé go lán sásta as san amach, agus faoi chompord.

Agus beannacht Dé le hanamanna na marbh. Agus fuaireas-sa an méid sin ó m'athair féin. Go dtuga Dia fuascailt inniu ar a anam agus ar anaman na marbh go léir a d'fhág sinn, anamacha na bhfiréan ar fad.

THE STORY OF THE LITTLE WHITE GOAT

A good many years ago there was a farmer, and he had one daughter. Yes. A white goat used to come to the door every day of the week to her, and eventually she fell in love with the goat.

And he went away. And she went after him. And if she did, she followed him all the time.

They went into a fine mansion. He spoke to her then.

'*Wisha*, yes, now,' said he, 'which would you prefer now,' said he, 'me to be a goat during the night, or a man at night and a goat during the day?'

'Oh, to be sure,' she said, 'I'd prefer company at night, you to be a man at night and a goat during the day.'

That's how it was. They stayed together for a while. In a year she had a son. And he told her not to cry or shed a tear if anything happened to that child, because if she shed a tear, that she would not have him, that he would have to leave her. Yes. When the child was born it wasn't long until the child was taken away from her out of the bed, and she became a bit upset. But she remembered that she had no business shedding a tear, then when he came to her:

'Your child has been taken from you,' he said, 'but if he has,' he said, 'that doesn't matter at all,' he said, 'as long as you have me,' he said, 'for company.'

That's how it was.

A year from that day she gave birth to another son, and he told her not to shed a tear if anything happened to the child, because if she shed a tear he would not stay with her. The child left her. He was taken from her bed, and she felt sad, but she remembered that she had no business shedding a tear and she did not. Another year from that day she gave birth to another son and he told her not to shed a tear if anything happened to her or to the child. If the child went from her, to be pleased with that, because if she was not pleased, she would not have him. She considered, and when the child left her she was unable to prevent herself from shedding a tear. And she put a little pocket handkerchief up to her eyes so that he wouldn't see that they were wet. And that is how it was. When he came to her:

'Yes, now,' he said, 'you won't have me,' he said, 'for another day. If you could only keep your eyes dry,' he said, 'you would have little need,' he said, 'to shed tears ever again. You have no chance now,' he said, 'of having me,' he said. 'I have to leave you.'

'If you go,' she said, 'I will follow you.'

'There is no point in doing that,' he said, 'because you have no chance of getting me.'

He went, and she got up and followed him. During the day that followed she was torn and worn by the briars, and he going ahead of her, but she was trying to keep him in sight so that she would know where he was. *When the dew fell and evening came upon her, the terrier was seeking the shade of the dockleaf and the dockleaf was eluding him, and the fox was going into his own little den.*[1]

Night fell on her, and he sat down on a tussock and waited for her. That's how it was.

'You've little business chasing after me,' he said.

'I can't help it,' she said. 'I'll follow you through water and fire,' she said.

'There's a house down there,' he said, 'and go down there and look for a night's lodging,' he said. 'If you don't get a welcome,' he said, 'ask for the night's lodging for the sake of the little white goat.'

That's how it was.

'And will you wait for me?' she said.

'I'll wait here for you,' he said, 'until morning.'

She went down, and she asked for shelter until morning, and she wasn't getting it.

'Wisha,' she said, 'if you please,' she said, 'give me the night's lodging,' she said, 'for the sake of the little white goat.'

'You will get it, and a thousand welcomes to you, for his sake,' the woman said. 'Sit down,' she said.

She sat down. She got food and drink, and a bed to sleep in, and breakfast in the morning. And when she was leaving in the morning the woman gave her a comb so that she could comb her hair and so that she would get the most beautiful hair that a young girl ever had. She went off and he was waiting for her in the same place.

'You've little business to be chasing after me,' he said to her.

'I can't help it,' she said. 'I will follow you,' she said.

'You won't follow me,' he said, 'because you won't know how,' he said. 'It would be far better for you to go back home,' he said, 'and go home to your father.'

'Ah, I've no business going home to my father,' she said, 'but to come looking for you, and I will follow you.'

She went after him and he himself went, and he went through every bit of undergrowth, and through every briar, to make her turn back. *And she was torn and worn by the briars until the dewfall and night came upon her, the terrier seeking the shade of the dockleaf and the dockleaf eluding him, and the fox going into his own little den, small blame on the gentle fox.*

He sat down on a tussock and waited for her.

'You are tired out,' he said, 'and it does you little good,' he said, 'to be chasing after me,' he said. 'It would be as well for you,' he said, 'to return home. There is a house down there,' he said, 'and go down,' he said, 'and look for lodging there till morning,' he said. 'And I will wait for you until you come. If you are unwelcome,' he said, 'ask for it,' he said, 'for the sake of the little white goat,' he said, 'and you will get it.'

That's how it was.

She asked for the night's lodging and the woman did not give her much of a welcome.

'Oh, if you please,' she said, 'would you give me the night's lodging,' she said, 'for the sake of the little white goat?'

'You'll get it and welcome,' she said, 'for his sake.'

She got food and drink, a bed to sleep in, and when she got up in the morning she got her breakfast. And when she was going the woman gave her a little scissors.

'There's a little scissors for you,' she said, 'and when you cut the rags you have on you,' she said, 'you will get the finest clothes a young girl ever wore.'

That's how it was.

She went and he was ahead of her, and he was waiting for her in the same place. That was the second day.

'Yes, now,' he said, 'you'd be better off,' he said, 'going back home — do me a favour now —' he said, 'go to your mother and father's house.'

'I haven't a chance of finding my father or mother,' she said, 'and I will never see them,' she said. 'Since I followed you, I'll follow you,' she said, 'wherever you go.'

---

1. A formulaic 'run' describing nightfall.

'You have little chance of getting me,' he said, 'only today. You'll have no chance of getting me,' he said, 'any other day.'

She went after him, and he'd go through every bit of undergrowth and every glen, and through every briar, so that she might turn back, and she worn and torn. *And the dewfall and the end of the afternoon and night were coming upon her, the terrier seeking the shade of the dockleaf and the dockleaf eluding him, and the red fox going to his own den, small blame on the gentle fox.*

He sat down on a tussock and he waited for her and he said to her:

'If you had sense,' he said, 'you would have gone home,' he said, 'the first day you followed me.'

'I won't go home now, wisha,' she said.

'There is a house down there,' he said, 'and go down there until morning, and that's as good as you'll get,' he said. 'And ask for shelter,' he said, 'for the sake of the little white goat, until morning. I'll wait here until you come,' he said. 'But if I do,' he said, 'that's as much as you're going to get.'

She went down and looked for shelter for the sake of the little white goat. She got it, and a thousand welcomes, food and drink and a bed for the night. And when she got up in the morning she noticed three little children around the house. And she couldn't take her eyes off these children.

'What business have you looking at those little children?' said the woman of the house.

'Wisha, I've no reason to be looking at those little children at all,' she said, 'because I haven't a clue who they are, but I think they're nice,' she said, 'and I like to be looking at them,' she said. 'I've no special reason for looking at them,' she said.

'Put a stop to it now,' the woman said, 'looking at those three children,' she said.

The woman gave her a tablecloth. When she spread out the tablecloth all kinds of food came to her on the cloth, enough to eat and drink. And she went off.

When she came to him:

'Yes, now,' he said. 'It's doing you no good,' he said, 'to chase after me, and it would be as well for you to go home,' he said. 'You can't expect me to be waiting for you any other evening, apart from yesterday evening,' he said, 'to give you any help. Go home,' he said.

'Ah, I won't go home at all,' she said. 'I don't care,' she said. 'I'll follow you.'

'What good will it do you,' he said, 'following the one,' he said, 'that you will not see from this moment,' he said, 'ever again?'

'I don't care,' she said. 'I will follow you,' she said, 'through fire, through water, through valleys and through every kind of undergrowth, until we can manage to settle down together somehow.'

That's how it was.

He went ahead of her and she followed him. And he didn't stop at all during the day as he had done every other day, but continued onward all the time. And she was exhausted, dead with trying to keep him in view, to see where he would stop. And she was keeping her eyes on him all the time, continuing on until she saw him stopping at the top of a cliff. But he disappeared, and from the moment she saw him stop, she didn't know in the wide world what place had swallowed him up. But she kept her eyes fixed to that patch of ground. She came to that patch, but there was nothing there. Nothing but a patch of grass. There was no way to go down or up, east or west, nothing but the green patch on the top of the cliff. She sat down. She began to cry and scream.

'What am I to do now?' she said. 'Or where will I go or what will I do?'

A man came up to her, and the man asked her why she was crying.

'Oh, I couldn't tell you my sorry tale!' she said. But she began to tell him the story anyway, and she told him everything.

'I'll go home. I'll bring back a spade with me,' the man said, 'and I'll be able to find out for you if you have any chance,' he said, 'of getting down there.'

He went home and he brought back a spade with him and he started digging, digging away all the time. And after a lot of digging he hit a big strong slab of stone. He raised the slab, and saw beneath him a flight of stairs, going down as far as he could see.

'There are some stairs,' he said, 'that are going somewhere,' the man said to her.

'Wisha, maybe with the help of God,' she said, 'I'll get down on them,' she said.

'You'll be able to get down, all right,' he said, 'but will you find any land down there underneath?'

'I'll find something,' she said, 'with the help of God.'

She went on down the stairs, down and down and down. And she began to doubt that she'd ever hit land. In the heel of the hunt she was at the bottom, however, and there was a place there. And she began to walk. And after a while she came to a little cottage and she went into it, and there was an old couple inside the cottage. And she greeted them and they greeted her and asked her why she had come.

'Oh, I don't know,' she said, 'except that I have landed myself here,' she said, 'and I don't know,' she said, 'if I should go eastwards or westwards now.'

She sat down with the old couple and she told them her story from beginning to end.

'God love you, you poor girl,' said the old man. 'You are to be pitied. You stay with us,' he said, 'and you'll get food and drink from us.'

'Ah, wisha,' she said, 'I don't need, 'she said, 'to depend on you,' she said, 'to give me food and drink. Thank you very much,' she said. 'I'm carrying food and drink,' she said, 'plenty for me, and for you as well,' spreading out the tablecloth.

Every imaginable kind of food appeared on the tablecloth, and they sat down together, the three of them, and started eating. And if they had been eating ever since they wouldn't gobble up all that was on the cloth.

'You've got a good thing there that will last you all your life,' said the old fellow.

'Wisha,' said she, 'I'd rather,' said she, 'have my little white goat than anything that comes on that cloth,' she said.

'Go out tomorrow,' the man said to the girl, the man in the cottage. 'And maybe . . . ,' he said. 'There is an old hag under a spell in a castle over beyond,' said he to her. 'And that old hag's daughter is the Scabby Crow, and her son,' he said, 'is the little white goat. That old hag has three other daughters too, and it was from one of them that you got the tablecloth. She is one of her daughters, and she gave her the magic tablecloth, the scissors and the comb. She only had to comb her hair with it to have the most beautiful hair any young girl ever had.'

That's how it was. They told her all that, the old man and the old woman, they told her to go out tomorrow, and that she might see the Scabby Crow, and maybe she would help her.

She went out the next day walking around the place sadly, and eventually she saw the Scabby Crow. And she started cutting the rags she had on her with the scissors, and her rags turned into the finest suit of clothes you ever saw. And the Scabby Crow saw the fine clothes and ran to her.

'Wisha, will you give me that scissors?'

'I would give you the scissors, wisha,' said she, 'and welcome, if I could spend the night with the little white goat.'

'Ah, it is not for me to arrange that for you,' she said, 'but I'll do my best for you. The old witch would have to do it,' she said.

'I won't give you the scissors,' she said, 'until I get that,' she said.

The Scabby Crow went off to the witch, and she told her she could get the girl's magic scissors.

'When she cut off her rags a fine suit of clothes appeared on her, and she told me she'd give it to me,' she said, 'if she only got to spend the night with the little white goat.'

'Tell her she will,' said the witch.

That's how it was. The Scabby Crow came to the girl and got the scissors, and that night the girl went to the witch's castle and the witch ordered her into a bedroom and told her that he would stay with her until morning.

The girl went into the room and lay down on the bed, and fell asleep. Then the little white goat came to the castle. The witch gave him food and drink and then gave him a sleeping draught. And when he went to bed, it was all the same to him who was in the bed with him. He didn't know if it was a man or a woman. The girl talked to him all night but he didn't pay the slightest bit of attention to her. And when she got up in the morning, she was just as sad and downhearted as she had been before. She left the castle and returned to the cottage of the old man and old woman. She told them what had happened.

'Ah, she is up to something, the old whore,' said the old man, said he. 'May a long wandering be the lot of that old woman,' he said, 'the horrible hag. That's the way it is with her,' he said. 'Go out again tomorrow,' said the old man, 'and the Scabby Crow will meet you — and bring that little comb with you,' he said.

She went out, and she saw the Scabby Crow, and she went up to her, and took out the comb. And she was combing her hair, and when she combed her hair she got the most wonderful head of hair you could possibly imagine.

'Wisha,' said the Scabby Crow, 'would you give me that?'

'I'd give it,' she said, 'and welcome,' she said, 'if I could spend tonight in the company of the little white goat.'

'I'll find out for you,' she said.

She left her, and went to the castle, and she told the old witch that she could have the girl's wonderful comb if the girl could spend the night with the little white goat.

'Tell her she will,' said the witch.

The Scabby Crow went off and got the comb, and when night came the poor girl came to the castle again. And the old witch ordered her to go to the bedroom. She went, and she lay down on the bed.

Later on, the little white goat came to the witch's castle. He got food and drink from the old witch, and he also got a sleeping draught. And when he went to bed, he was so sleepy that he didn't know whether it was a man or a woman he had as a companion. She was prodding him, prodding him, prodding him, all through the night, talking to him, and at him, and she couldn't get a single word out of him.

She was so depressed and sad the next morning that she started crying. She returned to the cottage where the old man and old woman were.

'Wisha, my tale is a miserable one,' she said.

'I suppose it is, you poor girl,' said the old man. 'That's the sort of carry-on you get from that old hag,' he said. 'Tomorrow now,' said he, said the old man to her, 'it's no good going to her or giving anything to her,' he said, 'unless you get this much out of the Scabby Crow. Tell her to tell the servant boys that such-and-such a girl is coming every night to bed with the little white goat — that his wife has been in bed with him for the past two nights — but he hasn't a clue whether she's there or not. She should tell them that he has been getting a sleeping draught from the old witch, and that when he gets it tonight, he must spill it and pretend he has drunk it. That poor girl has been greatly troubled, and greatly to be pitied, and she has spent two nights with him, without his knowing it. Tell her to say all that, and if they could tell it to him, then you might have some chance,' the old man said.

She went out and she pulled out the tablecloth. The Scabby Crow came up to her, and there was the tablecloth spread out, with every kind of food on it that your mouth could want or that you might like to eat. And when she saw the wonderful cloth the girl had, and all the food on it, she was amazed.

'Wisha,' she said, 'would you give me that?' she said.

'I would give it to you,' she said, 'in exchange for being with the little white goat tonight. But it's useless for me,' she said, 'going and giving you things in order to be with the little white goat, for the poor man hasn't a clue whether I'm there or not. And you'll have to go,' she said, 'to the servant boys who are working out in the field, and tell them that he has been getting a sleeping draught from the old witch, and that when he gets it tonight, he must spill it. And that his wife has been in his room, in his bed, when he got there, and that she has been there two nights, without his knowing it.'

'I'll do that for you,' said the Scabby Crow, 'and a thousand welcomes,' she said. 'And I'm more than willing to do it for you.'

'You will get the tablecloth, in that case,' she said.

The Scabby Crow went to the hag and asked her if the girl could come to the little white goat tonight, that she had a fine tablecloth, with every kind of food your mouth could want on it.

'Tell her she can spend the night with him' said the witch.

She came back to the girl.

'Yes, now,' said she, 'are you promising me?' said she. 'I'm making a promise to you, so are you promising me that you will say that to the boys, to tell the little white goat?'

'Oh, I swear to you,' she said, 'from my heart out,' said she, 'that I will go to them, myself,' said she, 'tonight, and I will say it to them.'

She left her, and she gave her the tablecloth. When night fell she set out and went to the castle.

'Go to the room and go to bed,' said the old hag to her.

No food or drink did she give her. She went to bed, and she was in the bed when the little white goat came home. He got food and drink from the old hag, but he did nothing except fling it down on the floor — the sleeping draught — and go to bed. And he gave the girl a big hug then, and asked her how she had managed to come.

'You had a lucky journey,' he said, 'to imagine that you found me,' he said, 'in the condition I am in, and that I came here and you following me,' said he, 'and you having no idea where I was.'

'But look,' said she, 'I knew how to find you,' said she. 'God was helping me.'

'Oh, be that as it may,' he said. 'But everything is as miserable as ever it was, if you can't find out,' said he, 'from the Scabby Crow,' he said, 'how that old witch can be put to death,' said he. 'If we don't find out,' said he, 'a way to kill the old hag,' said he, 'we will remain under the magic spell, and we'll all be under the spell of that old hag,' said he. 'But if the Scabby Crow is fond of you at all she will help you to this extent, that she will tell you all she can find out from the old witch about where the sod of her death is. And tell her that, and that you will still be good to her.'

So it was. She went off to the cottage where the old couple had been that morning, and whatever she had done the day before, she had no food or drink to spread out today, because she had given away the tablecloth. But the old couple had a little food, and she got food from them. And she told them. She told them everything.

'The Scabby Crow will do her best for you,' said the old man. 'Because you were good to her, and she will keep trying. But when she comes to you tomorrow, call her aside and tell her that you will take the place of a sister or a brother for her forever, if only she finds out from the hag where her sod of death is, so that she can be put to death.'

'I'll do my best for you,' said the Scabby Crow. And that was good.

And the following day she said to the old hag:

'I'm very frightened, Mother,' said she, the Scabby Crow, 'I'm very frightened that you are going to die,' she said, 'and what will I do then?' she said. 'Who will help me?'

'Dear love,' said the old hag. 'Dear bright love,' she said, 'you needn't worry that I am going to die,' she said, 'because there is nothing that can kill me.'

'Oh, is there anything at all [that can]?' said the Scabby Crow. 'Or will you remain like that forever?' said she. 'That is what I want.'

'Yes,' said she. 'But leaving that aside,' she said, 'my death is in that block there outside,' she said, 'and there is no chance that anyone will ever break that block,' she said.

The next day the Scabby Crow started to put posies and things on the block, to wash it and clean it, and to put every sort of paint and things on the block, letting on that it was the sod of death of her mother, the old hag.

'Oh, you are greatly to be pitied,' said the old hag. 'You are greatly to be pitied,' she said. 'My death is not there, and don't bother about that.'

'And where is your death then?' asked she. 'I must look after it,' said she, 'and I am getting frightened. You are moving towards the end of your life,' she said, 'and I am afraid,' said she, 'not to get ready for it, but tell me, where is your death, even if it is never going to happen,' said she. 'Not that I want it to.'

'No one will ever be able to put me to death,' said she, 'and don't be afraid about that. In the field,' said she, 'where the servant boys are working,' said she, 'that is the place where my death is,' said she. 'And there is no finding it, ever. There is a big stone slab there,' said she, 'and it takes at least four men to lift that slab,' said she. 'And there is a wether[2] underneath,' said she, 'and that wether would climb out. And the wether would throw away a duck, and the duck would throw away an egg. And where is the person who can catch that egg as soon as the duck throws it away? Catch it and hit it?' said she. 'Look at that black spot on my right side,' said she. 'They would have to hit that with it,' said she. 'Who could ever do it?' said she. 'It won't happen. Never fear.'

'Ah, that's what I want to hear,' said she.

She started to wash and bathe her, so that she could see where the spot was. She would be washing her every single day, and she went to the servant boys and she told the servant boys she would do anything for them, if they dug in that place, and found the slab. And she said:

'The slab is in that field where you are working,' she said. 'And you should lift it and then I will do anything at all for you, anything you want,' she said, 'if you do that much,' she said. 'And when the wether climbs out, he will throw away a duck, and the duck will throw away an egg, and if you could get the egg and give it to me?'

---

2. A castrated ram.

So it was. They said they would do their best and they did. And they brought the egg to her. And she hit her with the egg on the black spot on her side and she was turned into a big lump of salt. And there she remained.

Yes. That was good. And I left her behind me.[3]

Before that she had made her tell how to remove the magic spell from all of them, and the witch had said:

'After my death,' she said, 'and that's a long time away, there is a magic wand hidden under the cupboard,' she said, 'and you should give three slaps of that wand to the little white goat,' she said, 'and he will be turned into a fine big man,' she said. 'And if you get three slaps of it as well,' she said, 'you will become a fine big girl. And give three slaps of it to each of your three sisters,' she said — that was those three women — 'and the magic spell will be removed from them,' she said. 'But now,' she said, 'you don't need to know that, because I will never die.'

She died. She was made into a lump of salt. But I said that before. I'd better say it again.

That was good. And when she was turned into a lump of salt, the Scabby Crow was happy to have news to tell the little white goat when he came home for the night. And when the little white goat came home she said:

'Yes, little brother,' she said. 'I'm able now,' she said, 'to call you brother. You have some luck now,' she said. 'Give me the little magic wand that is in there under the cupboard. Give it to me in my hand.'

He went gladly, and gave it to her, into her hand, and she hit the little white goat three blows with the little magic wand, and turned him into a fine big boy.

'Now, brother,' she said, 'hit me three blows with it, and I won't be a Scabby Crow any more.'

He did. And she was turned into a fine big girl. And there were no scabs or anything on her as there had been. They didn't show any more; she was a big fine woman. And they were there happily together for a while. And the little white goat said:

'Yes, now, everything is fine now,' he said, 'thanks be to God. And it is this girl here who is responsible for giving us this gift,' he said. 'That was planned for her. She has had a good taste of hardship. It is many a trough and bramble she went through while she was running after me, but look,' he said, 'thanks be to God that she has me now. And let us go,' he said, 'and remove the magic spell from our three sisters and from my three children. My three children,' he said, 'are waiting for me, and they're well,' he said, 'except that one of them has lost an eye, more's the pity.'

'He hasn't,' said the girl. 'I have it here,' she said, 'in my pocket-handkerchief, where I caught it,' she said, 'when I let a tear fall. I was afraid of you,' she said, 'afraid you would leave me. I caught it in my pocket-handkerchief and it's in there still.'

They set off. He gave the Scabby Crow in marriage to one of the servant boys and made them a present of the castle and all the treasures that were in it, and he arranged a comfortable living for the old man. He and his wife had been under the spell as well, but the little white goat removed it, and they lived happily from then on.

He went to the three sisters, and he took home his three children. And they lived happily ever after that, and in comfort.

And the blessing of God on the souls of the dead.

I heard that from my own father, may God bless his soul and the souls of all the dead who have left us, the souls of all the dead.

---

3. Here, as the story comes to an end, the storyteller interjects herself into the action.

MÁIRE MHIC FHIONNLAOICH

(b. 1873)

from:

IRISH FOLKLORE COLLECTION MS NO. 509 (1938)

[This tale is a sub-type of the Bluebeard story, which is not very common in Ireland; only thirty-one versions are listed in Ó Súilleabháin and Christiansen's *Types of the Irish Folktale*. It is an unusual fairytale type, falling outside the pattern in which all the events of the story lead to a happy marriage. The theme of this fairytale, which must be defined as such on account of its imagery and characterization, is the danger of marriage, at least marriage for money, rather than its desirability. In Máire Mhic Fhionnlaoich's version, the hero's role is played by a brother rather than a suitor; it concludes with the breakup of three marriages and the subsequent happy cohabitation of a family of siblings with their mother.

The narrator's sympathy lies with the point of view of the mother, who wishes to keep all her children with her for ever. The story emphasizes the conflict between love (in this case, filial and parental, rather than sexual) and greed, but the narrator clearly feels that material prosperity, or at least comfort, is very important: the wives of the 'monsters' are relieved to have their husbands killed, but reluctant to give up their opulent homes. The attitude that material comfort is at least as desirable as emotional fulfilment is quite marked in many Irish fairytales.

Collected by Seán Ó hEochaidh in May 1938, when the storyteller was sixty-five years old. A version of AT 312, 'The Giant-killer and his Dog (Bluebeard)'. From IFC 509: 194–205. Translation and headnote by E. Ní D.]

[THE CASTLE OF PENNIES]

Bhí fear agus bean ann uair amháin agus bhí triúr nigheanach acu. Bhí siad iontach bocht agus ní raibh slí bheatha ar bith acu ach ag dhul na coille a bhaint brosna agus á ndíol. Bhí carr agus asal aige agus nuair a bhaineadh sé lód thugadh sé isteach 'na bhaile mhóir é.

Bhí sé lá amháin ag baint sa choillidh agus tháinig fear galánta chuige. D'fhiafraigh sé dó a raibh iníon ar bith aige. Dúirt seisean go raibh triúr.

'Bhal, má chuireann tú an bhean is sine acu chugamsa amárach bhéarfaidh mé lán dó charr de phighneacha duit uirthi.'

'Maith go leor,' dúirt an fear.

Tháinig sé aníos abhaile agus dúirt sé:

'Beidh sí seo liom amárach go gcuidigh sí liom. Bainfidh muid níos mó ár mbeirt agus beidh muid ábalta ar níos mó a thabhairt 'na bhaile mhóir.'

Ach rinne an bhean a ba shine de na nighneacha réidh an lá seo agus chuaigh sí leis. Tháinig an fear uasal fá na coinne. Thug sé lán a chart de phighneacha dó uirthi agus chuaigh sí leis. Chuaigh sé 'na bhaile an oíche sin agus d'fhiafraigh an mháthair dó cá raibh a nighean.

'O, d'fhan sí insa a choillidh,' a deir sé, 'b'fhada léi an siúl 'na bhaile agus b'fhearr léi fuireacht ins a choillidh go maidin. Ach bhéarfaidh mé í seo eile liom amárach.' Chuaigh sé na bhaile innseoir a bhean agus dúirt sé leis an bhean go dtabharfadh sé í seo eile leis amárach, agus go gcuideodh an bheirt níos mó a bhaint. Thug sé leis í agus nuair a chuaigh sé 'na coilleadh, tháinig an fear seo chuige agus thug sé lán a chart de scillingeacha dó. Tháinig fear eile ansin agus dúirt sé dá dtugadh sé an tríú bean chuige go dtabharfadh sé lán a chart dó ghinidheacha dó uirthi. 'Maith go leor,' a dúirt an fear.

Chuaigh sé abhaile an oíche sin agus d'fhiafraigh a bhean dó cá raibh na nigheanacha. D'inis sé daoithe ansin go raibh siad insa a choillidh agus go gcaitheadh sé an tríú bean a thabhairt leis amárach.

B'fhíor é. Thug sé leis an bhean a b'óige lá thar na bhárach agus chuaigh sé 'na coilleadh agus nuair a chuaigh sé ansin tháinig fear roimhe agus lán a chart de ghinidheacha leis. Bhí na trí lód aige ansin agus chuir sé na nighneacha ar shiúl. Fill sé na bhaile an oíche sin agus lán a chart de ghinidheacha leis chuig na bhean. D'fhiafraigh an bhean dó cá raibh na nighneacha. Dúirt sé léi gur dhíol sé an bhean a ba sine ar lán a chart de phighneacha. Agus d'fhiafraigh sí ansin cá raibh an darna bean. Agus dúirt sé gur dhíol sé an darna bean ar lán a chart de scillingeacha, agus gur dhíol sé an tríú bean ar lán a chart de ghinidheacha. Thug sé an trí lód ansin 'na bhaile, agus ní raibh sin ag sásamh na máthar ar chor a bith. Bhí sí buartha fá na nighneacha. Bhí sí ansin agus bhí sí ag caoineadh achan lá fá na nighneacha.

Bhí gasúr beag ansin acu, agus bhí an gasúr ag coimhead ar a mháthair achan lá ag caoineadh agus ní raibh a fhios aige goidé bhí uirthi.

'A mháthair,' arsa seisean aon lá amháin. 'Tá mé ag coimhead ort ag caoineadh achan lá ó thóg mé mo chos ón talamh, agus níl a fhios agam goidé atá ort agus tú ag caoineadh achan lá.'

'Bhal, tá sé chomh maith agam é innse.'

Thosaigh sí agus d'innis sí dó go raibh triúr deirfiúracha aige agus gur dhíol a athair an triúr. An bhean ba sine ar lán a chart de phighneacha, an dara bean ar lán a chart de scillingeacha, agus lán a chart de ghinidheacha ar an tríú bean.

'Bhal, mo dhún is mo dhorn ormsa,' arsa seisean, 'nach bhfhaghaim suaimhneas go bhfaghaidh mé amach iad.'

'O,' a dúirt an mháthair, 'ní choróchaidh tusa uaim. Tá tú beag go leor agam féin.'

Ní dhéanfadh sin gnoithe. Chaitheadh seisean imeacht.

'Déan réidh *trifle* lóin damhsa,' a deir sé, 'agus rachaidh mé a gcuartadh amárach.'

Rinn sí réidh dhá bhonnóg aráin agus d'fhiafraigh sí dó cé acu a b'fhearr leis, an bhonnóg bheag agus a beannacht nó an bhonnóg mhór agus a mallacht.

'Is fearr liom an bhonnóg bheag agus do bheannacht.'

D'imigh sé leis ansin agus an bhonnóg leis. Shiúil sé leis ansin go dtí go dteachaidh sé go dtí coillidh mhór. Chuaigh sé isteach sa choillidh agus chonaic sé solas beag í bhfad uaidh, agus tharraing sé ar an tsolas. Ní raibh astoigh ansin ach seanduine mór. D'fhiafraigh an seanduine dó goidé bhí ag cur buartha air. D'inis sé dó ó thús go dtí na dheire go raibh sé ar siúl ag iarraidh a chuid deirfiúracha.

'Bhal,' a dúirt an seanduine, 'fan agamsa go maidin agus b'fhéidir go dtabharfainn eolas amárach duit.'

D'fhan sé ag an tseanduine go dtáinig an lá agus nuair a d'éirigh siad ar maidin chuir an seanduine each dubh leis nach mbainfeadh ribe den ghaoith agus nach mbaineadh an ghaoth ribe de. 'Agus bhéarfaidh an t-each dubh fhad leis an fhathach a bhfuil an chéad bhean de do chuid deirfiúracha [aige] thú.'

Shiúil leis go dtáinig sé fhad le caisleán agus bhí cumhdach pighneacha uilig go léir ar a chaisleán. Tháinig sé den bheathach agus d'imigh an beathach uaidh. Chuaigh sé go dtí an doras ansin agus ligeadh isteach é. Tháinig an *lady* í féin go dtí é agus d'fhiafraigh sé daoithe ar b'í a bhí ann, agus dúirt sí gurbh í. 'Bhal, mise do dheartháir,' a dúirt sé.

'O, nach trua mise ag amharc ar an fhathach do [do] mharú,' arsa sise.

'Bhal,' a dúirt sé, 'troidfidh mise an fathach.'

Ach bhí go maith. Chuir sí í bhfolach é, agus tháinig an fathach. 'Mothaím boladh an Éireannaigh atá í mo chaisleán anocht,' a deir sé.

'O, beidh sin agat fhad agus bhéas mise agat,' a dúirt sise.

Bhí go maith go dtáinig an lá. D'éirigh seisean agus chuartaigh sé an teach agus fuair sé an stócach í bhfolach í gcúl na comhlach. Tharraing sé amach é. 'Caithfidh tú mise a throid amárach,' a deir sé. *Chuaigh an bheirt le chéile agus bhí siad ag troid go dtearn siad criogán don bhogán agus bogán don chriogán, agus dá mbeadh fear ó íochtar an domhain go huachtar an domhain gur ar a dís a thiocfas sé a dh'amharc. Nuair a bhí neoin agus deireadh an lae ann thug an stócach fáscadh dó, agus an darna ceann steall sé an chloigeann dó. Thug sé léim idir an cholainn agus an chloigeann.*

'Char bhac duit,' arsan fathach. 'Ach go b'é go dtearn tú sin, dá bhfaighinn ar ais, feara fáil nach scarfadh é.'

Bhí go maith. Chuaigh sé abhaile chuici-se ansin. Agus ní raibh sise ag brath é a ligean uaithe níos mó. Dúirt sé go gcaithfeadh sé a dhul go dtí go bhfaigheadh sé an bheirt eile. D'imigh leis ar maidin lá ar na bhárach agus nuair a chuaigh sé amach tháinig an t-each caol dubh seo go dtí é, agus chuaigh sé a mharcaíocht air agus thug sé go dtí an caisleán é a raibh cumhdach na scillingeacha air. Bhí fathach mór ansin a bhí í bhfad ní ba mhó ná an chéad fhathach. Chuaigh seisean isteach agus d'inis sé do na dheirfiúr goidé mar bhí.

'O, nach trua mé a choimhead ar an fhathach do [do] mharú!' arsa sise.

Dúirt seisean go mairfeadh seisean é. Chuaigh sé í bhfolach í gcúl na comhlach agus tháinig an fathach agus thosaigh an cuartú agus tharraing sé amach as cúl na comhlach é.

'Caithfidh tú mise a throid anois,' arsa seisean. Chuaigh an bheirt le chéile. Rinn siad mar rinn siad an chéad lá agus nuair a bhí neoin agus deireadh an lae ann fuair an buachaill bua ar an fhathach agus steall sé an chloigeann dó. Thug sé léim idir an cheann agus an cholainn.

'Char bhac duit,' a dúirt an fathach, 'ach go b'é go dtearn tú sin, dá bhfuigheadh an ceann ar an cholainn arais feara Éireann nach scarfadh é.'

Chuaigh sé chuici-sé ansin agus ní raibh sise fá choinne é ligean ar siúl ní b'fhaide. Ach dúirt seisean go gcaithfeadh sé an tríú bean a fháil. D'imigh sé lá ar na bhárach agus an t-each caol dubh seo leis, agus níor stad sé go raibh sé ag an teach a raibh cumhdach na nginidheacha air. Chuaigh sé go dtí an teach agus ligeadh isteach é, agus d'inis sé daoithe-se an rud céanna. Bhí lúcháir iontach uirthi roimhe agus dúirt sí leis go mairbhfeadh an fathach é. Dúirt seisean nach mairbhfeadh. Tháinig an fathach trathnóna agus dúirt sé: 'Mothaím boladh an Éireannaigh astoigh anseo anocht agat.'

Chuaigh sé síos agus chuartaigh sé an teach agus tharraing sé amach as cúl na comhlach é. 'Caithfidh tú mise a throid amárach,' a deir sé. 'Maith go leor,' a dúirt an buachaill. Chuaigh an bheirt le chéile ar maidin lá ar na bhárach agus throid siad go dtáinig neoin agus deireadh an lae. Nuair a bhí neoin agus deireadh an lae ann steall an buachaill a cheann dó. Thug sé léim idir a cheann agus a cholainn. 'Char bhac duit,' arsan fathach, 'dá bhfuighinse ar an cholainn ar ais, feara Éireann nach scarfadh é.'

Bhí an triúr marbh ansin aige. Fill sé ansin go dtí an áit a raibh ise. Dúirt sise go raibh áit ghalánta anseo aicise agus gur mhór an trua é a fhágáil. Dúirt seisean: 'Bhéarfaidh muid linn ár sáith agus cead ag an chuid eile a bheith ansin agus rachaidh muid abhaile chuig ár muintir.'

Thug siad leo an méid a tháinig leo den ór ansin agus níor stad siad go raibh siad ag an chaisleán a raibh na scillingeacha air. Bhí lúcháir uirthise rompu agus dúirt sí 'Fanfaidh sibh anseo agamsa.'

'Ní fhuinneochaidh ar chor ar bith' a dúirt an buachaill, 'rachaidh muid 'na bhaile chuig ár n-athair agus chuig ár máthair agus beidh lúcháir mhór orthu romhainn.'

Ach thug siad leobhtha an méid a thiocfadh leobhtha de gach ollmhathas dá raibh insa chúirt. D'imigh leobhtha. Nuair a chuaigh siad go dtí an

bhean a raibh an cumhdach pighneacha uirthi bhí lúcháir iontach uirthi rompu agus dúirt sí 'Is fearr dúinn fanacht uilig anseo feasta.'

Ní dhéanfadh siadsan sin ar chor ar bith. Chaitheadh siad a dhul 'na bhaile. Thug siad leobhtha ansin an méid ollmhathais a bhí san chúirt seo agus d'imigh siad 'na bhaile chuig a n-athair agus a máthair. Tháinig sé 'na bhaile agus a thriúr deirfiúracha leis. Agus ní raibh duine faoin áit a bhí leath chomh saibhir leobhtha on lá sin go dtí an lá inniu.

TRANSLATION

Once upon a time there was a man and a woman, and they had three daughters. They were very poor and they had no way of making a living other than going to the woods gathering kindling and selling it. He had an ass and cart and when he would collect a load he'd bring it into the town.

One day he was gathering in the wood and a fine man came to him. He asked him if he had any daughter. He said he had three.

'Well, if you send the eldest of them to me tomorrow I'll give you the full of your cart of pennies for her.'

'Very well,' said the man.

He came up home and he said:

'She can come with me tomorrow to help me. We'll gather more if there are two of us and we will be able to bring more to the town.'

So the eldest of the daughters got ready this day and she went with him. The nobleman came for her. He gave him the full of his cart of pennies for her and she went with him. He went home that night and the mother asked him where her daughter was.

'Oh, she stayed in the wood,' he said. 'She thought the walk home was too long, and she'd rather stay in the wood until morning. But I'll take this other one with me tomorrow.'

He went home to his wife and he said to his wife that he would take this other one with him tomorrow, and that the two would help to gather more. He brought her with him and when he went to the wood this man came to him and he gave him the full of his cart of shillings for her. Then another man came and he said that if he brought the third girl to him he would give the full of the cart of guineas for her. 'Very well,' said the man.

He went home that night and his wife asked him where the daughters were. He told her then that they were in the wood and that he would have to bring the third girl with him tomorrow.

It was true for him. He brought the youngest girl the next day and he went to the wood and when he went there the man came before him bringing the full of his cart of guineas with him. He had the three loads then and he sent off the daughters. He returned home that night and the full of his cart of guineas with him to his wife. The wife asked him where the daughters were. He told her that he had sold the eldest girl for the full of his cart of pennies. And then she asked where the second girl was. And he said that he had sold the second girl for the full of his cart of shillings, and that he had sold the third girl for the full of his cart of guineas. He brought home the three loads then, and that didn't please the mother at all. She was worried about the daughters. She was there and she was crying every day about the daughters.

They had a little boy, and the boy was looking at his mother crying every day and he did not know what was wrong with her.

'Mother,' he said one day, 'I am watching you crying every day since I was born, and I don't know what's wrong with you, crying every day.'

'Well, I might as well tell you.'

She started and she told him that he had three sisters and that his father had sold the three — the eldest girl for the full of his cart of pennies, the second girl for the full of his cart of shillings, and the full of his cart of guineas for the third one.

'Well, blow me!' he said, 'I won't have any peace until I find them.'

'Oh,' said his mother, 'you won't stir from me. You are small enough to stay with me.'

That wouldn't do. He would have to go.

'Get ready a bit of lunch for me,' says he, 'and I'll go looking for them tomorrow.'

She got ready two loaves of bread and she asked him which he would prefer, the small loaf with her blessing or the big loaf with her curse.

'I prefer the small loaf with your blessing.'

He went off then, taking the loaf with him. He walked along until he came to a big wood. He went into the wood and he saw a little light far away from him, and he went towards the light. There was nobody in there but a big old fellow.

The old man asked him what was worrying him. He told him from beginning to end that he was out looking for his sisters.

'Well,' said the old man, 'stay with me until morning and maybe I would give you some information tomorrow.'

He stayed with the old man until it was day, and when they got up in the morning the old man gave him a black steed that would not catch a rib of hair from the wind and from which the wind would not catch a rib of hair. 'And this black steed will bring you as far as the giant who has the first one of your sisters.'

He went on until he came as far as a castle, and the castle was covered all over with pennies. He got down from the horse, and the horse went away from him. He went to the door and was let in. The lady herself came to him and he asked her if it was herself. And she said it was. 'Well, I'm your brother,' he said.

'Oh, am I not to be pitied, having to watch the giant kill you!' she said.

'Well,' he said, 'I will fight the giant.'

That was all right. She hid him and the giant came. 'I get the smell of an Irishman in my castle tonight,' says he.

'Oh, you'll be getting that smell as long as you have me here,' she said.

It was all right until day came. He got up and searched the house and he found the young lad hiding behind the door. He dragged him out. 'You have to fight me tomorrow,' he said. *The two went together and they were fighting until they made the soft place hard and the hard place soft, and if there was a man from the top of the world to the bottom of the world it is at that pair he would come to look. When it was evening and the end of the day, the young lad knocked him down, and the second thing he did was to knock the head off him. He leapt between the body and the head.*

'*It's well for you,*' said the giant. '*If you hadn't done that, if I had got it back again, the men of Ireland would not cut it off.*'[1]

That was all right. He went home to her then. And she wasn't planning to let him leave her ever again. He said he would have to go to get the other two. He went off the following day and when he went out, the slender black steed came

---

1. Traditional 'run' describing a fight with a giant. Shorter versions occur later in the story.

to him, and he went riding on it and it carried him to the castle which was covered all over with shillings. There was a big giant in there who was twice the size of the first giant. He went inside and told his sister what the situation was.

'Oh, am I not to be pitied, watching the giant kill you!'

He said that he would kill him. He went hiding behind the door and the giant came and started the search and dragged him out from behind the door.

'You must fight me now,' he said. The two went together. *They did what they had done on the first day, and when it was evening and the end of the day the boy overcame the giant and knocked off his head. He leapt between the head and the body.*

'*It was well for you,*' *said the giant, 'if you had not done that, if I had got the head on my body again, the men of Ireland would not cut it off.*'

He went to her then and she didn't plan to let him away again. But he said that he would have to get the third girl. He went the following day with the slender black steed, and he did not stop until he was at the house which was covered with guineas. He went to the house and he was let in, and he told her the same thing. She was very happy to see him and she told him that the giant would kill him. He said he would not kill him. The giant came in the afternoon and he said: 'I get the smell of an Irishman inside here tonight with you.' He went down and searched the house and he pulled him out from behind the door. 'You must fight me tomorrow,' says he. 'Very well,' said the boy. *The two went together on the morning of the following day and they fought until evening and the end of the day came. When it was evening and the end of the day the boy knocked the head off him. He made a leap between the head and the body.*

'*It was well for you,*' *said the giant, 'if I got it on the body again, the men of Ireland would not take it off.*'

He had the three dead then. He returned then to the place where [his sister] was. She said that she had a lovely place here and that it would be a great pity to leave it. He said: 'We will take with us as much as we want and the rest can stay here, and we will go home to our own people.'

Then they took with them as much as they could of the gold and they didn't stop until they came to the castle covered with shillings. [His second sister] was delighted to see them, and she said: 'You'll stay here with me.'

'Indeed and we will not,' said the boy. 'We will go home to our mother and our father and they will be overjoyed to see us!'

So they took with them everything good that was in the court. And off they went. When they came to the daughter who had the castle covered with pennies, she was happy to see them, and she said, 'It's best if we stay here from now on.'

But they would not do that on any account. They really wanted to go home. They brought with them then all of the good things in the court and they went home to their father and mother. He came home and his three sisters with him. And there was not one person in the district who was half as rich as they were from that day until this.

SORCHA MHIC GHRIANNA

(b. 1875)

from:

IRISH FOLKLORE COLLECTION MS NO. 289 (1936)

[Collected in Rinn na Feirste, County Donegal, on 30 September 1936, by Aodh Ó Duibheannaigh, a local schoolteacher and part-time collector for the Irish Folklore Commission. This is AT 313, 'The Girl as Helper in the Hero's Flight', one of the most often told, or collected, fairytales in Ireland: 644 versions are listed in S. Ó Súilleabháin and R. Christiansen's *Types of the Irish Folktale*.[1] It is a version of a popular international story, some of whose central episodes were first documented in classical mythology, in the stories of the Labours of Hercules and of Jason and Medea. Uniquely among fairytales, it features both a male and a female protagonist in equally active roles. In the first section (as in the majority of fairytales) the hero is active, while the heroine takes over about halfway through. From IFC 289: 328–46. Translation and headnote by E. Ní D.]

1. Only 'The Dragon Slayer' (AT 300) has been collected more frequently.

RÍ NA FÁSAIGHE DUIBHE[2]

Bhí rí i gConnachta aon uair amháin, agus ní raibh aige ach aon ghasúr amháin, nuair a fuair a bhean bás. Bhí droch dhóigh ar é féin agus ar an ghasúr agus d'imigh sé agus phós sé bean eile. Ní raibh an bhainríon og ina ceann rómhaith don dílleachta, ach bhí an rí féin ag coinneáil súil air, agus á thabhairt leis ansiúd agus anseo, go dtí gur fhás an gasúr aníos ina bhuachaill ábalta go raibh sé bliain agus fiche de aois.

'A Athair,' ar seisean, 'níor fhág mé na fraitheacha ariamh gan duine inteacht a bheith liom, agus nár chóir go ligfeá amach inniu mé go bhfeicim luí na tíre.'

'Ligfidh cinnte,' adeir an t-athair.

Thug sé leis beathach capaill agus d'imigh sé leis. Bhí sé ar shiúl go dtí gur shíl sé go raibh sé rófhada ar shiúl, agus tháinig sé fhad le coillidh. Dar leis go ligeadh sé don bheathach greim beag a ithe, agus thug sé cead a chinn dó isteach fríd an choillidh. Chuaigh sé féin ag spaisteoireacht thart, agus á bhreathnú, agus tchí sé seanduine beag ina shuí ag bun crainn agus é ag imirt cardaí.

Chuir an seanduine fáilte roimhe, agus d'iarr air a theacht agus cluiche a bheith aige. Siúd an bheirt a dh'imirt agus níorbh fhada gur chuir mac rí Chonnachta cluiche ar an tseanduine.

'Iarr achainí anois,' arsan seanduine.

'O, ní fiú domh é,' ar seisean.

'Bhail, achainí ar bith dá n-iarrfaidh tú, gheobhaidh tú í,' arsan seanduine.

'Bhail,' ar seisean, 'iarraim achainí cloigeann gabhair a bheith ar mo leas-mháthair, gur mian liomsa é a bhaint duithe.'

D'imigh sé leis ag tarraingt ar an bhaile. Nuair a tháinig sé ar amharc an toigh, bhí muintir an bhaile uilig cruinn thart fá theach an rí, agus an rí é féin amuigh agus é ag fáscadh a chuid lámh. Ní dhearn seisean iontas de dhath ar bith, agus ní dhearn sé ach a bheathach a chur ar stábla, agus a ghabháil isteach agus a ghabháil a luí.

Dá luaithe agus d'éirigh sé ar maidin, thug sé leis an bheathach agus d'imigh sé ar ais, agus shiúl sé leis go dtáinig sé fhad leis an choillidh chéanna a raibh sé aici an lá roimhe sin. Thug sé cead a chinn don bheathach, agus tchí sé an seanduine beag céanna ina shuí ag bun an chrainn agus é ag imirt chardaí.

Chuir an seanduine fáilte roimhe, agus d'iarr air a theacht agus cluiche a bheith aige. Siúd an bheirt a dh'imirt agus níorbh fhada gur chuir mac rí Chonnachta cluiche ar an tseanduine.

'Iarr achainí anois,' arsa an seanduine.

'O, ní fiú domh é,' ar seisean.

'An bhfuair tú an achainí a d'iarr tú inné?' arsa an seanduine.

Dúirt mac an rí go bhfuair.

'Bhail, iarr achainí eile inniu,' arsa an seanduine.

'Bhail,' ar seisean, 'tá mé ag iarraidh achainí páirc sé n-acra atá ag m'athair a bheith lán de eallach choimhitheach, gan beirt ar bith acu a bheith cosúil le chéile agus iad a bheith ansin choíche gur mian liomsa a gcur ar shiúl.'

'Gheobhaidh tú d'achainí,' arsa an seanduine.

Bhain mac an rí a bhaile amach, agus nuair a bhí sé ag tarraingt ar an bhaile, tchí sé an pháirc uilig lán de eallach choimhitheach, agus cuid seirbhíseach an rí uilig amuigh ag iarraidh iad a chur ar siúl. Ní luaithe a chuireadh siad bó fhad leis an gheata nó bheadh sí i lár na páirce. Sa deireadh d'iarr an rí iad a fhágáil, go gcaitheadh sé gur rud iontach a bhí Dia a dhéanamh orthu. Rinne seisean a shuipéar, nuair a chuir sé an bheathach ar stábla, chuaigh a luí agus níor lig dada air.

Nuair a d'éirigh sé ar maidin, bhí deifre air ag déanamh réidh agus ag imeacht, agus rinne sé dearmad den bheiste bheag a chur air. Bhí leabhar phóca sa bheiste bheag agus fhad agus bheadh sí ar iompar leis, ní thiocfadh le duine ar bith cluiche a chur air.

Shiúl sé leis go dtáinig sé go dtí an choillidh chéanna. Bhí an seanduine beag ina shuí ag bun crainn agus é ag imirt.

'Bhfuil tú agam inniu arais?' ar seisean.

'Tá,' arsa mac rí Chonnachta.

'Bhail, goitse go raibh cluiche againn,' ar seisean.

Shuigh siad síos a dh'imirt, agus níorbh fhada gur chuir an seanduine cluiche ar mhac rí Chonnachta.

'Bhail, anois,' ar seisean, 'cuirim-sa thusa faoi gheasaibh gan dhá oíche a chaitheamh in aon teach go bhfaghaidh tú amach caidé mar tá caisleán Rí na Fásaighe Duibhe déanta.'

Thug mo dhuine bocht léim ar dhroim a bheithigh agus bhain a bhaile amach. Nuair a

---

2. MS has *Rí na Fásaigh Duibhne.*

tháinig sé isteach shuigh sé ar chathaoir, rinne sé osna, agus níor fhan cnaipe ar a bheiste nár réab.

'A mhic,' arsa an rí, 'is cosúil d'osna le hosna mac rí faoi gheasaibh.'

'O, mac rí mise faoi gheasaibh anocht,' ar seisean.

Nuair a d'éirigh sé ar maidin, d'iarr a athair air an bheathach a b'fhearr sa stábla a thabhairt leis.

'Bhail, sul a n-imím-sa,' ar seisean, 'iarraim achaní a cloigeann féin a bheith ar mo leasmháthair, agus an t-eallach coimhitheach imeacht, agus achan chineál san teach a bheith mar is ceart.'

Thug sé léim ar dhroim a bheithigh, agus d'imigh leis. Bhí sé ar shiúl go raibh an neoin bheag agus deireadh an lae ann. Shuigh sé síos a ghlacadh a scíthe, agus tchí sé cnap ceo ag tarraingt air sa spéir.

Dar leis, 'más ag gabháil ag cuidiú liom atá tú, is feairrde domh é, agus más in m'éadan atá tú is dona mé.'

Caidé tháinig amach as an cheo ach iolar mór.

'Bhail,' arsan t-iolar, 'dá dtabharfá domhsa an beathach, sé a bheadh a dhíobháil orm, nó tá mo chuid iolair bheaga ag fáil bháis leis an ocras agus ní bheidh siad beo ar maidin.'

'O! Caidé mar bhéarfainnse mo bheathach duit agus gan a fhios agam féin cá fhad go deireadh m'astair?' arsa mac an rí.

'Bhal,' arsa an t-iolar, 'má thugann tusa an bheathach domhsa tiocfaidh mise ar ais agus cuideoidh mé leat.'

'Seo, bhail,' ar seisean, 'ardaigh leat é.'

'Bhail, ná corraigh tusa as sin,' arsa an t-iolar, 'go dtarraidh mise ar ais, agus ní bheidh mé ach dhá uair go leith uilig.'

D'éirigh an t-iolar anairde san aer, ar eiteogaí, agus tháinig sé ar ais gur chuir sé a chuid spur isteach insan bheathach, agus d'ardaigh leis é. Siúd an bhuachaill bocht ag amharc i ndiaidh an bheithigh, go dteachaidh sé féin agus an t-iolar as amharc. Shuigh sé ansin tamall mór fada dar leis, seal ag meabhrú, agus seal ag amharc uaidh sna spéarthaí, agus é ar fad ag feitheamh leis an iolar a fheiceáil ag tarraingt air. Sa dheireadh tchí sé é[3] ag tarraingt air faoi dheifre iontach. Tháinig sé chun talaimh agus sheasaigh ag taobh mhac an rí.

'Arú, nárbh fhada a bhí tú amuigh,' arsa mac an rí.

'Dar liomsa,' arsan t-iolar, 'go raibh mé níos fearr ná mo chuid ama. Is doilig liom a rá go bhfuil sé dhá uair go leith ó d'fhág mé seo.'

'Maise, shíl mise,' arsa mac an rí, 'go raibh tú ar shiúl le cúig nó sé huaire, ach ar ndóigh, is fearr go mall féin nó go bráth.'

D'inis sé a scéal don iolar.

'Gabh ar mo dhroim,' arsa an t-iolar.

Chuaigh, agus d'imigh an bheirt leo, go dtáinig said fhad le teach beag baoideach.

'Sin teach,' arsa an t-iolar, 'agus gabh isteach ann agus tá an seanduine iontach eolach, más féidir a fháil amach cá bhfuil caisleán Rí na Fásaighe Duibhe, beidh a fhios ag an seanduine sin é.'

Tháinig sé isteach chuig an tseanduine agus chuir an seanduine míle fáilte roimhe. D'inis sé a shiúl dó.

'Bhail, níor chuala mé trácht ariamh ar Rí na Fásaighe Duibhe,' arsa an seanduine, 'ach déan do shuipéar, gabh a luí agus amharcóidh mise fríd mo chuid leabhar go maidin.'

Ar maidin dúirt sé nach raibh tuairisc chaisleán Rí na Fásaighe Duibhe le fáil aige, 'ach,' ar seisean, 'tá deartháir domhsa in a leithéid seo d'áit, agus tá sé leabhar níos faide chun tosaigh na mise, agus b'fhéidir go mbeadh seisean ábalta a thuairisc a fháil duit. Seo péire buatais agus bhéarfaidh na buataisí thú go doras theach mo dhearthára[4] agus nuair a bhéas tú ansin, bain díot iad, tionntaigh a n-aghaidh ormsa, agus tiocfaidh na buataisí chugamsa anseo arís.'

Chuir mac rí Chonnachta air na buataisí, agus d'imigh leis.

Shiúl sé leis go raibh an neoin bheag agus deireadh an lae ann, go dtáinig sé go dtí teach beag. Bhain sé dó na buataisí, tionntaigh iad agus d'imigh leo arais chuig an tseanduine. Tháinig sé isteach agus ní raibh aon duine istigh roimhe ach seanduine beag. Chuir sé sin céad míle fáilte [roimhe], agus d'iarr air suí.

D'inis mac rí Chonnachta a shiúl. Dúirt an seanduine nár chuala sé iomrá riamh ar chaisleán Rí na Fásaighe Duibhe. 'Ach,' ar seisean, 'déan dó shuipéar, gabh a luí, agus amharcóidh mise fríd mo chuid leabharthach go maidin.'

Ar maidin dúirt an seanduine nach raibh caisleán Rí na Fásaighe Duibhe i bprionnta ar

<hr/>

3. MS, í.

4. MS, *dheartháireacha.*

bith dá raibh aige. 'Ach seo dhuit péire buatais,' ar seisean, 'agus bhéarfaidh siad go doras theach mo dhearthára thú, agus tá seisean leabhar níos faide chun tosaigh na mise, agus má tá a leithéid de chaisleán ar dhroim an domhain, beidh a fhios aige-san cá bhfuil sé. Nuair a rachas tú go deireadh do rása, tionntaigh aghaidh na mbuatais ormsa, agus tiocfaidh said féin 'na bhaile.'

Chuir mac an rí air na buataisí, shiúl leis go raibh an neoin bheag agus deireadh an lae ann, nó go dtáinig sé go dtí teach an tseanduine. Bhain sé dó na buataisí, tionntaigh a n-aghaidh an bealach a tháinig sé agus d'imigh siad leo 'na bhaile. Chuaigh seisean isteach agus ní raibh Críostaí ansin roimhe, ach seanduine beag. Chuir an seanduine céad míle fáilte roimhe, agus d'iarr air suí aníos chun na tine, gurbh olc an áit a bhí aige-san fá choinne a leithéid. Dúirt mac rí Chonnachta go raibh a áit agus a ionad maith go leor, nach b'iad a bhí ar a umhal ach tuairisc chaisleáin Rí na Fásaighe Duibhe.

'Char chuala mé iomrá ariamh air,' arsa an seanduine, 'ach déan do shuipéar, agus gabh a luí, agus amharcóidh mise fríd mo chuid leabharthach go maidin.'

Shuigh an seanduine go maidin ag léamh, agus ar maidin dúirt sé nach raibh a thuairisc in aon leabhar ar an domhan.

'Bhail,' arsa mac rí Chonnachta, 'caithfidh sé a bheith ar an domhan in áit inteacht.'

Chuir an seanduine feadóg ina bhéal, agus sheinn sé trí huaire í. I bhfaiteadh na súl chruinnigh a raibh de iasc san fharraige taobh amuigh den doras, an chuid ba lú in aice an dorais agus iad ag éirí mór de réir mar bhí siad ag imeacht uaidh, sa dóigh go mbeadh sé ábalta iad a fheiceáil uilig. D'fhiafraigh sé díobhtha ar chuala ceann ar bith acu iomrá ariamh ar chaisleáin Rí na Fásaighe Duibhe. Dúirt siad nár chuala.

'Bhail,' ar seisean, 'sé a dtig liomsa a dhéanamh, tú fanacht anseo go dtí am dinnéara, agus gabh síos go dtí an loch bheag sin thíos. Agus sin síos teach níocháin, agus gabh isteach ann. Tiocfaidh trí eala bheaga bhána chun na locha á ní féin. Tá ceann acu a mbíonn brat beag glas uirthi agus baineann sí duithe é agus fágann ar chloich sa chladach é, fhad agus bhíonn sí á ní féin. Anois coinnigh tusa an brat go dtí go dtéigh sise ag caint leat, agus b'fhéidir go mbeadh a fhios aicese rud inteacht faoi chaisleán Rí na Fásaighe Duibhe.'

Chuaigh seisean síos agus chuaigh i bhfolach i dteach an níocháin, agus níorbh fhada go bhfaca sé na trí eala bheaga ag tarraingt air. Bhain ceann acu brat beag glas a bhí uirthi duithe, agus d'fhág sa chladach é. Thug seisean leis an brat agus chuaigh isteach i dteach an níocháin leis ar an chasán. Nuair a nigh na trí eala iad féin, chuaigh an ceann seo a chuartú a brat. Ní raibh sé le fáil aici, agus d'amharc sí isteach sa teach bheag seo, agus chonaic sí an buachaill ina shuí istigh.

'An tú a chonaic mo bhrat beag?' ar sise.

Dúirt sé gurb é, agus go raibh sé aige istigh anseo. D'iarr sí air é a thabhart duithe, agus dúirt sé nach dtabharfadh go dtiocfadh sí isteach ag caint leis. Tháinig sí isteach agus d'fhiafraigh sé duithe an raibh a fhios aici a dhath faoi Rí na Fásaighe Dhuibhe. D'fhiafraigh sí dó cad chuige a raibh sé ag cur tuairisc Rí na Fásaighe Duibhe. Dúirt sé go raibh sé faoi gheasaibh choíche go bhfaghadh sé amach caidé mar bhí caisleán Rí na Fásaighe Duibhe déanta.

'Bhail, tabhair domhsa mo bhrat beag,' ar sise, 'agus déanfaidh mé mo dhícheall duit.'

Thug sé duithe an brat, agus chuir sí thart ar a muinéal é. Bhuail sí buille de shlaitín draíochta uirthi féin, agus rinne eala iontach mhór duithe féin.

'Gabh ar mo dhroim anois,' ar sise, 'agus coinnigh greim maith orm.'

Chuaigh sé ar a droim, agus d'imigh said leo trasna na farraige, go dtí go dtáinig siad fhad le cladach agus caisleán, agus lig sí anuas ansin é.

'Sin thuas teach,' ar sise, 'a bhfuil fathach ina chónaí ann, agus gabh isteach ann agus iarr obair, ach ná hinis go bhfaca tú mise.'

D'imigh sé leis suas le taobh an chaisleáin go raibh sé ag doras an toigh. Bhuail sé buille ar an doras agus tháinig an fathach é féin gur oscail sé an doras dó. D'fhiafraigh an fathach dó caidé thug anseo é.

'Nuair a d'éirigh mé ar maidin,' ar seisean, 'léim mé ar dhroim an tuar cheatha, agus d'fhág sí mo sheasamh amuigh anseo mé.'

'Buachaill gasta thú,' arsa an fathach.

'Buachaill gasta cinnte mé,' arsa an buachaill.

'Caidé atá ag cur buartha ort anois?' arsa an fathach.

'Tá mé go díreach ag cuartú oibre,' ar seisean.

'Bhéarfaidh mise sin duit,' arsa an fathach, 'ach caithfidh tú achan rud á n-iarrfaidh mise ort a dhéanamh, sin nó an ceann a chailleadh.'

'Bhail, ar ndóigh, déanfaidh mé mo dhícheall air,' arsa mac rí Chonnachta.

'Bhail, gabh síos ndaidh[?] a luí,' arsan fathach.

Níor fhiafraigh sé de cé acu bhí ocras air nó nach rabh. Ar maidin nuair a d'éirigh an buachaill, chuaigh sé chuig an fhathach, agus d'iarr air éirí suas as sin agus a chuid oibre a thabhairt dó.

'B'fhéidir gur dá luathas duit,' arsa an fathach, 'a tchífeá í.'

'Ó, bhail,' ar seisean, 'creidim go bhfuil sé go maith agam a ghabháil in a ceann go luath.'

'Bhail, an bhfeiceann tú an caisleán mór sin thall?' arsa an fathach.

'Tchím,' ar seisean.

'Bhail, leag an caisleán sin. Caith na clocha uilig amach san fharraige, agus fág an áit ionas nach n-aithneodh súil dá deachaidh i gceann go raibh aon chaisleán ariamh ann,' arsa an fathach.

Chuaigh mo dhuine bocht amach agus ní raibh sé ábalta barr na seimléirí a fheiceáil, bhí sé chomh hard sin. Ní raibh a fhios aige caidé an dóigh a dtiocfadh sé air. Níorbh fhada go dtáinig an eala bheag go dtí é.

'Caidé a d'iarr sé ort a dhéanamh inniu?' ar sise.

'Tá mo sháith inniu agam,' ar seisean. 'Tá an caisleán sin le leagan agam, agus le caitheamh amach san fharraige sa dóigh nach dtig éinne go raibh aon teach ariamh ann.'

'An bhfuair tú do bhricfeasta?' ar sise.

'Ní bhfuair mé bricfeasta nó suipéar nó aon ghreim ó tháinig mé anseo,' ar seisean.

Spréidh sí amach brat beag a bhí léi, agus bhí achan chineál bidh agus dí ansin dá bhfaca tú ariamh.

'Suigh anois,' ar sise, 'agus ith dó sháith.'

'Bhail, caidé an mhaith a ghabháil a dh'ithe,' ar seisean, 'agus go mbeidh an chloigeann domh ar ball.'

'Déan do chuid ar scor ar bith,' ar sise.

Shuigh seisean a dh'ithe, agus thoisigh sise ar an chaisleán, agus nuair a bhí an béile caite aigesan, bhí an caisleán uilig leagtha aicese. Ní raibh cloch nó carnán ar áit na dubhshraith!

'Ó, a Dhia, is maith thú,' ar seisean.

'Bhail, ar do bhás,' ar sise, 'agus ná hinis go bhfaca tú mise.'

Tháinig sé isteach agus d'fhiafraigh an fathach dó an dearn sé sin agus dúirt go dearn.

'Bairfinn buachalla atá ionat,' arsa an fathach. 'Gabh a luí anois mar a bheadh buachaill maith ann.'

Nuair a d'éirigh an duine bocht ar maidin, d'fhiafraigh sé cá raibh a chuid oibre. D'iarr an fathach air a ghabháil amach agus gach uile chloch dár chaith sé san fharraige a thógáil an lá sin, agus an caisleán a fhágáil sa dóigh nach n-aithneodh aon duine beo gur baineadh dó. Chuaigh sé amach agus do shuigh sé os cionn an áit a raibh na clocha sa chladach. Ní raibh aon chloch amháin acu le feiceáil. Dar leis, 'Beidh an ceann anocht domh ar scor ar bith.'

Níorbh fhada go bhfaca sé an eala bheag ag tarraingt air. D'fhiafraigh sí dó caidé a bhí aige le déanamh inniu.

'Tá mo sháith,' ar seisean. 'Tá an caisleán seo le tógáil go húr nua mar a bhí ariamh, agus tá eagla orm go mbeidh seal air de mo thairbhesa.'

'An bhfuair tú aon ghreim le hithe?' ar sise.

Dúirt sé nach bhfuair, gurbh í féin a thug an greim deireannach dó. Spréidh sí amach brat beag a bhí léi, agus bhí achan chineál bidh agus dí ansin dá bhfaca tú ariamh.

'Siúd anois,' ar sise, 'agus ith dó sháith.'

'Bhail, caidé an mhaith domh a ghabháil a dh'ithe,' ar seisean, 'agus go mbeidh an chloigeann domh roimhe an oíche.'

'Ith do chuid ar scor ar bith,' ar sise.

Shuigh seisean a dh'ithe, agus thosaigh sise ag tógáil an chaisleáin, agus nuair a bhí a chuid déanta aigesan bhí an caisleán tógtha aicese, agus é sa dóigh agus nach n-aithneodh aon duine beo gur leagadh barr méir air ariamh.

'Ó, a Dhia, is maith thú,' ar seisean.

'Bhail,' ar sise, 'ar dó bhas, na hinis go bhfaca tú mise.'

'Cha n-insim leoga,' ar seisean.

D'imigh sise agus ní raibh ann ach é go raibh sí ar shiúl nuair a tháinig an fathach thart.

'Ó, maith thú,' ar seisean. 'Tá obair mhór déanta agat. Gabh isteach anois agus gabh a luí mar a bheadh buachaill maith ann.'

Nuair a d'éirigh sé ar maidin d'fhiafraigh sé den fhathach caidé an obair a bhí faoi na choinne inniu.

'Tá tobar síos ansin,' arsa an fathach, 'nár glanadh le céad bliain, agus tá fáinne ar a thóin a bhí ag mo mháthair mhór tá céad blian ó shin, agus caithfidh tú an fáinne a fháil roimh an oíche nó mise an ceann a bhaint duit.'

Chuaigh sé síos go dtí an tobar, agus ní fheicfeadh amharc ar shúil síos go híochtar an tobair, bhí sé chomh domhain sin. Sheasaigh sé agus ní raibh a fhios aige caidé a b'fhearr dó a dhéanamh. Le sin tchí sé an eala bheag ag tarraingt air.

'Caidé a d'iarr sé ort a dhéanamh inniu?' ar sise.

'Tá,' ar seisean, 'fáinne a chaill a mháthair mhór, tá céad blian ó shin, agus tá sé ar thóin an tobair seo, agus caithfidh mise é a fháil roimh an oíche, nó an ceann a chailleadh.'

'Tá eagla orm,' ar sise, 'go bhfuil ár sáith ós ar gcoinne inniu, nó tá an fáinne sin thíos in ifreann agus earcan nimhe lúbtha thart air. Ach, an bhfuair tú aon ghreim bricfeasta inniu?' ar sise.

'Ní bhfuair mé aon ghreim,' ar seisean, 'ó thug tú féin an greim deireannach dom.'

'Bhail, suigh síos anois,' ar sise, 'go ndéanaidh tú do chuid.'

Spréidh sí brat beag geal faoi, a raibh achan chineál bidh agus di air. Rinne sí cearc uisce duithe féin agus d'imigh sí síos go tóin an tobair, agus bhí sí tamall fada amuigh. Sa deireadh tchí sé buileogógaí beaga ag teacht aníos ar bharr an uisce agus deora beaga fola ag teacht aníos ina dhiaidh.

Dar leis 'A chréatúir, maraíodh thú.'

Sa deireadh tháinig sí chuige, an fáinne léi in a gob agus a heiteog agus a cois briste.

'Á. Tá mé chomhair marbh,' ar sise, 'ach seo dhuit an fáinne anois, agus gabh suas agus taispeán don fhathach é, ach ná tabhair dó ina lámh é. An fathach sin a tchí tusa achan lá, bhail sin m'athair, agus tá sé faoi gheasaí a bheith choíche ina fhathach go bhfaigheadh sé an fáinne seo, agus mise agus an dá eala eile a thriúr nigheanach, agus beimid inár gcailíní anois mar a bhí ariamh, nó tá na geasaí dúinn uilig. Anois, nuair a thaispeánaidh tusa an fáinne do m'athair beidh na geasaí dó, agus déarfaidh sé leatsa go bhfuil triúr nigheanach aige agus go bhfaighidh tú do rogha den triúr le pósadh. Ach creidim nach nglacann tú mise nó tá mo lámh agus mo chos briste.'

'Ni phósfaidh mé aon bhean choíche ach tú,' ar seisean.

'Bhail,' ar sise, 'cuirfidh m'athair isteach i dteach dhorcha muid agus seasóidh mise ag taobh an dorais, agus nuair a leagas tusa do lámh orm dhéanfaidh mise scread. Abair thusa ansin gur seo an ceann a bheas agat.'

Tháinig sé isteach agus thaispeáin sé an fáinne don fhathach.

'B'é sin é?' ar seisean.

'Sé,' arsa an fathach, 'agus is maith an buachaill thú. Buíochas do Dhia,' ar seisean, 'tá na geasaí domh féin agus de mo chuid girseach inniu.'

Caidé a bhí ann ach Rí na Fásaighe Duibhe, a cuireadh faoi gheasaí, agus ba é sin caisleán Rí na Fásaighe Duibhe a leag an eala, agus a chuir sí i gcionn a chéile ar ais sa dóigh go bhfaca Mac Rí Chonnachta caidé mar bhí caisleán Rí na Fásaighe Duibhe déanta.

'Anois,' arsa an Rí, 'tá an triúr nigheanach agam is deise ar shoilsigh grian ariamh orthu, agus gheobhaidh tú do rogha bean den triúr le pósadh, ach cuirfidh mé isteach i seomra druidte, dhorcha iad, agus an chéad cheann a mbeirfidh tú uirthi, sin an ceann a gheobhas tú.'

'Maith go leor,' arsa Mac Rí Chonnachta. 'Is cuma liomsa, cé acu a gheobhaidh mé.'

Cuireadh an triúr isteach i seomra druidte dhorcha, agus sheasaigh sí seo anall i n-aice an dorais. Nuair a tháinig seisean isteach bhuail sise í féin anonn in a éadain, agus bheir seisean greim uirthi. Rinne sise scread.

'Seo mo bheansa,' arsa mac an rí.

'Á, ní phósfaidh aon duine mise,' ar sise, 'agus mo lámh agus mo chos briste.'

'Bhail, a leanbh,' arsan t-athair, 'bhéarfaidh mise an dochtúir chugat go leigheasfaidh sé thú.'

Tugadh an dochtúir chuici, agus cuireadh dóigh uirthi. Nuair a fuair sí biseach maith pósadh an bheirt. Rinneadh bainis mhór leo. Chuir an rí mála óir agus airgid leo anall go Connachta. Bhí áthas mór ar Rí Chonnachta nuair a chonaic sé an bheirt ag teacht, agus rinne sé féin bainis eile leo. Thóg sé caisleán breá daobhtha, agus chuaigh an bheirt a chónaí ansin. Chaith siad saol breá, suaimhneach, neamh-airceach, agus sin mo scéal-sa, agus codlaigh.

THE KING OF THE BLACK DESERT

There was a king in Connacht once upon a time, and he had only one son, when his wife died. The boy and himself were not managing very well and he went and married another woman. The young queen wasn't very good to the orphan, but the king himself kept an eye on him, and brought him here and there, until the boy had grown into a competent fellow of twenty-one.

'Father,' he said, 'I've never left the walls without some companion or other, and shouldn't you let me out today, so that I can see the lie of the land?'

'I'll let you, surely,' says the father.

He got a horse and went off. He was away until he felt he had been too long away, and he came as far as a wood. He decided he would let the horse eat a bit, and he set him loose in the wood. He himself went walking about, and looking, and he saw a little old man sitting at the foot of a tree, playing cards.

The old man greeted him, and asked him to come and have a game. So the two of them played, and it wasn't long until the son of the King of Connacht beat the old man in a game.

'Make a wish now,' said the old man.

'Oh, it is not worth my while,' said he.

'Well, any wish you make, you'll get it,' said the old man.

'Well,' he said, 'I wish my step-mother had the head of a goat, that [only] I can take off her.'

He set off home. When he came within view of the house, all the people of the town were gathered around the king's house, and the king himself was outside, wringing his hands. The son passed no remark on anything. All he did was put his horse in the stable and go to bed.

As soon as he got up the next morning he took the horse and went off again, and he went until he came to the wood where he had been the day before. He set the horse loose, and he saw the same little old man sitting at the foot of a tree, playing cards.

The old man welcomed him, and asked him to come and have a game. So the two of them played and it wasn't long until the son of the King of Connacht had beaten the old man.

'Make a wish now,' said the old man.

'Oh, it's not worth it,' said he.

'You got the wish you made yesterday?' said the old man.

The king's son said that he had.

'Well, make another wish today,' said the old man.

'Well,' said he, 'I wish the six-acre field that my father owns to be full of strange cattle, no two of them the same, and that they will be there always until I want to get rid of them.'

'You'll get your wish,' said the old man.

The king's son came home, and when he was approaching home he saw the park full of strange cattle, and all the king's servants out trying to chase them away. But no sooner would they have driven a cow as far as the gate than she was back in the middle of the park. Finally the king asked them to leave them there, that it must be something odd that God was doing to them. The son ate his supper when he had stabled the horse, went to bed and didn't let on that he knew a thing.

When he got up in the morning he was rushing to get ready and get away, and he forgot to put on the little vest. There was a pocket book in the little vest and as long as he was carrying that, nobody could beat him in a game.

He went on until he came to the same wood. The little old man was sitting at the foot of a tree, playing.

'Are you here again today?' he said.

'I am,' said the King of Connacht's son.

'Well, come here and we'll have a game,' he said.

They sat down to play, and it wasn't long before the old man had won a game on the King of Connacht's son.

'Well, now,' he said, 'I'll put you under a spell not to spend two nights in any one house until you find out what way the castle of the King of the Black Desert is built.'

The poor fellow jumped onto the back of the horse and went home. When he came inside he sat on a chair, let out a sigh, and there wasn't one button on his vest that didn't snap off.

'Son,' said the king, 'your sigh is like the sigh of a king's son under a spell.'

'Oh, I am a king's son under a spell tonight,' said he.

When he got up in the morning, his father asked him to take the finest horse in the stable with him.

'Well, before I go,' said he, 'I wish my step-mother to have her own head on her, and that the strange cattle will go away, and that everything in the house will be as it should be.'

He jumped onto the horse's back and went off. He was going until the end of the day. He sat down to take a rest, and saw a cloud of fog approaching him from the sky.

He said: 'If you are coming to help me,' he said, 'all the better for me, and if you are against me then it is too bad.'

What came out of the fog but a great eagle.

'Well,' said the eagle, 'if you would give me that horse, I could do with it, because my little eagles are dying of hunger and they won't be alive tomorrow.'

'Oh, how could I give you my horse, since I don't know how far it is to the end of my journey?' said the king's son.

'Well,' said the eagle, 'if you give me the horse I will come back and help you.'

'Here, then,' said he, 'take it away.'

'Well, don't you stir from there,' said the eagle, 'until I come back, and I won't be longer than two and a half hours in all.'

The eagle went up into the air, on wings, and then came back to put his claws into the horse, and he took it with him. So there was the poor boy looking at his horse until he and the eagle disappeared from view. He sat there then for a very long time, as it seemed to him, sometimes thinking, sometimes staring up at the skies, and all the time waiting to see the eagle returning to him. Eventually he saw him approaching in a great hurry. He landed, and stood beside the king's son.

'Aru, weren't you away a long time?' said the king's son.

'In my opinion,' said the eagle, 'I was better than my estimate. I would hardly say that it is two and a half hours since I left here.'

'Musha,' said the king's son, 'I thought you were away for five or six hours, but of course it's better late than never.'

He told his story to the eagle.

'Get up on my back,' said the eagle.

He did, and the two of them went until they came to a little tiny house.

'There is a house,' said the eagle, 'and go in there, and the old fellow is extremely learned. If it's possible to find out where the castle of the King of the Black Desert is, that old fellow will know it.'

He came in to the old fellow and the old fellow welcomed him warmly. He told him of his quest.

'Well, I never heard of the King of the Black Desert,' said the old fellow. 'But eat your supper, go to bed and I will search through my books until morning.'

In the morning he said that he had been unable to find out anything about the castle of the King of the Black Desert. 'But,' he said, 'I have a brother in such a place, and he is a book ahead of me,[1] and maybe he would be able to find out something about him for you. Here is a pair of boots; these boots will bring you to the door of my brother's house, and when you get there, take them off, turn them towards me, and the boots will return to me.'

The son of the King of Connacht put on the boots and set off. He kept going until the close of day, when he came to a little house. He took off the boots and turned them around and they went back to the old fellow. He came in and there was nobody inside but a little old man. He welcomed him warmly and invited him to sit down.

The son of the King of Connacht told of his quest. The old fellow said he had never heard of the castle of the King of the Black Desert. 'But,' he said, 'eat your supper, go to bed, and I will look through my books until morning.'

In the morning the old fellow said that the castle of the King of the Black Desert was not in any publication that he possessed. 'But here is a pair of boots,' he said, 'and they will bring you to the door of my brother's house, and he is a book ahead of me, and if there is such a castle on the face of the earth, he will know where it is. When you come to the end of your journey, turn the toes of the boots towards me, and they will come home themselves.'

The king's son put on the boots and walked until the close of day, when he came to the old man's house. He went in and there was no Christian there in front of him, apart from an old man. The old man gave him a warm welcome, and asked him to sit by the fire, although his house was a poor one for the likes of him. The King of Connacht's son said that the place was fine, that he was not concerned about that, but about information concerning the castle of the King of the Black Desert.

---

1. The stages of primary education in Ireland were formerly measured in 'books', as students progressed through graduated readers.

'I never heard tell of it,' said the old man, 'but eat your supper and go to bed, and I will look through my books until morning.'

The old man sat up reading until morning, and in the morning he said that there was no information about it in any book on earth.

'Well,' said the King of Connacht's son, 'it must be somewhere in the world.'

The old man put a whistle in his mouth and blew on it three times. In the blink of an eye all the fishes in the sea gathered outside the door, the smallest ones near the door and the others gradually increasing in size the further away from him they were, so that he was able to see all of them. He asked them if any one of them had ever heard tell of the castle of the King of the Black Desert. They said that they had not heard of it.

'Well,' he said. 'What I can do is have you stay here until dinner time, and then send you down to the little lake down below. And there is a wash-house down there, and go into it. Three little white swans will come to the lake to wash. One of them wears a little green cloak, and she takes it off and leaves it on a rock on the beach while she is in washing herself. Now, you keep that cloak until she comes and talks to you, and maybe she would know something about the King of the Black Desert.'

He went and hid himself in the wash-house, and it wasn't long until he saw the three little swans approaching. One of them took off the green cloak she was wearing and left it on the beach. He took the cloak and went into the wash-house with it immediately. When the three swans had washed, this one went looking for her cloak. She couldn't find it, and she looked into this little house, and she saw the boy sitting inside.

'Is it you who saw my little cloak?' she said.

He said that it was, and that he had it inside. She asked him to give it to her, and he said he wouldn't until she came in and talked to him. She came in and he asked her if she knew anything at all about the King of the Black Desert. He told her that he was under a spell until he could find out what way the castle of the King of the Black Desert was built.

'Well, give me my cloak,' she said, 'and I'll do my best for you.'

He gave her the cloak and she wrapped it around her neck. She hit herself with a magic wand, and turned herself into an enormous swan.

'Get up on my back now,' she said, 'and hold on tightly!'

He got up on her back, and they went off across the sea, until they came as far as a shore and a castle, and she let him down then.

'There is a house up there,' she said, 'and a giant lives in it. And go in and ask for work, but don't say that you saw me.'

He went up along the side of the castle until he came to the front door. He knocked on the door and the giant himself came to answer it. The giant asked why he had come.

'When I got up this morning,' he said, 'I jumped on the back of the rainbow, and it left me standing out here.'

'You are a smart boy,' said the giant.

'I certainly am a smart boy,' said the boy.

'What is worrying you now?' asked the giant.

'I'm just looking for work,' he said.

'I'll give you that,' said the giant, 'but you have to do everything I ask, or else lose your head.'

'Well, of course I'll do my best,' said the son of the King of Connacht.

'Well, go to bed now,' said the giant.

He didn't ask him if he was hungry or not.

Next morning when the boy got up, he went to the giant and asked him to get up out of that and give him some work.

'Maybe when you see it you will think it is too early.'

'Oh well,' he said, 'I believe it is as well for me to start early.'

'Well, do you see that big castle over there?' said the giant.

'I see it,' he said.

'Well, knock down that castle. Throw all the stones out into the sea, and leave the place in such a state that no eye would recognize that a castle ever stood there,' said the giant.

The poor fellow went out and he wasn't able to see the tops of the chimneys, it was so high. He didn't know how he would reach it. It wasn't long until the little swan came to him.

'What did he ask you to do today?' she said.

'I have plenty to do today,' he said. 'I have to knock down that castle, and throw it into the sea, so that nobody will know that there ever was a house there.'

'Did you get your breakfast?' she said.

'I didn't get breakfast or supper, or any bite at all, since I came here,' he said.

She spread out a little cloak she had, and on it was every kind of food and drink that you ever saw.

'Sit down,' said she, 'and eat your fill.'

'Well, what's the good of eating,' he said, 'if I am to lose my head later on?'

'Eat up anyway,' she said.

He sat down to eat, and she started on the castle, and when he had eaten the meal, she had the whole castle knocked down. There wasn't a stone or a heap of stones in the place.

'Oh God, you are kind!' he said.

'Well, on pain of death,' she said, 'don't say that you saw me.'

He came in and the giant asked him if he had done it and he said that he had.

'You are a gem of a boy,' said the giant. 'Go to bed now like a good boy.'

When the poor fellow got up the next morning he asked him where he was to work. The giant asked him to go out that day and take every single stone that he had thrown into the sea, and to leave the castle in such a state that nobody would know it had ever been tampered with. He went out and sat above the place where the stones were on the shore. And not one of the stones was to be seen. 'I'll lose my head tonight anyway,' he said.

It wasn't long until he saw the little swan approaching him. She asked what he had to do today.

'I have plenty to do,' he said. 'I have to build this castle up as brand new as ever it was, and I am afraid it will take me quite a while.'

'Did you get a bite to eat?' she asked.

He said that he did not, that it was she who had given the last bite to him. She spread out the little cloak that she had with her, and she had every kind of food and drink that you ever saw.

'There now,' she said. 'Eat your fill.'

'Well, what good will it do me to eat,' he said, 'when I am to lose my head tonight?'

'Eat up anyway,' she said.

He sat down eating, and she started to build the castle. And when he had finished eating, she had built the castle in such a way that no living soul would guess that anyone had ever laid a finger on it.

'Oh God, you are kind!' he said.

'Well,' she said, 'on pain of death, don't say that you saw me.'

'To be sure I won't,' he said.

She went, and she had just gone when the giant came around.

'Good for you,' he said. 'You've done a good job. Go inside now and go to bed like a good boy.'

When he got up in the morning he asked the giant what work he was to do today.

'There is a well down there,' said the giant, 'which has not been cleaned for a hundred years. And there is a ring at the bottom of it that belonged to my grandmother a hundred years ago, and you have to get that ring by nightfall, or I will take the head off you.'

He went down to the well, and no eye could see to the bottom of the well, because it was so deep. He stood there and he didn't know what he should do. With that he saw the little swan coming towards him.

'What did he ask you to do today?' she said.

'There is a ring,' he said, 'that his grandmother lost a hundred years ago, and it is at the bottom of this well, and I have to get it before nightfall, or lose my head.'

'I am afraid,' she said, 'that we have enough to do today, because that ring is down in hell, and a poisonous serpent is twisted around it. But did you get any breakfast today?' she said.

'I didn't get a bite,' he said, 'since you gave me the last bite.'

'Well, sit down now,' she said, 'until you get something to eat.'

She spread out a little white cloth for him, on which there was every kind of food and drink. She turned herself into a water hen and went down to the bottom of the well, and she was away for a long time. In the end he saw little bubbles rising up at the top of the water and little drops of blood coming up behind them, and he said:

'You poor thing! You have been killed!'

In the end she came to him, the ring in her beak and her wing and leg broken.

'Ah! I am nearly dead,' she said. 'But here is the ring for you now. And go up and show it to the giant, but do not give it to him into his hand. That giant that you see every day, that is my father, and he is under a spell to remain a giant until this ring is found, and I and the other two swans are his three daughters, and we will be girls again now as we always were before, because we have all been released from the spell. Now, when you show the ring to my father he will be released from the spell, and he will tell you that he has three daughters and that you can choose whichever of them you like, to marry. But I don't believe you'll want me now that my arm and leg are broken.'

'I will marry no other woman but you,' he said.

'Well,' she said. 'My father will put us into a dark house, and I will stand beside the door. And when you touch me I will scream. And then you say that this is the one you want!'

He came in and showed the ring to the giant.

'Is that it?' he asked.

'It is,' said the giant, 'and you are a good boy. Thank God,' he said, 'I and the girls are free of the spell today.'

Who was it but the King of the Black Desert, who had been under a spell, and that was the castle of the King of the Black Desert that the swan had knocked down, and put together again, so that the son of the King of Connacht would see how the castle of the King of the Black Desert was built.

'Now,' said the king, 'I have three daughters who are as lovely as any the sun ever shone upon,

and you can have your pick of the three to marry. But I will put them in a closed, dark room, and the first one you catch, she is the one you will get.'

'All right,' said the son of the King of Connacht. 'It's all the same to me which of them I get.'

The three of them were put into a dark locked room, and she stood over behind the door. When he came in she bumped herself into him, and he grabbed her. She screamed.

'This is my wife!' said the king's son.

'Ah, nobody will marry me,' she said, 'with my broken arm and broken leg.'

'Well, child,' said the father, 'I will get the doctor for you and he will cure you.'

The doctor was brought to her and she was fixed up. When she was quite well the pair were married. They had a big wedding. The king sent a bag of gold and of silver with them over to Connacht. The King of Connacht was delighted when he saw the two of them coming, and he held another wedding for them. He built a fine castle for them and the two went to live in it. They had a fine, peaceful, untroubled life. And that is my story, and you go to sleep!

ANNA UÍ SHIGHIL

(b. 1867)

from:
IRISH FOLKLORE COLLECTION MS NO. 626 (1939)

[Cinderella, probably the best known of all fairytales in the modern children's storybook tradition, is one of a cluster of stories from international oral tradition which involve a similar heroine and similar motifs. A number of tale types in the Cinderella Cycle were known and told in Ireland. This example belongs to the main type (AT 510A), of which 302 Irish versions are known.[1] With its focus almost entirely on female characters, the story might be expected to appeal particularly to women storytellers. However, of

97 versions in the collection (Main Manuscripts), only 27 were told by women. This may reflect an imbalance between collected material and the actual tradition, but it does suggest that speculation about the predilection of either gender for particular kinds of tale is risky.

In a sample of versions told by women in Kerry, Galway, Mayo and Donegal, the role of the helper, played by the 'fairy godmother' in Charles Perrault's influential and well-known literary version, is variously performed by a cat, a sheep or a little old woman, usually stated to be the heroine's dead mother.[2] The ballroom is often replaced, as in Anna Uí Shighil's version, by Sunday mass. The heroine is generally less passive than in the Perrault version of the tale; in some Irish versions, she actively solicits the help of her dead mother by going to her grave and asking for assistance. In others, such as this one, the Cinderella

---

1. See S. Ó Suilleabháin and R. Christiansen, *Types of the Irish Folktale*.

2. Charles Perrault, *Contes de ma Mère l'Oy* ['Tales of Mother Goose'] (Paris, 1697). Translated into English by Robert Samber, 1729.

figure wins help by carrying out an act of kindness which her sisters have refused. She does not simply sit in the cinders, weeping, as in the Perrault version, but takes some responsibility for her own destiny. Neither Irish nor other oral versions of Cinderella can be described as radically feminist, but given the social and psychological assumption underlying every fairytale (that human fulfilment is best found in a happy and prosperous marriage), the oral versions tend to present heroines who are more independent and sturdy than those in storybooks. Like Anna Uí Shighil's version, the oral variants of 'Cinderella' are also frequently humorous. This one was collected by Seán Ó hEochaidh, in Cluain Dá Choircigh, County Donegal, on 23 June 1939. From IFC 626: 552a–70. For literary treatments of the Cinderella story, see pp. 1156–64. Translation and headnote by E. Ní D.]

NÍ MHAOL DHONN, NÍ MHAOL FHIONN, AGUS NÍ MHAOL CHARACH

Bhí bean ann uair amháin agus bhí triúr nigheanacha aici. Ní Mhaol Dhonn, Ní Mhaol Fhionn, agus Ní Mhaol Charach. Bhí Ní Mhaol Dhonn dóighiúil, agus bhí Ní Mhaol Fhionn dóighiúil i gceart fosta, ach bhí Ní Mhaol Charach — ní raibh meas ar bith acu uirthi ar chor ar bith ach ina luí ins an chlúdaigh istoigh sa luaidh.

Caidé an diabhal ach aon mhaidin amháin Dé Domhnaigh, bhí an tine as, agus d'iarr siad ar Ní Mhaol Dhonn a dhul agus aibhleog³ a fháil nó go mbeadh siad mall ag an Aifreann. Chuaigh sise chuig cailleach agus nuair a chuaigh sí chuig Cailleach na gCearc, nuair a bhí sí ag dul thar *dhrain* a bhí ann, labhair an biolar agus deir an biolar: 'Bain biolar, ith biolar agus beir biolar leat.'

'Mhaise, cha mbainim biolar, cha n-ithim biolar agus cha dtugam biolar liom.'

Shiúil sí giota eile go dtáinig sí fhad le spíonóg.

'Bain spíonóg, ith spíonóg agus beir spíonóg leat.'

'Mhaise cha mbainim spíonóg, cha n-ithim spíonóg agus cha dtugam spíonóg liom.'

Chuaigh sí isteach chuig Cailleach na gCearc. Deir sí: 'tá aibhleog de dhíobháil orm.'

'Bhail,' adeir Cailleach na gCearc, 'má gheibh tú an sreadán dearg atá i gcúl mo chluaise gheobhaidh tú aibhleog.'

'Bhail, spreaghadh ort féin agus ar do chuid sreadáin shalacha: coinnigh do shreadán.'

'Bhail,' adeir sí, 'coinneoidh mé mo aibhleog fosta.'

B'éigin daoithe a dul 'na bhaile ansin agus cha raibh aibhleog ar bith léi.'

D'iarr an mháthair ar Ní Mhaol Fhionn a dhul ansin. D'imigh Ní Mhaol Fhionn ansin. Labhair an biolar léi an dóigh chéanna agus labhair an spíonóg léi agus cha dtabharfadh sí léi aon chuid acu. Nuair a chuaigh sí an fad sin ansin d'iarr Cailleach na gCearc uirthi an sreadán a bhaint amach as cúl a cluaise agus cha ndéanfadh. Ansin tharla nach dtabharfadh . . . ní thabharfadh sí aibhleog ar bith daoithe.

D'iarr siad ansin ar Ní Mhaol Charach a dhul. D'éirigh Ní Mhaol Charach agus chraith sí í féin, agus chraith sí píce luatha buí aisti féin. Chuaigh sí fhad leis an bhiolar.

'Bhain biolar agus ith biolar, agus beir biolar leat.'

'Mhaise bainfidh mé biolar. Íosfaidh mé biolar agus béarfaidh mé biolar liom.'

Labhair an spíonóg.

'Bain spíonóg, ith spíonóg agus beir spíonóg leat.'

'Mhaise bainfidh mé spíonóg, íosfaidh mé spíonóg agus béarfaidh mé spíonóg liom.'

Chuaigh sí isteach chuig Cailleach na gCearc.

'Tá aibhleog a dhíobháil orm,' adeir sí.

'Bhail má bhaineann tú amach an sreadán dearg atá i gcúl mo chluaise gheobhaidh tú an aibhleog.'

Dúirt sise léi go mbainfeadh, agus bhain.

'Anois,' adeir sí, nuair a bhain sí amach an sreadán dearg as cúl a cluaise, 'anois' a deir sí, 'chomh luath agus imtheothas siad 'un Aifreann tar thusa anuas chugamsa. Tá gnoithe agam leat.'

Chomh⁴ luath géar agus d'imigh siadsan 'un Aifreann d'imigh sise síos agus chuir sí isteach i dtubán í agus thug sí folcadh breá daoithe. Agus chóirigh sí suas í. Chuir sí culaith bhreá ansin uirthi, agus thug sí each caol dubh amach as an stábla, agus chuir sí Ní Mhaol Charach a mharcaíocht ar an each chaol dubh agus chuaigh sí go teach an phobail.

Nuair a tháinig siad abhaile as teach an phobail bhí sise sa bhaile agus an t-éadach uilig daoithe agus a cuid bratóg uirthi, agus an dinnéar thíos aici. 'An raibh iontas ar bith i dteach an phobail inniu?' arsa sise le Ní Mhaol Dhonn.

---

3. MS, *uibhleóg.*

4. MS, *cómh.*

'Tá fios a dhíth ort!' arsa sise.

D'fhiafraigh sí de Ní Mhaol Fhionn é ansin agus dúirt sise an rud céanna.

D'fhiafraigh sí de n'a máthair ansin é.

'Bhí,' adeir sí, 'bhí an cailín i dteach an phobail inniu a ba deise ar shoilsigh grian uirthi agus bhí each caol dubh léi agus bhainfeadh sí ribe den ghaoith agus cha mbainfeadh an ghaoth ribe daoithe. Agus bhí sí taire an mheasardhacht.' (Caidé bhí anseo ach Ní Mhaol Charach í féin.)

An darna huair d'iarr Cailleach na gCearc uirthi a dhul síos, agus chuaigh. Chóirigh Cailleach na gCearc í agus bhí culaith níos fearr uirthi an darna lá agus each caol gorm léi an lá sin. Nuair a tháinig siad 'na bhaile ansin d'fhiafraigh sí an raibh scéal nua ar bith leofa.

'Ó, cé d'inseodh a dhath duitse!' adeir Ní Mhaol Dhonn.

'An bhfuil scéal nua ar bith leatsa?' adeir sí le Ní Mhaol Fhionn.

'Ó, cé d'inseodh a dhath duitse,' adeir Ní Mhaol Fhionn. D'fhiafraigh sí de n'a máthair ansin é.

Dúirt an mháthair go raibh, go raibh cailín ag teach an phobail inniu agus nach raibh a leithéid le fáil, agus go raibh sí seachtain sa lá inniu fosta ann agus go mbeadh garda ag mac an rí ar gheaftaí teach an phobail le breith uirthi an darna lá.

Bhí seo go maith ansin. Chuaigh Ní Mhaol Charach síos ansin agus d'inis sí seo do Chailleach na gCearc. D'iarr Cailleach na gCearc uirthi a dhul síos breá luath ar maidin nuair a d'imtheodh siadsan go teach an phobail. Rinne sí sin, agus chóirigh sí í, agus bhí sí deich n-uaire chomh galánta an lá sin. D'imigh sí amach agus each deas caol buí a bhí léi an lá sin. Chuaigh a mharcaíocht, a chailleach, agus caidé an diabhal a bhí ach mac an rí agus a gharda le greim a fháil uirthi. Ach thug sise léim ar an bheathach agus d'imigh an beathach mar bheadh an ghaoth ann. Ach bhain sé an bhróg daoithe.

D'imigh sé ansin agus an bhróg leis agus garda leis, agus bhí sé ag féachaint achan nduine ansin go bhfeiceadh sé an bhfreagródh an bhróg seo iad. Chuaigh sé isteach ins an teach seo agus ins an teach seo eile agus cha raibh teach ar bith a raibh sé ag dul isteach ann, cuid acu a bhí ag gearradh píosa de na sála díobhtha féin, agus cuid ag gearradh na ladhra díobhtha féin, a dhéanamh go ndéanfadh an bhróg gnoithe

díobhtha. Nuair a chuirfeadh siadsan ortha an bhróg, rachadh an chos a chur fola, agus bheadh a fhios aige-san gur bréag a bhí ann agus gur gearradh an chos. Chuaigh sé isteach ins an teach a raibh Ní Mhaol Charach ina cónaí ann. Chuir siad Ní Mhaol Charach faoi bhairille nuair a insigh siad ag teacht é. Bhí Ní Mhaol Fhionn agus Ní Mhaol Dhonn ansin ach má bhí féin, caidé an diabhal an mhaith a bhí ansin. Ghearr duine acu an ladhar mhór daoithe féin agus cha raibh a dhath a mhaith ann. Agus ghearr bean eile giota den tsál daoithe féin agus cha raibh a dhath a mhaith ann.

Thosaigh sise a scríobadh, scríobadh astoigh faoin bhairille.

'Caidé atá astoigh anseo agaibh?'

'Tá sin muc bheag a cheannaigh muid,' a dúirt sise, 'agus tá sí astoigh ansin agus má ligeann muid amach í rachaidh sí í bhfeadham.'

'Lig amach í,' adeir mac an rí, 'chan fhacaidh mise aon mhuc ariamh agus ba mhaith liom í a fheiceáil.

'Bhail, chan fheiceann tú í ar chor ar bith,' adeir an tseanbhean, 'cha dtiocfadh linn a ligint amach ar chor ar bith.'

'O, bhail, caithfidh mise í a fheiceáilt sula bhfágaidh mé an teach.'

Thosaigh sise ag scríobadh léi agus shaoilfeá go raibh sí díolta ar a shon. Ins an deireadh fuair sí amach. Thug seisean an bhróg daoithe agus, ó a chailleach! Cha raibh a dhath ar an tsaol a d'fhoir daoithe chomh maith leis an bhróg sin.

'Tchím, tchím,' adeir sé, 'gur tú atá fá mo choinne.'

'Ó, bhail,' adeir sise, 'caithfidh mise a dhul amach bomainte beag.'

Chuaigh sise amach agus chuaigh sí síos chuig Cailleach na gCearc gur chóirig sí í, agus cá bith mar bhí sí Dé Domhnaigh, bhí sí dhá uair chomh deas an lá sin. Thaitin sí go breá leis ansin agus nuair a chonaic sé an chéad uair í caidé bhí le fáil aige ach *lady* astoigh faoi bhairille agus thit a lámha faoi na chrios, ach nuair a chonaic sé ar ais í agus an t-éadach breá a bhí uirthi, agus chomh breá agus d'amharc sí, bhí sé breá sásta. D'imigh said ansin agus pósadh iad agus bhí bainis acu ansin a mhair lá agus bliain agus b'fhearr an lá deireannach ná an chéad lá.

Agus nuair a bhí an bhainis agus achan rud thart ansin, thug sé Ní Mhaol Charach 'na bhaile.

Nuair a bhí sí ansin lá agus bliain, deir sí, 'Caithfidh mé a dhul a dh'amharc ar mo dheirfiúr go bhfeicidh mé caidé mar tá sí.'

'Bhail cinnte,' adeir an mháthair.

Chuaigh siad síos 'na fairrge ansin á ní féin agus caidé an diabhal ach nuair a fuair Ní Mhaol Dhonn ise á ní féin astoigh insa an uisce caidé rinne sí ach í a choinneáil astoigh agus chuir sise a cuid éadaigh uirthi agus fill sí 'na bhaile, agus d'inis sí do mhac an rí gur ise Ní Mhaol Charach, tá a fhios agat. Bhíodh mil ag sileadh as a cuid méara achan oíche agus ba ghnáthach leis a bheith ag diúl a cuid méara, agus cha raibh a dhath meala i méara na mná eile. Agus dúirt seisean nár b'í a bhí ann, agus dúirt sise gurbh í, ach chomh luath agus chuaigh sí isteach insan lán mara gur imigh an mhil as a cuid méara.

Bhí buachaill síos ag mac an rí ag buachailleacht agus nuair a thiocfadh sé 'na bhaile, ó, bhí sé chomh ramhar le ministir, agus cha raibh sé ag ithe a dhath ar chor ar bith. Dúirt mac an rí leis, 'Caidé an seoirt saoil atá agat, nó caidé atá tú a dhéanamh ar chor ar bith? Níl tú ag ithe a dhath agus tá tú ag spréachadh as a chéile?'

'O tá,' adeir sé, 'shlug péist mo mháistreás nuair a chuaigh sí isteach ins a lán mhara, agus ghabh sí amach uair achan lá agus tá mise ag diúl a cuid méara agus níl rud ar bith a dhíobháil orm.'

'Bhail,' adeir mac an rí, 'rachaidh mise síos amárach go bhfeicidh mé caidé mar tá.'

Chuaigh, agus caidé an caitheamh a bhí ach an bhean s'aige-san. Shlug an phéist í ach má shlug féin ligeadh sí amach í achan lá. Chuaigh sé síos agus chonaic sé caidé mar bhí. Agus deir sise: 'Mura dtógaidh tusa cloch agus an phéist a bhuaileadh insan chamóg-ghearach, dóifidh sí an saol, agus tabhair tusa aire mhaith amárach nuair a thiocfas tú anuas, agus bíodh an chloch leat agus buail insan áit cheart í nó mura ndéanaidh,' adeir sí, 'tá mise agus tusa réidh.'

Choimhéad seisean lá ar na mhárach agus nuair a fuair sé seans ar an phéist, bhuail sé insan chamóg-ghearach[5] í leis an chloch, agus mharbh sé í agus thug sé an bhean s'aige féin 'na bhaile. Bhí an bheirt ansin aige: Ní Mhaol Dhonn agus Ní Mhaol Charach agus bhí fios aige gurbh í Ní Mhaol Dhonn a rinne an dáinséar, agus a chuir ise chun siúil ag iarraidh í a bháthadh.

Agus d'imigh sé agus fuair sé coillidh bhrosnaí. Chroch sé in airde í agus chuir sé tine leis na brosnaí. Thug sé a bhean féin 'na bhaile leis agus choinnigh sé í on lá sin go dtí an lá inniu, agus an uair dheireannach a chonaic mise iad bhí siad chomh reamhar — bhí maróg orthu. Bhí siad ag iarraidh orm a dhul a dh'amharc orthu, ach cha dteachaidh mé ariamh ó shin.

MISS BROWN, MISS BLONDE, AND MISS PLEASANT

Once upon a time there was a woman, and she had three daughters: Miss Brown, Miss Blonde, and Miss Pleasant. Miss Brown was pretty, and Miss Blonde was very pretty too, but Miss Pleasant — they had no time at all for her, and had her stuck at the fireplace in amongst the ashes.

What the devil anyway, but one Sunday morning the fire went out, and they asked Miss Brown to go and get a light or they would be late for Mass. She went to an old hag. And when she went to the Hag of the Hens,[1] she was passing a drain that was on the way and the watercress spoke. And the watercress said:

'Pick watercress, eat watercress and take watercress with you.'

'Musha, I'm not picking watercress, I'm not eating watercress, and I'm not taking watercress with me!'

She walked another bit until she came to a gooseberry bush.

'Pick a gooseberry, eat a gooseberry, and take a gooseberry with you.'

'Musha, I'm not picking a gooseberry, I'm not eating a gooseberry, and I'm not taking a gooseberry with me.'

She went in to the Hag of the Hens. She says: 'I need a light.'

'Well,' says the Hag of the Hens, 'if you get the red nit that's at the back of my ear you'll get your light.'

'Well, hump you and your dirty nits. Keep your nit!'

'Well,' says she, 'I'll keep my light as well.'

---

5. MS, chamóg-ghearaigh.

1. *Cailleach na gCearc*, the Hag of the Hens, or the Henwife, occurs frequently in fairytales.

She had to go home and she didn't have a light with her.

Her mother asked Miss Blonde to go then. Miss Blonde went. The watercress spoke to her just as before, and the gooseberry spoke to her, and she wouldn't take either of them with her. When she went that far then, the Hag of the Hens asked her to take the nit from behind her ear. And she wouldn't. So she wouldn't give her a light.

Then they asked Miss Pleasant to go. Miss Pleasant got up and shook herself, and she shook a peck of yellow ashes off her. She went as far as the watercress.

'Pick watercress and eat watercress, and bring watercress with you.'

'Musha, I'll pick watercress, I'll eat watercress and I'll bring watercress with me.'

The gooseberry spoke.

'Pick a gooseberry, eat a gooseberry, and bring a gooseberry with you.'

'Musha, I'll pick a gooseberry, I'll eat a gooseberry and I'll bring a gooseberry with me.'

She went in to the Hag of the Hens.

'I need a light,' says she.

'Well, if you take out the red nit that's at the back of my ear you will get the light.'

She told her she would take it out, and she did.

'Now,' says the Hag, when she had taken the red nit from behind her ear, 'now,' says she, 'as soon as they go to Mass you come down to me. I want to talk to you about something.'

The very minute they went to Mass she went down. And the Hag put her into a tub and gave her a good bath. And she tidied her up. Then she put a fine suit on her, and took a slender black horse out of the stable, and put Miss Pleasant riding on the slender black horse, and she went to the chapel.

When they came home from Mass she was at home, and all the clothes removed, and her rags on her, and the dinner cooking. 'Was there anything strange in the chapel today?' she asked Miss Brown.

'Aren't you inquisitive?' said she.

She asked Miss Blonde then, and she said the same thing. Then she asked her mother.

'Yes,' says she, 'there was a girl in the chapel today, and she was the most beautiful girl the sun ever shone on. And she had a slender black horse that could snatch a hair from the wind but the wind would not snatch a hair from it. And she was amazing.' (Who was it but Miss Pleasant herself!)

The Hag of the Hens asked her to go down a second time, and she went. The Hag of the Hens tidied her up and she had a better suit the second day than the first, and she had a slender grey horse with her that day. When they came home then she asked them if there was any news.

'Oh, who'd be bothered telling you!' says Miss Brown.

'Do you have any news?' says she to Miss Blonde.

'Oh, who'd be bothered telling you?' says Miss Blonde.

She asked her mother then.

The mother said that there was news, that there was a girl in the chapel today whose beauty had no match. And besides, the king's son planned to have guards at the gate of the chapel a week from today, to catch her the next day.

That was all right, then. Miss Pleasant went down then and she told this to the Hag of the Hens. The Hag of the Hens asked her to go down good and early in the morning, when they'd go to the chapel. She did that, and she tidied her up, and she was ten times as elegant that day. She went, and she had a slender golden horse with her that day. She went riding, my old woman! And who the devil was there but the king's son and a guard out to seize her! But she leaped up on the horse and the horse ran like the wind. But he grabbed her shoe.

He went off then with the shoe, and the guard with him. And he was checking everyone to see if the shoe would fit them. He went into this house and that house and every house he went into, some of them were cutting bits off their heels and some bits off their big toes to get the shoe to fit them. When they'd put on the shoe their feet would start bleeding, and he would know then that they were deceiving him and that the foot had been cut.

He went into the house where Miss Pleasant lived. They put Miss Pleasant under a barrel when they heard he was coming. Miss Brown and Miss Blonde were there but what the devil use was that? One of them cut the big toe off herself but it was no good. And the other woman cut a bit of her heel off, and that was no good. She started scratching, scratching in under the barrel.

'What do you have in here?'

'That's a little pig we've bought,' she said, 'and she's in there and if we let her out she runs away.'

'Let her out,' says the king's son. 'I never saw a pig before and I'd like to see her.'

'Well, you won't see her at all,' says the old woman. 'We can't let her out at all.'

'Oh well, I have to see her before I leave the house.'

She started scratching so hard you would think she was being paid to do it. Finally she got out. He gave her the shoe, and, oh my old woman, there was nothing in the world suited her as well as that shoe.

'I see, I see,' says he, 'that you must be the one for me.'

'Oh well,' says she, 'I need to go out for a wee minute.'

She went out, and down to the Hag of the Hens so that she could do her up, and however lovely she was on Sunday she was twice as nice that day. He liked her very much then. The first time he saw her, when he saw that it was a lady in under the barrel, his face dropped. But when he saw her again and the fine clothes that she had on her and how lovely she looked, he was well satisfied.

They went then and they were married. And they had a wedding then that lasted for a year and a day, and the last day was better than the first. And when the wedding and everything was over then he took Miss Pleasant home. When she was there a year and a day, she said:

'I have to go and visit my sister to see how she is.'

'Well, of course,' says the mother.

They went down to the sea then to wash themselves, and what the devil, when Miss Brown got her washing herself in the water what did she do but keep her there. And she put on her clothes and she went home, and she told the king's son that she was Miss Pleasant. Do you understand?

Miss Pleasant used to have honey dripping from her fingers every night, and he used to suck her fingers. And there was no honey in the other woman's fingers. And he said that she wasn't herself, and she said she was but that as soon as she went into the sea that the honey had left her fingers.

The king's son had a boy herding cows, and when he came home he was as fat as a minister, even though he wasn't eating a thing. The king's son said to him: 'What sort of a life do you lead, or what are you doing at all? You never eat a thing but you're fit to burst.'

'Oh yes,' says he. 'A monster swallowed my mistress when she went into the sea, but she comes out once a day and I suck her fingers, and I don't need a thing.'

'Well,' says the king's son. 'I'll go down tomorrow to see what is going on.'

He went, and who was there but his own wife. The monster had swallowed her, but even so, she[2] let her out every day. He went down and saw how it was. And she says: 'If you don't take a stone and hit the monster in the temple she will destroy the world. And you take care tomorrow when you come down, and have the stone, and hit her in the right spot, because if you don't,' says she, 'you and me are finished.'

He watched the next day, and when he got a chance he hit the monster in the temple with the stone, and he killed her. And he brought his own wife home. He had the two of them then: Miss Brown and Miss Pleasant. And he knew it was Miss Brown who had done the damage, who had sent her off and tried to drown her. And he went and got a bundle of twigs. And he hung her up and he lit the twigs.

He brought his own wife home and he kept her from that day to this. And the last time I saw them they were so fat — they had puddings on them. They were asking me to come and call on them, but I've never gone since then.

---

2. The words *péist*, *piast* and *ollphéist*, all derived from Latin *bestia*, are feminine.

PEIG SAYERS

(1873–1958)

from:
SCÉALTA ÓN MBLASCAOD
(1968)

[Formal in style as befits the wonder tale, and indicative of Peig Sayers's exceptional verbal artistry, this long and elaborate version of 'Cinderella'[1] is an excellent example of Peig's skill as a storyteller. Themes from other international folktales such as, for example, the substituted bride (AT 403 [IV]) and the calumniated wife (AT 707 [II]) have been skilfully woven into the main fabric of Peig's tale to form a logical and coherent whole. The heroine's mother appears as helper under the guise of a little grey cat, and Peig's devotion to, and feeling of loss for her own mother, are perhaps indicated in the concluding lines which state that the cat on being disenchanted 'was a mother to Móirín for the rest of her life'. Kenneth Jackson transcribed stories from Peig Sayers between 1932 and 1937 and published them as 'Scéalta ón mBlascaod' in *Béaloideas*, vol. 8 (1938).[2] Robin Flower and Marie-Louise Sjoestedt also collected folklore material from Peig Sayers while she lived on the Great Blasket Island. After her return to Baile Bhiocáire on the mainland in 1942, Seosamh Ó Dálaigh, full-time collector for the Irish Folklore Commission, began to collect her repertoire. Over nine years he collected about 375 tales of which 40 were long *Märchen*. He also recorded four Fenian tales from her, forty songs and a considerable body of socio-historical material.[3]   Translation and headnote by P. L.]

AN CAITÍN GEARR GLAS

Do bhí rí ann aon uair amháin, agus rí cumhachtach saibhir dob ea é. Do phós sé bean óg uasal go raibh mórán saibhris aici; ní le grá di a phós sé í, ach le dúil ina cuid saibhris. Do bhíodar trí bliana pósta, agus ní raibh aoinne clainne acu; ach ag déanamh isteach ar an gceathrú bliain do saolaíodh iníon óg di. Ba mhór go léir an lúcháir a bhí ar an máthair; ba chuma léi cad é an maoin ná saibhreas a bhí ag an rí, dob fhearr léi aon leanbh ná saibhreas an tsaoil.

Do bhí an páiste seacht mbliana d'aois nuair a thug bean an rí fé ndeara ná raibh sé chomh ceanúil ná chomh hurramach di is ba cheart do rí a bheith. Do tháinig fén mar do thiocfadh sórt éada uirthi agus do bhí sí ag faire ina dhiaidh; ach is gairid go raibh deimhin aici go raibh an fhírinne sa scéal. Aon lá amháin do bhíodar suite síos chun boird, ach má bhíodar, do bhí an rí ag féachaint go stuacach mallaithe. Ach do labhair sí go cneasta.

'Is mise tá ag déanamh na gcros, a rí, ach ní bhead feasta.' Ansin d'éirigh sí ón mbord agus do bhuail doras an tseomra amach, agus ní fhacaigh aoinne beo ná marbh ag imeacht í, ná ní raibh a fhios acu cár thug sí a haghaidh. Do bhí draíocht go flúirseach ins an tír san am sin.

Do bhí an dinnéar ar an mbord, ach ní raibh an bhanríon ag teacht ná níor tháinig. Do bhí an páiste go brónach agus go huaigneach i ndiaidh a máthar.

Ach, aon tráthnóna amháin i gceann cúpla lae, do bhí sí ina seasamh sa doras, agus do chonaic sí chúichi caitín glas agus gach aon mhíamha aige.

'Mo ghreidhin tú, a chaitín,' arsa an páiste, 'nach deas an caitín tú! Nach trua ná fanfá agamsa mar pheata.'

Do dh'fhan an caitín, agus níl aon áit go dtéadh an páiste ná bíodh an caitín in éineacht léi.

Do bhí sí ag éirí suas nó go dtí go raibh sí dhá bhliain déag d'aois. Do phós a hathair an bhean a bhí uaidh, baintreach ab ea í, agus do bhí beirt iníon aici féin. Nuair a tháinig an leasmháthair don tigh agus a beirt iníon níor fhan aon mheas acu ar an ndílleachtaí, do bhíodh gach ceann trom uirthi, agus pé ní a bhíodh le déanamh is í chaitheadh é a dhéanamh.

Ach an rí a bhí i gCúige Connacht, do bhí an t-aon mhac amháin aige, agus do theastaigh

---

1. AT 510 A (and 403, 707): see Anna Uí Shighil's version, pp. 1247–52. Jackson mentions further printed versions of this folktale from Peig Sayers (1968, pp. 85–6).
2. A collection of international tales, romantic tales and adventures, anecdotes, moral tales, tales of saints and miracles, tales of the supernatural and traditional ballads, made by Kenneth Jackson on the Great Blasket Island, County Kerry, 1932–7. Thirty-seven narratives are from Peig Sayers. Jackson collected the remaining three (nos 18, 20, 35) from her son Micheál Ó Gaoithín (p. 85). Originally taken down and published in a modified form of the International Phonetic script, the text is rendered into standard orthography for the present publication.
3. J.H. Delargy, 'The Gaelic Storyteller', p. 15.

uaidh rogha a bhaint as mna óga ina chúige. Do cuireadh fógra amach go raibh fleá le bheith ar siúl i gcúirt an rí, agus do fuair gach duine gur mhian leis dul ann cuireadh, agus go mórmhór na mná óga uaisle. Do fuair beirt leasiníon an rí cuireadh chomh maith le cách, is do thugadar an tseachtain á gcóiriú féin chun dul go dtí an féasta. Do bhí an dílleachtaí agus í go cúramach ag fáil gach ní ullamh dóibh.

Bhí an oíche tagtha agus iad ullamh chun dul go cúirt an rí. D'fhéach an dílleachtaí ina ndiaidh agus iad ag fágaint an tí.

'Mo bhrón,' ar sise, 'mise i gcúinne na luaithe agus clann mo leasmháthar ag imeacht i gcóiste ornáideach!' Do shuigh sí síos agus do bhí sí ag gol go dúch, nuair a bhuail an caitín chúichi an t-urlár aníos.

'Éirigh i do shuí, a stóirín,' arsa an caitín, 'téanam liom amach go dtí an gairdín; seo slaitín draíochta duit, agus buail buille beag dó ar an gcrann béithe agus tiocfaidh chughat amach each caol donn agus culaith bhreá éadaigh.'

Do rug an dílleachtaí ar an slaitín draíochta agus chuaigh sí mar a raibh an crann béithe. Do bhuail sí buille beo den tslat ar an gcrann, agus ní túisce sin ná do tháinig chúichi amach each caol donn féna shrian agus iallait óir greanta; agus an t-éadach do bhí aici le cuir uirthi, níorbh fhéidir le haon tsúil féachaint air, mar do bhí sé ag taithneamh ar nós an airgid ghil. Do bhí mar bharr ar an scéal péire de bhróga gloine.

'Cuir ort suas an t-éadach sin anois, a dhalta,' arsa an caitín, 'agus téirigh ag marcaíocht ar an gcapall seo, agus béarfaidh sé leis tú go dtí cúirt an rí. Dein do chuileachtan ann chomh maith agus is féidir leat, ach ná fan aon neomait tharna dó dhéag a chlog ann, mar má fhanann tú ní bheidh ionat ach gioblacháinín gan bhrí. Dein rud orm, imigh anois agus bua leat. Nuair a dh'fhillfidh tú níl agat le déanamh ach buille don tslaitín a bhualadh ar an gcrann seo, agus raghaidh do chapall is do chuid éadaigh chun coimeádta ann.'

D'imigh Móirín, agus í ina banríon amach agus amach; agus níor dhein sí aon stad nó gur bhain sí cúirt an rí amach. Do chonaic an lucht faire an ríon uasal ag teacht, agus do bhí iontas mór orthu ná facadar a leithéid d'óigbhean riamh roimhe sin. Do chuaigh duine acu go dtí mac an rí.

'A mhic an rí,' ar seisean, 'tá ríon óg uasal aige an ngeata, is go deimhin do bhain a háilneacht mo mheabhair díom.' D'imigh mac an rí agus do chuaigh sé go dtí an geata, agus má chuaigh, do bhí an óigbhean ann roimis. Do shín sé a lámh chúichi agus do thóg anuas den chapall go haicillí í. Do thug sé ordú an capall a chur chun coimeádta. Do thóg sé leis isteach an bhean óg, agus do bhí gach aon neach dá raibh sa rítheaghlach ag féachaint uirthi. Níor fhéach mac an rí siar ar aon chailín eile dá raibh sa chúirt ach uirthi. Do thug sé rince, agus do bhí ceol agus caitheamh aimsire agus cuideachta acu i dteannta a chéile, nó go dtí go raibh sé buailte lena dó dhéag a chlog. Do ghaibh sí buíochas le mac an rí, agus dúirt sí leis go gcaithfeadh sí féin a bheith ag imeacht anois. Is é a bhí go brónach, an ní nach iontach. Do thionlacaigh sé í go dtí an geata, agus do thug cúnamh di chun dul ar marcaíocht. D'fhág sí slán aige, agus as go brách léi. Ní mór an mhoill a bhí an t-each donn á tabhairt abhaile. Ní mór an chuileachtan a bhain mac an rí as an gcuid eile den oíche.

Nuair a tháinig na leasdeirfiúracha abhaile, is amhlaidh a fuaireadar Móirín agus í ina suí cois na tine agus gur dhóigh leat nár chorraigh sí as an áit sin. Do bhí sí ag cur cuntais ar na cailíní conas mar do bhí an oíche acu, an raibh cuileachta acu. Do bhíodar ag insint di, agus dúradar léi ná raibh aoinne is mó ná b'iontaí ná ríon uasal tharna bearta do tháinig go dtí an gcúirt.

'Ó,' arsa Móirín, 'ar dh'aithníobhair í?'

'Níor dh'aithníomar,' ar siad, 'agus is dóigh linn nár aithin aoinne dá raibh sa tigh í. Pé scéal é,' ar siad, 'do bhí mac an rí go han-mhór léi. Ba chuma leis aon ní mar gheall ar aoinne eile ach í.'

'Muise mo thrua é,' arsa Móirín; 'n'fheadar an mbeidh an féasta aon oíche eile ann,' ar sise.

'Is dóigh linn go mbeidh, mar is maith le mac an rí an bhean óg d'fheiscint arís.'

'Nach trua chráite,' arsa Móirín, 'nach féidir liomsa dul ann.'

'Ó, tá cúram agat ann,' arsa na deirfiúracha léi.

Do tháinig an tráthnóna amáireach, agus do tháinig an caitín agus a slaitín draíochta, agus do chuir sí Móirín i dtreo chun dul go dtí tigh an rí. Do bhí an oíche go compordach aici agus í suite i dteannta mhic an rí, go dtí gur tháinig an t-am céanna, agus do ghaibh sí leithscéal leis an gcuideachtan agus d'fhág an chúirt.

Ach an tríú hoíche, do bhí sé beartaithe ina aigne ag mac an rí gan í a ligean uaidh an oíche sin gan a fhios a bheith aige cad as í nó cér díobh í. Nuair a bhí sé an-bhuailte lena dó dhéag do bhí imní ar Mhóirín ar eagla go mbeadh an t-am caite. Do bhí mac an rí ag faire ag an ngeata, agus nuair a chuaigh sí ar marcaíocht ar an each donn, ní raibh am aige chun aon chaint a dhéanamh léi; ach le linn di a bheith ag imeacht tharais do thug sé snap ar an mbróig a bhí ar a cois, agus d'fhág ina diaidh í agus d'imigh sí léi.

Nuair a tháinig mac an rí isteach níor inis sé d'aoinne cad a d'imigh air; ach do bhí an bhróigín aige, agus ba luachmhar an tseoid í. Do chuir sé gairm scoile amach, ná beadh aon bhean go deo aige ach an bhean go 'riúnódh an bhróg a bhí aige í. Nuair a chuaigh an scéal amach, sin é an uair a bhí an phramsáil ag na mná óga, féach ciocu acu go mbeadh an t-ádh air; ach do bhí scéal fuar acu. Ansin do ghaibh mac an rí agus garda saighdiúirí leis. Ní raibh aon bhean óg ná go raibh cead aici an bhróg a thástáil, ach ní bhíodh sí oiriúnach d'aoinne. Cad a dhein na leasdeirfiúracha ach Móirín a chur fé bhéal comhra móir a bhí sa chistin, ar eagla go mbeadh sé de mhí-ádh uirthi gur di a bheadh an bhróg oiriúnach. Nuair a tháinig mac an rí chomh fada le tigh Mhóirín, do tháinig sé isteach agus do thug sé cead dosna mná óga an bhróg a thástáil; ach sin a raibh de mhaith dhóibh ann.

Chomh luath is do tháinig mac an rí isteach do phreab an caitín in airde ar an gcomhra, is do thosnaigh sé ar a bheith ag miamhlaigh agus ag scríobadh. Do shamhlaigh sé do mhac an rí gurb é an glór a bhíodh sa mhiamhlaigh aige ná 'Móirín, Móirín fé bhéal comhrín, is go 'riúnódh an bhróigín í.'

D'iompaigh mac an rí sall mar a raibh an comhra.

'B'fhéidir,' ar seisean, 'go mbeadh aoinne fén gcomhra i gan fhios dúinn.'

Do thóg sé in airde an comhra, agus is amhlaidh bhí an créatúirín agus í leathmhúchta.

'Cuir ort an bhróg seo,' ar seisean. Do rug sí ar an mbróigín gloine, agus do chuaigh sí ar a cois gan mórán trioblóide.

'Is tusa mo ghrá agus mo chéile,' ar seisean.

'Faghaim pardún agat, a mhic an rí,' ar sise, 'ní féidir liom dul leat go fóill, ach téanam liom go dtí an gairdín.'

D'ardaigh sí léi é, agus is amhlaidh bhí an caitín suite ag bun an chrainn. Do fuair sí an tslaitín draíochta, agus do tháinig chúichi amach

as an gcrann an t-each caol donn, culaith d'éadach sróil, agus a seoide gloineach. Nuair a bhí sí gafa suas, is maith an té ná tugfadh taitneamh aige dhi. Do thóg sé leis í, agus stad níor dheineadar nó gur bhaineadar an chúirt féin amach.

I gceann beagán aimsire do pósadh Móirín agus mac rí Chonnacht. Do bhíodar go sásta agus go compordach ansin. Do tháinig formad agus éad ar na leasdeirfiúracha léi, ach níor ligeadar orthu é. Do chuadar go dtí an chúirt mar a raibh sí, agus do dhein sí mná uaisle cúirte dhóibh. I gceann lae agus bliana do saolaíodh leanbh óg di; agus cad a dhein na leasdeirfiúracha ach an naíonán do thógaint leo agus é a chaitheamh síos le faill; agus thugadar leo coileán óg agus do ligeadar orthu gurb shin é a bhí ann. Ach ar maidin amáireach nuair a tháinig mac an rí ar thuairisc na mná, dúradar leis go raibh an bhean go maith ach ná raibh aon ní eile.

'Is cuma sin,' arsa mac an rí, 'táim sásta ón uair go bhfuil sí féin go maith.'

Do bhí an scéal ag imeacht mar sin go dtí go raibh triúr páistí aici; ach ní raibh a dtamhasc ná a dtuairisc le fáil ag mac an rí ná aige na máthair ach chomh beag. Is beag an choinne a bhí aici gurb iad na leasdeirfiúracha a bhí ag déanamh na díobhála.

Ach nuair a chonacadar ná raibh aon chuir ina coinne ag mac an rí, ná aon ghráin aige uirthi mar gheall ar a raibh tite amach, do cheapadar seift eile. Lá breá agus Móirín suite ina cathaoir shuaimhnis, do thánadar chúichi isteach dhon pharlús agus do bhíodar ag caint chomh cneasta, chomh deas léi. Dúirt duine acu léi,

'Tánn tú ag féachaint bán mílítheach, a mhnaoi uasail, agus teastaíonn aer uait. Dá mb'áil leat tú féin a dhéanamh suas, is go rachfá ag siúl tamall linne.'

'Ba mhaith liom,' arsa Móirín.

Do ghléas sí í féin in éadach uasal. Do bhuaileadar amach agus stad níor dheineadar nó go dtí gur bhaineadar amach barr na faille, san áit díreach gur chaitheadar an triúr naíonán le fána. Bhíodar suite ansin tamall, agus do labhair duine dosna leasdeirfiúracha léi:

'Mhuise, is álainn an t-éadach é sin ort, a ríon,' ar sise, 'nuair atá an ghrian ag taitneamh; n'fheadar dhon tsaol,' ar sise, 'conas d'fhéachfainnse dá mbeadh sé orm.'

'Cuir ort é,' arsa Móirín, 'agus beidh a fhios againn an dtiocfaidh sé go maith duit.'

Do bhí an ghrian ag taitneamh go soilseach.
Do bhain sí dhi an clóca agus ar lean é, agus do
chuir an leasdeirfiúr uirthi féin é. Ní túisce sin ná
bhéic an ceann eile, 'Ó, Ó, Ó,' ar sise, 'cad é siúd
thíos?' agus ionadh uirthi, mar dhea.

D'éirigh Móirín ina seasamh ar bharr na faille
go bhfeicfeadh sí cad a bhí ann; ach mo chreach,
do thug sí a dhá láimh léi, is do chaith sí síos í.

'Is ea,' ar sise, 'tá do ghnó déanta anois. Beidh
saol maith againn i dteannta mhic an rí.'

Nuair a thánadar abhaile do lig an leasdeirfiúr
uirthi mar dhea gurb í féin Móirín, ach do bhí a
fhios ag mac an rí go raibh rud éigint bunoscionn
sa scéal; ach níor lig sé aon ní air.

Chomh luath agus do caitheadh síos Móirín,
do bhí an caitín féna bun, agus do ghaibh sí í, fé
mar do ghaibh sí an triúr páistí. Do thóg sí léi í
go hoileáinín uaigneach aerach. Ní raibh a fhios
a seoid ag Móirín nó go dtí go raibh sí ina
seasamh i dtigh ghleoite ornáideach, agus gach
uile ní a bhí ag oiriúint do bhanríon ann.

'Ó, cá bhfuilim?' arsa Móirín.

'Tánn tú aige baile, a chailín,' arsa an caitín;
'ná bíodh aon bhrón ort.'

Pé féachaint a thug sí thairsti, do chonaic sí an
triúr páistí ba ríúla agus ba uaisle féachaint agus
gnaoi dá bhfaca sí riamh. 'Agus na páistí deasa?'
arsa Móirin agus ionadh uirthi.

'Is iadsan do pháistí féin,' arsa an caitín.

Níorbh fhéidir léi a thuiscint cad a bhí tite
amach. Ansin d'inis an caitín di conas mar do
dhein a leasdeirfiúracha an feall uirthi, agus gur
chaitheadar a leanaí le fána na haille, agus ansin
gur chaitheadar í féin ann.

'Ach do bhíos-sa, a iníon ó, ro-mhaith dhóibh;
agus an bhfuil a fhios agat cad é an cara dhuit
mise?'

'Níl a fhios agam,' arsa Móirín.

'Is mise do mháthair, a iníon ó,' ar sise; 'ní
bhfuaireas bás in aon chor, ach le barr feirge do
chuir d'athair orm do chuireas fé dhraíocht mé
féin i riocht cait. Is mé do tháinig chughat an
chéad lá, agus táim leat ó shin anuas. Tá do
leanaí saor agam, agus tánn tú féin saor agam;
agus b'fhéidir go saorfainn d'fhear céile leis.'

Do bhí Móirín go sásta, í féin agus a leanaí i
dteannta a chéile, ar feadh tamaill mhaith.

Aon lá amháin do tháinig an caitín isteach
chúichi.

'Níl aon ghnó againn,' ar sise, 'a thuilleadh
folaigh do dhéanamh. Tá mac an rí chun pósadh,

agus níl aon ghnó agatsa a bheith anseo agus é a
ligeant le bean eile. Téanam liom amáireach.'

Do bhuaileadar síos chun na trá lá arna
mháireach go himeall an uisce. Do bhuail sí
buille dá slaitín dhraíochta ar bhuilcín adhmaid,
agus do bhí sé ina churacháinín báid ar snámh.
Do phreab an caitín isteach sa bhád, agus do shín
Móirín isteach an triúr páistí, agus do chuaigh sí
féin isteach ansin. An fhaid a bheifeá ag bualadh
do dhá bhois le chéile do bhíodar ar barr na faille
mar a caitheadh síos iad.

'Anois,' arsa an caitín, 'tá tigh beag thall ansin
agus tá aoire muc ann; is é an ainm atá air, Micí
na Muc. Is é an t-aoire atá ag an rí é le fada.
Gaibhse suas agus fiafraigh dó mar seo: 'A Mhicí
na Muc, an sileann bhur méireanna mil, nó an
seineann an chruit ceol, an gcuireann an t-each
caol donn suas dá chuid, nó an bhfuil buairt ró-
mhór ar an rí óg?'

'Agus', arsa Móirín, 'cad fáth an méid sin?'

'Tá, a iníon ó,' arsa an caitín, 'níor deineadh
aon deoch sa rítheaghlach ó dh'fhágais é, agus
níorbh fhéidir aon cheol a bhaint as an gcruit,
agus níor ith an t-each caol donn aon ghreim bia
ó dh'fhágais an áit.'

Do bhí sé de bhua ag Móirín ó bhí sí ina rud
bheag, le barr draíochta a máthar go ndeinfeadh
sí deoch i bhfoirm beorach dosna huaisle a
bhíodh ag teacht go dtí rítheaghlach an rí; agus
níor ith an capall blaiseadh bia ach óna dhá láimh
mhín féin.

Do bhuail sí suas agus do chuaigh sí isteach go
tigh Mhicí na Muc. Do tháinig ionadh air sin
nuair a chonaic sé an ríon álainn óg agus an triúr
páistí ba dheise dá bhfacaigh a dhá shúil riamh.
Ní fheadair cá has gur thánadar, níor aithnigh sé
í; dúirt sé léi suí. Do shuigh sí ar bhinsín luachra
a bhí ar thaobh an tí.

Ní fada a bhí sí istigh nuair a labhair sí le Micí,
'Muise, a Mhicí,' ar sise, 'an sileann bhur
méireanna mil, nó an seineann bhur gcruit ceol,
an gcuireann an t-each caol donn suas dá chuid,
nó an bhfuil buairt ró-mhór ar an rí óg?'

'Mhuise, a mhnaoi uasail,' dá freagairt, 'is
dóigh liom go bhfuil gach ní atá ráite agatsa fíor
go leor; tá buairt ar mhac an rí, ach is dóigh liom
go bhfuil sé chun bean chéile eile do thogha sara
fada.'

'Is trua sin,' ar sise, agus níor labhair sí a
thuilleadh ach bualadh an doras amach; agus
d'éirigh Micí go bhfeicfeadh sé cá raibh sí ag

tabhairt a haghaidh, ach is amhlaidh do chonaic sé i féin agus na páistí ag imeacht as a radharc le fána na faille síos.

Chomh luath agus do bhí an scanradh agus an t-ionadh imithe de Mhicí, 'Imeoidh mé,' ar seisean, 'agus 'neosfaidh mé an scéal do mhac an rí. Is dócha ná creidfidh sé mé, ach mar sin féin.' Stad níor dhein sé nó go dtí gur bhain sé amach mac an rí. 'A mhic an rí,' ar seisean, 'tá scéal iontach agam le hinsint duit; ach ná bí feargach liom nuair a chloisfidh tú é.'

'Ní bhead, a Mhicí,' arsa mac an rí; 'inis do scéal.'

Ansin d'inis Micí dhó mar gheall ar an ríon agus ar na páistí; agus is ar éigean do chreid mac an rí é.

'Má mhaireann tú beo,' arsa Micí leis, 'tar chugham amáireach, agus cuirfidh mé i bhfolach fén luachair tú, agus má thagann sí cífidh tú féin le do shúile í.'

'Tá go maith, a Mhicí,' arsa mac an rí, 'raghaidh mé ann.'

Ar maidin amáireach níor dhearúid mac an rí gan dul go dtí tigh Mhicí; agus do chuaigh sé i bhfolach fén luachair i dtreo go raibh radharc maith aige uirthi nuair a thiocfadh sí isteach. Do bhí sé ag feitheamh go mífhoighneach, ach fé dheireadh do bhraith sé na páistí ag teacht agus iad ag súgradh dhóibh féin. Do tháinig sí isteach agus do shuigh sí mar a raibh sí suite inné roimhe sin. Do bhí mac an rí á tabhairt fé ndeara i gan fhios di; ach do labhair sí go brónach, 'Mhuise, a Mhicí na Muc, an sileann bhur méiríní mil, nó an seineann bhur gcruit ceol, an gcuireann an t-each caol donn suas dá chuid, nó an bhfuil buairt ró-mhór ar an rí óg?'

'Mhuise ambaiste,' arsa mac an rí, 'is air atá sé!' ag preabadh amach ón áit go raibh sé i bhfolach. Do rug sé lombharróg uirthi, agus do thug sé deocha póg di. 'Ó a ríon,' ar seisean, 'conas mar tá an scéal seo go léir tite amach, nó cé leis na páistí gleoite seo?'

'Liomsa agus leatsa, a mhic an rí,' ar sise; 'mo leasdeirfiúracha fé ndeár an obair seo go léir, ach do bhí cara dílis agamsa do dhein díon dom féin agus dom leanaí.'

Do thóg sé leis abhaile í féin agus a clann, agus Micí lena gcois. Do hadaíodh tine cnámh i lár páirce, agus nuair a bhí sí dearg do ceanglaíodh an bheirt leasdeirfiúracha agus do caitheadh isteach dhon tine iad, agus dódh agus loisceadh iad. Do bhí fleá agus féasta ins an rítheaghlach in onóir do Mhóirín agus dona triúr leanbh a theacht fé bhua agus fé mhaise go dtí an rítheaghlach arís.

Is mó lá grámhar cneasta do chaitheadar i bhfochair 'na chéile ina dhiaidh sin, agus níor ghá do Mhicí aon mhuc ná caora d'aoireacht as sin go dtí lá a bháis. Do bhí urraim duine uasail aige ó Mhóirín agus ó mhac an rí, agus ba mhaith an ceart é. D'imigh an draíocht den gcaitín agus do bhí sí ina máthair ag Móirín an chuid eile dá saol.

THE LITTLE GREY CAT

There was a king one time, a powerful and rich king. He married a young noblewoman who had a lot of wealth; it was not for love of her that he married her but for her riches. They were married for three years and they had no family, but at the approach of the fourth year a young daughter was born to her. The mother was overjoyed; she did not care how much wealth or riches the king had; she preferred a child to the wealth of the world.

The child was seven years old when the king's wife noticed that he was not as fond or respectful of her as a king should be. She got sort of jealous and began to watch him. It was not long until she was sure that the story was true. One day they were sitting at the table, and if they were, the king was looking really ill-tempered. But she spoke kindly, 'It is I who am making mischief, king, but I will not from now on.' Then she rose from the table and went out the door of the room, but nobody at all saw her leaving, and they didn't know where she headed. Magic was plentiful in the country at that time.

The dinner was on the table, but the queen was not coming, and she did not come. The child was sad and lonely after her mother. But one evening a few days later she was standing at the door and she saw a little grey cat, mewing. 'God love you,' said the child, 'aren't you the nice little cat! Isn't it a pity you wouldn't stay with me as a pet?' The cat stayed, and everywhere the child went the cat accompanied her. She was growing up, and when she was twelve years old her father married the woman he wanted, a widow with two daughters of her own. When the stepmother and the two daughters came to the house they had no regard for the orphan. She was bullied and had to do everything that needed to be done.

But the king of Connacht, he had one son, and he wanted to choose someone from among the young women in his province. It was announced that a feast was to be held in the royal court, and everyone who wished to go there was invited, especially the young noble ladies. The king's two stepdaughters got an invitation just like everyone else, and they spent the week preparing themselves to go to the feast. The orphan was busy preparing everything for them.

The night had come, and they were ready to go to the royal court. The orphan gazed after them as they left the house. 'Alas!' said she, 'I am in the chimney-corner and my stepmother's children are leaving in a fancy coach.' She sat down, and she was crying sadly when the little cat came along the floor to her.

'Stand up, my dear,' said the cat, 'and come with me to the garden. Here is a little magic wand for you. Give the birch tree a little tap with it, and a slender brown steed and a fine suit of clothes will come out to you.'

The orphan took the little magic wand and went to where the birch tree was. She gave the tree a little tap with the wand, and no sooner had she done so than a slender brown horse with reins and saddle of burnished gold came out to her. And the clothes she had to put on her, no eye could look at them, for they were shining like bright silver. To top all there was a pair of glass shoes.

'Put on the clothes, now, dear child,' said the little cat, 'and mount this horse, and he will take you to the royal court. Enjoy yourself as much as you can there, but don't stay a moment past midnight, because if you do you'll only be an insignificant tattered little person. Do what I say, go now and may luck be with you. When you return all you have to do is strike the tree with the little wand, and the horse and your clothes will go for safe keeping into it.'

Móirín went, just like a real queen, and she didn't stop until she reached the royal court. The sentries saw this noble lady coming, and they were very surprised that they had not seen such a young woman ever before. One of them went to the king's son. 'King's son!' said he, 'there is a

young noble lady at the gate, and truly, her beauty has taken my mind away.'

The king's son went to the gate, and if he did, the young woman was there before him. He stretched out his hand to her and smoothly helped her to dismount. He ordered the horse to be stabled. He brought in the young woman and everyone in the royal household was looking at her. The king's son didn't look at any other girl in the court but her. He danced with her, and they had music and recreation and fun together until it was almost midnight. She thanked the king's son and told him that she would have to be going then. He was sad, and no wonder. He accompanied her to the gate and helped her to mount the horse. She said goodbye to him and off she went.

It didn't take the brown steed long to get her home. The king's son didn't get much enjoyment from the rest of the night. When the stepsisters came home they found Móirín sitting by the fire as if she hadn't moved from that place. She enquired of the girls how their night was, did they enjoy it? They were telling her, and they said the strangest thing was a wonderful noble lady who came to the court.

'Oh!' said Móirín, 'did you recognize her?'

'We didn't,' said they, 'and we have the impression that nobody in the court recognized her. At any rate,' said they, 'the king's son was very taken with her. He didn't care anything about anyone else but her.'

'Poor man!' said Móirín. 'I wonder will there be a feast there any other night?' said she.

'We think there will be, as the king's son would like to see the young woman again.'

'Isn't it a terrible pity that I can't be there?' said Móirín.

'Oh! what business would you have there!' said the sisters to her.

The following evening came, and the little cat came with her little magic wand and got Móirín ready to go to the king's house. She had a comfortable evening sitting with the king's son, until the same time came, and she excused herself to the company and left the court.

But the third night the King's son had decided not to let her leave him until he had found out where she came from and who her people were. When it was almost twelve o'clock Móirín was anxious in case the time would be up. The king's son was watching at the gate, and when she mounted the brown steed he did not have time to speak to her, but as she went by him, he snapped at the shoe on her foot. She left it behind and off she went.

When the king's son came in he didn't tell anyone what had happened to him. But he had the little shoe and it was a precious object. He issued a proclamation that the only wife he would ever have would be the woman that the shoe would fit. When the story became known it was then the young women were prancing to see which of them would be lucky. But it was useless for them. Then the king's son went out, accompanied by a guard of soldiers. Every young woman had the right to try on the shoe but it didn't fit anyone. What did the stepsisters do but put Móirín underneath a big chest in the kitchen, for fear she would have the misfortune that it was she the shoe would fit!

When the king's son came as far as Móirín's house he came in, and he allowed the young women to try on the shoe. But that was all the good it was to them.

As soon as the king's son came in, the cat jumped up on the chest and began mewing and scraping. It appeared to the king's son that what it was saying while mewing was 'Móirín, Móirín, under a little chest, and the little shoe would fit her!' The king's son turned over to where the chest was. 'Perhaps,' said he, 'there might be someone under the chest unknown to us.' He lifted up the chest, and there was the poor little creature, and she half smothered. 'Put on this shoe,' said he. She took the little glass shoe and it went on her foot without much trouble. 'You are my love and my wife,' said he.

'Pardon me, king's son,' said she, 'I can't go with you yet, but come with me to the garden.' She took him with her, and there was the cat, sitting at the foot of the tree. She got the little magic wand, and the sleek brown horse, and a satin suit of clothes, and her glittering jewels came out of the tree to her. When she was dressed up it was a strong person who would not be attracted to her. He took her with him and they did not stop until they reached his own court.

In a short while, Móirín and the son of the king of Connacht married. They were satisfied and comfortable then. The stepsisters became envious and jealous of her, but they did not let this be known. They went to the palace where she was and she made noble court ladies of them. At the end of a year and a day a young child was born to her. And what did the stepsisters do but take the infant and throw him down a cliff, and they brought a young pup and pretended that was what had been there.[1] But on the following morning when the king's son came asking after his wife, they told him that the woman was fine but that nothing else was.

'That doesn't matter,' said the king's son, 'I'm satisfied so long as she herself is all right.' The story was like that until she had three children, but neither the king's son, nor their mother even, could find track or trace of them. Little did she suspect that it was the stepsisters who were doing the damage.

But when they saw that the king's son didn't object, or have any hatred for his wife because of what had happened, they thought up another trick. One fine day as Móirín sat in her easy chair they came to her in the parlour, talking ever so kindly and nicely to her. One of them said, 'You are looking pale and sickly, noble lady, and you need air. Maybe you would like to get yourself ready and to walk a while with us.'

'I would,' said Móirín. She dressed herself in fine clothes. They went out and they didn't stop until they reached the top of the cliff, the very same place where they had thrown the three children down the cliff. They were seated there for a while, and one of the stepsisters spoke to her. 'Indeed that is a lovely outfit you have on, Lady!' said she, 'when the sun shines on it. I wonder,' said she, 'how it would look on me.'

'Put it on,' said Móirín, 'and we will know if it suits you well.' The sun was shining brightly. She took off the cloak and its attachments and the stepsister put it on herself.

Immediately the other one shouted, 'Oh! oh! oh! what is that below?', pretending to be surprised!

Móirín stood up on top of the cliff to see what was there, but alas! the stepsister put her two hands to her and threw her down. 'Yes,' said she, 'you're finished now. We will have a good life with the king's son.'

1. i.e. that she had given birth to a pup.

When they came home the stepsister pretended she was Móirín; the king's son knew that there was something odd going on, but he didn't let on.

As soon as Móirín was thrown down the cliff, the little cat was underneath her, and caught her just as she had caught the three children. She took her with her to a lonely lofty little island. Móirín did not realize a thing until she was standing in a delightful ornate house with everything that was suitable for a queen there.

'Oh! where am I?' said Móirín.

'You are at home, girl,' said the little cat, 'don't worry!'

Whatever look she gave sideways, she saw the most kingly, and noble-looking, and beautiful children she had ever seen. 'And the nice children?' said Móirín, with surprise.

'They are your own children,' said the little cat.

She could not understand what had happened. Then the little cat told her how her stepsisters had deceived her, and that they had thrown the children down the cliff, and that they had thrown herself down then. 'But I was too smart for them, dear girl! And do you know what friend I am to you?'

'I do not,' said Móirín.

'I am your mother, dear girl; I did not die at all, but because your father made me so angry I put myself under enchantment in the shape of a cat. It was I who came to you the first day and it is I who have been with you from then on. I have your children safe and now I have you safe, and perhaps I will save your husband also.'

Móirín was happy, she and her children together for a good while. Then one day the little cat came in to her. 'We have no business,' she said, 'to hide any longer. The king's son is to marry, and you have no business being here and letting another woman have him. Come with me tomorrow.'

They went down to the strand the following day to the very edge of the water. She struck a small piece of wood with her little magic wand and it became a little *currach*[2] floating on the water. The little cat jumped into the boat, and Móirín handed in the children, and she went in

herself then. While you would be clapping your hands together they were on the top of the cliff from where they had been thrown down.

'Now,' said the little cat, 'there is a small house over there, and there is a swineherd in it. His name is Mící na Muc [Mickey of the Pigs]. He has been the king's swineherd for a long time. Go up to him and enquire of him as follows: Mící na Muc, do your fingers drip honey, or do the harps play music, does the sleek brown steed refuse his food, or is there too great a sorrow on the young king?'

'And,' said Móirín, 'why that?'

'It is this, dear girl,' said the little cat, 'no drink has been made in the royal household since you left it, and no music has been got from the harp, and the sleek brown steed has not eaten a bit of food since you left the place.' Since she was a child, and because of her mother's magic, Móirín had the gift of making a drink like beer for the nobles who used to visit the king's royal household. And the horse only ever tasted food from her own two fine hands.

She went on up and into Mící na Muc's house. He was surprised when he saw the lovely young lady and the three nicest children his two eyes had ever seen. He didn't know from where they came; he did not recognize her. He told her to sit down. She sat on a bunch of rushes that was at the side of the house. She was not long in the house when she spoke to Mící na Muc.

'Mící,' said she, 'do your fingers drop honey, or do your harps play music, does the sleek brown steed refuse his food, or is there too great a sorrow on the young king?'

'Indeed, noble lady,' said he, answering her, 'I think everything you have said is true enough; the king's son is sad, but I think he is going to choose another wife before long.'

'That is a pity,' said she, and she spoke no more, but went out the door. And Mící got up to see where she headed, but all he saw was her and the children going out of sight down the cliff slope.

As soon as Mící got over the fright and wonder, 'I will go,' said he, 'and I will tell the king's son the story. I suppose he won't believe me, but all the same.' He didn't stop until he reached the king's son. 'I have a wonderful story for you, king's son!' said he, 'but don't be angry with me when you hear it.'

---

2. A small keel-less boat made of tarred canvas stretched on a wooden frame.

'I will not, Mící,' said the king's son; 'tell me your story.' Then Mící told him about the noble lady and the children, and the king's son hardly believed him.

'If you live,' said Mící to him, 'come to me tomorrow and I will hide you under the rushes, and if she comes you will see her with your own eyes.'

'All right, Mící,' said the king's son, 'I will.' The following morning the king's son didn't forget to go to Mící's house, and he hid under rushes so that he would have a good look at her when she came in. He was waiting patiently, but at last he heard the children playing as they approached. She came in and sat where she had the day before. The king's son was watching her without her knowing it. But she spoke sadly, 'Mící,' said she, 'do your fingers drip honey, or do your harps play music, does the sleek brown steed refuse his food, or is there too great a sorrow on the young king?'

'Well, indeed,' said the king's son, 'it is on him it is!' jumping out from where he was hiding. He hugged her tightly and smothered her with kisses. 'Oh noble lady!' said he, 'what has happened, and whose are those lovely children?'

'Yours and mine, king's son!' said she. 'My stepsisters are responsible for all this, but I had a loyal friend who protected me and my children.'

He brought her and her family home with him, and Mící along with them. A bonfire was kindled in the middle of a field, and when it was red the two sisters were tied and thrown into the fire, and they were burned and destroyed. There was feasting and drinking in the royal household to honour Móirín and the three children who came in victory and comeliness to the royal household again. They spent many a gentle loving day together afterwards, and Mící did not have to herd any pig or sheep after that to the day he died. He got a gentleman's respect from Móirín and the king's son, and rightly so. The enchantment was lifted from the cat, and she was a mother to Móirín for the rest of her life.

Biographies/Bibliographies

Máire Ruiséal

LIFE. Storyteller Máire Ruiséal was born in Cill Mhaolchéadair (Kilmaceadar), County Kerry, in 1856, and lived until the middle of the 1940s. She never went to school, and at the age of nine went into domestic service, where she was paid one pound a year. She continued in service until she married Seán Ó Lúing when she was twenty-two. It was an arranged match, but according to what she told folklore collector Seosamh Ó Dálaigh, she arranged it herself, without having seen her future husband, breaking off a previous engagement to a weaver in Dingle for reasons which were entirely pragmatic: she considered Seán Ó Lúing, a farmer, with cow and horse, a better prospect than the weaver. She had eight children, all but one of whom went to America. Her husband died when she was quite young and for much of her life she was a widow, living initially on the family farm and, in old age, with her daughter, Mrs Sheehy in Dunquin. She was famed for her physical strength, and boasted that as a girl she had been able to lift a sack of meal weighing twenty stones (280 lb) (IFC 965, 271–7).

Máire Ruiséal belonged to a family of storytellers. She told Seosamh Ó Dálaigh that she had heard a lot of stories from her father when she was a girl. Her sister, Cáit Ruiséal, was a good storyteller, and Cáit's granddaughter Cáit 'Bab' Feirtéar is one of the best storytellers living today. 'Bab' Feirtéar has told Eilís Ní Dhuibhne that she remembers visiting Máire as a child, describing her as a woman with a good sense of humour — 'bean ana-phléisiúrtha' (in contrast with her sister Cáit, who was serious and fond of religious tales).

Máire Ruiséal had a reasonably large repertoire; at least twenty different stories, as well as much larger quantities of seanchas, prayers, etc., have been collected from her.

CHIEF WRITINGS. Proinsias Ó Raghalla, 'Dhá Scéal ó Dhún Chaoin, Co. Chiarraighe', Béaloideas, vol. 2 (1929), pp. 53–4.

Máire Mhic Fhionnlaoich

LIFE. Storyteller Máire Mhic Fhionnlaoich, 'Máire Mhicí', was born in 1873 in An Bun Beag (Bunbeg), County Donegal, where she continued to live all her life. She was married, and probably had responsibility for a farmhouse. She was straightforward, fluent and articulate, like many storytellers in her part of Donegal, and had a wide repertoire, including songs, legends and seanchas, as well as several folktales. She often cited her father as the source of her tales. Seán Ó hEochaidh, full-time collector, collected most material from her, between 1938 and 1955, using an Ediphone recording machine. Brian Ó Riain and Séamas Ó Dubhgáin also collected from her.

Sorcha Mhic Ghrianna

LIFE. Born in 1875, Sorcha Bean Mhic Ghrianna, or Sorcha Chonaill, was one of the best-known storytellers in Rinn na Feirste (Rannafast), County Donegal. She was connected by marriage with the Mac Grianna family of writers and storytellers, the best-known members of which were Seosamh and Séamas, novelists and short story writers (see Anna Nic Ghrianna, pp. 491–2). Two cousins, Aodh Ó Domhnaill and Aodh Ó Duibheannaigh, schoolteachers and part-time folklore collectors, recorded substantial quantities of material from her wide repertoire for the Irish Folklore Commission, including fairytales, jokes and anecdotes, and legends.

Her fluent and rather formal and literary style is characteristic of narrators in her area of Donegal, who often knew their stories by heart (unlike narrators in most other parts of Ireland). The Mac Griannas also tended to write their oral folktales down and publish them in literary magazines, a practice which undoubtedly influenced their oral narrative style.

BIOGRAPHY AND CRITICISM. Gordon W. MacLennan, *Seanchas Annie Bhán/The Lore of Annie Bhán*, ed. and trans., Alan Harrison and Máiri Elena Crook (Dublin: Seanchas Annie Publication Committee, 1997).

Anna Uí Shighil

LIFE. Anna Uí Shighil, of Cluain Dá Choircigh (Clondahorkey), County Donegal, was not a well-known storyteller, yet the Irish Folklore Commission archive contains some 400 pages of material, covering *seanchas*, legends and some folktales, collected from her by Seán Ó hEochaidh. Her occupation is listed as 'housewife'. She was born in 1867.

Peig Sayers

For biography and bibliography, see Volume IV, p. 1212

BAIRBRE NÍ FHLOINN, *Editor*

Storytelling Traditions of the Irish Travellers[1]

Mother tells stories in the dark black roads
Poking the stick fire, afraid of the ghost.
Talking of hell, the Lord up above.
Me waiting to lie at my mother's toes.

from 'Musha Mary Daughter', Chrissie Ward.

Tales travel.
Folktales are the Travellers of literature.
Travellers are in a constant state of flux and
    movement.
They do not abide by the usual rules and
    expectations, or by the usual conventions.
They have their own dynamics.
They adapt themselves to suit the situation.
They exist outside the usual norms and
    structures.
They lack a fixed and final form or structure,
    and so they are difficult to label and control.
They have no fixed abode.
They are impermanent.
They lack respectability.
They are a threat to the established order.
As constantly changing Travellers, they can
    hardly be regarded as literature.
They have no vote.
Officially, they are almost invisible.

At the start of the twenty-first century, Irish
Travellers are still frequently subjected to
intolerance, prejudice and bigotry. Attitudes are
changing, however, and that change brings the
attendant danger of romanticization. Neither
extreme does Travellers or their culture any
favours.[2]

In the days when few settled people were
interested in Travellers, the Irish Folklore
Commission was almost unique in acknowledging both their existence and their culture by
collecting material from and about them. Much
of the IFC's work already dealt with individuals
and with communities who were marginalized,
either by language, physical location or economic
circumstances, or because of colonization.
Travellers, however, were on the edge of that
margin.[3]

As early as 1932, Séamus Ó Duilearga wrote
an editorial note to an article on Irish Travellers
by Pádraig Mac Gréine, published in *Béaloideas*,
the journal of the Folklore of Ireland Society:

> This paper . . . is, to our mind, one of the
> most important contributions made to this
> journal during the five years of its
> existence. In congratulating Mr. Mac
> Gréine on his work in an almost untilled
> field we hope that he will continue his
> researches, and that others may be
> encouraged to follow his example, and by
> their study of the 'traveller-folk,' their
> manners and customs, language and
> traditions, provide material to folklorists
> and others interested in the study of Irish
> popular traditions.[4]

---

1. Some of the material in this essay also appears in Bairbre Ní Fhloinn, 'Irish Travellers and the Oral Tradition' in Nóirín Ní Laodhóg (ed.), *A Heritage Ahead: Cultural Action and Travellers* (Dublin: Pavee Point Publications, 1995), pp. 63–85.

2. Cf. Gearóid Ó Riain (ed.), *Traveller Ways, Traveller Words* (Dublin: Pavee Point Publications, 1992), p. 10.
3. Cf. G. Ó Riain, ibid.
4. Note to P. Mac Gréine, 'Irish Tinkers or "Travellers"', *Béaloideas*, vol. 3 (1932), p. 185.

Pádraig Mac Gréine was a schoolteacher who used his free time to carry out valuable collecting work for the IFC among Travellers in his native County Longford. It was he who recorded the long folktales and legends of Nora 'Oney' Power (see pp. 1271–1279), and her son John. Mac Gréine also noted many words and phrases in the secret language of the Travellers, known as 'shelta' or 'cant', in which he was especially interested, and he wrote too of the customs and beliefs of the travelling people he knew. Much of his material has appeared in print over the years, in the pages of *Béaloideas*, and more recently in the book of Traveller stories edited by George Gmelch and Ben Kroup, *To Shorten the Road*.[5]

Mícheál Mac Énrí, later a full-time collector in west Mayo, recorded material from Mayo Travellers which was published in *Béaloideas* in 1939.[6] Some years later, Seán Mac Craith recorded valuable material on Traveller language and traditions in south Clare.[7] In the same county in the 1930s, Séamus Ó Duilearga made a collection of folktales from a travelling chimney sweep called Paddy Sherlock.[8]

In 1950 the IFC circulated a detailed questionnaire on the subject of Travellers to the network of correspondents it had established all over the country. It enquired about the terminology, names, appearance, customs, itineraries, habits, language, songs, etc., of travelling people. The response yielded over eight hundred pages of material. Of course, all the respondents were settled people, whose sympathy towards Travellers varied, so the resulting information is very much the settled community's view of Travellers. Indeed, as an indication of relations between Travellers and settled people at the time, the material has considerable value. It is also worth noting that in 1950 Travellers still had an acknowledged and clear-cut function to perform in the traditional economy, as tinsmiths (whence the name 'tinker'), pedlars, chimney sweeps, horse dealers and casual labourers. Ireland was on the brink of entering the consumer society, however, and profound changes were about to take place. With the arrival of mass-manufactured plastics, the need for the tinsmith disappeared. With mechanization on the farm, there was not the same need for horses and donkeys or for casual labour. With modern transport, there was no need for the pedlar, and with the advent of television and radio, the need for the storyteller and the news-bringer disappeared.

In the 1970s Jim Delaney, full-time collector for the IFC's successor, the Department of Irish Folklore, UCD, recorded some stories from a Traveller in Athlone called Mickey Green, as well as a great deal of material about the love of Mickey's life — horses and their care. Three of these stories appear in Gmelch and Kroup's *To Shorten the Road*.

IFC collectors Kevin Danaher and Leo Corduff recorded some of the most famous Traveller musicians, among them the Donegal fiddle-player Mickey Doherty and the travelling piper Johnny Doran, whose playing has had a significant influence on many of the younger generation of pipers.[9] Throughout the late 1960s and 1970s Tom Munnelly collected songs from Travellers all over Ireland, uncovering a huge wealth of material in the process (see subsection 'The Song Tradition', pp. 1312–1364).

Apart from these substantial collections, material on Travellers in the IFC archive consists of descriptions of them by settled people, many of which clearly illustrate their marginal position. Time and again, Travellers emerge as poets, as healers, as holders of supernatural power of one kind or another (whose curse is to be feared), or as physically disabled. Either way, they are different from the settled community and are set apart, as foreigners or outsiders are in many societies.

5. P. Mac Gréine, 'Irish Tinkers or "Travellers"', pp. 170–86; 'Further Notes on Tinkers' "Cant"', *Béaloideas*, vol. 3 (1932), pp. 290–303; three riddles, *Béaloideas*, vol. 3 (1932), p. 414; 'Some Notes on Tinkers and their "Cant"', *Béaloideas*, vol. 4 (1934), pp. 259–63; George Gmelch and Ben Kroup (eds), *To Shorten the Road* (Dublin: O'Brien Press, 1978).

6. M. Mac Énrí, 'Ceant agus saoghal na dtincéirí', *Béaloideas*, vol. 9 (1939), pp. 219–29.

7. See indexes to the Main Manuscripts Collection, Department of Irish Folklore, University College Dublin.

8. P. Shearlock [*sic*], 'The Three Wishes', ed. Séamus Ó Duilearga, *Béaloideas*, vol. 3 (1932), p. 434; 'Clare Folk Tales', *Béaloideas*, vol. 5 (1935), pp. 24–7; 'The Beauty of the World', *Béaloideas*, vol. 15 (1946), pp. 263–72; 'Paddy Sherlock's Stories', *Béaloideas*, vol. 30 (1964), pp. 1–75.

9. Both musicians can be heard on cassette tapes published by Comhairle Bhéaloideas Éireann (The Folklore of Ireland Council): *The Gravel Walks: The Fiddle Music of Mickey Doherty* (CBÉ 002, Dublin, 1990), and *The Bunch of Keys: The Complete Recordings of Johnny Doran* (CBÉ 001, Dublin, 1988).

The image of the Traveller as storyteller and disseminator of stories is related to some of the traditional stereotypes mentioned above. The following example, from the Bannow area of County Wexford, illustrates the importance of this function in an age before mass communications:

> In those days, poor travelling men and women were nearly always welcome to a bed on the settle . . . Where there was no settle, a comfortable bed of straw was laid near the fireplace. In those days, there was no question of not keeping a poor traveller for the night. Each poor traveller had a certain house to face and stop in every night, and when they came at night they were welcomed almost as a member of the family whom they had not seen for some time. For the people liked to hear the news the poor traveller had brought from outside districts, and listen to the long fireside stories. They had some fine old stories then, but all the old people are gone and, alas, the most of the fine old *scéalta* with them.[10]

In the past, travelling people seem to have bedded down in the houses or outhouses of the settled community; apparently only in the early years of this century did they start to sleep in tents and wagons of their own. This change in accommodation habits must certainly have had an effect on Traveller relations with the settled community, and can only have resulted in reduced contact and social intercourse between the two groups. It must also have had a detrimental effect on the role of the Traveller as disseminator of stories.

Travellers were known to have a considerable wealth of stories. Pádraig Mac Gréine has written:

> There are among the tinkers many fine storytellers . . . The family sat around the camp fire listening to the elders telling stories. The good storyteller was a person of note and his fame widespread. In the telling of certain stories he was without

equal, and for years after his death his name was spoken of with respect and regret.[11]

Unfortunately, tales collected from travelling people represent only a tiny fraction of the thousands of folktales and stories in the IFC archives and a huge amount of material must have been lost.[12] Much greater resources have been available for the study of Traveller traditions in Scotland, resulting in a rich harvest of traditional narrative of all kinds, especially in the archives of the School of Scottish Studies at Edinburgh University, and there is every reason to believe that Irish Travellers could have produced a similar richness.[13]

In more recent years the Dublin Travellers Education and Development Group at Pavee Point has worked to reinforce Travellers' sense of identity, partly by focusing on their traditions and culture. Traveller participants have conducted a number of interviews in which other Travellers talk about themselves and their lives, and tell their own stories. This is a refreshing change from the previous line of folklorists, anthropologists and sociologists, and the material published in *Traveller Ways, Traveller Words* adds a new and valuable dimension to our knowledge.[14] Although this book is primarily biographical and descriptive, it also contains a number of more structured narratives and stories.

Irish Travellers have also travelled outside Ireland, most noticeably to Britain and to the United States. In both places, many of them have continued to maintain a separate identity. In London, Jim Carroll and Pat Makenzie have collected songs and stories of Irish travelling people.[15] In the United States, Jared Harper, Mick Moloney and others have worked with

---

10. IFC 107: 45–46. See also p. 1207 above.

11. P. Mac Gréine, 'Irish Tinkers or "Travellers"', p. 175.
12. The same could be said of other areas of tradition also, for similar reasons.
13. For details of work done in the 1960s and 1970s by American anthropologists George and Sharon Gmelch and by Alen MacWeeney and Artelia Court, see G. Gmelch and B. Kroup, *To Shorten the Road*, and Artelia Court, *Puck of the Droms: The Lives and Literature of the Irish Tinkers* (Berkeley, Los Angeles, London: University of California Press, 1985). Extracts from Court's *Puck of the Droms* appear below.
14. G. Ó Riain (ed.), *Traveller Ways, Traveller Words*.
15. See, for example, J. Carroll, 'Irish Travellers Around London', *Folk Music Journal*, vol. 3, no. 1 (1975), pp. 31–40.

communities of Irish Travellers, Harper making a special study of their language.[16]

What makes Travellers different? The question itself is loaded, assuming as it does that settled people represent the norm, and that Travellers represent a deviation from that norm.[17] Why do so many settled people dislike and fear Travellers? Is it simply because they are seen to be different?[18]

The superficial differences between Travellers and the settled community are obvious and easy to see, but perhaps more important differences lie at a deeper level. Several commentators have written about differences in fundamental values and attitudes between Travellers and settled people. Travellers live more for the present, and in the present. Traditionally, when a Traveller died, his or her caravan and belongings were burned. Travelling people cannot afford to burden themselves with things which they do not need. Chrissie Ward, two of whose poems appear on p. 1282, explains:

> . . . an' so the wagon would be always left up in a yard in the summer. And we'd take the pony an' four-wheeler an' we'd carry a very light load because you might be goin' up mountains and hills and you couldn't bring an extraw pilla or heavy mattress an' you couldn't bring extraw clothes or anything like that. So you had to just bring the bare enough that you got around the country with. So some o' the young girls sometimes use' ta . . . hide a pillow under the, d'ye know a pillow, because if you couldn't carry an extraw pilla, say there was ten childer you'd have to have ten pillas, so you couldn't put ten pillas in the pony an' car.[19]

Unlike settled people, Travellers do not accumulate property and material possessions. They often swap possessions or give them away. Sharon Gmelch writes: 'John Maugham once praised a pair of boots he had purchased, "I had 'em for nine months and they were still as good as the day I bought them." When asked what happened to the boots, he replied, "I gave 'em away . . . just got tired of looking at 'em."'[20] Pádraig Mac Gréine comments: 'This exchange of articles, together with the constant movement from place to place . . . is the colour in [Travellers'] lives.'[21]

Travellers are not obsessed by outward appearance. They judge a person not by his or her material possessions but by the person's quality of life and the extent to which he or she enjoys life. Settled people, on the other hand, are often trapped by their possessions, and choked by them. As Victor Bewley puts it, our possessions own us, rather than the other way around.[22] Yet we cling on to them ever more desperately, locking them up and insuring them for all we are worth (living as we do in a culture of insurance). And all the while we live in fear of the ultimate loss of our material possessions, and of the ultimate journey which faces us all (living as we do in a culture which cannot cope with death).[23]

Travellers do not always order their world in the same way as settled people do, and this difference can sometimes find physical expression. In terms of vernacular building traditions, the Travellers' lack of any house at all could be seen to represent the ultimate development of the so-called direct-entry house, with its communal layout and lack of compartmentalization.[24] Unlike people living in the hearth-lobby houses of the south-east of Ireland, which appear to have been an architectural expression of the beginning of a quest for privacy, Travellers traditionally had hardly any barrier at all between

16. See, for example, Pat Bond, 'The Irish Travellers in the United States', *Sinsear: The Folklore Journal*, no. 5 (1988), pp. 45–58; J. Harper, 'The Irish Travellers of Georgia', Ph.D. dissertation, University of Georgia, 1977.

17. Compare language use and convention with regard to the use of the masculine pronoun 'he' as the unmarked form.

18. On this point see Sinéad ní Shuinéar, 'Why Do Gaujos Hate Gypsies So Much Anyway?' in T. Acton (ed.), *Gypsy Politics and Traveller Identity* (Hatfield: University of Hertfordshire Press, 1997), pp. 26–53, and S. ní Shuinéar, '"Othering" the Irish (Travellers)', in R. Lentin and R. McVeigh (eds), *Racism and Anti-racism in Ireland* (Belfast: Beyond the Pale Publications, 2002, pp. 177–92).

19. In G. Ó Riain (ed.), *Traveller Ways, Traveller Words*, p. 44.

20. In Sharon and George Gmelch and Pat Langan, *Tinkers and Travellers* (Dublin: O'Brien Press, 1975), p. 96.

21. P. Mac Gréine, 'Some Notes on Tinkers and their "Cant"', p. 260.

22. Victor Bewley, 'The Travelling People in Ireland', in *Travelling People*, ed., V. Bewley (Dublin: Veritas Publications, 1974), p. 35.

23. Thanks to Deirdre Cox for her ideas on this point.

24. For a description of the direct-entry house and the hearth-lobby house in Ireland, and for a discussion of the social implications of the internal layout of both, see Alan Gailey, *Rural Houses of the North of Ireland* (Edinburgh: John McDonald Publishers, 1984), chaps. 8 and 9.

themselves and the rest of the community, or between each other. This was not without its own symbolic importance.

Is it possible that some settled people dislike Travellers because they represent not only a threat to accepted attitudes et cetera, but also a challenge? In post-colonial Ireland, settled attitudes to Travellers are often indistinguishable from English attitudes to Irish people in the not-so-distant past.[25] So the oppressed lean all the more heavily on the next ones down. In post-colonial Ireland, Travellers may be an uncomfortable reminder of an uncomfortable past, which we would prefer to forget, or at least to site where we would not have to see it. In the not-so-distant past, a huge number of Irish people lived in abject poverty. Vast numbers of our near ancestors were utterly destitute. Perhaps today we are not sufficiently aware of the extent of that poverty, and of the effect it has had on our development as a people.

Whatever its source, Travellers today undoubtedly suffer from misunderstanding and fear on the part of the settled community, a problem they share with other minority groups in Ireland and abroad. They encounter censure, prejudice and romanticization, and the disadvantages of being subjected to analysis of various kinds (the irony of which is not lost here).

Traveller women's position is particularly complex. It would be easy to see them as suffering a double oppression, as the oppressed of the oppressed. However, we must take account of differences between the experiences of individual Traveller women, resisting the appeal of the simplistic stereotype, which has in the past been applied to Irish women in general, and has done us as little service. Nan Joyce's often idyllic account of life as a young Traveller girl, despite the dreadful hardships she and her family suffered (see pp. 1205–1208), contrasts with Nan Donahue's harrowing descriptions of life with a man who regularly battered her.[26] On the subject of domestic violence it is worth noting that Travellers necessarily live more publicly than the rest of us do. When a Traveller man attacks his wife, he often does so for all the world to see and to throw its hands up in horror. The settled professional, however, has the decorum and discretion to do so in the privacy of his house, so that the rest of us need never know. Patricia McCarthy's believable, down-to-earth and readable account of life with travelling people, points out that, although wife-beating occurs among Travellers, 'husband-beating is not unknown either'. However, Patricia McCarthy also writes that 'generally the women and children suffer most in the deprivations of their lives.'[27]

The huge preoccupation with 'respectability' in Ireland in the recent past must also have a bearing on society's attitudes to Traveller women. Many settled — especially married — women seem to have felt that their lives should revolve around home and family: respectable women simply did not go out much. To describe a married woman as being 'a great one for the road' was a definite slight on her character, but Travelling women had no such inhibitions; they lived on the road. Much worse than that, however, they even dared sometimes to drink and to get drunk in public, and to be seen enjoying themselves with abandon. This represented the antithesis of married respectability. Could they sometimes have been envied by their settled, 'respectable' sisters? At least the Traveller women had their moments.

It is worth noting that many spokespeople for the travelling community who have emerged in recent years have been women. A National Traveller Women's Forum has worked with considerable success since 1988. Traveller women have been in the forefront of the struggle for Travellers' rights, and in bringing the concerns of Travellers to the attention of the public.

In any discussion of folktales collected from travelling people, Oney Power must be given prominent mention. Pádraig Mac Gréine, who collected Power's stories from her, describes his first meeting with her as follows:

> I was cycling around a bye-road one day. It must have been in the mid-1920s, and I saw this poor dilapidated tent. A poor tent

25. See Ní Shuinéar, 'Why Do Gaujos Hate Gypsies So Much Anyway?'.
26. Nan Joyce, *Traveller: An Autobiography*, ed., Anna Farmar (Dublin: Gill and Macmillan, 1985); Sharon Gmelch, *Nan: The Life of an Irish Travelling Woman* (London: Souvenir Press, 1986).
27. P. McCarthy, 'Life with the Travelling People', in *Travelling People*, p. 69.

on the roadside and a little old woman sitting by a stick fire. I stopped for curiosity more than anything else and I started to talk to her. So I asked her who she was and she told me, 'A Power.' I said, 'Do you know any stories?' 'Ah,' she says, 'I could tell you stories from this day to this day week.'[28]

Oney Power's stories are clear evidence that storytelling among Travellers was not confined to men. Like stories collected from other Travellers, they often portray women as strong characters, very much in charge of their own destiny, and even in a dominant position. Autobiographical accounts by Traveller women mention storytelling around the campfire at night among women's activities: 'Well in the evenin' time maybe the men'd go fishin'. The childer'd skip, mebee, or the men'd hunt. The women'd have conversations around the fire, makin' cups o' tae . . . They'd be tellin' stories, maybe makin' flowers. They always had something to do. Travellers never was idle.'[29]

Travellers' stories do not differ substantially from those of settled people, at least with regard to subject matter.[30] Travellers shared an environment, a language, a religion and a general historical experience with the settled community. There was always considerable intercourse between the two groups, so this common pool of stories is hardly surprising. However, Máire Mac Aongusa writes:

> The folktale as told by the Traveller is basically the same as the folktale told by the seanchaí.[31] We recognise in it some of the poetic formulae which are direct translations from the Irish. Whereas the seanchaí proceeds at a measured pace, meticulously repeating formulae and ornate descriptive passages which add to the mystery and otherworldliness of those typically Märchen stories, the Traveller

storyteller does not always follow the traditional episodic style. S/he often prefers to make 'a long story short and a short story merry.' Consequently, s/he condenses and concentrates the action, melodeon like, to produce a more muscular and rumbustious version of the story in which the sequence of events is less clear than in the story of the seanchaí.[32]

Those differences which do exist between the repertoires of Travellers and settled people appear to be ones of style and emphasis, rather than of content. Máire Mac Aongusa has examined the traditional stories of Travellers as part of her analysis of Traveller values and perceptions in general, noting the necessity of understanding

> . . . the metamorphosis which takes place when Oney Power internalizes the motifs [of the story]. She makes her own of them and her spoken version reveals the grinding reality of her people's daily existence. When you read her stories, you hear not only about the physical differences in the circumstances of her life, but also about the felt pain of hunger, the resignation of enforced parting, the humiliation of rejection, the anger at upstart arrogance etc. Her stories are an evocation of a culture which is still with us today and which is still grossly misunderstood. Could we say that her storytelling reveals the soul of her people?[33]

A number of stories recorded from Travellers extol the virtue of charity, illustrating the notions that we should give generously to the less well-off, and that such generosity will bring its own rewards. Oney and John Power's stories are full of examples of the rich getting their come-uppance, while the poor end up doing well. The folktale 'The Fiery Dragon' (pp. 1271–1276) illustrates this idea.

The business of travelling also features prominently in many Traveller stories; the Powers' stories are full of accounts of people setting off

28. G. Gmelch and B. Kroup, *To Shorten the Road*, p. 39.
29. Chrissie Ward, quoted in G. Ó Riain (ed.), *Traveller Ways*, p. 52.
30. T. Munnelly, Introduction to vol. 7 ('Folktales and Folk Music') of Aileen L'Amie's 'The Irish Travelling People: A Resource Collection', held in the library at the University of Ulster, Jordanstown. The same, we are told, holds true for the gypsy storytelling tradition (see Dora E. Yates, *A Book of Gypsy Folk-Tales* [London: Phoenix House, 1948], p. 7).
31. Irish traditional storyteller.
32. Máire Mac Aongusa, *The Alienation of Travellers from the Educational System* (Dublin: Sociological Association of Ireland, n.d.), pp. 40–1.
33. Thanks to Máire Mac Aongusa for this valuable personal communication.

on journeys. Mother-love is graphically illustrated in Oney Power's story 'Jack from Tubberclare', where the hero of the tale brings his wife home to his mother at the end of the story:

> So, Jack and the lady came along in the coach till they came to the poor old mother's door. 'Are you there, mother?'
>
> 'I am.'
>
> 'Well, I have a wife home with me, and I brought her to be your humble servant all the days of your life.' So, he brought her into the little house. 'Go on now, mother,' says he, 'and sit down. There's a crown on your head all the days of your life. She'll have to do everything in this house, for I only brought her to be your maid.'[34]

Other stories reflect men's traditional dominance. One man in a story by Oney Power threatens to disgrace another by revealing to the world at large that he has slept with the other man's wife,[35] while one of John Power's stories tells us that the hero of the story 'starts to cry because a woman hit him; he only wished it was a man'.[36] The importance of family and children is expressed less seriously in the common formulaic ending found in several Travellers' stories: 'So they got married, and lived united, and had family in basketfuls and threw them out in shovelfuls.'[37]

Travellers tell many stories of the supernatural,[38] while the emphasis they place on religious faith and practice can be detected in stories such as 'The Fiery Dragon'. People in occupations of stress or risk have been shown to have a higher level of luck beliefs than those in non-risk occupations; times of uncertainty and change are guaranteed to make us look to the supernatural or the spiritual in some shape or form. We should hardly wonder that the Traveller, whose life is often lived at a considerable level of uncertainty, should show a particular interest in otherworld and spiritual matters.

Travellers have adapted the details of individual stories to suit their own circumstances, so in the legend of the banshee's comb, the banshee is said to approach the Travellers' campfire at night in her attempt to retrieve the comb, rather than appearing outside the house of the person who has taken it.[39]

The vibrant and colourful language of Traveller storytellers can be seen clearly in the stories of Oney Power. Like settled people, Travellers often made use of 'runs' in storytelling. These consist of a string of stock, formulaic descriptions, usually involving elaborate and highly decorative use of language: verbal gracenotes which invite comparisons between storytelling and the musical style of some travelling pipers:

> Out o' that they did hear the Black Dog coming from the other end of the world, with the oul' trees breaking and the young trees shaking, till they made the hard ground soft and the soft ground hard, till they drew spring-water through the green flags, until the cock crew in the morning, until the Black Dog of the Wild Forest had to retire back again![40]

Elsewhere, the same storyteller, Paddy Sherlock, gives a poetic account of the hero being chased by his enemies:

> They turned themselves into seven hawks, and they flew after the pigeon. The pigeon was right over the sea, and he looked back and he seen the seven hawks coming after him. He had nothing to do but to turn himself into an egg. He dropped right to the bottom of the sea, and they turned theirselves into seven whales, and they went down after him. They came so convenient to the egg that he came to the top of the water again, and the seven whales to the top after him. He turned

---

34. IFC 81: 280; also in G. Gmelch and B. Kroup, *To Shorten the Road*, p. 68.

35. IFC 81: 259; also in G. Gmelch and B. Kroup, *To Shorten the Road*, p. 60.

36. IFC 81: 21; also in G. Gmelch and B. Kroup, *To Shorten the Road*, p. 161.

37. See, for example, IFC 81: 281; also in G. Gmelch and B. Kroup, *To Shorten the Road*, p. 69.

38. Cf. similar material from the oral tradition of settled people in the subsection 'Legends of the Supernatural', pp. 1303–1304.

39. P. Mac Gréine, 'Further Notes on Tinkers' "Cant"', p. 302. For stories of the banshee see pp. 1303–1304.

40. S. Ó Duilearga, 'Paddy Sherlock's Stories', p. 59. Similar 'runs' are a prized feature of hero-tales in Irish, usually told by men. See the subsection 'International Folktales', pp. 1216, 1219.

himself into a pigeon again, and flew into the cloud . . .[41]

For sheer poetic exaggeration, however, the following description from one of John Power's stories of the hero striking a blow must reign supreme: 'Jack hit him. And whether he ever fell or not, I can't tell you. He's going yet, I think.'[42]

The fantastic is mixed with the familiar in John Power's account of the hero's brother setting out on a journey:

So, the son goes. And before he goes, he leaves a cup of water on the table. 'If anything happens me again twelve months,[43] that cup of water'll turn into human blood.' 'Righto,' says the brothers, 'off ye pop.'[44]

Not for the Traveller storyteller the safe use of language and convention. Instead, Traveller stories are full of energy, colour and movement. Which brings us back to our opening point, and brings the wheel full circle, as befits a Traveller.

41. S. Ó Duilearga, 'Paddy Sherlock's Stories', p. 14.
42. IFC 81: 66; also in G. Gmelch and B. Kroup, *To Shorten the Road*, p. 135.

43. i.e., within twelve months.
44. IFC 81: 27–8; also in G. Gmelch and B. Kroup, *To Shorten the Road*, p. 138.

ANONYMOUS

from:
PUCK OF THE DROMS: THE LIVES AND LITERATURE OF THE IRISH TINKERS (1985)

[The following fortune was recorded by Alen MacWeeney and Artelia Court from an anonymous travelling woman in County Wicklow, and published in Court's book *Puck of the Droms: The Lives and Literature of the Irish Tinkers* (Berkeley, Los Angeles, London: University of California Press, 1985), pp. 69–70. The date of collection is unclear. From the context, however, it seems likely that this piece was recorded in the late 1960s or early 1970s.

Like many other nomadic peoples, Travellers often told fortunes to supplement their incomes.   B. Ní F.]

TELLING A FORTUNE

Now, I can see by the straight line of your hand, Dear, that is your line of life. Your line of life runs wide and deep; you've got a long life to live. You're a person is not fond of rows or arguments, but you've got a hasty temper when your temper's risen. You're fond of brightness and bright surroundings, Dear, but you're a peculiar person, it's very hard to please you at times, isn't that so?

Your past life wasn't all sunshine for you, isn't that so? You have worked and toiled hard in the past, and you haven't gained much riches or prosperity through your past life. But there is brightness ahead of you, that you do not least expect.

You're a straightforward person, Dear, and you're fond of amusements. You're well liked, not for your appearances alone, but for your trustworthy and your honesty. Where you show your face once, you can always show it a second time, isn't that so?

Now, Dear, you had a little darkness in your past. You parted with one in your family that caused a drawback in your own life, isn't that so? You're a person that's fainthearted, you shed tears over slight matters that don't concern you at times. It's easy to worry you, if you can understand me plainer. But you don't have to worry, Dear. There is nothing to worry you. Your darkness will come, Dear, even that you worry. Otherwise, there is brightness.

You are mostly interested, and you're very anxious, that you'll have the pleasure of rocking a cradle, isn't that so? Well, you will have that pleasure, Dear, in the space of three. Your firstborn will be a baby boy, which will cause a lot of happiness between you and your husband both. More of your time will be taken up rocking a cradle than it will to go outdoors.

Now, I'm going to ask you a very serious question. You did have a relative abroad that you haven't been in close contact with for a number of years, isn't that so? Well, in a very short time you are to receive news from that particular person. Well, it is going to be hasty. I'm sorry to have to tell you the truth: you'll come in contact with this particular person through a death, Love. But through it you're going to gain a piece of money. Now you tell me the truth, there is a relative in your relationship bear a *J* in his initial, a gentleman? You'll have to sign large government forms and you'll make arrangements to divide this money with four. The first of the four is this particular gentleman. The money doesn't trouble you much. You're not anxious for money, but you are going to gain it through a death, Love. Outside that you don't have to be upset as you usually do be.

You don't have to take life seriously, Dear, it's only just come and go, as we call it. You're interested in the gentleman you changed your life for and he's interested in you, Dear, and that's all that counts in this life. Well, wish on something good anyhow.

Now, I want you to be straightforward and truthful in what I repeat to you. When you took that wish you didn't wish for eatables, drinkables, wearables, or money, isn't that so? No, you did not. Your particular wish is to be lucky and successful, to have luck with yourself, luck with your fiancé in life, and you do wish to rock that cradle, Dear, isn't that so? Isn't that particularly your wish?

You'll be very lucky, happy, and successful in the near future, Dear. You'll rock a cradle that will make both you and your fiancé very lucky.

Now, are you quite satisfied to part with this bit of silver here? You're quite happy about this bit of silver? Good enough, and I'm very thankful to you.

NORA 'ONEY' POWER

(1861–1937)

from:
IRISH FOLKLORE
COLLECTION MS NO. 81
(1930)

[The following folktale was recorded by Pádraig Mac Gréine from Nora 'Oney' Power near Ballinalee in County Longford, in 1930. It is a good example of a type of narrative usually referred to as *Märchen* by folklorists, meaning a tale of wonder, often with a strong magical content (see subsection 'International Folktales', pp. 1214–1262). These stories enjoyed great popularity across Europe from the Middle Ages, but had virtually disappeared from western Europe by the middle of the twentieth century.

The present story, AT 300,[1] was popular throughout Europe, and nowhere more than in Ireland, where several hundred versions have been recorded from oral tradition, showing it to be one of the most popular stories of its kind. This version contains a number of characteristics and themes often found in the stories of Oney and John Power.

They include an emphasis on the importance of mother-love and of religious practice, and the idea that generosity brings its own reward. The story also contains characteristically colourful use of language, including a number of traditional formulae and proverbial expressions. A number of stock storytelling motifs are also used, including the inversion of the well-known 'Cinderella' motif of the search for the owner of a shoe.

Another version of this story was recorded by Séamus Ó Duilearga from Paddy Sherlock, a travelling chimney sweep in County Clare, in the 1930s, and published in *Béaloideas*, vol. 30, 1962, pp. 2–10, under the title 'The Seven-year-old Child'; the present version can also be found in Gmelch and Kroup, *To Shorten the Road* (1985), pp. 88–95. From IFC 81: 169–90. B. Ní F.]

THE FIERY DRAGON

There was once and once and very good times, and 'twas neither my time nor your time, but 'twas somebody's time, there was a poor woman and she lived in a very lonely place in the forest. She had but one son, for her husband died when she was a very young widow [*sic*]. She kept on

1. A. Aarne and S. Thompson, *The Types of the Folktale.*

this gossoon[2] going to school, and doing the best she could for him, for to give him education, but the world couldn't do anything with him. All that was for him to be out with cows or with a country man. He couldn't learn no learning, nor he could do nothing.

So it happened to be that it came on, and when he was about twelve or thirteen, he was a very good gossoon. And there was a farmer near, and he came on, and he says, 'Well Mary, will you give me that gossoon, and I'll train him on, and make a ploughman out of him, and he'll be better nor he is with you. Aren't you killed feeding him and looking after him?' 'All right,' says she.

So bedad, when the gossoon came home, she told him.

'All right, Mother,' says he, 'sure, you won't be lonely?' (He was very fond of his mother.)

'All right,' says she, 'I won't.'

So the next morning he went up to the farmer, and the first thing he bought for him was a pair of boots and a suit of clothes. 'Now,' he says, 'again[3] you have them wore, you'll have the price of them earned from me.'

'It's all right,' he says. So begorras, he continued for a year and he was a very good boy, and another year. So it happened the third year the master died. The missus didn't want him, so she says: 'You'll have to go home to your mother.'

So home he comes. And he got a bit of money from her [his mistress] and thanked her. 'Now, Mother,' he says, 'I'll leave you this bit of money, and in the name of God, I'll go and seek my fortune. And I won't forget you, no matter where I be, so don't fret for me.'

'All right, Jack,' says she, 'God give you luck.' So, away grey with him.[4] 'Oh, Jack,' she says, 'wait till I roll up this bit of bread and meat for you, for it might be long enough till you get another bit.'

'All right, Mother,' says he. He rolled up the bit of bread, a bit of oaten bread, and a little bottle of milk, and away grey with him.

He came a long way and he never thought of the bit of bread. He began to get hungry, and he says, 'My mother gave me a bit of bread and a bottle.' So he sat down. He was going across a

field, and there was a rock in the middle of it. So he sat down and took out the bit of bread and the bottle and a little bit of piatae.[5] And 'twasn't long till a little bird flew up one side of him, and she says, 'Will you give me the crumbs that falls from your table?'

'Ah, the crumbs is too small. I'll give you the half of what I have.' So begorras, he broke the bit of bread and left the half of it over to her, and he says, 'What'll I give you the sup of milk with?'

'Look behind you there,' she says, 'and you'll see a cup.' So he did, and he lifted the grandest cup you ever seen in the world.

'Now Jack,' she says, 'look behind you and give me a drop of that water, the milk is little enough.' So he did, and he lifted her a drop in the cup.

'Now Jack,' she says, 'you're going to seek your fortune?'

'I am.'

'Well, you have a great lot of troubles and trials before you. Come over here and rise up[6] my wing, and take that feather that you see loose under my wing.' So he did.

'Now,' she says, 'put that around your waist.'

'How will I put a feather around my waist?' He put it to his waist and it went round him like a belt.

'Now Jack,' she says, 'wherever you go, don't leave that behind you. Always bring it with you, nor never give it to no one, if you get thousands for it. Whenever you're in any trouble, move a hole in the belt[7] and call upon me.'

'All right,' says Jack. 'Goodbye.'

Away grey poor Jack goes, and the belt around his waist, till he came to a farmer's place with a big white wall all round it and a lot of cows in the yard. 'Begorra, I might get work here,' says he. In he goes, and he met the master.

'Well, my good boy,' says he, 'what's troubling you?'

'I'm in want of a job,' says Jack.

'Can you mind cows?'

'I never done anything else,' says Jack.

'Well, there's twenty-four cows here, and I'll give you the job to look after them, but there was thirteen [boys] here before you, and they were all killed by giants that lives up in the wood.'

2. 'A young boy', from Fr. garçon via Irish garsún.
3. 'by the time'.
4. i.e. off he went.

5. potato.
6. Lift up.
7. Tighten the belt.

'What matter,' says Jack.

So the next morning, he got up, and says the master, 'Now Jack,' says he, 'take care would you go in to the wood, or the giants'll kill you.'

'Sorra fear,'[8] says Jack, and away grey with him, driving the cows before him.

'Twasn't long till he came to a gap in the wall, and he drove the cows out into the wood. And after a while, down comes a terrible big giant:

'Foo faw fum, I smell the blood of an Irishman. Be him dead, or be him alive, I'll have his bones for stepping stones, his puddings for my garters and his blood for my morning dram!'

'Ah, go easy, would you,' says Jack, 'as big as you are, I was no stable-boy in my own father's house.'

'Well,' he says, 'you'll have to fight me.'

'I may try to do that too,' says Jack.

'Well,' he says, 'which'll you fight me with: swords, or with gloves?'

'Ah well,' says Jack, 'I never knew how to fight with swords or gloves, but,' he says, 'I always had[9] collar and elbow, and whichever got the first fall in wrestling wins.'

'Oh, but I mean to kill you,' says the giant.

'Well,' says Jack, 'let the best cock crow on the dunkle.'[10]

Well, Jack tightened three holes in his belt. And the first twist, he had the giant on his knees, and the next, to his shoulders [in the ground].

'Bedad,' says he, 'you're a tough lad, Jack. Spare my life and I'll give you a Suit of Darkness, and a Sword of Sharpness.'

'Where is it?' says poor Jack.

'Behind that tree,' he says.

'Where'll I try it?' says Jack.

'On that butt of a tree there.'

'Devil a better butt nor your own head,' says Jack, giving it a sweep, and putting it in adams[11] up in the air.

'Oh, then, Jack, if I could get on the body again, you wouldn't get me off that easy.'

'Remember,' says Jack, 'I was never a sleepy fellow in the morning. I was always up early and knew my work.' So he put a small little whistle in his mouth, and here comes every one of the cows, out on the gap, and they bursting with milk.

8. 'No fear'.
9. Fought.
10. dunghill.
11. atoms (?).

Well, the master was looking out to see if there was any sign of Jack and the cows coming. 'Oh missus,' he says, 'here's the boy and the cows, and I don't know what we'll do, for they're bursting with milk.'

'Ah then, sure, I knew he'd come back,' says she, 'for I knew he was a good boy, and I seen him doing good turns when he got up this morning, and saying his prayers.'

'Well Jack,' says she, 'how did you get on?'

'All right,' says he.

[They] milked the cows, and, sure, there was hardly vessels enough to hold all the milk they had.

Now, the next morning, Jack was away for himself. And [the farmer] says, 'Now Jack, take care would you let the cows into that domain.'

'Ah no,' says Jack. So he started, and let them go in at the gap. And after a half an hour or so, here comes a giant, and the roars of him shook the whole domain: 'Foo faw fum, I smell the blood of an Irishman. Be him dead or be him alive, I'll have his bones for stepping stones, his puddings for garters, and his blood for my morning dram!'

'Ah, be easy with yourself,' says Jack.

'Well,' he says, 'are you the little impudent cur that killed my brother yesterday? I'll squeeze you between my finger and thumb.'

'Ah, be easy with yourself,' says Jack.

'Well,' he says, 'what way will you fight me?'

'I'll fight you,' says he, 'collar and elbow, what I learned in my youthful days.'

'Ha ha! You villain! You used that on my poor brother,' says he.

'Well, if I didn't use it on him, he'd use it on me.' Jack gave his belt a pull, and to it with them. And the first twist he gave him, he landed him on his two knees, and the second landed him to his shoulders.

'Oh Jack,' he says, 'spare me my life, and I'll give you a Suit of Darkness and a Sword of Sharpness, and as much money as will do you your life.'

'Where is it?' says Jack.

'Hanging behind that tree.' So he got it.

'What'll I try it on?' says he.

'That old stump of a tree.'

'Your own two old heads is the best.' (I forgot to tell that this giant had two heads!)

So he gave a sweep and knocked the two heads off him, clean at the shoulder. One of them tried to get back, but he gave it a kick and sent it adams up in the air.

'Oh then, Jack,' he says, 'if I got on the body again, all the Jacks of your name wouldn't take me off of it.'

'You done your best,' says Jack. And he put the little whistle in his mouth, and the cows came, and off Jack went home with them. And there wasn't vessels to hold all the milk.

Well, the next morning, to make a long story short and a short one merry, away grey with him and the cows. And he drove them in again. And he wasn't long within, till up comes a big giant with three heads on him. Well, he shook the forest! He shook the castle! He shook all![12] Oh dear! Oh dear!

'You're too big for one pinch of snuff, and you're too little for two,' says he to Jack, 'but I'll squeeze you between my finger and thumb.'

'Your brothers said that too,' says Jack. Jack gave a squeeze to the belt, and begorras, he was getting it hard, so he shouted, 'Help! Help!'

'Jack! Squeeze, squeeze!' says the little bird. And Jack touched the belt, and begorras, he got the giant to his shoulders.

'Jack, spare me my life, and I'll give you my castle and a half a million.'

'I'd rather have my own house,' says Jack.

'Well, I'll give you a Suit of Darkness and a Sword of Sharpness.'

'Where is it?' says Jack.

'Behind that tree.'

Over he went and got it. He made a clout of the sword at the first head, and the second, but he got it very hard to knock the three of them off. And wasn't one of the heads trying to get back, when the little bird shouted out of the tree.

'Oh Jack, Jack!' she says, 'look out, look out!'

Jack looked, and he made a stroke at the head, and knocked smithereens out of it.

So Jack blew his whistle and the cows came, and they went home.

'Jack,' says the master, 'do you ever go in to the giants' wood?'

'Arrah, what'd bring me there?' says Jack.

'Well,' says he, 'there's three giants that used to give three roars every day, and I didn't hear them these last few days.'

'I don't know anything about them,' says Jack.

So the next morning, Jack started, and left the cows in the wood and went up to the castle. He went in, and there was a big old woman at the fire, and a big long tooth coming out of her mouth, and making a rope for her body, and a stick to stir the stirabout with.

'Oh ho! Good morrow to you, you villain. You're the spalpeen,'[13] she says, 'that killed my three poor gossoons; one a hundred, and the other two hundred, and the other three hundred. But I'm the colleen[14] of four hundred that'll settle you. I've a nail here, and if I get one scratch at you, you'll never forget it all the days of your life.' So she made a crack at Jack with the old tooth. And as soon as she did, he drew a Sword of Sharpness.

'Well,' he says, 'I don't like to kill you, but I must do away with you.'

'Don't come near me, or I'll give you a prod of this that'll poison you,' and she took up the long stick of a tooth that she was stirring the stirabout with. Jack made a crack of the sword at her and knocked the tooth out of her head, and all her enchantments fell away from her.

'Jack,' she says, 'spare me my life and I'll be your humble servant all the days of my life.'

'I'll have nothing to do with you,' says he, pitching her out in the yard. 'You can stay abroad there and do as you like. Anyone that likes can come and see you, for I wouldn't have the sin of killing you.'

So away grey with him. And he went over to the barn, and in the first was a Cloak of Darkness, and a Sword of Sharpness, and a lovely black horse. The cloak and the horse was for the giants flying through the air and all over the world, and they could go a hundred miles, maybe, in an hour. He went into the other [barn], and he saw the same, and into the next, and saw the same — one exceeding the other. One was a red [cloak], the other a blue, and the other a white.

So it happened, he came home in the evening. And the man says to him, 'Why Jack, the giants must be dead or sick. I don't hear any shouts this evening.'

'Ah, I don't know,' says Jack, 'I never seen any of them.'

---

12. Mac Gréine adds a note here: 'Told in tones of wonder by storyteller.'

13. A migratory labourer, from Irish *spailpín*.

14. A young girl, from Irish *cailín*.

'Oh, Jack,' he says, 'I nearly forgot to tell you. There's going to be a great fiery dragon tomorrow, and will you come to it?'

'And what's that, sir?' says he.

'Oh, there's a lady going to be devoured with [by] a fiery dragon. And it'll be the awfulest scene in the wide world, for they'll be coming,' says he, 'from all over the world to see the lady devoured.'

'It would be cruel,' says Jack. 'And how could she be saved?' says Jack.

'Oh, if there was anyone there that'd fight the fiery dragon. You ought to come, Jack,' says he.

'Indeed, I'll not,' says he. 'I'll go and mind my cows. It'd be more in my way. I hired with you to mind your cows, and to be honest and faithful, and I'm not going to do any other thing.'

So when they were gone, Jack went up to his castle and got out his Cloak of Darkness and his Sword of Sharpness, and mounted a horse, and away to where the lady was. He came flying down and went over to where she was tied in an iron chair.

'Well, my lady, you're waiting for your end,' he says.

'I am,' she says.

'Will you let me lay my head on your lap?' he says.

'Why not?' she says. And he did. And when he left his head down, didn't she take a little scissors she had, and cut a lock of his hair and put it in her pocket.

So, here comes the fiery dragon [the next day]. And as soon as ever he did, Jack stood up, and into it with Jack and the fiery dragon. So to it with them both, fighting, and they kept at it from ten o'clock in the morning till nine that night. And they put stones and scraws flying, and bored holes in the ground, but neither of them got the better. So, they put it [the fight] back till the next morning, at ten o'clock. So the lady was let home till tomorrow morning.

And now, we'll follow Jack and leave them all. Jack flew home through the sky and was at home before the master, and had the cows home and the half of them milked, when the master and missus came home.

'Oh Jack, in all the beautiful places ever you seen or known! Didn't there come a beautiful man dressed in armour, on a beautiful horse. And he flew down out of the sky, and here he dropped beside the lady. And he fought the fiery dragon, and he's to come at ten o'clock tomorrow.[15] You'll have to come, Jack.'

'Sorra one foot I'll go,' says Jack. 'What an eegit[16] I'd be, looking at foolish things while I have my house to mind. I'm faithful to the bargain I made with you, till you'd put me away.'

'Well, I'll never say a word to you, Jack.'

'Ah, I'd rather stay where I am,' says Jack.

'Oh, all right,' says he [the master].

So they went away. And they weren't long gone, till Jack went up to the castle, and got another horse and the second cloak — scarlet — and flew like a bird right to where the lady was.

'Oh, good morning, Miss,' says he.

'Oh, good morning most kindly. It's a bad place your feet brought you.'

'Well, bad or not now, I'll try and get success for you.'

'Oh, I wouldn't like to see you killed.'

'Don't fret,' says he.

Here, didn't the fiery dragon come, and into it with them. And they made the hard ground soft and the soft ground hard, until ten o'clock that night, without any of them getting the better. So they put it back to ten o'clock the next morning. And he got up to go. And he had slippers on him, and didn't she pull one of them off his foot. And he flew up over the whole lot of them, and away grey with poor Jack.

Now, Jack was home, and had everything done and the cows half milked, when the master and missus got home. And the master says, 'Now Jack, you'll have to come tomorrow. I don't care what anyone says, you'll have to come. For I couldn't bear to see you at home without seeing such a wonderful sight. Ah, such a beautiful sight! Sure, it must be an angel, coming down out of the sky, horse and all. You'll have to come tomorrow and see it all.'

'Ah, indeed then, I won't,' says Jack. 'I'd sooner be out minding my cows, and watching the little birds flying about and courting, and seeing my cows eating the grass.'

'Oh, please yourself, Jack,' says he.

So the next day, they started. And sure, Jack was there before them, in his blue cloak. And this day, he killed the dragon. Just when he was going

15. Mac Gréine adds: 'Related in tones of wonder.'
16. idiot.

away, didn't the lady pull the glove out of his hand. And Jack flew up in the air and away home, and had the cows milked when the master got back.

'Oh Jack,' he says, 'the dragon's killed and you'll have to come tomorrow, for the lady is going to marry the fellow that killed him. For she has a bit of his hair, and his slipper and glove.'

'Sorra go I'll go,' says he, and he wouldn't.

Well, all the great men was there [the next day], and they doing all sorts, but the glove or shoe wouldn't fit. The trial went on the next day, and was just the same. The next morning, says the master, 'Well Jack, no matter what happens, high up or low down, you'll have to come today.'

'Arrah, where would the like of me be going, a poor cowboy like me?'

They kept at him, and in the heel of the reel he agreed. And off they started on the car, or trap, or whatever they had.

When they got there, there was fellows cutting bits off their heels, and cutting off their big toe, trying to get on the shoe, and cutting bits off their fingers, trying to get on the glove, but 'twas no good. Poor Jack was standing behind, with the corner of his shirt sticking out of his trousers and his sleeve out of his coat,[17] and no one passing any remarks on him.[18]

The lady saw him. 'Come over here, my man.' He came over. She asked him to put out his foot, and when he did, the shoe flew on it, and the glove flew on his hand, and the lock of hair to his head. Them all gathered round and looked at Jack. So he asked leave to go for an hour, and they let him.

He came flying back with his three cloaks and his horse and swords, and landed in the middle of them all. He told them all that his good luck came from a little bird, because he divided what he had with her. 'And never,' says he, 'refuse help to the poor.' He brought over his old mother, and got married to the lady. And they all went to live in the giants' castle.

So, put down the kettle and make tay, and if they don't live happy, that we may.

from:
IRISH FOLKLORE COLLECTION MS NO. 1498 (1932)

[The following story was recorded from Oney Power by Pádraig Mac Gréine in 1932. Stories of encounters with the fairies are rarely told in the first person as is the case here. The story contains a good deal of the Travellers' own language, or cant, and offers an excellent illustration of the way in which the skilled Traveller storyteller could adapt a story to suit the circumstances of her own lifestyle. Here, the storyteller approaches the enchanted house because she and her family are in need of straw as bedding for the night. The story also illustrates the fears and anxieties inherent in life on the road. Tom Munnelly has written that: '"The Enchanted Man" captures well the aura of fear generated by such encounters (real, or imagined to be real) and tells us much of the sense of isolation felt by travellers on strange or hostile circuits.'[1] The story finishes with the commonly found motif of fairy goods disappearing on the morning after the supernatural encounter. From IFC 1498: 2–13.[2]   B. Ní F.]

THE STRANGE ADVENTURE OF THE STORYTELLER WITH THE ENCHANTED MAN

Well, this is only a few words I'm going to tell you about the beginning of my life. When I got married first I was very poor. I had neither ways or means to go travel, and myself and my husband went away a-through the country, and we came on to a place called Frenchpark in the Co. Roscommon. And to be sure, we met a lot of travellers. Some of them was my friends, and more of them was his friends. So bedad, we waited a while, and took a sup of drink — 'twas cheap them times, only tuppence a pint — and 'twas easy getting a drink for two.

So begorras, the night was coming on, and says I, 'We have very bad ways [of travelling],' thinking of the long way we had to go.

---

17. Torn out.
18. No one taking any notice of him.

1. T. Munnelly, Introduction to vol. 7 of Aileen L'Amie's 'The Irish Travelling People', p. 4.
2. Also published in *Béaloideas*, vol. 3 (1932), 294–8. Notes to the story are almost all by Pádraig Mac Gréine, taken from the original manuscript of the story.

'Oh,' says they, 'we'll be all going now in a minute.' So begorras, they got another drink, and we all came on out, about four miles from the town to a place called Fairymount, one side between Castlerea and Frenchpark. They used to inhabit an old empty house there, so we all came — a whole family party — there that night. But the devil a wisp of bedding we had. So I didn't know what to do so. 'Mary, will you come?' says I, 'will you *tóri* with my *jeel* for a *milk* of *grisk*?'[3]

'I will,' she says. 'What'll you do with the *goya*?'[4]

'Ah, I'll leave it with your *naderum* till I *tóri arais*.'[5]

So away grey with us till we got out on the road, and says I, 'Where'll we go, Mary? This is my first visit here and by God if I live till morning, it'll be my last. For,' says I, 'it's the wildest-looking country ever I seen.'

'Well, sure we'll go down here.'

'We'll go down,' says I, 'in the name of the Father, Son and Holy Ghost. We'll turn to the left.' So down we goes, and sure if we were going since we wouldn't meet a house or a home.

'Ah God, I'll go no farther,' says I, and I stood, 'till I get the lie of the ground.' And I seen the beautifulest white gate that ever you left an eye upon. And I looked up, and what did I see but a whole lot of lights, beautiful lights. 'God,' says I, 'this must be a farmer's place. This is like a place we'd get a bed, surely.'

So up we goes, and we came into the yard. There was a light in every window, and we didn't know what door to go to. 'Ah,' says I, 'we'll go to this one with the knocker on it.' I was always a little bit forward. I went to the door and I knocked it, and the voice says inside, 'Come in.'

Says I, 'God save all here.'

'God hear your prayer,' says she. And says I, 'I came up, missus, to see if you could oblige me with a wisp to make a bed tonight?'

'Wait till the boss comes in,' she says, 'and he'll get it for you.'

'Thanks.'

'Sit down,' she says.

We sat down, and we were there for ten minutes, and there was a big pot of piates[6] in the corner, and they steaming.

'Ah *Dhalún*,' says the *lacín*, 'if I could get a few of them *cullions*! I'm *corrib'd* with the *clórusc*.'[7]

'Oh,' says I, '*ní jésh*. If you *salc* any of them we'll be *corrib'd*.[8] If you're caught,' says I, 'we'll *bog* no *grisk*.'[9]

So begorras, 'twas all right now, the door got a knock, and in comes a fine big man, as big as today and tomorrow, and he says, 'Goodnight, women. Oh missus, you have visitors.'[10]

'Oh, I have,' she says, 'two poor women that came up for a bed. Two poor women,' she says, 'that came up for a bed.'

So begorra-sa-war, 'Mollie,' says he, 'did you give them anything to ate?'

'No sir,' says she, 'not till you'd come in.'

'Well,' he says, 'give them out the spuds.'

So begor, the big pot was brought over afore him, and she left down the basket, and he threwn out about two stone of spuds. Poor Mary, God help her, thought she'd never get enough of the spuds.

So he stood looking at us, and says Mary, 'Oh, this is a queer *céna*.[11] We'll be *corrib'd* tonight.'

'Oh, *ní jésh*,' says I, 'but don't *tári*. The *gleoch* has a *gami* appearance.'[12]

'Wait now,' he says, 'till I get yous some "kitchen".'[13]

So begorras, he got a big knife and leaped up on top of the table. And I looked up, and what did I see but a big dog, and he hanging down out of the top of the house. So here he pulls out a cork, and let down the full of a plate of lard, and stuck up the cork again. 'Twas only the hide of the dog was there, and it full of lard. So, when I used to ate a piate, I used to let the lard fall on me lap, but Mary ate the whole lot. I was a bit cleverer than Mary.

'Oh Mary,' says I, 'this is a *céna ly*.'[14] So she was laughing.

'Don't *tári*,' says I, 'or we're *corrib'd*.'[15] I was trying to keep her from laughing, but the devil wouldn't keep her from it.

---

3. 'Will you come with me for a bundle of straw?'
4. child.
5. 'I'll leave it with your mother till I come back.'
6. potatoes.
7. 'Ah God,' says the girl, 'if I could get a few of them potatoes! I'm dead with the hunger.'
8. 'Oh,' says I, 'no. If you steal any of them we'll be killed.'
9. 'we'll get no straw'.
10. Mac Gréine tells us, in a note, that the storyteller shouts this in a high-pitched voice.
11. house.
12. 'Oh no,' says I, 'but don't talk. The man has a bad (or queer) appearance.'
13. Flavouring for the potatoes.
14. A queer house.
15. 'Don't talk,' says I, 'or we'll be killed.'

So at any rate now, when we had enough ate, I said, 'We have enough ate now, God bless you.'

'Well,' he says, 'eat enough now, and give the house a good name. Wait till I get you a good drink of buttermilk.' So he went over to the dresser and he pulled the cork out of a bottle, and there was nothing in it, and he pulled the cork out of another jar and there was nothing in it. He pulled the cork out of a third one, and the milk ran up out of it, it was so sour. So he filled an old noggin of buttermilk and he handed it to Mary, and Mary took a good drink out of it. So he filled it and handed it to me, and I pretended to drink it and let it run down on my apron. I was afraid to drink it for I knew he was an enchanted man. So he took it, and it was half empty.

'Did you drink it?' he says.

'I did,' says I. So he threw the milk into my face.

'If you haven't it inside, you'll have it outside,' he says.

He knew well I didn't drink it, and he knew Mary did.

So I took up my old apron and wiped myself the best way I could, and he says to me, 'Are you long married?'

'I'm about a year and a half, sir,' says I.

'Did you ever ride a horse?' says he.

''Deed, I did not, sir,' says I. 'I wish to God I had a horse.'

'Or an ass?'

'I have neither one or the other, sir,' says I.

'And what have you?'

'The high road and my chances.'

'Well,' he says, 'you'll come out and ride my grey mare now.'

'Now,' says I, 'the *gleoch'll corrib* my *jeel*, he's not *tari'n* to your *jeel* at all.'[16]

So it was all right now, he brought me out and he called the little white mare out. He says, 'Come on out.' So she came out. 'Get up there,' he says.

'Ah no, sir,' says I.

'By this and by that,' he says, 'if you don't get up there, you'll be no more alive, and you'll never see a sight of your husband again.'

I got up on the horse at any rate, and he [*sic*] brought me through the whole fields, till he came to where there was a drain. And didn't the horse fall. So the horse fell, but I didn't fall off.

'Oh, that God Almighty may bless us and save us,' says I, '*gur a mo chaistin.*'[17]

So the little grey horse turned round and he says, 'That's a good word you said. In the beginning and you coming,[18] you started "In name of the Father, Son and Holy Ghost", and that's what saved you.'

So he got up and he let me down, and back we went to the house where we were, and there was Mary and the two bundles of straw.

'*Orra Dhálún seek súdil!*[19] Where were you, and where'd the *gleoch misli?*'[20]

'Oh, don't *tári*,' says I.

So we started, and we were no length going back.

'Begor, yous weren't long away,' says they. Sure I thought 'twas a long time.

'Did the child quit crying?' says I.

'She never wakened since you went,' says she. So we divided the straw with three or four other travellers, and went to bed, and when we got up in the morning, there wasn't a bit of the straw under any of us. But I forgot what the little horse said. 'You were in an enchanted house,' says he, 'and that man was the King of the Fairies.[21] And any time,' he says, 'that ever you go astray, think on me,' he says, 'and say "God be with the time I was on the little grey horse", and you'll be all right. And any time you're in need of anything, I'll give you a gift to call on me, and you'll get it. And now,' says he, 'God be with you.'

And I came home and we divided the straw, and in the morning we hadn't a wisp under us. So says I, 'Musha, *Sréni*,' says I, '*tori* down the *tobera* till we *súni* the big *céna* we were in last night.'[22] So down we went.

'Arra, *mídil cena* there, *beoir*,'[23] says she.

'Oh, *Dhálún*,' says I.

'Oh, come on,' says Mary, 'he was a *gleoch ly*.'[24]

---

16. 'Now,' says I, 'the man will kill me, he's not talking to you at all.'
17. Meaning unclear.
18. 'When you were coming.'
19. 'Good God Almighty!'
20. 'where did the man go?'
21. Note that the women's adventure is set in a place called Fairymount.
22. 'Musha, Mary,' says I, 'come down the road till we see the big house we were in last night.'
23. 'Arra, devil a house there, woman.'
24. 'He was a queer fellow.'

So from that day to this, me and Mary has the story to tell about one another. Only I went through it, for when I was on the horse, she was getting the straw. So there's the old story now,

and it's a good story, for not one word of that but's the truth, for I went through it.

So put down the kettle and make tay, and if they weren't happy, that we may.

NELLIE JOYCE

(1942–92)

from:
TRAVELLER WAYS,
TRAVELLER WORDS (1992)

[The legend of the old woman who could turn herself into a hare is very common in Ireland (another version, from a settled woman, is given on p. 1308).[1] It illustrates a number of folk beliefs, including one that such hares could suck milk from a cow, stealing both the milk and the owner's butter profit. In an age when milk and butter-making were of considerable economic importance, this was a serious matter. The offending hare was often hunted in the manner described here. Usually, however, the story ends with the discovery of the hare's true nature and of the witchery involved. The version reproduced here is unusual in that it ends with the death of most of the hunters.

This story was recorded from Nellie Joyce in Blanchardstown, County Dublin, in 1991 by the Dublin Travellers Education and Development Group, and published in G. Ó Riain (ed.), *Traveller Ways, Traveller Words*, pp. 193–4. B. Ní F.]

THE ENCHANTED HARE

An' she[2] said that there was three Travellin' men one time an' they went out huntin'. This was a tradition because they were doin' it for their way o' life. They use' to eat the hares accordin' as they'd kill them.

So they went out huntin' in this land one day. An' they met a farmer. They couldn't rise any hares. So they met a farmer. An' he said to them, 'Is the dogs any good?' An' one o' the men said,

'Yeah, they are good dogs,' he said, 'is there any hares about?'

So he said, 'There's one hare in this field but your dogs won't kill him.'

He said, 'How do you make that out?'

He said, 'Well he's here in years an' no dog ever kilt him. He hasn't been caught yet.' So the Travellin' man said, 'Well show us where he is an' we'll find out very shortly whether he'll get him or not.'

So he brought them out to a bush, which was very unusual. Because you'd never get a hare in a bush. You always get them in a form in the middle of a field. An' he shook the bush an' a white hare jumped out. So the dogs took after the hare an' they coorsed[3] him 'round the field. But they didn't ketch him. One dog happened to ket up[4] on him an' took a bite out of his hip. An' the Travellin' men knew that the dog cotch[5] him but had to let go again.

So he disappeared into the walls of a house an' the min[6] followed him in an' they looked for him but they couldn't find any hare. So they searched around and in the corner of an old wall, it used to be a house one time, an' there was an old woman sittin' down. She was all in black.

And he said, 'Excuse me, madam, did you happen to see a hare comin' in here?'

She said, 'No hare came in here. Get out of here at wanst![7] You're not supposed to be here.'

So he said, 'Well, we're not doin' any harm, mam,' he said. 'I hope we're not doin' any harm,' he said. 'All we want to do is find the hare.'

1. See also Éilís Ní Dhuibhne, '"The Old Woman as Hare": Structure and Meaning in an Irish Legend', *Folklore*, vol. 104 (1993), pp. 77–85.
2. The storyteller's mother.
3. coursed (chased).
4. catch up.
5. caught.
6. men.
7. at once.

She said, 'There isn't any hare in here, you better layve.'[8]

So the dogs was barkin' very viciously around where the woman was sittin' down. An' one of the men walked over an' picked her up. And when he did there was a pool o' blood where she was sittin'.

So there was a bite gone out of her hip an' her big long black skirt. An' they knew right away what was wrong. They knew it was somethin' to do with witchery. An' she said, 'Get out of here because this time twelve months neither you nor your dogs'll hunt.' An' one o' the men turned around to look for the farmer to aks [sic] his advice. But he was gone as well. He wasn't there. So be God the min got an awful fright an' they flew home an' the dogs.

The next mornin' they got up one o' the min was snow white in the hair. An' the three dogs were dead. But the other two men didn't live very long after that. They died also. One man lived for years. The man with the grey hair. But he had the grey hair 'til he died. It never changed. It's an actual true story.

8. leave

PATRICK STOKES

(c. 1940–   )

from:
PUCK OF THE DROMS: THE LIVES AND LITERATURE OF THE IRISH TINKERS (1985)

[The legend of the man who married the mermaid is known in many parts of the Atlantic seaboard of north-west Europe. Versions in Irish and English are widespread in the oral tradition of coastal areas of Ireland, and folkloristic analysis has distinguished several regional types among them.[1] Seamus Heaney's poem, 'Maighdean Mara', based on an Irish-language version from County Donegal, underlines the metaphorical richness of stories like this one as it mourns the suicide by drowning of a young married woman.[2] Most versions of the 'Man Marries Mermaid' story depict the woman who recovers her stolen cloak as gratefully escaping from the husband who has captured her, regretting only the loss of her children. In this telling by a man, however, the woman has no wish to leave.

The story is related to the commonly held belief that certain families were descended from a union between a man and a mermaid, or between a man and a seal. There are several surnames to which this belief is strongly attached, including Conneely in the west of Ireland and O'Shea in County Kerry.[3]

Alen MacWeeney and Artelia Court recorded this story from Patrick Stokes in the late 1960s, later publishing it in *Puck of the Droms*, pp. 63–4. Patrick Stokes would have been described officially as a tinsmith and labourer. He described himself thus: 'Some of them calls us Travellers, Gypsies, or mumpers. Maybe, itinerants, tramps, or wasters. I heard them say no-goods, scoundrels, and *nackers*. But I'd say we're *minkers*, puck o' the droms. But you are what you are.'[4]   B. Ní F.]

THE MAN WHO MARRIED THE MERMAID

They say this is true, about this man one time and he fought a mermaid. This man was a farmer and every morning he used to see this mermaid abroad[5] in the grass field. Every morning she come, you know, eating grass or combing her hair, and he seen her there. And he fell in love with her. 'I'll get you,' says he, 'longer nor shorter.' She was a lovely looking girl.

1. See Bo Almqvist, 'Of Mermaids and Marriages. Séamus Heaney's "Maighdean Mara" and Nuala Ní Dhomhnaill's "An Mhaighdean Mhara" in the Light of Folk Tradition', *Béaloideas*, vol. 58 (1990), pp. 1–74.
2. Seamus Heaney, *Selected Poems 1965–1975* (London: Faber and Faber, 1980), pp. 146–7.
3. See David Thompson, *The People of the Sea: A Journey in Search of the Seal Legend* (London: Turnstile, 1954; rev. Barrie and Rockliff, 1965; repr. Paladin, 1980), and Bairbre Ní Fhloinn, 'Tadhg, Donncha and Some of their Relations: Seals in Irish Oral Tradition', in P. Lysaght, S. Ó Catháin and D. Ó hÓgáin (eds), *Islanders and Water Dwellers* (Dublin: DBA Publications Ltd, 1996), pp. 223–45.
4. In A. Court, *Puck of the Droms*, p. 87.
5. out.

One day he come along, anyway, and he went down behind the deal ditch[6] and he started to steal and steal and steal down a-through the field, 'til he got to the turn in the river that run through the field. She seen him then and she run to the river, but he grabbed her. Into it with the two of them, they fell in the water, and they fought, but he bested her. And, begad, he brings her up to the house. He takes the cloak of scale off her then. Her feet was only stuck into this cloak like a fish's tail, but she was a plain woman within. He takes the cloak and he hides it above in the thatch, and she never knew where he hid it.

He gets the girl anyways, and he loved her. She had a family then, three in number, and she lived happy. It was about ten years after, and one day the little girl, the youngest, come to her and says, 'Oh Mammy, do you know what I seen today? I was atop,' says she, 'up in the loft and I seen a remarkable sort of thing with scales on it, something, now, like a fish.'

'Where'd you see it?' says the mother.

'Up in the loft,' says the child.

Up the woman goes and she gets it. It was in a little loft in this thatched house, where only just the man was used to go. Well, you see, she had to get it, and once she got it she was enchanted again, as soon as she got the cloak of scale. She had to go back to the sea then, and the roaring of her and the crying of her as she didn't want to go! She brought the three childer with her down to the strand, and she took them into the water.

Well, your man was above ploughing the field, and he seen them going down. Ah, he left ploughing and helter-skelter with him to the river, but he wasn't fast enough. Just when he got there they were turned into mermaids, all four of 'em!

The woman didn't want to ever find this cloak, you know. When she got into the sea she calls back to him, 'For all those years I'm married to you, and you never did away with me cloak! Why didn't ya burn it? Now, sure, we're separated same as the first day.'

Then she went away out in the sea and sat on top of a big rock and started combing her hair and, sure, singing. 'Come in,' she says. 'Come in to me.' And she kept calling to him to come.

He'd see her every morning on this rock, but if he'd ha' go in to her she'd have drownded him, you see. And it'd be a couple of mile out to sea anyway, and he couldn't get to her.

6. 'A ditch . . . surmounted by a wooden barrier or fence of boards or sticks' (A. Court, *Puck of the Droms*, p. 256).

ELLIE CARR

(1912–2002)

from:
TRAVELLER WAYS, TRAVELLER WORDS (1992)

[In *The Year in Ireland* (Cork: Mercier Press, 1972), Kevin Danaher points out that the first day of May was one of the four most important festivals of the year in Irish tradition. It marked the beginning of summer and many of the customs and traditions associated with it are concerned with the safety and fertility of the growing crops. May Day and May Eve were also believed to be a time of great supernatural activity. The present piece illustrates the overlap and interplay found throughout Irish folk tradition between pre-Christian/non-Christian and Christian traditions.

This piece was recorded from Ellie Carr in County Longford in 1991 by the Dublin Travellers Education and Development Group. We are told that the narrator has a great deal of information on the customs and traditions of travelling people in general. G. Ó Riain (ed.), *Traveller Ways, Traveller Words*, p. 86. B. Ní F.]

THE MAY DEW

Well a May mornin', we'd all get out an' wash our faces in the dew. The May dew, the mornin' dew. You'd want to be out aroun' five o'clock though. An' we'd get the shout from me mother, God resht her. An' all th'ould people an May Day, we'd have the tints[1] then covered with flowers for

1. tents.

the Blessed, honourin' the Blessed Virgin.[2] That's all ever I knew now. 'Tis lucky t'honour the Blessed Virgin an' you'd never get your skin peeled. Your skin wouldn't get peeled for the whole hot summer 'round about now. And do you know if you were out at four o'clock of a May mornin' you'd see the sun an' moon dancin'. And they said that never shall be. And ya would. I never saw it. I'd be runnin' for the grass! I might never get out at four o'clock you know for to see it. But 'twas the truth though. I knew people that did see it. They looked out an' their caravans in the winda, in the back winda, people that was wakened and they seen the sun and moon dance. But that's the only people I ever heard talk o' seein' it, so now.

2. Compare Rosaleen Ferguson's account of throwing primroses on the house roof 'for luck and plenty', p. 1211.

CHRISSIE WARD

(1947–)

from:
PAVEE PICTURES (1991)

[Chrissie Ward's poetry echoes the oral storytelling with which she grew up, and comments on Travellers' contemporary lives. These poems appear in Derek Speirs, *Pavee Pictures* (Dublin: Dublin Travellers Education and the Development Group, 1991), pp. 23, 48.   B. Ní F.]

Woman's Work

Washing my clothes, scrubbing away.
They are so dirty, I can't get them clean.
Dragging cold water from the tap,
Hard it is to live a life like that.
I can't get any bubbles, it seems so strange
All of this washing powder washes the same.
Breaking my nails.
Bleach destroying my clothes.
What shall I do, nobody knows.
Wasting my time and a pain in my back.
These bones in my knees go crack crack.
Hurrying to boil dinner, wasting too much time.
Scrubbing those clothes seems like miles.
Washing is over and no further on.
Tomorrow I travel the same road again.

Musha Mary Daughter

Musha Mary daughter since I came to this city
My goats won't milk no more,
Or my chicks won't lay no more,
There's not a tree to tie my mare.
Traveller women bare necked
Their skirts up to their knees.

My poor Johnny, his wife has him starved
With tins of red beans.
Women spend their time putting on that yoke
    called make up.
No older women to talk to,
If I don't get out of here
Surely I'll lose him
Sure I cursed the day that I moved away
From that narrow country road.

Oh dear God give me the power to go back
To my little narrow country road,
My lonely campfire on a summer's night,
Watching bright stars from Heaven on high.
Some stars fly so fast
They're souls gone in the past.

Mother tells stories in the dark black roads
Poking the stick fire, afraid of the ghost.
Talking of hell, the Lord up above.
Me waiting to lie at my mother's toes.

In the night, her heart was so full of fear
Swearing from her eyebrows, wishing morning
    was here
Morning comes and the sun breaks through
    green trees
The night still in our eyes, Oh how it feels.
Think of last night, of dreams of hell
And angry mad ghosts.

Biographies/Bibliographies

Nora 'Oney' Power

LIFE. Traveller storyteller Oney Power was born in Boyle, County Roscommon, in 1861. Her name before she married was Ward — one of the most common of all Traveller names in the west of Ireland. Oney Power died in 1937.

CHIEF WRITINGS. George Gmelch and Ben Kroup, *To Shorten the Road* (Dublin: O'Brien Press, 1978); Pádraig Mac Gréine, 'Further Notes on Tinkers' "Cant",' *Béaloideas*, vol. 3 (1932), pp. 290–303.

Nellie Joyce

LIFE. Nellie Joyce, a Traveller and a storyteller, was born in Ennis, County Clare, in 1942, and died in 1992, leaving fourteen children.

CHIEF WRITINGS. Gearóid Ó Riain (ed.), *Traveller Ways, Traveller Words* (Dublin: Pavee Point Publications, 1992).

Patrick Stokes

LIFE. Born *c.* 1940, Patrick Stokes grew up in a Traveller family in various parts of the west of Ireland, and worked as a tinsmith and labourer. In the 1960s Alen MacWeeney and Artelia Court interviewed him and recorded some of his storytelling. No further information is available.

CHIEF WRITINGS. Artelia Court, *Puck of the Droms: The Lives and Literature of the Irish Tinkers* (Berkeley, Los Angeles, London: University of California Press, 1985).

Ellie Carr

LIFE. Born in 1912, Traveller Ellie Carr, also known as Mrs Ellen Lawrence, was consulted in County Longford in 1991 by the Dublin Travellers Education and Development Group, and contributed a great deal of information on the customs and traditions of travelling people to the project published as *Traveller Ways, Traveller Words*. She died tragically in a fire in her house in Longford town in March 2002.

CHIEF WRITINGS. Gearóid Ó Riain (ed.), *Traveller Ways, Traveller Words* (Dublin: Pavee Point Publications, 1992).

Chrissie Ward

LIFE. Poet Chrissie Ward, a Traveller, was born in 1947 and spent much of her childhood in Northern Ireland. She has been writing and publishing poetry for a number of years. Her sister, Nan Joyce, features in the subsection 'Life Stories', pp. 1205–1208.

CHIEF WRITINGS. Derek Speirs, *Pavee Pictures* (Dublin: Dublin Travellers Education and Development Group, 1991); Gearóid Ó Riain (ed.), *Traveller Ways, Traveller Words* (Dublin: Pavee Point Publications, 1992).

ANGELA BOURKE and PATRICIA LYSAGHT, *Editors*

Legends of the Supernatural

Legends differ from folktales in purporting to be true.[1] Instead of the far away and long ago of folktale, they deal with a more-or-less recent past; instead of princes, princesses, widows' daughters and giants, they deal with 'real' people, often very similar to the members of their audience, and often named.[2] Legends of the supernatural appeal to the credulity of listeners with detailed descriptions of familiar environments, life and work; they are valuable repositories of practical information therefore, but their central 'plot' is usually an extraordinary encounter of some kind. Most legends are short, and easily remembered, although some talented storytellers, like Éamon a Búrc (pp. 1296–1303), spin them out at great and elaborate length.

Women are sometimes said to be better at the telling of legends, especially ghost stories and stories about fairies, than men are; certainly there is no restriction on the telling of such stories by women, as there is in the case of hero-tales and *Fiannaíocht*.[3] As the examples given here illustrate, however, the telling of legends does not require the sustained attention and semi-formal setting which longer folktales do, so that in rural Ireland in the past it was perhaps more easily accommodated to women's routine of constant domestic activity.

The rural society which has produced most of the oral verbal art recorded in Ireland is over-whelmingly Catholic, with most of its members subscribing to belief in an afterlife of heaven or hell, and deriving their morality from the Christian God. Legends of the supernatural are told and heard against this background, some-times apparently independent of it; occasionally in tension with it; more often, subtly moulded to fill the spaces left in Christian discourse or to mediate its occasional contradictions.[4]

Legends are told about animals ('The King of the Cats'), about human shape-shifters ('The Old Woman as Hare'), about the banshee and other death-omens,[5] but the great bulk of Irish tradition of the supernatural deals with the fairies.[6] They are known by a variety of euphemistic aliases, 'the good people', 'little people', 'hill-folk', or 'wee gentry',[7] and are represented as living alongside humans, often inside particular hills, or in the circular earthworks which archaeologists call ringforts. Some also live in the air and under the sea.

The fairies are like 'us' in important ways, but are nevertheless fundamentally different; unpredictable and powerful, and essentially amoral, they are the invisible neighbours who must not be offended. They inhabit that part of the landscape which is not domesticated, and impinge on human life at those points where it is least amenable to social control.[8] Their associations are with boundaries — in the

---

1. For an overview of the state of scholarship on the legends discussed here, see Bo Almqvist, 'Irish Migratory Legends on the Supernatural: Sources, Studies and Problems', *Béaloideas*, vol. 59 (1991), pp. 1–43. The same issue, titled *The Fairy Hill Is On Fire*, contains several essays on important aspects of the legend tradition.
2. Cf. the subsection 'International Folktales', pp. 1214–1217.
3. Ibid.
4. Cf. the subsection 'Spirituality and Religion in Oral Tradition', pp. 1399–1420.
5. See also the subsection 'Storytelling Traditions of the Irish Travellers', pp. 1263–1283.
6. See Peter Narváez (ed.), *The Good People: New Fairylore Essays* (New York: Garland, 1991); Barbara Rieti, *Strange Terrain: The Fairy World in Newfoundland* (St John's: ISER Books, 1991).
7. For a comprehensive list, in Irish and English, see Máire MacNeill's Introduction to Seán Ó hEochaidh, Máire MacNéill and Séamus Ó Catháin, *Siscéalta ó Thír Chonaill/Fairy Legends from Donegal* (Dublin: Comhairle Bhéaloideasa Éireann, 1977), several selections from which appear below, pp. 1286–1290, 1293–1296.
8. See Séamus Ó Catháin and Patrick O'Flanagan, *The Living Landscape: Kilgalligan, Erris, Co Mayo* (Dublin: Comhairle Bhéaloideas Éireann, 1975).

landscape, in time, and in human life — while the people who encounter them are often marginal or in transition: widows, children, young women, and lonely single men. The most common places for these meetings include mountainsides, the seashore between the marks of high and low tide, and badly kept houses. The fairies belong to twilight, and wintertime, and are particularly present at Hallowe'en and May Eve, which are the boundaries between the light and dark halves of the year. Accidents and sudden illnesses, whether of humans or of livestock, are attributed to their agency, and anyone whose behaviour is puzzling or unacceptable may be referred to, either jocularly or seriously, as being 'away with the fairies'. Discipline is one of their major functions: despite their preoccupation with the invisible, they serve to warn children and adults about real physical dangers, like high cliffs, open water and mountain fog, and they caution listeners against antisocial behaviour.

Individual fairy-belief stories connect with each other in interlocking systems of great complexity to provide a conceptual model of social and economic life, which is mapped onto a familiar landscape and yet remains sufficiently abstract to be flexible. The boundaries depicted and contemplated in stories about the fairies are fluid and fuzzy: vast areas of grey between society's accepted ideas of black and white. Such grey areas, characterized by anxiety, become sources of creative expression.

Fairy legends add value to places, particularly those not already densely inscribed with human activity; they make them at once more interesting and more knowable, and help to locate them on the mental maps of an oral culture. They honour the expertise of skilled workers, describing their tools and techniques, and often using details of their practice as the hinges of narrative. They detail the terrifying fates which may befall those who do not conform to society's rules, but they also offer an imaginative freedom from social and familial constraint, and a system of metaphor with which to confront ambiguity, ambivalence and paradox.

Many legends of fairy encounter focus on women and girls. The intensely patriarchal society which produced them did not assign places or roles to women in their own right; instead, it expected women to fit into whatever

gaps might open in the system of economic and social relationships between men, and to disappear somehow when those gaps closed. So land passed from fathers to sons, but rarely to daughters; marriages were negotiated chiefly among male members of the families involved, and could be effectively repudiated if no male heir appeared. And yet women's labour was essential to the effective running of households and smallholdings, and once she acquired a firm footing, either through marriage or through keeping house for bachelor or widowed brothers or elderly parents, a woman was a fully functioning and highly respected member of society. Much ambiguity still surrounded her position, however, especially in cases of rivalry between families, where sibling bonds were often expected to take precedence over sexual partnerships, and great unhappiness could result. Physical abuse was not unknown, but like other grievances, could not be openly discussed. The discourse of fairy-belief legend offered a system of metaphor and oblique reference which individual storytellers negotiated according to their own preoccupations; like money, it was a currency, neutral in itself, but capable of facilitating important interventions.[9]

The fairies steal healthy children and young adults and leave withered, sickly, ill-tempered (or lifeless) changelings in their place. This theme of fairy abduction, which is central to the tradition, offers both a fantasy of escape and, in cases of sudden infant death, accident or the formerly prevalent tuberculosis, a consolation for the bereaved.

'Fairy doctors', practitioners of vernacular or folk medicine, many of whom were women, are often said to derive their skill from the fairies, as are exceptionally talented musicians and poets.[10] The fact that a person taken by the fairies may sometimes be rescued or redeemed means too that episodes of depression, alcoholism or mental

9. See Richard P. Jenkins, 'Witches and Fairies: Supernatural Aggression and Deviance Among the Irish Peasantry', *Ulster Folklife*, vol. 23 (1977), pp. 33–56; rev. in P. Narváez (ed.), *The Good People*; C.M. Arensberg and S.T. Kimball, *Family and Community in Ireland*, pp. 136–7 and *passim*. For sibling loyalty, see also Robin Fox, *The Tory Islanders* (Cambridge: Cambridge University Press, 1978), and compare the laments below, pp. 1390, 1393, in which women boast that husbands can be replaced, but not brothers.
10. For traditions about the fairies collected by Lady Gregory early in the twentieth century, including stories of the famous healer Biddy Early, see the subsection 'Writing Oral Traditions', pp. 1435–1445.

illness can later be relegated to a place outside the individual's responsibility.[11]

Storytelling is an interaction between teller and audience, which often has the characteristics of a game. Many storytellers and listeners sincerely believe that at least some of the strange occurrences narrated in these legends are true,

but often only the most credulous are expected to believe, while other listeners enjoy the play between verisimilitude and fantasy, or simply relish the patterning of narrative. Notwithstanding the laconic or perfunctory way in which they are sometimes told, however, fairy legends treat of some of the most intense and emotionally charged moments of human life. Further examples of fairy legend, collected and published by Lady Augusta Gregory, will be found in 'Writing Oral Traditions', pp. 1435–1445.

ANGELA BOURKE

11. For further discussion of these topics, see Angela Bourke, *The Burning of Bridget Cleary: A True Story* (London: Pimlico, 1999; New York: Viking, 2000; Penguin, 2001); 'Reading a Woman's Death: Colonial Text and Oral Tradition in Nineteenth-Century Ireland', *Feminist Studies*, vol. 21, no. 3 (1995), pp. 553–86; 'The Virtual Reality of Irish Fairy Legend', *Éire-Ireland*, vol. 31, nos 1 and 2 (1996), pp. 7–25.

ANNA NIC AN LUAIN

(1884–1954)

from:
SÍSCÉALTA Ó THÍR CHONAILL (1977)

[Fairy lore from Donegal, like Irish fairy lore in general, describes the fairies as living much as human beings do: they eat, drink, have children, sow crops, own animals, play music, sing, and quarrel among themselves. While certain places in the landscape are recognized as the abodes of the fairies and are thus 'gentle' or sacred, generally the boundary between the human and the fairy worlds is not clearly defined, giving rise to tension and interaction between the two worlds. The following legends from Anna Nic an Luain's repertoire suggests a lively perception of an immediate 'otherworld' and a 'hill folk' in the Donegal glen that was her *petite patrie*, yet she achieves a subtle element of distancing in time and space by setting the narratives in a neighbouring parish or in the distant past.

As in the human world, faction fighting, it seems, occurred in the fairy world, with occasional conflicts taking place after mass on Sunday, near the church where the local communities had gathered. This fairy legend has the typical combination of realistic circumstance and illusion. The story and the two which follow are taken from *Síscéalta ó Thír Chonaill/Fairy Legends from Donegal* (Ó hEochaidh, MacNeill, Ó Catháin, 1977, pp. 260–1, 278–81, 286–91). The translations are by Máire MacNeill; headnotes, P. L.]

BRUÍON AMHRA

Chualaí mé an seanbhunadh dá rá gur ghnách le bunadh na gcnoc troid eatarthu féin corruair nuair a thigeadh tuitim amach ínteacht eadar dhá dhream acu. Is é an t-ainm a thugadh siad ar an troid seo Bruíon Amhra.

Deirtear go rabh troid acu seo eatarthu thoir ag Cill Taobhóige fad ó shin. Domhnach amháin nuair a bhí na daoine ag teacht amach as teach an phobail, shíl na mná go rabh na fir uilig ag marbhadh a chéile, agus shíl na fir gurbh iad na mná a bhí ar ghreim mullaigh cinn le chéile. Ní rabh duine ar bith ag baint le chéile ach b'iadsan a bhí fá chéile, agus chuir siad geasrógaí de chineál ínteacht ar shúile an phobail.

THE WONDERFUL STRIFE

I heard the old people say that the hill-folk used to fight among themselves sometimes when a dispute arose between two factions. The name they had for this fight was 'the Wonderful Strife'.

It is said that they had a fight east at Cill Taobhóige long ago. One Sunday when the people were coming out of church, the women thought that the men were killing each other and the men thought that it was the women who were at each other's heads. It was not the people at all but 'those ones' who were fighting, and they put come kind of spell on the eyes of the congregation.

AN CHOILL UASAL

[That certain places in the landscape were regarded as the special property of supernatural beings is evident from this legend, which also combines realistic setting and fantastic happening.]

Tá áit ar an Éadan Anfa a dtugtar an Choillidh air, agus deirtear ariamh anall nach bhfuil an darna háit i bparóiste Inis Caoil atá comh huaigneach uasal leis. Chonaictheas na daoine beaga ann go minic, agus bhí taibhsí agus solais le feiceáil ann in amannaí eile. Bhí sé comh holc agus gur dhoiligh le morán daoine a ghabháil an bealach ann i ndiaidh na hoíche ar chor ar bith.

Bhí beirt bhuachaill ag gabháil suas bealach an Éadain oíche amháin a dh'áirneál. Bhí rún acu nuair a d'fhág siad an bhaile le gabháil chuig faire a bhí sa chomharsanacht, ach dar leo go ndéanfadh siad tamall áirneáil an chéad uair. D'imigh siad suas bealach Choillidh an Éadain, agus nuair a bhí siad ag tarraingt suas an bealach chonaic siad an tine thall sa choillidh a ba mhó a chonaic siad ariamh. Bhí sí ag gabháil suas go glinntí an aeir, agus shíl siad go rabh an choillidh uilig le tine. Tharraing siad ar an teach áirneáil a rabh siad ag gabháil ann, agus d'inis siad do bhunadh an toighe fán tine, agus dúirt siad nach mbeadh morán fágtha ar maidin ag an fhear ar leis an áit.

Bhí go maith. Chuaigh siad chun na faire, agus shuidh siad ansin go rabh an lá geal ann — ba é sin an gnás ins na háiteacha seo uilig go dtí le gairid. Ar an mbealach chun an bhaile ar maidin, smaoitigh siad go rachadh siad ar amharc na tine go bhfeiceadh siad an scrios a bhí déanta aici. Chuaigh, ach nuair a chuaigh siad chun talaimh ar cheart don tine a bheith, ní rabh lorg ar bith le fáil uirthi. Chuartaigh siad, ach ní rabh smál féin le fáil acu.

Tá na daoine ag smaoitiú ariamh ó shin gur tine a bhí ag bunadh na gcnoc ann nuair nach rabh aon dath le fáil dóite ar maidin.

THE FAIRY WOOD

There is a place on Éadan Anfa known as the Wood, and it is always said that there is not another place in the parish of Iniskeel as eerie or gentle as it is. Often the wee folk were seen there, and at other times ghosts and lights. It was so bad that many would not go that way at all after night-fall.

Two boys who were going visiting went up the Éadan road one night. When they left home they had intended to go to a wake in the neighbourhood, but they thought they would go visiting first. When they were approaching Éadan Wood they saw the greatest fire that they had ever seen. It was going up into the firmament and they thought the whole wood was on fire. They went to the visiting house and told the people there about the fire and said the man who owned the place would have little left by morning.

Well and good. They went to the wake and stayed there until daylight: that was the custom always at wakes until recently. On their way home in the morning they thought they would go and see what damage the fire had done. When they went to the land where the fire would have been there was no trace of a fire to be seen. They searched but could find no ashes.

Ever after, people believed it was a fairy fire since there was no sign of burning to be seen next morning.

CIAPÓGAÍ AN AISTIR AISTIGH

[Several legends tell of journeys taken with the fairies. Exceptionally, in this version of the legend of 'The Marvellous Journey Illusion', a man is abducted into the fairy world to nurse a human child. A central motif is his illusion of being a mother; however, he seems to abandon the child when he comes to his senses, and one loose thread remains: after the farmer comes back from fairyland the little girl, who has accompanied him, disappears from the narrative. Two other versions of this story have been recorded from male storytellers in County Donegal. Both of them tell of a man changed into a woman, who breastfed an infant, a king's daughter; one of them adds that s/he went on to have another child by the same king. Both identify a young girl, present when the man tells his story, as the child who came back with him in the boat, now grown up.[1]]

1. See Énrí Ó Muirgheasa, 'Mac Uí Néill [Sgéal ó Thír Chonaill]', *Béaloideas*, vol. 1 (1927–8), pp. 84–9.

Bhí fear ann fad ó shin, agus bliain amháin bhí mórán arbhair curtha aige. D'éirigh sé mall air le baint an arbhair, agus d'iarr sé meitheal fá choinne an tSathairn a bhí ag teacht. Ní tháinig leis na fir a theacht ar an tSatharn, agus thosaigh siad a theacht ar an Luan agus gan iad réidh fána gcoinne. Ní raibh a sáith aráin déanta acu; agus arán mine choirce uilig a bhí ag gabháil san am. Ní raibh an t-uisce féin istigh, agus d'iarr an cailín ar fhear an toighe a ghabháil amach agus stópa uisce a thabhairt isteach chuici as an tsileán a bhí ag teacht anuas fá ghiota den teach.

Chuaigh an fear sin amach, agus nuair a chuir sé an stópa faoin tsileán, sheas sé go mbeadh an stópa lán. Agus nuair a d'amharc sé uaidh síos bhí an fharraige ag tarraingt air aníos, agus an coite beag báid uirthi a ba deise a chonaic sé riamh. Bhí seanduine beag ribeach rua ina shuí i ndeireadh an bháid agus éadach breacdhearg air; trí *bhall* bheaga bhuí leis, agus é dá gcaitheamh san aer agus dá gceapadh ar ais. Tháinig an bád isteach aníos go raibh sí ag cosa fhear an stópa. Thosaigh an bád á bhualadh ins na loirgneacha agus chuir sí mothú feirge air, agus thóg sé a bhróg, agus thug sé iarraidh cic uirthi. Níor luaithe sin déanta aige ná tógadh isteach chun an bháid é, agus ar shiúl leis an bhád chun na farraige arís. Chuaigh an bád ar aghaidh léithi, agus nuair a bhí an tráthnóna dubh dorcha ann bhuail sí talamh ar an taoibh eile den fharraige.

Bhí go maith agus ní raibh go holc. Chuaigh sé i dtír anseo. Bhí áit an-áimhréiteach ann, agus ba bheag an siúl a bhí déanta aige go dtug sé fá dear go raibh rud ínteacht dá chreapall. D'amharc sé síos air féin agus caidé a bhí air ach éadach mná. Cá bith mar bhí, shiúil sé leis. Chonaic sé solas beag i bhfad uaidh, agus tharraing sé ar an tsolas. Chuaigh sé isteach chun toighe, agus bhí buachaill agus cailín istigh ansin, agus chuir siad caint air. Shíl siadsan, ar ndóiche, gur bean a bhí ann, agus ins an am bhí siad ag gléas le ghabháil chun faire a bhí ar an bhaile. D'fhiafraigh siad an rachadh 'sí' leofa agus dúirt seisean go rachadh.

D'imigh siad leofa chun na faire, agus sí an fhaire a bhí ann bean a fuair bás i ndiaidh linbh. Anonn san oíche chuaigh an leanbh a chaoineadh, agus thóg bean de na mná amach as an chliabhán é. Bhí sé ag gabháil ó bhean go bean, ach ní raibh bean ar bith ábalta ciall a chur ann ná baint faoi. D'iarr fear an toighe orthu a

thabhairt don 'bhean' choimhthíoch. Thug, agus ba ghairid gur chodlaigh an páiste.

Ar maidin lá tharna mhárach nuair a bhí lucht na faire ag scabadh, dúirt fear an toighe é féin cá bith rud a rinn an bhean choimhthíoch sin a chuir an páiste a chodladh nach gcorróchadh sí go dtógfadh sí an páiste. Ar an bhomaite ar dhúirt fear an toighe sin rinn an fear eile dearmad den bhaile s' aige féin, agus ó sin amach ní raibh aon dath ag cur bhuartha air ach ag gabháil don leanbh. Páiste girsí a bhí inti, agus ba bheag an aois a bhí sí uilig go dteachaigh sí a shiúl. Bhí sé ann go raibh an ghirseach seacht mbliana.

Bhí sé féin agus an ghirseach amuigh ag siúl aon lá amháin. Chuaigh siad síos a chois na farraige, agus rud nár mhothaigh sé riamh go dtí sin, bhuail an-chumhaidh é, agus chuaigh sé ag smaoitiú go corr ar an bhaile. Níorbh fhada dó go bhfaca sé an bád beag chuige ins an chumadh chéanna a bhí uirthi an chéad uair a tharraing sí air. Nuair a tháinig sí chuige bhuail sé cic uirthi an dóigh chéanna, agus níor mhothaigh sé gur tógadh isteach chun an bháid é féin agus an ghirseach bheag. D'imigh an bád beag, agus bheireadh sí ar an ghaoith a bhí roimpi, agus ní bheireadh an ghaoth a bhí ina dhiaidh uirthi, agus níor mhothaigh sé go raibh sé arais ag an áit a raibh an stópa faoin tsileán. D'fhág sé féin agus an ghirseach an bád, agus nuair a dhearc sé fá dtaobh de bhí an stópa ansin go díreach mar d'fhág sé é. Rug sé ar an stópa, agus thug sé leis chun toighe é.

Bhí an cailín ina seasamh i lár an urláir, agus scála na mine aici go díreach mar bhí sé nuair a d'imigh sé.

'Nach fada a bhí tú amuigh!' a deir sí.

Is ansin a smaoitigh sé gurbh aistíoch an rud a d'éirigh dó agus dar leis go n-imeochadh sé agus nach gcodlóchadh sé dhá oíche ar aon leaba go bhfeicfeadh sé caidé a tháinig air ar chor ar bith.

D'imigh sé leis, agus bhí ag siúl leis go tráthnóna. Chonaic sé teach beag fá dheireadh istigh i lár caoráin. Nuair a tharraing sé air dar leis gur mhothaigh sé callán mór istigh. Chuaigh sé isteach, agus nuair a chuaigh bhí dhá chliabhán ansin — ceann ar gach aon taoibh den tine, agus bhí cailleach in achan chliabhán. Bhí súgán trasna eadar an dá chliabhán, agus iad ag bogadh a chéile, agus an bheirt ag caoineadh leofa. D'fhiafraigh sé caidé ba chiall daofa a bheith ag caoineadh.

'Tá muid marbh leis an ocras,' arsa siadsan. 'Tá bóraí amuigh ó mhaidin,' arsa siadsan, 'agus níor phill sí, le greim a thabhairt dúinn ó d'imigh sí ar maidin.'

'Agus cá bhfuil bhur máthair mhór?' arsa seisean.

'Tá sí thíos ar an tráigh ag cur amach feamnaí.'

Smaoitigh sé go gcaithfeadh an mháthair mhór a bheith gearraosta nuair a bhí an bheirt a bhí ins na cliabháin comh haosta, agus dar leis go mb'fhéidir dá bhfaghadh sé chun cainte leis an tseanbhean seo go mbeadh sí ábalta eolas ínteacht a thabhairt dó. Tharraing sé ar an fharraige ansin, agus nuair a chuaigh sé ar amharc na trá bhí sí chuige aníos, agus ualach uirthi a mbeadh sáith gearráin ann. Bhuail sí béal an chléibh a raibh an t-ualach ann faoi agus shuigh sí ar thóin an chléibh, agus thosaigh an seanchas aici.

'Caidé atá ag cur bhuartha ortsa,' a deir sí, 'ná caidé a ruaig an bealach seo thú?' arsa sise.

Thosaigh seisean gur inis sé a scéal dí ó thús go deireadh: fán dóigh ar tharraing an fharraige aníos air nuair a bhí an stópa faoin tsileán aige, agus ar tógadh isteach chun an bháid é a rabh an seanduine beag ribeach rua ina shuí ar a deireadh.

'Níor bhog tú ariamh as áit do bhoinn!' arsa an tseanchailleach. 'Shíl tú féin gur bhog, ach cuireadh ciapógaí ort mar cuireadh ar go leor eile. Tháinig an slua aerach ort, agus siúd is gur shíl tú gur tógadh isteach chun an bháid thú, mar tá mé i ndiaidh a rá leat, níor fhág tú amach áit do bhoinn. Gabh ar ais abhaile anois, agus ná luaigh a n-ainm go bráth gan a rá go ndiúltaíonn tú dá gcuideachta, agus ní chuirfidh siad buaireamh ar bith ort níos mó!'

'Bhail, dhéanfaidh mé do chomhairle,' arsa seisean, 'ach sula bpillfí mé ba mhaith liom fios a fháil caidé mar d'éirigh leat a leithéid d'fhad saoil a fháil?'

'Tá, maise, inseochaidh mé sin duit,' arsa sise. 'Ní theachaidh mise a luí ariamh go mbínn ag tuitim i mo chodladh, agus níor ith mé aon ghreim go mbinn chóir a bheith réidh leis an ocras; agus chaith mé mo shaol uilig ag obair mar tí tú mé. Níl duine ar bith dá ndéanfaidh sin nach bhfaighidh saol fada.'

Phill sé abhaile ansin, agus ón lá sin go lá a bháis níor chuir an dream beag aerach buaireamh ar bith air.

THE MARVELLOUS JOURNEY ILLUSION

There was a man long ago and one year he had planted a lot of corn. It was getting late for reaping and he engaged a group of reapers for the following Saturday. The men could not come on Saturday and so they arrived on Monday and nothing was prepared for them. There was not enough bread made for them, and it was all oatmeal bread at that time. Even the water had not been brought in. The maid asked the man of the house to go out and bring in a pail of water from the stream which came down near the house.

The man went out, put the pail under the flow and stood while it was filling. When he looked down, the sea was rising up towards him and on it the prettiest little boat he had ever seen. There was a little old red-haired man sitting in the stern of the boat: he was dressed in speckled clothes and juggling with three little yellow balls. The boat came in up to the man's very feet, and began to beat against his shins. In a rush of rage he lifted his foot and made a kick at it. No sooner had he done so than he was taken into the boat which went off to sea and kept going until in the darkness of evening it reached land on the other side of the ocean.

Well and good. He went ashore on very rough ground and had not gone far before he felt something was hampering him. He looked down and what was he wearing but woman's clothes! He walked on, however, until he saw a small light far away and he went towards it. He went into the house and there was a boy and girl inside who spoke to him. They thought, of course, that he was a woman. They were dressing to go to a wake in the townland. They asked if 'she' would go with them and he said he would.

They went off to the wake which was for a woman who had died in childbirth. During the night the infant began to cry and one of the women lifted it out of the cradle. It was being handed from one woman to another, but none of them was able to soothe it. The man of the house asked them to give it to the strange woman. They did, and very soon the child fell asleep.

Next morning when people were leaving the wake-house, the man of the house declared that whatever it was that the strange woman had done to put the child asleep, she was not to leave without the child. The moment the man of the house said this, the other man forgot all about his own home and from that on was only concerned with attending to the child who was a girl and was able to walk at a very early age. He stayed there until the girl was seven years old.

He was out walking with the girl one day by the seaside and a great loneliness came over him that he had not felt before and he began to think of his home. Before long he saw the little boat coming towards him the same way as it did the first time. And like the first time when it reached him he gave it a kick and before he realized, he and the little girl were taken into the boat. It went at such a pace it could catch up on the wind before it and the wind behind it could not catch up with it, and in no time he was back where his pail was under the flow of the stream. He and the little girl got out of the boat, and when he looked about him, the pail was just exactly as he had left it. He caught hold of it and brought it into the house.

The maid was standing in the middle of the floor with the measure of meal, just as she had been when he left. 'Isn't it long you have been out!' she said.

It was then he thought that it was a very strange thing that had happened to him and he decided that he would set out and that he would not sleep two nights on the same bed until he understood what had happened.

He set out and was walking until night fell. At last he saw a little house in the middle of a moor. As he approached it he thought he could hear great noise inside. He went in and saw two cradles, one on each side of the fire, and an old woman lying in each cradle. A straw rope was stretched between the cradles and the old women were rocking each other with it and crying. He asked them why they were crying.

'We are killed with hunger,' said one of them. 'Granny has been out since morning and she never came back to give us a bit to eat.'

'And where is your grandmother?' he asked.

'She is down on the strand spreading seaweed.'

He thought that the grandmother must be very ancient when the pair in the cradles were so old, and perhaps if he could speak to her she could give him some knowledge. He went towards the sea and when he came in sight of the strand she

was coming towards him carrying a load that would tax a horse. She turned the basket in which she was carrying it mouth down and sat on its bottom, and began to converse with him.

'What is troubling you,' she said, 'and what sent you this way?'

He told her his story from beginning to end, how the sea had come on him while he was filling the pail under the flow of the stream and how he had been taken into the boat in which the little red-haired man was sitting in the stern.

'You never moved from the place you were standing!' said the old woman. 'You thought you did, but you were under enchantment, as many others have been. The airy host came upon you, and as I said, although you thought you were taken into the boat you did not move from where you were standing. Go back home now and never mention their name without saying that you shun their company, and they will never trouble you again!'

'Well, I will follow your advice,' said he, 'but before I go, I would like to know how you managed to live so long?'

'Musha, indeed, I will tell you that,' said she. 'I never lay down until I was falling asleep, and I never ate a bite until I was famished with hunger, and I spent my whole life working, as you see me. Anyone who does that will have a long life.'

He returned home then and from that day until his death the airy ones did not bother him.

from:
NA CRUACHA: SCÉALTA AGUS SEANCHAS (1985)

[Stories of supernatural or phantom funerals occur frequently in Irish oral tradition and their purpose is explained in a number of ways. Experienced by day or night, they are variously regarded as a funeral to the family graveyard of a family member buried elsewhere in Ireland or abroad, or in the wrong cemetery or grave; or the funeral from fairyland of an abducted mortal who died there; or, as in the present narrative, as an omen of death.[1]

---

1. See Seán Ó Súilleabháin, *A Handbook of Irish Folklore* (Detroit: Singing Tree Press; Dublin: Folklore of Ireland Society, 1942, 1970), pp. 491–2.

Here the omen is experienced by the person about to die and its import and the tension of the situation is heightened by the crying and lamenting sound — a traditional foreboding of death in Anna Nic an Luain's family (the Wards/Clann Mhic an Bhaird), which she describes in this personal experience narrative. Although she does not attribute the crying sound to the banshee, the experience, as she describes it, bears similarities to that tradition.[2] From Áine Ní Dhíoraí, *Na Cruacha: Scéalta agus Seanchas* (Baile Átha Cliath: An Clóchomhar, 1985), pp. 126–7. Translation and headnote, P.L.]

TÓRRAMH SÍ

Tá mé ag éisteacht leis an tseanbhunadh ariamh dá rá go bhfaigheann daoine áirid comharthaí roimh bhás duine. Tá daoine anseo a chaointear roimh an mbás agus chualaigh mé mo mháthair féin dá rá go gcaointí Clann Mhic an Bhaird fada ó shin. Bhí deartháir óg agam féin a fuair bás nuair a bhí sé ina fhear agus thiocfadh liom mionnú gur caoineadh é roimh a bhás.

Bhí mé oíche amháin anseo agus tháinig m'athair ón chnoc go mall (go ndéana an Rí grásta orthu, tá siad uilig marbh anois); ní raibh tobaca ar bith aige agus nuair a bhíodh sé mar sin bhíodh sé mar bheadh easóg agus ní mó nó go dtiocfadh le duine amharc air mura mbeadh toit aige. Thug mo mháthair cogar domsa agus dúirt sí go mb'fhearr dom labhairt le cailín beag eile a bhí thiar anseo i dtoí na comharsan agus muid araon a dhul siar chun an Éadáin fá choinne giota tobaca dó. Ní raibh de dhíth ormsa ach an leideadh a fháil agus ní raibh eagla nó uaigneas orm a dhul chun siúil nó ar an chailín a bhí liom. Bhí oíche gheal ann agus bhí sé chomh ciúin agus dá dtitfeadh pionna as an aer go mothófá é ag bualadh an talaimh. Chuaigh muid siar chun an Éadáin agus fuair muid an tobaca agus tháinig muid aniar ar ais agus leoga ní raibh deifre ar bith orainn — coiscéim anois agus arís agus is trua Mhuire gan mise chomh neamh-mbuartha inniu agus a bhí mé an oíche sin!

Ag teacht aniar dúinn os coinne Chruach an Airgid mhothaigh mise an caoineadh a ba thruacánta a mhothaigh mé ariamh. Sheas mé go tobann agus d'éist mé agus nuair a sheas mé stad

2. For the banshee, see examples 'The Banshee's Comb', pp. 1303–1304, and P. Lysaght, *The Banshee: The Irish Supernatural Death-Messenger* (Dublin: Glendale Press, 1986).

sé. Shiúil mé liom agus d'fhiafraigh an cailín eile díom an bhfacaigh mé dadaidh. 'Ní fhacas,' arsa mise, 'ach chualaigh mé rud inteacht. An gcualaigh tusa dadaidh?' arsa mise.

'Níor chualaigh,' arsa sise, 'caidé a chualaigh tusa?'

'Chuala mé caoineadh, agus caoineadh truacánta!' arsa mise.

Sin a raibh de sin. Shiúil muid linn agus ní theachaigh muid céad slat gur mhothaigh mise an rud céanna. Stad sé ar ais agus níor mhothaigh sise é ach oiread. Bhí muid ag dul ó ghiota go giota agus ní raibh giota slat ar bith a raibh muid ag dul nach raibh mise ag éisteacht leis an chaoineadh. Sa deireadh tháinig muid aniar ar amharc an bhaile agus leis sin féin chuaigh an caoineadh thart fá fhad bata dúinn agus bhí mise ag éisteacht leis go dteachaigh sé suas taobh na Cruaiche Goirme agus i rith an ama níor chualaigh an bhean a bhí liom é.

Bhí go maith, tháinig muid chun an bhaile agus bhí sé ag tarraingt anonn ar am luí an uair sin agus bhí cúpla duine de bhunadh an bhaile istigh ag airneáil. Thug mo mháthair fá deara orm féin go raibh mé tógtha agus cuma scanraithe i gceart orm. D'fhiafraigh sí díom ar lean duine ar bith mé nó an bhfacaigh mé dadaidh. D'inis mé daoithi caidé mar bhí. 'Bhail, níor mhaith liom sin,' arsa sise agus níor chuir sí an scéal ní b'fhaide.

Bhí mo dheartháir istigh, agus an tráthnóna céanna bhí seisean suas fán Leamhach ag amharc fá ghráinnín caorach a bhí thuas ansin againn. Bhí seisean ag éisteacht liom fosta. 'Bhail, a mháthair,' arsa seisean, 'caithfidh sé go bhfuil rud inteacht le héirí do dhuine inteacht againne gan mhoill. Chonaic mise rud uafásach tráthnóna inniu thuas ar mhalaidh na Leamhaigh ach ní raibh súil agam trácht air nó shíl mé gur ar mo shúile a bhí sé.'

'Caidé a chonaic tú?' arsa sise.

'Tá maise, chonaic mé an tórramh a ba chorpartha a chonaic mé ariamh ag ardú suas taobh thoir díom. Bhíthear ag iompar na cónra agus an gleo agus an callán a bhí acu bhí sé mór le rá. Choimheád mé iad tamalt agus ansin thóg mé mo shúil daofu agus nuair a d'amharc mé ar ais ach oiread agus dá slogfadh an talamh iad ní raibh aon amharc agam le feiceáil orthu. Shíl mé ansin gur ar mo shúile a bhí sé ach tá a fhios agam anois nach ea.'

Bhí go maith, ní raibh sé an-fhada ina dhiaidh sin gur ghlac an deartháir céanna tinneas agus go dteachaigh sé a luí agus níor éirigh sé ariamh go bhfuair sé bás. Rinneadh a chaoineadh agus chonaic sé a thórramh féin an lá céanna a rinneadh a chaoineadh.

A PHANTOM FUNERAL

I've always heard the old people say that certain people experience a death-foreboding before someone dies. Some people here are cried for before death, and I heard my own mother say that the Wards used to be cried for long ago. A young brother of my own died when he was a man, and I can swear that he was cried for before his death.

I was here one night and my father came home late from the hill (may God be merciful to them, they are all dead now!). He had run out of tobacco and he was like a weasel as a result — one could hardly look at him if he didn't have a smoke. My mother gave me the nod and told me to have a word with another little girl in the neighbouring house and the two of us to go west to Edenfinfreagh[1] for a piece of tobacco for him. I was only waiting for the opportunity, and I wasn't a bit afraid to go and neither was the other girl who was with me. It was a bright night and so calm that if a pin dropped from the sky you would hear it hitting the ground. We went west to Edenfinfreagh and got the tobacco and came on home, and indeed we weren't in any hurry — a step now and again, and it is a pity that I'm not as carefree today as I was on that night!

As we came eastwards opposite Croaghanarget I heard the most pitiful cry I have ever heard. I stopped suddenly and listened, and when I did, it stopped. I walked on and the other girl asked if I had seen anything. 'I didn't,' said I, 'but I heard something.' 'Did you hear anything?' said I.

'I didn't,' said she, 'what did you hear?'

'I heard lamenting, a pitiful lamenting!' said I.

That was that. We walked on and we hadn't gone a hundred yards when I heard the same thing again. It stopped again and she didn't hear it then either. We kept going bit by bit and every yard or so we went I was listening to the lamenting. Finally we came within sight of home and even with that the lamenting passed within a rod's length of us, and I was listening to it until it went up the side of the Blue Stack,[2] and during all this time the girl who was with me didn't hear it.

Well and good! We came home and it was around bed-time then and there were a few people from the townland in the house, night-visiting. My mother noticed that I was excited and looking very frightened indeed. She asked me if anyone had followed me or if I had seen something. I told her what had happened. 'Well, I don't like that,' said she, and she said no more.

My brother was there in the house, and the same evening he had been up around Lavaghmore looking after a handful of sheep we had up there. He was listening to me too. 'Well, mother,' said he, 'something must be going to happen to some one of us soon. I saw a terrible thing this evening up on the side of Lavaghmore, but I hadn't bothered to talk about it as I thought I had only imagined it.'

'What did you see?' said she.

'Well, I saw a funeral that looked as real as I have ever seen coming up over beyond me. They were carrying the coffin and making a great noise and clamour. I observed them for a while and then I took my eye off them, and when I looked again I couldn't see them — it was as if the ground had swallowed them! I thought then that I had imagined it but I now know that I hadn't.'

Well and good! It wasn't too long after that that the brother got ill and took to his bed and stayed there until he died. He had been cried for and he saw his own funeral the same day he was lamented.

1. For the anglicized form of the place-names in the text, see end map in S. Ó Catháin, *Uair an Chloig Cois Teallaigh/An Hour by the Hearth: Stories Told by Pádraig Eoghain Phádraig Mac an Luain* (Dublin: Comhairle Bhéaloideas Éireann, 1985).

2. A mountain in Donegal, near the storyteller's home.

MÁIRE NÍ BHEIRN

(b. *c*. 1890)

from:
SÍSCÉALTA Ó THÍR CHONAILL (1977)

[A woman being carried through the air by the fairies is released from their power when a man below utters a Christian blessing. The woman's passivity and silence are perhaps the most striking features of this legend, but it does reflect the economic basis of marriage in rural Ireland in the late nineteenth and early twentieth centuries. Men ideally remained on the farms where they had grown up, while women, whose work was essential to the smooth running of a small farm, were drafted in through marriage. Unmarried, they were placeless, but without children, their married status was in jeopardy.[1] Fairy legend provides a wealth of metaphorical expression for the difficult situations which could arise when personal desires were subjected to economic necessity. This story is assigned No. 900 in Ó Súilleabháin and Christiansen, *The Types of the Irish Folktale*. From *Síscéalta ó Thír Chonaill/Fairy Legends from Donegal* (Ó hEochaidh, MacNeill, Ó Catháin, 1977), pp. 54–7; translated by Máire MacNeill. Headnote, A.B.]

AN BHEAN A THUIT ÓN SPÉIR

Bhí fear ina chónaí istigh i nGleann fad ó shin, agus fuair a bhean bás go han-tobann. An lá céanna a cuireadh í, bhí fear thiar i gConnachta amuigh ins an chuibhreann i gcionn a spáide. Chualaí sé an tormán ag tarraingt air fríd an spéir, agus nuair a dhearc sé fá dtaobh de bhí bean ag tarraingt air san aer.

'Do Dhia is do Chriost thú!' arsa seisean, nuair a d'aithin sé gur bean shaolta a bhí inti, agus leis sin thuit sí ag na chosa. Bheir sé uirthi, agus thug sé chun toighe í, agus choinnigh sé ansin í ag obair léithi fán teach.

Bliain ón am sin chuaigh fear na mná seo siar go *Carney* a cheannacht caorach, agus ar an

1. See Conrad M. Arensberg, *The Irish Countryman* (Gloucester, Mass.: Peter Smith, 1959 [1937]), p. 91; Richard Breen, 'Dowry Payments and the Irish Case', *Comparative Studies in Society and History*, vol. 26, no. 2 (1984), p. 292; and Angela Bourke, *The Burning of Bridget Cleary: A True Story* (London: Pimlico, 1999; New York: Viking, 2000; Penguin, 2001).

bhealach bhain sé faoi ins an teach a rabh an bhean choimhthíoch seo ann. Ní rabh áimear ar bith dá rabh sé a fháil nach rabh sé ag amharc uirthi faoina shúil, agus é ag rá ina intinn féin nach bhfaca sé aon bhean ariamh a bhí comh cosúil lena bhean féin léithi seo. Thug fear an toighe fá dear é fá dheireadh, agus labhair sé:

'Títhear domh,' arsa seisean, 'go bhfuil tú ag breathnú na mná seo go han-ghéar,' arsa seisean.

'Tá,' arsa fear Ghlinne, 'ach ná bí i mo dhiaidh orm. Bliain is an t-am seo cuireadh mo bheansa, agus ní fhacaí mise ariamh cúpla ar bith comh cosúil le chéile leis an bheirt.'

'Cén lá den mhí a bhfuair sí bás agus ar cuireadh í?' arsa an Connachtach.

D'inis sé do.

'Bhail, an lá céanna sin,' arsa seisean, bhí mise amuigh i gcionn mo ghnoithe ins an chuibhreann, agus chonaic mé an bhean seo ag tarraingt orm fríd an aer mar bheadh éan ar eiteog. Dúirt mé 'Do Dhia is do Chríost thú!' nuair a chonaic mé í, agus níor luaithe a dúirt mé na focla sin ná thuit sí anuas ag mo chosa. Thug mé liom chun toighe í, agus tá sí anseo ó shin, agus má mheasann tusa gurb í do bhean féin í, ar ndóiche, bíodh sí leat chun an bhaile!'

Nuair a tháinig sé ar ais as *Carney* tháinig sé bealach an toighe, agus bhí a bhean leis isteach go Gleann, agus tá siad beo beitheach ó shin ann!

THE WOMAN DROPPED FROM THE AIR

Long ago there was a man living in the Glen whose wife died very suddenly. On the same day that she was buried, a man west in Connacht was digging in his field. He heard noise approaching through the sky and and when he looked up he saw a woman in the air coming towards him.

'God and Christ to you!' he said when he recognized that she was a woman of this world, and with that she fell at his feet. He took hold of her and brought her to his house and he kept her there to do the housework.

A year later the woman's husband went west to Carney to buy sheep and, on his way, he stopped at the house where this strange woman was. There was no opportunity he could get that he did not steal a look at her and think to himself that he had never seen a woman so like his own wife. The man of the house noticed this at last and said:

'It seems to me that you are looking very keenly at this woman.'

'I am,' said the man from the Glen, 'but do not blame me. It is a year since my wife was buried, and I have never seen twins as alike as the two of them.'

'Which day of the month did she die?'

He told him.

'Well, on that same day I was out working in the field and I saw this woman coming towards me in the air like a bird in flight. I said, "God and Christ help you!" when I saw her, and no sooner had I said the words than she fell down at my feet. I brought her to the house and she has been here since, and if you think she is your own wife take her home with you!'

He came back to the house on his return from Carney, and his wife went with him to the Glen, and they are alive and well since then!

CONALL Ó BEIRN

(b. *c.* 1904)

from:
SÍSCÉALTA Ó THÍR CHONAILL (1977)

[This short legend, told in 1954 to Seán Ó hEochaidh, is densely packed with references to a wide range of fairy belief, and rich in implications about social relations. The 'good people', 'hill-folk', or fairies are normally invisible. They live a life of ease and luxury inside hills, but are often understood to be infertile, so that they steal human babies, or abduct pregnant women to bear children for them, calling on human midwives to aid them. The many legends which tell of such encounters reflect the midwife's important and anomalously independent position in rural Irish society.[1]

Unlike other women, whose work was centred on the house and its immediate surroundings, the midwife was regularly required to leave home alone, often at night or for days on end, and sometimes with strangers. While most women taken by the fairies are depicted as victims, the midwife is a powerful person, who usually negotiates her own safe return. Presiding over one of the most important boundaries in human life, she is also a liminal figure — a prime candidate for dealings with the fairies — while the cliff which mysteriously opens to admit her to the fairy dwelling in the hill offers a metaphor for childbirth. Here, she foils the fairies' attempt to steal her own child, but

later pays with the loss of her eye. The suggestion seems to be that had she not rescued her child, she would have returned home to find the dead one in its place: a changeling left by the fairies. This may reflect anxiety or resentment about conflicting demands on a midwife's time, and the possibility that her work might cause her to neglect her own children.

People taken by the fairies are often said to suffer some physical blemish, by which they may be identified. While the loss of an eye is clearly part of this discourse on disability, the punishment in this story appears also to carry a metaphorical message about the midwife's need to turn a blind eye to things she may see in the homes she visits.[2] From *Síscéalta ó Thír Chonaill/Fairy Legends from Donegal* (Ó hEochaidh, MacNeill, Ó Catháin, 1977), pp. 62–5; translation by Máire MacNeill. Headnote, A.B.]

BEAN GHLÚN A CHAILL AMHARC NA LEATHSHÚILE

Bhí bean thall anseo ar an Bhaile Bhuí aon am amháin. Bean ghlún a bhí inti, a bhíodh ag freastal ar mhná a bhíodh i ngéibheann thall is abhus. Oíche amháin, tháinig marcach chun dorais chuici, agus d'iarr sé uirthi bheith ina suí go rabh gnoithe aige léithi. Dúirt sí gur dhoiligh léithise an teach a fhágáil fán am seo d'oíche, agus gan fios aici cá rabh sí ag gabháil.

---

1. For a study of these legends (variants of ML 5070), see Críostóir Mac Cárthaigh, 'Midwife to the Fairies (ML 5070): The Irish Variants in Their Scottish and Scandinavian Perspective', *Béaloideas*, vol. 59 (1991), pp. 133–43.

2. For an exploration of this theme from folklore in modern fiction, see the short story by Éilis Ní Dhuibhne, 'Midwife to the Fairies', in her *Blood and Water* (Dublin: Attic Press, 1988), pp. 25–34.

'Na bíodh eagla ná uafás ar bith ort!' arsa an marcach léithi. 'Fágfaidh mise slán sábháilte anseo ag do dhoras féin thú roimh an lá amárach!'

Ghléas sí uirthi, agus shuidh sí ar a chúlaibh ar an bheathach. D'imigh siad leofa, agus ní rabh fhios aicise caidé a shiúil siad — b'fhéidir go dteachaidh siad isteach sa dara paróiste — ach, fá dheireadh, tháinig siad ionns ar bhéal creige. D'fhoscail doras ansin, agus chuaigh siad isteach. Shiúil siad leofa go dtáinig siad fhad le caisleán mór, agus bhí an áit sin lán daoine, agus iad uilig ag ithe agus ag ól. Thug sé an bhean seo fhad le háit a rabh seomra, agus bhí bean ansin i dtinneas clainne. Ar ball rugadh leanbh daoithi, agus bhí an leanbh marbh. Cuireadh i leataobh é, agus tamall beag ina dhiaidh sin tí sí páiste eile, agus cé an páiste a bhí ann ach an páiste a d'fhág sí féin ina diaidh sa bhaile!

'Come, come!' arsa sise, 'fágaigí an páiste seo arais!'

'Ní fhágfaidh, maise,' arsa fear acu, 'ach bí thusa ag imeacht amach as seo comh tiubh agus a thig leat!'

Chuaigh an bhean fá dtaobh den pháiste, agus bhí cineál ínteacht soithigh crochta a chois an dorais, agus tíodh sí iad ag cur na méar ann nuair a bhíodh siad amach is isteach ar an doras. Chuir sí féin a méar ins an tsoitheach bheag seo, agus thóg sí braon uisce a bhí ann, agus chuir sí ar a bathais é. Tháinig sí abhaile agus an páiste léithi.

Bhí go maith agus ní rabh go holc. Coicís ina dhiaidh sin bhí aonach i mBaile an Droichid, agus smaoitigh sí go rachadh sí chun aonaigh go bhfeiceadh sí caidé bhí ag gabháil. Ag gabháil síos an Caiseal daoithi mhothaigh sí an t-an-challán, agus mar bheadh séideán gaoithe móire ar an aonach. Caidé a bhí ann ach bunadh na gcnoc. Chuaigh sí síos agus isteach fríofa, agus cé a thug sí fá dear ina measc ach an fear céanna seo a dtearn sí freastal ar a bhean. Tharraing sí air, agus d'fhiafraigh sí de caidé mar bhí bean an toighe. Sula dtug sé freagar ar bith uirthi, ní thearn sé ach a lámh a thógáil agus steall sé an tsúil aisti.

'Anois,' a deir sé léithi, 'ní fheicfidh tú mise ná aon duine dá mbainí domh an dá lá shaol a bheas agat!'

Is cosúil nuair a chuir an bhean seo an t-uisce a bhí sa tsoitheach ar a bathais, gur shil cuid de anuas ina súil, agus ba leis an tsúil sin a chonaic sí eisean. Ní fhacaí sí é leis an tsúil eile, agus ní fhacaí duine ar bith eile é ach oiread. Mhair an ghaoth mhór bunús an lae, agus bhí an scairteach agus an callán agus an gleo le cluinstin i rith an lae acu agus gan fios acu caidé a bhí ann.

THE MIDWIFE WHO LOST AN EYE

There was a woman beyond here at Baile Buí one time. She was one of those midwives who used to attend women in childbirth. One night a horseman came to her door and aroused her, saying he had need of her. She said she was loath to leave the house at that hour of the night without knowing where she was going.

'Don't be in the least afraid,' said the horseman to her. 'I will leave you back safe and sound at your own door before tomorrow morning!'

She got ready and sat up behind him on the horse. Off they went and she did not know how far they had gone — perhaps they had gone into the next parish — but at last they came to the face of a crag. A door opened and they went in. They rode on until they came to a big castle which was full of people all eating and drinking. He took her to a room where there was a woman in labour. After a while the child was born, a dead child. It was put aside, and shortly afterwards she saw another child and what child was it but her own that she had left at home!

'Come, come,' said she, 'leave this child back!'

'I will not, indeed,' said one of them, 'but go you out from here as quickly as you can!'

The woman went to the child. There was a vessel of some sort hanging beside the door, and she had seen them putting their fingers into it as they went in and out. She herself put her finger in this little vessel and took a drop of water from it and put it on her forehead.[1] She came back home with her child.

Well and good. A fortnight later there was a fair at Kilcar, and she thought she would go to the fair and see what was going on. Going down by Caiseal she heard a great noise as if there was a big blast of wind at the fair. What was it but the

---

1. Compare the small ceramic holy-water fonts fixed inside the doors of many Irish Catholic homes, and the custom of dipping the fingers and blessing oneself before going out.

hill-folk! She went down amongst them, and who did she see but the very man whose wife she had attended. She went up to him and asked him how his wife was. Before he made any reply to her, he raised his hand and gouged her eye out.

'Now,' said he to her, 'you will not see me or anyone belonging to me as long as you live!'

It is likely that when this woman put the water from the vessel on her forehead some of it trickled into her eye, and it was with this eye she

saw him. She did not see him with the other eye, and no one else saw him either.[2] The big wind lasted most of the day, and a howling noise and clamour was heard without people knowing what caused it.

---

2. Other versions of this legend say that the midwife delivered a healthy child, and was given an ointment to rub to its eyes, before being brought safely home. She also rubbed some on her own eye, and this later enabled her to see the fairy man at the fair.

ÉAMON A BÚRC

(1866–1942)

from:
ÉAMON A BÚRC: SCÉALTA
(1983)

Peadar Ó Ceannabháin, *Éamon a Búrc: Scéalta* (Dublin: An Clóchomhar, 1983), pp. 267–73. Translation and headnote, A.B.[2]]

[Much longer than the average Irish legend of the supernatural, this is a master-storyteller's account of a young woman taken by the fairies. It uses repetition, formulaic passages, lengthy description and other techniques more often found in folktale to achieve its length, but also provides a thoughtful account of the psychological dilemmas which are more often implicitly than explicitly treated of in fairy legends. Stories like this one reinforce the restrictions placed on young people's freedom, and place special emphasis on the dangers which await young women if they are allowed out alone; however, they can also offer an imaginative escape from domesticity and the constraints of family. Here the young woman's parents treat her brusquely, but she finds sympathy, as well as danger, when she stumbles into the fairies' dwelling. Storytellers constantly emphasize the importance of not eating food offered by the fairies, an injunction which carries meaning at several levels. It protects children and adults against food which may be poisonous or rotting, offers guidelines for people's obligations of hospitality towards others, and reinforces the most prevalent message of fairy legend: the need to be vigilant about boundaries of all kinds. Here, the young woman's refusal of food becomes a battle of wills with an older woman, and is strikingly reminiscent of modern descriptions of eating disorders, while her months of illness after a thorn has pierced her leg may be read as a metaphor for pregnancy following rape.[1]

BEAN ÓG A TUGADH SA mBRUÍN

Insa tseanaimsir anseo i gConamara bhí lánúin a phós agus bhí beirt mhac acu agus iníon agus beirt fhear bhreá agus ní raibh bean ar bith insa tír ba dathúla ná an iníon nuair a tháinig sí suas ina bean óg. Lá, ghabh duine de na fir óga amach chun cnoic ag baint ualach fraoigh agus nuair a ghabh sé i mbun an fhraoigh dá bhaint bhí aill ann agus bhí fraoch an-bhreá air, agus suas leis i mullach na haille ag baint an fhraoch (sic). Agus dúirt an rud insan aill: 'Céard tá tú a dhéanamh ansin?'

'Ag baint fraoigh,' a deir an fear óg.

'Déarfainnse leat,' a deir an rud insan aill — an duine — 'a fhágáil agus go mbadh é ab fhearr duit.'

Agus d'fhág. Agus ar an mbealach ag teacht abhaile dó bhí an t-ualach ar a dhroim, agus leagadh é, agus labhair an glór de bhean a tháinig ina dhiaidh taobh thiar de:

'Ní hé sin muis,' a deir sí, 'do chuid de fós: níl muide réidh fós leat chor ar bith. Lig tú an

---

1. See Angela Bourke, 'Fairies and Anorexia: Nuala Ní Dhomhnaill's "Amazing Grass"', *Proceedings of the Harvard Celtic Colloquium*, vol. 13 (1993 [1995]), pp. 25–38.

2. An earlier version of this translation has appeared in Paul Brennan and Catherine de Saint Phalle (eds.), *Arguing at the Crossroads: Essays on a Changing Ireland* (Dublin: New Island Books, 1997), pp. 67–74, and in *Gender and Sexuality in Modern Ireland*, Anthony Bradley and Maryann Valiulis (eds.) (Amherst: University of Massachusetts Press/American Conference for Irish Studies, 1997), pp. 299–314.

bháisteach aníos agus anuas orainn agus d'fhága tú réidh muid.'

Chaith sé an t-ualach de agus rith sé agus d'fhága sé ansin é, agus tháinig sé abhaile agus d'inis sé an scéal. Agus nuair a d'inis, dúirt an t-athair agus an mháthair leis nár cheart dó, ó chuala sé an chéad ghlór, é a leanúint suas ná bacadh leis ní ba mhó.

'Tá an t-ualach fágtha i mo dhiaidh agam,' a deir sé, 'insan áit ar leagadh mé agus ar labhair an bhean liom.'

'Má tá,' a deir an t-athair agus an mháthair, 'fág ansin é.'

Agus d'fhága agus níor chorraíodar riamh é.

Bhí go maith agus ní raibh go holc. Bhí beithigh ar chnoc acu agus théidís gach uile mhaidin ag bleán na mbeithíoch chun an chnoic, agus duine ar an *turn* den chlann mhac. Agus bhí siad imithe lá ón mbaile ar ócáide gnotha, ag déanamh rud éigin eile lá, agus bhí an lá ag fás deireanach agus an tráthnóna ag teacht agus dúirt an t-athair leis an mbean óg éirí agus a dhul amach ag bleán na mbeithíoch. Agus ní raibh aon fhonn ar an mbean óg a dhul ann. Dúirt sí go raibh sé ag fás deireanach.

'Déan deifir,' a deir an mháthair, 'agus ná lig níos deireanaí ort féin é.'

Ach bhí an ghrian go hard. Rug sí ar a canna agus ar naigín — is iad a bhíodh ag imeacht san am sin. Agus ghabh sí amach agus nuair a ghabh, is é an t-ainm a bhí ar an áit a dtáinig sí imleach agus bhí na beithigh ina seasamh ar thaobh tamhnóg ar mhullach an imligh. Leag sí an canna lena hais. Agus nuair a leag sí an canna lena hais, thug sí an sean-naigín léi agus chuaigh sí ag bleán na bó sa naigín. Agus nuair a bhíodh an naigín sin bhainne blite i gcónaí aici, bheireadh sí ar an naigín agus dhóirteadh sí sa *tin can* í. Ach bhí sí mar sin riamh ó naigín go naigín ag bleán na mbeithíoch go raibh an canna lán — canna mór millteach líonta de bhainne agus lán.

Nuair a d'iompaigh sí thart ag dul ag tiomáint na mbeithíoch roimpi, ní raibh an canna le feiceáil aici agus ní raibh a fhios aici ó Dhia na ngrást cá raibh sí. Bhí sí dá tuairteáil agus an tráthnóna ag teacht agus dhorchaigh an lá suas le ceo, agus dá mbeadh sí ó shoin ann ní bhfaigheadh sí aon channa agus ní bhfaigheadh sí naigín ó leag sí uaithi é. Bhí sí ag imeacht roimpi nó go raibh sé ina oíche. Agus nuair a bhí sé ina oíche dhubh thosaigh sí dá leagan agus dá

tuairteáil trí chnoic agus sléibhte agus bogachaí agus ag dul go básta in aibhneachaí, agus ní raibh a fhios aici ó Dhia na ngrást cá raibh sí go bhfaca sí solas tamall maith uaithi:

'Mó ghrá chugam!' a deir sí, 'marab sheod teach éigin agus mara dtrialla mé air níos túisce ná gheobhas mé bás anseo. Agus siúráilte má bhím ag siúl mar atá mé agus an drochúsáid atá mé a fháil, bog báite mar atá mé, ní bheidh aon bheochas ar maidin ionam.'

Rinne sí ar an teach a bhfaca sí an solas ann, agus ní raibh ann ach go raibh sí in ann a cosaí a chur thar a chéile de bharr a cuid éadaí a bheith fliuch báite agus neart puitigh orthu. Nuair a tháinig sí isteach chonaic sí daoine ag dul trína chéile, agus bia agus beatha agus bord leagtha i lár an urláir, agus bean rua ina seasamh ag dul tríd an mbeatha agus bean dubh í féin ina seasamh an taobh eile. Agus nuair a chonaic an bhean dubh í seo ag triall isteach go dtí an doras, ghabh sí go dtí an doras agus dúirt sí léi gan aon ghreim beatha a ithe dá dtairgeofaí di go deo go dtéadh sí féin dá roinnt agus dá thabhairt di:

'Ar a bhfaca tú riamh agus ar a bhfeicfidh tú go brách aon bhlas den bheatha atá an bhean rua ag dul tríd ná caith thusa é go deo go dté mise agus go n-abraí mé leat a dhul ag ithe beatha agus ansin caithfidh tú é agus ní bheidh aon dochar duit ann.'

Nuair a tháinig sí isteach cuireadh céad míle fáilte roimpi ina hainm agus ina sloinneadh. Agus ní i bhfad nó go dtáinig banríon bhreá anuas, de bhean an-bhreá, as an seomra agus chuir sí féin céad míle fáilte roimpi agus d'ordaigh sí don bhean rua seo a suipéar a leagan anuas ag an mbean a tháinig isteach. Ghabh agus leag. Agus nuair a bhí an bia dá réiteach chroith an bhean dubh a ceann uirthi gan a dhul ag an mbord ná aon bhlas de a ithe — i ngan fhios. Nuair a bhí an bia leagtha anuas ag an mbean rua dúirt sí léi suí isteach. Agus dúirt sí ná raibh aon ocras uirthi, nach n-íosfadh sí aon bhlas beatha anocht go maidin.

'Is aisteach an rud é sin,' a deir an bhean rua seo, 'ith beatha agus is maith duit a fháil. Agus tá a fhios ag gach uile dhuine duine ar bith atá ag siúl ó mhaidin inniu i gcás go dteastaíonn bia anois uaidh.'

'Ní theastaíonn is níl mé in ann aon bhlas a ithe,' a deir an bhean shaolta.

Tháinig an mháistreás anuas arís, agus badh i

máistreás na bruíne í. Insa mbruín a bhí sí agus dúirt sí léi beatha a leagan anuas aici.

'Leag mé cheana anuas aici é,' a deir an bhean rua, 'agus ní íosfadh sí uaim é.'

'Leag arís anuas aici é nó go n-ithe sí beatha,' a deir an bhean mhór ramhar seo a tháinig as an seomra anuas, 'le m'ordúsa,' a deir sí, 'abair léi a dhul dá ithe.'

Leag agus nuair a leag, dúirt sí nach n-íosfadh sí aon bhlas de, ná raibh aon ocras uirthi agus nach raibh sí in ann aon bhlas a ithe.

'Tá sé chomh maith duit ithe,' a deir an bhean rua, a deir sí, 'níl aon mhaith duit ag caint, caithfidh tú bia a ithe agus is mór an peaca duine a bheith ina throscadh agus neart bídh agus beatha anseo le n-ithe agus le n-ól aige má theastaíonn sé uaidh.'

'Ní theastaíonn sé uaim, go raibh maith agat agus fad saoil!' a deir an bhean shaolta.

As sin go ceann tamaill ghabh sí ina bun arís agus dúirt sí léi a dhul ag ithe beatha.

'Ní ghabhfad,' a deir sí, 'níl mé in ann.'

Agus níl aon uair a d'ordaíodh an bhean rua don bhean shaolta a dhul ag ithe na beatha nach gcroithfeadh an bhean dubh, a bhí ag dul tríd an teach taobh thall, a ceann uirthi gan ithe. Nuair a bhí an bhean rua sáraithe agus nach n-íosfadh sí aon bhlas uaithi, dúirt an bhean rua:

'B'fhéidir go leagfadh Bríd beatha aici go n-íosfadh sí é,' agus ba sheod í an bhean dubh.

'Leag bia chuici,' a deir banríon na bruíne, ag cur aniar a ceann as an seomra, 'a Bhríd, thusa.'

D'éirigh Bríd agus leag sí anuas bia agus beatha aici agus d'ith sí é. Agus nuair a d'ith bhí sí ceart. Ach dúirt Bríd léi ansin — an bhean a dtugadar Bríd uirthi — dúirt sí léi ag an mbord, i gcogar:

'Ar a bhfaca tú riamh,' a deir sí, 'agus ar a bhfeicfidh tú go brách ná hith aon bhlas beatha insan áit a bhfuil tú ach an bia a leagfas mise chugat anuas le n-ithe, nó má itheann, seo ní fhágfaidh tú go brách.'

Bhí go maith agus ní raibh go holc. Lá arna mhárach badh é an cás céanna é. Badh í an bhean rua a leag an beatha aici is ní íosfadh sí é. Agus nuair a tháinig lá arna mhárach níor tháinig sí abhaile agána muintir agus ghabhadar dá tóraíocht chun an chnoic agus ní raibh aon fháil uirthi. Bhí an bheirt dearthár dá tóraíocht feadh na hoíche agus feadh an lae lá arna mhárach, agus fuaireadar an canna agus é lán le bainne ar

an tamhnóg bhán seo a bhí ar an imleach agus an naigín leagtha lena ais. Ar ndóigh, thugadar abhaile an bainne, is dócha liom, ní hé go leor suim a bhí acu ann, bhí siad ag caitheamh i ndiaidh na deirfíre chomh mór sin. Agus ní raibh a fhios acu ó Dhia na ngrást cé ndeachaigh sí. Bhí siad gach uile lá dá raibh sí ar iarraidh feadh sé lá na seachtaine dá tóraíocht, gur dhúradar gurb é an chuma a ndearna sí ar siúl léi féin — ar chaith sí in abhainn nó i loch í féin agus gur bháigh sí í féin. Ní raibh aon tuairisc uirthi abhus nó thall. Agus is é an áit a raibh sí coinnithe istigh insa mbruín feadh na sé lá agus na sé oíche agus gan iadsan ag déanamh cónaí ná stad oíche ná lá, ná codladh, ach ag caoineadh agus dá tóraíocht, agus na bailte.

Bhí go maith go dtí an séú oíche. Bhí sí coinnithe istigh agus nuair a bhí sí coinnithe istigh, bhí Bríd — mar a dúradar féin le Bríd a bhí sa mbruín — bhí sí ina seasamh sa doras agus chonaic sí fear ag teacht.

'Mh'anam,' a deir sí, 'go bhfuil Seán Rua ag teacht.'

Agus ní raibh a fhios ag an mbean shaolta cérb é Seán Rua. Agus mhaisce, tháinig sé isteach. Agus badh éard a bhí ann — bhí sé básaithe leis an fhad seo aimsire — agus badh éard a bhí ann col ceathar den bhean shaolta bhí istigh. Agus nuair a tháinig sé isteach insa mbruín chuir sé cúl a chos leis an áit a raibh an tine agus bhreathnaigh sé ar a chol ceathar a bhí istigh insa mbruín.

'Céard a thug tusa,' a deir sé, 'isteach anseo?' ag breith ar ghualainn uirthi agus dá caitheamh amach.

Dúirt sí ná raibh a fhios aici.

'Gabh amach anois,' a deir sé, 'agus téighre abhaile go beo!'

'Ní ghabhfaidh,' a deir an bhean rua.

Agus tháinig an bhanríon anuas í féin agus dúirt sí nach ngabhfadh. Agus dúirt sé seo go ngabhfadh. Agus d'ionsaigh bualadh agus marú idir Seán Rua agus Bríd a chúnamh dó, agus iad féin ag marú a chéile.

'Tá sé chomh maith,' a deir an bhanríon, 'í a chur abhaile.'

Rugadh uirthi agus caitheadh amach ar an tsráid í, agus ghabh Seán Rua agus Bríd in éineacht léi go dtug sé tamall ón teach í agus go dtug sé cóngarach go leor dá teach féin í. Agus nuair a thug, ní raibh ann ach go raibh Seán Rua scartha léi agus Bríd nuair a cuireadh ar cheartmhullach a cinn í i ngar don teach agus ghabh bior géar suas ina glúin mar a bheadh snáthad mhór ann. Agus bhí sí ag teacht agus pian uirthi insa nglúin agus má bhí féin, dar fia, tháinig sí isteach. Agus nuair a tháinig sí isteach níor dhúirt sí aon bhlas faoi, ach d'fhiafraíodar di céard a d'éirigh di agus ghaireadar agus choiscreadar í agus thugadar im agus salann di agus gach uile shórt dár fhéadadar. Agus d'inis sí óna thús go dtína dheireadh dóibh ansin an scéal, agus ní ar leagan ná ar ghortú ná ar rud ar bith eile a bhí caint acu nó go raibh sé ina lá ar maidin.

Agus nuair a bhí sé ina lá ar maidin bhí an-phian ina glúin. Agus tráthnóna lae lá arna mhárach ní raibh sí in ann éirí ina seasamh ar an urlár le pian. An tríú lá b'éigean di fanacht sa leaba uilig, nó leaba fúithi sa gclúid agus daoine ag tabhairt aire di, agus gach aon sian aici agus scréachaíl — ag béiciúch chomh hard agus a bhí ina ceann le pian.

D'at a glúin suas. Bhí dochtúirí ag teacht go dtí í, bhí an sagart ag teacht go dtí í, ag iarraidh í a leigheas. Agus bhí gach uile shórt dá chaitheamh léi agus dá chur ar an gcois — plástair agus gach uile ní, agus ceiríní agus luibheannaí — agus ní raibh aon mhaith le déanamh di; nó go raibh sí mar sin go raibh sí ráithe, agus is é an chuma a raibh a cos ag méadú agus ag at go raibh sí ar ball chomh mór agus ná raibh duine ar bith in ann a cos a láimhsiú, bhí sí chomh mór chomh hataithe sin suas go dtí bun a ceathrú.

Chaith sí an-ghar do bhliain agus gach aon bhéic aici le pian feadh na haimsire ar chúl a cinn sa leaba, gan aon ghair ag duine cos ná lámh a leagan uirthi ach ag screadach le pian agus le piolóid; go dtí oíche a dtáinig seanbhean isteach — seanbhean siúil — agus bhí sí sa gclúid. Agus nuair a bhí:

'Muise,' a deir sí, 'an miste dúinn a fhiafraí céard tá ar an mbean atá ag béiciúch mar seo?'

'Ní miste,' a deir máthair na mná, ag inseacht di mar a d'insigh mé díbhse — gach uile shórt ní dár éirigh di agus an áit a raibh sí insa mbruín agus an bealach a dtáinig sí abhaile agus an bealach ar imigh sí ón mbaile ar dtús ag bleán na mbeithíoch.

'Hm,' a deir an tseanbhean.

'Agus is é an chuma ar airigh sí ar dtús é, leagadh í agus ghabh mar a ghabhfadh bior géar suas ina glúin agus d'at a glúin suas agus níl aon leigheas ina cionn agus creidim nach mbeidh go deo go bhfaighidh sí bás.'

'Dá mbeadh an lá ann,' a deir an tseanbhean, a deir sí, 'bheadh a fhios agamsa é, agus caithfidh muid fanacht go dtige an lá.'

Agus ar maidin chomh moch agus a d'fháinnigh an lá d'éirigh an tseanbhean agus ghabh sí amach roimh éirí gréine, agus pé ar bith asarlaíocht a bhí aici le luibheannaí, ghabh sí amach agus dúirt an luibh léi — agus thug sí isteach idir a dhá méir í — agus dúirt sí go n-éireodh.

'Huga leat anois,' a deir an tseanbhean, 'agus an áit a bhfuil an tine chnámh anois,' a deir an tseanbhean — an tráth den bhliain a bhí ann aimsir na Féile San Seáin, bhí tine chnámh ar an mbaile — agus dúirt an tseanbhean leo insan áit a raibh an tine chnámh a dhul ann agus dá bhfaighidís aon bhlas de na cnámhaí, na luaithreamáin féin, agus cuid de na sméara dóite a bhí sa tine a thabhairt leo abhaile:

'Agus an luibh seo,' a deir sí, 'a chur tríothu atá agamsa anseo agus a chur le glúin na mná sin idir dhá éadach, mara leigheasfaidh sé sin í níl a fhios agamsa,' a deir an tseanbhean, 'céard a leigheasfas í.'

Ghabh a máthair amach agus na deartháireacha agus mar a dúirt an tseanbhean leo rinne siad é. Agus nuair a rinne, bhí an luibh bainte ag an tseanbhean dóibh agus nuair a bhí, chuireadar suas trína chéile na cnámhannaí a bhí dóite ina smúdar agus na haithinneacha a bhí sa tine chnámh agus an luibh trína chéile, idir dhá éadach, agus leagadar isteach idir dhá éadach ar a glúin é.

'Ná corraigí é sin anois,' a deir an tseanbhean, a deir sí, 'go dtí maidin amárach. Pé ar bith pian nó pionós a bheas uirthi go dtí sin ná bíodh lámh ná cos agaibhse ann, agus nuair a bheas, rachaidh mise i mbannaí díbh go mbeidh sí leigheasta ar maidin amárach chomh luath agus a éireos grian. Beannacht libh,' a deir sí, 'tá mise ag dul ag imeacht,' a deir an tseanbhean.

'Ní féidir,' a dúirt bean an tí, 'go bhfuil.'

'Táim,' a deir sí, 'níl mé ag dul ag fanacht agaibh níos faide.'

Ghabh sí amach.

'Ba cheart duit,' a deir fear an tí agus an chlann, 'rud éigin a thabhairt don tseanbhean sin.'

Agus nuair a ghabh bean an tí amach ina diaidh i gcionn tamaill le íocaíocht a thabhairt di agus ní raibh sí le fáil abhus ná thall aici.

'Níl a fhios agam ó Dhia na ngrást,' a deir sí, 'cá ndeachaigh sí.'

Ach ó cuireadh an ceirín seo — an plástar — le glúin na mná óige, ní raibh aon uafás faoi luí na gréine ach an phian a bhí uirthi, ag béiciúch go raibh sé ina lá geal. Ach rinneadar mar a d'ordaigh an tseanbhean, agus nuair a rinne ghabhadar roimh éirí gréine ar maidin go dtí í agus scaoileadar anuas na ceirteachaí seo di agus gur thógadar amach an plástar a bhí acu curtha léi, agus tháinig fad do mhéire nó níos mó de shnáthad mhór amach as a glúin in éineacht leis an éadach ar maidin, le feiceál ag gach uile fhear. Agus níl aon phointe ón am sin amach ná raibh sí ag feabhsú, ach faoi cheann seachtaine bhí sí in ann éirí a chois na tine. Agus faoi cheann míosa bhí sí in ann a dhul timpeall an tí. Ach faoi cheann ráithe bhí sí chomh maith agus a bhí sí riamh.

Níl aon bhréag ansin. D'éirigh sé i gConamara anseo insa tseanaimsir.

Beannacht dílis Dé agus na hEaglaise le hanam na marbh agus go mba seacht gcéad míle fearr a bheas sinn féin agus an comhluadar bliain ó anocht.

A YOUNG WOMAN TAKEN BY THE FAIRIES

Long ago here in Connemara there was a couple who got married. They had two sons and a daughter: two fine men, and there wasn't a more beautiful woman in the country than the girl when she grew up. One day, one of the young men went out to the hill for a load of heather.[1] When he started to cut, he was beside a cliff, and he noticed lovely heather growing on top of it, so up he went, cutting away. Suddenly a voice in the cliff said, 'What are you doing there?'

'Cutting heather,' said the young man.

'I'm telling you,' said the thing in the cliff — the person — 'you'd better stop, if you know what's good for you.'

He stopped. But on his way home with the load on his back he tripped, and a woman's voice spoke behind him:

'You've not heard the last of this, you know! We're not finished with you at all. You let the rain in on us from every side and you've left us in a terrible state.'

He threw down his load and ran, and left it there. He came home and told his story. When he told it, his father and mother said he'd had no business, once he heard the first voice, staying there at all, or having anything more to do with it.

'I left the load behind me,' he said, 'where I fell, and where the woman spoke to me.'

'Well then,' said the father and mother, 'leave it there.'

And he did, and they never moved it.

Well and good. They had cows out on the hill, and every morning they used to go out to milk them, the sons taking turns. Then one day they were away from home on some business, something they had to do one day. It was getting late, evening was coming, and the father told the young woman to go out and milk the cows. She didn't want to go. She said it was getting too late.

'Hurry up,' said the mother, 'and don't let it get any later.'

The sun was still fairly high. She took her can and her naggin measure — that's what they used in those days — and out she went, and the place she came to was an *imleach*, a little hill, with the cows standing on a grassy patch on the top. She put down the can and left it on the ground, and then she took the old naggin with her and went around milking the cows into it. Every time the naggin was full she carried it over and poured it into the tin can. She went on like that, naggin by naggin, until the can was full: a great big can full to the top with milk.

But when she turned around then to drive the cows ahead of her, she couldn't see the can, and she didn't know where in God's name she was. She was tripping and falling, and it was getting dark, and foggy, and if she was there till now she couldn't find the can, or the naggin, from the moment she left it out of her hand. She was going on like that until night fell, falling and stumbling in the black darkness among hills and mountains and bogs, and going up to her waist in rivers, with no idea where in God's name she was, until she saw a light in the distance:

---

1. Used for animal bedding.

'I declare to goodness,' she said, 'that must be a house, and I'd better head for it sooner than die here! If I keep walking like this, taking the knocks I'm taking, and wet to the skin as I am, there'll surely be no life left in me by morning.'

She headed for the house where she saw the light, but she could hardly move one foot in front of the other, her clothes were so wet and so full of mud. When she got to the house, she saw people moving around inside, and food and drink on a table set in the middle of the floor. A red-haired woman was serving the food, and a black-haired woman was by her side. As soon as the black-haired woman saw this girl coming to the door, she came over and told her not to eat any food whatsoever that might be offered to her until she herself divided it and gave it to her:

'For the sake of all you ever saw or ever will see, don't taste a bite of the food the woman with the red hair is serving, until I come and tell you to eat. You can eat then and it will do you no harm.'

When the young woman came into the house, people called her by her own name and surname and made her heartily welcome. And it wasn't long before a fine queen came in from the other room — a beautiful woman — and she made her welcome as well, and ordered the red-haired woman to set out a supper for this woman who had just arrived. The red-haired woman set to work. But while the food was being got ready, the black-haired woman shook her head at her, to remind her not to go to the table or eat anything. The red-haired woman laid out the food then and told her to sit down. But she said she wasn't hungry, that she wouldn't eat anything until morning.

'That's very strange behaviour,' said this red-haired woman. 'Eat! It's good for you. Everyone knows that a person who's been walking since morning needs food by now.'

'I don't,' said the earthly woman, 'I can't eat anything.'

The mistress came in again — the mistress of the fairy-fort, for that's where she was — and told the woman to give her something to eat.

'I already did,' said the red-haired woman, 'but she wouldn't eat it.'

'Serve her again so she eats a meal,' said a big fat woman who came down from the other room. 'My instructions. Tell her she has to eat it.'

The red-haired woman brought the food again, but the young woman said she wouldn't eat; she wasn't hungry and she couldn't eat anything.

'You may as well eat,' said the red-haired woman. 'Talking won't do any good. You have to eat; it's sinful for a person to fast when there's so much food and drink here for anyone who wants it.'

'I don't want it, thank you very much and long life to you,' said the earthly woman.

She kept at her for a while even after that, trying to persuade her to eat.

'No,' the young woman kept saying, 'I can't.' And every time the red-haired woman ordered the earthly woman to eat, the woman with the dark hair would shake her head as she passed along the other side of the house, telling her not to. At last, when she still wouldn't eat, the red-haired woman gave up:

'Maybe if Bríd served her she'd eat.' — That was the dark-haired woman.

'Serve her food,' said the queen of the fairy fort, putting her head out the door of the other room. 'You, Bríd.'

Bríd got up and placed food in front of her, and she ate it, and when she had eaten she felt fine. But Bríd — the woman they called Bríd — whispered to her as she sat at the table, 'For the sake of all you ever saw or ever will see, don't taste any bite in this place except what I put in front of you, for if you do you'll never be able to leave.'

Well and good. The next day the same thing happened. The red-haired woman served her and she wouldn't eat. And when the next day came and she didn't come home to her family, they went out to the hill to look for her, but they found no sign of her. All that night and all the next day her two brothers searched. They found the can full of milk on the little hill, with the naggin laid down beside it. They took the milk home of course, though I don't suppose they had much interest in it, they were so upset about their sister. They didn't know where in the name of God she'd gone. Six days that week they searched for her, every day that she was missing, until they decided that she must have done away with herself — thrown herself into a lake or a river and drowned. There was not a sign of her anywhere. But she was being held in the fairy fort all that time, six days and six nights, and they didn't stop or sleep, day or night, but mourned and searched for her all over.

That went on until the sixth night. She was being kept indoors, but while she was inside, Bríd — the woman they called Bríd in the fairy fort — was standing at the door, and she saw a man approaching.

'Well I declare,' she said, 'here's Seán Rua.'

And the earthly woman didn't know who Seán Rua was, but in he came. And who was he — he'd been dead a certain length of time — but a first cousin of her own! He came into the fairy fort and stood with his back to the fire, looking at his first cousin who was being held there.

'What brought you here?' he asked, taking her by the shoulder and shoving her towards the door.

She said she didn't know.

'Get out right now,' he said, 'and go home.'

'She will not,' said the red-haired woman.

And the queen herself came out and told her not to go, but she said that she would, and then a fight broke out: Seán Rua, with Bríd helping him, against those others, and they were killing each other.

'We'd better let her go home,' said the queen.

They grabbed her and threw her out onto the ground. Seán Rua and Bríd went with her some of the way from the house, until she was fairly close to her own home. But no sooner had Seán Rua and Bríd left her than she fell down near the house and a sharp spine, like a big needle, went right into her knee. She kept on walking, though her knee was very sore, and sure enough, she made it home.

When she came in, she didn't say anything about it, but they asked her what had happened to her, and blessed her and praised her and gave her butter and salt and every other kind of thing they could. She told them the story from start to finish, and they had other things to talk about besides falls and injuries and things of that kind from then until morning.

But when the morning came, she had a terrible pain in her knee, and by the next afternoon it was so bad she couldn't stand on the floor. By the third day she had to stay in bed altogether. They had to make up a bed for her beside the fire, and people had to nurse her, and all the time she moaned and screamed — screeching at the top of her voice with pain.

The knee swelled. Doctors came to her, the priest came to her, trying to cure her. They tried everything: plasters and everything, poultices and herbs, but nothing could be done for her, until she'd been there three months, and the leg was still swelling, and getting so big that no one could lift it, it was so swollen, all the way up to the top of her thigh.

She spent nearly a whole year lying on her back in bed, screaming all the time with pain. No one could lay a finger on her, or she screamed with pain and agony, until one night an old woman — an old travelling woman — came in and sat by the fire.

'Is it any harm to ask what ails the woman who's screaming?' she asked.

'No harm at all,' said the young woman's mother, and she told her what I've told you: everything that had happened to her, how she had been taken into the fairy fort, and had made her way home, and how she had gone out milking in the first place.

'Hm,' said the old woman.

'And the first thing she felt was when she fell down, and something like a sharp spine went up into her knee, and the knee swelled up. There's no cure for her, and I'm afraid there won't be now until she dies.'

'If it was daylight,' said the old woman, 'I could do something. We'll have to wait for daylight.'

Next morning, as soon as the day dawned, the old woman got up and went out before the sun was up, and whatever secret way she had with herbs, she went out and the herb told her — she brought it in between two fingers — told her it would work.

'Now,' said the old woman, 'off you go to where the bonfire is' — it was around St John's Eve, so there was a bonfire in the village.[2] She told them to go to the bonfire site and look for some trace of bone, even ashes, and to bring home some of the burnt embers from the fire.[3]

'And mix them with this herb here and put them on her knee between two cloths,' said the old woman, 'and if that doesn't cure her, I don't know what will.'

2. 23 June, the custom of lighting bonfires on St John's Eve was once widespread in Europe. It continues in parts of Ireland.
3. For magical uses of embers from a bonfire, cf. M. Carbery, *The Farm by Lough Gur*, p. 163.

The mother and the two brothers went out and did everything the old woman had told them. The old woman had picked the herb for them, so they mixed up the bones that were burnt to ashes and embers in the bonfire with the herb, wrapped it all up, and laid it between two cloths on her knee.

'Don't move that now,' said the old woman, 'until tomorrow morning. Whatever pain or torment she suffers until then, don't lay a finger on her, and I guarantee she'll be healed by morning as soon as the sun rises. Goodbye to you now,' she said, 'I'm off.'

'Oh,' said the woman of the house, 'you can't be going.'

'I am,' she said. 'I'm not staying here any longer,' and out she went.

'You know,' said the father and the sons, 'you should give that old woman something.'

But when the woman of the house went out after her a few minutes later, to pay her something, she couldn't see her anywhere.

'I don't know where in the name of God she's gone,' she said.

But from the moment the plaster — the poultice — was put on the young woman's knee, there never was such a horror under the sun as the pain she felt, or the way she screamed, until day broke. But they did what the old woman had told them. Before sunrise in the morning they went to her, and when they took away the rags and lifted off the plaster that morning, a needle as long as your finger, or longer, came out of her knee along with the cloth, for every man to see. From that moment on she improved. By the end of a week she could sit by the fire; at the end of a month she could move around the house, and after three months she was as well as she had ever been.

That's no lie. It happened here in Connemara in the old days. The blessings of God and the Church on the souls of the dead, and may we and the company be seventeen hundred thousand times better a year from tonight!

SÉAMUS Ó CEALLA

(fl. 1937)

from:
THE BANSHEE (1986)

[Stories are told all over Ireland about the banshee (*bean sí*, literally, fairy woman), a solitary supernatural death-messenger who is said to 'follow' certain families, especially those whose names begin with O' or Mac, crying or appearing to foretell their members' deaths. Her most consistent features are her unearthly screaming and her long hair. The legend of the banshee's comb is found in complementary distribution with the coastal legend of 'The Man who Married the Mermaid' (pp. 1280–1281).[1] Both feature otherworld women combing their long hair, and are sometimes told to discourage children from picking up old combs they may find. Patricia Lysaght

points out in *The Banshee* (p. 167) that: 'The unusual length of this version has been achieved by a variety of devices. Certain motifs and episodes, such as the beetle[2] and the dramatic pursuit, have been borrowed from another legend current in the area. Runs,[3] formulas and other stylistic ornaments more commonly found in folktales . . . than in legends have been used, for example, *You'd think the March wind before him couldn't keep before him.* Explanations and discourses only marginally relating to the plot are lavishly supplied.' The description of the different uses of bog deal is typical. Headnote, A.B.]

THE BANSHEE'S COMB

I used to hear my father saying (the bed of heaven to his soul) that there was an old man of the Regans who lived here in Killeen[4] a good many

1. See Patricia Lysaght, *The Banshee*, 1986; distribution maps of the 'Mermaid' and 'Banshee's Comb' stories appear on pp. 158, 161 and 162; the story text is on pp. 164–7; it was collected by Seán Ó Flannagáin in 1937. See also Patricia Lysaght, *A Pocket Book of the Banshee* (Dublin: O'Brien Press; Niwot, Colorado: The Irish American Book Company, 1998), pp. 76–7.

2. A wooden paddle, used in washing clothes. Another legend depicts the *bean sí* as a washer of clothes.
3. Formulaic passages.
4. County Galway.

years ago. There were no candles or lamps going in them times but 'twas how everyone used to go to the bog and root up a good thick block of bog deal timber[5] and bring it home with him. He'd get his hatchet then and split that block up into *sliseóg*s,[6] nice thin long *sliseóg*s. Them *sliseóg*s then used to be dipped into tallow that they'd get out of the cattle or sheep they'd kill and then whenever they'd want a light they used one of them and someone would hold them in his hand or maybe they'd put it standing in the middle of a heap of potatoes while they'd be eating them for supper. Them *sliseóg*s that they used to burn that way were called *caisne*s or *caisnín*s. They usen't have the *caisnín*s burning all the night like the lamps are burning now. Devil a long they'd hould if they'd be wasting them like that. They'd use them only while they'd be putting down a pot or taking up a pot or if they were looking for something around the house. For the rest of the time they'd be sitting around the fire and 'tis how they'd be telling stories to one another and putting down on the ould times. The light of the turf fire was enough for them and there was some of the old people and they could hould telling stories forever. Well, this ould man of the Regans — he'd be Pateen Regan's great-grandfather, so that'll tell you that it must be a good long while ago — he had a big stump of bog deal like beyant[7] in Carrachán Bog, just at the foot of the mountain or in the mountain, as you might say. He had the stump rooted up and all, had it thrown up in the bank ready to bring home and as soon as night had fallen he made over across towards Carrachán. There is a stream running down this side of Carrachán and didn't he hear the beetling going on, on the top of the big flag that you'd pass going over. He was a kind of harum-scarum of a young man then and the devil one if he'd care for either *deamhan*[8] or *deabhal*.[9] He had that cutting in him.[10] He made over across to where he heard the beetling going on and sure enough he saw her[11] there and she having the beetle in one hand and a lovely rack [comb] in the other. He stepped

lightly in behind her, snapped the rack out of her hand and made one leap for the other bank and away with him home, and look here, the March wind before him couldn't keep up with him, he was that quick on his foot.

Away with the *bean sí* hither after him and every scream out of her worse than one another. She caught the beetle that was in her hand and flung it after him and I suppose that 'twas God that saved him or that he didn't give her the power to hit him, but anyways the beetle went whistling out by his poll and if he got it in the poll he was a dead man. Regan was a great runner and maybe 'twas how that Almighty God didn't give her the footing that he'd gave to Regan, but anyways, he was always able to keep before her. When she came up to the beetle she caught it the second time and Regan could hear it whistling out by his ear and I suppose it was promised to him, but anyways, it missed him the second time. The banshee came up with the beetle the third time and as soon as she caught it Regan was just turned in home at his own gable-end and didn't the banshee fire the beetle for the third time. Regan was just landed inside his own door when the beetle struck the gable-end and shook the house from head to bottom. He bolted the door and secured it from the inside with the *maide éamainn*[12] that they used to have in them times to secure the door in the time of a storm. They were all sitting down within at home and wasn't the heart put across them when they heard the scream outside the door. She told them in Irish to put the rack to her or that she'd knock the house. Regan rose and he took the spade and he left the rack on the top of the spade and caught the spade by the *feac* [handle] and pushed the rack out under the door to her. Half the iron of the spade was outside the door and the other half was inside. She caught the rack and half of the iron that was outside and brought the rack and half the spade with her. When they pulled in the spade again wasn't half of it gone! Next morning when they got up and went outside didn't they find the gable-end of the house split in two even halves from thatch to ground and any day that you go over to see Regan's ould *cabhail* [ruin] you'll see the gable-end split in two even halves and that's how it happened.

5. Wood from fallen trees, preserved in the acid bog; much used for building and fuel after deforestation.
6. Thin strips.
7. beyond.
8. demon.
9. devil.
10. That was his temperament.
11. i.e. the banshee.

12. A bar across the doorframe, used to keep the door closed.

MAIRÉAD NÍ FHEARFHIA

(b. 1844)

from:
CHILD MURDERESS AND DEAD CHILD TRADITIONS: A COMPARATIVE STUDY (1991)

[Petticoat Loose is the name of a malevolent female spirit known to speakers of Irish and English in the southeast of Ireland. She is said to be a woman whose life was so evil that no place could be found for her after death in either heaven or hell. She accosts men on the road and first tries to seduce them, but then the unbelievable weight of her sins makes the men and even their horses collapse. When interrogated by a priest, she gives a catalogue of her sins, and usually the priest declares that none of them would have damned her if she had not killed an unbaptized child. She is finally banished, to the Dead Sea (as here) or to the Red Sea, where she is condemned for all eternity to bail the sea with a bottomless cup, or to make ropes of sand. In this version, from County Waterford, Petticoat Loose's most heinous sin was drinking alcohol instead of attending mass. This legend was recorded in 1931 by Pádraig Ó Fionníosa from 87-year-old Mairéad Ní Fhearfhia of Glenahiry, Kilronan, Ballymacarbry, County Waterford (IFC 85: 257–60). From Anne O'Connor, *Child Murderess and Dead Child Traditions: A Comparative Study* (Folklore Fellows Communications, No. 249) (Helsinki: Academia Scientiarum Fennica, 1991), pp. 225–7. Translation by Anne O'Connor; headnote, A.B.]

PETTICOAT LOOSE

Bhí sí ina cónaí i gCoiligán, dosna Hanagáin ab ea í, ach *Petticoat Loose* an leasainm a bhí uirthi. Drochbhean ba ea í in gach aon slí; bhíodh sí ag bualadh a hathar is a máthar, mharaigh sí páiste a bhí aici is chrom sí ag déanamh suas le fear eile is mharaíodar ansan an chéad fhear. Ansan bhíodh sí ag ól i measc na bhfear síos ag 'Pike an Bhrúnaigh' i gCoiligán.

Fuair sí bás i dtigh ósta 'An Pike' idir dhá bhairille beathuisce aimsear an chéad aifrinn. As san amach bhíodh sí á taispeáint í féin. An oíche a cuireadh í bhí daoine ag ól ag an 'Pike' is dúradar 'Tá sé ana-uaigneach anocht mar ná fuil Petticoat inár measc'. Nuair a chuadar amach ar an mbóthar bhí sí ann rompu is caitheadar

filleadh thairsti nó bheadh siad marbh aici. Bhíodh sí ag marú na ndaoine ansan is tháinig fear léi oíche is d'iarr sé uirthi suí isteach sa trucall is gan fhios aige cé bhí aige. Shuigh sí is ní bhfaigheadh an capall coiscéim a chuir de.

'Dia linn,' arsa an fear, 'cad atá ar an gcapall agus is é an capall is fearr sa cheantar é.'

'Ó is mise atá ag déanamh an ualach go léir,' is ansan dúirt sí leis gurb í féin Petticoat is go raibh an oiread san tonnmhaí ar an láimh a bhíodh ag bualadh a hathar is a leath ar an láimh bhíodh ag bualadh a máthar, is ar sí leis,

'Mharóinn tusa anois ach feabhas d'fhear tú ach tá an capall tabhartha is beidh sí caillte ar maidin, is tá peidléir ag gabháil an bhóthair sa tSeanphobal is beidh sé agam i d'áit.'

Fuaireadh an peidléir marbh ar an mbóthar ar maidin. Níorbh fhada ina dhiaidh san gur tháinig sí le fear eile is bhí sí chun é mharú ach chuir sé guí comh truamhéalach i láthair an Tiarna fóirithint air gur lig sé an tAthair Seán Ó Maonaigh, sagart ón áit sin, ósna Flaithis á fhuascailt.

'Cén sórt bean í sin,' arsa an tAthair Seán leis an bhfear. 'Bean a tháinig liom, a Athair,' ar seisean.

'Bhuel, is olc an bhean í sin,' ar sé, ag iompú léi siúd.

'Cad a dhamnaigh tusa a dhiabhail?'

'Mharaigh mé páiste,' ar sí.

'Níor dhamnaigh sin tú, a dhiabhail,' ar sé.

'Bhínn ag bualadh m'athar is mo mháthar,' ar sise.

'Níor dhamnaigh sin tú, a dhiabhail,' ar sé.

'Mharaigh mé mo chéile,' ar sí.

'Ní hé sin féin a dhamnaigh tú, a dhiabhail,' ar sé.

'Bhínn ag ól is fuair mé bás in aimsear an aifrinn, ag an "Pike".'

'Sin é a dhamnaigh tú, a dhiabhail, is fág an áit sin anois,' ar sé.

'Ní fhágfaidh,' ar sise.

'Bhuel, cuirfidh mise diachair ort fágaint is cuirfidh mé amach sa bhfarraige tú go Lá an Bhreithiúnas,' ar sé.

'Beidh mé ag iompu na n-árthaí,' ar sí.

'Bhuel cuirfidh mé san bhfarraige thú ná beidh long ná árthach ag imeacht,' ar sé.

Cuireadh amach sa bhFarraige Marbh í, is tobán miotail anuas uirthi is beidh sí ann go lá bhrátha, ag déanamh súgán breá den ghainimh.

TRANSLATION

She was living in Colligan. She was one of the Hannigans but she was nicknamed Petticoat Loose. She was a bad woman in every way. She used be hitting her father and mother. She killed a child she had and she went off with another man. And the two of them killed her first husband. Then she used be drinking with the men down at 'Pike an Bhrúnaigh' in Colligan.

She died in the hostelry called the 'Pike' between two barrels of whiskey during the first mass. From that she used be showing herself. On the night she was buried, there were people drinking in the 'Pike' and they said, 'It's very lonesome tonight because Petticoat isn't among us.' When they went out on the road she was there before them and they had to return or she would have killed them. She used be killing the people then.

A man met her one night and he asked her to sit into the car without knowing who he had. She sat in and the horse couldn't move a step.

'God bless us,' said the man, 'what's wrong with the horse? And he's the best horse in the locality.'

'Oh, it's I who is making all the load,' said she, and she told him that she herself was Petticoat, and she told him that there were so many tons in her hand, that used be beating her father, and half the same on the hand that used be beating her mother, and said she to him, 'I would kill you, irrespective of how good a man you are, but

the horse is finished and he'll be dead in the morning, and there is a pedlar going this road to Seanphobal[1] and I'll have him instead of you.'

The pedlar was found dead on the road in the morning. It wasn't long after that until she met another man, and she was going to kill him, but he prayed so piteously to the Lord to save him, that he [God] let Father Seán Ó Maonaigh, from that place, down from heaven to release him.

'What sort of woman is that?' said Father Seán to the man.

'A woman that I met,' said he.

'She's a bad article,' said he, and turning to her, he said, 'What damned you, you devil?'

'I killed a child,' said she.

'That didn't damn you, you devil,' said he.

'I used to be beating my father and my mother,' she said.

'That didn't damn you, you devil,' said he.

'I killed my husband,' said she.

'It's not that even that damned you, you devil,' said he.

'I used to be drinking, and I died at mass-time, drinking in the "Pike".'

'That's what damned you, devil, and leave that place now,' said he.

'I won't,' said she.

'Well I'll compel you, and I'll put you out in the sea till the Day of Judgement,' said he.

'I'll capsize all the ships,' said she.

'Well I'll put you in a sea where there won't be a ship or a vessel going,' said he.

She was put out into the Dead Sea, with a metal tub down on top of her, and she'll be there till the end of time, making ropes of the sand.

---

1. In Ring, County Waterford. Literally, 'the old parish'.

JENNY McGLYNN

(1939–   )

from:
ORIGINAL RECORDINGS
(1976–81)

[Brought up in an essentially English-language environment and cultural milieu, Jenny McGlynn is an exponent of folk traditions known and transmitted through the medium of English in the eastern midlands of Ireland. Her exposure to the oral tradition of her native place occurred as recently as the 1940s, and continued in her home environment during the 1950s, and in her new surroundings after her marriage in 1961.

Jenny McGlynn, now a housewife in her early sixties, has described the hospitable home where she lived with her in-laws as 'a place to go for a chat and a laugh and a cup of tea to break the monotony of the night . . .'[1] It was in this environment that she gradually began to perform her narratives for appreciative adult audiences. She describes storytelling sessions in the 1960s when large groups of people gathered in the kitchen at night while she and her husband sat at either side of the fire; her husband would open the session by telling a story if the circumstances required it. Jenny's descriptions of the ensuing sessions indicate that they were occasions of participation and interaction between teller and audience; no one narrator necessarily dominated the performance, but each person present was welcome to contribute if he or she so wished. Jenny, as the woman of the house, was often the only female present on these occasions, and when called upon by the predominantly male audience to contribute she would do so if the theme under discussion was suitable. Her preferred genre was, and is, supernatural lore in all its variety and complexity, especially ghost lore, and she is regarded as an expert in this branch of tradition. At large sessions she usually told only one story, in order to give the others present an opportunity to participate.

Legends of the *leipreachán* are common in Irish folklore. Depicted as a solitary, diminutive, male supernatural being, the *leipreachán* is an artisan, usually a shoemaker.[2] He is also a treasure guardian, possessor of great riches in the form of a crock of gold or an inexhaustible magic purse. He is clever and particularly adroit at evading human attempts to capture him and gain possession of his treasure. Commonly, the *leipreachán* tricks his captor into averting his gaze and thus escapes with his wealth intact; or, as in the following story, told to Jenny McGlynn as a child by her grandmother, he apparently marks the location of his riches and is released, but in the absence of the captor who has gone to fetch a spade to dig up the treasure, he multiplies the marker to such an extent that it is impossible to distinguish the original. This and the following eight items are from original recordings made by Patricia Lysaght between 1976 and 1981. Headnotes, P.L.]

1. P. Lysaght, 'Fairylore from the Midlands of Ireland', p. 53.
2. For a study of this legend in Irish folk tradition see D. Ó Giolláin, 'Capturer of Fairy Shoemaker Outwitted: The Multiple Marker Versions (MLSIT [Migratory Legend Suggested Irish Type] 6011)', *Béaloideas*, vol. 59 (1991), pp. 161–6; see also D. Ó Giolláin, 'The *Leipreachán* and Fairies, Dwarfs and the Household Familiar: A Comparative Study', *Béaloideas*, vol. 52 (1984), pp. 75–150, in which he regards the *leipreachán* as an Irish expression of a wider tradition of supernatural artisan dwarfs shared by many European peoples. Cf. also P. Lysaght, 'A Tradition-Bearer in Contemporary Ireland', in *Storytelling in Contemporary Society*, eds, L. Röhrich and S. Wienker-Piepho (Tübingen: Günter Narr Verlag, 1990), pp. 119–214, and 'Fairylore from the Midlands of Ireland', p. 25.

THE LEIPREACHÁN'S POT OF GOLD

My granny used to tell the story that if you caught a *leipreachán* or fairy you'd have to ask them for their wealth. And they usually had a crock of gold and it was buried under a *buachallán* [ragwort]. And there was a lot of *buachalláns*, but this one was the biggest *buachallán* in the field. And the man dug it up and saw that it was the fairy gold. He tied a piece of his red handkerchief around the *buachallán*, and went home for to get a spade for to dig down deeper to see if there was anymore there. And when he came back with the spade every *buachallán* in the field was tied up with red string!

ATTEMPTED ABDUCTION OF A BRIDE

[This legend acknowledges the rite of passage involved in bethrothal and marriage. The interval between the two (*idir dáil agus pósadh*) could be quite short — perhaps only a week — but was considered a dangerous time for the bride-to-be. Her status was ambiguous during the period of transition between unmarried and married life and she was thought to be particularly at risk of abduction by the fairies, who often seek the assistance of a human helper for this purpose.[1] The attempted abduction of the bride usually takes place during the wedding meal, but is invariably foiled by the human helper. Usually, conscious of traditional precepts, he utters a pious exclamation (for example, *Dia linn!*, God with us!) when the bride sneezes for the third time; the fairies must then vanish. In the following version the storyteller has given a modern setting and rationale to the legend.[2]]

Well, they had this man helping them for to get at the bride so that they could take her, and he was there and they were having high tea the evening before the wedding. And she was to fit on her clothes and let them all see her — the family that is — before she went to church next day. And the little people, you see, got in while the old man [the human helper] was making his greetings and they were up in the rafters. And they used do terrible funny things, you see, to

1. That the fairies are dependent on a human agent for the successful conclusion of certain activities is a widespread belief in Irish oral and literary tradition.
2. For a Donegal version of this legend see S. Ó hEochaidh, M. MacNeill, S. Ó Catháin, *Síscéalta ó Thír Chonaill*, pp. 52–5. Cf. also P. Lysaght, 'A Tradition-Bearer in Contemporary Ireland', pp. 211–12, and 'Fairy Lore from the Midlands of Ireland', p. 36.

distract the neighbours and family from the bride so as to be able to take her. And one of them was moving over, and seemingly there was dust, and she sneezed and the fairies vanished. So they couldn't take her; you see, they wouldn't take her unless she was perfect. They couldn't have anyone that was sickly in their tribe because otherwise they'd all get sick. So they had to have everyone perfect, especially the humans they had taken.

THE OLD WOMAN AS A HARE

[Like the version told by Traveller Nellie Joyce ('The Enchanted Hare', pp. 1279–1280), this legend of the milk-stealing hare suggests that, in certain economic situations in which they have a primary role such as milk- and butter-production, women may engage in shape-shifting and detrimental magic, and in these circumstances that physical aggression towards them may be sanctioned by society.[1]]

The cow would be out in the fields and every morning when the man would go to get the cow to milk it, she'd be dry. They had the vets with them and they couldn't find out what was wrong. Then an old man came — he was a tramp of the road — and asked them did they ever notice was there anything at the cows at night? So the old man and the farmer went out and they sat out all night long. And this hare came on the scene and no matter how they tried to catch it, they couldn't. So they decided anyway that they'd lay a trap for it. And 'twas a big she-hare. And they met this old woman in the mornings; she used to be walking up and down the roads. They were telling her and they said they were going to catch the hare and she asked them not to . . . 'don't kill it'. They said they had to because it was leaving them without any milk for the children.

It was going on anyway for three or four weeks at a time. This night the farmer and his son went out and his son had a gun. As soon as the hare saw them coming, she ran away. And as she did, the young lad let off with the gun and shot her. And with that she let an unmerciful scream and staggered away, anyway. So they followed it on to see where it would go, to make sure it was dead.

It went into a little old hut. And when they got to the hut there was no hare, but there was an old woman lying on the ground and her ribs all shattered with pellets from the shotgun. It happened that she was after being enchanted in some way and she was able to change into a hare at night, something to that effect.

THE DEAD COACH

[Jenny McGlynn has many beliefs and legends about death-omens and rituals. The spectral coach known as the 'dead coach' (cóiste bodhar), or more commonly the 'death coach', or 'headless coach' (cóiste gan cheann), is a well-known omen of death in Irish tradition, and, according to the storyteller, haunted the road near the McGlynn family home. Characteristically, it was a black coach drawn by headless horses which were usually driven by a headless coachman. Occasionally associated with particular families, it was also thought to frequent some roads, especially those leading to old graveyards. One such road wound past Jenny's house, and among her personal experience narratives concerning omens of death is the following one about the 'dead coach'. Compare Anna Nic an Luain's story of 'A Phantom Funeral', pp. 1291–1292.]

I have heard the coach, sitting down by the fire. One night I heard it. I heard it myself, yeah; me mother-in-law and I were sitting, one at either side of the fire. She didn't be well, you know, and I used to sit up with her. It was before Catherine was born. That's about fourteen year ago and . . . the time was half past one. Our men was working in the bog at the time and they were on the night shift, and we were waiting for them to come home. She was sitting by the fire. She wasn't too well . . . And she thought when she heard it first that it was her time [to die] and, she said, 'Bless yourself, for that is the dead coach.' And I listened: I could only hear the wind first and then I heard the noise. It was the very same as a pony's trap[1] . . .

Well, I went very cold and I thought, if it is the dead coach it is one of us that are going to go, especially like when we were in bad health and me . . . being expecting the child and that, you know?

A woman further up the road died that time, Mrs Geoghan.

---

1. See also the notes to Nellie Joyce's 'The Enchanted Hare', p. 1279

1. A two-wheeled light vehicle with springs, usually drawn by a pony and formerly used for family transport.

GUSH OF WIND AS OMEN OF DEATH

[In particular circumstances a sudden gust of wind can be regarded as an omen of death. Jenny vividly describes her physical, emotional and psychological condition in the following personal experience narrative, as she tells of the incidents which she still regards as signs of her mother-in-law's death; the details of the time of death which Jenny subsequently heard confirmed the omens for her.]

When my mother-in-law died I was in hospital. It was April, the first of April, and I was in hospital on the birth of the last child. And I got word earlier in the day that she wasn't too well. I wasn't told that she was bad, or that she was dying, but that she wasn't too well. And I was after getting sleeping tablets from the nurse. About half past eleven or a quarter to twelve, an awful blast of wind came and it opened up the windows — you know the windows in the hospital that open down, the small little windows, they open down? It fell in, and the curtain went right up to the roof, and the next morning I got the nurse to 'phone up the hospital, you know: 'I'd like to find out how the mother-in-law was' — and she had died at the time that the blast of wind came to me . . . Probably it was because I was thinking of her, but I thought I saw her at the foot of me bed after the blast of wind. I had to call the nurses and everything. I really was upset over it, and . . . she had died that exact time that I thought she was there with the blast of wind. It definitely happened to me.

DEAD MOTHER REVISITS HER CHILDREN

[This legend, common in Ireland, suggests that a mother's love, concern and support for her family extend even into eternity.[1]]

Yes. I heard tell of a story about four children — they were between the ages of a month and five years old. And the father had to work to keep going, to keep the house going, and to keep the children fed. And he couldn't get over how the children were able to manage, have the house

clean and the fire lit and a meal ready for him every evening. So he asked the eldest girl one night how did she do it. They were sitting in the dark with the fire lighting and the meal cooked. And they said that they didn't do it, that Mammy had been there with them; she had been with them for two or three years before he realized that she had been there. She definitely was there helping them, because they were too small to be left on their own.

DEVIL DELAYS PRIEST ON A SICK CALL

[A popular narrative in Irish oral tradition, this legend portrays the devil as seeking to win a soul by delaying the priest on his journey to the dying person's house. It reflects people's intense desire for a happy death, having received the consolation of the Catholic church's last rites.[1]]

Well, he's supposed to be on the road here, down here — a country road. And he won't let people pass by. There was a woman dying one night and a man came in for the priest. And at that time the priests used to go on horses. And they went up this laneway — it was the shortest way to the woman's home. And it was a moonlit night and there was two crowns shining on the ground. Now, the priest, of course, had his stole on him, especially when he was going to visit the sick.[2] And he says to the man, 'Keep the horse going,' he says, 'and don't stop, you can get your crowns coming back.' So the man was very reluctant, of course, when he saw the two crowns there lying on the ground and he very badly off — he needed money. But he went on anyway, he done the priest's bidding, and when they were coming back, the priest stopped the horse himself and told him to go down and get the crowns. And it was two horseshoe nails that had taken the shape. And he said 'twas the devil was there trying to stop him from getting there on time to save the woman's soul.

1. Extreme unction, now known as the Sacrament of the Sick. Formerly, as people wished to be anointed only *in extremis*, it was important that the priest should attend the death bed as quickly as possible.
2. The stole is defined by the *New Catholic Encyclopedia* (1967) as: 'a band of material worn by bishops, priests, and deacons for all liturgical services; bishops and priests wear it about the neck and with the ends loose or crossed over the breast; deacons across the breast . . . It must be worn by all clergy when they administer any sacrament or exercise their order during any liturgical function.'

1. Cf. 'The Children of the Dead Woman', in Seán O'Sullivan (ed.), *Folktales of Ireland*, pp. 176–9.

THE CARDPLAYERS AND THE DEVIL

[Found in many countries, especially in northern Europe, this legend is also fairly common in Ireland. It reflects antipathy towards card-playing, which is considered the devil's pastime. The legend may be set indoors, or may have an outdoor setting, late at night, as in the following example. Typically, the devil is recognized by his cloven foot.[1]]

It happened not too far away from here, really, about the playing of the cards. There was a few men that were in [town] on a fair day and they had a few drinks too many and they used to stay out too late. And one night they were going home and there was this man sitting at a table at the bull corra gates playing cards. And a candle on the table, and he invited them to play with him. So they got into the game and were playing away. He let them win. There was a whole lot of sovereigns flying every way. About twelve o'clock one of the men sneezed and a card fell. And when they stooped down to pick up the card they saw that this man had a cloven foot. Of course everyone broke up. The next morning they found that the sovereigns they had won were only leaves.

1. This international migratory legend which is fairly common in Ireland is listed as type 3015 in R. Th. Christiansen, *The Migratory Legends: A Proposed List of Types with a Systematic Catalogue of the Norwegian Variants* (Folklore Fellows Communications, No. 175) (Helsinki: Academia Scientiarum Fennica, 1958; 2nd printing 1992). For a study of Irish versions see É. Ní Anluain, 'The Cardplayers and the Devil (ML 3015)', *Béaloideas*, vol. 59 (1991), pp. 45–54.

THE KING OF THE CATS

['The King of the Cats' — a subtype of the so-called 'Legend of Pan', named from a story told by the Greek writer Plutarch — indicates that a human being can act as an intermediary between supernatural beings to communicate tragedy in the spirit world.[1]]

1. This international migratory legend, which is popular in Ireland, is listed as type 6070 B in R. Th. Christiansen's *The Migratory Legends*. For a study of this legend see E. R. Ó Néill, 'The King of the Cats (ML 6070 B). The Revenge and Non-Revenge Redactions in Ireland', *Béaloideas*, vol. 59 (1991), pp. 167–88; cf. also P. Lysaght, 'A Tradition-Bearer in Contemporary Ireland', pp. 209–10; 'Pan ist Tot' (Aa Th 113A), in *Enzyklopädie des Märchens*, Band 10, Lieferung 2 (Berlin, New York: Walter de Gruyter, 2001), pp. 492–7.

There was a man coming home from work late at night. It was in the winter nights and those times he used to work until maybe ten or eleven o'clock. And the man was making his way home and the road was completely blocked with cats. He had to step through them. And just as he was going past the last cat, one shouted, 'When you go home, tell Muggins that Juggins is dead. We have to elect a new king.'

So he went home, and he was a bit frightened over it. And the wife was sitting at the side of the fire and he says, 'I'm after getting the fright of me life,' he says, 'I thought I heard a cat saying, "When you go home tell Muggins that Juggins is dead".' And the minute he said it the cat that was on the hearth let a roar, 'Let me out, that's me uncle!'

Biographies/Bibliographies

Anna Nic an Luain

LIFE. Born Anna Nic an Bhaird (Anna Ward) in Cruach Thiobraid in the Bluestack Mountains of County Donegal in 1884, Anna Nic an Luain was known as Anna John Chiot (Kit's son John's Anna) in her native area. Her husband was John Mac an Luain. She was one of the most important storytellers from whom full-time collector Seán Ó hEochaidh recorded songs, tales, legends, local history and other lore over a period of almost twenty years until her death — some two hundred songs and fifty long stories in all. Scholars of language and folklore, journalists and photographers, visited her from all parts of Europe. A photograph taken by Caoimhín Ó Danachair (Dr Kevin Danaher), of the Irish Folklore Commission, appears as Plate 4 of *Síscéalta ó Thír Chonaill/Fairy Legends from Donegal*. It shows her standing by a spinning wheel, outside a thatched house. She died in 1954.

CHIEF WRITINGS. *Béaloideas*, vol. 23 (1954), p. 141; *Béaloideas*, vol. 27 (1959), pp. 20–3; Seán Ó hEochaidh, Máire MacNeill and Séamas Ó Catháin, *Síscéalta ó Thír Chonaill/Fairy Legends from Donegal* (Dublin: Comhairle Bhéaloideas Éireann, 1977), nos 107, 108, 109, 117, 120; Áine Ní Dhíoraí, *Na Cruacha: Scéalta agus Seanchas* (Baile Átha Cliath: An Clóchomhar, 1985).

BIOGRAPHY AND CRITICISM. Obituary, *Derry People*, 6 February 1954; Áine Ní Dhíoraí, *Na Cruacha*; Seán Ó hEochaidh, 'Tomhasannaí ó Thír Chonaill', *Béaloideas*, vol. 19 (1949), pp. 1–28; Patricia Lysaght, 'Traditional Storytelling in Ireland in the Twentieth Century', in Margaret Read MacDonald (ed.), *Traditional Storytelling Today* (Chicago and London: Fitzroy Dearbon, 1999), pp. 264–72 (here 268–9).

Máire Ní Bheirn

LIFE. Little information available. Storyteller, known as Máire an Ghréasaí (the shoemaker's daughter), born County Donegal *c.* 1890. Unmarried. Lived in Iomaire Mhuireanáin, near Teileann, south-west Donegal, where Seán Ó hEochaidh recorded legends about the fairies on Ediphone cylinders from her and from her brothers Conall (q.v.) and Peadar (1895–1954), in 1954.

CHIEF WRITINGS. *Béaloideas*, vol. 23 (1954), pp. 148–9, 152, 178–9, 182, 203–4, 215–16; Seán Ó hEochaidh, Máire MacNeill and Séamas Ó Catháin, *Síscéalta ó Thír Chonaill/Fairy Legends from Donegal* (Dublin: Comhairle Bhéaloideas Éireann, 1977), nos 9, 12, 33, 37, 50, 68.

Conall Ó Beirn

LIFE. Fisherman and noted *seanchaí*, born *c*. 1904, from whom Seán Ó hEochaidh recorded many legends of the fairies. He lived in Iomaire Mhuireanáin, near Teileann, County Donegal.

CHIEF WRITINGS. *Béaloideas*, vol. 23 (1954), pp. 139–40, 156, 167–8, 171–4, 176–8, 185–8, 195–8, 203, 217, 221–4; Seán Ó hEochaidh, Máire MacNeill and Séamas Ó Catháin, *Síscéalta ó Thír Chonaill/Fairy Legends from Donegal* (Dublin: Comhairle Bhéaloideas Éireann, 1977), nos 1, 2, 15, 28, 29, 30, 34, 41, 44, 47, 48, 56, 58, 60, 67, 70, 74, 80, 81, 84, 87, 92, 93.

Éamon a Búrc

LIFE. Born in Carna, County Galway, in 1866, master storyteller Éamon a Búrc was also known as Éamon Liam (Liam's son Éamon). When he was fourteen he emigrated with his family to the United States; they were among 309 people from Gaeltacht areas of Galway and Mayo whom John Ireland, Catholic Archbishop of St Paul, Minnesota, had invited to settle in Graceville, Minnesota, in 1880. The scheme, badly conceived, was not a success. At seventeen, jumping on and off trains, Éamon lost a leg, and his parents brought him back to Ireland where he was apprenticed to a tailor. He later also kept a small shop, but preferred sailing and fishing, at which he was highly skilled, and became renowned as the finest storyteller in his area. IFC collector Liam Mac Coisdeala (1907–96) met him in 1928, and from then until Éamon's death in 1942 recorded hundreds of stories from him, including the longest folktale ever recorded in Ireland, 'Eochair, Mac Rí in Éirinn', which ran to 34,000 words, told over three evenings in 1938.

CHIEF WRITINGS. Seán O'Sullivan, *Folktales of Ireland* (London: Routledge, 1966), nos 13, 26, 29, 32, 34, 35; *Legends from Ireland* (1977), nos 35, 46, 64 and 71B; Caoimhín Ó Nualláin/Kevin O'Nolan, *Eochair, Mac Rí in Éirinn/Eochair, a King's Son in Ireland* (Dublin: Comhairle Bhéaloideas Éireann, 1982) (includes editor's translation and a six-page essay on the storyteller by Liam Mac Coisdeala, 'Fear Inste an Scéil'); Peadar Ó Ceannabháin (ed.), *Éamon a Búrc: Scéalta* (Dublin: An Clóchomhar, 1983).

BIOGRAPHY AND CRITICISM. Liam Mac Coisdeala, 'In Memoriam, Éamonn (Liam) a Búrc (Aill na Brón, Cárna, Co. na Gaillimhe)',*Béaloideas*, vol. 12 (1942), pp. 210–14, and 'Im' Bhailitheoir Béaloideasa,' *Béaloideas*, vol. 16 (1946), pp. 141–71; Angela Bourke, 'The Virtual Reality of Irish Fairy Legend', *Éire-Ireland*, vol. 31, nos 1 and 2 (1996), pp. 7–25, and 'Economic Necessity and Escapist Fantasy in Éamon a Búrc's Sea-Stories', in *Islanders and Water-Dwellers*, eds, Patricia Lysaght, Séamas Ó Catháin, Dáithí Ó hÓgáin (Dublin: DBA, 1999), pp. 19–35.

Séamus Ó Cealla

LIFE. Little information available. In 1937 Séamus Ó Cealla was a farmer living near Kiltartan, County Galway, when Seán Ó Flannagáin collected the banshee legend from him.

CHIEF WRITINGS. *Béaloideas*, vols 42–4 (1977), pp. 116–18; Patricia Lysaght, *The Banshee: The Irish Supernatural Death-Messenger* (Dublin: O'Brien Press, 1996; Boulder, Colorado: Roberts Rinehart, 1997 [Dublin: Glendale Press, 1986]). See also Patricia Lysaght, *A Pocket Book of the Banshee* (Dublin: O'Brien Press; Niwot, Colorado: The Irish American Book Company, 1998), pp. 76–7.

Mairéad Ní Fhearfhia

LIFE. Little information available. Mairéad Ní Fhearfhia was aged eighty-seven in 1931, when Pádraig Ó Fionníosa collected the story of 'Petticoat Loose' and another legend of a 'bad' woman from her. Her address was Glenahiry, Kilronan, Ballymacarbry, County Waterford. The texts as collected are in IFC 85: 257–60.

CHIEF WRITINGS. Anne O'Connor, *Child Murderess and Dead Child Traditions: A Comparative Study* (Folklore Fellows Communications, No. 249) (Helsinki: Academia Scientiarum Fennica, 1991), pp. 178, 225–8.

Jenny McGlynn

LIFE. Born in 1939, Jenny McGlynn has lived all her life in Mountmellick, the County Laois town where she was born. Both her parents' house and the home she later shared with her husband's family were noted 'rambling houses', where neighbours were made welcome, and stories were told. During the formative years of her repertoire formation, her family lived with her maternal grandmother, from whom Jenny learned many of her narratives. She also heard stories from her mother, who entertained the children with storytelling on rainy days. As she grew up, other types of situation had a bearing on her repertoire formation, such as the years she spent in domestic service in houses in the town and her contact with and work for local farming families. In 1961, aged twenty-two, she married and moved to the other side of her home town. Her mother-in-law, who had a large store of supernatural lore, became an important influence, as did her father-in-law, who encouraged her to relate the traditions she already knew. In this way she became an active bearer of tradition. Her emergence as a storyteller in her own right was an important social and psychological achievement for her, as it gave her confidence and a sense of belonging in her new surroundings. Lore of the supernatural in its diverse manifestations is her preferred narrative genre.

CHIEF WRITINGS. Patricia Lysaght, *The Banshee: The Irish Supernatural Death-Messenger* (Dublin: O'Brien Press, 1996; Boulder, Colorado: Roberts Rinehart, 1997 [Dublin: Glendale Press, 1986]; Patricia Lysaght, *A Pocket Book of the Banshee* (Dublin: O'Brien Press, 1998; Boulder, Colorado: Irish American Book Company, 1998).

BIOGRAPHY AND CRITICISM. Patricia Lysaght, 'A Tradition-Bearer in Contemporary Ireland', in *Storytelling in Contemporary Society*, eds L. Röhrich and S. Wienker-Piepho (Tübingen: Günter Narr Verlag, 1990), pp. 119–214; 'Fairylore from the Midlands of Ireland,' in *The Good People: New Fairylore Essays*, ed. Peter Narváez (London and New York: Garland, 1991), pp. 22–46; 'A Contemporary Irish Tradition Bearer: Beliefs and Narrative', *Acta Ethnographica Hungarica*, vol. 39, nos 3–4, 1994, pp. 419–41 (Budapest); 'Traditional Storytelling in Ireland in the Twentieth Century', in *Traditional Storytelling Today: An International Sourcebook*, ed. Margaret Read MacDonald (Chicago and London: Fitzroy Dearborn, 1999), pp. 263–72 (see pp. 269–70).

RÍONACH UÍ ÓGÁIN and TOM MUNNELLY, *Editors*

The Song Tradition

It is not easy to identify or isolate 'women's songs' as a type or genre of traditional song in Ireland. Women sing and have sung all kinds of songs in Irish and in English, including, among other types, love-songs, religious songs, comical songs, political songs, lullabies, dandling songs and drinking songs.

The home was the most important venue for the oral transmission of song and story until comparatively recently, when greater financial independence and easier availability of transport led people to seek entertainment elsewhere. This erosion was vastly accelerated by the introduction of radio and television. Social gatherings moved to the public house or were dominated by the television in private houses. However, Irish tradition is conservative by nature, and women continued for a long time to make their own entertainment. They played an active part in passing on the old songs and stories to the children of the household and to other relatives and friends.

The following selection is an illustrative sampler, focusing on women, from various sources within the English- and the Irish-language singing tradition. The songs selected are examples of material which has been collected over the years from both women and men. While most of the examples quoted were recorded from women, songs have also been included which were recorded from men but which indicate a possible female composer or a female point of view. Others offer representations of the female in the song text. Although each song is an independent unit, it is also an example of a particular song-type or may illustrate a particular aspect of women's lives as expressed through the singing tradition. Various song-types sung by women are included here, as a way of indicating that female singers do not see themselves as the tradition bearers exclusively of songs about women.

Some of these songs are available on commercial recordings; others, from archive sources, are published here for the first time. We have chosen to emphasize the songs themselves and the messages they convey. An important feature of all of this material is that it indicates how women expressed and express themselves through song and also how women are perceived in song by others, presumably by both women and men, as most of the songs are anonymous. The songs also reflect women's perception of society and how women are perceived by that society, as no song can survive which is not consistent with contemporary outlook. Humorous songs and satire often survive because of their deliberately contradictory stance.

The songs selected here are from all parts of Ireland, both from the Gaeltacht and from English-speaking areas. At the time most of the songs in Irish were composed (roughly 1650–1850), Irish was spoken in most counties in Ireland. These songs were therefore part of a more widespread tradition than they are today, when the Irish language as a vernacular survives only in comparatively small districts. Many of the Irish-language songs were collected from singers whose repertoire included songs in both languages. As a general rule though, Gaeltacht singers, who sing mostly in Irish, will inevitably also sing a few songs in English, whereas singers from outside the Gaeltacht, whose song repertoires are in English, will be less likely to sing in Irish.

In keeping with the tradition of other countries, Ireland's store of documented traditional song contains a very high percentage of love-songs, and these form the largest single genre in most singers' repertoires. Songmakers use the full range of their skills to try to put into physical terms the intangible emotion of love. In Ireland, in both languages, classical allusion and comparisons with nature are frequently used devices. In referring to females, comparison with swans is a recurring theme, so the girl in the well-known 'My Lagan Love' goes 'homeward with one star awake, / As the swan in the evening moves over the lake', while another song runs:

> Not the swan on the lake or the foam on the
> shore
> Can compare with the charms of the maid I
> adore
> Not so white is the new milk that flows o'er
> the pail,
> Or the snow that is showered from the
> boughs of the vale.[1]

Songs which dwell on the attributes of the male, real or imagined, are not numerous, although there are examples like the moving English-language version of 'An Draighneán Donn' ('The Blackthorn') sung by Maggie McDonagh of Fínis Island, County Galway:

> My love he is far fairer than a bright
> summer's day,
> His breath is far sweeter than the new moon
> ray.[2]
> His hair shines like gold when exposed to the
> sun,
> He is fairer than the blossoms early on the
> *draighneán donn.*

Even more intensely expressive is the girl who sings of her love for her 'Greenwood Laddie':

> If you had seen my dearest
> Whose eyes shine the clearest,
> His cheeks like the red blood
> That's new-dropped in snow.
> He is neat, tall and handsome,
> And his hands warm and tender,
> He'll be my Greenwood Laddie
> Till time is no more.[3]

Adultery is usually treated lightly in songs sung in English in Ireland. There are occasional exceptions such as 'The Red-Haired Man's Wife', a direct translation from the Irish 'Bean an Fhir Rua', and 'The Old Man Rocking the Cradle', whose narrator sings:

> When first that I married your inconstant
> mother
> I thought myself happy to be blessed with a
> wife.
> But for my misfortune, sure I was mistaken
> She proved both a curse and a plague on my
> life.
>
> Hi-ho, hi-ho, my laddie, lie aisy,
> For perhaps your own daddy might never be
> known.
> I'm sittin' and sighin' and rockin' the cradle
> And nursin' the baby that's none of my own.[4]

This song, known throughout Britain and North America, is often accompanied in Ireland by a tradition that the old man who rocks the cradle is Saint Joseph, as yet unsure who is the father of Mary's child. This fits in well with the suspicious Joseph of 'The Cherry Tree Carol', sung in Ireland in both Irish and English. The cuckolded husband has been a figure of fun in literature and folklore throughout Europe since the Middle Ages. He receives no sympathy and is seldom given credit for much intelligence. Tailors and weavers are often cited in these songs as the wife's seducers (as in 'The Bold Trooper', pp. 1333–1334). These tradesmen were under suspicion, as they were often alone in the house with women while other menfolk were in the fields; folk tradition commonly portrays them as puny, contemptible figures.

There is a considerable difference in the English-language song tradition in Ireland between overt and implicit sexuality. Most of the more explicit songs come from Britain. Irish tradition is by no means lacking in songs of seduction, but focuses more on the interplay between the characters and the consequences of their actions than on the act of seduction itself.[5]

---

1. Sam Henry, *Sam Henry's Songs of the People*, eds G. Huntington, L. Herrmann and J. Moulden (Athens, Ga, and London: University of Georgia Press, 1990), p. 227, 'Not the Swan on the Lake'. For another song from this collection, see 'The Flower of Gortade', pp. 1327–1328.

2. i.e. new-mown hay.

3. Maighread Ní Dhomhnaill, *Gan Dhá Phingin Spré: No Dowry* (Dublin, Gael Linn, CEF CD 152, 1991). Cf P. Kennedy (ed.), *Folksongs of Britain and Ireland* (London, Cassell, 1975), p. 306.

4. From the singing of the late Johnny Doherty of Donegal. See P. Kennedy (ed.), *Folksongs of Britain and Ireland* (London: Cassell, 1975), p. 469.

5. Compare, however, English collections such as Frank Purslow (ed.), *Marrowbones: English Folk Songs from the Hammond and Gardiner MSS* (London: EFDS Publications, 1965) and *The Wanton Seed: More English Folk Songs from the Hammond and Gardiner MSS* (London: EFDSS Publications, 1968), which contain a number of songs in which love is not only requited but immediately consummated. This is consistent with the English West Country songs collected by Cecil Sharp and Sabine Baring-Gould. See also Purslow's *The Constant Lovers: More English Folk Songs from the Hammond and Gardiner MSS* (London: EFDS Publications, 1972); *The Foggy Dew: More English Folk Songs from the Hammond and Gardiner MSS* (London: EFDS Publications, 1974).

Songs directly relating sexual encounters do not seem to act as a source of inspiration for many Irish songmakers, although songs of this nature were imported. Of the overtly bawdy songs which enjoy a widespread currency, 'Brave O'Donohue', 'One-Eyed Reilly', 'The Jolly Tinker' and 'The Sea Crab' are among the most popular.[6]

Many characteristics of the love-song are universal. Those Irish songs sung in English share traits with songs found in Britain and there is also a substantial volume of shared repertoire. Continual reference to the British song tradition is therefore inevitable, particularly in the case of ballads, or narrative songs. Of the 305 classic ballads published in Francis James Child's *The English and Scottish Popular Ballads*, more than one third are concerned with straightforward love stories.[7] If the scope is broadened to include stories in which crimes of violence are motivated by factors such as jealousy and sexual attraction, about one half of Child's collection may be categorized as love-songs.

Many Irish love-songs are simple courtship dialogues which move to their conclusion with little argument. A very high proportion adhere to the formula 'love declared: obstruction raised: obstruction overcome'. The English-language songs are usually more specific in outlining the difficulties which impede the path of true love. Common impediments are: (a) religion and politics, as in 'The Holy Church of Rome' (pp. 1336–1337); (b) class: numerous songs depict a poor man or woman who marries a rich, noble person; the output of the broadsheet presses suggests that hundreds of songs of this type were current at any time in the last couple of centuries; (c) parental disapproval: the reasons for their censure are also social and financial; (d) rival suitors ('As I Roved Out', pp. 1338–1339).

Approximately 65 to 70 Child ballads have been noted from oral tradition in Ireland.

6. Vance Randolph, *Roll Me in Your Arms: 'Unprintable' Ozark Folksongs and Folklore*, vol. 1, *Folksongs and Music*, ed. G. Legman (Fayetteville: University of Arkansas Press, 1992), p. 71. A recording of *The Crabfish* is published on the cassette *Songs of the Irish Travellers* (Dublin: European Ethnic Oral Traditions, 1983).

7. Francis James Child, *The English and Scottish Popular Ballads*, 5 vols (Boston and New York: 1882–98; repr. New York: Dover Publications, 1965). This definitive collection of old British ballads with hundreds of variants is the cornerstone of English-language ballad study. The texts are classified numerically and are generally referred to as 'Child ballads'.

Although sound recording as a means of collecting traditional song is a fairly recent arrival, some forty-four individual Child ballads have been recorded. Of these, at least thirty-four have love as their theme. In the Child ballads the lovers' relationship may culminate in sexual intercourse, but the sexual act may also be performed without the presence of love. Sometimes there is a mutually satisfactory ending, sometimes not. Whereas some ballads display considerable brutality, great tenderness is also found. The emotions expressed are primeval, although often expressed in beautiful language. A lover is prepared to give his or her life for the desired partner and is also prepared to take the life of anyone who may obstruct a perfect union. These songs in English are narrative and descriptive in style.

In Irish, on the other hand, most love-songs are of the lyrical, non-narrative kind. They express emotion directly — in most cases, deep pain due to unfulfilled love — and the vast majority are extremely unhappy. For reasons which are not clear, most, though by no means all, describe man's love for woman, rather than woman's for man. Some songs can be ascribed to either men or women and the singing tradition imposes no rules regarding who may sing what. Thus men sing songs ascribed to women and vice versa. 'Mainistir na Búille' (pp. 1322–1324) is usually a woman's song, but is here sung by a man, and changed accordingly. In a version of this song collected from Sorcha Ní Ghuairim, and ascribed to a woman, she says:

Is tá mo chroí-sa chomh haerach le leanbh insan gcliabhán,
Nó le úlla i mbarra géagáin lá gréine is é ag gíoscán,
Nó le long i lár léige is gan aon chóir dá tiomáint,
Is cuirim beannacht, a stór, is céad leat, nuair nár fhéad mé thú choinneáil.

[My heart is as airy as a child in a crib,
Or as apples on a high branch, creaking on a sunny day,
Or a ship on the high sea with no wind driving it,
And my blessing to you my darling, and a hundred, since I could not keep you.]

This expression of forgiveness and lack of bitterness is characteristic of the lyrical love-songs. Despite the speaker's sorrow at her lover's departure, her emotion is intense and she finds extreme happiness in her love, just as the lack of love produces such intense sorrow in other songs, such as 'Dónall Óg', v. 7 (see pp. 1320–1322). However, in another song, 'Thug Mé Grá Duit is Mé Beag Bídeach', closely related to 'Dónaill Óg', the woman is so bitter at having been left pregnant that she curses her lover, saying:

> Ach a ghiolla úd siar a bhfuil an chulaith
>   ghearr ort,
> Ó, bheirimse mo mhallacht duit is ná raibh an
>   t-ádh ort.
> Ó, leaca lom agat ar bheagán fáltais,
> Óra seisear dall agat is iad gan máthair!

> [But my lad yonder, in the short suit,[8]
> Oh, I curse you and may you not be lucky,
> May you have bare rocks and little profit,
> And six blind children without a mother.]

This last verse seems to originate in the idiom of lament, which often includes lavish curses phrased in this way (see subsection 'Lamenting the Dead', p. 1371). The lyrical nature of the love-songs in Irish, and the fact that much of the imagery and phraseology is the same throughout the genre, means that songs can change a great deal from singer to singer and from region to region, while verses are relatively easily borrowed or adapted from one song to another. Tradition is in a constant state of change. However, in both English and Irish, certain versions of songs are regarded as 'good' by singers and tend to take precedence over others.

The love-songs in Irish equate love with sexual intercourse. Marriage is rarely mentioned and when it is, this is usually because it is unhappy or is preventing another desired relationship from taking place (but see 'Mainistir na Búille', p. 1322). Much of the imagery used is of a standard form and is repeated or only slightly changed from song to song and from type to type within the general love-song genre. Erotic song in Irish seems to be lacking, although the imagery is quite explicit in sexual terms, with numerous references to flowers and gardens, for example, in relation to virginity or loss of virginity. References to rape are also relatively few, although 'Maile Ní Maoileoin' (pp. 1348–1350) is a notable exception. The song 'Dónall Ó Maoláine' also includes what is apparently a coded reference:

> Idir an Caiseal agus an Úrchoill tharla orm an
>   chúileann,
> Agus í go ró-mhúinte dhul tharam sa ród,
> Bheir mé greim ghúna uirthi, agus chuir mé ar
>   mo ghlúin í,
> Is d'fhág mé a croí brúite aici is í ag sileadh na
>   ndeor.

> [Between Caiseal and Úrchoill I met the
>   beautiful girl,
> She was very polite as she passed me on the
>   road,
> I caught her by the dress, and I put her on my
>   knee,
> And I left her with her heart bruised, in tears.][9]

Although most of the love-songs in Irish are lyrical in nature, some have a narrative or descriptive element and a few, all in dialogue form, are ballads which are part of the Child classification system. In these instances, the 'story' or background to the songs is often included by the singer as an integral part of the performance.[10]

It is important to bear in mind that songs change over the years, particularly the songs in Irish, which are lyrical by nature. A song collected in the Gaeltacht in the 1930s is often the result of a long development. Today, however, we encounter the remnants of a tradition which was once more vibrant and widespread, but which has now become confined and therefore less susceptible to change.

In Irish and English alike, the songs must be seen in their own emotional, social and textual context. The moral standards, behaviour and attitudes to sexuality which they portray are far removed from those at the start of the twenty-

---

8. Probably a jacket and matching short woollen trousers, worn by boys until recent years.

9. Énrí Ó Muirgheasa, *Dhá Chéad de Cheoltaibh Uladh* (Dublin: Government Publications, 1934, 1974), pp. 110–11.
10. Hugh Shields, 'Old British Ballads in Ireland', *Folk-Life: Journal of the Society for Folk Life Studies*, no. 10 (1972), pp. 68–103; see also his *Narrative Singing in Ireland*.

first century. The examples selected here are from performers who are esteemed by other traditional singers. These singers and songs represent the finest examples available since the documenting of traditional song began. The criteria we have used in selecting the material are based to a large degree within the tradition itself and to a lesser degree on the work of the collectors, scholars and other documenters of traditional song.

Borrowing between languages and cultures is a feature of all oral tradition. The idiom of love-songs in Irish, which has been traced authoritatively to influence from French *troubadour* poetry,[11] was later extended through oral tradition to songs in English. The Gaelic poetic tradition also influenced song forms, idioms and syntax in the English-language songs, many of which travelled to other English-speaking countries, where they were absorbed into singers' repertoires. Other songs were brought from England and became a part of Irish singers' repertoires, among them songs from the ballad tradition, which flourished throughout Europe from the Middle Ages. Although none of these ballads of medieval ancestry originated in Ireland, and, with a few exceptions, the ballad form did not cross the language barrier into Irish, examples of the genre found a willing audience. Some ballads flourished among Irish singers long after they had disappeared from the memory of song carriers in Britain. Broadsheet collections from Ireland and Britain over the last couple of centuries reveal many songs which were familiar on both sides of the Irish Sea, while Scottish collections taken from rural people at the turn of the twentieth century show a very high percentage of songs of obvious Irish origin.[12]

Migrant workers from Ireland travelled regularly to Britain, to Scotland in particular, and brought songs with them in both directions. Neilí Ní Dhomhnaill (1907–84), of Rinn na Feirste in County Donegal (see subsection 'Lamenting the Dead', pp. 1388–1390), contributed a large body of songs to the IFC, many of which were brought back to her area by seasonal workers. She often recalled for her niece, singer Maighread Ní Dhomhnaill, that when a suitor of her own mother, Maggie Chonaill, was departing for seasonal work on the harvest, he asked what he could bring her back from Scotland. Maggie's request was that he would bring her back a song.

Today, traditional singing in Ireland is on the decline; singing as an ordinary social pastime is declining to an even more rapid degree in English than in Irish. As time goes on, it becomes more and more difficult to analyze the true nature and spread of traditional singing in Ireland. Individual, unaccompanied singing in Irish and in English is usually ornamented to varying degrees, with certain regional variations. A highly ornamented style, closely associated with slow songs in Irish and also with some slow songs in English, is usually referred to by English- and Irish-speakers alike as *sean-nós*, literally, 'old way', or 'old style'. Due to the individual and often highly ornamented nature of the music of the songs and also because of their free rhythm, it is difficult to apply standard music transcription and notation methods.[13]

The songs are part of a living tradition and have survived for many reasons and combinations of reasons. Among these are their aesthetic qualities in matters of lyrics, textual content, language, music, and linguistic and musical style. Their creation, development, continued existence and retention in the tradition are part of a communal decision which is both involuntary and conscious at the same time.

The following selection reflects some of the history of the song tradition and of song collecting in Ireland. The material which is commercially available was recorded for the most part in recording studios, while that from the IFC was collected by full-time, part-time and occasional collectors, the majority of whom were men. The song-texts identified below by the prefix IFC/FMS come from the Folk Music Section of the IFC. Those which include the initials T.M. were collected by Tom Munnelly; songs collected by Ríonach uí Ógáin are marked R.Ó. Some women, like Sarah Makem, of Keady,

---

11. Seán Ó Tuama, *An Grá in Amhráin na nDaoine* (Dublin: An Clóchomhar, 1960).
12. See, for example, John Ord, *The Bothy Songs and Ballads of Aberdeen, Banff and Moray, Angus and the Mearns* (Paisley, 1930; repr. Edinburgh: John Donald (n.d.)).
13. Seóirse Bodley, 'Technique and Structure in "Sean-Nós" Singing', *Éigse Cheol Tíre/Irish Folk Music Studies*, no. 1 (1972–3), pp. 44–53.

County Armagh (pp. 1351–1352), Elizabeth (Bess) Cronin (Éilís Uí Chróinín), of Baile Mhic Íre, Baile Bhuirne, County Cork (pp. 1354–1355) and Neilí Ní Dhomhnaill had very large repertoires. These women may not have been exceptional in the past, but others like them do not appear to have been documented or recorded. In the early years of formal or organized collecting, comparatively little song material in English was collected, as the heaviest emphasis was placed on material in the Irish language, which was perceived as being in more immediate danger of being lost.

Some collectors' names occur repeatedly among the examples given here. Séamus Ennis (1919–82) was a full-time collector of music and song with the IFC from 1942 to 1947. He collected songs, music and lore in west Munster, in counties Galway, Mayo, Cavan and Donegal, and in the Gaidhealtachd of Scotland. In later years he worked with Radio Éireann and the BBC and often returned to the informants from whom he had recorded material during his years with the IFC. Tom Munnelly, based in County Clare, works as a full-time collector with the Department of Irish Folklore, University College Dublin. The thousands of Irish traditional songs in English which he has collected form a substantial part of the Folk Music Section of the IFC. He has published and lectured widely on the English-language song tradition in Ireland. Ríonach uí Ógáin, based in Dublin, is lecturer/ archivist in the same department.[14] Hugh Shields, formerly a senior lecturer in French at Trinity College Dublin, has written widely on the subject of old British ballads in Ireland; his *Narrative Singing in Ireland* (1993) is a major contribution to the study of the song tradition.

These last three scholar/collectors are also members, or former members, of the Board of the Irish Traditional Music Archive, Dublin, founded in 1987 under the auspices of An Chomhairle Ealaíon/The Arts Council. Almost all of the material given in this selection was collected in the twentieth century although some of the song-texts themselves may be hundreds of years older. The names given at the heads of the various entries are those of the singers. To convey a sense of traditional song as sung, a number of these texts are followed by original music transcriptions, while others include references to sound recordings and to published transcriptions of their music. Text transcriptions and English translations of songs in Irish, unless otherwise stated, are by Ríonach uí Ógáin. Songs in English which were collected by Tom Munnelly were transcribed by him. Music transcribed by Marian Deasy, Joan Dempsey and Thérèse Smith.

14. Both Tom Munnelly and Ríonach uí Ógáin have written and published extensively on the song tradition, and have produced and edited many tapes and CDs. References to their published work and to recordings which are available commercially will be found in the notes below and in the Biographies/Discographies/Bibliographies which follow.

KATE 'DINEERY' DOHERTY

(1902–92)

from:
IRISH FOLKLORE
COLLECTION RECORDING
(1984)

['Broken-token' ballads have found immense popularity throughout Ireland and Britain: parting lovers break a ring or some other token before one of them (usually the male) sails away on a lengthy voyage. After an absence of several years he returns and proposes marriage to the waiting girl, who does not recognize him. More often than not, he brings false news of her lover's death. She vows loyalty to her lover, whereupon he identifies himself by producing his half of the token. They are immediately united in wedlock.

Such tales do not seem so far-fetched if we take into account the great length of sea voyages in the nineteenth and preceding centuries. A parting of several years was not unusual and, as one lover admits, 'Seven years make a great alteration / With the raging seas between you and me'. In a number of songs about similar partings, the female either offers to wear, or actually does wear, men's clothes to sail away with her lover. Recorded by Tom Munnelly, October 1984: IFC/FMS TM 8/1 (1984). A version of Laws N 35.[1] T.M.]

The Dark-eyed Sailor

It's of a charming young maiden fair
Roved out one evening for to take the air,
She met a sailor along the way
And I paid attention, and I paid attention
To hear what they would say.

Said Willie, 'Fair maid, why do you roam?
The day is done and the night has come.'
She sighed while tears to her eyes did flow,
'It's my dark-eyed sailor, it's my dark-eyed sailor,
The cause of all my woe.'

1. G. Malcolm Laws Jr, *Native American Balladry* (rev. edition, Philadelphia: American Folklore Society, 1964) [Letters A–I] and *American Balladry From British Broadsides* (Philadelphia: American Folklore Society, 1957) [Letters J–Q]. The catalogues of G. Malcolm Laws Jr list ballads of American and British origin found in oral tradition in North America. In spite of the American orientation of these catalogues they are extremely useful tools for folksong research in Ireland. Laws's references are used to identify later 'post-Child' broadsheet ballads.

'Oh,' said the young man, 'drive him from your mind,
Another sailor, as good, you'll find.
For love turns aside and cold does blow
Like a winter's morning, like a winter's morning,
When the hills are clad with snow.'

'Oh,' said the lady, 'what do you mean?
A tarry sailor would treat me the same.
You may drink his health with a chink of coin,
For my dark-eyed sailor, for my dark-eyed sailor
Does claim this heart of mine.

'His cherry cheeks and coal-black hair,
His two blue eyes they did me ensnare.
Genteel he was, not a rake like you,
To invite a fair maid, to invite a fair maid
To forsake her jacket blue.

'It's seven long years since he left the land,
He took a gold ring off my right hand,
He broke the token, left half to me,
Whilst the other's rolling, whilst the other's rolling
At the bottom of the sea.'

THE DARK-EYED SAILOR

Then half the ring did young Willie show,
She seemed distracted between joy and woe,
Saying, 'You're welcome, Willie, I have gold in
   store
For my dark-eyed sailor, for my dark-eyed
   sailor,
A maid I'll live and die.'

So now this couple's married, right well does
   agree,
They live in a cottage all along the sea.
Be true, fair maids, when your love's away,
For a cloudy morning, for a cloudy morning
Brings forth a pleasant day.

JAMES KEANE

(1793–c. 1878)

from:
OLD IRISH FOLK MUSIC
AND SONGS (1909)

[Performers usually give love and fear of parting as reasons why female characters in songs adopt male disguise. The woman disguises herself as a man and goes in search of her lover and/or of adventure in a genre classified as 'female warrior' songs. This type of song gained credibility from several authenticated accounts of women who had served in the navy or army for many years before their sex was disclosed or discovered.[1]

Perhaps surprisingly, the songmaker's approval of such direct and forceful action as occurs in the final verse is manifest in an additional verse which P.W. Joyce does not give: 'When the captain came to hear it, of the deed that she had done, / He made her a ship's commander, over a vessel for the Isle of Man.'[2] Cross-dressing in the other direction does not figure in traditional song in Ireland, except in 'The Seducer Outwitted', a Dublin broadsheet ballad recorded from oral tradition in Derry: the seducer is confounded when the girl he would debauch convinces him that she is a man disguised as a maid![3] From P.W. Joyce (ed.), *Old Irish Folk Music and Songs* (Dublin: Hodges, Figgis, 1909; repr. New York, 1965), no. 424, pp. 235–6 (includes music transcription). A version of Laws N 11.2. T.M.]

1. For a study of this genre, see Dianne Dugan, *Warrior Women and Popular Balladry, 1650–1850* (Cambridge: C.U.P., 1989). For cross-dressing in literature and memoirs, compare the section 'Sexuality 1685–2000', pp. 776–778.
2. Version from Louth tradition sung by Gerry Cullen, Fran McPhail and Phil Callery, 'Many's the Foolish Youth' (Dublin: Faetain Records, SPIN 996, 1987).
3. Hugh Shields, *Shamrock, Rose and Thistle: Folk Singing in North Derry* (Belfast: Blackstaff Press, 1981), pp. 100–1, 114.

Willie Taylor

Willie was a youthful lover full of heart and full
   of play;
Soon his mind he did discover to a youthful
   lady gay.

Chorus (after every verse):
*Oh, the vows, oh, the breezes: vows and breezes pass
   away!*

When her parents came to hear it they were
   filled with wrath and spite,
Soon they'd prove young William's ruin — rob
   him of his heart's delight.

Four and twenty British sailors met him on the
   king's high road,
As he went for to be married: pressed he was
   and sent abroad.

She dressed herself in sailor's garments, went on
   board a ship of war;
Her pretty fingers long and slender all
   besmeared with pitch and tar.

In this ship there was a skirmish, she among the
   rest did fight:
Her jacket burst the silver buttons; her breast
   was bared all snowy white!

Then the captain did inquire, 'What misfortune
   drove you here?'
'Sir, I'm seeking Willie Taylor; pressed he was
   by you last year.'

'If you rise tomorrow early, if you go at break of
day,
There you'll see your Willie Taylor with another
lady gay.'

Then she rose at early morning; out she went at
break of day;
There she saw her Willie Taylor walking with a
lady gay.

'Oh, false Willie, you've deceived me, you
promised to make me your wife;
She that bought you shall not keep you, for this
hour I'll have your life.'

Soon she got a case of pistols, sore she mourned
and sore she cried;
There she shot false Willie Taylor and the lady
by his side.

MÁIRE ÁINE NÍ DHONNCHADHA

(1919–91)

from:
DEORA AILLE: IRISH SONGS FROM CONNEMARA (1970)

[In 'Dónall Óg', probably the best known of the love-songs
in Irish ascribed to women, a woman addresses her
beloved, who has betrayed her. The devastation which
follows his broken promise is absolute, and she presents
her inconsolable grief in rural, pastoral imagery. This
imagery, the first-person address, and the theme of
suffering because of love, are typical of the lyrical love-
song tradition in Irish, but the near-suicidal desperation
expressed in the final verse is unsurpassed elsewhere in the
tradition. In other songs the woman may implore the man
to stay with her, or ask him to take her with him, as in the
first verse given here.

Other motifs which occur repeatedly in the love-songs
include the idea, also found in Dante, that the only reason to
go to mass is to see the beloved (v. 3). 'Dónall Óg' is one of
the very few songs originally composed in Irish which is sung
in English translation today. Lady Gregory's translation
featured as a recitation in John Huston's film *The Dead*
(1987), although it does not appear in James Joyce's story
of the same name in *Dubliners* (1914). From Máire Áine
Ní Dhonnchadha, *Deora Aille: Irish Songs from Connemara*
(Dublin: Claddagh Records, CC6, 1970). R.Ó.]

Dónall Óg

A Dhónaill óig, má théir thar farraige,
Tabhair mé féin leat is ná déan do dhearmad,
Beidh agat féirín lá aonaigh agus margaidh,
Agus iníon Rí Gréige mar chéile leaptha agat.

Gheall tú dhomsa agus rinne tú bréag liom
Go mbeifeá romhamsa ag cró na gcaorach;
Lig mé fead agus dhá bhlaoi dhéag ort,
Is ní raibh romham ach na huain agus iad ag
méilí.

Siúd é an Domhnach a dtug mé grá dhuit,
An Domhnach díreach roimh Domhnach
Cásca,
Is thú ar do ghlúine ag léamh na Páise
Is ea bhí mo dhá shúil ag síorthabhairt grá dhuit.

Nuair a théimse féin go Tobar Phádraig[1]
Ag tabhairt an turais ar son mo ghrá geal,
Níl mo shúil leat inniu nó amárach,
Agus a mhuirnín dílis, mo chúig chéad slán leat.

Nuair a théimse féin go Tobar Bhríde
Suím síos ann ag ligean scíthe,
Sileann mo shúile ar nós na díleann,
Tá mo cheann dubh bán le mo dhubhsmaointe.

Nuair a théim isteach go teach an tsuaircis
Suím síos ann ag déanamh buartha,
Nuair a fheicim an saol is nach bhfeicim an
buachaill
Go raibh scáil an ómair i mbarr a ghruanna.

A ghile na finne is a ghile na ruaichte,
A ghile an domhain is tú d'fhága mé buartha,

1. People went regularly to holy wells and performed patterns or
pilgrimages there on the feast day of the relevant saint, or to pray
for a cure or favour.

Nuair a chloisim trácht ar na mná dá lua leat
Titeann an bun dhíom agus barr na gruaige.

Tá mo chroí-sa chomh dubh le airne
Nó le gual dubh a dhóifí i gceárta,
Nó le bonn bróige ar hallaí bána,
Agus tá lionn dubh mór os cionn mo gháire.

Bhain tú thoir agus bhain tú thiar dhíom,
Bhain tú a raibh romham is i mo dhiaidh
    dhíom,
Bhain tú an ghealach is bhain tú an ghrian
    dhíom,
Ach is rí-mhór é m'fhaitíos gur bhain tú Dia
    dhíom.

DÓNALL ÓG

'Dhó—nai—ll ói—g má théir thar fa————rrai—ge,

Tabhair mé féi—n leat is ná dé—an do dhear-mad, (a) Beidh a-ga—t féi—rín—

lá——ao——naigh 'gu—s ma——rgaidh, a—gus

inío-n Rí——Gréi——ge——mar

chéi——le——leap-tha 'gat.

Young Dónall

Oh, Dónall Óg, if you go across the sea
Take me with you and do not forget,
You shall have a present every fair and market
    day
And the daughter of the King of Greece as bed
    companion.

You promised me but told me a lie
That you would meet me at the sheep-shed.
I whistled and called twelve times
But my only reply was the lambs bleating.

That was the Sunday I gave my love to you,
The Sunday just before Easter Sunday,
And you on your knees reading the Passion
My two eyes were loving you forever.

When I go to St. Patrick's well,
Doing the pattern[1] for my fair love,
I do not expect you today or tomorrow
And my darling, five hundred farewells.

1. Pattern, from English 'patron [saint]'. Cf. note 1, p. 1320.

When I go to St. Brigid's well,
I sit down to rest,
My eyes shed tears like the flood:
My black head is white with dark thoughts.

When I go into the house of gaiety,
I sit down there and I am sorrowful,
When I see everyone and I don't see the boy
Whose amber-coloured locks were reflected in
his cheeks.

Oh, brightest of the fair, Oh, brightest of the
red-haired,
Oh, brightest of the world, you left me sorrowful:
When I hear other women mentioned with you,
I lose heart and my hair falls down.

My heart is as black as a sloe,
Or black coal burning in a forge,
Or the soles of shoes in white halls
And there is black sorrow over my laughter.

You've taken east from me; you've taken west
from me,
You've taken what was before me and what was
after me,
You've taken the moon and you've taken the
sun from me
But my fear is great, that you've taken God
from me.

CÓILÍN Ó CUALÁIN

(c. 1950–)

from:
IRISH FOLKLORE
COLLECTION RECORDING
(1986)

[Very often the song 'Mainistir na Búille'[1] tells the story of a
pregnant girl who awaits the return of her beloved. However,
as Cóilín Ó Cualáin sings it, it tells of the man who is unable
to sleep as he waits for his sweetheart. This version shows the
flexibility of the lyrical love-song and the ease with which a
'woman's song' can become a 'man's song' by merely
changing the personal pronouns. An unusual feature in this
song is the reference to marriage as the ideal situation and
the aspiration that the priest will marry the speaker and his
lover. From IFC/FMS RÓ 18C (1986). R.Ó.]

Mainistir na Búille

Chaith mé seacht seachtainí i Mainistir na Búille,
Ar mo luí ar mo leaba is ní in mo chodladh ach
i mo dhúiseacht,

Ag súil leat gach uile leathuair go dtabharfá an
sagart faoi rún leat,
Ó, bhí tú do mo mhealladh is gur chaill mé mo
chliú leat.

Mar bhláth bán insa ngairdín a bhíonns mo
ghrása i dtús an tsamhraidh,
Nó na faoileáiníní bána a bhíonns ag snámh ar
Loch Éirne,
Nó mar long os cionn an tsáile a mbeadh a
dealramh ag dul timpeall
Agus sin mar a bhíonns mo ghrá bán ag teacht
ag rámhaillí i m'intinn.

Chuaigh mo mhuintir go Baile an Róba ag cur
mo chónra dhá déanamh,
Is chuaigh an chuid eile acu go coilltí Eochaill
ag baint mo chróchair de bharr géaga.
Tá súil le Rí na Glóire agam go bhfuil siad uilig
bréagach
Is go mbeidh mise is mo mhíle stóirín seal ag ól
lena chéile.

1. The town of Boyle, County Roscommon. This version of the song
is also published in R. uí Ógáin, 'The Love-Songs of Conamara',
Dal gCais: The Journal of Clare, no. 3 (Miltown Malbay, County
Clare: Dal gCais Publications, 1991), pp. 111–23.

Is nach aoibhinn don chábán a dtéann mo
   ghrása ag ól ann,
Is nach aoibhinn don chosán a leagann sí bróig
   ann,
Is nach aoibhinn don ógfhear a gheobhaidh í le
   pósadh
Réalt eolais na maidne is crann soilse an
   tráthnóna.

Nár ba fada nó go bhfágha mé uait litir is scéala
Nár ba fada nó go bhfágha mé lena oscailt is le
   léamh í,
Nár ba fada nó go bhfeice mé an sagart ina
   léine
Ór buí inár bpócaí is muid pósta le chéile.

MAINISTIR NA BÚILLE

Chaith mé sea—cht sea—chtain-í
i Main—is—tir na Búi—lle,
Ar mo luí ar mo lea-ba
ní in mo—chod—ladh ach 'mo dhúis—eacht,
A—g súi—l leat gach uil—e
leath—uair go dtabhar—fá'n sa—gart faoi rún leat
Ó bhí tú do mo mheall- adh is gur
chaill—mé—mo chliú leat.

The Town of Boyle

I spent seven weeks in the town of Boyle,
Lying in bed; not asleep, but awake
And hoping every half-hour you would come
  with the priest, in secret
Since you enticed me so that I lost my honour
  by you.

My love is like a white flower in the garden at
  the start of summer
Or the little white gulls swimming on Lough
  Erne,
Or like a ship on the sea turning in brightness,
And that is how my bright love makes my mind
  delirious.

My people went to Ballinrobe[1] to order my coffin,
The rest of them went to Eochaill woods to
  make my bier from the tops of the branches,

1. A town in County Mayo.

I hope to God that they are all lying
And that I and my darling will drink together a
  while.

How lucky the cabin where my beloved goes
  drinking,
How lucky the path where she places her shoe
  treads,
How lucky the young man who will have her to
  marry,
The guiding star of the morning, and a torch in
  the evening.

I hope it won't be long until I get a letter and
  news from you,
I hope it won't be long until I get it to open and
  to read,
I hope it won't be long until I see the priest in
  his vestments
Bright gold in our pockets and we married to
  each other.

BRÍD NÍ CHONAIRE

(1959–)

from:
IRISH FOLKLORE
COLLECTION RECORDING
(1986)

[Bríd Ní Chonaire learned this song, about a young woman's love for a celibate priest, in Ros Muc, County Galway, from a member of her husband's family. She sings it on IFC V 1988. It is also known as 'Tiocfaidh an Samhradh' ('Summer Will Come'); 'Bideoigín' (a girl's name); 'An Cumann Gearr' ('Short-lived Love'); and 'Deas an Sagairtín é Stór mo Chroí' ('My Darling Is a Nice Priest'). Oral tradition remembers that the young woman was in love with the young man before he left home. On his return as a priest, she did not realize that he had been ordained. The song expresses her distress that he is not destined for her. It takes the form of a dialogue, where the young woman proclaims her love and he explains that he is not meant for any woman but that he hopes to baptize her child some day (from IFC 1280: 367).

In Sorcha Ní Ghuairim's version of this song the young woman laments the fact that she is no longer a virgin and that until apples grow on cows' horns she will never be one again — a common formula in the love-songs. Cf. R. uí Ógáin, 'The Love-songs of Conamara', pp. 111–23. R.Ó.]

An Sagairtín

Tá an oíche seo dorcha is tá sí fuar
Tá sí ag goilliúint ar mo chroí go mór,
Mo stór a d'imigh uaim is nach bhfuil le fáil
Is a bheidh ag goilliúint orm go bhfaighfidh mé
  bás.

Nach deas an sagairtín é stór mo chroí,
Nach beannaithe an pobal a dtéann sé tríd,
Tá beannacht ó Mhuire air is séala ó Chríost,
Is tá sé ag triall ar choláistí.

Éist a chailín ó, is ná sil aon deor,
Mar níor dhuit a rugadh mé ná d'aon bhean
    beo,
Ach baistfidh mé do leanbh dhuit le cúnamh Dé,
Is dá mbeadh breith ar m'aiféala agam ba leatsa
    mé.

Tháinig mé aréir ag doras an *hall*
Chun cogar a thabhairt do mo mhíle grá,

Is é an rud a dúirt a hathair liom nach raibh sí
    ann,
Go raibh sí imithe go Meiriceá.

Dúirt a máthair liom is í ag gol go hard,
Go raibh sí sínte i gcónra chláir,
A Íosa Chríost nach mór an feall,
Bheith i ngrá le mnaoi is gan í agam le fáil.

AN SAGAIRTÍN

Tá an oíche seo dorcha agus tá sí fuar, Tá sí ag goilliúint ar mo chroí go mór, Mo stór a d'imigh uaim is nach bhfuil le fáil, Is a bheidheas ag goilliúint orm go bhfaighfidh mé bás.

The Little Priest

The night is dark and cold;
It breaks my heart.
My darling has left me and cannot be found,
And this will make me unhappy until I die.

My darling is a fine priest;
The people he serves are blessed.
Mary blesses him and Christ has given him his
    seal,
And he is going to college.

Listen, my girl, and do not cry,
I was not born for you or for any living woman,
But I will baptize your child for you, please
    God,
And if I could change things I would be yours.

I came last night to the hall door,
To give a secret message to my love.

Her father told me she was not there,
That she had gone to America.

Her mother told me as she wept loudly
That she was stretched in a coffin.
O God, isn't it a terrible shame
To be in love with a woman, when she cannot
    be mine!

SINÉAD CAHER

from:
THE FLOWER OF MAGHERALLY (1978)

[This love-song's popularity in oral tradition today is due to a recording made in 1947 by Séamus Ennis of Elizabeth Cronin (see pp. 1354–1355). Though Mrs Cronin's version is exquisitely sung, her text is somewhat corrupt, so the more coherent version sung on a commercial recording, *The Flower of Magherally*, by another fine singer, Sinéad Caher, is given here (Dublin: Sruthán Records, LUN A333, 1978). This song would appear to be of Scots origin, as several items in Mrs Cronin's repertoire were.

See, for instance, 'O Gin I Were at the Top of Yon Mountain', in E.B. Lyle (ed.), *Andrew Crawfurd's Collection of Ballads and Songs*, vol. 1, no. 33 (Edinburgh: The Scottish Texts Society, 1975), p. 82.[1]   T.M.]

1. Thanks to John Moulden for this reference.

The Bonny Blue-eyed Lassie

How can I live upon
The top of a mountain,
With no money in my pocket
And no gold for to count it?

THE BONNY BLUE-EYED LASSIE

How __ can I live up-on The __ top __ of a moun-tain With no __ mo-ney __ in __ my poc-ket And no __ gold for to count it? I would let the __ mo __ ney go All for to ____ please __ her __ fan-cy And __ I will mar _____ ry no one But my - own true _blue _eyed las __ - sie.

I would let the money go,
All for to please her fancy
And I would marry no-one
But my own true blue-eyed lassie.

She's my own true blue-eyed lassie
With an air so sweet and tender,
Her walk like swan that floats
And her waist so small and slender,
Her golden hair in ringlets fair
Lies o'er her snow-white shoulder
And I'd ask her for to marry me
And there's no man could be bolder.

And there's some people say
That she is very low in station,
And there's other people say
She'll be the cause of my ruination.
But let them all say what they will,
To her I will prove constant still.
Till the day that I die
She will be my own lovely lady.

O sweetly swims the swan
O'er the dark waters of Eochaill
And blithely sings the nightingale
So happy to behold her,
But the wind may blow and moorcocks crow,
The moon can shine so sweetly,
But sweeter by far
Is my love for my own lady.

THOMAS H. STEWART

(*fl.* 1927)

from:
SAM HENRY'S SONGS OF
THE PEOPLE (1990)

[Sam Henry collected this song from a fiddle-player called Thomas H. Stewart, of Mayoghill, Garvagh, County Derry, and printed it in the *Northern Constitution*, a weekly newspaper published in Coleraine, on 9 April 1927. The song was composed by a 'blind poet Kane, in honour of his sister'. Kane, or O'Kane, was a native of Gortade about a mile from Tirgarvil, County Derry. Sam Henry notes that 'The classical references were a feature of songs of that period [nineteenth century] and may be traced to the influences of McCloskey's Academy at Tirgarvil from which over 300 students graduated and obtained degrees, including the renowned Dr. George Sigerson, the poet.'[1] Many Irish rural people would have understood these references to Greek and Roman deities, but the composer of 'The Flower of Gortade' seems to have attempted to include the entire pantheon. Published with music transcription in G. Huntington, L. Herrmann, J. Moulden,

Sam Henry's Songs of the People, pp. 233–4. Sung by Len Graham on *Chaste Muses, Bards and Sayes* (Derby: Free Reed Record No. 007, 1976).   T.M.]

The Flower of Gortade

Descend, ye chaste muses, ye bards and ye sages
With Orpheus, who tamed roaring beasts with
    his lyre;
You ancient historians that's dead many ages,
I hope you'll awake and my genius inspire:
You great men of learning, give your approbation,
Ye gods and philosophers, lend me your aid
In praise of a female who's leaving our nation:
She's the bright star of Erin and the flower of
    Gortade.

Oh, was I as Homer, the prince of the writers
Who sang of Athenians and Spartans so bold,
Could I paint with the skill of a Roman inditer,
The praise of this fair one can never be told.
Fair Penelope, Venus, Diana or Flora,
Whose beauty and chastity never can fade,
Fair Helen, Lucretia or famous Aurora;
All these could not equal the flower of Gortade.

1. For George Sigerson, see Volume III, pp. 563–5. For classical references in Irish popular culture, compare Brian Friel's play *Translations*, Volume III, pp. 1207–36.

Unrivalled she stands 'mongst the daughters of
  Erin,
For wit or for beauty none can her excel;
On the third of September her vessel she's
  steering
Far, far from the place she did formerly dwell.
The consorts of Hector that's mentioned in
  story,
Susanna, whose virtues are still undecayed,
Queen Dido, who reigned with her sovereign in
  glory:
Even those do not equal the flower of Gortade.

Adieu to old Erin, the land of my childhood,
Where luxury, pomp and magnificence rove,
No more I'll traverse o'er the plains or the wild
  wood
Or listen to the mavis that sings in the grove;
No more by the creeks or promontories I'll
  wander
In search of the wild rose in beauty displayed,
No more in romances my memory shall ponder
Alongst with my comrades that dwell in Gortade.

Adieu to my mother, my sisters and brothers,
My cousins, my comrades and neighbours so
  kind;
When I'm far away from this old Irish nation,
They'll all join in chorus and bear me in mind,
And if to Columbia God sends me safe over,
I'll write a few lines to my dear comrade maid,
Who does constantly mourn with my friends
  and true lover
Since Margaret O'Kane has abandoned
  Gortade.

Since destined by fate to forsake Erin's nation,
I hope that my mother no longer will mourn,
I pray that the Lord may send her consolation
Till I to this island again do return,
For then will all sorrow and sadness be ended
And for all her trouble she'll then be repaid
When she in fond raptures with her arms
  extended
Will welcome her daughter once more to
  Gortade.

BILL DONEGAN

(b. 1906)

from:
IRISH FOLKLORE
COLLECTION RECORDING
(1975)

[When marriage is the subject of a song, it is more often
than not unhappy. Songs of unhappy marriage can be
broadly categorized as either poignant or comical. In the
latter, love is usually dead or has never existed; in the
former, love may still exist, but that love is not for the
marriage partner. Lord Randal (Child No. 12) regrets his
marriage for the very valid reason that he has been
poisoned by his wife. The Orangeman's wife wishes she
had never been born when she discovers her husband was
the leader of a gang of Wreckers who slew her father. In
Laws P27, Caroline of Edinburgh Town regrets marrying
Henry, and drowns herself when he deserts her and goes
to sea. Even more instant despair comes to the bride in
'The Nobleman's Wedding' who dies of remorse on the
very night of her wedding. From IFC/FMS TM 374/A/2; a
version of Laws P 31.   T.M.]

The Nobleman's Wedding

Last night I was invited to a nobleman's
  wedding
All by a lady who proved so unkind,
And now she begins to bewail all her follies
For her former true lover still runs in her mind.

After the wedding dinner and toast it was all
  over
Everyone there had to sing a love song,
And who should begin but her former true lover?
And the song that he sung to the bride did
  belong.

Sayin', 'How can you sleep on another man's
  pillow?
And I to be your true love that you loved of late?
Or are you goin' to leave me to wear the green
  willow?
And quite discontented sure I am for your sake.

'Or are you goin' to leave me to wear the green
  willow?
It shall be only for one month or two,
And then I will throw it by and I will wear a red
  rose
And I will go a-courting as all young men do.'

The bride she sat at the head of the table
An' every word was spoke she remarked it right
  well.
But to bear it any longer she was not well able
And down at the foot of the bridegroom she
  fell.

Sayin': 'This one request, love, I am goin' to ask
  of you,
It is the first and it may be the last:
To give me this night for to lie with my Mama,
And the remainder of my lifetime, I'll spend it
  with you.'

'This one request, love, it's hard to be granted.
Why didn't you think of yourself, love, in time?

I know very well, love, of what is the matter —
Your former true lover still runs in your mind.'

But after great persuading the gift it was
  granted.
Sobbing and crying this maid went to bed.
And early, oh early, the very next morning,
The bridegroom arose, found his new bride was
  dead.

He raised her up in his lily-white arms.
He laid her down on the bank so green,
Covered her over with pink and red roses
Thinking she might come to her colours back
  again.

Oh, this willow tree bears a very handsome
  blossom
Only in springtime, the season of the year
When young men an' maidens go kissing and
  courting
And talking of their love tales but can't be the
  same.

SEOSAMH Ó hÉANAÍ

(1919–84)

from:
Ó MO DHÚCHAS (1976)

[This item often combines song and prose narrative. The international prose tale 'Na Trí Chomhairle' or 'The Three Pieces of Advice' (AT 910B)[1] is sometimes given as background explanation to the song. The good counsels given vary, but one consistently found in the folktale is that when one is angry, one should repeat the Lord's Prayer. This seems to occur in the background to the Irish versions of the song. In the international ballad classification system the ballad is 'Our Goodman', Child No. 274. Some versions in English contain a strong element of humour based on the concept of cuckolding — possibly introduced by migratory labourers. As it occurs in Irish, the ballad assumes that the audience knows that Peadar has been married for six months when his wife tells him he must earn money, as she is expecting a child. He hires himself to a farmer some distance away for twenty-one

years. Finally, he leaves the farmer and returns to his wife. The farmer persuades him to accept three pieces of advice. The final one is 'Never do at night what you may regret in the morning.' In the song, the faithful wife is rewarded when she explains her innocence during her husband's absence. This song is often performed by a man and a woman who sing alternate verses. Seosamh Ó hÉanaí, *Ó Mo Dhúchas* (Dublin: Gael Linn Records, CEF CD 051 1976).   R.Ó.]

Peigín is Peadar

'A Pheigín na gcarad, a Pheigín mo chroí,
Ce hé an fear fada údan sínte leat síos?
*Ó a ó, a ó mhaithín ó, a ó mhaithín ó, a stóirín mo
  chroí.*

Is a Pheigín na gcarad, is a Pheigín na gcroí
Cé hé an fear fada údan sínte leat síos?
*Ó a ó, a ó mhaithín ó, a ó mhaithín ó, a stóirín mo
  chroí.'*

1. A. Aarne and S. Thompson, *The Types of the Folktale*, p. 313.

'Muise, a Pheadair na gcarad, is a Pheadair mo
    chroí
Sin é do leanbh nach bhfaca tú riamh.
*Ó a ó, a ó mhaithín ó, a ó mhaithín ó, a stóirín mo
    chroí.'*

'Muise, shiúil mise thoir agus shiúil mise thiar,
Ach féasóg ar leanbh ní fhaca mé riamh.
*Ó a ó, a ó mhaithín ó, a ó mhaithín ó, a stóirín mo
    chroí.*

Muise, a Pheigín na gcarad, is a Pheigín mo chroí
Éirigh in do sheasamh agus réitigh greim bia.
*Ó a ó, a ó mhaithín ó, a ó mhaithín ó, a stóirín mo
    chroí.'*

'Is a Pheadair na gcarad, is a Pheadair mo chroí
Níl insan teach againn greim mine bhuí.
*Ó a ó, a ó mhaithín ó, a ó mhaithín ó, a stóirín mo
    chroí.'*

'Is a Pheigín na gcarad, is a Pheigín mo chroí,
In íochtar mo mhála tá cáca mine bhuí.
*Ó a ó, a ó mhaithín ó, a ó mhaithín ó, a stóirín mo
    chroí.'*

'Muise, a Pheadair na gcarad, is a Pheadair mo
    chroí
Tá an cáca seo agat lán de ghineachaí buí.
*Ó a ó, a ó mhaithín ó, a ó mhaithín ó, a stóirín mo
    chroí.'*

'Is a Pheigín is a mhaicín suífimid síos
Ní fhágfad an baile chúns mhairfeas mé aríst.
*Ó a ó, a ó mhaithín ó, a ó mhaithín ó, a stóirín mo
    chroí.'*

Peigín and Peadar

'Oh, dearest Peigín, Peigín my heart,
Who is that tall man lying down beside you?
*Oh, a oh, a owa-heen oh, a owa-heen oh, darling of
    my heart.*

Oh, dearest Peigín, Peigín my heart,
Who is that tall man lying down beside you?
*Oh, a oh, a owa-heen oh, a owa-heen oh, darling of
    my heart.'*

'Well, dearest Peadar, Peadar my heart,
That is your child that you have never seen.
*Oh, a oh, a owa-heen oh, a owa-heen oh, darling of
    my heart.'*

'Well, I have walked east and I have walked
    west,
But I never before saw a beard on a child.
*Oh, a oh, a owa-heen oh, a owa-heen oh, darling of
    my heart.*

Well, dearest Peigín, Peigín my heart,
Get up and prepare a bite to eat.
*Oh, a oh, a owa-heen oh, a owa-heen oh, darling of
    my heart.'*

'And dearest Peadar, Peadar my heart,
There is not a bit of Indian meal in the house.
*Oh, a oh, a owa-heen oh, a owa-heen oh, darling of
    my heart.'*

'Well, dearest Peigín, Peigín my heart,
There is a cake of Indian meal in the bottom of
    my bag.
*Oh, a oh, a owa-heen oh, a owa-heen oh, darling of
    my heart.'*

'Well, dearest Peadar, Peadar my heart,
This cake is full of yellow guineas.
*Oh, a oh, a owa-heen oh, a owa-heen oh, darling of
    my heart.'*

'And Peigín and little son, let us sit down,
I won't leave home again as long as I live.
*Oh, a oh, a owa-heen oh, a owa-heen oh, darling of
    my heart.'*

NONIE LYNCH

(*c.* 1910–   )

from:
IRISH FOLKLORE
COLLECTION RECORDING
(1992)

[Ballads of revenge for adultery are not numerous, and although there are exceptions in which women are punished, generally women who cuckold their husbands receive remarkably little explicit censure from the song-makers. However, in a few songs, such as 'My Good-looking Man', women take immediate, dramatic action on discovering an unfaithful husband.[1] IFC/FMS TM 1289D/23 (1992).   T.M.]

My Good-looking Man

When I was sixteen years of age,
A damsel in my prime,
I daily thought on wedded life
And how I'd spend my time;
I daily thought on wedded life,
Its beauties I did scan.
I sighed and sobbed both night and day
To get a nice young man.

The wish I wanted, soon I got
One Sunday afternoon
As home from church I gaily walked,
Sure I met this fair *garsún*.[2]
He looked so neat about his feet,
To win him it was my plan
And that very day I fell in love
With my good-lookin' man.

He pledged to me the words of love
And I said his bride I'd be.
He pressed me fondly to his breast
Saying 'Oh, you are my dear.'
He pressed me fondly to his breast
As to the church we ran,
And there and then I got wed
To my good-lookin' man.

Scarcely were we wed three months,
One Sunday afternoon,
My gentleman he did step out
Just on our honeymoon.
I did not go along with him,
For to watch him it was my plan,
And soon a flashing young lass I saw
With my good-lookin' man.

He pledged to her the words of love,
Just as he had done with me,
He pressed her fondly to his breast
Saying 'Oh, you are my dear,'
He pressed her fondly to his breast
As to my home I ran,
And there I patiently did wait
For my good-lookin' man.

The clock was just on the stroke of ten
When my gentleman stepped in.
'Where have you been, oh Johnny dear,
Where have you so long been?'
'To church, to church, kind love,' he said,
But this I could not stand.
By Heavens! the tongs I did let fly
At my good-lookin' man.

I blackened his face, I broke his nose,
In ribbons I tore his clothes.
I seized the poker from the stove
And hit him across the nose.
He looked just like a chimney-sweep
As out the door he ran.
Ah-hah, the divil a girl fell in love again
With my good-lookin' man.

1. For a study of humorous English and German ballads on adultery, which includes a version of this song, see Klaus Roth, *Ehebruchschwanke in Liedform* (München: Wilhelm Fink Verlag, 1977), esp. pp. 427–8.
2. Irish, a boy; from French, *garçon*.

MAGGIE McDONAGH

(*c*. 1911)

from:
THE COLUMBIA WORLD LIBRARY OF FOLK AND PRIMITIVE MUSIC, VOL. 1: IRISH FOLK SONGS (1995)

[The title of this song as published, 'Amhrán Fosaíochta', translates as 'Herding Song', but it is safe to assume that Maggie McDonagh happened to sing it while herding cattle, rather than that it was composed specifically to suit the rhythm and pace of that work. Songs like 'Dúín Dú' are very suitable to extempore composition because of the frequent nonsense vocables which keep them in constant motion. Stylistically, this resembles another song, 'Óró a Mhíle Grá' ('O My Thousand Loves'), sung very often in an entirely extempore style and frequently consisting of an amusing, sometimes bawdy, commentary on local and national events of the day, and taking the form of a game. In Ireland this type of verse appears to occur in Irish only. For another example, see 'Dúnadán Dorcha Donn' (p. 1423). A new recording of 'Dúín Dú' (called 'Dóín Dó') may be heard on Peadar Ó Ceannabháin, *Mo Chuid den tSaol: Traditional Songs from Connemara* (Indreabhán: Cló Iar Chonnachta, CICD131 1997). *The Columbia World*

Library of Folk and Primitive Music, vol. 1, *Irish Folk Songs*, recorded and edited by Séamus Ennis and Alan Lomax (USA: Columbia Records, SL-204, 1955). R.Ó.]

Dúín Dú

Dúín dú ó deighdil ó
Agus tá mo stór chomh deas
Dúín dú ó deighdil ó
Is nach bhféadaim éirí as.
Is dúin dú, dú ó deighdil lom.

Dúin etc.
Agus tá mo stór chomh cóir,
Dúin etc.
Le gloine i dteach an óil.
Is dúin dú etc.

Dúin etc.
Is nach neantóg is bláth buí,
Dúin etc.
Atá ag fás ar áit mo thí.
Is dúin dú etc.

DÚÍN DÚ

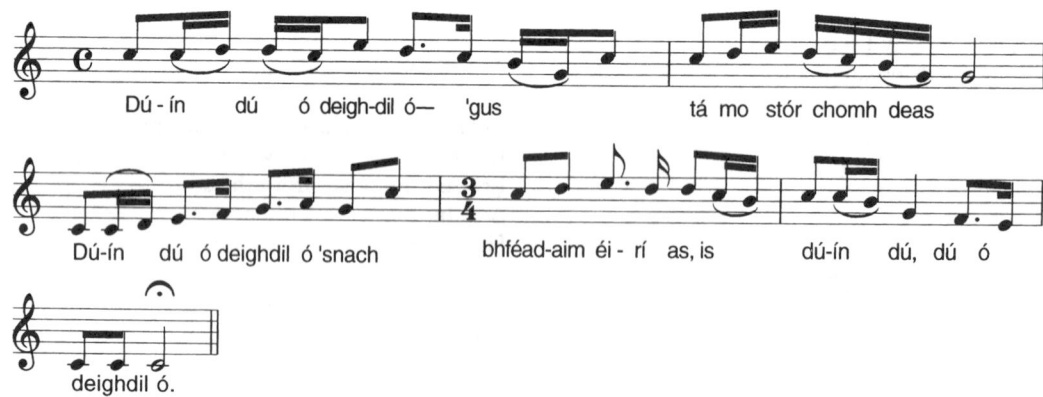

Doo-Een Doo

Doo-een doo, oh didle oh
And my love is so nice
Doo-een doo, oh didle oh
That I cannot give him up.
And doo-een doo, doo oh didle oh.

Doo-een doo, oh didle oh
My love is as good

Doo-een doo, oh didle oh
As a glass in the drinking house.
And doo-een doo, doo oh didle oh.

Doo-een doo, oh didle oh
Is it not nettles and yellow flowers
Doo-een doo, oh didle oh
That are growing on the site of my house.
And doo-een doo, doo oh didle oh.

NORA CLEARY

(1927–88)

from:
IRISH FOLKLORE
COLLECTION RECORDING
(1975)

[A song sung throughout Ireland, which might also have appealed to the more liberal of Chaucer's pilgrims, is known as 'The Wee Croppy Tailor' or 'The Bold Trooper'. Tom Munnelly has encountered very little bawdy song material in twenty-five years of collecting and research. Alan Lomax seems to be correct in his statement that: 'Bawdy ballads are rare in Ireland, common in England and universal in the English-speaking parts of Scotland, where Calvinism seems to have had no effect on a much older tradition.' Bawdy stories, however, were and are frequently found in oral tradition in Ireland.[1] Recorded by Tom Munnelly, 4 July 1975: IFC/FMS TM 416/B/3 (1975).   T.M.]

The Bold Trooper

Oh, there was an oul' merchant near London
  did dwell,
And he had a fine daughter, he loved her quite
  well.
She was pretty and witty and could not be
  excelled,
And her husband he was a bold trooper.

Chorus (after each verse):
Singing fal de riddle aye, riddle aye, riddle aye,
Singing fal de diddle aye, riddle addy, I do.

There was an oul' tailor that lived nearby
And on this pretty damsel he soon cast an eye.
'Four guineas I'll pay for my lodgings tonight
If your husband is gone to stand duty.'

T' oul' trooper went out, and that before long,
And they went into bed and began for to fun.
They went into bed and began for to fun
And never since thought of the trooper.

The trooper he came at the dead hour of night,
He knocked at the door, which caused them
    great fright.
'Oh hide me! Oh hide me!' the tailor he cried,
'For I hear the bold knock of the trooper.'

'There is an oul' cupboard behind the room's
    door
And there you may lie both safe and secure.
I'll go downstairs and I'll open the door
And I'll welcome my husband, the trooper.'

She went downstairs and let him in
And with kisses and compliments she did begin.
'[For] your kisses and compliments I don't give
    a pin,
But light me some fire,' said the trooper.

---

1. Another recording of Nora Cleary singing this song was published on the long-playing record *The Lambs on the Green Hills: Songs from County Clare* (London: Topic Records, 12TS369, 1978). See also 'The Wee Croppy Tailor' in Robin Morton (ed.), *Folksongs Sung in Ulster* (Cork: Mercier Press, 1970), pp. 80–1.

'I have no fire, nor no fire-stuffs,
But come up to bed, we'll be warm enough.'
'There is an oul' cupboard behind the room's
    door.
I'll burn it tonight,' said the trooper.

'Oh husband, oh husband, oh grant my desire,
That useless oul' cupboard is too good for fire.
Besides, there I do keep my game-cock I
    admire.'
'Show me your game-cock!' says the trooper.

T' oul' trooper went up behind the room's door
And there found the tailor safe and secure.
He gave him a halt in the middle of the floor.
'Is this your game-cock?' says the trooper.

The trooper he sent for a pair of sharp shears
And with it he cut off the tailor's two ears.
And for his night's lodging, he paid for it dear,
And away went the poor croppy tailor.

[A version of Child No. 272, 'The Holland Handkerchief'
is a much more widespread ballad of a dead lover's return
than 'Jimmy Whelan' (pp. 1353–1354). Nora Cleary
learned the song from her father. In it a girl is brought on
a midnight ride by her true love after her father has killed
him. Recorded by Tom Munnelly, 10 July 1975:
IFC/FMS TM 421/B/2 (1975).][1]

The Holland Handkerchief

There was a lord that lived in this town
And a lord of high renown.
He had a daughter and a beauty bright
And the name he called her was his heart's
    desire.[2]

Many's the lord who came courting her
But none of them could her favour gain
Till there came a man of low degree
And above them all, sure, she fancied he.

And when her father came this to know
For fifty miles he sent her away,
For fifty miles he sent her away
For to deprive them of their wedding day.

One night as Mary was going to bed
An' just slipping off her gown
She heard a voice of a deadly sound
Saying 'Loose the bonds, love, that we have
    bound.'

Her father's steed she did well know,
Her mother's mantle she knew also.
She dressed herself in rich attire
And away she went with her heart's desire.

'Twas with her love she rode behind,
They went far swifter than any wind
For about an hour and a little more,
He cried, 'My darling, my head is sore.'

A Holland handkerchief she then pulled out
And around his head she twisted about.
She kissed his lips and those words did say:
'My love, you're colder than any clay.'

An' when she came to her father's hall
'Who is that? Who is that?' her father called.
''Tis I, dear father, did you not send for me
By such a messenger?' — naming he.

He vowed an' swore that young man was dead,
He tore the grey hairs down off his head.
He wrung his hands and he cried full sore,
And this young man's darling cried ten times
    more.

'Twas early, early at the dawn of day
They went to the grave where that young man
    lay.
Although he was nine long months dead
A Holland handkerchief was around his head.

'It's a warning now,' her father said,
'To all young men and all fair maids.
For once their hearts an' their vows they give
That they ne'er shall part 'em so, while they
    live.'

---

1. For a study of this and related ballads see Ríonach uí Ógáin and
   Anne O'Connor, 'Spor ar an gCois is gan an Chois Ann',
   Béaloideas, vol. 51 (1983), pp. 87–125.
2. Usually 'delight'.

JOHN REILLY

(1926–69)

from:
ORIGINAL RECORDING
(1967)

[See the Introduction to the subsection 'Storytelling Traditions of the Irish Travellers', pp. 1263–1270, for a discussion of the Traveller society to which John Reilly belonged. 'The Well Below the Valley' (Child No. 21, 'The Maid and the Palmer') is an international ballad which survived among Irish Travellers after it had passed out of the repertoires of singers in the rest of the English-speaking world. It tells the story of Christ and the Samaritan woman, as told in the New Testament (John 4: 1–42), with the addition that the balladmaker has developed the woman who refuses Christ a drink into a Magdalen figure, whose history includes incest and infanticide.

The refrain of this song is printed in full after each couplet or line as sung, in order to reproduce the hypnotic effect of John Reilly's performance. Line 2 in verse 5 has been introduced by the collector from other versions in order to make the story clearer. From a recording by Tom Munnelly (1967).[1]   T.M.]

The Well Below the Valley

A gentleman was passing by.
He axed[2] a drink as he got dry
At the well below the valley O.
Green grows the lily O,
Right among the bushes O!

My cup it is in overflow
And if I do stoop I may fall in.
At the well below the valley O.

1. The text given here is substantially the same as that printed by Bertrand Harris Bronson, *The Traditional Tunes of the Child Ballads*, vol. 4 (Princeton, NJ: Princeton University Press, 1959–72), pp. 457–9. See also Tom Munnelly, 'John Reilly, the Man and His Music', in *Ceol*, vol. 4, no. 1 (January 1972), pp. 2–8. John Reilly may be heard singing this song on *The Bonny Green Tree: Songs of an Irish Traveller* (London: Topic Records, T 12T359, 1978). For yet another transcription see *Ceol*, vol. 3, no. 3 (June 1969), pp. 66–8. The popular Irish folk group Planxty perform this song on *The Well Below the Valley* (Dublin: Polydor Records, 2383 232, 1973). For a discussion of this ballad in Ireland and another full text collected in Achill Island, County Mayo, from Anna Ní Mháille, aged 86, see Anne O'Connor, *Child Murderess and Dead Child Traditions* (Helsinki: Academia Scientiarium Fennica, 1991), pp. 85, 119–20.
2. Asked.

Green grows the lily O,
Right among the bushes O!

Well, if your true love was passing by
You'd fill him a drink if he got dry.
At the well below the valley O.
Green grows the lily O,
Right among the bushes O!

She swore by grass and swore by corn
That her true love was never born.
At the well below the valley O.
Green grows the lily O,
Right among the bushes O!

I say, fair maiden, you're swearin' wrong
[For full five children you have borne.]
At the well below the valley O.
Green grows the lily O,
Right among the bushes O!

Well, if you're a man of that noble fame
You'll tell to me the father o' them.
At the well below the valley O.
Green grows the lily O,
Right among the bushes O!

Two o' them by your father dear.
At the well below the valley O.
Green grows the lily O,
Right among the bushes O!

Two more o' them came by your Uncle Dan.
At the well below the valley O.
Green grows the lily O,
Right among the bushes O!

Another one by your brother John.
At the well below the valley O.
Green grows the lily O,
Right among the bushes O!

Well, if you're a man of the noble fame
You'll tell to me what happened them.
At the well below the valley O.
Green grows the lily O,
Right among the bushes O!

There was two o' them buried by the kitchen
  fire.
At the well below the valley O.
Green grows the lily O,
Right among the bushes O!

Two more o' them buried by the stable door.
At the well below the valley O.
Green grows the lily O,
Right among the bushes O!

The other was buried by the well.
At the well below the valley O.
Green grows the lily O,
Right among the bushes O!

Well, if you're a man of the noble fame
You'll tell to me what will happen mysel'.
At the well below the valley O.
Green grows the lily O,
Right among the bushes O!

You'll be seven years a ringin' a bell
At the well below the valley O.
Green grows the lily O,
Right among the bushes O!

You'll be seven more a-portin' in Hell.[3]
At the well below the valley O.
Green grows the lily O,
Right among the bushes O!

I'll be seven long years a-ringin' the bell
But the Lord above might save my soul
From portin' in Hell
At the well below the valley O.
Green grows the lily O,
Right among the bushes O!

3. Sometimes 'a porter in Hell'.

PADDY 'TORPEY' KILLOUGHRY

(1892–1967)

from:
ORIGINAL RECORDING
(1962)

[A high proportion of love-songs take the form of the *pastourelle* and *débat*, as the lovers meet in a sylvan setting and a debate follows. *Pastourelle* was a branch of courtly poetry, already described as ancient in twelfth-century France, which described an encounter between a knight and a shepherdess. In Irish examples, courtship dialogue takes the form of an initial rebuff followed by further entreaties and eventual acquiescence or sometimes rejection. In many instances, politics and religion are aligned when patriotic girls ward off attacks on their virtue and their politics, as in 'The Gay Galtee Mountains' and 'The Girl and the Policeman'. Or the young woman may swear undying love to her Orange hero and to his cause, as occurs in 'The Purple Boy'. If the couple are of different religious persuasions, however, reconciliation can only come about if one of them takes the religion of the other. In almost all cases this means that one of them becomes a

Roman Catholic.[1] From a recording by Dr Ivor Browne (1962) (copy in IFC/FMS1).[2]   T.M.]

The Holy Church of Rome

As I roved out one evening
All in the month of May
When the birds were sweetly singing
And the lambs did sport and play
I heard a couple talking
As they walked hand and hand
And to hear their conversation
I eagerly did stand.

1. This comes about only after convoluted theological wrangling, for example as in 'The Pride of Dundalk Town', 'The Star of Donegal', 'The Star of Townley Hall' or 'The Banks of Dunmore'. A less familiar song of this type is known in oral tradition as 'The Holy Church of Rome', although broadsheets call it 'The Lady's Conversion to Catholicity'. James N. Healy (ed.), *The Mercier Book of Old Irish Street Ballads*, vol. 1 (Cork: Mercier Press, 1967), pp. 197–9.
2. Reproduced by kind permission of Dr Browne.

'Well,' said the young man, 'I'm a Roman
That ne'er denied my faith,
And you, my dear, a Protestant
All of the Saxon Race.'
To hear their conversation
I drew near to a bush.
'Well,' he says to her, 'my charmer,
I thought I had my wish.'

This fair one was quite angry,
Those words to him did say:
'If you think that I'm a heretic,
Young man you're going astray,
For I'm as loyal to my church
As you are to your creed,
So therefore as you went so far,
I'm of the proper seed.'

'Well, how can it be,' said Johnny,
'You're of the proper seed?
You sprang from Bess and Harry
Who inflicted wicked deeds.
Since Luther's Reformation
You are left in the lurch.
Don't you know he was a friar
That revolted from the church?'

This fair one being quite angry,
She made him this reply:
She said, 'My dearest Johnny,
I know he was a friar.
He said it was by the Roman creed
That he was led astray
Until an angel from the Lord
Had showed him the right way.'

'No, my dear, 'twas Satan tempted him
To invent that wicked plan,
He thought to tempt our Blessed Lord,
But He made him begone.
He tempted our first mother,
By which you see we die
For touching the forbidden fruit,
That same you can't deny.'

'Now there is another objection,
My love, I will relate,
Your creed all worship images,
And that's but little faith.'

'We do adore no images
Of either red or blue
But we keep it dear in memory
Of what our Lord went through.

'Now come all you dukes and officers,
My love, I will relate,
That goes before Her Majesty
And do salute her chair,
But is that chair to be compared
To the Shepherd and His flock
He keeps within His holy church,
Built on Saint Peter's rock?'

'Now don't talk to me about Peter,
He had but little faith,
He did deny our Saviour,
I mean for to relate.
He did deny our Saviour
One night among the Jews
So therefore go no further,
His power is little use.'

'Well, if Peter denied our Saviour,
I'll tell you the reason why,
Now the Lord Himself foretold it,
And He never told a lie.
But when Peter seen what he had done
He went and wept full sore
And he has the keys of Heaven now
And will forever more.'

Now she said, 'My dearest Johnny,
If all you say be true
I think it's but a folly
To go so far with you.
I will forsake my religion
And friends I will disown,
And while I live I'll be content
With the Holy Church of Rome.'

Those couple they got married
In hopes to gain success
And in spite of friends and relatives
One creed they do profess.
She did forsake her religion
And friends she did disown
And while they lived they were content
With the Holy Church of Rome.

BRIGID TUNNEY

(1896–1975)

from:
BRITISH BROADCASTING CORPORATION RECORDING
(1953)

[A great many love-songs deal with rejection by a lover. Like 'The Nobleman's Wedding' (pp. 1328–1329), 'As I Roved Out' ('The False Bride') is concerned with ill-fated marriage. The title is derived from the formulaic opening lines, also found in 'The Holy Church of Rome', above. Recorded in August 1953 by Sean O'Boyle and Peter Kennedy for the BBC (BBC Sound Archive 20026). See also *Where Linnets Sing: Three Generations of the Tunney Family and Their Songs* (Dublin, Comhaltas Ceoltóirí Éireann Records, CL44, 1993), and Paddy Tunney, *The Stone Fiddle* (Dublin: Gilbert Dalton, 1979), pp. 78–9.   T.M.]

As I Roved Out

As I roved out of a bright May morning
To view the flowers and meadows gay,
Who did I spy but my own true darling
As she sat under yon willow tree.

I took off my hat and I did salute her,
I did salute her courageously,
When she turned around and the tears fell from her
Saying: 'False young man, you have deluded me.'

'For to delude you, how can that be, my love,
It's from your body I am quite free.
I'm as free from you as the child unborn is
And so are you, my dear Jane, from me.

'[A] three-diamond ring, sure, I own I gave you,
Three-diamond ring to wear on your right hand.'
'And the vows you made, sure, you went and broke them
And married the lassie that had the land.'

'If I married the lassie that had the land, my love,
It's that I'll rue till the day I die;
Where misfortune falls, sure, no one can shun it,
I was blindfolded I'll ne'er deny.

AS I ROVED OUT

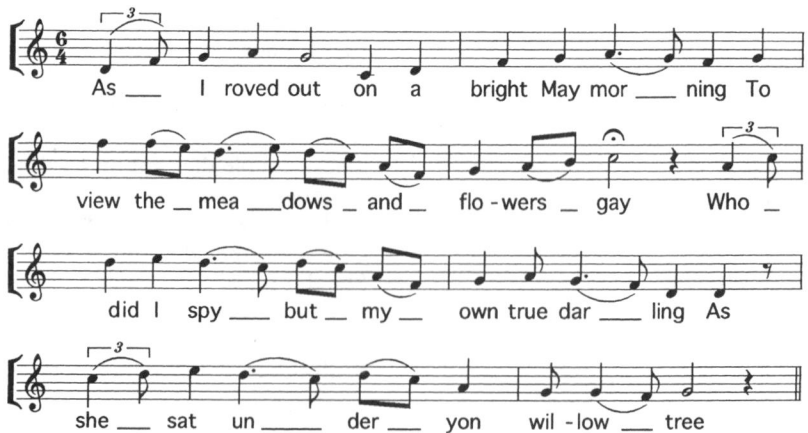

As __ I roved out   on   a   bright May mor __ ning   To
view the _ mea __ dows _ and _ flo -wers _ gay   Who _
did I   spy __ but _ my _   own true dar __ ling   As
she _ sat   un __ der _ yon   wil - low _ tree

'At night when I go to my silent slumber
The thoughts of my true love run through my
    mind;
When I turn around to embrace my darling,
Instead of gold, sure 'tis brass I find.

'I wish the Queen would call home her armies
From England, Scotland, America and Spain,
And every man to his wedded woman,
In hopes that you and I may meet again.'

SÍLE NÍ GHALLCHOBHAIR

(c. 1860–1956)

from:
BRITISH BROADCASTING
CORPORATION RECORDING
(1953)

[Most songs of women's unhappy marriage are complaints of a young woman married to an older man: frequently in a 'match' arranged by her parents. Here the woman wishes her husband dead and anticipates his wake with delight, for she will be free to associate with younger men. Some versions of 'An Seanduine' or 'An Seanduine Dóite' are explicit about the husband's sexual inadequacy. In a version recorded from Jane Nic Ruairí, Glenlark, County Tyrone, by Radio Éireann in 1951, the woman accuses the man of marrying her for money: 'Pósadh eisean mar gheall ar an tsaibhreas' (He got married because of wealth); then mocks him as he comes home at night lighting his pipe: 'Dhá chois aige mar bheadh maide sníofa ann, / Troid agus raic is gan faic ina bhríste' (His two legs like two woven sticks, / Fighting and uproar and nothing in his trousers.) Another version blames the priest for the marriage: 'Comhairle is ea fuaireas amuigh ar an mbóthar, / Ó rógaire sagairt an seanduine a phósadh; / Ba chuma leis é ach go méadóinn a phócaí, / Is mé bheith fada ag brath ar na comharsain' (The advice I got out on the road, / From a rogue of a priest, was to marry the old man. / He didn't care so long as I added to his pockets, / And I could spend the rest of my life depending on the neighbours).[1] This song is followed by a short narrative in English. From BBC 8/1953[2] (IFC/DISC 2253). R.Ó.]

1. Donal O'Sullivan, *Songs of the Irish* (Cork: Mercier Press [1960], 1981).
2. BBC Radio Sound Archive, London.

An Seanduine Dóite

Chuir mé mo sheanduine isteach insa chónra
Ag ól bainne ramhair is ag ithe aráin eorna,
Dá gcuirfeadh sé a cheann amach, bhainfinn an
    tsrón de
Agus d'fhuígfinn an chuid eile ag na cailíní óga.

Curfá 1:
Is óró 'sheanduine, 'sheanduine dhóite
Is óró 'sheanduine, is mairg a phós thú.
Is óró 'sheanduine, 'sheanduine dhóite,
Cúradh agus mealladh ort, is mairg a phós thú.

Dá bhfaighinnse mo sheanduine báite i bpoll
    mhóna,
A mhuineál a bheith briste is a chos a bheith
    leointe,
Théinn abhaile is thabharfainn aire dá
    thórramh,
Shiúlfainn amach leis na buachaillí óga.

Curfá 2:
Is óró 'sheanduine, 'sheanduine dhóite,
Is óró 'sheanduine, is mairg a phós thú,
Is óró 'sheanduine, 'sheanduine dhóite
Dá mbeinn ag an doras nár bheire mé beo ort.

Chuir mé mo sheanduine go Sráidbhaile an
    Róba,
Bhí coc ina hata is bhí búclaí ina bhróga,
Bhí triúr á mhealladh is ceathrar á chóiriú,
Is chuala mé i nGaillimh nach rachadh sé leofa.

Curfá 2

Chuir mé mo sheanduine siar go Díoraic(?)
An áit a raibh corradh agus dhá chéad cliabh
    air,
Chrap a chuid 'leggings' agus thit a chuid fiacla,
Agus tháinig sé chun an bhaile ina bhromaistín
    bliana.

Curfá 1

Chuir mé mo sheanduine go Tír na hÓige,
D'imigh mé liom ag dul mo phósadh,
Ag filleadh chun an bhaile dom ard tráthnóna,
Cé bhí romham ach an seanduine dóite.

Curfá 1

This old man, this old man, she married the old
man, she didn't like him. And she was, she was
thinking she would get him drowneded. That she
would take him home. And make his wake, and
walk out with the young fellows. Well, she came.
She put him in to the big chest and if he put out
his nose, she would take the nose off him and she
would walk out with the young fellow. True. She
wanted to put him away, where she would never
see him, that he would come home, without his
teeth nor nothing, she would be glad to get rid of
him. Well the first, she put him away to
someplace, and there were a lot of young girls
wanting to go with him, and she heard in
Gaillimh,³ I don't know if that's in Connacht,
that he wouldn't go with them. Next thing, she
put him away, to Tír na hÓige,⁴ that's where the
people used to go long ago, I don't know, and
when she come home, she went away to get
married I think, and when she come home, who
was on the corner but the *seanduine dóite*. He
seems to be a very old, old man: he was too old
for her. She didn't like him. [Laughs] Some old
funny things on the go. She didn't like him. She
would rather get a young fellow you see. It was a
young fellow she was wanting like some of the
old fools. [Laughs] I don't know now.

The Withered Old Man

I put my old man into the chest
Drinking thick milk and eating barley bread,
If he stuck his head out, I would take off his nose
And I'd leave the rest to the young girls.

Chorus 1:
And oh, old man, withered old man,
And oh, old man, woe to whoever married you,
And oh, old man, withered old man,
A scourge and disappointment to you, woe to
*   whoever married you.*

If I found my old man drowned in a bog hole,
His neck broken and his leg wounded,
I would go home and tend to his wake;
I would walk out with the young boys.

Chorus 2:
And oh, old man, withered old man,
And oh, old man, woe to whoever married you,
And oh, old man, withered old man,
If I were at the door, may I not catch you alive.

I sent my old man to the village of Ballinrobe,
He had a cock in his hat and buckles in his
    shoes,
There were three enticing him and four looking
    after him,
And I heard in Galway that he would not go
    with them.

Chorus 2

I sent my old man back to Díoraic¹
Where he was carrying more than two hundred
    creels.
His leggings shrank and his teeth fell out
And he came home a year old colt.

Chorus 1

I sent my old man to the Land of Youth,
I went off to get married,
As I came home in mid-afternoon,
Who was before me but the withered old man.

Chorus 1

---

3. Galway.
4. Also called Tír na nÓg: the land of eternal youth.

1. Obscure: probably a place-name.

LABHRÁS Ó CADHLA

(1889–1961)

from:
IRISH FOLKLORE COLLECTION RECORDING (1954) AND RADIO TELEFÍS ÉIREANN RECORDING (n.d.)

[A number of songs take the form of a conversation between a daughter and her mother: the mother gives advice or the daughter complains about her parents' attitudes to her sexual behaviour or their choice of husband for her. Comparatively few songs in the Irish language mention social attitudes to sex, but this is one of a small number in which the girl complains that she has been too long a virgin and wants to have a man. This type originated in the medieval French tradition (cf. S. Ó Tuama, *An Grá in Amhráin na nDaoine*, p. 51). The final verse refers with evident familiarity to customs of matchmaking and dowries. The song begins with a spoken introduction. Recorded by Leo Corduff, IFC/DISC 1250B (1954). The final verse in parentheses is taken from a Radio Éireann[1] archive recording (copy in IFC/DISC 1445).   R.Ó.]

1. The Irish national radio station, set up in 1926. Now combined with national television stations in Radio Telefís Éireann (RTÉ).

A Mhamaí, Nach Tú an Cladhaire!

Bean agus a hiníon agus iad ag argóint. Theastaigh ón iníon buachaill óg a phósadh ach níor theastaigh ón tseanabhean cead a thabhairt di go fóill.

Is a mhamaí, nach tú an cladhaire,
Nár dh'insigh do mo dhaidí i dtráth,
Ó, go rabhas-sa breoite, tinn,
Agus mé millte le dairte grá?
Ó, go mbím san oíche ag taibhreamh,
Gur i mo mhaighdean le fada atháim.
Is mura bhfaighfear fear gan mhoill dom,
Is deimhneach go raghad i mo bhá.

Ó, a Nóra, bíse foighneach,
Ní bhfaighfidh tú aon fhear go fóill;
Tá an cíos ag glaoch gan mhoill orainn,
Is gan puinn againn le cuir ina chomhair;
Tá broid agus ceant gach ló orainn
Is ár ngabháltachas ró-bheag go deo;
Agus d'athair bocht drochshláinteach,
Is an máistir ró-dhian go deo.

IS A MHAMAÍ, NACH TÚ AN CLADHAIRE!

A mhamaí, bíse tuisceanach
Do dhuine bheadh i bpian mar atáim,
Tá plámás míle duine ionat,
Ach ní thuigeann tusa cé hé mo chás;
Dá gcuirfinn mo scéal i dtuiscint duit
Cárbh ionadh leat dá raghainn i mo bhás.
Mura bhfaighfear fear faoi Inid dom,
Bead curtha sul dá dtiocfaidh an Cháisc.

Ó fan go bhfaighfidh mé húda dhuit
Gúna agus parasól;
Handkerchief trí chúinne
A mbeidh súil ann den bhfaisean nua.
Cuir búclaí i do bhróga,
Teannfaidh siad do chosa i gcóir,
Agus gheobhaidh tú buachaill ceansa
Gan amhras a chailín óig.

(Nach maith a fuaireabhar fear do Shíle
A raibh caora aige agus ba go leor,
Ó, ní bhfaighfinnse an gamhainín buí uaibh,
Dá laghad é ná luach na mbróg.
Tá mo *habit-shirt* gan ní
Le trí mhí agam de dheasca *soap*,
Is mar a mheasaimse ní bhfaighfidh mé
Uaibh saibhreas ná fear go deo.)

Mammy, Aren't You The Rogue!

A woman and her daughter, arguing. The daughter wanted to marry a young lad but the old woman didn't want to allow her do so yet.

Oh, Mammy, aren't you the rogue
That you didn't tell my daddy then,
That I was sick and weary,
And destroyed by love's darts?
That my sleep is disturbed at night as I dream
That I am a long time a virgin,
And if you don't find a man for me soon,
I'll definitely go and drown myself.

Oh, Nora, be patient
You won't get any man yet;
We have to pay the rent very soon,
And we don't have anything to put towards it,
Every day we are pressed and we auction
    something,
And our holding is much too small;
And your poor father is in bad health
And the master is far too severe.

O, Mammy, try to understand,
A person suffering like me,
You can flatter a thousand people,
But you don't understand my position;
If I were to explain my story to you,
You wouldn't be surprised that I would die,
If you don't find a man for me before
    Shrovetide,[1]
I'll be buried before Easter comes.

Oh, wait until I get a hood for you,
A dress and a parasol,
A three-cornered handkerchief
With eyelet embroidery of the new fashion,
Put buckles on your shoes,
They will tie your feet up properly
And you will get a gentle boy,
Without doubt, young girl.

(How well you found a man for Síle
Who had sheep and a lot of cows!
I wouldn't even get the yellow heifer from you,[2]
Though it's worth less than a pair of shoes,[3]
My habit-shirt[4] hasn't been washed
For three months for lack of soap,
And I think I will never get
Wealth or a man from you.)

---

1. The period before Lent: the traditional time for celebrating marriages.
2. Wordplay: 'scéal an ghamhna bhuí' (the tale of the yellow heifer) is used to describe a rambling story that never ends or continues for a long time.
3. Wordplay: 'luach na mbróg' (the price of shoes): a metaphor for virginity. See also 'An Sceilpín Draighneach', pp. 1345–1348.
4. A long, loose-fitting shirt or shift.

PATRICK A BÚRC

(1924–96)

from:
IRISH FOLKLORE
COLLECTION RECORDING
(1986)

['Bean Pháidín' is a light, mocking song in a fast style. A chorus is a feature of many of these songs in 6/8, or jig, time, which are ideally suited to lilting. The verses are frequently comical. This woman wants her loved one's wife to die so that she can marry him. The ills she wishes on the other woman are clearly stated: broken bones, legs and neck.[1] From IFC/FMS RÓ 16C (1986). R.Ó.]

Bean Pháidín

Is gabhfaidh mé siar Tóin an Roisín
Is tiocfaidh mé aniar Barr an tSáilín,
Isteach tí Mhaitiais Uí Chathasaigh
Ar shúil is go bhfeicfinn bean Pháidín.

1. R. uí Ógáin, 'The Love-Songs of Conamara', pp. 111–23.

Curfá:
Nach trua ghéar nach mise, nach mise
Nach trua ghéar, nach mise bean Pháidín,
Nach trua ghéar nach mise, nach mise
Is an bhean atá aige a bheith caillte.

Is gabhfaidh mé aniar Tóin an Roisín
Is tiocfaidh mé aniar Barr an tSáilín,
Is breathnóidh mé isteach ar na fuinneoga
Ar shúil is go bhfeicfinn bean Pháidín.

Agus ghabhfainn go Gaillimh, go Gaillimh,
Agus ghabhfainn go Gaillimh le Páidín,
Is ghabhfainn go Gaillimh, go Gaillimh
Agus thiocfainn abhaile sa mbád leis.

Curfá

Is go mbrisfear do chosa, do chosa,
is go mbrisfear do chosa a bhean Pháidín,
Go mbrisfear do chosa, do chosa
Go mbrisfear do mhuineál is do chnámha.

Curfá

BEAN PHÁIDÍN

Páidín's Wife

And I'll go west to Tóin an Roisín,[1]
And come back by Barr an tSáilín,[2]
Into Maitias Ó Cathasaigh's house
Hoping to see Páidín's wife.

Chorus:
Isn't it a great pity, a great pity,
Isn't it a great pity I'm not Páidín's wife,
Isn't it a great pity, a great pity,
And that his wife is not dead?

1. Literally, 'the bottom of the little wood'; a place near Carna, County Galway.
2. Literally, 'the top of the headland'; a place near Carna.

And I'll go west to Tóin an Roisín,
And come back by Barr an tSáilín,
And I'll look in the windows
Hoping to see Páidín's wife.

And I'd go to Galway, to Galway,
And I'd go to Galway with Páidín,
And I'd go to Galway, to Galway,
And come home with him in the boat.

Chorus

And may your legs, your legs, be broken,
And may your legs be broken, Páidín's wife,
May your legs, your legs, be broken,
May your neck and your bones be broken!

Chorus

MARY SEALE

from:
IRISH FOLKLORE COLLECTION RECORDING (1973)

[This melodramatic murder ballad is a version of Laws P 37. Many murder ballads survive in the repertoire of traditional singers today, and although the seducers and slayers of rural maidens are sometimes squires and earls, most of the ballads are journalistic and reflect a more ordinary way of life. Recorded by Tom Munnelly, 13 June 1973: IFC/FMS TM 166/1. T.M.]

The Old Oak Tree

The night was dark, cold blew the blast
And thickly fell the rain,
As Bessie left her own dear home
And came not back again.
She left her widowed mother's side,
Not fearing rain or cold,
The girl was young and fair to see,
But love had made her bold.

The night being past, the day did dawn
And Bessie was not home,
Which made her weeping friends to think
Where Bessie dear could roam.
At length her mother started up
And cried in accents wild:
'I'll search the world o'er and o'er
To find my darling child.'

For three long weary weeks she spent
In searching up and down.
Her journey proved of no avail,
For Bessie was not found,
And for to reach her lonely home
The aged mother tried.
All broken down with grief and tears
She, broken-hearted, died.

But at the end of all the scenes
The owner of the ground,
Young James McCullough, came one day
To hunt with all his hounds.
Up hill, down dale they boldly rode
In a gallant company
Until at last they lost the fox
Beneath the old oak tree.

And here the hounds began to yell,
To sniff and tear the clay,
But all that horns and whip could do
Could not drive those dogs away.
The gentlemen all gathered round,
They called for pick and spade.
They dug the ground and there they found
The missing murdered maid.

The grave, to prove the horrid deed,
It was a shocking sight;
The worms were creeping from her eyes
That was once so blue and bright.
Her bosom once was sparkling fair,
Now black from wounds and blows
And from the corpse fresh blood did flow
And sprinkled through her clothes.

A knife revealed, stuck in her side,
And to his grief and shame
The gentlemen upon the haft,
Read James McCullough's name.
'Since I've done the deed,' McCullough cried,
'My soul is food for Hell.
Oh hide her cold corpse from my sight
And I the truth will tell.

'It is true I loved young Bessie long,
And by my cunning art
I gained her to my vicious views
And I broke her mother's heart.
When we would meet she used to say:
"Oh make me quick your bride."
But I laughed at all her griefs and tears,
I was hardened in my pride.'

'And thus she coaxed until at last,
And as it seemed to me,
The Devil whispered, "Take her life
And then you shall be free!"
The knife that did my dinner cut
I plunged into her side
And with great might I knocked her down,
I need not tell the rest.'

And here he stood and looked upon
Her corpse with a look of pain.
He drew a pistol from his side
And fired right through his brain.
He was buried where he fell,
No Christian's grave got he;
Or no priest was found to bless the ground
Beneath the old oak tree.

SORCHA NÍ GHUAIRIM

(1911–76)

from:
IRISH FOLKLORE
COLLECTION RECORDING
(1940)

[In 'An Sceilpín Draighneach', a man walking early in the morning is hit by a fairy dart; he can be cured only by the woman he loves. This is a *pastourelle*, a song type related to the *aisling*.[1] One oral account describes this song as a conversation between a man and a woman in which he tries to persuade her that he will give up drinking if she will marry him (IFC 1280: 357). In the notes which accompany the text given here, Sorcha Ní Ghuairim recalled that this song was sung so frequently while she was growing up that she could not but learn it. Seán Ó Súilleabháin recorded her singing it on disc (IFC/DISC 52A 1940), but for reasons of limited space, could only include the first two verses. The remaining verses, in parentheses, come from the manuscript transcription.[2]   R.Ó.]

1. In the *aisling* the poet meets with a beautiful woman, who is sometimes Ireland personified, and a discussion ensues. Cf. 'Dreams of Love and Freedom', Volume I, pp. 292–7. For the importance of the *pastourelle* form in Irish, see S. Ó Tuama, *An Grá in Amhráin na nDaoine*, pp. 14–29.

2. See also R. uí Ógáin, 'The Love-Songs of Conamara', pp. 111–23.

An Sceilpín Draighneach

Ar maidin chiúin dár éiríos amach faoi bharra
  coillte
Is ea go cinnte caitheadh an saighead liom is
  mo leigheas nach raibh le fáil,
Nó gur dhearc mé an bhruinneall mhoiglí faoi
  bhruach an sceilpín draighnigh
Is gur gheit mo chroí le meidhre ach níor éirigh
  liom í a fháil.

Muise, a stóirín, tuige nach scríobhann tú litir
  in aghaidh na míosa,
Go cén caladh cuain le mbíonn tú faoi
  dhraíocht nó bhfuil tú beo?
Bím amach faoi bharra coillte is tá mil ar feadh
  do radhairc ann,
Bím i ngleanntáin dhorcha, choigríocha, is nach
  tú an cladhaire nach dtéann ann?

[Is nach trua gan mé in mo smóilín; is deas a
  leanfainn thríd an ród thú,
Mar gur thusa bláth na hóige is go dtóigfeá suas
  mo chroí,
Is bheinnse ag seinm cheoil duit ó mhaidin go
  tráthnóna
Is níor bhaol duit choíche aon dólás, aon bhrón
  ná briseadh croí.]

[Is a stóirín, tabhair do láimh dom, i ngan fhios
  do do mháithrín,
Is aithris do do ghrá bán ins gach áit dá mbíonn
  tú tinn.
Do chúilín soilseach is do bhéilín tanaí, tláth,
  deas,
Is más fíor go bhfuil tú i ngrá liom, cuir do
  láimhín tharam siar.]

[Is a stóirín ó, ná tréig mé mar gheall ar bha ná
  ar chaoirigh,
Is a ghaireacht is a bheidís ag éaló uainn in
  imeacht bliain nó dhó.
Dá mba liomsa dúiche an Phaoraigh ba tú mo
  rún, dá bhféadfainn,
Is gur in aois mo dhá bhliain déag dom a chuir
  mé eolas ort ar dtús.]

[Tá mo ghrása ar chúl an ghairdín is í an chú, is
  í an luath, is í an láir í,
Is is í is gile bráide dá bhfaca aon fhear ariamh,
Is é mo thrua nach bhfaighfinn aríst í, is é mo
  léan ní bhfaighfead ná choíchin,
Is nach geall le spile ar spíon mé, is nach cloíte
  an galra é an grá?]

[Is nach minic a d'ól mé píosa coróin, scilling is
  sé pínne,
Is tá tart ó shiúl na dtíortha orm, is nach
  cladhartha, bocht mo scéal?
Nuair a bhíonns mo phócaí líonta, bíonn fáilte
  romham is míle.
Is nuair a bhíonns mo sparán spíonta,
  dheamhan a bhfaighfinnse lán mo bhéil.]

[Ach feasta beidh mé críonna is ní ólfaidh mé
  dhá phínn rua,
Ach beidh mé ag déanamh tíobhais is nach
  bhfuil sé óg go leor!
Beidh mná na leanna ag caoineadh is nár fhóire
  orthu Íosa,
Is iad a d'fhág mo sparán spíonta is gan pínn as
  luach na mbróg.[3]]

[Is má théann tú chun an aonaigh, bíodh an
  chaora agat is an t-uan,
Is má théann tú ag déanamh tíobhais, bíodh do
  mhian agat ar láimh,
Ná santaigh an chaoirín fhómhair is ná pós an
  cailín Domhnaigh,
Is í mo ghrása an bhean ar fónamh nár cailleadh
  leis an mbród.]

[Ó, is éireoidh mise amárach is rachaidh mé
  thar sáile,
Le dhul san arm Ghallda, is ann a chaith mé tús
  mo shaoil,
Is ní thiocfaidh mé go hÉirinn go labhraí an
  chuach ins gach réigiún
Is go mbeidh caisleáin Chlanna Míle dhá
  ndéanamh as an nua.]

3. Cf. p. 1342 n3.

AN SCEILPÍN DRAIGHNEACH

Ar mai—din chiúin dá—r éi—rí—os a—mach faoi bharr—a coill———te, 'Sea go cinn———te caith————eadh an saigh-ead liom is mo leigheas nach raibh le fáil, nó gur dhearc mé mo bhruinn———eall mhoig——lí- faoi bhruach an sceil——pín draigh————nigh, is gur gheit mo chroí le meidh———re ach níor éir————igh liom í a fháil.

The Thorny Little Rock

One quiet morning I went out to the woods
A dart was thrown at me certainly, and I could not be cured,
When I saw the gentle girl at the edge of the thorny little rock,
And my heart jumped for joy, but I could not get her.

My darling, why don't you write a letter to me every month,
To tell me in what harbour you are bewitched, or whether you are alive?

I go to the woods where there is honey everywhere,
I go to the dark, strange valleys and aren't you the rogue that won't go there?

[Isn't it a pity I'm not a thrush, for I'd follow you on the road,
Because you are the flower of youth and you would lift my heart,
And I would play music for you from morning until evening,
And you would never be in danger of sorrow, sadness or heartbreak.]

[My darling, give me your hand, without your
  mother's knowledge,
And tell your fair love wherever you are ill,
Your shining hair and your fine, tender little
  mouth,
And if it's true that you're in love with me, put
  your dear arm around me.]

[My darling, oh, do not leave me for the sake of
  cows or sheep!¹
How easily they would pass away from us within
  a year or two,
If I owned de Paor's land, you would be my
  darling if I could manage it,
And I was twelve years old when I first knew
  you.]

[My beloved is at the back of the garden; she is
  the hound, swiftness, and the mare,
She has the fairest form that any man ever saw,
It is my pity that I could not have her again, my
  sorrow that I will not now, nor ever,
Am I not like a burnt-out spill,² and isn't love
  an enervating disease?]

[Didn't I often drink a crown, a shilling and a
  sixpence,
I'm thirsty from walking constantly, and is my
  story not poor and cowardly?
When my pockets are full, I'm given a thousand
  welcomes,
And when my purse is drained, I wouldn't get a
  mouthful.]

[But from now on I will be wise; I won't drink
  two coppers' worth,
But I will set up house, and he is young enough:
The women in the ale houses will be weeping,
  and may Jesus not assist them,
It was they left my purse drained and without a
  penny for the price of our shoes.]

[If you go to the fair, have the sheep and the
  lamb with you,
If you are setting up house, have your beloved
  with you,

Do not covet the little autumn sheep, and do
  not marry the showy girl,
My love is the good woman who did not die of
  pride.]

[I will get up tomorrow and will go across the
  sea,
To join the English army, where I spent my
  early life,
And I will not come to Ireland until the cuckoo
  sings in every part,
And until the Milesians' castles³ are being built
  anew.]

---

3. Milesians: descendants of Milesius, a fictitious Spanish king whose
  sons are said to have conquered Ireland *c.* 1300 BC.

from:
SORCHA NÍ GHUAIRIM
SINGS TRADITIONAL SONGS
(1957)

[Sorcha Ní Ghuairim learned 'Maile Ní Maoileoin' from
her father, who used to tell the story as related in the song
before singing it. The verses in parentheses were transcribed
from Ní Ghuairim, but not included on the record. The
scene of outdoor seduction is familiar from *pastourelle*-type
songs such as 'An Sceilpín Draighneach' (pp. 1345–1348).
The narrative is clear and heartbreaking, most of it in the
form of dramatic dialogue: Maile (Molly) pleads for her
life, but her lover proceeds to rape and then murder her;
later she returns to haunt him. Descriptive murder songs
are very rare in Irish, although relatively common in
English (see 'The Old Oak Tree', pp. 1344–1345), while
such an explicit account of rape is unusual. From *Sorcha
Ní Ghuairim Sings Traditional Irish Songs* (New York:
Folkways Records, FW 861, 1957). R.Ó.]

Maile Ní Maoileoin

'An dtiocfá baint an aitinn liom, a Mhaile Ní
  Maoileoin?'
'Muise, thiocfainn is dhá cheangal leat, a chuid
  den tsaol is a ruain,
Agus rachainnse chun an Aifrinn leat agus ní le
  grá do m'anam é,
Ach mar shúil is go mbeinn ag breathnú ar do
  bhaibín catach romham.'

---

1. Probably a reference to items for a dowry, or marriage settlement.
2. A spill is a thin piece of wood used for lighting a fire.

('Is an dtiocfá don choill chraobhaigh liom, a
Mhaile Ní Maoileoin?'
'Muise, thiocfainn faoin gcoill chraobhaigh leat,
nó céard a bheadh muid a dhéanamh ann?'
'Ag baint úll i mbarra géagán, is ag manaois
lena chéile,
Is ag damhsa ar hallaí gléigeala nó go n-éiríodh
an lá bán.')

'An dtiocfá ar chúl an teampaill liom, a Mhaile
Ní Maoileoin?'
'Muise, thiocfainn ar chúl an teampaill leat, nó
céard a bheadh muid a dhéanamh ann?'
'Ag éisteacht leis an dántaireacht ag ministéaraí
Gallda
Nó go socraíodh muid an cleamhnas úd le
Maile Ní Maoileoin.'

Thug mé liom ar chúl an teampaill í, mo chúig
mhíle grá,
Agus d'éist sí le mo dhradaireacht, mo chuid
den tsaol is mo stór,
Ó d'ísligh mise síos uirthi, agus tharraing mé
amach scian ghlas,
Nuair a lig mé fuil a croí léi, go dtí lascaí a cuid
bróg.

['Muise, a chomrádaí na dílse, ó, go céard seo
atá tú a dhéanamh?
Lig m'anam liom, is ná déan sin, is ní fheicfidh
tú aríst choíche mé.
Lig m'anam liom an oíche seo, is ní fheicfidh tú
arís choíche mé
Is go siúlfainn na seacht ríochta le do leanbáinín
ó.']

[Thug mé liom isteach sa ngairdín í, mo chuid
den tsaol is mo stór,
Is rug mé i ngreim barr láimhe uirthi is bhain
mé di dhá phóg,
Níor lig mé as an áit sin í gur bhain mé di mo
shásamh,
Is ansin is ea rinneas feall ar phlúr na mban óg.]

Tháinig Maile bhán ar cuairt chugam trí huaire
roimh an lá,
Agus leag sí a béal anuas orm, is nárbh fhuaire é
ná an bás,
'An i do chodladh atá tú, a bhuachaill, mar is
mithid duitse gluaiseacht,
Tá an tóir seo ag teacht anuas ort faoi bhás
Mhaile Ní Maoileoin.

[Is cén chaoi a bhfuil do mháithrín, a ógánaigh
óig?'
'Muise, tá sí buartha, cráite mar bheas sí lena
ló,
Ach ní hé sin féin is cás léi ach a buachaillín
deas, mánla,
Atá ag dul sa gcré amárach faoi bhás Mhaile Ní
Maoileoin.]

['Muise, sínigí go domhain sa bhfuaigh mé is
braillín gheal ar m'uachtar.
Is nár mhaith í an aithrí an uair sin, té
dhéanfadh í in am.]

Maile Ní Maoileoin

'Would you come cutting furze with me, Maile
Ní Maoileoin?'
'Indeed I would come and tie it with you, love
of my life and my dear,
And I would come to Mass with you and not
for the sake of my soul,
But hoping to look at your curly hair before me.'

['Would you come to the branchy wood with
me, Maile Ní Maoileoin?'
'Indeed, I would come to the branchy wood
with you, and what would we do there?'
'Pick apples from the tops of the branches and
dally with each other,
And dance in bright halls until the break of day.']

'Would you come behind the church with me,
Maile Ní Maoileoin?'
'Indeed, I would come behind the church, and
what would we do there?'
'Listen to the singing of Protestant ministers
Until we arrange that match[1] for Maile Ní
Maoileoin.'

I brought her behind the church, my five
thousand loves,
And she listened to my chatting, my life's love
and my dear,
I lowered myself down upon her, and I pulled
out a grey knife,
So I let her heart's blood drip down to the ties
of her shoes.

1. A 'match' was an arranged marriage.

['Indeed, my dear friend, what are you doing?
Let me live and don't do that, and you will
    never see me again.
Leave me my life tonight and you will never see
    me again,
And I would walk the world over with your little
    child.']

[I took her into the garden, the love of my life
    and my dear,
And I took hold of the top of her hand and I
    took two kisses from her,
I did not let her leave that place until I took my
    fill from her,
And it was then I did the treacherous deed to
    the flower of young women.]

Fair Maile came to visit me three hours before
    the dawn,
And she put her mouth down on me and it was
    colder than death,
'Are you asleep my lad? It is time for you to
    move on,
You are being hunted for the death of Maile Ní
    Maoileoin.

[And how is your mother, young fellow?'
'Indeed she is worried and tormented, and will
    be as long as she lives,
But that is not what bothers her, but her nice,
    gentle son
Who'll be buried tomorrow for the death of
    Maile Ní Maoileoin.']

[Indeed, lay me deep in the grave, with a bright
    sheet over me,
And is repentance not a good thing for the one
    who repents in time.]

[Sorcha Ní Ghuairim had a number of songs of this kind —
fast, light songs for amusing children. The chorus consists of
lilted nonsense syllables. She called this a song for 'dancing
and matchmaking'. She only ever heard it from her mother,
who sang it to amuse Sorcha's sister's children. She said she
would not have heard it, 'marach gur bhain sé don ócáid'
(except that it belonged to the occasion).]

Digeas, ó, Deabhas, ó

Curfá:
Digeas, ó, deabhas, ó, deabha, digeas, ó, deabhas,
*   ó deam,*
Digeas, ó, deabhas, ó, deabhas, ó, deabhas, ó, digeas,
*   ó, deabhas, ó deam.*

Goirim i gcónaí, gcónaí,
Goirim i gcónaí an bhean,
Goirim i gcónaí, i gcónaí, i gcónaí,
Is m'anam Dé Luain an fear.

Curfá

Buachaill aniar, aniar,
Buachaill aniar an fear,
Buachaill aniar, aniar, aniar,
Is cailín ó shliabh a bhean.

Curfá

Buachaill maith súiste, súiste,
Buachaill maith súiste an fear,
Buachaill maith súiste, súiste, súiste,
Is cailín deas túirne í an bhean.

Curfá

Diggis oh Dows

Chorus:
Diggis oh dows, oh dow, diggis oh dows oh dum,
Diggis oh dows, oh dows, oh dows oh, diggis oh dows
*   oh dum.*

I always, always love,
I always love the woman,
I always, always, always, love,
And on Monday I love the man.

Chorus

The man is a boy from the west,
A boy from the west, from the west,
A boy from the west, from the west, from the
    west,
And the woman is a mountain girl.

Chorus

The man is a boy who is good with the flail,
A boy who is good with the flail, with the flail,
A boy who is good with the flail, with the flail,
    with the flail,
And the woman is a girl who is handy with a
    spinning wheel.

MARY ANN CUNNINGHAM

(*fl.* 1955)

from:
CEOL: A JOURNAL OF IRISH MUSIC (1963)

['The Factory Girl', with its mutation of shepherdess to young factory worker, shows how the *pastourelle* (cf. 'An Sceilpín Draighneach', above) evolved to suit prevailing circumstances. Notated by Hugh Shields from the singing of Mary Ann Cunningham in Annalong, County Down, and published by him in *Ceol: A Journal of Irish Music*.[1] As Shields suggests: 'It is doubtless to [our] Gaelic legacy that we owe the existence of rather more songs of the *pastourelle* type in Anglo-Irish tradition than may be found in the English of Britain.'[2] Another splendid recording of this song, by Sarah Makem from Keady, County Armagh, can be heard on *Mrs Sarah Makem: Ulster Ballad Singer* (London: Topic Records, 12T 182, 1968).   T.M.]

The Factory Girl

As I went out walking one fine summer's morning
The birds in the bushes did warble and sing;
I spied lads and lasses, and couples were sporting
Going down to yon factory their work to begin.

I spied one among them more fairer than any,
The rose in her cheek that few could excel;
And her skin like the lily that grew in yon valley;
And she was a hard-working factory girl.

I kindly stepped to her all seeming to view her:
On me she cast a look of disdain,
Saying, 'Young man, have manners and do not
    come near me,
The more you're a poor girl I think it no shame.'[3]

'It's not for to scorn you, fair maid, I adore you,
Would you grant me one favour, love, where do
    you dwell?'
'Oh young man, excuse me, for now I must
    leave you,
For yonder's the sound of my factory bell.'

'Well I have fine houses adorned with ivy,
Gold in my pockets and silver as well,
And if you'll come with me, a lady I'll make you,
And no more will you need yon poor factory
    bell.'

'Love and temptation are our ruination,
Go find a lady, and may you do well,
For I am an orphan, neither friend or relation,
And forbye, I'm a hard-working factory girl.'

With these words she vanished and then she did
    leave me,
All for her sake, I'll go wander away,
And in some deep valley where no one will
    know me
I will mourn for the sake of my factory girl.

1. Hugh Shields, 'A Latter-Day Pastorelle', *Ceol: A Journal of Irish Music*, vol. 1, no. 3 (1963), pp. 5–10.
2. Ibid., p. 5.
3. Usually, 'Although I'm a poor girl, I think it no shame.'

SARAH MAKEM

(1900–85)

from:
MRS SARAH MAKEM: ULSTER BALLAD SINGER (1968)

[Logic has little place in traditional love-song. The enormously popular ballad of 'Barbara Allen', catalogued by

Child as No. 84, ends with both lovers dead. The final verse contains the widespread ballad motif of two graves from which rose and briar grow entwined. From *Mrs Sarah Makem: Ulster Ballad Singer* (London: Topic Records, 12T 182, 1968). For a version of this ballad by County Clare singer Tom Lenihan (1905–90), with the singer's comments, see Tom Lenihan, *The Mount Callan Garland: Songs from the Repertoire of Tom Lenihan*, collected and edited by Tom Munnelly, with music transcriptions by Marian Deasy (Dublin: Comhairle Bhéaloideas Éireann, 1994), pp. 29–31. Cf. Eleanor Long, '"Young Man, I Think You're Dyin'"': The *Twining Branches* Theme in the Tristan Legend and in English Tradition', *Fabula: Journal of Folktale Studies*, vol. 21, nos 3–4 (1980), pp. 184–99.   T.M.]

Barbara Allen

Michaelmas Day bein' in the year
When the green leaves they were fallin',
When young Jemmy Grove from the North
     Countrie
Fell in love with Barbara Allen.

He sent his servants out one day
To see if she was comin';
'One word from you will bring me to,
If you be Barbara Allen.'

'Get up, get up,' her mama said.
'Get up and go and see him.'
'Oh Mama dear, do you not mind[1] the time
That you told me how to slight him?'

'Get up, get up,' her father said,
'Get up and go and see him.'
'Oh Dada dear, do you not mind the time
That you told me how to shun him?'

Slowly, slowly, she got up
And slowly she put on her,
And slowly went to his bedside
And slowly looked upon him.

'You're lyin' low, young man,' she said,
'And almost near a-dyin'.'
'One word from you will bring me to,
If you be Barbara Allen.'

'One word from me you never will get,
Nor any young man breathin',
For the better of me you never will be
If your heart's blood was a spillin'.'

'Look at my bed-foot,' he said,
'And there you'll find them lyin';
Bloody sheets and bloody shirts
I sweat for Barbara Allen.

'Look at my bed-head,' he said,
And there you'll find it tickin',
My gold watch and my gold chain
I bestow to Barbara Allen.'

As she went over her father's green
She heard the dead-bell ringin',
An' every chop the dead-bell gave
It was 'Woe to Barbara Allen.'

As she went over her father's hall
She saw the corpse a-comin'.
'Lay down, lay down those[2] weary corpse
Till I get lookin' on them.'

They lifted the lid up off the corpse,
She bursted out with laughin'
An' all his wearied friends around
Cried, 'Hard-hearted Barbara Allen!'

As she went into her father's house;
'Make my bed long and narrow,
For the dead-bell did ring for my true-love today,
It will ring for me tomorrow.'

Out of one grave there grew a red rose,
And out of the other a briar.
For they both twisted into a true-lover's knot,
And there remained forever.

1. recall.

2. that.

MARY DOLAN

(b. 1889)

from:
IRISH FOLKLORE
COLLECTION RECORDING
(1971)

[County Cavan seems to be the only region in Ireland in which 'Jimmy Whelan' has been collected. Found mainly in Canada, the influence of Irish and oral tradition is manifest.[1] Whelan returns after his death by drowning to visit his grieving lover. Along with other French song forms, Irish tradition has absorbed the *aube*, or *alba*, songs of the night-visit which must end with dawn. In literary versions such as 'The Spinning Wheel' or 'The Whistling Thief' the visiting lover has to contend with watchful, even if blind and sleepy, grandparents. In 'The Bonny Wee Window' (Laws O 18) and 'Barney's Courtship' (Laws O 21) the form descends into gauche Paddywhackery, with the clod-hopping Barney Brallaghan courting his coy Kate through the bedroom window. 'When a Man's in Love' (Laws O 20) and 'Who Comes Tapping at My Window?' (Laws M 4) are more serious ballads, also found in current oral tradition, which use the same format. While the visiting lover in these songs is clearly terrestrial, in songs like 'Willie-O', 'Fly Up My Cock', or

'Here's a Health to All True Lovers', the visiting lover may be a revenant from beyond the grave.[2]

Female revenants include the deserted pregnant girl who has committed suicide in 'It's of a Sailor of Whom I Write' (Laws P 34A). Her ghost returns to drag her lover to hell from his becalmed ship. Molly Bán Lowery (Laws O 36) comes back to prove that her lover mistook her for a swan and shot her by accident. 'Maile Ní Maoileoin' (p. 1350) has another female revenant. Among the male visitors from the dead is Sweet William's Ghost (Child No. 77), who comes to return his plighted troth in a ballad rare in Irish tradition. Even rarer is 'The Unquiet Grave' (Child No. 78). In this exquisite ballad, the sole Irish version of which was noted in Waterford in the 1940s, the dead lover is disturbed by his sweetheart's grief. IFC Main Mss, vol. 696, pp. 292–3. Cf. 'The Holland Handkerchief', p. 1334. Recorded by T. Munnelly, 10 November 1971: IFC/FMS TM T 19/A/10 (1971). A version of Laws C 8.   T.M.]

Jimmy Whelan

One evening of late as I went walking,
Watching the sunbeams as evening drew near,
It's onwards I rambled, I spied a fair maiden
Who was weeping and wailing with many a sigh,

---

1. See Phillips Barry, *Bulletin of the Folk-Song Society of the Northeast*, no. 11 (Cambridge: Mass., 1936), pp. 4–7, and G. Malcolm Laws Jr, *Native American Balladry*, p. 151. See also Edith Fowke, *The Penguin Book of Canadian Folksongs* (Harmondsworth, Middlesex: Penguin, 1973), p. 71.

2. For an overview of revenant ballads in Ireland, see Hugh Shields, 'The Dead Lover's Return in Modern English Ballad Tradition', *Jahrbuch für Volksliedforschung*, vol. 17 (1972), pp. 62–71, and his '*The Grey Cock*: Dawn Song or Revenant Ballad?', in *Ballad Studies*, ed., E[mily] B. Lyle (Cambridge: Cambridge University Press, 1976), pp. 67–92.

JIMMY WHELAN

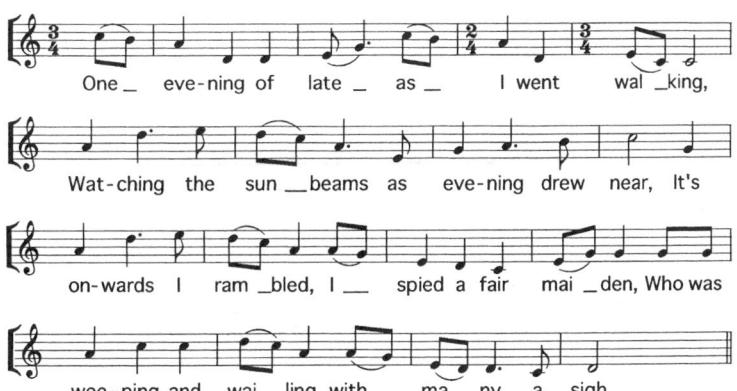

One _ eve-ning of late _ as _ I went wal _king,
Wat-ching the sun _beams as eve-ning drew near, It's
on-wards I ram _bled, I _ spied a fair mai _den, Who was
wee-ping and wai _ling with _ ma-ny a sigh.

For one that is gone and now lying lonely,
Lonely for one that no mortal can tell.
The deep rolling waters roll swiftly around him
And the grass it grows green o'er Jimmy's grave.

'Jimmy,' she said, 'don't go and leave me,
Don't go and leave me to mourn here alone.
Take me, oh take me along with you, darlin'
Down to your grave and your cold silent tomb.'

'Darling,' he said, 'you are asking a favour
That no mortal person could grant unto thee,
For death was the dagger that tore us asunder
And wide is the grave, love, between you and
    me.

'But as oft times as you do wander by the banks
    of the river
My spirit will meet you to guard and to keep
My spirit will hover and ever fly over
To protect you, my darling, from a cold silent
    tomb.'

'Jimmy,' she said, 'don't go and leave me,
Don't go and leave me to mourn here alone.
Take me, oh take me along with you, darlin'
Down to your grave and your cold silent tomb.'

ELIZABETH (BESS) CRONIN

(1879–1956)

from:
BRITISH BROADCASTING
CORPORATION RECORDING
(1947)

[This dandling song is one which Bess Cronin sang to her own children. The last verse consists of lilted nonsense syllables. Macaronic songs, which in Ireland combine the Irish and English languages, are found in all Irish-speaking districts but are particularly strong in Munster. From BBC 1947 (IFC/FMS 710A). Some verses of this song are included on *The Columbia World Library of Folk and Primitive Music*, vol. 1, recorded and edited by S. Ennis and A. Lomax (USA, SL-204, 1955 [AKL 4941]). Another version collected from the same singer appears as No. 41 in the comprehensive collection of her songs (some 200 in all), assembled and edited by her grandson, and recently published as a large-format paperback book with two CD records: Dáibhí Ó Cróinín (ed.), *The Songs of Elizabeth Cronin, Irish Traditional Singer* (Dublin: Four Courts Press, 2000), pp. 91–2. R.Ó.]

Cuc-A-Neaindí

Hups, a Sheáin, a bhráthair, fuair do mháthair
    bás
Ó, ní bhfuair, ní bhfuair do chuaigh sí suas an
    tsráid.

Hups, a Sheáin, a bhráthair, fuair do mháthair
    bás
Ó, ní bhfuair in aon chor, chuaigh sí suas an
    tsráid.

Cuc-a-neaindí-neaindí, cuc-a-neaindí-ó
Cuc-a-neaindí-neaindí, cuc-a-neaindí-ó
Cuc-a-neaindí-neaindí, cuc-a-neaindí-ó
Poirtín Sheáin an tsíoda is iníon Philib an
    cheoil.

He didn't dance, dance, and he didn't dance today,
He didn't dance, dance, no, nor yesterday
He didn't dance, dance, no, nor yesterday.

Throw him up, up, throw him up high,
Throw him up, up, and he'll come down by and by.
Throw him up, up, and he'll come down by and by.

Throw him over, over, throw him over sea.
Throw him over, over, he'll be here today.
Throw him over, over, throw him over sea.
Throw him over, over, he'll be here for tea.

Didil í aigh, dí aigh dí, didil í aigh dí am,
Didil í aigh dí, aigh dí, aigh dí aigh dí am,
Dó dil í dil í dil, dó dí aigh dí am,
Didil í aigh dil amh dil, damh dí aigh dí am.

CUC-A-NEAINDÍ

Hups, a Sheáin, a bhráth-air,   fuair do mháthair bás   Ó ní bhfuair, ní bhfuair do

chuaigh sí suas an tsráid.   Hups, a Sheáin, a bhráth-air,   fuair do mháthair bás

ó ní   bhfuair in aon chor,   chuaigh sí suas an tsráid.   Cuc-a-   nan-dy nan-dy, cuc-a-

nandy ó,   cuc-a-   nan-dy nan-dy,   cuc-a-nan-dy   ó,   Cuc-a-

nandy nan-dy, cuc-a-   nan-dy ó   Poir-tín Sheáin an tsíoda's

in-íon Phi-lib a'   cheoil ——

Cuc-A-Nandy

Hups, Seán, my brother, your mother died,
Oh, she didn't, she didn't, she went up the street,
Hups, Seán, my brother, your mother died,
Oh, she didn't at all, she went up the street.

Cuc-a-nandy-nandy, cuc-a-nandy-o
Cuc-a-nandy-nandy, cuc-a-nandy-o
Cuc-a-nandy-nandy, cuc-a-nandy-o
The little tune of Seán of the silk and the
    daughter of Pilib of the music.

He didn't dance, dance, and he didn't dance
    today,
He didn't dance, dance, no, nor yesterday
He didn't dance, dance, no, nor yesterday.

Throw him up, up, throw him up high,
Throw him up, up, and he'll come down by and
    by.
Throw him up, up, and he'll come down by and
    by.

Throw him over, over, throw him over sea.
Throw him over, over, he'll be here today.
Throw him over, over, throw him over sea.
Throw him over, over, he'll be here for tea.

Diddly eye-dee, eye-dee, diddly eye-dee am,
Diddly eye-dee, eye-dee, eye-dee, eye-dee, am
Doodle eedle eedle, doo dee eye-dee am,
Diddle-ee idle, owdle, dowdy eye-dee am.

CÁIT NÍ MHUIMHNEACHÁIN

(1918–49)

from:
IRISH FOLKLORE COLLECTION RECORDING (1941)

[Songs in praise and celebration of drink are quite common in the Irish tradition. This recording was made by Seán Ó Súilleabháin: IFC/DISC 77 1941. For the lines in parentheses, see *Béaloideas*, vol. 7 (1937), pp. 39–40. R.Ó.]

An Jug Mór is é Lán

Tá scéilín breá nua agam le hinsint,
Is is cóir é chraobhscaoileadh ins gach áit,
Go bhfuil biotáille gach lá dul i saoire,
Agus áthas i mo chroí orm dá bharr.
Dos na sárfhir do b'fhearr liom é insint,
Bíonn ag tálamh na dí ar ceann cláir,
Go bhfaighfí lán cáirt ar *thirteen* de,
Agus cairdeas trí mhí chun reicneáil.

Ó chuaigh sé i saoire chomh mór san,
Ní foláir liom suí suas ar ceann cláir,
Agus suíochán d'fháil ann chun fuaire,
Agus go lá geal Dé Luain bead dá fháil.

AN JUG MÓR IS É LÁN

Mo chairde bheith láimh liom fé thuairim,
Is níorbh fhearr liom bheith cur cruach ar sparán,
Níl gnó agam bheith ag trácht thar aon
    bhuaireamh,
Ach mo ghrása an *jug* mór is é lán.

Nách ró-bhreá an t-oideas dochtúra
Fuiscí breá cumhra is é saor,
Mar tógann sé an ceo agus an smúit leis,
Agus déanann sé súgach gach n-aon,
An tseanbhean bhíonn ag luí insan chúinne,
Le seacht mbliana ina súsa i bpéin,
[Nuair ólann sé [*sic*] cúpla piont de
Is ard is is lúfar a léim.]

[Is ná creidigí gur bladar mo ráite,
Chun go n-insead fios fátha in aghaidh an scéil;
Mar is mó fear leathan groí láidir
Atá curtha le trí ráithe insa chré.
An té nár ól riamh a scilling i dtigh an tábhairne,
Ach ag cnuasach an sparáin bhoicht go léir,
Is mairg ná baineann an chéad lá as
Is gan an t-airgead bheith spártha ina dhéidh.]

[A bhuachaillí óga na dúiche
Sin comhairle do thabharfainn díbh fós
Dul go tigh an leanna le fonn díbh
Is bheith ag mealladh na gcúileann deas óg.
Glaoigí ina chárt is ina phiont é
Is scaipigí bhur bpunt is bhur gcoróin.
Fágaigí an chailleach ag búirthí,
Nuair a chnuasóidh sí chugaibh a cuid óir.]

[Greadadh ar an gcnagaire gránna
Mar is ní é nár ghrádhas-sa fós riamh,
Ach mara dtugainn do ainnir ina láimh é,
Go leanfadh sí an tsráid soir i mo dhiaidh.
B'fhearr liom é thomhas ina chártaibh,
Is é riarú ar an gclár go breá fial.
Is mairg ná baineann an chéad lá as,
Is gan an t-airgead a bheith ina dhiaidh.]

The Big Jug when it is Full

I have a fine new story to tell,
And it should be passed around everywhere,
That liquor is getting cheaper each day,
And my heart is happy because of it.
I had better tell it to the best of men,
Who take the drink at the bar,

You could get a quart full for thirteen [pence]
And three months' credit to settle.

Since it became so cheap,
I must sit at the bar,
And get a seat there to become cool,
And I will get it until daylight on Monday.
My friends around me for that reason,
I need not tighten the purse,
I have no business talking about any worry,
But my love is the big jug when it is full.

Isn't it a very fine doctor's prescription!
Fine, fragrant, cheap whiskey,
Because it lifts cloud and gloom,
And makes everybody merry,
The old woman lying in the corner
In pain for seven years on a blanket,
[When she drinks a few pints of it
Her jump is an agile one.]

[And do not think that what I am saying is
    nonsense,
Until I tell you the reason for the story,
Because many a solid, fine, strong man,
Has been buried in the ground in the last three
    seasons.
The person who never drank a shilling in the
    drinking house,
But has been gathering it all into a purse,
It is sad that he will not spend one day there,
And not leave the money after him.]

[Young boys of the district,
This is the advice I would give you:
Go happily to the drinking house,
And entice nice young girls.
Order it in quarts and in pints,
And spend your pounds and your crowns,
Leave the hag roaring,
When she gathers her gold from you.]

[Bad luck to the horrible noggin
Because it is something that I have never loved,
And if I didn't give it to the beautiful girl in her
    hand,
She would follow me all down the street.
I would prefer to measure it in quarts,
And to share it generously around the counter,
Pity the person who can't enjoy it for a day,
Instead of leaving the money there after him.]

CÁIT NÍ AILÍOSA

(b. *c.* 1897)

from:
RADIO TELEFÍS ÉIREANN
RECORDING (pre-1976)

[Tomás Rua Ó Súilleabháin (1785–1848) was a contemporary and acquaintance of Daniel O'Connell, known as the Liberator; both came from Derrynane, County Kerry. Ó Súilleabháin composed this song in praise of O'Connell and in anticipation of the winning of Catholic emancipation, which was achieved in 1829.[1]

The broadcaster and music collector Ciarán Mac Mathúna was introduced to Cáit Ní Ailíosa, who lived just outside Waterville, County Kerry, by Fionán Mac Coluim (1875–1976), a folklore and folksong collector and an Irish-language enthusiast who collaborated with him on over fifty radio programmes. No recording date is given for this song, which comes from Radio Telefís Éireann Traditional Music Archives, Dublin: RTE MC 102 1987.

Fionán Mac Coluim told Mac Mathúna that it was customary to dance a few steps with the chorus. The sound of his dancing steps can be heard on the recording along with occasional words of encouragement for the singer, such as '*maith thú!*' (good on you!). Such interjected words and phrases are a feature of singing in Irish. A version of this song has been published on audio cassette with accompanying translation and notes in Tim Dennehy, *A Thimbleful of Song* (Dublin: Góilín, 002, 1989. Now on CD [Sceilig Records, Mullagh, Co. Clare, 1996]). See also Deirbhile Ní Bhrolcháin, *Smaointe* (Dublin: Gael-Linn, CEF CD 147, 1990). R.Ó.]

Is é Dónall Binn Ó Conaill Caoin

In Uíbh Ráthach thiar tá an dragún dian
Ár sciath ar iarthar Éirinn,
Go bhfágfar iad go brách faoi chiach,
An t-ál seo shéan an éide.
Is é Dónall binn Ó Conaill caoin
An prionsa fíor den Ghaeilge;
Is é do chuir an chúis ar bun
Is tabharfaidh sé an rud daor chugainn.

---

1. Ríonach uí Ógáin, *Immortal Dan: Daniel O'Connell in Irish Folk Tradition* (Dublin: Geography Publications, 1995), pp. 69–118, and Diarmuid Breathnach agus Máire Ní Mhurchú, *1782–1881: Beathaisnéis a Sé* (Baile Átha Cliath: An Clóchomhar, 1999), p. 137.

Curfá:
Is an daigh al de dal dal, right *fal de dal dal,*
Right *fal de dal dal déril dil ídil*
Right *fal de dal dal, dal dal dal dal,*
Right *fal aigh ral éri.*

Sa bhfómhar seo chugainn is ea dhófam poirt
Le glór na n-údar naofa,
Beidh Seoirse dubhach gan choróin, gan chlú
Gan sólás boird gan féasta.
Ólfam lionn is beoir le fonn
Is comhsheinfeam tiúin den Ghaeilge,
Beidh bróga dubha ar gach ógfhear clúil,
Cé gur fada dhúinn á n-éagmais.

Curfá:
An right *fal de daigh raigh,* right *fal daighdil*
Right *fal de daighdil dé ril dadil dí dil*
Right *fal de daigh ral daigh ral daigh ral*
Right *fal aigh ril éri.*

Beidh ministrí gan strus gan phoimp,
Is ní rithfid chugainn mar a théidís,
Ní bhainfear cíos de Chaitlicigh,
Mar cuirfear síos na méirligh.
Beidh Dónall choíche ar a dtí,
Go nglanfar cruinn as Éire iad,
Nuair a bheidh an dlí fúinn féin arís,
Ar theacht an *Emancipation.*

Curfá:
An right *fal de dé raigh,* right *fal dídil,*
Right *fal de dídil é dil adail dídil*
Right *fal de díril* right *fal dí dil*
Right *fal íril éri.*

Daniel O'Connell, Gentle and Kind

The mighty dragon is in Uíbh Ráthach,
Protection for us in the west of Ireland,
May they be left forever in oppression,
Those who denied the faith.
Daniel O'Connell who is gentle and kind
The true prince of the Irish language,
It was he who started the movement,
And he will bring the costly event to us.

Chorus:
And the die ol de dol dol, right fol de dol dol,
Right fol de dol dol die ril a dil eedil,
Right fal de dol dol, dol dol dol dol,
Right fol I rol airee.

Next autumn we will burn the harbours,[1]
According to the voice of the holy writers,[2]
King George will be sorrowful without crown or
   honour,
Without good things to eat, without a feast.
Let us drink ale and beer with good humour,
And let us join in a tune in Irish,
Each man of honour will wear black shoes,

Although we have been without them for a long
   time.

Chorus:
The right dol de die rye, right fol die dil
Right fol de die dil, dae ril dadil dee dil,
Right fol de die rol die rol die rol
Right fol aye ril airee.

Ministers will be without wealth, without pomp,
And they will not run to us as they used to,
They will not take rent from Catholics,
Because the scoundrels will be put down.
Daniel will keep after them,
Until they are cleared out of Ireland,
When we will have control of the law again,
When Emancipation comes.

Chorus:
The right fol de dae rye, right fol dee dil,
Right fol de deedil, ae dil adil deedil,
Right dol de deeril, right fol deedil,
Right fol eeril airee.

---

1. In the eighteenth and nineteenth centuries, the belief was prevalent among the Irish that the French would come to their assistance; the ships in the harbours would be set on fire to prevent the British navy from putting to sea.
2. Refers to works such as those by Pastorini (Charles Walmsley, 1722–97), which foretold the downfall of the English monarchy. In James Fenton, *Amhráin Thomáis Ruaidh/The Songs of Tomás Ruadh O'Sullivan* (Dublin: M.H.Gill, 1922), an additional verse refers to Pastorini's prophecies, sold at fairs and markets.

BRÍD UÍ GHALLCHOBHAIR

(*fl.* 1956)

from:
IRISH FOLKLORE
COLLECTION RECORDING
(1956)

['Abhainn Mhór' was composed about 1810 by Séamus Mac Coscair from Erris, County Mayo, where his songs are still popular.[1] According to tradition, the poet had had to leave home and wander through the country following a disagreement over a young woman. Failing to find lodgings for the night in Tralee, County Kerry, he sat down and composed aloud this song of homesickness for his native district. When the people of Tralee heard it they offered him lodgings. The final verse, as sung by Bríd Bean Uí Ghallchobhair (IFC/DISC 2300 10/1956), occurs in other songs, such as 'Amhrán Rinn Mhaoile', 'Béal an Átha Buí' and 'Ceaite na gCuach'. Songs in praise of place, often combined with themes of emigration, play an important role in song repertoires; they are a very real part of life in rural Ireland.   R.Ó.]

Abhainn Mhór

Ó, is céad slán dhuit, Abhainn Mhór, nach é mo
   bhrón gan mé anocht le do thaobh,
A liachtaí bóithrín caol, uaigneach bheith fós ag
   gabháil idir mé is í,
Nach ann a gheobhainn spórt tráthnóna is go
   mall tíocht na hoíche,
An ghloine ar cheann an bhoird ann agus
   comhluadar geanúil le suí síos.

---

1. See Micheál Ó Gallchobhair, 'Amhráin ó Iorrus', *Béaloideas*, vol. 10 (1940), pp. 210–84.

Tá mé tuirseach, sáraithe, ó, is go céad
    mb'fhearr liom dá mbristí mo chroí,
Ag ísliú agus ag ardú an mháilín idir dhá thigh,
I bhfad ó mo chairde is gan áit agam a
    ndéanfainn mo scíth,
Ach le cúnamh ó Rí na nGrásta ní bheidh fán
    orm ach tamall, is cén bhrí.

Tá mo rúitíní gearrtha, ó, gan áireamh, tá
    m'ioscaidí lag,
Tá mo loirgní stróicthe ag siúlóid na mbóithrí
    amuigh go mall,
Ní fhéadaim an máilín seo a ardú leis an bpian
    atá in mo dhroim,
Ó, is níl ball ar bith slán dom nach bhfuil fágtha
    agus ag éagaoin de bheith tinn.

Ó, agus bhéarfaidh mé móide is tá dúil agam
    nach mbrisfidh mé í,
I gcomhluadar ban óg go deo, deo ní shuífidh
    mé síos,
Mar is mé a labhair leofa i dtús m'óige mo
    chreach mhaidine, faraor,
Ó, is gurb iad mná Bhun an Bhóthair a mhúin
    an t-eolas dom isteach go Trá Lí.

Cuan Galún(?), cinnte, mo léan gan mé anocht
    le do thaobh,
Is níor insíodh dhom féin nach dtréigfinn cúige
    Chonnacht aríst,
Níl maidin a n-éirím nach réabtar míle osna in
    mo lár,
Is mé síorchuimhneamh air, céad faraor géar
    nach bhfeicfead go brách.

Tá mé i mo shuí ó d'éirigh an ghealach aréir,
Ag cur tine síos go mall is dá fadú dom péin,
Tá muintir an tí uilig ina gcodladh ar leabaidh
    chlúmhach éin
Tá na coiligh ó, uilig ag glaoch agus an tír uilig
    ina gcodladh ach mé.

Abhainn Mhór [The Big River]

Oh, a hundred farewells to you Abhainn Mhór,
    my grief is that I am not beside you tonight,
Many the lonely, narrow little road comes
    between it and me,
Isn't it there I would have sport in the evening
    and late when night came,

And a glass at the head of the table and
    pleasant company sitting there!

I am tired and exhausted and I would prefer a
    hundred times if my heart were broken,
Lowering and lifting a bag between two houses,
Far from my friends, with nowhere to rest,
But with the help of the King of Graces, I will
    be astray only for a while, and what matter.

My ankles are cut, and without counting that,
    the backs of my knees are weak,
My shins are torn from walking the roads late at
    night,
I cannot lift the little bag because of the pain in
    my back,
And there is no part of my body that is not
    neglected and complaining of pain.

Oh, and I will make a vow and I hope I won't
    break it,
I will never, ever sit in the company of young
    women,
Because I spoke to them at the start of my
    youth, and woe is me, alas,
It was the women of Bun an Bhóthair[1] who
    taught me the way into Tralee.

And Galún[2] harbour, certainly my sorrow is that
    I am not beside you tonight,
I wasn't told that I wouldn't leave the province
    of Connacht again,
There is not a morning that I get up that I do
    not sigh a thousand heartrending sighs,
And I think all the time of it; alas I'll never see
    it again.

I have been up since the moon appeared last
    night,
Putting down a fire late at night and kindling it
    all by myself,
The people of the house are all asleep in beds of
    birds' feathers,
The cocks are all crowing and the whole
    country is asleep but me.

---

1. Bun an Bhóthair: the old road, or way, through the hills from Baile
   Uí Fhiacháin (Newport) to Bangor in County Mayo.
2. The recording is unclear: place-name unknown.

Biographies/Discographies

Kate 'Dineery' Doherty

LIFE. Born near Clonmany, County Donegal, in 1902. Tom Munnelly recorded her singing in October 1984, when she was eighty-two. She died on 24 April 1992.

James Keane

LIFE. Born 1793. Singer, Kilkee, County Clare, aged eighty-three in 1876, when Patrick Weston Joyce (1827–1914) transcribed three songs from his singing which later appeared in his major work, *Old Irish Folk Music and Songs.* Joyce writes, p. 32: 'James Keane's memory was richly stored with Irish music, and with songs both in Irish and English. He told me at the time, with the greatest confidence and cheerfulness, that he had two more years to live, as his father, grandfather and great-grandfather all died at 85.' In the heading to song 424, 'Willie Taylor', Joyce refers to the singer as 'Old James Keane'.

BIBLIOGRAPHY. P.W. Joyce (ed.), *Old Irish Folk Music and Songs* (Dublin: Hodges, Figgis, 1909 [rpr. New York, 1965]), pp. 19, 32, 235–6.

Máire Áine Ní Dhonnchadha

LIFE. Born in Cnoc na hAille in the Gaeltacht district of Cois Fharraige, west of Galway city, in 1919, she was the youngest child of two singers. Educated at boarding-schools in County Galway and at Mary Immaculate College of Education, Limerick, she qualified as a primary school teacher in 1941. She won a gold medal at Oireachtas na Gaeilge in 1950, and Corn Uí Riada, the premier prize for *sean-nós* singing, in 1974. In addition to making a reputation as a fine singer, she actively encouraged younger people to sing in the traditional style. She lived in Dublin for about forty years until her death in 1991.

DISCOGRAPHY. *Deora Aille: Irish Songs from Connemara* (Dublin: Claddagh Records, CC6, 1970); *Traditional Music of Ireland,* vol. 1 (with Seán 'ac Dhonncha and Willie Clancy) (CIC 033); *Claddagh's Choice: An Anthology of Irish Traditional Music* (Dublin: Claddagh Records, CC40\65CD, 1998).

BIOGRAPHY AND CRITICISM. Liam Mac Con Iomaire, 'Ní Dhonnchadha, Máire Áine' in *The Companion to Irish Traditional Music,* ed. Fintan Vallely (Cork: Cork University Press, 1999), p. 266.

Cóilín Ó Cualáin

LIFE. Born *c.* 1950 in Maínis, Carna, County Galway, Cóilín Mháirtín Sarah, as he is known, sings and plays the flute at home and at local sessions, but does not take part in singing competitions and rarely sings on formal occasions. He spent a number of years in England before deciding to return to his native district to settle. He is deeply interested in the folklore and traditions of the area and proud of this heritage.

Bríd Ní Chonaire

LIFE. Traditional singer, Ráth Cairn, County Meath, born 1959. A niece of the well-known singer Darach Ó Catháin (1922–87), Bríd Ní Chonaire has a number of songs, learned from her neighbours in the Gaeltacht of County Meath, and from singers in Conamara, County Galway. Ráth Cairn became a Gaeltacht area when twenty-seven families transferred there from Conamara in 1935, with government assistance. Similar transfers took place from Gaeltacht areas of Kerry and Donegal around this time but only the Ráth Cairn Gaeltacht survives as a vibrant, Irish-speaking community.

Sinéad Caher

LIFE. Born in Belfast in 1947, Sinéad Caher learned many songs from her parents, both of whom were singers. She trained as a teacher at St Mary's College, Belfast, and went to live in Dublin in 1972. She married John Slattery in 1977 and moved to Carlow. She now lives and teaches in Cork.

DISCOGRAPHY. *The Flower of Magherally* (Dublin: Sruthán Records, LUN A333, 1978).

Thomas H. Stewart

LIFE. Fiddle-player, Mayoghill, Garvagh, County Derry, from whom song collector Sam Henry wrote down 'The Flower of Gortade' about 1927. No other information available.

BIBLIOGRAPHY. S. Henry, *Sam Henry's Songs of the People,* eds G. Huntington, L. Herrmann, J. Moulden (Athens, Georgia, and London: University of Georgia Press, 1990).

Bill Donegan

LIFE. Born 1906. In March 1975, when Tom Munnelly recorded songs from him, he was a retired labourer, in poor health, and lived on Quarry Road, Shillelagh, County Wicklow.

Seosamh Ó hÉanaí

LIFE. Traditional singer Seosamh Ó hÉanaí (Joe Éinniú, Joe Heaney) was born on 1 October 1919 in An Aird Thoir, Carna, County Galway, an Irish-speaking area rich in singing and storytelling. He was awarded a scholarship to a preparatory college for teachers, but did not finish the course. In 1942 he won first prize in the *sean-nós* singing competition at the Oireachtas in Dublin. He emigrated to Glasgow, Scotland, in 1947, and later moved to England, where he spent a number of years working as a labourer on building sites. He made a number of important and influential recordings for Gael Linn in Dublin during the 1960s. In 1966 he emigrated to the United States, where he worked as a doorman in New York. Well known among folk singers such as the Clancy Brothers and Bob Dylan, in the early 1980s he was appointed to teach and lecture on traditional singing in Irish at the University of Washington, Seattle, where he remained until his death in 1984. His remains were brought home for burial in Maoras, near Carna.

DISCOGRAPHY. *Seosamh Ó hÉanaí* (Dublin: Gael Linn, CEF 028, 1971); *Come All You Gallant Irishmen* (CIC 020 [NWAR CD 001]); *Joe and the Gabe* (GLCD 1018); *Ó Mo Dhúchas* (CEFCD 051); *Joe Heaney* (Cambridge, Mass.: Philo 2004, 1975); *Joe Heaney: Seosamh Ó hÉanaí: The Road from Connemara* (Indreabhán: Cló Iar-Chonnachta, CICD 143, 2000).

BIOGRAPHY AND CRITICISM. Liam Mac Con Iomaire, 'Ó hÉanaí, Seosamh', in *The Companion to Irish Traditional Music,* ed. Fintan Vallely (Cork: Cork University Press, 1999), pp. 277–8; Steve Coleman, 'Joe Heaney Meets the Academy', *Irish Journal of Anthropology,* vol. 1 (1996), pp. 69–85.

Nonie Lynch

LIFE. Born about 1910, Mrs Nonie Lynch, of Mount Scott, Mullagh, County Clare, was described as a housewife when Tom Munnelly recorded songs from her on 9 January 1992. In December 2000 he described her as 'still very much alive and singing'.

Maggie McDonagh

LIFE. Born *c.* 1911, Maggie McDonagh (Meaigí Sheáinín Choilmín Nic Dhonncha) of Fínis, near Carna in the Gaeltacht of County Galway, belonged to one of the best-known families in Irish song tradition. Fínis is a tiny island, just off the coast, and can be reached on foot at low tide from Roisín na Mainiach, the home of singer Sorcha Ní Ghuairim (q.v.). Séamus Ennis, collector for the Irish Folklore Commission, has described (IFC 1295: 225) how enthralled he was on arriving on the island in August 1942, when Maggie and her two sisters spent a whole afternoon entertaining him with their singing. Maggie, then in her thirties, appears to have preferred the lighter, faster and more amusing songs. She later moved to the mainland, where she died. Her brother Cóilín 'ac Dhonncha, singer and maker of songs, was the last person to live in Fínis, much of which had become covered in sand by the burrowing of rabbits. He remained there until the 1970s.

DISCOGRAPHY. *The Columbia World Library of Folk and Primitive Music*, vol. 1, *Irish Folk Songs*, recorded and edited by Séamus Ennis and Alan Lomax (USA: Columbia Records, SL-204 [AKL 4941] 1955); *The Alan Lomax Collection*, vol. I, *Ireland* (various artists) (Rounder CD 1742).

Nora Cleary

LIFE. Singer, born 1927. Worked for some time as a waitress. Her repertoire, which Tom Munnelly recorded for the Department of Irish Folklore, UCD, in the mid-1970s, included old ballads, songs from broadsides, local and topical songs and her own compositions. He notes that her cottage, at The Hand, Doonogan, County Clare, on the road from Mullagh to Miltown Malbay, was 'a renowned gathering place for singers and musicians'. She died in 1988.

DISCOGRAPHY. *The Lambs on the Green Hills: Songs from County Clare* (various artists) (London: Topic Records, 12TS369, 1978).

BIOGRAPHY AND CRITICISM. Tom Munnelly, 'Cleary, Nora', in *The Companion to Irish Traditional Music*, ed. Fintan Vallely (Cork: Cork University Press, 1999), p. 74.

John Reilly

LIFE. John Reilly, also known as Jacko, was born into a family of Travellers from Carrick-on-Shannon, County Leitrim, in 1926. He had seven sisters and one brother, Martin. Both of his parents were singers, from whom he learned many of the traditional songs in his rich repertoire. The Reilly family travelled the roads of Sligo, Leitrim and Roscommon, and moved to Northern Ireland after the Second World War, where they lived mostly around Belfast and John worked as a tinsmith. He also worked as a thatcher and chimney sweep. In 1962 he settled in Boyle, County Roscommon, where Tom Munnelly recorded him singing the very rare ballad 'The Well Below the Valley' in 1967. He died aged forty-four in 1969, and is buried beside his mother in Ballaghaderreen, County Roscommon.

DISCOGRAPHY. John Reilly, *The Bonny Green Tree: Songs of an Irish Traveller* (London: Topic Records, 12T 359, 1978); (Cassette) *Songs of the Irish Travellers*, ed. T. Munnelly (Dublin: European Ethnic Oral Traditions, 1983); cf. Planxty, *The Well Below the Valley* (Dublin: Polydor Records, 2383 232, 1973).

BIOGRAPHY AND CRITICISM. Tom Munnelly, 'John Reilly, the Man and His Music', *Ceol*, vol. 4, no.1 (1972), pp. 2–8.

Paddy 'Torpey' Killoughry

LIFE. Paddy 'Torpey' Killoughry, Doonagore, Doolin, County Clare, traditional singer, recorded by Dr Ivor Browne in 1962, but made no commercial recordings. Born 1892; died November 1967.

Brigid Tunney

LIFE. Brigid Tunney (née Gallagher) was born in Pettigo, County Donegal, in 1896, but lived most of her adult life in Garvery, Belleek, County Fermanagh. She came from a family of renowned singers and passed on her tradition to her own family, the most celebrated of whom is her son, Paddy Tunney (1921–). She died in 1975.

DISCOGRAPHY. *Where Linnets Sing: Three Generations of the Tunney Family and Their Songs* (two-cassette and booklet set, Dublin: Comhaltas Ceoltóirí Éireann Records, CL44, 1993).

BIOGRAPHY AND CRITICISM. Paddy Tunney, *The Stone Fiddle* (Dublin: Gilbert Dalton, 1979).

Síle Ní Ghallchobhair

LIFE. Síle Ní Ghallchobhair, of Dobhar Láir, An Bun Beag, County Donegal, had a large repertoire of songs in Irish and English, together with stories explaining them, and was also highly regarded as a traditional dancer. Born about 1860, she worked in Scotland for some years, where she learned many songs in English. The recording of 'An Seanduine Dóite' was made when she was ninety-three years of age. She died in 1956.

Labhrás Ó Cadhla

LIFE. Born in 1889 to an Irish-speaking family in Scairt na Draighní (Scartnadriny), County Waterford, in the Gaeltacht area known as Na Déise, Labhrás Ó Cadhla lived for a time in the Irish College in Ring but spent most of his life in Sliabh gCua, Cappoquin. He spent many years as a teacher of Irish in his native county and cycled to classes in different areas throughout the Second World War. Acknowledged as one of the finest singers of his generation, he was sought after as an exponent of the Déise style of *sean-nós*. Séamus Ennis recorded songs from him on acetate discs in 1948, Ciarán MacMathúna made further recordings on tape during the 1957 Fleadh Ceoil in Dungarvan and these, together with songs made by Breandán Ó Cnáimhsí in 1958, were remastered in 2000 by Radio Telefís Éireann for a commercial CD produced by Peter Browne. Labhrás Ó Cadhla had hundreds of songs and was said often to have been tearful when he sang the sad ones. Nicknamed Labhrás Binn ('the melodious'), he was a noted lilter and also played the uilleann pipes and the tin whistle. He was a close friend of the Sliabh gCua poet and songmaker Pádraig Ó Milleadha (1877–1947), and is credited with selecting the tunes for many of his compositions. He remained single throughout his life and died on 15 January 1961, in Dungarvan hospital.

DISCOGRAPHY. Labhrás Ó Cadhla, *Amhráin Ó Shliabh gCua* (Baile Átha Cliath: RTÉ CD 234, 2000).

BIOGRAPHY AND CRITICISM. Micheál Mac Cárthaigh, *Feasta* (Márta, 1961); Diarmuid Breathnach and Máire Ní Mhurchú, *1882–1992: Beathaisnéis a Trí* (Baile Átha Cliath: An Clóchomhar, 1992), pp. 70–1.

Patrick a Búrc

LIFE. Patrick a Búrc (Patrick Phádraig Liam a Búrc), of Aill na Brún, Cill Chiaráin, County Galway, died in 1996, aged 72 or 73. He had a large repertoire of songs, most of which he sang in a definite, rhythmic style. Many of them were composed locally and are not often heard outside the Conamara Gaeltacht. Patrick learned many of his songs from two local poets, brothers Vail Bheairtle and Michael Bheairtle Uí Dhonncha (Ó Donncha). He was a nephew of the celebrated storyteller Éamon a Búrc (q.v.) pp. 1296–1303.

Mary Seale

LIFE. Born Mary Kilkenny, Mary Seale, of Birch Grove, Ballinasloe, County Galway, was well known in the 1960s and 1970s among competitors at the singing competitions in Fleadhanna Ceoil (music festivals) held throughout Ireland.

Sorcha Ní Ghuairim

LIFE. Singer, teacher and journalist. Born 1911 in Roisín na Mainiach, Carna, County Galway, a Gaeltacht area noted for singing and story-telling. She spent two years at University College Galway before moving to Dublin, where she lived until about 1955, teaching Irish and writing. She was involved in the Irish-language revival movement, was a regular participant at sessions of music, singing and storytelling associated with it, and wrote articles on Irish language and literature. Noted for her passionate idealism and devotion to language rights, as well as for her vivid beauty and magnificent singing voice, she appears to have suffered from depression as a young woman. In 1935 she became editor of *An t-Éireannach*, an Irish-language socialist newspaper for the Gaeltacht. The paper ceased publication in 1937, the same year that her close friend Eamonn McGrotty was killed in battle at Jarama in Spain. In 1941 she was appointed lecturer in spoken Irish at Trinity College Dublin, and in 1947 was conferred with an MA *jure officii* by the university. She also worked as a journalist and columnist ('Coisin Shiúlach' — Wandering Foot) with the *Irish Press*, but apparently became disillusioned with life in Ireland and the position of her native language. She moved to England, where she worked in relatively menial jobs, but also visited her brothers in America twice or three times, recording a collection of songs there for Folkways Records in 1957. She died in England in December 1976, and was brought back to Carna for burial on Christmas Eve. A programme about her life and background was broadcast on Raidió na Gaeltachta on 14 April 1980.

DISCOGRAPHY. *Sorcha Ní Ghuairim Sings Traditional Irish Songs* (New York: Folkways Records, FW 861, 1957), reissued as *An Chéad Dólás* (Indreabhán: Cló Iar-Chonnacht, 1990); *Sorcha: Amhráin Shorcha Ní Ghuairim: Traditional Songs from Conamara* (Baile Átha Cliath: Comhairle Bhéaloideas Éireann/Gael-Linn, CEFCD 182, 2001).

BIOGRAPHY AND CRITICISM. Diarmuid Breathnach and Máire Ní Mhurchú, *1882–1992: Beathaisnéis a Ceathair* (Baile Átha Cliath: An Clóchomhar, 1994), pp. 125–6; Éamonn Ó Ciosáin, *An t-Éireannach 1934–37: Nuachtán Sóisialach Gaeltachta* (Baile Átha Cliath: An Clóchomhar, 1993).

Mary Ann Cunningham

LIFE. Mrs Mary Ann Cunningham, traditional singer, was originally from County Armagh. She lived on the Longstone Road, Annalong, County Down, in the 1950s, when Hugh Shields noted 'The Factory Girl' from her singing with pen and paper.

BIBLIOGRAPHY. Hugh Shields, 'A Latter-Day Pastourelle', *Ceol: A Journal of Irish Music*, vol. 1, no. 3 (1963), pp. 8–9. Recorded by Hugh Shields.

Sarah Makem

LIFE. Born 1900 in Keady, County Armagh, Mrs Sarah Makem was one of the finest traditional singers ever recorded in Ireland, with a repertoire of over five hundred items in various genres. Recorded by the American singer and song collector Jean Ritchie, she was heard on the BBC radio programme *As I Roved Out* in the 1950s, and became well known and much sought after by younger singers and folksong scholars, although she had not previously performed outside her local area. Her mother, from whom Sarah learned most of her songs, came from a family well known for generations for its singing. Her husband, Peter, was a fine fiddle-player, and their five sons inherited their parents' music and singing tradition. One of them, Tommy Makem, became internationally famous with the Clancy Brothers singing group; the family's musical career is traced on its website, www.makem.com. Sarah Makem died in 1985.

DISCOGRAPHY. *Mrs Sarah Makem: Ulster Ballad Singer* (London: Topic Records, 12T 182, 1968).

BIOGRAPHY AND CRITICISM. David Hammond, 'Makem, Sarah', in *The Companion to Irish Traditional Music*, ed. Fintan Vallely (Cork: Cork University Press, 1999), pp. 224–5.

Mary Dolan

LIFE. Born in 1889, Mrs Mary Dolan, of Blacklion, County Cavan, was aged eighty-two and resident in the Cavan County Home when Tom Munnelly recorded her singing in November 1971.

Elizabeth (Bess) Cronin

LIFE. Usually known as Bess, Mrs Cronin is sometimes referred to in Irish as Eilís Uí Chróinín. She was the daughter of a schoolmaster and was born in 1879 in the Gaeltacht of West Cork, near the Kerry border, and after her marriage lived most of her life at Carraig an Adhmaid, Baile Mhic Íre (Ballymakeera), County Cork, in a house known as 'The Plantation'. She had a vast repertoire of folklore, including large numbers of songs in Irish and in English. In 1947 Séamus Ennis, with Brian George of the BBC, began to record her songs for the Irish Folklore Commission. Despite her age when many of the recordings were made, her sensitivity as a singer is evident, and her individual style has influenced a number of singers (see 'The Bonny Blue-eyed Lassie', pp. 1326–1327). She became well known internationally in the 1950s, when her songs were heard on the BBC radio series *As I Roved Out*, and on commercial recordings. Several members of her family have achieved distinction in Irish studies and traditional arts. They include her sons Irish scholar Donncha Ó Cróinín and folklore collector Seán Ó Cróinín (1915–65), her grandson Dáibhí Ó Cróinín, historian, and her grandnephew, singer Iarla Ó Lionaird. Bess Cronin died in 1956.

DISCOGRAPHY. Eilís Uí Chróinín's singing may be heard on a number of records in the Topic series *The Folk Songs of Britain*, vols 1–10. See also Elizabeth Cronin, *Cucanandy* (Devon: Folktracks, FSP60-160, 1981) (cassette), and *The Columbia World Library of Folk and Primitive Music*, vol. 1, *Irish Folk Songs*, recorded and edited by Séamus Ennis and Alan Lomax (USA, SL-204 [AKL 4941], 1955). The two CDs which accompany Dáibhí Ó Cróinín's book listed below contain respectively thirty songs originally recorded on disc and twenty-nine songs from tape.

BIBLIOGRAPHY. Dáibhí Ó Cróinín (ed.), *The Songs of Elizabeth Cronin, Irish Traditional Singer* (Dublin: Four Courts Press, 2000. Book and two CDs).

Cáit Ní Mhuimhneacháin

LIFE. A member of a very musical Irish-speaking family, from Béal Átha an Ghaorthaidh, Múscraí Thiar, County Cork, traditional singer Cáit Ní Mhuimhneacháin was born in 1918. Her singing was recorded on disc on a number of occasions by the IFC, the BBC and Radió Éireann. She won first place in the competitions for both slow singing and lively singing at Oireachtas na Gaeilge in 1942. Uí Thuama by marriage, she died in 1949, aged thirty-one. Her brother Aindrias Ó Muimhneacháin was a well-known figure in Irish-language circles in Dublin until his death on 14 November 1989.

DISCOGRAPHY. *Ireland/Irelande: Musiques Traditionelles d'Aujourd'hui/Traditional Musics of Today* (Gentilly: Auvidis/UNESCO, D8271, 1997); *An Joga Mór: Sean-nós Singing from County Cork/Amhráin Cháit Ní Mhuimhneacháin* (Dublin: RTÉ/RBÉ, RTÉ 242, 2001).

Cáit Ní Ailíosa

LIFE. Traditional singer from An Dromaid, near Waterville, County Kerry, born about 1897. The broadcaster and music collector Ciarán Mac Mathúna was introduced to her by Fionán Mac Coluim (1875–1976), a folklore and folksong collector and an Irish-language enthusiast who collaborated with him on over fifty radio programmes. Heard on RTÉ Radio, *Ciarán Mac Mathúna Introduces Music from Clare and Kerry.*

Bríd Uí Ghallchobhair

LIFE. Singer Bríd Bean Uí Ghallchobhair, Achill, County Mayo. Recorded by Leo Corduff in 1956 for the IFC. No other information available.

ANGELA BOURKE, *Editor*

Lamenting the Dead

It is unlikely that any of the lament-poets featured in this subsection composed their laments exactly as they are printed here.[1] Laments composed in the eighteenth and nineteenth centuries were usually written down only after they had become famous within oral tradition, either for the excellence of their expression or because of the circumstances which produced them. The first three texts given here qualified on both counts: in each case the dead man was a prominent Catholic whose early death became a focus of resistance to Protestant or English rule, and the oral *caoineadh* was only one of several memorials which served to concentrate popular memory and rhetoric in the years that followed his death.[2]

The Irish *caoineadh* (anglicized as 'keen', 'keening'), was chanted or sung. It was a central theatre of women's expression in the Irish language, its characteristic diction found as early as the eighth-century *Poems of Blathmac*.[3] Unlike other forms of public utterance, it offered its composers and performers a certain protection as they challenged those in authority: by convention, the *bean chaointe*, or lament-poet, was a woman crazed with grief, whose appearance and behaviour expressed disorder and loss of control. In fact, however, her performance, like that of a tragic actor, required considerable intellectual stamina, as well as great reserves of emotion. Anger and invective were central to the traditional lament in Ireland, as elsewhere; in these examples they are directed eloquently at named individuals, many of them people in authority, who are accused of murdering, injuring or betraying the dead hero.[4]

The playwright J.M. Synge, in his account of the Aran Islands, off the coast of Galway, in the early years of the twentieth century, describes two scenes of lamentation. The funeral of an old woman was conducted with deliberate formality, then:

> While the grave was being opened the women sat down among the flat tombstones, bordered with a pale fringe of early bracken, and began the wild keen or crying for the dead. Each old woman, as she took her turn in the leading recitative, seemed possessed for the moment with a profound ecstasy of grief, swaying to and

1. For studies of the Irish lament tradition see Rachel S. Bromwich, 'The Continuity of the Gaelic Tradition in Eighteenth-Century Ireland', *Yorkshire Celtic Studies: The Yorkshire Society for Celtic Studies, Transactions*, vol. 4 (1947–8), and 'The Keen for Art O'Leary, Its Background and Its Place in the Tradition of Gaelic Keening', *Éigse*, vol. 5 (1948), pp. 236–52; Seán Ó Tuama, 'Caoineadh Airt Uí Laoghaire [The Lament for Art Ó Laoghaire]' (Dublin: An Clóchomhar, 1961), and 'The Lament for Art O'Leary and the Popular Keening Tradition' in his *Repossessions: Selected Essays on the Irish Literary Heritage* (Cork: Cork University Press, 1995), pp. 78–100; Seán Ó Coileáin, 'The Irish Lament: An Oral Genre', *Studia Hibernica*, vol. 24 (1998), pp. 97–117; Breandán Ó Buachalla, *An Caoine agus an Chaointeoireacht* (Baile Átha Cliath: Cois Life, 1998).
2. For the political implications of lament-poetry's dissemination, see L.M. Cullen, 'The Contemporary and Later Politics of Caoineadh Airt Uí Laoire', *Eighteenth-Century Ireland*, vol. 8 (1993), pp. 7–38.
3. For the music of *caoineadh* see Breandán Ó Madagáin, 'Irish Vocal Music of Lament and Syllabic Poetry', in Robert O'Driscoll, ed., *The Celtic Consciousness* (Portlaoise: The Dolmen Press; Edinburgh: Canongate, 1982), pp. 311–31. See also Angela Bourke, 'Performing, not Writing: The Reception of an Irish Woman's Lament', in *Dwelling in Possibility: Women Poets and Critics on Poetry*, eds Yopie Prins and

Maeera Shreiber (Ithaca, NY, and London: Cornell University Press, 1997), pp. 132–46. For Blathmac, see James Carney, *Poems of Blathmac, Son of Cú Brettan* (Dublin: Irish Texts Society, 1964).
4. Ritual lamentation is a feature of funeral practice in many societies. See Maria Leach (ed.), *Standard Dictionary of Folklore, Mythology and Legend*, 2 vols (New York: Funk and Wagnalls, 1949). Cf. Margaret Alexiou, *The Ritual Lament in Greek Tradition* (Cambridge: Cambridge University Press, 1974), and Aili Nenola-Kallio, *Studies in Ingrian Laments* (Folklore Fellows Communications, No. 234) (Helsinki: Academia Scientiarum Fennica, 1982).

fro, and bending her forehead to the stone before her, while she called out to the dead with a perpetually recurring chant of sobs.[5]

Later Synge attended the funeral which must have inspired his play *Riders to the Sea*. The drowned body of a young man had been washed ashore, and, he tells us, 'the keen lost a part of its formal nature, and was recited as the expression of intense personal grief by the young men and women of the man's own family'. Young men did take part, but the major responsibility fell to the women:

> When a number of blackened boards and pieces of bone had been thrown up with the clay, a skull was lifted out, and placed upon a gravestone. Immediately the old woman, the mother of the dead man, took it up in her hands, and carried it away by herself. There she sat down and put it in her lap — it was the skull of her own mother — and began keening and shrieking over it with the wildest lamentation . . . [Later she] got up and came back to the coffin, and began to beat on it, holding the skull in her left hand. This last moment of grief was the most terrible of all. The young women were lying among the stones, worn out with their passion of grief, yet raising themselves every few moments to beat with magnificent gestures on the boards of the coffin.[6]

To the extent that it offers women a licence to speak loudly and without inhibition, and frequently to defend their own interests against those of men, *caoineadh* may be read as feminist utterance. It is an art in which women collaborated with other women, both synchronically — taking turns to weep over the same dead body, joining in a chorus of stylized sobbing, such as *Ochón agus ochón ó!* — and diachronically: remembering and quoting each other's laments, often over many generations. We should not,

however, be surprised to find within the tradition of lament-poetry another voice, which in today's terms is distinctly anti-feminist. Oral verbal art is typically combative or adversarial in tone. The person lamented was most often a man, and his dead body, particularly if he was young and well known, could become a site of contest between factions or families in the concentrated and emotionally charged time between death and burial. The lament-poet's repertoire included scathing insults and withering curses, frequently directed at women, as well as at men.[7]

Synge and other eyewitnesses describe the lament-poet as rocking back and forth with eyes closed, repeating certain words in a low voice before beginning her loud public performance.[8] The metre is simple, with short, rhymed lines of two or three stresses, in stanzas of varying length. The themes are traditional: lavish praise of the dead person's beauty, bravery and generosity, and of his home and lineage; equally lavish castigation of his enemies; exhortations to him to get up and come home; descriptions of the lamenter's grief. Established verbal formulae act as mnemonics for the common themes and as building blocks of composition. The rocking or swaying of the lamenter's body undoubtedly helped to establish metrical rhythm, but she may also have used it as a way of altering her consciousness: of tuning in to particular areas of emotion, memory and experience. *Caoineadh* was a performance, and entailed taking possession of space and demanding attention, as much as arranging words in order.[9]

Lament-poets were grief therapists, as well as inciters of public outrage. Analysis of their various rhetorical stances shows them dealing with all the stages of what modern psychology recognizes as a process of grieving: denial, anger, bargaining, sadness and acceptance.[10]

The poetry of *caoineadh* is formulaic: the method of composition in performance was

5. John Millington Synge, *The Aran Islands* (Oxford and New York: Oxford University Press, 1907, 1979), pp. 36–7. See also, Angela Bourke, 'Keening as Theatre: J.M. Synge and the Irish Lament Tradition', in *Interpreting Synge: Essays from the Synge Summer School, 1991–2000*, ed. Nicholas Grene (Dublin: Lilliput, 2000), pp. 67–79.

6. Ibid., pp. 143–4.

7. See Angela Bourke, 'More in Anger than in Sorrow: Irish Women's Lament Poetry', in *Feminist Messages: Coding in Women's Folk Culture*, ed. Joan N. Radner (Chicago: University of Illinois Press, 1993), pp. 160–82.

8. See, for example, R.S. Bromwich, 'The Keen for Art O'Leary', p. 243.

9. See A. Bourke, 'Performing, not Writing', pp. 132–46.

10. See A. Bourke, 'The Irish Traditional Lament and the Grieving Process', *Women's Studies International Forum*, vol. 11, no. 4 (1988), pp. 287–91.

apparently similar to that described by Albert B. Lord as used by (male) oral poets in the former Yugoslavia, whose expertise was achieved through long immersion in the themes and verbal formulae of their tradition.[11] The same lines and groups of lines, the same ideas and images, are found not only in a number of different lament-poems, but also in other, related areas of oral poetry. Songs about drownings and other tragic deaths differ in structure from the ritual laments performed at funerals, but share with them a use of stark and shocking contrasts, among other verbal techniques. The song 'Liam Ó Raghallaigh' includes the lines *'Tá do shúile ag na péiste is tá do bhéilín ag na portáin, / Tá do dhá láimhín gheala ghlégheala faoi ghéarsmacht na mbradán'* (Oh, the crabs have devoured your mouth, love, the eels have feasted upon your eyes, / And your white hands so strong and tender are now the salmon's proudest prize).[12] Such a deliberate and public dwelling on the more horrifying aspects of death might do much to diminish private nightmares during grieving.

In Scotland, songs sung while 'waulking', or thickening woven cloth, belonged, like *caoineadh*, to communal occasions when women worked in groups; many of them also echo the formulaic

diction of laments, as do the religious laments ascribed to the Virgin Mary (see the subsection 'Spirituality and Religion in Oral Tradition', pp. 1410–1412).[13] The significance of lament-poetry in traditional society may be gauged by the extent to which it was parodied: wakes, particularly those of old people, could be occasions of Rabelaisian celebration, and several texts survive in which conventional expressions of grief are turned upside down, inverting the messages and subverting the agendas of ritual praise and mourning.

Even within the ritual lament for the dead, however, the messages conveyed could be coded; they could make political points under the guise of personal grief, or protest publicly at domestic situations for which no other remedy was available, as in the lament for Diarmaid Mac Cárthaigh (pp. 1384–1388).[14] In the formulaic composition of the original Irish, adjectives and other words sometimes serve metre, rather than meaning. The English translations which follow therefore depart occasionally from the literal meaning, in order to convey the rhythm which is an integral part of the originals.

11. Albert B. Lord, *The Singer of Tales.*
12. See Volume II, pp. 96–7.

13. See John Lorne Campbell and Francis Collinson, *Hebridean Folksongs*, 3 vols (Oxford: Oxford University Press, 1969, 1977, 1981).
14. See also Bourke, 'More in Anger than in Sorrow.'

SIR JAMES COTTER'S NURSE

(*fl.* 1720)

from:
MURPHY MS NO. 9, NATIONAL UNIVERSITY OF IRELAND, MAYNOOTH

[Sir James Cotter the younger (1689–1720), of Carrigtwohill, County Cork, was the son of Sir James Cotter (*c.*1630–1705), a leading Jacobite in the south of Ireland. Still a minor at the time of his father's death in 1705, he was now an orphan (his mother having died in 1698), and the Penal Laws dictated that he would be educated as a Protestant and would repudiate his Catholic heritage as a condition of inheriting his ancestral lands.

Such was the influence of his father's supporters, however, that instead he emerged in adulthood as the chief hope of the Catholic Jacobite cause. He was hanged in Cork on 20 May 1720, having been found guilty of 'ravishing Elizabeth Squibb, a Quaker' — a charge generally believed at the time to be unfounded. Several poets of the literary tradition composed elegies after his death, and at least one black-letter English-language broadside was printed, possibly for sale at his public execution.[1] The lament given

1. See Breandán Ó Conchúir, *Scríobhaithe Chorcaí 1700–1850* (Baile Átha Cliath: An Clóchomhar, 1982), p. 215 and *passim*; Brian Ó Cuív (ed.), *Párliament na mBan* (Dublin: Dublin Institute for Advanced Studies, 1970), p. xxxix. A copy of a black-letter broadside elegy on his death is pasted to the endpaper of Murphy MS no. 9, National University of Ireland, Maynooth.

here, which displays many characteristics of oral composition, is attributed to his old nurse. A transcription by
'Fiachra Éilgeach' (Risteárd Ó Foghludha, 1871–1957)
was published in the *Irish Press*, Monday 27 April 1936.
Translation and headnote, A.B.; the spelling has been
modernized.]

Caoineadh Shéamuis Mhic Choitir

Mo chéad chara tú
Is breá thíodh hata dhuit,
Claíomh cinn airgid,
Bhíodh sráid dá glanadh dhuit,
Bóithre dhá ngealadh dhuit,
Cóiste ocht gcapall duit
Is Sasanaigh ag umhlú go talamh duit,
Is ní le taitneamh duit
Ach le haonchorp eagla.

Greadadh oraibh is brón,
A lucht na mbolg mór,
Fanaidh siar go fóill
Is leogaidh Séamus romhaibh
Mar is dó ba chuí is ba chóir.

A mhná ó! Mo scairt,
Druididh uaim amach
Chun go bhféachfad san aird aneas,
Go bhfeicfinn an Ridire críonna ag teacht,
Nó Séamus Óg a mhac,
Srian béil óir na n-each,
Claíomh cinn óir ina ghlaic
'S a choisí roimis amach
Ag dul go deimhin sa chath;
Do dhéanfadh sé díobh spreas
nó gheobhadh sé díol ina mhac.

A dhianghrá lár na gcarad,
Is iomaí dailtín smeartha
Ó do chistin gonat halla
Do gheobhadh bean in aisce,
Nó bean ar chairt leanna,
Ní áirím bean gan baiste,
Gan ionladh, gan aiste,
Nár chrom a glúin chun sagairt
Is ná dúirt riamh a paidir
Ach Beití Sciobbs a hainm

Táine anall thar caise
Chun mo lao-sa a thachtadh,
Is nárab Dé n-a beatha!

The Lament for Sir James Cotter

My very first friend,
You looked well in a hat,
With your silver-hilted sword.
They used to clear the street for you,
Whiten the roads for you,
Your coach had eight horses,
And the English bowed down to you,
Not that they liked you;
They were frightened to death of you!

Bad cess to you and sorrow,
You with the big bellies!
Stand back out of the way,
And let Sir James in front,
As is his right and due.

Women-o I cry!
Stand back away from me;
Let me look south,
To see the old knight come,
Or young James, his son.
Gold bits and bridles,
Golden-hilted sword,
His footman before him,
Racing into battle.
He'd chop them down like firewood,
Or he'd avenge his son.

Dear friend and love,
Any dirty kitchen-lad
Or servant from your hall
Could get a woman free,
Or for a quart of ale
— Not to mention a pagan,
Unwashed and unshriven,
Who never knelt to priest
And never said her prayer.
Her name was Betty Squibb,
Who came across the sea,
To strangle my own love,
And may God not reward her!

CÁIT DE BÚRCA

(*fl.* 1766)

from:
FEASTA (1956)

[Nicholas Sheehy (1728–66), parish priest of Clogheen, County Tipperary, and described as 'a symbol of the marginality on many levels of contemporary Catholicism',[1] was hanged, drawn and quartered in Clonmel, County Tipperary, on 15 March 1766. He was descended from prominent, well-off Catholic families and, like other priests of his time, had been educated abroad (at the Irish College in Louvain in Belgium). Active in support of parishioners who opposed tithe-collecting, he was suspected of sedition. In February 1765 he was proclaimed on a charge of high treason, with a price of £300 on his head,[2] and fearing a conspiracy against him in Tipperary, gave himself up to the authorities in Dublin, where he was tried and found not guilty almost a year later. However, he was immediately brought back to Clonmel under heavy guard, arrested on a trumped-up charge of murder, found guilty, and executed. His case provoked widespread outrage and extensive commentary in oral tradition, as well as in print. After his execution his head was left impaled on a spike above the prison gate for twenty years, until his sister Cáit de Búrca was allowed to remove it for burial: a dramatic detail also told of other executed men and the women who lamented them.

Like other laments with political overtones, this one, attributed to Nicholas Sheehy's sister (perhaps the same Cáit de Búrca who recovered his severed head), is a memorial designed to keep anger and outrage alive. Its formulaic construction, elaborate invective, and naming of names ensured that the dead man's enemies and those who had betrayed him would continue to be vilified, while the injustice perpetrated against him remained vivid in popular memory. The text was unpublished and feared lost in 1956 when Séamus Ó Néill (1892–1974), a senior Garda Síochána officer, supplied it as transcribed from his wife, nationalist poet and teacher Áine Ní Fhoghludha (1880–1932), who had most probably learned it in her native Ring, County Waterford. It appeared in *Feasta*, February 1956, p. 2. Translation and headnote, A.B.]

---

1. Maurice Bric, 'The Whiteboy Movement in Tipperary, 1760–80,' in William Nolan and Thomas G. McGrath (eds), *Tipperary: History and Society* (Dublin: Geography Publications, 1985), p. 158.
2. Ibid., p. 157. The Whiteboy movement, which began in County Tipperary in 1761, used secrecy and violent action to oppose oppressive policies, such as the fencing of common land and the imposition of tithes.

An tAthair Nioclás Mac Síthigh:
Caoineadh do chum a dheirfiúr

A Athair Niocláis, mo chás id luí thú,
Atá do chomhlucht go buartha gan aoibhneas,
Atá Clanna Gael fé ghéarsmacht do
    chaoineamh,
Ó ghlacadar na Black Townsends le fonn a gcroí
    thú —
Aodhagán is Créach a dhíol tú;
Bagwell is Maude a chráigh an croí ionat,
Nuair chuireadar an córda féd' scornach nár
    thaoiligh;
An diabhal dá dtachtadh — gus is dealbh an
    díol é!

Mo chreach ghéar fhada is m'atuirse nimhneach!
An treas lá Samhraidh agus é 'na shaoire,
Dainid cruaidh do chomhlucht 'na luí é!
Cuirfidh sé ar a thuilleadh acu briseadh agus
    scaoileadh,
Aimsir féile agus glaoite an chíosa,
Ní leigfeadh an bhroid i gcomhair a' tí cúcha
Go dtagadh laogh in aos a dhíol' dóibh,
Go gcuiridís an t-im sa *price* b'aoirde,
Go ndéanaidís bréidín olann na gcaoire,
Agus a cholann gan cheann, mo chantla id
    luí tú!

Mo chreach ghéar agus mo chás,
A shagairt an urla bháin!
Agus ní bréag domsa é rá
Gur fada chuaigh do cháil
San bhFrainc is san Spáinn
Gus go Droichead Geal na mBán.[3]
Míle altú le Rí na nGrás,
Ní raibh acu leat a rá
Ach gur tú captaon na bhFear mBán,
    a dhriotháir ó!

Mo chreach ghéar fhada ghoirt,
A shagairt an urla ghil!
Agus ní bréag domhsa sin,
Gur bhinne liom do ghuth,

---

3. Glossed, 'an Róimh'.

'S an ceol binn do bhí i mbarr do ghoib
Id' sheasamh os cionn coirp,
Ná an chéirseach 's ná an druid,
Ná an chuach i mbarr an toir,
Cé go mbeidh do cheann bán anocht go dubh
Ar spair an phríosúin thoir, a dhriotháir ó!

Mo chreach ghéar agus mo thuirse,
Nár ghlac an tAthair Nioclás 'ac Síthigh a
      bhriseadh,
Agus dul uathu thar uisce,
Sar do dhein Maude é mhilleadh,
Agus an cucól ná raibh gnó leis chun cloinne!
Céad léan ort, a thréinis⁴ Mac Mhuire,
'Gus a dhaorais an t-aon úd dár gcineadh
Thiocfadh ar ár n-éileamh go minic!
      a dhriotháir ó!

A Bhagwell óig, go n-imidh Dia ort!
Nár thagaidh an rós i ngort ná an síol chughat,
An chruithneacht dhearg nár thagaidh i gcriaidh
      chughat,
Nár bheiridh do bhean mac ná iníon duit.
Má bheireann cheana go raibh sampla don
      saol agat
Crúb chapaill agus earball caoire
Agus gob lachan a chartfadh an t-aoileach
Ar eagla gur rógaire tú a mharódh daoine.

Bagwell gránna na cnaige,⁵
Diabhal fhuadfadh mar fhuadaigh t'athair
Fásach ag táirseach do halla
Crann cárthainn in áit do leapan,
Tobar uaithne agus nead dubhán-fhalla,
Neantóga agus feochadáin ghlasa
Ar an slí romhat agus a dhá ceann i dtalamh
Cuirim féin go bráth gan driotháir gan sagart.

Máire Ní Dhoinnléi go n-imídh Dia ort,
Stríopach choiteann clogar na mílte,
Thug na trí boinneáin as ceart lár na tíre
A chroch an dá Shéamas is Nioclás 'ac Síthigh
Dá mbeinn im muilleoir do mheilinn gan
      díol tú
Chráifinn chomh cráite lem chroí tú
Ar leac na bpian ag an diabhal mar chíste.⁶

---

4. Obscure: cf. *crinnim*, I erode, gnaw.
5. Source has *cuaige*, but *cnaige* fits better for rhyme and sense.
6. Source: *ciste* (treasure/chest), but both metre and sense are better served by *císte* (cake/small round loaf).

Mo chreach ghéar fhada is m'atuirse chráite
'Gus ní crann duilleabhar aon ná fásfaidh
'S ní ó chrann na n-úll bhfiain a d'fhás sé
Ach ó phlúr na buairne báine
Déinídh slí dó tríd an mbearnain
Mar a bhfuil fearantas a athar is a mháthar
Go gcuire Séamus Óg roimhe fáilte
Mar is iad a dá iciú le díograis tál ort
      a dhriotháir ó!

Father Nicholas Sheehy: A Lament Composed by His Sister

Father Nicholas, alas that you lie there!
Your household has been deprived of all
      pleasure,
The native Irish have grieved and lamented you
Since the Black Townsends were so quick to
      arrest you —
Egan¹ and Creagh² were the ones to sell you;
Bagwell³ and Maude⁴ the two to torment you,
When they put the rope around your innocent
      neck;
May the devil choke them — small
      compensation!

My long bitter sorrow, my poisonous grief!
The third day of summer, a holiday too:
Hard affliction for the ones who are sleeping!
A shattering blow for others as well:
When the gale-day came and rents were due,
He wouldn't let demands come near their
      houses⁵
Until they had a calf of a saleable age,
Or their butter was priced in the highest range,
Or their wool was woven to make the best cloth
And dear headless corpse, I grieve for your fall!

---

1. Dr William Egan, parish priest of Clonmel, later bishop of Waterford and Lismore. Sheehy called on him to testify on his behalf in Clonmel, but Egan refused to become involved.
2. Bishop of Waterford.
3. John Bagwell, MP for Tulsk, and his brother William, prominent in the campaign against Sheehy.
4. Sir Thomas Maude, of Dundrum, County Tipperary, said to have led a party of horsemen who intimidated witnesses during Sheehy's trial (M. Bric, 'The Whiteboy Movement', p. 158).
5. Thanks to Dáithí Ó hÓgáin and Diarmaid Ó Muirithe for help with this translation.

My bitter grief and sorrow,
Priest with the fair forelock,
I tell no lie in saying
That your fame spread far:
To France and to Spain
And the White Bridge of the Lea.[6]
A thousand thanks be to God,
The worst name they could call you
Was captain of the Whiteboys,
      brother dear!

My long bitter sorrow,
Priest with the shining forelock!
And I tell no lie,
The sound of your voice,
And the music you sang,
Standing over a corpse,
Was sweeter to me
Than blackbird or starling
Or the cuckoo perched high,
Although east of here tonight,
Your fair head will turn black
On a pole outside the jail,
      brother dear!

My bitter sorrow and sadness,
That Father Sheehy didn't escape
Across the water from them,
Before Maude did him in
Along with that impotent cuckold!
A hundred curses on you, who injured the Son
    of Mary
And hanged the one man of our race
Who would often answer our call,
      brother dear!

Young Bagwell, may God forsake you!
May your fields not produce either linseed or
    any seed,
May the red wheat never again grow on your
    land,
May your wife never bear either daughter or son,
But if she does, may the child be a freak,
With horse's hoof and tail like a sheep,

And a bill like a duck, to poke in the dunghill,
For fear of you, rogue, and killer of people.

Ugly Bagwell, you scowler,
May the devil take you as he took your father,
May a wasteland extend from your hall door,
A rowan tree[7] grow in the place of your bed,
Green slime in your well, and spiders' webs.
May twice-rooted nettles[8] and thistles grow
    green
Across your path, and choke it forever,
And may you not have a brother, or a priest
    when you need him.

Molly Dunlea,[9] may God forsake you!
A common whore with a bad reputation,
Took three slender lads from the heart of the
    country;
Hanged two called James,[10] and Nicholas Sheehy.
If I were a miller, I'd grind you for free,
I'd crush you to bits, as the heart's crushed in
    me,
On the agony-slab,[11] to make bread for the devil.

My long, sharp grief, my tortured sadness,
A tree that won't grow has no leaves or branches,
But his was no stock of wild crab-apple;
He came from the flower of fairest women.
Make way for him, going through the gap,
To the ancestral lands of his father and mother,
Where his young brother James will make him
    welcome
For those two were suckled with great affection,

---

6. Glossed in source: Rome.

7. Rowan or mountain ash, native to Irish mountainsides, is associated with the fairies.
8. Briars (but not nettles or thistles) make new roots where they touch the ground. Plants which appear to be rooted at both ends have sinister connotations in oral tradition; the phrase 'a dhá cheann i dtalamh' is formulaic.
9. A prostitute whose conduct Sheehy had publicly denounced, and who was one of the chief witnesses against him.
10. James Farrel of Rehill and James Buxton of Killroe, 'men of good circumstances and connections', were charged with complicity in the murder for which Sheehy was hanged and, on 3 May 1766, sentenced to be executed. See M. Bric, 'The Whiteboy Movement', p. 159. Sheehy had by then been dead for many weeks; the reference shows how a lament-poem, traditionally composed directly after a death, could be added to and edited later.
11. A formulaic phrase, meaning hell.

EIBHLÍN DUBH NÍ CHONAILL

(c. 1743–c. 1800)

from:
FERRITER MS NO. 1, UNIVERSITY COLLEGE DUBLIN

[Eibhlín Dubh Ní Chonaill's lament for her husband Art Ó Laoghaire (Ó Laoire, O'Leary), shot dead on 4 May 1773 near Carraig an Ime (Carriganimmy), County Cork, is by far the best-known text of its kind in Irish.[1] Published in a scholarly edition in 1961 by Seán Ó Tuama, it has since been included in countless anthologies (including Frank O'Connor's translation in Volume I, pp. 309–13), and is often invoked as the pinnacle of Irish women's literary achievement in the eighteenth century. In fact, internal evidence of metre and diction, and comparison with other laments, show that this composition owes little or nothing to writing. The versions printed here differ significantly from the standard edited text and illustrate something of the flexibility of the tradition through which poetry like this was composed, performed and remembered.

Eibhlín Ní Chonaill came from a prosperous and educated family, whose male members, at least, were highly literate and fully bilingual in Irish and English; however, when her headstrong young husband was shot as an outlaw, instead of *writing* about her grief and anger, she expressed both through the medium most readily available to women in the Irish-language tradition: the oral lament, composed in performance.

Laments were designed to be remembered, by their composers and by others who were expert in the art of *caoineadh* and adept in the use of its metre and diction. Eibhlín Ní Chonaill's composition makes use of lines and groups of lines which also occur in texts said to have been composed earlier, such as 'The Lament for Sir James Cotter' and 'Father Nicholas Sheehy: A Lament Composed by His Sister'. Similarly, for years after her own death, long passages of her lament for her husband were quoted, often by women whose own business it was to keen over the dead. The two longest versions which survive were written down many years apart, from the dictation of Nóra Ní Shíndile (Norrie Singleton), who lived near Millstreet, County Cork, close to where Art Ó Laoghaire died in 1773. She was known as a keening woman (*bean chaointe*) and died about 1870 at a great age.

Ó Tuama's edition (source of almost all the translations found in anthologies) is based largely on the earlier of these, with interpolations from other texts.

The first text given here is that of Ní Shíndile's later version, from University College Dublin Library, Special Collections, Ferriter MS, no. 1, pp. 298–305. It was written in Tralee, County Kerry, in 1894 by Pádraig Feirtéar (Patrick Ferriter), who transcribed it from a manuscript borrowed from his fellow Land League member Domhnall Mac Cába (Daniel McCabe) (1818–1903), of Banteer, County Cork. Mac Cába had written down the lament many years previously from the recital of Nóra Ní Shíndile, and Pádraig Feirtéar appended to it a number of lines which he had heard from his own kinswoman, Mairéad Ní Fhionnagáin (Margaret Finnegan), in Baile an Chalaidh, near Ballyferriter, County Kerry, on 28 September 1893. This second text is also given below.

Pádraig Feirtéar was born in An Baile Uachtarach, near Ballyferriter, in 1856, and was lame from childhood. He was a strong supporter of Charles Stewart Parnell, and his Land League activities, directed against local landowner Lord Ventry, led to his rejection for a position as relieving officer in Dingle, to four terms of imprisonment totalling two years, and to his family's eviction from their smallholding in 1887. He kept a small shop in Dingle from 1887, and began to collect folklore throughout County Kerry and to borrow manuscripts and make copies of them. In 1896 he emigrated to the United States. He lived first in Chelsea, Massachusetts, near Boston, later moving to New York, where he lived in poor circumstances but continued to read, to contribute to Irish periodicals, and to acquire and copy Irish manuscripts. On his death in 1924, he bequeathed his valuable manuscript collection to University College Dublin, in recognition of the National University's adoption of Irish as a matriculation requirement. MS no. 1, which includes this text, is the largest of the manuscripts. Translation and headnote, A.B.]

Tórramh-Chaoineadh Airt Uí Laoghaire

Mo chara go daingean tú!
Do thug mo shúil aire duit,
Do thug mo chroí taitneamh duit
Agus d'éalaíos óm charaid leat.
Is domsa nárbh aithreach:
Do chuiris párlús dá ghealadh dhom,
Seomraí dá nglanadh dhom,
Bácús dá dheargadh dhom,
Bríc dá ceapadh dhom,
Róst dá bhreacadh dhom,

---

1. Eibhlín's and Art's names are anglicized as Eileen O'Connell and Art O'Leary respectively.

Riaradh is glacadh dom,
Boird dá leathadh dhom,
Fíon dá tharraingt dhom,
Mairt dá leagadh dhom,
Muca dá bhfeadadh dhom,
Mná fuinneach reannta dhom,[2]
Mná glactha leastar dhom,
Codladh i gclúmh lachan dom,
Go dtíodh an t-eadartha,
Nó thairis dá dtaitneadh liom.
Cé gurb é a leathadh ort,
Má bhíteá ceachartha,
Ní bhíteá ach tamall beag.
Ba mise faoi ndeara san:
Tá fhios ag an Athairmhac
Go mb'fhiú fear t-ainme
Súd do mhaitheamh duit,
A mharcaigh an mhallroisc.[3]

Mo chara go daingean tú,
Is breá thíodh hata duit,
Faoi bhanda d'ór tharraingthe,
Agus claidheamh cinn airgid.
Coiscéim bhalarach[4]
Ag each caol ceannann fút,
D'umhlaídís Sasanaigh
Síos go talamh duit,
Agus ní ar mhaithe leat
Ach le haonchorp eagla,
Cé gur leo a cailleadh tú.

A mharcaigh na mbánghlac,
Is breá thíodh ráib duit,
'S holón faoi cháimbric
Is hata faoi lása.
Tar éis teacht thar sáile,
Ghlantaí an tsráid dhuit,
Is ní le grá duit
Ach le haonchorp gráine ort.

Mo chara tú go daingean,
Agus nuair a thiocfaidh chughamsa abhaile
Conchubhar beag an cheana
Agus Fear Ó Laoghaire an leanbh,

Fiafróid díom go tapaidh
Cár fhágas féin a n-athair.
Inneosad dóibh faoi mhairg
Gur fhágas i gCill na Martar.
Glaofaidh siad ar a n-athair
Agus ní bheidh sé acu le freagairt.

Mo chara agus mo ghamhain tú,
Gaol Iarla Antraim
Is Barraigh ón amhchoill,
Is breá thíodh lann duit,
Hata faoi bhanda,
Bróg chaol ghallda,
Is culaith den abhras
A rinntí thall duit.

Mo chara go daingean,
Agus níor chreideas riamh do mharbh
Gur tháinig chugham do chapall,
Agus fuil do chroí ar a leacain,
Siar go diallait ghreanta
Mar a mbíteá id' shuí agus id' sheasamh.
Thugas léim go tairsigh;
An tarna léim go geata;
Agus an tríú léim ar mo chapall.
Do liús agus do screadas;
Do bhuaileas go luath mo bhasa;
Do bhaineas as na reathaibh
Chomh maith agus do bhí sé agam,
Go bhfuaireas romham tú marbh
Mar bheadh bó nó capall,
Faoi thár thoirín aitinn,
Gan pápa gan easpag,
Gan cléireach gan sagart,
A léifeadh ort an tsailm,
Ach seanbhean chríonna chaite
A leath ort binn dá fallaing.

Mo ghrá tú go daingean,
Is éirigh suas id' sheasamh
Agus tar liom féin abhaile
Go gcuirfimid mart dá leagadh,
Go gcuirfimid róst dá bhreacadh,
Go gcuirfimid trianta dá leathadh,
Go nglaofam ar chóisir fhairsing,
Go mbeidh againn ceol dá spreagadh,
Go gcóireód fút leaba
Faoi bhratachaibh líonda geala
Agus faoi chuilteanna breátha breaca
A bhainfidh asat allas
In ionad an fhuachta 'ghlacais.

<hr />

2. Cf. *An Gaodhal: mná fuintes rannta dom* (Ó Tuama, *Caoineadh Airt Uí Laoghaire*, p. 55).
3. These lines about Art's anger are repeated below, after *mná ceannaithe*. Ó Tuama notes this repetition (pp. 66–7), but prefers the reading given by Feirtéar, scribe of this MS, in his edition published in *An Gaodhal* (June–August 1899), which completely omits the lines.
4. Read *bhollaireach*, 'boastful'?

Deirfiúr Airt:
Mo chara agus mo stór tú
Agus níl ainnir bhreá chórach
Ó Chorcaigh na seolta
Go droichead na dTóime,
'Ga mbeadh a cuid airgid cnósta
Agus a macha breá bó aici,
A raghadh a chodladh ina seomra
Oíche do thórraimh,
A mharcaigh na n-órfholt.

Eibhlín Dubh:
Mo chara agus m'uan tú,
Agus ná creidse siúd uathu,
Ná an cogar a fuairis,
Ná an scéal fir fuatha,
Gur a chodladh do chuas-sa.
— Níor throm suan dom
Ach do bhí do linbh róbhuartha
Agus do theastaigh sé uathu
Iad do chur chun suaimhnis.
Agus nár léige Dia suas
An bhean thug fúm tuairim,
Agus í thabhairt ar tuathal.

A dhaoine na n-ae istigh,
A' bhfuil aon bhean in Éirinn
Ó luí na gréine
A shínfeadh a taobh leis,
Do bhéarfadh trí lao dó,
Ná raghadh le craobhachaibh,
Ach mé féinig,
I ndiaidh Airt Uí Laoghaire,
Atá anso traochta
Ó mhaidin inné agam?

Órrú a *Mhorrison* léan ort!
Fuil do chroí agus t'ae leat!
Do shúile caochta,
Do ghlúine réabtha,
Do mhairbh mo laosa,
Agus gan aon fhear in Éirinn
Do ghreadfadh na piléir leat!

Mo chara tú agus mo shearc,
Is éirigh suas a Airt!
Léimse in airde ar t'each,
Éirigh go Maigh Chromtha isteach,
Is go hInse Geimhleach tar n-ais,
Buidéal fíona id' ghlaic,

Is buidéal eile ag teacht,
Cur ribíní i gcúl na mban,
Mar a mbíodh i *room* do Dhaid.

M'fhadachreach léirghoirt
Ná rabhas-sa taobh leat
Nuair a lámhachadh an piléar leat!
Go ngeobhainn é im thaobh deas,
Nó i mbinn mo léine,
Go léigfinn cead sléibhe leat,
A mharcaigh na réghlac.

Mo chreach ghéarchúiseach
Ná rabhas-sa ar do chúlaibh
An uair lámhachadh an púdar!
Go ngeobhainn é im chom deas,
Nó i mbinn mo ghúna,
Go léigfinn cead siúil leat,
A mharcaigh na súl nglas
Mar is tú b'fhearr léigean chucu.

Mo chara thú agus mo shearcmhaoin,
Agus is gránna an chóir ag cur ar ghaiscíoch:
Comhra agus caipín,
Ar mharcach an deachroí,
Bhíodh ag iascaireacht ar ghlaisíbh
Agus ag ól ar hallaíbh
Farradh mná na ngealgcíoch,
Agus mo mhíle mearaí
Mar do chailleas do thaithí!

Greadadh chughat is díth,
A *Mhorrison* ghránna an fhill
A bhain díom fear mo thí,
Athair mo chlainne gan aois,
Dís acu ag siúl an tí
Agus an tríú duine istigh im chlí,
Agus is dócha ná cuirfead díom.

Mo chara tú is mo thaitneamh,
An uair a ghabhais amach an geata,
D'fhillis tar ais go tapaidh.
Do phógais do dhís leanbh,
Do phógais mise ar bharra baise
Dúrais "Eibhlín, éirigh id' sheasamh,
Is cuir do ghnó chun taisce
Go luaimneach is go tapaidh.
Táimse ag fágáil an bhaile;
Ní móide go deo go gcasfainn.'
Níor rinneas dá chaint ach magadh
Mar bhíodh dá rá liom go minic cheana.

Mo chara tú agus mo chuid,
A mharcaigh an chliatháin ghil,
Éirigh suas anois
Is cuir ort do chulaith
Éadaigh uasail ghlain:
Cuir ort do bhéabhar dubh,
Taraing do lámhainní iomat.
Siúd í in airde t'fhuip,
Sin í do láir amuigh,
Buailse an bóthar caol sin soir,
Mar a maoileoidh romhat na toir
Mar a gcaolóidh romhat an tsruith
Agus mar a n-umhlóidh duit mná agus fir,
Má tá a mbéasa féin acu,
Agus is baolach liomsa nach bhfuil⁵ anois.

Mo chara tú agus mo chumann,
Agus ní hé a bhfuair bás dem chine,
Ná bás mo thriar clainne,
Ná Dhomhnaill Mhóir Uí Chonaill,
Ná Chonaill a báthadh sa tuile,
Ná bean na bliana is fiche
A chuaigh anonn tar uisce
Déanamh cairdeasaí Críost le rithibh
— Ní hiad go léir atá agam dá ngairm,
Ach Art do bhaint aréir dá bhonnaibh:
Marcach na lárach doinne
Atá agam féin anso go singil
Ar Inse Charraig an Ime.
Nár mhaire sí a hainm ná a sloinne,
Mar nár rinneadar mná beaga riabhacha an
    Mhuilinn sileadh
Go bhfacadar mise
Ar buile, a ghrá na muirne!

Mo chara agus mo lao tú,
A Airt Uí Laoghaire
Mhic Conchubhair mhic Céadaigh
Mhic Laoisigh Uí Laoghaire
Aniar ón nGaortha
Agus anoir ón gCaelchnoc,
Mar a bhfásann caora
Agus cnó buí ar ghéagaibh,
Úlla 'na slaodaibh
'Na n-am féinig.
Cárbh ionadh liom féinig
Dá lasfadh Uíbh Laoghaire
Agus Béal Átha an Ghaorthaidh
Agus an Guagán naofa

I ndiaidh mharcaigh na réghlac
Níodh an fiach do thraochadh
Ón nGreanaigh ar saothar
Nuair stadaidís caolchoin
Is marcaigh na gclaonrosg?
Nó cad 'imigh aréir ort?
Óir do shíleas féinig
Ná maródh an saol tú
An uair cheannaíos duit éide.

Mo chara tú agus mo ghrá,
Gaol mhághshlua an stáit
Na mbíodh hocht mbanaltrana déag ar aon
    chlár
Go bhfaighidís go léir a bpá:
Loilíoch agus láir,
Cráin agus a hál,
Muileann ar áth,
Ór buí agus airgead bán,
Síoda is *velvet* bhreá,
Píosa talaimh is stáit,⁶
Go nídís cíocha thál,
Ar lao na mascalach mbán.

Mo ghrá is mo rún tú,⁷
Is mo ghrá mo cholúr geal,
Cé ná tángas-sa chughatsa
Is nár thugas mo thrúip liom,
Ba chúis náire súd liom
Mar bhíodar i gcúngrach
I seomraí dúnta
Agus i gcónraí cunga
Agus i gcodladh gan mhuscailt.

Mura mbeadh an bholgach
Agus an bás dorcha
Agus an fiabhras spotaitheach
Agus gach ní eile a ghortaigh mé,
Bheadh an mághshlua bhrollaigh ghil
Agus a srianta á gcroitheadh acu
Ag déanamh fothraim
Ag teacht id shochraid
A Airt an bhrollaigh ghil.

Mo ghrá tú go daingean
A ghaoil an mhághshlua ghairbh,
A bhíodh ag lorg an ghleanna
Mar a mbaintí astu casadh

---

6. Cf Ó Tuama 41: 'píosa talamh eastáit'.
7. These lines are usually attributed to Art's sister.

5. MS has *nách bh-fuil*, perhaps pron. *ná fuil*.

Dá mbreith isteach don halla,
Mar a mbíodh péatar ag scréachaigh fá
    sceanaibh,
Muiceoil nach ndiúlaidís na bainbh,
Caoireoil nach gcomhaireofaí a heasna,
Coirce craorag ramhar
A bhainfeadh sraoth as eachaibh.
Capaill ghruagacha
Is buachaillí na n-aice,
Is dá bhfanfaidís siúd seachtain,
Ná bainfí díol ina leaba
Ná as fásach a gcapall,
A dheartháir lár na gcarad.

Mo chara agus mo lao tú
Is aisling trí néaltaibh
A rinneadh aréir dhom
I gCorcaigh go déanach
I leaba im aonar
Gur thit an chúirt aolda
Gur chríon an Gaortha
Agus nár fhan friotal id chaolchoin
Ná binneas ag éanaibh,
Nuair a fuaradh tú traochta
Ar bholg an tsléibhe amuigh,
Gan sagart gan cléireach
Ach seanbhean aosta
Do leath binn dá bréid ort,
Nuair a fuadh den chré tú,
A Airt Uí Laoghaire,
Agus do chuid fola ina slaodaibh
I mbrollach do léine.

Mo ghrá agus mo rún tú
Agus is breá thíodh súd duit:
Stoca chúig dhual duit,
Buatais go glúin duit,
Caroline cúinneach,
Is *whip* go lúfar
Ar ghillín tsúgach.
Is mó ainnir mhodhúil mhúinte
Bhíodh ag féachaint sa chúl ort.

Mo ghrá go daingean tú,
Agus nuair théiteá sna cathracha
Daora daingeana,
Bhíodh mná ceannaithe
Ag umhlú go talamh duit,
Óir do thuigidís ina n-aigne
Gur bhreá an leath leapa tú
Nó béalóg chapaill tú

Nó athair leanbh tú,
Go dtíodh an fhearg ort,
Agus í go hannamh ort,
Is ba mise fá ndeara san.
Tá 'fhios ag an Athairmhac
Go mb'fhiú fear t'ainme
Súd do mhaitheamh duit
A mhuirnín m'anama.

Tá fhios ag Íosa Críost
Nách mbeidh caidhp ar bhaitheas mo chinn
Ná léine chnis lem thaoibh
Ná bróg ar thrácht mo bhoinn
Ná trioscán ar fuaid mo thí
Ná srian leis an láir ndoinn
Ná go gcaithfead féin le dlí,
Is go rachad anonn tar toinn
Ag comhrá leis an rí,
Is mura gcuirfidh ionam aon tsuim,
Go dtiocfad tar n-ais arís
Go bodach na fola duibhe
A bhain díom féin mo mhaoin.

A mhná so amach ag gol,
Stadaí ar bhúr gcois.
Tá an tigh tábhairne anso,
Go nglaofaidh Art mac Conchubhair deoch,
Go ndíolfaidh sé aisti scot,
Agus go dté sé isteach don scoil
    — Agus ní ag foghlaim léinn ná port
Ach ag iompar cré agus cloch
I dtuama daingean docht,
Go Mainistir na gCor.

Cion an chroí seo agamsa
Ar mhnáibh beaga riabhacha an Mhuilinn
I dtaobh a fheabhas a níd siad sileadh
I ndiaidh mharcaigh na lárach doinne
Atá agam féin anso go singil
Ar Ínse Charraig an Ime!

Greadadh croí crua ort
A Sheáin Mhac Uaithne!
Más breab a bhí uaitse,
Nár tháinig fám' thuairim
Is go dtabharfainn duit mórchuid:
Capaill ghruagacha
A dhéanfadh tú a fhuadach trísna sluaitibh
An lá ba chrua dhuit;
Nó macha breá buaibh duit,
Nó caoire ag breith uan duit,

Nó talamh chun tuaire,
Nó culaith le m'uan geal
Do shíneadh suas liom,
Gidh gur mhór an trua liom
Í do bheith thuas ort,
Mar cloisim dá luachaint
Gur boidichín fuail tú,
Fé mar ba dhual duit.

A mharcaigh na mbánghlac,
Ó leagadh do lámh leat,
Éirigh go dtí Baldwin,
An spreallairín gránna,
An fear caol crágach,
Is bain de sásamh
In ionad do lárach
Is úsáid do ghrá geal.
Gan an seisear mar bhláth air,
Gan olc do Mháire,
Agus ní le grá di,
Ach mar do rinne mo bhanaltra tál uirthi.

D'éis an tsaoil, a Mháire
Molaim go deo tú.
Molaim go brách tú.
Rug leat Baldwin,
Marcaigh na mbánghlac,
Is ní le gráin ort,
Ach le lánchorp grá dhuit,
Is giorracht do chairde orm,
Ó inniu go dtí amáireach.

Mo chara tú is mo chumann,
A Mháire mhaith Ní Duibh,
Is dá fheabhas atá do thigh
Is dá fheabhas atánn tú ann,
Ní rabhas le dhá bhliain déag id thigh.
Ní raibh aon ghnó agam ann.
Do bhí ordú agam féin ar mo thigh:
Scagadh do chur ar an mil,
Leamhnacht do chur ar an bpeic,
Agus an tsaill ar an mbior.
Rachadsa siar anois
Má tá aon ghnó agam ann,
Agus is baolach liomsa nach bhfuil anois.

Mar bharr ar mo mhairg,
Mo leanbh do dhul tar caise,
Baint a aráin as an Laidin,
Gidh gur beag a saoileadh dó tamall,
Ná go mbeadh cumhacht aige ar bhailtibh,

Agus ceann síos ar Ghallaibh,
Mar a mbíodh ag a athair.

Mo chara tú go daingean
A ghaoil Uí Laoghaire do b'fhearra
Is Airt ó Ghuagán Barra
Is Thaidhg mheirgigh na scaball,
Agus an ghaiscígh ghléigil cheannais
Bhíodh agam féin i gceangal,
Fuarthas uaim in aisce
In imeall sléibhe gan sagart. Críoch.

Críochnaithe agamsa Patric Feirtéar, i dTrá Lí,
Dé Domhnaigh an chéad lá de Aibreán 1894, as
macleabhar a fuaireas i bhfaradh a leabhar ó
Dhónall mhic Cáib a scríobh síos an caoineadh
seo ó bhéalrá Nóra Ní Shíndile ón mBuaile Mór.

Do bhí Art ó Laoghaire in arm Austria, agus
air thairiscint chúig bpúnt na diandlí dó ar a
chapall, do lámhach sé Morris, Sasanach ó
Chorcaigh, trér fógraíodh Art, agus do lámhach
saighdiúirí a bhí i bpóna Charraig an Ime é. Do
chónaigh sé ag Ráth Luigheach óna bhfuil
Carraig an Ime sé mhíle ó thuaidh agus sé mhíle
aduaidh ó Shráid an Mhuilinn.

Ag so cuid den gcaoineadh nach raibh scríofa
ag Dónall mhic Cáib agus a fuaireas óm bhean
ghaoil Máraed Ní Fhionnagáin i mBaile an
Chalaidh, taobh thiar de Dhaingean Uí Chúise,
an 28.9.1893.

Deirfiúr Airt:
Mo thaisce agus m'uan tú,
Agus is mó bean óg uasal
As so go Ruachtach,
Agus go Corcaigh na gcuanta,
A thabharfadh macha fá bhuaibh duit,
Caoire geala ag breith uan duit,
Is ór ina chruachaibh,
Agus ná raghadh a chodladh uaitse.

Eibhlín Dubh:
A Chonchubhair Uí Laoghaire a ghrá,
Is fiú tusa urraim d'fháil
Bhíodh chúig bhanartlacha déag ar aon chlár,
[Go bhfaighidís go léir a bpá:
Loilíoch agus láir,
Cráin agus a hál,
Muileann ar áth,
Ór buí agus airgead bán,
Síoda is *velvet* bhreá

Píosa talaimh is stáit,][8]
D'fhonn na gcíní thál
Ar lao na mbachall mbán
Atá agam anocht fé chlár
— A dhein mo chroí do chrá
Agus a chuir mé féin chun fáin.

Mo ghrá tú agus mo dhalta,
Agus éirigh suas id sheasamh,
Agus téanam féin abhaile
Go cistin mhór na dtreanadh,
Go párlúistí na n-aiteas,
Agus go gairdíní na bhfearann,
Mar a bhfuil úlla cumhra ar chrannaibh
Agus cnó buí le cnagadh
Agus ceol binn ag meachaibh
Ag éirí amach ar maidin
Ar chuileann mhaol gan dealg.

Léan agus ár ort,
A mhac mic Bhaldwin
An fear caol gágach
Do gheobhfá ní b'fhearr é
Ach le taitneamh do Mháire
A thug leaba ina lár duit
Ar feadh trí ráithe
Agus mise a bhí láimh léi. (Cúpla í féin agus
   Máire)

8. MS refers readers to these lines *supra* ('mar tá ar bhun leathanaigh
   301').

The Funeral Lament for Art Ó Laoghaire

Dear firm friend,
My eye took note of you,
My heart took joy from you,
I escaped from my kin with you,
Without regret.
You had a parlour whitewashed and
Bedrooms cleaned for me,
An oven heated for me;
Bread was made for me,
And meat was roasted.
Managing your household,[1]
I had tables spread for me,
Wine drawn for me,
Beef slaughtered for me,

1. Literally 'Distributing and accepting were my [responsibility]'.

Pigs butchered for me,
Women to knead for me,
Women to pour for me,[2]
I could sleep in duckdown
Until midmorning,
Or later if I wanted to.
Although it was said of you
That you were stingy
It was only sometimes,
And I was to blame,
For the Son of God knows
That a man of your nature
Can be excused that much,
Dear soft-eyed horseman.

Dear firm friend,
You looked well in a hat
With a band of gold around it;
A silver-hilted sword
And the proud high step
Of your white-blazed horse.
The English would bow
Down to the ground to you,
Not out of love for you
But because of their fear of you,
And yet through them you died.

Dear white-handed horseman,
Who so beautifully galloped,
Dressed in Holland and cambric,
With a lace-trimmed hat;
When you came from abroad
They used to clear the street for you,
— Not that they loved you,
— They hated your guts.

My dear firm friend,
When the children come home:
Sweet little Conor
And baby Farr Ó Laoghaire,
They'll ask me straight away
Where I've left their father, and
I'll have to tell them sadly
That he's in Killnamartyr.
They'll be calling for their daddy,
But he won't be there to answer.

Dear friend and beloved,
Kin to Earls of Antrim

2. Literally 'Women to accept vessels from me'.

And to Barrys from the wild woods,
You looked well with a sword
And a hat with a band;
Narrow continental shoes
And a suit of fine yarn
That was spun for you abroad.

Dear firm friend,
I didn't credit your death
Till your mare came back, streaked
With your heart's blood, from her cheek
To your tooled leather saddle,
Where you rode astride and standing.
I took one leap to the doorstep,
A second to the gate
And the third up on her back.
I yelled and I screamed,
And beat my hands together,
And pressed the mare to gallop
As fast as she could travel,
Till I found you, lying dead,
Like a cow or a horse,
Beneath a clump of furze
With no pope or bishop,
No clerk, no priest
Who could read a psalm above you;
Just a weary old woman
Who had spread her cloak across you.

Dear love indeed,
Now rise up on your feet
And come back home with me,
And let us slaughter beef
And roast a joint of meat
And spread a great feast
For a retinue of guests.
We'll have musicians play,
And I'll make you a bed
With white linen sheets
And fine patchwork quilts
That will make you sweat with heat
Instead of this awful cold.

Art's sister:
Dear friend and treasure,
There's not a single fine young woman
From Cork with its sails,
To the bridge at Toome,
With her dowry-money gathered
And her fine field of cows,
Who'd sleep in her bedroom

On the night of your wake,
Dear golden-haired horseman.

Dark-haired Eileen:
Dear friend and dear lamb,
Now don't believe them:
The things they whisper;
Their gossip so malicious,
That I went to lie down.
— I wasn't sleepy at all,
But your children were upset
And they needed me with them
To put them to sleep.
And may God not forgive
That woman who judged me,
But set her astray.

Dear friends all,
What woman in Ireland
From the time the sun sets,
If she had shared her bed with him
And borne him three children,
Would not go crazy,
Apart from me,
With grief for Art Ó Laoghaire
Who is laid out here
Since early yesterday?

Oh Morrison,[3] may you suffer
— Bleed from heart and from liver!
May your eyes be blinded,
And your kneecaps shattered,
For you killed my darling
And there's no man in Ireland
To fire the shot at you.

Dear friend and loved one,
Rise up, Art.
Jump on your horse's back
And ride into Macroom
And over to Inchigeela;
A bottle of wine in your hand;
And another coming back;
Tying ribbons in women's hair,
As you did in your father's room.

---

3. Abraham Morris was a near neighbour and opponent of Ó Laoghaire,
a former high sheriff, and a prominent supporter of the anti-
Catholic political interest. This MS, however, gives his name as
Morrison. See L.M. Cullen, 'Contemporary and Later Politics',
pp. 15 ff.

It's my bitter, lasting sorrow
That I wasn't beside you
When the shot was fired,
To catch it in my right side, or
In the skirt of my shift,
And let you ride free,
Dear even-handed horseman.

It's my keenly-felt sorrow
That I wasn't riding pillion
When the powder was fired.
I'd have caught it in my waist,
Or in the skirt of my gown,
And let you go safe,
Dear grey-eyed horseman:
Only you could take them on.

Dear friend and treasure-love,
It's a poor show for a hero,
To lie white-capped, in his coffin
— This good-hearted horseman
Who used to fish the streams,
And drink in the halls
With the white-breasted woman —
And my thousand distractions,
I'm bereft of your company!

Bad cess to you, and lack,
Ugly treacherous Morrison!
You took my husband,
My babies' father:
Two toddlers in the house,
And the third still in my body,
Will hardly go full term.

Dear friend and delight,
When you went out the gate
You turned and came back;
You kissed your two children;
You blew a kiss to me;
Said, 'Eileen, stand up,
And order your affairs;
Be efficient and quick,
For I'm leaving the house,
And I probably won't be back.'
I took it for a joke,
Like so many times before.

Dear friend and loved-one,
Fair-bodied horseman,
Rise up now
And put on your suit

Of clean noble clothing:
Take your black beaver hat;
Pull on your gloves;
Your whip's hung up there
And your mare's at the door.
Take the narrow road east, where
The bushes will bend for you,
The stream grow narrow for you,[4]
Men and women will bow to you,
If they have any manners,
Though I fear now they've none.

Dear friend and lover,
It's not my dead kinsfolk,
Or my three lost babies,
Or Big Dan O'Connell,
Or Conall who drowned,
Or the girl of twenty-one
Who went over the sea,
To find an Empress as godmother —[5]
They're not the ones I grieve,
But Art, felled last night;
The brown mare's horseman,
Who lies here so sadly
On the grass of Carriganimmy.
— May it have no luck, since
The freckled little mill-women
Never wept, till they saw me
Distraught, my darling!

Dear friend and pet,
Dear Art Ó Laoghaire,
— Son of Conor, son of Céadach
Son of Laoiseach O'Leary,
From the Geeragh in the west
And the steep hills in the east,
Where the berries grow,
And the nuts on the branches,
And apples in clusters,
In their proper season —
It would not surprise me
If Iveleary blazed up,
Likewise Ballingeary,
And holy Gougane Barra

---

4. At the bottom of the MS page, Ferriter notes that a stream in Ventry, County Kerry, near his own home, was said to grow narrow when anyone of noble blood attempted to cross.

5. Eibhlin's sister 'Gobinette' (Ir. Gobnait, usually rendered as Abigail) married an officer in the service of the Empress Maria Theresa, later godmother to her first child. See Mrs M.J. O'Connell, *The Last Colonel of the Irish Brigade*, vol. I, p. 102, and cf. S. Ó Tuama, *Caoineadh Airt Uí Laoghaire* (Dublin: An Clóchomhar, 1983), p. 91.

To mourn the even-handed horseman
Who could wear out the hunt
All the way from Grenagh
When the sleek hounds gave up,
And the horsemen lowered their eyes.
But last night, what happened?
For I always thought
That nothing could kill you
When I bought clothes for you.

My dear friend and lover,
Kin to the country's greatest,
Eighteen wet-nurses
Were paid at one time:
Paid a milch cow, a mare,
And a sow with her litter,
A mill by a ford,
Yellow gold and white silver,
Silk and fine velvet,
A landed estate
Just for feeding from their breasts
The strong fair women's pet.

Dearly beloved,[6]
Dear white turtle-dove,
Though I didn't come to you,
And didn't bring a troop to you,
To my great shame, it was
Because they were lying
In darkened rooms,
And in narrow coffins
And asleep beyond rousing.

Were it not for the smallpox,
The black death,
The spotted fever,
And all my other hurts,
Those white-breasted riders
Would be tossing their reins,
Setting up a commotion
On their way to your funeral,
Dear white-breasted Art.

Dear steadfastly-loved one,
Kin to the rough horsemen
Who hunted the valley,
Where you turned them around, and
Brought them home to the hall,
Where knives scraped on pewter,
With pork from virgin pigs,

Endless racks of lamb,
And plump ripe oats
That would make horses sneeze.
There were heavy-maned horses
With boys to groom them, but
If they stayed a whole week,
They never paid for their beds
Or for foddering their horses,
Dearest brother of all.

Dear friend and pet,
A dream in my sleep
Came before me last night
In Cork, very late,
As I lay in my bed:
That our whitewashed home crumbled,
That the Geeragh had withered,
That your sleek hounds were silenced
And birds stopped their singing,
When you were discovered
On the slope of that hill,
With no priest or cleric,
Just a feeble old woman
Who spread her cloak over you
When you bit the dust,
Art Ó Laoghaire,
With your blood soaking out
Through the front of your shirt.

Dearly beloved,
How well you looked:
In a five-pleated stock,
With boots to the knee, and
A Caroline hat;
Your whip at the ready
To keep tipsy lads steady.
Many a well-bred maiden
Followed you with her eyes.

Dear steadily-loved one,
When you went to town,
To expensive, proud places,
The wives of the merchants
Would bow to the ground,
For they knew in their hearts
You were great as a lover,[7]

6. The lines which follow are usually attributed to Art's sister.

7. Cf Mrs M.J. O'Connell, *The Last Colonel of the Irish Brigade*, vol. I, p. 245, where O'Connell, apparently unaware of the frankness of the original, adds the following note: "'The merchants' wives would show you great respect." (This verse is defaced. I suppose she must have described his buying costly goods and and bringing them to her.)'

As a foreman[8] on horseback,
As a father of children,
Until something angered you,
Which wasn't so often,
And I was to blame,
For the Son of God knows
That a man of your nature
Can be excused that much,
Dear heart of my soul.

Jesus Christ is my witness,
I'll have no cap on my head,
No shift next my skin,
No shoe on my foot,
No goods in my house,
No rein on the brown mare,
That I won't spend at law,
But I'll cross the sea
To interview the King, and
If he won't hear my case,
Then I'll come back here,
To that black-blooded ruffian
Who murdered my dear.

Dear women out there weeping,
Hold on a moment here,
Outside the tavern.
Con's son Art will call a drink
And pay for it himself,
Then he'll go into the school,
— Not for learning or music —
But to hold up the stony clay
Of a tightly closed grave
In the crooked-walled abbey.[9]

My heart's affection
To the freckled little mill-women,
Whose weeping was excellent
For the brown mare's horseman
Who lies so sadly here
On the grass of Carriganimmy.[10]

My heart's hard curse on you,
Sean Mac Uaithne[11]

If a bribe was what you wanted,
You could have asked me!
I'd have given you the lot:
The heavy-maned horses
To carry you safely
Through crowds of people
When you had to get out;
Or a fine field of cows,
Or ewes all in lamb,
Or a green to bleach linen,
Or a suit of my darling's
Who used to lie down with me,
However much it pained me
To see you wear it,
For I hear it said, you're
A wretched specimen,
Which is what I'd expect.

Dear white-handed horseman,
Now your arm has been stilled,
Rise up against Baldwin,[12]
That ugly-looking misery,
That skinny, grasping man,
And get satisfaction
For the loss of your mare and
The way he treated me, and
May his six be no joy to him,
— No harm to Máire —
And that's not for love of her,
But the same woman suckled us.

Still and all, Máire,[13]
I praise you for good, and
I praise you forever,
Take Baldwin away,
And the white-handed horsemen,
It's not that I hate you,
I have wholehearted love for you,

---

denunciation of the man believed to have betrayed Art Ó Laoghaire for a reward.

12. Husband of Eibhlín's twin sister Máire, James Baldwin was a Protestant who was said to have co-operated with the authorities after Art's death to the extent of handing over the dead man's valuable mare. The 'six' referred to below seem to be their children. Cf. reference to 'Thug Me Grá Duit is Mé Beag Bídeach' in the introduction to 'The Song Tradition', p. 1315, where a woman curses her unfaithful lover, wishing him 'six blind children without a mother'.

13. S. Ó Tuama, *Caoineadh Airt Uí Laoghaire*, pp. 86–7, gives the rest of this text as his 'Aguisín III' (Appendix III: 'Extra verses composed by Eibhlín Dubh Ní Chonaill'). These verses occur as an appendix to version A1'). The present text is his A1, however nothing in the MS gives these lines the status of 'Appendix'. By contrast, the text from Mairéad Ní Fhionnagáin, given here and referred to by Ó Tuama (p. 47), is clearly appended.

8. Ibid., p. 34. The 'foreman' was the horseman behind whom a woman rode pillion.

9. See S. Ó Tuama, *Caoineadh Airt Uí Laoghaire*, p. 70, i.e. Kilcrea Abbey, 'from the numerous corners and windings of its walls'.

10. Lament-poetry was designed to be remembered and repeated. It therefore often includes corrections of the record, as here, where Eibhlín apparently regrets her earlier scathing comment about the women of the mill.

11. Formulaic lines about plenty are here turned into a withering

For our close connection
Both today and tomorrow.

Dear friend and companion,
Good Máire Ní Duibh,[14]
Though your house is so fine,
And you run it so well,
It's twelve years since I've stood in it,
For I had no business there.
I had my own house to manage:
With honey to strain,
And milk to skim,
And bacon to hang,
But I'll go over now,
If I have any business there,
Though I fear that I've none.

As if that were not enough,
My child will go abroad
To earn his bread with Latin.
Though once it was imagined
He would rule over towns
Where the English knew their place,
When his father was there.

Dear firm friend,
Kin of noblest Ó Laoghaire,
Of Art from Gougane Barra,
Of cranky Tadhg of the breastplates,
Of the shining, leading hero,
Who was married to me,
Till his fate overtook him,
On a hillside, with no priest.

Finished by me, Patrick Ferriter, in Tralee,
Sunday the first day of April, 1894, from a copy
I obtained along with his books from Daniel
McCabe, who transcribed this lament from the
recital of Nora Singleton, An Buaile Mór.
Art Ó Laoghaire was in the Austrian army, and
when offered his penal-law entitlement of £5 for
his horse, he shot Morris, an Englishman from
Cork, for which act he was proclaimed, and later
shot by soldiers from the Carriganimmy pound.[15]
He lived at Raleigh, six miles south of

Carriganimmy, and six miles north of Millstreet
[County Cork].
Here is part of the Lament, not written down
by Daniel McCabe, but which I obtained from
my own kinswoman Margaret Finnegan, in Baile
an Chalaidh, west of Dingle [County Kerry], on
28.9.1893.

Art's Sister:
Dear treasure and lamb,
Many a noble young woman,
From here to Ruachtach
And to Cork of the harbours,
Would have brought you fine cows,
Ewes in lamb,
Gold in heaps,
And would not have gone to sleep.

Dark-haired Eileen:
Darling [son of] Con Ó Laoghaire
You well deserve respect
Fifteen wet-nurses
[Were paid at one time:
Paid a milch cow, a mare,
And a sow with her litter,
A mill by a ford,
Yellow gold and white silver,
Silk and fine velvet,
A landed estate][16]
Just for feeding their breast-milk
To the curly-headed pet, who's
Here tonight, in his coffin,
Leaving my heart tormented and
My mind set astray.

Dear love and darling,
Come rise up and stand,
And let us go home
To our kitchen full of food,
To our parlours full of comfort,
To our landed gardens,
Where the trees bear sweet apples
And nuts ripe for knocking,
And the bees hum melodious,
Going out in the morning
To the gentle thornless holly.

---

14. Mother of Eibhlin Dubh, mistress of a large household and a well-known oral poet in her own right.
15. Ferriter here repeats the commonly held belief that Art Ó Laoghaire's death was the result of a quarrel over the insultingly low price offered for his horse by a Protestant, under the terms of the Penal Law of 1695. See L.M. Cullen, 'Contemporary and Later

Politics of Caoineadh Airt Uí Laoghaire', for a discussion of the complex political issues underlying this tradition. Cullen makes clear (p. 24) that Ó Laoghaire was, in fact, never technically an outlaw; this was, however, the common perception.
16. The MS refers to these lines in the main text (above, p. 1381).

Affliction and agony
On you, Baldwin's grandson!
You skinny-legged misery
—You'd get more of the same
But for love of Máire

Who bore you in her body
For three times three months
And that I assisted her.[17]

17. The MS adds a note: 'She [i.e. Eibhlín] and Máire were twins.'

MOTHER OF DIARMAID MAC CÁRTHAIGH

(fl. c. 1850)

from:
ÉIGSE (1939)

[Three versions of this lament were published in the first volume of *Éigse: A Journal of Irish Studies*, in spring, summer and autumn 1939. All had recently been taken down from oral recital in west Cork and east Kerry. The lament was once well known in the west Cork Gaeltacht, and even more highly regarded, according to some accounts, than that for Art Ó Laoghaire (see pp. 1372–1384). The version given here was remembered by an old woman called Casey from Cullen, County Cork, and written down by Seán Ua Cadhla, retired local schoolteacher, from whom it passed to Caitlín Ní Bhuachalla and then to Gerard Murphy, editor of *Éigse*. It appeared in *Éigse*, vol. 1 (1939), pp. 185–90.

Mac Cárthaigh, known as Diarmaid mac Eoghain na Toinne, was a prosperous butter-merchant in Cork city who was killed in a fall from his horse about 1860. Oral tradition has preserved an image of his mother which echoes other descriptions of the keening woman: heroically dishevelled and fearless, expressing, and ultimately containing, the disorder brought about by death. At her home some twenty miles away to the north-west, she is said to have heard the news of her son's death while milking. She set off immediately and walked across the hills to Cork, still wearing her milking clothes and carrying the spancel rope she had used to restrict the movement of each cow's hind legs.[1] Her lament berates the city people who dare to remark on her appearance, and bewails her son's death, but it also details the fate that has befallen her daughter, married to a violent and stingy man.[2] It shows the flexibility of lament-rhetoric, whose repertoire of formulaic utterance, praise and blame she turns to deal with issues and emotions much broader than those the literate mind may associate with mourning. Headnote and translation, A.B.]

1. See Tomás Ó Concheanainn (ed.), *Nua-Dhuanaire III* (Baile Átha Cliath: Institiúid Ardléinn, 1978), pp. 9–13.
2. See A. Bourke, 'More in Anger than in Sorrow'.

Caoine ar Dhiarmaid Mac Cárthaigh ó Ráth Dubháin, a bhí 'na Cheannuighe Ime i gCorcaigh

Mo chara is mo rún tú,
Is dá mbeifeá id dhúthaigh
Ní mustart ná túrann
Ná stoca beag lúba
Do bheadh orthu mar chúram;
Ach idir bhóithre ba chúng dóibh,
Ag fir ag búirthigh,
Ag mná ag liúirigh
Ag teacht chun do chuarta,
A mharcaigh na súl nglas.

Mo ghrá is mo chumann tú,
Agus ansúd a milleadh tú,
Ag Páil an Ridire,
Mar a ghnáthadh fireannaigh
Agus fia á chluicheadh acu,
Gan Dia i gcumar dóibh
Nar leaghfadh fuinneamh leat
A mharcaigh an iarainn ghlais![3]

Mo ghrá is mo thaisce,
Tá na mná óga ag siosarnaigh
De chionn a rá gur oileas thú:
Dá ngabhaidís siúd Muisire
Agus Cóngar na gCurraithe
Agus gach slí dar thugas-sa,
Ba rómhór m'amhras-sa
Nárbh fhalsa na liobair iad!

Mo ghrá is mo chumann thú,
Is róbhreá a mheasas duit
Go mbeadh bóithre dá nglanadh romhat,

3. These last three lines appear to be corrupt.

Fallaí dá ngealadh romhat,
Súirt dá leathadh romhat
Ag tabhairt mná abhaile leat,
Seachas tú bheith ar an aiste seo
Idir búrthaí Sasanaigh
Agus clann ceannaithe,
Id ualach ceathrair
Ag fágáil na cathrach —
Gura maith agaibhse
Ó ráiníos eadraibh,
Ó bhí sé d'easpa orm —
Ach Rí na Fairsinge!

Mo ghrá is mo thaisce thú,
Is dá mbeadh agam teachtaire
Nó coisí meanmnach
A raghadh cois Mainge siar,
Is mó bean bhreá mhascalach
Agus marcach breá ceannasach
Lena n-iallaití dearga
Agus a mbéalbhachaí airgid,
Ag trá agus ag tarrac ort,
Do bhainfeadh tine chreasa amach
Ag fágáil na cathrach.

Mo ghrá is mo chumann thú,
Ó tánn tú ag dul chun luite
Gearr-se cóngar slite,
Agus ná dearmhad Tigh na Croise,
Glaoigh ar an dá bhruinneall
Agus ar Dhiarmaid mhac Eoghain na Toinne.
'Sé dúirt a dteachtaire liomsa
Go raibh a gcuid éadaí nua gan chumadh,
Is go raibh a srianta briste
Is a n-iallaití gan giorta,
Agus gur imigh a n-eacha ar buile
Chun fiántais fésna cnocaibh,
Agus ná raibh aon ghabha ina n-ionad
Do chuirfeadh iad i bhfoirm
I gcomhair an fhiaigh is an chluichidh!

Mo chara thú is mo stór,
A Mháire dheas, iníon Eoghain,
Ná raibh beag ná mór
Is a bhí sa múnla cóir:
Do stopadh na fir dá ngnó
Na leanaí suas den spórt,
Agus na capaill do bhíodh sa bhfód,
Ag éisteacht le fuaim do cheoil
Maidin aoibhinn fhómhair
Sa mhacha ag crú na mbó.

Mo ghrá thú is mo chumann,
A ghamhain na gamhnaí bige,
A bhruscair na saille,
Agus a shúlach an ime,
Nár cáineadh riamh agamsa
(Agus má cáineadh, níor thuigeas),
Chun gur chuais-se uaim chun suite
Ag bun Chloch Bhuaile Bige,
Go dtí Maití Sín na Circe
Do chuirfeadh srian led chuislinn,
Ag riar agus ag fuineadh
Agus ag cur na seisreach chun suite,
Is ná faighfeá féin ina ionad
Ach sáspan an linbh.
Do thógadh sé an t-im den chuiginn
Agus tusa id shuí ag an tine,
Agus chuireadh na cearca chun nide.

Mo chara is mo chiall thú,
Is do ghabhadh sé den tsrian ort,
Is d'fhuip naoi n-iall ort,
Is den mhaide ina ndiaidh sin;
Níor insis-se riamh é,
Go bhfuaireas-sa a rian ort
Ar an leaba tar éis bliana ort.

Mo ghrá is mo thaisce thú,
Thugas fiche bó bhainne dhuit,
Tarbh chun dártha dhuit,
Losaid chun fuinte dhuit —
Mo mhallacht ina ionad duit,
Ní id stoc ná id iothlainn,
Ná i dtinteán na tine istigh,
Ach id chroí agus id chuisleanna
Ag iarraidh do chiorraithe,
A bhodaigh an domlais!

Mo chara thú is mo mhaoin,
Is do théadh do litir go cruinn
Go Parlaimint an Rí
Is go Corcaigh na seolta síos,
Mar a bhfaigheadh do theachtaire ithe agus
    fíon,
Mar a mbíodh do chomhrá cruinn,
A dhalta ghil agus a mhaoin.

Mo chara thú is mo mhaoin,
Is b'fhuirist dom do bhaile a chur síos,
Siar go Ciarraí an ghrinn,
Thar n-ais aniar arís
Go pobal Chuilinn Uí Chaoimh,

Is go hÁthán na meathán mín,
Is go Driseán an chaisleáin aird,
Is go Prothus tall an troim,
Is go Ráth Cumhaill an ghrinn,
Is go Gort Breac na liag,
Agus an Bhuaile Mhór lena thaobh —
Do dhearmhadas duit a chur síos,
Agus fillim ar ais arís
Ar Dhroim na Bó Duibhe.

Mo chara is mo lao thú,
Agus raghair liom féinig
Go Driseán aolmhar
An chaisleáin ghléigil
Is breátha in Éirinn,
Dá mbeadh cuan éisc ann.
Mura bhfuil san féin ann,
Tá ann mil bhuí agus céir bheach
Agus cruithneacht ina slaodaibh
Thar bráidibh a chéile;
Agus mar bharr ar gach aon rud,
Go bhfuil sé naofa!

Mo chara is mo rún tú,
Béarfad liom thú
Go Driseán cumhra
An chaisleáin chúinnigh —
Caora cumhra,
Meas go glúine,
Ba boga ag búirthigh
Maidin bhog dhrúchta
Ag iarraidh a gcrúite!

Mo ghrá is mo chumann thú,
Is romhór m'amhras, a chumainn,
Gur rúimín íseal clochmhar
Atá ar an dtaobh thoir den reilg
Gurb é do rogha chun luite.

A Lament for Diarmaid MacCarthy of Ráth Dubháin, Who Was a Butter-Merchant in Cork

Dear friend and darling,
If you were at home,
Neither worsted or spinning,
Nor the socks they were knitting
Would be their concern,
But the roads too narrow

For the roaring men
And the screaming women
Coming to see you,
Dear grey-eyed horseman.

Dear love and sweetheart,
Your downfall was there,
At the Knight's Paling,
Where the men used to gather
When they hunted the deer —
May God not protect them;
They hadn't half your energy,
Dear iron-stirruped horseman.[1]

Dear love and treasure,
The young women wonder
That the likes of me reared you:
If they'd walked over Mushera
And the short-cut through the Curraghs,
And all the paths I've taken,
I'd be very surprised if
They didn't look as rough.

My love and my dear one,
I had great hopes for you:
That roads would be cleared for you,
That walls would be whitewashed,
Swards spread before you,
As you brought a woman home;
Not like this, surrounded
By boors from England
And the children of merchants,
Carried by four men
Out of the city —
But my thanks to all of you,
Since I've come among you
For I needed help —
Dear King of Bounty.[2]

Dear love and dear treasure,
If I had a messenger,
Or a spirited runner
To go west along the Maine[3]
Many a fine sturdy woman,
Many a proud stately horseman,

---

1. These last three lines are obscure in the original.
2. The lamenter's sudden change of attitude in this passage may be compared with a similar reversal in the lament for Art Ó Laoghaire (pp. 1380, 1382), where the 'freckled little mill-women' are first castigated, then thanked. *Caoineadh* was designed to be remembered, so the record was often corrected in this way.
3. A river in north Kerry.

With their saddles all crimson
And their horse-bits of silver,
Would be galloping towards you,
Knocking sparks from the rocks,
As they left the city.

Dear love and dear treasure,[4]
If you're going to bed,
Take the quickest way home,
And don't forget Tig na Croise:
Call the two lovely girls,
And Diarmaid, son of Eoghan na Toinne.
Their messenger told me
Their new clothes weren't ready;
That their bridles were broken,
And their saddles lacked girths;
That their horses had run away
Wild in the hills, and
No blacksmith was there
Who could get them all ready
For the hunt or the chase.[5]

Dear love and precious one,
Sweet Máire, daughter of Eoghan,
Who was neither small nor big,
But perfectly shaped;
Who would halt the men from work,
Or the children from their play,
Or the horses in the field,
Listening to your song,
On a lovely autumn morning,
As you milked the cows outdoors.

Dear love and beloved,
Dear little calf's calf,
Dear delicious crumbs of bacon,
Dear juice of the butter,
Whom I never criticized
(Or if I did, didn't realize),
Till you left me, and settled
Below in Cloghboley,
With Maití Sín na Circe,
Who would curb your heart's blood,
With his fussing and organizing,
And harnessing his plough-team;
All you got for your trouble

Was the baby's leftovers.
He'd take the butter from the churn
While you sat at the fire;
He'd shut the hens in at night.[6]

My friend and my dear one,
He beat you with the bridle,
With the nine-thonged whip,
And then with a stick;
But you never told me,
Till I found the marks on you
In bed a year later.[7]

Dear love and dear treasure,[8]
I gave you twenty milking cows
Along with a bull, and
A trough to knead bread in —
But now instead I curse you,
Not your livestock or harvest;
Not the fire on your hearth,
But your heart and your veins,
To leave you maimed,
You bilious lout!

My love and my precious,
You wrote to the King's parliament,
And to Cork of the sailing ships.
Where they wined and dined your messenger,
And enjoyed your conversation,
Dearest child and precious one.

Dear love and precious,
I could name your townlands
All the way to lovely Kerry,
And all the way back
To the parish of Cullen:
Áthán with its smooth saplings,
Drishane with its high castle,

6. Buttermaking and care of hens were properly the woman's responsibility, and income deriving from them should have been hers. See Caoimhín Ó Danachair, 'Marriage in Irish Folk Tradition', in Art Cosgrove (ed.), *Marriage in Ireland* (Dublin: College Press, 1985), pp. 99–115, esp. pp.109–10, and cf. Joanna Bourke, 'Women and Poultry in Ireland, 1891–1914', *Irish Historical Studies*, vol. 25, no. 99 (1987), pp. 293–310; 'Poultry-Rearing', chapter 6 in her *Husbandry to Housewifery: Women, Economic Change, and Housework in Ireland, 1890–1914* (Oxford: Oxford University Press, 1993), pp. 169–98. This lament-poet seems to suggest that her son-in-law's stinginess extended to depriving his wife of her only source of income.
7. For violence in lament, see A. Bourke, 'More in Anger than in Sorrow', see also pp. 1395, 1396.
8. This stanza opens with the formulaic affectionate address, although its substance is invective against the lamenter's son-in-law.

4. Although opening with the conventional term of endearment, this stanza is apparently addressed to someone in the crowd who has begun to move away: a common feature of laments.
5. Compare the excuses attributed to the dead man's sister in Caoineadh Airt Uí Laoghaire, above.

Far Prothus with its elder-tree,
Rathcoole for good company,
Gortbrack with its headstones,
And Booleymore beside it,
And one I forgot to mention,
So I turn and go back
To the Black Cow's Ridge.

Dear love and pet,
You'll come with me
To limewashed Drishane
With its dazzling castle,
The finest in Ireland,
If it only had a harbour.
But even without one,
It has honey and beeswax,
Wheat in thick swathes
Overlapping on the ground,

And besides all that,
The place is a holy one!

My friend and my darling,
I'll take you with me
To fragrant Drishane
With its four-cornered castle —
With sweet-smelling berries,
Beech-nuts knee high,
Gentle cows lowing
On a fine dewy morning,
Ready for milking.

My love and my dear!
I very much fear
That a low stony cell
In the graveyard's east side
Is where you've chosen to lie.

NEILÍ NÍ DHOMHNAILL

(1907–84)

from:
CEOL: A JOURNAL OF IRISH MUSIC (1982)

[A song from County Donegal, whose diction and dramatic shape are drawn from the tradition of *caoineadh*. Songs in Irish are more often lyrical than narrative, but are frequently accompanied by stories, although these are not included in every performance. The story told with or about a song may explain its background, or may be extrapolated from the song; it may also be assimilated to patterns familiar elsewhere in storytelling tradition, while either song, or story, or both, may incorporate and serve to legitimate proverbs and other sayings.[1]

The song 'Eoin Búrcach' resembles the English ballad 'Bruton Town' in telling of a young serving man who marries his employers' daughter, but is then killed by her outraged brothers. Well-known musician Mícheál Ó Domhnaill recorded this version from his aunt, Neilí Ní Dhomhnaill, of Rinn na Feirste, County Donegal, in 1974, for the Irish Folklore Collection. Cathal Goan edited it, with a music transcription and comprehensive notes in Irish ('Dhá Amhrán ó Neilí Ní Dhónaill'), in *Ceol*, vol. 5, no. 2 (March 1982), pp. 38–42, and vol. 6, no. 1, pp. 2–4. Lorcán Ó Muireadhaigh (1883–1941), a Catholic priest who used his travels as an inspector of religious education in schools (1922–37) to collect folklore in Irish, had earlier taken down both story and song from Méadhbh Tharlaigh Mhóir of Rinn na Feirste, and published them first in *An tUltach*, vol. 4, nos. 11–12 (December 1927), p. 13, and later, together with a music transcription by Uinnsean Mac Suibhne, in his *Amhráin Chúige Uladh* (Dublin: Gilbert Dalton, 1927, 1977), pp. 73, 142–3.[2]

Songs on the same theme are found elsewhere in the Irish-language tradition, most of them giving the young man's name as Burke and purporting to be the lament composed by his wife. Most of them express the conflict of loyalties which marriage entails by the motif found also in Herodotus, of one woman telling another that while a husband is replaceable, a brother is not.[3] Other motifs familiar from the ritual lament include the young woman's exhorting her mother to lament as is proper, and the line beginning 'A Bhean úd thall atá ag déanamh gáire' ('You over there, the woman laughing'), found also in the 'waulking' songs of Scottish Gaelic.[4]

---

2. Other versions (with music): *Journal of the Irish Folk Song Society*, vol. 7 (1909) (from a manuscript of Edmund Bunting), and vol. 19 (1922). See also Séamus Ó Duilearga, 'Seán do Búrc', *Éigse*, vol. 1, no. 4 (1939), pp. 235–6; Michael Tierney, 'An Ancient Motif in the Lament for Seán do Búrc', ibid., pp. 236–8; Seán Ó Súilleabháin, 'An Bhean do Thogh a Driotháir', *Éigse*, vol. 2, no. 1 (1940), pp. 24–30.
3. M. Tierney, 'An Ancient Motif'; cf. 'You Down There in the Silk Dress', pp. 1393–1395.
4. Cf. 'A Bhean úd thíos . . .', p. 1393.

---

1. See Hugh Shields, 'Old British Ballads in Ireland', *Folklife*, vol. 10 (1972), p. 71.

The story told here is remarkable in its depiction of a young woman who lives wild and naked in the woods after being abandoned there by her family. It bears a striking resemblance to the 18th-century text, *Scéal Mis agus Dubh Rois* (see pp. 239–241). That story too has close connections with lament tradition, recording that Mis, a king's daughter, after whom Slieve Mis[5] is said to be named, went mad when lamenting her dead father and drinking his blood on the battlefield, and then lived wild on the mountainside until tamed by the harper Dubh Rois, whom she married. Headnote and translation, A.B.]

EOIN BÚRCACH

Seo daoine agus bhí siad iontach saibhir agus bhí cuid mhór talamh acu agus eallach agus caoirigh agus achan chineál mar sin. Agus bhí rud ann fad ó shin a dtabharfadh siad *An Deoch Bhuí* air — bhail, rud pisreogach a bhí ann — creidim nach raibh a leithéid ann. . . . ach ba mhaith leis na daoine a raibh saibhreas mór acu rud éigin a thabhairt suas don *Deoch Bhuí* i gcónaí. Agus nuair a tháinig an ghirseach bheag seo ar a tsaol, thug siad suas don *Deoch Bhuí* í fá choinne ádh a bheith orthu. Bhí siad ag déanamh mura dtabharfadh siad a dhath suas don *Deoch Bhuí*, nach mbeadh ádh ar bith orthu, de thairbhe eallaigh nó daoine nó a dhath mar sin. Agus d'fhág siad an ghirseach bheag seo amuigh sa choillidh, i bhfad ón bhaile.

Bhí buachaill fostaithe acu a raibh *Eoin Burke* air, agus is é a bhí ag amharc i ndiaidh an eallaigh agus i ndiaidh achan rud agus bheadh sé ar shiúl giota fada ón teach, ag amharc i ndiaidh an eallaigh agus caorach agus achan chineál mar sin. Ach lá amháin chonaic sé an ghirseach seo insa choillidh, agus d'imeodh sí ina rith nuair a chífeadh sí eisean. Ach fá dheireadh bhí seisean ag caint léi agus ní raibh sí ábalta a thuigbheáil ach *bhlanderáil* sé leis í go dtí go bhfuair sé í a mhealladh. Agus bhí sé ag comhrá léi achan lá, agus nuair a tháinig sé isteach go dí an teach a raibh sé ar fastóidh ann, d'inis sé dóibh fá'n ghirseach a bhí amuigh sa choillidh. Agus bhí a fhios acu ansin gur a n-iníon féin a bhí ann a thug siad suas don *Deoch Bhuí* blianta roimhe sin. Agus dúirt siad leis dá dtiocfadh leis í a mhealladh in sa dóigh go dtiocfadh leis í a thabhairt isteach 'na bhaile, go dtabharfadh siad dó le pósadh í. Agus ar ndóigh, bhí seisean fá'n choillidh achan lá agus

é ag comhrá léi agus ag caint léi. Agus rinne sé éadach dithe amach as duilleogaí na gcrann agus fá dheireadh fuair sé í a mhealladh sa dóigh go dtug sé isteach go dtí teach a muintire í. Agus ar ndóigh, pósadh an bheirt, í féin agus Eoin Burke. Ach nuair a bhí siad pósta, bhí siad ag déanamh nach raibh Eoin maith go leor aici, mar chéile, as siocair go raibh sé ag obair acu agus nach raibh sé saibhir go leor, nó a dhath mar sin. Agus rinne siad amach eatarthu féin go rachadh siad ag iascaireacht agus go dtabharfadh siad Eoin leofa — agus go mbáfeadh siad é nuair a bheadh sé amuigh ansin. Chuaigh siad amach an lá seo, iad féin agus Eoin, agus, ar ndóigh, tháinig beirt deartháireacha na girsí seo ar ais [agus] ní raibh Eoin leo. Agus seo mar a dúirt siad — mar adúirt an mháthair leis an iníon:

Ó fuist, a iníon is ná bí cráite,
Nár fusa duit fear a fháil ná dís deartháir;
Tá súil as an Rí agam gurb iad mo chlann a tháinig
Is gurb é an Búrcach a' chúil doinn a fágadh.

Ó tá súil as an Rí agam gurb iad do chlann a fágadh,
Donnchadh Fionngeal 'chéad mhac mo mháthara;
Agus an Búrcach a theacht ón ghábhadh,
Ó ná's leis féin ba thrua mo chás-sa.

Ó's a Mháithrín dhíleas, ó can mar is cóir duit,
Nach é do chliamhain uasal óg é?
Ní hé mac mná na mbailteach' mór' é,
Is gur ina chliamhain ag an Iarla ba chóir é.

'S nach tú a dhéanfadh mo cheann a dheisiú,
'S nach tú a dhéanfadh mo bhróg a bhreacadh,
Nach leat a dhéanfainnse casaoid m'ocrais
Ó nuair nár dhual dom féin a ghlacadh.

Ó's a bhean úd thall atá ag déanamh gáire,
Nárb é fada go raibh agat fios m'ábhair,
Do cheann (a) cromtha 's do chroí cráite,
Is do dhá lámh teanntaithe fa mhac mo mháthara.

Ó druidigí thart, a mhná na gclócaí,
Seo feoil chugaibh agus ní feoil chóir í;
Ní feoil muice í nó caorach rósta,
Ach an Búrcach uasal a bhí i dtús a óige.

---

5. A mountain in County Kerry.

TRANSLATION

There were these people who were very rich, and they had a lot of land and cattle and sheep and that sort of thing. And there was something long ago that they called the *Deoch Bhuí*[1] — well, it was a superstition — I don't believe there was any such thing, really . . . but anybody who had great wealth always wanted to give something up to the *Deoch Bhuí*. And when this little girl was born, they gave her up to the *Deoch Bhuí* so that they would have good luck. They believed that if they didn't give something up to the *Deoch Bhuí*, they would have no luck as regards their cattle or their people or anything like that. So they left this little girl out in the woods, far from her home.

They had a hired boy who was called Eoin Burke, and it was he who used to take care of the cattle and that sort of thing, and he used to work a long way from the house, herding cattle and sheep and everything. Then one day he saw this girl in the woods. Every time she saw him, she would run away, but in the end he managed to speak to her. She didn't understand him, but he blandished her and coaxed her until he got her confidence, and he used to talk to her every day. When he came back to the house where he was employed, he told them about the girl in the woods. They realised then that it was their own daughter, whom they'd given up to the *Deoch Bhuí* years before. And they told him that if he could gain her confidence enough to bring her back home, they would give her to him in marriage. And of course he was out in the woods every day, talking to her and making conversation. And he made clothes for her out of the leaves of the trees, and in the end he managed to gain her confidence enough to bring her back to her family's home. And of course the two got married, the girl and Eoin Burke. But after they were married, her people decided that Eoin wasn't good enough for her, as a husband, since he was working for them and he wasn't rich enough, that sort of thing. So they made up their

minds to go fishing, and to take Eoin with them, and to drown him out at sea. They went out this day, themselves and Eoin, and of course this girl's two brothers came back, but Eoin didn't. And this is what they said — this is what the mother said to her daughter [as the boat approached]:

Hush, daughter, and don't be tormented,[2]
A husband is easier replaced than two brothers.
I hope to God that my sons have been saved,
And that brown-haired Burke is the one left
    behind.

I hope to God, Mother, it was your sons who
    drowned,
Fair-haired Donnchadh, my mother's firstborn,
And that Burke has come safely out of the
    danger,
For if he were dead, I'd be a pitiful case.

Mother dear, you should be keening,
Wasn't he your noble young son-in-law;
He wasn't the son of some woman from the
    town,
He could have married the daughter of an earl.

It was you who used to tidy my hair,
You who used to embroider my shoes,
You I complained to when I felt hungry,
When it didn't come naturally to me.[3]

You over there, the woman laughing,
May it not be long until you know what ails me:
Your head bent, and your heart tormented,
With your two arms clasped around my
    mother's son![4]

Gather round me, you women wearing cloaks,
Here is meat for you, but no ordinary meat,
This is not pork, or roasted mutton,
This is noble Burke, in the flower of his youth.

---

1. The literal meaning, 'yellow drink', is meaningless in this context, but compare the equally obscure word *Deachma* found in certain folktales, where it is used, as here, to explain the sacrifice of one child in a large family. Both words would appear to derive from *deachmha*, 'tithe', and to reflect the distress experienced by poor people who had formerly to pay tithes to the Established Church.

2. Compare a similar line in the 'Mary's Lament' (see p. 1412).
3. The last line here is obscure. These lines are more commonly associated with laments of daughters for their mothers, but are here explained by the narrative.
4. These lines are found often in lament-songs. The speaker shows the extent of her anger at her sister-in-law's lack of sympathy by wishing her own brother dead.

MÁIRE RUISÉAL

(1856–c. 1945)

from:
BÉALOIDEAS (1929)

[A story about death, or pretended death, provides the context for the Rabelaisian inversion of many lament themes. Máire Ruiséal's 'An Tórramh Bréagach', 'The Fake Wake' (AT 1350, 'The Loving Wife'), though told as a memorate, or personal-experience narrative, is a folktale of the type classified by Aarne-Thompson as 'Stories about Married Couples'. In its cynicism, misogyny, and tragicomic tone, it is not untypical of the many folktales which tell of marriage rather than of weddings. 'An Tórramh Bréagach' is full of ethnographic detail, giving a good picture of Irish wake customs — laying the corpse out on the table, eating a supper of bread and boiled fowl — together with details about the fittings and furniture of the Irish country house: food kept in a cupboard, door secured with a hasp, water carried in a can. This is a folktale which has many of the characteristics associated with legends: an excellent example of a story which crosses the genre boundaries. Its realism, and its density of naturalistic detail, is much more typical of legends than of folktales. J.M. Synge based his play *The Shadow of the Glen* (1905) on a version of this tale, which he heard in the Aran Islands. Published in 'Dhá Scéal ó Dhún Chaoin, Co. Chiarraighe' by Proinsias Ó Raghalla, *Béaloideas*, vol. 2 (1929), pp. 53–4. An editorial note by Séamus Ó Duilearga gives the date of collection as 1917. Headnote and translation, Eilís Ní Dhuibhne.]

AN TÓRRAMH BRÉAGACH

Chuas in aimsir nuair a bhíos naoi mbliana d'aois go dtí an Boghléireach. Sé cúram a chuir sé orm ag aoracht caorach, agus duairt sé liom má leigfinn aon cheann dosna caoire bhuam gan teacht chuig an tigh.

Nuair a shíos cois an chluí, i mbun na gcaorach, do thuit mo cholla orm, agus nuair a dhúisíos bhí ceann dosna caoire imithe bhuam. Do dh'imíos ag lorg an chaoira bhí imithe as na caoire bhuam. Nuair a thána leis an gcaoira bhí an chuid eile imithe bhuam, agus do dh'imíos orm ansan, agus ní ligfeadh sgannra dhom dul go dtí an tigh chuige.

Casadh isteach i dtigh mé, agus duart leo mé fhágaint istigh do lá. Dúradar liom go bhfágaidís agus míle fáilte mura mbeadh go raibh tigh eile thíos go raibh an fear marbh, is ba mhaith léi me bheith aice mar chuileachta. Do dh'imíos orm is do chuas isteach chúihe agus d'fhiarhuíos an bhfágfadh sí istigh me, agus duairt sí go bhfágfadh. Bhí canna ar a cromán aici chun dul ag triall ar uisge. Duairt sí liom suí thuas sa chúinne go dtiocfadh sí leis an gcanna uisge. Nuair a bhí sí ag imeacht chuir sí an lúb ar an ndoras.

Ní fada bhíos suite sa chúinne nuair a chonoc an fear a bhí marbh ar an mbord ag corruí. Do tháinig sgannra orm, is dá bhfaghainn aon pholl sa bhalla do raghainn amach tríd — ach ní raibh. Duairt sé liom, 'Tá eagal ort!'

'Tá mo dhóthain!' aduart-sa.

Duairt sé liom gan a bheith. Duairt sé liom dul isteach don chupard agus an bhulóg a bhí ann a thúirt liom agus an coileach dearg a bhí beirithe ar an bpláta. Duart-sa leis go raibh eagal orm go maródh bean an tí mé. Duairt sé liom ná déanfadh sí aon ní liom.

Sea, do thugas chuige iad ar an mbord agus duairt sé liom féin teacht á ithe, mar ná gheóinn aon ní le n-ithe go maidin. Do chuamar ag ithe agus d'itheamair leath na bulóige agus leath an choileach dearg. Sea, duairt sé liom iad do chur isteach sa chupard arís. Duairt sé liom dul suas 'on tseomra agus an taobhán a bhí fén leaba a thúirt liom agus é a bhuala ar an dtaobh istigh ar an mbord, agus an báirdlín (braithlín) a shocarú anuas air. Bhí sé socair ansan agam. Duairt sé liom go gcloisfinn scéal nua fé mhaidin, agus gan aon eagal a bheith orm féin.

Ní rabhas ach suite sa chúinne nuair a bhain sí an lúb den ndoras agus canna uisce aice. Bhí óganach fir in éineacht léi. Do dhein an t-óganach isteach ar an bhfear marbh, agus tharraig sé trí buille dhorn anuas ar an gcroí ar an bhfear a bhí marbh, [a rá]: 'Mhuise, tuille mar an tubaiste chút bheith sínte annsan!'

Chuaigh sí féin isteach don chupard ag triall ar an mbulóg agus ar an gcoileach dearg. Nuair a chonaic sí an bhulóg ite tháinig uathás is olc aice chúm. 'Mhuise gan tú mhór a leigint dom. Mara agat a bhí an ghoile — leath na bulóige do dh'ithe agus leath mo choileach dearg!'

Duairt an t-ógánach léi eisteacht, dá mbeadh ocras uirthi féin go¹ n-íosfadh sí é. 'Tá do dhóthain fós ann!' aduairt sé.

D'imíodar suas don tseomra ag ithe an aráin. Nuair a bh'am leis an bhfear marbh iad a bheith ina [g]colla d'éirigh ó'n mbord, riug sé leis an taobhán, chuaigh sé ag triall ortha, agus bhí sé ag gabháil orthu an fhaid a bhí aon teas ionnta. Nuair a bhíodar leath-mharbh aige tharraig sé leis anuas iad, tharraig sé don tintean síos iad agus an doras amach iad. Bhuail sé amach ar an mbuaile iad, agus do tháinig corruí éigin san óganach is bhí sé bailithe leis nuair a tháinig an lá.

Ghaibh sé an capal ar maidin, agus riug sé abhaile go dtí a muinntir fein í. Duairt sé leó í chimeád aige baile — ná raibh aon ghnó aige féin di. Chimeádfadh sé mé féin mar chailín dá bhfanfainn aige, ach níor fhanas.

1. MS, *do.*

THE FAKE WAKE

When I was nine years of age I went into service with Bowler. The job he gave me was to herd sheep, and he told me that if I allowed any of the sheep to go astray, I was not to return to the house. When I sat down beside the ditch, looking after the sheep, I fell asleep, and when I woke up one of the sheep had strayed. I went in search of the sheep that had strayed. And when I came back with that sheep all the rest had gone too, and I went away then, and fear would not let me return to the house to him.

I turned in to a house, and asked them if I could stay until daybreak. They said I could, and a thousand welcomes, if it were not that there was another house nearby where the husband was dead, and that the woman would be glad of my company. I left, and went in to her, and I asked if she would let me in, and she said she would. She had a can on her hip, on her way to fetch water. She told me to sit up in the corner until she would come back with the can of water. When she was going she put the hasp on the door.

I was not long sitting in the corner when I noticed the man who was dead on the table moving about. I got a fright, and if there had been any hole in the wall, I would have escaped through it, but there was not. He said to me, 'You are afraid!'

'I am frightened enough!'

He told me not to be frightened. He told me to go into the cupboard and to take out of it the loaf that was inside and the red cockerel that was boiled on a plate. I told him I was afraid that the woman of the house would kill me. He said she would do me no harm.

Yes. I brought them to him on the table and he invited me to come and eat myself, because I would not get another bite until morning. We set to and we ate half the loaf and half the red cockerel. Yes. He told me to put them back in the cupboard again. He told me to go up to the room and to take the plank that was under the bed and to put it beside him on the table, and to conceal it with the sheet. I arranged it all neatly. He told me I would hear a new story before morning, and not to be afraid myself.

I was just sitting in the corner when the woman took the hasp off the door, and she was carrying a can of water. There was a young man with her. The young man went up to the dead man, and gave three blows of his fist to the dead man's heart, saying: 'Wisha, more bad luck to you, lying there dead!'

She herself went to the cupboard, looking for the loaf of bread and the red cockerel. When she saw the loaf half-eaten she became very angry. 'Wisha you couldn't be left alone! Isn't it you have the big appetite! To have eaten half the loaf and half the red cockerel!'

The young man told her to be quiet, that if she had been hungry she would have eaten it too. 'You have enough left anyway,' he said.

They went up to the room, eating the bread. When the dead man thought they would have fallen asleep he got off the table, grabbed the plank, and went after them, and he beat them as long as there was any heat in them. When he had half-killed them he dragged them down to the hearth and out the door. He threw them out in the yard, and the young man came to and by morning he was gone.

He took out the horse in the morning and he took her home to her own people. He told them to keep her at home — that he didn't want her any more. He would have kept me on as a hired girl if I'd wanted to stay, but I didn't.

ANONYMOUS

from:
AN SEANCHAIDHE
MUIMHNEACH (1932)

[This traditional stave-anecdote (story incorporating
verse) was submitted by Caitlín Ní Úrdail of Derrycairn
School, Adrigole, County Cork, for publication in the
bilingual periodical *An Lóchrann* in 1911 (vol. 4, p. 3) and
later anthologized in *An Seanchaidhe Muimhneach* by its
editor, Pádraig Ó Siochfhradha 'An Seabhac'.[1] It preserves
several tags of lament-poetry prized for their wit, and
known in many versions, especially in Munster. Also
included is the motif noted in 'Eoin Búrcach'
(pp. 1388–1390), that a husband can be replaced, while an
adult brother cannot. Its frame is the tale of the man who
outwitted his unfaithful wife by pretending to be dead
(AT 1350; compare 'An Tórramh Bréagach', p. 1391).
Lamenting the dead was a sacred duty, which the dead
man's sister accuses his wife of neglecting, as happens also
in the lament for Art Ó Laoghaire (p. 1379). The man in
this case is shown as a *cliamhain isteach*: living in his wife's
rather than his parents' house, and therefore occupying,
and placing his family of origin in, a somewhat ambiguous
social role. The lines attributed to him at the end are very
like some of those used by the mother of Diarmaid Mac
Cárthaigh (p. 1387), similarly asserting economic and
social rights within the system of arranged marriages and
dowries.[2] The forceful speech of the single woman to both
her sister-in-law and the priest contrasts strongly with the
disapproving voice of the framing narrative: an illustration
of how subversive messages may be conveyed with
apparent innocence.[3]   Headnote and translation, A.B.]

[A BHEAN ÚD THÍOS GO BHFUIL AN SÍODA ORT]

Do bhí lánú óg ann fadó — agus is fadó riamh do
bhí. Ní rabhadar ag gabháil ró mhaith le chéile;
má 'seadh dob í an bhean fé ndeara san.

Nuair do bhraith an fear go raibh aigne na
mná ionntuithe 'na choinnibh tháinig buairt agus

1. Pádraig Ó Siochfhradha 'An Seabhac' (ed.), *An Seanchaidhe
   Muimhneach .i. Meascra de Bhéaloideas Ilchineál ó An Lóchrann
   1907–1913* (Dublin: Institute Béaloideasa Éireann, 1932),
   pp. 278–80.
2. For arranged marriages and dowries, see C. Arensberg and
   S. T. Kimball, *Family and Community in Ireland*.
3. See A. Bourke, 'More in Anger than in Sorrow'.

brón air. Lá do leog sé air bheith breoidhte, agus
do luigh sé go diachrach chun na leabthan. Do
bhí sé ag dul i laige i n-alt a chéile i
gcómhnaidhe, go dtí fé dheireadh go bhfuair sé
bás mar 'dheadh.

Níor tugadh aon dochtúir chuige, mar is dócha
ná rabhadar chómh hiomadúil an uair sin agus
táid anois agus, 'na theannta san, is dócha ná
raibh aenne 'na chúram. Ar a shon san féin, do
chuir a bhean scéala a bháis chun deirfiúr a céile
do bhí tamall uaithi.

Tháinig sí sin agus do bhí a deartháir
tonnachta, leogtha amach roimpi. Do luigh sí go
díombádhach chun é do chaoineadh. Nuair do
chuir sí dhi an chéad tocht, d'fhéach sí timcheall
uirthi; agus ní fheaca sí aenne 'na teannta 'á
chaoineadh.

Chonnaic sí a bhean thíos insa phárlús, agus a
cos ar a leathghlúin aici agus í ag deargadh a
phíopa.

Dubhairt an deirfiúr léi:

'A bhean úd thíos go bhfuil an síoda ort.
'Do chos ar do leathghlúin agat agus tú ag
    deargadh do phíopa,
'Ná tiocfá aníos agus t'fhear a chaoineadh.'

'Ó,' arsan bhean thíos:

'Gheobhad-sa fear mara bhfuilim críona,
'Agus deartháir ní bhfaghair-se go bráth ná
    choidhche.'

Sé dubhairt an deirfiúr annsan:

'A dheartháir ó! is a dheartháir na gcarad,
'Tá rian na drochmhná go hárd ar do leacain,
'Tart na hoidhche agus fuacht an earraigh,
'Easpa 'n éadaigh agus an céalacan fada.'

Le linn na bhfocal so do rádh tháinig an sagart
isteach chun na liodáin do léigheadh ar an
marbh. Nuair do chualaidh sé an spídiuchán
gránna tháinig gráin aige ar an gcailín singil, agus
dubhairt sé:

'Éist! Éist! a bhraobaire caille.'

'Éist féin, a bhraobaire sagairt,' ar sise,
Léigh na liodáin ar na mairbh,
Tuill do réal agus buail abhaile,
Agus leog dom féin mo dheartháir d'fhaireadh.'

D'fhan sí annsan chun gur imthigh an sagart abhaile. Annsan dubhairt sí,

'Is mithid dómh-sa dul abhaile,
Chun go 'nneosad dom mháithrín is dom athair,
Gur gol mná aonair do bhí aréir ar a leanbh.'

'Dar fiadh,' arsan fear marbh ag preabadh 'na shuidhe, 'bead-sa i n-éinfheacht leat.' Nuair do bhí sé idir dhá lígh an dorais, 'sé dubhairt sé:

'Táim ag fágaint fiche bó bhainne agat,
Tarbh chun durtha agat,
Tobán na coiginne agat;
Má fhágaim a thuille agat,
Mo mhallacht 'na n-ionad agat,
A chailligh an toirmisc.'

Ba mhaith an slán beo d'fhág sé aici i ndeireadh a saoghail, ach is dócha ná dubhairt sé léi ach mar do bhí tuillte aici. Ní fheadar cad é an chrích do rug 'na dhiaidh san iad.

YOU DOWN THERE IN THE SILK DRESS

There was a young couple long ago, and it was a long time ago. They were not getting on very well, and it was all the woman's fault.

When the man noticed that the woman's mind had turned against him, he was worried and sad. One day, he pretended to be sick, and took to his bed, complaining miserably. He kept getting weaker, until eventually he died, or so it appeared.

Nobody fetched a doctor; they may not have been so plentiful in those days as they are now, and in any case, probably nobody was taking care of him. Even so, the wife sent news of the death to her husband's sister, some distance away.

When she arrived, she found her brother already washed and laid out, and she began sorrowfully to lament him, but when she had finished the first spate of keening, she looked around and saw that nobody was weeping with her.

She saw the wife below in the parlour, sitting with one foot across the other knee, lighting a pipe. The sister said to her:

'You down there in the silk dress,
With your foot on your knee, lighting your pipe,
Would you not come up and lament your man?'

'Oh,' said the woman below,

'I can get another man, for I'm still young,
But you won't have a brother ever again.'[1]

Then the sister said:

'Brother dear, and dearest brother,
I can see by your face that you had a bad wife,
Thirsty at night, and cold in the spring,
Not enough clothes, and long hours fasting.'

As she was saying these words, the priest came in, to read the litanies over the dead man. When he heard this abusive language he was disgusted with the single woman, and said:

'Stop that at once, you insolent girl!'

'Stop yourself, you insolent priest,' she answered,
'Read the litanies over the dead man;
Earn your sixpence and be off home,
And let me have a proper wake for my brother.'[2]

She waited until the priest had left. Then she said:

'It's high time for me to go back home
To tell my mother and my father
That only one woman keened their son last
    night.'[3]

'By God,' said the dead man, jumping up, 'I'll come with you!' Then standing in the doorway, he said:

'I leave you twenty milch cows,
A bull to service them,

1. This motif, of the irreplacability of an adult brother, is common in lament-poetry, and has been traced in European literature to the Greek historian Herodotus (5th century BC).
2. Disputes between keening women and priests about who is to preside at funerals are often couched in economic terms.
3. At least three women should be present to lament together: *gol mná aonair*, the weeping of a lone woman, was a deeply felt disgrace.

And the tub for churning;
If I leave you any more,
My curse on you instead,
You obstructive old hag!'

That was a fine way that he left her at the end of her life, but he probably only said what she deserved. I don't know what became of them after that.

ANONYMOUS

from:
JOURNAL OF THE IRISH FOLK SONG SOCIETY (1922)

[Another example of the fake wake, in which women's poetry appears to be parodied for men's amusement. Wilfrid Brown transcribed the music of this joking lament, published in the *Journal of the Irish Folk Song Society*, vol. 19 (1922), from the singing of An Seabhac, who notes that he learned both words and music in 1903 from Seán Bán Ó Conchubhair (aged then about sixty), of An Bóthar Buí, near Dingle, County Kerry. He was a noted singer, and used regularly to entertain the young men who gathered nightly in winter in the local blacksmith's house. He often sang this 'lament', contextualizing it with the story which An Seabhac gives below.

This example, which both parodies the genre and underlines the resources it provides for the expression of discontent, gives pride of place to the vituperation found to some extent in almost all lament-poetry. References to stinginess and domestic violence, cautiously expressed elsewhere in the tradition, are central. The terms of endearment, with which several stanzas begin, strike an odd note, but are the essential 'starter motors' of formulaic composition, and occur in a similar context in the lament for Diarmaid Mac Cárthaigh (p. 1387, notes 4, 8). For a similarly jocular, but pointed, text see Angela Partridge [Bourke], 'Is Beo Duine tar éis a Bhuailte: Caoineadh Aorach as Béara', *Sinsear*, vol. 3 (1981), pp. 70–6. Headnote and translation, A.B.]

Caoine Magaidh

Ó moladh mór le Muire,
Mar tá cliathán mo thíse cluthar,
Agus cruach mhóna im' chistin,
Is m'fhear tí ag dul don reilg.
        A Sheáin óig, a rúin!

A Sheáin, trí lár mo chroí anonn!
Do chosa fada buí

Sínte síos le taobh do thí,
        A Sheá..á..á..áin
        trí lár mo chroí a...nonn!

Gol a gol ó, gol ó, gol ó;
Gol ó, gol ó, gol ó, gol;
Gol a gol ó, gol ó, gol ó;
        A Sheáin, trí lár mo chroí a...nonn!

Mo thaisce is mo rún tú!
Is do bhuailtheá mé le craobh is rúta,
Is le ceann ramhar an tsúiste;
Is moladh bhéarfad don Úrmhac
Mar ba dhuitse ba thúisce,
        A Sheáin óig a rún!

Mo ghrá thú is mo thaisce!
Do thugthá dhom an taobh ba chrua den leaba,
An chuid ba chaoile den bheatha,
Is an ceann ba raimhre den bhata,
        A Sheáin óig a rúin!

Mo ghrá thú is mo chumann!
Do chuirtheá na cearca chun nide
Do thógthá an t-im den chuiginn,
Is mise sa chúinne ag sileadh,
        A Sheáin óig a rúin!

Mo ghrá thú is mo chiall!
Is tá féasóg ar do ghiall,
Gan tú féachaint soir ná siar,
Is t-anam gléigeal ag an ndiabhal,
        A Sheáin óig a rúin!

Mo chreach mór is mo lot!
Nuair a gheobhair-se uaim amach
Is braitlín bán id' ghlaic,
Is tairne síos id' chab
Do chuallacht suas let' ais,
Is mise rompu amach,

Mo ramhainn agam is mo shluasaid
Chun clúdaithe anuas ort,
   A Sheáin óig a rúin!

Cuirfead leac le cúl do chinn,
Is leac eile le trácht do bhoinn,
Dhá leac déag nó trí
Anuas ar aghaidh do chroí,
Ná ligfidh duit éirí aníos,
   A Sheáin óig a rúin!

Ach ní chreidfinn féin ón ríocht
Ná go bpreabfá fós id' shuí,
Is bheadh bata glas ón gcoill
Go hard ós cionn mo chinn
   A Sheáin óig a rúin!

Fuaireas an Caoine seo — ceol agus focail — ó
Sheán Bán Ó Conchubhair .... B'é scéal a bhí
aige 'na thaobh ná seo: fear ná réidhtigheadh a
bhean is é féin, leig sé air bás d'fhághail chun go
gcloiseadh sé cad déarfadh sise nuair bheadh sé
féin, dar léi, tar éis bháis. Nuair a bhí sé fé chlár
do chaoin sí é mar ba ghnáth an uair sin. Ní
ró-mhaith an cháil a thug sí air, má b'fhíor di.

A Joking Lament

Oh praise be to Mary,
My little house is cosy,
A stack of turf in the kitchen,
And my man on his way to the graveyard,
   Dear Johnny, oh!

Oh, John, straight through my heart!
Your long yellow legs
Stretched out at the side of your house,
   Dear Johnny o-o-o-oh
   Straight through my hea-a-art!

Gol a gol ó, gol ó, gol ó;
Gol ó, gol ó, gol ó, gol;
Gol a gol ó, gol ó, gol ó;
   Oh, John, straight through my hea-a-art!

My treasure and darling!
You beat me with root and branch,
And with the thick end of the flail,
And I'll praise the Son of God,
Because you died before me,
   Dear Johnny, oh!

My love and my treasure!
You gave me the hard side of the bed,
The thin side of the food,
The thick end of the stick,
   Dear Johnny oh!

My love and my precious!
You used to shut in the hens,
And take the butter from the churn,
While I wept in the corner,[1]
   Dear Johnny oh!

My love and my darling!
There are whiskers on your jaw,
But you're not looking east or west,
And the devil is welcome to your soul,
   Dear Johnny oh!

My great grief and sorrow!
When you go before me
In a white sheet, with clasped hands,
Your toothless mouth nailed shut,
Your relatives up beside you,
I will walk in front,
With my shovel and my spade,
To cover you with earth,
   Dear Johnny oh!

I'll put a stone above your head
And another at your feet,
Twelve more or thirteen
I'll lay across your heart,
So you won't get up again,
   Dear Johnny oh!

But I still can't believe
That you won't yet jump up,
With a green stick from the woods
To brandish over my head,
   Dear Johnny oh!

I learned this lament — words and music — from
Seán Bán Ó Conchubhair . . . This is the story he
told about it: a man and his wife who did not get
on; he pretended to die, so as to hear what she
might say when she thought he was dead. When
he was laid out, she lamented him according to
the custom of the time. She didn't say anything
very good about him, by all accounts.

---

1. For the significance of the man's occupying himself with hens and
butter, see the lament for Diarmaid Mac Cárthaigh, p. 1386, note 6.

ANONYMOUS

from:
AN SEANCHAIDHE MUIMHNEACH (1932)

[Originally published in *An Lóchrann*, vol. 7 (1908), this stave-anecdote celebrates the quick wit and ready retort at which keening women excelled. It is another example of lament-poetry which wittily expresses tensions between in-laws, attributed here to a woman from Inch, County Kerry, on the death of her father. The lines quoted are known also from other sources. This text is from Pádraig Ó Siochfhradha 'An Seabhac' (ed.), *An Seanchaidhe Muimhneach* (1932), pp. 277–8. Headnote and translation, A.B.]

BEAN ÍNSE AG CAOINEADH A ʜATHAR

San tseanaimsir agus indiu féin sa Ghaedhealtacht, nuair a chaillfí duine, bheadh mná ag déanamh ranna molta dhóibh agus iad fá chlár i dtigh an tórraimh. Do dhéanfaidís iad ar an nóimeat san gan aon chuimhneamh roimh ré, nó, mar adéarfá, extempore . . .

Do cailleadh seanduine timcheall Ínse agus tháinig inghean leis go tigh an chuirp. Bhí sí pósta i nÍnse. Bhí bean mhic ag an seanduine, leis agus ó Ínse ab eadh í. Dubhairt inghean an tseanduine nuair a tháinig sí isteach os a chionn:

Mo ghrádh thú is mo thaisce,
Is ba mhór le rádh thú tamall,
Nuair a báthtaí muc id chuid bainne,
Idir dhá Chéadaoin an Earraigh,
Nuair a bhíodh muinntir Ínse dealbh.

Dubhairt bean a mhic 'á freagairt:

Léan ort agus lagar!
A sraoile bhuidhe 's a chaile,
Is ná cuir bréag go deo ar mhairbh,
Is go mórmhór ar t'athair,
Mar níorbh mhuc é ach banbh,
Is níor leis féin an bainne,
Ach é bhailiú ar fuaid na mbaile.

HOW A WOMAN FROM INCH LAMENTED HER FATHER

In the old days, and even today in the Gaeltacht, when somebody would die, women would make verses praising them while they lay in state in the wake-house. They would compose them straight away, without thinking about them beforehand, or as you might say, *extempore* . . .

An old man died around Inch [County Kerry], and one of his daughters came to the wake. She was married, and living in Inch. The old man had a daughter-in-law as well, who was from Inch. When the old man's daughter came in, she went and stood at his head where he lay, and said:

'My love and my treasure,
You were once well-known,
When you milked enough to drown a pig,
Between two Wednesdays in spring,
While the people of Inch had nothing.'

The son's wife retorted:

'Bad luck to you and weakness!
You sallow slut, you hag;
Don't tell lies about the dead,
And especially not your father
That was no pig, just a *banbh*,[1]
And he didn't own the milk,
He collected it around the villages.'

1. A young pig, sometimes spelt 'bonham' in English, but pronounced 'bon'v'.

Biographies/Bibliographies

Sir James Cotter's Nurse

LIFE. The name of the woman who composed an oral lament in Irish for Sir James Cotter the younger at the time of his execution in Cork in 1720 has not been recorded. She was said to be his old nurse.

CHIEF WRITINGS. 'Fiachra Éilgeach' [Risteárd Ó Foghludha, 1871–1957], 'Cé Cheap an Caoine?', *Irish Press*, Monday 27 April 1936.

Cáit de Búrca

LIFE. Cáit de Búrca (Mrs Kate Burke) is named as the woman who was given permission to remove the severed head of her brother, Father Nicholas Sheehy, from the gate of Clonmel jail, County Tipperary, twenty years after he was executed there on 15 March 1766. The oral lament composed at the time of his death is also attributed to his sister, though it is not certain that the same sister is meant. The Sheehys were a prominent Tipperary family in the eighteenth century.

CHIEF WRITINGS. *Feasta* (February 1956), p. 2.

BIOGRAPHY AND CRITICISM. Maurice Bric, 'The Whiteboy Movement in Tipperary, 1760–80,' in *Tipperary: History and Society*, eds. William Nolan and Thomas G. McGrath (Dublin: Geography Publications, 1985), pp. 158–62; Dáithí Ó hÓgáin, *Duanaire Thiobraid Árann: Cnuasach d'Fhilíocht na nDaoine ó Oirdheisceart an Chontae* (Dublin: An Clóchomhar, 1981), pp. 88–9; William P. Burke, *History of Clonmel* (Waterford, 1907), pp. 361–405, 496–7.

Eibhlín Dubh Ní Chonaill

LIFE. Born about 1743 and brought up in Derrynane House, near Waterville, County Kerry, Eibhlín was the daughter of Dónall Mór Ó Conaill (d. 1770), a prosperous Catholic gentleman who was also a smuggler, and Máire Ní Duibh, a well-known poet and personality in the oral tradition. She and her sister Máire were twins; her twenty other siblings (ten of whom survived) included Dónall, the so-called 'Last Colonel of the Irish Brigade', and the father of another Dónall, Daniel O'Connell MP (1775–1847). This nephew later came to national prominence as 'The Liberator', credited with achieving Catholic emancipation in 1829. Máire married James Baldwin, a landowner, of Macroom, County Cork, and Eibhlín is said to have first seen her future husband, Art Ó Laoghaire, of Raleigh, near Macroom, while visiting her. Eibhlín had already been married, at fifteen, to an elderly man called O'Connor, of Firies, County Kerry, but was widowed six months later. She married Ó Laoghaire on 19 December 1767. They had two sons, Conchubhar and Fear, and Eibhlín was pregnant again, according to her own account, when her husband was shot dead on horseback by crown forces in 1773, when he was twenty-six. Eibhlín is remembered as the composer of the most famous oral lament in Irish tradition. She died *c*. 1800.

CHIEF WRITINGS. Seán Ó Tuama (ed.), *Caoineadh Airt Uí Laoghaire* (Dublin: An Clóchomhar, 1961); trans. Frank O'Connor, 'The Lament for Art O'Leary', in *Kings, Lords and Commons: An Anthology from the Irish* (Dublin: Gill and Macmillan, 1970), pp. 109–19 (see extract, Volume I, pp. 309–13); trans. Eilis Dillon, 'The Lament for Arthur O'Leary', *The Cork Anthology*, ed. Seán Dunne (Cork: Cork University Press, 1993), pp. 354–66.

BIOGRAPHY AND CRITICISM. Mrs Morgan John O'Connell, *The Last Colonel of the Irish Brigade: Count O'Connell and Old Irish Life at Home*

and Abroad 1745–1833 (1892; rpr. Cork: Tower Books, 1977, vol. 2); Rachel S. Bromwich, 'The Keen for Art O'Leary, its Background and its Place in the Tradition of Gaelic Keening,' *Éigse*, vol. 5 (1948), pp. 236–52; Seán Ó Coileáin, 'The Irish Lament: An Oral Genre', *Studia Hibernica*, vol. 24 (1984–88), pp. 97–117; L.M. Cullen, 'The Contemporary and Later Politics of Caoineadh Airt Uí Laoire', *Eighteenth-Century Ireland*, vol. 8 (1993), pp. 7–38; Seán Ó Tuama, 'The Lament for Art O'Leary', in his *Repossessions: Selected Essays on the Irish Literary Heritage* (Cork: Cork University Press, 1995), pp. 78–100; Breandán Ó Buachalla, *An Caoine agus an Chaointeoireacht* (Baile Átha Cliath: Cois Life, 1998); Angela Bourke, 'Performing, not Writing: the Reception of an Irish Woman's Lament', in *Dwelling in Possibility: Women Poets and Critics on Poetry*, eds. Yopie Prins and Maeera Schreiber (Ithaca, NY, and London: Cornell University Press, 1997), pp. 132–6; Declan Kiberd, 'Eibhlín Dubh Ní Chonaill: The Lament for Art Ó Laoghaire', in his *Irish Classics* (London: Granta Books, 2000), pp. 161–81.

Mother of Diarmaid Mac Cárthaigh

LIFE. No biographical information available on this woman from County Cork, said to have composed a famous lament for her son on his death in 1860.

Neilí Ní Dhomhnaill

LIFE. Singer, storyteller and maker of new songs, born 1907 in Rinn na Feirste, County Donegal, she suffered from poor eyesight, becoming totally blind in later life. Her brother Aodh (Hiúdaí Mhicí Hiúdaí), later a teacher in Kells, County Meath, was a noted collector of folklore in Donegal in the mid-twentieth century, while his children, Maighréad and Tríona Ní Dhomhnaill and Mícheál Ó Domhnaill, are well-known singers and musicians. Performing solo, together, and as members of Skara Brae, the Bothy Band, Touchstone and other groups, they have recorded many songs learnt from her. In the 1970s, Mícheál Ó Domhnaill recorded dozens of songs from his aunt Neilí Ní Dhomhnaill for the Irish Folklore Collection. She died in 1984.

DISCOGRAPHY. *Ireland/Irlande* (compilation) (Auvidis, UNESCO D8271).

BIBLIOGRAPHY. Cathal Goan, 'Dhá Amhrán ó Neilí Ní Dhónaill', *Ceol*, vol. 5, no. 2 (1982), pp. 38–42, and vol. 6, no. 1 (1983), pp. 2–4; 'An Fial Athair Dónaill', *Ceol*, vol. 7, nos 1 and 2 (1984), pp. 46–9; Hugh Shields, Douglas Sealy, Cathal Goan, *Scéalamhráin Cheilteacha* (Baile Átha Cliath: An Clóchomhar, 1985), pp. 15–17; Fintan Vallely (ed.), *The Companion to Irish Traditional Music* (Cork: Cork University Press, 1999), pp. 265–6.

Máire Ruiséal

For biography and bibliography, see p. 1261.

ANGELA BOURKE and PATRICIA LYSAGHT, *Editors*

Spirituality and Religion in Oral Tradition

In Ireland's oral culture, especially in Gaeltacht areas, women have been the acknowledged experts and specialists in the whole area of vernacular religion, its theory and practice.[1] Until late in the twentieth century, especially in old age, women versed in religious tradition were accorded an authority in rural areas that was largely independent of the institutional church. Many of them would discuss doctrine and prayer intensely among themselves and speak of their heritage of religious poetry and narrative as their greatest intellectual and spiritual treasure. Legends about local saints, their lives, and the miracles attributed to them, are an important component of a sense of place, developed over generations. Women telling such stories to children and adults enlisted the features of the familiar landscape to give immediacy to the lessons they taught about behaviour, while stories about the Virgin Mary, who is often depicted as visiting the homes of the rural poor, gave dignity to the daily round of life.[2] While such stories preach the value of virtues like charity and forbearance, they also offer consolation in adversity and tacit support for resistance to oppressive authority.

The strength of the Catholic church in Ireland during the period after Catholic emancipation (1829) was reflected in a growing centralization of authority, and depicted in the architecture of large churches or 'chapels', many of which became the nuclei of new villages in the countryside.[3] The priest's authority reigned supreme in the system they represented; he insisted on regular attendance at Sunday mass and the sacraments, and often on the congregation's dressing 'respectably' — meaning, in shop-bought clothing.[4] Throughout Ireland, vernacular patterns of spirituality gradually gave way to those imported from continental Europe.[5] The dedications of new chapels, like the names given to children, reflected the growing popularity of European saints, and changes in the cult of the Virgin Mary. These new patterns were disseminated by a priesthood drawn mostly from the English-speaking 'strong farmer' class of rural Ireland and educated at the seminary founded in Maynooth, County Kildare, in 1795.[6] Although large sections of the population spoke only Irish until after the Famine, the language of this institutional Catholicism was English; the printed word its medium. The oral tradition of spiritual practice and religious teaching, of which women were the chief practitioners, became largely unheard in English-speaking areas, but continued in the Gaeltacht.[7]

3. See Kevin Whelan, 'The Catholic Parish, the Catholic Chapel and Village Development in Ireland', *Irish Geography*, vol. 16 (1983), pp. 1–15.
4. Cf. Caitriona Clear, *Nuns in Nineteenth-Century Ireland* (Dublin: Gill and Macmillan; Washington, D.C.: Catholic University of America Press, 1987), p. 18, for an anecdote of children expelled from school for lack of 'respectable shop clothes'.
5. S.J. Connolly, *Priests and People in Pre-Famine Ireland 1780–1845* (Dublin: Gill and Macmillan; New York: St Martin's Press, 1982), ch. 3, 'Popular and Official Religion'; Desmond J. Keenan, *The Catholic Church in Nineteenth-Century Ireland: A Sociological Study* (Dublin: Gill and Macmillan; Totowa, New Jersey: Barnes and Noble, 1983); James O'Shea, *Priest, Politics and Society in Post-Famine Ireland: A Study of County Tipperary 1850–1891* (Dublin: Wolfhound Press; New Jersey: Humanities Press, 1983).
6. J. O'Shea, *Priest, Politics and Society*, pp. 13–42.
7. See Margaret MacCurtain, 'Fullness of Life: Defining Female Spirituality in Twentieth-Century Ireland', in *Women Surviving: Studies in Irish Women's History in the 19th and 20th Centuries*, (eds) Maria Luddy and Cliona Murphy (Dublin: Poolbeg, 1990), pp. 233–63.

1. For the written expression of women's spirituality and religion, see the section 'Religion, Science, Theology and Ethics, 1500–2000', pp. 459–753.
2. See Pádraig Ó Héalaí, 'Moral Values in Irish Religious Tales', *Béaloideas*, vols 42–4 (1974–6), pp. 176–212.
3. See Kevin Whelan, 'The Catholic Parish, the Catholic Chapel and Village Development in Ireland', *Irish Geography*, vol. 16 (1983), pp. 1–15.

Like the lamenting of the dead (see pp. 1365–398), the maintenance and transmission of vernacular spirituality and religion guaranteed a certain — if sometimes marginal — authority and prestige to those who were expert in it. Prayers, practices and religious narratives accompanied life's daily routines, and offered support and consolation during its most frightening and painful moments. Some people who had inherited the vernacular system could, like Peig Sayers, accommodate their spirituality without apparent conflict to the often authoritarian Catholicism administered by a male priesthood; other cases, however, saw confrontations between priests and the practitioners of non-institutional religion, as the teachings of the sixteenth-century Counter-Reformation were finally implemented throughout Ireland.[8]

All across Christian Europe, before the Protestant Reformation, religion was taught through narrative. Educated people read scripture and the lives of the saints in Latin; others heard of them in sermons, illustrated by the iconography of religious painting in churches. Religious tales became an important part of the oral storyteller's repertoire. 'Apocryphal' gospels supplied details about the lives of Christ and his apostles not found in the canonical New Testament, and could resemble the modern soap opera in their drama and complexity.[9] *Exempla* were tales told by clergy to stress points of morality by dramatic and sometimes lurid example.[10]

Prayers (direct appeals to God) and charms (verbal formulae believed to be efficacious in themselves) were known by heart, or written down and carried as talismans, often by those who could not read. There were prayers for all occasions; charms for a variety of ailments and problems. Many of them drew on incidents from scripture, canonical or apocryphal, and charms especially were closely guarded secrets. They could be lucrative, although their owners rarely accepted rewards of money, and were transmitted to a chosen member of the next generation, usually a person of the opposite sex.

In the late Middle Ages, growing interest in the humanity of Christ and of his mother led to a cult of the Passion, which dwelt in detail on the sufferings of both. Across Europe, from Greece, to Germany, to Ireland, songs about Good Friday depicted the Virgin Mary not as the stoic and steadfast mother of the Latin hymn, 'Stabat Mater', but as a woman lamenting her crucified son according to vernacular traditions: angry, energetic, dishevelled and eloquent.[11] In Irish, such songs have survived, finding a new role in institutional Catholic practice since the 1960s, when vernacular languages replaced Latin, and new liturgies began to be used in church. Until then they had been identified almost exclusively with domestic spirituality and with the older women who made it their special business to remember and transmit them, along with prayers and religious narratives. Unlike love-songs and other kinds of oral poetry, which are rarely performed without being sung, these religious songs could be, and were, recited as devotional poems.

Religious songs described, and also elicited, intense emotion: 'I never heard anything so moving in my life,' one man from Kerry told folklore collector Seosamh Ó Dálaigh, 'as Peig Sayers reciting a lament of the Virgin Mary for her son, her face and voice getting more and more sorrowful. I came out of the house and I didn't know where I was.'[12] Similar responses to other performers are recorded from other places, and it was not unusual for a singer to weep copiously as she recounted details of the Crucifixion.[13] The recurring chant of stylized sobs which punctuates many of these songs is borrowed from the lament tradition and seems to have worked as a releaser of emotion.

Songs of the Virgin's lamentation were commonly sung during Lent, especially on Good Friday. Teenage boys and young men who entered houses during this period, expecting an evening

---

8. Cf. Keith Thomas, *Religion and the Decline of Magic* (London: Weidenfeld and Nicolson, 1971; Penguin Books, 1973).

9. See M.R. James, *The Apocryphal New Testament* (London: Oxford University Press, 1924; rpr. 1980).

10. The primary reference work for this narrative genre is F.C. Tubach, *Index Exemplorum: A Handbook of Medieval Religious Tales* (Folklore Fellows Communications, No. 204) (Helsinki: Academia Scientiarum Fennica, 1969, 1981); see also, P. Ó Héalaí, 'Moral Values in Irish Religious Tales'.

11. See M. Alexiou, *The Ritual Lament in Greek Tradition*, pp. 55–82; Angela Partridge, *Caoineadh na dTrí Muire: Téama na Páise i bhFilíocht Bhéil na Gaeilge* (Baile Átha Cliath: An Clóchomhar, 1983), pp. 68–85.

12. Quoted in Peig Sayers, *An Old Woman's Reflections*, p. xiii.

13. A. Partridge, *Caoineadh na dTrí Muire*, p. 91.

of night-visiting, sometimes found the grandmother authoritatively leading the household in prayer — in which they were expected to join. Religious songs were also heard at deathbeds and at wakes, where songs of the Virgin's lamentation apparently fulfilled some of the functions of *caoineadh* or ritual lament after that practice had been abandoned.[14] Church opposition to the *caoineadh* did not extend to the Virgin's laments, but several singers have asserted that their songs vindicate the practice; in them the Virgin Mary keens her son, and the son, from his place on the Cross, blesses women who lament.[15]

Modern liturgies use quite short versions of traditional religious songs, and confine themselves to those which conform to orthodox religious teaching, but versions collected from oral tradition can be up to and over one hundred lines long, sung slowly, and with a refrain after each line. Some of them contain startlingly precise detail about the indignities inflicted on the suffering Christ: one long prayer, probably written down in County Cork or County Waterford early in the twentieth century, mentions a total of 5,475 red and painful wounds on his body — the same number as specified in artists' manuals published in France in 1493 and 1495.[16] The women who preserved these songs also frequently specialized in stories about Christ, his mother and the saints, pointing out connections between items of

tradition and drawing inferences from them for daily life. Women who had been married in their teens or early twenties to much older men often spent long years as widows. Many who had reared sons placed special emphasis on the relationship between Christ and his mother, explaining the intensity of emotion expressed in terms of their own lives: 'Mo ghrá thú, a Mháthair!' — 'Mother, you are my love!' — Christ says on the Cross, according to Irish religious song; Mary's reply is 'Mo sheacht ngrá thusa, a Mhic', 'Son, you are my seven loves!' This is the reason, singers sometimes explain, why every mother loves her son seven times more than he loves her.[17] This story is just one of a large group of aetiological legends which focus on the Crucifixion as mythic time, when features of the world as we know it came to be.

The religious verbal art and the spiritual practices, through which pious women situated themselves *vis-à-vis* eternity, consolidated their authority in old age, and contrived to chart both space and time without the aid of writing, had almost died out in their traditional form and context by the end of the twentieth century. A growth in local studies, however, together with a strong revival of 'Celtic' spirituality means that they are unlikely to be forgotten.[18]

ANGELA BOURKE

14. Ibid., pp. 101–3.
15. Ibid., pp. 99–101.
16. A. Partridge, *Caoineadh na dTrí Muire*, pp. 70, 275; Émile Mâle, *L'art religieux de la fin du moyen âge en France* (Paris, 1908, 1922), p. 89, n. 6.

17. A. Partridge, p. 230; cf. S. Ó Súilleabháin, *Scéalta Cráibhtheacha* (Baile Átha Cliath: An Cumann le Béaloideas Éireann, 1951–2), pp. 7–8.
18. See John O'Donohue, *Anam Chara: Spiritual Wisdom from the Celtic World* (London, New York, Toronto, Sydney, Auckland: Bantam, 1997).

PEIG SAYERS

(1873–1958)

from:
MACHTNAMH SEANA-MHNÁ
(1939)

[One critic has said of Peig Sayers's autobiography, *Peig* (1936), extracts from which appear elsewhere in this volume, that the religion it depicts is like Valium: a

panacea for all life's ills, which deprives her narrative of the assertiveness that would have made it a better book.[1] In her mid-sixties, the famous storyteller from the Blasket Island in County Kerry dictated a second volume, in which she described herself as an old woman, close to

1. Cathal Ó Háinle, 'Peig, Aonghus Ó Dálaigh agus MacBeth', in *Oidhreacht an Bhlascaoid*, ed. Aogán Ó Muircheartaigh (Baile Átha Cliath: Coiscéim, 1989), pp. 253–69, at 259.

death. This elegiac reminiscence is at once depressive and lyrical, but shows the centrality of religion to Peig's world-view, and the strong spiritual element in her aesthetic appreciation of her natural surroundings on the island, with its high hill and cliffs, white beach, and view of the mainland opposite. Peig Sayers lived for almost twenty years after *Machtnamh Seana-mhná* was published, only beginning to work with Seosamh Ó Dálaigh, her most important collector, after she moved back to the mainland in 1942. The translation is by Séamus Ennis (1919–82), the noted musician and folklore collector, some of whose collecting of songs in Irish is documented in the sub-section 'The Song Tradition', p. 1317. See Séamus Ennis, *An Old Woman's Reflections*, with an introduction by W.R. Rodgers (London: Oxford University Press, 1962). Headnote, A.B.]

AN CHAIBIDIL DHEIREANNACH

Tá mo thréimhse ar an mbinsín seo beagnach críochnaithe. Is doilbhir dubhach agus is uaigneach atáim ó bheith ag scaradh leis. Da fhad é an lá tagann an oíche, agus, foraíl! tá an oíche ag teacht domsa leis.

Táim ag scaradh leat, a lantáinín aoibhinn, a ghrian mo bheatha. Ag daoine eile a bheidh do shólás feasta, ach beadsa i bhfad i gcéin uait i ríocht nach eol dom. Ní bheidh Peig Mhór, mar a thugann na páistí orm, ann níos mó, ach b'fhéidir go mbeidh bean is fearr ná í. Ach ní bhainfidh sí a oiread sóláis as mar dá mhéid mo bhrón is mo chrá croí, thug Dia na Glóire is a Mháthair Bheannaithe cabhair dom. Ba mhinic mé i mo sheasamh anseo ag déanamh staidéir ar oibreacha an Chruthaitheora agus ag blaiseadh a mhilseachta ríúla i mo chroí.

Gach ní dár chruthaigh sé, ba shólás dom é, go fiú an bhróin féin is amhlaidh a chuireadh sé ag machnamh níos doimhne mé. Dar liom ní raibh i nithe an tsaoil seo ar fad ach an dealús — an áit seo lán inniu agus é folamh amárach — ná raibh sé le feiscint go soiléir agam. Na daoine a raibh aithne agam orthu i m'óige, ba mhinic an chloch sa mhuinchille acu dá chéile. Bhíodar láidir misniúil teannfhoclach, ach thiteadar go léir; glanadh as an saol iad. Ba é an cóiriú céanna a fuair an dream a bhí ann rompu, agus go bhfóire Dia orainn, cá bhfuil a saothar inniu? Daoine eile a bheith ina n-ionad, agus gan an chuimhne is lú acu orthu siúd. Is baois, dar liom, gach ní ach grá a thabhairt do Dhia.

Táim anois in achrann daingean na mblianta agus is iomdha rud a chonac. Gach rud a chuireas spéis ann, níor ligeas amú é. Bainfidh daoine eile caitheamh aimsire as mo shaothar nuair a bheadsa ar shlí na fírinne. Déarfaidh duine anseo agus duine ansiúd, b'fhéidir, 'Cérbh í an Pheig Sayers úd?' ach beidh Peig bhocht faid a nglaoidh uathu. Beidh an binsín glas seo mar a ndeineadh sí staidéar ina bhall cónaithe ag éanlaith an fhásaigh, agus an teach beag mar a mbíodh sí ag ithe is ag ól, ní dócha go mbeidh a rian ann.

Is uaigneach na smaointe iad seo atá á nochtadh i mo chroí inniu. Ní taitneamhach liom iad ach níl aon leigheas agam orthu. Seo chugam iad ina mílte — is cosúil le saighdiúirí iad. Faoi mar a chuirim an briseadh orthu tagann siad le chéile arís. Ní haon mhaith dom a bheith leo — tá buaite acu orm. Mo bheannachtsa agus beannacht Dé leis an óige. Agus mo chomhairle do gach n-aon an iasacht a bhaint as an saol seo mar ní luaithe spól ag casadh ná é. Tá mo shaolsa caite ar nos coinnile agus tá mo shúil in airde gach lá go nglaoifí orm isteach sa ríocht síoraí.

A Dhia atá ar neamh, tá mo mhuinín is mo dhóchas go hiomlán asat. Go ndéine tú treoir dom ar an mbóthar fada seo nár ghabhas fós. Is minic i gcaitheamh mo shaoil a thug tú treoir dom ar an mbóthar fada seo nár ghabhas fós. Is maith is eol domsa an chabhair naofa mar ba mhinic mé gafa ag brón agus gan dul as agam. Nuair ab airde a bhíodh an gábh sin é an uair a leagtá do shúil thrócaireach orm agus thagadh lonradh mar a bheadh taitneamh na gréine arís ar m'aigne bhuartha. Bhíodh na néalta bróin imithe agus gan a rian ann: ina leaba bhíodh aoibhneas spioradálta nach féidir liomsa a mhilseacht a léiriú anseo.

Ach tá an méid seo agam le rá, go raibh comharsain mhaithe agam. Chuidíomar féin le chéile agus ar scáth a chéile a mhaireamar. Gach rud a bhíodh ag teacht dorcha orainn nochtaímis dá chéile é agus chuireadh sin sólás aigne orainn. Ba í an charthanacht an phréamh ba dhaingne a bhí inár gcroí.

Is mar a bheadh róisín in uaigneas a d'fhásas féin suas, gan de chuideachta agam ach na seoidíní seo a cheap Dia na Glóire, moladh go deo leis. Gach maidin mhoch sa tsamhradh nuair a nochtadh an ghrian a haghaidh aníos de dhroim Shliabh an Fhiolair ba mhinic mé ag dearcadh uirthi agus san am céanna mé ag déanamh ionaidh de na dathanna a bhíodh ar an aer timpeall. Is cuimhin liom go maith go mbíodh gaithíní buí órga ina mbóithríní caola ag teacht orm anoir ó bharr an tsléibhe agus go mbíodh an sliabh dearg agus crios mór de gach uile dhath, idir bhán is bhuí is dhubh, timpeall na spéireach, agus gach dath ag tabhairt a chosúlachta féin ar an muir mhór bhraonach. Dar liom go mbíodh fáilte i gcroí gach créatúra roimh lonradh na maidine.

Tá daoine ann agus is dóigh leo gurb áit uaigneach aerach an t-oileán seo. Is fíor dóibh sin ach tá síocháin an Tiarna ann. Táimse i mo chónaí ann le breis is daichead bliain agus ní fhaca beirt de na comharsain ag troid ann fós. Ba gheall le mil do mo chroí bocht cráite éirí suas ar ghualainn sléibhe ann ag cnuchairt na móna agus ag bailiú na bhfód ar a chéile. Ba rómhinic a chaithinn mé féin siar sa fhraoch ghlas ag tógaint mo scíthe. Ní le cnámhleisce a dheininn é ach le háilleacht na gcnoc agus dordán na dtonn a bhíodh ag caoineachán siar uaim i gcuaiseanna dorcha mar a mbíodh róinte na farraige ag déanamh cónaí — iad sin agus an spéir ghorm gan néal á siúl, a bhí os mo chionn — sin iad a chuireadh d'fhiachaibh orm é mar b'in iad na pictiúirí ba thaitneamhaí le mo chroí agus is orthu is mó a bhí taithí agam.

Déaradh duine, b'fhéidir, gur simplí an saol a bhí againn á chaitheamh, ach ná measadh aoinne go raibh ár saol sámh. Lean ár n-anró féin sinn. Ba mhinic sinn i reachtaibh dul le heagla agus le scanradh, mar nuair a thagadh an geimhreadh ní cneasta mín ba ghnáth leis teacht. Bhíodh an mhuir mhór ag gabháil sa mhullach orainn agus tréan-neart na gaoithe ag cuidiú léi. Ní bhíodh le déanamh againn ach ár nguí a chur go dúthrachtach chun Dé gan aoinne a leagadh tinn ná breoite. Bhíodh ár mbun féin againn leis sin mar ní raibh sagart ná dochtúir láimh linn gan dul trasna an ghóilín mara, agus bhí an góilín sin suas le trí mhíle ar fad. Ach bhí Dia i bhfábhar dúinn, moladh go deo leis; mar le mo chuimhnese níor cailleadh aoinne gan an sagart le stoirm an gheimhridh.

Slán le beartaibh an tsaoil seo anois agus go mórmhór leis an aimsir aoibhinn aerach atá caite agam anseo. Is baolach liom ná déanfad a thuilleadh saothair feasta ar mhaithe le teanga na sárfhear. Ach tá cion duine déanta agam,

b'fhéidir. Dhéanfainn a oiread eile, agus ba chroí liom é, ach tá an cairde caite.

Guígig dom, a chairde is a chlann ó, Dia a thabhairt cabhair dom i gcomhair an bhóthair fhada.

THE LAST CHAPTER

My spell on this little bench is nearly finished. It's sad and low and lonely I am to be parting with it. Long as the day is, night comes, and alas, the night is coming for me, too.

I am parting with you, beautiful little place, sun of my life. Other people will have your pleasure in future, but I'll be far away from you in a kingdom I don't know. Big Peig, as the children call me, will be there no more, but maybe a better woman would. But she won't have as much pleasure as I had, because great as was my sorrow and heart-torment, God of Glory and His Blessed Mother helped me. I was often standing here studying the works of the Creator and tasting his royal sweetness in my heart. Everything He created was a consolation to me even unto grief itself, it would make me think deeper. I thought there was nothing in the things of life but poverty — this place full today and empty tomorrow — hadn't I got it to be seen, clearly. The people I knew in my youth, it was often they had the stone in the gauntlet for each other. They were strong, courageous, strong worded, but they all fell, they cleared out of the world. It was the same do the people who were there before them got, and may God have mercy on us, where is their work today? Other people to be in their place, without the slightest thought for them. I think everything is folly except for loving God!

I am now at tight grips with the years, and many a thing I saw. Everything I was interested in I didn't let it astray. Someone else will have pastime out of my work when I'm gone on the way of truth. A person here and a person there will say, maybe, 'Who was that Peig Sayers?' but poor Peig will be the length of their shout from them. This green bench where she used to do the studying will be a domicile for the birds of the wilderness, and the little house where she used to eat and drink, it's unlikely there'll be a trace of it there.

These thoughts appearing in my heart today are lonely. They are not pleasant for me but I can't help them. Here they are towards me in their thousands; they are like soldiers. As I scatter them, they come together again. It's no good for me to be at them. They have beaten me. My blessing of God be with Youth; and my advice to everyone is to borrow from this life, because a spool is no faster turning than it. My life is spent, as a candle, and my hope is up every day that I'll be called into the eternal kingdom.

O God who is in heaven, my trust and my hope is fully in you! May you guide me on this long road I have not travelled before! It's often during my life you helped me. Well I know your holy help, because I was often held by sorrow, with no escape. When the need was highest, it was then you would lay your merciful eye on me, and a light like the shining of the sun would come on my troubled mind. The clouds of sorrow would be gone without trace; in place there would be some spiritual joy whose sweetness I cannot describe here.

But I have this much to say, that I had good neighbours. We helped each other and lived in the shelter of each other. Everything that was coming dark upon us, we would disclose it to each other, and that would give us consolation of mind. Friendship was the fastest root in our hearts.

It was like a little rose in the wilderness that I grew up: without for company only those gems that God of Glory created, eternal praise to Him! Every morning in the summer when the sun would show its face over the top of Eagle Mountain[1] I was often looking at it and at the same time making wonder of the colours in the sky around us. I remember well that there used to be little yellow, golden rays as slender roads coming to me from the top of the mountain, and that the mountain used to be red and a big belt of every colour, between white, yellow and black, around the sky and every colour giving its own appearance on the great, wet sea. I think there was welcome in the heart of every creature for the sparkling of the morning.

There are people and they think that this island is a lonely airy place. That is true for them, but the peace of the Lord is in it. I am living here for more than forty years, and I didn't see two of the neighbours fighting in it yet. It was like honey for my poor tormented heart to rise up on the shoulder of the mountain footing turf or gathering the sods on each other.[2] Very often I'd throw myself back in the green heather, resting. It wasn't for bone-laziness I'd do it, but for the beauty of the hills and the rumble of the waves that would be grieving down from me, in dark caves where the seals of the sea lived — those and the blue sky without a cloud travelling it, over me — it was those made me do it, because those were the pictures most pleasant to my heart, and it's those I was most used to.

A person would say, maybe, that it was a simple life we were living, but nobody would say that our life was comfortable. Our own hardships followed us. It's often we were in a way to go with fear and fright, because when winter came it wasn't its habit to come gentle and kind. The great sea was coming on top of us and the strong force of the wind helping it. We had but to send our prayers sincerely to God that nobody would be taken sick or ill. We had our own charge of that because there wasn't a priest or doctor near us without going across the little strait and the little strait was up to three miles in length. But God was in favour with us, eternal praise to Him! For with my memory nobody died without the priest in winter-time.

Farewell to the things of this life now, and especially to the pleasant, gay time I have spent here. I'm afraid I'll do no more work in future for the language of the superior men, but I have done a person's share, maybe. I would do as much more, and have the heart for it, but the time is spent.

Pray for me, friends and dear people, that God will give me help for the long road!

---

1. On the mainland, visible across the Blasket Sound.

2. Sods of turf (peat) are cut for fuel and propped together to dry in the sun and wind (footed) before being stacked and transported home.

MÁIRE NÍ GHUITHÍN

(c. 1905–88)

from:
BEAN AN OILEÁIN (1986)

[This short account of a woman's life on the Great Blasket Island, County Kerry, by a younger neighbour of Peig Sayers, devotes one chapter to the traditional prayers and blessings which featured in the life of a child growing up. Tasks which had to be performed with care, such as lighting or dousing a lamp or setting a pot-oven over an open fire, were accompanied by short prayers; other prayers taught to children calmed them during such minor crises as tripping and falling, or having dust in the eye. No clear distinction is drawn here between practical, social and religious precepts. The priest emerges as a trusted authority figure, but is set clearly apart from the lay people to whom he ministers.   Translation and headnote, A.B.]

PAIDREACHA

Nuair a lasadh mo mháthair an solas, deireadh sí i gcónaí:

'Solas na bhFlaitheas chugainn agus a ghrásta beannaithe.' Nuair a mhúchadh sí é, deireadh sí: 'Nár mhúchadh Dia solas na bhFlaitheas ar ár n'anam.'

Nuair a dhéanfá sraoth, déarfaí leat: 'Dia linn is Muire is do shláinte.'

Dá mbeifeá breoite agus go ndéanfá sraoth, déarfaí leat: 'Dia linn is Muire agus tar i do shláinte.'

Deiridís sraoth na hoíche nár mhaith í nuair a bheifeá breoite ach sraoth na maidine go mbíodh sí go maith mar gur briseadh ar an mbreoiteacht í agus go mbeifeá ag dul i bhfeabhas gach lá eile.

Dá ndéanfaí taibhreamh duit istoíche agus tú i do chodladh agus go n-eachtrófá ar maidin é, déarfaí leat tú féin a choisreacan agus a rá: 'Breith maith ag Mac Mhuire ar mo thaibhreamh agus go ndeona le Dia is le Muire é sin inniu.' Ansan tú féin a choisreacan arís agus an phaidear san a rá trí n-uaire agus tú féin a choisreacan roimpi is ina diaidh agus nár bhaol go dtiocfadh aon drochní as do thaibhreamh.

Nuair a bhíodh an Choróin Mhuire á rá agus sinne inár leanaí beaga agus go ndéanfadh aoinne againn gáire, déarfaí linn: 'Cuimhnigh cé leis atánn tú ag caint,' nó 'An bhfuil a fhios agat cé leis atánn tú ag caint?'

Nuair a bhímis ag dul ag ithe, chaithimis sinn féin a choisreacan agus tar éis a bheith ite againn chomh maith. Bhaineadh na fearaibh agus na garsúin a gcaipíní díobh ag dul ag ithe, an t-aon uair amháin a bhainidís díobh sa tigh iad, ach nuair a bhídís ag dul a chodladh.

Thógaidís in airde ábhairín a gcaipín dá gceann ag beannú don sagart. Bhíodh an-ómós ag fad ag na seandaoine san oileán don sagart agus ag an seanghlúin go léir ins gach áit, is dócha. Aon ní a thagadh trasna orthu nó a bheadh ag cur tinnis orthu chuiridís dá gcroí leis an sagart é agus dheineadh a chomhairle maitheas dóibh anso. Teachtaire Dé ar an dtalamh a deiridís. Nuair a bhídís ag insint scéil dá chéile, deireadh na seanmhná: 'Tá sé sin chomh fíor anois is gurb é an sagart a déarfadh leat é.' B'é an sagart a nDia beag ar an talamh.

Bhí rud éigin faoi leith ag baint leis an ndúchas a bhí sna seandaoine. Bhí múineadh is deabhéasa éigin nádúrtha ó Dhia saolaithe leo, cé go raibh a lochtaí féin orthu chomh maith le duine. Ach bhí tuiscint agus fírinne agus féachaint rompu iontu, agus carthain. Déarfainn dá mbeidís beo inniu gurbh ait leo an saghas saoil atá ann agus go mbeadh seanbhlas acu air. Bíonn an roth ag iompú, a deirtear.

Rud eile a deiridís: 'Cabhair leis an laige i gcónaí mar ní maith í an éagóir ná an feall.'

Seanfhocail a bhíodh acu: 'Is fada siar a théann iarsma na drochbhirte' agus 'Filleann an feall ar an bhfeallaire.'

Deiridís dá ndéanfadh duine drochbheart, mara n-agródh Dia air féin é ar an saol so, go n-agrófaí ar a shliocht é. Deiridís leis, 'Duine íogair is ea an sagart — ní mar a chéile é agus aoinne eile agus ní maith d'aoinne é a chur i bhfeirg.' Sin aon ní a dhéanamh ina choinne a chuirfeadh fearg air . . .

Seo paidear a deirtí linn a rá dá mbeadh cáith choirce, síol féir nó rud éigin istigh faoinár súil.

Ar dtúis, sinn féin a choisreacan. Ansan an fabhra thuas a chur ar an bhfabhra thíos is a rá:

'Tá rud faoi mo shúil, Dia os mo chionn, Muire faoi mo dhá ghlúin is go mbaine Dia an rud ó mo shúil.' Ansan fíor na croise a dhéanamh arís agus an phaidear a rá trí huaire.

Bheadh greim agat ar an bhfabhra thuas le do láimh dheis á choimeád anuas ar do shúil ar an bhfabhra thíos. Ansan nuair a bheadh an phaidear ráite trí n-uaire bhogfá den bhfabhra thuas, rithfeadh uisce amach as do shúil is thiocfadh pé rud a bheadh istigh fúithi amach.

Dá mbeadh luaith nó gainimh istigh faoin súil, chuirfeadh bean barra na teanga isteach fúithi agus bheadh sí soir siar go héadrom cneasta le fíorbharra na teanga go dtí go mbaileodh sí amach an luaith nó an ghainimh a bheadh istigh. Uaireanta eile, chuirtí cúinne de chiarsúr síoda isteach faoin súil d'iarraidh pé rud a bheadh istigh a bhailiú amach.

Nuair a bhítí ag cur cearc ar gor deirtí: 'Cearca go tiubh is coiligh go fánach.'

Nuair a fhaightí bainne ó thigh na gcomharsan tar éis a mbó a bhreith, chuirtí gráinne salainn mhín is scilling san áras go bhfaighfeá an bainne ann; mara mbeadh aon airgead oiriúnach agat chuirfeá ubh circe ina ionad. Agus déarfá leis an duine a thug chugat an bainne: 'Go méadaí Dia bainne agus a mháithreacha chugat.'

Na chéad scealláin a ghearrfaí do na prátaí síl, sara dtógfaí amach as an dtigh iad le cur, bhaineadh fear an tí de a chaipín agus bheadh buidéal uisce coisreacan ina láimh chlé. Chroithfeadh sé lena láimh dheis braon beag den uisce coisreacan air féin ar dtús, is déanfadh sé Fíor na Croise air féin. Ansan chroithfeadh sé ar pé duine eile a bheadh istigh é agus ansan ar scealláin na bprátaí síl. Bhuailfeadh uaidh buidéal an uisce coiscreacan ansan agus chuirfeadh air a chaipín, bhuailfeadh thiar ar a dhrom mála na sceallán is raghadh 'on ghort á sá.

Bhaintí an-úsáid as an uisce coisreacan san oileán. Ní raghadh aoinne ar an gcnoc ann a bheadh ag dul síos sna faillteacha i ndiaidh na gcaorach ná caithfeadh braon uisce coisreacan air féin ar dtús sara bhfágfadh sé an tigh.

Bhí an-mhuinín ar fad acu as agus as Fíor na Croise a dhéanamh leis. Fiú amháin, dá mbeadh pian ort, déarfaí leat: 'Cuimil braon uisce coisreacan de is coisric tú féin is leighisfidh Dia thú.'

Dá sleamhnófá nó dá dtitfeá, dhéanfá cros a tharraingt san áit a thitis le cloch is dhéanfá Fíor

na Croise trí n-uaire ar phátrún na croise sin a tharraingís is déarfá: 'In Ainm an Athar agus a Mhic agus an Spioraid Naoimh,' trí n-uaire is deirtí ná sleamhnófá is ná titfeá arís san áit sin.

Seo seanphaidear a déarfá tar éis dul isteach sa leaba chun dul a chodladh istoíche:

Síocháin ár dTiarna Íosa Críost,
Trí bhrí a Pháise Beannaithe, Tódal
    Cairéanach,[1]
Íosa na Nasairéanach, Rí na nGiúdach.
Maighdean is Muire Mháthair,
Coimirce na Naomhaingeal,
Eadraí na nUile fhíréan idir mé is mo
    namhdaibh go léir,
Istigh is amuigh. Áiméan.

Nuair a bhíodh císte san oigheann ag mo mháthair is í ag cur tine dhearg anuas ar an gclúdach, deireadh sí i gcónaí nuair a bhíodh an teas ag breith ar a láimh: 'Go saora Dia sinn ar thine na bpian.'

Bhíodh Dia i gcónaí i mbéal agus i ráite na seandaoine. Deiridís: 'Go maithe Dia ár gcionta, ár gcortha is ár bpeacaí dúinn. Go bhféacha Dia orainn is nach le feirg é.'

Dá ndéarfadh duine leo rud éigin nár thaitin leo, déarfaidís: 'Nár agraí Dia ort é.'

---

1. Last two words obscure.

PRAYERS

When my mother lit the lamp, she would always say: 'May the light of Heaven and its blessed graces be with us.' When she extinguished it, she would say 'May God never extinguish the light of Heaven in our souls.'

Whenever you sneezed, someone would say: 'May God and Mary and your health be with us.'

If you sneezed when you were ill, they would say: 'May God and Mary be with us; get well.'

They used to say that sneezing at night was not a good sign if you were ill, but sneezing in the morning was good. It meant the sickness was breaking and you would improve every day from then on.

If you had a dream in bed at night and told it in the morning, you would be told to bless yourself[1] and say: 'May the son of Mary judge my dream to be good and may it please God and Mary today.' Then bless yourself again and say that prayer three times, blessing yourself before and after, and nothing bad would come of your dream.

While the Rosary was being said when we were small, if any one of us laughed, we would be told, 'Remember to whom you are speaking, or do you realise to whom you are speaking?'

When we began to eat, we had to bless ourselves, and again when we had finished. The men and boys took off their caps while eating, the only time they did so indoors, except when they were going to bed.

They would lift their caps a little from their heads when greeting the priest. The old people in the island had tremendous respect for the priest, as the older generation did everywhere, I suppose. When anything bothered them or worried them, they used to unburden themselves to the priest about it, and his advice would do them good. They called him God's messenger on earth. When the old women were telling each other something, they would say 'Now that's as true as if the priest told it to you.' The priest was their little God on earth.

There was something very special about the old people's nature. They were born with natural good manners and courtesy from God, although they had their faults, the same as anybody. But they had understanding and truthfulness and foresight, as well as charity. I'd say if they were alive now they would find today's world strange; I don't think it would appeal to them. The wheel goes round, they say.

Something else they used to say: 'Always help the weak, for injustice and betrayal are not good.'

They had a proverb: 'The effects of a bad turn go a long way,' and another one, 'Treachery returns to the traitor.'

They used to say that if someone did something wrong, if God did not punish him in this life, his descendants would suffer for it. And they said, 'The priest is a touchy person — not like anybody else — and it's not good for anyone to anger him.' That is, to do anything that might annoy him . . .

Here is a prayer we were told to say if a bit of oats, or a grass-seed, or anything like that got into our eye.

First, we had to bless ourselves. Then draw the top eyelid over the bottom one saying, 'There's something in my eye, God above me, Mary under my two knees, and may God take the thing out of my eye.' Then make the Sign of the Cross again and say the prayer three times.

You would be gripping the top eyelash with your right hand, holding it down over the eye on the bottom lid. Then when you had said the prayer three times, you let go the top eyelash; water ran out of your eye, and whatever was in there came out.

If you had ash or sand in your eye a woman would put the tip of her tongue into it, and lick over and back ever so gently with the very tip of her tongue until she took out the ash or the sand. Sometimes too, they would put the corner of a silk handkerchief into the eye to get rid of whatever was there.

When they were setting a hen to hatch eggs they would say: 'May the hens be plentiful and the roosters scarce!'

When you got milk from the neighbours' house after their cow had calved, you would put a grain of salt and a shilling in the vessel you got the milk in; if you didn't have any money handy, you would put in a hen's egg instead. And you would say to the person who had brought the milk, 'May God increase your milk and your cows.'[2]

When the first seed potatoes were cut for sowing, before they were taken out of the house, the man of the house would take off his cap, and he would have a bottle of holy water in his left hand. With his right hand he would first sprinkle a small drop of the holy water on himself, and make the Sign of the Cross on himself. Then he would sprinkle it on whoever else was in the house, and then on the cut-up seed potatoes. He would leave down the bottle of holy water then, put on his cap, take the bag of seed-potatoes on his back and go to the field to sow them.

Holy water was used a lot on the island. Nobody would go to the hill intending to climb down the cliffs after sheep, without sprinkling a drop of holy water on himself first, before leaving the house.

1. With the sign of the Cross, touching the right hand to the forehead, the breast, and the left and right shoulders.

2. Literally, 'your milk and its mothers'.

They had a lot of faith in it, and in making the Sign of the Cross. Even if you had a pain, you would be told: 'Rub a drop of holy water on to it and bless yourself, and God will cure you.'

If you slipped or fell, you would use a stone to draw a cross [on the ground] in the place where you'd fallen, and make the Sign of the Cross three times on the mark of the cross you had drawn, and say: 'In the name of the Father and of the Son and of the Holy Ghost' three times, and they used to say you would never slip or fall in that place again.

Here is an old prayer you would say after getting into bed, to go to sleep:

> The peace of our Lord Jesus Christ
> Through the meaning of his Blessed
>   Passion,

Jesus of the Nazarenes, King of the Jews.
Virgin and Mary Mother,
Protection of the holy angels
Mediator of all the righteous between me
  and all my enemies
Within and without. Amen.

When my mother had put a cake in the pot-oven and was piling red embers on the lid, as the heat caught her hand she always said: 'May God preserve us from the painful fire [of hell].'

God was always on the lips and in the sayings of the old people. They would say: 'May God forgive us our crimes, our faults and our sins. May God look at us, but not angrily.'

If anyone told them something that did not please them, they would say: 'May God not punish you for it.'

ANNA NÍ BHAOILL

(b. 1894)

from:
BÉALOIDEAS (1936)

[Dozens, if not hundreds, of versions have been collected of the short prayer said while 'saving' the household fire at night. The open hearth of the traditional Irish house was always placed centrally at the base of the gable or an internal wall parallel to it. It was the literal focal point of indoor living, and the special responsibility of the 'woman of the house'. Last thing at night, she would gather the glowing embers together and arrange them carefully, covering them with ashes so as to conserve the fire until morning, and marking the ashes with a cross. This prayer was written down in Rinn na Feirste, County Donegal, and published in Béaloideas, vol. 6 (1936).[1] Translation and headnote, A.B.]

Nuair a Bhíonn Tú ag Coigilt na Teineadh

Coiglim-se an teine seo i n-ainm Chríost
  lághaigh
Go raibh Muire ar dhá cheann an toighe agus
  Brighid ina lár;
Gach a bhfuil de naoimh is d'aingle i gcathair
  na ngrást,
Go raibh ag cosaint 's ag coimhead an toighe
  seo go lá.

1. 'Adhamhnán', 'Cnuasach Sean-phaidreacha ó Rann na Feirsde', in Béaloideas, vol. 6 (1936), p. 50.

Prayer as You Save the Fire

I save this fire in the name of generous Christ
May Mary be at each end of the house, and
  Brigid in the middle;
May every saint and angel in the city of graces[1]
Keep and protect this house until day.

1. heaven.

ANNA NÍ GHRIANNA

(1893–1963)

from:
BÉALOIDEAS (1936)

[A popular prayer called 'The White Paternoster' is referred to in various European languages in texts that date from before the Protestant Reformation of the sixteenth century; it has also been collected extensively from oral tradition. Irish versions are usually called 'An Phaidir Gheal', but the noun and adjective are inverted in County Donegal. From *Béaloideas*, vol. 6 (1936), p. 53. Translation and headnote, A.B.]

An Gheal-Phaidir

A Gheal-Phaidir bheannuighthe, cá'r chodail tú
   'réir?
Chodail mé ar Neamh.
Cá gcodlochaidh tú anocht?
Fá chosa Chríost.
Caidé sin romhat?
Na haingle
Caidé sin id do dhiaidh?
Na haspail.
Caidé sin in do láimh deis leat?
Uisce coisreactha a chuir Muire liom a
   dhéanamh eolais go toigh Phárrthais.

Is léir liom an dabhach udaigh thall
a bhfuil an choinneal ghearach lasta 'n-a lár

Bríghid fá n-a brat
Muire fá n-a mac
Mícheál fá n-a sciath,
Dhá láimh Dé trasna fá m'anam.

The White Paternoster

Blessed White Paternoster,
Where did you sleep last night?
I slept in heaven.
Where will you sleep tonight?
Under Christ's feet.
What is that in front of you?
The angels.
What is that behind you?
The Apostles.
What are you holding in your right hand?
Holy water, that Mary sent with me, to show
   the way to the house of Paradise.

I can see the vat over there
with the tallow candle lighting in the middle.
Brigid with her cloak,[1]
Mary with her son,
Michael with his shield,[2]
The two hands of God placed across my soul.

1. Saint Brigid's most persistent attribute in medieval iconography, as well as in oral tradition, is her cloak or mantle.
2. Michael the archangel, depicted as a warrior.

MARY BARNABLE

(1854–*c.* 1957)

from:
ROMANTIC SLIEVENAMON IN HISTORY, FOLKLORE AND SONG (1955)

[Mary Barnable, of Walshbog, Killusty, on the slopes of Slievenamon in County Tipperary, was one hundred years old when this prayer was recorded from her in 1954. It is one of the latest examples of the Irish language recorded from that county. James Maher, *Romantic Slievenamon in History, Folklore and Song* (Mullinahone, Co. Tipperary: Kickham St., 1955), p. 285.   Translation and headnote, A.B.]

[A Rí na nGrást]

A Rí na nGrást, beidh mé go bráth ag súil leat;
A Rí 'na Mhac, beidh mé sa chúirt leat.

A Pheadair agus Phóil agus Mhichíl naomhtha,
A Eoin geal bhaiste agus Mhuire ghléigeal,
A bhfuil de Naoimh is d'Aingil ins na Flaithis le
    chéile
Déanaoighidh síothcháin leis an Athair
    naomhtha.
Cómhnuighfimid dáil ins na bFlaithis Lá
    Déidheann[ach]

Translation

King of Graces, I place my hope in you forever,
King with your Son, I shall be in the court with
    you.
Peter, Paul and holy Michael,
Fair John the Baptist and purest Mary,
All the saints and angels in heaven together
Make peace with the holy Father.
We shall meet in heaven on the last day.

ANNA NÍ RAGHALLAIGH

(1858–1936)

from:
CAOINEADH NA dTRÍ MUIRE
(1983)

[The longest versions of the song known through
commercial recordings and print as 'Caoineadh na dTrí
Muire', 'The Lament of the Three Marys', come from
County Mayo. This one was written down in 1903, when
the singer was forty-five, by Mícheál Ó Tiománaidhe. In
August 1941, in Glais, Erris, County Mayo, Séamus
Ó Duilearga wrote another, very similar, version from
Anna Ní Raghallaigh's daughter, Anne Cawley. She told
him that her mother had always said it was proper to
lament the dead, for the Virgin had asked the other women
to come and keen her son with her: 'D'abruíodh sí gur
cheart an marbhánach a chaoiniú, mar gur iarr an
Mhaighdean ar na mrá a theacht a' caoiniú a mic héin
leich.'[1] Original text in IFC 1650: 62–3. Translation and
headnote, A.B.]

Caoineadh na Maighdine

Nach mithid domsa féin féin dul chun an
    tsléibhe!
        Ochón ó agus ochón eile [*I ndiaidh gach líne*]
Nach mithid domsa féin féin dul agus mo
    leanbh éagcaoint!
Ó casadh Peadar Easpuig dom, ag siúl dhá lae,
'Ó a Pheadair Easpuig, an bhfaca tú
    m'aonmhac?'

'Ó a Mhaighdean, pill abhaile. Chonaic mé inné
    é agus é gabhtha lena námhaid'.
Ansin do scaoil sí a gruaig le fánaidh,
Níor airigh sí clocha míne an bhóthair á gortú
    ná á gearradh.
Ghearr sí an aicearra thríd an bhfásach,
An chéad léim a thug sí, sgoith sí an garda,
An dara léim go Gairdín Pharrthais,
Is an tríú léim go Crann na Páise.
'Ó cé sin thuas i gCrann na Páise?
Nó an é sin thuas mo mhaicín a d'iompair mé
    na trí ráithe?'
'Nó an ea nach n-aithníonn tú mé, a Mháthair?
    ar seisean',
'Ó cé an chaoi a n-aithneoinn thú, a Mhíle Grá
    geal,
Do shúilín briste agus do bhéilín gearrtha,
Agus do chuid fola uaisle anuas thríd leacrachaí
    na sráide?'
Ansin d'aithnigh siad gurb í a mháthair í;
Thóg siad suas é ar ghuailleacha arda,
Agus bhuail siad anuas é ar leacracha na sráide.
'Ó buailigí mé féin agus ná bainigí le mo
    mháthair!'
'Ó maróimid thú féin agus buailfimid do
    mháthair!'
'A Eoghain Baiste, tabhair leat mo mháthair,
Sul a bhfeice sí an splíníocht a gheobhas mo
    chnámha.'
'Ó an é sin an casúr a thiomáin na tairní?
Nó an í sin an tsleigh nimhe a chuaigh thríd do
    thaobh deas?
Nó an é sin an pionsúr a phioc an fheoil de na
    cnámha

---

1. See *Béaloideas*, vol. 12 (1942), pp. 203–5. For a comprehensive
study of the Virgin's laments in Irish, see A. Partridge, *Caoineadh na
dTrí Muire*; for this text, pp. 18–19, 150–3.

Nó an é sin a caipín splíníocht a chuaigh ar do
    cheann?'
Ansin d'iarr sé deoch orthu, agus gléasadh
    dragún, agus nimh ar súite,
Thóig sé ar a dheasláimh é, agus rinne sé fíon
    folláin de.
'Ó gabhaigí aníos, a Mhná, go gcaoine sibh liom
    an t-ár seo!
'Ó gabhaigí aníos, a Mhná, go gcaoine sibh liom
    mo pháistín!'
Ó cén rud a chaoinfeas muid mura gcaoine
    muid na cnámha?'
'Ó foighid, foighid, a Mháthair', ar seisean —
    'anocht agus amárach!
Caoinfidh na haspail mé, agus caoinfidh na
    bráithre mé,
Agus caoinfear go fóill fóill mé ar Oileán
    Pharrthas.
Agus níl éinne a chaoinfeas leat do pháistín,
Nach geal í a leaba i gcúirt na ngrásta.'

The Virgin's Lament

I myself must go to the mountain!
    Ochón and again, ochón! [*after every line*]
I must go and lament my baby!
Oh I met Peter the Bishop[1] walking by day,
'Oh, Bishop Peter, have you seen my only son?'
'Oh, Virgin, go home. I saw him yesterday,
    captured by his enemies.'
Then she let her hair hang loose.
She didn't feel the small stones of the road hurt
    and cut her,
She took a short cut through the wasteland,
The first leap she took, she passed the guard,
The second leap, to the Garden of Paradise,
The third leap, to the crucifixion tree.
'Oh, who is that, hanging on the crucifixion tree?
Or is that my little son, that I carried for nine
    months?'
'Can it be that you don't know me, Mother?' he
    said,
'Oh how could I know you, my Thousand White
    Loves,

With your little eye split and your little mouth
    cut,
And your noble blood flowing between the
    flagstones of the street?'
Then they realised that she was his mother;
They lifted him high on their shoulders,
And they threw him down on the stones of the
    street.[2]
'Oh, beat me if you wish, but don't touch my
    mother!'
'Oh, we will kill you, and we'll beat your mother
    too!'
'John the Baptist, take my mother away,
Before she sees the torture inflicted on my
    bones.'
'Oh, is this the hammer that drove the nails?
Or is this the poisoned spear that pierced your
    right side?
Are these the pincers that pulled the flesh from
    your bones?
Is this the cap of thorns that was put on your
    head?'
When he asked for a drink, they prepared
    dragon's bile, with poison soaked in it.
He took it in his right hand and made good
    wine of it.
'Oh come up here, Women, and help me keen
    this slaughter!
Come up here, Women, and help me keen my
    son!'
'Oh what can we keen, unless we keen the
    bones?'
'Oh patience, patience, Mother,' he said,
    'tonight and tomorrow,
The Apostles will keen me, and the friars will
    keen me,
And I'll be keened yet on the Island of
    Paradise.[3]
Every person who helps you to keen your little
    child
Will have a white bed in the Court of the
    Graces.'[4]

---

1. Saint Peter, said to have been the first bishop of the Christian church. Other versions have *Peadar Aspal*, 'Peter the Apostle'.

2. Versions from other singers say that the Virgin, too, was lifted high and thrown onto the stones.
3. Other versions have *Oileán Phádraig*, '[Saint] Patrick's Island', i.e. Ireland.
4. Heaven.

MÁIRE NÍ FHLANNCHADHA (MRS KEADY)

(fl. 1904)

from:
AN CLAIDHEAMH SOLUIS
(1904)

[This text was first published by Patrick Pearse in September 1904 in the weekly Irish-language newspaper *An Claidheamh Soluis*, whose editorship he had taken over eighteen months earlier. He had transcribed it from the singing of Máire Ní Fhlannchadha, in Moycullen, County Galway, at Feis Chonnacht, an Irish-language cultural festival which sponsored competitions in traditional verbal arts. He described Máire Ní Fhlannchadha's performance as 'the finest thing seen or heard at the Feis', and later added, 'I have heard nothing more exquisite than her low sobbing recitative, instinct with a profoundly felt emotion. There was a great horror in her voice at "'S an é sin an casúr [Is that the hammer]?" etc., and with the next stanza the chant rose into a wail. She cried pitifully and struck her breast several times during the recitation.'[1] After Pearse was executed following the Easter Rising of 1916, this text, entirely in dialogue and much shorter than many from oral tradition, including the one given above, became a mainstay of anthologies of Irish-language poetry, especially those aimed at schoolchildren.[2] Translation and headnote, A.B.]

Caoineadh Mhuire

'A Pheadair, a Aspail, an bhfaca tú mo ghrádh geal?'
    M'óchón agus m'óchón ó [I ndiaidh gach líne]
'Chonaic mé ar ball é, i láthair a námhad.'
'Gabhaidh a leith, a dhá Mhuire, go gcaoinfidh sibh mo ghrádh geal!'
'Céard tá le caoineadh againn muna gcaoineamuid a chnámha?'
'Cia hé an fear breágh sin ar Chrann na Páise?'
'An é nach n-aithnigheann tú do mhac, a Mháthair?'
'Agus an é sin an maicín a d'iomchur mé trí ráithe?

1. Patrick Pearse, 'Caoineadh Mhuire,' *Irish Review*, vol. 1 (March 1911).
2. It was republished at least seventeen times, with minor editorial changes, between 1915 and 1936, and also forms the basis of several sung recordings. See A. Partridge, *Caoineadh na dTrí Muire*, pp. 158–63.

Nó an é sin an maicín do rugadh san stábla?
Nó an é sin an maicín do hoileadh in ucht Mháire?
Agus an é sin an casúr do bhuail thríot na táirgní?
Nó an í sin an tsleagh do chuaidh trí do lár geal?
Nó an í sin an choróin spíonta chuaidh ar do mhullach áluinn?'
'Maise, éist, a Mháithrín, agus ná bí cráidhte,
Tá mná mo chaointe le breith go fóilleach,
Níl aon duine chaoinfeas thú in Oileán Pharrthais,
Nár gheal í a leaba i bhFlaithis na ngrásta.'

Mary's Lament

'O Peter, Apostle, have you seen my darling?'
    M'óchón and m'óchón ó! [after every line]
'I saw him just now, in the presence of his enemies.'
'Come here, you two Marys, and keen for my darling.'
'What have we to keen for, unless we keen his bones?'
'Who is that fine man, on the crucifixion tree?'
'Mother, can it be that you do not know your son?'
'Can that be the son I bore for nine months?
Can that be the child who was born in the stable?
Can that be the child who nursed at Mary's breast?
And is that the hammer that drove the nails into you?
Or is that the spear that pierced your white body?
Are those the thorns that crowned your lovely head?'
'Listen, Mother, hush — don't be distraught,
Women who will keen for me have yet to be born.
No one you lament in the island of Paradise [*sic*]
Will lack for a white bed in Heaven of the Graces.

SIUBHÁN NÍ MHAOLÁIN

(fl. 1932)

from:
BÉALOIDEAS (1932)

[Gearóid Ó Murchadha, who wrote down this prayer in Baile Bhúirne, County Cork, says of his informant, 'Siubhán learnt the prayer, when a child, from an old woman who was kept in her parents' house out of charity.' 'The Virgin's Dream' is known in various European languages, where, as in Ireland, it was recited as a charm against nightmares. Its structure, a narrative of encounter, is common in charms, where personages from Christian tradition have sometimes replaced the deities of earlier mythologies. The 'slender dark rider' mentioned here is Longinus, a common character in Christian folklore. He is first named in the apocryphal gospel of Nicodemus, where he is identified as a blind Roman soldier who was the only person prepared to pierce Christ's side with a spear as he hung on the Cross. His sight was miraculously restored when Christ's blood splashed on his eyes. In English tradition, Longinus is known as Lance the Holy. The same incident is remembered in 'Ortha na Fola', the charm against bleeding.[1] Published in *Béaloideas*, vol. 3 (1932), p. 237.   Translation and headnote, A.B.]

Aisling na Maighdine

''Ní Dhia dhuit, a Mháthair''[2]
''Ní Dia dhuit 's Pádraig'

1. See A. Partridge, *Caoineadh na dTrí Muire*, pp. 60–2; 74–5.
2. i.e. 'Go mbeannaí Dia dhuit'.

'Cad 'na thaobh ná codlann tú, a Mháthair?'
'Ní fhéadfainn é, a ghrá ghil'
'Cad 'na thaobh san, a Mháthair?
'Aisling a dineadh trím shuan dom:
marcach caol dubh ar each caol donn,
an tsleá dhearg ina dheasláimh,
an fhuil ghlórmhar á dhórta amáireach.'
'Is fírinne t'aisling, a Mháthair'
An té déarfadh é trí huaire
T'r éis luighe ar leabuidh shuain do,
Gheobhadh sé Flaithis Dé mar dhualgas
Agus bheith lem ghualainnse go brách.'

The Virgin's Dream

'God bless you, Mother!'
'God and Patrick bless you!'
'Why are you not sleeping, Mother?'
'I can't sleep, dear Love.'
'Why is that, Mother?'
'I had a dream as I slept:
A slender dark rider on a sleek brown steed,
The red spear in his right hand,
The glorious blood being spilled tomorrow.'
'Your dream is true, Mother.

'Anyone who recited it three times
After lying down to sleep
Would get the Kingdom of God as reward,
And a place at my side forever.'

MRS LINES

(fl. 1912)

from:
JOURNAL OF THE IRISH
FOLK SONG SOCIETY (1912)

[A version of the well-known English religious ballad 'The Seven Joys of Mary', recorded in 1912 in Portlaw, County Waterford, on an Edison phonograph by Charlotte Milligan Fox, honorary secretary of the London-based Irish Folk Song Society. Milligan Fox made a special journey to County Waterford, by chauffeur-driven car, in search of old songs. This one was recorded in the local convent school, where local priest 'Rev. Father Power' brought several old people after Sunday mass, 'the Mother Superior being particularly delighted with Mrs Line's [*sic*] "Seven Rejoices of Mary," which she said she remembered hearing in her childhood'. 'The Seven Joys of Mary' is found also in Irish-language versions. It appears to have been composed on the model of another religious song, the 'Seven Sorrows of the Virgin' (in Irish, *Seacht nDólás na Maighdine*). Mary's seven sorrows were depicted in Flemish art from the early fifteenth century as seven swords piercing her heart.[1] A music transcription is given with this text in the *Journal of the Irish Folk Song Society*, vol. 12 (1912), pp. 24–5. The collector adds: 'The Seven Rejoices of Mary — sung by Mrs. Lines of Portlaw, who learnt the song from her mother, a native of Kille. The ballad seems to be the production of some hedge schoolmaster. Mrs. Lines had a fine loud voice, and the song made a very good record. When she heard the record repeated, she turned to Father Power, saying, "I've not been much good, but I have done one thing well in remembering this song."'   Headnote, A.B.]

The Seven Rejoices of Mary

The first rejoice our Ladye got,
  It was the rejoice of one;
It was the rejoice of her dear Son,
  When he was born young.

Chorus:
Glory may he be,
And blessed now is she,
And those who sing the seven long verses
In honour of our Ladye.

Sing Alleluia, sweet Alleluia;
Sing Alleluia, the heavens are true;
Sing Alleluia!

1. É. Mâle, *L'art religieux*, p. 123.

The second rejoice our Ladye got,
  It was the rejoice of two;
It was the rejoice of her dear Son,
  When he was sent to school.

The third rejoice our Ladye got,
  It was the rejoice of three;
It was the rejoice of her dear Son,
  When he led the blind to see.

The next rejoice our Ladye got,
  It was the rejoice of four;
It was the rejoice of her dear Son,
  When he read the Bible o'er.

The next rejoice our Ladye got,
  It was the rejoice of five;
It was the rejoice of her dear Son,
  When he raised the dead to life.

The next rejoice our Ladye got,
  It was the rejoice of six;
It was the rejoice of her dear Son,
  When he carried the crucifix.

The next rejoice our Ladye got,
  It was the rejoice of seven;
It was the rejoice of her dear Son,
  When he opened the gates of heaven.

Sing Alleluia, sweet Alleluia;
Sing Alleluia, the heavens are true;
Sing Alleluia!

ANNA NIC AN LUAIN

(1884–1954)

from:
NA CRUACHA: SCÉALTA AGUS SEANCHAS (1985)

[Religious tales, mainly medieval in origin, have been extremely popular with Irish storytellers and their audiences down the centuries. Especially favoured were the dramatic stories dealing with severe penances either voluntarily undergone or imposed by a priest or a bishop, or even by the Pope, to expiate some heinous act, or unfilial or self-righteous behaviour.[1] The punishment often involved marginalization and isolation from the community, such as wandering as a beggar or living on a deserted island until some miraculous act of nature

1. See Types 756, 756 A in A. Aarne and S. Thompson, *The Types of the Folktale*, and S. Ó Súilleabháin and R. Christiansen, *The Types of the Irish Folktale*. For other tales of severe penances see S. Ó Súilleabháin, *Scéalta Cráibhtheacha*, pp. 106–26; (*Béaloideas*, vol. 21); and *Storytelling in the Irish Tradition* (Cork: Mercier Press, for the Cultural Relations Committee, 1973), pp. 18–19, 41–4; D. Ó hÓgáin, *Myth, Legend and Romance: An Encyclopaedia of the Irish Folk Tradition* (London: Ryan, 1990), pp. 372–4.

occurs, like a dry stick blossoming,[2] or, as in the following folktale, until the birds have flown from a nest constructed unawares on the penitent's outstretched palm.[3] The story provides an origin for the traditional *turas*, or pilgrimage, in Inis Caoil, Inishkeel Island, County Donegal. Text from Áine Ní Dhíoraí, *Na Cruacha: Scéalta agus Seanchas* (Baile Átha Cliath: An Clóchomhar, 1985), p. 79; translation and headnote, P.L.]

BREITHIÚNAS AITHRÍ NAOMH CONAILL

Chualaigh mé an seanbhunadh ag trácht go minic ar bhreithiúnas aithrí a cuireadh ar Naomh na paróiste seo fada ó shin — Naomh Conall Caol. Is cosúil gur peata gan chomhairle a bhí ann agus chnag sé a athair le smután aon lá amháin. Chuaigh sé ar faoistin ionsar shagart agus dúirt an sagart leis nach mbeadh maithiúnas aige choíche ó Dhia mura dtéadh sé amach ar oileán fásaigh agus a bheith ansin go dtigeadh éan de chuid an aeir agus go ndéanfadh sé nead ar chroí a bhoise agus nuair a d'imeochadh na héanacha óga as an nead go mbeadh maithiúnas aige ó Dhia.

Ba chruaidh an bhreithiúnas aithrí é ach shiúil Conall leis agus níor stad sé go dtáinig sé go hInis Caoil thiar anseo ag an fharraige. Deir siad gur chaith sé seacht mbliana ansin agus gan greim aige le hithe ach bia trá. Ar an seachtú bliain tháinig samhradh an-te, agus lá amháin bhí sé ina luí amuigh agus thit sé ina chodladh, agus ní raibh a fhios caidé an codladh a rinne sé ach nuair a mhúscail sé bhí soipín na neide ar a bhois agus an t-éillín ar shiúl. Bhí a bhreithiúnas aithrí istigh ansin agus bhí a fhios aige go raibh maithiúnas aige ó Dhia fosta ach ní raibh sé sásta

2. This tale is included under Type 756 D 'Other Tales of Severe Penances' by S. Ó Súilleabháin and R. Christiansen in *The Types of the Irish Folktale*.

3. Collected by Seán Ó hEochaidh, 6 December 1947. Compare Seamus Heaney's poem 'St Kevin and the Blackbird', in *The Spirit Level* (London and Boston: Faber and Faber, 1996), pp. 20–1, which is based on a similar legend about a County Wicklow saint.

ina intinn mar sin féin agus dar leis go gcaithfeadh sé an chuid eile dá shaol i gcionn oibre Dé. Thoisigh sé ansin agus chaith sé an chuid eile dá shaol ag déanamh turais agus ag beannú achan seort. Rinne sé turas mór in Inis Caoil agus níl bliain ar bith ó shin nach dtéid na céadta ann a shiúl an turais agus leoga leigheasadh daoine go leor ann fosta.

SAINT CONALL'S PENANCE

I often heard the old people talking about a penance put on a saint from this parish — St Conall Caol — a long time ago. It seems he was an undisciplined fellow who knocked his father with a block of wood one day. He went to confession to a priest who told him that he would never get forgiveness from God if he didn't go to a deserted island and stay there until a bird of the air made a nest in the centre of his palm, and when the young birds left the nest he would be forgiven.

It was a hard penance, but Conall kept journeying on foot and didn't stop until he reached Inis Caoil to the west here by the sea. It is said that he spent seven years there with only shore-food[1] to eat. The summer of the seventh year was very hot and one day when he was lying outside he fell asleep, and he didn't know how long he slept but when he awoke the straws of the nest were in his hand and the brood had flown. His penance was finished then and he knew also that he had forgiveness from God. But still he wasn't happy in his mind and thought he would spend the rest of his life in God's service. He began then and spent the rest of his life making pilgrimages and blessing everything. He made a great pilgrimage to Inis Caoil and every year since, hundreds go there on pilgrimage and indeed plenty of people have also been cured there.

1. Shellfish and edible seaweed.

CÁIT ('AN BHAB') FEIRTÉAR

(1916–   )

from:
ORIGINAL RECORDINGS
(1975)

[Many apocryphal legends are told about Christ, the Virgin Mary and the saints. The many variants of 'The Virgin's Visit' occurring in Irish folk tradition emphasize the importance of charity and the reward — including earthly reward — which follows its giving. Recorded by Patricia Lysaght from Cáit ('An Bhab', or 'Bab') Feirtéar, Baile na hAbha, Dún Chaoin, County Kerry, in 1975. Another version of the story was published in 1952, as told by Mrs Máire Uí Dhuinnshléibhe, aged sixty-one, of Baile Ícín, in the same parish in September 1936.[1] Her version adds the explanation, not given here, that the mysterious visitor was the Virgin Mary.   Translation and headnote, P.L.]

CUAIRD NA MAIGHDINE

Bhí baintreach bhocht fadó ann is bhí sí féin agus a hiníon ag maireachtaint ar thaobh cnoic i mbotháinín bocht, fuar, dealbh. Ní raibh aon ní sa tsaol acu agus bhídís ag maireachtaint ar thorthaí na gcrann agus nuair a bhíodh an lá breá — mar bhí an cailín óg — théadh sí amach agus bhailíodh sí na torthaí go dtína máthair agus d'itheadh an bheirt acu iad is mhairidíst leo. Ach tháinig trí lá splanncach is toirneach is uisce agus ní fhéadfadh éinne corraí agus bhí na créatúirí bochta i ndealbh na gcás gan aon ní le n-ithe acu agus dúirt an mháthair, 'B'fhearra dhúinn, a Bhrídín, a chroí,' a dúirt sí, 'b'fhearra dhúinn dul a chodladh.'

'A Mhuire Mháthair,' a dúirt sí, 'cad ab áil linn a chodladh nó conas a raghaimid a chodladh le bolg folamh?'

'Mo chroí,' a dúirt sí, 'dá ligimís ár dtoil le toil Dé b'fhéidir go gcodlóimis chomh sásta is a chodlaíomair aon oíche riamh.'

'Is cuma liom,' a d(úirt) an cailín beag, 'Caithimid dul is dócha.'

Ach chuadar a chodladh agus ar maidin nuair a gheal sé bhí sé ag stealladh báistí fós.

---

1. No. 23 in S. Ó Súilleabháin, *Scéalta Cráibhtheacha*, pp. 28–31, 286 (source details), 307 (English summary).

'B'fhearra dhúinn éirí, a chroí,' arsa an mháthair.

'Dhera,' arsa an cailín, 'cad ab áil linn ag éirí. Níl aon ní le cur ar an dtine againn.'

'Tá an tine againn le cur síos. Bhuel,' a dúirt sí, 'nach bhfuil sé ráite riamh, "Leath bídh is ea tine."' 'Éireodsa,' a dúirt sí, 'agus cuirfidh mé síos an tine agus beirse ag éirí im' dhiaidh.'

'Ó! n'fheadar, a Mham,' a dúirt sí, 'níl aon fhonn orm éirí nuair ná fuil aon ní againn le beiriú.'

Ach d'éirigh an mháthair agus chuir sí greadhnach thine síos, agus ní fada a bhí an tine lasta suas nuair a tháinig sruithín de bhean bheag isteach go dtí béal an dorais agus í fliuch báite.

'Druid aníos,' arsa an bhaintreach léi, 'a bhean bhocht, tánn tú fliuch báite.'

'Táim, mhuis', a chroí,' a dúirt sí.

'Druid aníos is triomaigh tú féin,' a dúirt sí. Dhruid sí aníos agus shuigh sí cois na tine.'

'Ó táim breá tirim anois,' a dúirt sí.'

'Tánn tú, a chroí,' arsa an bhaintreach, 'ach tá náire orm ná féadfainn aon ní a halthú leat. Is náireach an rud é a rá,' a dúirt sí, 'níl aon bhia sa tigh.'

'Dhera, mhuis',' a dúirt sí, 'an bhfheadaraís, bíonn cabhair Dé ar an mbóthar i gcónaí,' arsa an bhean siúil léi. 'Ní bheadh a fhios agat ná go mbeadh bhur ndóthain agaibh. Téirigh síos,' a dúirt sí, 'cois an dorais agus cíonn tú an mhealbhóg bheag san thíos,' a dúirt sí, 'cuir do lámh isteach ann.'

Chuir sí a lámh isteach ann agus gach aon uair a chuireadh sí isteach a lámh ná beadh cúpla práta amach chuichi. Is bhí sí mar sin go dtí go raibh stán breá prátaí bailithe aici. Chuir sí ar an dtine iad agus chuir sí ag fiuchadh iad. Agus nuair a bhíodar ag fiuchadh d'fhiafraigh an bhean siúil di: 'An bhfuil aon anlann agaibh?'

'Ó, ní gá dhúinn é, a chroí,' a dúirt sí, 'nílimid ag iarraidh aon anlann. Tá ár ndóthain anois againn.'

'Téirigh síos arís,' a dúirt sí.

Chuaigh sí síos arís is chuir sí a lámh sa mhealbhóg is tháinig spóla breá feola amach chuichi.'

'Buail san oighean é sin anois,' arsa an bhean siúil léi. Agus bhuail.

Agus nuair a bhí san déanta do shuigh triúr acu go dtí an mbord mar d'éirigh an cailín beag fonnmhar nuair a bhraith sí an bia ar siúl agus shuíodar go dtí an mbord agus d'itheadar agus dúirt an bhean siúil léi: 'An bhfuil aon deoch againn anois,' a dúirt sí.'

'Ó, níl, a chroí,' a dúirt sí, 'níl aon deoch agam is tá náire orm mar ní fhéadaimis dul amach,' a dúirt sí, 'chun na torthaí dh'fháil.'

'Téir síos arís,' a dúirt sí.

Chuaigh sí síos agus fuair sí stuif éigin ar chuma an tae is dócha athá againn anois agus chuir sí san uisce é agus dhein sé deoch bhreá dhóibh.'

'Ó, anois', a dúirt an bhaintreach léi, 'caithfidh tú fanacht inár dteannta.'

'Ó, a chroí,' a dúirt sí, 'ní dh'fhanaimse ach oíche amháin in aon tigh. Fanfaidh mé anocht in bhur dteannta,' a dúirt sí, 'ach sin uile.'

'Sea, anois,' a dúirt an bhaintreach, 'faighidh tú leaba in éineacht linn féin.'

'Ó, ní chuas riamh i leabaigh in éineacht le aon duine,' a dúirt sí, 'agus ní raghaidh mé go deo,' a dúirt sí. 'Ní haon mhaitheas duit a bheith liom. Ach fanfaidh mé anso,' a dúirt sí, 'ar shoipín anso sa chúinne.'

Dheineadar tathant na mílte uirthi, is níorbh aon mhaitheas a bheith léi. Chuaigh an bheirt acu a chodladh agus chuaigh an bhean bhocht a chodladh cois na tine. Agus nuair a dh'éirigh sí ar maidin dúradar léi 'fanfaidh tú in ár dteannta lá eile.'

'Ó, níor dh'fhanas riamh in aon tigh thar oíche,' a dúirt sí, 'níor thugas thar oíche in aon tigh riamh agus ní thabharfaidh mé anois.'

'Ach beir leat an mhealbhóigín anois,' a dúirt an bhaintreach léi, 'agus go raibh Dia na nGlór id bhóthar,' a dúirt sí, 'mar beidh ár ndóthain againn, mar tá sé ag gealadh agus is dócha go bhfuil aimsir bhreá air.'

'Ní dhéanfad, mhuis',' a dúirt sí. 'Fágfaidh mé agaibh an mhealbhóigín anois agus an fhaid a mhairfidh sibh aríst,' a dúirt sí, 'beidh bhur ndóthain agaibh; ach ná tagadh aon éirí in airde chugaibh,' a dúirt sí, 'ach bí ag tarraingt ar an mhealbhóg agus bí ag maireachtaint fé mar bhéibhir go dtí so.' Sin a chuala-sa.

THE VIRGIN'S VISIT

There was a poor widow one time and she and her daughter were living in a poor, cold, poverty-stricken little hut on the side of a hill. They had nothing in the world and they were living on the fruits of the trees. When the day was fine the daughter — because she was young — would go out and collect the fruits for her mother, and the two of them ate them and they survived. But three days of thunder, lightning and heavy rain came and nobody could move out. And the poor creatures were utterly destitute without anything to eat. And the mother said, 'It is best for us, Brídín, my dear,' said she, 'it is best for us to go to sleep.'

'Oh Mother Mary!' said she, 'what is the use of going to bed and how would we go to sleep on an empty stomach?'

'My dear,' said she, 'if we accept the will of God maybe we will sleep as contented as we have slept any night ever.'

'All right,' said the little girl, 'I suppose we will have to.'

They went to bed, and in the morning when it brightened it was still pouring rain.

'It is best for us to get up, my dear,' said the mother.

'Yerra,' said the girl, 'what is the use of getting up, we have nothing to put on the fire.'

'We have a fire to put down. Well,' said she, 'hasn't it always been said that a fire is half sustenance? I will get up,' said she, 'and I will put down the fire, and let you get up after me.'

'Oh I don't know, Mother!' said she, 'I have no desire to get up when we do not have anything to boil.'

But her mother got up and she put down a bright fire and the fire was not long lighting when a nifty, small little woman came to the doorway, drenched wet.

'Move up [to the fire], poor woman,' said the widow to her, 'you are drenched wet.'

'I am indeed, my dear,' said she.

'Move up to the fire and dry yourself,' said she.

She moved up and sat down by the fire.

'Oh I am fine and dry now!' said she.

'You are, dear,' said the widow, 'but I am ashamed that I cannot share anything with you. It is a shameful thing to say,' said she, 'there is no food in the house.'

'Indeed,' said she, 'do you know, God's help is always on the way,' said the travelling woman. 'Maybe you will have enough. Go over,' said she, 'near the door, and you see that small bag there below. Put your hand into it.'

She put her hand into it, and every time she put in her hand she took out a few potatoes. And she was going on like that until she had a fine tin can of potatoes. She put them on the fire to boil. And while they were boiling the travelling woman asked her, 'Have you anything tasty to put with the potatoes?'

'Oh we don't need it, dear!' said she, 'we don't need any condiment.[1] We have enough now.'

'Go over again,' said she.

She went over again and she put her hand in the small bag and out came a fine joint of meat to her.

'Put that in the oven now,' said the travelling woman to her, and she did.

And when that was done the three of them sat down to the table — the young girl had got eager when she realized there was food. And they sat down to the table, and they ate, and the travelling woman said to her, 'Do we have anything to drink now?'

'We don't,' said she, 'there is nothing to drink, and I am ashamed; we could not go out,' said she, 'to get the fruit.'

'Go over again,' said she.

She went over, and she got some stuff like the tea, I suppose, that we have now, and she put it in water and she made a fine drink for them.

'Oh!' said the widow, 'now you will have to stay with us.'

'Oh my dear!' said she, 'I only stay but one night in any house. I will stay with you tonight but that's it.'

'Now,' said the widow, 'you will sleep with ourselves.'

'Oh I never went into a bed with anyone ever, and I never will!' said she. 'There is no point pressing me about it. But I will stay here,' she said, 'on a wisp of hay here in the corner.'

They tried to convince her, but it was no use pressing her. The two of them went to bed, and the poor woman went to sleep by the fire. And when she got up in the morning they said to her: 'Stay with us for another day.'

'Oh I never stayed more than one night in any house,' said she, 'and I won't now.'

'But take the little bag with you now,' said the widow to her, 'and may the God of Glory be with you on your way,' said she, 'for we will have enough because the day is brightening and I suppose good weather is coming.'

'I will not, indeed,' said she, 'I will leave you the little bag now, and as long as you live,' said she, 'you will have enough. But do not become proud,' said she, 'but be drawing from the bag and continue living in the same way as you did up to now.' That's what I heard.

from:
ORIGINAL RECORDINGS
(1975)

[Heavenly reward for charitable deeds is another popular theme in Irish religious legends. In the following *exemplum*,[1] the dead person who returns on the invitation of the priest to tell of his position in the next world demonstrates the power of charity for gaining admittance to heaven. A sunbeam miraculously supports his cloak in the church — a sign for the priest and the congregation that he has been saved. The motif of the cloak on the sunbeam is popular in Irish legendry as well as in early literary works. In a seventh-century biography of Saint Brigid, it appears to be a borrowing from an apocryphal life of Christ.[2] Collected by Bo Almqvist, 1975. Translation and headnote, P.L.]

AN CÓTA MÓR AR AN ɴGA GRÉINE

Ó! réic é sin a bhí ag maireachtaint leis féin . . . Dhera, fear bocht, ba chuma leis. Bhíodh sé ag goid, is ag foghail is ag fuadach ach ní ghoidfeadh sé ó aoinne ach ó dhuine éigin go raibh a fhios aige go mbeadh a dhóthain á cheal aige, agus bhí

---

1. 'Condiment', Irish *anlann*, sometimes translated 'kitchen': tasty, often salty, food eaten with bread or potatoes.

1. See F.C. Tubach, *Index Exemplorum*.
2. Cf. D. Ó hÓgáin, 'Migratory Legends in Medieval Irish Literature', *Béaloideas*, vols 60–1 (1992–3), pp. 63–4. The narrative is included as Type 759 B, 'Holy Man Has His Own Mass', in A. Aarne and S. Thompson, *The Types of the Folktale*, and in S. Ó Súilleabháin and R. Christiansen, *The Types of the Irish Folktale*. For other printed versions of this story see S. Ó Súilleabháin, *Scéalta Cráibhtheacha*, no. 101, pp. 224–6 (299, 332), translated in Seán O'Sullivan, *Legends from Ireland* (London: Batsford, 1977), pp. 100–1, 165.

sé ag maireachtaint leis. Ach nuair a bhí an fear bocht ag dul chun bháis chuaigh duine éigin des na comharsain agus thug sé an sagart chuige. Agus nuair a bhí an sagart ag cur an ola dhéanach air, dúirt an sagart leis: 'An bhfuileann tú sásta?'

'Táim,' a dúirt sé. 'Ach cá raghad?'

'Ó,' arsa an sagart, 'n'fheadar cá raghair, is ró-bhaolach ná raghair in aon áit chóir,' a dúirt sé, 'mar chuiris ana-dhrochshaol isteach. Bhí sé agat ag foghail is ag fuadach,' a dúirt sé, 'agus níl sé sin ceadaithe de réir dlí Dé agus na hEaglaise,' arsa an sagart leis.

'Ach, dheineas, is dócha,' arsa an fear bocht.

'Ach an bhfuil a fhios agat,' arsa an sagart, 'pé áit a raghair, más féidir leat in aon chor, tar chughamsa le cúntas, is tabhair cúntas chugham ar chonas mar a thá agat i saol eile.'

'Ó, mhuise, déanfad,' a dúirt sé, 'sin í achainí dhéanach a dhéarfaidh mé anois,' a dúirt sé, 'ar Dhia na Glóire, mar ní fiú mé go bhfaighinn aon achainí.'

Ach cailleadh an fear bocht, agus ráithe ina dhiaidh sin, maidin bhreá gréine, bhí an sagart ag rá Aifrinn agus tháinig ga iontach gréine isteach tríd an bhfuinneog aige bun na haltóra agus lena linn sin do ghabh an fear tríd an sáipéal aníos. Bhain sé dho a chasóg agus d'fhéach sé timpeall, thall 's abhus agus ní fhaca sé aon áit go gcrochfadh sé a chasóg. Agus cad a dhein sé ná an chasóg a chaitheamh ar an nga gréine agus d'fhan sí ann. Léigh an sagart an tAifreann agus ansan do labhair sé leis an bpobal agus dúirt sé: 'Níl dabht ar domhan,' a dúirt sé, 'ná gur fear naofa atá inár measc. Ach dá bé a thoil é,' a dúirt sé, 'an dtiocfadh sé chun cainte liom tar éis an Aifrinn?'

Níor labhair fear na casóige aon fhocal. Ach nuair a dh'imigh an pobal d'fhan sé sa tsáipéal agus chuaigh sé ag caint leis an sagart.

'Agus ní dh'aithníonn tú mé, is dócha,' a dúirt sé, 'ach do gheallsa dhuit go dtiocfainn thar n-ais ón saol eile,' a dúirt sé, 'agus táim tagaithe.'

'Mise Cian na mBeann Óir
Gur shia mo lón ná mo shaol
Níor chuireas aoinne riamh as mo thigh,
Agus níor cuireadh mise as tigh Dé.
Ach is baolach an áit go ndúraís-se a
    raghainn-se
Gur baolach gurb ann a raghair féin,'

a dúirt sé. 'Mar a bhfuil fhios agat,' a dúirt sé, 'bhíos-sa ag goid, is ag foghail, is ag fuadach, ach do ghoideas ón té go raibh sé aige, agus do thugas dos na bochtáin é, agus níor chuireas aon fhear déirce riamh óm dhoras,' a dúirt sé, 'ach tánn tusa,' a dúirt sé, 'ag maireachtaint ar na bochtáin chomh maith leis na daoine saibhre agus is cuma leatsa,' a dúirt sé, 'cé dhíolfaidh cess na Nollag ná na Cásca leat ach an t-airgead do dh'fháil,' a dúirt sé, 'agus mar gheall air sin is dócha go gcaithfidh tú féachaint chugat féin,' a dúirt sé, 'más maith leat aon ní cóir a dh'fháil ón dtaobh eile.'

THE GREATCOAT ON THE SUNBEAM

Oh! He was a rake who was living alone; indeed, a poor man, and he did not care about anything; he was thieving and plundering and spoiling. But he only stole from people who he knew could do without it, and he was going on living. But when the poor man was dying one of the neighbours brought the priest to him. And when the priest was anointing him he said to him, 'Are you satisfied?'

'I am,' said he, 'but where will I go?'

'Oh!' said the priest, 'I don't know where you will go, but it is doubtful that you will go to any right place,' said he, 'because you have lived a very bad life. You were plundering and spoiling,' said he, 'and that is not allowed according to the law of God and the Church,' said the priest to him.

'I suppose I was,' said the poor man.

'But do you know?' said the priest, 'wherever you go, if you can at all, come back to me with an account, and give me an account of how things are with you in another world.'

'Oh indeed, I will!' said he, 'that is a last petition I will make,' said he, 'of the God of Glory, for I am not worthy to receive any request.'

But the poor man died, and three months later, on a fine sunny morning when the priest was saying Mass, a wonderful sunbeam came through the window at the bottom of the altar, and with that the man came up along the church. He took off his coat and he looked around, here and there, but did not see anywhere he could hang his coat. And what did he do but throw his coat on the sunbeam and it stayed there. The priest read the Mass and then spoke to the people; he said: 'There is no doubt in the world,' said he, 'but that the man in our midst is a holy man. And if it be his will,' said he, 'would he come to talk to me after Mass?'

The man with the coat did not speak one word. But when the congregation left, he stayed in the church, and he began talking to the priest.

'And you don't recognize me, I suppose,' said he, 'but I promised you that I would come back from the other world,' said he, 'and I have come:

'I am Cian of the Golden Locks
Whose supplies are longer than his life,
I never put anyone out of my house
And I was not put out of God's house,
But I fear, the place you said I would go,
I fear you will go there yourself,'

said he. 'As you know,' said he, 'I was stealing, plundering and spoiling. But I stole from him that had it and I gave it to the poor, and I never turned a beggar man from my door,' said he. 'But you,' said he, 'are living off the poor as well as the rich people, and you do not care,' said he, 'who will pay the Christmas or Easter cess,[1] except to get your money,' said he, 'and because of that I suppose you had better take heed to yourself,' said he, 'if you wish to get any just reward from the other side.'

1. Presumably the Christmas or Easter dues, payable to the church, are meant here.

Biographies/Bibliographies

Peig Sayers

For biography and bibliography, see p. 1212.

Máire Ní Ghuithín

LIFE. Born on the Great Blasket Island, County Kerry, c. 1905, daughter of Maidhc Léan Ó Guithín (Ó Gaoithín). Helped her parents in looking after scholars who visited the island in summer to learn Irish, and acquired the habit of making written notes about the way of life there. Later published two books in Irish. Moved to mainland and married Labhrás John Larry Ó Cíobháin. Two daughters, Caitlín and Máirín. Went to live with her brothers Maidhc, Muiris and Seán after the death of her husband. Died 29 October 1988.

CHIEF WRITINGS. (as Máire Ní Ghaoithín) An tOileán a Bhí (Baile Átha Cliath: An Clóchomhar, 1978); (as Máire Ní Ghuithín) Bean an Oileáin (Dublin: Coiscéim, 1986).

Anna Ní Bhaoill

LIFE. Born in Rinn na Feirste (Rannafast), County Donegal, c. 1894. Her brother was the well-known storyteller Micí Sheáin Néill Ó Baoill (1901–81). Date of death unknown.

Anna Ní Ghrianna

LIFE. Known as Annie Bhán (white-haired Annie) and born into a family renowned for mastery of oral storytelling, Anna Ní Ghrianna lived all her life (1893–1963) in Rinn na Feirste (Rannafast), in the Donegal Gaeltacht. Like her brother, storyteller Seán Bán Mac Grianna, she suffered from poor eyesight, which Gordon W. MacLennan suggests as the chief reason she never married. The IFC archive contains some 2,800 pages of oral tradition (folktales, local legends and history, religious and humorous narratives) collected from her in the 1930s, while MacLennan recorded seven folktales from her in October 1961. Annie Bhán's other brothers were the Irish-language writers Seosamh Mac Grianna (1901–90) and Séamus Ó Grianna (1891–1969) (see Volume III, pp. 816, 845–9).

CHIEF WRITINGS. Gordon W. MacLennan, Seanchas Annie Bháin/ The Lore of Annie Bhán, ed. and tr., Alan Harrison and Máire Elena Crook (Dublin: The Seanchas Annie Bháin Publication Committee, 1997).

Mary Barnable

LIFE. Mary Barnable was a native speaker of Irish who lived to the age of one hundred and three. In 1954, aged one hundred, she lived at Walshbog, Killusty, County Tipperary.

Anna Ní Raghallaigh

LIFE. 1858–1936. No further information available.

Máire Ní Fhlannchadha (Mrs Keady)

No biographical information available.

Siubhán Ní Mhaoláin

No biographical information available.

Mrs Lines

LIFE. Portlaw, Co. Waterford. No further information available.

Anna Nic an Luain

For biography and bibliography, see p. 1310.

Cáit ('An Bhab') Feirtéar

LIFE. 'Bab' Feirtéar, of Baile na hAbha, Dún Chaoin, County Kerry, is one of the best-known storytellers in Ireland. She was born in 1916, and her grandmother and grand-aunt were Cáit Ruiséal and Máire Ruiséal (q.v. pp. 1219–1232, 1391–1392). She has a large repertoire of fairytales, religious tales, legends and rhymes, and is frequently heard on Raidió na Gaeltachta.

CHIEF WRITINGS. Roibeard Ó Cathasaigh, 'Bab Feirtéar', in Scothsmaointe (Luimneach: Coláiste Muire gan Smál, 1995), pp. 4–12.

ANGELA BOURKE, *Editor*

Work and Play

Like quilts, cakes and other forms of traditional art, the kinds of singing, rhyming and storytelling considered here are designed for use as much as for decoration. Certain kinds of oral verbal art act directly: the subsection 'Spirituality and Religion in Oral Tradition' includes a charm against nightmares, for instance, while the poetry in 'Lamenting the Dead' was an essential part of funeral ritual. Songs and stories teach or amuse children, soothe them, or put them to sleep; prayers bring blessings and peace; and curses do damage. But songs and stories also accompany work and play, or did before radio, and later piped music, became a feature of the workplace, and before personal stereos allowed everyone to carry their choice of recorded music. Children have their own folklore, preserved for generations, but they learn it from other children and rarely remember it as adults.[1]

Nostalgic accounts of 'good old times' look back in some wonder at quiet streets that rang to the sound of children's chanting, and at farm dairies or city factories filled with women's voices singing. Many songs of the streets, factories and countryside have disappeared, but some have moved to a different environment. They have entered the mass media through the folksong revival, and often feature innovative and exciting musical arrangements. Although observers have romanticized them as the happy outpourings of a docile workforce or of innocent childhood, work songs and street songs in every culture express the concerns of the people who sing them. Little girls in Ireland skip rope and play ball games while singing of bloodthirsty violence or speculations

about sex; women's work songs express frustration at working conditions, as well as pride in work and a range of attitudes to sexuality, childbearing, friendship and other issues.

Men sang at work too, of course: sea-shanties and chain-gang songs are among the best-known examples of the classic work song, in which a soloist is answered every line or two by the other workers singing in unison. Such songs assist heavy, repetitive, shared work by regulating its rhythm, and counteract its often brutal monotony with the pleasure of music and poetry.[2] As Roger Abrahams has remarked of the corn-shucking songs of the American south, their antiphonal structure 'not only embodies the very way in which the work is organized. By centering and coordinating the group's combined energies, the singing empowers the captain to speak for the group and to make whatever commentary he might wish to make on the proceedings, on slave life in general, and on the nonsensical goings-on he has noticed in Big House life.'[3] This is no less true of certain kinds of women's oral poetry in the Gaelic tradition.[4] The oral tradition of Scottish Gaelic, closely related to Irish, includes hundreds of 'waulking songs' which reflect the concerns of women's lives some two hundred years ago. These were sung by women as they 'waulked' or worked in groups on newly woven woollen cloth to thicken it, passing a heavy, sodden length of tweed from hand to hand around a wooden board

---

1. For children's folklore, see Eilis Brady, *All In! All In!: A Selection of Dublin Children's Traditional Street Games with Rhymes and Music* (Dublin: Comhairle Bhéaloideas Éireann, 1984 [1975]); *Green Peas and Barley O: Children's Street Songs and Rhymes from Belfast Collected by Brendan Colgan*, ed. D. Hammond (Belfast: Arts Council of Northern Ireland, LPS 3018, 1974 (LP record)).

2. See A.L. Lloyd, *Folksong in England* (London: Lawrence and Wishart, in association with the Workers' Music Association, 1967), pp. 269–96, 'The Sea Shanties', and cf. pp. 297–387, 'The Industrial Songs'.
3. Cf. Roger D. Abrahams, *Singing the Master: The Emergence of African-American Culture in the Plantation South* (New York: Penguin, 1992), pp. 124–5.
4. See Joan N. Radner (ed.), *Feminist Messages: Coding in Women's Folk Culture* (Chicago: University of Illinois Press, 1993), esp. pp. 160–82: Angela Bourke, 'More in Anger than in Sorrow: Irish Women's Lament Poetry'.

and beating it repeatedly; no men were admitted, and both work and music became closely identified with women and women's concerns.[5] As with sea-shanties and laments, soloists in the waulking song tradition originally sang extempore, at least to some extent, drawing on a well-known stock of themes and formulae. In more recent times, however, as the tradition became less widespread and less productive, texts became relatively more fixed.

Although the rich lyrical tradition of the waulking song, with its variety of themes, is not found in Ireland, a number of tunes and formulae do survive with which young women formerly accompanied handwork done in groups. Many allow for extemporized solo lines, and most consist of mutual teasing and mocking, generally about boyfriends, or potential boyfriends. They closely resemble the party or playground games of more leisured societies. In the west of Ireland these are called lúibíní ('loops', or 'rounds'). Eight such songs were published in the Journal of the Irish Folk Song Society, vol. 21 (1924), pp. 36–46, from a manuscript written in 1876 by Proinnsias Ó Catháin (Francis Keane), of County Clare, then resident in Dublin. The editor, Donal J. O'Sullivan, quotes him as follows on the 'Singing of Dialogues in Irish':[6]

> This melodramatic amusement is very popular among the female peasantry . . . These dialogues are sung in parts by the women while spinning, knitting, sewing, etc., to some curious old Irish airs.[7] The women assemble by appointment in certain houses to discharge the 'comhar' or mutual co-operation which they have agreed upon; but in all cases the work is cheerfully accompanied by a musical dialogue, one commencing the dialogue, another replying, usually with the intervention of a chorus to afford time to prepare an extempore verse in succession.[8] And thus the dialogue is prolonged by two successive singers — praising or dispraising the young men whose names are introduced, until they have all sung their parts to their own amusement, as well as to the gratification or otherwise of the young men and the rest of their audience.

Some of the texts published early in the twentieth century were arranged afterwards for choirs and for harp accompaniment, moving some considerable distance from the atmosphere of hilarity in which they were first sung, and were later widely taught in these genteel forms to children in primary schools. Improvisational songs are still sung for amusement by adults in the Gaeltacht of County Galway, however, and in recent years Raidió na Gaeltachta has fostered a revival by sponsoring competitions for lúibíní, where two singers (often male) alternate in extemporizing witty or topical lines. 'Dúin Dú', see pp. 1332–1333, sung in the mid-twentieth century while herding cattle, is closely related to this kind of song.

Betty Messenger's study in industrial folklore, Picking up the Linen Threads, details the extent to which women workers in the linen mills and factories of Belfast accompanied their work with song in the first three decades of the twentieth century. The makers of mill songs borrowed from music-hall and from hymns, but created a tradition all of their own.[9] The women lived close to each other in streets of small houses near the mills. They were often related to each other, and many of them were very young. As soon as they left school, often at thirteen or fourteen, girls entered the mills where their aunts and older sisters worked. Much hilarity and ribaldry surrounded the initiation of young girls into the women's topics of discussion.[10] The noise of the machines did not permit conversation, but the women could make themselves heard by singing loudly in unison as

---

5. See John Lorne Campbell and Francis Collinson, Hebridean Folksongs, 3 vols (Oxford: Oxford University Press, 1969, 1977, 1981). In the Scottish communities of Canada, the work of thickening cloth, now called 'milling', fell to men, and the songs lost their woman-centred world-view, although they retained their strong rhythm and tunefulness, and many of their themes.

6. Journal of the Irish Folk Song Society, vol. 21 (1924), p. 37. Proinnsias Ó Catháin's manuscript is in the Royal Irish Academy, Dublin, MS 12 Q 13 (ibid., 36).

7. The editor adds the following note: By 'parts' Keane no doubt means 'sections'; it is unlikely there was any part-singing.

8. For traditions of co-operative work, see Anne O'Dowd, Meitheal: A Study of Co-operative Labour in Rural Ireland (Baile Átha Cliath: Comhairle Bhéaloideasa Éireann, 1981), esp. pp. 40–9.

9. Betty Messenger, Picking up the Linen Threads: A Study in Industrial Folklore (Austin: University of Texas Press, 1975, 1978; Belfast: Blackstaff Press, 1980). See also Vol. v, pp. 539–542.

10. Storyteller Maggi Peirce, from Belfast, now living in Massachusetts, speaking about her work as a 'mill girl' at the University of Amherst, Massachusetts, 2 February 1994.

they worked. 'The Doffing Mistress', included below, survived until the folk revival of the 1960s and may be heard in several recorded versions.

The work of childcare is accompanied by a rich repertoire of verbal art, both sung and spoken. 'Digeas Ó Deabhas' (p. 1350) and 'Cuc-a-nandy' (pp. 1354–1355) are Irish-language nonsense songs with strong rhythm, sung to amuse or distract babies and toddlers, while 'A Bhean Úd Thall', given below, has a typical lullaby refrain. Such soothing songs, whose main and evident function is to send children to sleep, often carry secondary messages for adult listeners, taking advantage of their apparently trivial form to convey serious personal or political meaning.[11] This short selection ends with a formula tale which is at once a tongue-twister and a feat of memory, as told by Anna Nic an Luain, who also features in the subsection 'Legends of the Supernatural', pp. 1286–1292.

11. Cf. Radner, *Feminist Messages*, and Bess Lomax Hawes, 'Folksongs and Functions: Some Thoughts on the American Lullaby', *Journal of American Folklore*, vol. 87, no. 344 (1974), pp. 140–8.

ANONYMOUS

from:
JOURNAL OF THE IRISH FOLK SONG SOCIETY (1924)

[This dialogue-song was one of those printed in the *Journal of the Irish Folk Song Society* in 1924 from Proinnsias Ó Catháin's manuscript of 1876. The editor of *JIFSS*, D[onal] J[oseph] O'S[ullivan] notes differences between versions, characteristic of this type of song: 'Keane's version of "Dúnadán Dorcha Donn" as given to [George] Petrie is contained in the Complete Petrie Collection (No. 1, 174);[1] it differs in some respects from the version printed here, and this is the case with Petrie's versions of Keane's other tunes, referred to infra. I have compared these, as given in the Complete Petrie Collection, with the originals in the Petrie MSS., now in the National Museum, and have found them to be faithful copies.' For another tune to the above title, also from County Clare, see Petrie No. 1, 473. Translation, A.B.]

Dúnadán Dorcha Donn

1st Girl   Dúnadán dorcha donn,
Do rachainnse féin do léim thar abhainn.
2nd Girl   Dúnadán dorcha donn,
Tomás Ó hÉagarta do léimfeadh leat ann.
1st Girl   Do chuirfinn san abhainn é, is cloch ar a cheann.

1. See George Petrie (ed.), *The Petrie Collection of the Ancient Music of Ireland I & II* (London: Gregg International [facsimile], 1969 [1855, 1882].)

2nd Girl   Do rachainnse féin a chodladh ar a' ngleann.
1st Girl   Seaghan Ó Catháin do chuirfinn leat ann.
2nd Girl   Photátaí is feoil do thabharfainn dó ann.
1st Girl   Do rachainnse féin thar fairrge anonn.
2nd Girl   Cé hé an fear óg do chuirfinn leat ann?
1st Girl   Diarmaid Ó Cealla ar thugas dó greann.
2nd Girl   Do mairidh tú i bhfad le do chéile ann.

Translation

1st Girl   Dúnadán dorcha donn,
I would go and jump across the river.
2nd Girl   Dúnadán dorcha donn,
Thomas Hegarty would jump over with you.
1st Girl   I would throw him into the river, with a stone on his head.
2nd Girl   I would go and sleep in the valley.
1st Girl   I would send John Keane along with you.
2nd Girl   I would give him potatoes and meat there.
1st Girl   I would go across the sea.
2nd Girl   What young man should I send along with you?
1st Girl   Dermot O'Kelly, whom I love.
2nd Girl   Long life to you and your husband.

ANONYMOUS

from:
PICKING UP THE LINEN THREADS: A STUDY IN INDUSTRIAL FOLKLORE (1975)

[In the Belfast linen mills, 'full bobbins of spun yarn were *doffed* from each machine and replaced with empty bobbins to be filled'.[1] The doffing mistress, who might be as young as fourteen, was selected for her quickness and efficiency, and for her ability to get on with the women whose work she co-ordinated. Betty Messenger's text of 'The Doffing Mistress' is taken from a typescript collection of street songs and rhymes made in Belfast by schoolmaster Hugh Quinn about 1920. Messenger writes of versions she heard from informants in Belfast: 'Numerous respondents sang the song, and never was it presented the same way twice. Verses were omitted or sung in a different order, and within the stanzas phrases and words were altered constantly.' Another version, sung by revival singers June Tabor and Maddy Prior, may be heard on *Silly Sisters* (Ho-Ho-Kus, NJ: Shanachie Records 79040, 1984). See Vol. IV, pp 539–542.]

The Doffing Mistress

Oh, do you know her, or do you not,
This new doffin' mistress we have got?
Ann Jane Brady, it is her name,
And she hangs her clothes up on the highest
frame.

1. B. Messenger, *Linen Threads*, p. 30.

Chorus:
Raddy rightful rah, raddy rightful ree.

On Monday morning when she comes in,
She hangs her clothes on the highest pin,
She turns around for to view her girls,
Saying, 'Dang you doffers, lay up your ends.'

Chorus

Lay up our ends, we will surely do,
Our hands are steady, and our touch is true,
Lay up our ends, we will surely do,
All for Lizzie Murphy, and not for you.

Chorus

Oh, Lizzie Murphy, are you going away?
Is it tomorrow, or is it today?
You'll leave us then with a broken heart,
For there's no one left that now will take our
part.

Chorus

Oh, Lizzie Murphy, when you've gone away,
Every night, it's for you we'll pray,
We'll send for you when you're far away,
And we'll bring you back, and we'll make you
stay.

Chorus

ANONYMOUS

from:
IRISLEABHAR NA GAEDHILGE/THE GAELIC JOURNAL (1905)

[This lullaby, which is not common although versions of it have been recorded in various parts of Ireland, purports to

have been first heard near a *lios* or fairy dwelling, as a woman who had been abducted by the fairies attempted to attract the attention of her sister or another woman.[1] In this version she gives her name as Máire Ní Mheachain, and

1. For traditions about the fairies, including their abduction of humans, see pp. 1284–1311, 1435–1445 and Angela Bourke, *The Burning of Bridget Cleary: A True Story* (London: Pimlico, 1999; New York; Viking, 2000). For a discussion of this song, and a music transcription, see H. Shields, *Narrative Singing in Ireland*, pp. 75–7.

tells how she was taken from her home and forced to tend children in the *lios*. She gives the listener a message for her lover: if he will come to the *lios* with a black-handled knife and call her name, he can rescue her. The lullaby refrain, *Seoithín seó*, is repeated between the lines and expresses the singer's own loneliness and homesickness even as she tries to soothe the child in her arms — an ironically poignant touch, as some of the mothers who sang it would have been girls married against their will to much older men.

This text is one of a number of lullabies collected by Amhlaoibh Ó Loingsigh (1872–1947) and entered for competition in An tOireachtas, the Irish-language cultural festival, in 1902. Ó Loingsigh, from Baile Bhúirne, County Cork, later became one of the best-known storytellers in Ireland.   Translation, A.B.]

A Bhean Úd Thall

Deirtear gur istigh i lios do chualathas an rann so. Is follus ar an rann féin gurab amhlaidh do ghoid na sidheóga leó an bhean agus go raibh sí ina bean altruim aca, agus go raibh sí ag leigint scéala chum a fir teacht ag fortacht uirthi.

A bhean úd thall ar lic an átha,
    Seoithín seó, seoithín seó —
Abair lem dhian-ghrádh teacht i mbáireach,
    Seoithín seó, seoithín seó.

Scian choise duibhe do thabhairt n-a ghlaic leis;
    Seoithín seó, seoithín seó —
Gabháil trí huaire timcheall an leasa,
    Seoithín seó, seoithín seó.

Glaodhach go hárd ar Mháire Ní Mheachain,
    Seoithín seó, seoithín seó —
Nó beidh an téarma dúbaltha ormsa an lá san;
    Seoithín seó, seoithín seó.

Siúd é thall mo thigh mór gealsa;
    Seoithín seó, seoithín seó —
Is iomdhó bean óg ag beathughadh mac ann.
    Seoithín seó, seoithín seó.

Is iomdhó cruadh-laoch do chaill a neart ann;
    Seoithín seó, seoithín seó —
Agus sean-bhean chríona chlaoidhte, lag, ann,
    Seoithín seó, seoithín seó.

Annso atáim ag feidhilt na leanbh,
    Seoithín seó, seoithín seó —
Is mór gur bh'fheárr liom bheith sa bhaile.
    Seoithín seó, seoithín seó.

Translation

They say these verses were heard coming from a *lios*. It's clear from the text itself that the woman had been abducted by the fairies and that she was working for them as a foster-mother, and trying to send a message to her husband to come and rescue her.

Woman over there on the stony ford,
    Shuheen-sho, shuheen-sho —
Tell my love to come tomorrow,
    Shuheen-sho, shuheen-sho —

Tell him to bring a black-handled knife,
    Shuheen-sho, shuheen-sho —
And to walk three times around the *lios*,
    Shuheen-sho, shuheen-sho —

And to call out loud for Máire Mahon,
    Shuheen-sho, shuheen-sho —
Or I'll have to stay here twice as long,
    Shuheen-sho, shuheen-sho —

Over there is my big white house,
    Shuheen-sho, shuheen-sho —
Where many young women are feeding children,
    Shuheen-sho, shuheen-sho —

Where many young heroes have lost their vigour,
    Shuheen-sho, shuheen-sho —
And many old women are weak and helpless,
    Shuheen-sho, shuheen-sho —

And this is where I nurse the children,
    Shuheen-sho, shuheen-sho —
Although I'd far rather be at home,
    Shuheen-sho, shuheen-sho.

SIOBHÁN LYNCH

(1965–   )

from:
BÉALOIDEAS (1979)

[In 1977–8, folklorist Geraldine Lynch made a study of the games and rhymes known by her younger sister Siobhán, then aged twelve. 'The Farmer Wants a Wife' is one of the most popular of girls' school playground games. From G. Lynch, 'The Lore of a Wicklow Schoolgirl', *Béaloideas*, vol. 45–7 (1979), pp. 52–3. Cf. Eilís Brady, *All in! All in!* (1984), pp. 101–2.[1]]

THE FARMER WANTS A WIFE

In the game 'The Farmer Wants a Wife', the number of people inside the circle gets bigger as the game progresses. The children all form a circle and hold hands: one is chosen to be the 'farmer', and [s]/he stands in the middle of the circle. The others walk around clockwise saying [or chanting] the first verse. The 'farmer' closes his eyes and chooses a 'wife' who joins him in the circle, etc. During the last verse the 'bone' is slapped on the back by all the other children.

The farmer wants a wife,
The farmer wants a wife,
Ee-eye add-i-o
The farmer wants a wife.

The wife wants a child,
The wife wants a child,
Ee-eye add-i-o
The wife wants a child.

The child wants a nurse,
The child wants a nurse,
Ee-eye add-i-o
The child wants a nurse.

The nurse wants a dog,
The nurse wants a dog,
Ee-eye add-i-o
The nurse wants a dog.

The dog wants a bone,
The dog wants a bone,
Ee-eye add-i-o
The dog wants a bone.

We all clap the bone,
We all clap the bone,
Ee-eye add-i-o
We all clap the bone.[2]

1. Other children's games and rhymes from Ireland are included in Alice Bertha Gomme, *Traditional Games of England, Scotland and Ireland* (London, 2 vols, 1894–8; rpr., 1 vol., Thames and Hudson, 1984), and Iona and Peter Opie, *The Lore and Language of Schoolchildren* (London: Oxford University Press, 1959).

2. Other versions have 'the bone won't break'.

ANONYMOUS

from:
CNIOGAIDE CNAGAIDE: RAINN TRAIDISIÚNTA DO PHÁISTÍ (1988)

[A game played by girls outdoors in the Conamara Gaeltacht. Like many of the games played in English in streets and school yards, it requires a high level of co-operation. From Nicholas Williams, *Cniogaide Cnagaide: Rainn Traidisiúnta do Pháistí* (Baile Átha Cliath: An Clóchomhar, 1988), pp. 162–3.   Translation, A.B.]

BEAN AN TÍ

Cluiche do chailíní atá anseo agus is amuigh faoin aer a imrítear é. Roghnaítear beirt chailíní. Is í 'bean an tí' duine acu. Téann sí síos ar a dhá glúin agus ligeann sí uirthi féin gur ag séideadh tine atá sí. Tá na cailíní eile ar cúl an dara cailín agus greim acu ar a chéile. Labhraíonn an dara cailín ('an chearc') le bean an tí agus bíonn an comhrá seo leanas acu:

Céard tá tú a dhéanamh ansin?
Ag séideadh na tine.
Cad chuige an tine?
Chun uisce a bheiriú.
Cad chuige an t-uisce?
Chun mo sceana a ghlanadh.
Cad chuige na sceana?
Chun do shicíní a mharú.
Cad chuige mo shicíní a mharú?
Mar d'ith siad mo choirce.
Níor ith siad agus ní bhfaighir iad.
D'ith siad agus gheobhad iad.
Caithfidh tú troid liomsa.
Troidfidh mé thusa.

Ansin tosaíonn bean an tí ag iarraidh breith ar na sicíní (na cailíní eile) agus bíonn an chearc ar a seacht ndícheall ag iarraidh iad a chosaint uirthi. Nuair a bheir bean an tí ar shicín, cuireann sí é ina luí marbh mar dhea cois na tine. Nuair atá na sicíní go léir marbh, tá deireadh leis an gcluiche.

THE WOMAN OF THE HOUSE

This is a game played outdoors by girls. Two girls are chosen. One of them is 'the woman of the house'. She kneels down and pretends to blow on a fire. The other girls line up behind the second girl, each holding onto another. This second girl ('the hen') speaks to the woman of the house as follows:

What are you doing there?
Blowing the fire.
What's the fire for?
To boil water.
What's the water for?
To clean my knives.
What are the knives for?
To kill your chickens.
What will you kill them for?
Because they ate my corn.
They didn't, and you won't get them.
They did, and I will get them.
You'll have to fight me.
I'll fight you.

Then the woman of the house tries to catch the chickens (the other girls), and the hen does her best to protect them. Every time the woman of the house catches a chicken, she leaves it lying by the fire, pretending to be dead. The game ends when all the chickens are dead.

JOHN BUCKLEY

from:
THE IRISH TIMES (1982)

[This short article was written by photographer John Buckley to accompany his images of girls' street games in Ireland. His photographs of games which involve rhymes were exhibited in Cork and Dublin in 1982. From *The Irish Times*, 24 September 1982.]

CINDERELLA DRESSED IN YELLA WENT UPSTAIRS TO KISS HER FELLA

Rhymes reflect a child's view of the world, a world often beyond the realm of adult under-standing or imagination. But children's rhymes often make incursions into the adult world, involving references to birth and death.

The single theme which has enormous and widespread appeal is that dealing with love, involving as it does in contemporary society, boyfriend and marriage. Rhymes dealing with romantic encounters in great variety can be found the length and breadth of Ireland in rural and urban society.

Red rosy apples lemon pie,
Tell me the name of your sweet pie.
(Limerick city)

Strawberry custard, cream on top,
Tell me the name of your sweetheart.
(Listowel, County Kerry)

Blackberry, gooseberry, blackcurrant jam,
Tell me the name of your young man.
(Athy, County Kildare)

These three rhymes are sung while skipping and the letters of the alphabet are shouted to find out the initials.

And in Tralee [County Kerry], Cinderella is taken from her world of banquets and Prince Charmings, to meet her 'fella' in:

Cinderella dressed in yella
Went upstairs to kiss her fella.
By mistake she kissed a snake.
How many doctors did she need?'

In the reference to boyfriend, found in the rhyme 'My boyfriend gave me apples,' the boyfriend is not the kind and loving sort. This is a well-known rhyme throughout the country, sung while handclapping. The Clonmel [County Tipperary] version goes:

My boyfriend gave me apples,
My boyfriend gave me pears,
My boyfriend gave me kiss kiss kiss
And kicked me down the stairs.
He kicked me over London
He kicked me over France
He kicked me over Mexico
And he lost his underpants.

Meanwhile in Cork city, the boyfriend is more loving, soft and romantic, as this rhyme suggests:

Under the apple tree
My boyfriend said to me
Kiss me, hug me,
Tell me you will marry me.
Dumb didi um dum sexy.

Underneath trees or in trees are acknowledged as popular spots for courting couples, according to the following rhymes:

Under the shade of the blackberry tree,
True love for you my darling,
True love for me.
We will get married,
We'll have a family,
A boy for you, girl for me,

A girl for you, boy for me.
Dumb didi um dum — success.
(Westport, County Mayo)

And in Cork city we have:

John and Joan up a tree
K-I-S-S-I-N-G
First comes love,
Then comes marriage,
Then comes baby in a carriage.

And still on kissing we have the following from Donegal town:

Who stole the kisses from the boy next door?
Was it you? No. 1?
Who, me?
Yeah, you.
Couldn't have been.
Then it must have been No. 2,

and so on. And in Carraroe,[1] West Galway, we have:

Bluebells, cockleshells, eevy ivy over.
How many boys did you kiss last night?
1-2-3-4-5-6-7 etc.

These rhymes are sung while skipping, playing with a ball against a wall, handclapping and going round in a circle, and sung by girls, consequently the references to boyfriends. One called 'I've got a boyfriend' is heard on streets in Cork, Dublin, Kilkenny, Cahir [County Tipperary] and Donegal town.

In all versions the boyfriend comes from New York and almost anything is done to keep him alive, despite the fact that the boyfriend might have 'two hairy legs just like two hard-boiled eggs' (Cahir version) or that 'he has a pair of feet just like O'Connell Street' (Dublin version).

All the money earned seems to go on the boyfriend, but in the version found in the southside of Cork city, the boyfriend, because of his hairy legs (which were just like his mammy said), is having to get used to being alone.

In some areas however — Tralee being one — the reference is to a girlfriend, who again is from New Yorka [sic] . . . while in Waterford the girlfriend is from Cork and goes to Unislim,[2]

1. A Gaeltacht, or Irish-speaking, area.
2. A commercial weight-loss organization.

because, I suppose, she has a pair of legs just like two hard-boiled eggs. In Ennis [County Clare], the reference is to a girl who has a pair of knees like O'Connell Street.

Here is the Cahir version:

I've got a boyfriend.
He's from New Yorker.
I do most anything to keep him alive.
He's got two hairy legs,
Just like two hard-boiled eggs.
That's where all my money go-es.

EILÍS BRADY

from:
ALL IN! ALL IN!: A SELECTION OF DUBLIN CHILDREN'S TRADITIONAL STREET GAMES WITH RHYMES AND MUSIC (1984)

[Eilís Brady recorded the street games of the neighbourhood where she grew up and still lives, within a half-hour's walk of Dublin city centre. Among them are many skipping rhymes, some of which prescribe complicated movements for the child as she skips. With the 'Charlie Chaplin' rhyme, Brady tells us, 'At *cross-bars* she must cross her feet; at *kicks* she must kick out one leg; at *twirl-around* she must twirl right around skipping all the time; at *splits* she stops with the rope between her feet.' From Eilís Brady, *All in! All in!: A Selection of Dublin Children's Traditional Street Games with Rhymes and Music* (Dublin: Comhairle Bhéaloideas Éireann, 1984 [1975]), pp. 84–5.]

SKIPPING RHYMES

Teddy bear, teddy bear,
Tip the ground.
Teddy bear, teddy bear,
Twirl around.
Teddy bear, teddy bear,
Show your shoe,
Teddy bear, teddy bear,
That will do.
Teddy bear, teddy bear,
Go up the stairs.
Teddy bear, teddy bear,
Say your prayers.
Teddy bear, teddy bear,
Put out the light
Teddy bear, teddy bear,
Say goodnight.

Charlie Chaplin
Went to France
To teach the ladies
How to dance
And this is the way
He taught them:
First you do your cross-bars,
Then you do your kicks.
Then you do your twirl-around,
And then you do your splits.

ANNA NIC AN LUAIN

(1884–1954)

from:
NA CRUACHA: SCÉALTA AGUS SEANCHAS (1985)

[This amusing formula tale of the sort told to children in many cultures links together a chain of objects which must be procured before an objective can be reached. The quest for a stick to beat the culprit who stole berries is in vain until three riddlefuls of water are brought to millers. The formula is then complete and a chain reaction is precipitated which enables the objective to be achieved. Collected by Seán Ó hEochaidh for the IFC in 1947; published in Áine Ní Dhíoraí, *Na Cruacha: Scéalta agus Seanchas* (1985), pp. 106–7.   Translation and headnote, P.L.]

MURCHADH MÓR AGUS MURCHADH BEAG

Beirt ghasúr a bhí ann i bhfad ó shin agus is fada ó bhí, nó bhí caint ag achan seort san am udaí. Murchadh Mór agus Murchadh Beag arbh ainm daofu. Bhí siad amuigh ag baint sú craobh lá. Bhí barraíocht bainte ag Murchadh Mór agus thug sé do Mhurchadh Beag iad le taiscidh. In áit a gcur i dtaiscidh is é an rud a d'ith Murchadh Beag iad. Rinne Murchadh Mór amach ansin go bhfaigheadh sé slat a sciúrfadh é.

Chuaigh sé ionsar an tslat. 'A shlait,' a deir sé, 'an sciúrfaidh tú Murchadh Beag a d'ith mo chuid sú craobh aréir?'

'Ní bhfaighidh tú mise,' arsa an tslat, 'go bhfaighidh tú tuaigh a ghearrfas mé.'

Chuaigh sé a fhad leis an tuaigh. 'Tuaigh a ghearrfadh slat,' a deir sé, 'slat a sciúrfadh Murchadh Beag a d'ith mo chuid sú craobh aréir.'

'Ní bhfaighidh tú mise,' a deir sé, 'go bhfaighidh tú cloch a líomhfas mé.'

Chuaigh sé a fhad leis an chloch. 'Cloch a líomhfadh tuaigh, tuaigh a ghearrfadh slat, slat a sciúrfadh Murchadh Beag a d'ith mo chuid sú craobh aréir.'

'Ní bhfaighidh tú mise,' a deir an chloch, 'go bhfaighidh tú uisce a fhliuchfas mé.'

Chuaigh sé a fhad leis an uisce. 'Uisce a fhliuchfadh cloch, cloch a líomhfadh tuaigh, tuaigh a ghearrfadh slat, slat a sciúrfadh Murchadh Beag a d'ith mo chuid sú craobh aréir.'

'Ní bhfaighidh tú mise,' arsa an t-uisce, 'go bhfaighidh tú fia a shnámhfas mé.'

Chuaigh sé a fhad leis an fhia. 'Fia a shnámhfas uisce, uisce a fhliuchfadh cloch, cloch a líomhfadh tuaigh, tuaigh a ghearrfadh slat, slat a sciúrfadh Murchadh Beag a d'ith mo chuid sú craobh aréir.'

'Ní bhfaighidh tú mise', arsa an fia, 'go bhfaighidh tú gadhar a ruaigfeas mé.'

Chuaigh sé a fhad leis an ghadhar. 'Gadhar a ruaigfeadh fia, fia a shnámhfadh uisce, uisce a fhliuchfadh cloch, cloch a líomhfadh tuaigh, tuaigh a ghearrfadh slat, slat a sciúrfadh Murchadh Beag a d'ith mo chuid sú craobh aréir!'

'Ní bhfaighidh tú mise,' arsa an gadhar, 'go bhfaighidh tú im do mo chosa.'

Chuaigh sé a fhad leis an im. 'Ní bhfaighidh tú mise,' arsa an t-im, 'go bhfaighidh tú luchóg a scríobfas mé.'

Chuaigh sé a fhad leis an luchóg. 'Ní bhfaighidh tú mise,' arsa an luchóg, 'go bhfaighidh tú cat a ruaigfeas mé.'

'Cat a ruaigfeadh luchóg, luchóg a scríobfadh im, im i gcosa gadhair, gadhar a ruaigfeadh fia, fia a shnámhfadh uisce, uisce a fhliuchfadh cloch, cloch a líomhfadh tuaigh, tuaigh a ghearrfadh slat, slat a sciúrfadh Murchadh Beag a d'ith mo chuid sú craobh aréir!'

Chuaigh sé a fhad leis an chat. 'Ni bhfaighidh tú mise,' arsa an cat, 'go bhfaighidh tú trí bhraon bainne ó na gamhna.'

'Trí bhraon bainne le tabhairt don chat, cat a ruaigfeadh luchóg, luchóg a scríobfadh im, im i gcosa gadhair, gadhar a ruaigfeadh fia, fia a shnámhfadh uisce, uisce a líomhfadh tuaigh, tuaigh a ghearrfadh slat, slat a sciúrfadh Murchadh Beag a d'ith mo chuid sú craobh aréir!'

'Ní bhfaighidh tú aon bhraon bainne,' a deir na gamhna, 'go bhfaighidh tú trí phunann arbhair ó na buailteoirí.'

Chuaigh sé ionsar na buailteoirí. 'Ní bhfaighidh tú aon phunann arbhair uainne,' a deir na buailteoirí, 'go bhfaighidh tú trí bhonnóg aráin ó na bróinteoirí.'

'Ní bhfaighidh tú aon bhonnóg aráin uainne,' a deir na bróinteoirí, 'go dtugaidh tú trí rideal uisce chugainn.'

Chuirfeadh sé síos an rideal agus ar ndóiche nuair a thógfadh sé aníos í ní bhíodh deoir inti. Chuaigh feannóg thart os a cheann. 'Cuir lóib leis an rideal,' arsa an fheannóg.

Rinne sé sin agus thóg sé lán na dtrí rideal agus thug an t-uisce chucu. Thug na buailteoirí na trí phunann arbhair do na gamhna. Bhligh seisean trí bhraon bainne ó na gamhna. Thug sé na trí bhraon bainne don chat. Ruaig an cat an luchóg. Scríob an luchóg an t-im. Chuaigh an t-im i gcosa an ghadhair. Ruaig an gadhar an fia. Shnámh an fia an t-uisce. Fhliuch an t-uisce an chloch. Líomh an chloch an tuaigh. Ghearr an tuaigh an tslat.

Bhí sé ag sciúradh Murchadh Bhig leis an tslat go raibh sé tuirseach agus ca bith a d'éirigh daofu ina dhiaidh sin níor chualaigh mise aon iomrá orthu ón lá sin go dtí an lá inniu!

BIG MURCHADH AND LITTLE MURCHADH

Two boys who lived long ago, and it is long ago since they did, as everything could talk in those times. Big Murchadh and Little Murchadh were their names. They were outdoors one day picking raspberries. Big Murchadh had picked too many and he gave them to Little Murchadh to store, but instead of storing them Little Murchadh ate them. Big Murchadh decided that he would get a rod to trounce him.

He went to get the rod. 'Rod,' said he, 'will you trounce Little Murchadh who ate my raspberries last night?'

'You won't get me,' said the rod, 'until you get an axe to cut me.'

He went along to the axe. 'Axe to cut rod,' said he, 'rod to trounce Little Murchadh who ate my raspberries last night.'

'You won't get me,' said the axe, 'until you get a stone to sharpen me.'

He went along to the stone. 'Stone to sharpen axe, axe to cut rod, rod to trounce Little Murchadh who ate my raspberries last night.'

'You won't get me,' said the stone, 'until you get water to wet me.'

He went along to the water. 'Water to wet stone, stone to sharpen axe, axe to cut rod, rod to trounce Little Murchadh who ate my raspberries last night.'

'You won't get me,' said the water, 'until you get a deer to swim me.'

He went along to the deer. 'Deer to swim water, water to wet stone, stone to sharpen axe, axe to cut rod, rod to trounce Little Murchadh who ate my raspberries last night.'

'You won't get me,' said the deer, 'until you get a dog to chase me.'

He went along to the dog. 'Dog to chase deer, deer to swim water, water to wet stone, stone to sharpen axe, axe to cut rod, rod to trounce Little Murchadh who ate my raspberries last night.'

'You won't get me,' said the dog, 'until you get butter for my paws.'

He went along to the butter. 'You won't get me,' said the butter, 'until you get a mouse to scrape me.'

He went along to the mouse. 'You won't get me,' said the mouse, 'until you get a cat to chase me.'

'Cat to chase mouse, mouse to scrape butter, butter on the dog's paws, dog to chase deer, deer to swim water, water to wet stone, stone to sharpen axe, axe to cut rod, rod to trounce Little Murchadh who ate my raspberries last night.'

He went along to the cat. 'You won't get me,' said the cat, 'until you get three drops of milk from the calves.'

'Three drops of milk to give to the cat, cat to chase mouse, mouse to scrape butter, butter on dog's paws, dog to chase deer, deer to swim water, water to wet stone, stone to sharpen axe, axe to cut rod, rod to trounce Little Murchadh who ate my raspberries last night.'

'You won't get any drop of milk,' said the calves, 'until you get three sheaves of corn from the threshers.'

He went along to the threshers. 'You won't get any sheaf of corn from us,' said the threshers, 'until you get three loaves of bread from the grinders.'

'You won't get any loaf of bread from us,' said the grinders, 'until you bring us three riddlefuls of water.'

He kept dipping the riddle,[1] but of course when he took it up there wasn't a drop of water in it. A raven went by overhead. 'Put mud on the riddle,' said the raven.

He did that, and raised three riddlefuls of water, and brought it to them. The threshers gave the three sheaves of corn to the calves. He milked three drops of milk from the calves. He gave the three drops of milk to the cat. The cat chased the mouse. The mouse scraped the butter. The butter went on the dog's paws. The dog chased the deer. The deer swam the water. The water wet the stone. The stone whetted the axe. The axe cut the rod.

H e trounced Little Murchadh with the rod until he was tired, and I never heard from that day to this what happened to them afterwards.

---

1. A coarse sieve.

Biographies/Bibliographies

Siobhán Lynch

LIFE. Born 1965, in County Wicklow, Siobhán Lynch was twelve years of age when her sister Geraldine, a folklore scholar, made a systematic collection of games and lore from her, using Eilís Brady's *All In! All In!*

(1975) and Iona and Peter Opie's *The Lore and Language of Schoolchildren* (1959) as templates. Siobhán had attended national schools in the village of Ashford and in Wicklow town, and Geraldine Lynch collected some hundred pages of material from her, which she later deposited as IFC 1920: 1–100. The material published in *Béaloideas*, vols 45–7, is drawn from that collection.

CHIEF WRITINGS. Geraldine Lynch, 'The Lore of a Wicklow Schoolgirl', *Béaloideas*, vols 45–7 (1977–9), pp. 46–62.

John Buckley

LIFE. Photographer. In 1982 he exhibited a collection of his photographs of children's games which involve rhymes, first in Cork, and later at the Grapevine Arts Centre, Dublin. No other information available.

Eilís Brady

LIFE. Born in Dublin, Eilís Brady (Ní Bhrádaigh) has lived all her life in the house where she grew up, and has made a lifelong study of the children's folklore of her area. This research produced a valuable collection of material now in the Department of Irish Folklore, UCD, and an important book, *All In! All In!* (1975). Her professional life was spent on the editorial staff of the Department of Education's Publications Branch. A lexicographer, bilingual in Irish and English, she has worked on three major dictionaries of the Irish language (the third still in preparation).

CHIEF WRITINGS. *All In! All In!: A Selection of Dublin Children's Traditional Street Games with Rhymes and Music* (Dublin: Comhairle Bhéaloideas Éireann, 1984 [1975]).

Anna Nic an Luain

For biography and bibliography, see p. 1310.

PATRICIA LYSAGHT, *Editor*

Writing Oral Traditions

Folklore was in fashion in nineteenth-century Ireland among creative writers, members of antiquarian societies, the Irish literary renaissance and the language revival movement.[1] Anglo-Irish novelists were drawing heavily on the oral tradition: William Carleton in *Traits and Stories of the Irish Peasantry* (two series, 1830, 1833), Samuel Lover in two series of *Legends and Stories of Ireland* (1830, 1834) and Gerald Griffin in *Tales of the Munster Festivals* (1827) and *Tales of the Jury Room* (n.d.). Antiquarian interest in the subject was much in evidence, and numerous, more or less amateur enthusiasts were at work gathering and publishing collections of Irish tales and legends.

Thomas Crofton Croker (1798–1854), born in Cork, the son of an English army major, but based in London for most of his life, set the ball rolling in 1825 with the publication of his substantial *Fairy Legends and Traditions of the South of Ireland* — which the Grimm brothers translated into German as *Irische Elfenmärchen* within a year. Next in importance is the bookseller Patrick Kennedy (1801–73), whose many works relate to County Wexford in the

southeast of Ireland, an area from which relatively little folklore was subsequently collected. Influenced by the work of Croker in Ireland, the Grimms in Germany, Peter Christen Asbjörnsen and Jörgen Moe in Norway and John Francis Campbell of Islay in Scotland, he published an important collection of tales, *Legendary Fictions of the Irish Celts* (1866), parts of which were expanded in *The Fireside Stories of Ireland* (1870) and *The Bardic Stories of Ireland* (1871).

With Jeremiah Curtin (1838–1906), an American anthropologist and linguist from Wisconsin, the geographical focus of Irish folk narrative collecting broadened to include the Gaeltacht areas along the Atlantic seaboard counties of the west of Ireland, and a Gaeltacht perspective has informed Irish folklore collecting ever since. Of Irish-speaking parents from Cork and Limerick, Curtin knew some Irish but required the services of an interpreter during his collecting trips to Ireland, and the tales and legends he recorded were published in English. As a result of a series of visits between 1887 and 1893, he published three collections of tales: *Myths and Folk-Lore of Ireland* (1890), in which he does not name his informants, *Hero-Tales of Ireland* (1894), and *Tales of the Fairies and of the Ghost World Collected from Oral Tradition in South-West Munster* (1895). Curtin states in *Tales of the Fairies* (p. 144) that he was told three of the stories by Maggie Doyle, 'an old woman leaning on a staff'; he was moved to write the following about female tradition bearers:

> It is not out of place to refer here to a certain popular error. It is supposed by many persons that women are the chief depositories of tales touching fairies and other extra-human characters, but they are not. It is a rare thing to find a woman in

---

1. The following are general surveys of the interest shown in Irish folklore in nineteenth- and twentieth-century Ireland and the key figures, collections and studies involved: Douglas Hyde, *Beside the Fire: A Collection of Irish Gaelic Folk Stories* (London: David Nutt, 1890; rpr. Dublin: Irish Academic Press, 1978); Richard M. Dorson, Foreword in S. O'Sullivan, *Folktales of Ireland* (London: Routledge and Kegan Paul, 1966; rpr. 1969), pp. v–xxxii, and 'The Antiquary-Folklorists' and 'The Celtic Folklorists — Ireland', in *The British Folklorists: A History* (London: Routledge and Kegan Paul, 1968), pp. 44–57, 431–9; Patricia Lysaght, 'Hyde, Douglas', in *Enzyklopädie des Märchens*, Band 6, Lieferung 4/5 (Berlin, N/York: Walter de Gruyter, 1990), and 'Irland', in *Enzyklopädie des Märchens*, Band 7, Lieferung 1 (Berlin, N/York: Walter de Gruyter, 1991), pp. 273–83; Bo Almqvist, *The Irish Folklore Commission: Achievement and Legacy* (Dublin: Comhairle Bhéaloideas Éireann Pamphlet, 3, 1979), 21pp (rpr. from *Béaloideas*, vols. 45–7 [1977–9], 1979, pp. 6–26), and 'Irish Migratory Legends of the Supernatural: Sources, Studies and Problems', *Béaloideas*, vol. 59 (1991), esp. pp. 5–24. See also Letitia McClintock, pp. 1169–72.

possession of wonderful tales of the best quality. During researches extending over a number of years, I have found among Indians in the United States only one woman who could be classed with the very best tale-tellers. In Ireland I have found few women who can tell tales at all, and none who can compare with the best men. I believe this is so in all countries.

William Larminie (1849–1900) — encouraged by Douglas Hyde — also collected tales in the Gaeltacht areas of Galway, Mayo and Donegal, and he too translated the tales into English for his compilation *West Irish Folktales and Romances* (London, 1893; rpr. Shannon, 1972), an important contribution to the scientific collecting and publication of Irish folktales. He names his informants, all of whom are male.

It was Douglas Hyde (1860–1949), a founder member of the language revival movement, first president of the Gaelic League (founded in 1893), and later first president of Ireland, 1938–45, who most firmly linked the cultural regeneration of Ireland to the language and culture of the contemporary Gaeltacht, concentrating his attention on the oral traditions of native Irish-speakers in Connacht. His *Leabhar Sgeulaigheachta* (Book of Storytelling), published in 1889, was the first collection of folktales in the Irish language, and in 1890 another small collection, *Cois na Teineadh*, was published, along with a companion volume in English, *Beside the Fire*. These were followed by the large and important collection of *Märchen*, *An Sgeuluidhe Gaodhalach* (The Gaelic Storyteller) published initially in *Annales de Bretagne*, vols 10–18 (1895–1901), with French translations by Georges Dottin, and republished in book form in 1901. In *Scéalta Thomáis Uí Chathasaigh/Mayo Stories Told by Thomas Casey* (1939), Hyde brought together the repertoire of one male storyteller.

Throughout most of the nineteenth century, as the most important published collections show, collecting the tales and legends of Ireland was the pursuit of men, while women figured only rarely as their informants. It is not until the closing decade of the nineteenth century — when the Irish language was also in fashion — that an important and assiduous female collector and

compiler of works on Irish folklore emerges. This was Lady Isabella Augusta Persse Gregory (1852–1932), mistress of Coole, a country estate in the barony of Kiltartan, County Galway. A central figure in the Irish literary renaissance, she was drawn to folklore initially through the work of W.B. Yeats (1865–1939). Looking back after more than a decade of fruitful folklore collecting, mainly in Galway and Clare, she recalls the sense of excitement and mission she felt when she read his *Celtic Twilight* (London, 1893):

> The Celtic Twilight was the first book of Mr. Yeats that I read, and even before I met him, a little time later, I had begun looking for news of the invisible world; for his stories were of Sligo and I felt jealous for Galway. This beginning of knowledge was a great excitement to me, for though I had heard all my life some talk of the fairies and the banshee (have indeed reason to believe in the last), I had never thought of giving heed to what I, in common with my class, looked on as fancy or superstition . . .[2]

In 1897 Lady Gregory first met Hyde at Tullira, the home of Edward Martyn in County Galway. That same year she had successfully begun to learn Irish, and that, together with her membership and active involvement in the Gaelic League, led to her friendship with Hyde. She understood the importance of the league for Ireland and for herself. For Ireland, 'It was an upsetting of the table of values, an astonishing excitement. The imagination of Ireland had found a new homing place.' For Lady Gregory, it was the beginning of her discovery of a hidden Gaelic Ireland at her doorstep.[3]

When the Folklore of Ireland Society was founded in 1927, Lady Gregory was in her mid-seventies. With the establishment of the Irish Folklore Commission in 1935, the collecting of folklore became a job for professionals, not amateurs, and in keeping with normal employ-

---

2. *Visions and Beliefs in the West of Ireland Collected and Arranged by Lady Gregory: With Two Essays and Notes by W.B. Yeats*, 2nd ed. (Gerrards Cross: Colin Smythe, 1970 [1920], p. 15.
3. Patricia Lysaght, 'Perspectives on Narrative Communication and Gender: Lady Augusta Gregory's Visions and Beliefs in the West of Ireland (1920)', *Fabula: Journal of Folktale Studies*, 39 (1998), Heft 3/4, pp. 256–76.

ment practice at the time, those hired to travel the country as collectors were all male. Fifty years after Curtin wrote that he had found few women who could tell tales, J.H. Delargy, the IFC's founder and honorary director, commented further on the gender aspect of Irish storytelling in terms of the main and most skilful narrators of particular genres of tradition, in his well-known monograph 'The Gaelic Storyteller' (1945).[4] With the benefit of his considerable experience in the field and the evidence of the accumulating collections of the IFC, he modified one of Curtin's more sweeping pronouncements by stating that women excelled in the branch of tradition called *seanchas*, which included 'many tales of a short realistic type about fairies, ghosts, and other supernatural beings'. Being of the opinion, however, that the Gaelic storyteller, that is, the teller of the *seanscéal* (*Märchen*: Wonder Tale) was usually a man, he was in essential agreement with Curtin's statements that only few women could tell tales and that it was 'a rare thing to find a woman in possession of wonderful tales of the best quality'. Considering the IFC's rich collections from gifted female storytellers such as Peig Sayers and Anna Nic an Luain, however, whose repertoires contained a substantial number of *Märchen*, he could hardly have agreed with Curtin — though he does not seem to have subsequently expressed an opinion on it — 'that none could compare with the best men'.

Máire MacNeill was employed in the IFC in Dublin. She spent a period in Sweden where she

received training in archival and research methods. Surveying regional newspapers for folklore items led her to noticing the occurrence of similar celebrations in a variety of places in Ireland about the beginning of August, and to the painstaking and inspired research which resulted in the publication of *The Festival of Lughnasa* some twenty years later in 1962. She was not officially expected to conduct independent research or to publish, but records in a Foreword her gratitude to the Commission's director Séamus Ó Duilearga for facilitating both: 'He made a vanished world visible to me when he gave me the opportunity of becoming familiar with Irish folklore and folklore research methods, and he encouraged me to set out on my own venture in this undertaking.'

Based on her analysis of existing sources, a questionnaire about Lughnasa traditions was prepared and sent out to the IFC's network of correspondents in July 1942. Three hundred and sixteen replies were received, which she then proceeded to analyse, along with material in the manuscript archive, and in printed books and journals. The result was a classic of folklore scholarship in some 700 pages.

MacNeill's IFC colleague Bríd Mahon also conducted her own research in the Commission's archive and library, publishing articles and books, mostly on food and clothing, and becoming well known as a journalist.

Since the 1970s, when folklore became a university discipline in Ireland, women folklorists have attained national and international repute in academia and in many other areas of Irish life. A number of them have contributed to this volume.

4. The Sir John Rhŷs Memorial Lecture. British Academy (London: The Proceedings of The British Academy, vol. 31, 1945, rpr. Chicago: American Committee for Irish Studies, 1969).

LADY GREGORY

(1852–1932)

from:
VISIONS AND BELIEFS IN THE WEST OF IRELAND (1920)

[*Visions and Beliefs in the West of Ireland*, published in two volumes in 1920, is Lady Gregory's most substantial and

powerful collection of folklore, one which provided much inspiration and material for the Irish Literary Renaissance.[1] Women figure prominently in *Visions and Beliefs,* as daughters, wives and mothers; daughters who may be suspected of being changelings, wives who are said

1. London and New York: Putnams, 1920; Gerrards Cross: Colin Smythe, 1970.

to have been 'touched' by the supernatural and to have been 'away', mothers who have watched children die in their prime. Lady Gregory's characterization of her female dramatis personae is one of the outstanding characteristics of *Visions and Beliefs*, and bears testimony not only to her genius as a collector of this genre of tradition, but also to her honesty and democracy towards other, and not necessarily socially similar or likeminded, women.[2]

The powerful women she describes inhabit boundary zones, geographically, socially or personally. Mary Glynn, a practitioner with adherents of her 'Mountain Theology', is poised between Galway and Clare; living near the boundary river with stepping stones in it, 'she can cross from Connaught to Munster when she has a mind' . . . 'And Mrs. Casey comes and looks at the stepping stones now and again, for she is a Clare woman; and though she has lived fifty years in Connaught, she is not yet quite reconciled to it.'[3]

Familiar with the woods and other wild places of the Coole demesne and its neighbourhood, 'Mrs. Sheridan', 'old, wrinkled and half blind', is also on the edge of things. Having 'paid the penalty' of blindness to the fairies because of her 'knowledge' of their ways, gleaned when she 'used to be away among them', she is also, however, empowered by that 'knowledge', and thus her status *vis-à-vis* the supernatural and human worlds is ambiguous.

But it is undoubtedly Biddy Early, the nineteenth-century *bean feasa* or 'wise woman of Clare' who epitomizes power and marginalization in *Visions and Beliefs*.[4] As a mediator of supernatural knowledge, she was a folk healer prepared to exercise her power for the good of the community. This was in contrast to the clergy, who possessed a similar power according to popular belief but were unwilling to use it. The tension which thus ensued between Biddy and the church authorities led to notoriety and social isolation for her.

Lady Gregory's comprehensive collection of traditions surrounding Biddy Early (c. 1798–1874) illustrates the central aspects of the traditions about the well-known healer. Her renowned psychic and curative powers are attributed to contact with supernatural forces, and many of her principal characteristics, especially her clairvoyance, can be compared to similar traits of healers in other cultures. In the following extract Lady Gregory describes the expedition she made in the mid-1890s to find out about Biddy Early through original field research, driving across the mountains in the old-fashioned phaeton which had been a wedding gift from her brother some fifteen

years before. This is followed by the material she collected, which she wrote as though spoken by her informants.

The account of Biddy Early attributed to Daniel Shea describes the clergy's attitude to her, as well as her reputed faculty of clairvoyance. This personal narrative also incorporates the theme of the fairy abduction of humans, and other related beliefs. Biddy Early's attribution of the illness of the boy 'that some strange thing had been put upon' to supernatural forces emanating from the local fairy fort is clarified as abduction in the course of the narrative. Aspects of the abduction process are also mentioned: the role of the human agent, the child's stumbling and injury on the threshold — 'a numinous spot between the earthly and spirit realms'[5] — during his parents' absence from the house, and the boy's subsequent condition of irreversible decline. His father's fearful reaction to his son and the patterns of behaviour (typical of changelings in Irish and European folk belief) attributed to him by a neighbour after his death, further confirm the boy's status as a changeling.[6] The temporary recovery of the boy is attributed to Biddy Early's intervention and his subsequent 'death' to a breach of her instructions.

Biddy Early's antagonist, the priest, is also credited with the power of healing. The contrasting sources and mediation processes of their powers are strikingly illustrated in O'Shea's narrative. Unlike Biddy Early, whose exercise of psychic and curative powers is associated with the a-Christian tradition through the medium of her magic bottle (*buidéal draíochta*), the priest is the direct mediator of the Christian power of healing; consequently, according to folk tradition, he must pay a penalty for the exercise of that power, in the form of physical or mental suffering or other kinds of loss.[7]

2. P. Lysaght, 'Perspectives on Narrative Communication and Gender', op. cit.

3. Lady Gregory, *Poets and Dreamers* (1974), p. 84.

4. See pp. 31–49 (1970); for the traditions of Biddy Early see Nancy Schmitz, 'An Irish Wise Woman – Fact and Legend', *Journal of the Folklore Institute*, vol. 14, no. 3 (1977), pp.169–79, and works quoted there. Cf. also M. Ryan, *Biddy Early: The Wise Woman of Clare* (Cork: Mercier Press, 1978); E. Lenihan, *In Search of Biddy Early* (Cork: Mercier Press, 1987).

5. W.D. Hand, *Boundaries, Portals, and Other Magical Spots in Folklore* (London: The Folklore Society, 1982; The Katharine Briggs Lecture No. 2, delivered 2 November 1982), p. 3; for further discussion of the significance of the threshold as a setting for a large body of folk belief and custom, see also pp. 10–12.

6. For a discussion of the physical and behavioural characteristics of the changeling, and modes of recognition and banishment in Irish oral tradition, see S. Mac Philib, 'The Changeling (ML 5058): Irish Versions of a Migratory Legend in Their International Context', *Béaloideas*, vol. 59 (1991), pp. 121–31. For suggestions of a strong relationship between changeling lore and children born with congenital diseases, see S. Schoon Eberly, 'Fairies and the Folklore of Disability: Changelings, Hybrids, and the Solitary Fairy', in P. Narváez (ed.), *The Good People*, pp. 227–50; in the same volume J. Underwood Munro compares the medical concept of 'failure to thrive' in infants with traditional changeling accounts ('The Invisible Made Visible: The Fairy Changeling as a Folk Articulation of Failure to Thrive in Infants and Children', pp. 251–83).

7. See P. Ó Héalaí, 'Cumhacht an tSagairt sa Bhéaloideas', *Léachtaí Cholm Cille VIII* (Má Nuad: An Sagart, 1977), pp. 115–18. Also, *Visions and Beliefs*, p. 39 ('. . . Father Flynn said to me . . . if I do them I let the devil into me. But there was Father Carey used to do them, but he went wrong, with the people bringing too much whiskey to pay him — and Father Mahony has him stopped now'); p. 41 ('. . .The priests can do cures by the same power that she had, but those that have much stock don't like to be doing them, for they are sure to lose all.').

Sudden illnesses or infections occurring without obvious cause, as in Mrs Locke's account, were often ascribed to fairy agency or malevolent forces. These afflictions were attributed to a *poc sí* — 'fairy dart' or 'elf-shot', 'fairy stroke' or 'blast' — which was said to leave a mark of some kind on the the victim's body.[8] Water taken from the point where three townlands or farms met (*uisce na dtrí teorann*) was considered exceptionally potent in relation to the supernatural; many cultures have recourse to running water for the divestment and sweeping away of disease and magical substances.[9] Extracts are from pp. 31–2 , 36–7, 38, 42–3, 45–6. Headnote, P.L.]

SEERS AND HEALERS

Biddy Early

In talking to the people I often heard the name of Biddy Early, and I began to gather many stories of her, some calling her a healer and some a witch. Some said she had died a long time ago, and some that she was still living. I was sure after a while that she was dead, but was told that her house was still standing, and was on the other side of Slieve Echtge, between Feakle and Tulla.[10] So one day I set out and drove Shamrock, my pony, to a shooting lodge built by my grandfather in a fold of the mountains, and where I had sometimes, when a young girl, stayed with my brothers when they were shooting the wild deer that came and sheltered in the woods. It had like other places on our estate a border name brought over from Northumberland, but though we called it Chevy Chase[11] the people spoke of its woods and outskirts as Daire-caol,[12] the narrow Oak Wood, and Daroda,[13] the Two Roads, and Druim-da-Rod,[14] their Ridge. I stayed the night in the low thatched house, setting out next day for Feakle 'eight strong miles over the mountain'. It was a wild road, and the pony had to splash his way through two unbridged rivers,[15] swollen with

the summer rains. The red mud of the road, the purple heather and foxglove, the brown bogs were a contrast to the grey rocks and walls of the Burren[16] and Aidhne, and there were many low hills, brown when near, misty blue in the distance; then the Golden Mountain, Slieve nan-Or,[17] 'where the last great battle will be fought before the end of the world'. Then I was out of Connacht into Clare, the brown turning to green pasture as I drove by Raftery's Lough Greine.[18]

I put up my pony at a little inn. There were portraits of John Dillon[19] and Michael Davitt[20] hanging in the parlour, and the landlady told me Parnell's likeness had been with them, until the priest had told her he didn't think well of her hanging it there.[21] There was also on the wall, in a frame, a warrant for the arrest of one of her sons, signed by, I think, Lord Cowper, in the days of the Land War.[22] 'He got half a year in gaol the same year Parnell did. He got sick there, and though he lived for some years the doctor said when he died the illness he got in gaol had to do with his death.'

I had been told how to find Biddy Early's house 'beyond the little humpy bridge,' and I walked on till I came to it, a poor cottage enough, high up on a mass of rock by the roadside. There was only a little girl in the house, but her mother came in afterwards and told me that Biddy Early had died about twenty years before, and that

8. Cf. 'The Midwife Who Lost an Eye' in the subsection 'Legends of the Supernatural', pp. 1294–1296.
9. See in this connection W.D. Hand, *Boundaries, Portals, and Other Magical Spots in Folklore*, p. 6.
10. Villages in east County Clare.
11. 'Chevvy Chase Cottage' is marked on the first edition Ordnance Survey maps 1835, Galway, sheet 129 (OS 129, 1835).
12. Irish *Doire*, 'oak-wood'; *caol*, 'narrow'.
13. Irish *D[h]á ród*, 'two roads'.
14. Irish *Droim dá ród*, 'ridge of two roads'.
15. One of the rivers which Lady Gregory forded on the road from Chevy Chase Cottage can probably be identified as the Owendalulleegh on the border between Galway and Clare, which bears the legend 'Ford' (OS 129, 1835) at the point where the road running by Chevy Chase Cottage crosses it.
16. The Burren plateau in north-west County Clare is one of the finest barren karstlands in western Europe, famous for its flora. This large karst area of carboniferous limestone with bare surface-rock has underground drainage and many cavities. Boundary walls in the area are also built of this grey stone. (Cf. J.W. O'Connell and A. Korff, *The Book of the Burren* (Newtownlynch, Kinvara, County Galway: Tír Eolas, 1991).
17. Irish, *Sliabh an Óir*.
18. Loch Gréine, 'Lough Graney', in north-east County Clare lies close to the Clare–Galway border and is mentioned by the Mayo poet Antaine Ó Raifteari (Anthony Raftery) (1779–1835) in a number of poems. It has associations too with the Clare poet Brian Merriman, author of *Cúirt an Mheán Oíche*, 'The Midnight Court'.
19. John Dillon (1851–1927), prominent nationalist MP, campaigner for tenant farmers, leader of the Irish Parliamentary Party, 1918. See Maurice Manning, *James Dillon: A Biography* (Dublin: Wolfhound Press, 1999).
20. Michael Davitt (1846–1906), founder of the Irish National Land League, 1879.
21. Charles Stewart Parnell (1846–91), charismatic leader of the Irish Parliamentary Party, 1880; fell from grace in 1890 when he was cited in the divorce case of Katherine O'Shea, whom he married shortly before his death.
22. For Dillon, Davitt and Parnell, see T.W. Moody, 'Fenianism, Home Rule, and the Land War 1850–91', in T.W. Moody and F.X. Martin (eds), *The Course of Irish History* (Cork: Mercier Press, 1993; rpr. of revised edition, 1984), pp. 275–93.

after they had come to live in the house they had been 'annoyed for a while' by people coming to look for her. She had sent them away, telling them that Biddy Early was dead, though a friendly priest had said to her, 'Why didn't you let on that you were her and make something out of them?' She told me some of the stories I give below, and showed me the shed where the healer had consulted with her invisible friends. I had already been given by an old patient of hers a 'bottle' prepared for the cure, but which she had been afraid to use. It lies still unopened in a shelf in my storeroom. When I got back at nightfall to the lodge in the woods I found many of the neighbours gathered there, wanting to hear news of the 'Tulla Woman' and to know for certain if she was dead. I think as time goes on her fame will grow and some of the myths that always hang in the air will gather round her, for I think the first thing I was told of her was, 'There used surely to be enchanters in the old time, magicians and freemasons. Old Biddy Early's power came from the same thing.'[23]

The Little Girl of Biddy Early's House: The people do be full of stories of all the cures she did. Once after we came to live here a carload of people came, and asked was Biddy Early here, and my mother said she was dead. When she told the priest he said she had a right to shake a bottle and say she was her, and get something from them. It was by the bottle she did all, to shake it, and she'd see everything when she looked in it. Sometimes she'd give a bottle of some cure to people that came, but if she'd say to them, 'You'll never bring it home,' break it they should on the way home, with all the care they'd take of it.

She was as good, and better, to the poor as to the rich. Any poor person passing the road, she'd call in and give a cup of tea or a glass of whiskey to, and bread and what they wanted.

She had a big chest within in that room, and it full of pounds of tea and bottles of wine and of whiskey and of claret, and all things in the world. One time she called in a man that was passing and gave him a glass of whiskey, and then she said to him, 'The road you are going home by, don't go by

it.' So he asked why not, and she took the bottle — a long-shaped bottle it was — and looked into it, holding it up, and then she bid him look through it, and he'd see what would happen him. But her husband said, 'Don't show it to him, it might give him a fright he wouldn't get over.' So she only said, 'Well, go home by another road.' And so he did and got home safe, for in the bottle she had seen a party of men that wouldn't have let him pass alive. She got the rites of the Church when she died, but first she had to break the bottle.[24]

It was from her brother that she got the power, when she had to go to the workhouse, and he came back, and gave her the way of doing the cures.

An Old Midwife: Tell me now is there anything wrong about you or your son that you went to that house? I went there but once myself, when my little girl that was married was bad, after her second baby being born. I went to the house and told her about it, and she took the bottle and shook it and looked in it, and then she turned and said something to himself [her husband] that I didn't hear — and she just waved her hand to me like that, and bid me go home, for she would take nothing from me. But himself came out and told that what she was after seeing in the bottle was my little girl, and the coffin standing beside her. So I went home, and sure enough on the tenth day after, she was dead.

Daniel Shea: It was all you could do to get to Biddy Early with your skin whole, the priests were so set against her. I went to her one time myself, and it was hard when you got near to know the way, for all the people were afraid to tell it.

It was about a little chap of my own I went, that some strange thing had been put upon. When I got to her house there were about fifty to be attended to before me, and when my turn came she looked in the bottle, a sort of a common greenish one that seemed to have nothing in it. And she told me where I came from, and the shape of the house and the appearance of it, and of the lake you see

---

23. Lady Gregory here shows an awareness of what modern folklore scholars call 'motif attraction' between powerful traditional figures. She makes a similar comment in relation to Daniel O'Connell in *The Kiltartan History Book*, p. 149.

24. According to Nancy Schmitz, Biddy Early at her death 'readily consented to give up her magic bottle . . . and was reconciled to the church'. N. Schmitz, 'An Irish Wise Woman — Fact and Legend', p. 173. Cf. also M. Ryan, *Biddy Early*, and E. Lenihan, *In Search of Biddy Early*.

there, and everything round about. And she told me of a lime-kiln that was near, and then she said, 'The harm that came to him came from the forth[25] beyond that.' And I never knew of there being a forth there, but after I came home I went to look, and there sure enough it was.

And she told me how it had come on him, and bid me remember a day that a certain gentleman stopped and spoke to me when I was out working in the hayfield, and the child with me playing about. And I remembered it well, it was old James Hill of Creen, that was riding past, and stopped and talked and was praising the child. And it was close by that forth beyond that James Hill was born.

It was soon after that day that the mother and I went to Loughrea, and when we came back, the child had slipped on the threshold of the house and got a fall, and he was screeching and calling out that his knee was hurt, and from that time he did no good, and pined away and had the pain in the knee always.[26]

And Biddy Early said, 'While you're talking to me now the child lies dying,' and that was at twelve o'clock in the day. And she made up a bottle for me, herbs I believe it was made of, and she said, 'Take care of it going home, and whatever may happen, don't drop it'; and she wrapped it in all the folds of my handkerchief. So when I was coming home and got near Tillyra I heard voices over the wall talking, and when I got to the Roxborough gate there were many people talking and coming to where we were. I could hear them and see them, and the man that was with me. But when I heard them I remembered what she said, and I took the bottle in my two hands and held it, and so I brought it home safely. And when I got home they told me the child was worse, and that at twelve o'clock the day before he lay as they thought dying. And when I brought the bottle to him, he pulled the bed-clothes up over his head, and we had the

work of the world to make him taste it. But from the time he took it, the pain in the knee left him and he began to get better. Biddy Early had told me not to let many days pass without coming to her again, when she gave me the bottle. But seeing him so well, I thought it no use to go again, and it was not on May Day, but it was during the month of May he died. He took to the bed before that, and he'd be always calling to me to come inside the bed where he was and if I went in, he'd hardly let me go. But I got afraid, and I didn't like to be too much with him.[27]

He was but eight years old when he died, but Ned Cahel that used to live beyond there then told me privately that when I'd be out of the house and he'd come in, the little chap would ask for the pipe, and take it and smoke it, but he'd never let me see him doing it. And he was old-fashioned in all his ways.

Another thing Biddy Early told me to do was to go out before sunrise to where there'd be a boundary wall between two or three estates, and to bring a bottle, and lay it in the grass and gather the dew into it. But there were hundreds of people she turned away, because she'd say, 'What's wrong with you has nothing to do with my business.'

There was a Clare woman with me when I went there, and she told me there was a boy from a village near her was brought tied in a cart to Biddy Early, and she said, 'If I cure you, will you be willing to marry me?' And he said he would. So she cured him and married him. I saw him there at her house. It might be that she had the illness put upon him first.

The priests don't do cures by the same means, and they don't like to do them at all. It was in my house that you see that Father Gregan did one on Mr. Phayre.[28] And he cured a girl up in the mountains after, and where is he now but in a madhouse. They are afraid of the power they do them by, that it will be too strong for them. Some say the bishops don't like them to do cures

25. A ringfort, defined as a circular space surrounded by a bank and a fosse. These are the most common and widely distributed ancient monuments in Ireland (S.P. Ó Riordáin, *Antiquities of the Irish Countryside* [London: Methuen, 1976; rpr. of 4th edition 1965], p. 1). In traditional belief ringforts are considered the dwelling places of supernatural beings such as the fairies (S. Ó Súilleabháin, *A Handbook of Irish Folklore*, pp. 467–70). See also Matthew Stout, *The Irish Ringfort* (Dublin: Four Courts Press, 1997).
26. Cf. 'A Young Woman Taken by the Fairies' in the subsection 'Legends of the Supernatural', pp. 1296–1303.

27. Parents' fearful reaction to children whom they suspect of being 'overlooked' or abducted into the fairy world because of their continuing physical decline is further strikingly illustrated in the personal account of 'A Hillside Woman', who tells of her inability, for that reason, to respond to her dying infant (*Visions and Beliefs*, p. 143). Underlying the fear was the notion that the child was fated to 'die', otherwise something else, perhaps even an adult member of the family, would have to 'die' in his place.
28. Daniel Shea is referring to his own house, which was visible to Lady Gregory as he spoke.

because the whiskey they drink to give them courage before they do them is very apt to make drunkards of them. It's not out of the prayer-book they read, but out of the Roman ritual, and that's a book you can read evil out of as well as good.

Mrs. Locke: It was my son was thatching Heniff's house when he got the touch, and he came back with a pain in his back and in his shoulders, and took to the bed. And a few nights after that I was asleep, and the little girl came and woke me and said, 'There's none of us can sleep, with all the cars and carriages rattling round the house.' But though I woke and heard her say that, I fell into a sound sleep again and never woke till morning. And one night there came two taps at the window, one after another, and we all heard it and no one there. And at last I sent the eldest boy to Biddy Early and he found her in the house. She was then married to her fourth man. And she said he came a day too soon and would do nothing for him. And he had to walk away in the rain. And the next day he went back and she said, 'Three days later and you'd have been too late.' And she gave him two bottles, the one he was to bring to a boundary water and to fill it up, and that was to be rubbed to the back, and the other was to drink. And the minute he got them he began to get well, and he left the bed and could walk, but he was always delicate. When we rubbed his back we saw a black mark, like the bite of a dog, and as to his face, it was as white as a sheet.

I have the bottle here yet, though it's thirty year ago I got it. She bid the boy to bring whatever was left of it to a river, and to pour it away with the running water. But when he got well I did nothing with it, and said nothing about it — and here it is now for you to see. I never let on to Father Folan that I went to her, but one time the Bishop came, McInerny. I knew he was a rough man, and I went to him and I made my confession, and I said, 'Do what you like with me, but I'd walk the world for my son when he was sick.' All he said was, 'It would have been no wonder if the two feet had been cut off the messenger.' And he said no more and put nothing on me.[29]

[While fear of going astray in lonely places at night has no doubt given rise to many legends of encounters with the fairies, supernatural beings, according to traditional belief, might also be met with in certain parts of wild nature, such as forests, woods, mountains or other remote areas, even in daytime. Although it is unclear whether the boy in Mrs Sheridan's narrative, which follows, belongs to the category of the restless dead or is to be considered an abducted human being, his supranormal status, indicated by his increasing size and sudden disappearance near subterranean caves, would be immediately evident to a traditional audience.

These narratives also attribute heightened powers of perception to Mrs Sheridan, especially an ability to observe the behaviour of supernatural beings, and her striking descriptions of modes of abduction — as well as her partial loss of sight — are linked to that capacity. In the narrative, her partial blindness is placed in the context of the common folk idea of fairy retribution against humans who pry into the fairy world. The 'blinding of one eye' motif commonly occurs in relation to the midwife who is enabled to see the fairies at will by virtue of her having come into contact with a forbidden substance (for example, ointment) while delivering a child in fairyland.[1] The abduction methods — flight through the air and drowning — though told in the first person, are not unique to this particular narrative, being firmly based on received oral tradition. Here they serve to explain the sudden and untimely death of Mrs Sheridan's own child and two other young boys. The traditional notion of 'temporary abduction' or being 'in the fairies' is also drawn on to explain possible strange behaviour on her part during her early married life.   Headnote, P.L.]

MRS. SHERIDAN

Mrs. Sheridan[2]
Mrs. Sheridan, as I call her, was wrinkled and half blind, and had gone barefoot through her lifetime. She was old, for she had once met Raftery, the Gaelic poet,[3] at a dance, and he died before the famine of '47. She must have been comely then, for he had said to her: 'Well planed you are, the carpenter that planed you knew his trade', and she was ready of reply and answered him back, 'Better than you know yours,' for his fiddle had two or three broken strings. And then he had spoken of a neighbour in some way that

---

29. Penance, which in the Roman Catholic and Orthodox Churches is an act of penitence imposed by a priest in confession, was, surprisingly, not imposed in this case.

1. This motif occurs in one of the two major redactions of the migratory legend 'Midwife to the Fairies'; see 'The Midwife Who Lost an Eye', p. 1296.
2. The extracts are from pages 50–1, 52–3, 56–7, 62.
3. Antaine Ó Raiftearai (Anthony Raftery), 1779–1835.

vexed her father, and he would let him speak no more with her. And she had carried a regret for this through her long life, for she said: 'If it wasn't for him speaking as he did, and my father getting vexed, he might have made words about me like he did for Mary Hynes and for Mary Brown.'[4] She had never been to school she told me, because her father could not pay the penny a week it would have cost. She had never travelled many miles from the parish of her birth, and I am sure had never seen pictures except sacred ones on chapel walls; and yet she could tell of a Cromwellian castle built up and of a drawbridge and of a long-faced, fair-haired woman, and of the yet-earlier round house and saffron dress of the heroic times . . .

I was told by Mrs. Sheridan:
. . . I was led astray myself one day at Coole when I went to gather sticks. I was making a bundle of them, and I saw a boy beside me, and a little grey dogeen[5] with him, and at first I thought it was William Hanlon, and then I saw it was not. And he walked along with me, and I asked him did he want any of the sticks and he said he did not, and he seemed as we were walking to grow bigger and bigger. And when he came to where the caves go underground he stopped, and I asked him his name, and he said, 'You should know me, for you've seen me often enough.' And then he was gone, and I know that he was no living thing.

There was a child I had, and he a year and a half old, and he got a quinsy[6] and a choking in the throat and I was holding him in my arms

beside the fire, and all in a minute he died. And the men were working down by the river, washing sheep, and they heard the crying of a child from over there in the air, and they said, 'That's Sheridan's child.' So I knew sure enough that he was *taken*.[7]

Come here close and I'll tell you what I saw at the old castle there below (Ballinamantane). I was passing there in the evening and I saw a great house and a grand one with screens (clumps of trees) at the ends of it, and the windows open — Coole House is nothing like what it was for size or grandeur. And there were people inside and ladies walking about, and a bridge across the river. For they can build up such things all in a minute. And two coaches came driving up and across the bridge to the castle, and in one of them I saw two gentlemen and I knew them well and both of them had died long before. As to the coaches and the horses I didn't take much notice of them for I was too much taken up with looking at the two gentlemen. And a man came and called out and asked me would I come across the bridge, and I said I would not. And he said, 'It would be better for you if you did, you'd go back heavier than you came.' I suppose they would have given me some good thing. And then two men took up the bridge and laid it against the wall. Twice I've seen that same thing, the house and the coaches and the bridge, and I know well I'll see it a third time before I die.[8]

One time when I was living at Ballymacduff there was two little boys drowned in the river there, one was eight years old and the other eleven years. And I was out in the fields, and the people looking in the river for their bodies, and I saw a man coming away from it, and the two boys with him, he holding a hand of each and leading them away. And he saw me stop and look at them and he said, 'Take care would you bring them from me, for you have only one in your own house, and if you take these from me, she'll never come home to you again.' And one of the little chaps broke from his hand and ran to me, and the other cried out to him, 'Oh, Pat, would you leave me!' So then he went back and the man led them away. And then I saw another man, very tall

4. Somewhat similar lines attributed here by Lady Gregory to Mrs Sheridan occur in Douglas Hyde's edition of Raftery's poems, *Abhráin atá Leagtha ar an Reachtúire* or *Songs Ascribed to Raftery* (Baile Átha Cliath: Gill, 1903), pp. 18–19. (Hyde acknowledged Lady Gregory's substantial contribution to the collection by dedicating the book to her.) In the extract quoted here it is quite correctly stated that Raftery composed a praise poem for Mary Hynes (Máire Ní Eidhin), said to have been a very beautiful woman from Ballylee in the parish of Kiltartan, County Galway, who died young of a broken heart. (C. Ó Coigligh, *Raifteraí: Amhráin agus Dánta* (Baile Átha Cliath: An Clóchomhar, 1987), pp. 84–5, 177, no. 21; Hyde, op. cit. ('Máire Ní hEidhin nó An Pósae Glégeal'), pp. 324–35). It was, in fact, Marcus Ó Callanáin, one of two brothers who were poets in the parish of Craughwell, County Galway, who composed the song for Mary (Molly) Brown (Máire Brún) (cf. S. Ó Ceallaigh, *Filíocht na gCallanán* [Baile Átha Cliath: An Clóchomhar, 1967], pp. 47–8, 86–91).

5. A small dog: '-een' is from the Irish diminutive -*ín*, frequently suffixed to English nouns in Ireland, especially by Irish-speakers.

6. 'An inflammation of the throat, especially an abscess in the region around the tonsils' (COD).

7. i.e., abducted by the fairies, Irish *tugtha as*.

8. In a lengthy footnote (note 12, pp. 348–50), W.B. Yeats, who knew Mrs Sheridan through Lady Gregory, gives various theories and explanations of visions.

he was, and crooked, and watching me like this with his head down and he was leading two dogs the other way, and I knew well where he was going and what he was going to do with them.

And when I heard the bodies were laid out, I went to the house to have a look at them, and those were never the two boys that were lying there, but the two dogs that were put in their places. I knew this by a sort of stripes on the bodies such as you'd see in the covering of a mattress, and I knew the boys couldn't be in it, after me seeing them led away.

And it was at that time I lost my eye, something came on it, and I never got the sight again. All my life I've seen *them* and enough of them. One time I saw one of the fields below full of them, some were picking up stones and some were ploughing it up. But the next time I went by there was no sign of it being ploughed at all. They can do nothing without some live person is looking at them, that's why they were always so much after me.[9] Even when I was a child I could see them, and once they took my walk from me, and gave me a bad foot, and my father cured me, and if he did, in five days after he died.[10]

But there's no harm at all in them, not much harm . . .

. . . I know that I used to be away among them myself, but how they brought me I don't know, but when I'd come back I'd be cross with the husband and with all. I believe when I was with them I was cross that they wouldn't let me go, and that's why they didn't keep me altogether, they didn't like cross people to be with them. The husband would ask me where was I, and why I stopped so long away, but I think he knew I was *taken* and it fretted him, but he never spoke much about it. But my mother knew it well, but she'd try to hide it. The neighbours would come in and ask where was I, and she'd say I was sick

in the bed — for whatever was put there in the place of me would have the head in under the bed-clothes. And when a neighbour would bring me in a drink of milk, my mother would put it by and say, 'Leave her now, maybe she'll drink it tomorrow.' And maybe in a day or two I'd meet someone and he'd say, 'Why wouldn't you speak to me when I went into the house to see you?' And I was a young fresh woman at that time. Where they brought me to I don't know, or how I got there, but I'd be in a very big house, and round it, the walls far away that you'd hardly see them, and a great many people all round about. I saw there neighbours and friends that I knew, and they in their own clothing and with their own appearance, but they wouldn't speak to me nor I to them, and when I'd meet them again I'd never say to them that I saw them there. But the others had striped clothes of all colours, and long faces, and they'd be talking and laughing and moving about. What language had they? Irish of course, what else would they talk?

[Lady Gregory adds:]

She died some years ago and I am told:

'There is a ghost in Mrs. Sheridan's house. They got a priest to say Mass there, but with all that there is not one in it has leave to lay a head on the pillow till such time as the cock crows.'[11]

11. That ghosts and revenants must disappear at cockcrow or daybreak is a commonly held traditional belief, and according to this belief, a 'March cock' (born from an egg laid on the first Tuesday in March and hatched out on a Tuesday of the same month) could protect the dwelling house against the devil and other evil forces (cf. S. O'Sullivan, *Folktales of Ireland*, p. 276, and *Legends from Ireland*, pp. 29–31).

[Lady Gregory tells of collecting folklore further from home, in County Mayo and in the Aran Islands of Galway Bay. Stories of the fairies abound, together with the belief that if harm is avoided by one person or thing, it will pass to another.

The evil eye belief referred to in Margaret Bartly's account has been defined as 'primarily the belief that someone can project harm by looking at another's property or person'.[1] It is found in many parts of the

9. That fairies are dependent on the help of a human agent in order to carry out certain activities is a widespread traditional belief. The assertion that the fairies need to be observed by a human before they can perform any activity is an adaptation and generalization of that belief, and further emphasizes the link between Mrs Sheridan's declared ability to see the fairies and her loss of sight in one eye.

10. Mrs Sheridan adds elsewhere (p. 62) that her father was 'taken', i.e., abducted into the fairy world in her stead, and gives concrete expression to that idea by means of a narrative detailing an encounter with the fairy world on the road to Kinvara when her father pleaded on her behalf: 'and my father said, "Spare the girl!" "I will do that, I will spare her," said the man. He went away then, and within a week my father was dead.'

1. For the evil eye, see C. Maloney (ed.), *The Evil Eye* (New York: Columbia University Press, 1976), p. v. See also Alan Dundes (ed.), *The Evil Eye: A Folklore Casebook* (New York, London: Garland Publishing, 1981), and for Gaelic Scotland see R.C. Maclagan, *Evil Eye in the Western Highlands* (London: David Nutt, 1902).

world, including Ireland, where it is also termed 'blinking' or 'overlooking'. According to traditional belief, a person might possess the evil eye without being aware of it; it was therefore always considered necessary to utter the precautionary 'God Bless!' in order to protect an object of praise or attention (for example, a child, animal or crop) from even an inadvertent use of the evil eye.

The belief in fairy abduction is drawn on once again by a mother in the Aran Islands to account for the death of family members in their prime. Behind the matter-of-fact description of her son's and daughter's physical ailments — which may well have been caused by cancer — probably lies the notion that their condition is the result of attempts to abduct them into the fairy world. In traditional belief, mothers in childbirth were considered to be particularly vulnerable to supernatural influences, and legends point out that human mothers who had supposedly 'died' in childbirth have been recognized in fairyland by the human midwife brought into the fairy fort to deliver a child.[2] This extract also indicates the role which the community could play in identifying the cause of illness or death. Extracts are from pp. 80–2, 92–3. Headnote, P.L.]

THE EVIL EYE — THE TOUCH — THE PENALTY

There was one visit I have always been a little remorseful about. It was in Mayo where I had gone to see the broken walls and grass-grown hearthstone that remain of the house where Raftery the poet was born.[3] I was taken to see an old woman near, and the friend who was with me asked about 'Those.'[4] I could see she was unwilling to speak, and I would not press her, for there are some who fear to vex invisible hearers; so we talked of America where she had lived for a little while. But presently she said, 'All I ever saw of *them* myself was one night when I was

going home, and they were behind in the field watching me. I couldn't see them but I saw the lights they carried, two lights on the top of a sort of dark oak pole. So I watched them and they watched me, and when we were tired watching one another the lights all went into a blaze, and then they went away and it went out.' She told also one or two of the traditional stories, of the man who had a hump put on him,[5] and the woman 'taken' and rescued by her husband, whom she had directed to seize the horse she was riding with his left hand.[6]

Then she gave a cry and took up her walking stick from the hearth, burned through, and in two pieces, though the fire had seemed to be but a smouldering heap of ashes. We were very sorry, but she said 'Don't be sorry. It is well it was into it the harm went.' I passed the house two or three hours afterwards; shutters and doors were closed, and I felt she was fretting for the stick that had been [to] 'America and back with me, and had walked every part of the world,' and through the loss of which, it may be, she had 'paid the penalty.'[7]

I told a neighbour about the doctor having attended a man on the mountains — and how after some time, he found that one of the children was sick also, but this had been hidden from him, because if one had to die they wanted it to be the child.

'That's natural,' he said. 'Let the child pay the penalty if it has to be paid. That's a thing that might happen easy enough.'[8]

Margaret Bartly: There was a woman below in that village where I lived to my grief and my sorrow, and she used to be throwing the evil eye, but she is in the poorhouse now — Mrs. Boylan her name is. For she threw it on, not children but

2. See in this connection legend no. 16 in S. Ó hEochaidh, M. MacNeill, S. Ó Catháin, *Siscéalta Ó Thir Chonaill/Fairy Legends from Donegal*, pp. 64–5, in which a human midwife is brought into the otherworld to deliver the child of a human mother which she had failed to deliver when the mother fell into a faint. For further examples of the legend 'Midwife to the Fairies', see ibid., nos 14, 15, pp. 60–5; 'The Midwife of Listowel', in J. Curtin, *Tales of the Fairies and of the Ghost World Collected from Oral Tradition in South-West Munster* (New York: Lemma Publishing Corporation, 1970; Dublin: Talbot Press, 1974; reprints of 1st edition, London 1895), pp. 42–5; and C. Mac Cárthaigh, 'Midwife to the Fairies (ML 5070)', *Béaloideas*, vol. 59 (1991), pp.133–43.
3. Near Killedan, Kiltimagh, County Mayo.
4. A variety of euphemisms including 'the good people', 'the little people', 'the wee folk' and 'the people of the hills' were used when referring to the fairies.

5. This is most likely a reference to the international folktale, well known in Ireland, listed as Type 503, 'The Gifts of the Little People. Dwarfs take a hump from a hunchback and place it on another man' (see A. Aarne and S. Thompson, *The Types of the Folktale*, and S. Ó Súilleabháin and R. Christiansen, *The Types of the Irish Folktale*).
6. A number of story types tell of the rescue of women from the fairies; the reference here is probably to the type known to scholars as 'Rescue from the Fairy Cavalcade'. For a version of this see S. Ó hEochaidh, M. MacNeill, S. Ó Catháin, *Siscéalta Ó Thir Chonaill*, pp. 46–53.
7. Presumably for discussing the fairies.
8. This is one of the starkest expressions of the idea that when someone is healed, someone else, or something else, has to pay the penalty, and, as is evident from Lady Gregory's accounts, it can be a human being or an animal that 'dies' instead of the healed person.

big men, and they lost the walk and all, and died. Maybe she didn't know she had it, but it is no load to anyone to say 'God Bless you.' I faced her one time and told her it would be no load to her when she would see the man in the field, and the horses ploughing to say 'God bless them,' and she was vexed and asked did I think she had the evil eye, and I said I did. So she began to scold and I left her. That was five years ago, and it is in the poor-house in Ballyvaughan[9] she is this two years; but she can do no harm there because she has lost her sight.

An Old Woman in an Aran Village: I'll tell you what happened a son of my own that was so strong and so handsome and so good a dancer, he was mostly the pride of the island. And he was that educated that when he was twenty-six years, he could write a letter to the Queen. And one day a pain came in the thigh, and a little lump came inside it, and a hole in it that you could hardly put the point of a pin, and it was always drawing.[10] And he took to his bed and was there for eleven months. And every night when it would be twelve o'clock, he would begin to be singing and laughing and going on. And what the neighbours said was, that it was at that hour there was some other left in his place. I never went to any one or any witchcraft, for my husband wouldn't let me but left it to the will of God; and anyway at the end of the eleven months he died.

And his sister was in America, and the same thing came to her there, a little lump by the side of the face, and she came home to die. But she died quiet and was like any other in the night.

And a daughter-in-law of mine died after the second birth and even the priest said it was not *dead* she was, he that was curate then. I was surprised the priest to say that, for they mostly won't give in to it, unless it's one that takes a drop of drink.

9. A village in north-west County Clare.
10. Suppurating.

[Mrs Roche's personal narrative strikingly indicates that pressure might be brought to bear on a family by the community to identify the cause of illness of a child in obvious physical decline, and illustrates the possible

dilemma which could arise for the family in relation to their child as a result. The use of *lus mór* (foxglove, *Digitalis purpurea*) to cure 'fairy strokes' (lumps) or to discover changelings is widely attested.[1]

The most common method of banishing a supposed changeling, according to popular tradition in Ireland and elsewhere, was by means of fire, or the threat of fire. Community responsibility for the mother's attempt to get rid of the changeling by fire is hinted at in the narrative of the Policeman's Wife. Extracts are from pp. 128, 146. Headnote, P.L.]

AWAY

Mrs. Roche: . . . I was delicate one time myself, and I lost my walk, and one of the neighbours told my mother it wasn't myself that was there. But my mother said she'd soon find that out, for she'd tell me that she was going to get a herb that would cure me, and if it was myself I'd want it, but if I was another I'd be against it. So she came in and she said to me, 'I'm going to Dangan to look for the *lus-mór*, that will soon cure you.' And from that day I gave her no peace till she'd go to Dangan and get it; so she knew that I was all right. She told me all this afterwards.

The Policeman's Wife: There was a girl in Co. Clare was away, and the mother used to hear horses coming about the door every night. And one day the mother was picking flax in the house, and of a sudden there came in her hand an herb with the best smell and the sweetest that ever was smelt. And she closed it with her hand, and called to the son that was making up a stack of hay outside 'Come in, Denis, for I have the best smelling herb that ever you saw.' And when he came in she opened her hand, and the herb was gone clear and clean. She got annoyed at last with the horses coming about the door, and some told her to gather all the fire into the middle of the floor and to lay the little girl upon it, and to see could she come back again. So she did as she was told, and brought the little girl out of the bed and laid her on the coals. And she began to scream and call out, and the neighbours came running in, and the police heard of it, and they came and arrested the mother and brought her to the Court-house before the magistrate, Mr.

1. Cf. N. Williams, *Díolaim Luibheanna* (Baile Átha Cliath: Sáirseal-Ó Marcaigh, 1993), pp. 104–5.

MacWalter, and my own husband was one of the police that arrested her. And when the magistrate heard all, he said she was an ignorant woman, and that she did what she thought right, and he would give her no punishment. And the girl got well and married. It was after she was married I knew her.[2]

2. Cf. S. Mac Philib, 'The Changeling', 1991, and Angela Bourke, *The Burning of Bridget Cleary*.

from:
THE KILTARTAN HISTORY BOOK (1909)

[With *The Kiltartan History Book* (1909), which she called the 'Book of the People',[1] Lady Gregory broke new ground. This is a compilation of the folk history of the people of the barony of Kiltartan and other parts of County Galway, and it comments on the mythic history of Ireland as well as major historical events and personages from the coming of the Norsemen to the Anglo-Irish War (1919–21). Accordingly, narratives of the mythic figures Fionn mac Cumhail and Méadhbh of Connacht, and the divine smith, the Gobán Saor, for example, take their places alongside traditions of Saint Patrick, the Anglo-Normans, Cromwell, the Stuarts, the Battle of the Boyne, the Battle of Aughrim, and the 'Wild Geese', and mingle also with memories of the nineteenth-century Great Famine (1845–9), political movements such as the Fenian Rising (1867) and figures such as Charles Stewart Parnell and Daniel O'Connell. Lady Gregory also shrewdly comments on the heroic process already in action in relation to O'Connell, who had died only some sixty years previously (p. 149).

Probably to be identified with Goibhniu, the ancient god of smithcraft, the Gobán Saor (*saor*: 'artificer') is mainly portrayed in Irish folklore as a master builder and craftsman whose trademark is a two-tailed cat.[2] Included in a cycle of narratives about the Gobán Saor in Irish folk

1. Dublin: Maunsel, 1909; London: Fisher Unwin, 1926; Gerrards Cross: Colin Smythe, 1971.
2. For lore concerning the Gobán Saor in Irish literature and folklore see D. Ó hÓgáin, *Myth, Legend and Romance*, pp. 241–3. Cf. also S. Ó Súilleabháin, *A Handbook of Irish Folklore*, pp. 496–7, 575. The motif of the two-tailed cat is also linked to a famous poetic figure in Irish folk tradition, Cearúl Ó Dálaigh, who, like the Gobán Saor, was said to be a master craftsman. See in this regard: S. Ó Duilearga (ed.), *Leabhar Sheáin Í Chonaill* (Baile Átha Cliath: Comhairle Bhéaloideas Éireann, 1977 [1948]), pp. 325, 440 (notes, references and international comparisons), 488 (English summary); cf. also pp. 287, 403 in the English translation of this book by Máire

tradition are the following very popular stories about his shrewd and clever daughter-in-law.[3]   Headnote, P.L.]

THE GOBÁN SAOR

A Witty Wife[4]

The Gobán Saor was a mason and a smith, and he could do all things, and he was very witty. He was going from home one time and he said to the wife, 'If it is a daughter you have this time I'll kill you when I come back'; for up to that time he had no sons, but only daughters. And it was a daughter she had; but a neighbouring woman had a son at the same time, and they made an exchange to save the life of the Gobán's wife. But when the boy began to grow up he had no wit, and the Gobán knew by that he was no son of his. That is the reason he wanted a witty wife for him. So there came a girl to the house one day, and the Gobán Saor bade her look round at all that was in the room, and he said, 'Do you think a couple could get a living out of this?' 'They could not,' she said. So he said she wouldn't do, and he sent her away. Another girl came another day, and he bade her take notice of all that was in the house, and he said, 'Do you think could a couple knock a living out of this?' 'They could if they stopped in it,' she said. So he said that girl would do. Then he asked her could she bring a sheepskin to the market and bring back the price of it, and the skin itself as well. She said she

MacNeill: *Seán Ó Conaill's Book* (Baile Átha Cliath: Comhairle Bhéaloideas Éireann, 1981); see also J. Doan, 'Cearbhall Ó Dálaigh as Craftsman and Trickster', *Béaloideas*, vol. 50 (1982), esp. pp. 59–68, 87–9; D. Ó hÓgáin, *Myth, Legend and Romance*, pp. 336–7.

3. The three narratives are from *The Kiltartan Books Comprising the Kiltartan Poetry, History and Wonder Books by Lady Gregory*, Coole Edition IX (Gerrards Cross: Colin Smythe, 1972), pp. 77–9. See also Lady Gregory's 'Notes', pp. 148–9. These three anecdotes about the Gobán Saor were taken down by the Danish philologist Holger Pedersen on Inishmore, Aran Islands, in 1895 — see Ole Munch-Pedersen (ed.), *Scéalta Mháirtín Neile. Bailiúchán Scéalta ó Árainn. Holger Pedersen a thóg síos sa bhliain 1895* (Baile Átha Cliath: Comhairle Bhéaloideas Éireann, 1994), pp. 190–4 (text), p. 319 (notes and references), p. 392 (English summary). For County Kerry versions of the second and third anecdotes, see S. Ó Duilearga, *Leabhar Sheáin Í Chonaill*, pp. 263–5; for further references see pp. 430–1, and p. 480 for English translation; cf. also M. MacNeill, *Seán Ó Conaill's Book*, pp. 226–7, 393–4.

4. This narrative is related to the international tale Type 875 'The Clever Peasant Girl' in A. Aarne and S. Thompson, *The Types of the Folktale*, and in S. Ó Súilleabháin and R. Christiansen, *The Types of the Irish Folktale*. Cf. also S. Ó Súilleabháin, *A Handbook of Irish Folklore*, p. 575.

could, and she went to the market, and there she pulled off the wool and sold it and brought back the price and the skin as well. Then he asked could she go to the market and not be dressed or undressed. And she went having only one shoe and one stocking on her, so she was neither dressed or undressed. Then he sent her to walk neither on the road or off the road, and she walked on the path beside it. So he said then she would do as a wife for his son.

An Advice She Gave

One time some great king or lord sent for the Gobán to build a *caisleán* for him, and the son's wife said to him before he went, 'Be always great[5] with the women of the house, and always have a comrade among them.' So when the Gobán went there he coaxed one of the women the same as if he was not married. And when the castle was near built, the woman told him the lord was going to play him a trick, and to kill him or shut him up when he had the castle made, the way he would not build one for any other lord that was as good. And as she said, the lord came and bade the Gobán to make a cat and two-tails, for no one could make that but himself, and it was meaning to kill him on it he was. And the Gobán said he would do that when he had finished the castle, but he could not finish it without some tool he had left at home. And they must send the lord's son for it — for he said it would not be given to any other one. So the son was sent, and the Gobán sent a message to the daughter-in-law that the tool he was wanting was called 'When you open it shut it.' And she was surprised, for there was no such tool in the house; but she guessed by the message what she had to do, and there was a big chest in the house and she set it open. 'Come now,' she said to the young man, 'look in the chest and find it for yourself.' And when he looked in she gave him a push forward, and in he went, and she shut the lid on him. She wrote a letter to the lord then, saying he would not get his son back till he had sent her own two men, and they were sent back to her.

Shortening the Road

Himself and his son were walking the road together one day, and the Gobán said to the son,

'Shorten the road for me.' So the son began to walk fast, thinking that would do it, but the Gobán sent him back home when he didn't understand what to do. The next day they were walking again, and the Gobán said again to shorten the road for him, and this time he began to run, and the Gobán sent him home again. When he went in and told the wife he was sent home a second time, she began to think and she said, 'When he bids you shorten the road, it is that he wants you to be telling him stories.' For that is what the Gobán meant but it took the daughter-in-law to understand it. And it is what I was saying to that other woman, that if one of ourselves was making a journey, if we had another along with us, it would not seem to be one half as long as if we would be alone. And if that is so with us, it is much more with a stranger, and so I went up the hill with you to shorten the road, telling you that story.

[The historical event referred to in this narrative, which Lady Gregory heard as oral tradition around Kiltartan and Coole Park, is the abduction, or supposed abduction,[1] of Dervorgilla, wife of Tiernan O'Rourke, Prince of Breifne, by Dermot MacMurrough, King of Leinster, in 1152, and the role which that event played in the Anglo-Norman invasion of Ireland (1169). One of the great Norman leaders in Wales from whom MacMurrough sought assistance was Richard FitzGilbert de Clare, Earl of Strigoil, better known as 'Strongbow', who agreed to assist him to regain power in Leinster on condition that Dermot gave him his eldest daughter in marriage, and the right of succession to the kingdom of Leinster.[2] Headnote, P.L.]

THE QUEEN OF BREFFNI

Dervorgilla was a red-haired woman, and it was she put the great curse on Ireland, bringing in the English through MacMurrough, that she

---

5. i.e. very friendly.

1. According to Irish and Anglo-Norman accounts it was Dervorgilla herself who arranged the abduction (F.X. Martin, 'The Normans: Arrival and Settlement', in T.W. Moody and F.X. Martin (eds), *The Course of Irish History*, pp. 123–4; F.X. Martin, 'Diarmait Mac Murchada and the Coming of the Anglo-Normans', in A. Cosgrove (ed.), *A New History of Ireland*, II, Medieval Ireland 1169–1534 (Oxford: Clarendon Press, 1987), pp. 50–1).
2. F.X. Martin, 'The Normans: Arrival and Settlement', in T.W. Moody and F.X. Martin (eds.), *The Course of Irish History*, p. 127. For the Anglo-Norman invasion of Ireland, see ibid., pp. 123–43, and F.X. Martin, Chapters 2–5, in A. Cosgrove (ed.), *A New History of Ireland*, II, pp. 43–155.

went to from O'Rourke. It was to Henry the Second MacMurrough went, and he sent Strongbow, and they stopped in Ireland ever since. But who knows but another race might be worse, such as the Spaniards that were scattered along the whole coast of Connacht the time of the Armada. And the laws are good enough. I heard it said that the English will be dug out of their graves one day for the sake of their laws. As to Dervorgilla, she was not brought away by force, she went to MacMurrough herself. For there are men in the world that have a coaxing way, and sometimes women are weak.

[Oliver Cromwell (1599–1658), English parliamentary leader and Lord Protector of the British Commonwealth, ranks as probably the most notorious folk villain in Irish folklore,[1] and the imprecation 'the curse of Cromwell' (*scrios Chromail*) is considered to be of the worst kind. His brutal and inhumane nine-month campaign in Ireland (1649–50), and the severity of the confiscations which followed (1652–3), are indelibly etched in the Irish Catholic folk memory.[2] In the following narrative, which combines fairy belief-narrative with oral history, Cromwell appears to be portrayed as an Irishman, although the storyteller may have lost the thread of the story at this point, failing to distinguish between cobbler and blacksmith. The more usual and more logical version of the story, which was widely known in the west of Ireland, is connected with the Duhallow (County Cork) chieftain MacAuliffe, who dreamt that a cobbler in England called Cromwell would one day rule all Ireland. He travelled to England to obtain the signature of the cobbler to a covenant securing MacAuliffe in his lands in Ireland, and Cromwell is said to have subsequently honoured his signature by leaving MacAuliffe in possession of his lands. The name 'Howley' in the following story is a version of the Irish Mac Amhlaoibh — MacAuliffe.[3] Extracts are from pp. 11–13. Headnote, P.L.]

1. See S. Ó Súilleabháin, 'Oliver Cromwell in Irish Oral Tradition', in L. Dégh, H. Glassie, F.J. Oinas (eds), *Folklore Today: A Festschrift for Richard M. Dorson* (Bloomington: Indiana University Press, 1976), pp. 473–83.
2. For the Cromwellian campaign in Ireland and the suppression of the Rebellion of 1641 and the Nine Years War, see P.J. Corish, chapters 13–14, in T.W. Moody, F.X. Martin, F.J. Byrne (eds), *A New History of Ireland*, III, Early Modern Ireland 1534–1691 (Oxford: Clarendon Press, 1976), pp. 353–86.
3. See in this connection D. Ó hÓgáin, *Myth, Legend and Romance*, pp. 128–31.

THE TRACE OF CROMWELL

I'll tell you now about the trace of Cromwell. There was a young lady was married to a gentleman, and she died with her first baby, and she was brought away into a forth by the fairies, the good people, as I suppose. She used to be sitting on the side of it combing her hair, and three times her husband saw her there, but he had not the courage to go and bring her away. But there was a man of the name of Howley living near the forth, and he went out with his gun one day, and he saw her beside the forth, and he brought her away to his house, and a young baby sprang between them at the end of a year. One day the husband was out shooting and he came in upon Howley's land, and when young Howley heard the shooting he rose up and went out and he bade the gentleman to stop, for this was his land. So he stopped, and he said he was weary and thirsty, and he asked could he rest in the house. So young Howley said as long as he asked pardon he had leave to use what he liked. So he came in the house and he sat at the table, and he put his two eyes through the young lady. 'If I didn't see her dead and buried,' he said, 'I'd say that to be my own wife.' 'Oh!' said she, 'so I am your wife, and you are badly worthy of me, and you have the worst courage ever I knew, that you would not come and bring me away out of the forth as young Howley had the courage to bring me,' she said. So then he asked young Howley would he give him back his wife. 'I will give her,' he said, 'but you never will get the child.'[4] So the child was reared, and when he was grown he went travelling up to Dublin. And he was at a hunt, and he lost the top of his boot, and he went into a shoemaker's shop and he gave him half a sovereign for nothing but to put the tip on the boot, for he saw he was poor and had a big family. And more than that, when he was going away he took out three sovereigns and gave them to the blacksmith, and he looked at one of the little chaps, and he said, 'That one will be in command of the whole of England.' 'Oh, that cannot be,' said the blacksmith, 'where I am poor and have not the means to do anything for him.' 'It will be as I tell you,' said he, 'and write me out a

4. Cf. 'An Bhean a Thuit ón Spéir'/'The Woman Dropped from the Air' in the subsection 'Legends of the Supernatural', pp. 1293–1294.

docket,' he said, 'that if ever that youngster will come to command Ireland, he will give me a free leg.' So the docket was made out, and he brought it away with him. And sure enough the shoemaker's son listed, and was put at the head of soldiers and got the command of England, and came with his soldiers to put down Ireland. And Howley saw them coming and he tied his handkerchief to the top of his stick, and when Cromwell saw that, he halted the army, 'For there is some poor man in distress,' he said. Then Howley showed him the docket his father had written. 'I will do some good thing for you on account of that,' said Cromwell; 'and go now to the top of that high cliff,' he said, 'and I'll give as much land as you can see from it.' And so he did give it to him. It was no wonder Howley to have known the shoemaker's son would be in command and all would happen him, because of his mother that got knowledge in the years she was in the forth. That is the trace of Cromwell. I heard it at a wake, and I would believe it, and if I had time to put my mind to it, and if I was not on the road from Loughrea to Ballyvaughan, I could give you the foundations of it better.

[King James II of England (1633–1701), deposed by his daughter Mary and her husband William of Orange, was defeated by William on Irish soil at the Battle of the Boyne in 1690.[1] He is remembered for his cowardly flight from the battle, leaving his army leaderless, and for his attempt to blame his Irish allies for his defeat. His supposed encounter with Lady Tyrconnell, the wife of his chief of staff, on his arrival in Dublin in the course of his flight from the country, probably gave rise to the following legend.[2]   Headnote, P.L.]

THE STUARTS

As to the Stuarts, there are no songs about them and no praises in the West, whatever there may be in the South.[3] Why would there, and they running away and leaving the country the way they did? And what good did they ever do it? James the Second was a coward. Why didn't he go into the thick of battle like the Prince of Orange? He stopped on a hill three miles away, and rode off to Dublin, bringing the best of his troops with him. There was a lady walking in the street at Dublin when he got there, and he told her the battle was lost, and she said, 'Faith you made good haste, you made no delay on the road.' So he said no more after that. The people liked James well enough before he ran; they didn't like him after that.

[As a lawyer, politician and leader of his people, Daniel O'Connell (1775–1847) was the outstanding Irish figure of the first half of the nineteenth century. The movement for Catholic emancipation, which he led from 1823, achieved its objective in 1829, introducing the mass of the Irish people to the democratic process.[1] In the following legend O'Connell is given a heroic birth, while his cleverness as an advocate and his enemies' attempts to destroy him, are highlighted.[2] Headnote, P.L.]

DANIEL O'CONNELL

O'Connell's Birth

O'Connell was a grand man, and whatever cause he took in hand, it was as good as won. But what wonder? He was the gift of God. His father was a rich man, and one day he was out walking he took notice of a house that was being built. Well, a week later he passed by the same place, and he saw the walls of the house were no higher than before. So he asked the reason, and he was told it was a priest that was building it, and he hadn't the money to go on with. So a few days after he went to the priest's house and he asked was that true, and the priest said it was. 'Would you pay back the money to the man that would lend it to you?' says O'Connell. 'I would,' says the priest. So with that O'Connell gave him the money that was wanting — £50 — for it was a very grand house. Well, after some time the priest came to

---

1. J.G. Simms, 'The War of the Two Kings, 1685-91', in T.W. Moody, F.X. Martin and F.J. Byrne, *A New History of Ireland*, III, pp. 478–508.
2. D. Ó hÓgáin, *Myth, Legend and Romance*, pp. 261–2.
3. The Munster poets of the eighteenth century still saw deliverance from English oppression in terms of native kingship and turned to the exiled Scottish Stuarts for a symbol of their deliverance. See P. Mac Cana, *Celtic Mythology* (London: Hamlyn, 1973; 2nd impression), p. 117; Breandán Ó Buachalla, *Aisling Ghéar* (Baile Átha Cliath: An Clóchomhar, 1997).

1. D. McCartney, *The Dawning of Democracy in Ireland 1800–1870* (Dublin: Helicon, 1987), pp. 110–66; J.H. Whyte, 'The Age of Daniel O'Connell 1800–47', in T.W. Moody and F.X. Martin (eds), *The Course of Irish History*, pp. 248–62.
2. Cf. the song, 'Is é Dónall Binn Ó Conaill Caoin', in the subsection 'The Song Tradition', pp. 1358–1359.

O'Connell's house, and he found only the wife at
home, so, says he, 'I have some money that
himself lent me.' But he had never told the wife
of what he had done, so she knew nothing about
it, and says she, 'Don't be troubling yourself
about it, he'll bestow it on you.' 'Well,' says the
priest, 'I'll go away now, and I'll come back
again.' So when O'Connell came, the wife told
him all that had happened, and how a priest had
come saying he owed him money, and how she
had said he would bestow it on him. 'Well,' says
O'Connell, 'if you said I would bestow it, I will
bestow it.' And so he did. Then the priest said,
'Have you any children?' 'Ne'er a child,' says
O'Connell. 'Well, you will have one,' says he. And
that day nine months their young son was born.
So what wonder if he was inspired, being, as he
was, the gift of God.[3]

The Man [who] was going to be Hanged
I saw O'Connell in Galway one time, and I
couldn't get anear him. All the nations of the
world were gathered there to see him. There were
a great many he hung and a great many he got off
from death, the dear man. He went into a town
one time, and into a hotel, and he asked for his
dinner. And he had a frieze[4] dress, for he was very
simple, and always a clerk along with him. And
when the dinner was served to him, 'Is there no
one here,' says he, 'to sit along with me; for it is
seldom I ever dined without company.' 'If you
think myself good enough to sit with you,' says
the man of the hotel, 'I will do it.' So the two of
them sat to the dinner together, and O'Connell
asked was there any news in the town. 'There is,'
says the hotel man, 'there is a man to be hung tomorrow.' 'Oh, my!' says O'Connell, 'what was it
he did to deserve that?' 'Himself and another that
had been out fowling,' says he, 'and they came in
here and they began to dispute, and the one of
them killed the other, and he will be hung
tomorrow.' 'He will not,' says O'Connell. 'I tell
you he will,' says the other, 'for the Judge is to
come to give the sentence.' Well, O'Connell kept
to it that he would not, and they made a bet, and
the hotel man bet all he had on the man being

hung. In the morning O'Connell was in no hurry
out of bed, and when the two of them walked
into the Court, the Judge was after giving the
sentence, and the man was to be hung.
'*Maisead*,'[5] says the Judge when he saw
O'Connell, 'I wish you had been here half an
hour ago, where there is a man going to be hung.'
'He is not,' says O'Connell. 'He is,' says the
Judge. 'If he is,' says O'Connell, 'that one will
never let anyone go living out of his hotel, and he
making money out of the hanging.' 'What do you
mean saying that?' says the Judge. Then
O'Connell took the instrument out of his pocket
where it was written down all the hotel-keeper
had put on the hanging. And when the judge saw
that, he set the man free, and he was not hanged.[6]

The Cup of the Sassanach[7]
He was over in England one time, and he was
brought to a party, and tea was made ready and
cups. And as they were sitting at the table, a
servant girl that was in it, and that was Irish,
came to O'Connell and she said, 'Do you
understand Irish? *An dtuigeann tú Gaedhilge*,
O'Connell?' '*Tuigim*,' says he, 'I understand it.'
'Have a care,' says she, 'for there is in your cup
what would poison the whole nation!' 'If that is
true, girl, you will get a good fortune,' said he. It
was in Irish they said all that, and the people that
were in it had no ears. Then O'Connell quenched
the candle, and he changed his cup for the cup of
the man that was next him. And it was not long
till the man fell dead. They were always trying to
kill O'Connell, because he was a good man . . .

5. *Más ea*, 'if so, even so'.
6. For further versions and discussion of this story, see R. uí Ógáin, *Immortal Dan*, pp. 122–4.
7. Cf. *The Kiltartan Books*, pp. 101–2. See also R. uí Ógáin, *An Rí Gan Choróin*, pp. 244–50, no. 43.

3. For a discussion of this legend and further versions, see Ríonach uí Ógáin, *Immortal Dan: Daniel O'Connell in Irish Folk Tradition* (Dublin: Geography Publications, 1995), pp. 179–81.
4. 'Coarse woollen cloth with nap usually on one side only' (COD).

[Charles Stewart Parnell (1846–91), charismatic
champion of Home Rule and leader of the Irish
Parliamentary Party, is here given a common attribute of
the folk hero, when it is suggested that he has not really
died. The woman referred to in this passage is Katharine
O'Shea, whom he married following her divorce, shortly
before his death. See pp. 1435–37. Headnote, P.L.]

PARNELL[1]

Parnell was a very good man, and a just man, and if he had lived to now, Ireland would be different to what it is. The only thing ever could be said against him was the influence he had with that woman. And how do we know but that was a thing appointed for him by God? Parnell had a back to him,[2] but O'Connell stood alone. He fought a good war in the House of Commons. Parnell did a great deal getting the land. He wouldn't like at all that you'd wrong the poor. I often heard he didn't die at all — it was very quick for him to go. I often wondered there were no people smart enough to dig up the coffin and to see what was in it. At night they could do that. No one knows in what soil Robert Emmet was buried, but he was made an end of sure enough. Parnell went through Gort one day, and he called it the fag-end of Ireland, just as Lady Morgan called the North the Athens of Ireland.

1. *The Kiltartan Books*, pp. 116–17. For Parnell and the Land War, Home Rule and his association with Mrs O'Shea, the ostensible cause of his political downfall, see T.W. Moody, 'Fenianism, Home Rule, and The Land War (1850–91)', in T.W. Moody and F.X. Martin (eds), *The Course of Irish History*, pp. 283–93.
2. i.e. had many supporters.

from:
THE KILTARTAN WONDER
BOOK (1910)

[*The Kiltartan Wonder Book*,[1] comprising folktales and legends, is a more conventional volume of folklore than the *History Book*. It has its drawbacks, however: it is not evident who the narrators are or in what language the stories were told, and the neatly trimmed folktales, in particular, contrast with later and more robust tellings in the Irish language collected from County Galway by the Irish Folklore Commission.[2]

The following is an example of an international folktale common in Ireland. Under the title 'Guarding the Door' it is listed as tale Type 1653 A in A. Aarne and S. Thompson,

1. Dublin: Maunsel, 1910; Gerrards Cross: Colin Smythe, 1971. Extract p. 192.
2. Lady Gregory acknowledged splicing passages from different tales (even from different regional versions) in a 'Note' to the volume (p. 210, 1971 ed.).

The Types of the Folktale, and in S. Ó Súilleabháin and R. Christiansen, *The Types of the Irish Folktale*. While Lady Gregory's version is a well-rounded narrative, containing all the essential elements of the tale and faithfully reflecting folk tradition, it is nevertheless only about one-third as long as Irish-language versions from County Galway.[3] Headnote, P.L.]

THE WOMAN THAT WAS A GREAT FOOL

There was a woman was a great fool. She had meal to sift one day, and the hens were bothering her, coming over to the door. And it was outside in the field she went sifting it, that it was brought away with a blast of wind that rose, till there wasn't one grain left on the top of another, but it was brought away with the wind into the fields and over the grass. And when the husband came back in the evening he asked where was it, and it was all spent. 'Sure you have money in the bag to buy more,' says she. 'I have not,' says he; 'for what is in the bag I have to keep for the Grey Scrape of the Spring.'

Well, the next day an old beggarman came asking for money, and when the woman looked at him and saw that he was grey: 'That should be the Grey Scrape of the Spring,' she said. And she gave him all the money was in the bag.

When the husband heard that, he didn't say much, for he was a quiet man. But he went and he killed the cow that was all he had left, and he cut it up and put it in a barrel, and put salt on it. 'That will be enough to grease the cabbage anyway,' says he.

So the next day the wife brought out every bit of beef, and she put a bit of it on top of every head of cabbage was in the garden. Well, when the night came and they were in bed, there came a thousand dogs fighting for the meat was in the garden, and barking, and calling and roaring. And when the husband went out they had it brought away, and all the cabbage destroyed and broken.

So he said then it was as good for them to go wandering. And he went out of the house, and the woman following him. 'Let you draw the door after you,' says he — that is that she should close it. What she did was to rise it off the hinges, and to draw it after her along the road till they

3. See, for example, a version collected in the parish of Ross, County Galway, in 1935 (IFC 112: 213–19).

came to a wood. And they went into the branches of a tree to pass the night, and she bringing the board with her.

It happened there came some robbers under the tree, dividing a great deal of gold and silver they were after robbing from a castle. And when the man and the woman saw that, they dropped the door down on them with a great noise, and the robbers were afrighted and ran away, leaving all they had robbed after them. And the man and the woman got it for themselves and they were rich from that day.

MÁIRE MacNEILL

(1904–87)

from:
THE FESTIVAL OF LUGHNASA (1962)

Gort an Choirce (Gortahork), County Donegal. Máire MacNeill, *The Festival of Lughnasa: A Study of the Survival of the Celtic Festival of the Beginning of Harvest* (Dublin: Comhairle Bhéaloideas Éireann, 1982 [1962]), pp. 140–2. Headnote, P.L.]

[*The Festival of Lughnasa* is one of the most significant works in the fields of Irish and European folklore studies. It was the first study of one of the quarterly feasts of the old Irish year and established that the harvest festival in Ireland was a survival of Lughnasa, the Celtic festival held on the first of August. From the methodological and theoretical points of view, it is a landmark work in its use of folklore as primary source material to provide a comprehensive study of a single festival over the last two hundred years. It established the particular value of the questionnaire system used by the Irish Folklore Commission as a means of assembling a representative body of source material for an in-depth study.[1] Making a clear distinction between ascertained facts and their interpretation, Máire MacNeill's painstaking synthesis of the large body of oral sources sets out the principal characteristics of the festival as it was until recent times in Ireland. Her analysis of the customs and of folk legends about the origin of the festival and the assembly sites enabled the dominant myth of the festival to be brought to light. In this work Máire MacNeill is at once a source, a collector and a scholar.

Lughnasa, the Celtic festival of the beginning of harvest, was celebrated in Ireland on the last Sunday of July or the first Sunday of August. A meal of the first fruits of the year was eaten and assemblies were held at certain traditional sites on heights, at wells, river-banks and lakeshores. Two elevated sites on which Lughnasa assemblies were held were Carn Treuna, near Gaoth Dobhair (Gweedore), and Cnoc na Bealtaine (Beltany Hill), near

Carn Treuna is a hill north of Gweedore in the extreme northwest corner of Ireland. Across the valley from it to the east are the mountains of Errigal and Muckish and five miles northward the view opens on to the Atlantic. Until the mid-nineteenth century young men and women of the surrounding countryside used to resort there on the first Sunday of August, known locally as Domhnach na bhFraochóg (Bilberry Sunday).

Four miles down the valley nearer the sea and overlooking Ballyness Bay and the village of Gortahork there is a small hill called Beltany in English, from the Gaelic Croc [Cnoc] na Béaltaine. Here also there was a gathering of young people. In 1942, an eighty-five year old woman of Beltany told the Folklore Commission's collector all she remembered having heard of both these gatherings. She had not been at them herself but she had often heard her mother recall her girlhood memories of them. The old countrywoman's simple description re-creates for us a festival of rare and idyllic charm. Translated from Gaelic it runs as follows:

> As I remember it, I heard the old people say that it was on the first Sunday of the month of Lughnasa they used to have a great day on the tops of the hills about here looking for bilberries. This Sunday was set out specially for the young people to go off to the hills as soon as the mid-day meal was

1. A questionnaire (in Irish and English), entitled *Domhnach Chrom Dubh/*'Garland Sunday', was issued by the Irish Folklore Commission in July 1942, and the response from 316 correspondents amounted to over a thousand pages of text.

eaten and they would not return again until twilight had fallen. There were two hills on the nearer side of the parish of Cloghaneely that the people used to go up, the hill of Beltany and Carn Treuna. It has been always held that there is a 'gentleness' (*uaislineacht*)[2] belonging to the hill of Beltany, but I cannot say whether or not that is so of Carn Treuna. The hill of Beltany is about a mile and a half south of Gortahork. Carn Treuna is about five miles to the Gweedore side of Gortahork. The people used to come from every part of the parish to spend this day on the hills. Those nearer Beltany went to the top of that hill, and, in the same way, people living near Carn Treuna went there. Indeed the young boys used to go to whichever place their girls would be.

As well as I can understand, in the time these outings were made to the hill-tops the people had little to choose in clothes and they used to wear the best of what they had on this Sunday. They wore no boots, because few in this district had any boots to wear in those days.

After reaching the top of the hill they would sit and eat their lunches. They used to bring flat cakes of oatmeal and milk for the day. They would eat and then sit around resting. Then they would go here and there over the hill looking for bilberries. Sometimes they would scatter in pairs — boys and girls — and other times they would go in groups.

When they returned with their gathering of bilberries they had a strange custom. They all sat down on the hill-top and the boys began to make bracelets of bilberries for the girls. They had brought short threads in their pockets for the purpose. They would pick hard stalks on their way to the hill and with these they would put thread through the bilberries. Each man would compete with another as to which would make the best and prettiest bracelet for his own girl.

When that was done, a man or maybe a girl would be named to sing a song. The melody would begin then and would go round from one to another, and anyone who had a note of music at all in his or her head would have to keep the fun going. They used to tell stories and plenty of verses as well. After the singing they would begin the dancing. According to the old talk, they had no instrument for music at all; they had to make do with lilting.[3] In those days boys and girls were good at lilting and they would make enough music for those who were dancing.

When all was over then and they were preparing to go home, the girls would take off the bilberry bracelets and leave them on the hill-top. Whatever meaning there was to that, none of the old people were able to tell me, but they all knew it and they heard from their elders that it was customary for them to do that. They would all come down then and go home.

It is a long time since people stopped going to Carn Treuna for the bilberries. An odd one here and there used to go until about thirty years ago, but the old people consider that it is between eighty and a hundred years since they went up in crowds.

This old woman's re-telling of her mother's memories is the most charming evocation of a Lughnasa festival which we possess. There is a primeval innocence about these barefooted boys and girls exchanging their tender courtesies on the summer hills, singing and dancing to the music of their own lips, so free of worldly possessions and so happy, as if the serpent had not yet entered Eden. We may be glad that no harsh note has lingered here, that no legend of ancient conflict or mysterious peril is told of these hills, for all their nearness to a scene of the drama of Lugh's mythological struggle with his grandfather Balor. Tory Island, which was Balor's stronghold and the birthplace of Lugh, can be seen in the northern sea, and nearby on the mainland Balor killed Lugh's father and was later killed by Lugh.

2. A connection with fairies.

3. Also called 'mouth-music' in Ireland, and by musicologists 'vocalization', lilting is a kind of singing, using meaningless syllables, often used for dancing, as a memory-aid for musicians, and in refrains.

from:
BÉALOIDEAS (1971–3)

[Máire MacNeill's essay on connections between traditional narratives and a dramatic feature of the Irish coastal landscape was published in a volume dedicated to Séamus Ó Duilearga, founder of the IFC. It demonstrates the same striking combination of meticulous scholarship with poetic imagination, common sense and modesty which MacNeill demonstrated in *The Festival of Lughnasa*. As in the longer work, she here draws on linguistic and literary evidence, as well as on the systematic study of oral narrative, using her own observation of natural landscape features to illuminate connections between them. Headnote, A.B.]

POLL NA SEANTUINNE AND POLL TIGH LIABÁIN [1]

Thomas J. Westropp pointed out that several places on the north Mayo coast were known as Poulnashantona (*Journal of the Royal Society of Antiquaries of Ireland*, XLII, 1912, pp. 102–3, 197, 204, 209–10). These places are natural features sometimes described as 'blow-holes' or 'puffing-holes', i.e. they are holes in the cliff roof over sea caverns. When high winds and tides coincide the sea is dashed into the caverns with such force that fountains of spray rise through the holes, sometimes accompanied by great noise.

One of the most remarkable of these is Poll na Seantuinne on Downpatrick Head, a place associated with the local legend of St. Patrick's victory over the representative of paganism. One version of this legend was recorded from Dean Lyons by John O'Donovan in 1838 and is preserved in the Ordnance Survey Letters; it was edited by T.F. O'Rahilly in *Gadelica* I (1913), pp. 171–6. Dean Lyons, describing the hole, said:

> Agus is uathfásach amharc síos anns a' bpoll úthfialta so air a' bhfarraige ag oibriughadh ann; agus a n-aimsir séine tiomaintear an t-uisce chomh teann sin go sceartann sé suas anns a' spéir fríd a bhfosgladh seo a bhfad asteach ós cionn talmhana, agus, is uaidh sin is dóich a thugtar Poll na Seantuine air.

[And it is terrifying to look down through this dreadful hole at the sea churning below; in stormy weather the water is driven in so powerfully that it shoots up towards the sky through this opening, reaching far inland. This seems to be why it is called *Poll na Seantuine*.[2]]

O'Rahilly's note on the name as given in O'Donovan's recording is as follows:

> *Poll na Seantuine: Seantuine* is variously explained. Dean Lyons in his legend does not make clear what meaning he attached to it; but O'Donovan in translating the passage *is uaidh sin* etc., attributes to him the curious derivation of *síon* + *tonn*: 'from which circumstance it has received the name of Poll na Siontuinne, meaning "the hole of the stormy waves"'.

> M[icheá]l Mhag Ruaidhrí explains it as = *sean* + *tine* (*Lúb na C[aillighe]*, p. 37). O'Connor writes the name *Poll na sean tŏna* (Mayo O. Letters i, 283). But that the word was originally *Seantuinne* (from *sean* + *tonn*) there can be little doubt. Cf. *Bun Seantuinne* and *Loch Seantuinne* on the Derry coast. (Hogan[3] is mistaken in spelling the former *Bun Sentuine*, as may be seen from ZCP,[4] iv. 312 and F[our] M[asters],[5] iii, 109.) Other chasms elsewhere on the Mayo coast are also called *Poll na Seantuine*. The single *n* seems due to a kind of dissimilation, owing to the double *n* (*nt* = *nnt*) preceding; the Cork *pingin* for *pinginn* might perhaps be compared.

From this it appears that O'Rahilly was of opinion that the word meant 'Hole of the Old Wave'.

There is, however, an alternative to be considered, the archaic word *seanntuinne* meaning old woman. Indeed the *Ordnance Survey Namebook* for the district has this notation: 'Poll na Sean Tona (al. Tuine, hole of the hag).' This

---

1. *Béaloideas*, vols 39–41 (1971–3), pp. 206–11.

2. Translation by Angela Bourke.
3. Edmund Hogan SJ (1831–1917), author of *Ononmasticon Goedelicum* (Dublin: Four Courts Press, 1993 [1910]).
4. *Zeitschrift für Celtische Philologie*, (Halle and London).
5. Four Masters. *Annals of the Kingdom of Ireland by the Four Masters*, vol. III, p. 109 (note), (ed.) John O'Donovan (Dublin: Hodges and Smith, 1851).

meaning was tentatively put forward by Seósamh Laoide in *Lúb na Caillighe* (1910), p. 78 and appears to be that accepted by Dinneen.[6]

The Loch Seantuinne referred to by O'Rahilly is identified as Loch Feabhail (Lough Foyle) in *Ononmasticon Goedelicum*; and Bun Seantuinne, which suggests a river-mouth, is described in Mánus Ó Domhnaill's *Betha Colaim Cille* (A. O'Kelleher and G. Schoepperle, p. 84) as being on the east of Lough Foyle near Derry city and in Cluaine (Clooney townland). These places, while part of or near the sea, do not seem to support the *tonn* (wave) component of the placename in the same sense that the blow-holes might be thought to do. The problem could be more easily solved if more information was available about places which have *seantuinne* in their names. Since it occurs in placenames as far apart as Derry and north Mayo it is to be expected that it has, or had, a wide distribution.

There is a place of the name in the centre of Clare. It is marked Poulnashantinna on the six-inch map (Clare 17), and is in Lismuinga West townland in the parish of Ruan. It is a deep circular chasm in a limestone plateau reaching down to a pool far below the level of the surrounding land. The river Fergus flows about one-third of a mile to the north, and the pool may be part of an underground stream. The owner of the land pumps water from it for his farming needs. I have been told that his elders disapproved of this innovation as the place had a fairy reputation. It is awe-inspiring. There is a wall built round it — a necessary precaution because of the abruptness of the cavity. Bushes have grown inside the wall and also around the upper reaches of the cavity itself. These increase the shadowiness of the water below. This place has certain, but not complete, resemblances to the north Mayo instances in the abrupt enclosed chasm over water below and the general awesomeness. But it does not support the 'wave' explanation of the name. The local pronunciation of the name, as nearly as I can reproduce it, is Poll na Seannt're [poul nə ˈʃountrɛ].[7]

The probability of the name having a mythological origin and of the *seantuinne* being

no ordinary old woman is strengthened by the fact that the places so named resemble several other places formerly known as Poll Tighe Liabáin, the mythological nuance of which cannot be doubted. Poll Tighe Liabáin as a synonym for Hell or a place of great depth was a commonplace in proverbial sayings recorded widespreadly where Irish was spoken. Seósamh Laoide first heard it in a song sung for him by a Meath Irish speaker he met casually while walking by the Boyne, and this sparked his curiosity about it. As a result he wrote an article on it in *Irisleabhar na Gaedhilge* XII, May 1902, pp. 66–74. He also contributed a useful note on it in *Lúb na Caillighe*, pp. 78–9. Since then the collections of the Irish Folklore Commission provide further data.

Poll Tighe Liabáin was the name of specific places known to people who lived in certain districts, but it was also widely known as an entrance to the underworld or an abyss of unfathomable depth by people who had no notion of its whereabouts. It turns up, curiously enough, in a few versions of the international folktale [Aarne–Thompson] Type 1535, 'The Rich and Poor Peasant', recorded in County Galway, both in the region north-west of Lough Corrib bordering on County Mayo and in Claregalway east of Lough Corrib. This tale was very popular with country people, no doubt because of its comically outrageous plot: it tells how a rich, ruthless, gullible and avaricious man is tricked out of his possessions by his poor, clever and equally ruthless neighbour. In the last episode the trickster persuades his dupe that there are herds to be got at the bottom of a deep pool; the dupe leaps in and is drowned. The pool is named Poll Tighe Labáin by the north-west Galway storytellers. The Claregalway storyteller called it Poll Tighe Liabáin, and added '*pébí cá'il Poll Tighe Liabáin,*' [wherever Poll Tighe Liabáin may be]. Éamon Ó Tuathail recorded a folktale in Glengevlen,[8] a version of [Aarne–Thompson] Type 130 B, 'The Animals in Flight from Threatened Death' (*Béaloideas*, IV, Supplement, p. 11, note, p. 45). In this tale foolish people and animals are thrown into Poll Toigh Liabáin and never heard of again.

---

6. Reverend Patrick Dinneen (1860–1934), lexicographer.
7. I am indebted to Professor Conn R. Ó Cléirigh for the phonetic rendering.

8. County Cavan.

In addition to these references in folktales, oral tradition has legendary tales[9] to account for the origin of the place. One elaborated version with the title 'Poll Tighe O Leó Leobáin' told by Mícheál Mhag Ruaidhrí, was printed in *Lúb na Caillighe*. In this instance the storyteller said the old people of his district always maintained that it was in County Roscommon on the border of County Mayo, a good distance from his native Lacken by Killala Bay. The origin legends fall into two categories; in one of which retribution is made for a murder, in the other for an act of impiety. In the murder versions a man murders his partner in order to get money to marry a woman who shares his guilt, they prosper for a while (sometimes seven generations) and then suddenly their house is swallowed into the ground leaving only a bottomless hole on the site where it had been. This form of the legend I have not found allied to a specific place. The other category in which the house is engulfed because of an act of impiety is told of a Poll Tighe Liabáin on the south coast of Valentia Island, County Kerry, in Bray townland between Faill na n-Iath (Foilenea Cliff) and Dún na Ruadha (Doonroe Cliff), (IFC MS 25: 371). There is another Poll Tighe Liabáin in Valentia on the north coast between Rinn Gharbh (Reengarriv Point) and Tráigh Dhonnáin (Trawaginnaun) in Dohilla townland.

Seósamh Laoide mentions two instances in Galway in the Gort[10] district. One of these must indeed have been famous in times past, as Keating[11] mentions it as a well-known place:

> . . . agus leabaidh Dhiarmada Uí Dhuibhne agus Ghráinne ag Poll Tighe Liabháin i nUíbh Fiachrach Eidhne, dá ngoirtear Dúthaigh Uí Sheachnasaigh aniú, agus mar sin do mhorán d'áitibh eile in Éirinn.

> [. . . and the bed of Diarmaid Ó Duibhne and Gráinne at Poll Tí Liabáin, in Aidhne, which is today called O'Shaughnessy territory, and many other places in Ireland the same.[12]]

9. Type 960 B in S. Ó Súilleabháin and R. Christiansen, *The Types of the Irish Folktale*.
10. County Galway, the town nearest to Lady Gregory's home at Coole Park.
11. Geoffrey Keating (*c*.1580 – *c*.1644), writer in Irish. He was a Catholic priest, historian, poet and author of spiritual texts. He was of Anglo-Norman extraction.
12. Translation by Angela Bourke.

Laoide printed a report by Tomás Ó hEidhin of Gort who said it was one of the holes of the Gort river about two hundred yards from the hole known as Poll Dubh, that it was better known as Poll an Fheadha but that Poll Tighe Liabáin, as its name, was not forgotten by the old people. He gave the origin legend: St. Fiachain, who was travelling with St. Patrick, blessed a rod and set it in the ground and prophesied that it would grow into a tree covering a quarter of land, which prophecy was fulfilled; in course of time Liabán, a carpenter, began to take bits of the blessed tree for his work materials and because of doing so he and his house were swallowed into the ground. A somewhat different version (IFC MS 354: 252–3) attributes the catastrophe to a couple who refused hospitality to St. Patrick.

Tomás Ó hEidhin also reported that the spot where the Ballylee river goes underground was known as 'Liabán's Gulf'.

Laoide gives a graphic description of a Poll Tighe Liabáin which he was shown on the cliff near Malinbeg opposite Rathlin O Birne Island on the Donegal coast. It is a blow-hole with a narrow edge on the sea side and slopes rather like a funnel to its open bottom over the waves.

Poll Tighe Liabáin then appears to be applied to the same kind of natural features as Poll na Seantuinne, to deep and awesome holes in the ground over watery bottoms. They occur inland as well as by the sea.

It is reasonable to assume that there must be, or have been, many more places of these names or names of similar import in Ireland. The proverbial phrases, the adventitious occurrences in folktales, the origin legends even in the atrophied forms in which they survive, all point to a formerly stronger and more explicit belief. It would be tempting to compare them with the tales in our older literature of Liban the sea woman and of suddenly engulfed dwellings, but this must be left to experts in the field. Here it is intended only to bring forward one small example of the manifold riches for research of Irish popular tradition and to add a mite of recognition to Séamus Ó Duilearga, who has salvaged so much of it from the wreck of time.

POSTSCRIPT

The identification of the Poll Tighe Liabháin mentioned by Keating remains a problem. The place indicated by Tomás Ó hEidhin of Gort in his contribution of 1902 seems to be the cavity marked 'Ladle' on the six-inch map (Galway 128), but there is an indecisiveness in his account. He states that most of the old people of the district had heard of Poll Tighe Liabháin and told him that it was near the Poll Dubh (known in English as Black Water and marked on the same six-inch map), but he found only two boys and an old man who could tell him which hole it was. Quite close to Poll Dubh is the much more remarkable and extensive circular chasm known now as the Punch Bowl and marked on the half-inch map as well as on the six-inch (Galway 129). In size and impressiveness it would seem much more likely than the Ladle to merit widespread fame and be known to Keating many miles away in south Tipperary. It is in a wooded glade and close to the

gorge made by the river draining Lough Cutra before it goes underground. The water in its bottom is a re-appearance of the river. The Irish name on the signpost is 'An Daibhchín', a diminutive which seems inappropriate for such an impressive landmark but which must have tradition behind it as the surrounding townland is named Rindifin. I think it probable that there was some confusion in the information given to Ó hEidhin but I must also admit that it would have been strange for his informants to disregard the well-known Punch Bowl if, in fact, the tradition had originally been associated with it. Nevertheless, the Punch Bowl is such an outstanding example of the type of natural feature to which the mythological name was given that I incline to the opinion that it is the place Keating had heard of as Poll Tighe Liabháin.

BRÍD MAHON

from:
LAND OF MILK AND HONEY: THE STORY OF TRADITIONAL IRISH FOOD AND DRINK (1991)

[In a book aimed at the general reader, Bríd Mahon draws on the work of her Irish Folklore Commission colleagues, both collectors and scholars, to describe the practice of transhumance — moving milk cattle to mountain and moorland areas for summer grazing — known as *buailteachas*, 'booleying', in Ireland. The young women who tended the cows lived in groups, away from their families, in temporary dwellings. They herded the grazing animals and made butter, but they also found time for entertainment. The practice of transhumance was described in Irish for some areas along the Atlantic seaboard in *Béaloideas*, vol. 13 (1943), pp. 130–72, and the custom was surveyed in a questionnaire on milk and milk products circulated by the Irish Folklore Commission in 1955–8. Mahon quotes from what she calls 'Perhaps the most descriptive and attractive account we have of booleying in living memory', recorded in Irish in 1943 by full-time folklore collector Seán Ó hEochaidh from Niall Ó Dubhthaigh (b. 1874), an Bhealtaine, Gort an Choirce,

County Donegal, and published in the 1943 article (pp. 130–56) as 'Buailteachas i dTír Chonaill'. It was translated by ethnologist Caoimhín Ó Danachair and published in 1983 as 'Summer Pasture in Donegal', an appendix to his authoritative introduction to the practice, 'Summer Pasture in Ireland' in *Folk Life. A Journal of Ethnological Studies*, vol. 22 (1983–4), pp. 36–54. Ó Dubhthaigh's account includes an aetiological religious legend: typical of the way oral tradition incorporates such material into narratives of daily life (cf. p. 1399). See also E. Estyn Evans, *Irish Folk Ways* (London: Routledge and Kegan Paul, 1957), pp. 27–38. Extract is from pp. 100–2. Headnote, A.B.]

On May morning the whole village set out together to accompany the local girls to the booley where they would spend the summer months tending the cattle. Provisions had to be brought along, everything the girls would need from needle and thread to soap and hairbrush. The moorland tracks were too rough for carts, so donkeys, panniers slung across their backs, as well as pack horses, were used as transport; what the beasts could not carry the men did. They brought with them milking-cans, tubs and butter-churns, bed linen and stools, pots and pans, crockery, knives and spoons, wool for spinning, and iron rations[1] of flour, potatoes, oatmeal, and salt fish. On the journey the cattle were herded along the mountain track by excited young boys and barking dogs, while each girl carried her own spinning-wheel, combs, and knitting-needle[s]. On November Day, when the potatoes were gathered and the harvest was in, they would leave the mountains and return to their homes . . .

Life on the heights was simple but pleasant. Each little shieling contained a window, a fireplace with a turf-basket, three-legged wooden stools, heather hassocks, and a carpet of green rushes on the floor. The girls slept on beds of rushes, heather, bracken, and black mountain sedge, covered with woven linen sheets, woollen blankets and quilts. Black sedges were said to make such a comfortable mattress that a legend grew up around them.

When the Blessed Woman and St Joseph were walking the roads and without a place to lay their heads they were forced to spend the night in a stable, and it was there between the ox and the ass that the Child Jesus was born. The bed of the Holy Family was made of black sedges from the mountains and it was said that ever since anyone sleeping on such a bed never suffered sleeplessness, pain or anxiety but arose the following morning fresh and rested.

The months on the mountains were remembered as idyllic. The girls rose with the dawn and spent their days tending the stock, milking the cows, making butter and cheese, spinning wool and knitting. Food was simple but wholesome. To drink they had an abundance of sweet milk and buttermilk, and to eat oat cakes hot from the griddle with freshly churned butter, as well as curds, oatmeal porridge, potatoes, meat and eggs brought from home, fish from mountain streams and lakes, and occasionally rabbits, hares or game snared or brought down by the young men from the townland, who visited them on Sundays or holiday evenings. Life on the heights could sometimes be adventurous. A tale is told in several places of the killing of 'the last wolf in Ireland in a summer pasture'.

Butter was made by the girls in common, and in his account of booleying on a Donegal

mountain, Niall Ó Dubhthaigh tells us that when the butter was sold at the Letterkenny market, whatever the yield, each girl was paid according to the number of cows her family owned. None of the butter went astray; it was packed into tubs and safely stored in little underground houses lined with flagstones, which the men built and which were as cold as ice-houses. Neither sun, wind nor rain could penetrate the walls and all summer the butter remained as hard and firm as an icicle.

In the evenings when the day's work was done, the girls gathered to spin and tell stories, or sing and dance with the young men who joined them at weekends or on the great festival of the Assumption, 15 August.[2] Years later the girls, now grown old, remembered with delight and nostalgia those sunlit days at the booleying.

2. *Lá Fhéile Muire Mhór sa bhFómhar*, 'Great Lady Day Harvest'.

Biographies/Bibliographies

Lady Gregory

For biography and bibliography, see Volume II, p. 560 and above, p. 914.

Máire MacNeill

LIFE. Born in Dublin in 1904, Máire MacNeill was the youngest daughter of Eóin Mac Neill (1867–1945), scholar, Irish revivalist and founder of the Irish Volunteers (see Volume II, p. 368). A student of University College Dublin, she obtained a BA degree in Celtic Studies from the National University of Ireland in 1923. In 1935 she became a staff member of the Irish Folklore Commission, a position she held until 1949 when she moved to Boston, Massachusetts, on her marriage to the Harvard academic and poet John L. Sweeney. Like her colleagues in the Irish Folklore Commission, she went to Lund and Uppsala in Sweden to study archival and research methods, and also received training in ethnological cartography — all of which she subsequently put to good use in her monumental work on the harvest festival of Lughnasa. At Harvard, she taught courses in Irish language and folklore, and continued her scholarly research.

On her husband's retirement, the couple returned to Ireland, to Corofin, County Clare, where she continued to live and work after his death. Máire MacNeill's celebration of the Irish landscape and its sacred places, evident in *The Festival of Lughnasa* (1962), is manifested again in her sensitive Introduction to and translations for *Síscéalta ó Thír Chonaill/Fairy Legends from Donegal* (1977). Her posthumously published book on Máire Rua O'Brien, chatelaine of Leamaneh Castle, near Inchiquin, marks her commitment to the heritage of County Clare. When Máire MacNeill died on 15 May 1987, she bequeathed her valuable collection of paintings to the National Gallery of Ireland.

1. Iron rations: staple foods.

CHIEF WRITINGS. *The Festival of Lughnasa: A Study of the Survival of the Celtic Festival of the Beginning of Harvest* (London: Oxford University Press, 1962; rpr. Dublin, 1982); (with Seán Ó hEochaidh and Séamas Ó Catháin), *Síscéalta ó Thír Chonaill/Fairy Legends from Donegal* (Dublin: Comhairle Bhéaloideas Éireann, 1977); *Seán Ó Conaill's Book* [translation] (Dublin: Comhairle Bhéaloideas Éireann, 1981); *Máire Rua, Lady of Leamaneh*, ed. Maureen Murphy (Whitegate: Ballinakella Press, 1990).

BIOGRAPHY AND CRITICISM. Bo Almqvist, 'Dr Máire MacNeill-Sweeney (1904–87). In Memoriam', *Béaloideas*, vol. 56 (1988), pp. 221–3; Brid Mahon, *While Green Grass Grows: Memoirs of a Folklorist* (Cork: Mercier Press, 1998), pp. 62–3; Maureen Murphy, 'Máire Mac Neill (1904–1987): An Appreciation', in *Máire Rua, Lady of Leamaneh*, ed. Maureen Murphy (Whitegate: Ballinakella Press, 1990), [pp. vii–ix].

Bríd Mahon

LIFE. Bríd Mahon's family have been Dubliners for many generations. From the early 1940s until her retirement in 1986 she worked with the Irish Folklore Commission, succeeding Máire MacNeill as secretary in 1949. She has also worked as a theatre critic and written plays, short stories and dramatizations for radio, as well as historical novels and books for children. In the 1960s she wrote a weekly column for the *Sunday Press*.

CHIEF WRITINGS. *Irish Dress* (Dublin: Folens, 1975); *Land of Milk and Honey: The Story of Traditional Irish Food and Drink* (Dublin: Poolbeg Press, 1991); *Dervogilla* (novel) (Dublin: Poolbeg Press, 1994); *While Green Grass Grows: Memoirs of a Folklorist* (Cork: Mercier Press, 1998).

Index includes only those names that have particular importance for the texts in this volume. Names of translators are included. Bold numerals indicate text selections; italic numerals indicate biographical and bibliographical references. Names beginning with 'Mac' and 'Mc' are ordered as if they were spelled 'Mac'.